THE COLUMBIA ENCYCLOPEDIA OF MODERN DRAMA

THE COLUMBIA ENCYCLOPEDIA OF

Modern Drama

Edited by **GABRIELLE H. CODY** and **EVERT SPRINCHORN**

Volume 1

COLUMBIA UNIVERSITY PRESS

New York

Columbia University Press

Publishers Since 1893

New York Chichester, West Sussex

Library of Congress Cataloging-in-Publication Data

The Columbia encyclopedia of modern drama / edited by
Gabrielle H. Cody and Evert Sprinchorn.

p. cm.

Includes bibliographical references and index.

ISBN 978-0-231-14032-4 (set : alk. paper)

978-0-231-14422-3 (v. 1 : alk. paper)

978-0-231-14424-7 (v. 2 : alk. paper)

1. Drama—Bio-bibliography—Dictionaries. 2. Drama—20th century—History and criticism. 3. Theater—History—20th century— Encyclopedias. I. Cody, Gabrielle H., 1956– II. Sprinchorn, Evert.

PN1861 C65 2007

809 2003—dc22 2006051841

Columbia University Press books are printed on permanent and durable acid-free paper.

This book is printed on paper with recycled content.

Printed in the United States of America

C 10 9 8 7 6 5 4 3 2 1

CONTENTS

EDITORIAL BOARD

PREFACE

The Columbia Encyclopedia of Modern Drama covers the period from 1860 to the present. It was in the 1860s that the Norwegian dramatist Henrik Ibsen (1828–1906) wrote his epic dramas *Brand* and *Peer Gynt*, which, for their philosophical content alone, can be seen as giant pillars raised at the entrance to the modern drama. Later, in his realistic plays, such as *A Doll's House* (1879), he converted the theater into a place where the most serious ideas could be discussed. His position as the "father" of modern drama, both as regards technical mastery of dramatic art and the impact of his plays on society, is unquestioned. Thanks in large part to his radical innovations and to the inspiration he gave to those who followed him, the last one hundred fifty years constitute one of the great eras in the history of drama, rivaling that of ancient Greece and the Renaissance.

The distinctive feature of this encyclopedia is the emphasis it places on the cultural context of dramatic works and their authors. They are treated in their relationship to significant movements, whether political or philosophical, artistic or religious. There is consequently less concern with detailed plot summaries than in many comparable reference works. *The Columbia Encyclopedia of Modern Drama* is structured as a compendium of substantive articles and differs conceptually from previous and existing works of reference by engaging conventional as well as experimental, established as well as emerging authors on a global scale. While Ibsen's paternity as founder of modern European or Western drama remains unquestioned, the important work of many women, authors of color, and non-Western dramatists has often been neglected. We have tried to fill these lacunae by emphasizing the multiplicity of aesthetic genres, viewpoints, and voices that animate the modern and contemporary dramatic landscape. With the invaluable help of our advisors, we have placed 540 individual plays, 640 playwrights, and over 60 countries in their cultural and historical context. Significant dramatists who are not given separate entries are covered in the national surveys or in articles devoted to movements or currents of thought, such as political theater, the avant-garde, philosophy and drama, and apocalyptic currents in drama. Such surveys are of special value in providing a broad cultural context that cannot be accommodated in the shorter biographical entries. Cross-references set in capital and small capital letters cue the reader to these surveys.

Standard reference works in this field, such as John Gassner and Edward Quinn's *The Reader's Encyclopedia of World Drama* and Myron Matlaw's *Modern World Drama: An Encyclopedia*, have been devoted almost exclusively to the literary drama or have given equal space to both the written drama and theatrical practice (*The Oxford Encyclopedia of Theatre and Performance*, edited by Dennis Kennedy). *The Columbia Encyclopedia* differs from them in stressing the written drama while also providing informative articles on theater practice; for instance, biomechanics in Russia and Takarazuka in Japan. Entries on practitioners such as Konstantin Stanislavsky, Mei Lanfang, or Ariane Mnouchkine remind us of how much the drama is inseparable from its theatrical presentation.

One of the characteristics of the modern era is that the printed play is often no more than a representation of a work in progress, intended only as a guide to performance. With this in mind, we have also included entries for those theatre practitioners, actors, directors, designers, or scenographers whose creative work has had a significant impact on the drama. The theatrical presentation of a play often has a lasting effect on the way it comes to be understood, an outstanding example being Stanislavsky's interpretation of Anton Chekhov's plays, or Joint Stock Theatre Group's team of collaborating artists whose working strategies are now inseparable from the brilliance of Caryl Churchill's dramatic structure during the late 1970s and early 1980s.

We have also grappled with the fact that modern literary drama is fundamentally Anglo-European, since much non-Western drama is orally transmitted rather than recorded as "literature," and therefore exists *between* drama and performance. From a global perspective, then, the very term *modern drama* must reflect the specific cultural and political history that has shaped it, *locally*. The purpose of our national surveys is to contextualize the drama within a particular cultural tradition and to directly address the ways in which "drama" is often a biproduct of colonial incursions. Just as European colonialism wiped out indigenous traditions at the start of the modern era in drama, rendering modernity for many cultures synonymous with colonial values, the *avant-garde* is also a term that must be reexplored and taken out of a strictly European context. Much of the artistic energy that informed the European avant-garde at the turn of the nineteenth century came from the adoption of so-called primitive non-Western aesthetics. Modernist movements such as Dadaism or Futurism sought to foreground the more populist "theatrical" over the more patrician "literary," often making the case for performance as more accessible and democratic; such that the antitextual aspects of avant-garde drama have, over time, rendered the terms *text* and *performance*, *drama* and *theater* difficult to distinguish over the course of the 20th century. We have tried to incorporate as many articles as possible on Western as well as non-Western avant-garde movements and aesthetic genres, in order to underline this point.

It is the fate of reference works that despite their attempts to be comprehensive certain areas will remain underdeveloped. It was for instance beyond the scope of this work to include the vast field of musical theater, though we do touch briefly on this important literature in an extensive survey on librettists.

We wish to thank Donna Sanzone and Cheryl Clark for their generous encouragement and perseverance; Karen Casey and her staff for their superb editorial support, and our extraordinarily patient and steadfast advisors and contributors for their faith in this project.

Gabrielle H. Cody
Evert Sprinchorn
Poughkeepsie, New York, January 2007

AADHE ADHURE *See* HALFWAY HOUSE

ABDALLAH, MOHAMMED BEN (1944–)

Writer Mohammed Ben Abdallah was born in April 1944 in Kumasi in the Ashanti region of Ghana to Muslim parents and, through his maternal grandfather, traces part of his roots to North Africa. He claimed to feel no particular attachment to any ethnic group but, rather, saw himself as a Pan-Africanist more than anything else. Some of his plays imaginatively explore African history, and it is sometimes difficult to locate them in one particular African country, demonstrating his Pan-Africanist tendencies. His play *The Slaves*, although set in a dungeon at Elmina Castle, uses characters from all over Africa. There is Dikko, "a slave woman from the Fouta Jalon Mountains"; Margan, "The fiery Mossi slave"; The Old Priest, an old "Yoruba slave"; and Segou, "A Malinke slave." Similarly, *The Witch of Mopti* has a constellation of characters from different parts of the African continent. Abdallah acknowledges the influences of great Pan-Africanist writers such as Amilsan Cabral, Kwame Nkrumah, and Frantz Fanon on his life and writing.

Abdallah received his early education in Kumasi but moved to Accra to live with his uncle in Nima, a highly populated slum area, when his father died. He later trained as a teacher at the Wesley College in Kumasi, where he joined the drama club and participated in the regular drama competitions held among student residence halls. To avoid teaching for a while after completing his training, he enrolled in the School of Music and Drama at the University of Ghana (now the School of Performing Arts) in Legon, where his interests in theater were galvanized. He wrote his first play, *The Alien King*, in 1972, during his final year at the university; *The Slaves* and *Verdict of the Cobra* were also written that year. Abdallah went on to earn an M.A. in playwriting at the university of Georgia and then a Ph.D. at the University of Texas at Austin. His play *The Trial of Mallam Ilya* had its premiere at the University of Georgia.

Back in Ghana in 1982, where, despite the hardships of daily life, Abdallah successfully produced *The Trial of Mallam Ilya* with students in the School of Performing Arts. He regarded *The Trial* as a landmark production, as it brought together staff and students from all three departments of the school: music, dance, and drama. Abdallah believed that these three elements of the performing arts should come together in a true experience of African theater. In the preface to the first publication of a collection of his plays, *The Trial of Mallam Ilya and Other Plays* (1987), he indicates his deliberate search for what could be called an "authentic 'African theatre.'" He acknowledges his use of "traditional story-telling and the techniques of Africa's revered Griots" and "elements of African religious practices." This collection includes *The Alien King*, which uses the storytelling framework, and *Verdict of the Cobra*, which incorporates music, mime, and dance. The title play, which is based on an actual trial, is expansive in its use of African traditional elements. Abdallah deliberately attempts to engage audiences in dialogue by using direct address and planting actors in the audience. *The Trial* includes an interlude of dances and extensive use of mime.

Abdallah's second collection of three plays, *The Fall of Kumbi and Other Plays* (1989), includes *The Slaves* and *The Witch of Mopti*. The latter play, which was written for Abibigromma, the resident theater company of the School of Performing Arts, is innovative in its structure and use of language. Abdallah employs both Fante and English in a kind of progressive translation of each other. In production (and even in reading), non-Fante speakers are generally able to follow the play, as much of what is said in Fante is also said in English. Here his concept of *Abibigoro* (loosely translated as "black performance"), which builds on Sutherland's *Ananse-goro*, comes of age. Again, he fuses mime, music, dance, and storytelling and uses multiple storytellers to relate the story to the audience. *The Land of a Million Magicians* (1993), which is a loose reworking of BERTOLT BRECHT's *Good Woman of Sechuan*, takes *Abibigoro* to even higher heights. Here Abdallah draws on his knowledge of Nima and creates an intriguing drama of prostitutes and ordinary folk seeking to make ends meet in a situation where those in authority appear not to care about their living conditions. The first production of the play was a large-scale, successful collaboration among a number of performance groups, including the Abibiman Concert Party, the Amore Cultural Troupe, and Abibigromma. Music was provided by Lord Bob Cole, a popular concert party musician. *Song of the Pharaohs*, which as of this writing was unpublished, has been long in coming and is scheduled to be produced in Accra.

[*See also* Africa]

PLAYS: *The Alien King* (1987); *The Trial of Mallam Ilya* (1987); *Verdict of the Cobra* (1987); *The Fall of Kumbi* (1989); *The Slaves* (1989); *The Witch of Mopti* (1989); *The Land of a Million Magicians* (1993); *Song of the Pharaohs* (20)

FURTHER READING

Abdallah, Mohammed Ben. *The Trial of Mallam Ilya and Other Plays*. Accra: Woeli, 1987.

——. "On Plays and Playwriting: Interview by Anastasia Agbenyega and James Gibb." In *Fontomfrom: Contemporary Ghanaian Literature, Theatre, and Film*, ed. by Kofi Anyidoho and James Gibb. Atlanta: Rodopi, 2000.

Banham, Martin, and Jane Plastow, eds. *Contemporary African Plays*. London: Methuen, 1999.

Breitinger, Eckhard, ed. *Theatre and Performance in Africa*. Bayreuth: Bayreuth Univ., 1994.

Awo Mana Asiedu

ABE KŌBŌ (1924–1993)

Abe Kōbō, a Japanese SHINGEKI playwright born in Tokyo, is considered one of the leading postwar dramatists, as well as a top director and theater teacher. His works explore themes such as alienation, loss of identity, and societal divisions. Blending techniques from *shingeki* and theater of the absurd, Abe created powerful stage images and challenged traditional Japanese theater.

Shortly before graduating from the medical school at Tokyo Imperial University in 1948, Abe became involved with Night Group (Yoru noKai), a loose confederation of Japanese writers, philosophers, and intelligentsia led by the writer Hanada Kiyoteru. The group sought to blend AVANT-GARDE writing and communist ideology, leading Abe to join the Japan Communist Party in 1951. In 1948 he published his first major work, *To the Sign at the End of the Road*.

His output increased in the 1950s bringing recognition from critics and scholars. In 1954 his play *The Uniform* (*Seifuku*) was published, *Slave Hunting* (*Doreigari*) was staged in 1955, and in 1957 a broadcast of *The Man Who Turned into a Stick* (*Bō ni Natta Otoko*) won the Geijutsusai Shōrei Prize. In 1958 Abe won JAPAN's highest drama award, the Kishida Kunio Drama Prize, for *The Ghosts Are Here* (*Yūrei wa Koko ni Iru*).

In 1961 Abe and twenty-seven other literary figures declared their opposition to the Stalinist policies of the Japan Communist Party. To a great degree, his opposition came as a result of a trip through HUNGARY in 1956 and his dismay at the treatment of the Hungarian independence movement. Because of his opposition to these policies Abe was expelled from the party in 1962. Four months after his expulsion, Abe's most famous novel, *Woman in the Dunes* (*Suna no Onna*), was published to great acclaim.

Abe continued to write plays throughout the 1960s, including some of his best-known works, FRIENDS (*Tomodachi*) and *Enomoto Dance* (*Enomoto Būyo*) in 1967 and *Stick* (*Bō*) in 1969. Though he continued to write through the 1970s, most of his artistic attention focused on the creation of his own acting studio. The Abe Kōbō Studio (Abe Kōbō Sutajjio) was formed in 1973 with the aim of training actors in avant-garde movement techniques and developing work based in the collaborative rehearsal process. The group produced works such as *Image Exhibition Kidnappers* (*Imeiji no Tenkrankai Hitosarai*, 1978) and *The Little Elephant Is Dead* (*Kozō wa Shinda*, 1979).

Although the Abe Kōbō Studio dissolved after seven years, Abe continued to write essays and novels until his death in 1993. Abe's legacy is a rich body of dramatic literature that blends absurdist humor with existentialist pathos.

SELECT PLAYS: *The Uniform* (*Seifuku*, 1954); *Slave Hunting* (*Doreigari*, 1955); *The Man Who Turned into a Stick* (*Bō ni Natta Otoko*, 1957); *The Ghosts Are Here* (*Yūrei wa Koko ni Iru*, 1958); *You, Too, Are Guilty* (*Omae ni mo Tsumi ga aru*, 1965); *Enomoto Dance* (*Enomoto Būyo*, 1967); *Friends* (*Tomodachi*, 1967); *Stick* (*Bō*, 1969); *Involuntary Homicide* (*Mihitsu na Koi*, 1971); *Fake Fish* (*Nise Sakana*, 1973); *The Green Stocking* (*Midoriiro no Stokkingo*, 1974); *Ūē: The New Slave Hunt* (*Ūē: Shin Doreigari*, 1975); *Image Exhibition Kidnappers* (*Imeiji no Tenkrankai Hitosarai*, 1978); *Guidebook IV: The Crime of S. Karma* (*S. Karma-shi no Hanzai*, 1978); *The Little Elephant is Dead* (*Kozō wa Shinda*, 1979)

FURTHER READING

Abe Kōbō. *Abe Kōbō no Gekijō–Shichinen no Ayumi* [The Abe Kōbō Theater–Seven Years]. Tokyo: Sōrinsha, 1979.

——. *Abe Kōbō Zenshū* [Complete Works of Abe Kōbō]. 30 vols. Tokyo: Shinchōsa, 1997.

Iles, Timothy. *Abe Kōbō: An Exploration of his Prose, Drama and Theatre*. Fucecchio, Italy: European Press Academic Publishing, 2000.

Shields, Nancy. *Fake Fish: The Theater of Kobo Abe*. New York: Weatherhill, 1996.

David Jortner

ABE LINCOLN IN ILLINOIS

On October 15, 1938, *Abe Lincoln in Illinois*, written by ROBERT SHERWOOD, opened at the Plymouth Theatre in New York City, the first production of the Playwrights' Company, which had been founded the previous July by Sherwood and four other dramatists. The play was a tremendous success. Hailed by critics as "the great American drama" (Heywood Broun), "the living truth of America" (Brooks Atkinson), and "one of the great achievements of the American theater and the American spirit" (Richard Watts, Jr.), it had 472 performances, won a Pulitzer Prize, and earned Sherwood a fortune. Revived for a five-week run in New York in 1963, the play suffered from the passage of time. While it was honest, direct, and persevering in its objective and in its idealism—a good illustration of Sherwood the man—the production's reception clearly reveals that one generation's passion can inspire a later generation's cynicism.

A peak and turning point in Sherwood's writing career, *Abe Lincoln in Illinois* was a happy combination of the man, the moment, and the material—much of that inspired by Carl Sandburg's *The Prairie Years* and based on Sherwood's considerable research. Composed of three acts divided into 12 scenes, *Abe Lincoln in Illinois* traces Abraham Lincoln's developing character from a young man to president-elect, as he departed from Springfield, Illinois, for Washington, D.C., on February 11, 1861. From the first scene, set in Salem in 1833, Sherwood presented Lincoln as a man of many moods—strong for liberty and union, worried about his business failures and personal debts, a man "so friendly, at the same time so misanthropic." He could be somber and melancholy, and although there may be no historical evidence that

Lincoln ever read the poem, Sherwood creates for his Abe a fascination with John Keats's "On Death" to establish the central thread of the play: "How strange it is that man on earth should roam, / And lead a life of woe, but not forsake / His rugged path."

Plotting Lincoln's fretful and difficult path over the next 28 years, Sherwood dramatized Abe's introduction to political life, his heart broken by the news of his beloved Ann Rutledge's death, the intertwining of his longing for love and his sense of humanity with his indecisiveness and his fears. Just as he cannot make up his mind whether to marry Mary Todd, Lincoln finds deep contradictions in his fundamental beliefs: He is as opposed to slavery as he is to war. But he and Mary do get married; he debates Stephen Douglas; he wins a crucial election with the help of cynical politicians; and gloomy and uncertain, he sets off for Washington. The setting is 1861, but it might as well be 1938, for many of the moods and emotional conflicts assigned to Lincoln were in fact Sherwood's own. Lincoln's final words as he leaves Springfield give voice to the playwright's heartfelt desires: "Let us live to prove that we can cultivate the natural world that is about us and the intellectual and moral world that is within us."

For the published versions of his dramatic works, Sherwood wrote interesting and usually entertaining introductions. For this play he contributed a long and thoughtful essay, "The Substance of *Abe Lincoln in Illinois*," detailing his sources and providing a scene-by-scene explanation of what he hoped to accomplish in the play. While it is an illuminating introduction, *Abe Lincoln in Illinois* must, like all plays, stand alone, appreciated only by what takes place on stage.

[*See also* United States, 1920–1940]

FURTHER READING

Brown, John Mason. *The Worlds of Robert E. Sherwood: Mirror to His Times, 1896–1939*. New York: Harper & Row, 1965.

Meserve, Walter J. *Robert E. Sherwood: Reluctant Moralist*. New York: Western, 1970.

Sherwood, Robert E. "The Substance of *Abe Lincoln in Illinois*." In *Abe Lincoln in Illinois*. New York: Scribner, 1939.

Walter J. Meserve

ABELL, KJELD (1901–1961)

Danish theatre of today is not of today. Most of all it reminds me of the good old dish: porridge, a strange liquid without one single prune, representing a point of view.

—Kjeld Abell, *Danish Theatre*, 1936

Kjeld Abell was the most important innovator in the Danish theater, a multitalented artist whose works included plays, ballets, and scenography. Abell was born on August 8, 1901, in Ribe, Denmark. Although he graduated in political science in 1927, he knew his forte did not lie in politics; in 1920, as a young student, he witnessed MAX REINHARDT's guest performance in Copenhagen of AUGUST STRINDBERG's THE GHOST SONATA and realized theater was his passion. With his pronounced visual imagination, Abell decided to become a scene painter after graduation. He went to Paris, where he worked for two of the leading French theater directors, Louis Jouvet and Charles Dullin. The Russian dancer and choreographer Georges Balanchine was attracted by Abell's light and graceful style and chose him as a scenographer for the Russian ballets he presented at the Royal Theatre in Copenhagen in 1930. Four years later the theater performed Abell and Harald Landers's ballet *The Widow in the Mirror* (*Enken i Spejlet*), with sets and costumes by Abell himself.

The crucial breakthrough came in 1935 with the revue comedy *The Melody That Got Lost* (*Melodien, der blev væk*), presented on a tiny stage in Riddersalen. The comedy was a result of the teamwork among several young leftist artists: Abell was responsible for the dialogues and the sketches for sets and costumes; Sven Møller Kristensen wrote the song texts; and Bernhard Christensen and Herman D. Koppel composed the music. The comedy—the story of an employee named Larsen who leaves his trivial, petit bourgeois life and finds the lost melody of life—broke down the barriers between scene and auditorium, hitting the rhythm and tempo of a new time and becoming the greatest Danish theater success of the 1930s. It was also performed in other Scandinavian countries, France, and England; performances in the United States and Canada were canceled because of economic disagreements. Abell's next comedy, a solo effort, *Eve Serves Out Her Childhood* (*Eva aftjener sin Barnepligt*), a satire of bourgeois upbringing, was performed at the Royal Theatre 1936. In 1940 he returned to Riddersalen, and the revue comedy with *Dyveke* was performed shortly after the German occupation. It met with success similar to that of *The Melody*, especially owing to the song texts of Poul Henningsen whose protests against the German occupants could easily be heard between the lines.

As the political situation during the 1930s deteriorated, Abell's plays struck a more serious note. A dominant theme was the need for personal courage to stand up against tyranny, most directly expressed in ANNA SOPHIE HEDVIG (1939), more blurred in *Queen on Tour* (*Dronning gaar igen*, 1943). Following the murder of fellow dramatist Kaj Munk by the Gestapo in 1944, Abell showed great courage when he interrupted a performance at the Royal Theatre and, from the stage, invited the audience to commemorate Munk who, from his pastorate in the small Jutland town Vedersø, had spoken and written against the German occupation. After that, Abell had to go underground. In 1946 he returned to theater with *Silkeborg*, a critical and far-from-flattering commentary on Denmark during the occupation years.

In the shadow of the Cold War, with East and West mutually suspicious, Abell wrote a series of formally innovative plays, mingling dream and reality—*Days on a Cloud* (*Dage paa en Sky*, 1947), *Vetsera Does Not Blossom for Everybody* (*Vetsera blomstrer ikke for enhver*, 1950), and *The Blue Pekinese* (*Den blaa Pekingeser*, 1954)—plays showing kinship with dramatists such as Strindberg, JEAN GIRAUDOUX, and JEAN-PAUL SARTRE. The hope for a human community is still alive, but the optimism of the 1930s has given way to an increasing feeling of isolation and despair. Abell died on March 5, 1961, in Copenhagen.

PLAYS: *The Widow in the Mirror* [ballet] (*Enken I Spejlet*, 1934); *The Melody That Got Lost* (*Melodien, der blev væk*, 1935); *Eve Serves Out Her Childhood* (*Eva aftjener sin Barnepligt*, 1936); *Thorvaldsen* [ballet] (1938); *Anna Sophie Hedvig* (1939); *Dyveke* [revue] (1940); *Judith* (1940); *Spring* [ballet] (*Vaaren*, 1942); *The Queen on Tour* (*Dronning gaar igen*, 1943); *Silkeborg* (1946); *Days on a Cloud* (*Dage paa en Sky*, 1947); *Miss Plinckby's Patience* (*Miss Plinckby's kabala*, 1949); *Vetsera Does Not Blossom for Everybody* (*Vetsera blomstrer ikke for enhver*, 1950); *The Blue Pekinese* (*den blaa Pekingeser*, 1954); *The Lady of the Camellias* (*Kameliadamen*, 1959); *The Scream* (*Skriget*, 1961)

FURTHER READING

Days on a Cloud. In *Genius of Scandinavian Theatre*, ed. by Evert Sprinchorn with an essay by Elias Bredsdorff. 1964.

Heje, Alice Bryrup. *I Kjeld Abells dramatiske verden* [In the dramatic world of Kjeld Abell]. Copenhagen: Gyldendal, 1989.

Madsen, Børge Gedsø. "Leading Motifs in the Dramas of Kjeld Abell." *Scandinavian Studies* 33 (1961).

Marker, Frederick. *Kjeld Abell*. Boston: Twayne Publishers, 1976.

Kela Kvam

ABIE'S IRISH ROSE

Abie's Irish Rose, written by Anne Nichols, opened on Broadway at the Fulton Theatre on May 23, 1922, closing more than five years later on October 22, 1927, chalking up 2,327 performances, at the time a Broadway record. The story behind its success is theater legend. Nichols had heard of an incident in which a Jewish boy married an Irish girl and unsuccessfully attempted to pass her off as Jewish to his parents. Nichols took only three days to write the play, five more to revise it, but over three years to interest a producer. Finally, Oliver Morosco agreed to give *Abie's Irish Rose* a California production, only after Nichols offered to stand the entire loss if it failed. The play ran for forty-four weeks.

Nichols returned to New York, put a company together, rehearsed them, and eventually opened to reviews that lambasted the production. The play floundered and almost closed. Determined, the playwright mortgaged her home, sold her jewels, and borrowed $30,000 to keep the show afloat. After two months, mostly through word of mouth, the play began to catch on with the public. Ultimately, the play's phenomenal success made Anne Nichols a millionaire several times over.

Abie's Irish Rose centers on Abraham Levy, Jewish, and Rose Mary Murphy, Irish, who have married in a Methodist ceremony. When they arrive at his father's store, Abie introduces Rose Mary as Rosie Murpheski. Solomon Levy and his friends, the Cohens, assume the young people are betrothed, so Solomon, eager to see his son married, insists on planning a wedding for the following week with the rabbi officiating. In act 2, as the wedding comes to a close in the next room, Patrick Murphy, thinking his future son-in-law is a fine Irish boy, arrives from Chicago with his old friend Father Whalen. Both fathers are aghast to discover the truth of the situation. While the fathers rail at one another, Rabbi Samuels and Father Whalen learn that they both ministered to troops during the last war. In a spirit of harmony, the rabbi suggests that since "the young folks have made a business of getting married," Father Whalen wed them according to Roman rites. Solomon and Patrick pause long enough in their bickering to hear the priest conclude a third ceremony. "My God! They've done it again!" Murphy exclaims.

The last act occurs on Christmas in the young couple's apartment. Having learned of the birth of a grandchild, the fathers arrive—first Patrick sneaks in with gifts for a granddaughter; then Solomon appears with presents for a boy. Abie and Rose Mary appease both fathers by presenting them with twins, a boy named for Patrick and a girl, Rebecca, for Solomon's late wife. As the grandfathers hold the babies, bells ring. "Vod iss it? A fire?" asks Solomon. "A fire!" retorts Patrick. " 'Tis Christmas! Merry Christmas, Sol!" "Good Yonteff, Pat!" Solomon responds, grinning.

Abie's Irish Rose possesses a simple plot, based on ethnic humor and character disagreements, but even in modern revivals, audiences still relate to its underlying sentimentalities.

[*See also* United States, 1860–1929]

FURTHER READING

Abramson, Doris, and Laurilyn Harris. "Anne Nichols: $1,000,000 Playwright." In *Women in Theatre*, ed. by Helen Krich Chinoy and Linda Walsh Jenkins. New York: Theatre Communications Group, 1981, 1987.

Braggiotti, Mary. "Abie's Rose Grows an Olive Leaf." *New York Post* (June 26, 1943): 6.

Israel, Lee. "The Hit They Love to Hate." *Theatre Week* (August 5–11, 1991): 25–27.

Sherry D. Engle

ABSOLUTE PROHIBITION

After a short, general introduction about the history, meaning and purpose of windows, their misuse is strictly forbidden.

—Adam, Part 1, Scene 1

Absolute Prohibition (*Absolútny zákaz*, 1968) is one of Peter Karvaš's best satirical works, along with *A Big Wig* (1965) and *Experiment Damokles* (1967). *Absolute Prohibition* premiered at the Slovak National Theatre on December 20, 1969, a little more than a year after the Soviet invasion, but it was removed from the repertory after several performances.

Karvaš masterfully develops a simple plot, revealing a musical ability to vary motifs as in jazz improvisation. The decree prohibiting the misuse of windows is the central comedic paradox. Grotesque hyperbole results when the inhabitants of the house, scarred by their experience of the totalitarian regime, not only are afraid to protest the nonsensical decree but actively interpret it themselves. They finally come to the absurd conclusion that the decree prohibits looking out of windows. Karvaš creates a model situation of conflicting views that reveals the different attitudes of the characters. The family drama becomes a powerful satire on the regime as well as a comedy of human nature, not dissimilar to the VÁCLAV HAVEL and György Schwajda type of Theater of the Absurd.

In *Absolute Prohibition* Karvaš attacks the very essence of the regime, which lies in creating an atmosphere of fear, manipulating the people, and dividing them into two categories: the faithful and devoted or the traitors and saboteurs. Mather and Father are simple people who know that it is better to obey under any circumstances. Adam, Mather's brother who lives with them in the flat, is a type who successfully survives all regimes. Only the young revolt and ask unpleasant questions: Andrej, a neighbor and a painter, and Ann, his blind girlfriend, the daughter of Mather and Father. Ann serves as a reminder of reality and brings a tragic element into the play, although the actual story comes to an absurd conclusion. Ironically, those punished are the innocent and harmless who are isolated in their own worlds: blind Ann, who in protest "confesses" to watching out the window, and Andrej, the painter of subjective, unrealistic pictures. Finally, the people in the house wall in their windows: They are not enthusiastic about having to get their oxygen and electricity on allotment, but they accept it. After some time has passed, Adam, who has a good nose for coming changes in society, begins knocking windows into the walls. It is confirmed by a new decree, which, as Gonda, an agent-controller, says, has already been on the books for quite a long while. On Adam's advice, the family leaves the bricks from the holes made in the walls in the apartment, in case they may be needed again in the future. Then, as they watch in surprise, a new, high wall is erected several feet from their windows. The wall may represent the border between free and unfree worlds, between knowledge and darkness; it is another element of violence directed against the citizens. In *Absolute Prohibition* Karvaš not only depicted the political situation in SLOVAKIA; he also prophetically predicted future developments.

FURTHER READING

Felix, Jozef. "Slovo o Petrovi Karvašovi. Doslov" [A word about Peter Karvaš: An epilogue]. In *Absolútny zákaz* [The Absolute Prohibition], by Peter Karvaš. Bratislava: Tatran, 1970.

Štefko, Vladimír. "Znovuobjavený dramatik? Doslov" [A reclaimed dramatist? An epilogue]. In *Veľká parochna a iné hry* [A Big Wig and Other Plays]. Bratislava: LITA, 1990.

Juraj Sebesta

ABSOLÚTNY ZÁKAZ See ABSOLUTE PROHIBITION

ABSURDISM

A world that can be explained by reasoning, however faulty, is a familiar world. But in a universe that is suddenly deprived of illusions and light, man feels a stranger. His is an irremediable exile, because he is deprived of memories of a lost homeland as much as he lacks the hope of a promised land to come. This divorce between man and his life, the actor and his setting, truly constitutes the feeling of Absurdity.

—Albert Camus, *The Myth of Sisyph us*

In modern philosophy and literature, the tenets of existentialism have considerably expanded the sense of the term *absurd* beyond its original application in philosophy to describe logical impossibilities or, in more common parlance, to refer to something ridiculous or untrue. Cast in its most widely recognized and influential mold in JEAN-PAUL SARTRE'S *Nausea* (1938) and *Being and Nothingness* (1943) and ALBERT CAMUS'S *The Myth of Sisyphus* (1942) and its companion novel *The Stranger* (1942), the concept of absurdism became a broadly encompassing framework for portraying the experience of estrangement, uncertainty, isolation, and despair produced by a modern, secularized world in which human existence no longer seemed to make sense. Building on the legacy of Søren Kierkegaard, FRIEDRICH NIETZSCHE, Martin Heidegger, Fyodor Dostoevsky, Franz Kafka, and André Malraux, among other important 19th- and 20th-century precursors, existentialism portrayed absurdism as a condition arising from confrontation with an illogical, nonresponsive universe that condemns humanity to solitude, violence, insignificance, and unanswered metaphysical queries in the face of an inevitable, meaningless death.

Existentialist depictions of irrational, unjustified existence and what Camus termed the "unreasonable silence of the world" reverberated forcefully in the mid-20th century as traditional social, political, moral, and religious values collapsed in a world ravaged by two world wars, heinous Nazi crimes, the explosion of the atomic bomb, perversion of the idealism of the French Resistance into bourgeois Gaullist politics, revelations of the atrocities of Joseph Stalin's regime, rapid expansion of dehumanizing technologies, and the Cold War's ideological divisions, nuclear threats, and devaluing of language by propaganda and jargon.

In the 1950s and early 1960s, absurdism was given another defining and indelible dimension by an international, although predominantly Paris-centered, AVANT-GARDE theater phenomenon widely known as the Theater of the Absurd. The label was invented by drama critic Martin Esslin as the title for his pioneering study of the enigmatic, highly physical, irrational, antipsychological, and linguistically, socially, and culturally irreverent avant-garde plays of SAMUEL BECKETT, EUGENE IONESCO, ARTHUR ADAMOV, JEAN GENET, and HAROLD PINTER, as well as a number of other playwrights working in a similar vein, including WITOLD GOMBROWICZ, FERNANDO ARRABAL, Boris

Vian, JEAN TARDIEU, MAX FRISCH, EDWARD ALBEE, VÁCLAV HAVEL, TOM STOPPARD, and SAM SHEPARD. The label was chosen to highlight the commonality of these otherwise highly diverse plays as compellingly visceral, anti-intellectualizing, blackly comic renderings of the alienation described in less immediate, more cerebral terms by Sartre and Camus.

The principal absurdist playwrights resisted the critical link to existentialist tenets. Ionesco's proposed label "Theater of Derision" captures an essential difference of the "New Theater" (Nouveau Théâtre), as it was often called in France, from existentialism's intellectual emphasis on resistance, revolt, and liberation. In contrast to Sartre's and Camus's attention to a potential human nobility permitting at least a limited transcendence of the "absurd" by means of lucid political or humanitarian choices, absurdist theater depicts farcically derelict misfits, somnambulistic victims of society, bad luck, and manipulative or empty language, and is concerned not with collectivity and authenticity but with individual survival in a brutal, violent—a violence to which they frequently contribute—world. Placelessness, banally interchangeable dialogues and identities, stultifying repetitiveness, and Beckettian "ballast of habit" characterize this theater. Its primary roots are not philosophical or political but the burlesque physicality of ALFRED JARRY'S UBU TRILOGY, the pratfalls and rapid-fire patter of vaudeville and the Marx Brothers, the haunting pathos of Charlie Chaplin's little tramp, DADA's linguistic revolt, SURREALISM's experiments with automatic writing and the oneiric, and especially in its innovative staging, ANTONIN ARTAUD's Theater of Cruelty.

Paradoxically, in this seemingly "dehumanized" theater that draws on darkly irrational sources and eschews linear time, coherent plots, dialogue, and character development, the anguish of absurdism took on its most convincing human dimensions. It portrays as no rationally developed philosophical text could the appalling existential state poignantly described by Adamov: "All I know of myself is that I suffer. And if I suffer, it is because at the origin of myself there is mutilation, separation."

FURTHER READING

Blocker, H. Gene. *Metaphysics of Absurdity*. Washington, D.C.: Univ. Press of Am., 1979.

Bradby, David. *Modern French Drama, 1940–1990*. Cambridge: Cambridge Univ. Press, 1991.

Camus, Albert. *The Myth of Sisyphus and Other Essays*. Tr. by Justin O'Brien. New York: Vintage, 1991.

Esslin, Martin. *The Theatre of the Absurd*. New York: Vintage, 2004.

Gaensbauer, Deborah. *The French Theater of the Absurd*. Boston: Twayne, 1991.

Oaklander, L. Nathan, ed. *Existentialist Philosophy: An Introduction*. Englewood Cliffs, N.J.: Prentice-Hall, 1992.

Serreau, Genvieve. *Histoire du "nouveau théâtre"* [History of "New Theater"]. Paris: Gallimard, 1966.

Deborah Gaensbauer

ACCIDENTAL DEATH OF AN ANARCHIST

DARIO FO'S farce *Accidental Death of an Anarchist* was a response to a bombing outrage in a bank in Milan, Italy, on December 12, 1969, that left sixteen people dead. Later it was shown that the massacre was the work of neofascist extremists, but the police at the time, headed by Luigi Calabresi, blamed anarchists and arrested Pino Pinelli. On the night of December 15 or 16, while still in custody, Pinelli met his death in circumstances that have never been clarified. Official sources suggested, first, that the death was suicide motivated by recognition of guilt and, later, that it was an accident.

Fo's play was the first work staged by La Comune, an acting cooperative established by Fo after his break with "bourgeois theater" in 1968 and the disagreements with Communist Party policy, which led to the schism with his other acting group, Nuova Scena. While written with wit and brio, the play was a highly politicized act of counterinformation, aimed at discrediting media reports of anarchist complicity and at presenting the bombing and Pinelli's death as part of a right-wing threat to Italian democracy. Fo drew material from a court case brought by Calabresi against the left-wing journal *Lotta Continua*, which had mounted a campaign implicating him in Pinelli's death. The trial opened in October 1970, and Fo's play, which changed day by day to incorporate material from the court case, premiered in December of the same year. Calabresi was himself assassinated by terrorists in 1972.

In structure, *Accidental Death* is an imaginary investigation of police conduct held in the very offices where the interrogation of Pinelli, who is never named, took place. The transforming device is that the investigation is conducted by a madman with a genius for disguise and impersonation, who passes himself off as an examining magistrate. All the other characters in the play have their equivalents in the real-life affair—the Inspector being clearly based on Calabresi—but the madman is pure invention, perhaps a Harlequin in modern dress. He hilariously but devastatingly disconcerts the officers by dismantling their story, offering them support to manufacture increasingly extravagant new versions, then reverting to the role of prosecutor. His supposed madness provides an excuse for farcical tumbling and knockabout but does not conceal the guile and cunning with which he makes the policemen contradict themselves. If they were telling the truth, the victim must have had three feet, he concludes at one point. When the journalist, based on the investigative reporter Camilla Cederna, enters, he adopts seemingly ludicrous disguises, as forensic expert or bishop, which are also subtle means of incriminating elements of church and state.

Fo's play has been performed all over the world and has been savored by audiences who know nothing of the circumstances of its conception, largely because of the cleverly constructed and plotted comic mechanisms. But this is tragic farce, a bold and innovative device that revolutionized the nature and range of political theater. The issues are the death of an innocent man and the conspiracy of police and politicians against the people. Farce allowed Fo to combine "laughter with anger" and gave him a means of avoiding catharsis, which he abominated as causing the dissipation of anger, and holding an audience's attention while serious ideas were presented to them.

FURTHER READING

Farrell, Joseph. *Harlequins of the Revolution: Dario Fo and Franca Rame.* London: Methuen, 2001.

Farrell, Joseph, and Antonio Scuderi. *Stage, Text, and Tradition.* Carbondale: Southern Illinois Univ. Press, 2000.

Mitchell, Tony. *Dario Fo: The People's Court Jester.* London: Methuen, 1999.

Joseph Farrell

ACKLAND, RODNEY (1908–1991)

Rodney Ackland died poor and bitter on December 6, 1991, in Surrey, his dramatic canon neglected. His playwriting career basically ended in 1956. Ackland had been seen, negatively, as a dated writer: Like other dramatists who predated the post-1956 theatrical "revolution," he became overlooked by myopic commentators. However, when Ackland died, interest in his work was increasing. Actors, critics, and directors—including Tom Conti, Judi Dench, Nicholas Dromgoole, Sheridan Morley, and Hilary Spurling—were regularly expressing admiration for his unromantic worldview. Revivals of his better-known plays have mushroomed from the mid-1980s onward; Ackland's best-known play *Absolute Hell* (1988) was filmed (in a shortened version) by the British Broadcasting Corporation (BBC) in 1991; and well-introduced, attractively presented editions of his plays are in print.

Ackland, in his eighties, was called on to write new dialogue for *Absolute Hell*. Originally called *The Pink Room* (1952), the play's explicit language and overt homosexual content had been mercilessly excised because of Britain's pre-1968 censoring strictures. Ackland, in effect, executed a sort of inverse bowdlerization. Critics now realize that the unpatriotic, feckless, drink- sodden milieu of *Absolute Hell* has much affinity with, for example, the gin-soaked seediness that Archie Rice's family "enjoy" in JOHN OSBORNE'S THE ENTERTAINER (1957). Ackland's plays retain a gritty, social realism that other prewar plays generally lack.

Born in Essex on May 18, 1908, Ackland's real name was Norman Ackland Bernstein. His mother was a traveling performer, calling herself Ada Rodney; his father was a Jewish businessman, who went bankrupt when Ackland was very young. Never financially fastidious and forgetful about taxes, Ackland always lived in varying states of financial precariousness. Often unconventional, Ackland converted to Buddhism in the late 1940s. He had significant homosexual relationships but married Mabby Poole (died 1972) in 1952. Ackland acted from his teens and wrote plays from the late 1920s until 1956, when *Dead Secret*, his last West End play, was staged. He also acted in films and, more successfully, wrote screenplays, the most acclaimed being the 1949 Thorold Dickinson–directed, Faust-influenced film *The Queen of Spades*. Perhaps because his co-writer Elspeth Grant was a film critic, Ackland's 1954 memoir *The Celluloid Mistress* focuses more on his film career than on the theater. Alfred Hitchcock scholars plunder *The Celluloid Mistress* for anecdotes about Hitchcock, on whose early films Ackland often collaborated.

Ackland dramatized Russian works by MIKHAIL BULGAKOV, FYODOR DOSTOEVSKY, and ALEKSANDR OSTROVSKY. His 1949 theatrical version of WILLIAM SOMERSET MAUGHAM's story "Before the Party," about the fraught wife of an abusive drunk, was reviewed coldly. Other than *Absolute Hell*, Ackland's most famous original play is *Strange Orchestra* (1932). Although *Strange Orchestra*, which features a quest for purposefulness among a group of seemingly aimless Chelsea socialites, received mixed reviews, it is noted as the first major play that John Gielgud directed. Gielgud insisted that Ackland "deals with real people" in his plays. Altogether Ackland wrote sixteen original plays in various genres, a dozen or so screenplays, and around a dozen theatrical adaptations. The original plays in particular are now finding a readership and an audience that were absent between 1956 and 1985.

[*See also* England]

SELECT PLAYS: *Strange Orchestra* (1932); *The Pink Room* (1952); *Dead Secret* (1956); *Absolute Hell* (1988)

FURTHER READING

Chothia, Jean. *English Drama of the Early Modern Period, 1890–1940.* London: Longman, 1996.

Dromgoole, Nicholas. Introduction to *Absolute Hell*, by Rodney Ackland. London: Oberon, 1995.

——. Introduction to *Plays: One*, by Rodney Ackland. London: Oberon, 1997.

Duff, Charles. *The Lost Summer: The Heyday of the West End Theatre.* London: Nick Hern, 1995.

Hastings, Michael. Introduction to *Plays: Two*, by Rodney Ackland. London: Oberon, 2000.

Kevin De Ornellas

ACTING

HARLEY GRANVILLE-BARKER, actor, playwright, and director, said in *On Dramatic Method* (1931) that the "history of the theater could be viewed as a never-determined struggle between dramatist and actor for pre-eminence." He went on to say that in this struggle the dramatist is the first into the field. "The great periods in drama, the periods of renascence and development, have almost invariably been dominated by dramatists who knew so much of the theater and of actors and their acting that they had no illusions left about them" (1931).

Nothing better demonstrates the truth of his remarks than the revolution in drama and theater that occurred in the 19th century, when the art of acting underwent a revolutionary change, a change that was imperative because of the demands of the realistic and naturalist playwrights. One reason that HENRIK IBSEN is commonly thought of as the father of modern drama is that his characters and subtle plots required a new kind of acting. Similarly, AUGUST STRINDBERG with his *MISS JULIE* (1888) and ANTON CHEKHOV with his *THE SEAGULL* (1895) called for actors who would not simply play or perform but who would be the character.

Before Ibsen, well-trained actors learned techniques that would allow them to be seen and heard and understood, often in theaters that were large and cavernous with stages that were poorly lit. Good vocal delivery and standardized gestures provided the means for clear communication. Actors did not incarnate their characters; they presented their characters to the audience. If they had tried to create the illusion of complete reality, they would at times have had to lower their voices to the point of inaudibility or turn their backs on the audience. To be real in the artificial world of the theater was (and is) quite difficult, requiring avoidance of old techniques and development of new ones. It took two generations of actors to develop them. In FRANCE, EMILE ZOLA, chief advocate of NATURALISM, complained about "theatre voice" and "false recital" of lines, the product of academic training in acting schools or conservatories. In Russia, KONSTANTIN STANISLAVSKY complained about actors who made themselves the center of attention, destroying the illusion of reality. Stars "made their entrances amidst ovations and began their performances by thanking the audience. There was applause again on their exit and they would return to take their bows." The first task confronting Stanislavsky as director was to break the actor's habit of "looking across the footlights at the audience, exchanging compliments with them and intoxicating himself with declamatory speech and theatrical poses" (Stanislavsky, tr. 1924).

Some of the more successful, innovative productions were those that did not rely on academically trained actors. Stanislavsky in Moscow and ANDRÉ ANTOINE in Paris worked with talented (or at least aspiring) amateurs who were not classically trained.

The mature, realistic plays of Ibsen, beginning with *A DOLL'S HOUSE* (1879), became the testing ground for actors who hoped to advance their art. Accordingly, for those who liked the old ways and loved the theater as a place of artifice, Ibsen was a bane. Said one of them: "This crazy apothecary will ruin our whole theater." But for those who wanted to advance the frontiers of acting, Ibsen was a rewarding challenge. German actress Louise Dumont said in 1909 that the old theater world had to collapse in order for a new one to arise. The actor had to express the deepest emotions without resorting to the flowery language or the tempestuous speeches that might transport the audience; the actor had to use the plain, simple language of ordinary speech. Dumont put the actor's problem very succinctly: Ibsen "demands the greatest self-denial on the part of the actor, the profoundest grasp of the poet's intentions along with the abandonment of all the actor's freedom. There is the conflict that will not easily nor quickly be resolved."

The greatest actress of her generation, Eleanora Duse had said the same thing a few years earlier.

> To save the theater, the theater must be destroyed, the actors and actresses must all die of the plague. They poison the air, they make art impossible. It is not drama that they play, but pieces for the theater. . . . We must bow before the poet, even when it seems to us that he does wrong. He is a poet, he has seen something, he has seen it in that way; we must accept his vision, because it is vision.

Inevitably, new schools of acting arose, replacing the academies of classic acting and emphasizing complete identification with the part. Stanislavsky, who established the MOSCOW ART THEATER, was by far the most articulate of the new teachers, and his theories and practices were adopted and modified, especially in America, by Richard Boleslavsky (1889–1937), Lee Strasberg (1901–1982), Stella Adler (1901–1992), and others, under a program of actor training that came to be known as "The Method," in distinction to Stanislavsky's "System." The Method put an even heavier emphasis on psychology, the psychology of both character and actor.

In the struggle between the actor and the dramatist, the best actors soon found that the realistic theater, instead of limiting them, offered new opportunities for creativity. By complete immersion in the part, the actor often displayed an artistic vision that complemented the author's. Granville-Barker remarked on the power of good acting to transform the written script into superb drama. "I have seen a performance of Tchekov's 'Cherry Orchard' in Moscow, and to read the play afterwards was like reading the libretto of an opera—missing the music. Great credit to the actors; no discredit to Tchekov" (*The Exemplary Theatre*, 1922).

Sometimes the actor, having immersed himself or herself in the part, finds means unknown to the author of filling in the blanks left in the script. Because of insightful acting, the play in performance may be quite different from the play as read.

Ibsen has often been faulted for not making believable the transition in Nora from the playful wife of the first act of *A Doll's House* to the independent woman she suddenly becomes at the end. In the last act, Nora realizes she has never really known her husband. Threatened with scandal, he blames her for having caused it. But the scandal was the result of her having saved his life, and she expects him to take the blame. Recognizing how little she has understood her husband, she is transformed. Her voice, playful and teasing in the first act, now turns cold and hard. Her once smiling lips now express ice-cold disdain. When at her insistence they exchange their wedding rings, hers falls to the floor, and he picks it up. She thanks him with a curt nod.

This is how Eleanora Duse played the scene in 1892. But most of it is not in the script. The long discussion between the spouses was supposed to explain what lay behind the change.

To Duse, however, the change was not an intellectual process; it was emotional. Her Nora was a woman who had been slapped in the face by the man she thought she knew and loved. Duse's knowledge of human behavior told her that emotion precedes thought, and she made the most of the hint contained in Ibsen's stage direction: Nora speaks "with a stiffening expression."

Sometimes the sensitive actor, having in weeks of rehearsal re-created the author's character, can justifiably violate an important stage direction. In Chekhov's THE CHERRY ORCHARD (1904), at the end of the third act news comes in the middle of a dance party that the orchard has been sold. In Chekhov's script, Madame Ranevskaya, the owner of the estate, breaks down and sobs. In the performance at the Moscow Art Theater, she sat unmoving, not crying, while the dance whirled about her, and the new owner exulted in his acquisition. Yet by her silence and inaction, Ranevskaya completely dominated the scene.

On occasion the actor is most eloquent when silent. Those who saw Helene Weigel's silent scream in BERTOLT BRECHT's MOTHER COURAGE (1951) will never forget it. And those who witnessed Duse's blush in HERMANN SUDERMANN's *Magda* (1895) could only marvel at the actress's complete involvement with the character.

Either through their particular stage presence (star quality) or their insight into the part, actors can greatly affect the audience's interpretation of the play. A notable example is the way in which Marlon Brando enlarged the role of Stanley in A STREETCAR NAMED DESIRE (1947) from the mere brute and rapist he is in TENNESSEE WILLIAMS's script to a vital, life-giving human being. As a result, the play became more disturbing and more tragic. As written, Blanche represents culture, civilization, the tender feelings, love in the higher sense, but Brando won the sympathies of many in the audience by incarnating life itself, especially the generative drive. Reviewing the play before its New York premiere, a critic in one Philadelphia newspaper said the play was about a happy marriage destroyed by a neurotic woman, an interpretation quite contrary to Williams's intentions. On the subconscious level, the average spectator prefers the healthy animal to the neurotic creature. Blanche calls Stanley an ape, but played by Brando, he was the embodiment of vitality. When he swept the plates off the table and sent them crashing to the floor, a violent act that anticipates the rape scene, many in the audience broke out into loud applause.

Oswald in Ibsen's GHOSTS (1883) is suffering from syphilis. August Lindberg, who created the part in Scandinavia, was not a classically trained actor, and to present a naturalistic portrait, he consulted doctors and observed patients. He adopted a slightly shambling walk characteristic of the last phase of the disease, a physical symptom that Ibsen does not mention. This sensationalist performance made Oswald rather than his mother, Mrs. Alving, the central character and changed the whole slant of the play. Rather than being a drama play about the battle within the mother, it became a deterministic, naturalistic drama about the inescapable force of the past and her son's decline into dementia.

Inevitably, the proponents of THEATRICALITY reacted against the naturalistic theater. Two of Stanislavsky's pupils, VSEVOLOD MEYERHOLD and Eugene Vakhtangov, led the rebellion, directing productions in which the audience never forgot for a moment that they were in a theater. It was not, of course, the old theater of declamation and standardized gestures. It was an immensely creative theater, calling for actors of great physical skill.

Vakhtangov, in his diary, contrasted the new revolutionary theater with Stanislavsky's Chekhovian theater: "The crushing of theatrical banality by means of the conventional theater has led Meyerhold to true theatricality. Hence the formula: the audience must not for a moment forget that it is in a theater. Stanislavsky, through his demolition of banality, has arrived at the formula: the audience must forget that it is in a theater" (1934).

The Russian Revolution inspired the new theatricality—a revolution in the theater that paralleled the Communist revolution. Vakhtangov spelled it out, declaring, "Meyerhold has never felt 'today,' but he has felt 'tomorrow.' Stanislavsky has never felt 'tomorrow;' he has only felt 'today.' " While the techniques associated with realistic acting were based largely on psychology, Russian theatricalism was oriented toward politics. The development of realistic acting in the Western world coincided with the rise of the middle class. The movement away from it—the return to theatricality—was encouraged by the rise of communism.

The anti-Stanislavsky movement spread to Germany and influenced ERWIN PISCATOR and Bertolt Brecht, both advocates of political revolution. They were in tune with the Russian avant-garde in deemphasizing the element of illusion but differed from them in regarding the actor essentially as a mind rather than as a body. Actors distanced themselves from their roles emotionally in order to engage with them intellectually. Brecht's theories of acting, especially what he called the ALIENATION EFFECT, exercised a profound effect on theater in the latter half of the 20th century. But on the whole, in the Western world, Stanislavsky has remained the dominant force.

[*See also* Directing Plays; Dramatic Dialogue; Epic Theater; Realism]

FURTHER READING

Cima, Gay Gibson. "Discovering Signs: The Emergence of the Critical Actor in Ibsen." *Theatre Journal* 35, no. 1 (March 1983): 5–22.

Cole, Toby, and Helen Crich Chinoy, eds. *Actors on Acting*. Rev. ed. New York: Crown, 1970.

Lewes, George Henry. "On Natural Acting." In *On Actors and the Art of Acting*. New York: Grove, n.d.

Stanislavsky, Konstantin. *Stanislavsky on the Art of the Stage*. Tr. by David Magarshack. New York: Hill & Wang, 1961.

Evert Sprinchorn

ADAMOV, ARTHUR (1908–1970)

Playwright, translator, essayist, and poet Arthur Adamov is remembered primarily as a contributor to the Theater of the Absurd, Martin Esslin's term for the radical new DRAMATURGY of mid-20th-century French playwrights.

Adamov was born in Kislovodsk, Russia, on August 23, 1908, to a wealthy oilman of Armenian descent. His family moved to GERMANY when he was four, then to SWITZERLAND after the outbreak of World War I. The family fortunes were destroyed after their Russian oil wells were nationalized following the 1917 Revolution. Despite his varied cultural influences, Adamov wrote in French and considered it his first language.

Adamov settled in Paris in 1924, where he associated with the surrealists, including JEAN COCTEAU and ANTONIN ARTAUD. In 1938 Adamov suffered a nervous breakdown and began his first major literary endeavor, *The Confession* (*L'Aveu*, published in 1946), a confessional autobiography that reveals the author's profound sense of alienation in an antagonistic world. Part of *The Confession* was written while Adamov was in a concentration camp in Argelès. He returned to Paris after the liberation in 1941. In 1947 he met Jacqueline Trehet, who became his wife in 1961 and with whom he later collaborated on radio plays.

His career as a playwright began with the completion of his first major play, *The Parody* (*La Parodie*), in 1947. It was not produced until 1952, after the premiere of *The Invasion* (*L'invasion*), his second play.

Adamov's plays examine man's frustrating and ultimately futile attempt to locate meaning. He dramatizes this continuous, desperate search through absurd and darkly comic stage action, which he conceived as a literal representation of the unconscious and the conscious and which depended heavily on sound and visual effects. For example, a handless clock hovers over figures preoccupied with time in *The Parody*, and the pinball machine in *Ping Pong* (*Le Ping-Pong*, 1955) serves as the play's locus of action and its central metaphor.

Adamov's episodic dramaturgy reveals links to EXPRESSIONISM, SURREALISM, Franz Kafka's fiction, Artaud, AUGUST STRINDBERG, and BERTOLT BRECHT. In *The Invasion* Adamov folds the irrational into a seemingly realistic form, a tactic related to the dreamlike logic of Strindberg's A DREAM PLAY (1901). *The Big and Small Maneuver* (*La grande et la petite manoeuvre*, 1950), *The Professor Taranne* (*Le Professeur Taranne*, 1951), and others share an affinity with Strindberg's innovative use of dramatic structure.

In 1957, Adamov stepped away from the abstraction and introspection of his earlier plays and engaged directly with contemporary politics in *Paolo Paoli* (1957), a play indebted to Brecht's *Saint Joan of the Stockyards* (1929). *Spring of '71* (*Le Printemps 71*, 1961), and *The Politics of Waste* (*La Politique des restes*, 1962) follow this political trend. In the 1950s and 1960s, Adamov began translating and adapting classic plays by Strindberg, Georg Büchner, Nikolai Gogol, ANTON CHEKHOV, and Heinrich von Kleist.

Adamov died in Paris of a barbiturate overdose on March 16, 1970, having never received international recognition at the level of SAMUEL BECKETT or EUGENE IONESCO, but his achievements nonetheless secured his reputation as a central figure of the absurdist movement. His plays are still occasionally produced in France but are left largely to academic study abroad.

[*See also* Absurdism]

SELECT PLAYS: *The Parody* (*La Parodie*, 1947); *The Invasion* (*L'invasion*, 1949); *The Big and Small Maneuvers* (*La grande et la petite manoeuvre*, 1950); *Disorder* (*Le Désordre*, 1950); *The Direction of the March* (*Le Sens de la marche*, 1951); *The Professor Taranne* (*Le Professeur Taranne*, 1951); *All Against All* (*Tous contre tous*, 1952); *As We Were* (*Comme nous avons eté*, 1953); *The Recoveries* (*Les Retrouvailles*, 1953); *Ping Pong* (*Le Ping-Pong*, 1955); *Paolo Paoli* (1957); *The Lament of the Ridiculous* (*La Complainte du ridicule*, 1958); *The Apoliticals* (*Les Apolitiques*, 1958); *Intimacy* (*Intimité*, 1958); *I Am Not French* (*Je ne suis pas Français*, 1959); *Dead Souls* (*Les Ames mortes*, 1960); *Spring of '71* (*Le Printemps 71*, 1961); *Present Time* (*Le Temps vivant*, 1962); *The Politics of Waste* (*La politique des restes*, 1962); *Finita la commedia* (1964); *Saint Europe* (*Sainte Europe*, 1966); *Mister Moderate* (*M. le Modéré*, 1967); *Off Limits* (1968); *Ferdinand de Lesseps* [incomplete] (1970); *If Summer Should Return* (*Si l'été revenait*, 1970); *The Two Marys* (*Les Deux Marie* [incomplete], 1970)

FURTHER READING

Adamov, Arthur. *Théâtre*. Vol. 1–4. Paris: Gallimard, 1953–1968.
Bradby, David. *Adamov*. London: Grant & Cutler Ltd., 1975.
Dukore, Bernard F., and Daniel C. Gerould. *Avant-Garde Drama: A Casebook*. New York: Bantam, 1969.
Esslin, Martin. *The Theatre of the Absurd*. New York: Anchor Bks., 1961.
McCann, John J. *The Theater of Arthur Adamov*. Chapel Hill: Univ. of North Carolina Press, 1975.
Reilly, John H. *Arthur Adamov*. New York: Twayne, 1974.

Wendy A. Weckwerth

ADDING MACHINE

The Adding Machine, ELMER RICE's only expressionist play, was originally produced by the Theatre Guild. The first production, directed by Philip Moeller and featuring landmark scenography by Modernist American designer Lee Simonson, opened on March 19, 1923.

In seven scenes the play dramatizes the descent of Mr. Zero, a neurotic accountant who is henpecked by his strident wife. His only joys seem to be watching women through windows and bickering with his female colleague Daisy. On the 25th anniversary of his employment, Zero is told he is being replaced by an adding machine. Enraged, he kills his boss and is ultimately executed for the murder. Unlike nearly all other expressionist plays, both German and American, *The Adding Machine* does not end at the moment of the protagonist's death.

The last three scenes take place in Zero's afterlife—first at his gravesite and later in the Elysian Fields, a pastoral location of peaceful rest for the dead which Rice has borrowed from Greek mythology. He discovers that Daisy committed suicide after his execution because she was secretly in love with him. Zero reveals that in life he, too, had tender feelings for her. The two share a brief idyllic fantasy in the Elysian Fields before Zero leaves her to try and work his way back into life. Finally we see Zero in a purgatorial office where he returns to his job of accounting, this time on an adding machine. There he works for another 25 years, hoping for release or reward for his efforts; instead, he is sent back to Earth to be born again and live out the same servile life he has lived ever since his soul was new.

> Well—time's up! Back you go—back to your sunless groove—the raw material of slums and wars—the ready prey of the first jingo or demagogue or political adventurer who takes the trouble to play upon your ignorance and credulity and provincialism.

Rice presents Zero as voyeuristic, adulterous, cowardly, petty, and racist. He is the ignoble modern American Everyman trapped by capitalism and ignorance.

> A waste product. A slave to a contraption of steel and iron. The animal's instincts, but none of his strength and skill. The animal's appetites, but not his unashamed indulgence of them.

This depiction of the dehumanization of modern man is a common theme in expressionist drama.

Spectacle is especially interesting in *The Adding Machine*. When Zero is fired, Rice describes the stage revolving wildly, flooding with theatrical sound effects: "the wind, the waves, the galloping horses, the locomotive whistle, the sleigh bells, the automotive siren. . . . The noise is deafening, maddening, unendurable. Suddenly it culminates in a terrific peal of thunder." These chaotic visual and aural effects serve to express Zero's shock at losing his place in life. Another example of Rice's theatrical use of sound is the mysterious offstage noise of "a sharp clicking such as is made by the operation of the keys and levers of an adding machine." Only Zero hears the sound, a ghostly reminder of the adding machine that took away his livelihood in life and enslaved him in the afterlife.

[*See also* United States, 1860–1929]

FURTHER READING

Burroughs, William S. *The Adding Machine: Selected Essays*. New York: Seaver Bks., 1986.

Koritz, Amy. "Drama and the Rhythm of Work in the 1920s." *Theatre Journal* 53, no. 4 (December 2001): 551–567.

Rice, Elmer. *Minority Report: An Autobiography*. New York: Simon & Schuster, 1963.

DeAnna M. Toten Beard

THE ADMIRABLE CRICHTON

James Matthew (J. M.) BARRIE's *The Admirable Crichton* was first performed in 1902. To critics and audiences, it was clear that the play challenged existing social hierarchies.

The action begins in London, in the household of Lord Loam, where Loam regularly compels his servants to dine as equals with their employer. Loam's butler Crichton believes, however, that nature dictates in all societies a division into master and servants. Two months later, all of the household's members find themselves wrecked on a tropical island. On the island, Crichton establishes his leadership: It is he who can most effectively hunt, cook, build, and organize. Over the next two years, Crichton becomes uncrowned king of the island, which he eventually equips with various modern conveniences. In the final act, though, the party is shown back in London, having been rescued by a passing ship. The upper classes, we discover, have rewritten events to erase Crichton's leadership—to their narrative, Crichton mysteriously, perhaps even tragically, assents.

The Darwinian background to the story is clear. The island is a natural environment in which the struggle for survival selects the fittest members of the human species. Indeed, to the struggle against the environment Barrie adds an element of sexual selection. On the island, the upper-class fop, Ernest Woolley, is an irrelevance to the womenfolk. Instead, Tweeny the maid and Loam's daughters Mary and Agatha compete with each other to be Crichton's "mate."

How seriously to take this thesis is another matter. The play seems to argue that British society has become decadent, enslaved to a hereditary caste whose supremacy is preserved only artificially. Only a cataclysm, of which the island is a scaled-down version, can install a new and deserving ruling class.

On the other hand, there is much in the play—comic and objectionable—that challenges this reading. Crichton's development of the island is beyond plausibility: In two years, he installs a dam, a sawmill, and electric lighting. Does Barrie here bolster, or simply mock, the "Robinson Crusoe" self-image of a middle-class audience that feels unjustly rewarded by the British aristocracy?

Crichton's rule is also rather sinister to 21st-century eyes. One of his first actions is to duck Ernest's head in water for speaking out of turn. This dictatorial bent intensifies. By the end of act 3, when he is on the verge of marrying Lady Mary, Crichton even suspects he may be an ancient king, reincarnated in modern society. Many will also have difficulties accepting the submissiveness to Crichton of the females on the island. Lady Mary, for example, like the other women, adores Crichton and longs to sit by his feet as his servant.

Indeed, whatever the play's overall meaning, it displays an eerie prescience. Just over a decade after *The Admirable Crichton*'s first performance, European society was shaken to the core by the cataclysm of the Great War. From this chaos there ensued a more just distribution of rewards in society; yet also, of course, there came the rise of European dictators Francisco Franco,

Benito Mussolini, and Adolf Hitler. Where the enigmatic Crichton himself stands between the poles of meritocracy and fascism is a matter of continued and fascinating debate.

[*See also* England, 1860–1940]

FURTHER READING

Geduld, Harry M. *Sir James Barrie*. New York: Twayne, 1971.

Jack, R. D. S. *The Road to the Never Land: A Reassessment of J. M. Barrie's Dramatic Art*. Aberdeen: Aberdeen Univ. Press, 1991.

Ormond, Leonée. *J. M. Barrie*. Edinburgh: Scottish Acad. Press, 1987.

Gavin Miller

ADVENT

The five-act *Advent: A Mystery Play* (*Advent: Ett mysterium*) was written by AUGUST STRINDBERG in 1898 and published together with CRIMES AND CRIMES in 1899 in a volume titled *At Higher Court* (*Vid högre rätt*); it was first performed at the Kammerspiele in Munich in 1915. When subtitling his play *ett mysterium*, Strindberg wished to activate both meanings of the Swedish noun: "a medieval play based on biblical material" and "a reality that cannot be understood, but is the object of belief."

At the play's opening, the Judge and his Wife sit in their vineyard in front of a mausoleum built as a symbol of their lives. Self-righteously, they praise their own good fortune and rejoice at the misfortunes of others. A procession of shadows comes out of the mausoleum: Death with his scythe, a beheaded sailor, the Judge with a rope about his neck, and many more. The Devil, dressed as a poor schoolteacher, beats the couple with a rod. A hailstorm destroys their harvest. The Wife is taken to a ball with chalky-white guests. The Judge is brought before a court and condemned without anyone being present. In the end the Wife freezes to death in a marshland, and the Judge is stoned to death by those he has condemned unjustly. The couple meet in Hell, where they receive, as a Christmas present, a children's peep-show theater in which they can see all their evil deeds. Chastened at last, they discover the star of Advent and the manger with the Christ child.

In Strindberg's words, "a fairy tragedy with mysticism," *Advent* is a strange mixture of childish and even sentimental elements, in the tradition of Charles Dickens and Hans Christian Andersen, and Swedenborgian elements such as corrective spirits charged with the devastation and regeneration of erring humankind.

As Jacobs (1991) has pointed out, the play opens with a striking contrast in vision:

> The Judge and the Wife look very different to us than they do to each other and to themselves: his costume, dating from the 1820s, links him with his double, the Unjust Judge, who was once executed on the spot where the mausoleum now stands; the Wife (with her kerchief, cane, glasses, and snuffbox) is identical with her double, the Witch, whose ballgown she later borrows. As if we were looking at X-rays of the Judge and the Wife, we see their inner corruption.

A striking symbol is the dancing sunbeam, the *solkatt* in Swedish, meaning literally "sun-cat." For the double protagonist the sun-cat eventually becomes a searing spotlight. The Judge sees the Wife for the witch she is, and his criminal nature is revealed to her. In the conciliatory ending the sun-cat is transformed into the star of Bethlehem.

Expressionistically grotesque is the ghostlike ball in the Waiting Room, peopled by cripples, beggars, and criminals as well as by the seven deadly sins. A Swedenborgian place where people are brought to be tested after death, the Waiting Room is a pregnant symbol with repercussions in later drama (PAR LAGERKVIST, JEAN-PAUL SARTRE, SAMUEL BECKETT).

[*See also* Sweden]

FURTHER READING

Jacobs, Barry. "Strindberg's *Advent* and *Brott och brott*: Sagospel and Comedy in a Higher Court." In *Strindberg and Genre*, ed. by Michael Robinson. Norwich: Norvik Press, 1991.

Ollén, Gunnar. *Strindbergs dramatik* [Strindberg's plays]. Stockholm: Sveriges Radios förlag, 1982.

Stockenström, Göran. *Ismael i öknen: Strindberg som mystiker* [Ishmael in the desert: Strindberg as mystic]. Uppsala: Acta Universitatis Upsaliensis, Historia Litterarum, 5, 1972 [English summary].

Egil Törnqvist

ADVENT: ETT MYSTERIUM *See* ADVENT

THE ADVENTURES OF A BLACK GIRL IN SEARCH OF GOD

> *Heaven is Negro Creek.*
> —Abendigo, Act 2

DJANET SEARS's play *The Adventures of a Black Girl in Search of God*, first performed in February 2002 in an Obsidian Theatre Company production directed by Sears herself, reflects many theatrical influences. With their rounded characterization, individual scenes owe a debt to 19th-century NATURALISM. Moments of high farce—such as the flawed refurbishment of a dismantled replica dinosaur skeleton—recall 20th-century entertainments. The extensive use of a large, mobile chorus echoes the dramatic traditions that Sears witnessed in Benin, Africa. Significant facts are detailed—including the history of Canada's pioneering black resident Oliver Le Jeune, the role of Captain Runchy's Colored Militia in 1812's war against the United States, and the racist murder of James Byrd—in a manner reminiscent of the didactic EXPRESSIONISM of BERTOLT BRECHT.

Politically, the play is centered on the context of the real-life, mid-1990s controversy surrounding the Holland Township decision to rename Negro Creek Road, a symbolically important highway in western Ontario. Septuagenarian blacks, including

Abendigo, the title character, Rainey's terminally ill father, resolve to confront the Township's decision. Supposedly motivated by political correctness, the authorities plan to rename the road after a white settler. This is seen as an attack on black history, one as equally racist as the desecration of Pastor Michael's church. The actions of Abendigo and his ailment-suffering, aged cohorts are laughable: They steal objects that they believe demean the black man—they steal 357 black garden gnomes. But a more meaningful theft is executed when they "reclaim" a uniform worn by a black soldier of 1812 from a museum. The "heist" is successful, and Abendigo is buried with a strip from the uniform. He has always stressed the continuity between the various generations of Negro Creek communities. For Abendigo, "Negro Creek is heaven," a place where the souls of the dead and the living unite: Fighting the whites' name-changing violation is worth breaking any law for, he insists.

Despite the medically trained Rainey's horror at her father's exertions, she is ultimately inspired by his rousing defense of black identity. She begins to confront her own demons. Rainey's loss of her young child Janie caused the breakdown of her marriage to Pastor Michael, her departure from medical practice, an eating disorder, and her loss of religious faith. The play's title is an ironic allusion to George Bernard Shaw's novella *The Adventures of the Black Girl in Her Search for God* (1932). Shaw's African heroine finds (albeit problematic) fulfillment, but Rainey, Sears's North American African heroine, loses her spiritual direction. A recurrent complaint of Rainey is the failure of God to prevent suffering in the world, such as that of Rainey's meningitis-racked daughter and the horrendous murder of Byrd. Rainey even intends to write a thesis called "The Death of God and Angels."

The decision to rename Negro Creek Road is reversed: The play ends with black dignity triumphantly intact and with a coincident romantic reunion for Rainey and Michael, but the characters cannot believe in the redemptive powers of God. Even Pastor Michael admits that although he sees the church as a vital support mechanism, he does not believe his own message about God's benevolent omniscience.

[*See also* Canada]

FURTHER READING

Breon, Robin. "Interview with Djanet Sears: A Black Girl in Search of God." *Aislesay Toronto*, 2004. http://www.aislesay.com/ONT-SEARS.html.

Filichia, Peter. "Theatre in Toronto [including review of *The Adventures*]." *TheaterMania.com*, 2003. http://www.theatermania.com/content/news.cfm?int_news_id=4175.

King, Joyce. *Hate Crime: The Story of a Dragging in Jasper, Texas*. New York: Pantheon Bks., 2002.

Sears, Djanet. *The Adventures of a Black Girl in Search of God*. Toronto: Playwrights Canada Press, 2003.

Shaw, George Bernard. *The Adventures of the Black Girl in Her Search for God*. London: Constable, 1932.

Kevin De Ornellas

AFGHANISTAN

Although three decades of war in Afghanistan have inspired a number of Western playwrights to address its causes and effects in very moving plays, the extended period of conflict has also discouraged the development of any dramatic tradition among Afghan writers. As in many of the Islamic countries of southwest Asia, there has been no native tradition of formal dramatic literature in Afghanistan. Where an interest in drama has taken root in the broader region, it has been a product of colonialism. As a result, in postcolonial societies, either interest in drama has waned or the Western traditions have become transformed through some synthesis with native cultural and literary traditions.

The lack of any dramatic tradition in Afghan literature can be traced to several factors that have actually predated the recent series of conflicts. Much of the country is very rural and remote, if not wholly inaccessible, and the few cities are small and isolated. Although cosmopolitan centers are not absolutely necessary to the development of a dramatic tradition, their absence is a major impediment. In addition, the country has never been as thoroughly colonized as others have been, and the nation is composed of distinct tribal groups, with often competing cultural traditions that are connected most pointedly by their shared suspicion of outside influences.

Afghanistan has not been, in any sense of the word, a "playful" place, even discounting the series of wars that have completely disrupted its political, economic, and social life. Ironically, the Soviets might have encouraged the development of drama in Afghanistan if the insurgency had not made any public gatherings extremely hazardous. Following the victory of the *mujahideen* over the Soviet-backed government and the emergence of the Taliban as the governing force in Afghanistan, staging a theatrical production was unthinkable and would have been treated as a criminal enterprise subject to severe, if not capital, punishment.

Somewhat ironically, this latest chapter in Afghanistan's history of conflict has attracted the most attention in the West, where the Taliban's code of fundamentalist Islamic justice has been perceived as outrageously unjust. Not surprisingly, given the political and media attention to the Taliban's brutal repression of women, the three most acclaimed plays treating the recent conditions in the country, as well as several of the less widely known plays on the topic, have featured female characters.

Tony Kushner's first play since his great success with *Angels in America* (1991–1992), *Homebody/Kabul* (2001) was actually written and in pre-production before the terrorist attacks of September 11, 2001, and the subsequent American campaign in Afghanistan against the Taliban and Al-Qaeda.

The play is divided into the two sections separated by the slash in the title. In *Homebody*, a woman sits alone in her living room somewhere in the United Kingdom and in an hourlong monologue reveals a good deal about her circumstances and her eccentricities. She is dependent on prescription medications that she takes for chronic depression, and she amuses herself by discovering odd words with a limited currency. But her major preoccupation is a fascination with Afghanistan that has evolved to include a romantic adventure with an Afghan haberdasher. In *Kabul*, her husband and daughter are introduced as they search for her in the Afghan capital. She has apparently gone off in search of her haberdasher and has disappeared among the material and cultural wreckage of the country. Her husband and daughter become acquainted with a series of characters, some Afghans and other foreigners, who eccentrically manifest the effects of continuous civil turmoil, random terror, and dislocation felt on many levels. The play juxtaposes Western and Central Asian views of the world, but in the Homebody's disappearance into an environment as seemingly hopeless as her own obsessions, the play suggests the strange cultural synergy between escapist fantasy and bleak reality that has long defined Afghanistan to outsiders.

Bina Sharif is a Pakistani American playwright who has accumulated impressive credits as a performer in her own works as well as those of other playwrights. She has presented her one-woman drama *Afghan Woman* (2002) at community and university theaters throughout the United States and Europe. Written after the September 11 attacks, the play presents a portrait of a representative Afghan woman who describes her long struggle to survive with some dignity through the series of tumultuous conflicts that led up to the even more terrible repression of women's rights under the Taliban. During the entire performance, this woman speaks from behind a *burqa* or veil. In another of her plays, *Democracy in Islam* (2002), Sharif focuses on the responses of a Pakistani American family to the pervasive anti-Islamic sentiment in America following the terrorist attacks.

William Mastrosimone's *The Afghan Women* (2003) focuses on three Afghan women who have been made homeless by the almost incessant violence of the last three decades. Loosely modeled on the classic Greek drama *The Trojan Women*, Mastrosimone's play explores the paradox that while women have been terribly victimized by the violence in Afghanistan and in many ways have been treated as scapegoats for the country's instability, it is the determination and perseverance of Afghan women that have kept the country from falling into such anarchy that any vestige of community might have ceased to be a possibility.

FURTHER READING

Davis, Tracy C. "Extremities and Masterpieces: A Feminist Paradigm of Art and Politics." In *Feminist Theatre and Theory*, ed. by Helene Keyssar. New York: St. Martin's, 1996.

Lafferty, Mera Moore. "From Islamabad to New York City: Bina Sharif's Spiritual Politics." *Text and Presentation: The Journal of the Comparative Drama Conference* 23 (April 2003): 57–69.

Minwalla, Framji. "Tony Kushner's *Homebody/Kabul*: Staging History in a Post-Colonial World." *Theater* 33, no. 1 (2003): 29–43.

Reston, James, Jr. "A Prophet in His Time: Premonition and Reality in Tony Kushner's *Homebody/Kabul*." *American Theatre* 19 (March 2002): 28–30, 50–53.

Martin Kich

AFRICA

The term *modern drama* is a particularly complicated idea within which broad historical and cultural issues conflict and contest each other. In Africa, dramatic literatures, theories regarding their interpretations, and the performance traditions with which they engage their audiences are as diverse as the continent's peoples, cultures, and nations. All cultural practices in Africa illustrate the varied contacts of African peoples with themselves as well as with others from other worlds, thereby complicating any simple classifications of drama on the continent. However, what dramatic literatures and the theatrical traditions they enunciate have in common is that they constitute a frontier within which cultures—varieties of indigenous forms and foreign ones, the literary and oral, the secular and religious—intertwine, conflict, or are integrated into the cosmopolitan outlook of each society. Such a premise suggests that Africa's endogenous historical movements, as well as the exogenous cultures they encountered, frame and direct the particular identity of its ancient and modern drama. The drama of the griots (court historians who, using their oratorical and musical skills, document as well as contextualize the ruling king in the history of his people) in countries we know today as Guinea, Mali, and Senegal is heavily mediated by the exploits of various emperors who ruled the Songhai and Mali empires, just as the nationalist drama of Nigeria's FEMI OSOFISAN contests the neocolonial politics of his country. However, regardless of these generalizations, Africa's particular historical entry into what we know as the "modern world" broadly informs what we also call "modern drama."

If to be "modern" is to be readable and understood within the discourses and languages of European modernity, then Africa's entry into that framework brings special historical and cultural inflections to what *modern* and *modern drama* mean. Various types of cultural interactions ranging from commerce in human and other commodities, colonization, and neocolonial relations characterize Africa's incorporation into European modernity. Systems of knowledge developed within such contexts were never complimentary; rather, they degenerated into Europe's "othering" of Africa and Africans as its inferior "other" that must be streamlined and assimilated into the very margins of European modernity.

The colonial period that formally began in 1885 is illustrative of the most systematic period and process of incorporating Africa into European forms of knowledge, their cultures, and their values. The colonization of Africa was itself part of the larger story of European power rivalries—an often violently competitive quest for markets, raw materials, and sites for the investment of surplus capital. In a landmark meeting presided over by German Chancellor Otto Von Bismarck in Berlin between December 1884 and January 1885, the European nations at the conference table formally developed a more organized structure for integrating African lands as well as its diverse people into European modernity. By that token, Africa's "modernization" was equated with colonization by dominant European nations whose mission included assimilating such distant lands and peoples into its own frames of cultural and political reference.

Similarly, anything qualified as "modern" implies either tacit acceptance of or acts of refusal to the themes and values of European modernization. The Berlin meeting effectively framed the "Scramble for Africa" by defining spheres of political influence and economic interest that various European powers would subsequently consolidate by force and chicanery. Using commerce, culture, and its own notions of civilization to define Africa, European colonization combined military might with economic relations to produce "colonial nationalisms"—processes of acculturating Africans into subservient forms of European nationalisms and cultural traditions derived from them. Colonial nationalism not only helped to name and place Africans into nations subordinate to their European patrons; it also firmly aided European nations and nationalism in defining themselves by the mutations and assimilations of their culturally "significant others" into European identities. For the Africans, becoming Nigerian, South African, or Egyptian meant becoming citizens of a nation within a European nation—an alienating situation that modern African dramas not only named but also sought to contest.

Resistance to colonial nationalism developed various forms of anticolonial nationalisms with which Africans defined themselves in the modern world, particularly after World War II. The structural and historical changes that reorganized the world into definite colonial and postcolonial nation–states after World War II further complicated the roles of drama and theater as cultural practices that either enunciated nationalist themes or contested them. For most of Africa, nation–states and national identities have historically remained contestatory, and cultural practices such as drama and theater are caught within the interstices of such contests. What the Kenyan state calls its "national theater" was seriously contested by the Kamiriithu Cultural and Community Association's play *I'll Marry When I Want* (*Ngahika Ndeenda*, 1977) thereby questioning the legitimacy of such categories as "national theaters." Similarly, classifying performance traditions as simply "traditional theater" raises serious questions within dynamic cultural processes in which people and communities reinvent themselves. These assertions do not in any way diminish the categories of inquiry and information outlined here; rather, they underscore their tentativeness and possible limitations despite their immediate usefulness.

INFLUENCE OF EUROPEAN LANGUAGES

European languages became the most enduring mode of communicating and socializing Africans into colonial modernity. Achieving literacy within such languages went hand in hand with assimilation into colonial nationalism and modernity—a paradoxical situation that anticolonial intellectuals and writers such as Franz Fanon, NGUGI WA THIONG'O, Chinua Achebe, and WOLE SOYINKA articulated eloquently in their thoughts and cultural practices. Modern African dramas are largely written in French, English, and Portuguese—hence such classifications as Francophone, Anglophone, and Lusophone, respectively. Apart from signifying the European colonial origin and linguistic heritages of the language of cultural production, literacies within such languages also meant proximity to the cultural histories and conventions of representations within them—hence the site within which African dramatists contest their colonial subordination. Fanon's (1967) assertion that "[t]o speak means to be in a position to use a certain syntax, to grasp the morphology of this or that language, but it means above all to assume a culture, to support the weight of a civilization" paved the way for most modern African writers seeking to consciously articulate the burden of writing and thinking in European languages. The playwright Ngugi wa Thiong'o's decision to begin developing literacy in Gikuyu was partly influenced by Fanon, whose writings challenged not only colonialism but also the limited scope of postcolonial nationalism. Apart from his apparent ethnonationalist approach, Ngugi also sought a Marxist approach to issues of disengagement from colonial capitalism. For dramatists like Wole Soyinka, writing in English was a subversive act within which the conventions of the language and its epistemological assumptions are subverted, its tenor compacted and within it the inscription of anticolonial becoming. The two, among others, illustrate how colonial languages became arenas for developing countermodernist and anticolonial attitudes.

Beyond the issue of language, dramatic conventions employed by most dramatists also became sites for anti-Eurocentric dissent. Adaptations of Aristotelian tragedy in plays by Nigeria's Ola Rotimi or SURREALISM by TEWFIQ AL-HAKIM or Jerzy Grotowski's "POOR THEATER" by MBONGENI NGEMA, Percy Mtwa, and Barney Simon are cases in point. Dramatic conventions derived from African folklore and other modernities also feature prominently in their hybrid forms in contemporary dramas of Africa.

Though the critical establishment contributed to various ways of questioning and highlighting contradictions of producing dramatic literatures in European languages, its various schools were equally implicated in using such languages to produce even countermodernist thought and criticisms. European languages became the forum for articulating ideas ranging from the Marxists to Afrocentrics, the so-called evolutionists, and relativists, and the ethno-nationalists (see Ogunbiyi, 1982). Beyond the issue of the language of engaging Eurocentric ideas of Africa, some of the critical schools were themselves extensions of movements resisting and counteracting foundations of European modernity in Europe. Marxism became particularly important as a countercolonial and anticapitalist philosophical movement for most writers and critics of drama and literature in general. Mixed with ethno-nationalism, it became a clarion call for drama that was not only non-Eurocentric but borrowed a lot from other modernities that stressed Africa's other ethnicities and possibly new intramodernist identity.

Apart from Marxism, which sought to interpret colonialism as the consequence of European capitalism, there were various shades of Afrocentrisms seeking to revive pre-European African forms, particularly in areas of black Africa. Negritudism, which originated as a Pan-Africanist artistic and political movement, fits into the spectrum of Afrocentrisms that stressed aesthetics celebrating Africa before its external contacts with Europe. In West Africa, the evolutionists and relativists were two critical schools in which the former sought dramas that evolve in similar historical trajectories as Europe's. For the evolutionists, mimicry of European drama from its ritualistic to its modern variations was necessary for dramatists writing in European languages. The latter is their opposing school that stressed the relative independence of African drama based on its own unique social developments that must be appropriately translated into European languages. In Maghrebian Africa such as Tunisia, Morocco, and Libya, there were calls for representations, language, and conventions predating Arab and European colonialisms. These critical schools played significant roles in enabling playwrights to respond to the specific issues in their various countries and regions and their homes from the early days of anticolonial agitations to moments of contending with the neocolonialism that has always been present at colleges and universities.

Within the universities, Marxism and residual forms of anticolonial nationalism offered analytical frameworks for mounting critical challenges to Nigeria's corrupt dominant class and the unitary nationalist ideology it deployed to buttress its regime. Sometimes contesting, at other times complementing each other as they confronted the national government, countercultural activists ranged from passionate ethnocentrists to mimics of European political radicalism. Marxist scholarship highlighted issues of class and the neocolonial economic structure and presented strategies for defining and empowering working-class identities.

AFRICAN DRAMA AND MODERNITY

The question of what kind of modernity the works of Wole Soyinka, Ngugi wa Thiong'o, or AMA ATA AIDOO represent always comes up when the term *modern drama* is used.

Despite the colonizing implications of classifying any cultural practice in Africa as "modern," the term in itself draws attention to a complex cultural and political landscape within which Africans thematically articulate their marginalization in European modernity, as well as a site from which they enunciate a spectrum of what can be loosely termed *countermodernist* tropes. Colonial nationalism as an instrument of "modernizing" Africans also produced a marker of limits to the absorption of Africans into European modernity. Epistemologies and cultural traditions that Africans were supposed to move into also had denigrating notions of Africans and Africanness in which varieties of anthropological ideas on race and ethnicity limited assimilation. The boundary, or limits, of colonial assimilation may be described an "intermodernist" landscape (Amkpa, 2003). It is from within such a landscape that cultural alienation of "educated" Africans, revivalist impulses such as "Negritudism" and Afrocentrism, and other forms of countermodernist ideologies were inaugurated. Anticolonial nationalism, decolonization, and calls for independent African nations were also launched from within the intermodernist landscape. For dramatists, it involves not only writing within European languages and their conventions of representation but also using such to express social and political alienation and calls for a liberating culture and political independence. Most of what we would call "modern African drama" is indeed framed within intermodernist landscapes; as such thematic preoccupations and use of language, characterization, and settings engage readers and spectators in calls for a more liberating modernity that counters, contradicts, and limits European modernity. In addition to writing, other infrastructures of producing dramatic literature were also implicated in such contradictions. What phenomena described "modernity" within African cultures? What roles have they played in thematizing African modernities and modernisms?

A singular modernity such as "European modernity" is insufficient in describing the breadth and depth of cultures, traditions, and modes of representation in Africa. Indeed, the ability to imagine contrarian global systems derived from African contacts with itself alludes to the existence of "overlapping modernities" within the continent. This suggests knowledge of cultural traditions and values that were not European inspired varieties of revivalism that furthered decolonization from European modernity. It also suggests most Africans are indeed residents between the overlaps of modernities—being Mandigo or Yoruba as well as being Senegalese and Nigerian.

Furthermore, just as "educated" Africans saw their limits from within intermodernist landscapes, African societies had to contend with their own redefinitions. Using consciousness of overlapping global systems, Africans also found themselves in a parallel scenario—the "intramodernist landscape." Within it, African countries, as newly independent from their European founders, had to develop new relations and cultures of their independence. Issues and crises of national renaming, belonging, and identity were all part of the intramodernist landscape—a cultural context within which relations with each other had to be renegotiated. This also means that what we call "modern drama" in Africa responds simultaneously to intermodernist and intramodernist issues. Ama Ata Aido's *Anowa* (1970), Wole Soyinka's DEATH AND THE KING'S HORSEMAN (1976), and Tewfiq al-Hakim's *Fate of a Cockroach* (1966) all exemplify the simultaneous responses to intermodernist and intramodernist issues in their themes and indeed conventions within which they expressed themselves. The intramodernist landscape completes the picture of what new forms of relationships and cultures Africans have developed as they borrowed from other modernities as well as engaged Euro-modernity. The intramodernist crises of civil wars and anomies within Africa are best contextualized within such frameworks.

However, the themes of decolonization and anticolonialism developed from both the intermodernist and intramodernist landscapes did not maintain the momentum for social justice and equality in most of Africa. Recessions within anticolonial movements and regressions into new colonial relations with mutations of European modernity continue to network Africans to discourses of exploitation and cultural domination. Such regressions led to the formation of neocolonial nationalisms that, on one hand, kept the external affects of anticolonialism and, on the other, separated the nation–states from their peoples. Once described as "the worst form of imperialism" by Kwame Nkrumah, Africa's leading Pan-Africanist and erstwhile leader of postindependent Ghana, neocolonialism is a political and cultural phenomenon in which for "those who practice, it means power without responsibility and for those who suffer from it, it means exploitation without redress." It is a phenomenon that continues to split the ideas of nationhood between the political state and its citizens as well as the focus of most contemporary dramatic literatures in Africa.

Modern African dramas such as Ngugi wa Thiong'o and Ngugi wa Mirii's *I'll Marry When I Want* (1977) exemplify how dramatists engage neocolonialism by referencing anticolonial moments as well as other modernities that once upon a time gave them senses of justice and communal belonging. Such are the contexts of the themes and styles of modern African drama as they broadly engage the complexities of cultural and political issues that make them modern. Issues of the overlapping modernities describing Africa, varieties of nationalisms (colonial, anticolonial, and neocolonial), ideas of citizenship and democracy, conventions derived from indigenous performance traditions—all pervade the spectrum of dramatic literature from Africa.

FURTHER READING

Amkpa, Awam. *Theatre and Postcolonial Desires*. London: Routledge, 2003.

Breitinger, Eckhard, ed. *Theatre and Performance in Africa*. Bayreuth: Bayreuth African Studies, 1993.

Fanon, Franz. *Black Skin, White Mask*. New York: Grove, 1967.

Kerr, David. *African Popular Theatre from Pre-colonial Times to the Present Day*. London: Heinemann, 1995.

Nkrumah, Kwame. *Neo-Colonialism: The Last Stage of Imperialism*. London: Nelson, 1965.

Ogunbiyi, Y., ed. *Drama and Theatre in Nigeria: A Critical Source Book*. Lagos: Nigeria Magazine, 1982.

Owomoyela, Oyekan. *African Literatures: An Introduction*. Waltham, Mass.: African Studies Assoc., 1979.

Awam Amkpa

POSTCOLONIAL DRAMA

Chinua Achebe, Nigerian novelist, states that what Nigeria is today would never have come into existence without colonialism and that he and his colleagues are a by-product of colonial intervention. Edward Said, Palestinian critic and cultural philosopher, emphasizes that colonialism altered the perception of "the Other" and, more important, determined the response of the colonized to the colonial experience. Terry Eagleton, British literary critic, refers to the importance of the English literature syllabus in the recruiting of civil servants; familiarity with "The Great Tradition" provided colonial officers with the attitude of superiority to carry out their missions on the peripheries. Russian born Nobel Laureate poet, Joseph Brodsky, in his introduction to DEREK WALCOTT's poems, speaks of the decline of the imperial centers, when the people of the "provinces" take over and "language, not legions," guarantee continuity. Homi Bhabha, Indian born theorist of postcolonialism, sees the main feature of postcolonial cultures in their hybridity. Postcolonial theater in Africa is a good illustration of issues and methods.

The metropolitan discourse on postcolonial theater in Africa was long dominated by the question of whether precolonial indigenous theater ever existed. In the Western concept of theater (written script, purpose-built venue, professional actors performing to a paying audience), the answer was definitely no. Colonialist discourse devalued indigenous performance; colonial practice often banned it. Missionaries in Uganda banned the Ganda wedding dance because of obscenity; WOLE SOYINKA refers in *Death and the King's Horseman* (1975) to the banning of Egungun masquerades by the British. Recently, a broader concept recognizes the importance of ritual performances, seasonal and cultural festivals, song, and dance. Thus, the theatrical is incorporated into the concept of the performance text (also known as the cultural text), a concept that can accommodate both pre-scribal and literate traditions.

Colonial mentality rested on the conviction that to be in possession of the hegemonial texts is to be culturally superior; thus, the inevitable schoolday productions of "Scenes from Shakespeare," as well as later, more critical efforts, are excellent examples of the hybrid character of much postcolonial theater. The response to William Shakespeare's plays has ranged from true-to-the-script productions to deconstructive rewrites. But even "true" interpretations cause unexpected effects with colonial audiences. A 1969 school production of *Romeo and Juliet* in Uganda nearly ended in a riot because Asian parents would not accept that an African Romeo should publicly kiss an Asian Juliet. Colonial racism interfered with the "true" Shakespeare envisaged by the British teacher. Since the francophone West Indian AIMÉ CÉSAIRE rewrote *The Tempest* (*La Tempête*, 1969), the idea of "writing back," of shifting the perspective from the colonizer (Prospero) to the colonized (Caliban, Cannibal) has become a favored method. Favorite postcolonial rewrites are *Othello*, *Julius Caesar*, *Macbeth*, and the history plays. Race, succession, good governance, the morality of political revolt, and even regicide lent themselves to critical assessment of the colonial regime within colonialism's own cultural paradigms. Translocating the Elizabethan setting into the postcolonies, the adaptation of the War of the Roses to postcolonial politics became the major strategy of deconstructing colonial cultural hubris and initiating a critique of postcolonial regimes. Bole Butake, Cameroonian dramatist and director (of theater and television), and others used the Elizabethan history play formula to write their own histories, in which precolonial rulers, abuse of power, and intrigues about succession are used to portray the shortcomings of the current government.

The other corpus of dramatic texts favored for rewritings, intertextual adaptation, and hybridization are classical Greek plays, also pillars of Western cultural hegemony. Wole Soyinka adapted *The Bacchae* in 1973, Nigerian Ola Rotimi reset *Oedipus Rex* into the Yoruba context as *The Gods Are Not to Blame* in 1968, and FEMI OSOFISAN rewrote *Tegonni, An African Antigone* (1994). Transposing plot and setting from classical Greece to colonial Nigeria signifies an appropriation of world theater tradition and hegemonic success for postcolonial theater.

The most striking forms of rewriting are the metatheatrical plays that reveal conflicts and fusions of cultural traditions. ATHOL FUGARD's *The Island* (1973) deals with two political prisoners who rehearse *Antigone* for a "concert" performance for the other prisoners on the notorious Robben Island. In Derek Walcott's *Pantomime* (1980), a British ex-actor and a Trinidadian ex-Calypso musician prepare a Robinson Crusoe playlet. In such metatheatrical plays, the struggle to produce the play opens the situation of the actors and audiences to multiple, contradictory perspectives that shed a different light on the canonical text, its relevance to the postcolonial context, and theatrical discoursivity and hybridity. Soyinka foregrounds this revalorization of indigenous cultures in *Death and the King's Horseman*. His essay "The Fourth Stage" (1976) elaborates a concept of African TRAGEDY on an equal level with classical Greek tragedy.

Postcolonial theater concentrates on theatrical practice but is fully aware of the classical canon and both Western and—to a lesser degree—Eastern drama theories. The preferred method of creating plays is improvisation preceeding writing the scripts. "Total theater," that is, the combination of song, dance, music, and ritual, ranges before "dialogue" theater.

FURTHER READING

Balme, Christopher B. *Decolonizing the Stage*. Oxford: Oxford Univ. Press, 1999.

Banham, Martin, ed. *A History of Theatre in Africa*. Cambridge: Cambridge Univ. Press, 2004.

Johnson, Lemuel. *Shakespeare in Africa (and Other Venues)*. Trenton, N.J.: Africa World Press, 1998.

Kerr, David. *Popular Theatre in Africa from Pre-Colonial Times to the Present*. Oxford: Oxford Univ. Press, 1995.

Eckhard Breitinger

EAST AFRICA

The three East African countries of Kenya, Tanzania, and Uganda possess diverse indigenous cultural and political structures, from the feudal hierarchies of the landlocked kingdom of the Baganda to the internationally oriented Swahili coast to Zanzibar with its cultural and commercial links to the Arab peninsula. Differences in colonial practices are significant, too, and continue into the postcolonial era: Tanzania, under its charismatic president Julius Nyerere, experimented with African socialism (*Ujamaa*); Kenya gained independence after a fierce armed struggle but installed an exploitive capitalist system, whereas Uganda relapsed into ethnic policies under the notorious dictatorships of Milton Obote and Idi Amin. All three countries can look back to indigenous performance traditions. The Swahili practiced a dramatized form of epic recitation. Uganda boasted a rich tradition of royal music and performance at the Kabakka court but also popular dance and narrative traditions. The Luo cherished their song tradition. The countries also share the denigration or banning of such practices, with people in urban centers having submitted to the "civilizing" mission of colonialism.

The Little Theatre Movement in Dar-es-Salaam (1947) and Arusha (1953) mollified the cultural onslaught of European hegemony by bringing modern plays onto the stage, but the fact remains that scripts, venues, and adjudicators were all British and strongly inclined toward a theatrical tradition of Victorian REALISM and of aesthetic standards set in the 1920s and 1930s. The colonized were thus made to believe that there exists only one theater form and one theater tradition; African traditions were discarded as worthless. However, indigenous theatrical groups organized along different lines. In Tanganyika, the union-affiliated Tanganyika Textile Drama Group and Friendship Textile Drama Group became the principal theatrical activists in the 1960s, whereas in Uganda, each ethnic group established separate groups, the Asians gathered in distinct Muslim and Hindu groups, and the Catholic Goans operated their own cultural groupings. Each catered to specific audiences and tastes.

All three countries can boast internationally known dramatists who had an impact on the development of theater in Africa: Ebrahim Hussein (Tanzania), critical *Ujamaa* socialist, writing in Kiswahili; the Marxist NGUGI WA THIONG'O (Kenya), who first wrote in English before he opted for his native Gikuyu; and Bugandan royalist ROBERT BALLAMINO SERUMAGA (Uganda), writing in English before he resorted to a theater without words.

In a 1969 interview (published in 1972) with Okot p'Bitek, the first Ugandan director of the National Theatre, Serumaga, argued that "theater should not start from the National Theatre in the city and then spread outwards, but should start from the villages, and build up to the National Theatre in the city." This concept of reversing the colonial top-down trickle of culture was realized by Ngugi wa Thiong'o and Ngugi wa Mirii at the Kamiriithu cultural center outside Nairobi. Ngugi wa Thiong'o began his writing career with contributions to the Makerere Inter Hall Drama Competition. His involvement in the Kamiriithu Cultural Project with *I Marry When I Want (Ngaahika Ndeenda*, 1977) initiated a new strategy for popular theater activities. According to Ngugi, he was only the "secretary" of the project; the creative forces were the peasants and workers of Kamiriithu. They decided on the topic and developed scenes and setting, while Ngugi wa Thiong'o and Ngugi wa Mirii wrote. The topic, however, reflects Ngugi wa Thiong'o's own political agenda, especially the land issue, central both to the Gikuyu struggle and independent Kenya. Here, the peasant Kiguunda is driven from his land by the *nouveau riche* Kioi. He demands that Kiguunda and his wife Wangeci have a Christian wedding before he can agree to his son's marrying Kiguunda's daughter. Kioi offers a loan, knowing that Kiguunda cannot pay it back. He thus manages to grab Kiguunda's land, which he sells to an international company for the construction of an insecticide factory. The villagers brought their dances, wedding ritual, old resistance songs and new lyrics, Ngugi wa Thiong'o adding a plotline of almost Victorian domestic MELODRAMA, thus camouflaging the political message. Still, the Kenyan government intervened; after nine performances, the show was banned and Ngugi was detained for over a year. It was exactly this popularity and popular participation that made the Kamiriithu experiment into a model for the rapidly growing Theatre for Development movement in Africa.

Ebrahim Hussein from Tanzania made his strongest impact with *Kinjeketile* (1969), about the Maji-Maji resistance against German colonialism. Hussein is rooted in the cultural tradition of the coastal Swahili, familiar with the genre of *taraab*, the satiric sketches of *vicheksho*, and the epic narrative of *haditi*. At university, he learned about BERTOLT BRECHT'S EPIC THEATER. After the Arusha Declaration of *Ujamaa* socialism in 1967, independent Tanzania needed popular theatrical support for its socialist project and a historical perspective that could link the postcolony to precolonial times in support of national identity. Hussein chose a precolonial hero of resistance to "narrate the nation." *Kinjeketile*, when first performed at the University of Dar-es-Salaam, demonstrated Hussein's rejection of proscenium-stage dramaturgy. He presents the story of the Maji-Maji revolt, spirit possession, and the captivity and martyrdom of Kinjeketile in an episodic structure. During the first act, Kinjeketile's tribesmen, the Wamatumbi, discuss his involvement with the Water Spirit, dance his spirit possession, and sing about his prophecy of the return of Sultan Seyyid Said. Act 2 shows Kinjeketile in a state of possession as we hear about armed struggle against the Germans. In Brechtian style, Kitunda as narrator addresses the audience directly. The final act, with Kinjeketile as prisoner, opens the play for a dialectical struggle between terrorist/witch doctor on the one side and martyr/liberator/prophet on the other. Although the historical plot ends with clear closure—the execution—the national epic is open-ended. *Kinjeketile* is Hussein's most popular play, often performed outside Tanzania in English. In his plays *Mashetani* (1971) and *Arusi* (1980), Hussein shifts attention from national identity to *Ujamaa* ideology as enforcing cultural conformity and aesthetic uniformity. Having encountered DARIO FO and HEINER MÜLLER in Europe, Hussein has departed from traditional folklore, introducing parallel narrative strands, loading narration with metaphorical images and an open-ended plot structure, and changing the tone from one-dimensional cultural affirmation to a critical discussion without solutions. Penina Muhando, Hussein's colleague in Fine and Performing Arts at the University of Dar-es-Salaam, with *Lina Ubani* (1979) and *Harakati za Ukombouzi* (1982, with Amandina Lihamba), also presents critical views of the socialist experiment before going into the popular Theatre for Development (TfD) practice. TfD has since become the most prolific theater activity; it aims to communicate development messages (health, [HIV], sanitation, land use, democratization) to the grass roots, preferably with the participation of the target communities. Mostly funded by nongovernmental organizations (NGOs), TfD provides employment for theater practitioners as facilitators.

Drama in local language played an important role in East African cultural politics. In 1977 Byron Kawadwa represented Uganda at the Festival of Black and African Arts in Lagos with his opera *Song of the Cock (Oluyimba Lwa Wankoko)*. *Song of the Clock* deals with the same issue as WOLE SOYINKA'S *A Dance of the Forests* (1963): the false idealization of the precolonial past for propagandistic purposes in the period of cultural nationalism. Kawadwa's Wankoko arrives at the Kabaka court as the "new man" from the up-country, just like Prime Minister Milton Obote. He is a talented schemer and mass mobilizer, wins the confidence of Prince Suuna, establishes himself as leader of the palace workers, gains control over the royal court, and tilts the political system of the monarchy. Kawadwa chose a 19th-century historical situation, but the characters point directly to the current political situation in independent Uganda. Kawadwa paid special attention to the accuracy of the historical atmosphere, first performing in public the song of the

Palace Guards ("Ffe basajia ba Kabaka"—"We are the Kabaka's men, we eat from his hand") and ritual court performances. Kawadwa, as royalist, was breaking the most cherished taboos in Ganda culture: presenting royal court music and dances in public. However, this was itself a political statement against Obote, who had destroyed the Baganda monarchy. Thus, the use of royal music and dance in the piece must not be seen as a traditionalist pose but as an indictment of a new class of politicians. In this way, Kawadwa reshaped traditional Ganda performance into a modern and politically relevant form.

Robert Serumaga trained as an economist in Ireland, where he encountered the Theater of the Absurd. Back in Uganda, Serumaga submitted his actors to a rigorous KONSTANTIN STANISLAVSKY training that emphasized body, movement, and voice as essential theatrical elements. *Majangwa* (1971) deals with onetime successful performers Majangwa and Nakiriji, who now perform pornographic shows on roadsides. The hourlong play consists of a single scene in which the two characters speak to their betrayed expectations, illusions, and frustrations, "setting out for new horizons beyond the reaches of small minds" and performing a sex act as "a promise of rain." In the last minute of the piece, a car passes by and a dead body is dumped. Ugandan political reality suddenly intrudes, existentialist angst transforms into moral degradation, and serious performers degrade into peep-show dancers and willing executioners for the regime, ready to burn the body and destroy the evidence. Nakijira assesses their degeneration: "Shadows of ourselves, that's what we are."

With *Renga Moi*, Serumaga relocated a legend from the Acholi North to the "village of the seven hills" (Kampala), a story of rival loyalties and moral obligations. Again, Serumaga merges ritual performance, traditional legend, and the political realities of the day—random killings under the Amin dictatorship. In Serumaga's last, brief play, *Where Dead Dogs Are Thrown* (*Amayirikiti*), only seventeen words are spoken or, rather, stammered by a dumb coffin maker. Thus enforced, deadly silence is the pervasive sense of the play. The rest consists of dance, movement, and action frozen before a scaffold backdrop on which lifeless bodies are hung. Serumaga experiments here with theatrical idiom to carry his message of horror beyond words, an idiom Amin's killers could not grasp. He fooled Amin himself, who invited him to perform the play at the 1975 Organization of African Unity meeting in Kampala.

Rose Mbowa's *Mother Uganda and Her Children* (1986) marked a new beginning for theater in Uganda. It attempts to merge dramatic folk performance with Brechtian parable structures. Mbowa revived the interdisciplinary *Imbalu* project at Makerere University in the 1960s. Students were sent to study indigenous performance traditions, and their findings were mounted in a collage revealing the rich diversity of ethnic cultures. The piece takes the spectator on an ethnographic tour through the country: the circumcision rites of the Bugiso, the wedding rituals among the Acholi, the planting season, and harvest celebrations. It marks not only different cultural spaces and regions but also the stations in the life of an ordinary Ugandan from initiation through marriage, childbearing, and seasonal rituals. Ethnic specificity is thus summarized in a life experience of a typical Ugandan beyond ethnic boundaries. Mbowa also brings politics to bear, welding the diverse ethnic performances into a politically charged plot with Tabusana (Swahili for "troublemaker") as the protagonist. Tabusana abuses traditional rituals that fortify ethnic harmony and identity in order to sow discord among neighbors and benefit from their conflicts. He represents the ethnocentric Ugandan politician that has plagued the country in the past. In the end, Mother Uganda succeeds and converts Tabusana into a responsible citizen. Mbowa thus succeeds in fusing ritual performance, folk tradition, and a contemporary political plot line with an inclusive theatrical idiom that allows space for ethnic specificity within the framework of a common language of national unity.

East African dramatists have responded directly to the political situations in their countries. Domestic farces constitute one platform used by semiprofessional but purely commercial urban theater groups to escape political pressures. Indigenous performance traditions, both popular and feudal, are used in support of political statements. African languages and code switching between colonial and indigenous languages are used to "decolonize the mind" (Ngugi) or to assert the cultural plurality of the nation. Independent of their ideological orientation, most dramatists have adopted Brecht's parable style into their syncretistic theatrical idiom.

FURTHER READING

Balme, Christopher B. *Decolonizing the Stage*. Oxford: Oxford Univ. Press, 1999.

Banham, Martin, ed. *African Theatre History*. Cambridge: Cambridge Univ. Press, 2004.

Breitinger, Eckhard, ed. *Uganda: The Cultural Landscape*. Kampala, Uganda: Bayreuth African Studies, 1999.

Cook, David, and Michael Okenimkpe. *Ngugi wa Thiongo: An Exploration of His Writings*. Oxford: Oxford Univ. Press, 1997.

Kerr, David. *Dance, Media Entertainment and Popular Theatre in East Africa*. Kampala, Uganda: Bayreuth African Studies, 1998.

Ricard, Alan. *Ebrahim Hussein: Swahili Theatre and Individualism*. Dar-es-Salaam, Tanzania: Mkuki na Nyota Pub., 2000.

Eckhard Breitinger

CENTRAL AND SOUTHERN AFRICA

In southern and central Africa there was no indigenous tradition of literary drama, but there were a rich variety of performing arts containing strong theatrical elements in masquerades, dance-mimes, rituals, and oral narratives. Masquerades such as *Makisi* (Lunda word for ancestral spirits and for the masquerade performance that represents them) (modern Zambia and Angola) and *Gule wa Mkulu* (Chewa word meaning "the big dance," referring to the masquerade performance by members of the Nyau cult) (modern Malawi, Zambia, and Mozambique) portrayed ancestral spirits either as sacred animal structures—which recreated a period of prelapsarian harmony between humans, animals, and God—or satirical human masks, presenting vices for the audience to avoid. Initiation ceremonies such as *Bogwera* (Tswana name for male initiation ceremonies) and *Bojale* (Tswana name for female initiation ceremonies) (Botswana), *Chisungu* (Bemba word for female initiation ceremonies) (Zambia), and *Jando* (Yao word for male initiation ceremonies) and *Chinamwali* (Nsenga/Chewa word for female initiation ceremonies) (Malawi, Zambia, and Mozambique) used play skits, rituals, dances, and oral narratives to educate initiates about sexual hygiene and morality. Spirit possession rituals such as *Mapira* (Shona word for spirit possession ceremony, meaning appeasement of spirits) (Zimbabwe), *Mashabe* (Shona word, meaning spirits, referring to a spirit possession dance) (Zimbabwe and Zambia), *Ukuvumisa* (Swati word, meaning "Do you agree?" for a spirit possession dance) (Swaziland), and *Vimbuza* (Tumbuka word for a spirit possession dance) (Malawi and Zambia) contained strong dramatic elements when "possessed" dancers spoke in foreign tongues or mimed the actions of possessing spirits. Throughout the region, oral narratives allowed for the narrator to dramatize various voices and for the audience to respond through songs or narrative interventions.

Indigenous precolonial performance tended to be marked by strong elements of collective creativity, audience participation, and a highly sophisticated coordination of plastic arts (masks, costumes, ritual paraphernalia), dance, choreography, song, and narrative fantasy. Although the performances were very functional, in that they provided a source of moral and community identity, they were perfectly capable of reflecting historical changes. These include migration, as in the ceremony of *Umutomboko* (modern Zambia and Congo), re-creating the historical crossing of the Luapula river by the Lunda people, or invasion, as in the way Tumbuka patients in *Vimbuza* dances were possessed by the spirits of Ngoni or Bemba invaders.

The slave trade conducted by Arab, British, and Portuguese forces from the 17th century onward had an important impact on indigenous performance. These alien influences became even stronger after the arrival of trading companies, such as Cecil Rhodes's British South African Company in the mid-19th century. Although Portugal occupied Angola and Mozambique as early as the 17th century, it was the Lochner concession of 1888 that opened up much of the southern African region to formal British colonialism. Many southern African performing arts used the potential of their satirical stereotyping as a form of cultural resistance. In *Gule wa Mkulu*, for example, dancers created several new mask-characters to lampoon colonial whites. Other forms (such as *Mashabe*) attempted to incorporate the power of the invaders into the psychotherapy of their performances.

A rather different phenomenon arising from colonial conquest was the creation of hybrid forms. The opposition of Christian missionaries to dances and rituals that they perceived as pagan or obscene led peoples who were closely affected by Christianity to create syncretic forms, such as *Jerusarema* (Shona corruption of the word "Jerusalem," referring to an entertainment dance in 1920s Zimbabwe) as an alternative to the more frankly sexual dance of *Mbende*. Likewise, throughout the urban areas, Christian "kitchen parties" came to replace indigenous initiation ceremonies. At a more secular level, creators of dances such as *Beni* (Swahili word, used as a loan word in many other Southern and East African languages, for a militaristic mime dance) (Tanzania and Malawi), *Malipenga* ("trumpets" in Tumbuka and Chewa languages, used as the name in Malawi for a militaristic mime dance)/*Muganda* (Nyanja name used in Zambia for Malipenga dance) (Malawi and Zambia), and *Kalela* (Bemba name for a militaristic mime dance, different from Muganda) (Zambia and Congo) used colonial-style uniforms and marching steps, along with indigenous traditions of drumming, dance, and song, to create choreographed mimes that sometimes drew inspiration from colonialism but eventually developed into satirical attacks upon it. Finally, in some cultures old traditions were revived or reinvented in order to challenge colonialism. In 1921, for example, Sobhuza, the new king of Swaziland, revived the 18th-century ritual offering of first fruits to the king (*Incwala*; Swati, Zulu, Ndebele, and Ngoni word for first fruits harvest festival in Swaziland, South Africa, Zimbabwe, and Zambia).

The theater introduced by colonialists into southern Africa tended to be of a reactionary kind. Jingoistic vaudeville shows were imported from Europe to Zimbabwe as early as 1892. Imported or locally written and produced plays tended to offer nostalgic solace to white settlers in an alien environment. All-white theater clubs and organizations prevented African penetration into this field. Theater (and film) aimed at Africans, which became popular from the 1930s onward, were mainly forms of propaganda aimed at domesticating African populations and integrating them within the colonial political economy.

The first stirrings of an indigenous African literary drama emerged in the latter days of the colonial era. Most of these were literary texts (often not intended for performance), written mainly in vernacular languages for mission-oriented Literature Bureaus. Some prominent playwrights in this mode include Michael Seboni and Leetsile Raditladi in Botswana and N. M. Khaketla in Lesotho. A more innovative field was that of radio drama beamed from Lusaka to the British colonies of northern and southern Rhodesia and Nyasaland. In the late 1940s and early 1950s, Zambian broadcasters such as Edward Mungoni and Stephen Mpashi, with their respective radio drama series *Malikopo* (siTonga, the language of Tonga) and *Mwa Shimwamba Kopolo* (chiBemba, the language of Bemba), found ways of incorporating African collective traditions of improvisatory narrative into the colonial form of radio drama. The only major play broadcast in English at that time (1957) was Andreya Masiye's epic critique of imperialism, *Kazembe and the Portuguese*. During the Chimurenga war against the Ian Smith regime, indigenous *Mapira* spirit possession rituals were used by guerrilla fighters to mobilize the civilian population, as was a syncretic form—the *Pungwe* (all-night entertainment)—which mixed speeches, oral poems, songs, dances, and dramatic sketches.

A huge increase in the writing and production of plays occurred soon after independence, which most countries in the region achieved in the mid-1960s, with the exceptions of Zimbabwe in 1980 and Namibia in 1990. These authors were often associated with universities in the early period and particularly with the university traveling theater movement. Later, however, independent theater troupes emerged as centers of writing and production.

The styles and genres of the plays depended to a large extent on the political and economic systems in the various countries. In Zambia, with its tradition of hosting liberation movements and its official socialist policy of humanism, playwrights such as Masautso Phiri, Dickson Mwansa, Zimbabwean exile Stephen Chifunyise, and choreographers such as Mapopa Mtonga explored themes of social injustice and national liberation. All of these were associated with the University of Zambia's Chikwakwa Theatre, and many with the later independent group Tikwiza Theatre. Important Tikwiza plays produced in the late 1970s and early 1980s included the collective, satirical epic *Freedom in Ndongo* (*Uhuru wa Ndongo*) (1977), Dickson Mwansa's socialist MELODRAMA *The Cell* (1982), and Masautso Phiri's tribute to the schoolchildren of Soweto, in the rhetorical style of South African black consciousness poetry, *Soweto Flowers Will Grow* (1978). In Malawi, by contrast, where censorship and dictatorship made writing and play production a riskier occupation, plays tended toward allegory and metaphor. Steve Chimombo used both techniques in his precolonial, neoritual epic *The Rainmaker* (1976) and his chiChewa (the language of Chewa) social parable *Who Has Seen It?* (*Wachiona Ndani?*, 1983). James Ng'ombe also used myth and history to explore themes of power and sexuality in such plays as *The Banana Tree* (1974) and *The King's Pillow* (1975).

In Zimbabwe and Namibia, nations that gained their independence later after extensive wars of liberation, a rather different theater style emerged. In Zimbabwe, several plays celebrated the Chimurenga war or linked the antiimperialist struggle to that against apartheid in South Africa. The multilingual, collectively created plays of the theater company Zambuko-Izibuko (in which Robert McClaren was an important creative force) were particularly prominent in this genre. Stephen Chifunyise, on his return to Zimbabwe, continued to explore a vein of social realistic didacticism in such plays as *I Am Not for Sale* (1982). As disillusionment against the Zimbabwe African National Union (ZANU) regime of Robert Mugabe began to set in, however, plays indirectly critical of the post-1980 government began to be produced, many of them collaborations between black and white artists. These include *The Nyola Tree* (1988) and *The Rise and Shine of Comrade Fiasco* (1990) by Andrew Whaley and a whole series of plays by the Bulawayo-based group Amakosi, under the directorship of Cont Mhlanga, some in SiNdebele (the language of Ndebele, similar to Zulu) (such as *Here Is the Man* [*Nansi le Ndoda*, 1986]), others in English or a mixture of languages. The most controversial was his 1986 play about labor exploitation and race relations, *Workshop Negative*. Daves Guzha, artistic director of Rooftop Productions, has continued that critical and intercultural tradition into the 1990s and the 21st century.

In Namibia, a similar pattern can be identified. University lecturer Dorian Haarhoff wrote a trilogy of plays—*Orange* (1988), *Skeleton* (1989), and *Guerrilla Goatherd* (1990)—about events leading to Namibia's independence struggle and the contradictions they created. Probably the most prominent playwright in Namibia is Frederick Philander; his plays range from celebration of popular struggle against apartheid (*Katatura 59*, 1989) to satirical dissection of Namibia's postindependence sociopolitical landscape. A younger playwright, Victor Hangula, has written a controversial, intertextual, postmodernist critique of the South West Africa People's Organization (SWAPO) regime, *The Show Isn't Over Until . . .* (1998).

One very influential theater movement throughout the region has been what is usually called Theatre for Development. This movement started in Botswana in the mid-1970s with the Laedza Batanani project, which tried to link theater to community development and to such issues as poverty, gender discrimination, and social deprivation. This style of theater, which rapidly spread through Africa in the 1980s, was influenced both by indigenous, collective, community performance traditions and by the theories of AUGUSTO BOAL. At its worst, it merely offers predictable instrumentalist messages preplanned by nongovernmental organization (NGO) development agencies. At its best, it allows communities to create their own plays (usually in conjunction with facilitators) to comment upon or challenge existing social attitudes, structures, and hierarchies. Such performances are linked to programs or institutions initiating social transformation. The performance style has also affected conventional theater in the region. The Zimbabwe Association of Community Theatres, the Namibian Bricks Theatre Collective, and Reetsenang Group of Community Theatres in Botswana all engage in improvised, collective Theatre for Development and in more formally produced plays of a socially progressive nature. Often, commissioned Theatre for Development projects help to subsidize experimental theater for more formal venues.

The liberation of South Africa climaxing in the democratic elections of 1994 had an impact on drama throughout the region. Plays tended to concentrate less on antiimperialist themes and to seek more variety, often through critiquing entrenched governments. The introduction of multiparty democracy in some previous one-party regimes, at about the same time, had a similar liberatory impact. In Malawi, Du Chisiza, Jr., wrote plays such as

Democracy Boulevard (1993) mocking both the previous Malawi Congress Party (MCP) regime and some of the new shibboleths of democracy. In Botswana, groups like Magosi Dedicated Artists and UBE423 created plays attacking aspects of government policy. The impact of acquired immunodeficiency syndrome (AIDS) was also reflected in drama, not just in the proliferation of plays (many sponsored by donor organizations) about the pandemic but also in the increase in plays about women's issues. This coincided with increased confidence among female playwrights, directors, and facilitators, some of whom included Norah Mumba in Zambia, Tisa Chifunyise in Zimbabwe, Tania Terblanche and Laurinda Olivier-Sampson in Namibia, Zondwa Sithebe in Swaziland, and Gertrude Kamkwatira in Malawi.

By the dawn of the new millennium, the increased networking among theater artists through workshops and festivals was allowing the exchange of new ideas, styles, and ideologies. For example, integration of both African and Western styles of dance or narrative into drama productions became normal. Such changes have made experimental theater, which challenges old concepts, more attractive to both artists and audiences.

FURTHER READING

Gunner, Liz, ed. *Politics and Performance: Theatre Poetry and Song in Southern Africa*. Witswatersrand: Witswatersrand Univ. Press, 1994.

Kamlongera, Chris, Mike Nambote, Boston Soko, and Enoch Timpunza-Mvula. *Kubvina: An Introduction to Malawian Dance and Theatre*. Zomba: Univ. of Malawi, 1992.

Kerr, David. *African Popular Theatre in Sub-Saharan Africa from Pre-Colonial to the Present Day*. London: Heinemann, 1995.

——. *Dance, Media Entertainment & Popular Theatre in South East Africa*. Bayreuth: Bayreuth Univ. Press, 1997.

——. *African Theatre*. Vol. 4, *Southern Africa*. Oxford and Cape Town: James Currey & David Philip, 2004.

Matusse, Renato, ed. *Past, Roles and Development of Theatre Arts in SADC*. Gaborone: SADC House, 1999.

Mda, Zakes. 1993. *When People Play People: Development Communication through Theatre*. Witswatersrand: Witswatersrand Univ. Press & Zed Books, 1993.

Rohmer, Martin. 1999. *Theatre and Performance in Zimbabwe*. Bayreuth: Bayreuth African Studies, 1999.

Zeeman, Terence, ed. *New Namibia Plays*. Windhoek: New Namibia Books, 2000.

David Kerr

WEST AFRICA

Modern West African theater is a marriage of two theatrical traditions, indigenous African and Western inspired. This article looks at the experimentation and challenge to the aesthetics of REALISM by West African playwrights. It focuses on Anglophone and Francophone West Africa because the theater in the former Portuguese colonies is in a nascent stage.

GHANA

Ghanaian theater was started by nationalists who were not professional playwrights; therefore, the plays were literary and philosophical: Ferdinand Kwasi Fiawoo's *The Fifth Landing Stage* (1943), Joseph Boakye Danquah's *The Third Woman* (1943), and Kobina Sakyi's *The Blinkards* (1916). Even in this pioneering phase, one sees the impetus toward the AVANT-GARDE, as demonstrated in Danquah's use of Akan folklore in dramatizing the Akan myths of origin. Similarly, the bold experimentation in *The Blinkards*—using both Fante and English in satirizing the Gold Coast elite for their slavish imitation of British habits—is unconventional for the period.

EFUA SUTHERLAND and Joe de Graft (1924–1978) solidified the Ghanaian theater. Playwright and director Sutherland was interested in researching and experimenting with the rich theatrical traditions of the Akan, especially *Anansesem* (Ananse stories). She collaborated with the people of Atwia-Ekumfi to build a community theater—*Kodzi dan* (storytelling house)—and also employed the resources of *Anansesem* in *The Marriage of Anansewa* (1975). Sutherland departs from Western convention and employs an African-Ghanaian aesthetic. The play uses the multigeneric features of *Anansesem*—narrator, *mmoguo* (songs used for creation of character, atmosphere, and suspense), dance, and the character of Ananse (the Spider)—in dealing with themes of national unity, greed, and avarice. Even in Sutherland's otherwise realistic play *Foriwa* (1967), Sintim's absurd speech to his goat exemplifies what Christopher Innes (1993) sees as one of the tenets of the avant-garde—illogicality of language.

After Sutherland and de Graft came a new generation—AMA ATA AIDOO, Asiedu Yirenkyi, MOHAMMED BEN ABDALLAH, and Martin Owusu. Aidoo has the widest international recognition. *The Dilemma of a Ghost* (1965) deals with the clash of cultures, represented by the marriage of Ato (Ghanaian) to Eulalie (American). Aidoo examines this by grounding her play in the *Anansesem* tradition. Although not as bold as Sutherland, Aidoo frames the play with a storyteller, ensuring poetic license by making her refer to herself as the "Bird of the Wayside." This manner of depicting the narrator as a stranger helps us to understand the inability of the characters to resolve their conflicts. Aidoo's *Anowa* (1969), considered one of the masterpieces of African drama, is her greatest achievement yet. It deals with the impact of the transatlantic slave trade on the psyche of the Gold Coast of the 1870s. Anowa, the heroine of the play, confronts her patriarchal society and questions its involvement in the traffic of human souls. As in the first play, Aidoo manipulates the function of the storyteller of *Anansesem* in the form of a choric prologue.

Yirenkyi's reputation rests on his collection titled *Kivuli and Other Plays* (1980), but undoubtedly it is in *Amma Pranaa* (1980) that Yirenkyi resorts to *Anansesem*. This play is unique among those constructed in the *Anansesem* tradition, especially the talking drums employed to signify the start and create the fictive world of the performance. The drum language enhances the play as a whole.

Abdallah is the most prolific playwright in the contemporary Ghanaian theater. All his plays have been staged by Abibigroma, the resident company of the School of Performing Arts. *The Fall of Kumbi* (1989) deals with the fall of the ancient Ghana empire, and its precursor, *The Trial of Mallam Ilya* (1987), examines in epic proportions the sociopolitical repercussions of Kwame Nkrumah's overthrow. In *Mallam Ilya*, we see *Anansesem* theater in its use of music, dance, and the versatility of the narrator. It is through this performance mode (Brechtian, in a sense) that Ilya reveals his complicity in various postindependence governments to amass wealth. Playwright and critic Martin Owusu deserves mention for his adept use of *Anansesem* in *The Story Ananse Told* (1971).

NIGERIA

Nigeria has produced over half of the continent's output of dramatic literature; its theater was dominated by the literary giant WOLE SOYINKA, as well as John Pepper Clark-Bekederemo and Ola Rotimi. Playwright, poet, novelist, critic, and Nobel Prize laureate (1986) Soyinka is noted for his use of Yoruba religion and folklore, establishing a theory of Yoruba-African tragedy and attacking despotic regimes in Africa. Yoruba metaphysics are explored in THE ROAD (1965), DEATH AND THE KING'S HORSEMAN (1975), and *A Dance of the Forests* (1963; commissioned for Nigeria's independence in 1960). The satiric comedies include *The Lion and the Jewel* (1963), *The Trials of Brother Jero* (1964), and *A Play of Giants* (1984), which indicts African dictatorship and the complicity of the United States and the Soviet Union. From the earlier *A Dance of the Forests* to his later *King Baabu* (2002), Soyinka has shocked the sensibilities of his audiences by exposing the intolerable rate of corruption and rejecting the glorification of the African past. In *A Dance of the Forests*, Soyinka destroys the myth of a glorious African past as preached by the Negritudinists. Instead of "glorious and illustrious ancestors," the play is peopled with gory and violent ancestors. *King Baabu*, a mixture of ALFRED JARRY's UBU and William Shakespeare's *Macbeth*, uses burlesque, storytelling, and theatricality to indict Sani Abacha's regime. In *The Baachae of Euripides* (1973), he returns to the spirit of regeneration: Contextualizing Euripides for the modern stage celebrates Ogun, his favorite god in the Yoruba pantheon. Soyinka alters the ending of the play, infusing it with fecundity and regeneration—the head of Dionysus spurts wine, not blood.

Rotimi is best known for his plays *The Gods Are Not to Blame* (1971) and *Our Husband Has Gone Mad Again* (1977). In terms of experimentation, his greatest contribution is *Holding Talks* (1979), which uses illogical language, such as when the self-absorbed Man, for example, claims to see with his own eyes "loud and clear." Clark-Bekederemo, poet, novelist, playwright, and critic, comes from the Niger Delta, and his plays reflect the rich riverine culture of the region. His earlier plays *Song of a Goat* (1961) and *Ozidi* (1966) deal with the need to subsume an individual's pride and self-esteem in favor of the continuity and growth of the community. He uses traditional Ijaw narrative and performance forms that allow the stylization of stage props and characters such as a huge pestle and the spirits of diseases.

During the oil boom of the mid-1970s, a new generation of Nigerian playwrights—more radical and bolder in utilizing and experimenting with traditional forms—emerged. Prominent among them are Zulu Sofola, TESS ONWUEME, FEMI OSOFISAN, Kole Omotoso, Stella Oyedepo, and Bode Sowande. Osofisan's plays are popular in Nigerian universities because of their innovative theatricality (actors revealing themselves as actors) and entertainment value. Awam Amkpa (2004) notes that "music in its residual and emergent mode, dances in their innovatory forms, and storytelling traditions steeped in Yoruba mythology define the esthetics of his plays." His major plays examine brutality, corruption, and kleptomania ensconced in his country: *Once Upon Four Robbers* (1980), *The Chattering and the Song* (1977), *Moroundodun* (1980), and *Farewell to a Cannibal Rage* (1986).

The leading female Nigerian dramatist, Onwueme clothes her work in the signifiers of traditional Igbo culture, but she manipulates these to subvert the hegemonic patriarchy. In *The Reign of Wazobia* (1988), for example, the heroine boldly asserts, "I, Wazobia, have tasted power and will not go" and insists, "Henceforth, women will have equal representation in rulership." In conflict with the conservative men in the play, the women strip naked, destroying "the gyno spectatorial prism" through which they are seen (Amkpa, 2004). *Shakara: The Dance Hall Queen* (2000) adopts an antiillusionist play-acting device in the manner of Osofisan. Her characterization of coupling and doubling African names with prominent black names from the diaspora such as Traveler X, Marcus Mandela, Winnie Ida, and Sojourner Nkrumah in *Riot in Heaven* (1996), is dramatically effective in dealing with the exploitation of Africans in history and in the contemporary world.

An important new voice emerging in the Nigerian theater is Stella Oyedepo. Like other Nigerian dramatists, Oyedepo sees Nigerian society as divisive, corrupting, and alienating. Her *Worshippers of the Naira* (1994) lambastes the materialism that has engulfed Nigerian society in the 1990s. Episodes in this play are interspersed with dances around a Naira Idol. Zulu Sofola employs traditional elements to examine patriarchal society in *Wedlock of the Gods* (1972), *The Sweet Trap* (1977), *King Emene* (1974), and *Song of a Maiden* (1991). On the other hand, Sowande's plays exhibit Brechtian techniques of dislocation as well as incorporation of music, song, dance, and role-play. His major contributions are his trilogy *The Night Before*, *Farewell to Babylon*, and *Flamingoes* (1972–1982), *Monkey's Gold* (1993), and *Tornadoes Full of Dreams* (1990).

FRANCOPHONE AND OTHER INFLUENCES

Francophone African drama, since its inception in the William Ponty School in the early 1930s, has dealt principally with three themes: history, society, and politics. The history play, a fairly recent phenomenon in Anglophone drama, has been a watershed in African theater of French expression: Cheikh Ndao

(L'Exil d'Albouri, 1967), Jean Pliya (*Kondo le requin*, 1966), and Seydou Badian (*Le Mort de Chaka*, 1962). The political and social satires of Guillaume Oyono-Mbia, Maxime Ndebeka, and Tchicaya U'Tamsi are worth noting. However, it is in the plays of Nicole Werewere-Liking, Zadi Zaourou, and Senouvo Zinsou that we find the bold experimentation with the rich and versatile traditional theatrical forms and rituals that abound in West Africa.

Werewere-Liking's theater, Katheryn Wright (1995) aptly observes, "combines dance, music, song, speech, and traditional spatial arrangements and concentrates on eliciting an emotional response to engender an intellectual one." Her plays depart significantly from the conventions of the Western theater; instead, they are firmly rooted in her native Basa healing, initiation, or death rituals. Werewere-Liking's theater is predicated on the belief that contemporary African theater should confront and propose African problems using African symbols and performance techniques. For her, the only way of restoring the spectator-celebrant to a healthy spirit is to encourage complementarity in modern Africa. These concerns are well depicted in *Touareg* (1992). Her other significant works are *The Devil's Tail* (*La Queue du diable*, 1979), *The Power of Um* (*La Puissance d'Um*, 1979), *A New Land* (*Une Nouvelle Terre*, 1980), *Of the Unjust Sleep* (*Du sommeil injuste*, 1980), *Hands Have Meaning* (*Les Mains veulent dire*, 1987), and *The Rainbow Measles* (*La Rougeole arc-en ciel*, 1987).

Senouvo Zinsou is a Togolese playwright and former head of the National Company for the Performing Arts who combines Togolese theater traditions and the techniques of the modern concert party. His major contribution to the spirit of innovation and experimentation is his play *We Are Playing Comedy* (*On joue la comedie*, 1975). The play sees theater as a "game" and is a reflection on the art of creating a play.

Bernard Zadi Zaourou has been involved in invigorating the Ivorian theater since the 1970s. *The Eye* (*L'Oeil*, 1974) effectively utilizes several modes of theatrical language such as speech, drum language, silence, and mime. *The Anthill* (1979) is an initiation play based on the principles of the hunter narratives of his Bete people, the *didiga* (art of the unthinkable). Rationally illogical but mystically significant, it uses SYMBOLISM and surreal poetry. Some of Zaourou's plays include *Sory Lambre* (1968) and *The Hair* (*Les Tignases*, 1984).

Although this article has focused primarily on plays in English and French, there is a vibrant theater tradition in the local languages. These theaters, whether *Apidan* (Yoruba), *Yankamanci* (Hausa), *Anansesem* (Akan), *Okumkpa* (Ibo), or *Koteba* (Bamana), continue to provide material and inspiration for those in the vanguard.

FURTHER READING

Amkpa, Awam. *Theatre and Postcolonial Desires*. New York: Routledge, 2004.

Anyidoho, Kofi, and James Gibbs, eds. *FonTomFrom: Contemporary Ghanaian Literature, Theatre and Film*. Amsterdam: Rodopi, 2000.

Banham, Martin, et al., eds. *The Cambridge Guide to African and Caribbean Theatre*. Cambridge: Cambridge Univ. Press, 1994.

——, eds. *African Theatre: Women*. Bloomington: Ind. Univ. Press, 2002.

Boateng, Alex. "Theater: Anglophone Western Africa." In *Encyclopedia of Africa South of the Sahara*, ed. by John Middleton. 4 vols. New York: Scribner, 1997.

Conteh-Morgan, John. *Theatre and Drama in Francophone Africa*. Cambridge: Cambridge Univ. Press, 1994.

Dunton, Chris. *Nigerian Theatre in English: A Critical Bibliography*. London: Hans Zell, 1998.

Hamilton, Russell. "Portuguese Language Literature." In *A History of Twentieth Century African Literatures*, ed. by Oyekan Owomoyela. Lincoln: Univ. of Nebraska Press, 1993.

Innes, Christopher. *Avant Garde Theatre 1892–1992*. New York: Routledge, 1993.

Wright, Katheryn. "Werewere-Liking: From Chaos to Cosmos." *World Literature Today* 69, no. 1 (1995): 56–63.

Alex Boateng

AFTER THE FALL

ARTHUR MILLER's *After the Fall*, produced by the Lincoln Center Repertory Company, opened in New York at their temporary quarters, the ANTA-Washington Square Theatre, on January 23, 1964. It ran for 208 performances, part of the time in repertory with Miller's *Incident at Vichy* (1964). The object of titillation for both audiences and the press was that Maggie, the protagonist's second wife, a vulnerable, demanding, suicidal singer, was obviously based on Marilyn Monroe, who had died of an overdose of sleeping pills two years before and who was still very much alive in the minds and memories of the public. Many people who saw the play—or who only heard about it—assumed that it was Miller's attempt to absolve himself of any blame for the collapse of his marriage to Monroe, which was ironic since the play was about learning to accept one's guilt and to live with it.

The opening stage direction of the play reads: "The action takes place in the mind, thought, and memory of Quentin." This may suggest DEATH OF A SALESMAN (1949), in which the audience invades the head of Willy Loman, but in the earlier play, the disintegration of Willy is dramatized; all the events, real and imagined, take place in the present. *After the Fall* is an extended analysis or self-analysis in which Quentin settles into a chair at the front of the stage and explains his multiple dilemmas to a device called the Listener, bringing up fragments of his past by way of illustration. In a foreword to the play when it was first published in *The Saturday Evening Post* (February 1, 1964), Miller wrote, "The 'Listener,' who to some will be a psychoanalyst, to others God, is Quentin himself turned at the edge of the abyss to look at his experience, his nature and his time in order to bring to light, to seize and—innocent no more—to forever guard against his own complicity with Cain." It is clear that for all the recollected figures in his life—Maggie, his downtrodden father and brother, his rancorous mother, his accusatory overpsychoanalyzed first wife, his old Communist friends—he has transferred whatever blame lay in their relationships so that he could always come out of the ugliest situation with his innocence intact. Now he wants to embrace his life, guilt and all, an insight that will presumably free him to commit to Holga, the woman he now loves. So he does, but in doing so, he continues to sidestep personal blame by generalizing guilt. The tower of a concentration camp hovers over the stage, about which he says, "My brothers died here . . . but my brothers built this place." While the play was still running, Miller wrote "Our Guilt for the World's Evil," an article for the *New York Times Magazine* (January 3, 1965) in which he insisted on the need "to discover our own relationship to evil, its reflection of ourselves." Miller presumably wants his very long play to make a serious point, but it comes across as a cop-out for Quentin and—given the autobiographical core of the play—for Miller as well.

[*See also* United States, 1940–Present]

FURTHER READING

Miller, Arthur. *The Theater Essays of Arthur Miller*. Ed. by Robert A. Martin. New York: Viking, 1978.

——. *Timebends, A Life*. New York : Grove, 1987.

——. *Echoes down the Corridor, Collected Essays, 1944–2000*. Ed. by Steven R. Centola. New York: Viking, 2000.

Weales, Gerald. *The Jumping-Off Place, American Drama in the 1960's*. New York: Macmillan, 1969.

Gerald Weales

AFTER THE REUNION

Adapted by Chen Renjian (1913–1995) from a traditional Chinese play titled *Regret of the Father and Son* (*Shi Tianwen*; also known by the title *Fu zi hen*), *After the Reunion* (*Tuan yuan zhi hou, puxian xi*) depicts the tragedy of a family trying frantically to preserve its honor. A strong condemnation of traditional Confucian ethics, the play was written and staged in 1956 and was enthusiastically applauded by some Chinese government leaders when it was first performed in Beijing in 1959. The play was made into a movie a year later.

Deeply in love with her cousin Zheng Sicheng, Ye was forced by her parents to marry Mr. Shi when she was already two month's pregnant with Zheng's child. Shi died soon after their marriage; Ye continued her relationship with Zheng, and together they brought up their son Shi Yisheng. The play begins when Shi Yisheng, now coming out first in the imperial examination, arrives home to marry his fiancée Liu and to present his mother with this imperial honor to acknowledge her chasteness for all those years. Fearful of offending the honor once her affair with Zheng comes to light, Ye secretly meets Zheng to end their relationship. Their last rendezvous, however, is seen by Liu, now Ye's daughter-in-law; consequently, Ye hangs herself in shame. Afraid that the truth about his mother's death may be known, Shi asks his wife to falsely admit her guilt in causing her mother-in-law's death. Nevertheless, a county official reveals the truth. Knowing that his mother's name may be sullied, Shi can only think of death and decides to take poison. While he is bidding his mother farewell at her spirit tablet (a tablet erected in a mourning hall for people to pay homage to the recent dead), he sees none other than his uncle Zheng, who is grieving. Knowing that Zheng has been his mother's lover all along, Shi angrily forces him to take the poison. Just before he dies, in tears, Zheng reveals that he is really Shi's father. Filled with remorse and sorrow, Shi acknowledges Zheng as his parent and swallows the remaining poison himself, dying with his father before Ye's spirit tablet. At the end of the play, Liu also commits suicide by hitting her head against the wall of a pavilion built by the local officials in honor of her loyalty and filial piety.

Closely knit in structure and full of twists in plot, the play is a rare tragedy in traditional Chinese drama. Different from its original, which promotes feudal ethics, the adapted play conveys profound social significance in exposing the hypocrisy of the Confucian code of ethics. In staging the play, Chen Renjian made innovative use of several traditional ways of expression in Chinese drama. For example, the "butterfly steps" by the young female protagonist help to express the emotional depths of the character. The dance choreography with *cangues* (heavy wooden yokes carried on the shoulders, which enclose the neck and arms) suggests the punishment being meted out. And percussion instruments echo plot development.

Chen Renjian also wrote another influential play, *Chuncao Forces Her Way into the Judge's Court* (*Chuncao chuan tang*, 1960).

[*See also* China]

FURTHER READING

Chen Renjian. *Chen Renjian xiqu xuan* [Selected plays by Chen Renjian]. Beijing: Zhongguo xiju chubanshe, 1981.

——. "Qiu xin, qiu shen, qiu zhen—huiyi 'Tuan yuan zhi hou,' 'chun cao chuang tang' and 'Song kou si' de xiezuo" [To be novel, profound and truthful: Recalling the writing of "After the Reunion," "Chuncao Forces Her Way into the Judge's Court" and "The Legend of the Inspector at Songkou"]. *Juben* [Play Scripts] 2 (1982).

Li Guoting. *Chen Renjian ping zhuan* [A biography of Chen Renjian with commentary]. Beijing: Zhongguo xiju chubanshe, 1988.

Ma Jianhua and Lin Daoxing. " 'Tuan yuan zhi hou' de beiju texing guankui" [A glimpse of the tragic features in "After the Reunion"] *Fujian xiju* [Fujian Drama] 1 (1987).

Tian Han. "Du 'Tuan yuan zhi hou' " [Reading "After the Reunion"]. *Juben* [Play Scripts] 11 (1959).

Hongchu Fu and Cai Xingshui

AGITATION-PROPAGANDA

Agitation-propaganda drama, or "agit-prop," arose in the aftermath of the Russian Revolution when, in 1923, students from the Institute of Journalism created the Blue Blouse, the first agit-prop troupe. Inspired by oral newspapers and drawing on VSEVOLOD MEYERHOLD's Biomechanics, Sergei Eisenstein's cinematic montage, popular performance, and propaganda poster art, they created a theatrical style whose goal was to inform the mostly illiterate masses about unfolding political events while engaging them in class struggle and creating solidarity. Their work spawned five professional companies and nearly 7,000 amateur groups throughout the USSR.

Agit-prop performers sought a theatrical style that moved away from bourgeois REALISM, that was mobile and entertaining, and that could convey practical information. Troupes of ten to twelve players took performances to the clubs and halls where peasants and workers gathered. They used few props and dressed in workers' blue shirts and black pants. Their program took the form of a living newspaper, beginning with headlines followed by news reports on major events, editorials, local issues, and cartoons. They combined AVANT-GARDE and popular performance styles of the day, using speaking choruses, living posters in which actors poked their heads through painted canvases, folk verse with musical accompaniment, vaudeville, cabaret, music hall, and acrobatics to make performances as engaging as possible. Although agit-prop was the most widespread theatrical form of the postrevolutionary period, political pressure led to its demise in favor of SOCIALIST REALISM around 1928.

The Blue Blouse's 1927 tour of GERMANY inspired the creation of numerous German troupes such as the Red Megaphone and the Red Blouses. Over 400 troupes were affiliated with the German Communist Party, Communist Youth League, and Worker's Theatre League by 1930. Their pieces contrasted German woes with a utopian vision of the USSR, with the militant goal of trying to foster revolution. The influence of German agit-prop can be seen in the political theater of BERTOLT BRECHT.

In the 1930s, agit-prop spread to workers' theaters around the world. As in the USSR, networks of troupes shared scripts and ideas at meetings and in publications. In both Britain and America, agit-prop competed with Socialist Realism. The Workers' Theatre Movement (1926–1935) in Britain adopted agit-prop as their primary style, as did New York's Shock Troupe, whose members trained in Biomechanics and lived communally to be available to perform at strikes and rallies at any time. American agit-prop uniquely addressed a multiracial workforce. New York's GROUP THEATRE's successful production of CLIFFORD ODETS's *WAITING FOR LEFTY* (1935) fused agit-prop and Socialist Realism, as did large-scale living newspapers created under the Federal Theatre Project (1935–1939) such as Arthur Arent's *One Third of a Nation* (1938).

In SPAIN, Rafael Alberti and his wife Maria Teresa León developed agit-prop plays dramatizing working-class life. They mixed the Soviet model with Spanish popular forms and toured to rural areas. During the Spanish Civil War (1936–1939), they helped the National Theatre Council's GUERRILLA THEATER division mobilize "urgency theater" against fascism. Short, didactic pieces like *Crush Franco!* (1938) inspired people to support the Republican cause, sometimes boosting morale close to the fighting itself.

A new American agit-prop emerged out of the turbulent 1960s. The short, didactic "actos" of EL TEATRO CAMPESINO drew from popular Chicano performance traditions to educate immigrant farmworkers about their class position and encourage them to support the United Farm Workers' Union. The company took their plays out to the fields on the back of a flatbed truck. The San Francisco Mime Troupe, founded by Ron Davis, created more elaborate pieces, using *commedia dell' arte*, vaudeville, minstrelsy, and other popular forms as their model. Through comedy, music, and caricature, they protested the Vietnam War and supported civil rights. Peter Schumann's Bread and Puppet Theatre made its mark integrating silent but visually eloquent papier-mâché masks and giant puppets into anti–Vietnam War marches. Schumann drew inspiration from the popular traditions of his German homeland transmitted through his unique sculptural style. In the BLACK ARTS MOVEMENT, ED BULLINS and Ben Caldwell promoted a black revolutionary agenda. The LIVING THEATRE adopted an Artaudian Theater of Cruelty aesthetic for their political agitation.

In the early 21st century, giant puppets, wild costumes, and other performance elements are an expected part of political protest. Leftist activist-performers like The Billionaires, Art and Revolution, the Surveillance Camera Players, and Reverend Billy capitalize on visual imagery, sound bytes, and irony to compete with corporate propaganda, bringing agit-prop into the media age.

FURTHER READING

Bablet, Marie-Louise, and Denis Bablet, eds. *Le Théâtre d'agit-prop de 1917 à 1932.* [Agit-prop theatre from 1917 to 1932]. Work Collective: Claude Amey et al. Vols. 1–4. Lausanne: La Cité-L'Age d'homme, 1977.

Bodek, Richard. *Proletarian Performance in Weimar Berlin: Agitprop, Chorus, and Brecht.* Columbia, S.C.: Camden House, 1997.

Bradby, David, and John McCormick. *People's Theatre.* Totowa, N.J.: Rowman & Littlefield, 1978.

Orenstein, Claudia. "Agitational Performance, Now and Then." *Theater* 31 (2001): 139–151.

Samuel, Raphael, Ewan MacColl, and Stuart Cosgrove, eds. *Theatres of the Left, 1880–1935: Worker's Theatre Movements in Britain and America.* London: Routledge & Kegan Paul, 1985.

Stourac, Richard, and Kathleen McCreery. *Theatre as a Weapon: Workers' Theatre in the Soviet Union, Germany and Britain, 1917–1934.* New York: Routledge & Kegan Paul, 1986.

Wikler, Ruth Juliet. "Popular Army, Popular Theater: Spanish Agitprop during the Civil War, 1936–1939." *Theater* 31 (2001): 78–105.

Claudia Orenstein

AGRA BAZAAR

Written and directed by HABIB TANVIR and first performed in the open-air theater at Jamia Millia University, New Delhi, in 1954, *Agra Bazaar* is an entertaining and meaningful play. It is one of Tanvir's most popular and repeatedly performed plays and one of the most important plays of the 1950s. This musical production deals with the poetry and times of Urdu poet Nazir Akbarabadi, who lived in Agra during the historically and economically difficult period of the late 18th and early 19th centuries. Quite remarkably for his time, Nazir not only wrote about ordinary people and their everyday concerns, but he wrote in a style that often ignored the orthodox, elitist norms of poetic idiom and subject matter.

Using a mix of educated, middle-class urban actors and more or less illiterate folk and street artists, Tanvir virtually brings alive on stage a whole bazaar teeming with shopkeepers, vendors, prostitutes, street entertainers, performing bears, and monkeys. The play depicts the economic hardships faced by the common people of Agra and shows how Nazir's poetry helped them in their struggle. Tanvir divides the stage into two cultural and social polarities. At one end is a kite-shop where the plebeian admirers of Nazir's poetry gather. At the opposite end, there is a bookstore that attracts those writers and critics who represent the cultural orthodoxy of the time and who look down on Nazir, on his association with the "vulgar" culture of the people, and above all, on his use of popular idiom in his poetry. This conflict of two contrary standpoints constitutes the play's thematic core. It uses the example of Nazir's poetry and his plebeian appeal to challenge orthodox, elitist literary canons.

Agra Bazaar has an episodic structure. There is no overarching story or conflict of the conventional kind. The profusion of poetry, music, festive scenes, and polemical debates about the nature and function of art makes it an assertion and a celebration of a democratic approach to culture.

[*See also* India]

FURTHER READING

Tanvir, Habib. *Agra Bazaar*. Tr. by Javed Malick. Kolkata: Seagull Bks., 2006.

Javed Malick

AIDOO, AMA ATA (1942–)

No man made a slave of his friend and came to much himself. It is wrong. It is evil.

—Ama Ata Aidoo

Ghanaian writer Ama Ata Aidoo is better known as a novelist and writer of short stories than as a playwright. Her works include the novels *Our Sister Killjoy or Reflections from a Black-Eyed Squint* (1977) and *Changes* (1991) and two collections of short stories, *No Sweetness Here and Other Stories* (1970) and *The Girl Who Can and Other Stories* (1997). Aidoo is an adept storyteller with a unique experimental style that gives her prose a dramatic quality. She has said that she writes her stories to be heard and often imagines them as oral performances. This quality of her stories gives a hint of the dramatist in her. She has to her credit two major plays, *Dilemma of a Ghost* (1965) and *Anowa* (1970).

Both of Aidoo's plays deal with the issue of the slave trade directly and indirectly. *Dilemma of a Ghost* was written and produced while Aidoo was in her final year at the University of Ghana in 1964. Ato, the oldest son of the family, returns from his studies in the United States with an African American wife, much to the chagrin of his family, who are initially unable to accept her slave ancestry. Ato's wife, Eulalie, sees her marriage and "return" to Africa as a way of reconnecting with her past. The main conflict in the play, however, revolves around the couple's decision to delay having children until they feel ready. Ato's family, unaware of their decision, assume Eulalie is barren. Ato, who is expected to play a mediating role, is totally confused and unable to adequately handle the situation. In the end, Ato's mother reaches out to her daughter-in-law in compassion, and Ato is chided for his lack of understanding of and sensitivity to both his family and his wife.

Anowa more directly addresses the slave trade from a woman's point of view. It is an imaginative reworking of an old Ghanaian legend about a girl who defies her parents and rejects all acceptable suitors, to marry a man of her own choice, but lives to regret it. In Aidoo's play, Anowa and her chosen husband, Kofi Ako, are very happy the first years of their marriage, selling animal skins from town to town. As they become rich, Ako decides to buy slaves to help them in their business, much against Anowa's vehement opposition. Her deep dissatisfaction with this situation, coupled with their inability to have children, turns Anowa into a shadow of her former vivacious self. The reason for her deep feelings against buying slaves is revealed in a moment of intimacy with the audience where she relates a terrifying dream she had had as a little girl, after her grandmother had told her a story about how people had been sold as slaves to white strangers. The play ends tragically with both committing suicide.

Aidoo's concern with the state of the African woman permeates her works, giving them a feminist edge. She recently founded Mbasem (literally meaning "women's affairs" or "women's words"), a nongovernmental organization, in Accra, which aims, among other things, at encouraging women writers.

[*See also* Africa]

PLAYS: *Dilemma of a Ghost* (1965); *Anowa* (1970)

FURTHER READING

Kerr, David. *African Popular Theatre from Pre-colonial Times to the Present Day*. London: James Currey, 1995.

Awo Mana Asiedu

LES AIGUILLES ET L'OPIUM See NEEDLES AND OPIUM

AKIMOTO MATSUYO (1911–2001)

Akimoto Matsuyo, a Japanese SHINGEKI playwright, is the most important female dramatist JAPAN has produced. Her play *Kaison the Priest of Hitachi* (*Hitachibō Kaison*, 1964) is a landmark in the transition of modern drama in Japan from modernist conventions to a form with an original voice.

Akimoto was born in Yokohama in 1911. Sickly as a child, she had no more than a grade-school education. She was a voracious reader, however, and was encouraged in her studies by her two elder brothers. Her mastery of the Japanese language in all of its regional inflections and her love of the Japanese classics, reflected in such works as *Akaigo's Love* (*Akaigo no Koi*, 1956), *Prince Karu and His Sister* (*Karu no Taishi to Sono Imōto*, 1959), and the highly successful *A Tale after Chikamatsu* (*Chikamatsu Monogatari*, 1979), came from her early immersion in books.

Akimoto's career began when she joined MIYOSHI JŪRŌ's newly established Drama Workshop (Gikyoku Kenkyūkai) in 1945. Miyoshi was a disillusioned former Communist and humanist playwright who immediately recognized and nurtured Akimoto's talent.

Throughout her career, Akimoto was concerned with the problem of death. In play after play, she took up the various solutions the Japanese had devised for conquering death and found them imperfect. *Mourning Clothes* (*Reifuku*, 1949), which defines the problem and was Akimoto's first produced work, concerns a fractious family pulled apart by their inability to mourn the death of their mother. In *The Life of Muraoka Iheiji* (*Muraoka Iheiji-den*, 1960), the efficacy of the Japanese emperor system as an immortalizing system is questioned. And in *Thoughts on Our Lady of Scabs* (*Kasabuta Shikibu-kō*, 1968), the saving power of a typical Japanese saving cult (a term that refers to the *shinko shukyo* or "new religions" that were founded in the mid-19th century and their numerous descendants) is critically examined. Akimoto is less interested in criticizing the various systems the Japanese have devised to deal with death than she is in depicting the human suffering that leads desperate people to resort to them.

Kaison the Priest of Hitachi is the finest example of Akimoto's approach. The play describes the plight of a group of young boys evacuated from Tokyo to northeastern Japan in October 1944. Isolated in the region's interminable winter and brutalized by Japan's death-drenched wartime ideology, the boys are completely bereft when they learn that their parents have been killed in the firebombing of Tokyo on March 10, 1945. Unable to deal with this reality, the weakest and most vulnerable boy, Keita, escapes into the embrace of a local shamaness and the cult of Kaison, an immortal savior figure who is reputed to wander perpetually, taking upon himself the sins and suffering of all those in need. The Kaison cult offers Keita a way to transcend death—but at a terrible price. He is exploited mercilessly and driven to the brink of madness by the old shamaness and her granddaughter, who succeeds the former as the rapacious head of the cult. The way the play stages the Japanese premodern imagination demonstrates its continuing power in the present and holds it up to critical scrutiny is what made *Kaison* a milestone in the transition from *shingeki* to ANGURA in the 1960s.

SELECT PLAYS: *Fine Dust* (*Keijin*, 1946); *Mourning Clothes* (*Reifuku*, 1949); *Silent Women* (*Monoiwanu Onna-tachi*, 1954); *Akaigo's Love* (*Akaigo no Koi*, 1956); *Prince Karu and His Sister* (*Karu no Taishi to Sono Imōto*, 1959); *The Life of Muraoka Iheiji* (*Muraoka Iheiji-den*, 1960); *Kaison the Priest of Hitachi* (*Hitachibō Kaison*, 1964); *Thoughts on Our Lady of Scabs* (*Kasabuta Shikibu-kō*, 1968); *A Tale after Chikamatsu* (*Chikamatsu Monogatari*, 1979)

FURTHER READING

Akimoto Matsuyo. *Akimoto Matsuyo Zen Sakuhinshū*. 3 vols. Tokyo: Yamato Shobō, 1976.

——. *Kaison the Priest of Hitachi*. Tr. by David G. Goodman. In *The Return of the Gods: Japanese Drama and Culture in the 1960s*, by David G. Goodman. Cornell East Asia Papers 116. Ithaca, N.Y.: Cornell East Asia Program, 2003.

Inoue Yoshie. "Nanpō no Monoiwanu Onna-tachi: Gūshū no Gensō, *Muraoka Iheiji-den*" [Silent women of the South: The delusion of the foolish, "The Life of Muraoka Iheiji"]. In *Baishun to Nihon Bungaku* [Prostitution and Japanese literature], ed. by Okano Yukie et al. Tokyo: Tokyodō Shuppan, 2002.

Morii Naoko. "Akimoto Matsuyo *Kasabuta Shikibu-kō*" [Akimoto Matsuyo's "Thoughts on Our Lady of Scabs"]. In *Nijusseiki no Gikyoku II: Gendai Gikyoku no Tenkai* [Twentieth century plays II: The evolution of contemporary plays], ed. by Nihon Kindai Engekishi Kenkyūkai. Tokyo: Shakai Hyōronsha, 2002.

David G. Goodman

AKINS, ZOË (1886–1958)

Primarily known for her work as a dramatist, Zoë Akins was also a poet, a novelist, an adapter of French and Hungarian plays, and a screenwriter. Akins was born on October 30, 1886, in Humansville, Missouri. When she was 12, her wealthy family moved to Saint Louis, where she completed her studies in a private school. Three years later William Marion Reedy offered to publish Akins's poems, short stories, book reviews, and criticism in his journal *Mirror*. After recovering from tuberculosis and some preliminary failures in her profession, she moved to New York in 1909 and eventually began to write plays. The production of *The Magical City* (1916), an experimental melodrama and a love story in free verse, was first performed by the Washington Square Players and marked the beginning of a fruitful career. Her next work, the three-act satire *Papa* (1913), ran on Broadway with modest success. Akins's first successful play on Broadway, *Déclassée* (1919), starring Ethel Barrymore, deals with the decline of Lady Helen Haden, a married woman who falls in love with a man who is not her husband.

Akins's concern with women and contemporary ethics is clearly reflected in her subsequent plays, including *Daddy's Gone A-Hunting* (1921), about marital unfaithfulness; *The Varying Shore* (1921), in which Madame Leland, an old lady, recalls her disastrous love life ever since she was forced to get married when she was seventeen; *Greatness* (1922, published as *The Texas Nightingale*), a comedy about an opera singer; and *O Evening Star!* (1936), based on the life of Canadian-born actress and Hollywood star of the 1930s Marie Dressler. Akins's experimental mode of writing was not appreciated by audiences. For instance, she wrote *The Varying Shore* with the third act placed at the beginning, and she was forced to rewrite the play. Her most celebrated play is *The Old Maid* (1935), a dramatization of Edith Wharton's novel of the same title, which earned Akins a Pulitzer Prize for drama. This noteworthy play deals with the quarrelsome relationship between Delia Lovell and her cousin Charlotte. After giving birth to an illegitimate daughter with the man both of them loved, Charlotte is fated to trust her child, Tina, to Delia. It is on the day of Tina's wedding that these two cousins finally come to terms with themselves and reach a better understanding of each other.

Akins moved to California in the early 1920s, owing to health problems. There, several filmmakers became interested in her work, producing some of her earlier plays, including *Déclassée*, filmed as *Her Private Life*, and *The Moon Flower* (1924), filmed as *Eve's Secret*. As a screenwriter, Akins continued to focus her attention on women's concerns in contemporary society, such as in *Sarah and Son* (1930), *Anybody's Woman* (1930), and *Once a Lady* (1931).

In 1932 Akins married Captain Hugo Rumbold, an artist who died one year after their wedding. Her most representative screenplays were *Morning Glory* (1932), for which Katharine Hepburn won an Oscar for best actress; *Camille* (1936), starring Greta Garbo; and *Zaza* (1938). She also wrote numerous adaptations of other writers' novels, such as Gilbert Frankau's *Christopher Strong*. Among her last works are the novel *Forever Young* (1941) and a film that she wrote after a six-year hiaitus, *Desire Me* (1947). Akins died on October 29, 1958, in Los Angeles, California.

[*See also* United States, 1920–1940]

PLAYS: *Papa* (1913); *The Magical City* (1916); *Déclassée* (1919); *Foot-loose* (1919); *Daddy's Gone A-Hunting* (1921); *The Varying Shore* (1921); *The Texas Nightingale* (1922); *A Royal Fandango* (1923); *The Moon-Flower* (1924); *First Love* (1926); *The Crown Prince* (1927); *The Furies* (1928); *The Love Duel* (1929); *The Greeks Had a Word for It* (1930); *The Old Maid* (1935); *O Evening Star!* (1936)

FURTHER READING

Bradley, Jennifer. "Zoë Akins and the Age of Excess: Broadway Melodrama in the 1920s." In *Modern American Drama: The Female Canon*, ed. by June Schlueter. London: Associated Univ. Presses, 1990.

Shafer, Yvonne. *American Women Playwrights 1900–1950*. New York: Peter Lang, 1995.

Sutherland, Cynthia. "American Women Playwrights as Mediators of the 'Woman Problem.'" *Modern Drama* 21, no. 3 (1978): 319–335.

Estefania Olid-Peña

ALBANESI, MEGGIE (1899–1923)

Margherita Cecilia Brigida Lucia Maria Albanesi (Meggie) was born on October 8, 1899, in London, England, her mother popular novelist Effie Rowlands, her father Carlo Albanesi, professor at the Royal Academy of Music. She studied the violin but moved in 1915 to the Academy of Dramatic Art, winning the Bancroft Gold Medal in 1917. She began professional life among respected conservative practitioners, as Lucy in Sydney Grundy's *A Pair of Spectacles*, understudy in J.M. BARRIE's DEAR BRUTUS, and touring with Fred Terry. After the war, she worked more experimentally in London, acclaimed in the Pioneer Players' production of Herman Heijerman's *The Rising Sun*. In 1920 she joined Basil Dean's theater company ReandeaN, based in the St. Martin's, committed to producing challenging modern plays. She had instant success as Jill Hillcrist in JOHN GALSWORTHY's *The Skin Game*, a role offering scope for her greatest strengths: emotional intensity allied to modernity.

She enlarged her experience of comedy in Alice Duer Miller's *The Charm School*, playing opposite matinee idol Owen Nares, returning to ReandeaN in early 1921 for the role that made her famous, Sydney in Clemence Dane's *A Bill of Divorcement*. A tomboyish, flippant young girl confronting a tragic fate, the character fitted both her naturalistic intensity and her comic gift. The play ran for 401 performances; the audience, mostly young, found their experience of the postwar world reflected, and Albanesi became a cult figure. It placed ReandeaN on a more secure footing, and Dean launched a series of experimental matinees like Galsworthy's *The First and the Last*, in which Abanesi played a refugee prostitute opposite Nares, anxious to develop his reputation as a serious actor. Critically acclaimed, they began an affair, but Nares's wife intercepted a letter, and he brutally split with Albanesi.

Two long runs followed—Galsworthy's *Loyalties* and Dean's first major commercial production, WILLIAM SOMERSET MAUGHAM's *East of Suez* at His Majesty's. The role of Daisy, a rootless half-Chinese girl who makes an unsatisfactory marriage, was demanding but old-fashioned in its conception. Despite good reviews, Albanesi was frustrated by the role and dogged by illness. To the concern of her friends, she had begun a frenzied nightlife. After visiting her sister in New York, she collapsed, recovering in June to play a "flapper" who hooks her husband by imitating Victorian manners in *The Lilies of the Field*, the comedy success of 1923. In the summer she worked on

ReandeaN's experimental Playbox matinees, notably John Masefield's *Melloney Holtspur*; her performance as a modern young woman surrounded by ghosts was described by Masefield as "one of the wonders of our stage." Albanesi's health suffered throughout this period. Her role in Brown's *A Magadalen's Husband*, the wife of a violent man whose lover is hanged, was seen by the company as a great leap forward.

She died suddenly on December 9, 1923, in Broadstairs, Kent, England, probably the result of a botched abortion.

[*See also* England, 1860–1940]

Frances Gray

ALBEE, EDWARD (1928–)

Each play is an act of aggression against the status quo. Too many playwrights let the audience off the hook instead of slugging them in the face, which is what you should be doing.

—Edward Albee, 2004

Considered by many to be the natural successor to ARTHUR MILLER, TENNESSEE WILLIAMS, and even EUGENE O'NEILL, and by others as closer in style to SAMUEL BECKETT, HAROLD PINTER, and the European Theater of the Absurd, Edward Albee and his early plays explored the pain and disillusionment of the transitional years between the solid postwar security of the Eisenhower era and the burgeoning creative diversity of the 1960s. Albee's work challenged American postwar complacency and questioned the cozy sense of stability that pervaded the society of the period.

THE EARLY YEARS

Born on March 12, 1928, in Washington, D.C., and adopted as a child into an affluent family with theatrical origins (his adoptive grandfather, after whom he was named, was the highly successful vaudeville producer E. F. Albee), Albee was educated first at the Lawrenceville School in New Jersey, at Pennsylvania's Valley Forge Military Academy, and then at the Choate School in Connecticut. His first exposure to mainstream theater at the age of seven—a visit to the Broadway show *Jumbo*, starring Jimmy Durante—provided little indication of the impact that he would later make on the Broadway theater of the 1960s.

He began writing poetry at the age of eight, although he waited several years before he saw his first published poem, "Eighteen," appear in a Texas literary magazine in 1945. He had written his first full-length play, *Aliqueen*, at age twelve, and his first published play, *Schism*, appeared in the Choate school magazine during his final year. He graduated in 1946, then spent a year at Trinity College in Hartford, where he gained his first practical theater-making experience as an actor.

An unpublished three-act play, *The City of People*, was completed in 1949. But Albee's engagement with dramatic writing was symptomatic of the growing split between the young Albee and his parents. In spite of his mother's attempts to secure him a stable profession and integrate him into a solid social circle, Albee chose to spend his time with artists and writers and, at the age of twenty, moved to Greenwich Village in New York City. To supplement the small allowance from his grandfather's estate, he undertook a variety of jobs: office boy, record salesman, book salesman for Bloomingdale's department store, and messenger for Western Union. His first paid writing job was to pen continuity announcements for a New York radio station. However, Albee continued to develop his serious writing, and a meeting with THORNTON WILDER in 1953 inspired him to concentrate on the theater. He later dedicated his one-act verse play *The Making of a Saint* (1953/54) to Wilder.

Albee completed his first successful play, THE ZOO STORY, over a three-week period in 1958. Shortly afterward he received a sizable inheritance from his grandmother's estate, which alleviated many of the stresses suffered by the archetypal "struggling writer." Having been rejected by several New York producers, *The Zoo Story* was staged at the Schiller Theater in Berlin in the following year as part of a double-bill with Beckett's KRAPP'S LAST TAPE. The play was then staged at the Provincetown Playhouse in January 1960, marking Albee's American debut. The playwright directed the subsequent national tour of *The Zoo Story* himself and, a year later, also led a South American tour, setting a creative precedent that was to continue throughout his career.

Albee's early plays provided evidence of a facility to adapt to a range of contrasting theatrical styles: The existentialism of his first play, *The Zoo Story*—in which a rootless young man enacts a disturbing premeditated suicide with the unwilling participation of an innocent bystander—shocked audiences by its illustration of the violent response of a new generation alienated and disillusioned by postwar society.

His exploration of the death of the legendary black blues singer Bessie Smith in his second play, *The Death of Bessie Smith* (1960), explored the already sensitive area of race relations in America, shortly to be even more vividly and actively illustrated on the streets of American cities and towns. *The Sandbox* (1960) and *The American Dream* (1961) saw Albee moving recognizably into the area of absurdist theater, and Martin Esslin, in *The Theatre of the Absurd* (1962), described *The American Dream* as a "brilliant first example of an American contribution" to that influential genre. In the same year, Albee experimented with musical staging, collaborating with composer William Flanagan on an operatic adaptation of Herman Melville's *Bartleby the Scrivener.*

The Death of Bessie Smith and *The American Dream* both opened off-Broadway in 1961. Although both plays were met with mixed reviews, they enjoyed relatively long runs.

FORAY INTO CONTEMPORARY REALISM

With roots firmly embedded in the European absurdist tradition, Albee continued to develop a reputation as a writer of provocative, socially aware plays that examined the anxiety of contemporary American society. However, the rapidly changing society of the early 1960s frequently overtook the writer by providing even more graphic evidence of social change than Albee's theatrical vision could provide.

Albee's stylistic departure into the realm of contemporary REALISM, however, brought him his first major critical and popular success in 1962 with *WHO'S AFRAID OF VIRGINIA WOOLF?*—a play whose uncomfortably raw and realistic view of family life and marital relationships provoked inescapable comparison with Eugene O'Neill. The premiere production, starring Uta Hagen and Arthur Hill, marked Albee's Broadway debut and ran for two years. It won for Albee the prestigious New York Drama Critics Circle Award as Best Play of the Year, and five Tony Awards, including Best Play and Best Production. The play was nominated for a Pulitzer Prize but did not win the award: Some of the Pulitzer trustees took exception to what they considered obscene dialogue. Two of the Pulitzer Committee members consequently resigned in protest. Stanley Kauffmann suggested that the principal couple in the play should actually have been men, emphasizing the fact that several homosexual writers had thinly disguised gay relationships in their portrayal of heterosexual characters. Albee, however, refuted this, pointing out that if the characters had been gay men, it would hardly have been possible for one to suffer a phantom pregnancy.

Albee's future career seemed assured, and *Virginia Woolf* was given several productions in Europe and South America. The play continues to be one of his most popular and still frequently performed works, with several television adaptations and a highly successful movie version directed by Mike Nichols in 1965, which drew memorable performances from Elizabeth Taylor, Richard Burton, George Segal, and Sandy Dennis.

Albee's commitment to writing for the theater also found an outlet in the activities of the New York Playwrights' Unit Workshop, which he co-founded in 1963 to support the work of new young writers. Over the next eight years the Workshop enabled the production of more than 100 new works by writers such as MART CROWLEY, TERRENCE MCNALLY, and SAM SHEPARD.

Albee's next two plays, *The Ballad of the Sad Café* (1963, based on the novel by Carson McCullers) and *Tiny Alice* (1964), both enjoyed successful Broadway runs, and the latter production also won both the Drama Critics Circle Award and a Tony. *Tiny Alice* is considered to be one of Albee's most densely metaphysical plays, dealing as it does with the subject of unconsciousness. Albee's ambivalence toward critics may well originate from his experience with this play: He once stated that audiences appeared to have no problem understanding the complexities of *Tiny Alice* in previews until the play opened and the critics insisted on emphasizing how difficult it was to understand the play.

In 1966, Albee returned again to a domestic theme in *A Delicate Balance*, which he had completed during a trip to Europe. Here we are presented with an almost archetypal theatrical portrait of the dysfunctional American family. As the characters try ever harder to avoid confronting painful issues, so the issues become increasingly painful. The principal themes of suppressed emotions, lost opportunities, and regret for potential unfulfilled find their focus in the portrayal of a retired suburban couple whose lives are turned upside down in one weekend when they are exposed to the emotional insecurities of their family and friends. This, in turn, exposes the painful hidden insecurities in their own lives. The play premiered at the Martin Beck Theatre and won the Pulitzer Prize for Drama.

Continued success, however, was not unconditionally guaranteed for Albee, and a series of uncharacteristic adaptations—including a 1966 musical version of Truman Capote's *Breakfast at Tiffany's*, which closed during previews, and a 1981 dramatization of Vladimir Nabokov's controversial novel *Lolita*—all failed to attract the approval of either critics or audiences.

Perhaps in response to this, *Box* and *Quotations from Chairman Mao* (1968), *All Over* (1971), and *Seascape* (1975, directed by the author) saw Albee returning to his more accustomed experimental approach to theater making. The last of these won him a second Pulitzer Prize.

The year 1976 witnessed a further departure in Albee's experimental one-act play for radio, *Listening: A Chamber Play*, which was produced in England by the BBC. In the following year, Albee staged the play with another one-act, *Counting the Ways*, at London's National Theatre. Later that same year, he directed a highly successful Broadway revival of *Virginia Woolf*, with Colleen Dewhurst and Ben Gazzara in the leading roles. Now in increasing demand as a director of his own plays, Albee was invited to stage a touring season of his work in 1978, under the collective title *Albee Directs Albee*, and in 1980 he was appointed co-director of the Vivian Beaumont Theater at Lincoln Center in New York.

The Lady from Dubuque (1980) and *The Man Who Had Three Arms* (1982), both of which harkened back to the writer's earlier styles and preoccupations, failed to generate very wide interest, even though the first of these was awarded a Gold Medal by the American Academy and Institute of Arts and Letters. This marked what seemed to be at least a partial withdrawal from theater writing—punctuated only by *Envy* (1985) and *The Marriage Play* (1987)—for almost a decade, during which Albee concentrated primarily on directing productions of his own work.

A NEW PERIOD OF CREATIVITY

This fallow period came to an end in 1991 with the premiere of *THREE TALL WOMEN* at the English Theatre in Vienna, in which the three characters portrayed at the beginning of the play turn out to represent one woman at three different stages of her life. Here Albee succeeds in presenting a witty and totally unsentimental picture of the sensitive subject of aging and the increasing frailty that it brings. The play was staged off-Broadway in 1994 and was hugely successful, winning Albee his third Pulitzer Prize and the New York Drama Critics Circle and Outer Critics Circle Awards for Best Play.

Three Tall Women marked the beginning of a new period of creativity in Albee's writing career: *The Lorca Play* premiered at the Alley Theatre in Houston in 1992, and *Fragments* in Cincinnati the following year. The Signature Theater in New York staged an entire season of Albee plays in 1993–1994. Further awards followed: the Kennedy Center Commendation for Lifetime Achievement (1996) and the National Medal of Arts (1997).

The Play about the Baby, which was described by Donald Lyons in the *New York Post* as "an absurd meditation on marriage, trust and fertility," provided yet another exploration of marriage and relationships. Although it premiered in London in 1998, it did not receive an OFF-BROADWAY production until three years later, when it enjoyed a respectable run. Set in an abstract version of Eden, the play involves two characters simply named Boy and Girl, who are evidently deeply in love. It is not until the arrrival of two older, more cynical and "knowing" characters, Man and Woman, that their idyllic relationship is placed under pressure.

In 2002, Albee returned yet again to the theme of marriage in his controversial play *The Goat, or Who Is Sylvia?* The play, which opened at the John Golden Theater in February of that year, explores the romantic relationship that develops between an apparently happily married man and a goat. The exploration of marital strife seen in *Virginia Woolf* here moves on forty years later to an even bleaker and less forgiving view of contemporary society's take on relationships between the sexes. Albee pushes the boundaries of acceptability once again and confronts a new audience with difficult and perhaps unpalatable questions. *The Goat* won the Tony Award for Best Play, and Albee was once again nominated for a Pulitzer Prize.

Although some might have viewed *The Goat* as a return to more familiar territory for this writer, Albee's next new project represented yet another new departure. *The Occupant*, staged off-Broadway by Signature Theatre, was a biographical dramatization of the life of distinguished sculptor Louise Nevelson, a close friend of the author. Nevelson, a Russian-born Jew, as a young child immigrated with her family to Maine, experiencing the harsh life of an unwelcomed outsider. The victim of a loveless marriage and years of poverty, Nevelson's eventual triumph as a creative and individual artist who finally found her expression in sculpture provided an inspiring character for the distinguished actress Anne Bancroft to portray. Talking about the play, Albee stated that his interest was "how we invent, reinvent and create ourselves, and the difference between the private person and the public image."

Albee next returned to his earliest work by writing *Homelife*, a "prequel" to *The Zoo Story*. Both plays were joined together as 1 and 2 of *Peter and Jerry*, which premiered at the Hartford Stage in 2004.

As Albee's career progressed, some commentators felt that his writing had developed from the challenging to the inaccessible and that perhaps the writer's own personal language failed to communicate as directly with his audience as it once had. However, it is equally possible to interpret this as the author's unwillingness to simplify his themes and viewpoints to pander to the requirements of an ever-less intellectual commercial theater, increasingly dominated by popular art forms such as the big-budget musical.

Albee's contributions to screenwriting have been limited: Early television versions of several plays made in France, Sweden, and the United States gave him some exposure in this area, but it was not until 1970 that he produced his first full-length original screenplay for Tony Richardson's biographical movie *Nijinsky*, with Rudolph Nureyev in the title role.

A rather labored and static screen version of *A Delicate Balance*, also directed by Richardson, followed three years later. It starred Katharine Hepburn and Paul Schofield, although it failed to make any significant critical or popular impact.

With the exception of Ernest Lehman's work on *Virginia Woolf*, screen adaptations by other writers have also failed to capture the particular qualities of Albee's writing: *The Ballad of the Sad Café*, directed by Simon Callow in 1991, is a particular example, failing dismally in spite of the efforts of a distinguished cast that included Vanessa Redgrave and Rod Steiger.

Although he has not always retained his popularity, Edward Albee is a writer who has continued to pose challenges and push boundaries, when others might have chosen to live off the fruits of their earlier successes. He has made major contributions to the development of theater writing through his involvement with the Playwrights' Workshop, as founder of the William Flanagan Center for Creative Persons in Montauk, New York, and as a contributor to numerous arts organizations in the United States. For the past fifteen years he has also been a much-valued teacher, delivering highly successful seminars at the School of Theatre at the University of Houston, where he holds the post of Distinguished Professor of Theater, and lectures in colleges throughout the United States.

Perhaps there is no better description of Albee's work than one that he offers himself when he describes his plays as "an examination of the American Scene, an attack on the substitution of artificial for real values in our society, a condemnation of complacency, cruelty, and emasculation and vacuity, a stand against the fiction that everything in this slipping land of ours is peachy-keen."

[*See also* United States, 1940–Present]

PLAYS: *The Zoo Story* (1959); *The Death of Bessie Smith* (1960); *Fam and Yam* (1960); *The Sandbox* (1960); *The American Dream* (1961); *Bartleby* (with James Hinton, Jr., from a story by Herman Melville, 1961); *Who's Afraid of Virginia Woolf?* (1962); *The Ballad of the Sad Café* (from the story by Carson McCullers, 1963); *Tiny Alice* (1964); *Breakfast at Tiffany's* (from the story by Truman Capote, 1966); *A Delicate Balance* (1966); *Malcolm* (from the novel by James Purdy, 1966); *Everything in the Garden* (from the play by Giles Cooper, 1967); *Box and Quotations from Chairman Mao* (1968); *All Over* (1971); *Seascape* (1975); *Counting the Ways* (1976); *Listening: A Chamber Play* (1977); *The Lady from Dubuque* (1980); *Lolita* (1981); *The Man Who Had Three Arms* (1982); *Envy* (in *Faustus in Hell*, 1985); *The Marriage Play* (1987); *Three Tall Women* (1991); *The Lorca Play* (1992); *Fragments: A Concerto Grosso* (1993); *The Play about the Baby* (1998); *The Goat, or Who Is Sylvia?* (2002); *The Occupant* (2003); *Peter and Jerry* (2004)

FURTHER READING

Gussow, Mel. *Edward Albee: A Singular Journey*. London: Oberon Bks., 1999.

McCarthy, Gerald. *Edward Albee*. London: Macmillan Modern Dramatists, 1987.

Roudane, Mathew. *Understanding Edward Albee*. Columbia: Univ. of South Carolina Press, 1987.

Paul E. Fryer

ALBERTINE, EN CINQ TEMPS See ALBERTINE IN FIVE TIMES

ALBERTINE IN FIVE TIMES

One of MICHEL TREMBLAY's most acclaimed works, *Albertine in Five Times* (*Albertine, en cinq temps*, 1984) is a unique journey through a woman's life. It offers at once a unified vision and a fractured reality, as Albertine takes to the stage as five separate women, each playing the title role at a different stage of her life, from ages thirty to sixty.

At seventy, Albertine has been consigned to a retirement home, where she is haunted by memory. The five Albertine "alter egos" appear onstage to confront each other, often arguing, other times playing out for both the audience and the elder Albertine some moment of her life. Taking place in a single long act, these Albertines describe the events of their shared life with differing degrees of perspective and bitterness. As her husband leaves her, as her daughter becomes a prostitute and faces an ugly end, and as her son is committed to a psychiatric institution, the Albertines face a bitter and confused personal history, full of shame and betrayal. The only counterpoint voice is that of Madeleine, Albertine's sister, who serves as confidante and supporter.

We meet Albertine at 30, slowly recognizing her lost innocence and guilt-ridden soul after brutally assaulting her young daughter. At 40 we encounter her sinking into depression, caught between a mother driving her mad and two very troubled teenagers. The 50-year-old Albertine, having turned away from her family, seems to almost find happiness before it is ripped away from her, while at 60 the character lies medicated and near-insane in the hospital. In the eldest, Albertine-at-70, we return to a character who has established an internal calm and acceptance of her past. She is resigned to herself and to the present and looks no further than the next moment.

Short-listed in 1984 for the Governor General's Award for Drama, *Albertine* premiered at the National Arts Centre in October of that year. Among Tremblay's most frequently staged works, notable productions include the Chalmer's Award–winning English-language Tarragon Theatre production (1986) and a critically acclaimed revival at Montreal's Espace Go (1995).

Albertine represents the beginning of a new period in Tremblay's writing. Where earlier pieces, like SISTERS IN LAW (*Les Belles Soeurs*, 1968) centered themselves in the gritty realism of Montreal's east end and its working class, in *Albertine* the playwright experiments with ideas of time, memory, perspective, and identity that will inform later works.

In the piece Tremblay remains committed to tackling the issues of economic and emotional despair in contemporary francophone Quebec, its search for cultural unity and identity within Canada, and its confrontation with a contentious and fractured understanding of its own history. Albertine faces herself at five separate ages and so comes to understand a true personal narrative, rather than the more comfortable story on which she had perhaps sold herself.

As in other works, here Tremblay shows us that only when we challenge our self-deception and mythologizing can we reconcile the past.

[*See also* Canada]

FURTHER READING

Anthony, Geraldine, ed. *Stage Voices: Twelve Canadian Playwrights Talk About Their Lives and Work*. Toronto: Doubleday Canada, 1978.

Brisset, Annie. *A Sociocritique of Translation: Theatre and Alterity in Quebec, 1968–1988*. Tr. by Rosalind Gill and R. Gannon. Toronto: Univ. of Toronto Press, 1996.

Linteay, Paul-André, et al. *Quebec since 1930*. Tr. by Robert Chodos and E. Garmaise. Toronto: Lorimer, 1991.

Smith, Douglas Burnet. *Voices of Deliverance: Interviews with Quebec and Acadian Writers*. Tr. by Larry Shouldice. Toronto: Anansi, 1986.

Daniel Goldberg

AL-HAKIM, TAWFIQ (1898–1987)

Tawfiq al-Hakim was the playwright most responsible for establishing drama as a serious literary form within the Arab world. Well into the 20th century, Arabic literature fell into two exclusive categories: a formal tradition and a popular tradition. Although staged entertainments had a long history within the popular tradition, dramas that required written scripts; that treated serious themes in a complex manner; and that relied on sophisticated language, painstakingly executed motifs, and subtle turns of action simply did not exist in the formal literature before al-Hakim. In the process of reworking these expectations, al Hakim liberated the formal tradition from its increasingly anachronistic constraints.

In attempting to create a dramatic tradition in Arabic, al-Hakim faced a conundrum similar to that confronted by Yehuda Amichair and the Israeli poets of his generation, who had find a way to treat contemporary issues in Hebrew, a language that for centuries had been used only in religious writings, recitations, and discussions. In al-Hakim's case, he had to write his dramas, at least initially, in the rather limiting language of the formal tradition in order to have them accepted as serious literary efforts; yet that language was unsuitable to treating the contemporary issues that would give his dramas dimension and appeal. Al-Hakim gradually brought a more flexible syntax into the language of the formal tradition and then began to expand the diction.

Using Western dramas as models, al-Hakim adapted their forms to stories drawn from Arabic history, classical literature, and folklore. Some earlier directors of popular theatrical troupes had tried to rewrite Western classics for an Arabic audience, but these efforts were so superficial and self-conscious that the results seemed more like parodies than credible adaptations. In contrast, Al-Hakim became expert in the intricacies of dramatic forms. Indeed, during the course of a career in which he wrote some seventy plays, he experimented across the whole spectrum of available forms, from the dramatic pageant to the theater of the absurd. The degree to which al-Hakim was breaking new ground is indicated pointedly by the fact that his early plays were published first as books. Their popularity in printed form created a demand for venues in which they could be appropriately staged. In 1935, the National Theater Troupe was founded in EGYPT, and its first production, al-Hakim's *The People of the Cave*, created a sensation.

Al-Hakim had first been exposed to Western literature and culture in a consequential way when he went to Paris in 1925 to pursue a law degree. Three years later, he returned to Cairo without legal credentials but with a passion for drama. A prolific author, al-Hakim earned a considerable reputation and income as a novelist, a writer of short stories, an essayist, and a memoirist, as well as a dramatist. Yet, despite his great commitment to literature, he took pains to insure that he had a regular income outside of his literary efforts by working as a journalist or in the government bureaucracy. Generally, he kept the two arenas of his life separate, but in 1945, he did write a series of short plays that were published first in the newspaper for which he was working and then in book form.

[*See also* Egypt]

SELECT PLAYS: *Before the Ticket Office* (*Amam Sheebak Al Tazaker*, 1926); *The Return of the Spirit* (*Awdet Al Rouh*, 1928); *The People of the Cave* (*Ahl al-Kahf*, 1933); *Scheherazade* (*Shahrazad*, 1934); *Pygmalion* (1942); *Solomon the Wise* (*Sulayman al-hakim*, 1943); *King Oedipus* (*Al-Malik Udib*, 1949); *Soft Hands* (*Al-Aydi al-na'imah*, 1954); *The Deal* (*al-Safqah*, 1956); *The Sultan's Dilemma* (*al-Sultan al-ha'ir*, 1960); *The Tree Climber* (*Ya tali'al-shajarah*, 1962); *The Fate of a Cockroach* (*Masir sarsar*, 1966); *Anxiety Bank* (*Bank al-qalaq*, 1967)

FURTHER READING

al-Shetawi, Mahmoud. "The Treatment of Greek Drama by Tawfiq al-Hakim." *World Literature Today* 63 (Winter 1989): 9–14.

Hamouda, Abdel-Aziz. "Modern Egyptian Theatre: Three Major Dramatists." *World Literature Today* 53 (1979): 601–605.

Hutchins, William Maynard. *Tawfiq al-Hakim: A Reader's Guide*. Boulder: Rienner, 2003.

Megally, Fuad. "*Fate of a Cockroach* and Other Plays by Tewfik Al-Hakim." *Ba Shiru: A Journal of African Languages and Literature* 4, no. 2 (1973): 91–93.

Rudnicka, Dorota. "Futurological Problems in the Dramas of Tawfik al-Hakim." *Folia Orientalia* 22 (1981–1984): 259–266.

Salama, Mohammad R. "The Aesthetics of 'Pygmalion' in G. B. Shaw and Tawfiq al-Hakim: A Study of Transcendence and Decadence." *Journal of Arabic Literature* 31, no. 3 (2000): 222–237.

Martin Kich

ALIENATION EFFECT

This is great art! Nothing is self-evident!

—Bertolt Brecht, "Vergnügungstheater oder Lehr theater?", 1936

The complex meaning of the German word *Verfremdung* is only partially rendered into English as "alienation." This translation is particularly vexing because it has as one of its many connotations its use in Marxist theory, where it describes the objectionable process by which industrial workers become "alienated" from their product owing to the division of labor. The product confronts the workers like another being, that is, not as the result of their own work. Brechtian *Verfremdung*, however, has the opposite intention: to destroy the appearance of history and human interactions as unalterable. BERTOLT BRECHT's alienation effects are intended to allow the theatrical audience to reappropriate the process presented to them on the stage so that they can deconstruct the events and make visible again their constructedness—while at the same time realizing their own role in the process. Thus, in Brecht's EPIC THEATER, historical events confront the spectator not as alien phenomena but as products of their own (possible) actions.

It is useful to view the alienation effect as the element that replaces empathy in Aristotelian theater. "To 'alienate' (*verfremden*) an event or a character simply means to take away from the event or character what is self-evident, familiar, obvious and to generate astonishment and curiosity about it" (Brecht, 1939). The spectators watch the apple fall to the ground not as a natural phenomenon but as an event that warrants some further thought. Like scientists, they investigate a process in isolation as if for the first time. All previous assumptions have to be put aside, which makes the *Verfremdungseffekt* so important. Nothing should appear to occur "naturally" on the stage, which has been turned into a laboratory.

Brecht believed he had found a theatrical practice—a "theater for the scientific age"—that could rival the modern revolutions in the natural and social sciences. For Brecht the Marxist, the model of scientific thinking was Karl Marx and Friedrich

Engels's dialectical and historical materialism. While the bourgeois social scientist needs to affirm the present state of social relations as the "naturally occurring" one, the dialectical materialist aims to reveal its constructedness as a set of power relations between classes, a configuration that can be replaced by another. Thus *Verfremdung* also means demonstrating that historical events could have taken another turn and that the present state of things can be changed.

One arrives at the concrete techniques of the *Verfremdungseffekt* by reversing the tenets of psychological realism dominating the Anglo-American theater: Everything that serves to create the illusion that the events on stage are real has to be avoided. Actors step out of their roles and reflect on their actions as actors. The set can be taken from a completely different time than that of the plot. The plot, in turn, is not a web of psychologically motivated actions and their countereffects but a fable containing a lesson that can be applied to different time frames. Elements such as posters and songs that are external to the events on the stage comment on and represent the events from various angles. In short, the spectators will not be submersed into the action but confronted with it.

FURTHER READING

Brecht, Bertolt. "A Short Organum for the Theater." In *Brecht on Theatre: The Development of an Aesthetic*, ed. and tr. by John Willett. New York: Hill & Wang, 1964.

——. "Über experimentelles Theater" [About the Experimental Theater] (1936). In *Schriften 2* [Writings Two], ed. by Werner Hecht, Jan Knopf, Werner Mittenzwei, and Klaus-Detlef Müller. Grosse Kommentierte Berliner and Frankfurter Ausgabe [Great annotated Berlin and Frankfurt Edition]. Vol. 22.1. Berlin und FrankFurt/M.: Aufbau and Suhrkamp, 1993.

Grimm, Reinhold. "Brecht's Theater of Alienation." *Halcyon* 13 (1991): 51–66.

Schoeps, Karl Heinz. "From Distancing Alienation to Intuitive Naivete: Bertolt Brecht's Establishment of a New Aesthetic Category." *Monatshefte* 81, no. 2 (1989): 186–198.

Friedemann J. Weidauer

ALISON'S HOUSE

According to historian John L. Toohey, SUSAN GLASPELL's *Alison's House* (1930) holds the dubious distinction of being "the rankest outsider ever to win the Pulitzer Prize." New York critics loathed the drama, dismissing it as too literary and only of interest to a coterie audience. The furor over the 1931 award, combined with the vociferousness of the reviewers' rejection of the play and its production by Eva Le Gallienne's Civic Repertory Theatre, probably damned *Alison's House* to theatrical obscurity. However, Glaspell's dramatic study in biography posed moral, social, artistic, and personal questions against a backdrop of America's cultural history; these questions are why the play stood out for the Pulitzer adjudicators. *Alison's House* exemplifies the original award criteria as an "American play . . . which shall best represent the educational value and power of the stage in raising the standard of good morals, good taste, and good manners."

Glaspell based her drama on details from the life and work of Emily Dickinson and her family, but renamed the characters and changed the setting. Reviewers nevertheless knew that the Dickinson legend lay behind the play, a fact the Civic Rep also advertised. The critical slighting of *Alison's House*, the second Pulitzer drama by a woman, thus reflects the ongoing debate about a work's breadth of appeal when it centers on a female character.

The action occurs on December 31, 1899, 18 years after the death of renowned poet Alison Stanhope, and features the discovery of some of her theretofore-unknown love poems. The Stanhope family, stung by a scandal surrounding niece Elsa's personal life, must decide whether to publish or to destroy the cache of verse, which reveals that Alison, too, had loved but renounced a married man. The drama chronicles Alison's living legacy and debates the question of who controls a cultural icon.

Glaspell's calculated choice to set the play on the brink of a new millennium resonates both stylistically and thematically. Early reviewers did not grasp the aptness of Glaspell's deployment of the 19th-century well-made play form, itself about to give way to the dramaturgical advances of modernism. Nor did they perceive the relationship of the play's form to its content; the characters' convictions similarly split along generational lines, the older holding fast to traditional ideas while the younger see the new century as a time of change and promise.

Alison's House, like such earlier dramas as *Trifles* (1916) and *Bernice* (1919), features a hallmark of Glaspell's dramaturgy—the depiction of an "absent center" figure who never appears on stage but who is central to the action. These individuals serve as foils; we come to know Alison through the other characters we encounter. In that process we learn much about the late poet, but even more about those whose lives her artistry touched. Glaspell's engagement with issues of the individual and society, refracted through her representation of one prominent American woman artist, gives *Alison's House* significance that supersedes its initial theatrical reception.

Alison's House has recently come back into print in *Worthy But Neglected: Plays of the Mint Theater Company* (2002), which revived the play in 2000.

FURTHER READING

Ben-Zvi, Linda, ed. *Susan Glaspell: Essays on Her Theater and Fiction*. Ann Arbor: Univ. of Michigan Press, 1995.

Gainor, J. Ellen. *Susan Glaspell in Context: American Theater, Culture, and Politics, 1915–48*. Ann Arbor: Univ. of Michigan Press, 2001.

Makowsky, Veronica. "Susan Glaspell and Modernism." In *The Cambridge Companion to American Women Playwrights*, ed. by Brenda Murphy. Cambridge: Cambridge Univ. Press, 1999. 49–65.

Ozieblo, Barbara. *Susan Glaspell: A Critical Biography*. Chapel Hill: Univ. of North Carolina Press, 2000.

Papke, Mary. *Susan Glaspell: A Research and Production Sourcebook*. Westport, CT: Greenwood, 1993.

Toohey, John L. *History of the Pulitzer Prize Plays*. New York: Citadel, 1967.

Worthy But Neglected: Plays of the Mint Theater Company. New York: Granville, 2002.

J. Ellen Gainor

ALL GOD'S CHILLUN GOT WINGS

We're never free—except to do what we have to do.

—Jim, Act 1

EUGENE O'NEILL's *All God's Chillun Got Wings* was first produced by Kenneth Macgowan, ROBERT EDMOND JONES, and O'Neill at the Provincetown Playhouse on May 15, 1924, with Paul Robeson in the role of Jim Harris.

In a poor, biracial neighborhood in New York, a group of children play marbles, and because Jim, a black boy, and Ella, a white girl, are "soft" on each other, the others tease them. She wishes she were black so the children would not call her "Painty Face," and he has been drinking chalk in order to become white.

Nine years later, Mickey, a white boxer, claims Ella as his "goil." He derides the quiet, sensitive Jim for aspiring to become a lawyer. Jim begs him to treat Ella "square," but she denies remembering when they were playmates.

Another five years pass, and Ella is alone; Mickey has abandoned her and their baby, who dies, and Jim struggles with his law courses. They decide to marry in spite of the neighbors' iron disapproval.

After two years in France, Ella becomes increasingly withdrawn, and Jim comes to regret being a "quitter," so they return to the States. Ella seems oddly anxious and distracted, quick to notice racial difference to the detriment of Jim and his sister Hattie, a dignified schoolteacher; Ella screams in fright when she sees the Congo mask that Hattie has given Jim. She assures Jim that she hopes he will pass his examinations, but when she is alone, she sneers to the Congo mask that he will never pass.

Ella develops schizophrenia, calling Jim a "dirty nigger" and vowing never to bear his child because it will be born black. Alone, she rants to the Congo mask, revealing her fear that Jim might pass his exams, but Jim, failing yet again, ironically declares that for a black man to become a lawyer would be "against all natural laws." She confesses, in her dementia, that she had wandered the apartment with a carving knife to prevent him from getting enough rest to study effectively; her fondest wish is that they play together as children again. Their marriage has become a nightmare in the manner of the plays of AUGUST STRINDBERG, while the Congo mask introduces an expressionistic technique and heightens the THEATRICALITY of the corrosive race prejudice that torments the couple.

The mixed marriage and the investigation of race relations inspired threats from the Ku Klux Klan, and because the mayor refused to issue the permits required to use child actors in the opening scene, director Jimmy Light read it aloud to the audience. Ludwig Lewisohn reported in *The Nation* (June 4, 1924) that "O'Neill has at last hit upon tragedy. He has the theme, the intensity, the terror and exaltation." Heywood Broun dismissed the piece as a "downstroke" for the playwright, and John Corbin called it "a painful play." Edmund Wilson wrote in the *New Republic* (May 28, 1924):

> [It] is one of the best things yet written about the race problem and among the best of O'Neill's plays. Two of O'Neill's chief assets as a dramatist seem to be, first, a nervous driving force which carries the audience inescapably along, and second, a gift for writing eloquently the various forms of the American vernacular.

George S. Scott directed a 1975 revival, with designs by Ming Cho Lee.

[*See also* United States, 1860–1929]

FURTHER READING

Brucher, Richard. "O'Neill, Othello and Robeson." *Eugene O'Neill Review* 18 (Spring–Fall 1994): 45–58.

Haque, Anisul. "Eugene O'Neill's Earnest Gesture: *The Dreamy Kid, The Emperor Jones, All God's Chillun Got Wings*." *Journal of American Studies* 28 (Winter–Summer 1998): 71–78.

Holton, Deborah Wood. "Revealing Blindness, Revealing Vision: Interpreting O'Neill's Black Female Characters in *Moon of the Caribbees, The Dreamy Kid* and *All God's Chillun Got Wings*." *Eugene O'Neill Review* 19 (Spring–Fall 1995): 29–44.

Maufort, Marc. "The Legacy of the American Romance in O'Neill's Expressionist Drama." *English Studies* 5 (1994): 32–45.

Jeffrey D. Mason

ALL MY SONS

ARTHUR MILLER's *All My Sons* opened at the Coronet Theatre in New York on January 29, 1947, and ran for 328 performances. It appeared at a time when the veterans of World War II, like Chris Keller in the play, were still returning home, when there was a general sense that the victory had not been over just GERMANY and JAPAN but over the narrow worldview of a self-absorbed, family-absorbed American society. Miller distrusted that feeling; as he said in the introduction to *Collected Plays*: "[M]y personal experience was daily demonstrating that beneath the slogans very little had changed." In *All My Sons*, he sets out to illustrate that fact through his protagonist, Joe Keller.

Joe is a self-made businessman, but the self he has made is his society's image of the good husband and the good father, one who believes, as he mistakenly says that his dead son Larry did, that his world "had a forty-foot front, it ended at the building line." Chris expects more than that of him. Inadvertently predicting the end of the play, Joe says, "I'm his father and he's my son, and if there's something bigger than that I'll put a bullet in my head!" Admitting his debt to HENRIK IBSEN, Miller begins the action at the end of the story, letting the past unfold in the process of revealing the fatal secret. When Joe's factory shipped out cracked cylinder-heads during the war, causing the death of pilots, he was charged but found not guilty, having managed to shift the blame to his partner. Back home, accepted by the neighbors who may believe him guilty but who accept his cleverness, his home is a simulacrum of small-town domestic content, one in which the returning son might sink comfortably if it were not built on a lie and if his mother, who refuses to believe in Larry's death, did not produce a continuing sense of tension. She refuses to accept Ann, Larry's old girlfriend, as Chris's intended wife, for that would be to admit that Larry was dead and that Joe was guilty. Ann produces a letter—a convenient device that is an example of the excessive neatness that mars an otherwise forceful play—in which Larry says that he is going to purposely crash his plane in his distress at what he sees as his father's guilt. Joe at first tries to justify his action by explaining, "I'm in business, a man is in business," the unthinking shift from first to third person suggesting that the sins of the business community excuse personal guilt. But at the end of the play, he recognizes what Chris and Larry's letter have been trying to tell him: "But I think to him they were all my sons." In the introduction, Miller wrote that "Joe Keller's trouble, in a word, is not that he cannot tell right from wrong but that his cast of mind cannot admit that he, personally, has any viable connection with his world, his universe, or his society."

[*See also* United States, 1940–Present]

FURTHER READING

Martin, Robert A., ed. *Arthur Miller, New Perspectives*. Englewood Cliffs, N.J.: Prentice-Hall, 1982.

Miller, Arthur. *Collected Plays*, New York: Viking, 1957.

——. *The Theater Essays of Arthur Miller*. Ed. by Robert A. Martin. New York: Viking, 1978.

——. *Timebends, A Life*. New York: Grove, 1987.

Weales, Gerald. *American Drama since World War II*. New York: Harcourt, 1962.

Gerald Weales

ALL THAT FALL

> *Have been asked to write a radio play [for the BBC] and am tempted, feet dragging and breath short and cartwheels and imprecations from the Brighton Rd to Foxrock station and back, insentient old mares in foal being welted by the cottagers and the Devil tottered in the ditch—boyhood memories.*
>
> —Letter from Samuel Beckett to Aidan Higgins, July 1956

All That Fall is not only SAMUEL BECKETT's first play for radio (he was to write six more and adapt another by ROBERT PINGET), it is his first play written in English. Beckett settled on the title, a fragment from Psalm 145, late in the process of composition—his working title had been "Lovely Day for the Races." The plot is tripartite and uncomplicated: Mrs. Rooney (née Maddy Dunne, a rheumatic lady in her seventies and later described by her husband as "two hundred pounds of unhealthy fat") sets out from her home to walk, with painful dragging steps, a country road to the local Boghill station to meet her husband as he returns home from his place of business after a half-day's work—the play is set on a Saturday in June. She wants to surprise her blind husband, Dan, because it is his birthday.

On her way she has three encounters. The first is with Christy, who offers her the load of sty-dung in the cart drawn by a hinny—the progeny of a she-donkey and a horse—he is leading by the snaffle. The second is with Mr. Tyler, a retired bill-broker, who overtakes her on his bicycle. The third is with the clerk of the racecourse, Mr. Slocum, who offers her a lift in his car. From each Mrs. Rooney hears of the ill health of their loved ones. Mrs. Rooney herself notes that "it is suicide to be abroad" but to be at home is "a lingering dissolution." Throughout the play, references to death, ill health, and suffering permeate the dialogue. Black comedy is wrung from these encounters. Christy's hinny refuses to move despite being "welted" three times. The back tire on Mr. Tyler's bicycle is flat despite having been pumped hard as iron, causing him to curse God and man and the wet Saturday afternoon of his conception. Mr. Slocum's car refuses to start until he decides "to choke her."

When she arrives at the station Mrs. Rooney is assisted up the steps to the platform by the wonderfully named Miss Fitt, whose "Protestant" piety is witheringly presented. As she helps Mrs. Rooney she hums a hymn in which Mrs. Rooney joins, wondering if it is the one sung by the victims of the *Lusitania* or the *Titanic* disasters. The play lightly insists that faith and good works are without efficacy in a diseased and dying world—Mrs. Rooney at one point is moved to exclaim, "Christ what a planet!"

Dan's train arrives fifteen minutes late, but no explanation for the delay is offered by the station staff beyond reference to "a hitch." Man and wife, the halt leading the blind, set off for home as the wind rises and the rain starts to fall. A confrontation with jeering children causes Dan to ask his wife if she has ever felt the desire to kill a child, to "nip some young doom in the bud." Mrs. Rooney reads the announcement of the text for tomorrow's sermon, "The Lord upholdeth all that fall and raiseth up all those that be bowed down." This causes them to break into wild laughter. Dan twice refuses to tell his wife why the train was delayed, but the explanation is given in the last lines of the play by the boy Jerry, Dan's usual escort from the station, when he tells of a child falling from a carriage onto the line and under the wheels. The play deftly implies Dan's part in the "accident," but, as is usual with Beckett, judgment is left to the listener. The play ends in a tempest of wind and rain.

[*See also* Apocalypse in Modern Drama; Ireland; Philosophy and Drama]

FURTHER READING

Gontarski, S. E., ed. *On Beckett: Essays and Criticism*. New York: Grove, 1986.

Pountney, Rosemary. *Theatre of Shadows: Samuel Beckett's Drama 1956–1976*. Gerrard's Cross: Colin Smythe, 1988.

Zilliacus, Clas. *Beckett and Broadcasting*. Åbo, Finland: Åbo Akademi, 1976.

Gerry Dukes

ALMIGHTY VOICE AND HIS WIFE

Of nearly a dozen plays by DANIEL DAVID MOSES, *Almighty Voice and His Wife*, a structural assault on traditional TRAGEDY, is the most commonly anthologized and published. It is a two-act reimagining of the misfortunes of Cree Kisse-Manitou-Wayou, also known as Jean Baptiste and in Moses's drama called Almighty Voice. Act 1, set on the Saskatchewan Prairie, from October 1895 to May 1897, trails the courtship and marriage of Almighty and his wife and the incidents that lead Almighty Voice to murder and his own ultimate execution at the hands of 100 mounted officers and white volunteers. In the second act, set in the auditorium of an abandoned industrial school, Moses demolishes the exposition/climax/denouement arrangement of tragedy, which he views as one part of an unhealthy triad of native performance (with white guilt and romanticism). In a grotesque adaptation of the minstrel show, Moses provides an experimental theatrical context for his characters to deal adequately with their collective wounds and potentially transcend their tragedy. It was first produced in 1991 by Ottawa's Great Canadian Theatre Company.

According to Richard Knowles and Monique Mojica (2003), *Almighty*, like other Moses dramas, is "obsessed with watching, looking, seeing, and being seen." Throughout the first act, the daughter of Old Dust (White Girl) repeatedly insists that Almighty see her and that she, in turn, see him. Placards at the start of each scene announce various moons (Midwinter Moon, Honeymoon, Hunting Moon), marking temporal motion toward the inevitable and also gesturing to the viewing lens of nature, the eye of the sky world. White Girl has a vivid dream of her husband's demise, a tipi that shatters with the sound of a gunshot. Moses rounds out the obsession with a series of personal displays, brief alliterative poems on the power of nature spoken as dramatic monologues.

Robert Appleford (1993) compares *Almighty* to classic comedies in which lovers overcome obstacles to reunite at the close of the play. In the second act, the obstacle is a thematic memory of native history articulated through minstrelsy. White Girl becomes Interlocutor; Almighty Voice becomes Ghost. Interlocutor tries to engage Ghost in comic repartee. Angered by his use of Cree, she resorts to racial epithets in comic form ("I'll sell you a cigar store"). This sets the tone for the act, scenes incorporating racist jokes ("Chief Shitting Bull") interspersed with scenes of unsatisfying romanticism (a song retelling Almighty's death that is based loosely on "Three Little Indians" and the "Hollywood Indian" War Dance). The final scene permits their reconciliation. They recognize each other and share a final look. Ghost returns to a melancholy dance of healing; Interlocutor bids him farewell. Appleford explains that their obstacles are "texts which reify themselves at the expense of the bodies that enact them." Moses assaults white guilt by exposing racism in an experimental theatrical context, challenges romanticism by portraying characters of questionable moral character, and drives native dramatic conventions beyond the sanitizing closure of tragedy by permitting his characters space to heal their wounds.

[*See also* Canada; Highway, Tomson; Ross, Cree Ian]

FURTHER READING

Appleford, Robert. "The Desire to Crunch Bone: Daniel David Moses and the 'True Real Indian.' " *Canadian Theatre Review* 77 (1993): 21–26.

Knowles, Richard. " 'Look. Look Again.' Daniel David Moses' Decolonizing Optics." In *Crucible of Cultures: Anglophone Drama at the End of the New Millennium*, ed. by Marc Maufort and Franca Bellarsi. New York: Peter Lang, 2002.

Knowles, Richard, and Monique Mojica, eds. *Staging Coyote's Dream: An Anthology of First Nations Drama in English*. Toronto: Playwrights Canada Press, 2003.

Moses, Daniel David. "How My Ghosts Got Pale Faces." In *Speaking for the Generations: Native Writers on Writing*, ed. by Simon J. Ortiz. Tucson: Univ. of Arizona Press, 1998.

Moses, Daniel David, and Terry Goldie. *An Anthology of Canadian Native Literature in English*. 2nd ed. New York: Oxford Univ. Press, 1998.

Ben Fisler

ÁLVAREZ QUINTERO, JOAQUÍN (1873–1944), AND SERAFÍN ÁLVAREZ QUINTERO (1871–1938)

Joaquín and Serafín Álvarez Quintero were brothers and early-20th-century Spanish dramatists who collaborated on over 200 theatrical works. Born in Utrera (near Seville) (Joaquín in 1873 and Serafín in 1871), sons of a government functionary, they demonstrated theatrical talent from an early age—their first play was performed in 1888, when Serafín was not yet seventeen years old. The family moved to Madrid the following year, and the brothers turned to theater as a way of aiding their family's precarious financial situation. Most of their early works were one-act plays, designed to exploit the vogue for short theatrical works then at its height in Madrid. A significant portion of their output before 1910 took the form of ZARZUELA libretti; these attracted Spain's most talented and popular theatrical composers, notably Ruperto Chapí and José Serrano. Even as the brothers turned their primary output toward full-length comedies, they continued to write shorter pieces and monologues. Thus, between 1910 and 1936 the brothers usually managed to premiere an average of four to eight plays per year—two or three of which would be full-length works, the rest shorter or occasional pieces.

The decade and a half before the Spanish Civil War marked the apex of the careers and reputations of the Álvarez Quinteros. The brothers were elected to the Real Academia de la Lengua—Serafín in 1920, Joaquín in 1925—and their plays reached the peak of popularity. There were numerous productions of their work abroad, most notably of the English translations by HARLEY and Helen GRANVILLE-BARKER (two of which served as vehicles for a young John Gielgud). The brothers also had the privilege of seeing a monument dedicated to them in Madrid's Retiro Park in 1934. Although Serafín died in 1938, Joaquín continued to attribute his new plays to both brothers. Joaquín's death six years later served as the official national period of mourning for their passing, as Serafín's passing had been overshadowed by the Civil War.

The strengths and weaknesses of the Álvarez Quinteros' plays all stem from the same basic source: their ability to please an audience. The brothers were first and foremost commercial playwrights, concerned with pleasing and entertaining their public; the plays teem with gentle humor and genial characters, and even their more serious works are filled with such delicate touches. Critics of their work tend to find the plays facile and formulaic, often pandering to bourgeois taste. More positive views concern themselves with the plays' sure dramatic structure, their vivid characterizations, and their shrewd use of local color. The plays of the Quinteros have also been singled out for their realistic and accurate depictions of Spanish mores and customs of their times. In this regard, the defining facet of their work is its focus upon the region of Andalucia; over half their plays are set in somewhere in southern Spain and depict the customs of the region with knowing accuracy. Although today their work may seem somewhat dated, it provides a fine exemplar of popular theatrical taste in SPAIN during the first third of the 20th century.

SELECT PLAYS: *The Moorish Queen* (*La reina mora*, with music by José Serrano, 1903); *The Mad Muse* (*La musa loca*, 1905); *The Homeland* (*La patria chica*, with music by Ruperto Chapí, 1907); *The Daughters of Cain* (*Las de Caín*, 1908); *Doña Clarines* (1909); *The One Hundred Year Old Man* (*El centenario*, 1909); *Hollyhock* (*Malvaloca*, 1912); *Marianela* (1916); *That's How They Write History* (*Así se escribe la historia*, 1917); *Passion Flower* (*Pasionera*, 1921); *As the World Turns* (*Las vueltas que da el mundo*, 1922); *The Wedding of Quinita Flores* (*La boda de Quinita Flores*, 1925); *The Daughters of Abel* (*Las de Abl*, 1926); *One Hundred Comedies and a Drama* (*Cien comedias y un drama*, 1929); *Five Little Wolves* (*Cinco lobitos*, 1934)

FURTHER READING

Losada de la Torre, José. *Perfil de los hermanos Álvarez Quintero* [Profile of the brothers Álvarez Quintero]. Madrid: Editora nacional, 1945.

Sánchez del Arco, Manuel. *Algo más que Andalucia (Estudio del teatro quinteriano)* [Something more than Andalucia: A study of Quinterian theatre]. Madrid: Prensa española, 1945.

Sánchez de Palacios, Mariano. *Serafín y Joaquín Álvarez Quintero* [Serafín and Joaquín Álvarez Quintero]. Madrid: Gráficas Valera, 1971.

Clinton D. Young

AMERICAN BUFFALO

Businessmen left it muttering vehemently about its inadequacies and pointlessness. But they weren't really mad because the play was pointless—no-one can be forced to sit through an hour-and-a-half of meaningless dialogue—they were angry because the play was about them.

—David Mamet on the audience response to *American Buffalo*

One of DAVID MAMET's first full-length plays, *American Buffalo* was first produced by Chicago's Goodman Theatre in late 1975 and had its New York premiere at the St. Clements Theatre in 1976, where it earned an Obie Award as Best New American Play (a distinction it shared with another Mamet play, SEXUAL PERVERSITY IN CHICAGO [1973]). A 1977 Broadway production, although only a moderate commercial success (135 performances), it received the New York Drama Critics' Circle Award and cemented Mamet's reputation as one of the leading playwrights of his generation. The play, revived on Broadway in a limited engagement starring Al Pacino in 1983, has since been produced countless times in professional and university theaters around the world, and was adapted to the movie screen in 1996.

American Buffalo takes place in a junk shop over the course of a single Friday. In act 1, we learn that Don, the shop's middle-aged proprietor, is planning to steal a collection of rare coins (the play's title refers to the buffalo-head nickel prized by collectors). He has invited his friend and associate Teach to collaborate with him in the burglary. The two men disagree over whether to include Bob, Don's errand boy, in their plans. Teach's doubts about Bob's reliability eventually prevail over the boy's protests, and Don and Teach agree to make their associate Fletcher (who never appears on stage) the third man on the job. In act 2, set late that night, Don, Teach, and Bob have returned to the junk shop, and the audience watches their plan unravel before the crime can even begin. In frustration, the characters exchange harsh words that soon escalate to physical violence. The play ends with both the crime and the relationships between the characters unresolved.

Early critics praised *American Buffalo* for its grittily realistic depiction of the *demimonde* of petty thieves and junkies, particularly in terms of the characters' speech. The play's liberal use of "fuck" and other vulgarities, while not unprecedented on the Broadway stage, would come to be seen as Mamet's trademark, a sign of his work's raw and unsentimental flavor. The repetitive and often banal dialogue struck reviewers as simultaneously poetic and authentic, though some complained that the playwright's skillful use of language masked an underdeveloped plot.

Very quickly, however, critics and audiences came to recognize *American Buffalo* as an allegorical exploration of American ethics and the degree to which those ethics have been corrupted by a business mentality, a theme Mamet would take up in such subsequent plays as *The Water Engine* (1977) and GLENGARRY GLEN ROSS (1983). Influenced by a false sense of entrepreneurial self-righteousness, Don, Teach, and Bob see their friendship for one another eroded by avarice, competition, and the desire to get something for nothing. In the failure of the planned heist, we see the failure of our society.

[*See also* United States, 1940–Present]

FURTHER READING

Kane, Leslie, ed. *David Mamet in Conversation*. Ann Arbor: Univ. of Michigan Press, 2001.

Roudane, Matthew. "Betrayal and Friendship: David Mamet's *American Buffalo*." In *The Cambridge Companion to David Mamet*, ed. by Christopher Bigsby. Cambridge: Cambridge Univ. Press, 2004.

Schlueter, June, and Elizabeth Forsyth. "America as Junkshop: The Business Ethic in David Mamet's *American Buffalo*." *Modern Drama* 26, no. 4 (December 1983): 492–500.

Henry Bial

THE AMERICA PLAY

SUZAN-LORI PARKS's *The America Play* grapples with the elusiveness of history—in particular, of the history of African Americans in the UNITED STATES. Few events occur; there is no plot in the traditional sense. To the extent that there is any dramatic development at all, it occurs through characters' manipulation of language and through Parks's subtle modification of repeated scenes, themes, and phrases.

Act 1 takes place in "a great hole," which, we are told, is an exact replica of an East Coast theme park known as "The Great Hole of History." The act consists mostly of a monologue spoken by "the Foundling Father," whose name immediately provides an example of the type of wordplay Parks employs throughout the script: The audience member recalls the phrase "Founding Father," along with the idea of the father as origin, the personification of national roots, but now hears "foundling," orphan, a youth without parents—and hence without history or roots. "The Foundling Father" is Parks's name for a black man who, having been told that he bears a close resemblance to Abraham Lincoln, discovers he can earn a living by charging people a penny to pretend to assassinate him. At the end of the act, some of these assassinations are staged, with participants choosing different phrases to shout after committing the deed, ranging from a white man exclaiming, "Thus to the tyrants," to a black woman who ambiguously yells, again and again, "Lies!"

Act 2 takes place after the Foundling Father has died. Now, Lucy, his widow, and Brazil, his son, appear in the great hole, and they are digging for artifacts, traces of the Foundling Father. The act is interrupted several times in order to show brief excerpts of *Our American Cousin* (1858), the play that Lincoln was watching in the theater where he was shot. Parks, in her stage directions, calls these reenactments "echoes"; and even when the reenactments are not being staged, the sounds of gunshots, referred to by characters as echoes, interrupt Brazil's digging. When Brazil finds an artifact related to his father, he places it in a "Hall of Wonders." By the end of the drama, the Hall contains, among other things, a jewel box with an A. L. monogram, Washington's wooden teeth, a marble bust of Lincoln, and medals for bravery, honesty, "makin do," and "fakin."

The America Play received its premiere under the direction of Liz Diamond at the Yale Repertory Theatre in 1994 before moving on to the New York Shakespeare Festival. Critical reception was mixed, with *New York*'s John Simon calling the play "a farrago of undigested Beckett and distantly ogled Joyce" and *Variety*'s Markland Taylor citing it as a symptom of "the emperor's-new-clothes syndrome." The script has found more support in academic publications; David Rose, in *Theatre Journal*, praised the play for its "restrained mode" and "Beckettian minimalism," while Frank Haike, in *American Drama* (2002), described it as "complex" and "multi-layered," a work that deliberately "chases its own meaning." The Booth–Lincoln motif would surface later in *Topdog/Underdog*, the play for which Parks won the Pulitzer Prize in 2002.

[*See also* United States, 1940–Present]

FURTHER READING

Drukman, Steven. "Suzan-Lori Parks and Liz Diamond: Doo-a-Diddly-Dit-Dit." *The Drama Review* 39, no. 3 (1995): 56–75.

Haike, Frank. "The Instability of Meaning in Suzan-Lori Parks's *The America Play*." *American Drama* 11, no. 2 (2002): 4–22.

Ryan, Katy. " 'No Less Human': Making History in Suzan-Lori Parks's *The America Play*." *Journal of Dramatic Theory & Criticism* 13, no. 2 (1999): 81–94.

Daniel Mufson

EL AMIGO MANSO

See OUR FRIEND MANSO

ANATOL

As I felt the warm breath of her mouth on my hand, I experienced the whole thing as a memory. It was actually already over with.
—Anatol, "Episode"

ARTHUR SCHNITZLER wrote *Anatol* between 1888 and 1891. Set in turn-of-the-century Vienna, the seven scenes that make up this cycle are loosely connected by the eponymous protagonist Anatol, his friend Max, and Anatol's lovers. Each scene was published separately (1889–1891) and premiered singly in the 1890s. The complete cycle appeared in 1893 with a prologue written by Loris (the pseudonym of HUGO VON HOFMANNSTHAL), and in 1910, five of the scenes were performed together as a cycle in Berlin and Vienna. Schnitzler also wrote an alternative final scene, "Anatols Größenwahn" (Anatol's Megalomania), starring an aging Anatol, that was not included in the series and was neither published nor performed until after the author's death.

The bachelor hero of this play pursues a playboy's life; he is an egotistical, self-centered, and melancholic (so-called) lady-killer. Many of his comic situations entertain the audience—for example, his effort to try to get rid of his girlfriend Ilona on the morning of his wedding to another woman or the one-upmanship that he displays when breaking up with Annie ("Abschiedssouper" [Farewell Supper]). At the same time, however, *Anatol* also has a serious side and presents issues central to Schnitzler's work and representative of his times. The play portrays concerns with such abstract concepts as truth and illusion, unity and multiplicity, and stability and impermanence, all viewed within the context of love relationships. Anatol's assorted episodes demonstrate that these relationships are actually just a series of superficial love affairs in various stages of impermanence and infidelity. Although Anatol fantasizes about love and constancy, he ironically tries to demand faithfulness from his lovers while being unable (or unwilling) to make the same commitment himself. He recognizes the elusive nature of love relationships—and of life in general. Indeed, his doubts and suspicions mirror fundamental questions of *fin de siècle* Vienna: What is reality, truth and dream, illusion? What do words (or actions) denote if they are void of meaning? Yet when Anatol has the opportunity to use hypnosis to discover Cora's true nature ("Die Frage an das Schicksal" [Questioning Fate]), he refuses; he not only would rather hold on to his illusions, but he also concludes that words, even from the subconscious, can be misconstrued. Is truth really truth if it is only the truth of the very moment? Anatol wants to know the truth but is unable to tolerate it, so he moves from one woman to the next in search of that (unreachable) ideal love. The fleeting nature of his relationships blurs the boundaries of time so that past and future become disconnected from the present, and as Anatol obsesses about his lovers' past and future relationships, he becomes unable to live in the present.

The general public as well as critics frequently identified Schnitzler with his melancholic bachelor hero who dallied in superficial love affairs. The author therefore tried to distance himself from this early work, even though its success had propelled him onto the major stages of Vienna and Berlin.

[*See also* Austria]

FURTHER READING

Kenny, Joseph M. "The Playboy's Progress: Schnitzler's Ordering of Scenes in *Anatol*." *Modern Austrian Literature* 27, no. 1 (1994): 23–50.

Roche, Mark W. "Schnitzler's *Anatol* as a Philosophical Comedy." *Modern Austrian Literature* 22, nos. 3–4 (1989): 51–63.

Seyler, Athene, and Stephen Haggard. *The Craft of Comedy*. New York: Theater Arts, 1946.

Walton, Luverne. "*Anatol* on the New York Stage." *Modern Austrian Literature* 2, no. 2 (1969): 30–44.

Elizabeth Ametsbichler

ANDERSON, CLARA ROTHWELL (1871–1958)

The plays of Clara Rothwell belong to the tradition of amateur theater that was developing at the beginning of the 20th century. Between 1915 and the early 1920s she published twelve plays and a novel, *John Matheson* (1923). All save *Aunt Sophie Speaks* were written during her tenure as the wife of a Presbyterian minister.

She was born Clara Rothwell in Listowel, Ontario, the third of six children of Benjamin Rothwell and Sarah Cozens. Still a girl when her mother died in 1888, it was her Irish immigrant father who had the greatest influence on her education. Benjamin Rothwell, who founded Listowel's first public school and was clerk and treasurer of the municipality, fostered his daughter's love of literature; he loved to spin a yarn, quoted the classics by the page, and took his young daughter to performances of Shakespeare and the Chautauqua Institute. Clara studied music with the local organist and graduated from the Toronto Conservatory of Music. She then took the position of soprano soloist at Trinity Methodist Church in Toronto, followed by a short stint as choir leader in a church in Chatham. During this period she met and married Peter William Anderson, a student of theology at Knox College. Clara had already given birth to her first son when in 1904 her husband accepted the pastorate of New Edinburgh Presbyterian Church. There she spent the next 30 years of her life, had two more children, and produced all but one of her published works. Anderson died in Ottawa, Ontario, in 1958.

In their dissemination of Christian values, Anderson's plays shared in the evangelical spirit of the Social Gospel movement that swept Canada and the United States between 1880 and 1920 and galvanized women's organizations like those that produced them. Her plays were written, by and large, for women actors and always first staged by the Ladies' Aid of MacKay Presbyterian Church, for whom they helped raise money. But Anderson, who was her own literary agent and retained her own copyrights, also sold plays for performance to women's organizations throughout Canada and the United States. In terms of genre, Anderson's plays fall into two types: domestic feminist comedies and character sketch entertainments. The former are highly conventional and conform to the type of comedy passed down from the New Greek tradition, except that in them women are redemptive heroes. *Joggsville Convention* and *An Old Time Ladies' Aid Business Meeting at Mohawk Crossroads* are feminist parodies that stage women's meetings to critique a variety of issues relating to women's organizational ability and political acumen.

[*See also* Canada]

PLAYS: *An Old Time Ladies' Aid Business Meeting at Mohawk Crossroads* (1912); *Minister's Bride* (1913); *The Young Village Doctor* (1915);

Afternoon Tea in Friendly Village, 1862 (1917); *Aunt Susan's Visit* (1917); *Aunt Mary's Family Album* (19-?); *The Joggsville Convention* (19-?); *Let Mary Lou Do It* (19-?); *Martha Made Over* (19-?); *Wanted—A Wife* (19-?); *The Young Country Schoolm'am* (1920); *Marrying Anne?* (192-?); *Aunt Sophia Speaks* (1940)

FURTHER READING

Bird, Kym. "Instructive and Wholesome: Domestic Feminism, Social Gospel, and the Protestant Plays of Clara Rothwell Anderson." In *Redressing the Past: The Politics of Early English-Canadian Women's Drama, 1880–1920*. Kingston, Ontario: McGill–Queen's Univ. Press, 2004.

Edwards, Margaret Bunel, ed. *Highlights from MacKay's History*. Ottawa: LoMor Printers, 1975.

Kym Bird

ANDERSON, MAXWELL (1888–1959)

Maxwell Anderson's father was a Baptist preacher whose vocation entailed an itinerant life for the growing family from 1890 until they settled in Jamestown, North Dakota, in 1907. Anderson was born on December 15, 1888, in Atlantic, Pennsylvania. After graduating from the University of North Dakota in 1911, Anderson married his classmate, Margaret C. Haskett, who bore him three children before succumbing to stroke in 1931. In 1913 he attended graduate school at Stanford University and between 1914 and 1918 was a teacher of English, first in a high school in San Francisco and later at Whittier College. For the next five years, until his first theatrical success, he worked as a journalist for, among others, *The New Republic* and *New York World*.

After an ineffectual first play, *White Desert* (1923), he joined fellow journalist Laurence Stallings in 1924 to produce the riveting, antiwar blockbuster WHAT PRICE GLORY? His success allowed him to become a full-time playwright, one whose reputation, penchant for tragedy, and prolific output were to be matched on the modern American stage only with that of EUGENE O'NEILL. In the course of his evolution as a formidable, popular, and eclectic playwright who was attempting to create a new poetic language for the theater, Anderson was lucky in finding collaborators like Stallings and Kurt Weill, who opened up new vistas for him in matters of experience as well as artistic expression.

Anderson married Gertrude (Mab) Maynard, an actress, in 1933, the year he received the Pulitzer Prize for *Both Your Houses*. But the unhappy outcome of the marriage moved through estrangement to the eventual suicide of Mab in 1953. A year later, his marriage to Gilda Oakleaf corresponded with his last Broadway success, *The Bad Seed*.

In a stage career spanning four decades, Anderson progressed from a literary idealism geared by classical and Renaissance paradigms to a modest yet fulfilling realization of his dreams of a heroic, poetical, and humanist theater in a variety of plays: ELIZABETH THE QUEEN (1930), *Both Your Houses* (1933), *Mary of Scotland* (1933), WINTERSET (1935), *High Tor* (1937), *Key Largo* (1939), *Barefoot in Athens* (1951). He won the Drama Critics' Circle Award in 1936 for *Winterset* and in 1937 for *High Tor*.

Indeed, there are few American playwrights in the first half of the 20th century who could be said to rival Anderson's prodigious literary output. He experimented widely with dramatic themes and structures but stressed the necessity of developing the genre of poetical drama, especially in both historical (*Elizabeth the Queen*, *Mary of Scotland*, *Anne of the Thousand Days* [1948]) and contemporary TRAGEDY (*Winterset*); musical comedy (*Knickerbocker Holiday* [1938]); antifascist plays (*Key Largo*, *Candle in the Wind* [1941]); and philosophical drama (*Barefoot in Athens*). From the early 1920s to the late 1950s, he wrote about thirty published and twenty unpublished plays; three books of verse; masques; some fiction; two books of criticism (*Off-Broadway*, 1947; *The Essence of Tragedy*, 1939); seventy odd articles on drama and related fields; radio plays; screen plays (*Joan of Arc*, 1948; *All Quiet on the Western Front*, 1930); and adaptations of novels—such as *Lost in the Stars* (1949), based on Alan Paton's *Cry the Beloved Country*, through which he achieved a lifelong desire to "state the position and perhaps illustrate the tragedy of our Negroes."

The measure of his success, of course, varied considerably. In his grateful note of appreciation to his alma mater, the University of North Dakota, "Love Letter to a University," Anderson modestly remarked that he had not "achieved very much" and revealed an acute antipathy to American capitalism. But, fortunately, Anderson felt that he had had the regenerative, compensating experience of being associated with a university milieu that could consider "the life of the mind more important than banking."

In the "godless" 1920s, when Anderson "stumbled upon" the only religion he adopted, the theater, he came to realize and define on his own the constitutional rules of that faith: A play is the manifestation of the inner workings of the mind and heart of a man or woman; its action is geared by the conflict of the forces of good and evil within a single individual who, representing the former, should be able to vindicate its cause amidst a healthy moral atmosphere; the protagonist must be exceptional and yet not perfect in the first place; and then, in the end, he must emerge as a more admirable being than he was when he went in, in terms of moral excellence rather than material uplift and with the strengths of character and conviction. This amounts to what he defines as "the essence of tragedy or even serious play," being "the spiritual awakening or regeneration of the hero" (Anderson, 1939). It is only in a few plays—like *Mary of Scotland* and *Winterset*—that Anderson achieves the realization of most of these precepts.

Anderson had always been averse to talking about himself through interviews. But he divulged the varied literary influences on him. Starting with his childhood association with the classic 19th-century novelists that he discovered on the shelves of his father's modest library—Charles Dickens, Robert Louis Stevenson, Sir Walter Scott, Alexandre Dumas, and James Fenimore Cooper—he progressed into the magical world of poetry: John

Keats, Percy Bysshe Shelley, and William Shakespeare and, later, Alfred Lord Tennyson, Robert Browning, and Algernon Swinburne. He was to realize the nature of "a major revolution" in his life, the dynamic relativity and cadence of words in the conceptual wake of a modern poetical resurgence in the theater, which to him essentially constituted "the central artistic symbol of the struggle of good and evil" (Anderson, 1947).

Anderson laid stress on the search for truth and beauty through the dramatic conflict that theater promotes. And though he sought to identify this search with a modern poetical discourse, he did not subscribe to a limited conception of poetic drama but discovered, as well, the poetical and dialectical principles within vital prose drama that could reach superior heights of human relevance. Anderson refers to GEORGE BERNARD SHAW's lifting of the art of debate to a high level that transcended dialectic, that "pushed dialectic into the realms of the spirit" (Anderson, 1947).

At the end of an eventful life (Anderson died on February 28, 1959, in Stamford, Connecticut) comprising myriad trials and successes, Maxwell Anderson did not waver from his original view that "the theatre at its best is a religious affirmation, an age old rite restating and reassuring man's belief in his own destiny" (Anderson, 1939).

[*See also* United States, 1860–1940]

PLAYS: *What Price Glory?* (with Laurence Stallings, 1924); *First Flight* (with Stallings, 1926); *Saturday's Children* (1927); *Hell on Wheels* (musical, with Jack Niles, 1928); *Elizabeth the Queen* (1930); *Night over Taos* (1932); *Both Your Houses* (1933); *Mary of Scotland* (1933); *Valley Forge* (1934); *Winterset* (1935); *Masque of Kings* (1936); *Wingless Victory* (1936); *High Tor* (1937); *Star-Wagon* (1937); *Knickerbocker Holiday* (musical, with Kurt Weill, 1938); *Key Largo* (1939); *Journey to Jerusalem* (1940); *Candle in the Wind* (1941); *The Miracle of the Danube* (1941); *The Eve of St. Mark* (1942); *Storm Operation* (1944); *Joan of Lorraine* (1946); *Truckline Café* (1946); *Anne of the Thousand Days* (1948); *Lost in the Stars* (musical, with Kurt Weill, 1949); *Barefoot in Athens* (1951); *The Bad Seed* (1954); *The Masque of Pedagogues* (1957)

FURTHER READING

Anderson, Maxwell. *Dramatist in America: Letters of Maxwell Anderson, 1912–1958*. Ed. by Laurence G. Avery. Chapel Hill: Univ. of North Carolina Press, 1977.

——. *The Essence of Tragedy*. New York: Russell & Russell, 1939.

——. *Off-Broadway. Essays about the Theatre*. New York: W. Sloane Associates, 1947.

Bailey, Mabel Driscoll. *Maxwell Anderson: The Playwright as Prophet*. London: Abelard-Schuman, 1957.

Clark, Barrett H. *Maxwell Anderson: The Man and His Plays*. New York: French, 1933.

Gerstenberger, Donna. "Verse Drama in America: 1916–1939." *Modern Drama* (December 1963): 309–322.

Halline, Allen G. "Maxwell Anderson's Dramatic Theory." *American Literature* (May 1944): 68–81.

Prior, Moody E. *The Language of Tragedy*. Bloomington: Indiana Univ. Press, 1947.

Shivers, Alfred S. *The Life of Maxwell Anderson*. New York: Stein & Day, 1983.

Rupendra Guha-Majumdar

ANDORRA

It is a misreading to construe MAX FRISCH's *Andorra* (1957) as a historical drama, even though many in the audience at the 1961 Zurich premiere could hardly have avoided that. A play in which a community's latent anti-Semitism gathers strength until it is unleashed in the murder of an innocent scapegoat had to remind people of their own recent past and of the millions of Jews and other victims murdered at the hands of ordinary citizens. The parallels between Frisch's invented Andorra and the years 1933 to 1945 could be drawn too easily. Anticipating such a reaction, the perspicacious critic Hans Magnus Enzensberger declared in the performance program: "*Andorra* is not an historical drama. . . . The 'Blacks' are not the SS, the Jew-Inspector is not [Adolf] Eichmann, and not even the Jew is a Jew."

Frisch's original title for the play had been *Model Andorra*, reflecting his training as an architect. Models show how something is built, revealing elements and forces the clad structure will hide. In the world of *Andorra*, the elements are familiar and mundane emotions: love, joy, cowardice, jealousy, and fear. The deeds are likewise domestic: adultery, betrayal, indifference, and denial. The space of the action is a small community where everybody knows everyone else, and that is what makes the tragedy so compelling. Like any great play, *Andorra* gives evil a familiar face and makes the unspeakable crime into an ordinary event.

The plot centers on Andri, a young man ensnared by his father's lie. Rather than confessing his affair with a woman from the "Blacks"—the Andorrans' supposed foe in the neighboring country—the father tells everyone that the child he brought back is Jewish. Initially, the Andorrans are pleased to show their tolerance for the rescued child's otherness, but over time their prejudices become clearer and firmer. In every little interaction they let Andri know that for them he is a Jew—and therefore alien. As their prejudices are imprinted upon Andri, he comes to believe that he must be a Jew since everyone treats him so cruelly. The community feels increasingly threatened by the "Blacks," and they displace their irrational fears and rage upon Andri. Finally, they murder him.

The play is organized as a series of twelve episodes, short snippets of the story that move forward in time. Between them are brief interludes in which accused members of the community address the audience and explain why they treated Andri as they did. The majority still feel they are not to blame; their attitudes have not changed despite the crime they have evidently committed. The character "Someone" speaks for all those who saw and heard no evil: "What the soldiers did with him, when they took him away, I don't know, we only heard his cry. . . . At some point one just has to be able to forget, it seems."

Without experiencing the horrors of his own era, Frisch could not have written *Andorra*. But his analysis of what drives ordinary people to violate the sanctity of human life aligns the play with the sequence of tragedies that begins with Sophocles. *Andorra* shows how easily people can slip into inhumanity, a lesson that extends far beyond two decades in the middle of the 20th century.

[*See also* Germany]

FURTHER READING

Butler, Michael. *Frisch: Andorra*. London: Grant & Cutler, 1985.

Feinberg, A. "*Andorra*: Twenty Years On." *New German Studies* 10, no. 3 (1982): 175–190.

Huyssen, Andreas. "The Politics of Identification: 'Holocaust' and West German Drama." *New German Critique* 19 (Winter 1989): 117–136.

Löb, Ladislaus. "Insanity in the Darkness: Anti-Semitic Stereotypes and Jewish Identity in Max Frisch's *Andorra* and Arthur Miller's *Focus*." *Modern Language Review* 92, no. 3 (1997): 545–558.

Arnd Bohm

ANDREEV, LEONID (1871–1919)

Born on August 9 (21), 1871, in Oryol, Leonid Andreev (Andreyev; also Andreyeff) had established himself as one of Russia's leading writers of prose long before he turned to drama. His early stories reflect a realist manner, and he was close to MAKSIM GORKY and the group of writers allied with the Znanie publishing house; however, his themes often bear the veneer of the *fin de siècle* and underscore Andreev's kinship to nonrealist groups, particularly the symbolists. This tension, coupled with his disillusionment after the 1905 Revolution and the death of his beloved first wife, led him away from the Znanie group and toward the symbolists, whose almanac *Sweetbriar* he edited from 1907 to 1909. This period of transition roughly coincides with Andreev's first attempts at drama.

The inner tension in his work was never completely resolved, and Andreev's plays fall into one of two categories: Plays of the first sort, such as *Anfisa* (1909) and *Ekaterina Ivanovna* (1912), are generally realistic, sometimes naturalistic, in theme and resemble his early stories in their frank treatment of sex, licentiousness, murder, abortion, and similar themes. Such plays tended to reinforce the perception of Andreev as a writer who achieved notoriety by shocking his audience. However, his best work in this vein rests on psychological REALISM and owes a considerable debt to ANTON CHEKHOV and, to a lesser extent, Gorky.

Andreev's plays of the second variety veer away from realism toward more general philosophical themes and often come to resemble Russian symbolist drama contemporary to Andreev. Such plays as *Tsar Hunger* (1907), *Anathema* (1909), and *Black Masks* (1908) exhibit certain traits that are common in MONODRAMAS, inasmuch as the internal psychic conflict of the protagonist is reified on the stage. Mythic patterns and emblematic settings lead the audience beyond the parameters of realism. It was with this type of drama that Andreev achieved his greatest success as a playwright THE LIFE OF MAN (1906), for example, was seen by some, including the author, as the beginning of a new type of drama. Toward the end of his life, Andreev created his most famous drama, HE WHO GETS SLAPPED (1915), which shows Andreev's strengths as a playwright to good effect.

Major directors recognized Andreev's importance as a playwright. VSEVOLOD MEYERHOLD staged both *To the Stars* and *The Life of Man*. In their search for a post-Chekhov theater, KONSTANTIN STANISLAVSKY and Vladimir Nemirovich-Danchenko put on productions of both *The Life of Man* and *Anathema* at the MOSCOW ART THEATER.

Because of his early death (September 12, 1919, in Kuokkala, Finland) and staunch opposition to Bolshevism, Andreev was ignored in Russia through much of the Soviet era. This neglect owes only in part to politics. Critics have often faulted Andreev for his overly abstract and schematic treatment of philosophical problems and for his lurid themes; however, it is easy to overlook Andreev's influence on succeeding generations of playwrights, particularly in Western Europe. Andreev, in his strident secularism, was one of the first to treat the problem of humankind stripped of belief in God. His work anticipated existential themes. In his nonrealist technique, Andreev also provided an important model for later playwrights, particularly for the expressionists, whose work often betrays a familiarity with Andreev.

Andreev's plays number nearly thirty and include generally realistic dramas, such as *Days of Our Lives*, and also symbolic, if not symbolist, dramas, such as *The Life of Man* (1917).

[*See also* Russia and the Soviet Union; Symbolism]

PLAYS: *The Life of Man* (*Zhizn' cheloveka*, 1906); *Tsar Hunger* (*Tsar' Golod*, 1907); *Black Masks* (*Chernye maski*, 1908); *Days of Our Lives* (*Dni nashei zhizni*, 1908); *Anathema* (*Anatema*, 1909); *Anfisa* (1909); *Ekaterina Ivanovna* (1912); *Gaudeamus* (1912); *Professor Storitsyn* (1912); *The Mark of Cain (Thou Shalt Not Kill)* (*Kainova pechat'* [*Ne ubii*], 1913); *He Who Gets Slapped* (*Tot, kto poluchaet poshchechiny*, 1915); *Requiem* (*Rekviem*, 1916)

FURTHER READING

Andreev, Leonid. "Letters on the Theater." In *Russian Dramatic Theory from Pushkin to the Symbolists*, ed. and tr. by Laurence Senelick. Austin: Univ. of Texas Press, 1981.

——. (Several essays on theater). In *The Symbolist Theatre: An Anthology of Plays and Critical Texts*, ed. and tr. by Michael Green. Ann Arbor: Ardis, 1986.

Kaun, Alexander Samuel. *Leonid Andreyev: A Critical Study*. 1924. Reprint. New York: Books for Libraries Press, 1969.

Newcombe, Josephine Marjorie. *Leonid Andreyev*. 1972. Reprint. New York: Ungar, 1973.

Woodward, James B. *Leonid Andreyev: A Study*. Oxford: Oxford University Press, 1969.

Timothy C. Westphalen

ANGELS IN AMERICA: A GAY FANTASIA ON NATIONAL THEMES. PART ONE: MILLENNIUM APPROACHES

The Great Work Begins!

—The Angel, Act 3

Millennium Approaches, the Pulitzer Prize–winning first play of TONY KUSHNER's two-play epic *Angels in America: A Gay Fantasia on National Themes*, inspired critical acclaim and intense controversy beginning with its debut at San Francisco's Eureka Theatre in 1991, under the direction of Oskar Eustis. Written with the partial support of a National Endowment for the Arts grant, this first production was followed by revised versions produced at Los Angeles's Mark Taper Forum and the Royal National Theatre of Great Britain prior to a yearlong run at New York's Walter Kerr Theatre. The Broadway production won the 1993 Tony Award as Best Play. In an unprecedented event, the second *Angels* play, *Perestroika*, won the Best Play Tony Award the following year. A long and complex work mixing drama and comedy with elements of history, politics, and fantasy, *Angels* weaves together diverse strands of late-20th-century American life.

Set in the mid-1980s shortly after Ronald Reagan's reelection to the U.S. presidency, *Millennium Approaches* follows two fictional couples and one icon from post–World War II American history, Roy Cohn, the conservative New York lawyer who served as an aide to Wisconsin's Senator Joseph McCarthy during the Communist "witch hunts" of the 1950s. Joe and Harper Pitt, a Mormon couple, move to New York City where Joe has a job as a law clerk for a conservative judge. Struggling to be true to his Mormon upbringing while coming to the realization that he is a closeted gay man, Joe battles with Harper, who is treating a deep depression with Valium and a vivid imagination, agonizing over her suspicions about Joe's true sexuality. Cohn, who, by 1985, is a disreputable divorce lawyer on the verge of disbarment, intends to secure a position for Joe in the Reagan administration's Justice Department in Washington, D.C., where Cohn, who learns he is suffering from AIDS, hopes that Joe will serve as his informant.

Prior Walter and Louis Ironson, a committed gay couple, learn that Prior is HIV-positive. Louis, a liberal court reporter working in the same building with Joe, fears he will not be able to live up to the requirements of caring for Prior as the disease takes its toll. Louis abandons Prior and spirals downward into despair and self-recrimination. Prior turns for support to a close friend, Belize, an African American nurse who is also a sometime drag queen. Meanwhile, Joe, finally accepting his sexuality, telephones his mother, Hannah, to tell her. He leaves Harper to pursue Louis, whom he met earlier in the men's room of the Criminal Courts Building.

The physical conditions of Prior and Cohn worsen as *Millennium Approaches* moves forward. Delirious from his illness, Prior meets an overdosed Harper in a mutual hallucination, while Cohn is haunted by the specter of another historical figure, Ethel Rosenberg, who, along with her husband Julius, was executed in the early 1950s for allegedly selling atomic secrets to the Soviet Union. Cohn reveals to Joe that he had illegally pressured the judge in the Rosenberg case to give them the death sentence. Cohn refuses to acknowledge his homosexuality—gay men, in his opinion, are powerless and faceless people—and despite his weakening condition, he seems more concerned with preventing his disbarment. Louis, after a punishing anonymous sexual encounter in Central Park, again meets Joe, and they run off together as Harper sinks more deeply into depression and drugs. Prior is haunted by the ghosts of two ancestors—"prior Priors"—both of whom have died of plagues in previous eras, and he intermittently hears the voice of an Angel calling him "prophet." In the play's final scene, the Angel crashes through the ceiling of Prior's bedroom, announcing that "The Great Work Begins."

In and around the personal crises of the characters, *Millennium Approaches* explores late-20th-century attitudes about American history, sexuality, race, religion, and the traditional poles of conservative and liberal politics. Kushner was inspired in part by Walter Benjamin's essay "Theses on the Philosophy of History," which, in turn, was inspired by Paul Klee's *Angelus Novus*, a painting depicting the Angel of History being blown into the future by the winds of progress while glancing back at the rubble of history. Using that image as a thematic inspiration, Kushner employs an EPIC THEATER style drawn from his admiration for ERWIN PISCATOR's theories and BERTOLT BRECHT's plays, weaving his variation of epic form with American lyric REALISM in the manner of TENNESSEE WILLIAMS. Over three and a half hours long in performance. *Angels* has been produced in over forty countries. *Perestroika* picks up where *Millennium Approaches* leaves off, continuing to track the same set of characters as the Angel, Hannah, and Belize evolve from secondary characters to figures as significant as Joe, Harper, Prior, Louis, and Cohn. A majority of critics found *Angels* to be one of the most significant dramas of the late 20th century and applauded its theatricalized exploration of the perplexing and challenging issues of the last half of the 20th century, while also offering a model for an overt brand of American political drama.

[*See also* Gay and Lesbian Drama; United States, 1940–Present]

FURTHER READING

Brask, Per, ed. *Essays on Kushner's Angels*. Winnipeg: Blizzard Pub., 1995.

Fisher, James. *The Theater of Tony Kushner: Living Past Hope*. New York: Routledge, 2001.

Freedman, Jonathan. "Angels, Monsters, and Jews: Intersections of Queer and Jewish Identity in Kushner's *Angels in America*." *PMLA* (January 1999): 90–102.

Geis, Deborah R., and Steven F. Kruger, eds. *Approaching the Millennium: Essays on Angels in America*. Ann Arbor: Univ. of Michigan Press, 1997.

Norden, Edward. "From Schnitzler to Kushner." *Commentary* 99 (January 1995): 51–58.

Savran, David. "Ambivalence, Utopia, and a Queer Sort of Materialism: How *Angels in America* Reconstructs the Nation." *Theatre Journal* 47 (May 1995): 207–227.

James Fisher

ANGOLA See AFRICA

ANGRY YOUNG MEN

The people I should like to contact—if I knew how—aren't likely to be reading this book, anyway. If they have ever heard of me, it is only as a rather odd-looking "angry young man."

—John Osborne

The opening night of JOHN OSBORNE's *LOOK BACK IN ANGER* at the Royal Court Theatre in London on May 8, 1956, is one of the most mythical occasions in postwar British drama. Not only has it been credited with bringing about a revolution in new writing for the stage overnight, but it also unleashed the myth of the "Angry Young Men." Originally, the phrase "Angry Young Man" (AYM) was used in 1951 by the Christian apologist Leslie Paul to title his autobiography, and Osborne reported that it was the Royal Court's part-time press officer George Fearon who first used it to describe the playwright. Although the phrase may thus belong to the history of publicity rather than that of drama, its origins were not accidental. Anger is certainly one of the attributes of Jimmy Porter, the antihero of *Look Back in Anger*, and although Osborne took time to decide on the play's evocative name—the manuscript includes six discarded titles—most were variations on the theme of anger, including *Farewell to Anger*, *Angry Man*, and *Man in a Rage*.

By late summer 1956, newspaper journalists were using the AYM label to describe almost anyone who was loudly critical of what was then called "The Establishment." It was most commonly applied not only to Osborne but also to novelist Kingsley Amis and philosopher Colin Wilson. Soon, it also enveloped other writers, such as John Wain and John Braine. Cartoons and feature articles spread the word about these disaffected artists. Then, in 1958, Kenneth Allsop rushed into print with *The Angry Decade*, although a more accurate title would have been "The Angry Eighteen Months." He argued that although *anger* advertised these emergent talents, a better word for their "new spirit" was *dissentience*, a dissent from "majority sentiments and opinions."

All the individuals who were labeled Angry Young Men may have enjoyed the resulting publicity, but they all quickly dissociated themselves from the label and from each other. In 1957, when Tom Maschler edited *Declaration*, a volume of essays—which included Osborne's "They Call It Cricket"—by cultural protagonists such as Lindsay Anderson, Kenneth Tynan, and Doris Lessing, he denounced the label as a product of a "lower level of journalism." Its role, he argued, was to defuse the writers' "indignation against apathy," and he mocked the fact that it had been applied to author Nigel Dennis, "over forty, the father of teen-age children, and the mildest of men."

Cultural myth is a combination of historical truths and popular distortion, and the myth of the Angry Young Men took the form of what Robert Hewison (1981) calls a "compelling slogan." The AYM became a composite fictional character, a mixture of "outsider" and "rebel." After all, the landmark review of *Look Back in Anger* by Kenneth Tynan, the critic of *The Observer*, suggested that Osborne was a left-wing playwright. So the Angry Young Men were constantly criticized for their lack of commitment to serious left-wing causes, which irritated them because they did not think of themselves as a group, let alone a movement. In fact, they felt more allegiance to their craft than to a political ideology, even if their combination of youth, ambition, and dissatisfaction did generate a certain creative energy.

Although Osborne was soon part of the larger phenomenon of "new wave" or "kitchen-sink" playwrights—which included women (SHELAGH DELANEY and ANN JELLICOE) as well as men (ARNOLD WESKER, JOHN ARDEN, and HAROLD PINTER)—there was no female equivalent of the AYM. And at the time of the Suez Crisis, Osborne's bad-boy image had less to do with politics than with misogyny: In the *Daily Mail*, for example, he blustered, "What's gone wrong with WOMEN?" Anger, in the cultural imagination of the late 1950s, was a man's business.

Ironically, the myth's most surprising asset was Osborne himself, ever happy to play up to the role of being "the angriest young man of them all." An early example of the rent-a-quote personality, Osborne enjoyed castigating anything from the monarchy to suburban pastimes and the H-bomb. But having played up to the myth, he found it hard to shake off the label and, as he got older, was condemned for turning into the highly individualistic right-wing reactionary he arguably had always been. Media labels, it could be said, make good servants but bad masters.

[*See also* England, 1940–1960]

FURTHER READING

Allsop, Kenneth. *The Angry Decade: A Survey of the Cultural Revolt of the Nineteen-Fifties*. London: P. Owen, 1958.

Carpenter, Humphrey. *The Angry Young Men: A Literary Comedy of the 1950s*. Harmondsworth: Penguin, 2002.

Hewison, Robert. *In Anger: Culture in the Cold War 1945–60*. London: Methuen, 1981.

Maschler, Tom. *Declaration*. London: MacGibbon & Kee, 1957.

Osborne, John. *Damn You, England: Collected Prose*. London: Faber, 1994.

Ritchie, Harry. *Success Stories: Literature and the Media in England, 1950–1959*. London: Faber, 1988.

Aleks Sierz

ANGURA AND SHŌGEKIJŌ

Angura, from the Japanese pronunciation of "underground," was a theater movement that began in Tokyo about 1960 and succeeded in integrating Western-style modern theater with aspects of the premodern Japanese tradition. Also known as the post-SHINGEKI or the little theater (*shōgekijō*) movement, *angura* was a revolt against theatrical modernism that centered on small, alternative theater spaces (coffee shops, basements, tents) and took its inspiration from the underground and OFF-OFF-BROADWAY theaters of Europe and the United States.

By the late 1950s *shingeki* had become the theatrical establishment in Japan. The postwar generation of theater practitioners, those born about 1940, rebelled against this establishment. As critic Tsuno Kaitarō (1978) put it, "*Shingeki* has become historical; it has become a tradition in its own right. . . . *Shingeki* no longer maintains the dialectical power to negate and transcend; rather, it has become an institution that itself demands to be transcended."

Angura was the theatrical expression of the noncommunist New Left political movement that emerged in Japan following the failure of mass demonstrations in 1960 to prevent renewal of the U.S.-Japan Mutual Security Treaty, which permits U.S. military bases on Japanese soil. Young artists wanted to assert Japan's cultural autonomy even if the treaty compromised its political autonomy. *Angura* revolted against the universalistic humanist ideology of theatrical modernism and insisted on the particularity of Japan's cultural experience.

Angura was also a revolt against the *shingeki* production system, which was dominated in the late 1950s by three major troupes: the People's Art Theatre (Mingei), the Actors Theater (Haiyū za), and the Literary Theater (Bungaku za). By narrowly defining modern theater as theater performed on proscenium arch stages and controlling access to these theaters through such organizations as Workers Theatre Councils (Rōen), a network of local theater appreciation societies modeled after the German *Volksbühne*, the major *shingeki* companies exercised an effective monopoly over modern theater audiences and what they were allowed to see. This had to end. As one underground troupe put it in a typical manifesto, "Ultimately it is our intention to destroy *shingeki* as an art, *shingeki* as a system and in its place present before you a concrete alternative contemporary theater distinct from *shingeki*" ("Engeki Sentaa ni Tsuite," 1972).

The guiding principle of the underground movement was to use the premodern imagination to transcend the modern. This did not mean abandoning modern theater in favor of premodern forms. Rather, it meant reaffirming in a critical fashion the religious and aesthetic principles that had animated premodern theater but that had been abandoned in the struggle to create a modern theater for Japan. *Angura* sought to create a new, hybrid form of contemporary theater that was both modern and authentically Japanese. Plays such as AKIMOTO MATSUYO's *Kaison the Priest of Hitachi* (*Hitachibō Kaison*, 1964) provided models for this effort.

Several troupes founded in the early 1960s spearheaded the underground theater movement. The Youth Art Theatre (Seigei), an offshoot of the People's Art Theatre, mounted its first production in 1960. Led by the playwright FUKUDA YOSHIYUKI, the troupe introduced a politically engaged, activist theater inspired by BERTOLT BRECHT. Fukuda's play *Find Hakamadare!* (*Hakamadare wa Doko da*, 1964) was among the pioneering works of the underground movement. Seigei served as a training ground for many other young innovators, and both KARA JŪRŌ and SATOH MAKOTO apprenticed with the troupe.

Kara's Situation Theatre (Jōkyō Gekijō) grew out of the Experimental Theatre club at Meiji University, where Kara was a student. After graduation Kara, his then wife Ri Reisen, and Maro Akaji (who would go on to found the Dairakudakan *butō* troupe in 1972) created the Situation Theatre, named for JEAN-PAUL SARTRE's theater of situations. In October 1966, the group performed Kara's *Petticoat Osen: A Tale of Forgetfulness* (*Koshimaki Osen Bōkyakuhen*, 1966) in an outdoor band shell in the Toyamagahara section of Tokyo. The group also performed street theater in the urban hubs of Ginza and Shinjuku. The actual breakthrough came on August 5, 1967, however, when the troupe pitched its newly acquired red tent theater in the precincts of Shinjuku's Hanazono Shinto Shrine. Kara conceived his theater in the premodern mold of *kabuki* and his actors as "riverbed beggars" (*kawara kojiki*), a reference to the pariah status of premodern *kabuki* performers. Kara's tent theater challenged *shingeki*'s hegemony over theater spaces; and his introduction of immortal characters who defied death and transcended history broke decisively with the secular, realistic paradigm of modern theater. Images of the Situation Theatre's performances of the time form the centerpiece of Ōshima Nagisa's 1968 film *Diary of Shinjuku Thief* (*Shinjuku Dorobō Nikki*, 1968); and *John Silver: The Beggar of Love* (*Jon Shirubaa: Ai no Kojiki*, 1970) is representative of Kara's playwriting style.

The Black Tent Theater (BTT, or Kuro Tento) built its tent theater in 1969, inspired by the example of the Situation Theatre. The troupe, founded as Theatre Center 68/69 after British playwright ARNOLD WESKER's Theatre Center 42, grew out of an alliance between graduates of the Actors Theatre Training School (Haiyū za Yōseijo), including Satoh Makoto, Kushida Kazuyoshi, Saitō Ren, and Yoshida Hideko, and former members of student theater clubs at Waseda and Tokyo Universities, including Tsuno Kaitarō, Saeki Ryūkō, Muramatsu Katsumi, and Yamamoto Kiyokazu. Satoh quickly emerged as the leading playwright of the troupe. Strongly influenced by Brecht, the BTT was and remains the most overtly political of the underground troupes; but Satoh's plays, like Kara's, reject homogenous time and linear plots in favor of multilayered, ahistorical dramas reminiscent of *kabuki*. Among the most successful of these were Satoh's *Nezumi Kozō: The Rat* (*Nezumi Kozō Jirokichi*, 1969); *The Dance of Angels Who Burn Their Own Wings* (*Tsubasa o Moyasu Tenshi-tachi no Butō*, 1970); and the trilogy *The World of Shōwa: A Comedy* (*Kigeki Shōwa no Sekai*, 1972–1979). The BTT also published two pioneering magazines, *Dōjidai Engeki* (*Contemporary Theatre*) and *Concerned Theatre Japan*, in Japanese and English respectively.

The Waseda Little Theatre (Waseda Shōgekijō) grew out of a student theater group at Waseda University. It opened on April 3, 1962, with a production of founder BETSUYAKU MINORU's *The Elephant* (*Zō*, 1962), an absurdist play about survivors of Hiroshima. The director Suzuki Tadashi and the actor Ono Hiroshi were cofounders of the troupe. In 1966, the troupe moved to the converted second floor of a coffee shop. Until his departure from the troupe in August 1968, Betsuyaku was the troupe's main playwright, and his 1967 play *Little Match Girl* (*Matchi-uri no Shōjo*) was the first post-*shingeki* work to receive the prestigious Kishida Kunio Drama Prize. Betsuyaku's departure was precipitated by artistic differences with Suzuki, who was preparing to stage *On the Dramatic Passions I* (*Gekiteki-naru Mono o Megutte*, 1969), a collage of dramatic scenes from works ranging from 19th-century *kabuki* to *WAITING FOR GODOT*. This production, staged in April 1969 and followed by a second version in 1970, was a revolutionary inquiry into the nature of acting and theatricality that placed Western and Japanese works on the same plane, something inconceivable in orthodox modern theater. With the significant help of the actress Shiraishi Kayoko, Suzuki developed from these experiments a series of actor-training exercises that came to be known as the Suzuki Method. In 1976 the Waseda Little Theatre left Tokyo for the isolated mountain village of Toga, eight hours away; and in 1984 it changed its name to SCOT (Suzuki Company of Toga). Between 1982 and 1999, SCOT sponsored the Toga Festival, Japan's first international theater festival.

The troupe Tenjō Sajiki (sometimes translated as Peanut Gallery but derived from Children of Paradise, after Marcel Carne's 1945 film *Les Enfants du Paradis*) was founded in 1967 by TERAYAMA SHŪJI. Unlike the other underground troupes, Tenjō Sajiki did not grow out of student theater clubs or existing *shingeki* companies. Born in 1935, Terayama was an established poet and playwright closely identified with the classical European avant-garde. Terayama did not share the other post-*shingeki* troupes' intense ambivalence toward the West, and his troupe made almost annual appearances at European theater festivals beginning in 1969 and continuing until his untimely death. Tenjō Sajiki was the most protean of the underground troupes, performing street theater and happenings as well as more traditional plays, virtually all authored by Terayama. The environmental theater piece *Knock* (*Nokku*, 1975), for example, involved 1,000 participants who visited 33 places in Tokyo over a period of 30 hours, guided by directions provided by the troupe. Tenjō Sajiki was more interested in shocking the bourgeoisie than in recapturing Japan's premodern imagination, but it did exploit the premodern in plays like *Heresy* (*Jashūmon*, 1971), which was performed in several European countries and became Tenjō Sajiki's most acclaimed production.

Once the hegemony of *shingeki* was broken and it became clear that the premodern Japanese imagination could be drawn on to inform modern theater, the floodgates were open. The 1960s were the beginning of a theatrical renaissance in Japan; and as Japan's rapidly expanding economy became able to support them, more and more troupes were founded, emphasizing various aspects of the new theater paradigm. By 1995 an average of 4.3 new contemporary theater productions were opening every day in Tokyo, serving an audience of more than 3.3 million people. *Angura* was the beginning of this efflorescence.

[*See also* Japan; *Shingeki*; *Shin Kabuki*]

FURTHER READING

"Engeki Sentaa ni Tsuite" [About Theatre Center]. Quoted in Senda Akihiko. "Kaisetsu" [Commentary]. In *Gendai Nihon Gikyoku Taike* [Compendium of contemporary Japanese plays]. Vol. 8. Tokyo: San'ichi Shobō, 1972.

Goodman, David G. *After Apocalypse: Four Japanese Plays of Hiroshima and Nagasaki*. Cornell East Asia Papers 71. Ithaca, N.Y.: Cornell East Asia Program, 1994.

——. *Concerned Theatre Japan: The Graphic Art of Japanese Theatre, 1960 to 1980*. CD-ROM. Champaign: Krannert Art Museum, Univ. of Illinois, 1998.

——. *Angura: Posters of the Japanese Avant-Garde*. New York: Princeton Arch. Press, 1999.

——. *The Return of the Gods: Japanese Drama and Culture in the 1960s*. Cornell East Asia Papers 116. Ithaca, N.Y.: Cornell East Asia Program, 2003.

Rolf, Robert T., and John K. Gillespie, tr. and eds. *Alternative Japanese Drama: Ten Plays*. Honolulu: Univ. of Hawaii Press, 1992.

Senda Akihiko. *Nihon no Gendai Engeki* [Japan's contemporary theatre]. Tokyo: Iwanami Shoten, 1995.

Tsuno Kaitarō. "The Tradition of Modern Theatre in Japan." Tr. by David G. Goodman. *Canadian Theatre Review* (Fall 1978): 8–19.

David G. Goodman

ANNA CHRISTIE

Only dat ole davil, sea—she knows!

—Chris, Act 4

A revision of EUGENE O'NEILL's own *Chris Christopherson* (1920), *Anna Christie* opened at the Vanderbilt Theatre in New York on November 2, 1921, produced and directed by Arthur Hopkins and designed by ROBERT EDMOND JONES.

The longshoremen gather at Johnny-the-Priest's, a saloon where Chris Christopherson, a Swedish coal barge captain, waits for his daughter Anna. He has not seen her for fifteen years, and he imagines her growing up in decent circumstances in Minnesota, but she turns out to be "a tall, blond, fully developed girl" who is a prostitute. She believes that her father is a janitor, and she resents him for leaving her with cousins who worked her "to death like a dog" on their farm. Chris blames "dat ole davil sea" for all his misfortunes, and Anna is disgusted at the prospect of joining her father on a barge.

Ten days on the barge transform Anna—she even loves the fog—but Chris warns her against the men she will find on the sea. They assist an Irish sailor named Mat Burke, who spent five days in an open boat after his steamer was wrecked. Mat flirts with Anna, and she cannot quite resist him, but he agrees with Chris about men and women and the sea: "It's a hard and lonesome life, the sea is. The only women you'd meet in the ports of the world who'd be willing to speak you a kind word isn't women at all."

Although Anna cryptically assures Chris that she is not good enough for Mat, the Irishman confirms Chris's suspicions when he tells the captain that he intends to marry his daughter. Ashamed of her past, Anna refuses to accept Mat's proposal, even though she loves him. Pressed, she tells both men how one of her cousins seduced her; because none of the young men in St. Paul regarded her as a marriage prospect, she went to work in a brothel. Furious, Mat repudiates her.

The men go on a two-day binge and return to find Anna packed and ready to resume her old life. Both Chris and Mat and have decided to return to the sea, and by coincidence, they have signed to ship out on the same steamer. They reconcile, and Anna plans to keep a little house so they have a home where they might return. Unlike the sailors in the O'Neill's four one act plays known as the S.S. *Glencairn* plays, Anna and her men have made a grudging peace with the sea that holds them.

Kenneth Macgowan declared in the *New York Globe and Commercial Advertiser* (November 3, 1921):

> O'Neill has never so fully achieved his dramatic purpose. None of his plays so completely realizes its characters. None of his plays is so full-bodied. None of his plays plough through the tragedy and suffering of life to such an affirmation of its eternal vitality. . . . In the end life goes on as it has gone from the beginning. It is not the hopeless, inescapable tragedy of living on and on. . . . It is the acceptance of suffering and happiness lived out into new life.

Maide Castellun, of the *New York Call* (November 4, 1921), mentioned its "sordid commonplace" and its "magnificent fatalism."

The Roundabout Theatre Company revived the play in 1993 with Liam Neeson, Natasha Richardson, and Rip Torn.

[*See also* United States, 1860–1929]

FURTHER READING

Brietzke, Zander. "Tragic Vision and the Happy Ending in '*Anna Christie*.'" *Eugene O'Neill Review* 24 (Spring–Fall 2000): 43–60.

Codde, Philippe. "'Dat Ole Davil, Sea': Cowardice and Redemption in Eugene O'Neill's '*Anna Christie*.'" *Eugene O'Neill Review* 22 (Spring–Fall 1998): 23–32.

Garvey, Sheila Hickey. "Anna Christie and the 'Fallen Woman Genre.'" *Eugene O'Neill Review* 19 (Spring–Fall 1995): 67–80.

Holmberg, Arthur. "Fallen Angels at Sea: Garbo, Ullman, Richardson, and the Contradictory Prostitute in '*Anna Christie*.'" *Eugene O'Neill Review* 20 (Spring–Fall 1996): 43–63.

Jeffrey D. Mason

ANNA SOPHIE HEDVIG

> *It is the usual—we are neither for nor against—we always understand both sides of a case—that is our glaring weakness in relation to the others who stand firmly on theirs' without the slightest doubt—they walk straight ahead—and we only give up—pleading to be so humane.*
>
> —John, Act 3

KJELD ABELL'S *Anna Sophie Hedvig* was staged in January 1939 at the Royal Theatre of Copenhagen at a time when German pressure on DENMARK was growing. It is Abell's most directly political play. He has left the playful, satirical style of his earlier antibourgeois comedies and returned to the drawing-room drama, so familiar to the Danish theatergoer of the time, but only to relate the drawing room to the outside world and to show that it is no longer merely harmlessly trivial but already infected by Nazism.

In *Anna Sophie Hedvig* Abell described a milieu he thoroughly knew—an upper-middle-class milieu where words are used to conceal rather than reveal and where any controversial or dangerous subject is avoided by talking about something else, a mode of conversation perfectly unfolded by the nervous and superficial chitchat of the Lady of the House. This bourgeois world of appearances is provoked from a rather unexpected quarter—a poor relation, Anna Sophie Hedvig—an elderly, provincial schoolmistress who arrives unannounced in the middle of the preparations for a dinner party and reluctantly is asked to stay. When the guest of honor, Director Hoff, an important business connection of the host, during the meal asks the rhetorical question if anybody around the table would ever be able to use violence, Anna Sophie Hedvig is the only one to answer yes. While the others try to overhear the fatal answer, Hoff insists on a further questioning during which it is revealed that this apparently anonymous and gray little lady has committed murder by spontaneously pushing the coming headmistress of her school, a relentless and power-seeking person, down a staircase because she was threatening everything good and valuable in life. It is Abell's perhaps somewhat hard-drawn point that Anna Sophie Hedvig's impulsive act to liberate her own little world from a ruthless dictator and the fight for freedom on the greater political stage are one and the same.

Early in the play a picture in the newspaper of a young condemned freedom fighter standing before a wall makes a strong impression on Anna Sophie Hedvig and John, the son in the family and a representative of the young intellectuals with progressive opinions but bereft of the ability to act by their bourgeois upbringing. At the end of act 1 the picture is presented as a *tableau vivant*, and in the very last scene of the play, Abell makes Anna Sophie Hedvig join the freedom fighter, thus breaking down the walls between the two worlds. On the realistic level, Anna Sophie Hedvig is not condemned to death but handed over to the police on the initiative of Hoff, who is later assaulted by John and revealed as a dubious character willing to use any means to reach his ends. By her example the anonymous schoolmistress has made a difference, and she leaves behind her a transformed family.

Anna Sophie Hedvig is not only Abell's most political play but also his most realistic. Because his aim is not a psychological inner drama, he breaks away from the closed dramaturgy of the traditional drawing-room play by using a flashback technique, known from film, with frequent leaps in time and space, combined with scenes of a purely symbolic nature.

Kela Kvam

ANOUILH, JEAN (1910–1987)

Jean Anouilh stands as France's most prolific and popular playwright of the mid-20th-century. His nearly fifty plays reflect a wide range of influences: the comic spirit of Molière, the linguistic refinement of Alfred de Musset and Pierre de Marivaux, the literary polish of JEAN GIRADOUX, the meta-theatricality of LUIGI PIRANDELLO, and the existentialism of JEAN-PAUL SARTRE and ALBERT CAMUS. Anouilh's voice is consistently tragicomic—a quintessential postwar pessimism lightened with abundant playfulness. He shares his generation's despair over the frustrations and paradoxes of modern society, but retains an amused sympathy for those forced to muddle through life's absurdities. Some critics have balked at the conservative aesthetics and primarily apolitical, upper-class tenor to his dramaturgy. But Anouilh never aspired to politicize or to revolutionize the stage; he was content to seduce and entertain his audiences, while exposing the uncertainties, contradictions and pretenses of their world.

Jean Anouilh was born on June 23, 1910, in Bordeaux, FRANCE. He was the son of a hard-working tailor, from whom he learned discipline and attention to detail; years later, he remarked, "I write plays . . . the way my father used to cut his suits." Anouilh's mother was a musician in a local casino orchestra. She would permit her son to watch the first acts of operettas she accompanied, fueling in the boy an appreciation for showmanship and a curiosity about the intricacies of plots and their resolutions. As a young adult Anouilh enrolled in law school, but quickly withdrew and took a job writing advertising copy, a trade he credited with teaching him "lessons of precision and ingenuity. . . . A slogan presupposes a precision of words within a phrase that resembles the strictness necessary for lines in a play." While employed at the agency, Jean became friendly with fellow copywriter and aspiring dramatist George Neveux, who introduced his colleague to Parisian director Louis Jouvet. Jouvet hired Anouilh as his personal secretary in 1929, but was uninterested in his assistant's attempts at playwriting. Thus Anouilh's first productions occurred through other companies, including *The Ermine* (1932) at the Théâtre de l'Oeuvre (staged by Aurélien Lugnè-Poë), and the critical success *There Was a Prisoner* (1935) at the Théâtre des Ambassadeurs. The latter drew disappointing audiences, but garnered enough accolades to bring Anouilh a Hollywood contract for the film rights. (The picture was never made.)

Two years later Jouvet's rival, Georges Pitoëff, staged Anouilh's first popular success, *Traveler Without Luggage* (1937), a drama depicting an amnesiac war veteran's search for his identity. With this triumph, a busy and prosperous period of output had begun. Anouilh's drama would dominate the Parisian stage for the next quarter-century, when scarcely a year transpired without the debut of a major new work. The rise of ABSURDISM brought Anouilh's more conventional dramaturgy into disfavor, and perhaps as a result he turned his attentions from writing to directing for most of the 1960s. He returned to playwriting later in the decade and composed new dramas regularly until the early 1980s, but never again enjoyed the acceptance of his earlier career. He died in Lausanne, Switzerland, on October 3, 1987.

Anouilh organized his oeuvre into specific tonal categories. The somber, pessimistic "black plays" (*pièces noires*) include adaptations of Greek tragedies. His version of Sophocles's *Antigone* was enormously popular in occupied Paris during World War II, interpreted by many as a veiled protest against the Vichy government's collaboration with the Nazis. In contrast, the "pink" plays (*pièces rosées*) are filled with romance, fantasy, and masquerade. The "brilliant plays" (*pièces brilliantes*) depict aristocratic splendor and the backstage intrigues of the theater. The more unsettling "abrasive plays" (*pièces grinçantes*) dramatize soured romantic and familial relationships. Anouilh is best known in the English-speaking world for his "costume plays" (*pièces costumées*), which revisit familiar historical episodes with a decidedly modern sensibility. Two of these have been successful both on stage and in film: *Becket, or The Honor of God* (1959), which explores the friendship between Thomas à Becket and England's King Henry II, and *The Lark* (1953), a retelling of the heresy trial of Joan of Arc. In both of these historical dramas the title characters emerge as more than divinely chosen martyrs; they are human idealists who dare to live purely within corrupt worlds that hold no tolerance for idealism.

Anouilh categorizes other works as "farcical plays" (*pièces farceuses*), "baroque plays" (*pièces baroques*), "secret plays" (*pièces secrètes*), and more humbly, "my failures" (*mes fous*). He also produced numerous film scenarios, as well as acclaimed French adaptations of William Shakespeare, OSCAR WILDE, EUGENE O'NEILL, Heinrich von Kleist, and other foreign playwrights.

[See also *Antigone*; *Eurydice*; *The Waltz of the Toreadors*]

SELECT PLAYS: *Humulus the Mute* (*Humulus le muet*, with Jean Aurenche, 1929); *The Mandarin* (*La mandarine*, 1929); *The Ermine*

(*L'hermine*, 1932); *Jezebel* (*Jézabel*, 1932); *Theives' Carnival* (*Le bal des voleurs*, 1932); *There Was a Prisoner* (*Y avait un prisonnier*, 1935); *Dinner with the Family* (*Le rendez-vous de senlis*, 1937); *Traveler Without Luggage* (*Le voyageur sans bagage*, 1937); *Time Remembered* (*Léocadia*, 1939); *Eurydice* (1942; also performed in English under the titles *Point of Departure* [1950] and *Legend of Lovers* [1951]); *Antigone* (1944); *Medea* (*Médée*, 1946); *Romeo and Jeanette/Fading Mansions* (*Roméo et Jeannette*, 1946); *Ring Round the Moon* (*L'invitation au château*, 1947); *Ardele, or the Cry of the Peacock* (*Ardèle, ou la Marguerite*, 1948); *The Rehearsal* (*La répétition, ou l'amour puni*, 1950); *Mademoiselle Colombe* (*Colombe*, 1951); *The Waltz of the Toreadors* (*La valse des Toréadors*, 1952); *The Lark* (*L'alouette*, 1953); *Poor Bitos, or The Masked Dinner* (*Pauvre Bitos, ou le díner de têtes*, 1956); *The Fighting Cock* (*L'hurluberlu, ou le rèactionnaire amoureux*, 1958); *Becket, or The Honor of God* (*Becket, ou l'honneur de Dieu*, 1959); *Catch as Catch Can* (*La foire d'empoigne*, 1962); *The Orchestra* (*L'orchestre*, 1962); *The Baker, His Wife and Their Apprentice* (*Le boulanger, la boulangère et le petit mitron*, 1964); *Dear Antoine* (*Cher Antoine, ou l'amour raté*,1969); *Don't Awaken Madame* (*Ne réveillez pas madame*, 1970); *The Goldfish, or My Father the Hero* (*Les poissons rouge, ou mon père ce hèros*, 1970); *You Were So Nice When You Were Young* (*Tu ètais si gentil quand tu ètais petit*, 1972); *Monsieur Barnett* (1974); *The Arrest* (*L'arrestation*, 1975); *Dear Birds* (*Chers oiseaux*, 1976); *The Scenario* (*Le scénario*, 1976); *The Breeches* (*La Culotte*, 1978); *Long Live King Henry IV* (*Vive Henri IV*, 1978); *The Navel* (*Le nombril*, 1981)

FURTHER READING

Falb, Lewis W. *Jean Anouilh*. New York: Ungar, 1977.

Guicharnaud, Jacques. *Modern French Theatre from Giradoux to Genet*. New Haven: Yale Univ. Press, 1967.

McIntyre, H. G. *The Theatre of Jean Anouilh*. London: Harrap, 1981.

Pronko, Leonard. *The World of Jean Anouilh*. Berkeley: Univ. of California Press, 1961.

Smith, Christopher. *Jean Anouilh, Life, Work, and Criticism*. Fredericton: York, 1985.

Thody, Philip. *Anouilh*. London: Oliver & Boyd, 1968.

Jonathan Shandell

ANTIGONE

Antigone is JEAN ANOUILH's retelling of the final tragedy in Sophocles's Theban trilogy. Following Oedipus's death, his brother-in-law Creon rules Thebes. After the death of Oedipus's son Polyneices, Creon declares that Polyneices was a traitor to the state and decrees that the body must remain unburied, in a state of dishonor. When his sister Antigone defies Creon and ritualistically covers her brother with dust, the king sentences her to death. As guards take her to the cave where she will be buried alive, Creon's son Haemon implores his father to release Antigone because he is in love with her. Finally, Creon accepts; Haemon rushes to Antigone, only to find she has committed suicide. Haemon and his mother Eurydice kill themselves, and Creon is left alone.

Often read and adapted as a political play, Sophocles's *Antigone* features clear themes of honor, guilt, and the clash between the laws of the state and the laws of the gods. First published in 1942, Anouilh's *Antigone* premiered in 1944 in Paris at the Théâtre de l'Atelier during the Nazi occupation of FRANCE, in a production directed by André Barascq.

In recasting the Sophoclean material, Anouilh adheres to the plot essentials but differs in his style and characterization. Creon is more clearly a villain in Sophocles, while Anouilh's king is a more ambiguous, human, and "political" creature. Sophocles' heroine never wavers in her determination to defy Creon; Anouilh's Antigone is soul-searching. She rejects Creon's formula for obedience and happiness; happiness is a human goal unworthy of her idealistic sacrifice, yet in the end, she is not sure if her belief is worth dying for. Sophocles' characters act; Anouilh's deliberate, act, and then analyze the repercussions. Anouilh also transforms the Chorus from a group of Theban elders into an often witty narrator who reminds the audience that they are watching a play. Anouilh also has his Eurydice, a negligible force in the Greek version, sit and knit throughout the play until it is time for her suicide. Anouilh's additions add humanity and immediacy to the material and showcase his literary skills. He is unique among French writers of the period in that he manages to serve as a link between the erudite polish of JEAN GIRAUDOUX's work and the more overtly engaged existential dramas of JEAN-PAUL SARTRE.

Like Sartre's THE FLIES, *Antigone* is a fatalistic wartime adaptation of a classical text that proved popular with French and German audiences alike. What is exceptional about Anouilh's play is the multiple interpretations it allows. Creon's abuse of power led some to view the play as an indictment of the Nazi occupation. Yet, at the same time, Anouilh's more sympathetic and multidimensional portrayal of the king led other critics to read it as a defense of the tainted Vichy government. Anouilh offers no simple parable, telling instead a complex story of loyalty, loss, and human accountability. His particular emphasis on the consequences of personal actions led Sartre to claim him as an existentialist. The play is frequently revived in Europe and the United States.

FURTHER READING

Bradby, David. *Modern French Drama: 1940–1980*. Cambridge: Cambridge Univ. Press, 1984.

McIntyre, H. G. *Theatre of Jean Anouilh*. Totowa, N.J.: Barnes & Noble, 1981.

Steiner, George. *Antigones*. New Haven, Conn.: Yale Univ. Press, 1996.

Kate Bredeson

ANTOINE, ANDRÉ (1858–1943)

Credited with founding the independent theater movement that swept across Europe and America in the early 20th century, André Antoine created the model for developing new writing and performance methods outside a mainstream system of commercial profit. His workshop style aimed at nurturing young writers and exploring the possibilities and limitations of theatrical "REALISM."

Antoine was born on January 31, 1858, in Limoges, FRANCE. After being rejected from the prestigious Conservatoire and acting with an amateur troupe, Antoine founded the Théâtre-Libre. The opening performance took place on March 29, 1887, with four one-acts; Léon Hennique's *Jacques Damour*, adapted from a story by EMILE ZOLA, attracted large crowds and much interest for its naturalistic detail. At his "Free Theatre," Antoine directed 124 plays by 114, mostly new, playwrights, and despite the theatre's financial ruin, it saw seven years of rousing success and faithful audiences. Antoine would eventually pass between the Théâtre de l'Odéon and the Théâtre des Menus Plaisirs (renaming it the Théâtre-Antoine), always leaving behind the same blend of financial loss and artistic triumph, constantly seeking, in his words, "a modern theatre which lives by and for French literature."

While other theaters served mostly as producing houses, Antoine responded to Zola's call for a theater of simplicity and proportion, truth and conflict. In doing so, he exposed the tension inherent in developing a playwrights' theater, in which the text was supreme, and a director's theater, in which one creative mind exerted control based on his or her own analysis and imagination. The model Antoine developed at the Théâtre-Libre and replicated thereafter was of a single organizing consciousness. For Antoine, the stage environment was a visible character. Taking his cue from the Duke of Saxe-Meiningen's company in GERMANY, Antoine skewed the traditionally flat angles of the stage, creating an active playing space in perspective. Under motivated lighting, he organized objects and people to construct a "fourth wall" between the actors and the audience. No longer playing to or for the audience, the actors' focus was inward, creating a more credible illusion, the impression of spontaneity, and a heightened sense of realism. Direct address and asides were rejected in favor of expressive subtext created through nuance, intonation, and silence. Antoine was discovering the behavioral motivations behind the use of the playing space; the modern concept of "blocking" was solidified under his method.

With Antoine's own acting as a model, his actors absorbed themselves into their characters' lives with an intelligence and a vigor that established the mode of 20th-century drama. The body was an instrument, the voice its tool, and the formal gestures of the Conservatoire gave way to individual movements that indicated age, class, and mood; actors were even responsible for their own costumes, makeup, and hair. For these reasons, Antoine is known as the father of the modern *mise-en-scène*, combining psychological absorption and extreme physical awareness to emphasize the text in a way it never had been before; the modern interest in playwrights and their development began in earnest. Antoine acted as the bridge between RICHARD WAGNER's *Gesamtkunstwerk* ("total artwork") and KONSTANTIN STANISLAVSKY's psychology, providing today's model, artistically successful if not financially so, of cohesive and relevant drama.

FURTHER READING

Antoine, André. *Memories of the Théâtre-Libre*. Tr. by Marvin A. Carlson. Ed. by H. D. Albright. Coral Gables: Univ. of Miami Press, 1964. Originally published as *Mes souvenirs sur le Théâtre-Libre*. Paris: A. Fayard & cie, 1921.

———. *Antoine, L'invention de la mise en scène* [Antoine, the invention of staging]. Ed. by Jean-Pierre Sarrazac and Philippe Marcerou. Paris: Actes-Sud, 1999.

Chothia, Jean. *André Antoine*. Cambridge: Cambridge Univ. Press, 1991.

Waxman, Samuel. *Antoine and the Théâtre-Libre*. Cambridge: Harvard Univ. Press, 1926.

Matt Di Cintio

AOMORI-KEN NO SEMUSHI OTOKO

See THE HUNCHBACK OF AOMORI

APOCALYPSE IN MODERN DRAMA

As the millennial year 1900 approached, artists in many fields turned to the imagery of apocalypse, a narrative structure found in the Hebrew and Christian Bibles and most notably in Revelation but which in modern literature and social discourse has appeared in many nontheological forms.

At the end of the 19th century, images of the End—such as the final battle between good and evil and the emergence of a utopian new order—answered to contemporary anxieties about radical, and possibly catastrophic, transformations of the condition of life in the century to come. Nowhere was this tendency in art more pronounced than in MODERNIST theater.

Scenarios of the end of the world had stirred relatively little interest in theatrical representation between the Last Judgment plays of the Middle Ages and the conflagration of Valhalla in Götterdämmerung. In the 1890s, however, apocalyptic motifs began to appear regularly in experimental European drama. Some plays expressed a Nietzschean defiance against conventional Christianity, such as Oskar Panizza's scandalous *Council of Love* (1893)—which stages a universal plague of syphilis invented by the devil—and AUGUST STRINDBERG's miniature *Coram Populo!*, portraying an evil god who destroys his own experiment of life on earth. Originally intended as a puppet play-within-a-play in the epilogue to the verse edition of MASTER OLOF (1878), this playlet took on a more menacing quality in the French version published with *Inferno* in 1898.

Influenced by Ernest Renan's historical analysis of the SYMBOLISM of Revelation, ALFRED JARRY wrote a youthful work indebted to Revelation titled *The Four Horsemen of the Apocalypse* (1888). Apocalyptic imagery resurfaced in Jarry's symbolist mystery play *Caesar-Antichrist* (1895), in the third act of which the notorious Père Ubu makes his debut as the Antichrist.

ANTON CHEKHOV, too, contributed to the *fin de siècle* DRAMATURGY of apocalypse. Treplev's little mystery play of act one in *The Seagull* (1895) is set millennia beyond the present time in a frozen wasteland where life has been extinguished. In a speech inspired by Revelation, the World Spirit predicts a final battle with the Devil, after which "mind and matter will merge in a beautiful harmony and the Kingdom of Cosmic Will will come into being." Chekhov's anticipation of a terminal global ice age—a theme also touched in *Coram Populo!*—echoed widespread late-19th-century fears of planetary death by solar extinction, given powerful credence by Lord Kelvin's second law of thermodynamics.

In EMPEROR AND GALILEAN (1873), HENRIK IBSEN proposes the idea the "third empire," a culminating phase of human civilization that would succeed the pagan and Christian eras. This idea has been linked by Reeves and Gould (1987) to the "Joachite" branch of millennialist thinking, which underwent a revival in the 19th century. Joachim, abbot of Fiore in the 12th century, interpreted Revelation not as a poetic vision describing remote events outside human history but as a trinitarian progress of three ages unfolding within human history. Ibsen's long fascination with a tripartite spiritual evolution of human consciousness takes on the specific coloration of Revelation in his final play, *WHEN WE DEAD AWAKEN* (1899), with images of the Great Beast (suggested by the bestial Ulfheim), of the redemptive "child," of apocalyptic destruction, and of the rising of the dead.

The 19th century ended, as has often been observed, not as the 20th began but in the landscapes of death of the first world war. W. B. YEATS's famous comment ("After us, the savage God") on attending the 1896 opening of *Ubu Roi* has often been read as an intuition not only about the "primitivist" turn in literature and the fine arts in the next decade but about the violence of the century that was unleashed by the war. Human-made, historical forms of the end of the world—for instance, the destruction of European civilization by war—became a recurring preoccupation of expressionist playwrights, as did the complementary idea of the emergence of the "New Man" through an ecstatic social transformation.

The German-language plays predicting and later reacting to the war took grim satisfaction in matching the iconography of the canonical apocalyptic texts with the enormity of historical events. Carl Hauptmann, older brother of the more famous GERHART HAUPTMANN, published the astounding *War: A Te Deum* in 1914, a few months before the war began. A strange blend of REALISM, neoromanticism, EXPRESSIONISM, and prophecy, the play is an hallucinatory vision of the approaching European conflagration. Among the many restatements of the classical apocalyptic vision of destruction and salvation in the play are those uttered by the Escaped Visionary, a self-described personification of "the Great War," who promises to drive his coach "through streams of human blood . . . into the new dawn."

Other well-known apocalyptic World War I dramas are ERNST TOLLER'S *TRANSFIGURATION* (1917), with its dance of death and its ecstatic, world-salvation rhetoric; GEORG KAISER'S *Gas* trilogy, the final play of which, *Gas II* (1920), depicts a modern technological war of total destruction leading to the final tableau of jumbled gravestones in a world without survivors; and the Austrian KARL KRAUS'S monumental *The Last Days of Mankind* (1918), written "for a theater on Mars." At the end of Kraus's several-hundred page text God rains down fiery destruction on the earth as punishment for its four-year killing spree. All the apocalyptic World War I plays depict a redeemer-child, a seeming stand-in for the Christ figure of Revelation. If the child is a figure of hope in Toller and Kaiser, and of skepticism in Hauptmann (the child will turn into Cain and resume the cycle of violence), it is a figure of such outrage in Kraus that it becomes the Unborn Child who refuses to come into the world.

The twin enthusiasms for the destruction of the old order and the creation of the new often appear in the manifestos of the AVANT-GARDE art movements of the early 20th century. The ITALIAN FUTURISTS and the Vorticist circle around the British Wyndham Lewis (including Ezra Pound) attacked the "Babylon" of bourgeois decadence and celebrated speed, technology, and the "new." (Pound's famous injunction "MAKE IT NEW" appears in the first issue of Lewis's *BLAST*.) In a rush of millennarian optimism the Russian Cubo-Futurists turned the feared apocalypse of solar death on its head. Dependence on the unreliable sun would be shaken off in the victory of electricity over nature, according to the 1913 Russian avant-garde opera *Victory over the Sun*. The sixth and final act of VLADIMIR MAYAKOVSKY'S *MYSTERY-BOUFFE* (1918) translates the image of the New Jerusalem in Revelation into a new Moscow swathed in electric light and bursting with modern trains, streetcars, and automobiles. A heavenly choir of hammers, needles, saws, and tongs welcomes workers to the "great blacksmith shop of the new paradise."

Apocalyptic and millennialist strains run through the drama of the late 1920s and 1930s. ANTONIN ARTAUD invoked the extremity of apocalypse at full strength: Theater must be staged at the limit of experience, signaling through the flames of its own incineration. Despite its origin in parody, *The Spurt of Blood* (1926) relies directly on the canonical imagery and structure of Revelation, moving through a cycle of paradise, fall, earthly life, apocalyptic destruction, and restored life.

The language of millennialism suffuses revolutionary rhetoric from the French Revolution on. BERTOLT BRECHT'S *Lehrstücke* (translated as "LEARNING PLAYS" by some, "teaching plays" by others), such as THE MEASURES TAKEN (1930) and THE MOTHER (1931), exhibited millennialist confidence that the world could be made anew through revolution. Polish playwright STANISŁAW WITKIEWICZ, on the other hand, frequently depicted a world moving toward a violent, apocalyptic transformation or end, as in *The New Deliverance* (1921) and in arguably his darkest play, *The Shoemakers* (1934).

POST–APOCALYPTIC PLAYS AFTER WORLD WAR II

After World War II, playwrights did not, for the most part, depict apocalypse as an event; rather, apocalypse was presented as coming after the event, as a chronic postapocalyptic condition characterized by ruined landscapes and failing life. SAMUEL BECKETT'S *WAITING FOR GODOT* (1949), ENDGAME (1954–1956), and HAPPY DAYS (1960) are all set in end-of-the-world landscapes. In *Endgame* earth and sea outside the windows are "corpsed," and in the half-interred bunker onstage, the central figure Hamm and his two aged parents are breathing their last. Whether the very principle of life can survive is in doubt. Yet even in this postapocalyptic world a trace of the Christian redeemer-child remains in the Christmas Day appearance of the young Boy on the landscape (or in his figure in Hamm's story of the Boy).

In its depiction of a ruined Europe and its invocation of a dead Hamlet, HEINER MÜLLER'S *HAMLETMACHINE* (1977) bears some striking similarities to *Endgame*. Most of Müller's plays—for instance, *The Slaughter* (1951/rev. 1974), *Germania Death in Berlin* (1956/71), *Gundling's Life Frederick of Prussia Lessing's Sleep Dream Scream* (1977), and *Despoited Shore Medeamaterial Landscape with Argonauts* (1982)—are organized around apocalyptic premises, whether depicting the end of GERMANY, of the artist and art, or the environment. Revolutionary enthusiasm and hope of social transformation are at best distantly bruited in Müller, as in *The Task* (1979) and in *Hamletmachine*, where, after "fiercely enduring millenniums," a world revolution of the oppressed begins in the heart of darkness, and threatens to sweep away the detritus of both socialism and capitalism.

If there was any corner of Western theater from which a revival of millennialist utopianism might emerge after the war, it was destined to be found in the United States. In 1968, the LIVING THEATRE unveiled *Paradise Now* at the Avignon Festival. Trained young in ERWIN PISCATOR'S New School workshop, Julian Beck and Judith Malina created a work much indebted to German expressionism. And yet the Living's heterogenous mix of Kaballah, yoga, anarchist revolution, alchemy, and a Joachite faith in a progressive earthly transformation was thoroughly American.

The group described the performance as a "vertical ascent toward Permanent Revolution," a progression up "rungs" of consciousness and action that was to be both interior and exterior, spiritual and political, in the course of which actors ripped off their clothes and invited audience members to join them. When Beck and Malina wrote the piece down after performing it for a year, it was outlined, like classical apocalypse, as a series of "visions," hinged in the middle by a condition they named *Apokatastasis* after a line in a poem by Allen Ginsberg. The term was used by both Ginsberg and the Living to signify a reversal of consciousness, a transformation of demonic into celestial forces.

Though even his early dramatic works had catastrophic trajectories, in his last works TENNESSEE WILLIAMS turned to undisguised end-of-the-world scenarios, as in *The Red Devil Battery Sign* (1975–1980), which depicts civilization threatened by a hellish political conspiracy, and the one-act *The Chalky White Substance* (1980) set "a century or two after . . . the great thermonuclear war" in which the deity himself dies. At the end of the play his pulverized bones begin to drift down from the sky. At his death Williams was working on a new play, *The Lingering Hour* (1982). An existing fragment shows Williams creating a global apocalypse from a Vesuvius-like eruption, to the offstage anguished cries of "fine del mondo!"

Toward the end of the century, entering an age of the AIDS pandemic and with fears of urban chaos and total war, American playwrights returned to the theme of apocalypse. Undisguised religious imagery returned, often rendered with a gritty documentary texture. However, apocalypse as a religious concept no longer carried the overwhelming effect of the sublime experienced in plays earlier in the century.

In ADRIENNE KENNEDY'S *Motherhood 2000* (1994), an African American female narrator describes an apocalyptic urban war that brings refugees from New Jersey fleeing across the Hudson River to New York City. The play veers off to become a fantastic revenge play in which the narrator murders the leading actor of a homeless roving theater troupe as he is performing the role of Jesus Christ in a medieval passion play. Before society broke down—a mordant irony—he was the white law officer who once criminally assaulted her son.

In TONY KUSHNER'S two-part *ANGELS IN AMERICA: A GAY FANTASIA ON NATIONAL THEMES* (1992) and Jose Rivera's *Marisol* (1994), angels return to earth on a mission of salvation in the absence of a departed God. Rivera's setting is the urban jungle of the South Bronx. Kushner's epic play combines a multistrand soap opera plot with the heaven-earth-hell registers of the medieval mystery. In both plays, God has vanished, leaving the angels to cope with a degraded world. Arguing for quiet persistence, human goodness, and "more life" in the face of plague, Kushner engages the rhetoric of apocalypse and millennium theatrically but not ideologically.

Finally, in the millennial year 2000 itself, came the British CARYL CHURCHILL'S corruscating *FAR AWAY*. This one-act play culminates in the image of a terminal global war that engulfs all people, all species, and inanimate nature. Even the rivers take sides. "The cats have come in on the side of the French," Churchill writes, and the "elephants have gone over to the Dutch." Utterly without the salve of redemption, it is a play of apocalyptic despair about the state of life on the planet as the human calendar enters the 21st century.

FURTHER READING

Bull, Malcolm. *Apocalypse Theory and the Ends of the World*. Oxford: Blackwell, 1995.

Fuchs, Elinor. "The Apocalyptic Ibsen: *When We Dead Awaken*." In "Literature and Apocalypse," ed. by James Berger. Special issue, *Twentieth Century Literature* 46, no. 4 (Winter 2000).

——, ed. "The Apocalyptic Century." Special issue, *Theater* 29, no. 3 (Fall 1999).

Kermode, Frank. *The Sense of an Ending: Studies in the Theory of Fiction*. Oxford: Oxford Univ. Press, 1967.

Reeves, Marjorie, and Warwick Gould. *Joachim of Fiore and the Myth of the Eternal Evangel in the Nineteenth Century*. Oxford: Clarendon Press, 1987.

Scherpe, Klaus R. "Dramatization and De-dramatization of 'the End': The Apocalyptic Consciousness of Modernity and Post-Modernity." Tr. by Brent O. Peterson. In "Modernity and Modernism, Postmodernity and Postmodernism." Special issue, *Cultural Critique* no. 5 (Winter 1986–1987).

Elinor Fuchs

APOLLINAIRE, GUILLAUME (1880–1918)

Without Guillaume Apollinaire, there would be no SURREALISM, at least in name. He invented the term in 1917 while writing the program notes for JEAN COCTEAU's *Parade*. He was also among the first to defend cubism and to imagine the creative potential of the new art form, cinema.

Wilhelm Albert Wladimir Alexandre Apollinaris de Kostrowitzky was born in Rome, ITALY, on August 25 or 26, 1880. The date remains uncertain, as does Apollinaire's parentage. His mother was Angelica de Kostrowitzky, a rebellious Polish refugee. His father was probably an Italian officer, but Apollinaire, with typical embellishment, boasted he was a descendant of Napoleon, or perhaps the pope.

The young Apollinaire found solace in the symbolist poets Stéphane Mallarmé and MAURICE MAETERLINCK. He began to write his own poems, gradually developing a distinctive, lyrical style, free of punctuation. In 1899, before finally settling in Paris, the family sought refuge in the tiny Belgian town of Stavelot. When his mother could not pay the hotel bill, she warned her sons to leave town quietly. Apollinaire and his younger brother, Albert, fled at midnight, an escapade that inspired Apollinaire's first play, the one-act *The Moonlit Flight* (*A la cloche de bois*), completed in 1900.

In Paris Apollinaire took up hackwork to survive, toiling as a ghostwriter, an erotic novelist, even an ersatz stockbroker. In 1902 he helped found a short-lived journal, *Fesin d'Ésope*. That spring he also published his first story, adopting the pen name Guillaume Apollinaire.

Those early years were lean but not lonely. Apollinaire befriended many emerging leaders of the AVANT-GARDE—Pablo Picasso, Max Jacob, Henri Matisse, and Georges Braque. In 1908 he began a turbulent affair with painter Marie Laurencin. Roger Shattuck (1968) has described this era in Paris as "the banquet years," a feast of artistic innovation. The insatiable Apollinaire had a seat at the head of the table, rebelling with his associates against the strictures of REALISM, seeking to represent multiple dimensions of time and space at once. This simultaneity fascinated Apollinaire. He wrote the first serious study of Picasso in 1905, and in 1913 he published *The Cubist Painters* (*Les Peintres cubistes*), which remains a definitive work.

As Apollinaire's criticism attracted attention, so did his poetry. In 1912 he published his great poem *Zone*, followed the next year by an anthology, *Alcools*, which scandalized readers with its lack of punctuation and erotic themes.

With the outbreak of World War I in 1914, Apollinaire eagerly sought to enlist, and he was eventually promoted to the rank of officer. His military career was cut short in 1916, when he was struck in the head by a shell fragment. He recovered but lost his spark, becoming secretive and irritable.

During his convalescence Apollinaire finished a play he claimed to have begun in 1903, *The Breasts of Tiresias* (*Les Mamelles de Tirésias*). The play emulates the zany anarchy of Apollinaire's idol, ALFRED JARRY. It was not produced until June 1917, overshadowed by the debut of Cocteau's *Parade* one month earlier. He described the ballet's bizarre style as *sur-naturalisme*, but on the advice of an editor, he changed to *sur-realisme*.

At the time of his death in Paris on November 9, 1918, Apollinaire was working on two more plays and film scenarios. Their dreamlike scene changes anticipated surrealist experiments. Apollinaire would have shunned categorization, however, preferring to emphasize the varied alternatives to realism he had championed throughout his career.

[See also France]

PLAYS: *The Moonlit Flight* (*A la cloche de bois*, 1900); *The Breasts of Tirésias* (*Les Mamelles de Tirésias*, possibly begun 1903, completed 1916); *Casanova* (text by Apollinaire completed 1918, score by Henri Defosse and others, completed 1920); *Mood of the Age* (*Coleur du temps*, 1918)

FURTHER READING

Adéma, Marcel. *Apollinaire*. London: Heinemann, 1954.

Breunig, L. C. "The Laughter of Apollinaire." *Yale French Studies*, no. 31 (1965): 66–73.

Davies, Margaret. *Apollinaire*. London: Oliver & Boyd, 1964.

Schumacher, Claude. *Alfred Jarry and Guillaume Apollinaire*. London: Macmillan, 1984.

Shattuck, Roger. *The Banquet Years: The Origins of the Avant-Garde in France 1885 to World War I*. Rev. ed. New York: Vintage, 1968.

Steegmuller, Francis. *Apollinaire, Poet among the Painters*. Harmondsworth: Penguin, 1973.

Heather Jeanne Violanti

ARBUZOV, ALEKSEI (1908–1986)

Aleksei Nikolayevich Arbuzov, a Russian, was a playwright of the Soviet era whose ability to straddle the line between artistic independence and official acceptance for more than a half century made him supremely influential. His settings, characters, and themes generally corresponded to the stylistic requirements of SOCIALIST REALISM. When the Moscow metro was being built, he wrote *The Long Road* (1936) about subway construction crews; when the authorities encouraged writers to respond to international topics after World War II, he wrote *European Chronicles* (1952) about the moral struggles of European intellectuals; when a much-publicized hydroelectric plant was built in Siberia, he wrote the love story *It Happened in Irkutsk* (1959). His heroes and heroines usually were builders of Soviet society—students, construction workers, engineers, doctors, journalists, and artists. Superficially, their lives were happy and rewarding; their fates seemed to be in their own hands. But this was the key element differentiating Arbuzov from other dramatists of his time. Occasionally compared to HENRIK IBSEN and ANTON CHEKHOV, Arbuzov examined the quotidian details of common lives, quietly revealing how drastically they could be altered by even the most routine choices people make. This prompted some to speak of Arbuzov's "cruelty" to his characters, whereas the scholar Konstantin Rudnitsky defined his style as "honest but modest REALISM." Morality—though not moralizing—was a dominant factor in his oeuvre. In *The Choice* (1971), a scientist is faced with choosing between two potential wives and two potential employers. The play's two acts develop the divergent courses his life would take, depending on which choices he makes.

Arbuzov favored large dramatic canvasses revealing subtle changes in characters over time. He frequently involved representatives of various generations less to expose generation gaps than to demonstrate the continuity of human nature. He often employed a modern version of the Greek chorus, in which people stepped forward to comment on events. He routinely began plays on a carefree note before introducing dramatic conflicts by way of almost imperceptible shifts in the worlds of his characters.

Tanya (1939), which established his fame, was one of the most popular of all Soviet plays. In it a young woman decides she will be happiest if devoting herself entirely to her husband. Instead she loses him, her child, and her self-esteem before rehabilitating herself. *Years of Wandering* (1954), hotly debated when staged, examined a flawed hero who brings pain and suffering to those who love him over an eight-year period from 1937 to 1945. *The Happy Days of an Unhappy Man* (1968) observes a dying man who believes his life was ruined by two of the happiest days in his life decades ago. One of Arbuzov's best and most curious plays, apparently a parody of Soviet drama as well as of his own, is *What a Lovely Sight!* (1972), in which a constellation of aggressively happy people is undaunted by their crumbling lives. Many of his plays enjoyed significant success abroad, including London and New York, between the 1960s and 1980s. From 1938 until his death in 1986, he conducted various playwriting studios from which many prominent Soviet dramatists emerged, among them Aleksandr Galich, Lyudmila Petrushevskaya, Viktor Slavkin, and Aleksei Kazantsev.

[*See also* Russia and the Soviet Union; Socialist Realism, Soviet Union]

SELECT PLAYS: *Facing the Industrial Financial Plan* (*Litsom k Promfinplanu*, 1930); *Class* (*Klass*, 1931); *The Fortunate Patrol* (*Schastlivy dozor*, 1935); *Six Favorites* (*Shestero lyubimykh*, 1935); *The Long Road* (*Dal'naya doroga*, 1936); *Tanya* (1939; rewritten 1946); *The Town at Dawn* (*Gorod na zare*, 1940); *The Immortal One* (*Bessmertny*, with Aleksandr Gladkov, 1942); *The Little House in Cherkizovo* (*Domik v Cherkizove*, 1943; rewritten as *The Little House on the Outskirts* [*Domik na okraine*], 1954); *A Meeting with Youth* (*Vstrecha s yunostyu*, 1947; reworked substantially as *Once Again—A Meeting with Youth* [*I vnov'—vstrecha s yunostyu*], 1964); *On the Eve* (*Nakanune*, after Ivan Turgenev, 1948); *European Chronicles* (*Yevropeiskaya khronika*, 1952); *Years of Wandering* (*Gody stranstvii*, 1954); *It Happened in Irkutsk* (*Irkutskaya istoriya*, 1959); *The Night before Immortality* (*Noch' pered bessmertiyem*, 1959); *The Twelfth Hour* (*Dvenadtsaty chas*, 1959); *The Lost Son* (*Poteryanny syn*, 1960); *We are Expected Somewhere* (*Nas gde-to zhdut*, 1962); *My Poor Marat* (*Moi bedny Marat*; a.k.a. *The Promise*, 1965); *Nocturnal Confession* (*Nochnaya ispoved'*, 1967); *The Happy Days of an Unhappy Man* (*Schastlivye dni neschastlivogo cheloveka*, 1968); *Tales of the Old Arbat* (*Skazki starogo Arbato*; a.k.a. *Once Upon a Time*, 1970); *The Choice* (*Vybor*, 1971); *In This Pleasant Old House* (*V etom milom starom dome*, 1972); *What a Lovely Sight!* (*Moyo zaglyadeniye*, 1972); *Evening Light* (*Vechernii svet*, 1974); *An Old Fashioned Comedy* (*Staromodnaya komediya*; a.k.a. *Do You Turn Somersaults?* 1975); *Expectation* (*Ozhidaniye*, 1977); *Cruel Games* (*Zhestokiye igry*, 1978); *The Involuntary Witness* (*Nechayanny svidetel'*, 1980); *Memory* (*Vospominaniye*, 1981); *The Victorious Woman* (*Pobeditel'nitsa*, 1983); *The Guilty Ones* (*Vinovatye*, 1984)

FURTHER READING

Segel, Harold B. *Twentieth-Century Russian Drama from Gorky to the Present*. Rev. ed. New York: Performing Arts Journal Pubns., 1993.

Selected Plays of Aleksei Arbuzov. Tr. by Ariadne Nicolaeff. New York: Pergamon, 1982.

Vasilinina, Irina. *Teatr Arbuzova* [The theater of Arbuzov]. Moscow: Iskusstvo, 1983.

John Freedman

ARCADIA

I thought my hermit was a perfect symbol. An idiot in the landscape. But this is better. The Age of Enlightenment banished into the Romantic.

—Hannah Jarvis, Act 2

TOM STOPPARD's intellectual cleverness and playfulness always please, but sometimes his highly sophisticated structures can become challenging mazes with distracting side tangents. His play *Arcadia*, however, seems an ideal balance of his theatrical strengths—mind-teasing puzzles and fresh perspectives, advanced through razor-sharp humor, frequent surprises, and dazzling dialogue.

Arcadia premiered in April 1993 at London's Royal National Theatre, directed by Trevor Nunn and featuring first-rate performers. With few exceptions, the comedy was warmly embraced by critics and audiences who observed that Stoppard apparently had returned to his strong suit of brilliant comedy and language such as in earlier hits including ROSENCRANTZ AND GUILDENSTERN ARE DEAD (1966), *Jumpers* (1972), and TRAVESTIES (1974). *Arcadia* transferred in 1994 to New York's Lincoln Center, where it earned equally high praise and three Tony nominations. One reservation voiced on both sides of the Atlantic concerned a coolness in *Arcadia*'s intellectual feast, with characters more spokespersons for concepts than representing humans. More chilling, beneath the sparkling give-and-take about the physical universe stands a sobering conclusion. Thomasina, the play's brilliant 13-year-old mathematical prodigy, is charming, bright, and therefore very attractive to audiences. But it is her discovery of what was to become the second law of thermodynamics that portends an eventual end of the universe.

In broadest outline, *Arcadia* is a two-act work composed of seven scenes. Within those scenes, Stoppard projects two stories from two eras but both set in the same room. Stoppard shuttles action between the two time periods, focusing on the Coverly family in the early 19th century and the Coverly clan living in today's world. The setting, a room in a large country house in Derbyshire, changes little as the two stories are alternated. Stoppard's goal is to use the play to discuss momentous teleological matters regarding the universe—what designs exist in nature that can be confirmed. Audiences learn standard scientific beliefs at the turn of the 18th century by way of young Thomasina Coverly's studies taught by her handsome tutor Septimus Hodge. Their lessons and conversations cover vast concepts of accepted physics and mathematics of the time, but their interchanges also establish the intuitive genius of the girl. Along with her lessons, Thomasina independently arrives at the law of physics—only to be codified years later—that all energy will be dissipated and all light and life extinguished.

In the plot concerning today's times, the present-day Coverlys live on the same estate. Much of the action involves two scholars—Hannah Jarvis and Bernard Nightingale—who come to research lives of the prior Coverlys, particularly Thomasina and Septimus's acquaintance Lord Byron. Lending spice to both stories are cases of misguided love. Stoppard deftly moves the two story lines closer to each other, suggesting that little changes over time in human nature. To underscore that fact, he places characters from both plots on stage at the same time for a thrilling final scene. Overlaying the entire play is a fascinating commentary about neoclassical and Romantic aesthetics, achieved by considerations of taste changes in landscape gardening—thus the play's title.

[*See also* England, 1940–Present]

FURTHER READING

Demastes, William W. "Re-inspecting the Crack in the Chimney: Chaos Theory from Ibsen to Stoppard." *New Theatre Quarterly* 10 (August 1994): 242–254.

———, ed. *British Playwrights, 1956–1995: A Research and Production Sourcebook*. Westport, Conn.: Greenwood Press, 1996.

Greene, Alexis. Review of *Arcadia*. *Theatre Week* (April 17, 1995): 23–24, 33.

Gussow, Mel. *Conversations with Stoppard*. New York: Grove, 1995.

Innes, Christopher. *Modern British Drama: The Twentieth Century*. Cambridge: Cambridge Univ. Press, 2002.

Kelly, Katherine E., ed. *The Cambridge Companion to Tom Stoppard*. Cambridge: Cambridge Univ. Press, 2001.

C. J. Gianakaris

THE ARCHITECT AND THE EMPEROR OF ASSYRIA

The Architect and the Emperor of Assyria, FERNANDO ARRABAL's AVANT-GARDE play, was written in 1965 and first staged in Paris on March 18, 1967. The work exists as a commentary on institutions such as government, organized religion, and family. Through the two characters' dialogue and interactive play, Arrabal examines the human condition. In reverberant and nonsensical conversation, the characters display constant changing personalities, expressing realities of sadomasochism, incest, and sacrilege as well as vulnerability and tenderness. The play is characterized as "Theater of the Absurd," a term originally coined by French philosopher ALBERT CAMUS. These collective plays are characteristic of ambiguous plots and repetitive dialogue portraying the individual as insignificant and out of sync in relation to the universe.

Referring to his work as "Panic Theater," Arrabal incorporates elements of sadomasochistic behavior such as love and cruelty. The characters relate in a schizophrenic babble in which they abuse one another, provoking irony and shock. In this manner, Arrabal expresses his personal abhorrence of repression, social apathy, media control, and the destruction of war. In *The Architect and the Emperor of Assyria*, Arrabal considers the formation of societal roles. The story commences with an airplane accident on an isolated island inhabited by a solitary man. His character represents the "primitive savage." Startled by the explosion, he buries his head in the sand and expresses himself by a series of grunts and incoherent garble. The second character appears suddenly, falling out of the sky. He implores help from the other: "Help me sir! I am the only survivor of the accident." The other, terrified, flees aghast. This concludes the first scene.

Scene 2 takes place two years later. The character who had fallen from the sky calls himself "the emperor of Assyria" and assigns the other the "architect." It is immediately apparent that the emperor has assumed the role of teacher to the architect in a relationship similar to Robinson Crusoe and Friday. Like Robinson Crusoe, the emperor takes the liberty to provide the architect with the means and knowledge he deems as necessary. The architect eagerly takes on the role of protégé and absorbs the information.

The arrogance and self-confidence of the emperor are ever present throughout his superfluous accounts of his past life as a revered and feared monarch. He continually scoffs at the architect's keen sense and is often threatened by his rapid ability to learn. These moments are realized by play-acting and dress-up performances in which the two are pitted against each other in an interchange of emotional chess. Throughout the play the emperor expresses deep adoration and hatred toward his mother. The play comes to an end when the two act out a trial in which the emperor is accused of killing his mother. The plot runs in a cyclical revolution: The roles of the two characters are exchanged as the architect devours the emperor and is transformed into him. They become one and the same.

FURTHER READING

Arrabal, Fernando. *El Cemeterio de Automoviles/El Arquitecto de Asiria* [The Automobile Cemetery/The Architect of Assyria]. Madrid: Catedra, 1987.

Cassanelli, Rino. *El cosmos de Fernando Arrabal: Lo cósmico-cíclico en El arquitecto y el emperador de Asiria* [The cosmos of Fernando Arrabal: The cosmic cycle in The Architect and The Emperor of Assyria]. New York: Peter Lang, 1991.

Geen, Renee. "Arrabal's The Architect and Emperor of Assyria." *Romance Notes* 19 (1978): 140–145.

Huerta Calvo, Javier. *Historia del Teatro Español* [The history of Spanish theater]. Madrid: Gredos, 2003.

Puig, Montserrat Roser. "Moral Games and Corrupting Justice in Fernando Arrabal's The Architect and the Emperor of Assyria." *European Studies: A Journal of European Culture, History, and Politics* 17 (2001): 209–224.

Rash, Robin. "Man's Eternal 'Tilt' in Arrabal's L'Architecte et l'empereur d'Assyrie." *LitteRealite* 5, no. 1 (Spring 1993): 97–104.

Nicole Baran Lucero

ARDEN, JOHN (1930–)

British playwright John Arden was born in Yorkshire on October 26, 1930. He studied architecture at King's College at Cambridge and the Edinburgh College of Art, then served in the military in Scotland. His plays, most notably SERJEANT MUSGRAVE'S DANCE (1959), are reminiscent of Brechtian drama and use poetry, song, and fractured REALISM to inject political commentary into a theatrical venue. Plays such as *The Waters of Babylon* (1957), *Soldier Soldier* (1960), *The Workhouse Donkey* (1963), and *Armstrong's Last Goodnight* (1964) revolve around questions of patriotic right and blunder as well as moral obligation to the state and its visceral and dangerous ramifications. His work focuses primarily on the political structure and its insidious pervasion of British rural politics.

A political activist, Arden championed the Irish in the 1970s and castigated overly zealous criticism of their perceived danger as instigators of political strife; denounced the United States by disrespecting its flag after his accusation that *The War Carnival* (1967) had been elicited as a tool by the Central Intelligence Agency (CIA) to discover antiwar activists; and caused a boycott by using nonprofessional actors in *The Royal Pardon* (1966). In addition, his noted collaboration with fellow playwright Margaretta D'Arcy on such works as *The Island of the Mighty* (1972), based on the universality of the Arthurian legends, and *The Business of Good Government* (1960) attest to lifelong concerns with political responsibility and activism.

While Arden's plays have enjoyed critical acclaim, they have never garnered box-office appeal. In addition to his achievements as a playwright, he has written prose including the novels *Silence Among the Weapons: Some Events at the Time of the Failure of a Republic* (1982) and *The Book of Bale* (1988); an autobiography with Margaretta D'Arcy, *Awkward Corners: Essays, Papers, Fragments* (1988); as well as theatrical review and criticism such as *To Present the Pretense* (1979) and *Sean O'Casey: A Collection of Critical Essays*.

Arden began his career as an architect's assistant in London but quickly moved on to a fellowship in playwrighting at Bristol University (1959–1960); a visiting lectureship in drama and politics at New York University (1967); Regent's Lecturer, at the University of California at Davis (1973); and writer in residence at New England University in Australia (1975). He moved his home base from London to Galway, Ireland, in 1968. His theatrical writing also includes commissions by the British Broadcasting Corporation (BBC) that were shelved owing to political tensions in Northern Ireland (*The Non-Stop Connelly Show*) and radio plays such as *Bagman* (1970), *Pearl* (1978) and *Garland for a Hoar Head* (1982).

[*See also* England, 1940–Present]

FURTHER READING

Arden, John. *Awkward Corners: Essays, Papers, Fragments*. London: Methuen, 1989.

Rebecca R. Basham

ARENA THEATER OF SÃO PAULO

The Arena Theater of São Paulo (Teatro Arena de São Paulo), an experimental theater group from São Paulo, BRAZIL, served as an incubator for playwrights, set designers, and actors who were exploring questions of national identity, political engagement, and theatrical innovation in the mid-20th century. Established in 1953 by José Renato and graduates of the Dramatic Art School in São Paulo, the group's plays from its nearly twenty-year history engage with key moments in Brazil's recent past.

The Arena Theater began as a traveling group performing European and American classics. Its first major innovation was the adoption of the theater-in-the-round or arena format. By 1955 the troupe had acquired a permanent playhouse, merged with a student theater group, and begun to explore the idea of developing plays with Brazilian themes. AUGUSTO BOAL joined the Arena Theater as co-director in 1956. His theater training at Columbia and his desire to explore new ways to stage Brazil's changing political and economic landscape were in harmony with the members of the struggling troupe. The Arena Theater's efforts took on more definition and direction in 1958 when founder and co-director José Renato chose to stage GIANFRANCESCO GUARNIERI's first play (*Eles não usam black-tie*, THEY DON'T WEAR BLACK-TIE, 1958). Although the play was meant to be a swan song, its resounding success not only provided for the group's solvency, but it also shaped its agenda for the next two years. Guarnieri's study of an industrial strike that pits a union leader father against his son captured the tensions of a working-class family in language and actions that had not previously appeared on a Brazilian stage. Renato's use of a simple set and the realistic, gritty portrayal of the actors were surprisingly powerful for the audience, especially when set in the intimacy of an arena stage. During the next two years the group sponsored a weekly workshop that studied and developed plays using *Black-Tie* as a model. These workshops nurtured ten plays from budding dramatists such as ODUVALDO VIANNA FILHO, Roberto Freire, Edy Lima, Ruy Barbosa, Flávio Migliaccio, Francisco de Assis, and Augusto Boal.

Arena Theater's progressive political orientation, focusing on the working classes and encouraging activism from the audience, was in agreement with the nationalistic and populist trends of its time. Just as the Arena Theater was establishing its creative direction in 1956, Juscelino Kubitchek was elected president. The president energized the country with his plans to build the modern capital of Brasília in the interior of the country and to improve economic development. Nationalist policies became more radical with the election of Jânio Quadros in 1960. As the year advanced the growing divisions between leftist populists and conservatives were exacerbated by Joâo Goulart, who inherited the presidency from Quadros when he resigned unexpectedly. Although the Arena Theater lost key individuals such as Oduvaldo Vianna Filho in 1960 and José Renato in 1962, it gained greater cohesion in political and artistic terms under the direction of Boal.

From 1962 to 1964 the Arena Theater reworked and even rewrote classic European plays in order to highlight similarities to the unrest in Brazil. The unstable political environment in Brazil reached its climax with a military coup in 1964. The Arena Theater responded in 1965 with the musical *Arena Tells the Story of Zumbi* (*Arena conta Zumbi*), written by a team of playwrights and musicians. In an expansion of its earlier comparative approach, Arena employed an event from Brazilian history, the destruction of escaped slave communities during the 1600s, to encourage its audience to resist the coup that had taken its freedom. *Arena Tells the Story of Zumbi* was the greatest box-office success in Arena's history, in part because of its theatrical innovation and in part because of its political protest that attracted disaffected student activists and intellectuals.

The Arena Theater's second effort to link Brazilian history with the dictatorship, *Arena Tells the Story of Tiradentes* (*Arena cona Tiradentes*), opened in 1967. The play experimented with a more complex framework, later formalized by Boal as the *coringa* ("joker") system, but repeated the same theme of freedom. It advocated heroism through its portrayal of the revolutionary leader Tiradentes (Joaquim José da Silva Xavier) who attempted to overthrow the Portuguese in the late 1700s. Even though political clashes on the streets were worsening, inside the Arena Theater theatrical protests continued without interdiction. Then, in April 1968, the military regime declared a dictatorship and imposed a wide range of repressive measures, including many that had a direct impact on the theater. In spite of the harsh new environment, the Arena Theater continued its experiments in three more plays during 1970–1972. However, in 1971 after Boal was picked up and tortured by the police, then went into exile, the group became fragmented and dispersed. In 1977, when the playhouse's name was changed to the Eugênio Kusnet Experimental Theater (Teatro Experimental Eugênio Kusnet), the Arena Theater's contribution to Brazilian theater was relegated to history.

Scholarship on the Arena Theater began to appear in the United States and Brazil in the early 1980s. The studies written in Portuguese examine the political theory and practice of the group, its application of Brechtian techniques, its use of realism and the arena stage, and the theories of Boal. Although no complete analysis has been produced yet in English, there are two monographs and four dissertations that treat some aspects of the group's work.

The history of modern Brazilian theater was greatly influenced by the Arena Theater. Many renown theater professionals in Brazil developed their careers there. The group is also important for its model of theater work and its experimentation with collective creation. Its plays introduced a new image of Brazilian life to audiences. In its early years the group's investigation and experimentation with speech, movement, and psychological detail produced moving representations of working-class characters and their struggles. Its later work employed the past as a metaphor for the present and became a common approach for plays written during the difficult years of censorship. The Arena Theater's attempts at consciousness-raising and outreach also have served as a point of reference for other groups. Finally, Boal launched an international career from the Arena Theater that continues to influence theater and politics in Brazil and beyond.

FURTHER READING

Bissett, Judith I. "Consciousness-Raising Dramatic Structures in Latin American Theater of Commitment." Ph.D. diss., Arizona State Univ., 1976.

Damasceno, Leslie H. *Cultural Space and Theatrical Conventions in the Works of Oduvaldo Vianna Filho.* Detroit: Wayne State Univ. Press, 1996.

Ellis, Lorena B. *Brecht's Reception in Brazil.* New York: Peter Lang, 1995.

Fonseca-Downey, Elizabeth. "The Theater of Gianfrancesco Guarnieri as an Expression of Brazilian National Reality." Ph.D. diss., Univ. of Iowa, 1982.

George, David. *The Modern Brazilian Stage.* Austin: Univ. of Texas Press, 1992.

Milleret, Margo. "Teatro Arena and the Development of Brazil's National Theater." Ph.D. diss., Univ. of Texas, Austin, 1986.

Quiles, Edgar H. "The Theater of Augusto Boal." Ph.D. diss., Michigan State Univ., 1981.

Margo Milleret

ARGENTINA

As early as the 18th century there existed in the Río de la Plata territory a theater that reflected the political, social, and cultural environment of the colonial viceroyalty. The year 1717 saw the presentation in Santa Fe of the first theater piece, *In Praise of Santa Fe* (or *Homage to Santa Fe—Loa a Santa Fe*), a eulogistic prologue written by native-born author Antonio Fuentes de Arcos. It was intended to keynote any and all cultural events in homage to the royal ruler, at that time Philip V. In Buenos Aires, in 1789, at the Settlement Theater (Teatro de La Ranchería), the five-act tragedy *Siripo* premiered, placing its author, Manuel José de Lavardén, among the earliest pioneers in the dramatic arts of the Río de la Plata region. At that time, various European circuses toured the entire national territory, presenting rudimental humorous and popular theater pieces.

Toward the end of the 1800s, the most prolific playwright was Pedro Echagüe, who in 1860 first staged his work *Roses* (*Rosas*) in Buenos Aires at the Victory Theater (Teatro de la Victoria; today the Columbus Theater, or Teatro Colón). In 1884, in Buenos Aires the Podestá Circus presented the pantomime *Juan Moreira* by Eduardo Gutiérrez, considered to be the beginning of the drama in the history of Argentine theater. Converted into a *gauchesque* ("cowboylike") mime drama, it marks a historical milestone by its incorporation of the *gaucho* ("cowboy"), a social and moral prototype of a nationality in the process of defining itself.

Around 1853, as immigration policies relaxed, the *gauchesque* theater began giving way to a new genre called GROTESCO CRIOLLO ("creole grotesque"), a fusion of contradictory elements reflecting the frustrations of the foreign immigrant, which debuted with the rural drama *Mother Earth* (*Madre tierra*, 1920) by Alejandro Berruti, *Tenement of the Pigeons* (*El conventillo de la palomo*) by Alberto Vaccarezza, and *Mateo* by ARMANDO DISCÉPOLO (1923). Reality became totally absorbed in *criollismo* ("nativism") and found affirmation on the native stage. At the helm of testimonial and critical drama writing was Roberto J. Pairó, who produced plays that explored deep sociological concerns. *Above the Ruins* (*Sobre las ruinas*) and *Marco Severi* (1905), both sharply socially critical, are his best works. FLORENCIO SÁNCHEZ, an outstanding dramatist of the realist theater of the Río de la Plata region, portrayed characters taken from real life. His finest work, *My Son the Doctor* (*M'hijo el dotor*), appeared in 1903, garnering vociferous acclaim on Buenos Aires stages. *Downhill* (*Barranca abajo*, 1905), *Papergirl* (*Canillita*, 1902), *The Foreign Woman* (*La gringa*, 1904), and *In the Family* (*En familia*, 1905) are among his principal works.

Three writers for the national stage stand at the vanguard of the most productive period in the evolution of Argentine drama: Gregorio de Laferrère, comedic playwright of this "golden age" of the native theater, wrote the comedies *Jettatore* (1904), which brims with satirical humor, and *The Women from the Gulley* (*Las de Barranco*, 1908), a portrayal of the manners of society's upper classes. Other representative dramatists also contributed their works: Pedro E. Pico, José León Pagano, Julio Sánchez Gardel, Vicente Martínez Cuitino, and Carlos Mauricio Pacheco portrayed universal character types such as the boor, the dimwit, the livewire, the big spender, and the big talker, but with local coloring.

By the mid-20th century ethnic transformations had changed the physiognomy of society, revealing the farcical side—the comic mask—of the immigrant. Nemesio Trejo, Ezequiel Soria, and Enrique García Belloso are masters of the genre. The figure of the immigrant became a fundamental medium on the theatrical palette. Writers found inspiration in the interplay of passions in the working-class tenements and housing projects, featuring the native-born *criollos* ("creoles"), Italians, Syrians, Jews, and Spaniards. Among the more successful dramatists, Samuel Eichelbaum wrote memorable short comic pieces such as *The Tamed Wolf* (*El lobo manso*) and *A Handsome Man of 900* (*Un guapo del 900*, 1940). As part of this "typecasting" approach, Jewish Argentinian writers such as César Tiempo, Germán Rozenmacher, and Jorge Goldenberg depict the immigrant Jew on the basis of their personal experiences. *Nobody Ever Met Her* (*Nadie la conoció nunca*) and *Aaron the Jew* (*El judío Aaron*) by Eichelbaum, and *Creole Bread* (*Pan criollo*) by Tiempo, are prime examples of this approach. The plays of Carlos Schaeffer Gallo, including *The Jewish Cowboy* (*El gaucho judío*, 1920), and *Neighborhood of the Jews* (*El barrio de los judíos*, 1919) by Alberto Vacarezza, delighted their audiences. In this same genre, José Rabinovich categorized moral and symbolic-religious values in his *Conceived in Sin* (*Con pecado concebida*), which appeared in 1975.

The transition to modern times revamped theatrical forms. The generation of the 1960s produced important writers of the independent theater, which lasted until 1976. Roberto Arlt, an innovator, sought to capture the individuality of his characters. In 1936 he penned two works: *The Ghost Manufacturer* (*El fabricante de fantasmas*) and *Saverio the Cruel* (*Saverio el cruel*). In 1938 he introduced *A Sensitive Man* (*Un hombre sensible*), *The Desert Island* (*La isla desierta*), and *Africa* (*África*), and his last play, *The Festival of Hiero* (or *Hiero's Party—La fiesta de Hiero*), was mounted in 1940.

The stultifying pressure of the military dictatorship (1976–1983) impacted the most diverse forms of art. Drama and research also suffered devastating effects. The abolition of the course titled "History of the Argentine Theater" at the National School of Dramatic Arts mobilized the idea of creating an Open Theater, which materialized in 1981 and lasted until 1983. Deaths, torture, and the "disappeared" (*los desaparecidos*) colored the dramatic texts of OSVALDO DRAGÚN, GRISELDA GAMBARO, Eduardo Pavlovsky, RICARDO HALAC, CARLOS GOROSTIZA, Mauricio Kartún, and Roberto Cossa. Clearly political in its agenda, the Open Theater was the first massive gesture, on the artistic level, of repudiation of the military process. People of the theater reopened the path toward an esthetic and political restoration, risking their lives in the face of censorship and repression. Important works of that period are *The Jack's Leg* (*La pata de la sota*, 1967) and *La nona* (1977) by Cossa; *Spiderwebs* (*Telarañas*, 1977) by Pavlovsky, banned as "insolent, indecent and aberrant"; and *Distant Promised Land* (*Lejana tierra prometida*, 1981) by Halac. *Marathon* (*Marathón*, 1980), by Ricardo Monti, premiered during the dictatorship, in 1980. During this period many dramatists were blacklisted and compelled to leave the country. Resistance continued, against all odds. Dramatist Aída Bortnik wrote the screenplay for the film *The Official Story* (*La historia oficial*), directed by Luis Puenzo; its subject matter had international transcendence, and actress Norma Aleandro was awarded an Oscar for her performance in it. At this time, drama was in the service of REALISM. Major texts were *The Old Servant/Butler* (*El viejo criado*, 1980) by Cossa; *The Showoffs* (*Los compadritos*, 1985) and *Anniversary Concert* (*Concierto de aniversario*) by Eduardo Rovner; *The Closed Mouth* (*La boca cerrada*, 1984) by Juan Carlos Badillo; and *Ulf* (1989) by Juan Carlos Gene. Griselda Gambaro, a pioneer in a new kind of playwriting, wrote *Bad Blood* (*La malasangre*, 1981), in which she disguised reality in order to render it visible, and *True Envy* (*Real envido*, 1982), which was banned and attacked relentlessly by the censors.

The collapse of the ideas of modernism at the end of the 20th century produced a genuine change in prevailing thought. Early in the new millennium, as in any theatrical system, there were a number of currents. While many playwrights continue to deploy realist techniques, others experiment with a postmodern intertext theater. Influenced by European and U.S. dramatists seeking to reveal the core climate of our society, playwrights like Griselda Gambaro have created works such as *Furious Antigone* (*Antígona furiosa*), an adaptation of Sophocles's *Antigone* in the tradition of the grotesque that seeks to indict Argentine society's complicity in the atrocities of the "Dirty War." Gambaro joins other theatrical innovators such as Javier Daulte, Sergio Bizzio, Daniel Guebel, Rafael Spreguelburd, Daniel Veronese, and Alejandro Tantanian, who are continuing to map the landscape of Argentine theater into the 21st century.

[*See also* Avant-Garde Drama]

FURTHER READING

Arancibia, Juana Alcira, and Zulema Mirkin. *Teatro argentino durante el proceso, 1976–1983*. Buenos Aires: Editorial Vinciguerra, 1992.

Castagnino, Raúl H. *Sociología del teatro argentino*. Buenos Aires: Ed. Nova, 1963.

Dragún, Osvaldo, and Rubens Correa. *Reapertura del Teatro del Pueblo. El regreso de la utopia*. El Periodista de Buenos Aires [The Buenos Aires Reporter], 1987.

Graham-Jones, Jean. *Exorcising History: Argentine Theatre under Dictatorship*. Lewisburg, Pa.: Bucknell Univ. Press, 2000.

Ordaz, Luis. *Historia del teatro argentino* [History of Argentine theater]. Buenos Aires: Instituto Nacional del Teatro, 1999.

Pavlovsky, Eduardo. *Apuntes para una obra de teatro. El teatro de Eduardo Pavlovsky*. Buenos Aires: Ediciones Búsqueda, 1986.

Taylor, Diana. *Disappearing Acts: Spectacles of Gender and Nationalism in Argentina's Dirty War*. Durham, N.C.: Duke Univ. Press, 1997.

Marta de Paris

ARIA

Although very little critical attention has been paid to TOMSON HIGHWAY's semi-monodrama *Aria*, at least compared to *The Rez Sisters* (1986) and DRY LIPS OUGHTA MOVE TO KAPUSKASING (1989), it is a provocative showcase of archetypal native women and a tempting vehicle for an exceptional actor. The "Woman" plays seventeen characters throughout the event, including a mother, a child, a Diva with an animal spirit, and an aging prostitute. The second performer is her accompanist. The play was originally produced in 1986 by Native Earth Performing Arts at the Native Canadian Centre, in Toronto. Inuit mask dancer Makka Kleist and Highway himself (a London-trained concert pianist) filled the roles.

Similar to *Rez Sisters*, *Aria* elevates everyday experiences to the level of poetry. Each scene, beginning with "Ko-Kum" and ending with "The Earth," circulates themes of institutionalized racism, the spirit of all living things, and the notion that "pain becomes power" (uttered periodically in the text). Ko-Kum is housebound but remembers when she taught 12 children and would float through the miracle of nature. Birth describes blood that sprays as the light of the sun. The Lover of Men tries to forget Cree so she will not be punished for speaking it in school. Wife's home is destroyed by a Weetigo, an evil spirit in native belief. Indian Woman speaks a mostly Cree text (all but "those trees"), reflecting on the deep spirit of trees. White Woman cannot find the spirit in the taxis, traffic, stores, and cement of city life. Secretary dreams of success, donning the white woman's uniform (navy blue "Veritable soldierette" costume). As Executive Secretary, she internalizes the culture of wealthy European-descended civilization ("horses are an asset"). The Executive criticizes the failures of the Native Courtworker Program and requests increased funding, dreaming of the "dental, medical, optical, family, and other benefits, rent-a-car credit card, and darned good business lunch [that the money will provide for] the members of the executive committee." In her first scene, Diva is brutally murdered by her husband for making love to 10,000 snakes. In her second, she refuses to die, turning into an undead beast that tears the throats of her husband and sons. The Prostitute deplores the lights that shine in her eyes, until she discovers one might be her next john. The Earth remembers the snakes, the pain, and the enduring female spirits. Concluding the event as Cree, she becomes the spiritual repository of cruelty, suffering, injustice, and enduring will.

Although staged as a grand, prima donna recital with the protagonist wearing what Highway describes as a "Turandot-type diva gown," *Aria* is an averted concert. The scenes are never sung. Only in the final moments, after the pianist descends into an aggressive bel canto, does Woman summon her strength to sing. However, as she forms her lips to sing her inaugural note, the lights fade and the play comes to an unsatisfied musical conclusion. In *Aria*, the burdens of life as woman or native, or both, stifle all but the inaudible hope of a song.

[*See also* Canada]

FURTHER READING

Gilbert, Helen, ed. *Postcolonial Plays: An Anthology*. New York: Routledge, 2001.

Heath, Sally Ann. "The American Indian Community House." In *American Indian Theater in Performance: A Reader*, ed. by Hanay Geiogamah and Jaye T. Darby. Los Angeles: Univ. of California Press, 2000.

King, Thomas. "Native Literature in Canada." In *Dictionary of Native American Literature*. New York: Garland, 1994.

Knowles, Richard, and Monique Mojica, eds. *Staging Coyote's Dream: An Anthology of First Nations Drama in English*. Toronto: Playwrights Canada Press, 2003.

Taylor, Drew Hayden. "Alive and Well: Native Theatre in Canada." In *American Indian Theater in Performance: A Reader*, ed. by Hanay Geiogamah and Jaye T. Darby. Los Angeles: Univ. of California Press, 2000.

Ben Fisler

ARIYOSHI SAWAKO (1931–1984)

Japanese playwright, screenwriter, producer, and director, Japanese classical dance choreographer, and novelist Ariyoshi Sawako was born in Wakayama, Japan. As the daughter of a prominent banker, she spent most of her childhood years abroad, where her experiences contributed to her appreciation of traditional Japanese literature and performing arts as well as to her commitment to broad socioeconomic and sociopolitical issues, as seen in her works.

In the early 1950s, while studying English literature at Tokyo Women's College, Ariyoshi wrote stage reviews for the theater periodical *Engekikai* (Theatre World). After graduation, in 1954 and 1956 she accompanied Japanese classical dancer Azuma Tokuho and her troupe on tours to the United States and Europe. In the 1950s, she wrote exclusively for Tokuho scripts for such dance dramas as *The Damask Drum* (1956) and *The Village of Eguchi* (1958), the latter inspired by a 1924 two-act play *The Courtesan Aizen and the Petty Thief Tarō of Mumyō*, by Tanizaki Jun'ichirō, and *Rain*, by WILLIAM SOMERSET MAUGHAM. *The Village of Eguchi* was based on the story of the Nō play *Eguchi* as well as the Japanese dance *Shigure Saigyō* (Showers and Saigyō)—depicting an encounter in the rain between the 12th-century priest poet Saigyō and a courtesan named Eguchi in a village of Eguchi—but was developed into a relationship between a Catholic priest and a geisha set in contemporary times.

In 1958 Ariyoshi wrote the lyrics for the ballad-drama *Homura*, which won prestigious recognition by the Ministry of Education on the occasion of the annual arts festival, proving her talent not only as a playwright but also as a lyric writer of the traditional, powerful, and expressive *gidayū*-style, rhythmic, dramatic narrative associated with the *bunraku* puppet theater.

In 1959, while studying comparative literature at Sarah Lawrence College in Bronxville, New York, Ariyoshi was particularly impressed by the OFF-BROADWAY drama *The Trial of the Catonsville Nine* by Jesuit priest and poet Daniel Berrigan. In 1971 she translated, produced, and directed her version of Berrigan's play at a theater in Tokyo to wide success.

After 1960, Ariyoshi wrote her best-known fiction, including *The River Ki* (1960), *The Doctor's Wife* (1967), and *The Ecstatic One* (1972). Ariyoshi adapted many such works for stage and screen. In their examination of sociopolitical issues of contemporary Japan, they met with wide popular success and critical acclaim. Plays such as *The Doctor's Wife* and *The Ecstatic One* brought to the foreground issues relating to arranged marriage, traditional views of women ("good wife, good mother"), cancer awareness, aging, and Japanese traditional family values.

In 1972 Ariyoshi wrote her notable play *American Rain Won't Wet My Sleeves*, a tragic love story involving an American sailor, a Japanese prostitute and her geisha friend, and a young Japanese interpreter of Dutch, set in a Yokohama brothel in the early Meiji period (1868–1912). The play has been shown repeatedly in SHINGEKI theaters, recently in 2003, when famed *kabuki* actor Bandō Tamasaburō V directed it, to mark the customary December conclusion to the theater year.

[*See also* Japan]

SELECT PLAYS: *The Damask Drum* (*Aya no Tsuzumi*, 1956); *The Snowfall on the Lake* (*Yukia ya Kon Kon Sugata no Mizuumi*, a *bunraku* puppet play,

1956); *The Village of Eguchi* (Eguchi no Sato, 1958); *Rock Garden* (Ishi no Niwa, 1959); *The River Ki* (Ki no Kawa, 1960); *Empress Kōmyō* (Kōmyō Kōgō, 1962); *Perfume and Flower* (Kōge, 1963); *The River Arita* (Arita Gawa, 1964); *Akaiko* (Akaiko Monogatari, 1967); *The Doctor's Wife* (Hanaoka no Seishū no Tsuma, 1967); *Kabuki Dancer* (Izumo no Okuni, 1967–1969); *American Rain Won't Wet My Sleeves* (Furu Amerika ni Sode wa Nurasaji, 1972); *The Ecstatic Ones* (1972); *The Twilight Years* (Kōkotsu no Hito, 1972); *Three Grandmothers* (San Baba, 1973); *Omine of Masagoya* (Masagoya Omine, 1975); *Her Royal Highness Princess Kazu* (Kōjo Kazu no Miya, 1979); *The First String* (Ichi no Ito, 1981)

FURTHER READING

Ariyoshi Sawako Senshū. 13 vols. Tokyo: Shinchō sha, 1970–1971.

Ariyoshi Sawako Senshū. 13 vols. Tokyo: Shinchō sha, 1977–1978.

Ariyoshi, Tamao. *Migawari: Haha Ariyoshi Sawako to no Nichinichi* [My mother Ariyoshi Sawako and her daily life]. Tokyo: Shinchōsha, 1989.

Keene, Donald. *Dawn to the West: Japanese Literature of the Modern Era: Fiction.* New York: Holt, 1984.

Samuel, Yoshiko Yokoichi. "Ariyoshi Sawako." In *Japanese Women Writers: A Bio-Critical Sourcebook,* ed. by Chieko I. Mulhern. Westport, Conn.: Greenwood Press, 1994.

Rokuo Tanaka

ARMS AND THE MAN: AN ANTI-ROMANTIC COMEDY

Arms and the Man: An Anti-Romantic Comedy was written by GEORGE BERNARD SHAW in 1893–1894 and first performed at Florence Farr's Avenue Theatre on April 21, 1894, in a double billing with W. B. YEATS's *The Land of Heart's Desire.* With a first run of fifty performances, this production gave Shaw his first real taste of success as a playwright. There are several records of the sensational opening night, about which Shaw wrote in a letter to Henry Arthur Jones (December 2, 1894): "I had the experience of witnessing an apparently insane success, with the actors and actresses almost losing their heads with the intoxication of laugh after laugh, and of going before the curtain to tremendous applause" (Shaw, 1965). When Shaw appeared for a curtain call, a solitary voice from the gallery booed as the rest of the audience laughed and cheered. The person who booed was J. Golding Bright—later a drama critic and eventually one of Shaw's theatrical agents—to whom Shaw gave his famous response: "My dear fellow, I quite agree with you, but what are we two against so many?" After reporting his version of this riposte, Yeats wrote, "[F]rom that moment Bernard Shaw became the most formidable man in modern letters, and even the most drunken of medical students knew it" (Yeats, 1955).

The play is set in Bulgaria at the time of the Serbo-Bulgarian war of 1885–1886 and takes its title from the opening line of John Dryden's translation of Virgil's *Aeneid.* Glorification of war and military valor and idealized conceptions of human love are twin targets of ridicule in a play that, despite its subtitle, displays a basic structure of romantic comedy. The play's heroine, Raina Petkoff, is betrothed to the dashing cavalry officer Sergius. But in the course of the action her affections change to the pragmatic and commonsensical, but self-admittedly "romantic," professional soldier Bluntschli, who, finding them more useful in the field, carries chocolates in his holster instead of pistols and ammunition. Sergius, in turn, becomes enamored of the pert maidservant Louka (first played by Florence Farr), who is also engaged to another. Both Raina and Sergius discover the self-delusions associated with their initial devotion to what they term "the higher love." In a cultural and historical context in which Alfred Lord Tennyson's "The Charge of the Light Brigade" and the soldiers' chorus in Charles Gounod's *Faust* reflected more normal attitudes, the play's satirical demolition of romanticized attitudes to war and military valor seemed extraordinarily eccentric to some members of its first audiences, which included on one occasion the Prince of Wales and the Duke of Edinburgh. The play's treatment of love relationships can be seen as part of Shaw's general critical and creative engagement with Victorian gender stereotypes and romantic ideals.

While the main plot is an original creation by Shaw, the act 1 scene in which Bluntschli is afforded refuge in the enemy Petkoff household echoes similar episodes in Giuseppe Verdi's romantic opera *Ernani* (1844) and William Gillette's popular American Civil War play *Held by the Enemy* (1887). The phrase "the chocolate soldier" became identified with the work from publicity about it in the days of its first production. Without Shaw's permission, the play was adapted by Oscar Strauss as an operetta, *The Chocolate Soldier* (*Der tapfere Soldat*), which was first performed in 1908.

[*See also* Ireland]

FURTHER READING

Crompton, Louis. "*Arms and the Man.*" In *Shaw the Dramatist.* Lincoln: Univ. of Nebraska Press, 1969.

Gibbs, A. M. "Romance and Anti-Romance in *Arms and the Man.*" In *The Art and Mind of Shaw: Essays in Criticism.* London: Macmillan, 1983.

Kiberd, Declan. "George Bernard Shaw: *Arms and the Man.*" In *Irish Classics.* Cambridge: Harvard Univ. Press, 2001.

Shaw, Bernard. *Bernard Shaw: Collected Letters 1874–1897.* Ed. by Dan H. Laurence. London: Max Reinhardt, 1965.

Yeats, W. B. *Autobiographies.* London: Macmillan, 1955.

A. M. Gibbs

ARMY FORMATION

Army Formation (*Chakravyuha,* 1984) is RATAN THIYAM's most famous production, the one that "put him on the map" theatrically. In *Army Formation* Thiyam uses an episode from the epic poem *The Mahabharata* (*The Great War of the Bharatas*) to make analogies between the bloody war depicted in the tale and current events in Manipur. In the play, army generals, with their elegant robes and soft voices, seem rational and noble—until they pump their young nephew Abhimanyu into a bloodthirsty frenzy of false heroism. They send him into war knowing he will be slaughtered.

In the first scene the Kauravas convince their guru Drona to unleash the powerful *chakravyuha* (an undefeatable military formation). In the opposing Pandava camp, two of the five brothers, Yudhishthira and Bhima, are worried because their brother Arjuna is the only one who knows how to penetrate the formation, and he is engaged in battle elsewhere. Arjuna's 16-year-old son Abhimanyu claims he knows how to break into the formation. He learned how to defeat the *chakravyuha* because, as a child in the womb, he overheard his father tell his mother Subhadra the secret. But Subhadra fell asleep in the middle of the conversation, so Abhimanyu does not know how to get out of the formation once he has broken into it. Yudhishthira deceitfully promises to solve the problem by sending reinforcements that will rescue the boy from the *chakravyuha*. Seen this way, the play is about the older generation sacrificing their children in battles they cannot or would not fight themselves. It is about how war wastes youth. As Abhimanyu lies dying on the battlefield, he says: "Oh great kings and emperors of this world, ensconced under canopies of power . . . you have polluted this fair and pure earth with your blind egos and criminal use of power." In *Army Formation* Thiyam makes political issues personal and highlights the way people in power knowingly commit heinous acts to protect their own selfish interests.

At another level, *Army Formation* is the story of an individual who pits himself against "the system" in all its strength and power—personified by the seven charioteers (*saptarathis*) of the *chakravyuha*—and is crushed. Thiyam describes Abhimanyu as "a young man who has learnt everything but experienced nothing." The boy gets trapped in a *chakravyuha* of mature, experienced warriors through his own naive eagerness to prove himself in battle.

Finally, *Army Formation* is an attack on nationalism. In the prologue, flagbearers from both the Kaurava and Pandava sides perform a dance. Using steps choreographed by a martial arts teacher, they stomp and thrust their way in and out of various military formations in a display of martial skill and opposing "national" prides. Some of their steps are meant to intimidate, some to appease, some to threaten, some to retreat. As they wave their flags proudly, the narrator proclaims that "national flags conceptualize politics. . . . This is a war of flags. . . . This is a war of power grabbers."

Army Formation has been performed all over India and won Edinburgh's Fringe First Award in 1987.

[*See also* India]

FURTHER READING

Katyal, Anjum. "Of War and Peace: The Theatre of Ratan Thiyam." In *Arts International* (Winter, 1999): 39–43.

Mee, Erin. "Star of India." *American Theatre Magazine*. July/August, 2000.

Thiyam, Ratan. "The Audience is Inside Me." *Seagull Theatre Quarterly*, no. 14/15 (1997): 62–72.

——. *Chakravyuha*. Kolkata: Seagull Books, 1998.

——. "Interview with Kavita Nagpal." In *Contemporary Indian Theatre*. Delhi: Sangeet Natak Akademi, 1989.

——. "Uttar-Priyadarshi: Theatre of Manipur." *International Gallerie*, no. 2 (1999), 2: 41–49.

Erin B. Mee

EL ARQUITECTO Y EL EMPERADOR DE ASIRIA See THE ARCHITECT AND THE EMPEROR OF ASSYRIA

ARRABAL, FERNANDO (1932–)

Bilingual playwright Fernando Arrabal is perhaps best known as a founding member of the Theatre of Panic, an eclectic movement embracing elements from ANTONIN ARTAUD, SAMUEL BECKETT, and JEAN GENET. A prolific and politically conscious artist, Arrabal is also a novelist, poet, screenwriter, sculptor, and film director.

Arrabal was born in 1932, in Spanish Morocco, shortly before the outbreak of the Spanish Civil War. The war divided his family. In 1936 Arrabal's mother betrayed her husband to the police. He was arrested, jailed, and sentenced to death, although he managed to escape. Arrabal never saw his father again, nor did he forget his mother's betrayal. His plays are populated by domineering, treacherous maternal figures, as seen in the sadistic mothers of *The Two Executioners* (1958).

After his father's arrest, Arrabal's family returned to Spain. Only a small boy, Arrabal began to display an interest in drama, constructing a theater out of cardboard boxes, with actors cut from newspaper. As a teenager Arrabal hitchhiked to France to see BERTOLT BRECHT's Berliner Ensemble. He spent his nights at the cinema, immersed in the films of Charlie Chaplin, Buster Keaton, and Laurel and Hardy. Like FEDERICO GARCÍA LORCA, and later Samuel Beckett, these films inspired Arrabal, who would use their comedic tropes in his work.

By 1953 Arrabal had written two plays—*Picnic on the Battlefield* and *The Tricycle*. Arrabal entered the latter in a contest in Barcelona; the judges, believing he had plagiarized Beckett, awarded him second prize. Unhappy with Spanish censorship, Arrabal sought refuge in France. He won a three-month scholarship to Paris in 1955. Shortly after his arrival, he developed tuberculosis, a diagnosis Arrabal eventually considered a blessing, since it allowed him to stay in Paris indefinitely after his recovery.

In 1957 Arrabal met director Jean-Marie Serreau, who agreed to put on his plays. The following year Arrabal won a lifetime contract from the Julliard publishing house. Two years later he earned international acclaim for his next Parisian production, *Picnic on the Battlefield*. He won a Ford Foundation grant to study theater in the United States, a nation he found too conformist in outlook.

Arrabal's theater is intended to shock, surprise, and move people. He explained his ideas in a series of "Panic" manifestos, beginning with "Panic Texts" (*Textes paniques*) in 1962. The Panic movement began half in jest, as a surrealist stab against pretentious academics. Gradually, however, the Theatre of Panic evolved into a sincere concept. Inspired by Pan, the Greek god of confusion, Arrabal called for an eclectic theater that mixed tragedy with comedy, the sublime with the Guignol.

Over the course of 50 years Arrabal's drama has embraced everything from vaudevillian clowning to grand ceremonials. His work demonstrates an obsession with the darker aspects of childhood, as seen in *The Solemn Communion* (1967), where the Communion ritual parallels a young girl's sexual initiation.

Arrabal has received many international awards for his writing and commitment to human rights. He was named a Chevalier des Arts et des Lettres in 1983 and won the Croatian order of Marko Marulic in 1997.

[*See also* France]

PLAYS: *Picnic on the Battlefield* (*Pique-nique en campagne*, written 1952, published 1961); *The Tricycle* (*Le tricycle*, written 1953, published 1961); *The Car Cemetery* (*Le cimetière des voitures*, 1958); *Fando and Lis* (*Fando et Lis*, 1958); *Orison* (*Oraison*, 1958); *The Two Executioners* (*Les deux bourreaux*, 1958); *The Condemned Man's Bicycle* (*La bicyclette du condamné*, 1961); *Guernica* (1961); *The Labyrinth* (*Le labyrinthe*, 1961); *The Grand Ceremonial* (*Le grand cérémonial*, 1965); *The Architect and the Emperor of Assyria* (*L'architecte et l'empereur d'Assyrie*, 1967); *Has God Gone Mad?* (*Dieu est-il devenu fou?*, 1967); *The Solemn Communion* (*La communion solennelle*, 1967); *A Tortoise Named Dostoevski* (*Une tortue nommée Dostoïevski*, 1968); *They Put Handcuffs on the Flowers* (*. . . Et ils passèrent des menottes aux fleurs*, 1969); *God Tempted by Mathematics* (*Dieu tenté par les mathématiques*, 1972); *The Great Twentieth Century Revue* (*La grande revue du XXe siècle*, 1972); *Heaven and Crap* (*Le ciel et la merde*, 1972); *The Tower of Babel* (*La tour de Babel*, 1978); *Heaven and Crap II* (*Le ciel et la merde II*, 1980); *The King of Sodome* (*Le roi de Sodome*, 1980); *The Crazy Success of Jesus Christ, Karl Marx and William Shakespeare* (*L'extravagante réussite de Jésus-Christ, Karl Marx et William Shakespeare*, 1982); *Stand Up and Dream* (*Lève-toi et rêve*, 1982); *Love Breviary of a Weight Lifter* (*Bréviaire d'amour d'un haltérophile*, 1985); *The 'Cucarachas' from Yale* (*Les "cucarachas" de Yale*, 1988); *The Red Madonna* (*La madonne rouge*, 1988); *A Virgin for a Gorilla* (*Une pucelle pour un gorille*, 1988); *The Crazy Crusade of an Obese Revolutionary* (*L'extravagante croisade d'un révolutionnaire obese*, 1989); *The Uncontrolled Laughter of the Lilliputians* (*Le fou rire des liliputiens*, 1994); *Like a Lily among Thorns* (*Comme un lis entre les épines*, 1996); *Like a Supplicant Chinaman* (*Comme un supplice chinois*, 1999); *Love Letters* (*Lettre d'amour*, 1999)

FURTHER READING

Arrabal, Fernando, and Francisco Torres Monreal. *Teatro pánico* [Panic theater]. Madrid: Cátedra, 1986.

Arrata, Luis Oscar. *The Festive Play of Fernando Arrabal*. Lexington: Univ. of Kentucky Press, 1981.

Donahue, Thomas John. *The Theater of Fernando Arrabal: A Garden of Earthly Delights*. New York: New York Univ. Press, 1980.

Farmer, R. L. "Fernando Arrabal's Guerrilla Theatre." *Yale French Studies*, no. 46 (1971): 154–166.

Fletcher, John, ed. "Towards a New Concept of the Theatre: Adamov, Beckett, and Arrabal." In *Forces in Modern French Drama: Studies in Variations on the Permitted Lie*. London: Univ. of London Press, 1972.

Monreal, Francisco Torres. *Introducción al teatro de Arrabal* [Introduction to Arrabal's theater]. Murcia: Editorial Godoy, 1981.

Orenstein, Gloria. *The Theatre of the Marvelous*. New York: New York Univ. Press, 1975.

Podol, Peter L. *Fernando Arrabal*. Boston: Twayne, 1978.

Heather Jeanne Violanti

ART

In her famous play *Art*—originally published in 1994 and translated into more than thirty languages—French dramatist YASMINA REZA creates an absurd situation with a focus on the existential issues of friendship, authenticity, and the futility of life. Serge has bought an expensive modernist painting that consists only of a white canvas. His friend Marc considers this purchase to be an act of provocation. From his view, the painting is nothing but "white shit." The ensuing conflict between Serge and Marc successively departs from the painting itself and touches upon the very foundation of their friendship. The third character, Yvan, who seeks to mediate between the opponents, is increasingly drawn into the conflict. Serge finally inspires Marc to destroy the artwork by overpainting it with a blue marker. Yet after deciding to renew their endangered friendship, Serge and Marc manage to cleanse the painting.

Reza's play is in part an entertaining satire on modern art and the selling mechanisms of the market. Yet its essential concern consists less in aesthetic considerations than in the fundamental challenges of human relations. The quarrels about the expensive painting reveal unresolved tensions in a seemingly intact friendship. Having set aside the restraints of politeness, the friends reproach each other with envy, lack of compassion, and absence of humor. These tensions are mainly based on the characters' obsession with the futility of their personal lives. Serge's compulsive attachment to his painting, Marc's aggressiveness, and Yvan's nervous conformism are the outer symptoms of existential dissatisfaction. The characters suffer from a lack of meaning that cannot be moderated either by marriage or by psychological treatment. Nevertheless, the final attempt at a renewal of their friendship leaves it up to the reader's interpretation whether the play ends with the hope of a new beginning or with perpetuated misunderstanding.

Reza's play creates an atmosphere in which futility and humorous reflection coexist. It is thus located in between TRAGEDY and COMEDY, provoking the audience to laugh at the absurd interaction. An alternation of dialogues and soliloquies, a play of repetition, and Reza's concise language add to the artistic quality of *Art*.

After its premiere in Paris in 1994, *Art* became famous both in Europe and in the United States. It received, among others, the Molière Award in 1995 and the Tony Award in 1998. This overwhelming popularity may be a response to the genuine combination of tragedy and humor, which makes the play appealing to a larger audience. Yet several critics have argued that *Art* lacks intellectual profundity and philosophical impact and that it generally remains on a rather shallow level.

[*See also* England, 1940–Present]

FURTHER READING

Blot-Labarrere, Christiane. "Yasmina Reza: Mesure du Temps" [Yasmina Reza: Measure of time]. In *Nouvelles ecrivaines: Nouvelles voix?* ed. by Nathalie Morello and Catherine Rodgers. Amsterdam: Rodopi, 2002.

Carroll, Noel. "Art and Friendship." *Philosophy and Literature* 26, no. 1 (April 2002): 199–206.

Danto, Arthur C. "Yasmina Reza's Art." In *The Madonna of the Future: Essays in a Pluralistic Art World*. New York: Farrar, Straus, 2000.

Hattenstone, Simon. "Art and Artifice." *The Guardian*, January 1, 2001. http://www.guardian.co.uk/g2/story/0,3604,416658,00.html.

Reza, Yasmina, *Art*. Tr. by Christopher Hampton. London: Faber, 1996. Originally published in French as *Art*. Arles: Actes Sud, 1994.

David Wachter

ARTAUD, ANTONIN (1896–1948)

Theater, which is no one thing, but uses all languages (gestures, words, sound, fire, and screams), is to be found precisely at the point where the mind needs a language to bring about its manifestations.

—Antonin Artaud, *The Theater and Its Double*, 1938

Antonin Artaud, a writer, actor, and director for the theater, inaugurated postwar modernity with a fiery culmination of the historical AVANT-GARDE moment. His oeuvre, spread out over more than twenty volumes of correspondence, manifestos, poetry, prose, critical essays, reviews, and scenarios, is less a body of dramatic theory than an impassioned call to renovate Western civilization (which he termed "syphilization") using theater. His ideas reverberate profoundly in the fields of modern art, psychology, and philosophy as well as drama. A constellation of convictions unify his work, including the impossibility of authentic expression, the gap between true experience and everyday life, and the need for violence to reconnect spiritual and material existence.

Artaud's painful obsession with the radical divorce between thought and language first appeared in *Correspondence with Jacques Rivière* (1923), a series of letters analyzing why Rivière rejected Artaud's poems from the journal *Nouvelle Révue Française*. Early collections of prose, poetry, and theatrical writings (*The Umbilicus of Limbo*, *Art and Death*, *Fragments from a Diary in Hell*, *The Nerve Meter*, all written between 1925 and 1927) articulated this paradigmatic rupture between body and mind and attracted the notice of the surrealists, who shared Artaud's desire to revolt against traditional forms of expression, to "smash language in order to touch life." Artaud joined the surrealist ranks from 1924 to 1926, directing the Bureau of Surrealist Investigations in 1925. His short play, THE JET OF BLOOD demonstrates the influence of SURREALISM in this period, as Artaud embarked upon alogical, nonnarrative, and highly imagistic modes of writing. Clashes over the theater (which the surrealists viewed as a bourgeois commercial enterprise) and the nature of revolution (which Artaud believed should be purely spiritual and not political or aesthetic) proved fatal to their alliance.

In his short theatrical acting career (1921–1923), Artaud sought noncodified means to convey information in character, often going far beyond the already innovative methods of his directors, including Aurélien Lugné-Poe, Georges Pitoëff, and Charles Dullin. From 1923 to 1936, he acted in films directed by Abel Gance, Carl Dreyer, Fritz Lang, and Georg Wilhelm Pabst. He believed strongly in the power of cinema to convey the hidden world of dreams, but he renounced it completely in favor of live theater when he determined that the film industry was becoming a commercial vehicle for spectacle and psychological narrative.

In 1926 Artaud founded, with ROGER VITRAC and Robert Aron, the Théâtre ALFRED JARRY, mounting four productions between 1927 and 1929, with Artaud as director, producer, and writer of scenarios and manifestos. He likened his ideal theater to a police raid on a brothel, carrying the same violence, urgency, implication of the spectator, and intense physical presence. The theater would be a "a real operation involving not only the mind but also the very senses and flesh" (Artaud, 1971). The Jarry Theater foregrounded the director as the organizing element of theatrical production, breaking with the primacy of the text. As director, Artaud experimented with puppets, masks, simple concrete stage objects, and antinaturalist lighting and sound effects, creating, inasmuch as his limited resources allowed, *mises-en-scène* that reflected his interest in materially creating on stage a "world tangential to the real" (Théâtre Alfred Jarry, 1980). He directed the premieres of AUGUST STRINDBERG'S French translation of *A* DREAM PLAY (1928) and Vitrac's *Les Mystères de l'amour* (1927) and *Victor, ou le pouvoir aux enfants* (1929).

A performance of Balinese dancers in Marseilles's 1931 Colonial Exposition crystallized Artaud's belief in the ability of theater "to speak its own concrete language" (Artaud, 1976). Under this influence, Artaud wrote several essays arguing for a theatrical language "halfway between gesture and thought" that would operate via a system of signs and utilize performers as "moving hieroglyphs" (Artaud, 1958), forming the foundation for his arguments about *mise-en-scène* published in *The Theater and Its Double* (1938). This, Artaud's single most influential work, brings together his disgust with theatrical standards and Western civilization, arguing that both are divided from essential reality by psychology and tradition. Masterpieces, "good for the past but not for us" (Artaud, 1958), emblematize society's tendency to elevate empty forms above the vitality of creative presence. Society must be reconnected with its lost spirit through a violent, overwhelming crisis like the plague, which "unravels conflicts, liberates powers, unleashes potential" (*Oeuvres complètes d'Antonin Artaud IV*, 1980), radically transforming the individual as well as the social order. The "Theater of Cruelty" would play this role, jolting the spectator into a "crucible of fire." "Cruelty" is necessary rigor, a merciless push of the spirit "toward the source of its conflicts" (*Oeuvres complètes d'Antonin Artaud IV*, 1980). Artaud's attempt to establish such a company resulted in one production in 1935, *The Cenci*, which Artaud adapted, directed, and starred in.

Encountering numerous obstacles in his financial and artistic life, Artaud voyaged to Mexico, where he explored the rituals of the Tarahumara Indians. His mental health, always shaky, thoroughly deteriorated during a trip to Ireland. He spent the years 1937 to 1946 in various asylums and underwent electroshock therapy. He was transferred to a clinic near Paris in 1946 and greeted with enthusiasm by European artists who had read his work while he was confined. In 1947, Artaud wrote *To Have Done with the Judgement of God*, a radio play that united his spiritual and physical concerns in a collage of invented language, percussion, multiple voices, and poetry; it was banned on the eve of its transmission.

Artaud's influence permeates American experimental theater of the 1960s (*The Theater and Its Double* was translated in 1958), especially the work of the LIVING THEATER, The Performance Group, the Open Theater, and much performance art. European playwrights ARTHUR ADAMOV, JEAN GENET, and FERNANDO ARRABAL and directors Jean-Louis Barrault, Roger Blin, Charles Marowitz, and Peter Brook testify to his strong influence. His desire to free theater from its conventions in order to unleash its "power to influence the aspect and formation of things" (Artaud, 1958) echoes throughout modern experimental theater: "I am an enemy / of the theater. / I have always been that. / As much as I love the theater, / As much am I, for that very reason / its enemy."

[*See also* France]

PLAYS: *Jet of Blood* (*Le Jet de sang*, c. 1925); *The Cenci* (*Les Cenci*, an adaptation from Shelley, 1935); *To Have Done with the Judgement of God* (*Pour en finir avec le jugement de dieu*, a radio play, 1947)

FURTHER READING

Artaud, Antonin. *The Theater and Its Double*. Tr. by Mary Caroline Richards. New York: Grove Weidenfeld, 1958.

——. *Collected Works II*. Trans. Victor Corti. London: Calder & Boyars, 1971.

——. *Selected Writings*. Tr. by Helen Weaver. Ed. by Susan Sontag. New York: Farrar, Straus and Giroux, 1976.

——. *Oeuvres complètes d'Antonin Artaud IV, nouvelle édition revue et augmentée* [Complete works of Antonin Artaud IV, new revised and augmented edition]. Paris: Gallimard, 1980.

——. "Le Théâtre Alfred Jarry" [Alfred Jarry Theater]. In *Oeuvres complètes d'Antonin Artaud II, nouvelle édition revue et augmentée* [Complete works of Antonin Artaud II, new revised and augmented edition]. Paris: Gallimard, 1980.

Bermel, Albert. *Artaud's Theatre of Cruelty*. New York: Taplinger Pub. Co., 1977.

Brau, Jean-Louis. *Antonin Artaud*. Paris: La Table Ronde, 1971.

Costich, Julia F. *Antonin Artaud*. Boston: Twayne, 1978.

Esslin, Martin. *Antonin Artaud*. London: John Calder, 1976.

Greene, Naomi. *Antonin Artaud: Poet Without Words*. New York: Simon & Schuster, 1970.

Innes, Christopher. *Avant-Garde Theatre 1892–1992*. New York: Routledge, 1993.

Virmaux, Alain. *Antonin Artaud et le théâtre* [Antonin Artaud and the theater]. Paris: Seghers, 1970.

Kimberly Jannarone

ASADAH KA EK DIN *See* ONE DAY IN ASADA

THE ASCENT OF F6

The Ascent of F6 was one of three plays co-written by W. H. AUDEN and his close friend CHRISTOPHER ISHERWOOD: Each of these plays attempted to overthrow theatrical and political complacencies in the mid-1930s. *The Ascent of F6* was first produced by the GROUP THEATRE in London, an AVANT-GARDE company, in 1937, drawing on the talents of director Rupert Doone and composer Benjamin Britten. The play was notable first of all in being largely in verse, and in being broadly poetic, political, and mystical, rather than conceived of in the conventional realistic/melodramatic theatrical modes of the time.

The play concerns the conquest of a mountain, F6, on the borders of British and Ostnian Sudoland. There are three sets of characters: the British colonial officials who are concerned about the possibility of a pro-Ostnian uprising in Sudoland, the group of British climbers famous for their daring ascents, and the Everyman figures Mrs. A and Mr. A. The first group has a range of colonial types (deliberately presented as stereotypes): the nameless General, the civil servant Sir James Ransom, the newspaper owner Lord Stagmantle, and the representative of colonial womanhood, Lady Isabel Welwyn. The climbers include Sir James's brother, Michael Ransom (based on the polar explorer

Scott and on the contemporary poet/mountaineer Michael Roberts), and an assortment of adventurous types—such as the utterly honest Shawcross and the utterly unreliable Gunn. Mr. and Mrs. A represent the audience whose opinion the ruling classes are anxious to control: They are always shown listening to the radio, that new organ of government. Expanding the usual techniques of the stage, Mr. and Mrs. A are shown in a theater box on one side of the stage, while the radio announcer is shown reading the news in a box on the other side of the stage. It is clear that both theater boxes have a secondary relation to the "reality" that is represented on the main stage and represent the controlling role of the mass media in forming ordinary people's opinions.

Sir James Ransom and his colleagues, in the face of colonial rivalry from Ostnia, are keen to exploit a "native" superstition that whoever first climbs F6 will be the ruler of Sudoland. They ask Michael Ransom to attempt the formidably difficult climb for the sake of "England." He initially refuses but is persuaded to make the attempt by his mother. He initially accuses her of always preferring his brother James, but she tells him (in a brief summary of Auden/Isherwood's ideas about "the truly strong man") that in fact she gave him less attention so that he would become a hero.

As the climbers ascend F6, their true natures are revealed, and at the very peak, they face a trial presided over by the abbott of the monastery lower down on the slopes of F6. The ending of the play is complex (some think overly so), as the trial attempts to bring together all the ideas raised in the play in a short space. Nevertheless, the play certainly attempted something new, especially in its portrayal of how heroic acts of exploration, though partly motivated by individual bravery, might be linked to imperial ideologies and to the need to divert the discontents of the ordinary people at home.

[*See also* England, 1860–1940]

FURTHER READING

Berg, James, and Chris Freeman. *The Isherwood Century: Essays on the Life and Work of Christopher Isherwood*. Madison: Univ. of Wisconsin Press, 2000.

Hoggart, Richard. *W. H. Auden*. London: Longmans, 1961.

Mendelson, Edward. *The English Auden: Poems, Essays and Dramatic Writings 1927–1939*. London: Faber, 1977.

Smith, Stan. *W. H. Auden*. Oxford: Blackwell, 1985.

Chris Hopkins

THE ATAMI MURDER CASE

The Atami Murder Case (*Atami Satsujin Jiken*, 1973) is a Japanese play by TSUKA KŌHEI that shared the Kishida Kunio Drama Prize of 1974 with *When We Go Down the Heartless River* (*Bokura ga Hijō no Taiga o Kudaru Toki*, 1972) by SHIMIZU KUNIO. Shimizu was an established playwright, but Tsuka was just starting out, and the prize secured his reputation. Tsuka went on to create other successful plays, but *The Atami Murder Case* probably remains his most popular work. Tsuka encouraged improvisation in later productions of his work, and when remounting his plays, he created new versions for performance and publication. Hence, there are several published versions of *The Atami Murder Case*; among them is the *Monte Carlo Version*, most recently restaged by the Tsuka Kōhei Company in July 2002.

Tsuka's works often deal with the politics of how one person may perform various identities, and *The Atami Murder Case* may be the quintessential example. During the course of the play, the four characters—three police detectives and a murder suspect—go through a process of confronting and altering how they perform their identities. In the process, Tsuka calls into question performance on stage and in society.

The play involves the police interrogation of a young factory employee named Ōyama Kintarō on suspicion of murdering a female co-worker in the seaside resort town of Atami, south of Tokyo. Interrogating him are the soon-to-retire chief detective Kimura Denbei, legendary for his ability to solve cases; his competent female assistant, Hanako; and the brash young Kumada Tomekichi, freshly transferred from the countryside and looking to make a name for himself.

Ōyama's guilt or innocence is of no interest to the police. Their only concern is to construct the performance of the crime and its investigation so that it will play well in the news. Tsuka has Detective (director) Kimura "stage" and "rehearse" the events of the murder, using music to heighten the mood, until all the characters get it right. At first Ōyama insists on his innocence and will not "cooperate" with the investigation. Gradually, however, he gets into his role and eagerly anticipates his forthcoming fame as a criminal. Detective Kumada must be persuaded that Kimura's methods are more appropriate to a successful law-enforcement career than standard police procedure. In Tsuka's hypertheatrical world, Kumada and Ōyama eventually grow into their roles.

As Ōyama begins to master his part, the truth of the murder starts to come out. He and the young woman, Akiko, were from the same rural town. Ōyama still held to traditional rural values, while Akiko was becoming urbanized and losing interest in him. The rural/urban split mirrored the condition of Japanese society as it rapidly modernized after World War II.

Each version of the play brings up different aspects of performed identity. The *Monte Carlo Version* incorporates differences of class and sex ual identity.

[*See also* Japan]

FURTHER READING

Japan Playwrights Association, ed. *Half a Century of Japanese Theatre. Vol. 5, 1970s*. Tokyo: Kinokuniya, 2003.

Kazama Ken. *Shōgekijō no Fūkei* [The Little Theatre Landscape]. Tokyo: Chūō Kōronsha, 1992.

Powell, Brian. *Japan's Modern Theatre: A Century of Change and Continuity.* London: Japan Library, 2002.

Senda Akihiko. *The Voyage of Contemporary Japanese Theatre.* Tr. by J. Thomas Rimer. Honolulu: Univ. of Hawaii Press, 1997.

John D. Swain

ATAMI SATSUJIN JIKEN See THE ATAMI MURDER CASE

AT THE HAWK'S WELL

At the Hawk's Well, a one-act verse play by W. B. YEATS, was privately performed in Lady Cunard's (the hostess) London drawing room on April 2, 1916 (T. S. ELIOT was in the small audience), and two days later, semipublicly, at Lady Islington's, to an "audience composed exclusively of crowned heads and divorcées" (Ezra Pound). It was constructed as a dance-play to be performed by masked actors with an attendant chorus of musicians, after the manner of Japanese Nō plays, to which Yeats had been introduced by Ezra Pound. The masks and music were created by Edmund Dulac, a leading artist, and the dance was performed by Michio Ito, a Japanese disciple of Russian ballet star Vaslav Nijinsky.

In the brief action of the play, the Irish hero Cuchulain comes as a young man to a magic well in search of immortality. An old man has been waiting by the well for years, but each time the waters bubble up, the guardian of the well—a hawk-shaped creature—puts him to sleep. Cuchulain, too, is led astray by this "bird, witch, or woman," who performs a spellbinding dance while the waters rise and once again run away. From the musicians' song, we learn that Cuchulain "has lost what may not be found / Till men heap his burial mound"; in other words, his immortality will not be endless days of peace and quiet but fame after death in battle.

In its simplicity and clarity of image, the poetry of the play is among the most successful dramatic verse of the 20th century. The play was deliberately aesthetic and elitist; Yeats was tired of trying to please an Abbey Theatre audience. It also relied for a successful production on talents not often found among the regular staff of a repertory theater company; the play requires a composer of original music, musicians who can both play instruments and sing, and a female dancer of genius, for the dance was meant to be the climax of the theatrical experience. The form proved more suitable to Yeats's powers than the double-plotted Shakespeareanism of his earlier blank verse plays, such as *On Baile's Strand* (1904). Most of his later dramatic work followed from this first experiment with the Nō spirit plays. *At the Hawk's Well* influenced both T. S. Eliot (see "Ash Wednesday") and SAMUEL BECKETT, who admitted he took "a sup from the Hawk's Well." The absence of scenery—other than a verbal evocation of a bare tree and well long choked up and dry—and theme of waiting passionately for what never comes are some of the elements of Yeats's play that may have found their way, much transformed, into Beckett's *WAITING FOR GODOT*.

[*See also* Ireland]

FURTHER READING

Clark, David R. *W. B. Yeats and the Theatre of Desolate Reality.* Dublin: Dolmen Press, 1965.

Foster, R. F. *W. B. Yeats, a Life: The Arch-poet, 1915–1939.* Oxford: Oxford Univ. Press, 2003.

Sekine, Masaru. *Yeats and the Noh: A Comparative Study.* Gerrards Cross: Colin Smythe, 1990.

Skene, Reb. *The Cuchulain Plays of W. B. Yeats.* New York: Columbia Univ. Press, 1974.

Adrian Frazier

AUDEN, WYSTAN HUGH (1907–1973)

W. H. Auden, a dynamic, prolific, and technically skilled poet, is considered among the major literary figures of the 20th century. Auden was born in 1907 in York, ENGLAND. Although educated at Christ Church, Oxford, his poetry was quite accessible, written in everyday language. His subject matter addressed politics, modern psychology, and Christianity. Auden's earliest works were not well received. In fact, his first collection of poetry was rejected by T. S. ELIOT at Faber and Faber Publishing. Auden, like many of his contemporaries, found liberation from English mores in the bohemian and sexually liberated atmosphere of 1930s Berlin. He became involved with a leftist literary group that included CHRISTOPHER ISHERWOOD and Stephen Spender. Auden and Isherwood collaborated on three verse plays, including *Journey to a War* (1939), which recorded their experiences in China.

Auden gained public attention in 1930 with his short verse play "Paid on Both Sides," which was published in Eliot's periodical, *The Criterion*. *Poems*, Auden's first commercially published book, avoided romantic self-expression. These poems were short, untitled, and cryptic, pointing to a new method of writing on love and desire. Auden's journey as a leftist intellectual continued as he showed interest in the economic and social theories of Marx and Freud's psychoanalytic work. Auden's early work was politically passionate and socially astute as illustrated in *Look, Stranger!* (1936).

In the late 1930s Auden shifted to a less radical political perspective. He seemed to accept and address suffering and injustice as a part of ordinary life. The last works from this decade astonished readers with their light comic tone and domesticity. Auden's personal politics were just as radical and socially aware as demonstrated by his marriage to Thomas Mann's daughter Erika Mann, a lesbian actress and journalist, to assist her in securing a British passport. Perhaps in relation to his shift in poetic tenor, Auden emigrated to the United States in 1939 with Isherwood and became a citizen in 1946. Auden taught at many U.S. colleges and universities. From 1956 to 1961, Auden was professor of poetry at Oxford. Subsequently he lived in a number of countries, including Italy and Austria, and in 1972 he returned to England. He was awarded the National Medal for Literature in 1967.

Auden's mature period is best illustrated by *About the House* (1965), a technically adventurous and intellectually dynamic work. The poems in the book corresponded to the rooms of Auden's Austrian house and his own ecological and biographical boundaries. Auden also wrote opera librettos with the American poet Chester Kallman, who was eighteen when Auden fell in love with him. The two lived together for more than twenty years. In 1972, Auden left New York and returned to Oxford, living in a cottage provided by Christ Church. He died of a heart attack after giving a poetry reading in Vienna on September 29, 1973, and was buried in nearby Kirchstetten.

[*See also* The Ascent of F6]

PLAYS: *The Orators* (1932); *On the Frontier* (with Christopher Isherwood, 1938); *Journey to a War* (with Christopher Isherwood, 1939); *The Age of Anxiety* (Pulitzer Prize, 1947); *Elegy for Young Lovers* (libretto, 1961); *City Without Walls* (1969)

FURTHER READING

Carpenter, Humphrey. *W. H. Auden, A Biography*. Boston: Houghton Mifflin, 1981.

Fuller, John. *W. H. Auden: A Commentary*. Princeton: Princeton Univ. Press, 2000.

Hendon, Paul, ed., *The Poetry of W. H. Auden*. New York: Palgrave Macmillan, 2002.

McDiarmid, Lucy. *Auden's Apologies for Poetry*. Princeton: Princeton Univ. Press, 1990.

Mendelson, Edward. *Early Auden*. Cambridge: Harvard Univ. Press, 1983.

——. *Later Auden*. New York: Farrar, Straus and Giroux, 1999.

Smith, Stan. *W. H. Auden*. Oxford: Blackwell, 1985.

Spears, Monroe Kirklyndorf. *The Poetry of W. H. Auden; The Disenchanted Island*. New York: Oxford Univ. Press, 1963.

Shanté T. Smalls

AUDIBERTI, JACQUES (1899–1965)

Ranked among the most important practitioners of the New Poetic Theater (Théâtre poétique noveau), Jacques Audiberti was a prolific writer. In addition to 26 plays, he penned several poems, novels, and theater reviews. His drama shows a distinct symbolist influence while anticipating the playful cruelty of the Theater of the Absurd.

Audiberti was born on March 25, 1899, in the small town of Antibes, FRANCE. A shy, dreamy child, he was intrigued by his village's legendary history. The contrast between such grandeur and the crass tourists who invaded Antibes each summer never failed to startle him. The disjuncture between ancient legend and the brutality of modern life was a theme that would later haunt his writing.

Having difficulty adjusting at school, Audiberti retreated into a world of books. He immersed himself in the works of Pierre Benoit, Stéphane Mallarmé, Anatole France, and Victor Hugo. He began to write his own poems and stories, developing a florid style that biographer Constantin Toloudis (1980) has described as "cataclysmic lyricism."

Audiberti moved to Paris in 1924, working as a writer for *Le Journal*, a suburban newspaper. He struggled to find a publisher for his poetry. Finally, in 1930 Audiberti's first book of poems was published, *The Empire and the Trap Door* (*L'Empire et la Trampe*). In 1935 Audiberti won his first of many awards, the Prix Mallarmé.

He turned to playwriting late in his career. Audiberti was forty-seven when his first play, *Quoat-Quoat*, was produced, almost by chance, by André Reybaz and Catherine Toth in 1946. As a result, Audiberti met Georges Vitaly, an up-and-coming director known for the "shock theater" he produced on the Left Bank. Vitaly agreed to direct his next work, *Evil Is Spreading* (*Le mal court*), in 1947. The production was sparsely attended, but a revival staged in 1955 at the Théâtre de la Bruyère proved a triumph. Audiberti was now established as a major new force in the theater. His subsequent plays toured AVANT-GARDE venues and student festivals throughout Paris. In 1962 he achieved iconic status when *Pins and Needles* (*La Fourmi dans le corps*) was presented at the Comédie Francaise. Two years later he won the prestigious Grand Prix des Lettres by unanimous vote.

Audiberti's plays are characterized by rich, baroque poetry, bordering on discursive delirium. Reminiscent of the playwright MICHEL DE GHELDERODE, the musicality of Audiberti's language also demonstrates another influence—that of opera. Indeed, he wrote three opera libretti—*Altanima*, and *Spoken Opera* (*Opéra parlé*) (both 1956), and *The Opera of the World* (*L'Opéra du monde*, 1965).

Like Ghelderode's dramaturgy, Audiberti's focuses on the struggle between good and evil, an evil caused less by the devil than by inhumanity to others. This is perhaps illustrated most chillingly in *Patients* (*Les Patients*, 1961), in which a young girl is dismembered and raped by invading soldiers while her family helplessly looks on. The plays also interweave elements from myth and French legend with elements of contemporary life, such as *The Maid of Orleans* (*La Pucelle*, 1950), a modern retelling of the Joan of Arc story. Audiberti died on July 10, 1965, in Neuilly-sur-Seine.

[*See also* France]

PLAYS: *Quoat-Quoat* (1946); *Evil Is Spreading* (*Le mal court*, 1947); *The Ox's Women* (*Les femme du boeuf*, performed 1948); *Black Festival* (*La fête noire* [originally *The Black Beast* (*La bête noire*)], 1949); *The Maid of Orleans* (*La Pucelle*, 1950); *The Natives of Bordelais* (*Les naturels de Bordelais*, 1953); *Doctors Are Not Plumbers* (*Les médicins ne sont pas des plombiers*, published 1954); *The Landlady* (*La Logeuse*, published 1954); *Altanima* (opera libretto, 1956); *Spoken Opera* (*Opéra parlé*,

1956); *Le Ouallou* (1957); *The Small Falcon* (*La Hoberaute* [a reworking of *Spoken Opera*], 1958); *The Glapion Effect* (*L'Effet Glapion*, 1959); *The Classical Cupboard* (*L'armoire classique*, 1961); *Heart to Be Cooked* (*Coeur à cuire*, 1961); *Patients* (*Les Patients*, 1961); *Pins and Needles* (*La Fourmi dans le corps*, 1962); *The Soldier Dioclès* (*Le soldat Dioclès*, 1961); *A Very Beautiful Child* (*Un bel enfant*, 1961); *Apple, Apple, Apple* (*Pomme, Pomme, Pomme*, 1962); *Baton and Ribbon* (*Bâton et ribbon*, 1962); *La Brigitta* (1962); *The Closed Boutique* (*Boutique fermeé*, 1962); *The Lone Knight* (*Le cavalier seul*, 1963); *The Opera of the World* (*L'Opéra du monde*, 1965)

FURTHER READING

Guicharnaud, Jacques, and June Guicharnaud. *Modern French Theatre from Giraudoux to Genet*. Rev. ed. New Haven, Conn.: Yale Univ. Press, 1967.

O'Connor, Garry. *French Theatre Today*. London: Pitman, 1975.

Pronko, Leonard Cabell. *Avant-Garde: The Experimental Theatre in France*. Berkeley: Univ. of California Press, 1966.

Toloudis, Constantin. *Jacques Audiberti*. Boston: Twayne, 1980.

Heather Jeanne Violanti

DER AUFHALTSAME AUFSTIEG DES ARTURO UI

See THE RESISTIBLE RISE OF ARTURO UI

AUSTRALIA

At the beginning of the 21st century Australia acknowledges the legacy of two performance traditions, one transplanted from European theater and the other developed within indigenous Aboriginal culture. The momentum of innovation over the last three decades brought together these areas in the development of a distinctly Australian theater that reflects the diversity of a multicultural society. The advent of new wave drama in the 1970s provided the foundation for this unique theater exploring what it means to be Australian.

1860–1945

Improvised theater and music were plentiful in the early colonial period, but the discovery of gold in 1851 brought the world to Australia, and it joined AFRICA, INDIA, and Southeast Asia as a destination for acting troupes. Impressive theaters were built. George Coppin, British comedian and entrepreneur, imported a prefabricated 1,150-seat theater to the colony's financial center, Melbourne. Stars, such as Irish tragedian Gustavus Brooke and Irish soprano Catherine Hayes, were showered with gold and diamonds. Balladeer Charles Mathews and Shakespeareans Charles and Ellen Kean published memoirs of the goldfields.

American actors Joseph Jefferson and Edwin Booth began their careers in Australia. Older performers settled and worked as teachers. While traveling was long and hard, life in the cities provided comfort and entertainment. The first blackface minstrel show, the Virginia Minstrels, arrived in 1843. Circus entertainment began in the 1840s: The equestrian May Wirth and the Aboriginal low-wire walker Con Colleano became internationally famous.

Local stage writers were active, writing melodramas, comedy, and pantomime. Surviving texts lampoon authority and celebrate the superiority of the Australian over the "new-chum" Englishman. But it was not until the 1870s, when Australian-born citizens began to reach a majority, that the concept of a national identity was asserted.

Most of the early playwrights were journalists. Colonial rule and convict transportation from England until the 1840s had entrenched censorship; however, burlesque provided an ideal platform for political satire in the years leading up to the Federation of Australian states in 1901. Prominent among these satirists were William Mower Akhurst, Walter Cooper, Marcus Clarke, and Garnet Walch. Actor-manager-playwrights such as George Darrell and Alfred Dampier introduced horses, train rides, and river crossings into productions. A golden period began, with the arrival in 1874 of American entrepreneur J. C. Williamson with his wife Maggie Moore. He founded an empire that dominated Australian theater until 1976.

A growing bourgeoisie provided audiences for opera, operetta, classical ballet, girls chorus, and historical drama. Shakespearean George Rignold settled in Sydney in 1884. Robert Brough and Dion Boucicault, Jr., created a taste for polite comedy following their tour in 1885 with Irish playwright Dion Boucicault, Sr. But the greatest stars were in operetta: Nellie Stewart and Gladys Moncrieff.

Cinema put an end to popular melodrama, but one working-class form survived: variety. The cockney comedian Harry Rickards and his Tivoli variety circuit encouraged local artists, notably the great Jewish comedian Roy Rene.

World War I and the 1930s Depression provided opportunities for the rise of an amateur repertory movement that produced writers such as Louis Esson, and George Landen Dann and particularly women writers such as DYMPHNA CUSACK, Betty Roland, Catherine Shepherd, Mona Brand, and Oriel Gray. They were mostly middle-class socialists. Australian theater was not considered fully professional until Sumner Locke Elliott's army comedy, *Rusty Bugles* (produced 1947), which achieved notoriety in 1948 when it was banned (for the use of blasphemous and swear words) by the chief secretary of New South Wales.

FURTHER READING

Brisbane, Katharine, ed. *Entertaining Australia, An Illustrated History*. Sydney: Currency, 1991.

Fitzpatrick, Peter. *Pioneer Players: The Lives of Louis and Hilda Esson*. Melbourne: Cambridge Univ. Press, 1995.

Jordan, Robert. *The Convict Theatres of Early Australia, 1788–1840*. Sydney: Currency, 2002.

Love, Harold, ed. *The Australian Stage, A Documentary History*. Sydney: Univ. of NSW Press, 1984.

Osric (Humphrey Hall and Alfred John Cripps). *The Romance of the Sydney Stage* (1789–1864). Sydney and Canberra: Currency and National Library of Australia, 1996.

Parsons, Philip, with Victoria Chance, eds. *Companion to Theatre in Australia*. Sydney: Currency, 1995.

Williams, Margaret. *Australia on the Popular Stage 1829–1929*. Melbourne: Oxford Univ. Press, 1983.

Katharine Brisbane

1945–1969

The years succeeding World War II were rich ones for Australian theater, with the country committed to developing a homegrown drama, if ambivalent about its implications. The government-commissioned Guthrie Report (1949) identified the deficiencies of the professional industry as it then stood: a lack of artistic personnel; a lack of actor training institutions; a lack of locally written plays; and above all, a lack of an alternative to commercial managements (particularly J. C. Williamson's) and their reliance on foreign fare. Over the following decade the calls for a "national theater" became ever stronger and led, in 1954, to the establishment of the Australian Elizabethan Theatre Trust (AETT), a quasi-independent agency marking the beginnings of ongoing government subsidy of the arts.

The fruits of these activities were immediately felt. Armed with a guarantee against loss, a recently founded Union Repertory (later Melbourne) Theatre Company premiered RAY LAWLER's *Summer of the Seventeenth Doll* (1955) to great acclaim. The production toured around the country before transferring to first London and then New York. Such success for an Australian play was unprecedented, and the aftereffects were both galvanizing and complex. On the one hand, it turned the spotlight on local dramatists, clearing the way for plays like Richard Beynon's *The Shifting Heart* (1960), Peter Kenna's *The Slaughter of St. Teresa's Day* (produced 1959), Alan Seymour's *The One Day of the Year* (1962), and Alan Hopgood's *And the Big Men Fly* (1963). On the other, it affirmed stage REALISM and the reproduction of the Australian vernacular as the overdetermining goal for all serious playwrights. This led to a string of realist plays set in slums (the "*Doll* clones," as critic Harry Kippax dubbed them) and the neglect of writers at odds with the dominant trend—for example, Hal Porter's *The Tower* (1964), Douglas Stewart's *Ned Kelly* (1943), and Patrick White's drama. White, perhaps Australia's best-known novelist, found a difficult reception. In 1961 *The Ham Funeral* was rejected by the Adelaide Festival, while *The Season at Sarsaparilla* (produced 1962) and *A Cheery Soul* (produced 1963) met with critical indifference and box-office failure. Such experiences for local playwrights were not atypical.

As the 1960s wore on, it became clear that despite the impact of the AETT and the success of the *Doll*, no substantial body of staged Australian plays was appearing. However, noncommercial theater did acquire an infrastructure. Professional repertory theaters were established in most states and provided a basis for the state theater (mainstream) companies in the 1970s, while a new National Institute of Dramatic Art (founded 1958) ensured a steady supply of trained actors and production personnel. Some companies made efforts to support Australian writers. Jane Street Theatre was a studio attached to the Old Tote Theatre, which from 1966 onward developed plays by Rodney Milgate and novelist Thomas Keneally. While experimental seasons did not compensate for neglect of Australian plays, they did act as models for the explosion of NEW WAVE drama, which seismically erupted in the following decade and created the substantial artistic movement that has since become Australian drama and theater.

FURTHER READING

Fitzpatrick, Peter. *After the Doll*. London: Edward Arnold, 1979.

Guthrie, Tyrone. "Report on Australian Theatre." *Australian Quarterly* 21 (June 1949): 9–30.

Holloway, Peter, ed. *Contemporary Australian Drama*. 2d ed. Sydney: Currency, 1987.

Inglis Moore, T. "A Chequered Story: The Creation of a National Drama." *Meanjin* 33, no. 2 (1974): 193–197.

Meyrick, Julian. "Sightlines and Bloodlines: The Influence of British Theatre on Australia in the Post-1945 Era." In *Playing Australia*, ed. by Elizabeth Schafer and Susan Pfisterer. Amsterdam: Rodopi, 2003.

Rees, Leslie. *The Making of Australian Drama*. Vol. 1. Sydney: Angus and Robertson, 1973.

Sumner, John. *Recollections at Play—A Life in Australian Theatre*. Melbourne: Melbourne Univ. Press, 1993.

Ward, Peter. *A Singular Act: Twenty-five Years of the State Theatre Company of South Australia*. South Australia: Wakefield Press, 1992.

Julian Meyrick

DRAMA FOR YOUNG PEOPLE

Before 1960, Australian young people's theater consisted mostly of imported pantomimes, the schools' repertoire of the Young Elizabethan Players, and the touring work of Joan and Betty Rayner's Australian Children's Theatre. During the 1960s, new companies such as the Australian Theatre for Young People, Arena, and Patch were established, and in the 1970s, dramatic writing for young people became influenced by models of Theatre-in-Education (TIE) introduced by expatriate British artists Roger Chapman, Barbara Manning, and DAVID YOUNG. With increased government subsidy for youth-specific arts and the concomitant growth of participatory community theater in the 1980s, writers became adept at traversing the fields of both writing for and with young people. Key works of this period include *Year 9 Are Animals* (produced 1981), by Richard Tulloch; *Wolf Boy* (1985), by Peter Charlton; *No Worries* (1989) and *The Small Poppies* (1989), by David Holman; *Honey Spot* (1987), by JACK DAVIS; and group-devised plays such as Magpie Theatre's

Hey Mum, I Own a Factory (1985) and Salamanca Theatre's *Thirst* (produced 1989). In the early 1990s, dramatic adaptations of Australian novels for young readers became an increasingly popular mode of playwriting for young audiences.

Prominent writers whose work has spanned these developments include Richard Tulloch, winner of numerous Australian Writers' Guild (AWGIE) awards. His plays include *Hating Alison Ashley* (1987), adapted from an original book by Robin Klein (1984); *Body and Soul* (1997); and a collection of plays based on the stories of novelist Paul Jennings titled *Stage Fright* (1996). In 2003, Tulloch's puppet theater piece *Twinkle Twinkle Little Fish* opened on Broadway. Debra Oswald's *Dags* (produced 1985) received an AWGIE award in 1986 and was followed by *Gary's House* (1996) and, more recently, *Sweet Road* (2000). Peta Murray, well known for her feminist adult drama *Wallflowering* (1992), won an AWGIE for *The Keys to the Animal Room* for Junction Theatre Cin in 1994. Murray's *Spitting Chips* (produced 1989) and *Blueback*, an adaptation of the novel by Tim Winton, won an AWGIE award for Best Play for Young People in 2000. Murray's adult plays include the multiaward-winning *Salt* (2001) and *One Woman Song* (produced 1993). Mary Morris has written adaptations of Robin Klein's *Boss of the Pool* (1993) and novelist Morris Gleitzman's *Blabber Mouth* (1996) and *Two Weeks with the Queen* (1997).

In the late 1990s, as government subsidy for young people's arts became more attuned to youth cultures, and as multimedia capabilities in theater expanded, a trend toward more multi-artform and collaborative performance-writing for young audiences developed. Examples are the work of writer David Brown with *Keep Everything You Love* (produced 1999) for Toadshow; Tom Lycos and Stefo Nantsou's *The Stones* (produced 1999) for Zeal Theatre; Chris Thompson's *The Bridge* (produced 2002) for HotHouse Theatre; and writer-director Rose Myers's work with Arena Theatre, including *Autopsy* (produced 1998); *Eat Your Young*, with Julianne O'Brien (produced 2000); and *Play Dirty*, with STEPHEN SEWELL (produced 2002).

FURTHER READING

ASSITEJ (International Association of Theatre for Children and Young People). *Theatre Childhood and Youth* (Special Focus Issue on Australia). Paris: ASSITEJ, 1987.

Australia Council. *Ideas, Facts and Futures: Youth and the Arts*. Redfern: Australia Council, 1991.

Fitzgerald, Michael. *Young People's Theatre in Australia*. Sydney: Australia Council for the Arts, 1987.

Gallasch, Keith. "Promise and Participation: Youth Theatre in Australia." *New Theatre Quarterly* 2, no. 5 (1986): 90–94.

Hunter, Mary Ann. "Contemporary Australian Youth-Specific Performance and the Negotiation of Change." *Drama Australia* 24, no. 1 (2000): 25–35.

——. "Anxious Futures: Magpie2 and 'New Generationalism' in Australian Youth-Specific Theatre." *Theatre Research International* 26, no. 1 (2001): 71–81.

O'Toole, John, and Penny Bundy. "Kites and Magpies: TIE in Australia." In *Learning Through Theatre: New Perspectives on Theatre in Education*. Ed. by Tony Jackson. London: Routledge, 1993.

Mary Ann Hunter

NEW WAVE DRAMA

By 1968 there had been two decades of conservative government in Australia. It was an increasingly affluent, urban society; it was also waking to the vigorous call of the women's movement, and it had troops involved in the Vietnam War. A general feeling of social unrest was palpable, especially among an increasingly tertiary-educated younger generation opposed to the war in Vietnam, to stiflingly conservative social attitudes, and to the foreign domination of most cultural institutions. The young generation wanted broad public affirmation of Australia's independence as a nation (politically and culturally) and—especially—a reflection of its increasingly confident national identity on the stage and screen.

The fruit of this protest movement was soon seen in the theater—initially in small alternative venues that opened in the late 1960s, providing spaces for mostly younger-generation local writers (including recent university graduates) to give voice to an aggressive sense of national identity. In Melbourne, Jack Hibberd (a medical doctor) immediately contributed plays like *White with Wire Wheels* (1967), about immature males and their sexual ambitions, and DAVID WILLIAMSON, who would become the most produced playwright of the next three decades, portrayed similar characters in *The Coming of Stork* (1970) and portrayed police violence in *The Removalists* (1971). JOHN ROMERIL wrote street theater against the Vietnam War and domestic drama about working-class battlers. In 1970 Hibberd and Romeril co-wrote *Marvellous Melbourne*, a hybrid music theater piece in epic narrative style that was critical of Australia's past and present. In Sydney, Alex Buzo wrote realistically about racism (and challenged censorship laws) in *Norm and Ahmed* (produced 1968) and farcically about conflicts among urban officeworkers in *The Front Room Boys* (produced 1969). Michael Boddy and Bob Ellis's *The Legend of King O'Malley* (produced 1970) pioneered a new knockabout style of music theater and a new style of satirizing Australia's present by depicting its past.

The playwrights and the major plays that dominated the repertoire of drama in the 1970s included Hibberd with, in particular, *A Stretch of the Imagination* (produced 1972); Romeril, Buzo, and Williamson (with nine major plays each through the decade); ALMA DE GROEN (six plays); Ron Blair with *The Christian Brothers* (1975); Jim McNeil with *How Does Your Garden Grow?* (produced 1974); and DOROTHY HEWETT with *The Chapel Perilous* (produced 1971). Following huge instant success in alternative theaters, Williamson and Buzo were immediately absorbed into the mainstream, while other playwrights were to enjoy mainstream success later, through new works and revivals.

Ironically, in a movement to establish a strong sense of national identity, these plays satirically exposed weaknesses and deep-seated fears in the—mainly male—Australian psyche. All brilliantly exploited Australian linguistic idiom and character stereotyping and touched on "taboo" issues like sexual politics, racial tensions, and religion. The new movement was also notable for its rejection of REALISM and the well-made play of earlier decades, with its increasingly common and confident mastery of forms such as MONODRAMA and drama with songs and EPIC THEATER.

[*See also* Nowra, Louis; Sewell, Stephen]

FURTHER READING

Brisbane, Katharine, ed. *Plays of the 70s*. Vols. 1–3. Sydney: Currency, 1998.

Fitzpatrick, Peter. *After the "Doll."* London: Edward Arnold, 1977.

Hainsworth, John, ed. *Hibberd*. Sydney: Methuen Australia, 1987.

Holloway, Peter, ed. *Contemporary Australian Drama*. 2d ed. Sydney: Currency, 1987.

McGillick, Paul. *Jack Hibberd*. Amsterdam: Rodopi, 1988.

Radic, Leonard. *The State of Play: The Revolution in the Australian Theatre Since the 1960s*. Melbourne: Penguin, 1991.

Geoffrey Milne

NEW WAVE PRODUCTIONS

The "New Wave" of Australian drama in the 1970s arose with the activities of smaller companies—most notably Nimrod Theatre in Sydney and the Australian Performing Group (APG) in Melbourne—but its roots were more broadly based. A new generation of playwrights writing about Australian identity demonstrated a polyglot stage aesthetic and a rejection of the "well-made play" of earlier decades. Songs, audience participation, improvisation, and an epic narrative approach went hand-in-hand with a critical attitude to Australia's past and present. As the decade wore on, the activities of alternative theaters such as Melbourne's La Mama, based on Ellen Stewart's New York original, and Sydney's Jane Street Theatre brought forth a range of talented writers who quickly became more widely known. These playwrights were well served by a new generation of actors and directors, trained in Australia and dedicated to the idea of a locally derived theater. Jim Sharman, John Bell, Richard Wherrett, and Graeme Blundell—and in the 1980s, Neil Armfield, Gale Edwards, and Rodney Fisher—were directors who staged imaginative productions of Australian work for alternative and mainstream companies alike. Other forms of theater challenged the preponderance of Anglo-style verbal drama: the APG-affiliated Women's Theatre Group, Circus Oz, Anthill Theatre, and Rex Cramphorn's Performance Syndicate were just some of the groups exploring new forms of physical, visual, circus, or classics-related theater.

Underpinning all this activity lay a number of important changes to the industry. The election in 1972 of a Labor government under the culture-loving prime minister Gough Whitlam led to the doubling of public subsidy to the arts and the establishment of the Australia Council in 1973, the statutory successor to the Australian Elizabethan Theatre Trust. The Council's specialist arts boards were an effective force in extending subsidized support to all manner of innovative projects. In a few short years the country's noncommercial theater sector boomed. Around a core of, by now, well-established state theaters arose a ring of "second-string" high-profile companies offering more challenging fare. Troupe Theatre in Adelaide, Company B (Belvoir Street) in Sydney, Black Swan in Perth, the Darwin Theatre Company in the Northern Territory, Playbox in Melbourne, and La Boite in Brisbane were high-turnover, low-cost venues dedicated to the production of new Australian writing. By the end of the decade, noncommercial theater in Australia had changed, structurally and behaviorally, in almost every feature. In the 1980s the industry came under pressure again from both decreasing real levels of public assistance and falling attendances.

A series of government reports—most notably the Rotherwood Plan in 1982 and the McLeay Report in 1986—sought to restructure Australian subsidized theater by introducing, among other measures, a cap on levels of subsidy and new accountability procedures. These interventions were only partially successful, and the 1990s became a time of downsizing, with both the numbers of theater companies and their rate of production falling over the decade, though the increasing importance of arts festivals have encouraged the development of some new work.

FURTHER READING

Holloway, Peter, ed. *Contemporary Australian Drama*. 2d ed. Sydney: Currency, 1987.

Jones, Liz, and Betty Burstall. *La Mama. The Story of a Theatre*. Melbourne: Penguin, 1988.

Meyrick, Julian. *Nimrod and the New Wave, 1970–1985*. Sydney: Currency, 2002.

Milne, Geoffrey. *Theatre Australia (Un)Limited: Australian Theatre since the 1950s*. Amsterdam: Rodopi, 2004.

Radic, Leonard. *The State of Play: The Revolution in the Australian Theatre Since the 1960s*. Melbourne: Penguin, 1991.

Rees, Leslie. *The Making of Australian Drama*. Vol. 2. Sydney: Angus & Robertson, 1978.

Robertson, Tim. *The Pram Factory: The Australian Performing Group Recollected*. Melbourne: Melbourne Univ. Press, 2001.

Tait, Peta. *Original Women's Theatre*. Melbourne: Artmoves, 1993.

Theatre Australia. August/September 1976 to May 1982.

Julian Meyrick

GENDER AND SEXUALITY IN DRAMA AND PHYSICAL THEATER

The drama that flourished after 1970 in Australia explored national identity through domestic relationships, using realist dialogue; male playwrights reflected iconoclastic masculinity, and female playwrights searched for new perspectives on female identity. The breakdown of family relationships and gender issues became common themes. The realist dialogue of HANNIE RAYSON's *Hotel Sorrento* (1990) synthesized questions of gender, national, and cultural identity.

In the 1980s a genre of body-based performance developed that does not use written plays and realist dialogue but instead is nonrealistic, visual, image-based, and impressionistic. The best work was typified by Sydney Front's annual productions (1987–1993). Female performance writers found imaginative ways to show gender identity physically. The Home Cooking Company's 1986 production of *Running Up a Dress*, by Suzanne Spunner in collaboration with group members, delivered images of women sewing in explorations of the cultural and economic value of clothing and the molding of female identity. Body-based performance also drew on training methods from southern and northeastern Asia during the 1980s. For example, Thérèse Radic's *Madame Mao* (produced 1986), about Jiang Qing and the Chinese Revolution, was staged with acrobatics by a new circus (animal free theatrical circus), Circus Oz, itself influenced by Chinese acrobatics. Highly physicalized productions expanded the representations of gender and sexual identity in theater.

Dramatic representations of homosexual identity coincided with explorations of gender and encompass 1970s realist dialogue plays through to the 1990s nonverbal physical theater. Male homosexuality is depicted in the 1970s plays of Peter Kenna, including *Mate*; Steve J. Spears's Obie-winning *The Elocution of Benjamin Franklin*; and Clem Gorman's *A Manual of Trench Warfare*, set in Gallipoli in World War I, which explores precepts of national and family identity, and masculinity and sexuality. These themes continue in, for example, Alex Harding's *Blood and Honour* (produced 1990). From the 1980s there is professional drama about lesbians, including Alison Lyssa's *Pinball*, about a lesbian couple seeking custody of children; Sandra Shotlander's *Framework*, about a lesbian relationship; and well-known performer, Robyn Archer's *The Pack of Women*, which celebrates women's history with songs. The Vitalstatistix theater company specializes in producing female-centered drama, including Margaret Fischer's *The Gay Divorcee*, about lesbian relationship breakups. Gay and lesbian subcultures produce numerous nonprofessional performances, first, because of an absence, then a sparseness of theater productions. The Sydney Gay and Lesbian Mardi Gras generated a major arts festival during the 1990s.

Australia's distinctive style of new circus and physical theater has been internationally recognized since the early 1990s. Groups like Rock 'n' Roll Circus, renamed Circa, and Club Swing presented outrageous and Queer identity. This style originated in 1970s animal-free, thematically unified new circus such as Circus Oz and 1980s physical theater groups such as Legs on the Wall, which use acrobatics and trapeze work. Their offshoots are community and women-only circuses promoting social justice themes. Identity is created bodily with, for example, images of muscular females. In 2002, Keith Gallasch and Virginia Baxter (of Open City with ten productions—1987–1997) identify 55 companies specializing in body movement performance. These artists make strongly visual theater with minimal speech and radical, physicalized images of gender and sexual identity.

FURTHER READING

Allen, Richard, and Karen Pearlman, eds. *Performing the Unnameable*. Sydney: Currency/RealTime, 1999.

Australia Council/RealTime. *A Guide to Australian Contemporary Performance*. Comp. by Keith Gallasch and Virginia Baxter. Sydney: Australia Council, 2002.

Grehan, Helena. *Mapping Cultural Identity in Contemporary Australian Performance*. Brussels: P. I. E.–Peter Lang, 2001.

Kelly, Veronica, ed. *Our Australian Theatre in the 1990s*. Amsterdam: Rodopi, 1998.

Parr, Bruce, ed. *Australian Gay and Lesbian Plays*. Sydney: Currency, 1996.

"Performance Studies in Australia." Special issue, *Australasian Drama Studies* 39 (October 2001).

Tait, Peta. *Converging Realities: Feminism in Australian Theatre*. Sydney: Currency, 1994.

——, ed. *Body Show/s: Australian Viewings of Live Performance*. Amsterdam: Rodopi, 2000.

Peta Tait

MALE PLAYWRIGHTS, 1980–1990S

After 1993, Australian subsidized theater was organized into two tiers according to budget. Each state (seven states) has 1 major company and at least 1 other high-profile company subsidized by the Australia Council. As well, there are about 30 smaller companies, most in the eastern states, that are minimally subsidized. State companies produce a male-dominated repertoire of classic drama, Sondheim musicals, contemporary foreign plays, and some new work by established Australian playwrights, while the smaller companies are mainly responsible for the development and creation of new Australian work in many different forms and the majority of productions of women's drama. State governments also subsidize companies. Through the 1990s, Australian works accounted for about sixty five percent of total national productions, more than half being new work.

Issues and themes preoccupying many playwrights included gender relations, world politics, the increasing gap between the affluent and an underclass of the poor, and reconciliation between non-Indigenous and Indigenous Australians dispossessed of land. REALISM had increasingly given way to fragmented and discontinuous styles of writing, especially outside mainstream theater.

DAVID WILLIAMSON continues to write entertaining satires about topical issues affecting middle- and upper-class characters for the state theater companies. The younger Daniel Keene wrote more than 30 new works for smaller theaters in the 1990s—half of them full-length plays and the rest short pieces in double and triple bills. His breadth of interest is illustrated by *Low* (produced 1991), a grim comedy about two inept petty criminal outcasts like Bonnie and Clyde but entirely without glamour, and *Because You Are Mine* (produced 1994), a bleak, highly stylized portrayal in discontinuous vignettes of horrific events in the Balkan war. His short plays of the late 1990s range from highly personalized reflections of the Holocaust, including *Kaddish*, *The Violin*, and *The Rain* (produced 1998), to portrayals of derelicts, down-and-outs, and drifters. The 1998 triple bill of *Neither Lost nor Found*, *Untitled Monologue*, and *Night, a Wall, Two Men* was produced in a charitable organization's furniture warehouse, surrounded by goods that, like the characters, had been cast off by affluent society.

Another prominent playwright of the 1990s is Andrew Bovell, who has written for mainstream and smaller theaters on widely divergent themes, also mostly in nonrealistic style. *Scenes from a Separation* (produced 1995), co-written with HANNIE RAYSON, has each writer contributing a totally different view of a marriage breakup in two separate acts. Bovell's *Ballad of Lois Ryan* is a play with songs about an industrial accident and its impact on a union activist's family and toured workplaces in 1988, while his ambitious *Ship of Fools* (produced 1989) seamlessly juxtaposed scenes from a medieval tale of outcasts banished on a river barge with a group of present-day unemployed people bussed to the bush on an aimless work-experience scheme. Bovell's *Holy Day* (2001) dealt with 19th-century outback outcasts and a horrific Aboriginal massacre. Recently he has written for international films.

Most Australian playwrights of the 1990s responded vigorously to social and political issues, writing for mainstream major companies and for smaller theaters.

[*See also* Gow, Michael; Nowra, Louis; Sewell, Stephen]

FURTHER READING

AusStage. *Gateway to the Australian Performing Arts*. http://www.ausstage.edu.au/.

Kelly, Veronica, ed. *Our Australian Theatre in the 1990s*. Amsterdam: Rodopi, 1998.

Milne, Geoffrey. *Theatre Australia (Un)limited*. Amsterdam: Rodopi, 2004.

Parsons, Philip, and Victoria Chance. *Companion to Theatre in Australia*. Sydney: Currency, 1995.

Geoffrey Milne

WOMEN PLAYWRIGHTS BEFORE 1970

Women were significant playwrights in Australia before 1970, motivated by political concerns and their desire to address Australian themes. They were the mainstay of Australia's alternative to commercial and mainstream theater.

In the early 20th century the quest for female suffrage shaped expatriate Inez Bensusan's playwriting in England, and her play *The Apple* (produced 1909) championed gender equality. Other suffrage playwrights included novelists Katharine Susannah Prichard and Miles Franklin.

The 1917 Russian Revolution, the rise of fascism, and the formation of the international Popular Front led to the creation of much left-wing theater in Australia. The best known was the New Theatre movement, which had branches across Australia from the early 1930s. Writers such as Catherine Duncan, Prichard, and Betty Roland used their playwriting to intervene in political debates: to plead for peace in Duncan's *The Sword Sung* (produced 1938) or for workers' rights in Duncan's co-authored play *Thirteen Dead* (produced 1937) and Prichard's *Forward One* (produced 1935). Roland wrote many AGITATION-PROPAGANDA (agit-prop) sketches (published in *Communist Review* [1938–1939]) and a now-lost hymn to the Communist Party, *Are You Ready, Comrade?* (produced 1938).

As the political climate shifted during World War II, plays remembered wartime sacrifices, such as Duncan's *Sons of the Morning* (1945), or appealed to nationalism in Oriel Gray's *Lawson* (produced 1944). DYMPHNA CUSACK, the most important female playwright in the mid-20th century, paid particular attention to women's experience of war and work. Later the Cold War and the war in Vietnam provided the impetus for the creation of satirical revues like Mona Brand's *Out of Commission* (produced 1955) and were exemplified by *On Stage Vietnam* (produced 1967) by Brand and Pat Barnett.

Many playwrights addressed the harshness of pioneering life and women's lives in rural Australia: Roland's *The Touch of Silk* (produced 1928), Henrietta Drake-Brockman's *Men Without Wives* (1938), and Prichard's *Brumby Innes* (produced 1927). Roland's *Granite Peak* (written 1952; never produced) was one of a number of plays whereby women questioned Australia's treatment of its Indigenous people; others included Gray's *Had We But World Enough* (produced 1948) and *Burst of Summer* (produced 1960), Brand's *Here Under Heaven* (produced 1948), and Nance McMillan's *The Painter* (produced 1960). Other plays looked outside Australia to comment on decolonization struggles in Asia, such as Brand's *Strangers in the Land* (produced 1952) and McMillan's *Christmas Bridge* (produced 1950), or on concerns about the nuclear threat, such as Cusack's *Pacific Paradise* (produced 1955). Some told stories of Australia's past, for example, Dorothy Blewett's *The First Joanna* (produced 1948), Catherine Shepherd's *Jane My Love* (produced 1951), and Gray's *The Torrents* (produced 1956).

A number of talented playwrights, such as Shepherd, earned a living writing radio plays; others, such as Lynn Foster, Kathleen Carroll, and most famously Gwen Meredith, wrote serial dramas. Meredith's plays include *Wives Have Their Uses* (produced 1938) and *Cornerstone* (produced 1955). She wrote two of the longest-running serials for Australian Broadcasting Commission radio: *The Lawsons* (1944–1949) and *Blue Hills* (1949–1976).

FURTHER READING

Arrow, Michelle. *Upstaged: Australian Women Dramatists in the Limelight at Last*. Sydney: Pluto Press and Currency, 2002.

O'Loughlin, Iris. "Four Australian Women Playwrights." *Australian Feminist Studies* 21 (Autumn 1995): 129–151.

Pfisterer, Susan. *Tremendous Worlds: Australian Women's Drama 1890–1960*. Sydney: Currency, 1999.

Pickett, Carolyn, and Susan Pfisterer. *Playing with Ideas: Australian Women Playwrights from the Suffragettes to the Sixties*. Sydney: Currency, 1999.

Michelle Arrow

WOMEN PLAYWRIGHTS, 1980–1990S

In the 1970s and 1980s women writers in Australia had limited access to mainstream theater production. In the 1990s their presence became more established, although their drama still represented no more than twenty percent of mainstream programs. Despite this limited access, plays written by women are among the most successful work produced by major Australian theater companies. Half the drama produced in smaller and community theaters is by women writers. Australian women playwrights, though a diverse grouping, have collectively made a significant contribution to the theatrical representation and examination of Australian life. Regardless of the breadth of differences in their styles of writing and preoccupations, there is an overriding commonality evident in the often humorous insights into human relationships.

Another distinguishing feature of women's writing in the 1980s and 1990s is that many women have not restricted themselves to one type of theater. Katherine Thomson is a multi-award-winning writer, and her plays include the comedy *Barmaids* (1991), the bleakly realist *Diving for Pearls* (1991), and the music-drama *Mavis Goes to Timor* (2002). The subject matter of Thomson's work is the experience of ordinary people as seen in their social and working lives. Strong characters are key features of her writing. Thomson writes for mainstream and smaller theaters and television.

Another award-winning woman playwright is Beatrix Christian. Her work is quirky and offers often blackly comic insights into human relationships. Christian's plays include *Blue Murder* (produced 1994), based on the Bluebeard fairy story; the comedy *Fred* (2000); and the historically based *The Governor's Family* (2001).

Novelist Tobsha Learner writes about relationships. She has made use of the monodrama form with her very successful *S.N.A.G.* (produced 1992); the title stands for "sensitive new age guy." Her plays include *Wolf* (1990) and *The Glass Mermaid* (1994). Like Christian, her work is a quirky examination of human relationships, and like Thomson, Learner has written for both smaller and mainstream stages.

Joanna Murray-Smith is noted for sparse, stylized dialogue and the close examination of human interactions within middle-class society. Her plays include *Love Child* (1994), *Honour* (1995), *Redemption* (1997), *Nightfall* (2002), and *Rapture* (2002). Murray-Smith has also written libretti for operas such as *Love in the Age of Therapy* (produced 2002).

The list of women playwrights making a substantial contribution to Australian theater is extensive. Sarah Hardy's plays include the award-winning *Vita!—A Fantasy* (1991) and *She of the Electrolux* (produced 1995). Heather Nimmo's works include *One Small Step* (1993) and *The Other Woman* (produced 1997). Jill Shearer's work includes *Shimada* (1992) and *Georgia* (1997). Some women writers have focused primarily on issues of equity and social justice, such as Melissa Reeves's *Road Movie* (1996) and Patricia Cornelius's *Platform* (produced 1998). The commitment to writing plays for a variety of audiences and theatrical forms is equally apparent in emerging women writers. This is demonstrated in work such as Catherine Zimdahl's *Clark in Sarajevo* (produced 1995) and Jodi Gallagher's *Elegy* (2000).

Cumulatively, these women represent a cross section of Australian women playwrights writing across a broad range of cultural and economic interests.

[*See also* Kemp, Jenny; Rayson, Hannie]

FURTHER READING

Fensham, Rachel, and Denise Varney. *The Doll's Revolution: Australian Theatre and the Cultural Imagination*. With Maryrose Casey and Laura Ginters. Melbourne: Australian Scholarly, 2005.

Gilbert, Helen. *Sightlines: Race, Gender and Nation in Contemporary Australian Theatre*. Ann Arbor: Univ. of Michigan Press, 1998.

Milne, Geoffrey. *Theatre Australia (Un)limited: Australian Theatre since the 1950s*. Amsterdam: Rodopi, 2004.

Tait, Peta. *Converging Realities: Feminism in Australian Theatre*. Sydney: Currency, 1992.

Tait, Peta, and Elizabeth Schafer, eds. *Australian Women's Drama*. Sydney: Currency, 1997.

Thomson, Helen. "Recent Australian Women's Writing for the Stage." In *Our Australian Theatre in the 1990s*, ed. by Veronica Kelly. Amsterdam: Rodopi, 1998.

Tompkins, Joanne, and Julie Holledge, eds. *Performing Women/Performing Feminisms: Interviews with International Women Playwrights*. Brisbane: Australasian Drama Studies Assoc., 1997.

Maryrose Casey

INDIGENOUS PERFORMANCE

Indigenous (Aboriginal) traditional song and dance performance expresses religious beliefs, and myths known as the Dream-time stories, from a culture going back 40,000 to 60,000 years. These performances are part of secret ceremonies and have traditional owners. Selected myths, however, are performed with permission in adaptations of traditional performance for public audiences. In a social context where Indigenous Australians have been marginalized and mistreated, contemporary Indigenous theater artists use nontraditional live performance to demonstrate their complex society, its history, and its survival. In the process they change the representations of Indigenous Australians and make a substantial contribution to Australian theater. Within their own communities, they have performed topical sketch comedy such as *Jack Charles Is Up and Fighting* (produced 1972), presenting the non-Indigenous audience with a different perspective on racism and colonization.

In the 1970s, dramas by Indigenous writers were produced by the first Indigenous-controlled theater companies, such as Nindethana in Melbourne and Black Theatre in Redfern, Sydney. They featured innovative explorations of form. Throughout the 1980s and 1990s Indigenous artists continued to push the boundaries in their theatrical practice. Mudrooroo's *Aboriginal Demonstrators Confront the Declaration of the Australian Republic on 26th January 2001 with the Production of Der Auftrag by Heiner Müller* (1993) frames and plays with HEINER MÜLLER's post-modern text. This layering of form and content in performance, drawing from the present and the past and different sources, continues. Shows such as *Bidenjarreb Pinjarra* (produced 1994), which tells the story of the Pinjarra massacre in Western Australia in 1834, are loosely scripted and improvised with the audience.

Indigenous-controlled theater companies have played a major role developing new work, exemplified by the Bangarra Dance Company, which mixes traditional and contemporary styles under the creative guidance of Steven and David Page. Companies such as Ilbijerri Aboriginal and Torres Strait Islanders' Theatre Co-operative in Melbourne, Kooemba Jdarra in Brisbane, and Yirra Yaakin in Perth have provided a forum whereby community stories can be translated into a theatrical context; productions include *King Hit* (1997), *Cruel Wild Woman* (produced 1997), and *Stolen* (1998). Sydney's Festival of the Dreaming in 1997 was the first of the Olympic Games Arts Festivals and featured work ranging from text-based performances such as *Up the Ladder* (1997) to Koori clowning troupes such as the Oogadee Boogadees, as well as classic texts such as William Shakespeare's *A Midsummer Night's Dream* with an all-Indigenous cast.

In the 1990s a major new development was in monologues, particularly by writer-performers, and include Ningali Lawford's award-winning show *Ningali* (produced 1994), Deborah Cheetham's *White Baptist Abba Fan* (produced 1997), well-known television performer Deborah Mailman's *The 7 Stages of Grieving* (1995), and Leah Purcell's *Box the Pony* (1997). These semibiographical texts use many of the elements that have marked Indigenous playwriting: storytelling, music and song, shifts in style and time, and use of Aboriginal languages. In the 2000s, work by Indigenous artists continues to expand and is encouraged by directors such as Wesley Enoch and Andrea James working in mainstream theaters.

FURTHER READING

Casey, Maryrose. "Performing Indigenous Women." *Hecate's Australian Women's Book Review* 11 (1999): 41–43.

——. *Creating Frames: Contemporary Indigenous Theatre 1967–97*. Brisbane: Univ. of Queensland Press, 2004.

Grehan, Helena. "Faction and Fusion in *The 7 Stages of Grieving*." *Theatre Research International* 26, no 1. (2001): 106–116.

Milne, Geoffrey. "The Festival of the Dreaming." *Australasian Drama Studies* 37 (October 2000): 27–39.

Thompson, Liz, ed. *Aboriginal Voices: Contemporary Aboriginal Artists, Writers and Performers*. Brookvale, New South Wales: Simon & Schuster, 1990.

Thomson, Helen. "Aboriginal Women's Staged Autobiography." In *Siting the Other: Revisions of Marginality in Australian and Canadian Drama*, ed., by Marc Maufort and Franca Bellarsi. Brussels: P. I. E.–Peter Lang, 2001.

Maryrose Casey

INDIGENOUS PLAYWRIGHTS

One of the main features of Indigenous (Aboriginal) playwriting is the use of multiple layers of storytelling within one text. In the 1970s, using explorations of form that combined song, dance, poetry, and dialogue, the first plays by Indigenous Australian playwrights to be produced outside Indigenous communities were primarily concerned with contemporary issues of survival from poverty and discrimination. Many playwrights are identified by the names of their regional communities. Works from Koori writers, such as Kevin Gilbert's *The Cherry Pickers* (written 1968, published 1988), Robert Merritt's *The Cake Man* (1977), Gerry Bostock's *Here Comes the Nigger* (1977), and from Nyoongah writers, such as JACK DAVIS's *Kullark* (1983), individually and collectively altered the range of representations of Indigenous Australians within drama. In doing so, they increased awareness of issues affecting Indigenous people and demonstrated their strong ongoing cultures. Faced with an overwhelming silence within the dominant Australian culture, they set out to tell collective stories.

In the 1980s the number of playwrights achieving prominence increased significantly, and the most acclaimed, Nyoongah Jack Davis, wrote his major works. Another Nyoongah playwright is Richard Walley, and his works include *Coordah* (1988) and *Munjong* (produced 1990). Plays from Koori writers include Jimmy Everett's *Cultural Lesson* (produced 1987) and Bill Bennett's *Backlash* (produced 1987). From Murri writers there is work such as Roger Bennett's *Up the Ladder* (first performed 1989). Bob Maza wrote *Mereki* (produced 1986) and *The Keepers* (1988). Eva Johnson, of the Mulak Mulak people, presented the first Indigenous woman's perspective with her play *Murras* (produced 1988).

With each decade the range of subjects explored within the plays has broadened. The plays of the 1980s built on the foundation established in the 1970s, expanding the types of stories from collective and historical stories to individual and autobiographical stories. In the 1990s a new generation of Indigenous writers began developing these themes further. In the eastern states, Koori writers such as John Harding with *Up the Road* (1997) and *Enuff* (2002) and Goori writer Ray Kelly with *Get Up and Dance* (produced 1989) and *Somewhere in the Darkness* (produced 1996) present and explore the problems facing young Indigenous men. In central Australia, Merrill Bray's *Mechanics of the Spirit* (produced 1994) presents the issues facing many young Indigenous women. In Western Australia, Jimmy Chi's *Bran Nue Dae* (1990) used the musical form to explore the search for identity. Other writers such as Jane Harrison explore new ways to tell collective stories in work such as *Stolen* (1997). Melodie Gibson explores the possibilities of violent action in *Uprising* (produced 1997).

In the 1990s and 2000s, new work also explores themes with wide social relevance. Jimmy Chi's *Corrugation Road* (produced 1995) focuses on the experience of mental illness. In Ningali Lawford and Kelton Pell's *Solid* (produced 2000), attention is focused on the ways in which Aboriginal people relate to each other. Jadah Milroy's *Crowfire* (2002) and Richard J. Frankland's *Conversations with the Dead* (2002) deal with the continuing injustices Indigenous people suffer and the struggle for identity and dignity.

FURTHER READING

Casey, Maryrose. "From Wings to Centre Stage." *Australasian Drama Studies* (October 2000): 85–98.

——. *Creating Frames: Contemporary Indigenous Theatre 1967–97*. St. Lucia, Brisbane: Univ. of Queensland Press, 2004.

Davis, Jack, and Bob Hodge, eds. *Aboriginal Writing Today*. Canberra: Australian Institute of Aboriginal Studies, 1985.

Gilbert, Helen. *Sightlines: Race, Gender and Nation in Contemporary Australian Theatre*. Ann Arbor: Univ. of Mich. Press, 1998.

Milne, Geoffrey. "Black and White in Australian Drama." *Meridian* 9, no. 1. (1990): 33–44.

Saunders, Justine, ed. *Plays from Black Australia*. Sydney: Currency, 1989.

Shoemaker, Adam. *Black Words, White Page: Aboriginal Literature 1929–1988*. St. Lucia, Brisbane: Univ. of Queensland Press, 1989.

Maryrose Casey

MULTICULTURAL IDENTITIES IN DRAMA

Multicultural drama in Australia focuses on exploring racial and ethnic identities of migrants from most countries in the world now living in Australia. Its aim is not to present a static idea of cultures of origin but to highlight the ways in which people negotiate cultural diversity and national belonging. Multicultural drama has undergone considerable changes since its emergence in the 1970s and 1980s. Early work focused on the experiences of first-generation migrants and utilized techniques such as multiple languages, storytelling, humor, playing with stereotypes and mistranslation, and a concern with preserving or recuperating the idea of home. More recent work in the 1990s, which is often created by second-generation and third-generation migrants, is more diverse in terms of form and content and extends earlier techniques by drawing from a range of genres and styles. These include fragmented or multiple narratives, singing, dance, acrobatics, stand-up comedy, and multimedia.

Since the 1980s, Doppio Teatro, the professional Italo-Australian theater group, has focused on the difficulties of living between two cultures that many first-generation Italian migrants experienced. Key multicultural writers of the 1990s include Tes Lyssiotis, Noelle Janacweska, and William Yang. Lyssiotis's plays deal with generational shifts, the complexity of belonging, and mother-daughter relationships. Her trilogy composed of *A White Sports Coat*, *The Forty Lounge Café*, and *Blood Moon* (1996) centers on three generations of women in one Greek family affected by migration from Greece to Australia. In the most important, *The Forty Lounge Café*, Elefteria, a young Greek migrant, experiences the difficulties associated with achieving a sense of home in a new land. Lyssiotis plays with language within the text, employing broken English and Greek to highlight the complexity of translation and mistranslation. Noelle Janacweska's *Historia* (1997) documents the search for identity in a shifting landscape of cultures and histories. Through the homosexual love affairs of an anthropologist (based on Bronislaw Malinowski) and an artist, and of Zoe and Zosia, issues of identity, technology, and sexuality emerge in an experimental and poetic play with sparse and poignant language. William Yang's *Sadness* (1996) depicts, through the juxtaposition of photography and storytelling, his experiences of growing up in a remote region of Australia and coming to terms with both his sexuality and his identity and heritage as Australian Chinese.

Multicultural drama has played an important role in Australia's cultural maturation by representing a range of stories that had previously been silenced or marginalized. Plays emerging in the 2000s that deal with multicultural concerns include Anna Yen's *Chinese Take Away* (2000), Indija Mahjoeddin's *The Butterfly Seer* (2000), Binh Duy Ta's *The Monkey Mother* (2000), and Duong Le Quy's *Meat Party* (2000). These works present rich nonstereotypical stories of mostly second-generation migrants. While still concerned with issues of identity and cultural diversity, current works tend to focus less on storytelling and negotiating ideas about home countries than on the intersections of class, race, and representation in the lives of young Australians with access to diverse racial and ethnic heritages.

FURTHER READING

Batchelor, Don, ed. *Three Plays by Asian Australians*. Queensland: PlayLab Press/Queensland Univ. of Technology, 2000.

Gilbert, Helen. *Sightlines: Race, Gender, and Nation in Contemporary Australian Theatre*. Ann Arbor: Univ. of Michigan Press, 1998.

Grehan, Helena. *Mapping Cultural Identity in Contemporary Australian Performance*. Brussels: P. I. E.–Peter Lang, 2001.

Lo, Jacqueline. "Beyond Happy Hybridity: Performing Asian-Australian Identities." In *Alter/Asians: Asian-Australian Identities in Art, Media and Popular Culture*, ed. by Ien Ang et al. New South Wales: Pluto Press, 2000.

Lyssiotis, Tes. *A White Sportscoat & Other Plays*. Sydney: Currency, 1996.

Mitchell, Tony. "Maintaining Cultural Integrity: Teresa Crea, Doppio Teatro, Italo-Australian Theatre and Critical Multiculturalism." In *Our Australian Theatre in the 1990s*, ed. by Veronica Kelly. Amsterdam: Rodopi, 1998.

Pickett, Carolyn. " 'The Past Is Here': An Interview with Tes Lyssiotis." *Australasian Drama Studies* 28 (1996): 79–85.

Tompkins, Joanne. "Inter-referentiality: Interrogating Multicultural Australian Drama." In *Our Australian Theatre in the 1990s*, ed. by Veronica Kelly. Amsterdam: Rodopi, 1998.

Helena Grehan

AUSTRIA

Any discussion of Austrian drama from the latter part of the 19th century to the end of the 20th necessarily entails examining a political, geographical, and cultural entity—Austria—and a literary form—drama—that have undergone significant transformations in the process of modernization. The small, largely alpine, politically stable, and seemingly politically insignificant Second Republic of Austria was established at the end of World War II. Located in the heart of Central Europe, contemporary Austria consists of 32,374 square miles (83,848 sq km) and is home to approximately 8 million predominantly German-speaking people. In the 1860s, in contrast, Austria constituted the political and cultural center of the vast Habsburg Empire, a powerful multiethnic and multilingual entity that stretched from Lake Constance in the west to beyond Lemberg (Lvov) in the east, from above Prague in the north to below Dubrovnik in the south. The lands of the empire encompassed more than 260,000 square miles (673,397 sq km), within which lived 53 million people speaking 15 different languages. In addition to the Austro-Germans, the population of the Habsburg Empire included Czechs, Slovaks, Slovenes, Croats, Serbs, Italians, Magyars, Romanians, Ruthenians, and Poles.

The traumas and dislocations of two world wars transformed Austria from the center of a great empire (one of the Habsburgs once remarked that the empire is so large that the sun is always shining on at least one part of it) to a relatively peripheral "rump nation." In the course of the 20th century, these transformations have been accompanied by two significant historical myths. Looking back on the lost imperial grandeur of the Habsburg monarchy, many have come to idealize the empire as a harmonious multiethnic state (*Vielvölkerstaat*), thus overlooking the divisive ethnic and national conflicts that played a crucial role in the empire's demise. More recently, in the aftermath of World War II, political officials of the Second Austrian Republic, aided by the Allies' 1943 Moscow Declaration, were more than willing to propagate the myth of Austria as the "first victim" of Nazi aggression. Since both of these myths have found various forms of critical representation in Austrian fiction, we can thus dispel yet another pervasive Austrian myth: that the country's literature, including its significant contributions to the development of modern drama, is essentially escapist and apolitical.

THE RISE OF MODERN AUSTRIAN DRAMA AND THE FALL OF AN EMPIRE

The emergence of modern drama in Austria and Vienna's development into a modern metropolis both coincide with the unraveling and eventual end of the Habsburg Empire. Ironically, it was precisely Vienna's relative backwardness in the middle of the 19th century that enabled it to become a vibrant center of cultural modernity by century's end, home to such important modernists as painter Gustav Klimt (1862–1918), composer Arnold Schönberg (1874–1951), architect Otto Wagner (1841–1918), and psychoanalyst Sigmund Freud (1856–1939). The glacis, a large tract of undeveloped land encircling the city center and physically separating it from Vienna's suburbs, had been used until mid-century for both recreational and military purposes. Despite all assertions and appearances to the contrary, the military might of the imperial army continued to decline, and in 1866 the army suffered a devastating defeat by the Prussians at the Battle of Königgrätz. As a result, Austria forever lost its long-held place as the dominant power in German-speaking Europe. To counteract such losses, to reaffirm the grandeur of the monarchy and its capital city, and in anticipation of hosting a world's fair in 1873, large-scale development of the glacis began. Vienna's Ring (Ringstraße), the grand boulevard that served to connect the city center with its outer areas, thus took shape, expanding both the city's boundaries and its architectural character. While the baroque nature of the inner city was preserved, the imposing representational buildings strategically located along the Ring were constructed in a variety of architectural styles, a historicist attempt to match form and function. The Ring became the site of such important buildings as the new Parliament, constructed in Greek style, the new University (Renaissance), the State Opera House (early Renaissance), and Vienna's City Hall (Gothic). Across the Ring from City Hall, the Burgtheater (Imperial Theater) was built, with its early baroque style commemorating, according to Carl E. Schorske (1979), "the era in which theater first joined together cleric, courtier, and commoner in a shared aesthetic enthusiasm." To this day, the Viennese Burgtheater maintains its position as one of the most prestigious stages in the German-speaking world.

The birth of modern drama in Germany, and in Berlin in particular, is largely synonymous with the breakthrough of literary NATURALISM. To be sure, naturalism had its practitioners in Austria as well, the most prominent of whom was the poet, short-story writer, and playwright Karl Schönherr (1867–1943). Born in Tirol, Schönherr came to Vienna to study medicine. He remained in the capital city, working as a doctor and a writer. Despite spending his adult life largely in the urban metropolis, Schönherr situates many of his plays in alpine milieux. Dramas such as *The Woodcarvers* (*Die Bildschnitzer*), which premiered at Vienna's Deutsches Volkstheater (German Popular Theater) in 1900, and *Solstice Day* (*Sonnwendtag*), first performed at the Burgtheater in 1902, typify Schönherr's representation of politically and economically oppressed peasants speaking in Tirolean dialect. His attention to questions of local color and regional speech evidence his naturalist tendencies, as does his concern for the sociopolitically disadvantaged. At the same time, such qualities also signify Schönherr's general affinity with the tradition of the Austrian VOLKSSTÜCK (popular drama) and with the dramas of Ludwig Anzengruber (1839–1889) in particular. In the early 1870s, Anzengruber enjoyed great success with a series of *Volksstücke* depicting rural life: *The Parish Priest of Kirchfeld* (*Der Pfarrer von Kirchfeld*, 1870); *The Farmer Forsworn* (*Der Meineidbauer*, 1871); *They Signed with Three Crosses* (*Die Kreuzelschreiber*, 1872); and *The Worm of Conscience* (*Der G'wissenswurm*, 1874).

While the majority of Schönherr's dramas have contemporary settings, he also wrote a number of historical plays. His first drama, *Judas of Tirol* (*Der Judas von Tirol*), premiered in 1897 and depicts the betrayal of Andreas Hofer (1767–1810), the Tirolean patriot who was eventually executed on orders from Napoleon Bonaparte. Set amid the struggle for Tirolean independence in the early 19th century, the play interestingly focuses not on the folk-hero Hofer but rather on his down-and-out countryman Franz Raffl. *Faith and Fireside* (*Glaube und Heimat*), first performed at Vienna's Deutsches Volkstheater in 1910, also focuses on political struggles in Tirol, although from an earlier era. The play takes place during the Counter Reformation and valorizes those Tiroleans who bravely defy foreign authorities for the sake of their religious and political beliefs. The play is noteworthy in the development of both Schönherr's work and Austrian drama in that it constitutes a departure from the determinism informing naturalist dramaturgy.

Schönherr's plays explicitly represent important periods in Tirolean history, but they can also be read in terms of more contemporaneous events, such as the increased demands by the various ethnic groups within the empire for greater political freedom and autonomy. Schönherr's final drama, *The Flag Is Waving* (*Die Fahne weht*, 1937), again takes up the theme of Tirolean resistance to French occupation. The drama contains a number of passages comparing Napoleon to Adolf Hitler and thus functions as a protest against the impending annexation of Austria by Nazi Germany.

Schönherr's naturalist dramas made a significant mark upon the Austrian stage, and his works continue to be periodically performed today. However, it was the group of writers known as Jung-Wien (Young Vienna) that collectively created what has become canonized as a quintessentially Viennese form of modern literature. The Young Vienna group regularly met at the Café Griensteidl, a traditional Viennese coffeehouse located in the heart of the city close to the imperial Habsburg palace. Members included Peter Altenberg (1859–1919; born Richard Engländer), Raoul Auernheimer (1876–1948), Hermann Bahr (1863–1934), Richard Beer-Hofmann (1866–1945), Felix Dörmann (1870–1928; born Felix Biedermann), Hugo von Hofmannsthal (1874–1929), Karl Kraus (1874–1936), Felix Salten (1869–1945; born Siegmund Salzmann), and ARTHUR SCHNITZLER.

Altenberg authored a large number of literary sketches and is considered by many to be the epitome of the turn-of-the-century coffeehouse bohemian. Having twice interrupted his university studies (initially law, subsequently medicine), he eventually found a doctor to attest to his "oversensitive nervous system" and thus his inability to work. Altenberg combined a strict vegetarian diet with excessive consumption of alcohol and pills. Salten, who immigrated to Switzerland in 1939, is best known to American readers as the author of *Bambi* (1923); in the German-speaking world he is primarily known as the author of *Josefine Mutzenbacher* (1906), a novel that chronicles the life and work of a Viennese prostitute. Dörmann wrote novels, novellas, libretti, and two dramas—*Single People* (*Ledige Leute*, 1897) and *Lodgers* (*Zimmerherren*, 1900). He played an important role in the emerging Austrian film industry by founding the Vindobona-Film company ("Vindobona" was the name the Romans gave to their encampment in what is now the city of Vienna) and working as a film producer until the outbreak of World War I.

The spokesperson for the Young Vienna group was clearly Hermann Bahr, a prolific author whose works include numerous novels, multiple volumes of essays, studies in theater history, and 34 dramas. Having worked in a variety of literary genres, Bahr's involvement with the theater was similarly multifaceted. His plays include comedies (e.g., *The Domestic Woman* [*Die häusliche Frau*, 1893] and *The Concert* [*Das Konzert*, 1909]); dramas representing issues of women's emancipation (*The Fool* [*Das Tschaperl*, 1898]) and indicting political corruption and incompetence (*The Apostle* [*Der Apostel*, 1901]); and a satire (*The Monster* [*Der Unmensch*, 1919]) of social conditions in the immediate aftermath of World War I. In addition to writing his own plays, Bahr spent a considerable amount of time reviewing those of others. Bahr's commentaries on the theater of his time are contained in the volumes *Wiener Theater: 1892–1898* (*Viennese Theater, 1892–1898*, 1899); *Premièren: Winter 1900 bis Sommer 1901* (*Premieres: Winter 1900 to Summer 1901*, 1902); *Rezensionen* (*Reviews*, 1903); and *Glossen zum Wiener Theater* (*Glosses on the Viennese Theater*, 1907). His *Burgtheater* (1920) stresses the importance of Austria's baroque tradition in the theater, and *Die Schauspielkunst* (*The Art of Acting*, 1923) reiterates his frequently articulated claim that the actor is the most important element in the theater. Bahr served as an adviser to Max Burckhardt (1854–1912), the director of the Burgtheater in the 1890s; worked with director MAX REINHARDT, from 1906 to 1908; and in 1918 was appointed director of the Burgtheater for six months at the end of World War I.

The so-called *Mann von übermorgen* (man of the day after tomorrow), Bahr contributed to the development of Austrian drama in a variety of ways. His greatest contribution, however, lies not in any particular play, review, or directorial post but, rather, in his unceasing efforts to champion the cause of modernity. Criticized as a shallow chameleon by his detractors and hailed as the consummate modernist by his supporters, Bahr worked as a cultural entrepreneur and aesthetic advocate on behalf of three important modernist movements: naturalism, impressionism, and EXPRESSIONISM. (In contrast to Germany, Austria produced relatively few expressionist playwrights, the most famous of whom is painter and author OSKAR KOKOSCHKA. Kokoschka played a pivotal role in the rise of expressionist drama owing to his "Viennese trilogy": *Sphinx and Strawman* [*Sphinx und Strohmann*, 1907]; *Murderer, Hope of Women* [*Mörder, Hoffnung der Frauen*, 1909]; and *The Burning Bush* [*Der brennende Dornbusch*, 1911].)

Bahr lived in Berlin from 1889 to 1890, just as naturalism was beginning to assert itself on the German stage. In the German capital, Bahr became acquainted with such major figures of the naturalist movement as GERHART HAUPTMANN, Arno Holz (1863–1929), and OTTO BRAHM, and Bahr expresses his enthusiasm for naturalism in his essay "Zur Kritik der Moderne" (On the Critique of Modernity, 1890). Bahr ultimately tried to challenge Brahm for the editorship of *Freie Bühne* (Free Stage), a journal devoted to promoting naturalist drama and theater. When that challenge failed, Bahr went briefly to Russia, whence he returned to Vienna and began to champion the cause of literary impressionism.

In 1891 Bahr completed his essay "Die Überwindung des Naturalismus" (The Overcoming of Naturalism), at the outset of which he programmatically declares: "The supremacy of Naturalism is over, its role has been played out, its spell broken." Bahr calls for a new form of modernity, one commensurate with his understanding of "modern man." "When Classicism says 'man,' it means reason and feeling," Bahr contends. "And when Romanticism says 'man,' it means passion and the senses. And when Modernism says 'man,' it means the nerves." Bahr advocates a "nervous Romanticism," one that would reject naturalism's slavish reproduction of external reality and focus instead on the subjective and inner realms.

Bahr's impressionist polemics imply a turn away from the tenets of Marxism and Darwinism, important underpinnings of naturalism, and a move toward literary appropriation of the theories of Sigmund Freud and scientist Ernst Mach (1838–1916). Abandoning naturalism's emphasis on biological determinism and the socioeconomic conditioning of the individual, impressionist writers sought to give literary expression to Freud's examination of the unconscious and the sexual drives that animate and plague it. Freud's social scientific explorations into the workings and constitution of the self found a corollary in the natural sciences in the writings of Mach, a physicist who, in the course of his career, held university positions in Graz, Prague, and Vienna. Mach developed his critical positivism in such works as *Die Analyse der Empfindungen und das Verhältnis des Physischen zum Psychischen* (*The Analysis of Sensations and the Relation of the Physical to the Psychical*, 1900) and *Erkenntnis und Irrtum. Skizzen zur Psychologie der Forschung* (*Knowledge and Error: Sketches on the Psychology of Enquiry*, 1906). Of particular importance to literary impressionism is Mach's contention that everything we know about the world is derived from and can be reduced to elements of sensation. These elements, in turn, exist in a state of constant flux, forever combining and recombining themselves in interdependent relationships with other elements. Hence, according to Mach, there can be no point of view that has absolute validity, no such thing as a false perception, and no right or wrong. Similarly, Mach posits that there is no such thing as a fixed and stable ego. His dictum "Das Ich ist unrettbar!" (The ego is unsalvageable!) was enthusiastically greeted by impressionist authors who shared Mach's belief in the fluidity of the ego and his desire to reclaim the immediacy of experience.

The moral relativism underlying Mach's work and Freud's preoccupation with Eros and Thanatos find particularly lively expression in the dramas of Arthur Schnitzler. Schnitzler's cast of highly memorable characters includes Anatol, the title figure of a work completed in 1891. An egotistical *Augenblicksmensch* (man of the moment), Anatol proceeds from one superficial relationship to another, unable to make any kind of real or lasting connection. The rapid exchange of partners in the search for physical gratification propels the plot in Schnitzler's *Reigen* (1896–1897) as well. The drama consists of a series of ten dialogues—between types drawn from all of Vienna's social classes, from the soldier and the whore to the young bourgeois wife and the count—that culminate in sexual intercourse. The male partner from scene 1 reappears with a different female partner in scene 2, who, in turn, is featured with another male partner in scene 3, until the circle is completed in scene 10, when the female partner of scene 1 reappears with a different man. A modernist take on the medieval dance of death, it would appear in *Reigen* as if sex, and not death, were the great leveler. Yet this is not completely the case. While all of the characters are united in their lust for sexual activity, Schnitzler simultaneously differentiates them by levels of language, for example, and by the degree to which they do or do not respect social conventions in their pursuit of sexual gratification.

The seemingly endless recombination of partners in these plays gives dramatic expression to Mach's notion of elements in a state of constant flux. Indeed, the episodic structure of impressionist drama stands in sharp contrast to the naturalist attempt to represent a specific external milieu as comprehensively as possible. The action of Hauptmann's BEFORE DAYBREAK (*Vor Sonnenaufgang*, 1889), for instance, is restricted to a period of hours in and around one particular household, and the stage directions provide extensive details concerning the appearance of the characters and their setting. The Silesian peasants speak Silesian dialect; the more educated characters speak standard High German. The drama's five acts are nowhere divided into smaller scenes, and the rigid ethical and biological beliefs of the protagonist ultimately compel him to abandon the woman he loves once he discovers that although she herself is not an alcoholic, many members of her family are. In Schnitzler's *Undiscovered Country* (*Das weite Land*, 1910), in contrast, the settings are much more expansive and the time between acts much less defined. An extensive array of characters all speak standard German, whether they are in a fashionable spa town in the vicinity of Vienna or high in the Tirolean Alps. Each of the drama's five acts is broken down into a series of smaller scenes, with scene changes typically marked by a reconfiguration of speakers. Games of tennis, both literal and metaphoric, serve to underscore the casual way in which adulterous affairs begin and end in the play, seemingly without consequence. Indeed, the self-absorbed protagonist, Friedrich Hofreiter, a wealthy factory owner, cannot comprehend how his wife's sense of virtue could actually prohibit her from having an affair with a man to whom she feels attracted. Doctor Aigner's explanation of how he was able to commit adultery despite his profound love for his wife echoes Freud, Mach, and the impressionists in its conception of the human psyche and its implications for interpersonal relationships: "So much coexisits within us—! Love and betrayal . . . fidelity and infidelity. . . . While we may try to create internal order as best we can, that order is simply artificial. . . . The natural thing . . . is chaos."

As Schnitzler and his fellow impressionists continued their dramatic investigations into the chaotic state of human affairs, the chaotic state of the Habsburg Empire was entering its final phase. Despite the unifying force of Kaiser Franz Joseph (1830–1916), escalating ethnic and national conflicts and an outmoded bureaucracy unable and/or unwilling to respond to the demands for greater democracy plunged the empire—and the continent—into World War I. Assurances of a swift and certain Habsburg victory were soon dashed, and the casualties of the "Great War," including the end of over 600 years of Habsburg rule, were far greater than anyone was able to imagine at the war's outset.

THE DRAMA OF INTERWAR AUSTRIA

Following the end of World War I, the vast territory of the Habsburg Empire was carved up to form a number of nation-states, largely, although not exclusively, along linguistic lines. Karl, the last Habsburg emperor, abdicated in November 1918, and in the following year, the imperial family immigrated to Switzerland. The former Habsburg crown lands were ceded to Czechoslovakia, Poland, Romania, and Yugoslavia, and the Austrian province of South Tirol was given to Italy. According to French foreign minister Georges Clemenceau (1841–1929), "L'Autriche, c'est ce qui reste" (Austria, that is what is left over); it was a rump nation soon to be known as "the state that no one wanted."

Given the immense loss of human and natural resources resulting from the breakup of the empire, many Austrians questioned the political and economic survivability of a small, independent Austria. Hence, the founding of the First Austrian Republic in the aftermath of World War I was accompanied by calls from leading politicians and from substantial segments of the population for a union with Germany. This desire was explicitly expressed in the name "Deutsch-Österreich" (German-Austria) and in the constitution of the new republic. Article 1 read, "German-Austria is a democratic republic," while Article 2 stated, "German-Austria is a constituent part of the German Republic." The victors of World War I, however, fearing the political consequences of a strong Greater Germany, expressly forbade such a union. According to the terms of the Treaty of St. Germain, the peace treaty negotiated with Austria and reluctantly signed by the Austrian delegation on September 10, 1919, the new nation was simply to be called "Austria," and any union between it and Germany was strictly prohibited.

The political and economic instability that many feared would plague the new republic in fact soon came to characterize it. Hyperinflation and significant unemployment debilitated the interwar economy. The ideologically rigid "camp mentality" of Austria's major political parties, the proliferation of parties on the Radical Right, and a growing desire for a return to the imperial grandeur of the past severely undermined the nascent republic. In light of all of the political uncertainty, the dramas of ÖDÖN VON HORVÁTH (author of TALES FROM THE VIENNA WOODS) asked just how long and to what extent the fragile and flawed interwar democracy would survive. Horváth sought to revitalize the tradition of the *Volksstück* in the 1920s and 1930s, advocating a socially critical form of theater supported by the broad masses.

The title character in Horváth's *Sladek or The Black Army* (*Sladek oder Die schwarze Armee*, 1928) is young, poorly educated, and unemployed. Unable to find his way among the social and economic upheavals following World War I and incapable of imagining peace, Sladek ultimately joins the "Black Army," an underground organization of the extreme Right. Membership in the group, Sladek hopes, will provide him with a sense of belonging and a way to overcome his social alienation. In the end, however, Sladek becomes just another victim of the brutal Black Army, while the republic is further undermined by a judiciary and military that refuse to acknowledge the acute political threats emanating from the Right.

Horváth's *The Italian Evening* (*Italiensiche Nacht*, 1930) dramatizes the ineffectual pseudodemocratic activities of the "Republikanischer Schutzverband" (Association for the Preservation of the Republic), a group supposedly committed to defending the republic against the growing fascist threat. But instead of formulating and executing an effective plan of political action, the members of the association appear incapable of political solidarity. Although better educated than the likes of Sladek, association members spend most of their time drinking beer, playing cards, and spouting Marxist rhetoric and Freudian jargon. Intent on denouncing each other's imagined psychosexual "perversions," they thereby fail to address the real perversion of social democracy confronting them. The group's shortsightedness and petty infighting serve only to splinter an already weak political organization even further, thus strengthening the position of the fascists.

An unwavering commitment to strengthen democracy and counteract fascism also informs the work of Jura Soyfer (1912–1939), who was born in what is now the Ukrainian city of Kharkov. Soyfer's parents were Russian Jews; his father, a wealthy businessman, decided the family should flee the Bolshevik Revolution. Emigrating via Georgia and Turkey, the family settled in Vienna in the early 1920s. A committed Socialist, Soyfer experienced firsthand the far-reaching social welfare programs instituted by Vienna's "red" interwar city government, programs that included extensive municipal housing projects. At the same time, he also witnessed the undermining of those very programs by both the Austro-fascists and the Nazis. Deeply disappointed by the inability of the Austrian Socialists to offer an effective opposition to Austro-fascist dictator Engelbert Dollfuß (1892–1934) and his call for a "social, Christian, German state of Austria organized on a corporate basis with strong authoritarian leadership," Soyfer joined the outlawed Austrian Communist Party following the Austrian Civil War in 1934.

As a political journalist, Soyfer called for international solidarity, attacked the Austro-fascists, and warned against both the Austrian and German Nazi parties. These same tendencies inform his six dramas, five of which have been preserved: *The End of the World* (*Der Weltuntergang*, 1936); *Trip to Paradise* (*Der Lechner Edi schaut ins Paradies*, 1936); *Astoria* (1937); *Vineta* (1937); and *Broadway Melody 1492* (*Broadway-Melodie 1492*, 1937). During his lifetime, Soyfer's plays were performed not in Vienna's large venues such as the Burgtheater or Volkstheater but rather in what was then the city's thriving *Kleinkunstbühnen* (little theaters), in particular the ABC and Literatur am Naschmarkt. Such venues, located in the basements of coffeehouses, typically seated no more than 49 spectators and offered politically oppositional fare. The performers were either Austrian actors who had lost their jobs during the Depression or German actors who fled to Austria in the early years of the Nazi regime.

Broadway Melody 1492 is an adaptation of *Christopher Columbus or the Discovery of America* (*Christoph Kolumbus oder die Entdeckung Amerikas*, 1932), by WALTER HASENCLEVER and Kurt Tucholsky (1890–1935). In Soyfer's version, the Spanish conquest of America serves as a metaphor for the Nazi "conquest" of Austria. Soyfer himself never saw this play performed. Three days before its premiere in November 1937, Soyfer was arrested by the Austrian secret police and imprisoned three blocks from the theater in which *Broadway Melody 1492* was playing to great audience acclaim. Soyfer was released in February 1938 as part of a general amnesty for political prisoners. His freedom, however, did not last long. On March 12, 1938, German troops marched into Austria and not a single shot was fired. Three days later, greeted by hundreds of thousands of cheering Austrians in Vienna's Heldenplatz (Heroes' Square), Hitler proclaimed Austria as the newest bastion of the Third Reich. The incorporation of Austria into Greater Germany, which so many Austrians had wanted in 1918, had finally come to pass.

Soyfer, meanwhile, tried to flee across the border to Switzerland on March 13, 1938, but was arrested and immediately sent to the concentration camp in Dachau, Germany. Six months later he was transferred to Buchenwald, where he died of typhoid fever on February 16, 1939, a few days after his release for emigration had been granted.

STAGING HISTORY IN AUSTRIA'S SECOND REPUBLIC

In 1943, four years after World War II began and two years before its conclusion, the Allies issued the Moscow Declaration in which they identified Austria as the "first victim" of Nazi Germany's war of aggression. The Allied pronouncement was intended, in part, to strengthen the small but committed Austrian resistance movement, which did not grow significantly as a result. At the same time, the Allies were also looking to the future, and their declaration provided a means for differentiating Germany and Austria in the post–World War II political landscape. To be sure, there were Austrians who actively opposed national socialism, many of whom paid for their opposition with their lives. But to declare Austria the "first victim" of Nazism constitutes a significant historical distortion and ignores the large number of Austrians who actively and willfully participated in the National Socialist regime.

The myth of Austrian victimization provided a convenient escape hatch for the nation's citizens. It enabled them to evade their ethical and historical responsibilities and supplied the necessary precondition for creating a postwar Austrian identity that was distinctly anti-German, that is, anti-Nazi. Indeed, during the initial decades of the Second Republic, public officials repeatedly invoked the Moscow Declaration's useful half-truth in their attempts to reconstitute Austria as a political and cultural nation. The representation of Austria as first victim figured prominently in the proclamation of Austrian independence from Nazi Germany issued on May 1, 1945. Similarly, the Austrian State Treaty of 1955, which reestablished the country's sovereignty and resulted in the complete withdrawal of all occupying troops, also includes, in the preamble, a revised version of the myth of Austrian innocence. History finally caught up with the Second Republic, however, during the presidential election campaign of 1986, when Kurt Waldheim (born 1918), the former secretary general of the United Nations (1971–1981), ran for the largely ceremonial presidency as the candidate of the Austrian People's Party. Having previously remained silent about his activities in the German Wehrmacht, Waldheim, in the course of the campaign, was accused, among other things, of having participated in Nazi atrocities in the Balkans. The presidential election thus exploded into numerous national and international controversies, and for the first time on a large-scale basis, Austrians were forced to confront and acknowledge the nation's fascist past.

Long before the "Waldheim Affair" erupted, however, Austrian dramatists had presented a number of nuanced and critical depictions of the nation's recent history. Fritz Hochwälder (1911–1986), whose parents were murdered in the Nazi concentration camp in Treblinka, immigrated to Switzerland in 1938, where he remained until his death. Highly influenced by the traditions of the Viennese Volkstheater (popular theater), Hochwälder's plays examine such issues as exile (*The Fugitive* [*Der Flüchtling*, 1944]), the power of the state, and those who simply follow its orders (*The Holy Experiment* [*Das heilige Experiment*, 1942] and *The Public Prosecutor* [*Der öffentliche Ankläger*, 1948]). Hochwälder's popular comedy *The Raspberry Picker* (*Der Himbeerpflücker*, 1964) is his most explicit treatment of Austria's Nazi past. Set in the town of Bad Brauning (symbolizing the Austrian town of Braunau, Hitler's birthplace), the play unmasks the continuing devotion to Nazism among the community's leading citizens, who owe their postwar prosperity to the gold removed from concentration camp prisoners' teeth.

The most vituperative critic of postwar Austria and its fascist past is surely THOMAS BERNHARD (author of EVE OF RETIREMENT). Dubbed the "Alpine Beckett," Bernhard wrote a great number of tragicomic plays in which the emotional, social, and political deformations resulting from an unexamined legacy of national socialism (deformations frequently represented in terms of physical disabilities) play a crucial role. Through long and highly theatrical monologues, Bernhard's characters expose the deceit and duplicity lying at the core of postwar Austrian identity. Bernhard's final play, HELDENPLATZ (1988), caused such a scandal before its premiere that the author became the subject of parliamentary debates as well as the object of death threats.

The works of ELFRIEDE JELINEK have also elicited strong reactions from contemporary Austrian audiences. Jelinek's aesthetic and social critiques are often aimed at undermining the "Austrian ideology" from a feminist point of view. Her dramas, such as *What Happened after Nora Left Her Husband: or Pillars of Society* (*Was geschah, nachdem Nora ihren Mann verlassen hatte. oder Stützen der Gesellschaft*, 1979) and *Clara S.: A Musical Tragedy* (*Clara S. Musikalische Tragödie*, 1982), frequently examine the historical exclusion of women from the production of culture in the public sphere. The complicity of Austria's premiere theatrical institution with the National Socialist regime is the subject of Jelinek's *Burgtheater* (1985). Her most recent drama to date, *The Work* (*Das Werk*, 2003), combines postmodernist spectacle with documentary materials from postwar Austria to dramatize the political issues surrounding the building of a hydroelectric power station in alpine Kaprun in the 1950s, a massive and costly undertaking intended to signal unequivocally Austria's postwar reconstruction.

The widespread revival of the *Volksstück* tradition that began in the 1960s and 1970s has provided another important means for representing issues of Austrian history. PETER TURRINI's *Swine* (*Sauschlachten*, 1971) dramatizes fatal continuities between the Third Reich and the postwar republic, while his *Alpine Glow* (*Alpenglühen*, 1992) examines the role and power of the theater in a society in which history has become completely mythologized. Another *Volksstück* dramatist, Tirolean Felix Mitterer frequently bases his plays on actual historical events. Mitterer's *There's Not a Finer Country* (*Kein schöner Land*, 1987) documents the rise of fascism in a Tirolean village, highlighting political splits within families and the ways in which the villagers willingly betray their neighbors to the Nazis. Mitterer's *In the Lion's Den* (*In der Löwengrube*, 1998) dramatizes the story of Leo Reuss, a Jewish actor fired from the theater in the early years of the Nazi regime who then returns to the stage by adopting the identity of an "Aryan" Tirolean farmer whom directors, critics, and audiences alike hail as a "natural."

PETER HANDKE constitutes a prominent exception to those authors intent on using the institution of the theater to explore institutionalized myths of the past. In response to calls for a literary *Vergangenheitsbewältigung* (coming to terms with the past), Handke polemically declared that the only past he was interested in coming to terms with was his own. Drawing on the linguistic philosophy of Ludwig Wittgenstein and the work of French poststructuralists, Handke has created an extensive dramatic corpus that attempts to dramatize and simultaneously subvert the very conventions of theater itself.

FURTHER READING

DeMeritt, Linda C., and Margarete Lamb-Faffelberger, eds. *Postwar Austrian Theater: Text and Performance.* Riverside, Calif.: Ariadne Press, 2002.

Landa, Jutta. *Bürgerliches Schocktheater: Entwicklungen im österreichischen Drama der sechziger und siebzier Jahre* [Bourgeois shock theater: Developments in Austrian drama in the 1960s and 1970s]. Frankfurt am Main: Athenäum, 1988.

Robertson, Ritchie, and Edward Timms, eds. *Theatre and Performance in Austria: From Mozart to Jelinek*. Edinburgh: Edinburgh Univ. Press, 1993.

Schorske, Carl E. *Fin-de-siècle Vienna: Politics and Culture*. New York: Knopf, 1979.

Steinberg, Michael P. *Austria as Theater and Ideology: The Meaning of the Salzburg Festival*. Ithaca, N.Y.: Cornell Univ. Press, 2000.

Yates, W. E. *Schnitzler, Hofmannsthal, and the Austrian Theatre*. New Haven, Conn.: Yale Univ. Press, 1992.

——. *Theatre in Vienna: A Critical History, 1776–1995*. Cambridge: Cambridge Univ. Press, 1996.

Craig Decker

AVANT-GARDE DRAMA

Since its inception in the early 1800s, the avant-garde has had an ongoing but troubled relationship with drama. The 1830 production of Victor Hugo's *Hernani* is emblematic. The play tells a tale of Romantic yearning and rejects the strict rules of classical drama, employing techniques from popular MELODRAMA and opera. But the text—and the theatrical production—ultimately proves secondary to what happened in the auditorium. There, supporters of Hugo, most notably Théophile Gautier, splendid in a bright crimson sash, positioned themselves in the theater to battle the rearguard of classicism. This kind of tension between drama and performance is long-lived, informing debates about popular entertainment, cultural chauvinism, and academic priorities to our own times. ANTONIN ARTAUD's manifesto "No More Masterpieces" (1933) is probably the best known articulation of the antidramatic line: "All words, once spoken, are dead and function only at the moment when they are uttered." In line with Artaud, drama has been viewed as affording "master emplotments" that deny difference and reproduce the status quo. On the other hand, performance has been viewed as subversive, the "people's form," and better able to address the performative structures of society. In general, each side of the debate has been ungenerous and insufficiently inattentive to the other.

The tradition of avant-garde drama and theater possesses four broad tendencies: MODERNIST, AGITATION-PROPAGANDA, experimental, and postmodern. The "modernist" is defined best by philosopher Theodor Adorno and art critic Clement Greenburg: studied attention to form as immanent criticism of and refuge from modernity. The "happenings" staged by Polish artist and theater directer Tadeusz Kantor in the 1960s meditate profoundly on the relationship of form, ideological correctness, and the unpresentable. SAMUEL BECKETT's *WAITING FOR GODOT* (1958) is an excellent example of modernist attention to form: Plot is merely form in this play about the impossibility of achieving narrative progress or closure. Beckett's later, shorter works are even more provocative.

Agitation-propaganda (agit-prop) is defined as art that is topical, goal directed, overtly political. The Blue Blouse movement in the early Soviet Union is a good example: Their staged skits reported and editorialized current events (i.e., *New and Old Holidays* [1924], which staged a battle of old religious and new revolutionary calendars). Agit-prop drama was the forte of a number of groups in the United States during the 1960s: EL TEATRO CAMPESINO, which began its career in support of migrant farmworker issues; the San Francisco Mime Troupe, deeply involved in the antiwar effort; and the one-man Black Power movement, Ben Caldwell, perhaps the single most prolific composer of such works.

The "experimental" trend in avant-garde drama and theater constructs situations to test theses and/or technologies. The "Acid Tests" of the 1960s explored new musical, lighting, and sound technologies, supplemented by liberal amounts of the drug lysergic acid diethylamide (LSD). EUGENE O'NEILL's *THE GREAT GOD BROWN* (1926) attempts to reflect and dramatize Sigmund Freud's model of the conflicted self. Experiment is risky; some of the worst examples of avant-garde theater belong to the trend.

The postmodern tendency in drama and theater challenges the basic assumptions of both the avant-garde and drama, viewing them as hopelessly entrenched in the status quo. Coco Fusco and Guillermo Gomez-Peña's *Two Undiscovered Amerindians Visit . . .* (1992) placed them in a busy Madrid square dressed as residents of an American island overlooked by the Europeans. Emblematic of the postmodern trend, it utilizes cutting-edge presentational forms while criticizing those forms for shoring up racist-colonialist ways of seeing: The "visitors" are in a golden cage. We might turn to the Wooster Group for other examples of deconstructed drama. This postmodern trend is grounded, in part, in a critique of avant-garde Eurocentricity. It is difficult to deny the association: The avant-garde is derived from a style of warfare devised by the French; was first utilized as a metaphor of modernity by a French utopian philosopher; was first popularized by the French press; and is, of course, a French word. However, the avant-garde model has proven highly soluble and put to good use around the globe, often to critique Eurocentric culture and institutions, including the avant-garde itself. Currently, avant-garde studies, itself an increasingly diverse and international community, has taken the Eurocentric bias of criticism to task. A reassessment is under way to consider avant-garde theater more equitably, with the European and bourgeois traditions playing a significant but far from central part, as many of the following articles demonstrate.

[*See also* Absurdism; Dadaism; Surrealism]

FURTHER READING

Bürger, Peter. *Theory of the Avant-Garde*. Tr. by Michael Shaw. Minneapolis: Univ. of Minnesota Press, 1984.

Calinescu, Matei. *Five Faces of Modernity: Modernism, Avant-Garde, Decadence, Kitsch, Postmodernism*. Durham, N.C.: Duke Univ. Press, 1990.

Egbert, Donald Drew. *Social Radicalism and the Arts: Western Europe*. New York: Random House, 1970.

Goldberg, RoseLee. *Performance Art: From Futurism to the Present*. New York: Thames & Hudson, 2001.

Harding, James. *Contours of the Theatrical Avant-Garde*. Ann Arbor: Univ. of Michigan Press, 2000.

Mann, Paul. *Theory-Death of the Avant-Garde*. Bloomington: Indiana Univ. Press, 1991.

Poggioli, Renato. *Theory of the Avant-Garde*. Cambridge: Harvard Univ. Press, 1990.

Shattuck, Roger. *The Banquet Years: The Origins of the Avant-Garde in France, 1885 to World War I*. New York: Vintage, 1955.

Mike Sell

ARGENTINA

Experimentation in Argentinean theater is too easily characterized as derivative of Euro-American theater. Although *vanguardismo* is a term often reserved for the early 20th century's modernist moment, Argentines customarily use *vanguardia*, often in the plural, to refer to experimentation taking place during the 70-year period deemed the "historical" avant-garde. A port city with a long history of immigration, Buenos Aires is generally regarded as the most "European" of Latin America's cultural centers, and its experimental theater scene has benefited from close cultural contact with Europe and North America. Nevertheless, throughout the 20th century, Argentina (especially its capital city) placed its own stamp on theatrical experimentation and innovation during the first and second waves of the Buenos Aires theatrical avant-garde—the 1930s and the 1960s.

At the beginning of the 20th century, during Río de la Plata theater's "golden age," Buenos Aires audiences enjoyed both the naturalistic bourgeois theater associated with FLORENCIO SÁNCHEZ's rural *gaucho* ("cowboy") tragedies (e.g., *Down the Ravine* [1905]) and the more "popular" SAINETE *criollo* (one-act MELODRAMA with music and local immigrant character-types). After Sánchez's death in 1910, both forms deteriorated, and the decline in theatrical innovation and quality—if not in quantity—continued until the 1920s and the development of another local one-act form, the GROTESCO CRIOLLO ("creole grotesque"). The *grotesco criollo* evolved but also diverged from the *sainete criollo* in critical ways. While both forms centered on the problems encountered by immigrants, the *sainete*'s melodrama of cultural encounter and miscommunication turned tragic in the *grotesco*'s extreme situations of frustration and failure, frequently ending in the protagonist's martyrdom. *Grotescos* by ARMANDO DISCÉPOLO (*Mateo* [1923] and *Stéfano* [1928]) and Francisco Defilippis Novoa (*I've Seen God*, [1930]) required a new acting style to unmask the *sainete*'s externalized performances. The 1920s *grotesco criollo*—with its ties to immigrant expectations and misfortunes and its innovations in text and performance—would directly influence Argentina's first avant-garde wave.

At its height, the *grotesco criollo* attracted some 7 million spectators annually; by 1935, attendance was reduced by half, and many of the neighborhood theaters had closed. The year 1930 saw Argentina's first military coup of the 20th century, and the ensuing 10 years were known as the "Infamous Decade" for their political corruption and repression, nationalistic xenophobia, and anti-Semitism. Unsurprisingly, early Argentine avant-garde artists aligned themselves with either the politically committed "Boedo" socialist realists (a political literary group in Buenos Aires) or the apolitical "Florida" Europeanists, each with their own journal (*Claridad* and *Martín Fierro*, respectively) and figurehead (Roberto Arlt and Jorge Luis Borges). Out of such a polarized environment emerged Buenos Aires's influential Independent Theatre. The Independent Theatre movement, responding to commercial theater's growing mediocrity and waning audiences, sought to rejuvenate the Argentine stage through "theater in service to art," in the words of Leónidas Barletta, theatrical producer, director, and member of the Boedo group. Founded in 1930, Barletta's collectively run People's Theatre (a reference to Romain Rolland's concept of theater as a living art) staged plays by new local authors as well as European and North Americans. Today it is difficult to regard as "avant-garde" the Independent Theatre movement: It idealized a pure "art theater," rejected local commercialization and Europeanized experimentation for its own sake, sought to replace naturalistic acting with "realistic" performance, and attempted to increase spectator competency. However, the movement's anticommercial mix of theatrical forms and collaborative philosophy regarding playwright, actor, designer, and spectator merit consideration as *vanguardista*. The Independent Theatre's blend of sociopolitical criticism, innovative theatrical aesthetics, and redefinition of the spectator laid the foundation for not only Argentina's later realistic theater but also future experiments in popular, engaged performance. The movement quickly spread to Uruguay, Chile, Bolivia, Paraguay, and Peru; in Argentina it established a vital noncommercial theater scene continuing to this day.

In 1932, Barletta convinced fellow Boedo member, established novelist and journalist Roberto Arlt, to write for his theater. Arlt wrote eight plays, five of which Barletta premiered before the author's death in 1942: *300 Million* (1932), *Proof of Honor* (1932), *Saverio the Cruel* (1936), *The Maker of Ghosts* (1936), *The Desert Island* (1937), *Africa* (1938), *The Feast-Day of Steel* (1940), and *The Desert Comes to the City* (1942). Not unlike his *grotesco* predecessors, Arlt staged the tragic plight of the proletarian or petit bourgeois "loser" in a terrifyingly modern world. In fusing daily reality with his protagonists' grotesque dreams, illusions, and fantasies, Arlt became the representative author of the 1930s Argentinean avant-garde.

Much of the Independent Theatre's work—in particular, its socialist realist goal of making theater indispensable to national life—evinced a more realistic (albeit nonnaturalistic) aesthetic of streamlined acting styles and carefully designed sets, lights, and costumes. The Independent Theatre also opened possibilities for more abstract theatrical endeavors by combining aesthetic experimentation with social, political, and historical analysis. Thus, by 1960, two ostensibly opposed paths led from the earlier Independent Theatre movement; they are often dichotomized as simply *realismo* ("realism") and *vanguardismo*. By the late 1950s, the New Theatre dominated the Buenos Aires cultural scene with its critical realism, introduced in 1949 with *The* BRIDGE by CARLOS GOROSTIZA and followed by works from the period's leading playwrights, especially OSVALDO DRAGÚN. During the 1960s, Argentina was once again under military dictatorship, and the *realistas* ("realists") became increasingly "reflective." Like their U.S. contemporary ARTHUR MILLER, RICARDO HALAC, Roberto Cossa, Carlos Somigliana, Germán Rozenmacher, and Ricardo Talesnik (known collectively as the "60s Generation") exposed Argentinean middle-class obsessions and the frustrated but complicitous individual.

In the 1960s Buenos Aires also enjoyed an active avant-garde theater and performance scene, frequently categorized as either "absurdist" or "experimental." From 1958 to 1970, the downtown Torcuato Di Tella Institute was the symbolic home to *vanguardista* music, visual arts, film, theater, and performance. Most theatrical activities took place in the Institute's Center for Audiovisual Experimentation. Participants in dance/theater performances, cabarets, musical parodies, experimental group performances, and HAPPENINGS brought experiences ranging from local New Theatre groups to the internationally renowned LIVING THEATER. Playwright GRISELDA GAMBARO premiered her earliest works (*The Blunder* [1965] and *The Siamese Twins* [1966]) in the downtown Institute. Elsewhere in the city, Eduardo Pavlovsky wrote and performed in his early "absurdist" plays *The Tragic Wait* (1962) and *Robot* (1966). Buenos Aires had bars, workshops, and communal living-performance spaces where intellectuals, visual artists, actors, and musicians congregated to stage exhibits, create events, and debate ideas. Nevertheless, the period's so-called absurdist playwrights saw the larger theater community dismiss their works as "European," or as apoliticized drafts for later, more "political" plays. Pavlovsky's early productions, with their underidentified characters' frustrated attempts at communication and use of taped recordings and projected images, were excoriated for lacking ideas and ideology. Gambaro's first plays were not only categorized as derivative and apolitical; they were also condemned for premiering in the Di Tella, a target of avant-garde and realist artists alike. For *vanguardistas*, the Institute's strong international market ties to foreign art galleries, museums, and foundations denied it vanguard status; the *realistas* found such Di Tella events as their world-renowned Happenings frivolous and irresponsible.

Such divisions notwithstanding, theater practitioners frequently crossed boundaries and worked in commercial, independent, and experimental productions. Socioaesthetic blurring, coupled with the outright militancy and social upheaval of the late 1960s, resulted in "parricidal" plays like Ricardo Monti's *An Evening with Mr. Magnus & Sons* (1970) and Guillermo Gentile's *Let's Talk Frankly* (1969). In their politicized theatricalism, early 1970s plays foregrounded the theatrical event itself by mixing genres, metaphors, and structures and reflected the powerful aesthetic-political shift taking place in conjunction with Argentina's brief return to democracy. Group theaters and collaborative experiments escalated, and by the early 1970s, *creaciones colectivas* (collaborative works) were commonplace. Gambaro's focus shifted from the complicitous victim's experience to "the drama of disappearance," and Pavlovsky became more overtly revolutionary. By the mid-1970s, even the 60s Generation's reflective realism had evolved into a "critical realism," as Cossa's *The Granny* transformed the *grotesco criollo* into a savage allegory of the filicidal destruction of the Argentine middle class at the repressive order's hands. The 1970s Buenos Aires "political" theater and performance successfully built upon multiple local—arguably antithetical—models of realism and avant-garde to create a theater of resistance.

[*See also* Argentina; Socialist Realism, Soviet Union]

FURTHER READING

Foster, David William. *The Argentine* Teatro Independiente, *1930–1955*. York, S.C.: Spanish Lit. Pub. Co., 1986.

——. "The Argentine 1960s." In "Vectors of the Radical: Global Consciousness, Textual Exchange, and the 1960s." Special issue, *Works and Days* 20, nos. 39–40 (2002): 120–41.

Graham-Jones, Jean. "Transculturating Politics, Realism, and Experimentation in 1960s Buenos Aires Theatre." *Theatre Survey* 43, no. 1 (2002): 5–19.

Kaiser-Lenoir, Eva Claudia. *El grotesco criollo: Estilo teatral de una época*. Havana: Casa de las Américas, 1977.

King, John. *El Di Tella y el desarrollo cultural argentino en la década del sesenta*. Buenos Aires: Gaglianone, 1985.

Longoni, Ana, and Mariano Mestman. *Del Di Tella a "Tucumán Arde": Vanguardia artística y política en el '68 argentino*. Buenos Aires: Ediciones El Cielo por Asalto, 2000.

Pelletieri, Osvaldo, ed. *Teatro argentino de los '60s polémica, continuidad y ruptura*. Buenos Aires: Corregidor, 1989.

Taylor, Diana. *Theatre of Crisis. Drama and Politics in Latin America*. Lexington: Univ. of Kentucky Press, 1991.

Jean Graham-Jones

CHINA

The emergence of avant-garde drama and theater in China is generally traced to the period following the Cultural Revolution (1966–1976). The postrevolutionary years witnessed unprecedented intellectual freedom and cultural debate, as well as firm rejection of the authoritarianism and utilitarian views of art and literature that had dominated the previous decades.

Since the early years of Communist rule, the official guidelines of the party, based on the principles formulated by Mao Zedong in his *Talks at the Yan'an Forum on Literature and the Arts* (1942), emphasized the role of drama as a powerful weapon for revolutionary struggle, political education, and social change. Mao's stress on the integration of the arts with the masses initially produced a considerable growth in creativity and popular participation. New dramatic genres emerged as well as several forms of amateur and proletarian theater that emphasized the active involvement of the people in the process of artistic production.

Besides the composition of new works exposing the abuses of the old social system and celebrating the new political order, the Communist reform also involved an extensive revision of the traditional theatrical heritage, further intensified after the establishment of the People's Republic in 1949. The repertoire of Beijing opera and other regional styles was amended according to the new cultural directives, while ancient forms such as folk songs and dances were revived and endowed with revolutionary content.

Nevertheless, the authoritarianism of cultural institutions and the repressive policies of the regime increasingly restricted intellectual freedom and individual creativity. The subordination of aesthetic criteria to ideological concerns, moreover, led to a progressive qualitative decline, and drama gradually turned into a mere instrument of mass indoctrination and promotion of political campaigns.

Since the early 1960s, and particularly after the outbreak of the Cultural Revolution in 1966, with the increased political radicalism and the drastic drama reform endorsed by Mao's wife Jiang Qing, the theatrical stage became a battleground for factional struggles, and artistic production almost came to a standstill. Most dramatic genres and performing styles were suppressed, artists persecuted, and troupes disbanded. The whole decade was dominated by the so-called revolutionary model operas, originally five Beijing operas, two dance dramas, and a symphony portraying flawless proletarian heroes and extolling the glorious accomplishments of the Communist leadership.

The end of the Cultural Revolution and its ultraleftist policies inaugurated a new era of resurgence for Chinese drama. A wide range of styles emerged, fostered by the introduction of Western theories and models such as BERTOLT BRECHT, ANTONIN ARTAUD, and the Theater of the Absurd. Theater workers embarked on an extensive process of experimentation, attempting to produce new paradigms capable of dealing with recent national traumas and current sociopolitical changes. Besides the assimilation of foreign influences, a further phenomenon of such artistic renaissance was the rediscovery of native performing traditions that had been violently suppressed, and almost destroyed, in the previous decade.

The development of the postrevolutionary avant-garde was marked by a fundamental break with the earlier propagandistic trends, which involved both issues of formal innovation as well as a substantial redefinition of the sociopolitical functions of drama. The former was symbolized by a rejection of the dominant aesthetic orthodoxy, primarily the eulogistic modes of model operas and SOCIALIST REALISM, as well as the theater of illusion and verisimilitude that constituted mainstream practice since the early 20th century. The latter was embodied in the avant-garde's reaction against the institutional role of art as a tool of ideological indoctrination and state-sponsored propaganda.

In the early 1980s, new dramatists emerged with unconventional, often controversial plays such as *If I Were for Real* (SHA YEXIN, 1979), *Hot Currents Outside* (MA ZHONGJUN and Jia Hongyuan, 1980), *Investigation and Analysis of Fifteen Divorce Cases* (Liu Shugang, 1983), *The Dead Visiting the Living* (Liu Shugang, 1984), *WM* (Wand Peigong, 1985), and *Rubik's Cube* (Tao Jun, 1985). Other representative works of the decade include the experimental Sichuan opera *Pan Jinlian* (WEI MINGLUN, 1986) and *Stories of Mulberry Village* (Chen Zidu and others, 1988).

In terms of form, most of these "explorative" works, as they were called at the time, experimented with antirealistic devices such as fragmented temporalities, superimposed spaces, inner monologues, and multiple narrative voices. The investigation of the characters' psyches, moreover, displayed a degree of complexity that contrasted with the Manichean polarizations and the superhuman heroes of revolutionary drama. They did not aim at producing utopian mythologies and providing the audience with "correct" interpretations but at deconstructing the grand narratives of party–state discourse by exposing corruption, oppression, and empty promises.

The most aesthetically daring and politically provocative works were those resulting from GAO XINGJIAN's cooperation with director Lin Zhaohua, *Absolute Signal* (1982), *Bus Stop* (1983), and *Wild Man* (1985), now regarded as both origin and culmination of the initial phase of the Chinese dramatic and theatrical avant-garde. *Bus Stop*, particularly, aroused great controversy for its supposed antisocialist implications and was officially denounced as the most subversive play since the establishment of the People's Republic. After the difficulties encountered with *The Other Shore* (1986), Gao went into exile to FRANCE, where he took permanent residence after the authorities' condemnation of *Escape* (1990), which focused on the Tiananmen Square Incident of 1989. He was awarded the Nobel Prize for Literature in 2000.

Gao's exploration of the notions of "theatricism," "hypotheticality," and "triplication of the actor," moreover, provided the movement with a new theoretical basis, contributing to the formation of a concept of the avant-garde that does not merely exist as a derivation of Western practices but whose *raison d'être* is deeply embedded in the indigenous cultural context. These principles, rooted in traditional Chinese opera and to some extent reminiscent of Brecht's notion of "alienation," refer to anti-illusionistic techniques of exposing the fictitious nature of the theatrical event and the "traces" of the actor's craft. The concept of triplication describes Gao's idea of the three identities of performers, who are simultaneously themselves, their roles, and a "neutral actor," a transitional state between their own person and the characters they create. Theatricism and hypotheticality aim at dispelling the illusion of realism by reminding the audience that what they see onstage is artificial, thus unreal. The performance does not represent an authentic simulation of reality but a "hypothetical resemblance" to it.

Following a temporary interruption provoked by the post-Tiananmen repression, in the 1990s, the Chinese avant-garde witnessed further radical developments, primarily through the contribution of Mou Sen and Meng Jinghui. After working with the Frog Experimental Troupe and Lin Zhaohua's Theater Research Studio, in 1993 Mou founded the Garage Theater, the first independent theatrical group in China. In cooperation with poet Yu Jian and choreographer Wen Hui, he created some of the most groundbreaking texts of the decade, marked by new experiments with performance art, improvisation, and training methods reminiscent of Polish vanguardist Jerzy Grotowski.

A Grammatical Discussion of the Other Shore (1993), an exercise in linguistic deconstruction and physical performance based on Gao's play, was produced with a group of nonprofessional actors after months of physically and psychically exhausting training. The internationally acclaimed *File Zero* (1994), based on Yu's poem, denounced the dehumanization of the individual in the Chinese state machinery and is often read as an allegory of the mechanical violence of Tiananmen. In the same year the group presented *Things Related to AIDS*, an almost entirely improvised performance in which actors cooked and talked, mentioning AIDS only in passing. Mou's later works include *Red Herring* (1995), *The Hospital* (1996), and *Baring My Heart* (1997).

Meng Jinghui's *I Love So and So* (1994) represents an analogous attempt at establishing an indigenous (anti)theatrical canon, reworking a number of Western avant-garde motifs (loss of meaning, lack of plot, illogical speech) into an original Chinese script. The play, an obsessive litany of over 700 sentences all starting with the phrase "I love," aroused great controversy owing to its unconventional structure and politically sensitive content.

In 1993, Meng produced *Longing for Worldly Pleasures*, a collage of a Ming dynasty opera about the earthly desires of a nun and a monk and two novellas from Giovanni Boccaccio's *Decameron*, inaugurating a tendency toward disfiguration of the classics and hybridization of tradition. Similar intertextual techniques are central to his later works with the Central Experimental Theater Company, for instance, *Put Down Your Whip, Woyzeck* (1995), a pastiche of a wartime street theater piece and Georg Büchner's classic; *Comrade Ah Q* (1996), a parody of Lu Xun's novella; and *Bootleg Faust* (1999). His co-productions with the Hong Kong avant-garde group Zuni Icosahedron, *The Eighth Year of One Hundred Years of Solitude—Viva!* (1996), *Journey (To the East)* 99 (1999), and *Experimental Shakespeare: King Lear* (2000), represent further examples of these trends. In the late 1990s, Meng Jinghui significantly contributed to the reformulation of the avant-garde in terms of popularization and stage-audience communication and is now regarded as the foremost representative of contemporary Chinese experimental theater.

[*See also* China]

FURTHER READING

Chen Xiaomei. *Acting the Right Part. Political Theater and Popular Drama in Contemporary China, 1966–1996*. Honolulu: Univ. of Hawaii Press, 2002.

Conceison, Claire. "Hot Tickets. China's New Generation Takes the Stage." *Persimmon* 3, no. 1 (2002): 18–27.

Huot, Claire. "Away from Literature II: Words Acted Out." In *China's New Cultural Scene. A Handbook of Changes*. Durham: Duke Univ. Press, 2000.

Meng Jinghui, ed. *Xianfeng xiju dang'an* [Files of the Avant-Garde Theater]. Beijing: Zuojia Chubanshe, 1999.

Salter, Denise. "China's Theatre of Dissent: A Conversation with Mou Sen and Wu Wenguang." *Asian Theatre Journal* 13, no. 2 (1996): 218–228.

Zhao, Henry Y. H. *Towards a Modern Zen Theatre. Gao Xingjian and Chinese Theatre Experimentalism*. London: School of Oriental and African Studies, 2000.

Rossella Ferrari

EASTERN EUROPE

The interwar period in Eastern Europe was a time of anxiety and foreboding—for many artists, millenarian hope. From the start, the Bolshevik Revolution of 1917 and its aftershocks shaped thinking about that most social and political of all the arts, the theater. The proposition that the artistic avant-garde and the political revolution shared goals and could be fused in actual practice—long a dream of writers and intellectuals—would finally be put to the test. Fired by utopian visions, the leftist vanguard, to which the great majority of writers, painters, and musicians belonged, embraced collectivism.

Rejecting the official institution of theater as trivial class entertainment, the avant-gardist sought to redefine the space of performance and the function of audiences. Instead of mirroring the smug bourgeois spectators in flattering guises, the theater had to go out into life itself if it hoped to include the masses. A playing area was needed that could accommodate active audience participation. To bring about these transformations, new styles and new players were required. Above all, new forms—new forms not only reflect new content; they create it. On this latter point all the avant-gardists—communist and noncommunist, collectivist and individualists—were in agreement.

In the former Austro-Hungarian and Russian empires, the experience of war, revolution, and social upheaval from 1914 to

1918 created a sense of crisis conducive to the emergence of a theatrical avant-garde. Change was everywhere in evidence. As a result of the Treaty of Versailles the map of Europe had been redrawn. Poland had recently been reborn as a sovereign nation after more than a century of partition; CZECHOSLOVAKIA had just come into existence as a modern state; and following the Treaty of Trianon, HUNGARY lost a third of its former territory and 3 million become refugees. The Soviet Union, forged in a chaotic revolution and bloody civil war, was a huge experiment without firm foundation or historical precedent.

The theatrical avant-gardes in Eastern Europe did not find congenial soil upon which they could grow, despite some outstanding triumphs in the early 1920s in the USSR. Hostile ideologies of the Right and the Left and a general turn toward "REALISM" in the 1930s produced an atmosphere in which nonconformist plays could neither be performed nor published. Authors fled, went into interior exile, committed suicide, or were sent to concentration camps.

The appearance in the 1960s of theatrical avant-gardes in Poland, Hungary, Czechoslovakia, Romania, and Yugoslavia surprised and delighted visitors from the West. The sources of this brilliant flourishing of drama from 1956 to 1989 were to be found in the experiments of the 1920s, which had been suppressed, buried, and temporarily forgotten. EUGÈNE IONESCO (a Romanian familiar with fascism and communism) made the point that from *fin de siècle* SYMBOLISM to the 1950s Theater of the Absurd the European avant-garde is a single movement twice disrupted by world war and revolution.

After the Thaw in 1956, the interrupted avant-garde of the 1920s resurfaced, vindicated and triumphant, in lavishly financed state theaters in Eastern Europe and, to a lesser degree, in the Soviet Union. In order to promote theater as an international showcase of socialist culture, the communist regimes, reluctantly and censorously, gradually permitted the avant-gardes of the 1920s to be revived, rehabilitated, and officially supported. The theatrical avant-garde was now becoming classic, except in cases of severe political repression, as in Czechoslovakia after 1968. It has been through this legacy that the West has come to know the interwar theatrical avant-garde in Eastern Europe.

THE AVANT-GARDE IN HUNGARY

Of all the countries of Eastern Europe during the interwar years, Hungary was the least well situated socially and politically for the development of avant-garde drama. After the defeat in World War I of the Austro-Hungarian empire, an ill-fated Hungarian Soviet Republic, led by Béla Kun, was proclaimed, filling neighboring countries with fears of the spread of Bolshevism. An invasion by Romanian troops ended the regime four and a half months later and led to the creation of the reactionary kingdom of Admiral Miklos Horthy, in power to the end of World War II.

The Hungarian Soviet Republic immediately announced its intentions of nationalizing all theaters but was soon forced to abandon these grandiose plans. During the 133 days of the regime, children's theaters were established, and traveling companies went out to rural audiences, factory workers, and soldiers in army camps. A union for performers was established, with Bela Lugosi as its secretary. The People's Commissar for Culture and Education, György Lukács, drew up guidelines for the arts. Béla Balázs was put in charge of theater; Béla Bartók, Zoltán Kodály, and Erno Dohnányi of music; and Lajos Kassák and Tibor Déry of literature. As Kun turned increasingly dictatorial, strict censorship was invoked.

Once the republic was crushed, counterrevolutionary white terror was unleashed. Leftist intellectuals and artists were forced to emigrate or hide. Freed of the communist agenda, the Hungarian theater reverted to frivolous prewar fashions. The bourgeoisie did not want to be challenged in its prejudices or made to think about unpleasant realities. As a keystone of its cultural policy, the Horthy regime promoted a commercial theater of entertainment typified by FERENC MOLNÁR's sophisticated comedies depicting a world of luxury and glamour.

Denied a theater and driven underground, the Hungarian avant-garde disappeared. VSEVOLOD MEYERHOLD's theater was not allowed to perform. Plays by LUIGI PIRANDELLO and THORTON WILDER were attacked as immoral by the reactionary Catholic and rightist press. Between 1919 and 1922, the leftist theorist János Mácza published four articles titled "Total Theatre" in Lajos Kassák's avant-garde journal *MA* (Today), which had to move from Budapest to Vienna after Kun's defeat.

The only experimental theater able to thrive between the wars was cabaret. The best writers and artists contributed to the programs of the 18 cabarets that flourished in Budapest. The humorist Fryges Karinthy (1887–1938) composed such outstanding skits as *The Long War* and *The Singing Lesson*, anticipating Ionesco and the Theater of the Absurd. His long one-act *The Magic Chair* (1917) is a masterpiece of theatricalist sleight-of-hand, exposing the ubiquity of lies, including that practiced by the playwright and performers.

A few leftist artists battled to create a socialist theater linked to the working class. Using whatever makeshift spaces he could find, Odon Palasovszky experimented with choral recitation and movement that directly involved the audience. He staged VLADIMIR MAYAKOVSKY's poetry, put on revues, and organized dance dramas, combining Egyptian funeral ceremonies, Tibetan devil-dances, and texts by Nikolai Evreinov and ERNST TOLLER. These semiclandestine performances were frequently stopped by the police. After World War II, Palasovszky was effectively forced off the stage—this time by the communist regime.

Avant-garde drama was written by authors in exile: Zsigmond Remenyik (1900–1962), who immigrated to America; Dadaist Sándor Barta (1897–1938), who fled to the Soviet Union and was liquidated there; and János Lékai (1896–1925), who participated in the Third International in 1921 in Moscow where his three one-act plays *Prisoner*, *Revolution*, and *Salvation* were performed on the same program with Mayakovsky's *Mystery-Bouffe*.

The outstanding avant-garde playwright was Tibor Déry (1894–1977). From a well-to-do bourgeois family, Déry became a communist in 1919, was jailed by many different Hungarian governments, and lived much of his life in exile, forced to move from country to country. Although better known as a novelist, Déry made original experiments with Dadaist drama. Hungarian DADA, born of a lost war and a lost revolution, was written by men on the run from the White Terror. Their experiences were comparable with those that produced the Theater of the Absurd after World War II; anger, disgust, and despair were their prime sources of inspiration. In his 1921 study of Dadaism, Déry wrote, "Dead as we are . . . let us live on, because there is no help for us. . . . Dada sees that all efforts are abortive, that any system is good only for a while. . . . there's no aim . . . there's no ideal . . . there are no laws, there are no truths."

While in Italy in 1926, Déry wrote his Dada plays *The Giant Baby*, *The Blue Bicyclist*, and *What Are You Having for Breakfast?* His masterpiece *The Giant Baby* is a Dadaist version of Everyman's circular journey from nothing to nowhere. Immediately after birth, Newborn escapes from his crib, fully grown and able to speak. He soon discovers that every man is a murderer; coming into the world, he has killed his mother. Now he must confront a senseless world in which freedom and order, the individual and society, are eternally at war. Déry's grotesque tragifarce is compounded with nonsense rhymes, everyday clichés, advertising jingles, and poetic speech. Powerful visual effects are produced by the use of silent film and slide projections, animated objects, masks, and a chorus of life-size puppets.

The Giant Baby was given an amateur production in 1969, it was first published in 1971, and it has received two professional performances, in 1978 and 1991, only after the author's death. The discovery of Déry's richly inventive Dadaist drama came too late for it to have any direct impact on the evolution of Hungarian drama. But its very existence indicates that the seeds of a vital Hungarian avant-garde theater had been sown in the interwar years.

THE AVANT-GARDE IN CZECHOSLOVAKIA

Compared to Hungary, the First Republic of Czechoslovakia seemed favorable to the development of a popular democratic avant-garde theater. Centrally located between East and West, Prague was open to the influence of the many international artistic movements freely circulating in a Europe at peace.

Russian FUTURISM was propagated by Mayakovsky's friend Roman Jakobson. Italian futurist Enrico Prampolini spent several months in Prague in 1921, bringing with him sets from the Teatro Sintetico Futurista, whose principles of simultaneity influenced subsequent Czech staging. Prague was also a cosmopolitan asylum for artistic refugees fleeing tyranny. Despite Slovak discontent, problems with ethnic minorities, and the growing menace of German fascism, the new republic prospered under President Tomáš Masaryk. The Czech half of the country was an advanced liberal democracy with a large, educated bourgeoisie, always the breeding ground and primary source of support for the avant-garde.

The arts in Prague flourished. The best-known playwright of the period, KAREL ČAPEK, was avant-garde in artistic orientation, but his apocalyptic *R.U.R.* (1921), about the dangers of technology and mechanization, was a science-fiction MELODRAMA, making it accessible to audiences at Prague's National Theatre and ensuring worldwide success.

Opposing the large state-financed institutionalized theater (which, in Karel Hilar, had a director of genius of the expressionist school) were dozens of small studios pursuing antirealist, anti-illusionist, antistylized, and antiexpressionist programs, first under the banner of constructivism, then of poetism, and finally of SURREALISM. A decisive influence on the development of avant-garde theater in the interwar years was the leftist arts group Devetsil (Nine Forces, or Nine Muses), consisting of young poets, critics, writers, painters, actors, directors, musicians, and sculptors.

Devetsil's revolutionary manifesto of 1922 contained a theoretical piece on the proletarian theater by the communist intellectual (and future semiotician) Jindřich Honzi, a director known for his staging of mass choral recitations of workers' poetry. By 1924, the heavy rhetoric of Marxism was abandoned for pietism—pure poetry, devoid of propaganda, even thought. Drawing on architecture, film, dance, technology, circus, and music-hall, the theorists of poetism argued that the stage should be a play of fancy expressing the joy of life and dreams of beauty. Stale ideas would be replaced by images, words, music, and movement.

Honzi, who had visited the Soviet Union and fallen under the spell of Meyerhold and Alexander Tairov, opposed a literary conception of theater and considered the text only as a starting point. In the mid-1920s, Honzi joined forces with Jiří Frejka (1904–1952), known for his *commedia dell'arte* productions, to found the Liberated Theatre as part of Devetsil. Based on Soviet constructivism, the Liberated Theatre was small, devoid of decoration and scenery, where the harmony of word, gesture, music, dance, pantomime, and visual effect created pure spectacle. Staged were French surrealist and protosurrealist works by Georges Ribemont-Dessaignes, GUILLAUME APOLLINAIRE, and ALFRED JARRY, as well as Czech plays by poets like Vitězslav Nezval's lyrical *Telegrams on Wheels* (1926).

In 1927, two former law students, Jiří Voskovec and Jan Werich, created the Vest-Pocket Revue, which quickly became the most popular avant-garde theater. The duo was soon sponsored by the Liberated Theatre, which they eventually took over, calling it "The Liberated Theatre of V+W" and moving into larger quarters. Voskovec and Werich wrote, produced, and acted their own "jazz revues." The best young actors in Czechoslovakia appeared in supporting roles. The jazz-inspired music was by Jaroslav Ježek, and Honzi directed the shows. The circus and silent-movie slapstick and the parodies of famous film and theater sequences created irreverent fun in a "camp" style that appealed to youth. After Adolf Hitler's rise in 1933, Voskovec and Werich directed their barbs against the fascist threat. The caricature of Hitler in *Ass and Shadow* (1933) brought protests from the German embassy, and *Executioner and Fool* (1934) led to fights between rightist students and the majority of the spectators. The last two productions, *Heavy Barbara* (1937) and *A Fist in the Eye* (1938), were their most complex and satisfying; both alluded to the Sudeten crisis of 1938, when Hitler wanted to take over the Sudeten land in Czechoslovakia. After the demise of the republic at Munich in 1938, the Liberated Theatre was closed by the police; Voskovec and Werich fled.

In 1927, Frejka formed his own Theatre Dada and invited composer, musician, and actor Emil Frantisek Burian to join him as co-director. It was then that Burian produced Voiceband, a form of syncopated choral recitation and chant using 32 players, mostly amateurs. In 1933, Burian created his own small theater collective, D34 ("D" from the Czech word for *theater*, and the number of the current year). Music organized a montage of poetry, movement, and light that united acting and dancing. Burian radically simplified theatrical structure by use of light and music he composed himself. He presented the world premiere of Bruno Jasienski's *Mannequins' Ball* in 1933. He often wrote his own material, such as *War* (1935), a poetic antimilitary scenario set in a Czech village and based on popular ballads. Burian regarded every text as a libretto that he then must execute as composer, orchestrator, and conductor. In 1935, he invented a Theatergraph combining live actors and film projections, anticipating the Laterna Magika of the 1950s.

After the economic crash of 1929 and the growing threat of fascism, the Czech avant-garde became more engaged politically, as did the state theaters. In the struggle against Hitler, the avant-garde abandoned its extreme experimental stance for performances that would reach a larger public. And avant-garde directors began to work in the state theaters. The Czech theater was united in defense of Czech culture and the republic. The National Theatre joined the struggle with its productions of Čapek's last two plays, the antitotalitarian *White Plague* (1937) and MOTHER (1938).

The direct descendants of the avant-garde studio theaters of the interwar years were the little stages of Prague that VÁCLAV HAVEL found so exhilarating in the 1960s. In 1989, it was the Czech theaters that led the way in the Velvet Revolution (known initially as the "Actor's Revolution"), which overthrew the communist regime nonviolently. Havel discovered in the little theaters of Prague the "tradition of free humor, of poetic shorthand, clown shows and the like" that comes directly from the avant-garde of the interwar years. Above all, it is the tradition of the avant-garde that made Czech theater "a place for social self-awareness," "a seismograph of the times," "an area of freedom, an instrument of human liberation."

[*See also* Czechoslovakia; Hungary]

FURTHER READING

Burian, Jarka M. *Modern Czech Theatre: Reflector and Conscience of a Nation.* Iowa City: Univ. of Iowa Press, 2000.

——. *Leading Creators of Twentieth-Century Czech Theatre.* London: Routledge/Harwood, 2002.

Stanislawski, Ryszard, and Christoph Brockhaus, eds. *Europa, Europa: Das Jahrhundert der Avantgarde in Mittle-und Osteuropa.* [Europe, Europe: The century of the Avant-garde in Middle and Eastern Europe]. Vol. 2, *Theater.* Bonn: Kunst-und-Ausstellungshalle der Bundesrepublick Deutschland, 1994.

Daniel Gerould

ISRAEL—PALESTINE

Israeli theater is of recent vintage, defined as "Israeli" since 1948, the year of the founding of the State of Israel. Although there was theater in Israel–Palestine before 1948, the amount of theatrical activity has increased dramatically since then; prior to 1948, theater in Hebrew was also a relatively new phenomenon. While there were scattered examples of Jewish plays written in classical Hebrew after the Renaissance and many plays were written and performed in Yiddish during the 19th century, it was only toward the turn of that century that the Hebrew language itself was revived and once again became a spoken language, reconnecting Jewish identity with the language of the Bible and with the idea of the (promised) Land of Israel. Reviving the language was part of Zionist ideology, underpinning the secularization of Jews in Europe and Israel and forming an essential tool for the maturation of the theater.

ROOTS OF ISRAELI THEATER

The performance of Szymon Ansky's *The* DYBBUK, (first titled *Between Two Worlds*, translated from Yiddish by Chaim Nachman Bialik, Israel's national poet) is considered to be the formative production. It premiered in Moscow in 1922, directed by Evgeny Vakhtnagov, and was performed by the members of the Habima Theatre (the Stage Theatre), founded in 1917. The Moscow Habima Theatre was part of KONSTANTIN STANISLAVSKY's studio system, which encouraged the development of theater based on specific ethnicities and cultures. The play tells the story of a young bride about to be married to Menashe in an arranged marriage but whose wedding is disturbed when the ghost (the *dybbuk*) of her dead lover speaks from her throat. The attempts to exorcise the *dybbuk* result in Leah's death, and she is united with her real love. The unification of the couple symbolized rejection of the old religious culture and a quest for revolution. In 1926, after Joseph Stalin came to power, the Habima group left Moscow.

After successfully touring the world with *The Dybbuk* and in spite of a split in 1928, the group, led by actors Nachum Zemach,

Menachem Gnessin, and Hanna Rovina, settled in Tel Aviv in 1931. Soon after, the Habima Theatre became the National Theatre of Israel, a title it still holds, gradually changing from an avant-garde and experimental company to a state-subsidized, mainstream repertory theater.

Two other important theaters already existed before 1948. The Ohel Theatre (the Tent Theatre) was founded in 1925 by Moshe Halevi as a workers' theater promoting a socialist agenda. It focused on biblical plays and was closed in 1967. In 1944, actor-director Yosef Milo founded the Cameri Theatre (the Chamber Theatre) against the styles of the Habima and Ohel theaters. The Cameri, also located in Tel Aviv, became the second largest repertory theater in Israel. Opposed to what Milo and his young friends considered to be a European and pompous acting style and to a repertory mostly based on Hebrew diasporic materials, the Cameri Theatre depicted the local and more realistic scene of Israeli culture. The play that typified this ideology was Moshe Shamir's *He Walked in the Fields* (*Hu Halach baSadot*, 1948), the first Israeli play to depict topical issues in a realistic manner, reflecting collective identification with the price that had to be paid for independence—sacrificing the sons. Uri, the protagonist, is Israeli born and a kibbutz member. He falls in love with Mika, a Holocaust survivor, but is unaware of her past; she cannot understand why he is so willing to sacrifice his life for the collective. When Uri goes on a mission, he gets killed and Mika discovers she is pregnant. The stylistic and thematic novelty of the play was only the beginning of the complex process of creating Israeli theater.

Less than a century old, Israeli theater is still theater in search of identity. Beyond the lack of a dramatic tradition, the gradual naturalization of the Hebrew language is still ongoing, and most critically, Israel's borders are still in dispute. There has been at least one war every decade since 1948, and the historical development of Israeli theater and society can be traced according to the changes that each war brought with it. It is hard to avoid oversimplifications, but there are central tenets in drama and theater as well as recurring themes and questions. Until 1973, the year of the Yom Kippur War, which utterly shattered the victorious and euphoric optimism of Israeli society, a general sense of collectivity characterized the drama. Since 1973, however, Israeli drama has continued to be political in the sense that it is almost always concerned with collective questions such as the survival and struggle of Israeli society, differences between Jewish and Israeli identities, the burden of the Holocaust, relations with the Arabs and the Palestinians, schisms between western Ashkenazi Jews and Mizrahi Jews, conflicts between new immigrants and old ones, and the role of the army in Israeli society.

The playwrights of the 1950s (the generation of "Tashach"—1948 according to the Jewish calendar) wrote sociorealistic dramas—though full of stereotypes—that told and retold stories about the wars with the Arabs, moral conflicts, and settlement. Some of the prominent plays are Yigal Mossinsohn's *In the Plains of the Negev* (*Be'arvot Hanegev*, 1949); Natan Shacham's *They'll Arrive Tomorrow* (*Hem Yagiu Machar*, 1949); and Shulamit Bat-Dori's *Huts and the Moon* (*Tzrifim ve Yareach*, 1952). Although the Holocaust is an event of mythical dimensions in Israeli consciousness, penetrating almost every level of Israeli culture and theater, many years passed before Israeli drama began to grapple with it. Three early plays that bring up the subject are Lea Goldberg's *The Lady of the Castle* (*Ba'alat Haarmon*, 1955); Aharon Meged's *Chana Senesh* (1958); and Ben-Zion Tomer's *Children of the Shadow* (*Yaldei Hatzel*, 1962).

THE QUEST FOR "NORMAL" THEATER

Differing from the heroic drama of the 1950s, many escapist plays were written in the 1960s, expressing a quest to have "normal theater" in a "normal country." Many world masterpieces were translated into Hebrew, and influenced by world trends such as the drama of the absurd, Nissim Aloni wrote his metatheatrical *The American Princess* (*Hanesicha haAmerikait*, 1963) and his poetic *The Bride and the Butterfly Hunter* (*Hakala ve Tzayad Haparparim*, 1967). Plays based on biblical themes, such as Meged's *Genesis* (*Bereshit*, 1962) and Yehuda Amichai's *Journey to Nineveh* (*Massa le Ninveh*, 1964), replaced the epic and heroic worlds of earlier biblical plays with existentialist social allegories. The sweeping victory of Israel in the 1967 Six-Day War increased national euphoria, and it was only Hanoch Levin, a very young playwright at the time, who wrote visionary satiric revues such as *You and Me and the Next War* (*At ve Ani ve Hamilchama Habaah*, 1968) and *Queen of the Bathtub* (*Malkat ha Ambatia*, 1970), specifically alluding to Prime Minister Golda Meir. Both plays sharply and ruthlessly criticize the death of so many soldiers in the ongoing "War of Attrition" and were the first to raise questions about the recently occupied territories. The plays were targeted at the militaristic hubris and included scenes such as "The Victory Ceremony of the 11 Minute War," in which a Major General talks to an empty court, praising his soldiers who did not return from the war.

The euphoria and confidence following the Six-Day War were harshly shattered in 1973. Although Israel eventually won the war, the war became an unhealed scar that would nurture Israeli drama and theater for many years to come. During the 1970s, playwrights continued to develop styles from the 1960s, for example, Yosef Mundi's *It Turns Around* (*Ze Mistovev*, 1970), in which Theodor Herzel and Franz Kafka meet each other in a sanatorium.

Levin, who was becoming one of Israel's most appreciated playwrights and directors, now turned to grotesque domestic comedies such as *Object* (*Hefetz*, 1972), *Young Varde'le* (*Neurei Varde'le*, 1974), and *Shitz* (1975)—each using the petit bourgeois family as political allegory. In the 1970s, there was once again an interest in realistic drama, typified by soul searching and reexamination of values, such as in A. B. Yehoshua's *A Night in May* (*Laila beMai*, 1969), which portrays a family on the verge of crisis and the Six-Day War; Avraham Raz's *Mr. Shefi's Night of Independence* (*Leil haAtzmaut shel Israel Shefi*, 1972), which dealt with parental guilt feelings for sending their son to die in the war; Yosef Bar-Yosef's Chekhovian *Hard People* (*Anashim Kashim*, 1973); and Danny Horowitz's *Dress Parade* (*Cherli Ka Cherli*, 1977), an ironic adaptation of the Israeli ceremony *masechet*, in which he put together a collage of images that represented the fragmentation that the image of the *tzabar* was undergoing.

Another significant aspect of the mid-1970s was the social and political theater created by American-born director Nola Chilton at the Haifa Municipal Theatre. She based her productions on documentary materials from everyday life and was the first to foreground images and problems of "other" Israelis such as Arabs, Mizrahi Jews, women, and people from development towns. The peace agreement with Egypt in 1978 also allowed Israeli drama to turn its gaze inward; it was only in the late 1970s that Arab characters ceased to be absent.

DRAMA AS A PROTEST TOOL

Although there were signs of deconstructing the self-confident image of Israeli society, it was not until after the 1982 Lebanon war—the first nonconsensual war in Israeli history—that theater and drama became overtly political, not only representing collective traumas and topical events but also serving as a tool of protest. Side by side with Levin, now writing mythical tragicomic spectacles of doom such as *The Sorrows of Job* (*Yisurei Iyob*, 1981), *The Great Whore of Babylon* (*HaZona HaGdola MiBavel*, 1982), and *The Lost Women of Troy* (*HaNashim HaAvudot MiTroya*, 1984), Yehoshua Sobol, artistic manager of the Haifa Theatre with Gedaliah Besser, wrote political dramas, often based on historical events, that grapple with questions of Jewish and Israeli identity. His most famous play is *Ghetto* (1984), a metatheatrical drama about theater in the Vilna ghetto and about the moral dilemma of Jews who cooperated with Nazis in order to save other Jews. Some of his other plays are *The Soul of a Jew* (*Nefesh Yehudi*, 1982), based on the real character of Otto Weininger and dealing with the meaning of being Jewish and Israeli, *The Palestinian Woman* (*Palestinait*, 1985), one of the first plays in Israel to feature a Palestinian protagonist; and *The Jerusalem Syndrome* (*Syndrom Yerushalaim*, 1987), which drew an analogy between the fall of the second Temple in the biblical era and the contemporary situation of Israeli society, suggesting that the Jews are (and were) responsible for the destruction. After producing this apocalyptic play, both Sobol and Besser were forced to leave the Haifa Municipal Theatre.

Other important plays from the 1980s are Shmuel Hasfari's *Sanctification* (*Kidush*, 1985), the first part of a trilogy that criticizes Ashkenazi religious society in Israel; Motti Lerner's *Kastner* (1985), a docudrama about the dilemma of cooperating with the Nazis during the Holocaust; Emil Habibi's *The Opsimist* (*HaOpsimist*, 1986), an adaptation of Emil Habibi's novel about the existential inner struggle of an Israeli Palestinian, performed by Arab actor Muhammad Bakri for a Hebrew-speaking audience; Yitzchak Laor's *Ephraim Returns to the Army* (*Ephraim Chozer la Tzava*, 1987), about an Israeli military governor in the Occupied Territories who treats women and Palestinians alike; and Shulamit Lapid's *Deserted Property* (*Rechush Natush*, 1987).

Two other significant moments of the 1980s were the foundation of the Acre Festival for Alternative Theatre in the Arab-Jewish city of Acre in 1980, initiated by Oded Kotler, in which amateur, avant-garde, and new voices in theater and drama compete in an annual contest, and the professionalization of the repertory theaters, which began to import successful plays and musicals from Broadway and the West End. The latter process created a place for new directors, stage designers, and performance techniques, but it also marked the disengagement of the large theaters from the ideological role they had traditionally taken.

In 1987 the first Intifada (Palestinian uprising) broke out, exploding the illusory sense of near-tranquility that had characterized the Occupied West Bank and Gaza Strip and leading Israeli society to realize the necessity of a peace process, while confronting the vicious cycle of terror and retaliation. Hanoch Levin, who, during the 1990s, wrote mostly poetic drama, also wrote a straightforwardly political play, *Murder* (*Retzach*, 1997), which poignantly depicted this cyclical situation. Ilan Hatzor's *Masked-Faced Terrorists* (*Reulim*, 1990) was the first Israeli play to deal directly with the Intifada. Other plays examined social differences and schisms within Israeli society, such as Hillel Mittelpunkt's *Gorodish: The Seventh Day* (*Gorodish: Hayom Hashvii*, 1993), about the militaristic society that bred General Gorodish, one of those responsible for the Yom Kippur fiasco.

The 1990s were, however, years full of experimental theater. One could say that almost all theater in Israel up until the 1990s was "experimental," but it was the fact that the repertory theaters had become so mainstream that created the need for groundbreaking and avant-garde theater. The Acre Festival allowed new and alternative voices to be heard. In 1991, Dudu Ma'ayan's *Arbeit macht frei vom Toitland Europa* premiered. This monumental performance, five hours long, performed for no more than 30 spectators at a time, was a journey into the impact of the Holocaust on contemporary Israeli identity, daringly suggesting parallels between the Holocaust and the ongoing conflict with the Palestinians. The performance takes place in two parts, the first as a site-specific theater in the Holocaust museum, reflecting on Israeli memorial rituals, and the second part in the Acre Theatre Center, where the spectators were seated in a small room, unable to stand, in which Zelma, a Holocaust survivor, unfolds her story, which is the Israeli story. Eventually, the audience climbs up into a nightmarish hell full of horrific scenes performed by the actors and a collage of Israeli images.

Another Israeli director who flourished in the 1990s is Rina Yerushalmi, who in 1989 founded the Itim Ensemble as a theater laboratory dedicated to classical texts. Her most important work to date is her 1996–1998 Bible Project, *And He Said, and He*

Walked, and They Bowed, and He Feared (*Va Yomer, Va Yelech, Va Yishtachu, Va Yerra*), an eight-hour-long epic performance based on excerpts from the Hebrew Bible, reedited to offer a secular examination of the role of the Bible in contemporary Israeli identity and culture. The biblical Exodus and conquering of the Land of Israel were compared with the 20th-century travails of the Jewish nation, and the performance ended with the apocalyptic prophecies of Jeremiah, implying that the contemporary State of Israel might also turn into a temporary phase in the history of the Jewish nation.

In 1991, Israel's newest theater, Gesher (Bridge), was established. Its company was composed entirely of Russians who had recently immigrated to Israel and who were led by director Yevgeny Arye, whose artistic style and theatricality quickly became admired. Many of the Gesher productions relied on Russian materials, and for many years the company performed both in Russian and in Hebrew. Two of their most successful productions, however, were of Israeli plays that dealt with collective themes. Sobol's *Village* (*Kfar*, 1996) was about Israel's War of Independence experienced from the viewpoint of a young boy, and Yoram Kanyuk's *Adam Son of a Dog* (*Adam ben Kelev*, 1993) dealt with a man turned into an amusement dog in the Holocaust. This performance took place in a circus tent and has been performed annually since 1993 during the weeks before Holocaust Memorial Day.

PALESTINIAN THEATER

Although Israeli theater is still evolving and changing, it is already an established phenomenon. Palestinian theater, on the other hand, is very much at its beginning. Before 1948, there were about 30 troupes of Palestinian performers that mostly presented didactic adaptations of English and French plays in the schools. Between 1948 and 1967 a few small amateur groups continued to perform in clubs in East Jerusalem and in Ramallah, and Israeli-Arabs/Palestinians were either connected to Israeli communist groups or performed plays that adhered to the patronizing establishment. The first Palestinian play that was written and performed in Arabic in Israel was Mishil Haddad's *Darkness and Light* (*Zalam wa-Nur*, 1954), about the struggle of a student who wants to study despite his father's blindness and poverty.

In Israel, Arabic theatrical activity was centered in Haifa and Nazareth, and there was very little activity outside of Israel. Somewhat paradoxically, after 1967 and after Israel conquered the West Bank and the Gaza Strip, the volume of Palestinian theater increased dramatically, partially because the Israeli-Arabs and the Palestinians were reunited. Before 1967, Egyptian and Jordanian censorship limited theatrical activity in the territories. After 1967, Palestinian national consciousness started to rise, but poverty stood in the way of mounting professional theater until the mid-1970s.

In 1977, the Al-Hakawati Theatre (Itinerant Storyteller Theater) was established in East-Jerusalem by François Abu-Salim as a joint project of Arab dramatists, directors, and actors from Israel and East-Jerusalem. It is to date the most important development in Palestinian professional theater. Its agenda was aimed at resisting the occupation, but it also produced plays that criticized Palestinian society. Some of the plays staged in this theater were Emil Habibi's *Luka' the Son of Luka'* (*Luka' ibn Luka'*, 1980) and Abu-Salim's *In the Name of the Father, the Mother, and the Son* (*Bismi al-Ab wa-l-Umm wa-l-Ibn*, 1978), *Mahjub, Mahjub* (1980), and *A Thousand and One Nights of the Nights of a Stone Thrower* (*Alf Layla wa-Layla min Layali Rami al-Hijara*, 1987).

After the Intifada broke out, the Al-Hakawati Theatre changed its name to al-Masrah al-Watani al-Filastini (Palestinian National Theater), and it has become the central framework for Palestinian theater. Two plays that deal with the Palestinian tragedy are *The Gravedigger* (*'Adnan Tarabsha's al-'Akash*, 1991) and Antwan Shalhat's *The Electricity Pole* (*Amud al-Kahraba*, 1992). In a recent production of Ephraim Gotthold Lessing's utopian *Nathan the Wise* (2004), Israeli actor, director, and translator Doron Tavori gathered Jewish and Arab actors from theaters throughout Israel who voluntarily worked together to stage the play. We can only hope that the play's ideology will realize itself in the near future.

[*See also* Israel; Palestine; Yiddish Theater]

FURTHER READING

Avigal, Shosh. "Patterns and Trends in Israeli Drama and Theater, 1948 to Present." In *Theater in Israel*, ed. by Linda Ben-Zvi. Ann Arbor: Univ. of Michigan Press, 1996.

Ben-Zvi, Linda, ed. *Theater in Israel*. Ann Arbor: Univ. of Michigan Press, 1996.

Levi, Shimon, and Korina Shoef. *The Israeli Theatre Canon: One Hundred and One Shows*. Tel Aviv: Hakibbutz Hameuchad, 2002 [in Hebrew].

Rokem, Freddie. "Hebrew Theater from 1889–1948." In *Theater in Israel*, ed. by Linda Ben-Zvi. Ann Arbor: Univ. of Michigan Press, 1996.

———. *Performing History: Theatrical Representation of the Past in Contemporary Theatre*. Univ. of Iowa Press, 2000.

Snir, Reuven. "Palestinian Theatre: Historical Development and Contemporary Distinctive Identity." *Contemporary Drama Review* 3, no. 2 (1995): 29–73.

Urian, Dan. *The Arab in Israeli Drama and Theatre*. Tr. by Naomi Paz. Amsterdam: Harwood Acad. Pubs., 1997.

———. *The Judaic Nature of Israeli Theatre*. Tr. by Naomi Paz. Amsterdam: Harwood Acad. Pubs., 2000.

Sharon Aronson-Lehavi

JAPAN

If rejection of the past and opposition to tradition are hallmarks of the avant-garde, there is something distinctly paradoxical about the avant-garde in Japan. To the extent that it has risen above mere imitation of the West and succeeded as an indigenous phenomenon, the avant-garde in Japan has served as a vehicle to access the past rather than to imagine the future.

Modern theater developed in Japan not as a creative modification of premodern tradition but through a rupture with it. When OSANAI KAORU, the leading figure in SHINGEKI, the Japanese modern theater movement, wrote the following words in 1926, he could not have been more explicit about his intentions.

> Above all, the enemy we must fight against in our effort to establish the *national* theater we hold as our ideal is the traditional theater, that is, *kabuki* drama. . . . We must first wage war on this *tradition*. We must destroy *kabuki patterns*; we must create completely separately *our own theater art* new and free!

If avant-garde movements are characterized by their rejection of the past and worship of the new, then *shingeki* certainly qualifies as an avant-garde movement. But it is typical of the Japanese avant-garde that at the same time Osanai was making these belligerent remarks, he was also moving to recapture the essence of *kabuki* and reincorporate it into Japanese modern theater.

European trends such as EXPRESSIONISM, DADAISM, and SURREALISM washed over Japan in succeeding waves after World War I. Osanai perceived them, among other things, as means to recapture the essence of premodern tradition without surrendering to it. The essence of *kabuki* was nonsense, Osanai argued, and Western avant-garde techniques were ways to reinject nonsense and the irrational into modern theater. Osanai became enthralled with the theatricalism of MAX REINHARDT. He developed a plan (never realized) to create a Japanese version of Nikita Baliev's cabaret theater *The Bat* in Japan. He was an early and enthusiastic advocate of expressionism. And his last project before his untimely death in 1928 at the age of 47 was an eclectic adaptation of Chikamatsu Monzaemon's 1715 play *The Battles of Coxinga*, using techniques learned from VSEVELOD MEYERHOLD (who had himself learned much from *kabuki*) and combining, among other things, Chinese, Indonesian, and Mongolian theater techniques.

In short, from the outset, the Japanese avant-garde theater incorporated the paradoxical longing to reaffirm and recapture the very theater tradition it was rejecting. And Western avant-garde techniques were perceived as a means to this end.

Not everyone perceived European avant-gardism in this way. As in Europe following the success of the Russian Revolution, the avant-garde in Japan became bound up with political radicalism; artists like SENDA KOREYA and MURAYAMA TOMOYOSHI, who had spent time in Germany in the early 1920s, cleaved closely to their militant European models. Mavo, the group of artists and designers that Murayama founded about 1923, was the epitome of this politicized European-style avant-garde. In short order, avant-garde artists such as Murayama, who had begun as anarchistic iconoclasts, converted to Marxism; when the Union of Soviet Writers declared "SOCIALIST REALISM" the desired literary method in 1932, they toed the Soviet line, albeit with some face-saving modifications. In 1933, however, Murayama, like many other left-wing artists and intellectuals, was forced to commit political apostasy (*tenkō*), proclaiming Marxism inappropriate to Japan's imperial system. In 1940, left-wing troupes were ordered to disband, and more than 100 of their leaders, including Senda and Murayama, were arrested and imprisoned. Avant-garde theater in the prewar period was over.

After the war, the major *shingeki* figures picked up where they left off, and the troupes they created immediately established hegemony in the modern theater world. This hegemony was the result of the major troupes' ability to dominate audiences and access the limited number of theater spaces available. They achieved this through their relationship with the Workers Theater Council (Rōen), the Japanese Communist Party (JCP)–affiliated organization, modeled after the German Volksbühne, that assembled audiences through labor unions. The remarkable success of this system in the years after the war is indisputable, but it also led to a homogeneous repertory of realist plays. After 1956 and Nikita Khrushchev's revelation of Joseph Stalin's crimes, and then with increasing clarity in the wake of the failure of JCP-led demonstrations against renewal of the U.S.-Japan Mutual Security Treaty in 1960, this alliance of the major theater companies, the JCP, and the labor unions presented itself to the younger generation of the nascent New Left as distinctly unholy.

One member of this younger generation, Kan Takayuki, described his sense that the *shingeki* system had become a monolith that enforced "realism" as a pernicious orthodoxy:

> The realism . . . that is the orthodox theory of the *shingeki* movement . . . is naturally antagonistic to all "avant-garde" tendencies in the arts that might be considered virulent or subversive, and it indicates a theory of art that remains within the frame of Socialist Realism (in its contemporary revisionist guise) that would repress all such tendencies.

The critic Tsuno Kaitarō explained the situation in more theatrical terms:

> *Shingeki* has become historical; it has become a tradition in its own right. The problem of the younger generation has been to come to terms with this tradition. . . . Beneath *Shingeki*'s prosperous exterior there is decadence. It has lost the antithetic élan that characterized its origins. *Shingeki* no longer maintains the dialectical power to negate and transcend; rather, it has become an institution that itself demands to be transcended.

Tsuno proposed to use the premodern paradigm of art and theater to free theatrical creativity from the strictures and prescriptions of modernity. In the characteristic slogan of the 1960s, the avant-garde aimed "to use the premodern imagination to transcend the modern":

> We feel that although Shingeki's break with classical Nō and Kabuki was both justified and inevitable, it nonetheless cut us off from the sources of our tradition and trapped us within

> the restrictive confines of a static, bourgeois institution. . . . We . . . are attempting to reaffirm our tradition, even when we find it distasteful, in order to deal directly and critically with it. Our hope is [to] transcend the enervating clichés of modern drama and revolutionize what it means to be Japanese.

In terms that recall Osanai Kaoru's rejection of *kabuki*, the new theatrical avant-garde, known variously as "the LITTLE THEATER MOVEMENT" (SHŌGEKIJŌ UNDŌ) and "the underground" (ANGURA), blasted *shingeki*:

> Ultimately it is our intention to destroy *shingeki* as an art, *shingeki* as a system and in its place present before you a concrete alternative contemporary theater distinct from *shingeki*. . . . What we lack in money we will make up for with our wits, and where we lack experience we will rely on a new sensitivity and on concrete acts; we will explore modes of expression different from *shingeki* and give them form; we will explore different production systems from *shingeki*, different ways of organizing ourselves, different ways of relating to our audiences, and we will give these form as well.

Three troupes in particular shared these views and were central to the 1960s movement. The Situation Theater (Jōkyō gekijō) was founded in 1963 by KARA JŪRŌ, his wife Ri Reisen, and Maro Akaji (who studied with the radical choreographer Hijikata Tatsumi and founded the Dairakudakan Butoh troupe in 1972). Theater Center 68/69, which later came to be known as the Black Tent Theater (BTT), was an eclectic group that brought together graduates of Tokyo and Waseda Universities and the conservatory program of the Actors Theater (Haiyūza). It was the most overtly political troupe and included Tsuno Kaitarō, SATOH MAKOTO, Yamamoto Kiyokazu, and Saeki Ryūkō, among others. The Waseda Little Theater (Waseda Shōgekijō), which subsequently evolved into SCOT (Suzuki Company of Toga) and produced the so-called Suzuki Method of actor training, was founded by director SUZUKI TADASHI, playwright BETSUYAKU MINORU, and actor Ono Hiroshi in 1966. TERAYAMA SHŪJI's Tenjō Sajiki, founded in 1967, which is usually included in this list, belongs to a slightly different lineage and began as a more classically European-style avant-garde troupe.

Angura's retrospective revolt against modernism and its reclamation of the premodern imagination succeeded, radically expanding the possibilities open to the theater. To accommodate the newly popular form, numerous theaters were built; and by 1995 an average of 4.3 new contemporary theater productions were being opened in Tokyo every day of the year, serving an audience of more than 3.3 million people. In the mid-1980s, government spending on the arts rapidly increased, culminating in 1997 with the construction of a multimillion-dollar New National Theater devoted to modern theater. Abroad, "traditionalists" like Suzuki Tadashi and Butoh troupes like Sankai Juku, descended from Maro Akaji's Dairakudakan, came to be regarded as the most cutting-edge representatives of the Japanese avant-garde.

Today, the hybrid variations in Japanese theater seem endless. Anything is possible, and experimentation is everywhere. In this environment, it is difficult to anticipate from what direction the next avant-garde might appear.

[*See also* Japan]

FURTHER READING

Goodman, David G. *Angura: Posters of the Japanese Avant-Garde*. New York: Princeton Arch. Press, 1999.

——. *The Return of the Gods: Japanese Drama and Culture in the 1960s*. Ithaca, N.Y.: Cornell East Asia Program, 2003.

Munroe, Alexandra, ed. *Japanese Art after 1945: Scream against the Sky*. New York: Abrams, 1994.

Powell, Brian. *Japan's Modern Theatre: A Century of Continuity and Change*. London: Japan Library, 2002.

Soda Hidehiko. *Osanai Kaoru to nijusseiki engeki* Tokyo: Bensei shuppan, 1999.

Weisenfeld, Gennifer. *Mavo: Japanese Artists and the Avant-Garde, 1905–1931*. Berkeley: Univ. of California Press, 2002.

David G. Goodman

RUSSIA AND THE SOVIET UNION

SYMBOLISM, introduced to Russia from FRANCE in the mid-1890s, found a receptive welcome in the theater, where directors such as KONSTANTIN STANISLAVSKY, VSEVELOD MEYERHOLD, and Yevgeny Vakhtangov, seeking to go beyond the confines of REALISM, staged both foreign and Russian works in the new Maeterlinckian mode in the period up to the outbreak of World War I. Fyodor Sologub (1863–1927) with *The Triumph of Death* (1907) and ALEKSANDR BLOK with *The Fairground Booth* (and *The Stranger*) were the outstanding playwrights of the movement, whose works were brilliantly staged by Meyerhold. FUTURISM, which followed as the next dominant avant-garde, gave rise to VLADIMIR MAYAKOVSKY's *Vladimir Mayakovsky, a Tragedy* (1913) and Aleksei Kruchenykh's *Victory over the Sun* (1913), both presented with sets by Kazimir Malevich together on alternate nights in 1913. None of these productions reached large audiences or left a living legacy.

The year 1917 was a time of theatrical uncertainty. Nowhere did political revolution seem to offer greater hope for artistic innovation than in Russia. Theater artists like Meyerhold who embraced the Bolshevik cause believed that communism would in turn promote the avant-garde. In fact, the first decade of Soviet theater was an era of unprecedented experimentation, and the groundbreaking productions of Vakhtangov, Meyerhold, and Aleksandr Tairov have been seminal in the formation of modern stagecraft throughout the world.

The development of Soviet drama lagged far behind that of theater. Political revolution did not call forth exciting new plays, and avant-garde writers, unlike their counterparts in the theater arts, found themselves immediately at odds with the regime and its cultural ideology. In the first period of revolutionary theater, the most innovative stagings were not of new Soviet works but of foreign plays and Russian classics. The one striking exception is Mayakovsky, who, in his collaboration with Meyerhold, was the creative force of the Russian avant-garde.

An immediate problem for the Soviet authorities was the total lack of a revolutionary repertory. After 1917, the same bourgeois plays and playwrights dominated the stage. An innovative form of theater that departed totally from traditional dramaturgy was the mass spectacle that reconstructed principal events in the history of world revolution or reenacted on site central episodes of the Russian Revolution. Inspired by the festivals of the French Revolution and Romain Rolland's Théâtre du peuple (Theater of the People), Soviet mass spectacles drew on traditions of Russian carnivals, fairs, and religious holidays, which they were designed to replace.

To celebrate the first anniversary of the October Revolution in 1918, pageants, demonstrations, and AGITATION-PROPAGANDA shows were organized for soldiers, workers, and students, but the professional theater world still maintained a guarded neutrality and ignored the government's request to join in the festivities. The only purely theatrical event for the celebrations was Meyerhold's production of Mayakovsky's MYSTERY-BOUFFE (1918), subtitled "A Heroic, Epic, and Satiric Representation of Our Era." The first Soviet play, it provided a model for the revolutionary avant-garde—bright, cheerful, militant, popular in spirit, blending high and low, and inviting active participation from the audience. An allegory of the triumph of the international proletariat, *Mystery-Bouffe* is an irreverent mixture of old and new, combining Aristophanic comedy, biblical mystery, and futurist poetry. Revolution is presented as a second flood annihilating the old world. In the course of their journey to the Promised Land, the Seven Pairs of the Unclean—workers wearing identical blue blouses and chanting slogans in unison—inherit the industrial future. The Clean—capitalists and imperialists—attempt to highjack the revolution but are thrown overboard from the ark. At the end of the play, the audience was invited to come on stage and join the revolutionary workers in a joyous celebration of the World Commune.

A seminal work for the Russian avant-garde, *Mystery-Bouffe* is a storehouse of innovative forms, containing almost all the new Soviet genres and styles that would be developed during the 1920s: drama of revolutionary class struggle, montage of attractions, living newspaper, Blue Blouse acrobatics, political revue, and mass spectacle. With his defiant restoration of flamboyant spectacle, subversive carnivalization of culture, and impudent parading of circus tricks, Mayakovsky defined the new aesthetic sensibility of the period. The "poster aesthetics" that underlies *Mystery-Bouffe* has its roots in Russian popular culture: the traditional *lubok* woodcut (Russian folk pictures) and fairground puppet plays.

No new Soviet play was staged in any professional theater until 1921 when Meyerhold's successful revival of the revised *Mystery-Bouffe* played in Moscow for over two months. A professional circus clown appeared as one of the devils, making an acrobatic entrance sliding down a rope. The violent side to Mayakovsky's carnivalesque inversion of values appears in the updated version where the civil war is repeatedly invoked to justify exterminating class enemies.

Mayakovsky opened the way for the creation of an aggressive new political and propagandist theater aimed at large popular audiences. Owing much to the allegorical cartoon figures of *Mystery-Bouffe*, the most famous mass spectacle, *The Storming of the Winter Palace*, was performed in 1920 on the anniversary of the revolution. Some 10,000 sailors and soldiers, cocoordinated by a team of five directors headed by Nikolai Evreinov, reenacted the events before an audience of 100,000.

When Mayakovsky returned to the theater, the New Economic Policy (1921–1928)—designed to foster limited private enterprise—had produced a class of opportunistic capitalists, and his last two plays, THE BEDBUG (1929) and THE BATHHOUSE (1930), are satires on a corrupt and hypocritical system. Both plays utilize the science-fiction device of time travel and express Mayakovsky's ever-present concern with immortality and resurrection at the same time that they directly confront vices and foibles of Soviet reality. The first exposes the sterile, joyless socialist future by identifying the audience with the unregenerate parasitic clown Prisypkin; the second shows the betrayal of revolution by a soulless bureaucracy with its double-speak and entropic mechanisms. *The Bathhouse* was savagely attacked by party critics, and after Mayakovsky's suicide (caused in part by his political disillusionment) on April 14, 1930, his plays did not appear in the Soviet theater for over 20 years. After SOCIALIST REALISM became compulsory for writers in 1932, Mayakovsky's theatrical legacy was completely rejected by the cultural authorities. When in 1935 Joseph Stalin declared Mayakovsky the greatest poet of the Revolution, it was—in Boris Pasternak's words—the writer's second death.

In the 1950s, Mayakovsky's plays returned to the Soviet stage, and to the theaters of Eastern Europe, as a prime agent for change in the battle against socialist realism. The rehabilitation of the avant-garde of the 1920s accompanied the post-1956 thaw and opened the way for rebellious young playwrights like Vasily Aksyonov to experiment with dramatic form in his fantastic satire *Always on Sale* (1965), although his later plays were banned, and he was forced to immigrate to America.

During the interwar years, other avant-garde playwrights fared less well than Mayakovsky. One of the most promising young writers, Lev Lunts (1901–1924), a leading member of the Serapion Brotherhood (an alliance of twelve artists), wrote four plays, including *Beyond the Law* (1929) and *City of Truth* (1929), stark historical tragedies and dystopian fables, but his dramas could not be staged in the Soviet Union.

Yevgeny Zamyatin, author of the anti-utopian novel *We* (1920–1921), wrote a number of plays before leaving the Soviet Union for Paris in 1929, but only *The Flea* (1926), an adaptation of a Nikolai Leskov story, was staged. The Soviet playwright who has been the most highly esteemed and most often performed worldwide after the fall of communism is MIKHAIL BULGAKOV, whose career was plagued by censorship. His first play, *The Days of the Turbins* (1926)—an adaptation of his novel *The White Guard*—was a great success at the MOSCOW ART THEATER but is conventional in form. Controversial because of its sympathetic portrait of a White family in Kiev during the civil war, the play was at one point banned but remained a favorite of Stalin, who saw it 18 times. More experimental in its structure of seven "dreams," *Flight* (1928), an account of the experiences of White émigrés, was never allowed to reach the stage, and Bulgakov's other plays had no chance in the theater. His complex study of the position of the artist and the tyrant, *Moliere* was in rehearsal for many years at the Moscow Art Theater and finally received only seven performances in 1936.

Radical avant-garde theatrical experimentation in the composition of new dramatic texts was undertaken by the group of poets, painters, and musicians known as Obyedineniye Realnogo Isskustva (OBERIU, a playful Russian acronym for the Association for Real Art), which managed to put on performances in Leningrad from 1926 to 1930 until government persecution curtailed their public activities. Two of the group's leading authors, DANIIL KHARMS and Aleksandr Vvedensky, were arrested in 1941 and liquidated shortly thereafter.

The theatrical section of OBERIU presented unusual shows that combined poetry and acrobatics and exploited the techniques of the circus, music hall, and fairground puppet show. The plays ridiculed dramatic and linguistic conventions, drawing inspiration from futurism, Russian folklore, and the nonsense verse of Edward Lear. Kharms's grotesque one-act comedy *Elizabeth Bam*, which was publicly performed in 1927, anticipates EUGÈNE IONESCO in its probing of the absurdity of existence through the clichés and non sequiturs of daily life. Vvedensky's *Christmas at Ivanovs'* (1938) is a macabre parody of a holiday play full of Dadaist violence and black humor. Because of its ruthless suppression by the Soviet authorities in the 1930s, this small but significant body of experimental avant-garde Russian drama remained virtually unknown until the 1960s.

[*See also* Russia and the Soviet Union]

FURTHER READING

Rudnitsky, Konstantin. *Russian and Soviet Theatre: Tradition and the Avant-Garde*. London: Thames & Hudson, 2000.

Russell, Robert. *Russian Drama of the Revolutionary Period*. Totowa, N.J.: Barnes & Noble, 1988.

Segel, Harold. *Twentieth-Century Russian Drama*. 2d ed. New York: Columbia Univ. Press, 1993.

Tolstoy, Vladimir. *Street Art of the Revolution*. New York: Vendome, 1990.

Worrall, Nick, *Modernism to Realism on the Soviet Stage: Tairov-Vakhtangov-Okklopov*. Cambridge: Cambridge Univ. Press, 1989.

Daniel Gerould

SOUTH AFRICA

South African avant-garde theater challenges the politics of race and class, the ideological and repressive role of the state, perceptions of history and colonization, and questions of identity. There is a strong tradition of being oppositional to the status quo using extremely diverse theatrical forms. Specifically, artists have aimed to fuse two seemingly opposed aesthetics: African traditional performance forms and 20th-century Western approaches. A striking example of this is "township theater," which integrates improvisation, song, dance, music, narration, spoken word, hybrid languages, mime, one actor in multiple roles, fantastic leaps in time and place, and emphasis on physical energy in performance.

South African avant-garde theater can be divided into two categories: 1950–1994, the apartheid era, and 1994 to the present, the postapartheid period. Protest theater directly challenged apartheid ideology. Many works were banned and the writers arrested. Prominent playwrights/groups included Workshop 71 with *Survival* (1976), which employed township forms to depict the harsh realities of urban life; and Maishe Maponya's *The Hungry Earth* (1979), *The Nurse* (1983), and *Gangsters* (1984). Inspired by the Black Consciousness movement, Maponya's plays combined township theater forms with aspects of REALISM. Similar in style and influence, Matsamela Manaka's *Egoli—City of Gold* (1978) reveals the hardships of migrant laborers working in Johannesburg's gold mines.

The protest play *Woza Albert!* (1981) by MBONGENI NGEMA, Percy Mtwa, and Barney Simon was created in workshops. Its premise: What would happen if Christ returned to apartheid-era South Africa? It combines township styles with direct political satire. The many characters are played by two actors in an empty space using few props. Polish innovator Jerzy Grotowski's influence is demonstrated by the dynamic physicality of the performers and the minimalist aesthetic. Other protest plays include Ngema's *Asinimali—We Have No Money!* (1984), about rent boycotts, and Mtwa's *Bopha–Arrest!* (1983), which focuses on the lives of black police collaborators. *Cincinatti—Scenes from City Life* (1979) and *Born in the RSA* (1984), workshopped by Barney Simon, represent the intensely contradictory lives of ordinary people. ATHOL FUGARD, John Kani, and Winston Ntshona's workshop produced *The Island* (1973), which employs township-theater styles as political prisoners try to stage *Antigone* in the Robben Island prison where Nelson Mandela and others were kept.

Combining Brechtian notions with historical narrative, Junction Avenue Theatre Company's *Randlords and Rotgut* (1978) represented gold mine owners and the rotgut beer fed to black mineworkers. *Sophiatown* (1986) focused on the forced removal of blacks in the 1950s to the townships. *Tooth and Nail* (1989) reflected social conflict in a fragmented, disorientated structure. In *Horn of Sorrow* (1988), the Theatre for Africa Company applied their physical skills to storytelling, creating wild animals to provide social critique. James Whyle's *National Madness* (1982) and David Peimer's *Serpent's Mate* (1982) focus on white males forced to serve in the army. They employ the Theatre of Images (Bonnie Marranca's term) with emphasis on the visual. Peimer adapted HEINER MÜLLER's *The Task* (1991) along the same lines, though infused with African aesthetics.

Satirist Pieter Dirk-Uys staged *Paradise Is Closing Down* (1977) and *God's Forgotten* (1977) after the 1976 mass revolt by schoolchildren, exploring the violent end of apartheid and the lives of marginalized people of mixed race.

In postapartheid South Africa, artists expressed personal experience while also provoking politically. They incorporate many aesthetic innovations, ranging from POSTMODERNISM to traditional African forms. Reflecting the diversity of cultures, pressures, and creativity unleashed in this rare moment of historical transformation, there is no single dominant avant-garde style.

During the late 1990s, William Kentridge created *Woyzeck on the Highveld* (1992), *Ubu and the Truth Commission* (1996), and *Faust in Africa* (1995). He is highly innovative in his use of puppets, music, and animation to focus on the legacy of apartheid, the Truth Commission, and the history of colonization. Lara Foot-Newton's *Ways of Dying* (2000) is rooted in imagistic storytelling, and *Baby Tsepang* (2002) is about the baby-rape crisis. Andrew Buckland's *The Well Being* (2003) demonstrates the influence of physical theater and township performance styles.

Inspired by Pina Bausch, choreographer Robyn Orlin deconstructs dance. Her many works include *Naked on a Goat* (1995), about sexual politics; *Daddy, I've seen this piece six times before and I still don't know why they're hurting each other* (1999), concerning current violence in South Africa; and *We must eat our suckers with the wrappers on* (2002), about the AIDS pandemic. Brett Bailey's *iMumbo Jumbo* (1996) and *Ipi Zombi* (1998) combine African singing and dance in rituals, trance, real *sangomas* (traditional healers/diviners), and powerful physical energy with kitsch, satire, and postmodern juxtaposition of images to interrogate "witchcraft," corruption, and dictatorship. Xoli Norman fuses township jazz and blues with narrative, focusing on crime in *Hallelujah!* (2001) and the conflict between the black apartheid generation and their children in *Our Father, Ma's Got the Blues* (2002). In *I Mike What I Like* (2003) and *Thy Condom Come* (2000), Kgafela oa Magogodi's "spoken word poetry in performance" infuses traditional praise poetry with social critique and gritty urban language. Using smell as a medium, Monkey's Wedding Theatre Company's *Scavenger's Dream* (2002) combines installation art with a surreal, visual, and African physical/singing performance style to explore European and African perceptions of the "other." Using "shock" performance art, Steven Cohen provokes questions about sexuality and religion. Athena Mazarkis incorporates mime and surreal expressions of violence in *Breaking News* (2003). Deconstructing realism, Reza de Wet's *Crossing* (1994) shows characters interacting with the dead. Echoing protest theater, Aubrey Sekhabi's *On My Birthday* (2000) and *Not without My Gun* (2001) focus on domestic and gun violence.

True to its roots in the apartheid era, South African avant-garde theater remains provocative and continues to embrace both contemporary and traditional African performance forms and Western avant-garde aesthetics. This embrace sometimes produces a raw collision, sometimes a haunting fusion. But within the mutual mirroring of "otherness," perhaps what is most inspiring is the creative diversity and the radical tradition of opposition to the status quo.

[*See also* South Africa]

FURTHER READING

Crow, Brian, and Chris Banfield. *An Introduction to Post-Colonial Theatre.* Cambridge: Cambridge Univ. Press, 1996.

Etherton, Michael. *The Development of African Drama.* New York: Africana, 1982.

Graver, David, ed. *Drama for a New South Africa.* Bloomington: Indiana Univ. Press, 1999.

Hauptfleishch, Temple, and Ian Steadman. *South African Theatre.* Pretoria, South Africa: Haum Educational Publs., 1984.

Kavanagh, Robert Mshengu. *Theatre and Cultural Struggle in South Africa.* London: Zed Bks., 1985.

Maponya, Maishe. *Doing Plays for a Change.* Witwatersrand, South Africa: Witwatersrand Univ. Press, Johannesburg, 1995.

Ndlovu, Duma, ed. *Woza Afrika! An Anthology of South African Plays.* New York: Braziller, 1986.

Soyinka, Wole. *Myth, Literature, and the African World.* Cambridge: Cambridge Univ. Press, 1976.

David Peimer

SOUTHEAST ASIA

Avant-garde drama and theater in Southeast Asia vary widely among individual nations and often within each country. The cultural diversity and complexity of the region, its many languages, and the differing imprints left by European colonialism all contribute to a range of practices that divide the region into roughly two groups: (1) the formerly colonized countries of SINGAPORE, MALAYSIA, and the PHILIPPINES, which have been much influenced by the colonizer's educational system and theatrical traditions; and (2) the remaining countries either where colonization did not occur (THAILAND) or where the theatrical traditions of the colonizer had little influence on practice (VIETNAM, CAMBODIA, LAOS, BURMA/Myanmar). In the case of these countries, traditional performance practices—often altered by modern technology—continue to be most vital.

The only exception is INDONESIA, where a body of drama emerged in the late 1960s that challenged social constructs and political authority in ways that traditional performance practices did not. As the only country in the region not subjected to colonization, Thailand continues to revere traditional performance forms while also embracing commercial, Western-influenced theater practice.

Avant-garde theater practices found in Southeast Asian countries generally fall into three categories: (1) AGITATION-PROPAGANDA (agit-prop) and socially conscious theater that confronts existing political, economic, and social structures; (2) dramatic literature influenced by, or that shares similar features with, theater movements in the West such as ABSURDISM and POSTMODERNISM; and (3) staging practices such as ENVIRONMENTAL THEATER that are influenced by or parallel to avant-garde theater practices that were popularized in the 1960s by New York–based groups such as the LIVING THEATRE, the Open Theatre, and the Performance Group. These strands will be examined on a country-by-country basis.

INDONESIA

Indonesia, a vast nation of some 13,670 islands that lies astride the equator, is the most populous country in the region and the world's largest predominantly Muslim nation. Indonesians have historically maintained strong performance traditions; many of them predate the arrival of Islam in the country in the 13th century. During the colonial era, the Dutch—unlike the British in Singapore and Malaysia—never succeeded in fully imposing their educational structures on a culturally and linguistically diverse population. The avant-garde drama and staging practices that have emerged in the country since 1968 have generally been limited to theaters in urban areas where education and relative economic prosperity have created an audience receptive to such work.

Following the political and social upheavals of the final years of the Achmed Sukarno era, Thojib Suharto's New Order government, established in 1966, brought increasing political stability to Indonesia, though not without continuing repression. Nevertheless, the late 1960s witnessed the emboldening of a generation of young Indonesians to use theater as a tool for criticizing the country's top-down political style, corruption, and oppressive social forces. The radical spirit of the post-1968 era found its strongest initial expression in poet and playwright W. S. RENDRA. After returning from the United States in 1967, Rendra established his theater workshop Benkel in a working-class area of the university city of Yogyakarta. His earliest productions were nonlinear and featured little dialogue, in line with New York avant-garde practices of the time. By the mid-1970s, Rendra created the works for which he is best known, *The Mastodon and the Condor* (*Mastodon dan Burung Kondor*, 1973), THE STRUGGLE OF THE NAGA TRIBE (*Kisah Perjuangan Suku Naga*, 1974), and *Regional Secretary* (*Sekda*, 1977). All three plays criticize political repression in artfully indirect ways through analogy, FARCE, and traditional performance forms such as *wayang kulit*, known in the West as shadow puppetry. Rendra's success encouraged others to create politically conscious theater companies in Yogyakarta, among the most significant of which were Dinasti, Gandrik, and Jeprik.

Other playwrights who have expanded the boundaries of expression in Indonesian theater include PUTU WIJAYA, ARIFIN C. NOER, and NANO RIANTIARNO. Wijaya's Jakarta-based Teater Mandiri, formed in 1971, is known for staging spectacles, or *tontonan*, that feature the use of found objects and stunning stage pictures to create a spirit of collective meditation linking the performer and the audience. Noer's reputation rests largely on his poetic masterpiece MOTHS (*Kapi-Kapi*, 1970), a work that speaks to the dehumanizing forces of political and social repression. Riantiarno runs Jakarta's Teater Koma, and his most important work, THE COCKROACH OPERA (*Opera Kechoa*, 1985), combines Western-influenced rock music with traditional Indonesian performance forms in telling the story of individuals struggling to survive on the streets of Jakarta. Also significant is the arts center, Taman Ismail Marzuki (TIM), located in Jakarta, which once nurtured the more adventurous work of Rendra, Putu, and Arifin, though today it offers theater more in line with safe, middle-class sensibilities.

PHILIPPINES

The colonization of the Philippines, the only predominantly Christian nation in Asia, was marked by a lengthy process of acculturation, first by the Spanish in the 16th century, then by the Americans following the Spanish-American War of 1898. From the early days of the 20th century, Filipinos have used theater as an instrument to press for political and social change, first as they criticized American colonialism in works such as Aurelio Tolentino's *Yesterday, Today and Tomorrow* (*Kapahon, Ngayo, at Bukas*, 1903) and later as they took on the Ferdinand Marcos family with plays such as BONIFACIO ILAGAN's *The Nation's Worship* (*Pagsambang Bayan*, 1977). Ilagan's play, written in the midst of the martial law years (1972–1981), uses the structure of the Catholic liturgy to call for liberation. During the Marcos era, the work of agit-prop theater artists who staged street skits critical of the regime constituted an important element in the fight against the political cronyism and injustice of the American-backed regime.

Embodying this fighting spirit is the PHILIPPINE EDUCATIONAL THEATER ASSOCIATION (PETA), founded in 1967 by Cecile Guidote-Alvarez. More than any theater group in the region, PETA has provided an important model for the use of theater as an instrument of social change. The company's process-oriented theater, similar in design to the "Theater of the Oppressed" model of Brazilian AUGUSTO BOAL, has a long, successful history working with communities facing particular social or economic problems and dramatizing the issues in order to affect change. In addition to performing in and around metropolitan Manila, the company has frequently toured to rural areas to deal with subjects such as poverty, violence against women, and the plight of Filipinas working overseas in unskilled, low-wage jobs. Among the many significant plays that have come out of PETA is MALOU JACOB's *Juan Tamban* (1979), a searing drama that looks at the plight of a Manila street kid. The company's staging practices are minimalist, as the demands of touring require, and the audience is acknowledged and even implicated in many of their performance works.

SINGAPORE AND MALAYSIA

In the former colonies of Singapore and Malaysia, the British model of education meant that for the generation of potential playwrights coming of age during the 1960s models of dramatic construction were very much influenced by European practices. Because political debate in both countries is tightly controlled by the parties that have ruled throughout the postindependence era, political criticism is generally muted or couched in metaphors. Nevertheless, playwrights in both countries have created works that challenge the complacency of fellow citizens while critiquing an authoritarian political landscape.

In Malaysia, among the most significant voices to emerge during the 1980s were playwrights Kee Thuan Chye and K. S. Maniam. Drawing parallels with George Orwell's book, Kee's *1984: Here and Now* (1985) suggests that his compatriots accepted a system of repression without being fully conscious of the degree to which thought and speech are regulated. Maniam is best known for his play *The Cord* (1984), which shows a member of Malaysia's relatively disadvantaged ethnic Indian minority laying claim to his personal power. Emerging a few years later was playwright LEOW PUAY TIN, who uses minimalist, Brechtian staging and epic narrative structures to explore Chinese Malaysian identity in her plays *Three Children* (1988) and *Family* (1996). The epicenter for the most progressive and challenging theater in English and Malay has been Kuala Lumpur's Five Arts Centre, where well-respected director Krishen Jit has been instrumental in bringing much of this work to the stage.

Singaporean playwright KUO PAO KUN is best known for his two much-produced one-act monologues THE COFFIN IS TOO BIG FOR THE HOLE (1985) and *No Parking on Odd Days* (1986), which slyly and skillfully critique the dehumanizing forces of an inflexible bureaucracy in the wealthy metropolis of contemporary Singapore. Less direct in its criticism is his *Descendants of the Eunuch Admiral* (1995), which employs castration as a metaphor for the losses Singaporeans have endured for a life of wealth and comfort. In spite of having been detained by the government from 1976 to 1980, Kuo never stopped demanding that Singaporeans consider the trade-off between material comforts granted by political masters and the more leisurely and diverse lifestyles of earlier times. His artistic home, the Practice Performing Arts School, was formed in 1965, and along with his wife, choreographer Goh Lay Kuan, Kuo provided important training in avant-garde theater practice to two generations of Singaporeans. The company with the longest and most consistent history of bravely tackling Singapore's most pressing social problems through theater is the Necessary Stage, formed in 1987 by artistic director Alvin Tan and featuring the work of resident playwright Haresh Sharma.

Singapore is also the one country in the region where staging practices for contemporary drama have been the most aggressively avant-garde, running the range from environmental theater in found spaces to high-tech performances incorporating mixed media. During the 1990s, the company Theatre Works, under the artistic direction of ONG KENG SEN, emerged as a regional leader, utilizing modern technology while blending elements of the Western avant-garde with a range of Asian performance traditions. Among their best-known works in this style are *Broken Birds* (1995), *Lear* (1997), and *Desdemona* (2000). Ong is the region's best-known director and has emerged as in important figure in the development of a contemporary, Pan-Asian theater practice.

BURMA, CAMBODIA, LAOS, VIETNAM, AND THAILAND

Burma (Myanmar), Cambodia, Laos, and Vietnam all have long-standing performance traditions generally far removed from practices that might be called avant-garde. In the case of Thailand, Laos, Cambodia, and Burma, traditional court dance forms (*khon* and *lakon fai nai* in Thailand and Laos, *zat gyi* in Burma, *lakon kabach boran* in Cambodia) have endured as core performance traditions, while in Vietnam, *hat bôi*—similar to what is known as Chinese opera in the West—remains important. French colonization in Vietnam, Laos, and Cambodia left little imprint on the country's performance traditions, owing to the relative insularity of French culture and the disruptive effects of what is known in the region as the "American War."

In the case of Thailand, spoken drama has a lengthy tradition extending from the reign of King Rama VI (1910–1925), a prolific writer of romantic melodramas. During the 1970s, a more experimental practice emerged with a growing middle-class audience of potential patrons. The three companies that pushed for a more radical theater practice in terms of staging and content—Kamron Kunadilok, Shakdao, and Thawanplueng—died a quick death after the right-wing coup of 1976. For the most part, modern theater in Thailand today means Western plays or musicals staged for a relatively wealthy, elite audience in Bangkok. A practice that fuses indigenous dramaturgy with Western theater practices of the sort found in Singapore has not yet emerged.

THE NEW AVANT GARDE FOR SOUTHEAST ASIA

Indonesia, the Philippines, Singapore, and Malaysia stand out as the four countries in the region with the most clearly identifiable avant-garde practices in terms of playwriting and the staging of drama. While the Philippines is the regional leader in the use of theater as an instrument of political and social change, Singapore emerged during the 1990s as an important regional center for intercultural theater through the development of staging practices that draw broadly from traditional

Asian and Western avant-garde sources. The future is likely to see the further development of a distinctly Asian avant-garde theater practice, especially in wealthier Southeast Asian nations such as Singapore and Malaysia.

FURTHER READING

Brandon, James. *The Cambridge Guide to Asian Theatre*. Cambridge: Cambridge Univ. Press, 1993.

Fernandez, Doreen G. *Palabas: Essays on Philippine Theater History*. Manila: Ateneo de Manila Univ. Press, 1996.

Lo, Jacqueline. *Staging Nation: Postcolonial English Language Theatre in Malaysia and Singapore*. Hong Kong: Hong Kong Univ. Press, 2004.

Necessary Stage. *Nine Lives: 10 Years of Singapore Theatre, 1987–1997*. Singapore: Author, 1997.

Peterson, William. *Theatre and the Politics of Culture in Contemporary Singapore*. Middletown, Conn.: Wesleyan Univ. Press, 2001.

Van Erven, Eugène. *The Playful Revolution: Theatre and Liberation in Asia*. Bloomington: Indiana Univ. Press, 1992.

William Peterson

UNITED STATES

Avant-garde drama in the United States begins in earnest after World War II through what is broadly thought of as artistic experimentation; however, there are earlier high modernist influences. This article focuses on the historically self-aware American avant-garde, meaning theater artists whose aesthetic experimentation was self-conscious, intentional, and innovative enough that, in its cultural moment, it shocked audiences.

In terms of a high modernist avant-garde, a beginning point is often set with the sensational New York Armory Show in 1913, which introduced the public to modernism through over 1,300 paintings, sculptures, and drawings, including the work of cubists, Fauvists, and American modernists. The exhibition is considered a radical break with tradition out of which emerged vital art and drama. Both Marsden Hartley and Alfred Maurer, exhibitors at the Armory Show, had been introduced to cubism through GERTRUDE STEIN. Stein and her brother were among the first collectors of cubist art, and their Paris home was a popular salon. While Stein's dramas were not widely available until later, her influence on the European avant-garde was paramount.

Designer ROBERT EDMOND JONES was influenced by the Armory Show. Jones would later lead a movement called the New Stagecraft, inspired by European design. As early as 1913, Jones created an expressionistic set design for the "Pageant of the Paterson Strike." Held at Madison Square Garden, this pageant was the brainchild of journalist Jack Reed and was designed to raise both consciousness and money for the striking silk workers of Paterson, New Jersey. While not a political success, the pageant did engage politics and theater and raise the morale of 1,200 striking silk workers who participated in this massive pageant.

Jones later became the designer for playwright EUGENE O'NEILL, and his plays THE HAIRY APE (1921) and EMPEROR JONES (1921) typified what came to be called American EXPRESSIONISM. Expressionism externalized the subjective world of emotions, thoughts, and ideas. SOPHIE TREADWELL'S *MACHINAL* (1928), about the Snyder-Gray murder trial of 1927, is another example, as is SUSAN GLASPELL'S TRIFLES (1920). O'Neill's work was first produced by one of the earliest "little theaters," the Provincetown Players. Modeling themselves after the French Art Theater movement, the Little Theater movement offered subscribers amateur seasons of artistic plays. By 1917, there were 50 little theaters in the country.

In the 1930s and 1940s, politically engaged companies like Theatre Union, the GROUP THEATRE, many groups funded by the FEDERAL THEATRE PROJECT, and playwrights such as JOHN HOWARD LAWSON and ELMER RICE continued to interrogate sociopolitical injustices. European influence played a crucial role as European expatriates came to the United States in search of refuge from the Nazis. The most influential of these were BERTOLT BRECHT and ERWIN PISCATOR. Piscator's overtly political Dramatic Workshop at the New School for Social Research (1939–1951) trained hundreds of socially minded practitioners.

Black Mountain College in North Carolina had an extremely progressive arts program modeled on the Bauhaus, the modernist architecture and art school in Germany. In the summer of 1952, composer John Cage, dancer Merce Cunningham, and painter Robert Rauschenberg produced an untitled, mixed-media event that became an originary moment for self-aware aesthetic experimentation. Alan Kaprow's work, particularly in *18 Happenings in Six Parts* (1959), was influenced by Cage. Kaprow divided the rooms of the Reuben Gallery in New York into three rooms with plastic walls. The visitors' tickets directed them to specified seats in each room at particular times and with strictly choreographed movements and witnessed, among other events, a girl squeezing oranges, an artist lighting matches and painting, and an orchestra of toy instruments. Although tightly scripted and planned, Kaprow's early happenings possessed an air of unstructured spontaneity.

Black plays and theater were a source of both innovation and agitation in the 1960s. JEAN GENET'S THE BLACKS (1955) was directed by Gene Frankel at the St. Mark's Playhouse (1961) with a cast that included Maya Angelou, James Earl Jones, Cicely Tyson, and Roscoe Lee Brown. It ran for 1,408 performances. *The Blacks* involves the ritualized murder of a white woman by an African American court, and while the play interrogates racism, it was both written and directed by whites. Many cast members wanted to find their own voices and went on to work for the first all African American company, the Negro Ensemble Company, formed by Robert Hooks and Douglas Turner in 1963. Another extremely important playwright, and co-founder of the BLACK ARTS MOVEMENT was Leroi Jones, later Imamu AMIRI BARAKA. Baraka helped start the Black Arts Repertory Theatre/School in 1965, after his powerful play DUTCHMAN (1964) won the Obie Award for Best Play in 1964. ADRIENNE KENNEDY also won an Obie the same year for her play *Funnyhouse of a Negro* (1964). Perhaps the most avant-garde in terms of her representational style, Kennedy's plays rejected REALISM's unified characters and instead created split subjects that demonstrate her views on internalized racism. Other black avant-garde playwrights are ED BULLINS, Sonia Sanchez, and Ben Caldwell.

In New York, the OFF-BROADWAY movement began in the early 1950s in response to the commercialization of Broadway. Certain theaters in the off-Broadway movement can be thought of possessing an avant-garde impulse inasfar as they rejected the star system of Broadway and attempted to run as collectives, such as Circle in the Square. The earliest off-Broadway house, Judith Malina and Julian Beck's the LIVING THEATRE, began in 1946 and continued to be extremely radical throughout the tumult of the 1960s. Their production of JACK GELBER's *The Connection* (1959) involved heroin addicts waiting for a fix from their connection, playing jazz, and making seemingly pointless small talk. Kenneth Brown's *The Brig* (1963) focused on the cruelty of Marine Corps prisons. Both productions were informed by ANTONIN ARTAUD's *The Theater and Its Double*, which was first translated in the United States in 1959. This text was of tremendous importance to theater practitioners from the 1960s onward. The Living Theatre is often considered AGITATION-PROPAGANDA (agit-prop) in its political engagement, particularly their collectively created improvisational piece *Paradise Now* (1968). Other agit-prop theaters were Peter Schumann's Vermont-based Bread and Puppet Theater, LUIS VALDEZ's California-based EL TEATRO CAMPESINO, and Ron Davis's San Francisco Mime Troupe. All of these companies were invested in making theater that worked for social change.

As the 1960s continued, operating costs made innovative work almost impossible, and newer, smaller theaters called OFF-OFF-BROADWAY houses were opened. The most visionary producer was Ellen Stewart, whose playwright's theater La Mama opened in 1961 in a converted basement. Stewart encouraged young playwrights to develop their craft, and in her 1967 season, more plays were produced at La Mama than on all the Broadway stages combined. Playwrights whose work was fostered by La Mama include ROCHELLE OWENS, Paul Foster, and Jean Claude Van Italie.

Van Italie's collaborative style of creation was influenced by another off-off-Broadway company, the Open Theater. Their production of *The Serpent* (1969) was created through seven weeks of improvisational exercises with actors. The play that resulted involved cultural myths such as the Garden of Eden combined with the assassination of heroes like Martin Luther King, Jr., and Robert Kennedy. Richard Schechner' Performance Group was also an important company and perhaps most renown for their adaptation of Euripides' *The Bacchae*, titled *Dionysus in '69* (1969). The Performance Group later became the Wooster Group and launched the careers of SPALDING GRAY, Willem Dafoe, and Kate Valk.

While the regional theater movement is often considered traditional, at least one company breaks that mold. The Actor's Workshop of San Francisco was started by Herbert Blau and Jules Irving in 1952, and the impulse behind their choice of plays was avant-garde and brought them national attention. They produced the American premieres of Bertolt Brecht's MOTHER COURAGE (written in 1939 and produced in 1956), HAROLD PINTER's THE BIRTHDAY PARTY (written in 1957 and produced in 1960), and MARIA IRENE FORNES's very first play, *Tango*, then called *There! You Died* (1963). In 1963, Martin Esslin made the company his poster child for his book *The Theatre of the* by opening his book with a description of their production of SAMUEL BECKETT's WAITING FOR GODOT at San Quentin Prison (1957). This was the first production to be done in a maximum security prison. Herbert Blau's book *The Impossible Theater, A Manifesto* (1964) remains one of the most important articulations about American theater to date. Other important regional theaters in the avant-garde tradition are those of the BLACK ARTS MOVEMENT: BLKARTSWEST, Concept East, the New Lafayette Theatre, and Black House among them.

The American avant-garde is thought by many to have ended in the early 1970s. Primarily this end intersects with the rise of POSTMODERNISM and the proliferation of forms considered avant-garde, which, because there are so many, are no longer innovations but re-creations. Since part of the impulse behind the avant-garde is to shock or make new, both these ideas become less possible within the postmodern moment. The current avant-garde might be more suitably called the popular "experiment" and includes work that is, according to Schechner (1993), "forward-looking, tradition-seeking, and intercultural."

FURTHER READING

Blau, Herbert. *The Impossible Theater, A Manifesto*. New York: Macmillan, 1964.

Brockett, Oscar. *Century of Innovation*. New York: Allyn, 1973.

Graver, David. *The Aesthetics of Disturbance*. Ann Arbor: Univ. of Michigan Press, 1995.

Harding, James, ed. *Contours of the Theatrical Avant-Garde, Performance and Textuality*. Ann Arbor: Univ. of Michigan Press, 2000.

Hobbes, Stuart. *The End of the American Avant-Garde*. New York: N.Y. Univ. Press, 1997.

Sayre, Henry. *The Object of Performance: The American Avant-garde since 1970*. Chicago: Chicago Univ. Press, 1989.

Schechner, Richard. "Introduction: Jayaganesh and the Avant-Garde." In *The Future of Ritual*. New York: Routledge, 1993.

Kara Reilly

WESTERN EUROPE

To represent avant-garde drama in Western Europe as a linear genealogy is problematic. The influences and alliances of artists and movements in Western Europe's avant-garde drama and theater constitute a complicated and intertwined web of influence. Artists traveled widely throughout Western and Eastern Europe and to the Americas, making national demarcations misleading at best. Yet nearly all of Europe's experimental drama written between 1890 and 1945 shares the perspective of a world in chaos or what expressionist playwright Gottfried Benn called "reality disintegration." Drama in the historical avant-garde followed several common (if not uniform) thematic trends, most notably the negation of faith in God and nonrepresentational language but also political and social revolution. Drawing on Sigmund Freud's theories of sexuality and dreams and cinema's fragmentation, avant-garde drama developed an aesthetic vernacular for articulating the transformations of the early 20th century that was expressly antirealistic.

BEGINNINGS

These cultural, social, and political changes first emerged in NATURALISM and REALISM, which drew heavily on the theories of Charles Darwin and Freud and their secular, though entirely causal, explanations of the universe and humanity's role within it. In the wake of Friedrich Nietzsche's pronouncement "God is dead," HENRIK IBSEN, EMILE ZOLA, and AUGUST STRINDBERG attempted to make up for this loss of divinity by adapting scientific analysis and positivist explanations like those of August Comte and Social Darwinism (with all its racist and gendered implications) to the existing form of the well-made play. However, the "avant-garde," as conceived by French socialist Henri de Saint-Simon, sought to transform society through science and art. This term *avant-garde* (also translated as *avangard*, or *vanguard*) was quickly absorbed into mid-19th-century political discourse, appearing in Karl Marx's *Communist Manifesto* (1848) and later in Vladimir Lenin's *What Is to Be Done?* (1902) and inspiring the experiments of Russians VSEVOLOD MEYERHOLD and Boris Youjanin and the German EPIC THEATER, first introduced by ERWIN PISCATOR and later adopted by BERTOLT BRECHT. In FRANCE, JACQUES COPEAU's Théâtre du Vieux-Colombier (what Piscator called "the true avant-garde of French theatre") sparked further political and social experimentation among French directors such as Charles Dullin, Louis Jouvet, and Georges Pitoeff, as well as Michael St. Denis and the London Theatre Studio. The political avant-garde became widely known as "agit-prop" (AGITATION-PROPAGANDA) and was briefly popular in American theater collectives.

Such utopian visions ultimately may prove less influential than the negation for which the avant-garde has more often been known. SYMBOLISM, for example, rejected scientific explanation in favor of fate, mysticism, and the supernatural. French symbolists like Charles Baudelaire, Villiers de l'Isle-Adam, Stéphane Mallarmé, and MAURICE MAETERLINCK wrote poetic plays that increasingly turned inward, eventually favoring the CLOSET DRAMA over the public theater. Maeterlinck's titles echo the private world he sought to create in *The Intruder* (1890), *The Blind* (1890), and *Interior* (1894). OSCAR WILDE's *Salomé* (1892) exhibits the self-conscious autonomy that Mallarmé associates with art, and even Strindberg displays the influence of Maeterlinck in his later work. Following the symbolists, Strindberg rejected realistic representation in favor of dreams, ghosts, and mystical experience in plays such as *TO DAMASCUS* (Parts I and II, 1898; Part III, 1900–1901), *A DREAM PLAY* (1901), and his chamber play *GHOST SONATA* (1907). In addition to such converts as Strindberg, French symbolism also ignited a parallel movement in Russia. Valery Briusov became a leading figure in Russian symbolism through plays like *The Earth* (1905) and *The Wayfarer* (1910), arguing against the realistic style of the MOSCOW ART THEATER.

It was between the diverse impulses of positivist social change and symbolist rumination that the avant-garde's most rambunctious experiments occurred. Although ALFRED JARRY's *Ubu Roi* (1896) first appeared in the symbolist Théâtre de l'Oeuvre, its aim was no less transformative than that of the political theater to follow. Like the military shock troops for whom the avant-garde was named, *Ubu Roi* was a calculated—and effective—attack on its bourgeois audience. In stark contrast to the symbolists' ruminations, Jarry's protagonist Père Ubu was a loud, boisterous assault on his audience's good taste, openly blaspheming God, usurping the fictional king of Poland, and flushing the nobility down a toilet. According to most accounts, the first word of the play, *merdre* (a slurring comparable to *shitre*, suggesting excrement), caused a riot such that the play abruptly stopped. As W. B. YEATS reflected on the performance, "After us the savage gods."

Such assaults on reason and morality have become virtually clichéd in the history of avant-garde drama, but their significance should not be underestimated. Following the example of Jarry's excrement-laden torch, subsequent avant-garde drama began to breach the barrier between actor and audience, fantasy and reality, art and life. Perhaps the best-known example of this in drama is LUIGI PIRANDELLO's *SIX CHARACTERS IN SEARCH OF AN AUTHOR* (1921), but he was by no means the first Italian to attack the easy divisions between art and life. Italian futurists had already begun using their audiences as unwitting (and unwilling) collaborators. Like Jarry, Italian futurist FILIPPO TOMMASO MARINETTI came to modernism through symbolism, founding the symbolist journal *Poesia* in 1905. As a symbolist, he wrote two full-length plays, *King Glutton* (1905), modeled on Jarry's *Ubu Roi*, and *Electric Dolls* (1909). Though avowedly symbolist in inspiration, the latter play marks the direction Marinetti would follow in FUTURISM. That same year, Marinetti wrote the first futurist manifesto, espousing the virtues of machines, speed, and war. As futurism developed in the years leading up to World War I, playwrights adopted the form of the *sintesi*: extremely short, forceful plays designed to create the maximum effect with a minimum of language and time.

For futurism, language gave way to violent gesture, and their drama violated all previous definitions of a "play." Franceco Cangiullo's *sintesi Detonation* (1915), for example, raises the curtain, fires a gun, and lowers the curtain. Manifestos, a principal art form in futurism (and throughout avant-garde drama), quickly became combined with *sintesi*, as in Bruno Corra and Emilio Settimelli's *Dissonance* (1915). Corra's *Alternation of Character* (1915) signaled a formal end to cohesive character by creating a couple, each of whom changed with each line of dialogue. Following the Bolshevik Revolution in 1917, futurism quickly spread east to Russia. VLADIMIR MAYAKOVSKY's MYSTERY-BOUFFE (1918), for example, has been called both the greatest Bolshevik and the greatest futurist drama.

Emerging in concurrence with futurism, German EXPRESSIONISM followed the internalizing impulses of symbolism but turned such interiorities outward, expressing the anguish of the modern psyche not in privately understood dreams but through the transformation of physical environments. Perhaps the first major work in German expressionism came from neither a playwright nor a German but from the Russian-born painter Wassily Kandinsky. In the same year that *Ubu Roi* premiered (1896), Kandinsky arrived in Munich to study painting. Beginning in 1908, he began painting expressionistic landscapes, and his first play, the visually inspired *Yellow Sound* (1909), would follow just a year later. His abstract plays clearly indicate his primary medium—*The Green Sound* (1909), *Black and White* (1909), and *Violet* (1911)—and his alliance to Der Blaue Reiter (The Blue Rider), an artistic group dedicated to the expression of the inner life of the artist.

DEVELOPMENTS FOLLOWING WORLD WAR I

As Europe edged ever closer to war, representations of this inner life became increasingly darker. Austrian painter OSKAR KOKOSCHKA wrote *Sphinx and Strawman: A Curiosity* (1907) and *Murderer, Hope of Women* (1909), a play that foreshadows the phenomenon of Lüstmord (sexual murder) in post–World War I painting and film. Plays like REINHARD SORGE's *The Beggar* (1911) and GEORG KAISER's *FROM MORNING TO MIDNIGHT* (1917) used episodic structure to depict characters engaged in seemingly endless, futile searches for meaning. Like the futurists, violent, aggressive language, often directed at women, became the vernacular for such plays as August Stramm's *Sancta Susanna* (1911), Gottfried Benn's *Ithaka* (1914), and WALTER HASENCLEVER's THE SON (1916). Expressionist design became as important as dramatic structure, with exaggerated facial features, shadows, and costumes standing in for characters' distorted and disturbed interior sensibilities. Such internal distortions would eventually give way to actual horror in the world's first fully mechanized war and its assault on the sensibilities of Europe through trench warfare, machine guns, tanks, and bombs. Such morbid technology and its effect on a mechanized humanity were plainly evident in plays like ERNST TOLLER's *Machine Wreckers* (1922) and Bertolt Brecht's early works DRUMS IN THE NIGHT (1922), *Jungle of Cities* (1923), and BAAL (1923).

As World War I broke out in 1914, various threads of the avant-garde were beginning to coalesce in Zurich, SWITZERLAND. Although some avant-garde drama was written in ENGLAND—Wyndham Lewis's *Enemy of the Stars* (1914), for example—the high concentration of European artists escaping the war created a primary center for theatrical and artistic experiment. Drawing on symbolism, expressionism, and futurism, Hugo Ball, Emmy Hennings, Richard Huelsenbeck, Marcel Janco, Hans Arp, YVAN GOLL, and Tristan Tzara gathered at the Cabaret Voltaire in 1916 to create spontaneous performances and poetry readings they titled "DADA," a deliberately nonsensical title. As Dada progressed, it transcended expressionism and futurism, becoming its own unique entity, which has become known as "anti-art." Reacting against both the self-focused intensity of expressionism and the violent dehumanization of World War I, Dada plays became experiments in collisions of sounds and images. Dada produced few texts (Ball's *A Nativity Play* [1916] is more poetry than drama), but notable among them are Tristan Tzara's *The First Celestial Adventure of Mr. Antipyrine, Fire Extinguisher* (1917) and *The Gas Heart* (1920), Kurt Schwitters's *Dramatic Scene* (1919), Georges Ribemont-Desaignes's *The Mute Canary* (1919), André Breton and Philippe Soupault's *If You Please* (1920), and Francis Picabia's *No Performance* (*Relâche*, 1920). It is also worth noting that Dada and later SURREALISM included women artists, though hardly as equals. In addition to Hennings, sometimes playwright Mina Loy and photomontage artist Hannah Höch were included in Dada shows, and surrealism contained a number of women, though few playwrights.

In the years following World War I, Dada gave way to surrealism in France, although the details are debatable. Following Freud explicitly, Breton formally broke ranks in 1922, declaring the unconscious mind the primary source for artistic expression. In 1924, he published the *First Surrealist Manifesto*. *Surrealism*, a term first used by GUILLAUME APOLLINAIRE in his preface to THE BREASTS OF TIRESIAS (1917), denoted a nonrepresentational or heightened view of reality. It is generally accepted that such experiments were more successful in poetry and film than in live performance, but surrealists produced several noteworthy dramas, including JEAN COCTEAU's *Parade* (1917) and *The Wedding on the Eiffel Tower* (1921), ROGER VITRAC's *The Mysteries of Love* (written 1924; produced 1927) and *Victor, or The Children Take Over* (1928), and ANTONIN ARTAUD's *Spurt of Blood* (1924).

Following his early experiments in surrealism and his expulsion from the Parisian group, Artaud crafted his Theater of Cruelty as a potent blend of dream theory, antiestablishment aggression, and orientalist impressions of Balinese theater. His *The Theater and Its Double* (1938) became a seminal theatrical text for the 20th century. In SPAIN, novelist RAMÓN DEL VALLE INCLÁN experimented with surrealist techniques in his *Farce of the True Spanish Queen* (1920), as did Miguel de Unamuno in his *Dream Shadows* (1931) FEDERICO GARCÍA LORCA borrowed heavily from surrealism in the second act of his otherwise naturalist BLOOD WEDDING (1933), and he devoted two plays to total experiment: *The Public* (1934–1936) and *Play Without a Title* (c. 1934).

In 1933, almost simultaneously, Western European dramatic experiment ceased. With Adolf Hitler's rise to power, artistic experiments like the Bauhaus in GERMANY abruptly closed. Many artists fled, some only to be confronted again in occupied France or fascist ITALY. In 1934, purging by the Communist Party had begun, and by 1941, Joseph Stalin would emerge as the undisputed head of the Soviet government, declaring SOCIALIST REALISM as the only acceptable dramatic form and imprisoning and executing avant-garde artists. The Spanish Civil War of 1936 would similarly claim the lives of playwrights, most famously Lorca. Though drama was profoundly changed by the mass destruction of World War II, the impact of the early avant-garde has continued to influence experimental and avant-garde drama around the world.

FURTHER READING

Brockett, Oscar, and Robert R. Findlay. *Century of Innovation: A History of European Drama and Theatre Since the Late Nineteenth Century*. 1973. 2d ed. Boston: Allyn, 1991.

Cardullo, Bert, and Robert Knopf, eds. *Theater of the Avant-Garde: A Critical Anthology, 1890–1950*. New Haven, Conn.: Yale Univ. Press, 2001.

Dukore, Bernard F., and Daniel C. Gerould, eds. *Avant-Garde Drama: A Casebook*. New York: Crowell, 1976.

Eng, Jan van der, ed. *Avant-Garde: Interdisciplinary and International Review*. Amsterdam: Rodopi, 1991.

Goldberg, Roselee. *Performance Art: From Futurism to the Present*. Rev. ed. Originally published as *Performance: Live Art, 1909 to the Present*. 1979. New York: Abrams, 1988.

Innes, Christopher. *Avant-Garde Theatre, 1892–1992*. Rev. ed. of *Holy Theatre: Ritual and the Avant-Garde*, 1981. New York: Routledge, 1993.

Melzer, Annabelle Henkins. *Dada and Surrealist Performance*. Baltimore, Md.: Johns Hopkins Univ. Press, 1994.

Shattuck, Roger. *The Banquet Years: The Origins of the Avant-Garde in France, 1885 to World War I*. 1958. Rev. ed., 1968. Freeport, N.Y.: Books for Libraries, 1972.

Sarah Bay-Cheng

AWAKE AND SING!

In February 1935 *Awake and Sing!* established CLIFFORD ODETS as a powerful figure who could take on the problem of the Depression in a truly socially oriented drama with a strong impact on the sophisticated audiences of the commercial theater.

Odets's portrayal of the lower-middle-class Berger family struggling to hold together in a society crumbling around them is a play lacking any semblance of a conventional plot. In its concept of ensemble acting, there is no central character around whom the action evolves; all on stage are of equal importance, receiving equal dramatic emphasis. There is no typical plot progression toward a climactic resolution of a critical issue or the solving of a problem. The "problem" is the Depression, and it affects everyone; there is no solution. In action and dialogue, and in the setting itself, the spectators are watching a scene that could take place in numberless homes in the city around them in which the empathetic response extends to every character without distinction. And everything that happens is the fault of everybody—the small group in the crowded New York apartment and the larger society outside. The emotions aroused in watching are genuine, completely uncontrived.

Throughout *Awake and Sing!* there is constant awareness of the individual private frustrations of the characters as they speak to each other or, quite often, as they talk past each other and seem, at times, to be conversing only with themselves. The result is a unique sense of observing reality, obviously carefully planned for dramatic effect but tremendously moving. Simultaneously, the audience develops sympathy and understanding in spite of some unthinking acts and even cruelty practiced by the family members.

It is impossible not to identify with twenty-two-year-old Ralph, who must sleep on the front room daybed and cannot afford to buy a pair of black and white shoes. We cannot fault the physically attractive twenty-six-year-old Hennie, whose strong will and independence have trapped her into a loveless forced marriage. There is genuine sympathy for the hapless Sam Feinschreiber, totally unaware that Hennie's child is not his. And it is impossible to condemn the maimed Moe Axelrod who can offer Hennie the love she deserves.

Equally successful in creating audience sympathies are the members of the family's older generation. Myron Berger, inept, unable to support the family, strives for a modicum of dignity. Old Jacob, the patriarch, reduced to a life of playing his Caruso records, sees a future only in terms of a Marxist society. Bessie, the actual head of this faltering household, may well arouse considerable audience antipathy for her dominating behavior, forcing Hennie's marriage and smashing Jacob's prized records among other things; not a monster, she is really the only effective force that keeps the family from breaking apart.

"Awake and sing, ye who dwell in the dust," says the prophet Isaiah. Ultimately, despite all, the play does heed these words and does look toward a better future, as Moe and Hennie flee with Ralph's blessing, while he, in a totally upbeat curtain speech, vows to carry on as urged by his deceased grandfather to do "what is in the heart." He stands tall in the doorway as Moe and Hennie depart and the curtain falls.

Possibly Odets's best play, and probably his best known, *Awake and Sing!* makes its social point not by overt condemnation and Far Left advocacy but by highly effective underplaying.

Its appeal remains permanent, easily transcending its original time.

FURTHER READING

Clurman, Harold. *The Fervent Years: The Story of the Group Theatre and the Thirties.* 1945. New York: Hill & Wang, 1957.

Goldstein, Malcolm. *American Drama and the Theatre of the Great Depression.* New York: Oxford Univ. Press, 1974.

Weales, Gerald. *Clifford Odets, Playwright.* New York: Pegasus, 1971.

Jordan Miller

AYCKBOURN, ALAN (1939–)

I think how to tell the story to me is always very important. And I always look for new ways. I am peculiarly attracted to the stage. . . . And particularly I'm fascinated by things like how it presents time, and how its space can be changed, and the peculiarity which it possesses that when you warp time on stage, you're warping time for an audience as well as for the actors—you're doing it positively, in front of people's eyes.

—Alan Ayckbourn

A prolific playwright and director, Alan Ayckbourn is one of England's most successful theater practitioners. Born in Hampstead on April 12, 1939, he has penned more than sixty plays, including musicals and children's drama, most of which he also directed. After joining Scarborough's Library Theatre in the Round (later the Stephen Joseph Theatre) as an actor in 1957, he turned to writing and directing at the behest of the theater's founder, Stephen Joseph. It was for the Library Theatre that Ayckbourn wrote *Relatively Speaking* (1967), his first play to transfer to London, thus beginning a pattern of Scarborough premieres and London transfers that would continue for over thirty years. During the 1960s Ayckbourn was also a founding member of the Victoria Theatre in Stoke on Trent and drama producer for the BBC (British Broadcasting Corporation) in Leeds. In 1970 he became the artistic director of the Library Theatre in the Round, and except for a two-year leave to direct for the National Theatre in 1987–1988, Scarborough has remained his home base.

While his plays resemble FARCES because of their focus on marriage and infidelity in suburban England, Ayckbourn's work defies narrow categorization. In these comedies of quiet desperation, his characters actually feel the pain that usually bounces off cartoonlike farce characters, yet their anguish is also the source of much humor. Darker undertones emerge more fully in Ayckbourn's later plays, which nonetheless retain hilariously comic moments.

Ayckbourn's work is also characterized by remarkable formal experimentation with space and time. *Taking Steps* (1979) represents three stories of a house simultaneously set on one stage, and in *A Small Family Business* (1987), one set serves for four households. *Time of My Life* (1992) moves forward and backward in time to complete a story that starts in the middle. *Communicating Doors* (1994) jumps decades each time a character passes through doors that connect suites in a hotel. Narrative playfulness is also present in *Intimate Exchanges* (1982), a play with sixteen story variations depending on choices made by the actors. Similarly, the plot of *Sisterly Feelings* (1979) is determined by the flip of a coin onstage.

Ayckbourn's success has also allowed him to realize ambitious large projects. *The Norman Conquests* (1973), a trilogy, depicts the same set of events during a weekend house party from three different locales. The two plays of *House and Garden* (1999) revisit this idea with the added complication of performing both plays simultaneously in two adjacent theaters; some actors must make exits in one auditorium to make entrances in the other. Most notoriously, *Way Upstream* (1981) calls for a working cabin cruiser afloat on a river. (The fiberglass water tank built for this play at the National Theatre cracked, flooding electrical equipment; after several canceled previews, Ayckbourn reluctantly opened without the water.) Ayckbourn's innovative dramaturgy, however, is rarely a mere gimmick: In his best plays, such *coups de théâtre* illuminate his themes. Recognition of this skill has made Ayckbourn one of the most critically respected of commercially successful playwrights and has garnered him numerous awards.

PLAYS: *Absurd Person Singular* (1972); *The Norman Conquests* (1973); *Bedroom Farce* (1975); *Taking Steps* (1979); *Way Upstream* (1981); *A Chorus of Disapproval* (1984); *Woman in Mind* (1985); *Henceforward* (1987); *A Small Family Business* (1987); *By Jeeves* (1996); *House and Garden* (1999); *Comic Potential* (2000); *Snake in the Grass* (2002); *Sugar Daddies* (2003); *Private Fears in Public Places* (2004); *Improbable Fiction* (2005); *If I Were You* (2006)

FURTHER READING

Allen, Paul. *Alan Ayckbourn: Grinning at the Edge.* London: Methuen, 2001.

Watson, Ian. *Conversations with Ayckbourn.* London: MacDonald Futura Ltd., 1981.

Melissa Dana Gibson

B

BAAL

BERTOLT BRECHT wrote *Baal*, his first play, in 1918 when he was twenty, revised it in 1919, and published the drama in 1922. In 1955 Brecht altered the opening scene of the 1922 version and restored a previously cut final scene to create the text as we now know it.

Named after a Canaanite fertility god whose yearly death and resurrection were frequently celebrated by human sacrifice and ritual prostitution, *Baal* chronicles the life of its eponymous hero, a drunken, bisexual poet who murders his best friend and dies of debauchery. The play premiered in Leipzig in 1923 amid critical and moral controversy. One reviewer called it a "mud-bath," while the mayor of the city ordered its removal from the theater's repertory. Following productions in Munich and Vienna, the play finally reached Berlin in 1926 for a single performance directed by the author.

A loosely connected sequence of scenes, the play opens with a lengthy "chorale" narrating Baal's passage from "the white womb of his mother" to "the dark womb of the earth," a journey that takes place under a "huge . . . calm . . . pallid" sky seemingly indifferent to human affairs. Subsequent scenes show Baal drinking himself into a stupor; seducing respectable young women; fraternizing with teamsters; swindling peasants; visiting taverns; wandering in the forest; embracing a corpse; making love to his male friend Ekart; killing Ekart; fleeing from the law; and lying on a filthy deathbed while being insulted by drunken gamblers. All the while, Baal plays his guitar, sings his songs, and grows grossly fat.

A variety of literary influences lie behind *Baal*. In March 1918 Brecht had expressed a desire to write a play about François Villon, the 15th-century French poet, vagabond, and murderer. Shortly thereafter, Brecht was repelled by HANNS JOHNST's *The Lonely One* (*Der Einsame*, 1917), an expressionist play about the dissolute romantic dramatist Christian Dietrich Grabbe (1801–1836). Loathing the sentimentality and verbal abstraction of *The Lonely One*, Brecht set out to create in Baal a figure who would capture the outcast experience of Villon in vivid and concrete poetry. He drew not only on Villon himself but also on Arthur Rimbaud (1854–1891), whose sexually charged poetry Brecht had admired since his school days. The influence of Georg Büchner (1813–1837), another favorite of the young Brecht, is apparent in the play's *Woyzeck*-like disjunctive structure and its atmosphere of erotic violence.

In many ways, *Baal* reflects the guitar-toting, bisexually promiscuous, bohemian persona of the pre-Marxist Brecht. The author was later confronted with the problem of reconciling the nihilism of his first play (and, presumably, his early life) with his subsequent political beliefs. This he attempted to do by characterizing Baal as one who resists "a world whose form of production is designed for exploitation rather than usefulness."

[*See also* Alienation Effect; Epic Theater]

FURTHER READING

Brecht, Bertolt. *Baal*. Tr. by William E. Smith and Ralph Manheim. In *Bertolt Brecht: Collected Plays*, vol. 1., ed. by John Willett and Ralph Manheim. New York: Pantheon Bks., 1971.

Ewen, Frederic. *Bertolt Brecht: His Life, His Art, and His Times*. New York: Citadel Press, 1969.

Fuegi, John. *Bertolt Brecht: Chaos, According to Plan*. Cambridge: Cambridge Univ. Press, 1987.

Speirs, Ronald. *Brecht's Early Plays*. Atlantic Highlands, N.J.: Humanities Press, 1982.

Martin Andrucki

THE BABY BLUES

The Baby Blues is a two-act comedy by DREW HAYDEN TAYLOR, first produced at Arbour Theatre, Peterborough, Ontario, on February 21, 1995. The second part of Taylor's "Blues Quartet," this "Native version of a British sex farce" brings together one "white" and five Native figures at a powwow in Ontario. At the logistic center of the play is Amos, a Mohawk elder and chef whose food stand serves as a gathering point of refreshment and advice for all characters. His fortune scones, culinary hybrids of Chinese and Native cultures that contain little sayings of debatably profound extent, provide the structural outline as well as the leitmotifs of the plot. Conflicts begin when Jenny, a single Ojibway mother, tries to prevent her seventeen-year-old daughter Pashik from traveling to see the world, and Pashik defiantly tries to catch a ride to Connecticut with a visitor. Two visitors—thirty-eight-year-old Noble (short for "Noble Savage"), who struggles with his aging body, and twenty-year-old tricksterlike Skunk—use the opportunity to enter a rivalry of conquering females. Skunk, basically a younger version of Noble, gains advantages when Summer enters the scene: a naive anthropology student, she is in search of her 1/64th indigenous heritage and an easy prey to Skunk's "traditional" approaches before Noble tries to win her over. In the following Oscar Wildean regrouping of romantic constellations, act 1 ends with Pashik's discovery that Noble, who had been hoping for an affair with her, is actually her father. As Jenny recognizes in him the same fancy dancer who had left her behind without child support, she confronts him and sabotages his car to keep him from escaping again. Suddenly faced with paternal responsibility, Noble now finds himself changed, strongly disapproving of Skunk's advances on Pashik.

As most of Taylor's plays, *The Baby Blues* offers a satirical discussion of universal human values in the specific local context of an Ojibway reserve. Summarizing the central issues of place and the quest for oneself, Jenny instructs Pashik, "Being grounded can have two different meanings. The other is knowing who you are and where you belong." Identity is paramount but always in the making, continuously (re)constructed through negotiation and mutual understanding in a complex social network. In the particular context of Native identity, Taylor ironizes the notion of authenticity most effectively through Summer, the classical "wannabe" Native who speaks Cree, Ojibway, and Mohawk more fluently than any tribal character and who even manages to reinterpret a fortune scone joke—telling her to "check the authentic Native totem pole for a 'Made in Korea' label"—as an indigenous spiritual truth. The play's larger philosophical implication that all positions are relative culminates in the final punch line, when Noble discovers that in addition to being a father, he is Amos's son.

With a form that consistently follows the play's message, Taylor mainly relies on dialogue to tell his story. Combining Native humor with references to Western popular culture (such as Rod Stewart, *The Cosby Show*, or *Dances with Wolves*) while simultaneously deconstructing all common stereotypes of Nativeness, *The Baby Blues* is a hybrid celebration of both Native life and interculturality. It won the Native Playwrights Award from the University of Alaska in 1996.

FURTHER READING

Nunn, Robert. "Hybridity and Mimicry in the Plays of Drew Hayden Taylor." *Essays on Canadian Writing* 65 (Fall 1998): 95–119.

——, ed. *Drew Hayden Taylor: Essays on His Works*. Toronto: Guernica, 2005.

Taylor, Drew Hayden. "Storytelling to Stage: The Growth of Native Theatre in Canada." *The Drama Review* 41, no. 3 (Fall 1997): 140–152.

——. "Laughing Till Your Face Is Red." In *Furious Observations of a Blue-Eyed Ojibway: Funny, You Don't Look Like One Two Three*. Penticton, B.C.: Theytus Bks., 2002. 89–97.

Wasserman, Jerry. "Where Is Here Now? Living the Border in the New Canadian Drama." In *Crucible of Cultures: Anglophone Drama at the Dawn of a New Millennium*, ed. by Marc Maufort and Franca Bellarsi. Dramaturgies 4. Brussels: Peter Lang, 2002. 163–173.

Birgit Däwes

BACK TO METHUSELAH

A five-part play cycle on evolutionary themes by GEORGE BERNARD SHAW, *Back to Methuselah* was written in 1918–1920 and first performed in 1922. The play displays great inventiveness and imaginative reach but has had a mixed critical reception. Shaw regarded it as his masterpiece, and in 1946 it was published in the Oxford University Press *World's Classics* series. Science fiction–like fantasy, parodic versions of Christian and classical mythology, historical pageant, and satirical COMEDY are the main components of the complex mixture of ingredients in the work. The enormous length and technical demands of *Back to Methuselah* make it a difficult work to produce onstage, but it has been quite frequently revived with some success.

The carnage and futility of World War I are strong influences on the work, which can be seen partly as a manifesto of Shaw's "religion" of creative evolution and partly as radical, Swift-like satire on human folly. A key notion played with in *Back to Methuselah* is that in its present state of evolution the life span of the human species is too short to enable its members to gain sufficient wisdom for proper self-government: a return to the state of extreme longevity attributed to Methuselah and other Old Testament patriarchs is needed.

The first play of the cycle is set in the Garden of Eden, where a female Serpent tells Adam and Eve (products of the primal, androgynous creature Lilith) that the motivational forces of change in the universe are the imagination, desire, and the will. As the cycle unfolds, the population of the world gradually divides into ordinary "short-livers" and the more highly evolved "long-livers." Part 2 reflects directly on the recent world war, and two brothers named Barnabas put forward their idea of going "back to Methuselah" so that the human race can have time to develop wisdom. They propose this "gospel" to two politicians whose characters are based on those of British politicians Herbert Asquith and David Lloyd George. Amid much satirical comedy, part 3, titled "The Thing Happens," shows the miracle of exceptional longevity actually occurring in two characters who had previously appeared as a curate and a parlor maid. A device used by the characters in part 3 for communicating with one another visually and verbally at long distance anticipates the use of television communication by satellite; and a tuning fork that is used for distance communication in part 4 anticipates the mobile phone.

In part 4, "The Tragedy of an Elderly Gentleman," set in Galway Bay in the year A.D. 3000, a clash between an old-fashioned English gentleman and a society of more highly evolved, but sinister, long-livers ends with the extermination of the former by a female Oracle who deploys her powerful mesmeric field against him. The long-livers in part 4 have completely lost track of conventional human value systems and the language used to describe them. Primitive marital and parental relations have completely disappeared, words such as "father," "Miss," and "Mrs." have fallen out of polite use, and blushing is unknown. A "landlord" is an extinct creature.

The temporal setting of part 5, "As Far as Thought Can Reach," is the year A.D. 31,920. Here the action is dominated by two immensely old humans, the He-Ancient and the She-Ancient, who spend almost all of their time in contemplation, abstracted from the pleasures and squabbles of the younger people, one of whom is hatched out of an egg as a fully grown and pretty girl of seventeen. The He-Ancient memorably counsels a youth with the saying "Life is not meant to be easy, my child; but take courage: it can be delightful." But the extremely ascetic and, in ordinary terms, joyless life of the Ancients adds a negative dimension to the evolutionary fantasy. Part 5 concludes with an appearance of Lilith who projects the idea of a final transition of humanity into a state of pure intelligence, a "vortex freed from matter." A lengthy preface to *Back to Methuselah* supplies Shaw's fullest nondramatic essay on the idea of creative evolution.

[*See also* Ireland; Philosophy and Drama, 1860–1960]

FURTHER READING

Gahan, Peter. "*Back to Methuselah*: An Exercise of Imagination." In *Shaw and Science Fiction*, ed. Milton T. Wolf. Shaw Annual, Vol. 17. University Park: Pennsylvania State University Press, 1997.

Morgan, Margery M. "*Back to Methuselah*: The Poet and the City." In *The Shavian Playground: An Exploration of the Art of George Bernard Shaw*. London: Methuen, 1972.

Wolf, Milton T., ed. *Shaw and Science Fiction*. Shaw Annual, Vol. 17. University Park: Pennsylvania State University Press, 1997.

A. M. Gibbs

BAGNOLD, ENID (1889–1981)

Enid Bagnold was born in Rochester, Kent, ENGLAND, in 1889 and educated in the cosmopolitan and bohemian atmospheres of England, SWITZERLAND, and Paris. She studied painting with Walter Sickert, and during World War I she worked as a nurse and an ambulance driver in FRANCE. The latter experience provided material for both novels and plays and perhaps partly explains her preoccupation with families of strong women surviving without men.

She wrote novels, poetry, and plays, and her reputation largely rests on her novel *National Velvet* (1935), which she rewrote as a stage play (1946). It was later made into a highly successful film (1944) and dramatized for BBC radio (2002).

Her best-known stage play, *The Chalk Garden*, was produced in New York in 1955 and appeared in London in 1956, the watershed year in British theater when JOHN OSBORNE's *LOOK BACK IN ANGER* marked fundamental changes in drama.

Despite the aristocratic and somewhat dated aura that surrounds her (critic Kenneth Tynan described her dialogue as "building ornamental bridges of metaphor"), certain themes permeate all her plays, and their style and form show a sensitivity to social change.

Lottie Dundass (1943), the first of her eight plays, sets out these themes: at its center is a young woman on the edge of adult life, reaching for independence. Her plays consistently feature the elderly (most often women) coming to terms with a changing world. Tensions are played out through intergenerational conflict—between mothers and daughters, granddaughters and grandmothers, daughters and fathers, town and country—with the sea as an evocative backdrop. All the plays are set in the houses of the upper middle class, whose security is subject to the strains of social change.

The fragility of life is symbolized by either murder or suicide in the backdrop of characters' lives, or by role reversals, where elderly servants are looked after and governesses come from the same stratum as their employers. Social and familial displacement is reflected in the unfolding dramas.

The Chalk Garden ran for over two years in London's West End and was the most commercially successful play in the West End in 1956. On the surface, this is a drawing room drama, built round the metaphorical chalk garden that mirrors the aridity of the family's relationships. Three generations of women, a bedridden butler, and a governess who turns out to be a duke's daughter, once tried for murder, struggle to make sense of their lives. The threat of TRAGEDY is subtly reversed into a suggestion of a new flowering—both horticultural and human.

Bagnold's last play, *Call Me Jacky*, produced in 1968, the year British censorhip law was repealed, shows an awareness of its social context. A kitchen sink onstage accompanies left-wing politicians, a mixed-race marriage, lesbian and gay couples, and an elderly aristocratic lady.

Bagnold's plays would repay revival, with their impeccable stagecraft and quicksilver dialogue, with only the occasional melodramatic moment. Along with Agatha Christie, she maintained a slender—but important—presence for women playwrights in the first half of the 20th century.

[*See also* England, 1940–1980]

PLAYS: *Lottie Dundass* (1943); *National Velvet* (1946); *Poor Judas* (1946); *Gertie (Little Idiot)* (1953); *The Chalk Garden* (1955); *The Last Joke* (1960); *The Chinese Prime Minister* (1964); *Call Me Jacky* (1968)

FURTHER READING

Bagnold, Enid. *Enid Bagnold's Autobiography*. Boston: Little, Brown, 1970.

Berney, K. A., ed. *Contemporary British Dramatists*. Detroit: St. James Press, 1994.

Griffiths, Trevor, and Margaret Llewellyn-Jones. *British and Irish Women Dramatists Since 1958*. Philadelphia: Open Univ. Press, 1993.

Sebba, Anne. *Enid Bagnold: The Authorised Biography*. London: Weidenfeld & Nicholson, 1986.

Michelene Wandor

BAI FENGXI (1934–)

Born in Wen'an, Hebei Province, Bai Fengxi attended North CHINA People's Revolutionary University in 1949 and became an actress in the China Youth Theater in 1954. Writing exclusively about women's issues since 1981, Bai is best known for *The Women Trilogy*, which depicts the concerns of intellectual women in the transitional period from Maoist China (1949–1976) to post-Maoist (1976–present) China.

Her first play, *First Bathed in Moonlight (Mingyue chu zhao ren*, 1981), remarkable for the absence of men onstage, represents a miniature cultural history of women of the People's Republic of China through the life experiences of three generations of mothers and daughters who struggle between their official roles and their private identity in search of love and happiness. The grandmother raised her daughter by herself after her husband's betrayal. She also supports her daughter's choice to become a successful official in the Women's Federation, a government institution. Fang Rouming, the mother, however, meets with challenges of a different kind. Although she is eager to help countryside women in arranged marriages regain their rights to free love, she is nevertheless against her two daughters' free choice in love. By the end of the play, Fang Ruoming puts aside her own sorrow in support of her daughters.

Bai's second play, *An Old Friend Returning on a Stormy Night (Fengyu guren lai*, 1983), probes more deeply into women's multiple protests against the sexist society that glorifies fathers who make both their leaving and staying home impossible. Xia Zhixian represents a typical dilemma in Maoist China, which believed that "women can hold up half of the sky." Women were expected to be equal to men in their professional careers, in addition to their domestic duties as loving wives and mothers. Xia's successful career as gynecologist is therefore achieved at the expense of her family life—she lives alone after her husband found it hard to support her total devotion to her career. As the play unfolds, her daughter faces a similar dilemma: she is under pressure to give up her opportunity to study abroad in favor of her husband since a family with a Ph.D. husband is more acceptable than a family with a Ph.D. wife. Xia encourages her daughter to pursue her journey abroad with her famous stage line: "A woman is not a moon. She does not need to depend on someone else's light to glow." Bai Fengxi's play touched a sensitive spot in the experience of many contemporary Chinese women. Her play exerted an influence in raising the consciousness of women's issues.

Her third play, *Where Is Longing in Autumn (Buzhi qiusi zai shui jia*, 1986), staged a group of courageous women whose daring unconventional decisions in marriage and career shocked contemporary Chinese audiences. Su Zhongyuan was puzzled by the choice of her children. Her elder daughter divorced her husband because she wanted to take care of herself while rejecting the roles of good wife, mother, and daughter-in-law. Her second daughter did not mind being a spinster in her mid-thirties and wondered why people were more tolerant of a married couple without love than they were of a single woman. Her son refused to take the college entrance examination in favor of a business career. The seemingly irreconcilable dramatic conflicts between mother and children suggest the moral tribulations of a nation departing from traditional paths and embarking on modernization, Westernization, and commercialization. The much-criticized images of fashion models, divorcees, and single women—now quite conventional in China—accounted for the popularity of the play, which connected the historical agencies of the audience members with the very current subjects that were much on their minds.

PLAYS: *First Bathed in Moonlight (Mingyue chu zhao ren*, 1981); *An Old Friend Returning on a Stormy Night (Fengyu guren lai*, 1983); *Where Is Longing in Autumn (Buzhi qiusi zai shui jia*, 1986)

FURTHER READING

Bai Fengxi. *Bei Fengxi juzuo xuan* [Selected plays of Bai Fengxi]. Beijing: Zhongguo xiju chubanshe, 1988.

——. *The Women Trilogy*. Tr. by Guan Yuehua. Beijing: Panda Bks., 1991.

Chen, Xiaomei. "A Stage of Their Own: The Problematics of Women's Theater in Post-Mao China." *The Journal of Asian Studies* 56, no. 1 (1997): 3–25.

——. *Acting the Right Part: Political Theater and Popular Drama in Contemporary China*. Honolulu: Univ. of Hawaii Press, 2002.

Sheng, Ying, et al. *Ershi shiji nuxing wenxuan shi* [A history of twentieth-century women's literature]. 2 vols. Tianjin: Tianjin renmin chubanshe, 1994.

Tung, Constantine. "Tensions and Reconciliation: Individualistic Rebels and Social Harmony in Bai Fengxi's Plays." In *Drama in the People's Republic of China*, ed. by Constantine Tung and Colin MaKerras. Albany: State Univ. of New York Press, 1987. 233–353.

Xiaomei Chen

BAIMAN NÜ, GEJU See WHITE-HAIRED GIRL

BAISHE ZHUAN, JINGIU See THE WHITE SNAKE

BAITZ, JON ROBIN (1961–)

> *What makes [Hedda Gabler] a masterpiece, not just of feminist theatre, but a linchpin of modern drama, is this play, like all great works, offers the opportunity to glimpse the real, horrible, yet often comic mechanics of emotional violence at very close range.*
> —Jon Robin Baitz

Born in Los Angeles in 1961, Jon Robin Baitz grew up privileged and somewhat isolated as the child of a father who worked in a large, multinational corporation. Stops along the way, before the return of the family in 1978 to Los Angeles, included Brazil, South Africa, Amsterdam, and London. Baitz's first success, *The Film Society* (1988), derived from his experiences as a private school student in South Africa during the apartheid era. Before production, one reader of the play assumed the author was a college professor in his fifties. Instead, Baitz was a hip, young man in sunglasses and a leather jacket.

Consciously a literary playwright who uses a DRAMATURGY of what David Savran has called "exact and exacting forms," Baitz has acknowledged earlier influences as coming from English playwrights (TOM STOPPARD, HOWARD BRENTON, and DAVID HARE) rather than American (DAVID MAMET and SAM SHEPARD). Simply ignoring the experimental tradition of OFF-OFF-BROADWAY and elsewhere, Baitz's work can be called structurally austere with stylistically accomplished dialogue and subtle characterizations of depth and complexity. The friction and tension of the plotting also allow for an analytical look at the emotional depth of ideas. Diplomats, expatriates, corporate officers, and the odd wife or child (young adults; rarely are his characters under thirty) move about the globe in an upper-class mode of both assumed power and the contingent paranoia that is the result of the morally ambiguous high stakes being played out.

Baitz's *The Substance of Fire* (1991) employs a clash over control of a "quality publishing house" between the fiery, intellectual father, uninterested in profits, and his more "practical" sons and daughter. *The End of the Day* (1992) delineates the difficulties of an aristocratic English doctor "adapting" to America. Ultimately his ideals crumble, and he ends up quite successful and happy in a life of high-status West Coast crime. The writer's *Mizlansky/Zilinsky* (1998) is a scathing and very funny look at tax-shelter selling, filmmaker "schmucks" on the way down. Other plays of distinction include *Three Hotels* (1993), *A Fair Country* (1996), and *Ten Unknowns* (2001).

Predictably, perhaps, some critics have found the plays "talky" and criticized Baitz's "tendency to moralize." This may explain the comparison, positive and negative, with ARTHUR MILLER. Most critics acknowledge the eloquence of his writing and the substance of his ambition. Joel Hirschhorn, citing in *Variety* certain reservations about *The Paris Letter* (2004) (questions of continuity and transitions), remarks that if "corrected," the play "has the potential to rank beside the works of Arthur Miller and Tennesee Williams."

Initially, Baitz began writing plays in Los Angeles but then relocated to New York City. He was a founding member of off-off Broadway's Naked Angels, and in one brief piece presented there in 1991, *Coq au Vin*, Baitz abandoned his "traditional dramaturgy" and has "lights come up on two people in chicken suits, center stage."

SELECT PLAYS: *The Film Society* (1988); *Dutch Landscape* (1989); *The Substance of Fire* (1991); *The End of the Day* (1992); *Three Hotels* (1993); *A Fair Country* (1996); *Mizlansky/Zilinsky* (1998); *Ten Unknowns* (2001); *Chinese Friends* (2004); *The Paris Letter* (2004)

FURTHER READING

Hitchcock, Laura. *The Paris Letter* (Los Angeles production, December 23, 2004). *CurtainUp*. http://www.curtainup.com/.

Ibsen, Henrik. *Hedda Gabler*. Adapted by Jon Robin Baitz, from a translation by Anne-Charlotte Hanes Harvey. New York: Grove Press, 2000.

L.A. Theatre Works. http://www.latw.org/.

Naked Angels Theater Company. http://www.nakedangels.com/.

Savran, David. "Jon Robin Baitz." In *The Playwright's Voice: American Dramatists on Memory, Writing and the Politics of Culture*. New York: Theatre Communications Group, 1999.

Stanley R. Richardson

BAKER, GEORGE PIERCE (1866–1935)

George Pierce Baker was a pioneer educator who raised the legitimacy of theater studies in American universities. Born in Providence, Rhode Island, he earned his undergraduate degree at Harvard (1887), became acquainted with CLYDE FITCH, and returned as an instructor in 1888. During the early 1890s, he wrote five one-act "commediettas" and two full-length plays, but he was unable to get any produced and so gave up playwriting in 1895 except for three collaborations with Thornton M. Ware.

He introduced drama into the Harvard curriculum with a course on the history of the English drama before the Puritan revolution (1890) and a Radcliffe course on contemporary drama (1897). In 1903, four graduating women submitted original plays, in lieu of the traditional theses, to the Radcliffe English Department. Baker began developing what became his standard progression of playwriting assignments: a one-act adaptation of a novel or short story, an original one-act, and an original three-act play.

Baker introduced his groundbreaking playwriting course as Harvard's English 47, "The Technique of the Drama" (1906), and the first group of ten men included Van Wyck Brooks and EDWARD SHELDON. Subsequent students included EUGENE O'NEILL, George Abbott, SIDNEY HOWARD, S. N. BEHRMAN, PHILIP BARRY, Brooks Atkinson, Kenneth Macgowan, Frederick Koch, Glen Hughes, Elia Kazan, and Thomas Wolfe.

Baker taught his students to plan each play by establishing background, characters, relationships, setting, structure, and the nature of the play: "whether it merely tells a story, is a character study, a play of ideas, a problem play, or a fantasy" (Baker, *Dramatic Technique*). He coached them in exposition, dramatic action, characterization, dialogue, suspense, and climax, and he urged the need for economy, for engaging and building the audience's attention, and for bringing down the curtain immediately following the climax.

Leaving Harvard after years of often inadequate support, Baker helped found the Yale School of Drama. The school's 1925 *Bulletin* included Forms of the Drama, Playwriting, History of Stage Design, Practice and Theory of Stage Design, Stage Lighting, History and Practice of Costume Design, Dramatic Criticism, Pageantry, and The Technique of Drama (Drama 47) but no courses on acting. The institution built a complex including a 750-seat theater, a studio theater, a laboratory theater, and various support spaces. From 1926 to 1932, Baker directed 17 productions at Yale, including HENRIK IBSEN'S BRAND, William

Shakespeare's *The Winter's Tale*, and O'Neill's THE EMPEROR JONES. In 1933, Baker retired, and Yale began offering a Master of Fine Arts degree with options in stage design, stage lighting, and directing. Baker died on January 6, 1935, in New York City.

FURTHER READING

Baker, George Pierce. *The Development of Shakespeare as a Dramatist*. New York: Macmillan, 1907.

——. *Dramatic Technique*. Boston: Houghton, 1919.

——. "The One-Act Play." In *Types of Modern Dramatic Composition*, ed. by LeRoy Phillips and Theodore Johnson. Boston: Ginn, 1927.

Bogard, Travis. *Contour in Time: The Plays of Eugene O'Neill*. 1972. Rev. ed. New York: Oxford Univ. Press, 1988.

Fawson, Diane. "George Pierce Baker: His Influence Upon Selected Educational Theatre Systems in the United States." Master's thesis, Univ. of Oregon, 1966.

Kinne, Wisner Payne. *George Pierce Baker and the American Theatre*. Cambridge: Harvard Univ. Press, 1954.

Jeffrey D. Mason

BALAGANCHIK *See* THE PUPPET SHOW

LE BALCON *See* THE BALCONY

BALCONVILLE

Balconville, produced at Montreal's Centaur Theatre in 1979, was the biggest hit in playwright DAVID FENNARIO's career. Touted as Canada's first bilingual play, *Balconville* struck a chord with audiences in Montreal, Toronto, and Vancouver, eventually taking Fennario to London's Old Vic and the Grand Opera House in Belfast in 1981.

Balconville is set on the balconies and on the street in front of an apartment building in the Pointe Saint Charles district of Montreal during a hot summer in which the baseball team loses, apartment buildings burn down, and local politicians try to get reelected. The plot revolves around three families who live in the building. The hard-working paterfamilias of the francophone famliy, Claude Paquette, is waited on by his complacent wife Cecile and has difficulty interacting with his attractive young daughter Diane. His anglophone neighbor, Johnny, is an aging, angry young man whose wife is fed up with supporting him while he blames "separatists" for his inability to get a job. The third family is composed of Muriel Williams and her son Tom, who seems to be a younger version of Johnny. The cast is rounded out with a simple-minded delivery boy, Thibault, and a callous politician, Gaetan Bolduc, who passes through knocking on doors. Frustration brought on by unemployment and political hopelessness leads to tension between the French- and English-speaking neighbors. Johnny calls Paquette a "pepper"; and as relations deteriorate, Thibault yells, "Fuck the Queen," and Paquette refuses to speak English ever again. A suggestion of romance between Tom and Diane implies hope for the younger generation. The play ends bleakly, however, with the families working together to save their belongings as the neighborhood burns but turning to the audience in despair to ask as one: "Qu'est-ce qu'on va faire? What are we going to do?"

The play is punctuated with raw, often crude humor, which accounted for much of its audience appeal, but actor Peter MacNeill, who played Johnny, felt that Fennario was afraid that the comedy would undercut the political message. The play's ending was a bone of contention among author, director, and cast throughout its long run and tour. The published version of the text contains the final tableau and Brechtian direct address, but director Guy Sprung and actors from the company insist that they never performed the play with Fennario's ending. Relations between the company and playwright also soured when Fennario insisted on walking the picket line with striking ushers at Montreal's Place des Arts during the run of the show.

Balconville represented the zenith of Fennario's career. After *Balconville* he rejected traditional theater venues and modes of production, choosing to stage politicized COMMUNITY THEATER instead. In his one-man show *Banana Boots* he recounts the experience of touring *Balconville* to Belfast, where he experienced a kind of artistic and political epiphany when comparing his play to the theater of local Belfast activists. True to his socialist convictions, his work has concentrated on political action and community-based theater ever since.

FURTHER READING

Fennario, David. *Banana Boots*. Vancouver: Talonbooks, 1998.

Wallace, Robert, and Cynthia Zimmerman. *The Work: Conversations with English-Canadian Playwrights*. Toronto: Coach House Press, 1982. 292–303.

Donald Cameron McManus

THE BALCONY

JEAN GENET's *The Balcony* (*Le Balcon*), published in 1956, first produced in 1957, is a study of power hierarchies in sex and politics. The action takes place in a deluxe brothel called the "Grand Balcony." Under the eye of the proprietress, Madame Irma, who calls her brothel a "House of Illusions," the male customers, including top public officials, act out fantasies of domination and submission in order to achieve sexual fulfillment. Meanwhile, outside the brothel, the country faces revolutionary turmoil.

The play opens with three scenes in which a Bishop, a Judge, and a General stage their sexual fantasies in elaborate settings assisted by brothel staff. Irma supervises and watches the clock for them, worried because signs of rebellion and street fighting are growing in the city. The Chief of Police, long a protector of the brothel, arrives to ask hopefully if any clients have pretended to be him—thus offering a tribute to his social status and power. He also checks on the progress of a new room designed for his own use as a monumental tomb where he can fulfill his fantasy of eternal glory.

An envoy from the court arrives at the brothel, reporting that the Queen, endangered by the civil unrest, may be dead. He asks that Irma appear as the Queen for a show of government stability in front of the unruly citizens. Irma, the Chief of Police, and her clients, the Bishop, Judge, and General, present themselves on the brothel's balcony before the restless crowd. The citizenry is appeased by their appearance, and the revolution is halted.

The young man who led the failed revolution now comes to the brothel, seeking to act out the fantasy of being Chief of Police. The action ends when he castrates himself during his brothel session, thus taking a shortcut to resembling the impotent, aged men his revolution had sought to replace. In a final, lyrical monologue, Irma puts out the lights and tells the theater audience that the whole process will begin again the following day.

The fact of the Chief of Police being the most recent addition to the brothel's, and society's, symbolic figures of power may derive, in part, from Genet's favorite play, *The Eaglet* (*L'Aiglon*, 1900) by EDMOND ROSTAND, in which bureaucratic police officers, at the drama's end, show themselves to have greater power than the Old Regime nobility conspiring with Napoleon Bonaparte's son, the "eaglet" of the title.

Genet reworked *The Balcony* more than any of his other plays and published several versions of the French script between 1956 and 1968. Differences among them are so great that scholars sometimes refer to multiple plays sharing the same title, and various combinations of these versions are now in publication and production. The 1957 world premiere, directed by Peter Zadek, occurred in London because of censorship issues in FRANCE. Genet disrupted Zadek's dress rehearsal and was denied entry to the premiere. The 1960 Paris premiere was directed by Peter Brook, whom Genet had approached after seeing Brook's famous 1957 production of William Shakespeare's *Titus Andronicus* during its Paris run; Genet nonetheless disliked this staging as well, describing it as not "equivocal" enough.

The Balcony enjoyed a successful OFF-BROADWAY New York run, opening at the Circle in the Square in March 1960; it ran for 672 performances, the longest run for any off-Broadway play until then. It would eventually be overtaken in its off-Broadway record by Genet's THE BLACKS (*Les Nègres*), which opened a year later and ran for 1,408 performances.

Genet sold the film rights to *The Balcony* in 1961 to the American director Joseph Strick, and the two worked closely together on the script for the film that was released in 1963. In 2002, Hungarian composer Peter Eötvös premiered an operatic version of the play at Aix-en-Provence.

With THE MAIDS (*Les Bonnes*), *The Balcony* is the most frequently revived of Genet's plays. First interpreted as a political allegory, *The Balcony* is now also viewed as a depiction of how desire is entangled with public status and how the power granted to an individual by society at large can be manipulated through imagery created for mass consumption.

FURTHER READING

Corvin, Michel, and Albert Dichey, eds. *Théâtre complet de Jean Genet* [Complete theater of Jean Genet]. Bibliothèque de la Pléiade. Paris: Gallimard, 2002.

Guicharnaud, Jacques, with June Guicharnaud. *Modern French Theatre from Giraudoux to Genet*. Rev. ed. New Haven: Yale Univ. Press, 1967.

White, Edmund. *Genet: A Biography*. New York: Knopf, 1993.

David Pelizzari

THE BALD PRIMA DONNA *See* THE BALD SOPRANO

THE BALD SOPRANO

[The Bald Soprano] *is an experiment in abstract or nonrepresentational drama. . . . The aim is to release dramatic tension without the help of any proper plot or any special subject.*

—Eugène Ionesco

Romanian-born, French dramatist EUGÈNE IONESCO was a founding father—with JEAN GENET and SAMUEL BECKETT—of the Theater of the Absurd. Influenced by the surrealists and the Marx Brothers, Ionesco wrote in the French FARCE tradition.

He obtained the idea for *The Bald Soprano* (*La Cantatrice chauve*, 1949) from an English-French primer, in which he discovered "that there are seven days of the week . . . that the floor is below us, the ceiling above." Using such "profound statements" as dialogue, he set his one-act parody in a middle-class English household (claiming that if he had been studying Spanish, he would have set it in SPAIN).

At lights up, a clock strikes seventeen, and Mrs. Smith announces, "There, it's nine o'clock," and delivers a monologue that skates between the banal and the ridiculous ("Yogurt is excellent for the stomach, the kidneys, the appendicitis, and apotheosis"). Looking up from his newspaper, Mr. Smith reports that Bobby Watson has died. Subsequent conversation indicates that Bobby Watson has been dead for two years, a year and a half, three years, and/or four years and that his wife, children, aunts, uncles, and cousins are all named Bobby Watson. Such is the power of language that talking about them makes the Bobbies multiply.

Upon arriving for a visit, the Martins discover—through a "courtship" of intensive inductive reasoning (they live in the same city and house, sleep in the same bed, have the same daughter)—that they must be married. Both couples break into a chorus of non sequiturs and incongruous associations. Having three times answered the doorbell in vain, Mrs. Smith refuses to respond a fourth time ("Experience teaches us that when one hears the doorbell ring, it is because there is never anyone there"). But the Fire Chief is there—and initiates a round of inane storytelling, which is interrupted by the maid's throwing herself on his neck ("It was she who extinguished my first fires").

When the Chief takes off for a fire that will ignite "in exactly three-quarters of an hour and sixteen minutes," the two couples descend into a cacophony of arbitrary aphorisms, climaxing in hostile, frenzied screaming of nonsense syllables, halted by a blackout. When the lights come back up, the Martins, seated like the Smiths at the play's beginning (suggesting the couples' interchangeability), recite the opening lines.

Ionesco dubbed *Soprano* an "anti-play" and considered it "pure drama, anti-thematic, anti-ideological, anti-social-realist, anti-philosophical, anti-boulevard-psychology . . . the rediscovery of a new free theatre" (1964). He described the characters as "puppets" and called the play "a satire of a . . . universal petite bourgeoisie" whose conformity to fixed ideas and slogans is revealed by mechanical language (1964).

The Bald Soprano was first produced at the Théâtre des Noctambules, Paris, in 1950 by Nicholas Bataille. Audiences were not amused. But shortly after, it was revived on a double bill with *The Lesson* in the tiny, Left-Bank Théâtre de la Huchette, where it ran for over forty years. It reached London as *The Bald Prima Donna* in 1956 and New York as *The Bald Soprano* in 1958.

[*See also* Absurdism; France]

FURTHER READING

Bloom, Harold. *Eugene Ionesco* (Bloom's Major Dramatists). Ed. by Robb Erskine. Broomall, Pa.: Chelsea House, 2002.

Coe, Richard. *Eugene Ionesco: A Study of His Work*. New York: Grove, 1968.

Gaensbauer, Deborah B. *Eugene Ionesco Revisited* (Twayne's World Author Series, No. 863). New York: Twayne, 1996.

Ionesco, Eugène. *Four Plays: The Bald Soprano, The Lesson, Jack or the Submission, The Chairs*. Tr. by Donald M. Allen. New York: Grove, 1958.

——. *La Cantatrice Chauve, La Leçon*. New York: French and European Publications, 1972.

——. *Notes and Counternotes*. Tr. by Donald Watson. 1964. New York: Riverrun Press, 1984.

Patricia Montley

BALDWIN, JAMES (1924–1987)

> *I knew that out of the ritual of the church, historically speaking, comes the act of the theatre, the communion which is the theatre. And I knew that what I wanted to do in the theatre was to recreate moments I remembered as a boy preacher, to involve the people, even against their will, to shake them up, and, hopefully, to change them.*
> —James Baldwin

Primarily known as a novelist and poet, James Baldwin also wrote plays, essays, and criticism. His plays had an enormous influence on American protest theater of the 1960s. Baldwin is considered by many to be the leading literary spokesman for the civil rights movement in the United States. Through his plays *Blues for Mister Charlie* (1964) and *The Amen Corner* (1955), he exposed the suffering and abuse of African Americans and challenged his audiences to confront these issues.

Much of Baldwin's writing is based on his early life growing up in poverty in Harlem, New York, and his time as a boy preacher. Born in Harlem on August 2, 1924, Baldwin was raised in a strict religious family headed by a stepfather who was a storefront preacher from New Orleans. As a high school student, Baldwin became involved in the school's literary club, whose adviser was the important Harlem Renaissance poet Countee Cullen. Cullen was an important role model for Baldwin. In 1938, Baldwin began to preach at the Fireside Pentecostal Church in Harlem but renounced the ministry upon graduating from high school in 1942. Then Baldwin moved to New Jersey, where he wrote while working at several defense factories. During this period, Baldwin witnessed the violence between whites and blacks who had migrated from the South in search of employment opportunities. Baldwin returned to Harlem in 1943, and over the next five years he began to write book reviews for such periodicals as the *Nation* and the *New Leader*. In 1948, Baldwin moved to Paris, where he continued writing.

Although Baldwin found tremendous success with his 1953 novel *Go Tell It on the Mountain*, he decided to shift from writing novels to writing plays in what he would later call a "desperate and even irresponsible act." He wrote *The Amen Corner* in 1955. Similar in theme to *Go Tell It on the Mountain*, *The Amen Corner* is a play about the dilemmas faced by his parents, who were trying to survive during a time of intense racism and poverty. It was not published until ten years after it was written. At first, only small theater companies throughout the United States performed the drama. Finally, it was given a Broadway debut in 1965.

Baldwin's second play, *Blues for Mister Charlie* (1964), has received more critical attention, although *The Amen Corner* is critically considered the most theatrically effective of Baldwin's two plays. Some critics believe that *Blues for Mister Charlie* has received more critical attention because it more readily appeals to white audiences. *Blues for Mister Charlie* was first produced on Broadway in 1964 and is based on the murder of a young black man, Emmett Till. The accused murderer is a white man who is tried and acquitted of the charges. After the acquittal, he brags about actually performing the deed. When it was first produced, the play received harsh reviews from nearly all the theater critics.

Baldwin's plays were written during the beginning of his participation in the civil rights movement in the 1960s, when his role as a literary spokesman for the movement was at its height. After the assassinations of Martin Luther King, Jr., and Robert Kennedy, Baldwin returned to Paris because he believed that his own life was in danger. He continued to write from his home in FRANCE. Baldwin died on December 1, 1987, in Saint-Paul-de-Vence.

[*See also* Black Arts Movement; Political Theater in the United States; United States, 1940–Present]

PLAYS: *The Amen Corner* (1955); *Blues for Mister Charlie* (1964)

FURTHER READING

Campbell, James. *Talking at the Gates: The Life of James Baldwin*. Boston: Faber, 1991.

Miller, Quentin, ed. *Re-viewing James Baldwin: Things Not Seen*. Philadelphia: Temple Univ. Press, 2000.

Stanley, Fred L., and Nancy Burt, eds. *Critical Essays on James Baldwin*. Boston: G. K. Hall, 1988.

Ellen Anthony-Moore and Christopher Moore

BALODIS, JANIS (1950–)

Janis Balodis has worked as a freelance writer, DRAMATURG, and director, including at the Melbourne Theatre Company (1987–1993), and dramaturg-in-residence at Queensland Theatre Company (1995–1996). His first play, *Backyard* (produced 1980), mordantly describes small-town life in the 1960s with humor and poetic warmth. Two productions based on Grimms' fairy tales with extensive use of music followed: *Happily Never After* in 1982 and *Summerland* in 1984. A third, *Wet and Dry* (1991), is an ambitious play with contrasting themes of fertility and barrenness, nature and the metaphorical and actual aridity of Australian experience. Located in Darwin, a northern tropical town destroyed by a cyclone in 1974, and Sydney, the leading commercial city, Balodis's play uses the climatic polarities of wet and dry, climate and landscape, to delve into the loneliness of contemporary life. In her introduction to the Currency edition, Katherine Brisbane notes: "The heart of Janis Balodis's work has always lain in the uneasy tension between the past and the future and *Wet and Dry* offers, beneath the wit, both an indictment of civilisation as we know it and a way forward to a healthier and happier community."

Balodis's most significant work is *The Ghosts Trilogy* (1997), which examines the implications of history. The son of Latvian parents who fled Europe during World War II, Balodis draws on these experiences in *Too Young for Ghosts* (1985), where displacement is both a theme and a technique, interweaving a narrative of seven Latvian émigrés arriving in Australia in 1945 with a speculative account of explorer Ludwig Leichhardt's ill-fated expedition from the Gulf of Carpentaria to Perth in 1847. The play is audacious and assured in its nonrealistic devices and multicultural themes. His modern characters must contend with grief for lost language, culture, and history just as Leichhardt, with his sextant, considers the vast, forbidding geography, which eventually overwhelms him. *Too Young for Ghosts* has been widely performed and well received critically.

In the second part of the trilogy, *No Going Back* (produced 1992), the refugees have floundered in later life after the initial promise of their new beginnings. The play was greeted positively as adding complexity to the circumstances of *Too Young for Ghosts* and as a perceptive portrait of characters under duress. The third play, *My Father's Father* (produced 1996), was criticized for its handling of the dual narratives of the refugees and history, and Balodis removed the Leichhardt story.

Balodis's drama brings a unique and probing aspect to Australian life and culture, highlighting the culture of northern Queensland and the Darwin region. His commitment to regional theater has continued with the Northern Rivers Theatre Company in the state of New South Wales, where he has collaborated with the opera singer and director Lyndon Terracini. His account of the immigrant experience, and the melancholy underlying it, has usefully tempered the jaunty, sometimes complacent nationalistic optimism of his contemporaries.

[*See also* Australia]

PLAYS: *Backyard* (1980); *Happily Never After* (1982); *Summerland* (1984); *Too Young for Ghosts* (1985); *Wet and Dry* (1991); *No Going Back* (1992); *My Father's Father* (1996)

FURTHER READING

Balodis, Janis. *The Ghosts Trilogy*. Sydney: Currency, 1997.

Brisbane, Katharine. *Contemporary Dramatists*. Ed. by K. A. Berney. London: St. James Press, 1993.

Kelly, Veronica. "Falling Between Two Stools—The Theatre of Janis Balodis." *Ariel* 23, no. 1 (January 1992): 115–131.

Murray Bramwell

THE BALTIMORE WALTZ

If just one grandchild of George Bush caught this thing during toilet training, that would be the last we'd hear about the space program.
—Carl, Scene 2

The Baltimore Waltz, PAULA VOGEL's breakthrough drama, won an Obie Award for best OFF-BROADWAY play of 1992. Celebrated primarily as an AIDS play, Vogel's danse macabre is perhaps more accurately described as a journey of expiation arising from feelings of loss and guilt. In 1988 Vogel's brother Carl died from AIDS. He had earlier asked Vogel to accompany him on a trip to Europe, but Vogel declined, unaware of her brother's HIV status and assuming that there would be other opportunities to make such an expedition. In *The Baltimore Waltz* the trip does take place, at least in the mind of the female protagonist Anna—only this time it is she who is suffering from an incurable disease.

Vogel's DRAMATURGY usually takes the road less traveled in approaching any given subject. True to character, *The Baltimore Waltz* is a dark, satiric COMEDY in which death and disease are effectively explored through the medium of the bizarre and humorous. In Anna's attempt to deny the painful realities of life, the first-grade teacher retreats into fantasy. Through a surreal, fragmented, cinematic narrative, she imagines she has "ATD"—Acquired Toilet Disease, picked up from classroom toilet seats—and sets off on a trip to Europe in search of a cure, accompanied by her brother Carl and his fluffy rabbit.

While *The Baltimore Waltz* is primarily about coming to terms with loss, it nonetheless offers a strong and angry comment on attitudes toward AIDS and the U.S. government's handling of the crisis. In Vogel's play, little is known about ATD, even though it is the fourth major cause of death in single elementary schoolteachers. There is no cure, and it is a paltry eighty-sixth on the list of government health-care priorities. Moreover, the government does not consider itself responsible for education about ATD, and news of the disease is downplayed, lest it provoke widespread panic and calls for costly checks of toilet seats. Carl notes bitterly, "If just one grandchild of George Bush caught this thing during toilet training, that would be the last we'd hear about the space program."

It is no coincidence that Vogel chooses a chaste, elementary schoolteacher—an icon of respectability—to comment about attitudes toward AIDS; nor that Anna greets death with a new lust for life and sleeps her way across Europe. Other seemingly bizarre references, another trait characteristic to Vogel, also fit this paradigm. The stuffed rabbit that Carl surreptitiously carries with him at all times is a reference to his (homo)sexuality. As a boy, Carl was not allowed to play with dolls, so his substitute was a stuffed rabbit, and in *The Baltimore Waltz*, it symbolizes his secret sexuality. In many ways, it is also Carl's lifeline, something the Third Man is anxious to acquire. The figure of the Third Man recalls Graham Greene's unscrupulous Harry Lime from Greene's novel *The Third Man*, whose exploitation of the new wonder-drug penicillin made him less someone who promised new life than an ominous specter of death. Poignantly, in Vogel's play the Third Man morphs into all the other characters that Carl and Anna meet, including the ineffectual doctor at the Baltimore hospital, a German quack whose name is German for "death rattle," and Harry Lime himself.

[*See also* Feminist Drama in the United States]

FURTHER READING

Bigsby, Christopher. *Contemporary American Playwrights*. Cambridge: Cambridge Univ. Press, 1999.

Osborn, Elizabeth M. *The Way We Live Now: American Plays and the AIDS Crisis*. New York: Theatre Communications Group, 1990.

Solomon, Alisa, and Franji Minwalla. *Queerest Art: Essays on Lesbian and Gay Theater*. New York: New York Univ. Press, 2002.

Vogel, Paula. *The Baltimore Waltz and Other Plays*. New York: Theatre Communications Group, 1996.

Olivia Turnbull

A BANKRUPTCY

Nanna, now life is founded on truth. Now I feel that our home is blessed.

—Mr. Tjælde, Act 4

As the first full-fledged realist drama, *A Bankruptcy (En Fallit)* by BJØRNSTJERNE BJØRNSON is a watershed in the history of Norwegian and European drama. It premiered in Stockholm in 1875 and enjoyed enormous success at home and abroad. Together with Bjørnson's drama *The Editor*, also 1875, *A Bankruptcy* was hailed by AUGUST STRINDBERG as the signal rocket of a new era for drama. It was embraced by Danish critic Georg Brandes, who claimed that Bjørnson's two plays were the long-awaited proofs that Scandinavian literature finally had become contemporaneous and modern.

The play confronted its audience with a realistic and witty analysis of the consequences and ravages of unchecked capitalism. Equally topical and progressive was its critique of the institutions of marriage and family and thus, and no less directly, of the relations between the sexes.

A Bankruptcy explores partly tested, partly unknown territory; it does not invent REALISM, and it is not the first literary text to deal with issues such as ethics and finance or the question of marriage and the transformation of women's roles. But as a realist drama it represents a first in its combined effect of contemporary themes, stage decor, and technique and especially in its characterizing and often humorous use of everyday language, allowing for the expression not only of individual psychological traits but equally those of class and professional status. The use of the glass veranda, later so central to HENRIK IBSEN'S DRAMATURGY, makes its debut in Bjørnson's *A Bankruptcy*.

The play's tendentiousness, the heavy-handed yoking of realism and idealism, of art and morality, has become the very cause for its lack of holding power over subsequent generations. In recreating its own times by concentrating so heavily on the period's contemporary political, social, and ethical currents, the play ends up discussing and moralizing rather than rendering a sense of the universal, the ineffable, and the incontrovertible.

The action takes place in the luxurious family house (glass veranda, living room, dining room, and office) of the wealthy merchant Tjælde. Noteworthy is Bjørnson's concrete scenic representation of the intimate sphere of the upper middle class. The small coastal town is dominated by and dependent upon Tjælde's involvement in local and international business. Unbeknown to his family and the workers, Tjælde is experiencing serious financial problems. In order to stave off his creditors Tjælde engages in dishonest transactions, by fraudulently securing additional loans through well-connected acquaintances. But his creditors are in the know and send a representative, the moral and wise laywer Mr. Berent, to prevent the transaction from taking place. Berent forces a panicked Tjælde to confront his deceitful behavior and encourages him to come clean, not only to society but, importantly, to himself and to his own family.

In the highly charged and effective confrontation between Tjælde and Berent in the office, where Tjælde crumples under Berent's stern but empathetic unveiling of the true state of affairs, private and public, the play dips over into the melodramatic (Tjælde's threat of murder, of suicide, and finally, his attempt to flee the country to seek capital abroad). Berent, wise and sagacious, convinces Tjælde to stay and face the public humility of bankruptcy. With renewed understanding of truth and responsibility to self, family, and society, Tjælde, with the support of his eldest daughter Valborg and the substantial financial loan of his trusted office manager Sannes, rises from the ashes, a new man, and with his family as his strongest support and with the "idealistic" marriage of Valborg and Sannes as the building block for a new understanding between the sexes.

[*See also* Norway]

FURTHER READING

Lunde, Johs. "Økonomisk krise og moralsk drama. *En Fallit* i lys av Bjørnsons inntrykk fra den økonomiske krisen i Bergen 1857–59" [Financial crisis and moralistic drama, bankruptcy in light of Bjornson's impressions of the economic crisis in Bergen 1857–59]. *Edda* 2 (1967): 90–106.

Sanaker, John Kristian. "Bjørnstjerne Bjørnsons *En Fallit* som realistisk drama" [Bjørnstjerne Bjørnson's *A Bankruptcy* as realist drama]. In *Drama-analyser fra Holberg til Hoem* [Drama analyses from Holberg to Hoem], ed. by Leif Longum. Oslo: Universitets forlaget, 1977. 29–48.

Pål Bjørby

BANYA *See* THE BATH HOUSE

BARAKA, AMIRI (1934–)

The reason I'm not a violent man—that's what I'm trying to say in Dutchman—is that art is the most beautiful resolution of energies that in another context might be violent to myself or anyone else.

—Amiri Baraka

Born Everett LeRoi Jones in Newark, New Jersey, in 1934, Amiri Baraka is a leading figure in the BLACK ARTS MOVEMENT, which revolutionized black theater in America. Baraka came to the forefront of the American literary scene in the 1960s as a poet, playwright, and essayist concerned with forging a political and cultural revolution for African Americans and increased awareness of black arts.

Following his education at Rutgers and Howard universities, Baraka moved to New York City's Greenwich Village in the 1950s and worked with Beat poets Jack Kerouac, Allen Ginsberg, and Charles Olson. Along with his wife, Hetti Cohen, he co-founded and edited the AVANT-GARDE literary magazine *Yugen* in 1958 that continued until 1963. In 1965 Baraka established the Black Arts Repertory Theatre and School, which brought music, poetry, and performance to the street corners of Harlem. The theater was aimed at developing techniques for improving ghetto life, furthering black rights, and fostering pride in the African American community.

Baraka's reputation as a playwright was established with the production of DUTCHMAN at the Cherry Lane Theatre in New York in 1964. This drama concerns a fatal confrontation on a New York City subway between Lula, a seductive and sadistic Caucasian woman, and Clay, a black, middle-class, intellectual man. The same year, Baraka wrote a succession of one-act plays examining black repression, empowerment, and revolution in America including *The Baptism* and *The Slave*. Also in 1964, Baraka wrote *The Toilet*, set in an urban high school bathroom, about the brutal beating of a homosexual boy, Karolis, as a result of a love letter he wrote to Foots, the leader of a black gang.

The assassination of Malcolm X and the Watts riots in Los Angeles propelled Baraka increasingly toward black militancy and the politics of black nationalism in plays such as *A Black Mass* (1966), *The Great Goodness of Life (A Coon Show)* (1967), and *The Death of Malcolm X* (1969). In rejecting white culture he became a Kawaidi Muslim minister in 1968 and adopted the Muslim name Imamu Amiri Baraka. Baraka's work has provoked both passionate praise and intense controversy. Some critics argue that while his wit is razor sharp and his poetry profound, his separatist views and hostility toward whites perpetuate racial hatred.

Throughout the 1970s and 1980s, Baraka became interested in Marxism and the exploitation of the poor under capitalism. He was made poet laureate of New Jersey in 2002 and was later removed from the post following public outcry over a poem that implied that Israel had foreknowledge of the September 11, 2001, terrorist attacks on New York City and Washington, D.C. Baraka remains a forceful voice of the Black Arts movement, which emphasizes the particular experiences of African Americans, the relationship between ethics and aesthetics, and the responsibility of artists to their communities.

[*See also* Political Theater; United States, 1940–Present]

SELECT PLAYS: *A Good Girl Is Hard to Find* (1958); *The Baptism* (1964); *Dutchman* (1964); *The Slave* (1964); *The Toilet* (1964); *Insurrection* (1969); *Resurrection in Life* (1969); *Bloodrites* (1970); *Black Power Chant* (1972); *The Motion of History* (1977); *What Was the Relationship of the Lone Ranger to the Means of Production: A Play in One Act* (1979); *Dim'crackr Party Convention* (1980); *Boy and Tarzan Appear in a Clearing!* (1981); *Song: A One Act Play About the Relationship of Art to Real Life* (1983); *Primitive World* (1984)

FURTHER READING

Baraka, Amiri. "The Revolutionary Theatre." In *Home: Social Essays*. New York: Morrow, 1966.

——. *The Autobiography of LeRoi Jones/Amiri Baraka*. New York: Freundlich, 1984.

Benston, Kimberly W., ed. *Imamu Amiri Baraka (LeRoi Jones): A Collection of Critical Essays*. Englewood Cliffs, N.J.: Prentice-Hall, 1978.

Brown, Lloyd W. *Amiri Baraka*. Boston: Twayne, 1980.

Hudson, Theodore R. *From LeRoi Jones to Amiri Baraka: The Literary Works.* Durham, N.C.: Duke Univ. Press, 1973.

Reilly, Charlie, ed. *Conversations with Amiri Baraka.* Jackson: Univ. Press of Mississippi, 1994.

Molly Castelloe

BARKER, HOWARD (1946–)

Let me state here unequivocally that theatre is without use, is the abnegation of use-value, and defies annexation or appropriation, being neither a diversion from the tedium of common life nor a palliative for deformed social relations, and therefore it reconciles no one either to his neighbor or his fate.

—Howard Barker

Born in South London in 1946, Howard Barker attended Battersea Grammar School before going on to study history at Sussex University, where he received his M.A. The son of a bookbinder and trade unionist, Barker's early plays reflect the left-wing idealism of his socialist upbringing. Unlike other writers of his generation (i.e., HOWARD BRENTON, CARYL CHURCHILL, and DAVID HARE), Barker's writing quickly abandoned overt ideology, in favor of a more complex and ambiguous approach, a contemporary form of TRAGEDY that he calls "Theater of Catastrophe." The author of more than fifty plays, Barker has long been derided by critics for his dark subject matter and difficult intellectual content, while earning praise from actors who relish his raw yet poetic dialogue and the intensity his roles require.

Barker's plays from the 1970s display a strong socialist concern, if not a direct agenda. *No One Was Saved* (1970) shows his early willingness to engage with others' work by blending The Beatles' "Eleanor Rigby" with EDWARD BOND's SAVED and then adding his own violent twist to the mix for a relentless look at working-class frustrations. *Claw* (1975) and *Fair Slaughter* (1977) both explore the power of institutions to crush the ambitions of individuals who would dare rise above their social class.

The shift away from both ideology and REALISM is clear in Barker's plays from the 1980s onward, as he refined his theory of catastrophic theater. His most popular success, *Scenes from an Execution* (1984; originally a radio play, later adapted for the stage), set in the 17th century, explores the social and political responsibilities imposed on artists by state sponsorship. *The Castle* (1985) features a knight returning home from the Crusades, who finds that his faithless wife has established a feminist community in his absence. The knight's efforts to restore a patriarchal order, symbolized by the erection of the largest castle ever, fail to resolve the gender conflict. Helen of Troy's body is both erotic fetish and mutilated object of vengeance in *The Bite of the Night* (1988), as the survivors of Troy conspire with a classics professor of an abandoned contemporary university to create new Troys, resulting in the inability to negotiate between the will to knowledge and the desire for social stability.

The unique nature of Barker's Theater of Catastrophe is most clear with his daring revisions to works from the dramatic canon. With *(Uncle) Vanya* (1996) Barker not only rewrites ANTON CHEKHOV; he makes him a character. Barker even takes on William Shakespeare's most revered tragedies, with his prequel *Seven Lears* (1989) and with his radical transformation of the Hamlet myth in *Gertrude—The Cry* (2002).

The increasing neglect of his work by the major national theaters of Britain is countered by the success of The Wrestling School (the company founded in 1988 exclusively for the production of plays by Barker) and the positive reception his work enjoys in continental Europe. The influence of Barker on the younger generation of British dramatists (especially SARAH KANE) is well documented and proof that his prophetic appeals for theatrical reform have not gone unheard.

[*See also* England, 1940–Present]

SELECT PLAYS: *No One Was Saved* (1970); *Claw* (1975); *Fair Slaughter* (1977); *Victory* (1983); *Scenes from an Execution* (1984); *The Castle* (1985); *The Bite of the Night* (1988); *Seven Lears* (1989); *The Europeans* (1993); *Hated Nightfall* (1994); *Judith* (1995); *(Uncle) Vanya* (1996); *Gertrude—The Cry* (2002)

FURTHER READING

Barker, Howard. *Arguments for a Theatre.* 3d ed. New York: Manchester Univ. Press, 1997.

"Howard Barker." Special issue, ed. by Tony Dunn, *Gambit* 41 (1984).

Lamb, Charles. *Howard Barker's Theatre of Seduction.* Amsterdam: Harwood Acad. Pubs., 1997.

Rabey, David Ian. *Howard Barker: Politics and Desire.* New York: St. Martin's, 1989.

The Wrestling School [Web site of the company devoted exclusively to the production of Barker's plays]. http://www.thewrestlingschool.co.uk/tws.html.

David Kilpatrick

BARNES, DJUNA (1892–1982)

Recent evidence suggests that for many years Djuna Barnes was engaged in an incestuous relationship with her maternal grandmother Zadel and that at the age of sixteen, her notoriously libertine father compelled her to have sexual relations with a male neighbor three times her age. Ironic celebrations of libertinage and lesbianism mark her early work, while the rape became a recurring theme in her later, more serious work both as novelist and playwright.

Barnes was born on June 12, 1892, in Cornwall-on-Hudson, New York. Between 1913 and 1921, Barnes developed a reputation as a brilliant journalist, theatrical reviewer, and short-story writer, interviewing and befriending such luminaries as James Joyce, Frank Harris, and Mabel Dodge Luhan. Among

Barnes's friends at this time were the founding members of the Provincetown Players, including SUSAN GLASPELL, George Cram Cook, and EUGENE O'NEILL. For the Players, Barnes wrote at least sixteen short, witty, often highly stylized plays; these, which focus very much on women, are derivative of styles she admired, imitating by turns OSCAR WILDE and J. M. SYNGE. In some she dispenses with classical concepts of dramatic "action" and explores the intricacies of dialogue alone, conjuring the ABSURDISM of EUGÈNE IONESCO and SAMUEL BECKETT. Reviews of this stage of her work range from "impenetrable" and "unactable" (Scott, 1976) to S. J. Kaufman's more charitable "near to being great. . . . [T]he incalculable depth of it has us enthralled" (Messerili, 1995). In the 1920s, Barnes completed, but never published, two three-act plays: *Biography of Julie von Bartmann* and *Ann Portuguise*.

In 1921, *McCall's* magazine sent Barnes to Paris as a correspondent; there she was to become the darling of the Left Bank "salon" crowd of expatriate American writers and artists. In the 1930s, she returned to New York where she became a founding member of the THEATRE GUILD and worked on her most famous novel, *Nightwood* (1936), which would make her a highly celebrated, if controversial, author. Barnes then succumbed to a lifelong struggle with alcoholism and depression. Heiress and art patron Peggy Guggenheim supported her during this period but refused to enable her addictions: Barnes was sent to various sanitariums to "dry out" and later lived on Guggenheim's charity in a small flat in Greenwich village.

In 1952, Barnes began writing *The Antiphon*, a full-length bitter revenge drama in complex Jacobean-style verse that brutally lashes out at her family and their complicity in the horrors of her youth. The play was completed in 1956, but Barnes had difficulty finding a publisher. This was due in part to her friend T. S. ELIOT's halfhearted endorsement: "It might be said of Miss Barnes, who is uncontestably one of the most original writers of our time, that never has so much genius been combined with so little talent" (qtd. in Herring, 1995). Nevertheless, this play, premiering at Stockholm's Royal Dramatic Theatre in 1961, would afford Barnes her greatest popularity as a dramatist. The remaining decades of Barnes's life were plagued with health problems, and she died on June 19, 1982, in New York City.

[*See also* United States, 1929–Present]

PLAYS: *The Death of Life* (1916); *At the Roots of the Stars* (1917); *Maggie of the Saints* (1917); *Madame Collects Herself* (1918); *A Passion Play* (1918); *Three from the Earth* (1919); *Kurzy from the Sea* (1920); *An Irish Triangle* (1921); *Little Drops of Rain* (1922); *The Beauty* (1923); *Five Thousand Miles* (1923); *She Tells Her Daughter* (1923); *Two Ladies Take Tea* (1923); *Water-Ice* (1923); *The Dove* (1929); *To the Dogs* (1929); *The Antiphon* (1958); *Ann Portuguise* (unpublished); *Biography of Julie von Bartmann* (unpublished)

FURTHER READING

Barnes, Djuna. *The Selected Works of Djuna Barnes*. New York: Farrar, Straus, 1962.

Broe, Mary Lynn, ed. *Silence and Power: A Reevaluation of Djuna Barnes*. Carbondale: Southern Illinois Univ. Press, 1991.

Field, Andrew. *Djuna: The Life and Times of Djuna Barnes*. New York: Putnam, 1983.

Galvin, Mary E. *Queer Poetics: Five Modernist Women Writers*. Westport, Conn.: Praeger, 1999.

Herring, Philip. *Djuna: The Life and Work of Djuna Barnes*. New York: Viking, 1995.

Messerli, Douglas, ed. *At the Roots of the Stars: The Short Plays of Djuna Barnes*. Los Angeles: Sun & Moon, 1995.

Scott, James B. *Djuna Barnes*. Boston: Twayne, 1976.

Michael M. Chemers

BARRIE, J. M. (1860–1937)

Writer Sir James Matthew (J. M.) Barrie was born in 1860 in Kirriemuir, Forfarshire (Angus), SCOTLAND, the ninth of ten children of a weaver and a housewife. Small and slight, whereas other boys his age were tall and athletic, Barrie found solace in hearing and creating stories. His mother, Margaret Ogilvy, would read all of the children stories of adventures in the evening. Perhaps this is where Barrie began to develop his art and love for storytelling. When James, or Jamie as his family called him, was seven, his brother David died in a skating accident. David Barrie had been the mother's favorite; she had even intended for him to be a minister. As a result of his death, Ogilvy fell into a deep depression, never again to be the same. Often children who endure this particular type of tragedy excel at attempting to rectify the loss by creating fantastic adventures.

At the tender age of thirteen, James left his home to attend school. There, he grew his passion and interest in stories and storytelling, reading the works of authors such as Jules Verne and James Fenimore Cooper with fierce adoration. Much has been made of Barrie's seeming disaffection for women. He did not seem so much a misogynist as a perpetual young boy, which perhaps led him to writing his most famous work, PETER PAN (1904). Barrie attended Dumfries Academy and then the University of Edinburgh. Barrie received his master's degree in 1882 and made his way to London, working first as a freelance journalist. Barrie was fortunate to fall in with a crowd of contemporary and future luminaries such as GEORGE BERNARD SHAW and H. G. Wells, whom he would satirize in his writing.

Barrie wrote and published two novels, *Auld Licht Idylls* (1888) and *The Little Minister* (1891), both enormous critical and commercial successes. Barrie focused mostly on writing for the theater despite the success of his novels. Barrie married actress Mary Ansell in 1894, the couple having met when she starred in his production *Walker, London*. The couple divorced in 1909 after Ansell revealed an affair with writer Gilbert Cannan. Barrie's perpetual "boyness" and his recurrent theme of man-boy relationships would inspire production of his most famous, loved, and lasting work, *Peter Pan*, first produced at the Duke of York's Theatre, London, in 1904. The work is believed to have evolved from stories Barrie told to the five young sons of friend Sylvia Llewelyn Davies, who died of cancer on June 19, 1937, in London. Barrie became the guardian of the five boys after their mother's death.

[*See also* The Admirable Crichton; Dear Brutus; England, 1860–1940]

SELECT PLAYS: *Ibsen's Ghost* (1891); *Quality Street* (1901); *The Admirable Crichton* (1902); *Peter and Wendy* (1911); *Dear Brutus* (1917); *What Every Woman Knows* (1917); *Peter Pan, or The Boy Who Would Not Grow Up* (1928); *Boy David* (1936); *When Wendy Grew Up* (1954)

FURTHER READING

Aller, Susan Bivin. *J. M. Barrie: The Magic Behind Peter Pan*. Minneapolis: Lerner, 1994.

Asquith, Cynthia. *Portrait of Barrie*. London: J. Barrie, 1954.

Birkin, Andrew. *J. M. Barrie and the Lost Boys*. London: Constable, 1979.

Ormond, Leonée. *J. M. Barrie*. Edinburgh: Scottish Acad. Press, 1987.

Rose, Jacqueline. *The Case of Peter Pan, or, The Impossibility of Children's Fiction*. London: Macmillan, 1984.

Shanté T. Smalls

BARRY, PHILIP (1896–1949)

Philip Barry experimented with a variety of forms during his twenty-five year career as a playwright. A gifted writer of novels, short stories, and poetry, he enjoyed most success when employing the form of American high COMEDY or comedy of manners.

Barry was born on June 18, 1896, in Rochester, New York. He entered Yale University after completing parochial high school. While at Yale, his short stories and poetry were published in the *Yale Literary Magazine*. After World War I caused a brief interruption in his studies, he returned to the States in 1919 and enrolled in GEORGE PIERCE BAKER's Workshop 47 at Harvard. Professor Baker mentored his development as a playwright. In 1922, he married society debutante Ellen Semple, and the marriage produced two sons. Speculation about the accomplishments of a daughter, who died in infancy, and his relationship with her had she lived, may have prompted Barry's creation of what would become a signature character, "the Barry Girl."

In 1922, *The Jilts* received the Herndon Prize, which provided a Broadway production. Retitled *You and I*, Barry's debut offering opened in New York on February 19, 1923, and ran for 170 performances. For the next twenty years, Broadway seldom lacked a Philip Barry play.

Barry's comedies of manners were uniquely American. Characterized by a mode of equitable resolution, these plays feature witty, wealthy characters who exhibit entitlement as a result of successful pursuit of the American dream. They epitomize the American urban "smart set" (of which Barry was a member), as it existed in the 1920s and 1930s. Lacking a prescribed code of conduct characteristically ridiculed in European comedies of manners, Barry's characters exhibit manners patterns born of ideological conviction. Usually, the lesson to be learned focuses on the individual who acquires such a solid sense of self that he or she can exhibit tolerance toward those whose manners do not match their own. While many of Barry's American high comedies such as *Paris Bound* (1927), HOLIDAY (1928), and *The Animal Kingdom* (1932) enjoyed success, THE PHILADELPHIA STORY remains his most popular work. *The Philadelphia Story* boasts innumerable productions since its premiere in 1939 as well as a remarkable film version and a less-popular musical adaptation titled *High Society*. It is responsible for reviving the career of actress Katharine Hepburn.

Perhaps driven by a need to respond to the Depression, Barry explored other forms for his plays. While most did not meet with the critical acclaim that his comedies enjoyed, scholars are now beginning to develop a new appreciation for this work. His 1925 play *In a Garden* reveals his experimentation with Freudian concepts, which he developed further in *Hotel Universe* (1930) and *Here Come the Clowns* (1938), two works that place him in the forefront as a writer of psychodrama.

Barry made his mark on modern theater by creating a distinctly American genre of comedy of manners that continues to delight audiences around the world. He died on December 3, 1949, in East Hampton, Long Island.

[*See also* United States, 1860–1929]

PLAYS: *Autonomy* (1919); *A Punch for Judy* (1921); *You and I* (1923); *The Youngest* (1924); *In a Garden* (1925); *White Wings* (1926); *John* (1927); *Paris Bound* (1927); *Cock Robin* (1928); *Holiday* (1928); *Hotel Universe* (1930); *Tomorrow and Tomorrow* (1931); *The Animal Kingdom* (1932); *The Joyous Season* (1934); *Bright Star* (1935); *Spring Dance* (1936; adapted from Eleanor Golden and Eloise Barrangon's play); *Here Come the Clowns* (1938); *The Philadelphia Story* (1939); *Liberty Jones* (1941); *Without Love* (1942); *Foolish Notion* (1945); *My Name Is Aquilon* (1949; adapted from Jean Pierre Aumont's play); and *Second Threshold* (1951; revised by Robert E. Sherwood)

FURTHER READING

Broussard, Louis. *American Drama: Contemporary Allegory from Eugene O'Neill to Tennessee Williams*. Norman: Univ. of Oklahoma Press, 1962.

Gild, David C. "Psychodrama on Broadway: Three Plays of Psychodrama by Philip Barry." *Markham Review* 2 (1970): 65–74.

Meserve, Walter J. "Philip Barry: A Dramatist's Search." *Modern Drama* 13 (1970): 93–99.

Roppolo, Joseph Patrick. *Philip Barry*. Twayne's United State Authors Series. New York: Twayne, 1965.

Sievers, David W. *Freud on Broadway*. New York: Hermitage House, 1953.

Judith Midyett Pender

THE BATHHOUSE

VLADIMIR MAYAKOVSKY wrote his last play, *The Bathhouse* (*Banya*), in 1930. In it, he created a scathing satire of Soviet society but also a problematic play. The success of his previous play THE BEDBUG led to high expectations, which were not rewarded in full.

The play depicts a stifling bureaucracy that has ground society to a halt. This stagnation finds its fullest expression in the character of Comrade Pobedonosikov, who rules by means of edicts, memoranda, circulars, and the like. His very name conjures up a totalitarian and repressive atmosphere since it suggests a "nose for victory" but sounds suspiciously like Pobedonostsev, one of the most reactionary politicians of the 19th century. Because of Pobedonosikov's preoccupation with power, human creativity struggles to find an outlet. When the inventor Chudakov creates a time machine, his industrious assistant Velosipedkin looks for official backing but has trouble even getting an audience with Pobedonosikov. Time is indeed of the essence because Mr. Pont-Kitsch, a British capitalist, wants to buy the invention for his own purposes. A demonstration is forced upon Pobedonosikov at his private apartment. Inadequate funding notwithstanding, the time machine hurtles a Phosphorescent Woman, a denizen of the distant future and a perfect society, right onto the landing of Pobedonosikov's apartment. The Phosphorescent Woman speaks about the future and assures the group that the future will accept only those of their characteristics that are consonant with communist society and will reject the rest. Pobedonosikov announces his intention to rule over the future in the same manner he rules over the present. The time machine—a kind of temporal bathhouse that sanitizes the future—spits him out. The play closes with a moment that recalls both *The Bedbug* and Nikolai Gogol's *Inspector General*. Mayakovsky lays bare the artifice of the fourth wall, as Pobedonosikov addresses the audience directly, asking whether or not he and they are necessary to the future.

The great strength and, at the same time, the great weakness of *The Bathhouse* lies in Mayakovsky's language. At its worst, the play is replete with dull, repetitive, and unimaginative didacticism. Nearly all of Pobedonosikov's speeches fall into this category, and this applies with a vengeance to the future-speak of the Phosphorescent Woman. On the other hand, Pont-Kitsch's language is imaginative and delightful and has earned Mayakovsky much deserved praise. The poet worked in close collaboration with translator Rita Rait to fashion Pont-Kitsch's language in such a way that each of his utterances is roughly intelligible, if wildly divergent in meaning, in both Russian and English. Though a tour de force, it is not enough to redeem the play's slack dramatic structure and frequent longueurs.

These weaknesses contributed to the failure of *The Bathhouse* on the stage. Although VSEVOLOD MEYERHOLD championed the play and staged it compellingly, the play often bored the audience and often offended Party officials. (The actual premiere of the play, which was directed by Vladimir Liutse, preceded Meyerhold's production by a month and a half.) Those who attended the first performances recount a deadly silence throughout the first two acts. Mayakovsky's enemies launched vicious attacks, which Joseph Stalin is said to have encouraged.

The demise of *The Bathhouse* exacerbated Mayakovsky's personal and professional problems. He committed suicide less than a month after the premiere of Meyerhold's production.

FURTHER READING

Brown, Edward J. *Mayakovsky: A Poet in the Revolution*. Princeton, N.J.: Princeton Univ. Press, 1973.

Markov, Vladimir. *Russian Futurism: A History*. Berkeley: Univ. of California Press, 1968.

Mayakovsky, Vladimir. *The Bathhouse*. In *Twentieth Century Russian Drama*, ed. and tr. by Andrew MacAndrew. New York: Bantam, 1963.

———. *The Bathhouse*. In *Selected Works in Three Volumes*. Vol. 3, *Plays, Articles, Essays*, ed. by Alexander Ushakov. Moscow: Raduga Pubs., 1987.

———. *Plays*. Tr. by Guy Daniels. Evanston, Ill.: Northwestern Univ. Press, 1995.

Terras, Victor. *Vladimir Mayakovsky*. Boston: Twayne, 1983.

Timothy C. Westphalen

BEAN, RICHARD (1956–)

Richard Bean took up playwriting after having spent twenty years working in industry. He has recently received a great deal of recognition as an important new voice in theater. Within the space of over a year, his works were commissioned by the National Theatre, the Royal Court, and the Bush, honors achieved by few playwrights. Over the last few years, he has written several plays for stage and radio.

Born in 1956, Bean was raised in Hull, where he studied psychology at Loughborough University. Following completion of his studies, he spent six years as a personnel officer and ten years as a freelance occupational psychologist working for nongovernmental organizations (NGOs). The comic skills that would mark his plays were honed during these years as Bean spent his spare time as a stand-up comedian. From there he went on to be a writer and performer with the sketch comedy troupe Control Group Six on BBC radio. The quality of the troupe's work was recognized with a Writers Guild Award nomination.

In 1995 Bean wrote the libretto for the Stephen McNeff opera *Paradise of Fools*, which premiered at the Unicorn Arts

Theatre. His first full-length play, *Of Rats and Men* (1992), was produced at the Canal Cafe Theatre before moving to Edinburgh. A BBC radio adaptation of the play was nominated for a Sony Award. Another Sony Award nomination was received for Bean's radio play *Unsinkable*, broadcast by BBC Radio 3 in 2000.

In his forties, Bean gave up his career to devote himself full-time to playwriting. His first major play, *Toast* (1999), drew on Bean's experiences working at a bakery during his student days. After *Toast*, which played Upstairs at the Royal Court, Bean received a Pearson residency at the National Theatre's Studio.

Following a stint as writer-in-residence at the National Theatre, where *Mr. England* (2002) was produced, Bean returned to write *The Mentalists* (2001), which was produced at the Lyttleton Loft in 2002 as part of the Transformations Season. After a tour of Britain the play opened OFF-BROADWAY to a full production by New York's New Group in 2004.

His fifth play, UNDER THE WHALEBACK, won Bean the George Devine Award for Most Promising Playwright in 2002 and opened at the Royal Court Theatre in 2003. The year 2003 also saw the production of *The God Botherers* at the Bush as well as the premiere of *Smack Family Robinson* at Live Theatre in Newcastle. The latter play offers a sympathetic depiction of a family of drug dealers in Whitely Bay. After initial discussions with the author, the BBC decided not to pursue a television adaptation of the controversial story. In 2004, a new play, *Honeymoon Suite*, produced by Stephen Unwin's English Touring Theatre, was presented Downstairs at the Royal Court.

In his fight against prevailing orthodoxy that would smother dissent, Bean effectively deploys black COMEDY to say serious things about society. Even a story like *Under the Whaleback*, which deals with the tragic deaths of twenty men and the loss of fishing communities and ways of living, is held together with a thread of comedy. Indeed, this humor in times of distress reflects the "gallows humor" often expressed by working-class people struggling with the difficulties and anxieties that accompany job loss and economic uncertainty.

Bean's reputation as a working person's playwright is well deserved. The wide-ranging themes pursued in his works are expressive of his concerns and perspectives as a libertarian socialist. Bean's earlier life as a worker in Hull has informed all of his writing. His plays offer poignant reflections on the decline of working-class employment and communities in the era of neoliberal socioeconomic restructuring. Bean, who has expressed frustration with the lack of attention given to people's working lives in contemporary plays, has brought working-class concerns to center stage in a rich body of works that chart the transformation from industrialism to postindustrialism in Britain.

[*See also* England, 1940–Present]

SELECT PLAYS: *Of Rats and Men* (1992); *Toast* (1999); *Mr. England* (2000); *The Mentalists* (2001); *The God Botherers* (2003); *Smack Family Robinson* (2003); *Under the Whaleback* (2003); *Honeymoon Suite* (2004)

FURTHER READING

Fisher, Philip. "Richard Bean: Hot New Playwright." *The British Theatre Guide*. 2001. http://britishtheatreguide.info/otherresources/interviews/RichardBean.htm.

Writernet. "Richard Bean and the Work Plays." 2004. http://www.writernet.co.uk/.

Jeff Shantz

BECKETT, SAMUEL (1906–1989)

Success and failure on the public level never mattered much to me[;] in fact I feel more at home with the latter, having breathed deep of its vivifying air all my writing life up to the last couple of years.
—Samuel Beckett, letter to Alan Schneider

EARLY YEARS

Samuel Beckett's paternal ancestors arrived in Ireland from France sometime in the late 17th or early 18th century, fleeing the persecution of Huguenots by the French Catholic monarchy. The Huguenots were an industrious people and brought with them the skills of poplin weaving and glassmaking and ancillary trades. Their assimilation into the Protestant middle class was speedy and uncomplicated.

By the early 19th century the Becketts had successfully diversified into architecture and building construction; some of the major civic buildings in Dublin were designed and built by them. With the construction of railways radiating from Dublin city, opportunities for suburban housing development were created, and the Becketts joined in this work. Beckett's father (William; 1871–1933) worked for and later led a firm of Dublin quantity surveyors (construction cost consultants); he had sufficiently progressed in his profession to have a substantial suburban villa designed and built soon after his marriage, at the turn of the century, to May Roe (1871–1950).

The Roe family was English in origin and had arrived in Ireland as part of the Cromwellian plantations of the mid-17th century. By the middle of the next century, the Roes occupied lands to the west of Dublin and had become successful grain farmers and millers. The family seat was at the village of Leixlip in County Kildare, and the manor house was called Cooldrinagh (an anglicization of a Gaelic phrase meaning "behind the blackthorn hedge"). William and May Beckett were to adopt this name for their suburban home some years later. The Roe family fortunes went into decline from about the middle of the 19th century as the price of grain fell sharply under the pressure of cheap imports from North America. Samuel Roe (the future writer's maternal grandfather, after whom he was named) died in his early fifties, while his daughter May was still in her teens, and she was propelled into employment as a nurse in the Adelaide hospital in central Dublin. There she met William Beckett as he was recovering from a bout of pneumonia.

William and May Beckett moved into their new house in the suburb of Foxrock in south County Dublin early in 1902. Their first son, Frank (1902–1954), was born there as, four years later, on Good Friday, April 13, 1906, was Samuel. Cooldrinagh was (and is) a large and gloomy detached house, mock-Tudor in style, situated on an acre of ground. There were lawns, a kitchen garden, a small copse, a tennis court, a double garage—William Beckett was an avid motorist—and various outbuildings, including a stable for the family donkey. Local gardeners were hired to tend the grounds, and there were indoor servants as well, among them a succession of maids and nannies for the children.

Cooldrinagh was close to all amenities. The Dublin and South Eastern Railway (known to its users as the Slow and Easy) served Foxrock station, a few minutes' walk from the house. The Church of Ireland (Anglican) parish church where the Beckett family had a pew was close by. Essential provisions could be ordered by telephone from nearby Connolly's Stores for delivery by van. Sea bathing was available at the Blackrock Seawater baths or at the famous Forty-Foot bathing place (gentlemen only) in Sandycove, both a leisurely bicycle ride away, and at the resort of Bray, at the end of the Slow and Easy. There were two golf courses in the vicinity, and the foothills of the Dublin and Wicklow mountains to the south and west provided an ideal venue for recreational walking. Samuel Beckett's home, then, was the epitome of Protestant middle-class security; comfort without ostentation, prosperity without opulence.

Beckett's education followed the pattern established earlier for his older brother. His first schooling was at a local kindergarten, where he learned to read, write, and play the piano. After a few years he followed his brother to Earlsfort House school in central Dublin, commuting daily on the Slow and Easy, the city terminus of which was only a few hundred yards from the school. It is likely that location was the reason for the parents' choice of school, although the school was exceptional for the time in that its enrollment was multidenominational and its curriculum liberal. Here Beckett had his first experience of organized sports, and he participated fully in rugby football, cricket, and track athletics. Later on he also participated in boxing, swimming, motorcycling, and chess.

Just after his fourteenth birthday, in 1920, Beckett was enrolled as a boarder at Portora Royal School in Enniskillen, in County Fermanagh in the north of the country. Portora was closely modeled on the better English public (in American usage, private) schools and was patronized mainly by middle-class Protestant families of a staunchly Unionist political orientation.

The apparently even tenor of Beckett's formative years was frequently interrupted by tumultuous political events in Ireland. His attendance at Earlsfort House School was temporarily halted after Easter in April 1916 because the center of Dublin had become a battleground. Militant Irish nationalists operating as a provisional government proclaimed a republic, and the British army was sent in to quell the uprising. Hundreds died in the fighting and in the artillery barrages used to dislodge the rebels. Later in life Beckett recalled, with horror, being taken to the foothills of the mountains to look north to the city center in flames. The dirty Anglo-Irish war, the so-called Troubles, broke out in 1919 and only came to an end with a truce between the Irish Republican Army and the British government in July 1921. Traveling back to Portora after the Christmas school holiday in January 1921, Beckett would have discovered that Enniskillen was now in a different country, anomalously called Northern Ireland. The following year he would have found that Dublin was no longer a provincial city in the United Kingdom of Great Britain and Ireland but the capital of the Irish Free State. The ratification of the Anglo-Irish Treaty, which established the Free State, was followed by a yearlong brutal civil war that ended just before Beckett entered university. Some of Beckett's most formative years were spent in a country in considerable turmoil when it was not literally at war.

Beckett's school career was not distinguished by high academic achievement and gave no hint of his talents. His athletic prowess guaranteed his popularity and status among his schoolmates, although he did not achieve the position of senior prefect, as his brother had. In fact, all through his life he deliberately avoided the limelight, preferring to protect his privacy.

1923–1929

Beckett entered Trinity College, Dublin, in the fall of 1923 and registered for an arts degree. While he read modern languages (French and Italian) for his degree, he also took mathematics and English literature programs in his first two years, and he read intensively in philosophy for his own edification. He had no clear idea as to what career he might pursue, indicating to his tutor that he might aim for law or accountancy. While he had the option of working in his father's firm after graduation, the necessity for doing so did not arise because his brother was already studying engineering and would in due course join the family firm. In later life Beckett jokingly bemoaned not taking his father's advice to apply for a clerkship in Guinness's brewery, where duties would be light and security assured.

Beckett lived at the family home for the first three years of his university program, commuting daily. He continued his participation in college sports but suffered the embarrassment of a reprimand from his tutor at the end of his first year for irregular attendance at classes. He took this to heart, and by the end of his second year, his grades had greatly improved. The improvement continued in his third year to such a level that he gained a college scholarship, entitling him to rooms on campus, reduced fees, and a small stipend. In the vacation before his final year, Beckett went to FRANCE for the first time, taking a bicycle tour through the Loire Valley and improving his spoken French. Another trip the following year, this time to Italy, was undertaken a few months before his final examinations. He gained first among firsts and was awarded a gold medal.

Trinity College had an exchange fellowship with the École Normale Supérieure (ENS) in Paris. During Beckett's final year the incoming fellow was Alfred Péron, with whom Beckett struck up a friendship that was to have momentous consequences for both men during World War II. Expecting that Beckett would score highly in his finals, Trinity College authorities nominated him as the outgoing fellow in 1927, on the understanding that he would join the staff of the French department when he had completed the exchange. An administrative hitch arose preventing Beckett taking up the fellowship until late 1928, so he spent a "limbo year" (his phrase) producing a research essay on a French literary movement—no copy has yet come to light—and teaching English and French at a boys' boarding school in Belfast. He found Belfast dull and the task of teaching tedious. He was glad to get away to Paris in the fall of 1928.

In the summer before his departure, he met and fell in love with his first cousin Peggy Sinclair, who was on holiday in Ireland. He had not seen her since her family had immigrated to GERMANY in the early 1920s. His parents disapproved of the relationship, but he persisted, despite their protestations. Heated arguments between Samuel and his parents marked the first rift in the family. The relationship lasted intermittently for about two years and then fizzled out. (Beckett presented a thoroughly fictionalized version of it in his first novel, *Dream of Fair to Middling Women*, written in 1931–1932 and posthumously published in 1992.)

Beckett went to Paris for a year but stayed for two. His experience there radically altered his expectations and liberated him in many ways. He was fortunate to have as a colleague at ENS an older Irishman named Thomas MacGreevy, who became his closest friend and confidant for many years. Within days of Beckett's arrival in Paris, MacGreevy introduced him to James Joyce, whom Beckett was eager to meet. The two men quickly discovered a shared enthusiasm for the work of Dante Alighieri and, more important, for the plays of J. M. SYNGE. Joyce was greatly impressed by Beckett's breadth of literary knowledge. Within a short time Joyce enlisted Beckett as one of the "12 apostles" (MacGreevy was another) to contribute to a symposium on "Work in Progress" (finally published as *Finnegans Wake* in 1939), which was then appearing in monthly installments in the magazine *Transition*. The symposium, titled *Our Exagmination Round His Factification for Incamination of Work in Progress*, was published by Shakespeare and Company, the first publishers of Joyce's *Ulysses*. Another one of the contributors to *Our Exagmination*, Eugene Jolas, who was also the editor of *Transition*, thought so highly of Beckett's essay that he published it, accompanied by Beckett's first short story, in June 1929. Beckett's career as a writer, which was to continue for nearly 60 years, had begun.

1930–1937

Beckett's duties at the ENS were light, and the teaching methodology (one-to-one tutorials at times convenient for both tutor and student) suited him admirably. It allowed him time for extensive reading and note taking, a practice he had started as a student in Trinity. In early 1930 he was reading René Descartes and taking notes. One afternoon MacGreevy heard that the Hours Press in Paris was offering a £10 prize and book publication for a poem of no more than 100 lines on the theme of time. He told Beckett, who promptly reviewed his notes and worked up a poem, titled *Whoroscope*, of 98 lines, completing it at three o'clock the following morning and delivering it to the publisher's office. Beckett won the prize and achieved his first individual publication.

Again at MacGreevy's prompting, Beckett spent much of the summer of 1930 writing a critical monograph on Marcel Proust's multivolume novel *In Search of Lost Time and Remembrance of Things Past (Á la recherche du temps perdu)*, which was accepted by Dolphin Books (an imprint of Chatto and Windus) and published in London in 1931. Simultaneously, Beckett was collaborating with Alfred Péron on a translation into French of Joyce's *Anna Livia Plurabelle*, but he had to break off the work before its completion to return to Ireland to take up his junior lecturership at Trinity College.

Beckett was now launched on a respectable academic career. He had been a brilliant student, had worked abroad at a prestigious institution, and had a growing list of critical publications. Nevertheless, he lacked the communication skills essential for academic teaching. As a student he had been a member of the college debating society but had never spoken at meetings. His shyness made public speaking difficult, and his commitment to scrupulous precision and his suspicion of the trickery of simplification meant that his lectures were pithy and went over the heads of most of his students. He stuck to the job but lasted a mere four academic terms before he fled to Germany, from where he cabled his resignation to the college in January 1932.

Beckett had other difficulties as well. He found writing almost impossible and was disappointed by anything he did achieve. One piece (exactly which is not known) was read by his mother and so shocked her that she expelled Beckett from the family home in 1931. Intercession by his brother and father did not succeed in effecting a reconciliation. The delivery of a spoof lecture on a fictitious French poet to the Modern Languages Society at Trinity and his participation in *The Kid (Le Kid)*, a grotesque parody of Pierre Corneille's play (it ran for three nights at the Peacock Theatre in Dublin—the only known occasion on which Beckett played in a theatrical piece), probably did little to lift his stock with his colleagues in the French department. His health was becoming shaky, surprising in view of his athleticism, and, more worryingly, he began to experience panic attacks, night sweats, and tachycardia. These latter afflictions were probably psychosomatic because they eased when he was away from home.

After resigning from Trinity, Beckett moved to Paris to set up as a professional writer. He had friends there he could turn to for support, and the lively literary scene might afford occasions for small earnings. He was also probably in receipt of "small charitable sums" of money (as is the central character in the novel *Murphy* that Beckett was to write a few years later) sent by his father, with whom he remained on good terms despite the family difficulties. He worked intensively and almost exclusively on the novel *Dream of Fair to Middling Women* and had the finished typescript with him when he moved to London in July. *Dream* was rejected by any publisher he could persuade to read it, and possibilities for literary earnings were scarcer than in Paris, so he lapsed homeward in August, having received the fare home from his parents. He was back in Cooldrinagh with no prospects, no job, no money, and an unpublishable book.

Dream is erudite and sly, precocious and scabrous, and makes few concessions to readability. Belacqua Shuah (a name redolent of Dante and the Book of Job), the protagonist, "a penny maneen of a low-down low-church Protestant high-brow," is a thoroughly skewed portrait of the artist as a narcissist in flight from the demands and messy complications of the real world. The presentation of character and incident is determinedly antirealist or surrealist. The book fails to cohere, being too episodic in structure. It was this failure that Beckett seized on as he dismembered the text into separate substories, added a few more newly written stories, and submitted the reassembled book to Chatto and Windus under the title *More Pricks than Kicks*. It was published in 1934 and received some reasonable reviews, but sales were disappointing.

Work on this book proceeded slowly and was interrupted twice while Beckett was hospitalized—his health was failing again. He was in the hospital when he received the news of Peggy Sinclair's death from tuberculosis in May 1933, and the following month his father suffered a heart attack that incapacitated him. Late in the month William Beckett suffered a second attack that proved fatal.

His father's death was a severe blow for Beckett. They had had an easy and loving relationship, with many interests in common. Beckett was fully aware that he owed everything to his father and had been able to count on his overt and covert support in the recent difficult years. His mother's mourning was elaborate and lengthy. The blinds were down for months, making the house gloomier still. Piano playing, a relaxation for Beckett, was strictly forbidden, and all conversation had to be properly solemn. Beckett was driven to set up a makeshift writer's studio in the attic of his late father's offices in central Dublin and, after much struggle, completed *More Pricks than Kicks*. He then suffered a breakdown for which his doctor prescribed psychotherapy.

In 1934 such treatment was not available in Dublin, so Beckett had to undergo his therapy in London. He had no money to fund the treatment, and he had to look to his mother for financial help. She, of course, gave it to him: It must have pained and mystified her that her younger son had willfully given up his chances of a respectable and secure profession for the production of writings that shocked her when she found them comprehensible. But his health came first, and she was unstinting in her support.

Beckett took lodgings in London and attended the Tavistock Clinic as an outpatient for the best part of two years. His therapist was a Dr. Bion, whom he met two or three times a week, with occasional breaks of a month or so. Progress was slow and often painful. The analysis revealed that Beckett's psychological and social problems—his debilitating shyness, inability to mix, and volatility in his difficult relationship with his mother—were generated by a sense of superiority inculcated by her high expectations of him. His failure to meet these led to frustration and generalized irritability, and his suppression of these feelings led inevitably to his nagging physical ailments. The analysis showed that he could have a reasonable relationship with his mother but only from a distance, a notion corroborated by the general improvement in his condition when he was away from home.

Beckett made good use of his extended stay in London. He did the rounds of the public art galleries and deepened his knowledge and appreciation of painters and painting, a practice he had engaged in since his student days. He attended concerts and recitals when he was in funds and went to the cinema often. He responded to a request from George Reavey for a book of poems by making a rigorous selection of those he had written from 1928 onward, revising thirteen of them and sending them to Paris. They were published by the Europa Press as *Echo's Bones and Other Precipitates* in 1935. He read widely and deeply in the available literature of psychology and psychoanalysis and deployed some of his research in the novel *Murphy*, which he began in the fall of 1935. Beckett ended his attendance at the Tavistock Clinic in December 1935 and returned home, having gained little apparent benefit.

Murphy is regarded as Beckett's first fully achieved creative work. Erudition is in evidence again but now deployed for comic effect. The narrative is playfully saturated with detail of no particular help to the reader, while essentials can only be retrieved with very close reading or guesswork. Beckett distributes aspects of his own experiences and characteristics among the characters and implies a set of severe judgments. He had considerable difficulty in controlling the clotted detail that the novel required—in his early monograph on Proust, he had castigated realists as "chartered recountants" who indulge in the "penny-a-line vulgarity of a literature of notations"—but he stuck to the task and completed the novel in 1936. It was circulated to some forty publishers in England and the United States; all rejected it. It was finally accepted by Routledge in late 1937, but only after Beckett's friend, the painter Jack Yeats, wrote to the publisher pointing out that his young friend was "the real thing." *Murphy* finally appeared in 1938. Again, sales were disappointing, despite a few respectful reviews.

No royalties had yet accrued from any of Beckett's published work, and his only income was a small annuity from his father's estate. The strain between him and his mother seemed to have eased, but Beckett sensed that to stay at home without employment was to court disaster. His long-suffering mother was again persuaded to fund her son, this time for a tour of galleries, art collections, and artists' studios in Germany. She thought that Beckett could use his experience in Germany for some kind of journalism that would yield a return. She may well have realized that separation was necessary for both their sakes and that the expense of the trip was money well spent. Beckett set off in late September 1936 and was away for six months.

The German tour was important in at least two areas. Beckett conceived a hearty dislike for national socialism that was to find practical expression in a few years' time, and his exposure to the various kinds of visual art he so intensively visited informed and consolidated dimensions of his own aesthetic thinking, later carrying over to his own practice. Briefly, he came to realize that the artist's sole responsibility is to the work; that the meaning of the work is encoded in its making; that authentic work arises only from its own inner necessities; and that the reception and interpretation of the work are of little or no concern to the artist. This kind of thinking was to bear spectacular fruit, but not yet.

Beckett arrived back in Dublin in time to celebrate his thirty-first birthday but with nothing to show for his protracted and expensive tour. His brother Frank married Jean Wright and moved out of Cooldrinagh. Beckett and his mother were left to make the best of it together, but it was not to last. There were flare-ups between them, each one worse than the last. He moved to Paris for good in October 1937.

1938–1945

While touring Germany, Beckett had begun working on a stage play based on the relationship of Dr. Samuel Johnson and Hester Thrale. Prior to leaving Dublin he had reread Johnson's work and taken copious notes on the secondary literature generated by it. He filled three notebooks with material but, in the end, abandoned the project, titled *Human Wishes*, having written—perhaps as late as 1940—a fragment of a scene of what he called in some letters the "Johnson blasphemy" and a "red herring." The significance of the piece is that it marks Beckett's first declaration of an interest in theatrical writing. He had been interested in many forms of theater, from plays to variety turns, since boyhood. Given his lack of success with either prose or poetry to that date, it is unsurprising that he should consider other possibilities.

Beckett's lack of success with his work in English also led him to consider changing his language of composition. Thus, in the late 1930s he began to write poetry—exactly how much is currently a matter of dispute among scholars—and art criticism in French. He did not abandon English yet; that was a decision he deferred until 1946.

In January 1938 Beckett was the victim of a late-night random assault on a Paris street. His assailant stabbed him in the left side with a knife. The blade barely missed Beckett's heart and lung, and he soon lost consciousness through loss of blood. At the hospital it was thought his life was in danger, but he pulled through. News of the incident spread quickly. One of the first to arrive at the hospital was James Joyce, who insisted that Beckett be moved to a private room and put under the care of Joyce's own personal physician. Joyce also paid all Beckett's hospital bills, and he was very helpful to Beckett's mother, Frank, and Jean, both when they came to Paris and later, reporting on his recovery when they had gone home and Beckett was out of danger. The proofs of *Murphy* arrived at the hospital, and Beckett corrected them as he was recovering.

Among Beckett's other visitors was a woman with whom he had played occasional games of tennis during his first extended stay in Paris in the late 1920s. She was Suzanne Deschevaux-Dumesnil, six years older than he. After his release they met frequently, and within a short time, she moved into his small flat on the rue des Favorites. They lived together for the rest of their lives, marrying in 1961. Beckett survived her death in 1989 by six months.

In the final prewar years, Beckett's circle of friends in Paris expanded. Many of his friends were painters. Among them the van Velde brothers, Geer and Bram, were the most influential for Beckett. Both painters were pushing toward abstraction, emptying their paintings of representation and rejecting the "tyranny" of the factual object. These strategies meshed with Beckett's evolving aesthetic and were to underpin much of his later work. Beckett was also collaborating with Alfred Péron on translating *Murphy* into French, another indication that he saw his future as a French writer. The translation was interrupted at the outbreak of war, but Beckett completed it in 1946, and it was published, dedicated to Péron—who did not survive the war—in 1947.

Beckett was visiting his mother when war was declared in September 1939. He immediately returned to Paris, later saying that he "preferred France in war to Ireland in peace." Theoretically, he was fairly safe; Ireland remained neutral in the war, and Beckett had retained his Irish citizenship and held a valid residence permit (*carte de séjour*) as a resident alien in France. Nevertheless, as the Germans advanced toward Paris in May 1940, Beckett and Suzanne, along with thousands of others, fled south. They stopped in Vichy, where Beckett met Joyce for the last time, and then moved to the west coast, just north of Bordeaux. As the situation in France stabilized, with the Vichy government in the Unoccupied Zone meshing seamlessly with the Nazi occupation in the rest of the territory, many of those who had fled from Paris returned home. Beckett and Suzanne returned in September, but Beckett did not long remain a "neutral" bystander. Alfred Péron soon recruited him into the Resistance.

Beckett later dismissed his participation as "boy scout stuff," but it was essential and dangerous work for which he was decorated. He acted as a collator of intelligence concerning troop and freight movements in the north of France. He typed up the information and brought the pages to a local restaurant, where a chef microfilmed them for transmission to London. The cell to which Beckett was attached required a substantial number of members, with the result that security was problematic. It was breached in 1942, and Beckett and Suzanne got away just ahead of a Gestapo raid. They were secreted in "safe" locations until they were smuggled into the Unoccupied Zone in the fall of 1942. They arrived in the village of Roussillon in the southern Vaucluse with very little baggage. Nevertheless, Beckett had the ongoing translation of *Murphy* and a set of notebooks containing the manuscript in progress of a new novel in English.

Beckett subsisted in the Vaucluse for two years, working on local farms and in vineyards in exchange for food and other essentials. The makeshift nature of daily life there provided him with models of existence that were to inform much of his subsequent writings, both prose and drama. One day monotonously followed another; the wait for something of significance to happen seemed endless and pointless. Such experience Beckett folded into the text of the novel he was writing, along with withering criticism of rationalist thinking and systems. *Watt*, written "to keep his hand in," as Beckett later said, explores a world characterized by radical uncertainty.

Beckett and Suzanne were able to return to Paris early in 1945 as the war front moved eastward. Shortly afterward Beckett traveled on to Dublin to visit his mother, whom he had not seen for nearly six years. Cooldrinagh had been sold, and she had moved to a more modest house close by. The typescript of *Watt* was finalized there and sent out to publishers, to no avail. Extracts appeared in Irish literary journals in the early 1950s, and it was finally published in book form by Olympia Press in Paris (1953). *Watt* was promptly banned in Ireland, more likely because of the notoriety of the imprint rather than the novel's content.

As he was preparing to return to Paris, Beckett discovered that currency restrictions did not permit taking the accrued sum of his annuity with him and that the provisional French government had imposed severe entry restrictions on aliens. Just as he had achieved a modest independence to pursue his writing career, he was debarred from his home, partner, and place of work. He extricated himself from this impasse by being appointed on a six-month contract as interpreter and storekeeper attached to the Irish Red Cross humanitarian mission to Saint-Lô in Normandy. The mission (funded by donations and a sweepstakes) was to build, equip, and run a hospital in the Normandy town that had become known as the "Capital of the Ruins," having been almost flattened in bombing raids prior to the D-Day landings. Beckett arrived there in August 1945 with the advance party to oversee the construction. The fact that he could speak German as well as French was a distinct advantage when it came to communicating with German prisoners of war who assisted with the project. He was happy when his contract came to an end: writing to MacGreevy, he said, "If I don't feel myself quite free again soon, freedom will never again be any good to me."

1946–1950

Beginning in February 1946 Beckett experienced what he later called the "siege in the room" and a "frenzy of writing." Between then and January 1950, he produced four novellas, four novels, and two full-length plays. The feature common to these works was the language of composition: French in all cases. The first of them, a novella titled *Suite* but retitled later as *The End* (*La Fin*), was begun in English, but Beckett drew a line across a manuscript page and continued in French, doubling back at the end to rewrite the earlier, English-language part in French. This and the other three novellas—*The Expelled* (*L'Expulsé*), *First Love* (*Premier amour*), and *The Calmative* (*Le Calmant*), all 1946—and the so-called trilogy of novels—*Molloy*, *Malone Dies* (*Malone meurt*), and *The Unnamable* (*L'Innommable*), all 1947 to 1950—all share the first-person, subjective narrative form. Taken as a whole, the sequence presents, among many other things, a set of excavations of the self under circumstances of increasing degradation and alienation, shot through with scathing satire, bracing hilarity, and acute awareness of suffering.

The novel *Mercier and Camier* (*Mercier et Camier*, 1946) lies outside the sequence; it employs an omniscient narrator, offers synopses of its chapters, and extensively "records" the dialogue of its main characters. In creative terms it is a small step from this to the writing of dramatic dialogue, a step that Beckett was soon to take with the plays *Eleutheria* (1947) and WAITING FOR GODOT (*En attendant Godot*, 1948–1949). Beckett chose to withhold the novel from publication until 1970 and did not permit publication of his first play during his lifetime.

1950S AND BEYOND

In the midst of this "frenzy," the firm Bordas published *Murphy*, but the sales were so small that they lost interest in Beckett's other work. His breakthrough came in 1950 when Jérôme Lindon of Les Éditions de Minuit read *Molloy* and immediately contracted to publish everything that Beckett might produce. Beckett was extricated from Bordas, and Minuit became his exclusive French publisher. *Molloy* and *Malone Dies* were issued in 1951 to considerable critical acclaim. *Waiting for Godot* was published the following year but had to wait until 1953 for a stage production. Within two months the play had been translated into German with Beckett's assistance, and by the fall a number of productions were running in Germany, ahead of Beckett's finalized translation of the play into English. Thus, after a quarter of a century of creativity, personal difficulties, and unrewarding obscurity, Beckett was an "overnight" success on the Continent. It took two more years for the penny to drop in the anglophone world.

During the latter half of the 1940s, Beckett continued to visit his mother for at least a month every summer. As she aged, the ravages of Parkinson's disease became ever more evident, and she died in 1950 with Beckett in helpless attendance. KRAPP'S LAST TAPE (1958), perhaps Beckett's most accessible play and the one he most often directed in English (the language of composition), French, and German, deploys that experience to unsentimental and moving effect. Four years later he was back in Dublin to be with his brother as Frank succumbed to cancer.

In 1952 Beckett built a plain cottage in Ussy, twenty-five miles east of Paris, with a portion of his legacy from his mother. He used this cottage right up the the early 1980s as a writer's retreat and refuge from the publicity generated by the worldwide success of *Godot* and his later plays. Beckett had mixed feelings about the success of *Godot*, claiming that he had written it as a relaxation from the "awful prose" of the trilogy. He found the stage to be a "habitable space," for which he was to write over twenty plays and to branch into dramatic writings for radio, television, and film.

The major stage plays that followed *Godot* show a restless interrogation of the possibilities of theater, progressively reducing the actors' mobility and their room for maneuver, simplifying the scenic design, sacrificing comprehensibility for speed of delivery, reducing visibility and audibility so as to compel the closer attention of the spectator, animating the lighting design as an agent in the play—this listing is merely indicative. Beckett never evolved a particular theatrical style; the mode of staging for each play is intrinsic in the conception of the piece. As Beckett said in his first published essay, on Joyce, in 1929: "Here form is content, content is form. . . . His writing is not *about* something; *it is that something itself*."

After much struggle Beckett completed ENDGAME (*Fin de partie*) in 1956. It opened in London but was played in French, and he reported to Alan Schneider that "it was like playing to mahogany, or rather teak." Incomprehension marked the initial responses to many of his plays, but this arose because audiences expected to be entertained rather than challenged. Beckett's theater is a modest one; it does not seek to communicate meanings or enlist the audience's sympathy; rather, it orchestrates an experience that connects directly with *being*. Take, for example, Winnie's situation in HAPPY DAYS (1961). In the first act she is buried up to her waist in a mound of scorched earth; in the second, up to her neck. Beckett specifies that Winnie be "About 50, well-preserved, blonde for preference, plump, arms and shoulders bare, low bodice, big bosom, pearl necklace." The second act deprives the audience of this fleshy spectacle and offers a dramatic image that is suggestive rather than explicit: to be living is to be gradually buried in the accumulation of hours and days.

Compression and brevity mark Beckett's dramatic output following *Happy Days*. The plays become increasingly pure distillations requiring consummate skills for their presentation. From the mid-1960s on, Beckett himself increasingly participated in productions of his plays, first as adviser and later as director. His involvement in theater affected his production of prose and poetry, leading to the development of abbreviated forms he called "residua" and "fizzles." The worldwide respect his work commanded was recognized in 1969 with the award of the Nobel Prize for Literature. In the late 1970s he reduced his directorial involvement and, in the space that opened up, produced four more prose texts, *Company* (*Compagnie*, 1979), *Ill Seen Ill Said* (*Mal vu mal dit*, 1981), *Worstward Ho* (1983), *Stirrings Still* (*Soubresauts*, 1988), and a poem, *What Is the Word* (*Comment dire*, 1988). Beckett died on December 22, 1989, and is buried with his wife in the Cimetière Montparnasse in Paris.

[*See also* Absurdism; Apocalypse in Modern Drama; Beckett, Samuel: Short Plays and Dramaticules; Ireland; Philosophy and Drama]

SELECT PLAYS: *Waiting for Godot* (*En attendant Godot*, 1952, French; 1954, English); *All That Fall* (1957); *Endgame* (*Fin de partie*, 1957, French; 1958, English); *Krapp's Last Tape* (1958); *Happy Days* (1961); *Play* (1964); *Come and Go* (1967); *Not I* (1973); *Footfalls* (1976); *That Time* (1976); *A Piece of Monologue* (1979); *Ohio Impromptu* (1982); *Rockaby* (1982); *Catastrophe* (1984); *Quad* (1984); *What Where* (1984)

FURTHER READING

Bair, Deirdre. *Samuel Beckett*. New York: Harcourt, 1978.

Cohn, Ruby. *A Beckett Canon*. Ann Arbor: Univ. of Michigan Press, 2001.

Cronin, Anthony. *Samuel Beckett: The Last Modernist*. London: HarperCollins, 1996.

Dukes, Gerry. *Illustrated Lives: Samuel Beckett*. London: Penguin, 2001.

Gontarski, S. E. *The Intent of Undoing in Samuel Beckett's Dramatic Texts*. Bloomington: Indiana Univ. Press, 1986.

Harmon, Maurice, ed. *No Author Better Served: The Correspondence of Samuel Beckett and Alan Schneider*. Cambridge, Mass.: Harvard Univ. Press, 1998.

Knowlson, James. *Damned to Fame: The Life of Samuel Beckett*. London: Bloomsbury, 1996.

O'Brien, Eoin. *The Beckett Country*. Dublin: Black Cat Press, 1986.

Pilling, John. *Beckett Before* Godot. Cambridge: Cambridge Univ. Press, 1997.

Gerry Dukes

BECKETT, SAMUEL: SHORT PLAYS AND DRAMATICULES

My work is a matter of fundamental sounds (no joke intended), made as fully as possible, and I accept responsibility for nothing else. If people want to have headaches among the overtones, let them. And provide their own aspirin.

—Samuel Beckett, letter to Alan Schneider

Short plays and "dramaticules" (dramaticule—meaning a minuscule or insignificant drama) occupy a central place in the canon of SAMUEL BECKETT's work. He found these forms, onstage and in radio and television, congenial and hospitable to his abiding thematic concerns. The first such play, *Act Without Words 1* (1955), is a mime that effortlessly distills the themes of WAITING FOR GODOT and ENDGAME, the play he was struggling to complete at the time, into a brief, wordless recapitulation. A man is "flung" onto the stage and soon learns there is no exit. Various items are flown in from the flies above, only to hang tantalizingly out of reach, despite the man's best efforts, or to be withdrawn and so frustrate his intentions. The mime is of a piece with what Beckett described (in his monograph on Proust, in 1931) as "the poisonous ingenuity of Time in the science of affliction."

Mime engaged Beckett's creative attention all through his dramatic career. *Act Without Words 2* (1959), for two players and a "goad" on wheels, offers a brief meditation on optimism, pessimism, and necessity. *Breath*, a forty-second piece for light, sound, and "miscellaneous rubbish," enacts the brevity of human life; in *Quad* (1981), for four players or dancers, light and percussion bring rigorous geometry and choreography to bear on the perilous zones of living. When Beckett directed the piece for color television in Stuttgart, he added a second, monochrone version with no percussion as a second act.

Following the success of *All That Fall* for BBC radio, Beckett wrote four more radio pieces that, in various ways, exploit the spectral quality radio makes possible, where the distinction between "real" and imagined voices is not marked, where cutting from outer to inner worlds can be seamless. He carried these effects over to his first television play, *Eh Joe* (1965), for a male actor and a female voice-over. After a lengthy opening mime, Joe sits on the side of his bed, facing a single camera. At this point the female voice (presumably in Joe's head) begins to talk to and harangue him about his past treatment of others, especially women. In the nine pauses in the voice-over the camera closes in on Joe's face so that it fills the entire screen at the end. Image and voice fade out in one of those moments of ambiguity that are characteristically Beckettian.

Beckett's only deviation into film occurred in 1963, in response to a request from Barney Rosset, his American publisher. He wrote the scenario for *Film* and the following year went to New York for the filming. The final cut was arrived at in 1965, and Beckett professed himself pleased with the work, which featured Buster Keaton in the central role.

Writing for radio, television, and film did not deflect Beckett from his commitment to theater, and each successive stage play is marked by audacity in conception and tireless creativity. *Play* (published in 1964, revised edition 1968) typifies these features. The plot is clichéd and conventional and features a man, wife, and mistress—M, W1, and W2 in the text. What makes Beckett's play extraordinary is his method of staging. The players' heads protrude from urns; each player speaks only in response to an inquisitorial spotlight that swivels at speed from face to face, gleaning what it can and impatiently moving on. The resulting action is, for the audience, confusing and disorienting and carefully calculated by Beckett. When the action is completed, it is then repeated (either exactly or with very slight variation in intensity of light and speed of delivery), but this time the effect is harrowing—the clichéd plot contains real suffering.

An inquisitorial light is also used as the agent of provocation in *Not I*, begun in 1963 but put aside and completed in 1972. This time Beckett reduced the female player to an illuminated Mouth, upstage right and eight feet above stage floor level. The life story Mouth tells is so insupportable that she vehemently refuses to acknowledge it as hers, and the play fades to an end after her fifth refusal. Similar "fade-outs" mark the conclusions of *Footfalls* (1975) and *Rockaby* (1981), plays that offer brief but compelling images of distress. Distress and doomed bravery are central to the dramaticule *Come and Go*, written for three female players in 1965. All Beckett's late plays offer arresting theatrical images of pain and distress and of human persistence. The opening line of *A Piece of Monologue* (1979) is a succinct statement of Beckett's vision: "Birth was the death of him."

FURTHER READING

Acheson, James, and Kateryna Arthur, eds. *Beckett's Later Fiction and Drama*. London: Macmillan, 1987.

Gontarski, S. E., ed. *The Theatrical Notebooks of Samuel Beckett*. Vol. 4, *Shorter Plays*. New York: Grove, 1999.

McMullan, Anna. *Theatre on Trial: Samuel Beckett's Later Drama*. London: Routledge, 1993.

Gerry Dukes

BECQUE, HENRY (1837–1899)

Although his first plays were "splendid failures" at replicating the successes and styles of DUMAS FILS and Émile Augier, Henry Becque was finally attacked and praised for disregarding the currents of his day. Though heralded as a pioneer of NATURALISM, Becque sought to create a "bleeding reality" rather than depict a "slice of life." He attempted a new REALISM without doctrine or philosophy, exhibiting life without analyzing or debating it. Indeed, his most popular play, *The Vultures* (1882), a cynical study in which an unprincipled notary ruins the family of his dead business partner, became the whipping horse of ÉMILE ZOLA and his naturalist followers.

With a comic sense, Becque created strong, reflective characters and savored their full development over consistent and vigorous dramatic action. Characters remained his focus throughout his career, but he showed them no sympathy or mercy. In fact, his treatment of them is so macabre, cynical, and indignant that Becque was accused of being dispassionate about them. He observed them pursuing their passions and placed them in situations to highlight those passions. In this sense, Becque followed Molière, whose creations, such as Tartuffe, follow journeys to logical absurdity: Becque's plays end only when he has extracted from his characters all their passions will lead them to do. Although reminiscent of dramatic naturalism, Becque's work was more concerned with how characters' reactions were determined by immediate situations, not predetermined by heredity, historical moment, and milieu.

Becque's plays are leaps in action, composed of juxtaposed tableaux and scenes with few characters. Contemporary detractors called his structures incoherent, but they are merely dispersed for the sake of character study. There is nothing broad, planned, or contrived: for Becque, observation sufficed. Anything else, including the frivolous subject matter often chosen by his contemporaries, was deceitful. Understanding a play was to be heard, not read, he replaced the classical tirade with conversational speeches; his focus was mood and rhythm, not event. He presented both COMEDY and drama with detached irony: the former is neither hilarious nor sentimental; the latter is neither pathetic nor tragic. This balance made Becque a forerunner of TRAGICOMEDY; both ANTON CHEKHOV and AUGUST STRINDBERG would express their debt to him.

Becque's skeptical, sober realism was a contrast to the artificiality of popular art. He could be said to have offered social criticism: simplicity acting as a check to the opulence of the Second Empire and Third Republic, but the dramatist himself would never have espoused such dogma. The starkness descended even to the level of his characters' language: caustic, direct, devoid of any well-made wit. Critics bemoaned Becque's lack of imagination, thinking he squandered his potential in trivialities, sarcasm, and empty philosophies. However, as early as the 1890s, ANDRÉ ANTOINE was developing an acting style to suit the dramatist's acerbic realism. Although later writers eclipsed Becque, he was openly credited with giving birth to the "vicious" (*rosse*) style, a form of comedy that depicts a "golden age in reverse," a casual delight in decadence. This tonal influence would spread across Europe in the 20th century.

[*See also* France]

SELECT PLAYS: *Sardanapalus* (*Sardanaple*, 1867); *The Prodigal Son* (*L'enfant prodigue*, 1868); *Michel Pauper* (*Michel Pauper*, 1870); *The Abduction* (*L'enlèvement*, 1871); *The Merry-Go-Round* (*La navette*, 1878); *The Virtuous Women* (*Les honnêtes femmes*, 1880); *The Vultures* (*Les corbeaux*, 1882); *The Woman from Paris* (*La Parisienne*, 1885). Also, *An Execution* (*Une exécution*), *The Quiet Game* (*Le domino à quart*), *Widowed* (*Veuve*), *The Departure* (*Le départ*), and *The Puppets* (*Les polichinelles*) were all written in the late 1890s but were performed and published posthumously.

FURTHER READING

Chandler, Frank Wadleigh. *The Contemporary Drama of France*. Boston: Little, Brown, 1920.

Descotes, Maurice. *Henry Becque et son théâtre* [Henry Becque and his theater]. Paris: Minard, 1962.

Filon, Augustin. *The Modern French Drama*. Tr. by Janet E. Hogarth. London: Chapman, 1898. Originally published as *De Dumas à Rostand: Esquisse du mouvement dramatique contemporain* [Of Dumas with Rostand: Outline of contemporary dramatic movement]. Paris: A. Fayard & cie, 1898.

Hyslop, Lois Boe. *Henry Becque*. New York: Twayne, 1972.

Parigot, Hipploythe. *Le théâtre d'hier* [The theater of yesterday]. Paris: Lecène, Oudin, 1893.

Matt Di Cintio

BED

Bed, the second of JIM CARTWRIGHT's plays to be produced, was first performed at the Royal National Theatre in London in 1989. Cartwright's first play, ROAD, had initially been praised as a "state of the nation" play, catching a dissenting zeitgeist in the same way that JOHN OSBORNE's LOOK BACK IN ANGER had thirty years previously. *Bed*, though in several places returning to the matter of England ("Oh Britannia, / Doing anything to get fat. / Morally sparse"), draws more heavily on absurdist DRAMATURGY, particularly that of SAMUEL BECKETT, and on SURREALISM more generally.

Most of the play's action takes place in a giant bed, which at the play's opening contains seven elderly people: Captain, Charles, The Couple, Bosom Lady, Marjorie, and Spinster. The play opens with the seven falling asleep. The transition between scenes is often accomplished by the characters falling back to sleep, then one or more waking. The first major scene has Charles taking the others out for a mimed drive, at the end of which they reach a disco. Their fun is disrupted by the hitherto unseen Sermon Head, static in the shadows outside the bed, who complains that he cannot sleep. The Couple leave the bed for a glass of water for Marjorie, climbing a pile of armchairs that then swing out over the bed itself. The bed becomes a boat, and the others sleep as the Captain soliloquizes. After this the Couple get a short scene, and Sermon Head addresses the audience on the different kinds of sleep ("One's is brittle. One's is see-through. One's is alchemical. One's is passed around"). The Spinster awakes and has a solo speech about herself and England. The Couple continue their search for a glass of water, waking the Spinster, who discovers a patch of earth in the bed and digs things out that she passes to the others, who cry into a handkerchief, which is then wrung out into the Couple's glass. Bosom Lady wakes, covers the bed with bras, and has a short routine with Sermon Head, now in the bed. The final soliloquy is Marjorie's, reminiscing about her marriage, and the play ends with the characters (apart from Sermon Head) huddling under an umbrella to shelter from a heavy fall of feathers.

Bed's linguistic style and episodic narrative structure bear comparison with DYLAN THOMAS's *Under Milk Wood*. In the conceit of a bed set in a dream world, Cartwright finds a structure enabling his genius for poetic language to flourish. The focus here, as in much of Cartwright's work, is on memory, loss, and what can be rescued from both. As Bosom Lady explains, "I do know when I exit through sleep, I make my entrance onto a little 'stage.'" Though some elements of the play, particularly Marjorie's closing soliloquy, work with a demotic REALISM, these are always framed within the surreal visuals and abrupt narrative shifts of Cartwright's sleep world.

[*See also* England, 1940–Present]

FURTHER READING

Billington, Michael. *Jim Cartwright*. British Contemporary Dramatists. London: St. James Press, 1994.

Dromgoole, Dominic. *The Full Room*. London: Methuen, 2000.

Peacock, D. Keith. *Thatcher's Theatre: British Theatre and Drama in the Eighties*. Westport, Conn.: Greenwood Press, 1999.

Stephen Longstaffe

THE BEDBUG

Although VLADIMIR MAYAKOVSKY set out in 1928 to write a satire of bourgeois elements left over in Soviet society, the play that resulted, *The Bedbug* (*Klop*), took a course quite different from the one the poet had originally intended.

A "spectacle comedy" (*feericheskaia komediia*) in nine tableaux, *The Bedbug* contrasts Soviet society in 1928 (in the first four tableaux) with the perfect communist society fifty years hence. As the play opens, the protagonist, Prisypkin, has dumped his proletarian girlfriend, Zoya Berezkina, for the petit bourgeois hairdresser, Elzevira Renaissance. In broad, satiric strokes, Mayakovsky paints Prisypkin as a materialistic snob who has betrayed true revolutionary principles for creature comforts. Prisypkin has gone so far as to change his name to Pierre Skripkin (Violin), which becomes an emblem of his affectation. Prisypkin and Elzevira busy themselves with preparations for a bourgeois wedding, all the time mouthing Soviet platitudes. Meanwhile, Zoya is so heartbroken that she attempts suicide. Despite the Soviet veneer, the wedding turns out to be a bourgeois affair, as the guests behave ostentatiously and get drunk. The situation gets out of hand, and a fire breaks out. Everyone perishes, except Prisypkin, whose frozen body is discovered in 1979. Mayakovsky's society of the future is reminiscent of Yevgeny Zamyatin's dystopia in *We* in its rational and collective structure. After much debate, Prisypkin is revived through the good services of the Institute of Human Resurrections, although doubt remains about the wisdom of such an act. Prisypkin bears within him the contagion of love, which has been eliminated in the society of the future. Nor does his weakness for alcohol help matters. In order to contain the contagion and the bedbugs that infest his body and clothing, officials decide to keep Prisypkin in a zoo, where he will be exhibited. The pathos of Prisypkin's predicament is affecting: his innate sympathy for the society he helped to create is undermined by his profound alienation from it. Nowhere does Mayakovsky give better expression to this alienation than at the end of the play, when Prisypkin addresses the audience directly and asks why he is in the cage alone. The device brings to mind Nikolai Gogol, whose drama clearly influenced Mayakovsky.

The Bedbug is generally considered Mayakovsky's best play, and it certainly was his most successful. VSEVOLOD MEYERHOLD directed the first production at the theater that bore his name and brought together some of the best talent the Soviet Union had to offer: Mayakovsky helped coach the actors in the delivery of his verse, Dmitry Shostakovich composed the score, and Aleksandr Rodchenko contributed to the set design. Igor Ilyinsky won great praise for his Prisypkin. The production proved immensely popular despite official criticism and dozens of other productions followed.

The Bedbug has been staged throughout the world with particularly notable productions in New York (1931) and Paris (1959). It remains one of the finest examples of Soviet satire.

[*See also* Avant-Garde Drama; Russia and the Soviet Union]

FURTHER READING

Brown, Edward J. *Mayakovsky: A Poet in Revolution*. Princeton, N.J.: Princeton Univ. Press, 1973.

Markov, Vladimir. *Russian Futurism: A History*. Berkeley: Univ. of California Press, 1968.

Mayakovsky, Vladimir. *The Bedbug*. In *Selected Works in Three Volumes*. Vol. 3, *Plays, Articles, Essays*, ed. by Alexander Ushakov. Moscow: Raduga Pubs., 1987.

——. *Plays*. Tr. by Guy Daniels. Evanston, Ill.: Northwestern Univ. Press, 1995.

Terras, Victor. *Vladimir Mayakovsky*. Boston: Twayne, 1983.

Timothy C. Westphalen

BEFORE DAYBREAK

> *You Miss and you Hoffmann don't seem to know what horrible role alcohol plays in our modern life.*
>
> —Loth, Act 1

Few theater events in GERMANY have attracted more attention than the premiere of GERHART HAUPTMANN's first play, *Before Daybreak* (*Vor Sonnenaufgang*), a "social drama" in five acts. The play was staged in Berlin, and before its opening night in October 1889, two camps had already been formed. One group considered the play a masterpiece, seeing in Hauptmann a German equal to HENRIK IBSEN, ÉMILE ZOLA, and LYOV TOLSTOY, while the opposing camp saw nothing in the drama but a decadent attack on established rules and morals. The controversial work made Hauptmann famous overnight. *Before Daybreak* presents a whole range of themes deemed inappropriate for the stage at the time, for example, alcoholism, incest, eugenics, and female emancipation. In addition, the language was considered "low," with its use of dialect and vulgarities.

The main characters are Alfred Loth and Helene Krause. Loth is a socialist who has traveled to a coal-mining district to write about the plight of the miners. He stays there with an old friend, Hoffmann, who has married into a nouveau riche farming family—their wealth resulting from coal deposits on their property. The money has corrupted the family, which is now utterly dysfunctional. Hoffmann's wife and father-in-law are alcoholics, and the father-in-law's new wife has an incestuous relationship with her nephew. The only family member who appears to have escaped the decadence is Helene, Hoffmann's sister-in-law. Having been educated at a boarding school, Helene dreams of a life away from her destructive family. She falls in love with Loth, who, in turn, promises her eternal devotion. However, Loth is a firm believer in eugenics, and when he discovers that Helene's family is plagued by alcoholism, he abandons her and she commits suicide.

Most critics regard *Before Daybreak* as a profoundly naturalist drama in which social and biological determinism defines the course of the action. The drama's major themes, the use of dialect, and the attempt to present a highly detailed "slice of life" without a true resolution support such an interpretation. At the same time, however, *Before Daybreak* contains striking antinaturalist elements such as epic narration, lyric interludes, and symbols. Perhaps the most compelling argument against a strict naturalist interpretation lies in the fact that Loth, the character who most clearly expresses a naturalist viewpoint, is presented as a very unsympathetic and heartless figure. Not only does he break his promise and thus is ultimately responsible for Helene's death, but his tirades against the hereditary nature of alcoholism are contradicted by Helene's example as well as by his old friend Schimmelpfennig, a doctor in the area. The characterization of Helene also speaks against a naturalist interpretation. She has proven that the presumed laws of heredity and environment are flawed; however, she ultimately becomes a victim of the belief in naturalist dogma.

Before Daybreak has continued to appear on stages in many countries and is considered a classic in Germany.

[*See also* Naturalism]

FURTHER READING

Gaddy, Kerstin T. "Elements of 'Novelization' in Gerhart Hauptmann's *Vor Sonnenaufgang*: Bakhtin as a Perspective on the Modernity of German Naturalist Drama." *Excavatio: Emile Zola & Naturalism* 13 (2000): 112–121.

Mellen, Philip. "Gerhart Hauptmann's *Vor Sonnenaufgang* and the Parable of the Sower." *Monatshefte* 74, no. 2 (1982): 139–144.

Osborn, John. "Gerhart Hauptmann's *Vor Sonnenaufgang*: Zwischen Tradition und Moderne" [Between tradition and modernity]. *Der Deutschunterricht* 40, no. 2 (1988): 77–88.

Kerstin T. Gaddy

BEFORE THE NEW BUREAU DIRECTOR CAME

A COMEDY of satire by He Qiu (b. 1921), *Before the New Bureau Director Came (Xin juzhang lai dao zhi qian, huaju)*, a one-act play, was premiered in 1955 by CHINA Youth Art Theater, and the playscript was published in the monthly *Juben* (Play Scripts) of the same year. Warmly accepted by readers and audience alike, the play was once performed especially for Chinese leaders such as Mao Zedong and Zhou Enlai. In 1956 the play won first prize for one-act plays from the *Juben* monthly for the year 1954–1955. Because of its popularity, it was subsequently made into a movie, translated into English and Russian, and even adapted into several local dramas for performance.

The play starts with the news of the arrival of the new bureau chief, Zhang Yuntong. In order to curry favor with Zhang, Liu Shanqi, director of the general affairs department of the bureau, tries every means within his power, even embezzling government funding, to remodel Zhang's office and to purchase new office furniture for it. At the same time, he turns a blind eye to the loss of the government property and to the hardship borne by ordinary people. As a satirical play against certain government officials and their behavior in the society, it has achieved its goal by designing a specific situation—the arrival of the new bureau chief—and by employing a series of cases of plausible misunderstanding among the characters, together with their hyperbolic, witty, and yet lively language. The successful portrayal of the protagonist Liu Qishan as a low-level government functionary given to boasting and flattering adds to the power of the play. In contrast, the play also eulogizes the moral attitude of those who fight resolutely with Liu.

A native of Guangdong province, He Qiu developed his interest in theater early in his life. He started writing when he was a teacher in a normal school. His one-act play *Before the New Bureau Director Came* won him a reputation as one of the promising young playwrights of the time. As one of the early satirical plays after the founding of the People's Republic of China in 1949 and for its role of muckraking, however, the play was severely criticized along with its author during the Anti-Rightist movement launched by Mao Zedong in 1957 for its critical attitude by innuendo toward some Chinese officials. As a result, He Qiu was labeled a rightist during the political campaign. He continued his playwriting after that, but his second play, *Luck Upon the Grand Opening*, in five acts, did not appear as successful as his first one. He was active in the writers' circle in

Guangdong for some years and has been silent since the early 1960s.

FURTHER READING

Ho Ch'iu (He Qiu). *Before the New Bureau Director Came*. Tr. by Doris Sze Chun and Howard Goldblatt. In *Literature of the People's Republic of China*, ed. by Kai-yu Hsu and Ting Wang. Bloomington: Indiana Univ. Press, 1980.

Xiang Hong. "Tan *Xin juzhang lai dao zhi qian*" [On *Before the New Bureau Director Came*]. *Juben* (Play Scripts) 11 (1955).

Cai Xingshui and Hongchu Fu

BEG *See* FLIGHT

BEGGAR ON HORSEBACK

MARC CONNELLY and GEORGE S. KAUFMAN reached the zenith of their stage collaborations in the COMEDY *Beggar on Horseback*, which was first produced in New York City on February 12, 1924. The journalists-turned-playwrights adapted on their own terms the German expressionistic play *Hans Sonnenstossers Hollenfahrt* by Paul Apel. A year earlier, ELMER RICE's THE ADDING MACHINE had played along similar lines of an urban individual's (Mr. Zero) overt reaction to the pressures of materialism. But Rice's play had not displayed the prospective rainbow on the horizon, as *Beggar on Horseback* does.

In *Beggar on Horseback*, Kaufman and Connelly view from a typically American social perspective the predicament of a poor but talented composer, Neil McRae, and the nightmare of his marriage of convenience to a rich man's daughter, Gladys Cady. It is actually Cynthia Mason, the pleasant girl next door, that he loves. Ironically, it is not only his old friend Dr. Albert Rice from Chicago but Cynthia as well who prompt Neil to clinch the union with a most eager Gladys. Unhappy and confused about the grim yet pragmatic advice that his closest friends have proffered, Neil gets engaged to the girl over the phone.

In a dream sequence that swells with Rabelaisian effusion, Neil undergoes the exorcism of, first, his temptation to easy riches and, then, his impulse to kill off the entire Cady family with a giant paper-cutting knife after he has realized the absurdity of wealth as an end in itself. A "trial" in court and sentence of "Guilty" follow.

The play's action in the expressionistic sequence is significantly blurred and individuated, with dialogues becoming monologues—as two, four, or more people speak simultaneously; and body movements proceed on a similar pattern of jostling motion. Invisible "friends" are introduced and addressed; look-alike butlers multiply in numbers from two to twelve. Money, too, multiplies—into hyperbolic millions at every turn of phrase, with Neil's frail pleas of wanting to write his great music punctuating the blare.

As REALISM replaces EXPRESSIONISM at the very end, awareness dawns on Neil and Gladys that theirs is a sorry misalliance. Liberated from the unholy tryst, which he had subconsciously invoked and had seriously needed to resolve, albeit in the terms of COMEDY, Neil re-aligns with Cynthia in a romance about the devoted women of wayward sons, reminiscent of HENRIK IBSEN's PEER GYNT.

Kenneth McGowan (1924) was critical of the play's dearth of any "living and dynamic pattern" despite its "good satire." Others like Barrett Clark ("the first genuinely imaginative satire of its kind") and JOHN GALSWORTHY ("a fine satire on the America of the times") were more generous in their praises (qtd. in Pollack, 1988). In 1964, John Mersand included *Beggar on Horseback* in his anthology *Three Plays About Business in America*, believing that it was "breaking new ground in the American theatre."

[*See also* United States, 1860–1929]

FURTHER READING

Lewisohn, Lewis. "Beggar on Horseback." *Nation* 118 (February 27, 1924): 238–239.

McGowan, Kenneth. "From the Four Corners of American Art." *Theatre Arts* 8 (April 1924): 215–228.

Nolan, Paul T. *Marc Connelly*. New York: Twayne, 1969.

Pollack, Rhoda-Gale. "Enter Marc Connelly." Chap. 2 in *George S. Kaufman*. Boston: Twayne Publishers, 1988.

Young, Stark. "Beggar on Horseback." *New Republic* 38 (March 5, 1924): 45–46.

Rupendra Guha-Majumdar

BEHAN, BRENDAN (1926–1964)

Soldier: "Brendan Behan, he's too anti-British."

Officer: "Anti-Irish, you mean. Bejasus, wait till we get him back home. We'll give him what for for making fun of the Movement."

Soldier: [To the audience] "He doesn't mind coming over here and taking your money."

Pat: "He'd sell his country for a pint."

—Act 2, *The Hostage*

Brendan Behan wrote plays, short stories, poems, and memoirs. But his fame is largely due to his public drunkenness and reckless lifestyle, which culminated in his death from illnesses related to alcoholism in 1964.

Behan was born in Dublin, IRELAND, in 1926, shortly after the conclusion of the Irish War of Independence and Civil War. His family members were sympathizers with the losing side of the Civil War, the Republicans—a group seeking the unification of Northern Ireland and the Irish Free State that ultimately developed into the illegal Irish Republican Army (IRA). From an early age, Behan involved himself in Republican activities, writing patriotic verse, and joining the Fianna, the youth organization of the IRA, in 1937.

In 1939, Behan traveled to Britain, apparently without the approval of the IRA, and was arrested for possession of bomb-making equipment. He spent the following two years in jail, being deported to Ireland in 1941. He soon found himself back in prison, after he shot at an Irish policeman, spending the period 1942–1946 at the Curragh, where he learned Irish, read voraciously, and began to write plays. After his release in 1946, he wrote poetry and traveled widely, though he spent two further short spells in jail in 1948 and 1950.

In the early 1950s, Behan's literary reputation began to grow. His radio plays *Moving Out* and *A Garden Party* were produced by Radio Éireann in 1952, and his journalism became popular. His first theatrical success, THE QUARE FELLOW, premiered at the Pike Theatre, Dublin, in November 1954. Set in an Irish prison the night before an inmate's execution, the play was well received by Dublin audiences, but it did not achieve international recognition until it was produced by Joan Littlewood at Stratford East in May 1956. In the period between these two productions, Behan married Beatrice Salkeld, a young Irishwoman—though it should be noted that recent scholarship has indicated that Behan was probably gay and certainly bisexual.

In 1958, Behan produced his famous memoir *Borstal Boy*. He was also commissioned to write a play in Irish and produced *The Prisoner (An Giall)* in Dublin in June 1958. An English adaptation of that play, retitled *The Hostage*, was presented by Joan Littlewood at Stratford East in November of the same year. The original version of the play is a conventional tragedy, presenting the killing of an English soldier held hostage in a Dublin brothel by the IRA. The English version differed in many ways: It drew heavily from the British tradition of music hall comedy and featured contemporary references, songs, and even new characters. These changes are widely regarded as having been more the work of Littlewood than Behan.

During the remaining six years of his life, Behan struggled to produce work of producible or publishable quality. His radio play *The Big House* (broadcast by the BBC in 1957) was adapted for the stage and produced at the Pike in 1958, but Behan produced no further original drama—instead earning notoriety for his drunkenness, both in Britain and New York. He returned to Ireland in 1963, where his wife gave birth to a daughter. He died the following year from cirrhosis of the liver. His funeral was attended by thousands and included an honorary ceremony by the IRA.

Many of Behan's works were produced or adapted in the years following his death. The unfinished *Richard Cork's Leg* appeared at the Abbey Theatre in 1972—but audiences appear more interested in Behan's life than his work, as shown by the enduring popularity of the stage adaptation of the autobiographical *Borstal Boy*, first presented in 1967.

Behan's reputation has declined since his death. Controversy over the extent of Littlewood's contribution to *The Hostage* continues, and there has been much debate about the importance of Behan's sexuality. And as concern in Ireland has grown about the damaging social effects of alcohol abuse, Behan has fallen from favor somewhat. His artistic reputation has similarly declined, though there is evidence that a reappraisal of his work is underway, with some arguing that his writing is one of the earliest examples of revisionism, an Irish intellectual movement that set out to critique the historical roots of Irish nationalism and Republicanism. This shift from Behan's life to his work may do much to preserve—and perhaps enhance—his reputation.

PLAYS: *The Quare Fellow: A Comedy-Drama* (1954); *The Hostage* (1958); *The Prisoner (An Giall*, 1958); *Richard Cork's Leg* (1972)

FURTHER READING

Brannigan, John. *Brendan Behan: Cultural Nationalism and the Revisionist Writer*. Dublin: Four Courts Press, 2002.

Kearney, Colbert. *The Writings of Brendan Behan*. Dublin: Gill and Macmillan, 1977.

Mikhail, E. H., ed. *The Art of Brendan Behan*. London: Vision, 1979.

O'Sullivan, Michael. *Brendan Behan: A Life*. Dublin: Blackwater, 1997.

Simpson, Alan. *Beckett and Behan and a Theatre in Dublin*. London: Routledge, 1962.

Patrick Lonergan

BEHRMAN, S. N. (1893–1973)

Samuel Nathaniel (S. N.) Behrman's life is recounted in *People in a Diary: A Memoir*, published in 1972, the year before his death. Born on June 9, 1893, in Worcester, Massachusetts, Behrman grew up in a poor Jewish neighborhood, but while not a rich man, his father "was learned in the sacred books and did have standing." Fears of being poor haunted his dreams (of being in hotel rooms without money to pay the bills). He went to Clark University for two years, then went to Harvard to study playwriting with GEORGE PIERCE BAKER and then to Columbia for an M.A. There he took a memorable seminar on the well-made plays of Eugène Scribe and VICTORIEN SARDOU, taught by drama scholar Brander Matthews. Behrman died on September 9, 1973, in New York City.

After graduation he wrote plays with J. Kenyon Nicholson, then worked for two years at the *New York Times* and then as a publicity agent, finally for Jed Harris, until his first play was successfully produced by the THEATRE GUILD in 1927, *The Second Man*, starring Alfred Lunt and Lynn Fontanne. He subsequently wrote other plays, as well as adaptations, for the Lunts. In addition, Ina Claire starred in several of his plays, as did Laurence Olivier. On the heels of his first success, he also became a writer for Harold Ross's *New Yorker*, doing a profile of George Gershwin as his first piece. Kenneth T. Reed (1975) thinks Behrman a late bloomer, who only became a good playwright in the 1930s and an accomplished prose writer in the 1940s; he picks his best work as *The Cold Wind and the Warm* (1958). His work for *The New Yorker* led to the publication of four nonfiction books as well as the collection *The Suspended Drawing-Room*, and though he went on to write plays after World War II, his most significant work was done before the war.

As a playwright, he developed two techniques that reinforced each other in his best plays. First, he found a plot—*The Second Man* sets the pattern—a love triangle with an older woman, a younger woman, and an artistic man caught in the middle. In BIOGRAPHY (1932) he reverses the genders, and Marion is the older woman with a younger man, Richard Kurt, whom she abandons at the end of the play. Orrin Kinnicott is her older suitor. In *Rain from Heaven* (1934), Lady Lael Wyngate is poised between the naive explorer, Rand Eldridge, and the worldly wise refugee from a German concentration camp, Hugo Willens. The genders reverse again in *No Time for Comedy* (1939), where Gay Easterbrook is the center caught between his wife, realist actress Linda Paige, and naive idealist Amanda Smith. In all of these plays, the artist finds a balanced position between the extremes. The men return to the older, wiser women they came in with and forsake the younger, wilder idealists who think they can be much more than they are. When Behrman places a woman at the center, however, she concludes the play alone. Hugo leaves Lael Wyngate and returns to Germany to fight the Nazis, but Marion drops all the men to avoid losing her independence and her "tolerance." It is this kind of balance, a desire to maintain "tolerance" or something like it, that gave Behrman the reputation of sophisticated detachment. He positioned himself, as Robert Gross (1992) notes, as "a late inheritor of Enlightenment values. He believed in liberalism, individualism, democracy, and clarity." One difficulty with Behrman, however, is that his elegant prose is so beautifully balanced and clever that it must be read aloud to be appreciated fully—and he rarely gets a hearing today.

In his essay on his art "What Makes Comedy High," in Horst Frenz's *American Playwrights on Drama* (1965), he argues that "it is well for a high comedy if it has a tragic core." This makes the stakes in finding balance much more significant in his plays: How does one find balance in the face of German concentration camps in 1935, or the Spanish Civil War in 1939? Or socialist ideals during the Depression as in *Biography* and *The End of Summer* (1936)? But Behrman the enlightenment rationalist argues that the general horror can only be grasped in a specific instance; the story of one concentration camp survivor is more gripping than that of millions starving in Russia. And most important, in his view: "The ability to laugh at its own pretensions and shortcomings is the true mark of the civilized nation, as it is of the civilized man." This is the solution he provides his playwright hero in *No Time for Comedy*, when his wife argues that those struggling for survival are not able to exercise the freedoms of civilization and that his duty as an American (this is before entry into the war) is to keep up the writing of comedies: "Isn't there this for you to insist on? That the more inhuman the rest of the world, the more human we. The grosser and more cruel the others, the more scrupulous, and fastidious, the more precisely just and delicate we."

SELECT PLAYS: *Bedside Manners* (1923); *The Second Man* (1927); *Meteor* (1929); *Serena Blandish* (1929; adapted from the novel by Enid Bagnold); *Brief Moment* (1931); *Biography* (1932); *Rain from Heaven* (1934); *End of Summer* (1936); *Amphytrion 38* (1937; adapted from the play by Jean Giraudoux); *Wine of Choice* (1938); *No Time for Comedy* (1939); *The Talley Method* (1941); *The Pirate* (1942; from a play by Ludwig Fulda); *Jacobowsky and the Colonel* (1944; adapted from a play by Franz Werfel); *I Know My Love* (1949; adapted from *Auprès de Ma Blonde* by Marcel Achard); *Jane* (1952; from a story by Somerset Maugham); *Let Me Hear the Melody* (1952); *Fanny* (1955); *The Cold Wind and the Warm* (1958); *Lord Pengo* (1962); *Whom Charlie* (1964)

FURTHER READING

Behrman, S. N. *The Worcester Account*. New York: Random House, 1954.

——. "What Makes Comedy High." In *American Playwrights on Drama*, ed. by Horst Frenz. New York: Hill & Wang, 1965.

Gross, Robert F. *S. N. Behrman: A Research and Production Sourcebook*. Westport, Conn.: Greenwood Press, 1992.

——. "High Ambivalence: S. N. Behrman's Disembodiment Project." *Journal of Dramatic Theory and Criticism* 15, no. 2 (Spring 2001): 145–161.

Klink, William R. *S. N. Behrman: The Major Plays*. Amsterdam: Rodopi, 1978.

Reed, Kenneth T. *S. N. Behrman*. Boston: Twayne, 1975.

Weales, Gerald. "S. N. Behrman Comes Home." *Commentary* 27, no. 3 (March 1959): 256–260.

David Sauer

BELASCO, DAVID (1853–1931)

Methods and fashions on the stage are variable . . . the theatre always reflects the taste and proclivities of its own time.
—David Belasco

As playwright, actor, manager, and producer, David Belasco was a commercial and artistic leader of the American theater of his time. Born on July 25, 1853, in San Francisco, California, soon after his parents emigrated from England, Belasco appeared onstage while still a boy and later toured as Uncle Tom in blackface, Fagin in *Oliver Twist*, and in various female impersonations. Too short and stout for leading roles, he moved into stage managing and working with dramatists DIONYSIUS BOUCICAULT and JAMES HERNE. He learned that "the successful play is not written, but rewritten."

After two failed attempts to break into the New York market with his own plays, he took the position of stage manager at the Madison Square Theatre in 1882 and built his reputation by devising effects like the battle scene with hundreds of men and horses for *Not Guilty*. Two years later, he scored with his own play, *May Blossom* (1884), a story of romantic love during the Civil War. Future success followed a proven formula: melodramatic love stories paired with realistic sets and increasingly spectacular stage effects.

"The essential thing," wrote Belasco, "is to create illusion and effect." For *Under Two Flags* (1901), the effect was a raging sandstorm; for *Du Barry* (1901), he imported all of the stage furnishings from France; and *The Governor's Lady* (1921) included a reproduction of a Child's Restaurant, accurate down to the smell of their famous pancakes.

His success defined the director as the single artist joining set, lights, costumes, music, and acting into a unified whole. Writing that "lights are to drama what music is to the lyrics of a song," his newly built Belasco Theatre (1907) featured a three-story lighting board where dozens of technicians labored through each performance. In *Madame Butterfly* (1900), a fourteen-minute lighting sequence moved the audience from night to morning, without action or sound, as the abandoned Cho-Cho-San waited for her lover. A climactic prairie sunrise cost Belasco $5,000 in THE GIRL OF THE GOLDEN WEST (1905), one of his greatest successes.

For all of his commitment to REALISM onstage, Belasco was never able to move beyond melodramatic plots based on coincidence and fate and romantic love between idealized and sentimental characters. He frequently used war as the backdrop for his love stories: the Franco-Prussian war in *Marie-Odile* (1915, by Edward Knoblauch), an Indian uprising for *The Girl I Left Behind Me* (1893), and the Civil War for *The Heart of Maryland* (1895).

Although he publicly defended art against commercialism, Belasco pandered to his public with Blanche Bates's striptease in *Naughty Anthony* (1900) and Mrs. Leslie Carter's scandalously bare feet in *Du Barry*.

In over 355 productions, Belasco staged but a single William Shakespeare play (*The Merchant of Venice*, in 1922) and never directed anything by EUGENE O'NEILL, ANTON CHEKHOV, or HENRIK IBSEN. Following World War I, audiences seeking realistic plots found Belasco old-fashioned. Unable by temperament or training to embrace the new theater led by such authors as O'Neill and ELMER RICE, he became increasingly out of step but continued to write and produce until his death on May 14, 1931, in New York City.

[*See also* United States, 1860–1929]

SELECT PLAYS: *The Haunted House* (1877); *Chums* (1879, later *Hearts of Oak*, adapted with James Herne from Henry J. Leslie's *The Mariner's Compass*); *The Creole* (1881); *The Stranglers of Paris* (1883); *May Blossom* (1884); *The Girl I Left Behind Me* (1893, with Franklin Fyles), *The Heart of Maryland* (1895); *Zaza* (1899); *Madame Butterfly* (1900); *Du Barry* (1901); *The Girl of the Golden West* (1905); *The Rose of the Rancho* (1906, with R. W. Tully); *The Return of Peter Grimm* (1911); *Laugh, Clown, Laugh* (1923, with Tom Cushing); *Mima* (1928)

FURTHER READING

Belasco, David. *The Theatre Through Its Stage Door*. New York: Harper, 1919.

——. *Six Plays*. Boston: Little, Brown, 1929.

Marker, Lise-Lone. *David Belasco: Naturalism in the American Theatre*. Princeton, N.J.: Princeton Univ. Press, 1975.

Timberlake, Craig. *The Life and Work of David Belasco: The Bishop of Broadway*. New York: Library Pubs., 1954.

Winter, William. *The Life of David Belasco*. Freeport, N.Y.: Books for Libraries Press, 1918.

Philip Zwerling

BELGIUM

EARLY HISTORY

Although the nine provinces that make up Belgium are very ancient, the Belgian nation as such is quite recent. The southern Lowlands endured a history of successive occupations and annexations—Romans, Burgundians, then the Hapsburgs; then Spain, followed by the Austro-Hungarian Empire; then France under Napoleon; and lastly by the United Provinces, the northern Netherlands. It was in 1830, following a brief but effective homegrown revolt, that the great powers of Europe founded the Belgian nation as a neutral buffer state to confound imperial incursions. This artificial fusion resulted in a long-term unhappy marriage between two language communities: the Flemish in the north, where a variant of Dutch is the vulgate, and French in Wallonia to the south. The formula of polarization does not take into account the great complexities of linguistic and economic interchange that have been undergone by the two peoples over the course of centuries. For example, while Flemish (a language that varies widely in both accent and grammar) was the language of the common people throughout Flanders, Brabant, and Limburg in the 19th century, the bourgeois class distinguished itself by speaking and writing in French. Thus, French, throughout the 19th and early 20th century, was the cultural language of the entire Belgian nation, and Flemish the despised parlance of the oppressed lower classes in the north. Flemish was kept alive by the Chambers of Rhetoric, where medieval plays were performed, and the popular "dialect" theaters of Ghent, Antwerp, and Brussels staged FARCES, MELODRAMAS, and vaudevilles in local argot that were enjoyed by the masses. When exceptional playwrights, such as Cyriel Buysse, presumably educated and cultivated, wrote plays in Dutch, it was understood as a political gesture, one bent on the return of dignified status to a formerly legitimate means of expression, though one sunk in disrepute. The Flemish movement, which agitated for Flemish linguistic emancipation, lurched to each successive phase of vindication in a series of convulsive shudders over the course of many decades, first galvanizing into active form in 1870, completing its mission over 100 years later.

In contrast to chiefly Calvinist Netherlands, Belgium, following the Spanish occupation, remained intensely Catholic, particularly in Flanders, and an astonishing number of Belgian plays are concerned with the spiritual inner conflicts of clerics or of lay Catholics' religious crises. Even such anti-ecclesiastical authors as MICHEL DE GHELDERODE and HUGO CLAUS are in dialectic with Church doctrine, albeit in a position antithetical to it.

The bulk of Belgian DRAMATURGY of the fin de siècle period, though, consisted of romantic epics or well-made comedies and melodramas of little distinction in the mode of Eugene Scribe, following idioms co-opted from France and the Netherlands. In any case, there was precious little encouragement for native Belgian writing when the audiences were in the habit of flocking to see touring companies of French actors performing French plays. The chronic inferiority complex endemic to Belgian arts was the natural consequence of the little nation's tardy genesis and close proximity to the cultural beacons that are Paris and Amsterdam.

The Belgian playwriting (and artistic production in general) that stands out in relief from this mediocre picture was the work of certain French-speaking Belgians of Flanders. Indeed, the triumvirate of internationally recognized Belgian dramatists—MAURICE MAETERLINCK, FERNAND CROMMELYNCK, and Michel de Ghelderode—are all in this category. The young Belgian "francophones" at the turn of the century were questing after a literary and dramatic identity that, even though texts were to be declaimed in the French language, was distinctly Flemish in flavor. Maurice Maeterlinck and his friend, also from the francophone bourgeoisie of Ghent, Charles Van Lerberghe (1861–1907), found their voice at the proverbial "knee" of symbolist poet Stéphane Mallarmé and were founders of the symbolist school as practiced in the theater. Maeterlinck with such short, atmospheric pieces as *The Blind* (*Les Aveugles*, 1890), *The Intruder* (*L'Intruse*, 1890), and *Pelléas and Melisande* (1893), and Van Lerberghe with his one-act tour de force *The Wanderers* (*Les Flaireurs*, 1889), took the world by storm with plays suggesting the imminence of the realm of spirits impinging on the material world. Relying on static dramatic action, hieratic visual imagery, staccato dialogue redolent of the unspoken, and a rich array of sound effects, these plays revived the theater of the Middle Ages. The most powerful force is an invisible death. Another Flemish francophone symbolist, Georges Rodenbach (1856–1898), author of the seminal novel *Bruges the Dead* (*Bruges-la-Morte*, 1892), which he adapted into a play with the title *The Mirage* (*Le Mirage*, staged 1903), also wrote a neurasthenic short, decadent play, *The Veil* (*La Voile*, 1895), both of which played in Paris.

Van Lerberghe branched out from SYMBOLISM with his landmark play *Pan* (1906). This full-length work takes the form of a modern-day fable in which the ancient Greek demigod Pan washes up on the shores of modern-day Belgium. As he accrues converts by the score, all of whom rediscover their elemental selves in a pagan fever, the agents for social status quo, priests, teachers, and government officials, make feeble, pedantic attempts to maintain their dead order. Their series of forays against Pan are exceedingly drole, revealing their essential impotence in the face of an authentic living force and unmasking present-day society as bankrupt and false.

Writing on contemporary social issues, poet Emile Verhaeren (1855–1916) wrote several plays that had an international impact, notably, his verse drama *The Dawns* (*Les Aubes*, 1904), an epic, polemic work that dramatizes the conflicts between rural and urban oppressed workers whose climax celebrates a utopian ideal of their ultimate unification against the reigning bourgois authority. This exalted work became legendary as a result of a brilliant Russian production by VSEVOLD MEYERHOLD. His other play, *The Cloister* (*Le Cloître*, 1900), is an allegorical play whose intrigue pits various monks against each other, as their individual pasts undermine their spiritual authority.

One contemporaneously writing in Flemish who embraced the naturalistic school was Cyriel Buysse (1859–1932), making a sensation with his landmark *The Van Paemel Clan* (*Het Gezin Van Paemel*, 1905), a social play depicting a Flemish peasant family indentured to the local, French-speaking squire.

A quintessentially Belgian work, albeit in a typically boulevard mode, was Frantz Fonson (1870–1924) and Fernand Wicheler's (1874–1936) perennial favorite, *Miss Bullberg's Marriage* (*Le Marriage de Mlle. Bullemans*, 1910). A COMEDY of manners, written out of the Era of Good Feeling, followed an intrigue recognizable from the theater of Georges Courteline and Eugène Marin Labiche but whose social context is extremely local. The Brussels beer manufacturer Bullemans welcomes a young Parisian upstart into his home to learn the beer trade. The latter promptly falls in love with Bullemans's pragmatic daughter Suzanne, who is being paid court by the young Seraphin Meulemeester, a maladroit homegrown Bruxellois. The Brussels characters not only are coarse-mannered nouveaux riches but spout the savory local dialect of French, which joins crude reworkings of normal usage with Flemish outcroppings. They deride the young Parisian, misinterpreting his natural aplomb and ease of expression for snobbery. The play plots the difficulties and eventual triumph of the young Parisian, who claims his ladylove by achieving mastery over the low-class Brussels dialect! This signature work still draws appreciative crowds when it is revived today, as it is on a regular basis.

WORLD WAR I REALITIES

The high-brow public had tired of the symbolist wave by the time World War I broke out, thrusting cruel and concrete realities of a political nature into the lives of all Belgians, putting a decisive end to art for art's sake in the theater. Belgium, which served as a military theater for so much of the Western Front, was particularly brutalized by the German invasion and was rendered for the umpteenth time in its history an occupied state.

World War I further complicated the linguistic quagmire. The bulk of Belgian commanding officers were francophone, whereas the rank and file, who were being thrown into the fray as cannon fodder, tended to be Flemish. Conversely, there was a certain amount of sympathy in certain Flemish circles for the German occupant, with whose Teutonic language they felt more kinship than with the romantic French that epitomized their oppressed status. In the theater it meant that if Flemish writers still wrote in French, a language that promised a potentially larger audience, a growing number, moved by feelings of solidarity, were tempted to pen at least a part of their oeuvre in Flemish.

The sequel to the war brought with it an explosion of dramatic experimentation, as Belgium partook of the European tendency to break the bounds of both well-made tradition and NATURALISM. The Between-the-Wars period thus saw the theatrical debuts of two giants: Fernand Crommelynck and Michel de Ghelderode. We also find experimentalists like Clément Pansaers (1885–1922), a devotee of Dada and follower of Tristan Tzara; another Dada practictioner, the hermetic painter Paul Joostens (1889–1960); and Michel Seuphor (1901–1999), who attempted to create a theater denuded of subject matter but that emulated a nonobjective arrangement of rectilinearly deployed lines and shapes reminiscent of his friend Piet Mondriaan's paintings. The Surrealist Group of Brussels, whose founding preceded that of André Breton's Parisian Groupe Littérature, in its earlier incarnation as Groupe Correspondance, also produced a certain amount of theater. For example, its chief theoretician, Paul Nougé (1895–1967), wrote a little music hall work titled *The Other Side of the Cards* (*Le Dessous des Cartes*, 1926).

The propensity for EXPRESSIONISM, so powerful in GERMANY, had its echo in Belgium as well. The Flemish expressionist school of painting, with many extraordinary talents, such as Fritz van den Berghe, Frans Masereel, James Ensor, and Constant Permeke, tending toward the satirical, pastoral, and primitivist, rivaled its German counterparts in brilliance. These visual artists were seconded by theatrical artists. Many of Michel de Ghelderode's earlier plays bore the expressionist stamp. So did his contemporary Géo Norge (1898–1990) in his curious AVANT-GARDE work *Tom-Tom* (1926), whose performance is more famous for the storm it provoked than for its inherent value. The well-attended performance of *Tom-Tom* was interrupted by catcalls and proclamations from members of the Belgian surrealist group who had insinuated themselves into the auditorium, so that the play could scarcely be heard. In fact, *Tom-Tom* is a very interesting work recounting, in fragmentary and distorted fashion, the recent slaughter of World War I and predicting further butchery.

Other expressionists included Max Deauville (1881–1966), whose play *Nothing but a Man* (*Rien qu'un Homme*, 1926) dealt with the theme of capital punishment; Henri Soumagne (1891–1951), remembered for his *The Other Messiah* (*L'Autre Messie*, 1923), a fantasy about a Jewish hero, David Kellerstein, whose rejection of God leads to a confrontation in a dream with various deities representative of the world's religions, as well as for his lighter two-character work *The Dancers of Gigue* (*Les Danceurs de Gigue*, 1925); and the young Hermann Closson (1901–1982), with *Basement* (*Sou-sol*, 1925), a refreshingly earthy MONODRAMA about a woman who cleans toilets. Closson later went on to write high-blown hieratic works on subjects from history, including ancient Flemish national heroes, such as *The Four Brothers Aymon* (*Le Jeu des Quatre Frères d'Aymon*, 1946) and *Godefroid de Bouillon* (1932).

A theatrical giant in his own way was Herman Teirlinck (1879–1967). Teirlinck was primarily a great theoretician and pedagogue, lobbying for a modern Flemish theater whose maturity would equal the francophone theater of Belgium. His early plays *Man Without a Body* (*De Man Zonder Lijf*, 1925), *Slow Motion Movie* (*De Vertraagde Film*, 1922), and *Magpie on the Gallows* (*Ekster op de Galg*, 1937) integrate flashbacks, stop-action, commedia dell'arte, and jazz, attempting to apply contemporary experiments such as those of Gordon Craig and ERWIN PISCATOR. In his later works, he aimed for a monumental theater, a Wagnerian opera without the music.

WORLD WAR II AND BEYOND

The occupation of Belgium through World War II was even more traumatic than that of World War I. Alongside an active Resistance flourished a virulent Collaboration. Germany controlled all means of communication, including radio stations, publishing houses and newspapers, and theaters. Following the war, there was an energetic, sometimes peremptory and unjust "cleansing." As a corollary, King Leopold III, who had remained in Brussels during the war, even as his government fled to London, was charged with collaboration. He lingered in exile, while the Belgian populace heatedly argued his fate. The very existence of Belgian royalty was in jeopardy as a plebiscite resulted in an even 50/50 split, with half the country (predominantly the southern half) calling for his abdication, followed by riots in the streets as Leopold prepared to return. The "Royal Question" was ultimately resolved as late as 1954 when he abdicated in favor of his son Baudouin, and the royal line was preserved.

Nuanced shadings of collaboration had been so common early in the war, when it was expected that Adolf Hitler would triumph and that adaptation was shrewder than resistance, that many of Belgium's writers and artists tended, once the worm had turned, to banish the war as a subject from their writing. As a kind of amnesia set in, the dramaturgy of the 1950s became what has been called Belgian "neoclassicism." This generation opted for exalted, abstracted subjects entirely removed from the sullied immediate past of collaboration and linguistic conflict. The plays are often set in nebulous unidentified lands or in some murky past; the heroes are typically confonted with some moral decision that brings about a tragic end. The intellectual diction coupled with the distantiation produces an effect of cold exaltation and has rendered the majority of these plays quite dated.

Chief among the neoclassicists were Suzanne Lilar (1901–1992), whose *The Burlador* (*Le Burlador*, 1945) is a reworking of the Don Juan legend, her *All Roads Lead to Heaven* (*Tous Chemins Mènent au Ciel*, 1947) is set in a 16th-century beguinage, where one of the holy sisters attempts to reconcile her physical and spiritual needs. Charles Bertin's (1919–2003) *Christopher Columbus* (*Christophe Colomb*, 1958) was well received. Georges Sion (1913–2003) is most noted for *The Voyager of Forceloup* (*Le Voyageur de Foreloup*, 1952), a moral drama in which a good samaritan figure sacrifices his own spiritual faith to another, as well as the pseudo-classical comedy *The Matron of Ephesus* (*La Matronne d'Ephèse*, 1943). Jean Mogin (1921–1986) wrote *To Each According to His Hunger* (*À Chacun Selon sa Faim*, 1950), another drama of moral crises among Catholic clerics. On the Flemish side in the postwar period, Herwig Hensen (1917–1989) and Johan Boonen (b. 1939), among others, were producing their own version of neoclassicism.

A notorious collaborator, Louis Carette (b. 1913) recreated himself in France under the name Félicien Marceau, where he ultimately was even named to the Académie Française! His escapist entertainments enjoyed great success in postwar Paris, most notably *The Egg* (*L'Oeuf*, 1956), in which the hero, Magis, relives his life in reverse order, trying to ascertain the source of his basic malaise. The latter work even enjoyed a successful run in New York in 1959. Another reformed collaborator, who has known success latterly, is Henri Bauchau (b. 1913), whose epic *Genghis Khan* (1960) was staged at the Théâtre National.

A distinguished playwright whose career spanned from the 1950s to the 1990s, PAUL WILLEMS managed to transcend the cold abstraction of the neoclassicists, authoring a theater of magic and enchantment.

Concurrently, SAMUEL BECKETT and EUGÈNE IONESCO's Theater of the Absurd was having its impact, and we find the young HUGO CLAUS (b. 1929) and Tone Brulin (b. 1921) experimenting with its forms before they each found their own voices. Both Claus, beginning with his early masterpiece *Bride in the Morning* (*Een Bruid in de Morgen*, 1955), and Brulin went far beyond these early experiments. Other young writers such as Pieter De Prins (b. 1926) and Marcel Van Maele (b. 1931), with his baroque experiment *Revolution* (*Revolutie*, 1966), also dabbled in Theater of the Absurd.

While the neoclassicists were producing their chaste works of academic perfection, Belgium was beginning to undergo yet a new period of turmoil. By 1960 the formerly rich territory of Wallonia, with its mines and factories and a tradition of socialist syndicalism, had become outdated and outstripped by the now industrial Flanders. Its decline was marked by a series of crippling mass strikes. Other social upheavals included the achievement of independence by the Congolese colony. And the linguistic battle, ever ready to boil over, finally did. By the 1970s, the Ministries of Culture and Education were separated forever after into a Flemish one and a francophone one. The newly autonomous administrative situation brought both financial and artistic changes to both language communities. The formerly dominant francophones of Flanders were ever more residual, their very existence in question, and the literature and arts of the communities became separate in more pronounced and irremediable ways.

In Wallonia, the playwright who is most identified with a workers' theater is Jean Louvet (b. 1934). Beginning with his AGITATION-PROPAGANDA work growing directly out of the strikes of the 1960s, his *Good Lord's Train* (*Le Train du Bon Dieu*, 1962) was followed up by his masterpiece *Conversation in Wallonia* (*Conversation en Wallonie*, 1976). Louvet manages to transcend the EPIC THEATER of BERTOLT BRECHT, as he integrates a dialectic with an abstract aesthetic surface and rarified, even lyrical mood. Other key works include *The Man Who Had the Sun in His Pocket* (*L'Homme Qui Avait le Soleil Dans sa Poche*, 1982), one of the only plays about the Royal Question and the role played by Julien Lahaut, who shouted "Long live the Republic" at the crowning of King Baudouin only to be assassinated one week later. *The Furnishings* (*L'Aménagement*, 1984) dramatizes the dysfunction in the relationship between a wealthy woman and her lower-class lover. Jean Sigrid (1920–1998), who reached his mature period in the 1970s, was prominent for a stripped-down Pinteresque way with dialogue. He took on the collaboration elliptically with *The Sound of Your Steps* (*Le Bruit de Tes Pas*, 1979) and the generation conflict with *The Hitchhiker* (*L'Auto-stoppeur*, 1977) and successfully revives the Maeterlinckian mood of death's imminence with the lyrical *Angel Knife* (*L'Ange Couteau*, 1980). The poet Liliane Wouters (b. 1930) created the popular *Teachers' Room* (*La Salle des Profs.*, 1983), a boulevard comedy about secondary school education; drawing from Belgium's historical bad conscience, she wrote *Charlotte or the Mexican Night* (*Charlotte ou la Nuit Mexicaine*, 1989) about the Empress Carlotta, a finely wrought play about the insanity of emperor of Mexico Maximilian's ill-treated widow. Another attempt to grapple with history and the national bad conscience, the domination of the Congo by Belgium, was essayed by Anita Van Belle (b. 1960) with *Wanderings, the Interior Voyage of Patrice Lumumba* (*Errances, le Voyage Intérieur de Patrice Lumumba*, 1999). A seminal figure in the Flemish theater was Tone Brulin, who founded the Otrabanda Theatre in America, studied with Jerzy Grotowski, and collaborated with ATHOL FUGARD. Under the twin influences of Brecht and ANTONIN ARTAUD, his time in Africa proved particularly fruitful, as he took on subjects like apartheid in such works as *Now That the Town Doesn't Exist* (*Nu het Dorp Niet Meer Bestaat*, 1955) and *The Dogs* (*De Honden*, 1960).

Later, in the 1970s, he founded TIEDRIE (Theater of the Third World in Europe) with an international company of actors and put on plays like *The Tale of the Mah-Meri* (1975) and *BaAnansi*

(1980), taking off from African and Asian myths and folktales and producing works of great theatrical ingenuity and social value.

Another important Flemish dramatist is Walter Van Den Broeck (b. 1941), whose *Greens from Balen* (*Groenten uit Balen*, 1972) is about the destructive effects of a workers' strike on the relationships within one family. Hesitating between a naturalistic sketch of local color and social pamphleteering, the play ends on a triumphant note as family members realize they need only depend on themselves to determine their future.

CONTEMPORARY VOICES

Since the 1970s, in the final phases of the Flemish movement's forward march, the nation has edged toward ever increasing federalism, which in Belgium means stricter division and autonomy. The language communities live in willed ignorance of each other's activities despite promotion of sporadic exchanges. The most recent transformation has come with the identification of Brussels as the capital of the European Community, which has put formerly obscure Belgium into the spotlight, brought about extensive renewal of its capital (with a concomitant loss of quaint atmosphere), and created a sense that Belgian artists are first and foremost European; they do in fact, more than ever, strive for European and international recognition.

The extremely original RENÉ KALISKY set the tone for a wave of innovative, international dramaturgy. Under the sway of HEINER MÜLLER and other German postmodernists, Michèle Fabien (1945–2001) wrote a series of loosely structured works—such as the monologue *Jocaste* (1981), which recenters the Oedipus myth on the figure of the mother/sister—that are essentially linguistic explorations with emphasis on utterance rather than other facets of theatricality and attempt to deconstruct the well-made mold, obliterating even the well-crafted sentence. And while Jean-Marie Piemme (b. 1944) at first shared a similar project for declamatory theater in such plays as *Snow in December* (*Neige en Décembre*, 1987) and *No Lies* (*Sans Mentir*, 1989), he has more recently matured into a dramaturgy that is at once more visceral and theatrically exciting. His play *Patriot's Café* (*Café des Patriotes*, 1998), for example, which takes on the Extreme Right and its purveyors, pairs an originality of language with singular characters whose longings are both universal and local. From Paul Emond, and his whimsical intellectualism, to Pascal Vrebos (b. 1952), and his accessible, sometimes vulgar situations, to Jacques DeDecker (b. 1945), and his with-it domestic comedies, the spectrum of contemporary Belgian writing covers many bases in its present renaissance. Half Belgian, half Iranian Jew, the novelist and film scenarist Philippe Blasband (b. 1964), whose multicultural background enriches his work, is equally adept in the dramatic form, notably *Where Are You, Sammy Rebenski?* (*Où-Es Tu, Sammy Rebenski?* 2001). One of the works that has excited the most interest on the francophone side of late is actually the work of a theatrical ensemble, Groupov, led by Jacques Delcuvellerie (b. 1946). Taking on the painful subject of the slaughter in Rwanda, the ensemble collectively created a documentary work—*Rwanda 1994* (2002)—that has toured to many festivals and had staggering impact.

The ever more thrilling theatrical work on the Flemish side of the language divide has come out of such collectives, for example, De Blauwe Mandaag Compagnie, De Tijd, and Arne Sierens (b. 1959) and Alain Platel (b. 1956). The latter two, a writing/directing team, are perhaps the most original voices in Belgium since Maeterlinck; in the theater, they rival the brilliant reception of Belgian choreographers such as Anna-Teresa DeKeersmaker and have forged a synthesis between high culture avant-garde and populist. With an original dramaturgy where the set design precedes the writing of the script, their shows vaguely recall the trends of Anne Bogart in America. With large-cast shows, often in local dialect and sometimes site-specific settings—such as *Bernadetje* (1997), set in an actual bumper-car race course; *My Blackie* (*Mijn Blackie*, 1998), a local fresco of life in a small town replete with an omnipresent live black dog on a leash; and *The Soldier Postman and Rachel* (*De Soldaat Facteur en Rachel*, 1986), in which two old folks reminisce about the German Occupation—they produce works that are freewheeling and, loosely structured and yet incredibly disciplined in their use of sophisticated theatrical means.

Other highly original contemporary voices include journalist and politician Tom Lanoye (b. 1958), author of the notorious *In the War* (*Ten Oorlog*, 1997), a ten-hour deconstruction of William Shakespeare's history plays, and Peter Verhelst (b. 1962), the foremost linguistic stylist writing in Flemish today.

FURTHER READING

André, Luc, and Paul Van Morckhoven. *The Contemporary Theatre in Belgium. Belgian Review*. Brussels: The Belgian Information and Documentation Inst., 1970.

Glasheen, Anne-Marie. *Four Belgian Playwrights, Gambit: International Theatre Review*, nos. 42–43. London: John Calder Pubs., 1986.

Knapp, Bettina, ed. *An Anthology of Modern Belgian Theatre: Maurice Maeterlinck, Fernand Crommelynck, and Michel de Ghelderode*. Troy, N.Y.: Whitston, 1982.

Kourilsky, Françoise, ed. *New French-Language Plays: Martinique, Quebec, Ivory Coast, Belgium*. New York: Ubu, 1993.

Kourilsky, Françoise, and Catherine Temerson, eds. *Gay Plays: An International Anthology*. New York: Ubu, 1991.

Lilar, Suzanne. *The Belgian Theater Since 1890*. New York: Belgian Government Information Center, 1962.

Willinger, David, ed. *An Anthology of Contemporary Belgian Plays: 1970–1982*. Troy, N.Y.: Whitston, 1984.

——. "Belgium." *Western European Stages* 13, no. 1 (Winter 2001): 15–28.

——, ed. *Three Fin-de Siècle Farces*. New York: Peter Lang, 1990.

——, ed. *Theatrical Gestures of Belgian Modernism: Dada Surrealism, Futurism and Pure Plastic in Twentieth-Century Belgian Theatre.* New York: Peter Lang, 2002.

David Paul Willinger

LES BELLES SOEURS See SISTERS IN LAW

BENAVENTE, JACINTO (1866–1954)

Jacinto Benavente y Martínez, one of SPAIN's foremost 20th-century playwrights, wrote 172 plays spanning a sixty-year period. He adopted a diversity of styles and techniques but is credited especially for introducing Spaniards with his early works to late-19th-century European REALISM. With *The Intruder* (*El nido ajeno,* 1894) and *Well-Known People* (*Gente conocida,* 1896), appearing when Romanticism's influence still prevailed in Spain, Benavente set new parameters for playwrights by emphasizing psychology over MELODRAMA and by adopting dialogue instead of verse. Benavente wrote various plays for Spain's leading actresses—María Guerrero, Rosario Pino, and Margarita Xirgu—thus helping to establish new standards for acting as well, whereby psychological depth and the natural representation of human behavior would replace the lofty, declamatory style of the past. The portrayal of strong-willed women struggling against a web of social forces is frequent in Benavente's work and suggests the dramatist's possible role as precursor to FEDERICO GARCÍA LORCA.

A native of Madrid and son of a prominent pediatrician, Benavente gained childhood exposure to the various social groups, most notably (but not exclusively) the bourgeoisie and upper classes, whose mores and thinking would form the basis for many of his plays. He is an ideologically complex figure who betrays facile classifications. Averse to conflict, he lived through years of often violent upheaval and of political instability that resulted in various changes of regime: a monarchy (Alfonso XIII, 1902–1931) punctuated by dictatorship (Miguel Primo de Rivera, 1923–1929), the 2nd Republic (1931–1939) that was truncated by Civil War (1936–1939), and renewed totalitarianism (Francisco Franco, 1939–1975). During World War I he aligned himself politically with Antonio Maura and, as may be seen in *The Happy, Confident City* (*La ciudad alegre y confiada,* 1916), Benavente embraced the conservative statesman's faith in the ability of a morally superior upper class to effect meaningful change "from above" ("revolución desde arriba"). Such stances, along with his allegedly contradictory efforts at remaining neutral in an increasingly polarized world and his adherence to traditional modes of writing and thinking in the AVANT-GARDE era, gained him the reputation of a conservative—his occasional denunciations of inequality, his anticlericalism, and his inclination toward social satire notwithstanding. Some contemporary critics acknowledged Benavente's earlier contributions to the Spanish stage while criticizing his election as Spain's Nobel Laureate in 1922.

Benavente's notoriety today derives primarily from such early successes as *The Bonds of Interest* (*Los intereses creados,* 1907), *Stones and Saints* (*Señora ama,* 1908), and *The Passion Flower* (*La malquerida,* 1913), plays that enjoyed successful runs in Spain and abroad and that, to a greater or lesser degree, reflect a proclivity toward social satire that draws comparisons with HENRIK IBSEN, OSCAR WILDE, and GEORGE BERNARD SHAW. In the first play, considered his masterpiece, Benavente employs the conventions of the commedia dell'arte to highlight such vices as greed and hypocrisy. The latter two are rural social dramas, the second patterned along the lines of the Phaedra myth. Relentlessly attentive to contemporary social issues, Benavente continued producing plays until the year of his death. Critics, however, tend to overlook his later output in assessing his influence on the history of Spanish theater.

SELECT PLAYS (*indicates plays for which an English translation exists): *The Intruder* (*El nido ajeno,* 1894); *Well-Known People* (*Gente conocida,* 1896); *The Governor's Wife** (*La gobernadora,* 1901); *Saturday Night** (*La noche del sábado,* 1903); *Autumnal Roses** (*Rosas de otoño,* 1905); *The Evildoers of Good** (*Los malhechores del bien,* 1905); *The Bonds of Interest** (*Los intereses creados,* 1907); *Stones and Saints** (*Señora ama,* 1908); *The Passion Flower** (*La malquerida,* 1913); *Field of Ermine** (*Campo de armiño,* 1916)

FURTHER READING

Diaz, José A. *Jacinto Benavente and His Theatre.* Long Island City, N.Y.: Las Americas, 1972.

Lázaro Carreter, Fernando. Introduction to *Los intereses creados* [The bonds of interest]. 17th ed. Madrid: Cátedra, 2003.

Peñuelas, Marcelino C. *Jacinto Benavente.* New York: Twayne, 1968.

Ruiz Ramón, Francisco. *Historia del teatro español, siglo XX* [History of the Spanish theater, 20th century]. 12th ed. Madrid: Cátedra, 2001.

Sheehan, Robert Louis. *Benavente and the Spanish Panorama, 1894–1954.* Chapel Hill, N.C.: Estudios de Hispanófila, 1976.

Vila Selma, José. *Benavente, fin de siglo* [Benavente, turn of the century]. Madrid: Rialp, 1952.

Bernardo Antonio González

BENNETT, ALAN (1934–)

Alan Bennett, born in Leeds, England, was known as an actor well before he made his mark as a dramatist and man of letters. His debut performance was in the *Beyond the Fringe* COMEDY revue, which he performed at Edinburgh, then at London's West End and in New York with Dudley Moore, Jonathan Miller, and Peter Cook in the early 1960s. Born in 1934, he was the son of a butcher. He once joked that he would go down in literary history only for once having delivered meat to T. S. ELIOT's mother-in-law.

Educated at Exeter College, Oxford, he wrote concert sketches that went on to become part of the revue *Beyond the Fringe* (1960).

Bennett often uses FARCE and music hall techniques as in *Habeas Corpus* (1973). He has written widely for television and radio and penned some film scripts. Nominated for an Oscar for the screenplay adaptation of THE MADNESS OF GEORGE III (1991), Bennett has been described as "a miniaturist" both for his precise acting as well as his prose writing in the semiautobiographical *Writing Home* (1994). He is the winner of several awards, including the Tony Award, the Hawthornden Prize, and the Olivier Award.

Famous as a dramatist for his MONODRAMA series TALKING HEADS I and II (1987 and 1998), presaged by the one-woman script *A Woman of No Importance* (1982), widely popular on television, radio, and the stage besides audio CD and video, Bennett is also famed as a commentator on the 20th century as he relates incidents, amusing and ironic, about real people in his *Diaries 1980–1990*. The monodrama, which is a one-act piece with a single speaking character, was the dramatic monologue extended, in the 20th century, as a genre or dramatic structure by SAMUEL BECKETT with KRAPP'S LAST TAPE (1958). However, it is Bennett who achieved national fame for writing monodramas that feature ordinary women and men from northern England, making him known as "the bard of the drab." The Bennettian monodrama typically portrays the individual as trapped; it then widens to admit the whole picture to the audience. His observations, mediated through his characters, reveal the scene in a gently quickening series of perspectives that make the situation clear to the audience but not necessarily to the characters themselves. We simultaneously see the characters through a double perception: first, the authorial comic vision, which is at once satirical and humane, and second, through the self-deluded eyes of the character who never sees himself or herself as he or she is viewed by the audience, making for comic pathos. Bennett's monologues are so intensely descriptive that several reviewers have felt the characters who figured in the speaking character's reverie actually appeared on the stage.

The gamut of his writing, from his earliest plays to his *Diaries* and prose, contains trenchant and ironic observations about life and the people of northern England, rendering them lifelike in the richness of their language and diction and portrayed with a wry ironic wit. Bennett proves a master artist in the portrayal of minor lives that are sketched wittily, in depth, and almost with a love for the characters that enables the audience to come to know and feel for them as the monodrama draws to a close. Bennett's is a high art and a skillful one, which fulfills the aims of true comedy, fusing laughter and grief in his portrayal of lives that contain deep sadness or keen disappointment.

[*See also* England, 1940–Present; *The History Boys*]

PLAYS: *Better Late* (1959); *Beyond the Fringe* (1960); *Forty Years On* (1968); *Sing a Rude Song* (1969, co-writer); *Getting On* (1971); *Habeas Corpus* (1973); *The Old Country* (1977); *Enjoy* (1980); *Kafka's Dick* (1986); *A Visit from Miss Prothero* (1987); *Single Spies* (An Englishman Abroad and A Question of Attribution) (1988, writer and director); *The Wind in the Willows* (1990); *The Madness of George III* (1991); *Talking Heads* (A Chip in the Sugar, Bed Among the Lentils, A Lady of Letters, Her Big Chance, Soldiering On, A Cream Cracker Under the Settee) (1992); *The History Boys* (2004)

FURTHER READING

Bergan, Roland. *Beyond the Fringe . . . and Beyond: A Critical Biography of Alan Bennett, Peter Cook, Jonathan Miller, and Dudley Moore*. London: Virgin Bks., 1990.

Kendle, Burton S. "Alan Bennett." In *Contemporary Dramatists*, ed. by K. A. Berney. 5th ed. London: St. James, 1993.

Wu, Duncan. *Six Contemporary Dramatists: Bennett, Potter, Gray, Brenton, Hare, Ayckbourn*. London: St. Martin's, 1995.

Dimple Godiwala

BENT

MARTIN SHERMAN's *Bent* demonstrates that homosexuals suffered their own Holocaust under Nazism. Given a stage reading at 1978's EUGENE O'NEILL Playwrights' Conference at Waterford, Connecticut, *Bent*'s renown snowballed after the production was first staged at London's Royal Court Theatre in May 1979. That production, directed by Robert Chetwyn, starred Ian McKellen as the lead character Max. A subsequent Broadway production featured Richard Gere playing Max. McKellen reprised his role as Max in an acclaimed Sean Mathias–directed 1990 revival at the National Theatre in London; he played the smaller role of Uncle Freddie in the film version of *Bent* (1997, also directed by Mathias). The film version has made Sherman's play—and the persecution of homosexuals under the Nazis—even better known. The play itself has been performed regularly since 1980. Sherman's greatest success to date, *Bent* figures prominently in the canons of both Holocaust literature and gay drama.

The play opens in a milieu of carefree decadence. Max's partner, Rudy, has to remind Max about Wolf, the youth that he has seduced and brought home. In his drunken excess, Max has quite forgotten about Wolf. The lovers' unconventional, but peaceful, homosexual lives are violently halted by Nazis who come to arrest Wolf, slitting his throat when he resists. The lackadaisical days of the Weimar era are now unambiguously over. Max and Rudy flee Berlin. Despite help from another "fluff," Uncle Freddie, the rampantly homophobic Nazis soon capture them. Max and Rudy are transported to the labor camp at Dachau. Rudy is savagely beaten. On the advice of another prisoner, Horst, Max hides his emotions, denying his character, to join in the beating of Rudy, who soon dies. Max can survive because he is prepared—at first—to subjugate much of his personality. He wears the yellow triangle, symbolizing his Jewishness, rather than the homosexuals' pink. He even copulates with a dead teenage girl to "prove" his manliness to his Nazi captors.

Life gets no easier in the labor-intensive camp, where the pointlessness of the tasks combines with their physical relentlessness to break the despised prisoners' bodies and spirits. Max strives for human contact and enjoys a brief, but meaningful, moment of psychologically enabled eroticism. Horst and Max have become close. Each is desperate for an interpersonal closeness that is impossible in an environment where showing tenderness will be fatal—the characters know that the Nazis "hate it if anyone [even] looks at each other." Still carrying stones, Max and Horst arouse each other verbally, both managing to climax without even touching. Later, the ailing Horst's temperature is mentally raised as Max vocally pretends to be cradling him. These moments of tender respite are transient, but the newfound defiance of the Nazi intolerance for homosexuality is cemented when Max takes the dead Horst's pink triangle and proudly wears it. That act is a prelude to suicide, but what matters is that when confronted with the most hostile oppression imaginable, Max and Horst are, eventually, able to maintain the dignity and legitimacy of their homosexual identity.

[*See also* England, 1940–Present; Gay and Lesbian Drama]

FURTHER READING

Hammermeister, Kai. "Inventing History: Toward a Gay Holocaust Literature." *German Quarterly* 70, no. 1 (1997): 18–26.

McClum, John M. *Still Acting Gay: Male Homosexuality in Modern Drama*. New York: St. Martin's, 2000.

Plant, Richard. *The Pink Triangle: The Nazi War Against Homosexuals*. New York: Owl Bks., 1988.

Reviews of *Bent*. *Theatre Record* 10, no. 2 (1990): 90, 99–106.

Schulman, Michael, and Eva Mekler, eds. *Great Scenes and Monologues for Actors*. New York: St. Martin's, 1998.

Sherman, Martin. *Bent*. Ashover: Allen Lane, 1979.

Kevin De Ornellas

BENTLEY, ERIC (1916–)

". . . Critic . . . playwright . . . do you think of yourself as mainly one thing?"

"Yes: a writer."

—Eric Bentley, in an interview on *Voice of America*

Born in Lancashire, England, on September 14, 1916, Eric Bentley went to school at Bolton, then Oxford, and earned a Ph.D. at Yale University. He become an American citizen in 1948 and, though widely traveled, remained based in the United States throughout his career. Renowned as a theater critic and theorist of drama, two of his many books on theater, *The Playwright as Thinker* (1946) and *The Life of the Drama* (1964), had a great influence on several generations of dramatists and theater practitioners and are surely to remain classics. He is perhaps most widely known in the popular sense because of his translations of plays by BERTOLT BRECHT and LUIGI PIRANDELLO. Bentley worked directly with Brecht in America and, after World War II, in Europe.

Bentley's most acclaimed and widely produced play, *Are You Now or Have You Ever Been?* (1972), is based entirely on transcripts from the House Un-American Activities Committee hearings from the McCarthy period (1950–1954). The methods of dramatic construction within the play, then, are those of transposition, abridgement, and arrangement. Bentley considered this last element, the order in which the scenes are presented, to be the most important, and he used juxtaposition and COLLAGE to create effect.

Bentley has stated that his "playwriting happened in a sequence that had to do with translation." Although he remarked in the early 1950s that "adaptation is a racket," it was just such adaptation that led to his own dramatic work later on. Finding that a strict literal translation of Brecht's poetry did not make sense, he more and more moved toward free adaptation. Two early plays, *A Time to Die* (1967) and *A Time to Live* (1967), were derived from dramas by Euripides and Sophocles. Bentley's intriguing triptych *The Kleist Variations: Concord, The Fall of the Amazons,* and *Wannsee* (1982) is derived from or suggested by German texts of Henrich von Kleist.

Other plays of Bentley, *The Recantation of Galileo Galilei* (1972), *From the Memoirs of Pontius Pilate* (1976), and *Expletive Deleted* (1974), are based on found materials (the Nixon tapes or historical episodes), and in this he is clearly following his mentor Brecht, both in terms of method (Brecht told Bentley "Anyone can be creative, what takes time is re-writing someone else") and in an emphasis on politics and ideas.

Bentley's legacy is various and substantial. Seeing the dramatist as an engaged scholar, translator, and adaptor who occasionally writes originally as well, he has pointed out that this was the working method of William Shakespeare and the Elizabethans, as well as the Greek tragedians. It is hard not to think of the careers of such writers as RICHARD NELSON and TONY KUSHNER, in America, or EDWARD BOND, David Edgar, and DAVID HARE, in Britain. They are better playwrights, but Bentley's example of the German idea of playwright as dramaturg (from Doris Lessing to Friedrich Schiller, Johann Wolfgang von Goethe, and Brecht) has surely been suggestive both to playwrights and producers. National Theatre literary manager Kenneth Tynan wrote after reading *The Life of the Drama*, "My writing will owe even more to Bentley in the future than it has in the past." Bentley was a strong advocate of the playwright as most important in theater, then the actor, and then everybody else. This position in a period where directors and designers were deemed dominant was important. The supposition that dramatists needed to work with ideas as well as emotional content continues to resonate.

Bentley received a Lifetime Achievement Obie Award in 2006.

[*See also* Dramatic Criticism; Political Theater in the United States; United States, 1940–Present]

SELECT PLAYS: *Orpheus in the Underworld* (libretto, 1956); *Roaring All Day Long* (1957); *A Time to Die* (1967); *A Time to Live* (1967); *Are You Now or Have You Ever Been?* (1972); *The Recantation of Galileo Galilei* (1972); *Expletive Deleted* (1974); *From the Memoirs of Pontius Pilate* (1976); *Lord Alfred's Lover* (1981); *The Kleist Variations* (1982)

FURTHER READING

Bentley, Eric. *The Playwright as Thinker*. New York: Reynal & Hitchcock, 1946.

——. *The Life of the Drama*. New York: Atheneum, 1964.

——. *The Brecht Memoir*. Evanston: Northwestern Univ. Press, 1989.

Sullivan, Patrick. "Author Eric Bentley Still Shaping Theater." *Sonoma County Independent* (September 24–30, 1998). Metro Publishing. http://www.metroactive.com/papers/sonoma/09.24.98/bentley-9838.html.

Stanley R. Richardson

BERGMAN, HJALMAR (1883–1931)

Maybe a dramatist is in fact a dwarfed actor.
—Hjalmar Bergman

Swedish novelist and playwright Hjalmar Bergman was married to Stina Lindberg, the daughter of prominent stage director August Lindberg. For many years the couple lived mostly abroad, although they spent summers in the Stockholm archipelago.

Best known for such novels as *God's Orchid* (*Markurells i Wadköping*, 1919), *Thy Rod and Thy Staff* (*Farmor och vår Herre*, 1921), and *The Head of the Firm* (*Chefen fru Ingeborg*, 1924), the extremely productive and versatile Bergman was, along with PÄR LAGERKVIST, the most gifted Swedish playwright of his generation.

In his first published play, *Mary, Mother of Jesus* (*Maria, Jesu moder*, 1905), a CLOSET DRAMA, the title figure is one of the many strong women in Bergman's work. Seeing her hopes quenched, she rebels against an unjust world order. The much more actable *Parisina* is a colorful Tristan and Isolde story.

In the three *Marionette Plays* (1917) Bergman continues the tradition of MAURICE MAETERLINCK's symbolist mood pieces and AUGUST STRINDBERG's chamber plays in his own, innovative manner. Rather than outline characters, these plays illustrate a fatalistic view of life. In the first of these, *Death's Harlequin* (*Dödens Arlekin*), a pillar of a small society, Consul Broman, lies dying backstage behind closed doors. Like so many other Bergman characters, Broman has suppressed what was once genuine and tender in him. His imminent death in various ways affects his surroundings. The title refers to the idea that Harlequin, when jingling his bells, may cause Death to lose its grip. The second play, *A Shadow* (*En skugga*), deals with the old motif of the young girl who is being sacrificed to a rich, ailing, aged bridegroom. The shadow represents both the bridegroom's jealous fantasies and the bride's hopes. The same motif is found in the third play, *Mr. Sleeman Is Coming* (*Herr Sleeman kommer*), where an innocent young girl finds herself trapped between the young forester she loves and the rich but old, syphilitic Sleeman she detests but whom her aunts have chosen to be her husband. At the end of this fateful and grim "fairy" drama, the romantic lover is sadly replaced by the cynical wooer of reality.

Another significant landmark is the three short plays published in 1923. *The Gambling House* (*Spelhuset*), written in 1916, is an early experiment in expressionistic technique. The gambling house is a transparent symbol of life, the gamblers, searching for happiness, of mankind. Two young lovers escape destruction in this diabolical story. In the fairy-talish *The Weaver of Baghdad* (*Vävaren i Bagdad*), Orient and Occident are contrasted. In *The Portal* (*Porten*), written in 1920, reasoned self-restraint is a central concept. On the other side of the portal of death, through which Henrik is to pass, he finds that his view of himself and others has changed.

Bergman's dramatic breakthrough came in 1925 with *Swedenhielms*, a COMEDY with serious undertones. The family name indicates that we are introduced to a family that is an incarnation of supposedly Swedish qualities: frivolity, extravagance, honesty. Swedenhielm Sr., a prominent scientist, learns almost simultaneously that one of his sons has falsified his name and that he himself has received the Nobel Prize. When it appears that not the son but the housekeeper—the most likeable character in the play—is guilty of the falsification, Swedenhielm feels rehabilitated and can receive the prize. The success of this play prompted Bergman to dramatize three of his novels, most successfully *God's Orchid*, as a play called *Markurells of Wadköping* (1930, stage).

The posthumously published and performed *The Legend* (*Sagan*, 1942) reveals, as often with Bergman, the conflict between two families, that is, two ways of life, and is thematically akin to Alfred de Musset's proverb "There is no trifling with love" (*On ne badine pas avec l'amour*).

The late comedy *The Rabble* (*Patrasket*, 1928) according to Bergman himself is intended as a study of Jewish fantasy. It has a protagonist, Joe Meng, who as a dreamer cannot get his ideas to harmonize with reality. In addition to radio plays, Bergman has written a number of film scripts, assembled posthumously in *Film* (1940).

[*See also* Sweden]

SELECT PLAYS: *Parisina* (1915); *Death's Harlequin* (*Dödens Arlekin*, 1917); *Mr. Sleeman Is Coming* (*Herr Sleeman kommer*, 1917); *A Shadow* (*En skugga*, 1917); *The Gambling House* (*Spelhuset*, 1923); *The Portal* (*Porten*, 1923); *The Weaver of Baghdad* (*Vävaren i Bagdad*, 1923; 1936, Germany); *Swedenhielms* (1925); *The Rabble* (*Patrasket*, 1928); *Makurells of Wadköping* (1929, radio; 1930, stage); *The Baron's Will* (*Hans nåds testamente*, 1939; 1929, radio; 1931, stage); *The Legend* (*Sagan*, 1942)

FURTHER READING

Ek, Sverker R. "*Marionettspel*: En studie i Hjalmar Bergmans experimenterande dramatik" [Marionettes: A study of Hjalmar Bergman's experimental theater]. In *Kring Hjalmar Bergman* [Around Hjalmar Bergman], ed. by Sverker R. Ek. Stockholm: Wahlström & Widstrand, 1965. 142–184.

Linder, Erik Hjalmar. *Hjalmar Bergman*. Tr. Catherine Djurklou. Boston: Twayne, 1975.

Sprinchorn, Evert. "Hjalmar Bergman." *Tulane Drama Review* 6, no. 2 (1961).

Törnqvist, Egil. "Hjalmar Bergman: *Herr Sleeman kommer* (1917)" [Mr. Sleeman is coming]. In *Svenska dramastrukturer* [Swedish drama structures]. Stockholm: Prisma, 1973. 58–84.

Wirmark, Margareta. *Spelhuset: En monografi över Hjalmar Bergmans drama* [The gambling house: A monograph on Hjalmar Bergman's drama]. Stockholm: Raben & Sjögren, 1971 [English summary, 208–213].

Egil Törnqvist

BERGMAN, INGMAR (1918–)

My films are only a distillation of what I do in the theater.
—Ingmar Bergman

World famous for numerous films and stage productions, Ingmar Bergman actually started out as a dramatist. It was Bergman's contact with amateur theater groups that first stimulated him to write for the stage. In 1942 he directed his own *The Death of Punch* (*Kaspers död*). Kasper leaves his wife for a life of debauchery when death suddenly overcomes him. This early play already demonstrates an affinity with PÄR LAGERKVIST's metaphysical anguish, HJALMAR BERGMAN's view of mankind as marionettes pulled by unseen strings, and AUGUST STRINDBERG's view of life as an inferno. In 1948 he published the three *Morality Plays* (*Moraliteter*) he had earlier staged. The first, *Rachel and the Cinema Doorman* (*Rakel och biografvaktmästaren*) was later used for one of the episodes in his film *Secrets of Women* (*Kvinnors väntan*). The second, *The Day Ends Early* (*Dagen slutar tidigt*), about an old lady who has heard a voice ordering her to tell five people that they are to die the following day, is thematically akin to Bergman's film *The Seventh Seal* (*Det sjunde inseglet*). The third, *To My Terror . . .* (*Mig till skräck . . .*), is a discussion drama with two mythic figures representing contrary moral forces within the protagonist. Closer to the medieval morality play than these dramas is *Wood Painting* (*Trämålning*, 1954), written as a dramatic exercise for Bergman's students at the Malmö City Theater. A theatrical counterpart of the church murals found in medieval Swedish churches, the playlet anticipates *The Seventh Seal*. The central character and Bergman's alter ego in *The City* (*Staden*, 1951), written for the radio, is called Joakim Naken. The second name, meaning "naked," suggests an unmasked person and is an early example of Bergman's perennial concern with the mask-face dichotomy.

In recent years Bergman has again devoted himself to playwriting. His radio play *A Matter of the Soul* (*En själslig angelägenhet*, 1992), a portrait of a woman in which dream and reality come together, won the jury's special Prix Italia. The scripts in *The Fifth Act* (*Femte akten*), Bergman says, "were written without any thought of presentational medium." *After the Rehearsal* (*Efter repetitionen*, 1984), seen on television, deals with an aging director's memory of his relationship to an actress, now dead, who is the mother of the young actress he is presently in love with. It vivifies the enduring Bergmanian theme of art versus life and the intermingling of stage roles and life roles.

In the Presence of a Clown (*Larmar och gör sig till*, 1997), broadcast on television, is in part a sequel to Bergman's film *Winter Light* (*Nattvardsgästerna*). Bergman here in the character of Carl combines an inventive and artistic life with an ambivalent attitude toward death, the sexually ambiguous Rigmor, a compound of "rigor mortis" and the Swedish word for "mother," *mor*. The original title of the play, literally meaning "struts and frets," is a quotation from the Swedish translation of Macbeth's tomorrow soliloquy. A television production, titled *Saraband*, a follow-up of *Scenes from a Marriage* (*Scener ur ett äktenskap*, 1973), appeared in 2003.

[*See also* Sweden]

SELECT PLAYS: *Jack Among the Actors* (*Jack hos skådespelarna*, 1946); *The Day Ends Early* (*Dagen slutar tidigt*, 1948); *Rachel and the Cinema Doorman* (*Rakel och biografvaktmästaren*, 1948); *To My Terror . . .* (*Mig till skräck . . .*, 1948); *The City* (*Staden*, 1951; 1951, radio; 1955, stage); *Wood Painting* (*Trämålning*, 1954, radio; 1955, stage; 1955, tr. by Randolph Goodman and Leif Sjöberg, *Tulane Drama Review* 6 [1961]); *After the Rehearsal* (*Efter repetitionen*, 1984, TV); *A Matter of the Soul* (*En själslig angelägenhet*, 1992; 1990, radio; tr. by Gunilla Anderman, 1992); *In the Presence of a Clown* (*Larmar och gör sig till*, 1997, TV)

FURTHER READING

Gado, Frank. *The Passion of Ingmar Bergman*. Durham, N.C.: Duke Univ. Press, 1986.

Marker, Lise-Lone, and Frederick J. Marker. *Ingmar Bergman: A Life in the Theatre*. Cambridge: Cambridge Univ. Press, 1992.

Sjöman, Vilgot. *L 136: A Diary with Ingmar Bergman*. Tr. by Alan Blair. Ann Arbor: Karoma, 1978.

Steene, Birgitta. *Ingmar Bergman*. Boston: Twayne, 1968.

Törnqvist, Egil. *Between Stage and Screen: Ingmar Bergman Directs*. Amsterdam: Amsterdam Univ. Press, 1995.

Egil Törnqvist

BERMAN, SABINA (1953–)

I find in theatre the experience of freedom, of escaping a personal destiny and assuming many destinies, and I am able to play.
—Sabina Berman

Sabina Berman, a playwright of Polish Jewish descent, is also a novelist, a poet, and a film director who has had both commercial and critical success. Her plays fill theaters to capacity throughout Latin America, and scholars all over the United States study them diligently.

Berman got hooked on the theater while studying psychology at the Universidad Iberoamericana. She started her theatrical career in 1974 by acting in and directing *Butterfly* (*Mariposa*). In 1985, several of her first plays—*The Torture of Pleasure* (*El suplicio del placer*, 1976), *Yankee* (1979), *Conundrums* (*Rompecabezas*, 1981), *Heresy* (*Herejía*, 1983), and *Eagle or Sun* (*Aguila o sol*, 1984)—were published in a volume titled *Theater of Sabrina Berman* (*Teatro de Sabina Berman*). The last three are based on historical events. *Eagle or Sun* examines the conquest and grants La Malinche the power to create and recreate through translation. *Heresy*, a play about colonial Mexico and the Inquisition, depicts a gentile who profits handsomely by assuming a Jewish identity, but his impersonation costs him his life. *Conundrums* stages two different versions of Leon Trotsky's death to challenge the notion of a true history. She has also published *Sudden Death* (*Muerte súbita*, 1988), *The Crack* (*La grieta*, 1990), *Krisis* (1996), *Between Villa and a Woman Undresses* (*Entre villa y una mujer desnuda*, 1993), *Molière* (2000), and *Happy New Century, Doctor Freud* (*Feliz nuevo siglo, doktor Freud*, 2001). Her plays are the direct result of her keen observations of male/female relationships as well as of a well-grounded knowledge of dramatic literature and scholarship. Her goal is to obliterate patriarchal stereotypes by obfuscating gender difference, challenging long-held historical truths, and testing fixed notions of identity.

She has received Mexico's coveted National Award for Theatre four times. Award-winning plays include: *Yankee*, *Conundrums*, *The Wonderful History of the Pingüica Boy* (*La maravillosa historia de niño pingüica*, 1982), and *Heresy*. In 1986, *The Smoke Tree* (*El árbol de humo*) won the Celestino Gorostiza Award for Children's Theatre.

Berman has also authored movie, television, and dance scripts. In 1979, she received the Ariel Award (Mexico's equivalent of the Oscar) for the year's best movie script, *Aunt Alejandra* (*Tía Alejandra*), co-authored with Delfina Careaga. The film version of her play *Between Villa* won the audience award at the Guadalajara Film Festival and earned Jesús Ochoa an Ariel for Best Supporting Actor for his performance of Villa. Also in 1995, her short film *The Music Tree* (*El árbol de la música*) was chosen as Mexico's submission to the Latin American Children's Film Festival.

Berman's dance scripts *One Moon One* (*Una luna una*) and *Neither Doors nor Windows* (*Ni puertas ni ventanas*) were staged in 1987 with noted success. Her poetic production includes two volumes: *Water Poems* (*Poemas de agua*, 1987) and *Moons* (*Lunas*, 1988). In 1990 she published her first novel, *Bubbeh* (*La bobe*, 1990), a recollection of her childhood memories and Judaic family traditions. Her short stories have been collected in *A Grain of Rice* (*Un grano de arroz*, 1994). Her most recent novel, *Lover of Other's Possessions* (*Amante de lo ajeno*, 1997), returns to the topic of homosexuality, addressed earlier in *The Torture of Pleasure* and in *Moons*.

In 2000, Berman was awarded the Premio Nacional María Lavalle Urbina, which named her woman of the year for her literary work and for her role as a public intellectual who takes up issues of sex and gender in Mexico. Thus, her productivity, her creativity, and her commitment to social change have earned her a well-deserved national and international reputation.

[*See also* Mexico]

PLAYS: *The Garden of Delights, or The Torture of Pleasure* (*El jardín de las delicias or El suplicio del placer*, 1976); *Bill or Yankee* (1979); *A Good Worker of Piolet or Conundrums* (*Un buen trabajador de piolet or rompecabezas*, 1981); *The Wonderful History of the Pingüica Boy* (*La marvillosa historia del niño pingüica*, 1982); *Anathema or Heresy* (*Anatema or herejía*, 1983); *Sudden Death* (*Muerte súbita*, 1988); *The Crack* (*La grieta*, 1990); *The Cultured War* (*La guerra culta*, 1991); *The Thieves of Time* (*Los ladrones del tempo*, 1991); *Between Villa and a Woman Undresses* (*Entre villa y una mujer desnuda*, 1993); *The Smoke Tree* (*El árbol de humo*, 1993); *Krisis* (1996); *Molière* (2000); *Happy New Century, Doctor Freud* (*Feliz nuevo siglo, doktor Freud*, 2001)

FURTHER READING

A'Ness, Francine. "Diálogo con Sabina Berman." *Sediciosas seducciones: sexo, poder y palabras en el teatro de Sabina Berman* [Seditious seductions: Sex, power and words in Sabina Berman's theater]. Ed. Jacqueline E. Bixler. Mexico City: Escenologia, 2004.

Bixler, Jacqueline Eyring. "The Postmodernization of History in the Theatre of Sabina Berman." *Latin American Theatre Review* 30, no. 2 (Spring 1997): 45–60.

——. "Power Plays and the Mexican Crisis: The Recent Theatre of Sabina Berman." In *Performance, pathos, política de los sexos: Teatro postcolonial de autoras latinoamericanas* [Performance, pathos, politics of the sexes: Postcolonial theater of Latin American authors], ed. by Heidrun Adler. Madrid: Vervuert-Iberoamericana, 1999. 83–99.

Burgess, Ronald D. "Sabina Berman's Undone Threads." In *Latin American Women Dramatists: Theater, Texts, and Theories*, ed. by Catherine Larson and Margarita Vargas. Bloomington: Indiana Univ. Press, 1998. 145–158.

Gladhart, Amalia. "Playing Gender." *Latin American Literary Review* 24, no. 47 (January–June 1996): 59–89.

Hind, Emily. "Entrevista con Sabina Berman" [Interview with Sabina Berman]. *Latin American Theatre Review* 33, no. 2 (Spring 2000): 133–139.

Magnarelli, Sharon. "Tea for Two: Performing History and Desire in Sabina Berman's *Entre Villa y una mujer desnuda*." *Latin American Theatre Review* 30, no. 1 (Fall 1996): 55–74.

Merithew, Charlene. "Berman, Sabina." http://www.hope.edu/latinamerican/berman.html.

Margarita Vargas

BERNHARD, THOMAS (1931–1989)

Thomas Bernhard was born on February 9, 1931, in Heerlen, Holland, the son of an unwed mother who went from her father's hometown in rural AUSTRIA to Holland to find a job and deliver her baby. Bernhard died in 1989, one year after the fiftieth anniversary of Austria's annexation to Adolf Hitler's Third Reich. Bernhard's development as a writer coincided with Austria's emergence from the devastation of World War II and its shameful involvement in the Holocaust. His works reflected, challenged, and in turn affected the process. Though deeply rooted in Austrian culture, Bernhard became his country's most ferocious critic. His contribution to the commemoration of the fiftieth anniversary of the Anschluss in 1988 was the play HELDENPLATZ, which turned out to be his last. Commissioned by CLAUS PEYMANN, the artistic director of the world-renowned Viennese Burgtheater at the time, *Heldenplatz* triggered an unprecedented nationwide political scandal months before its premiere. While Bernhard's literary career was marked by international acclaim, it was marred at home by public outrage over his unrelenting attacks on Austria's ongoing politics of denial and self-(re)construction following World War II. In his will, Bernhard expressly forbade the posthumous performance of his works in Austria for the duration of the legal copyright, but ten years after his death, his heirs lifted the ban.

EARLY CAREER PATHS

Bernhard's childhood experiences of the bombings of Salzburg and his infection with tuberculosis as an adolescent are arguably the two decisive events that shaped his obsession with death and disease as the leitmotif of his work, for which he was soon acknowledged as an heir to Franz Kafka (1883–1924) and SAMUEL BECKETT (1906–1989). Bernhard never finished high school. He chose to be a grocer's apprentice instead, while taking private singing lessons. His early training as an opera singer, though stopped short by lung disease, is reflected both in the musicality and the performative force of his language, in his plays as well as in his prose texts.

By his own account, his grandfather, novelist Johannes Freumbichler (1881–1949), was his most important teacher. He introduced Bernhard to the great writers and philosophers and became a model for his grandson's portrayals of older men driven by their idea of greatness and perfection.

Bernhard started out as a poet and journalist, before he studied acting and directing at Salzburg's renowned Mozarteum conservatory. After graduation, his brief association with Austria's AVANT-GARDE artists led him to write some short experimental librettos. His roman à clef *Woodcutting* (*Holzfällen*, 1984) is a scathing attack on his friends of that period, their early commitment to artistic and political integrity, and their subsequent compromises with local politics to assure funding, awards, and status.

Before Bernhard turned to writing full-length plays, he had already established himself as one of the most promising writers of the second half of the 20th century, owing to his major (and arguably best) prose texts, beginning with his breakthrough novel *Frost* in 1963, followed by *Amras* in 1964 and *Gargoyles* (*Verstörung*) in 1967. Early in his career he received several distinguished awards. His acceptance speeches often caused an uproar due to their criticism of contemporary politics, culture, and often the very institution honoring him.

Already in *Frost* he began to explore a language of performance rather than description, a language perfected in the DRAMATURGY of his later novels, such as *Concrete* (*Beton*, 1982), *The Loser* (*Der Untergeher*, 1983), *Old Masters* (*Alte Meister*, 1985), and *Extinction* (*Auslöschung*, 1986). Typically, Bernhard's novels feature a narrator who attempts to reconstruct a deceased person from his papers, remembered conversations, or gossip. In *Frost*, a student of medicine has been assigned to observe a mad painter. As he writes down his observations, he increasingly adopts the painter's fragmented language together with his vision ("picture") of an insanely moribund world. The process of writing is performative: the text contains the speech of another; writing becomes an enactment of the other.

Bernhard's next major narrative, *Amras*, chronicles the extinction of a family. Ostensibly written by one of the two sons who survived a family suicide pact, the text includes correspondence, journal entries, and notes by both brothers, compiled by one who documents and describes the other's road to suicide while his own mental deterioration is inscribed in the increasingly disjointed grammar of his writing. Syntax vividly connotes the performance of the mind. In that sense, all of Bernhard's texts are performance texts. Not surprisingly, he resisted the term "novel" for his longer prose narratives.

In *Gargoyles*, a country doctor and his visiting son, an engineering student, make the rounds among a bizarre array of patients in the mountainous, wooded hinterlands of Austria. Their last encounter is with a mad prince in the spectacular setting of his castle atop a steep cliff. In what amounts to a virtuoso solo performance, which basically makes up the second half of the book, the prince monologizes about disease and degeneration, a process that intimately intertwines human and natural history. His obsessive speech acts and philosophical fixations make him the forerunner of Bernhard's stage characters.

MAJOR THEMES

Bernhard's plays usually feature one dominant speaker and one or more quiet partners. Power relationships, the traditional stuff of drama, are no longer established by physical action—Bernhard's leading figures are often old or ill—but rather by the performative force of speech. Like the prince's title, language is inherited. It "speaks us." Like a theatrical text, language has been rehearsed to perfection, as it has been passed on through generations and refined in the daily rituals of familial interactions or professional training.

The play *The Ignoramus and the Madman* (*Der Ignorant und der Wahnsinnige*, 1972) features the blind father of an opera singer, a young doctor (her admirer), and the singer, introduced only as the Queen of the Night (the role she performs in Mozart's *The Magic Flute* [*Die Zauberflöte*, 1791)] while the other two are waiting in her dressing room). None of the characters are mentioned by name. They are defined only by their roles as the Father, the Young Doctor, and the Queen of the Night. The father keeps drinking, while the doctor alternately describes to him in minute detail the dissection of a corpse and the mechanism of a perfect performance as demonstrated by the singer, who rushes in from time to time in extreme agitation to change her costume. After the performance, she finally collapses in a restaurant. The perfect mechanism of her performative genius, stretched beyond its limits, breaks down when there is no more role to play, no more text to perform.

In *Force of Habit* (*Die Macht der Gewohnheit*, 1974), Caribaldi, the director of a small circus, rehearses Schubert's Trout Quintet with his troupe but is never able to get past the first few notes. Drawing on an old stand-up comedy routine, breaking off at the beginning also means that there is still something left to play. The rehearsals—that is, life—can go on.

In EVE OF RETIREMENT (*Vor dem Ruhestand*, 1979), Rudolf, a retiring judge and former Nazi concentration camp commander, annually celebrates Heinrich Himmler's (1900–1945) birthday with his two sisters. The ritual includes Rudolf's dressing up in his old SS uniform and putting his younger, anarchist sister, paralyzed as a child in an American bombing raid, in a camp inmate's uniform. As Rudolf and his older sister, Vera, nostalgically remember their parents' family values—which led them to embrace national socialism—the children also assert the perverted ideals in their own lives. Speech is reenactment. Its performative force carries the past into the present, where it continues to fester. In the words of the performance artist Laurie Anderson (b. 1947): "Language is a virus."

Bernhard's late play *Ritter, Dene, Voss* (1984) is inspired by the philosopher Ludwig Wittgenstein (1889–1951) and his two sisters. The title refers to the names of the actors for whom Bernhard wrote the play: Ilse Ritter (b. 1945), Kirsten Dene (b. 1943), and Gert Voss (b. 1941). Only Ludwig is introduced by name. He is a composite of the philosopher and his nephew Paul, a friend of Bernhard whom the author remembered in his quasi-autobiographical narrative *Wittgenstein's Nephew* (*Wittgensteins Neffe*, 1982). In *Ritter, Dene, Voss*, Ludwig's sisters are mediocre actresses. That is to say, they have not made a name for themselves. His older sister's speech is informed by their patrician family, by her brother whom she desires, and by the doctor in the mental institution, who takes care of Ludwig during his frequent stays there. The line between Ludwig's clinical insanity and his mad performance is blurred. Speaking the fool's language, he is the only one who can effectively disrupt and thereby threaten family tradition. His linguistic power is grotesquely visualized in his wildly wolfing down the famous Viennese pastry his sister has baked from an old family recipe. Stuffing many pieces at once into his mouth, he nearly chokes to death. The act is suicidal on the linguistic level as well: stopping his speech. The philosopher has thus performed his own (Ludwig Wittgenstein's) famous dictum "Whereof one cannot speak, thereof one must be silent" to its absurdly logical end.

Bernhard's last play, *Heldenplatz*, demonstrates the intricate, hidden processes by which the language of the persecutor is iterated by the persecuted and passed on from master to servant.

Bernhard's stage characters do not only quote at length the persons they love, admire, or hate. Quite often they quote themselves, which makes for the many repetitions and variations so characteristic of his work. Cutting the works for production, which is frequently done, not only disrupts the tightly composed rhythmical structure of his plays but also eliminates an essential aspect of his approach to the construction of identity through the performative force of language. His characters do not reveal themselves in action according to the Aristotelean model; they are always shown in the often tedious process of constructing themselves through language. They hold on to their speech habits as to scaffolding they have constructed around themselves—until the structure collapses. Emotional responses are embedded in grammar. Identity asserts itself only in the iteration of speech. In Bernhard's view, people cling to the gestures and poses of high culture, even though that culture has already destroyed itself through two world wars. In his memoirs (published in five volumes in German [*An Indication of the Cause* (*Die Ursache*, 1975), *The Cellar* (*Der Keller*, 1976), *Breath* (*Der Atem*, 1978), *In the Cold* (*Die Kälte*, 1981), and *A Child* (*Ein Kind*, 1982)] and as one, *Gathering Evidence*, in English), Bernhard remembers his early experience in a tuberculosis ward, where patients are suspended on drips like marionettes. The image informs his vision of contemporary society as consisting of puppets dangling on the strings of language.

Skepticism and critical vigilance toward language and its many abuses have a long tradition in Austrian literature and can be found in abundance in the comedies of Johann Nestroy (1801–1862). Nestroy was a favorite of Ludwig Wittgenstein, who, in turn, had a significant impact on post–World War II Austrian writers from Ingeborg Bachmann (1926–1973) to PETER HANDKE (b. 1942) and ELFRIEDE JELINEK (b. 1946).

In his play KASPAR, Handke also uses the theater as a model for the mechanisms underlying the construction of identity. While Bernhard begins near the end, as it were, when that mechanism is about to break down, Handke starts at the beginning, with the acquisition of language. A chorus of prompters drills Kaspar in media speak. Jelinek goes even further in her ferocious attacks on the abuse of language. In her later plays, she sets up blocks of text that are no longer assigned to individual speakers. They are composites of quotes that track the long, intricate chain of linguistic contamination from the German classics perverted into Nazi propaganda and further subverted and abused in contemporary culture and politics. Jelinek leaves it up to her directors to assign individual actors or choruses to the textual passages, thus implicating them in the process she set up. The director's identity manifests itself in the arrangement and rearrangement of preexisting texts.

Bernhard, however, wrote for specific performers. To him life itself was a performance act against death. The characters he created for the few actors he admired were all accomplished self-performers. In Bernhard's ongoing battle against lung disease, he himself became the supreme self-performer as a "survival artist." In his collisions with the Austrian government and the public, which felt itself attacked without having read his books or seen his productions, he took on the role of the Shakespearean fool.

Bernhard's career as a playwright is intricately linked to the director CLAUS PEYMANN, who staged the acclaimed premiere of Bernhard's first full-length play, *A Party for Boris* (*Ein Fest für Boris* 1970), at the renowned Hamburg Schauspielhaus in 1970. As artistic director of the major theaters in Stuttgart and Bochum and Vienna's Burgtheater, Peymann produced and directed the world premieres of most of Bernhard's plays. Together with the set designer Karl-Ernst Herrmann, Peymann developed an aesthetic that was considered definitive during Bernhard's lifetime: expansive rooms with elongated walls, doors, and windows together with a few select pieces of furniture reflected the cultural context and perception of the main character, who usually is driven by one obsessive vision that excludes the perspectives of others.

The reception of Bernhard's plays in the German-language press was usually mixed. Given such contexts as the aftermath of the Holocaust, the division of GERMANY, the Cold War, and student rebellions in the 1960s, some critics missed a political perspective. Others resisted the wordiness and repetitiousness. Bernhard's supporters, meanwhile, praised the power and musicality of his language and his portrayal of single-minded, authoritarian figures as the last representatives of a dying patriarchy.

As was the case with Kafka and Beckett, it took some time before Bernhard's humor was acknowledged amid the essential darkness of his vision. His sense of COMEDY asserts itself most strongly in his late prose texts, which at times are reminiscent of stand-up routines. Elfriede Jelinek imagines him standing at a typewriter, speaking—that is, performing his prose texts as he types them. The narrator writes in a speaking voice, watching himself in the act of writing or, as in *Concrete*, putting off the act of writing a study of the composer Felix Mendelssohn-Bartholdy (1809–1847). The procrastination becomes a hilarious performance act, which then becomes the subject of his writing, leading him to a completely different, tragic story about the death of a young woman.

Following Bernhard's death on February 12, 1989, in Gmunden, Austria, the theatrical thrust of his prose texts was discovered for the stage. Hermann Beil (b. 1941), Claus Peymann's longtime dramaturgical collaborator and co-artistic director, adapted *Wittgenstein's Nephew*, *Concrete*, *Woodcutting*, and *The Voice Imitator* (*Der Stimmenimitator*, 1978) as solo performance texts, some of which Beil himself performs. They are most frequently presented at the Berliner Ensemble, where Peymann became artistic director in 1999. *Old Masters* has been adapted into different, more conventional French and German dramatizations.

Ironically, while Bernhard's plays are generally considered secondary to his major literary accomplishments as a novelist, his major prose texts are intrinsically more theatrical than his stage works. His plays exploiting the theatrical mechanism to magnify the mechanism of human existence tempt directors to indulge in absurd abstractions at the expense of the behavioral REALISM underlying Bernhard's exaggerations. At the same time, adopting a psychological approach to underplay the hyperbole destroys the theatricality, which is central to Bernhard's understanding of the art of survival.

Some of Bernhard's best plays were written and originally produced in response to a specific place and/or time, such as the Salzburg Festival (*The Ignoramus and the Madman*, 1972; *Force of Habit*, 1974; and *Arrived* [*Am Ziel*, 1981]), the postwar employment of former Nazis in the highest government positions (*Eve of Retirement*), or the anniversary of Hitler's triumphant arrival in Vienna (*Heldenplatz*). When performed, Bernhard's plays are dependent not only on an understanding of the cultural and political contexts that generated them but, in some instances, also on the immediacy of the audience's shared experiences of those very contexts at the moment of production.

SELECT PLAYS: *A Party for Boris* (*Ein Fest für Boris*, 1970); *The Ignoramus and the Madman* (*Der Ignorant und der Wahnsinnige*, 1972); *Force of Habit* (*Die Macht der Gewohnheit*, 1974); *The Hunting Party* (*Die Jagdgesellschaft*, 1974); *The President* (*Der Präsident*, 1975); *The Famous* (*Die Berühmten*, 1976); *Minetti* (1976); *The German Lunch Table* (*Der deutsche Mittagstisch*, 1978); *Immanuel Kant* (1978); *Eve of Retirement* (*Vor dem Ruhestand*, 1979); *Arrived* (*Am Ziel*, 1981); *Over All the Mountain Tops* (*Über allen Gipfeln ist Ruh*, 1981); *Appearances Are Deceiving* (*Der Schein trügt*, 1983); *Histrionis* (*Der Theatermache*, 1984); *Ritter, Dene, Voss* (1984); *Claus Peymann Buys Himself a Pair of Pants and Takes Me to Lunch* (*Claus Peymann kauft sich eine Hose und geht mit mir essen*, 1986); *Simply Complicated* (*Einfach kompliziert*, 1986); *Claus Peymann and Hermann Beil on Sulzwiese* (*Claus Peymann und Hermann Beil auf der Sulzwiese*, 1987); *Elisabeth II* (1987); *Heldenplatz* (1988)

FURTHER READING

Dittmar, Jens. *Thomas Bernhard: Werkgeschichte* [A history of his works]. Frankfurt am Main: Suhrkamp, 1990.

Höller, Hans. *Thomas Bernhard*. Reinbek bei Hamburg: Rowohlt, 1994.

Honegger, Gitta. *Thomas Bernhard: The Making of an Austrian*. New Haven, Conn.: Yale Univ. Press, 2001.

Huguet, Louis. *Chronologie. Johannes Freumbichler/Thomas Bernhard* [A chronology: Johannes Freumbichler/Thomas Bernhard]. Weitra: Bibliothek der Provinz, 1995.

Konzett, Matthias, ed. *A Companion to the Works of Thomas Bernhard*. Rochester, N.Y.: Camden House, 2002.

Gitta Honegger

DER BESUCH DER ALTEN DAME

See THE VISIT OF THE OLD LADY

BETRAYAL

I mean, just because my name is Downs and your name is Downs doesn't mean that we're the Mr. and Mrs. Downs that they, in their laughing Mediterranean way, assume we are. We could be, and in fact are vastly more likely to be, total strangers.

—Robert to Emma, Act 2

HAROLD PINTER's innovative and realistic character play *Betrayal* was first produced at the National Theatre, London, in November 1978. Critical reception of Peter Hall's stage debut of *Betrayal* in both London and New York was mixed. Objections were directed to the play's regress to REALISM and the conventional love triangle; praise centered on Pinter's novel framework of reversed time sequences and the play's sparse, understated dialogue, which produced forced emotional restraint.

Perhaps Pinter's most accessible play, *Betrayal* centers on a conventional love triangle involving three young, middle-class friends: Robert, a Prufrockian book publisher; Emma, Robert's lovely but restless wife; and Jerry, Robert's best friend and publishing colleague. The first of *Betrayal*'s nine scenes takes place in 1977: a meeting between Jerry and Emma two years after their affair has ended. The following scenes largely move backward in time to the very moment when the triangle of deceit begins in 1968. This reverse time strategy portrays the long friendship between Robert and Jerry, the hideaway apartment used by Jerry and Emma to carry on their afternoon trysts, parties between the two families, and the climatic moment when Robert discovers his wife's infidelity, two years before the affair ends.

Structurally and thematically, the central scene is scene 5, in which Robert finally wrests the truth about the affair from Emma. He has found an Ibsenesque surprise letter to Emma from Jerry. But Pinter treats Robert's absurd reaction not as HENRIK IBSEN might have but more in the manner of EUGÈNE IONESCO in THE BALD SOPRANO: "I mean, just because my name is Downs and your name is Downs doesn't mean that we're the Mr. and Mrs. Downs that they . . . assume we are." Robert, who, surprisingly, shows no outrage at Emma's affair, offers his implied consent, both when he discovers the tryst and years earlier, when the affair begins. It is the problematic sublimation of emotion and passion onstage that seizes or troubles audiences. There are no emotional outbursts or denunciations. Emotion is practically silenced. These are characters without passion and rage. One expects vituperative outbursts on the order of those in EDWARD ALBEE's *WHO'S AFRAID OF VIRGINIA WOOLF*, but *Betrayal*'s verbal exchanges are misleadingly polite. These various scenes paint a picture of friendship and love changed by the rough edge of duplicity.

A Pinteresque light verbal mist in the form of half-statements and vague implications, reminiscent of SAMUEL BECKETT's indirectness, fogs the stage, carefully veiling the characters' motivations from direct view. It seems that all the characters and their spouses are engaged in secret affairs: Robert, Jerry's wife Judith, and Emma are keeping secret liaisons. The proliferation of affairs spreads to the audience. While the act of betrayal in the play involves romantic liaisons, Pinter has in mind a broader pattern of deceit. He centers the notion of betrayal on the friendship of the two men, involving their male bonding and thwarted ideals from their college years.

In typically Pinteresque fashion, the friendship between the two men continues, while Emma's marriage to Robert ends. A fresh treatment of the female role allows Emma, like Ibsen's Nora, to shed her primary role as wife and love object and to pursue instead her work as the owner of an art gallery. In the present time of the first scene, Emma has moved on to a new life, while Robert and Jerry have returned to their old friendship and betrayed principles.

What makes this play unique in Pinter's oeuvre is clearly its reversed time sequence. The backward progress, which amplifies the Proustian notion that memory is degraded by time, allows Pinter to reveal carefully scripted, fragmented tableaux of the affair rather than to present fluid linear, forward action in time. Each of the nine vignettes is a study of emotional emptiness, psychological bewilderment, and loss. Jerry, in particular, has flawed memories of the events of the affair. *Betrayal* is richly clothed in autobiographical garments from Pinter's own seven-year affair.

Betrayal, from Pinter's middle playwriting period, represents a stylistic shift back to the sharper camera lens of realism and away from the blurred images of the earlier THE BIRTHDAY PARTY and HOMECOMING with their AVANT-GARDE sense of inexplicable menace, gaps in characters' backgrounds and motivations, and mysterious causality. *Betrayal*'s counterclockwise motion adds an important dimension to the recognized Pinteresque convention of challenging how memory creates, recreates, and often falsifies one's sense of the past and existence. Marcel Proust's exploration of time and memory in *Remembrance of Things Past (À la recherche des temps perdu)* directly influences this play.

[*See also* England]

FURTHER READING

Billington, Michael. *The Life and Work of Harold Pinter*. London: Faber, 1996.

Esslin, Martin. *The Peopled Wound: The Work of Harold Pinter*. Garden City, N.Y.: Doubleday, 1970.

——. *Pinter: The Playwright*. 4th ed. London: Methuen, 1984.

Sakellaridou, Elizabeth. *Pinter's Female Portraits*. London: Macmillan, 1988.

Michael D. Sollars

BETSUYAKU MINORU (1937–)

Betsuyaku Minoru, a Japanese playwright, was born in 1937 and raised in Manchuria. He experienced the privations of war and his father's death. In 1946 he was repatriated with his mother and siblings to Japan and a bleak postwar existence. He entered Waseda University in 1958 to study journalism but instead was caught up in its hotbed of theater studies and the leftist political ferment of the counterculture, including the nationwide demonstrations against the renewal of the U.S.–Japan Mutual Security Treaty in 1960. He was so intensely involved that when the demonstrations failed and the treaty was renewed, he dropped out of Waseda and focused his political fervor on opposing the establishment of a missile base on an island near Tokyo. This commitment generated a life-changing experience: living among the island's farmers, he saw firsthand that standard Marxist class-conflict rhetoric had no impact on their lives. Betsuyaku shaped his idea of theater accordingly, eschewing ideology for unrestricted expression.

Remaining close to his former Waseda classmates, director SUZUKI TADASHI and actor Ono Seki, Betsuyaku wrote THE ELEPHANT (Zō) in 1962, the first play for their troupe Free Stage (Jiyū Butai). It was his first major success and became the young company's signature work. Betsuyaku continued to work with Suzuki and Ono, and in 1966 the three founded the influential Waseda Little Theater (Waseda Shōgekijō). By 1968, however, Betsuyaku, a playwright grounded in the sanctity of words, found himself at odds with Suzuki, a director given to reducing the primacy of text. Betsuyaku became independent, wrote prolifically (nearly a hundred plays), and garnered widespread recognition, including the prestigious Kishida Kunio Drama Prize for *The Little Match Girl* (*Matchi-uri no Shōjo*, 1966) and *Landscape with Red Bird* (*Akai Tori no Iru Fūkei*, 1967) in 1967. He is one of the most prominent playwrights to emerge from the Japanese counterculture of the 1960s.

Given the disruption and hardship of Betsuyaku's upbringing and postwar Japan's headlong drive toward economic success, it is hardly surprising that his plays often embody the ubiquitous theme of contemporary Japanese theater: coming to terms with personal and national identity. Reflecting that challenge, his characters are nameless types: Father, Mother, Soldier 1, Soldier 2, Man, Woman. He found in absurdist theater—he has acknowledged SAMUEL BECKETT's influence—techniques congenial to his stage vision. Like Beckett's plays, Betsuyaku's are spare, his stage mostly bare but for a trademark focal point of a tree, a telephone pole, or bus stop standard—features reminiscent of Beckett's barren tree in WAITING FOR GODOT. A telephone pole or bus stop may imply human connection, but his characters—often juxtaposed, like Vladimir and Estragon, in symbiotic pairs—valiantly try yet invariably fail to communicate; as in *Godot*, the bus never arrives. Identity remains elusive.

Unlike his contemporaries, Betsuyaku does not write exercises in exuberant theatricality but, rather, plays characterized by silence, subtle exchanges, and quiescence. These qualities constitute the touchstones of his dramatic tension and, ironically, reveal the tortured intensity of his characters' feelings. Betsuyaku's genius leaps out here, his sensual, unremarkable language penetrating the quotidian so unremittingly as to transcend it and raise the particular to universal proportions.

[*See also* Angura and Shōgekijō; Japan; Shingeki]

SELECT PLAYS: *The Elephant* (*Zō*, 1962); *The Little Match Girl* (*Matchi-uri no Shōjo*, 1966); *Landscape with Red Bird* (*Akai Tori no Iru Fūkei*, 1967); *I Am Alice* (*Ai Amu Arisu*, 1970); *The Move* (*Idō*, 1971); *The Legend of Noon* (*Shōgo no Densetsu*, 1973); *Bubbling and Boiling* (*Aabukutatta, Niitatta*, 1976); *Thirty Days Hath September* (*Ni Shi Mu Ku Samurai*, 1977); *Water-Bloated Corpse* (*Umi Yukaba Mizuku Kabane*, 1978); *The Cherry in Bloom* (*Ki ni Hana Saku*, 1980); *Red Elegy* (*Sekishoku erejii*, 1980); *The Snow Falls on Tarō's Roof* (*Tarō no Yane ni Yuki Furitsumu*, 1982); *The Incident of the Salad Murder* (*Sarada Satsujin Jiken*, 1986); *Letters from the Wildcat—The Legend of Iihatōbo* (*Yamaneko kara no Tegami—Iihatōbo Densetsu*, 1990)

FURTHER READING

Betsuyaku Minoru. *The Story of the Two Knights Travelling Around the Country* [Shokoku o Henrekisuru Futari no Kishi no Monogatari]. Tr. by Yuasa Masako. Leeds, England: Alumnus, 1990.

Goodman, David G., tr. *After Apocalypse: Four Japanese Plays of Hiroshima and Nagasaki*. New York: Columbia Univ. Press, 1986.

Ozasa, Yoshio. *Dōjidai Engeki to Gekisakkatachi* [Contemporary plays and playwrights]. Tokyo: Gekishobō, 1980.

Rolf, Robert T., and John K. Gillespie, trs. and eds. *Alternative Japanese Drama: Ten Plays*. Honolulu: Univ. of Hawaii Press, 1992.

Senda, Akihiko. *The Voyage of Contemporary Japanese Theatre* [Gendai Engeki no Kōkai]. Tr. by J. Thomas Rimer. Honolulu: Univ. of Hawaii Press, 1997.

Takaya, Ted T., tr. *Modern Japanese Drama: An Anthology*. New York: Columbia Univ. Press, 1979.

John K. Gillespie

BETTI, UGO (1892–1953)

Ugo Betti, the Italian playwright, short-story writer, and poet, was born in Camerino, Marche, on February 4, 1892. In 1901 his family moved to Parma. In 1914 he graduated with a doctorate in law; the year after, convinced that war would bring about socialism in ITALY he volunteered, distinguishing himself for the bravery that won him a medal before he was captured. He remained a prisoner until the armistice, after which he embraced pacifism.

In 1923, the year he became a judge, he published *The Thoughtful King* (*Il re pensieroso*), the first of his four books of poetry. In 1925 he composed *The Mistress of the House* (*La padrona*), the first of his twenty-five plays; in 1928 he published *Cane* (*Caino*), the first of his three story collections. In 1930 he married and transferred to Rome, where in 1950 he was nominated to the court of appeals.

Meanwhile, he pursued his true vocation as a playwright: his work was considered second only to LUIGI PIRANDELLO's in the Italian drama of the first half of the 20th century. In 1953, with the Paris production of his masterpiece *Crime on Goat Island* (*Delitto all'Isola delle capre*, 1946), he achieved worldwide fame. He died on June 9, learning of his acclaim on his deathbed.

Betti's best plays remind some critics of the world of HENRIK IBSEN, Luigi Pirandello, and Franz Kafka. Although his muse is at times hindered by his mannered rhetoric, in his more successful plays he convincingly dramatizes a relentless interrogation of a seemingly bottomless self and struggles "to understand," as he wrote in the preface to *The Mistress of the House*, "the tremendous, bewildering incongruity that we see between our existence and what it ought to be according to our soul's aspiration, to understand why life is the marvelous tranquil iniquity that it is . . . the tortuous roots" of every human act "swallowed by the shadow." This statement epitomizes Betti's theater.

Eight of Betti's plays take the form of a legal investigation, the most famous being *Landslide* (*Frana allo Scalo Nord*, 1932), *Corruption in the Palace of Justice* (*Corruzione al Palazzo di Giustizia*, 1945), and *The Inquiry* (*Ispezione*, 1946). In some others the investigation is sparked by the arrival of a stranger, as in *Crime on Goat Island*, or by the protagonist's quest for self-discovery, as in *Struggle Till Dawn* (*Lotta fino all'alba*, 1947) and in THE QUEEN AND THE REBELS (*La Regina e gli Insorti*, 1949). The purpose of the investigation is not uncovering facts but rather excavating the individual psyche: the revelation, as in *Corruption in the Palace of Justice*, of a collective consciousness of shared guilt; or, as in *The Inquiry*, the indictment of such obvious social myths as respectability, success, and familial and romantic love. Some of Betti's protagonists achieve salvation through pity (*Landslide*) or through their acceptance of punishment (*Corruption in the Palace of Justice*). Some remain in an anguished and lonely state of being (*The Fugitive* [*La fuggitiva*, 1953] and *A Night in the Rich Man's House* [*Notte in casa del ricco*, 1938]). Others reach freedom and dignity only through suicide (*Innocent Irene* [*Irene innocente*, 1947] and *The Queen and the Rebels*).

PLAYS: *The Mistress of the House* (*La padrona*, 1924); *An Inn on the Harbor* (*Un albergo sul porto*, 1930); *Landslide* (*Frana allo Scalo Nord*, 1932); *Summertime* (*Il paese delle vacanze*, 1937); *A Night in the Rich Man's House* (*Notte in casa del ricco*, 1938); *The Night Wind* (*Il vento notturno*, 1941); *Husband and Wife* (*Marito e moglie*, 1943); *Corruption in the Palace of Justice* (*Corruzione al Palazzo di Giustizia*, 1945); *Crime on Goat Island* (*Delitto all'Isola delle capre*, 1946); *The Inquiry* (*Ispezione*, 1946); *Innocent Irene* (*Irene innocente*, 1947); *The Queen and the Rebels* (*La Regina e gli Insorti*, 1949); *The Gambler* (*Il giocatore*, 1950); *The Burnt Flower-Bed* (*L'aiuola bruciata*, 1952); *The Fugitive* (*La fuggitiva*, 1953)

FURTHER READING

Arnett, Lloyd A. "Tragedy in a Postmodern Vein: Ugo Betti Our Contemporary?" *Modern Drama* 33 (December 1990): 543–552.

Licastro, Emanuele. *Ugo Betti, an Introduction*. Jefferson, N.C.: McFarland, 1985.

McWilliam, G. B. "Interpreting Betti." *Tulane Drama Review* 5 (December 1960): 15–23.

Rizzo, Gino. "Regression-Progression in Ugo Betti's Drama." *Tulane Drama Review* 8 (Fall 1963): 101–129.

"Ugo Betti: Essays, Correspondence, Notes." Tr. by William Meriwether and Gino Rizzo. *Tulane Drama Review* 8 (Spring 1964): 51–86.

Usmiani, Renate. "The 'Felix Culpa' Motif in the Drama of Ugo Betti." *Humanities Association of Canada Bulletin* 21 (Winter 1970): 39–44.

Emanuele Licastro

BEYOND HUMAN POWER

Answer me in front of God—try your last, most fragile belief and answer me: is it the miracle, what we have experienced here?
—Elias, Act 2

Beyond Human Power (*Over Ævne. Andet Stykke*) had its premiere in Paris in 1894 and in Norway and Denmark in 1899. It is one of BJØRNSTJERNE BJØRNSON's strangest plays. An important context of the play is discussions Bjørnson started in 1876 about Christianity and its role in modern society. Earlier Bjørnson had been a strong advocate of the teachings of N. F. S. Grundtvig (1783–1872), a Danish poet, political activist, and liberal theologian, who sought to give each congregation its own authority. But during the 1870s Bjørnson studied the writings of Charles Darwin, Herbert Spencer, and John Stuart Mill and grew more critical of Christianity and the clergy.

The drama is situated in a Nordland fjord landscape. The idealistic "miracle vicar" Adolf Sang has called home his two children. He wants them to join him in a "prayer chain," in order to heal his wife. She is the only person he has not managed to cure through prayer and the laying on of hands. It turns out that the children no longer share their father's belief. Sang starts to pray and sing alone in the church that lies next to their home, while hundreds of people gather outside, waiting for a miracle. A group of clergymen use the vicarage living room to discuss how they should react to a possible miracle. In the end Sang's prayers seem to be granted: Klara rises and walks toward her husband—but then she falls down and dies. Adolf Sang utters the words: "But this wasn't the intention . . . Or?"—and he dies also. A significant part of the drama text is an endnote where the author refers to two contemporary French studies (1881), one on the nervous system by Dr. J. M. Charcot (whom Bjørnson met during his stay in Paris, 1882–1887) and one on hypnosis and hysteria by Dr. P. Richer. It is obvious that this information relates to Klara's illness. Yet it is not obvious how these references are meant to influence the interpretation.

The play can be read as a drama of *character*: the main focus is on the personality and belief of Adolf Sang and the various kinds of relations between him and other characters in the drama. The play shows similarities to TRAGEDY. The most important tragic elements are the hybris/nemesis theme and tragic irony at work when Sang's acts lead to the opposite result: he wants to cure his wife, but she dies from his attempt. It is also relevant to talk about a hamartia, a significant flaw in Sang's character, but it is not easily identified.

Bjørnson was concerned about treating the dramatic matter so that a devoted Christian would not be offended. The play can in fact be comprehended as a religious drama, presenting miracles from God in the human world. The Bible is an important intertext of the drama. The last scene where Klara has risen from her bed and comes walking resembles the story of the awakening of Lazarus. Because of the religious dimension, the play's interpretative potential seems to exceed Bjørnson's possible intentions.

The gathering of clergymen in the long "Fourth meeting" (second part) works as a kind of comic relief, and yet serious issues are debated. The extensive use of stage effects, SYMBOLISM, and poetical expressions connects the play to romantic tragedy like the ones by William Shakespeare, Friedrich Schiller, and Adam Gottlob Oehlenschläger.

FURTHER READING

Downs, Brian W. *Modern Norwegian Literature 1860–1928*. Cambridge: Cambridge Univ. Press, 1966.

Grøndahl, Illit, and Ola Raknes. *Chapters in Norwegian Literature*. Copenhagen: Gyldendal, 1923.

Hemmer, Bjørn. "Bjørnsons *Over evne 1*: Konflikten mellom intensjon og dramaturgi". In *Ibsen og Bjørnson—essays og analyser*. Oslo: Aschehoug, 1978.

Alvhild Dvergsdal

BEYOND THE HORIZON

I'm happy at last—free—free!—freed from the farm—free to wander on and on—eternally!

—Robert, Act 3

Beyond the Horizon by EUGENE O'NEILL opened at the Morosco Theatre in New York on February 3, 1920; in June, the play received the Pulitzer Prize. O'Neill explores the complex ties between man and the land, and he presents the land and the sea as metaphors for each other.

Robert Mayo is about to leave his family farm to follow his dreams on a three-year voyage with his uncle, while his brother, Andrew, is a born farmer and glad to stay on the land. They are both in love with Ruth, whose family owns the neighboring farm, but when Robert reveals his feelings, she first assures him that she cares for only him, even though she spends so much time in Andrew's company, and then insists that he stay on the farm. When Robert breaks the news to his family, Andrew, deeply disappointed at losing Ruth, decides to accompany his uncle in Robert's place. O'Neill's treatment of the two brothers demonstrates the influence of T. C. Murray's *Birthright*, which the playwright saw when the Abbey Theatre toured to New York in 1911.

Three years later, both farms are deteriorating under Robert's inept management, and Ruth cherishes the letters she receives from Andrew while openly criticizing her husband. Andrew returns with fascinating tales of the sea, but he plans to settle in Argentina to pursue success in the grain business. Ruth reveals that she had been hoping that he would stay on the farm and run it properly, but she cannot quite disclose that she now prefers him to Robert; their marriage has become a self-destructive prison after the example of such AUGUST STRINDBERG plays as THE FATHER and THE DANCE OF DEATH.

After five more years, the farm is falling to ruin, and Robert is suffering from pleurisy and consumption. He now believes that the farm has destroyed his life, and he begs Ruth to come to the city with him and make a fresh start. Andrew returns, horrified to find how poorly his family is faring, and he brings a specialist who predicts that Robert has only a very short time to live. Ruth confesses her love for Andrew, while he, the born farmer, admits that he has been making money speculating in wheat prices. Each brother has lived the other's dream and failed; as in O'Neill's earlier plays, the displaced suffer.

Heywood Broun wrote in the *New York Tribune* (February 4, 1920) that "the fundamental tragedy of the play lies in the fate of the incompetent dreamer forced to battle with the land for a living against every inclination and ability. . . . The power of the play is tremendous, and there is no sense of the author's arbitrarily moving pawns about into implausible situations to thrill an audience. It is as honest and sincere as it is artistic." Alexander Woollcott argued in the *New York Times* (February 4, 1920) that the play "rehearses the tragedy of a man whose body and mind need the open road and the far spaces, but who, by force of wanton circumstance and the bondage of a romance that soon burns itself out, is imprisoned within the hill-walled boundaries of a few unyielding acres, chained to a task for which he is not fitted, withheld from a task for which he was born." In the *New York Post* (February 4, 1920), J. Rankin Towse called the play "poignant domestic American tragedy" and "a realistic study of actual life."

[*See also* United States, 1860–1929]

FURTHER READING

Black, Stephen A. "America's First Tragedy." *English Studies in Canada* 13 (June 1987): 195–203.

Murphy, Brenda. "*Beyond the Horizon*'s Narrative Sentence: An American Intertext for O'Neill." *Theatre Annual* 41 (1986): 49–62.

Regenbaum, Shelly. "Wrestling with God: Old Testament Themes in O'Neill's *Beyond the Horizon*." *Eugene O'Neill Newsletter* 8 (Winter 1984): 2–8.

Jeffrey D. Mason

BHAGAT, DATTA (1945–)

The central themes of Bhagat's plays are essentially social. But the core of these plays makes us uneasy, raises uncomfortable questions, highlights the very things which we want to ignore, interrogates us, allows us no easy escapes; you cannot escape these questions through easy laughter and tears.

—Vijay Tendulkar on Datta Bhagat

Datta Bhagat (born on June, 13, 1945, in Vaghi, Nanded, Maharashtra, INDIA) is a Dalit writer, but his plays avoid populist, conventional, or verbose interpretations of Dalit issues, concentrating instead on the complex interconnections between social processes and human motives through individuals and the events they live through. Bhagat focuses on the issues arising out of the hierarchical power relations between the Dalits, members of the lowest caste in India, and the upper castes, as well as the issues arising out of the equally hierarchical relations among the Dalit communities themselves.

With *The Broken Ship* (*Jahaj Phutle Ahe*, 1982) Bhagat made his first statement as a political playwright. The backdrop of the play is postindependence India—a period in which there was a great deal of resentment against Dalits because of a government policy in which posts in jobs and educational institutes were reserved for Dalits as a way of creating political and social equality. The politically and culturally powerful dominant upper castes often took this as an affront to their dominance and held the Dalits responsible for the large-scale unemployment of an underdeveloped society. This resentment often found violent expression in anti-Dalit riots. In *The Broken Ship*, Bhagat sensitively delineates the world of five young, educated, unemployed friends of different castes in search of a job. One old man offers them the job of saving his sinking ship. There is competition among the friends. Gradually resentment and anger poisons their world of youthful relations. They are so busy fighting over caste issues that they are never able to unite and take on the task of keeping the ship afloat. The ship becomes a metaphor for a society disintegrating under caste oppression and caste prejudice. The play's statement is clear: sympathetic political understanding is required to resolve caste issues.

The Alienated Woman (*Ekti*, 1982) presents the alienation of an educated young Dalit woman from her Mahar community as well as from the upper castes whose parochial ways of thinking she refuses to endorse and accept. This play is the first sensitive expression of the angst felt by young modern educated Dalit women and their rebellion against those patriarchal ideologies that are shared by both upper castes and Dalits.

The Defeated One (*Paranhhute*, 1982) portrays the turmoil within a traditional, caste-bound village when a Brahmin doctor invites his Dalit friend to live with him. The play dramatizes the difficulties of doing away with caste even when sensitive individuals from among both the Dalit and high caste communities try to reject it.

These one-act plays paved the way for Bhagat's full-length plays, *The Manipulator* (*Khelia*, 1986), *The Piece of Stone* (*Ashmak*, 1985), and *Routes and Escape Routes* (*Wata Palwata*, 1986). Both Bhagat's political concerns and his language found sharper expression in these plays, which have more clearly defined structures and settings. In *The Manipulator*, first performed by "Droppers" in Pune, Bhagat portrays the sociocultural strategies employed by so-called progressive high caste leaders to contain and control the aspirations of young men in suppressed Dalit communities.

In *The Piece of Stone* Bhagat is concerned with exposing the politics of power that forces rationality and intelligence into a mute acceptance of slavery. The power struggle is presented through the conflict between two ideologically opposed attitudes: a ruler seeks power by offering his subjects material wealth in exchange for their ability to reason. He is opposed by Chakshu, a man who believes that reason is what separates man from animal. The plot is a thinly disguised discussion of the politics of "reservations for Dalits" in India. Places (in jobs and in educational institutions) have been reserved for Dalits as a way of reversing years of discrimination in education and in the marketplace. However, the policy of reservations indirectly compels Dalits to assimilate into the very discourse of power that they seek to challenge and overthrow.

Bhagat's ROUTES AND ESCAPE ROUTES became a milestone in Marathi (the language of the Indian state of Maharashtra) theater because its theme, the Dalit movement, was a completely uncharted territory for the established Marathi stage. While Bhagat has made use of traditional performance genres such as tamasha and dindi in his earlier plays, most of his later plays are written in naturalistic style. He has chosen this style for his later plays both because it is the form that yields itself best to the expression of his preoccupations and because he is a people's playwright and wants to use a theater form and idiom with which they are familiar.

Bhagat has received many awards in Maharashtra such as the Natya Darpan Award in 1978 and the Dalit Mitra Award (Best Friend of Dalits) in 2000. His plays have been translated into Telugu, Hindi, and English.

PLAYS: *The Alienated Woman* (*Ekti*, 1982); *The Broken Ship* (*Jahaj Phutle Ahe*, 1982); *The Defeated One* (*Paranhhute*, 1982); *Routes and Escape Routes* (*Wata Palwata*, 1986)

FURTHER READING

Bhagat, Datta. *Routes and Escape Routes*. In *DramaContemporary—India*, ed. by Erin B. Mee. Baltimore: Johns Hopkins Univ. Press, 2000.

Maya Pandit

BILLY BISHOP GOES TO WAR

Researched and developed between 1976 and 1978, *Billy Bishop Goes to War* premiered November 3, 1978, at the East Culture Centre in Vancouver, British Columbia. The play was extremely popular in CANADA, touring the nation and enjoying a lengthy run. When the play made the transition to Broadway under the guidance of producer Mike Nichols, however, it fared disappointingly—much to the chagrin of a Canadian media highly invested in the play's success abroad. Since its debut, *Billy Bishop* has been staged several times in North America and Europe and has been filmed for television. In 1982 *Billy Bishop* brought JOHN GRAY the Governor General's Award for drama.

The play was written in collaboration with actor Eric Peterson and based on the exploits of Canadian World War I flying ace William Avery Bishop. While the two men were in Ottawa performing for Theatre Passe Muraille, Peterson discovered Bishop's memoir *Winged Warfare* in a local bookshop. Gray was struck by the book's dramatic possibilities: "As representatives of a generation of Canadians who had never been anywhere near a war, we regarded the man with apprehension and curiosity. Was he a homicidal maniac? What was going on in that war? What was it like to be a Canadian then? Why were more top aces Canadian than any other nationality?" (1994).

Gray structured the play as a one-man show with intermittent songs. Peterson played all eighteen parts; Gray sang and accompanied Peterson on piano. Gray also elected to have Billy address the audience directly as an informal raconteur. This decision to eliminate theater's "fourth wall" grew out of Gray's experience on the barn circuit of southwestern Ontario, where he observed that "Canadians don't much like listening in on other people's conversations" (1994). Gray's stylistic and staging decisions—the collaboration between playwright and actor, the minimalist set, the emphasis on direct performance—reflected the alternative theater movement flourishing in Canada at the time. The choice to ponder the nature of Canadian heroism and colonial identity was also in keeping with this alternative theater's interest in uncovering a national mythology.

The play shows Bishop's progression from his inauspicious beginning as Royal Military College's worst student to his enlistment in the Canadian Expeditionary Forces cavalry in World War I, his eventual decoration as Canada's top aviator, and his emergence as a colonial figurehead. Bishop's seminal moment comes when he sees a fighter plane touch down "like a dragonfly" amid the "mud, sweat, and horse manure" of his camp. Seeking to avoid being buried alive in the mud, Billy takes the aviator's advice to heart: "The only way out is up." After this point Bishop becomes an ace pilot, accumulating kills at an astonishing rate. Several factors motivate Bishop, including the colonial's yen to prove himself, but his strongest motivation for success is his desire to survive the war.

Although the play has been criticized for glorifying war, it is worth taking note of Billy's resistance to the role of colonial figurehead, self-deprecation, and constant deflation of romantic visions of war. Gray's musical score adds further layers of tonal complexity. The play concludes with the older Bishop, on the eve of World War II, "wondering what it was all for? But then, we're not in control of these things, are we?"

FURTHER READING

Billy Bishop Goes to War. In *Canadian Drama and the Critics*, ed. by L. W. Conolly. Vancouver: Talonbooks, 1987.

Bressai, Diane. "Discovering the Popular Audience." *Canadian Literature* 118 (1988): 7–27.

Gray, John. Introduction to *Billy Bishop Goes to War*. In *Modern Canadian Plays*. 3d ed. Vol. 2, ed. by Jerry Wasserman. Vancouver: Talonbooks, 1994.

Usmiani, Renate. *Second Stage: The Alternative Theatre Movement in Canada*. Vancouver: Univ. of British Columbia Press, 1983.

Zimmerman, Cynthia. "John Gray." In *The Work: Conversations with English-Canadian Playwrights*, ed. by Robert Wallace. Toronto: Coach House Press, 1982.

Andrea R. Stevens

BIOGRAPHY

S. N. BEHRMAN's *Biography* was presented by the Theatre Guild, opening on December 12, 1932, and running for 238 performances. Ina Clare starred as Marion Froude, who returns to New York after some years abroad as a leftist portrait artist who knows everyone in the belle monde. She painted famous Bolsheviks in Moscow—Vladimir Lenin and others. This is revealed as her old friend Feydak the composer stops to see her on his way to Hollywood from Vienna. He was mistaken for his more famous brother by a producer and hired to do movie scores—just like the real-life Richard Falls whose brother Leo was the successful one as described in *People in a Diary*. When Leander Nolan enters, Marion fails to recognize him. "Bunny" was her first love from Tennessee, now risen to be candidate for the Senate, with a prospective father-in-law of great power. As he leaves, impatient young editor Richard Kurt arrives and offers a $2,000 advance for Marion's autobiography. At first she demurs, but she needs money and is intrigued by the idea of taking "a good, straight, clear-eyed look" at her life. As she writes, however, and as the biography is promoted, Nolan, who commissioned a portrait, is outraged and fearful that she will reveal their early affair and ruin his prospects for marriage and the Senate. Kurt resists pressure from Nolan's wealthy father-in-law but is dismissive of Marion and her work because it seems trivial to him. Marion, however, argues the exercise is invigorating. At the end of the act, Kurt "sinks to his knees beside her, his arms around her" and confesses his love for her.

In the third act, Nolan, his father-in-law-to-be Kinnicott, and daughter Slade arrive in order to kill the biography. Marion, however, charms them all. Slade looks up to her as a role model, the independent woman who can go anywhere and do anything. Nolan is outraged that she will not give in to his demands, but Kinnicott thinks he has won her heart and asks her to his penthouse the following night for dinner where he will win the concession he wants from her. Once they leave, however, Marion burns the manuscript, sends Nolan back to Slade, and breaks off with Kurt in an act of self-sacrifice, because she realizes he hates her essential quality, her tolerance of others, and that she would teach him tolerance herself and destroy his essential quality, his anger and hate of privilege and injustice. As a result, despite her love, she must send him away. Financially, however, she is saved at the last minute by a telegram from Feydak, who has commissions for her among the Oscar winners in Hollywood. The play, therefore, achieves a Behrmanesque balance between rich privilege and desire for radical reform—reconciling them with tolerance. *The Cambridge Guide to American Theatre* (1993) notes, "In opting for the middle way between conservatism and radicalism, Marion encapsulates the situation of many mainstream American playwrights of the 1930s."

FURTHER READING

Kessely, Urs. *S. N. Behrman's Komödien: Spiel und Konflikt. Untersuchungen zu einem Gattungsberiff und sum Verhältnis der Geschlechter* [Behrman's comedies: Play and conflict. Examinations of a concept of genre and the relationship between the sexes]. Bern: Herbert Lang, 1972.

Sievers, W. David. *Freud on Broadway: A History of Psychoanalysis and the American Drama*. New York: Hermitage House, 1955.

Waldau, Roy S. *Vintage Years of the Theatre Guild: 1928–1939*. Cleveland, Ohio: Case Western Reserve Univ. Press, 1972.

Wilmeth, Don B., ed. *The Cambridge Guide to American Theatre*. New York: Cambridge Univ. Press, 1993.

David Sauer

THE BIRD LOVERS

Lucifer's highest virtue was obedience to God always and under every circumstance. Who was therefore the first to demand obedience to the authorities? [Silence] Who was evil—God or Lucifer?

—Piccolino, Part 2

In *The Bird Lovers* (*Fugleelskerne*, 1966) Norwegian poet, novelist, and playwright JENS BJØRNEBOE examines personal responsibility and individuals' evil actions under the pressure of society. Written in a mood of grotesque humor and with an irony of despair, the drama is set in an Italian village two decades after World War II. A group of German bird lovers visits the village with the prospect of turning it into a tourist paradise for ornithologists. Their leaders, Greifenklau and Johannes, are soon recognized as war criminals by former partisans, who capture them and improvise a court-martial with the intention of hanging the Germans. Caruso, who during the war was sentenced by Greifenklau and unsuccessfully executed by Johannes, gives the role of mock defender to the former priest Piccolino. In a spirit of justice and compassion Piccolino unexpectedly takes his role seriously and embarks on a philosophical defense where bestiality is seen an integral part of the history of civilization—a motif typical of Bjørneboe. However, his townsmen ignore his unveilings of an evil god and the shared guilt of all humankind, and Piccolino, as a last resort, successfully evokes their greed. Only Caruso remains unmoved by the prospect of prosperity through German tourism. As his friends pardon Greifenklau, Caruso enters the now-empty gallows in disgust of all humanity, but his courage fails him, and the play ends with Caruso climbing down and asking forgiveness of his former executioner. The last strong individual thereby succumbs to the immorality of the group, and Caruso comes to embody the moral weakness of human beings: "The main thing is that the juicy, dear, good Caruso is the real villain," Bjørneboe later commented in a letter.

Both thematically and technically the play is influenced by BERTOLT BRECHT, whose works Bjørneboe studied carefully. From 1959 onward, Bjørneboe had extensive contact with the Berliner Ensemble, and their conductor Hans-Dieter Hosalla wrote music for the Brecht-like songs in *The Bird Lovers*. Another member of the ensemble, Charly Weber, staged the play for the first time in Oslo in 1966. An early version titled *Ornitofilene* had already been produced by the experimental Odin theater under Eugenio Barba, with whom Bjørneboe had close collaboration. Uncomfortable with the many comparisons to Brecht, Bjørneboe himself emphasized that Brecht did not invent the musical genre and furthermore that Brecht's own plays, too, often chose to opt for ideology rather than facing the darkness of truth. However, these comments do not change the fact that Bjørneboe's long-lasting admiration for Brecht is evident both in the dark humor and the social criticism of the play, alongside other influences, such as fascination with pantomime and a sense of a "high, mystical truth" incarnated in the paradoxes of art.

The Bird Lovers was an instant success, and Hosalla's production was invited to the theater festival in Venice in 1967, an opportunity the theater declined, much to the author's dismay. Still, Bjørneboe enjoyed early international success as his plays were translated into a number of European languages during the 1960s.

FURTHER READING

Bjørneboe, Jens. *The Bird Lovers*. With tr.'s introduction. Los Angeles: Sun & Moon Press, 1994.

Garton, Janet. *Jens Bjørneboe. Prophet Without Honor*. Westport, Conn.: Greenwood Press, 1985.

Martin, Joe. *Keeper of the Protocols: The Works of Jens Bjørneboe in the Crosscurrents of Western Literature*. New York: Peter Lang, 1996.

Jørgen Sejersted

THE BIRTHDAY PARTY

It's only necessarily necessary! We admit possibility only after we grant necessity. It is possible because necessary but by no means necessary through possibility. The possibility can only be assumed after the proof of necessity.

—Goldberg, Act 2

In *The Birthday Party* HAROLD PINTER shows the meaninglessness of life by depicting the absurd nature of the human condition in a godless world. The play opened in Cambridge in 1958 and moved to London later that year, where it was savaged by critics and closed after one week.

The three-act play revolves around themes of power and identity in a hostile Kafkaesque world. With its main character Stanley as a modern Everyman figure, the play may be seen as an allegory on birth and death similar to medieval morality plays.

The play begins with Petey and Meg, the owners of a seaside boardinghouse, talking over breakfast. After Petey leaves for work, Meg tells Stanley, their pianist lodger, to expect two new lodgers that day. This upsets Stanley. Meg goes shopping, and the two, Goldberg and McCann, arrive. Stanley slips out of the room without being seen. The two discuss whether this is the place where they have a "job to do." Meg returns and tells them it is Stanley's birthday. Goldberg plans a party for him and leaves with McCann. Meg tells an uneasy Stanley about the planned party and gives him a present of a toy drum. Act 1 ends with Stanley marching round the room, beating the drum, initially in strict time and then in a "savage and possessed way."

In act 2 Stanley meets McCann and Goldberg and tries to persuade them to leave. Instead, they interrogate him with disconnected, often absurd questions that become increasingly menacing until Stanley begins to break down.

Meg enters in a party dress, beating the toy drum. Goldberg flirts with her and her friend Lulu, and it becomes apparent that there might be a connection between his and Stanley's past lives. In a game of blind man's buff, McCann breaks Stanley's glasses and trips him up. A blindfolded Stanley tries to strangle Meg, and in an electrical blackout, McCann's flashlight reveals Stanley giggling and bending over an unconscious Lulu whom he has positioned, spread-eagled on the table. Stanley seems to have gone out of his mind, and the shadowy figures of Goldberg and McCann converge on him.

Act 3 opens on breakfast the following morning with Meg mentioning to Petey that McCann and Goldberg are still with Stanley in his room. Goldberg enters, announcing that Stanley has suffered a mental breakdown. Petey and Meg leave, and McCann enters with packed suitcases, eager to "finish the bloody thing" and leave. Lulu arrives and is treated badly by Goldberg and McCann. McCann then ushers in a neatly dressed Stanley. Goldberg and McCann attempt to cajole him into coming with them but eventually escort an incoherent and broken Stanley to Goldberg's car. The play ends with Petey and Meg at the breakfast table.

The Birthday Party, Pinter's second play, is a product of the postwar British cultural revolution. Although possibly influenced in style and structure by pre- and early postwar theater, it clearly rejects the polished poise and thriller elements in plays by then popular writers like NOËL COWARD, TERENCE RATTIGAN, and Agatha Christie, aligning itself instead with the works of SAMUEL BECKETT and EUGÈNE IONESCO.

[*See also* England, 1940–Present]

FURTHER READING

Burkman, Katherine H., and John L. Kundert-Gibbs, eds. *Pinter at Sixty*. Bloomington: Indiana Univ. Press, 1993.

Esslin, Martin. *Pinter the Playwright*. 4th ed. London: Methuen, 1977.

Raby, Peter, ed. *The Cambridge Companion to Harold Pinter*. Cambridge: Cambridge Univ. Press, 2001.

Thompson, David T. *Pinter: The Player's Playwright*. London: Macmillan, 1985.

Gregory Hacksley

BISHANG LIANGSHAN *See* FORCED UP MOUNT LIANG

BJØRNEBOE, JENS INGVALD (1920–1976)

It is compassion that is most important,—subsequently to transform compassion into action.

—Unfinished autobiography, 1976

Dramatist and writer Jens Ingvald Bjørneboe was born in Kristiansand, NORWAY, in 1920. At age fifteen, he was decisively influenced by the German actor and writer Wolfgang Langhoff's disclosure of the atrocities of the concentration camps

(*The Bog Soldiers* [*Die Moorsoldaten*, 1935]), and descriptions of evil, together with the will to denounce actual abuse of power, resonate throughout Bjørneboe's writings.

Bjørneboe started his artistic career as a painter but made his literary debut as a poet in 1951. Before this, his first drama, *Before the Cock Crows* (*Før hanen galer*, 1950), describing medical experiments carried out by the Nazis, was turned down. Disappointed by the rejection, Bjørneboe rewrote the play as a novel, a genre he was later to pursue with considerable success.

Bjørneboe maintained his theatrical interest and published essays on a number of dramatists, BERTOLT BRECHT, in particular, but also FRIEDRICH DURRENMATT, Georg Büchner, and AUGUST STRINDBERG and actors such as Marcel Marceau and Klaus Kinsky. In 1959 he visited the Berliner Ensemble in East Berlin, where he became acquainted with key members. This proved a decisive impetus for his work as a dramatist. In 1965 he had success with the play *Many Happy Returns* (*Til lykke med dagen*), describing the sufferings of the young prisoner Tonnie, who is driven to suicide by an inhumane system. The play marks the beginning of Bjørneboe's lifelong war against the Norwegian penal system. Both formally and thematically this play shows inspiration from Brecht, but Bjørneboe himself emphasized that the Brecht-like poetic songs are detached from the plot, as in the overall tradition of musical comedy. Also unlike Brecht, the Rudolf Steiner– and FRIEDRICH NIETZSCHE–inspired Bjørneboe valued poetical and philosophical mystery above clear-cut ideology, a tendency that is recognizable in the ethical paradoxes of his next play, *The Bird Lovers* (1966).

In *Semmelweiss* (1968), the *Verfremdungs* (distancing) technique is maintained as students rush onto the stage at the beginning of the play, initially the idea of experimental theater manager Eugenio Barba, with whom Bjørneboe had close collaboration. The historical figure of the Hungarian doctor Ignaz Semmelweiss (1818–1865), who discovered that childbed fever could be controlled through disinfection, constitutes a typical Bjørneboian hero, the solitary individual who at great personal expense challenges authority. Semmelweiss has the energy to hold on to his convictions, even as his enemies slowly drive him toward apathy. This faintly optimistic element is subdued when the play stresses how this anti-authoritarian hero, after his death, is used as a symbol by the following authoritarian rulers—in Bjørneboe's view, a destiny parallel to that of Norwegian dramatist HENRIK IBSEN.

In the last of his major plays, *The Torgersen Case* (*Tilfellet Torgersen*, 1972), Bjørneboe explores the dramatic potential of a criminal case and further develops the documentary aspect of his novels and plays, giving a detailed account of the murder trial of Torgersen, a famous convict. Among his main projects is also an unfinished play based on the life of Russian anarchist Emma Goldmann (1869–1940). In anarchism Bjørneboe saw a promising combination of socialism and freedom for the individual.

Throughout his life, Bjørneboe was a controversial figure in Norway, and despite considerable international acclaim, his plays are not regularly produced on Norwegian stages. Depressed and sick from abuse of alcohol, in 1976 Bjørneboe committed suicide at the age of fifty-six—a destiny prefigured in his writings.

PLAYS: *Many Happy Returns* (*Til lykke med dagen*, 1965); *The Bird Lovers* (*Fugleelskerne*, 1966); *Semmelweiss* (1968); *Amputation* (*Amputasjon*, 1970); *The Torgersen Case* (*Tilfellet Torgersen*, 1972); *Levi's* (*Dongery*, 1976); *Red Emma* (*Røde Emma*, 1976)

FURTHER READING

Garton, Janet. *Jens Bjørneboe. Prophet Without Honor.* Westport, Conn.: Greenwood Press, 1985.

Martin, Joe. *Keeper of the Protocols: The Works of Jens Bjørneboe in the Crosscurrents of Western Literature.* New York: Peter Lang, 1996.

Jørgen Sejersted

BJØRNSON, BJØRNSTJERNE (1832–1910)

But for each individual what is most important is to be in truth.
—Bjørnstjerne Bjørnson, 1877

Bjørnstjerne Bjørnson was born on December 8, 1832, at Kvikne, NORWAY, and died on April 26, 1910, in Paris. His dramatic oeuvre as a whole constitutes a continuous response to the notions of honesty and truth challenging. All his writing, a seeming barometer of everything that swirled around him, new ideas and debates, political and aesthetic, testifies to his willingness to abandon preconceived notions when found to stand in the way of rationality, positivism, and scientific truth.

Bjørnson's apprenticeship as a theater director and a writer of drama took place in Bergen (1857–1859) and in Christiania (now Oslo) (1865–1867). In the early years, the foremost concern was to promote a kinship between contemporary Norway in the figure of the free peasant and the heroic age commemorated in the sagas. In order to develop a cultural history and a national cultural sense of self, he turned to the Norwegian past—the saga literature and Snorri Sturluson's history of the Norwegian medieval kings.

His first historical play, *Between the Battles* (*Mellem Slagene*, 1856), recreates the historical saga period with the single purpose of throwing light on his awakening nation. By evoking a sense of continuity between past and present, he expected the audience to take new pride in Norway and to gather around the need for national identity, purpose, and solidarity. The main character of King Sverre can easily be seen as a prototype for Bjørnson's male leads in the ensuing array of historical plays written between 1856 and 1872: a sensitive man, with great confidence in his vision for the future nation and with a determination to do what is good, is forced to realize that his own people fail to understand him. Of particular note, the effective use of the pithy saga style—short, terse phrases pregnant with meaning and an accompanying sense of reticence—gave birth to a dramatic language that comes across as realistic and direct but also as laconic and doom laden.

Central among Bjørnson's historical dramas is also the trilogy *Sigurd Slembe* (1862), where the arena is no longer limited to that of the medieval North but is widened to encompass the European Middle Ages and the spirit of the Crusades.

A Lesson in Marriage (*De Nygifte*, 1865) is an epoch-making work in Scandinavian drama. The play announces Bjørnson's growing dissatisfaction with historical themes and romantic visions and marks his turn to contemporary REALISM with an increasing emphasis on the everyday life of the bourgeoisie. By the mid-1870s, positivism has taken root, and the natural sciences define Truth. Bjørnson reads Charles Darwin, John Stuart Mill, Herbert Spencer, Hippolyte Taine, Ernst Renan, and Georg Brandes. By the end of the decade, he undergoes his religious crisis. In the years immediately preceding that crisis, however, Bjørnson embarked upon a series of the first major realistic plays of Scandinavian drama, *The Editor* (*Redaktøren*) and *A* BANKRUPTCY (*En Fallit*), both published in 1875, and *The King* (*Kongen*, 1877). *The King* remains an underrated play: the king has realized there is a lie at the core of the monarchy. He seeks to bring both church and the people into line with his own ideals. The ensuing failure represents the very opposite of the sentimentality and theatricality of *A Bankruptcy*. The king has realized the falseness of his position as king, and his flawed attempt to democratize the monarchy by "dressing" his citizens in the mantle of "royalty," against the will of the church and the state and the middle class, lends a sense of sublimity to the play.

Bjørnson's deepening realism grows with his focus on the woman question and especially in his unrelenting protest against a "sick" society's destructive hold over institutions of education and marriage. Distrusting any claim of inherent dignity and decency in "the common man and woman," he calls for greater self-reliability and self-responsibility in plays such as *Leonarda* (1879) and *The New System* (*Det ny system*, 1879).

His plays of the 1880s and 1890s can be divided into two distinct groupings: those that deal with the private conflicts of the individual in society and those that focus on the individual's relation to spiritual or supernatural authority. Central to both groupings is the impossible and often degraded position of woman subjected to sexist conventions, institutions, and laws; to the abuse and iniquities of the double standard; and importantly, to her own lack of knowledge of her body and sexuality. *A Gauntlet* (*En hanske*, 1883) with its theme of sexual purity before marriage, for both women and men, was meant as an antidote to the Modern Breakthrough's radical notion of free love for both sexes. The play sparks the beginning of the Scandinavian morality debate that raged throughout the 1880s. The play was a great stage success in Scandinavia but was derided by both radical and conservative critics alike. Bjørnson tried in vain to protest that the purity issue was not the central question of the play but, rather, that man and woman both must learn to live in truth. In addition to *A Gauntlet*, the first group is represented by the plays *Geography and Love* (*Geografi og kjærlighed*, 1885), *Laboremus* (1901), *At Hove Manor* (*På Storehove*, 1902), and *Land of Dag* (*Daglannet*, 1904).

The second grouping of plays is represented by BEYOND HUMAN POWER (*Over ævne I*, 1883) and *Beyond Human Power II* (*Over ævne II*, 1895), *Paul Lange and Tora Parsberg* (*Paul Lange og Tora Parsberg*, 1898), and *When the New Wine Blooms* (*Når den ny vin blomstrer*, 1909).

As *A Gauntlet* remains the dramatic achievement of the first group, *Beyond Human Power*, the most classic of Bjørnson's plays, remains the central play of the second grouping. Viewed by most as an anti-BRAND play, *Beyond Human Power* is a poised, laconic drama of two acts—taut, concentrated, effective in its damning critique of religious supernaturalism, in part the result of Bjørnson's visit to Dr. Charcot's hospital La Salpêtrière in Paris and their conversations about hypnotism and hysteria. To Bjørnson the mystical aspects of Christianity, or any religion, are literally too much for the human being as portrayed in the character of pastor Sang, with his abstract and ecstatic flight from reality. This theme is further elaborated in *Beyond Human Power II*, but the object of study this time is that of fanatic idealism combined with unrealistic political utopian objectives (the play centers on the bombing and killing of industrial magnates gathered at a hotel). The "terrorist" is pastor Sang's son.

Bjørnson further explores the power and fateful hypocrisy of politics in *Paul Lange and Tora Parsberg*, a thinly disguised play about the political and personal attack that led to the suicide of one of Norway's ministers, Ole Richter, in Stockholm in 1888.

In his last play, *When the New Wine Blooms*, written with self-irony and wistfulness, Bjørnson returns the dramatic action to the home, only to create a protagonist, a woman this time, who takes leave of both home and marriage to pursue a career abroad.

Bjørnson's dramatic genius was not that of Heinrich von Kleist, Georg Büchner, HENRIK IBSEN, or AUGUST STRINDBERG, that is, the sort of genius that leaves its unequaled imprint on the history of drama in terms of innovative form and technique or that produced a lasting contribution to the issue of aesthetics. He did not plumb the human psyche so as to create unrivaled dramatic character portraits. Rather, his importance lies in his bringing to the theater and to drama the very tumultuousness and the important questions of his own times. He did so in ways that made him read and staged all over Europe. A fearless combatant for causes he supported and principles he cherished throughout his critical and creative life, he made the theater and the reading of drama both relevant for his contemporaries and highly anticipated events. For these reasons, and more, he remains an essential chapter in the history of Scandinavian and European theater.

PLAYS: *Between the Battles* (*Mellem Slagene*, 1856); *Lame Hulda* (*Halte-Hulda*, 1857); *King Sverre* (*Kong Sverre*, 1861); *Sigurd Slembe* (*Sigurd Slembe*, 1862); *Mary, Queen of Scots* (*Maria Stuart i Skotland*, 1864); *A Lesson in Marriage* (*De Nygifte*, 1865); *A Bankruptcy* (*En Fallit*, 1875); *The Editor* (*Redaktøren*, 1875); *The King* (*Kongen*, 1877); *Leonarda* (1879); *The New System* (*Det ny system*, 1879); *Beyond Human Power* (*Over ævne I*, 1883); *A Gauntlet* (*En hanske*, 1883); *Geography and Love* (*Geografi og kjærlighed*, 1885); *Beyond Human Power II* (*Over ævne II*, 1895); *Paul Lange and Tora Parsberg* (*Paul Lange og Tora Parsberg*, 1898); *Laboremus* (1901); *At Hove Manor* (*På Storehove*, 1902); *Land of Dag* (*Daglannet*, 1904); *When the New Wine Blooms* (*Når den ny vin blomstrer*, 1909)

FURTHER READING

Bull, Francis, Fredrik Paasche, and A. H. Winsnes. *Norsk litteraturhistorie* [Norwegian literary history] 4 (1937).

Grøndahl, Illit, and Ola Raknes. *Chapters in Norwegian Literature*. 1923. repr. Freeport, N.Y.: Books for Libraries Press, 1969.

Næss, Harald. *A History of Norwegian Literature*. Lincoln: Univ. of Nebraska Press, 1993.

Pål Bjørby

BLACK ARTS MOVEMENT

Called by Larry Neal (1989) "the aesthetic sister of the Black Power concept," the Black Arts movement (BAM) is one of the most controversial movements in the modern era. A radical movement, it carried through W. E. B. Du Bois's 1926 call for art "for us, about us, near us, and by us." Initiated in the early 1960s, though rooted in a black radical tradition dating back at least to the Haitian Revolution of 1791, it flourished, suffered significant setbacks in the mid-1970s from federal harassment and economic downturn, and continues today on campus and neighborhood block.

Theater and drama played a major—arguably, preeminent—role. Again, according to Neal (1989), "[T]heater is potentially the most social of all the arts. It is an integral part of the socializing process." Much inspiration was supplied by LORRAINE HANSBERRY'S *A RAISIN IN THE SUN* (1959). Even more significant were AMIRI BARAKA'S *DUTCHMAN* (1964) and the cultural institution he helped found in 1965, Harlem's Black Arts Repertory Theatre/School. A generation of playwrights was fostered in centers such as Black Arts West, Black House, The New Lafayette Theatre, and Concept East.

Three significant influences on BAM drama and theater can be described. First was a focus on popular and folk culture inspired by Du Bois, Alain Locke, Antonio Gramsci, C. L. R. James, ZORA NEALE HURSTON, and Mao Zedong. Malcolm X (1970) was perhaps most influential in this respect: "Our cultural revolution must be the means of bringing us closer to our African brothers and sisters." This is a matter of content. For instance, Ron Milner's *Who's Got His Own* (1967) is a typical, highly moving example of black MELODRAMA—a genuine hit, too. Production conditions are also important—where, by whom, and for whom the drama is written and staged. The BAM's successful response to this issue is clear when we view it as a regional theater movement. It is also a matter of technique: Kimberly Benston (2000) argues the primacy of methexis ("communal helping-out of the action by all assembled") over mimesis ("the representation of an action"). In practice, this meant (1) participatory events such as the National Black Theatre's *A Revival! Change! Love! Organize!* (1969); (2) a call to action, as in the razor-sharp AGITATION-PROPAGANDA plays of Ben Caldwell; or (3) overt invitation to the audience to discuss and criticize during and/or after the performance.

Another crucial resource was radical theology, the assumption being that the most invidious effect of slavery and colonialism was spiritual. As James T. Stewart (1968) asserts, "[E]xisting white paradigms or models do not correspond to the realities of Black existence. It is imperative that we construct models with different basic assumptions." Ritual drama, in particular, dominated the stages and periodicals of black theater in the late 1960s, attracting Baraka (*Bloodrites*, 1972), Joseph Walker (*Ododo*, 1973), Marvin X (*The Resurrection of the Dead*, 1969), Paul Carter Harrison (*The Great MacDaddy*, 1973), and ADRIENNE KENNEDY (*An Evening with Dead Essex*, 1973). Generally, such pieces blend bold dramatic structure with deeply affecting references to texts, movements, cadences, intonations, and props of diverse religious traditions. Religion was not universally appreciated; Caldwell shows no sympathy for the theologically minded in *Prayer Meeting, or, The First Militant Minister* (1969). It depicts a hilarious bit of subterfuge by a quick-on-his-feet burglar and a hopelessly gullible liberal preacher who mistakes the intruder for God.

The significance of music—both popular and avant-garde—on black drama and theater must be noted. It enabled the vital dynamic of tradition and innovation called for by cultural revolutionaries such as Kwame Nkrumah, Jomo Kenyatta, Mao, and X. The blues, rhythm and blues, gospel music, and JAZZ were considered the "key," as Neal (1969) put it, to expanding the movement's connections to local, national, and international currents.

Baraka utilizes music thematically and structurally in many of his works and has been composing full-fledged musicals since the mid-1970s. Baraka collaborated closely with Sun Ra and Archie Shepp on two works (*A Black Mass*, 1967; *Slave Ship*, 1967) and has attested to how much the former influenced his thinking in general.

Too often, Robinson (1983) has demonstrated, the continuity of the black radical tradition has been obscured. As in black music, continuity exists not only between BAM artists and their artistic forebears but also to the post-BAM generation—NTOZAKE SHANGE, Thulani Davis, Aishiah Rahman—and the current surge of hip-hop musical theater. The controversy caused in 1997 by AUGUST WILSON when he called for renewed attention to the importance of plays written and produced by and for African Americans only confirms the continuing importance of the Black Nationalist position in U.S. arts and letters.

[*See also* Avant-Garde Drama, United States; Baldwin, James; Grimké, Angelina Weld; Hughes, Langston; Identity Theater; Political Theater in the United States]

FURTHER READING

Benston, Kimberly. *Performing Blackness: Enactments of African-American Modernism*. New York: Routledge, 2000.

Cruse, Harold. *The Crisis of the Negro Intellectual*. New York: Quill, 1967.

Gayle, Addison, Jr., ed. *The Black Aesthetic*. Garden City, N.Y.: Anchor Bks., 1972.

Kelley, Robin D. G. *Freedom Dreams: The Black Radical Imagination*. Boston: Beacon Press, 2002.

Malcolm X. "The Organization of Afro-American Unity: For Human Rights and Dignity." In *Black Nationalism in America*, ed. by John H. Bracey Jr., August Meier, and Elliott Rudwick. Indianapolis: Bobbs, 1970.

Neal, Larry. "And Shine Swam On." In *Black Fire: An Anthology of Afro-American Writing*, ed. by LeRoi Jones and Larry Neal. New York: Morrow, 1968.

——. "Any Day Now: Black Art and Black Liberation." *Ebony* 24 (August 1969): 54–62.

——. "The Black Arts Movement." In *Visions of a Liberated Future*, ed. by Michael Schwartz. New York: Thunder's Mouth Press, 1989.

Robinson, Cedric J. *Black Marxism: The Making of the Black Radical Tradition*. London: Zed Press, 1983.

Sell, Mike. "The Black Arts Movement: Performance, Neo-Orality, and the Destruction of the 'White Thing.'" In *African American Performance & Theatre History: A Critical Reader*, ed. by Harry Elam Jr. and David Krasner. New York: Oxford Univ. Press, 2001.

Stewart, James T. "The Development of the Black Revolutionary Artist." In *Black Fire: An Anthology of Afro-American Writing*, ed. by LeRoi Jones and Larry Neal. New York: Morrow, 1968.

Mike Sell

THE BLACKS

The fourth of five plays written by French author JEAN GENET, *The Blacks* (*Les Nègres*) is a grotesque, allegorical spectacle of racial hatred and resentment featuring exaggerated characters and a destabilizing rapport between audience and actors, a play best described by its subtitle: "un clownerie" (a clown show).

As with his other plays, Jean Genet uses the stage to demonstrate his frustration with and hatred for the mendacities of organized society. A homosexual "outlaw" with a criminal past, Genet asserted that he was a "black whose skin happens to be pink and white." As a study of race, justice, and power written during an era of heightened racial tension in both France and the United States, *The Blacks* constructs a particularly provocative landscape of fear and alienation.

The play presents a group of black actors, some with hierarchical, colonialist roles to embody (reminiscent of Genet's THE BALCONY)—Queen, Valet, Missionary, Judge—performing for a white audience. The blacks reenact the murder of a white woman, an event that has happened before the beginning of the performance. Her coffin, draped in a white sheet, stands at center stage throughout the play. Genet complicates the situation by introducing not only another group of spectators (a group of blacks in white masks assuming the guise of a European court) but also an important offstage subplot in which a black man is being tried for treason.

Distinct from other absurdist playwrights like EUGÈNE IONESCO and SAMUEL BECKETT, Genet revels in the ritualistic dimensions and potential of the stage. Using sardonically poetic language, elaborate costumes, stylized movement, exaggerated makeup and masks, and a persistent blurring of the line between reality and illusion, Genet provokes the audience throughout the performance. The masks in particular serve to conflate the audience-performer dynamic with the master-slave relationship. Near the end of the play, the coffin at center stage is revealed to be nothing more than a white sheet hung on a pair of chairs. It is further revealed that the onstage performance was a ruse to distract the white audience from the "true" offstage spectacle of the black traitor. Every supposed truth in the performance is exposed as a sham.

Roger Blin directed the premiere of *The Blacks* at the Théâtre de Lutèce, where it attracted considerable attention and ran several months. Its New York debut took place in 1961 at the St. Mark's Playhouse and featured a cast including James Earl Jones, Louis Gossett, Cicely Tyson, and Maya Angelou. This OFF-BROADWAY production ran for an unprecedented three years and sparked much controversy. In direct response to *The Blacks*, American playwright LORRAINE HANSBERRY (*A RAISIN IN THE SUN*) wrote a more realistic play about colonial oppression in Africa titled *The Whites* (*Les Blancs*). An acclaimed revival by the Classical Theater of Harlem in 2002 demonstrates *The Blacks*' enduring ability to agitate and exhilarate.

FURTHER READING

Bradby, David. *Modern French Drama: 1940–1980*. Cambridge: Cambridge Univ. Press, 1984.

Esslin, Martin. *The Theater of the Absurd*. 3d ed. London: Methuen, 2001.

Genet, Jean. *The Balcony*. Tr. by Bernard Frechtman. New York: Grove, 1958.

Guicharnaud, Jacques. *Modern French Theatre from Giraudoux to Genet*. New Haven, Conn.: Yale Univ. Press, 1967.

Hansberry, Lorraine. *Les blancs* [The whites]. New York: Vintage, 1994.

White, Edmund. *Genet: A Biography*. New York: Vintage, 1993.

Kate Bredeson

BLASTED

The world don't exist, not like this. Looks the same but—Time slows down. A dream I get stuck in, can't do nothing about it.

—Cate, Scene 1

SARAH KANE's *Blasted* was one of the most sensational British plays of the 1990s. When it opened at the Royal Court Theatre Upstairs in London in January 1995, it created a storm of controversy. Attacked as a "disgusting feast of filth" (by the *Daily Telegraph*) and championed as a revolutionary masterpiece (by writers like HAROLD PINTER and EDWARD BOND), the play earned its then twenty-three-year-old author instant notoriety. An unflinching exploration of human extremes, *Blasted* takes place in a posh Leeds hotel room. In the first scene, Ian, a forty-five-year-old journalist/hit man dying of lung cancer, tries to seduce Cate, his former lover, a young woman who stutters and is prone to fainting fits. She resists his advances, saying she no longer loves him. The second scene takes place the following morning, and the audience learns that during the night Ian has raped Cate. She locks herself in the bathroom, and the play's reality shifts: a Soldier enters with a rifle, and a bomb blows the room apart. In the third scene, the Soldier tells Ian how his girlfriend was raped, killed, and mutilated. He rapes Ian and sucks out his eyes, then shoots himself. Cate returns in the fourth scene, clutching a baby. Ian tries to kill himself, but his revolver is empty. The baby dies, and Cate buries it under the floor. She leaves to find food, and the play dissolves into short scenes showing Ian reduced to his most basic essence: he masturbates, defecates, laughs, cries, and ultimately, eats the dead baby. When Cate comes back, she gives him food and comforts him; he thanks her, and the lights fade.

Blasted presents a considerable challenge for audiences, who must watch the play's horrors unfolding before their eyes. Kane's purpose in putting such violence onstage is not for gratuitousness or mere shock value, as some theater critics claimed in reviews of the original production. The play suggests a connection between a rape in a Leeds hotel room and the use of rape as a weapon of war. In particular, Kane draws a comparison between Ian's rape of Cate and the mass rapes perpetrated during the Yugoslavian civil war, showing that they are at root the same act. Kane deliberately disrupts the unities of time and action while retaining the unity of place to show that the comfort and security of civilization can be blown apart at any time, just as the mortar bomb destroys Ian and Cate's hotel room. The play's antecedents are the nihilistic dramas of William Shakespeare and SAMUEL BECKETT: the blind, bleeding Ian evokes the sufferings of Lear and Gloucester, and the final moment of connection and comfort between Ian and Cate recalls the hope that gives meaning to Beckettian Theater of the Absurd. Although *Blasted* was initially vilified as much as it was praised, it is now regarded as one of the most important contemporary British plays, both for its willingness to descend into physical and psychic depths and for its experimentation with dramatic form.

[*See also* England, 1940–Present; Gay and Lesbian Drama]

FURTHER READING

Buse, Peter. *Drama + Theory: Critical Approaches to Modern British Drama*. Manchester: Manchester Univ. Press, 2001.

Greig, David. *Introduction to Sarah Kane: Complete Plays*. London: Methuen, 2001.

Saunders, Graham. *"Love Me or Kill Me": Sarah Kane and the Theatre of Extremes*. Manchester: Manchester Univ. Press, 2002.

Sierz, Aleks. *In-Yer-Face Theatre: British Drama Today*. London: Faber, 2000.

Stephenson, Heidi, and Natasha Langridge. *Rage and Reason: Women Playwrights on Playwrighting*. London: Methuen, 1997.

Elizabeth Klett

BLESSING, LEE (1949–)

As an artist I see myself as an adventurer, that part of my self-exploration that makes me want to try different forms.

—Lee Blessing, 2005

Playwright Lee Blessing was born in Minneapolis, Minnesota, in 1949, and the Midwest had a recognizable impact on his work as a writer. He received his bachelor of arts degree from Reed College in Portland, Oregon, and a master of fine arts degree from the University of Iowa. It was as a graduate student in Iowa that the focus of his work shifted from poetry to playwriting. His plays examine a broad range of themes and subjects from AIDS to spelling bees, politics to baseball. Decidedly, the scope of Blessing's work extends far beyond the American Midwest.

He first came to national attention with the production of his play *A Walk in the Woods* (1987). The play presents the relationship between a pair of nuclear arms negotiators during the Cold War. Over the course of a year, the young American negotiator learns from his wiser Russian counterpart. Loosely based on a actual negotiation in 1982 in Geneva, Blessing's ability to truthfully portray the evolving relationship between these men, as well as capturing the political ramifications of their story, earned the play a nomination for the Pulitzer Prize. It also received a Tony nomination for Best Play in 1988.

Blessing's ability to be both politically resonant and provocatively human is also apparent in plays such as *Flag Day* (2004), *Two Rooms* (1988), and *Whores* (2002). The play *Two Rooms* also illustrates Blessing's ability to weave together human and political drama. Blessing sets the play in a room in Beirut where Arab terrorists are holding an American hostage and a second room in the United States that the hostage's wife has stripped of furniture so that she can symbolically share her husband's suffering. As the story unfolds, the role of the government and the media influence the resolution of the drama. *Time* magazine chose *Two Rooms* as Best Play of the Year in 1988.

While Blessing can be politically provocative, in plays like *Eleemosynary* (1985), his work is more personal and less political. Framed against the backdrop of the National Spelling Bee, *Eleemosynary* embodies Blessing's ability to use wit and a simple set to portray the complex family relationship of three women. In the play an obsessive mother, her precocious daughter, and her grandmother quietly confront a shattered family dynamic, ultimately finding the ability to move forward and heal. With plays like *Fortinbras* (1992), a fantasy on what happens after William Shakespeare's *Hamlet*, and *Cobb* (1989), which explores issues of race by presenting four different depictions of the famous baseball player Ty Cobb, Blessing's plays resist categorization. He was one of the most prolific writers of the last half of the 20th century. He was chosen as the inaugural playwright for the Signature Theatre Company in New York City in 1992 and has developed and presented plays at the EUGENE O'NEILL Center National Playwrights Conference, the Sundance Institute, New Dramatists, and The Playwright's Center in Minneapolis.

[*See also* United States, 1940–Present]

PLAYS: *Authentic Life of Billy the Kid* (1979); *Nice People Dancing to Good Country Music* (1982); *Oldtimers Game* (1982); *Independence* (1984); *Eleemosynary* (1985); *Riches* (1985); *A Walk in the Woods* (1987); *Two Rooms* (1988); *Cobb* (1989); *Down the Road* (1989); *Fortinbras* (1992); *Lake Street Extension* (1992); *Patient A* (1993); *Chesapeake* (1999); *The Winning Streak* (1999); *Thief River* (2002); *Whores* (2002); *Flag Day* (2004)

FURTHER READING

Hatcher, Jeffrey. *The Art & Craft of Playwriting*. Cincinnati, Ohio: Story Press, 1996.

Ellen Anthony-Moore and Christopher Moore

BLITHE SPIRIT

It's disconcerting to think how many people are shocked by honesty and how few by deceit.

—Charles Condomine, Act 1

Blithe Spirit was NOËL COWARD's comedic response to the bombing of his home in London in 1941. Written during a five-day span, the play was an instant success after its opening in July 1941 at London's Picadilly Theatre, with a staggering 1,997 performances, a successful New York run, and a well-received film in 1945. While the war raged, audiences delighted in the antics of Coward's characters as they worked their way through his latest work of "improbable farce," as he termed it. As John O'Hara (1941) noted at the time, "The author just about never falters," and most critics did not disagree.

Blithe Spirit depends more on plot to make its appeal than on any psychological depth or razor-sharp repartee. The drama is pared down to allow its device—a ménage à trois between a man, his wife, and his dead wife—adequate leverage for impact. The writer Charles Condomine invites a medium, the effervescent Madame Arcati, to his home one evening for a séance from which he hopes to glean valuable notes for a book. As Condomine's sturdy wife, Edith, and his drab friends, the Bradmans, look on, the spiritualist conjures forth the shade of the deceased Elvira Condomine. The problem is that only Charles can see and hear his ex(pired)-wife, and she is anything but pleased to find her husband remarried. After considerable hi-jinks, the jealous Elvira develops a plot to kill Charles and thus steal him away from Edith. Unfortunately, tragic misplacement results in Edith dying instead and joining Elvira in tormenting their husband. A repentant Madame Arcati eventually returns to the scene, and the two termagants are banished as Charles, free from female domination, resolves to travel the world in celebration.

Misogynistic overtones are certainly present in *Blithe Spirit*. Charles enjoys a less stressful life after disposing of his wives, but his cavalier attitude toward heterosexual intimacy often grants him a rather appealing homosexual flair, so it is difficult to castigate him when he strides offstage into peregrination. Beneath the misogyny, however, is a message that Coward likely had embedded in his mind after his Blitz experiences: England will endure its tormentors (Hoare, 1999). After all, Charles is nothing if not highly English as he compartmentalizes his wives' taunts into distanced specimens for study, dissection, and speedy disposal. He pays his harpies all the heed they deserve, and then he departs for untold delights. If Charles is England, then his wives are GERMANY (ruthless and efficient, respectively), and the conclusions are inescapable after that. Of course, the message of England's inevitable longevity reaches beyond the context of World War II when one considers the influence of Madame Arcati. Where Charles is England in its reserved shell, she is the same country in the archetypal perfumed springtime. Indomitable in the face of ridiculous adversity, capably crisp, and bubbling over with silly goodwill, one is severely hard-pressed to imagine her ever downtrodden and dusted over (Gray, 1987). Hers is the blithest spirit in the play, and it comforts as warmly as the proudest national sentiment.

[*See also* England, 1929–1940]

FURTHER READING

Coward, Noël. *Blithe Spirit. Three Plays: Blithe Spirit, Hay Fever, Private Lives*. New York: Vintage, 1999.

Gray, Frances. *Noël Coward*. New York: St. Martin's, 1987.

Hoare, Philip. Introduction to *Three Plays: Blithe Spirit, Hay Fever, Private Lives*, by Noël Coward. New York: Vintage, 1999.

Kindley, Joseph. "Noël Coward." In *British Writers*. New York: Scribner, 1992. 139–158.

O'Hara, John. "Out of This World." *Newsweek* (November 17, 1941): 57.

Brian C. Billings

BLITZSTEIN, MARC (1905–1964)

Known for writing convincing music for the theater reflecting American vernacular speech, Marc Blitzstein wrote most of his own librettos and lyrics for his mature works. A student at the University of Pennsylvania and the Curtis Institute in the 1920s, he studied further with Nadia Boulanger in Paris and Arnold Schoenberg in Berlin. In early piano works and string quartets he showed an angry, experimental, polytonal demeanor; his jazzy settings of homoerotic Walt Whitman texts also revealed his dismissal of received styles and willingness to challenge authority.

In *Triple-Sec* (1928), a dadaistic farce, he had his characters multiply onstage as the presumed audience became ever more inebriated; it ran in a Broadway revue for 150 performances. *The Harpies* (1931) is a lusty satire of Igor Stravinsky's neoclassicism. With *The Condemned* (1932), an unperformed choral opera somewhat based on the 1920–1927 Nicola Sacco and Bartolomeo Vanzetti case, Blitzstein first approached the socially conscious themes that characterize his later theatrical works.

By the mid-1930s Blitzstein developed a pro-labor, antifascist politics, abandoning a beaux arts aesthetic for a populist, more tonal language influenced by Kurt Weill and Hanns Eisler. The primary exemplar of this new phase was THE CRADLE WILL ROCK (1936), a proletarian "play in music" in ten scenes, whose cartoonlike style derives from American vaudeville and popular music forms. Often revived and given several complete recordings and a film treatment by Tim Robbins (*Cradle Will Rock*), this musical is emblematic of Blitzstein's lifelong project: he would abandon the transparent agenda of agit-prop (AGITATION-PROPAGANDA) but would retain the drive to make the theater both more sophisticated musically and more attentive to social issues. The relative absence of love stories in his work testifies to what he felt was the pointlessness of adding more romance to the Broadway stage when so many other topics in American society went chronically unaddressed. A Communist Party member from the late 1930s until 1948, he is often remembered as the social conscience of American music and became an advocate of African American performers.

No for an Answer (1936–1940; first performance, 1941), a full-length opera about immigrant workers, their middle-class supporters, and the proto-fascist elements in America lined up against them, is also based on popular musical styles but treats its characters in greater depth than in *Cradle* and employs the chorus powerfully. It was the first American opera to employ a split stage depicting simultaneous events and, in a nod to film noir, the first to include the technique of flashbacks. After a musical career as an enlisted soldier based in London during World War II, he based his opera *Regina* (1949) on LILLIAN HELLMAN'S THE LITTLE FOXES. Debuting on Broadway in 1949, it has become an often-staged modern American operatic classic, as much about race and the evolution of American music as about a rapacious family exploiting the poor and each other in 1900 Alabama.

Blitzstein's translation of Weill's *Die Dreigroschenoper* debuted OFF-BROADWAY as THE THREEPENNY OPERA in 1954 with Lotte Lenya as Jenny. It ran for six years and became the standard performing version. In 1955 his *Reuben Reuben* with Eddie Albert and Evelyn Lear was an allegory about the failure of communication in contemporary society; although its score is perhaps his most lush and ecstatic, the message got lost. *Juno* (1957–1959), a musical based on SEAN O'CASEY'S *JUNO AND THE PAYCOCK*, uses traditional Irish melodies orchestrated in rich, Britten-like harmonies that sounded too advanced for Broadway. With a book by Joseph Stein, it starred Melvyn Douglas and Shirley Booth, with choreography by Agnes de Mille. Small-scale revivals have not yet brought out the durable effect a major production might reveal.

At the end of his life, Blitzstein left incomplete three operas: a full-scale opera on Sacco and Vanzetti commissioned by the Metropolitan Opera and two one-acts based on Bernard Malamud stories, *Idiots First* and *The Magic Barrel*.

Blitzstein's reputation rests largely on *The Cradle Will Rock* and *Regina*, but his broader legacy is a lifelong body of creation reaffirming the artist's rightful concern with social issues. In an age when Broadway and American operatic composers drew heavily on European models, there were few composers searching for an American voice who fused classical and popular styles, or who fitted to music the many accents of the American language, as well as Blitzstein. In these ways he influenced succeeding generations of composers and librettists for the American musical stage.

[*See also* Political Theater in the United States]

PLAYS: *Triple-Sec* (1928); *Parabola and Circula* (1929); *The Harpies* (1931); *The Condemned* (1932); *The Cradle Will Rock* (1936); *I've Got the Tune* (1937); *No for an Answer* (1941); *Regina* (1949); *Reuben Reuben* (1955); *Juno* (1959); *Idiots First* (completed by Leonard J. Lehrman)

FURTHER READING

Dietz, Robert James. "The Operatic Style of Marc Blitzstein in the American 'Agit-Prop' Era." Ph.D. diss., Univ. of Iowa, 1970.

Gordon, Eric A. *Mark the Music: The Life and Work of Marc Blitzstein*. New York: St. Martin's, 1989. Reprint, Lincoln, Nebr.: iUniverse, 2000.

Houseman, John. *Run-through*. New York: Simon & Schuster, 1972.

Talley, Paul Myers. "Social Criticism in the Original Theatre Librettos of Marc Blitzstein." Ph.D. diss., Univ. of Wisconsin, 1965.

Eric A. Gordon

BLOK, ALEKSANDR (1880–1921)

One of RUSSIA'S greatest poets, Aleksandr Blok was also the foremost playwright of Russian SYMBOLISM. He was born into Russia's cultural elite and made his name as a poet even before graduating from St. Petersburg University. Although many elements of the dramatic enter into Blok's early verse, not until well into the second phase of his career did he turn to drama proper in search of a language that better reflected the reality around him, particularly after the 1905 Revolution.

Blok's first play, A PUPPET SHOW (*Balaganchik*, 1906), issued from the abortive attempt of a group that frequented the poet Viacheslav Ivanov's "Tower" to create a miscellany and theater, *Torches*. VSEVOLOD MEYERHOLD took the play to the fledgling Komissarzhevskaia Theater and created one of the most important productions in the history of MODERNIST DRAMA. In *A Puppet Show*, Blok combined and parodied elements of past traditions, such as the commedia dell'arte and Greek classical TRAGEDY, juxtaposing them with a prescient use of devices of estrangement. Meyerhold seized on Blok's innovations and availed himself of Nikolai Sapunov's set design and the poet Mikhail Kuzmin's musical score as he elaborated his THEATER OF THE GROTESQUE.

The second of Blok's trilogy of "lyric dramas," *The King on the Square* (*Korol' na ploshchadi*, 1906), is problematic, and Blok dealt more successfully with its social and political themes in the dramatic dialogue *Of Love, Poetry, and Governmental Service* (*O liubvi, poËzii, i gosudarstvennoi sluzhbe*, 1906), which grew directly out of the play. Despite its shortcomings, Meyerhold saw potential in the play and, as late as 1919, intended to stage it.

By contrast, Blok created another small masterpiece in his third play, *The Unknown Woman* (*Neznakomka*, 1906), based on the eponymous poem. Organized according to a thoroughgoing use of doubles and structural parallelism, the play exhibits an organic symbology and some of Blok's sharpest social satire. Despite the early objections by the censor, Meyerhold persevered and staged *The Unknown Woman* in 1914 at the Tenishevsky school on a double bill with *A Puppet Show*. The production proved pivotal because it marked the beginning of Meyerhold's constructivist phase.

Dissatisfied with the genre of "lyric drama," Blok sought "healthy realism" in his next play, *The Song of Fate* (*Pesnia sud'by*, 1907–1908; revised 1919). The play's rambling structure is reminiscent of romantic and epic drama, while Blok's approach to psychology takes on distinctly Chekhovian tonalities. The play was not produced; however, KONSTANTIN STANISLAVSKY and Vladimir Nemirovich-Danchenko considered it seriously for the Moscow Art Theater, and Meyerhold did his best to stage it at the Aleksandrinsky. Late in life, Blok radically revised the play to tighten its structure.

Blok set *The Rose and the Cross* (*Roza i krest*, 1912), his last play and one of the finest plays of the symbolist era, in Languedoc during the Albigensian Crusade. The play represents Blok's most successful treatment of the personal and the social in dramatic form. Stanislavsky and Nemirovich-Danchenko hoped to stage it at the MOSCOW ART THEATER, but the Revolution intervened. Although the play went through more than 200 rehearsals, it was not staged. Modernist directors, including Meyerhold and Alexander Tairov, also wished to stage the play but were discouraged by Blok, who still sought "healthy realism."

Obscured during the Soviet era for ideological reasons, Blok's dramatic legacy is only now receiving a full and fair assessment.

[*See also* Avant-Garde Drama]

PLAYS: *The King on the Square* (*Korol' na ploshchadi*, 1906); *Of Love, Poetry, and Governmental Service: A Dialogue* (*O liubvi, poËzii, i gosudarstvennoi sluzhbe. Dialog*, 1906); *A Puppet Show* (*Balaganchik*, 1906); *An Unknown Woman* (*Neznakomka*, 1906); *The Song of Fate* (*Pesnia sud'by*, 1907–1908; revised 1919); *The Rose and the Cross* (*Roza i krest*, 1912); *Ramses* (*Ramzes*, 1919)

FURTHER READING

Berberova, Nina. *Aleksandr Blok: A Life*. Tr. by Robyn Marsack. Manchester: Carcanet, 1996.

Blok, Aleksandr. "On Drama." In *Russian Dramatic Theory from Pushkin to the Symbolists: An Anthology*, ed. and tr. by Laurence Senelick. Austin: Univ. of Texas Press, 1981.

——. *The Puppet Show* and *The Rose and the Cross*. In *The Russian Symbolist Theatre: An Anthology of Plays and Critical Texts*, ed. and tr. by Michael Green. Ann Arbor: Ardis, 1986.

——. *A Puppet Show, The King on the Square*, and *The Unknown Woman*. In *Aleksandr Blok's Trilogy of Lyric Dramas: A Puppet Show, The King on the Square, and The Unknown Woman*, tr. by Timothy C. Westphalen. London: Routledge, 2003.

Chukovsky, Kornei. *Alexander Blok as Man and Poet*. Tr. by D. Burgin and K. O'Connor. Ann Arbor: Ardis, 1982.

Mochulsky, Konstantin. *Aleksandr Blok*. Detroit: Wayne State Univ. Press, 1983.

Orlov, Vladimir. *The Life of Alexander Blok*. Moscow: Progress Pubs., 1980.

Pyman, Avril. *The Life of Aleksandr Blok, Volume I: The Distant Thunder 1880–1908*. Oxford: Oxford Univ. Press, 1979.

——. *The Life of Aleksandr Blok, Volume II: The Release of Harmony 1908–1921*. Oxford: Oxford Univ. Press, 1980.

Westphalen, Timothy C. *Lyric Incarnate: The Dramas of Aleksandr Blok*. London: Harwood Acad. Pubs., 1998.

Timothy C. Westphalen

BLOOD, SWEAT AND FEARS

MARIA OSHODI's play *Blood, Sweat and Fears* was premiered by Harmony Theatre at Battersea Art Centre, London, in May 1988 and toured in England. The title, a modification of Winston Churchill's famous lines, refers to the main themes of the play: a young black man who suffers from sickle cell anemia (a blood disorder that affects about ten percent of black people and that has not been fully explored by the medical establishment) and tries to cover up the symptoms of his disease with pain killers because he is afraid of coming to terms with his disability. Oshodi, herself black and suffering from "disabling" blindness, interviewed young sickle cell anemia sufferers at a center in Lambeth with the intention of representing how "its victims perceived themselves as disabled people" and "exploring the agonising tensions surrounding invisible disability" (Oshodi, 1989).

The play is set mainly in a Star Trek Café, the fast-food store serving as a metaphor for "our increasingly competitive society's sometimes dismissive, or superficial, attitude to disability." The eighteen-year-old Ben, who suffers from sickle cell anemia, but was misdiagnosed until the age of nine, is polarized in his emotions between revealing and concealing his suffering, between suppressing his awareness of his illness and tackling it actively. His girlfriend Ashley tries to force him to face his condition and to take positive steps in order to alleviate it by healthy food, by abstention from alcohol and tobacco, and by alternative medicine. Her involvement and suffering and Ben's obstinate refusal to collaborate with her efforts—"I don't care because the disease don't care"—create a rising tension, which culminates in Ben's breakdown shortly before an important exam that would allow him to fulfill his dream of becoming a chef. Ben's mother Tessa teaches Ashley not to sacrifice her own life for Ben but instead to wait for him to develop a responsibility toward his own body.

Oshodi draws a critical portrait of the British medical system: doctors talk merely to themselves and their assistants in incomprehensible medical terminology, reducing Ben to an interesting case; the hospital neglects a patient in pain for a whole hour; an incompetent nurse gives morphine to a patient who explains that he is allergic to it; a young girl looks for an abortion in the private sector but is unable to afford it. Ben's only "friend," Curtis, a macho character who steals money and who forces his girlfriend to have an abortion, is dismissive of Ben's illness, offering him cigarettes and simply trying to ignore that Ben is suffering at all when he visits him in the hospital. The reaction of the (white) boss at the Star Trek Café when he watches Ben collapsing is revealing in its heartless ignorance: "What?! And he's been working here? In my branch? With my food? And he's got that? I didn't know he was that way inclined. I thought he was your boyfriend. God. I'm surrounded by crooks and perverted cripples." He obviously confuses anemia with HIV and betrays his homophobia and prejudice. The play ends on a rather hopeful note, Ben being offered a job as a commis chef that his college teacher has obtained for him, despite his disability and his not having taken the exams. In the end, Ben is shown reading for the first time the forms he needs to fill out to be certified as "disabled" and thereby entitled to certain privileges.

The language of the play ranges from the colloquial to the poetic, with the most poetic parts being given to Ben: soliloquies and flashback scenes in which he remembers the traumatic experiences of his life, being shunned at school and excluded from the normal life of a child. The focus of the play is on a problem particular to young black people, which, however, is presented in such a way that it can stand for those of the disabled in general.

[*See also* England, 1940–Present]

FURTHER READING

Aston, Elaine, and Janelle Reinelt. *The Cambridge Companion to Modern British Women Playwrights*. Cambridge: Cambridge Univ. Press, 2000.

Brewer, Mary F. *Race, Sex, and Gender in Contemporary Women's Theatre: The Construction of "Woman."* Brighton: Sussex Acad. Press, 1999.

Griffin, Gabriele. *Contemporary Black and Asian Women Playwrights in Britain*. Cambridge: Cambridge Univ. Press, 2003.

Oshodi, Maria. *Blood, Sweat and Fears*. In *Black Plays: Two*, ed. by Yvonne Brewster. London: Methuen Drama, 1989.

Heike Grundmann

THE BLOOD KNOT

Written in 1961 about two brothers with the same black mother and different fathers, one black and the other white, *The Blood Knot* opened on October 22 in a makeshift performance venue called Dorkay House in Johannesburg. ATHOL FUGARD acted the brother with a white father—Morrie—while his roommate and actor Zakes Mda played the black brother—Zachs. Classified as "coloreds," the one with the lighter skin had potential room for achieving subjectivity, while the darker skin one has no options to produce himself as a subject of history and culture. Morrie returns to his brother Zachs after some years apart with a business proposal of setting up a jointly owned farm. Zach's desire for female companionship prompts his brother suggesting he take a pen pal. Ethel—the pen pal—turns out to be a white woman, thereby setting off an immediate conflict in South Africa's apartheid setting. When Ethel promised to visit, Zach had to persuade his brother Morrie to play his role as well as acquire "white" behavior to suit the occasion. The process of one brother entering into the other's existential limitations through role-playing gives audiences access to the interiority of alienation felt by both brothers in their society. The brothers dropped off the idea of playing each other when Ethel canceled the trip; they decided instead to focus on their relationship as siblings in their social context.

At the core of the story is how the bodies of these two signify in a social setting within which the color of a person's skin is an absolutist identity sanctioned not to interact by a state that believed in the superiority of one race over the other. Set in a poor shanty at the outskirts of Port Elizabeth, the play sheds particular light on class and race as identities in South Africa. Like Fugard himself, white privilege in racist South Africa did not necessarily trickle down to poor rural-based Afrikaners in shacks and shantytowns. The play broadens the racial issue to explore ideas of desire and subjectivity of these different but related bodies. Morrie's role is paradoxical. It is he who had the capacity to leave as well as conceptualize possibilities of farm ownership or even desiring a woman. Foisting his dreams on his brother, Morrie transforms Zachs's futureless life with one burdened by hope. The play boldly stresses the collective victimization of all South Africans—those whose bodies are demonized and those forced to witness their marginalization. According to Fugard (1979): "[T]he essence of *The Blood Knot* is the problem of one person trying to cope with the reality of another existence, of someone else whose pain he feels, whose suffering he witnesses. It is the existentialist's dilemma of one person trying to relate to another."

Like most of Fugard's plays, there are certain ludic qualities to this play—from the letters to the car ride. The playwright draws attention to the games that frame existential quests and uses them to seduce audiences into the play's narrative structure.

[*See also* Africa, East Africa]

FURTHER READING

Benson, Mary, ed. *Notebooks 1960/1977 Athol Fugard*. London: Faber, 1983.

Fugard, Athol. "The Family Plays of the Sixties." In *South African Literature: An Introduction*, by Stephen Gray. Cape Town: David Phillips, 1979.

Awam Amkpa

BLOOD RELATIONS

SHARON POLLOCK's *Blood Relations* is an imaginative, well-researched dramatization of the infamous Lizzie Borden story. It premiered in Edmonton in 1980 and has won the Governor General's Award. An earlier version, titled *My Name Is Lisbeth*, was produced in 1976. The blood of this later title refers to the murder of Lizzie's father and stepmother, a crime for which Lizzie was acquitted. This play is sympathetic to Lizzie but does not try to exonerate her. However, the external pressures on Lizzie that came from her family and the wider society, and that decided how a gentlewoman should behave, are highlighted here. The irony of this play and of her acquittal is that the role of the feminine is what imprisoned her yet also gave her freedom, as, according to the defense, no gentlewoman could have committed such a crime. *Blood Relations* is influenced by feminist thinking and critiques the patriarchal and class values that controlled Lizzie and, by implication, other women of her class around the time the play is set.

By setting the play in two time zones, in 1892 and 1902 (in the time directly preceding the axe murders and ten years later), Pollock is able to explore the aftermath of the murders and emphasize how this is a fictional re-creation of an actual event. The play begins ten years later, with Lizzie (Miss Lizzie) talking to The Actress who is playing her role in a theater. Together they reimagine the past as Lizzie acts the role of Bridget the maid, and The Actress plays Lizzie, which distances Lizzie from her accused actions. The play is framed by these two as Lizzie finally accuses The Actress of the murders. The past is emphasized as being a reconstruction, but it is also a memory as Lizzie (as Bridget) initially prompts The Actress when she plays her part.

Lizzie, played by The Actress, asks rhetorically if there is a magic formula for being a woman. Lizzie is depicted as a misfit in her family and within society because she has no desire to marry simply because it is expected of her. Her family is pointedly a microcosm of the outside world that is never seen here in the play but is only referred to.

Because Pollock uses a historical event for dramatic purposes, she is able to investigate the social factors that could have led to these murders if Lizzie were guilty. These factors are channeled through her father's patriarchal authority and in the realization by Lizzie, played by The Actress, that she is expected to be a mirror: "I'm supposed to reflect what you want to see but everyone wants something different. If no one looks in the mirror, I'm not even there. I don't exist." The ironic use of metadrama means that The Actress is potentially speaking as an actress and as Lizzie simultaneously, implying that Lizzie has always been trying, but failing, to act the part of the dutiful daughter and sister.

[*See also* Canada]

FURTHER READING

Clement, Susan, and Esther Beth Sullivan. "The Split Subject of Blood Relations." In *Upstaging Big Daddy: Directing Theatre as if Gender and Race Matter*, ed. by Ellen Donkin and Susan Clement. Ann Arbor: Univ. of Michigan Press, 1993.

Salter, Denis. "Biocritical Essay. (Im)possible Worlds: The Plays of Sharon Pollock." In *First Accessions*, ed. by Apollonia Steele and Jean Tener. Calgary: Univ. of Calgary Press, 1989.

Julie Ellam

BLOOD WEDDING

Blood Wedding (*Bodas de sangre*), written by FEDERICO GARCÍA LORCA in 1933, is the first of three rural plays that make up a trilogy in which Lorca creates a cultural imagery of Andalusia linked to sexual repression, violence, and death—what has been called "Tragic Andalusia." Spanish writer Azorín (José Martínez Ruíz) had previously used this term in the early 20th century to refer to the socioeconomic conditions present in rural Andalusia and the strong anarchist revolts that took place as a consequence of those conditions. Lorca's tragic Andalusia, however, was not built with this historical referent in mind. Lorca constructs his tragic imagery by incorporating popular rites like weddings, burials, and pilgrimages and by using the concept of destiny from classical tragedy, as well as the figure of Christ and the concept of honor from Spanish morality plays.

Blood Wedding revolves around a wedding rite. In an Andalusian village two middle-class families—landowners—fix the marriage of their son and daughter and start the wedding preparations. The play's atmosphere is strongly determined by The Mother of the Groom's tormented remembrances and bad premonitions—her husband and eldest son had been killed in vendettas with another family in the village. The play is also marked by the strong sexual attraction between The Bride and Leonardo, her ex-boyfriend and member of the family responsible for the death of The Groom's brother and father. In the middle of this tension, the wedding finally takes place. During the wedding banquet, The Bride runs away with her ex-boyfriend Leonardo. The Mother of the Groom claims vengeance and incites her son to clean the family's honor. The play ends tragically with the deaths and funerals of both Leonardo and The Groom.

Besides the wedding rite, the burial is another crucial rite in *Blood Wedding*. Lorca represents the burial rite through a symbolic union between The Mother, constantly identified in the play with the earth, and her dead eldest son, linked to the figure of Jesus Christ through his spilled blood. At the same time, this symbolic relationship of Mother-Son is identified with the wedding rite throughout the play.

This identification takes us right into the topic of incest, so characteristic of classical TRAGEDY. However, unlike in the case of classical tragedy, the characters in *Blood Wedding* never consummate their sexual desires: the married couple never gets to consummate the wedding night, and the lovers do not have sexual relations; in fact, at the end of the play The Bride proudly announces that her honor is intact because she is still a virgin. By extension, this symbolically represents the lack of sexual consummation in the Mother-Son relationship. Consequently, in opposition to classical tragedy, Lorca creates his vision of tragic Andalusia by identifying the sacred function of the wedding rite with the taboo of incest and with the sexual repression it generates. This idea points directly to the psycho-anthropological studies by Sigmund Freud and his theory about the link between pagan and Catholic rites and about the origin of the taboo of incest, marriage, and social institutions.

[*See also* Spain]

FURTHER READING

Anderson, Andrew A. *¿De qué trata Bodas de sangre?* [What is *Blood Wedding* about?]. Toulouse: Univ. Toulouse–Le Mirail, 1982.

Basterra, Gabriela. "The Grammar of Fate in Lorca's Bodas de sangre." *Journal of Romance Studies* 3, no. 2 (2003): 49–68.

Edwards, Gwynne. "The Way Things Are: Towards a Definition of Lorcan Tragedy." *Anales de la Literatura Espanola Contemporanea* 21, no. 3 (1996): 230, 271–290.

MacMullan, Terence. "Federico García Lorca's Critique of Marriage in Bodas de sangre." *Neophilologus* 77, no. 1 (1993): 61–73.

Martínez Masdeu, Edgar. "Bodas de sangre y Federico en el tiempo: Obsesión por el sino" [Blood Wedding and Federico throughout time: Obsessed by destiny]. *Revista del Ateneo Puertorriqueno* 3, no. 8 (1993): 183–194.

Tirumalesh, K. V. "History, Criticism, and Lorca: The Curious Case of Blood Wedding." *Central Institute of English and Foreign Languages Bulletin* 7, nos. 1–2 (1995): 225–237.

Maribel Parra-Domínguez

BOAL, AUGUSTO (1931–)

The Theater of the Oppressed, in all its various modalities, is a constant search for dialogical forms, forms of theatre through which it is possible to converse, both about and as part of social activity, pedagogy, psychotherapy, politics.

—Augusto Boal, *Legislative Theatre*, 1998

Brazilian director Augusto Boal has gained international renown for work he began in the 1950s and 1960s on the Theater of the Oppressed, an interactive theater approach that engages communities in dialogue about their issues and stories. This nonscripted, preliterary theater form fosters a communal space for exchange that Boal sees as providing an antidote to Aristotelian tragic theater, which is typically derived from preexisting literary texts and aimed at purging the audience member of socially unacceptable behavior. Central to Boal's technique is the use of the "spect-actor," a method in which an audience member can interrupt an unfolding scene and demonstrate his or her ideas for action in the scene. Consequently, this technique engages communities in an interactive dialogue approach and serves as a vehicle for grassroots activism.

By the early 1970s and shortly after the publication of his first book, *The Theatre of the Oppressed*, Boal's work was increasingly seen as a political threat. Arrested and tortured, Boal was exiled to Argentina, where he continued to work on Forum Theater, Image Theater, and Invisible Theater. He exiled himself to Paris in 1976, where he developed a series of techniques for introspection that draw from dramatic psychotherapy—work later published in *The Rainbow of Desire* (1995). While in Paris, Boal established several centers for the Theater of the Oppressed and held the first International Theater of the Oppressed Conference in 1981. After the military junta in BRAZIL was removed in 1986, Boal returned to Brazil and established a center. In 1992 Boal's book *Games for Actors and Non-Actors* was published. He subsequently extended his work into a new phase, what he calls "Legislative Theater," the focus of his book *Legislative Theatre: Using Performance to Make Politics*. This work chronicles Boal's invitation by the vice governor of Rio de Janeiro to return and set up the Integrated Centres for Popular Education, where Boal's theater company developed plays on unemployment, health, and housing in order to provide education and dialogue for a number of disenfranchised communities in Rio. After the vice governor lost the election, Boal and his company collaborated with the Worker's Party; in order to strengthen the work, Boal ran for election and won. Serving as a councilman from 1992 to 1996, Boal used his interactive theater techniques to engage disenfranchised communities in interactive theater techniques in order to articulate what laws they would like to see passed. This approach has met with success in Brazil; thirteen laws have been passed. It has also been implemented in city council work in Vancouver, Canada, through Headlines Theater, a community-based theater group.

Boal's work has had a profound impact on hundreds of community-based theater companies around the world. Boal's international travels to lead workshops and give talks now include extensive travel in the United States. In 1997, Boal was awarded the Career Achievement Award by the Association for Theater in Higher Education.

[*See also* Avant-Garde Drama; Poor Theater]

FURTHER READING

Boal, Augusto. *The Theatre of the Oppressed*. New York: Urizen Books, 1979.

——. *Games for Actors and Non-Actors*. New York: Routledge, 1992.

——. *The Rainbow of Desire*. New York: Routledge, 1995.

——. *Legislative Theatre: Using Performance to Make Politics*. New York: Routledge, 1998.

Cohen-Cruz, Jan, and Mady Schutzman. *Playing Boal*. New York: Routledge, 1994.

Heritage, Paul. "The Courage to Be Happy: Augusto Boal, Legislative Theatre, and the 7th International Festival of the Theatre of the Oppressed." *The Drama Review* 143 (Fall 1994): 25–36.

Paterson, Douglas L. "We Are All Theater: An Interview with Augusto Boal." *High Performance* 72 (Summer 1996): 18–23.

Taussig, Michael, and Richard Schechner. "Boal in Brazil, France, and the USA: An Interview with Augusto Boal." *The Drama Review* 34 (Fall 1990): 50–65.

Kanta Kochhar-Lindgren

BODAS DE SANGRE *See* BLOOD WEDDING

BÖDELN *See* THE HANGMAN

BOGART, ANNE (1951–)

Born in 1951 to a navy family, Anne Bogart developed an interest in theater at an early age as she moved from school to school. After attending three colleges, Bogart graduated from Bard College in 1974, where she joined a student-created theater company, Via Theater, which was dedicated to the practical study of Jerzy Grotowski's work and method. Upon its dissolution, Bogart moved to New York City, where she went to New York University, obtaining a master's degree in theater history.

As a young and untried director, Bogart had to search for opportunities and quickly became known for unconventional staging—on rooftops, basements, store window, discos, and so on. In 1979, because of her experimental work, she was asked to teach at the Experimental Theatre Wing (ETW), an innovative undergraduate theater program at New York University. At ETW, Bogart was introduced to Mary Overlie, a choreographer and founder of the Six Viewpoints. Bogart eventually built on Overlie's Six Viewpoints to develop a unique approach to training and working with actors. She briefly served as artistic director of Trinity Repertory Company (1989–1990) but resigned over a budget dispute. Bogart served as president of Theatre Communications Group from 1991 to 1993. In 1992, she co-founded the Saratoga International Theatre Institute (now known simply as the SITI COMPANY) with Japanese director TADASHI SUZUKI, artistic director of the Suzuki Company of Toga (SCOT). Bogart serves as artistic director for the SITI Company and teaches at Columbia University.

SITI combines the Viewpoints training with the Suzuki method. Viewpoints is a technique for improvisation that originated in postmodern dance to develop a group's ability to work together spontaneously. The Suzuki method is a rigorous discipline that trains the actor to be fully present emotionally and physically in each moment. The company is dedicated to three principles: creating new work, training young theater artists, and international collaboration. Utilizing these two training systems, SITI has created several critically acclaimed works including *Small Lives/Big Dreams* (1994), *Culture of Desire* (1997), *Cabin Pressure* (1999), and the trilogy on American artists *Bob* (1998), *Room* (2000), and *Score* (2002).

Bogart has worked with several respected contemporary playwrights including MAC WELLMAN (1951, 1986), Tina Landau (*American Vaudeville*, 1992), PAULA VOGEL (*THE BALTIMORE WALTZ*, 1992; *Hot 'N' Throbbing*, 1994), and CHARLES MEE (*bobrauschenbergamerica*, 2001).

Committed to teaching her craft to young artists, Bogart teaches master classes at many colleges and universities around the country and teaches at SITI's intensive summer workshop at Skidmore College, Sarasota Springs, New York.

Bogart is the recipient of numerous awards including a Guggenheim Fellowship (2000–2001), two Obie Awards (1988, 1990), the New York Dance and Performance Award (1984), the Villager Award (1980), a National Endowment for the Arts Artistic Associate Grant (1986–1987), and the Bard College Kellog Award (2001). In 1995, Actors Theatre of Louisville named her a "Modern Master" at its 10th annual Classics in Context Festival.

[*See also* United States, 1940–Present]

FURTHER READING

Bogart, Anne. *A Director Prepares: Seven Essays on Art and Theatre*. London: Routledge, 2001.

Dixon, Michael Bigelow, and Joel A. Smith, eds. *Anne Bogart: Viewpoints*. Lyme, N.H.: Smith & Kraus, 1995.

J. Briggs Cormier

BOHEMIAN LIGHTS

Bohemian Lights (*Luces de Bohemia*, 1920, 1924) by RAMÓN MARIA DEL VALLE-INCLÁN tells the story of Max Estrella's night pilgrimage through early-20th-century Madrid. The play offers a view of the political and social panorama of 1920s SPAIN. Estrella, a drunken, blind poet, playwright, and newspaper collaborator, is accompanied by his alter ego, Don Latino de Hispalis, on his journey through a bookstore where Estrella is scammed; a dirty tavern where he meets a young prostitute and her pimp; a jail cell where Estrella is taken after being arrested and where he meets a young man who awaits his own death with cold resignation; the office of the home secretary, who turns out to be an old friend of Estrella's who traded the bohemian life for politics; a café where Estrella and Don Latino converse with *modernista* poet Rubén Darío (the most representative and acclaimed poet of *modernismo*, the poetic movement prevailing at the end of the 19th century in the Hispanic letters).

The characters finally arrive at Estrella's building doorstep where he tragically dies of hypothermia. However, the journey does not end with Estrella's death. The action continues and the reader-spectator witnesses the protagonist's wake and funeral. Not without black humor and irony, the last scenes in the play serve as a final tribute to Estrella. *Bohemian Lights* is the greatest example of the Esperpento (which means "grotesque" or "ugly"), a style that Valle-Inclán himself created and named in order to reflect the distortion and deformation of Spanish social conventions of the early 20th century as if placed in front of a concave mirror. Along the journey in *Bohemian Lights*, the author presents a parade of figures that have no future and, at times, no expectations. Thus, the protagonist is a bohemian who does not belong anymore to that society and the ludicrous world of political corruption and mediocrity. At the very end of his life, Max concludes: "The tragic sense of Spanish life can only be rendered through an aesthetic that is systematically deformed. . . . Spain is a grotesque deformation of European civilization." In this sense, the Esperpento serves as a vehicle for social and political satire, even as Max Estrella serves as the channel to voice this general complaint, which is not addressed to institutions or individuals in particular; on the contrary, this total lament is one in which a collective criticism can be seen for the first time, as Alonso Zamora Vicente pointed out in *Luces de Bohemia* (Valle-Inclán, 1990). Through Max, the bohemian life, so inoperative and sterile, is ridiculed.

Language in *Bohemian Lights* is complex, multiple, and varied. One can find literary language as well as popular jargon, used by rogues and prostitutes, or *madrileñismos* (words and expressions of the colloquial Spanish spoken in Madrid's slums). A parody of certain literary styles is also present, for example, in the mockery of the affected expression of the *modernistas*.

In sum, *Bohemian Lights* attacks the entire society, thus the manifold repertoire of characters, lexicon, and social classes caricatured in the play.

FURTHER READING

Almeida, Diane. *The Esperpento Tradition in the Works of Ramón del Valle-Inclán and Luis Buñuel.* Lewiston, N.Y.: Edwin Mellen Press, 2000.

Servera Baño, José. *Luces de Bohemia. Ramón del Valle-Inclán.* [Lights of Bohemia. Ramón del Valle-Inclán]. Palma de Mallorca: Monograma, 1994.

Valle-Inclán, Ramón del. *Luces de Bohemia. Esperpento.* [Lights of Bohemia. Esperpento]. Ed. by Alonso Zamora Vicente. Madrid: Espasa-Calpe, 1990.

———. *Three Plays.* Tr. and introd. by María M. Delgado. London: Methuen Drama, 1993.

María Dolores Morillo

BOLT, ROBERT (1924–1995)

> *It is not easy to know what a play is "about" until it is finished, and by then what it is "about" is incorporated in it irreversibly and is no more to be separated from it than the shape of a statue is to be separated from the marble. Writing a play is thinking, not thinking about thinking; more like a dream than a scheme—except that it lasts six months or more, and that one is responsible for it.*
> —Robert Bolt

Robert Bolt achieved his greatest artistic fame as author of the highly successful play *A Man for All Seasons* (1960) and as the screenwriter for such films as *Lawrence of Arabia* (1962) and *Doctor Zhivago* (1965). He also wrote several other stage plays, film scripts, radio plays, and one novel. In his most notable works, he focuses on the conflict between the conscience of the individual and the opposing forces of that individual's environment. Although his treatment of this conflict never engages directly with religious ethics, not even in his dramatization of Sir Thomas More's fatal confrontation with Henry VIII, Bolt's preoccupation with the psychological threat posed by ethical compromise dominates his work.

After serving in the armed forces in World War II, Bolt completed a degree in history at Manchester University and began teaching and writing plays for radio and for the stage. His first successful stage play, *Flowering Cherry* (1957), featured Sir Ralph Richardson in the leading role and established Bolt as a playwright of significant ability. His next play, *The Tiger and the Horse*, was finished by 1958 and was produced in 1960 shortly after Bolt's *A Man for All Seasons*, a revision of a 1954 radio play that had been televised by the BBC in 1957, had begun playing. With both of these dramas enjoying long performance runs, Bolt's reputation grew, and his success with the historically based *A Man for All Seasons* led to his being asked to write a revised screenplay for the Sam Spiegel and David Lean film *Lawrence of Arabia*. Although Bolt's 1963 stage play *Gentle Jack* was poorly received by audiences, his screenplay for *Lawrence* was an artistic and financial success that brought him new opportunities in the film genre.

A series of film projects followed: *Doctor Zhivago* (1965), Bolt's own *A Man for All Seasons* (1966), *Ryan's Daughter* (1970), *Lady Caroline Lamb* (1972), *The Bounty* (1984), and *The Mission* (1986). Although much of his energy was engaged in these projects, Bolt continued when possible to work on plays, with two more historical dramas appearing in the 1970s. With *Vivat! Vivat Regina!* (1970) he returned to the 16th century, portraying the conflict between Elizabeth Tudor and her cousin Mary, Queen of Scots. He moved to the early 20th century for *State of Revolution* (1977), which dealt with the interaction of the leaders of the Soviet Revolution in Russia.

In 1979, Bolt's busy career was interrupted by a stroke and other medical problems, and though he eventually recuperated sufficiently to resume some of his work for the screen, his career as playwright was effectively ended. He died in 1995, having won Academy Awards for his screenplays for *Doctor Zhivago* and *A Man for All Seasons*.

Much criticism of Bolt originates from those who see his work as insufficiently ideological or excessively conventional. His commercial success and the popularity of *A Man for All Seasons* appear to have been particularly irksome to those drama critics who disdain the opinions of ordinary people. Bolt himself was usually modest and candid about his achievements, and he acknowledged the influence of BERTOLT BRECHT while preserving an appreciable distance between his own DRAMATURGY and that of the activist German. Bolt had been in youth a member of the Communist Party and remained a public opponent of nuclear armament, but in his most insightful artistic work, he adroitly evaded the predictabilities of factional commitment.

[*See also* England, 1940–Present]

SELECT PLAYS: *A Man for All Seasons* (radio version, 1954; televised, 1957; produced, 1960); *The Last of the Wine* (radio version, 1955; produced, 1956); *The Critic and the Heart* (1957); *Flowering Cherry* (1957); *The Tiger and the Horse* (written by 1958; produced, 1960); *Gentle Jack* (1963); *The Thwarting of Baron Bolligrew* (1965); *Vivat! Vivat Regina!* (1970); *State of Revolution* (1977)

FURTHER READING

Atkins, Anselm. "Robert Bolt: Self, Shadow, and the Theater of Recognition." *Modern Drama* 10 (1967): 182–188.

Barnett, Gene A. "The Theatre of Robert Bolt." *Dalhousie Review* 48 (1968): 13–23.

Bolt, Robert. Preface to *A Man for All Seasons*. New York: Vintage Books, 1990.

Harben, Niloufer. *Twentieth-Century English History Plays: From Shaw to Bond*. Totowa, N.J.: Barnes & Noble, 1988.

Hayman, Ronald. *Robert Bolt*. London: Heinemann, 1969.

Palmer, Richard H. *The Contemporary British History Play*. Westport, Conn.: Greenwood Press, 1998.

Prüfer, Sabine. *The Individual at the Crossroads: The Works of Robert Bolt, Novelist, Dramatist, Screenwriter*. Frankfurt am Main: Peter Lang, 1998.

Robert Haynes

BOND, EDWARD (1934–)

Human consciousness is class consciousness.

—Edward Bond, in a letter to Tony Coult, 1979

As a writer for world stages, Edward Bond typically arouses sharply divided reactions. Some observers sympathize with the insistent anticapitalistic polemics underlying his three dozen plays. Others do not accept Bond's single-minded politics, particularly when his political parables are punctuated with seemingly arbitrary violence. Bond has remained a notable influence in contemporary drama despite a modest following in England and even less in the United States, where his plays are not widely known. For other playwrights, he has expanded what is permissible and playable on stages.

Born into a working-class family in 1934, Bond attended state schools until he was fourteen, entered the army, and married in 1971. Evident early in his career was a dedication to using the theater as a discussion forum and teaching podium. Bond's position regarding the individual and community has been straightforward: class-structured societies cause social damage. Using Marxist vocabulary, his characters engage in dialectical exchanges ranging across many moral issues. Primarily, Bond focuses on the corrupting power of capitalism on society, causing self-interest to supersede communal well-being.

Like the German playwright BERTOLT BRECHT, whom he greatly admires, Bond does not integrate spectators into action through REALISM but rather distances them with song interludes from the story and characters, to better argue the ethics concerned. The result often is phantasmagorical, with rapid shifting of settings and chronology. *Restoration* (1981) offers a useful example.

Bond employs theater to depict painful and disturbing images of the world. His early career was closely aligned with London's Royal Court Theatre, with his reputation defined by his enormously controversial drama SAVED, which premiered there in 1965. The play made British legal history as the last drama successfully prosecuted by the Lord Chamberlain using powers of censorship. Yet governmental objections to *Saved* were not exclusively based on its revolutionary politics. The drama's pervasive violence evoked public outcry. Especially criticized was a horrifying scene in which teen-aged London thugs torment, torture, and then stone to death an infant in a baby carriage. Violent acts have become standard in Bond's works, with human mutilation common. His bloody rewriting of William Shakespeare's *King Lear*, titled *Lear* (1971), contains seemingly gratuitous physical horrors far exceeding Shakespeare's original carnage. In his preface to the play, Bond anticipated complaints: "Violence shapes and obsesses our society, and if we do not stop being violent, we have no future." For Bond, physical violence is a didactic tool to gain audience attention and understanding.

Bond's works cover wide terrain and expanses of time but without dramatic realism. *Early Morning* (1968) is a surrealistic fantasy regarding an imaginary lesbian affair between Queen Victoria and Florence Nightingale. Shakespeare himself is given a radical reinterpretation as a wealth-mongering Stratfordian landowner in *Bingo* (1973). Bond's writings include a half-dozen stage adaptations of works including *Three Sisters* and *The White Devil*, as well as radio and movie scripts (*Blowup*, 1967, for Michelangelo Antonioni's acclaimed film); opera librettos; and a ballet scenario. Given his abundant writing in many formats and on widely diverse themes, Bond has proven himself a genuine man of letters who disavows compromises in the subjects and style of his work.

[*See also* England, 1940–Present]

SELECT PLAYS: *The Pope's Wedding* (1962); *Saved* (1965); *Early Morning* (1968); *Narrow Road to the Deep North* (1968); *Black Mass* (1970, part of *Sharpeville Sequence*); *Lear* (1971); *Passion* (1971); *Bingo* (1973); *The Sea* (1973); *The Fool* (1975); *We Come to the River* (1976, opera libretto); *A-A-America* (1976); *Stone* (1976); *The Bundle* (1978); *The Woman* (1978); *The Worlds* (1979); *Restoration* (1981); *Derek* (1982); *Summer* (1982); *The Cat* (1983, opera libretto); *Choruses from After the Assassinations* (1983); *Burns* (1986, for children); *Human Cannon* (1986); *Jackets II* (1989); *September* (1989); *In the Company of Men* (1992); *Olly's Prison* (1993); *Coffee* (1996); *At the Inland Sea* (1997); *Chair* (2000)

FURTHER READING

Coult, Tony. *The Plays of Edward Bond*. London: Methuen, 1979.

Eagleton, Terry. "Nature and Violence: The Prefaces of Edward Bond." *Critical Quarterly* 26 (1984): 127–135.

Hirst, David L. *Edward Bond*. Modern Dramatists Series. New York: Grove, 1985.

Innes, Christopher. *Modern British Drama: The Twentieth Century*. Cambridge: Cambridge Univ. Press, 2002.

Roberts, Philip, and Malcolm Hay. *Bond, a Study of His Plays*. London: Methuen, 1980.

Spencer, Jenny S. *Dramatic Strategies in the Plays of Edward Bond*. Cambridge: Cambridge Univ. Press, 1992.

C. J. Gianakaris

BONDAGERS

Fields aye need folk.
—Maggie, Act 1

In a hundred years—more—
We'll be ghosts in the fields,
But we'll cry out in vain,
For there'll be no one there.
—Sara, Act 2

First peformed in 1991 at the Traverse Theatre, Edinburgh, and winner of the LWT New Plays on Stage Award, the reviewer for *Scotland on Sunday* recognized SUE GLOVER's *Bondagers* as "one of the finest plays of the modern Scottish theatre" (Glover, 1997). It has played around the world, in the original and in translation, and appears on academic reading lists wherever contemporary Scottish playwriting is studied.

The play follows the cycle of one farm year in the lives of female laborers on SCOTLAND's great 19th-century Border farms, where no man would be employed unless he brought with him a female laborer, either a relative or a bondager hired by him at the local fair. The women of Blackshiels farm include Ellen, the former bondager who married the master; Liza, in her first season away from her family; and Sara, struggling to support her simple daughter, Tottie. Glover has set the piece during a period of rapid economic development, when the agrarian revolution has changed the way the land is worked and the yield it brings, but mechanization has not yet stripped the farms of their communities of laborers. This is no rural idyll. Glover portrays unflinchingly the dirt, cold, monotony, and ever-present fear of poverty and hunger that dominates the characters' lives. The whispered litany "Barley means bread, oats means bread, pease means bread / Bread of carefulness / Never enough bread" (Voices, act 1, scene 6) makes poignant Tottie's vision of a future abundance of bread bought at the cost of the emptying of the land. It is only Tottie who sees the continuum from the ox ploughs of the ancient fields—the lang syne, or olden-day, rigs—to modern machines that "scorn to wait on the moon for light to reap."

Focusing on the female laborers, Glover emphasizes their lack of self-determination by having no male characters appear onstage. Instead, the women speak repeatedly of the men who dominate their lives, economically or emotionally—the farmer, Maister Elliott; the "hind" (farmhand) Andra; and Kello, the black-eyed ploughman, who will precipitate a major crisis in the play, raping Tottie, only to die later at her hands. In the introduction to the 1997 Methuen edition of the play, Glover explains how these two characters relate to her wider vision of our present stewardship of the landscape: "Tottie . . . stands for the land. And Kello stands for our (sometimes criminal) carelessness."

The women's world is shaped by the seasons and the weather, punctuated by songs and dance, storytelling, and superstition. There is celebration, too, of the strength gained by women coming together to support each other and to celebrate their lives. Only Ellen, who has moved out of her class, and Liza, too inexperienced to understand where the true economic power lies, comment on the wider political picture. As Adrienne Scullion (1995) has pointed out, however supportive the community of women might appear, "the range of character-types is limited, and there remains a traditionalist tendency to value the stoical woman." At the last, offered a chance to leave the area by Ellen, Sara refuses, saying, "These fields are my calf-ground."

FURTHER READING

Bain, Audrey. "Loose Canons: Identifying a Women's Tradition in Playwriting." In *Scottish Theatre Since the Seventies*, ed. by Randall Stevenson and Gavin Wallace. Edinburgh: Edinburgh Univ. Press, 1996.

Glover, Sue. *Bondagers & The Straw Chair*. London: Methuen, 1997.

Horvat, Ksenija, and Barbara Bell. "Sue Glover, Rona Munro and Lara Jane Bunting: Echoes and Open Spaces." In *Contemporary Scottish Women Writers*, ed. by Aileen Christianson and Alison Lumsden. Edinburgh: Edinburgh Univ. Press, 2000.

Poggi, Valentina, and Margaret Rose. *A Theatre That Matters: Twentieth-Century Scottish Drama and Theatre*. Milan: Editzioni Unicopli, 2000.

Scullion, Adrienne. "Feminine Pleasures and Masculine Indignities: Gender and Community in Scottish Drama." In *Gendering the Nation*, ed. by Christopher Whyte. Edinburgh: Edinburgh Univ. Press, 1995.

——. "Contemporary Scottish Women Playwrights." In *Modern British Women Playwrights*, ed. by Elaine Aston and Janelle Reinelt. Cambridge: Cambridge Univ. Press, 2000.

Barbara A. E. Bell

LES BONNES *See* THE MAIDS

BOOTHE, CLARE (1903–1987)

You can do anything in the world if you're prepared to take the consequences, and consequences depend on character.

—Clare Boothe, 1942

Clare Boothe was born on April 10, 1903, in New York City. The first of her many careers was in journalism. She initiated it in 1930 by wangling a job as a routine staff writer for *Vogue*. The following year she moved to *Vanity Fair*. Both magazines were published by Condé Nast. For *Vanity Fair* she wrote a series of satirical sketches on New York's high society. These were published as a book, *Stuffed Shirts*. She so impressed Nast that he named her managing editor of *Vanity Fair* in 1933. Within a year she left this prestigious post to seek fame as a playwright.

Abide with Me (1934), her first play to be produced, recalled her unhappy years with George Brokaw, whom she married in 1923 and divorced in 1929. Damned by reviewers, it closed after thirty-six performances. Undaunted, she quickly wrote three more plays, all resounding successes. In THE WOMEN (1936) she examined the lives of Park Avenue wives and divorcées. *Kiss the Boys Goodbye* (1938), loosely based on David O. Selznick's search for the right actress to portray Scarlett O'Hara in *Gone with the Wind*, was unconvincing as the allegory of fascism in America that she intended it to be but pleased audiences as an exposé of the manners of East Coast literati and West Coast filmmakers. With *Margin for Error* (1939) she expressed in sharp satire her contempt for the Nazi regime in GERMANY.

Boothe's later works for the theater were disappointing. *Love Is a Verb* (1942), written in collaboration with Alexander King, was staged briefly by Virginia's Barter Theater and not heard of again. Her last play, *Child of the Morning* (1949), closed in Boston en route to Broadway and failed again in a production OFF-BROADWAY in 1958. After the death of her only child, Ann Brokaw, in 1944, Boothe turned to Roman Catholicism for consolation. Her newfound faith became the dominant force in her life, as was evident in *Child of the Morning* and her screenplay for the well-received film *Come to the Stable* (1949), both on religious themes. The screenplay was nominated for an Oscar.

With her marriage in 1935 to Henry R. Luce, one of the founders of *Time* magazine, Boothe developed an interest in public affairs. As a correspondent for *Life*, Luce's picture magazine, she traveled to Europe in 1940. From this came a book, *Europe in the Spring*. Increasingly conservative, she was elected to Congress from Connecticut in 1942 and 1944 as a Republican. Although she chose not to run for a third term, she continued to speak out on political issues. In 1953 President Dwight D. Eisenhower appointed her ambassador to ITALY, a post she held until 1956, when illness forced her to resign. She was less active in politics after the death of Luce in 1967, but in her last years she served on President Ronald Reagan's Intelligence Advisory Board. Boothe died on October 9, 1987, in Washington, D.C.

[*See also* Feminist Drama in the United States; United States, 1929–1940]

PLAYS: *Abide with Me* (1934); *The Women* (1936); *Kiss the Boys Goodbye* (1938); *Margin for Error* (1939); *Love Is a Verb* (with Alexander King, 1942); *Child of the Morning* (1949)

FURTHER READING

Fearnow, Mark. *Clare Boothe Luce: A Research and Production Sourcebook*. Westport, Conn.: Greenwood Press, 1995.

Martin, Ralph G. *Henry and Clare: An Intimate Portrait of the Luces*. New York: Putnam, 1991.

Morris, Sylvia Jukes. *Rage for Fame: The Ascent of Clare Boothe Luce*. New York: Random House, 1997.

Malcolm Goldstein

BORCHERT, WOLFGANG (1921–1947)

His health destroyed by alternating stints as a conscript in Adolf Hitler's armies in Russia—two separate tours of duty including a punitive one—and as an accused traitor arrested, interrogated, and tried on four separate occasions, twenty-year-old Wolfgang Borchert died on November 20, 1947, of a liver ailment in a hospital in Basel, SWITZERLAND, exactly one day before his only drama had its premiere on the stage. It had been broadcast some months earlier, on February 13, 1947, as a *Hörspiel* (radio play), but on that evening the electricity had gone out in his Hamburg neighborhood, so the author never heard or saw his work performed.

And yet Borchert, who was born on May 20, 1921, in Hamburg, GERMANY, is arguably one of the most important dramatists of 20th-century German literature, and his drama *The Man Outside* (*Draußen vor der Tür*, staged 1947) is one of the most oft-performed, memorable, and influential plays of postwar Germany. (Borchert's collected works consist of only 300 pages in total.)

Though still performed widely onstage, deep down *The Man Outside* is clearly a radio play, relying almost entirely on the power of the spoken word—together with minimal sound effects such as the gurgling of water in the river, the "tick-tock" made by the crutches of a one-legged man, or the slamming of a door—all of which resonate in the fantasy of the listener.

In a kind of prologue, for example, "God," a pathetic old man whose children ignore his teachings, speaks with "Death," here portrayed as a grossly obese undertaker. Death's acoustical signature includes a grotesque stream of continuous belching. "God" finally demands to know why this is. "Well, I've put on a bit of fat in this century," "Death" replies. "Business has been good. One war leads to the next one. Like flies! Like flies the dead . . . lie stiff and dry on the windowsill of our times."

The protagonist proper, Beckmann, is a limping veteran. Having spent a thousand days outside in the cold, including time as a prisoner of war in Siberia, he returns to Hamburg to find his parents dead, his wife living with another man, and his young son crushed under rubble from the bombing and firestorm in which nearly all of Hamburg was destroyed.

In a kind of dream sequence, Beckmann attempts suicide by drowning himself in the Elbe river, but the Elbe—personified as a gruff, profane old woman, yet with a kind heart—orders her water sprites to throw him out again on the sand so that he can start life over again, for in her view he has much suffering yet to experience before he can sleep with the fishes.

But our visionary hero—paradoxically his bizarre gas-mask eyeglasses are a symbol not for his myopia but for his farsightedness—with his symbolic limp marking him as a modern-day Jacob who has wrestled with the gods of war and emerged with higher insights, has a great challenge surviving in and educating a postwar society desperate to forget the past and to ignore the causes of war and holocaust that he is forced to see so clearly.

In scene after scene, he stands outside the doors of individuals who have been calloused and hardened, blinded rather than endowed with higher ethical vision. When he attempts to return to a colonel the responsibility given to him for 11 men, for example, Beckmann describes to his old commanding officer in his comfortable home in the bosom of his adoring family how he has suffered sleeplessness for years because of a recurring nightmare wherein he sees the horrible host of the dead rise from their graves each night at the behest of an old general who plays martial music on a xylophone made of human bones.

Naturally the colonel laughs at Beckmann's nightmare and at his visionary literalness: "My dear Beckmann, it wasn't intended that way!" "Yes it was, Colonel Sir, it has to have been intended that way! Responsibility is not just a word, a chemical formula, according to which bright human flesh is transformed into dark earth. One can't let human beings die for an empty word!"

This and other scenes show that Borchert's magnum opus attempts to create an ethical foundation for postwar German society by seeking out the root causes of fascism and militarism. Each of Beckmann's negative experiences with evil or even simply thoughtless people becomes one more "thou shalt not" in Borchert's pragmatic mandate for a better Germany after Adolf Hitler.

PLAY: *The Man Outside* (*Draußen vor der Tür*, 1947)

FURTHER READING

Fickert, Kurt J. "The Christ-Figure in Borchert's *Draußen vor der Tür*." *The Germanic Review* 54 (1979): 165–169.

Keele, Alan Frank. "'. . . Through a (Dark) Glass Clearly': Magic Spectacles and the Motif of the Mimetic Mantic in Postwar German Literature from Borchert to Grass." *The Germanic Review* 57 (1982): 49–59.

Koepke, Wulf. "German Writers After 1945: Wolfgang Borchert." *German Studies Review* 2, no. 1 (1979): 49–62.

Nelson, Donald F. "To Live or Not to Live: Notes on Archetypes and the Absurd in Borchert's *Draußen vor der Tür*." *The German Quarterly* 48 (1975): 343–354.

Reid, J. H. "*Draußen vor der Tür* in Context." *Modern Languages* 61 (1980): 184–190.

Willson, A. Leslie. "The Drowning Man: *Draußen vor der Tür*." *Texas Studies in Literature and Language: A Journal of the Humanities* 10 (1968): 119–131.

Alan Keele

THE BOSS

The Boss by EDWARD SHELDON was first produced at the Garrick Theatre in Detroit, Michigan, on January 9, 1911, and in New York City at the Astor Theatre on January 30, 1911, directed by Holbrook Blinn and William Brady and running eighty-eight performances.

Sheldon took his cue for *The Boss* from the social problems of the day. The play addresses issues of turn-of-the-century class, politics, and business, and it became the third in Sheldon's realistic studies of American life SALVATION NELL and *The Nigger*.

Michael R. Regan is a coarse Irish immigrant who has worked his way up from the lower classes to a position of significant power as "The Boss." Through bullying and intimidation, he gains control of the grain trade in a lake port of eastern New York. His deceit, thievery, and ruthlessness allow him to underpay his workers and drive his competitors out of business.

Regan meets with James and Donald Griswold, father and son merchants who face economic ruin if they cannot reach a compromise. Regan offers the Griswolds a controlling interest in his grain business if James will give his daughter, Emily, in marriage. The Griswolds immediately refuse, but Emily, concerned about the welfare of the poor who stand to suffer because of unscrupulous loans that James has made to his own business, accepts Regan's offer. The Boss keeps his word, but James and Donald incite his workers to strike, an action that begins to topple his grain empire. During a rally, one of Regan's men, Porky MacCoy, in a fit of anger, throws a brick and nearly kills Donald; a riot breaks out and leads to Regan's arrest on charges of attempted murder. He gives up his business and his future to offer to take the blame for the incident, and Emily leaves him while he awaits the inevitable judgment. When MacCoy confesses to the crime, Regan is set free. Donald survives, and Emily, to whom Regan has deeded the mortgages of the houses of the poor, willingly reconciles with her husband because he is now redeemed.

The play conforms to many traditional elements of the melodramatic form it follows, but it deviates significantly because of the characters' complexities, which help to carry Sheldon's social messages. Regan, unlike the traditional villain of MELODRAMA, shows humanity at points throughout the play, and while Emily is an archetypal melodramatic female, concerned with the downtrodden and dependent on men to care for her, she does nonetheless have depth in her idealism and a willingness to challenge both family and husband.

As part of his social message, Sheldon highlights the conflict between new and old money. In choosing Regan as the representative of the lower classes, Sheldon played on the largely upper-class theatergoing audience's stereotypes of the lower classes while elaborating the lower class's honor and virtue despite initial appearances. However, Sheldon's realistic portrayal of the lower classes attracted poor reviews from critics; Regan's foul language challenged upper-class sensibilities. Regardless, Sheldon's work stands as a milestone in the later development of American REALISM.

FURTHER READING

Barksdale, Richard K. "Miscegenation on Broadway: Hughes's *Mulatto* and Edward Sheldon's *The Nigger*." In *Critical Essays on Langston Hughes*, ed. by Edward J. Mullen. Boston: G. K. Hall, 1986. 191–199.

Metcalf, J. E. "Not Putting Our Best Foot Forward." *Life* 57 (February 9, 1911): 308–309.

Ruff, Loren K. *Edward Sheldon*. Boston: Twayne, 1982.

Sirkin, Elliot. "Vita: Edward Sheldon: Brief Life of a Secret Dramaturge: 1886–1946." *Harvard Magazine* 103 (March–April 2001): 32–33.

Eric-Michael MacCionnaith

BOUCHARD, MICHEL MARC (1958–)

Born in 1958 in Lac St. Jean, CANADA, Michel Marc Bouchard's childhood underlies many of the themes and situations that his plays explore. In an interview (Ouzounian, 2004), Bouchard comments that he was a "curious child," a child aware of the differences that set him apart from others. "I can't say I knew that I was gay," he recalls, "but I was aware that my impulses, my desires, were different." But Bouchard was equally aware of his talents and quick to take advantage of them. Growing up in his widowed grandmother's house, Bouchard quickly began to exploit his gift of storytelling and was soon publicly staging comic sketches. Bouchard attended the University of Ottawa to study theater, and the sometimes blatant political commentary that infuses his later plays found its origin in the concurrent rise of the Parti Québécois.

After graduation in 1980, Bouchard worked briefly as an actor, but he soon found his true calling as a playwright. An early play, *Water Carriers* (*Les Porteurs d'eau*, 1981), was soon followed by three more major plays. The third of these, *Les Feluettes ou la Répétition d'un drame romantique* (1987), brought Brouchard critical acclaim and attention. Linda Gaboriau translated the play as *Lilies; or, The Revival of a Romantic Drama* and has continued to translate many of Bouchard's later works. Released as a film in 1996, *Lilies* reveals many of the motifs that repeatedly appear throughout Bouchard's plays. Dealing with homosexuality, repression, treachery, violence, and betrayal, the film version of the play won the 1996 Genie for best film. Notably, the female characters in *Lilies* are played by men; the play itself revolves around a play within a play, as the main character, Bishop Jean Bilodeau, witnesses a reenactment of past events while visiting a penitentiary. Bouchard's next play, the 1989 work *The Orphan Muses* (*Les muses orphelines*), contained equally disturbing and controversial overtones; the play is both a political allegory and a story of the lasting effects of abandonment. Although the play has been mildly criticized by Mira Friedlander (1998) as "so much a writer's play that the actors seem like puppets following a complicated set of instructions," she also applauds Bouchard for the play's "colorful characters."

Despite the adult themes and situations present within *Lilies* and *The Orphan Muses*, Bouchard's most critically acclaimed play to date was written for a younger audience. However, *The Tale of Teeka* (*L'histoire de l'oie*, 1991) nevertheless deals with a controversial and contentious subject: child abuse and victimization. Bouchard's THE CORONATION VOYAGE (*Le voyage du couronnement*, 1995), one of his most politically sensitive plays, also focuses on the failure of parents to protect and nurture children and on the victimization of unwary children by predatory adults. On another level, the play is an allegory of French Canada, suggesting its desire and need to break away from a damaging "parental" influence and authority.

Bouchard continues to write and is presently vice president of the Théâtre d'Aujourd'hui; if his plays have sometimes been criticized for their absurd and controversial elements, they are nonetheless successful at highlighting social and political issues that might otherwise be neglected.

SELECT PLAYS: *Water Carriers* (*Les Porteurs d'eau*, 1981); *The Counter Nature of Chrysippe Tanguay, Ecologist* (*La contre-nature de Chrysippe Tanguay, écologiste*, 1984); *Beyond Twenty Years* (*De haut de ses vingt ans*, 1985); *Pelopia's Doll* (*La poupée de Pélopia*, 1986); *Lilies; or, The Revival of a Romantic Drama* (*Le Feluettes ou la Répétition d'un drame romantique*, 1987); *Rock'n'roll for a Drone* (*Rock pour un faux bourdon*, 1987); *The Orphan Muses* (*Les muses orphelines*, 1989); *The Tale of Teeka* (*L'histoire de l'oie*, 1991); *Heat Wave* (*Les grandes chaleurs*, 1993); *The Coronation Voyage* (*Le voyage du couronnement*, 1995); *Jade and Ebony* (*Le jade et ebène*, 1997); *The Unfinished One—Exercise on Pride* (*L'inachevé—exercise sur l'orgueil*, 1997); *Down Dangerous Passes Road* (*Le chemin des passes—dangereuses*, 1998); *The Moth* (*Les papillon de nuit*, 1999); *Written on Water* (*Sous le regard des mouches*, 2000)

FURTHER READING

Benson, Eugene, and William Toye, eds. *The Oxford Companion to Canadian Literature*. New York: Oxford Univ. Press, 1997.

Duchesne, Scott. "Michel Marc Bouchard." *The Literary Encyclopedia*. http://www.litencyc.com/.

Friedlander, Mira. Rev. of *The Orphan Muses*. *Variety* 369, no. 11 (January 26, 1998): 78.

Godin, Jean Cléo, and Dominique Lafon. *Dramaturgies québécoises des années quatre-vingt: Michel Marc Bouchard, Normand Chaurette, René-Daniel Dubois, Marie Laberge* [Quebec playwrights of the eighties: Michel Marc Bouchard, Normand Chaurette, René-Daniel Dubois, Marie Laberge]. Montreal: Leméac, 1999.

Morissette, Brigitte. "Michel-Marc Bouchard livre aux Mexicains quelques secrets de son succès au théâtre" [Michel-Marc Bouchard delivers some secrets of his success to the Mexicans]. *La Presse* (July 30, 2001): C2.

Ouzounian, Richard. "Playwright in Character." *Toronto Star* (Canada) (January 25, 2004).

Winter S. Elliott

BOUCHER, DENISE (1935–)

Canadian poet, playwright, and lyricist, Denise Boucher was born in Victoriaville, Quebec, on December 12, 1935. She graduated from the University of Sherbrooke with a degree in pedagogy and started her career teaching. In the 1960s, she turned to journalism and began working for several newspapers and as a freelance journalist for Radio-CANADA. She started publishing her poetry in 1976. Initially, her writing was influenced by such poets as Claude Gauvreau, Gaston Miron, and Gilbert Langevin and the painters Jean-Paul Mousseau, Ozias Leduc, Ulysse Comtois, and Guido Molinari. But in the 1970s, Boucher discovered postmodern culture, and since then she has became a multidisciplinary author celebrated widely in Montreal's poetry, rock music, political, and theatrical circles.

Her first well-known work *Recut* (*Retailles*), a collaboration with Madeleine Gagnon, was published in 1977. It was followed by *Cyprine* in 1978. Boucher is best known for her feminist drama, *The Fairies Are Thirsty* (*Les fées ont soif*, 1978), which was translated into English by Alan Brown. The play opened at the Théâtre du Nouveau Monde in 1978, starring Louisette Sussault, Sophie Clement, and Michele Magny. The premiere was directed by Jean-Luc Bastien. Interrogating the stereotypes of a housewife, a whore, and the Virgin Mary, the play touched on the sensitive issue of gender and the role of the Catholic Church in the oppression of women. *The Fairies Are Thirsty* stirred instant controversy, and it was loudly protested by various Catholic groups, some of whom went so far as to picket the theater and to recite the rosary during the shows. Despite the scandal, or perhaps because of it, *The Fairies Are Thirsty* was translated into several languages and produced around the world.

In 1996, *The Divine Ones* (*Les Divines*) was produced at the Théâtre d'Aujourd'hui. Boucher has also authored a rock opera, *Pink Rose* (*Rose Ross*) and another unproduced play, *Jézabel*, a gospel tragedy written in collaboration with Gerry Boulet. She also wrote two collections of poetry, *Paris Polaroid* (*Paris Polaroïd*, 1990) and *Natural Size* (*Grandeur nature*, 1993), and numerous songs. In 1985, she received the Charles-Cros Prize with Pauline Julien for their collaboration on the song "Or Can One Touch You?" ("Où peut-on vous toucher?"). In 1988, she received the Felix Prize with Gerry Boulet for the song "Soft Appointment" ("Rendez-vous doux"). In 1994, she received the Trophy of the SOCAN for the song "A Beautiful Large Boat" ("Un beau grand bateau"), which was the song played most often on the radio that year. Boucher's songs are performed on stages throughout the world, from New York to Paris. In 2002, she received the prize of Poet of the Year, given by the Marché de la poésie de Montréal. From November 1998 to December 2000, Boucher was president of the Union of Quebec Writers. She lives and works in Montreal.

PLAYS: *The Fairies Are Thirsty* (*Les fées ont soif*, 1978); *The Divine Ones* (*Les Divines*, 1996); *Jézabel* (unproduced; Gerry Boulet, collaborator)

FURTHER READING

Boucher, Denise. *The Fairies Are Thirsty: A Play*. Vancouver: Talonbooks, 1989.

Ripley, Gordon, and Anne Mercer, eds. *Who's Who in Canadian Literature 1987–88*. Toronto: Reference Press, 1987.

Weinmann, Heinz, and Roger Chamberland, eds. *Littérature québécoise, des origines à nos jours* [Quebec literature, from its origins to our times]. Montreal: Hurtubise HMH, 1996.

Magda Romanska

BOUCICAULT, DIONYSIUS (1820–1890)

Instead of a blundering blockhead, with jigs, howls, and shillelaghs, we we have the true son of the son represented, bold and courageous even to recklessness, with all his virtues and virtuous errors, ready to sacrifice his life to save that of a fellow creature.

—Dionysius Boucicault, promotional statement for *The Colleen Bawn*, Dublin, 1861. Quoted by Christopher Morash, *A History of Irish Theatre 1601–2000*, 2002

Actor and playwright Dionysius (Dion) Boucicault, illegitimate son of Dr. Dionysius Lardner, was reportedly born on December 26, 1820, in Dublin, IRELAND, to a family of Huguenot descent. From the age of seven he was educated in England. His natural father wanted him to become a railway engineer, but he left school for the provincial stage. Encouraged by the manager of Covent Garden to write a modern play, Boucicault, then just twenty years old, wrote *London Assurance*, which ran for sixty-nine nights in 1841.

Subsequently, he lived in France, married and then lost his wife, returned to England, went bankrupt, became resident playwright at Charles Kean's Princess Theatre in London, and in 1852 went to America with a promising actress, Agnes Robertson. She became a star and bore the playwright six children.

Boucicault had a talent for brewing a MELODRAMA out of a contemporary issue and also a talent for conceiving of stage sensations to climax the melodrama. He also thought of ways in which pretty young actresses, wearing breeches or short skirts, could be pathetically mauled by one man and delightfully rescued by another. *The Octoroon* (1859), for instance, successfully brought together race problems and melodramatic thrills on the eve of the American Civil War.

Two years later, Boucicault staged the first of his "Irish plays," *The Colleen Bawn* (1860), based Gerald Griffin's popular novel *The Collegians*. Following its New York success, Boucicault invented the touring company in order to make the most of his property. Earlier, performers had gone from London to New York, or New York to Dublin, but the rest of the cast was normally recruited from local repertory companies. Boucicault took the whole show on the road and, innovatively working for a percentage of the gate rather than a straight fee, gathered profits as author, star, and stage manager.

During the Irish Revival at the turn of the 20th century, Boucicault's Irish plays were condemned as the vehicle of the "stage Irishman," a caricature of natives of the country that made the Irish the laughing stocks of English audiences, who drew the comforting conclusion that such people were unworthy of self-government. Nevertheless, Boucicault's stereotypical Irishmen are actually idealized. The men are witty, noble-hearted, and deep thinking, if not urbane and educated. The female Irish characters, especially in *Arrah-na-Pogue* (1864), are neither slovenly nor vulgar but pure-hearted and sensitive. One of the most enjoyable of Boucicault's Irish plays is *The Shaughraun*, which opened in New York in 1874, a favorite of GEORGE BERNARD SHAW and J. M. SYNGE. Here the fun-loving, tricky Irishman—a part Boucicault wrote for himself—became the title role. The background to the plot is the Fenian uprising in Ireland, an insurrectionary movement supported by Irish Americans and suppressed by the British government. The play's action gives a daring gesture of support for an illegal movement. Boucicault's profits from *The Shaugraun* amounted to half a million dollars.

Boucicault was one influence Irish playwrights George Bernard Shaw, J. M. Synge, and SEAN O'CASEY all had in common, yet his background was international—French, Irish, English, American—and he had a theater man's natural talent for capitalizing on populist emotions wherever he found himself. He is accorded a place in theater histories of America and England as well as Ireland.

SELECT PLAYS: *London Assurance* (1841); *An Irish Heiress* (1842); *Peg Woffington or The State Secret* (1845); *The Corsican Brothers* (1852); *Andy Blake or The Irish Diamond* (1854); *The Poor of New York* (1857); *The Octoroon* (1859); *The Colleen Bawn* (1860); *Arrah-na-Pogue* (1864); *Rip Van Winkle* (1865); *The Rapparee or The Treaty of Limerick* (1870); *The Shaughraun* (1874); *Robert Emmet* (1884)

FURTHER READING

Fawkes, Richard. *Dion Boucicault: A Biography*. London: Quartet Bks., 1979.

Harrington, John. *The Irish Play on the New York Stage 1874–1966*. Lexington: Univ. Press of Kentucky, 1997.

Krause, David, ed. *The Dolmen Boucicault*. Dublin: Dolmen Press, 1964.

Parkin, Andrew, ed. *Selected Plays: Dion Boucicault*. Washington, D.C.: Catholic Univ. of Am. Press, 1987.

Adrian Frazier

BOWLES, JANE (1917–1973)

I'm not all that keen on the theater: cannot sit through most plays once; nevertheless, I saw In the Summer House *three times, and not out of loyalty to the author, but because it had a thorny wit, the flavor of a newly tasted, refreshingly bitter beverage. . . . My only complaint against Mrs. Bowles is not that her work lacks quality, merely quantity.*

—Truman Capote, 1966

Although Jane Bowles turned to the stage late in her short career, her experiments with drama proved to be highly original in subject matter and style, ranking in the company of GERTRUDE STEIN and Carson McCullers. Jane Bowles's life—her marriage to Paul Bowles, her celebrity friends and lesbian lovers, her bout with alcohol and drugs, and her ultimate madness—eclipsed her literary innovations and made her a cult figure before she died in 1973. Her writing finally started to receive critical interest during the 1980s when her collected works were reissued, her letters and a biography were published, and a new generation of academic critics contextualized Bowles's achievements within feminist and experimental frameworks.

She was born Jane Auer on February 22, 1917, in New York City, and after her father died when she was thirteen, the family moved to a Long Island suburb that she came to despise. Early on, Jane learned to stage her sense of "otherness" as Jewish, lesbian, and communist and even nicknamed herself the "kike dyke" and "crippie" (to ward off comments about her permanently locked knee). Sent to a Swiss sanatorium at the age of fifteen to recover from tuberculosis, she avidly read works by André Gide, Marcel Proust, Louis-Ferdinand Céline, and Henry de Montherlant. Though she was resolute about becoming a writer and completed her first novel, *The Hypocritical Phaeton (Le Phaeton Hypocrite*, written in French, no manuscript survives), in 1935, Jane had a tortuous relationship with her writing throughout her life.

In 1938, Jane married writer and composer Paul Bowles, then a protégé of Virgil Thomson and Aaron Copland. As a couple, they were part of the bohemian art circles of New York (where Paul wrote operas and other music for theater and served as theater critic for the *New York Herald Tribune*), as well as the expatriate art communities of Paris, Taxco (Mexico), and Tangier (Morocco). Their infamously open marriage served as a magnet for an artistic salon wherever they found themselves and included William Burroughs, W. H. AUDEN, Oliver Smith, Benjamin Britten, Peter Pears, Alice Toklas, TENNESSEE WILLIAMS, Truman Capote, and Ned Rorem, as well as Paul and Jane's various lovers.

Despite her anxieties about writing, Bowles managed to complete a small body of distinctive work. She first made her mark as a writer of fiction, including her novel *Two Serious Ladies* (1941); several short stories, among the best of which are *A Stick of Green Candy* (1949) and *Plain Pleasures* (1946); and a novella, *Camp Cataract* (1948). The theatrical designer and producer Oliver Smith greatly admired her talent and urged her to shift her focus to drama. After he produced OUR TOWN on Broadway in 1943, he subsidized her while she wrote and constantly revised IN THE SUMMER HOUSE over the next decade. *In the Summer House* is her only full-length play, and it was mounted on Broadway in 1953 under the direction of José Quintero, with Judith Anderson, Mildred Dunnock, and Jean Stapleton in the cast. Though it received mixed reviews, the play, which ruthlessly explores mother-daughter relationships, was lauded for its expressive atmosphere and candid dialogue and was published in Louis Kronenberger's *Best Plays* series.

Her only other finished theater work is a puppet play, *A Quarreling Pair*, which was performed in 1945 with puppets created by the artist Kurt Seligmann and music by Paul Bowles. The play was written for John Myers, an editor of *View*, a surrealist magazine, and extended her experimentation with nonrealistic theater styles. All her work was completed by 1957 when she suffered a stroke and became physically debilitated, in addition to her continuing emotional problems. She left hundreds of pages of notebooks and other writings unfinished, including an opera in collaboration with Paul.

[*See also* Feminist Drama in the United States; United States, 1940–Present]

PLAYS: *A Quarreling Pair* (1945); *In the Summer House* (1947)

FURTHER READING

Bowles, Jane. *My Sister's Hand in Mine: An Expanded Edition of the Collected Works of Jane Bowles*. Intr. by Truman Capote. New York: Ecco, 1978.

——. *Out in the World: Selected Letters of Jane Bowles 1935–1970*. Ed. by Millicent Dillon. Santa Barbara: Black Sparrow, 1985.

——. *The Portable Paul and Jane Bowles*. Ed. and intro. by Millicent Dillon. New York: Penguin, 1994.

Dillon, Millicent. *A Little Original Sin: The Life and Work of Jane Bowles*. Berkeley: Univ. of California Press, 1998.

Green, Michelle. *The Dream at the End of the World: Paul Bowles and the Literary Renegades of Tangier*. New York: HarperCollins, 1991.

Skerl, Jennie, ed. *A Tawdry Place of Salvation: The Art of Jane Bowles*. Carbondale: Southern Illinois Univ. Press, 1997.

Mary Fleischer

BOY MEETS GIRL

Skewering the pretensions and absurdities of the Hollywood studio system was a favorite Broadway sport in the 1920s and 1930s: comedies like *Merton of the Movies* and *Once in a Lifetime*, both written by GEORGE S. KAUFMAN with different collaborators, not only titillated audiences with "backstage" glimpses of an exotic culture but implicitly affirmed the superiority of sophisticated theatrical folk over the rubes of the rushes. BELLA AND SAM SPEWACK's *Boy Meets Girl*, which opened on November 27, 1935, was not the first of the genre but was the most successful. Directed by George Abbott, which contributed mightily to its zany anarchy, the play ran for 669 performances.

The Spewacks, husband and wife who had gravitated to theater from the newspaper business, had written four unremarkable Broadway plays before making it big with this mad FARCE about a pair of wisecracking screenwriters loosely based on Ben Hecht and Charles MacArthur. Unlike some of their fellow Broadway satirists of Hollywood, the Spewacks had actually spent time in the film business, and their experience informs *Boy Meets Girl* in everything from its stage directions to its loopy dialogue to its scattershot pace.

The involved plot revolves around the two screenwriters, Law and Benson, attempting to create a vehicle for a dimwitted, has-been cowboy star, Larry Toms, and his harassed producer, "C.F." Friday. When a pregnant waitress, Susie, appears in the producer's office and proceeds to give birth, the boys have their inspiration: the new film (and its dreamed-of sequels) will star her actual baby, named Happy, thereby both charming audiences and relegating Toms to the second-banana status he richly deserves. But with Toms's wily agent sniffing around the writers' power of attorney over the tyke, it is only a matter of time before the show-biz futures of Happy, his naive mother, and the two scenarists are all endangered.

Complications, of course, ensue, some involving a shy young man who turns out to be an English lord and is the agent by which the play comes to embody the cheerful, pragmatic Benson's immutable formula: "Boy meets girl. Boy loses girl. Boy gets girl." (Responds the more cynical Law: "The great American fairy tale. Sends the audience back to the relief rolls in a happy frame of mind.") But plot accounts for only part of the appeal of *Boy Meets Girl*; the rest derives from the frenzied atmosphere of Friday's office: the comings and goings of assorted sycophants, composers, technicians, and other eccentric denizens of what Benson calls "an accidental business in an accidental world."

Critics generally loved *Boy Meets Girl*; the *New York Times*' Brooks Atkinson (Beckerman, 1973) termed it "an extraordinarily hilarious comedy" that "fills the evening with impudent vertigo and glee." The film version, for which the Spewacks wrote the screenplay, appeared in 1938.

[*See also* United States, 1940–Present]

FURTHER READING

Beckerman, Bernard, and Howard Siegman, eds. *On Stage: Selected Theater Reviews from the New York Times 1920–1970*. New York: Arno Press, 1973.

Schatz, Thomas. *The Genius of the System: Hollywood Filmmaking in the Studio Era*. New York: Pantheon, 1989.

Spewack, Bella. *Streets: A Memoir of the Lower East Side*. New York: Feminist Press at the City Univ. of New York, 1995.

Clifford A. Ridley

BRACCO, ROBERTO (1861–1943)

Roberto Bracco, born in Naples, ITALY, on November 10, 1861, began his career as a journalist and author of short stories, articles, reviews, and poetry in Neapolitan dialect. Appointed drama and music critic for the *Corriere di Napoli*, he promoted the theater of HENRIK IBSEN and the music of Richard Wagner. His first play, *Do Not Do unto Others* (*Non fare ad altri*), was produced in 1886, followed in 1892 by *A Woman* (*Una donna*). *The Masks* (*Le Maschere*) and other works dealing especially with the social roles of women soon appeared. Like Marco Praga, Giovanni Verga, and Giuseppe Giacosa, Bracco gave a newly united Italy plays based on themes of family relations, work, wealth, and social behavior. On stage, the drama of adultery—husband, wife, and lover, which in the words of Clotilde in *Him, Her, Him* (*Lui, lei, lui*) "present an infinite series of combinations, comic and tragic"—interested the country's developing middle class. By the turn of the century, Bracco was the most highly regarded Italian playwright both in Italy and abroad. The famous actresses Eleanora Duse and Emma Grammatica performed his female roles. His personal acquaintances included Matilde Serao, Arturo Toscanini, GABRIELE D'ANNUNZIO, Praga, MAKSIM GORKY, Nino Martoglio, Giacosa, and LUIGI PIRANDELLO.

From 1913 to 1923 Bracco approved the transposition of his best-known works into film. An eleven-volume edition of his *Teatro* (Theater) was published in 1927 in Palermo. That same year *The Little Saint* (*Il Piccolo Santo*) was performed in New York City in English. There are several of Bracco's plays in English translation in the New York Public Library Theatre Collection. A twenty-five-volume edition of his *Opera omnia* (Collected works), including comedies, dramas, monologues, texts for music, and idylls, was published by Lanciano in 1935–1942. Before his death in 1943, however, Bracco's fame was eclipsed by the ascendancy of Luigi Pirandello, and Bracco's public voice was silenced by the fascist regime.

His last play, *Madmen* (*I pazzi*), written in 1917, was performed after twenty-seven postponements in June 1929 at the Teatro Fiorentino of Naples with the permission of Benvenuto Mussolini, obtained by Emma Grammatica. Although the Neapolitan audience appreciated the play, the press berated the author for his intransigence as an "intellectual antifascist." A month later fascists shouted down the play's Roman debut. Thereafter, Bracco's work was banned from performance, and he was excluded from journalistic, literary, and cinematographic activities. His correspondence was regularly intercepted. Culturally, *Madmen* opened a polemic that praised Pirandello as champion of a new kind of theater and saw in Bracco an exponent of the old guard, allied with Ibsenism, verismo, socialism, and psychological drama.

His works range from veristic plays admired for their acute representations of women in the roles of wives, lovers, and mothers to experimental approaches taken most effectively in *The Little Saint* and *Madmen*, where Bracco sought to move beyond dialogue in order to produce, as he says in his prologue to *Madmen*, "a synthetic combination of meaningful signs" that contains the reality hidden below the surface. His contribution to dialect theater is augmented by Peppino DeFilippo's transposition of *Do Not Do unto Others* and *A Travel Adventure* (*Un'avventura di viaggio*) into Neapolitan dialect and Eduardo DeFilippo's Neapolitan version of *The Little Saint*.

SELECT PLAYS: *A Woman* (*Una donna*, 1893); *Unfaithful* (*Infedele*, 1894); *The Triumph* (*Il trionfo*, 1895); *Don Pietro Caruso* (1895); *The End of Love* (*La fine dell'amore*, 1896); *The Soul's Tragedies* (*Tragedie dell'anima*, 1899); *The Right to Live* (*Il diritto di vivere*, 1900); *Lost in the Gloom* (*Sperduti nel buio*, 1901); *Motherhood* (*Maternita*, 1903); *The Unripe Fruit* (*Il frutto acerbo*, 1904); *Snowy Night* (*Notte di neve*, 1905); *The Hidden Source* (*La piccola fonte*, 1905); *Ghosts* (*I fantasmi*, 1906); *Nellina* (1908); *Perfect Love* (*Il perfetto amore*, 1910); *The Little Saint* (*Il Piccolo Santo*, 1912; written in 1909); *The Distant Lover* (*L'amante lontano*, 1916); *The Cradle* (*La culla*, 1918); *Madmen* (*I pazzi*, 1929; written in 1917)

FURTHER READING

Alonge, Roberto. *Teatro e spettacolo nel secondo Ottocento* [Theater and performance in the second half of the nineteenth century]. Bari: Laterza, 1988.

Di Nallo, Antonella. *Roberto Bracco e la Società Teatrale Fra Ottocento e Novecento.* [Robert Bracco and the theatrical society between the nineteenth and twentieth centuries]. Lanciano: Rocco Carabba, 2003.

Iaccio, Pasquale. *L'Intellettuale Intransigente: Il Fascismo di Roberto Bracco.* [The intransigent intellectual: The facism of Roberto Bracco]. Naples: Guida editori, 1992.

Pullini, G. "Eclettícismo nel teatro di Roberto Bracco" [Eclecticism in the theater of Roberto Bracco]. In *Teatro italiano fra due secoli: 1850–1950* [Italian theater from two centuries: 1850–1950]. Florence: Parenti Editore, 1958. 165–192.

Stäuble, Antonio. *Tra Ottocento e Novecento. Il teatro di Roberto Bracco.* [Between the Nineteenth and Twentieth century. The theater of Roberto Bracco]. Turin: Ilte, 1959.

Nancy Dersofi

BRAHM, OTTO (1856–1912)

And immediately we sensed the first realization of a new poetic world. . . . From the first moment we belonged to this new real-world art, and [so] our aesthetic life had received its content.
—Otto Brahm, 1904 (explaining his reaction to seeing Henrik Ibsen's *Pillars of Society* for the first time in 1878)

If any one person should be credited for the success of modern drama on the German stage, it would be Otto Brahm. As a critic, as chairman and co-founder of the Freie Bühne (Free Stage) theater society, and as director of the Deutsches Theater and the Lessingtheater, Brahm strove to introduce and promote both foreign and domestic modern playwrights in GERMANY.

Brahm was born on February 5, 1856, in Hamburg, Germany. He began his career as a theater critic for the *Vossische Zeitung* in 1881. Eight years later, he became chairman of the Freie Bühne theater club, responsible for selecting plays, hiring actors, finding a stage, and fund-raising. Modeled on the Théâtre Libre in Paris, the private theater club could circumvent government censorship.

The first two performances of the Freie Bühne were HENRIK IBSEN'S GHOSTS and GERHART HAUPTMANN'S BEFORE DAYBREAK (*Vor Sonnenaufgang*). The success of the undertaking was immediate: within two months the society had 900 members. The board of directors subsequently launched a literary journal, *Die Freie Bühne*; Brahm became its editor as well as a prolific contributor. In his articles, he described how the theater club must bring the new art, that is, NATURALISM, to the stage.

Brahm served as the chairman of the Freie Bühne for five years. During that time he also became a member of the board of directors of the Freie Volksbühne, a sister stage that performed the same type of plays as the Freie Bühne but charged less for its ticket prices in order to attract the lower classes into the theater in greater numbers. Brahm realized his ambition of becoming a theater director in 1894 by renting the Deutsches Theater. Prior to his directorship, the Deutsches Theater had primarily staged the classics, but during the decade in which Brahm directed the theater, it became Germany's leading stage for contemporary playwrights. In addition to Ibsen and Hauptmann, Brahm actively promoted such authors as HUGO VON HOFMANNSTHAL, MAURICE MAETERLINCK, EDMOND ROSTAND, ARTHUR SCHNITZLER, and HERMANN SUDERMANN.

Following internal strife in 1904, Brahm left the Deutsches Theater and rented the Lessingtheater, where he continued to promote and stage contemporary works. However, his standing as the leading theater director in Berlin was soon challenged by MAX REINHARDT, who had begun his career as an actor under Brahm at the Deutsches Theater. Reinhardt became director of the Deutsches Theater in 1905, when it once again became a stage devoted primarily to the classics. Traditional acting combined with spectacular sound and lighting effects attracted an audience that preferred to be entertained rather than confronted with the miseries of contemporary life.

Brahm and Reinhardt competed not only for spectators but also for actors and authors. The case of Hauptmann is illustrative. No one had done more to advance Hauptmann's career than Brahm. Nevertheless, Hauptmann gave Reinhardt the rights to perform his neo-romantic plays, which he felt needed the theatrical effects Reinhardt championed. This almost led to a schism between Hauptmann and Brahm, but they agreed on a compromise whereby Brahm continued to stage Hauptmann's naturalist plays. Although Brahm foresaw the overcoming of naturalism by other literary styles, he continued his naturalist stagings until his death from cancer on November 28, 1912, in Berlin, Germany.

FURTHER READING

Brahm, Otto. *Kritiken und Essays* [Critiques and essays]. Zurich: Artemis, 1964.

——. Kritische Schriften über Drama und Theater [Critical writings on drama and theater], vol. 1, Berlin: Fischer Verlag, 1913.

Claus, Horst. *The Theater Director Otto Brahm.* Ann Arbor: UMI Research Press, 1981.

Sprengel, Peter. "Literaturtheorie und Theaterpraxis des Naturalismus: Otto Brahm" [Naturalist literary theory and theatrical practice: Otto Brahm]. *Der Deutschunterricht* 40, no. 2 (1988): 89–99.

Kerstin T. Gaddy

BRAND

Brand is HENRIK IBSEN'S first major work after he moved to ITALY in 1864, and it also marks his entry into world literature. Inspired by a strong personal feeling of frustration at DENMARK'S isolation during the recent war with Prussia and Austria, as well as by the overwhelming experience of St. Peter's Cathedral in Rome and the art of Michelangelo, Ibsen has created a dramatic work that surmounts its own political, satirical, and prophetic impulses, standing forth as a tragic drama comparable to the works of William Shakespeare and the Greek masters: five acts with dialogues and monologues in rhymed verse, and with a hero at its center who has both fascinated and repelled generations of readers and theater audiences.

Brand is a dynamic and intransigent young priest with strong willpower and an equally strong vocation: supported by a utopian vision of a New Humanity, he has devoted himself to the furtherance of human perfection—a new world populated with forceful and uncompromising men and women, able to transcend the infirmities of The Old Adam. Descending from the mountains like a precursor of FRIEDRICH NIETZSCHE's Zarathustra, and making a stop in the small and poor community of his childhood where he has no intention to stay, he meets Agnes, his veritable soul mate, and they decide to start their work by devoting themselves to the spiritual needs of the narrow fjord village below the darkening mountains. This decision brings them into a series of temptations and ordeals that they have to pass in order to approach the state of perfection that is their vocation. Brand has to refuse his dying mother the last sacraments, he has to sacrifice his own son, and finally, he has to suffer the loss of his wife. Agnes, on the other hand, not only loses her only son but is also forced by her uncompromising husband to rid herself of every material thing that reminds her of little Alf. Finally, having left every rest of her old affections behind, she enters a peculiar state of joy and freedom, which, paradoxically, can only be realized in death. In the final act, Brand is rejected by his seemingly faithful congregation and enters total isolation. Chased by the stone-throwing mob into the mountains where he came from, his only company will be the crazy gypsy girl Gerd, who leads him into the frozen landscape of the Ice Church. Here, in an enigmatic final scene, they are both swept away by an avalanche released by Gerd when she fires a shot at her imaginary black hawk. At the moment of his death, Brand insists in his faith in man's will of perfection, which for the last time is put against the Christian idea of merciful love and compassion that he has been accused of lacking. The last words of the play, however, are the declaration "He is deus caritatis," which emanates from a mysterious voice through the roaring thunder of the avalanche.

This final scene and the titanic character that the entire drama gravitates around have from the very beginning divided critics, readers, stage directors, and theater audiences into two opposite blocks and continue to do so. For the majority, Brand is Ibsen's critical portrayal of religious fundamentalism and its disastrous consequences, and Agnes is the pitiful victim of masculine brutality. But a minority of critics and readers have read Brand and Agnes as real tragic characters whose positive qualities lead to their disaster and who can only realize their freedom and ultimate humanity in death. To judge from his own commentaries on Brand, Ibsen himself belongs to this minority group. "Brand is myself in my best moments," he once wrote in a letter.

There exists a draft that shows that Ibsen first planned to write an epic poem based on a character, Koll, who later became the Brand of the dramatic poem. And like PEER GYNT, the drama was originally not meant for the stage. *Brand* had to wait until 1885 for its first performance, which took place in Stockholm and lasted six and a half hours. Ibsen himself waited even longer. In 1898, as part of the celebration of his seventieth birthday, he attended a gala performance of his masterpiece in Copenhagen. This first stage experience of Brand touched him deeply and probably also inspired him when, in the following year, he wrote his dramatic epilogue *WHEN WE DEAD AWAKEN*, which also ends with the main characters being swept away by an avalanche high up in the Norwegian mountains.

[*See also* Norway]

FURTHER READING

Durbach, Errol. "Brand: A Romantic Exile from Paradise." *Contemporary Approaches to Ibsen* 8 (1994): 71–82.

Johnston, Brian. *To the Third Empire. Ibsen's Early Dramas*. Minneapolis: Univ. of Minnesota Press, 1980.

Lyons, Charles R. *Henrik Ibsen. The Divided Conscience*. Carbondale: Southern Illinois Univ. Press, 1972.

Sohlich, Wolfgang. "Ibsen's *Brand*: Drama of the Fatherless Society." *Journal of Dramatic Theory and Criticism* 3, no. 2 (1989): 87–105.

Atle Kittang

BRANNER, HANS CHRISTIAN (1903–1966)

Man has his deepest roots in the earth of defeat, man is the creature who grows through his defeats and dies from his victories. The eternal crisis seems to be a vital necessity—now as ever we are living in an apocalyptic time.

—Hans Christian Branner, *The Crisis of Humanism*, 1950

Hans Christian (H. C.) Branner was a central figure in the postwar cultural and ethical debate in DENMARK. His literary work, including novels, short stories, essays, and plays, centers on concepts of guilt, responsibility, and human fellowship. In the essay *The Crisis of Humanism* (1950) he calls for a new humanism in a time of chaotic darkness that is marred by feelings of defeat and treason. As an author Branner was influenced by Freudian psychoanalysis and French existentialism, matched with a growing preoccupation with myth and religion. Branner will probably be remembered primarily for his novels and short stories, but he also wrote a few plays that made a deep impression on the contemporary public.

Branner's first work for the theater, *The Horseman* (*Rytteren*; staged 1950 in Stockholm, 1952 in Copenhagen), is built on his 1949 novel of the same title and is an in-depth psychological reckoning with Nazism and Nietzschean worship of the Superman.

The play centers on the departed Hubert, a riding master and a charismatic and domineering person, totally controlled by his instincts, with whom all the persons onstage have been involved. The main character of the play is Susanne, Hubert's mistress who denies accepting his death, but in the end she overcomes her erotic obsession with the help of the weak and guilt-haunted humanist Clemens.

While *The Horseman* is rich in symbols and mythological associations, Branner's next drama, *The Siblings* (*Søskende*; staged in Stockholm 1951, in Copenhagen 1952), is a purely Ibsenite psychological play without much action. Three siblings meet, after many years' separation, in the home of their childhood where their father, a much respected but callous and authoritarian judge, is dying. The judge's three children are all more or less emotionally impaired: Arthur, the hampered man of duty who has taken over his father's identity without having ever had his love; Michael, the sailor who after his mother's death fled from his home to an illusionary freedom; and finally Irene, who is married to a wealthy businessman with a dubious past during the German occupation and compensates for her conventional and childless marriage by taking a much younger lover. The reunion briefly makes the three siblings dream of a shared future by trying to relive the state of innocence of their childhood. But when the nurse announces their father's death, the spell disappears, and they part to return to their separate lives.

In *Thermopylae* (1958), taking place immediately before and during the German occupation, a destructive father is the main character. Stefan is an idealistic humanist whose tolerance and belief in freedom of choice have driven his two sons into the arms of totalitarian movements—Nazism and communism—and made his daughter, who admires him blindly, unable to love other men. While the martyr Stefan stubbornly refuses to leave the country, everything around him falls apart.

Branner is a dramatist of ideas, but apart from *The Siblings* his plays are weighed down by symbols and religious associations that often make his characters untrustworthy—e.g., the alcoholic artist Kristoffer, in *Thermopylae*, who walks the streets at night "carrying God on his back." Unlike KJELD ABELL, Branner never broke the frames of the naturalistic drama in his plays for the stage. In his radio play *A Play on Love and Death* (*Et Spil om Kærligheden og Døden*, 1960), however, he moved much more freely in time and space and used a stream-of-consciousness technique that gave the play a lyric flow and showed potential for a new drama.

PLAYS: *The Horseman* (*Rytteren*, 1950); *The Siblings* (*Søskende*, 1951); staged as *The Judge* in New York, 1958); *Thermopylae* (1958); *A play on Love and Death* (*Et Spil om Kærligheden og Døden*, 1960)

FURTHER READING

Branner, H.C. *Humanismens Krise* [The Crisis of Humanism]. Copenhagen: Hans Reitzels Forlag, 1950.

Frederiksen, Emil. *H. C. Branner*. Olso: Gyldendal, 1966.

Jarlby, Janne. *H. C. Branner—splittelse og kontinuitet* [H.C. Branner—Disintegration and continuity]. Odense: Sydansk Universitets forlag, 2003.

Markey, T. L. *H. C. Branner*. New York: Twayne, 1973.

Kela Kvam

BRASCH, THOMAS (1945–2001)

Why play: To render this question superfluous / to create a counter-world / to present dreams of fear and hope to a society that dreamlessly works towards its own destruction / to not let the dead rest / to not let the living rest / to cast roots / to tear out roots / to make money / to give a sign of life.

—Thomas Brasch, "Why Play" (an Essay), in Hanf, 2004 1983

Thomas Brasch (born on February 19, 1945, in Westow, Yorkshire, ENGLAND, emerged in the 1970s in East GERMANY as one of the most significant, prolific, and controversial playwrights. Born in Britain to exiled German Jewish communists, he was originally destined to follow in the footsteps of his father, who became a high-ranking party functionary in the newly established German Democratic Republic (GDR). Brasch soon, however, fell afoul of the GDR authorities for adopting an anti-ideological stance to the left of the regime. In 1965, he had to leave Leipzig University because of his "existentialist attitudes," and in 1968, he was expelled from the Babelsberg film academy and jailed for distributing leaflets protesting the suppression of the Prague Spring by Warsaw Pact troops. Menial jobs (including punitive labor in industry) alternated with a stint at the Brecht Archives in East Berlin as a protegé of BERTOLT BRECHT's widow Helene Weigel. None of his theater projects—from a 1966 Vietnam War program banned for "left radical tendencies" to various experiments in children's theater in the 1970s—made it past a second performance. Apart from a slim volume of poems, *Poetry Album 89* (*Poesiealbum 89*, 1975), Brasch's works could not be published, and he was unable to attend the first production of one of his plays in the West, *The Paper Tiger* (*Der Papiertiger*, 1976), in Austin, Texas. In December 1976, during the crisis surrounding the forced expatriation of dissident singer-songwriter Wolf Biermann, Brasch was allowed to leave East Germany. Arriving in the West with a suitcase full of manuscripts, he achieved considerable success with his plays, adaptations, and translations (notably of ANTON CHEKHOV and William Shakespeare), and three feature films. Despite being showered with literary awards, Brasch remained critical of the West no less than he had been of the East.

Brasch's creative output centers on the efforts of individuals to cope with or to escape preassigned or self-defined roles. The stories in *The Sons Die Before the Fathers* (*Vor den Vätern sterben die Söhne*, 1977), the poetic fragments in *Cargo: 32nd Effort to Escape One's Own Skin* (*Kargo: 32. Versuch aus der eigenen Haut zu kommen*, 1977), and the emblematic debut film *Angels of Iron*

(*Engel aus Eisen*, 1981) highlight issues of intergenerational conflict, rebellious nonconformity, and the incompatibility of individual desire and societal demands—measured against an anarchic, utopian individualism. In his plays, Brasch merges the dense poetic language of Heinrich von Kleist (1777–1811) and the German expressionists with the fragmentary, often phantasmagoric DRAMATURGY of Georg Büchner (1813–1837), early Bertolt Brecht, and HEINER MÜLLER. The various characters' flirtations with crime, violence, insanity, and wish-fulfilling role-playing emerge as survival strategies in response to societal strictures. *Rotter* (1977) is a study of an "authoritarian personality," a man equally adaptable to national socialism as to the emerging East German communist state. *Lovely Rita* (1978) centers on a young woman who, after being raped by an occupation officer after World War II, turns fantasies of movie stardom into aggressive ambitiousness. *Dear George* (*Lieber Georg*, 1980) presents a kaleidoscope of fragmented scenes surrounding the failure of expressionist poet Georg Heym (1887–1912). Brasch's most frequently performed play, *Mercedes* (1983), a kind of postmodern variant of SAMUEL BECKETT's *WAITING FOR GODOT*, concerns two bored unemployed youngsters in a postindustrial wasteland who experiment with compensatory fantasies of affluence and success. *Women: War: Comedy* (*Frauen. Krieg. Lustspiel*, 1988), a dazzlingly complex collage of scenes involving shifting identities and alternate scenarios, has two bereaved women act out the quest for a soldier missing in World War I, who may or may not have been the husband of one and lover of the other woman.

The collapse of communism in 1989 plunged Brasch, who had in the 1980s acquired a British passport, into a profound creative crisis revolving around his identity as a Jewish leftist writer in a reunified, market-driven Germany—issues he had anticipated in his films *Domino* (1982) and *Der Passagier—Welcome to Germany* (1988). For years, Brasch virtually fell silent as a playwright in his own right, focusing his public energies almost entirely on translations and reworkings of Shakespeare. He reemerged in the late 1990s with a series of publications and productions: the libretto to an experimental multimedia opera by Georg Hajko, *The Plunge or, The Crack* (*Der Sprung*, 1997); the slim novella *Girl Murderer Brunke* (*Mädchenmörder Brunke*, 1999); and the play *Boot Has to Die* (*Stiefel muß sterben*, 1999) about the 1819 murder of conservative playwright August von Kotzebue by a nationalist student. After a long struggle with cancer, Brasch died in Berlin on November 3, 2001, his extraordinary artistic promise only partially fulfilled.

PLAYS: *She Is Leaving, She Isn't* (*Sie geht, sie geht nicht*, 1970); *The Exemplary Life and Death of Peter Goring* (*Das beispielhafte Leben und der Tod des Peter Göring*, 1971); *Galileo Galilei—Pope Urban VIII* (*Galileo Galilei—Pabst Urban VIII*, 1972); *Report on the Passing of Musician Jack Tiergarten* (*Bericht vom Sterben des Musikers Jack Tiergarten*, 1973); *Eulenspiegel* (1974); *Rooster's Head: A Jazz Oratorium* (*Hahnenkopf. Ein Jazz-Oratorium*, 1975); *The Paper Tiger* (*Der Papiertiger*, 1976); *Argentinian Night* (*Die argentinische Nacht*, 1977); *Rotter* (1977); *Lovely Rita* (1978); *Dear George* (*Lieber Georg*, 1980); *Mercedes* (1983); *Dead Man, Height 304* (*Toter Mann, Höhe 304*, 1985); *Women: War: Comedy* (*Frauen. Krieg. Lustspiel*, 1988); *Love, Power Death* (*or Love Makes Death*) *or The Play of Romeo and Juliet* (*Liebe Macht Tod oder das Spiel von Romeo und Julia*, 1990); *The Plunge/The Crack: Description of an Opera* (*Der Sprung. Beschreibung einer Oper*, 1997); *Boot Has to Die* (*Stiefel muß sterben*, 1999); *Sophocles's Women of Trachis, or Power Love Death* (*or Does Love Make Death?*) (*Die Trachinierinnen des Sophocles oder Macht Liebe Tod*, 1999); *Women's War: Three Paintings-Over* (*Frauenkrieg. Drei Übermalungen*, 2000)

FURTHER READING

Frölich, Margrit. *Between Affluence and Rebellion: The Works of Thomas Brasch in the Interface Between East and West*. New York: Peter Lang, 1996.

Hanf, Martina, and Schulz, Kristin, eds. *Das blanke Wesen. Arbeitsbuch Thomas Brasch* [The exposed being. Thomas Brasch workbook]. Berlin: Theater de zeit, 2004.

Häßel, Margarete, and Richard Weber, eds. *Arbeitsbuch Thomas Brasch* [Thomas Brasch workbook]. Frankfurt/M.: Suhrkamp, 1987.

Janssen-Zimmermann, Antje. *Träume von Angst und Hoffnung: Untersuchungen zum Werk Thomas Braschs* [Dreams of fear and hope: Investigations into the work of Thomas Brasch]. Frankfurt/M.: Peter Lang, 1995.

Ponath, Jens. *Spiel und Dramaturgie in Thomas Braschs Werk* [Play and dramaturgy in Thomas Brasch's work]. Würzburg: Königshausen & Neumann, 1999.

Christian Rogowski

BRAZIL

Unlike many cultures in which theater evolved naturally from the fabric of society, Brazilian theater developed from Portugal's already long-standing tradition. It arrived in all of its baroque glory, depicting the ecclesiastical conflicts of early colonial times. From these beginnings, Brazilian theater blended subaltern cultural expressions, thus becoming more authentic. Indeed, the evolution of Brazil's theater has been one characterized by a dichotomy between foreign influence and cultural nationalism. Its creative energy emanates from this attempt at reconciling conflicting worlds, the process of defining a national identity in an increasingly complex, heterogeneous society, and an underlying historical tendency of incorporating social themes.

In the mid-19th century, REALISM divided Brazilian theater into two periods: The first, from 1855 until 1884, was shaped by impresario Joaquim Heliodoro Gomes dos Santos's company the Dramatic Gymnasium (O Ginásio Dramático). The company's rehearsal leader and director, Emílio Doux, imported the most modern plays of the era from his native France. The French realist theater brought to the stage social issues relevant to the era. The enactment of *The Mandarin* (*O Mandarim*) in 1884 by playwright Arturo Azevedo was also a turning point. Azevedo had a knack for improvisation and is credited with having fused the genre of revues with that of serious drama. The second period, which lasted from 1884 until the 20th century, was marked by the popularity of the operetta and the revue.

Faced with cultural transformations in the wake of the Industrial Revolution, Brazilian theater blossomed during the 20th century. The comedies and vaudevilles, which marked the 19th century, gave rise to a deeper sense of social commitment on the national front. This kind of theater had its roots in modernism (*modernismo*)—an artistic movement of the AVANT-GARDE—that rejected the classic mode. In 1922 it became evident that during the Modern Art Week (Semana de Arte Moderna) a new current was about to redefine Brazilian theater. MODERNIST DRAMA's most representative writers were Oswald and Mário de Andrade.

But it was not until the 1940s and 1950s that Brazilian theater really flourished artistically through the efforts of groundbreaking companies and directors such as Zbigniev Ziembinski, a war refugee from Poland who introduced European EXPRESSIONISM to Brazilian theater, and Adolfo Celi, an Italian immigrant who incorporated sophisticated European stagecraft. In 1943, the Comedians (Os Comediantes), the country's first modern company, broke the outdated mold of comedy-of-manners theater that had been dominant since the 19th century by staging NÉLSON RODRIGUES's *WEDDING GOWN* (*Vestido de Noiva*), directed by Ziembinski. Rodrigues (1912–1980) is the most innovative and provocative figure in Brazilian DRAMATURGY. His detailed stage instructions and the remarkable structure of his plays inspired other directors and led to stagings that changed the course of Brazilian theater.

In the 1950s the Brazilian Comedic Theatrical Company (Teatro Brasiliero de Comédia [TBC]), the country's largest theater school, established a tradition of stagecraft based on Italian models. In 1956 the Arena Theater (Teatro de Arena), founded by José Renato, spearheaded the new theater and attempted to Brazilianize certain Brechtian principles. The company was a forum for AUGUSTO BOAL's plays. Boal, who was one of the most influential practitioners of political theater in Latin America, later created the Theater of the Oppressed in an effort to convert theater from the "monologue" of traditional performance into a "dialogue," a give-and-take between the audience and stage. Boal experimented with many kinds of interactive theater. While working at the grassroots level, he used theater as a vehicle for social reform.

In the 1960s vibrant companies and cutting-edge playwrights continued to push the envelope. Office Theater's (Teatro Oficina) José Celso deconstructed classic works by BERTOLT BRECHT, ANTON CHEKHOV, and Brazilian modernist (*modernista*) playwright Oswald de Andrade. The company came to represent Brazilian counterculture; its most noteworthy production was 1967's THE CANDLE KING (*O rei da vela*). Also during this decade, the People's Center of Culture (Centro Popular da Cultura), led by progressive playwright ODUVALDO VIANNA FILHO, concentrated on educating people through art. However, the center was shut down in 1964 by a repressive military government that had come to power through a coup d'état. The authoritarian regime influenced the creation of a type of theater known as "Contestation Theater," which, much like Boal's innovative approach, brought theater to the general public and encouraged their participation, especially students and people who were politically active.

Female playwrights also made substantial contributions during the 1960s. Hilda Hilst, who is mostly known as a poet and fiction writer, wrote eight plays between 1967 and 1969. She won an important playwriting award, the Anchieta Prize, for her *The Executioner* (*O Verdugo*). However, it was Renata Pallotini who became the first woman in Brazil to establish a lengthy career as a playwright. She wrote her first play in 1958 and received the Anchieta Prize in 1968 for *The Scorpion of Numancia* (*O escorpião de Numância*), inspired by Miguel de Cervantes's TRAGEDY *The Siege of Numancia*. Like many of her contemporaries who wrote under the military dictatorship, Pallotini became skilled at using metaphors of resistance that sent a clear message to the opposition.

In the 1970s the military dictatorship continued to censor artistic expression in Brazil. Antunes Filho picked up the pieces of the cultural wasteland, becoming the "upstart par exellence" (*encenador par excellance*), with his internationally acclaimed production in 1978 of a text by Andrade. Filho controlled every phase of production, paid special attention to design, and subordinated the verbal text to audiovisual elements. Another theatrical rebirth came in 1979 when Filho's Macunaíma Group (Grupo Macunaíma) staged the adaptation of the seminal modernist work of the same name—*Macunaíma*. The production is a celebration of carnival as the unofficial, grotesque universe described by Russian theorist Mikhail Bakhtin.

Celso and Filho are considered to have planted the seed of postmodernist theater in Brazil. But there were hurdles along the way that had to be overcome. As if the stifling atmosphere imposed by the military regime was not enough to hinder the freedom of artistic expression, economic uncertainty loomed, and the popularity of prime-time soap operas (*telenovelas*) threatened the survival of Brazilian theater. Its demise, according to many critics and commentators, seemed eminent and unavoidable. Yet in the face of adversity, the country's theatrical scene reinvented itself yet again.

The late 1980s and the 1990s saw the resurgence of a new generation of directors, upstarts (*encenadores*) who like Filho wielded total control over their productions. The names that stand out most are Bia Lessa, whose best-known works are literary adaptations, Gabriel Villela, Márcia Vianna, and Moacyr Góes. Since 1985, theatrical plays that were previously relegated to the underground have been slowly coming out of hiding, accompanying the slow redemocratization of the country. In the following decade the tendency of stressing imagery over text was accompanied by a gradual return to the word through the production of classics. The experimentalist theater continued to boom and attain popular and critical acclaim with the plays *Paradise Lost* (*Paraíso Perdido*), in 1992, and *Job's Books* (*O Livro de Jó*), in 1995, by Antonio Araujo. Regional theater also thrived in the 1990s. In Pernambuco, Antônio Nóbrega's comedic art was well received. An actor, musician, and dancer, Nóbrega explored the playful side of stage direction, employing local songs and dances.

Brazilian national theater continues to devise new forms of theatrical expression. While it is true that art thrives in a free society, adversity can also function as an incentive with results that are no less worthy of critical acclaim. To this extent, amateur theater has an important role in today's scene. Inherently linked to popular culture, amateur theater is at the forefront of cultural expression in Brazil's theater of the 21st century. Productions can be followed in the innumerable theater festivals around the country. Most noteworthy are productions from the Northeast, the most marginalized part of Brazil, plagued by droughts and poverty. With its fusion of high culture and street life, Northeastern theater exemplifies the unique beauty that sometimes arises from hardship.

[*See also* Castro, Consuelo de; Guarnieri, Gianfrancesco]

FURTHER READING

Ellis, Lorena B. *Brecht's Reception in Brazil*. New York: Peter Lang, 1995.

George, David Sanderson. *The Modern Brazilian Stage*. Austin: Univ. of Texas Press, 1992.

——. *Flash and Crash Days: Brazilian Theater in the Postdictatorship Period*. Austin: Univ. of Texas Press, 2000.

Magaldi, Sábato. *Panorama do teatro Brasileiro* [Panorama of Brazilian theater]. São Paulo: Difusão Européia do Livro, 1962.

Sousa, J. Galante de. *O teatro no Brasil* [The theater in Brazil]. Rio de Janiero: Ministério da Educação e Cultura, Instituto Nacional do Livro, 1960.

Lissette Corsa

BREAK THE HEART

Break the Heart (*Rasga Coração*), ODUVALDO VIANNA FILHO's (Vianinha) last play, unanimously considered his masterpiece, was concluded at his deathbed in 1974 and represented his most ambitious project, having demanded extensive and detailed historical research. It was conceived as a form of homage to the generation of the old-time Left militants Vianna had come to know through his own parents' militancy and deals with three generations of a small middle-class family in Rio de Janeiro, from the early 1900s to the early 1970s. Some seventy years of the country's history are shown in a dramaturgical panel combining epic techniques and expressionist use of time frame.

The protagonist, Custódio Manhães, informally known as Manguary Pistolão, is a middle-aged militant who dreams of introducing Luca, his seventeen-year-old son, to the importance of political struggle. Luca, a hippie who shares the ideals of the flower-power generation, studies in a middle-class school that has banned wearing long hair. This event gives his father the idea of using this prohibition to introduce the boy to the importance of political organization against authoritarianism, but the debates conducted in the students' get-togethers indicate that Manguary's tactics do not meet the expectations of the student leaders, who aim at confrontation and direct action.

Vianna used the plot to produce implicit references to the different factions of the Left and to the clash between the old-time militancy and the post-1968 young radicals, who defended armed struggle and criticized the older generation as being reformist and complacent.

The play makes interesting use of simultaneous actions in present and past levels, exposing the way different generations tend to repeat certain patterns of reaction in the face of similar experiences and facts. The new ideas are not always revolutionary, warns Vianna in the introduction to the play, and the revolutionary ideas are not always new. Manguary's youth memories, evoked during his sleepless nights or even during the moments of confrontation with Luca, produce instances of paradoxical similarity and, at times, of undeniable (yet unconscious) contradiction.

Other important characters of the play are Lord Bundinha, Manguary's bohemian friend who had died in the 1930s; Camargo Velho, a former militant companion who had given up the pleasures of youth to give priority to political militancy; his young nephew, Camargo Moço, who happens to be Luca's schoolmate; and Luca's girlfriend, Milena, a passionate advocate of armed resistance and direct action.

Even having been awarded the first prize in the country's most important competition of original plays, *Break the Heart* was censored and could only be staged at the end of the military period, in 1979, when the country started to gradually return to the democratic regime.

[*See also* Brazil]

FURTHER READING

Damasceno, Leslie H. *Cultural Space and Theatrical Conventions in the Works of Oduvaldo Vianna Filho*. Detroit: Wayne State Univ. Press, 1996.

Maria Sílvia Betti

THE BREASTS OF TIRESIAS

The Breasts of Tiresias (*Les mamelles de Tirésias*) was the first surrealist drama. It was written by GUILLAUME APOLLONAIRE and performed only once during his lifetime, on June 24, 1917.

This brief play's rollicking, grotesque style is signaled by the stage directions for the entrance of Therese, her face painted blue, attired in a "long blue dress decorated with painted monkeys and fruit." Bemoaning her husband's endless sexual advances, Therese dreams not of love but of masculine adventure: she wants to be anything a man can be—soldier, artist, chemist, president of the state.

Suddenly she opens her dress, and her breasts, large balloons, detach themselves and rise into the air. As she gleefully pops them with a cigarette lighter, she finds herself growing a mustache. Announcing she has become a man, she wrestles her stunned husband into her former skirts and renames herself Tiresias (after the ancient Greek seer who had lived as both a man and a woman). A policeman arrives and is less interested in keeping the peace than in flirting with the husband. As a chorus of women chant, "No more babies!" Therese's husband announces that he himself will produce progeny. The curtain falls.

At the top of act 2, the husband raves about the joys of fatherhood, having given birth to 40,049 children. He brags of their accomplishments—one is a novelist, another is a scientist—and how much they have earned. But the policeman announces that this rash of new children has created a food shortage. A fortune-teller shows up to predict a grim fate for the childless policeman and an idyllic one for the fecund husband. Then she rips off her costume, revealing herself as Therese/Tiresias, now commander in chief of the army. The couple reconciles, and everyone agrees: "It can be fun to switch / Just mind you get it right."

Apollinaire claimed that the play was a serious call for repopulation, but its wildly anarchic style—reminiscent of ALFRED JARRY's *King Ubu* (*Ubu Roi*, 1896)—seemed to subvert all bourgeois values of home and family. Whatever Apollinaire's intentions, the play's scandalous premiere marked a turning point in modern art. Audience members included Henri Matisse, JEAN COCTEAU, Russian ballet impresario Serge Diaghilev, and poet André Breton, who did not think much of the production but wrote later that "never before, as I did on that evening, had I measured the depth of the gap that would separate the new generation from the one preceding it" (quoted in Polizzotti, 1995).

As a piece of literature, the play proved less influential than its preface, which discusses the concept of SURREALISM, a word Apollinaire first used in program notes for Cocteau's ballet *Parade* (February 1917). In his own preface, Apollinaire defended his radical style: "When man resolved to imitate walking, he invented the wheel, which does not look like a leg. In doing this, he was practicing surrealism without knowing it. . . . theatre is not life, any more than a wheel is a leg. Consequently, I feel it is legitimate to bring to the theatre new and striking aesthetic ideas." Apollinaire's play later inspired Francis Poulenc's opera of the same name.

[*See also* France]

FURTHER READING

Mackworth, Cecily. *Guillaume Apollinaire and the Cubist Life*. London: John Murray, 1961.

The Mammaries of Tiresias. In *Three Pre-Surrealist Plays*. Tr. with an intro. by Maya Slater. Oxford: Oxford Univ. Press, 1997.

Polizzotti, Mark. *Revolution of the Mind: The Life of André Breton*. New York: Farrar, Straus, 1995.

Schumacher, Claude. *Alfred Jarry and Guillaume Apollinaire*. Basingstoke: Macmillan, 1984.

Charlotte Stoudt

BRECHT, BERTOLT (1898–1956)

Food is the first thing. Morals follow on.

—Bertolt Brecht, *The Threepenny Opera*, 1928

A few years before his death on August 14, 1956, in East Berlin, Bertolt Brecht is reputed to have exclaimed in mock despair that he would be remembered in the annals of literary and theater history for the above line from the song "How to survive" from his (and Kurt Weill's) spectacular hit THE THREEPENNY OPERA (*Die Dreigroschenoper*, produced 1928), which, in the MARC BLITZSTEIN version, opened in New York City in March 1954 and had a seven-year run with a total of 2,611 performances—then a record for "musicals." To be sure, the quote's underlying assumption that social injustice is the sole cause of human depravity and thus will disappear in a just society is indicative of the materialist aesthetic and Marxist convictions that Brecht began to espouse around 1926; however, reducing a complex and voluminous work encompassing thirty volumes (in the latest, copiously annotated German edition) of drama, poetry, prose fiction, essays, and theoretical writings to a single line hardly does justice to Brecht's achievements. Arguably, he remains the preeminent dramatist of the 20th century whose plays continue to be staged worldwide, and he must also be counted among the great innovators and practitioners of the theater who redefined the relationship between actors and audience and, particularly during the last phase of his life, put his theories into practice in widely acclaimed and imitated productions of his plays.

FROM MUNICH TO BERLIN, 1917–1933

Brecht was born on February 10, 1898, in Augsburg, GERMANY. Apart from a stint as an orderly at a military hospital in his hometown of Augsburg, the young Brecht was not seriously affected by World War I. As a not particularly eager student of medicine and philosophy at the University of Munich, he wrote his first major play, BAAL, in 1918; he revised the play repeatedly afterward. The young playwright went against prevailing artistic norms by creating in Baal an aggressively antibourgeois, grossly materialistic, insatiably promiscuous, homoerotically inclined, but extraordinarily gifted poet—the very antithesis of the idealized, visionary artist figures and lonely geniuses that populated the then influential expressionist drama. *Baal* was not produced until 1923; the production in the city of Leipzig caused the first of several scandals at Brecht premieres, owing to the play's unconventional, episodic structure and its highly unorthodox protagonist who offended spectators' sensibilities. Today, the play is not likely to give offense; it is generally recognized as a powerful and poetic representation of a poet who, conceived under the influence of the philosopher FRIEDRICH NIETZSCHE, appears to have cast off all ethical moorings.

Brecht's position as a bystander and observer rather than an active participant in the revolutionary events following World War I is, in part, reflected in his second major play, DRUMS IN THE NIGHT (*Trommeln in der Nacht*). Protagonist Kragler, a soldier returning from the war, is faced with the choice of fighting on the barricades in support of the revolutionary Berlin Spartacus movement in January 1919 or of securing a modest bourgeois existence. He ultimately opts for the latter and denounces any idealistic desire to make the world a better place. He retreats to the domestic sphere with his former girlfriend, who is pregnant with a child from another man, and extols the pleasures of the "big, white, broad bed." The 1922 Munich premiere was the first production of a drama by Brecht; in recognition of its merits, he was awarded the prestigious Kleist Prize. The play includes some devices that suggest to the spectators that they are in the theater rather than witnessing "life"; hence, it may be considered an early precursor of EPIC THEATER. More than thirty years later, when Brecht was a resident of East Berlin, he reworked the play in a halfhearted attempt to counterbalance Kragler's "shabby" betrayal of the revolution by adding references to a positive hero, a class-conscious worker.

THE WEDDING (*Die Hochzeit*, produced 1926) is the best-known one-act play among several that Brecht wrote in the fall of 1919—in part influenced by the grotesque humor of the Munich folk comedian Karl Valentin. The play lampoons the pretensions to middle-class respectability on the part of the young newlyweds; the bride turns out to be pregnant, the homemade furniture collapses, and the wedding guests abandon all sense of propriety. Brecht's third major play, *In the Jungle of Cities* (*Im Dickicht der Städte*), a dense and not easily accessible drama, overtaxed the patience of the conservative Munich audience at the 1923 premiere and caused another scandal. The setting—the cold, big, and semimythical city of Chicago—was inspired by literary sources such as the German translation of Upton Sinclair's novel *The Jungle* (1906). The play presents an "inexplicable [figurative] wrestling match" between two men; the younger and stronger man rejects the homoerotic advances of the older one. There are moments of great poetic intensity and compelling depictions of the individual's alienation and lack of human contact in the jungle of the city.

Although the Bavarian capital offered a cultural environment that was conducive to facilitating the beginning of Brecht's career, he was eager to become established in Berlin, the undisputed artistic and cultural center of the Weimar Republic. The 1924 premiere of *The Life of Edward the Second of England* (*Leben Eduards des Zweiten von England*), a joint translation and adaptation of Christopher Marlowe's *Edward II* (1592) with his friend and mentor Lion Feuchtwanger, was the last Munich production in which Brecht actively participated. Dismissing the inevitability of TRAGEDY and employing narrative devices to diminish suspense, the adaptation may be considered another forerunner of the "epic theater."

In the mid-1920s, Berlin's theater scene was vibrant. There were nearly fifty stages that produced plays, three opera houses, and a considerable number of cabarets and variety theaters. Creative directors such as the legendary MAX REINHARDT and the politically oriented ERWIN PISCATOR with his multimedia productions established their artistic authority; famous actors such as the first Oscar winner Emil Jannings added luster; and well-known theater critics such as Herbert Ihering (a Brecht supporter) and Alfred Kerr (a Brecht opponent) were widely read. Brecht's appointment to a minor position at Reinhardt's Deutsches Theater in 1924 marked the beginning of the playwright's productive Berlin career that was to end with the demise of the Weimar Republic. Brecht actively participated in the debates about the function and future of the theater; he advocated a productive approach to the new mass entertainment phenomena of film, radio, operetta, revues, and boxing matches, which in part emanated from America. He was attuned to the sober, unpretentious style and emphasis on the here and now of the NEW OBJECTIVITY that was replacing the pathos and utopianism of EXPRESSIONISM as the dominant mode in literature and drama.

The "asphalt city" and urban mass society, which fostered the individual's loss of autonomy, left their mark on Brecht's comedy *A Man's a Man* (*Mann ist Mann*, produced 1926), a play in which the predilection for technical innovation among adherents of the New Objectivity is carried to an absurd extreme. Brecht posits that the social conditioning of human beings can be perfected to the point of losing one's identity. Dockworker Galy Gay is subject to an astonishing process of machinelike transformation: once meek and gentle, he turns into ferocious Jeraiah Jip, "the human fighting machine." The loss of identity is not presented as tragic; rather, the play relies on comic and farcical elements, especially in the interlude *The Baby Elephant* (*Das Elefantenkalb*). "Epic" devices such as actors stepping out of their roles are indicative of the direction in which Brecht's theater was heading.

The play takes place in a remote, curiously exotic and vague Indo-Chinese milieu that was derived from the writings of Rudyard Kipling about the British imperial world. Brecht became acquainted with Kipling's work through Elisabeth Hauptmann, an aspiring writer whom he had met in 1924. She became Brecht's collaborator on *A Man's a Man*, and she was the first of his three important female co-workers cum lovers—there has been much speculation about Brecht's "polygamous" nature—who contributed significantly to his work. Lately, there have been unconvincing attempts to elevate the positions of Hauptmann and the two other major female collaborators, Margarete Steffin and Danish actress Ruth Berlau, at the expense of Brecht by portraying them as the actual authors of his works and presenting them as exploited victims. But despite Brecht's reliance on teamwork, a mode of production that invalidated traditional notions of the author as the sole originator of specific works, he was clearly and unambiguously acknowledged as the dominant voice and motivating force in his theater collective.

In 1926, Brecht began to read Karl Marx for a projected, uncompleted play, *Jae Fleischhacker in Chicago* (*Jae Fleischhacker in Chikago*), about the transactions of the Chicago Wheat Exchange. Brecht's acceptance of Marxism has been attributed by Martin Esslin (1984) to Brecht's "divided nature," which induced him to overcome the undisciplined hedonism of his younger years by subjecting himself to rigid party discipline. Conversely, Klaus Völker (1978) argues that Brecht studied Marx in order to be able to adequately represent on stage an increasingly complex social reality. Brecht's Marxist studies coincided with the gradual evolution and theoretical formulation of the concept of "epic theater," a term he first used in conjunction with Piscator's political theater. In retrospect, Brecht deemed the Berlin premiere of *The Threepenny Opera* in August 1928 a "most successful demonstration of the epic theater." Apart from visual, short scene descriptions to minimize suspense, the special song lighting and the illumination of the organ were intended to prevent the seamless merging of speech and singing so as to foreground the aspects of performance. Yet the extraordinary popular success of the "opera," which deliberately violated the time-honored norms of the genre, is largely attributable to its "culinary," entertaining qualities. Weill's catchy tunes, foremost among them the evergreen "Mack the Knife" (a song extant in numerous adaptations and used in the 1980s in a television advertisement for McDonald's), tended to overshadow both the intended social criticism and theatrical innovations of the work.

The Threepenny Opera is loosely based on John Gay's ballad opera *The Beggar's Opera* (1728), which was translated by Hauptmann. Brecht retained the original London setting in his attempt to equate its underworld of 1900 with respectable bourgeois society. His unacknowledged use of lyrics resulted in a charge of plagiarism; Brecht provocatively professed his "fundamental laxity in matters of intellectual property"—a statement that reaffirmed his rejection of the conventional view of the author and implicitly posited cooperative endeavors as the new mode of production. As a "monument of Weimar popular culture," *The Threepenny Opera* has been credited with perfectly expressing the effervescent spirit and turmoil of that brief period before the arrival of Adolf Hitler that witnessed an exceptional flourishing of the arts.

Brecht and Weill again cooperated on *Rise and Fall of the City of Mahagonny* (*Aufstieg und Fall der Stadt Mahagonny*, produced 1930). The premiere at the Leipzig Opera House resulted in yet another theater scandal because the "opera" gravely disappointed the expectations of those accustomed to operatic tradition in general and Wagnerian opera in particular. Mahagonny, the city of nets that seeks to catch all comers and deprive them of their hard-earned money via unlimited and unrestricted pleasures, is located somewhere in the southern part of the North American continent. The warnings of lumberjack Jim Mahoney (later renamed Paul Ackermann) regarding the seductive power of false hopes go unheeded; in a society based on greed, he is sentenced to death for lack of money.

Brecht formulated his theory of the "epic theater" in "Notes to the Opera *Rise and Fall of the City of Mahagonny*" ("Anmerkungen zur Oper *Aufstieg und Fall der Stadt Mahagonny*," 1930, revised 1938), and declared: "The modern theater is the epic theater." Juxtaposing the characteristics of "epic theater" (and "epic opera") with their "dramatic" equivalents induced critics to conceive of the two types as absolute opposites rather than as related, yet distinct, forms. Brecht assigned a new role to the audience, aiming to prevent spectators' identification with the characters and emotional involvement with the action. As critical, rational observers, Brecht argued, theatergoers could attain novel, liberating insights into the workings of society. Brecht also sought to break open the closed form of drama by emphasizing the relative independence of individual scenes, a use of montage, and a deviation from linear action. In the 1935 essay "Alienation Effects in Chinese Acting" ("Verfremdungseffekte in der chinesischen Schauspielkunst"), he defined his key concept, the "ALIENATION EFFECT." The term has gained wide currency; it essentially entails Brecht's endeavor to enable the audience, whose perception has been dulled by the habitual observation of recurring phenomena, to open its collective mind to new possibilities and keen solutions via presenting our everyday world in an unfamiliar, estranging light.

A new phase in Brecht's productivity began with the "LEARNING PLAYS," which, for the most part, originated between 1928 and 1931. Although set to music by various composers, they, unlike the operas, dispense with "culinary" elements and foreground their Marxist orientation in an attempt at a novel form of communication through spectator involvement. In the 1960s, the "learning plays" were praised by some Brecht scholars as Brecht's ultimate dramatic achievement. The contemporaneous reception was less effusive; in particular, THE MEASURES TAKEN (*Die Maßnahme*, 1930) proved to be highly controversial. The play presents a stylized trial situation; three agitators from Moscow explain their killing of a young comrade, albeit with his consent, before an anonymous control chorus representing the party. The young comrade had endangered their mission in China because he had ignored party discipline and repeatedly reacted impulsively and emotionally. The intended demonstration of the hypothetical, extreme consequences of politically incorrect behavior did not find favor with either the Right or the Left: the play was condemned as "right-wing opportunism" as well as an anticipation and glorification of the Stalinist show trials of the late 1930s.

Written during the worldwide economic crisis resulting from the Wall Street stock market crash of October 1929 that ended the prosperity of the "golden twenties," *Saint Joan of the Stockyards* (*Die heilige Johanna der Schlachthöfe*) was broadcast on Berlin radio in 1932 but not produced until after Brecht's death. It dispensed with the sparseness of the "learning plays" in favor of a conventionally staged, complex drama. Naive and guileless Joan Dark, a lieutenant in the Salvation Army and latter-day Joan of Arc figure, explores the causes of the abysmal working and living conditions of the Chicago stockyard workers. She encounters the "giant of [meat] packers/king of the stockyards" Pierpont Mauler, a truly Faustian character and the industrial-age equivalent of the absolute rulers of yore, who fittingly prefers an elevated mode of speech—Shakespearian blank verse. Joan Dark is expelled from the Salvation Army—an organization that Brecht considered a front for the establishment—and fails to support the striking workers. Dying, she denounces the capitalist system and advocates violence as the only means to cause its downfall. But her message falls on deaf ears; in the highly theatrical final scene her feeble voice is drowned out by those who sing her praises in a successful attempt to render her harmless by coopting and canonizing her. In its condemnation of capitalism in the United States, the play is a far cry from Brecht's former enthusiasm for a vigorous, youthful America that, after World War I, provided important impulses in technology, mass entertainment, and sports.

The January 1932 Berlin premiere of THE MOTHER (*Die Mutter*), an adaptation of MAKSIM GORKY's novel by the same name (1907) with Helene Weigel, Brecht's actress wife, in the lead, was the last Brecht play in which he was actively involved before the Nazis seized power. The drama presents the development of Pelagea Vlasova from a simple worker's mother, one initially distrustful of her son Pavel's revolutionary activities, to a genuine activist. She learns to read and, after her son has been shot, starts printing and distributing illegal flyers and organizes antiwar demonstrations during World War I. In her resilience, maturity, and level-headedness, Pelagea Vlasova represents one of those mother figures that Brecht was to employ in his later plays.

On January 30, 1933, Hitler was appointed chancellor of a coalition government; about a month later, the building of the parliament, the Reichstag, was ablaze—an event that served the Nazis as justification for increasing the terror against political opponents. Brecht, accompanied by Weigel and son Stefan, left Berlin and Germany in February 1933; his exile was to last nearly fifteen years.

EXILE IN EUROPE AND THE UNITED STATES, 1933–1947

The Danish isle of Fyn, where Brecht lived in Skovbostrand near the city of Svendborg from December 1933 to April 1939, served as his first refuge. The ballet *The Seven Deadly Sins* (*Die sieben Todsünden der Kleinbürger*) was his first work written in exile (in collaboration with Weill); it premiered in Paris in June 1933. The two sisters Anna 1 and Anna 2 actually represent different facets of the same personality. Their family in Louisiana sends them away to make their fortune in the big cities. Anna 1 (the singer) markets her artistically gifted sister (the dancer); the normative Christian ethic of the medieval seven deadly sins (such as pride and sloth) is subverted in the service of acquiring wealth.

Brecht considered it one of his main tasks to attack Hitler via literary means. In March 1934 Brecht, Steffin, and composer Hanns Eisler began revising *Roundheads and Pointed Heads* (*Die Rundköpfe und die Spitzköpfe*), a play whose origins date from 1932 and one that was eventually produced in the fall of 1936 in a Danish translation in Copenhagen. Brecht turned the original adaptation of William Shakespeare's *Measure for Measure* (1604) into a parable play about the divisiveness of racial theories. For selfish reasons, farmer Callas joins the movement of the racist demagogue Iberin—who faintly resembles Hitler—in the mythical country of Yahoo. Iberin proclaims that the shape of one's head (in analogy to physical characteristics used to establish racial difference) determines one's status, that is, inferior or superior. As Callas belatedly realizes, Iberin functions merely as a tool of the ruling classes; he is used by them to obfuscate the status quo of harsh class divisions. Callas's refusal to join his exploited fellow tenant farmers in the uprising of the Sickle results in the defeat of the Sickle and perpetuates social injustice. Somewhat questionably, the play tends to reduce the complex causes of racism and anti-Semitism to socioeconomic factors.

Señora Carrar's Rifles (*Die Gewehre der Frau Carrar*)—Weigel played the lead role in the enthusiastically received play—and FEAR AND MISERY OF THE THIRD REICH (*Furcht und Elend des III. Reiches*; translated by ERIC BENTLEY, Brecht's chief promoter in the United States, as *The Private Life of the Master Race*) were performed by and for German exiles in Paris, in 1937 and 1938, respectively. *Fear and Misery* is based on accounts from Nazi Germany and takes place inside the Third Reich; *Señora Carrar's Rifles* is set in Spain at the time of the Civil War in the mid-1930s. Similar to the protagonist of *The Mother*, Señora Carrar progresses from a passive figure who abhors violence to a determined combatant who fights against General Francisco Franco and his counterrevolutionary forces. *Fear and Misery* consists of twenty-seven scenes; some are self-contained one-act plays. In particular, spineless bourgeois intellectuals such as the judge in "In Search of Justice," the teacher in "The Informer," and the non-Jewish physician husband in "The Jewish Wife" are exposed to derisive laughter because of their futile endeavors to please their new masters. Conversely, in several scenes, members of the working class act in accordance with their political convictions and engage in acts of genuine resistance. In both plays, Brecht made a deliberate effort to deemphasize "epic" elements in favor of a more realistic portrayal of the threat emanating from fascism.

In 1937, Brecht began to write those plays that greatly enhanced his reputation and that are now part of the Brecht canon and the repertory of the world's stages. In a rather short period, he completed the first version of THE LIFE OF GALILEO (*Leben des Galilei*, 1939), MOTHER COURAGE AND HER CHILDREN (*Mutter Courage und ihre Kinder*, 1939–1940), *The Good Woman of Szechwan* (*Der gute Mensch von Setzuan*, 1939–1940)—all of which premiered in neutral SWITZERLAND's Zurich during World War II when Brecht was no longer in Europe—and *Mr. Puntila and His Man Matti* (*Herr Puntila und sein Knecht Matti*, 1940). These plays, in which Brecht returned to the "epic" mode and did not refer explicitly to contemporaneous, political developments, added considerably to the extant body of his dramas. Their theatricality and presumed lack of an overt ideological message were to facilitate their reception in the West during the Cold War.

The Life of Galileo, of which there are three versions, posits the question as to the independence of science in the face of political demands for its instrumentalization. In the parable play THE GOOD WOMAN of SZECHWAN, Shen The, the Chinese prostitute with a golden heart, is visited by the gods. They have come to Earth to find at least one good person; if they fail to do so, there is no justification for the world to continue to exist. Shen The is able to open a small business, but she is beset by poor and greedy relatives as well as avaricious neighbors. She finds out that she will only be able to survive and protect her unborn child by masquerading as her fictive, ruthless male cousin Shui Ta. In an operatic ending, the impotent gods, spouting pious platitudes, ascend to heaven and leave Shen The, who is desperately seeking an answer as to how to be good in an evil world, helplessly behind. Religion does not offer any solutions to the problems of this world, and the epilogue, which is addressed directly to the audience, draws the conclusion that societal conditions in which good people cannot flourish must be changed.

Mother Courage and Her Children takes place during the Thirty Years' War (1618–1648) in Central Europe. Ostensibly a religious conflict between Protestant and Catholic countries, the war is really fought because of the political and economic interests of the participating powers. Mother Courage, a down-to-earth camp follower and small-scale trader, comments irreverently from her plebeian perspective on the foibles and true motives of the mighty and powerful, yet she deludes herself into thinking that she will be able to profit from the war. She does not pretend to be good; Brecht envisioned her as a "hyena" of the battlefields whose commercial instincts win out over her love for her three children, all of whom she loses. Yet post–World War II audiences were inclined to perceive her not as a small-time, incorrigible, and ultimately unsuccessful war profiteer but, rather, as a tragic mother figure and a victim of war who carries on indomitably. Such a perception blunted Brecht's intended message that war was the cause of Mother Courage's downfall and had to be prevented at all costs.

Because of the imminent threat of a German invasion of DENMARK, Brecht and family left for SWEDEN in April 1939 and settled near Stockholm. In April 1940, after the German occupation of Denmark and NORWAY, the Brecht entourage left Sweden for FINLAND, their last European refuge. Finnish writer Hella Wuolijoki provided materials for Brecht's only VOLKSSTÜCK, *Mr. Puntila and His Man Matti*, which was not produced until after World War II. Finnish estate owner Puntila is given to drunken bouts during which he expansively seeks to overcome differences in social status by fraternizing with his chauffeur Matti, a class-conscious, albeit not a revolutionary, proletarian. When sober, however, Puntila shows his true self and turns businesslike, becoming a hard-hearted exploiter. Matti rejects his boss's daughter as unfit for a proletarian existence; in parting, he pronounces the moral: servants will become their own masters once there will be no more masters. The great theatrical potential of Puntila's role, particularly in his intoxicated, effusive state, often resulted—contrary to Brecht's intent—in Puntila stealing the show.

As Europe began resembling a trap during his Finnish exile, Brecht chose not to settle in the Soviet Union—on the surface, a logical step given his Marxist convictions—but rather in the UNITED STATES. In view of the prevalent artistic doctrine of SOCIALIST REALISM under Stalin, a doctrine far removed from Brecht's stylized "epic theater," which shunned the surface REALISM of mimetic representations and naturalistic productions, Brecht had reason to be concerned. During the so-called debate on EXPRESSIONISM (*Expressionismusdebatte*), which was inconclusively conducted in the Moscow-based, German-language periodical *Das Wort* (The Word) during the late 1930s, Brecht had run afoul of official doctrine by insisting on the variety and diversity of realistic modes of representation; he rejected prescriptive models such as those advocated by the influential critic György Lukács.

In preparing for the United States, Brecht completed a project in 1941 that was explicitly intended for American audiences, THE RESISTIBLE RISE OF ARTURO UI (*Der aufhaltsame Aufstieg des Arturo Ui*). The play was designed to elucidate the connections between capitalism, mobsters, and Nazism as well as to demonstrate that Hitler's rise to power was not at all inevitable. *Arturo Ui* incorporates significant historical events such as the burning of the Reichstag in February 1933 and the annexation of AUSTRIA in March 1938. Brecht endowed his Hitler figure with traits of gangster Al Capone and again chose Chicago as the setting so as to expose Hitler as a highly dangerous perpetrator of "great political crimes" rather than as an inspired, charismatic political leader. But the mixture of grand classical style and

Chaplinesque elements detracted from the intended analogy of Hitler and Al Capone. After Germany had declared war on the United States in December 1941, an American production of the play no longer appeared necessary or appropriate; it was not performed until 1958.

In May 1941, Brecht's party (including Berlau) left Finland by train via Moscow (where Steffin had to be left behind; she died shortly afterward) to Vladivostok in Siberia, whence they embarked for the journey to the West Coast and took up residence in Santa Monica. Brecht's seven-year American sojourn was a period of substantial productivity but resulted in few stage productions of his plays, publications, or completed film projects. Completely unaccustomed to the working conditions and attitudes prevailing in Hollywood, Brecht resented the crass commercialism and the low regard in which writers were held; at the same time, the behavior of some of his fellow exiles in California (such as the scholar Theodor W. Adorno) provided material. Brecht classified them as "Tuis," a neologism and pun derived from the word "intellectuals." "Tuis" represented a caste of lenders of intellect to the highest bidder—an activity that was particularly flourishing in America, where everything had become a salable commodity. After returning to Germany, Brecht reworked the "Tui" materials into *Turandot* (*Turandot oder Der Kongress der Weißwäscher*, 1953), a play set in a mythical China that satirizes those intellectual apologists of all political persuasions who defend an unjust order. The play was neither published nor staged during Brecht's lifetime.

The fight against Hitler remained a priority for Brecht. He actually achieved a measure of (financial) success for his significant contribution to Fritz Lang's anti-Nazi film *Hangmen Also Die* (1943), but Brecht's repeated efforts to have his plays produced on Broadway proved futile. The first play he completed in America, a collaborative effort with his old Munich friend Feuchtwanger, portrays French resistance to the German invasion in World War II. *The Visions of Simone Machard* (*Die Gesichte der Simone Machard*, produced 1957) takes place in June 1940. Adolescent and impressionable Simone, a hardworking, exploited maid, reads a book about Joan of Arc. She begins to identify with FRANCE's national heroine in a sequence of dream scenes, which are interspersed with "real" scenes, and hears voices that exhort her to resist the aggressors. Her boss, a hotel proprietor and eager collaborator who wants to preserve his possessions, supports Simone's punishment for burning the gasoline supplies that would have facilitated the rapid advance, the Blitzkrieg, of the German army. For her patriotic act she is confined to an asylum controlled by brutal nuns. Yet the play, in which historical events are seen through the eyes of an innocent young girl unaffected by material interests, ends on an optimistic note: Simone's example has inspired the people to begin to resist the occupation.

The ongoing war continued to occupy Brecht. He had worked on the script for Piscator's production of *Schweyk*, an adaptation of Jaroslav Hasek's novel *The Good Soldier Schweik* (1921–1923), in the late 1920s and returned to the project in 1943 by transposing the protagonist from World War I and the Austro-Hungarian Empire to World War II and Nazi-occupied Prague as well as the Russian front. Schweyk is the exemplary, shrewd, and nonheroic survivor who uses his feigned lack of intelligence as a cover but, at the same time, adheres to a subversive, idiosyncratic kind of folk wisdom that tends to foil the grandiose plans for world conquest on the part of Hitler and other Nazi bigwigs who are represented as oversized caricatures. They do not sufficiently take into account the little man who is supposed to carry out their insidious plans. In contrast, Mrs. Kopecka's inn The Flagon, with its ambiance of warm hospitality, offers a refuge for the little man. "The Song of the Moldau" (the play was set to music by Hans Eisler) gives poetic expression to the inevitability of change and the inexorable downfall of the mighty. Again, the drama was not produced until after Brecht's death.

THE CAUCASIAN CHALK CIRCLE (*Der kaukasische Kreidekreis*, 1943–1944) had its origins in an old Chinese play that, in the 1920s, was adapted into German. Brecht was familiar with the adaptation but did not begin work on his own *Chalk Circle* until after he had left Germany. Among the plays that Brecht wrote in the United States, it is unquestionably the drama that received the highest accolades on account of both its poetic qualities and its skillful use of the elements of epic theater. Notably the "Singer," who is distinct from the characters in the play and directs as well as narrates the simultaneously occurring stories of Grusha and Azdak successively rather than in parallel fashion, represents an innovative feature. In addressing questions of motherhood, property rights, and justice, the play appears to deal with genuinely American topics. Yet these concepts are subject to incisive scrutiny. Crafty and unorthodox, Azdak, a "disappointed revolutionary," became a judge during a brief, "golden" period when, in revolutionary times, feudal Georgia's system of class justice was temporarily suspended. Azdak awards the male child to the socially useful, kind, and motherly Grusha rather than to his biological, avaricious mother. In the famous chalk circle test, the biological mother shows her propensity for hurting the child in order to achieve her materialistic ends. Conversely, Grusha acts entirely in the interest of the child; the fact that she is indisputably the better mother implicitly advances a new definition of motherhood.

Again, the intended premiere on Broadway did not materialize (the play was not produced in New York City until 1966); instead, the play opened (in Bentley's translation) in March 1948 in Northfield, Minnesota, after Brecht's departure from the United States. A potential ideological stumbling block turned out to be the "Prologue," in which, at the end of World War II, the farmers of two agricultural collectives in Soviet Georgia settle their property dispute about a fertile valley agreeably and reasonably. Brecht deemed the "Prologue" an integral part of the play, but Western critics denounced it as communist propaganda. In the drama's first productions, the "Prologue" was simply omitted.

With the second, American version of *Galileo*, on which he cooperated with actor Charles Laughton (who also played the role of Galileo in the Beverly Hills [July 1947] and New York City [December 1947] productions), Brecht achieved one of the rare, modest successes during his years in the United States. After the dropping of atomic bombs on Hiroshima and Nagasaki in August 1945, Brecht began to reexamine the role of Galileo and concluded that it was no longer adequate to pursue scientific research without considering to which ends it might be used. He no longer viewed Galileo's recantation at the sight of torture instruments as a shrewd ploy to mislead the church authorities so as to be able to complete his work and have it smuggled out of Italy; rather, in his self-condemnation Galileo blames himself for cowardice and for having established a pattern for subordinating science to authority instead of advancing knowledge in the service of humankind.

In October 1947, Brecht testified before the House Un-American Activities Committee that investigated the alleged communist infiltration of Hollywood. He had rehearsed his testimony well and is generally assumed to have outwitted his interrogators who, however, were hardly familiar with Brecht's work and political convictions. One day after this potentially dangerous, but ultimately uneventful, brush with the authorities, Brecht left the United States.

RETURN TO EUROPE: ZURICH AND EAST BERLIN, 1947–1956

Brecht spent the first few years after returning to Europe in Zurich, where another of his major plays, *Mr. Puntila and His Man Matti*, premiered in June 1948. In the late 1940s and 1950s, the drama was staged to great acclaim in West Germany, in part because of the erroneous—and ironic—assumption that it lacked the ingredients of class antagonism. In Zurich, Brecht finished his theoretical treatise *A Short Organum for the Theatre* (*Kleines Organon für das Theater*), an important work that set forth the aesthetics of his "theater of the scientific age" in opposition to "Aristotelian" drama, which lacked an appeal to the spectators' critical faculties. In January 1949, *Mother Courage and Her Children* opened at the Deutsches Theater in East Berlin with Weigel in the leading role, an event that brought into sharp focus the contradictory tendencies underlying the formation of a new, socialist theater in the Soviet Occupation Zone and, as of October 1949, the German Democratic Republic (GDR). Communist dramatist FRIEDRICH WOLF, who returned from exile in the Soviet Union and was an adherent of "Aristotelian," cathartic theater, criticized the play for being pessimistic, but eventually Mother Courage prevailed and became an international triumph. Wolf's objections were reminiscent of the expressionism debate of the 1930s and highlighted Brecht's dilemma subsequent to taking up permanent residence in East Berlin in May 1949: on the one hand, he was considered one of the chief cultural representatives of the GDR; on the other, he was constantly running the risk of being accused of violating the aesthetic norms of socialist realism.

Brecht had opted for East Berlin in part because of the prospect of having at his disposal a theater of his own. He envisioned a representative role, one transcending the political division of Germany, by having his plays staged in both the East and the West. The vehicle for promoting his design was the Berliner Ensemble, a troupe headed by Weigel, with Brecht serving as chief director. The Berliner Ensemble obtained a permanent home in 1954 at the Theater am Schiffbauerdamm (the venue for the 1928 triumph of *The Threepenny Opera*) and eventually developed into one of the GDR's premiere cultural institutions. After a war that had wreaked massive physical destruction and perverted the moral and aesthetic underpinnings of the theater, Brecht considered it his chief responsibility to rebuild the repertory with socially progressive plays from the German and international stage, including adaptations of Shakespeare, Molière, and others. Yet there was a price to be paid for the considerable benefits of working in a theater that was financially secure and allowed Brecht and his team of young co-workers and future dramatists virtually unrestricted rehearsal time for his "model" productions. For instance, in March 1951 the trial run of the opera *The Trial of Lucullus* (*Das Verhör des Lukullus*), originally a radio play written at the beginning of World War II, met with severe criticism on the part of cultural functionaries who suspected "formalist" and pacifist deviations from the party line. Brecht and composer Paul Dessau appeared to acknowledge the criticism; they called their reworked version *The Condemnation of Lucullus* (*Die Verurteilung des Lukullus*) to stress the point that Roman general Lucullus was deservedly sentenced for his criminal wars of aggresssion.

Guest appearances by the Berliner Ensemble (which Weigel continued to manage after Brecht's death until her own in 1971) in Paris and London paved the way for Brecht's rise in the West to the position of a "modern classic," one whose craft transcended his politics. Brecht's ascendancy was briefly interrupted by West German boycotts of his plays following the workers' uprising in East Berlin and the GDR on June 17, 1953, in the wake of Joseph Stalin's death in March of the same year. Brecht responded ambiguously to the uprising; he was accused of abject servitude to an unpopular, oppressive regime. Further boycotts occurred during the Hungarian uprising and its suppression by the Soviet Union in 1956 as well as upon the construction of the Berlin Wall in August 1961. In the intolerant atmosphere of the Cold War, the playwright was posthumously held responsible for these events.

Brecht's reputation has withstood further challenges. The unprecedented attention the media paid to Brecht on the occasion of his 100th birthday provides an indication of his stature: At the beginning of the 21st century, there is general agreement that he remains one of the great innovators and practitioners of the theater who has contributed a remarkable array of plays to the repertory of the international stage—plays that seek both to enlighten and to entertain.

PLAYS: *Baal* (1918; revised 1926); *The Wedding* (*Die Hochzeit/Die Kleinbürgerhochzeit*, 1919); *Drums in the Night* (*Trommeln in der Nacht*, 1919–1920; revised 1953); *In the Jungle of Cities* (*Im Dickicht der Städte*, 1921–1923; revised 1927); *The Life of Edward the Second of England* (*Leben Eduards des Zweiten von England*, 1923–1924; with Lion Feuchtwanger); *A Man's a Man* (*Mann ist Mann*, 1924–1926); *Rise and Fall of the City of Mahagonny* (*Aufstieg und Fall der Stadt Mahagonny*, 1927–1929; music by Kurt Weill); *The Threepenny Opera* (*Die Dreigroschenoper*, 1928; music by Kurt Weill); *Saint Joan of the Stockyards* (*Die heilige Johanna der Schlachthöfe*, 1929–1930); *The Measures Taken* (*Die Maßnahme*, 1930; revised 1931); *The Mother* (*Die Mutter*, 1931); *Roundheads and Pointed Heads* (*Die Rundköpfe und die Spitzköpfe*, 1932–1936); *The Seven Deadly Sins* (*Die sieben Todsünden der Kleinbürger*, 1933; music by Kurt Weill); *Señora Carrar's Rifles* (*Die Gewehre der Frau Carrar*, 1936–1937); *Fear and Misery of the Third Reich*, also translated as *The Private Life of the Master Race* (*Furcht und Elend des III. Reiches*, 1937–1938); *The Life of Galileo* (*Leben des Galilei*, 1939; revised 1944–1947; revised 1955–1956); *The Trial of Lucullus/The Condemnation of Lucullus* (*Das Verhör des Lukullus/Die Verurteilung des Lukullus*, 1939; music by Paul Dessau; revised 1949–1950); *The Good Woman of Szechwan* (*Der gute Mensch von Setzuan* 1939–1940); *Mother Courage and Her Children* (*Mutter Courage und ihre Kinder*, 1939–1940); *Mr. Puntila and His Man Matti* (*Herr Puntila und sein Knecht Matti*, 1940); *The Resistible Rise of Arturo Ui* / (*Der aufhaltsame Aufstieg des Arturo Ui* (*Der Aufstieg des Arturo Ui*, 1941); *The Visions of Simone Machard* (*Die Gesichte der Simone Machard*, 1942–1943; with Lion Feuchtwanger; revised 1946); *Schweyk in the Second World War* (*Schweyk/Schweyk im Zweiten Weltkrieg*, 1943); *The Caucasian Chalk Circle* (*Der kaukasische Kreidekreis*, 1943–1944); *Turandot* (*Turandot oder Der Kongress der Weißwäsche*, 1953)

FURTHER READING

Bentley, Eric. *Bentley on Brecht*. Rev. 2d ed. New York: Applause, 1999.

Esslin, Martin. *Brecht: A Choice of Evils. A Critical Study of the Man, His Work and His Opinions*. 4th rev. ed. London: Methuen, 1984.

Fuegi, John. *Brecht and Company: Sex, Politics, and the Making of the Modern Drama*. New York: Grove, 1994.

International Brecht Society. http://polyglot.lss.wisc.edu/german/brecht/.

Lyon, James K. *Bertolt Brecht in America*. Princeton, N.J.: Princeton Univ. Press, 1980.

Mews, Siegfried, ed. *A Bertolt Brecht Reference Companion*. Westport, Conn.: Greenwood Press, 1997.

Völker, Klaus. *Brecht. A Biography*. Tr. by John Nowell. New York: Seabury, 1978.

Siegfried Mews

BRENTON, HOWARD (1942–)

Born in Portsmouth, ENGLAND, Howard Brenton wanted to be an archaeologist but ended up reading English at Cambridge, which he loathed. His first play, *Ladders of Fools*, was produced at Cambridge University in 1965.

A controversial voice in British postwar political theater, Brenton has written or co-written more than forty plays, as well as newspaper articles, essays, poetry, a novel and television drama, including thirteen episodes of the BBC's award-winning *Spooks*. Brenton's drama is political, both in form and content; his writing challenges the traditional values of capitalist Britain, juxtaposing theatrical shocks, verbal and visual humor, overt sexuality, and language at once elevated and crude. His plays are shaped by characters from different perspectives and value systems encountering (often violently and brutally) their differences.

Brenton frequently portrays England mired by cultural crisis characterized by the demands of competing sociopolitical binaries: order and anarchy, capitalism and socialism, individual experience and social need, historical inheritance and utopian vision. Brenton's early short plays, such as *Gum and Goo* (1969), *Heads* (1969), and *The Education of Skinny Spew* (1969), capture events through action that explodes in disorienting and rapidly shifting images, rather than through psychology and explanation. *Revenge* (1969), a seriocomic two-act play, undermines assumptions concerning social rectitude and the legitimacy of legal institutions, rendering law-breaker and law-enforcer equally corrupt and violent. *Christie in Love* (1969) comically exposes the sham of conventional social and moral values and expands the controlled aggressiveness of his earlier plays. During this period, Brenton also experimented with plays for public places, writing for nontheatrical environments including a skating rink (*Scott of the Antarctic*, 1971) and a Methodist church (*Wesley*, 1970). *Lay-By* (1971), a collaboration with six other playwrights including HOWARD BARKER, DAVID HARE, and Stephen Poliakoff, exemplifies Brenton's continued investment in experimentation.

Brenton explores a world heading for disaster; characters acquiesce and become corrupt or, alternatively, violence erupts on the scene. While resident playwright at the Royal Court Theatre in London (1972–1973), Brenton began work on a series of full-length plays constructed in short scenes. *Magnificence* (1973) shows the tragedy of a group of squatters attempting to revolutionize the government's housing policy. *Brassneck* (1973), written with David Hare, explores the survival of a family of corrupt local politicians, offering a satirical attack on capitalist greed and corruption. *The Churchill Play* (1974) offers a dystopian vision, deconstructing the patriotic myths Britain has constructed about itself since the Second World War. *Epsom Downs* (1977) celebrates ordinary folks on Derby Day, unwittingly participating in the class structure that promotes horse racing as "the sport of kings." *The Romans in Britain* (1980) controversially equates the invasion of Britain by the Romans with the British "occupation" of Northern Ireland. *Pravda* (1985), written with David Hare, is a nuanced black COMEDY about the British newspaper industry of the mid-1980s, caricaturing the social and economic changes in Margaret Thatcher's Britain.

Brenton develops BERTOLT BRECHT's epic style, creating alienation effects and historicizing the incidents of the narrative; deliberately questioning and puncturing popular conceptions of history, provoking audiences to recognize and act on possibilities for political and social change.

He won the *Evening Standard* award in 1976 for *Weapons of Happiness*, and in 1985, the *London Standard* award and Plays and Players award for best new play for *Pravda: A Fleet Street Comedy*.

SELECT PLAYS: *A Sky Blue Life* (1966); *Christie in Love* (1969); *The Education of Skinny Spew* (1969); *Gum and Goo* (1969); *Heads* (1969); *Revenge* (1969); *Wesley* (1970); *Lay By* (1971); *Scott of the Antarctic: Or, What God Didn't See* (1971); *Hitler Dances* (1972); *How Beautiful With Badges* (1972); *Magnificence* (1973); *The Churchill Play* (1974); *Government Property* (1975); *The Salvia Milkshake* (1975); *Weapons of Happiness* (1976); *Epsom Downs* (1977); *Deeds* (1978); *Sore Throats* (1979); *The Life of Galileo* (1980); *The Romans in Britain* (1980); *A Short Sharp Shock!* (1980); *Thirteenth Night* (1981); *Conversations in Exile* (1982); *Danton's Death* (1982); *The Thing* (1982); *The Genius* (1983); *Sleeping Policemen* (1983); *Blood Poetry* (1984); *Pravda* (1985); *Greenland* (1988); *H.I.D. (Hess Is Dead)* (1989); *Iranian Nights* (1989); *Moscow Gold* (1990); *Berlin Bertie* (1992); *Faust: Parts One and Two* (1995); *Ugly Rumours* (1998); *Collateral Damage* (1999); *Snogging Ken* (2000); *Paul* (2005)

FURTHER READING

Bennett, Susan. "At the End of the Great Radical Tradition? Recent Plays by Howard Brenton." *Modern Drama* 33, no. 3 (1990): 409–18.

Boon, Richard. *Brenton the Playwright*. London: Methuen, 1991.

———. "Retreating to the Future: Brenton in the Eighties." *Modern Drama* 33, no. 1 (1990): 30–41.

Evendon, Michael. " 'No Future Without Marx': Dramaturgies of the End of History in Churchill, Brenton, Barker." *Theatre* 29, no. 3 (1999): 100–113.

O'Connor, John. "Disrupting the Spectacle: French Situationist Political Theory and the Plays of Howard Brenton." *Theatre Symposium* 9 (2001): 86–94.

Wilson, Ann, ed. *Howard Brenton: A Casebook*. New York: Garland, 1992.

Yoo, Kim. "Insoluble Gaps Between Reality and Vision: Howard Brenton's Bloody Poetry." *Journal of Modern British and American Drama* 15, no. 1 (2002): 101–135.

Zeifman, Hersh. "Making History: The Plays of Howard Brenton." In *British and Irish Drama Since 1960*, ed. by James Acheson. New York: St. Martin's, 1993. 130–145.

Kerry Moore

THE BRIDGE

The Bridge (*El Puente*) premiered at the Teatro La Máscara on May 4, 1949. At the time, the debate raging within Argentine theater circles concentrated less on aesthetics than on the antagonism of commercial versus independent theater.

This first work by CARLOS GOROSTIZA would prove a determining factor in the future evolution of such a debate. *The Bridge* renewed a unique national tradition, marked by a forceful critical impulse, that extended back to Leónidas Barletta's Teatro del Pueblo/People's Theatre and to such popular theatrical genres as the FARCE and the THEATER OF THE GROTESQUE (*el grotesco*). The play also transcended this tradition to establish the foundation for a reflective/introspective REALISM (*realismo reflexivo*) that came to dominate the Argentine theatrical scene in the decades to come.

The plot centers on the anticipated return of two individuals—an engineer (Luis) and his assistant (Andresito)—who are at work constructing a bridge and who have not communicated with their friends and relatives in days. The foreboding atmosphere that characterizes the play (*la desgracia*) is reflected not only in the increasing tension of the dialogue but also in the sounds that prefigure an ultimate tragedy: the pealing of church bells, the ringing of a telephone, and ultimately, the siren of an ambulance.

Spatially, Gorostiza depicts class divisions by situating the action within two distinct environments. The first is the engineer's home, inhabited by his wife, son-in-law, and brother-in-law. The second is the street, along which Andresito's mother and sister continually pass and where his friends meet up. Rich and poor thus establish a counterpoint wherein every exchange between the two classes is doomed to failure and the levels of moral virtue and wealth are inversely proportional to one another. For instance, Andresito's downtrodden friends take it upon themselves to collect the money that his mother needs to avoid eviction, while the engineer's wife embodies the superficiality and the selfishness of an aristocracy that feels threatened by the advance of Peronism.

The play is rife with social and historical allusions. In the characters' conversations with one another, soccer and the *milonga* (a form of tango popular in Buenos Aires at the time) share space with the "Crisis of '29," the consequences of the war (such as the rising cost of bread), unemployment, poverty, and limited educational opportunities. While the characters may generate sympathy or antipathy among the audience, the play avoids a didactic tone. Such is the reflective/introspective quality that distinguishes Gorostiza's unique brand of realism.

The drama unfolds within the context of Peronist hegemony in the latter half of the 1940s and its ostensible efforts to overcome the deep social divisions that had characterized the nation up to that time. To this end, the finale establishes Death as the great equalizer: in an ironic twist of fate, the corpses of Luis and Andesito are confused and delivered to the wrong families.

Meanwhile, the handful of money that Andresito's mother drops—after having gone through so much suffering and humiliation to attain it—ultimately serves as a powerful symbol of the pettiness and injustice characteristic of this materialistic world.

The Bridge initiated a substantial transformation in Argentine theater. Gorostiza found a voice rich with the colloquialisms and idioms of Buenos Aires's citizens. Yet this reality transcended its immediate environment, to take on a universal character that would help independent theater to liberate itself from the straightjacket of costumbrism (*costumbrismo*).

[*See also* Argentina]

FURTHER READING

Forster, Merlin H. *The Theater of Carlos Gorostiza.* In *Dramatists in Revolt: The New Latin American Theater*, ed. by Leon Lyday and George Woodyard. Austin: Univ. of Texas Press, 1976. 110–119.

Laurent, Madeleine. *Personajes, referencias socials y símbolos en el teatro de Carlos Gorostiza* [Personages, social references, and symbols in the theater of Carlos Gorostiza]. Ottowa: National Library of Canada, 1991.

Norberto Cambiasso (Tr. by Gabriel Milner)

BRIDIE, JAMES (1888–1951)

Born Osborne Henry Mavor to a middle-class Glasgow family on January 3, 1888, James Bridie became one of the influential playwrights and promoters of the theater in twentieth-century SCOTLAND. Educated first at Glasgow Academy, he later studied medicine at Glasgow University. After graduating in 1913, he worked at the Glasgow Royal Infirmary before serving as a doctor in France and the Middle East during World War I. He returned to civilian life after the war, got married, and joined the staff of Glasgow's Victoria Infirmary in 1923. Shortly thereafter he began putting his energies into writing plays under pseudonyms adopted to avoid problems with his patients. He retired from medicine in 1938 to focus on the theater, where his influence extended beyond his plays. During this period he helped found the Glasgow Citizens' Theatre (1943) and served as its first president; was named to the committee that would become the Scottish Arts Council and served as its chair (1947); and founded the College of Drama in the Royal Scottish Academy of Music, Glasgow, the first such institution in Scotland (1950). For his dedication to Scottish drama, he was granted an honorary Doctor of Laws degree by the University of Glasgow in 1939 and was made a Commander of the British Empire in 1946. He died on January 29, 1951, in Edinburgh.

Bridie experimented in the theater during his university days, when his experiences of Glasgow Repertory productions inspired him to write plays for his classmates. His first serious foray came in 1922 with *The Switchback*, a play inspired by his experiences as a physician that concerned the conflict between individual creativity and community constraints. However, it was not until 1928 that one of his works would make it to the stage: *The Sunlight Sonata*, an allegorical satire on middle-class Glaswegian mores. His first true success was *The Anatomist* (1930), a historical drama centering on Dr. Knox, the infamous nineteenth-century physician whose exploits with the body-snatchers Burke and Hare Bridie painted in Faustian tones. After its run in Edinburgh, the production moved to London in 1931, where it became the first in a string of West End triumphs. With his success in England in the 1930s, Bridie returned to writing for the Scottish stage; of the twenty scripts first produced after 1940, including one revision, twelve premiered in Glasgow (nine under the aegis of the Glasgow Citizen's Theatre) and three more in Edinburgh.

Bridie's debts to classical and medieval models and to the pantomime tradition are evident. Many of his plays employ biblical characters, angels and devils, and allegory to address modern themes; however, Bridie's works often end on an ambiguous note. At the close of *Mr. Bolfry* (1943), the characters convince themselves that they have not been visited by the devil (Bolfry)—at which point the titular character's umbrella exits of its own accord. In *Daphne Laureola* (1949), the romantic young Ernest's infatuation with the uninhibited Lady Pitts is crushed when she spurns him in favor of her late husband's chauffeur. At the end of *The Queen's Comedy* (1950), Jupiter, the universe's ultimate authority, acknowledges that he is motivated by forces beyond his comprehension. Despite the threads of allegory that tie many of Bridie's plays together, they are typically open-ended, a feature that stymied some early theatergoers but has assured his works' continued popularity in repertory.

PLAYS: *The Sunlight Sonata, or To Meet the Seven Deadly Sins* (by "Mary Henderson," 1928); *The Switchback* (1929, originally written 1922, revised with James Brandane); *What It Is to Be Young* (1929); *The Anatomist: A Lamentable Comedy of Knox, Burke and Hare, and the West Port Murders* (1930); *The Girl Who Did Not Want to Go to Kuala Lumpur* (1930); *Tobias and the Angel* (1930); *The Dancing Bear* (1931); *The Amazed Evangelist* (1932); *Jonah and the Whale: A Morality* (1932, later produced as *Jonah 3*); *The Proposal* (1932, adapted from Anton Chekhov's *Predlozhenie*); *A Sleeping Clergyman* (1933); *Colonel Witherspoon, or The Fourth Way to Greatness* (1934); *Marriage Is No Joke* (1934); *Mary Read* (1934, with Claud Gurney); *The Black Eye* (1935); *Storm in a Teacup* (1936, adapted from Bruno Frank's *Stürm in Wasserglass*, later produced as *Storm over Patsy*); *Susannah and the Elders* (1937); *Babes in the Wood* (1938); *The King of Nowhere* (1938); *The Last Trump* (1938); *The Golden Legend of Shults* (1939, revised 1948); *What Say They?* (1939); *A Change for the Worse* (1942); *The Dragon and the Dove* (1942); *The Holy Isle* (1942); *Mr. Bolfry* (1943); *The Forrigan Reel* (1944, revised 1945); *It Depends What You Mean* (1944); *Hedda Gabler* (1945, adapted from Henrik Ibsen's *Hedda Gabler*); *Lancelot* (1945); *The Wild Duck* (1946, adapted from Henrik Ibsen's *Vildanden*); *Dr. Angelus* (1947); *John Knox* (1947); *Gog and Magog* (1948); *Daphne Laureola* (1949); *The Tintock*

Cup (1949, with George Munro); Mr. Gillie (1950); The Queen's Comedy (1950); Red Riding Hood (1950, with Duncan Macrae); The Baikie Charivari (1952); Meeting at Night (1954, revised by Archibald Batty)

FURTHER READING

Bannister, William. *James Bridie and His Theatre: A Study of James Bridie's Personality, His Stage Plays, and His Work for the Foundation of the Scottish National Theatre*. London: Rockliff, 1955.

Leary, Daniel. "James Bridie." In *Modern British Dramatists, 1900–1945*, ed. by Stanley Weintraub. Vol. 10 of *Dictionary of Literary Biography*. Detroit: Gale Research, 1982. 66–75.

Low, John Thomas. *Doctors, Devils, Saints, and Sinners: A Critical Study of the Major Plays of James Bridie*. Edinburgh: Ramsay Head Press, 1980.

Luyben, Helen L. *James Bridie: Clown and Philosopher*. Philadelphia: Univ. of Pennsylvania Press, 1965.

Mavor, Ronald. *Dr. Mavor & Mr. Bridie: Memories of James Bridie*. Edinburgh: Canongate, 1988.

Tobin, Terence. *James Bridie (Osborne Henry Mavor)*. Boston: Twayne, 1980.

Jason A. Pierce

BRIEUX, EUGÈNE (1858–1932)

Born in Paris on January 19, 1858, Eugène Brieux took part in the moralistic tradition begun in the 1750s by Denis Diderot and continued by Émile Augier and ALEXANDRE DUMAS FILS. His work's modern relevance demonstrated the form's durability, reacting against artifice during a time when many believed that current institutions and principles were decaying. Brieux presented contemporary facts, not eternal truths, working with the immediate situations of his characters, not their innate tendencies. Brieux is considered a successor to HENRIK IBSEN, writing from a democratic conscience as a means of serving his audience and attacking specific social systems.

Brieux combined Diderot's social interests with Dumas fils' "thesis-play" didacticism. He studied general conditions, not individual passions, and if he shared Ibsen's public conscience, he shared nothing of his mastery of construction or psychology: the problem's exposure was more significant than the lives of its characters or the style through which they are portrayed. Brieux's structures are a "polyphony of themes," each thesis studied individually with warmth and vigor. The plays comprise processions of characters in which the acceptance of powerlessness is often the resolution. In the best cases, the dramatist shows such concern for his characters he allows them to pursue any paths they wish, across the bounds of style and logic. In the worst cases, the characters are merely puppets in a quest for rectitude. To compound this, Brieux's style is inconsistent, even within each play: scenes move rapidly from manners to dark despair to desolate calm. Character development is impeded, often leaving caricature to fulfill the duty of sermonizing; the application of the criticism to the general public consequently falters. There are some vivid characters (Julie of *The Three Daughters of Monsieur Dupont* [*Les trois filles de Monsieur Dupont*, 1897]), but they are rare. Still the action is rousing, the suspense is nearly melodramatic, and the satire is always biting.

Brieux's highest polemic comes midcareer (1897–1903). We find shrewd arguments presented in strong language devoid of affectation. No happy ending is necessary; indeed, at times, no ending at all is necessary. Brieux sets out to identify a problem—for example, arranged marriages (*The Three Daughters of Monsieur Dupont*), a corrupt legal system (*The Red Dress* [*La robe rouge*, 1900]), dishonest charities (*The Benefactors* [*Les bienfaiteurs*, 1896]), venereal disease (*Damaged Goods* [*Les avariés*, 1901])—and probe its effects on representative characters. Because he treats the familiar material with a sympathy that approaches apology, the works inherently offer forgiveness. Brieux believed fundamentally in the good of man, who commits evil when he does not realize his social responsibility. He said, "Humanity is perfectible, the world is improving, and we may as well do all we can to hasten that evolution, which nothing can prevent or stop" (Scheifly, 1917). He wished to stir the conscience of the masses and inspire them to hygienic living: each play shows a form of man's malpractice, and the remedy lies in the practice depicted. Brieux died in Nizza on December 6, 1932.

Called a "public servant," Brieux stages social propaganda through debates between characters, in scenes that mirror the author's debate with his audience. Even if he is accused of "jettisoning the artistic in order to salvage the useful," Brieux helped reawaken drama to a sense of social accountability, offering the option of public service over contemporary frivolity.

[*See also* France]

SELECT PLAYS: *Artists' Families* (*Ménage d'artistes*, 1890); *Blanchette* (1892); *The Chain* (*L'engrenage*, 1894); *The Benefactors* (*Les bienfaiteurs*, 1896); *The Escape* (*L'évasion*, 1896); *The Three Daughters of Monsieur Dupont* (*Les trois filles de Monsieur Dupont*, 1897); *The Cradle* (*Le berceau*, 1898); *The Red Dress* (*La robe rouge*, 1900); *Damaged Goods* (*Les avariés*, 1901); *The Substitutes* (*Les remplaçantes*, 1901); *Maternity* (*Maternité*, 1903); *False Gods* (*La foi*, 1909); *The Woman on Her Own* (*La femme seule*, 1912)

FURTHER READING

Bacourt, Pierre de, and J. W. Cunliffe. *French Literature During the Last Half-Century*. London: Macmillan, 1923.

Chandler, Frank Wadleigh. *The Contemporary Drama of France*. Boston: Little, Brown, 1920.

Courtney, W. L. *Old Saws and Modern Instances*. Freeport, N.Y.: Books for Libraries Press, 1969.

Filon, Augustin. *The Modern French Drama*. Tr. by Janet E. Hogarth. London: Chapman & Hall, 1898. Originally published as *De Dumas à Rostand: Esquisse du mouvement dramatique contemporain* [From Dumas to Rostand: Outline of the contemporary dramatic movement]. Paris: A. Fayard & cie, 1898.

Scheifly, William H. *Brieux and Contemporary French Society*. [New York]: Putnam, 1917.

Thomas, Penrhy Vaughan. *The Plays of Eugene Brieux*. Boston: J. W. Luce, 1915.

Matt Di Cintio

BROCH OTT BROCH *See* CRIMES AND CRIMES

BRONNEN, ARNOLT (1895–1959)

Hailed as a "raw" and "explosive talent" by critic Herbert Ihering after the premiere of the scandalous one-act expressionist drama *Patricide* (*Vatermord*, 1915) in Berlin on May 14, 1922, Arnolt Bronnen had no fewer than seven plays reach the German stage from 1922 to 1926. His earliest works are left-wing, expressionist, and anarchistic, but during the interwar period his texts shifted to reflect nationalist and ultimately to glorify fascist ideology. Bronnen's legacy is largely overshadowed by his literary and ideological opportunism.

Bronnen was born on July 19, 1895, in Vienna, AUSTRIA, to a middle-class Jewish family. He volunteered for military service in World War I, but unlike most, he never lost his enthusiasm for his wartime experiences, even after being wounded and taken prisoner in ITALY (1916–1919). He chafed under the humiliation of Austria's defeat in 1918 and worked as a sales clerk before the success of *Patricide*. In Bronnen's violently amoral play, the Oedipal conflict is taken to its logical extreme when the son Walter Fessel (i.e., Walter Schackle) breaks free from the chains of the violent and repressed world of the father by engaging in an incestuous act with his mother and killing his father. "I blossom" are his final words. The play's violent psychopathological tendencies and brutal eroticism prompted a riot on opening night. Other works quickly followed, such as *The Bird of Youth* (*Die Geburt der Jugend*, 1922), *Excesses* (*Die Exzesse*, 1923), *Anarchy in Sillian* (*Anarchie in Sillian*, 1924), which also highlighted the talents of the AVANT-GARDE theater group The Young Stage (Die junge Bühne), the three-act antimilitarist drama *Catalunian Battle* (*Katalaunische Schlacht*, 1924), and his MONODRAMA of Frederick the Great titled *East Pole Expedition* (*Ostpolzug*, 1926). For a time, Bronnen and the surreal, naturalist qualities of his epic dramas, influenced by the revolutionary staging techniques of ERWIN PISCATOR's Proletarian Theater, placed him ahead of BERTOLT BRECHT as the most promising German playwright.

Bronnen's disillusionment with literary EXPRESSIONISM and his marked turn to national socialism is seen in the nationalistic drama *Rhineland Rebels* (*Rheinische Rebellen*, 1925), which protests the French occupation of the Rhineland. His novels *OS* [*Oberschlesien*] (1929; Upper Silesia) and *Roßbach* (1930) protest the annexation of Upper Silesia to Poland and glorify Adolf Hitler's Beerhall Putsch of 1923, respectively; the publication of *OS* led to a friendship with Nazi propaganda minister Joseph Goebbels (1897–1945). Impressed with the power of mass media, Bronnen became dramaturge for the UFA Film Studio and the Dramatic Radio Hour (Dramatische Funkstunde) in Berlin (1928–1933). Bronnen tried to prove (unsuccessfully) his Aryan heritage, but he fell out of favor with the Nazi leadership, was expelled from the Nazi writers' organization in 1937, and was declared politically unreliable in 1940; his books were banned in 1942. After the war, he turned to communism and was briefly mayor of Bad Goisern in the Soviet-occupied portion of Austria before serving as cultural editor of the communist paper *Neue Zeit* (New Age) in Linz (1945–1950) and then (1955) as theater critic for the East German *Berliner Zeitung* (Berlin Newspaper). Bronnen's later works, impossible to publish or stage during the war, include *N* (1935–1936), the COMEDY *Gloriana* (1940–1941), and *The Kolin Chain* (*Die Kette Kolin*, 1950). Bronnen died on October 12, 1959, in East Berlin, German Democratic Republic.

[*See also* Germany]

PLAYS: *Patricide* (*Vatermord*, 1920); *The Bird of Youth* (*Die Geburt der Jugend*, 1922); *Excesses* (*Die Exzesse*, 1923); *Anarchy in Sillian* (*Anarchie in Sillian*, 1924); *Catalunian Battle* (*Katalaunische Schlacht*, 1924); *Rhineland Rebels* (*Rheinische Rebellen*, 1925); *East Pole Expedition* (*Ostpolzug*, 1926); *Reparations* (*Reparationen*, 1926); *Michael Kohlhaas* (1929); *Gloriana* (1941); *The Kolin Chain* (*Die Kette Kolin*, 1950)

FURTHER READING

Aspetsberger, Friedbert. *Arnolt Bronnen: Biographie* [Biography]. Vienna: Böhlau, 1995.

Gadberry, Glen W. "Arnolt Bronnen's Austro-Expressionist War Plays." In *Text and Presentation: The University of Florida Department of Classics Comparative Drama Conference Papers, X*, ed. by Karelisa Hartigan. Lanham, Md.: Univ. Press of America, 1990. 35–51.

Scheit, Gerhard. "Dramatik der Inneren Emigration oder 'Nationale Verdauungs-Störungen.' Über Arnolt Bronnens Stücke seit den dreißiger Jahren" [Drama of inner emigration or "national indigestion": On Arnolt Bronnen's plays of the 1930s]. In *Literatur der "Inneren Emigration" aus Österreich* [Literature of "inner emigration" from Austria], ed. by Johann Holzner and Karl Müller. Vienna: Döcker, 1998. 127–140.

Szekendi, Nóra. "Arnolt Bronnens frühe Dramen. Ein Einzelfall innerhalb des Expressionismus?" [Arnolt Bronnen's early dramas: An exception of the expressionist movement?]. In *Lauter Einzelfälle. Bekanntes und Unbekanntes zur neueren österreichischen Literatur* [Nothing but exceptions: Familiar and unknown aspects of recent Austrian literature], ed. by Karlheinz F. Auckenthaler. Bern: Peter Lang, 1996. 257–274.

Christa Spreizer

BROOKS, DANIEL (1958–)

Canadian director, playwright, and actor Daniel Brooks was born in Toronto, CANADA, in 1958. He graduated from the University College Drama program at the University of Toronto in 1981 before studying various performance disciplines in New York, Paris, ARGENTINA, and BRAZIL. Since the mid-1980s, he has been one of the most versatile and influential alternative theater practitioners in Toronto, working with many of Canada's most innovative performers and writers, especially DANIEL MACIVOR, Don McKellar, Tracy Wright, and GUILLERMO VERDECCHIA.

Brooks's work is characterized by intellectual depth and an interrogative attitude to performance itself. This attitude often emerges in the highly theatrical nature of his presentations, which have drawn on improvisation, dance, and realistic acting. While not all his productions are as overtly political as *The Noam Chomsky Lectures* (1992), he remains concerned with questions of political, social, and theatrical authority.

Brooks has said of his Augusta Company's approach to script work: "The written word has attained a kind of reverence in theatre. We're interested in spreading authority around" (Sherman, 1991). This fluid approach to creation is reflected in the fact that most of his writing credits are shared with other performers.

Although Brooks has directed plays by other contemporary Canadian dramatists, such as Greg Morrison and Lisa Lambert's *The Drowsy Chaperone* (2001), MacIvor's *House* (1992), and JOHN MIGHTON's *Possible Worlds* (1998) and *Half Life* (2004), he has also directed modern and early classics, including William Shakespeare's *Measure for Measure* (1989), SAMUEL BECKETT's ENDGAME (1999), Johann Wolfgang von Goethe's *Faust* (1999), HAROLD PINTER's BETRAYAL (2000), Jean Racine's *Phaedra* (2003), and Euripides' *The Bacchae* (with Verdecchia, 2003).

Much of Brooks's influence in Canadian theater stems from the sheer volume of his output and from his links with key Toronto companies. Besides co-founding the Augusta Company and his membership in da da kamera, he has a continuing relationship with Soulpepper Theatre and has served as associate artist at Buddies in Bad Times Theatre (1993–1995) and as artist-in-residence at the Tarragon Theatre (1995–2002). In 2003, he replaced Richard Rose as artistic director of Necessary Angel Theatre.

Brooks's wide critical acclaim includes winning the Chalmers Award, the Dora Mavor Moore Award, the Edinburgh Fringe First Award, and the Capital Critics Award and three nominations for the Governor General's Award. In 2001, he won the inaugural Elinore and Lou Siminovitch Prize in Theatre.

PLAYS: *The Return of Pokey Jones* (1985); *Indulgence* (1989, with Don McKellar and Tracy Wright); *Drinking* (1990, with McKellar and Wright); *Red Tape* (1991, with McKellar and Wright); *The Book of Rejection* (1992, with McKellar and Wright); *The Lorca Play* (1992, with Daniel MacIvor); *The Noam Chomsky Lectures* (1992, with Guillermo Verdecchia); *86: An Autopsy* (1995, with McKellar and Wright); *Here Lies Henry* (1996, with MacIvor); *Insomnia* (with Verdecchia, 1997); *Monster* (1998, with MacIvor); *Cul De Sac* (2002, with MacIvor); *The Good Life* (2002); *Bigger Than Jesus* (2003, with Rick Miller)

FURTHER READING

Brooks, Daniel. "Some Thoughts about Directing *Here Lies Henry*." *Canadian Theatre Review* 92 (1997): 42–45.

Sherman, Jason. "The Daniel Brooks Lectures." *Canadian Theatre Review* 67 (1991): 17–21.

Robert Ormsby

THE BROWNING VERSION

Originally produced at the Phoenix Theatre in London, starring Eric Portman, Mary Ellis, Peter Scott, and Hector Ross, *The Browning Version* was performed as the first half of an evening of two short plays titled *Playbill* and established TERENCE RATTIGAN as a dramatist of significance in 20th-century English-speaking drama. Having proven himself a successful crafter of numerous comedies and one dramatic masterpiece, *The Winslow Boy* (1947), with this play Rattigan solidified his ability to triumph in a more serious medium. Rattigan wrote *The Browning Version* with the actor John Gielgud in mind for the central character (Rattigan often wrote his plays with specific actors in mind), but because of Gielgud's reluctance and schedule conflicts, Eric Portman instead played Andrew Crocker-Harris, a middle-aged classics teacher. Gielgud was not to play the role until eleven years later, in 1959.

The play takes place in the sitting room of the lodgings of a public school classics instructor and his wife. After eighteen years at the school, due to a heart problem Andrew Crocker-Harris is about to retire to the country to teach at a private crammer's school. A brilliant scholar who took the highest honors while at Oxford, Crocker-Harris has since found life a dismal disappointment. He is mocked and feared by his students, his attractive wife indulges in a string of affairs with younger, more popular professors, and now he has little to look forward to with scant pay for teaching at a school for remedial students. The school to which he has given eighteen years of his life refuses him a pension, and the headmaster asks him to give way in his valedictory speech to a presentation by the cricket master. The only bright spot in this desolation comes when a current student brings him the gift of a secondhand copy of Browning's translation of the *Agamemnon* by Aeschylus. The gift is spoiled when his wife claims it was merely a bribe for a passing grade. When Crocker-Harris chooses instead to believe that it was a gift of sincere appreciation, he finds his dignity and the courage to claim his rightful precedence over the cricket master at the end-of-term proceedings.

The play, like its central character, demonstrates a masterful restraint; the play is a paradigm of Rattigan's characteristic architecture of understatement. Critics in England were unanimous in their praise for the premiere production of *The Browning Version*, and it won Rattigan his second Ellen Terry Award (1948). The play did not fare as well across the Atlantic, where Maurice Evans played Andrew Crocker-Harris, but it has become a classic of enduring popularity, receiving periodic major productions each decade following its original creation.

The Browning Version was adapted for the screen in 1951, starring Michael Redgrave as Andrew Crocker-Harris and directed by Anthony Asquith. The film received the 1951 Cannes Film Festival Award for Best Screenplay. In 1994 Mike Figgis, under Paramount Pictures, remade the play as another film, starring Albert Finney as Crocker-Harris.

[*See also* England, 1940–Present]

FURTHER READING

Darlow, Michael, and Gillian Hodson. *Terence Rattigan: The Man and His Work*. London: Quartet Bks., 1979.

Rusinko, Susan. *Terence Rattigan*. Twayne's English Author Series 366. Boston: Twayne, 1983.

Antonia Sophia Krueger

BUERO VALLEJO, ANTONIO (1916–2000)

Antonio Buero Vallejo, born in Guadalajara, SPAIN, on September 29, 1916, is generally considered Spain's first serious dramatist of social concern since the Spanish Civil War of 1936–1939. Although Buero was not a combatant during the war (he was a medic and a pro-Republican propaganda artist), he was sentenced to death by the victorious Nationalist regime. His sentence was commuted to six years in prison, and he quickly took to theater upon his release. The Civil War and postwar nationalist repression had a profound impact on Buero's literary career, and pacificist themes run throughout his works.

Buero broke away from the escapism theater that characterized Spanish drama in the early postwar years. He insisted on plays of social criticism and substance even though he often fell victim to pro-Franco censors. His signature TRAGEDY, *Story of a Stairway* (*Historia de una escalera*, 1949), relates the lives and tribulations of three generations of tenement dwellers in post–Civil War Madrid. Each generation is seemingly as miserably poor and hopeless as the other, and *Story of a Stairway* has generally been understood as a veiled attack on the vacuous nature of Franco regime Spain. For *Story* he won the prestigious Lope de Vega Prize, which won him a loyal following among liberal literary circles as well as made him the subject of literary attacks by conservative pro-Franco critics.

Though accused of being fatalistic and pessimistic, Buero implored his Spanish dramatist colleagues to "cultivate a sincere theater where life—our anxieties, pessimism, and, also, our hopes—are revealed without falsification" (Buero Vallejo, 1951). His plays were concerned with the dignity and nobility of individuals as they trudge through tremendous difficulties. He hoped that his spectators would find catharsis, which he defined as transforming or elevating emotions from a primitive to a moral or ethical plane. Buero believed that the Spanish had accepted the tragic (*lo trágico*) as a major component of their lives and that the tragic sense of life was seen in the works of Spain's greatest writers and dramatists. He hoped, however, that through his works of social justice the apathetic spectator would leave the theater with a strong desire to ameliorate societal injustices.

Buero Vallejo's serious theater made him popular not only with Spain but throughout the world; several of his plays have been performed and translated throughout Europe, North America, and Asia. In 1966 the author was invited by the U.S. Department of State to be a participant in the International Visitors program, and he lectured at major universities across the United States. In 1971, Buero was elected to the Spanish Royal Academy. Though he did not seek the honor and though he was sponsored by liberal elements within the Academy, his election was unanimous, indicating a substantial change in the relationship between liberal and conservative Spain. The election acknowledged Buero as an activist and proponent of a theater of substance. He died in Madrid on April 29, 2000.

SELECT PLAYS: *In the Burning Darkness* (*En la ardiente oscuridad*, 1946); *The Words in the Sand* (*Las palabras en la arena*, 1948); *Story of a Staircase* (*Historia de una escalera*, 1949); *The Dream Weaver* (*La Tejedora de sueños*, 1950); *Irene, or the Treasure* (*Irene, o el tesoro*, 1954); *Today's a Holiday* (*Hoy es fiesta*, 1955); *A Dreamer for His People* (*Un soñador para un pueblo*, 1958); *The Ladies-in-Waiting* (*Las Meninas*, 1960); *The Double Case of Doctor Valmy* (*La doble historia del doctor Valmy*, 1964); *The Basement Window* (*El tragaluz*, 1966); *The Sleep of Reason* (*El sueño de la razón*, 1967); *Judges in the night* (*Jueces en la noche*, 1979); *Lazarus in the Labyrinth* (*Lázaro en el laberinto*, 1986)

FURTHER READING

Buero Vallejo, Antonio. "El teatro como problema" [The theater as problem]. In *Almanaque de teatro y cine* [Almanac of theater and cinema]. Madrid, 1951.

Halsey, Martha T. *From Dictatorship to Democracy: The Recent Plays of Buero Vallejo*. Ottawa: Dovehouse Editions Canada, 1994.

Iglesias Feijoo, Luis, and Mariano de Paco, eds. *Antonio Buero Vallejo. Obra completa*. [Antonio Buero Vallejo. Complete works]. 2 vols. Madrid: Espasa Calpe, 1994.

Nicholas, Robert L. *The Tragic Stages of Antonio Buero Vallejo*. Chapel Hill, N.C.: Dept. of Romance Languages, Univ. of North Carolina Press, 1972.

Paco, Mariano de, and Francisco Javier Díez de Revenga, eds. *Antonio Buero Vallejo, dramaturgo universal*. [Antonio Buero Vallejo, universal dramatist]. Murcia: CajaMurcia/Obra Cultural, 2001.

Enrique A. Sanabria

BUFO THEATER

Bufo theater (*teatro bufo*) is a popular theatrical form in CUBA that flourished in the mid- to late 19th century and is considered the first manifestation of Cuban national theater. *Bufo*, derived from an Italian verb meaning to "puff out one's cheeks in mockery," was entertainment that appealed to the masses because of its humor and the prominence of music and dance. It is an offspring of Italian commedia dell'arte, the Spanish one-act FARCES (*sainetes*), and the traveling minstrel shows of the United States. *Bufo* performances were brief and centered on parodied portrayals of the customs of Cuba's lower classes, from the poor farmer to the freed black. Often, the plot was secondary to the music and dance. Critics credit Cuban actor Francisco Covarrubias (1775–1850) as the founding father of the *bufo* theater movement with his initiative to Cubanize theatrical forms brought over from SPAIN. Other important authors and performers of this genre are the Spaniard Bartolomé Crespo y Borbón (1811–1871), performing as his character Creto Gangá, and playwright Ignacio Sarachaga (1952–1900). With the advent of *bufo* theater, Spanish aesthetic influence began to disappear from the island's theaters.

Bufo has been historically reexamined as an example of Cuban nationalism in the face of Spanish colonial rule. *Bufo* theater represents the first time Cuban characters graced the stage in the guise of the sexy mulatta, the naive farmer (*guajiro*), the freed black man (*negrito*), the ignorant Spaniard (*gallego*), and the cunning Chinese man (*chino*). Although racism influenced many of these exaggerated representations, critics still emphasize the appearance of these characters as a crucial step toward the formation of a Cuban national identity. Other important nationalistic aspects of *bufo* theater are the use of colloquial Cuban language, instead of the more formal Castilian from Spain, and the essentially Cuban rhythms and dances that became a vital part of these productions. *Bufo* theater introduced its audience to the *guaracha*, among other dances of African influence that soon became staples of Cuban popular culture. Also important was the humor and satire that made these performances enjoyable for a wide variety of audience. Often, *bufo* performers poked fun at Spain and Spanish colonial rule to the delight of the pro-independence Cubans. Threatened by the nationalistic impulses manifested in *bufo* theater, Spanish colonial authorities prohibited it for ten years, beginning with the first war of independence in 1868, fearing it would incite rebellious sentiments among its audience. In essence, *bufo* theater helped move the nation toward independence.

Bufo theater was definitive to the independence movement and in the formation of Cuban national identity; yet these performances also helped create the racial stereotypes that have plagued the island for a better part of its history. For example, Cuban theater critic Rine Leal points out that with the abolition of slavery in 1880 the portrayal of black characters changed radically to represent them as uneducated, stupid, and superstitious. This change reflected the overall preoccupation many Cubans felt over the recently freed slaves, who accounted for almost fifty percent of the population of the island. The representations of the black man and the sensual mulatta eventually adopted and disseminated by the national press, novels, and society in general added to the racism and discrimination already widespread in Cuba at the time. Toward the end of its artistic life, *bufo* theater eventually declined into semipornographic skits that were just for men with a tendency to promote stereotypes that provoked what Leal calls "negrofobia," or fear of blacks (Leal, 1982).

Bufo theater has only recently received the critical attention it deserves as an important cultural phenomenon in Cuba. It has been a difficult genre to investigate since there are few extant examples of these plays, because only a small percentage were ever published. All that remains of many *bufo* plays are newspaper reviews and eyewitness accounts of performances but no print version. Additionally, for years literary critics ignored *bufo* theater, owing to the poor artistic quality of these plays. Through the important critical and preservation work of Leal, who has edited and published studies and anthologies of *bufo* theater, this genre has been reevaluated not necessarily for its artistry but for its importance in Cuban theatrical, cultural, and political history.

FURTHER READING

Frederik, Laurie Aleen. "The Contestation of Cuba's Public Sphere in National Theater and the Transformation from *Teatro Bufo* to *Teatro Nuevo*." *Gestos: Revista de Teoría y Práctica del Teatro Hispánico* 16, no. 31 (2001): 65–97.

Leal, Rine, ed. *Teatro bufo, siglo XIX* [*Bufo* theater, 19th century]. Havana: Arte y Literatura, 1975.

———. *La selva oscura* [The dark jungle]. 2 vols. Havana: Arte y Literatura, 1982.

Río Prado, Enrique. *La Venus de Bronce: Hacía una historia de la zarzuela cubana* [The bronze Venus: Toward a history of Cuban zarzuela]. Boulder, Colo: Society of Spanish and Spanish-American Studies, 2002.

Suarez Duran, Esther. "El teatro vernaculo: Trayectoria de la cubanidad" [Vernacular theater: Cuban trajectory]. In *De las dos orillas: Teatro cubano* [Of the two borders: Cuban theater], ed. by Heidrun Adler and Adrian Herr. Madrid and Frankfurt: Vervuert—Iberoamericana, 1999. 131–137.

Teatro del siglo XIX [Theater of the 19th century]. Havana: Letras cubanas, 1986.

I. Carolina Caballero

BUKAN LALANG DITIUP ANGIN See IT IS NOT THE TALL GRASS BLOWN BY THE WIND

BULGAKOV, MIKHAIL (1891–1940)

Mikhail Bulgakov (b. 1891 in Kiev; d. 1940 in Moscow) was a Russian novelist, short-story writer, and probably RUSSIA's finest playwright of the 20th century. Bulgakov abandoned his profession as a doctor and turned to literary work. He adapted his novel *The White Guard* (1925) for the Moscow Art Theatre as DAYS OF THE TURBINS (*Dni Turbinykh*, 1926), the eventual success of which owed much to Joseph Stalin's approval of the play. The reception of Bulgakov's other plays was, by contrast, less happy. *Zoya's Apartment* (*Zoykina kvartira*, 1926), a satire on prostitution and financial shady dealings characteristic of the limited free market economy of the 1920s, was given an extended run before being banned. *The Crimson Island* (*Bagrovy ostrov*, 1927), his satire on revolution and Soviet censorship, was banned before the premiere, as was *Flight* (*Beg*, 1927), the sequel to *Days of the Turbins*.

Despairing of life in the Soviet Union (his short stories had also been banned for exhibiting anti-Soviet tendencies), Bulgakov applied to live abroad for a limited period. However, with the unexpected help of Stalin himself, he found work at the Moscow Art Theatre as an assistant director. "In the broad field of Russian literature in the USSR, I was the lone literary wolf. I was advised to dye my coat. It was absurd advice. Dye its fur or cut it, a wolf will still not look like a poodle" (from Bulgakov's letter to Stalin, March 28, 1930). He continued to write plays, only one of which (plus an adaptation) was staged at the theater, the remainder being either banned or staged posthumously. At the Art Theatre, Bulgakov's personal relations with KONSTANTIN STANISLAVSKY proved rather fraught, leading to the satirical depiction of the director in his *Theatrical Novel*, also known as *Black Snow* (1936). His adaptation of Nikolai Gogol's *Dead Souls* (1932) was staged but, owing to disagreements with Stanislavsky, not in the way Bulgakov had imagined. The same was true of his play about his literary hero, Molière, *A Cabal of Hypocrites* (*Kabala Svyatosh*, 1929), in which Molière's relationship to the court of Louis XIV can be seen to have parallels with Bulgakov's own relationship to the Soviet Communist Party. Bulgakov's short stories of the 1920s, especially *Heart of a Dog* and *The Fatal Eggs*, showed evidence of their author's interest in fantasy and science fiction, and a series of plays in the 1930s also reflected this vein of Bulgakov's creativity. These include *Adam and Eve* (*Adam i Eva*, 1931), which foresees a devastating world war; the satirical *Bliss* (*Blazhenstvo*, 1933), which involves time travel to the year 2222; and *Ivan Vasil'yevich* (1935), which reworks the material of *Bliss* into another play about time travel—from the present back to the days of Ivan the Terrible in the 16th century.

His play about Alexander Pushkin, titled *The Last Days* (*Posledniye dni*, 1935), portrays the poet's death in a duel, less as a consequence of romantic jealousy than as state-aided assassination. It was performed in 1943. His final play, *Batum* (1939), was written to celebrate Stalin's 60th birthday and concerns the dictator's early life as a Georgian revolutionary. Stalin is reported to have said, with mock modesty, that there was no need for plays about "the young Stalin," and it remained banned until the late 20th century. Bulgakov's novel about the devil's visit to Moscow, *Master and Margarita*, completed before his death but only published in 1966, was adapted for the stage in the 1970s, as was *Heart of a Dog*. He also wrote film scripts of Gogol's *Dead Souls* and *The Government Inspector* and adapted LYOV TOLSTOY'S *War and Peace* and Miguel de Cervantes's *Don Quixote* for the stage.

PLAYS: *Days of the Turbins* a.k.a. *The White Guard* (*Dni Turbinykh*, 1926); *Zoya's Apartment* a.k.a. *Madame Zoyka* (*Zoykina kvartira*, 1926); *The Crimson Island* (*Bagrovy ostrov*, 1927); *Flight* a.k.a. *On the Run* (*Beg*, 1927); *A Cabal of Hypocrites* a.k.a. *Moliere* (*Kabala Svyatosh*, 1929); *Dead Souls* (*Myortvyye dushi*, 1930); *Adam and Eve* (*Adam i Eva*, 1931); *Halfwitted Jourdain* (*Poloumny Zhurden*, 1932); *War and Peace* (*Voina I mire*, 1932); *Bliss* (*Blazhenstvo*, 1933); *Ivan Vasil'yevich* (1935); *The Last Days* (*Posledniye dni*, 1935); *Don Quixote* (*Don Kikhot*, 1938); *Batum* (1939)

FURTHER READING

Bulgakov, Mikhail. *Early Plays of Mikhail Bulgakov*. Tr. and ed. by Carl R. Proffer and Ellendea Proffer. Bloomington: Indiana Univ Press, 1972.

——. *Flight & Bliss*. Tr. by Mirra Ginzburg. New York: New Directions, 1985.

——. *Six Plays*. Tr. by Michael Glenny, William Powell, and Michael Earley, with an intro. by Lesley Milne. London: Methuen, 1991.

Milne, Lesley. *Mikhail Bulgakov: A Critical Biography*. Cambridge: Cambridge Univ. Press, 1990.

Smeliansky, Anatoly. *Is Comrade Bulgakov Dead? Mikhail Bulgakov at the Moscow Art Theatre*. Tr. by A. Tait. London: Methuen, 1993. An abridged version by the author of his *Mikhail Bulgakov v Khudozhestvennom teatre* [Mikhail Bulgakov at the Art Theatre]. 2d ed. Moscow: Iskusstvo, 1989.

Wright, Colin A. *Mikhail Bulgakov: Life and Interpretation*. Toronto: Univ. of Toronto Press, 1978.

Nick Worrall

BULGARIA

Bulgarian theater and drama saw the light of day during the last decades of the National Revival—a period, spanning from 1762 to 1878, that helped bring the 500-year Turkish occupation of Bulgaria to an end. Conceived and developed as one of the main vehicles for the resurgence of national consciousness, Bulgarian drama at its dawn displayed all the main characteristics of the time: it was educational and uplifting, explicitly didactic and fervently patriotic, aiming to revive memories of Bulgaria's glorious past. The first significant play of the kind was *Ivanko* (1872) by Vassil Drumev, one of the founding fathers of Bulgarian drama. However, it was Ivan Vazov, the doyen of Bulgarian literature known as the national poet, who, at the turn of the last century, brought the genre of the romantic historical play to such a professional height that his plays—*Revolutionaries* (1884), *On the Brink of the Precipice* (1910), *Under the Yoke* (1911), adapted from his very popular novels—dominated the repertory of Bulgarian theaters for many years.

The conception of the stage "as a teacher" was so deeply ingrained in the audiences' perception during the last thirty years of the 19th century that it became one of the major "genres" of both Bulgarian theater and drama—a "genre" so strong that even today theatrical works that are mere entertainment are not likely to be taken seriously. It is taken for granted that no matter what genre is being presented onstage, it is supposed to address significant problems and convey some kind of moral.

This applies to COMEDY as well—a very popular genre that again was born and matured during the National Revival. The first full-fledged original comedy, *Civilization Misunderstood* (1872), by Dobri Voinikov, satirizing the fascination with and adoration of everything foreign, is still in the repertory of Bulgarian theaters, topical for today's mores as well. It was again Ivan Vazov, however, who developed the genre of comedy to a truly professional level. His *Duel* (1902) and *Job-Hunters* (1903) are still played today in Bulgaria because of their outstanding craftmanship and because of their never-ending topicality. The same applies to the next eminent Bulgarian comic playwright, St. L. Kostov, and his *Men-Hater* (1914), *Golemanov* (1927), and *Vrajalez* (1933).

The secret of the great Bulgarian comedies' everlasting success is the particular brand of the absurd they feature. They sound absurd, yet they are entirely realistic, the absurd here is deeply rooted in reality, and in most cases, it is simply one of the faces of reality. Therefore, any small exaggeration of that reality already seems to dwell in the territory of the impossible.

This very typical characteristic of Bulgarian comedy was excellently displayed in the 1970s and 1980s in Stanislav Stratiev's works (*Roman Bath*, 1974; *Suede Jacket*, 1976; *Bus*, 1980) and today in the plays by Hristo Boytchev, the most globally produced Bulgarian playwright of all time. Boytchev's *That Thing* (1985) and *The Underground Man* (1988) opened the door to a new wave of absurd plays that cross the border between the comic and the philosophical and depict a reality that, in its improbability, is ultimately too sad to laugh at. His *The Colonel Bird* (1997), a hilarious satire of NATO's (North Atlantic Treaty Organization) role in the Balkans, has already been staged in nearly thirty countries. Another contemporary playwright, highly inventive in transferring the absurd of everyday life to the stage, is Kamen Donev, whose scenariolike plays have introduced to Bulgarian theater a genre reminiscent of the revue.

Reflections of and on alternate realities, belonging to ancient times and the unseen world beyond the materialistic here and now, and expressed in ritual, old beliefs, and folklore, are at the base of another strong line in Bulgarian drama, established again in the beginning of the 20th century. Its pioneer was P. Y. Todorov, the plots of whose *Builders* (1889), *Elf* (1903), and *Dragon's Wedding* (1910) involve or evolve around daunting superstitions or fairy creatures that people are transformed into, fall in love with, or simply have to come to terms with. In *Deer Kingdom* (1934), G. Raichev continued the same tradition, which in the second half of the 20th century reached its apex in the works of Yordan Radichkov—a brilliant storyteller whose idiosyncratic style, deeply rooted in the Bulgarian identity and bordering on the naive and the absurd, renders his fiction a challenge to translators, yet his plays, especially *January* (1973), *Lazaritza* (1978), and *Trying to Fly* (1979), have all the qualities of universal masterpieces.

Despite its various "detours," modern Bulgarian drama has, for the most part, followed one major line: that of psychological REALISM. Apart from Vazov and P. Y. Todorov, who also worked in this vein, other eminent contributors to it were Anton Strashimiriov (*Vampire*, 1903), the great poet Peio Yavorov with his Ibsen-like *In the Outskirts of Vitosha* (1911) and *When Thunder Strikes, How the Echo Dies Down* (1912), and Racho Stoyanov (*Masters*, 1927). This trend was strongly reinforced by the introduction of The Method to Bulgarian theater by N. O. Massalitinov, a co-worker of KONSTANTIN STANISLAVSKY, who in 1923 became head of the National Theatre and stayed there for thirty years.

For the theater, the "silver lining" of the fifty years following 1944 was the Aesopean metaphoric language Bulgarian drama had to adopt in its dialogue with the audiences, since it actually enriched the texture of realism onstage. In the late 1950s and 1960s a pinch of poetry was thrown into that mixture by a new generation of poets who successfully tried their hand at playwriting: Ivan Peichev, Valeri Petrov, Ivan Radoev, Nedialko Yordanov, and Stefan Tzanev. The down-to-earth one-act dramas of the great writer Nikolai Haitov (1968) added a special nuance to the whole picture of Bulgarian drama at that time and so did the historically metaphorical dramas of Nikola Russev (late 1970s and 1980s). *The Last Night of Socrates* (1987) and *The Other Death of Jean of Arc* (1989) by Stefan Tzanev and *Easter Wine* (1879) and *Nirvana* (1982) by Konstantin Iliev, which played to full houses in Bulgaria and abroad throughout the 1980s and early 1990s, are examples of world-class drama that defies the limits of time and place. After the untimely death of Radichkov (2004), Tzanev and Iliev remain the only living classic authors of Bulgarian drama.

Among the younger playwrights who have begun their careers after 1989 as followers of the realistic trend, those who stand out are Teodora Dimova (also an interesting novelist), Yana Dobreva, Elin Rahnev (a poet with a cult status), and Yuri Datchev (a critic and successful scriptwriter). All of them are eager to experiment with form and genre and at times inevitably resort to the absurd. Yet they have already developed their own distinctive voices as playwrights: Dimova as a relentless dissector of the traumas of Bulgarian society; Dobreva as a shrewd connoisseur of women's problems; Rahnev with his splendid mixture of earthy realism and soaring poetry; Datchev with a language and sensitivity reminiscent of TENNESSEE WILLIAMS. Their plays, along with the masterpieces of their predecessors, form a whole trove of magnificent made-in-Bulgaria drama that has yet to take the place it deserves in the hearts of theater lovers worldwide.

FURTHER READING

Contemporary Bulgarian Drama. [Sofia]: Antract, 2002.

Stefanova, Kalina, ed. *Contemporary Bulgarian Theatre*. Vol. 1–2. Amsterdam: Harwood Acad. Pubs., 1998.

——, ed. *Eastern European Theatre After the Iron Curtain*. Amsterdam: Harwood Acad. Pubs., 2000.

Kalina Stefanova

BULLINS, ED (1935–)

It's very strange that some people will say that I'm a raving radical and others will say that Bullins doesn't stand for anything. I don't write the kind of plays they want me to, because I believe in trying to come at the audience fresh.

—Ed Bullins, 1973

Controversial African American playwright Ed Bullins was born in Philadelphia, Pennsylvania, on July 2, 1935, and was raised in the slums of that city. As a young man Bullins dropped out of high school and joined the navy from 1952 to 1955. After leaving the Navy he finished school and moved to Los Angeles in 1958. There he observed the interracial relationships that evolved against the background of the growing Black Nationalism movement. The theme of race relations would occupy a central role in many of Bullins's plays.

His professional playwriting career began in 1965 with the production of *How Do You Do, Dialect Determinism (or The Rally)*, and *Clara's Ole Man* at the Firehouse Repertory Theatre in San Francisco. In 1967 Robert Macbeth invited Bullins to New York City to write plays for the New Lafayette Players. He accepted the invitation and success quickly followed. From 1968 to 1972, Bullins had fifteen plays produced in New York City. In 1968 he premiered *In the Wine Time*, the first play in his Twentieth-Century Cycle, which focused on a group of friends coming of age in the 1950s. The complete cycle includes *The Corner* (1968), *In New England Winter* (1969), *The Duplex* (1970), *The Fabulous Miss Marie* (1971), *Home Boy* (1976), and *Daddy* (1977). Since his earliest plays, critics and audiences have responded positively to Bullins's unique style. While his plays reflect the turbulent times in which he writes, confronting issues of race and class in an uncompromising tone, they also retain a unique focus on the inner constraints limiting his characters' freedom. Bullins earned critical praise for his remarkable ability to capture the language and poetry of urban life, without sanitizing its profanity. With *We Righteous Bombers* (1969), Bullins ignited a controversy by challenging black revolutionaries in New York City. The play was produced under a pen name, and Larry Neal later revealed that it had been taken from ALBERT CAMUS's *The Just Assassins*.

As the editor of *Black Theatre Magazine*, Bullins was a powerful force in encouraging the growth of other black plays and playwrights. Collaborators and contributors to the magazine included Larry Neal and AMIRI BARAKA (Leroi Jones). In 1970, he was given an Obie award for *The Fabulous Miss Marie*. In his celebrated play *The Taking of Miss Janie* (1975), Bullins explores the dynamics and downfall of an interracial group of political idealists. The play was honored with the New York Drama Critics Circle Award. Other awards for Bullins include a Venice Biennial Drama Prize, and the National Black Theatre Festival Living Legend Award. A prolific playwright, he also served as the Minister of Culture for the Black Panther Party in the 1960s. Bullins remains active in theater as a playwright, director, mentor, distinguished professor, producer, and outspoken authority on black culture.

[*See also* Black Arts Movement; Political Theater; United States, 1940–Present]

SELECT PLAYS: *Clara's Ole Man* (1965); *The Theme Is Blackness* (1966); *In New England Winter* (1967); *The Corner* (1968); *The Electronic Nigger* (1968); *In the Wine Time* (1968); *We Righteous Bombers* (1969); *The Devil Catchers* (1970); *The Fabulous Miss Marie* (1970); *Street Sounds* (1970); *House Party* (1973); *The Taking of Miss Janie* (1975); *Home Boy* (1976), *Steve and Velma* (1980); *Leavings* (1980).

FURTHER READING

Gates, Henry Louis, and Nellie McKay, eds. *Norton Anthology of African American Literature*. New York: Norton, 1996.

Hay, Samuel. *Ed Bullins: A Literary Biography*. Detroit, Mich.: Wayne State Univ. Press, 1997.

Sanders, Leslie Catherine. *The Development of Black Theatre in America*. Baton Rouge: Louisiana State Univ. Press, 1988.

Ellen Anthony-Moore and Christopher Moore

BURIED CHILD

I know you've got a secret. You've all got a secret. It's so secret in fact, you're all convinced it never happened.

—Shelly, Act 3

Buried Child (1978) by SAM SHEPARD ingeniously exploits many of the structural devices of the conventional "well-made" realistic play, while at the same time subverting the genre with Shepard's own brand of theatricality. Who is the buried child? Shepard does not resolve the mystery and instead heightens it through a fusion of idiomatic language, vivid stage images, and ritual patterns to explore a dark, disturbing view of the American family.

The play is set in the living room of a rundown farmhouse in Illinois, where we first discover Dodge, the ailing patriarch, ensconced on the couch, zoning out to the sounds of pelting rain, the blue flicker of the television, and a mix of medications and whiskey; his wife, Halie, unseen in the upstairs bedroom, henpecks him. Their oldest son, Tilden, enters from the muddy backyard with his arms overflowing with fresh-picked corn, and we watch as he proceeds to clean it, tossing the husks on the floor and the ears into a metal bucket. Halie demands to know "the meaning of the corn," since nothing has been planted since 1935, and even suggests that Tilden has stolen it; but he keeps shucking away. By allowing this and other actions to upstage the conventional imperatives for exposition, Shepard theatricalizes the corn as an image that leads us to the thematic concerns of the play. At the end of the act, Tilden methodically buries the sleeping Dodge in cornhusks and retreats outside.

Bradley, the younger son and a sadistic bully, barges into this wakelike atmosphere and violently shears Dodge's hair with electric clippers, while Dodge strangely remains asleep.

At the opening of act 2, grandson Vince, a jazz musician, returns with his California girlfriend Shelly, who is eager to meet his typically American, "Norman Rockwell" family. None of the family recognize Vince, and all his attempts to jog their memories fail. Vince runs off to buy Dodge more whiskey, while Shelly cuts up the armload of carrots Tilden has harvested from the garden, and he tells her the story of a baby that Dodge had killed and buried.

In act 3, the rain has stopped, and Dodge explains how Halie had a child "on her own," which Tilden loved, and how Dodge had to kill it "because it made everything we'd accomplished look like nothin'." Vince bursts in, drunk, to find that everyone now recognizes him, and he relates a haunting vision of the patriarchal line embodied in a "mummy's face" that beckoned him back to the farm. The play closes as Dodge quietly dies, Vince takes stock of his dubious inheritance, Halie remarks that the backyard is full of vegetables, and Tilden mounts the stairs with the muddy corpse of the child as Halie's disembodied voice repeats from upstairs, "Maybe it's the sun."

Buried Child was first produced at the San Francisco's Magic Theatre in 1978, then at the Theatre for the New City in New York. It won the *Village Voice*'s "Obie" Award for Best Play of 1979 and was the first OFF-BROADWAY play to be awarded the Pulitzer Prize for Drama in 1979. In 1995, Chicago's Steppenwolf Theatre Company mounted a revival for which Shepard revised the script. The production moved to Broadway in 1996, which brought Shepard critical acclaim and national attention.

[*See also* United States, 1940–Present]

FURTHER READING

Marranca, Bonnie, ed. *American Dreams: The Imagination of Sam Shepard*. New York: Performing Arts Journal Publications, 1981.

Roundané, Matthew, ed. *The Cambridge Companion to Sam Shepard*. Cambridge: Cambridge Univ. Press, 2002.

Shepard, Sam. *Buried Child*. In *Sam Shepard: Seven Plays*. New York: Bantam, 1981.

———. *Buried Child*. New York: Dramatists Play Service, 1997. [This edition is Shepard's revised script for the 1996 Broadway revival.]

Mary Fleischer

BURMA

Drama in modern Burma (Myanmar) derives from Buddhist performances of *jataka* (stories of previous lives of the Buddha), which at court were presented in marionette versions (*yokthe pwe*). These puppet shows were developed in the reign of Mindon Min (1853–1878) and became the model for human performance in a dance-drama style called *zat pwe* (classical dance-drama on *jataka* or historical themes). The repertoire also included materials such as *Enaung*, the story of the Indonesian Prince Panji, and *Yama*, the Burmese version of the *Ramayana*—a story of Rama, an incarnation of Vishnu who fights a demon king.

Dramas written by U Kyin U (d. 1853) and U Pon Nya (1807–1866) were the most notable early dramatic achievements. Plots abound in the murderous struggles for power that characterize Burmese history. U Pon Nya's plays take their titles from the name or labor of the main character. *Pauduma* features a sensual and murderous heroine. *Vessantara Jataka* tells of a virtuous man who gives away his children, his long-suffering wife, and his wealth. In *The Water Seller* a ruler impressed by the integrity of a poor water seller makes him crown prince. But the water seller, realizing he is tempted to kill the king, renounces his title and becomes a hermit. *Wizaya* tells of a rebellious prince of Ceylon who is expelled by his father. U Pon Nya's own involvement in court intrigues ended with his execution in 1866.

As court support for it ended with the fall of the Konbaung dynasty in 1885, dance-drama took to the villages. Performance outside the palace was also fed by religious and festival performance styles. *Nibhatkin* were religiously motivated *jataka* performances given for temple festivals. Drum dance involved comic theatricals featuring a drum prince, a drum princess (played by a female impersonator), and a clown. By the late 1890s the impacts of court theater, religious performance, and drum dance were seen in *myai-wang* (earth circling) troupes that roved the countryside. Dance, song, and emotional narratives attracted the public. *The History of Thaton* (1877), by Saya Yaw, was a popular MELODRAMA showing the relations between hill-tribe Shan and Burmese lowlanders. A reincarnation of a murdered Shan girl reconciles her brother and husband. U Ku's story of children born to a king and baboon, *Baboon Brother and Sister* (1877), was also a resounding success, as was his Rama play of 1880. Saya Hau Thaw's *Saw Pha and Saw May* was a lighthearted love story of the same period.

Western influences on Burmese drama include performing on a raised stage, charging admission, and using movable scenery. These innovations were introduced around the turn of the century. Although works of William Shakespeare, Molière, and ANTON CHEKHOV were translated, they had no impact in professional theater circles. The main performer usually plays the refined male lead (prince, *mintha*). He, the writer, and the chief musician are the major personnel. From the early 20th century, female dancers and even all-female troupes were found. Ma Thein May was the first female to take the part of the prince.

Major stars of the stage included Aungbala (1882–1913), a popular female impersonator; Sein Kadon, who was known for costumes covered with electrical lights; and Po Sein (1880–1952), who staged chilling plays such as *Hti Lat Po U*, in which the villain removes the fetus from his lover's womb. *Shin Thu Dain* was the story of a son who becomes a monk against his mother's wishes. Po Sein was active until his death in 1952, and his son Kenneth Sein was a prominent performer in the late 20th century.

The state schools of fine arts at Mandalay and Rangoon became the major training site for performers after their founding in 1953. To the present, the *zat pwe* remains the major offering on a typical theater program. But modern troupes have also found that their audiences hunger for *pya zat*—modern stories that take contemporary events and common characters for their theme. Violence, eroticism, and patriotism are recurring features. In addition to a traditional orchestra, performances now require Western drums and electrical guitars.

Major troupes in the late 20th century included Golden Mandalay Troupe (Shwe-Man-thabin), led by Bo Win, noted for his romantic performances; Golden Mandalay (Shwe-Man), led by Kyaw Aung; and Capital (Myo-daw), directed by Thein-Aung, both popular for their modern plays; while the Great Sein Troupe (Sein-Maha-tha-bin) carries on the tradition of excellence begun by Po Sein. All troupes tour at least the surrounding countryside, and major groups tour nationally. Insurgency and political instability and repression since the 1970s have, however, impeded the free movement and expression of troupes.

FURTHER READING

Brandon, James. *Theatre in Southeast Asia*. Cambridge, Mass.: Harvard Univ. Press, 1967.

Foley, Kathy. "Burma." In *Cambridge Guide to Asian Theatre*, ed. by James Brandon. Cambridge: Cambridge Univ. Press, 1993.

Maung Htin Aun. *Burmese Drama: A Study, with Translations, of Burmese Plays*. 1937. Reprint, Westport, Conn.: Greenwood Press, 1978.

Sein, Kenneth, and Joseph Withey. *The Great Po Sein*. Bloomington: Indiana Univ. Press, 1965.

Singer, Noel. *Burmese Dance and Theatre*. Kuala Lumpur: Oxford Univ. Press, 1995.

Kathy Foley

BUTTERFLY KISS

Martha. Listen to me. My mother asked me to kill her.

—Lily, Act 1

With *Butterfly Kiss* (1994) PHYLLIS NAGY firmly established herself as a powerful new, theatrically innovative voice in the British theater. At the same time, she found herself placed among a new wave of young British playwrights identified by critic Aleks Reisz (2001) as in-yer-face writers, including SARAH KANE, MARK RAVENHILL, and Joe Penhall. A significant difference between Nagy and these writers, however, is her nationality. While the in-yer-face writers cast profanely violent and critically disparaging looks at a 1990s ENGLAND horrifically misshapen by the policies of Prime Ministers Margaret Thatcher and John Major, Nagy offers a similar perspective on her native country, the UNITED STATES, challenging the 1990s facade of the American dream.

Nagy drafted the first version of the play while a student at New York University in 1983 and revised it six years later. The play underwent its final transformation with its Almeida Theatre (London) production in 1994.

Like PETER SHAFFER's *Amadeus* (1979) and DAVID HENRY HWANG's *M. Butterfly* (1988), *Butterfly Kiss* is set in a prison cell and focuses on the life of Lily Ross, imprisoned for the murder of her mother. Unlike Shaffer and Hwang, however, Nagy does not tell her story chronologically. Instead, the play interweaves past and present scenes depicting her mother's hypochondria; her grandmother fourcing Lily to watch her mother and father make love; her affair at age fourteen with her father's best friend; her blossoming lesbian relationship with Martha; her meetings with her lawyer; her mother's attempts to dance with her; and her father's abandonment of the family to live with his lover, a countess. Adding an additional level of complexity to the story, Nagy also depicts imagined scenes from Lily's past, present, and future. In so doing, Nagy eschews a linear narrative that would provide a clear rationale for Lily's murder of her mother. Instead, by providing a COLLAGE of scenes about Lily, Nagy forces the audience to make a decision not only about the truth of Lily's character but also about her matricidal motivations. To make the audience's decision even more challenging, Nagy ends the play with the disturbing image of Lily patiently and lovingly combing her mother's hair, first with a brush and then with a gun. As the stage fades to black, a gunshot is heard.

In addition to showcasing Nagy's theatrical skill, *Butterfly Kiss* focuses on matricide, a topic not often discussed, and indicts the American family, which postures behind the so-called normalness of the American dream. From the outside the Ross family represents the embodiment of the American norm, but Nagy slices away at the image of the family and its individual members to show the emotional, psychological, and physical depravity and damage that exist underneath. Nagy's play overlaps theatrically and thematically with PAULA VOGEL's *How I Learned to Drive*, produced in 1998, but Nagy's work is much darker, more structurally challenging, and more critical of the American experience than Vogel's Pulitzer Prize–winning play.

FURTHER READING

Barnett, Claudia. "Phyllis Nagy's Fatal Women." *Modern Drama* 42, no. 1 (1999): 28–44.

Kenyon, Mel, and Phyllis Nagy. "Seasons of Lad Tidings." *The Guardian* (December 4, 1995): 2.

Nagy, Phyllis. "Hold Your Nerve: Notes for a Young Playwright." In *State of Play: Playwrights on Playwriting*, ed. by David Edgar. London: Faber, 1999.

Reisz, Aleks. *In-Yer-Face Theatre: British Drama Today*. London: Faber, 2001.

William C. Boles

BYGMESTER SOLNESS

See THE MASTER BUILDER

C

CALIGULA

For the dramatist the passion for the impossible is just as valid a subject for study as avarice or adultery. Showing it in all its frenzy, illustrating the havoc it wreaks, bringing out its failure—such was my intention.

—Albert Camus

Generally considered ALBERT CAMUS's best play, *Caligula*, originally titled *Le sens de la mort*, is the dramatic parallel of his *The Myth of Sisyphus (Mythe de Sisyphe)*. This existential essay examines "the walls of absurdity" (death is inevitable; reality is incomprehensible; suffering is omnipresent) that lead us to consider suicide. Thus imposing rationality on a nonrational world is absurd. Rather, we must love life despite its incomprehensibility, seek happiness despite its impossibility, and, like Sisyphus, persistently roll our boulders upward knowing that there will be no rest.

Absurdist in theme if not in form, and written while Camus was wrestling with tuberculosis, *Caligula* is based on Suetonius' account of the fourth Caesar. At the outset Caligula rages, distraught over the death of his sister/mistress and tormented by his realization that grief does not last. Indeed, "Nothing lasts." Rather, "Men die; and they are not happy." This discovery impels him to rebel against the limits of his human condition by trying to capture the moon.

Caligula determines to exercise complete freedom by demolishing the moral values and faith in reason of all around him. He insists that they be logical. When an official complains that the Treasury is low, Caligula decrees that every patrician disinherit his children and will his money to the state; then they will be killed as the needs of the Treasury require. He kills the sons and fathers of his friends and rapes their wives. He closes the public granaries and decrees a famine. He establishes a National Brothel and awards Badges of Civic Merit to its patrons. Far from showing remorse for these outrages, he dresses as a grotesque Venus and demands worship. His final act is to strangle his faithful mistress while whispering in her ear, "I live, I kill. . . . this is happiness." But just before being assassinated, Caligula realizes his failure: "I have chosen a . . . path that leads to nothing. My freedom isn't the right one." He has not overcome the power of a hostile universe. In his preface Camus describes *Caligula* as the "story of a superior suicide. . . . Unfaithful to mankind through fidelity to himself, Caligula accepts death because he has understood that . . . one cannot be free at the expense of others."

Camus wrote *Caligula* in 1938 for the Théâtre de l'Équipe, but the war delayed production until 1945, when a revised version, directed by Paul Oettly and featuring Gérard Philipe in the title role, opened in Paris at the Théâtre Hébertot. Although its depiction of the perils of absolutism resonated with audiences all too familiar with political tyrants, and critics praised its theatrical appeal, it ran for only some two hundred performances. Despite revivals during Camus's lifetime—Embassy Theatre, London (1949), Théâtre Hébertot (1950), Festival d'Angers (1957), Petit Théâtre de Paris (1958), 45th Street Theatre, New York (1960)—*Caligula* was faulted for its rhetoric and two-dimensional characters and has not enjoyed a long history of successful, professional runs. Yet its tragic, existential antihero has earned it inclusion in modern anthologies and its creator a place in theater history.

[*See also* Absurdism; France; Philosophy and Drama, 1860–1960]

FURTHER READING

Brée, Germaine. *Albert Camus*. New York: Columbia Univ. Press, 1964.

Camus, Albert. *Caligula, and Three Other Plays*. 1958. Tr. by Stuart Gilbert. New York: Random House, 1962.

——. *The Myth of Sisyphus, and Other Essays*. 1955. Tr. by Justin O'Brien. New York: Vintage, 1991.

Cruickshank, John. *Albert Camus and the Literature of Revolt*. London: Oxford Univ. Press, 1959.

Ellison, David R. *Understanding Albert Camus*. Columbia: Univ. of South Carolina Press, 1990.

Patricia Montley

CAMBODIA

Modern isn't foreign.

—Chheng Phon, Khmer playwright, educator, and minister of culture, as quoted by Ly Daravuth and Ingrid Muan, 2001

Khmer modern spoken drama (*lakhaoun niyeay*) is distinguished by textual primacy, contemporary settings, and proscenium staging. Developed under French influence in the colonial period, it is an urban genre that was embraced by artists of the postcolonial period as a forum for critique of the modernization process. Begun in the 1920s and developed after World War II as French-educated Khmers experimented with performance of European scripts, modern drama rose to popularity only in the 1950s.

Cambodia has a long tradition of theater, including the court arts—female dance-drama (*lakhaoun krabach boram*), large leather puppetry (*nang sbek thom*), and mask dance (*lakhaoun khaol*)—and village genres, such as the small-puppet theater (*ayang*) and popular folk theaters such as the Thai-influenced *yike* or Vietnamese-derived *lakhaoun bassac*. These genres present a repertoire based on the *Reamker* (the Cambodian version of India's *Ramayana* epic), legends, or popular tales. The performances highlight music and dance, with limited emphasis on text, which is sometimes improvised by actors in performance. These are actor-centered genres. Characterization is stylized, and staging is often in-the-round with little attention to REALISM. Modern drama allowed more realistic staging, often using a proscenium stage, and invited a more direct critique of contemporary social and political problems. In contrast to the traditional arts, modern drama gives author and director central roles. *Lakhaoun niyeay*'s creators saw drama as a tool to confront modern realities.

In the 1950s Guy Porée, French cultural attaché to the Cambodian monarch, founded a theater school that later became the National Theatre under the support of Queen Sisowath Kossamak Nearireath (1903?–1975), an important patron and developer of the arts from the 1940s to the 1970s. Students were sent to study in FRANCE, the United States, or CHINA. Hang Thun Hak (1924–1975), called the "second Molière," returned from Paris in 1951. He taught at Lycée Sisowath, where he translated Molière and William Shakespeare and created his own scripts through the 1950s. He directed a large-cast *Life of Buddha* (1957) for the 2,500th birthday of the Buddha. Hang Thun Hak's productions criticized the corruption that plagued the developing nation: *Dancing Stone* (*Thama Raom*), created in this period, attacked by implication the complicity of officials in the illegal marketing of Khmer antiquities on the international art market.

Another author of this period was Meas Kok, whose works include *The Guy Son and the Girl Mom*, a rural love story, and *One Blood*, which shows siblings fighting over political ideology. The latter work highlighted the partisan politics that laid waste the newly independent country and contributed to a power vacuum that was eventually filled by the Khmer Rouge. Other authors included Prince Norodom Sihanouk (1922–), a monarch who both wrote drama and directed films. Pich Tum Kravel, vice minister of culture and fine arts in the 1990s, was another important figure.

Chheng Phon, who directed the Royal University of Fine Arts and served as minister of culture in the 1980s, explored a movement away from European-inspired realism toward indigenous models. In the 1960s he scripted the popular love story *Tum Teav*, based on an improvised version of *lakhaoun bassac* performed by Look Ta Ki. Chheng Phon, with the support of the queen, researched folk genres and reinterpreted them for modern audiences. For this popular production he took the normally improvised folk story and carefully scripted it, highlighting conflicts implicit in the plot. This rethinking of traditional material in the 1960s was facilitated by consolidation of traditional and modern performing-arts training in Cambodia at the Royal University of Fine Arts, where, as of 1965, folk arts, court traditions, and modern theater were taught side by side.

The turmoil of the Vietnam War brought all art activities to a standstill. In 1975 Khmer Rouge leader Pol Pot, inspired by China's Cultural Revolution, began a purge of intellectuals and artists. The "killing field" became the destination of many artists, and many others fled the country during this period. After the defeat of the Khmer Rouge by Vietnamese troops in 1979, the country was reconstructed. Reclaiming an endangered cultural heritage became a prime artistic mission of the next decades.

Beginning in the 1980s, the curriculum of the Royal University of Fine Arts was painstakingly restored. Masters who survived were sought out to train a new generation. Older artists joined ranks to document and return strength to the arts and the nation. Younger artists became interested in examining their threatened heritage. The National Theatre's modern and traditional drama troupes were reestablished.

During his decade as minister of culture, Chheng Phon created many historical pieces, including *The Development of the Nation of Kampuchea* (1983), *The Development of the Nation of Laos* (1984), *The Blood of the Nation of Kampuchea* (1989), and *The Life of the Nation of Cambodia* (1993). Reexamination of history and society was appropriate for the time.

In later years a new generation trained at the Royal University of Fine Arts has started to mix traditional and modern elements and to explore across disciplines. Mann Kosal (1960–) became interested in the then-defunct puppet tradition after study of *lakhaoun bassac* in school. His troupe Sovanna Phum, based in Phnom Penh, is reviving both court and village puppet styles while addressing modern problems in terms of content. Pieces look at the trafficking in children (1996), AIDS (*Chantu and Champa*, 1997), and issues of child labor (*The Global March*, 1998). He and two other Khmer survivors of the Pol Pot era worked with Singaporean director Ong Keng Sen to co-create a piece based on their personal experiences during those years in *The Continuum—Beyond the Killing Fields* (2000). The work had giant puppets enveloped by fire: "The flames symbolize . . . the Pol Pot regime, when everything was destroyed, snuffed out, burnt to cinders, ashes," noted the puppet artist (in an unpublished interview with Kathy Foley in 2002).

Another later intercultural exploration was *Samritechak* (2000), a Cambodian classical dance-drama version of Shakespeare's *Othello* by Sophiline Cheam Shapiro (1957–), a Los Angeles–based artist trained at the Royal University of Fine Arts. The large-scale work involved both a male and a female chorus. Iago was presented using "monkey" movement technique.

Despite this vitality, considerable challenges remain. The burning of the National Theatre in 1994 dealt a blow to theater arts by eliminating the most important performance venue in Phnom Penh. The economy and political situation have remained unstable. Nevertheless, troupes are active in Phnom Penh, Kandel, Takeo, Prey Veng, and Svay Rieng provinces. Competition from videotapes has reduced the number of live performances, and actors work in radio, video, and television more frequently than in live theater. Yet Khmer artists are actively exploring across class, cultural, and artistic borders to create a lively modern drama that speaks to the present.

[*See also* Avant-Garde Drama; South East Asia]

FURTHER READING

Brandon, James. *The Theatre in Southeast Asia*. Cambridge, Mass.: Harvard Univ. Press, 1967.

Foley, Kathy, and Tony Shapiro. "Cambodia." In *The Cambridge Guide to Asian Theatre*, ed. by James Brandon. Cambridge: Cambridge Univ. Press, 1993.

Ly Daravuth and Ingrid Muan. *Cultures of Independence: An Introduction to Cambodian Arts and Culture in the 1950s and 1960s*. Phnom Penh: Reyeum, 2001.

Phim, Tony Samanth, and Ashley Thompson. *Dance in Cambodia*. Kuala Lumpur: Oxford Univ. Press, 1999.

Kathy Foley

CAMINO REAL

The violets in the mountains have broken the rocks!
—Block 16

At the height of his career, after triumphs with THE GLASS MENAGERIE and A STREETCAR NAMED DESIRE, TENNESSEE WILLIAMS indulged himself in the most experimental of his many plays, *Camino Real*. Even admiring critics and audiences found it a strange and disturbing oddity when it opened at Broadway's Martin Beck Theatre on March 19, 1953, under Elia Kazan's direction. Set against a stream of historical and cultural landmarks and drawing on the classics of literature for many of its characters, *Camino Real* appropriated elements from Spanish folklore, Christian tradition, and classic Hollywood films to impressionistically illuminate the lives of the defeated and discarded beings found along the Camino Real.

Kilroy, the play's protagonist and an embodiment of the mythical all-American G.I., arrives in a fantastic plaza where the privileged and powerful mingle with the poor and weak along the Camino Real. In an imaginary netherworld populated with humanity's refuse, Williams's characters reveal his fascination with the perilous struggle of the sensitive, the artistic, and the damaged to survive in a harsh and godless world. "The violets in the mountains have broken the rocks," exclaims Cervantes's Don Quixote, as Williams's literary misfits (also including Casanova, Marguerite Gautier, Lord Byron, and Proust's Baron de Charlus) discover that a romantic outlook is necessary to survive life's brutal realities.

Williams's literary skid row is revealed in sixteen scenes (or "blocks") on a phantasmagoric Camino Real. The cynical Gutman, a character inspired by Sydney Greenstreet's memorable screen characterizations in *The Maltese Falcon* and *Casablanca*, narrates encounters between the golden-hearted Kilroy, who has pawned his prized boxing gloves to come there, and Esmeralda, a Gypsy's daughter, with whom he becomes enamored. Longings for connection and redemption are central among the play's cascading themes as the characters seek to defeat their own demons, the callousness of the world, the decay of their bodies, and death itself.

Part EPIC THEATER, part absurdist carnival, *Camino Real* profits from Williams's characteristic mastery of poetic imagery, language, and symbols, all set in bold relief against the play's otherworldly landscape. Williams had originally written the play in one-act form in 1948 as *Ten Blocks on the Camino Real*. After the performance of scenes at New York's Actors Studio, director Kazan encouraged Williams to expand the play into a full-length work. Critics and scholars have numbered Dante, ANTON CHEKHOV, EUGENE O'NEILL, BERTOLT BRECHT, AUGUST STRINDBERG, T. S. ELIOT, Franz Kafka, JEAN-PAUL SARTRE, SAMUEL BECKETT, and the art of M. C. Escher among the myriad influences on *Camino Real*, but Williams confirmed few influences. He was, however, inspired by current events. The play assaults the social conformities of the early 1950s, and the cynical opportunism depicted reflects Williams's reaction to Senator Joseph McCarthy and his Communist "witch-hunt," which was in full flower during the years Williams worked on the play.

Camino Real was deemed a failure in its original Broadway production. It had a short run (the first true commercial failure for Williams on Broadway) and few critical supporters. Most critics found the play obscure, and audiences generally seemed to share their confusion. Williams challenged the negative critical response in a *New York Times* essay and was deeply disappointed by the play's cold reception. Since 1953, however, *Camino Real*'s theatricality, lyricism, and literary underpinnings have won for it a growing critical appreciation and occasional productions. After its New York run *Camino Real* was produced in London in 1957 before a New York revival directed by José Quintero in 1960. In 1966 an National Educational Television (NET) adaptation starring Lotte Lenya and a young Martin Sheen won critical plaudits. *Camino Real* was revived again at Los Angeles's Mark Taper Forum in 1968 and at New York's Vivian Beaumont Theatre in 1970, with a strong cast led by Al Pacino, Jean-Pierre Aumont, and Jessica Tandy. England's Royal Shakespeare Company produced *Camino Real* in 1998 as its first-ever production of a Williams play. Numerous regional theaters across the United States continue to perform the play, and a major movie version was under consideration in the first years of the new millennium.

Williams's least characteristic work, *Camino Real* paved the way for departures from the brand of American lyric REALISM of which he was a prime exemplar. In the last four decades of the 20th century, leading U.S. playwrights increasingly expanded their definition of realism by making bolder use of imaginary and imaginative elements. Therefore, *Camino Real* emerges as a prescient work, an important early demonstration that American dramatists could effectively explore serious themes in forms other than realism.

[*See also* United States, 1940–Present]

FURTHER READING

Balakian, Jan. "*Camino Real*: Williams's Allegory About the Fifties." In *The Cambridge Companion to Tennessee Williams*, ed. by Matthew C. Roudané. Cambridge: Cambridge Univ. Press, 1997. 67–94.

Cless, Downing. "Alienation and Contradiction in *Camino Real*: A Convergence of Williams and Brecht." *Theatre Journal* 35 (March 1983): 41–50.

Jenckes, Norma. " 'Let's Face the Music and Dance': Resurgent Romanticism in Tennessee Williams's *Camino Real* and *Clothes for a Summer Hotel*." In *The Undiscovered Country: The Later Plays of Tennessee Williams*, ed. by Philip C. Kolin. New York: P. Lang, 2002. 181–193.

Parker, Brian. "A Developmental Stemma for Drafts and Revisions of Tennessee Williams's *Camino Real*." *Modern Drama* 39 (Summer 1996): 331–341.

Turner, Diane E. "The Mythic Vision in Tennessee Williams's *Camino Real*." In *Tennessee Williams: A Tribute*, ed. by Jac Tharpe. Jackson: Univ. Press of Mississippi, 1977. 237–251.

Williams, Tennessee. "On the Camino Real." *New York Times* (March 15, 1953): Sec. 2, pp. 1, 3.

Wolf, Morris Philip. "Casanova's Portmanteau: *Camino Real* and Recurring Communication Patterns of Tennessee Williams." In *Tennessee Williams: A Tribute*, ed. by Jac Tharpe. Jackson: Univ. Press of Mississippi, 1977. 252–276.

James Fisher

CAMPBELL, BARTLEY (1843–1888)

Bartley Campbell was born on August 12, 1843, in Allegheny City (now part of Pittsburgh), Pennsylvania. He worked in his father's brickyard as a boy, then entered a law office. He became a newspaper reporter in 1858, helped found the *Pittsburgh Leader* in 1865 and became its drama critic, and founded the short-lived *Southern Monthly Magazine* in New Orleans in 1869. He wrote stories, sketches, poems, and novels before turning to playwriting in 1871. He worked as a "literary attaché" (i.e., resident playwright) for Hooley's Theatre during 1872–1875, and during the summer of 1874 the company toured to San Francisco, where Campbell became a member of the Bohemian Club and met Mark Twain, BRET HARTE, and JOAQUIN MILLER. He organized a company to produce his own plays during 1876–1878 but fared poorly and nearly gave up the theater before a string of successes that opened during the last four months of 1879: MY PARTNER, *The Galley Slave*, and *Fairfax*. Through 1885, during the height of his popularity, Campbell directed his own productions in New York and on tour, but he suffered a breakdown, possibly in response to overwork and financial difficulties, and in 1886 he was committed to the State Hospital for the Insane in Middletown, New York, where he remained until his death on July 30, 1888.

My Partner is set in the Siskiyous in California, near the Oregon border, where the Edenic landscape shapes the action and the relationships. Two miners—the partners—are in love with the same woman, but one has sexual relations with her and then falls to the villain's knife before he can marry her. The others arrest his partner but acquit him when the comic "Chinee" produces a torn shirt that incriminates the villain.

The Galley Slave follows the romance of Sidney Norcott, an artist who anticipates a lavish inheritance, and Cicely Blaine, who is already wealthy. A French baron courts Cicely but has fathered a child by Sidney's model, but Cicely misunderstands that Sidney is the wayward lover. Falsely accused of robbery, Sidney goes to the gallows to save Cicely's honor. The baron is finally revealed as a phony, and the true lovers are reunited.

In *Fairfax*, Gladys is married to a wastrel who neglects her and their baby; when they struggle over some money that a stranger gave her, he shoots himself. The child dies, and she goes to work as a governess for Fairfax, a well-to-do widower who falls in love with her, but before they may wed, she must confess the "murder" and he must forgive her.

The White Slave moves one step beyond DION BOUCICAULT's *The Octoroon* (1859) by developing the sensational potential in the situation of a white woman raised as the child of an octoroon and so supposed by all to be legally black and therefore a slave. The heroine survives not only being sold to a villainous Mississippi plantation owner but also a burning riverboat, but in the end she establishes her true racial identity and marries the hero.

[*See also* United States, 1860–1929]

PLAYS: *Through Fire* (1871); *Peril* (1872); *Fate* (1873); *Hearts* (1873); *Little Sunshine* (1873); *Risks* (1873); *The Orphans* (1874); *The Virginian* (1874); *Bulls and Bears* (1875); *Grana Uaile* (1875); *On the Rhine* (1875); *A Heroine in Rags* (1877); *How Women Love; or, The Heart of the Sierras* (1877); *My Foolish Wife; or, A Night at Niagara* (1877); *Struck Oil* (1877); *Clio* (1878); *The Vigilantes; or, The Heart of the Sierras* (a revision of *How Women Love*, 1878); *Fairfax* (1879); *The Galley Slave* (1879); *My Partner* (1879); *Matrimony* (a revision of *Peril*, 1880); *My Geraldine* (1880); *Government Bonds* (1881); *Friend and Foe* (a revision of *On the Rhine*, 1882); *Siberia* (1882); *The White Slave* (1882); *Ardendale* (1884); *Separation* (1884); *Paquita* (1885)

FURTHER READING

Bank, Rosemarie. "Frontier Melodrama." In *Theatre West: Image and Impact*, ed. by Dunbar H. Ogden, with Douglas McDermott and Robert K. Sarlós. DQR Studies in Literature 7. Amsterdam: Rodopi, 1990. 151–160.

Campbell, Bartley. *The White Slave, and Other Plays*. Ed. by Napier Wilt. America's Lost Plays 19. Princeton: Princeton Univ. Press, 1941.

Mason, Jeffrey D. "*My Partner* (1879) and the West." In *Melodrama and the Myth of America*. Bloomington: Indiana Univ. Press, 1993. 127–154.

Meserve, Walter J. "The American West of the 1870s and 1880s as Viewed from the Stage." *Journal of American Drama and Theatre* 3 (Winter 1991): 48–63.

Wattenberg, Richard. "Americanizing Frontier Melodrama: From *Davy Crockett* (1872) to *My Partner* (1879)." *Journal of American Culture* 12 (Spring 1989): 7–16.

Jeffrey D. Mason

CAMPBELL, WILLIAM WILFRED (1861–1918)

Born in Berlin (now Kitchener), Ontario, in 1861, Wilfred Campbell is remembered for his work as a poet, playwright, and historian. Campbell studied at Toronto's University College (1881–1882) and Wycliffe College (1882–1883), then continued his clerical training at the Episcopal Theological School in Cambridge, Massachusetts. After he married in 1884, he worked as a rector in New Hampshire and New Brunswick until he left the ministry in 1892 (accounts differ on whether it was a "retirement" or a "crisis of faith" that precipitated his departure). After that he worked for the Ottawa civil service.

Campbell published regularly throughout his life, beginning with *Snowflakes and Sunbeams*, a collection of verse, in 1888. Eight more volumes of Campbell's poetry were published in his lifetime. In addition, in the early 1890s he contributed regularly to the "Mermaid Inn" literary columns in the *Toronto Globe*. He also published two novels, four verse dramas, and four historical works, including *The Beauty, History, Romance, and Mystery of the Canadian Lake Region* (1911).

Of Campbell's four verse dramas, *Mordred* and *Hildebrand* were the best known. The first, based on Sir Thomas Malory's telling of the Arthurian legend, reflects Campbell's strong interest in mythology and his love of British history and culture. For Campbell, the story of Arthur and Mordred was one of the great stories of mankind, filled with the types of themes that resonate in all timeless tragedies, from the Greeks to the Bible to William Shakespeare. Though Campbell's second best-known drama, *Hildebrand*, takes on a disparate subject matter with its emphasis on Pope Gregory VII and eleventh century Rome, it is tied to *Mordred* by its similar exploration of the never-ending struggles of the human spirit and the battle to preserve the human soul, a favorite topic of Campbell's. Campbell's remaining two tragedies also range broadly in subject matter, with *Daulac* chronicling the story of the Canadian hero Daulac, Sieur des Ormeaux, and *Morning* centering on more metaphysical issues of whether faith, hope, and belief can (or even should) be sustained in a modern world.

Wilfred Campbell was elected to the Royal Society of Canada in 1892/1893. In 1906 he represented the Royal Society of Canada at the Aberdeen University Quarter-Centenary and was there awarded an honorary doctor of laws degree and presented to King Edward and Queen Alexandra. He died near Ottawa, Ontario, in 1918.

Campbell's dramatic legacy consists solely of his four verse dramas. *Mordred* and *Hildebrand* were penned in 1893 and published together in 1895. The composition dates for *Daulac* and *Morning* are uncertain, although they received their first publication with the reprinting of Campbell's two other dramas in the 1908 volume *Poetic Tragedies*. Campbell's reputation as a poet still shines, and he is remembered for collections of verse such as *Snowflakes and Sunbeams* (1888), *Lake Lyrics and Other Poems* (1889), *The Dread Voyage* (1893), *Beyond the Hills of Dream* (1899), *The Collected Poems* (1905), and *Sagas of Vaster Britain* (1914). He is also remembered for his historical works chronicling Canadian life, including his history *The Scotsman in Canada* (1911).

[*See also* Canada]

PLAYS: *Hildebrand* (1895); *Mordred* (1895); *Daulac* (1908); *Morning* (1908)

FURTHER READING

Klinck, Carl F. *Wilfred Campbell: A Study in Late Provincial Victorianism*. Toronto: Ryerson, 1942.

Wicken, George. "William Wilfred Campbell (1858–1918)." In *Canadian Writers and Their Works*, ed. Robert Lecker, David Jack, and Ellen Quigley. Toronto: ECW, 1993. 45–47.

——. "William Wilfred Campbell (1858–1918): An Annotated Bibliography." *Essays on Canadian Writing* 9 (1977–1978): 37.

Kate Maurer

CAMUS, ALBERT (1913–1960)

I continue to believe that this world has no superior meaning. But I know that something in it has meaning: it is man, because man is the sole being to insist upon having a meaning.

—Albert Camus, *Camus' Lettres à un ami allemand*, 1984

Born in Mondovi, Algeria, in 1913, Albert Camus claimed that he grew up "half-way between poverty and the sun," a juxtaposition that provided perhaps the greatest influence on his work (1958). While he was a scholarship student at the Lycée d'Alger, soccer consumed his energy, and a philosophy teacher opened his mind to the perishability of the beautiful. This lesson hit home when an attack of tuberculosis forced him to disrupt his studies.

After a very brief membership in the Communist Party, in 1935 he founded the Théâtre de l'Équipe, dedicated to bringing good plays to the working classes, as well as the elite. By 1938 he had completed his doctoral studies in philosophy, relocated to FRANCE, and become a reporter and literary critic for the left-wing *Alger Républicain*, where he took issue with JEAN-PAUL SARTRE's philosophy and insisted on the need to go beyond absurdity.

When, at the outbreak of the war, he was rejected for military service, he joined the French Resistance and edited a clandestine newspaper, *Combat*. During the war years, although plagued by recurrent attacks of tuberculosis, he became an editor at Gallimard publishing house in Paris. After the war he made lecture tours of the United States and South America. Camus died on January 4, 1960, in Sens.

Camus's major works are divided into two cycles. The Sisyphus Cycle or Cycle of the Absurd of the prewar years includes a novel, *The Stranger*; a play, CALIGULA; and an essay, *The Myth of Sisyphus*. In these he examines humankind's loss of a system of moral values beyond the self and the consequent hubris of individuals that leads to chaos. The Prometheus Cycle or Cycle of Revolt of the postwar years includes a novel, *The Plague*; an essay, *The Rebel*; and three plays, *State of Siege*, *The Just Assassins*, and *The Possessed*. In these he depicts the individual's desire to live in freedom and work creatively being frustrated by the larger society's massive injustice and violence. Serving as a transition between the two is *The Misunderstanding*, a modern TRAGEDY.

As a playwright, Camus is absurdist in philosophy, but not in form. He exposes the irrationality of the human condition, but uses logical dialogue to do so—sometimes too much. For while critics are fascinated by his philosophical development, they fault his language for lapsing into distended rhetoric, his plots for lacking dramatic tension, and his characters for lacking complexity. Yet their respect for his passion and honesty—and for his fiction masterpieces—often make them forgiving in their criticism.

In 1957 Camus received the Nobel Prize in Literature for "his important literary production, which with clear-sighted earnestness illuminates the problems of the human conscience of our time." Two years later the promising young writer was appointed minister for cultural affairs of the French government and director of the new, state-supported experimental theater. The next year he was killed in an automobile accident, just a few years after his admission that, after twenty years of writing, "I continue to live with the notion that my work is not begun."

[*See also* Philosophy and Drama, 1860–1960]

PLAYS: *Caligula* (1938); *The Misunderstanding, or Cross Purpose* (*Le malentendu*, 1943); *The State of Siege* (*L'état de siège*, 1948); *The Just Assassins* (*Les justes*, 1949); *The Possessed* (*Les possédés*, 1959)

FURTHER READING

Barnes, Hazel E. *Humanistic Existentialism: The Literature of Possibility*. Lincoln: Univ. of Nebraska Press, 1962.

Bloom, Harold. *Albert Camus*. Bloom's Biocritiques. Broomall, Pa.: Chelsea House, 2003.

Brée, Germaine. *Albert Camus*. New York: Columbia Univ. Press, 1964.

Camus, Albert. *Caligula, and Three Other Plays*. Tr. by Stuart Gilbert. New York: Random House, 1962.

———. *L'envers et l'endroit* [Betwixt and Between]. Paris: Gallimard, 1958.

———. *Notebooks, 1935–1951*. Tr. by Philip Malcolm Waller Thody and Justin O'Brien. New York: Marlowe, 1998.

Ellison, David R. *Understanding Albert Camus*. Columbia: Univ. of South Carolina Press, 1990.

Patricia Montley

CANADA

This survey of Canadian drama is presented in two parts, "Canadian Drama, English Language" and "Canadian Drama, French Language."

CANADIAN DRAMA, ENGLISH LANGUAGE

Although theater in Canada predates the arrival of the Europeans, it is difficult to speak of "modern" Canadian drama, in either English or French, until the years between the two world wars. The barriers to the development of a national drama in Canada have been formidable. Canada is a vast land, sparsely populated and rural until the mid-20th century and lacking the urban centers and wealth that theater has relied on since Aeschylus's Athens. The religious establishment, in both French- and English-speaking Canada, was also traditionally puritanical and antitheatrical. Added to this, however, has been the bilingual nature of the country throughout its history: as a result, English-language literature and the literature of Quebec developed separately, and there is still a critical tendency (continued in the present volume) to discuss English- and French-language literature separately.

As a result of these obstacles, drama arose late in Canada: the first published plays in English appeared in the late 1850s, most notably the verse drama *Saul* by Charles Heavysege (published in 1857). CLOSET DRAMA was the order of the day, with most plays fitting into three categories: imitators of William Shakespeare such as Heavysege, dramas of small-town life such as *The Female Consistory of Brockville* (1856) by the pseudonymous Caroli Candidus, and historical-patriotic dramas such as Charles Mair's *Tecumseh* (1886). Performance was dominated by British and American touring companies. Only a handful of Canadian plays before 1900 received more than a single performance. Of these, the only national success was William Henry Fuller's *H.M.S. Parliament* (1880), a satiric adaptation of Gilbert and Sullivan's operetta *H.M.S. Pinafore*. Only *Tecumseh* has seen significant revivals in the late 20th century. The most financially successful writer was the actor-producer McKee Rankin, who epitomized another challenge to a national drama that persists to the present: the opportunity to earn more money and fame in ENGLAND or, especially, the UNITED STATES, where Rankin's career was based.

None of the new forms of European drama, including REALISM, showed any influence in Canada until the 1920s: by European standards, it is easy to agree with Northrup Frye's judgment that the drama of the 19th century was "as innocent of literary intention as a mating loon."

A vibrant amateur theater movement in the years after World War I fostered the first "modern" Canadian drama. In 1919 Hart House Theatre was founded in Toronto by Vincent Massey, who later became an important advocate of the arts as Canada's first native-born governor general. Devoted to the ideals of the international LITTLE THEATER MOVEMENT, the company produced plays of the European AVANT-GARDE, as well as Canadian writers, including MERRILL DENISON and HERMAN VOADEN.

Denison wrote realist plays set in rural Ontario. Most of his plays are one-acts, such as *Brothers in Arms* (1921), produced at Hart House Theatre, which became one of the most produced plays in Canada, but his reputation is based mostly on *Marsh Hay*, his most enduring work (unperformed until 1975), which is darker and closer to the naturalist tradition.

Voaden also set his plays in rural Ontario. But Voaden, who had studied in Europe and the United States, created a style combining poetry, music, and dance that he termed "Symphonic Expressionism." He directed and produced his plays himself, such as *Murder Pattern*, first in Sarnia, Ontario, and later at Toronto's Central High School for Commerce, where he served as chair of the English Department for thirty years.

Voaden was important not only as a playwright and producer, but also as a theorist. His "Sarnia Idea" recognized that a genuinely Canadian drama could not develop in the professional theater of the time, dominated by British and U.S. works, and he urged the amateur theaters to adopt the highest professional standards in their work. The establishment of the Dominion Dramatic Festival in 1932, the first national showcase for little theaters (with international judges), offered further encouragement to Canadian playwrights. The creation of the Governor General's Award for Literature in 1936 provided additional recognition and encouragement for Canadian dramatists.

What unifies Denison and Voaden is a theme that was later termed by pianist Glenn Gould "the Idea of North," which critic Brian Parker characterized as "the individual's confrontation with raw nature" (Parker, 1977). Some critics have seen this national myth as an obstacle to the development of Canadian drama, centering on an abstraction that is inherently undramatic in traditional terms.

The other significant playwright of this period was the prairie writer GWEN PHARIS RINGWOOD (1910–1984). Like Voaden, Ringwood studied playwriting in the United States, in this case at the Carolina Playmakers in North Carolina, a program dedicated to producing "folk plays," serious dramas in dialect about contemporary rural life. His plays, of which *Dark Harvest* (1939) is the most important, are excellent examples of this style.

A professional Canadian theater began in the 1950s. The most successful playwright of the period was ROBERTSON DAVIES (1913–1995), better known for his novels. Some of Davies's plays received Broadway and London West End productions. A man of many talents, Davies was also a theater historian who felt that the economic hardships of the Great Depression and World War II made the postwar rise in Canadian drama possible by sharply curtailing tours by British and U.S. companies, allowing the amateur theaters more attention and the beginnings of a truly professional Canadian theater. The first major theater was the Stratford Festival in the Ontario town of the same name. Although the festival has focused on Shakespeare as its prime reason for being, from its early years it also provided workshops and premieres of Canadian works.

It was not until the 1960s, however, that a broad-based "Canadian" drama began to emerge, fueled by a surge of nationalism sparked by Canada's belated evolution from a dominion of the British Crown to independent nationhood. The excitement of independence brought about an increase in government support for the arts and culture, which fostered the creation of professional theaters across the country.

JAMES REANEY was the first of the new generation of English-language playwrights to come to prominence. Reaney began his career as a poet and wrote his first plays for children. His plays show both influences, focusing on language and the transformative abilities of actors, using minimal design elements. Like Denison and Voaden, Reaney's work uses rural southwestern Ontario as its setting. Reaney is closer to Voaden in style and temperament: a former student of Northrup Frye, he finds poetry and mythic resonance in its history and geography. His best work is the historical trilogy *The Donnellys* (1972–1975), which exhibits remarkable parallels to Voaden's *Murder Pattern*.

Other playwrights of note in the 1960s included GEORGE RYGA, who expanded the dramaturgical terrain to First Nations (Native American) topics with his play *The Ecstasy of Rita Joe*, and John Herbert, whose prison drama *Fortune and Men's Eyes* (1967) premiered in New York and became the first U.S. success by a Canadian playwright.

In the wake of celebrations for the Centennial Year (1967), an alternative theater movement grew out of dissatisfaction with what was seen as the continued dominance of the professional stage by U.S. and British imports. Young companies sprang up that championed Canadian writers: in Toronto, Theatre Passe Muraille (1968), Factory Theatre Lab (1970), and Tarragon Theatre (1971); in Montreal, Centaur Theatre (1969). Tarragon also championed Quebec drama in translation, especially the work of MICHEL TREMBLAY, who proved almost as much an inspiration for English-language drama as he had for French. Although Centaur has always programmed a larger percentage of British, American, and Irish work than the Toronto theaters, it bridged the cultural gap with the bilingual plays of DAVID FENNARIO (such as ON THE JOB and BALCONVILLE), as well as productions for Tremblay and other French-language playwrights in translation.

Additional opportunities for production were provided by government restrictions on support based on the percentage of Canadian content (including both works by Canadians and the use of Canadian actors, directors, etc.) in programming. The creation of Playwrights' Cooperative (now the Playwrights Union of Canada) generated further support, including a commitment to publishing Canadian plays.

The 1970s saw a flowering of playwrights with a wide range of styles, including Carol Bolt, JOHN GRAY, Rick Salutin, GEORGE F. WALKER, DAVID FRENCH, Bernard Slade, DAVID FREEMAN, Herschel Hardin, Joanna McClelland Glass, SHARON POLLOCK, and JOHN MURRELL. Several of these writers have achieved international success and reputations, most notably George F. Walker. The decade also saw the rediscovery of Denison's and Voaden's work, leading to the belated premiere of *Marsh Hay* and the first publication of Voaden's work.

In the late 1970s Canada entered an economic recession from which it has not yet recovered. Cultural funding was cut back by the national governments of Brian Mulroney and Jean Chrétien, following the pattern set by Ronald Reagan and Margaret Thatcher in the United States and the United Kingdom. As a result, Canadian drama retrenched. Large-scale work such as Reaney's *The Donnellys*, Theatre Passe Muraille's *The Farm Show*, or Rick Salutin's *Les Canadiens* was displaced by plays for small casts and more commercial topics. One-person shows (such as LINDA GRIFFITHS and PAUL THOMPSON's MAGGIE AND PIERRE) became popular.

As a result, the leading Canadian venues have remained small in comparison with their counterparts in other nations. The Tarragon's mainstage is just 200 seats, Theatre Passe Muraille's is 170, each significantly less than the smallest venue at the Royal National Theatre in London. This makes it almost impossible for a Canadian playwright to earn a living from stagewriting without repeated international productions: the options of writing for film or television are also fewer and less remunerative than for his or her British and American counterparts unless the writer chooses to move to those countries. There is a secondary effect of the Canadian situation on the development of an internationally prominent profile for its drama: even great plays have usually required championing by great actors or directors. For English-speaking Canadian actors, there are few incentives, in terms of money or fame, to stay in Canada if the opportunity arises to work in London or Hollywood. Although there have been many talented English-speaking Canadian directors, none has established an international reputation while remaining in Canada, and several very talented ones, including John Caird and Des McAnuff, have chosen to pursue their stage and film careers in the United Kingdom or United States, respectively.

Despite these handicaps, Canadian drama has continued to progress. JOHN KRIZANC's environmental play TAMARA—conceived to be staged in a house—became the most internationally successful Canadian play, with long runs in New York, Los Angeles, London, and Buenos Aires. The 1980s also saw the development of a more culturally diverse DRAMATURGY, led by the emergence of First Nations playwrights, most notably TOMSON HIGHWAY, whose plays, including *The Rez Sisters* and DRY LIPS OUGHTA MOVE TO KAPUSKASING, explore life on a reservation on Manitoulin Island in Lake Huron. DREW HAYDEN TAYLOR's work has also met with success, and numerous First Nations troupes across the nation are producing quality work in English, French, and tribal languages. Although more productions and greater commercial recognition can be wished, the extent to which this element of the Canadian experience has found a place onstage far exceeds that of Native American drama in the United States.

Because of the late development of Canadian drama, female playwrights have always been a presence since the 1960s. The first generation, led by Bolt, Pollock, and Glass, has been joined by many others, including ANNE-MARIE MACDONALD, JOAN MACLEOD, and JUDITH THOMPSON. Gay and lesbian theater developed at roughly the same time as in New York and London. The most prominent company has been Buddies in Bad Times. The first gay playwright to gain national and international attention was SKY GILBERT; in the 1990s BRAD FRASER became one of Canada's most internationally successful playwrights to date. Afro-Canadian playwrights have emerged, most notably DJANET SEARS. A wave of immigration from other parts of the British Commonwealth has led to plays with West Indian and South Asian themes and characters by writers such as Sunil Kuruvilla. And, of course, straight white men have continued to write good plays, including JASON SHERMAN, David Gow, JOHN MIGHTON, and Michael Healey.

Brian Parker's 1977 question whether "Canadian drama" has the same sort of meaning as "American," "French," "British," or "German" drama remains important for English-language drama. Canada has produced no new style of drama. No Canadian playwright has built an undeniable international reputation, although George F. Walker came close in the late 1980s and early 1990s, and Brad Fraser premiered a play in the United Kingdom in 2003 before its first Canadian production. But British and U.S. productions remain rare, Broadway and West End productions rarer still, and European productions almost nonexistent. The style of Canadian plays varies widely: apart from First Nations writers such as Highway and Taylor, it is almost easier to define "Canadian dramaturgy" by contrast with its British and U.S. contemporaries. From the 1970s to the mid-1990s, Canadian drama was probably more likely to have political, historical, and international themes and settings than U.S. drama, although the success of playwrights such as AUGUST WILSON, TONY KUSHNER, and SUZAN-LORI PARKS in the United States and continuing economic crisis in Canada have largely eliminated this difference. But politically and historically concerned Canadian playwrights are still more dialectical in their thinking and more willing to present a range of viewpoints than most of their colleagues to the south. Canadian plays also, in the main, have been more interested in ideas and less in strong emotions than U.S. writing, which may reflect a difference in national character in an era in which the United States has emerged as the only superpower while Canada has identified itself internationally as one of the largest suppliers of peacekeeping forces for UN missions.

English-language Canadian drama since the late 1960s bears many resemblances to British drama, apart from the specific subject matter. This is especially true for history plays: in both nations one can speak of a "history play culture," a situation where Canadian plays about history have begun to acknowledge a tacit conversation with their audience about other history plays about Canada. Indeed, one of the most popular recent Canadian plays has been Michael Healey's *The Drawer Boy*, which draws not only upon Canadian history, but also the history of the creation of Theatre Passe Muraille's *The Farm Show*. In contrast to their British counterparts (Edward Bond, Caryl Churchill, Howard Brenton, John McGrath, Robert Bolt, and others), Canadian writers such as Reaney, Carol Bolt, Pollock, Salutin, or Sherman seem more attuned to personal passions and less passionate about personal ideology. This has resulted in wonderfully complex works that usually lack the intellectual fieriness of Cloud Nine, *Bingo*, or *The Romans in Britain*, to name three prime examples from the British theater. Among naturalist plays, works such as Walker's *East End Plays* or the plays of Judith Thompson or Brad Fraser are obviously more "American," much rawer emotionally and more closely related to Sam Shepard and David Mamet than to David Hare, for instance. Here again, some of this distinction has been disappearing in recent years with a younger generation of British playwrights, such as Sarah Kane, Mark Ravenhill, and Patrick Marber, and emerging black English writers such as Debbie Tucker Green, Roy Williams, or Kwame Kwei-Armah.

FURTHER READING

Athabasca University. *Encyclopedia of Canadian Theatre*. http://www.canadiantheatre.com/.

Edwards, Murray. *A Stage in Our Past*. Toronto: Univ. of Toronto Press, 1968.

Glaap, Albert-Reiner. "Constructing a New Diversity: Contemporary Plays in English." In *New Worlds: Discovering and Constructing the Unknown in Anglophone Literature*, ed. by Martin Kuester, Gabriele Christ, and Rudolf Beck. Munich: Verlag Ernst Vögel, 2000.

Grace, Sherill, Eve D'Aeth, and Lisa Chalykoff, eds. Introduction to *Staging the North: Twelve Canadian Plays*. Toronto: Playwrights Canada Press, 1999.

Historica. *The Canadian Encyclopedia*. http://www.thecanadianencyclopedia.com/.

Parker, Brian. "Is There a Canadian Drama?" In *The Canadian Imagination*, ed. by David Staines. Cambridge, Mass.: Harvard Univ. Press, 1977.

Saddlemyer, Ann, ed. *Early Stages: Theatre in Ontario, 1800–1914*. Toronto: Univ. of Toronto Press, 1990.

Saddlemyer, Ann, and Richard Plant, eds. *Later Stages: Essays in Ontario Theatre from the First World War to the 1970s*. Toronto: Univ. of Toronto Press, 1997.

Walter Bilderback

CANADIAN DRAMA, FRENCH LANGUAGE

Although theatrical traditions predated the arrival of Europeans in Canada, a wide range of obstacles prevented the development of any strong dramatic tradition until well into the 20th century. The general conditions are sketched out in the part on English-language drama. For Francophone Canada, some of these conditions were mitigated: the geographic area is much more limited, and the province of Quebec (which constitutes the bulk of French-speaking Canada) has long possessed two urban centers, Montreal and Quebec City, while English-speaking Canada lacked any until Toronto emerged as a major city in the mid-20th century. In other ways, French-speaking Canada had more obstacles. While Marc Lescarbot's *Théâtre de Neptune en la Nouvelle-France* (performed in 1606, published in 1609) is one of the earliest European dramatic works written, performed, or published in the Western Hemisphere, it is also one of only three dramatic texts that predate the fall of French Canada (1763), because of the absence of a single printing press in the colony. French colonization did not lead to the development of urban centers, so it was only after England gained control that Montreal and Quebec began to develop. Religious opposition to drama, strong in English-speaking Canada, was even stronger in Quebec: all theater was banned by the Catholic Church in the late 17th century after a performance of Molière's *Tartuffe*, and excommunication was still being threatened to theatergoers well into the 20th century. In addition, the official dominance of English culture until the Quiet Revolution of the 1960s meant that the vast majority of theatrical activity in Montreal, the cultural center of the province, was performed in English.

Leonard E. Doucette divides 19th-century drama into three categories: religious/pedagogic, political, and "social" (Historica). The first was often written by clergymen and was not subject to church intervention; as a result, according to Doucette, it "was the source of most live theatre in the first two-thirds of the 19th century." Political plays were often printed in newspapers, appearing in clusters with each new political controversy. Some received performance, notably Elzear Labelle's *Conversion of a Nova Scotia Fisherman*, which received multiple revivals from 1868 to 1899. "Social" drama, dedicated only to entertainment, lagged behind the other forms until the last part of the century, when it began a dominance in performance that was not challenged until the 1960s.

The most significant literary figure of the 19th century was Louis-Honoré Fréchette, whose historical play *Félix Poutré* (1862) was a huge success. Fréchette's work, which also included *Papineau* (1880, often considered the first important Canadian play in French), was lyrical, melodramatic, and patriotic, straddling the political and "social" categories. Fréchette was also a Parliamentarian, like the other significant French-language playwright of the century, Félix-Gabriel Marchand. (A sizable number of the English-language plays of the century were also written by politicians to publicize their causes.) Marchand eventually became the first French-speaking premier of Quebec; he was also the first French-language playwright to draw inspiration from the contemporary French stage, although his model was the Boulevard rather than ÉMILE ZOLA or HENRY BECQUE. His verse comedy *The False Wits* (produced posthumously in 1905) is the only play of the period to receive a modern revival.

In the last third of the 19th century "social" drama (including a heavy focus on operettas and burlesques of the European variety) increasingly dominated the French-speaking stage, while native playwrights continued to stress patriotic and historical themes. As a result, the percentage of published plays that actually received performances declined throughout the period. (The situation in English-speaking Canada during this period was very similar.)

Although English-speaking drama began to emerge in the 1920s with the work of writers such as MERRILL DENISON, HERMAN VOADEN, and GWEN PHARIS RINGWOOD, popular taste and the power of the church prevented any serious developments until 1938, when a priest, Emile Legault, founded the Compagnons de Saint-Laurent in Montreal. Legault had just returned from France, where he had been inspired by the work of JACQUES COPEAU and his studio. He imbued this amateur troupe with the sort of professionalism Voaden had urged in his "Sarnia Idea," and the repertoire shifted from religious plays to the classics and modern plays. This company provided the basis for the later professionalization of Quebec theater. When the company disbanded in the early 1950s, several members founded Théâtre du Nouveau Monde (TNM, 1951), one of the first true professional troupes in Montreal.

The late development of serious drama in Quebec meant that radio drama developed simultaneously with stage drama, and many dramatists earned a living from radio before they achieved stage success (a phenomenon that would repeat in the 1950s with writers such as Marcel Dubé and Jacques Languirand, with television joining the mix as well). The two most significant such writers in this period were Françoise Loranger, later to become an important early feminist dramatist in the 1960s, and Gratien Gélinas.

Gélinas was the first truly modern Quebec dramatist. An actor, as well as a dramatist, he adapted his Everyman character Fridolin to the stage in a series of popular annual sketches, collectively known as *Les Fridolines* (which have been successfully revived on numerous occasions since their publication in the early 1980s). Gélinas wrote in *joual*, the working-class slang of Montreal. In 1948 Gélinas wrote his most important work, *Tit-Coq*. This tale of a working-class bastard who does not want to be the father of a bastard received over 200 performances over the next few years and even opened on Broadway (where it closed after three performances). Gélinas was active into the 1980s; as a translator, he brought George Ryga's *The Ecstasy of Rita Joe* and the American rock musical *Hair* to the Quebec stage. His work remains popular to this day among an older generation of working-class Canadians.

On the heels of Gélinas's success came the precocious Marcel Dubé, who established his reputation at twenty-three, when his company Jeune Scène won the Dominion Drama Prize with Dubé's play *Zone*. Dubé's career also continued into the 1980s.

The late 1940s and 1950s also saw the birth of serious professional theaters in Montreal, including Théâtre du Rideau Vert (1948), TNM, and Théâtre Quatre-Sous (1955). While much of their repertoire was dedicated to the classics and contemporary foreign work, they also provided opportunities for native dramatists. Gélinas himself founded a company, the Comédie-Canadienne (1958–1970), dedicated to producing new Canadian works.

These theaters, the success of Gélinas and Dubé, and, in the 1960s, a rising sense of Quebecois identity fostered a generation of writers, many of them with political leanings, including Languirand, Claude Gavreau, Loranger, Jacques Ferron, and Robert Gurik, all important for what was to come later, but most working within what were clearly European models. Nothing prepared people for what would happen when Théâtre du Rideau Vert decided to produce, among a season of modern classics, a play by an unknown twenty-six-year-old named MICHEL TREMBLAY.

The premiere of THE SISTERS-IN-LAW (*Les belles-soeurs*) remains the single most important event in Canadian theater history. As *The Encyclopedia of Canadian Theatre* puts it, "it introduced a theatre that was from here and could not be mistaken for theatre from anywhere else." Like Gélinas, Tremblay's characters spoke in *joual*, but spoke it with a casual vulgarity that had never been heard on the stage before. His characters were often anticlerical and expressed an openness about sexuality that was also shocking and new. Later plays such as HOSANNA and *La duchesse de Langeais* introduced gay characters to the Quebec stage. Perhaps most important, the plays were equally strong whether read as vibrant, native-born NATURALISM or as complex, multilayered symbolic works: the oppression under which Tremblay's "belles-soeurs" and transvestites live could easily been seen (and was) as paralleling the situation of all Quebec.

Even had his works remained confined to French Canada, Tremblay's importance would be great. But it extended to Canada at large. Tremblay became one of the first heroes of the gay movement in Canada. Theatrically, his plays had as great an impact on English-speaking drama as on French. And he is one of the few Canadian playwrights to achieve critical and box-office success outside Canada, with productions throughout the Americas, Europe, and even the Middle East.

Tremblay's use of *joual* encouraged other serious playwrights. Jean Barbeau, Jean-Claude Germain, Victor-Lévy Beaulieu, and Michel Garneau (who has also translated Shakespeare into *joual*) all wrote significant works, which in turn provoked debate among the cultural and intellectual elite, occasionally leading to controversies over provincial and municipal funding, most notably the decision not to financially support a production of *Les belles-soeurs* in FRANCE.

Native Quebec drama soon accounted for a major percentage of dramatic production in the province, with playwrights (especially Tremblay) regularly represented in translation in English-speaking theaters. Doucette notes two trends of importance in the 1970s: "a decline in traditional authored texts" and the development of women writers such as JOVETTE MARCHESSAULT and DENISE BOUCHER, growing out of a number of women's troupes created in the decade (Historica). Explicitly political work nearly vanished after the electoral victory of the Parti Quebecois in 1976.

Among the companies not producing "traditional authored texts," the most important is probably Gilles Maheu's Carbone 14. Because of its continuing connections with French theater French-language drama includes more multimedia and nonverbal work than its English-speaking counterpart, although this type of work has also been seen as an heir to the vision of Herman Voaden. More important still is the work of playwright-director-actor–film director Robert Lepage: although his reputation is greater as a director than as a playwright, much of it stems from works both epic (*The Seven Streams of the River Ota*) and intimate (*Needles and Opium*, *Vinci*) that he has also written. Lepage is probably the second most important creator of Canadian drama after Tremblay, although he is still virtually unknown in the United States outside the Brooklyn Academy of Music.

French-language drama in Canada remains vibrant. Significant writers who have emerged since the 1980s include Larry Tremblay (no relation to Michel), René-Daniel Dubois, MICHEL MARC BOUCHARD, Victor-Lévy Beaulieu, Carole Fréchette, Normand Chaurette, and Marie Laberge. Non-European writers, such as Lebanese-born WAJDI MOUAWAD, have also begun to establish themselves.

FURTHER READING

Athabasca University. *Encyclopedia of Canadian Theatre*. http://www.canadiantheatre.com/.

Donohoe, Joseph I., Jr., and Jonathan M. Weiss, eds. *Essays on Modern Quebec Theater*. East Lansing: Michigan State Univ. Press, 1995.

Historica. *The Canadian Encyclopedia*. http://www.thecanadianencyclopedia.com/.

Jack, Belinda. *Francophone Literatures: An Introductory Survey*. Oxford: Oxford Univ. Press, 1996.

Moss, Jane, and Jonathan Weiss, eds. *French-Canadian Literature*. Bowling Green: Association for Canadian Studies in the United States, 1996.

Nardocchio, Elaine F. *Theatre and Politics in Modern Quebec*. Edmonton: Univ. of Alberta Press, 1986.

Walter Bilderback

THE CANDLE KING

The Candle King (*O rei da vela*) was written in 1933 by Oswald de Andrade (1890–1954), one of the main representatives of Brazilian modernism in literature and author of the two manifestos that defined this movement of arts and ideas: *Manifesto of Brazil-Wood Poetry* (*Manifesto da poesia pau-Brasil*, 1924) and *Anthropophagous Manifesto* (*Manifesto antropófago*, 1928).

Starting as a "Week of Modern Art" organized by intellectuals and artists in São Paulo in 1922, the Modernist movement contested the academic taste in Brazilian art and literature and its imprisonment in imported models that had nothing to do with a truly Brazilian art. Andrade's *Manifesto of Brazil-Wood Poetry* criticizes the "doctoral side" of the Brazilian intellectual elite and advocates poetry based on native originality, on the legacy of the indigenous people, Brazil's original inhabitants. The modernist language is stripped of grandiloquence and of academicism; its syntax is fragmented, its narrative often telegraphic, marked by parody, derision, and sarcasm.

Anthropophagous Manifesto further radicalizes the ideas of *Brazil-Wood Poetry* and proposes cannibalism as a way of reversing colonization. Instead of being devoured by the colonizers, BRAZIL should devour them, as was the custom among certain Indian tribes. Cannibalization meant resistance to the history imposed by the colonizers, to their aesthetic and cultural values. Parodying William Shakespeare, Andrade asserts that for Brazilians the real question is Tupi or not Tupi (a reference to an Indian nation). Either they assume their authentic nature and reinvent themselves or stay culturally colonized.

The Candle King sets the *Anthropophagous Manifesto* in action. It takes place during the 1930s, when the Brazilian economy, based on the exportation of coffee, was hit hard by the crash of 1929, and the rural oligarchy was eclipsed by an ascendant urban bourgeoisie. The revolution of 1930 consolidated this power change, centralizing decisions in the hands of a federal government and promoting the country's industrialization.

Abelardo I, the Candle King, built his fortune selling candles during the blackouts caused by the closing of the electric company in 1929. He is also a loan shark, profiting from the disgrace of his clients, kept in a cage that serves as a waiting room. Abelardo II, his assistant, dresses as a lion tamer and executes delinquent clients.

His fiancée, Heloisa of Lesbos, is a member of a traditional but penniless family of the coffee "aristocracy." In contrast to the romantic love of the famous medieval couple, their marriage is strictly a business: Heloisa needs money, and Abelardo I wants a traditional family name. The play is a fierce critique of capitalism and of the values and morals of patriarchal society. With ruthless humor, Andrade subverts and reorganizes sexualities, genders, and social roles. This is clearly exemplified by Heloisa's family: her sister Joana's nickname—João dos Divãs (John of the Couches)—points to her alleged lesbianism. However, she competes with her gay brother, Totó Fruta do Conde, for the attention of another man. Heloisa is sexually emancipated and, despite her name and her way of dressing "as Marlene," uses her sexuality as currency for seducing powerful men. Her fascist brother, Perdigoto, is an inveterate drunk and a gambler.

Contrasting with his harsh and brutal behavior toward his clients, Abelardo I is a subservient lackey of imperialism, represented by Mr. Jones, an American businessman. He even offers Mr. Jones the first night with Heloisa, as was the custom in medieval times.

The second act of the play takes place on a tropical island, the exotic New World as imagined by the colonizers (and neocolonizers). The cannibalistic metaphor, present in the play at many levels, reaches its peak in this act. Abelardo I, who in the first act economically devours his clients and employees, now sexually devours (or attempts to) his mother-in-law and her sister. Totó Fruta do Conde devours many "fishes," and Heloisa is devouring and being devoured by Mr. Jones, who devours the whole country—plus his male driver.

The third act takes us back to the usury office, where Abelardo I, bankrupted after being robbed by Abelardo II, shoots himself. However, history does not change. As Abelardo I dies with a candle in his hand, we hear the bridal march and see Abelardo II and Heloisa receiving congratulations for their wedding. The American has the last words: "Oh, good business!"

The play broke with the ideas and the theatrical conventions of the Brazilian stage at that time. Cannibalizing AVANT-GARDE ideas and mixing expressionistic, futuristic, and surrealistic elements with popular, folkloric, and carnivalesque manifestations, Andrade created a unique Brazilian form that theater director José Celso Martinez Corrêa later defined as "Brazilian pop." The boldness of the play and the timing of its publication—1937, a little before the establishment of the authoritarian Estado Novo (New State)—may explain why the play was considered "unstageable" by its contemporaries.

It was staged for the first time in 1967 by Teatro Oficina, one of Brazil's most important theater groups. The alliance of the military dictatorship with big international capital, the valorization of imported cultural products, and the rapid spread of news communication brought a renewed meaning to Andrade's text. In the hands of Oficina's director José Celso Martinez Corrêa, the play became a live political-cultural manifesto. Following the modernist spirit, he carried the allegories, the parody, and the derision to their extreme, diving deeply into the baroque spirit of Andrade's work. The aesthetic shock caused by the performance was in large part responsible for the emergence of Tropicalismo, a short-lived but extremely significant movement that erupted in music, theater, cinema, and visual arts.

FURTHER READING

Candido, Antonio, and José Aderaldo Castello. *Modernismo—história e antologia*. Rio de Janeiro: Bertrand Brasil, 1997.

George, David. *Teatro e antropofagia*. Rio de Janeiro: Global, 1985.

Johnson, Randal. "Tupy or Not Tupy: Cannibalism and Nationalism in Contemporary Brazilian Literature." In *Modern Latin American Fiction: A Survey*, ed. by John King. London: Faber, 1987.

Magaldi, Sábato. *Teatro da ruptura: Oswald de Andrade*. São Paulo: Global, 2004.

Stam, Robert. *Subversive Pleasures—Bakhtin, Cultural Criticism, and Film*. Baltimore: Johns Hopkins Univ. Press, 1992.

Ana Bernstein

LA CANTATRICE CHAUVE *See* THE BALD SOPRANO

CAO CAO AND YANG XIU

The newly written historical play (*xinbian lishiju*) *Cao Cao and Yang Xiu* (*Cao Cao yu Yang Xiu, jingju*) is one of the most renowned and influential *jingju* (Beijing/Peking "opera") created since the end of the Cultural Revolution. Written by Chen Yaxian (b. 1948), with production impetus from the actor Shang Changrong and direction by Ma Ke, the play premiered in 1988 to considerable controversy and critical acclaim and then entered the permanent repertory of the Shanghai Jingju Company, where it has been further revised and remounted several times since. Extraordinarily popular, it has won numerous awards and has been widely toured and televised with Shang Changrong as Cao Cao and Yan Xingpeng, Guan Huai, and He Shu as Yang Xiu. The play is groundbreaking in many respects. Its creation process was one of the most extensive early post–Cultural Revolution experiments in the development of free-agent artistic enterprise in *jingju*, involving the collaboration of major artists from several different institutions. Its approach to traditional subject matter is also strikingly original. Cao Cao—one of the principal rulers in the third-century Three Kingdoms period, comparable in cultural importance to the Arthurian era in the English-speaking world—is traditionally dramatized as a two-dimensional villian. Earlier 20th-century attempts to reverse this interpretation were considered equally unbelievable. But in *Cao Cao and Yang Xiu* both major characters are complex, three-dimensional beings, and this warts-and-all approach is fundamental to the politically and philosophically daring themes of the overall piece.

The play is based on a few brief incidents in chapter 72 of the Mao Zonggang edition of Luo Guanzhong's novel *The Romance of the Three Kingdoms* (*Sanguozhi tongsu yanyi*). In the novel Yang Xiu is a somewhat prideful officer whose intellectual brilliance is both useful and threatening to Cao; when Yang, after publicly urging Cao to retreat, correctly interprets Cao's evening password as indicating the intent to do so and begins preparations for retreat ahead of any formal orders, Cao seizes the opportunity and has Yang beheaded for destroying the morale of his soldiers. A central premise of the much-expanded *jingju* plot is that Cao actively recruited Yang as part of a grand campaign to seek out worthy men of ability to serve his cause. Initially close comrades in arms, the two are driven apart by suspicion and arrogance. Both are principled, yet dangerously impetuous and inflexible, and each makes numerous attempts to bring the other to his point of view. Even on the execution ground Cao invites Yang to join him in a genuine—and very moving—heart-to-heart conversation. But Yang cannot stop himself from trying to save Cao by continuing to argue for retreat, and Cao cannot bring himself to pardon Yang in the face of such public insubordination. In the end, Cao orders the ax to fall. The relationship between the two characters has been seen as a clear parallel for the one between Mao Zedong and Peng Dehuai just before the opening of the Cultural Revolution, and although the play premiered a year earlier, for the one between Deng Xiaoping and Zhao Ziyang just before June 4, 1989. Official criticism has generally concurred that the play explores the perpetual nature of human conflict and reveals the tragedy inherent in being unable to transcend the concerns of self.

Cao Cao and Yang Xiu is the first major play by Chen Yaxian. His later plays include *Cao Cao and Chen Gong* (*Cao Cao yu Chen Gong*), *The Mayor's Wife* (*Shizhang furen*), *Hujia* (an ancient tribal reed instrument), and, with Chen Jianqiu, part two of the award-winning *jingju* series *Chancellor Liu the Hunchback* (*Zaixiang Liu luoguo*).

[*See also* China]

FURTHER READING

Chen Yaxian. *Xiqu bianju qiantan* [On xiqu playwriting]. Taipei: Wenjin chubanshe, 1999.

Davis, Edward, ed. [Entries on Ma Ke and Shang Changrong]. In *Encyclopedia of Contemporary Chinese Culture*. London: Routledge, 2005.

Mackerras, Colin. *Peking Opera*. Hong Kong: Oxford Univ. Press, 1997.

Wichmann-Walczak, Elizabeth." 'Reform' at the Shanghai Jingju Company and Its Impact on Creative Authority and Repertory." *Drama Review* 44, no. 4 (Winter 2000): 96–119.

Elizabeth Wichmann-Walczak

CAO CAO YU YANG XIU *See* CAO CAO AND YANG XIU

CAO YU (1910–1996)

Born in Tianjin in September 1910 and originally known as Wan Jiabao, Cao Yu began to study at Nankai Middle School in 1922, where, as a lover of theater since he was little, he joined and became an active member of the famed Nankai New Drama Troupe in 1925. He entered Nankai University in 1928 to study politics, but two years later he transferred to Tsinghua University, where he began exploring Western classics and was especially drawn to Greek TRAGEDY and to plays by William Shakespeare, HENRIK IBSEN, ANTON CHEKHOV, and EUGENE O'NEILL. In 1933, while still a student at Tsinghua, he wrote his maiden work, *Thunderstorm* (*Leiyu*), a play in four acts that opened a new chapter in Chinese drama. Two years later, another play, *Sunrise* (*Richu*), came out that, together with *Thunderstorm*, has made him the most prominent playwright in modern Chinese drama. After Cao Yu established his fame in the 1930s, he started to teach in Baoding and Tianjin and at the National Institute of Dramatic Art in Nanjing. Meanwhile he continued writing plays such as *The Wilderness* (*Yuanye*), *Metamorphosis* (*Tuibian*), and *Peking Man* (*Beijing ren*). He also adapted Ba Jin's novel *Family* (*Jia*) as a play with the same title. During the post-1949 period Cao Yu wrote a film script, *Bright Sky* (*Yan yang tian*), and two historical plays, *Gall and Sword Piece* (*Dan jian pian*) and *Wang Zhaojun* before his death in December 1996.

Heavily influenced by the antifeudal and anti-Confucian spirit of the May Fourth movement, Cao Yu started his playwriting by exploring the social issues of women's freedom and family ethics in a feudal hierarchy. Although his plays were mainly realistically written in a Chinese setting, Western theatrical influence on him was obvious in his early plays. A Greek sense of tragedy and an Ibsenian mission for social justice were mixed with a mystic idea of fate in *Thunderstorm*, which created a complex set of relationships bordering on incestuous love between members of two families unbeknownst to themselves until the very end. The instant success of the play was also attributed to its tightly knit structure with the dramatic techniques Cao employed to play up the atmosphere. Plays Cao wrote in the 1940s, except *Peking Man* (*Beijing ren*), were, however, more practically produced to fit the need of the political situation during the time. *Peking Man*, powerful in both characterization and use of symbols, was considered by some to be one of the masterpieces of modern Chinese drama. After 1949 Cao's creativity in drama was shown mainly in the two historical plays by his own interpretation of such historical figures as Gou Jian of the State of Yue and Wang Zhaojun. By common consent, Cao Yu's achievements and his reputation rest primarily on his four early plays, *Thunderstorm*, *Sunrise*, *The Wilderness*, and *Peking Man*.

Cao Yu was one of the first Chinese dramatists who consciously and extensively drew upon Western philosophical concepts and dramatic techniques to serve the Chinese reality that they tried to portray. Marking a milestone in modern Chinese drama, the intricate and well-knit structure and the profound dramatic conflict, as well as the sharp character portrayal in Cao's plays, have influenced many later Chinese dramatists.

[*See also* China]

PLAYS: *Thunderstorm* (*Leiyu*, 1933); *Sunrise* (*Richu*, 1935); *The Wilderness* (*Yuanye*, 1936); *Metamorphosis* (*Tuibian*, 1939); *Let Me Think* (*Zheng zai xiang*, 1940); *Peking Man* (*Beijing ren*, 1940); *Family* (*Jia*, 1942); *Bridge* (*Qiao*, 1946); *Clear, Bright Day* (*Minglang de tian*, 1954); *Gall and Sword Piece* (*Dan jian pian*, 1961); *Wang Zhaojun* (1978)

FURTHER READING

Cao Yu. *Thunderstorm* [*Leiyu*]. Tr. by Wang Tso-liang and A. C. Barnes. Peking: Foreign Languages Press, 1958.

——. *Bright Skies* [*Minglang de tian*]. Tr. by Chang Pei-chi. Peking: Foreign Languages Press, 1960.

——. *Sunrise* [*Richu*]. Tr. by A. C. Barnes. Peking: Foreign Languages Press, 1960. 2d ed., 1978.

——. *The Consort of Peace* [*Wang Zhaojun*]. Tr. by Monica Lai. Hong Kong: Kelly & Walsh, 1980.

——. *The Wilderness* [*Yuanye*]. Tr. by Christopher C. Rand and Joseph S. M. Lau. Hong Kong: Hong Kong Univ. Press, 1980.

——. *Peking Man* [*Beijing ren*]. Tr. by Leslie Nai-Kwai Lo with Don Cohn and Michelle Vosper. New York: Columbia Univ. Press, 1986.

Hu, John Y. H. *Ts'ao Yü*. New York: Twayne, 1972.

Lau, Joseph S. M. *Ts'ao Yü, the Reluctant Disciple of Chekhov and O'Neill: A Study in Literary Influence*. Hong Kong: Hong Kong Univ. Press, 1970.

Tian, Benxiang. *Cao Yu zhuan* [Biography of Cao Yu]. Beijing: Beijing shiyue wenyi chubanshe, 1988.

Wang, Aixue. *A Comparison of the Dramatic Work of Cao Yu and J. M. Synge*. Lewiston, N.Y.: Edwin Mellen Press, 1999.

Hongchu Fu

ČAPEK, KAREL (1890–1938)

Born on January 9, 1890, in Malé Svatonovice, Bohemia, to a provincial doctor, Karel Čapek brought international attention to Czech drama in the early 20th century with his provocative stage parables. He was a many-sided literary figure whose life was closely bound to the new state of CZECHOSLOVAKIA, a creation of World War I. A journalist, novelist, essayist, travel writer, and translator in addition to his theater work, Čapek was a cosmopolitan who studied in Berlin and Paris while completing his doctorate in philosophy at Charles University in Prague. Yet his roots were deeply Czech, and he came to be identified with the ideals of democracy and justice embodied by Czechoslovakia's first president, Thomas G. Masaryk, with whom Čapek was familiar as an unofficial biographer. Čapek's work in theater extended beyond playwriting to include directing and DRAMATURGY, and he occasionally collaborated with his brother Josef, an important artist and stage designer. Čapek died in Prague, Czechoslovakia, on December 25, 1938.

The First Republic lasted barely twenty years (1918–1938), but they were the very years in which Čapek produced his major plays and other literary work. The plays as a group are less notable for their style and technique than for their unconventional subject matter and their challenging themes. After some youthful, fanciful short plays written in part with his brother (*Love's Fateful Play*, a piece in the commedia dell'arte mode; and *The Brigand*, a wry study of youth's rash excesses), Čapek burst upon the theater world with his R.U.R. (1920), a theatrically effective, prototypal sci-fi MELODRAMA about the creation of a race of robots and the resulting near extinction of humanity at their hands. Inherent in the action are issues of technology and industrialism and the ethical dilemmas in mass-producing an expendable species designed exclusively for labor. The play received successful productions throughout Europe and America.

Written with Josef Čapek almost concurrently and produced a year after R.U.R., THE INSECT COMEDY (*Ze života hmyzu*, 1921) is an expressionistic fantasy depicting human follies in the form of the insect world, within the frame of a vagrant's hallucinatory dream. Its Prague premiere was directed by the greatest Czech director of the time, Karel Hugo Hilar, and designed by Josef Čapek. Three episodes focusing on butterflies, assorted bugs and beetles, and killer ants, respectively, provide both comic and distressful views of human greed, destructiveness, and other vanities, offset by glimpses of life-redeeming activity. Čapek imbued the play with a vitality and color that made it a more fully entertaining theatrical experience than R.U.R., and another international hit.

In *The Makropulos Affair* (*Věc Makropulos*, 1922) Čapek explores the implications of extending human life by hundreds of years. In the course of a legal dispute it is revealed that Emilia Marty, a glamorous opera singer, is actually over 300 years old by virtue of an elixir developed by her father in the 16th century. The practical and philosophical issues of an indefinitely prolonged life are debated among the characters, each guided by his or her own personality. Emotionally exhausted and bored, Emilia herself finally realizes that she has no desire for added years, and Čapek suggests that a normal life span is more reasonable and preferable for human beings. *Makropulos* was one of eight productions directed by Čapek himself during his two-year tenure as dramaturge and director at the Vinohrady Theatre in Prague; it was also the basis of Leoš Janáček's opera of the same name.

Čapek next joined with his brother Josef in writing *Adam the Creator* (*Adam stvořitel*, 1927), a fantastical story that shows how a man's attempts to start a new world from scratch ultimately produce a world rather worse than the one that was rejected. The play had a stimulating concept and more overt comedy than most of Čapek's other works, but it did not sustain an action that held most audiences' interest.

As in the rest of the world, so in Czechoslovakia the transition to the 1930s was painful. Economic depression was reinforced by the rise of fascistic dictatorships in Europe and the growing threat of a second world conflict. After some ten years of nontheatrical activity Čapek, a humanist and civilized person of reason, responded with two dramas that acutely reflect the increasing tension of the times. *The White Disease* (*Bílá nemoc*, 1937) is a dramatic allegory of the confrontation of aggressive militarism by a special form of passive resistance. A plague is devastating a nameless land headed by a general. Doctor Galen has discovered a cure, but he steadfastly refuses it to anyone who supports an imminent war, including the general, until the general agrees to cease his belligerent activity. The play ends with the agonizing irony of the doctor being slain by a hysterical mob in support of the war before he is able to reach the desperate general. The deeply pessimistic ending echoed Čapek's premonition of the war to come. That premonition was markedly strengthened by the time Čapek wrote *The Mother* (*Matka*, 1938), produced only a month before the German Anschluss of Austria in March 1938. In a wartime situation the mother is alone with one surviving son, having lost her husband and other sons, all of whom appear in the play as if alive, debating issues of honor, courage, and war. The mother, an instinctive pacifist, resists all inducements to have her surviving son participate in the conflict until she learns of the death of children in the war at the hands of the enemy, at which point she hands her son a rifle and tells him, "Go!" The melodramatic and otherwise awkward elements of the plot were transcended by the strength of the parallel to what was threatening the Czechs at the time, and it was clear that Čapek's inherent abhorrence of aggression was overcome by his realization that evil must be resisted by force. A half year later, in September 1938, Czechoslovakia lost its autonomy at Munich when its French and English allies caved in to Adolf Hitler. Čapek's death three months later on Christmas Day was undoubtedly hastened by the extinction of Czech independence.

[*See also* Topol, Josef]

SELECT PLAYS: *Love's Fateful Play* (*Lásky hra osudná*, written with Josef Čapek, 1910); *The Brigand* (*Loupežník*, 1920); *R.U.R.* (*Rossum's Universal Robots*) (1920); *The Insect Comedy* (*Ze života hmyzu*, written with Josef Čapek, 1921); *The Makropulos Affair* (*Věc Makropulos*, 1922); *Adam the Creator* (*Adam stvořitel*, written with Josef Čapek, 1927); *The White Disease* (*Bílá nemoc*, 1937); *The Mother* (*Matka*, 1938)

FURTHER READING

Bradbrook, Bohuslava R. *Karel Čapek: In Pursuit of Truth, Tolerance, and Trust*. Portland, Ore.: Sussex Academic Press, 1998.

Harkins, William E. *Karel Čapek*. New York: Columbia Univ. Press, 1962.

Jarka M. Burian

CARAGIALE, ION LUCA (1852–1912)

Playwright, writer, and actor Ion Luca (I. L.) Caragiale is undeniably the most important figure in Romanian literature. Though he wrote two collections of short stories and collaborated as journalist and essayist at many Romanian newspapers and periodicals, he established his fame with four plays that have become permanent classics in the Romanian repertoire.

He was born in Haimanale, a little village near Bucharest, on January 30, 1852. At the age of eighteen he graduated from school and became, at the request of his father, a clerk at the county court, a position he did not hold for long. After his father's death in 1870 he became the sole support for his mother, Ecaterina, and his younger sister, Lenci. He tried his hand at many jobs as journalist, substitute teacher, and prompter until the opening in 1879 of his first comedy, *A Stormy Night* (*O noapte furtunoasa*), at the National Theatre in Bucharest. Five years later his masterpiece, the comedy *A Lost Letter* (*O scrisoare pierduta*) opened in November 1884 to unanimous acclaim. Two more plays followed, the comedy *A Carnival Absurdity* (*D-ale carnavalului*) in 1885 and his only drama, *The False Accusation* (*Napasta*), in 1890.

I. L. Caragiale's comedies are sharp satires of the mores and foibles of his contemporaries. His characters, crazed with politics, will stop at nothing for a government appointment; they lie, steal, blackmail, and bribe. In his comedy *A Lost Letter*, a provincial politician, running for a seat in Parliament, uses a lost love letter, addressed to the adulterous wife of the local head of the opposition party in power, as a foil to force him into supporting his candidacy. *A Stormy Night* is a sharp analysis of the petty bourgeoisie and their hypocritical exaggeration of morality. Master Dumitrache, a petty shopkeeper, who is very keen on his "family honor," puts his entire trust in his assistant while the latter is having a clandestine affair with his wife.

Caragiale's contemporaries criticized him bitterly and accused him of being an enemy of the people and his views an insult to the nation and its institutions. Despite all criticism, Caragiale continued to ridicule the powerful of the entire political spectrum, thus thwarting his own political aspirations. Except for a brief and controversial tenure as artistic director of the National Theatre in Bucharest and a short period as school inspector, he barely eked out a living. Things got so bad that he had to open a beer pub at the train station in a provincial town. Finally, disgusted with his Romanian contemporaries, he took advantage of a small inheritance to go into voluntary exile and settled in Berlin for the last seven years of his life. He died in 1912 at the age of sixty.

EUGÈNE IONESCO made the following backhanded compliment about Caragiale in *Notes and Counternotes*: "I. L. Caragiale is perhaps the greatest among the unknown dramatic authors" (Ionesco, 1962).

[*See also* Jonah; Romania; Sorescu, Marin]

PLAYS: *A Stormy Night* (*O noapte furtunoasa*, 1879); *Master Leonida Facing the Opposition* (*Conu Leonida de Fata Cu Reactiunea*, 1880); *A Lost Letter* (*O scrisoare pierduta*, 1884); *A Carnival Absurdity* (*D-ale carnavalului*, 1885); *The False Accusation* (*Napasta*, 1890)

FURTHER READING

Caragiale, Ion Luca. *Teatru*. Bucharest: Biblioteca Pentru Toti, 1960.

Cioculescu, Serban. *Viata Lui I. L. Caragiale: Caragialiana*. Bucharest: Editura Eminescu, 1977.

Ionesco, Eugène. *Notes et contre-notes*. Paris: Gallimard, 1962.

Moshe Yassur

THE CARETAKER

Published and staged in 1960, *The Caretaker* was HAROLD PINTER's first commercial triumph. A three-act play, *The Caretaker* focuses on the emerging conflict among three working-class men. Alan Pryce-Jones summarizes the plot in a 1960 *Observer* review: "They talk, fail to communicate with one another, and break into moments of violence which reflect the despair of the world." Pinter uses the interactions of these characters—Aston, in his early thirties; Mick, his younger brother; and the old man Davies—to explore power dynamics and identity. Critics praise Pinter's ability to inspire sympathy for both the manipulative Davies and the slow, quiet Aston; Pryce-Jones admires those "moments of the utmost eloquence in which nothing happened." In Pinter's drama, silence and action convey meaning that cannot be related through language.

The Caretaker reflects Pinter's concern with existential themes and yet also incorporates political responses to racial and class tensions in 1950s Britain. Homeless and unemployed, Davies lacks control over his life. Aston rescues the old man from a fight and offers him a place to stay. Davies enters, complaining about his lot and expressing racist hate. Davies's character is also associated with imprecise identity through his need to travel to Sidcup and collect papers to establish "his real identity." When Aston wakes Davies in the morning, he complains about noises the old man made while sleeping. After Aston departs, Davies begins searching the room. Mick enters and throws the old man to the floor.

As the second act opens, Mick interrogates Davies about his presence. Aston returns with Davies's bag, left at the café the previous night, and the two brothers toss the bag between themselves out of Davies's reach. After Mick leaves, Aston explains that he is working on the house for his brother, and he offers Davies a job as caretaker. Later Davies enters the dark room and realizes that someone else is there. The loud sound of a machine frightens Davies; the lights reveal Mick standing on Aston's bed, holding a vacuum cleaner plug. Mick complains to the old man about Aston's laziness and offers Davies the caretaker position, contingent upon acceptable references. Davies again mentions his need for shoes in order to go to Sidcup. The next morning Aston reminds Davies of this plan. Aston recalls his time in a psychiatric hospital, where he was kept against his will and subjected to electric shock therapy. In his monologue Aston describes the side effects from that treatment.

Two weeks later Davies complains about Aston while Mick describes renovation plans. Aston arrives with shoes, which are ungratefully accepted by Davies. That night Aston wakes Davies to complain about his groaning. The old man threatens to return Aston to the psychiatric hospital. Undaunted, however, Aston packs Davies's belongings. The old man leaves to find Mick. When Mick and Davies return, Mick grows angry as Davies discusses Aston's psychiatric treatment. Mick tells Davies to leave. Davies then approaches Aston, but Aston silently turns his back on the old man. Both Davies and Mick use violence and language in search of power, but Aston's ultimate power lies in silence.

[*See also* England, 1940–1960]

FURTHER READING

Esslin, Martin. *Pinter: The Playwright*. 6th ed. London: Methuen, 2000.

Scott, Michael, ed. *Harold Pinter: The Birthday Party, The Caretaker, The Homecoming: A Casebook*. London: Macmillan, 1986.

Sykes, Alrene. "*The Caretaker* and 'Failure of Communication.'" In *Critical Essays on Harold Pinter*, ed. by Steven H. Gale. Boston: G. K. Hall, 1990.

Robin Seaton Brown

CARL XII

Carl XII, a historical play in five acts by AUGUST STRINDBERG, was written and published in 1901 and first performed at the Royal Dramatic Theater in Stockholm in 1902. Depicting the last phase in the life of King Carl XII (1682–1718), *Carl XII* opens as the king, after fifteen years of warring abroad, returns to SWEDEN. He encounters an impoverished country and a dissatisfied people. An attempt to improve the economy by means of emergency coins fails. In a tableau loosely connected with the rest of the play, the bachelor-king's relations to women, notably to his sister Ulrika Eleonora, are demonstrated. Carl finally decides to march on NORWAY, where he is killed while besieging the fortress of Fredriksten. Recognizing that the king had made himself guilty of hubris, Emanuel Swedenborg (Swedish scientist, philosopher, theologian, and visionary) points to heaven and says that even if the fatal shot came from the fortress, in a deeper sense it came from heaven. (Strindberg does not stress the widespread rumors that Carl was assassinated by one of his own people.)

The action covers a period of about three years, from the king's return to Sweden in December 1715 until the deadly shot on November 30, 1718. The whole play is one long waiting. What the king in the last instance waits for and finally elicits is his own death; in Strindberg's words: "The kingdom is ruined, and only an honorable suicide remains. So—to Norway!"

"My *Carl XII*," Strindberg claims, "is a drama of character and catastrophe, i.e. the last acts of a long story, and in this following somewhat the classical tragedies where everything has already happened" (Strindberg, 1959). However, unlike the situation in analytical drama, the action in *Carl XII* does not consist of a reconstruction of the past but of the problems facing the king in the present. Nevertheless, although the play is arguably the least historical of all Strindberg's historical plays, a certain knowledge of Swedish history greatly helps one understand it.

Carl is on the whole a rather passive, remarkably taciturn, and morally inflexible character, with little trace of penitence or sense of guilt. A static character, he incarnates "a dead man whose body walks about as a ghost." Although his violent death may seem to be a nemesis for his hubris, it may as well, in view of his death urge, be seen as a blessing. This explains why, unlike the situation in most of Strindberg's other post-*Inferno* plays, the title figure in *Carl XII* hardly puts up a battle with the Powers.

Next to the historical characters, a few anonymous ones, together forming a "chorus" representing the Swedish people, appear: the Man, the Woman, a Malcontent, the Sailor. A novelty in the play that has hardly been observed is the dramatist's tendency to phrase his acting directions in such a way that the reader rather than the spectator is favored.

FURTHER READING

Brantly, Susan. "The Formal Tension of Strindberg's *Carl XII*." In *Strindberg and History*, ed. by Birgitta Steene. Stockholm: Almqvist & Wiksell International, 1992. 121–137.

Johnson, Walter. *Strindberg and the Historical Drama*. Seattle: Univ. of Washington Press, 1963.

Lamm, Martin. *August Strindberg*. Tr. and ed. by Harry G. Carlson, New York: Blom, 1971.

Stockenström, Göran. "*Charles XII* as Historical Drama" and "*Charles XII* as Dream Play." In *Strindberg's Dramaturgy*, ed. by Göran Stockenström. Minneapolis: Univ. of Minnesota Press, 1988. 41–55, 223–244.

Strindberg, August. *Open Letters to the Intimate Theater*. Tr. and ed. by Walter Johnson. Seattle: Univ. of Washington Press, 1959.

Törnqvist, Egil. "Visual and Verbal Scenery in Strindberg's Historical Plays: *Carl XII* as Paradigmatic Example." In *Strindberg and History*, ed. by Birgitta Steene. Stockholm: Almqvist & Wiksell International, 1992. 103–112.

Egil Törnqvist

CARPA

Speakers of Spanish in MEXICO and ethnic Mexican communities in the United States have long applied the word *carpa* to tents and similar structures, particularly those intended for theatrical performance. The term has then been extended to the performances that have taken place in such structures and even to a rough-and-tumble style of acting associated with those performances. Artists who have worked in tent shows have often been called *carperos*, although a stigma associated with the shows has led some performers to shun the label. Those who write about the *carpa* usually refer to commercial variety shows for working-class audiences that centered on the antics of versifying clowns and comedians who developed variants on a comic hobo character called the *pelado* or *peladito* (literally, "naked one"). These shows combined circuslike entertainments with song and dance, magic, ventriloquism, puppet shows, topical sketch COMEDY, and other types of acts. However, it is worth noting that drama, MELODRAMA, ZARZUELA, musical revues, and other theatrical forms also occurred in the tent shows. With the advent of film in the early 20th century, some *carpas* alternated film screenings with live performances. In Texas some ethnic Mexicans have even called Protestant religious revivals held in tents *carpas*.

Although the *carpa* was important throughout Mexico and the southwestern United States, the academic literature on the subject concentrates on Mexico City and southern Texas. In Mexico City sedentary *carpas* and *jacalones* (shacklike performance spaces) appeared in marginalized neighborhoods from at least the middle of the 19th century until approximately 1960. In Texas traveling *carpas* served similar neighborhoods during much of the same period. Few *carpas* in Texas survived World War II, and the form was more or less extinct in the United States by 1950. During the Mexican Revolution the sketches and musical revues of the *carpas* were an arena of political struggle, providing relatively uncensored news and political commentary to audiences whose members were often illiterate. After the revolution the *carpas* became a training ground for the nation's emerging entertainment industry. The beloved comedian Mario Moreno (known as Cantinflas) was the *carpa*'s most famous alumnus, but many other noted Mexican comedians and musicians also started out in the tent shows. In the United States the film industry's racial dynamics prevented the *carpas* from serving a similar function, although some *carperos* did make their way to large Anglo-owned circuses. The only U.S. actor associated with the tent shows to achieve notoriety in Hollywood was San Antonio's Ramiro ("Pedro") González-González, who played supporting roles in westerns with John Wayne during the 1950s. Competition from electronic media contributed to the *carpa*'s demise in both the United States and Mexico. Official censorship also played a significant role in Mexico. In the United States the pressure ethnic Mexican audiences faced to embrace "American" cultural forms was equally damaging. During the late 1960s and early 1970s performers associated with both the Mexican student movement and the Chicano movement sought to revive the *carpa* aesthetic as a noncommercial tool of political struggle. The *nuevo teatro popular* (new popular theater) that emerged from these movements remains influential today.

FURTHER READING

Covarrubias, Miguel. "Slapstick and Venom: Politics, Tent Shows, and Comedians." *Mexican Life* 15, 1939.

Granados, Pedro. *Carpas De México: Leyendas, Anécdotas E Historia Del Teatro Popular* [Carpas of Mexico: Legends, anecdotes and history of the popular Theater]. México, D.F.: Editorial Universo, 1984.

Kanellos, Nicolás. *A History of Hispanic Theatre in the United States: Origins to 1940*. Austin: Univ. of Texas Press, 1990.

María y Campos, Armando. *Los payasos, poetas del pueblo* [The clowns, poets of the people]. México: Ediciones Botas, 1939.

Merlín, Socorro. *Vida y Milagros de las carpas: La Carpa en México, 1930–1950* [Life and miracles of the carpas: The carpa in Mexico, 1930–1950]. México, D.F.: Instituto Nacional de Bellas Artes, Centro

Nacional de Investigación y Documentación Teatral Rodolfo Usigli, 1995.

Ybarra-Frausto, Tomás. "I Can Still Hear the Applause. La farándula Chicana: carpas y tandas de variedad [The Chicano entertainment world: Carpas and variety shows]. In *Hispanic Theatre in the United States*. Ed. by Nicolás Kanellos. Houston: Arte Público Press, 1984.

Peter Haney

CARR, MARINA (1964–)

There's some fierce wrong ya done that's caught up with ya.

—*By the bog of cats . . .*, Scene 3

Born in Dublin, IRELAND, on November 17, 1964, Marina Carr was brought up in Offaly, in the mainly rural Irish midlands. Her father Hugh is a dramatist and short-story writer; her mother Maura, who died when Carr was seventeen, was also an important influence.

Carr has received numerous awards for her writing that confirm her status as an important talent who since her emergence in the early 1990s has inspired countless other Irish women playwrights while becoming one of the major voices in contemporary drama.

Carr's first plays were produced between 1989 and 1991. The first to appear was *Low in the Dark* (1989), an absurdist treatment of gender and fertility and a witty and inventive piece of surrealism. *The Deer's Surrender* appeared in 1990, and *This Love Thing* in 1991; Carr has stated that both should be regarded as apprentice pieces, unworthy of significant attention. *Ulaloo*, having been given a rehearsed reading at the Abbey in 1989, was produced in 1991 but was quickly withdrawn. After the failure of these plays Carr broke off writing in an attempt to discover her own voice and to refine her technical skills.

She returned to the Irish stage in 1994 with *The Mai*, the first of a series of five plays set in the Irish midlands. These plays are notable for highly stylized language and violence and for a bleak representation of women's lives. In *The Mai* the title character commits suicide after her husband leaves her. The protagonist of *Portia Coughlan* also kills herself, in fulfillment of a suicide pact with her twin brother Gabriel. In *by the bog of cats . . .* Hester Swayne commits suicide, but first murders her daughter Josie. *On Raftery's Hill*, Carr's most brutal play, portrays a family suffering from horrendous abuse by their father and includes a shocking scene of incestuous rape. And in *Ariel* a politician murders his daughter for personal advancement before himself being killed by his wife, who is in turn murdered by their other daughter.

Considered exclusively from the point of v iew of plot, these plays may seem melodramatic, but, as Carr's use of ABSURDISM in her earlier work shows, she is a writer with a strong sense of the power of metaphor. She does not represent reality, but exaggerates it to underline and make unavoidable the actual conditions under which people live. An essential aspect of this style of writing is her use of legend: *The Mai* is grounded in Irish myth, *by the bog of cats . . .* closely resembles *Medea*, and *Ariel* draws heavily from *Iphigenia at Aulis*, *Electra*, and *Faust*.

Although Carr is very highly regarded, her work has been subjected to occasional criticism. Some believe that because she represents women from disadvantaged socioeconomic groups being controlled by fate, she is implying that such people are not in control of their own lives. Others feel that she has fully explored the dramatic potential of the Irish midlands and ought to attempt new work. Nevertheless, her writing is always intellectually challenging and highly dramatic and provides an original and unsettling critique of gender in society and theater.

PLAYS: *Low in the Dark* (1989); *The Deer's Surrender* (1990); *This Love Thing* (1991); *Ulaloo* (1991); *The Mai* (1994); *Portia Coughlan* (1996); *by the bog of cats . . .* (1998); *On Raftery's Hill* (2000); *Ariel* (2002); *Meat and Salt* (2003)

FURTHER READING

McGuinness, Frank. Introduction to *The Dazzling Dark: New Irish Plays*. London: Faber, 1996.

McMullan, Anna. "Marina Carr's Unhomely Women." *Irish Theatre Magazine* 1, no. 1 (1998).

McMullan, Anna, and Cathy Leeney, eds. *The Theatre of Marina Carr*. Dublin: Carysfort Press, 2003.

Ní Anluain, Clíodhna, ed. *Reading the Future—Irish Writers in Conversation with Mike Murphy*. Dublin: Lilliput, 2000.

Wallace, Clare. "Tragic Destiny and Abjection in Marina Carr's *The Mai, Portia Coughlan and By the Bog of Cats . . .*" *Irish University Review* 21, no. 2 (Autumn/Winter 2001): 431–449.

Patrick Lonergan

CARTWRIGHT, JIM (1958–)

Jim Cartwright was born in Farnworth, Lancashire, in 1958. His first play, ROAD, was an instant success at its premiere at London's Royal Court in 1986 and is now recognized as a contemporary classic. The ferocity of Cartwright's vision in *Road* is echoed in much of the in-yer-face theater of the 1990s; less obviously influential, because inimitable, is the originality and exuberance of his linguistic and theatrical imagination. Though social, sexual, cultural, and economic deprivation is Cartwright's home territory, the creativity and energy in the language he gives his characters, in company and alone, ensure that his plays function on many levels. Cartwright's plays are as concerned with SURREALISM and romance as they are with documentary: *Hard Fruit* (2000) places a man with a dummy talking cat on his head in the classic realist territory of the backyard of a northern terraced house.

BED (1989), setting seven elderly characters somewhere between sleeping and waking in a giant bed, signaled the extent of Cartwright's willingness to experiment with a range of theatrical modes. *To* (1989, later retitled *Two*) employs REALISM more sustainedly, focusing on a mutually hostile couple running a pub. The play, like *Road*, features a range of monologues and vignettes; like *Road*, its action occurs on a single night, building toward a cathartic climax. The often downbeat mood of the play is filtered through Cartwright's talent for comic dialogue and pacing and his capacity for sketching complex and sympathetic characters and relationships. The final scene, during which landlord and landlady finally confront the death of their child, ends with "I love you too." In the original production, and many subsequently, all parts were played by two performers who mimed setting and props. Such virtuosity is part of Cartwright's commitment to a reflexive theater, something often missed by critics who focus on his realism.

The Rise and Fall of Little Voice (1992) is also built around virtuoso performance; its central character, LV, is a shy and inarticulate young woman who can sing like Judy Garland, Shirley Bassey, Edith Piaf, Marilyn Monroe, and Gracie Fields. This is the first of Cartwright's plays to focus sustainedly on character development over more than a few hours and, in its ending focused on a young couple, is his most obviously "feel-good" play. It was followed by possibly Cartwright's grimmest piece, *I Licked a Slag's Deodorant* (1996), a short two-hander between a prostitute and a client who ends the play living underneath her bed. *Hard Fruit* (2000) centers on Choke, an aging gay virgin obsessed with physical culture. Its depiction of wrestling and working out makes it Cartwright's most immediately physical piece, and its themes of nostalgia and repressed potential align it most strongly with *Road*'s cameos of wasted lives. Choke is, however, part of a community; his sexual and personal isolation is self-inflicted rather than a necessity.

[*See also* England, 1980–Present]

PLAYS: *Road* (1986); *Bed* (1989); *Two* (1989); *The Rise and Fall of Little Voice* (1992; filmed as *Little Voice*, 1998); *I Licked a Slag's Deodorant* (1996); *Prize Night* (1999); *Hard Fruit* (2000); *Strumpet and Vacuuming Completely New in Paradise* (BBC TV, 2001)

FURTHER READING

Billington, Michael. "Jim Cartwright." In *Contemporary British Dramatists*, ed. by K. A. Berney. London: St. James, 1994.

Dromgoole, Dominic. *The Full Room*. London: Methuen, 2000.

Peacock, D. Keith. *Thatcher's Theatre: British Theatre and Drama in the Eighties*. Westport, Conn.: Greenwood Press, 1999.

Sierz, Aleks. *In-Yer-Face Theatre*. London: Faber, 2001.

Stephen Longstaffe

LA CASA DE BERNADA ALBA *See* THE HOUSE OF BERNADA ALBA

CASADH SÚGÁIN EILE *See* THE QUARE FELLOW

CASAS, MYRNA (1934–)

Like many Boricua artists, Myrna Casas depicts PUERTO RICO'S divided psyche caused by the duality of its Latin American heritage under American sovereignty, especially the conflicts of women; Boricua derives from Borinquen, the original name of Puerto Rico. In *Glass Shattered Through Time* (*Cristal roto en el tiempo*, 1960) an aging prostitute dwells in romantic fantasies to escape her past. In contrast, the protagonist in *Eugenia Victoria Herrera* (1963) fights personal and cultural degradation. The brothel setting and scorched hacienda allude to the ruined state of the island.

With *Absurdities in Solitude* (*Absurdos en soledad*, 1963), Casas turned to AVANT-GARDE COMEDY and metadrama, the recursive interplay between illusion and reality. In *The Trap* (*La trampa*, 1964) a docile wife leaves her family to search for life in all its contradictory richness. The world-as-stage metaphor in *The Impromptu of San Juan* (*El impromptu de San Juan*, 1966) derides the facile formulas of comedy. The humor in the outer play clashes with the failed rehearsal of the inner play. Unable to influence the action, the actors leave the stage to a foreigner, implying that unless Boricuas affirm their own culture, they risk dancing off into an abyss.

Later comedies share many anti-illusionary techniques. *Not All of Them Have It* (*No todas lo tienen*, 1974; rewritten in 1994) starts as a domestic FARCE but evolves into a parody of theater. Just as the ludic knot is about to unravel, the protagonist rips off her wig and refuses to continue; the denouement hurls everyone into turmoil and provokes uneasy amusement. Dropping the mask reveals the superficial values of the urban middle class, obliging spectators to question their own authenticity.

THE GREAT USKRANIAN CIRCUS (*El gran circo eucraniano*, 1988) is Casas's most compelling play. Beyond the double structure of circus-comedy and actor-character, one perceives the political and psychic confusion of Puerto Ricans. *This Country Does Not Exist* (*Este país no existe*, 1993) is similar in structure. The outer action represents the failure to stage a historical drama; the inner play reenacts a thwarted rebellion. Just as Boricuas loyal to Spain betrayed the rebels, today's obeisance to foreign values stifles national identity. *This Country* won the Miami Circle of Critics Award in 1993. *Voices* (*Voces*, 2000) attacks the lack of introspection and communication required to promote civility, even among professionals. Again, the theater-mirror metaphor reflects back to the past and forward toward the audience.

Versatility and experimentation mark the *ars poetica* of Myrna Casas. She portrays theater as invention; as spectators deconstruct the artful guises of the stage, they recognize the falseness in their lives. She mocks kinship obligations, patriarchal privilege, social alienation, and government incompetence with rapid-fire exchanges. The action, sometimes frenzied or ludicrous, keeps the audience alert to surprises. Despite their lunacy and private rituals, the lyrical revelations of her characters accentuate their humanity. Her anti-illusionary techniques, however, seek to provoke an intellectual reaction, not emotional attachment. The open endings call for action. Easy jocular solutions cannot mend a fractured psyche nor heal festering social diseases. Just as the players must collaborate to craft a meaningful performance, Puerto Ricans must cooperate to create a healthy society. Artists define the issues; society must resolve them.

SELECT PLAYS: *Glass Shattered Through Time: A Painful Pause in Two Acts and One Voice* (*Cristal roto en el tiempo: pausa dolorosa en dos actos y una voz*, 1960); *Absurdities in Solitude* (*Absurdos en soledad*, 1963); *The Trap* (*La trampa*, 1964); *Eugenia Victoria Herrera* (1964); *The Impromptu of San Juan* (*El impromptu de San Juan*, 1973); *Three* (*Tres*, 1974)—comprises a series of satirical skits: *Prologue* (*Loa*), *Lunch Will Not Be Served to Anita Millán or the Tragic Story of Plastic Flowers* (*No se servirá almuerzo a Anita Millán o La historia triste de las plantas plásticas*), *Get Away!* (*Quítatetu*), *There Were Three and Now There are Four* (*Eran tres y ahora son cuatro*); *Not All of Them Have One* (*No todas lo tienen*, 1975, revised 1994); *Forty Years Later: Drama Without Head nor Tail* (*Cuarenta años después: drama sin son ni ton*, 1975); *Aladdin I* (*Aladino I*, 1987); *The Great USkranian Circus* (*El gran circo eucraniano*, 1988); *This Country Doesn't Exist* (*Este país no existe*, 1993); *Adrift* (*Al garete*, 1995); *Voices* (*Voces*, 2000); *I Am So Suspicious!* (*¡Qué sospecha tengo!*, 2001); *Three Nights in the Tropics and a Lifetime in Hell* (*Tres noches tropicales y una vida de infierno*, 2004); *The Strange Case of the García de la Parra Triplets* (*El extraño caso de las triples García de la Parra*, 2004); *The Queens of Chanticleer* (*Las reinas del Chantecler*, 2006)

FURTHER READING

Casas, Myrna. *The Great USkranian Circus*. In *Women Writing Women: An Anthology of Spanish-American Theater of the 1980s*, ed. by Teresa Cajíao Salas and Margarita Vargas. Albany: State Univ. of New York Press, 1997.

Cypess, Sandra M. "*Eugenia Victoria Herrara* and Myrna Casas' Redefinition of Puerto Rican National Identity." In *Essays in Honor of Frank Dauster*, ed. by Kirsten Nigro and Sandra Cypess. Newark, Del.: Juan de la Cuesta, 1995. 181–194.

Feliciano, Wilma. "Myrna Casas: La mujer y el juego metadramático." *Revista del Ateneo Puertorriqueño* 4, nos. 10–12 (1994): 147–154.

Salas, Teresa Cajiao, and Margarita Vargas. "Women's Voices in Hispanic Theater." In *International Women Playwrights: Voices of Identity and Transformation*, ed. by Anna Kay France and P. J. Corso. Metuchen, N.J.: Scarecrow, 1993. 213–221.

Stevens, Camilla. "Traveling Troupes: The Performance of Puerto Rican Identity in Plays by Luis Rafael Sánchez and Myrna Casas." *Hispania* 85, no. 2 (May 2002): 240–249.

Unruh, Vicky. "A Moveable Space: The Problem of Puerto Rico in Myrna Casas's Theater." In *Latin American Women Dramatists: Theater, Texts, and Theories*, ed. by Catherine Larson and Margarita Vargas. Bloomington: Indiana Univ. Press, 1998. 126–142.

Vargas, Margarita. "Relational Identity in Myrna Casas' *El gran circo eucraniano*." *Latin American Theatre Review* 36, no. 2 (Spring 2003): 5–19.

Wilma Feliciano

CASTE

Notwithstanding that the progress of dramatic development in theatrical history has been assuredly slow, yet there are from time to time indications that an English school of dramatic writing is among the possibilities of no very remote future. . . . The latest instance took place at the Prince of Wales's Theatre, on Saturday, when a new play by Mr. T. W. Robertson was produced, under the monosyllabic title of "Caste," and achieved a remarkable success.
—*Illustrated London News*, April 13, 1867

This excerpt from a review in the *Illustrated London News* captures the importance of THOMAS WILLIAM ROBERTSON'S *Caste* (1867) as a turning point in Victorian theater. The phrase "cup and saucer drama" emerged from a scene in *Caste* and refers to Robertson's attention to domestic details. This designation, however, diminishes the play's thematic REALISM, which contributed to renewed respectability for the Victorian theater as it increasingly attracted middle-class audiences.

According to George Rowell, the "box set"—a self-enclosed realistic interior—with which Robertson became associated was first used by Vestris and Mathews at the Olympic Theatre and Covent Garden "twenty years earlier" than Robertson, but "they could find no Robertson to evolve a new school of comedy on which to lavish their scenic reforms" (Rowell, 1978). Allardyce Nicoll describes Robertson's plays as a form of "spiritual reality" and as "a deliberate attempt, through the medium of art, at dealing with the major problems of the day" (Nicoll, 1959).

In *Caste*, which was based on Robertson's short story "The Poor Rate Unfolds a Tale," the actress Esther Eccles marries Hon. George D'Alroy against the wishes of his mother. The play delineates the characters of Esther's father, sister, and sister's beau as vivid and humorous contrasts to George's genteel world. After George is sent to war in India and reported killed, Esther desperately maintains a home and fends off the attempts of the Marquise to take her son from her until George's unexpected return finally reconciles his wife and his mother. The play emphasizes its own realism when George's friend, Hawtree, tells him:

> My dear Dal, all those marriages of people with common people are all very well in novels and in plays on the stage, because the real people don't exist, and have no relatives who exist, and no connections, and so no harm's done, and it's rather

> interesting to look at; but in real life with real relations, and real mothers, and so forth, it's absolute bosh. It's worse—it's utter social and personal annihilation and damnation.

Hawtree foregrounds that Robertson's play echoes a cross-class romantic plot of many novels and plays, but, even as it employs melodramatic conventions, is more realistic because it addresses the problem of social disapproval of marriages that cross class lines.

The *Daily News* (April 8, 1867) review of *Caste* pointed out that in writing a "play 'with a purpose,'" Robertson produced "something more than a mere attempt to amuse the groundlings." Robertson's dramas, combined with the commercial strategies of Marie Wilton, who managed the Prince of Wales's Theatre where Robertson's plays were staged, changed the form of Victorian drama and the audiences that it attracted, and have been regularly revived for almost a century and a half.

[*See also* England, 1860–1940; Melodrama]

FURTHER READING

Barrett, Daniel. *T. W. Robertson and the Prince of Wales's Theatre*. New York: P. Lang, 1995.

Nicoll, Allardyce. *Late Nineteenth Century Drama, 1850–1900*. 1959. Vol. 5 of *A History of English Drama, 1660–1900*. Cambridge: The Univ. Press, 1952–59.

Robertson, T. W. *Plays by Tom Robertson*. Ed. by William Tydeman. Cambridge: Cambridge Univ. Press, 1982.

Rowell, George. *The Victorian Theatre, 1792–1914*. 2d ed. Cambridge: Cambridge Univ. Press, 1978.

Renata Kobetts Miller

CASTRO, CONSUELO DE (1946–)

Born in 1946 and raised in the state of Minas Gerais, BRAZIL, Consuelo de Castro moved to São Paulo to attend college in the 1960s. Castro was active in leftist student politics and used those experiences as the basis for her first two plays. She received attention as a participant in the short-lived movement known as *teatro novo* (new theater). This group of five young playwrights staged realistic plays that featured only two characters engaged in intense confrontations within a confined space. Their approach was novel when compared with the political protests against the dictatorship disguised in metaphor and history that dominated Brazil's theaters at the time. Castro's first play, *Test of Fire* (*À prova de fogo*, 1967), was censored for its portrayal of university students resisting a military invasion of their faculty building. It was finally performed in 1993 in the very building where its events took place. Castro's second play, *Skin Deep* (*À flor da pele*), was staged in 1969 and was later released as a movie in 1976. It critiques the failed leftist political agenda of the 1960s and particularly its co-opted leaders. Like the other plays written between 1968 and 1978, *Test of Fire* and *Skin Deep* follow a traditional theatrical structure that moves inevitably toward a tragic end. In these early dramatic conflicts the powerless, most of them women, are defeated or sacrificed in order to maintain the political and economic values of the status quo.

After the return to democratic government in the mid-1980s, Castro began trying out new themes and frameworks. Her most effective plays treat topics similar to those that marked her early career, but in a more experimental format. For example, *Script-tease* (1989) studies the differences between political action and accommodation as seen through the eyes of the main character, who appears as a younger and older version of herself in two different time planes. Castro's latest play, *Only You* (2000), can be seen as a synthesis of key concerns in the dramatist's long career. Two characters meet in a beach house during Easter weekend to remember the violence and destroyed ideals of Brazil's dictatorship (1964–1985). Castro's play provides a sympathetic and moving portrayal of these emotionally crippled human beings whose common bond is the memory of a woman from the leftist underground who disappeared and whose remains were never found. Her former husband has been trying to write a miniseries to document her life when he is visited by a young woman whose mental health depends on honoring the same missing activist. The play uses this simple romantic encounter, with its own process of discovery, to call for an accounting of the many physical and emotional losses caused by the dictatorship.

Consuelo de Castro has used her theater to dramatize the individual's struggle to live up to his or her highest political and social ideals in a less-than-perfect world. It is a struggle that she too has participated in throughout her life.

PLAYS: *Test of Fire* (*À prova de fogo*, 1967); *Skin Deep* (*À flor da pele*, 1969); *Homeward Bound* (*Caminho de volta*, 1974); *The Great Love of Our Lives* (*O grande amor de nossas vidas*, 1978); *Mad Ring of Desire* (*Louco circo do desejo*, 1985); *Walking Papers* (*Aviso prévio*, 1987); *Script-tease* (1989); *Medea: Memories of the Open Sea* (*Medéia: Memórias do mar aberto*, 1997); *Making-Off* (1999); *Only You* (2000)

FURTHER READING

Milleret, Margo. "Acting Radical: The Dramaturgy of Consuelo de Castro." In *Latin American Women Dramatists: Theater, Texts, and Theories*, ed. by Catherine Larson and Margarita Vargas. Bloomington: Indiana Univ. Press, 1998. 89–109.

——. "Lessons from Students About the Brazilian Dictatorship." *Hispania* 85, no. 3 (2002): 658–664.

Silva, Magda. "Consuelo de Castro and Brazilian Theater in the 1960s and 70s." Ph.D. diss., Univ. of North Carolina, 2000.

Szoka, Elzbieta, and Joe W. Bratcher III, eds. "Consuelo de Castro." In *3 Contemporary Brazilian Plays in Bilingual Edition*. Austin: Host Publications, 1988. 362–367.

Margo Milleret

CATALAN EXPERIMENTAL THEATER

The Catalan Experimental Theater (Teatro experimental catalan) is an innovative theatrical movement that originated in Catalonia, SPAIN, at the end of the 1970s. Experimentation in Catalan theater began in the so-called street theater. Els Comediants, La Cubana, La Fura dels Baus, and Xarxa Teatre are the most representative street-theater groups. Street theater is characterized by a new relationship between the actors and the public that distances itself from the Italian street theater; the integration of urban space into the scenic creation; the incorporation of diverse "plastic" elements (sound, music, noise, as well as objects, props, decorations, and wardrobe) that reduce or even eliminate the verbal elements; and itinerant shows that mimic parades, exploiting fully the relationship between scene and auditorium.

Another experimental wave of expression, more associated with Italian theatrical fashion, entails Brau Teatre, Dagoll-Dagom, Els Joglars, Grup d'Acció Teatral, Sémola Teatre, Teatre Lliure, and Tricicle. This wave encompasses the following changes in the mode of representation: an extremely provocative performance that attacks all institutions, including the church; a positive reassessment of the show as a collective enterprise of different art forms; a consideration of the play as secondary to spectacle; a parallel production of staging, seminars, and research papers; the use of private and independent playhouses, as opposed to commercial or public ones; and an absence of traditional theater professionals.

The three most accomplished Catalan theater groups in the last quarter of the 20th century are Els Comediants, La Fura dels Baus, and Els Joglars.

Els Comediants first emerged in 1972 with a show called *Non plus plis*, in which mimicry was the main component, along with the influence of the American group Bread & Puppet. From 1976 with Apoteosic soirée (*Apoteósic sarao*) and especially after 1978 with Sun; Little Sun (*Sol solet*) Els Comediants moved beyond an Italian style of theater and introduced a complex form of theater. Mostly this new variety involved explosions of vitality that required leaving the stage or creating an atypical relationship with the audience. *Wonders of Cervantes* (*Maravillas de Cervantes*, 2000) constitutes its latest show.

La Fura dels Baus developed the most imaginative and transgressive concept of theater of the 1980s. The festive personality of this group favors the expressive musical components and elements of the street theater. In 1983 the group premiered *Actions* (*Accions*). Its performances progressively moved toward new theatrical conceptions in which the most predominant components are noise, music, the scarcity of words, and plastic elements. Other shows by this group include *Suz/o/Suz* (1985), *Tier Mon* (1988), and *Noun* (1990).

Els Joglars is probably the oldest surviving experimental Catalan group. Its first performance was *Mimodrama* in 1963. It foregrounded pantomime, the visual "gag," and modern machinery full of surprising effects. In 1977 the performance of *La torna* led to the arrest of many of its members, who had to reunite in exile. Other shows by the group are The Odyssey (*L'Odissea*, 1979), *Teledeum* (1983), *Fontainebleau's Virtuous* (*Els virtuosos de Fontainebleau*, 1985), *Bye, Bye, Beethoven* (1987), *Columbus' Lapsus* (*Columbi lapsus*, 1989), and *The Retable of Wonders* (*El retablo de las maravillas*, 2004).

FURTHER READING

Berenguer, Ángel, and Manuel Pérez. "Tendencias del teatro español durante la transición política (1975–1982)." In *Historia del teatro español*, vol. 4. Madrid: Biblioteca Nueva, 1998.

Massip, Francesco. "Panorama del teatre catalá a finals del segon millenni." *Assaig de Teatre* (Barcelona: Associació d'Investigació i experimentació teatral) 32 (2002): 165–180.

Oliva, César. *Teatro español del siglo XX*. Madrid: Síntesis, 2002.

Pérez, Manuel. "Formas del teatro español actual: Génesis y renovación en el período transitorio." In *Teatro y antiteatro, la vanguardia del drama experimental: Actas de XV Congreso de Literatura Española Contemporánea*, ed. by Salvador Montesa. Málaga: AEDILE, 2002. 309–326.

Ragué-Arias, María José. *El teatro de fin de milenio en España (de 1975 hasta hoy)*. Barcelona: Ariel, 1996.

Sagarra, Joan de. "Entrevista a Albert Boadella." In *Teatro europeo de los 80*, ed. by Ángel Berenguer. Barcelona: Laila, 1983. 39–60.

Valázquez, Gerard. *El retratista*. Tarragona: Arola Editors, 2003.

Benito Gómez and Jorge Herreros

CATHLEEN NI HOULIHAN

Cathleen ni Houlihan is a political one-act play first performed in St. Teresa's Hall, Dublin, on April 2, 1902, with Maud Gonne, a famous beauty and anti-British agitator, in the title role. The performance is often taken as the beginning of the Irish National Theatre Society, later located at the Abbey Theatre. It is one of the first Irish plays to depict life in a peasant's cottage in a fashion that was understood to be neither comic nor sentimental.

The title of the play is one of the traditional names for IRELAND, imagined as a woman. It is set at the time of the 1798 rebellion of the United Irishmen against British rule and is located in a peasant's cottage near the place where French warships arrived to lend assistance to the rebellion. The son of the house, Michael Gillane, is about to be married when an old woman comes to the house. She is a mysterious, pained, and haunting figure. Her four beautiful green fields have been stolen by the stranger, she complains, but she warns that any man who helps her must be prepared to sacrifice everything. Many young men have died for her, many more will; the reward she promises is that they will be remembered forever. This transparent and incendiary allegory is puzzling to the other characters. Although his parents plead with him to stay home, Michael follows the old woman out as in a dream, as news comes that French troops have landed.

Out of all proportion to its length, the play had a powerful impact on Irish audiences throughout the period up to 1916, when there was a rebellion in Dublin. The play's logic of blood sacrifice and political martyrdom was praised and imitated by Irish writer and rebel Padraic Pearse. Since 1968 and the troubles in Northern Ireland the play has been condemned as a celebration of terrorism.

W. B. YEATS accepted praise as the author of the play. Certainly the idea for it was his, but manuscript evidence shows that most of the dialogue was the work of LADY GREGORY, who subsequently wrote quite similar plays, which Yeats never did. She ought to be at least credited as co-author of *Cathleen ni Houlihan.*

FURTHER READING

Gregory, Lady. *Lady Gregory: Selected Writings*. Ed. by Lucy McDiarmid and Maureen Waters. New York: Penguin, 1995.

Levitas, Ben. *The Theatre of Nation: Irish Drama and Cultural Nationalism, 1890–1916*. Oxford: Oxford Univ. Press, 2002.

Pethica, James. " 'Our Kathleen': Yeats's Collaboration with Lady Gregory in the Writing of *Cathleen ni Houlihan*." In *Yeats Annual* 6, ed. by Warwick Gould. London: Macmillan, 1988. 3–31.

Welch, Robert. *The Abbey Theatre, 1899–1999*. Oxford: Oxford Univ. Press, 1999.

Adrian Frazier

CAT ON A HOT TIN ROOF

I've lived with mendacity!—Why can't you live with it? Hell, you got to live with it, there's nothing else to live with except mendacity, is there?

—Act 2

TENNESSEE WILLIAMS received his second Pulitzer Prize in 1955 for the intense family drama *Cat on a Hot Tin Roof.* In the play the dramatist introduces a simplicity of form and clarity of theme not often present in his more complex "operatic" drama. The play, owing much to Freud's theories and the works of Williams's favorite writers, ANTON CHEKHOV and D. H. LAWRENCE, is set on the vast Pollitt plantation in the Mississippi Delta where the family patriarch, Big Daddy, is celebrating his sixty-fifth birthday with his wife, Big Mama, and their two adult sons, Gooper and Brick.

The joyful mood of the party is heightened by news that Big Daddy's recent ailments are not, as feared, stomach cancer, but merely a "spastic colon." The party's merriment is set against an undercurrent of marital strife, greed, and lingering fears about Big Daddy's health. Earlier, Brick, a former star athlete, attempted to jump hurdles in a drunken state. The resultant broken ankle has made him a captive in his bedroom, where Maggie, Brick's wife and a former beauty queen, exploits his immobility in an attempt to end their estrangement. Describing herself as a "cat on a hot tin roof," Maggie fears that Brick, the favored son of Big Daddy, will be disinherited should he fail to produce an heir. In fact, Brick, who displays no interest in Big Daddy's fortune or the feverish family machinations surrounding the battle for the estate, refuses to touch Maggie. Brick seeks only the "click" that comes when he has imbibed enough alcohol to render him senseless to the endless squabbles around him. His alcohol consumption is also an attempt to blot out the disturbing revelation that Skipper, his now-deceased team roommate, harbored homosexual desires for him. Questioning his own sexuality, Brick is mired in an alcohol-induced melancholic haze from which Maggie has been struggling to release him.

Meanwhile, Gooper, his wife Mae, and their children, described by Maggie as "no-neck monsters," are maneuvering to win Big Daddy's estate by highlighting Brick's incapacitating alcoholism and the assumption that no "son of Brick" will be forthcoming. Big Daddy confronts Brick about his drinking and general apathy to no avail. Both ruefully agree that "mendacity" is the way of the world, so Brick demonstrates his love for his father by leveling with the old man: Big Daddy does indeed have cancer. Big Daddy howls his rage and roars out into the stormy night, a Delta King Lear forced to face his mortality. In the play's final act the family comes together in Brick's room to battle out the future. In response to the barefaced greed of Gooper and Mae, Brick reluctantly goes along with a saving lie concocted by Maggie to comfort Big Daddy. She claims to be pregnant, and, therefore, the grandchild on whom Big Daddy has placed his hopes for the future will arrive in due course. The cat has leaped off the hot tin roof, and as the play ends, Maggie coaxes Brick back into their bed to make her lie into a truth.

Cat on a Hot Tin Roof opened for a long and critically applauded run at New York's Morosco Theatre on March 24, 1955. Under Elia Kazan's direction, the cast featured Barbara Bel Geddes as Maggie, Ben Gazzara as Brick, Mildred Dunnock as Big Mama, Pat Hingle as Gooper, Madeleine Sherwood as Mae, and Burl Ives in a memorable performance as Big Daddy. A significant disagreement between Williams and Kazan inspired a rewriting of the play's third act. In Williams's original Big Daddy does not reappear after dominating *Cat's* second act, which is essentially a long confrontation scene with Brick. Kazan persuaded Williams to find a way to bring Big Daddy back in the third act, fearing that his omission would disappoint the audience. This rewritten version was used for the original production, but in the subsequently published script Williams included both versions of the third act, inviting readers to decide on the most effective approach.

Cat on a Hot Tin Roof was awarded the Pulitzer Prize and numerous critics' awards. Although the homosexual issue in the play was removed entirely from *Cat's* 1958 film version starring Elizabeth Taylor, Paul Newman, and Burl Ives re-creating his stage performance, the film was critically well received and popular. *Cat* has often been revived on stage, most notably three times on Broadway. The play is one of Williams's most influential, paving the way for such later "Southern" dramatists as BETH HENLEY and HORTON FOOTE, as well as for playwrights from MART CROWLEY to TONY KUSHNER who, after the late 1960s, explored the previously taboo subject of homosexuality in their plays.

[*See also* United States, 1940–Present]

FURTHER READING

Bloom, Harold, ed. *Tennessee Williams's "Cat on a Hot Tin Roof."* Modern Critical Interpretations. New York: Chelsea House, 2002.

Crandell, George W. " 'Echo Springs': Reflecting the Gaze of Narcissus in Tennessee Williams's *Cat on a Hot Tin Roof*." *Modern Drama* 42, no. 3 (Fall 1999): 427–441.

Devlin, Albert J. "Writing in 'A Place of Stone': *Cat on a Hot Tin Roof*." In *The Cambridge Companion to Tennessee Williams*, ed. by Matthew C. Roudané. Cambridge: Cambridge Univ. Press, 1997. 95–113.

Loomis, Jeffrey B. "Four Characters in Search of a Company: Williams, Pirandello, and the *Cat on a Hot Tin Roof* Manuscripts." In *Magical Muse: Millennial Essays on Tennessee Williams*, ed. by Ralph F. Voss. Tuscaloosa: Univ. of Alabama Press, 2002. 91–110.

Parker, Brian. "A Preliminary Stemma for Drafts and Revisions of Tennessee Williams's *Cat on a Hot Tin Roof* (1955)." *Publications of the Bibliographical Society of America* 90, no. 4 (1996): 475–496.

Weimer, Christopher Brian. "Journeys from Frustration to Empowerment: *Cat on a Hot Tin Roof* and Its Debt to García Lorca's *Yerma*." *Modern Drama* 35 (1992): 520–529.

James Fisher

THE CAUCASIAN CHALK CIRCLE

BERTOLT BRECHT wrote *The Caucasian Chalk Circle* (*Der kaukasische Kreidekreis*) between 1943 and 1945 during his years as a refugee in the United States. In 1948 the play premiered at Carleton College in Minnesota in an English translation by Eric Bentley. *The Caucasian Chalk Circle* was first staged in GERMANY by the Berliner Ensemble in 1954 under the direction of the author.

The play begins with a prologue set in Soviet Georgia in the months after World War II. Two collective farms are contending for possession of a valley abandoned during the Nazi invasion. To celebrate the peaceful outcome of this dispute, the singer Arkadi Tscheide performs "The Chalk Circle," the story of a conflict between two mothers over the possession of a child.

The scene shifts to the "city of the damned" in ancient Grusinia, where the princes are organizing a coup d'état against the Grand Duke and his Governors. Meanwhile, Grusha, a servant, agrees to marry the soldier Simon.

During the coup the Governor's wife saves her finery but rushes off without her infant son, Michael. Grusha rescues the child and retreats with him to the northern mountains, encountering various perils on the way, including a band of Ironshirts who are trying to capture the Governor's heir. She flees across a decrepit bridge that collapses behind her, and finally finds refuge in a remote village. Simon tracks her down just as the Ironshirts arrive to carry her and Michael back to the capital, thus ending part 1.

Part 2 circles back to the day of the uprising. Azdak, a joking ironist and Brecht's mouthpiece in the play, inadvertently shelters the fleeing Grand Duke. Discovering his mistake, he runs to court to denounce himself, only to find that the judge has been hanged and the Ironshirts are in charge. As a joke they make Azdak the new judge. He promptly initiates a period of benign misrule during which he systematically discriminates in favor of the weak, the poor, and the victimized. However, the Grand Duke's faction returns to power, and Azdak is deposed and sentenced to death. At the last moment the Grand Duke himself, mindful of Azdak's earlier help, restores him to the bench.

Meanwhile, the Governor's wife, also restored to power, demands that Grusha return her son, heir to her husband's fortune. Azdak's reprieve allows him to judge the case, and once again he plays a joke on the system. He requires the contestants to stand in a chalk circle, each grasping one of Michael's arms, and perform a tug-of-war for possession of the boy. He then nullifies the physical victory of the Governor's wife and awards the child to the servant girl who rescued him.

Allegedly based on an ancient Chinese play, Brecht's text has little in common with the original. Instead, its antic humor and fairy-tale ending reflect the growing optimism of the period of its composition, the final years of the war, when the Nazi military machine was everywhere in retreat. *The Caucasian Chalk Circle* also looks forward to the postwar years, when Germany, torn between the competing political and economic systems of the East and the West, would be a prize claimed by irreconcilable adversaries, like the boy Michael himself. The Georgian prologue has been criticized on various counts. Some have taken offense at its implicit homage to Josef Stalin, a native of Georgia. Others have questioned its relevance to the rest of the play or have objected to its glowing portrayal of Soviet collective agriculture.

Particularly noteworthy is the two-part structure of the play: one half concentrating on Grusha, the other on Azdak. Many plays contain complementary and simultaneous story lines, but ordinarily, as in William Shakespeare, they are presented in alternating scenes. Brecht, in contrast, first tells Grusha's story and then circles back in time and tells Azdak's, connecting the two only at the end. This approach accentuates the contrasts in characterization and dramatic form between the two parts. The story of Grusha is largely narrated by the singer, who often speaks for the naïve servant girl in a voice more sophisticated than her own. The witty Azdak, on the other hand, speaks for himself. The Grusha story is thus more narrative in its presentation, the Azdak story more dramatic.

The 1954 production was an immense success both in Germany and abroad and helped secure Brecht's international reputation as a major playwright and director. For this staging Brecht sought the clarity, vitality, and energy of peasant art, specifically of the sort of nativity scene he recalled from his childhood, with its simple figures of Mary and Joseph and its richly arrayed Magi. Also notable was his use of masks to convey the "frozen faces" of the upper-class characters and his decision to have the actor Ernst Busch (1900–1980) double as the Singer and Azdak.

[*See also* Alienation Effect]

FURTHER READING

Esslin, Martin. *Brecht, a Choice of Evils: A Critical Study of the Man, His Work, and His Opinions*. 4th rev. ed. London: Methuen, 1984.

Fuegi, John. *Bertolt Brecht: Chaos, According to Plan*. Cambridge: Cambridge Univ. Press, 1987.

——. *The Essential Brecht*. Los Angeles: Hennessey & Ingalls, 1972.

Hayman, Ronald. *Brecht: A Biography*. New York: Oxford Univ. Press, 1983.

Martin Andrucki

CAVALCADE

Why is it that civilized humanity
Must make the world so wrong?
In this hurly burly of insanity
Your dreams cannot last long.
—Fanny Bridges, Part 3

After the success of PRIVATE LIVES NOËL COWARD wanted, in his words, to "test [his] production powers on a large scale" with a play about ENGLAND, inspired by old photographs and popular songs infused with his own memories of what had been a challenging past three decades for England. Premiering at the Theatre Royal, Drury Lane, in the autumn of 1931 and running for an incredible 405 performances, *Cavalcade* remains one of his most ambitious achievements, a chronicle of a waning empire grudgingly making the transition from the 19th century to the modern era. The play was marketed as "A Great Pageant" and boasted a cast of 250 performers, all dedicated to providing what Coward's biographer and friend Cole Lesley described as "an assault on the emotions and the senses" (Lesley, 1976).

Beginning on December 31, 1899, the dawning of a new century, the play chronicles major events in British history up to 1930 and allows the audience to view the Boer War, the death of Queen Victoria, the sinking of the *Titanic*, and World War I through the experiences of two families, the wealthy Marryots and the working-class Bridges clan. As matriarch Jane Marryot woefully remarks, "Time changes many things," and indeed, members of both families find their dreams dashed and desires unfulfilled in a world that seems increasingly out of their control and beyond their comprehension. Those who survive must deal with both the loss of loved ones and an image of their nation very much at odds with the modern world. *Cavalcade* concludes, appropriately enough, in a nightclub called Chaos and with a jazz rendition of Coward's song "Twentieth-Century Blues," whose lyrics are an evocative expression of the play's spirit and perhaps the feelings of Coward's generation, bewildered and bemused by the chaos of modern life: "In this strange illusion, / Chaos and confusion, / People seem to lose their way. / What is there to strive for? / Love, or keep alive for?" Among the ruins, Jane Marryot and her husband Robert endure with a measure of "hope that one day this country of ours, which we love so much, will find dignity and greatness and peace again," an optimism Coward certainly shared.

However, his concluding image, the entire company singing the National Anthem against a backdrop of a gigantic Union Jack, obscured the playwright's indictment of military imperialism. The play's initial audiences, witnessing potentially cataclysmic political maneuverings abroad and worldwide economic depression, seemed hungry for unabashed patriotism and greeted the play as a celebration of England's mythic (though perhaps now lost) past and its traditions, a response Coward later thought "cheapened" what he considered a more complex opportunity for cultural self-examination. Rather than awakening audiences to a crisis in social values and national definition, it was dismissed by many reviewers as mere conservative polemic, while enthusiastic viewers (including the king and queen and other members of the royal family) wept and applauded thunderously for a vision of England that was no longer tenable. An American film version was made in 1932; it won three Academy Awards, including Best Picture.

[*See also* England, 1860–1940]

FURTHER READING

Kaplan, Joel, and Sheila Stowell, eds. *Look Back in Pleasure: Noël Coward Reconsidered*. London: Methuen, 2000.

Lahr, John. *Coward, the Playwright*. London: Methuen, 1982.

Lesley, Cole. *Remembered Laughter: The Life of Noël Coward*. New York: Knopf, 1976.

Mander, Raymond, and Joe Mitchenson. *Theatrical Companion to Coward: A Pictorial Record of the Theatrical Works of Noël Coward*. 2d ed. London: Oberon Bks., 2000.

Christopher Wixson

CÉSAIRE, AIMÉ (1913–)

Poet, essayist, playwright, and politician Aimé Césaire was born in Basse-Point, Martinique, on June 25, 1913. As a scholarship student in Paris, he founded the literary journal *Black Student* (*Etudiant noir*) with Léopold Senghor. Heavily influenced by Arthur Rimbaud, SURREALISM, and the Harlem Renaissance, *Etudiant noir* gave rise to the *négritude* movement, which rejected FRANCE'S official policy of cultural assimilation and urged renewed pride in the heritage of Africa. Césaire's first major work was the prose poem *Notebook of a Return to My Native Land* (*Cahiers d'un retour au pays natal*, 1939). Césaire joined the French Communist Party and, returning to Martinique, was elected deputy mayor of Fort-de-France and deputy to the French Assembly, posts he held until 1993. During this time he became a major philosophical voice for anticolonialism, a position exemplified in his essay *Discourse on Colonialism* (*Discours sur le colonialisme*, 1950). Leaving the Communist Party in 1956, he founded the Martinican Progressive Party. Around this time his writing turned to drama. His first work was a stage version of a long dramatic poem, the intensely lyrical and surrealist *And the Dogs Were Silent* (*Et les chiens se taisaient*). This was followed in the 1960s by three plays that Césaire has described as a "triptych": *The Tragedy of King Christophe* (*Le tragédie du roi Christophe*), A SEASON IN THE CONGO (*Une saison au Congo*), and *A Tempest, After Shakespeare* (*Une tempête*), all of which were staged by the theater director Jean-Marie Serreau. Serreau's premature death in the early 1970s seems to have ended Césaire's interest in the drama, but many scholars consider these plays to be the high point of his literary output.

All of Césaire's plays feature black political rebels as their protagonists. In *And the Dogs* he is simply "the Rebel," a West Indian slave who has killed his master. The next two plays invoke historical figures: Jean Christophe, who founded a kingdom in northern Haiti after the death of Toussaint L'Ouverture, and, in *Congo*, the charismatic Patrice Lumumba, the first postcolonial leader of that nation. *A Tempest* takes the basic structure of William Shakespeare's late romance and, anticipating future productions and New Historicist readings of the play, makes the relationship between Caliban and Prospero the central metaphor of the play. All Césaire's protagonists except Caliban become martyrs to the cause of justice and humanity.

Césaire's stage work combines European DRAMATURGY, from Aeschylus to BERTOLT BRECHT, with elements of West African and Haitian voudon ritual. In *Christophe* Hugonin, the fool-character who remains by the protagonist's side, transforms in the end into an Ogoun, a god. Eshu, god of chaos, intrudes himself amid the Latin goddesses of Prospero's masque in *A Tempest*. Although *And the Dogs* is rarely performed today, the others receive regular revivals in France and elsewhere, and Césaire remains an essential figure in postcolonial studies: *A Tempest*, in particular, is a frequent subject of scholarly discussion on postcolonial drama.

PLAYS: *And the Dogs Were Silent* (*Et les chiens se taisaient*, 1956); *The Tragedy of King Christophe* (*Le tragédie du roi Christophe*, 1963); *A Season in the Congo* (*Une saison au Congo*, 1966, revised 1967); *A Tempest, After Shakespeare* (*Une tempête*, 1969)

FURTHER READING

Bailey, Marianne Wichmann. *The Ritual Theater of Aimé Césaire: Mythic Structures of the Dramatic Imagination*. Tübingen: Gunter Narr, 1992.

Césaire, Aimé. *A Season in the Congo*. Tr. by Ralph Manheim. In *Theater and Politics: An International Anthology*. New York: Ubu Repertory Theatre, 1990.

——. *A Tempest*. Tr. by Richard Miller. New York: Ubu Repertory Theatre, 1985.

Davis, Gregson. *Aimé Césaire*. Cambridge: Cambridge Univ. Press, 1997.

Palliser, Janis L. *Aimé Césaire*. New York: Twayne, 1991.

Walter Bilderback

CHAIKA See THE SEAGULL

CHAKRAVYUHA See ARMY FORMATION

CHALALONGKORA, KING See RAMA V

CHAMBER PLAYS

In a strict sense the term "chamber play" refers to five short plays by AUGUST STRINDBERG. *Thunder in the Air* (*Oväder*), *The Burned House* (*Brända tomten*), THE GHOST SONATA (*Spöksonaten*), and *The Pelican* (*Pelikanen*) were all written and published in 1907 and performed at Strindberg's own Intimate Theater in Stockholm in that year or, in the case of *The Ghost Sonata*, the year after. A fifth play, *The Black Glove* (*Svarta handsken*), written in 1908, was published and first performed in 1909.

Inspired by MAX REINHARDT's Kammerspiel-Haus in Berlin, which opened in 1906, Strindberg, together with the young director August Falck, founded the Intimate Theater in Stockholm in 1907. For this theater, which lasted only three years, he wrote his five chamber plays, as well as a stream of directorial notes. In a letter to Adolf Paul in January 1907 he explains that a chamber play should be "intimate in form, with a restricted subject, treated in depth, few characters, large points of view, free imagination, but based on observation, experience, carefully studied; simple, but not too simple; no great apparatus, no superfluous minor roles, no regular five-acters or 'old machines,' no long-drawn-out whole evenings" (Strindberg, 1992). And in his *Notes to the Members of the Intimate Theater* the following year he declares: "In drama we seek the strong, highly significant theme, but with limitations. We try to avoid in the treatment all frivolity, all calculated effects, places for applause, star roles, solo numbers. No particular form shall bind the author, for the theme dictates the form. Consequently, freedom in treatment, which is limited only by the unity of the concept and the feeling for style" (Strindberg, 1959). Seeing these plays as "chamber music transposed to drama," Strindberg provided each of them with an opus number and possibly meant their unnamed parts to recall the movements of chamber music. Also, the thematic orientation and the use of leitmotifs lead one's thoughts in the direction of chamber music.

In all the chamber plays a modern apartment house figures prominently, partly because Strindberg himself lived in such a house but more importantly because with its many separate dwellings and different inhabitants, it could serve as a fitting symbol for the world at large. The facade of the house functions as a pretty mask hiding all the shortcomings characteristic of mankind.

In *Thunder in the Air* the old Gentleman, Strindberg's alter ego, lives alone, attended by a young servant, Louise. His brother, the Consul, reveals to him that the new tenants upstairs, who disturb "the peace of old age," are the Gentleman's former wife, Gerda, her new husband, and Gerda's and the Gentleman's little daughter. When Gerda's present husband threatens to exploit the Confectioner's teenage daughter, the Gentleman, largely with the help of the Consul, manages to undo her husband's scheme. Gerda and her daughter are saved. At the end three old men wait for the first street lantern to be lit, the sign that autumn, death, is approaching.

The Burned House (also called *After the Fire*) is about the Stranger who after thirty years in America returns to the house of his childhood, only to find that it has just burned down. The house had been located in an area called the Swamp, where everybody is involved, mostly negatively, with everybody else until he or she ends up in the close-by cemetery. Various people are suspected of incendiarism, but the Stranger, more inclined to see the hand of "the World Weaver" in what has happened, believes that behind it all is a secret plan unknown to man. In the frequent soliloquies given to the Stranger, Strindberg abstains from the naturalistic motivation he pleaded for in the preface to MISS JULIE.

The pelican is said to give of its own blood to sustain its young ones. *The Pelican* shows the opposite, a mother who deprives her children of nourishment so that they grow weak, while she herself stuffs herself with food. Related to the Cook in *The Ghost Sonata*, the Mother in *The Pelican* is another vampire, sucking the life of others. At the end of the play the Son sets fire to the house. The Mother tries to save herself by jumping from the balcony. Her son and daughter prefer to die in the flames. As they are consumed by the fire, they regress to happy childhood memories of summers in the archipelago with their parents.

Lighter in tone and less important than the other chamber plays is *The Black Glove*, the story of a nasty young wife whose daughter is kidnapped by fairy creatures inhabiting the modern apartment house, which is patterned on Strindberg's last dwelling.

[*See also* Sweden]

FURTHER READING

Ekman, Hans-Göran. *Strindberg and the Five Senses: Studies in Strindberg's Chamber Plays*. London: Athlone Press, 2000.

Lindström, Göran. "Strindberg's Chamber Play, Opus 2, *After the Fire*." In *Essays on Strindberg*, ed. by Carl Reinhold Smedmark. Stockholm: Beckman, 1966. 49–64.

Sprinchorn, Evert. Introduction to *The Chamber Plays*, by August Strindberg. New York: Dutton, 1962. vii–xxiv.

Strindberg, August. *Open Letters to the Intimate Theater*. Tr. and ed. by Walter Johnson. Seattle: Univ. of Washington Press, 1959.

Strindberg, August. *Strindberg's Letters*. Tr. and ed. by Michael Robinson. Chicago: Univ. of Chicago Press, 1992.

Törnqvist, Egil. *Strindbergian Drama: Themes and Structure*. Stockholm: Almqvist & Wiksell International, 1982.

Wilkinson, Lynn R. "The Politics of the Interior: Strindberg's Chamber Plays." *Scandinavian Studies* 65, no. 4 (1993): 463–486.

Egil Törnqvist

CHAN, ANTHONY (1953–)

Anthony Chan (Chan Kam-kuen), a playwright, director, set designer, and translator for the stage in Hong Kong, was born in Hong Kong and graduated with his bachelor's degree and master's degree in theater studies and fine arts from the University of Colorado at Denver. He worked as art director at the Denver Children's Museum and, upon his return to Hong Kong, took up the post of stage manager with the Hong Kong Repertory Theatre. He started teaching drama at the Hong Kong Academy for Performing Arts and in 1994 was appointed head of directing and playwriting at the School of Drama at the academy.

Chan has written thirty-five original plays, adapted five plays from novels, and translated twenty-two scripts. He has also written six film scripts. Of his original plays, a short piece, *Hong Kong Heartbeat*, was staged as part of the Hong Kong Festival in London in 1992 and in Toronto in 1993. In 1992 Chan's *Nuwa Mends the Sky* (*Nuwa*) won the Outstanding Original Script Award from the Council for Performing Arts and then toured Tarascon and Bordeaux in FRANCE in the same year. In 1994 Chan received the Outstanding Achievement of the Decade Award from the Hong Kong Federation of Drama Societies. *The Call of the White Orchid* (*Bailan de huhuan*), which was workshopped in the Shenarts Playwright Retreat in Virginia, was one of the plays that received the Top Ten Most Popular Plays Award of 1997 when it was produced in Hong Kong. This play has remained one of Chan's plays that has received the most acclaim from critics. The story is set in 1977 against the true story of an incident of corruption in a school. The play conveys a sense of nostalgia for the sprit of the student movement in the colonial 1970s. It also offers a reflection on the disillusionment many of that generation felt toward the anticolonial idealism represented by this school that insisted on the use of Chinese rather than the colonial language of English as the medium of instruction. In 2001 Chan's play *The Legend of the White Snake* (*Xianshe jingmeng*) was performed in the Second Experimental Theatre Festival in Shanghai.

Chan demonstrates versatility in the handling of subject matter, as well as style. His early success *Metamorphosis Under the Stars* (*Xingguang xia de tubian*, 1986) is a short lyrical piece on personal relationships. In his *1841* (*Yibasiyi*, 1985) and *1941* (*Yijiusiyi*, 1986) he reviews in episodic scenes the history of Hong

Kong in light of the topical political issue of the return of Hong Kong's sovereignty to China. In *American House* (*Dawu*, 1991) the same topical issue for Chinese people living in Hong Kong and abroad is explored in a well-structured realistic drama. In his later plays such as *Nuwa Mends the Sky* and *The Legend of the White Snake*, which were performed outside Hong Kong and therefore before audiences not familiar with the Hong Kong Cantonese dialect, he chose to rework myths and legends and placed more emphasis on visual elements, sound, and movement than on speech. This versatility does not come as a surprise since Chan has rich experience in the translation and adaptation of plays for performance and is an experienced director and set designer, as well as teacher of drama.

[*See also* China]

SELECT PLAYS: *1841* (*Yibasiyi*, 1985); *Metamorphosis Under the Stars* (*Xingguangxia de tuibian*, 1986); *American House* (*Dawu*, 1990); *Hong Kong Heartbeat* (*Xianggang xin lian xin*, 1992); *Nüwa Mends the Sky* (*Nüwa*, 1992); *Johnny Got His Gun* (*Qingwei shengmingxian*, 1995); *1941* (*Yijiusiyi*, 1997); *The Call of the White Orchid* (*Bailan huhuan*, 1997); *Husband's Hideaway* (*Jinwu canggong*, 1999); *Formula of the Thunderstorm* (*Zhoumen jiashi*, 2000)

FURTHER READING

Chan, Anthony. *American House*. Tr. by H. L. Kwok. In *An Oxford Anthology of Contemporary Chinese Drama*, ed. by Martha Cheung and Jane Lai. Hong Kong: Oxford Univ. Press, 1997. 750–824.

Fong, Gilbert, and Hardy Tsoi, eds. *Xianggang huaju lunwen ji* [Essays on Hong Kong theater]. Hong Kong: High Noon Production Co., 1992.

Yeung, Jessica, ed. *Luodi kaihua: Xianggang xiju yijiujiujiu* [Down to earth: Hong Kong drama 1999]. Hong Kong: International Association of Theatre Critics, 2001.

Jane Lai and Jessica Yeung

CHAN, JOANNA (1939–)

Joanna Chan (Chan Wan-ying) was born in 1939 and grew up in Guangzhou, CHINA. She later moved to Hong Kong, where she studied at Chung Chi College of the Chinese University of Hong Kong, majoring in mathematics. She then studied theology in the Philippines and art and design at the Art Institute of Chicago. She received her M.A., M.Ed., and Ed.D. in theater and communications from Teachers' College, Columbia University, where she was appointed adjunct associate professor in 1982 and honored with a Distinguished Alumni Award in 1994.

Chan's theater career spans over thirty years in the UNITED STATES, CANADA, Hong Kong, China, and Taiwan. She was cofounder and artistic director (1970–1977 and 1983–1992) of the Four Seas Players in New York City and artistic director (1986–1990) of the Hong Kong Repertory Theatre. In 1992 she cofounded the Yangtze Repertory Theatre of America to produce works for and by Asian artists. The fifty productions written, adapted, and directed by her for arts festivals and major arts events in Hong Kong and elsewhere include *Othello*, *The Match Maker*, *The King and I*, *Cabaret*, *Dream of the Red Chamber*, and Hong Kong playwright RAYMOND TO's *Where Love Abides* (*Renjian youqing*), which she took to China in 1987.

Chan began writing plays in 1975. Her major works include *Before the Dawn Wind Rises* (*Shei xi guyuan xin*, 1985), a play that reflects the relationship between Hong Kong and China in view of the 1997 handover, commissioned by the Hong Kong Urban Council for the Tenth Asian Arts Festival, an English version of which has been published in *An Oxford Anthology of Contemporary Chinese Drama* (1997). Consistent with Chan's style shown in her other works, *Before the Dawn Wind Rises* is a realistic play. It tells the story of reunion between two brothers: one lives in Hong Kong and the other in mainland China in the years of turmoil during the early People's Republic. The complex relationship of the two territories is embodied in both the intimacy and the estrangement between the two brothers. Another play, *Crown Ourselves with Roses* (*Hua jin gaolou*, 1988), toured North America in 1989. It was cited by the *Asian Wall Street Journal* as "a tour de force of our time" and republished in Beijing in 1994. Her other works include *The Soongs: By Dreams Betrayed* (1992), a political drama published in Hong Kong and premiered in New York (2003); *Forbidden City West* (1994), a musical that examines 100 years of Chinese American experience; *The Story of Yuhuan* (1998); *Butterfly Dreams* (1999); and *OneFamilyOneChildOneDoor* (2000), a black COMEDY in both English and Chinese versions, set in southern China, about the problems of having one child. The play was named one of the top winners of the 2001 Jane Chambers Playwriting Award. A member of the Dramatists Guild in the United States, Chan is well known for her dedicated promotion of Chinese culture and the sharing of the Chinese experience in America, and in 1993 she was honored at "An All-Star Salute to Chinese American Cultural Pioneers" at city hall, New York City.

PLAYS: *Before the Dawn Wind Rises* (1985); *Crown Ourselves with Roses* (1988); *The Soongs: By Dreams Betrayed* (1992); *Forbidden City West* (1994); *The Story of Yuhuan* (1998); *Butterfly Dreams* (1999); *OneFamilyOneChildOneDoor* (2000)

FURTHER READING

Chan, Joanna. *Before the Dawn Wind Rises*. Tr. by Jane Lai. In *An Oxford Anthology of Contemporary Chinese Drama*, ed. by Martha Cheung and Jane Lai. Hong Kong: Oxford Univ. Press, 1997.

———. "Towards the Limpid Side of Life." In *Hong Kong Repertory Theatre 10th Anniversary*. Hong Kong: Urban Council, 1988.

Jane Lai and Jessica Yeung

CHANCE

Chance has been viewed in two seemingly mutually exclusive ways in the modern era. First, chance has been understood as a revelation of hidden order. This view has been favored by dramatists; after all, drama is threatened by unscripted events such as the collapse of an entrance ramp, the burning out of a stage light, or the absence of a page in the promptbook. In this respect chance serves as window dressing for fate. Sophocles' Oedipus wound up in Thebes by "chance"; AMIRI BARAKA's Lula and Clay meet by "chance" in a subway station in DUTCHMAN (1964). Even after the first pure chance artistic methods were tested by the Zürich dadaists during the 1910s, chance continued to be viewed as essentially unrandom. Carl Jung denied the randomness of chance with his notion of "synchronicity." Viola Spolin created theater games designed to take the chance suggestions of improvisation and maneuver them into compelling form. The Situationist International walked across Paris seemingly at random, searching for "psychogeographical situations" that might reveal the hidden order of capitalist repression. TOM STOPPARD's ROSENCRANTZ AND GUILDENSTERN ARE DEAD (1966) best captures the dramatic paradox of chance: two secondary characters in the grand tragedy of William Shakespeare's *Hamlet* marvel at a sequence of coin flips that keep coming up heads.

On the other hand is a less orderly notion of chance. Charles Baudelaire, Stéphane Mallarmé, FRIEDRICH NIETZSCHE, and Walter Benjamin all exercised the metaphor of gambling in their work. In response to the chaos of World War I, Tristan Tzara invented a poetic method in which a newspaper is cut into words and phrases, then reassembled at random. The surrealists were inspired by Sigmund Freud (the "accidental" slip of the tongue, the "arbitrary" use of the day's matter in the dreamwork) and Friedrich Engels (the "objective chance" that ties together historical tendency and accident). Under such influences they created critical-creative games such as "Exquisite Corpse," a blind group poem. A range of chance methods (*frottage*, *decalcomania*, *fumage*, and so on) were used by surrealist visual artists. GERTRUDE STEIN created CLOSET DRAMAS that demanded a high degree of attention and creativity from their readers, rendering chance situationally variable. John Cage and the creative communities of Black Mountain College, the New School for Social Research, and Rutgers University explored chance composition in the 1950s and early 1960s, often as a consequence of studying Eastern philosophy. For some, chance deobjectified the art work, turning it into a "happening." Allan Kaprow, the coiner of that term, and the Fluxus and mail-art communities used chance activity to defamiliarize objects, gestures, and everyday events, opening them to unexpected combinations. All of this is quite unlike the "dramatic" uses of chance.

Recent work in the fields of quantum and chaos theory has deconstructed these two perspectives. Apparently chance-governed events possess profound patterning structures; conversely, all things are prone to unpredictable crisis.

[*See also* Dadaism; Happenings and Intermedia; Surrealism]

FURTHER READING

Briggs, John C., and David F. Peat. *Turbulent Mirror: An Illustrated Guide to Chaos Theory and the Science of Wholeness*. New York: HarperCollins, 1990.

Demastes, William W. *Theatre of Chaos: Beyond Absurdism Into Orderly Disorder*. Cambridge: Cambridge Univ. Press, 1997.

Mike Sell

CHANDRAPRABHA, SOMPOP (1919–1987)

Soil engineer Sompop Chandraprabha grew up in a noble house where the theater tradition of the era of RAMA V (King Chulalongkorn) was alive, and his aunt was a famous novelist. Beginning in 1957, he wrote over fiftyeight plays, including fourtytwo 42 television dramas, that brought to life heroes of legend and history. His works show more interest in dramatic impact than strict historical accuracy. His writings include ten spoken dramas (*lakon phud*) in prose, twenty-two plays in the dance-operetta style (*lakon dukdamban*), and four spoken dramas enhanced by song and dance (*lakon phud slab ram*). He also adapted plays by others or from classical Thai literature. He established the television drama production company Chat Keo (Crystal Umbrella) in 1971. His play *Princess Supankalya* (*Supankalya*, 1970) impressed Queen Sirikit, who gave the company patronage, commissioning performances for soldiers and police during the royal family's annual visits to provincial palaces.

Sompop Chandraprabha's work is strongly nationalistic, a response to the Communist insurgency of the period. He targeted young adult audiences with his simple, bold language, his satire, and short, consecutive scenes. His costuming set a standard, using historically accurate clothing. Plays began with a long introduction of characters and context, built into quick scenes, and ended at a climax. He challenged the usual divinized portrayal of former rulers, presenting them with both positive and negative traits.

Pra Yod of Muang Kwang is an example of his spoken plays. Set in the 19th century as the French are trying to occupy Laos, then a vassal state of THAILAND, it shows the hero Pra Yod defeating the French in a battle. The French demand imprisonment of the hero, and King Chulalongkorn must reluctantly accede. Another work is *Crystal Umbrella* (*Chat keo*), a spoken drama with music and dance interludes, which depicts the abolition of slavery. In it Ho, a male slave with a brutal master, learns that King Chulalongkorn has abolished slavery and attempts to flee. Captured, the bleeding Ho dreams in the night of freedom in an interlude presented in modern dance style. *Nang Sueng*, named after its heroine, was done in *dukdamban* style with realistic sets and historically accurate costumes. It tells the story of Queen Sueng, who lived in the Sukhotai period (early 1800s). She helps her husband ward off Cambodian overlords who have seized Sukhothai and are conscripting Thais to build temples. This work of 1968 delivered a message of Thai independence as the Southeast

Asian war was escalating. Classicists took umbrage at the presentation of history, but audiences raved.

King Si Thammasokarat (*Si Thammasokarat*, 1972), one of Sampop's most frequently produced works, tells the story of Prince Si Thamma, who goes to pay tribute to the kingdom of Sriwijaya in Sumatra and falls in love with Princess Kusuma, who helps save his kingdom from invaders in her disguise as a male general. *Dis-united* (*Samakkipet*, 1977), a spoken drama with song to highlight emotional points, is based on a Buddhist chronicle. A-Chat-Satru, an Indian king, hopes to unify the states of Lit-Cha-Wee. He sends his minions to undermine these states and wins the war without a fight. Political strategies in politically complex worlds are the concern of many of Chandraprabha's works. Selected plays by him are performed to the present day, including *King Si Thammasokarat* and *Dis-united*.

SELECT PLAYS: *Pra Yod of Muang Kwang* (1973); *Nang Sueng* (1968); *Princess Supankalya* (*Supankalya*, 1970); *Crystal Umbrella* (*Chat keo*, 1967), *King Si Thammasokarat* (*Si Thammasokarat*, 1972); *Dis-united* (*Samakkipet*, 1977)

FURTHER READING

Duangpatra, Jackrit. "Plays by Sompop Chandraprabha" [in Thai]. Thesis, Sri Nakarindrawirot Univ. (Bangkok), 1989.

Surapone Virulrak

CHARANDAS CHOR

See CHARANDAS THE THIEF

CHARANDAS THE THIEF

Charandas the Thief (*Charandas Chor*), first performed in 1975, is the most acclaimed of HABIB TANVIR's plays. Its remarkable fusion of form and content and of fun and frolic and scathing social comment has made the play a classic of the contemporary Indian stage. It is adapted, with significant modifications, from a Rajasthani folktale. The production evolved from a protracted process of experimentation and improvisation and in close collaboration with village actors and poets from Chattisgarh. Thus it also represents an excellent example of the particular style of theater Tanvir has developed over the years.

The play tells the story of Charandas, an extraordinary thief who is truthful and honest. In gratitude to a religious guru who shelters him from the policeman, Charandas jokingly makes four pledges: never to allow himself to be taken in a grand procession, never to eat off a golden plate, never to marry a princess and become king, and never to tell a lie. Ironically, the thief finds himself in situations that compel him to live up to these promises. His last pledge of truthfulness costs him his life. The queen orders his execution for refusing to keep the fact of her amorous advances toward him a secret. The scene that follows Charandas's death dramatizes the devotion and reverence that he has evoked in the common people, who virtually deify him as they file past his shrine offering flowers. This gesture is put in a sharp social perspective by the concluding song—"A thief earned fame by his truthfulness"—by recapitulating the play's central irony: an honest and truthful thief in the midst of a degenerate and corrupt environment ruled by cruel landlords, greedy gurus, corrupt cops and officials, and a tyrannical queen. It is this irony that makes the play a subversive parable about our times. Since its first staging a number of outstanding folk actors have performed the title role and made Charandas memorable as a hilariously clever clown who holds a critical mirror to society.

Songs are a major element in the play. They have a simplicity of style and expression and are rich in humor, irony, and incisive social comment. They are set to delightful folk tunes and enhance the play's pleasurability in performance.

Charandas the Thief is Tanvir's most frequently performed and widely traveled production. In 1982 it received the Fringe First Award at the Edinburgh Festival in the United Kingdom.

[*See also* India]

FURTHER READING

Tanvir, Habib. *Charan the Thief*. Tr. by Anjum Katyal. Calcutta: Seagull Books, 1995.

Javed Malick

CHARLEY'S AUNT

Brazil . . . where the nuts come from.

—Repeated by multiple characters

The original production of (Walter) Brandon Thomas's three-act, ten-character FARCE *Charley's Aunt* ran for years; it has been translated and performed in many languages, including Afrikaans, Esperanto, Gaelic, and Zulu; several adaptations have been made for film and television; a musical version, *Where's Charley?* received audience approval; the text has been reprinted several times; constantly revived during the last century, the play continues to be regularly performed by both amateur and professional companies.

Charley's Aunt is the quintessential Victorian farce. Its endurance contrasts with the comparative failure of Thomas's dozen other plays. Rehearsals for the first production were fraught. At the eleventh hour Thomas used a solicitor's threats to prevent W. S. Penley (playing Lord Fancourt) from interpolating his own jokes. Thomas won this battle for his play's integrity, and the first performance took place at London's Royalty Theatre on December 21, 1892. Acting as Sir Thomas Chesney, Thomas saw the production receive immediate commercial success: the run lasted for four years. Thomas later played Lord Fancourt in a revival. The play is set in Oxford during 1892 and centers on the pleasure seeking of three undergraduates, Fancourt, Jack Chesney, and Charles (Charley) Wykeham. The latter two seek the hands of two young women: Amy and Kitty remain inaccessible to Charles and Jack because their ward, Stephen Spettigue, objects to the undergraduates' financial impecuniousness. But Charles has a rich aunt who resides in Brazil: she would promise wealth for Spettigue if Charles would marry. To acquire Spettigue's agreement, Fancourt, already dressed for a theatrical performance, is pushed into impersonating "Charley's Aunt." The farce thrives, as it is readily apparent to the audience that Fancourt mimics "Charley's Aunt" very unconvincingly (his dress slips, he is caught smoking a cigar when still in drag, and his only knowledge of Brazil is that it is "where the nuts come from"), but the young women and Spettigue are hoodwinked. Dramatic irony features heavily: Amy and Kitty enjoy "Charley's Aunt's" company, while Fancourt enjoys the tactile closeness to them that his female guise allows. The real aunt of Charley, Donna Luca, returns from Brazil and amusedly observes Fancourt's impersonation, then choreographs the happy ending: the play ends on a romantic high, with four marriage vows. But it is the two characters who do not get betrothed who represent the play's dark, loose ends. Spettigue, the victim of the hoax, has successfully proposed to Fancourt in his guise of "Charley's Aunt" and is distraught when he comprehends the deception. Malvolio-like, he ends the play swearing revenge. The carefulness, common sense, plain dealing, and resourcefulness of the butler, Brassett, contrasts with the mendaciousness and disorganization of the undergraduates. The disparity between the exploitation of Brassett and the lucky, work-free circumstances of Charles, Jack, and Fancroft suggests that the class system retains money and privilege for certain families, rewarding undeserving persons, whereas other, more useful members of society remain economically and socially marginalized. Despite this clear social comment, scholars generally ignore *Charley's Aunt*; theatergoers, contrarily, continue to be entertained by its fast-paced vivacity.

[*See also* Comedy; England, 1860–1940]

FURTHER READING

Abbott, G., and F. Loesser. *Where's Charley? A Musical Comedy*. London: Edwin H. Morris, 1964.

Davis, Jessica Milner. *Farce*. London: Methuen, 1978.

Souvenir of Charley's Aunt by Brandon Thomas, 1892–1952. London: Brandon Thomas Co., 1952.

Thomas, Brandon. *Charley's Aunt*. 1892. "Updated" ed. by Thomas's estate, 1935. Restored version, ed. by E. R. Wood. London: Heinemann, 1969.

Thomas, J. B. *Charley's Aunt's Father: A Life of Brandon Thomas*. London: D. Saunders, 1955.

Kevin De Ornellas

CHEKHOV, ANTON (1860–1904)

One of the world's greatest dramatists, Anton Chekhov was born on January 17/29, 1860, in provincial Taganrog, which on the surface seemed an inauspicious environment for a future playwright and short-story writer. Nor did his family background portend a literary career: His grandfather had been a serf, and his father had risen to become a merchant of the third guild by the time of Chekhov's birth. However, many of the qualities that later led to Chekhov's success originate in his family background. For example, his grandfather bought his family out of serfdom years before the emancipation, and Chekhov was heir to his grandfather's determination, independence, and capacity for hard work. Not every quality of his family affected Chekhov positively. His father was by all accounts an overbearing and sometimes brutal man, and Chekhov's intuitive revulsion against violence surely finds its origin here. The third of his parents' seven children, Chekhov often said that his childhood was no childhood.

Given all the problems at home, school offered, if not an escape, an alternative. Chekhov's father supported his children's education as a practical measure, convinced that an education would translate into lucrative jobs. Assessments of the quality of the *gimnaziia* in Taganrog differ sharply. What seems clear is that Chekhov received an education that was based on a classical model, yet severely restricted exposure to contemporary subjects with any political content, even literature. Although Chekhov did not excel as his elder brother Aleksandr did, he made a distinct impression on fellow students and teachers, who remembered him for his humorous and sometimes caustic witticisms.

The very existence of a *gimnaziia* in Taganrog points to the town's unusual resources, in part because of its significance as a port on the Sea of Azov, in part because of its ties to the tsar. Were it not Chekhov's birthplace, Taganrog would be best remembered as the city in which Aleksandr I died. Among its institutions was a theater, in which Chekhov's lifelong fascination with *Hamlet* and his acquaintance with the work of the great Russian dramatist ALEKSANDR OSTROVSKY began. Until his health interfered, Chekhov participated avidly in the town's amateur theatrical life, acting in such plays as Nikolai Gogol's *The Inspector General*.

With the failure of his father's business, the family moved to Moscow, but left Chekhov behind to finish the *gimnaziia*. He eventually joined them and enrolled in the medical school of Moscow University. His father never really recovered from the failure of his business, and responsibility fell increasingly on Chekhov's shoulders. In order to support himself and his family, Chekhov, like his elder brother, began to write comic pieces for humor publications, with his first pieces appearing in March 1880.

Even before his first publications he embarked on writing plays while still at the *gimnaziia*. His brother Aleksandr mentions the titles of three dramas in a letter from 1878. Despite the consistent effort this implies and perhaps because his last four dramatic masterpieces have garnered so much attention, a misconception about Chekhov as a dramatist has arisen. Critics sometimes portray the playwright as a short-story writer who turned to drama late in his career and adduce a half-dozen stories he dramatized as further evidence. In reality, Chekhov's engagement in theater and drama preceded his first forays into fiction by many years, and in many regards he was a dramatist who turned to prose fiction in order to support his family. His reliance on prose fiction for financial support owes in part to the state of theater at that time. No one, not even Ostrovsky himself, was able to make a living solely by writing for the stage.

This circumstance in no way dampened Chekhov's enthusiasm for theater. He continued to write drama, and his first surviving work for the stage dates from 1878. The manuscript of the play, which is usually called PLATONOV, was found among Chekhov's papers after his death. Although deeply flawed, *Platonov* sheds light on Chekhov's early conception of drama and demonstrates the enormous creative distance he traveled to reach a play like THE SEAGULL. Unlike the later masterpieces, *Platonov* relies on what has been called direct action, or the representation of overtly dramatic incidents, for its effect. The influence of the so-called well-made play is apparent in the way that each act ends with a shocking dramatic event. If the resulting play is somewhat hackneyed, it nonetheless contains many of Chekhov's later themes. Platonov is the first in a series of superfluous men—ineffectual nobleman who are keenly aware of their own lack of purpose—who parade through Chekhov's work. Tied to this is the play's examination of the decaying nobility. Yet in form the play is weak and ungainly, far removed from the economy of Chekhov's best work. The young playwright pinned his hopes for a production on the Maly Theater and took *Platonov* to the famous actress Maria Ermolova, who rejected it. Chekhov never returned to it.

In the meantime Chekhov continued to study medicine and to write humorous stories, anecdotes, and even a regular column. The early work is often characterized as ephemera; however, if the work was ephemeral, the process was not. The early work served as a creative laboratory in which Chekhov experimented with prose form and narrative technique. The rigor imposed by a punch line enforced an economy of means that, together with the concision and clarity of his exposition and the precision of his prose, would become a hallmark of Chekhov's later writing. Nonetheless, Chekhov saw writing in primarily utilitarian terms and signed most of these pieces with pseudonyms.

Chekhov's medical studies contributed significantly to his literary development. A dispassionate appraisal of symptoms coupled with a compassionate engagement in the patient's life characterizes not only Dr. Chekhov, but Chekhov the writer. Medical practice afforded him an intimate look into the lives of a wide range of people from throughout the socioeconomic spectrum. Chekhov had the opportunity to observe people and their reactions at moments of crisis. After his graduation in 1884 Chekhov's interest in medicine continued unabated, but he devoted himself more and more to writing.

Over time his prose grew in seriousness and purpose and quickly outgrew the humor magazines. Glimmers of this process became apparent in two early novels, *Unneeded Victory* (*Nenuzhnaia pobeda*, 1882) and a mystery, *The Shooting Party* (*Drama na okhote*, 1884–1885), which, although not on par with his later work, nonetheless demonstrate the young writer's growing ambition. With encouragement from the editor Aleksei Suvorin and the writer Dmitry Grigorovich, Chekhov tackled more complex themes in his stories, and his attitude toward himself as a writer changed as he began to take himself and his work more seriously. By 1886 he had begun to sign his work with his own name.

The transition from the early humorous pieces to genuine short stories occurred gradually, but most critics concur that Chekhov's so-called middle period begins in the mid-1880s. A decided shift in perspective defines the work of this period. Whereas the earlier writing treated characters from the outside for satiric purposes, the stories of the middle period explore characters' consciousness from within. Many seem to emanate from Chekhov's own experience of childhood abuse and concern the predicament and travails of the powerless, especially children. In stories such as "Vanka" (1886) and "I Need to Sleep" ("Spat' khochetsia," 1888), Chekhov's dispassionate approach paradoxically evokes a deeply emotional, yet unsentimental response. By 1884 book-length collections of his stories began to appear at regular intervals. Recognition soon followed, and Chekhov received the Pushkin Prize in 1887.

As his renown grew, so did the pressure. Increasingly critics saw Chekhov as the heir to the mantle of the great novelists Ivan Turgenev, Feodor Dostoevsky, and LYOV TOLSTOY and demanded a novel from the short-story writer. An error in critical judgment—the dominant genre for Chekhov's generation was the short story—it nonetheless exacted a real effect in Chekhov's increased interest in larger prose forms. The most notable result was the long story *The Steppe* (*Step'*, 1888). In it Chekhov drew on a trip undertaken in childhood with his brother to visit his grandparents to portray the consciousness of a young boy as he takes in a new and changing environment. The story's radical subjectivism in point of view and its diminishment of plot in favor of a drama of consciousness veer away from the conventions of the realist novel. Nonetheless, *The Steppe* marked an entry into literary journals proper.

Chekhov's passion for drama continued undiminished, and his development as a dramatist was analogous to his development as a short-story writer: After *Platonov* smaller and often comic forms provided the budding playwright a proving ground. From 1884 until the early 1890s Chekhov wrote nearly a dozen one-act plays, the majority of which he referred to as either "dramatic etudes" or "jokes in one act." Both generic markers point to the experimental nature of these works. In some instances Chekhov relied on earlier stories for source material. For example, *On the Highway* (*Na bol'shoi doroge*, 1884) derives from the story "In the Autumn" ("Osen'iu," 1883); *Swan Song* (*Lebedinaia pesnia*, 1886–1887, first performed at the Korsh Theater, 1888) from the story "Kalkhas" (1886); *A Tragedian in Spite of Himself*

(*Tragik ponevole*, 1889, first Moscow performance at the Theater of M. M. Abramova, 1889) from "One of Many" ("Odin iz mnogikh," 1887); *Jubilee* (*Iubilei*, 1891; revised, 1901; first major staging at the Aleksandrinsky, 1903) from "A Defenseless Creature" ("Bezzashchitnoe sushchestvo," 1887); and the unfinished *The Night Before the Trial* (*Noch' pered sudom*, early 1890s) from the 1886 story of the same title. One of Chekhov's most successful one-act plays, *The Wedding* (*Svad'ba*, 1889; revised, 1900; first major staging at the Aleksandrinsky, 1902), also belongs to this category. The play derives from two stories, "A Marriage of Convenience" ("Brak po rashchitu," 1884) and "A Wedding with a General" ("Svad'ba s generalom," 1884), but shares themes with two others, "Before the Wedding" ("Pered svad'boi," 1880) and "The Wedding" ("Svad'ba," 1887). *The Wedding* proved a very popular and funny play. Even in the austerity of his old age, Tolstoy is said to have "split his sides from laughter" while watching a performance.

Not all of Chekhov's one-act plays grew out of his stories. He wrote *Tatiana Repina* (1889), a sequel to Aleksei Suvorin's play of the same title, as a gift for his friend. Many critics regard the play as an essential stepping-stone along Chekhov's path to the play of indirect action because in it he eschews strong dramatic action in favor of an emotional and lyrical coloration. Chekhov also wrote completely autonomous one-act plays, and they include two of his most successful, *The Bear* (*Medved'*, 1888; first performed at the Korsh Theater, 1888, and then at the Aleksandrinsky, 1889) and *The Proposal* (*Predlozhenie*, 1888; stagings include one at the Aleksandrinsky, 1889, and another at the Maly, 1891). Both plays enjoyed great popularity, and it is worth noting that the role of Luka in *The Bear* served as a springboard for VSEVOLOD MEYERHOLD early in his career. Mention should also be made of the play *On the Injurious Effects of Tobacco* (*O vrede tabaka*, 1886; last revision, 1902), the numerous revisions of which have intrigued critics. Over the course of sixteen years Chekhov transformed a straightforward satirical piece into a highly affecting character study by stripping away outer action and concentrating on the main character's inner reaction to his circumstances. The revisions constitute a clear illustration of the evolution of Chekhov's poetics.

In addition to the one-act plays, Chekhov also undertook two more large-scale dramas toward the end of the 1880s. In the first, IVANOV (1887–1889), Chekhov returned to the problem of the superfluous man in the title character. Painfully conscious of the aimlessness of his existence, Ivanov comes to represent the quashed idealism of his generation, which had arisen with reforms of their childhood and fallen with the reaction of their adulthood. As in the earlier *Platonov*, Chekhov still relied on direct action to represent his characters and spoke of giving the audience "a punch in the nose" at the end of each act. Although Chekhov agonized over the productions of *Ivanov*—his correspondence on the topic is both anxious and amusing—the result was a popular success. Despite the success, Chekhov remained dissatisfied with the play and continued to revise it almost to the end of his life.

The other notable full-length drama of this period is *The Wood Demon* (*Leshii*, 1889). As in *Ivanov*, subtle changes in technique mark this play as a transitional piece. Chekhov's psychological portraiture is more assured and convincing, and signs of a different manner of handling dramatic material become apparent. A comparison of the murder in *Platonov* with the suicide in *The Wood Demon* is instructive. When Platonov is shot at the end of the play, the murder constitutes a melodramatic shock delivered for the voyeuristic pleasure of the audience. By contrast, Chekhov relegates the theme of suicide in *The Wood Demon* to a secondary character, Egor Voinitsky, whose dramatic death comes at a much earlier juncture and lacks the structural importance of Platonov's murder. On the other hand, Chekhov is still far from the delicate handling of the same theme in *The Seagull*. Caught between a poetics of direct action that Chekhov was abandoning and a poetics of indirect action that he was still trying to articulate, *The Wood Demon* was a failure and did not make it to the stage, except in private performance. However, the play became fodder for a later masterpiece, UNCLE VANYA.

Although literature dominated his life, Chekhov remained active as a physician. One of the most remarkable episodes in his life emanates, in fact, from the dissertation for his medical degree. In 1890 he embarked on a journey to Sakhalin Island, where he studied the socioeconomic, cultural, and medical condition of Russians and native peoples. He turned the raw material of his observations into a book-length study, titled simply *Sakhalin Island* (*Ostrov Sakhalin*, 1893–1895). Upon his return he continued to practice medicine through the famine and subsequent epidemics of the first half of the 1890s. His humanitarian pursuits were unflagging. However, he did not care for himself as he cared for others, and his tuberculosis, symptoms of which had appeared a decade earlier, continued to undermine his health.

Throughout this period a steady stream of stories issued from his pen. Critics often characterize them as "problem" stories. The problem as such is often no more than a premise, and Chekhov always took great care to create a fully realized fictional world in each work. Nonetheless, such themes as quietism in "Ward No. 6" ("Palata No. 6," 1892) or racism in "Rothschild's Violin" (1894) help shape these works. Other stories of this period reflect Chekhov's interest in Tolstoy, whose influence is perceptible in such stories as "The Duel" ("Duel'," 1891). Despite his great respect for Tolstoy, Chekhov remained independent and never allowed the Tolstoyan element to dominate his fiction. It is telling that in "The Duel" the Christian point of view remains just one of several contending voices.

In the second half of the 1890s Chekhov returned with renewed energy to drama and elucidated a startlingly innovative and influential poetics of drama. Abandoning direct action,

Chekhov instead focused on the drama of everyday interactions. Because of this emphasis on interactions between characters, the playwright abandoned the hero as such in favor of the ensemble of characters. The first fruit of this new poetics was *The Seagull* (*Chaika*, 1895), in which Chekhov explores the Oedipal drama that grows out of the relationship between the aspiring writer Treplev; his mother, the actress Irina Arkadina; and her lover, the already-accomplished writer Trigorin. Chekhov renders the drama not through confrontation, but primarily through failures of communication. As a final failure to connect with his mother, Treplev's suicide seems the inevitable resolution to the drama. *The Seagull* has also proved to be perhaps the most complex of Chekhov's dramatic texts. The inclusion of Treplev's quasi-symbolist play complicates its discourse and suggests its metatheatrical dimensions. The play's radical innovations contributed to its failure in 1896 at the Aleksandrinsky Theater, and its full significance was not recognized until KONSTANTIN STANISLAVSKY's historic production at the MOSCOW ART THEATER in 1898.

A second dramatic masterpiece, *Uncle Vanya*, followed *The Seagull*, probably in 1895/1896 (published in 1897), although the play has proven notoriously difficult to date. Chekhov returned to *The Wood Demon* and revised it so radically that a new and different play emerged, despite the nearly two acts' worth of shared material. The key difference between them is Chekhov's new poetics of indirect action, which clarified the insufficiently resolved dramatic material of *The Wood Demon*. Interaction, rather than action, defines the plot of the new play, which revolves around the resentment of Ivan Voinitsky, or Uncle Vanya, toward the husband of his now-deceased sister, Professor Serebriakov, who has exploited the family to further his own selfish interests. An undercurrent of tension between the two runs through the entire play and eventually leads to an overtly dramatic act when Vanya tries to shoot the professor. Chekhov's handling of this moment, however, demonstrates how much this episode differs from earlier murders: nothing comes of it. The professor escapes unscathed, and Vanya avoids any legal repercussions. The characters are left to contend in a drama of their own emotions. Despite Chekhov's misgivings, *Uncle Vanya* opened successfully at the Moscow Art Theater in 1899.

In the midst of the new plays, short fiction continued to appear and evolve, and many of the most perfect examples in the genre issued from Chekhov's pen in the last decade of his life. In them the coupling of the dispassionate, laconic narration and emotional engagement that characterized the earlier fiction reaches its culmination. Critics have often commented on the subtlety of works such as the so-called Little Trilogy, which consists of "The Man in the Case" ("Chelovek v futliare"), "Gooseberries" ("Kryzhovnik"), and "About Love" ("O liubvi," all 1898). Other masterpieces include "The Darling" ("Dushechka," 1899), "Lady with a Lapdog" ("Dama s sobachkoi," 1899), "In the Ravine" ("V ovrage," 1900), and "The Bishop" ("Arkhierei," 1902).

The turn of the century brought with it another dramatic masterpiece, THE THREE SISTERS, which continued to elaborate the new poetics begun in *The Seagull* and *Uncle Vanya*. The title already signals the ensemble work that is characteristic of Chekhov's last plays, and an oblique approach to dramatic action characterizes the plot. The setting is a provincial military town, and the drama of the play emanates from the sisters' collective nostalgia for Moscow, which renders them defenseless to the manipulation of their brother's wife Natasha and her lover, Protopopov. Chekhov again handles the most overtly dramatic events through indirect action, and a paradigmatic moment in the play comes in the muted reaction to Tuzenbakh's death in an offstage duel. The emotional fallout and the characters' inability to deal with it become the drama. *The Three Sisters* enjoyed considerable success in a 1901 staging at the Moscow Art Theater, Chekhov's qualms notwithstanding.

Chekhov finished his last dramatic masterpiece, THE CHERRY ORCHARD, in the autumn before his death. By this point tuberculosis had so ravaged his body that his creative output had dropped off markedly, and the completion of the play is a testament to Chekhov's determination and will. Like the three plays that preceded it, *The Cherry Orchard* reflects Chekhov's new poetics. The play's drama grows out of the interplay between a family from the nobility on the verge of losing its ancestral estate and the future owner, the descendant of their former serfs. The characters' emotional relations are complex, never deteriorating into mere antagonism, and the sale of the estate evokes a range of emotional response, from the nostalgia of Liubov Ranevskaia and her brother Gaev to the liberation felt by her youngest daughter Anya and the "eternal student" Trofimov to the ambivalence of Ranevskaia's eldest daughter Varya and the merchant and new owner Lopakhin. Although the production of *The Cherry Orchard* at the Moscow Art Theater in January 1904 enjoyed great success, the premiere marked Chekhov's last public appearance.

Despite the suffering of his last years, Chekhov enjoyed considerable happiness both professionally and personally. His marriage to Olga Knipper, a leading actress at the Art Theater, proved a rich experience for both husband and wife. His tuberculosis, however, was debilitating. He died in GERMANY while taking the waters on July 2/15, 1904. The return of his body to Russia became a major public event.

PLAYS: *Platonov* (1878–1881); *On the Highway* (1884); *On the Injurious Effects of Tobacco* (1886–1902); *Swan Song* (*Kalkhas*, 1886–1887); *Ivanov* (1887–1889); *The Bear* (1888); *The Proposal* (1888); *Tatiana Repina* (1889); *A Tragedian in Spite of Himself* (1889); *The Wedding* (1889–1900); *The Wood Demon* (1889); *Jubilee* (1891–1901); *The Night Before the Trial* (early 1890s); *The Seagull* (1895); *Uncle Vanya* (1895/1896?); *The Three Sisters* (1900); *The Cherry Orchard* (1903)

FURTHER READING

Allen, David. *Performing Chekhov*. London: Routledge, 1999.
Bloom, Harold, ed. *Anton Chekhov*. Philadelphia: Chelsea House, 1999.

Chekhov, Anton. *The Oxford Chekhov*. Ed. and tr. by Ronald Hingley. 9 vols., esp. vols. 1–3. Oxford: Oxford Univ. Press, 1964–1980.

——. *Anton Chekhov's Plays*. Ed. and tr. by Eugene W. Bristow. New York: Norton, 1977.

Clyman, Toby W., ed. *A Chekhov Companion*. New York: Greenwood Press, 1985.

Gilman, Richard. *Chekhov's Plays: An Opening into Eternity*. New Haven: Yale Univ. Press, 1995.

Gottlieb, Vera. *Chekhov and the Vaudeville: A Study of Chekhov's One-Act Plays*. Cambridge: Cambridge Univ. Press, 1982.

Jackson, Robert Louis, comp. *Chekhov: A Collection of Critical Essays*. Englewood Cliffs, N.J.: Prentice-Hall, 1967.

Magarshack, David. *Chekhov the Dramatist*. New York: Hill & Wang, 1960.

Peace, Richard. *Chekhov, a Study of the Four Major Plays*. New Haven: Yale Univ. Press, 1983.

Pitcher, Harvey J. *The Chekhov Play: A New Interpretation*. New York: Barnes & Noble, 1973.

Rayfield, Donald. *Anton Chekhov: A Life*. London: HarperCollins, 1997.

Senelick, Laurence. *Anton Chekhov*. Macmillan Modern Dramatists. London: Macmillan, 1985.

——. *The Chekhov Theatre: A Century of the Plays in Performance*. Cambridge: Cambridge Univ. Press, 2000.

Styan, J. L. *Chekhov in Performance: A Commentary on the Major Plays*. Cambridge: Cambridge Univ. Press, 1971.

Valency, Maurice. *The Breaking String: The Plays of Anton Chekhov*. New York: Oxford Univ. Press, 1966.

Timothy C. Westphalen

CHEN BAICHEN (1908–1994)

Born on March 1, 1908, in Jiangsu Province, CHINA, Chen Baichen, whose original name was Chen Zenghong, was a master playwright of COMEDY. His career was extraordinarily varied and embraced acting, directing, university teaching, and writing for stage, screen, and academics. He held many important posts in literary and academic fields, including the associate chair of the Theatre Association and the head of the Chinese Department of Nanjing University.

As a playwright, Chen Baichen was particularly known for his satirical and historical dramas. His sixty-year-long literary creations were closely associated with the political upheavals and social changes of 20th-century China, which was evidently reflected in his plays. Chen's early works showed strong marks of imitations of other writers. After 1933 Chen became a dramatist of the League of the Left Wing, and his plays were much influenced by the "Defense Drama," a school of drama of the early 1930s that aspired to call on dramatists with different political and ideological backgrounds to promote a drama of national defense against Japanese imperialist aggression. He instilled such nationalistic zest and spirit through a series of comedies. His keen satiric mind and much more skillful technical expertise allowed his drama of political satire to reach its zenith. After New China was founded in 1949, Chen Baichen focused his work primarily on historical drama, literary criticism, and filmmaking.

Heavily socially-politically oriented, *Promotion* (1945) secured his reputation and popularity and also heralded a new development of Chinese COMEDY. It was a satiric expressionistic play about a couple of bandits and a group of corrupt officials tempted to seek their promotions through evil tricks in a county during wartime. Chen stunningly used the techniques of allusion, exaggeration, and absurdity to depict the images of the venal officials and their insatiable avarice. Chen's dramatic depiction mocked philistinism and corruption of the time. He presented comic theatricality and political satire of the evil force so significantly in the play that his dramatization transcended its time and space. Even today we can still find it relevant to the historical present.

Based on the true account of the emperor Liu Bang of the Western Han dynasty (A.D. 206–225), *The Ode of the Wind* (1979), a seven-set historical drama, resulted from Chen's restless search for truth and peace during the ten-year turmoil of the Cultural Revolution in China (1966–1976). Chen remapped the turbulent events and political struggles between different parties at the high court of the time and emphasized that any governing body should always serve its people and satisfy their needs. That Chen made his historical drama directly deal with the national leadership greatly echoed people's longtime desire for stability and peace after enduring a decade of social chaos from the 1960s to the 1970s.

The 1981 cinematic adaptation of a great Chinese modern writer, Lu Xun's story titled *The True Story of Ah Q*, effectively proved Chen's success in employing his theatrical satire and comedy on the silver screen. The film received several international and domestic film awards and palpably displays his talent in filmmaking. Chen Baichen died on May 28, 1994, in China.

PLAYS: *Personal* (*Zheng hun*, 1935); *The Autumn Noon* (*Zhongqiu yue*, 1936); *Jintian Village* (*Jintian cun*, 1937); *The Den of Monsters* (*Moku*, 1938); *Men and Women in Wild Times* (*Luanshi nan nu*, 1939); *The Return of Spring* (*Dadi huichun*, 1941); *Arduous Years* (*Sui han tu*, 1945); *Promotion* (*Shenguan tu*, 1945); *The Dadu River* (*Dadu he*, 1946); *The Ode of the Wind* (*Da feng ge*, 1979)

FURTHER READING

Bu Zhongkang. *Chen Baichen zhuanji* [Special collection of Chen Baichen]. Huaiyin: Jiangsu renmin chubanshe, 1983.

Chen Baichen. *Chen Baichen ju zuo xuan* [Selected plays of Chen Baichen]. Chengdu: Sichaun renmin chubanshe, 1981.

——. *Men and Women in Wild Times*. [*Luanshi nan nu*]. Tr. by Edward Gunn. In *Twentieth-Century Chinese Drama: An Anthology*, ed. by Edward M. Gunn. Bloomington: Indiana Univ. Press, 1983. 126–173.

Chen Hong. *Chen Baichen ping chuan* [Chen Baichen's biography]. Chongqing: Chongqing chubanshe, 1998.

Dong Jian. *Chen Baichen chuangzuo licheng lun* [On the creative activities of Chen Baichen]. Beijing: Zhongguo xiju chubanshe, 1985.

Ge Yihong. *Zhongguo huaju tong shi* [A history of Chinese spoken drama]. Beijing: Wenhua yishu chubanshe, 1997.

Ping Fu

THE CHERRY ORCHARD

The last of ANTON CHEKHOV's four dramatic masterpieces, *The Cherry Orchard* (*Vishnevyi sad*, 1903) is, in many ways, the culmination of the new poetics of drama the playwright had initiated in THE SEAGULL. As the title suggests, it is the relation of the characters to the cherry orchard and to each other that interests Chekhov, not any single hero or heroine by him- or herself. The playwright emphasizes the ensemble of players. This emphasis led Chekhov away from the conventions of the so-called well-made play that held sway at that time. The demands imposed by such conventions—for example, the need for overt dramatic events at each curtain—inhibited the portrayal of real life. Chekhov instead turned to what has been called the play of indirect action as an alternative.

Critics often comment on the importance of mood and atmosphere in Chekhov's plays, and *The Cherry Orchard* is considered by many the zenith of the playwright's poetics. Although Chekhov eschews direct action, the play's metabasis, or reversal of fortune, nonetheless remains clear. The nobility who own the cherry orchard at the beginning of the play wind up in reduced circumstances at the end, while Lopakhin, the son of a former serf, rises to buy the estate. This schematic summary suggests how easily the material could have been handled through direct action, and certainly any number of works from the Soviet era formulate similar plots in terms of class conflict. Chekhov avoids this pitfall by maintaining a focus on each character's humanity. To no small degree, the class tension implied by the metabasis is attenuated by Lopakhin's affection for Liubov Ranevskaia and her brother Leonid Gaev. Chekhov took great pains to explain that Lopakhin should not be portrayed as a stereotypical merchant who is crude and crass, but as a sensitive and gentle soul. Although ambivalent, he too is implicated in the collective nostalgia for the world of the cherry orchard. All of the characters are acutely aware of the passing of that world. In a different context the poet ALEKSANDR BLOK would speak a few years later of the passing of the world of the hearth, and his conception of the problem suits *The Cherry Orchard* well. A world defined by domesticity and the intimacy of domestic relations gives way in *The Cherry Orchard* to a world defined by commerce and financial and legal relations.

This shift becomes apparent in the different attitudes the characters have toward the cherry orchard. Gaev, Ranevskaia, and, surprisingly, their manservant Firs are unambiguous in their love for the orchard, which represents the life they have known for good and bad. This is not merely a question of ownership, but a reality of their emotional life. For example, the loss of her son binds Ranevskaia to the cherry orchard in complex ways. Not everyone shares this attitude. At the other extreme are Ranevskaia's youngest daughter Anya and the "eternal student" Trofimov, who eagerly bid farewell to the world of the hearth and embark on a journey that will take them away from home. Somewhere between these two attitudes is the ambivalence expressed by Lopakhin and Ranevskaia's adopted daughter Varya. The hard work Varya puts into the management of the estate tempers her affection for the place, and the painful legacy of serfdom is too fresh for Lopakhin not to gloat a little when he becomes the new owner.

Despite their differing attitudes, none of the characters, not even Ranevskaia, experiences the sale of the cherry orchard as a tragedy. It is for all of them a loss. From this point of view, Chekhov's frequent and frequently reiterated admonitions to the actors of the MOSCOW ART THEATER that *The Cherry Orchard* is a COMEDY deserve consideration. The play follows, in many respects, the Aristotelian notion of a comedy in its portrayal of characters of a lower type, who are good, if slightly ludicrous. Gaev's impracticality, Trofimov's stridency, and Ranevskaia's nostalgia are the slightly ridiculous qualities of very decent people, and much of the play's comedy grows out of this disjuncture. Yet the comedy of *The Cherry Orchard* is not unadulterated, and it contains elements of poetic drama. The symbolists, for example, responded very strongly to the mysterious, evocative, and twice-repeated "sound of a breaking string."

The premiere of *The Cherry Orchard* at the Moscow Art Theater on January 17, 1904, was doubly the cause for celebration: The play, with Chekhov's wife Olga Knipper as Ranevskaia and the director KONSTANTIN STANISLAVSKY as Gaev, garnered considerable praise; and after the third act a veritable who's who of Moscow's artistic elite, including Sergei Rachmaninov, the poet Valerii Briusov, a young Andrei Bely, MAKSIM GORKY, and Fyodor Shaliapin, among others, came forward to pay homage to Chekhov on the twenty-fifth anniversary of his literary debut.

[*See also* Dramatic Dialogue; Russia and the Soviet Union]

FURTHER READING

Bely, Andrei. *The Cherry Orchard*. In *The Russian Symbolist Theatre: An Anthology of Plays and Critical Texts*, ed. by Michael Green. Ann Arbor: Ardis, 1986.

Chekhov, Anton. *The Cherry Orchard*. Tr. by Michael Frayn. Methuen student ed. London: Methuen, 1995.

Gilman, Richard. *Chekhov's Plays: An Opening Into Eternity*. New Haven: Yale Univ. Press, 1995.

Jackson, Robert Louis, comp. *Chekhov: A Collection of Critical Essays*. Englewood Cliffs, N.J.: Prentice-Hall, 1967.

Rayfield, Donald. *The Cherry Orchard: Catastrophe and Comedy*. Boston: Twayne, 1994.

Senderovich, Savely. "*The Cherry Orchard*: Chekhov's Last Testament." *Russian Literature* 35, no. 2 (1994): 223–242.

Valency, Maurice. *The Breaking String: The Plays of Anton Chekhov*. New York: Oxford Univ. Press, 1966.

Worrall, Nick. "Stanislavsky's Production Score for Chekhov's *The Cherry Orchard* (1904): A Synoptic Overview." Chekhov special issue, *Modern Drama* 42, no. 4 (Winter 1999): 519–540.

Timothy C. Westphalen

THE CHEVIOT, THE STAG AND THE BLACK, BLACK OIL

A whole culture was systematically destroyed—by economic power.
—Master of Ceremonies One, Act 1

In 1973 the magazine *Scottish International* held a conference titled "What Kind of Scotland" at which JOHN MCGRATH's company, 7:84 (Scotland), performed its new play. Delays in starting rehearsals meant that it presented "work in progress." McGrath records that at the end the audience stood, cheered, and then bombarded the company with their own suggestions for its improvement. This production was performed over 100 times to more than 30,000 people in one specific area of the United Kingdom.

The discovery of North Sea oil had created a boom in activity by companies moving into the Scottish Highlands, and the Scottish Nationalist Party (SNP) was running a campaign under the slogan "It's Scotland's Oil." Although McGrath's Marxist ideologies left little sympathy for nationalism as a cause, he could see that this represented a cycle of exploitation begun with the 19th-century Highland Clearances, when the valleys were emptied of people for the Cheviot sheep, and the later development of sporting estates that imposed a semifeudal state on those who remained.

Unlike BERTOLT BRECHT, McGrath emphasized the centrality of place, the local—particularly in terms of performance traditions. In *The Cheviot, the Stag and the Black, Black Oil* McGrath turned to the oral performance traditions of the ceilidh—a Highland gathering for song, music, and storytelling—which he combined with dramatic forms such as the double-act, the direct address to the audience, sketch, and parody, familiar from Scottish variety and pantomime.

There were techniques derived from left-wing agit-prop (AGITATION-PROPAGANDA)—caricature, strong visual elements such as the portable set, which was a giant pop-up book of Highland scenes, and the inclusion of factual information and figures from history, including Harriet Beecher Stowe, to contextualize the scenes. Scenes were short, the cast of characters was large, and actors stepped in and out of multiple roles to offer their documentary material at key moments. However, underpinning the whole was music, from a live ceilidh band, from community singing involving the audience, and from virtuoso Gaelic singing, whose haunting sound both celebrated Highland culture and recalled the banning of the Gaelic language.

The performance narrative ranged over 200 years of Highland history, jumping from one period to another to demonstrate the repeated exploitation by those too greedy, ignorant, callous, or inept to appreciate the unique qualities of Highland culture. These villains included absentee Scottish aristocrats, Lowland estate managers, and contemporary exploiters—the tourist entrepreneur, Andy McChuckemup, the ineffectual government minister, and Texas Jim, an oilman, whose energetic calling of a square dance began, "Take your oil-rigs by the score / Drill a little well just a little off-shore / Pipe that oil in from the sea / Pipe those profits—home to me."

The production traveled 17,000 miles in its 100 performances, almost all of which were in the Highlands; it crisscrossed by van and car ferry, usually playing in village halls. The "performance" began with the company's arrival. All aspects of the production from setup onward were visible, and the company carried low rostra staging to bring it nearer to the audience, which arrived to the sound of fiddle music and stayed, indeed had sometimes initially come, for the dance held immediately after the show. *The Cheviot* quickly became an audience favorite and is still widely studied as a key text in Scottish and UK political theater history.

[*See also* Scotland]

FURTHER READING

DiCenzo, Maria. *The Politics of Alternative Theatre in Britain, 1968–1990: The Case of 7:84 (Scotland)*. Cambridge: Cambridge Univ. Press, 1996.

Mackenney, Linda. "The People's Story: 7:84 Scotland." In *Scottish Theatre Since the Seventies*, ed. by Randall Stevenson and Gavin Wallace. Edinburgh: Edinburgh Univ. Press, 1996. 65–74.

MacLennan, Elizabeth. *The Moon Belongs to Everyone*. London: Methuen, 1990.

McGrath, John. *The Cheviot, the Stag and the Black, Black Oil*. Rev. ed. London: Methuen, 1981.

———. *A Good Night Out: Popular Theatre, Audience, Class and Form*. London: Methuen, 1981.

Patterson, Michael. *Strategies of Political Theatre: Post-war British Playwrights*. Cambridge: Cambridge Univ. Press, 2003.

Barbara A. E. Bell

CHIARELLI, LUIGI (1880–1947)

ITALY's Luigi Chiarelli (1880–1947) became active early in Roman literary circles and contributed verse, as well as prose, to various periodicals. In Milan he was acquainted with important theater groups and succeeded in having a few one-act plays staged, but recognition did not come until May 29, 1916, when the Compagnia Drammatica of Rome staged his *The Mask and the Face* (*La maschera e il volto*) at Teatro Argentina. The play was an immediate success in Italy, the Americas, and Europe. It is considered one of the first successful attempts to rejuvenate Italian and European theater.

Generally regarded as Chiarelli's masterpiece, this is an ironical COMEDY in three acts. The plot centers on the dilemma of a betrayed husband who, to avenge his honor, pretends that he has killed his wife: just the beginning of several absurd situations. Chiarelli satirizes conventional attitudes toward marital infidelity and the differences between what we preach and what we actually do, but what strikes us most is the originality of his approach: from an a priori distortion of reality to a *demonstratio per absurdum* of his theses.

Chiarelli characterized the genesis of his little masterpiece thusly: "*The Mask and the Face* was born of a critical as well as philosophical and polemical position . . . critical because it was subversive of all the rules of the old theatrical practice, shattering the prevailing threadbare norms on which European dramatic literature is based" (qtd. in Musti, 1942).

Thus the drama gives character and direction to a brief but significant movement called *grotesque;* this term refers to a genre of theater wherein the passions and tragedies of life are mechanically simplified or shockingly distorted. Grotesque incorporates also an unusual concept of ethics that leans toward a relativistic philosophy, but as a result these playwrights generally leave their protagonists in the midst of unresolved conflicts. This view of the world is made manifest in the works of Pier Maria Rosso di San Secondo, Luigi Antonelli, Enrico Cavacchioli, and others. As for *The Mask and the Face,* we notice some positive developments that change the lot of the protagonists and show what power love can have as a catalytic agent in the elimination of the conflict between form and reality, between the mask and the face.

Chiarelli therefore operates in an intellectual sphere closely related to LUIGI PIRANDELLO's. But The *Mask* is less pessimistic than most of Pirandello's plays: Chiarelli's conclusion seems to imply that a tolerant acceptance of life can be won through an understanding of its contradictions.

Chiarelli's contribution to modern theater was acknowledged by many authoritative witnesses, including Thomas Mann, FILIPPO T. MARINETTI, and Antonio Gramsci, while Pirandello not only supported the concepts of the grotesque but extended them in the multifaceted variations of his own production. Chiarelli's other plays were translated and performed on world stages. Chiarelli also wrote short stories and essays and translated numerous works from classical and modern languages. He enjoyed some success as a painter. In theatrical circles he exercised a great deal of influence, as evidenced by his long association with actor Virgilio Talli, his unique proposal for the establishment of a state theater in 1924, and his presidency of the Playwrights Union (the future Società Italiana degli Autori ed Editori [SIAE, copyright office]).

Clearly Chiarelli's social concerns and moral angst become an emblem of his theatrical self-reflexiveness; and the theater, as the place for simulations, improvisation, and conflict, offers the obvious artistic setting to exemplify such concerns. So, in dramatic form, he makes his attack on empty social conventions. His polemic, verging at times on tragic FARCE, is skillfully tinged with humor, fraught with paradox, and full of surprises. It lends itself to a rich development, typical of the postwar drama of the 1920s.

SELECT PLAYS: *The Mask and the Face* (*La maschera e il volto*, 1916); *Silken Stairs* (*La scala di seta*, 1917); *Chimeras* (*Chimere*, 1919); *Death of the Lovers* (*Morte degli amanti*, 1919); *Fireworks* (*Fuochi d'artificio*, 1922); *Jolly* (1928); *A Man to be Re-born* (*Un uomo da rifare*, 1931); *White Flash* (*Carne bianca*, 1934); *Magic Circle* (*Cerchio magico*, 1937); *A Mask* (*Pulcinella*, 1939); *Henry VIII* (*Enrico VIII*, 1940); *Aeneas Today* (*Enea come oggi*, 1938); *Being* (*Essere*, performed posthumously in 1953)

FURTHER READING

Bede, Jean-Albert, and William Edgerton, eds. [Article by Olga Ragusa.] *Columbia Dictionary of Modern European Literature.* New York: Columbia Univ. Press, 1980.

Bondanella, Peter, and Julia Conaway Bondanella, eds. *Dictionary of Italian Literature.* Westport, Conn.: Greenwood Press, 1979.

Grimm, R., and S. Garofalo. "Il teatro del grottesco." *Rivista Italiana di Drammaturgia*, no. 8 (August 1978). 80–116.

Lo Vecchio Musti, Manlio. *L'opera di Luigi Chiarelli* [The work of Luigi Chiarelli]. Roma: Cenacolo, 1942.

Ragusa, Olga. "Chiarelli, Luigi." *Columbia Encyclopedia of Modern European Literature.* Ed. Jene-Albert Bede and William Edgerton. New York: Columbia Univ. Press, 1980.

Thomson, Philip. *The Grotesque*, London: Methuen, 1972.

Vena, Michael, ed. *Italian Grotesque Theater.* Cranbury, N.J.: Fairleigh Dickinson Univ. Press, 2001.

Michael Vena

CHICHI KAERU

See THE FATHER RETURNS

THE CHILDREN'S HOUR

LILLIAN HELLMAN made an impressive stage debut with *The Children's Hour*, the story of two teachers accused of lesbianism. Loosely based on an actual incident that took place in 19th-century Scotland, the play opened on November 20, 1934, to overwhelmingly positive reviews. One critic called it "finely and bravely written"; the few negative comments focused on the drama's conclusion (Benchley, 1934). *The Children's Hour* ran for 691 performances in New York, the longest run for any Hellman play, although it faced censorship in Boston, London, and elsewhere. For the first film version of *The Children's Hour*, titled *These Three* (1936), Hellman was forced to change the plot to a heterosexual love triangle; the 1962 remake is more faithful to Hellman's original script.

Act 1 is set in a girls' boarding school run by Martha Dobie and Karen Wright. Mary Tilford, a spoiled child whose wealthy grandmother has long supported the school, runs away after being punished for lying. Act 2 takes place at Mrs. Tilford's home, where Mary, desperately trying to persuade her grandmother not to send her back, claims that her teachers have an "unnatural" relationship—a word used earlier by Martha's vindictive aunt Lily Mortar. Mrs. Tilford immediately calls all the parents and, despite protests from the teachers and Karen's fiancé, Joseph Cardin, spreads Mary's tale. The final act takes place after Karen and Martha have lost their libel suit against Mrs. Tilford. After a tearful confession that "maybe" she does harbor sexual feelings for Karen, Martha commits suicide only minutes before a remorseful Mrs. Tilford arrives to announce her discovery that Mary was lying.

Hellman repeatedly insisted that *The Children's Hour* was not "about lesbianism, but about a lie." The playwright herself directed a revival during the McCarthy era, when scores of Americans (including Hellman) were accused of being Communists. Her production focused on the danger posed by self-righteous "good" people like Mrs. Tilford who act on hearsay without considering the consequences of their deeds. Her wrath is also directed at those like the self-serving Lily Mortar, who knew that the young women were innocent of the charge of having "sinful sexual knowledge of one another" but avoided the trial because she feared being involved in a scandal.

Ironically, the very lesbianism that shocked audiences in 1934 has alienated some contemporary feminists. Where early viewers were appalled by Hellman's daring to address the topic at all—*The Children's Hour* reportedly lost the Pulitzer Prize because at least one judge was horrified by the subject matter—later critics have decried Martha's anguished confession and suicide. Why, they ask, does the play's resolution require the death of a lesbian? The drama's treatment of lesbianism is certainly ambiguous, but Martha's self-hatred is a reflection of American society's view, not necessarily Hellman's. At the very least, *The Children's Hour* perceptively explores society's fear of women's close friendship: the playwright knew which lie would most disturb her characters and her audience. Although marred by structural flaws attributable to Hellman's lack of theater experience, *The Children's Hour* remains a potent, thought-provoking drama.

[*See also* Gay and Lesbian Drama; United States, 1940–Present]

FURTHER READING

Benchley, Robert. "Review of *The Children's Hour*." *The New Yorker*. December 8, 1934.

Dolan, Jill. " 'Lesbian' Subjectivity in Realism: Dragging at the Margins of Structure and Ideology." In *Performing Feminisms: Feminist Critical Theory and Theatre*, ed. by Sue-Ellen Case. Baltimore: Johns Hopkins Univ. Press, 1990. 40–53.

Estrin, Mark W., ed. *Critical Essays on Lillian Hellman*. Boston: G. K. Hall, 1989.

Falk, Doris V. *Lillian Hellman*. New York: Ungar, 1978.

Griffin, Alice, and Geraldine Thorsten. *Understanding Lillian Hellman*. Columbia: Univ. of South Carolina Press, 1999.

Lederer, Katherine. *Lillian Hellman*. Boston: Twayne, 1979.

Wright, William. *Lillian Hellman: The Image, the Woman*. New York: Simon & Schuster, 1986.

Judith E. Barlow

CHILDRESS, ALICE (1916–1994)

As long as we are subliminally trained to recognize other racial feelings above our own, our ideas are in danger of being altered even before they are written. It becomes almost second nature to be on guard against the creative pattern of our own thought.

—Alice Childress, in *Black Women Writers, 1950–1980*, 1984

Alice White Childress was born on October 12, 1916, in Charleston, South Carolina. Her early years were spent with her mother, Florence. At the age of five she went to Harlem to live with her grandmother, Eliza White, who became her legal guardian in 1925. White exposed her to the arts and taught her the art of storytelling. When she died, the adolescent Alice was forced to leave high school and support herself through a variety of mundane jobs, including domestic work. During the 1930s she married Alvin Childress, who later starred as Amos in the 1950s television series *Amos 'n' Andy*. Their daughter, Jean, was born in 1935. After her divorce from Alvin Childress she married musician Nathan Woodard in 1957.

In 1940 Childress appeared as Dolly in John Silvera and Abram Hill's play *On Strivers Row*, based on the famous Harlem community of the same name. The following year she became a founding member of the American Negro Theatre and subsequently appeared in a number of its productions, including an adaptation of SOMERSET MAUGHAM's short story *Rain*. She received a Tony nomination for her performance as Blanche in *Anna Lucasta*, which had a two-year run on Broadway in the 1940s. Known primarily for her work in drama, Childress wrote several plays, including *Florence* (1949), which anticipated the drama of the BLACK ARTS MOVEMENT; *Just a Little Simple* (1950), a musical and dramatic restructuring of LANGSTON HUGHES's *Simple Speaks His Mind*; *Trouble in Mind* (1955); *Wedding Band: A Love/Hate Story in Black and White* (1966); and *Wine in the Wilderness* (1969). In 1952 her *Gold Through the Trees* became the first play written by an African American woman to be produced professionally. In 1956 *Trouble in Mind* had an OFF-BROADWAY run of ninety-one performances and received an Obie for Best Play, making Childress the first black woman playwright to receive the award. Childress also wrote novels: *A Hero Ain't Nothin' but a Sandwich* (1973), which was also made into a film in 1978; *A Short Walk* (1979); *Rainbow Jordan* (1981); and *Those Other People* (1989). Childress's work incorporates elements of history, African mythology, folk culture, feminist thought, and contemporary politics.

Florence established REALISM as Childress's chosen mode of dramatic expression and set the thematic stage for her full-length play, *Trouble in Mind*. The substance of *Florence* is a black mother's changing perspective on her daughter's right to realize her ambitions on the New York stage, despite the odds stacked against her. *Trouble in Mind*, a drama about actors rehearsing a Broadway play, focuses on the self-denying compromises that black actors must make in order to work in white-run theatrical productions. Childress develops her characters through the use of theme and argumentation and can be described as a traditionalist because she builds her plays by episodes, delineating a new scene by the arrival or departure of a character. Childress died on February 19, 1994, in New York City. She is remembered as an artist who used her writing to critique the failings of American democracy while championing the cause of the poor and the working class.

[*See also* Feminist Drama in the United States; United States, 1860–Present]

PLAYS: *Hell's Alley* (with Alvin Childress, 1938); *Florence* (1949); *Just a Little Simple* (1950); *Gold Through the Trees* (1952); *Trouble in Mind* (1955); *Wedding Band: A Love/Hate Story in Black and White* (1966; revised, 1972); *The Freedom Drum* (retitled *Young Martin Luther King*, 1969); *String* (1969); *Mojo: A Black Love Story* (1970); *The World on a Hill* (1970); *The Black Garden* (1971); *Wine in the Wilderness* (1971); *When the Rattlesnake Sounds* (1975); *Let's Hear It for the Queen* (1976); *Sea Island Song* (1977; revised as *Gullah*, 1984); *Moms: A Praise Play for a Black Comedienne* (1987); *A Man Bearing a Pitcher* (date unknown)

FURTHER READING

Abramson, Doris. *Negro Playwrights in the American Theater, 1925–1959*. New York: Columbia Univ. Press, 1969.

Brown-Guillory, Elizabeth. *Their Place on the Stage: Black Women Playwrights in America*. New York: Greenwood Press, 1988.

Evans, Mari. "Alice Childress." In *Black Women Writers, 1950–1980*. Garden City, N.Y.: Anchor/Doubleday, 1984.

Jennings, La Vinia D. *Alice Childress*. New York: Twayne, 1995.

Marsh-Lockett, Carol P., ed. *Black Women Playwrights: Visions on the American Stage*. New York: Garland, 1999.

Lovalerie King

CHINA

Generally speaking, there are basically two types of drama in China: the sung drama, or *xiqu*, and the spoken drama, *huaju*. In a *xiqu* play dialogues are interspersed with lyrics. Lyrics are largely sung on stage with distinctive and fixed music patterns, which are the main components that distinguish one *xiqu* form from another. For example, *jingju*, which has been traditionally translated as Beijing opera (or Peking opera), uses *pihuang* tunes for its sung lyrics, while *kunqu* employs a whole set of *taoqu* or *qupai* compositions for its singing part. Various *xiqu* dramas have their respective histories. For instance, *jingju* has a history of over 200 years, while *kunqu* had reached its mature form about 400 years ago. Historically, new *xiqu* forms kept emerging from the influences of older forms. Some *xiqu* forms such as *lüju* (in Shandong Province) have a relatively short history of fifty years or so. There are about 300 types of *xiqu* drama in China.

Most terms used to name various *xiqu* dramas have a similar syntactic structure: a word (of one or two characters) denoting the geographic place where a distinct *xiqu* form was first formulated precedes and modifies another word that is *ju* (drama), *xi* (show), *qu* (musical lyrics), or *qiang* (tune)—all having been generically translated as "opera." For instance, *jingju* has been translated as Beijing (Peking) opera, in which *jing* denotes Beijing, the birthplace of this music drama; *kunqu* has been translated as Kun opera, with *kun* referring to Kunshan, where this theatrical genre started in the 14th century; *qinqiang* refers to the music drama in and around the area of Shaanxi Province; *puxianxi* could be translated as "Puxian opera," with *puxian* indicating its birthplaces in Putian and Xianyou in Fujian Province. Some other nominative terms use descriptive adjectives to denote a genetic feature when a certain music drama first emerged. More and more scholars nowadays tend not to use English translations of these *xiqu* terms because the word "opera" carries different interpretive associations from *ju*, *xi*, *qiang*, *qu*, or other Chinese terms. Scholars nowadays prefer the usage of the original terms such as *jingju*, *huju*, *yueju*, and *huaiju* in both spoken and written texts of Western languages to avoid inaccurate or misleading interpretations that nominative translations in Western languages may cause.

In terms of geographic influences, some *xiqu* forms are called *da juzhong*, big theatrical genre, because they are regularly performed in more regional areas. *Jingju*, the biggest genre, reached its status as a national drama in the early 20th century. Most big and medium-sized cities in China have *jingju* troupes. Some *xiqu* forms are termed *xiao juzhong*, small theatrical genre, and they are only performed in one region or limited areas. However, with television and cinema as influential vehicles, the influence of an excellent play of a small theatrical genre may reach far and wide.

Xiqu drama has basically four categories of written texts: (1) published scripts of *zaju*, *nanxi*, and *chuanqi* handed down from the Yuan, Ming, and Qing dynasties (from the 13th to the 19th century), which were never fully staged in the 20th century, with rare exceptions; (2) performing scripts from the traditional repertoire of each *xiqu* drama, whose contents came from the sources of the earlier *zaju*, *nanxi*, and *chuanqi* plays, great novels, and well-known histories, and mostly do not have a full written text; (3) rearranged or adapted (*gaibian*) scripts by modern and contemporary dramatists with their new ideas (from the original repertoire), which have been performed and published since the early 1950s; and (4) scripts newly written by modern and contemporary dramatists about historical events and contemporary society. A *xiqu* play was usually written for one *xiqu* form. When it became successful on stage, some other *xiqu* forms tended to "transplant" (*yizhi*) or adapt it into their own music and dialectal forms. Nowadays a few plays have been written that are intented for more than one *xiqu* form. A *xiqu* play performed on the contemporary stage usually lasts two to three hours. A play of much shorter length is called *xiaoxi* (a short piece equivalent to a one-act play).

The other type of drama is called *huaju*, literally, spoken drama—a form that emerged around 1907 and followed the realistic mode of modern Western plays such as HENRIK IBSEN's. The play usually consists of dramatic dialogues written in modern vernacular language. The performance of a *huaju* play is usually done in *putonghua*, the standard common speech (Mandarin), which can be understood by all Chinese audiences because of the fact that *putonghua* or Mandarin has been taught in all schools and used in most television and radio programs and public communications. *Huaju* plays have been customarily performed in their full length.

Besides *xiqu* and *huaju*, there is another new genre called *geju*, a modern song drama that has a history of sixty years or so. The reason that *geju* does not belong to *xiqu* is that *geju* uses the Western music system to compose songs despite influences from the traditional theatrical music; its dialogues and songs are done in Mandarin; and its performing style is in the realistic mode. Although this genre as a whole is much less significant, some *geju* plays, such as WHITE-HAIRED GIRL (*Baimao nü*), were very influential in terms of social ideology and left a deep impression on Chinese audiences.

XIQU AND *HUAJU*: A HISTORICAL ACCOUNT SINCE 1860

The premodern, full-fledged drama developed in the forms of Song-Yuan *nanxi*, Yuan *zaju*, and Ming-Qing *chuanqi* from the 13th to the 19th century, which produced a rich body of dramatic literature. Examples from the northern *zaju* are *The Orphan of Zhao* (*Zhao shi gu'er*), which Voltaire adapted into his 1755 play *L'orphelin de la Chine*, and *The Chalk Circle* (*Hui lan ji*), which inspired BERTOLT BRECHT's play THE CAUCASIAN CHALK CIRCLE. The southern *nanxi*/*chuanqi* models include *The Story of the Lute* (*Pipa ji*), which was translated into the 1946 Broadway musical *Lute Song*, and *Peony Pavilion* (*Mudan ting*), which was transformed into Peter Sellas's 1998–1999 version combining the styles of *kunqu*, Western opera, and realistic plays. In China the bulk of these classical dramatic texts served as one of the major sources for the plays of numerous regional *xiqu* forms that enjoyed rapid growth in the mid- and late Qing dynasty. The content of the drama at the time was predominantly historical and traditional.

By 1860 China had experienced the Opium War (1840–1842), which marked China's entry into a modern period as a result of its military failure and its subjection to Western powers that forced their influences into coastal cities of China. From 1840 to 1919 the traditional society underwent drastic changes through its interactions with the Western military, economy, and culture and through the internal Taiping Uprising (1851–1864), the 1911 revolution that overthrew the Qing dynasty, and the May Fourth cultural movement in 1919 that called for science and democracy and a new culture, including the use of the vernacular language in writings. Chinese intellectuals began to question the causes for the weakness of China in the face of Western powers. They advocated social and cultural reforms. Drama, like other forms of literature, was urged to reform and, at the same time, used for advocating reforms. Before the birth of the spoken drama around 1907, in terms of the play scripts, the major forms of the drama were *zaju* and *chuanqi*, the two forms that were carried over from the Yuan, Ming, and early Qing periods, and the scripts for various regional theaters. About 300 *zaju* and *chuanqi* plays appeared from 1860 to 1949, the year that marked the end of these two genres. There was a peak of 172 plays published between 1902 and 1919, an important period for the advocacy of social reforms. The noted playwrights for the *zaju* and *chuanqi* in this period were Hong Bingwen (1848–1918), Lin Xu (1852–1924), Wu Ziheng (1855–1935?), Jiang Jixiang (1859–1924), Yuan Zuguang (1870–1912), Liang Qichao (1873–1929), and Wu Mei (1884–1939). The leading characteristic of the *zaju* and *chuanqi* plays during this period was their use of contemporary society as their dramatic content. For example, Hong Bingwen's *The Bell Tolls for Huang Di's Descendants* (*Jing huangzhong*) used allegories to awaken the Chinese to the situation of China's territory being carved up by Western powers; Zhong Zufen's *Opium Den* (*Zhao yin ju*) exposed the danger of opium smoking, reflecting a huge social problem at the time; and Yang Ziyuan's *Women's World* (*Nü jie tian*) portrayed eight outstanding Chinese and Western women to promote women's rights in China. This period was also notable for the first appearance of literary journals such as *New People's Journal* (*Xinmin congbao*), *New Novels* (*Xin xiaoshuo*), and *Twentieth-Century Grand Stage* (*Ershi shiji dawutai*), which featured new plays and articles with debates on theater reform. These seventeen years witnessed the last surge of the *zaju* and *chuanqi* plays. With the advent of spoken drama, these old genres were no longer relevant to the new culture and new literature that the modern society called for. These old forms were phased out in the next thirty years. By the time of the founding of the People's Republic of China, new *zaju* and *chuanqi* plays ceased to exist.

While the regional dramas of the *huabu* category were continuing as rising forces competing with one another, they were also inspired by the new cultural movement. Although the majority of the *huabu* scripts contained traditional dramatic content, progressive playwrights, especially those at the turn of the 20th century, wrote a significant number of new plays reflecting contemporary life, dealing with social issues, and promoting revolutionary ideas—all aiming at arousing a national spirit to make China strong. The vogue at the time was *shizhuang xinxi* (contemporary-costume plays), new plays about contemporary society, as opposed to the traditional plays in which characters wear ancient costumes. Among the most noted playwrights were Wang Xiaonong (1858–1918) and Xia Yueshan (1868–?) for *jingju*, Huang Ji'an (1836–1924) and Zhao Xi (1867–1948) for *chuanju*, Sun Yuan (1872–1943) and Fan Ninji (1878–1954) for *qinqiang*, and Cheng Zhaocai (1874–1929) for *pingju*, a brand-new *xiqu* genre that emerged around 1910 amid the drama reform movement. Among the most influential new plays of the regional dramas were *Wronged Ghosts in the Opium Den* (*Heiji yuanhun*) (*jingju*), *Mourning at the Ancestral Temple* (*Ku zumiao*) (*jingju*), *Dream of the Reform* (*Weixin meng*) (*jingju*), and *Yang Sanjie's Lawsuit* (*Yang Sanjie gaozhuang*) (*pingju*). Some well-known actors took the lead in experimenting with contemporary-costume plays. Mei Langfang was one of them and performed four new plays, *Billows in the Sea of Sins* (*Neihai bolan*), *Tides in the Sea of Officialdom* (*Huanhai chao*), *Deng Xiagu: A Young Woman for Freedom* (*Deng Xiagu*), and *A Strand of Hemp* (*Yi lü ma*), from 1913 to 1916.

The social and political situations in China during this period not only brought about reforms in the *zaju*, *chuanqi*, and regional dramas headed by *jingju*, but also led to the birth of *wenmingxi* (civilized drama), the early form of *huaju* (spoken drama). The genesis of the spoken drama lay in the amateur performances of Western plays by Chinese students in some Western missionary schools in Shanghai. These students were exposed to Western plays and acting styles and began to use the Chinese language to perform on social issues. Around 1907 Wang Zhongxian and Zhu Shuangyun organized an association of student actors in Shanghai for civilized performances (*Kaiming yanju hui*). The association once performed for three days on the theme of reforms. About the same time a group of Chinese students headed by Zeng Xiaogu and Li Shutong, who were studying in Japan and were exposed to the *Shinpai* (New Drama) of Japanese drama, organized a performing society titled Spring Willow Society (Chun liu she), with its first performances of DUMAS FILS *The Lady of the Camellias* (*La Dame aux Camélias*), and an adaptation of *Uncle Tom's Cabin* with the Chinese title *Heinü yutian lu*. Later the people associated with the Spring Willow Society, such as Lu Jingruo and Ouyang Yuqian, continued its activities in Shanghai under a new society called Society for New-Drama Comrades (Xinju tongzhi hu). In the same spirit Wang Zhongsheng organized Spring Sun Society (Chunyang she) in Shanghai. Ren Tianzhi organized the first professional troupe for civilized plays, called Evolution Troupe (Jinhua tuan). The 1911 revolution that overthrew the Qing dynasty and established the Republic of China pushed the *wenmingxi* to a new level. In the second decade of the 20th century the number of performance societies reached more than thirty in Shanghai. The names of the six leading professional societies reflected the purposes of the early spoken drama: New People Society (Xinmin she), People's Voice Society (Minming she), People-Enlightening Society (Qimin she), People Rising Society (Minxing she), Enlightenment Society (Kaiming she), and Spring Willow Theatre (Chunliu juchang). In addition to the societies in Shanghai, students in the Nankai School of Tianjin and those in the Qinghua University of Beijing played an important role in the early spoken drama movement. The most noted leaders in the North were Zhang Pengchun, TIAN HAN, and HONG SHEN. The birth of *huaju*, the spoken drama, resulted from the social calls for the reform of *xiqu* and, to a significant extent, from a reaction to the traditional forms of *xiqu*. Among the Western authors and playwrights whose work exerted tremendous influence on *huaju* was Ibsen. *New Youth* (*Xin qingniar*), the most influential journal in disseminating Western ideas at the time, devoted a whole issue (June 1918) to Ibsenism because the time needed "to create a new drama of the Western style, to raise the drama to the level of literature, to use vernacular language to write non-lyric drama . . . and also because Ibsen dares to attack the society," in the words of Lu Xun, the father of modern Chinese literature (qtd. in Chen Baichen and Dong Jian, 1989). Plays of GEORGE BERNARD SHAW, AUGUST STRINDBERG, Romain Rolland, ANTON CHEKOV, OSCAR WILDE, and other Western authors were also translated into Chinese.

1919–1949

From 1919 (marked by the May Fourth New Culture movement) on, *baihua wen* (the vernacular language) became the linguistic medium for most written materials, including most genres of literature. The year 1919 has been customarily used as a demarcation line to separate new culture and new literature from the old ones. The republic period of the new literature lasted up to 1949, when the Communist revolution drove the Nationalists to Taiwan and established the People's Republic of China over the mainland. As mentioned earlier, the *zaju* and *chuanqi* genres were phased out during this period. *Huaju* grew mature in this period and produced a great number of important playwrights such as Tian Han, OUYANG YUQIAN, Hong Shen, XIONG FOXI (Xiong Fuxi), GUO MORUO, DING XILIN, CAO YU, XIA YAN, LI JIANWU, LAO SHE, CHEN BAICHEN, and WU ZUGUANG, who are individually introduced in their respective entries in this encyclopedia. Besides these most productive playwrights, any further knowledge of the spoken drama in its different styles and movements in various periods of this time span requires a study of additional dramatists, including Hu Shi, Chen Dabei, Wang Zhongxian, Pu Boying, Bai Wei, Yuan Changying, Pu Shunqing, Yu Shangyuan, Xu Zhimo, Feng Naichao, Zuo Ming, Lou Shiyi, Shi Linhe, Zhang Min, Yao Shixiao, Yuan Muzhi, Gu Jianchen, Song Chunfang, Wang Wenxian, Yang Mei, Xu Yu, Chen Chuhuai, Yang Hansheng, A Ying, Yu Ling, Song Zhidi, Mao Dun, Zhang Junxiang, Shen Fu, Yang Jiang, Wu Tian, Gu Zhongyi, Yang Cunbin, Yao Ke (Yao Xinnong), Huang Zuolin, Ke Ling, Shi Tuo, Chen Quan, Sha Kefu, Li Bozhao, Wang Zhenzhi, Wu Xue, Du Feng, Yao Zhongming, Chen Bo'er, Cui Dezhi, Hu Ke, and Lu Mei.

All these playwrights' works not only represented a wide variety of subject matters, literary and social themes, and forms of dramatic expression, but also marked different phases and movements in the development of *huaju* closely related to the political history of its day. The predominant themes of this period centered around the predicament and emancipation of Chinese women, the empowerment of the nation, the exposure of various social problems, the awakening of a national heroic spirit to fight against the Japanese invaders, and the class oppression and rebellion heavily influenced by the leftist ideology. This period was also the most productive period for *huaju* as the result of the creation of many drama societies, such as the People's Drama Society in Shanghai (Shanghai minzhong xiju she, 1921–1923), the South China Society (Nanguo she, 1926–1930), and the Left-Wing Dramatists League (Zuoyi xijujia lianmeng, 1930–1936), and a series of drama movements, including the *aimei ju* (the term derived from the word *amateur*, which meant nonprofessional, and art theater, 1920–1925), the *guoju* movement (the national drama using Chinese materials to write Chinese plays, 1925–1927), the *guofang xiju* movement (national defense theater, 1936–1937) National Salvation Performance Teams (*jiuwang yanju dui*, 1937–1940), the Jiangxi Soviet District Drama (1930–1934), Chongqing Misty Season Drama Festivals (1941–1944), Drama Performance Movement in the Southwest Region (1936–1944), and the Yanan Liberated Area Drama (1937–1949). Throughout this period Western plays were further translated, adapted, and produced in the *huaju* form.

While *huaju* became more and more mature and its plays were considered as having more literary value, *xiqu* still remained a popular form for the majority of the Chinese people. The influence of the major regional dramas, especially *jingju*, reached far and wide, and new *xiqu* forms were still emerging in this period. Existing studies on modern Chinese drama have neglected the role of *xiqu* plays in terms of dramatic literature. Throughout this period most *xiqu* troupes performed traditional plays whose content was mainly stories and legends of imperial China. The most significant aspect of the *xiqu* genres was the new plays about contemporary society. The new plays in this period had three characteristics: (1) they had renowned artists participate in the productions and performances; (2) they tended to promote innovation in the existing genres; and (3) some of them remained as excellent plays in the repertoire of specific genres. In *jingju*, Shanghai was the major arena for plays with contemporary themes, of which *The Execution of Yan Ruisheng* (*Qiangbi Yan Ruisheng*, 1920) and *Huang Huiru and Lu Genrong* (*Huang Huiru yu Lu Genrong*, 1928) were based on actual events that happened in Shanghai in the same period, the former being a theatrical account of the murder of a high-class prostitute by a bank clerk, and the latter a story of a daughter of a Shanghai middle-class family falling in love with her family's servant against opposition from the family and society. It was during this period that the Zhejiang *yueju* developed into the only theatrical genre in China that exclusively cast female actors in female and male roles. The influential new plays performed by the *yueju* actresses included *Jiang Laowu Sacrifices Her Life for Love* (*Jiang Laowu xunqing ji*, 1940), *Xiangling's Wife* (*Xianglin sao*, 1946), and *Prodigal Son* (*Langdang zi*, 1947). *Huju*, the Shanghai music drama, was created as well during this period in Shanghai, a cradle for new ideas and reforms. *Huju* was the only *xiqu* genre that mainly produced plays of modern and contemporary themes. Only contemporary-costume plays survived as repertory plays in *huju*, such as *Under the Garnet Skirt* (*Shiliuqun xia*), *Rebellious Women* (*Panni de nüxing*), and *Heaven and Earth* (*Biluo huangquan*). In a sense, *huju* is a traditional *xiqu* form for modern themes. Other *xiqu* genres noted for new plays were *pingju*, *Hebei bangzi*, and *Henan yuju*, *quju*, and *chuanju*. Well-known plays of these genres include *Tears and Laughter in Predestined Relationships* (*Dixiao yinyuan*) (*Hebei bangzi*), *Divorce of Li the Harelipped* (*Li Huozi lihuan*) (*quju*), *Fighting on the Motherland* (*Da tudi*) (*Henan yuju*), *Deaf Husband and Charming Wife* (*Yafu yu jiaoqi*) (*chuanju*), and *Who Ruined Her?* (*Shi shei hai le ta*) (*chuanju*). Playwrights associated with creating new plays in the *xiqu* genres include Xia Chefeng, Fan Li, Xu Jin, Nan Wei, Xu Zuimei, Fan Qingfeng, Wang Mengliang, Zhao Yanshi, Ge Ge, Ye Zi, Zhang Shichuan, Cheng Zhaocai, Yang Yunpu, Wang Daotong, Wang Feiting, Wang Zhennan, and Liu Huaixu.

Special note should be made of the *xiqu* reforms in the Communist-controlled area in Shaanxi and Hebei provinces from the mid-1930s to 1949. Under the leadership of a group of Communist intellectuals, the traditional *xiqu* forms were consciously employed to promote the dissemination of new ideas. Emphasis was placed on the combination of the new cultural content with old national forms and on the inseparability of popularization and nationalization of the new culture. Two troupes were most influential: the People's Troupe (Minzhong Jutuan), headed by Ke Zhongping and Ma Jianling, and the Yanan Beijing Opera Troupe (Yanan Pingju Yuan) in close association with the Lu Xun Art Institute (Lu Xun Yishu Xueyuan). The former used *qinqiang* and *meihu*, the two most popular *xiqu* forms in the area, as theatrical vehicles for numerous new plays such as *The Hatred of Blood and Tears* (*Xuelei chou*) (*qinqiang*), *Poor People's Hatred* (*Qiongren heng*) (*qinqiang*), and *What All Like* (*Dajia xihuan*) (*meihu*). The latter contributed some outstanding new plays to *jingju*, and *Forced up Mount Liang* (*Bishang Liangshan*) set a good example for adapting traditional stories to new ideas and themes. Mao Zedong's famous "Talks at the Yanan Forum on Literature and Art" in May 1942 set the literary policy for reforms of drama in the decades to follow. The reforms of *qinqiang*, *meihu*, and *jingju* in the Communist-controlled area can be interpreted as the predecessor of the large-scale *xiqu* reforms in the 1950s and 1960s. The *geju* (song drama) *White-Haired Girl* (*Baimao nü*) was created as a new genre combining the traditional *yangge* (drum-dance-song) elements and Western music composition during this period and set a classic example for drama as an education form. The ideology of the class struggle between the oppressed and the oppressor influenced two or three generations of audiences.

During this period the traditional Chinese drama and theater was introduced to Western audiences by Chinese troupes' touring performances of Chinese plays. The most significant Chinese performances in the West were Mei Lanfang's 1930 performances in

New York and other U.S. cities and his 1935 lecture/performance in Moscow. Mei Lanfang's two trips exerted influences upon a group of Western dramatists and critics such as THORNTON WILDER, Stark Young, KONSTANTIN STANISLAVSKY, VSEVOLOD MEYERHOLD, Sergei Eisenstein, and, perhaps most of all, Bertolt Brecht. The aesthetic values of the Chinese drama and theater were elevated to the theoretical level in the West. They were practiced and absorbed in Western DRAMATURGY. On the Broadway stage alone, Western audiences saw *The Yellow Jacket* (1912), *The Flower of the Palace of Han* (1912), *Chalk Circle* (1925, 1930, 1933, 1941, 1945, 1947), *Lady Precious Stream* (1936), and *Lute Song* (1946)—all adaptations from Chinese sources. Wilder's OUR TOWN (1938) on Broadway and the world premiere of Brecht's *Caucasian Chalk Circle* (1948) at Carleton College were two classic examples that partly absorbed Chinese staging techniques and dramatic principles, and these plays have in turn exerted tremendous influence upon modern and contemporary Western nonrealistic plays. This period indeed saw a significant amount of exchanges between Chinese and Western dramas.

1949–1976

The period 1949–1976 covered two phases: the first seventeen years (1949–1966) of dramatic and theatrical experiences in the new People's Republic of China (PRC) and the ten-year experience in the Cultural Revolution (1966–1976). The most striking characteristic in this period was that drama and theater movements or activities were closely linked to Communist politics and to mass education via entertainment. Following the literary policies laid out in Mao Zedong's Yanan Forum talk, the government maintained the long revolutionary tradition in which drama's foremost mission is to serve the worker-peasant-soldier masses. The Ministry of Culture mobilized state-owned and semiprivate theater troupes to perform in the countryside, factories, construction sites, and military barracks. The number of performances for mass audiences kept increasing as time went by. At the same time, the government sponsored a series of performance festivals before fellow artists for the purpose of discussion and emulation (*guanmo huiyan*). The achievement as a whole in this period was that the drama (*xiqu*, *huaju*, and *geju*) reached a historical record of popularization.

Most playwrights working in *huaju* continued to be active in this period, but the plays they produced in this period did not surpass the high artistic quality of plays written in the periods before 1949 because of the limitations PRC politics imposed on their writings. The exceptions were Tian Han and Lao She. Tian Han, as one of the major leaders in modern Chinese drama and theater, continued to produce excellent plays such as THE WHITE SNAKE (*Baishe zhuan*) (*jingju*, 1952), *Guan Hanqing* (*huaju*, 1958), and *Xie Yaohuan* (*jingju*, 1961). Lao She, one of the best novelists before 1949, succeeded in producing a series of plays. His *Teahouse* (*Chaguan*, 1957), coupled with its excellent performance by the Beijing People's Art Theatre, has been regarded as the best *huaju* play in this period. (Its revival in the 1980s toured Europe with success.) In this period also emerged a group of new playwrights such as Chen Qitong, Lu Yanzhou, Sun Yu, Du Yin, Yang Lüfang, He Qiu, Hai Mo, Duan Chengbin, Du Shijun, Wang Lian, Fu Du, Chen Yun, Liu Chuan, Jin Shan, Shen Ximeng, Wu Yuxiao, Bai Reng, Ren Deyao, and Sha Se. Their plays reflected the political spirit of the time, following the literary policies of the Chinese Communist Party (CCP). Their subject matter portrayed heroic struggles of the previous revolutionary and war years, told stories in the factory and the countryside, promoted progressive ideas of the young people, and exposed the seamy side of the pre-1949 "old" society. In the early 1950s plays containing criticism of party officials did appear, but their playwrights were later criticized during the Anti-Rightist movement.

Toward the mid-1960s plays tended to focus on themes of class struggle. Those portraying "middle people" as leading characters, neither politically correct figures nor class enemies, were criticized. The dominant mode of expression was SOCIALIST REALISM and revolutionary romanticism. In *xiqu* genres this period saw a big boom in three areas: (1) the rearranged or adapted traditional plays (*chuantong ju zhengli*) raised the literary quality of and brought contemporaneity to the old plays; (2) a significant number of "newly written historical plays" (*xinbian lishi ju*) of high quality emerged; and (3) plays of modern or contemporary subjects and themes (*xiandaixi*) were systematically promoted. From 1949 to 1966 there were debates on policies for *xiqu* development centering on whether the emphasis should be on modern themes or historical themes. The policy favored by the majority was to develop evenly the three types of drama just mentioned. The authors of these plays include some of the most productive *xiqu* playwrights in this period, such as Tian Han, YANG LANCHUN, Chen Renjian, Xu Jin, Wen Mu, Hu Xiaohai, Huang Junyao, Gu Xidong, Chen Wu, Wang Ken, and Yang Ming. Some of the representative and most influential *xiqu* plays are introduced in their respective entries in this encyclopedia.

During the Cultural Revolution (1966–1976) most plays, like works of other literary genres, that had been created before 1966 were denounced as "poisonous weeds" of the feudalistic, capitalistic, and revisionist works and consequently banned. Most authors were criticized, and a significant number of them were persecuted. Jiang Qing, Mao Zedong's wife, represented the ultra-leftist ideas. She had been a *jingju* and film actress in the 1930s. She held an important position in leading the reforms of Beijing opera in the 1960s. She assigned some of the best actors, musicians, and writers to work on and rework some of the best contemporary *xiqu* plays (that had been produced in the early 1960s) according to her *san tuchu* theory (three emphases on positive characters, heroic characters, and the leading heroic character). As a result, the first batch of eight plays (most of which were Beijing operas) was labeled "Revolutionary Model Plays" (*geming yangban xi*) for their thematic content and artistic quality. The subject matters of these plays are the Chinese heroic spirit in wars against Japanese invaders or civil wars in the 1930s and 1940s and the class struggle between workers/peasants and the corrupted spirit of people with old ideas in the 1950s and 1960s. In terms of aesthetic values these plays did achieve a very high quality in combining traditional theatrical conventions with innovative staging techniques that conformed to the depiction of contemporary life and were influenced by the theatrical REALISM seen in the *huaju* or on the Western stage. At the same time, *huaju* and old *xiqu* drama were proclaimed "dead." There was a well-known saying: "There are EIGHT plays for the EIGHT hundred million people [China's total population at the time]!" (a criticism of the scarcity of the entertainment forms). The model plays were established for other plays-to-be to follow. By the end of the Cultural Revolution in the mid-1970s, the number of the model plays reached about eighteen. Most other *xiqu* genres "transplanted" some of these model plays into their regional styles. Model plays such as *Red Lantern* (*Hongdeng ji*) (*jingju*), *Shajiabang* (*jingju*), and *Taking Tiger Mountain by Strategy* (*Zhi qu Weihu shan*) (*jingju*) were staged, broadcast, and screened in their cinematic versions repeatedly in cities and the countryside. Arias from these model plays were so popularized that most people were able to sing them or hum their tunes.

1976–PRESENT

Soon after Mao Zedong passed away in 1976, Jiang Qing and her close colleagues in the Political Bureau of the CCP were arrested in October of the same year by their political opponents within the party, which signified the end of the Cultural Revolution. Jiang Qing and her ultra-leftist colleagues were accused of being responsible for the damaging policies and the atrocities that took place during the revolution. In the first three years immediately after the Cultural Revolution there was a fervor for reviving well-known *huaju* plays and traditional *xiqu* plays that had been banned for ten years. Old theater artists were respected again. Within a short period all Western dramatic and theatrical theories from antiquity to the 20th century were introduced in Chinese. Masterpiece plays from the West and other countries were translated into Chinese as the second big surge of translation since the early decades of the 20th century. Exchanges between Chinese artists and their Western counterparts became a reality in the true sense. Although there had been a long tradition of staging Western plays in Chinese on the *huaju* stage, events such as ARTHUR MILLER's direction of his DEATH OF A SALESMAN in Chinese in Beijing and Richard Schechner's roundtable discussion with Chinese dramatists in Shanghai were unprecedented. Inspired by some Western theoreticians and practitioners such as Wilder and Brecht who have sought nutrition from Asian traditions, *huaju* circles began to learn consciously from *xiqu* traditions (although some directors such as Huang Zuolin and Jiao Juyin had promoted such an intention in the 1950s and the 1960s, but had not received the attention, partly because of the dominance of Stanislavsky's method). In *xiqu* circles the important roles of playwrights and directors began to be emphasized and publicly recognized. In innovative productions directors who made their names known in the *huaju* genre were also invited to direct productions of *xiqu* plays. The interaction between *huaju* and *xiqu* has been more and more conscious and active. A new generation of playwrights has emerged in both *huaju* and *xiqu* who have produced a significant number of exciting plays.

Three phases in the development of new *huaju* plays can be identified since the New Period began. The first couple of years after the end of the Cultural Revolution saw a group of plays that belonged to the *shanghen* literature (literature of the wounded) to portray victims of the Cultural Revolution in condemnation of the Gang of Four (Jiang Qing and the other three ultra-leftists in the Political Bureau) and in praise of those who had been wrongly persecuted. Zong Fuxian's IN A LAND OF SILENCE (*Yu wu sheng chu*), SHA YEXIN's *Mayor Chen Yi* (*Chen Yi shizhang*), and Su Shuyang's *Noble Hearts* (*Danxin pu*) were among this category. These plays represented an emotional urge to condemn the Cultural Revolution. The second phase was characterized by a more somber need to look for the causes of the human disaster of the Cultural Revolution in the system of the party and the government. Sha Yexin's *If I Were Real* (*Jiaru wo shi zhende*), Xing Yixun's POWER VERSUS LAW (*Quan yu fa*), and LI LONGYUN's *Small Well Alley* (*Xiaojing hutong*) represented plays of "critical realism" with different sentiments. In terms of DRAMATURGY these two groups of plays shared the same mode of realism that had been dominant in the 1950s and 1960s along with the Stanislavsky system in acting. The third phase was marked by a departure from the traditional realism. A significant number of plays written in the 1980s and 1990s sought inspiration from different schools of Western drama, particularly the EPIC THEATER, the Theater of the Absurd, and EXPRESSIONISM, and from Chinese *xiqu* drama in order to create more modes of expression for the purposes of examining the historical past, probing into the deep structure of Chinese culture and mentality, and approaching a psychological reality. Plays that can be grouped under this category are numerous. Plays by the Nobel Prize winner GAO XINGJIAN such as *Bus Stop* (*Chezhan*) and *Wild Man* (*Ye ren*) belong to this group. Further examples are Liu Shugang's *A Dead Man's Interview with the Living* (*Yi ge sizhe dui shengzhe de fangwen*), Tao Jun and Wang Zhedong's *Magic Cube* (*Mo fang*), JIN YUN's *the Nirvana of Gou'er Ye* (*Gou'er Ye niepan*), Wang Peigong's *We* (*WM*), Jia Hongyun and MA ZHONGJUN's *Trendy Red Skirts* (*Jieshang liuxing hong qunzi*), Chen Zidu, Yang Jian, and Zhu Xiaoping's THE CHRONICLE OF SANGSHUPING (*Sangshuping jishi*), and most plays staged as *xiao juchang* or *xianfeng xiju* (LITTLE THEATER or AVANT-GARDE drama) by Lin Zhaohua, Mou Sen, and Meng Jinghui. Other active playwrights in this period include BAI FENGXI, GUO SHIXING, He Jiping, LIANG BINGKUN, Yang Limin, Xu Pinli, Zhang Mingyuan, and Zhang Xian. A new phenomenon should be noted: since the mid-1980s a new genre called *xiaopin* (skit) has been developed from the format of audition and has become a theater for mass entertainment. The *xiaopin* pieces performed on stage and television were mostly light satirical comedies in the *huaju* style as both creatures and critics of commercialism. Watching *xiaopin* pieces in gala performance has been a national pastime on every New Year's Eve.

Like *huaju*, *xiqu* also produced a good number of exciting plays. This period continued to see plays "rearranged or adapted" from the traditional *xiqu* repertoire. The most interesting ones were different new versions of the *nanxi*, *zaju*, and *chuangqi* masterpieces. The number of "newly written" historical plays is overwhelmingly bigger. The concept of this traditional term was broadened in this period: it included a new trend of inventing stories with premodern settings. The reasons for the emergence of a great number of plays of this type were that (1) playwrights wanted to reinterpret legendary, literary, and historical figures and traditional Chinese culture; (2) the *xiqu* forms with their theatrical conventions are more suitable for plays with premodern settings; and (3) playwrights had more freedom to relate their stories to contemporary society. In a sense, historicity was always mingled with contemporaneity in these plays. Well-known examples are Gu Xidong's *Five Daughters at the Birthday Party* (*Wu nü bai shou*) (*Zhejiang yueju*), Ma Shaobo's *Song of Righteousness* (*Zhengqi ge*) (*jingju*), Chen Yaxian's CAO CAO AND YANG XIU (*Cao Cao yu Yang Xiu*) (*jingju*), WEI MINGLUN's *Pan Jinlian* (*chuanju*), GUO QIHONG's *Reminiscences of Southern Tang* (*Nan Tang yishi*) (*kunqu*), LUO HUAIZHEN's *Golden Dragon and Mayfly* (*Jinlong yu fuyou*) (*huaiju*), ZHENG HUAIXING's *Tears at New Pavilion* (*Xinting lei*) (*puxianxi*), WANG RENJIE's *The Lament of a Chaste Woman* (*Jiefu yin*) (*liyuanxi*), XU FEN's *Sister Tian and Zhuang Zi* (*Tianjie yu Zhuang Zhou*) (*chuanju*), Guo Dayu and Xi Zhigan's XU JIUJING'S PROMOTION (*Xu Jiujing shengguan ji*) (*jingju*), Ye Yiqing and Wu Aojun's *The Case of Pregnancy* (*Ximai an*) (*Hunan huaguxi*), and Chen Canxia, Li Xiuzhen, and Liang Zhongqiu's *An Official's Demotion* (*Bianguan ji*) (*minju*).

Equally interesting are the plays on contemporary subjects. A new phenomenon for this type of plays was that playwrights turned to modern and contemporary fiction for thematic inspiration. A number of award-winning plays were adapted from novels or short stories on contemporary subjects. They include Wei Minglun's *The Fourth Daughter* (*Si guniang*) (*Chuanju*), He Shouguang, Xu Hengbin, and Song Zefu's *Strange Marriage* (*Qi hun ji*) (*huaiju*), Dong Zhenbo's *Romantic Widow* (*Fengliu guafu*) (*pingju*), Long Xueyi's *Jinzi* (*chuanju*), Zhong Wennong's *Camel Xiangzi* (*Luotuo Xiangzi*) (*jingju*), and Wei Zhong and Zhao Damin's *Hua Ziliang* (*jingju*). Among other well-received and critically acclaimed plays on modern subjects were Gan Zhengwen's *An Official at the Lowest Level* (*Bapin guan*) (*Hunan huaguxi*), Chen Zhengqing and Tian Jingzhi's *"Six-Pound" County Chief* (*Liujin xianzhang*) (*Shangluo huaguxi*), Peng Zhigan, Yu Xiaoyu, and Xie Lu's *Story of Medicine-God Temple* (*Yaowang miao chuanqi*) (*jingju*), and Yan Meikui's *Love at the Oil Mill* (*Zhayoufang fengqing*) (*Pingxiang caichaxi*). Most of these plays portrayed the lives of ordinary people in contemporary society, which signified a departure from the dramatic theory and practice that had been dominant during the Cultural Revolution (although some of the Revolutionary Model Plays enjoyed revivals in the late 1990s).

The *xiqu* circles also sought inspiration from Western drama and developed a vogue of adapting foreign plays. In a short span of twenty years or so, dozens of different productions of Western classics emerged in various *xiqu* forms with Chinese settings. These productions include plays by Aeschylus, Sophocles, Euripides, Shakespeare, EUGENE O'NEILL, and Brecht. Taking William Shakespeare, for example, there have been adaptations from *Macbeth*, *King Lear*, *Romeo and Juliet*, *Hamlet*, *The Merchant of Venice*, *Othello*, *Twelfth Night*, *Much Ado About Nothing*, and *The Winter's Tale*—all in eighteen different *xiqu* versions, not to mention their productions on the *huaju* stage.

It is also worthwhile to note that with the advent of television sets in Chinese families since the mid-1980s, television has created and popularized new forms of entertainment that took away many audience members from live theater of all genres. At the same time, television has also made various *xiqu* forms, which had been limited to specific regions because of their distinct dialectal features, reach a broader audience and adapt to more contemporary tastes. Most central and local television stations in China have either a designated channel or a fixed time slot for the *xiqu* theater. Thus, in addition to the telecasting of the best staged productions, a new genre has been created, *xiqu dianshi lianxuju* (television series of *xiqu* drama). The significance of the *xiqu* series on television is different from that of regular television serial drama: young members of the television audience are now exposed to *xiqu* theater, and different regional styles of traditional theater are known and appreciated by audiences of other regions.

TAIWAN AND HONG KONG DRAMA

Like any region or province in the mainland of China, Hong Kong and Taiwan have their respective regional *xiqu* dramas. Guangdong *yueju* (Cantonese opera) was a dominant form in Hong Kong, Guangdong Province, and part of Guangxi Province. Because Hong Kong, although a British colony until 1997, has never been completely separate from the mainland, the development of *yueju* in Hong Kong has shared similar characteristics with its counterpart in Guangdong except for the reforms that the mainland *xiqu* experienced in the 1950s and the 1960s. Similar connections between Taiwan and Fujian Province exist for *gezaixi*, the only *xiqu* form that originated in Taiwan from a type of folk song called *jinge* sung by immigrants from Zhangzhou, Fujian Province, and later, as theater, spread to Fujian. Other *xiqu* forms shared by both places were *liyuanxi*, *gaojiaxi*, and *minju*. Unlike Hong Kong, Taiwan's separation from the mainland was complete from 1949 until the 1980s, when dramatists and theater artists began to have mutual performance visits. In the 1950s, while *gezaixi* was developed into a more mature form and into *xiangju* in some areas of Fujian Province, it was not properly supported by the Taiwanese government, which paid more attention to the development of *jingju* in Taiwan. It is said that in order to better control the island, the Taiwanese government, which had just retreated from the mainland, did not want to see the local culture develop. Another setback was when film and television brought modern forms of entertainment; the number of *gezaixi* troupes was drastically reduced. Yet film and television in turn helped create new genres such as *dianying gezaixi* (cinematic *gezaixi*) and *dianshi gezaixi* (television *gezaixi*). The new genres changed some major conventions of *gezaixi*. An opportunity for further development came in the 1980s when literary authors, culture workers, and performing artists were actively promoting native culture, art, and literature. Both the government and intellectuals started to treat it as the cultural treasure of Taiwan. Since the 1990s *gezaixi* artists in Taiwan and Fujian Province have engaged in scholarly and artistic exchanges and cooperation in performance.

Huaju in Taiwan and Hong Kong did not thrive as early as in the mainland, although both places saw the earliest performances in the first and second decades of the 20th century. *Huaju* in Hong Kong from the 1930s to 1949 can be treated as part of the whole *huaju* movement in China because it was the mainland dramatists who spread the influence of modern spoken drama to southern China, including Hong Kong, in the 1920s. Theatrical activities in the 1930s and 1940s were mainly the anti-Japanese propaganda plays staged by drama teams from the mainland. During this period a good number of important playwrights went to Hong Kong either as refugees or as sojourners. Drama activities in Hong Kong were mainly associated with them.

Soon afterwards the founding of the People's Republic of China in 1949 brought another influx of refugees. Among them were some playwrights such as Yao Ke (Yao Xinnong, Yao Hsinnung) and Xiong Shiyi (Hsiung Shih-yi), who became the leading dramatists in the 1950s and early 1960s. They, together with local dramatists such as Hu Chunbing and Li Jueben (Lai Kok Bun), gradually started a Hong Kong drama scene that was separate from that of the mainland and Taiwan. Hong Kong was a unique place in its relations with the mainland and Taiwan. Both Communist and Nationalist elements coexisted there. The Hong Kong government wanted to keep them in balance. A censorship system was imposed to avoid politically sensitive materials. Therefore, most plays written in this period did not touch upon politics concerning the two parties. Playwrights tended to write plays based on traditional stories. Plays of this type include Yao Ke's *Xi Shi*, Li Jueben's DREAM OF THE RED CHAMBER and *The Orphan of Zhao*, Li Yuanhua's (Li Woon Wah) *Meng Lijun*, Bao Hanlin's *Three Smiles* (*San xiao yuan*), and Liu Cunren's *Nirvana: The Story of Wen Tianxiang* (*Niepan*). These plays are just a continuation of the dramatic tradition of historical plays in the mainland. These playwrights also turned to contemporary society of Hong Kong for dramatic content. The subject matters were mostly limited to familial life and ethics and love affairs, but a small number of plays began to deal with community problems such as drug addiction, the conditions of factory workers, and youth education. Among the plays with contemporary subjects are Yao Ke's *The Dark Alley* (*Lou xiang*), Yin Qingyuan's *Factory* (*Gongchang ranxi lu*), Weng Jintian's *The Son's Return* (*Zi gui*), and Wang Demin's *Divorce* (*Li hun*). According to a survey made by Chen Liyin of play scripts from 1950 to 1974, the total number of new plays published or staged during this period was fewer than 200, eight per year on average. From 1950 to 1966 (when college students entered the scene), fewer than six new plays per year were either published or staged, while there were about fifty stage productions each year. That is, the majority of performances were translated plays of Western drama, which has been a prominent feature on the Hong Kong stage, and older *huaju* plays written by mainland playwrights in the 1920s through the 1940s. Because Cantonese was the spoken dialect/language in Hong Kong and Mandarin was not promoted, performances of various plays in Cantonese were widespread.

The students' active participation in theater activities in the late 1960s and 1970s pushed Hong Kong drama further toward having its own identity. There were two significant student organizations: the Association of Hong Kong College Students (Xianggang Zhuanshang Xuesheng Lianhu) and the Drama Society for Secondary Schools (Xiaoxie Xiju She). They promoted regular interschool drama festivals, which began in 1966, and contests for play scripts. Through these activities students' short plays increased the total number of new plays, and they brought new perspectives to the creation and development of Hong Kong drama. Influenced by the spirit of postwar Western drama and the increased awareness of social problems through a series of social events of the period, dramatists, professional and amateur, produced plays that explored the meaning of life, examined social realities, and discussed Hong Kong's relation to the mainland. Representative plays on these three subjects were (1) Li Zhi'ang's *Running About* (*Ben*) and Liang Fengyi's *Night Farewell* (*Yebie*); (2) *School Certificate Exam 1974* (*Huikao yijiuqisi*, by the Xiaoxie Xiju She) and Xie Liyun's *Try Not to Be a "Man"* (*Quan jun mo zuo nanzihan*); and (3) *The Sun Rises and Sets* (*Ri chu ri luo*) and *Clouds Dispersed* (*Wusan yunkai*), two of the students' performances at the inter-school drama festival in 1974. The student drama activities also nurtured a number of dramatists who were to become the leading dramatists in the 1980s and 1990s and secured a basic and constant audience for *huaju*.

The 1980s and 1990s saw Hong Kong drama coming of age. After the 1967 social movement that made Hong Kong chaotic, the government tried to provide funds and resources to build cultural life for Hong Kong people. In June 1977 the Hong Kong Huaju Troupe was established with financial sponsorship from the government. It was a milestone in elevating the status of *huaju* in the cultural scene. In the next twenty years more and more troupes were set up. There were about thirty troupes active in

1997, and most of these professional or nonprofessional troupes had been subsidized by the government. The signing of the Sino-British Joint Declaration in 1984 for Hong Kong's return to China in 1997 urged Hong Kong people to tackle the question of identity and their relations with the mainlanders. They needed to reexamine the 100-year colonial history and their current conditions and to foresee or plan their future. All these issues provided the young dramatists with ample subjects to explore. These young dramatists, most of whom studied drama and theater in the West, produced a body of new plays with a true Hong Kong sensitivity. Notable playwrights and dramatists of this period include Chan Kam-kuen (Chen Ganquan, ANTHONY CHAN), Chan Wan-ying (Chen Yinying, JOANNA CHAN), Chen Zhihua, Lam Tai Hing (Lin Daqing), Pan Huisen, To Kwok-wai (Du Guowei, RAYMOND TO), Tsang Chui Chiu (Zeng Zhuzhao), Wu Jiaxi, Yuen Lap Fun (Yuan Lixun), and Yung Ning-tsun (Rong Nianceng, DANNY YUNG). Although each dramatist has had his or her own distinctive perspectives and modes of expression, their works shared some common characteristics: a conscious identification with Hong Kong, which is different from China and Britain; the building of connections with the Chinese tradition, cultural or theatrical; and an obvious influence from Western nonrealistic dramatic modes. The four most representative playwrights in relation to the current drama movement in Hong Kong are individually introduced in this encyclopedia.

Like the Hong Kong spoken drama, *huaju* in Taiwan did not have a really significant development until the 1960s, when the island's cultural atmosphere began to embrace the spirit of Western freedom and democracy and modernism in literature and art and when professors Li Man-kui and YAO YI-WEI actively promoted drama activities in schools and universities. As mentioned earlier, the first performances of spoken drama took place in Taiwan as early as the first decade of the 20th century. During the fifty-year Japanese occupation of the island (1895–1945), troupes from the mainland went to perform in Taiwan, and three local *huaju* societies also emerged at different times. But the Japanese rulers practiced heavy censorship, which prohibited the "new drama" that promoted new ideas leading to the awakening of the Taiwanese people. Therefore, during this colonial rule it was the *xiqu* forms such as *jingju*, *gezaixi*, and glove puppet shows with their traditional plays, rather than *huaju* drama, that appealed to mass audiences. After Taiwan's return to China as a province in 1945, the Shanghai New China Drama Troupe was invited to promote performances with some local societies. When Chiang Kai-shek's Nationalist government retreated to the island in 1949, Taiwan cut off all exchanges with the mainland for fear of the penetration of Communist ideas. Then *huaju* was mainly used for propaganda and for anti-Communist messages.

In 1960 a group of students from the Foreign Language and Literature Department of Taiwan University launched a journal titled *Modern Literature* (*Xiandai wenxue*), which opened the curtain of modernism in Taiwan literature. Five years later other students started two more journals titled The *Europe Journal* (*Ouzhou zazhi*) and *Theater* (*Juchang*). These three literary journals introduced Western modernism and existentialism. Various dramatic theories and theatrical movements such as the Theater of the Absurd, Epic Theater, the Theater of Cruelty, and the LIVING THEATER were intensely introduced into Taiwan and opened the horizon for the young generation and sowed seeds for the little theater movements later.

At the same time, the domestic and international situations also changed. At home, Taiwan achieved huge economic successes in the 1960s and 1970s and developed into a modern and cosmopolitan society from an agricultural island. The government funded a series of theater activities headed by Li Man-kui and Yao Yi-wei. *Huaju* began to develop in a more mature and diversified manner, including historical plays and plays on contemporary themes ranging from romances and reminiscences to moralistic didacticism. More important, Li Man-kui and Yao Yi-wei promoted theater education and popularization by mobilizing young people and students to engage in little theater activities that introduced world classics, as well as domestic plays.

Internationally, Taiwan lost its seat in the United Nations to the mainland and, accordingly, suffered a series of diplomatic setbacks in the 1970s. These events forced the Taiwanese people to experience a deep identity crisis. They needed to rethink their relation with the mainlanders and their role in the international world while dealing with new problems caused by the rapid process of industrialization and urbanization and the modernity of their society. To express the sentiments, views, and psychology of the Taiwanese people in these areas, dramatists of this period turned to new theatrical modes introduced from the West. Yet at the same time they were ambivalent toward the strong cultural influence from the Western powers, so they experimented with ways to combine their own traditions, cultural or theatrical, with the new modes they adopted from the West. Earlier examples frequently quoted include Yao Yi-wei's *One Suitcase* (*Yi kou xiangzi*), MA SEN's *Flower and Sword* (*Hua yu jian*), Huang Meishu's (Huang Meixu) *Fool Who Wins an Ass* (*Sha nüxu*), and Chang Hsiao-fen's (Zhang Xiaofeng) *Seats* (*Weizi*).

The development of Taiwan *huaju* drama in the 1980s and 1990s was characterized by two waves of the little theater movement. Under Yao Yi-wei's leadership as the director of the Chinese Huaju Appreciation Committee (Zhongguo Huaju Xinshang Weiyuanhu), five annual experimental theater festivals were held. Five plays were staged in 1980, of which Chin Shih-chieh's (Jin Shijie) *He Zhu's Marriage—A New Version* (*He Zhu xinpei*), produced by the Lan Ling Theatre Workshop, was well received. The play was freely adapted from a traditional Beijing opera into a satirical comedy about contemporary people's obsession with money. The success was also closely associated with the acting techniques learned at La Mama Experimental Theatre Club. With the successful example of the Lan Ling Workshop, new drama workshops were set up one after another. By 1987 there existed about forty such workshops or groups. In the 1990s some old workshops either dissolved, reorganized, or developed toward more commercial ones; new little theater workshops or troupes were still being established. By 1998 the total number increased to about fifty-five, in addition to seventeen children's troupes. Among the most notable experimental or little theater groups were LAI SHENG-CHUAN'S Performance Workshop (Biaoyan Gongzuo Fang), LEE KUO-HSIU'S (Li Kuo-hsiu, Li Guoxiu) Ping Feng Acting Troupe (Pingfeng Biaoyan Ban), and LIU CHING-MIN'S (Liu Jingmin) U Theatre Troupe (You Jutuan). Other dramatists who have contributed significantly to Taiwan spoken drama include Chung Ming-te (Zhong Mingde), Hu Chin-ch'uan (Hu Jinquan), Kung Min (Gong Min), Wu Ching-chi (Wu Jingji), and Yen Chen-ying (Yan Zhenying). As these dramatists and performance groups were striving for a Taiwanese sensitivity and identity, they shared two similarities: their works reflected a tradition of being antiestablishment politically, culturally, and theatrically, and most of their works blurred the divisions between scripts and acting, between *xiju* (drama) and *jutuan/jufang* (troupe/workshop), and between the traditional speaking and realistic aspects of *huaju* and the aspects of mixing dialogues, singing, music, and dance in *xiqu*.

The political and cultural atmosphere in the mainland of China, Hong Kong, and Taiwan has permitted dramatists of the three regions to engage in two-way and three-way exchanges and cooperations since the early 1980s. The venues for these exchanges and cooperations have been joint conferences and symposiums, performance tours, joint productions involving playwrights, directors, and actors from these two or three regions, and joint scholarly publications or publications of one region's authors by another region's publishing houses. Such trends have even reached more regions—the regions where drama is written and performed in Chinese such as Macau, SINGAPORE, and Chinese communities in the West and Southeast Asia. To be all-inclusive, a new term is being used, *huawen xiju* (Chinese-language drama).

FURTHER READING

Chen Baichen and Dong Jian, eds. *Zhongguo xiandai xiju shigao* [A history of Chinese modern drama]. Beijing: Zhongguo xiju chubanshe, 1989.

Chen Liyin. "Jianshu Xianggang de huaju juben chuangzuo (1950–1974)" [A brief account of the creation of huaju scripts in Hong Kong, 1950–1974]. Xiju [Drama] 4 (1998): 48–58.

Cheung, Martha, and Jane Lai. Introduction to *An Oxford Anthology of Contemporary Chinese Drama*, ed. by Martha Cheung and Jane Lai. Hong Kong: Oxford Univ. Press, 1997. xii–xxvi.

Du, Wenwei. *Bailaohui de Zhongguo ticai yu Zhongguo xiqu* [Broadway bound: Chinese subjects and Chinese *xiqu* theater]. Shanghai: Sanlian shudian, 2002.

Fang Zixun (Fong, Gilbert C. F.). "Jin ershi nian Xianggang huaju de fazhan (1977–1997)" [The development of Hong Kong *huaju* in 1977–1997]. Section 1: http://www.6art.net/2004/6-24/12259.shtml/; Section 2: http://www.6art.net/2004/6-24/12333.shtml/.

Gao Yilong and Li Xiao, eds. *Zhongguo xiqu xiandaixi shi* [A history of modern Chinese *xiqu* plays]. Shanghai: Shanghai wenhua chubanshe, 1999.

Ge Yihong, ed. *Zhongguo huaju tongshi* [A history of Chinese spoken drama]. Beijing: Wenyi yishu chubanshe, 1997.

Hu Xingliang. *Zhongguo huaju yu Zhongguo xiqu* [Chinese spoken drama and Chinese traditional music drama]. Shanghai: Xuelin chubanshe, 2000.

Mackerras, Colin, ed. *Chinese Theatre: From Its Origins to the Present Day*. Honolulu: Univ. of Hawaii Press, 1983.

Ma Sen. "Taiwan xiaojuchang de huigu yu qianzhan" [The retrospect and prospect of Taiwan little theaters]. *Xiju yishu* [Theater Arts] 1 (1999): 27–33.

Tian Benxiang, ed. *Xin shiqi xiju shulun* [On drama in the New Period]. Beijing: Wenhua yishu chubanshe, 1996.

Tung, Constantine, and Colin Mackerras, eds. *Drama in the People's Republic of China*. Albany: State Univ. of New York Press, 1987.

Yan, Haiping. "Theatre and Society: An Introduction to Contemporary Chinese Drama." In *Theatre and Society: An Anthology of Contemporary Chinese Drama*, ed. by Haiping Yan. Armonk, N.Y.: M. E. Sharpe, 1998. ix–xlvi.

Yu, Shiao-Ling. Introduction to *Chinese Drama After the Cultural Revolution, 1979–1989*, ed. by Shiao-Ling Yu. Lewiston, N.Y.: Edwin Mellen Press, 1996. 1–34.

Zhang Geng, ed. *Dangdai Zhongguo xiqu* [Contemporary *xiqu* drama]. Beijing: Dangdai Zhongguo chubanshe, 1994.

Zuo Pengjun. *Jindai chuanqi zaju yanjiu* [A study of modern *chuanqi* and *zaju* plays from 1840 to 1949]. Guangzhou: Guangdong gaodeng jiaoyu chubanshe, 2001.

Wenwei Du

CHLUMBERG, HANS (1897–1930)

Although hardly known today, playwright Hans Chlumberg had great success with his late expressionist antiwar drama *Miracle at Verdun* (*Wunder um Verdun*, 1930).

Born Hans Bardach, Edler von Chlumberg, on June 10, 1897, in Vienna, AUSTRIA, Chlumberg attended a military academy outside Vienna and saw action as a cavalry lieutenant in ITALY during World War I. Disillusioned by the carnage and destruction, as well as by the ensuing social and political chaos of the Hapsburg Empire, Chlumberg worked as a clerk to support himself while writing propaganda pieces and experimenting with various literary styles before finding success with *Miracle at Verdun*.

His earliest plays include *The Leaders* (*Die Führer*, 1919) and *Someday* (*Eines Tages*, 1922); the latter details the breakup of a marriage under the pressures of everyday life. Chlumberg's more whimsical and experimental five-scene play *Out of a Blue Sky* (*Das Blaue von Himmel*, 1928) is a light COMEDY centering on a domestic love triangle. But in this play within a play Chlumberg challenges the illusory NATURALISM of realist theater: the proscenium arch disappears as the director asks the audience for volunteers to improvise that evening's performance since the actors are nowhere to be found. The play was successful in GERMANY, Italy, SPAIN, SWITZERLAND, and CZECHOSLOVAKIA. It premiered as *Out of a Blue Sky* on February 8, 1930, in New York, but closed after just seventeen performances.

Chlumberg proved most effective using epic dramatic techniques and expressionist themes such as pacifism, universal brotherhood, and humanism. His thirteen-scene *Miracle at Verdun* premiered in October 1930 in Leipzig. It was staged widely in Germany, AUSTRIA, FRANCE, and Great Britian, was included in *Famous Plays of 1932 to 1933*, and became a staple of left-wing European theaters. An eight-scene adaptation in English titled *Miracle at Verdun*, with incidental music by the composer Aaron Copland, premiered in New York on March 16, 1931, and ran for forty-nine performances.

At a common mass graveyard in the Argonne Forest (the site of one of the bloodiest battles of the war) in August 1939, a group of tourists led by their guide, Mazas, commemorates the war's twenty-fifth anniversary with a crass blend of nationalist prejudice and consumerism. In the following scenes France, Germany, and Great Britain memorialize their war dead for political effect; the French president goes so far as to invoke them to arise. In scene 4 a Messenger from the Lord bids the war-ravaged soldiers to arise, and, now brothers, they march in a quest for peace, to the consternation of the state, the church, and their own families. In the 12th scene a summit conference debates the consequences of the thirteen million returning war dead; their deaths were a necessary economic corrective to capitalism, but now they imperil the international economy. In the final scene the soldiers return to their graves, weary of the chaos their presence has caused and rejected by all. Society has learned nothing and is now preparing for yet another "periodic war," one even deadlier and more destructive than the last.

During rehearsals for the play in Leipzig, Chlumberg suffered a concussion after a fall from the stage and died several days later, on October 25, 1930, never seeing his work performed.

PLAYS: *The Leaders* (*Die Führer*, 1919); *Someday* (*Eines Tages*, 1922), *Out of a Blue Sky* (*Das Blaue von Himmel*, 1928); *Miracle at Verdun* (*Wunder um Verdun*, 1930)

FURTHER READING

Branscombe, P. J. "Some Depictions of the First World War in Austrian Drama." In *Studies in Modern Austrian Literature: Eight Papers*, ed. by Brian O. Murdoch and Mark Ward. Glasgow: Scottish Papers in Germanic Studies, 1981. 74–86.

Pablé, Elisabeth. "Der vergessene Welterfolg: Hans von Chlumberg" [The forgotten world success of Hans von Chlumberg]. *Literatur und Kritik* 36–37 (1969): 382–394.

Christa Spreizer

CHONG, PING (1946–)

I look at things as a visitor. That's a dominant metaphor in all my work—someone not in society but visiting as an artist.

—Ping Chong

As a playwright and director, Ping Chong's style is experimental and eclectic, drawing from AVANT-GARDE precedents, a variety of Asian performance traditions, and other sources. Born in Toronto, Chong and his parents soon relocated to New York City, where he grew up in Chinatown. Both parents performed in Chinese opera, Chong's earliest artistic influence. He was also heavily influenced by film and received a degree in this subject from the School of Visual Arts. In 1970, he enrolled in a class with dancer/choreographer Meredith Monk and soon became a member of her company. While performing with Monk he also began creating independent theater works, beginning in 1972 with *Lazarus*, an imagistic mediation on the resurrected man transplanted from its biblical setting to a contemporary metropolitan environment. In 1975 he founded The Fiji Theatre Company, which was later renamed Ping Chong and Company.

Many of his plays utilize striking visuals, poetic language, and allegory in place of a traditional narrative. A recurring motif is the outsider, which finds expression in pieces such as *Humboldt's Current* (1977), about a visionary explorer on a journey through unknown territory; *A.M./A.M.—The Articulated Man* (1982), about a robot who escapes from a research facility and tries to live as a human; and *Kind Ness* (1986), which centers around an intelligent gorilla.

One of Chong's best-known projects is his East/West series. These works examine points of cultural contact between American and European cultures and those of Asia. Works in this series include *Deshima* (1990) about Japan, *Chinoiserie* (1995) about China, *After Sorrow* (1997) about Vietnam, and *Pojagi* (1999) about Korea.

In 1992 Chong began an ongoing project called *Undesirable Elements*. It started out as an art installation focusing on the ways that society deals with otherness, but soon incorporated a live theater component. For these pieces Chong selects a group of people, interviews them, edits their material, and ultimately produces a script based on their stories, but recombined in accordance with Chong's artistic vision. The first performance was at Artists' Space in New York City, and the process has since been repeated in cities such as Cleveland, Minneapolis, Seattle, Tokyo, and Washington, D.C.

Chong collaborates closely with designers and other artists, especially on the works that he directs. For example, *SlutForArt*

(1999) is the result of a close collaboration between Chong and dancer/choreographer Muna Tseng that was first performed at the 92nd Street YMCA in New York City. The piece centers around the relationship between Tseng and her deceased brother, the photographer Tseng Kwong Chi. Recordings of Chong's interviews with Tseng Kwong Chi's friends and family are utilized in the piece in addition to Muna Tseng's first-person narrative.

In 2000, Chong received an Obie Award for Sustained Achievement. He continues to produce an eclectic body of work that crosses disciplinary boundaries. He has worked in film and video, as well as in the visual arts. Occasionally Chong even appears onstage; he performed in several of his early works and took part in later performances like *Chinoiserie* and the tenth-anniversary installment of *Undesirable Elements* in 2002.

[*See also* United States, 1940–Present]

SELECT PLAYS: *Lazarus* (1972); *I Flew to Fiji, You Went South* (1973); *Fear & Loathing in Gotham* (1975); *Humboldt's Current* (1977); *Nuit Blanche* (1981); *Rainer & the Knife* (1981); *A.M./A.M.—The Articulated Man* (1982); *Anna Into Nightlight* (1982); *The Games* (1983); *A Race* (1983); *Astonishment and the Twins* (1984); *Angels of Swedenborg* (1985); *Nosferatu: A Symphony of Darkness* (1985); *Kind Ness* (1986); *Maraya—Acts of Nature in Geological Time* (1987); *Without Law, Without Heaven* (1987); *Quartetto* (1988); *Snow* (1988); *Brightness* (1989); *Noiresque—The Fallen Angel* (1989); *Skin—A State of Being* (1989); *Deshima* (1990); *Elephant Memories* (1990); *4am America* (1990); *I Will Not Be Sad in This World* (1991); *American Gothic* (1992); *Undesirable Elements* (1992); *Persuasion* (1994); *Chinoiserie* (1995); *98.6: A Convergence in 15 Minutes* (1996); *After Sorrow* (1997); *Nocturne in 1200 Seconds* (1998); *Kwaidan* (1999); *Pojagi* (1999); *SlutForArt* (1999); *Truth & Beauty* (1999); *Secret History* (2000); *EDDA: Viking Tales of Lust & Revenge* (2001); *Children of War* (2002); *OBON: Tales of Rain and Moonlight* (2002); *REASON* (2002); *BLIND NESS: The Irresistible Light of Encounter* (2004); *God Favors the Predator* (2004); *Cathay: Three Tales of China* (2005)

FURTHER READING

Banes, Sally. *Subversive Expectations: Performance Art and Paratheater in New York, 1976–85*. Ann Arbor: Univ. of Michigan Press, 1998.

Carroll, Noel. "A Selected View of Earthlings: Ping Chong." *The Drama Review* 27, no. 1 (Spring 1983): 72–81.

Lee, Josephine. *Performing Asian America: Race and Ethnicity on the Contemporary Stage*. Philadelphia: Temple Univ. Press, 1997.

Shimakawa, Karen. *National Abjection: The Asian American Body Onstage*. Durham, N.C.: Duke Univ. Press, 2002.

Dan Bacalzo

CHOUKRI, MOHAMED (1935–2003)

Moroccan author Mohamed Choukri is best known in the West for his memoir *For Bread Alone* (1973). It was translated initially into French and then into English by the American expatriate writer Paul Bowles, but it was banned from publication in Morocco for decades. The book was eventually translated into thirty-nine languages. After this notorious debut Choukri became a fairly prolific writer, producing several other volumes of memoirs, a novel, several collections of short stories and of other experimental and difficult-to-classify shorter writings, a collection of literary criticism, and the play *Happiness* (*Al-Saada*, 1994).

That Choukri would have become an author of any kind or stature was very unlikely. In *For Bread Alone* he describes his grindingly difficult childhood and adolescence. Born in Beni Chiker in the Rif Mountains, Choukri entered the world inauspiciously, during a severe famine. His impoverished family moved first to Tetwan and then to Tangier, looking for any work and income they could find. Eight of his siblings did not live to adulthood, dying very prematurely of disease exacerbated by malnutrition. As a young boy, Choukri himself was hired out by his father as a servant to French families touring Morocco, and at one point his father "sold" him to a café owner for thirty pesetas a month. By age eleven Choukri had had enough of his father's abuse and left his family. For the next decade he supported himself by any available means—working all sorts of menial jobs, committing petty crimes, and even prostituting himself.

Choukri was in his early twenties before he learned to read and write. Interestingly, although he had grown up speaking a Berber dialect and then had learned the idioms of Moroccan *darja*, he learned to read and write in standard Arabic. Eventually he acquired enough education to become a teacher, but he did not have the temperament to deal with children. His acquaintance with the poet Mohammed El-Sabbagh inspired him to devote himself to becoming a writer. His progress was interrupted by his troubling reunion with his family and his mother's death, by his periodic bouts of heavy drinking, and by emotional instability that culminated in his commitment to an insane asylum for four months. The writing of *For Bread Alone* served as a sort of purgation of much of this personal anguish and established Choukri as a leading AVANT-GARDE figure in Morocco and beyond. Despite the ban on his books in Morocco, his achievement was rewarded with a professorship in Tangier, which he held for two decades. For the last two decades of his life he worked as an editor and writer for MEDI I/Radio in Tangier. Besides Paul Bowles, Choukri became closely acquainted with such literary figures as JEAN GENET, TENNESSEE WILLIAMS, Edouard Roditi, and Juan Goytisolo. Although Choukri affected a bohemian appearance and manner in his public appearances, he lived rather simply, maintaining a modest household and a limited number of personal relationships.

PLAY: *Happiness* (*Al-Saada*, 1994)

FURTHER READING

Dawood, Ibrahim. "Review of *Streetwise* by Mohamed Choukri." *World Literature Today* 71 (Spring 1997): 440.

Gauthier, J. D. "World Literature in Review: Morocco." *World Literature Today* 67 (Summer 1993): 635–636.

Kirkup, James. "Obituary: Mohamed Choukri; Celebrated Figure of Literary Tangier." *Independent* (London) (November 19, 2003): 18.

"Moroccan Novelist." *Gazette* (Montreal) (November. 7, 2003): B6.

Tanoukhi, Nirvana. "Rewriting Political Commitment for an International Canon: Paul Bowles' *For Bread Alone* as Translation of Mohamed Choukri's *Al-Khubz Al-Hafi*." *Research in African Literatures* 34 (Summer 2003): 127–144.

Martin Kich

THE CHRONICLE OF SANGSHUPING

Premiered by the China Central Drama College in 1988, *The Chronicle of Sangshuping* (*Sangshuping jishi*) or *Sangshuping Chronicles*, written by Chen Zidu, Yang Jian, and Zhu Xiaoping, is one of the most successful experiments combining the realist tradition with the suggestive theater (*xieyi xiju*) of the ancient Greek and the Chinese operatic theater.

Based on Zhu Xiaoping's series of novels about Sangshuping, a small, isolated village in the northwestern part of CHINA, *The Chronicle of Sangshuping* presents the sorrows, tragedies, and daily routines of a poor village where ignorance, illiteracy, sexual suppression, a primitive lifestyle, and a brutal patriarchal structure have remained unchanged for thousands of years. The sense of futility in attempting to bring about any change is communicated by the bare, revolving stage, which alternately displays the different geographic features characteristic of the "yellow earth plateau," with its deep valleys, steep hills, soil erosion, and harsh living conditions. It provides a continuously moving performance space upon which singing and dancing chorus members portray villagers harvesting wheat or participating in local rituals, such as begging "the rain dragon" to fall on the neighboring village, while they, the villagers of Sangshuping, hasten to harvest the wheat in time. In one scene a woman is stripped naked by her insane husband in front of the villagers, who further insult and surround her, as if watching a caged animal. However, as the teasing crowd disperses, one sees a piece of marble representing the statue of a goddess standing in the woman's place, while the woman herself disappears into the singing chorus, who now meditate on the fate of an innocent girl drowned in the flowing river of history, but who left behind a frozen image in an infertile land inhabited by helpless men and women.

The play draws on the literary and dramatic trend known as "meditation on the historical and cultural past" (*lishi wenhua fansi*). According to its director, Xu Xiaozhong, it attempts to present a "living fossil" to symbolize the cultural and historical sentiments of the past 5,000 years as a way of calling for real change in contemporary China. This appeal is conveyed by stressing the changeless nature of the village. Li Jindou, a Communist production team leader, seems no different from the local despots depicted in pre-1949 literature. At once a slave to his immediate superior and a tyrant to the villagers, he rules as patriarch of his clan, and he imprisons Wang Zhike because he is an outsider with a different surname. The play imparts the message that the "sea of bitterness and misery of the poor people before liberation" is evident in the very landscape of contemporary China and will only grow worse with the unfolding events of the Cultural Revolution. Punctuating the play from beginning to end, the chorus's song, which acclaims and questions China's 5,000-year history (including that of the People's Republic of China), certainly leaves the impression that China still needs enlightenment and liberation. This critique, together with the play's stage design, acting talents, and creative directing, produced a classic piece of drama.

FURTHER READING

Chen, Xiaomei. *Acting the Right Part: Political Theater and Popular Drama in Contemporary China*. Honolulu: Univ. of Hawaii Press, 2002.

——, ed. *Reading the Right Texts: An Anthology of Contemporary Chinese Drama with a Critical Introduction*. Honolulu: Univ. of Hawaii Press, 2003.

Chen, Zidu, Yang Jian, and Zhu Xiaoping. *Sangshuping Chronicles*. Tr. by Cai Rong. In *Literature and Society: Anthology of Contemporary Chinese Drama*, ed. by Haiping Yan. Armonk, N.Y.: M. E. Sharpe, 1998. 123–261.

——. *Sangshuping jishi* [The chronicle of Sangshuping]. *Juben* 4 (1988): 4–28.

Lin, Haipo. *Jiushi niandai zhongguo xiju yanjiu* [A critical study of Chinese drama in the 1990s]. Beijing: Beijing guangbo xueyuan chubanshe, 2002.

Pan, Ping. "Triumphant Dancing in Chains: Two Productions of Chinese *Huaju* Plays in the Late 1980s." *Asian Theatre Journal* 16, no. 1 (Spring 1999): 107–120.

Yan, Haiping. "Theater and Society: An Introduction to Contemporary Chinese Drama." In *Literature and Society: Anthology of Contemporary Chinese Drama*, ed. by Haiping Yan. Armonk, N.Y.: M. E. Sharpe, 1998.

Xiaomei Chen

CHURCHILL, CARYL (1938–)

> *Playwrights don't give answers, they ask questions. We need to find new questions, which may help us to answer the old ones or make them unimportant, and this means new subjects and new form.*
> —Caryl Churchill

Caryl Churchill has been described by Benedict Nightingale, chief theater critic for the *Times* (London) and a contributor to the *New York Times*, as "uniquely important," whether or not she is, as he says, "the English-speaking world's greatest female dramatist." Churchill is unique: she is an innovative, collaborative, and socially conscious playwright whose style continues to evolve and cannot be easily categorized. And she is, arguably, the greatest (and most prolific) woman playwright in the English language.

Although some—including Churchill—might regret the implied sexism inherent in pairing the adjective "female" with the title "dramatist," especially in the 21st century, the modifier should not be construed as marginalizing or minimalizing. A self-proclaimed socialist-feminist playwright, Churchill consistently uses her intellect, artistry, and political engagement to create new forms in which she critiques the classism, sexism, violence, and oppression she locates in contemporary culture. She has been a prominent theatrical voice for more than thirty years, indisputably important as an English playwright, regardless of her gender, but also specifically significant as a woman playwright. Churchill was and is a leader in bringing women's issues to the stage. In a world where the writing of women remains undersupported, undervalued, and underproduced, Churchill's work has received widespread critical acclaim and has inspired countless theater makers, but has particularly influenced feminist practitioners and scholars. And at the same time Churchill's plays are produced in London (and other international) theaters, they appear regularly on university stages and syllabi; they are among the plays (still too few) by women to have entered the "canon" of Western dramatic literature.

Caryl Churchill was born in London on September 3, 1938, and spent most of her early childhood there, except for a brief period in the Lake District during the war. In 1948 she moved with her family to Montreal, CANADA, and lived there until 1955. Between 1957 and 1960 Churchill read English language and literature at Oxford University, where she received a B.A. in English. She wrote constantly throughout her childhood and, from the age of twenty or so, focused primarily on playwriting. While she was at Oxford, Churchill's early plays were produced by student groups. *Downstairs*, a one-act, was staged in 1958 and went to the Sunday Times/National Union of Students Drama Festival in 1959. *Having a Wonderful Time* received a student production at the Questors Theatre in Ealing in 1960, and *Easy Death* appeared at the Oxford Playhouse the following year. In this same period Churchill began writing plays for radio, one of which, *You've No Need to Be Frightened*, had a student sound production in 1961.

During the 1960s and into the early 1970s Churchill continued to write for the stage, but also for television and radio, the latter being the forum in which her plays were first professionally produced. Between 1962 and 1972, seven radio plays, all directed by John Tydeman, were broadcast on the BBC Third Programme: *The Ants* (1962), *Lovesick* (1966), *Identical Twins* (1968), *Abortive* (1971), *Not . . . not . . . not . . . not . . . not enough oxygen* (1971), *Schreber's Nervous Illness* (1972), and *Henry's Past* (1972). *The Judge's Wife* was televised on BBC-TV in 1972.

An intensely private person who rarely grants interviews, Churchill discloses little about her personal life. Her plays are never overtly self-referential; biography, therefore, plays little or no role in the critical reception of her oeuvre. She has said, in fact, that she sought to resist the "semi-autobiographical novels" that women in her generation were writing and to create a greater distance in her work. But this is not to suggest that Churchill does not write through her experiences as a woman. While she has noted, for example, that radio drew her partly because it held a greater market for plays in the early 1960s than did the theater, she has also noted that the short-form pieces she wrote during that decade, which made fewer demands on her time than the theater would, were compatible with the demands of her life as a woman. During the 1960s Churchill married David Harter (1961) and gave birth to three sons: Joe (1963), Paul (1964), and Rick (1969). Whether or not the juggling of marriage, motherhood, and career was, as a practical issue, reflected in the rhythm of Churchill's writing practices, her life as a working mother coincided with the women's movement, and feminist concerns began to influence the content and politics of her plays. Although she did not begin her career by thinking of herself as a "woman writer"—much less a feminist—she acknowledges that she "became increasingly interested in women's issues and consciously chose to write about those."

Churchill's career took an important turn in 1972, when *Owners* was presented by the Theatre Upstairs at the Royal Court in London. Although she had written approximately twenty plays by this time, *Owners* was the first full-length piece to receive a professional production. *Owners* began a new phase in Churchill's professional life, one in which she devoted herself primarily—and more directly—to work in the theater. *Owners* also commenced her long and continuing association with the Royal Court Theatre, where she was the first woman writer in residence in 1974–1975, and where her most recent play, *A Number*, was staged in 2002. Further, *Owners* can be said to prefigure much of Churchill's subsequent DRAMATURGY. It is first and foremost a darkly comic critique of capitalism, exposing the violence and greed of a culture that values ownership as a measure of human achievement. But the play also experiments with and subverts traditional gender roles.

Owners revolves around Marion, a real estate developer whose acquisitiveness is her means of controlling those around her and of achieving a sense of self-worth. Her husband, Clegg, is a "family butcher" who comically expects Marion to conform to his conventional expectations that she be a subservient wife, while she repeatedly cuckolds him and treats him with condescension. Marion's opposite is Alec, her Zen-like former lover, who wants nothing—nothing at all. The central action of the play concerns Marion's aggressive attempts to get the passive Alec back and, failing that, to get back at him. Using her employee, Worsely, as her henchman, she purchases the building in which Alec, his wife, Lisa, and their family live as tenants. When Marion's threats to evict Alec do not persuade him to become "hers," she manipulates Lisa into signing over her and Alec's newborn baby to Marion. The building, the spouses, and the baby are treated like pieces of property by the various characters (except Alec) who fight to claim ownership. The play culminates in an arson committed by Worsely at Marion's behest; Alec and another baby perish in the fire. The tone of *Owners* can be described as black humor; Churchill acknowledges the influence of JOE ORTON. Through increasingly outlandish and absurdly violent acts, the play points to the futility of human greed.

Owners might be said to be more of a socialist than a feminist play; its most poignant moments depict the helpless poverty of Lisa as she struggles to hold on to her home and family. But this play reveals an incipient feminism, for the central characters do not conform to traditional gender roles. Churchill's reading of Eva Figes's *Patriarchal Attitudes* influenced her writing of the buffoonlike Clegg. And though the play ostensibly explores the spiritual opposition of the "active, achieving attitude of 'Onward Christian Soldiers,'" embodied by Marion, to the spirit of a Zen poem, "sitting quietly, doing nothing," embodied by Alec, Churchill felt that it was crucial that the woman be active and the man passive, so that their actions would be seen for what they were and not be mistaken for traditional "masculine" and "feminine" behavior.

Marion, a character who possesses traits often associated with aggressive, male, and capitalist ruthlessness, clearly prefigures Marlene, the central character of TOP GIRLS. Written ten years after *Owners*, *Top Girls* expands upon the earlier play's socialist critique of capitalist culture, but does so with a more overtly feminist emphasis. First staged at the Royal Court Theatre in 1982, exactly a decade after *Owners*, *Top Girls* was written between 1980 and 1982, when the recent election of the first female prime minister in Great Britain seemed to evidence the significant advances made by women in society. *Top Girls* draws a direct parallel between the conservative Margaret Thatcher and Marlene, challenging the notion that the mere "advancement of women" solves social ills. Marlene, managing director of the Top Girls Employment Agency, enters into a personal and political argument with her working-class sister, Joyce, saying of Thatcher, "She's a tough lady, Maggie. I'd give her a job." To which Joyce retorts, "What good's first woman if it's her? I suppose you'd have liked Hitler if he was a woman. Ms. Hitler. Got a lot done, Hitlerina." Some critics have described the play as a "feminist critique of feminism," but what Churchill does is far more complex. She cuts across issues of gender and class, exposing a social structure without real "winners." No one in the play is happy. And in her customary fashion, Churchill asks questions but does not offer easy answers.

One might say that the "answers" Churchill offers are found within her playwriting innovations. *Top Girls* implies that women should make radical changes to the patriarchal system rather than replicate it, a connection Churchill makes to her own career. She says, "I remember before I wrote *Top Girls* thinking about women barristers—how they were in a minority and had to imitate men to succeed—and I was thinking of them as different from me. And then I thought, 'Wait a minute, my whole concept of what plays might be is from plays written by men.'" Although Churchill claims not to have been preoccupied by gender as a writer, she clearly broke both molds and barriers and created a dramaturgical style that has, in fact, become a model for feminist playwriting and production.

For feminist critics who champion disruptions of traditional (male) models of dramatic structure, one of the qualities that marks Churchill as an innovator is her tendency to work within collaborative structures. Although some of her best-known and most successful plays, such as *Owners*, *Top Girls*, and *Softcops* (1978), were written entirely on her own, a great many others were written in close collaboration with others: directors, actors, and composers and, more recently, choreographers and dancers. With only a few exceptions, Churchill has always functioned as the sole writer of her plays, but her writing has been greatly influenced by collaborative processes in which she has participated.

In 1976 Churchill embarked upon her first playwriting collaborations by working with two separate companies on two different plays, both set in 17th-century England. She wrote in 1982 that after these important experiments, "Though I still wanted to write alone sometimes, my attitude to myself, my work and others had been basically and permanently changed." The first experiment, *Vinegar Tom*, was conducted with MONSTROUS REGIMENT, a feminist theater collective. This particular project clearly reflected the feminist politics of the time, the group, and Churchill herself. Churchill first encountered members of Monstrous Regiment through political activism, at an abortion rally. The group was interested in creating a piece about witchcraft, a subject also of interest to Churchill. She had already read *Witches, Midwives, and Nurses* by Barbara Ehrenreich and Deirdre English when she was invited to attend the rehearsal of another Monstrous Regiment play. There they shared a list of books they were reading and generally discussed their ideas for working together. Churchill found the session "exhilarating." *Vinegar Tom*, the resulting piece, is, as Churchill describes it, "a play about witches with no witches in it; a play not about evil, hysteria and possession by the devil but about poverty, humiliation and prejudice, and how the women accused of witchcraft saw themselves." *Vinegar Tom* unfolds in twenty-one scenes, punctuated by modern songs sung by actors wearing contemporary dress. In the Brechtian style embraced by many feminist directors and critics, Churchill created a contemporary comment on the historical action, asking audiences, "Who are the witches now?" Which women—and people—does society scapegoat? Which single, sexual, and unruly women or nonconformists would have been hanged for witchcraft in the 17th century? (This time Churchill provides her audience with an answer: "Here we are.") Churchill worked with Monstrous Regiment again in 1978, contributing to its cabaret, *Floorshow*.

The second collaborative project Churchill undertook in 1976 was *Light Shining in Buckinghamshire*, a piece that began a long association with the Joint Stock Theatre Group and with director

Max Stafford-Clark, who also served as director on a number of Churchill's solo ventures, including *Top Girls* (1982), *Ice Cream* (1988), and *Blue Heart* (1997). Churchill's work on *Light Shining* overlapped with *Vinegar Tom* and explored the same time period. The Joint Stock Theatre Group had a preexisting process for the group creation of plays. It first selected a topic for exploration, then conducted a workshop period in which the group (including actors, director, and playwright) shared readings, conversation, games, and improvisation. On the basis of whatever emerged in the workshop period, the writer would independently create a script, then return to the company for a final period of rehearsal and revision. For *Light Shining in Buckinghamshire*, Stafford-Clark and Churchill chose to explore the millennial movement in the civil war: the utopian desires of those oppressed people who fought to overthrow the monarchy. But as Churchill says, "The play shows the amazed excitement of people taking hold of their own lives," when "soldiers fought the king in the belief that Christ would come and establish heaven on earth," but instead met with "an authoritarian parliament, the massacre of the Irish, the development of capitalism."

Like *Vinegar Tom*, *Light Shining in Buckinghamshire* made use of various theatrical strategies derived from BERTOLT BRECHT, strategies that have since become associated with feminist theater practice. In an unusual casting experiment that began as a joke between Churchill and Stafford-Clark, the characters wound up being played by different actors each time they appeared. The effect, as one critic said, was to root the play's history in a "*collective* consciousness which is its protagonist and hero." As in *Vinegar Tom*, Churchill's use of historicization cast light on contemporary conditions by asking audiences to make connections between past and present.

Churchill teamed with Joint Stock again in 1979 for CLOUD NINE, a play that explores what she describes as "the parallel between colonial and sexual oppression." This play followed the same process; this time actors were chosen for their personal, as well as acting, experiences and, during the workshop, shared stories about their sexual backgrounds and attitudes. The first act of *Cloud Nine* is set in Victorian Africa; the second is set in present-day (1979) London. Churchill's writing cuts across a number of social issues, exposing and connecting the oppression of colonized blacks, closeted homosexuals, and submissive women. And Churchill's text is enhanced by her staging experiments: In act 1 the characters are cast across racial and gender lines to highlight the social construction of these roles; in act 2 actors play characters of their own sex—different characters than in the first act. The play also tampers with time; the second act is set 100 years after the first, but only twenty-five years pass for the characters.

Another series of collaborative projects involved venturing into various communities and conducting oral research among living people. For FEN (1982), Churchill, Stafford-Clark, and the Joint Stock Theatre Group went out into the fens of East Anglia to talk with field workers; members of the company returned to "present" people they had met. Churchill says, "*Fen* is a play with more direct quotes of things people said to us than any other I've written." The play presents several generations of (primarily) women; it reveals the oppressive conditions of their lives as their hard labor is eternally exploited for the profit of others.

Serious Money (1987) took Churchill, Joint Stock, and Stafford-Clark to "the City," the financial center of London. The idea for the subject matter was Stafford-Clark's, but Churchill's biting, satirical attack on the greed and corruption at the very center of the capitalist system hit one of her favorite thematic targets at dead center. Stylistically, her inspiration to write the play in verse was another dazzling display of theatrical craft.

Mad Forest (1990) was another project conducted in the style of Joint Stock, this time organized by Mark Wing-Davey, a former member of the company. While director of the Central School of Speech and Drama, Wing-Davey had the idea to take students to Romania to create a piece about the recent revolution. Students lived with Romanian families and talked with people on the street; the play, *Mad Forest*, portrays the lives of two ordinary families from different social strata living under the oppression of the Communist regime and through the revolution and its aftermath. Here language becomes especially important as the characters are first afraid to speak freely, then effect political change through speech. *Mad Forest* continues Churchill's formal experiments, with doubled casting, realistic scenes mixed with scenes of high theatricality, and the embodied image of Romania's past as a blood-sucking vampire.

Formal experiments occupied Churchill throughout the 1990s as she began to work more extensively with music, song, and dance. *Lives of the Great Poisoners* (1991), written in collaboration with Orlando Gough and Ian Spink, incorporates song and dance with text, as does THE SKRIKER (1994). *Hotel* (1997), also written with Gough and Spink, consists of two parts, "Eight Rooms," which is entirely sung, and "Two Nights," which is danced.

Stephen Daldry, the director of several of Caryl Churchill's most recent plays, *This Is a Chair* (1997), FAR AWAY (2000), and *A Number* (2002), says that the playwright "has her finger on the pulse of time" and that her plays "always seem to prefigure the next important debate." Churchill has often been described as prescient, never more so, perhaps, than in *Far Away*. Written in 2000, *Far Away* captures the futile, escalating spiral of fear, hatred, and war; the play was even more chilling in its New York production in 2002, as it seemed to have anticipated the events of 9/11 and the "War on Terror." But Churchill has always traced the timelessness of greed, violence, fear, and oppression in human lives.

Churchill has also been prescient—or timely—in her stagecraft. She has been on the cutting edge of staging issues regarding gender and sexuality and in her examinations of the political and economic means through which human beings oppress one another. Subverting traditional dramaturgy in myriad ways, she writes nonlinear and episodic structures; she creates overlapping dialogue and overlapping roles. She explores a full range of acting styles. She often attacks the most serious subject matter with a humorous tone. Her plays typically do not have protagonists or antagonists; they are far more complex. She is a feminist playwright who does not create automatic sympathy for women or antipathy for men, but who examines sexual oppression as only one social ill among many. She does, however, always plead for the impoverished, the oppressed, and the victimized; she relentlessly exposes greedy and violent human behaviors, implicitly asking audiences to take a hard look—and to come up with their own answers.

[*See also* England, 1940–Present]

PLAYS: *Downstairs* (1958); *Having a Wonderful Time* (1959); *You've No Need to Be Frightened* (1959?); *Easy Death* (1960); *The Ants* (1962); *Lovesick* (1966); *Identical Twins* (1968); *Abortive* (1971); *Not . . . not . . . not . . . not . . . not enough oxygen* (1971); *Henry's Past* (1972); *The Judge's Wife* (1972); *Owners* (1972); *Schreber's Nervous Illness* (1972); *Moving Clocks Go Slow* (1973); *Perfect Happiness* (1973); *Turkish Delight* (1973); *Objections to Sex and Violence* (1974); *Light Shining in Buckinghamshire* (1976); *Traps* (1976); *Vinegar Tom* (1976); *The After Dinner Joke* (1977); *Floorshow* (contributor to, 1977); *The Legion Hall Bombing* (1978); *Softcops* (1978); *Cloud Nine* (1979); *Three More Sleepless Nights* (1979); *Top Girls* (1980–1982); *Crimes* (1981); *Fen* (1983); *Midday Sun* (with Geraldine Pilgrim and Peter Brooks, 1984); *A Mouthful of Birds* (with David Lan and Ian Spink, 1986); *Fugue* (with Ian Spink, 1987); *Serious Money* (1987); *Hot Fudge* (1988); *Ice Cream* (1989); *Mad Forest* (1990); *Lives of the Great Poisoners* (with Orlando Gough and Ian Spink, 1991); *The Skriker* (1994); *Thyestes* (translated from Seneca, 1994); *Blue Heart* (1997); *Hotel* (with Orlando Gough and Ian Spink, 1997); *This Is a Chair* (1997); *Far Away* (2000); *A Number* (2002)

FURTHER READING

Aston, Elaine. *Caryl Churchill*. London: Northcote House, 1997.
Aston, Elaine, and Janelle Reinelt, eds. *The Cambridge Companion to Modern British Playwrights*. New York: Cambridge Univ. Press, 2000.
Cousin, Geraldine. *Churchill the Playwright*. London: Methuen, 1989.
Fitzsimmons, Linda, comp. *File on Churchill*. London: Methuen, 1989.

Rosemary Malague

THE CIRCLE

Written in 1919 and premiered at the Haymarket, London, in 1921, the three-act COMEDY *The Circle* is SOMERSET MAUGHAM's most revived play, and, despite the fact that the play was booed by early audiences who did not understand some of the lines and were confused by the concluding elopement scene, it is also the one he considered his best. Maugham's comic characters and their all-too-human failings, combined with the star appeal of Fay Compton, Allan Aynesworth, and Ernest Thesinger, ensured *The Circle* a long run for the original production, wherein, according to *The Times of London* (March 4, 1921), "This brilliant play is brilliantly acted." The first New York production was similarly successful. Subsequent London revivals include productions in 1931, 1944—a production that featured John Gielgud and Leslie Banks, with decor by interior designers Sybil Colefax and John Fowler—and 1977, and the play has also been adapted for the screen: *The Circle* (directed by Frank Borzage, 1925) and *Strictly Unconventional* (directed by David Burton, 1930).

The Circle has a beguilingly simple moral: that each must make his own mistakes. It is a message well suited to the character-driven comedy that Maugham creates.

Thirty years before the action of the play, Lady Kitty Champion-Cheney left her husband, the Member of Parliament Clive Champion-Cheney, and her five-year-old son, Arnold, for her lover, Lord Hughie Porteus. Since then the pair has lived unmarried and in exile in Florence, part of the European demimonde, isolated from "respectable" society, gradually falling out of love and aging rather grotesquely. Arnold is now a Member of Parliament and is married to Elizabeth. They live in a fastidiously elegant house in which he indulges his interest in antique furniture. Elizabeth has grown tired of her husband and is set upon an affair with Teddy Luton, the intense but glamorous and successful manager of a Malayan rubber plantation. The comic plot depends not just on the paralleling of the two illicit love affairs—separated by several decades—and on the comic characters of Lord Hughie and Lady Kitty, but just as significantly on the strategy that Clive proposes to Arnold to prevent Elizabeth's elopement. Elizabeth must be allowed to make a free choice between two baldly put alternatives: a loveless but secure and respectable marriage or a life of exile tinged with scandal that is all too immediately represented by the decaying and fractious Lord Hughie and Lady Kitty. Both Clive and Arnold believe that, faced with the stark warning of the older couple, Elizabeth will balk at the risk.

The strategy, however, fails, and Elizabeth and Teddy elope. But, the play hints, their fate might be different from that of Lord Hughie and Lady Kitty. Maugham suggests that there is a chance of success for their relationship. While they ostensibly repeat the actions of the earlier generation, Maugham is clear that the characters involved are very different. Teddy, for example, has been utterly clear-eyed: he does not offer Elizabeth romance and happiness—which the example of Lord Hughie and Lady Kitty proves does not last—but real love with its attendant troubles and pain and unpredictability. And, daringly, Maugham also permits the possibility that society too might change to encompass different values. This was a bold proposition for 1920s Britain. The war was over and a new world order was being built, but divorce remained scandalous, and Maugham himself knew the cost of sex and sexuality that challenged conventional morality. But *The Circle* is a play that encompasses the potential of a vital, physical sexual affair; indeed,

Maugham celebrates characters who claim an active heterosexual life without the formal bonds of marriage. Unusually for him, this goal offers the prospect of true happiness and contentment. As Anthony Curtis summarizes, "In spite of all the awfulness, Maugham is saying, and all the degradation, if you do give up all for love, the world is well lost" (Curtis, 1982).

Despite the appeal of the comic situation, some of the play's comedy might now seem labored. Dramaturgically it is locked into a limitingly conventional take on structure and form. Linguistically it is located in a class and a society that barely made it to 1940, let alone into the postwar decades. But still the characters (and in particular the old and the new lovers) retain their appeal, and the play may indeed be described as achieving a "perfect balance of astringency and sentiment" (Curtis, 1982).

[*See also* England, 1860–1940]

FURTHER READING

Cordell, Richard. *Somerset Maugham: A Biographical and Critical Study*. London: Heinemann, 1961.

Curtis, Anthony. *The Pattern of Maugham: A Critical Portrait*. London: Hamilton, 1974.

——. *Somerset Maugham*. *Writers and Their Work*. Windsor: Profile Bks., 1982.

Morgan, Ted. *Somerset Maugham*. London: J. Cape, 1980.

Rogal, Samuel J. *A William Somerset Maugham Encyclopedia*. Westport, Conn.: Greenwood Press, 1997.

Whitehead, John. *W. Somerset Maugham: The Critical Heritage*. London: Routledge, 1987.

Adrienne Scullion

CIXOUS, HÉLÈNE (1937–)

Writer, philosopher, activist, successful playwright, proponent of *écriture feminine* (feminine writing), and founder of the first and only Women's Study Center in FRANCE, Hélène Cixous has made her mark in virtually every literary genre, as well as across institutions of education and justice. Born in French-controlled Algeria in 1937, Cixous grew up surrounded by a multiplicity of languages and cultural-political identities, a heightened awareness of bodies, and a prevailing sense of exile—experiences that are strongly reflected in all her writings. Her father was a Mediterranean Jewish doctor whose first language was French; her mother, a German-Czechoslovakian Jew who had fled GERMANY to escape Adolf Hitler and trained as a midwife after her husband's early death in 1948.

Cixous left Algeria for France in 1955. While studying James Joyce for her doctorate in the early 1960s, Cixous met Jacques Derrida, Jacques Lacan, and other key figures of poststructuralist thought, becoming influential as a philosopher and a spokesperson for the emerging student movement. In an extraordinary turn of events the French government charged the thirty-one-year-old Cixous with the task of creating an experimental university (University of Paris VIII) in 1968; she promptly hired such innovators as Michel Butor, Gérard Genette, Tzvetan Todorov, and Michel Foucault, with whom she also worked for Groupe Information Prison (GIP), an activist group focusing on police brutality and injustices within the judicial system.

In 1974 Cixous founded the first European doctoral program in "études feminines," which roughly translates as "feminine studies," a phrase Cixous did not choose and that has been vastly misinterpreted ever since. For Cixous, the feminine does not refer to any received cultural or biological definitions of woman, but rather an approach to writing, reading, teaching, and activism that emphasizes multiplicity of viewpoints, limitlessness of form and desire, and the pleasure of contradiction. The feminine describes the liberation of unconscious knowledge contained by the body of either sex, and Cixous frequently cites works by William Shakespeare, James Joyce, and JEAN GENET as examples of feminine texts.

Cixous's involvement in theater began when she met ARIANE MNOUCHKINE, artistic director of the Théâtre du Soleil, in 1972, in an effort to organize agit-prop (AGITATION-PROPAGANDA) performances with the GIP. However, their intensive, extended collaboration did not begin until 1975, when Cixous's play *Portrait of Dora*, a feminist reimagining of Sigmund Freud's famous case history, proved a surprise hit. Her subsequent works have an epic sweep, staging critical moments of decision and destiny in human history: THE TERRIBLE BUT UNFINISHED STORY OF NORODOM SIHANOUK, KING OF CAMBODIA (1983), *Indiade, or the India of Their Dreams* (1987), and *The Perjured City; or, The Awakening of the Furies* (1994), based on a health scandal in which French officials knowingly allowed HIV-tainted blood to be distributed to hospitals.

For Cixous the writer, plays offer an escape from the inwardness of prose; for Cixous the activist, the mission of theater is to produce "a state of incessant alert to responsibility." She believes plays to be the ideal artistic forum for humans to encounter and learn from one another, since "by showing us our crimes in the theater, in front of witnesses, plays accuse us and at the same time pardon us" (Cixous, 1989).

PLAYS: *The Pupil* (*La Pupille*, 1972); *Portrait of Dora* (*Portrait de Dora*, 1976); *The Arriver* (*L'Arrivante*, 1977); *The Name of Oedipus, Song of the Forbidden Body* (*Le Nom d'Oedipe, Chant du corps interdit*, 1978); *The Conquest of the School at Madhubai* (*La prise de l'école de Madhubaï*, 1984); *The Terrible but Unfinished Story of Norodom Sihanouk, King of Cambodia* (*L'histoire terrible mais inachevée de Norodom Sihanouk, roi du Cambodge*, 1985); *Indiade, or the India of Their Dreams* (*Indiade ou, l'Inde de leurs rêves*, 1987); *The Miraculous Night*, co-authored with Ariane Mnouchkine (*La nuit miraculeuse*, 1989); *No Leaving, No Returning* (*On ne part pas, on ne revient pas*, 1991); *The Perjured City* (*La Ville parjure ou le réveil des Erinyes*, 1994); *Black Sail White Sail* (*Voile Noire Voile Blanche*, 1994); *The Story (Never to be Known)* (*L'Histoire, [qu'on ne connaître jamais]*, 1994); *Drums on the Dam* (*Tambours sur la Digue*, 1999)

FURTHER READING

Cixous, Hélène. *The Hélène Cixous Reader*. Ed. by Susan Sellers. London: Routledge, 1994.

——. *The Terrible but Unfinished Story of Norodom Sihanouk, King of Cambodia*. Tr. by Juliet Flower MacCannell, Judith Pike, and Lollie Groth. Lincoln: Univ. of Nebraska Press, 1994.

——. "Writings on Theater." *Qui Parle* 3 (1989): 120–132.

Kiernander, Adrian. *Ariane Mnouchkine and the Théâtre du Soleil*. Cambridge: Cambridge Univ. Press, 1993.

Showalter, Elaine, ed. *The New Feminist Criticism: Essays on Women, Literature, and Theory*. New York: Pantheon Bks., 1985.

Charlotte Stoudt

CLARK, SALLY (1953–)

Born in Vancouver in 1953, Sally Clark moved to Toronto in 1973 and has been an active playwright for numerous companies across CANADA for the past thirty years. Clark has been a playwright-in-residence for the Theatre Passe Muraille, the Shaw Festival, Buddies in Bad Times, and Nightwood Theatre. She won the prestigious Chalmers Award in 1990, the Governor General's Award, and the Prix du Jury in 1992.

Coming out of the feminist movement of the 1970s and 1980s, Clark's work portrays female characters who refuse to be defined by gender stereotypes. Her characters are constantly, often physically, battling society's aim to put them in their place. Often Clark's heroines, Joan of Arc and Frances Farmer, among others, are forced to suffer ordeals because of their resistance to conventional pressure of how women should behave in society.

Clark often poses a feminist slant to historical and literary figures in her work. *The Trial of Judith K.* (1985) is a feminist version of Franz Kafka's novel *The Trial*; *Jehanne of the Witches* (1989) is a 15th-century story of Joan of Arc and Bluebeard. *Life Without Instruction* (1994) presents the tale of the female Renaissance Italian painter who was raped by her painting instructor; later she enacts her revenge by painting him as the biblical King Holofernes beheaded by a vindictive Judith. The image of victim turned to triumphant transcendence is one that Clark incorporates throughout her plays.

Clark's successful play *Moo* (1988), which won the Chalmers Award, is about a woman who is shot in the head, institutionalized, and finally abandoned by her husband. Despite her role as victim, however, Moo achieves a level of revenge by seducing her husband and also beating him up in various encounters with him. The play jumps through different stages of the characters' relationship from past to present as it documents Moo's tumultuous relationship and her triumph and despair over her relationship with her "rotter" husband.

Clark's portrayal of the tragic life of Frances Farmer, SAINT FRANCES OF HOLLYWOOD (1994), continues the theme of wrongful incarceration. Frances Farmer was a rising film star in the 1920s and 1930s; her promiscuity, outspokenness, and activity in the Communist Party proceeded to ruin her film career. Farmer's refusal to compromise her character is in conflict with both the Hollywood directors and her own mother, who ends up institutionalizing Farmer in an attempt at control. The story follows Farmer's raucous life to her lobotomy in 1949 and death in 1970.

An active film writer as well as playwright, Sally Clark was a resident at the Canadian Film Centre in 1992, where she wrote and directed her first short film, *Ten Ways to Abuse an Old Woman*, which won her the Prix du Jury award at the Henri Langlois International Short Film Festival in 1992. She also won the Bronze Award for Best Dramatic Short at the Worldfest Charlston Festival in 1993. She is currently a resident of Vancouver, where she continues to write and direct independent films.

PLAYS: *The Trial of Judith K.* (1985); *Moo* (1988); *Jehanne of the Witches* (1989); *Life Without Instruction* (1994); *Saint Frances of Hollywood* (1994); *Lost Souls and Missing Persons* (1998); *WASPS* (1998); *Wanted* (2004)

FURTHER READING

Clark, Sally. "(Re)Appropriation as Translation." *Canadian Theatre Review* 64 (Fall 1990): 22–31.

Conolly, L. W., ed. *Canadian Drama and the Critics*. Rev. ed. Vancouver: Talonbooks, 1995.

Holly Maples

CLAUDEL, PAUL (1868–1955)

In addition to being the brother of the famous sculptor Camille Claudel, Paul Claudel may be best known to English-language audiences through W. H. AUDEN's allusion in "In Memory Of W. B. Yeats," where he is numbered among those time will "pardon" because of his fine writing. Auden's misgivings about Claudel are indicative of a disparity in Claudel's critical reception: he is seldom performed in the United States or England, while he is regarded as one of the most important writers of the 20th century by much of continental Europe. Just as BERTOLT BRECHT's ties to Marxism have often prejudiced the reactions of his audience, so Claudel's devotion to Catholicism—and the proximity of his work to its dogmas—has dominated critical discussion of his work. Further, Claudel's conservative politics often invited attacks, particularly when he wrote an ode to Henri Pétain, head of the Vichy government, in 1940. Although Claudel, like Brecht, used alienating techniques and nonrealistic theatrical styles, this radical and innovative DRAMATURGY was put to the service of a devoutly conservative worldview.

Born Paul-Louis-Charles-Marie Claudel on August 6, 1868, in Villeneuve-sur-Fère-en-Tardenois, Claudel experienced a tumultuous early childhood, with frequent relocations required by his father's work. When his parents separated, his mother brought the children to Paris, where Paul attended the famous Lycée Louis-le-Grand. He went on to study Asian languages and law before pursuing a lifelong career in the diplomatic corps.

Shortly after receiving his *baccalauréat* in 1885, Claudel discovered the poetry of Arthur Rimbaud and recognized in Rimbaud's *A Season in Hell* echoes of his own feelings of despair. In 1886, at the Christmas Day Mass at Notre Dame Cathedral, Claudel was seized by religious fervor, although he waited until 1890, after completing his exams for the diplomatic service, before publicly converting to Catholicism. By 1887, however, he had begun to associate with the Parisian symbolists in Stéphane Mallarmé's circle, often attending the weekly salons at that poet's apartment. Aurélien Lugné-Poë at the Théâtre de l'Oeuvre, known for its symbolist work, was the first to stage one of Claudel's plays, *The Tidings Brought to Mary*, although this occurred as late as 1912.

Claudel's unconventional dramaturgy was influenced by his remarkable diplomatic career; he was posted to countries on four continents and spent more than fifteen years of his life in Asia. His interest in Japanese *kabuki* led to his collaboration with composer Kineya Sakichi on *The Woman and Her Shadow* (1922), and Asian influence is also evident in *The Book of Christopher Columbus* (1927). His reputation in FRANCE as a dramatist was rejuvenated in 1943 by Jean-Louis Barrault with a historic production at the Comédie Française of THE SATIN SLIPPER (1924), a play with an especially diverse mixture of theatrical techniques. Later in the century his work received acclaimed productions by directors Jean Vilar, Antoine Vitez, and Bernard Sobel.

For the last twenty years of his life, Claudel's literary output consisted mainly of essays, religious poetry and commentary, translations, adaptations of Japanese poetry, and literary correspondence. He was admitted to the Académie Française in 1947. Claudel died in Paris on Ash Wednesday, February 23, 1955, and was granted a state funeral.

PLAYS: *The Tidings Brought to Mary* (1892); *Break of Noon* (1905); *The Hostage* (1909); *Crusts* (1914); *The Humiliation of the Father* (1916); *The Satin Slipper* (1924); *The Book of Christopher Columbus* (1927)

FURTHER READING

Chaigne, Louis. *Paul Claudel: The Man and the Mystic*. Tr. by Pierre de Fontnouvelle. New York: Appleton-Century-Crofts, 1961. Originally published as *Vie de Paul Claudel et genèse de son oeuvre*. Tours: Mame, 1961.

Chiari, Joseph. *The Poetic Drama of Paul Claudel*. London: Harvill Press, 1954.

Ryan, Mary. *Introduction to Paul Claudel*. Dublin: Cork Univ. Press, 1951.

Daniel Mufson

CLAUS, HUGO (1929–)

Hugo Claus is generally acknowledged to be the finest Dutch-language playwright (and novelist and poet) of the 20th century. Even French-speaking Belgians admit that he is the greatest living writer of their bilingual nation. Born in Bruges on April 5, 1929, and brought up in the East Flemish town of Kortrijk, he passed his childhood during the German occupation of BELGIUM in World War II. He was profoundly marked by the experience, which penetrated into the very fibers of his family, as recounted in *The Sorrow of Belgium* (1983), his most renowned novel. As a young man he took off for FRANCE, working for a time in the sugar-beet fields and factories of the north, which provided material for his play *Sugar* (*Suiker*, 1958), then spending time in Paris. He became associated with the art movement Cobra (named after the three cities involved, Copenhagen, Brussels, and Amsterdam), whose most famous exemplars are Karel Appel, Asgr Jorn, and Pierre Alechinsky. In addition to several marriages, he had a notorious affair with the porn star (*Emmanuelle*) Sylvia Kristel. He has won the coveted Triennial Award for Theatre an unprecedented three times and is often mentioned as a candidate for the Nobel Prize.

An enormously prolific poet, novelist, cineast, and visual artist, he has in addition authored no fewer than fifty plays, many of which have achieved success in the theaters of Belgium, Holland, France, and GERMANY. While his poetry and prose reveal a certain consistency, with their signature mix, like their author, of the earthy and erudite, his dramatic output is marked by a protean variety. In early works, those that have brought him the greatest praise, he followed in the wake of such American naturalists as TENNESSEE WILLIAMS, ARTHUR MILLER, and John Steinbeck. With *Bride in the Morning* (*Een bruid in de morgen*, 1955), *Suiker*, and *Friday* (*Vrijdag*, 1969), Claus established his solid reputation in the theater. These are well-constructed and even traditionally constructed works, dependent on the colorfulness of their characters and the pathos of their situations, typically embroiled in impossible loves. Like the Mins, two elderly, bald twins who work in the sugar-beet factory, who, in effect, live for each other, all the principal characters of these works face the frustration of seeing their greatest passions thwarted.

Passing briefly through an absurdist phase that resurfaced in his later collaborative work, *Serenade* (1984), he was pulled by the polar attractions of the heroes of his generation: BERTOLT BRECHT and ANTONIN ARTAUD. He incorporates the cool distantiation of the former with the cruel grotesquery of the latter. Even in the early naturalistic works he cannot avoid dramatizing that which is twisted and sordid in human character. It is no accident that, when doing his famous adaptations of classics to modern contexts, he undertook plays such as the Roman Seneca's *Thyestes* and the Jacobean Cyril Tourneur's *Revenger's Tragedy*, plays that linger over grisly detail and gnarled human souls.

The taboo in sexual conduct is one of Claus's lingering preoccupations. In *Bride in the Morning* it is the suggestion that the semiretarded young hero and his sister are entertaining an incestuous relationship; in *Friday* it is the consummated sexual relationship of father and daughter; in *The Sacrament* (*Interieur*, 1971) the young hero cannot reconcile his homosexuality or attraction (which seems at some point to have been reciprocated) for his priest/uncle, Deedee. In a seemingly political play, written partly in verse reminiscent of W. S. Gilbert, such as *The Life and Works of Leopold II* (*Het leven en de werken van Leopold II*, 1970), Claus puts emphasis on the colonizer of the Congo's combined sexual envy and fascination with the African black men he subjugates and has transported in boxes, stuffed, to his palace in Brussels for close inspection, and on Leopold's insatiable lust for young females. The greed for territorial domination is equated with an equal hunger for human flesh. Even in a predominantly spiritual work such as *The Temptation* (*De verzoeking*, 1980) the extremely chaste elderly nun, Sister Mechtild, conducts an imaginary carnal liaison with her Lord, Jesus Christ. At the moment of most extreme spiritual ecstacy, her orgasm produces an unwonted stream of urine during the ceremony meant to celebrate her sainthood. The bathos and scatology of this dramatic "climax" is pure Artaudian Claus.

In a domestic drama (as expressed by its title), *Back Home* (*Thuis*, 1975), Claus uses the atmosphere of the ancient Flemish *klucht* or slapstick FARCE to dramatize an ostensibly ordinary Flemish family's peccadilloes. The colorless son comes home after an extended absence, his latest girlfriend in tow, who then obligingly lends her body to the old man's fantasies. But at the very moment when fulfillment could have been his, the father suffers a stroke and, incapacitated, crawls into bed alongside the ancient, senile crone whom he and his wife nurse in exchange for occupation rights.

PLAYS: *Bride in the Morning* (*Een bruid in de morgen*, 1955); *The Assassin's Song* (*Het lied van de moordenaar*, 1957); *Sugar* (*Suiker*, 1958); *Look Ma, No Hands!* (*Mama, kijk, zonder handen!* 1959); *The Heron's Dance* (*De dance van de reiger*, 1962); *Tijl Uilenspiegel* (1965); *(M)oratorium* (1966); *Thyestes* (1966); *The Golden Land* (*Het goudland*, 1967); *Maskeroon* (*Masscheroen*, 1968); *The Revenger's Tragedy* (*Wraak!* 1968); *Friday* (*Vrijdag*, 1969); *The Life and Works of Leopold II* (*Het leven en de werken van Leopold II*, 1970); *The Spanish Whore* (*De Spaanse hoer*, 1970); *Tooth by Tooth* (*Tand om tand*, 1970); *Oedipus* (1971); *The Sacrament* (*Interieur*, 1971); *The Fox Hunt* (*De vossejacht*, 1972); *Pas de Deux* (1973); *So-So* (*Blauw blauw*, 1973); *Back Home* (*Thuis*, 1975); *Orestes* (1976); *The House of Labdachos* (*Het huis van Labdakos*, 1977); *Jessica!* (1977); *Phaedra* (1980); *The Temptation* (*De verzoeking*, 1980); *An Anthem* (*Een hooglied*, 1981); *Hair of the Dog* (*Het haar van de hond*, 1982); *Blindman* (*Blindeman*, 1984); *Hamlet* (1984); *Serenade* (1984); *Gilles* (1988); *The Rocking Horse* (*Het schommelpaard*, 1988); *Under the Towers* (*Onder de torens*, 1993)

FURTHER READING

Claus, Hugo. *Hugo Claus: Four Works for the Theatre*. Ed. by David Willinger. New York: CASTA, 1990.

Willinger, David. "Belgium." *Western European Stages* 13, no. 1 (Winter 2001): 15–28.

——. "Introducing Hugo Claus." *Western European Stages* 2, no. 1 (Spring 1990): 45–48.

——, ed. *An Anthology of Contemporary Belgian Plays, 1970–1982*. Troy, N.Y.: Whitson, 1984.

David Paul Willinger

CLOSER

Closer, PATRICK MARBER's second play, first opened in the Cottesloe Auditorium of the Royal National Theatre in London on May 22, 1997. This production, directed by Marber, was later transferred to the West End Lyric Theatre, previewing on March 19, 1998. A New York production, also directed by the playwright, opened on March 9, 1999, at the Music Box Theater on Broadway. The play received critical acclaim, garnering the 1997 Evening Standard Best Comedy Award, the 1997 Critics' Circle Best Play Award, the 1998 Olivier Award for Best New Play, and the 1999 New York Drama Critics' Circle Award for Best Foreign Play.

Closer explores the sexual relationships of four characters whose professions thematically suggest a preoccupation with surface appearances. Dan, an obituary writer, and Alice, a stripper, meet and become lovers after she is mildly injured when she steps into the path of a cab he is riding in. Dan later pursues Anna, a photographer, who at first rejects him and befriends Alice.

In a scene that has been critically spotlighted as both explicit and comical, Dan then impersonates Anna on the Internet and meets Larry, a dermatologist. The two engage in anonymous virtual sex. Both men are seen at computer terminals in private spaces, Dan in his flat, Larry in his office. Neither speaks, but their obscene keyboard dialogue is projected at the rear of the stage.

In this pessimistic view of modern relationships, lies and sexual intimacies are the common means of exchange as partners struggle and fail to become close. Ultimately the play covers almost five years in the lives of the four characters. During this period Larry meets the real Anna and marries her, Dan and Anna have an affair, Anna and Larry sign divorce papers, Larry and Alice briefly become lovers, Dan returns to Alice, and Anna returns to Larry, having never mailed the divorce papers to her lawyer. By the final scene all four characters have parted ways, and Alice has been "knocked down by a car" in New York City, a death foreshadowed by the accident in scene 1.

More than any other character, Alice is objectified and used by her lovers. Marber highlights her abuse and her self-protective facades with frequent SYMBOLISM. Alice becomes the subject of Dan's novel and a popular photograph in Anna's gallery. She performs for Larry in a private room of the strip club. Larry demands that she strip her club persona as well as her clothes, and the final irony of the play is prepared as she makes an important personal revelation and he fails to believe her.

The play has been compared to NOËL COWARD's *PRIVATE LIVES* with its constant shuffling of partners and acerbic wit. The frequent one-liners are evocative of Marber's previous careers as a standup comedian and radio satirist. *Closer* includes scenes of violent passion and extreme profanity, but Marber tempers this fury with a plot structure that is intentionally contrived. The first meeting and last farewell of each pair of lovers are contained within the action of the play. Each scene can be characterized as a new tryst or a breakup of partners.

Marber also completed a screenplay version of *Closer*, which was directed by Mike Nichols and produced by Columbia Pictures in 2004. The film received several awards and nominations including a Golden Globe nomination for Best Screenplay.

[*See also* England, 1980–Present]

FURTHER READING

Eyre, Richard, and Nicholas Wright. *Changing Stages: A View of British and American Theatre in the Twentieth Century*. London: Bloomsbury, 2000.

Shellard, Dominic. *British Theatre Since the War*. New Haven: Yale Univ. Press, 2000.

Sierz, Aleks. *In-Yer-Face Theatre: British Drama Today*. London: Faber, 2001.

Steven C. Pounders

CLOSET DRAMA

I believe that literature . . . will give us a theater whose representation will be the truly modern cult: a book.

—Stéphane Mallarmé

The term "closet drama" refers to plays written to be read, not to be performed in a theater. Closet dramas thus imply a preference for solitary reading in a closet (i.e., in a private, secluded room) over a public performance. While in most cases dramatic texts are fully realized only when they are performed, closet dramas are fully realized on the page and constitute one literary genre among others, such as lyric poetry, the novel, or autobiography. But because any dramatic text necessarily evokes the possibility of stage representation, closet dramas do not simply ignore the theater, but often actively reject it. They thus belong to a history of antitheatricality, of opposition to the theater.

Throughout the history of the closet drama, playwrights chose to avoid the theater for a variety of reasons. One of the earliest writers of closet dramas was Plato, whose dialogues and dramas, such as *The Republic* (360 B.C.E.), attacked the theater on philosophical and pedagogical grounds, arguing that it tends to overwhelm the good sense of the audience and to simulate false worlds. Plato's dialogues initiated the tradition of the philosophical dialogue, which has continued to attract 20th-century philosophers such as Martin Heidegger and Paul Feyerabend. Theorists of the theater such as Edward Gordon Craig, OSCAR WILDE, and BERTOLT BRECHT have used philosophical dialogue to present provocative visions of a radically new theater. Craig's two dialogues on "The Art of the Theatre" (1911), Wilde's *The Decay of Lying* (1889), and Brecht's *Messingkauf* (1939–1942) are examples of dramatic dialogues about theater written not to be performed, though they use dramatic form.

Other writers chose to avoid the theater because they found the theater practices of their time incompatible with their art. To this group belongs the Roman playwright Seneca, but also 19th-century writers and poets. Percy Bysshe Shelley, Lord Byron, Johann Wolfgang von Goethe, Alfred Tennyson, and Algernon Charles Swinburne wrote plays they deemed too ambitious and literary for the theater, which they considered a vulgar form. This tradition of closet dramas acquired particular significance for early modernism, when poets and writers avoided the theater in order to preserve what they considered the purity of the written word. Gustave Flaubert's *The Temptation of St. Anthony* (1847), many symbolist plays such as Stéphane Mallarmé's *Hérodiade* (1869), and the poetic plays of HUGO VON HOFMANNSTHAL belong in this group.

Some modernist closet dramas are driven less by an aesthetic critique of the theater than by a recognition of its inherent limitations. KARL KRAUS's *The Last Days of Humanity* (1918/1919), which describes the degradation of public discourse before and during World War I, the long dramatic "Circe" chapter in James Joyce's quintessential modernist novel *Ulysses* (1922), and HENRIK IBSEN's PEER GYNT (1867) involve too many characters, demand too many changes of scene, and are simply too long to allow for stage representation. With changing conceptions of theatrical representation, however, many of these plays have found their way into the theater. A related group of closet dramas includes dramatic texts written by experimental writers of the 1920s and 1930s who similarly exceeded the actual or perceived limits of theatrical representation. Many of GERTRUDE STEIN's plays do not even have designated characters and settings and thus seem to ignore the most basic requirements of stage representation. Wyndham Lewis's *Enemy of the Stars* (1914), printed in the AVANT-GARDE journal *Blast*, is simply too unruly to invite a theatrical production.

Censorship has often forced plays that were written to be performed to become de facto closet dramas. Oscar Wilde's *Salomé* (1893) could not be performed in England because of a law forbidding the representation on the stage of biblical figures, and so Wilde decided to publish the play with elaborate drawings by Aubrey Beardsley instead. GEORGE BERNARD SHAW's *Plays Pleasant and Unpleasant* (1898) were also forced into the category of closet drama by the censor. Because closet dramas are defined by the absence of stage representation, what is or continues to be considered a closet drama thus depends on shifting aesthetic, economic, and legal notions governing the theater.

FURTHER READING

Barish, Jonas. *The Antitheatrical Prejudice*. Berkeley: Univ. of California Press, 1981.

Deak, Frantisek. *Symbolist Theater: The Formation of an Avant-Garde*. Baltimore: Johns Hopkins Univ. Press, 1993.

Puchner, Martin. *Stage Fright: Modernism, Anti-theatricality, and Drama.* Baltimore: Johns Hopkins Univ. Press, 2002.

Martin Puchner

THE CLOTHES THEY STOOD UP IN

First published in 1996, ALAN BENNETT's *The Clothes They Stood Up In* tells the tale of a typically dissatisfied older married couple. Like much of Bennett's work, it describes what happens to ordinary individuals when they are confronted with their own narrow lives and battle for, or fight against, transformation. For Bennett's characters, the journey of self-discovery is fraught with the struggle between the need for change and a strong desire to keep to the status quo.

Maurice and Rosemary Ransome are a middle-aged, middle-class couple who have nothing but opera to look forward to. "They had no children and but for Mozart would probably have split up years ago." On returning home from a production of *Così fan tutte* they discover that their home has been burgled. Rather than just taking the valuables, the unknown burglar appears to have taken everything. The house is empty of every item, every piece of furniture is gone, and the Ransomes are left with only the clothes on their backs.

Without their possessions, the Ransomes must try to start over; they find themselves changing the fabric of their lives along with their furniture. Mrs. Ransome begins to explore the neighborhood; she enjoys local shopping at the Pakistani market and is surprised to find her life changing for the better. Mr. Ransome, however, does not adapt as well as his wife does; he dreams of Mozart and the slow rhythm of their previous routine.

As the Ransomes begin to get used to their new lives, a disruption comes with a letter and the return of their possessions. Mrs. Ransome finds this as distressing an event as the loss of her material goods. While Mr. Ransome remains too old to change or learn from the experience, Mrs. Ransome discovers that "not the least of what they had lost in the burglary were their little marital deceptions." Their marriage, according to Mrs. Ransome, only continues out of habit. With the loss of everything, Mrs. Ransome suddenly sees through their veil of domestic amnesia and travels on her own "timorous voyages of discovery."

Bennett's plays and television dramas are often subtle, understated performances of the tragedies of daily life. Like ANTON CHEKHOV, Bennett concentrates on the family circle, class pretensions, and ordinary people contemplating the very things that make them ordinary. He presents much of his work on domestic British life. *The Clothes* is a subtle portrayal of the dissatisfactions of middle-class domestic life.

FURTHER READING

Bergan, Roland. *Beyond the Fringe . . . and Beyond: A Critical Biography of Alan Bennett, Peter Cook, Jonathan Miller, and Dudley Moore.* London: Virgin Bks., 1990.

Kendle, Burton S. "Alan Bennett." In *Contemporary Dramatists*, ed. by K. A. Berney. 5th edition. London: St. James, 1993.

Wolfe, Peter. *Understanding Alan Bennett.* Columbia: Univ. of South Carolina Press, 1999.

Wu, Duncan. *Six Contemporary Dramatists: Bennett, Potter, Gray, Brenton, Hare, Ayckbourn.* London: St. Martin's, 1995.

Holly Maples

CLOUD NINE

It'll be fine when you reach Cloud Nine. . . . Upside down when you reach Cloud Nine.

—Song, *Cloud Nine*

Written by CARYL CHURCHILL, directed by Max Stafford-Clark, and performed by the JOINT STOCK THEATRE GROUP in 1979, *Cloud Nine* has a significance that extends beyond its inherent value as a groundbreaking play about sexual oppression. Its creation represents a historic collaboration; its experiments in cross-gender, cross-racial, and double casting exemplify the power of embodied performance. Many subsequent theatrical and theoretical works investigating onstage representations of gender and sexuality have been modeled on or inspired by *Cloud Nine*.

Churchill had previously collaborated with Stafford-Clark and Joint Stock on *Light Shining in Buckinghamshire*; she joined them again for this project exploring "sexual politics." *Cloud Nine* followed Joint Stock's basic working method: the company conducted a three week workshop with Churchill, she wrote for twelve weeks, then returned for a six-week period of rehearsal and revision. Given the topic, actors were chosen for their personal, as well as acting, experiences and, during the workshop, shared stories about their sexual backgrounds and attitudes. They played improvisational games exploring power dynamics and role reversals, read books, and engaged outside contributors, including the mother of an actor and a woman who cleaned the rehearsal space. Using material generated in the workshop, and influenced by the writings of JEAN GENET, Churchill crafted a script manifesting what she describes as "the parallel between colonial and sexual oppression." The resulting play took a two-act form: the first is set in Victorian Africa, the second in present-day (1979) London.

Act 1 concerns the household of Clive, a British colonial administrator. The theatrical conceit is its cross-casting: some actors play characters of the opposite sex or another race, highlighting the social construction of gender and racial roles. Clive's wife, Betty (male actor), tries to be what men want her to be. Clive's black servant, Joshua (Caucasian actor), says that his "soul is white." Clive's gay son, Edward (female actor), can never be the man his father wants. Clive's daughter, Victoria (played not by a live actor but by a doll) is the seen-but-not-heard Victorian girl. Characters pursue one another with misdirected sexual desire while maintaining the facade of Victorian propriety. Clive chases Mrs. Saunders, who wants to be left alone; Ellen kisses Betty, who is oblivious to lesbianism; Betty desires Harry, who, secretly gay, has sex with Joshua and Edward. In a send-up of traditional comic endings, Harry, a homosexual, weds Ellen, a lesbian. The characters' cross-casting and cross-purposes make comically clear—yet also poignant—the difficulties of conforming to artificial roles and societal expectations.

Act 2 resumes the stories of Betty, Edward, and Victoria. Though 100 years have passed, they have aged only twenty-five. The biggest change, however, is that the actors switch characters, all but one playing roles of their own sex, further destabilizing notions of fixed identity. Clive and his paternalistic control disappear, and everyone changes; breaking free of conventional roles and relationships, they experiment with, and begin to accept, their sexualities. They *enjoy* sex more freely, putting them on "cloud nine." Betty changes most, allowing herself solitary sexual pleasure, becoming independent, and attempting new relationships. Her self-acceptance is embodied in the final image of the play, when she embraces the Betty of act 1.

A critical and popular success, *Cloud Nine* was immediately revived by the Royal Court Theatre in London in 1980 and received an Obie Award–winning production in New York in 1981. Currently regarded by some critics as a bit dated, *Cloud Nine* remains widely read, produced, and studied.

[*See also* England, 1960–1980]

FURTHER READING

Aston, Elaine. *Caryl Churchill*. London: Northcote House, 1997.

Aston, Elaine, and Janelle Reinelt, eds. *The Cambridge Companion to Modern British Playwrights*. New York: Cambridge Univ. Press, 2000.

Cousin, Geraldine. *Churchill the Playwright*. London: Methuen, 1989.

Fitzsimmons, Linda, comp. *File on Churchill*. London: Methuen, 1989.

Rosemary Malague

THE CLUB

Just because he is my son, I don't need to be a relative of his!

—The Mother, Act 3

JESS ØRNSBO's *The Club*, which premiered in 1995, was written for the small-stage Bådteatret (the Boat-Theatre) in Copenhagen, which disposed of only four actors for the production. This premise dictated the almost mathematical structure, which concerned the distribution of the parts on the two older and two younger actors, and at the same time implied the central thematical point: in the end it turns out that the many different parts actually are only four individuals. The fragmented narrative was typical of the time, known, for example, from BOTHO STRAUSS, and so far it reflected the postmodern trend. But, contrary to the deliberate search for absence of meaning, the scattered composition of *The Club* gradually creates patterns that in the end point to the typical Ørnsbo motifs: the family as a hate-love institution, and the father, mother, sister, and brother relations in all kinds of destructive and humiliating combinations, which make up a mosaic portrait of an actual way of living and of a cold and alienated society of the era. It may be compared with catastrophic or in-yer-face theater; however, the author developed his dramatic universe, with its characteristic absurd humour, much earlier.

The Club is made up of three very different acts. The first act consists of eleven scenes, small situations that in various ways treat meetings and confrontations between individuals of different ages and social classes, introduced by a scene in which a lonesome male individual tries to obtain access to an obscure "club." In a seeming mystification follow without further explanation episodes with the hateful mother, the schizophrenic child murderer, the cynical doctor who mocks his AIDS patients and sleeps with his secretary, who by the way recently has had an affair with one of the patients, the transvestite, the incestuous father, and others. Nevertheless, small hints indicate connections. In the shape of a short sound intermezzo, the second act draws a sketch of a perfect upper-class family with all kinds of energy resources. This is a significant contrast to the third act, which takes place in the barricaded flat of the mother (the different elderly women of the first act); it is Christmas, the family has been split, and gradually, as it is gathered again, while the different family members arrive, all the fragmented stories told in the first act merge into one single story about the insane and alcoholic mother, the incestuous, transvestite father, who is a former doctor, the criminal and psychotic brother, the AIDS-sick sister, who is a secretary, and so on. The "club" is the family, pervaded by an enormous mother fixation. With *The Club* Ørnsbo managed to reach another audience than that of the more institutionalized stages that mostly had shown his dramas, and thus to take a position in the very dynamic development of new Danish playwriting in the 1990s. The critics recognized the author's enormous, grotesque linguistic creativity. But, as has often been the case, several of them disliked his "monomaniac misanthropy" (Sørensen, 1995), declaring, for example, that "I don't need Ørnsbo's smashing, voluptuous whip . . . his sadism, hatred and obscenities" (Gade, 1995), even if they recognized his comic originality.

[*See also* Denmark]

FURTHER READING

Gader, Jonna. "Mors Eget Lille Gaskammer" [Mother's own little gas chamber]. *Ekstra Bladet* (March 20, 1995).

Kistrup, Jens. "Playwright for and Against Theatre." *Danish Literary Magazine* 5 (1993).

Sørensen, Viggo. "Ørnsbos Græsselige Familie" [Ørnsbo's horrible family]. *Jyllands-Posten* (March 3, 1995).

Theil, Per, and Lise Garsdal. *Hvem der? Scener fra 90erne* [Who's these? Scenes from the 90's]. Copenhagen: Høst og Søn, 2000.

Bent Holm

THE COAST OF UTOPIA

The Sovereign People are our invention.

—Alexander Herzen, Act 2, *Shipwreck*

Premiering in 2002 and consisting of *Voyage*, *Shipwreck*, and *Salvage*, the historical trilogy *The Coast of Utopia* features the great Russian intellectuals: noble-born anarchist Michael Bakunin, socialist reformer Alexander Herzen, and literary critic Vissarion Belinsky. Drawing from Isaiah Berlin's *Russian Thinkers* and E. H. Carr's *The Romantic Exiles*, TOM STOPPARD traces the maturation and disappointment of his characters' hopes for social transformation and individual fulfillment.

In *Voyage* the nineteen-year-old Bakunin returns from his military post to his familial estate outside Moscow, where his idealism conflicts with the staid opinions of his serf-owning parents. He denounces the passionless engagement of his sister Liubov to an aristocratic cavalry officer, which she eventually breaks off. Set in Moscow and St. Petersburg, as well as on the estate, the play intertwines the romantic concerns of Liubov and her three sisters with the philosophical debate and political agitation of Bakunin and his comrades, particularly Belinsky and Herzen. By the play's end Bakunin has abandoned his military post, has been stripped of his noble rank, and has fled to FRANCE to avoid forced labor in Siberia. *Voyage* establishes the trilogy's presiding tension between utopian aspiration and attainable, if compromised, personal happiness.

Shipwreck focuses on France between 1846 and 1852, where Herzen and his wife Natalie have settled in order to seek medical aid for their deaf son, Kolya. In the wake of the disillusioning defeat of the 1848 revolutions throughout Western Europe, Herzen endures personal catastrophe. During the summer of the revolution he learns of Belinsky's death. In 1851 he discovers that Natalie has had an affair with his friend, George Herwegh. The same year both Kolya and Herzen's mother drown. The loss of Kolya shatters Natalie, who dies in childbirth three months later, with the newborn also dying. Defying a state-issued decree for his return to Russia, Herzen embarks for England. In the penultimate scene he reunites with Bakunin on the Channel ferry, or dreams that he does (Stoppard leaves it unclear). Bakunin exults in the possibility of a successful peasant revolt in Russia. Having grown suspicious of revolution, Herzen responds by prophesying a civilization defined by the "collapse of law" and "fields left to rot."

Set between 1853 and 1868, *Salvage* concentrates upon Herzen in London amid other revolutionaries exiled from the Continent. He has an affair with the wife of his friend Ogarev, fathering a daughter by her. He also publishes and sends to Moscow *The Bell*, a journal committed to the emancipation of the serfs. Emancipation comes in 1861, but does so—as Herzen notes—without markedly improving the peasants' lives. Younger radicals denounce Herzen's support of gradual reform. Undaunted, Herzen affirms in the play's last scene a populist politics directed at the laborer's "personal happiness," ephemeral though this may be—a credo that encapsulates Stoppard's own liberal realism.

Several critics who saw the Trevor Nunn–directed premiere at Britain's National Theatre celebrated the trilogy for its moments of Chekhovian subtlety. Admiring reviews were often tempered by the observation that the work, with its nine-hour running time, sacrificed dramatic power to what the *London Times* described as "relentlessly protracted arguments."

[*See also* England, 1980–Present]

FURTHER READING

Berlin, Isiah, Sir. *Russian Thinkers*. Ed. by Henry Hardy and Aileen Kelly. New York: Penguin, 1979.

Carr, Edward Hallett. *The Romantic Exiles: A Nineteenth-Century Portrait Gallery*. New York: Octagon Bks., 1975.

Herzen, Aleksandr. *From the Other Shore and The Russian People and Socialism*. Tr. by Moura Budberg (*From the Other Shore*) and Richard Wollheim (*The Russian People and Socialism*). New York: Oxford Univ. Press, 1979.

Nadel, Ira Bruce. *Double Act: A Life of Tom Stoppard*. London: Methuen, 2004.

Nikolai Slywka

THE COCKROACH OPERA

Small-time criminals, prostitutes, transvestites, slum dwellers, petty officials, and journalists are among the stage characters in NANO RIANTIARNO's *The Cockroach Opera* (*Opera kecoa*) premiered in 1985 by his group, Teater Koma, at the Taman Ismail Mazurki, an arts complex in the center of Jakarta. The play, in the form of musical theater, is part of a trilogy that includes *Time Bomb* (*Bom waktu*, 1982) and *Julini's Opera* (*Opera Julini*, 1986).

At the premiere crowds jostled for tickets, box-office windows were smashed, and scalpers sold tickets for a considerable profit. Every performance was monitored by government security agencies. In the same year, when performed in the provincial capital of Bandung, West Java, *The Cockroach Opera* was subjected to a bomb threat. In December 1990 the play was scheduled for performance at the Jakarta Arts Building before a planned tour of four cities in Japan. A police warrant prevented further performances by Teater Koma of *The Cockroach Opera* in either INDONESIA or JAPAN, a current critic of Indonesia.

Julini, a transvestite, is the central character of the play. Her boyfriend, the small-time criminal Roima, works for the head criminal, Kumis, a former chief security officer. Roimi dreams of falling truly in love, but has to choose between Julini or Tuminah, a motherly prostitute to those of the slums, who dreams of a good life, of repenting, creating a household, and having children. Julini shares similar dreams; she is the inspiration of struggle for all the slum dwellers and their exasperation also when demonstrating for the rights of transvestites to have public toilets signposted as "Male" and "Female" include a "Transvestite" toilet.

Tuminah encourages the sexual liaison of one of her girls, Tarsih, with a high-ranking official in a position to negotiate overseas credit for the development and welfare of the people in the slums. He interests a Japanese creditor in a building project in the slums who is wooed by gifts and other pleasures while the press is kept at arm's length to protect the confidentiality of the project. Successful negotiations are completed on the golf course; the foreign credit is allocated to the pockets of officials. The slums are demolished; the development profits the wealthy; the poor are the victims. Julini dies, shot in a police raid, and Tarsih is killed at the time Kumis is murdered by Tibal out of revenge for his sister Tuminah, whose virginity Kumis had taken advantage of when promising to save her brother's house from demolition. The transvestites raise a monument to Julini.

The play is a satirical commentary about the unempowered classes, the street prostitutes and transvestites, the petty criminals, and the unemployed, all embroiled in a state of mental and physical terror and caught in the intrigues of corruption wrought by the Suharto regime. These are the classes referred by Nano as the "cockroach class." The play's satire is treated with broad humor, music, song, and dance. The work recalls popular Javanese theater genres such as *ludruk* and *ketoprak*, and plot is predicated on the astute social and political perceptions of Nano Riantiarno as playwright and director with his Brechian approach to theater.

FURTHER READING

Hatley, Barbara. Introduction to *Time Bomb and Cockroach Opera*, by Nano Riantiarno. Jakarta: Lontar, 1992. ix–xiv.

Vatikiotis, Michael R. J. *Indonesian Politics Under Suharto*. London: Routledge, 1993.

Zurbuchen, Mary. "Images of Culture and National Development in Indonesia: *The Cockroach Opera*." *Asian Theatre Journal* 7, no. 2 (1990): 127–149.

Ian Jarvis Brown

COCTEAU, JEAN (1889–1963)

In addition to plays and films, Jean Cocteau wrote novels, poetry, criticism, memoirs, and scenarios for ballets; designed stage scenery, clothing, and jewelry; and painted, sketched, acted, directed, and even managed the comeback of a champion boxer, a dizzying range of activities that led one critic to dub him "the first multimedia artist." He campaigned successfully for election to the French Academy, yet always considered himself an outsider. Although the surrealists denounced him, the word "SURREALISM" first appeared as a description of one of his works, and his play THE INFERNAL MACHINE and film *Blood of a Poet* stand as two of the foremost artistic representatives of the movement. Despite the wide range of his work, few of his contemporaries (or biographers) agreed with his estimation of himself as a genius in any of these fields; more than a few considered him a dilettante. What can be said is that the notions of theater and performance were central motifs for Cocteau's life; it is possible that Cocteau's true genius was as the chief exponent of a life of pure theatricality.

Cocteau was born on July 5, 1889, in Maisons-Lafitte, to a prosperous bourgeois family that moved to Paris after his father's suicide in 1899. There he fell in love with the Boulevard theater and the circus, a love he named "the red-and-gold disease." Cocteau did poorly in school, failing his *baccalauréat* three times. But he succeeded in ingratiating himself into the artistic world of Paris, first as an acolyte of the Boulevard star Edouard de Max, who in turn sponsored the first reading of Cocteau's poetry in 1907. Over the next few years Cocteau had a series of mentors, all successful "society" artists. The last of these (a somewhat reluctant one at that) was Sergey Diaghilev, who gave Cocteau the famous admonition "Astonish me!" Cocteau responded by devising a series of ballet scenarios, the most famous and important of which is *Parade* (1916). This work exuberantly juxtaposed elements of "high" and "low" culture. It took cubism from its self-imposed ghetto on the Left Bank and set it on the Paris stage through its famous costumes by Pablo Picasso; Erik Satie's score (which Cocteau may have had a strong hand in) incorporated the "found sound" of the Italian futurists (such as gunshots and sirens) with American jazz years before the first jazz band performed in Paris. Describing its style in a program note, GUILLAUME APOLLINAIRE coined the term "surrealism."

In the 1920s Cocteau's stage work developed toward playwriting. Influenced by his lover, the precocious and short-lived Paul Radiguet (1903–1923), he adopted a simpler, self-consciously metatheatrical style, often dealing with classic myths set in modern dress, such as ORPHEUS or *The Infernal Machine* (the most significant of several treatments of the Oedipus story by Cocteau). Most scholars agree that this combining of classic and contemporary is perhaps Cocteau's greatest contribution as an artist.

Cocteau's estrangement from the rest of the French AVANT-GARDE, particularly the surrealist movement, increased during this period. Many reasons for this have been put forward: rivalry between Cocteau and André Breton for public acclaim; Cocteau's abhorrence of politics and eagerness to associate with the haut monde, in contrast to the surrealists' movement toward communism; and Cocteau's open homosexuality, which offended the often belligerently heterosexual surrealists. Cocteau's rift with the avant-garde deepened in the late 1930s as his stage writing became more conventional in form and aimed directly at commercial success. The best of these works is *Les parents terribles*, an Oedipal MELODRAMA about a psychologically incestuous family, although *The Knights of the Round Table*, which features a major character played by a different actor in each act, might be possible to revive in the hands of a sensitive director.

Cocteau stayed in FRANCE throughout the German Occupation, remaining apolitical and writing little for the stage. During this time he did make the one really courageous action of his life, organizing artistic support for the young JEAN GENET when the poet/criminal faced a possible life sentence. Cocteau's passionate courtroom testimony was considered a turning point in the trial. After the war Cocteau's creative energies turned most strongly to filmmaking. He began shooting *Beauty and the Beast* within months of the war's end; he also filmed several of his plays, including *Les parents terribles* and *Orpheus*. These films are perhaps his greatest artistic achievement, providing inspiration for younger experimental filmmakers, such as François Truffaut in France and the American Stan Brakhage.

The two plays written after the war, *The Eagle with Two Heads* and *Bacchus*, return to some familiar themes of Cocteau's, including the primacy of poetry over politics and of innocence killed by "the World," but seem like overblown costume dramas judged alongside the contemporary work of JEAN-PAUL SARTRE, JEAN GIRAUDOUX, or JEAN ANOUILH. Despite the great differences in style and subject matter among his stage works, all the plays (as well as the novels and postwar films) put forward what one critic has called an "aesthetic of innocence": sophistication (often characterized as Death in the plays) inevitably destroys the artist or the pure of spirit. Alongside his writing and directing, Cocteau was also influential in raising the status of stage design in France, not only by bringing Picasso and Coco Chanel to the stage, but also through his own designs.

A series of debilitating heart attacks in the 1950s limited Cocteau's theatrical activities. His reputation continued to grow: election to the Belgian and French academies, an honorary degree from Oxford University, chair of the jury at the Cannes Film Festival. He died in Milly-la-Forêt of a heart attack on October 11, 1963, hours after learning of the death of his close friend, the singer Edith Piaf.

Cocteau's reputation has fluctuated since his death. In the 1960s it remained high; his films were mainstays of college film series, and his plays were regularly anthologized. Three major English-language biographies were published between 1968 and 1970 (none has appeared since). In the 1980s *Parade* was revived in New York (and subsequently elsewhere), redemonstrating Cocteau's influence on modern dance theater. His influence on "music theater" has been cited by many, especially composers Ned Rorem and Philip Glass. In the 1990s *Les parents terribles* was successfully revived in England and the United States under the title *Indiscretions*. The beginning of the 21st century has seen Cocteau's memory continue in ways he would have loved. In France the Centre Pompidou mounted a major exhibit devoted to Cocteau, presenting his work as an exemplar of 20th-century French culture; in the United States, at the same time, many readers were encountering Cocteau's name in a best-selling novel, *The Da Vinci Code*, as an alleged Grand Master of a secret society dedicated to defending the heirs of Jesus of Nazareth and Mary Magdalene.

PLAYS: *Parade* (scenario, 1916); *The Ox on the Roof* (scenario, 1920); *The Marriage on the Eiffel Tower* (1921); *Orpheus* (1926); *The Human Voice* (1929); *The Infernal Machine* (1932); *The Knights of the Round Table* (1933); *Indiscretions* (also known as *Intimate Relations*, 1938); *The Holy Terrors* (1939); *The Typewriter* (1940); *The Eagle with Two Heads* (1946); *Bacchus* (1951)

FURTHER READING

Anderson, Alexandra, and Carol Saltus. *Jean Cocteau and the French Scene*. New York: Abbeville Press, 1984.

Brown, Frederick. *Cocteau: An Impersonation of Angels*. New York: Viking, 1968.

Cocteau, Jean. *The Infernal Machine, and Other Plays*. New York: New Directions, 1963.

———. *Professional Secrets*. New York: Farrar, Straus & Giroux, 1970.

Knapp, Bettina. *Jean Cocteau*. New York: Twayne, 1970. Updated ed. Boston: Twayne, 1989.

Oxenhandler, Neal. *Scandal and Parade: The Theater of Jean Cocteau*. New Brunswick, N.J.: Rutgers Univ. Press, 1957.

Steegmuller, Francis. *Cocteau, a Biography*. Boston: Little, Brown, 1970.

Walter Bilderback

THE COFFIN IS TOO BIG FOR THE HOLE

Singaporean playwright KUO PAO KUN's dramatic monologue *The Coffin Is Too Big for the Hole* is one of his country's best-known and most performed works of theater. The English and Mandarin versions by the bilingual playwright were first performed in 1985, five years after Kuo had completed a four-year period of detention for writing and producing political plays that Singapore's authoritarian government deemed objectionable. *The Coffin Is Too Big for the Hole*, along with *No Parking on Odd Days* (1986), quickly established Kuo's reputation as a dramatist capable of grappling with the specifics of Singapore's complex social and political landscape using the deceptively simple, direct, and personal monologue form. The themes of loyalty and duty to family, the challenges of intergenerational communication, and the conflict between the individual and the state are played out with wit and humor, infused with a deep sense of our shared humanity.

The narrative voice of *The Coffin Is Too Big for the Hole* is provided by a grandson who recalls the events that transpired on the day of his grandfather's burial. As the eldest living male in a large, extended, ethnic Chinese Singaporean family, it is his responsibility to ensure that the grandfather is honored and that burial traditions are followed. With the family gathered at the graveside, it becomes clear that the grandfather's heavy, massive coffin will not fit in the standard-sized burial plot.

The undertaker, present at the ceremony, absolves himself of responsibility, using the opportunity to try to sell a smaller, substitute coffin. When the grandson suggests that the hole be expanded, he is told that digging a bigger hole might disturb the neighboring grave and is reminded of the regulation that says that "one dead is allotted one plot."

Emboldened by the massiveness of his grandfather's coffin, which becomes "a source of strength and inspiration," the grandson insists on taking the matter to the cemetery's officer in charge. The officer presents a series of unsatisfactory solutions, while the grandson insists that another burial plot be provided. The officer's response speaks as much to the general conditions of life in a populous, highly ordered state such as Singapore as it does to the specifics of this situation: "No, no, no, no! That will be running against our national planning. You are aware of the fact that we are a densely populated nation with very limited land resources. The consideration for humanity and sympathy cannot over-step the constraints of the state policy!"

Refusing to back down, the grandson delivers a stirring appeal to the humanity of the officer, concluding with a threat to camp out overnight in the cemetery with his entire family if another plot is not made available. To his surprise, the officer simply leaves the room, presumably to consult with his superior, returning with the news that under the circumstances, the cemetery has decided to expand the hole. On returning to the gravesite, the grandson discovers that a crowd of some 800 people has gathered, including newspaper, radio, and television reporters.

Ironically, the grandson later recalls, the event was voted "one of the Top 10 National News Stories of the Year," while the officer in charge was voted the "Most Humane Personality of the Year." The grandson's concluding remarks make it clear that this single instance of accommodating human needs will not alter social policy. Looking at the rows of standard-sized graves, he muses, "Now, with them all in the same size and the same shape, would my sons and daughters, and my grandsons and granddaughters after them, be able to find me out and recognize me? I don't know . . . I just don't know."

As is typical of Kuo's post-1980 work, *Coffin*'s criticism is not aimed directly at Singapore's authoritarian political establishment, but rather at a society complicit in this shift from the more human-centered values of a generation earlier to values based on a corporatist model. Singapore's dazzling economic success, especially relative to the plight of its regional neighbors, is often attributed to the willingness of its citizenry to accept microlevel political controls in all areas of life, presumably because they contribute to the greater social good and to the maximization of economic prosperity. Kuo's *Coffin* offers a counterweight to this dominant social and political narrative, reminding Singaporeans that wealth and a highly efficient, ordered, and law-abiding society have been purchased at the cost of individual expression.

The real beauty of Kuo's play is perhaps its disarmingly simple, straightforward style. An ordinary man with deep family obligations is torn between the necessity of honoring a much-loved relative and the demands of an inflexible bureaucracy. The twists and turns of the story are recounted in a charming, uncomplicated manner by a Singaporean Everyman who uses black humor and irony to draw the audience in. When he remembers how the coffin was "so damn heavy" that the workers "nearly dropped it to the ground when it got off the coach," the audience is given permission to laugh, remembering every time they may have been to a funeral where bizarre incongruities or accidents made them desperate to break through the solemnity of the occasion. Similarly, when the rule-bound, intransigent officer becomes the "Most Humane Personality of the Year," the sheer irony of the pronouncement elicits laughs of recognition. The accessibility and deeply satisfying theatricality of Kuo's play have contributed to its success on stage and its use as a school text in Singapore.

The Coffin Is Too Big for the Hole was initially performed in Mandarin by actor Choo Woon Hock, then later in the same year in an English-language production with actor Lim Kay Tong. It was presented in Malaysia in 1986, Hong Kong in 1987, and China in 1989. A significant revival of the play took place in the context of the 2000 Singapore Arts Festival, for which it was performed by Jack Neo in a double bill with *No Parking on Odd Days*.

FURTHER READING

Jit, Krishen. Introduction to *The Coffin Is Too Big for the Hole and Other Plays*, by Kuo Pao Kun. Singapore: Times Bks. Intl., 1990.

Kuo Pao Kun. *The Coffin Is Too Big for the Hole, and Other Plays*, Singapore: Times Bks. Intl., 1990.

——. *Images at the Margins: A Collection of Kuo Pao Kun's Plays*. Singapore: Times Bks. Intl., 2000.

Peterson, William. "Kuo Pao Kun." In *Contemporary Dramatists*, ed. by Thomas Riggs. 6th ed. New York: St. James, 1999.

——. *Theater and the Politics of Culture in Contemporary Singapore*. Middletown, Conn.: Wesleyan Univ. Press, 2001.

Seet, K. K. "Cultural Untranslatability as Dramatic Strategy: A Speculative Look at the Different Language Versions of Kuo Pao Kun's Plays." In *Beyond the Footlights: New Play Scripts in Singapore Theatre*. Singapore: UniPress, 1994.

William Peterson

COLLAGE

Widely viewed as the 20th century's "single most revolutionary formal innovation in artistic representation" (Ulmer, 1983), collage involves a metacritical technique of radical juxtaposition, according to Gregory Ulmer. It disrupts conventional meanings by an act of recontextualization that juxtaposes seemingly incongruous objects, images, and ideas. For example, Hannah Hoch juxtaposed African arts and contemporary photojournalism to challenge the stereotypical images of women in the early 20th century. At its most basic level, the techniques of collage foster the chance associations and "new possibilities of signification" that result, as Marjorie Perloff has noted, from "the transfer of [objects,] words and images from their original sources to the collage construction" (Perloff, 1983). Yet the historical significance of collage has less to do with the production of new associations or meanings than it does with raising fundamental questions, in an openly self-reflective manner, regarding representation and its limitations. In pasting a piece of a mirror to the canvas of *La lavabo* (1912), for example, Juan Gris drew attention to a world that defied painterly representation and questioned the limits of artistic expression.

In collage these questions center on issues of referentiality, linearity, and disciplinary thinking. Though often associated with graphic arts, the techniques of 20th-century collage are identifiable across disciplines. Indeed, the techniques of collage have had a particularly strong resonance in modern drama not merely because of the structural experiments with nonlinear narrative by GERTRUDE STEIN or in the episodic drama of Georg Büchner and BERTOLT BRECHT, but because the turn toward radical juxtaposition associated with collage largely coincided with a rethinking of the traditional relation of text to performance. The juxtapositions of collage parallel a rejection of the traditionally subservient role, or referential relation, assigned to performance vis-à-vis the literary dramatic text. Challenging the assumption that performance was merely a representation of that text, 20th-century theater artists set text and performance on an equal footing, conceptualizing their relation as a radical interdisciplinary juxtaposition of two autonomous art forms. As is the case with collage, the juxtaposition of text and performance on a nonhierarchical plane produced a disruptive, provocative dynamic, a staple of late 20th- and early 21st-century theater. The long performed silences in a production of a SAMUEL BECKETT play are potentially as significant as anything on the printed page of one of his dramas.

The collage aesthetic is also seen in the experimental notions of performance first explored by the dadaists and surrealists, cultivated by John Cage (especially his untitled event at Black Mountain College in 1952), and refined by happening and Fluxus artists. In the late 1960s these interdisciplinary modes of performance, which combined the graphic and performing arts and redefined theatrical space, were characterized as a "theatre of mixed means" by critics such as Richard Kostelanetz. Their eclectic sampling across the disciplines contributed to multimedia formats characteristic of much postmodern performance.

[*See also* Chance; Dadaism; Happenings and Intermedia; Philosophy and Drama, 1860–Present; Surrealism]

FURTHER READING

Kostelanetz, Richard. *Theatre of Mixed Means*. New York: Dial Press, 1968.

Perloff, Marjorie. "The Invention of Collage." *New York Literary Forum* 10–11 (1983): 5–47.

Ulmer, Gregory. "The Object of Post-Criticism." In *The Anti-aesthetic: Essays on Postmodern Culture*. Ed. by Hal Foster. Seattle, Wash.: Bay Press, 1983. 83–110.

James Harding

THE COLLECTED WORKS OF BILLY THE KID

Adapted into a play in 1973 from a book of poetry that won the Governor General's Award in 1970, *The Collected Works of Billy the Kid* by MICHAEL ONDAATJE is a work of history, fiction, and biography that jumps from the past to the present life of Billy the Kid, poet, outlaw, and legend. Ondaatje's story of Billy the Kid and his nemesis Pat Garrett is a TRAGICOMEDY that combines poetry, images of the violence found in the movies and legends of the Wild Wild West, and American pastiche.

The story dances between fact and legend; the characters contradict themselves and create an atmosphere of American mythology and western historiography. The subject of William H. Bonney, better known as Billy the Kid, combines historical and popular sources that Ondaatje uses to his advantage in the play. Drawing from the popular imagination of the Wild West, *The Collected Works* is a COLLAGE of poetic and historical images of gunslingers and their "histories."

The play is made up of Billy the Kid, Garrett, and the characters who ride in and out of their lives. A series of prose poems, images, and songs, *The Collected Works* is a nonlinear story of the outlaw's life. Ondaatje jumps between legend and unglamorous details of the sounds, smells, and violence of western life—"The smell of things dying flamboyant / smell stuffing up your nose / and up like wet cotton in the brain."

The characters of Billy and Pat Garrett are neither the villain nor the hero in Ondaatje's tale; as the character Sally Chisum describes the two in the play, "Both were worth knowing." Billy the Kid is seen in all his humanity, both good and bad, while the events of his life and that of his friend/pursuer Garrett are shown as any in life, difficult to pin down or take sides on.

The Collected Works is a performance piece for the postmodern era. Both self-reflexive and wittingly self-conscious, the play pushes the viewer to confront his or her own conceptions of the American past and the value of violence among the western legends. The characters contradict themselves and the events of their lives in a way that makes it difficult to believe what they say or wish to be said about them. Ondaatje's tale is tortuous; he jumps backwards and forwards in a Brechtian journey toward and away from the death of Billy the Kid.

FURTHER READING

Harrison, Keith. "Montage in *The Collected Works of Billy the Kid*." *Journal of Canadian Poetry* 3, no. 1 (Winter 1980): 32–38.

Jones, Manina. "The Collected Works of Billy the Kid: Scripting the Docudrama." *Canadian Literature* (Autumn–Winter 1989): 26–38.

Kamboureli, Smaro. "Outlawed Narrative: Michael Ondaatje's *The Collected Works of Billy the Kid.*" *Sagetrieb: A Journal Devoted to Poets in the Imagist/Objective Tradition* 7, no. 1 (Spring 1988): 115–129.

Holly Maples

THE COLLEEN BAWN

The Colleen Bawn; or, The Brides of Garryowen, DION BOUCICAULT's first "Irish play," opened at Laura Keene's Theatre, New York, on March 27, 1860, with the author in the role of Myles-na-Coppaleen (Myles of the Little Ponies). The play was based on Gerald Griffin's popular novel *The Collegians* (1829), which, in turn, had been founded on a sensational crime in the west of IRELAND, in which a young gentleman arranged for his boatman to murder his secret wife, a sixteen-year-old peasant beauty, and sink her body in the Shannon River. Into this sensational situation Boucicault introduced various sly, garrulous, and witty Irish characters, and he slightly sent up the blackmailing villain, the cold, stuck-up mother, and her deeply misguided gentleman son. The original crime is planned, but it does not succeed, so that the peasant girl and her aristocratic husband settle down happily at the end. The scene of the crime was relocated to the beautiful lakes of Killarney, so that painted backdrops amounted to large-scale tourist postcards of the Gap of Dunloe, the old Weir bridge, ancient castles, and other beauty spots. Interiors included those of an "authentic" peasant cottage, a castle ballroom, a cave beside the lakes, and a room in an artistocratic Anglo-Irish "Big House," in a vivid rendering of the extremes of 19th-century Irish society. Occasions for the singing of Irish songs—"Pretty Girl Milking Her Cow" and "Cruiskeen Lawn," among others—are introduced into the action.

The most successful invention, however, was that of Myles-na-Coppaleen, a character with no significant role in Griffin's novel who is turned into the hero of the play. Boucicault played him as a coaxing, blathering liar who charms one and all. He is a tramp, an ex-convict, and a horse thief; he illegally distills whiskey; he has no respect for church or castle, but he is the most natural, lovable, and attractive figure on stage. In the climax of the action, while distilling whiskey at his lakeside cave, Myles sees the boatman tumble the Colleen Bawn into the lake, so he shoots the boatman and dives into the water to rescue the heroine. In the final scene he effects the reconciliation and reunion of the maid with her gentleman husband. "Instead of a blundering blockhead," Boucicault said he wished to present his Irishman as "the true son of the sod, bold and courageous even to recklessness, with all his virtues and virtuous errors." His bold and clever victories over English propriety made Myles enormously popular with American and Irish audiences. The dreadful crime that became first a newspaper story, then a novel, and after that Boucicault's comic MELODRAMA, was next turned into a successful operetta, *The Lily of Killarney* (1862).

FURTHER READING

Fawkes, Richard. *Dion Boucicault: A Biography*. London: Quartet Bks., 1979.

Krause, David, ed. *The Dolmen Boucicault*. Dublin: Dolmen Press, 1964.

Morash, Christopher. *A History of Irish Theatre, 1601–2000*. Cambridge: Cambridge Univ. Press, 2002.

Adrian Frazier

COMEDY

In languages descended from Latin, the noun for *comedy* (*comédie*, *commedia*, and so on) has a specialized meaning, a *genre*, but also a general meaning, *play*. Associated as a rule with providing mirth and its fickle reward, laughter, comedy often generates in its audience more of a mixed feeling, which incorporates relief. Anyone who sits fondly through comedies will recognize the moments in the last act when two or more actors embrace one another, while spectators wipe away tears and try to gulp down a sudden lump in the gorge. Comedies nearly always contrive squabbles through most of the action between family members or next-door neighbors who hate one another or rivals for a job, a marriage partner, or a political constituency. But the final moments of harmony bring everyone in the cast into feelings of brotherhood, sisterhood, and outright love.

A comic structure, on its route to a happy ending, will finally invoke peacemaking or recruit a gifted mediator such as a psychiatrist or a psychic who advises rivals to remodel their conduct in public. Sometimes troublemakers even have to arrange for a personal armistice with themselves. Such reassuring consequences occur notably in most of the American comedies written by GEORGE S. KAUFMAN and MOSS HART: their collaborations during the 1930s and 1940s, such as *The American Way*, *ONCE IN A LIFETIME*, *The Man Who Came to Dinner*, and *YOU CAN'T TAKE IT WITH YOU*, still send spectators home chuckling and radiating goodwill.

Whether an audience laughs heartily or weakly, comedy puts emphasis on words and specifically on wit. Wit consists of exercises in verbal cleverness. The comic figures who utter witticisms mean them to be funny; sometimes they even take them well beyond funniness to cruelty. On occasion, characters with brutal wits seem to try not so much to hurt others as to put up a shield that will protect them against the wit of others.

In a FARCE, by contrast, we laugh not at wit, which is a technique for humiliating others, but at comic behavior, which is accidental, not purposeful. The accidents that take place in farce, it goes without saying, are not caused by clumsiness but by its opposite, the deployment of physical skills; a character in farce may move awkwardly, but the actor always looks nimble on his feet and eloquent with the rest of his body. The farceur does provoke laughter, but at his own expense, not at the expense of others. Although no necessary connection exists between comedy and laughter, laughs that arise from wit frequently helpfully accentuate a sardonic point such as a satirical thrust into someone else's pride.

In the modern era, starting in the early and middle 1800s, playwrights created theater against landscapes that were altering from mostly agricultural settings to mostly industrial, from countryside to city, from the intimacy of the family hearth to the more impersonal local community: scenes laid in factories and offices; aboard trains, cars, and ships; and, by the end of the following century, on enormous airplanes and space vessels. Some new comedies, tragedies, and MELODRAMAS did not quite free themselves from the patterns of the tried and partially true, most often well-made plays (*pièces bien faites*); but experimental productions explored less orthodox playmaking, under the sway of Johann Wolfgang von Goethe's monumental part 2 of *Faust* (1832) and the works of Christian Dietrich Grabbe, Heínrích von Kleist, and Georg Büchner, all from GERMANY; Alfred de Musset, Victor Hugo, and Honoré de Balzac from FRANCE; and Nikolai Gogol from Russia. Their plays and imitations of them not only attracted many among the theater public, but also supported a web of cooperating playhouses that introduced Europe to an international repertory of REALISM and poetic drama.

The most undaunted comic playwright in English of the 1800s and 1900s, GEORGE BERNARD SHAW, lifted comedy to a new pitch of wit, hilarity, and intellectual substance. Shaw met with some competition from an Irish woman, LADY GREGORY, and three other born Irishmen, DION BOUCICAULT, who ended his hyperactive career, made up of comedies and melodramas, in New York; JOHN MILLINGTON SYNGE, who invented a sonorous version of Irish stage poetry and one magnificent TRAGEDY in one act, RIDERS TO THE SEA; and OSCAR WILDE, who wrote some of the funniest plays of the time, culminating in THE IMPORTANCE OF BEING EARNEST. Shaw helped himself to just about every imaginable comic device bred and nurtured in the Victorian theater and earlier. His impeccably entertaining plays, with their ample jolts of healthy, impudent shock value, demonstrated that comedy could be enriched immeasurably by comic themes founded on a superlatively active conscience. He once told a friend that, although "I lean like the Tower of Pisa, I will never fall because I am held up by the force of levity."

The several dozen female roles created by Shaw extend from the motherly heroine in *Candida* and the pert Ann Whitefield in *Man and Superman* to the outrageous Epifania in *The Millionairess*, Lina Szczepanowska, the Polish woman pilot in *Misalliance*, and all the way up the moral scale to the saintly Joan of Arc. The dramatist treats them with a respectful and, in places, gleaming wit that draws forth his own incredulity, as if he had encountered them waiting for his permission to spring forth. Shavian men usually make worthy partners for these astonishing ladies, but they are not in quite the same class when it comes to comic characterization.

When Shaw turned away from writing dramatic criticism in magazines and relocated his criticism (theatrical, political, and economic) in his prefaces in order to give over a larger fraction of his working day to writing plays, comedy had settled itself in Great Britain and IRELAND on a secure, popular footing, thanks to the artistry of Douglas Jerrold, Edward Bulwer-Lytton, Tom Taylor, Sydney Grundy, and T. W. ROBERTSON, among other 19th-century figures.

After World War II several generations of playwrights made lasting, overlapping names for themselves. CHRISTOPHER FRY'S THE LADY'S NOT FOR BURNING, in rhyming couplets, marked what a famed actor-director, Laurence Olivier, referred to expectantly as a new Shakespearean age for England. HAROLD PINTER's spare dialogue in his comedies launched a long-lasting career with plays and screenplays that the *London Times* critic Irving Wardle christened "comedies of menace." ALAN AYCKBOURN wrote comedy—well over sixty plays at last count, three of them interpenetrating in *The Norman Conquests*—that he tried out with a tiny acting company of three women and three men in Scarborough on the coast of Yorkshire. He directed his plays himself and transferred most of them to London's West End and Broadway. TOM STOPPARD, a Czech-born wizard with English who broke into theater circles with ROSENCRANTZ AND GUILDENSTERN ARE DEAD, went on to compose a series of elegantly written comedies about the impact of science and scientists on the arts; one of his plays, TRAVESTIES, opens with a lecture that opens with the word "Secondly." MICHAEL FRAYN, who once specialized in comedies with farcical skeletons (*Voices Off*), has moved into a few solemn topics; his COPENHAGEN features a debate between two celebrated atomic physicists. *Comedians* (1967) by Trevor Griffiths is comedy in a new mode, a travesty of stand-up comics. CARYL CHURCHILL'S lighthearted CLOUD NINE, which made a plea on behalf of the world's feminine population, has given way in subsequent dramas like FAR AWAY to a horrific future, which younger writers may find imitable in its extraordinary, wide strides from scene to scene. The recent pleasing (and teasing) newer types of comedy invoke parody, irony, boulevard playfulness, pastiches, travesties, Gothic skits, evasive climaxes, comedies of crafty manners, antiliteralism, shrewd reawakenings of the classical unities (place, time, and action), followers of comic and melodramatic theatricalism by LUIGI PIRANDELLO, and excessively crafted plays.

Looking back over a season of typical performances on Broadway, its New York adjuncts, and counterparts elsewhere in the country, we find comedies shouldering aside other genres. Few of them alter opinions or stretch attitudes; otherwise, theater would have had a far more drastic impact on the American mind and sensitivity. Some of those who ply their wit in comedy boldly invite a cool reception, long-term neglect, and envy from critics who also write plays. Several Americans have supplied memorable work in the not-too-distant past. JACK RICHARDSON's *The Prodigal*, *Xmas in Las Vegas*, and *Gallows Humor*—the latter consisting of two acts written from the points of view of a hangman and the to-be-hanged—and Robert Hivnor's blithe *Too Many Thumbs*, about a primate with the brain of a genius and the affections of a Lothario, *The Ticklish Acrobat*, an archeological dig down to a wondrous past, and *The Assault Upon Charles Sumner*, a trip back into the career of an American idealist: these all exhibit learned wit that is exhilarating. So do JOHN GUARE's *The House of Blue Leaves*, *Six Degrees of Separation*, a title that has become an all-purpose mantra in some cultural circles, and *Four Baboons Adoring the Sun*. The playwright who has had an unrivaled success, that second most wanted experience on the Great White Way, after royalties, is NEIL SIMON. He has invented a surprising variety of boulevard comedies since *Come Blow Your Horn* (1961). Each one has something to teach aspiring dramatists.

French comedy has also relished its dealings with assorted comedies. Early in the 1800s Musset's "dramatic proverbs" (*No Trifling with Love* and *A Door Must Be Open or Closed* are two of the best) earned places in French literature for their charm wedded to gently jarring conclusions. But late in the century symbolist plays, their action driven by poetry, undoubtedly helped prepare the moods of the times for eruptions of Dada and SURREALISM. Younger poets dashed off short theatrical *manifestations*, in both senses of the French word: protests and demonstrations. In them the artist's id challenges its own moments of sanity during assaults from the unconscious. The id of the gifted young art critic-poet who renamed himself GUILLAUME APOLLINAIRE dared in THE BREASTS OF TIRESIAS to create a woman's role made up of both sexes. His id was pursued by those of André Breton, ANTONIN ARTAUD, and a group of painters such as Yves Tanguy and Louis Aragon (not to mention the Spaniards Salvadar Dalí and Pablo Picasso) who all, as one commentator remarked, "thought with their eyes."

Satirical drama in Polish, Russian, and German has poured into the mainstream of European comedy, defying official watchdogs even while the now-extinct Soviet empire tightened its political screws on Eastern Europe. As if to illustrate the comedies' defiance, STANISLAW-IGNACY WITKIEWICZ devised eye-arresting titles for his provocative THE MADMAN AND THE NUN, *The Crazy Locomotive*, and *The Beelzebub Sonata*. WITOLD GOMBROWICZ's *The Marriage* and Sławomir Mrożek's *Tango*, *Exiles*, and *Vatzlav* and his rich mix of one-acts show how an embrace of approval under a tyrannical regime becomes a stranglehold. Isaac Babel's *Marya* and *Sunset* pictured the lives of an astounding community, a Jewish gangster colony in Odessa. *YEVGENI LVOVICH SHVARTS*'s fables, which include *The Dragon* and *The Shadow*, and *LEONID ANDREEV*'s circus romp *HE WHO GETS SLAPPED* follow through on the same theme by stirring recipes for sane uncomfortable sanity into the laughter that greets their work.

More epochal plays before and after World War I came from ITALY. The FUTURISM movement, infatuated with machinery and speed as tokens of a more thrilling tomorrow, was led by FILIPPO MARINETTI. The Sicilian Pirandello compiled *SIX CHARACTERS IN SEARCH OF AN AUTHOR*, *TONIGHT WE IMPROVISE*, and some twenty other unsolvable mysteries about the arts of living and making theater. In AUSTRIA ARTHUR SCHNITZLER, a doctor who lived through Vienna's eminence in the arts and sciences, is remembered most readily today for *La Ronde*, made up of multiple love scenes. It has undergone adaptations galore in its periods, languages, costumes, sexuality, and comic anguish. Schnitzler's approximate contemporary, the Hungarian-born FERENC MOLNÁR, was the author of *Liliom* and other works that play neat tricks with the conventions of comedy; written in 1909, *Liliom* found a new source of fame when Rodgers and Hammerstein turned it into a musical, *Carousel* (1945), which still enjoys springhtly revivals.

But there is one comedy, *Knock; or, The Triumph of Medicine* (1923), by a philosopher-novelist, JULES ROMAINS, that wins out as the funniest play about doctors or any other calling since Molière's *The Imaginary Invalid* (1673). Dr. Knock starts out as a ship's doctor, that is, a doctor with a new degree but no practical experience. He is a medical scamp, though also a relentless moneymaker who understands the businessman's credo better than a banker. He takes over a sleepy practice in a French mountain village from a good-natured, retiring general practitioner who regularly forgot or did not bother to collect his fees. By the last scene of act 3 Knock has converted the south of France into one huge sick ward, where the anemic, feverish, and prostrate religiously obey the orders circulated from Knock, by this time a national luminary and probably a millionaire.

[*See also* Tragicomedy]

FURTHER READING

Bentley, Eric. "Comedy." In *The Life of the Drama*. New York: Atheneum, 1964.

Bermel, Albert. "Impulsive Behavior in Comedies." In *Shakespeare at the Moment*. New York: Heinemann, 2000.

Charney, Maurice, ed. *Comedy: New Perspectives*. New York: New York Literary Forum, 1978.

Kernan, Alvin B. *Modern Satire*. New York: Harcourt, Brace & World, 1962.

Sypher, Wylie, ed. *Comedy*. Containing George Meredith, "An Essay on Comedy," and Henri Bergson, "Laughter" (1900). Garden City, N.Y.: Doubleday, 1956.

Albert Bermel

COMIC MYSTERY

DARIO FO's *Comic Mystery* (*Mistero*), a series of sketches and monologues inspired by medieval sources, was premiered in

October 1969. The show became a central part of Fo's repertoire and a key to appreciating his views on the continuity of popular culture, his skills as a solo performer, his relation to tradition, and his identity as a writer.

When in 1968 Fo announced his intention to develop his own brand of political theater and become the "*giullare* [jester] of the people, not the bourgeoisie," public interest in the first part of the statement caused the second part to be overlooked. The *giullare* was a pre-Renaissance performer whom Fo took as an ideal and model, but there was dismay among politically committed members of Nuova Scena, the cooperative he and Franca Rame had established, when he proposed to tour as a 20th-century *giullare*, not with some exercise in contemporary agit-prop (AGITATION-PROPAGANDA) but with a series of one-man pieces featuring biblical tales ("The Marriage Feast at Cana"), miracles ("The Blind Man and the Cripple"), the oppression of the medieval poor ("The Birth of the Villeyn"), and the arrogance of long-dead Popes ("Boniface VIII"). Critics were scarcely mollified by Fo's belief in the value of historical awareness for activists, his insistence on the enduring vitality of popular culture, or his interpretation of those archaic religious pieces as a trenchant exposé of exploitation and the abuse of power. On stage Fo introduced each piece with a satirical preface, ridiculing contemporary politicians and churchmen and pointing to parallels between the problems of medieval peasants and those of industrial workers. The evening was rounded off with a public debate on the play and the politics of the day.

There is nothing philologically exact about the reconstruction of the individual scenes. The source material came from many countries, but was always substantially rewritten, or invented, by Fo. There are several extant versions of "The Blind Man and Cripple," but there are no known models for "The Birth of the Jester," which can be viewed as a manifesto for Fo's theater. A farmer whose family and livelihood had been destroyed by a local nobleman is on the point of suicide when a stranger, who turns out to be Christ in person, gives him the jester's gift of storytelling and charges him with the mission of expressing the rage of the downtrodden against injustice. In "The Raising of Lazarus" Christ is humanized as the grieving friend of Lazarus, while the crowd that flocks to witness the miracle contains con men out to make money from the purely lay spectacle Christ promises to perform. This dilution of the religious element caused Fo to be denounced for blasphemy, especially when the work was televised in 1977, but he never attacks Christian belief. His targets are the holders of power in state or church, as is clear from "Boniface VIII," where Christ on his way to Calvary meets the splendidly arrayed pope, but kicks him on the backside for having betrayed the gospel message of poverty.

Fo played all the parts, switching roles deftly in the course of each sketch and emerging as the reincarnation of the actor-author of Italian tradition.

[*See also* Italy]

FURTHER READING

Behan, Tom. *Dario Fo: Revolutionary Theatre*. London: Pluto, 2000.

Farrell, Joseph. *Dario Fo and Franca Rame: Harlequins of the Revolution*. London: Methuen, 2001.

Farrell, Joseph, and Antonio Scuderi. *Stage, Text, and Tradition*. Carbondale: Southern Illinois Univ. Press, 2000.

Mitchell, Tony. *Dario Fo: The People's Court Jester*. London: Methuen, 1999.

Joseph Farrell

COMMUNITY THEATER

No one is excluded from the theater. . . . Here is a workshop for every kind of workman.

—Louise Burleigh, 1917

Community theater refers to nonprofessional groups and productions as distinct from those of Broadway, regional theater, summer stock, and other professional companies. The term most commonly implies a locally run, permanent, amateur theater house that mounts a season largely consisting of familiar classical and contemporary plays and musicals.

Though evidence of communal performance stretches to antiquity (religious ceremonies, cycle plays, and so on), the community theater movement can be said to have emerged around 1900 in America thanks to the confluence of several factors: the reaction against the commercialization of professional theater, the influx of European and Russian theater theories and practices, and the emergence of theater courses in universities and high schools.

One of the first community theater initiatives was the Civic Theater movement, spearheaded by playwright PERCY MACKAYE. Moved to create a democratic, noncommercial American dramatic form, MacKaye encouraged towns and social groups to produce large-scale community pageants. These performances, some of which boasted a cast of thousands, featured allegorical celebrations of local history (*Pageant and Masque of Saint Louis*, 1914), meditations on classical Western works (*Caliban on the Yellow Sands*, 1917), or political statements (*The Patterson Strike Pageant*, 1913). Though pageants proved quite popular from 1908 to 1920, World War I dissipated Civic Theater's momentum, and by the mid-1920s pageantry had largely disappeared.

Closer to the present-day community theater model were the Little Theaters. Modeling themselves on European and Russian art theaters, Little Theaters sought to balance professional quality and popular appeal with artistic integrity and stylistic experimentation. Beginning with the Hull House Players in 1900, a variety of local groups sprang up around the country, notably the Washington Square Players, the Neighborhood Theatre, the Provincetown Players, and the Pasadena Playhouse. The LITTLE THEATER MOVEMENT fostered artistic innovation and professional training, opening the door to pathbreaking American talents such as EUGENE O'NEILL, SUSAN GLASPELL, and ROBERT EDMOND JONES.

Through the Great Depression, the Little Theater movement survived, aided by the New Deal's embrace of theater as a legitimate occupation. Rechristening themselves "community theaters" in the 1950s, these groups multiplied, formed national associations, sponsored festivals, and generally encouraged a widespread interest in amateur theater. Since the 1960s community theater's role as artistic innovator has been ceded to professional regional and OFF- or OFF-OFF-BROADWAY venues. Nevertheless, the movement continues to enjoy a robust existence under the organization of the American Association of Community Theatre, the primary networking resource for community theaters in the United States.

Recently "community performance" has taken on different connotations. Inspired by the grassroots performance activism of the civil rights era (such as the BLACK ARTS MOVEMENT, El Teatro Campesino, and AUGUSTO BOAL's Theatre of the Oppressed), many theater practitioners in the 1970s and early 1980s began experimenting with performance as a tool for social change and civic awareness. Rather than reproduce local versions of Broadway fare, some artists began working with local communities to create dramatic presentations about themselves—their histories, their makeup, their internal struggles, or their future—often drawing on community members to act out their own stories. The terms "grassroots" or "community-based" performance gained popularity as a label through which to differentiate such work from the more general "community theater." In the United States one of the best-known community-based troupes is Cornerstone Theatre Company, a Los Angeles–based professional ensemble of actors, playwrights, designers, and directors that works with communities to create and produce new works about them, either through adaptations of classical texts (such as 1996's *Central Ave. Chalk Circle*, based on BERTOLT BRECHT's THE CAUCASIAN CHALK CIRCLE, but adapted for the Watts community) or through original plays (such as 2001's *Growing Home*, about Fresno, California). Though professional expertise enhances the company's shows, the company takes pains to involve the community in every step of the production, from playwriting to rehearsal to performance. Recently Cornerstone has stretched its definition of community, pursuing projects based on communities of age, ethnicity, vocation, religious belief, and geography.

Today many professional and educational institutions regularly pursue occasional artistic collaborations with local communities, such as Stanford University's East Palo Alto Project. Other companies, such as Roadside Theater Company, Swamp Gravy, and the Mickee Faust Club, operate almost exclusively as community-based troupes. Internationally, community-based performance has proven highly effective as a means of preserving cultural memories, fostering political engagement, and generating local alternatives to Western dramatic canons. Representative troupes include Kenya's Free Traveling Theater, AUSTRALIA's Urban Theater Project, and ISRAEL's Eskesta Dance Theater.

[*See also* United States, 1940–Present]

FURTHER READING

American Association of Community Theatre. http://www.aact.org/.
Burleigh, Louise. *The Community Theatre in Theory and Practice*. Boston: Little, Brown, 1917.
Cohen-Cruz, Jan. "A Hyphenated Field: Community-Based Theatre in the USA." *New Theatre Quarterly* 16, no. 4 (2001): 364–378.
Community Arts Net. http://www.communityarts.org/.
Haedicke, Susan C., and Tobin Nelhaus, eds. *Performing Democracy: International Perspectives on Urban Community-Based Performance*. Ann Arbor: Univ. of Michigan Press, 2001.
Kuftinec, Sonja. *Staging America: Cornerstone and Community-Based Theatre*. Carbondale: Southern Illinois Univ. Press, 2003.
MacKaye, Percy. *Civic Theatre in Relation to the Redemption of Leisure*. New York: Mitchell Kennerley, 1912.
Van Ervin, Eugène. *Community Theatre: Global Perspectives*. New York: Routledge, 2001.

John Fletcher

THE CONDEMNED OF ALTONA

One of JEAN-PAUL SARTRE's most ambitious dramas, *The Condemned of Altona* (*Les séquestrés d'Altona*) involves not only questions of existential freedom and identity, but notions of war and criminality in the traumatic context of 20th-century political upheaval. The play centers on the postwar fate of privileged Frantz von Gerlach, a Nazi hero whose life and mind have been warped by historical and family pressures.

Like NO EXIT, *The Condemned of Altona* examines a confined world of characters grappling with their shameful pasts. The sprawling, soap-opera nature of its plot defies capsule summary. Upon learning that he is dying of throat cancer, old von Gerlach, shipping magnate and father to Frantz, announces that he is leaving his business in the hands of his son Werner under the condition that he continue to live at the family's estate in Altona. Johanna, Werner's wife, objects to this exercise of paternal control and seeks to remedy the problem at the source. Knowing that Frantz is furtively living in one of the upstairs wings, attended by his sister Leni, with whom he is having a halfhearted incestuous relationship, Johanna meets with him to request that he emerge from his hiding place and release the family from their obligation to the house.

Old von Gerlach facilitates Johanna's scheme in the hope that she can convince Frantz to meet with him before he dies. Frantz blames his father for being corralled into fighting on the Nazi side, where he committed crimes of torture that he can barely acknowledge to himself. Leni, who keeps Frantz in the dark about Germany's postwar economic recovery, refuses to let her father see him. She enjoys her cloistered intimacy with her brother, though its effects on his mental health are evident in the way he dictates into a tape recorder a poem dedicated to the "Crabs" who will one day stand in judgment on the human race. Frantz's newfound passion for his sister-in-law Johanna provokes Leni into telling her about her brother's heinous crimes. Aware that Johanna cannot tolerate this knowledge, Frantz discloses to his father his unfortunate story—an act of confession and indictment. Sharing the burden of the insupportable guilt, father and son recognize the entangled nature of their identities and resolve to end their lives together.

Frantz provides Sartre with an opportunity to explore the closed-world existential dynamics of his early drama with the more expansive historical concerns of his later work. One of Sartre's most fully realized characters, Frantz is both a victim and a perpetrator of history. Mad certainly, but charming and vulnerable, Frantz represents the intersection of individual will with larger historical forces. In this respect he is a synthesis of Sartre's literary and political ambitions.

The Condemned of Altona premiered at the Théâtre de la Renaissance on September 23, 1959, and was later adapted into a film by Vittorio de Sica, starring Sophia Loren, Maximilian Schell, and Robert Wagner, a version that Sartre apparently found distasteful.

[*See also* France; Philosophy and Drama, 1860–1960]

FURTHER READING

Howells, Christina. *Sartre: The Necessity of Freedom*. Cambridge: Cambridge Univ. Press, 1988.

Kern, Edith, ed. *Sartre: A Collection of Critical Essays*. Englewood Cliffs, N.J.: Prentice-Hall, 1965.

McCall, Dorothy. *The Theatre of Jean-Paul Sartre*. New York: Columbia Univ. Press, 1969.

Murdoch, Iris. *Sartre: Romantic Rationalist*. London: Vintage, 1999.

Sartre, Jean-Paul. *What Is Literature?* Tr. by Bernard Frechtman. London: Methuen, 1950.

——. *Sartre on Theater*. Tr. by Frank Jellinek. New York: Pantheon Bks., 1976.

——. *Basic Writings*. Ed. by Stephen Priest. London: Routledge, 2001.

Thody, Philip. *Jean-Paul Sartre: A Literary and Political Study*. London: Hamilton, 1960.

Wood, Philip R. *Understanding Jean-Paul Sartre*. Columbia: Univ. of South Carolina Press, 1990.

Charles McNulty

CONNELLY, MARC (1890–1980)

At the advent of modern American drama in the 20th century there were many playwrights whose contributions to its evolution were essentially in the nature of paired collaborations rather than as single authors. At the forefront of these duets appears the name of Marc Connelly, primarily in tandem with GEORGE S. KAUFMAN (e.g., BEGGAR ON HORSEBACK). Connelly later used Roark Bradford's southern folk tales, *Ol' Man Adam an' His Chillun*, as the basis for the much more sophisticated THE GREEN PASTURES. The unprecedented quality and character of these plays and their spectacular effect, for different reasons, on the contemporary theater audience on Broadway and across the nation confirmed that their creators were "in the vanguard of modernism in the American theatre" (Pollack, 1988).

Marc Connelly was, like EUGENE O'NEILL, an agnostic in search of a viable faith through the world of the stage. Both belonged to families in which theater constituted a primary and ongoing tradition rather than an incidental concern. Though Patrick Joseph Connelly, Marc's father of Irish lineage, was never as famous a figure as James O'Neill, the former was nonetheless talented as a stage singer and actor and along with his wife Mabel toured the country as an actor and manager with theater companies until Marc was born on December 13, 1890, in McKeesport, Pennsylvania. There they decided to settle down because of the tragic price they had had to pay a year earlier for their hectic, itinerant stage life in the death of their firstborn, a daughter.

Connelly's family life proved to be a harmonious one, especially in his affectionate relationship with his mother, to whom he was to dedicate *The Green Pastures*. The equanimity fostered by this harmony was also reflected in his own jovial and helpful nature. The family owned and lived in the White Hotel; through Joseph's connections it became the watering hole for many eminent actors and actresses of the time. The constant flow of artists provided a unique exposure for the young Marc, who was to recall meeting the great Buffalo Bill Cody (then touring the country with his Wild West show) and others such as Richard Mansfield and Minnie Maddern Fiske, from all of whom he received tips on the creation of a vital stage presence. As a boy he also sang regularly in the choir of St. Stephen's Episcopal Church, and his experience was to be used in his future compositions of musicals. In 1902, the year his father died, he matriculated at Trinity Hall in Washington, Pennsylvania, and after graduation he moved to Pittsburgh in 1907 to begin his career as a writer for papers such as the Sun and the *Gazette Times*.

In 1916 Connelly's first play, the musical *The Amber Empress*, opened at the Hippodrome Theatre on Broadway. In the following year he met George S. Kaufman, drama editor of the *New York Times*, with whom he was to collaborate in the composition of six Broadway comedies between 1921 and 1924: *Dulcy* (1921), *To the Ladies* (1922), *Merton of the Movies* (1922), *Helen of Troy, New York* (1923), *The Deep Tangled Wildwood* (1923), and *Beggar on Horseback* (1924). *Dulcy* proved to be their first Broadway success. It was selected by Burns Mantle for his *Best Plays of 1921–1922*. *Merton*, the story of Merton Gill, a despairing Hollywood aspirant, was an adaptation of the novel by Harry Leon Wilson and was included in the *Best Plays of 1922–1923*. Employing multiple sets and a cinematic approach to drama under the eyes of such veterans as ROBERT EDMOND JONES and Lee Simonson, *Merton* became a commercial and artistic success because it chastised the "vulgarization of art" (John Gassner) and was the first in a series of plays burlesquing Hollywood.

Beggar on Horseback, obliquely emulating the German expressionistic style, superbly satirizes American big business. With *The Green Pastures*, a modern miracle play, "the divine comedy of the modern theater" (Brooks Atkinson, *New York Times*, February 27, 1930), based on the Louisiana folktales and Bible stories of Roark Bradford, Connelly achieved a monumental feat that surpassed the recognition bestowed by the Pulitzer Prize in 1930. In performances over five years in 203 cities it grossed $3,000,000. It also ensured his alignment with a select tradition of white Anglo-Americans writing powerful folk (and urban) plays of black culture after World War I—Ridgely Torrence, EDWARD SHELDON, Eugene O'Neill, and PAUL GREEN. In 1935 Warner Brothers made *Pastures* into a film.

Connelly wrote several more plays on his own (*The Wisdom Tooth*, 1926; *Flowers of Virtue*, 1942) and in collaboration (*The Farmer Takes a Wife*, with Frank B. Elser, 1934; *The Wild Man of Borneo*, with Herman Mankiewicz, 1927). He also wrote for films and radio and published one novel. He accepted an associate professorship of playwriting at Yale University to teach Drama 47, succeeding Walter Pritchard Eaton and GEORGE PIERCE BAKER, the latter having been the pioneering creator of the course, first at Harvard in 1912 and later at Yale in the 1920s. In 1944 Connelly played the part of the Stage Manager in a production of THORNTON WILDER'S OUR TOWN.

In 1951 he accepted the position of U.S. commissioner to UNESCO, and in 1953 that of the president of the National Institute of Arts and Letters. Connelly died on December 20, 1980, in New York City.

Marc Connelly played a very significant, though limited, role in the development of modern American drama during the seventy years in which he was involved with the stage and the celluloid world as a playwright, director, actor, critic, and activist for the rights of theater. In his autobiography, *Voices Offstage* (1968), he was keen to affirm that the "stage instructs but is not a didactic teacher" and that "it is the best instrument man has ever devised."

[See also United States, 1929–1940]

SELECT PLAYS: *The Amber Empress* (music by Zoel Parenteau, 1916); *Dulcy* (with George S. Kaufman, 1921); *Merton of the Movies* (with Kaufman, 1922); *To the Ladies!* (with Kaufman, 1922); *The Deep Tangled Wildwood* (with Kaufman, 1923); *Helen of Troy, New York* (musical comedy, with Kaufman, 1923); *Beggar on Horseback* (with Kaufman, 1924); *Be Yourself* (musical comedy, with Kaufman, 1924); *The Wisdom Tooth* (1926); *The Wild Man of Borneo* (with Herman J. Mankiewicz, 1927); *The Green Pastures* (1929); *The Farmer Takes a Wife* (with Frank B. Elser, 1934); *The Mole on Lincoln's Cheek* (1941); *Flowers of Virtue* (1942); *The Portable Yenberry* (1961)

FURTHER READING

Bradford, Roark. *Ol' Man Adam an' His Chillun*. New York: Harper, 1928.
Brown, John Mason. *Dramatis Personae*. New York: Viking, 1963.
Connelly, Marc. *Voices Offstage*. New York: Holt, Rinehart & Winston, 1968.
"Divine Comedian." *Time* (May 19, 1949).
Goldstein, Malcolm. *George S. Kaufman: His Life, His Theater*. New York: Oxford Univ. Press, 1979.
Krumbleman, John T. "Marc Connelly's *The Green Pastures* and Goethe's *Faust*." *Studies in Comparative Literature* (Fall 1962).
Laufe, Abe. *Anatomy of a Hit: Long-Run Plays on Broadway from 1900 to the Present Day*. New York: Hawthorn Bks., 1966.
Mantle, Burns. *American Playwrights of Today*. New York: Dodd, Mead, 1929.
Nolan, Paul T. *Marc Connelly*. New York: Twayne, 1969.
Pollack, Rhoda-Gale. "Enter Marc Connelly." Chap. 2 in *George S. Kaufman*. Boston: Twayne Publishers, 1988.

Rupendra Guha-Majumdar

A CONSPIRACY OF FEELINGS

A Conspiracy of Feelings (*Zagavor chuvstv*, 1929) is a play by YURY OLESHA, based loosely on his novel *Envy* (1927), a landmark of early Soviet prose. Hailed by critics as quality drama but assailed for its ideological ambiguity, it had brief success at the Vakhtangov Theater in Moscow, where it was performed from 1929 to 1930. Like plays by NIKOLAI ERDMAN, MIKHAIL BULGAKOV, VLADIMIR MAYAKOVSKY, and others, it ran counter to prevailing cultural policies in the Soviet Union at the outset of the 1930s, when art increasingly was expected to glorify the Soviet way of life. Olesha sought to illuminate the mechanics of social progress but created a work that may be viewed as antiutopian. This explains its short life on the stage. New productions of it were inconceivable by the mid-1930s, the time of the buildup to the great purges and the rise of SOCIALIST REALISM.

Two of Olesha's key obsessions form the play's basis: his belief (troubled as it was) that youth and progress are right to push aside experience and custom, and his recognition that technology and social evolution might soon conquer such messy but crucial human emotions as love, hate, jealousy, heroism, and cowardice. It is structured on a triangle connecting three men: Andrei Babichev, the practical director of a food factory that has invented a new kind of sausage; his brother Ivan, the leader of a subversive "conspiracy" seeking heroes to defend "splendid," "old-fashioned" feelings against utilitarianism; and Nikolai Kavalerov, an educated, confused, and occasionally drunk romantic whom Andrei picks up off the street and whom Ivan encourages to kill Andrei. This trio is further united—and their relations further complicated—by Valya, Ivan's adopted daughter, who has run off to live with Andrei and is loved by both Andrei and Kavalerov. A key strength of the play is that while it employs characters as metaphors for specific problems, they do not represent a schematic dichotomy of "old versus new." The forward-looking Andrei is older than the retrograde Kavalerov, thus expressing Olesha's belief that youth and receptivity to progress are states of mind, not givens. The characters, clear-cut in their dramatic missions, are not stick figures: The practical Andrei is sufficiently sentimental to shelter and support Kavalerov; the emotional Kavalerov cannot do violence to his "benefactor"; and Ivan, a self-proclaimed poet and the "knight of a dying era," is so militant in his defense of emotions over machines that he appears more dangerous than Andrei. Ivan twice encourages murder and is the inventor of a machine called "Ophelia" that he claims can sabotage other machines by "being melancholy," "singing love songs," and "collecting flowers."

Not strictly a COMEDY, the play is written with humor and in natural, conversational language. Composed in seven discrete scenes that take place in Babichev's apartment, a communal apartment, a soccer stadium, and elsewhere, it includes a cast of twenty-three plus extras. This expands the work beyond MELODRAMA, introducing philosophical inquiry and timeless social commentary. Kavalerov certainly expresses Olesha's own thoughts when he tells Andrei, "You want everything to be useful, but I want to be useless."

[*See also* Russia and the Soviet Union]

FURTHER READING

Brown, Edward J. *Russian Literature Since the Revolution*. Cambridge, Mass.: Harvard Univ. Press, 1982.

Olesha, Yury. *The Complete Plays*. Ed. and tr. by Michael Green and Jerome Katsel. Ann Arbor: Ardis, 1983.

——. *The Conspiracy of Feelings*. Tr. by Daniel Gerould and Eleanor Gerould. In *Avant-Garde Drama: Major Plays and Documents Post World War I*, ed. by Bernard F. Dukore and Daniel Gerould. New York: Bantam, 1969.

——. *Envy*. Tr. by Clarence Brown. In *The Portable Twentieth-Century Russian Reader*, ed. by Clarence Brown. Harmondsworth: Penguin, 1993.

Tucker, Janet G. *Revolution Betrayed: Jurij Olesa's "Envy."* Columbus, Ohio: Slavica, 1996.

John Freedman

THE CONSTANT WIFE

Premiered in New York in 1926 (after an initial Cleveland tryout) with Ethel Barrymore and C. Aubrey Smith as the leads, SOMERSET MAUGHAM's comedy *The Constant Wife* was a major success, running for some 295 performances, followed by a one-year U.S. tour. But it achieved rather more moderate success on its London premiere in 1927, when Basil Dean and Fay Compton played John and Constance Middleton. Nevertheless, the play has been variously revived for the stage—including a London production in 2002—and was filmed as *Charming Sinners* (directed by Robert Milton, 1929).

After fifteen years of marriage Constance Middleton discovers that her respectable husband, the surgeon John Middleton, is having an affair with her friend Marie-Louise Durham. Constance seeks recompense neither through divorce nor even by way of an affair of her own. Instead, she sets a bold course for financial autonomy and emotional independence. At the conclusion of the play Constance not only has secured the former—she has become a successful interior designer—but is set to travel to Italy with her old flame Bernard Kersal. And her coup de grâce includes not only paying for her own holiday but also reimbursing John for her "board and lodging for the last twelve months" (act 3). Initially John declares that if she goes, she should not come back, but at the curtain he declares that despite everything, he remains fascinated by her, and she should indeed return to what will clearly become a very different partnership.

The Constant Wife revisits Maugham's favorite themes of the 1920s—the battle of the sexes, conventional marriage, and unconventional relationships. But this familiar territory is explored with a ruthlessness and perhaps even a protofeminist mien unexpected in the contemporary drawing-room COMEDY.

Constance realizes that she can only contemplate an affair when she has achieved financial security outside her marriage, no matter how "modern": "When all is said and done," she asserts, "the modern wife is nothing but a parasite" (act 2). Constance's logical deconstruction of marriage within her class brings her to the view that her husband "bought a toy, and if he no longer wants to play with it, why should he? He has paid for it" (act 2). This view of marriage as a physical and social exchange and, thereby, as emotionally belittling for both parties, but particularly for women, threads its way acerbically through the play as Maugham builds his case for a new kind of partnership: a meeting—legitimate or not—of emotional and sexual equals.

Throughout the play Maugham's humor is dry, the repartee lively, and the characters inviting. Constance, for example, presents the actress with a role of comic bravura combined with unexpected emotional, as well as linguistic, sophistication. One by one, she exposes and discards the conventions and the habits of marriage—simultaneously unpacking the similarly predictable conventions of the love affair—but in so doing she must create a new basis for her place in the world and her intimate and familial relations. The conventions of the drawing-room comedy perhaps constrain the psychological development of the characters, but there is no escaping the impact of Maugham's bold conclusion when Constance departs for an affair with Bernard, having briefed mother, sister, and husband of the arrangements. At the conclusion of the drama the audience has been convinced not only by Constance's logic but also by her desires and her acknowledged expectations of an emotional and sexual self. Such assertions had a wicked allure for West End and Broadway audiences, and Maugham capitalizes expertly on the piquancy of the situation. This is a comedy of manners, in the same vein as George Farquhar's *The Constant Couple*, and, as such, its goal is neither naturalism nor authenticity. But neither are the play and its characters to be seen as parodies, caricatures, and grotesques: as Richard Cordell comments in his rather hagiographic study of the author, "It is a play one can laugh at and enjoy without believing a word of it" (Cordell, 1961).

[*See also* England, 1860–1940]

FURTHER READING

Cordell, Richard. *Somerset Maugham: A Biographical and Critical Study*. London: Heinemann, 1961.

Curtis, Anthony. *The Pattern of Maugham: A Critical Portrait*. London: Hamilton, 1974.

——. *Somerset Maugham*. Writers and Their Work. Windsor: Profile Bks., 1982.

Morgan, Ted. *Somerset Maugham*. London: Jo. Cape, 1980.

Rogal, Samuel J. *A William Somerset Maugham Encyclopedia*. Westport, Conn.: Greenwood Press, 1997.

Whitehead, John. *W. Somerset Maugham: The Critical Heritage*. London: Routledge, 1987.

Adrienne Scullion

COOK, MICHAEL (1933–1994)

Born in London on February 14, 1933, Michael Cook was educated at boarding schools and then served for twelve years in the British military. After his discharge he enrolled in the Nottingham University College of Education. After completing a degree in English he emigrated to CANADA, where he worked first as a public school teacher before joining the faculty at Memorial University in St. John's, Newfoundland. He became a Canadian citizen in 1971. Cook died in St. John's, Newfoundland, in 1994.

Although not a native of Newfoundland, Cook made it the focal geographic and cultural location of his work. He was particularly concerned with two paradoxes that he felt defined contemporary life in Newfoundland. First, the economic prosperity that was dramatically improving the standard of living for most people in Newfoundland was eroding the distinct culture of the island, for one of the benefits of economic stagnation had been a cultural isolation that facilitated the preservation of local traditions and customs. Second, the people of Newfoundland have historically been unified by the continuing conflicts that have divided them; in particular, a central tension has long existed between the cultural emphases on hardy individualism and on responsibility to one's community. Cook received the Labatt Award for the best Canadian play for four of his plays: *The Head, Guts, and Sound Bone Dance* (1973), *Jacob's Wake* (1974), *On the Rim of the Curve* (1977), and *The Gayden Chronicles* (1978). His best-known play may be *The Head, Guts, and Sound Bone Dance*. Set in a "splitting room," where fish are commercially gutted and cleaned, the play works around the central irony that fish processing, which has been the emblematic industry of the local economy, has suddenly become moribund and anachronistic. The sense that something broader has gone off-kilter is reinforced by the eccentricities of the characters and by the terrible weirdness of the play's focal event, the drowning of a young boy.

In addition to his many plays for the stage, Cook wrote many plays for radio and television, as well as the novel *The Island of Fire* (1980). He also directed a large number of stage productions of works by other playwrights.

PLAYS: *The J. Arthur Prufrock Hour* (1968); *Colour the Flesh the Colour of Dust* (1972); *Tiln* (1972); *The Head, Guts, and Sound Bone Dance* (1973); *Jacob's Wake* (1974); *Quiller* (1975); *Not as a Dream* (1976); *On the Rim of the Curve* (1977); *Therese's Creed* (1977); *The Gayden Chronicles* (1978); *The Apocalypse Sonata* (1980); *The Deserts of Bohemia* (1980); *The Terrible Journey of Frederick Douglass* (1982); *The Great Harvest Festival* (1986)

FURTHER READING

Gygli, Karen L. "A 'Brave' New Newfoundland: *Jacob's Wake* by Michael Cook and the Significance of Past and Place." *McNeese Review* 35 (1997): 62–78.

Walker, Craig Stewart. "Elegy, Mythology and the Sublime in Michael Cook's *Colour the Flesh the Colour of Dust*." *Theatre Research in Canada/Recherches Théâtrales au Canada* 15, no. 2 (Fall 1994): 191–203.

——. "Ship of Death: Eschatology in Michael Cook's *Quiller*." *Theatre Research in Canada/Recherches Théâtrales au Canada* 16, nos. 1–2 (1995): 69–80.

Wallace, Robert. "Michael Cook." In *Profiles in Canadian Literature*, 4, ed. by Jeffrey M. Heath. Toronto: Dundurn, 1982. 109–116.

Martin Kich

COPEAU, JACQUES (1879–1949)

Considered the father of modern French theater, Jacques Copeau (born in Paris, February 4, 1879) reformed not only the art, but how it was studied and taught. He wished to "restore" drama by delving into Europe's theatrical heritage, particularly the Greeks, the Elizabethans, and Molière, searching for a truer sense of form and a stark theatricality to counter contemporary extravagance. Copeau opened the Théâtre du Vieux-Colombier in 1913, and its four seasons consisted of a repertoire ranging from Aeschylus to GEORGE BERNARD SHAW: plays with social, moral, and spiritual points of view. The high style of the classics and the extreme detail of contemporary plays provided Copeau a great range with which to develop his acting process. His 1914 adaptation of *The Brothers Karamazov* was seminal. Rehearsals consisted of improvisation, intense physical training, and reading exercises that focused on tonality, emphasis, and subtext. Copeau thought of the "text" as the whole of a play's potential as a theatrical event, and his goal was its hidden meaning. His greatest technique lay in working with performers' abilities and inadequacies. Seeking a blend of natural freedom and acquired discipline, he was a forerunner in the strategy of having his performers achieve their goals at the appropriate time.

When the Vieux-Colombier company re-formed in 1920, the space was remodeled on the basis of Elizabethan stages: the openness was itself a manifesto of Copeau's restoration. In the spirit of Elizabethan practices, Copeau formalized the relationship between the actor and the audience, making clear both parties' roles in the theatrical experience and thus inviting the audience's active, imaginative assistance. He continued to mix classics with new works, hoping that young writers would intuit their essential form and drive. Before long Copeau realized that he could never effectuate his reform on stage, and he turned his attention to the theater's school, a community unified by the belief in a new dramatic order. The potential of the human actor, independent of stage tricks or gimmicks, was celebrated for its strength and simplicity: slow, deliberate movements (often behind a neutral mask) were used to link action to psychic motivation. In a laboratory free of rehearsal constraints, Copeau's philosophies flourished, but the project became its own goal: no actor was able to incorporate the results into a rehearsal process.

In 1924 Copeau withdrew with a small company to the countryside in Burgundy, a locale rich in FARCE and commedia dell'arte traditions. They mimicked Greek performance, in which choric expression demonstrated that material and spiritual prosperity sprang from symbiosis with nature. When Copeau returned to Paris in 1929, writing and religious fervor took the place of theater; his pamphlet *The Popular Theater* became the cornerstone for postwar efforts to decentralize the French theatre. *The Miracle of Saint Uliva* (1933), *Savonarola* (1935), and *The Miracle of the Golden Bread* (1943) are considered his most successful later productions: syntheses of popular traditions, innovative but simple performance techniques, and a foundation in shared spirituality. In all his work, however, Copeau sought to explore the dimensions and potential of the theatrical art, discarding the naturalistic baggage of previous generations and inviting more liberal uses of dramatic form. He died in Côte d'Or on October 20, 1949.

[*See also* France]

SELECT PLAYS: *Improv of the Vieux-Colombier* (*Impromptu du Vieux-Colombier*, 1917); *The Brothers Karamazov* (adapted from Fyodor Dostoevsky's novel, 1921); *The Native Home* (*La Maison Natale*, 1923); *The Little Poor Man* (*Le Petit Pauvre*, 1941)

FURTHER READING

Borgal, Clément. *Jacques Copeau*. Paris: L'Arche, 1964.

Brown, Frederick. *Theater and Revolution: The Culture of the French Stage*. New York: Vintage, 1989.

Copeau, Jacques. *Copeau: Texts on Theatre*. Ed. and tr. by John Rudlin and Norman H. Paul. London: Routledge, 1990.

Doisy, Marcel. *Jacques Copeau, ou l'absolu dans l'art* [Jacques Copeau; or the absolute in art]. Paris: Le Cercle du livre, 1954.

Gignoux, Hubert. *Histoire d'une famille théâtrale* [History of a theatrical family]. Lausanne: Editions de l'Aire, 1984.

Kurtz, Maurice. *Jacques Copeau: Biography of a Theater*. Carbondale: Southern Illinois Univ. Press, 1999.

Rudlin, John. *Jacques Copeau*. Cambridge: Cambridge Univ. Press, 1986.

Whitton, David. *Stage Directors in Modern France*. Manchester: Manchester Univ. Press, 1987.

Matt Di Cintio

COPENHAGEN

Named after the locale of the quantum revolution in physics, MICHAEL FRAYN's *Copenhagen* conflates two materials of explosive dramatic energy: the discovery of scientific truths and the effects of war on individuals. As its final words indicate, the play points to the "final core of uncertainty at the heart of things," both material and human. In the years 1924–1927 the Danish physicist Niels Bohr and his younger collaborator Werner Heisenberg developed quantum mechanics. In World War II the two physicists found themselves in the awkward position of political enemies. Thus a central theme in the play is the difficulty of separating science from politics, a difficulty made especially acute during the development of the atomic bomb. The action consists of conversations between the two scientists, with Bohr's wife Margrethe as an active observer. Frayn does not subject the action to realistic limitations, and the conversations shift between different times—some during the war and others when the characters are "spirits of the past." The central questions in the play emerge from a real historical event: Heisenberg's enigmatic visit to Copenhagen in 1941. Did he come simply to talk to his old friend and mentor? Did he wish to warn him about the German nuclear program? Did he, on the contrary, try to glean information for the benefit of that program? The dramatization of these and other possibilities is Frayn's attempt to turn Heisenberg's great discovery—the uncertainty principle—into a principle of dramatic action and personality. Like a particle that exists as a wave function between interactions, containing many possibilities, Heisenberg is a man whose memories, actions, and motivations are enveloped in a cloud of ambiguity.

By applying a scientific concept to human action, *Copenhagen* exemplifies the imaginative impact of quantum mechanics on 20th-century theater. This impact does not come without the risk of taking scientific terms out of their context. Heisenberg's uncertainty principle, as Frayn acknowledges in his postscript, has a precise technical meaning that describes the possibilities and limitations of measurement during experiments. It does not make general claims about uncertainty in the world. In *Copenhagen*, however, uncertainty becomes a core principle of human, as well as of physical, reality. Politically, the focus on uncertainty lends validity to postmodern sensibilities that stress the difficulty of drawing moral distinctions between different sides engaged in war. While not minimizing the Holocaust, *Copenhagen* focuses at least equal attention on the immorality of the American atomic program. By focusing on possibility and uncertainty rather than on historical facts, the play runs the risk of creating a moral and historical vacuum in which questions of causality and necessity (was the atomic bomb a necessary evil required to bring an end to the crimes of World War II committed by Germany and its allies?) are made impossible to answer because of blurred distinctions. Thus great insights into physical nature—when turned into principles of dramatic action—do not necessarily lend themselves to accurate modes of historical and moral analysis and decision making.

[*See also* England, 1980–Present]

FURTHER READING

Frayn, Michael. " 'Copenhagen' Revisited." *New York Review of Books* 49, no. 5 (March 28, 2002): 22–24.

King, Robert L. "The Play of Uncertain Ideas." *Massachusetts Review* 42, no. 1 (Spring 2001): 165–175.

Rose, Paul Lawrence. "Frayn's 'Copenhagen' Plays Well, at History's Expense." *Chronicle of Higher Education* 46, no. 35 (May 5, 2000): B4–B6.

Ruddick, Nick. "The Search for a Quantum Ethics: Michael Frayn's *Copenhagen* and Other Recent British Science Plays." *Journal of the Fantastic in the Arts* 11, no. 4 (2001): 415–431.

Soto-Morettini, Donna. " 'Disturbing the Spirits of the Past': The Uncertainty Principle in Michael Frayn's *Copenhagen*." In *Crucible of Cultures: Anglophone Drama at the Dawn of a New Millennium*, ed. by Marc Maufort and Franca Bellarsi. Brussels: P. Lang, 2002. 69–78.

Stewart, Victoria. "A Theatre of Uncertainties: Science and History in Michael Frayn's *Copenhagen*." *New Theatre Quarterly* 15, no. 4: (November 1999): 301–307.

Gefen Bar-On

COPI (1939–1987)

The Argentine-French dramatist Raul Taborda Damonte (Copi) was born on November 20, 1939, in Buenos Aires, ARGENTINA, to a literary and journalistic family. His father, the editor of the left-wing journal *Critica*, was forced to flee with his family on the eve of the Perón revolution in 1945. Copi grew up largely in Uruguay, but visited Paris several times in his youth and settled there in 1962. He first garnered attention as an illustrator, creating "La femme assise," a full-page comic strip that ran from 1965 to 1975 in the French weekly *Le nouvel observateur*. During this time he also began writing for the theater. Among his early works, *Day of a Dreamer* (*La journée d'une rêveuse*, 1968) is a mild surrealist fantasy that has been compared to the work of Romain Weingarten. Copi's theatrical style veered into unique and unprecedented territory with *Eva Peron* (1969), a grotesque FARCE about the last days of the Argentine dictator's wife. Dying of brain cancer, she is deranged and abusive, is high on painkillers, and alternately seduces or derides everyone around her. (The scenery was demolished during an early performance when the theater was attacked by masked Argentine paramilitaries.)

Copi's next play was *The Homosexual: or, The Difficulty of Expressing Oneself* (*L'homosexuel ou la difficulté de s'exprimer*, 1971), set in a Siberia populated with drug-addled, transsexual refugees, which presented the first full development of the questions of identity that typify his work. Not easily categorized, Copi's plays stand out for their willingness to push the limits of indecency and their refusal to advocate any political or social position. *The Four Twins* (*Les quatre jumelles*, 1973) takes Copi's theater to an imaginary Alaska, where four women murder and rob each other repeatedly, between shots of heroin, camphor, and cocaine. Once again, identity is revealed as fluid (exchangeable by means of surgery or chemistry), twins and doubles abound, and life and death become volatile, mobile categories. Copi's theater is a zone of burlesque liberty, where the horrible is treated with a joyous lightness and comic touch (resurrection almost always follows close on the heels of death) that marks him as a satirist who looks upon society from far beyond the margins of acceptability, as illustrated in *Loretta Strong* (1974), a dramatic monologue in which the heroine is a space voyager who battles rats, drugs, murder, sex, birth, death, and a refrigerator, all while talking on the phone.

In the 1980s Copi returned to more recognizable backdrops of contemporary Paris, bringing his transvestite drug addicts and murderesses home to roost in *The Tower of La Défense* (*La tour de la défense*, 1978) and in the posthumous verse play *The Steps of Sacré Coeur* (*Les escaliers du Sacré-Coeur*, 1986). Perhaps Copi's most conventional work, *The Night of Madame Lucienne* (*La nuit de Madame Lucienne*, 1985), produced as part of the Avignon festival, is a Pirandellian murder mystery set in a theater. The semi-autobiographical *An Untimely Visit* (*Une visite inopportune*, 1988), also produced posthumously, marks a return to the themes of *Eva Peron*, twenty years later: the protagonist, this time dying of AIDS, is a relentless seducer, a dandy, a drug addict, and, above all, a performer of himself. He dies, is resurrected, and then dies for good. Copi was also the author of seven novels, as well as several collections of his "Femme assise" illustrations. Copi died of AIDS on December 14, 1987, in Paris.

[*See also* France]

SELECT PLAYS: *Day of a Dreamer* (*La journée d'une rêveuse*, 1968); *Eva Peron* (1969); *The Homosexual; or, The Difficulty of Expressing Oneself* (*L'homosexuel ou la difficulté de s'exprimer*, 1971); *The Four Twins* (*Les quatre jumelles*, 1973); *Loretta Strong* (1974); *The Pyramid* (*La pyramide*, 1975); *The Tower of La Défense* (*La tour de la défense*, 1978); *The Fridge* (*Le frigo*, 1983); *The Night of Madame Lucienne* (*La nuit de Madame Lucienne*, 1985); *The Steps of Sacré Coeur* (*Les escaliers du Sacré-Coeur*, 1986)

FURTHER READING

Damonte, Jorge. *Copi*. Paris: C. Bourgois, 1990.

Jeffrey M. Leichman

CORKER

Corker (1998) by WENDY LILL examines the liberal social and libertarian economic views of white upper-middle-class people in Nova Scotia. Following *All Fall Down* (1994), which explored the possible excessive puritanism in the accusation of child abuse, *Corker* examines the complacency of people who believe that all social problems have been solved. Premiering after Wendy Lill had become a sitting member of the Canadian House of Commons, the play bears a direct relation to the political currents of its era. Merit McPhee (the name satirizes the idea of the "meritocracy") is an ambitious career woman in Halifax. She and her husband Leonard Mills have a marriage oriented more toward their career pursuits than to traditional domestic concerns. They look down on Merit's younger brother, Galahad (or "Gal"), who, even though he has children, is in perpetually unsettled financial condition. Merit's sister, Serena, has killed herself, and Merit semiconsciously assumes that she has survived because she is ruthless, whereas Serena was more compassionate and imaginative. Merit's mother, Florence, is shattered by her younger daughter's death and stands in the play as a symbol of the residual compassion of the mid-20th-century social consensus that the younger, more ruthless and Darwinian generation has lost.

Until her death Serena had been taking care of Corker, a mentally disabled and childlike figure who cannot express himself in full sentences. After Serena's death he is placed in the care of Leonard and Merit. The couple tries to get rid of Corker, even laying out rat traps to obstruct his entry into their home. But, like the repressed, he keeps on returning. Albert Glenny, a social worker, tries to persuade the couple to be more compassionate toward Corker. Merit eventually realizes the limits of her ruthlessness and by the end of the play eschews her former careerism in favor of a more compassionate love of life modeled on her dead sister Serena's view of the world. As a character, Corker comes very close to fantasy; his disability is never explained; and, in contrast to the realistic depiction of the other characters, he seems to exist in a nonnaturalistic counterpoise. Lill is the mother of a son with Down's syndrome and has said that this play is her exploration of the theoretical side of disability issues. Corker, an outsider, teaches Merit and Leonard to be more respectful of difference and not rigidly adhere to conventional ideas of social and career success. The play, whose initial production at Halifax's Neptune Theatre starred Gay Hauser as Merit and Ryan Rogerson as Corker, was acclaimed for its frank interrogation of the complacency of contemporary elites. Lill's satiric portrait of the meritocratic career woman was especially striking in that she had been a consistent champion of feminist causes in her previous work, although some critics criticized Lill for Merit's sudden and rather too convenient repentance.

[*See also* Canada]

FURTHER READING

Hall, Michael. "*Corker*, by Wendy Lill." *Canadian Theatre Review*, no. 99 (Summer 1999): 92–93.

Nicholas Birns

THE CORN IS GREEN

EMLYN WILLIAMS's play *The Corn Is Green* (1938) was his most successful play. It struck a chord with London audiences and was also admired in Wales and the United States. The play was largely based on Williams's own experiences of cultural transformation (he played the character Morgan Evans in the first production). At school Williams received encouragement from his teacher, Miss Cooke, the model for Miss Moffat in *The Corn Is Green*. With her help Williams won a scholarship to Oxford University in 1923. That translation from Wales to England, Flintshire to Oxford, from working to upper class, was disconcerting: the play explores some of the ambiguities and difficulties of this "advancement." The teacher Miss Moffat is presented as a figure of beneficial progress, and though her (English) language is the voice of progress, the Welsh language is not correspondingly seen as its barbarous contrary. Some of the play's dialogue is in Welsh, and Miss Moffat treats Welsh with respect. However, she concentrates mainly on her practical purpose of changing the lives of the inhabitants. And her main transformations are from Welsh orality to English literacy. It is the power of Morgan Evans's Welsh English that draws Miss Moffat's attention to him. Morgan is asked to write an essay, which lends the play its title:

> The mine is dark. . . . If a light come in the mine . . . the rivers in the mine will run fast with the voice of many women; the walls will fall in, and it will be the end of the world. . . . when I walk through the . . . shaft, in the dark, I can touch with my hands the leaves on the trees, and underneath . . . where the corn is green.

This writing is seen by Miss Moffat as rooted in experience, with a strain of poetry and myth specific to its place and author. Miss Moffat determines to develop Morgan's talent. Miss Moffat's educational program, though, is strongly normative: he must learn Standard English. The play has a strong sense of loss running counter to the narrative of "progress." Miss Moffat adopts Morgan into her culture, but where and what is he now? He is no longer part of the Welsh community, but neither is he quite "English." Ironically, where Morgan at the opening of the play was highly articulate in his primal essay about escape, at the end he is reduced to inarticulacy. The imaginary is more powerful than the factual, but in becoming "educated," Morgan may have lost touch with his imaginative roots. This partly nostalgic critique of modern, standardized life may well be what gave the play its power for English and American audiences, as well as for Welsh ones.

[*See also* England, 1860–1940]

FURTHER READING

Dale-Jones, Don. *Emlyn Williams*. Cardiff: Univ. of Wales Press and Welsh Arts Council, 1979.

Harding, James. *Emlyn Williams: A Life*. London: Weidenfeld & Nicolson, 1993.

Stokes, Sewell. "Emlyn Williams." *Theatre Arts* 26 (1942): 697–705.

Trewin, J. C. *George: An Early Autobiography*. London: Hamilton, 1961.

——. "The Plays of Emlyn Williams." *Adelphi* 28 (1958): 431–437.

Williams, Emlyn. *Emlyn*. London: Bodley Head, 1973.

Chris Hopkins

THE CORONATION VOYAGE

MICHEL MARC BOUCHARD's politics frequently color the subjects and themes portrayed within his often controversial and startling plays, and *The Coronation Voyage* remains one of his most blatantly political works. Influenced by the rise of the Parti Quebecois, Bouchard's beliefs gradually aligned themselves with the sovereigntist movement. Consequently, *The Coronation Voyage* suggests French CANADA's yearning—and real need—to gain independence from a troubling, and potentially injurious, patriarchal power. But the play also remains true to motifs Bouchard returns to again and again: the victimization of the innocent, unresolved and irreparable pain, and betrayal.

First performed at Salle Pierre-Mercure, Centre Pierre-Péladeau, Montreal, on September 21, 1995, the play has since enjoyed both English and French performances. Like many of Bouchard's plays, it is set in the 1950s, but, unlike much of Bouchard's canon, it does not take place in the Canadian countryside. Instead, as its title suggests, the play concerns a number of passengers voyaging to Liverpool from Montreal to attend the coronation of Elizabeth II. Although Bouchard includes some COMEDY in the form of three girls, all named Elisabeth, who have won a competition based upon the similarity of their name and birthdate to that of the soon-to-be English queen, and in the speech of an officious official, the play never strays very far from its serious theme. At the center of the play is a family drama: The Chief, an ex-Mafioso who recognizes the evil facets of his character and wishes to rewrite history in his favor, is still willing to sacrifice his two sons, Étienne and Sandro, to ensure his own safety. The Chief is journeying to England to attend his own inauguration into a new life as Mr. Peacock, safe from the murderous attention of the thugs he has previously betrayed, for a hefty price, to the Canadian authorities. That future safety depends upon the three passports held by The Diplomat, who, having met Sandro, the Chief's innocent and compelling thirteen-year-old son, wants a "bonus" before he hands the passports over. In one of the play's most shocking moments, The Diplomat requests The Chief's permission, and his sanction, to seduce the young Sandro. The Chief never says no; his silence is his consent, and, indeed, his only corollary to the request, mentioned near the play's end, is that The Diplomat get Sandro drunk first. Étienne has also suffered because of his father; he was once a brilliant pianist, but his hands have been mutilated by two gangsters who sought vengeance upon his father. Although the play erratically speaks of forgiveness and forgetting, Étienne's attempt at reconciliation with his father comes to an abrupt and bitter end when he discovers that The Chief has sold Sandro to The Diplomat. Although Étienne and Sandro finally gain their passports to safety, The Diplomat does not have time to produce The Chief's—Étienne and Sandro "help" him fall overboard. *The Coronation Voyage* has sometimes been criticized for its MELODRAMA and its unrepentant lack of plausibility, characteristics that still contribute to its edgy and fascinating script. The play's success has ultimately depended upon how well audiences accept and engage with its more controversial aspects.

FURTHER READING

Bouchard, Michel Marc. *The Coronation Voyage*. Tr. by Linda Gaboriau. Vancouver: Talonbooks, 1999.

Ouzounian, Richard. "A Voyage on Stormy, Emotional Seas." *Toronto Star* (July 7, 2003).

——. "Playwright in Character." *Toronto Star* (January 25, 2004).

Winter S. Elliott

CORONA TRILOGY: CROWN OF SHADOW, CROWN OF LIGHT, CROWN OF FIRE

RODOLFO USIGLI's *Corona* trilogy is composed of three plays written over the course of almost twenty years: *Crown of Shadow* (*Corona de sombra*; written in 1943, produced in 1947), *Crown of Fire* (*Corona de fuego*, 1960), and *Crown of Light* (*Corona de luz*, 1963). *Crown of Shadow* dramatizes Emperor Maximilian and Empress Carlota's four-year reign in MEXICO. Historically, this period of Hapsburg rule was continually troubled, ending in Carlota's return to Europe and Maximilian's execution. Usigli's play opens when Erasmo Rodríguez, a young Oaxacan historian with a striking resemblance to Benito Juárez, arrives in Brussels to interview Carlota. Moving between Carlota and Erasmo's 1927 conversation about the events and scenes from their 1863–1867 Mexican rule in Mexico, Usigli's revisionist history depicts Maximilian as a secret democrat and admirer of Mexican culture, who considered co-ruling Mexico with Juárez. Its most dramatic scenes, however, are those between Carlota, Napoleon, and the pope, in which she fails to convince these powers to send troops to Mexico to defend Maximilian and the empire, resulting in her own insanity. The play ends when she comes to terms with this history and dies, effectively removing her "corona de sombra."

Crown of Fire, written as a verse TRAGEDY complete with Mexican and Spanish choruses, stages another important event in

Mexican history: Cortés's 1525 execution of indigenous warrior Cuauhtemoc. The play begins when, on his way to Honduras, Cortés encounters two indigenous groups, the Chontales and the Macuanes, who give him contradictory information about the Chontal leader's death. Ultimately discovering that the report was a lie, Cortés grows suspicious, assumes that an indigenous rebellion is on the horizon, and confronts the Chontales. Anticipating a battle, Cuauhtemoc, who has been taken along as a captive on the journey, reluctantly joins the Chontal leader Pax Bolom in a plan to attack Cortés. To guarantee his own safety, Cortés kills Cuauhtemoc by hanging him upside down. The silhouette of Cuauhtemoc's slain body, which resembles a cross, is *Fire*'s final image. In contrast to Cuauhtemoc's emergence as a Christ figure, Cortés is portrayed as a cruel tyrant, whose burning of the indigenous leader's feet before the trip to Honduras inspired the play's title.

The final work, *Crown of Light*, tells the story of the dark-skinned Virgin of Guadalupe's appearance on Juan Diego's *tilma* (cloak) in 1531. Act 1 takes place in SPAIN, focusing on conversations between King Carlos V and religious leaders about the problems religious leaders are having in New Spain. Act 2 takes us "behind the scenes" of this apparition where various 16th-century friars elaborate a plan to stage the Virgin of Guadalupe's miraculous appearance, so as to win the indigenous Mexicans' faith. Eventually they ask a young nun to impersonate the Virgin and ask a gardener to plant roses in the countryside so that she may present these flowers, unknown in the region, as evidence of her holiness. The last act depicts the Virgin's arrival. Her appearance, however, occurs earlier and at a different place than was planned. Friar Zumarrga, unsure as to whether the miracle was real or not, decides that he will let Spain take credit for staging the miracle, nonetheless arguing that the symbol will ultimately wrest Mexico from Spanish control. The play ends with his admission that "all at once I see these people [the Mexicans] crowned with light, with faith."

Usigli's trilogy was a crucial part of his larger mission of forging a truly Mexican theater. Each play formed a part of what he saw as the fabric of Mexican sovereignty: its creation of an indigenous Mexican religious icon, its articulation of political sovereignty vis-à-vis Maximilian and Carlota's fall, and its creation of a "material" national hero: Cuauhtemoc. In each case he chose to dramatize a controversial moment in Mexican history, with multiple and often contradictory accounts. While his works were far from being unique in choosing to treat historical subject matter (Miguel N. Lira's *Carlota de México* debuted before Usigli's *Shadow*, and Salvador Novo's *Cuauhtemoc* was nearly contemporaneous with *Fire*), his articulation of historiographical methodology was unique. He called the plays "antihistorical," claiming in a dedication to *Crown of Fire* that "[t]heatre is not history. A historical work is good, but it should be a history lesson, not a history class." Therefore, Usigli played fast and loose with his historical sources, inventing incidents and purposely including anachronisms within the works so as to get at the larger truth of Mexican identity. The trilogy, however, was as important to his attempt to build a Mexican theater as it was to his exploration of Mexican history. The antihistorical tenor of his tragedies implicitly referenced Aristotle's distinction between theater and history as the difference between "what has happened and what could happen," effectively linking Usiglian dramaturgy with a European classical tradition, which was one of his main goals. Despite his efforts, Usigli's drama won mixed responses in his home country.

Crown of Shadow is ranked today as one of his best works, having inspired GEORGE BERNARD SHAW to assure Usigli that "Mexico can starve you, but they can't deny your genius" (qtd. in Jones, 1971). *Crown of Light* also met recognition, winning the 1963 Latin American Play contest. *Crown of Fire*, however, was panned, the 1961 production at the Teatro Xola receiving negative reviews because of its stilted verse and static plot. Productions of *Shadow* met mixed success. While the first production of *Shadow*, which Usigli directed himself, closed after only one night, the second production, directed by the renowned Seki Sano, was lauded. Nevertheless, the trilogy has been regarded as one of the masterpieces of Mexican drama, *Crown of Shadow* being regarded by Hugo Argüelles, among others, as Mexico's premier tragedy. Unlike *Gesticulator* (1947), Usigli's most popular and widely produced play, the *Corona* trilogy's recognition stems from its contribution to Mexican national literature, rather than its success within the theater.

FURTHER READING

Beardsell, Peter. *A Theatre for Cannibals: Rodolfo Usigli and the Mexican Stage*. Rutherford, N.J.: Fairleigh Dickinson Univ. Press, 1992.

Finch, Mark. "Rodolfo Usigli's *Corona de sombra, Corona de fuego, Corona de luz*: The Mythopoesis of Anti-history." *Romance Notes* 22, no. 2 (Winter 1981): 151–154.

Jones, Willis Knapp. "Introduction." In *Two Plays: Crown of Light, One of These Days . . .* , by Rodolfo Usigli. Tr. by Thomas Bledsoe. Carbondale: Southern Illinois Univ. Press, 1971.

Layera, Ramón. *Usigli en el teatro: Testimonia de sus contemporaneos, sucesores y discipulos*. Mexico: CITRU, 1996.

Nigro, Kirstin. "Rhetoric and History in Three Mexican Plays." *Latin American Theatre Review* 21, no. 1 (1987): 65–73.

Vevia Romero, Carlos. *La sociedad mexicana en el teatro de Rodolfo Usigli*. Guadalajara: Univ. de Guadalajara, 1990.

Patricia Ybarra

COSI È, SE VI PARE *See* RIGHT YOU ARE

COSTA RICA

Costa Rican drama is a relatively recent phenomenon. Unlike dramatic production in colonial capitals such as Mexico City and Buenos Aires, Costa Rican national DRAMATURGY lacked a linear and cumulative development. During the period of Spanish colonialism a few *loas* (allegorical dramatic poems lauding a dignitary), *comedias* (entertaining dramas in the style of Lope de Vega), and *entremeses* (one-act comedies performed between acts of the featured light drama or COMEDY) were performed, yet no record is known of pre-Columbian drama. European theater dominated the colonial stage until the 20th century. Religious and historical themes and adaptations of European literature provided entertainment and didactic material during an era in which little was mentioned of native culture or local color.

Nineteenth-century Latin American countries lost the creative advantage of a common tradition and culture. *Costumbrismo*, the fictionalized slice of life depicting regional customs, dominated the stage. Bourgeois tastes of their select readership and audiences followed French formulas popularized during the economic expansion of the 19th century.

The first authentically Costa Rican play was performed in 1902. *Magdalena* was written by Ricardo Fernández Guardia. The nationalistic theme focused on the nascent middle class. Magdalena, the feminist and antipatriarchal protagonist, bridges the gap between *costumbrismo* and cosmopolitanism. She shuns marriage and a future on the coffee plantation in favor of a Parisian education. Despite the novel approach to gender roles, the major conflict occurs between national and foreign values, an issue revisited in contemporary dramas. The play was revived after seven decades and on its 100th anniversary. It remains popular for its contemporary style and identification with a native audience.

Because of the economic success of the Europeanized middle class, the Teatro Nacional (the National Theater of Costa Rica) was founded in 1897 to promote native, as well as foreign, productions. *Magdalena* heralded an era of original dramaturgy when its premiere took place in the National Theater. Teatro Variedades, built in 1891, featured entertainment of the *genero chico*, or short operettas. The variety venue popularized ZARZUELAS, or Spanish light operas, in the New World. Teatro Trébol also offered variety shows. Teatro Municipal, established around 1850, housed foreign productions. The prolific Eduardo Calsamiglia (1880–1918) wrote many plays for the Teatro Nacional. *Bronze Statues of Days Gone By* (*Bronces de antaño*) explored the romance of the wild frontier. Considered his best work, *The Battle* (*El combate*) deals with a doctor who discovers that his sick wife had deceived him while he treats and cures her illness. Calsamiglia's themes ranged from historical to *costumbrista*.

José Fabio Garnier's (1884–1956) style reflected stark REALISM with universal themes. *In the Shadow of Love* (*A la sombra del amor*) is a TRAGEDY about family loyalty and the conflict of a mother's affair with her daughter's fiancé. Garnier's simple and direct style is based upon action rather than psychological development.

Carlos Gagini (1865–1925) produced the popular zarzuelas *The Suitors* (*Los pretendientes*) in 1890 and *The Marquis of Talamanca* (*El marques de Talamanca*) in 1900. *Don Concepción*, his only prose work, performed during the same period, was recognized for its natural dialogue and engaging action as his best play.

Alfred Castro (1889–1966) concentrated on the psychological complexity of characters and plots based upon contemporary social issues. His works include *Deadlock* (*El punto muerto*), which personifies the conflict between totalitarian collectivism and individualism. *Black Water* (*Aguas negras*) portrays the power of nature over human actions and emotions.

The "generación del 40" (generation of the 1940s) focused on poetry and the novel. Proponents of social democracy suppressed reformist and Communist ideologies of the working classes. *Port of Limón* (*Puerto Limón*), written in 1950 by Joaquín Gutiérrez, focuses on the peasant uprisings and banana strikes of 1934. He viewed economic and political disparity as a result of the contradictory development of the working and middle classes who accepted their station as an inherent destiny that sometimes led to chaos or barbarism. Alfredo Catania paid homage to Gutiérrez in his musical staging of *Puerto Limón* with the Compañía Nacional de Teatro. He staged his original production in 1975. Catania's latest revival was honored as the best theatrical presentation of 2003.

The second half of the 20th century witnessed a resurgence of the performing arts. Motivated by political and social reforms, playwrights, directors, and theater ensembles searched for a national identity through the performance medium. Governmental support sustained their efforts. The resulting performing arts community thrived during the 1970s and 1980s.

The Teatro Nacional hosted the Primer Festival Cultural Centroamericano (First Central American Cultural Festival) in 1968. The Festival Internacional de Teatro por la Paz (International Theater Festival for Peace) expanded international representation from Central America to the global theater community. It featured new plays, as well as Costa Rican directors and performers. The Ministry of Culture has sponsored the international festival several times since its 1989 inception. Alberto Cañas led the *dramaturgos nacionales* (national dramaturges) to international recognition. After *The Hero* (*El héroe*, 1956), he published *Oldemar and the Colonels* (*Oldemar y los coronals*, 1957), *Those of Little Wisdom* (*Los pocos sabios*, 1959), *A Wife in the River* (*Una bruja el río*, 1959), *Something More than Two Dreams* (*Algo más que dos sueños*, 1963), *Stolen Mourning* (*El luto robado*, 1963), *In August It Will Be Two Years* (*En agosto hizo dos años*, 1966), *The Enchantress* (*La segua*, 1967), *Tarantela* (1976), *Operation TN . . . T* (*Operación TN . . . T*, 1978), *Uvieta* (1980), and *My House Is No Longer My House* (*Ni mi casa ya es mi casa*, 1982). Local and familiar situations are played out in the context of Costa Rican society and focus on the middle-class *josefino* (San José resident's) experience. The urban and rural working classes are generally viewed from an urban bourgeois perspective.

Samuel Rovinski believes that theater is a consequence of a dynamic society in constant flux, a necessary critique with an immediate and enduring impact. He identifies his dramas with social movements. They include *Atlantis* (*La Atlántida*, 1960), *Bedroom Government* (*Gobierno de alcoba*, 1961), *The Agitators* (*Los agitadores*, 1964), *The Labyrinth* (*El laberinto*, 1967), *The Busybodies of the Wide Way* (*Las fisgonas de Paso Ancho*, 1971), *A Model for Rosaura* (*Un modelo para Rosaura*, 1974), *The Blabbermouths* (*Los pregoneros*, 1978), *Compounded Interest* (*Los intereses compuestos*, 1981), *The Martyrdom of the Shepherd* (*El martirio del pastor*, 1983), *Saturday's Evensong* (*La víspera del sábado*, 1983), and *Sleeping Gulliver* (*Gulliver dormido*, 1985). Rovinski's "dramatización de lo inmediato" (dramatizing the immediate or present moment in time) reproduces reality within the parameters of the theater. He theorizes that performers positively transform their society through their role played within it. Rovinski incorporated his formal theories of comedy and tragedy as both writer and director of his plays.

Rovinski's masterpiece, *The Martyrdom of the Shepherd*, dramatized the assassination of Oscar Romero, bishop of San Salvador, by the Salvadoran military regime. Streaming multimedia images provide a continuous contemporary backdrop to the historical gunning down of Bishop Romero as he served Communion during Mass in the cathedral. Elements of Greek tragedy are evoked as a chorus responds to the protagonist and antagonists as they struggle toward their inevitable climax. The juxtaposition of classical and contemporary stylistic devices enhances Rovinski's immediate theme: the recurring struggle to overcome the evil that threatens a nation's psyche. *The Martyrdom of the Shepherd* won numerous international drama awards, including first place in New York's International Theatre Festival.

Daniel Gallegos is founder and director of the Departamento de Artes Dramáticas at the Universidad de Costa Rica. Gallegos was a professional actor and director before writing plays. His works include *That Something That Dávalos Has* (*Ese algo de Dávalos*, 1967), *The Hill* (*La colina*, 1969), *The Ignorant Ones* (*Los profanes*, 1969), *The House* (*La casa*, 1970), *Reference Point* (*Punto de referencia*, 1971), and *In the Seventh Circle* (*En el Séptimo círculo*, 1982). His plays reflect the most international perspective of the national playwrights. European speech, universal characterizations and situations, and AVANT-GARDE and absurd elements distinguish his work. The dramatic content exposes conflict that the reader or audience is left to resolve.

The Hill, the first Costa Rican play prohibited from performance by censorship, stirred up controversy after its premiere, despite extensive editing. The conservative majority that continues to dominate audiences protested its antireligious message. Gallegos critiqued religious icons, among other established institutions, with an abstract and absurdist style.

Collective grassroots theater companies have limited commercial success on the Costa Rican stage. Tierranegra, a cooperative ensemble, exemplified the ideological shift from its bourgeois origins in the capital to a direct connection with the diverse people of the regions. Most alternative theater companies, as well as contemporary playwrights, directors, and actors, emerged from professional training in the Teatro Universitario.

Sociohistorical events and their resulting conflicts ignited by national crises characterize the dramaturgy of Miguel Rojas. His corpus includes *Here We Are Below* (*Aquí abajo estamos*, 1984), *To Each His Own Flower* (*A cada quien su flor*, 1984), *Where the Sea Sings* (*Donde canta el mar*, 1984), *Take Up Arms* (*Armas tomar*, 1986), *The Peacock's Ring* (*El anillo del pavo real*, 1988), *Dark Clouds of Day* (*Los nublados del día*, 1991), and *The Sick Tree* (*El árbol enfermo*, 1996). Rojas seeks to re-create a unique Costa Rican dramaturgy in the context of crisis for a critical audience to relate its own experience to a national identity.

Guido Sáenz published *The Call of Time* (*La llamada del tiempo*) in 1992. A contemporary of the three national playwrights, Sáenz is a writer of all genres and a proponent of governmental support of the arts and its accessibility to all Costa Ricans. He is also a prominent critic of the performing arts.

The most recent generation to emerge from the Teatro Universitario and Taller Nacional de Teatro is generally known as Teatro joven (Young Dramatists) in the theater community. Ana Istarú is an internationally recognized poet, as well as writer, director, and actress. Her plays include *The Flight of the Crane* (*El vuelo de la grulla*, 1984), *Our Mother, Who Art on Earth* (*Madra nuestra, que estás en la tierra*, 1989), *Baby Boom in Paradise* (*Baby boom en el paraíso*, 1996), and *Men in Marinade* (*Hombres en escabeche*, 2000). Her protagonists are strong-willed and individualistic women who defy patriarchal, as well as matriarchal, structures. While conflict arises from typical Costa Rican situations, her themes relate universally to contemporary societies.

Guillermo Arriaga wrote *Latest News* (*Última noticia*, 1983), *Tenant* (*Inquilino*, 1984), and *War as a Consequence* (*La guerra como consecuencia*, 1986). His overtly political dramas criticize his society's political and social policy and the abuse of power. Victor Valdelomar used fables and folklore as material for his metaphorical plays, which include *The Parable of Wealth* (*La parábola de la riqueza*, 1981), *The Seed Is like the Pod* (*Como semilla e' coyol*, 1982), *Old Macedonio* (*Macedonia el viejo*, 1984), and *We All Love You So Much, Aurelia* (*Todos te queremos mucho, Aurelia*, 1988).

Other graduates of the Teatro Universitario and Taller Nacional de Teatro include Leda Cavellini and Lupe Pérez. Their play *Women in the Mill* (*Ellas en la máquila*, 1989) protested the governmental efforts to thwart the unionization of garment workers. Their activism exposed injustices to a receptive audience and influenced policy change. Jorge Arroyo criticized the status quo with his biting satire. His plays include *The Electronic Pacifier: TV or Not TV* (*La chupataelectrónica: TV o not TV*, 1986), *With Honor on the Wire* (*Con la honra en el alambre*, 1986), and *Yesterday, When You Told Me That You Loved Me* (*Ayer, cuando me decías que me queries*, 1986).

The Teatro joven continues to write, direct, and perform original dramas that seek a personal voice to express interpersonal, national, and universal concerns. National dramatist

Daniel Gallegos believes that it is not enough to know theater from a literary point of view. Creating each step as the genre unfolds is the primordial experience of the dramatist. He asserts, "No basta conocer el teatro desde el punto de vista literario, sino hay que vivirlo, y el vivirlo es la experiencia primordial del escritor del teatro" (It is not enough to know theater from a literary point of view, but it must be lived; and living it is the primordial experience of the dramatic writer) (Herzfeld and Salas, 1973).

FURTHER READING

Bonilla, Abelardo. *Historia de la literatura costarricense.* San José: Editorial Costa Rica, 1967.

Cortés, María Lourdes. "De Magdalena a Eva: Tres momentos en la dramaturgia nacional." *Escena* 11, nos. 23/24 (San José: Univ. de Costa Rica) (1989): 49–54.

——. *Lectura de la producción de sentido de la obra dramatúrgica de Alberto Cañas, Daniel Gallegos, y Samuel Rovinski.* San José: Univ. de Costa Rica, 1987.

Herzfeld, Anita, and Teresa Salas. *El teatro de hoy en Costa Rica: Perspectiva critica y antología.* San José: Editorial Costa Rica, 1973.

Rovinski, Samuel. "Dramatización de lo inmediato: El sentido de lo cómico." *Escena* 11, nos. 20/21 (San José: Univ. de Costa Rica) (1989): 126–133.

——. "Dramatización de lo inmediato: El sentido de lo trágico." *Escena* 10, nos. 19/20 (San José: Univ. de Costa Rica) (1988): 111–118.

Sandoval de Fonseca, Virginia. "Dramaturgia costarricense." *Rivista Iberoamericana* (Madrid: Artes Gráficas Benza) 1987: 173–192.

Urbano, Victoria. *El teatro en Centroamérica (desde sus orígenes hasta 1975).* Beaumont, Tex.: Lamar Univ., 1984.

Carole Anne Champagne

THE COUNT OF MONTE CRISTO

All is fortune and misfortune in this world.

—Morel, Act 2

Alexandre Dumas published *The Count of Monte Cristo* as a novel in 1845 and adapted the work for the stage under the title *Monte Cristo* three years later. Requiring two evenings for performance, the twenty-act, 221-scene play was a disaster when performed at Drury Lane in London. Another failure was the "Webster version," which opened on October 19, 1868, at the Adelphi Theatre with Charles Fechter in the leading role.

On September 12, 1870, the first "Fechter version" of *Monte Cristo* opened at the Globe Theatre in Boston, Massachusetts, with Fechter again in the lead. After several other revisions and cancellations, Charles Fechter's finished adaptation of *Monte Cristo* premiered at the Grand Opera House, New York City, in April 1873, and he made his last appearance in the play on December 17, 1877, at the Broadway Theatre, New York City.

John Stetson, successor to Arthur Cheney as proprietor of the Globe Theatre, acquired the script and announced the opening of Fechter's *Monte Cristo* on February 12, 1883, with James O'Neill as Edmund Dantès. Although critics panned the play, the run continued with O'Neill making many changes to the script and eventually buying the rights to the play for $2,000 and making Dantès his signature role. O'Neill's working copy is all that remains of Fechter's version.

Edmund Dantès is framed for treason by Ferdinand, who has designs on Dantès's betrothed, Mercédès. Along with Danglars, one of Dantès's shipmates, Ferdinand presents a forged letter to police chief Villefort, who, in order to cover up his brother's treasonous affairs, orders Dantès to spend eighteen years in prison.

While he is imprisoned in the Château d'If, a fellow inmate, the Abbé Faria, reveals the secret location of a treasure buried on the island of Monte Cristo, and before dying in prison, he helps facilitate Dantès's escape. Having believed her lover to be dead, Mercédès has married Ferdinand in order to protect the son she was carrying at the time of Dantès's imprisonment. On his way to Marseilles incognito as Abbé Busoni to exact revenge on Danglars, Ferdinand, and Villefort, Dantès learns of Mercédès's marriage to Ferdinand, who has taken the title of the Count de Morcerf.

Stopping at an inn on the way, accompanied by a soldier, he mentions that he is traveling to meet his brother, the Count of Monte Cristo. At the inn Villefort, to avoid capture for a theft gone wrong, kills himself, and Dantès exclaims, "One!" Arriving at Ferdinand's house disguised as the Count of Monte Cristo, Dantès learns that Albert, the soldier who accompanied him to the inn, is his son. In the heat of an argument Mercédès defends Dantès from Ferdinand, who, ashamed, runs into the hut and shoots himself, whereupon Dantès exclaims, "Two!" Dantès demands that Danglars defend himself, and the villain learns of Dantès's disguise before the hero runs him through. Shouting "Three!" Dantès is reunited with Mercédès, and Albert learns that his father is Dantès, the Count of Monte Cristo.

FURTHER READING

Clapp, Henry Austin. "Reminiscences of a Dramatic Critic." *Atlantic Monthly* 88 (1901): 494–499.

McLucas, Anne Dhu, ed. *Later Melodrama in America: "Monte Cristo."* Nineteenth-Century American Musical Theater 4. New York: Garland, 1994.

Russak, J. B., ed. *Monte Cristo, by Charles Fechter, as Played by James O'Neill, and Other Plays by Julia Ward Howe, George C. Hazelton, Langdon Mitchell [and] William C. De Mille.* America's Lost Plays 16. Bloomington: Indiana Univ. Press, 1940.

J. Nick Dickert

COWARD, NOËL (1899–1973)

Recent years have seen a major revival of interest in the work of dramatist, diarist, librettist, movie star, nightclub performer, nonfiction-prose writer, novelist, poet, revue compiler, short-story writer, songwriter, stage actor, and vocalist Noël Coward.

The centenary of Coward's birth alone does not account for renewed interest—an interest that has been directed primarily toward his large corpus of surprisingly diverse plays. Newfound critical realizations have inspired the rejuvenated scrutiny of Coward's massive playwriting oeuvre. These realizations include the enhanced awareness of Coward's vital contribution to gay culture; a rejection of the once-common assumption that all pre-1956 British drama was necessarily anodyne and escapist; and a realization, in difficult times for British theater especially, that Coward's commercialism was appropriate to at least get the public inside theaters. Above all, as a glut of revivals have proved, Coward's plays remain, simply, very effective, entertaining drama.

Even plays that failed in Coward's lifetime have been revived to considerable success in recent years. Sustained critical analysis by scholars such as Barry Day, Sean O'Connor, and Sheila Stowel has deepened awareness of the complexity of Coward's dramatic insinuations. Readings of the plays have been facilitated by a marvelous Methuen-published, multivolume edition of the plays—all introduced in detail by longtime Coward supporter Sheridan Morley. A comprehensive, extremely useful survey of Coward's dramatic work by Sarah Duerden has enabled scholars to comprehend the sheer longevity and success of Coward's plays. Together with these scholarly assessments and reprintings of Coward's plays, a number of biographies of Coward have appeared (or have been published in new, revised editions). Perhaps most significantly, the inclusion of a substantial entry on Coward in the sixty-volume *Oxford Dictionary of National Biography* (published in September 2004) enshrines Coward's status as a great Briton, one firmly canonized for his celebrity and for his dramatic achievements. As Coward's biographical circumstances have been so thoroughly and so recently been covered, it is appropriate here to give only essential details about Coward's life. The weight of any drama-focused account of Noël Coward must center on his most considerable, lasting achievement: his dozens of plays.

Born in Teddington, Middlesex, on December 16, 1899 (hence his given name, Noël), into a lower-middle-class family, Coward was acting professionally by 1911, when he played Prince Mussel in a fairy play called *The Goldfish*. Coward's theatrical precociousness was encouraged by his mother. Noël's parents were peripatetic, moving to homes in and around London, seeking work. But music and theater were constant ambitions for Noël. After 1911 Coward worked for Charles Hawtrey's company and with Italia Conti's group. Before the onset of war Coward played for two years in the role of Slightly in J. M. BARRIE'S PETER PAN. Having quickly come of age as an actor, Coward spent much of 1916 touring as Charley in *CHARLEY'S AUNT*. His very brief spell of World War I conscription saw him react to the call-up by suffering a breakdown and being placed in the First London General Hospital. There he witnessed the plight of seriously disturbed and maimed Great War veterans. After his quick military discharge Coward acted in more plays, with increasing success, but was also starting to write prolifically. Many unpublished and/or unperformed novels and plays date from this period. However, some minor productions of his stage pieces played in London: this was the beginning of a very long, very prolific, and very lucrative playwriting career (Coward died from a heart condition in Blue Harbour, Jamaica, on March 26, 1973).

Coward's major theatrical breakthrough as a writer came with *I'll Leave It with You*, which was written in 1921, but was performed with Coward himself starring in London and in Manchester. Other 1920s plays, such as *The Vortex* and HAY FEVER, received enormous public acclaim, but also moral condemnation in some quarters, because of their characters' sophisticated familiarity with sex. The Lord Chamberlain's Office frequently expressed unease about Coward's risqué material and even refused to license some of his plays. Coward's private life was also suspected: in 1925 Coward met the business-inclined New Yorker John (Jack) C. Wilson, who became his manager and lover for over ten years. It is widely accepted that Coward would have received a knighthood long before the final granting in 1970 were it not for his increasingly obvious homosexuality. Before World War II Coward also pursued now well-known affairs with the actors Louis Hayward and Alan Webb and the dramatist Keith Winter. In 1925 Coward had five different plays running in London, an extraordinary feat (one unimaginable today). But the price for personal and professional overreaching was severe: Coward suffered another breakdown in 1926; he soon recovered. Personal stress notwithstanding, Coward's songs, revues, short stories, and mannered, well-tailored image were becoming ubiquitous in British culture.

The highly contrived image of the well-dressed, carefree wit sold well in America too. PRIVATE LIVES (1930), which starred Coward himself and Gertrude Lawrence, brought Coward into a new league of superstardom in America and in Britain, although some critics desired more substantial material from a writer who was renowned for glibness and flippancy. Later defenders of Coward argue, convincingly, that Coward does not merely perpetuate moral laxity and verbal flippancy in his plays, but rather satirizes the flippancy that Coward thought defined a complacent and superficial generation. But Coward was a mainstream, commercial writer—he earned at least £50,000 per year from 1929 onward. *Private Lives*, initially a vehicle for Coward and Gertrude Lawrence as the wisecracking, divorced couple, Elyot and Amanda, ran for many hundreds of performances at several different theaters. A 1932 revival, directed by John Clements at London's Apollo Theatre, ran for a staggering 716 performances. Many major revivals have been produced since—a 1999 touring National Theatre production, starring Anton Lesser and Juliet Stevenson as Elyot and Amanda, was particularly spectacular and justly acclaimed. During the war Coward worked for the British services in propaganda (in Paris) and fact finding (in America). He excelled at neither task, but he shone as a morale-boosting entertainer. David Lean and Coward collaborated on a series of necessarily patriotic wartime films: *In Which We Serve*, *This Happy Breed*, *Brief Encounter*, and BLITHE SPIRIT—the last film made the British people laugh at least ephemerally, if not feel more confident about withstanding Hitler's onslaught. He also toured in a successful patriotic tour, the "Play Parade," which starred Coward himself in a rotating selection of his greatest crowd-pleasers. Coward considered distasteful many things about postwar Britain—Labour government taxes included. He built two homes in Jamaica in the late 1940s and settled down into a relationship with a South African actor, Graham Payn (born in 1918), who remained loyal to Coward for the rest of Coward's life and beyond. Although he spent much time in America, Bermuda, Britain, and SWITZERLAND at various periods after the war, Coward felt most relaxed and secure in Jamaica.

Coward's musicals and plays were no longer guaranteed successes: flops included the musicals *Pacific 1860* and *Ace of Clubs* and the serious play *Peace in Our Time*. The post-1956, Royal Court generation of playwrights denounced Coward as conservative, escapist, and irrelevant; Coward, in turn, railed against the kitchen-sink dramatists' focus on the mundane and the ordinary. Coward was an embodiment of a bygone theatrical age, but remained a major draw in cabaret, earning huge sums for (in retrospect) very camp stage performances at London's Café de Paris and Las Vegas's Desert Inn. But theatrical successes were periodically achieved by the supposedly washed-up Coward. He directed a revival of *Hay Fever* at London's National Theatre in 1964, and the triptych of new plays, *A Suite in Three Keys*, earned sometimes grudging but ultimately respectful reviews. The best-remembered play from the suite is *A SONG AT TWILIGHT*. The play concerns a declining old writer who confronts the dishonesty of his lifelong denial of homosexuality. Often thought to be loosely modeled on W. SOMERSET MAUGHAM, the portrait may be influenced by Coward's own struggles—he suffered greatly from his strenuous efforts to find gay love while also projecting an image of suave heteronormativity. Although buried in Jamaica, Coward has been honored with a memorial stone in Westminster Abbey. Many tributes were expressed to the ever-famous Coward, but perhaps the greatest tribute to Coward lies in the post-1990s academic and theatrical rediscovery of his work.

Long and varied as Coward's career was, it has to be conceded that his glory years as a creative playwright were between 1924 and 1941, a period bookended by the plays *The Vortex* and *Blithe Spirit*. The Coward-directed, Duchess Theatre, London, production of *Blithe Spirit*, an uproarious COMEDY about a tedious man's torture at the hands of an ex-wife's ghost, topped even *Private Lives* for commercial success. The production ran for 1,997 performances. *Blithe Spirit* has been revived frequently. One revival, starring Penelope Keith, pleased audiences during a lengthy UK tour in 2004. Coward's most commercial, enjoyable, and successful comedies were written during this time. However, Coward also wrote his most serious plays in this period. An examination of four plays from this period—*The Vortex*, *Easy Virtue*, *The Marquise*, and *Post-Mortem*—indicates that the clockwork depiction of Coward the easy, featherweight comic is woefully inadequate. In fact, Coward wrote anxious, challenging plays. Indeed, some of his plays were too challenging for their times. *The Vortex*, Coward's first great original play, first performed in late 1924, was controversial: the Lord Chamberlain almost did not grant it a license, and Sir Gerald du Maurier rounded on Coward's play in a general attack on the "immorality" of modern drama. On the actual day of the first performance Coward himself (who was playing a drug-addled youth, Nicky Lancaster, and co-directing) visited the Lord Chamberlain, convincing him that his play was a "moral" tract advertising the squalid horror that ensues when middle-aged women commit adultery, and when young men overlook women and pursue only male company and drugs instead. The play's themes are adult and serious, although the hypocrisy and shallowness of the Lancasters' guests causes much basic hilarity. For example, having drunk sufficient alcohol ("It's never too early for a cocktail," asserts the middle-aged, overdressed Florence Lancaster), Bruce Fairlight, a pretentious ("earnest") playwright, agrees to dance with Bunty. Self-effacingly, Bruce insists that "I'm no good" at dancing. The stage directions tell us that his dancing "confirms the truth of his warning." In Coward's drama this upper-class, decadent society is as clumsy and inelegant as it is inward-looking and narcissistic.

Having passed censorship, *The Vortex* was tested for twelve performances at London's Everyman Theatre—many Coward plays were tested in short provincial or smaller London theaters before opening for long West End runs. The first Royalty Theatre performance of *The Vortex* was staged on December 16, 1924, Coward's twenty-fifth birthday. A huge success, it ran for hundreds of performances before moving to London's Comedy and Little theatres. The play was also produced in the National Theatre, Washington, D.C., and in New York's Henry Miller Theatre during 1925. The play has been revived many times since: although the social setting of the Lancasters' drawing room and the characters' clothing, manners, and preoccupations very firmly date the play in the 1920s, the Oedipal themes in particular have transcended the ephemeral. The play's themes explain the censor's unease. Plot is rarely a significant feature in Coward's plays—he was fond of boasting that little actually happens in his plays as such. This holds true for *The Vortex*. In acts 1 and 2 Florence Lancaster cavorts with her latest young lover Tom Veryan, while her son disintegrates into drug-induced ignominy. In act 3 (practically a rewrite of *Hamlet*'s "closet scene") the son confronts his mother in her bedroom—both parties argue and then promise to eschew self-destructive, repugnant behavior and to embrace responsibility.

When we first see Nicky, he—the stage directions inform us—must be "tall and pale, with thin, nervous hands"; a later stage direction tells us that he is "strained and white." Physically shaky, mentally inert, and visibly wan, Nicky must even look like a drug addict. His later denial of drug use and subsequent admission that "I only take the tiniest little bit" are necessarily comic. His homosexuality is alluded to clearly. Nicky possibly loves romantically a young friend named John Bagot, to whom he has read personal letters—reading one's personal letters to a friend surely implies that a special intimacy exists. Replying to a question about when he will next see John, he replies, "Not until after Christmas." The use of the negative word "not" subtly implies that to Nicky "after Christmas" seems a long time away. Subtly, and with economic, precise dialogue, Coward tells us that Nicky pines for his male companion. The sporty Tom's contempt for Nicky is based on a notion that Nicky is less masculine than he: dismissively he describes Nicky as being "up in the air—effeminate." Nicky's subsequent, inexplicable rejection of his fiancée, Bunty Mainwaring, may also reflect his inherent homosexuality. Previously, bizarrely, Nicky has said that he has not "really noticed" whether or not Bunty is "pretty." Uninterested in females, he pays little attention even to someone whom he is supposed to marry—he has not even bothered to organize the acquisition of engagement rings. His piano-playing career has been lost to his drug taking. Frustrated personally and professionally, Nicky is left telling his distraught, ashamed mother that he has "grown up all wrong." The play ends soon after Nicky "buries his face in her lap"—to curb his drug taking and his mother's promiscuity, there is a reconciliation in which the son returns symbolically to the womb.

The Vortex ends on a moment of intense (but possibly short-lived?) reconciliation, when the son professes that he will give up drugs, and the mother insists that she will henceforth be faithful to her husband. Female promiscuity is an insinuation rather than a fact in *Easy Virtue*, which was written in 1923 and first produced in 1925. Allegations of promiscuity in *Easy Virtue* are unjust. Indeed, the play attacks misogynistic assumptions about female duplicity and fickleness. The title is sarcastic, because the heroine, Larita, is not at all prone to the "easy virtue" that she is so callously accused of. She is a divorcée, and her second marriage fails during the course of the play's action. The excesses of an abusive husband and a daring suitor have caused the failure of her first marriage; in the play it is the failure of the prejudiced, upper-class, country-dwelling Whittaker family to let her past go that causes the rift between her and her new husband, John Whittaker. Larita sincerely hopes that this second marriage will work: there is considerable pathos when she realizes in act 2 that John is "miles away from me already." Later John admits that he has been paying "pretty marked attentions" to another woman, Sarah Hurst, for "the last six months." Simply, the play is a defense of a wronged woman and clearly, at a time of suffragette-fearing misogyny, a defense of women in general. *Easy Virtue*'s title alone shocked some contemporary reviewers. Before playing in London, the play was staged in Manchester, where complaints forced the banning of the play's title on advertising posters: temporarily the play was given the vague, unsatisfactory title *A New Play in Three Acts*. After the scandal of *The Vortex*, outrage over this play's flagrantly adult theme of adultery and unfulfilled married life helped inspire a myth of Coward's personal decadence—one that he played up with masterful wit, inspiring valuable publicity.

Larita has a "past," one that is seized upon by John's harridan mother. Her past was the controversial divorce. Coward's sympathy is firmly with Larita, because her straightforward, dignified response to the Whittakers' suspicious coldness contrasts with the family's complacent, snobbish, and vicious disregard for outsiders. The audience cheers when Larita embarrasses the Whittaker family at a party. Her dress, "cut extremely low," is enough to cause apoplexy for Mrs. Whittaker. Ashamed of the presence of her unloved daughter-in-law in the house, Mrs. Whittaker has made it clear that Larita should not attend the party, and she tells the guests, dishonestly, that Larita is absent because of a "blinding headache." Quite publicly Larita excoriates Mrs. Whittaker for superciliously and untruthfully citing "this ridiculous fallacy of my being ill." Her victory is complete when a male guest proclaims that "I've never seen such an entrance in my life"; her dignity is enhanced when she refuses to dance with a young man, Hugh Petworth, who has made a bet that he can easily inveigle his way into this infamous woman's company. Larita gains unlikely support from Sarah, who, the family insists, should have been John's choice of spouse. The play ends—the action is dictated by Coward's typically careful stage directions—with Larita walking out through a door, preparing to leave for Paris, far away from the bigoted Whittakers. Her solitary, determined silence contrasts with the vacuous laughter from the partygoers, which continues as Larita leaves. Although wracked by "hopeless sadness," Larita gains the audience's respect and approval. The triumph of the wronged woman—and the triumph of Larita and Sarah's feminine integrity—over a vindictive family balances the play in favor of comedy. Otherwise, the failure of this second marriage would have rendered the play melodramatic or even tragic.

Easy Virtue played at the Broad Theatre, Newark, in November 1925 before transferring to New York's Empire Theatre in December, where it ran for 147 performances. After the troubled Manchester tryout in 1926, the play moved to Duke's Theatre, London, where it ran for a further 124 performances. The play has been revived only rarely, so it is not Coward's most significant play commercially, but *Easy Virtue* is highly significant in that it was filmed as the first major, full-length motion picture based on a Coward play. Most of Coward's major plays have been filmed, some more than once. Coward acted in many films written by others in a career that extended from a tiny part in the 1917 D. W. Griffith film *Hearts of the World* to his major, acclaimed role as a patriotic, decidedly camp, imprisoned crime boss in the 1969 British comedy-heist caper *The Italian Job*. Some of the many filmed Coward plays are *Bitter Sweet*, CAVALCADE, DESIGN FOR LIVING, and *The Vortex*. *Relative Values*, directed by Eric Styles in 2000, is the most recent film version of a Coward play. *Easy Virtue*, directed by Alfred Hitchcock in 1928, pioneered the use of Coward's plays by filmmakers. Although the film (which is silent and necessarily loses most of Coward's deceptively weighty dialogue) is famed more for Hitchcock's precocious technical mastery of mise-en-scène than for Coward's original concept, the play's progressive moral message remains intact: judge people on their present conduct, not on past notorieties.

In *The Marquise* another female character must confront prejudices about her conduct in the past. This play is significant for any appraisal of Coward's career because it was dismissed as a minor trifle in the 1920s and never received a Broadway or West End revival until 2004. *The Marquise* opened at London's Criterion Theatre on February 16, 1927. The production, starring Marie Tempest, whose performance thrilled Coward, ran for 129 performances. By Coward's 1920s standards, such a run constituted a comparative failure. But a major revival, which starred the celebrity actress Kate O'Mara in the central role of the Marquise Eloise De Kestournel, toured Britain and Ireland during 2004. This commercially successful revival suggested both that the play is hugely entertaining and that it has a moral code similar to that of *Easy Virtue*. *The Marquise* is set in 18th-century rural France. Eloise returns to the home of her former lover, the Compte Raoul De Vriaac, who leads an austere life, dominated by the memory of his pious, deceased wife, whose posthumous omnipotence is perpetuated by Raoul's devotion to a dour and "depressed" portrait of her. Initially very unwelcome, Eloise is disruptive, domineering, and presumptuous. She insults Raoul's dead wife ("she looks wretched") and humiliates a priest, forcing him to conduct a marriage ceremony at gunpoint. The apparently reckless conduct of Eloise, who has enjoyed a glamorous singing career in Paris, contrasts with the severity of life in Raoul's joyless household.

Eventually Eloise's comments about Raoul's life are vindicated: he admits that his religious wife "was a determined and unmitigated bore!" and his daughter, Adrienne, concedes that her deceased mother "never loved me." The dead woman was a sacred cow worth killing—the audience, because of the accuracy of Eloise's comments about the family's dreary life, and her sparkling audacity and wit, feels more and more sympathy for Eloise. The play ends in triumph when, after an improbable physical fight between the reinvigorated Raoul and his friend, Esteban (which is resolved amicably), Raoul admits that he loves Eloise and will welcome her back permanently. But *The Marquise* could have ended not in feel-good comedy but in incest-caused TRAGEDY. Adrienne has pursued a relationship with Esteban's son, Miguel. Eloise reveals that she is the mother of both Adrienne and Miguel. Raoul is seriously shocked when he is told that his daughter made a good decision in marrying the less moneyed Jacques instead of Miguel: "Miguel would not have been quite suitable. . . . He happens to be her brother." During the 2004 revival of *The Marquise* this revelation caused anxious laughter among audiences. Earlier in the play Adrienne and Miguel have admitted to each other that they are no longer in love—at this point, neither they nor the audience realize that Miguel is Adrienne's half brother. After admitting her fondness for another man, Adrienne is questioned aggressively by Miguel: "You haven't let him be your lover, have you?" After the revelation that the couple are closely related, the audience remembers this exchange and is chilled by its ambiguity. Does Miguel worry that Adrienne has had sexual relations with the other man because he as yet has not? Or is he worried that he has been only one of two or more sexual partners? Either interpretation would account for his possessive vituperativeness, but the suspicion that incestuous sex has indeed taken place between Adrienne and Miguel is not negated anywhere in the text. In fact, suspicions grow at the play's end. Eloise insists that Miguel should never know that Adrienne is his half sister—and vice versa. Adrienne has confided in Eloise about personal affairs. Has Adrienne told Eloise about physical lovemaking between herself and Miguel? If so, that would explain why Eloise insists that neither party should know that they are related to one another. Eloise gives no reason why the former couple should remain ignorant of their status as half siblings. The audience can only assume that Eloise demands confidentiality because she is determined to prevent a catastrophic revelation of incest. Initially castigated for perceived moral laxity, Eloise's ultimate contribution is not just to bring color and love back into Raoul's household, but—possibly—to ensure that revelations of incest do not damage her children. The wronged female, who, contrary to many insinuations, has only ever loved two men, Esteban and Raoul, proves to have a moral core that generates only love and propriety.

Critics have taken at face value Coward's typically self-effacing remarks about the flimsiness of *The Marquise* and about the irrelevance of its French setting. But the French setting at least allows William Shakespeare to be represented as an unknown foreigner. Eloise tells the assembled males that they "really must read" Shakespeare to "improve your minds." Eloise's impeccable literary taste—Coward admired Shakespeare immensely, although he found other Elizabethan playwrights bombastic and dull—underlines her actual maturity and wisdom. Setting the play in France may have eased the priest-baiting scene through censorship traps, but also, by showing that English drama (which Shakespeare still dominates) was not and is not the center of all cultures, Coward subtly attacks inward-looking jingoism. Not all people regard Shakespeare as the center of their universe—that seems to be a lesson that Coward in this post–World War I period asserts. Naïve assumptions about the universality of England's greatest dramatist are equivalent to chauvinistic notions of England's national superiority. Similar assumptions, shared by citizens of many nation-states, which at least partly caused the Great War, are attacked much more severely in another desperately underrated Coward play, *Post-Mortem*. Homosexuality, or, rather, fear of homosexuality, also raises its head in *The Marquise*. Excited by his new-found hopes of betrothal to Adrienne, Jacques propositions Raoul innocently: "You wouldn't care to dance with me, would you?" Raoul recoils in horror at the suggestion of a male dancing partnership, saying, "Go to bed, Sir, immediately." His shock is indicated by his use of the noun "Sir"—Jacques, his secretary, is his marked inferior. Coward also takes care to note that Raoul's rebuff is delivered "sternly." Piqued and disapproving of Jacques's informality, Raoul replies with excessive firmness to an innocuous suggestion—one with a very mild homoeroticism that repulses Raoul. Such hysterical fears about male companionship caused in part Coward's absence from Britain for many years.

Eloise praises Shakespeare because he was "a poet who was clever enough to persuade his own countrymen that he was only a playwright." Here Coward, speaking through his esteemed lead character, seems to be placing limits on the art of playwriting, as if drama is less profound than other art forms. But critics now see that Coward, to paraphrase Eloise, was a serious writer who was clever enough to persuade Britons that he was only a comic playwright. A complex man was concealed behind Coward's deflective quips and the debonair appearance and deportment. Coward's commercial image bore little relation to the depths of his important dramatic themes. In fact, the performance history of *Post-Mortem* indicates that Britain wanted its Noël Coward to be seemingly harmless and flippant. The British theater had abundant room for the comic Coward, but none for the angry, bitter Coward of *Post-Mortem*. In the mid-1920s Coward wrote several plays that could not have appealed to a mass audience. The Lord Chamberlain refused to give a license for 1926's *This Was a Man*—an adviser to the Lord Chamberlain claimed that the Soviets could use Coward's depiction of rampant British adultery as propagandist "proof" of Western decadence. That particular play was never performed in Britain, although it had a limited run on Broadway. Coward never even attempted to get the brazenly gay *Semi-Monde* (also 1926) past the censor. The play, which features hordes of gay and straight couples, was finally produced in Glasgow in 1977. It is clear, then, that Coward, at this point, had two playwriting identities: the crowd-pleasing, comic craftsman and the darker, serious writer who cared little for public approval. *Post-Mortem* derives from the latter aspect of Coward's identity.

Post-Mortem has been performed, but only in unusual circumstances: by British POWs in Germany in 1944; by Thame schoolboys in 1966; and broadcast on BBC Television (in edited form) in 1968. Although no major production of *Post-Mortem* has taken place, and very few read the published text, the play is outstanding as a polemical, vitriolic attack on British disregard for World War I victims. The play's episodic structure (the play is divided into eight scenes; most Coward plays have three acts) and large cast could not have attracted producers. The content of the play's dialogue is most significant. In the first scene the twenty-something John Cavan is shot dead in a vile trench in the spring of 1917. John has complacently downplayed allegations from a fellow soldier, Perry Lomas, that his father, Sir James Cavan, the editor of a major newspaper, has glorified the war, ignoring the consequences for the millions of young soldiers. In the remaining scenes John's Ghost visits family and friends, finding, to his horror, that lessons about chauvinistic destructiveness and belief in war's glamour have not been learned. He visits his mother, Lady Cavan. Their conversation is akin to that between a young boy and his mother—"Does it hurt terribly, my darling?" she asks of her dead son's wounds. John has not had the opportunity to grow into independent adulthood; he has also lost the chance to have an adult relationship with his sweetheart, Monica.

Perry Lomas has written a book titled *Post-Mortem*, exposing the truth of the conditions of Great War soldiers. But the English establishment—including John's father, still the editor of the million-selling daily—wants the book banned. John's mother treats the book as if it is a dangerous weapon: "Darling—don't open it—please put it down," she pleads. John then visits Monica, during scene 3, and despairs when he finds her empty-headed and blasé about crucial social issues. Her friend, Kitty, is equally superficial and trivial. For her, Lomas's book represents only a rare collector's item: "It's probably worth millions now!" she gushes, ignoring the book's incendiary content. Soldiers who have given everything to Britain are treated as a quaint, vague memory by a society that cannot care. Coward's contempt for the blandness and banality of society is clear and raw. This play's bitterness toward selfish, giggling blockheads illuminates his uncontroversial comedies—does Coward demonstrate similar contempt for the amoral, vapid Bliss family from *Hay Fever?* John's Ghost proceeds to meet the traumatized Perry in scene 4. In a virtual monologue that few interwar theatergoers could have endured, Perry complains about "poverty, unemployment, pain, greed, cruelty . . . crime . . . meanness, jealousy, money and disease." Perry sees this mistreatment of people as a way of preparing for another massive conflict—he even sees the Olympic Games tournaments as "superb preparation for the next War." Given the propaganda that mars all thoughts of the 1936 Berlin Olympics, Perry's words—and Coward's—have proved to be prescient.

Scene 5 of *Post-Mortem* dramatizes John's eavesdropping on a meeting involving his editor father and various other dignitaries, who all trash Perry's book and seek to have it banned because it undermines illusions about "the Great War for God." The attack on these self-appointed, myopic, and paranoid censors may have been inspired by Coward's mixed fortunes at the hands of the Lord Chamberlain. But the play's lacerating satire is more profound than a mere attack on censorship. The play ends with John and his fellows back in 1917, incarcerated in the hellish trenches. With intense bitterness the formerly naïve

John asserts, "You were right, Perry—[life is] a poor joke!" Exploited and remembered only in ludicrous fantasies about war, Britain's youth have been sacrificed to achieve nothing. Reading *Post-Mortem*, it is hard to reconcile Coward, the Angry Young Man, with the conservative figure who entertained World War II troops, whined nostalgically about the disappearing British Empire, and railed against the political leftism of the post-1956 dramatists. But reading *Post-Mortem* and many other similarly unpalatable works by Coward, one realizes that Coward did not, as his detractors have insisted, treat life as a mere "joke." Coward's diverse, enormous dramatic canon is as varied, as complex, and as open to interpretation as that of any other 20th-century dramatist. The fact that so many of the plays still hold the stage in such spectacular, entertaining fashion is just a bonus for those fortunate enough to study this difficult, multifaceted, fascinating man and playwright.

[*See also* England, 1840–1940; Gay and Lesbian Drama]

SELECT PLAYS: *I'll Leave It to You* (1920); *The Vortex* (1924); *Easy Virtue* (1925); *Fallen Angels* (1925); *Hay Fever* (1925); *The Marquise* (1927); *Bitter Sweet* (1929); *Private Lives* (1930); *Design for Living* (1933); *Tonight at 8:30* (1936); *Post Mortem* (1940); *Blithe Spirit* (1941); *This Happy Breed* (1943); *Nude with Violin* (1956); *Suite in Three Keys* (1966)

FURTHER READING

Coward, Noël. *Collected Plays*. 8 vols. London: Methuen, 1999–2000.

——. *Autobiography*. London: Methuen, 2003.

Day, Barry. *Coward on Film: The Cinema of Noël Coward*. Lanham, Md.: Scarecrow, 2004.

Duerden, Sarah. "Noël Coward." In *British Playwrights, 1880–1956: A Research and Production Sourcebook*, ed. by William W. Demastes and Katherine E. Kelly. Westport, Conn.: Greenwood Press, 1996. 81–96.

Hoare, Philip. *Noël Coward: A Biography*. New York: Simon & Schuster, 1995.

Kaplan, Joel, and Sheila Stowell, eds. *Look Back in Pleasure: Noël Coward Reconsidered*. London: Methuen, 2000.

Lahr, John. *Coward, the Playwright*. Berkeley: Univ. of California Press, 2002.

Mander, Raymond, and Joe Mitchenson. *Theatrical Companion to Coward: A Pictorial Record of the Theatrical Works of Noël Coward*. 2d ed. London: Oberon Bks., 2000.

O'Connor, Sean. *Straight Acting: Popular Gay Drama from Wilde to Rattigan*. London: Cassell, 1998.

Kevin De Ornellas

THE CRACKWALKER

The Crackwalker was an explosive debut for playwright JUDITH THOMPSON, so provocative that some theater patrons walked out on performances, repulsed by the characters and events represented on stage. Written in 1980, it was unlike any other play on the theater scene at the time: a gritty, evocative, painful REALISM that laid bare the "underneathness" of life in small-town, impoverished Ontario. The four main characters are trapped in cycles of abuse: Joe rapes Theresa and beats his wife, Sandy; Sandy retaliates by ripping Joe's back with her high heels. Sandy's and Joe's relationship is volatile—despite attempts to separate, they are always drawn back to each other. Theresa, the mentally challenged woman at the core of the play's action, finds her consolation for life's contradictions in chocolate donuts. Al is in love with Theresa, comparing her to the Madonna and insisting that they have a child together despite the social worker's advice to the contrary. Neither of them is capable of caring for Danny, the child they conceive, who has developmental challenges. Eventually Al breaks down. In a heart-wrenching scene near the end of the play, he strangles his own child. A fifth character, known only as The Man, prefigures a further descent for a character such as Al: he lives on the streets and speaks in a disconnected babble.

Intense, precisely defining monologues show us the inner contradictions and raw emotions of each of the characters. Al is in a constant struggle with the ugly thoughts that prevent him from sleeping. Sandy, though she presents a desperate bravado, suffers from constant anxiety and chronic stomach pains. Joe, in his extreme machismo, demonstrates his own moments of vulnerability. And Theresa, with her tenuous grasp on "truth," defies attempts at our containment: "You don't even know who I lookin like," she declares to the audience at the end of the play. The monologues are woven into emotionally true scenes of extreme human behavior as we see how Sandy both needs and despises Joe; how Theresa rises from banal circumstances to the status of a Greek tragic heroine. There is a violent, compelling energy to this play in the characters' struggle for definition and recognition.

In *The Crackwalker* some of Judith Thompson's ongoing obsessions are apparent: the short distance between love and hate; extraordinary actions by ordinary people; pregnancy and the baby as complex metaphors for both redemption and destruction. The stylistic markers that have come to define her style are also evident: monologues that are like arias; an acute ear for dialogue and dialect; realism that moves into the otherworldly. Robert Nunn, one of the most articulate critics of Judith Thompson, has analyzed her work with respect to the psychoanalytic motifs that permeate her plays. He describes how different levels of psychic and social realities are realized through Thompson's use of language and in the creation of visual images in performance. In this way Thompson addresses both social realities in the class struggles of these characters and their psychic distress as they attempt to appease and confront their own desires and actions.

[*See also* Canada]

FURTHER READING

Bessai, Diane. "Women Dramatists: Sharon Pollock and Judith Thompson." In *Post-colonial English Drama: Commonwealth Drama Since 1960*, ed. by Bruce King. New York: Macmillan, 1992. 97–117.

Nunn, Robert. "Spatial Metaphor in the Plays of Judith Thompson." *Theatre History in Canada* 10, no. 1 (Spring 1989): 3–29.

———. "Judith Thompson's Marginal Characters." In *Sitting the Other: Revisions of Marginality in Australian and English-Canadian Drama*, ed. by Marc Maufort and Franca Bellarsi. Brussels: P. Lang, 2001. 311–323.

Toles, George. " 'Cause you're the only one I want': The Anatomy of Love in the Plays of Judith Thompson." *Canadian Literature* 118 (Autumn 1988): 116–135.

Marlene Moser

THE CRADLE WILL ROCK

Inspired by a suggestion from BERTOLT BRECHT, *The Cradle Will Rock* by composer-LIBRETTIST MARC BLITZSTEIN is a savagely satirical examination of the ways in which the professional class has prostituted itself to the power of big business in a capitalist America. The setting of this "play in music" in ten scenes is Steeltown, USA, controlled by Mister Mister and populated by cartoon characters representing the arts, medicine, academia, the press, the clergy, and the proletariat. Stylistically it derives from vaudeville, WILLIAM SCHWENK GILBERT and Arthur Seymour Sullivan, HENRIK IBSEN, Kurt Weill, Brecht, and agit-prop (AGITATION-PROPAGANDA) street theater. Written in 1936 after the death of Blitzstein's wife Eva Goldbeck, *Cradle* was to receive its premiere in a FEDERAL THEATRE PROJECT production in New York City on June 16, 1937. Militant strikes in the steel industry and congressional fears that the New Deal theater had been taken over by left-wing elements resulted in a cancellation of the opening. Director Orson Welles and producer John Houseman quickly organized another venue, and the whole audience marched twenty blocks uptown for the performance, without sets, costumes, and orchestra. The actors sang from their seats, Blitzstein himself at a battered piano on stage. The runaway musical permanently established the composer's reputation as a rebel.

The Cradle Will Rock went on to a Broadway run, produced by Welles and Houseman as part of their Mercury Theatre. It is often revived as one of the most characteristic and telling examples of theater from the Angry Thirties, usually staged in the oratorio style originally presented on Broadway, with solo piano accompaniment. Rarely have producers included either full staging or the composer's orchestration, though this is more authentically what Blitzstein conceived.

Derived from familiar genres, the music of *Cradle* is several degrees more erudite and trickier to perform than standard Broadway shows of the period. Always the experimenter and challenger, Blitzstein sought to elevate the inherited forms of commercial theater and popular music into a higher art. At the same time, he wanted to raise public consciousness and bring into the theater everyday, workaday themes.

Though *Cradle* inspired working-class theatergoers in their ongoing struggles and still retains its power to do so, Blitzstein wrote it essentially for middle-class audiences, asking them, Which side are you on? Will you sell out to the lords of the land, or will you ally with the working class and its demands for a decent, free life? Tellingly, the triumphant hero belongs not to an ethnic or racial minority: Larry Foreman is clearly defined as an all-American small property owner with a Bible-quoting Aunt Jessie. His virtue stems purely from his conscious proletarian activity.

Blitzstein was certainly aware that *Cradle* is somewhat sentimental toward workers and was soon destined to become a period piece. Yet later productions have often revealed that audiences still find themselves "in the period" of sanctimonious moralism and hypocrisy, corruption, government intrusion, and corporate arrogance. Beyond being an emblematic capsule of an era and an apotheosis of vaudeville, *Cradle* has become a classic, inspiring later generations of socially engaged musicians and playwrights.

[*See also* United States, 1929–1940]

FURTHER READING

Dietz, Robert James. "The Operatic Style of Marc Blitzstein in the American 'Agit-Prop' Era." Ph.D. diss., Univ. of Iowa, 1970.

Gordon, Eric A. *Mark the Music: The Life and Work of Marc Blitzstein*. New York: St. Martin's, 1989. Repr., Lincoln, Nebr.: iUniverse, 2000.

Houseman, John. *Run-through*. New York: Simon & Schuster, 1972.

Talley, Paul Myers. "Social Criticism in the Original Theatre Librettos of Marc Blitzstein." Ph.D. diss., Univ. of Wisconsin, 1965.

Eric A. Gordon

CREDITORS

Creditors (*Fordringsägare*) is a TRAGICOMEDY in one act by AUGUST STRINDBERG, written in 1888, published in Danish in 1889, in Swedish in 1890, and first performed at the Dagmar Theater in Copenhagen in 1889.

Adolf, a sculptor and painter now physically in bad shape, and Tekla, his wife, are staying in a seaside resort hotel. While Tekla is away, Gustav, her former husband, tries to convince Adolf, who is unaware of Gustav's true identity, that he is being destroyed by Tekla's usurping nature. To prove this, he suggests that Adolf, hidden behind a door, witness the meeting between Gustav and Tekla upon her return. Adolf obeys. When he discovers Gustav's true identity and witnesses how Tekla plays up to him, he has an epileptic attack and dies. Filled with guilt, Tekla lovingly embraces her dead husband.

"In every play there is one real scene," Strindberg told Georg Brandes around this time. "That's the one I want. Why should I bother with the left-overs and give six or eight actors the trouble learning that stuff?" In the extremely compact *Creditors* he put this view into practice. *Creditors*, he claimed, was "better than MISS JULIE, with three persons, one table, two chairs, and no sunrise." Instead of placing a man between two women, Strindberg this time placed a woman between two men. Although the three unities are observed even more strictly than in *Miss Julie*, *Creditors* makes a less naturalistic impression since the three characters are more abstract cases than individuals rooted in a recognizable reality. Patterned on the real-life triangle of Carl Gustav Wrangel, Siri von Essen's first husband, Siri, and August Strindberg, her second husband, the three characters have also been characterized as the sadist (Gustav), the masochist (Adolf), and the vampire (Tekla).

Written shortly after the preface to *Miss Julie*, *Creditors* in many ways corresponds to what is stated in that preface, where Strindberg declares that what is experienced as tragic at present will in the future, when people have grown as strong as "the first French revolutionaries," make one feel relieved since what one sees is then merely "an incurably ill man finally die." In line with this, he told the actor playing the Darwinian evolutionist and Nietzschean superman Gustav to portray him as "playful and good-natured, which he as the superior person can afford to be. He plays with Adolf as the cat with the mouse. Never gets angry, never moralizes, never preaches."

The original title of the play, *Fordringsägare*, is ambiguous in that it can be understood either as singular or plural. The latter is the most natural, since both Adolf and Gustav are legitimate creditors with regard to Tekla. By taking revenge on her, the robust Gustav cancels her IOU, whereas the weaker Adolf succumbs to her.

Very striking is the use of eavesdroppers. Gustav eavesdrops on the conversation between Adolf and Tekla, whereupon Adolf eavesdrops on Gustav and Tekla. In either case the audience is in collusion with the men who have arranged the situation. The significance of these screen scenes is verbalized by Gustav when he tells Adolf, "You have never seen her [Tekla], when *you* haven't seen her! I mean when you weren't present!" The idea here is that the wife behaves differently when her husband is present and when he is absent, a worrying idea for Adolf since Tekla, as he knows, is very frivolous.

FURTHER READING

Jacobs, Barry. "Strindberg's *Creditors*: The Doppelgänger Motif and the Avenging Eye." *Annals of Scholarship* 9, no. 3 (1992): 257–278.

Johnson, Walter. "*Creditors* Reexamined." *Modern Drama* 5 (1962/1963): 281–290.

Robinson, Michael. *Studies in Strindberg*. Norwich: Norvik Press, 1998.

Rokem, Freddie. "The Significance of the Screen-Scenes in Strindberg's *Fordringsägare*: A Dramaturgical Reading." *Scandinavica* 34 (1995): 37–60.

Egil Törnqvist

CRIMES AND CRIMES

The "comedy" *Crimes and Crimes* in four acts by AUGUST STRINDBERG was published together with ADVENT in 1899 in a volume titled *At Higher Court* (*Vid högre rätt*) and was first performed at the Royal Dramatic Theater in Stockholm in 1900. With its happy ending, *Crimes and Crimes* (*Brott och brott*), a predominantly serious play, is a COMEDY mainly in a divine, Dantean sense. It has been variously relabeled TRAGICOMEDY, MELODRAMA, metacomedy, commedia, and dark comedy.

The title alludes to the fact that there are different kinds of crimes, those that are punished and those that are unpunished; at times people are even punished for crimes they have never committed. Another relevant distinction is the one between evil thoughts and evil deeds. For the "higher court" of the conscience and what Strindberg called the Powers, even those who nourish evil thoughts are culprits.

Maurice, a playwright living in Paris, falls in love with a sculptress, Henriette, and neglects his mistress, Jeanne, with whom he has a little daughter. Wanting to be free from responsibility so that he can devote himself to Henriette, Maurice wishes his daughter dead. His child dies, and he is haunted by guilt but is also suspected of having murdered the girl. Henriette and his friends leave him, and the performance of his play is postponed. A new autopsy shows that Maurice's daughter died a natural death. The Abbé, mouthpiece for the author, frees Maurice morally: "When providence has given you absolution, I can add nothing." The last act, Strindberg says in a letter to the Swedish writer Evert Gustaf af Geijerstam (1899), "is Swedenborgian with hell *déjà* on earth, and the hero, the plotter, is the Invisible One."

Many of the ingredients derive from Strindberg's own experiences. Like Maurice, he experienced a theatrical victory in Paris with *The Father* around this time. He also briefly fell in love with an English sculptress; the two met in Madame Charlotte's *crémerie*, faithfully reproduced in the play. Having manipulated his daughter's photo to cause her a slight illness, Strindberg felt persecuted by a Pole he knew who was accused of having murdered his ex-mistress and his two children.

As in many of his post-*Inferno* dramas, music plays an important role. When Maurice, having met Henriette, betrays Jeanne, his bad conscience is suggested as a pianist in a neighboring room plays Beethoven's Sonata no. 17 in D Minor ("The Tempest"), called "The Ghost Sonata" by Strindberg. According to Evert Sprinchorn, the whole play is structured with the sonata form in mind.

In a list of "Occult dramas—Nemesis dramas," Strindberg notes, "The evil will is punished just as the evil deed." However, far from being punished, Maurice is freed from suspicions at the end, where he decides to go to church the same evening "to settle this with myself—but tomorrow I'll go to the theater." Strindberg himself called the ending banal. Most critics have agreed.

FURTHER READING

Allan, J. L., Jr. "Symbol and Meaning in Strindberg's *Crimes and Crimes*." *Modern Drama* 9 (1966): 62–73.

Jacobs, Barry. "Strindberg's *Advent* and *Brott och brott*: Sagospel and Comedy in a Higher Court." In *Strindberg and Genre*, ed. by Michael Robinson. Norwich: Norvik Press, 1991. 167–187.

Sprinchorn, Evert. *Strindberg as Dramatist*. New Haven: Yale Univ. Press, 1982.

Stockenström, Göran. *Ismael i öknen: Strindberg som mystiker*. Acta Universitatis Upsaliensis, Historia Litterarum, 5. Stockholm: Almqvrist & Wiksell, 1972.

Strindberg, August. *Strindberg's Letters*. Ed. and Trans. by Michael Robinson. Chicago: Univ. of Chicago Press, 1992.

Egil Törnqvist

CROATIA

Coinciding with the ambitious and successful reforms introduced by Stjepan Miletić (1868–1908) in the theatrical practice and repertory of the national stage, the birth of modern Croatian drama is marked by a broadening of horizons characteristic of the two genres that reigned on the 19th-century Croatian stage: national-historical TRAGEDY and the folk play, either didactic or satirical, written according to predominantly Austrian models. Hence there was a turn to cosmopolitan topics and to the absorption of influences from Western and middle European cultures that has affected the development of modern Croatian drama to the present day. The plurality of its stylistic features, already discernible at the beginning of the 20th century, ranging from the conversational drama (Julije Rorauer, 1859–1912) and aestheticist accents (IVO VOJNOVIĆ, 1857–1929; Milan Begović, 1876–1948; Milan Ogrizović, 1877–1923) via NATURALISM (Vojnović; Begović; Sadan Tucić, 1873–1940) and SYMBOLISM (Vojnović; Begović; Fran Galović, 1887–1914; MIROSLAV KRLEŽA, 1893–1981) to EXPRESSIONISM (Josip Kosor, 1879–1961; Janko Polić Kamov, 1886–1910; Krleža; Kalman Mesarić, 1900–1983) and Pirandellianism (Vojnović; Josip Kulundžić, 1899–1970), make the first decades of its flourishing the most interesting and fruitful period of Croatian drama. During this period striking individuals battled against entrenched routines in playwriting, acting, and directing, because of which certain playwrights, such as the expressionists Krleža and Kamov, had to wait until long after World War II to have certain portions of their work duly recognized in the theater.

It was, however, also a period in which Croatian playwrights and directors closely followed European movements, some of them, for example, Milan Begović in Hamburg and Vienna, even actively participating in European theatrical life as literary advisers and performed playwrights. The fact that LUIGI PIRANDELLO'S *SIX CHARACTERS IN SEARCH OF AN AUTHOR* opened in Zagreb only three years after its premiere in ITALY indicates the vigor with which Croatian theatrical culture strove to react to contemporary trends. Of these, FRIEDRICH NIETZSCHE'S philosophy and Karl Marx's political analyses had a powerful impact, particularly on the oeuvre of Krleža. Sigmund Freud's psychoanalysis, in which Croatian Jewish intellectuals took an active part as members of Freud's circle and translators of his work, influenced both Begović (*An Adventurer at the Doors*, 1926) and Krleža (*Vucjak*, 1923). In the late 1920s, 1930s, and 1940s a return to Ibsenian "psychology" and social criticism was visible in the prevailing tendency of "analytic realism," whose major representatives remain Krleža (*Honorable Glembays*, 1928) and Begović (*Without the Third Party*, 1931), but which also embraced newcomers such as Miroslav Feldman (1899–1976), Marijan Matković (1915–1985), and Ranko Marinković (1913–2001), who was to rise to Krleža's level of genius in the ensuing decades. In fact, it was Marinković's politically allegorical "miracle" *Gloria* (1956) that, together with two plays using motifs from antiquity, Matković's *Hercules* (1958) and Krleža's incisive *Arethaeus* (1959), marked the beginning of "individualist dramaturgy" and the end of SOCIALIST REALISM, which had been, despite some promptly censored exceptions (e.g., Ivan Raos [1921–1987], *Two Crystal Glasses*, 1952), successfully imposed by the creators of the new regime's cultural policies after World War II and the victory of communism in Yugoslavia. Marinković came back again in the 1980s with his Shakespearean and Pirandellian *Desert* (1980), an intellectually demanding, eminently postmodern play.

The uprising of "the Croatian Spring" in the early 1970s, a revolt against the economic, cultural, and political dependence of Croatia on the federal government in Belgrade, brought new names to the Croatian stage. These authors, who wanted to break free of Krleža's "dialogue" primarily through the intentional disfigurement of his linguistic pathos, include Ivo Brešan (b. 1936), author of burlesque travesties of classical plays by William Shakespeare, Molière, and Racine, the first being his groundbreaking and ideologically challenging *Hamlet in the Village of Mrduša Donja* (1971), and a trio of playwrights: Boris Senker (b. 1947), Tahie Mujičić (b. 1947), and Nino Škrabe (b. 1947), who started as authors of light musicals for children and FARCES, but managed ultimately to blend crude wit and erudite references to Croatian culture at large, both historical and contemporary (*Domagoias*, 1979; *Histrionias*, 1982; *Histo/erias*, 1983; all written collectively by Senker, Mujičić, and Škrabe). Krleža's legacy—already called into question by the plays of Radovan Ivšić (b. 1921), a lonely proponent of a politically charged surrealistic poetics (*King Gordogan*, 1943) who emigrated to FRANCE—remains contested, having been self-consciously overtaken in the 1980s by Slobodan Šnajder (b. 1948), who in his "counterbiographies" of several exemplary Croatian cultural figures (Janko Polić Kamov, Vjeko Afrić, Gemma Boić) endeavored to maintain Krleža's high rhetorical, referential, artistic, intellectual, and political standards. Recently Krleža has also become the object of sympathetic irony and parodic revision (Senker). Lyrical drama (June Kaštelan, 1919–1990; Matković; Vesna Parun, b. 1922; Nikola Šop, 1904–1982) remained a rather isolated genre.

In contrast to the former obsession with historically grounded issues of political power and national or individual freedom (Antun Šoljan [1932–1993], *Diocletian's Palace*, 1969; Nedjeljko Fabrio [b. 1937], *Reformers*, 1967; Tomislav Bakarić [b. 1940],

Anno Domini 1573, 1974), sometimes also treated in a humorous vein (Ivan Kušan [b. 1933], *The End of Freedom*, 1970), the new generation of younger playwrights who emerged in the late 1980s is reluctant to root their imagination in concrete sociocultural contexts, oscillating between writing commercially successful, often mildly satirical well-made plays (Miro Gavran [b. 1961], the only living European playwright to whom an entire festival is devoted—"Gavranfest" in Slovakia) and, at the other extreme, exploring the crisis of the "decentered subject," also through the strategy of postmodern "remakes" of European and Croatian classic plays. An exception to the rule is the work of Mate Matišić (b. 1965), who continued Brešan's explorations of the linguistic crudeness of the rural ambiance (*A Flash of the Golden Tooth*, 1986).

In the 1990s female playwrights achieved distinction; one of the best plays on the situation both during and after the war in Croatia is *The Last Link* (1994) by Lada Kaštelan (b. 1961), a metatheatrical mixture of fantasy, dream, and public and private histories enacted on the stage of the female protagonist's conscience. The turn of the 21st century brought interest in the social margin, expressed in the fragmented DRAMATURGY and documentarism of the "new drama," but also ventures into writing of what H. Th. Lehmann calls "postdramatic theatre."

FURTHER READING

Senker, Boris. *Hrestomatija novije hrvatske drame.* [A reader of the modern Croatian drama]. 2 vols. Zagreb: Disput, 2000–2001.

Lada Cale Feldman

CROMMELYNCK, FERNAND (1886–1970)

Born on November 19, 1886, in Paris, Belgian Fernand Crommelynck was regarded in the 1920s and 1930s as one of the most innovative French-language playwrights of the period. Despite sporadic revivals of *The Magnificent Cuckold* (*Le cocu magnifique*), he is now studied chiefly as a historical figure whose work links Flemish mystic and sensual interests, as handled in the works of MAURICE MAETERLINCK and MICHEL DE GHELDERODE, with epistemological concerns about the perception of reality, in the mode of LUIGI PIRANDELLO.

Obsessive sexual jealousy is the most frequent engine of Crommelynck's plots. A central figure or couple plays out jealous misunderstandings in social contexts torn between the repressive virtues of Lent and the grotesque libertinage of Carnival or the Flemish kermis. Characterization is usually accomplished through traditional masks (character templates combining social roles with associated psychological syndromes). Secondary figures embody facets of the central figures' crude psyches, and a Boschian societal frenzy serves as background noise. The result is strident FARCE, complete with frequent chases and cudgels. Crommelynck said that his works could be produced either as tragedies or comedies, but the single term that other writers use most often in criticism of his work is neither "tragic" nor "comic," but "truculent."

Sexual jealousy provides title and plot to his most important play, *The Magnificent Cuckold*. Bruno, the village's public scribe, is married to the delicious young Stella. She cannot bear to be separated from her husband, and Bruno boasts about her beauty to the many villagers seeking his services. But in boasting about her attractions one day, he notices that the village's male population agrees and appreciates them as well. This ignites his own jealous doubts, which he decides to quash through achieving absolute certainty about Stella's faithfulness. The certainty he seeks, however, has the cruel turn of farce: he cannot be absolutely certain of her fidelity, so he will be absolutely certain of her infidelity. He now forces her to sleep, systematically, with every man in the village. Out of love for her husband, Stella obeys at first. But she eventually escapes her insane marriage with a village cowherd, and Bruno is left alone, crazed by his own self-fulfilling jealousy.

The most famous production of *The Magnificent Cuckold* was by VSEVOLOD MEYERHOLD at the Actors' Theater in Moscow in 1922—a production now studied for its constructivist set rather than for its script. After *Cuckold* Crommelynck wrote three more plays focusing on marital battles between libertinage and repression. By the end of the 1930s, however, he was no longer writing for the stage. He spent the war years in Brussels and Paris (where the occupying Germans permitted revival of his plays), turned his hand to now-forgotten screenplays, complained about his critics, and survived to die well after Pirandello, Maurice Maeterlinck, and Michel de Ghelderode. Memorably tagged by François Mauriac as a "drunken Molière," Fernand Crommelynck's name is known today chiefly because of his sons, founders of the printing studio Atelier Crommelynck in Paris, who served as Picasso's favorite engravers. Crommelynck died on March 17, 1970, in St. Germain-en-Laye.

[*See also* Belgium]

PLAYS: *The Sculptor of Masks* (*Le sculpteur de masques*, 1911); *The Magnificent Cuckold* (*Le cocu magnifique*, 1920); *The Childish Lovers* (*Les amants puérils*, 1921); *Golden Guts* (*Tripes d'or*, 1925); *Carine; or, The Young Woman Who Was Crazy About Her Soul* (*Carine ou la jeune fille folle de son âme*, 1929); *Hot and Cold; or, Monsieur Dom's Idea* (*Chaud et froid ou l'idée de Monsieur Dom*, 1934); *A Small-Hearted Woman* (*Une femme qu'a le coeur trop petit*, 1934)

FURTHER READING

Crommelynck, Fernand. *Théâtre*. 3 vols. Paris: Gallimard, 1967–1968.
Féal, Gisèle. *Le Théâtre de Crommelynck: Érotisme et spiritualité*. Paris: Lettres Modernes Minard, 1976.
Grossvogel, David I. *The Self-Conscious Stage in Modern French Drama*. New York: Columbia Univ. Press, 1958. Reissued under the title *20th Century French Drama*. New York: Columbia Univ. Press, 1961.

Knapp, Bettina L. *Fernand Crommelynck*. Boston: Twayne, 1978.

Piette, Alain, and Bert Cardullo. *The Crommelynck Mystery: The Life and Work of a Belgian Playwright*. Selinsgrove, Pa.: Susquehanna Univ. Press, 1997.

David Pelizzari

CROTHERS, RACHEL (1878–1958)

Rachel Crothers was born on December 12, 1878, in Bloomington, Illinois, the daughter of Eli Kirk and Marie Crothers, both physicians practicing in Bloomington. She began writing plays as a child but was determined to be an actress. Graduating from Illinois State Normal School, she studied elocution in Boston and then spent four years at the Stanhope-Wheatcroft School of Acting in New York, first as a student and then as a teacher. For several seasons she acted professionally with E. H. Sothern's company, but it was at Stanhope-Wheatcroft that she began writing one-act plays, staging a number of works with students in matinee productions. Thereafter, from *The Three of Us* in 1906 to *Susan and God* in 1937, she achieved twenty-five Broadway productions, the majority of which she cast and directed herself.

Crothers was the first American woman dramatist to consistently explore feminist themes. At the heart of all her work is the theme of modern woman's search for freedom in "a man's world." "If you want to see the sign of the times," asserted Crothers to the Drama League (Boston) in 1912, "watch women. Their evolution is the most important thing in modern life."

Early problem plays often depict the New Woman's struggle for independence, focusing on issues such as the unfairness of the double standard (*A Man's World* and *Ourselves*), conflicts between motherhood and career (*He and She*), and differences between generations of women (*Mary the Third*). Crothers's later social comedies employ satire, often showing sophisticates who alter their course: *When Ladies Meet* concerns two women who love the same man, but change their minds after they come to know each other, while *Susan and God* centers on a woman so obsessed with spiritual love that she neglects those dearest to her.

Most of Crothers's plays were critical and commercial successes. While reviewers often praised her ability to dramatize social problems and create believable, strong female characters, they sometimes complained that her male characters tended to be shallow and her realistic themes were not probed deeply enough. Crothers briefly spent time in Hollywood, working on films, one of which was her screenplay for *Splendor* in 1935; thirteen of her plays were made into films. Crothers worked on at least three Broadway-bound plays during the 1940s and 1950s, but for various reasons the projects were dropped.

Throughout her lengthy career Crothers remained a vital force in the theater community. In 1907 she joined with other women dramatists, who were not allowed into the American Dramatists' Club, to form the Society of Dramatic Authors. During World War I she led the Stage Women's War Relief. In the 1930s, when the Depression put theater people out of work, Crothers helped organize the Stage Relief Fund, which she led through 1951. In 1940 she served as founder and president of the American Theatre Wing War Service, which operated the Stage Door Canteen and entertained members of the armed forces through 1950. Her many honors include the Chi Omega National Achievement Award in 1939. Crothers died on July 5, 1958, at her home in Danbury, Connecticut.

[*See also* United States, 1860–1929]

PLAYS: *Criss-Cross* (1899); *Elizabeth* (1899); *Mrs. John Hobbs* (c. 1900); *A Water Color* (c. 1900); *Which Way* (c. 1900); *The Rector* (1902); *Nora* (1903); *The Three of Us* (1906); *The Coming of Mrs. Patrick* (1907); *Myself Bettina* (1908); *Katy Did* (1909); *Mrs. Molly* (1909); *A Man's World* (1910); *He and She* (originally *The Herfords*, 1920); *Ourselves* (1913); *Revenge; or, The Pride of Lillian Le Mar* (1913); *The Heart of Paddy Whack* (1914); *Young Wisdom* (1914); *Old Lady 31* (1916, novel by Louise Forsslund); *Mother Carey's Chickens* (with Kate Douglas Wiggin, 1917); *Once Upon a Time* (1917); *A Little Journey* (1918); *39 East* (1919); *Nice People* (1920); *Everyday* (1921); *Mary the Third* (1923); *Expressing Willie* (1924); *Peggy* (1924); *The Importance of Being Clothed, The Importance of Being Married, The Importance of Being Nice, The Importance of Being a Woman, Peggy, What They Think* (published in *Six One-Act Plays*, 1925); *A Lady's Virtue* (1925); *Venus* (1927); *Let Us Be Gay* (1929); *As Husbands Go* (1931); *Caught Wet* (1931); *When Ladies Meet* (1932); *Susan and God* (1937); *Valiant One* (1937); *Back in the Sun* (previously *Bill Comes Back*, 1945); *My South Window* (1950); *We Happy Few* (1955)

FURTHER READING

Gottlieb, Lois C. *Rachel Crothers*. Boston: Twayne, 1979.

Lindroth, Collette, and James Lindroth, eds. *Rachel Crothers: A Research and Production Sourcebook*. Westport, Conn.: Greenwood Press, 1995.

Murphy, Brenda. "Feminism and the Marketplace: The Career of Rachel Crothers." In *The Cambridge Companion to American Women Playwrights*, ed. by Brenda Murphy. Cambridge Univ. Press, 1999. 82–97.

Sherry D. Engle

CROUSE, RUSSEL

See LINDSAY, HOWARD, AND RUSSEL CROUSE

CROWLEY, MART (1935–)

> *"Well, why doesn't someone write a play in which there are gay men who are just gay men?" "Well, why not me?" . . . No one I knew had written this "uncloseted" play. Some people wouldn't speak to me anymore. Some wouldn't understand it. And most would think I was nuts. But I was broke and depressed.*
>
> —Mart Crowley

Playwright Edward Martino Crowley was born on August 21, 1935, in Vicksburg, Mississippi. He attended a Catholic high school there and graduated in 1957 from the Catholic University of America in Washington, D.C. After graduation he became involved in the California film and television industry and from 1964 to 1966 was secretary to actress Natalie Wood.

Crowley is best known for *The Boys in the Band*. First produced in 1968, the play stands as a landmark of OFF-BROADWAY theater, as well as gay theater history. A 1998 "end-of-the-century" issue of *Time* magazine went so far as to include the play as one of "six landmarks of (modern) drama." The story of a clique of gay friends who gather at their friend Michael's apartment for a birthday party, the play presents its characters unapologetically and is strongly influenced by EDWARD ALBEE's 1962 *WHO'S AFRAID OF VIRGINIA WOOLF?* in structure and tone. Critically praised and wildly popular for its then-provocative subject matter and bitchy banter, it ran for over 1,000 performances at what was then a high off-Broadway ticket price of ten dollars. The play's frank treatment of its characters' homosexuality was revolutionary and set the stage for a new generation of plays with gay characters and themes. In fact, many critics trace the beginning of gay theater to this play, just as the start of gay political consciousness is frequently traced to the Stonewall rebellion, which took place seven months after the play's premiere. Over the ensuing years the gay community alternately rejected and embraced the play for the attitudes it presents in its group portrait of pre-Stonewall gay men. The play was turned into a film in 1970, directed by William Friedkin and featuring the full original stage cast.

Some of Crowley's other plays continued to explore characters he first introduced in *The Boys in the Band*. In *A Breeze from the Gulf* (1973) Michael's childhood and relationship with his parents are explored. In *The Boys from the Men* (2002) Crowley brought the characters from *The Boys in the Band* back to Michael's apartment thirty years later for a wake for one of the original "boys." Crowley also added three new characters, all younger men representing contemporary gay attitudes. In addition to homosexuality, Catholicism also looms large in Crowley's plays. In *For Reasons That Remain Unclear* (1993) a man encounters and confronts the priest who molested him as a child of nine.

Crowley has also maintained an active career in television. He has written several made-for-television films, including *There Must Be a Pony* (1986), *Bluegrass* (1988), and *People Like Us* (1990), and from 1979 to 1984 served as producer for the television series *Hart to Hart*. After the death of Kay Thompson in 1998, Crowley finished the text for her last children's book, *Eloise Takes a Bawth* (2002).

[*See also* United States, 1940–Present]

PLAYS: *The Boys in the Band* (1968); *Remote Asylum* (1970); *A Breeze from the Gulf* (1973); *Avec Schmaltz* (1984); *For Reasons That Remain Unclear* (1993); *The Boys from the Men* (2002)

FURTHER READING

DeJongh, Nicholas. *Not in Front of the Audience: Homosexuality on Stage.* New York: Routledge, 1992.

Little, Stuart W. *Off-Broadway: The Prophetic Theatre.* New York: Coward, McCann & Geoghegan, 1972.

Sinfield, Alan. *Out on Stage: Lesbian and Gay Theatre in the Twentieth Century.* New Haven: Yale Univ. Press, 1999.

Joe E. Jeffreys

CROWN OF SHADOW; CROWN OF LIGHT; CROWN OF FIRE

See CORONA TRILOGY

THE CRUCIBLE

How may I live without my name?

—John Proctor, Act 4

ARTHUR MILLER's *The Crucible* opened at the Martin Beck Theatre in New York on January 22, 1953. A few weeks into the run Miller, who was never happy with Jed Harris's direction, restaged the work with some important cast changes, added a new scene, and replaced Boris Aronson's solid set with a simple black backdrop and immovable white lights. Even so, the play ran for only 197 performances. The critical reception was a mixed one; some negative reviews faulted the characters, who—even John Proctor—seem less vital human beings than representative figures. The main response to the play was a vigorous debate about whether or not the Salem witch trials provided a legitimate analogy for the government's search for subversives. Speaking at Harvard in 1999, Miller said, "It would probably never have occurred to me to write a play about the Salem witch trials of 1692 had I not seen some astonishing correspondences with that calamity in the America of the late Forties and early Fifties" (Echoes, 2000). The ideational opponents of the play insisted that there are no witches but that there are Communists, an argument that failed to keep most playgoers from recognizing the contemporary political implications of the play. An OFF-BROADWAY revival in 1958 ran for well over a year. Commenting on its belated success, Miller wrote in the introduction to the Compass edition of *A VIEW FROM THE BRIDGE* (1960), "With McCarthy dead it was once again possible to feel warmly toward the play, whereas during his time of power it was suspected of being a special plea, a concoction and unaesthetic." It had escaped its original context and become one of Miller's most successful plays.

Not simply a condemnation of the accusers, driven by ambition or greed or envy, the play has to establish a mood of mass hysteria in which guilt and confession become public virtues, the crucible in which John Proctor is to be tested. In a novelistic note in the published edition of the play, Miller describes Proctor as "a sinner not only against the moral fashion of the time, but against his own vision of decent conduct." Having committed adultery with Abigail, the servant girl, and having faced the icy contempt of Elizabeth, his wife, he is suffused with a guilt that, once he has been named in the investigation, becomes confused with the charge that he is a witch. Faced with the choice of confession or death and knowing that he is guilty of something, he is on the point of choosing to live when, as Miller's only romantic hero, he refuses to sign the confession and goes to the gallows. Elizabeth gets the last forgiving word: "He has his goodness now."

Miller wrote the screenplay for the film version of *The Crucible* (1996), directed by Nicholas Hytner and co-produced by the playwright's son, Bob Miller. It is a handsome film, but in opening up the play, it diluted the force of the original in which the sense of physical enclosure underlines the narrowness of Proctor's accusers.

[*See also* Political Theater in the United States; United States, 1940–Present]

FURTHER READING

Miller, Arthur. *The Crucible: Text and Criticism*. Ed. by Gerald Weales. New York: Viking, 1971.

——. *The Theater Essays of Arthur Miller*. Ed. by Robert A. Martin. New York: Viking, 1978.

——. *Timebends: A Life*. New York: Grove, 1987.

——. *Echoes down the Corridor: Collected Essays, 1944–2000*. Ed. by Steven R. Centola. New York: Viking, 2000.

Gerald Weales

CRUZ, MIGDALIA (1958–)

I started to write stuff down, hoping—if not to make sense of it, then to at least pay respect to the memory of it, of us, of a small time in history when all of us grew up too soon.

—Migdalia Cruz

Migdalia Cruz is one of the better-known and more provocative Latina playwrights to emerge in the United States in the late 1980s and 1990s. Born on November 8, 1958, in New York City and raised in the South Bronx, Cruz, of Puerto Rican heritage, has boldly interrogated her personal and cultural roots within the diverse styles of over thirty plays. Cruz received her master of fine arts degree from Columbia University's playwriting program in 1984. From 1984 to 1988 and in 1990 she worked under the tutelage of MARÍA IRENE FORNÉS in the Hispanic Playwrights Lab at INTAR (one of the oldest Latino theater companies in the United States) in New York City with Cherríe Moraga, Caridad Svich, Nilo Cruz, and others. Cruz noted Fornés's strict mentorship, as well as Moraga's outspoken politics, as important influences upon the development of her own aesthetic.

Cruz initially turned to writing to work through and pay tribute to her childhood experiences in such plays as *Sand* (1990), which tells of a community's rage and violence against a man who raped a young girl. In *The Have-Little* (produced at INTAR in 1991) young Lillian seeks redemption through the birth of a son after seeking comfort from a heroin addict. *Miriam's Flowers* (1988), regarded as Cruz's most controversial play, tells of a teenage girl coming to terms with the death of her younger brother. The title describes the shapes that the girl carves into her arm with a razor blade, an act of self-mutilation recalling the symbolic power of the Catholic Church and its adverse impact on women and girls in the barrio. Cruz's plays often defy REALISM while developing the spiritual and emotional resonances of her characters. For example, in *Dreams of Home* (published in 1993) a homeless couple living in the subway are taunted by Dolores, an "angel of death who looks like a Mexican movie star."

While some critics have accused Cruz of furthering negative portrayals of Latinos, others have lauded her ability to transform stereotypical roles with reverence and spiritually nuanced complexity. Critics have also noted Cruz's ability to write with grace about the realities and possible spaces for empowerment for women in American culture, and the special attention she has paid to the female body as a theatrical site of oppression and redemption. In addition to her many plays, Cruz has also written the book and lyrics for two Latin-jazz musicals and was the lyricist for *Frida: The Story of Frida Kahlo* (performed at the American Repertory Theatre in 1992, the Brooklyn Academy of Music in 1992, and the Houston Grand Opera in 1993).

Among other honors, Cruz was named a National Artist in Residence at the Classic Stage Company (1994), a playwright-in-residence at the Steppenwolf Theater Company (1996), a National Endowment for the Arts (NEA) Playwriting Fellow (1991 and 1995), and a writer-in-residence at the Latino Chicago Theater Company (1996–present).

[*See also* Feminist Drama in the United States; Identity Theater; United States, 1940–Present]

PLAYS: *Not Time's Fool* (1986); *Coconuts* (1987); *The Have-Little* (1987); *Loose Lips* (1987); *Sensible Shoes* (1987); *Lucy Loves Me* (1988); *Miriam's Flowers* (1988); *Welcome Back to Salamanca* (1988); *When Galaxy Six & the Bronx Collide* (1988); *The Touch of an Angel* (1989); *Frida: The Story of Frida Kahlo* (lyrics and monologues, 1991); *Fur* (1991); *Occasional Grace* (1991); *Street Sense* (1991); *Whistle* (1991); *Winnie-in-the-Citie* (1991); *Running for Blood No. 3* (radio play, 1992); *Cigarettes and Moby-Dick* (1993); *Dreams of Home* (published in 1993); *Rushing Waters* (1993); *Latins in La-La Land* (1994); *Another Part of the House* (1995); *Lolita de Lares* (1995); *Dylan & the Flash* (1996); *So . . .* (1996); *Che-Che-Che!* (1997); *Danger* (1998); *Featherless Angels* (1998); *Mariluz's Thanksgiving* (1998); *Salt* (1998); *Telling Tales* (1999); *Yellow Eyes* (1999); *Hamlet: Asalto a la inocencia* (2000); *Primer contacto* (2001); *El grito del Bronx* (2003); *X & Y Stories* (2003)

FURTHER READING

Lazú, Jacqueline. "Nuyorican Theatre: Prophecies and Monstrosities." Ph.D. diss., Department of Spanish and Portuguese, Stanford Univ., 2002.

López, Tiffany Ana. "Violent Inscriptions: Writing the Body and Making Community in Four Plays by Migdalia Cruz." *Theatre Journal* 52, no. 1 (2000): 51–66.

——. "Latina Dramatists: Irene Fornés; Cherríe Moraga; Migdalia Cruz." In *Reading U.S. Latina Writers: Remapping American Literature*, ed. by Alvina E. Quintana. New York: Macmillan, 2003.

Perkins, Kathy A., and Roberta Uno, eds. *Contemporary Plays by Women of Color: An Anthology*. New York: Routledge, 1996.

Sánchez-González, Lisa. *Boricua Literature: A Literary History of the Puerto Rican Diaspora*. New York: New York Univ. Press, 2001.

Gwendolyn Alker

CUBA

Cuban theater thrived during the 19th century, then stagnated until the third decade of the 20th century. Popular and critically acclaimed playwrights included Gertrudis Gómez de Avellaneda, José Jacinto Milanes, and José María de Heredia. Some exceptional European performers and productions appeared on the Cuban stage, but the majority of touring companies were commercially rather than artistically motivated.

The Cuban stage alternated between Spanish and other European repertory companies and BUFO THEATER, slapstick COMEDY routines. The popular *bufo* comic genre depended upon the actors and musicians rather than writers. Cubans personalized the ZARZUELA, or comic operetta, during the 1920s. The Alhambra Theatre featured a Cuban version of the zarzuela during the first four decades of the 20th century. Popular zarzuelas such as *Rosa, the Chinese Girl* (*Rosa la china*) and *The Coffee Plantation* (*El cafetal*) are still performed in Cuba. When the Alhambra Theatre's roof collapsed, other companies had short-lived success.

A flowering of creative activity in the performing arts was directly influenced by the innovations in post–World War II productions on the European stage. Grupo la Cueva, Teatro Universitario, and Academia Municipal de Artes Dramáticas represented the initiation of the movement. Theatralia, Prometeo, Las Máscaras, and Teatro Estudio characterized dramatic innovation in absurdist, symbolist, and a combination of other styles. During the late 1950s popularity assured the financial feasibility of many independent theater companies in the relatively small capital of Havana. Most of the national playwrights attended the Seminario de Arte Dramático or the Municipio de Artes Dramáticas in Havana. Directors also contributed to critically acclaimed productions. Francisco Morín, Andrés Castro, and Adolfo de Luís were renowned as directors of Cuban plays.

This creative environment inspired significant drama written by VIRGILIO PIÑERA, Eduardo Manet, Matías Montes Huidobro, Carlos Felipe, and Antón Arrufat, among other playwrights. Teatro La Cueva staged contemporary works. The Seminario de Artes Dramáticas of the Universidad of La Habana and the Academia de Artes Dramáticas promoted drama training during the 1940s. Directors, actors, and other performing arts professionals worked in a thriving arts community. The most prominent playwrights, Carlos Felipe and Virgilio Piñera, gained international recognition. Felipe wrote *The Chinaman* (*El chino*, 1947), *Caprice in Red* (*Capricho en rojo*, 1948), and *Naughty Jimmy* (*El travieso Jimmy*, 1951). Piñera wrote *Electra Garrigó* (1941), which gave him immediate success. *Jesús* and *False Alarm* (*Falsa alarma*) were published in 1948. Later works such as *Two Panicky Old Folks* (*Dos viejos pánicos*) expanded his international repertoire.

Playwrights, directors, and actors were able to earn a living from their work during the 1950s, and professional theater companies could be established with governmental and patron support. Between 1954 and 1958 small independent theaters, or *salitas*, offered performances every night. By the end of the decade ten small theaters operated in Havana. The theaters highlighted European classics and AVANT-GARDE works. Some theaters featured Broadway and commercial repertory comedies. National playwrights were not often highlighted, but they were able to stage most of their plays.

During the early 1960s national DRAMATURGY fell into two general styles. Realistic plays included *Theft of the Pig* (*El robo del cochino*, 1961) and *The Old House* (*La casa vieja*, 1964) by Abelardo Estorino, *With You, Bread, and Onions* (*Contigo pan y cebolla*, 1962) and *The Shabby Prize* (*El premio flaco*, 1964) by Héctor Quintero, and *Saint Camila of Old Havana* (*Santa Camila de la Habana vieja*, 1962) and *Saint Isidro's Rooster* (*El gallo de San Isidro*, 1964) by José R. Brene. Experimental plays included *Medea in the Mirror* (*Medea en el espejo*, 1960) and *Brotherhood Park* (*El parque de la fraternidad*, 1962) by JOSÉ TRIANA, *Zone Zero* (*La zona cero*, 1965) and *Living on Chicken* (*El vivo al pollo*, 1961) by Antón Arrufat, and *The Parakeets* (*Las pericas*, 1961) and *The Cardboard Palace* (*El palacio de los cartones*, 1962) by NICOLÁS DORR.

The prolific Virgilio Piñera staged new works every season: *Cold Air* (*Aire frío*, 1959), *The Skinny Guy and the Fat Guy* (*El flaco y el gordo*, 1959), and *The Philanthropist* (*El filántropo*, 1960). Carlos Felipe staged the critically acclaimed *Requiem for Yarini* (*Requíem para Yarini*, 1960). Its revival thirty years after the revolution reached a fresh audience. While playwrights were concerned with social inequities of the former regime, they did not address new conflicts from the Cuban Revolution. Fidel Castro and Che Guevara initiated the peasant revolt with a popularist platform in 1959 to overthrow the dictatorship of Fulgencio Batista. The proletariat, or disenfranchised lower classes, overthrew the bourgeoisie and wealthy ruling classes in the resulting polarized society.

The Cuban Revolution opened up opportunities to new dramatists. Playwrights such as José Triana, Abelardo Estorino, Julio Matas, and Héctor Quintero produced their works without initial opposition from the Union of Writers and Artists of Cuba (UNEAC). But many of these successful playwrights began to leave Cuba during the mid-1960s. After his "Palabras a los intelectuales" (words to the intellectuals) speech in 1961, Fidel Castro initiated a systematic and repressive regulation of the performing arts. Those artists who remained in Cuba suffered from the institutionalized sanctions on artistic freedom that expressed antigovernment themes. Piñera and Arrufat could not stage their works without extensive revisions, and René Ariza, who wrote *Return to the Apple* (*La vuelta a la manzana*) in 1967, endured censorship and imprisonment.

José Millán criticized the government throughout the 1960s in his plays *Going Back* (*Va de retro*), *The Taking of Havana by the British* (*La toma de la Habana por los ingleses*), and *Jehovah Again in the Story of Sodom* (*Otra vez Jehová en el cuento de Sodoma*). David Campas wrote *It Rains on the Parade* (*En la parada llueve*), and René Ariza wrote *The Banquet* (*El banquete*, 1968), an encore protest after *Return to the Apple*. All these playwrights were persecuted for their antigovernment messages.

Despite censorship, Cuban plays gained international recognition. *Night of the Assassins* (*La noche de los asesinos*, 1965) by José Triana, *Two Panicky Old Folks* by Virgilio Piñera, and *María Antonia* (1967) by Eugenio Hernández Espinosa won praise from many international performances and revivals. Triana's absurdist treatment of the underside of a society in transition, Piñera's approach to miscommunication and paranoia, and Hernández Espinosa's portrayal of society in conflict reflect the social crises of the 1960s.

The winners of the 1968 national literary competition had political repercussions on the arts. Antón Arrufat's play *Seven Against Thebes* (*Los siete contra Tebas*) and Heberto Padilla's poetry collection *Out of the Game* (*Fuera del juego*) were attacked by censors. An international panel of judges awarded prizes to these works despite the disapproval of the governmental sponsoring agency, the Union of Writers and Artists of Cuba. The National Congress on Education and Culture approved resolutions to restrict artistic influence from decadent Western societies, namely, Europe and the United States. The government enforced the resolution throughout the 1970s. Artists, intellectuals, directors, actors, and playwrights lost their jobs. Stages and drama schools and venues were destroyed, and plays were blacklisted.

After the Padilla case twelve theater professionals left Havana to form Grupo Teatro Escambray. They worked in the mountainous Escambray region with experimental collective creation and audience participation. In collaboration with the group, Alibio Paz created *The Showcase* (*La vitrina*, 1971), *Paradise Found* (*El Paraíso recobrado*, 1972), and *Evil Remedy* (*El mal de remedios*, 1976). Gilda Hernández wrote *Judgment* (*El juicio*) in 1973. Her work required audience participation for its success. Herminia Sánchez and Manolo Terraza returned to Havana to run their troupe Teatro de Participación with enthusiastic community involvement. Their plays *Storytellers* (*Cuenteros*), *The American Indies* (*Amerindias*), and *El macho y el guanajo* during the mid-1970s incorporated music, dance, and carnival images and fantastical elements. Major commercially successful productions included *The 23rd Breaks the Tree* (*El 23 se rompe el corojo*) and *How the Apostle St. James Came to Earth* (*De cómo Santiago Apóstal puso los pies en la tierra*). Another group, La Teatrova, broke away to perform similar spectacles, including *Pabobo* and *Little Pink Shoes* (*Los zapaticos de rosa*).

The Ministry of Culture organized the Theatre and Dance Directory in 1977. It declared the New Theater movement, Teatro Nuevo. This governmental agency devoted resources to theater of collective creation, to the exclusion of other styles. Despite the suppression of creative diversity, it enabled the followers of Teatro Escambray to perfect their art.

During the 1980s NATURALISM dominated the stage. Productions did not impact the public except for *Dying of the Story* (*Morir del cuento*, 1983) and *The Painful History of the Secret Love of José Jacinto Milanés* (*La dolorosa historia del amor secreto de José Jacinto Milanés*, 1974) by Abelardo Estorino. Directors revived popular works from the 1960s. Victor Varela directed experimental works, including *The Fourth Wall* (*La cuarta pared*, 1986), which was performed with only mime and incoherent sounds. This work affected experimentation with performance art and the fusion of different artistic media under the guise of theater. Carlos Díaz adapted familiar plays to his unique performance style, in which dialogue is reinterpreted through performance art.

During the 1990s the Ministry of Culture allowed performances that it had censored or forbidden during the 1970s. A new wave of directors revived performance. Varela and Díaz share the stage with Nelda Castillo, Carlos Celdrán, and Joel Sáez. New playwrights include Abilio Estévez, Joel Cano, and Reinaldo Montero.

The most famous Cuban exiled playwrights, Eduardo Manet and José Triana, write from Paris. Manet's *Les Nonnes*, or *The Nuns* (*Las Monjas*, 1970), was translated and performed all over the world. Triana's *Common Words* (*Palabras comunes*, 1980) was also performed internationally. The absurdist dialogues and disjointed plots reflected disillusionment, and the search for meaning conveyed immediate messages with universal appeal.

Other exiled dramatists work out of New York and Miami. The Cuban theater community founded La Ma Teodora and Teatro Avante, which initiated the International Festival of Hispanic Theatre in the late 1980s. EDUARDO MACHADO wrote a collection of plays titled *The Floating Island* series (1991). His *Broken Eggs* (1987) represented the experience of exile. Other exiled dramatists include Gloria González, with *Coffee with Milk* (*Café con leche*, 1984), and MARÍA IRENE FORNÉS, with *Tango Palace* (1971) and *The Danube*, *Mud*, and *Sarita* (1986). Montes Huidobro wrote prolifically, experimenting with a fusion of styles in plays such as *Exile* (*Exilio*, 1986) and *Funeral in Teruel* (*Funeral en Teruel*, 1990). Mario Martín's distinctive works include *Mama Is Eighty Years Old* (*Mamá cumple ochenta años*) and *Resurrection in April* (*Resurrección en abril*, 1981).

Cuban American Nilo Cruz won the Pulitzer Prize in 2003 for his play *Ana in the Tropics* (*Ana en el trópico*). The playwright arrived in Miami at the age of ten. From his childhood he wrote about the Cuban experience in South Florida. He joined other exiled artists producing their plays between New York City and Miami such as Matías Montes Huidobro and María Irene Fornés.

Playwrights publishing in the United States into the new millennium include Manuel Martín and Luis Santeiro.

FURTHER READING

Alder, Heidrun, and Adrián Herr, eds. *De las dos orillas: Teatro cubano.* Madrid: Iberoamericana, 1999.

Muguercia, Magaly. *El teatro cubano en vísperas de la revolución.* Havana: Editorial Letras Cubanas, 1988.

Pérez-Firmat, Gustavo. *Next Year in Cuba.* New York: Anchor Bks., 1995.

Stevens, Camilla. *Family and Identity in Contemporary Cuban and Puerto Rican Drama.* Gainsville: Univ. Press of Florida, 2004.

Valiño Cedré, Omar. *La aventura del Escambray: Notas sobre teatro y sociedad.* Havana: Editorial José Martí, 1994.

Carole Anne Champagne

CUMMINGS, E. E. (1894–1962)

And always I am repeating a simple and dark and little formula . . . "An artist, a man, a failure, MUST PROCEED."
—Him, *Him*

Poet, playwright, and artist Edward Estlin Cummings was a contemporary, colleague, and literary peer of Wallace Stevens, Robert Frost, and William Carlos Williams. Born on October 14, 1894, in Cambridge, Massachusetts, the son of Harvard's first professor of sociology, Cummings attended Harvard from 1911 to 1916, studying the classics, as well as modern literature, reading William Shakespeare under George Lyman Kittredge, serving as editor in chief of the *Harvard Monthly*, forming a lifelong friendship with John Dos Passos, and earning a bachelor's degree in literature and a master's degree in English. In 1917 he volunteered for the ambulance service and sailed for FRANCE, there to spend several weeks in Paris and later serve two months in a French prison for displaying an ambiguous attitude toward the German enemy. His first volume of poetry, *Tulips and Chimneys*, appeared in 1923, and in 1925 he received the Dial Award "for distinguished service to American letters," which brought a prize of $2,000, enough to support the poet for a year. Subsequent publications included & (1925) and is 5 (1926).

The first production of his play *Him* was by the Experimental Theatre at the Provincetown Playhouse on April 10, 1928. James Light directed the cast, with William Johnstone playing Him and Erin O'Brien Moore as Me.

The play examines the role of the artist within the context of human relations. Him's philosophical yet infantile nature frustrates his beloved, Me, and threatens to destroy their relationship, which is literally shown from various angles as the room rotates from one scene to the next. Interspersed between these strained conversations are scenes of various theatrical styles, vaudeville songs and dances, burlesques, detective whodunits, and minstrel shows. Presumably, these spectacles make up the play Him is writing, a play about "anything you like, about nothing and something and everything."

Three Weird Sisters open the play and reappear periodically, reminiscent of a Greek chorus, except that their non sequitur speech is more akin in style to Dada than to Aeschylus. One scene dramatizes the folk ballad "Frankie and Johnnie," complete with full chorus and a soloist who performs "the ground." Another scene reveals an Englishman carrying his unconscious in a trunk; another shows an ocean liner where two men pop each others' balloons and spout nonsense; while a third is a burlesque of Mussolini and ancient Roman decadence. The random series of surrealistic scenes confuses Me and, ultimately, the audience.

With its twenty-one scenes and 105 characters, *Him* made considerable financial demands on the production staff, but Cummings refused to alter the play. He deemed all the scenes integral to the psychic portrayal of the central character. According to Cummings, the play resolved "the distinction between time and eternity" and also explored the three mysteries of human life: "love, art, and self-transcendence or growing." The introspective conversations between Him and Me explore the paradoxical condition of the artist who seeks to be understood, but who fears that his message might be commonplace. The artist walks a tightrope between his fantastical imagination, on the one hand, and the banality of using a language the average person can understand. In order to be communicated, the artistic vision must be diluted, and thus the artist fails his own vision. The fragmentary nature of the play, filled with the energy and vitality of nontraditional theatrical forms, defies easy interpretation and thus resists this failure.

The play was generally disliked by the critics because of its ambiguity, but it did manage to collect an audience of supporters, chiefly theater critics and practitioners familiar with surrealist theater who lauded the experimental risk the Provincetown production had taken. Gilbert Seldes collected excerpts that summarized the critical debate between the two camps into a sixteen-page brochure and explained that not many understood the play's "tragic themes" when presented through the techniques of burlesque shows and the circus. For example, the last act's "freak show," in which a carnival barker introduces nine human oddities to an onstage audience consisting of earlier characters, shows Cummings's own preoccupation with the implicit theatricality of human life. As Him declares, "This play of mine is all about mirrors."

After *Him* Cummings's principal publications were *Viva* (1931), *No Thanks* (1935), 1 × 1 (1944), *XAIP?* (1950), and *95 Poems* (1958). In 1931 he gave his first major exhibition of his paintings and drawings at the Painters and Sculptors Gallery. He also published *Tom* (1935), an unproduced ballet based on *Uncle Tom's Cabin*, *Collected Poems* (1938), and *Poems, 1923–1954* (1954), which received a National Book Award citation and a Bollingen Prize. His second play, *Santa Claus* (1946), combines the Faust and Santa Claus stories. In 1952 he returned to Harvard to deliver the Charles Eliot Norton lectures. Cummings's poetry is notable for his unusual use of spelling and typography, as well as his creative modifications to syntax, but he frequently addresses traditional themes and demonstrates his connection with New England transcendentalism. Cummings died on September 3, 1962, in Conway, New Hampshire.

[*See also* United States, 1940–Present]

PLAYS: *Him* (1927); *Santa Claus* (1946)

FURTHER READING

Grossman, Manuel L. "Him and the Modern Theatre." *Quarterly Journal of Speech* 54 (1968): 212–219.

Kennedy, Richard S. *Dreams in the Mirror: A Biography of E. E. Cummings*. New York: Liveright, 1980.

Maurer, Robert E. "E. E. Cummings' Him." *Bucknell Review* 6 (May 1956): 1–27.

Seldes, Gilbert Vivian, ed. *"Him" and the Critics: A Collection of Opinions on Cummings' Play at the Provincetown Playhouse*. Provincetown, Mass.: Provincetown Playhouse, 1928.

Strickland, William Franklin. "E. E. Cummings' Dramatic Imagination: A Study of Three Plays and a Ballet." Ph.D. diss., Univ. of Florida, 1973.

Wagner-Martin, Linda. "Cummings' Him—and Me." *Spring: The Journal of the E. E. Cummings Society* 1 (October 1992): 28–36.

Miriam M. Chirico and Jeffrey D. Mason

CURSE OF THE STARVING CLASS

> *I don't think you begin from saying, "OK, I'm going to make this father figure an emblem for America," you know what I mean? . . . That's something I never really realized as a writer until I got into* Curse of the Starving Class, *and with* Curse *I began to realize that these characters were not only who they were in this predicament in this little subculture but they begin to have a bigger implication—there are ripples around them, particularly in the father.*
>
> —Sam Shepard

Written in 1976, *Curse of the Starving Class* is the first of SAM SHEPARD's full-length, mostly realistic "family dramas" of a period that includes BURIED CHILD (1978), TRUE WEST (1980), and FOOL FOR LOVE (1982). *Curse of the Starving Class* centers on an emotional and spiritual hunger that eats away at an American family and American life.

The Tate family, father Weston, mother Ella, and teenage children Emma and Wesley, is hardly starving on its rundown avocado farm somewhere in Southern California, but everyone wants to escape. Weston is a violent, noisy drunk who is an easy sucker for any scheme that comes his way, and Ella dreams of traveling to the Europe of "high art, paintings, castles, fancy food." The "fireball" Emma is wary of feminine roles, especially the "curse" of her first period, and attempts to bolt from the farm dressed in her western outfit, riding her horse down the freeway headed for Mexico, "just like that guy . . . who wrote *Treasure of Sierra Madre*." Although he wistfully dreams of moving to the Alaskan frontier that he presumes is "full of possibilities" and "undiscovered," Wesley is the only one who cares about keeping the family together and does what he can to shore up the chaos of the household.

Weston sobers up long enough to do everyone's laundry and cook up a full breakfast, but his newfound resolve to reclaim the farm cannot stand up to the criminal creditors who invade their home. Ella is seduced by a creepy lawyer who keeps her out on an overnight "business lunch" and persuades her to sell the farm, and Weston signs over his deed to a steak-house tycoon to pay off his gambling debts. The speculators are the "zombie invasion" that schemes to transform the West into a homogenized suburbia. Wesley tries to fight off the criminals, even spilling his own blood, and Emma dies in a car bombing that was meant to kill her father. A streak of violence and destruction reaches back through generations of Tates and extends to national proportions. When Weston pulls up in his car and drunkenly breaks down the door of their home, Wesley is lying in bed staring up at his model airplanes and connects the sounds of the car and his father's violence with a squadron of planes set to invade. "I was in the war, I know how to kill. . . . It's no big deal," Weston confesses to his son.

While the tone of the play is mordant and tragic, there are many absurd moments of black COMEDY. On a whim, Ella cooks and eats the chicken that Emma has raised over the past year for a 4-H presentation, and Wesley urinates on Emma's hand-colored chicken charts. Wesley cares for a maggot-ridden lamb in the middle of their kitchen, and Weston brings home bags of discounted artichokes to feed the family. Throughout the play family members repeatedly gravitate to the refrigerator, stare into it like a shrine, and turn away empty-handed.

Curse of the Starving Class was first performed in 1977 at the Royal Court Theatre (London) and in 1978 at the New York Shakespeare Festival's Public Theatre, which commissioned the play. Writing in *New York Magazine*, Ross Wetzsteon (November 24, 1980) described *Curse of the Starving Class* as "the finest 'family play' since *Long Day's Journey*," while Richard Eder of the *New York Times* (March 3, 1978) cited the play as a "remarkable piece of writing," but thought that it failed to achieve a balance between "the extremity of its images and violent symbolic functions of its characters" and "the characters' recognizable humanity." The play won the *Village Voice*'s Obie Award for Best Play of 1977.

[*See also* United States, 1940–Present]

FURTHER READING

Marranca, Bonnie, ed. *American Dreams: The Imagination of Sam Shepard*. New York: Performing Arts Journal Publications, 1981.

Roudané, Matthew. "Shepard on Shepard: An Interview with Matthew Roudané." In *The Cambridge Companion to Sam Shepard*. Ed. by Matthew Roudané. New York: Cambridge Univ. Press, 2002.

Shepard, Sam. *Curse of the Starving Class*. In *Sam Shepard: Seven Plays*. New York: Bantam, 1981.

Wilcox, Leonard, ed. *Rereading Shepard: Contemporary Critical Essays on the Plays of Sam Shepard*. New York: St. Martin's, 1993.

Mary Fleischer

CURZON, SARAH ANNE (1833–1898)

Canadian playwright, writer, and suffragist Sarah Anne Curzon was born in 1833 in Birmingham, England, a daughter of George Phillips Vincent, a rich manufacturer. Curzon received a private education and began contributing her writings early on to various family periodicals. In 1858 she married Robert Curzon, and four years later, in 1862, she immigrated with him to Toronto. In CANADA she contributed her essays and fiction to the *Canadian Monthly*, the *Dominion Illustrated*, *Grip*, *Week*, *Evangelical Churchman*, and the *Canadian Magazine*. An avid advocate of suffrage and women's education, Curzon published many essays on women's issues in British and U.S. newspapers. In November 1878 she became a founding member of the Toronto Women's Literary Club, a women's organization based on the model of the American Society for the Advancement of Women. After the death of her husband in 1878, Curzon supported herself by working as a freelance journalist. In 1881 she became associate editor of the *Canada Citizen*, Canada's first prohibitionist paper, for which she wrote a regular column on women's issues. She died in 1898.

Curzon is best known for her play about Laura Secord, *Laura Secord, the Heroine of 1812* (1887), a poetic account of Laura Secord's heroic actions during the War of 1812. Also in 1987 she wrote *Memoir of Mrs. Secord*, using the historical figure of Laura Secord to highlight the role of women in the political process. Secord crossed the enemy lines to warn the British of the upcoming American army. Considering Curzon's suffragist politics and solitary lifestyle, her creative manipulation and interweaving of historical details from Secord's life with Curzon's own personal narrative highlights issues for a woman's own life story. The play has been mostly forgotten, though recently some contemporary feminist critics have made attempts to see it in the light of modern gender theory as an ideological intersection of gender and nationhood. Curzon's only other play, *The Sweet Girl Graduate* (published in 1882 in *Grip-Sack*) is a closet comedy about a woman who cross-dresses as a man in order to attend the University of Toronto. The play had a political impact because it helped contribute to the 1884 order-in-council legislation that admitted women to the University College of Toronto.

PLAYS: *The Sweet Girl Graduate* (published in 1882), *Laura Secord, the Heroine of 1812* (1887)

FURTHER READING

Curzon, Sarah Anne. *Laura Secord* and *The Sweet Girl Graduate*. In *Women Pioneers*, vol. 2 of *Canada's Lost Plays*, ed. by Anton Wagner. Toronto: CTR, 1979.

Derksen, Celeste. "Out of the Closet: Dramatic Works by Sarah Anne Curzon; Part One: Woman and Nationhood: *Laura Secord, the Heroine of 1812*." *Theatre Research in Canada* 15, no. 1 (Spring 1994).

———. "Out of the Closet: Dramatic Works by Sarah Anne Curzon; Part Two: Re-dressing Gender Inequality: *The Sweet Girl Graduate*." *Theatre Research in Canada* 15, no. 2 (Fall 1994).

Gilbert, Sandra M., and Susan Gubar. *The Mad Woman in the Attic: The Woman Writer and the Nineteenth-Century Literary Imagination*. New Haven: Yale Univ. Press, 1979.

Magda Romanska

CUSACK, DYMPHNA (1902–1981)

Dymphna Cusack was born in Wyalong, New South Wales, AUSTRALIA, and received her early education in the New South Wales town of Armidale. She was a playwright, novelist, children's author, and travel writer. She received a B.A. with honors and a diploma of education (University of Sydney). At the university she met Florence James, who was to become a close friend and a collaborator on her most famous novel, *Come in Spinner* (1951). Cusack worked as a high-school teacher in New South Wales until her early retirement as a result of ill health in 1944.

Cusack's writing shows her interest in the plight of ordinary Australians. Her tendency to write about workers and the poor sprang from her strong socialist views. She had connections to the Communist Party and was a strong activist for social reform. Some of the typical thematic features that characterize her writing include gender conflicts, as well as issues of class and nationalism. She was a feminist who used her work to explore issues affecting women. Her best-known play, *Morning Sacrifice* (produced in 1942, published in 1950), covers thematic material that can also be seen in her other writing. She was concerned about the social pressures women felt to conform to "appropriate" standards of femininity. Repertory Theatre in Perth first produced *Morning Sacrifice* in 1942. The play is set in Easthaven Girls High School at the start of World War II and examines the way that the teachers at the school interact with each other. It features an all-female cast of characters who are a mixture of conservative teachers, interested in preserving the traditional values of the school, and progressive teachers, who want to change the system. Cusack had been openly critical of the New South Wales State Department of Education and its treatment of young women and was sent as a teacher to the small town of Bathurst.

Cusack was acutely concerned with issues of justice and was a strong advocate for peace, as is evident in plays such as *Pacific Paradise* (produced in 1955, published in 1963), which features a small island community that stands up to the rest of the world on the issue of nuclear weapons.

She won the Western Australian Drama Festival's prize for *Morning Sacrifice* in 1942 and for *Call Up Your Ghosts* in 1945. In 1955, after enjoying several productions in Australia, *The Golden*

Girls was produced in England, where it was awarded a British Arts Council grant.

A film adaptation of her play *Red Sky at Morning* was made in 1944. She edited and introduced a book titled *Caddie, the Story of a Barmaid* (1953), which was the basis for the 1976 film *Caddie*. The Australian Broadcasting Commission produced a miniseries of *Come in Spinner* in 1989.

Cusack won the Elizabeth II Coronation medal in 1953, and in 1981 her lifetime achievements in Australian literature were recognized when she was awarded the Australia Medal. She died in Sydney on October 19, 1981.

SELECT PLAYS: *Shallow Cups* (1933); *Morning Sacrifice* (1942); *Comets Soon Pass* (1943); *Red Sky at Morning* (1944); *Call Up Your Ghosts* (1945); *Shoulder the Sky* (1950); *Pacific Paradise* (1955); *Exit* (1957)

FURTHER READING

Freehill, Norman, and Dymphna Cusack. *Dymphna Cusack*. Melbourne: Nelson, 1975.

Lloyd, Vic. "Dymphna Cusack's *Morning Sacrifice*." *Australasian Drama Studies* 10 (1987): 67–77.

North, Marilla, ed. *Yarn Spinners: A Story in Letters; Dymphna Cusack, Florence James, Miles Franklin*. St. Lucia: Univ. of Queensland Press, 2001.

Thomson, Helen. "Dymphna Cusack's Plays." *Australasian Drama Studies* 32 (April 1998): 63–76.

Delyse Ryan

CYRANO DE BERGERAC

Seldom does a subtitle reveal more about an author's purpose than that of EDMOND ROSTAND's "heroic comedy in five acts in verse," otherwise known as *Cyrano de Bergerac*. First produced in 1897 to a rapturous reception, *Cyrano* is part of Rostand's quixotic campaign against NATURALISM in the theater.

Rostand's choice of subject is apt. The title character is inspired by the historical Cyrano, notable in life not for the size of his nose, but as a bold writer of plays and what are generally accounted the first works of science fiction. The setting is the Paris of 1640, of Cardinal Richelieu and the Musketeers, brimming with poetry and bravado suited to Rostand's aims.

Cyrano de Bergerac begins in a theater. An aristocrat's challenge occasions two of Cyrano's many famous speeches: the catalog of nasal insults ("The pure descriptive: 'From its size and shape, / I'd say it was a rock, a bluff, a cape— / No, a peninsula—how picturesque!' ") and the duel in rhyme, during which he defeats his opponent while composing an extemporaneous ballad. Shortly we learn that Cyrano loves his cousin Roxane, but despairs because he judges himself too ugly.

In act 2 Cyrano awaits Roxane, prepared at last to declare his love, but she preempts him, confessing that she loves the handsome young Christian de Neuvillette. Cyrano promises Roxane that he will protect Christian and have him write to her, but Christian reveals that he is incapable of romantic words. Cyrano has a love letter prepared for Roxane, and he offers it for Christian's use, initiating the master theme of the play's second half: Cyrano's self-sacrifice in affairs of the heart.

In the act 3 "balcony scene" Cyrano prompts Christian from the shadows as Roxane awaits expressions of love that the handsome young man is unable to produce. Finally, under cover of darkness, Cyrano takes over the conversation, speaking, unseen, the words of his own heart to the woman he loves.

The fourth act finds Cyrano and Christian at the siege of Arras. Cyrano carries out his promise of a daily letter—which he composes—inspiring a battlefield visit by Roxane, who declares her love for Christian's "soul," not his physical beauty. Christian insists that Cyrano tell Roxane the truth, but the battle is joined and Christian is the first to fall. As he dies in Roxane's arms, Cyrano, in another act of renunciation, reassures Christian that Roxane loves only him.

Act 5 occurs fifteen years later, in a convent where Roxane has taken refuge. She wears Christian's last letter close to her heart, but receives a weekly visit from Cyrano. On this day Cyrano is late for his visit because he has been grievously injured by a falling log. He finally appears and asks to see Christian's last letter. As the sun sets, Cyrano reads the letter aloud, reciting the last few lines in the darkness, from memory, revealing himself at last as the true object of Roxane's love. A poet to the end, he dies, declaring with his last words that what remains of him will be his "panache," literally the white plume of his hat, but metaphorically all the rich associations that have gathered around the word: style, dash, bravado, wit, excellence.

If *Cyrano de Bergerac* failed to usher in Rostand's hoped-for revival of heroic verse drama, it has succeeded profoundly in the theater and on film. The title role has become associated with famous actors from Constant Coquelin, who created the part, to Gérard Depardieu and many notable English-language Cyranos such as Walter Hampden, José Ferrer, Peter Donat, Christopher Plummer, and Derek Jacobi. The play, despite its large ensemble and stylistic challenges, remains a staple of American regional theater.

[*See also* France]

FURTHER READING

Cyrano de Bergerac, Savinien. *Other Worlds: The Comical History of the States and Empires of the Moon and Sun*. Ed. by Geoffrey Strachan. London: Oxford Univ. Press, 1965.

Rostand, Edmond. *Cyrano de Bergerac*. Tr. by Brian Hooker. New York: Bantam, 1950.

——. *Cyrano de Bergerac*. Tr. and adapted for the modern stage by Anthony Burgess. New York: Applause Theatre and Cinema Bks., 1996.

Rick Davis

CZECHOSLOVAKIA

Although the Czechs were still part of the Austro-Hungarian Empire at the beginning of the 20th century, Czech drama and theater by then had evolved from tentative beginnings in the early 19th century to a position approaching near parity with their longer-established European counterparts. Inspired by the establishment of their own National Theatre in the early 1880s, Czech playwrights and theater artists drew on their own resources, as well as those of German, French, and Russian theater. As the 20th century advanced through peace and war, concurrently with Czechoslovakia's birth as an independent republic (1918) and its fluctuating periods of repression and liberation, Czech theater and drama matured to the point of rivaling and at times even surpassing the achievements of its continental neighbors.

In the early years of the century Czech drama continued certain genres from the previous century, such as realistic plays dealing with Czech history and folk material. Alois Jirásek (1851–1930), primarily a novelist, wrote a number of plays about the Hussite Wars of the 15th century, chief among them *Jan Hus* (1911), but also *The Lantern* (1905), a classic folk fable of Czech village life that has held the stage to the present. Arnošt Dvořák's numerous historical works included *The Prince* (1908), drawn from legendary Czech history, as well as several plays of the Hussite era, of which *The Hussites* (1919) was perhaps the most effective theatrically. He also wrote an adaptation of Greek sources, *The New Oresteia* (1923), interesting in its use of Freudian psychology. Jaroslav Hilbert's (1871–1936) *Falkenštejn* (1903) and *Columbus* (1915) both dealt with strong, idealistic figures coping with resentful mediocrities. Hilbert's interest in moral and spiritual issues of the contemporary bourgeoisie was evident in *The Fist* (1905) and *The Other Shore* (1924). Jiří Mahen's (1882–1939) *Janošík* (1910) presented the Slovak folk hero as a complex figure who endures inner conflicts as a leader, and *The Dead Sea* (1918) dealt with religious faith and moral identity in historical Bohemia. Viktor Dyk (1877–1931), a poet, wrote *A Revolutionary Trilogy* (1907–1909), which presented three perspectives on the French Revolution, and *The Messenger* (1907), a drama of the era after the defeat of the Czechs by the Hapsburgs in 1620. Dyk also wrote *The Coming of Wisdom to Don Quixote* (1913), his most distinctive work, which revealed an ironic, disenchanted point of view about the archetypal failed idealist; a more positive tone marked two of Dyk's later works, *The Great Magician* (1915) and *Ondřej and the Dragon* (1919).

More lyrical and impressionistic than Dyk, Fráňa Šrámek (1877–1952) was another poet who turned his talents to drama. *Summer* (1915) is a paean to nature and youthful erotic attraction, while *The Moon Above the River* (1922) is a more moody, atmospheric study of youth grown older, an almost Chekhovian work in which elements of COMEDY are offset by a tone of melancholy resignation. *Hagenbek* (1920), a political, antimilitary satire, reflects conditions at the end of World War I, and *The Weeping Satyr* (1923) once again affirms the life force against all that would repress it. Akin in spirit to Šrámek was Vladislav Vančura (1891–1942), a lifelong opponent of bourgeois, establishment values. Both *Teacher and Pupil* (1927) and *The Ill Girl* (1928) were experimental in form and language, championing courage and action against passivity and fear. *The Alchemist* (1932) was a poetic celebration of Renaissance creativity and daring, and *Lake Ukereve* (1935) emphasized the humanistic nature of scientific work while attacking colonialism and racism.

It remained for two other writers of the interwar era, however, to bring world attention to Czech drama: KAREL ČAPEK (1890–1938) and, to a lesser degree, FRANTIŠEK LANGER (1888–1965). Čapek's strikingly imaginative subjects and provocative themes of universal concern transcended problems of linguistic and cultural translation. *R.U.R.* (1920), THE INSECT COMEDY (1921), *The Makropulos Affair* (1922), *The White Disease* (1937), and *The Mother* (1938), fantasies to a greater or lesser degree, contained the wit, philosophy, and dramaturgic skill to make them transportable to world stages. Langer, Čapek's contemporary and friend, wrote more realistic, often comedic plays, such as *Camel Through a Needle's Eye* (1923), *The Wrong Side of the Tracks* (1925), and *Angels Among Us* (1931); *The Mounted Patrol* (1935) was a more starkly serious work. His themes were less far-reaching than Čapek's, but his ability to create engaging characters and skillful plots also attracted audiences beyond the borders of Czechoslovakia in the 1920s and 1930s.

Although their stage creations were not conventional plays, Jiří Voskovec's (1905–1981) and Jan Werich's (1905–1980) revues (or plays with music and dance) were sophisticated, literate, and hugely successful with Czech audiences of the late 1920s and the 1930s, not only for their entertainment values but because they became acutely responsive to the increasing fascist threats to Czechoslovakia (and Europe) at the time. V+W's Liberated Theatre, in which they were producers, authors, librettists, and chief actors, was a rallying ground for Czechs confronting the strident demands of Adolf Hitler's Nazi Germany. Among their outstanding productions (more nearly plays than revues) were *Caesar* (1932), *Executioner and Fool* (1934), *Rag Ballad* (1935), and *Big Bertha* (1937).

From 1939 to 1945 Czechoslovakia was under the domination of Nazi Germany, and after a brief period of freedom following World War II, it fell under Soviet-style Communist rule from 1948 to 1989. During most of those fifty years Czech theater and drama (like Czech society) operated under conditions of restricted freedom. Nevertheless, stimulating work continued by playwrights, directors, and other production people. Among playwrights, VÁCLAV HAVEL (1936–) achieved the greatest recognition, recalling the international interest generated by the plays of Čapek. But other dramatists also produced interesting work that reflected the sociopolitical climate of the time and eventually helped improve it.

During the war years poet Vítězslav Nezval's (1900–1958) version of *Manon Lescaut* (1940) helped sustain the morale of Czechs with its highly poetic use of the Czech language, and the production of Jan Bor's (1886–1943) *Zuzana Vojířová* (1942) provided similar therapy by its depiction of a Czech hero of the Renaissance era. Immediately after the war Jan Drda's (1915–1970) comedy *Plays with the Devil* (1945) was extremely popular for its thinly veiled parallel between the devil and Hitler.

During the brief few years between Nazi and Communist domination, Vratislav Blažek's (1925–1973) *The King Dislikes Beef* (1947) was an effective social and political satire of the times. During the early years of the ensuing Communist regime, the most noteworthy playwright was Miloslav Stehlík (1916–1994), who managed to reflect the wartime years, the postwar recovery, and the transition to the new Communist society with relative objectivity and a degree of criticism in works such as *The Murderous Ravine* (1949), *Spring Thunder* (1949), *The Official Honorees* (1953), and *The High Summer Sky* (1956).

A number of new Czech playwrights first appeared on stages in the 1950s, a decade that started out in a harsh Stalinist climate that only gradually moderated, particularly after Joseph Stalin's death in 1953. The recently installed Communist regime (and its dogmatic insistence on SOCIALIST REALISM in the arts) imposed norms and goals that affected every aspect of life. All artists thereby gained a rich source of provocative material to respond to, with the knowledge that their audiences would be sensitive to their oblique comments, as long as the artists had the ability to operate within ideological restrictions in veiled terms.

Probably the most important new dramatist to develop in this period was JOSEF TOPOL (1935–), whose first play was a relatively apolitical history in verse, *Midnight Wind* (1955), but it was followed by a landmark work, *Their Day* (1959), a multiscene play in which Topol dealt subtly with familial and generational relations within the new society. An equally significant work was written by František Hrubín (1910–1971), an older, major poet who, like Topol, worked with National Theatre director Otomar Krejča in developing his play *A Sunday in August* (1958), a low-key, Chekhovian study of relations among characters indirectly reflecting the society of the time. Others in the 1950s who focused on contemporary, realistically depicted social and personal issues included František Pavlíček (1923–2004), whose sensitive, ethical perspective on the individual in relation to larger issues was evident in two closely linked plays, *I Want to Return* (1956) and *The Labyrinth of the Heart* (1959). Pavel Kohout (1928–), a prolific, talented writer with a great facility for varieties of theatrically effective forms, at first enthusiastically supported the new regime in *The Good Song* (1952), a verse comedy of the younger generation. In *September Nights* (1955) and *Farewell, Sorrow* (1957) he portrayed serious problems among individuals in military contexts but did not take a critical view of the larger system within which they operated. It was not until *Such a Love* (1957) that Kohout implied the current society's responsibility for certain personal tragedies. A concern with ethical and moral issues inherent in the new social context also occupied Oldřich Daněk (1927–2000) in *The Art of Departing* (1955) and *A Look Into the Eyes* (1959).

The 1960s were marked by increasing toleration of criticism of conditions in Czechoslovakia, always with the understanding that outright condemnation of the state or the Communist Party was taboo. The liberalization culminated in the 1968 Prague Spring, only to be crushed by the invasion of Soviet-bloc countries that August. During the more liberal period Václav Havel wrote his first three major works, *Garden Party* (1963), THE MEMORANDUM (1965), and *The Increasing Difficulty of Concentration* (1968), all of which imaginatively satirized the increasing mechanization and dehumanization of life in contemporary society. Havel's sense of absurdity, conveyed with notable metaphoric wit, gave his plays international resonance. In the 1960s, too, Josef Topol wrote his most powerful play, *The End of Carnival* (1963), drawing on folk ritual to enhance his study of the tragic dimensions of land reforms in the new society. Milan Uhde (1936–) wrote a popular satire in the 1960s, *King Vávra* (1964), a grotesque comedy of an Ubu-like ruler, and Ladislav Smoček's (1932–) *The Labyrinth* (1965) presented a menacing allegory of entrapment, followed by his *Cosmic Spring* (1969), an attempt to transcend the follies of the world by mystic vision. Pavel Kohout's *August, August, August* (1967) was a veiled condemnation of the regime in the form of a circus FARCE. Alena Vostrá (1938–1992) captured the spirit of aimless, alienated Czech youth in *When Your Number Comes Up* (1966), an ambivalent comedy.

Two other writers, primarily novelists, began to write plays in the 1960s: Milan Kundera (1929–) and Ivan Klíma (1931–). Kundera wrote a popular wartime MELODRAMA with a strong social comment, *The Owners of the Keys* (1962), and, in 1969, *Ptákovina*, a savage satire of power struggles that reflected the invasion of the previous year. Klíma's best-known works were *The Castle* (1964), a disturbing parable with echoes of Franz Kafka and Friedrich Dürrenmatt concerning obscure figures who liquidate anyone different from themselves, and *The Jury* (1969), which dealt with an all-powerful and cynical justice system. Before the end of the 1960s Klíma wrote a number of other plays reflective of the times (chiefly *Candy Shoppe Miriam*, 1969), but they were banned from production in Czechoslovakia, as were those of Havel, Topol, Kohout, and others during the officially designated "normalization" era after the August 1968 invasion.

Normalization lasted twenty years, during which theater and other arts again had to contend with repressive measures meant to assure a stabilized, muted culture. Exceptions to the pervasive blandness in theater occurred in two forms. First, nontraditional plays were developed collectively and improvisationally by new ensembles such as Studio Ypsilon and Theatre on a String in regions less closely monitored than Prague; second, critical new plays by individual playwrights began to be more tolerated in the course of the 1980s.

Of the new, traditionally written plays, several by Antonín Máša (1935–2001), Karel Steigerwald (1945–), Arnošt Goldflam (1946–), DANIELA FISCHEROVÁ (1948–), and Jan Antonín Pitínský (1955–) were of particular interest. Máša employed multimedia techniques in two plays that probed contemporary values and ethics: *Night Rehearsal* (1981) and *Vivisection* (1987). Steigerwald wrote a series of plays examining flaws in Czech society during several key eras, *Period Dances* (1980) and *Neapolitan Disease* (1984, produced in 1988) being the most effective. Arnošt Goldflam, a director as well as a playwright, composed several subjective plays blending whimsy and the grotesque, among them *Horror* (1980), *Agatomania* (1987), and *Sand* (1988). Fischerová brought a special touch of fantasy to plays that challenged ideological conformity: *The Hour Between Dog and Wolf* (1979) and *Princess T* (1986). Pitínský, a highly regarded director, wrote a harsh study of domestic cruelty reflecting society's values in *The Mother* (1987), as well as a fanciful study of society's abuse of a naïve outsider, *The Park* (1989).

Although their plays could not be produced in Czechoslovakia, already-known playwrights continued to write important new works during the twenty years before the Velvet Revolution of 1989, for example, Havel's *Beggar's Opera* (1972), *Largo Desolato* (1984), *Temptation* (1985), and *Urban Renewal* (1987) and Topol's *Farewell, Socrates* (1976) and *Voices of Birds* (1988). Others included Kohout's *Poor Murderer* (1972), Klíma's *Games* (1973), Smoček's *The Noose* (1972), and Daněk's *The Duchess of Wallenstein's Armies* (1980) and *You Are Jan* (1987), the last indirectly relating Jan Hus's ethics to contemporary Czech society.

With liberation from the Communist regime in 1989, restoration of social and artistic freedom, and a renewal of private enterprise in the 1990s, conditions seemed ripe for a new flowering of Czech playwriting. Although neither Havel nor Topol wrote anything new, and no single new play has stood out, established playwrights and some new ones have written plays worth noting. Steigerwald's *Sorrow, Sorrow . . .* (1990) reflected elusively on the abuses of humanity by tyrannical regimes of the 20th century; his *Nobel* (1994) depicted many disagreeable aspects of post-1989 Czech society; and his latest work, *Play Comedy* (2001), mocks the excesses of a media-driven age. Fischerová's morally centered contemporary plays include *The Massage Table* (1992) and *Fantomima* (1996). Máša's *Strange Birds* (1995) was an exposé of gangster-style corruption in the newly deregulated Czech Republic. Pitínský's *The Little Room* (1992) and *Buldocina* (1992) continued his neonaturalistic depictions of contemporary domestic callousness and violence. A tendency toward depiction of the more brutal, raw, and even criminal elements in the new society was also evident in Kohout's *Double Zeroes* (1997), which might have been inspired by MAKSIM GORKY's *Lower Depths*. Goldflam's *Blue Visage* (1992) was another rendering of distorted grotesque relations among individuals, while his *Sweet Theresienstadt* (1996) took a fresh look at the Holocaust phenomenon.

Among new playwrights, Tomáš Rychetský (1965–) gained attention for *The Innocent Are Innocent* (1991), a study of two young men whose boredom leads them to distressing adventures. David Drábek's (1970–) *Joan of the Park* (1994) and Jan Kraus's (1953–) *Softboiled Egg* (1994) were further variations on the theme of inauthentic, alienated contemporary lives. Lenka Lagronová (1963–) was praised for her sensitive study of total faith and love of God in *Terezka* (1996), as well as for the psychological depth in her lyrical fantasy centering on a mother-daughter relationship in *Antilopa* (1997). Two works by director-playwright Jiři Pokorný (1967–) won awards as best plays of the year: *Dad Kicks Goals* (1996) and *Rest in Peace* (1997); both reflected a fascination with forms of violence and aggression in a society seemingly taking its cue from lurid models flooding contemporary media.

FURTHER READING

Burian, Jarka M. *Modern Czech Theatre: Reflector and Conscience of a Nation*. Iowa City: Univ. of Iowa Press, 2000.

Goetz-Stankiewicz, Marketa. *The Silenced Theatre: Czech Playwrights Without a Stage*. Toronto: Univ. of Toronto Press, 1979.

Trensky, Paul I. *Czech Drama Since World War II*. White Plains, N.Y.: M. E. Sharpe, 1978.

Vocadlo, Otokar. "The Theater and Drama of Czechoslovakia." In *The Theater in a Changing Europe*, ed. by T. H. Dickinson. New York: H. Holt, 1937.

Jarka M. Burian

D

DACHNIKI *See* SUMMERFOLK

DADAISM

If you must speak of Dada, you must speak of Dada. If you must not speak of Dada, you must still speak of Dada.

—Jean Paulhan, 1920

Dadaism was the most explosive manifestation of the historic AVANT-GARDE. The movement flared up in World War I in Zurich, then reignited in capitals such as Berlin, Paris, and New York after the end of fighting; by the early 1920s, its flame was largely extinguished. Dada shared much of the spirit and style of movements such as FUTURISM, Cubism, and EXPRESSIONISM and was a precursor to the more long-lived SURREALISM. The frenzied and confrontational energies behind Dada also animated later cultural phenomena: 1960s situationism, Viennese actionism, and 1970s punk.

Though Dada did not last a decade, its impact on the art world is enormous. The movement's immediate engagement with its own moment transformed the turbulence of global conflict, the uncertainty of postwar economies, and the profound changes in the rhythms of everyday life wrought by new technologies into a source of cultural renewal. The significance of Dada beyond its historical origin lies in (1) the international connections made among artists; (2) its exploration of the boundaries between performers and audience and between scripted texts and embodied action; (3) the attention that dadaists brought to the interrelationship of media; and (4) the movement's focus on the revolutionary potential of creative activity, whether in political or more conventionally aesthetic terms.

Dada arose as an expression of protest against European tradition, which led, in the eyes of participants, to the horrors of World War I. The movement began in 1916 in politically neutral SWITZERLAND, when displaced persons and emigrés, largely from Central Europe, founded the Cabaret Voltaire. Named after the 18th-century French satirist and exponent of reason, the Cabaret Voltaire staged anarchic variety shows featuring readings of poetry in multiple languages (sometimes all at once), "negro" drumming and dancing, the spontaneous creation and destruction of paintings onstage, and political rants and declamations. The key figures in the Cabaret were Munich-born Hugo Ball (1886–1927), a former philosophy student with mystical tendencies formerly involved with MAX REINHARDT's experimental theater in Berlin; his consort Emmy Hennings (1885-1948), a chanteuse, dancer, and poet; the Rumanian poet Tristan Tzara (born Sami Rosenstock, 1896–1963); his countryman Marcel Janco (1895–1984), an architect who made masks and stage designs that fused ancient and modern forms; Hans Arp (1887–1966), an Alsatian painter; and a third Berliner, Richard Huelsenbeck (1892–1974), author and performer of aggressive nonsense poetry. The participants in the Cabaret Voltaire retitled their eponymous journal *Dada* within months of starting publication, and the name for the burgeoning movement was found. The uncertainties surrounding the origin and meaning of the word *Dada* are emblematic. Dadaists purposefully offered contradictory accounts of the name; some claimed the title of their movement was selected at random from a dictionary, and they delighted in finding new possibilities of what it really meant ("hobbyhorse" in French, "yes, yes" in Russian and Rumanian, "foolish naïveté and sexual obsession with a baby carriage" in German, and "the tail of a holy cow" in an "unspecified African language"). Clearly, *Dada* has no single, true signification. The word, like the movement, is a performative gesture of defiance and opposition that plays with the stability of symbolic orders.

With the end of armed conflict, Zurich Dada dissipated, and many participants returned to their native lands or moved on. However, the aftermath of war and the uneasiness of peace made artists elsewhere receptive to the jarring aesthetic of the Cabaret Voltaire. Berlin, Paris, Cologne, Hanover, and New York hosted distinct but related eruptions of Dada.

Berlin Dada, which began after the end of World War I when Huelsenbeck returned to GERMANY and met up with like-minded artists, displayed an aggressive character. Characterized by engagement with mass media, openly political pamphleteering, and confrontational events staged in public spaces, it was more visible and militant than its Swiss counterpart. The central figures of Berlin Dada were Raoul Hausmann, whom even fellow dadaist, experimental filmmaker, and chronicler of the movement Hans Richter (1888–1976) called a "fanatic" for his devotion to cultural anarchism; George Grosz (1893–1959), known for grotesque caricatures of obese bankers, mechanical military officers, and sadistic policemen; and the scathing collage artist John Heartfield (1891–1968). The group made the whole sphere of politics into its stage when it declared itself against the liberal Weimar Republic and elevated the *Oberdada* to "President of the Globe." Sporadic eruptions continued until 1923, but Berlin Dada had by then been in decline for years. Dada groups in Cologne (centered around Max Ernst, Johannes Baargeld, and Arp) and Hanover (where Kurt Schwitters founded the dadaesque Merz movement) retained their forces more fully for the same duration of time because of their more purely artistic and literary orientation.

The poet Tzara's editorship of the Zurich journal and his active participation in other publications (e.g., 391, published by Francis Picabia in SPAIN and New York; Theo van Doesburg's *Mecano* in the NETHERLANDS) were instrumental in establishing contacts and promoting the movement's expansion. In 1919, Tzara, the most voluble voice of Zurich Dada, left for Paris. Paris Dada, though based in the French capital, took place on an international stage, attracting artists from Zurich (Arp), Cologne (Ernst), New York (Man Ray), and beyond. The diversity of participants, who came by choice and not of necessity, and the political stability of postwar FRANCE tempered spirits and paved the way for the ascendancy of surrealism, which, under the guidance of André Breton (who, along with Louis Aragon and Georges Ribemont-Dessaignes, had contributed to the Zurich journal), transformed the violent spirit of Dada into a gentler movement with an often utopian cast.

Marcel Duchamp and Man Ray (born Emmanuel Radnitzky, 1890–1976), joined at regular intervals by the continent-hopping Picabia, formed the triumvirate of New York Dada. The American metropolis, like Zurich, offered an escape for European artists during World War I, but the form assumed was more contemplative, less militant. The group focused on challenging art and cultural institutions, not on effecting radical change in society, and never staged performances like its European counterparts. Indeed, members never officially called themselves or their activities Dada. Alfred Stieglitz's photo gallery 291 and his publication *Camera Work* provided the forum for the movement in its early days by showing works that challenged the primacy of realistic modes of representation in the pictorial arts, especially photography. Man Ray's photographs capture the play of light and shadow; images are not recordings of fact so much as evocations and suggestions of mental states and philosophical questions. Duchamp discovered the *ready-made*, a mass-produced object elevated into the spiritual realm when the artist transplants it from its everyday setting into a new context.

The spirit of negation and the will to disrupt tied together the many incarnations of Dada. Dada included the often near-nihilistic Berlin agitators, their starry-eyed counterparts in Paris, the playful activities of Merz in Hanover, and the quiet meditation of the New York group. The movement's lack of a constant geographical center stimulated the activities of its various manifestations, as did the absence of a centrally formulated program and leadership. However, the very features of Dada that assured its vitality in a wide range of settings over the short term limited the long-term viability of the movement. Without a base of operations and a codified program, the energies that had briefly coalesced into an extraordinarily dynamic cultural phenomenon dispersed. However, to dadaists, the process of transformation was more important than the creation of commodified products; they understood the destructive impulse animating the movement dialectically—that is, as an ultimately positive force.

In stage events, street actions, and publications, dadaists sought to break with established traditions by fusing heterogeneous forms and materials, such as political slogans, advertising jargon, verbal and visual images from "primitive" art, and decontextualized references to high culture. Indeed, the boundary separating performance and the concrete works (journals, paintings, sculpture, etc.) was often fluid. The works that are now displayed in museums are, to a large extent, objects and costumes that were employed in a performance setting. All Dada publications and image productions were conceived as a lever to dislodge entrenched views of art and its supporting institutions, not as an end unto themselves. Even in static form, Dada works are a kind of performance.

The lasting influence of Dada can be discerned not only in subsequent art that sought to revolutionize perception and disrupt institutions but also in cultural phenomena with a different ideological orientation. Pop art and, more broadly, the varied productions labeled "postmodern" operate with the irony and playful confusion of genres and forms that characterized Dada. Indeed, the fusion of heterogeneous styles and the staccato editing of images designed to strike the senses with a maximum level of intensity that characterize advertising culture in the 20th and 21st centuries attest to the enduring power of processes pioneered by dadaists to entirely different ends.

[*See also* Apollinaire, Guillaume; Avant Garde Drama, Western Europe]

FURTHER READING

Benson, Timothy O. *Raoul Hausmann and Berlin Dada*. Ann Arbor: UMI Res. Press, 1987.

Foster, Stephen C., ed. *Hans Richter: Activism, Modernism, and the Avant-garde*. Cambridge: MIT Press, 1998.

Gordon, Mel, ed. *Dada Performance*. New York: PAJ Publications, 1987.

Melzer, Annabelle. *Dada and Surrealist Performance*. Baltimore: Johns Hopkins Univ. Press, 1994.

Richter, Hans. *Dada: Art and Anti-Art*. Tr. by David Britt. New York: McGraw-Hill, 1965.

Willett, John. *Art and Politics in the Weimar Period: The New Sobriety, 1917–1933*. New York: Pantheon Bks., 1978.

Erik Butler

DADIE, BERNARD (1916–)

One of the important figures in the emergence of African literatures as national literatures, Bernard Dadie has authored noteworthy plays, as well as novels, several works of nonfiction, and collections of short stories, of updated African folktales, and of poems.

Born in Assinie, Ivory Coast, in 1916, Dadie grew up in the house of an uncle who enjoyed telling traditional folktales. Dadie's mother had lost her three previous children, believed herself to be accursed, and wished to protect her son from her ill-fated influence. Dadie attended École Primaire Superieure Bingerville, the Roman Catholic school in the Grand Bassam, and

École Normale William Ponty, a teachers' college where he pursued his interest in folklore and developed an interest in drama.

Having earned a civil servant's diploma in colonial administration, Dadie relocated to Senegal and took a position at the Institut Fondamental d'Afrique Noir, an educational institute that eventually evolved into the University of Dakar. Returning to the Ivory Coast a decade later, Dadie worked as a journalist for the newspaper published by the Parti Democratique de Cote d'Ivoire, which was in the forefront of the independence movement. At one point, Dadie was imprisoned for more than a year because of his political activism.

Since the Ivory Coast achieved independence, Dadie has held many high-ranking positions in the federal government, including first secretary of the Ministry of Education, director of Information Services, director of Cultural Affairs for the Ministry of National Education, inspector-general of Arts and Letters, director of Fine Arts and Research, and Minister of Culture and Information. He has also served as the director of the Commission Nationale de la Fondation Felix Houphouet-Boigny of the African Institute for Historical and Political Research and as president of the Conference Generale de l'Agence de Cooperation Culturelle et Technique.

In his plays, as in his fiction and poems, Dadie has been concerned with synthesizing African and Western literary forms and themes in order to create a literature that is modern and yet remains distinctly African. His plays have been very important in the development of Francophone drama, and a considerable body of criticism on the plays exists in French. But, unlike his short stories and updated folktales, Dadie's plays have had a limited impact on literature in English.

[*See also* Africa, West Africa]

PLAYS: *Cities* (*Les Villes*, 1934); *Assemien Dehyle, King of the Sanwi: Preceded by My Country and Its Theater* (*Assemien Dehyle, roi du Sanwi: Precede de Mon pays et son theatre*, 1936); *Min Adja-o* (1960); *Papassidi, Master-Swindler* (*Papassidi, maitre-escroc*, 1960); *Difficult Situation* (*Situation difficile*, 1965); *Pledge of Love* (*Serment d'amour*, 1965); *Beatrice of the Congo: Play in Three Acts* (*Beatrice du Congo: Piece en trois actes*, 1969); *Mister Thogo-gnini* (*Monsieur Thogo-gnini*, 1969); *Voices in the Wind* (*Les Voix dans le vent*, 1969); *Stormy Islands: Play in Seven Scenes* (*Iles de Tempete: Piece en sept tableaux*, 1973); *Mhoi-Ceul: Comedy in Five Scenes* (*Mhoi-Ceul: Comedie en 5 tableaux*, 1979)

FURTHER READING

Frederick, Patricia. "Quest and Sacrifice in Two Tales by Bernard Dadie." *Romance Quarterly* 40 (Fall 1993): 203–210.

Mudimbe-Boyi, Elisabeth. "Bernard Dadie: Literary Imagination and New Historiography." *Research on African Literatures* 29 (Fall 1998): 98–105.

Okafor, R. N. C. "Politics and Literature in Francophone Africa: The Ivory Coast Experience." *Okike: An African Journal of New Writing* 23 (August 1983): 105–121.

Smith, Robert P., Jr. "History and Tragedy in Bernard Dadie's Beatrice du Congo." *The French Review: Journal of the American Association of Teachers of French* 55 (May 1982): 818–823.

Martin Kich

DAGERMAN, STIG (1923–1954)

I wish to think of a drama imitating life even in such a way that it lacked an end and allowed the Action to couple with incidental Actions as freely and shamelessly as in reality. I believe, in short, that the dramatic art at least for an interim period would fare well by being dedramatized.

—Stig Dagerman, "Entrerepliker," 1948

Swedish novelist, dramatist, essayist, poet, and short-story writer Stig Dagerman was, from 1944 to 1946, the cultural editor of the syndicalist newspaper *Arbetaren* (The Worker). Although exceedingly productive for a short period, he committed suicide after five years of silence.

Dagerman made his debut in 1945 with the novel *The Snake* (*Ormen*; translated 1995). The intensity and artistry that characterizes this work can be sensed also in the collection of short stories *The Games of Night* (*Nattens lekar*; translated 1959) and in the highly symbolical *Island of the Doomed* (*De dömdas ö; translated* 1991), both published in 1946. In *German Autumn* (*Tysk höst*, 1947; translated 1951) Dagerman, unlike most of his contemporaries, shows concern for the suffering postwar civilian population in GERMANY. Self-deception is the theme in *A Burnt Child* (*Bränt barn*, 1948; translated 1950), his most popular novel.

The most talented dramatist of his generation, Dagerman brought an altogether new tone to Swedish drama. His first play, *The Condemned* (*Den dödsdömde*, 1947), deals with a man who has been condemned to death. When it appears that he is innocent and is set free, he is celebrated as a hero. He then commits a murder similar to the one for which he was earlier accused and is returned to the prison he has just left, undoubtedly awaiting execution. The mere fact that capital punishment was abolished in SWEDEN long ago should warn us that the play is not about the imperfection of legal justice but rather about the imperfection of human judgment and justice in general. At the heart of the play is the about-face from guilt to innocence. Unable to accept the idea that he is innocent, the Condemned's murder is an attempt to make the way others view him harmonize with the way he sees himself. He is a modern Everyman. In the wake of Franz Kafka and ALBERT CAMUS, Dagerman is concerned with the human condition. We are all guilty, all condemned. No one goes free.

In *The Shadow of Mart* (*Skuggan av Mart*, 1948) Gabriel lives in the shadow of his elder brother Mart, who was killed when resisting the occupants of his country. By contrast, Gabriel did not oppose the enemy. Others around him, notably the mother, never tire of reminding Gabriel of his cowardliness and Mart's heroism.

What Dagerman presents here is essentially a picture of a man who, given his authentic but weak nature, succumbs to the inauthenticity of the environment, resulting in a deed (matricide) that does not agree with his true self. In *The Shadow of Mart*, Dagerman has created a protagonist who is *not* ultimately courageous, who on the whole does *not* act; and when he finally does act, he does so in a destructive and inauthentic way. In short, Dagerman's protagonist is a victim rather than someone shaping his own fate. For what is his matricide other than a step toward an unavoidable suicide? We may wonder whether it was not in order to legitimate a suicide that Gabriel killed his mother. The protagonist as a substitutive suicide may well be the formula for Dagerman's branch of theatrical catharsis. Perhaps it was even a reason for him to turn to drama, the most palpably lifelike of the various genres he tried his hand at.

A few plays were yet to follow. *No One Goes Free* (*Ingen går fri*, 1949) is a moderately successful dramatization of *A Burnt Child*. *The Climber* (*Streber*, 1948) describes in a humorously bitter way how some workers attempt to run a garage in a syndicalist manner. In *The Day of Judgement* (*Den yttersta dagen*, 1952), a radio play about guilt in a rural setting, realistic and lyrical elements are subtly fused.

Dagerman's plays, it has been said, are written on a single note and draw their life from a single revelation: that of life's unbearableness. AUGUST STRINDBERG, who frequently depicts life as a hell in his post-*Inferno* plays, does not exclude the hope that there is a better life hereafter. Dagerman, writing after Kafka and JEAN-PAUL SARTRE, does not console us with such a hope.

SELECT PLAYS: *The Condemned* (*Den dödsdömde*, 1947); *The Explorer* (*Upptäcktsresanden*, 1947) *The Climber* (*Streber*, 1948); *The Shadow of Mart* (*Skuggan av Mart*, 1948); *No One Goes Free* (*Ingen går fri*, 1949); *The Day of Judgement* (*Den yttersta dagen*, 1952)

FURTHER READING

Dagerman, Stig. "Entrerepiker" ["Entrance Lines"]. *Prisma*, No. 2, 1948.

Perilleux, Georges, ed. *Stig Dagerman et l'Europe: Perspectives analytiques et comparatives* [Stig Dagerman and Europe: Analytical and comparative perspectives]. Paris: Didier Erudition, 1998.

Scobbie, Irene, ed. *Modern Swedish Literature*. 2d ed. Norwich: Norvik Press, 1999.

Thompson, Laurie, ed. "Stig Dagerman." Special issue, *Swedish Book Review* (supp. 1984).

Törnqvist, Egil. "Heroes and Hero-Worship: On Stig Dagerman's *The Shadow of Mart*." *Scandinavica* 32, no. 1 (1993): 69–78.

Egil Törnqvist

DALY, AUGUSTIN (1838–1899)

John Augustin Daly was a dominant force in late-19th-century theater as a dramatist, critic, theater manager, and director. Born on July 20, 1838, in Plymouth, North Carolina, at the age of eleven he moved to New York with his brother and widowed mother, and he soon became fascinated with the theater.

Daly began his professional work as a critic in 1859. During nine years he wrote thousands of essays and reviews, sometimes for five newspapers simultaneously. These pieces exhibit a strong aesthetic that would form the core of his managerial work in the years to come—innovative at the beginning of his career and rigidly conservative near its end.

As a dramatist Daly is primarily remembered for the sensational MELODRAMAS *UNDER THE GASLIGHT* (1867), featuring a victim tied to a railroad track, and *Horizon* (1871), a frontier drama. The vast majority of the plays he presented under his own name were adaptations of other works including ten novels, forty-four French plays, over thirty German plays, and old English and William Shakespeare's plays drastically cut and rearranged to suit his tastes and lavish scenic demands. Joseph Daly, his younger brother and later biographer, was a covert collaborator on virtually all of the plays.

Although it has been argued that Daly inspired Ambrose Bierce's teasing definition of a dramatist as "one who adapts plays from the French," both current and contemporaneous critics have expressed the opinion that Daly's stamp on his adapted works was truly authorial, adding morality, humor, and spectacular effects. He remade the foreign plays to be totally American and shaped all of the scripts to the talents of his acting company and the tastes of his carefully cultivated middle-class audience.

Daly exerted his strongest influence managing several theaters, in both New York and London, from 1869 to 1899. He was the first modern American director, unifying productions under one vision and his own absolute control. He supervised every aspect of production, introducing concepts that would become central to REALISM such as coordinating acting, sets, and costumes with each other and with period. Daly's training was the best acting school of its time. Actors were molded into a starless ensemble, although in the latter part of his career, he did promote the success of his "Big Four" who appeared together in thirty-one Daly productions: romantic leads John Drew and Ada Rehan (also Daly's mistress), supported by comics Mrs. G. H. Gilbert and John Lewis. Daly's methods have been recorded in the memoirs of numerous actors who worked under his strict control.

Daly's autocracy was motivated by a vision of theater as a civilized entertainment for the middle class. He controlled his actors' offstage behavior in an attempt to distance his company from rowdy, unrespectable thespians. His actresses behaved themselves and were dressed to be emulated; costume sketches were printed in local papers so matinee ladies could copy their fashionable designs. Daly wooed his audience with amusement, morality, and comfort. The theater lobby was a destination, sumptuously decorated to attract the refined audiences he sought. Daly composed every element of the theatergoing experience.

[*See also* United States, 1860–1929]

SELECT PLAYS: *Leah the Forsaken* (1862, from *Deborah*, by S. H. Mosenthal); *Judith* (1864); *Under the Gaslight* (1867); *A Flash of Lightning* (1868); *Griffith Gaunt; or Jealousy* (1868, from a novel by C. Reade); *The Red Scarf* (1868); *Frou-Frou* (1870, from H. Meilhac and L. Halévy); *Man and Wife* (1870, from the novel by Wilkie Collins); *Divorce* (1871, from a novel by Anthony Trollope); *Horizon* (1871); *Little Miss Million* (1892, from the German of O. Blumenthal); *The Countess Gucki* (1896, from the German of Franz von Schönthan and F. Koppel-Ellfeld)

FURTHER READING

Cullen, Rosemary, and Don B. Wilmeth, eds. and intro. *Plays by Augustin Daly*. Cambridge: Cambridge Univ. Press, 1984.

Daly, Joseph Francis. *The Life of Augustin Daly*. New York: Macmillan, 1917.

Felheim, Marvin. *The Theatre of Augustin Daly*. Cambridge: Harvard Univ. Press, 1956.

Hall, Roger A. *Performing the American Frontier, 1870–1906*. New York: Cambridge Univ. Press, 2001.

Marra, Kim. "Taming America as Actress: Augustin Daly, Ada Rehan, and the Discourse of Imperial Frontier Conquest." In *Performing America: Cultural Nationalism in American Theatre*, ed. by Jeffrey D. Mason and J. Ellen Gainor. Ann Arbor: Univ. of Michigan Press, 1999.

McConachie, Bruce A. *Melodramatic Formations: American Theatre and Society, 1820–1870*. Iowa City: Univ. of Iowa Press, 1992.

Shauna Vey

DAMONTE, RAUL TABORDA *See* COPI

THE DANCE OF DEATH

First performed at the Altes Stadttheater in Cologne in 1905, *The Dance of Death* (*Dödsdansen*) is a drama in two parts written by AUGUST STRINDBERG in 1900. The first part is one of Strindberg's most successful plays; the second part is rarely performed.

The Dance of Death was inspired by the marriage between Strindberg's sister Anna and Hugo Philp, who added "von" to his surname, affecting noble lineage. While Philp was seriously ill after a heart attack, Strindberg spent the night with him, and the two men talked about death.

In keeping with Strindberg's practice in his post-*Inferno* dramas, *The Dance of Death* lacks explicit division into acts or scenes. Instead, its parts are merely distinguished by asterisks. However, a division into four acts is easily surmised.

A prime example of the Strindbergian battle between the sexes, *The Dance of Death I* describes the marital struggle between Edgar, a Captain in the artillery, and his wife Alice. Married for nearly twenty-five years, both nourish longtime disappointments. The Captain has not received the promotion he expected. Alice feels that she has sacrificed a career as an actress when she married Edgar. Isolated from others on the island where they live, their married life has become exceedingly monotonous. When Alice's cousin Kurt arrives, both husband and wife try to monopolize him. Eventually, Kurt flees. After Edgar and Alice agree that Kurt is morally inadequate, they now find each other more likable by comparison and agree to celebrate their silver wedding anniversary.

The couple's living room is located in a "round tower," which once was a prison—symbolic not only of the nature of their marriage but also of humankind. The roundness of the room corresponds both to the globe and to the circular composition of the play: when it ends, we seem to be back at the beginning—as though time has stood still, life being characterized by endless repetition.

The Captain's health being precarious, his struggle also concerns death. Once he recognizes that he cannot beat this "enemy," he replaces his atheism with an anguished hope for a life beyond the grave. The realistic scenery with its cannons turned toward the sea and its sentinel guarding the tower suggest Edgar's struggle against death.

On a religious level, Edgar and Alice, Wirmark (1989) remarks, may be seen as counterparts of Adam and Eve expelled from Paradise, the sentinel's saber, glittering in the sunset, corresponding to the biblical "flaming sword" (Gen. 3:24). Allusions to liturgical drama, Kaynar (1986) shows, "are scattered all over the text."

The play's most dramatic moment occurs when Edgar, dancing to Alice's piano playing of Johan Halvorsen's *The Entrance of the Boyards*, collapses. The dance, meant to be a demonstration of virile strength, becomes instead a sign that Edgar, as he has earlier remarked, is "done with dancing." The dance of life becomes a dance of death.

Several scholars have pointed to Swedenborgian elements in the play, although, as Sprinchorn (1982) notes, "none of these correspondences can be made explicit in staging the play." It has even been argued that Edgar, after his fatal dance, goes on living as a ghost. But the Captain's vampirism in the latter part of the play should not be understood literally as emanating from the other side of the grave. It indicates, rather, his need to suck blood—life—from others when becoming aware that his own life is ebbing.

In act 4, after a severe stroke, Edgar dies. Alice notes that she has both loved him and hated him. Her and the play's last words are a conciliatory: "May he rest in peace!"

FURTHER READING

Brantly, Susan. "Naturalism or Expressionism: A Meaningful Mixture of Styles in *The Dance of Death* (I)." In *Strindberg's Dramaturgy*, ed. by Göran Stockenström. Minneapolis: Univ. of Minnesota Press, 1988. 164–174.

Kaynar, Gad. "A Rhetorically Oriented Analysis of Strindberg's *The Dance of Death*." *Assaph* 3 (1986): 109–134.

Plasberg, Elaine. "Strindberg and the New Poetics." *Modern Drama* 15 (1972): 1–14.

Robinson, Michael. *Studies in Strindberg*. Norwich: Norvik Press, 1998.

Sprinchorn, Evert. *Strindberg as Dramatist*. New Haven: Yale Univ. Press, 1982.

Törnqvist, Egil. *Strindbergian Drama: Themes and Structure*. Stockholm: Almqvist & Wiksell Intl., 1982.

Wirmark, Margreta. *Kampen med döden, En studie över Strindbergs Dödsdansen* (*The Battle with Death: A Study of Strindberg's Dance of Death*. Stockholm: Almqvist & Wiksell, 1989.

Egil Törnqvist

DANGEROUS CORNER

To lie or not to lie.

—Charles Stanton, Act 1

According to its author, the prolific JOHN BOYNTON PRIESTLEY, *Dangerous Corner*, his first solo play, was written during one week in 1932. The characters are allowed little depth or roundedness but, rather, represent typical bourgeois types from drawing-room FARCES. They talk airily and facetiously for the opening minutes, but trivial chatter about a musical cigarette box soon gives way to a searching investigation about the apparent suicide of Martin, the brother of one character, Robert Caplan. The play is metatheatrical—a radio play called *Let Sleeping Dogs Lie* is discussed. The "Sleeping Dog" is a hidden secret, one covered up by convenient lies. This reflects the major dilemma addressed by Priestley's *Hamlet*-alluding play—"To lie or not to lie." The conclusion seems to be that middle-class coteries need lies to thrive.

When characters begin to admit transgressions, a snowballing occurs, and a vast network of concealments and lethal secrets emerge. The major victim of the revelations is Robert: he learns that his unloving wife, Freda, has had an affair with her brother-in-law, Martin; that the married woman he does adore, Betty, is no ideal creature but a "greedy little cat on the tiles"; that his late brother was a doped-up, erratic "lunatic"; and that his friend, the married Gordon, is a homosexual—a "hysterical young pervert" who doted on Martin. Robert responds to this by shooting himself at the play's climax. Here, Priestley executes his major conceit—the action returns again to the beginning of the play. This time, however, the cigarette box is noticed, but no inquiries are made about it. Consequently, no unsavory truths emerge, and instead of pursuing ultimately fatal accusations and cross-examinations, the characters engage in a frivolous, harmless dance.

It was the first of many of Priestley's dramatic "time plays," in which standard chronological progression is eschewed. Priestley himself suggested that *Dangerous Corner* was "merely an ingenious box of tricks." Early reviewers were harsher. They panned the first, Tyrone Guthrie–produced performances at the Lyric Theatre (London, May 1932) with such vitriol that the backers withdrew their support. But the play lasted at the Lyric for 151 performances, and in October 1932, New York's Empire Theatre staged the first of its 206 performances. The same city's Waldorf Theatre put on ninety performances during 1933. For the American version, Priestley altered the script, making location and dialogue changes to render the play more palatable for American theater goers. In addition, the radio play was changed to a forthcoming novel, and a garden-visiting Owl was referred to—the ghostly bird being reminiscent of Martin, the deceased character who haunts the play.

A 1988 revival at the Shaw Festival, Ontario, received mixed reviews, as did a 2001 revival directed by Laurie Sansom at the West Yorkshire Playhouse, where high-profile television actress Dervla Kirwan took the role of the frustrated spinster, Olwen (the character who, it becomes apparent, has accidentally shot Martin). Reviewers lambasted Sansom's decision to tinker with and update both the dialogue and the action.

[*See also* England, 1860–1940]

FURTHER READING

Evans, Gareth Lloyd. *J. B. Priestley—The Dramatist*. London: Heinemann, 1964.

Holland, Ruth. *Dangerous Corner*. London: Hamish Hamilton, 1934 [novelized version, written with Priestley's permission].

Konkle, Lincoln. "J. B. Priestley." In *British Playwrights, 1880–1956: A Research and Production Sourcebook*, ed. by W. W. Demastes and K. E. Kelly. Westport, Conn.: Greenwood Press, 1996. 327–338.

Rogers, Ivor A. "The Time Plays of J. B. Priestley." *Extrapolation* 10 (1968): 9–16.

Sengupta, Supriya. *J. B. Priestley: A Study of His Major Novels and Plays*. Jaipur: Printwell, 1996.

Skloot, Robert. "The Time Plays of J. B. Priestley." *Quarterly Journal of Speech* 56 (1970): 426–431.

Young, Kenneth. *J. B. Priestley*. London: Longmans, 1977.

Kevin De Ornellas

D'ANNUNZIO, GABRIELE (1863–1938)

Ah! To decapitate the universe, and to dangle its head before the multitude from a stage, unforgettably. . . . Haven't you ever thought that a great tragedy could be likened to the enterprise of Perseus?

—Gabriele D'Annunzio, 1904

By the time Gabriele D'Annunzio began writing for the theater, he already had a Europe-wide reputation as the author of five major novels, among them *Child of Pleasure* (*Il piacere*, 1889), *The Victim* (*L'innocente*, 1892), *The Triumph of Death* (*Il trionfo della morte*, 1894), and *The Virgin of the Rocks* (*Le vergini delle rocce*, 1895); several collections of short stories, heavily abridged and anthologized forty years later in the English version *Tales of my*

Native Town (1920); as well as collections of poetry, beginning with the precocious *Spring* (*Primo vere*, 1879), *New Song* (*Canto Novo*, 1882), and *Roman Elegies* (*Elegie romane*, 1888). He continued to write prolifically after his theatrical debut, and other successful novels include *The Flame* (*Il fuoco*, 1904) and *Perhaps So, Perhaps Not* (*Forse che sì forse che no*, 1910), while his poetry reached a peak with the *Praises/Lauds* (*Laudi*, 1904).

D'Annunzio was born on May 12, 1863, in Pescara, ITALY. Between 1895, when he began his eight-year affair with the great Italian actress Eleonora Duse, and 1914, when he turned his talents to military exploits (and propaganda), he composed fourteen tragedies, seventeen of his operatic *Parisina*, the unfinished *Crusade of the Innocents* (*Crociata degli innocenti*), and the silent-film captions of the epic *Cabiria*. He was ambitious, in his new plays (eight of them in verse), to revolutionize what he considered Italy's banal theater, and he was aided by Duse's enthusiasm for novelty and by her considerable fortune, which, while it lasted, paid for lavish productions and guaranteed him a luxurious lifestyle.

The Dead City (*La città morta*), though written in 1895, was his third play to be produced three years later in Paris, starring Sarah Bernhardt. The clever plot, with its many undertones of the Orestes myth, involved the newspaper reports of Heinrich Schliemann's discoveries at Mycenae of a few years earlier, to which D'Annunzio added his reaction to the priceless finds that he had been able to examine in the archaeological museum in Athens. He transferred all these elements to a contemporary archaeological dig at Mycenae, which forms the background to the tragic love story of the four protagonists, Alessandro, Bianca Maria, Leonardo, and Anna, and, ultimately, to the murder of Bianca Maria by her brother Leonardo.

Angry that she had been passed over for her French rival, Eleonora Duse had to be assuaged by her lover with a play written for her alone. In 1897 D'Annunzio dashed off (in just ten days) his *A Spring Morning's Dream* (*Sogno d'un mattino di primavera*), allowing Duse to precede Bernhardt with a first D'Annunzio performance. In the play, set in a Tuscan villa, Giuliano, adulterous lover of Isabella, is murdered by her husband. After hugging Giuliano's body to herself all night, Isabella emerges the next morning drenched in his blood and insane. Her sister Beatrice is in love with Giuliano's brother Virginio, who in turn loves the mad Isabella and, in collaboration with her doctor, impersonates the dead Giuliano in order to shock her out of her insanity. The scheme fails, and desolation settles on all three characters. The play understandably had disappointing receptions in FRANCE and Italy, and in London it was banned by Lord Chamberlain's office.

A second "Dream," his *Dream of an Autumn Sunset* (*Sogno d'un tramonto d'autunno*), written in 1897 but not performed until 1905, had equally grotesque moments. Set near Venice, it shows the aging Dogoressa Gradeniga furthering her affair with an unnamed younger man by killing her husband the Doge, only to see her lover fall into the arms of the courtesan Pantea. She casts a spell on Pantea's ceremonial barge, the *bucintoro*, and her curse is worked out when noble Priamo Gritti and others in rival groups attack the barge and incinerate Pantea and her lovers. The two plays, their titles deliberately echoing William Shakespeare's *Midsummer Night's Dream* and their static qualities akin to the *drames statiques* of MAURICE MAETERLINCK, had been written too quickly, and their themes were too improbable even for an audience desirous of a revolutionary new theater.

Francesca da Rimini, written in 1901 and published the following year, was to have been the first in a trilogy of plays concerning the Malatesta family. (D'Annunzio was given to announcing such literary or dramatic trios; one other Maslatesta drama, *The Parisina* (*La Parisina*), was to be produced in 1913, set to music by Pietro Mascagni.) Adulterous love, a usual feature of D'Annunzio's theater, forms the basis for the *Francesca*, as D'Annunzio takes over from *Inferno*, canto 5, Dante Alighieri's version of Francesca's love for her brother-in-law Paolo. The play concludes when Gianciotto, Francesca's grotesque husband, slays the pair. Sadomasochistic actions of a Swinburnian kind help to complete the plot and add a medieval atmosphere. In 1914 the play was set to music by Riccardo Zandonai, with a libretto by Tito Ricordi, and had generous reviews.

D'Annunzio's best play, *Iorio's Daughter* (*La figlia di Iorio*), was written in 1904. Set in some far-off century, the play exploits the superstitions and primitive behavior of a tribal community in the author's native Abruzzi. Aligi, a shepherd newly betrothed to a village girl, has saved Mila di Codra, Iorio's daughter, from assault (and possibly worse) by a group of drunken farm laborers. Mila's presence in the family home is seen as a profanation, and Aligi, disregarding his vows for the moment, takes off with Mila into the hills, where they lead an apparently sexless existence. When his father Lazaro turns up to have his way with Mila, by then regarded even more as a public woman, Aligi kills him with his sculptor's axe. Condemned to a barbaric death, Aligi is saved when Mila "confesses" that she had bewitched him and that it has been she who had killed Lazaro. She truncates proceedings by leaping into a funeral pyre, and the TRAGEDY ends. Audiences in Italy still regard the play as a reflection of the primitive quality of life in southern villages.

The Light Under the Bushel (*La fiaccola sotto il moggio*), produced in Milan in 1905, further exploited D'Annunzio's knowledge of Abruzzese folklore, at the same time combining modern REALISM with echoes of the classical Clytemnestra-Electra conflict. Angizia, housekeeper of the Sangro castle, has (unknown to all) killed the wife of Tibaldo de Sangro in order to marry him herself. She simultaneously has an affair with Tibaldo's stepbrother Bertrando, planning with him to murder the sickly adolescent Simonetto, heir to the dynasty. Gigliola, Tibaldo's daughter, provokes Angizia into confessing the murder and resolves to kill her and then commit suicide. She plunges her hands into a basket of snakes, intending to murder Angizia before the venom can overcome her. She tells Tibaldo of Angizia's affair with Bertrando, and Tibaldo unknowingly anticipates Gigliola's plans by killing Angizia and then committing suicide himself. Too late, Gigliola discovers this as she dies from the inevitable end she has prepared for herself. As a background, D'Annunzio exploited the local folk cult of serpents, noted centuries before by Virgil and still very much alive in the 21st century.

The Ship (*La nave*) was produced in Rome in 1908 in the presence of the king and queen of Italy, who invited the author to join them in the royal box. The action is set in A.D. 552, when Venice was attempting to assert its independence from the Byzantine Empire. Marco and Sergio Gratico succeed in breaking the power of their imperial rulers by slaughtering the powerful rival Faledro family—only Basiliola, the beautiful daughter of the family, being saved. Through her wiles, she persuades Marco to kill his brother. Desolated by his action, to expiate his sin he decides to take the great ship that is being built in the Venetian dockyard and sail into exile, where he will perform heroic deeds. He arrests Basiliola, and she is about to be nailed to the prow of the ship in lieu of a figurehead when she breaks free and hurls herself into the flames of a nearby altar. The play, one of the most lavish productions ever seen in Italy, was taken to other Italian cities (including the Italian enclave of Fiume/Rijecka in present-day Croatia), where its nationalistic message had profound effects on local populaces.

Driven out of Florence and Italy by his many creditors in 1911, D'Annunzio spent the next four years in self-imposed exile in France. In May of that year, his *The Martyrdom of St. Sebastian* (*Le Martyre de Saint Sébastien*), a "mystery" in five "mansions" with a prologue, was put onstage at the Chatelet theater in Paris. In pagan Rome, Christian twins Marco and Marcellino are about to be put to death for their faith. Sebastian, captain of archers, a covert Christian, strengthens the resolve of the young couple and is in turn condemned to death; after pleas and an initial attempt by his men to save him, he dies. As his body slumps away from the tree to which he is bound, Sebastian is at once taken up into heaven and gathered with the saints in paradise.

In June 1913 D'Annunzio began to exploit the nascent silent cinema, collaborating with Giovanni Pastrone in revising the silent film *Carthage in Flames* (*Cartagine in fiamme*). D'Annunzio changed the title to *Cabiria* and rewrote the captions, using more grandiloquent expressions, typical of his rhetorical prose style. The epic was the precursor of the work of Sergei Eisenstein and D. W. Griffith. It also paid the impecunious D'Annunzio 50,000 lire for his trouble. D'Annunzio died on March 1, 1938, at the Vittoriale, his villa on Lake Garda, Italy.

PLAYS: *The Dead City* (*La città morta*, 1895); *Dream of an Autumn Sunset* (*Sogno d'un tramonto d'autunno*, 1897); *A Spring Morning's Dream* (*Sogno d' un mattino di primavera*, 1897); *La Gioconda* (1899); *Glory* (*La gloria*, 1899); *Francesca da Rimini* (verse, 1902); *Iorio's Daughter* (*La figlia di Iorio*, verse, 1904); *The Light Under the Bushel* (*La fiaccola sotto il moggio*, 1905); *More Than Love* (*Più che l'amore*, 1906); *Phaedra* (*Fedra*, verse, 1908); *The Ship* (*La nave*, verse, 1908); *The Martyrdom of St. Sebastian* (*Le Martyre de Saint Sébastien*, verse, 1911); *The Honeysuckle* (*Le Chèvrefeuille*, 1913); *La Parisina* (verse 1913); *Pisanella or Perfumed Death* (*La Pisanelle ou la Mort parfumée*, verse, 1913); *Cabiria* (1914); *The Crusade of the Innocents* (*La crociata degli innocenti*, verse, 1920, unfinished)

FURTHER READING

Bisicchia, Andrea. *D'Annunzio e il teatro, tra cronaca e letteratura drammatica* [D'Annunzio and the theatre, between current events and dramatic literature]. Milan: Mursia, 1991.

Klopp, Charles. *Gabriele D'Annunzio*. Boston: Twayne, 1988.

Valentini, Valentina. *La tragedia moderna e mediterranea: Sul teatro di Gabriele D'Annunzio* [The modern and Mediterranean tragedy: On the theater of Gabriele D'Annunzio]. Milan: Angeli, 1992.

Woodhouse, John. *Gabriele D'Annunzio, Defiant Archangel*. Oxford: Oxford Univ. Press, 2001.

John Woodhouse

THE DANTON CASE

Inspired by repeated readings of Georg Büchner's *Danton's Death* (1835), STANISŁAWA PRZYBYSZEWSKA undertook a serious study of the French Revolution. Soon she felt more at home in Paris under the Terror than in present-day Danzig. So deeply immersed was she in the tumultuous world of 1794 that she began to date her letters according to the revolutionary calendar and talked of Danton and Maximilien Robespierre as though they were her contemporaries.

Przybyszewska's ability to live intensely in the past was an incomparable strength, but rather than taking the spectators back to 1789, her aim was to bring past events and characters into the present. In *The Danton Case* (*Sprawa Dantona*, 1929), she set out to disclose a new image of the French Revolution, based on contemporary historiography (Albert Mathiez's revisionist rehabilitation of Robespierre) and seen through the lens of 20th-century experience (the Russian Revolution and its lurch toward Stalinist dictatorship).

Przybyszewska created masterful psychological portraits of the contrasting pair of revolutionary leaders, the sensual, charismatic manipulator Danton and the icy, incorruptible Robespierre, once allies but now implacable enemies caught in the revolutionary mechanism that will destroy them both.

By dealing with the same struggle for power between Danton and Robespierre that Büchner had dramatized, Przybyszewska made *The Danton Case* a rejoinder to *Danton's Death*. Her special accomplishment is to render Robespierre human and believable as a brilliant, highly principled statesman attempting to preserve the new Republic. Partly fashioned in her own image, Przybyszewska's Robespierre is a transsexual and suprapersonal genius striving to move in realms of pure thought. Absolute devotion to reason and refusal to compromise cause his alienation and lead to his downfall. The turning point comes in act 4 with Robespierre's tragic recognition that to save the revolution he must destroy it. By institutionalizing the Terror so that the government can survive, he knows he is bringing about his own death and sowing the seeds of dictatorship to be reaped by Napoleon Bonaparte.

In *The Danton Case* Przybyszewska anatomizes with great psychological, moral, and intellectual rigor the historical process that eventually leads to tyranny. Perceiving "revolution as the psychic condition of the twentieth century," Przybyszewska gives her characters a modern sensibility and has them speak a provocative up-to-date language; verbal anachronisms and Soviet-style acronyms emphasize continuity between 1789 and 1917.

Przybyszewska created a musical structure in *The Danton Case*, alternating tempestuous public gatherings with introspective scenes of private life. The dialogue moves easily from racy colloquialism to rhetorical eloquence, while the subtext is psychologically nuanced, rich in dark undercurrents and hidden erotic resonances. Precise, highly visual, and often cinematographic stage directions are addressed as much to readers as to theater practitioners.

Although a truncated version of *The Danton Case* was staged twice in the author's lifetime—in 1931 and 1933—the play had to wait until 1967 to be rediscovered by the Polish theater and launched on its triumphal career. Andrzej Wajda's austere, unadorned staging in 1975 turned the audience into participants in the action, while his post-Solidarity 1983 French film version called *Danton* shifted the balance of sympathy away from Robespierre to Danton.

FURTHER READING

Przybyszewska, Stanisława. *The Danton Case. Thermidor*. Tr. by Bolesław Taborski. Evanston, Ill.: Northwestern Univ. Press, 1989.

Jadwiga Kosicka Gerould

DAPHNE LAUREOLA

JAMES BRIDIE's quixotic 1949 play *Daphne Laureola* features one of his most familiar techniques: the interweaving of the modern and the quotidian with the mythical, the legendary, or the supernatural. In contrast to some of Bridie's other dramas—*The Queen's Comedy* (1950), for example—this play exists wholly in its contemporary and naturalistic settings: but still the mythical resonates. Here a young man's obsession with an older woman in the very contemporary setting of postwar London resonates with the mythical Apollo's obsession with the nymph Daphne, presciently transformed by Gaea into a laurel tree before she could be seduced. In this use of allusion one might see *Daphne Laureola*'s contemporary vernacular and contextual NATURALISM as being edged with the devices of the contemporary poetic drama—and, of course, CHRISTOPHER FRY and T. S. ELIOT are among Bridie's writing contemporaries.

Daphne Laureola premiered at Wyndham's Theatre, London, in 1949. It was directed by Laurence Olivier and featured Edith Evans as Lady Pitts, Felix Aylmer as Sir Joseph, her aging husband, and a youthful Peter Finch as Ernest Piaste, the young Pole lonely and isolated in postwar London and besotted of, and indeed fixated on, Lady Pitts. Evans revived the role for the Broadway premiere in 1950 when she played opposite Cecil Parker, who appeared as Sir Joseph.

Lady Pitts sits, at the very heart of the play's rather elusive and certainly somewhat elliptical narrative, as a challenge to both actress and critic. She is a woman of a certain age who finds herself in a dull marriage to an elderly, crippled, and ill baronet. We first meet her dining alone—and with greater application, drinking alone—in a Soho restaurant. As she becomes more inebriated, she becomes rather loud and indiscrete, attracting the attention of the other diners—an odd mix of choric characters, caricatured spivish low-lifes, boorish businessmen, and a group of energetic young people. At the close of the first act, Lady Pitts invites all the diners to her home, where the second act takes place. Later again Piaste aims to visit Lady Pitts alone, but he is intercepted by Sir Joseph. The latter reveals something of Lady Pitt's past: she was a brilliant scholar whose ambition was constrained by social convention; there was a tragic early marriage, a stalled career, and a dark middle period during which there is the suggestion of sexual indiscretion, as well as mental and physical breakdown. In the course of the conversation, Sir Joseph convinces Piaste that he must abandon all his desires for Lady Pitts. Reluctantly he agrees and leaves. There follows an intimate scene between Sir Joseph and Lady Pitts that ends with his gentle death. The play's fourth act is set several months later but again in the Soho restaurant, and—in a typical Bridie moment—all the same diners from act 1 are reunited. Lady Pitts arrives, and it is revealed that she has married the chauffeur Vincent. Piaste is shocked and even disgusted that his fantasy could be so fallen. Lady Pitts rejects him and his idealization of women in general and her in particular, and the play ends.

The play is part TRAGICOMEDY and part morality tale, but the plot is slight and the narrative allusive rather than direct: it is, according to one contemporary review, a "witty fantasy . . . neither a morality play nor a tragic-comedy but a tour-de-force which combines the flavors of both" (*The Tatler*, 1949). As ever with Bridie, the moral message is disquieting and tinged black.

[*See also* England, 1940–1960]

FURTHER READING

Banister, Winifred. *James Bridie and His Theatre*. London: Rockliff, 1955.
Low, J. T. *Doctors, Devils, Saints and Sinners: A Study of the Major Plays of James Bridie*. Edinburgh: Ramsay Head, 1980.

Luyben, Helen. *James Bridie: Clown and Philosopher.* University Park: Univ. of Pennsylvania Press, 1965.

Mardon, Ernest G. *The Conflict Between the Individual and Society in the Plays of James Bridie.* Glasgow: William MacLellan, 1972.

Mavor, Ronald. *Dr Mavor and Mr Bridie: Memories of James Bridie.* Edinburgh: Canongate, 1990.

Adrienne Scullion

DATTANI, MAHESH (1958–)

Mahesh Dattani, born on August 7, 1958, in Bangalore, INDIA, writes in English for an urban audience. English is dismissed by some in India as a foreign language, but it was one of the country's officially recognized languages until 1992 and is still used by people from different states (who speak different Indian languages) to communicate with one another. It is also used by the upper classes and is studied by those aspiring to be middle class—those for whom knowledge of English opens up a myriad of job possibilities. It is spoken, however, by a very small percentage (some say as small as five percent) of the population, most of whom live in cities. This is Dattani's audience.

English-language theater has for a long time been associated with the colonial enterprise. In the 19th century the British introduced modern theater to the colonial cities of Kolkata and Mumbai by touring productions to entertain their expatriate communities, by supporting amateur productions of English plays staged by the expatriates themselves, and by teaching English drama in Indian universities. From the mid-19th century, urban middle-class Indian intellectuals began to write their own plays in the style of the modern English drama to which they had been exposed, for a growing audience of English-educated Indian merchants and professionals. By the beginning of the 20th century, there existed a thriving middle-class Westernized urban theater. Since independence, plays written in English have stayed on the fringes of the theater scene because they are associated with mindless British drawing-room COMEDY and with an English-speaking elite. Dattani has done a great deal to change this.

Dattani takes as his subject the complicated dynamics of the modern urban family. His characters struggle for some kind of freedom and happiness under the oppressive weight of tradition, cultural constructions of gender, and repressed desire. Dattani is concerned with the "invisible issues" in Indian society. Homosexuality is a taboo subject, but Dattani takes it out of the closet and places it onstage for public viewing and dialogue. Specifically, Dattani deals with the ways in which homophobia destroys lives. *Bravely Fought the Queen* (first performed in 1991) centers around two sisters, one of whom is tricked into marrying the man who is having an affair with her brother in order to provide a cover for their relationship. She escapes by drinking heavily. *Seven Steps Around the Fire* (1999) focuses on the murder of Kamala, a *hijra* (the *hijra* are a community of male eunuchs who, dressed as women, sing and dance at weddings). It turns out Kamala was secretly married to the son of a wealthy government minister. The minister has Kamala killed and quickly arranges a "suitable" marriage for his son, who commits suicide at the wedding.

In other plays such as *Where There's a Will* (1988), *Dance Like a Man* (1989), and *Tara* (1990), Dattani deals with gender inequality. In *Final Solutions* (1993) he deals with communal hatred. In the two plays detailed under separate entries in this volume, THIRTY DAYS IN SEPTEMBER (2001) and ON A MUGGY NIGHT IN MUMBAI (1998), he deals (respectively) with incest and the place of gay culture in Indian society.

Dattani's work has occasionally been dismissed as "not Indian." This is in part because he writes in English, in part because his plays are performed on proscenium stages and retain other traces of Western influence, in part because he focuses on the complicated dynamics of the modern urban family in their domestic environment rather than on rural India, and in part because of the content of his work. "You can talk about feminism," Dattani says, "because in a way that's accepted. But you can't talk about gay issues because that's not India, it doesn't happen here" (quoted in Mee, 1997). In response to self-proclaimed liberals who complain about his subject matter, Dattani quips: "I have yet to meet a homosexual who says 'I have nothing against heterosexuals, but do we have to watch them on stage?' " (Dattani, 2000). Dattani's work claims a place for marginalized people onstage and by extension in society.

Dattani is the first playwright writing in English to be awarded the prestigious Sahitya Akademi award (in 1998) for his contribution to world drama. His plays are performed all over India and have been staged by the well-known directors Alyque Padamsee and Lillette Dubey.

SELECT PLAYS: *Where There's a Will* (1988); *Dance Like a Man* (1989); *Tara* (1990); *Bravely Fought the Queen* (1991); *Final Solutions* (1992); *Night Queen* (1996); *On a Muggy Night in Mumbai* (1998); *30 Days in September* (2001)

FURTHER READING

Dattani, Mahesh. "Of Page and Stage: An Interview with Mahesh Dattani." *Seagull Theatre Quarterly* 24 (December 1999):3–33.

Mee, Erin. "Contemporary Indian Theatre, Three Voices." *Performing Arts Journal* 19, no. 1 (1997):1–26.

Subramanyam, Lakshmi. "A Dialogue with Mahesh Dattani." In *Muffled Voices: Women in Modern Indian Theatre.* Delhi: Shakti Bks., 2002.

Erin B. Mee

THE DAUGHTER IN LAW

Marriage is like a mouse-trap, for either man or woman. You've soon come to th' end o' th' cheese.

—Mrs. Gascoigne, Act 1

Unproduced during the author's lifetime, D. H. LAWRENCE'S *The Daughter-in-Law* reflects the author's sustained interest in naturalistic representations of working-class life and marriage. Acclaimed for its presentation of complex human characters as opposed to JOHN GALSWORTHY'S more one-dimensional "mouthpieces" of working individuals, the play was written in 1912 alongside Lawrence's other so-called colliery plays. Steeped in dense Nottinghamshire dialect, *The Daughter-in-Law* explores tense relationships within a family set against the backdrop of a labor strike. From the start, it is evident that issues of money infuse every aspect of the Gascoigne family's existence. Mrs. Gascoigne resents the "superior airs" of her older son Luther's new wife, Minnie, who has brought a bit of money to the marriage. The situation is aggravated further by the news that Luther has impregnated another woman and that her mother has arrived for fiscal compensation. Initially, Luther and his brother scheme to keep this knowledge from Minnie, but a spousal spat that gathers intensity through act 2 drives Luther to reveal it when Minnie accuses him of being less a man than a "mollycoddled" boy.

Lawrence uses the struggle between husband and wife to illustrate the ways in which class and gender ideology intersect. Minnie subsequently feels responsible for Luther's indiscretion with Bertha, that she has not been enough of a conventional woman for him. Luther sees Minnie's money and upbringing as a threat to his masculinity and is desperate to prove his virility throughout the play, using every opportunity from a casual affair with Bertha to bullying Minnie to joining the labor strike. Although Lawrence satirizes Minnie's aspirations toward gentility with her nearly comic tearful outburst after her brother-in-law breaks a couple of her plates, he is careful to give Minnie complexity and poignancy in her attempts to put her marriage on a more equal footing, including spending her entire savings.

While it is clear that the dysfunctionality of the marriage is largely due to oppositional class affiliations, Minnie accuses Mrs. Gascoigne of dominating her sons and thus making them unable to be husbands because their "real caring" is for her. A resolution occurs at the end of the play when Mrs. Gascoigne softens toward Minnie (who ironically shares her perspective on the strike) and offers the young wife the benefit of her insight about relations with men. After her departure, which seems to mark her letting go of her grown-up son, Minnie steps into the role of mother-wife, as Luther pleads with her to "Ma'e what tha can o' me." Just as the play's first scene depicted mothers in control of domestic life, the final scene shoulders the responsibility for the man, the marriage, and the household squarely on the wife-mother's shoulders. As Luther and Minnie find themselves, in Mrs. Gascoigne's words, "at the end of the cheese" in the mousetrap of their marriage, the ambivalence that characterizes the play's open-ended conclusion is purposeful within Lawrence's commitment to NATURALISM, and he referred to it as "neither a comedy nor a tragedy—just ordinary." The effectiveness of the language and the vivid characterizations as well as the emotional situations have made the play (since its initial staging when it was hailed as a "masterpiece" in the 1960s) increasingly respected and revived.

[*See also* England, 1860–1940]

FURTHER READING

Sklar, Sylvia. *The Plays of D. H. Lawrence: A Biographical and Critical Study*. New York: Barnes & Noble, 1975.

Worthen, John. *D. H. Lawrence: The Early Years, 1885–1912*. Cambridge: Cambridge Univ. Press, 1992.

Christopher Wixson

DAVIES, ROBERTSON (1913–1995)

Best known for his novels and criticism, Robertson Davies has contributed richly to the arts and the humanities. Born in Thamesville, Ontario, on August 28, 1913, Davies was educated at Upper Canada College, Queen's University—which he left without taking a degree—and Balliol College, Oxford, which granted him a B. Litt. for his dissertation on William Shakespeare's boy actors. After he left Oxford, he joined the Old Vic Repertory Company as an actor, also giving lectures in the Old Vic drama school. Upon his return to CANADA at the outbreak of World War II, Davies, the son of a newspaperman, became literary editor of *Saturday Night Magazine* in 1940 and editor of the Peterborough *Examiner* in 1942. He was named first master of Massey College at the University of Toronto in 1961. Throughout this time he wrote essays, drama, and fiction, most notably the Salterton, Deptford, and Cornish trilogies. In 1986, Davies was shortlisted for both the Nobel Prize for Literature and the Booker Prize; although he lost both, the nominations confirmed Davies's international renown. Davies died in Orangeville, Ontario, on December 2, 1995.

Davies's earliest ambitions lay in acting and playwriting, although he never achieved wholesale success in these fields. At first he wrote for the London professional theater, and upon his return to Canada he wrote for amateur little theaters and then for the newly developing Canadian professional theater. Over the course of his career Davies wrote ten full-length plays, five one-act plays, and several masques and occasional pieces; the bulk of this corpus was written between 1944 and 1956. He was most successful during the 1940s and 1950s, winning Dominion Drama Festival awards in 1948 (*Eros at Breakfast*) and 1949 (*Fortune, My Foe*). In *Fortune, My Foe* he explored what was to become a central theme of his drama: Canada's cultural poverty, specifically its philistine attitude toward art. In this play the main character Nicholas must decide whether to abandon his Canadian roots for surer success in the States. In Canada, Nicholas feels "despised because [he] want things from life nobody else seem to miss." Davies's one-act play *Hope Deferred* (1948) also treats the theme of cultural deprivation: here the

Huron woman Chimene must return to FRANCE in order to achieve the artistic fulfillment she cannot find in Frontenac's New France: "My own land does not want me: I shall go where I am wanted." *Hunting Stuart* (1955) evinces Davies's growing interest in Jungian psychology and self-discovery, as does *General Confessions* (1956–1957). Based on Casanova's memoirs and described by Davies as "his best play and [his] favorite," *General Confessions* was never produced. An adaptation for Broadway of his novel *Leaven of Malice*, called *Love and Libel* (1960), closed after a few days.

After *General Confessions*, Davies's career as a dramatist slowed considerably. Many of his interests, in particular the Jungian psychology, were better pursued in novels. Moreover, Davies's "unanxiety of British influence" and preference for dialogue and exposition were out of step with the alternative theater movement sweeping Canada during the 1970s. Davies has been accused of not being Canadian enough; when he did use a Canadian setting, he often pointed out the inhospitableness of Canada's cultural scene. That he did so to enrich Canadian cultural life, and not to encourage flight elsewhere, is perhaps not sufficiently recognized.

SELECT PLAYS: *Overlaid* (1947); *At the Gates of the Righteous* (1948); *Eros at Breakfast* (1948); *Fortune, My Foe* (1948); *Hope Deferred* (1948); *At My Heart's Core* (1950); *King Phoenix* (1950); *The Voice of the People* (1950); *A Jig for the Gypsy* (1954); *Hunting Stuart* (1955); *General Confessions* (written 1956–1957; published 1972); *Love and Libel* (1960); *Pontiac and the Green Man* (1975); *Question Time* (1975)

FURTHER READING

Davies, Robertson. "A Dialogue on the State of Theatre in Canada." In *Canadian Theatre History: Selected Writings*. Ed. by Don Rubin. Toronto: Copp Clark, 1996. 155–175.

Diamond-Nigh, Lynne. *Robertson Davies: Life, Work, and Criticism*. Toronto: York, 1997.

Grant, Judith Skelton. *Robertson Davies: Man of Myth*. Toronto: Viking, 1994.

Mackay, Ellen. "Fantasies of Origin: Staging the Birth of the Canadian Stage." *Canadian Theatre Review* 114 (Spring 2003): 11–15.

Morley, Patricia. *Robertson Davies*. Toronto: Gage Educational, 1977.

Stone-Blackburn, Susan. *Robertson Davies, Playwright: A Search for the Self on the Canadian Stage*. Vancouver: Univ. of British Columbia Press, 1985.

Andrea R. Stevens

DAVIS, JACK (1917–2000)

Jack Davis, born in Perth, Western AUSTRALIA, in 1917, was brought up at the Yarloop and the Moore River Native settlements. He was a member of the Nyoongah Aboriginal community of the southwest of western Australia. Although he died in 2000, Davis remains the most prominent and successful Aboriginal playwright to date. Seven of his eight plays have been published. Davis was awarded the Order of Australia in 1985 and honorary doctorates from both Murdoch University and the University of Western Australia. His play *No Sugar* (1986) was awarded the Australian Writers' Guild Award (AWGIE) for best stage play in 1986. It also represented Australia at the Vancouver Expo in 1986. In *No Sugar*, the difficulties and hardships of life for the Millimurra family on the "Aboriginal Reserve" are addressed.

Davis's plays make important contributions to Australian history as well as to broadening what is meant by Australian drama. His most successful plays include *Kullark* (1982) and a trilogy about the Millimurra family comprising *The Dreamers* (1982), focusing on the interplay between urban hopelessness and the richness of Aboriginal tradition, *No Sugar* (1986), and *Smell the Wind* (*Barungin*, 1989), a more overtly political play, which deals with the failure of "white" justice in terms of land rights and deaths in custody.

Despite the fact that the themes of Davis's work are often bleak, the hardships and difficulties dealt to Aboriginal people, he encourages them to hold on to their cultural knowledge and traditions. *Kullark* centers on the story of the Yorlah family, and through this family tale it also presents the history of the colonization of the Nyoongah people and their attempts to counter white history. *In Our Town* (1992) deals with the segregation of Aboriginal and non-Aboriginal people and the issue of landownership in the period after World War II. Davis has also written two children's plays, *Honey Spot* (1987) and *Moorli and the Leprechaun* (1994). His play *Wahngin Country* (1992) is the only one that remains unpublished.

Davis's plays are multilingual and include Nyoongah words with a glossary at the back of the text, which are used to provide a non-Indigenous audience with some sense of the difficulties of not understanding, suggesting how foreign languages can be imposed on people through colonization. His plays use dream sequences and other staging techniques to link past and present. Davis gently subverts Western REALISM and expands theatrical form to present alternative views of space, time, and history. Despite the often traumatic historical events dramatized in his plays, devices such as humor, dance, song, and Aboriginal imagery are used to temper the political elements of the work and provide a picture of the complexity and richness of Aboriginal culture and the importance of survival in the face of even the most difficult circumstances.

Davis has been an inspiration to many younger Aboriginal playwrights and created alternative versions of history in his drama. His work is important as a historical record, as a challenge to Western realism, and for its sophisticated and innovative use of theatrical language and space.

PLAYS: *The Dreamers* (1982); *Kullark* (1982); *No Sugar* (1986); *Honey Spot* (1987); *Smell the Wind* (*Barungin*, 1989); *In Our Town* (1992); *Wahngin Country* (1992); *Moorli and the Leprechaun* (1994)

FURTHER READING

Dibble, Brian, and Margaret MacIntyre. "Hybridity in Jack Davis's *No Sugar*." *Westerly* 37, no. 4 (Summer 1992): 93–98.

Gilbert, Helen, and Joanne Tompkins. *Post-Colonial Drama: Theory, Practice, Politics*. London: Routledge, 1996.

Narogin, Mudrooroo. *Writing from the Fringe: A Study of Modern Aboriginal Literature*. Melbourne: Hyland House, 1990.

Turcotte, Gerry, ed. *Jack Davis: The Maker of History*. Sydney: Angus & Robertson, 1994.

Helena Grehan

DAVY CROCKETT

Davy Crockett; or, Be Sure You're Right, Then Go Ahead was first produced at the Opera House in Rochester, New York, on September 23, 1872. Written by Frank Hitchcock Murdoch (1843–1872) in collaboration with actor Frank Mayo, the play enjoyed little initial success. Mayo's enthusiasm for the piece, however, was undiminished, so he continued to revise and perform the melodramatic tale of the backwoodsman's wooing of Eleanor Vaughan. Eventually, the play became immensely popular, and Mayo enjoyed two decades of success as the play's eponymous hero.

Murdoch and Mayo's Davy Crockett is a noble and prodigiously able woodsman whose feats of strength and bravery are matched in intensity by his ardent commitment first to his mother and, later, to his sweetheart. The play is set in "a clearing in the forest," where Dame Crockett and her brood live a rough but virtuous life. When the play begins, Davy, having recently shot a bear, returns to the modest cottage with news of the imminent return of his childhood girlfriend. This Little Nell, now Eleanor, soon appears with her recently wounded guardian and fiancé in tow. Davy's ability to dress her guardian's twisted ankle, retrieve Eleanor's broken saddle, and offer down-home hospitality all make a favorable impression on the young lady, who is relieved to find herself back among people who remind her of her dear, departed father.

Davy is instantly smitten with the refined and educated Eleanor, but he is deeply embarrassed when she asks for his assistance in deciphering an ominous warning about her upcoming marriage, and he is forced to admit that he can neither read nor write. Davy, sensing danger ahead for Eleanor, retreats to his hunting lodge in the hills, where, days later, he rescues Eleanor and Neil, her fiancé, from a sudden winter storm. After tending to a delirious Neil, Eleanor reads Sir Walter Scott's ballad "Lochinvar" to Davy, which, he admits, stirs the smoldering fire in his "rough breast" to a blaze. Soon after, the house is surrounded by wolves, and Davy valiantly spends the night keeping the howling beasts at bay by barring the door with his body.

After the dramatic night, Eleanor and Davy resolve to part, but on her wedding day, Davy kidnaps Eleanor, and the two are married by a pastor held at gunpoint in the Crockett's humble cabin. The marriage foils a plot by Neil's uncle to recuperate the debts of Eleanor's guardian by marrying his nephew to the wealthy young woman.

Though the play capitalizes on the late-19th-century popularity of frontier-themed drama, it is more properly a MELODRAMA modeled on "Lochinvar" and James Fenimore Cooper's memorable character Natty Bumppo. Written while Murdoch was an actor with Louisa Lane Drew's Arch Street Theatre in Philadelphia, *Davy Crockett* is the most successful of his four plays; the others were *The Keepers of the Lighthouse Cliff* (date unknown); *Only a Jew* (1873); and *Bohemia, or The Lottery of Art* (1872).

[*See also* United States, 1860–1929]

FURTHER READING

"Frank Hitchcock Murdoch." In *Dictionary of American Biography*. Farmington Hills: Gale Group, 2003.

Hall, Roger A. *Performing the American Frontier, 1870–1906*. Cambridge: Cambridge Univ. Press, 2001.

Murdoch, Frank. *Davy Crockett & Other Plays*. Princeton, N.J.: Princeton Univ. Press, 1940.

Quinn, Arthur Hobson. *A History of the American Drama from the Civil War to the Present Day*. New York: F. S. Crofts, 1936.

Leah R. Shafer

A DAY IN THE DEATH OF JOE EGG

In Peter Nichols's *A Day in the Death of Joe Egg* (1967), the audience watches an evening in the life of Bri, a disillusioned thirty-something teacher, and his forbearing wife Sheila, as they try to care for their severely brain damaged daughter, Josephine, the eponymous "Joe Egg."

Nichols had been writing television plays since the late 1950s when his experiences with his own daughter, also born severely disabled, led him to turn to the theater to dramatize a subject that would never have been acceptable for the small screen. In the course of writing the play, he turned from the naturalistic style of his television plays and discovered his theatrical voice: one hinged on a playful opening up of the stage to embrace and, in Nichols's words, "cast" the audience.

In act 1, Bri and Sheila relate the difficult circumstances of Joe's birth. Originally written as lines to be delivered to other characters, in Nichols's final version the parents confide in and appeal directly to the audience in highly metatheatrical terms ("She is a wonderful woman, my wife. That girl upstairs. In the bedroom, off in the wings, wherever she is"). They invent improbable personae for Joe and act out a series of burlesque music hall sketches portraying their efforts to seek help for her condition. This apparent lightness of touch, which led many observers of earlier performances to incorrectly believe the actors were ad-libbing, is counterpoised by the closure of the act, a transcendental moment when Joe comes skipping onstage, transformed through her mother's imagination into all she might have been.

Act 2 takes place later the same evening, as Sheila returns home from her amateur dramatics rehearsals with Freddie and Pam, who have taken the couple under their wing and want to persuade them to put Joe into a home. Increasingly incensed by this well-meaning but preposterous couple, and by the arrival of his mollycoddling mother, Bri takes Joe outside in the cold where she collapses and is rushed to the hospital. The child survives, but the toll on Bri and Sheila has become clear; their play-acting cannot disguise the rift between them, and the play ends as, unbeknownst to Sheila, Bri walks out on his daughter and his marriage for the last time.

A play about a "vegetable" child, especially devoid of the usual gravitas, initially found little favor among the London theater managers and was unanimously rejected until director Michael Blakemore arranged a short run at Glasgow's Citizens' Theatre in May 1967. Mirroring the reluctance of the theater managers, the Lord Chamberlain's Office, responsible at this time for censoring all new plays, also worried about the appearance of a "spastic" child onstage and stipulated changes before issuing a license (a process dramatized by Nichols in *Blue Murder* [1996]). Subsequently, when the critics rushed to acclaim the work in Glasgow, Albert Finney (who was to play Bri in the first Broadway production of 1968) brought the play to the capital, where it won the Evening Standard Best Play Award, sealing its reputation and launching the theatrical career of its author. The play was filmed by Peter Medak in 1972 and has been performed since throughout the world.

[*See also* England, 1960–1980]

FURTHER READING

Foulkes, Richard. "'The Cure Is Removal of Guilt': Faith, Fidelity and Fertility in the Plays of Peter Nichols." *Modern Drama* 29 (1986): 207–215.

Kerensky, Oleg. *The New British Drama: Fourteen Playwrights Since Osborne and Pinter*. New York: Taplinger, 1979.

Nichols, Peter. *Feeling You're Behind: An Autobiography*. London: Weidenfeld & Nicolson, 1984.

——. "Introduction: Casting the Audience." In *Plays: One*. London: Methuen Drama, 1991.

Taylor, John Russell. *The Second Wave: British Drama of the Sixties*. London: Methuen, 1971.

Jamie Andrews

DAYS OF THE TURBINS

Days of the Turbins (*Dni Turbinykh*) (a.k.a. *The White Guard*) is a play in three acts by MIKHAIL BULGAKOV set in Kiev during the winter of 1918. The play is an adaptation, with significant changes of detail and incident, of Bulgakov's novel *The White Guard* (*Belaya gvardiya*), parts of which had appeared in 1925. It was staged by KONSTANTIN STANISLAVSKY at the MOSCOW ART THEATRE the following year in a cut version that excluded a violent episode in act 2, scene 2, which has still not been restored in some English versions of the play.

The historical background is complicated but reflects Bulgakov's own experience as an inhabitant of the capital of the Ukraine during the period in question. As he noted: "By the reckoning of the Kievans, they had eighteen violent changes of government. . . . I can state accurately that there were fourteen, and moreover I personally experienced ten of them" (Balint, 1976). In the play only one change is enacted, but a second is imminent at the end. At the beginning, the Ukraine is under German occupation as a consequence of the treaty that took Russia out of the 1914–1918 war. A puppet administration is headed by a Ukrainian "Hetman" who, during the course of the play, is ousted by a Ukrainian nationalist force led by Petlyura, who takes advantage of a power vacuum caused by the German decision to withdraw. In the course of resisting Petlyura, the anticommunist Colonel Aleksei Turbin, who really ought to keep his powder dry to fight the real enemy, the Reds, is killed, and his younger brother, the immature Nikolka, badly injured. A Colonel Talberg of the general staff who is married to the Turbins' sister, Yelena, opts to retreat with the Germans, thus unwittingly clearing the way for a fellow officer, Shervinsky, an aspiring opera singer, to flirt with his wife in his absence. Talberg is branded a coward and a traitor, but it emerges toward the end of the play that he is nothing of the kind, as he returns to his wife, vowing, together with another White officer, Studzinsky, who shares some of the dead Aleksei's fanaticism, to continue the fight against the Reds.

In a scene verging on FARCE, Talberg is shown the door by his wife and another rather feckless officer, Myshlavesky, who has a shaky grasp of politics, declaring he is "for the Bolsheviks, but against the communists." He is seconded by Lariosik, an unexpected visitor who appeared at the beginning of the play, having been sent by his mother to stay with his relations and having journeyed by train through the middle of a civil war with little in his suitcase other than underpants and some volumes of ANTON CHEKHOV.

In the play, which mainly takes place behind the "cream curtains" of the Turbin house, reality is revealed to be a combination of comic opera, pantomime, charade, farce, puppet show, circus, and real historical drama. The action partakes of all these modes, but the sense at the end is that the real historical drama is waiting in the wings. Because the production was construed as depicting the White forces too favorably, the play was removed from the Art Theatre's repertoire in 1929. However, by the late 1920s, the Party was inveighing against stereotypical propagandist plays that caricatured the Whites and other class enemies as superficial cardboard cutouts. By representing the forces that opposed Bolshevism in more substantial form, Bulgakov's play seemed to enhance the significance of the Bolshevik victory over them. At least it seemed so to Joseph Stalin, at whose request the play was restored to the Art Theatre's repertory in 1932 and who went to see the production fifteen times.

[*See also* Russia and the Soviet Union]

FURTHER READING

Balint, Judith. "Theatre Checklist No. 11—Mikhail Bulgakov." In *Theatrefacts: International Theatre Reference*, vol 3. London: TQ Publications, 1976.

Bulgakov, Mikhail. *The Days of the Turbins*. Tr. by Robert Daglish. In *Classic Soviet Plays*, ed. by A. Mikhailova. Moscow: Progress Pubs., 1979.

Curtis, J. A. C., ed. and tr. *Manuscripts Don't Burn: Mikhail Bulgakov—A Life in Letters and Diaries*. London: Bloomsbury, 1991.

Smeliansky Anatoly. *Is Comrade Bulgakov Dead? Mikhail Bulgakov at the Moscow Art Theatre*. Tr. by A. Tait. London: Methuen, 1993.

Wright, C. Colin. *Mikhail Bulgakov: Life and Interpretations*. Toronto: Univ. of Toronto Press, 1978.

Nick Worrall

DAYS WITHOUT END: A MODERN MIRACLE PLAY

> *He saw his God as deaf and blind and merciless—a Deity Who returned hate for love and revenged Himself upon those who trusted Him.*
>
> —Loving, Act 1

Written in 1932–1933, staged in Boston in 1933, and published in 1934, *Days Without End* proved to be one of EUGENE O'NEILL's most controversial plays. Critics were sharply divided over the religious content of the work. The Catholic journal *Commonweal* declared that O'Neill had "at last written the play which, in its spiritual content, some of us dared to hope would emerge from the deep conflicts within his poet's soul" (Shipley, 1956). In contrast, Gilbert W. Gabriel called the play "a religious tract clumsily tied to unpicturesque claptrap and most threadbare working" (Shipley, 1956). Some of the critics were clearly shocked by what they took to be O'Neill's return to the Catholicism of his childhood.

O'Neill himself called the work "a modern miracle play." The hero is a man who works his way through atheism, socialism, communism, and anarchism in a search for a faith that might replace Christianity. At the end of the play, however, he prostrates himself at the foot of the cross. *Days Without End* was intended to be the second play in a trilogy devoted to this search, the first play being *Dynamo*. The third play was never written.

O'Neill went about his search for a viable faith in a materialistic age rather methodically, asking himself what was the essence of a belief that could provide comfort for the human soul. In *Days Without End*, he finds this essence in the affirmation of love.

O'Neill expresses the divided soul of the hero John Loving by having him portrayed by two actors, one representing Loving, the cynical, atheistic aspect, and another representing John, the simple, good-hearted soul. At the beginning, Loving is dominant and, bored by John's quaint, old-fashioned attachment to his wife, sees to it that John Loving gets involved in an adulterous affair with the wife of his best friend. John hopes to redeem himself by writing an autobiographical novel about the affair, giving it a happy ending. Loving sneers at the idea, saying that honesty requires him to end the novel tragically.

To prove that he is right, John decides to relate the story to his wife, Elsa. However, she has heard the same story from a friend and quickly comes to the realization that John Loving has in fact been an unfaithful husband. Distraught, she dashes out into a storm, comes down with pneumonia, and is at the point of death.

In despair, John returns to the church of his youth, where the final struggle between John and Loving takes place. Loving tells John that God and love are illusions; there is only hatred and death. John overcomes him, asserting his belief in the lord of love. Loving surrenders to the cross, saying, "Thou hast conquered, Lord." John Loving is now at one with himself. Thereupon comes the news that Elsa will live.

O'Neill insisted that his play was not Catholic propaganda and described it as "a psychological study whose psychological truth would be the same, essentially, if a Buddhist or a Greek Orthodox hero were involved." (Halfmann) But the numerous revisions testified to the author's dissatisfaction with the play.

Most of the critics found *Days Without End* a great disappointment, ridiculing it as reactionary and as essentially dishonest. Even some Catholics denounced it for its favorable treatment of a divorced woman. Nevertheless, the book became a best-seller, and the play had a decent run.

[*See also* Dramatic Cycles]

FURTHER READING

Alexander, Doris. *Eugene O'Neill's Creative Struggle*. University Park: Pennsylvania State Univ. Press, 1992.

Bogard, Travis. *Contour in Time: The Plays of Eugene O'Neill*. New York: Oxford Univ. Press, 1972.

O'Neill, Eugene. *Eugene O'Neill: Comments on the Drama and the Theater*. Ed. by Ulrich Halfmann. Tübingen: Gunter Nan Verlag, 1987.

Scheaffer, Louis. *O'Neill: Son and Artist*. Boston: Little, Brown, 1973.

Shipley, Joseph T. *Guide to Great Plays*. Washington, D.C.: Public Affairs Press, 1956.

Sprinchorn, Evert. "O'Neill's Myth Plays for the God-Forsaken." *Theatre Three*, no. 5 (Fall 1988).

Evert Sprinchorn

DEAD END

The inspiration and epigraph for *Dead End*, SIDNEY KINGSLEY's second and most popular play, came from Thomas Paine: "The contrast of affluence and wretchedness is like dead and living bodies chained together." To dramatize his thesis that poverty deadens the spirit and breeds vice and crime, Kingsley set the 1935 drama at an inevitable point of collision between wealth and despair: a wharf on New York's East River where the rear entrance of a luxurious new apartment building abuts a row of grimy, rotting tenements.

The play's most visible and memorable characters are a gang of six filthy, foul-mouthed urchins who swim in the garbage-strewn water, play marbles, squabble, roast potatoes in tin cans, and harass the swells temporarily forced by a construction project to use their back door. The gang's informal leader is Tommy, a bright kid who, in the aftermath of harassing an apartment boy, stabs the boy's father in the hand and is put in danger of being sent to reform school.

Tommy is one focus of the multistranded plot; the other is Gimpty, a lame out-of-work architect who hangs around the wharf, tries to keep the boys out of trouble, and is in love with Kay, a kept woman who lives in the apartment building and eventually chooses the security of her sugar daddy over Gimpty's integrity. Himself a native of the slums, Gimpty encounters Baby-Face Martin, a childhood acquaintance turned vicious gangster. Martin has returned to the old neighborhood to see his mother, who bitterly rejects him, and his old girlfriend, who has become a diseased whore. In the end, Gimpty betrays Martin to the FBI and uses the reward money to help Tommy's labor-activist sister Drina hire the boy a lawyer.

The faint optimism of the ending notwithstanding, *Dead End* hammers home its deterministic message: given their environment, these slum kids are Baby-Face Martins in the making. Its language, which now can sound quaint because of its period slang, was shocking to some, but in fact it is the playwright's raw verisimilitude of speech and behavior, together with his evident compassion, that make *Dead End* work. Reviewing the premiere at Broadway's Belasco Theatre on October 28, critics noted the script's evident flaws, notably the cardboard texture of all the adult relationships, but mostly acclaimed the sprawling play as a whole; Whitney Bolton of the *Morning Telegraph* spoke for the majority in calling it "a thing of beautiful strength, of ferocity, contempt and possessed of a rolling, cumulative force" (Couch, 1995).

The production, directed by the playwright on a spectacular set by Normal Bel Geddes, received even greater applause. *Dead End* had 687 Broadway performances, which would be Kingsley's longest run, and ignited fierce debate about slum conditions. Eleanor Roosevelt saw it three times; contributions to the Boys Clubs of America tripled in its wake; and Senator Robert Wagner credited it with inspiring the first slum-clearance legislation introduced in the U.S. Congress.

The movie version starred Humphrey Bogart and the child actors from the Broadway production, who became so popular that they eventually appeared in more than eighty films as the "Dead End Kids."

[*See also* United States, 1929–1940]

FURTHER READING

Couch, Nena, ed. Sidney Kingsley: Five Prizewinning Plays, Columbus, Ohio: Ohio State Univ. Press, 1995.

MacNicholas, John, ed. Dictionary of Literary Biography, Vol. 7: Twentieth-Century American Dramatists. Detroit: Gale Research Co., 1996.

Clifford A. Ridley

DEAR BRUTUS

J. M. BARRIE's *Dear Brutus* gathers together an assortment of mainly unhappy characters to be guests of the strange elfin Lob at what a *Boston Herald* reviewer of the COMEDY called an "abnormal house party." After a first act in which the characters begin to reveal themselves as they try to figure out why they were invited, they are let loose in act 2 into a magic wood where they live out, on Midsummer Eve, their might-have-been fantasies. What they discover is that, in this imaginary place where they are given a second chance, they end up making the same mistakes they made in life. As one of the guests, the philanderer Purdie, says when the third act brings them together again in Lob's country house, "I feel there is something in me that will make me go on being the same ass, however many chances I get."

The Shakespeare allusions in *Dear Brutus* are ubiquitous. Lob is a present-day Puck, but the enchanted wood that springs up on Midsummer Eve outside his country house is associated with not only the wood in *A Midsummer Night's Dream* but also with the forest of Arden. Despite the title's suggestion, there is no Brutus in the cast of characters. The "Dear Brutus" of the title is Barrie's term for his "dear audience," but it also is meant to remind the viewer of the line from William Shakespeare's *Julius Caesar*, "The fault, dear Brutus, is not in our stars, / But in ourselves, that we are underlings." Indeed, the play dismisses the idea that some impersonal fate controls people's lives, demonstrating that it is character that determines choices.

But the play goes beyond showing its audience that while they might desire a second chance in life, it probably would not make any difference. According to a letter that he had an actor read to the audience in 1919 during the play's New York run, Barrie thought of the play as an allegory. He saw the childless painter Dearth as John Bull and the might-have-been daughter Margaret he meets in the wood as America; the two are given a "second opportunity" when they meet on the battlefields of FRANCE.

The play was regarded as a "triumphant success" in London, where it was first performed at Wyndham's Theatre on October 17, 1917, running for 365 performances. A few critics expressed delight that, with *Dear Brutus*, Barrie had left behind him the writing of war plays and had staged what some thought his best play. American reviewers called the comedy "whimsical" and "elfish." Those who disliked the play criticized its episodic action and its "interminable dialogue." Indeed, although PETER PAN had already set a new record in New York in 1905 for longest run, Barrie himself worried that *Dear Brutus* was too fantastic to be successful in New York, fears that proved to be unfounded. Barrie's talent at representing children convincingly is evident in the acclaim that greeted the powerful scene in act 2 where Dearth meets Margaret, the only promising encounter that takes place in the enchanted forest.

[*See also* England, 1860–1940]

FURTHER READING

Dunbar, Janet. *J. M. Barrie: The Man Behind the Image*. Boston: Houghton, 1970.

Mackail, Denis. *Barrie: The Story of J. M. B.* New York: Scribner's, 1941.

Wullschlager, Jackie. *Inventing Wonderland*. New York: Free Press, 1995.

Elaine Brousseau

DEATH AND THE MAIDEN

In Chilean poet, author, and playwright ARIEL DORFMAN's most celebrated work, *Death and the Maiden*, a woman named Paulina kidnaps and interrogates a stranger she suspects of having raped and tortured her fifteen years before. Paulina's only proof that Dr. Roberto Miranda is the man who abused her during the country's recent military regime is his voice, his smell, his vocabulary, and his love for Franz Schubert's *Death and the Maiden*, a piece of music that the doctor played while torturing her. Her husband Gerardo, a recent appointee to a commission investigating human rights violations, is forced to witness the impromptu interrogation; his skepticism and doubt about Paulina's claims and violent methodology to achieve justice reflects the ambiguity that faces the audience.

Set in a country where a democratic government is in the process of rebuilding after years of dictatorship, *Death and the Maiden* is Dorfman's response to the tremendous real-world violence that occurred during General Augusto Pinochet's dictatorship in Chile. This play asks a series of questions (and leaves them all unanswered) of both its characters and its audience. Is Miranda really the doctor who abused Paulina? Does Paulina's quest for revenge make her any less of a monster than her tormenters? How do we understand and punish crimes against humanity? Toward the end of the play, Paulina says, "I can only forgive someone who really repents, who stands up amongst those he has wronged and says, I did this, I did it, and I'll never do it again." *Death and the Maiden* imagines a world where the marginalized finally have an opportunity to tell their stories and demand justice and where a wounded country can begin to heal.

An early workshop production in Santiago, Chile, in March 1991 was not widely appreciated, perhaps because of a lack of critical distance; Chileans in a new, struggling democracy may have found that the play created more moral, ethical, and philosophical problems than it solved. *Death and the Maiden*'s world premiere at the Royal Court Upstairs in London on July 9, 1991, was highly acclaimed, however, and the play transferred to the Mainstage at the Royal Court Theatre only a few months later. Over the next few years it became one of the most popular plays in Europe, in part because its political sensibilities (the need to discover truth and move toward reconciliation) were so applicable to other contemporary events going on in Eastern Europe, the Persian Gulf, SOUTH AFRICA, and Northern IRELAND. *Death and the Maiden* opened at the Brooks Atkinson Theatre in New York on March 17, 1992, with Glenn Close, Richard Dreyfuss, and Gene Hackman. Mike Nichols's direction of this Broadway production was highly criticized, and the production was plagued with Equity disputes and protests by the Hispanic Organization of Latin Actors because of its lack of racial diversity in the cast. What success the New York production did enjoy was largely attributed to the name recognition of its stars, but it did ensure there was enough interest for a 1994 film version, which was directed by Roman Polanski and starred Sigourney Weaver, Stuart Wilson, and Ben Kingsley.

FURTHER READING

Barsky, Robert F. "Outsider Law in Literature: Construction and Representation in *Death and the Maiden*." *Substance: A Review of Theory and Literary Criticism* 26, no. 3 (1997): 53–65.

Crnkvoic, Gordana. "Film Review: *Death and the Maiden*." Film Quarterly 50, no. 3 (1997): 39–45.

Gregory, Stephen. "Ariel Dorfman and Harold Pinter: Politics of the Periphery and Theater of the Metropolis." *Comparative Drama* 30, no. 3 (1996): 325–345.

Morace, Robert A. "The Life and Times of *Death and the Maiden*." *Texas Studies in Literature and Language* 42, no. 2 (2000): 135–153.

Zachary A. Dorsey

DEATH OF A SALESMAN

ARTHUR MILLER's *Death of a Salesman* opened at the Morosco Theatre in New York on February 10, 1949, and ran for 742 performances. For the most part, the newspaper reviews were extremely positive. The play won the Pulitzer Prize and the New York Drama Critics' Circle Award. It quickly became and has remained one of the most successful and best American plays. It became a standard text in colleges and high schools and is almost constantly in production in some corner of the world (Miller directed it in Beijing, CHINA, in 1983). There have been sound recordings of the play, movie versions, and radio and television productions.

Shortly after the play was produced, it stirred up an academic brouhaha about whether or not it was a TRAGEDY. A failed salesman named Willy Loman (low-man as some critics liked to point out) was hardly a tragic figure in the Aristotelian sense, certainly not a hero who had fallen from an exalted place. Miller, who threw himself into the fray in several essays, said in "Tragedy and the Common Man," (Miller, 1978) written for the *New York Times* shortly after the play opened, "It is time, I think, that we who are without kings, took up this bright thread of our history and followed it to the only place it can possibly lead in our time—the heart and spirit of the average man." Willy Loman would not have liked that "average man," for as he said in his last big scene with his son Biff, "I am not a dime a dozen! I am Willy Loman, and you are Biff Loman!" Against all the evidence of his life, Willy continues to see the efficacy of those names as some people, unfortunately, think that a play gains or loses its substance according to whether or not it wears the label *tragedy*. Whatever generic sign one hangs on it, *Death of a Salesman* is a remarkable work of art because it is a richly textured account of a man at the end of his rope, drowning but still trying desperately to keep afloat, and that man, Willy Loman, is the most complex, exasperating, moving character in the Miller canon.

What the play offers us is the final disintegration of a man who has never even approached his idea of what he ought to have been. There are three father figures that suggest paths that Willy might have taken: his father, an itinerant flute-maker who walked off and left his family, represented in the play by haunting flute music (by Alex North in the original production); his adventurous robber baron of a brother ("Why, boys, when I was seventeen I walked into the jungle, and when I was twenty-one I walked out. And by God I was rich"); and Dave Singleman, the old salesman who at eighty-four could, through the strength of his personality, sit in a hotel room and command buyers. He imagines he takes Singleman's way, but he is closer to the conventional traveling salesman, the overeager man with a joke on his lips, incapable of reaching or recognizing the conflict in his twin ambitions—to be rich and to be well liked. It becomes obvious in the course of the play that, from the beginning, Willy has lied to himself, to his wife Linda, to his sons about the size of his sales and the number of friends he has in the business.

The working title of the play was "The Inside of His Head," which is where the play takes place—the immediate events, the evocations of the past, the fantasy memories. "There are no flashbacks in this play," Miller says in the introduction to *Collected Plays*, "but only a mobile concurrency of past and present" (Miller, 1978). The time is always now, and the crisis in racing toward the final, fatal end. His situation is exacerbated by his conflict with Biff, who refuses to accept Willy's belief that success in America is both possible and desirable ("He had the wrong dreams"). When the father and son reconcile in their final scene together, which ends in a pained and loving embrace, Willy goes to his suicide's death, his dreams still intact, for Biff now, not for himself. The final irony of the Requiem with which the play ends is that Biff, who believes that he has seen through Willy's and society's false dreams of success ("I know who I am, kid"), is still one of the lying Lomans, and his inheritance from his father is not the insurance money but the family's talent for self-delusion.

[*See also* United States, 1940–Present]

FURTHER READING

Centola, Steven R., ed. *The Achievement of Arthur Miller, New Essays.* Dallas: Contemporary Res. Press, 1995.

Miller, Arthur. *Death of a Salesman, Text and Criticism.* Ed. by Gerald Weales. 1977. New York: Penguin, 1996.

——. *The Theater Essays of Arthur Miller.* Ed. by Robert A. Martin. New York: Viking, 1978.

——. *Timebends, a Life.* New York: Grove, 1987.

Gerald Weales

DECONSTRUCTION

"They give birth astride of a grave"—with this declaration from WAITING FOR GODOT (1949), SAMUEL BECKETT not only eliminates the either/or dynamic from birth/life/death but offers an apt starting point to discuss deconstruction. As a form of philosophical and literary analysis built on the work of FRIEDRICH NIETZSCHE and Martin Heidegger, deconstruction was spawned by French philosopher Jacques Derrida in the late 1960s. While Derrida bristles at the notion of a singular definition, it is less a tangible methodology than a strategy of reading that actively pursues this type of Beckettian conjunction. As Barbara Johnson (1987) points out, Derrida's approach is conditioned by the fact that his writing "is always explicitly inscribed in the margins of some preexisting text" and that he is "first and foremost a reader who constantly reflects on and transforms the very nature of the act of reading."

Deconstruction is essentially a parasitic enterprise in which one needs something—a text, a philosophic premise, a work of art, a play, a performance—to deconstruct. This process brings nothing to the reading that is not already contained within the host subject. Since deconstruction acknowledges that texts are an intertextual weaving of other texts and that a singular stable meaning is ultimately impossible, there are always more interpretations than initially appear. Deconstruction, then, is a form of intellectual jujitsu that operates by concentrating on blind spots and contradictions within a given text.

This counterlogic is often employed to address a text's generally unquestioned binary oppositions (presence/absence, speech/writing, center/margin) in which one idea is always privileged by its negative opposition to the other. However, while the notion of absence may appear as the lack of presence, presence, a term so integral to performance, is contingent on the idea of absence to assert its presence. Signification, therefore, is a play of differences in which closure on a specific idea is suspended since meaning is inevitably deferred to its "opposite" (this is something that Derrida calls *différance*). Binary oppositions are constructed not on independent terms but, like Beckett's birth/life/death, on interlocked ideas fully dependent on each other. In exploring such dizzying logic, deconstruction does not seek to overturn the binary but to destabilize the entire notion of binaries and hierarchies by focusing on the tension or play between ideas. Creating open-ended dramatic structures, GERTRUDE STEIN, LUIGI PIRANDELLO, Beckett, and fellow absurdists EUGÈNE IONESCO and JEAN GENET clearly anticipate Derrida's deconstructive logic.

As an analytical tool employed by such theater critics as Elinor Fuchs, Herbert Blau, Gerald Rabkin, and Phillip Auslander, this process of reading focuses on the moment at which a text or performance begins to transgress its own laws. Explicating the deconstructive impulse in the work of ANTONIN ARTAUD, HEINER MÜLLER, ADRIENNE KENNEDY, BERTOLT BRECHT, RICHARD FOREMAN, and The Wooster Group, these critics establish a firm basis for deconstructive readings and performance strategies. By disrupting the assumed stability of dramatic and performance texts, deconstruction works to subvert from within the logic of the text that in a more traditional approach remains hidden.

[*See also* Philosophy and Drama]

FURTHER READING

Culler, Jonathan. *On Deconstruction*. Ithaca, N.Y.: Cornell Univ. Press, 1982.

Derrida, Jacques. *Writing and Difference*. Chicago: Univ. of Chicago Press, 1978.

Fuchs, Elinor. "Presence and the Revenge of Writing: Re-thinking Theatre After Derrida." *Performing Arts Journal* 9, nos. 2–3 (1985): 163–173.

Johnson, Barbara. *A World of Difference*. Baltimore: Johns Hopkins Univ. Press, 1987.

Norris, Christopher. *Deconstruction Theory and Practice*. New York: Routledge, 1982.

Rabkin, Gerald. "The Play of Misreading: Text/Theatre/Deconstruction." *Performing Arts Journal* 7, no. 1 (1983): 44–60.

Dean Wilcox

THE DEEP BLUE SEA

The Deep Blue Sea is the most intensely personal of TERENCE RATTIGAN's dramas, for he based it on the suicide of one of his former lovers, actor Kenneth Morgan, a man he had loved passionately but who had left Rattigan for an unhappy affair with another actor. When originally conceived, the play opened upon the corpse of a suicide, but in keeping with Rattigan's consistent commitment to life in the face of TRAGEDY, Rattigan instead soon transformed death into life, spinning the action of the play from the perhaps more challenging consequences of survival. In some ways the action of the play is a reflection on what might have happened had Kenneth Morgan survived. The drama was first produced at the Duchess Theatre on March 6, 1952. It was directed by Frith Banbury and starred Peggy Ashcroft, Kenneth More, Roland Culver, and Peter Illing. The show ran for 513 performances.

The Deep Blue Sea is a meditation on the soul-decimating consequences of obsessive passion. Set in post–World War II London, the play opens with Hester Collyer's landlords' discovery of her attempted suicide. As the action progresses, we learn that she has left her husband, a successful judge, for a young former Royal Air Force pilot, who has now forgotten to come home for her birthday dinner. Her husband, alerted to her circumstances by the landlords, pleads with her to return to him, but she refuses. While her passion for Freddie Page has driven her to desperate measures, she cannot turn away from it. When Freddie returns from the drinking binge that has kept him away from his lover, he determines that their relationship is far too destructive to both of them and decides to leave Hester for good. As the play closes, Hester once again turns to the gas meter that was to be her escape, but Mr. Miller, an upstairs tenant who treated Hester after her first attempt, steps in and persuades her to continue to live even without hope. This time she lights the gas fire.

When first approached to play the role of Hester Collyer, Peggy Ashcroft turned it down, claiming that if she disliked Hester, the audiences would be certain to despise the character. The role has since become, like Blanche DuBois or Mary Tyrone, one of the tests from 20th-century drama of the ability of a great actress. When the play opened in London, critics hailed Rattigan as the leading playwright of his time. The only adverse criticism came from Kenneth Tynan of the *Evening Standard*, who argued that Rattigan should have allowed his heroine to die at the end of the play. As so often for Rattigan's plays in New York, however, the play received only a lukewarm reception when it starred Margaret Sullavan in the leading role.

The Deep Blue Sea was adapted for the screen in 1955, starring Vivien Leigh as Hester Collyer and directed by Anatole Litvak. It has recently experienced an increase in artistic interest, receiving numerous productions at major theaters on both sides of the Atlantic.

[*See also* England, 1940–1960]

FURTHER READING

Rusinko, Susan. *Terence Rattigan*. Twayne's English Author Series 366. Boston: Twayne, 1983.

Wansell, Geoffrey. *Terence Rattigan*. London: Fourth Estate, 1995.

Young, B. A. *The Rattigan Version: The Theatre of Character*. New York: Atheneum, 1988.

Antonia Sophia Krueger

DE FILIPPO, EDUARDO (1900–1984)

The political, social, and cultural transformation of ITALY in the 20th century has its best expression in the works of a man who lived it and spoke passionately of it in the context of his theater. For Eduardo De Filippo, actor-author-director, theater was life and life was theater. De Filippo was the actor-son of an actor-father, born on May 24, 1900, to Eduardo Scarpetta, leader of a theater company, and Luisa De Filippo, niece of Scarpetta's legal wife.

The ten-year apprenticeship with Scarpetta, whom the son viewed as the greatest Neapolitan actor-author-director of the period, was fundamental in shaping the style of Eduardo's comic vein, inherited from the traditions of the Neapolitan variety show. Scarpetta, in attempting to reflect societal change, had renovated the Neapolitan COMEDY by making bourgeois some of the plebeian stock comic characters of his teacher, the actor-author Petito. Following in his father's footsteps, Eduardo, who worked for Scarpetta until 1928, started to modify the one-act plays of his family company because of his dissatisfaction with the themes he was bringing to the stage.

Some of the changes Eduardo made were the result of personal experience. He had left home at age eleven and for four years had worked for other theater companies that were experimenting with new genres in the form of musicless MELODRAMAS that would alternate with the familiar comedy routine. He was also influenced by new voices such as that of the Neapolitan poet Salvatore Di Giacomo, who was promoting a dramatic theater beyond the borders of Naples, and that of LUIGI PIRANDELLO, with whom he collaborated later on, whose work reflected the crisis of modern man in search of an identity but unable to communicate.

Eduardo found himself caught between tradition and innovation, past and present, regional and national. He knew that his father's formula of FARCE and caricatures was too narrow to reflect the array of social problems faced by contemporary man, yet he could not resist the temptation of making the public laugh, given that such a trait was an integral part of his heredity.

Ultimately he did not betray his father's work but rather used the familiar path of tradition to create a new language for a national theater in which the color of dialect becomes the most personal way to express human emotions.

In 1920 Eduardo went to Rome to serve in the military, and there he organized shows for the troops and began his career as an author by writing his first one-act play, *Pharmacy on a Rotating Shift* (*Farmacia di turno*).

Eduardo's second play, *Man and Gentleman* (*Uomo e galantuomo*, 1922), best reflects the social transformation of the times in the form of a new manipulation of the Pirandellian themes of "madness" as a tragic condition and of the "theater within the theater," in which the actor-protagonist lives his predicament.

However, in Eduardo's hands, the Pirandellian lesson takes a different turn.

If for Pirandello madness was a conceptualization played to uncover the despair of man, seeking truth in vain, in Eduardo it becomes a powerful dramatic instrument used to the extreme to produce pure stage play with comical effects in the Scarpettian tradition. At the same time it is intended to bring about a moralistic awareness of class differences.

Gennaro, the protagonist of *Man and Gentleman*, is the first of many characters in Eduardo's plays to represent the predicament of an actor's life. While in Pirandello the "theater within the theater" takes on philosophical undertones, in Eduardo things are more personal. He plunges into fiction to tell of a tortured reality that he himself lives daily and brings to the stage as a sign of his own *diversità* (difference), as he, actor-author, mixes the life of the stage and his own life.

Eduardo continues to explore the same themes in his next two plays. *Tell Him Always Yes* (*Ditegli sempre di si*, 1927) deals with the ambiguity of language, and *Sik Sik, the Magician* (*Sik Sik, l'artefice magico*, 1929) is a dramatic farce that touches again on the subject of the actor, but this time against a background of magic illusion.

The name Sik Sik (*secco secco* [thin thin] in Neapolitan) came to Peppino, Eduardo's brother, as he was watching the emaciated Eduardo play the role of the magician, a role with which Eduardo completely identified, as Sik Sik was the prototype of the actor-protagonist who reflects the difficulty and precariousness of being on the stage but who at the same time derives from his art his reason for being.

The success of the play led Eduardo, Peppino, and their sister, Titina, to form their own theater company, the Teatro Umoristico I De Filippo, whose first production was Eduardo's *Christmas in Naples* (*Natale in casa Cupiello*, 1931). Performed originally in one act, the first act later become the second one, and eventually the work developed into a three-act play.

Luca Cupiello lives in his own childlike reality, represented metaphorically by the Christmas crèche with its message of goodness and family values. Luca, however, stands in contrast to his family, who rejects his myth. When he is forced to face the external world through the discovery of his daughter's adultery, Luca, unable to confront that reality, succumbs to it. He falls ill and, ironically, after having united his daughter with her lover, taking him for his son-in-law, dies with a vision of a crèche larger than life in which order is restored and good triumphs over evil.

Christmas in Naples is the first play in which farcical representation becomes secondary to an ironic device of contrast between the protagonist and the other characters, as the drama of solitude and misunderstanding unfolds to reveal human suffering.

In 1944 Eduardo dissolved his company because of a traumatic break with Peppino, whose dreams of reforming the Neapolitan comedy contrasted with Eduardo's views of nationalizing his own theater. One year later the Teatro di Eduardo opened with *Naples Gets Rich* (*Napoli milionaria*, 1945), a play that shows the tragedies of postwar realities through a choral depiction of Naples, which is transformed into a stage on which the physical and moral destruction of a country and its people is played out.

Naples Gets Rich is the turning point for Eduardo's theater. The author-actor, faced with the ugliness of historical events, abandons farce as a genre, choosing instead to stress the dramatic conflicts between the individual-protagonist and the others-antagonists, using humor to denounce corruption, social hypocrisy, and conceit. Eduardo's later publication of his plays as theatrical novels, *The Song of the Odd Days* (*La cantata dei giorni dispari*) that includes plays from 1945 to 1973, and *The Song of the Even Days* (*La cantata dei giorni pari*) that includes plays from 1920 to 1944, confirms the author's awareness of his theatrical evolution from the "even" days of joy and laughter to the more contemporary "odd" days of anguish and strife.

Filumena (1946) is perhaps Eduardo's most famous play, written for Titina to compensate for the predominance of male protagonists in his other plays. Filumena, upon learning that her companion of twenty-five years has decided to marry a younger woman, pretends to be dying in order to persuade him to marry her instead. She succeeds, but when he wants to annul the marriage, she reveals to him that he is the father of one of her three sons.

Filumena's different roles in society, from prostitute to mother to wife, reveal a story of sacrifice and suffering, a story in which authentic values are never compromised. In *Filumena* Eduardo forges a new language that becomes his personal style, where experimentation with Neapolitan dialect and standard Italian brings about a poetic discourse as the former, belonging always to the protagonist, is contrasted with the latter, more prosaic, pertaining to the antagonists.

In *Those Damned Ghosts* (*Questi fantasmi*, 1946), *Grand Magic* (*La grande magia*, 1948), and *Inner Voices* (*Le voci di dentro*, 1948), Eduardo moves from the realistic theater to the fantastic one. Reality and illusion are juxtaposed amid the theme of the failure of human beings to understand one another. He extends this leitmotif to the microcosm of the family in *My Family* (*Mia famiglia*, 1955), *De Pretore Vincenzo* (*De Pretore Vincenzo*, 1957), and *Saturday Sunday and Monday* (*Sabato Domenica e Lunedi*, 1958), in which the economic boom has destroyed old values in favor of superficial gratification. Mirroring contemporary society, Eduardo explores topics such as the relationship between the old generation and the new in *The Son of Punchinello* (*Il figlio di Pulcinella*, 1958), and social injustice in *The Local Authority* (*Il sindaco del rione*, 1960).

Eduardo's last play, *The Exams Never End* (*Gli esami non finiscono mai*, 1973), is the summary of a man's life, which he recounts to his audience using the device of a fake bear that he changes three times to indicate the various stages of his life. When the man dies, his body, dressed in gala clothing, is his last word, acted in silence as he participates in his own funeral. This serves as contrast to the "fake" grief of the other participants and also as a denunciation of their hypocrisies.

Eduardo, who always chose to represent his times, also chose to conclude his work with silence. From loud farce to comedy in dialect to neorealism and ultimately to the drama of the modern world, no other playwright in Italy has succeeded as he has in bringing to the theater the humanity of the word acted on stage, dressed in Neapolitan clothing, to be sure, but universal nevertheless. Eduardo De Filippo died in 1984.

SELECT PLAYS: *Man and Gentleman* (*Uomo e galantuomo*, 1922); *Tell Him Always Yes* (*Ditegli sempre di si*, 1927); *Sik, Sik, the Magician* (*Sik, Sik, l'artefice magico*, 1929); *Christmas in Naples* (*Natale in casa Cupiello*, 1931); *Naples Gets Rich* (*Napoli milionaria*, 1945); *Filumena* (1946); *Those Damned Ghosts* (*Questi fantasmi*, 1946); *Grand Magic* (*La grande magia*, 1948); *Inner Voices* (*Le voci di dentro*, 1948); *My Family* (*Mia famiglia*, 1955); *De Pretore Vincenzo* (*De Pretore Vincenzo*, 1957); *Saturday Sunday and Monday* (*Sabato Domenica e Lunedi*, 1958); *The Son of Punchinello* (*Il figlio di Pulcinella*, 1958); *The Local Authority* (*It sindaco del rione*, 1960); *The Exams Never End* (*Gli esami non finiscono mai*, 1973)

FURTHER READING

Ciolli, Marco. *Theater of Eduardo De Filippo: An Introductory Study*. New York: Vantage, 1993.

Mignone, Mario. *Eduardo De Filippo*. Boston: Twayne, 1984.

Annalisa Sacca

DE GROEN, ALMA (1941–)

Alma De Groen, born in Foxton, NEW ZEALAND, on September 5, 1941, is one of AUSTRALIA's most produced playwrights who has won awards in CANADA and Australia. Her drama is known for its explorations of large concepts, in particular, the dilemmas facing women in the present, and insightful warnings about social trends through depictions of totalitarian futures. De Groen's daughter was two when she wrote a nonrealistic drama, *The Joss Adams Show* (produced 1970), about the delusions of postnatal depression. Her plays include: *The After-life of Arthur Cravan* (produced 1973), about a historical personality and self-invention; two realistic dramas, *Perfectly All Right* (1977) and *Going Home* (1977), depicting the problems facing women in domestic spaces and relationships; and *Chidley* (produced 1976), about a public health reformer. De Groen's best-known COMEDY is *Vocations* (1983), which is centered on a friendship between a writer, Joy, and an actress, Vicki, as Joy and Godfrey's marriage ends and Vicki meets her boyfriend biologist Ross and becomes pregnant. There are no straightforward resolutions when Ross will not accept that Vicki wants a career before motherhood, and Joy becomes an independent woman through circumstances.

De Groen's play *The Rivers of China* (1988) broke new ground, with both its exploration of form and content. Winner of the 1988 Premiers' Literary Awards for Drama, in New South Wales and in Victoria, this is an enduring play and studied widely. The play has two time sequences: a future where females dominate and men are subservient; and the 1920s world of the writer

Katherine Mansfield in the last years of her life and her meetings with spiritual philosopher (and possible charlatan) Gurdjieff. In the future sequences, Rahel is a doctor trying to save a suicidal character called Man, hypnotizing him to have Mansfield's memory in a gender reversal twist. *The Girl Who Saw Everything* (1993) is about a feminist historian who writes about biological determinism and who, with her husband, witnesses a fatal accident. It won the 1993 Australian Writers Guild award for best stage play. De Groen's radio plays are *Available Light* (1993) and *Invisible Sun* (produced 1997). *Woman in the Window* (1999) is a beautifully evocative play that returns to De Groen's concern with trends in society. It juxtaposes the world of poet Anna Akhmatova and her struggle to preserve her poetry from the Russian Stalinist secret police controlling her life, with a futurist, technologically advanced setting in Australia where books have been banished and women are in a subservient social position.

De Groen's play *Wicked Sisters* (2002) confirms her versatile use of form. This clever realist comedy presents four middle-aged, longtime women friends who meet after the death of Meridee's husband, a scientist who developed Alzheimer's in his last years. The revelations of the women's connections to him encompass the cultural schism between empathy and rationality in a clear synthesis of complex intellectual ideas that typify De Groen drama.

SELECT PLAYS: *The Joss Adams Show* (1970); *The After-life of Arthur Cravan* (1973); *Chidley* (1976); *Going Home* (1977); *Perfectly All Right* (1977); *Vocations* (1983); *The Rivers of China* (1988); *Available Light* (1993); *The Girl Who Saw Everything* (1993); *Invisible Sun* (1997); *Wicked Sisters* (2002)

FURTHER READING

Palmer, Jennifer, ed. *Contemporary Australian Playwrights*. Adelaide: Adelaide Univ. Press, 1979.

Perkins, Elizabeth. *The Plays of Alma De Groen*. Amsterdam: Rodopi, 1994.

Peta Tait

DELANEY, SHELAGH (1939–)

Shelagh Delaney, born in 1939 in Salford, Lancashire, in northern ENGLAND, wrote her first play script, *A Taste of Honey*, at the age of nineteen. The play, set in her tough and grimy working-class neighborhood of Salford, quickly gained popularity for its truthful representation of the desperate lives of people who struggle against the formidable barriers of poverty, illiteracy, race, and gender. The innovative British director Joan Littlewood, who had produced BRENDAN BEHAN and other emerging dramatists, first brought *A Taste of Honey* to her experimental Theatre Workshop. The play opened at the Theatre Royal in London's East End in May 1958 and was transferred to the West End the following year. Delaney's candid and raw portrayal of a dysfunctional mother-daughter relationship debuted in New York in 1960, winning the New York Drama Critic's Award. In 1961 the film adaptation of *A Taste of Honey* garnered four British Academy Awards, including one for Delaney's scriptwriting. That same year, *The Lion in Love*, her second full-length play, demonstrated much of the same remarkable gift for accurately capturing the voice and consciousness of postwar Britain.

The young Delaney had an inauspicious beginning in a literary career that would soon mark her as a leading young female playwright. After failing her grade school examinations, she later attended Broughton Secondary School in Salford, where she witnessed her first play, an amateur performance of *Othello*. The stage made a significant impact on the then-twelve-year-old Delaney. She went on to attend Pendleton High School, where she was heartily encouraged to write. After leaving school her interest in writing and drama continued while she held many brief jobs in her hometown of Salford, including store clerk, movie usherette, and research photographer. Delaney was only seventeen when she seriously began to pursue dramatic writing.

Delaney's literary accomplishments have shown gifted versatility, including popular film scripts (*The Railroad Station Man* and *Wide Sargasso Sea*), television plays (*Did Your Nanny Come from Bergen?*), radio plays (*So Does the Nightingale*), a short story collection (*Sweetly Sings the Donkey*), as well as her signature plays. Her writing, embodying the language, character, and challenges of the common person, reflects a dissatisfaction with the often superficial and stylized language and characters of GEORGE BERNARD SHAW, OSCAR WILDE, and TERENCE RATTIGAN, whose middle-class drawing-room plays continued their popularity in war-torn England in the 1950s. Delaney's denizens from the depths of the lower class in *The Lion in Love* reveal emotional decay, crushing poverty, vanishing hopes, and, surprisingly, acceptance of their lamentable conditions. Despite such hardships, her characters reveal a vibrant and authentic voice of this marginalized world—a voice of tempered, qualified optimism ironically kept afloat by the life belt of cynicism.

Her work often reflects the quarrelsome and savage realities evident in JOHN OSBORNE's groundbreaking LOOK BACK IN ANGER. Delaney's drama belongs to what has been widely categorized as "kitchen-sink drama" of the middle of the 20th century. And just as Osborne has been identified with the ANGRY YOUNG MEN of disillusioned postwar Europe, Delaney has become distinguished as one of the "Angry Young Women" of the same critical period.

Her main characters are often women who despite their shortcomings and inadequacies achieve a modicum of victory. The young pregnant Jo in *A Taste of Honey* must accept her abandonment by her boyfriend and mother. In *The Lion in Love*, the middle-aged Kit must deal with her chronic alcoholism and a wandering husband. This personal or family success is often recognized as a return to and acceptance of, albeit humble, the status quo of life marred by destitution and privation.

Ultimately, Delaney's characters, although rarely defeated, find no lessening of life's burdens. Her work, which has long achieved an international following, continues to probe life in her small northern English town of Salford in order to discover the hidden quintessence of the people and situations through which she can form universal statements that appeal to audiences worldwide.

[*See also* England, 1940–Present]

PLAYS: *A Taste of Honey* (1958); *The Lion in Love* (1961)

FURTHER READING

"It Won't Do, Luv" [review of *The Lion in Love*]. *Time* (May 3, 1963).

"Shelagh Delaney." Manchester Celebrities: Authors, Novelists, Writers & Poets. http://www.manchester2002-uk.com/celebs/authorsl.html.

Weiler, A. H. "'Taste of Honey' Arrives: British Drama Stars Rita Tushingham" [review of *A Taste of Honey*]. *New York Times* (May 1, 1962).

Michael D. Sollars

DENISON, MERRILL (1893–1975)

Journalist, writer, historian, one of CANADA's most important playwrights of the 20th century, Merrill Denison was born in Detroit, Michigan, on June 23, 1893. He grew up in Ontario and attended the University of Toronto. He died in San Diego, California, on June 13, 1975. Denison and his work occupied a key crossroad in the evolution of Canadian theater in the 1920s and 1930s and remain paradigmatic insofar as they concern the relationship of Canadian theater with American cultural power. Strikingly, his realist dramas and satires only recently came to the attention of critics. Denison wrote at the time of GEORGE BERNARD SHAW in the period when Canada was mostly rural and Canadian drama had just started to germinate in the larger urban centers. Denison got his beginnings in Little Theatre, but his works, with a few exceptions, remained largely unproduced until after his death. His plays deal predominantly with the sentimental image of Canada as the land of rugged mountains and brave pioneers. Denison's vision is highly antiromantic, as the title of his first collection of plays, *The Unheroic North* (1923), indicates.

The collection contained two of Denison's best-known plays, *Brothers in Arms*, produced in 1921 at Hart House Theatre in Toronto, and *Marsh Hay*. Set in a hunting lodge in 1919, *Brothers in Arms* is a COMEDY about the wealthy urban couple, a businessman husband and his ditzy wife, trapped in the wilderness and trying to get back to civilization for an urgent meeting.

Modeled on MAKSIM GORKY'S THE LOWER DEPTHS, *Marsh Hay*, a full-length drama, tells a tale of an impoverished farmer family ruled by an abusive, embittered father, John Serang, who is blaming everyone, including his wife and children, for his failure. Faced with the crisis of unwanted pregnancy of one of the daughters, the family's hopeless situation comes to full light, and despite the promise of a change, the play ends on the same despairing note that it started. Though there are some unconfirmed rumors that the play was staged in Kiev in the 1920s, it was not until spring 1974, a year before Denison's death, that it was produced at Hart House Theatre, under the direction of Richard Plant. *Marsh Hay* had its first professional production in 1996, at the Shaw Festival. It was directed by Neil Munro, with Michael Ball, Corrine Koslo, Elizabeth Inksetter, and Richard Farrell. Munro's production received mixed reviews.

Denison's other collection *Henry Hudson and Other Plays* (1931) was the first anthology of plays produced for radio. Denison's historical writings include: *Niagara's Pioneers* (1930), *Klondike Mike: An Alaskan Odyssey* (1943), *Harvest Triumphant: The Story of Massey-Harris* (1949), *The Barley and the Stream; the Molson Story; a Footnote to Canadian History* (1955), *Power to Go* (1956), and *The People's Power: The History of Ontario Hydro* (1960).

SELECT PLAYS: *Brothers in Arms* (1921); *From Their Own Place* (1923); *Marsh Hay* (written 1923, produced 1974); *The Weather Breeder* (1923)

FURTHER READING

Denison, Merrill. *The Unheroic North: Four Canadian Plays*. Toronto: McClelland & Stewart, 1923.

MacDonal, Dick, and Merrill Denison. *Mugwump Canadian: The Merrill Denison Story*. Montreal: Content Publishing, 1973.

New, William H., ed. *Dramatists in Canada: Selected Essays*. Vancouver: Univ. of British Columbia Press, 1972.

Magda Romanska

DENMARK

Danish drama in a professional sense was created by Ludvig Holberg (1684–1754) with significant inspiration from Molière and commedia dell'arte; from the beginning it was comic, ironic, and with some fondness for the burlesque, a rather special mix of reality and madness. Later on, another impact came from German ROMANTICISM, most significantly found in the lyrical tragedies by Adam Oehlenschlæger (1779–1850). Danish drama is placed between those two poles. However, ironic down-to-earth REALISM corresponds more with the general taste than grandiose, declamatoric drama does.

Realism was furthermore strengthened by an increasing American and English influence in the 20th century. Actually, the statues of the founding fathers, Holberg and Oehlenschlæger, are placed in front of the Royal Theatre in Copenhagen, the national stage of Denmark that apart from drama also includes opera and ballet. In the 19th century, Danish theater was to a great extent synonymous with the Royal Theatre. As a consequence of the fall of absolutism and the introduction of so-called constitutional monarchy, it inherited a bourgeois chief, the important critic and playwright J. L. Heiberg (1791–1860) in 1849. His charmingly satirical vaudevilles represented a "poetic realism" in opposition to Oehlenschlæger as well as a new, upcoming proper realism, with French inspiration. The Royal Theatre was seen as a leading cultural institution, and it possessed by law monopoly of the classical and serious repertoire. However, with the introduction of democracy, even a number of "secondary theaters" were allowed. They had to focus on more popular genres, but even an author like Hans Christian Andersen (1805–1875) wrote for those stages. Not until 1889 was the monopoly of the Royal Theatre significantly modified.

The last decades of the 19th century were dominated by the "modern breakthrough," an artistically and politically radical movement led by the brothers Georg (1842–1927) and Edvard Brandes (1847–1931), pleading for freedom of thought, attacking romantic epigonism, and claiming that modern literature and drama should "submit problems to debate." It is the period of NATURALISM. In an 1884 issue of the newspaper *Politiken* Edvard Brandes called for a new Danish drama marked by truth and courage, opposite the conventional well-made plot play: "The new drama is only written by an author, who has a meaning and answers for his words." The most significant contributions came from Norwegian playwrights such as BJØRNSTJERNE BJØRNSON and HENRIK IBSEN, not from Danish authors, although Edvard Brandes was a playwright, too, and authors like Otto Benzon (1856–1926) and Gustav Esmann (1860–1904) created satirical light comedies about the bourgeoisie of Copenhagen. Neoromantic plays like HOLGER DRACHMANN's (1846–1908) nationalist fairy tale *Once Upon a Time*, premiered 1887, were a reaction against Brandesianism. Naturalism did become the leading school—literally expressed in the foundation of the drama school of the Royal Theatre in 1886—and the impact of this cultural radicalism is felt even today. To the third generation of naturalist authors belonged satirist Gustav Wied (1858–1914) and HENRI NATHANSEN (1868–1944), whose play *Inside the Walls* (1912), pleading for reciprocal tolerance between Jews and Christians in the bourgeoisie of Copenhagen, is recurrently produced. The playwrights organized themselves in a Playwrights' Association in 1906, after the French model, in order to secure their copyright conditions.

THEATER IN THE 20TH CENTURY

The beginning of the 20th century was not marked by radical experiments typical of that epoch. Gordon Craig's staging of Ibsen's THE PRETENDERS at the Royal Theatre in 1926 was a resounding fiasco. Nevertheless, in a pamphlet, *The Decline of Drama*, from 1919, critic and author Svend Borberg (1888–1947) had asked for a modern drama that could reflect a new fragmented reality after the world war. Realism and psychology were lies: "The I is scattered and split, the Self doubts about itself, its only core is doubt." His drama *No One* (published 1920, premiered 1923) is one of the few Danish expressionist plays. In an astonishing way it anticipates LUIGI PIRANDELLO's discussion of the concept of identity. And typically enough, it could not really be accommodated within dominant conventions when it appeared onstage.

Real renewal in the theater did come from the playwrights, but it was a long process. More experimental names like Svend Clausen (1893–1961) were mostly played on small and experimental stages. But the 1930s and 1940s are marked by three great names who each uniquely represented renewal and connections with significant trends of the past: KAJ MUNK (1898–1944), CARL ERIK SOYA (1896–1983), and KJELD ABELL (1901–1961). Kaj Munk took Borberg's words in *The Decline of Drama* seriously when he called for "intoxication, ecstacy, the great visions . . . a place of revelation . . . a temple for intensified life"—a creed that can immediately be placed in the perspective of the great romantic drama deriving from William Shakespeare and Friedrich Schiller—the Oehlenschlæger line in Danish drama. The first play by Munk to be produced was *An Idealist* (premiered 1928), a bloodthirsty Old Testament drama—Munk was a pastor—about King Herod's maneuverings that nevertheless come to naught in the face of the infant Messiah. The first expressionist performance, at the Royal Theatre, was a famous fiasco. In a reply to his critics, in *Berlingske Tidende* 16.2. 1928 Munk said that "we want to strike all the mighty strings in the manifold harp of life with clenched fists and to listen intensely in the interval." Only when, ten years later, the play had been adapted to conform to a conventional realist pattern did it become a success. In his day Munk was able to relaunch both the lofty drama and the problem-debating naturalism of Ibsen, developing conservative and religious themes.

Soya wrote one of the most radical dramas of the time, THE PARASITES, which had its premiere in an experimental theater, the Royal Theatre having refused it for five years. It provides a glimpse into a callous world behind a petit bourgeois facade, with the estate agent Gruesen (*gru* = "horror") at its center, almost a kind of UBU TRILOGY in realistic dress. Naturalism's introduction of the subhuman was here endowed with a consistency that had a shocking effect, borne of a language that in its grotesque coarseness points back toward Holberg and Wied and forward to absurd-realistic writers such as JESS ØRNSBO and ERLING JEPSEN (see below). He claimed to create "neo-realism," more abrupt than well-made Ibsenism and aimed at disclosing the hypocrisy of bourgeois society and arguing for truth and honesty.

Abell was the author of the satirical musical game *The Melody that Disappeared* (1935), deriving its inspiration from BERTOLT BRECHT and from Pirandello's games with illusions, with a touch of French poetic esprit. But in its delightful poetry and musical charm, it also bears the hallmark of very Danish vaudeville, the genre created by Heiberg. It was presented at the small Riddersalen and became an enormous success. The main character, a kind of Mr. Everyman, has "lost the melody" and finds it again via a confrontation with his own petit bourgeois dreariness. To Abell, theater should be a "place of refuge for the imagination . . . the theatre should always be the fantastic place of refuge of the free thought (1948)"; he was part of the cultural radicalism that also expressed itself in vivid political revues that anticipate the politically committed theater of the 1960s and 1970s.

These three authors were performed in both private theaters and at the Royal Theatre. For decades after these giants, Danish drama had experimental theater as its special province, although authors like Knud Sønderby (1909–1966), Leck Fischer (1904–1956), and H. C. BRANNER (1903–1966), in various ways, continued or tried to renew problem-debating realism on the established stages. In the postwar period, the 1950s and 1960s, American realism, British social realism, French ABSURDISM, and Bertolt Brecht signaled significant impulses, often in continuation of Abell's cultural radicalism.

DRAMA IN THE 1960S

In the 1960s Danish drama came to be influenced by either social realism or absurdism, often displaying a mix of the two, as with Leif Petersen (1934–), with his main emphasis on realism, and Jess Ørnsbo (1932–), where the absurd predominates. Absurdism was particularly promoted by the Student Theatre, which acted as an experimental stage for young talents who later came to leave their mark on the professional theater. Ørnsbo is an example of an author who started at the Student Theatre whose works eventually were performed at regional theaters and the Royal Theatre. His production is radically, often shockingly grotesque; his characters are taken from a burlesque proletariat or a bizarre middle class, and they express themselves in fantastic lines placed in a linguistic zone between popular nonsense and proper SURREALISM. Ørnsbo insists in a quite un-Danish manner on an element of cruelty on the stage, pain released in comedy, which over the years has given a good deal of offense and scandal. To a high degree, he takes a position as the godfather of the new generation of playwrights of the 1990s, with its special mix of irony, absurdity, and everyday realism.

Even in student contexts, a kind of political revue was introduced at the beginning of the 1960s, based on inspiration from the cultural radicalism of the 1930s, as a kind of irreverent musical COMEDY. Important authors, all of them with professional careers, were Erik Knudsen (1922–) and Klaus Rifbjerg (1931–). Absurd as well as satirical drama flourished in the small professional theaters that emerged, the first of which was Fiolteatret (1962). In 1962 the political-satirical-musical trend even reached the Royal Theatre with *Teenagerlove* by ERNST BRUUN OLSEN (1923–), a fierce caricature of the emptiness of the pop industry. Bruun Olsen became the playwright who insisted on the critical comedy, very often in a rhetoric reminiscent of Abell.

In 1961 the establishment of a Ministry of Culture brought an end to the situation where the Royal Theatre belonged under the Ministry of Education and other theaters belonged under the Ministry of Justice. Conditions were improved for the provincial theaters and even for theater life outside the fixed institutional framework. Democratization and decentralization were important issues. A number of experimental or socially critical theater groups came into existence, addressing themselves to a different public from the established theaters, including younger people. As a point of orientation, the Odin Theatre, founded by Italian Eugenio Barba (1937–) in 1966, established itself in the small province town of Holstebro and has since gained world fame. International inspiration was offered during a number of seminars with the participation of, among others, DARIO FO and non-Western theater creators. The impact on not only Danish theater but also Scandinavian theater as a whole was considerable. The Odin Theater developed new ways of creating plays—for instance, by adapting and improvising texts by Danish authors into rather demanding avant-garde performances. The playwright's traditional role was under redefinition in those new ways of working.

The student revolution in 1968 meant an increasing politicization of the theater groups, besides collective working methods. A significant example of those radical redefinitions of drama and theater was the large-scale happening by the theater group Solvognen ("The Chariot of the Sun") in 1974. Named *Santa Claus' Army*, in this happening the capital was invaded by an army of men in red: a great number of Santa Clauses who installed a different kind of reality by, among other things, distributing goods from exquisite shops for free. No wonder the police interfered. A scandal emerged when the happening was awarded a prize from the Fund for the Endowment of the Arts under the Ministry of Culture for having, according to the prize committee, "expanded the conception of literature . . . by means of a linguistic action directly involving the audience into a critical and creative relationship to the tradition." Under mysterious conditions, the check for 20,000 Danish crowns disappeared on its way from the ministry to the theater. Only after acquittal in court for accusations of disturbing public order was the money paid out. This epilogue was of course considered part of the total staging, even if the kinds of provoked reactions were unpredictable.

DRAMA IN THE 1970S AND BEYOND

Part of the general breakup was the abolition of the Drama School of the Royal Theatre and the founding of the Danish National Theatre School in 1968, which was to train actors and subsequently directors, set designers, and technicians. This meant training in new ways of working together and mutual inspiration. From the beginning the idea was that a school for playwrights should be placed there, too. But, instead, in 1993 the school for playwrights was established at Aarhus Theatre, in the province of Jutland, as a three years' education for six students at a time. Different initiatives in the 1970s and 1980s had contributed to the professionalization of playwriting: workshops, studios, and courses, among others, dealing with writing for television and cinema. Since 1973 Aarhus Theatre has had a "playwright in residence." Aarhus Theatre has in general meant a lot to the development of new Danish drama, producing, for example, in the 1980s a number of plays by SVEND ÅGE MADSEN (1939–) greatly inspired by Pirandello's multifictionality. Also Folketeatret in Copenhagen has had a strategy that aimed at new Danish texts by, for example, Erik Knudsen, Sven Holm (1940–), Ulla Ryum (1937–), ASTRID SAALBACH (1955–), and Erling Jepsen (1946–). And when stage director Klaus Hoffmeyer (1938), who had all through his career focused on Danish authors, became head of Drama of the Royal Theatre, he dedicated his opening season in 1997 almost exclusively to Danish authors, some of them thus having their debut in the dramatic field. Not all the results were equally convincing.

The 1980s saw a tendency to abolish the drama of content and commitment and to turn to aesthetic research. Performance and dance theater came into focus. Hotel Pro Forma, founded in 1986 and led by artist Kirsten Dehlholm (1945–), produced strongly visual performances, incorporating multiple art forms, using nonlinear dramaturgical techniques without conventional priority to a literary text. It was a non- or anti-intellectual theater, in a certain sense representing the obscure or even "romantic" trend in Danish drama, even if pure formal experiments had precedence over emotional experience. It was the time of POSTMODERNISM and DECONSTRUCTION.

Regarding drama in a more plain sense, irony—sometimes accused of being arrogant or narcissistic—became a predominant feature as a new generation of playwrights took over and made the 1990s an extraordinarily dynamic era. In 1992, the young group The Desperate Renovation Show of Dr. Dante, led by stage director and playwright Nikolaj Cederholm (1963–), was granted the management of a theater in Copenhagen, a theater from then on called Dr. Dantes Aveny. They managed to attract a new, young audience, making theater in a quick, disrespectful way for those "who would prefer to go to the cinema." The most notable talent of that generation was LINE KNUTZON (1965–), who started off with an original mix of absurdism and realism in desperately grotesque portraits of juvenile confusion in a world showing the collapse of parental values and the painful escape from childhood. The line to Ørnsbo is obvious. Beneath her immediately comic texts is found a myriad of fairy-tale metaphors. In SOON THE TIME WILL COME (1998), she takes up the more mature issues of fear of aging and dying together with the obligatory couplehood theme in a refined game with time as an existential principle.

The period contained a lot of lifestyle satire, the generation's portraits of itself. But it also contained a whole group of more complicated plays—plays concentrated on dissolving borderlines between individuals, between inner and outer universes, sometimes including cultural criticism. That kind of dissolution of traceable meaning may be found in the work of Astrid Saalbach, Peter Asmussen (1957–), Morti Vizki (1963–), and Jokum Rohde (1970–). Erling Jepsen stands in a special position, with his grotesque plays from the neglected province or the suburban normality that turn out to hide cruelty and grotesque horror.

In the 21st century, a new opening has come as a consequence of the new global reality. Political issues are reappearing as demonstrations of the emptiness of political clichés or as another kind of political happenings, practiced by, for example, Claus Beck-Nielsen (1963–), strongly inspired by the new German POLITICAL THEATER. A trend toward "documentary" or "reality" theater is also seen, often dealing with multicultural issues.

FURTHER READING

Abell, Kjeld. *Teaterstrejf i paaskevejr* [Theatrical Roamings in Easter Weather]. Copenhagen: Thaning and Appel, 1948.

Holm, Bent. "Theatre and Drama." In *Denmark*. Copenhagen: Royal Danish Ministry of Foreign Affairs, 1996.

Kvam, Kela et al., eds. *Dansk teaterhistorie, vol. 2* [Danish Theater History, Vol. 2]. Copenhagen: Gyldendal, 1992.

Marker, Frederic and Lise-Lone. *The Scandinavian Theatre*. Blackwell: Rowman and Littlefield, 1975.

Mitchell, P. M. *A History of Danish Literature*. 2d ed. New York: Kraus-Thomson, 1971.

"Ny dansk dramatik" [New Danish Drama]. Special issue, *Peripeti* 3 (2005).

Paludan, Jacob, et al. *The Festival Arts: Danish Drama, Ballet and Music*. Copenhagen: Royal Danish Ministry of Foreign Affairs, 1958.

Rossel, Sven H., ed. *A History of Danish Literature*. Lincoln: Univ. of Nebraska Press, 1992.

Theil, Per, and Lise Garsdal. *Hvem der? Scener fra 90erne* [Who's There? Scenes from the 90's]. Copenhagen: Høst og Søn, 2000.

Bent Holm

D'ERZELL, CATALINA (1891–1950)

As for me, I support the woman's right to vote, for one reason only: so that the first of the women will not be less than the last of the men.

—Catalina D'Erzell, "El Feminismo," Radio Program, 1932

Catalina D'Erzell (pseudonym for Catalina Dulché Escalante, 1891–1950) was probably the first woman to gain significant notoriety in MEXICO's commercial theater industry. Her outstanding dramatic career helped pave the way for other female dramatists such as MARÍA LUISA OCAMPO (1899–1974), Amalia González Caballero de Castillo Ledón (1899–1950), and MAGDALENA MONDRAGÓN (1913–1988). She was born in Silao, Guanajuato, on July 29, 1891, to a Mexican mother and French father. At the onset of the Mexican Revolution (1910–1920), D'Erzell's family relocated to Mexico City. After the Revolution she became a journalist/columnist for national newspapers, often covering the women's rights movement. D'Erzell's interest in feminism would later resurface in her narrative, poetry, criticism, radio programs, and theater.

In 1923 D'Erzell began writing domestic MELODRAMA. Her plays featured outstanding actors, delighted audiences, and earned flattering reviews. With the famous actress Virginia Fábrigas in the lead role, D'Erzell's play *Those Men!* (*¡Esos hombres! (exclamation Maru* 1923) toured extensively in Mexico and beyond. International performances reached enthusiastic audiences as far north as Los Angeles, California, and as far south as Bogotá, Colombia. Willis Knapp Jones (1966) recalls that D'Erzell's hit plays received "more than a hundred performances apiece." Infused with feminist social commentary, *Those Men!* and her subsequent success *The Sin of Women* (*El pecado de las mujeres,* 1925) criticize the double standards in society that force women to act virtuously while giving men the freedom to do as they please. Both plays tell the tragic stories of women trapped in dishonest relationships as a result of the "machista" honor code.

D'Erzell's plays were so popular that some were made into movies in the 1930s and 1940s. These included *Those Men!*, *Maternity* (*Maternidad,* 1937) (changed to *Como todas las madres, Like all Mothers*), *The Reason for the Offence* (*La razón de la culpa,* 1927), and *That Which Only a Man Can Suffer* (*Lo que solo el hombre puede sufrir,* 1936). D'Erzell died on January 3, 1950.

PLAYS: *Chanito* (1923); *Snowy Peaks* (*Cumbres de nieve,* 1923); *Those Men!* (*¡Esos hombres!* 1923); *The Sin of Women* (*Pecado de las mujeres,* 1925); *The One Without Honor* (*La sin honor,* 1926); *The Reason for the Offence* (*La razón de la culpa,* 1927); *The Other Woman's Children* (*Los hijos de la otra,* 1930); *That Which Only a Man Can Suffer* (*Lo que sólo un hombre puede sufrir,* 1936); *Maternity* (*Maternidad,* 1937); *The Swamp* (*La Ciénaga,* 1941)

FURTHER READING

Jones, Willis Knapp. *Behind Spanish American Footlights.* Austin: Univ. of Texas Press, 1966.

Magaña Esquivel, Antonio, and Ruth S. Lamb. *Breve historia del teatro mexicano* [Brief history of Mexican theater]. Mexico, D.F.: Ediciones de Andrea, 1958.

Peña Doria, Olga Martha. *Digo yo como mujer: Catalina D'Erzell* [I speak as a woman: Catalina D'Erzell]. Guanajuato: Ediciones La Rana, 2000.

Schmidhuber, Guillermo. *El teatro mexicano en cierne: 1922–1938* [The blossoming Mexican theater: 1922–1938]. New York: P. Lang, 1992.

May Summer Farnsworth

DESIGN FOR LIVING

Design for Living by NOËL COWARD involves three and a half main characters: Otto, a painter; Leo, a playwright; Gilda, an interior decorator; and Ernest, an art dealer. The creative trio are all in love with one another; while Ernest is merely Gilda's husband. The play involves a series of disclosures over three acts and thus has been described as a sort of "anti-FARCE." Act 1 is set in Paris, where Otto is Gilda's proclaimed lover, and Leo her clandestine one. The disclosure of the latter relationship causes Otto to storm off, leaving Leo and Gilda together. Act 2 is set in London, where Leo and Gilda are living together in openly unmarried bliss. The arrival of Otto, after an absence of eighteen months, prompts Gilda to realize that she feels equally strongly about both Leo and Otto. Her inability to cope with this realization causes her to run away. The act ends with Leo and Otto getting drunk together and sobbing on one another's shoulders. Act 3 is set nearly two years later and sees Gilda now married to Ernest and living in New York. Otto and Leo turn up at a party hosted by Gilda while Ernest is away overnight. The following day Otto, Leo, and Gilda finally make the decision to live together in a ménage à trois. The play ends with Ernest's outraged reaction to this disclosure.

The play can be read either as a manifesto for or a satire on a particular kind of relationship. Either way, it involves a modernist approach in which the application of techniques analogous to those of the Bauhaus school are in this case directed toward the "design" of one's personal life.

The fact that the three central characters all operate in professional milieux that are rather separated from the everyday perhaps suggests that these three are also excused from having to observe the moral and sexual rules that might apply to people living more ordinary lives. There is a sense here that the three, having designed their ideal relationship, have then proceeded to pull the ladder up behind them, thus excluding the generality of humankind from participating in any similarly ideal arrangement. There is certainly something of cruelty and contempt in Leo's "Wave us goodbye, little Ernest, we're together again" toward the end of the play. This creative trio does not merely refuse to observe the moral standards of contemporary society; they openly express contempt for those who would seek to judge them on the basis of those standards.

There is an internal paradox to the play, in that it is open disclosure—a refusal to hide the unorthodoxy of their relationships—that drives Otto, Leo, and Gilda to a higher plane than the rest of the world. Yet any physical relationship between Leo and Otto could not be made explicit when the play was first produced in New York in 1933 and London in 1939. Nor indeed would Coward have countenanced any open display of or proselytizing about homosexuality. It was only with much later productions—an outstanding example being Sean Mathias's production of the play at the Donmar Warehouse in 1994—that the homosexual aspect of the central troilism was made explicit.

There appears to be an autobiographical aspect to the play, with the central characters representing Coward himself, Alfred Lunt, and Lynn Fontanne, the three of whom starred together in the original New York production. The play is said to have remained Coward's personal favorite among all his output. Perhaps more significantly, the play's bold wit and morality enable it to retain a widespread dramatic and ethical impact.

[*See also* England; Gay and Lesbian Drama]

FURTHER READING

Hoare, Philip. *Noel Coward*. 2d ed. London: Mandarin, 1996.

Kaplan, Joel, and Sheila Stowell, eds. *Look Back in Pleasure: Noel Coward Reconsidered*. London: Methuen, 2000.

Morley, Sheridan. *Introduction to Coward Plays: Three*. London: Methuen, 1994.

Andrew Wyllie

DESIRE UNDER THE ELMS

It's a jim-dandy farm, no denyin'. Wished I owned it!
—Sheriff, Part 3

EUGENE O'NEILL's *Desire Under the Elms* was first produced by Kenneth Macgowan, ROBERT EDMOND JONES, and O'Neill in New York on November 11, 1924, with Walter Huston as Ephraim Cabot. Jones directed and designed the production.

The central questions involve who will own the farm and how the land will then enslave its owner. In New England in 1850, old Ephraim Cabot marries for the third time, inspiring his older sons to sell their share of the inheritance to their younger, resentful half brother. Abbie, the new wife, longs for a home, so she competes with Ephraim and Eben while becoming a metaphor for fertility and sexuality.

Ephraim cleared the land, sifting out stone after stone, so he denies the right or the ability of even his own sons to take his place. He does promise that if Abbie bears him a son, "they hain't nothin' I wouldn't do fur ye."

Eben scorns Abbie as his new "Maw," and they quarrel repeatedly until she seduces him in his mother's parlor. She bears a child that Ephraim accepts unquestioningly as his own even though not a single neighbor believes in his paternity. The old man assures Eben that Abbie asked to have him cut out of the will, and since her lover resents the baby, she smothers the child to prove her loyalty. Shocked, Eben goes for the sheriff, and Abbie confesses all to Ephraim, who tells her that if she had truly loved him and the child had been his, he'd never have betrayed her. Eben returns to share in the guilt, and the lovers go to jail; Ephraim declares that God wants him to remain hard and unyielding, so he strides out to gather his stock.

O'Neill described the play as "a TRAGEDY of the possessive—the pitiful longing of man to build his own heaven here on earth by glutting his sense of power with ownership of land, people, money—but principally the land and other people's lives. It is the creative yearning of the uncreative spirit which never achieves anything but a momentary clutch of failing fingers on the equally temporal tangible" (O'Neill, 1988). The conflicts recall the classic myths of Oedipus (the son seeking to displace his father), Phaedra (the woman turning to her husband's son), and Medea (the mother sacrificing her children). From FRIEDRICH NIETZSCHE's *The Birth of Tragedy*, O'Neill drew the notion of the Dionysian search for awareness through rapture, staging it through the passion between Abbie and Eben that brought vitality to the farm. He positioned Ephraim as an Apollonian force in the Nietzschean sense, an emblem of control and restrictive will. Abbie is a powerful, dynamic woman drawn after the Strindbergian model as the antagonist to the men.

The incest and sexuality were provocative. Both the Actors' Association for Clean Plays and the Society for the Suppression of Vice attacked the play, and one critic denounced it as being as realistic as a sewer. In the *New York Times*, Stark Young hailed the "terrible beauty" and "unflinching realism," writing, "The minds of the people in this story are shaken and tinged with loneliness, with thwarted passion, with the trivial, the intense, the drab exaltation and denial of life" (Miller, 1965).

The José Quintero revival in 1963 featured George C. Scott, Colleen Dewhurst, and Rip Torn.

[*See also* Philosophy and Drama; Stage Directions and Stage Sets; United States]

FURTHER READING

Byrd, Robert E. "Unseen, Unheard, Inescapable: Unseen Characters in the Dramaturgy of Eugene O'Neill." *Eugene O'Neill Review* 24 (Spring–Fall 2000): 20–27.

Fambrough, Preston. "The Tragic Cosmology of O'Neill's *Desire Under the Elms*." *Eugene O'Neill Newsletter* 10 (Summer–Fall 1986): 25–29.

Mandl, Bette. "Family Ties: Landscape and Gender in *Desire Under the Elms*." *Eugene O'Neill Newsletter* 11 (Summer–Fall 1987): 19–23.

Miller, Jordan Yale. *Playwright's Progress: O'Neill and the Critics*. Chicago: Scott, Foresman, 1965.

Mossman, Mark A. "Eugene O'Neill and 'the Myth of America': Ephraim Cabot as the American Adam." *Eugene O'Neill Review* 23 (Spring–Fall 1999): 49–59.

O'Neill, Eugene. *Selected Letters of Eugene O'Neill*. Ed. by Travis Bogard and Jackson Bryer. New Haven: Yale Univ. Press. 1988.

Jeffrey D. Mason

THE DIARY OF A SCOUNDREL

See THE SCOUNDREL

DIKE, FATIMA (1948–)

Regarded as the "mother of South African theater," Fatima Dike has gradually gained an international reputation. Born Royline Fatima Dike in the black township of Langa in Cape Town in 1948, the future playwright was educated at church schools in Langa and then in Rustenburg in the Transvaal. Working in a bookstore gave Dike access to a broad range of literary works, and during the 1960s and 1970s, when the black consciousness movement swept through the South African townships, Dike began to read smuggled copies of books by American civil rights leaders such as Martin Luther King Jr. and by black radicals such as Eldridge Cleaver, H. Rap Brown, and Stokely Carmichael.

In 1972 Dike began her association with the Space Theatre, the primary mission of which was to provide a venue for the production of ATHOL FUGARD's plays. Robert Amato, a white writer and director, provided Dike with materials he had gathered on a king of the Gcalekas who had resisted the British colonizers. She shaped these materials into her first play, *The Sacrifice of Kreli* (1976), which was notable for being a bilingual drama, with dialogue in both English and Xhosa. It and her next three plays would be produced at the Space Theatre.

Dike continued her treatment of racial identity in SOUTH AFRICA in *The First South African* (1977). She integrated African folklore into *The Crafty Tortoise* (1978), a play primarily for children. In *Glasshouse* (1979), she focused on the relationship between a white and a black woman at a time of great civil unrest. It would be the last play staged at the Space Theatre, as the white government sought to suppress black expression of all kinds.

From 1979 to 1983, Dike went into exile in the United States. Although she attended many international conferences and was a visiting writing fellow at the Open University in the United Kingdom in 1996, she resided in South Africa after returning there in 1984. In 1991 one of her most popular plays was produced in South Africa and very much contributed to the revival of interest in the theater in the black townships. *So What's New?* is a COMEDY focusing on three black women who find ways of circumventing the oppression of blacks within the apartheid system. In striking contrast, *Street Walking and Company Valet Service* (2000) provides a stark treatment of the very troubling increase in drug addiction among young blacks in South Africa's cities.

Dike has directed the Siyasanga Cape Town Theatre Company and the Living Values Education Programme. In 2002 the National Arts Council of South Africa provided Dike with one of its ten annual grants, supporting her writing of the play *Our Struggle* (2003). In 2004 Dike was the head writer of *New Day*, a stage production celebrating the first decade of South African independence.

PLAYS: *The Sacrifice of Kreli* (1976); *The First South African* (1977); *The Crafty Tortoise* (1978); *Glasshouse* (1979); *So What's New?* (1991); *Street Walking and Company Valet Service* (2000); *Our Struggle* (2003); *New Day* (2004)

FURTHER READING

Banham, Martin et al., eds. *African Theatre: Women*. Bloomington: Indiana Univ. Press, 2002.

Flockemann, Miki. "On Not Giving Up—An Interview with Fatima Dike." *Contemporary Theater Review* 9, no. 1(1999): 17–26.

Gray, S. "The Theatre of Fatima Dike." *The English Academy Review* 2 (1984): 55–60.

Herber, A. "Fatima Dike, Playwright." In *Conversations*. Johannesburg, S.A.: Bateleur, 1979. 66+.

Martin Kich

DING XILIN (1893–1974)

Born on September 29, 1893, in Jiangsu Province, CHINA, Ding Xilin achieved the status of both great dramatist and noted scientist in his lifetime. Believing that science could save his country, Ding went to ENGLAND to study physics and mathematics at Birmingham University. While there, he expanded his interests to English literature and drama, which spawned his interest in drama. From then on, he engaged himself in the two worlds—science and drama. He returned to China in 1920 and started teaching physics at Peking University; there he became the head of the Physics Department and of the Research Institute of the central government. At the same time, he was already producing comedies.

If TIAN HAN and GUO MORUO were viewed as the pioneering playwrights of TRAGEDY in spoken drama (*huaju*), then Ding should be regarded as the father of COMEDY. His plays were generally characterized by one-act settings and well-charged satire. His unflagging sense of humor, his extraordinary gift of gab, and his masterful maneuver of vernacular language were well blended to display his burlesque on the socially ridiculous.

A Wasp (*Yi zhi mafeng*, 1923), a one-act love comedy and his debut, turned out to be the smash hit of the time and remains a favorite today. The success of the play garnered his reputation as an outstanding dramatist. This comedy depicted an old lady wholeheartedly trying to arrange marriages for her new-fashioned daughter and son with her old thinking and approaches. She attempted to marry her daughter to her nephew. Upon her daughter's rejection, she then attempted to betroth her nephew to Miss Yu, having no clue that Miss Yu was her son's love. In this play, Ding cleverly crafted comic tensions and effects through illustrating the old lady's mismatches and the young lovers' embarrassment and hesitation in revealing their true feelings. Under this comedic look at contemporary situations and characters, Ding was commenting on his strong opposition to arranged marriages and conveying a strong desire for change at the heart of his play.

Oppressions (*Yapo*, 1925) was another of Ding's highly celebrated works. Inspired by a true account of a single, male friend looking for a dwelling in Beijing, Ding portrayed an old-fashioned landlady who refused to rent rooms to unmarried men, fearing her daughter would date a bachelor tenant. The man argued that she was being unreasonable and refused to leave. Her young daughter, on the other hand, liked to rent rooms to singles. One day, a single male came to rent a room, and the daughter collected his deposit. When the landlady heard this, she returned the deposit, refusing to allow his tenancy. When they could not settle their disagreement, the landlady sent her maid for a policeman. While they waited for the policeman, a single woman stepped in to rent the room. When she realized the man's difficulties, she sympathetically proposed to the man that they pretend to be a couple and rent the room together. The conflict was finally resolved in this "indecent proposal." Chinese drama critics ranked Ding's *Oppressions* the best of all his plays.

Ding Xilin died in April 1974 in China.

PLAYS: *A Wasp* (*Yi zhi mafeng*, 1923); *Dear Husband* (*Qing ai de zhangfu*, 1924); *Flushed with Wine* (*Jiu hou*, 1925); *Oppressions* (*Yapo*, 1925); *Blind in One Eye* (*Xia le yi zhi yan*, 1927); *The Air of Beijing* (*Beijing de kongqi*, 1930)

FURTHER READING

Chen Shouzhu. *Lun Ding Xilin de xiju* [On the comedies of Ding Xilin]. Hong Kong: Huaju yanjiu she, 1976.

Li Xue. *Ding Xilin*. Beijing: Huaxia chuban she, 2000.

Shen Huiying. *Ding Xilin xiju zuopin xinshang* [The appreciation of Ding Xilin's comedies]. Hong Kong: Ke hua tu shu chuban gongsi, 2001.

Sun Qingsheng. *Ding Xilin yanjiu ziliao* [The materials of Ding Xilin studies]. Beijing: Zhongguo xiju chuban she, 1986.

Ping Fu

DINNER AT EIGHT

A play in three acts by GEORGE S. KAUFMAN and EDNA FERBER, *Dinner at Eight* was first produced by Sam H. Harris on October 22, 1932, at the Music Box Theatre in New York City. It ran for 232 performances. It was directed by Kaufman himself and starred Ann Andrews, Constance Collier, and Paul Harvey.

The playwrights call this play a "many-sided episode in New York life." The play begins in the home of Oliver and Millicent Jordan on Park Avenue and moves to six other locations around the city, including the office of the shipping company that Oliver's family has run for three generations, the office of his doctor Wayne Talbot, the hotel apartment of Wayne's lover Kitty and her husband Dan Packard, and the fancy hotel suite of Larry Renault, a declining Hollywood idol. By having seven sets (eleven scenes) for the play, the authors depict, with a cast of twenty-seven, the preparations and the related human entanglements in and around the lives of ten people attending a dinner in honor of a visiting English aristocrat. The play ends in the Jordans' drawing room, a moment before the dinner begins without the presence of the honored guest.

Dinner at Eight is notable for portraying independent, working women. Carlotta Vance, "a famous theatrical beauty and the mistress of millions," with "magnificent vitality and zest," is an example. Smaller parts like maid, cook, or office clerk are also colorfully portrayed. The best of all, Kitty Packard, a "dumb blond" type of a wife, when confronting her husband, becomes strong, independent, and funny. In George Cukor's 1933 film version, Jean Harlow made a big name playing Kitty.

The play features lively men as well, each doing his best the way people are expected to in the mobile and highly competitive New York City. Renault is middle-aged and, with the age of silent movies gone, senses that his "successful career" is past and steps out in a silent, dramatic way. In the 1933 film, John Barrymore brilliantly played the role, which is said to have been modeled on him.

The play is usually considered a COMEDY, owing to its wisecracking, sarcastic, ironic, or nonchalant exchanges of dialogue. Reviewers have called the play "a comedy of manners and morals" and "a biting satire of wealthy Americans during the Depression." However, the structured character list of the play indicates that *Dinner at Eight* is a good example of human drama, like ANTON CHEKHOV's *THE CHERRY ORCHARD*, although different in style. Both are placed at a time when society is going through a radical change, and ambitious lower-class people win over wealthier, so-called genteel people. Both plays indicate that old society is threatened by people coming from outside. *Dinner at Eight* shows more comic sides of human beings, but in the end, a change is shown, deftly enveloped in laughter.

[*See also* United States, 1929–1940]

FURTHER READING

Gilbert, Julie. *Ferber: Edna Ferber and Her Circle*. New York: Applause, 1999.

Goldstein, Malcolm. *George S. Kaufman: His Life, His Theater*. New York: Oxford Univ. Press, 1979.

Shafer, Yvonne. *American Women Playwrights 1900–1950*. New York: P. Lang, 1997.

Misako Koike

DIOSDADO, ANA (1938–)

In 1970 a young playwright by the name of Ana Diosdado staged her first original play, *Forget the Drums* (*Olvida los tambores*), in Madrid's Valle-Inclán Theater, captured the mainstream's public imagination, won the prestigious Mayte Prize in theater, and produced one of the season's major box-office hits with 450 consecutive performances. Those extraordinary events forever altered the face and characteristics of the male-dominated theater establishment and helped pave the way for an entire generation of women dramatists in SPAIN. Throughout thirty years of continuous success as playwright, actress, director, novelist, and television screenplay writer, Diosdado holds a privileged position in the legacy of contemporary Spanish theater who can claim the honor of heading an impressive list of "firsts" among her many accomplishments: first woman dramatist to achieve commercial success (1970) and be included in three volumes of F. C. Sainz de Robles's *Teatro español* (Spanish Theater), an annual anthology of the best Spanish plays of the season (Madrid: Aguilar, 1970–1971; 1972–1973; 1973–1974); first woman dramatist to have *the most* commercially successful play of a season, *The Eighties Are Ours* (*Los ochenta son nuestros*, 1987–1988); first author and star of two top-rated television hit series, the thirteen-hour-long *Wedding Rings* (*Anillos de oro*, 1983), and *Secondary Education* (*Segunda enseñanza*, 1986) that reached millions of viewers in Spain and Latin America and made her an international celebrity; and first woman to be elected president of Spain's dramatists' guild, Sociedad General de Autores y Editores (2002).

Ana Isabel Alvarez-Diosdado was born in Buenos Aires on May 21, 1938, into a vintage family of theater professionals that included her father, Enrique Diosdado, the distinguished actor and director, and stepmother, the actress Amelia de la Torre. At the age of six, Diosdado made her stage debut in Margarita Xirgu's production of FEDERICO GARCÍA LORCA's *Mariana Peneda*. Under the tutelage of three of Spain's most celebrated actors, Xirgu, Diosdado, and de la Torre, the young girl received an exceptional formative education in the art of drama, and soon after returning to Spain in 1950, she decided to make the most of her unique upbringing and develop her artistic and creative talents as a stage actress, novelist, and playwright.

One of the hallmarks of her theater is an overall sense of balance that integrates high-quality craftsmanship of the well-made play peppered with innovative theatrical techniques with stimulating thematic content presented from a multiplicity of perspectives. Whether setting her play in a historical, present-day, or futuristic period, Diosdado re-creates an identifiable reality inhabited by a socially diverse repertoire of characters speaking in a colloquial and vibrant language. Her work targets significant matters of contemporary immediacy that embrace issues of identity and personal relationships as well as broader concerns of political and social responsibility. Veering toward a feminist stance, her theater prompts new perspectives on past formulas as it unequivocally disputes and dismantles the sociopolitical dichotomy, deconstructs conventional paradigms of gender-assigned stereotypes by broadening the emotional and behavioral range of her characters, and strongly condemns materialism and consumer society and its degrading effects on the human spirit.

PLAYS: *Forget the Drums* (*Olvida los tambores*, 1970); *The Okapi* (*El okapi*, 1972); *Yours for the Asking* (*Usted también podrá disfrutar de ella*, 1973); *The Commoners* (*Los comuneros*, 1974); *And Shawls from Kashmir* (*Y de Cachemira, chales*, 1976); *Wedding Rings* (*Anillos de oro*, 1985); *Ballad* (*Cuplé*, 1986); *The Eighties Are Ours* (*Los ochenta son nuestros*, 1988); *The Silver Path* (*Camino de plata*, 1989); *Three Twenty-one, Three Twenty-two* (*Trescientos veintiuno, trescientos veintidós*, 1993); *Bohemian Crystal* (*Cristal de Bohemia*, 1995); *As We Were Saying Yesterday* (*Decíamos ayer*, 1997); *The Last Adventure* (*La última aventura*, 1999)

FURTHER READING

Lamartina-Lens, Iride. "Female Rage: Diosdado and Pedrero Deal with an Age-Long Problem in a New-Age Fashion." In *Entre Actos: Diálolgos sobre teatro español entre siglos* [Between acts: Dialogues on Spanish theater between centuries] ed. by Martha T. Halsey and Phyllis Zatlin. University Park, Pa.: Estreno, 1999. 63–68.

——. "Ana Diosdado." In *Modern Spanish Dramatists: A Bio-Bibliographical Sourcebook*, ed. by Mary Parker. Westport, Conn. Greenwood Press, 2002. 158–170.

O'Connor, Patricia W. "Women Playwrights in Spain and the Male-Dominated Canon." *Signs* 15, no. 2 (1990): 376–390.

Zatlin, Phyllis. "Ana Diosdado and the Contemporary Spanish Theater." *Estreno* 10, no. 2 (1984): 37–40.

——. "Ana Diosdado." In *Spanish Women Writers: A Bio-Bibliographical Sourcebook*, ed. by Linda Gould Levine et al. Westport, Conn.: Greenwood Press, 1993. 158–166.

Iride Lamartina-Lens

DIRECTING PLAYS

The rise of the director to prominence is a distinguishing characteristic of modern drama. Before the French Revolution, the directing of plays was usually in the hands of the principal actors and the author. In GERMANY directing was divided between the DRAMATURG and a stage manager. The first was responsible for interpreting the script and advising the actors about the characters they portrayed. The stage manager was in charge of "blocking" the play and overseeing the sets and costumes.

The advent of the play director coincided pretty much with the rise of the orchestra conductor. Large instrumental forces required a firm guiding hand, and the profoundly emotional works of composers like Ludwig van Beethoven necessitated the interpretative skills of an insightful leader.

In FRANCE, in the wake of the French Revolution, the popularity of MELODRAMA called for directors to manage the complicated physical action, such as the fight on a bridge over a rushing stream in Guilbert de Pixerécourt's *Coelina* (1800). Pixerécourt himself usually staged his own plays, continuing the old tradition of author as director.

The realistic drama, becoming increasingly popular in the middle of the 19th century, necessitated a new approach to acting, and often it was the director who forced the actors to give up their old ways. The chairs and tables that filled the stage in realistic plays were obstacles to the actors of the old school, who sought the brightest spot in the center of the stage. A. A. L. Montigny, who directed some of the plays of DUMAS FILS, had to put up with actors who would push a table out of the way to claim the space they thought was rightfully theirs.

In ENGLAND, WILLIAM SCHWENK GILBERT and THOMAS WILLIAM ROBERTSON enlarged the director's control of all aspects of stage production. Gilbert, who wrote the librettos for the popular Gilbert and Sullivan operettas, was a tyrannical director, paying attention to every detail. Similarly, Robertson, who was both an actor and a dramatist, brought a new degree of REALISM to the English stage by giving his actors instructions on how to make domestic scenes, such as a tea party in his CASTE (1865), ring true. His elaborate stage directions, which can be read in the published versions of his plays, show the extent to which Robertson advanced the technique of acting.

In Germany the Duke of Saxe-Meiningen (1826–1914), who had his own theater company, sought for greater realism, especially in historical dramas. His company was noted for the historical authenticity of sets and costumes and for the management of crowd scenes. The tours of this company to London, Paris, Moscow, and Berlin, beginning in 1874, encouraged directors like KONSTANTIN STANISLAVSKY in Moscow and ANDRÉ ANTOINE in Paris to break with old theatrical conventions. Both Stanislavsky and Antoine notably advanced the art of directing by instructing actors, most of them young and not academically trained, to a degree unheard of before. In Copenhagen, DENMARK, William Bloch (Marker) summed up the change that was taking place in the responsibilities of the director: "whereas before it only implied a logical arrangement of positions and settings, directing has now developed into an art which requires an intensive study of the individual roles, a minute working out of all the details." The production book for HENRIK IBSEN's ENEMY OF THE PEOPLE, as staged by Bloch at the Royal Theatre in Copenhagen in 1883, contains detailed instructions even for the supernumeraries who make up the crowd in act 4.

Until Stanislavsky formed his MOSCOW ART THEATRE in 1898, RUSSIA was behind the European nations in the responsibilities given to the director. Following the example of the duke of Saxe-Meiningen (and his co-director Ludwig Chronegk), he exercised absolute control over his actors and was able to bring a sense of unity to the play, which would have been impossible if he had had to work with star performers. The same was true of Antoine's first productions.

Stanislavsky's career as both director and teacher of acting reveals how influential the director has become in the modern theater. The director not only guides the actor through his part; he also interprets the script, sometimes to the extent of altering it in violation of the author's original intentions.

What the play says and how well the actors express it has become mainly the task of the director. In a novel, there are rich descriptive passages and elaborate explanations for a character's actions; in a play there are only stage directions supplementing the dialogue. The director has to supply what the novelist furnishes. To do that in a meaningful way, he has to work out what is known as the through-line, that is, the main theme of the play. The director Elia Kazan's through-line for TENNESSEE WILLIAMS's A STREETCAR NAMED DESIRE was the basis of a superb, never-bettered staging of the play: "We are shown the final dissolution of a person of worth, who once had great potential, and, who, even as she goes down, has worth exceeding that of the 'healthy,' coarse-grained figures who kill her." (Cole, 1976)

As dramatic characters became more psychologically complicated and the dramatic action more subtle, thanks largely to Ibsen, the director had to offer more guidance not only to the actors but also to the audience. Ibsen's THE WILD DUCK (1884) has several important characters, a number of intertwined stories, and a blurred moral atmosphere, all of which has to be sorted out by a director with a comprehensive overview and a full understanding of the play. The same is true of ANTON CHEKHOV's THE SEAGULL (1896). Significantly, both of these plays failed when first produced.

In plays like Chekhov's THREE SISTERS, Ibsen's ROSMERSHOLM and MAKSIM GORKY's THE LOWER DEPTHS, it is extremely difficult to establish a sense of theme and to draw a firm and clear through-line. Stanislavsky's difficulty in finding a through-line for *The Three Sisters* is vividly described in his *My Life in Art*.

As the director's authority over the play as staged increased, there were inevitably clashes between the playwright and the director, who on occasion not only reinterpreted the work but actually intervened in the writing of it. A notorious instance of the latter is Kazan's advice to Williams on the last act of CAT ON A HOT TIN ROOF. Kazan said the audience would not be satisfied with Williams's ending and would expect Big Daddy to reappear in the last act. Williams yielded to Kazan when the play was first staged, but he published the play with alternate endings. The version of OSCAR WILDE's classic COMEDY THE IMPORTANCE OF BEING EARNEST that triumphed on the London stage is very different from the version that Wilde originally handed the director, George Alexander, who suggested that Wilde cut the play radically.

Although Stanislavsky did not tamper with the text of Chekhov's *The Seagull*, he added a great many directorial touches that darkened the mood of the play. It had been only a modest success when first staged in 1896, and Chekhov decided he would not write any more plays. Under Stanislavsky's direction, however, the play became an extraordinary success two years later. Yet Chekhov, looking at the results thought Stanislavsky had misunderstood his play.

The EPIC THEATER of ERWIN PISCATOR and BERTOLT BRECHT required a different approach from the psychologically oriented, realistic theater. In epic theater the actor did not become his character: he presented the character, as if in quotation marks, to the audience. Here, too, the director, working in close collaboration with the actors, functioned as the main creative force. The extent to which some of Brecht's plays underwent changes during rehearsals is recorded in *Theaterarbeit*, edited by Ruth Berlau et al. (1952), a remarkable record of the process by which a script is realized onstage. The plays of CARYL CHURCHILL are in the Brechtian tradition in that they are created to a large extent in the process of being rehearsed.

Like Stanislavsky in his production of *The Seagull*, a director may justify his changes in the dramatist's script by claiming that he is clarifying in theatrical terms an element that might otherwise be lost or neglected. A stage direction in EUGÈNE IONESCO's THE LESSON notes that the professor, who has just savagely killed his young female pupil, puts on an armband that "perhaps" bears the Nazi swastika. In a production of the play in Stockholm in 1953, the director chose to change the "perhaps" into a certainty and achieved an extraordinary coup de théâtre by displaying on the walls of the studio theater huge photo murals showing thousands of Nazis assembled in endless ranks at Nuremburg, while the sound system blasted the theater with shouts of "Sieg Heil!" A play that is usually categorized as belonging to the Theater of the Absurd was transformed into an explicit parable about Nazism.

In his 1988 Stockholm production of EUGENE O'NEILL's *Long Day's Journey Into Night*, INGMAR BERGMAN violated O'Neill's unities by having the last act take place outdoors on the veranda of the house. This brought the action closer to the sea that serves as symbolic background to the drama. Also, Bergman's set for the first three acts was not realistic; its strangeness suggested that the characters had lost contact with reality through alcohol and drugs. But, one might ask, was it necessary to stress what is already obvious in O'Neill's script?

At the extreme end of the directorial spectrum are the directors who do not so much interpret a play as disassemble it and make it a different entity. VSEVOLOD MEYERHOLD, who was Stanislavsky's student, rebelled against his teacher and against the whole concept of realistic, psychological drama. In his view the word had taken over the theater, and he sought to create an art in which the theater spoke its own language—actors becoming gymnasts, sets becoming unrealistic constructions that were supposed to mirror the essence of the play and not its surface reality. For a few years after the Bolshevik Revolution, the innovative spirit in Russia allowed him to stage some of the most remarkable productions of the 20th century. His highly theatricalized production of ALEXSANDR OSTROVSKY's *The Forest* and his constructionist version of FERNAND CROMMELYNCK's *The Magnanimous Cuckold* would hardly be recognizable to their authors. The same could be said for Eugenio Barba's productions in Denmark in the 1960s and 1970s. Barba made a point of completely altering scripts, not to provide an insight into the author's intentions but, rather, often, to subvert the author's intentions or to emphasize an aspect that the author preferred to treat circumspectly.

[*See also* Acting; Stage Directions and Stage Sets]

FURTHER READING

Berlau, Ruth, et al., eds. Theaterarbeit [Theater-Work]. Dresden: VVV Dresdner Verlag, 1952.

Clurman, Harold. *On Directing*. New York: Collier, 1972.

Cole, Toby, and Helen Krich Chinoy, eds. *Directors on Directing*. New York: Macmillan, 1976.

Dietrich, Margret, ed. *Regie in Dokumentation, Forschung und Lehre* [Direction in documentation research and teachings]. Salzburg: Otto Müller, 1975.

Marker, Friedrich S., and Lise-Lone Marker, *The Scandinavian Theatre*. Oxford: Basil Blackwell, 1975.

Schneider, Rebecca, and Gabrielle Cody, eds. *Re: direction*. London: Routledge, 2002.

Evert Sprinchorn

DISCÉPOLO, ARMANDO (1887–1971)

Armando Discépolo reflected an age of extraordinary conflict and change in ARGENTINA and the world in his grotesque plays about Italian immigrants. Born to a Neapolitan musician and a woman of Genovese parentage in Buenos Aires on August 18, 1887, he was raised speaking Italian and listening to anecdotes about the thousands of immigrants who arrived in Argentina from the second half of the 19th century on. Due to the deaths of his father in 1906 and his mother in 1910, he abandoned school in the sixth grade to support the family, working at various menial jobs.

Discépolo claimed that he became a writer in 1909, when his mother discovered a little notebook in which he had written secrets in dialogical form, and she suggested, "Why don't you write plays?" He started out writing short plays, and in September 1910, he showed his first play, *In Between the Iron* (*Entre el hierro*), to the famous actor Pablo Podestá. This meeting launched not only Discépolo's dramatic career two months later, on December 12, 1910, but also a great friendship and working partnership that would last until Podestá's death in 1923. Discépolo also collaborated with other playwrights, especially at the beginning of his career.

His style moved from the external, social world of the SAINETE—minor plays that portrayed working-class stereotypes and their daily dramas of assimilation, acculturation, poverty, and political development—into the individual consciousness of the grotesque. He experimented with serious theater, minor genre (*género chico*), COMEDIES, and different kinds of sainetes and also wrote plays that he did not know how to name. This diversity is the reason his dramatic production cannot be classified under rigid parameters, but most of his plays belong to the poetic of REALISM.

Discépolo is the primary forefather of contemporary Argentinean theater. Playwrights like Roberto Cossa and GRISELDA GAMBARO have recognized his major influence in their writings. His master creations, all those plays belonging to the creole grotesque (GROTESCO CRIOLLO), opened a new discourse on the daily struggles of immigrants in Buenos Aires society by transforming and deepening the old *sainete*. The Italians in these plays are not just stereotypes who make the public laugh; they are individuals, lured to Argentina with promises of land and high wages, who found a hostile, unfamiliar place. His 1921 *Mustafá* delves into the immigrants' problems, but only in 1923 did he first characterize one of his plays, *Mateo*, as grotesque. *The Little Organ* (*El organito*, 1925), *Stephen* (*Stéfano*, 1928), *Cremona* (1932), and *The Watchmaker* (*Relojero*, 1934) complete the grotesque works. However, his dramatic production is very heterogeneous and includes minor pieces—such as *sainetes*, vaudevilles, and operettas—that have been overshadowed by the grotesques.

His creative years extend from 1910 to 1934. After 1934, Discépolo directed plays by Argentinean and European authors.

He died in Buenos Aires on January 8, 1971, at eighty-three, having written thirty-two dramatic plays in which he presents a glance, sometimes compassionate, sometimes comic, at human nature. He used the stage to accurately portray social problems, and his dramatic creation can also be seen as a testimony of the history of the nation during the first fifty years of the 20th century.

PLAYS: *In Between the Iron* (*Entre el hierro*, 1910); *Corner of the Kisses* (*El rincón de los besos*, 1911); *The Ring-Dove* (*La torcaz*, 1911); *The Forge* (*La fragua*, 1912); *Sea Foam* (*Espuma de mar*, 1912); *My Mother's Fiance* (*El novio de mamá*, 1914); *My Wife Becomes Bored* (*Mi mujer se aburre*, 1914); *Guard 323* (*El guarda 323*, 1915); *The Patio of the Flowers* (*El patio de las flores*, 1915); *The Continuous Movement* (*El movimiento continuo*, 1916); *The Science of Chance* (*¡¡La cience de la casualitat!!* 1916); *The Reverse* (*El reverso*, 1916); *The Bow-legged Pintos* (*El chueco Pintos*, 1917); *Conservatory "The Harmony"* (*Conservatorio "La armonía"* 1917); *The Sword of Damocles* (*La espada de Damocles*, 1918); *The Vertigo* (*El vértigo*, 1919); *The Nail of Gold* (*El clavo de oro*, 1920); *The Black Prince* (*El príncipe negro*, 1921); *Mustafá* (1921); *United Italy* (*L'Italia unita*, 1922); *Mateo* (1923); *Men of Honor* (*Hombres de honor*, 1923); *Giácomo* (1924); *Doll* (*Muñeca*, 1924); *Babylon* (*Babilonia*, 1925); *The Little Organ* (*El organito*, 1925); *The New Mother Country* (*Patria nueva*, 1926); *Stephen* (*Stéfano*, 1928); *Get Up and Walk!* (*Levántate y anda*, 1929); *Amanda and Edward* (*Amanda y Eduardo*, 1931); *Cremona* (1932); *The Watchmaker* (*Relojero*, 1934)

FURTHER READING

Dubatti, Jorge. "Una constante poética en la producción dramática de Armando Discépolo: Continuidad e innovación en el realismo" [An unchanging poetic in Armando Discépolo's Plays: Continuity and innovation in realism]. In *Cuartas Jornadas de Investigación Teatral* [Fourth occasion of theater investigation]. Buenos Aires: ACITA, 1987. 20–24.

Foster, David William. "Discépolo, Armando." In *Encyclopedia of Contemporary Latin American and Caribbean Cultures*. Vol. 1. London: Routledge, 2000.

Ordaz, Luis. "Frustraciones y fracasos del período inmigratorio en los 'grotescos criollos' de Armando Discépolo" [Frustrations and failures of the immigration period in the "creole grotesque" of Armando Discépolo]. *Espacio de crítica e investigación teatral* 3, no. 5 (1989): 43–51.

Sanhueza, María Teresa. "Armando Discépolo: Un obstinado transgresor de géneros" [Armando Discépolo: An obstinate transgressor of genres]. *Teatro. Revista del Complejo Teatral de Buenos Aires* 22, no. 65 (August 2001): 7–13.

Tálice, Roberto. *Armando Discépolo*. Buenos Aires. A-Z Editora S.A., 1986.

Ma. Teresa Sanhueza

DNI TURBINYKH See DAYS OF THE TURBINS

DOCUMENTARY DRAMA

It is only from the facts themselves that the constraints and the constant mechanisms of life emerge, giving a deeper meaning to our private fates.

—Erwin Piscator, *The Political Theatre*, 1929

The documentary drama constitutes a new form markedly different from the historical play. Documentary plays are written or compiled directly from "documentary" sources in order to increase their purchase on issues with the purpose of intensifying subsequent debate. Primary source material includes official reports, trial transcripts, newspaper articles, photographs, witness testimony, and the aural and visual evidence of the tape recorder and the film and video camera. "Documents" such as these were often regarded in the 20th century as almost unproblematical sources of facts and information, evidence of a widespread faith in facts derived from 19th-century positivism. "Documentary" is a quintessential 20th-century mode, the very concept linked with the history of visual technologies (especially film and photojournalism).

Documentary plays—on conventional and unconventional stages, written by both individuals and collectives—are often controversial, dealing as they do with contentious issues and/or events past and present. Documentary theater techniques were vital to oppositional political movements in many places between the two world wars and subsequently in the emerging nations/former imperial colonies after World War II. Usually nonnaturalistic, they embed documents within performance via direct address from both actors and what BERTOLT BRECHT termed "technological actors" (film, slide, and audio systems—nowadays, also video and digital technologies).

Documentary theater is something that groups and communities use in times of need. In postrevolutionary Russia, "Blue Blouse" troupes included the "living newspaper" (*zhivaya gazeta*) as both an agitational and educational tool in their performances. From the late 1920s, this methodology spread to communist and proto-communist groups in Europe and the United States (in New York, several immigrant groups imitated Blue Blouse methods). The work of major European theatrical innovators like Brecht and ERWIN PISCATOR was also central to documentary drama's development. Their use of technology and Brecht's "objective" acting style were part of the pioneering work. In *Rasputin* (1927), for example, Piscator analyzed the effects of the Russian Revolution on Weimar GERMANY partly by using projected material to present documents. These ideas were exploited in 1930s America by the FEDERAL THEATRE PROJECT (FTP) part of Franklin Delano Roosevelt's "New Deal" social and economic programs. The FTP's "Living Newspaper Unit" produced several provocative analyses of hard economic times, like *Triple-A Plowed Under* (1936, about agricultural policy) and *One-Third of a Nation* (1938, about housing). Hallie Flanagan, FTP's head, had studied theater in Europe as had Living Newspaper director Joseph Losey.

The House Un-American Activities Committee brought an end to the FTP in 1939, and the Cold War period ensured a climate inimical to documentary theater's usual political stance. It took a new period of heightened political awareness to revive the form. In West Berlin, Piscator embarked on a new series of documentary dramas, two of them about the Holocaust (ROLF HOCHHUTH's *The Deputy* [1963] and PETER WEISS's *THE INVESTIGATION* [1965]). In ENGLAND, Joan Littlewood's Theatre Workshop produced *Oh What a Lovely War* (1963), a review-style antiwar play, and the Royal Shakespeare Company produced US, a play about Vietnam (1966, directed by Peter Brook).

In 1960s America (with the anti–Vietnam War movement and the 1968 "student revolutions"), many theatrical experimenters used documentary material. Key groups included the San Francisco Mime Troupe and El Teatro Campesino; key works included Martin Duberman's *In White America* (1963, about race), Donald Freed's *Inquest* (1970, about the Rosenberg Trial), and Daniel Berrigan's *The Trial of the Catonsville Nine* (1970–1971, about the burning of draft cards). Responding to improvisational methodologies, the LIVING THEATRE produced documentary drama that was close to the heightened REALISM of film documentary. For example, with Jack Gelber's 1959 *The Connection* (about heroin addiction) the company approached a Gorkyesque NATURALISM (evident also in their 1963 production of Kenneth Brown's *The Brig*, about a U.S. Marine prison).

Inside and outside the developed world, within and without the mainstream, documentary drama continues to be useful as part of political opposition and/or community action. Brazilian director and activist AUGUSTO BOAL's Arena and "Forum" Theater methodologies are much used by community groups in South America, AFRICA, and Asia, for example, and mainstream productions by major directors like ARIANE MNOUCHKINE continue to use documentary material. In the United States, EMILY MANN and ANNA DEVEARE SMITH have used interview material to significantly extend the mode's performative possibilities. Smith's *Twilight: Los Angeles*, 1992, about the Los Angeles race riots, demonstrates the continuing power of the document in drama.

FURTHER READING

Dawson, Gary Fisher. *Documentary Theatre in the United States: An Historical Survey and Analysis of Its Content, Form, and Stagecraft*. Westport, Conn.: Greenwood Press, 1999.

Goldstein, Malcolm. *American Drama and Theater of the Great Depression*. New York: Oxford Univ. Press, 1974.

Paget, Derek. *True Stories: Documentary Drama on Radio, Screen and Stage*. Manchester: Manchester Univ. Press, 1990.

Piscator, Erwin. *The Political Theatre*. Tr. by Hugh Rorrison. London: Methuen, 1980.

Stott, William. *Documentary Expression and Thirties America*. New York: Oxford Univ. Press, 1973.

Taylor, Karen Malpede. *People's Theatre in Amerika*. New York: Drama Book Specialists, 1972.

Van Erven, Eugene. *Community Theatre: Global Perspectives*. New York: Routledge, 2001.

Derek Paget

DÖDSDANSEN *See* THE DANCE OF DEATH

A DOLL'S HOUSE

I'll try to discover who's right, society or I.

—Nora, Act 3

A Doll's House (*Et dukkehjem*) represents HENRIK IBSEN's international breakthrough and is still one of his most famous plays. It is in this play that Ibsen's retrospective technique, which is crucial for his way of composing dramas and for his psychological REALISM, can be said to be fully developed.

Published in December 1879, *A Doll's House* soon was one of the most frequently staged dramas in the world. Even today playing Nora is a great challenge to female actors all over the world. In Ibsen's time *A Doll's House* was received as a play about women's rights and female emancipation, and contemporary readers, audiences, and critics were either deeply shaken or really shocked by the ending of the play where Nora leaves her husband and her three children, and the soon very famous ending was widely discussed in heated debates. While some found Nora's final exit radical but both dramatically and historically necessary, others regarded it as extremely provoking and totally unconvincing. When German actress Hedwig Niemann-Raabe refused to play this ending and German theater directors were reluctant to stage the drama, Ibsen wrote an alternative ending for the Germans, where Nora chooses to stay.

A Doll's House is a three-act play. The setting is Nora and Torvald Helmer's middle-class living room, where several visitors, all closely related to the tightly woven plot, gather: Dr. Rank, Mrs. Kristine Linde, and Nils Krogstad. The play is generally considered a realistic PROBLEM PLAY, but it is also characterized by the overall metaphor of the doll house by which all of the characters in the play are seen as dolls playing with dolls. The story about Nora is based on the tragic real-life story of Laura Kieler, who did not, however, leave her husband. Ibsen in fact used the doll house metaphor to describe Kieler's at first seemingly happy marriage three years before he used it in his drama.

Nora, a beautiful, charming young woman, has been happily married for eight years to Torvald, when suddenly Krogstad arrives, threatening to reveal Nora's secret; when Torvald was seriously ill and needed a year in the South, she forged her father's signature to get a loan. When Torvald gets to know about the forgery, he is furious instead of—as Nora has been dreaming—grateful for what she has done. Nora has hoped and believed that Torvald, learning about what she secretly did to save his life, would take it as a declaration of love, but the laws of society and honor and reputation prove to be more important to Torvald. Her disappointment in him makes her realize that she does not know him at all, that he has never considered her as an equal, and that to him she has only been a doll he could play with. She also realizes that she cannot continue living together with him and that she has to leave him in order to try to find out who is right, Torvald and society or she herself, and thus become what she calls "a human being."

While Nora's decision to educate herself and to find out who is right can be understood in the light of the individualism of the time and the growing existentialist ideas, topics like genetic inheritance and parental influence can be understood in the light of the development of the natural sciences and Darwinism. The themes of identity and change are also expressed in key scenes in the play, that is, when Nora dances the tarantella. This "play within the play," which has been interpreted in various ways, is closely related not only to the subject of identity but also to the doll SYMBOLISM. What happens in this dance reflects the action of the play as a whole: Nora gradually shows herself to be different from the way Torvald wants to see her.

While most of the early critics clearly identified with Torvald, later critics tend to identify with Nora, or at least to regard her as the protagonist of the play. One decisive interpretative question commonly discussed is whether *A Doll's House* is a problem play about women and women's liberation or something more or other than that; for instance, whether, as Ibsen himself claimed, it is a play about people in general, that is, about human matters. Widely discussed is also Ibsen's portrait of Nora. Is she a *tragic* character? And is Ibsen's portrait of her a *coherent* one? Some critics find Nora's change from playful wife to truthseeking woman unconvincing and claim that Ibsen's portrait of Nora falls apart. Others respond that Nora is only playacting when she is Torvald's playful wife, his little "songbird," and "squirrel" and that she has a hidden—or gradually develops a new—more authentic self that is disclosed during the play's action.

[*See also* Norway]

FURTHER READING

Durbach, Errol. *A Doll's House. Ibsen's Myth of Transformation. A Reader's Companion to the Play*. Twayne's Masterwork Studies. Boston: Twayne, 1991.

McFarlane, James. "Drama and Society, 1875–1881." In *Meaning & Evidence. Studies, Essays & Prefaces 1953–1987*. Norwich: Norvik Press, 1987. 232–250.

Meyer, Michael. "A Doll's House: 1878–1880." In *Ibsen: A Biography*, 1967. London: Penguin, 1992.

Templeton, Joan. "The Poetry of Feminism." In *Ibsen's Women*, ed. by Joan Templeton. Cambridge: Cambridge Univ. Press, 1997. 110–145.

Lisbeth Pettersen Wærp

DONMAR WAREHOUSE

Built in the 1870s as a hop warehouse for a local brewery, the space was used in the 1920s as a film studio and then banana-ripening depot. Theater manager Donald Alberry and dancer Margot Fonteyn converted this former fruit warehouse in Covent Garden, London, into a theater in 1961, combining parts of their Christian names to come up with its name—Donmar, which they used as a rehearsal space for the London Festival Ballet, a company they founded. The Royal Shakespeare Company (RSC) took it over for rehearsals, and in 1964 it housed part of their "Theater of Cruelty" season. In 1977, when diversifying their venues, the RSC began using the Donmar as a studio theater. In 1981, when the RSC moved to the Barbican, the Donmar came under the management of Ian Albery and Nica Burns and provided performing space for touring companies.

Associated Capital Theatres (formerly the Maybox Group) acquired the Donmar in 1989 and changed it from a touring house to a fully producing house with annual eight-month seasons. Sam Mendes was brought aboard as artistic director. He oversaw the Donmar's redevelopment within a new shopping mall, maintaining the distinctive characteristics of the warehouse and its unique thrust stage while improving the backstage and front of the house, including adding two bars to the foyer. It reopened in 1992 with the Stephen Sondheim and John Weidman musical *Assassins*. Carol Newling, senior press representative of the RSC, joined him as executive producer. Under Mendes's leadership, the Donmar has been noted for the high quality of work produced there, especially for its contemporary plays and musicals. In 1999, Ambassador Theatre Group replaced Associated Capital Theatres as the Donmar's landlord. Michael Grandage succeeded Mendes as artistic director in 2002; Nick Frankfurt succeeded Newling as executive producer. Acclaimed revivals of Stephen Sondheim musicals include *Assassins* (1992), *Company* (1995), and *Merrily We Roll Along* (2000). Critically successful plays include NOËL COWARD's DESIGN FOR LIVING (1994), TENNESSEE WILLIAMS's THE GLASS MENAGERIE (1995), and TOM STOPPARD's THE REAL THING (1999). John Kander and Fred Ebb's *Cabaret* (1994) crossed the Atlantic to open at the Henry Miller Theatre in New York City in 1998; it later moved to Studio 54, where it won four Tony Awards. *The Real Thing* also crossed over to New York, opening at the Barrymore Theatre in 2000 and winning three Tony Awards.

In addition to offering student matinees, the Donmar offers its Write Now program in conjunction with the Mousetrap Foundation. This program is based around a new play premiering at the Donmar and encourages students to explore creative writing for the stage. Reaching out to college and university students, the Donmar offers its Student Rep Scheme where students become Donmar representatives to their university, promoting the Donmar to their fellow students. The Donmar Warehouse is located at 41 Earlham Street, Seven Dials, London.

[*See also* England, 1980–Present]

FURTHER READING

Wold, Matt. *Stepping Into Freedom*. London: Limelight Editions, 2003.

J. Briggs Cormier

DORFMAN, ARIEL (1942–)

In his introduction to *The Resistance Trilogy* (which contains the plays *Death and the Maiden* [1991], *Reader* [1995], and *Widows* [1987]), Chilean poet, author, and playwright Ariel Dorfman states, "My writing has been haunted, ever since I can remember, by twin obsessions, a central paradox that I cannot be rid of: on the one hand, the glorious potential and need of human beings to tell stories; and, on the other, the brutal fact that, in today's world, most of the lives that should be telling those stories are generally ignored, ravaged, and silenced."

Dorfman's life of exile led him to become a storyteller, using Spanish and English (his native and adopted languages) to document the atrocities committed in his own Chile and to work toward dreaming a path toward the reconstruction and healing of his country and his people. Born in ARGENTINA in 1942, Dorfman fled with his family to America only a few years later because of fascism. Scarcely a decade after that, Dorfman's family again was forced out of their home, this time because of the threat of McCarthyism. The family then moved to Chile, and Ariel Dorfman became a naturalized Chilean citizen in 1967. Dorfman studied at the University of Chile and the University of California at Berkeley, before returning to Chile to participate in the democratic movement that brought Salvador Allende to the presidency. After becoming a cultural adviser to the president's chief of staff, Dorfman only narrowly escaped the 1973 military coup led by General Augusto Pinochet, wherein many of Dorfman's colleagues and friends were tortured and killed.

Exiled from Chile, like many other writers, intellectuals, and politicians, Dorfman turned from writing scholarly nonfiction to novels, poetry, and plays that mostly centered around the consequences of dictatorships and political violence. In his 1987 play *Widows* (adapted from Dorfman's 1981 novel), a young Greek woman whose father, husband, and son have all disappeared takes a stand against the Nazis occupying her village and demands permission to bury an unidentifiable corpse that may be her father. In DEATH AND THE MAIDEN (a play in 1991 and a film in 1994), the wife of a lawyer kidnaps a man she suspects tortured and raped her fifteen years earlier and conducts his trial at gunpoint. In the 1995 play *Reader* (based on one of Dorfman's short stories), a government censor learns that the book he is about to ban predicts a horrible fate for his son. Even though each of these plays deals with abuse and violence, Dorfman titled this trilogy of plays *The Resistance Trilogy* to suggest the possibility that through speaking out as a means of rebellion, oppressive regimes can be overcome.

Though Dorfman is best known for writing *Death and the Maiden*, his greatest contribution may well be his role as a public intellectual. Teaching, publishing, and disseminating his views on contemporary global politics through the lens of his tumultuous relationship with his beloved Chile, Dorfman continues to call attention to the ways that cultures, governments, and societies must speak to each other to avoid the violence and senseless pain that befell Chile on the other 9/11—the overthrow of Allende's government on September 11, 1973.

PLAYS: *Widows* (1987; rev. with Tony Kushner, 1991); *Death and the Maiden* (1991); *Reader* (1995); *Mascara* (1998); *Who's Who* (1998); *The Other Side* (2005); *Purgatorio* (2005)

FURTHER READING

Dorfman, Ariel. *The Resistance Trilogy*. London: Nick Hern Bks., 1998.
——. "The Last September 11th." *Los Angeles Times* (September 21, 2001).
Postel, Danny. "Interview with Ariel Dorfman." *The Progressive* (December 1998). http://www.progressive.org/postel9812.htm.
Stavans, Ilan. "The Gringo's Tongue: A Conversation with Ariel Dorfman." *Michigan Quarterly Review* 34, no. 3 (1995): 303–312.

Zachary A. Dorsey

DORR, NICOLÁS (1947–)

Nicolás Dorr was born in Santa Fe, CUBA, on February 3, 1947. He became involved with the theater environment at the age of ten and was educated at Havana's Municipal Academy of Dramatic Arts. During this period, he performed his first presentation in theatrical representations at this academy.

On August 4, 1959, the well-known journal *Bohemia* made him known as a young poet, for his book of poetry *Tiempo inquieto* (Anxious Time) in an article by journalist Emma Pérez, titled "*Los que tienen doce años*" (*Those Who Are Twelve Years Old*). Two years later, Dorr joined the Cuban theatrical movement with the premiere of his first script *The Pericas* (*Las pericas*) at the Arlequin Theater on April 3, 1961; he was fourteen years old. With this premiere, he became the youngest drama writer ever within Cuban theater history. Two decades later, on October 24, 1982, *The Pericas* was presented as a classic ballet during the celebration of Havana's Eighth International Ballet Festival. This was the first time that a Cuban theatrical production was presented as a ballet script.

During the 1960s, he wrote four plays: *The Cartons' Palace* (*El palacio de los cartones*, 1961), *The Councilmen's Corner* (*La esquina de los concejales*, 1962), *Wonderful Inertia* (*Maravillosa inercia*, 1963), and *Sun's Key* (*Clave de sol*, 1965). From 1964 to 1970, he temporarily interrupted his drama career to study Hispanic language and literature at the University of Havana.

In 1972, in the José Martí Theater, he premiered *An Entertaining Trip* (*Un viaje entretenido*) and won a literary award sponsored by the Unión de Escritores y Artistes de Cuba (UNEAC) for his play *The Vibrant Claim Between an Author and an Angel* (*El agitado pleito entre un autor y un ángel*). In 1974, in the same theater, he presented the COMEDY *The Noisy Celebration* (*La chacota*). Four years later, he initiated his career as a theater director. During the 1980s, he achieved several honors and recognitions for the premiere of the following plays: *The Exciting Midday* (*Mediodía candente*, 1980); *A Colonial House* (*Una casa colonial*, 1981); *Confession in the Chinese Neighborhood* (*Confesión en el barrio chino*, 1984); *To Live in Santa Fe* (*Vivir en Santa Fe*, 1986), and *Confrontation* (*Confrontación*, 1989).

During the 1990s, he premiered three more scripts: *A Wall in Havana* (*Un muro en La Habana*, 1994), *Plants on the Roof of the World* (*Nenúfares en el techo del mundo*, 1997), and *The Eccentrics of the Night* (*Los excéntricos de la noche*, 1998). On April 14, 2001, the Department of Culture, the National Council for the Arts, and the National Theater of Cuba celebrated a special gala to commemorate forty years of Nicolás Dorr in performing arts, titled: Twenty Characters Reencounter Their Author (Veinte personajes reencuentran a su autor). During this celebration, Dorr received the title of Santa Fe's Illustrious Son. In June, an Argentine theater company presented his play *Dirty Games in the Basement* (*Juegos sucios en el sótano*, 1995) in the Nudo Theater in Buenos Aires.

Dorr has written more than twenty plays. All of them have been published and most of them premiered in several theaters all around the world in countries such as SPAIN, the UNITED STATES, the former Soviet Union, FRANCE, ITALY, POLAND, HUNGARY, Nicaragua, Panama, Colombia, VENEZUELA, ARGENTINA, and PUERTO RICO. He also has published essays on dramatic literature in journals such as *Cine Cubano* (Cuban Cinema), *Bohemia*, and *Gaceta de Cuba* (Gazette of Cuba).

Dorr has been invited as a visiting professor to a number of universities and lectured extensively at other universities. From 1992 until 1994, he offered theater seminars at the General Society of Authors of MEXICO's School of Literature. Currently, he is a full professor in the School of Audiovisual Communication at the Superior Institute of Art in Cuba. He is a member and founder of UNEAC; and he belongs to the Sociedad General de Autores y Editores (SGAE), under the category of drama and audiovisual author.

[See also Bufo Theater]

PLAYS: *The Cartons' Palace* (*El palacio de los cartones*, 1961); *The Pericas* (*Las pericas*, 1961); *The Councilmen's Corner* (*La esquina de los concejales*, 1962); *Three Anecdotes for the Trenches* (*Tres anécdotas para las trincheras*, 1962); *Wonderful Inertia* (*Maravillosa inercia*, 1963); *Sun's Key* (*Clave de sol*, 1965); *Letters on the Table* (*Cartas sobre la mesa*, 1968); *The Vibrant Claim Between an Author and an Angel* (*El agitado pleito entre un autor y un ángel*, 1971); *An Entertaining Trip* (*Un viaje entretenido*, 1972); *The Noisy Celebration* (*La chacota*, 1973); *With all the Ignited Stars* (*Con todas las estrellas encendidas*, 1975); *Action' Statements* (*Relatos de campaña*, 1976); *The Board's Door* (*La puerta de tablitas*, 1978); *The Golden Ages of Man* (*El hombre de la Edad de Oro*, 1978); *I Have a Diamond* (*Yo tengo un brillante*, 1978); *The Exciting Midday* (*Mediodía candente*, 1980); *A Colonial House* (*Una casa colonial*, 1981); *Confession in the Chinese Neighborhood* (*Confesión en el barrio chino*, 1984); *To Live in Santa Fe* (*Vivir en Santa Fe*, 1986); *Confrontation* (*Confrontación*, 1989); *A Wall in Havana* (*Un muro en La Habana*, 1994); *Dirty Games in the Basement* (*Juegos sucios en el sótano*, 1995); *Plants on the Roof of the World* (*Nenúfares en el techo del mundo*, 1997); *The Eccentrics of the Night* (*Los excéntricos de la noche*, 1998)

FURTHER READING

Consejo Nacional de las Artes Escénicas de Cuba [Cuban National Council for the Scenic Arts]. http://www.cubaescena.cult.cu.

Stevens, Camilla. *Family and Identity in Contemporary Cuban and Puerto Rican Drama*. Gainesville: Univ. of Florida Press, 2004.

Teatro y Revolución [Theater and revolution]. Havana: Editorial Letras Cubanas, 1980.

Unión Nacional de Escritores y Artistas de Cuba [Cuban National Union of Writers and Artists]. http://www.uneac.com.

Francisco Borja-Jimenez

DOUBT

Doubt, a parable by JOHN PATRICK SHANLEY, premiered at the Manhattan Theatre Club in late 2004. *Doubt* transferred to the Walter Kerr Theatre in March 2005 to popular and critical acclaim, winning four Tony Awards, including Best Play, Best Direction, Best Leading Actress, and Best Featured Actress, as well as the 2005 Pulitzer Prize for Drama.

Set in 1964, *Doubt* takes place at St. Nicholas parish, a Bronx parochial school overseen by the austere and stern principal Sister Aloysius, who watches both Donald Muller, the school's first African American student, and Sister James, a novice teacher, very closely. Sister James reports that Father Flynn, a popular young priest, has taken an interest in Donald, acting as his protector, and adds that Donald has been acting strangely. For Sister Aloysius, this information confirms her long-held suspicions that Father Flynn is molesting young boys at St. Nicholas. Despite Father Flynn's assurances to the contrary, Sister Aloysius is determined to protect the boy from Father Flynn and enlists the reticent Sister James in systematically casting suspicion against the young priest. Haunted by her own doubts, Sister James speaks to Father Flynn and becomes convinced of his innocence. Undaunted by the young nun's newfound belief in the priest, Sister Aloysius continues her unwavering attack. She calls in Donald's mother to relate her misgivings about the priest's relationship with the boy. However, Mrs. Muller sees Donald as a troubled child, disliked by other children and his own father for "being that way." She views the attention lavished on her son as a necessary evil, her only interest being Donald's graduation in June. After Mrs. Muller's visit, Father Flynn confronts Sister Aloysius. She lies to Father Flynn about speaking to a nun at his former parish who allegedly confirms her worst fears. Without denying the charges, Father Flynn resigns and ultimately accepts a transfer to another parish, leaving Sister Aloysius victorious but riddled with doubt about what she has done.

In light of the recent child abuse scandals within the Catholic Church, the story behind the play seems rather obvious. But if read carefully, the truth of what transpired between young Donald and Father Flynn is never revealed. The truth is obscured amid scandal (real, imagined, or exaggerated) and insufficient examination to further a specific agenda. In this way, Shanley uses *Doubt* as a parable to impart a pressing and thought-provoking comment on American society. *Doubt* asks whether conjecture and moral fortitude are enough to condemn dubious actions. This provides not only a captivating story but a charge for the audience to look at the doubt within their own lives.

FURTHER READING

Marks, Peter. "An Unshakable 'Doubt': New Work Puts Faith in the Church to the Test." *Washington Post* (December 16, 2004): C1. http://www.washingtonpost.com/wp-dyn/articles/A3514-2004Dec15.html.

Simonson, Robert. "John Patrick Shanley's *Doubt* Wins 2005 Pulitzer Prize for Drama." PLAYBILL (April 4, 2005). http://www.playbill.com/news/article/92095.html.

Gil Parkin

DRACHMANN, HOLGER (1846–1908)

I needed the world of legend and naivety after our modern conflicts. I believe myself that there is something sound, hearty, amiable in the fairy-tale comedy.

—Holger Drachmann in a Letter to Jacob Hegel, 1884

Holger Drachmann, born on October 7, 1846, in Copenhagen, DENMARK, started his career as a marine painter, but he was first and foremost a lyric poet. His poems are characterized by a musicality and a sensual imagery, which also mark his novels and plays. For a time Drachmann belonged to the circle around the Danish critic Georg Brandes, but in the beginning of the 1880s he turned away from the modern breakthrough. Before he did so, he wrote a clearly HENRIK IBSEN–inspired play, *Pupa and Butterfly* (*Puppe og Sommerfugl*, 1882), a variation of *A DOLL'S HOUSE*, followed by *Strandby People* (*Strandby Folk*, 1883), a naturalistic scene of life from the fishermen's town Skagen in Northern Jutland, then a magnet for Scandinavian painters.

Drachmann quickly got tired of the psychological REALISM of Henrik Ibsen and his followers who dominated the Danish stage. He wanted to revive the romantic drama, and in the Austrian Kärnten alps quite near the Italian border he wrote his fairy-tale COMEDY *Once Upon a Time* (*Der var engang*, published 1885, staged 1887), a play that he thought owned all the fine old Danish qualities: "good humour, delight in nature and men and with a flowing, perpetually young lyricism around it." Drachmann's play in which a haughty princess from the fictive country Illyrien is tamed by a Danish prince disguised as a Gypsy is inspired partly by a fairy tale from folklorist Evald Tang Kristensen's collections—the same source used by H. C. Andersen in *The Swineherd*—and partly by William Shakespeare's *The Taming of the Shrew*. When *Once Upon a Time* was Drachmann's greatest success on the stage, it was hardly because of the story itself or the play's not very progressive view of sexual roles but because of its lyric songs and neoromantic composer T. E. Lange-Müller's wonderful music. *Once Upon a Time* has served as an introduction to the theater for generations of Danish children, and its midsummer song is still heard at every Midsummer Eve bonfire around the country. The play was filmed three times: in 1907, 1922 (by Carl Th. Dreyer), and 1966.

After the success of *Once Upon a Time*, Drachmann wrote a long series of plays, many of which he characterized as MELODRAMAS (lyrical plays with music), but he often had difficulties with theaters that favored realist drama. Among his best plays are *Vølund Smith* (*Vølund Smed*, 1894, staged 1898), an epic drama based on the well-known Edda poem and ending with a scene where the old world is destroyed in an almost Wagnerian *Twilight of the Gods*; *Renaissance* (1894, staged 1901), a Venetian artists' drama; and *Gurre* (1899, staged 1901), on the love of Danish King Valdemar Atterdag and his mistress Tove. With the establishment of the open-air theater in Ulvedalene, north of Copenhagen, in 1910, Drachmann finally had a stage, posthumously (he died on January 14, 1908, in Hornbæk), perfectly fitted for his lyrical plays. When the theater was reopened in 1996 after having been closed from 1949, the two first performances were two national Danish classics: Johan Ludvig Heiberg's *The Hill of the Elves* (*Elverhøj*, 1928) and Drachmann's *Once Upon a Time*.

PLAYS: *The Princess and Half the Kingdom* (*Prinsessen og det halve Kongerige*, 1878); *East of the Sun and West of the Moon* (*østen for Sol og Vesten for Maane*, 1880); *Pupa and Butterfly* (*Puppe og Sommerfugl*, 1882); *Strandby People* (*Strandby Folk*, 1883); *Once Upon a Time* (*Der var engang*, published 1885, staged 1887); *Alkibiades* (1886); *Esther* (1888); *Renaissance* (*Renæssance*, 1894, staged 1901); *Vølund Smith* (*Vølund Smed*, 1894, staged 1898), *The Dancing at Koldinghus* (*Dansen paa Koldinghus*, 1895); *Gurre* (1899, staged 1901)

FURTHER READING

Boye, Ib. "Drachmann og teatret" [Drachmann and the theater]. Skagen: *Skagen Museum* (July 26, 1983).

Sigmund, Pia. "Holger Drachmann in America." *Scandinavian Studies* 65 (June 1993).

van der Liet, Henk. "A Fleeting Glimpse of Former Times. Holger Drachmann's Melodramas: 'Vølund Smed' and 'Renæssance.' " *Scandinavica* 33, no. 2 (November 1994).

Wamberg, Niels Birger. "Holger Drachmann og hans eventyr" [Holger Drachmann and his fairy tale]. In: *"Der var engang"* [*Once Upon a Time*] by Holger Drachmann, Sorgenfri: Green, 1998.

Kela Kvam

DRAGÚN, OSVALDO (1929–1999)

Osvaldo Dragún is one of the most acclaimed Argentine playwrights of the second half of the 20th century. He was born on May 12, 1929, in San Salvador, Entre Ríos, ARGENTINA. His theatrical vocation manifested itself in his university years. He soon abandoned studies in the law and enrolled in the theatrical group Teatro Popular Fray Mocho, with whom he premiered his first plays. As a playwright, Dragún addressed the socioeconomic problems that affected Latin America during his time. Dragún adopted a popular tone influenced by BERTOLT BRECHT and the Theater of the Absurd. However, Dragún has experimented widely with multiple dramatic styles, and thus his works resist simple aesthetic classification.

In his first plays, *The Plague Comes from Melos* (*La peste viene de Melos*, 1956) and *Tupac-Amaru* (1957), Dragún experiments with historical drama, leaving no doubt of his restless preoccupation with social topics. *Histories to Be Counted* (*Historias para ser contadas*, 1957) consists of three small plays; closely influenced by the style of the Italian commedia dell'arte, they expose the conventionalism and injustices of the bourgeois society of his time. In *Miracle in the Old Market* (*Milagro en el Mercado Viejo*, 1963), a tragic one-act influenced by the Argentine genre of the *sainete proteño*, Dragún explores the field of magic. Dragún's *Heroic of Buenos Aires* (*Heroica de Buenos Aires*, 1967) is an adaptation of Brecht's play MOTHER COURAGE.

Dragún's work in the theater is not limited to writing. In 1961 he moved to CUBA to direct and oversee the Cuban theater. He directed two important theatrical enterprises in Havana. First, he was in charge of the Seminario de Autores Dramáticos de La Habana, and years later, in 1988, he became involved with the Escuela Internacional de Teatro para América Latina y el Caribe. These projects proved to be a significant stimulant for Latin American theater, which had suffered at the hands of political dictatorships. The projects resulted in a proposal for theater renovation that attracted massive public support and evolved into new forms of expression that incorporated dance, poetry, and music. As a result of this collective effort, numerous plays by new and established authors came to light, including plays by Dragún, who premiered such plays as *My Dagger and I* (*Mi obelisco y yo*, 1981) and *Today They Eat the Skinny One* (*Hoy se comen al flaco*, 1981) at the time.

In 1980, when Argentina's military government had begun to weaken, Dragún became one of the inspiring leaders of the group *Teatro Abierto*, the first significant manifestation in the Argentine cultural sphere of an antidictatorship stance. Dragún died in Buenos Aires on June 14, 1999. He had dedicated his life to the theater, a life whose philosophy is perhaps best summed up by an observation he once made: "Theater is like a cork: it always floats. Although everything sinks and nobody throws out a rope, the passion remains alive. That's why, whether the impetus comes from the independent circles or the official ones, the task is to make sure it remains afloat." (http://usuarios.lycos.es/eitalc/osvaldo-dragun.htm)

SELECT PLAYS: *The Plague Comes from Melos* (*La peste viene de Melos*, 1956); *Tupac-Amaru* (1957); *The Garden of Hell* (*El jardín del infierno*, 1962); *Miracle in the Old Market* (*Milagro en el Mercado Viejo*, 1963); *Heroic of Buenos Aires* (*Heroica de Buenos Aires*, 1967); *History of My Corner*, (*Historia de mi esquina*, 1967); *Those of Table 10*, (*Los de la mesa 10*, 1967); *Histories to Be Counted* (*Historias para ser contadas*, 1967); *The Dough* (*El amasijo*, 1968); *And They Said That We Would Be Immortal*, (*Y nos dijeron que éramos inmortales*, 1968); *Miracle in the Old Market* (*Milagro en el Mercado Viejo*, 1968); *An Accursed Sunday!* (*¡Un maldito domingo!* 1968); *Histories with Jail* (*Historias con cárcel*, 1973); *And by Haven, In what Manner Can We Walk?* (*Y por casa, ¿cómo andamos?* 1980); *My Dagger and I* (*Mi obelisco y yo*, 1981); *Today They Eat the Skinny One* (*Hoy se comen al flaco*, 1981); *Arrive, Heart* (*Arriba, corazón*, 1987); *To Return to Havana* (*Volver a la Habana*, 1990)

FURTHER READING

Del Amo, Álvaro. "Conversación con Osvaldo Dragún." [Conversation with Osvaldo Dragún]. *Primer Acto*. 77 (1966).

Dauster, F. "Brecht y Dragún: teoría y práctica." [Brecht and Dragún: Theory and practice]. *Ensayos sobre teatro hispanoamericano* [Essays about Spanish-American theater]. México: Secretaría de Educación Pública, 1975. http://usuarios.lycos.es/eitalc/osvaldo-dragun.htm

Lyon, John E. "The Argentine Theater and the Problems of National Identity: A Critical Survey." *LATR*. 5/2 (1972): 14.

Pross, Edith E. "Open Theater Revisited: An Argentine Experiment." *LATR*. 18/1 (1984): 89.

Benito Gómez and Jorge Herreros

DRAMATIC CRITICISM

Drama critics might be divided into three categories, according to the amount of time they can devote to assessing a play. Reviewers who write for a daily newspaper must make an instant judgment. Critics who write for a weekly or monthly journal have more time to consider the merits of a play, as well as its failings. They are often selective in the plays they review, and tend to see the play in its cultural context. Then there are the scholars who write for learned journals. Their interests may be very broad or very narrow. They may focus on certain aspects of a particular work or dramatist, or they may set a group of plays in a broader context. And they may have spent months or years formulating their thoughts.

TYPES OF DRAMATIC CRITICISM

Reviewers who write for the daily press evaluate the immediate impact of the work. They situate the play in the present and necessarily concern themselves with a particular production, devoting as much space to the director, the actors, and the designers as to the dramatic content. Theirs is a special craft: they have to make a hurried judgment of the play, express their ideas in vivid language, all in a short space of time.

It might be thought that daily reviewers making snap judgments is the least reliable guide to a play's essential worth. This is not necessarily so. A play is intended to make an immediate impact on the audience, and the daily reviewer may be a better judge of this impact than the scholar who reads the play dozens of times. What the daily critics do best is to provide a consumer's guide to a particular product. They are the most powerful force determining the immediate success or failure of a play.

Although the daily critics often had to write their reviews hurriedly in order to meet the deadline for the morning edition of the paper, the best of them, usually those with years of theatergoing experience, often proved to be very insightful. Elliot Norton (1903–2003), the critic for a Boston newspaper, often saw plays in their out-of-town tryouts before they opened in New York. Producers and directors often heeded his advice, most famously in the case of NEIL SIMON's THE ODD COUPLE. Norton liked the play but not the ending. He wanted the Pigeon sisters to return in the third act. Simon saw the wisdom in that and rewrote the ending.

Brooks Atkinson, the theater critic for the *New York Times* for many years, was remarkably perceptive in his reviews of plays that went on to become classics. Although in order to meet his deadline he had to walk out of the theater before the curtain actually came down on the first night of A STREETCAR NAMED DESIRE, his evaluation of the play and his appreciation of the contrasting acting styles of Marlon Brando and Jessica Tandy still seems sound.

LITERARY CRITICISM

While the daily critics assess a play as a good value for time and money spent, those who write for highbrow publications try to keep their readers au courant and, if possible, try to see around the next bend in the road. Their function is to point out the social or political significance of a play and to recognize talent or genius in a young writer.

Georg Brandes, functioning as a literary critic, gave great encouragement to HENRIK IBSEN, when the playwright became the center of controversy. GEORGE BERNARD SHAW, one of the finest of all drama critics, helped establish Ibsen as a major force in the English-speaking world when Ibsen was being reviled by many reviewers. Herbert Jhering launched young BERTOLT BRECHT in GERMANY, awarding him the prestigious Kleist Prize when the leading critic Alfred Kerr treated Brecht, author of the notorious play BAAL, with disdain. ERIC BENTLEY became the ardent champion of Brecht in America, when Brecht's EPIC THEATER seemed to run contrary to everything that the American theater represented, both artistically and politically. Brooks Atkinson strove diligently to make SEAN O'CASEY a modern classic in America, but the playwright's avowed communist sympathies made the critic's task a daunting one.

While other critics expressed disappointment in EUGENE O'NEILL's THE ICEMAN COMETH when it premiered in New York in 1946, Atkinson recognized it as a master work, lavishing praise on it, while others deemed it too pessimistic and out of tune with the times (World War II had ended in 1945, and America was basking in the glow of victory). Atkinson called it one of O'Neill's best plays and in particular remarked on the power of O'Neill's dialogue when many literary critics were amazed that the playwright could have won the Nobel Prize for Literature. "It is good talk—racy, angry, comic drumbeats on the lid of doom, and a strong undercurrent of elemental drama silently washes the gloomy charnel-house where they [the habitues of the saloon] sit waiting" (Atkinson, 1946).

Most critics want to be more than reporters; they hope to be cultural arbiters, with the obligation of elevating the public's taste and powers of discrimination. It is their business to sense what has enduring value and to praise it and to dismiss what is shallow and trivial. The records abound in instances of both how right and how wrong critics have been in this regard. When EDWARD ALBEE's *WHO'S AFRAID OF VIRGINIA WOOLF?* opened in New York, the critic for the *New York Daily Mirror* called it "a sick play about sick people. They are neurotic, cruel and nasty. They really belong in a sanatorium for the mentally ill. . . . we loathed it [the play]. But we do not enjoy watching the wings being torn from human flies" (Coleman, 1962). This critic expressed an opinion widely held at the time. Though recommended for a Pulitzer Prize by the drama judges, the awarding committee rejected the recommendation.

The plays of CHRISTOPHER FRY provide an example of the opposite sort. Fry was for a while the critics' darling, who saw in him a man of religious yearnings who would revive poetic drama, and he was featured on the cover of a leading newsmagazine. But his plays have not aged well, and instead of acquiring a charming patina, they now seem more precious than poetic.

The ordinary theatergoer does not want brain puzzlers or plays that leave him feeling left out and intellectually snubbed. Critics who review plays regularly for the daily papers or popular weeklies write with this ordinary person in mind. Francisque Sarcey was the leading critic in Paris in the latter half of the 19th century. He knew what he liked and what his readers liked, and that was the well-made play acted by academically trained actors in handsome settings—the standard dramatic fare. When he saw the naturalist productions at Antoine's Théâtre-Libre, with untrained actors in plays that lacked proper dramatic structure in sets that were dimly lit, he was perplexed. When confronted with something radically new, like MAURICE MAETERLINCK's symbolist play *Pelléas and Mélisande*, he complained, "One leaves these dark shadows perfectly done in, as if one had a lead skull-cap on one's head."

By contrast, the English critic Arthur Symons, writing for connoisseurs, had an open mind about SYMBOLISM. Reviewing the first stage production (1898) of ALFRED JARRY's shocking "*comédie guignolesque, Ubu Roi*," he deemed it of "little importance in itself" but "of considerable importance as a symptom of tendencies now agitating the minds of the younger generation in France." (Symons, 1907) Instead of being scandalized by the play, he saw it as a serious FARCE about the human condition. "*Ubu Roi* is the brutality out of which we have achieved civilization, and those painted, massacring puppets the destroying elements which are as old as the world, and which we can never chase out of the system of natural things." (Symons, 1907)

CRITICAL REEVALUATION OF PAST WORK

The critical reception of Ibsen's works over a period of 150 years illustrates both how wrong critics may be at first and how long it may take them to be right. No dramatist in his own lifetime, not even Euripides, was both so reviled and so praised. At the end of his career, he was by far the most influential living dramatist. Hailed by some German critics as the equal of Sophocles and only a notch below William Shakespeare, he met a generally hostile reception in ENGLAND. The critics there launched a veritable campaign against Ibsen, as if he threatened the very minds and souls of good Englishmen. Even in Scandinavia, he was viewed by many as a baleful influence, and the Nobel Prize for Literature eluded him.

A primary function of critics is to reevaluate plays of the past. HEDDA GABLER (1890) puzzled its first critics, and Mrs. Ibsen had to remind them that it usually took twenty years for them to catch up with her husband's thoughts. Sixty or seventy years would have been a more realistic estimate.

The reevaluation of plays is a vital function of criticism, made necessary for two reasons: changing times allow the play to be seen in a different light, and there may be new insights into and revelations about what was in the play all along but had escaped notice. *Hedda Gabler* provides examples of both sorts of reevaluation, as do the works of Ibsen in general, when seen from the perspective of England and America. While still alive, he won worldwide fame as a social and political playwright. A few years after his death, a reaction set in. He was considered outmoded and passé; the social problem plays were treated like valuable heirlooms, handled with respect but not displayed. Then the psychological aspects of the dramas came to the fore, notably in Hermann J. Weigand's significantly titled *The Modern Ibsen: A Reconsideration* (1925). Subsequently, with the arrival of a new generation of critics, the realistic plays were seen in a new light. By a close examination of the stage directions, John Northam (1953) revealed a deeper level of symbolism in Ibsen's plays than anyone had previously been aware of. After yet another generation, Ibsen the philosophical thinker came to the fore in Brian Johnston's *To the Third Empire: Ibsen's Early Drama* (1980). This brought Ibsen criticism back to its starting point: in Scandinavia in the 1860s, Ibsen was viewed as a poet with a philosophical agenda.

Unfortunately, playwright and critic seldom engage in a dialogue. The critic usually has the first and last word, and often his last word is wrong. On those rare occasions when a dramatist forcefully challenged a critic, the results were memorable. When the leading Danish theater critic Clemens Petersen dismissed Ibsen's PEER GYNT as unpoetic, Ibsen told Petersen that the critic would have to change his standards and that if *Peer Gynt* was not poetry now, it would be. Ibsen knew better than the critic what the future would say because he was creating it. But later in his life, when he was a well-established writer, Ibsen did not deign to reply publicly to his critics, often to the harm of a real understanding of his works.

Georg Brandes did as much as anyone to support Ibsen, and yet at the end of his career, Ibsen said that Brandes had never really understood him. Because of George Bernard Shaw's growing fame, his *Quintessence of Ibsenism* became a standard guidebook to the works of the master. But its brilliance is due to Shaw's seeing himself mirrored in Ibsen. The result was a distortion of Ibsen, as much an explanation of the Irishman's PHILOSOPHY as of the Norwegian's.

One of the most meaningful confrontations of playwright and critic occurred in 1958 when EUGÈNE IONESCO, author of absurdist plays, responded to Kenneth Tynan, advocate of social REALISM. This was a debate that rose above personalities and styles; it brought out the great divide that characterizes modern drama, the divide between politics and metaphysics, between what Ionesco called the "didactic and ideological" (Brecht) and what Tynan described as a "phantom notion of art as a world of its own, answerable to none but its own laws" (Ionesco) (Ionesco, 1964).

The Spanish dramatist JACINTO BENAVENTE taught young playwrights on the need to say anything important in a play three times and explained why: first for bright members of the audience, second for the less bright, and the third time for the critics. In SAMUEL BECKETT's *WAITING FOR GODOT*, the ultimate insult is "Critic!"

Some of the criticism that is most helpful to students is contained in works that survey a broad field of drama or cover a specific genre. The best of these are written in an accessible style, acquaint the reader with the basic dramatic texts, allude to the standard or received opinions of them, and offer new insights into particular plays or authors. Among those that seem to have won a permanent place in dramatic criticism are Eric Bentley's *The Playwright as Thinker* (1946), Martin Esslin's *The Theatre of the Absurd* (1961), Maurice Valency's *The Flower and the Castle* (1963), Robert Brustein's *The Theatre of Revolt* (1964), and Raymond Williams's *Modern Tragedy* (1966). Also worth mentioning if only for its down-to-earth, anti-art-for-art's sake approach is Emma Goldman's *The Social Significance of the Modern Drama* (1914). Quite the opposite in tone is Peter Szondi's *Theory of the Modern Drama* (1965, English translation 1987), which employs postmodernist theory in discussing the historically significant characteristics of post-Ibsen drama.

The criticism that appears in learned journals is usually highly specialized, dealing with new developments in literary or dramatic theory, such as DECONSTRUCTION, or reflecting contemporary social issues, such as feminism or gay culture. The proliferation of these journals, especially after World War II, signaled a great shift in criticism, away from the well-informed broad discussion of a play or dramatist that the general reader could appreciate and toward a more hermetic criticism in which the latest theory is expounded to those who understand its jargon.

SCHOLAR-CRITICS

Scholars who study plays in minute detail sometimes discover aspects of them that had eluded critics with a broader perspective. Brecht specialists have called attention to the easily overlooked Christian symbolism in several of his plays. Cyrus Day (1958) discovered that in *The Iceman Cometh* O'Neill drew numerous parallels to the story of Jesus, the very title of the play being a perverse echo of "the bridegroom cometh" in the parable of the ten bridesmaids.

In instances like these the scholar-critic adds another dimension to familiar works and renews interest in them. Is that the reason why some dramatists keep much to themselves and leave it to the critics to discover the hidden text? Or is it because the dramatist wants to share the deeper meaning only with those who are wise enough or strong enough to appreciate the full meaning of the play? *The Iceman Cometh* is on the surface a play about the need the common man has for illusions. On the more profound level the play is about the end of Christian civilization, about the ineffectiveness of Jesus's love in a world driven by hate, a message of despair that most people do not want to hear.

The voice of the critic may sound loud and clear when first heard, but usually it fades away rather quickly with the passage of time, drowned out by newer voices. However, the student of drama can often learn a great deal from the best critics of the past, who being intimate with both the dramatist and his times can, like an old photograph, reveal the features of the subject in their true proportions.

James Huneker, not much read nowadays, can serve as an example of the finest sort of critic, one who understands the art of drama, one whose analyses throb with the pulse of new ideas and who writes about them in a language that anyone can understand. His 1905 essay on Ibsen's *Hedda Gabler* has hardly been bettered by later commentators and is worth quoting at some length.

> One merit of the piece is its absence of literary flavor. It is a slice of life. In his prose dramas, Ibsen throws overboard the entire baggage of "literary" effects. He who had worked so successfully in the field of the poetic legendary and historic drama; who had fashioned that mighty trilogy *Brand*, *Peer Gynt*, and *Emperor and Galilean*, saw that a newer rubric must be found for the delineation of modern men and women, of modern problems. So style is absent in his later plays—style in the rhetorical sense. Revolutionist that he is, he is nevertheless a formalist of the old school in his adherence to the classic unities. In Hedda Gabler the action is compressed within a space of about thirty-six hours, in one room, and with a handful of persons. One is tempted to say that the principal action occurs before the play or "off" the stage during its progress. We may see that Hedda does little throughout. Yet, through some magical impartment of the dramatist, we seem to be in possession of the characteristic facts of her nature before she arrives on the scene. Concision does not alone explain this, it may be noticed in other plays of the Norwegian. It is the dramaturgic gift raised to its highest power, though that power be expended upon base metal. . . .
>
> In Hedda Gabler all lyricism is sternly suppressed. As if the master had determined to punish himself for his championing of individualism in his earlier plays, he draws the portrait of one who might easily figure as a Nietzschean Super-Woman. Preaching that the state is the foe of the individual, that only revolution—spiritual revolution—can regenerate society, that the superior man and woman are lonely, that individual liberty must be fought for at all hazards,—liberty of thought, speech, action,—Ibsen then deliberately shows the free woman, one emancipated from the beliefs of her family circle and her country. She epitomizes the latter-day antisocial being and is rightfully considered by psychologists as a flaming sign of the times, a brief for the social democrats.

Most of the critical commentary of *Hedda Gabler* since Huneker's essay is an elaboration of what he says here. Hardly anything of significance has been omitted—Ibsen's technical mastery, the place of the drama in his oeuvre, its connection with new developments in philosophy and psychology—all either glanced at or dwelt on.

FURTHER READING

Atkinson, Brooks. Review of *The Iceman Cometh*. *New York Times* (October 10, 1946).

Coleman, Robert. "The Play You'll Love to Loathe." *New York Daily Mirror* (October 15, 1962).

Day, Cyrus. "The Iceman and the Bridegroom." *Modern Drama* 1 (May 1958): 3–9.

Huneker, James. *A Book of Dramatists*. New York: Charles Scribner's Sons, 1905.

Ionensco, Eugène. *Notes and Counter Notes: Writings on the Theatre*. New York: Grove, 1964.

Northam, John. *Ibsen's Dramatic Method*. London: Cambridge Univ. Press, 1953.

Symons, Arthur. *Studies in Seven Arts*. New York: Dutton, 1907.

Evert Sprinchorn

DRAMATIC CYCLES

Conventional dramatic structure centers on a critical moment, the climax. To maintain suspense and interest throughout the performance, most plays are short, compared to novels and epics. However, more ambitious dramatists sometimes wanted to encroach on the epic because their thoughts on a theme or subject could not possibly be contained in a three- or four-hour play. They created a series of plays on the specified subject.

Aeschylus seems to have been the first dramatist in the Western world to have created such a cycle. Greek tragedians vying for the prizes at the Dionysian festival in ancient Athens were required to submit three TRAGEDIES plus a satyr play. Evidently Aeschylus hit upon the idea of linking the three tragedies together, making them tell one story. He created several such cycles, but the only one that has survived complete is the *Oresteia*.

In the Middle Ages, plays based on the Bible stories and on religious subjects formed dramatic cycles, sometimes quite long, each play being relatively short.

Some cycles were not planned as such. William Shakespeare's history plays grew because the first ones proved to be popular. AUGUST STRINDBERG's cycle of a dozen plays based on Swedish history began with MASTER OLOF (1872), which is set in the 16th century, but Strindberg did not return to the subject until twenty-seven years later, when he composed *The Saga of the Folkungs*, set in the 14th century.

Preeminent among dramatic cycles is RICHARD WAGNER's *The Ring of the Nibelungs*, consisting of four operas, which together tell the story of the magical ring that bestows power on those who possess it. As first conceived, the *Ring* story was to focus on one hero, Siegfried, but Wagner soon found that Siegfried's story had to be prepared for by another drama. Wagner was directly inspired by the example of Aeschylus in extending his work. An avid student of Greek classics, he drew on Aeschylus and Homer as much as on Nordic and Teutonic legends in shaping his story. He ended up with a poem for the musical stage that tells of the world's beginning and its end. The *Ring* tetralogy is an awesome creation, about eighteen hours long in performance, the greatest of all dramatic cycles in the modern era, both by virtue of its original treatment of ancient legends and by the inventiveness of its music.

Many dramatic cycles take the form of trilogies, covering a relatively short period of time, the plays being linked together by a common theme. Strindberg's TO DAMASCUS tells of a man's spiritual journey; ARNOLD WESKER's political trilogy deals with a British family in the 20th century; and JEAN-CLAUDE GRUMBERG's trilogy pictures the plight of Jews in mid-century Europe.

Other cycles aspire to be serials or sagas, each play being an installment in a long story with many characters. HORTON FOOTE's "Orphans' Home Cycle" is about small-town life in Texas, while ED BULLINS in his seven-play "Twentieth-Century Cycle" dealt with race and class conflict among young blacks. AUGUST WILSON's ten-play cycle chronicles the life of African Americans over a hundred years. The ninth play, *Gem of the Ocean*, opened in New York in 2004.

After the success of his trilogy MOURNING BECOMES ELECTRA (1931), EUGENE O'NEILL planned other dramatic cycles. *Mourning* was a psychological drama inspired by Aeschylus's *Oresteia*; his next major project was to concern itself with religion in modern times. *Dynamo* (1929) was to be the first play in a trilogy in which the plays would not be linked together by story or character but by a broad theme—the search for a new faith in a faithless age. The second play, DAYS WITHOUT END met with a very mixed reception. He abandoned the planned trilogy and set to work on another cycle, turning his thoughts to the past, not to the future. Although it began as a trilogy, it quickly grew into a vast cycle as O'Neill outlined the plots and sketched the characters. The original three plays became eight, and finally eleven. O'Neill dreamed of a festival, surpassing Wagner's Bayreuth, devoted to this cycle, which would be performed over eight evenings and relate the rise and fall of the UNITED STATES from the French-Indian Wars to the 20th century by tracing the fortunes of two New England families. Ill health put an end to his dreams. Only one play from this cycle, A TOUCH OF THE POET, was completed by O'Neill, but another play, *More Stately Mansions* (next in the cycle), was sufficiently developed to be cut and adapted by others. The overall theme of the cycle ("A Tale of Possessors Self-Dispossessed") was stated by O'Neill in 1946: "Its main idea is that everlasting game of trying to possess your own soul by the possession of something outside of it, too. . . . We are the greatest example of 'For what shall it profit a man, if he shall gain the whole world, and lose his own soul?' " (O'Neill, 1987).

At the end of his life O'Neill created another kind of cycle by grouping his last four completed plays together, but not in the order in which they were written, indicating that a common theme ran through them. THE ICEMAN COMETH, he said, is "part of an interlocking series of plays. . . . The second is A MOON FOR THE MISBEGOTTEN, the third, *A Touch of the Poet*, and the fourth, LONG DAY'S JOURNEY INTO NIGHT" (Clark). O'Neill evidently saw these works as resonating with each other and as having a common theme.

GEORGE BERNARD SHAW wrote a cycle of five plays, BACK TO METHUSELAH (1921), which he called "a metabiological pentateuch." It tells the story of humankind from the time of Eden to a point 30,000 years in the future. Shaw thought it was his greatest work, but not even his admirers have agreed with him. He intended it as a summing up of his PHILOSOPHY, a bible for a new religion based on a belief in a life force. But this summing up was better accomplished earlier in three plays that Shaw himself grouped together as being a statement of his views on religion, politics, and economics: MAN AND SUPERMAN (1903), JOHN BULL'S OTHER ISLAND (1904), and MAJOR BARBARA (1905).

Anyone who reads HENRIK IBSEN's plays in the order in which they were written cannot help but notice that they form a kind of personal chronicle, each play growing out of the preceding one as regards theme. GHOSTS (1881) was obviously written in response to the criticism that A DOLL'S HOUSE was subjected to. Brian Johnston (1992) has argued that Ibsen deliberately in play after play worked out the philosophical ideas of Georg Hegel. That theory is much disputed. Ibsen himself, however, did refer to the plays from *A Doll's House* (1879) to WHEN WE DEAD AWAKEN (1899) as a connected series.

FURTHER READING

Clark, Barrett H. *Eugene O'Neill: The Man and His Plays*, rev ed. New York: Dover, 1947.

Johnson, Walter. *Strindberg and the Historical Drama*. Seattle: Univ. of Washington Press, 1963.

Johnston, Brian. *The Ibsen Cycle*. University Park: Pennsylvania State Univ. Press, 1992.

Lee, M. Owen. *Wagner's: Turning the Sky Round*. New York: Summit Bks., 1990.

O'Neill, Eugene. *The Calms of Capricorn*. Ed. by Donald Gallup. New Haven: Yale Univ. Press, 1982.

——. *Eugene O'Neill: Comments of the Drama and the Theater*. Ed. by Ulrich Halfmann, Tübingen: Gunter Narr Verlag, 1987.

Shaw, Bernard. *The Perfect Wagnerite*. 4th ed. London: Constable, 1922.

Evert Sprinchorn

DRAMATIC DIALOGUE

One of the difficulties in appreciating a play as it appears in print is because of the difference in the way information is processed by the ear and by the eye. What the eye takes in as it scans the page is different from what the ear takes in as it hears an actor speak. The difference is apparent when one compares the punctuation of a speech with its actual delivery. Punctuation on the page often does not convey the rhythms and stresses and pauses of the lines as uttered by the actor.

EUGENE O'NEILL remarked on the difference on dialogue that is meant to be heard and dialogue that is meant to be read. He said he wrote "primarily by ear for the ear, and that most of my plays, even down to the rhythm of the dialogue, had the definite structural quality of a musical composition. . . . I believe [this] to be a virtue, although it is the principal reason why I have been blamed for useless repetitions, which to me were significant recurrences of theme" (Cargill, 1961). O'Neill was often faulted for writing plays that seemed too long. But to cut O'Neill is like cutting a Mahler symphony. Of a 2003 production of MOURNING BECOMES ELECTRA in London, a critic wrote, "On the page, O'Neill often seems banal. But the layered effects, the repetitions and rhythms are transfixing in performance" (*Times Literary Supplement*, Dec. 12, 2003).

The difficulty in writing dialogue for a realistic play is that it must sound like real talk while being in fact quite artificial, saying much more than would be said in the actual circumstances. Of the dialogue in his DESIRE UNDER THE ELMS, O'Neill said it was "a synthetic dialogue which should be, in a way, the distilled essence of New England. . . . I wanted to express what [the characters] felt subconsciously" (O'Neill, 1990).

Good dialogue must not only sound right; it must also convey information rather rapidly, certainly much faster than in real life and even much faster than in novels. The expository scenes in realistic drama offer new bits of information in virtually every speech. These bits are processed much faster because in the theater eye and ear are fed simultaneously. Even when the actor is seemingly immobile, he is conveying information through his stance, manner, and facial expression. A description that might be spread out over a page or two in a novel requires in the theater only a stage direction and a line or two of dialogue.

It is no easy task to write dialogue that moves fast while at the same time sounding like real talk. ÉMILE ZOLA, the naturalist, who wanted his dramas to be as realistic as possible resisted "the claim that there is a special style [of language] for the theatre." "There is no such thing as 'theatre language'" (1880). But there is—if not in the actual words used (the vocabulary of ordinary life), then in the way they are arranged.

The drama critic and playwright William Archer insisted that writing realistic prose dialogue was more demanding than writing verse.

> The essential point is that the established custom of writing in verse, good, bad or indifferent, enabled and encouraged the dramatists to substitute rhetoric for human speech. It is immeasurably easier to make dramatic characters speak as men and women do *not* speak than to capture the true accent and the delicate interplay of actual talk, while at the same time condensing it, as drama must be condensed, and divesting it of superfluities (Archer, 1923).

HENRIK IBSEN would have agreed. He wrote his epic verse dramas BRAND and PEER GYNT at a furious speed. In contrast, his later realistic plays took longer to write, much of his time being spent on sharpening and honing the dialogue. Consistent with his aim of writing realistic dialogue, he allowed actors—even encouraged them—to "tweak" his lines so as to make them as vividly lifelike as possible (Ibsen, 1946).

The material of his realistic dramas is so rich and dense (they are like condensed novels) that virtually every sentence conveys a new bit of vital information. Conversation in real life is not like that. AUGUST STRINDBERG thought he could improve on Ibsen by letting conversations wander a bit, moving discursively from one topic to another.

Similarly, ANTON CHEKHOV sought to bring dialogue closer to offstage reality and to capture the randomness of everyday talk by having his characters suddenly say something that seems unmotivated and disconnected from what is going on. Reading his newspaper, Dr. Chebutykin in THE THREE SISTERS finds something significant in the fact that Balzac was married in Berdichev. The remark appears to have no connection with what has been said. But Chekhov was not one to waste time in his carefully constructed plays, and according to many commentators, Chekhov used apparently casual remarks as occasions for subtle authorial comment. His indirect dialogue often hints at much larger meanings that the actors must ferret out of the text.

The problem with realistic dialogue is that it dates very quickly. The way people speak in Ibsen's plays seems stilted to present-day readers and not true to life. But people did speak differently in the Victorian era; middle-class men and women used less slang, and they tended to speak in complete sentences. However, if a play adapter updates the dialogue it will not be in harmony with the 19th-century setting, the Victorian costumes, and the rigid social conventions—all part of the reality that the play intends to establish.

O'Neill's dialogue has often been faulted by literary critics as being strained, awkward, even illiterate. But his language in plays like BEYOND THE HORIZON was praised by theater critics of the time for its authenticity. Everyday dialogue with its modish expressions dates a play as much as the setting. The often lurching language of O'Neill's characters is more poetic—that is, evocative and haunting—than the language of, say, T. S. ELIOT in his dramas. DAVID MAMET is often praised for his ear for sharp, realistic dialogue, but one wonders how his plays will be accepted in the future.

Though most of modern drama employs dialogue that is terse and convincingly like speech in everyday life, there are plays that hark back to the days when grandiloquence was the essence of theater. GEORGE BERNARD SHAW and TOM STOPPARD often write bravura speeches meant to display the brilliance of both author and actor. In the devil's speech on man's destructiveness in MAN AND SUPERMAN Shaw brought to bear all the skill and experience he had acquired as a public speaker. The Don Juan in Hell scene is intensely theatrical when performed by actors trained in rhetorical techniques.

Although the economics of the realistic drama cannot accommodate many long speeches, when they do occur they become the center of interest, providing not only tours de force for actors but elevating the drama into the realm of poetry. Blanche Dubois's revelation of her past life in TENNESSEE WILLIAMS'S A STREETCAR NAMED DESIRE and James Tyrone's lament over his failure as an artist in O'Neill's LONG DAY'S JOURNEY INTO NIGHT rank among the finest moments that the modern theater has to offer.

These are exceptions, made memorable because of their rarity. The basic principle in writing stage dialogue is to be as economical as possible. It is usually better to cut than to add. In *The Three Sisters*, Chekhov wrote a speech half a page long in which Andrey complained about his marriage and the behavior of his wife. This occurs in the last act of the play, when the audience has seen for itself what has happened to Andrey's marriage. His marriage has turned sour, and the audience knows this. In rehearsals, Chekhov cut the speech, reducing it to one telling sentence: "A wife's a wife."

Slight changes can add enormously to effectiveness of dialogue, especially in COMEDY, where timing must be precise. Experienced actors often know better than dramatists how to make a good line even better. In the typescript of THE IMPORTANCE OF BEING EARNEST that OSCAR WILDE submitted to the actor-manager George Alexander, the famous interview scene in act 1 has this bit of dialogue.

Lady Bracknell: "Are your parents living?"
Jack: "I have lost both my parents."
Lady Bracknell: "Both? . . . To lose one parent may be regarded as a misfortune . . . to lose both seems like carelessness."

The George Alexander acting version reads:

"Are your parents living?"
"I have lost both my parents."
"Both? . . . That seems like carelessness."

The historical period can have a profound effect on the very rhythm of stage dialogue. O'Neill remarked on the fact that language is inevitably a reflection of its time. Of his TRAGEDY MOURNING BECOMES ELECTRA, O'Neill admitted it lacked great language and blamed the times as much as himself, saying that as a writer he had to express the "broken, faithless rhythm of our time."

After the horrors of World War I, which brought an end to the ideals of the Victorian era, some dramatists felt that the spirit of the age could be honestly expressed only in cries of anguish or in screams or in terse phrases, uttered abruptly (telegram style) as in Fritz von Unruh's *Plaza* (*Platz*, 1920) or in nonsensical drama, as in YVAN GOLL'S *Methuselah* (performed 1924), a play that anticipated the ABSURDISM of Ionesco after World War II.

After World War II there was a profound change in the very nature of stage dialogue. It was not so much the events on the battlefields that affected stage dialogue significantly as it was the revelation that millions had been systematically slaughtered in the concentration camps. The revelation of those horrors defied reason and made even the logic of language suspect. One result of this was a distrust of words as conveyors of knowledge or feeling. As Theodor Adorno said, "To write poetry after Auschwitz is barbaric."

To speak about the Holocaust in ordinary discourse was to give meaning to it, and from that it was only a short distance to explanation and from that to justification. There were thousands of people employed in the mass destruction and millions aware of it—all speaking the language of ordinary life as they carried on their business. To many sensitive writers in the postwar era, language, as an expression of the times, became morally tainted and divorced from reason and rationality. Playwrights like SAMUEL BECKETT in English, PETER HANDKE in German, and JON FOSSE in Norwegian all display a distrust of words as carriers of meaning. Theirs is a world entirely different from Ibsen's, in which every word added to one's understanding of human behavior. Their endeavor is a contrary one—to undercut any emerging sense of meaning. There is a perverse wizardry involved in keeping the audience involved while saying as little as possible. In Beckett's output one can see the result: plays becoming ever shorter as both plot and dialogue approach a vanishing point.

[*See also* Acting; Stage Directions and Stage Sets; Subtext]

FURTHER READING

Archer, William. *The Old Drama and the New: An Essay in Re-valuation.* Boston: Small, Maynard, 1923.

——. *Play-Making.* With introduction by John Gassner. New York: Dover, 1960.

Bentley, Eric. *The Life of the Drama.* New York: Atheneum, 1967.

Cargill, Oscar, N. Bryllion Fagin, and William J. Fisher, eds. *O'Neill and His Plays.* New York: New York Univ., 1961.

Ibsen, Henrik. *Samlede Verker. Hundreårsutgave.* Vol. 17. Ed. by Francis Bull, Halvdan Koht, Didrik Arup Seip. Oslo: Gylderelal Norsk, 1946

Lawson, John Howard. *Theory and Technique of Playwriting and Screenwriting.* New York: G.P. Putnam's Sons, 1949.

O'Neill, Eugene. *Conversations with Eugene O'Neill.* Ed. by Mark W. Estrin. Jackson: Univ. Press of Mississippi, 1990.

Zola, Émile. "Naturalism in the Theater." (1880) In *Documents of Modern Literary Realism*, ed. by George J. Becker. Princeton: Princeton Univ. Press, 1963.

Evert Sprinchorn

DRAMATIC STRUCTURE

The standard dramatic form in the Western world derives from ancient Greek TRAGEDY, Roman COMEDY, and the theories of Aristotle and Horace.

Aristotle said that a tragedy has three parts: a beginning, a middle, and an end. This seems simplistic and not very enlightening until one gives the three parts names—exposition, rising action, and resolution. Then the action of a tragedy acquires a drive leading to a climax, a moment of intense feeling—and a shape—the shape of a stepladder (*klimax* is the Greek word for ladder).

Aristotle provided another image of dramatic structure when he said that the first part of a tragedy was like the tying of a knot (several plot strands brought together), while the last part consisted in the untying of the knot. The French word for untying—denouement—became the standard term. Thus the last part of the drama could be regarded as both a falling action ("catastrophe" in Greek) and an untying.

A modern critic, Arthur Hopkins, saw the three parts, exposition, rising action, and denouement, as reducible to three punctuation marks—a question mark, an exclamation point, and a period. The first part raises the question, "What is going to happen?" The second part produces a surprise: "I didn't expect that!" The third part brings a resolution: "Everything is settled."

From Roman comedy and Horace came the idea that this three-part structure should be divided into five distinct acts. That allowed for a further refinement of the structure. Gustav Freytag (1894) in his highly influential analysis of play structure called these five parts: introduction, rising action, climax, falling action, and catastrophe.

Aristotle placed particular emphasis on the moment when the action is at its height—the top of the stepladder. It brings about the downward turn, the catastrophe—a term that acquired another meaning because of the terrible things that happened in the last part of most tragedies.

Crucial in the Aristotelian model is this moment when the action undergoes a violent change. He called it the *peripeteia*, anglicized as *peripety* and often rendered as *reversal*. This moment constitutes the heart of the action. Everything leads up to it; everything falls away from it. The image of the stepladder shows how crucial it is to the whole structure. Without it, there is no effective drama—only two ladders without any support.

To make it most effective (theoretically) three things are necessary—one hero, one action, one crisis. Having two central figures, each with his own agenda, would be like having two stepladders. The single moment that changes everything is of course what grips the audience—the exclamation point. The most famous example is Sophocles's *Oedipus Rex*. In one instant Oedipus learns that he himself is the criminal for whom he has been searching.

Aristotle also mentioned the need for a moment of recognition (anagnorisis)—the recognition by the hero of some significant truth behind the action, in Oedipus's case, the knowledge that he committed incest with his mother. Aristotle's perfect tragedy would have climax, peripety, and anagnorisis all occur simultaneously—as in *Oedipus*.

The classic model was revived in Renaissance ITALY and spread to FRANCE and ENGLAND. The French in their neoclassical drama adhered to it rigorously. On the other hand, the English dramatists of the early modern period—William Shakespeare and his contemporaries—found it too limiting. A major problem with it was that it derived from Greek tragedies that lasted about ninety to one hundred minutes. It is hard to hold the audience's interest for a long time when there is only one action. AUGUST STRINDBERG learned from the Greeks, and his long one-act tragedy MISS JULIE runs for about 100 minutes. The Elizabethan solution was double action—plot and subplot, violating Aristotle's basic rule.

The Aristotelian model has always been tampered with, even by the Greeks—witness Euripides' plays, which have often been faulted for having a double action or for having two leading characters.

In France, after the revolution, MELODRAMA, "tragedy for the people," became popular because of the exciting, suspense-filled action. The more highbrow dramatists tried to capture some of this excitement by appropriating one of its typical features—the seesaw action. Unlike Oedipus, battling with himself, the heroes of melodramas fight against villains. As the good guy takes on the bad guys, one side of the seesaw goes down for a while until a new bit of information or action reverses the swing of the seesaw. Each of these reversals is structurally akin to the overall structure of ancient tragedy. Imagine a seesaw superimposed on each step of the ladder. The dramas of VICTORIEN SARDOU (along with thousands of movies) afford excellent examples of this technique, which GEORGE BERNARD SHAW dismissively called "Sardoodledom." For an instance of the technique carried to an extreme, consider the execution scene in WILLIAM GILLETTE'S SECRET SERVICE.

In the first half of the 19th century the French dramatists perfected what came to be called the "well-made play." This form followed the rules while striking a compromise between melodrama and serious drama. To the standard recipe it added another ingredient—a physical object on which the plot depends, as in Sardou's A SCRAP OF PAPER. Or the two letters that bring about the denouement in HENRIK IBSEN'S A DOLL'S HOUSE.

Also characteristic of the well-made play was the *scène à faire*, a term coined by Francisque Sarcey, who understood and liked the well-made play to the practical exclusion of everything else. Translated into English (by William Archer) as the obligatory scene, it is the scene that the playwright is obliged to supply in order not to disappoint the audience. Usually it is the scene in which opposed parties are brought together. In DUMAS FILS'S *Camille*, it is the scene in which Armand embraces Camille just before she dies. In real life, he would probably have learned of her death without ever seeing her again. That real-life ending would please only a small group of hardheaded realists.

Practitioners of the well-made play often sought to emulate the Greeks in constructing plots that hinged on a single moment, the turning point, which occurs between the rising action and the falling action, the moment that unites reversal (peripety) with recognition (anagnorisis) with climax, as in *Oedipus*. ARTHUR PINERO achieves this in THE SECOND MRS. TANQUERAY, when the heroine, a married woman, says the simple line "How do you do" to her former lover. Her unsavory past has reentered her life, and she cannot escape it.

Reviewing HERMANN SUDERMANN'S *Magda* (*Heimat*), Shaw (1931) describes a similar moment.

> Magda, after many years of work and finally of great success as an independent woman . . . becomes reconciled to her father, a fanatical believer in the old ideals of family honor and manly supremacy. She has a child whose father turns up among the intimate friends of the family. Her father demands that she shall marry this man as a point of honor. She submits to this and to the sacrifice of her profession until the man demands also that she shall part with the child in order to save appearances. Magda then turns on him and overwhelms him with scorn. Her father insists. She defies her father, who attempts to kill her and is struck down by paralysis in the act.

And how is this motivated? By the utterance of a single line. "There are few strokes of drama more effective and convincing than the climax of the final scene between the father and daughter, when she at last asks him the terrible question, 'How do you know that he was the only one?' After that, the catastrophe comes quite inevitably."

For lovers of the well-made play, scenes like these constitute the very essence of good theater. But for those who preferred more REALISM and less theater, or more artistry and less carpentry, the well-made play had to be deconstructed. To them, life is messy and does not shape itself as a perfect tragedy. The rise of realism meant that the standard form had to be modified. It was too artificial to be real. It was acceptable for entertainment but not for serious thought.

Much of modern drama consists in attempts to break away from the standard model. In *A Doll's House*, Ibsen followed the formula up until the end, when he shattered expectations and ended the play with an exclamation point, not a period.

The rise of NATURALISM forced a redefinition of the exposition and denouement of a play. Jean Jullien in the preface to *The Date of Payment* (*L'Echéance*, 1890), responding to ÉMILE ZOLA'S view that a naturalist work should be "a corner of life seen through a temperament," said a play should be "a slice of life transferred to the stage with art." The exposition would be created "by the action itself and the denouement would be like a bus stop in the story line that would allow the play to offer an open field for the thoughts of the spectators."

Shaw took his inspiration as a dramatist from the discussion scene at the end of *A Doll's House* and soon was writing plays that were nearly all debate. ANTON CHEKHOV toned down the action and usually kept the melodrama offstage, as with the duel in THE THREE SISTERS. The climax is very quiet—the transfer of the keys of the house—and the ending is a question mark ("If only we knew . . .").

If the climactic scene is very quiet and subtle, it may fail to achieve its intended effect. In LYOV TOLSTOY'S THE POWER OF DARKNESS, the true climax is a soliloquy in which the hero sees the religious significance of what has happened to him, but the speech is likely to be overshadowed by the horrifying events leading up to it.

Others preferred to dispense with the rising action or held it to a minimum by writing short plays. The quarter-hour play, the *quart d'heure*, which had a vogue in the 1880s, was perfected by Strindberg in THE STRONGER. The Russian Kharms wrote skits only a page or two long. SAMUEL BECKETT, seeking to express meaninglessness, wrote a number of playlets. Of the more than twenty plays in his oeuvre, only four last longer than thirty minutes.

At the other end of the spectrum are the oversized structures, like O'Neill's last plays, each running to four or more hours, with plot and action held to a minimum. Yet the standard form is discernible in them. Even his five-hour STRANGE INTERLUDE in nine acts is constructed according to the standard formula, with the well-prepared climax occurring at the end of act 6.

Plays written according to the standard model expect the viewers to be familiar with the form, just as those who go to hear classical music are expected to know something about sonata form. An understanding of the play depends on knowing the form and being able to distinguish the significant action, which supports the main theme (the stepladder) from the byplay. One of the principal tasks of the director and the actors is to reveal the structure of the play to the audience. This is sometimes very difficult. One can read in KONSTANTIN STANISLAVSKY's *My Life in Art* of the problem he had in establishing the through-line for Chekhov's *The Three Sisters*, a drama with several intertwined stories.

Dissatisfaction with the standard form and the sense that it had exhausted all its possibilities led to experimentation—but also to loss of popular audience in the theater. The standard form, modified as necessary, prevailed in the movies. As testimony to the strength of the basic model are the careers of playwrights like SAM SHEPARD and SUZAN-LORI PARKS, who began by violating the rules but, after sowing their wild oats, came to embrace more conventional forms.

[*See also* Dramatic Cycles; Monodrama; Subtext]

FURTHER READING

Archer, William. *Play-Making*. With introd. by John Gassner. Reprint, New York: Dover, 1960.

Freytag, Gustav. *Freytag's Technique of the Drama*. Tr. by Elias J. MacEwan. Chicago: Scott, Foresman, 1894.

Lawson, John Howard. *Theory and Technique of Playwriting and Screenwriting*. New York: Putnam, 1949.

Montague, C. E. *Dramatic Values*. New York: Doubleday, 1925.

Shaw, George Bernard. *Our Theatres in the Nineties*. London: Constable, 1931.

Sprinchorn, Evert. "The Decline and Disappearance of Plot." In *20th-Century Plays in Synopsis*, ed. by Evert Sprinchorn. New York: Crowell, 1965.

Stanton, Stephen S. Introduction to *Camille and Other Plays*. New York: Hill & Wang, 1957.

Strindberg, August. "On Modern Drama and Modern Theatre." In *Selected Essays*, tr. by Michael Robinson. Cambridge: Cambridge Univ. Press, 1996.

Evert Sprinchorn

DRAMATURGY

EUROPEAN DRAMATURGY

Playwright-director HARLEY GRANVILLE-BARKER and critic William Archer were the first to include a detailed description in English of the roles of "dramaturg" and "literary manager" in their *A Scheme and Estimates for a National Theatre* (published 1908) in 1904. They defined the "literary manager" as "an official answering to the German *Dramaturg*," stating, "His duties should be to weed out new plays before they are submitted to the Reading committee; to suggest plays for revival and arrange them for the stage; to follow the dramatic movement in foreign countries, and to suggest foreign plays suitable for production; to consult with the scene painter, producers, etc., on questions of archeology, costume, and local color."

DRAMATURGY IN GERMANY

From the Greek *dramatourgos* ("maker of drama"), the dramaturg was originally the "dramatist" or "playwright," a meaning still preserved in the Spanish *dramaturgo* and the French *dramaturge* ("playwright" or "dramatist," as well as "dramaturg"). Originally a resident playwright or literary adviser, the dramaturg in the modern era has emerged as a distinct profession, and dramaturgy today specifically refers to the work of a resident or company dramaturg, "production dramaturg," or "literary manager." The professions of both dramaturg (1760s) and director (1860s) originated in German-speaking Europe. The modern profession of the director was an expansion of the role of theater manager (*generaldirektor* or *intendant*) with the addition of some duties previously the domain of the stage manager (*regisseur*).

Gotthold Ephraim Lessing (1729–1781) became dramaturg of the Hamburg Nationaltheater in 1765. His series of 104 dramaturgical notes to the company were published in 1769 under the title *Hamburg Dramaturgie*. The position of dramaturg (*theatersecretär*) was established for distinguished men of letters, such as playwright August von Kotzebue (1761–1819). Joseph Schreyvogel (1768–1832) was dramaturg from 1802 to 1804 and again from 1815 to 1832. Schreyvogel personally conducted all rehearsals, and he also worked closely with *theaterdichter* Franz Grillparzer (1791–1872) as his literary adviser and production dramaturg for fifteen years.

In 1791 Duke Karl August established a permanent professional company at the Weimar Höftheater and hired Johann Wolfgang von Goethe (1749–1832) as *intendant*. Friedrich von Schiller (1759–1805) joined him in 1795 as dramaturg, and by 1800 Weimar had become the literary center of GERMANY. Goethe gave Schiller notes on the drafts of his plays as he wrote them, and Schiller prepared the stage versions for Goethe's plays. It was in reference to Schiller's work at the Weimar theater that the word *dramaturg* was first used in the English language in an 1859 article in the *Times* of London, which described Schiller's function "as dramaturg or literary manager."

By 1800 German theaters included four key positions: the *intendant* (general manager), sometimes called the *generaldirektor*; the *dramaturg* (dramatist/literary adviser), sometimes called the *theatersecretär*; the *regisseur* (stage manager), who kept the *regiebuch* (promptbook); and the *theaterdichter* (theater-poet or resident playwright). Individual plays received only a few rehearsals. "Production dramaturgy" emerged from the collaboration between the dramaturg and other artists and staff. Increasingly, it has also included extensive documentation of production work.

Ludwig Tieck (1773–1853) became dramaturg of the Dresden Höftheater in 1824. From 1842 to 1853 he was dramaturg at the Königstheater in Berlin, where he staged a cycle of Greek plays while also editing the landmark August Schlegel–Dorothea Tieck translation of the complete works of William Shakespeare. Tieck and his protégé, playwright Karl Immermann (1796–1840), dramaturg at the Düsseldorf Town Theatre, re-created the first authentic Elizabethan stage (*Shakespearebühne*) for Tieck's 1842 production of *A Midsummer's Night Dream*.

As play production, experiments in dramatic form, and stage technology became more complex, the role of *intendant* also evolved, eventually transformed into the modern position of the specialist director. George II, duke of Saxe-Meiningen (1826–1914), *intendant* of the Meiningen Players from 1870 to 1895, was both head of state and head of his own theater. With an unlimited budget, he spent months of rehearsals on individual plays and created a powerful new authoritarian production model.

With the "new theater" movement, directors began to eclipse the other artists. In the early 20th century MAX REINHARDT introduced the practice of the directorial "concept"—an overriding theme or idea to which all aspects of the production were subordinated. The 20th century saw the growing dominance of the *auteur* director (*Regieführer*), first articulated by Edward Gordon Craig (1872–1966), claiming that only a single dominant voice (the director) could raise theater to the artistic level of music or poetry. By the late 20th century virtuoso directors would claim total autonomy from the playwright and performer. French director Roger Planchon (1941–) defined directing as *écriture scènique* (scenic writing).

DRAMATURGY IN RUSSIA

Russian actor-director KONSTANTIN STANISLAVSKY (1863–1938) was one of the first to become dissatisfied with the director-autocrat method of producing plays. Originally, as he put it, "I treated my actors as mannequins. I showed them what I saw in my imagination, and they copied me." At a famous eighteen-hour, all-night meeting at the Slavyansky Bazaar restaurant on June 22, 1897, he and critic-playwright Vladimir Nemirovich-Danchenko (1858–1943) decided to join forces and create a new theatrical venture where actors and artists would again become collaborators on productions. This became the Moskovskii Khudozhestvennyi Teatr (MOSCOW ART THEATRE, abbreviated as MKhAT or MAT), which produced their first play in 1898 with Stanislavsky acting and directing and Nemirovich-Danchenko as literary manager and dramaturg. Their collaboration is difficult to characterize in contemporary notions of director and dramaturg. For example, although Nemirovich-Danchenko gave lectures and critical notes to the company, he also often ran rehearsals based on handwritten notes from Stanislavsky. They both put great emphasis on dramaturgical background work. For their first production, Aleksai Tolstoy's *Tsar Fyodor*, designer Victor Simov and several other members of the company did extensive dramaturgical and historical research on 16th-century RUSSIA, including a field trip to the ancient city of Rostov.

Actor-director Alexandr Tairov (1885–1950) founded his Kamerny Teatr (Chamber Theater) in 1914 as an "acting collective" of co-creators and called for an end to "directorial despotism." He observed that "the actor had to yield to the newly powerful artist [i.e., the director], who began to lord it over the stage. And of course the actor only got in the way of the artist, who had transferred to the stage all the methods of easel painting."

Prolekult started in 1917 in order to create a totally new proletarian collaborative culture in all areas of literature and drama and swiftly sought to gain control of the new Theatrical Section (*teatralnyi otdel*), or TEO, of the Peoples' Comissariat for Enlightenment. Local Soviets also began to take direct control of municipal theaters, and in 1919 the MAT and other major theaters were nationalized. In 1920, actor VSEVOLOD MEYERHOLD (1874–1940) was named head of the newly created Tsentroteatr to supervise TEO with poet-playwright ALEXSANDR BLOK, the director of Repertoire, and director-actor Yevgeny Vakhtangov (1883–1922), director of Pedagogical Theatre for Workers and Peasants. Meyerhold immediately founded "Theatre No. 1 of the RSFSR" (Russian Socialist Federated Soviet Republic) and issued the call for a revolutionary "Theatrical October" (*teatralnyi Oktyabyr*) to create new collaborative theatrical forms. He declared an end to literature as private property and sought to collaborate with his company in reworkings and/or improvisations based on the texts.

Prolekult pioneered several unique forms of revolutionary theater, including the "living newspapers" and elaborately staged "mock trials" of class criminals such as *The Trial of Baron Wrangel* (April 1920). Prolekult's most dynamic creations, however, were the mass revolutionary pageant-spectacles. In 1920 revolutionary festivals were staged in many cities, most spectacularly in Petrograd. The greatest realization of this vision was NIKOLAI EVREINOV's mammoth production of *The Storming of the Winter Palace* on November 7 with over 10,000 performers, including many who had taken part in the actual events and 75,000 spectators in Petrograd on the actual sites of the events they were depicting.

The great actor Mikhail Chekhov (1891–1955), nephew of the playwright, took over the Moscow Studio Theatre in 1922. Rejecting the theory of the autocrat-director, he introduced the policy of "collective direction" in the company, requiring the collaboration of three or four different director-dramaturgs on each production, including *Hamlet* (1924, directors: Valentin Smyshlyaev, Vladimir Tatarinov, and Aleksandr Cheban). He left Russia in 1927, settling in the UNITED STATES in 1939.

Vladimir Lenin and Joseph Stalin had replaced the czarist system with an even more repressive and iron-fisted bureaucracy. Many of Russia's greatest artists were imprisoned and/or executed in the 1930s. Committed Bolshevik Vladimir Mayakovsky (1893–1930), who had been de facto poet laureate of the 1917 Revolution and author of the AGITATION-PROPAGANDA (agit-prop) masterpiece MYSTERY-BOUFFE, was denounced as counterrevolutionary, and he committed suicide. Even the dedicated Marxist Meyerhold, who had created the role of Tuzenbach in the original production of THE THREE SISTERS at the MAT in 1901 and had instituted the great "Theatrical October" in 1918, was arrested and executed by the KGB. Soviet dramaturgy, ironically mimicking and mirroring the system that was being set up in Nazi Germany by *Reichsdramaturg* Rainer Schlösser, became the dramaturgy of censorship.

DRAMATURGICAL COLLABORATION

The theatrical strides in early Soviet Russia made "dramaturgical collaboration" part of a wider political agenda throughout Europe. JACQUES COPEAU (1879–1949) founded the influential Théâtre du Vieux-Colombier in 1913. Copeau sought to return theater to a communal celebration, akin to religious ritual. In a 1938 speech he declared: "Let us hope for a dramatist [dramaturg] who replaces or eliminates the director." In 1936 he became a dramaturg at the Théâtre Française.

As *intendant* of the Proletarisches Theater and later the Volksbühne (people's stage) in Berlin, ERWIN PISCATOR (1893–1966) organized the dramaturgy department as a collective of playwrights, theorists, critics, and performers. In *The Political Theatre* (1929), he argued that "the dramaturg's task should not be limited . . . to drawing up the repertoire, making suggestions for casting the plays, looking for new scripts and cutting superfluous passages in the texts." Piscator saw the "dramaturgy collective" as the key to returning theater to its collaborative roots, destroying the "dictatorial principles" that had taken over the modern stage by creating "a democratic community" of "comrades who share a spirit of revolution and a concern for artistic matters."

The Second Spanish Republic in 1931 established two collaborative traveling companies: Teatro del Pueblo, headed by Alejandro Casona (1903–1965), and Teatro Universitario, known as La Barraca (The Booth), headed by FEDERICO GARCÍA LORCA (1898–1936). Lorca was dramaturg and resident playwright (*dramaturgo*) of the company that performed classics for the poor uneducated peasants in the Spanish countryside. In 1933 they began touring their enormously popular adaptation of Lope de Vega's *The Sheep Well* (*Fuente ovejuna*). Lorca's execution by a right-wing Falangist death squad in 1936 ended La Barraca. Casona fled SPAIN the following year.

More than any other individual BERTOLT BRECHT (1898–1956) fought to advance the profession of dramaturgy in the 20th century. Dramaturg at the Munich Kammerspiel and later at Berlin's Deutsches Theater, by the early 1930s he had developed a practical, working method of collaborative production. Brecht and Piscator both saw production as a learning experience—for the company as well as the audience—and they attacked the notion of a preconceived concept. Brecht saw the hegemony of modern directors and the authoritarian production model as creations of a capitalistic and fascist system.

After World War II Brecht settled in the German Democratic Republic, where he became founder and *chefdramaturg* of the Berliner Ensemble. In 1951 the Berliner Ensemble presented THE MOTHER, after months of rehearsal, and the result of the most extensive dramaturgical collaboration up to that time. Brecht introduced "preview" performances to the German theater as well as the dramaturgy *protocol*. Taking the *regiebuch* and dramaturgical research to a new level of sophistication, Brecht supervised the preparation of a series of *Modellbücher* ("model books" or dramaturgy logbooks/protocols), meticulously documenting his productions in ideological and critical terms.

The late 1960s were a time of great social upheaval. The year 1968 was the watershed year, with the "May Revolution" in Paris, the "Prague Spring," and the anti-Vietnam peace movement. As political institutions came under assault, traditional theatrical venues and means of production were attacked with increasing fervor.

ARIANE MNOUCHKINE (1934–) founded Théâtre du Soleil as a collective in 1964. As the political crisis of May 1968 intensified, theater artists from across FRANCE held an emergency weeklong "teach-in." Mnouchkine and others declared that theater had replicated the dysfunctional social-political order. Challenging the director's (*metteur en scene*) supremacy, she attacked it as both male dominated and fascist. She noted: "the director has already achieved the greatest degree of power he has ever had in history. And our aim is to move beyond that situation by creating a form of theatre where it will be possible for everyone to collaborate." Her company's work became a cause célèbre, known as "the collection creation" (*la création collective*). 1789 (1970), where *dramaturg* Elizabeth Brisson supervised the company of actor-dramaturgs, was an enormous success and validated the dramaturgical collective model. The subsidized French regional companies rapidly embraced the new model, and some dramaturgs began replacing both directors and playwrights as the primary force in French theaters. The collection creation model became so dominant that playwright MICHEL VINAVER submitted a report to the government in 1987 arguing that the occupation of playwright was in danger of extinction.

Following the May symposium in Paris, in July at a similar German conference, Peter Stein made himself spokesman for a new democratic, antifascist, dramaturgical collaborative theater. In the 1970s and 1980s at Berlin's Schaubühne, he put his theories into practice, collaborating with dramaturgs Dieter Sturm, BOTHO STRAUSS (1944–), and Marleen Stössel, insisting that the "role of dramaturg in the German theatre was an actual production collaborator rather than the more traditional peripheral consultant." Stein argued for the total elimination of the role of director, and most of his productions carried no credit for director. Stein and his dramaturgs often spent two years or more in preparation for a production. For their 1980 production of *The Oresteia*, production dramaturg Marleen Stössel prepared a 400-page dramaturgy protocol. Director CLAUS PEYMANN (1938–) joined Stein as the leader of a new generation of anti-authoritarian directors, collaborating with dramaturg Uwe Jens Jensen since the 1970s, and both moved to the prestigious Burgtheater in 1986.

DRAMATURGY IN POSTWAR EASTERN EUROPE

In postwar Eastern Europe, the repressive regimes in Eastern Europe funded theaters modeled on the concept of the worker collective, and ironically theater production in the East was more democratic than in the West. Dramaturgs and theater artists also were often at the forefront of antigovernment political events, such as the formation of "Solidarity" in POLAND and "Civic Forum in CZECHOSLOVAKIA.

VÁCLAV HAVEL (1936–) became dramaturg at the Divadlo Na Zábradlí (Theater on the Balustrade) in 1962, where he collaborated with dramaturg-director Jan Grossman (1925–1993). Havel and many other dramaturgs signed "Charter 77" in 1977, a declaration of human rights, and he openly challenged the government with his speeches and writings. Dramaturgs in Czechoslovakia saw themselves as the moral conscience of their nation, and many were leaders of the protests that bloodlessly toppled the communist government in November 1989, known as the "Velvet Revolution." Civic Forum, the organization founded by Havel, mobilized opposition to the government, holding its first meetings on the stage of the Činoherní Klub (Drama Club), until legendary designer Josef Svoboda made his Laterna Magika (Magic Lantern) the headquarters of Civic Forum. Dramaturgs stopped scheduled performances and used their theaters to disseminate the truth in the face of government control of television and radio. These included late-night lectures, sing-along versions of traditional Czech folksongs with new words, staged events from Czech history, and dramatized "living versions" of suppressed news events. Dramaturgs organized the protests and staged the mass-spectacle demonstrations. Havel was elected president of Czechoslovakia in 1990.

Collaboration had long been deeply instilled in the English dramatic tradition. In the Middle Ages, collective collaboration was the standard mode of creation of the biblical pageants staged every year. The Elizabethan-Jacobean era was also a time of enthusiastic collaboration. Many, if not most, plays of the period were jointly authored, some by as many as a half-dozen different hands. Script ownership by writers and the concept of "intellectual property" did not yet exist.

Actor-playwrights, such as Richard Brinsley Sheridan (1751–1816), and actor-managers, such as David Garrick (1717–1779), ran the British theater for the next two centuries. In the 19th century, theaters began employing literary advisers to read plays, such as George Gordon, Lord Byron (1788–1824), at Drury Lane. Actor-managers also started employing individual literary and historical advisers to ensure accuracy and document their work. Charles Kemble (1775–1854) for his *King John* (1823) at Drury Lane hired playwright J. R. Planché (1796–1880) as literary and historical adviser. Charles Kean (1811–1868) collaborated with historian George Godwin on *Macbeth* (1850), and for Byron's *Sardanapalus* (1852) he employed scholars and archeologists who had studied recent Assyrian excavations at Ninevah. Henry Irving (1838–1905) at the Lyceum Theatre employed scholars and critics as literary consultants and historical advisers.

Critic William Archer (1856–1924) prepared historical materials, attended rehearsals, and gave critical notes to the actors and directors for over two dozen different productions of plays by HENRIK IBSEN, each of which he had also translated. He was the first dramaturg to specialize in the work of an individual playwright and the first professional dramaturg in Great Britain. Harley Granville-Barker (1877–1946) ran the Royal Court and later the Savoy Theatre, with Oxford professor Gilbert Murray (1866–1957) as his literary adviser. Barker himself came out of retirement to dramaturg John Gielgud's production of *Hamlet* in 1940.

In 1929 Barry Jackson (1879–1961) founded the Malvern Festival dedicated to the plays of GEORGE BERNARD SHAW, with theater historian Allardyce Nicholl and playwright John Drinkwater (1882–1937) as literary advisers. George Devine (1910–1965) founded the English Stage Society at the Royal Court in 1954 as a "writers' theatre." The Royal Court began to employ playwrights as literary managers and dramaturgs, including N. F. Simpson, ANN JELLICOE (1927–), Christopher Hampton, and DAVID HARE (1947–). ENGLAND finally realized the dream of a national theater when the British government chartered and partially subsidized the Royal Shakespeare Company (1962) with Jeremy Brooks as literary manager and Peter Hall (1937–) as managing director, and the National Theatre (1963) with drama critic Kenneth Tynan (1927–1980) as literary manager and Laurence Olivier (1907–1989) as artistic director. In 1987 IRELAND's foremost theater, Dublin's Abbey, formally introduced its Literary Department and hired its first official dramaturgs and literary managers.

AMERICAN DRAMATURGY

America had no tradition of subsidized theaters, and its major impetus until the 20th century was commercial. As in England, actor-playwright-producers dominated the American stage in the 19th century, such as AUGUSTIN DALY (1838–1899), Irish-born DION BOUCICAULT (1820–1890), and playwright-impresario DAVID BELASCO (1853–1931).

In 1908 the New Theatre in New York hired critic John Corbin as the first official "literary manager" in America. The venture lasted only two years.

It took longer for the authoritarian concept of the director to take root in America because of its tradition of democratic institutions. American models of dramaturgical collaboration emerged in the early 20th century with the Washington Square Players (1915–1918), the Provincetown Players (1915–1929), the Neighborhood Playhouse (1915–1927), the THEATRE GUILD (founded 1919), the Group Theater (1931–1941), the Playwright's Company (1938–1960), and the Negro Ensemble Company (founded 1967). The Provincetown Players was perhaps the best example. Founded by George Cram Cooke, John Reed, and SUSAN GLASPELL (1876–1948), all of whom wrote plays for the company, they were quickly joined by the young EUGENE O'NEILL. Glaspell was head of the playreading committee and de facto literary manager. By 1925 they had produced almost one hundred new American plays, fifteen of them by O'Neill and eleven by Glaspell.

Theresa Helburn was the first literary manager for the Theatre Guild, followed by John Gassner (1903–1967). In the commercial theater, "play doctors," usually unbilled, were hired to "clean up" a play or to make changes in the script. GEORGE S. KAUFMAN, MOSS HART, George Abbott, and Abe Burrows especially excelled at this task. Harold Clurman, Kenneth MacGowan, and LILLIAN HELLMAN also were employed as playreaders for New York theaters to weed out or recommend scripts.

In 1951 Zelda Fichandler (1924–) became producing director of the Arena Stage in Washington, D.C., inaugurating the regional theater or resident theater movement in America. As the regional theater movement gained momentum in the 1960s, professional dramaturgy and literary management gained its first serious foothold in America. Theaters often turned to playwrights as literary managers to read scripts and supervise "new play development." Literary departments at the major regional theaters have expanded to include audience development, publication of programs, lobby displays, study guides and newsletters, educational outreach, and even grant writing. A number of contemporary American playwrights have served as "literary managers," including MEGAN TERRY, RICHARD NELSON, ERIC OVERMYER, Leon Katz, and Milan Stitt.

Founded by Lloyd Richards (1923–2006) in 1965, the National Playwrights Conference at the Eugene O'Neill Theater Center established a program for critics to work with playwrights as "dramaturgs," giving critical notes to the playwrights and leading postplay critiques of the work. These first dramaturgs included: Martin Esslin, Arthur Ballet, John Lahr, Edith Oliver, ED BULLINS, and Michael Feingold. The dramaturgs at the O'Neill were usually professional critics since no professional American dramaturgs existed when it was founded.

This situation would change when critic Robert Brustein (1927–) became dean of the Yale School of Drama from 1965 to 1979 and founder of the Yale Repertory Theatre (1969). Translator and critic Michael Feingold (1945–) was the first resident dramaturg of the Yale Rep. Brustein replaced Yale's Ph.D. in theater history with a D.F.A. in criticism, and in 1978 he instituted the M.F.A. in dramaturgy and criticism, the nation's first graduate degree program in dramaturgy, co-chaired by critics Richard Gilman and Stanley Kauffmann and later under successor Dean Lloyd Richard by Leon Katz. SUNY Stony Brook (now Stony Brook University), under the guidance of Polish-born critic-dramaturg Jan Kott (1914–2002), established the nation's second M.F.A. program in dramaturgy in 1984, on a more eclectic model. The first decade of the Yale program would have an enormous impact as the initial parameters of literary management, resident dramaturgy, and production dramaturgy were promulgated, with the M.F.A.s from Yale becoming its early disciples. Yale was especially influential in introducing the concept of "production dramaturg" (as distinct from resident or company dramaturg). Influenced by the German model, "production dramaturgs" collaborate on a single production with months of preproduction work, preparation of production histories and/or protocols, attendance at rehearsals, daily dramaturgy notes, and dramaturgy logbooks.

Today, there are more than fifty American programs in dramaturgy. Virtually all major American theaters have numerous staff dramaturgs or literary managers, and visiting production dramaturgs are more common. Even OFF-BROADWAY and Broadway theater now routinely include dramaturgs. Since the late 20th century, CANADA has also actively and prominently contributed to the development and practice of dramaturgy and literary management. However, debate continues as to whether the dramaturg is primarily a collaborative artist or an objective critic.

In 1985 the Literary Managers and Dramaturgs of the Americas (LMDA) was founded.

FURTHER READING

Archer, William, and Harley Granville-Barker. *A Scheme and Estimates for a National Theatre*. New York: Duffield, 1908.

Cardullo, Bert, ed. *What Is Dramaturgy?* New York: P. Lang, 1995.

Jonas, Susan, et al., eds. *Dramaturgy in America: A Sourcebook*. New York: Harcourt, 1997.

Piscator, Erwin. *The Political Theatre*. 1929. Tr. by Hugh Rorrison. London: Methuen, 1980.

Rudakoff, Judith, and Lynn M. Thompson, eds. *Between the Lines: The Process of Dramaturgy*. Toronto: Playwrights Canada Press, 2002.

Williams, David, ed. and comp. *Collaborative Theatre: The Théâtre du Soleil Sourcebook*. New York: Routledge, 1999.

Wolf, Stacy, ed. *Theatre Topics: Dramaturgy Special Issue* 13, no. 1 (March 2003).

Michael X. Zelenak

DREAM OF THE RED CHAMBER

Dream of the Red Chamber (*Honglou meng*) by Xu Jin is a "newly arranged drama" that belongs to the style Zhejiang Yueju, often called simply Shaoxing Opera. Because its most prominent artistic feature is all-female troupes, plays are civil and romantic, not military; the music tends to be gentle and melodious, compared with other styles; and the costuming is softer and more romantic.

Dream of the Red Chamber is among the most famous and typical examples of Shaoxing Opera. It is based on what is possibly CHINA's most famous novel, *Dream of the Red Chamber* (*Honglou meng*), most of it written by the Manchu Cao Xueqin (1715–1763). It is a novel of manners concerning the Jia family, reflecting how the upper classes lived in the 18th century. Although the novel is tremendously long and has innumerable characters, the basic plot concerns the young gentleman of the family, Jia Baoyu, and his relations with his two female cousins, Lin Daiyu and Xue Baochai.

Xu Jin's drama crystallizes the novel into an evening. Jia Baoyu's father wants him to study the Confucian classics in order to have an official career through the examination system prevalent at the time. However, Jia Baoyu loves to play in the family mansion's garden with his two female cousins, reading and writing poetry. The two young women are extremely different in character. Lin Daiyu is rather weak and sickly, introverted, and given to melancholy, but Xue Baochai is vivacious and charming. His family wants him to marry Xue, but it is Lin that Jia falls in love with. Knowing that he will never agree to wed Xue, his family attempts to trick him into marrying her, by telling him on his wedding day that his veiled bride is Lin, when in fact it is Xue. Thinking that Baoyu was actually willing to marry Xue Baochai, Lin Daiyu burns the poems they had written and dies of love and anguish. When Jia Baoyu discovers he has been deceived, he runs to find Lin, but it is too late—she is already dead. As a result, he flees the mansion and becomes a Buddhist monk, renouncing the world and its ills.

Xu Jin's drama is deliberately ideological. It is designed to emphasize the evils of pre–People's Republic of China society, especially the custom of arranged marriages that dictated that parents must decide on their children's spouses, not the marriage partners themselves. The end shows that it is personal reasons, mainly of disappointment in love or career, that drive men to enter Buddhist monasteries, not genuine religious feeling.

Dream of the Red Chamber has been dramatized in many different traditional Chinese opera styles. Xu Jin's Shaoxing Opera was premiered in 1957 by China's leading Shaoxing Opera troupe, the Shanghai Yueju Company (*Shanghai Yueju yuan*), and made into a film in 1962. Interestingly, the most famous actor in the lead role of Jia Baoyu is Xu Yulan, a woman.

FURTHER READING

Cao Xueqin. *The Story of the Stone, a Chinese Novel in Five Volumes*. Tr. by David Hawkes and John Minford. 5 vols. Harmondsworth: Penguin, 1973–1986; Bloomington: Indiana Univ. Press, 1979–1987.

Siu Wang-Ngai, with Peter Lovrick. *Chinese Opera, Images and Stories*. Seattle: Univ. of Washington Press, 1997 [contains summaries and colored illustrations].

Colin Mackerras

A DREAM PLAY

A Dream Play (*Ett drömspel*, written 1901, published 1902), a drama by AUGUST STRINDBERG, was first performed at Svenska teatern in Stockholm, SWEDEN, in 1907.

Strindberg began writing the play in September 1901 when Harriet Bosse, pregnant with their child, left him; he completed it after her return. "The play is of course about you!—Agnes—who is to let the prisoner out of the castle," Strindberg had written her in a letter. However, when Bosse played the Daughter at the world premiere six years later, she had divorced Strindberg.

In his "Author's Note" for the play, Strindberg (1998) writes:

> In this dream play the author has . . . attempted to imitate the inconsequent yet apparently logical form of a dream. Everything can happen, everything is possible and probable. Time and place do not exist; on an insignificant basis of reality the imagination spins and weaves new patterns: a blend of memories, experiences, spontaneous ideas, absurdities, and improvisations.
>
> The characters split, double, multiply, evaporate, condense, disperse, and converge. But one consciousness holds sway over them all, that of the dreamer; for him there are no secrets, no incongruities, no scruples, no law.

Soon after he completed the play, Strindberg (1965), inspired by Plato and Arthur Schopenhauer, wrote in his *Occult Diary* that it is doubtful "if in fact it [the world] exists at all—for it is really only a dream picture. (Consequently my *Dream Play* is a picture of life)." Viewed in this way, the much-debated question of whether the dreamer of the play is the author, Indra's Daughter, or the recipient can be answered easily. What Strindberg shows us is an image of life recognizable for anyone who shares his view that life is illusory, dreamlike.

The main action, modeled after Christ's life on earth, is simple. The daughter of the Indian god Indra descends to earth, where she is reborn as Agnes (cf. *agnus dei*, lamb of God), daughter of the Glazier. Gradually she becomes aware of man's miserable existence. She reaches a nadir when she experiences the most intimate form of human interaction, marriage, as imprisonment. She now longs for freedom and prepares to return to her Father in heaven. At the end, we witness her death through fire as she enters a burning castle, a symbolic ascension.

In her double role of character and "narrator," the Daughter is an unusual protagonist. Unlike the traditional outsider, she knows more than those she visits. And unlike them, she can see meaning in man's suffering. The Poet's exceptional position is indicated when she provides him alone with a kind of explanation for man's painful existence. In the course of the play, she frequently repeats, "Det är synd om människorna." Untranslatable in English, the expression means not only that mankind is to be pitied but also that mankind is rooted in sin. Taking it as her task to experience what it means to be a human being, the Daughter undergoes development from a little girl to a young woman to a mother to an aging woman—a metamorphsis hard for any actress to re-create.

A Dream Play describes life as a constant vacillation between illusion and disillusion. In a note for the play, Strindberg speaks of "the treacherous hope." What we hope for may well come true—but never in the way or to the extent we had hoped. The characters who symbolically represent humanity are in this respect all "such stuff as dreams are made on." Their hope, usually expressed in the form of endless waiting for something better, is constantly thwarted. The only hope that finally remains is the hope that death will be an awakening to a better existence.

With regard to the more important characters, Strindberg makes use of a pattern that, applying Kierkegaardian terminology, could be described as a change from an aesthetic stage (the Officer) via an ethical stage (the Lawyer) to a religious stage (the Poet)—development that signifies a widening from love for an individual via compassion for the repressed in society to compassion for all mankind. In the last instance, it is humankind, a product of Original Sin, that "is to be pitied."

Seemingly loosely structured, the play is thematically closely knit. The figure of the heroine is a unifier as well, since the Daughter figures in all the scenes.

One of the most obvious dream effects in the play is Strindberg's use of a technique resembling filmic dissolve. Thus some of the elements in the Theater corridor return in new contexts in the Lawyer's office and then in the Church. One of them is the linden tree; another, more important one is "*a door with an airhole in the shape of a four-leaved clover.*" The door reminds the Officer of a pantry door he saw as a child. In the Lawyer's office the door belongs to "*a filing cabinet*"; in the Church, it leads "*to the vestry.*" In all three scenes, the door clearly symbolizes what separates this life from what comes after it. This explains why the people in the Theater corridor, when the door is finally opened, can see nothing behind it. What is beyond life must remain an enigma to man. The four-leaved clover in the door, promising luck, has its counterpart in the Officer's hopeful waiting for his beloved Victoria (i.e., victory). But just as his red roses are doomed to wither until only the thorns remain, so the four-leaved clover is transformed into a cross when it becomes part of the vestry. The search for worldly success gives way to the insight that suffering is the meaning of life.

A Dream Play, it has often been said, is more cinematic than theatrical. It is true that the screen medium permits a playwright to move freely in time and space. It is also true that this medium allows swift and varied scene changes, promoting the dreamlike quality of the play. On the other hand, the play's mythical, parabolic nature is better served onstage.

[*See also* Expressionism; Philosophy and Drama; Symbolism]

FURTHER READING

Lamm, Martin. *August Strindberg*. Tr. and ed. by Harry G. Carlson. New York: Blom, 1971.

Lunin, Hanno. *Strindbergs Dramen* [Strindberg's drama]. Emsdetten: Lechte, 1962.

Müssener, Helmut. *August Strindberg, "Ein Traumspiel": Struktur- und Stilstudien* [August Strindberg, *A Dream Play*: Structure and style studies]. Meisenheim am Glan: Hain, 1965.

Quigley, Austin E. *The Modern Stage and Other Worlds*. New York: Methuen, 1985.

Sprinchorn, Evert. *Strindberg as Dramatist*. New Haven: Yale Univ. Press, 1982.

Strindberg, August. *From an Occult Diary: Marriage with Harriet Bosse*. Ed. and intr. and notes by Torsten Eklund. Tr. by Mary Sandbach. New York: Hill and Wang, 1965.

Strindberg, August. *Miss Julie and Other Plays*. Tr. and intr. and notes by Michael Robinson. Oxford-New York: Oxford Univ. Press, 1999.

Törnqvist, Egil. *Strindbergian Drama: Themes and Structure*. Stockholm: Almqvist & Wiksell Intl., 1982.

Egil Törnqvist

THE DREAMS OF CLYTEMNESTRA

DACIA MARAINI's *The Dreams of Clytemnestra* (*I sogni di Clitennestra*) won the prestigious Riccione Prize in 1978 and was performed for the first time in 1980 in the town in which it was set, Prato, known for its textiles. It was subsequently performed in Vienna, New York, and London. The play interweaves some of the Greek elements of Aeschylus's trilogy *The Oresteia*, from which it is drawn, with the modern story of an immigrant family during a crisis in the textile industry.

The overlapping of ancient and contemporary is a favorite technique in Maraini's plays. The device allows Maraini to search for the ancient roots of the modern condition, while showing that history repeats itself continuously. *The Dreams of Clytemnestra* restages "the passage from maternal rights to paternal rights" that many feminist critics see in *The Oresteia* (Cavallaro, 1995). The blending of new and ancient also underlines the loss of "maternal power" and a "defeat that reverberated down the centuries as a curse on the heads of women" (Maraini, 2000). Finally, the device also gives an epic tone to Maraini's condemnation of the injustices and violence of contemporary Italian life.

This TRAGEDY blends old and new through characterization, plot, and language. Each of the figures of Aeschylus's play has been given a contemporary profile. For example, Iphigenia is a pregnant teenager sacrificed to marriage by her father, Agamemnon. Orestes is rewritten as a homosexual. Electra, who in Aeschylus insists her brother Orestes avenge her father's death and defend patriarchal family rule, is recast in Maraini's play in the Freudian reading of a daughter obsessively in love with her father.

Maraini maintains dramatic tension through the juxtaposition of a violent classical plot and the unpredictability of the contemporary rendering of that plot. The intensity is further heightened by the disruption of "linear narrative" and the possibility of "more than one interpretation of the same event" (Cavallaro, 1995). This is caused by the layering of multiple narratives: the classical plot and the contemporary plot blend with the characters' dreams, some in sleep and some recited as if they were visions. The resulting oneiric atmosphere is underscored by linguistic repetition. "Go to sleep my love," Cassandra repeats soothingly to her lover, Agamemnon, as he recounts a dream in which he is murdered by his wife. The description of his murder coincides with his dying of a heart attack. Later, Clytemnestra recounts the same murderous dream. Maraini often uses such literary repetition as an "entry into the world of sleep and dreams" and the "unconscious." The interweaving of different registers of language further increases the play's complexity. Modern swear words and explicit language are interwoven with direct quotes from Aeschylus's play and Maraini's own poetic rhythm and verse.

At the center of the play is the fate of Clytemnestra, who refuses to keep chaste during her husband's emigration despite Electra's condemnation of her behavior. In the end, Orestes will in fact bury his mother alive by having her committed to an insane asylum. There, Clytemnestra will challenge the psychiatrist's narrow Freudian view of female sexuality, refuted by many feminists. (Note: The psychiatrist is a woman in the Italian play and a man in the English translation.) Rebellious unto death, Clytemnestra thus epitomizes the feminist struggle for independence and greater sexual autonomy.

[*See also* Italy]

FURTHER READING

Cavallaro, Daniela. "*I sogni di Clitennestra*: The *Oresteia* According to Maraini." *Italica* 72, no. 2 (Summer 1995): 340–355.

Cody, Gabrielle. "Remembering What the Closed Eye Sees: Some Notes on Dacia Maraini's Postmodern *Oresteia*." In *The Pleasure of Writing: Critical Essays on Dacia Maraini*, ed. by Rodica Diaconescu-Blumenfeld and Ada Testaferri. West Lafayette, Ind.: Purdue Univ. Press, 2000. 215–231.

Maraini, Dacia. *Stowaway on Board*. Bordighera, Italy: Bordighera, 2000.

Picchietti, Virginia. *Relational Spaces: Daughterhood, Motherhood and Sisterhood in Dacia Maraini's Writings and Films*. Madison, N.J.: Fairleigh Dickinson Univ. Press, 2002 [contains an analysis of Maraini's *Dreams of Clytemnestra*].

Wood, Sharon. "Women and Theater in Italy: Natalia Ginzburg, Franca Rame, and Dacia Maraini." *Romance Languages Annual* 5 (1993): 343–348.

Tommasina Gabriele

DIE DREIGROSCHENOPER

See THE THREEPENNY OPERA

ETT DRÖMSPEL

See A DREAM PLAY

DRUMS IN THE NIGHT

Stop that romantic staring!

—Kragler, Act 5

In the wake of the failed Spartacus revolt of 1919 and the resulting deaths of Rosa Luxemburg and Karl Liebknecht, BERTOLT BRECHT began writing a drama with the working title *Spartakus*. The play ultimately became *Drums in the Night* (*Trommeln in der Nacht*) and was first produced in 1922, the same year in which Brecht was awarded the prestigious Kleist Prize.

Although the drama's original title emphasizes the uprising of the Extreme Left, the revolution serves as the background of the drama and is represented by beating drums. The play unfolds in the collision between a returning soldier, Andreas Kragler, and civilian life, illuminating the status of Kragler and his comrades as outsiders in an astoundingly changed society where war profiteers prevail. The returning soldiers are perceived by the profiteers to be a threat, and by the revolutionaries as potential recruits.

The drama begins in the bourgeois milieu of the Balickes, as they set out to increase their immense profits by switching from the production of ammunition to the production of baby carriages. Balicke's daughter, Anna, having waited for four years for her fiancé Kragler to return, is now set to marry Friedrich Murk, a reckless opportunist. Kragler's unexpected return, however, not only threatens the marriage of Anna and Murk but also drastically affects the business relationship between Balicke and his future son-in-law. Pregnant by Murk, Anna first decides to stay with him. Her decision to abandon Kragler, in turn, drives him to join the communist revolution out of despair rather than conviction. Brecht perceived of Kragler as a petit bourgeois ready to betray the proletarian revolution and denounce revolutionary engagement as a romantic aberration. In the end, Kragler abandons his revolutionary ambition for a comfortable life with Anna as soon as she decides to leave Murk.

The genesis of the drama exemplifies Brecht's habit of significantly reworking his plays several times. With *Drums in the Night* Brecht vacillated about the ending, finally settling on a comedic happy end, a parody showing drunken romanticism and the ideal of the "great, wide, white bed." A second important change concerned his view of the revolution. Originally depicted as an event that lacked profound social and political significance, Brecht later emphasized the importance of the Spartacus revolt by introducing the character of the proletarian Paule. A true revolutionary who dies for his convictions, Paule was intended as a positive counterpart to the opportunistic Kragler.

Upon its premiere, the play was enthusiastically received as an example of a newly emerging spirit in the theater. Whereas some critics saw it as a play about the revolution, others called it a satire of a bourgeois TRAGEDY in which the heroine traditionally perishes as a result of her sexual transgression. Later approaches emphasize the features of the play that anticipate the ALIENATION EFFECTS of Brecht's EPIC THEATER, such as Kragler's famous appeal to the public: "Stop that romantic staring" (act 5). This appeal is intended to foster new viewing habits that are not steeped in romantic notions.

[*See also* Expressionism; Learning Plays]

FURTHER READING

Fraunhofer, Hedwig. "The Fascist Brecht? The Rhetoric of Alterity in *Drums in the Night*." *Brecht Yearbook* 22 (1997): 357–373.

Mews, Siegfried. "Trommeln in der Nacht" [Drums in the Night]. In *Brecht Handbuch* [Brecht handbook], ed. by Jan Knopf. Stuttgart: Metzler, 2001. 1:86–99.

Oesmann, Astrid. "The Theatrical Destruction of Subjectivity and History: Brecht's *Trommeln in der Nacht*." *German Quarterly* 70, no. 2 (1997): 136–150.

Maya Gerig and Cyrus M. Shahan

DRY LIPS OUGHTA MOVE TO KAPUSKASING

For the betterment and the advancement of this community.
—Big Joey, Act 1

So affected was TOMSON HIGHWAY by criticism of his play that he withdrew from playwriting for a number of years after its 1989 premiere in Toronto. *Dry Lips* is set on a fictional Indian reserve, Wasaychigan Hill, on Manitoulin Island, Ontario. Many reviews were positive; the play has been revived on several occasions; and the text has been subjected to much academic analysis. Despite the play's elaborate staging, careful choreography, amusing FARCE, imaginative musical accompaniment, unexpected twists, and linguistic variety, Highway was attacked for presenting very negative Indian characters—he was also accused of constructing female characters demeaningly. It is true that the characters are mostly unseemly: male and female characters pursue alcohol abuse, adultery, insincere piety, and self-interested acquisitiveness. However, Highway's scheme is to critique the reasons for this diminution of Indian dignity and togetherness.

The fracturing of Indian life derives largely from a feckless submission to white culture and religion. Christianity's influence is seen as insidious. Spooky laughably predicts, in his native Cree language (native speeches, which punctuate the play's mainly English dialogue, are translated in the published text's parentheses), that the world will end in 1990. He is accused, convincingly, by Big Joey of faking holiness to distract attention from his former transgressions. The corrosive influence of the White man's religion is symbolized by mute seventeen-year-old Dickie Bird's venomous act: he rapes a pregnant woman with a crucifix. Highway has said in interviews that the crime represents Christianity's patriarchal aggression overwhelming Indigenous Indian matriarchies. The act may also parallel the conquering of North American natives by European settlers who claimed religious zeal. In the play's dialogue, the crucifix is contested: Spooky reveres it, while other Indians mock what they see as idolatrous worship. Put simply, crucifix-focused Christianity causes divisions in Indian communities.

Big Joey, who fathered Dickie Bird illegitimately, looks on, passively acquiescing in the bloody violation. Years previously, he allowed Dickie Bird's mother to get drunk in a bar, causing the child's barroom birth and consequent handicap. Big Joey, rightly or wrongly, blames his inactivity on trauma caused by the FBI's brutality at Wounded Knee during 1973's siege. Big Joey strives to establish a radio station and blackmails the compromised adulterer, Zachary, who wants to open a bakery—they are business rivals because a license will only be given to one project. The men squabble for their selfish commercial interests: Big Joey's claim that "We work for the betterment and the advancement of this community" is blatantly hollow.

The play ends on moments of uplifting redemption. Zachary is reunited with his wife and their baby—his adulterous liaisons are over. The women's ice hockey team, set up to celebrate women's capacities outside of domestic life, flourishes despite the paranoid complaints of some men. But the beer-soaked laziness, individualist disunity and religious hypocrisy that characterizes the reservation's males will doubtless continue. Nanabush, an Indian spirit, causes much of the mischief in the play—but Highway's seedy characters are able to perpetuate fracturing violence without assistance.

[*See also* Canada]

FURTHER READING

Braz, Albert. "Nanabush's Return: Cultural Messianism in Tomson Highway's Plays." In *Changing Representations of Minorities, East and West: Selected Essays*, ed. by Larry E. Smith and John Reider. Honolulu: Univ. of Hawaii Press, 1996. 143–156.

Highway, Tomson. *Comparing Mythologies*. Ottawa: Univ. of Ottawa Press, 2003.

Innes, Christopher. "Dreams of Violence: Moving Beyond Colonialism in Canadian and Caribbean Drama." In *Theatre Matters: Performance and Culture on the World Stage*, ed. by Richard Boon and Jane Plastow. Cambridge: Cambridge Univ. Press, 1998. 76–96.

Lutz, Harmut. *Contemporary Challenges: Conversations with Native Authors*. Saskatoon: Fifth House, 1991.

Kevin De Ornellas

DUBILLARD, ROLAND (1923–)

An actor, director, and poet, as well as playwright, Roland Dubillard was born on December 2, 1923, in Paris. He began his theatrical career early, writing melodramatic sketches when he joined La Maison des Lettres in 1942, a hotbed of student resistance activities during the German occupation. During military service in Austria in 1946, he wrote his first play, *Thou Shall Not Drink Your Neighbor* (*Il ne faut pas boire son prochain*), and after his return to FRANCE, he composed and performed radio sketches for Jean Tardieu at Paris-Inter, creating an enduring comic duo, Grégoire et Amédée, who would reappear over time in stage shows called *Les Diablogues* (The Devilogues), *Le Gobe-Douille* (The Gobe-Casing), and *L'Eau en Poudre* (Powder Water).

His plays present a diversity of styles, ranging from the tale of a young boy captured by bloodthirsty monsters in *Thou Shall Not Drink Your Neighbor* to thematic variations on Beethoven's life in *The Beet Garden* (*Le Jardin aux betteraves*, 1969); from a parody of a symbolist drama involving a woman riding a bathtub across town—*If Camille Saw Me . . .* (*Si Camille me voyait . . .*, 1953)—to the rather naturalistic tableau of shopkeepers in *The Swallows* (*Naïves hirondelles*, 1961). The highly favorable reception of *The Swallows* in 1961 by critics, among them EUGÈNE IONESCO and JEAN ANOUILH, followed the next year by *The House of Bones* (*La Maison d'os*), a Kafkaesque drama of an old man delivered to phantom servants, cemented Dubillard's reputation.

Although not as verbally poetic as Dubillard's earlier works, these two later plays combine quotidian dramatic situation reminiscent of MARGUERITE DURAS's stripped-down theater with his trademark dialogue of hilarious discursive tics, hesitations, banalities, and repetition. It could be said that his characters speak without saying anything and watch their lives run down as they devote themselves to ridiculous projects and fall prey to pathetic mishaps with everyday objects. Dubillard's protagonists often exist in a suspended state, waiting for others: for instance, Séverine and Fernand wait for Bertrand and Germaine in *The Swallows*, the cellist Camoens and the violinist Milton wait for the rest of their quartet in *The Beet Garden*, the young man and his wife wait for a couple that rented their house in *The Crabs or The Hosts and the Guests* (*Les Crabes ou Les Hôtes et les hôtes*, 1970). A lack of overt dramatic action underlines the wordplay and the atmosphere of foiled communication. For example, in *The Crabs*, the younger and older couples stumble on the dual meaning of "hôtes" (French for both "guests" and "hosts"). Similarly, the word "monsieur" blurs the distinction between an indication of politeness or of status and confuses the servants of *The House of Bones*. In addition, the playwright's erratic line arrangement heightens confusion and often reduces his protagonists to simple onomatopoeia or rhythm-based nonsense.

Because Dubillard, under the stage name "Grégoire," acted in all of his premieres, and revivals without him have not fared nearly as well, critics and audiences alike have found it easy to confuse his protagonists with his own personality. Perhaps some time will have to elapse to see whether his particular brand of ABSURDISM will outlive its foremost interpreter.

PLAYS: *Thou Shall Not Drink Your Neighbor* (*Il ne faut pas boire son prochain*, 1946); *Furious Follies, Sweet Follies* (*Les Folies furieuses, les Folies douces*, 1952); *If Camille Saw Me . . .* (*Si Camille me voyait . . .*, 1953); *The Swallows* (*Naïves hirondelles*, 1961); *The House of Bones* (*La Maison d'os*, 1962, rev'd 1966); *The Beet Garden* (*Le Jardin aux betteraves*, 1969); *The Crabs or The Hosts and the Guests* (*Les Crabes ou Les Hôtes et les hôtes*, 1970); ". . . *Where the Cows Drink*" ("*Où boivent les vaches*," 1973); *The Devilogues* / *The Fiendialogues* (*Les Diablogues*, 1976)

FURTHER READING

Guicharnaud, Jacques. *Modern French Theatre: From Giraudoux to Genet*. New Haven, Conn.: Yale Univ. Press, 1967.

Klieger Stillman, Linda. "Doubling of Sign and Image in Roland Dubillard's *La Maison d'os*." *Sub-Stance* 22 (1979): 85–95.

Ruyter-Tognotti, Danièle. "La cohérence dans *La Maison d'os* de Dubillard: Une approache dialogique" [Coherence in *The House of Bones* of Dubillard: A dialogical approach]. *Neophilologus* 71 (1987): 210–226.

Lam-Thao Nguyen

ET DUKKEHJEM See A DOLL'S HOUSE

DUMAS FILS (1824–1895)

Alexandre Dumas, known as Dumas fils, was a 19th-century French playwright, novelist, and essayist. He developed the *pièce à thèse* (referred to as the social, problem, or thesis play), which dramatized a contemporary social problem and proposed a solution to the perceived ill. The social plays of Dumas fils owed a direct debt to the dramatic structure of the *pièce bien faite* (well-made play) developed by Eugène Scribe.

Dumas fils was born on July 27, 1824, in Paris, the illegitimate son of novelist and playwright Alexandre Dumas père and Marie-Catherine Labay, a dressmaker. Dumas père is remembered for his prolific literary output, of which the novels *The Three Musketeers* and *The Count of Monte Cristo* are the most familiar to contemporary readers. Dumas fils had a difficult childhood in a libertine environment and received little formal education. Many critics find significance in the moralistic bent of his plays in contrast to his own unconventional childhood.

His first considerable literary success came in 1848 with his novel *The Lady of the Camellias* (*La Dame aux camélias*). The plot of the novel resembles the author's relationship with Marie Duplessis, a famous courtesan with whom Dumas had a relationship and who died of tuberculosis in 1847. He adapted the novel into a play of the same name, and it was first performed in 1852. *Camille*, as the play is usually called in English, was a popular choice on 19th- and early-20th-century stages, due in large part to the appeal of its lead role, Marguerite Gauthier, to star actresses. Just a year after the *Camille*'s premiere, Guiseppe

Verdi's enduring opera version of the play, *La Traviata*, was first staged.

His plays encountered social problems in a new, more direct fashion than French audiences had come to expect. He merged the two dominant forms of drama on the French stage in the first half of the 19th century—the passion of Victor Hugo's romantic dramas and the structural efficiency and energy of the well-made plays of Scribe and VICTORIEN SARDOU. The social plays of Dumas fils, such as *The Demi-Monde* and *The Natural Son*, treat adultery, prostitution, and illegitimacy in a contemporary setting and with everyday language. His dramas fundamentally espouse the sanctity of marriage and family, but his plots exploit the darker side of these values.

The plays of Dumas fils are part of 19th-century drama's turn of focus toward middle-class life—as opposed to TRAGEDY or serious drama as the vehicle for noble figures. Émile Augier and ENGLAND'S THOMAS WILLIAM ROBERTSON, Dumas fils's contemporaries, were also fashioning more realistic dramas on European stages. This shift from elevated characters and highly romantic settings was a precursor of the NATURALISM of ÉMILE ZOLA and ANDRÉ ANTOINE. HENRIK IBSEN and GEORGE BERNARD SHAW expand the social play format in their plays—GHOSTS and MRS. WARREN'S PROFESSION being but two salient examples.

In 1861 Dumas married Nadeja Narischkine, a Russian woman, after the birth of the couple's daughter in the previous year. After his wife died, Dumas married Henriette Régnier, his mistress of several years. He was elected to the Academie Française in 1875 and admitted to the Légion d'Honneur in 1894. He died on November 27, 1895, in Marly-le Roi.

[*See also* France; Problem Play; A Scrap of Paper]

PLAYS: *The Queen's Jewel* (*Le Bijou de la Reine*, 1845); *Lady of the Camellias*, also translated as *Camille* (*La Dame aux camélias*, 1852); *Diana de Lys* (1853); *The Demi-Monde* (*Le Demi-Monde*, 1855); *The Money Question* (*La Question d'argent*, 1857); *The Natural Son*, also translated as *The Illegitimacy* (*Le Fils naturel*, 1858); *A Prodigal Father* (*Un Père prodigue*, 1859); *The Friend of Women* (*L'Ami des femmes*, 1864); *Madame Aubray's Ideas* (*Les Idées de Madame Aubray*, 1867); *Princess George* (*La Princesse Georges*, 1871); *A Wedding Visit* (*Une Visite de noces*, 1871); *Monsieur Alphonse* (1873); *The Wife of Claude* (*La Femme de Claude*, 1873); *The Strange Woman* (*L'Etrangère*, 1876); *The Princess of Bagdad* (*La Princesse de Bagdad*, 1881); *Denise* (1885); *Francillon* (1887); *The Road from Thebes* (*La Route de Thèbes*, unfinished, 1895)

FURTHER READING

Brockett, Oscar G., and Robert R. Findlay. *Century of Innovation: A History of European and American Theatre and Drama Since 1870*. Englewood Cliffs, N.J.: Prentice-Hall, 1973.

Maurois, André. *Three Musketeers: A Study of the Dumas Family*. Tr. by Gerard Hopkins. London: J. Cape, 1957.

Schwarz, H. Stanley. *Alexandre Dumas fils: Dramatist*. New York: New York Univ. Press, 1927.

Stanton, Stephen S., ed. *Camille and Other Plays*. New York: Hill & Wang, 1957.

Taylor, F. A. *The Theatre of Alexandre Dumas fils*. Oxford: Oxford Univ. Press, 1937.

Wendy A. Weckwerth

DUNCAN, RONALD (1914–)

Ronald Duncan is equally known today for his poetry, autobiographies, fiction, journalism, film script, and criticism as he is for his verse dramas. Indeed, the frequent comparison of Duncan's verse dramas with those of the more celebrated T. S. ELIOT and the rapid devaluation of verse drama in London as a valid and relevant dramatic genre after the 1950s have ensured the theatrical and critical neglect of one of the most prolific verse dramatists of his time.

Born in Rhodesia in 1914, Duncan moved to ENGLAND with his mother before he was a year old (his father died interned as an enemy alien during World War I). In his teens and early twenties, Duncan manifested a particular interest in the music of Franz Schubert, in poetry (he later claimed that he could find in Gerard Hopkins "Schubert in words"), and in the films of Charlie Chaplin, whom he credited with manifesting an ideal blend of pathos and beauty that Duncan later attempted to achieve in his own dramas. After reading English literature under F. R. Leavis at Cambridge, Duncan disguised himself temporarily as a working man in the Yorkshire coalfields. Convinced of the importance of social and political involvement, and determined to disseminate a pacifist philosophy, Duncan composed and distributed pacifist pamphlets, eventually accepting an invitation to visit Mahatma Gandhi. Despite his admiration for Gandhi and his conviction that his age needed "saints, not politicians," Duncan was unable to reconcile himself with Gandhi's disregard for the persuasive power of art. At this time, he also met Ezra Pound, whose poetic influence can be seen in his drama and poetry, and Benjamin Britten, who fostered in him an increased awareness of musical technique, and with whom Duncan would later work as the librettist for the oratorio *Mea Culpa* and the opera *The Rape of Lucretia*. While still in his early twenties, Duncan married Rose Marie Hansom. Together, they established a community farm for conscientious objectors during World War II (Duncan offers a full account of the farm and its eventual failure in *All Men Are Islands: An Autobiography*, 1964).

Often aligning himself with Eliot's intention to illuminate the spiritual beneath the apparent mundanity of modern life, Duncan adopted a verse style in his dramas that was much like Eliot's in its simplicity and directness but more explicitly indebted to the "sprung rhythm" of Hopkins. In their use of a contemporary setting and melodramatic plot, Duncan's *Stratton*

(1948) and *The Catalyst* (1956) evoke comparison with Eliot's later dramas such as *The Cocktail Party*, while the masque and antimasque *This Way to the Tomb* (1945), after the life of St. Anthony, is a deliberate reference to Eliot's MURDER IN THE CATHEDRAL. Nonetheless, Duncan's dramas are less explicitly allied to mythical subtexts and embrace a greater variety of subjects, from an almost naturalistic representation of colliers (*The Unburied Dead*, 1938), to a miracle play (*Ora Pro Nobis*, 1939), to an allusive and often humorous moralizing sequel to *Don Juan* (*The Death of Satan*, 1954). Despite his socialist interests, Duncan rarely represented those interests explicitly in his dramas, believing instead in the need to effect spiritual change that would influence social attitudes. Nonetheless, *The Unburied Dead* does address a collier strike, *Ora Pro Nobis* and *Pimp, Skunk and Profiteer* (1939) treat the impending war, and *Mea Culpa* responds to the bombing of Nagasaki.

A central theme in Duncan's work is the need and desire to surpass assumed limitations of our capacity to feel. Like Eliot, Duncan was concerned with the spiritual indifference he perceived in society. Unlike Eliot, Duncan is much less explicit about the existence of a specific transcendental deity. Instead, the "divine" can be located in humanity's honest and searching recognition of one's own potential for love of self and of others.

PLAYS: *Birth* (1937); *The Unburied Dead* (1938); *Ora Pro Nobis* (1939); *Pimp, Skunk and Profiteer* (1939); *The Dull Ass's Hoof* (1940); *This Way to the Tomb* (1945); *The Eagle Has Two Heads* (1946); *The Rape of Lucretia* (1946, libretto); *Stratton* (1948); *The Typewriter* (1948); *The Cardinal* (1949); *St. Spiv or Nothing Up Your Sleeve* (1950); *Our Lady's Tumbler* (1951); *Don Juan* (1953); *The Death of Satan* (1954); *The Portrait* (1954); *A Man Named Judas* (1955); *The Catalyst* (1956); *Three Times Two or The Seducer* (1957); *Playback* (1958); *Preface to America* (1959, television play); *Not All the Dead are Buried* (1960, television play); *The Rehearsal* (1960); *The Urchin* (1960); *The Comedy of Lovers* (1962); *The Seven Deadly Virtues* (1962); *The Rabbit Race* (1963); *O-B-A-F-G* (1964); *The Gift* (1966); *The Trojan Women* (1967)

FURTHER READING

Cairns, Krysia. *Ronald Duncan the Man and the Artist*. Plymouth: Univ. of Plymouth Press, 1998.

Haueter, Max Walter. *Ronald Duncan: The Metaphysical Content of His Plays*. London: Rebel Press, 1969.

Wahl, William B. *A Lone Wolf Howling: The Thematic Content of Ronald Duncan's Plays*. Salzburg: Institut für Englische Sprache und Literatur, 1973.

——. *Ronald Duncan: Dramatist and Poet Interviewed*. Salzburg: Institut für Englische Sprache und Literatur, 1973.

Irene Morra

DURANG, CHRISTOPHER (1949–)

Some people, I'm told, dismiss this play [The Marriage of Bette and Boo] as too angry; I don't agree with them and feel they may be denying something I've found to be true: that unless you go through all the genuine angers you feel, both justified and unjustified, the feelings of love that you do have will not have any legitimate base and will be at least partially false. Plus, eventually you will go crazy.

—Christopher Durang, 1997

Emerging from such eclectic influences as the ABSURDISM of EUGÈNE IONESCO, the anarchic iconoclasm of JOE ORTON, and the vivacity of classic Broadway musicals, Christopher Durang's manic dark comedies have documented the social upheavals of his time and connected with audiences consistently, even when critics have wavered. His prolific output of savage satires on taboo targets and outrageous parodies of theatrical genres have changed the landscape of the American stage COMEDY, paving the way for later controversial playwrights who would continue to push the boundaries of theatrical propriety.

Durang was born in Montclair, New Jersey, on January 2, 1949. While at the Yale School of Drama, he wrote, with classmate ALBERT INNAURATO, *The Idiots Karamazov* (1974), an epic send-up of Russian literature and much else. Robert Brustein, then head of the school, transferred the show to the affiliated Yale Repertory Theatre, which also premiered Durang's next solo effort, *The Vietnamization of New Jersey* (1977), a spoof of contemporary antiwar protest plays. His Broadway debut came in 1978 with *A History of the American Film*, another full-length panoramic travesty—this time of classic Hollywood movies.

By the 1980s Durang started relying less on his gifts for parody and wrote more thematically serious plays centered on deeply troubled yet hilarious characters. With *Sister Mary Ignatius Explains It All for You* (1981), he reached back to his Catholic school upbringing to mock the rigid teachings of the church in the person of one particularly tyrannical nun. The play enjoyed a two-year run OFF-BROADWAY, winning an Obie Award for best play, but sometimes met with controversy when it was produced regionally and church advocates denounced Durang as sacrilegious. *Beyond Therapy* (1982), a New York sex FARCE about the singles scene and psychoanalysis, has proven to be one of his most widely produced plays, despite an initial lukewarm reception on Broadway and a 1987 film version that Durang later disowned. *Baby with the Bathwater* (1983) and the autobiographical Obie-winner *The Marriage of Bette and Boo* (1985) provided grotesque glimpses of dysfunctional families that asked audiences to laugh as a way of understanding profound human failings. After *Laughing Wild* (1987), his duet of alternating monologues by neurotic city dwellers, Durang did not write a full-length play for nearly a decade. Critics then lambasted his next effort, *Sex and Longing* (1996), a political satire of the Christian Right, as a pale imitation of his earlier work. However, his subsequent take on tabloid television, *Betty's Summer Vacation* (1999), soon marked a return to critical favor and won Durang another Obie Award.

In addition to his eight full-length works to date, Durang has always been a master of the one-act and the comedic sketch. Many of these have become perennial favorites of amateur and professional companies alike—such as *'dentity Crisis* (1975), *The Actor's Nightmare* (1981), and the TENNESSEE WILLIAMS takeoffs *Desire, Desire, Desire* (1987) and *For Whom the Southern Belle Tolls* (1994). As a performer he has appeared in his own plays (in *Laughing Wild* and as the autobiographical narrator in *Bette and Boo*), as well as in films and in musical cabarets.

[*See also* United States, 1940–Present]

PLAYS: *The Idiots Karamazov* (1974, co-written with Albert Innaurato); *A History of the American Film* (1976–1978); *The Vietnamization of New Jersey* (1977); *Sister Mary Ignatius Explains It All for You* (1981); *Beyond Therapy* (1981–1982); *Baby with the Bathwater* (1983); *The Marriage of Bette and Boo* (1985); *Laughing Wild* (1987); *Sex and Longing* (1996); *Betty's Summer Vacation* (1999)

FURTHER READING

Durang, Christopher, *27 Short Plays*. Lyme: Smith & Kraus, 1995.
——. *Complete Full-Length Plays 1975–1995*. Lyme: Smith & Kraus, 1997.
Savran, David. *In Their Own Words: Contemporary American Playwrights*. New York: Theatre Communications Group, 1988.
Wetzsteon, Ross. *The Best of Off-Broadway: Eight Contemporary Obie-Winning Plays*. New York: Mentor, 1994.

Garrett B. Eisler

DURAS, MARGUERITE (1914–1996)

Novelist, journalist, playwright, screenwriter, and director Marguerite Duras was born Marguerite Donnadieu in 1914 in Gia Dinh, Indochina, the third child of French missionary parents stationed in Saigon. After her father's death from dysentery, Duras and her family lived in various parts of colonial Indochina where her mother taught in Indigenous schools. At the age of eighteen, Duras returned to FRANCE to pursue her studies. Duras first came to the attention of the French public as a novelist associated with the *nouveau roman* ("new novel") movement during the 1960s. Along with writers like Alain Robbe Grillet, NATHALIE SARRAUTE, Michel Butor, and ROBERT PINGET, Duras's novels are distinguished by their spare, first-person narratives and strong phenomenological bent: attention to things as they are perceived, rather than culled from objective reality.

Her first play, *The Square* (*Le Square*, 1957) is an adaptation of her 1955 novel by the same title in which, in the absurdist tradition, two unremarkable figures sitting on a park bench attempt for a moment to break surface communication only to return to their solitary condition. A major turning point in Duras's writing career came in 1959 with her film script *Hiroshima, My Love* (*Hirochima, Mon Amour*), co-written with director Alain Renais. The subjectivities of love and desire in the aftermath of Western history's failures remained central to Duras's work for over three decades. In 1965, Jean-Louis Barrault staged Duras's play *Days in the Trees* (*Des journées entières dans les arbres*), with Madeleine Renaud in the title role. In 1968, Duars directed two of her one-act plays, *Yes, Perhaps* (*Yes, peut-être*) and *Shaga* (*Le Shaga*), both critical of cultural and political imperialism and the Vietnam War. Starting with Duras's 1960 novel *Moderato Cantabile* (later adapted to the screen and directed by Peter Brook) and the play version of her novel *The English Lover* (*L'Amante Anglaise*, 1968)—and throughout the 1970s—Duras's increasingly uncategorizable texts began to challenge patriarchal assumptions about character and form and to foreground feminist concerns.

In 1972, Duras directed the film version of her play *India Song*. Set in a mythopoetic colonial Indochina, her multichanneled narratives about history and love emanate from different times and places, as unseen voices recount the life of Anne-Marie Stretter, the French ambassador's wife, before her suicide. Duras's 1977 play *Eden Cinema* (*L'Eden Cinéma*)—about her childhood in Indochina and her mother's madness as a result of colonial oppression—and three subsequent plays, *The Malady of Death* (*La Maladie de la mort*, 1982), *Savanah Bay* (1983), and *Vera Baxter, or the Atlantic Beaches* (*Vera Baxter; ou les plages atlantiques*, 1985), all feature female protagonists in a relationship of struggle with the representational frame and who speak back to a masculine symbolic. In 1984, Duras was awarded the Goncourt prize for her novel *The Lover* (*L'Amant*). Duras also undertook several adaptations during her theater career. Among them, Henry James's *The Aspern Papers* in 1961 and AUGUST STRINDBERG'S THE DANCE OF DEATH in 1970.

During her long life as a public intellectual—from the time of her return to France from Indochina to her subsequent and controversial involvement in the Resistance movement during the Nazi occupation (later chronicled in *The War*), and peripatetic relationship with the Communist Party—and until her death in 1996 in Paris, Duras remained an ardent political activist and critic of the status quo. Her novels, plays, and films dramatize an array of historical and political conflicts; Duras's articles for *Vogue*, *France-Observateur*, and *Liberation*, republished in a collection titled *Outside*, are compelling cultural documents that engage with equal passion and veracity topics as diverse as the Algerian War, Brigitte Bardot, and the art of making a good leek soup.

PLAYS: *The Square* (*Le Square*, 1957); *Days in the Trees* (*Des journées entières dans les arbres*, 1965); *The Department of the Environment* (*Les Eaux et Forêts*, 1965); *The Music* (*La Musica*, 1965); *Destroy, She Said* (*Détruire, dit-elle*, 1968); *A Man Came to See Me* (*Un homme est venu me voir*, 1968); *Shaga* (*Le Shaga*, 1968); *Suzanna Andler* (1968); *Yes, Perhaps* (*Yes, peut-être*, 1968); *India Song* (1972); *Eden Cinema* (*L'Eden Cinéma*, 1977); *Agatha* (1981); *The Malady of Death* (*La Maladie de la mort*, 1982); *Savannah Bay* (1983); *The Music II* (*La Musica deuxième*, 1985); *Vera Baxter, or The Atlantic Beaches* (*Vera Baxter; ou Les plages atlantiques*, 1985)

FURTHER READING

Bree, Germaine. "An Interview with Marguerite Duras." *Contemporary Literature* 13 (1972): 399–422.

Cody, Gabrielle. *Impossible Performances: Duras as Dramatist.* New York: NYU New Foundations, 2000.

Duras, Marguerite. *Outside: Selected Essays by the Author of The Lover.* Boston: Beacon Press, 1986.

Hill, Leslie. *Apocalyptic Desires.* London: Routledge, 1993.

Kristeva, Julia. "Pain and Sorrow in the Modern World: The Works of Marguerite Duras." Tr. by Katherine A. Jensen. PMLA 2 (1987): 138.

Gabrielle H. Cody

DÜRRENMATT, FRIEDRICH (1921–1990)

The worst thing I can imagine is to see a book displayed in a shop window: Consolation from Dürrenmatt.

—Friedrich Dürrenmatt in Conversation with Horst Bienek, 1961

SWITZERLAND's best-known dramatist of the 20th century is also its most troublesome. Friedrich Dürrenmatt's plays do not have happy endings. Bizarre coincidence, the prime mover in his dramatic universe, brings even his most courageous characters to a point diametrically opposite their desired goal. In an inherently unjust universe the individual can only hope to realize justice on an individual level. God is inaccessibly remote, and there is no salvation in ideologies, which are corrupt and interchangeable. TRAGEDY in the Aristotelian sense is no longer possible, because tragedy requires individual guilt and expiation. No one is guilty or responsible any more. We are too deeply mired in collective guilt. Only COMEDY can speak to us.

Born on January 5, 1921, in Konolfingen, Switzerland, as a pastor's son, Dürrenmatt was an artist, astronomer, philosopher, poet, novelist, and most important, internationally acclaimed dramatist. An undistinguished pupil, Dürrenmatt planned to attend an art academy. However, he refused to suppress his expressionistic tendencies in order to appease the judges and was denied admission. Thus he enrolled as a student of literature: first at the University of Zürich, where he enjoyed a bohemian lifestyle, and later at the University of Bern. Largely as a reaction to the Calvinism with which he was raised, Dürrenmatt changed his major to PHILOSOPHY.

In 1946, while preparing a dissertation on "Kierkegaard and the Tragic," he made the decision to become a writer. That same year he met and married Lotti Geißler, an actress in Basel. The following spring his first play, *It Is Written* (*Es steht geschrieben*, 1947), an expressionistic treatment of the 16th-century Anabaptist revolt in Münster, opened at the Schauspielhaus Zürich. Causing a scandal at its premiere, the play is important only insofar as it launched Dürrenmatt's career. He turned to comedy after a second attempt at serious drama, *The Blind Man* (*Der Blinde*, 1948), a play exploring the limits of Kierkegaardian absurd faith, ended in resounding failure.

In *Romulus the Great* (*Romulus der Große*, 1949), Dürrenmatt used a fictional account of the last Roman emperor Romulus Augustulus to illustrate a tenet of his dramatic theory that he would codify years later in his "Twenty-one Points to *The Physicists*" ("*21 Punkte zu den Physikern*," 1962). Romulus, like so many other tragicomic figures in Dürrenmatt's forty-year career as a dramatist, trips over "the worst possible turn of events," a coincidence so improbable that it thwarts the most carefully conceived plan. The play takes a controversial postwar stance on heroism. Romulus betrays Rome in a just cause, and his actions, while futile, are judged heroic.

Two popular detective novels, *The Judge and His Hangman* (*Der Richter und sein Henker*, 1951) and *The Quarry* (*Der Vedacht*, 1952), followed. Between 1946 and 1956 Dürrenmatt also wrote eight radio plays, two of which, *Traps* (*Die Panne*, 1955) and *Episode on an Autumn Evening* (*Abendstunde im Spätherbst*, 1956), he later adapted to stage plays. In 1952, *The Marriage of Mr. Mississippi* (*Die Ehe des Herrn Mississippi*) premiered in Munich. Swiss theaters thought the comedy of adultery and murder too scandalous. *The Marriage* is primarily a play about ideologies. As the Cold War superpowers were demanding doctrinal purity, Dürrenmatt revealed all ideologies to be equally destructive and completely interchangeable. The play was a success and established Dürrenmatt's reputation outside his homeland. While religion had been one of the ideologies critiqued in *The Marriage of Mr. Mississippi*, it is the primary target of *An Angel Comes to Babylon* (*Ein Engel kommt nach Babylon*, 1953), produced in Munich the following year. Here the author wrestled with the faith of his father, the Calvinism of his earliest plays. Originally intended as the first play in a trilogy about the Tower of Babel, *An Angel Comes to Babylon* examines the nature of God's grace, finding it too remote and exclusive to be of any relevance to the human race. The play makes evident Dürrenmatt's turn to agnosticism.

It was finally in 1956 with *The Visit of the old Lady* (*Der Besuch der alten Dame*) that Dürrenmatt gained acclaim outside German-speaking Europe. The TRAGICOMEDY that examines the nature of guilt and justice was a worldwide sensation. It was, therefore, almost inevitable that audiences would await his next play with exaggerated expectations. *Frank the Fifth: Opera of a Private Bank* (*Frank der Fünfte: Oper einer Privatbank*, 1959) was a disappointment. Gangsters murdered and sang their way through a lengthy comedy. Unfortunately, singing gangsters had already been done, and the play suffered by comparison with BERTOLT BRECHT'S THE THREEPENNY OPERA (*Die Dreigroschenoper*, 1928) to which it contains more than one intertextual reference. Dürrenmatt argued that William Shakespeare, not Brecht, had been the inspiration for the play.

Disillusioned, Dürrenmatt waited three years before venturing back to the stage. This time, instead of parodying Brecht superficially, he took issue with him philosophically and scored his second major theatrical triumph with the Cold War comedy THE PHYSICISTS (*Die Physiker*, 1962). The play enjoyed a three-day-long premiere in Zurich and raised expectations for the next play. Dürrenmatt created a major controversy in 1963 with *Hercules and the Augian Stables* (*Herkules und der Stall des Augias*). The setting in Ancient GREECE did little to mask the fact that the author was satirizing his own countrymen, their institutions, and their national myths. The Elian farmers have Swiss names. Despite a foolproof plan, Hercules fails to accomplish his task of cleaning the mountains of manure out of the land because he cannot secure permission from the even deeper layers of bureaucracy. This all-too-direct satire offended his audience, and the play failed.

Dürrenmatt returned to the stage in 1966 with *The Meteor* (*Der Meteor*), a two-act comedy that would be his last major success. Wolfgang Schwitter, a reprehensible individual who wants nothing more than to die, experiences the miracle of resurrection twice, while all those around him die or have their lives ruined by association with him. The outraged church played into the author's hands. The public debate that followed afforded Dürrenmatt his scandal, and the play enjoyed ongoing publicity.

During the next six years, Dürrenmatt dedicated most of his energy to adaptations. He began by adapting his own first play into the comedy *The Anabaptists* (*Die Wiedertäufer*, 1967). There followed adaptations of Shakespeare's *King John* in 1968, and AUGUST STRINDBERG's THE DANCE OF DEATH (1900) in 1969, which Dürrenmatt turned into the macabre FARCE *Play Strindberg*, the most popular and successful of his adaptations. Johann Wolfgang von Goethe's *Urfaust* (1775) and Shakespeare's *Titus Andronicus* followed in 1970, and Georg Büchner's *Woyzeck* (1837) in 1973. The one original composition during this time was the topical but unsuccessful *Portrait of a Planet* (*Porträt eines Planeten*, 1970), an experimental piece consisting of twenty vignettes on a bare stage, acted by four men and four women with biblical names. The Vietnam War, the drug culture, the space race, free love, and other issues of the late 1960s pass in review before an exploding supernova destroys the planet, like a giant camera taking one last flash snapshot of a pathetic society.

Dürrenmatt grew increasingly alienated from the medium through which he had achieved his greatest triumphs. He felt that the theater and its audiences had passed him by, especially after the failure of a play he considered one of his best: *The Collaborator* (*Der Mitmacher*, 1973), a gangster comedy much blacker than *Frank the Fifth* but with a similar premise. Society is so corrupt that those we call gangsters are merely servants of the real gangsters: the police, the government, and the military-industrial complex. The narrative Dürrenmatt wrote in defense of the failed play, "*The Collaborator*, a Complex: Afterword to a Comedy ("*Der Mitmacher*, ein Komplex: Nachwort zu einer Komödie," 1976), is four times longer than the play itself. There followed *The Grace Period* (*Die Frist*, 1977) about the protracted death of dictator Francisco Franco (1892–1975) and the corrupt government officials who keep him alive for their own political ends. Audiences, but not critics, responded more favorably to *Traps* (*Die Panne*, 1979), adapted from the successful radio play. Finally, Dürrenmatt ended his dramatic career with a failed but brilliantly conceived political comedy titled *Achterloo* (1983). The play takes place in an insane asylum, where the inmates play roles as therapy. The audience is faced with the dilemma of keeping four levels of reality separate as characters pretend to be characters playing other characters in a satire about a real political event. During the writing of the play, Dürrenmatt's wife Lotti died, and the following year he married the filmmaker Charlotte Kerr. He continued writing novels and novellas after bidding farewell to the theater. Throughout his career he authored numerous essays on the theory and practice of drama, among the more significant of which are "Problems of the Theater" ("Theaterprobleme," 1954) and "Sentences about the Theater ("Sätze über das Theater," 1970). He also wrote extensive program notes to several of his plays.

Dürrenmatt died on December 14, 1990, at his home in Neuchâtel, just three weeks before his seventieth birthday.

[*See also* Absurdism; Expressionism]

PLAYS: *It Is Written* (*Es steht geschrieben*, 1947); *The Blind Man* (*Der Blinde*, 1948); *Romulus the Great* (*Romulus der Große*, 1949); *The Marriage of Mr. Mississippi* (*Die Ehe des Herrn Mississippi*, 1952); *An Angel Comes to Babylon* (*Ein Engel kommt nach Babylon*, 1953); *The Visit* (*Der Besuch der alten Dame*, 1956); *Frank the Fifth: Opera of a Private Bank* (*Frank der Fünfte: Oper einer Privatbank*, 1959); *The Physicists* (*Die Physiker*, 1962); *Hercules and the Augian Stables* (*Herkules und der Stall des Augias*, 1963); *The Meteor* (*Der Meteor*, 1966); *The Anabaptists* (*Die Wiedertäufer*, 1967); *Play Strindberg* (1969); *Portrait of a Planet* (*Porträt eines Planeten*, 1970); *The Collaborator* (*Der Mitmacher*, 1973); *The Grace Period* (*Die Frist*, 1977); *Traps* (*Die Panne*, 1979); *Achterloo* (1983)

FURTHER READING

Crockett, Roger A. *Understanding Friedrich Dürrenmatt*. Columbia: Univ. of South Carolina Press, 1998.

Jenny, Urs. *Friedrich Dürrenmatt: A Study of His Plays*. Tr. by Keith Hamnet and Hugh Rorrison. London: Methuen, 1978.

Tiusanen, Timo. *Dürrenmatt: A Study in Plays, Prose, Theory*. Princeton, N.J.: Princeton Univ. Press, 1977.

Whitton, Kenneth. *The Theatre of Friedrich Dürrenmatt: A Study in the Possibility of Freedom*. London: Oswald Wolff, 1980.

Roger A. Crockett

DUTCH DRAMA *See* NETHERLANDS

DUTCHMAN

Let me be who I feel like being. Uncle Tom. Thomas. Whoever. It's none of your business. You don't know anything except what's there for you to see. An act. Lies. Device. Not the pure heart, the pumping black heart. You don't ever know that. And I sit here, in this buttoned-up suit, to keep myself from cutting all your throats.

—Clay, Scene 2

Dutchman is AMIRI BARAKA's (birth name LeRoi Jones) most acclaimed play, a one-act produced OFF-BROADWAY in 1964 and recipient of an Obie Award for best American play. This powerful drama indicts white racism in a murderous confrontation on a New York subway between Lula, a bigoted Caucasian woman, and Clay, a black, middle-class intellectual man. In this searing drama, Lula, haunted by distorted racist fantasies, provokes the rage of the repressed black revolutionary and then fatally stabs him. The *Dutchman* was a legendary ghost ship, a slave-trading vessel, condemned to sail the high seas until the Day of Judgment. Clay is the embodiment of a black poet who can find no safe shore on which to land.

Lula and Clay are archetypal figures representing racial and sexual mythologies. Lula is a cruel and seductive aggressor whose idea of African American experience is built on stereotypical fantasies of black identity. She calls Clay a "black Baudelaire" and reprimands him as a "dirty white man" for accommodating himself to middle-class American values. She finally provokes a response from Clay that releases all his pent-up racial hatred against whites. Yet he chooses to act with words rather than violence. In an angry climactic outburst, he argues that the jazz of Charlie Parker and Bessie Smith consists of sublimating African American lethal wrath: "Bird would've played not a note of music if he just walked up to East Sixty-seventh Street and killed the first ten white people he saw." Lula taunts Clay mercilessly until his initial attraction changes to bitter distain. He has, however, miscalculated the potential within his racist enemy for bloodshed and destruction.

The drama is a scathing critique of the middle-class assimilated black man. Between the white oppressor and the black rebel is the doomed Clay, the Uncle Tom, a shuffling servile traitor, also represented by the train conductor who enters the subway car at the end doing a soft-shoe dance as Clay's dying body is removed. The play also expresses an underlying intrigue with the sexual magnetism between a black man and a white woman.

Dutchman was written during the black militant phase of Baraka's work, in a year when race riots plagued the United States. This was a separatist period of the poet's writing, one that advocated division of the races, black political power, and racial pride. The play was generally well received, and critics praised its incisive poetry and ferocious wit. Others argued that it perpetuated interracial hatred and advocated violence as a means of resolving racism. Feminist criticism of the play addressed sexism among black men, remarking that black male empowerment often resulted in the subordination of African American women.

[*See also* Black Arts Movement; Political Theater; United States, 1940–Present]

FURTHER READING

Levesque, George A. "LeRoi Jones' 'Dutchman': Myth and Allegory." *Obsidian: Black Literature in Review* V, No. 3 (1979): 33–40.

Sarma, M. Nagabhushana. "Revolt and Ritual in the Plays of LeRoi Jones." *Osmania Journal of English Studies* XI, No. 1 (1974–75): 1–9.

Weisgram, Dianne H. "LeRoi Jones' 'Dutchman': Inter-Racial Ritual of Sexual Violence." *American Imago* 29, No. 3 (Fall 1972): 215–232.

Werner, Craig. "Brer Rabbit Meets the Underground Man: Simplification of the Consciousness in Baraka's 'Dutchman' and 'Slave Ship.'" *Obsidian: Black Literature in Review* V, No. 1 & 2 (1979): 35–40.

Molly Castelloe

DUTT, UTPAL (1929–1993)

Utpal Dutt's talents as a theater person—playwright, director, actor, and regisseur—were perhaps as multilayered as his politics and his positions on the practice of theater. His theatrical career began when he became a member of the English theater group Shakespeareana in 1947, just as INDIA became independent from British rule. However, indoctrinated by Marxist ideals, Dutt soon realized that theater in the English language had severe limitations in terms of audience outreach. In 1952, under Dutt's leadership, Shakespeareana became the Little Theatre Group (LTG) and started producing both Western and Indian classics in Bengali. Dutt wrote his first full-length play in 1958, launching a prolific career as a radical playwright and adding new dimension to his growing reputation as actor and director. Exploiting the already established form of the well-made play, and using elements of *jatra*, the Bengali popular theater, he used MAKSIM GORKY's idea of "amplification" to portray life not as it is but as it should be. Dutt's Marxist theater projects began in 1951 when he helped create a short AGITATION-PROPAGANDA (agit-prop) play about imprisoned Communist activists, called *Chargesheet*, for the IPTA or Indian People's Theatre Association.

In 1959, Dutt wrote and directed *Charred Coal (Angaar)* about the plight of exploited coal-mine workers and staged it with LTG at the Minerva Theatre. Witnesses still recount their sense of awe and horror when Dutt "showed" the mines being flooded and the workers dying. Understandably, the play became hugely popular. However, a decade later Dutt denounced *Charred Coal* as a nonrevolutionary play. With his 1965 play THE WAVE (*Kallol*), Dutt tried to bring the audience and the revolutionary closer. By the end of the 1960s, West Bengal was seeing the rise of a Maoist revolution led by a faction of the united Communist Party calling themselves the Naxalites. Dutt's play, produced in 1967 under his own direction, "tried to recount the . . . heroism of the peasant-guerilla and expose the brutalities of the soldiers and policemen sent . . . to the area (Gunawardana, 1971)." Dutt was arrested again.

In 1968, Dutt came back with a new play, *The Rights of Man (Maanusher Adhikaaré)* on the racist Scottsboro Trials that rocked the UNITED STATES in the 1930s. This play marked the dissolution of LTG and Dutt's entry into *jatra*.

A popular *jatra* performance typically plays for an audience of thousands. Its mass appeal, particularly in rural Bengal, is based on the way it uses song, dance, and drama to bring mythology to life. Dutt took full advantage of the "total performance" quality of *jatra*. In fourteen years, 1968 to 1982, Dutt wrote nineteen *jatra* plays, almost all of which were commercially successful. Of them *Rifle* (1968), *a JalianwalBag* (1969), and *Mao Tse Tung* (1974) stand out.

In 1971, Dutt reorganized his band of followers to form the People's Little Theatre (PLT). The PLT phase of his career was launched with a play about theater: *The Tin Sword* (*Tiner Talowar*, 1971). Set in 19th-century Kolkata, this play (situated in true historical fact) was about the inner contradictions and struggles of an imagined theater company, which in turn reflected the larger concerns of the time: colonial rule, social change, and nationalism. In 1974, in protest against Prime Minister Indira Gandhi's semifascist declaration of "emergency," Dutt staged *Nightmare-City* (*Duhswapner Nagori*), with the PLT, a gritty portrayal of Kolkata choking under Gandhi's oppressive regime.

After 1977, when the Left Front, led by the CPI(M), came into power, Dutt's career lost its edge. Now that the party with which he had aligned himself was in power, he had lost the need to be revolutionary. His notable plays of this period are *Blue, White & Red* (*Nil-Sada-Laal*, 1989), celebrating the French Revolution; *Walk Alone* (*Eklaa Chalo Ré*, 1989), a critical but sympathetic look at Mahatma Gandhi; and *The Red Bastion* (*Laal Durgo*, 1990), in defense of the declining socialist regime in Rumania. He said in a lecture in 1980, "We haven't yet risen to the level of revolutionary theatre. . . . We certainly have had a theatre movement, but not revolutionary theatre. In this regard, we need to be self-critical" (Dutt, 2001).

Dutt's theater stands as one of the best examples of its kind in India. However, Dutt's legacy endures in other ways as well. His books on acting are among the finest written in the Bengali language, and he was regarded very highly (albeit controversially) as a theater historian and scholar. His magnum opus *Shakespeare's Social Consciousness* (*Shakespearer Samajchetana*, 1972) is among the first and best books in Bengali on Elizabethan society and its theater. Dutt's English writings include two books, *Towards a Revolutionary Theatre* and *Girish Ghosh*, a monograph on the famous playwright/actor/regisseur of 19th-century Kolkata, and numerous articles. Lamentably, only two of his plays are readily available in English. Dutt was, until his death on August 19, 1993, in Kolkata, the editor of *Epic Theatre*, a Bengali theater journal.

SELECT PLAYS: *Charred Coal* (*Angaar*, 1959); *The Wave* (*Kallol*, 1965); *The Rights of Man* (*Maanusher Adhikaaré*, 1968); *Rifle* (1968); *JalianwalBag* (1969); *The Tin Sword* (*Tiner Talowar*, 1971); *Mao Tse Tung* (1974); *Nightmare-City* (*Duhswapner Nagori*, 1974); *Blue, White & Red* (*Nil-Sada-Laal*, 1989); *Walk Alone* (*Eklaa Chalo Ré*, 1989); *The Red Bastion* (*Laal Durgo*, 1990)

FURTHER READING

Banerjee, Himani. *The Mirror of Class: Essays on Bengali Theatre*. Kolkata: Papyrus, 1998.

Bharucha, Rustom. "The Revolutionary Theater of Utpal Dutt." In *Rehearsals of a Revolution: The Political Theater of Bengal*. Honolulu: Univ. of Hawaii Press, 1983.

Bhatia, Nandi. "Colonial History and Postcolonial Interventions: Staging the 1857 Mutiny as 'The Great Rebellion.' " In *Acts of Authority/Acts of Resistance: Theater and Politics in Colonial and Postcolonial India*. Ann Arbor: Univ. of Michigan Press, 2004.

Dutt, Utpal. "Rajnaitik Thietar o Saadhaaran Darshak" [Political Theater and the Public, Reprint of public lecture given in 1980]. Kolkata: *Pashchim Banga; Utpal Dutt Commemorative Issue*, Vol. 45–47, 2001.

Gunawardana, A. J. "Theatre as a Weapon: An Interview with Utpal Dutt," *The Drama Review: TDR* Vol. 15, No. 2 Theatre in Asia (Spring, 1971), pp. 224–237.

Jacob, Paul, ed. "Interview with Utpal Dutt." In *Contemporary Indian Theatre: Interviews with Playwrights and Directors*. New Delhi: Sangeet Natak Akademi, 1989.

Mukherjee, Sushil. *The Story of the Calcutta Theatres*. Kolkata: K. P. Bagchi & Co., 1982.

Raha, Kiranmay. *Bengali Theatre*. New Delhi: National Book Trust of India, 1985.

Sudipto Chatterjee

THE DYBBUK

Considered the Yiddish *Romeo and Juliet*, *The Dybbuk, or Between Two Worlds: A Dramatic Legend in Four Acts* (1918) centers on the love between Leah, the only daughter of a wealthy shtetl widower named Sender, and Khonon, a poor yeshiva student who takes possession of Leah's body in the form of a spirit or dybbuk on the eve of her wedding. The play takes place in 1860s southern Russia, the locus of Hasidism, a branch of Judaism infused with mystical teachings.

In act 1 Sender announces the betrothal of his daughter, which Khonon had been trying to prevent by practicing Kabbalah; on hearing the news, Khonon falls dead. In act 2, the day of her wedding, Leah visits a graveyard and returns "changed." When the groom moves to place the customary wedding veil on Leah, she tears it off, and from her mouth, Khonon's voice announces that he will not leave the body of his promised bride. In act 3, with the hope of exorcising him from Leah's body, Rabbi Azriel presides over a trial in which the living (Sender) and the dead (Khonon and his father Nissin) take part. The trial reveals that Sender ignored an oath he had made with Nissin that if one should have a daughter and the other a son, they would wed; Sender made the oath for wealth. He repents, and Khonon leaves Leah's body. Minutes before Leah is to be wedded, Khonon's disembodied voice beckons her to join him and she does, presumably in death.

Shloyme Zanv Rappoport, who wrote under the pseudonym S. Ansky, filled *The Dybbuk* with folk sayings and Hasidic tales. Born to a religious Jewish family in 1863 Vitebsk, Ansky became estranged from Jewish life for a time but by 1905 had experienced a cultural reconversion and had begun pursuing his interest in Jewish folklore. Ansky saw his ethnographic activity as a wellspring for secular Jewish art. Leah's decision to join Khonon at the end contradicts the preservation of life insisted upon by Azriel, and some critics have compared the play to a museum of Eastern European Jewish cultural life Ansky believed was growing extinct. Others see Leah's move as the triumph of love over death. According to one psychoanalytic reading, it indicates a return to infancy and the evasion of adulthood with its distinctions between life and death, male and female.

Ansky originally wrote the play in Russian for KONSTANTIN STANISLAVSKY, director of the MOSCOW ART THEATRE in 1917, who passed it on to the Hebrew theater troupe Habima, which persuaded poet Chaim Nachman Bialik to translate it. When Vladimir Lenin seized power in 1918, Ansky (an anti-Bolshevik socialist) fled Russia, losing the original Russian draft. Bialik's translation came to be the basis of the Yiddish version. Most critics agree that it is the greatest Yiddish drama. Ansky died in Warsaw two years later, never seeing the play produced. *The Dybbuk* was performed first by the Vilna Troupe in December 1920. In 1921, Maurice Schwartz introduced the play to America; a few months later, it saw its Moscow premiere.

[*See also* Yiddish Theater]

FURTHER READING

The Dybbuk and Other Writings. Ed. and intro. by David G. Roskies. Tr. by Golda Werman. New York: Schocken Bks., 1992.

Hoberman, J. "Repossessing the Dybbuk." *Pakn Treger* 28 (1998): 20–35.

Konigsberg, Ira. "The Only 'I' in the World: Religion, Psychoanalysis, and *The Dybbuk*." *Cinema Journal* 36 (Summer 1997): 22–42.

Alyssa Quint

E

EARTH SPIRIT

Earth Spirit (*Erdgeist*), by FRANK WEDEKIND, was intended to be part of a larger work, but his publisher anticipated problems with censors and divided it into two plays, *Earth Spirit* (1895) and *Pandora's Box, a Monster Tragedy* (*Die Büchse der Pandora, eine Monstertragödie*, 1902). The two plays make up Wedekind's Lulu plays. *Earth Spirit* consists of the first three acts of the original five-act work along with a new act between acts 2 and 3. The prologue was added in 1898 for the premiere in Leipzig, with Wedekind himself playing the role of Dr. Schön.

The plot of the play revolves around Lulu who, as a poor young girl, was taken in by the businessman Dr. Schön in a somewhat dubious act of charity. Schön has arranged Lulu's marriage to Dr. Goll, a sexually impotent but extremely jealous medical counselor. Goll soon collapses and dies after catching Lulu alone with the painter Schwarz, who has been painting her as Pierrot. Schön then arranges Lulu's marriage to Schwarz. He has benefited from Lulu's inherited wealth and become a successful painter, but Lulu complains to Schön about her husband's lack of interest in women. Schwarz cannot tolerate the sexual pressure and commits suicide. Lulu reverts to her earlier calling as a dancer but is frustrated by Schön's engagement to another woman. She orders Schön to write a letter canceling the engagement, which had been Schön's hope for achieving respectability. He then finds himself married to Lulu, who realizes that Schön has been using her all along. In a final argument, she shoots him dead.

Lulu has been traditionally interpreted as the embodiment of irrational and inherently destructive female sexuality in contrast to a male order based on reason and restraint. Some have seen this as a sign of women's sexual emancipation, while other interpretations stress the strong connection between the power of sexuality in achieving and maintaining socioeconomic status in bourgeois society. Certain critics, however, have taken issue with Wedekind's two-dimensional presentation of female sexuality.

Lulu's husbands refer to her by different names: she is Nelli for Goll, Eva for Schwarz, and Mignon for Schön. The name changes have been interpreted both as an illustration of Lulu's ability to adapt effectively and survive in changing situations and as the men's way of objectifying her to suit their particular needs.

The notion of an "earth spirit" has been traced to such sources as Johann Wolfgang von Goethe's *Faust* (1808) and Friedrich Schiller's *The Death of Wallenstein* (*Wallensteins Tod*, 1799). In both instances, the "earth spirit" represents a force of nature at odds with human order and comprehension. The figure of Lulu presents a similar challenge to civilization.

Although designated a "TRAGEDY," *Earth Spirit* combines the tragic with dark humor and absurd dialogue, thus skewing traditional dramatic categories.

[*See also* Expressionism; Germany]

FURTHER READING

Best, Alan. "The Rise and Fall of a Beautiful Dream: *Lulu*." In *Frank Wedekind*. London: Wolff, 1975. 82–97.

Hibberd, John. "The Spirit of the Flesh: Wedekind's *Lulu*." *Modern Language Review* 79 (1984): 336–355.

Lewis, Ward B. *The Ironic Dissident: Frank Wedekind in the View of His Critics*. Columbia, S.C.: Camden House, 1997.

Martins Masulis

THE EASIEST WAY

DAVID BELASCO's staging of Eugene Walter's *The Easiest Way* was the hit of the 1909 New York season, running an impressive two years. The first play about prostitution to be embraced by mainstream audiences, *The Easiest Way* was selected as the best play of 1909.

The Easiest Way portrays the decline of Laura Murdock, an aspiring actress. She becomes the mistress of Willard Brockton, a rich man with influential ties in the theater. While in Colorado on tour, Laura falls in love with John Madison in spite of his modest income. She returns to acting in New York, breaks up with Brockton, and waits for Madison to make his fortune out West. But Brockton sees to it that she is blacklisted. Penniless, and not having heard from Madison, Laura reluctantly returns to Brockton. Shortly after her reconciliation with Brockton, Madison appears in town.

Laura intends to marry Madison without telling him about her recent reunion with Brockton. In the final scene, just as Laura and Madison are about to depart, Brockton enters her apartment. The sound of the key in the door is a suspenseful moment that some scholars have compared to Nora's slamming of the door in *A DOLL'S HOUSE*. Laura tries desperately to defend herself, but Madison leaves. Rejected by both men and destitute, Laura turns to prostitution, telling her maid: "Get my new hat, dress up my body and paint up my face. It's all they've left of me. . . . I'm going to Rector's to make a hit, and to hell with the rest."

While in many ways *The Easiest Way* was a "familiar picture of the theater-woman, struggling for her virtue amid the alleged temptations of Broadway," as critic Alan Dale (1909) wrote, the play generated debates about the politics of women's work and prostitution. Many critics expressed moral condemnation of

Laura, whereas others took issue with the phrase "the easiest way" and defended Laura's impossible position.

Casting against type, Belasco used innocent-looking Frances Starr in the role of Laura. Belasco found in Starr a new type of actress, showing, as he put it, that "a little woman can play tragic scenes." Belasco's championing of Starr signaled a shift away from suffragist actresses with large presences (Olga Nethersole, Mary Shaw, Mrs. Fiske), toward smaller, frailer actresses.

Perhaps the most memorable aspect of *The Easiest Way* was Belasco's staging of a boardinghouse with the realistic exactitude that became his trademark. One review called it "the *pièce de résistance* in scenic accuracy." Belasco and his stage designer, Ernest Gros, located the shabbiest boardinghouse they could find and "bought the entire interior of one of its most dilapidated rooms . . . even the faded paper on the walls," and reassembled it onstage. As *Munsey's Magazine* (1909) reported, "Never before, probably, has there been seen on the stage such a striking example of that prodigal disarray of personal belongings that means poverty rather than wealth." Such unprecedented realism guaranteed a smash-hit success.

[*See also* United States, 1860–1929]

FURTHER READING

Belasco, David. *The Theatre Through the Stage Door.* New York: Harper, 1919.

Dale, Alan. "Eugene Walter's 'The Easiest Way.' " *New York American* (January 20, 1909).

Goldman, Emma. "*The Easiest Way*: An Appreciation." *Mother Earth* 4 (May 1909): 86–92.

"Miss Starr Triumphs in *The Easiest Way*." *New York Times* (January 20, 1909): 9.

"Pointers on *The Easiest Way*." *Munsey Magazine* 41 (1909): 878.

Katie N. Johnson

EASTER

Easter, (*Påsk*), a play in three acts by AUGUST STRINDBERG, was written in 1900, published in 1901, and first performed in 1901 at the Schauspielhaus in Frankfurt am Main.

The most remarkable figure in *Easter*, Eleonora, was inspired by Strindberg's sister Elisabeth, to whom he felt very close. She was taken to a mental hospital two years before the play was written.

Eleonora returns from the asylum to her family, the Heysts. Her father is in prison for embezzlement of funds. The family, supported by Eleonora's brother Elis, a schoolteacher, fears that the creditor Lindqvist, a Dickensian character who has returned to town, plans to visit them and demand payment. Lindqvist does pay a visit but only to reveal that he remits the debt.

The supernaturally sensitive Eleonora is a Christ figure, and her substitutive suffering is tied to one of the play's two basic themes: "suffering ennobles." The other theme concerns what Strindberg calls the benevolent nemesis; that is, the idea that good deeds are rewarded. Elis's father had once done Lindqvist a favor; therefore, Lindqvist, in his turn, is willing to overlook the family's debt.

The plot revolves around Elis's (and his mother's) change from implacability to conciliation, from belief in Old Testament justice to faith in New Testament forgiveness. By fulfilling the role of a benevolent deus ex machina, Lindqvist secures a happy ending.

Easter has all the characteristics of a CHAMBER PLAY. Although Eleonora thematically is the central figure, dramaturgically she is not. Being a Christ figure, she is not, like Elis, a divided character who undergoes an inner change. But Elis is a problematic protagonist because his rather vague conversion, more or less forced upon him, takes place exceedingly late in the play.

As one may suspect from the title, *Easter* is patterned on the Passion of Christ. In that sense, it is a modern mystery play. Temporally, Strindberg adheres to the station technique he had earlier used spatially. The first act plays on Maundy Thursday, the second on Good Friday, the third and last on Easter Eve. Each act has its own lighting. The play opens with a last ray of sun and ends with sunshine streaming into the Heyst living room, where all the acts are set. Related to Eleonora and to the light symbolism is the yellow Easter lily, sign of the return of the sun and of divine grace through the resurrection. Each act is preceded by a short part from Joseph Haydn's *The Seven Last Words of Our Savior on the Cross*, act 1 by the introductory maestoso adagio, act 2 by "Father, forgive them, for they know not what they do" (Luke 23:34) as largo, and act 3 with "I thirst" (John 19:31) as adagio. Although the Passion Plays at Oberammergau in Bavaria have probably served as an inspiration, Strindberg (1975), proud of his composition, declared: "the form is my invention."

[*See also* Expressionism; Philosophy and Drama, 1860–1960; Religion and Drama; Sweden]

FURTHER READING

Jacobs, Barry. "Strindberg and the Myth of the Androgyne: Christ Figures in *Easter* and *The Bridal Crown*." In *Strindberg's Post-Inferno Plays*, ed. by Kela Kvam. Copenhagen: Munksgaard, 1994. 92–105.

Lamm, Martin. *August Strindberg*. Tr. and ed. by Harry G. Carlson. New York: Blom, 1971. 305–326.

Ollén, Gunnar. *Strindbergs dramatik* [Strindberg's drama]. Stockholm: Sveriges Radios förlag, 1982.

Strindberg, August. *Dramas of Testimony*. Tr. and intro. by Walter Johnson. Seattle and London: Univ. of Washington Press, 1975.

Egil Törnqvist

EAST LYNNE

East Lynne was once a title as familiar to the general public as any Shakespearean play. Written by ELLEN WOOD and published as a three-volume novel in 1861, *East Lynne* caught the fancy of the reading public and generated a dizzying round of stage adaptations. The novel was republished in 2002 after falling out of critical and popular favor along with a host of other Victorian-era sensation novels featuring dramatic, sexually charged crimes. Sensation plots pit a tormented female heroine against a villain as well as conventional notions of morality, reflecting Victorian cultural anxieties about gender, sexuality and emerging modernity. Many of *East Lynne*'s adaptors found its plot congenial to that most popular form of Victorian theater, the MELODRAMA. Yet it also echoes William Shakespeare's *Othello* as it explores the destructive nature of jealousy and substitutes the contentious issue of class for the racial element in the original.

East Lynne is, on one level, a murder mystery. But the murder itself is a subplot and seems calculated to explore the larger issues of adultery and divorce that eventually shake up the bucolic notions of those who populate East Lynne. The main plot concerns Lady Isabel, an aristocrat who marries the admirable middle-class lawyer Archibald Carlyle, though her early confused affections are engaged elsewhere by the dashing Sir Francis Levison. Carlyle and Isabel have three children before Levison, functioning as Iago does in the plot of *Othello*, convinces Isabel that her husband loves someone else. Isabel runs away with Levison, who seduces and abandons her in the midst of a pregnancy. Friendless and alone, Isabel is injured and disfigured in a train wreck, and the illegitimate child is killed. Isabel conceives a plan to return to the family she loves but left behind. She disguises herself as Madame Vine, a governess, and becomes an employee in her own household, where she daily struggles to come to terms with her role in the destruction of her family. Thinking that Isabel was killed in the train wreck, Carlyle has remarried the very woman that Levison had convinced Isabel her husband really loved. Isabel watches her youngest son die in what is arguably the most famous sentimental child deathbed scene in all of 19th-century drama. This plot and the murder mystery come together when the killer is revealed to be Levison himself, and his role in Isabel's seduction is simultaneously made known. Isabel's health, however, has been weakened by her ordeal. She dies in a final reconciliation scene with Carlyle's full forgiveness.

In novel form, *East Lynne* was issued in twenty-four editions in the first ten years after its initial publication. Its subsequent life onstage, however, is even more astonishing with dozens of adaptations by both British and American playwrights, prompting claims at the turn of the 19th century that productions of *East Lynne* were almost continuously in performance, reaching a vast theater audience. The play lost its draw for audiences as the 20th century wore on, though it has been sporadically revived in both film and stage versions.

[*See also* England, 1860–1940]

FURTHER READING

Booth, Michael R. *English Melodrama*. London: Jenkins, 1965.

Cross, Gilbert B. *Next Week—East Lynne: Domestic Drama in Performance 1820–1874*. Lewisburg, Pa.: Bucknell Univ. Press, 1977.

Scullion, Adrienne, ed. *Female Playwrights of the Nineteenth Century*. London: Dent, 1996.

Wood, Ellen. *East Lynne*. Ed. Andrew Maunder. Orchard Park, N.Y.: Broadview, 2002.

Wynne, Deborah. "See What a Big Wide Bed It Is! Mrs. Henry Wood and the Philistine Imagination." In *Feminist Readings of Victorian Popular Texts: Divergent Femininities*, ed. by Emma Liggins and Daniel Duffy. Brookfield, Vt.: Ashgate, 2001. 89–107.

Julianne Smith

EBONG INDRAJIT

I've written many plays. I want to write many more. But . . . I know nothing about the suffering masses. Nothing about the toiling peasants. Nothing about the sweating coal-miners. Nothing about the snake-charmers. The tribal chieftains or the boatmen. There is no beauty in the people around me, no splendor, no substance. Only the undramatic material—Amal, Vimal, Kamal, and Indrajit.

—Writer, Act 1

The lines spoken above by the Writer in BADAL SIRCAR's celebrated play *Ebong Indrajit* (written in 1962, published 1965) expresses Sircar's own crisis as well as the sociopolitical crisis of a newly independent India. Postindependence disillusionment in INDIA placed Sircar in a consuming predicament: Why should he write? What should he write about? Whom should he write for? By the time he wrote *Ebong Indrajit*, Sircar was equally frustrated by the drawbacks of the proscenium stage, by his own class limitations, and by the ineffectiveness of theater to do anything about the political problems of the times. He chose to make his medium the message of his play.

Directed by Gobindo Ganguly in 1964, the play is about an ordinary man, Indrajit, who is about to become a commonplace man, a man with a name that rhymes with the Bengali equivalent of Tom, Dick, and Harry—Amal, Vimal, and Kamal. Indrajit can surrender to the routine of middle-class existence and become Nirmal. Instead, the Writer points Indrajit to the never-ending road that all human beings traverse, where the process of walking is the only product. Replacing the predictable dramatic tensions of the traditional well-made play with direct address to the audience and staged abstractions of the reality that surrounded him, Sircar makes Indrajit's dilemma the focal point of the play.

Ebong Indrajit shows the middle-class educated individual not as a vanguard of proletarian revolution but rather as a puerile entity trapped concentrically in its own spiraling drive for material gain and success. In doing this, Sircar found a way of dramatizing the crisis of the middle-class Indian, as well as the crisis of humanity at large. Four decades after it was first produced, *Ebong Indrajit* continues to have a huge impact on Indian theater and is the play most often translated from Bengali into other languages.

FURTHER READING

Bharucha, Rustom. *Rehearsals of a Revolution: The Political Theater of Bengal.* Honolulu: Univ. of Hawaii Press, 1983.

Crowe, Brian, and Chris Banfield. *An Introduction to Post-Colonial Theatre.* Cambridge: Cambridge Univ. Press, 1996.

Sircar, Badal. *The Third Theatre.* Calcutta: Badal Sircar, 1978.

——. *The Changing Language of Theatre.* Calcutta: Univ. of Calcutta Press, 1982.

——. *Voyages in the Theatre: Shri Ram Memorial Lectures, 1992.* Calcutta: BIT Blits, 1992.

——. *Ebong Indrajit.* Tr. by Girish Karnad. In *Modern Indian Drama: An Anthology*, ed. by G. P. Deshpande. Delhi: Sahitya Akademi, 2000.

Sudipto Chatterjee

ECHEGARAY, JOSÉ (1832–1916)

I never found in politics that innermost delight that mathematics and literature gave me.

Before becoming a dramatist, José Echegaray was a well-respected engineer, mathematician, and economist. Over the years he served in the Spanish government both as the minister of public works and as finance minister. He was also instrumental in the organization of the national Bank of Spain. He was still serving as finance minister when his first play, *The Avenger's Wife* (*La esposa del vengador*), was produced in 1874 under the pseudonym of Jorge Hayaseca. A staunch defender of free trade and liberalism, Echegaray enjoyed great intellectual, scientific, and political prestige by the time he was awarded the Nobel Prize for Literature in 1904, "in recognition of the numerous and brilliant compositions which, in an individual and original manner, have revived the great traditions of the Spanish drama." He was considered a dedicated statesman and an excellent mathematician. However, his literary accomplishments were not as universally acclaimed, despite the Nobel Prize.

The most notable of his critics were a group of young Spanish intellectuals, now referred to as the Generation of '98, who penned a manifesto against the conferral of the Nobel Prize, stating, among other complaints, that Echegaray represented a Spain "corroded by prejudice and fraud." The disdain for Echegaray in literary circles still exists today despite, or perhaps because of, his tremendous commercial success.

Although he began his literary career somewhat later in life at the age of forty-two, Echegaray became one of Spain's most successful dramatists. He saw sixty-seven of his works produced, thirty-four of which were written in verse; he was proud of being able to deliver at least two plays per year between 1874 and 1904. His mathematical exactitude is seen in his dramatic works, as their carefully precise structure was one of their most salient characteristics. His style varied little over the years, as he opted for tragic dramas, imbued with romantic and melodramatic characteristics: excessive emotion, excessive verbosity, and excessive situations. Wadda Ríos-Font (1997) claims Echegaray established the melodramatic standard in Madrid with its "esthetic of excess." Even when he attempted to model his plays after HENRIK IBSEN, AUGUST STRINDBERG, and other European naturalists, his PROBLEM PLAYS were little more than a continuation of his earlier style. Some of his more well known plays are *The Sword's Handle* (*En el puño de la espada*, 1875); *Madman or Saint* (*O lucura o santidad*, 1877); *The Stake and the Cross* (*En el pilar y en la cruz*, 1878); and *Conflict of Duties* (*Conflicto entre dos deberes*, 1882). THE GREAT GALEOTO (*El gran Galeoto*, 1881) is considered to be his best work. Later on in his career, we see him attempt to situate himself within the more realist contemporary European circles with such pieces as *Mariana* (1892), *The Son of Don Juan* (*El hijo de Don Juan*, 1892), *Spot that Cleans* (*Mancha que limpia*, 1895), and *The Madman Divine* (*El loco Dios*, 1900)—which suggest Ibsen's influence.

PLAYS: *The Avenger's Wife* (*La esposa del vengador*, 1874); *The Checkbook* (*El libro talonario*, 1874); *The Last Night* (*La última noche*, 1874); *A Sun Is Born and Dies* (*Un sol que nace y un sol que muere*, 1875); *The Sword's Handle* (*En el puño de la espada*, 1875); *The Gladiator of Ravena* (*El gladiator de ravena*, 1876); *It Begins as It Ends* (*Cómo empieza y cómo acaba*, 1876); *For Such Fault So Pain* (*Para tal culpa tal pena*, 1877); *Madman or Saint* (*O locura o sanidad*, 1877); *Peace Iris* (*Iris de paz*, 1877); *What Cannot Be Said* (*Lo que no puede decirse*, 1877); *In Pursuit of an Ideal* (*Correr en pos de un ideal*, 1878); *Sometimes Here* (*Algunas veces aqui*, 1878); *The Stake and the Cross* (*En el pilar y en la cruz*, 1878); *In the Bosom of Death* (*En el seno de la muerte*, 1879); *Ocean Without a Shore* (*Mar sin orillas*, 1879); *To Die as Not to Wake* (*Morir por no despertar*, 1879); *Tragic Weddings* (*Bodas trágicas*, 1879); *Death on the Lips* (*La muerte en los labios*, 1880); *The Great Galeoto* (*El gran galeoto*, 1881); *Haraldo the Norman* (*Haraldo el normando*, 1881); *The Two Curious Impertinent Ones* (*Los dos curiosos impertinentes*, 1881); *Conflict of Duties* (*Conflicto entre dos deberes*, 1882); *A Miracle in Egypt* (*Un milagro en Egipto*, 1883); *Happy Life and Sad Death* (*Vida alegre y muerte triste*, 1884); *If You Think the Worst, You Won't Be Far Wrong* (*Piensa mal . . . y acertarás*, 1884); *The Plague of Otranto* (*La peste de otranto*, 1884); *The Bandit Lisandro* (*El bandido lisandro*, 1886); *Of Bad Race* (*De mala raza*, 1886); *Count Lotario* (*El conde lotario*, 1887); *The Reality and the Delirium* (*La realidad y el delirio*, 1887); *Two Fanaticisms* (*Dos fanatismos*, 1887); *The Iron Son and the Son of Meat* (*El hijo de hierro y el hijo de carne*, 1888); *The Sublime in the Vulgar* (*Lo sublime en lo vulgar*, 1888); *The Rigid Ones* (*Los rígidos*, 1889); *Spring that Is Not Exhausted* (*Manantial que no se agota*, 1889); *Always Ridiculous* (*Siempre en ridículo*, 1890); *The Prologue of a Drama* (*El prólogo de un drama*, 1890); *Comedy Without Outcome* (*Comedia sin desenlace*, 1891); *An Incipient Critic* (*En crítico incipiente*, 1891); *Irene of Otranto* (*Irene de otranto*,

1891); *Bad Inheritances* (*Malas herencias*, 1892); *Mariana* (1892); *Sic vos non vobis, or Last Alms* (*Sic vos non vobis, o la última limosna*, 1892); *The Son of Don Juan* (*El hijo de don juan*, 1892); *The Power of Impotence* (*El poder de la impotencia*, 1893); *To the Border of the Sea* (*A la orilla de mar*, 1893); *The Spiteful* (*La rencorosa*, 1894); *The Birthmark* (*El estigma*, 1895); *The First Act of a Drama* (*El primer acto de un drama*, 1895); *Spot that Cleans* (*Mancha que limpia*, 1895); *The Street Singer* (*La cantante callejera*, 1896); *The Calumny by Punishment* (*La calumnia por castigo*, 1897); *Semíramis, or the Daughter of the Air* (*Semíramis, o la hija del aire*, 1897); *The Black Man* (*El hombre negro*, 1898); *The Doubt* (*La duda*, 1898); *Silence of Death* (*Silencio de muerte*, 1898); *Savage Love* (*Amor salvaje*, 1899); *The Madman Divine* (*El loco dios*, 1900); *The Perron of a Throne* (*La escalinata de un trono*, 1903); *The Unbalanced One* (*La desequilibrada*, 1903); *By Force of Crawling* (*A fuerza de arrastrarse*, 1905)

FURTHER READING

Cabrales Arteaga, José Manuel. "El teatro neorromántico de Echegaray" [Echegaray's neoromantic theater]. *Revista de Literatura* 51, no. 101 (January–June 1989): 77–94.

Martínez Olmedilla, Augusto. *José Echegaray: El madrileño tres veces famoso; su vida, su obra, su ambiente* [José Echegaray: The famous Madrid inhabitant three times: His life, his work, his environment]. Madrid: Imprenta Sáez, 1949.

Ríos-Font, Wadda C. *Rewriting Melodrama. The Hidden Paradigm in Modern Spanish Theater.* Lewisburg, Pa.: Bucknell Univ. Press, 1997.

Scanaro, Laura Rosana. "El modelo paródico como forma de enlace intertextual: De Echegaray a Valle-Inclán" [The parodic model as a form of intertextual connection: From Echegaray to Valle-Inclán]. *Letras de Deusto* 21, no. 49 (January–April 1991): 183–189.

Sobejano, Gonzalo. "Echegaray, Galdós y el melodrama" [Echegaray, Galdós, and melodrama]. *Anales Galdosianos* (1978): 91–117.

Jerelyn Johnson

EDWARDS, DIC (1952–)

Dic Edwards was born in Cardiff, Wales, in 1952 into an English-speaking, working-class family. He was educated at St. David's University College, Lampeter, and University College, Cardiff. Having held a variety of jobs, he now works as a writing tutor to support his playwriting. From 1981 onward, he has regularly written for Welsh theater companies such as Made in Wales Stage Company, Spectacle Theatre, Theatr Powys, and Sgript Cymru. His plays have also been performed in major venues throughout Britain.

Edwards's uncompromising language, his experimentation with form and style, and his willingness to express sometimes uncomfortable political views have meant that he has not received the recognition he is due. A writer who advocates a theater of ideas and debate over a theater that merely entertains, he tackles complex issues in his plays. He is committed to art as a disseminator of class politics, and all of his plays can be fruitfully discussed in terms of class. Another recurring theme is the madness of nationalism in whatever form: *Long to Rain Over Us* (1987) is set in an English prisoner-of-war camp during World War II and claims that English nationalism is indistinguishable from and just as perverted as German and Italian nationalism. In *Looking for the World* (1986), a Cardiff socialist and his wife become caught up in military events in junta-ruled Greece, and *Franco's Bastard* (2002) discusses the more unsavory characteristics of Welsh nationalism. The premiere of the play, whose main character is loosely based on Cayo Evans, the late leader of the Free Wales Army, was disrupted by angry demonstrators. Since the early 1990s, his plays have moved away from stage realism to be able to express his preoccupations through an idiosyncratic theatrical form. *Casanova Undone* (1992), a play about a Casanova past his prime, is an interrogation of image versus identity. *Wittgenstein's Daughter* (1993) deconstructs the post-modern preoccupation with language to reveal the need for humanity, passion, and political agency beyond a barren language ossified in cliché. *Utah Blue* (1995) is a highly antirealist play, which deals with serial killer Gary Gilmore and discusses how he might have been a symptom for the sickness of American society as a whole. Edwards's plays have been highly praised by, among others, EDWARD BOND, with whom he shares political convictions and ideas about the role of theater in society.

Edwards has also been involved in various Theatre in Education productions. He has also written opera libretti and an alternative pantomime, set during the American Depression, *Mother Hubbard* (1991). Edwards was awarded the Theatre in Wales Award for best new writing for *Franco's Bastard* in 2003.

[*See also* England, 1980–Present]

PLAYS: *Late City Echo* (1981); *At the End of the Bay* (1982); *Canned Goods* (1983); *Looking for the World* (1986); *Little Yankee* (1987); *Long to Rain Over Us* (1987); *Doctor of the Americans* (1988); *Low People* (1989); *The Fourth World* (1990); *Mother Hubbard* (pantomime, 1991); *Regan* (1991); *Casanova Undone* (1992); *The Beggar's New Clothes* (1993); *The Juniper Tree* (opera libretto, 1993); *Wittgenstein's Daughter* (1993); *Three Deaths of an Idiot* (1995); *Utah Blue* (1995); *The Idiots* (1996); *Lola Brecht* (1996); *The Man Who Gave His Foot for Love* (1996); *Idiots!* (1997); *Franco's Bastard* (2002); *Manifest Destiny* (opera libretto, 2003/2004)

FURTHER READING

Davies, Hazel Walford, ed. *State of Play: Four Playwrights of Wales.* Llandysul: Gomer, 1998.

Edwards, Dic. "Theatre for the Evicted." *Theatre in Wales* (August 31, 1997). http://www.theatre-wales.co.uk/critical/critical_detail.asp?criticalID-111.

Alyce von Rothkirch

EGLOFF, ELIZABETH (1953–)

In poetry you are following the metaphor. It leads you to the end of the poem. In plays, metaphor is secondary.
—Elizabeth Egloff, 1999

Elizabeth Egloff, a self-described late bloomer, was born on September 9, 1953, in Farmington, Connecticut, and grew up in a family of doctors and psychiatrists who encouraged introspection and an intellectualization of life. She began her literary career by majoring in poetry at Trinity College in Hartford. Following her 1975 graduation, Egloff worked briefly in publishing, then pursued a graduate degree at Brown University, where she met playwright and professor George Bass. This fortuitous meeting helped change Egloff's view of the world as a writer.

Prior to working with Bass, Egloff had viewed playwriting as a male dominion. She perceived men's thinking as more action oriented and more suited to drama than her "feminine" introspective focus on internal and psychological action. Seeing the potential for dramatic action in her own writing was a crisis-inducing shift that took Egloff several years to assimilate. After working in various jobs, including writing for a soap opera, Egloff sought to confirm her abilities by studying playwriting at the Yale School of Drama, graduating with an M.F.A. in 1989.

Another important influence in Egloff's career was her paternal grandmother, a Jungian psychoanalyst who worked with patients' dreams. Imagery figures strongly in much of Egloff's playwriting, and she often begins writing from a single image or action. Her first and most notable play, *The Swan*, began as a dream image of a swan crashing into a woman's picture window. Premiering at the Yale Repertory Theatre in 1989, and in New York City at the Public Theater in 1993, *The Swan* brought accolades to Egloff, including the Kesselring Prize for best new play and the Oppenheimer Award from *Newsday* for best New York City debut by an American playwright. *The Swan* continues to be her most frequently produced play.

During a difficult time in her personal life, Egloff chose to work on an adaptation of *The Devils*, based on Fyodor Dostoevsky's political novel. This adaptation won the 1994 Weissberger Prize, as well as the 1993 Lila Wallace–Reader's Digest Writers Award, which enables writers to create and run a three-year program of their choice. Egloff created The Legacy Project, a workshop for chronically ill writers, at the Public Theater. *The Devils* received its first professional production at the New York Theatre Workshop, directed by Garland Wright, in 1997. Other adaptations include *The Nose* (1988), inspired by Nikolai Gogol's *The Overcoat*; *Wolf-man* (1989), based on Sigmund Freud's famous case study; and *The Lovers* (1995), inspired by Ivan Turgenev's novel *On the Eve*.

Egloff received an Emmy nomination for the screenplay *The Reagans* and subsequently worked as screenwriter on *The Mystery of Natalie Wood* (2004), directed by Peter Bogdanovich.

[*See also* Feminist Drama in the United States; Political Theater in the United States; Symbolism; United States, 1940–Present]

PLAYS: *The Sin of Akaki Akakryevich* (1987); *The Nose* (1988); *Phaedra* (1989); *Wolf-man* (1989); *The Swan* (1990); *The Lovers* (1995); *The Devils* (1997); *Peter Pan and Wendy* (1997); *Community of Heaven* (forthcoming)

FURTHER READING

Cole, Susan Letzler. *Playwrights in Rehearsal*. New York: Routledge, 2001.

Greene, Alexis, ed. *Women Who Write Plays: Interviews with American Dramatists*. Hanover, N.H.: Smith & Kraus, 2001.

Turner, Benjamin Wardell. "*Swan Journal*." Master's thesis, Amherst College, 1995.

Marlys H. Johnson

EGYPT

The history of Egyptian drama was influenced by the existence of earlier dramatic and popular entertainments such as the medieval shadow theater, the wonder box, and folktales. However, it was in Beirut that Arabic drama was introduced by Marun al-Naqqash in 1847. Al-Naqqash's (1817–1855) first play was *The Miser* (*al-Bakhil*), based on Molière's *The Miser* (*L'Avare*). In 1876, the Lebanese playwright Salim (d. 1884)—al-Naqqash's nephew—and their Syrian imitator Abu Khalil al-Qabani (1833–1920) took their troupes to Egypt. There they joined Yaqub Sannu, an Egyptian Jew who studied in Italy and wanted to build an Arab theater similar to that of the Europeans. The Egyptian imitators joining the Lebanese and Syrian dramatists succeeded in making Arabic theater a landmark in Egypt, and by 1900, it constituted one of the main political forces in Egypt's nationalist struggle against the British occupation. By the 1952 revolution, Egyptian theater had its own national and artistic identity, and this theater movement was enhanced by the spread of modern Arabic literature, a move supported by the educated and middle class who wanted theater to reflect Egyptian social and political reality.

EGYPTIAN PLAYWRIGHTS

One of the most prominent early Egyptian playwrights was TAWFIQ AL-HAKIM (1898–1987), who at one point in his career hid the fact that he was a playwright, owing to the stigma associated with theater as a disreputable profession. Only when many educated patrons joined the theater did this stigma disappear. Al-Hakim's prolific career as a dramatist lasted from the 1920s until the 1970s, by which time he had written more than 80 plays. His first play, *Shahrazad*, written in 1927, was followed by *The Sleepers in the Cave* (*Ahl al-kahf*) in 1928 and was regarded a landmark in Arabic literature by scholar Taha Hussien. Al-Hakim's last play, *The World Is a Farce* (*al-Dunya Riwaya Hazliyya*), was produced in 1971. Al-Hakim wrote musical dramas, social satires on current political and social issues, and plays on women's emancipation. Al-Hakim's contribution to the Egyptian theater was joined by Mahmud Taymur (1894–1973) and by Ali Ahmad Bakathir (1910–1969).

After the 1952 revolution, a new generation of dramatists dominated the scene, and they were supported by the new regime, which recognized drama as a powerful tool of cultural propaganda. In 1960, the Ministry of Culture was established, and many theaters opened following the publication of *The Theater* (*al-Masrah*), publishing mainly in colloquial Arabic as the *new* medium for drama. However, other dramatists wrote verse drama, like Salah Abd al-Sabur's *Night Traveler*. A dramatist who influenced both Egyptian and Arab theater was Yusuf Idris (1927–1991) with his plays the *Flipflaps* and *The Striped Ones* (*al-Mukhattatin*, 1969)—a political satire written during the Nasser era.

Another prominent figure was Naguib Surur (1932–1978), known as a poet, critic, actor, and playwright who relentlessly attacked social and state corruption in Egypt. His work was meant to shock—and it did. Surur graduated from the Egyptian Institute of Acting in 1956, then traveled to Russia to earn a doctorate in drama. Returning to Egypt in 1964, he made his debut as a director at the Pocket Theatre with ANTON CHEKHOV'S THE CHERRY ORCHARD. He taught at the Academy of Theatrical Arts until the mid-1970s, when bouts of depression began to take their toll. But as Mahmoud el-Lozy argues in *Al-Ahram Weekly* (1998), he would never compromise his art in order to please the authorities: "He could not be bought, co-opted, corrupted, or bribed. If this is madness then Egypt is the sanest country in the world." Surur's fame came when he wrote a poem in the aftermath of the 1967 Arab-Israeli war. Though never formally published in Egypt, it was widely circulated and still has the power to make waves, even today.

Other dramatists followed such as Alfred Faraj and Ali' Salem, who attacked political dictatorship and tackled pressing social issues. Other dramatists continue to be inspired by Egyptian folktales and popular entertainment.

EGYPTIAN WOMEN AND THEATER

The changes in socioeconomic development in Egypt in the second half of the 19th century, the rise of the new social middle class, the migration from the rural areas to Cairo, and the opening of new entertainment and cultural venues were all factors that helped in paving the way for Egyptian women writers. During that period, Egyptian women started to demand education and social involvement. As for theater, women's participation can be traced to the days of Yaqub Sanu. Najwa Ibrahim Anus in the *Theater of Yaqub Sanu* (*Masrah Yaqub Sannu*, 1984) demonstrates how his scripts included two female roles only because female actors were rare. Anus reports that Sanu found two illiterate girls, and he taught them how to read, write, and act, thus creating the first female presence on the Egyptian stage. By the beginning of the 20th century, the women's movement was developing in Egypt, and by mid-century college-educated women ventured fully into the social and economic sector—not only in Egypt but also throughout the Arab world. Although in the late 19th century and early 20th century Egyptian women did contribute to the development of theater—some of them even had their own theater companies—it remained a male-dominated field. Yet one has to acknowledge the contribution of many female actresses as well as others who left their marks as patronesses, as supporters of theater, and later on as theater directors and playwrights.

The first Egyptian woman to appear onstage was Munira al-Mahdiyya in 1915 as a singer actress in Aziz Id's Arabic Comedy Troupe (1881–1942). She was so successful onstage that she decided to form her own company, becoming the first Muslim female to be an independent director and a star of a musical theater troupe. Owing to the rise of many troupes and the spread of the cinema industry, al-Mahdiyya dismantled her company.

Other females like Fatima al-Yusuf and Dawlat Abyad followed and reached stardom. Both of them started in 1917 with Aziz Id, who was working with the Najib Rihani Company. Al-Yusuf's fame came when she played the role of a seventy-year-old grandmother in one of Id's plays. Her success enabled her to move to the famous Ramsis Company and become a star from 1923 to 1925. Al-Yusuf, who was also known as Rose al-Yusuf, left the company in 1925 to dedicate herself to the publication of her own magazine, *Rose Al-Yousef*. The magazine is still considered one of the most widely read and influential political weekly magazines both in Egypt and the Arab world. As for Dawlat Abyad (1894–1978), after the introduction by Id in 1917, she joined a number of troupes and settled with George Abyad's Theatre Troupe. She was known for her successful roles in TRAGEDIES and MELODRAMA.

An example of the success of Egyptian women in theater as well as in cinema was Aziza Amin (1901–1952). In 1952, Aziz joined the Ramsis Company. After two years, she left to make a career in the new medium of filmmaking. However, she was ridiculed by her husband, family, and the media. She was the first woman to star in the first Egyptian silent movie, *Layla*, in 1927. Amin's determination paid off when her film became a hit. Her career continued, and she proceeded to make another 19 films. She preferred to make films focusing on social class issues—*The Laborer, My Daughter, My Countrymen*. Regarding the crisis of 1948 in Palestine, she made the film *A Girl from Palestine*.

Fatimha Rushdi (1908–1997) is yet another Egyptian women who became a star. Coming from a very poor but musical family, Rushdi made her first appearance on the stage in 1923, playing mainly boys' roles in the Ramsis troupe. However, illiteracy hindered Rushdi from earning leading roles. Id, noticing her talent, educated her and helped in developing her acting skills. After Rushdi and Id married, they left the Ramsis Company in 1927 and initiated their own Fatimha Rushdi. The company was successful, drew large audiences, won many critical accolades, and became the main competitor for Ramsis. Rushdi was also a pioneer in playing many male roles such as Hamlet and Mark Anthony. The determined Rushdi also directed her own films such as *Anna Karenina* and the *Resurrection*. She was the first Egyptian woman to own a theater troupe, direct and write her own films, and be a leading star both onstage and in the cinema.

The late Tahia Carioca (1920–1999), known as an accomplished Egyptian belly dancer, also became famous in theater and cinema. Carioca initiated her own theater troupe in 1962 with her husband Fayiz Halawa. The company earned its major success in 1972. During the presidency of Anwar Sadat (1970–1981), with his *infitha* policy (Sadat's Open Door Policy), state-sponsored theater in Egypt fell under strong censorship. Carioca's play *Long Live the Wafd! (Yaha al-Wafad)* was banned by the censors. She took her case to court, won, and performed her play to tremendous acclaim for its political satire.

In addition, under Sadat's regime, the Egyptian state-sponsored theater went into a state of steady decline where artists and playwrights could not triumph over the firm grip of censorship; many were forced to go into self-exile and silence. Sadat's Open-Door Policy encouraged foreign investment and private capital business, which helped private theaters to mushroom in Egypt. These theaters catered mainly to rich Egyptians and Arab tourists from oil-producing countries, and these tourists preferred comedy to political satire. The boom in education in the 1960s led many Egyptian women who graduated from universities and drama schools to start careers in the state-sponsored theaters. The publication of *The Hidden Face of Eve* (1981) by the well-known feminist Dr. Nawal el-Saadawi played a major role in boosting female representation in all walks of life as well as on the stage. El-Saadawi published her play *Isis* in 1981. During Sadat's regime el-Saadawi was put in prison more than once. Even today, she remains a controversial figure owing to her critical writings.

One of the most prominent stage actors since the 1960s is Samiha Ayyub, who in 1975 became the first Egyptian woman to direct the prestigious National Theatre of Egypt. Ayyub is known for her brilliant portrayals onstage and in the cinema. In 2004 *Al-Ahram* ran a critique of her role as a Palestinian mother in *Henna Nights (Leilat el-Henna)*, dedicated to Palestinian mothers—and written by yet another acclaimed Egyptian playwright, Fathiya El-Assal. Assal's writing has provided her with an effective public forum from which to disseminate her political ideals and fight "the twin devils of capitalism and patriarchy." For over half a century, in scores of radio and theater plays and television serials and dramas, El-Assal has persistently opposed the dominant structures of power and oppression, ruthlessly baring and questioning their underpinning values and assumptions. Her determination was finally recognized in 2004 when she was chosen by the International Theatre Institute (ITI) to address the world on International Theatre Day. Denied a regular education, confined at home on reaching puberty, and constantly watched and meticulously coached in the rituals of female obedience, El-Assal experienced oppression at a very early age. Her rejection of gender-specific roles gained political strength when, at seventeen, she married journalist and novelist Abdallah El-Toukhi, who encouraged her to educate herself and taught her leftist politics and Marxist theory.

Under President Hosni Mubarak (1981–), the Egyptian government has been trying to support and restore Egyptian state-sponsored theater. The government opened a new Opera House in 1988; the Ministry of Culture established the al-Hanajir theater to support young talents and sponsor the yearly Cairo film and theater festivals. During the last fifteen years, many Egyptian artists and playwrights have initiated a new kind of theater called "Free-Theatre." In this venue, free of convention, many women and men of the newer generations have made names for themselves. Among them is the late Nihad Jad (d. 1989) who relentlessly refused to depict one-dimensional female characters full of piety. Jad's first one-woman play was *Adila* in 1981, followed by *Azizah and Firdaws*. *The Pavement ('ala ar- Rasif)* also won critical acclaim. On the contemporary stage, the works of Nadia al-Banhawi—*The Glow (al- Wahj*, 1996) and *The Death and Love Sonata* (1997)—provide an example of a playwright who continues to have a serious professional career in theater. The contribution of Egyptian women to the theater is growing steadily and relentlessly, as is the case with their sisters around the Arab world.

FURTHER READING

Anus, Najwa Ibrahim. *Masrah Yaqub Sannu*. Cairo: al-Hayah al-Misriya al-Ammah lil-Kitab, 1984.

Badawi, M. M. *Modern Arabic Drama in Egypt*. Cambridge: Cambridge Univ. Press, 1987.

Cohen-Mor, Dalya. *A Matter of Fate in the Arab World as Reflected in Modern Arabic Literature*. Oxford: Oxford Univ. Press, 2001.

Jayyusi, Salma Khadra. *Short Arabic Plays. An Anthology*. New York: Interlink, 2003.

Jayyusi, Salma Khadra, and Roger Allen, eds. *Modern Arabic Drama. An Anthology*. Bloomington: Indiana Univ. Press, 1995.

Rudnicka-Kassem, Dorota. *Egyptian Drama and Social Change: A Study of Thematic and Artistic Development in Yusuf Idris's Plays*. Montreal: Enigma Press, 1993.

Zuhur, Sherifa, ed. *Images of Enchantment. Visual and Performing Arts of the Middle East*. Cairo: American Univ. in Cairo Press, 1998.

——, ed. *Colors of Enchantment. Theater, Dance, Music, and the Visual Arts of the Middle East*. Cairo: American Univ. in Cairo Press, 2001.

Hala Khamis Nassar

EIGHT REVOLUTIONARY MODEL PLAYS

Eight Revolutionary Model Plays is a collection of modern dramas, ballets, and music revised and reformed reportedly with Jiang Qing's supervision during the Chinese Cultural Revolution (1966–1976). They include five modern Beijing operas (*The Red Lantern* [*Hongdeng ji*], *Taking Tiger Mountain by Strategy* [*Zhiqu weihu shan*], *Shajiabang*, *On the Docks* [*Haigang*], and *Sweeping the White Tiger Regiment* [*Qixi baihutuan*]), two modern ballets (*The Red Detachment of Women* [*Hongse niangzi jun*] and *The White-Haired Girl* [*Baimao nu*]), and the symphony accompaniment (*jiaoxiang yinyue*) to *Shajiabang*. The official name came from an article from the *People's Daily* on December 26, 1966, when it attributed the above eight "revolutionary modern model works" to Jiang Qing's tutelage. Soon afterward there appeared more model plays. Toward the end of the Cultural Revolution in 1975, there were actually eighteen model plays in all, with eleven being Beijing operas.

Model plays (*yangban xi*) did not appear all of a sudden during the Cultural Revolution. Almost all of those model plays were revised and enhanced versions of existing modern Beijing operas or local operas to further stress the dominant theme of class struggle and to make a sharper distinction between friends and enemies. The revision of those model plays strictly followed the principle of "three highlights" (highlight positive characters from among all characters, highlight heroic characters from among all positive characters, and highlight the main heroic character from among other heroic characters). *The Red Lantern*, for example, originated from a Shanghai opera (*huju*) titled *Story of the Red Lantern* (*Hongdeng zhuan*), which in turn was based on the 1962 film *Successor to Revolution* (*Geming zihou houlai ren*). As the play finally appeared in Beijing opera form in 1964, the proletarian family structure of three distinct generations sharing a common revolutionary interest was evoked in place of the traditional blood relationship for a family. Mao Zedong personally went to watch the performance on November 6, 1964, and reportedly shed tears over the touching story.

The White-Hair Girl, a model modern ballet, was adapted from an earlier folk opera (*geju*) premiered in Yan'an in 1945. Recasting the two main characters Yang Bailao and his daughter Xi'er as unsubmissive to and fearlessly rebellious against the oppression of the feudal landlord, the ballet came to emphasize the themes of class struggle and armed struggle.

Aside from thematic revisions, model plays also underwent performance changes, the most noticeable of which was in the use of a huge orchestra including violins and pianos instead of the usual small musical group playing a few Chinese musical instruments. The use of face makeup was greatly reduced from that used in traditional Beijing operas even though some of the roles in the model plays were still classified as painted faces. The reforms in the performance of Beijing operas later led to the piano accompaniment (*gangqin bangchang*) of *The Red Lantern*, the symphony accompaniment (*jiaoxiang yinyue*) to *Shajiabang*, and the string quartet and piano (*xianyue gangqin wuchong zou*) of *On the Docks*, further experimentations in innovations using Western music.

[*See also* China]

FURTHER READING

Chen, Xiaomei. *Acting the Right Part: Political Theater and Popular Drama in Contemporary China*. Honolulu: Univ. of Hawaii Press, 2002.

Dai, Jiafang. *Yangban xi de fengfeng yuyu* [The wind and rain of model theater]. Beijing: Zhishi chubanshe, 1995.

Xie, Boliang. *Zhongguo dangdai xiqu wenxue shi* [A history of contemporary Chinese operatic theaters]. Beijing: Zhongguo shehui kexue chubanshe, 1995.

Hongchu Fu

THE ELEPHANT

The Elephant (*Zō*, 1962), a Japanese ANGURA play written by BETSUYAKU MINORU, was the first play produced by the Free Stage (Jiyū Butai), a troupe established by him, the director SUZUKI TADASHI and the actor Ono Seki as students at Waseda University and the forerunner of Waseda Little Theater. It was Betsuyaku's first major success and became the young company's signature masterpiece, marking the playwright, director and actor as key figures in the theater revolution that emerged from the counterculture of the 1960s. *The Elephant* remains one of the most important modern Japanese plays.

Betsuyaku's preoccupation in *The Elephant* involves the issue, conspicuous in modern Japanese literature, theater, and film of personal and national identity. That preoccupation is a reflection of JAPAN's development since the mid-19th century, when the country was an isolated backwater steeped in feudal values. Its subsequent history has taken it through virtually all of the social, political, and economic changes undergone in the West in the 500 years since the Renaissance. That dizzying compression, coupled with the trauma of World War II and the precipitous postwar drive to recover equilibrium and achieve wealth and technological sophistication, has conspired to open a rift between Japan's traditional and modern values.

That rift is central to *The Elephant*. The two main characters are a survivor of the Hiroshima atomic bomb and his nephew. The survivor, who has a huge keloid scar seared into his back by the bomb's radiation, struggles throughout the play to keep the signal experience of the bomb alive, principally by showing off his keloid scar in public. His effort is meant to crystallize the vivid reality of that frightful moment, hard and unchanging. In the same way as he gradually succumbs to the atomic disease, however, his experience inexorably recedes from public awareness. The nephew, convinced of the futility of such activism, urges his uncle not to struggle, but just to relax and to accept the inevitable. By the play's end, the nephew, too, has contracted atomic disease; his plight, it is clear, will be even less noticeable than his uncle's.

Betsuyaku renders here a convincing statement about contemporary Japan, whose people might be compared to blind persons attempting to describe an elephant by touching only that part of it immediately in front of them. Unable to embrace the whole, each can offer only a partial, highly subjective description—like the survivor and his nephew. In Betsuyaku's conception, not only has the impact of World War II faded; as well Japan's rich, vital cultural traditions are slowly being eroded. The impoverishment of experience rendered in the play is emblematic of the impotence of Japanese culture to reproduce itself, to mend the rift between traditional and modern values; the very means by which the Japanese people once arrived at a sense of individual and national identity are gradually fading away.

FURTHER READING

Goodman, David G., tr. *The Elephant*. In *After Apocalypse: Four Japanese Plays of Hiroshima and Nagasaki*. New York: Columbia Univ. Press, 1986. 185–248.

Nihon Kindai Engeki-shi Kenkyūkai, ed. *Nijusseiki no Gikyoku II: Gendai Gikyoku no Tenkai* [Twentieth-century plays II: The development of modern Japanese plays]. Tokyo: Shakai Hyōronsha, 2002.

Ozasa, Yoshio. *Dōjidai Engeki to Gekisakkatachi* [Contemporary plays and playwrights]. Tokyo: Gekishobō, 1980.

Powell, Brian. *Japan's Modern Theatre: A Century of Continuity and Change*. London: Japan Library, 2002.

Senda, Akihiko. *Gekiteki Runessansu—Gendai Engeki wa Kataru* [Theatrical renaissance: The modern theatre speaks]. Tokyo: Riburopōto, 1983.

John K. Gillespie

ELES NÃO USAM BLACK-TIE See THEY DON'T WEAR BLACK TIE

ELIOT, THOMAS STEARNS (1888–1965)

Birth, and copulation, and death
That's all the facts when you come to brass tacks.
—Sweeney Agonistes, "*Fragment of an Agon*"

Thomas Stearns (T. S.) Eliot, one of the most influential poets and critics of the modern era, won the Nobel Prize for Literature in 1948. Although he is known mainly as a poet for such works as *The Waste Land*, *Ash Wednesday*, and *Four Quartets*, Eliot wrote six plays.

Eliot was born in St. Louis, Missouri, in 1888, into an old New England family that reached back on his mother's side to the original Massachusetts Bay colonists. He distinguished himself at Harvard, studying with philosopher George Santayana and critic Irving Babbitt. He spent a year in France, studying with Henri Bergson and Alain-Fournier, then returned to Harvard to study Sanskrit and Indian philosophy. By 1914, Eliot had begun his important literary relationship with Ezra Pound. Eliot's first volume, *Prufrock and Other Observations*, which appeared in 1917, can be considered a pivotal moment in the 20th-century revolution in poetry.

His first marriage to ballet dancer Vivienne Haigh-Wood was not a success. From 1930 until her death in 1947, she was confined in mental institutions, which many view as a form of imprisonment her husband endorsed; he never visited her there. Carole Seymour-Jones has argued in *Painted Shadow: A Life of Vivienne Eliot* (2001) that Eliot may have been fundamentally homosexual. Michael Hastings's play *Tom and Viv* (also made into a film) is a dramatic interpretation of this messy marriage. In Eliot's play THE FAMILY REUNION (1939), Harry, the central character, expresses a homicidal wish—which may be a confession—about his dead wife who drowned during their ocean voyage, and Sweeney expresses the same desire in cruder terms: "Any man has to, needs to, wants to / Once in a lifetime, do a girl in."

Emily Hale, described as his "muse," idealized as purity and restraint, stood for Eliot at the opposite end of the female spectrum from wild, tormented Vivienne. Since Eliot's thousands of letters to Emily were sealed until 2019 and hers to Eliot destroyed (probably by him), it is difficult to know what their relation actually was; she is the hyacinth girl of *The Waste Land* and reappears as characters in *Ash Wednesday*, *The Cocktail Party*, *The Family Reunion*, *The Elder Statesman*, *Marina*, *Gerontion*, *The Four Quartets*, and *Old Possum's Book of Practical Cats*.

In 1957, Eliot would marry again, eloping with his secretary Valerie Fletcher, with whom he lived happily, by all reports, until his death from emphysema. His last play, *The Elder Statesman* (1958), is considered to be a metaphoric account of their courtship.

In 1927, Eliot became a British citizen and converted to the Church of England, a spiritual event crucial to both the early plays and much of the later poetry. In 1928, he took a vow of chastity ("The love of man and woman is only explained and made reasonable by the higher love, or else is simply the coupling of animals"). Some think he wished to be a saint but failed; his reputation has been clouded by accusations of racism, anti-Semitism, fascism, and misogyny.

Immensely influential in the practice of literary criticism, Eliot published some 600 essays ("the elucidation of works of art and the correction of taste") in which he rehabilitated the reputations of the metaphysical poets of the 17th century, especially Andrew Marvell and John Donne; the early essays in *The Sacred Wood* (1920), including the famous "Hamlet and His Problems," which contains his theory of the "objective correlative," and the much-quoted "Tradition and Individual Talent," argue for a depersonalized, deromanticized poetry ("The progress of an artist is a continual self-sacrifice, a continual extinction of personality"). His views and his taste helped create modern culture, and his pronouncements were often made—and heard—as though ex cathedra. In 1922 Eliot founded the *Criterion*, a quarterly review that he edited until the beginning of World War II. In 1925 he joined the publishing house of Faber and Gwyer (later Faber and Faber), becoming one of the firm's directors, where he lent powerful support to young writers, and from 1919 on, he was a regular contributor to the *Times Literary Supplement*.

The plays are in blank verse and spring from two basic tenets: "A verse play is not a play done into verse, . . . the poet with ambitions of the theatre, must discover the laws, both of another kind of verse and of another kind of drama" (Matthiessen, 1958); second, that a religious play "should be able to hold the interest, to arouse the excitement, of people who are not religious" (Matthiessen, 1958) Eliot's plays reveal varying degrees of success in meeting his own criteria.

MURDER IN THE CATHEDRAL (1935) and *The Family Reunion* have both had interesting and successful contemporary revivals. His invention of a new kind of blank verse dialogue and his attempt to revitalize the Greek Chorus as an element of modern drama are the distinguishing and often problematic elements of his dramaturgy. While *Murder in the Cathedral* takes up the martyrdom of Thomas Becket, *The Family Reunion* attempts to adapt Aeschylus's *Oresteia* to a modern family drama. The last three plays, written after World War II, are all COMEDIES of a sort, based on ancient Greek drama; *The Cocktail Party* (1949), which achieved some success, combines parlor farce with salvation and psychoanalysis.

It is surprising that Eliot was a practical joker (whoopee cushions and exploding cigars) and that he and Groucho Marx were both friends and mutual admirers. *Old Possum's Book of Practical Cats* (1939), Eliot's charming book of verse for children, has achieved worldwide success in a musical adaptation called *Cats*. He died in 1965, in London, England, and is buried in East Coker, memorial in Westminster Abbey.

[*See also* Philosophy and Drama; Religion and Drama]

PLAYS: *Sweeney Agonistes* (1926); *Murder in the Cathedral* (1935); *The Family Reunion* (1939); *The Cocktail Party* (1949); *The Confidential Clerk* (1953); *The Elder Statesman* (1958)

FURTHER READING

Eliot, T. S. *Poetry and Drama*. Cambridge: Harvard Univ. Press, 1951.

Gardner, Helen. *The Art of T. S. Eliot*. New York: Dutton, 1950.

Gordon, Lyndall. *T. S. Eliot: An Imperfect Life*. New York: Norton, 2000.

Matthiessen, F. O. *The Achievement of T. S. Eliot*. New York: Oxford Univ. Press, 1958.

Sencourt, Robert. *T. S. Eliot: A Memoir*. New York: Dodd, 1971.

Seymour-Jones, Carole. *Painted Shadow: A Life of Vivienne Eliot*. London: Robinson, 2001.

Tate, Alan, ed. *T. S. Eliot: The Man and His Work*. New York: Delacorte, 1966.

Toby Zinman

ELIZABETH THE QUEEN

The principle of TRAGEDY that MAXWELL ANDERSON devised at the seminal stage of his career reaches a maturity of expression in his "history" plays *Elizabeth the Queen* (1930), *Mary of Scotland* (1933), and *Anne of the Thousand Days* (1948). *Elizabeth*, which opened on Broadway on November 3, 1930, depicts the lovelorn Tudor monarch, way past her prime, in a passionate and tragic liaison with the Earl of Essex. Employing a casual blank verse laced with prose, Anderson achieves a fine balance between the demands of the historical and the modern through the portrayal of the conflict of power and love of a bygone era.

The three-act play begins with the conceptual aggrandizement of Essex as a potential "overreacher" in Elizabeth's court in romantic as well as political terms. Not only is he the lover of the queen, bypassing all other noblemen in her eyes, he is beloved of the common folk as well. He thereby proves a threat not only to his rivals Lord Cecil and Sir Walter Raleigh but also to the queen and sovereignty over the people. However, the queen's love for him will not make her compromise beyond a point, as Essex will discover to his cost.

The plot of Cecil and Raleigh to implicate Essex through the latter's ambition ("By right of name / And power and popular voice this is my kingdom") is clinched in act 2. Essex senses their motive yet is provoked to claim the generalship to the historically problematic IRELAND. As foreseen, the expedition swells into a rebellion following Cecil's effective alienation of the two lovers. Essex, with his army in tow, makes Elizabeth a captive in her own palace in London. In a riveting dialogue between the two, Essex's contention of equality in both love and power ("Must you be sovereign alone?") is countered by her self-esteem, shrewdness, and refusal to compromise. She tricks him into disbanding his army, gets him arrested for treason, and sends him to the Tower to await his doom. For, she has realized, as she tells him with Machiavellian objectivity, that he who would rule "must be / Quite friendless, without mercy, without love."

In act 3, Anderson suspends and subsequently disperses the romantic possibility of reconciliation between the lovers. Elizabeth, after waiting futilely for his appeal for pardon, summons him to her side for a last attempt at aligning their destinies. But he rationalizes with stringent honesty his own ambitious (and thus treasonous) nature and departs nonchalantly to his execution, ignoring her desperate offer of the crown and her love on his terms. His choice is an affirmation of self-dignity through death at the crossroads of temptation symbolized by a woman and her love. Essex's heroic, self-composed stature stands in contrast to the emotionally wrecked Elizabeth who will henceforth "be queen of emptiness and death."

FURTHER READING

Anderson, Maxwell. *The Essence of Tragedy*. Washington, D.C.: Anderson House, 1939.

Berkowitz, Gerald M. *American Drama of the Twentieth Century*. New York: Longman, 1992.

Gerstenberger, Donna. "Verse Drama in America: 1916–1939." *Modern Drama* 6 (December 1963).

Wall, Vincent. "Maxwell Anderson: The Last Anarchist." In *American Drama and Its Critics*, ed. by Alan S. Downer. Chicago: Univ. of Chicago Press, 1965.

Young, Stark. Review of *Elizabeth the Queen*. *The New Republic* 19 (1930): 19.

Rupendra Guha-Majumdar

ELKUNCHWAR, MAHESH (1939–)

Mahesh Elkunchwar, born on October 9, 1939, in Nagpur, Maharashtra, is one of the most famous Marathi playwrights. His plays reflect two distinct stages. The early plays, such as *The Oppressive Emperor* (*Sultan*, 1967), *Garbo* (1973), *The Tempestuous Rain* (*Rudravarsha*, 1974), *Period of Desire* (*Vasanakand*, 1974), and *Blood Flower* (*Raktapushpa*, 1979), are written in a more symbolic "experimental" mode and represent his preoccupation with the absurdity of existence, repressed desire, secret violence in human relationships, and creativity. They reflect a dark vision of life, and Elkunchwar himself has called them "shrill."

Garbo deals with the physical and psychological relationship among three male friends—Intuc (the Pseudo-Intellectual), Pansy (the Effete), and Shrimant (the Rich)—and Garbo, an ordinary film actress-cum-prostitute who wants to be "successful." Garbo's pregnancy gives them a purpose in life, but she aborts the fetus, because of her career, and the friends, plunged into a murderous rage, kill her.

Period of Desire presents a dark view of the creative process. It centers on the incestuous relationship between a young girl and her sculptor brother who exploits her body to create his vision of life in stone. The Censor Board banned the play on the grounds that it was obscene and that it posed a threat to the audience's moral well-being because of its portrayal of an incestuous relationship.

With *Party* (1975) Elkunchwar makes a transition from a symbolic to a more naturalistic theater idiom that evolves from his social concerns, though the characters are still pseudo-intellectuals and divorced from real life. The play depicts the world of the so-called elite through its portrayal of a party in which a group of writers, journalists, so-called progressive intellectuals, and society ladies interact to reveal their fake values, complacency, hypocrisy, and insensitivity.

It was, however, with OLD STONE MANSION (*Wada Chirebandi*, 1987) that Elkunchwar changed gear completely. *Old Stone Mansion* is like ANTON CHEKHOV'S THE CHERRY ORCHARD. This play and its sequels, *Engrossed on the Shores of the Lake* (*Magna Talyakathi*, 1994) and *End of an Epoch* (*Yuganta*, 1994), portray the accumulating contradictions in the lives of the members of an upper-caste Brahmin family from an agrarian village, who are caught between the stagnant, feudal ways of life and modernization. The intensely sensitive perception of familial relationships, especially among women, in a crumbling world is yet another feature that distinguishes these from his earlier pessimistic plays.

In his later play *Pratibimba* (1989), about a man who loses his reflection, Elkunchwar again takes an ironic, absurdist-modernist look at the predicament of an individual in the modern world. *Autobiography* (*Atmakatha*, 1988) explores the theme of gender relationships, marriage, and creativity. His most recent play *Sonata* (2000) explores loneliness in the lives of women.

Throughout his playwriting career, Elkunchwar has been most concerned with the complexity of human relationships in rapidly changing times.

[*See also* India]

SELECT PLAYS: *The Oppressive Emperor* (*Sultan*, 1967); *Garbo* (1973); *Period of Desire* (*Vasanakand*, 1974); *The Tempestuous Rain* (*Rudravarsha*, 1974); *Party* (1975); *Blood Flower* (*Raktapushpa*, 1979); *Old Stone Mansion* (*Wada Chirebandi*, 1987); *Autobiography* (*Atmakatha*, 1988); *Pratibimba* (1989); *End of an Epic* (*Yuganta*, 1994); *Engrossed on the Shores of the Lake* (*Magna Talyakathi*, 1994); *Sonata* (2000)

FURTHER READING

Gokhale, Shanta. *Playwright at the Centre: Marathi Drama from 1843 to the Present*. Calcutta: Seagull Press, 2000.

Elkunchwar, Mahesh. *Vinasat I and II*. New Delhi: Living Theatre, 1992.

Maya Pandit

EMPEROR AND GALILEAN

Emperor and Galilean (*Kejser og Galilœr*, 1873) is a play that HENRIK IBSEN himself referred to as his "opus major," claiming that this play contains his "positive worldview." The background of the last statement is that critics had accused Ibsen of merely exposing negative values in his writing, rather than providing a positive alternative. In spite of Ibsen's claim, many critics have found it exceedingly difficult to see any positive worldview in the play. The problem is that the presentation of the main character, Emperor Julian, and his dream of a new, freer, and better life, a "third empire," is fundamentally ambiguous and ironic; positive *and* negative, idealistic *and* skeptical. Accordingly the critical reception is generally characterized by confusion and ambivalence, and some critics accuse Ibsen of not being very successful as an author when he first idealizes Julian and his dream, then degrades him and perverts his dream of freedom, sovereignty, and authenticity, making both the portrait of Julian and the drama as a whole fall apart. In spite of this, *Emperor and Galilean* is regarded as an important play, first and foremost because of its philosophy but also in terms of drama history since Ibsen now abandons verse in order to write prose plays.

Emperor and Galilean is a two-play, ten-act historical drama set in the fourth century. The protagonist is Emperor Julian the Apostate, known for his attempts to return to pagan worship, and the plot is based on the conflict of the pagan and Christian worldviews. As the play opens, Julian is nineteen years old and a prince under the Christian emperor Konstanzios, who has killed almost all of Julian's family to secure his own position. Everyone believes Julian to be a good and pious Christian, and he pretends to be one, but even in the first act he reveals his doubt. Julian lives in constant fear not only of the increasingly paranoid emperor but also of the church, the priests, and God. He clings to his hope of a new, freer, and more authentic life; and together with Maximos the Mystic, he arranges a symposium with the spirits, where a spirit announces that there will be a new empire. Maximos the Mystic interprets the new empire as "the third empire"—"that empire which shall be established on the trees of knowledge and the cross together"—and claims that Julian is chosen to establish it. At the end of the first play Julian declares himself an apostate, and in the beginning of the second play, he has publicly abandoned his Christian faith and has even opposed the emperor by installing himself as emperor *before* the death of the real emperor. From an inferior position under both the emperor and God, he has risen to the position of apostate and emperor. Even though in the beginning he proclaims full religious freedom and claims that he wants a court free of hypocrisy, he is gradually struck by the same vanity, lust for power, and paranoia as his predecessor, and accordingly the attempt to create a new and better third empire is also perverted: he wants total power over the whole world and opens a war against the Persians not only in order to win more land for the Roman Empire but also to eliminate his own Christian soldiers because they see their god as more important than the emperor. In the last act Julian is killed in the war, stabbed by a Roman soldier, the Christian Agathon, using the Roman lance of Calvary, the lance the Romans are said to have used to stab Jesus the Galilean.

Ibsen's main interests with the drama were contemporary: Ibsen saw a parallel between Julian's time and his own, between Julian and modern man, between Julian's paganism and the secularization of modernity. The play is thus a depiction not only of a particular historical period but also of a historically recurring phenomenon: "a collision of two irreconcilable forces in the life of the world, which repeats itself in all eras." These two forces, the pagan, heathen or secular, and the Christian, are symbolically the *emperor* and the *galilean*.

[*See also* Norway]

FURTHER READING

Garborg, Arne. *Henrik Ibsen's "Kejser og Galilær." En kritisk Studie af G* [Henrik Ibsen's *Emperor and Galilean*. A critical study by G]. Christiania, 1873.

Johnston, Brian. *To the Third Empire, Ibsen's Early Drama*. Minneapolis: Univ. of Minnesota Press, 1980.

McFarlane, James. "Dramas of Transition: 1867–1875." In *Meaning & Evidence. Studies, Essays & Prefaces 1953–1987*. Norwich: Norvik Press, 1987.

Meyer, Michael. *Ibsen, a Biography*. Garden City, N.Y.: Doubleday, 1971.

Lisbeth Pettersen Wærp

THE EMPEROR JONES

I kills you, you white debil, if it's de last thing I evah does!

—Jones, Scene 4

The Provincetown Players produced EUGENE O'NEILL's *The Emperor Jones* on November 1, 1920, at the Playwrights' Theatre in New York. Charles S. Gilpin played the role of Brutus Jones, one of the first important roles written for a black actor even though it was a crap-shooting, arrogant Pullman porter. Director George Cram Cook built a plaster "dome," a quarter-sphere of white plaster that would respond to stage lighting by giving the illusion of virtually limitless space.

Brutus Jones has set himself up as the ruler of an island in the West Indies, where he makes the laws and steals on a grand scale. When he realizes that his "subjects" have deserted the palace, he runs away, carrying only a revolver loaded with five lead bullets and one silver one, the last to take his own supposedly charmed life in the event they corner him. A tom-tom starts at a normal pulse rate but accelerates through the rest of the play to reflect Jones's growing anxiety.

Jones reaches the edge of the forest, and as he seems to lose his way, "the Little Formless Fears creep out from the deeper blackness of the forest. They are black, shapeless, only their glittering little eyes can be seen." As Jones frets, from the formless fears come "a tiny gale of low mocking laughter like a rustling of leaves."

Jones meets the image of a fellow Pullman porter throwing dice; it is a man he killed with a knife. He sees a chain gang of black men working under a white prison guard; they move stiffly as though in a nightmare, and for a few moments the bewildered Jones joins them. In another clearing, a spectral auctioneer beckons Jones to stand on the block for an 1850s slave auction. He moves on to find two rows of seated, shackled men swaying as if in response to the motion of a slave ship. Guilt-ridden and exhausted, Jones joins in a primitive dance until the Congo witch doctor summons an enormous crocodile out of the river, and the runaway fires his last bullet—the silver bullet—at the apparition. In the end, Jones runs full circle through the forest and returns to where the waiting natives shoot him down. He has paid the price of pride in denying his own fallibility and mortality.

This expressionist play uses the tom-tom and the nightmarish visions to externalize what Jones is feeling. He does not "belong," so he is punished and destroyed; this is a motif that O'Neill explored in his early sea plays and BEYOND THE HORIZON and one to which he would return in several later plays. The drama recalls HENRIK IBSEN's PEER GYNT in the idea of the desperate fugitive and in the parallel between Jones's silver bullet and Peer's silver button, each serving as protective talisman to its bearer.

Alexander Woollcott called the play "an extraordinarily striking and dramatic study of panic fear" and asserted that "for strength and originality [O'Neill] has no rival among the

American writers for the stage" (Miller, 1973). The *New York Call* declared, "The Provincetown Players have done it again. . . . They are giving hundreds the most thrilling evening of their theatrical lives" (Miller, 1973). Kenneth Macgowan declared that the play "opens up the imagination of the American theatre" (Houchin, 1993).

[*See also* Expressionism; United States, 1860–Present]

FURTHER READING

Abdo, Diya M. "*The Emperor Jones*: A Struggle for Individuality." *Eugene O'Neill Review* 24 (Spring–Fall 2000): 28–42.

Houchin, John H. *The Critical Response to Eugene O'Neill*. Westport, Conn.: Greenwood Press, 1993.

Mendelsohn, Michèle. "Reconsidering Race, Language and Identity in *The Emperor Jones*." *Eugene O'Neill Review* 23 (Spring–Fall 1999): 19–30.

Miller, Jordan Yale. *Eugene O'Neill and the American Critic: A Bibliographic Check list*. 2d ed. Hamden, Conn.: Archon Books, 1973.

Siomopoulos, Anna. "The 'Eighth o' Style': Black Nationalism, the New Deal, and *The Emperor Jones*." *Arizona Quarterly* 58 (Autumn 2002): 57–81.

Steen, Shannon. "Melancholy Bodies: Racial Subjectivity and Whiteness in O'Neill's *The Emperor Jones*." *Theatre Journal* 52 (October 2000): 339–359.

Jeffrey D. Mason

EN ATTENDANT GODOT *See* WAITING FOR GODOT

ENDGAME

> *Have at last written another [play], one act, longish, hour and a quarter I fancy. Rather difficult and elliptic, mostly depending on the power of the text to claw, more inhuman than Godot. My feeling, strong, at the moment, is to leave it in French for a year at least, so tired of Godot and all the misunderstanding.*
>
> —Samuel Beckett, letter to Alan Schneider, 1956

SAMUEL BECKETT may have begun work on the play *Endgame* (*Fin de partie*) as early as 1952, the year before WAITING FOR GODOT was realized onstage. He made numerous drafts of mimes and sketches before editing or collapsing them into the "one act, longish" play he finalized in 1956. It was first performed in London in French in 1957, and the translation as *Endgame* was published in 1958. Beckett consistently referred to *Endgame* as his favorite among his plays.

The opening set is a bare interior with two small windows high in the back wall, an efficient cranial suggestion. To the right is a door into the kitchen of the factotum with Clov by it; at the front left are two ashbins touching each other and covered with a sheet. Center stage, seated in an armchair is Hamm, also draped in a sheet. The whole piece is played out under a uniformly gray light, but the opening routine performed by Clov suggests the beginning of a day. The action continues unbroken until it halts with a brief tableau, which is all the play provides as an "end."

The Hamm/Clov relationship—fraught with coldness, anger, and violence as well as moments of high comedy—that forms the core of the play is a compressed development of the interdependency of Estragon and Vladimir and of the master/slave relationship of Pozzo and Lucky in *Godot*. Despite having only one act the play nevertheless convinces us that we are witnessing an event that is merely one term in a lengthy but not interminable series. Things are running out—there is no more pap, no more painkillers, no more coffins, no more rugs or bicycle-wheels—and running down. The most startling image of deterioration in the play is provided by the characters Nagg and Nell, Hamm's parents, who are confined in the onstage ashbins. They are legless, having "lost their shanks" in a tandem crash on the road to Sedan in the Ardennes. Thus, pain and suffering are presented as essentially comic. It is Nell who says—in a sentence Beckett regarded as the most important in the play—"Nothing is funnier than unhappiness, I grant you that."

Beckett's typical refusal to be explicit is again in evidence throughout but balanced with ranges of suggestive hints. The names Nagg and Clov are almost puns on the German and French for "nail," while Nell's name is nearly a homophone. Three nails, familiar items in the iconography of crucifixion, require a hammer, and at the center of the play is Hamm. Clov's opening action of undraping the ashbins and Hamm and folding the sheets hints at a kind of daily resurrection, a removal of winding sheets. The language of the play is suffused with biblical echoes and allusions, but there is no promise of redemption or hope of salvation. Hamm's name recalls that of Noah's son in the Book of Genesis with its account of the Deluge and the subsequent repopulation of the earth by him and his brothers. Beckett's play runs counter to this procreative narrative. Outside the bare room, called "the refuge," there is only a "zero" landscape of earth and sea, a dying light sustaining nothing. When Clov discovers he has a flea in his trousers, there is a vaudevillian scene with a can of insecticide as he tries to kill it and has to have the difference between "lying" and "laying" explained to him by Hamm. The finding of a rat in Clov's kitchen immediately leads to efforts to exterminate it. Signs of life are invoked only to be ruthlessly canceled.

Hamm's principal preoccupation in the play is the composition of his "chronicle." His story is set on a Christmas Eve, that time replete with promise, when he was visited in the distant past by a man begging for sustenance for his son from Hamm's well-stocked granaries. The man's entreaties are met with refusal, Hamm saying, "Use your head, can't you, use your head, you're on earth, there's no cure for that!" Hamm's story is of a piece with his father Nagg's wonderful joke about botched creation and a tailor's perfect pair of trousers; both point to absence of life as the preferable condition. An exchange between father and son offers a succinct statement:

Hamm: Scoundrel! Why did you engender me?
Nagg: I didn't know.
Hamm: What? What didn't you know?
Nagg: That it'd be you.

[*See also* Absurdism; Ireland; Philosophy and Drama]

FURTHER READING

Gontarski, S. E. *The Intent of Undoing in Samuel Beckett's Dramatic Texts.* Bloomington: Indiana Univ. Press, 1985.

——, ed. *The Theatrical Notebooks of Samuel Beckett, Volume 2: Endgame.* London: Faber, 1992.

Harmon, Maurice, ed. *No Author Better Served: The Correspondence of Samuel Beckett and Alan Schneider.* Cambridge: Harvard Univ. Press, 1998.

Gerry Dukes

AN ENEMY OF THE PEOPLE

A political part—it's like a sausage grinder, it grinds all the heads up together into one mash.
—Dr. Stockmann, Act 5

Published one year after GHOSTS in 1882, HENRIK IBSEN's *An Enemy of the People* (*En folkefiende*) contains, among other things, Ibsen's determined response to the fervent protests against *Ghosts*. Dr. Stockmann, physician to the municipal spa, has had his suspicions regarding pollution of the water scientifically confirmed, and he informs his brother the mayor and the local newspaper that the baths have to be closed temporarily. Satisfied that he has done his hometown a great service, and initially supported by the newspaper editors, he is surprised to find that the support of his proposed remedial action is dwindling, as people begin to realize the public expense and the loss of houseowners' income that it will entail.

Dr. Stockmann proceeds with his cause, and the conflict hardens. The newspaper refuses to print his articles, and the mayor, who is also chairman of the board of the baths, warns his brother that as a member of the staff he cannot express his opinion regarding the sanitary conditions of the baths in public. The Doctor calls a public meeting to present his views on the matter. At the meeting the atmosphere is hostile against him, and he changes his subject to talk not about the pollution of the baths but about another discovery of his, "that all the sources of our spiritual life are polluted, and that our entire community rests on a muckheap of lies." The enemy of truth and freedom is the solid majority. The discussion leads to a vote to the effect that Dr. Stockmann is a public enemy.

In act 5 the windows of the Doctor's study have been shattered by stones thrown by the mob. Reports come in about the difficulty of the Doctor's family to continue to live in the town. The house owner has given them notice, Petra has lost her teacher's job, the boys have been mobbed at school, and the Doctor's practice will include only poor people from now on. Only Horster, an independent sea captain, is supportive, offering the family a house. Dr. Stockmann now wants to start a school for young boys to grow up to become free-spirited men. His final discovery is that the strongest man in the world is the one who stands most alone.

Doctor Stockmann is a staunch individualist, and he may seem naive regarding politics. Due to the cowardice and unfairness of his opponents, and the courage and independence of his few adherents, however, his position stands out as one of moral strength and incorruptibility in spite of the social ruin he has caused by his attitude.

[*See also* Norway; Political Theater]

FURTHER READING

Aarseth, Asbjørn. "Romantic Misanthropy: *An Enemy of the People.*" in *Ibsen at the Centre for Advanced Study*, ed. by Vigdis Ystad. Oslo: Scandinavian Univ. Press, 1997. 261–276.

Johnston, Brian. "The Poetry of *An Enemy of the People.*" *Scandinavica* 18, (1979): 109–122.

Rønning, Helge. "Individualism and the Liberal Dilemma. Notes Towards a Sociological Interpretation of *An Enemy of the People* by Henrik Ibsen." *Contemporary Approaches to Ibsen*, 3 (1977): 101–121.

Asbjørn Aarseth

EN FALLIT
See A BANKRUPTCY

ENGLAND

This composite entry explores four major periods of modern English drama, 1860–1940, 1940–1960, 1960–1980, and 1980–Present.

1860–1940

OVERVIEW

During the eighty years from 1860 to 1940, English theater began to take on the forms familiar to us today. The mid- to late-Victorian-era theater patron witnessed vast technological improvements in production design and technical effect. These innovations contributed to the revolutionary REALISM of the Victorian theater. This realism changed the way playwrights, producers, and actors saw their art; however, by the dawn of the 20th century, realism had become associated with the staid, old-fashioned values of the Victorian era. Although realism remained an important aspect of mainstream theater, movements like SYMBOLISM, EXPRESSIONISM, and SURREALISM would again revolutionize theater production. In the Victorian theater commercialism predominated, while as the 20th century progressed, more and more playwrights used the theater to convey a social message. Between 1860 and 1940, theater, performance, and playwriting changed dramatically in form, style, and structure. Too often, Victorian theater is glossed over in the rush to examine OSCAR WILDE and GEORGE BERNARD SHAW, but in order to understand theater of the late 19th and early 20th centuries, it is vital that the theater of the mid-Victorian period be examined.

The decades from 1860 to 1900 saw a revolution in British theater forms. In virtually every aspect of theater, realism took over from earlier styles, which emphasized artistry and artifice, and as Allardyce Nicoll argues in *A History of English Drama* (1959), this trend "proved to be the most determined and the most persistent of its age." This tendency can be seen in everything from design and technology to acting and playwriting. Methods of production underwent major changes, and a visit to the theater in 1900 bore little resemblance to the full evening of FARCE, short TRAGEDY or COMEDY, and burlesque or pantomime that early and mid-Victorians had enjoyed. By the 1890s, the middle classes had returned to the theater, and plays of literary merit were being produced in the large, opulent, commercial houses. Still, the theater of this period was predominantly a popular one, and as realism developed, sentimental comedy, formulaic MELODRAMA, and ridiculous farce remained popular.

Between 1860 and 1900, the British stage underwent a number of technical innovations. First used in 1817, gas lighting had become virtually universal by 1870. When coupled with limelight, gas enabled the production of spectacular effects and for the first time enabled theaters to darken the house, thus separating the performer from the audience. In the 1880s, electricity once again revolutionized stage lighting. The Savoy became the first fully electric theater, and others soon followed. Electric light allowed both greater realism and greater spectacle—even subtle effects, such as the light cues that mark the hero's entrances in ARTHUR PINERO's THE SECOND MRS. TANQUERAY (1893), show the impact of technological innovations on playwriting and production.

Set design was also transformed during this period. Early in the Victorian era, sets were painted on flats, and players had little interaction with the scenery around them. As melodramas with their spectacular effects grew in popularity, so too did the movement to create more realistic sets. Mid-Victorian melodramas relied on realistic effects for the catastrophic sensation scenes audiences came to expect, but this was very different from the realism that would develop in domestic plays. In the late 1860s, Marie Wilton became one of the first managers to concentrate on domestic realism. Her productions of THOMAS WILLIAMS ROBERTSON's plays at the Prince of Wales's Theatre were dubbed "cup-and-saucer dramas" because of the realistic sets. Productions at the Prince of Wales's were noted for employing real doors and actual paintings hung on the walls. Wilton and her husband, Squire Bancroft, paid careful attention to such details throughout their management, but Robertson is generally credited with this revolution because he was one of the first writers to insist on stage managing his plays. Audiences throughout the second half of the 19th century were fascinated with the real. Barnyard scenes used real animals, and sets reproduced everything from drawing rooms to public streets in detail.

The move toward realism can also be seen in the growing popularity of naturalistic acting styles. Early in the 19th century actors still played for points. For both audiences and actors, 18th-century theatrical styles emphasized the virtuoso performance over the accurate representation of a character. Stars such as Sarah Siddons were famous for their intense performances and the "tragedy and its persons mattered little; the artistry of the actress alone had significance" (Nicoll, 1959). As the theater community strove for respectability and greater realism, naturalistic acting and sincere stage emotions replaced stylized performance. Players presented a more realistic reflection of middle-class life, and theater began to be seen as an art form. These changes helped the upper echelons of performers begin to achieve respectability.

Early in her reign, Queen Victoria showed a marked interest in the theater. Theatricals were produced at Windsor, and the queen engaged a private box at the Princess's Theatre. The licensing restrictions that had been lifted in 1847 began to have a broad impact with a variety of new theater appearing throughout London. Society followed the example set by their queen. As more questionable entertainments like burlesques and pantomimes were diverted to music halls or tamed into holiday fare, the middle classes returned to the theater. With higher-class patronage, the social status of performers became significant. The increased respectability of performers brought new recruits to the profession from the middle classes. The culmination of Queen Victoria's patronage and the newfound respectability of the acting profession came in 1895 when Henry Irving was knighted for his work in the theater, beginning the tradition of rewarding outstanding performers with the title of knight or dame.

Perhaps the most notable effect of the changes in British theater between 1860 and 1900 is the playwriting renaissance of the 1890s, but this would have been impossible without the changes in production, performance, and playwriting that occurred throughout the period. For most of the Victorian era, playwriting was a fairly thankless profession. The Lord Chamberlain's authority over play production amounted to a system of censorship that persisted from 1747 to 1968. This censorship was originally designed to prevent theatrical attacks on the government, but it became infamous in the Victorian era and the early 20th century for its prudery and unpredictability. Playwrights were ill paid for their work, and formulaic adaptations dominated the stage. Generally, playwrights were paid a flat fee, regardless of their plays' success, had no recourse against plagiarism, and had little influence over changes made to their text by stars and managers. The low status of playwrights began to change in 1860 when DIONYSIUS BOUCICAULT was allowed to "share the terms" for the first British production of THE COLLEEN BAWN; *or, The Brides of Garryowen*. This deal would eventually earn him over £10,000. Long runs became common, and with the passage of the International Copyright

Act in 1887 and the American Copyright Act in 1891, playwriting became more lucrative and thus attracted talented writers.

By the end of the 19th century, light comedy and the problem play had risen to predominance, but earlier dramatic forms retained their hold on the popular imagination. Melodramas were the most popular theater form of the period. They tended to follow a strict formula with clearly defined roles for hero, heroine, and villain. Despite its formulaic nature, overblown characters, and sensational incident, even melodrama was influenced by the growing trend toward realism. Domestic melodramas with "familiar situations, settings and characters met with every day" began to replace the earlier forms like gothic, nautical, and eastern melodrama: "all served up, however, with thrills and happy endings *not* encountered in ordinary life" (Booth, 1965). Domestic comedies, such as the ones Robertson wrote for Wilton's Prince of Wales's company, became popular in the second half of the 19th century, but even these were influenced by the sentimentalism of melodrama. Music halls began to cater to the less respectable class of theater patrons, but legitimate theaters also continued to produce farce, pantomime, and burlesque. Still, realism was clearly the dominant force of the age.

Revolutionary Changes in British Theater, 1860s

A number of revolutionary changes that would begin to transform British theater occurred in the 1860s; thus, these years can be seen as among the most significant in 19th-century theater history. Melodrama was still the dominant form, but a new level of realism was beginning to impact both the style and practice of theater. Plays of the 1860s began to reflect the lives of the middle classes, and this in turn led to the social critique inherent in much late-Victorian theater. In 1860, Boucicault's transatlantic fame made him one of Britain's most popular playwrights. Boucicault was best known for his sensational melodramas. As a playwright, performer, and businessman, Boucicault was a consummate showman. *The Colleen Bawn* had been a hit in New York, so when it was accepted for production at the Adelphi in London, Boucicault was able to negotiate to "share the terms," thus beginning the changes that would make playwriting a far more profitable profession. *The Colleen Bawn* is an excellent example of the influence of realism on the melodramatic form. It is clearly a melodrama, with a noble hero, an endangered heroine, and an insidious villain; however, unlike many earlier examples, *The Colleen Bawn* purports to offer a realistic depiction of the life and character of Boucicault's native IRELAND.

The characters speak in vivid dialect, and the sets were noted for their spectacular depiction of the Irish countryside. As the 1860s progressed, even melodramatic playwrights like Boucicault had begun to move "towards reproducing the conditions of real life" (Nicoll, 1959).

Three years after *The Colleen Bawn*, another play appeared, furthering the influence of realism on the melodramatic form. Although THE TICKET-OF-LEAVE MAN did not earn THOMAS TAYLOR a share of the profits, this play, which ran for 407 consecutive performances, helped contribute to the growing popularity of the long run. Although based on a French play, *The Ticket-of-Leave Man* is notable both for its opening scene in a realistically depicted coffeehouse and for its introduction of a canny detective character, Hawkshaw. Taylor begins by introducing his audience to the underworld; this play "is one of the first melodramas to deal with the criminal life of London" (Nicoll, 1959). Taylor applies the melodramatic form to contemporary London life, furthering the importance of realism, but this is a realism of the poor and lower-middle class; the middle and upper middle classes had not yet seen themselves realistically depicted on the stage.

A significant moment in the move toward realism occurred in 1865 when the burlesque actress Marie Wilton took over the management of a small out-of-the-way theater and renamed it The Prince of Wales's. The Prince of Wales's Theatre would come to have a dynamic impact on Victorian acting, staging, and playwriting, making its name with Wilton's productions of Robertson's comedies. Both playwright Tom Robertson and actor-manager Squire Bancroft are credited with initiating the "cup-and-saucer" school of drama, but Wilton had begun the theater's move toward realistic representation of middle-class life before she married Bancroft or decided to produce Robertson's *Society*. Wilton's influence on Victorian realism is often underplayed, but as a star and an actress-manager, Robertson gave her a significant amount of control over his play texts. The plays considered to be his masterpieces—*Ours* (1866), CASTE (1867), and *School* (1868)—were all produced by Wilton's company and featured roles written to highlight her comedic skills. Although far from today's standards of realism, Victorians considered Robertson's comedies revolutionary, a fact illustrated by ARTHUR PINERO's thinly veiled dramatic portrait of Robertson and Wilton in *Trelawney of the "Wells"* (1898). Although often sentimental, Robertson's comedies offered a new direction for playwrights and represented middle-class life and manners in a way that was viewed as realistic by mid-Victorian audiences. Robertson's contribution to theater is not limited to his play texts; in fact, his creation of stage management is often seen as being more significant than his writing. Marie Wilton gave Robertson the freedom to superintend rehearsals, and the resulting productions presented a unified vision. Robertson's productions, with their realistic sets, ensemble casts, and attention to detail, offered a unique experience to Victorian audiences and began to extend the realism of the sets and acting style to the play's dialogue and theme.

1870s

The trend toward realism initiated in the 1860s continued through the 1870s, but its progress was not universal. In 1871, Leopold Lewis's *The Bells* became one of the most influential plays of the decade and made Henry Irving a star. With its haunted lead character and its staged dream sequences, *The Bells* seems to offer a gothic retreat from realism. Still, its exploration of a murderer's guilty conscience shows the movement toward psychological realism and clearly influenced the popularity of adaptations of sensation novels like T. A. Palmer's version of ELLEN WOOD'S EAST LYNNE (1874). This fascination with a guilty conscience also points to the problem plays of the 1890s. Another challenge to the dominance of domestic melodrama and sentimentality can be seen in the realm of comedy. Although widely panned by the critics, WILLIAM SCHWENK GILBERT'S *Engaged* (1877) presented a new kind of satirical society comedy. With its cast of reprehensible characters and its humorously unsentimental treatment of marriage, *Engaged* pokes fun at both the Victorian marriage market and at plays like Robertson's that center on the search for a mate.

Despite these deviations, domestic melodramas continued to dominate the stage. In many ways, H. J. Byron can be seen as a representative Victorian playwright. He was tremendously prolific, and his body of work includes farce, burlesque, comedy, and drama. Byron's *Our Boys* (1875) had a run of 1,366 nights, breaking the long-run record. Although it relies on stock characters and ends happily, *Our Boys* is neither a melodrama nor a typical comedy. There is no central villain; the two heroes, one an upper-class dilettante and the other an earnest product of upward mobility, oppose their domineering fathers and suffer for their principles. Sentimentality is central to the plot: both young men are motivated by a determination to marry the women they love, and both learn from their poverty as they attempt to make their way in the world. *Our Boys* focuses on a number of central Victorian preoccupations: class, education, and work. Some farcical moments lighten the last act, and the happy ending reinforces the message that a middle-class work ethic is preferable to inflexible snobbery and upper-class idleness.

1880s

As the 1870s drew to a close, the long run became the norm, and the stage grew ever more respectable. In 1879, this respectability led to the formation of The Theatrical Reform Association, the Church and Stage Guild, and the Shakespeare Memorial Theatre. In 1880, Marie Wilton and Squire Bancroft took over the larger and more fashionably located Haymarket Theatre where they created the "picture-box stage." The Bancrofts surrounded the Haymarket stage with a border resembling a picture's frame, thus further dividing the performers from the audience and emphasizing the theatrical illusion. The year 1880 also saw the first British production of HENRIK IBSEN'S *Quicksands*—later titled PILLARS OF SOCIETY—presented in a morning reading at The Gaiety. Electric light began to replace gas, and in 1881, the Savoy became the first fully electric theater. Although the flexibility of electric light was useful in producing realistic stage effects, the topsy-turvy Gilbert and Sullivan operetta *Patience* was the first production to use this technology.

Domestic melodramas like George Robert Sims's *The Lights o' London* (1881) and HENRY ARTHUR JONES'S *The Silver King* (1882) continued to dominate the stage. Farces remained popular, and some like Pinero's THE MAGISTRATE (1885) and *The Schoolmistress* (1886) centered on middle-class characters and settings. The fact that 1885 marks the formation of The Music Hall Artists' Association speaks to the continued importance of other forms of theatrical entertainment. As legitimate theaters and their playwrights catered to the middle class, music halls provided inexpensive, often bawdy entertainment to working-class patrons. In an attempt to further the mid- to late-Victorian quest for respectability, legitimate theater worked hard to differentiate between levels of performers. Actresses in particular were anxious to distance themselves from the women who performed in music hall reviews. By emphasizing the intellectual nature of their craft, the sincerity of their stage emotions, and the propriety of their offstage lives, stars of the legitimate theater attempted to make acting a respectable profession for middle-class men and women.

1890s

As the 1880s ended, realism had become the dominant form in the legitimate theater, and England was beginning to develop an alternative theater community. Female managers, playwrights, and performers were particularly active in this attempt to move British theater in new directions. The advent of the matinee was particularly useful in introducing playwrights like Ibsen to the British public. In 1888, Janet Achurch produced A DOLL'S HOUSE with her husband Charles Charrington, Mrs. Oscar Beringer produced *Pillars of Society*, and Elizabeth Robins performed her first Ibsen role. An American, Robins would go on to become one of Britain's most famous interpreters of Ibsen. In 1889, *A Doll's House* had its official London premiere, and in 1891, J. T. Grein founded the Independent Theatre Society (ITS). The goal of the ITS was to offer an alternative to the often banal popular entertainments of the day, but as Nicoll (1959) points out, a danger of the Independent Theatre was that it could become a highbrow society, extolling commercial failure as an artistic virtue. In this, the ITS seems to foreshadow the values and aesthetics of modernism. This company produced Ibsen's GHOSTS, *A Doll's House*, and HEDDA GABBLER, as well as original plays like *Alan's Wife* (1893) by Florence Bell and Elizabeth Robins. This short play explores the issue of infanticide and was so controversial its authorship was concealed.

There were few female playwrights in the 19th century, due in part to the fact that other forms of writing were far more profitable but also due to a prevailing prejudice against plays by women. Still, a few Victorian women did pursue playwriting. Earlier in the century, actresses like Fanny Kemble and Anna Cora Mowatt had some success as playwrights, and stage adaptations of women's novels were popular throughout the period. The use of pseudonyms was common; Pearl Craigie used the name John Oliver Hobbes when her plays were produced.

Craigie's *The Ambassador* (1898) shows the influence of 19th-century melodrama but begins to present more complex female characters and explores relationships between women in society. Craigie's play even examines a genuine friendship between a man and a woman.

The theater of the 1890s has been more widely studied than that of any other decade in the 19th century. The growing realism of English theater culminated in the problem play. Henry Arthur Jones and Arthur Wing Pinero wrote the most famous problem plays of the period. These plays, such as Pinero's *The Second Mrs. Tanqueray* (1893) and *The Notorious Mrs. Ebbsmith* (1895) and Jones's *Mrs. Dane's Defense* (1900), often center on a female character and thus offer actresses more interesting roles than those typical in melodrama. These roles, however, are often negative. Although the female characters are strong, their status as fallen women marks them as social outsiders. The characters of the new woman and the fallen woman became central to the problem play, but the 1890s was also the decade of aestheticism, decadence, and Oscar Wilde.

Wilde reintroduced British society to the comedy of manners. His light comedies both reflected and satirized the elite of his day. In contrast to Jones and Pinero, who were new to the society about which they wrote, Wilde was a member of the elite class about which he wrote, and his career was colored by his passion for style. In a few short years, Wilde produced some of the most memorable plays of the 19th century: LADY WINDERMERE'S FAN (1892), *A Woman of No Importance* (1893), *An Ideal Husband* (1895), and THE IMPORTANCE OF BEING EARNEST (1895). All share the same wit and comic depiction of society's foibles.

In the 1890s, George Bernard Shaw was just beginning his playwriting career. Despite the fact that the strict standards of what was deemed acceptable by the Lord Chamberlain's office had begun to expand, Shaw's MRS. WARREN'S PROFESSION (1893) was banned and could not be produced until the 1900s. Shaw's other early plays, such as ARMS AND THE MAN (1894), *The Devil's Disciple* (1897), and *You Never Can Tell* (1900), were produced but failed to achieve popular success. In one way or another, all these plays attack Victorian mores, and it seems that society was not quite ready for this brand of criticism. Despite these failures, Shaw still had a tremendous influence on the theater through his role as a critic.

Throughout the latter half of the 19th century, the British theater community continued its quest for respectability. In 1895, the same year that Wilde was tried for homosexuality, Henry Irving became the first actor to be knighted. The desire for respectability was not universal; some of the most famous actresses of the 1890s, Sarah Bernhardt, Ellen Terry, and Lily Langtry, were infamous for their offstage lives. But the flawless reputations of midcentury stars like Helen Faucit, Marie Wilton, and Madge Kendal had won a level of prestige for the profession, and acting had become, if not an entirely respectable profession, at least a respected art. The trend toward realism and the growing intellectualism of the theater community cannot be separated from performers' quest for respectability. Victorian realism is now viewed with some amount of skepticism, but as Nicoll (1959) points out: "In any art, when once virile conventions become stereotyped and hence bereft of meaning, only a return to realistic methods can produce sanity and fresh inspiration."

The End of Victorian Realism

Realism would continue to be the mainstay of theater production throughout the early 20th century, but between 1900 and 1940 various styles of playwriting, production, and performance would arise that offered an alternative to strict realism. As different as they were from the picture-box sets of the mid- to late-Victorian theater, these AVANT-GARDE experiments shared a key motivation with their realistic predecessors. Like the Victorian innovations, 20th-century theater experiments were often motivated by a quest for truth. Proponents of symbolism, expressionism, and even surrealism argued that these approaches offered a deeper truth than the surface effects of realism. Inspired by psychology and PSYCHOANALYSIS, these theatrical experiments began to explore the imagination. By the 1930s, elements of these movements had been integrated into mainstream theaters. Often, productions of even the most traditional plays employed at least some antirealistic elements.

Theater as Social Commentary

Another key aspect of the movement away from Victorian realism was the desire to make theater more useful. The first forty years of the 20th century were marked by economic depression and world wars. If the fin de siècle had revealed the shortcomings of Victorianism, the modernist period displayed utter disdain for the values and aesthetics of their predecessors. There was a movement away from the frivolous, escapist, entertainment-based Victorian theater. The value of art in the modern period was often assessed by the level of its inaccessibility rather than its popularity. Playwrights strove to offer political and social commentary in their works. One of the most notable of the sociopolitical playwrights in this period was clearly George Bernard Shaw, but ELIZABETH ROBINS, SOMERSET MAUGHAM, and others also used the theater to comment on and attempt to improve society. This shift arose, at least in part, out of the repertory movement, which replaced the touring and provincial stock companies that had been so significant in the early- to mid-Victorian period. With the long run, opportunities for new playwrights and performers were vastly limited. To an extent, the repertory movement helped alleviate this problem, while offering venues to more regional and progressive types of drama.

Throughout the late-Victorian period, the growing realism of playwriting and production had accompanied an increasingly naturalistic performance style. Popularized by the English productions of Ibsen, the problem plays of the late 19th and early 20th centuries introduced more psychologically complex characters, which furthered the need to explore new acting styles. Initiated by KONSTANTIN STANISLAVSKY and the MOSCOW ART THEATRE, method acting found its way to England in the 1920s and offered added depth to the realistic acting style that had become popular. Stanislavsky's method emphasized the use of genuine emotions in performance. In contrast, some progressive playwrights sought a way to challenge their audiences and break out of the illusions of the realistic tradition. This trend culminated in BERTOLD BRECHT'S ALIENATION EFFECT, which instructed performers to distance themselves from the role and used various tactics to keep the audience aware of the social message of the play.

The popularity of a few playwrights, such as Henry Arthur Jones and Arthur Wing Pinero, crossed the division between the centuries, but by 1910 the theater world belonged to a new group of representative playwrights. Jones faded because his single note of attacking hypocrisy began to seem old-fashioned to a new generation of theater patrons. Pinero's carefully written plays avoided such overarching ideas and thus held their appeal a bit longer, but like Jones, he was associated with the past, and the avant-garde condemned them both. Authors like George Bernard Shaw and J. M. BARRIE may have produced their first plays in the late 19th century, but their rise to fame would come in the first decades of the 20th century.

At the turn of the century much of British drama centered on romance—either in sparkling social comedies or in realism tinged with melodrama and sentiment. The popular theater often referred to by its prominent location in the West End of London, featured commercial playwrights who aimed to appeal to general audiences of fashionable people in search of amusement. These audiences did not crave intellectualism but excitement. The old melodrama lingered in the West End but was increasingly challenged by other forms as it faded into the detective play. Drama, rather than tragedy, became the main alternative to comedy, and both the problem play and the play of ideas moved from minority to mainstream. Whimsical fantasy plays and musicals were also fashionable early in the 20th century. The West End also featured the revue with its series of short sketches and musical numbers. Playwrights like NOËL COWARD often contributed to this genre. Coward's revue sketches have been lost, but many of his songs transcended the revue form and became well known. The growing popularity of film took audiences away from variety shows and music halls but did not seem to have a major impact on the legitimate theater, other than to add an element of the cinematic to some production styles. William Shakespeare also continued to be popular throughout the era. Many of the most renowned actors of the 20th century, such as Peggy Ashcroft, John Gielgud, Alec Guinness, and Laurence Olivier, first appeared in Shakespearean productions during the first four decades of the century.

As the 20th century progressed, the powerful actor- and actress-managers who had controlled Victorian theater began to disappear. In the years leading up to World War I, there was a theater building and remodeling boom. Actor-managers like Herbert Beerbohm Tree, Charles Wyndham, and George Alexander controlled the popular theater, and their talents and influence were rewarded with knighthoods. Yet as progressive theater arose to challenge the commercial West End, actor-managers were criticized because the range of plays they produced was limited by their own individual skills and prejudices. Gradually, the dominant actor- and actress-managers fell out of favor. They were replaced by the evolution of the director and producer, whose roles had developed out of the playwrights and stage managers who had helped control the look and feel of earlier productions. As Nicoll (1973) points out, directors first appeared in musical theater as stage managers began to take on an interpretive function. By 1920, directors had all but replaced actor-managers.

In contrast with the Victorian era, the early 20th century presented significant alternatives to popular theater. The progressive drama of this time emphasized the intellectual sometimes at the expense of the theatrical. These plays tended to be very serious. Even when comedy was evoked, there was a greater purpose. Progressive or minority drama often presented region-specific content and experimented with dialect. There were also a number of plays, like Elizabeth Robins's *Votes for Women* (1907), whose politics made them virtually propagandist. Progressive drama in this period often arose out of the proliferation of theatrical societies, clubs, and the growing repertory movement.

The repertory movement was inspired at least in part by W. B. YEATS and LADY GREGORY'S Irish Literary Theatre, and in England, SCOTLAND, and Wales, it came to replace the traveling stock companies that had been so important to the development of early-Victorian theater. Repertory companies offered new playwrights the opportunity to see their work onstage, provided young performers with valuable experience, and gave audiences an alternative to the long runs of London commercial houses. The late-Victorian matinees of intellectual plays also contributed to this movement. Theaters and societies like the Birmingham Repertory Theatre, the British Drama League, the Welsh National Drama Company, the Glasgow Repertory Theatre, the Liverpool Repertory Theatre, and the Scottish Repertory Theatre Company expanded the range of drama in this period. The Manchester Playgoers Society performances at Miss Horniman's Gaiety Theatre even lent their name to the social drama that evolved in the early years of the 20th century—The Manchester School.

Female playwrights continued to struggle for equality in the early 20th century, and their plays became increasingly feminist during this period. The politics of Elizabeth Robins's *Votes for Women* (1907) makes the otherwise unremarkable play interesting. The commercial settings in Cecily Hamilton's *Diana of Dobson's* (1908) and Elizabeth Baker's *Chains* (1909) both reveal the increasing numbers of women in the workforce and the social problems raised by employment inequalities and sexual double standards. GITHA SOWERBY'S RUTHERFORD AND SON (1912) incorporates both Marxism and feminism. Politics and playwriting combined with organizations like The Actresses' Franchise League and the Women Writers' Suffrage League. These early feminist plays reveal the changing role of women in British society and agitate for reform, but women's suffrage would not come until after World War I.

In a way, these political plays continued what the problem play had begun. Often the heroines fit into the fallen woman category, but in these plays, the heroines are outspoken and challenge the social values that condemned their predecessors. The feminist content of plays like Hamilton's *Diana of Dobson's* and STANLEY HOUGHTON'S HINDLE WAKES (1912) presented an alternative to the more traditional heroines and love plots shown on West End stages. It was also in this period that Shaw's 1896 play *Mrs. Warren's Profession* was produced at the New Lyric Club in 1902, but it would not be performed in a commercial theater until the 1920s. These plays show women who explore alternatives to marriage and who experiment with their sexuality in ways that challenged the Victorian double standards still clinging to Edwardian society. They centered on the conflict between older values and the new society that was evolving as the 20th century progressed.

PROGRESSIVE AND POPULAR DRAMA, PRE–WORLD WAR I

Difference and conflict were central to the common themes in both progressive and popular drama in the early 20th century. The conflict between the young and the old or between artists and mainstream society provided the core of many significant plays leading up to World War I. The figure of the artist in plays like Haddon Chambers's *The Awakening* (1901), H. H. Davies's *Cousin Kate* (1903), and JOHN GALSWORTHY'S *The Pigeon* (1912) allowed playwrights to question dominant social values. Another common motif that allowed for social criticism was the use of the "passer-by." Although the most significant use of this motif would not come until 1919 with A. A. MILNE'S somewhat satiric *Mr. Pim Passes By*, the early years of the century presented many variations on this motif. In these plays, the addition of an outsider moves the plot forward. This outsider forces change in the lives of the other characters. One of the most obvious instances of this motif as a central plot element can be found in Chambers's *Passers-By* (1911). Some of these characters were paupers or even burglars, drawing a link to the popular detective play. In J. K. Jerome's *The Passing of the Third Floor Back* (1908), the passer-by becomes mysteriously divine.

The years from the turn of the century through the beginning of World War I saw the introduction of many playwrights who would come to dominate theater in the first forty years of the 20th century. George Bernard Shaw finally gained widespread recognition, and major plays by J. M. Barrie, H. H. Davies, Stanley Houghton, Alfred Sutro, and Somerset Maugham appeared on London's stages. This was at least in part due to managements like HARLEY GRANVILLE-BARKER'S at the Court Theatre, which set out to encourage progressive drama. The play of ideas had taken hold in both progressive and popular theater, and playwrights like Granville-Barker, St. John Hankin, and John Galsworthy had their first hits during this period. Even Noël Coward, whose plays would flourish in the 1920s and 1930s, had a successful acting career by the start of the Great War.

George Bernard Shaw and J. M. Barrie would come to be the principal representative playwrights of the first fourteen years of the 20th century. Today known almost exclusively for PETER PAN (1904), Barrie was one of the best-loved writers of his day. Although there are clear notes of fantasy and whimsy throughout his works, Barrie's plays offered audiences unique observations about humanity. Barrie's first major successes *Quality Street* and THE ADMIRABLE CRICHTON both came in 1902. Unlike many of his contemporaries, Barrie did not seem to offer much serious purpose in his work. Although his last play, *The Boy David*, would not be presented until 1936, the height of Barrie's career clearly came before World War I.

In contrast, even when he presented an obvious sense of fun, Shaw's work had a serious purpose. The aggressive speaking style he developed on a soapbox in Speaker's Corner and in the Fabian Society is evident throughout his plays. The one major fault in Shaw's plays is that sometimes he is so fixed in the realm of ideas that his characters lose their humanity. As Richard Eyre and Nicholas Wright point out in *Changing Stages* (2001), "everything's on the surface: start worrying about the depths below and the boat will sink." Although he had had plays produced during the late-Victorian period, it was his association with Granville-Barker's management of the Court Theatre that brought Shaw to public attention. The Court was located in Sloane Square, well outside the fashionable West End Theatre district, and was set up as an experimental theater specializing in new and progressive drama. Granville-Barker's management also helped develop changes in play production; he has been called "the first modern British director." Between 1904 and 1906, Granville-Barker produced ten of Shaw's plays, including MAN AND SUPERMAN (1903), JOHN BULL'S OTHER ISLAND (1904), MAJOR BARBARA (1905), and *The Doctor's Dilemma* (1906). One of Shaw's most enduring successes, PYGMALION (1913), was also presented in the years leading up to World War I. World War I put a stop to most theater production in England, and Shaw's politics made him suspect during the war, but by the 1920s he had recovered his reputation and presented some of his finest work, including SAINT JOAN (1924). In 1925, Shaw received the Nobel Prize for Literature.

The years leading up to World War I also saw the early successes of a new establishment of playwrights. Maugham and Galsworthy eclipsed many of their contemporaries and would go on to influence the works of later playwrights like Coward. Like many of his contemporaries, Maugham worked to expose the absurdities and flaws of Edwardian and Georgian society, but his characters have more depth than those of his contemporaries. Maugham was an admirer of Ibsen and wanted to write dramas that confronted social issues. His early successes, *Lady Frederick* (1907) and *Mrs. Dot* (1908), seem to present the beginnings of a modern comedy of manners. After World War I, he would return to social criticism in plays like *The Sacred Flame* (1929) and *For Services Rendered* (1932).

Galsworthy's work was firmly situated under the heading of the play of ideas, but like Barrie, who had influenced him, Galsworthy's plays evince sympathy and compassion. His attempts to avoid the dullness that sometimes follows strict realism occasionally enter the realm of melodrama or sentimentality. Still, his plays such as *The Silver Box* (1906), *Strife* (1909), and *The Fugitive* (1913) offer interesting criticism of the British class system. Although he met with mixed success, his career continued between the wars with plays like *The Skin Game* (1920), *Windows* (1922), and *Exiled* (1929).

Theater Between the Wars

A major element of theater between the wars was the discussion of new methods and techniques among the British, European, and American theater communities. Although the Victorians had had some exchange of talent with Europe and the United States and had borrowed freely from French drama, it was not until the early 20th century that the public evinced a growing desire for the novelty of foreign experiments like NATURALISM and expressionism. The traditions of Japanese theater were discovered, studied, and performed. The Moscow Art Theatre toured London in 1928, but even before that Stanislavsky's "system" had been a topic of discussion in professional circles—an English translation of his *My Life in Art* was published in 1924, outlining the basics of his method. This method continues to influence acting styles to this day. Still, much of the British theater remained insular, apart from the great Irish playwrights like Wilde and Shaw who were generally seen as more-or-less English.

Between the wars, a new generation of playwrights came to the fore. John Drinkwater and ST. JOHN ERVINE came to the West End from minority theaters, while Coward and Milne had gained some prominence just prior to World War I and would achieve fame in the 1920s and 1930s. Today, A. A. Milne is most remembered for his creation of *Winnie the Pooh* (1926) and for his play *Mr. Toad of Toad Hall* (1929), adapted from Kenneth Grahame's book *The Wind in the Willows*. He was clearly an inheritor of Barrie's whimsical style of children's theater, but Milne's plays are quieter, contrasting reality and fantasy. His first success, *Mr. Pim Passes By* (1919), uses the passer-by motif as an excuse for the play's central portrait of a husband and wife. He wrote in a variety of styles from comedy and fantasy to detective plays. Plays like *The Truth About Blayds* (1921), *The Dover Road* (1921), *The Fourth Wall* (1928), *Success* (1929), and *The Ivory Door* (1929) show the originality of his structure and style.

Coward was truly a one-man theater: he wrote, acted, sang, danced, composed, and directed. His playwriting style was strongly influenced by Maugham. Despite his distaste for the comparison, his plays' light, satiric look at fashionable society reveal a connection to Wilde, as well. The law against homosexual acts was not abolished until 1967, and Coward was careful to avoid Wilde's fate. Coward's plays tease at revelations of his sexuality, but he did not formally come out of the closet. Coward's plays lack direct social criticism, but they are more than simply superficial entertainment. Raised in genteel poverty, the young Coward worked to gain entrée into the fashionable society he would later depict in his plays. His style is unique. As Nicoll (1973) reveals, Coward achieves his "comic effect from a condensation of ordinary talk and from exquisite pointing." Since Wilde, comedy had been marked by epigrams, but Coward's wit is integrated into the overall character development and dialogue; it becomes part of the character rather than an interjection by the playwright.

Coward's acting career was just getting started when World War I broke out. Initially, he was too young for the draft, but few major plays were produced during the war, and he had trouble finding work as an actor. Coward was drafted in 1918 but did not prove to be much of a soldier. After the war, he continued to have difficulty finding work as an actor, so he turned to playwriting. His first full-length West End play was *I Leave it to You* (1920), but it was *The Young Idea* in 1923 that won him both notoriety and esteem. His career in the 1920s was erratic. Major successes like *The Vortex* (1924) and HAY FEVER (1925) were followed by failures like *Home Chat* and *Sirocco*, both of which were produced in 1927. Even his successes differed greatly. Sparkling comedies like *Hay Fever* contrast sharply with the dark, voyeuristic examination of drug abuse in *The Vortex*. As the 1920s ended, Coward came into his own. His major plays include *This Year of Grace!* (1928), *Bitter-Sweet* (1929), PRIVATE LIVES (1930), and CAVALCADE (1931). According to Eyre and Wright (2001) DESIGN FOR LIVING (1932) was Coward's last great play. It explores bisexuality and celebrates a kind of "polymorphous perversity" characteristic of Coward's teasing revelations of his own proclivities.

As Europe suffered through the Great Depression and headed for World War II, theater continued on much the same trajectory. English theater and society had undergone profound changes since the days of Boucicault and Tom Robertson. Technology had created modern warfare and vastly altered everyday life. Women could now attend universities, hold a number of jobs, own property after marriage, and vote. Drama had undergone a staggering array of revolutions and counterrevolutions. Long runs replaced the stock system; technological innovations transformed set design and acting styles. The actor-manager rose and fell, replaced by the director and the producer. Realism was introduced, developed, and then challenged by experimental and progressive theater. The world had become increasingly international, yet despite challenges posed by music halls, censorship, and film, English theater thrived.

FURTHER READING

Booth, Michael. *English Melodrama*. London: Herbert Jenkins, 1965.

——. *Theatre in the Victorian Age*. Cambridge: Cambridge Univ. Press, 1991.

Eyre, Richard, and Nicholas Wright. *Changing Stages: A View of British and American Theatre in the Twentieth Century*. New York: 2001.

Nicoll, Allardyce. *A History of English Drama 1660–1900: Late Nineteenth Century Drama 1850–1900*. Vol. 5. Cambridge: Cambridge Univ. Press, 1959.

——. *A History of English Drama 1660–1900: The Beginnings of the Modern Period 1900–1930*. Vol. 6. Cambridge: Cambridge Univ. Press, 1973.

Robin A. Werner

1940–1960

English drama experienced many of its most emphatic innovations in the late 1950s. By the end of the decade, the first plays of JOHN ARDEN, HAROLD PINTER, and PETER SHAFFER were establishing a marked tone for the development of English drama that contrasted sharply with the drama that had preceded them only twenty years before.

In 1956, the Royal Court Theatre was taken over by the newly formed English Stage Company, under the artistic directorship of George Devine. Initially formed to promote new and experimental drama, the company soon established itself as the determinant of English dramatic developments. The Court's production of JOHN OSBORNE'S *LOOK BACK IN ANGER* (1956) has been held generally to mark a watershed in postwar British theater. Jimmy Porter, Osborne's working-class antihero, expresses a social rage and disillusionment that immediately identified the spirit of the "ANGRY YOUNG MEN" and "kitchen-sink drama." In its vehemence and frustration, this tone contrasted sharply with the polite interactions of the protagonists of TERENCE RATTIGAN, the spiritual and mythical explorations of THOMAS STEARNS ELIOT, or the flippant, privileged insouciance of NOËL COWARD'S characters. Upon exiting the theater on opening night, Rattigan himself told a reporter that the play should have been retitled, "Look how unlike Terence Rattigan I'm being." Nonetheless, to attribute to Osborne a radical rewriting of the dramatic English tradition does a disservice both to the plays that preceded *Look Back in Anger* and to the content and structure of the plays that are generally thought to bear his influence.

THEATER IN TRANSITION

That English theater was awaiting a transition in the 1940s is perhaps suggested by the fact that the most prominent postwar dramatists were the very same who had dominated the English stage in the 1930s. Noël Coward's *BLITHE SPIRIT* (1941), *Present Laughter* (1942), and *Relative Values* (1951) continued to manifest a similar interest in the self-theatricalizing leisure class epitomized by such earlier works as *HAY FEVER* (1925) and *PRIVATE LIVES* (1930). Nonetheless, in his characteristic use of an apparently minor situation between a set number of individuals (often within a single room), Coward maintains a link between his work and that of such dramatists as Pinter. Coward himself perceived in Pinter's work a superb craftsmanship with language; Pinter's technique resembles Coward's own use of language to establish and query power and identity in order to establish a fundamental sense of absurdity.

Despite their stylistic and structural relevance to later dramatic developments, Coward's plays persist in representing members of a society unchanged since *Hay Fever*. The war, the massive implementation of national social services that attempted to ensure greater economic, social, and educational equality, and the relatively rapid process of decolonization that began after the granting of self-government to INDIA, PAKISTAN, BURMA, and Ceylon in 1947–1949 ensured that society could no longer exist as a complacent norm. Dramatists and critics (if not audiences) began to demand a theater that would more accurately speak to a contemporary social reality.

The plays of JOHN BOYNTON PRIESTLEY were unafraid to address current social realities and the moral condition of England. Like GEORGE BERNARD SHAW, Priestley perceived drama as an educative tool; unlike Shaw, he sought less to provoke thought than to assert moral "truths." In his highly popular *AN INSPECTOR CALLS* (1946), Priestley manipulates a conventional detective thriller structure to expose the individual responsibility of various members of an Edwardian household for the imminent suicide of a young woman. The framing presence of a detective who acts as a metaphorical moral presence in the world of the Edwardian family and in the world of the reality that they have touched and the play's deliberate manipulation of linear sequences of time disprove critical contentions of Priestley's derivativeness. Nonetheless, Priestley's preference for Edwardian setting, his moral didacticism, and the popularity of almost all forty-nine of his plays over the decades in which they were produced helped to ensure his position as one of the primary targets for the NEW DRAMATISTS of the 1950s. Indeed, Osborne's Jimmy Porter singles Priestley out as "still casting well-fed glances back to the Edwardian twilight from his comfortable disenfranchised wilderness."

In the verse plays that followed *MURDER IN THE CATHEDRAL* (1935), T. S. Eliot, like Priestley, tended to adopt conventional dramatic settings. Eliot used these settings as a means through which to explore in a highly original manner the banality of social life and the potential for a more spiritual reality. In each of his plays, Eliot underpins conventional drawing-room or murder-mystery plots with Greek TRAGEDY; the events in *The Cocktail Party* (1949), for example, parallel those in Euripides's *Alcestis* and *Ion*. Eliot sought to establish a continuum between contemporary experience and antiquity that would give a greater significance to modern life. This emphasis on spirituality and myth, coupled with the perceived elitism of verse in drama, was deemed irrelevant and condescending by the mid-1950s, when the new generation of playwrights (and their critics) began to demand a REALISM, if not NATURALISM, explicitly allied to identified concerns of class and economic and social inequality. Although THE FAMILY REUNION (1939), *The Cocktail Party*, *The Confidential Clerk* (1953), and *The Elder Statesman* (1958) all undercut conventional dramatic forms to prove the illusory nature of reality, the very fact that they relied upon these forms ensured their eventual denigration by those advocating an entirely new drama.

CHRISTOPHER FRY's verse plays respond to some extent to objections to Eliot's verse drama. Whereas Eliot located his action in the context of a drawing-room mystery or adultery comedy, Fry tended to conform action to poetic imagery, often using historical settings and invoking pastoral traditions. While Eliot points to the banality of life and equates that with a spiritual malaise, Fry implicitly celebrates the trivialities of life in order to point to a benign spiritual presence and the constant potential for redemption. *A Phoenix Too Frequent* (1946), THE LADY'S NOT FOR BURNING (1948), *Venus Observed* (1950), and *A Sleep of Prisoners* (1951) are among Fry's more celebrated works, and all exemplify his poetic style with their wit, poetic conceits, and celebration of a joyously unpredictable divine order.

By the 1950s, such verse conceits may have remained popular with audiences and actors but were increasingly seen by critics as escapist and regressive. Indeed, despite being a cofounder of the English Stage Company, RONALD DUNCAN, a close successor to Eliot in his use of the structures of the "well-made play" to explore spiritual themes in verse drama, also found himself quickly ostracized from Royal Court productions. Osborne himself contended that the failure of Duncan's double bill in 1956 represented "a small but cruel revenge on Verse Theatre and Higher Thought." Duncan replied to such criticisms by asserting the ultimate regressiveness of the trend being established at the Royal Court: the socialist theater being implemented by the likes of Osborne and ARNOLD WESKER hearkened back to the theater of HENRIK IBSEN and George Bernard Shaw. With the existence of a welfare state in England, the dangers of nuclear warfare, and the need for humanity to seek other values, the realist and polemical drama at the Court should recognize the greater crisis of society as being spiritual, rather than material.

JOHN WHITING's prose dramas recognize the concerns of Duncan and Eliot and resemble verse drama in their manipulation of verbal and visual SYMBOLISM to suggest the existence of a reality beneath immediate consciousness. Unlike Eliot, Duncan, and Fry, however, Whiting emphasizes the mysteriousness of that reality, as it can only ever partially be recognized through the incomplete and almost unconscious articulations of characters. The surface reality of Whiting's characters is insecure, and the driving force beneath that reality is menacing both for its very existence and for its intangibility. One of the most original dramatists of his time, Whiting is also one of the most neglected. In 1948, Whiting's first play, *Saint's Day*, won first prize at the Festival of Britain, judged by Peter Ustinov, Christopher Fry, and Alec Clunes. While the play was popular with prominent directors and actors (including George Devine), it was condemned by the press. Devine's initial defense (which notably predated the realignment of his aesthetic following *Look Back in Anger*) did little to assert the importance of Whiting's position either at the Royal Court, among contemporary critics, or with English audiences. In its depiction of a decaying respectable household exposed to and eventually infiltrated by the mockery and menace of outside forces (both civilian and military), *Saint's Day* addresses contemporary insecurities about community, class position, and the role of the military in establishing historical and individual change. At the same time, however, it frames that social relevance with a vaguely defined symbolic context that often resembles AUGUST STRINDBERG's dream plays; the play is about locating, establishing, and maintaining identity in a chaotic inner world and the potential of human nature to wreak destruction within and on others. Whiting's establishment of a sense of paranoia that becomes increasingly justified by events that could be just as symbolic as "real," his isolation of the potential for menace within a variety of relationships (explored most thoroughly in *Conditions of Agreement* [1948–1949, staged 1965]), and his investment of particular visual objects and verbal reiterations with a surreal importance prefigure the very techniques for which ten years later Harold Pinter was to be first reviled, then acclaimed with THE BIRTHDAY PARTY (1958).

Similarly, the plays of Terence Rattigan, despite achieving significant popularity in their own time, have been unjustly ignored since *Look Back in Anger*. Rattigan's influence can be detected in subsequent English dramatic developments. While the plays of Pinter and TOM STOPPARD are as carefully crafted as those of Rattigan, the frequent absurdity of their plots and their redefinition of narrative event have helped critics too eager to assert a dramatic revolution in the 1950s and 1960s to ignore that indebtedness. *Look Back in Anger* follows a dramatic structure close to that of Rattigan's plays but situates its events in a working-class "drawing-room." Indeed, Osborne maintains a linguistic link with Rattigan; despite their working-class backgrounds, his characters use the language of the middle class.

Rattigan emerged as a serious dramatist after the war and helped to establish an early postwar dramatic aesthetic that examined the impossibility of complete communication, loneliness, and the simultaneous fragility and destructiveness of social conventions of behavior. In *Separate Tables* (*The Table in the Window*/*Table Number Seven*, 1954), a lonely spinster is unable to break from the domination of her mother, and an insecure man who has masqueraded as an upper-class major is about to be humiliated for propositioning women in a local cinema. While the drama explores the particular plight of these individual characters, in its evocation of a "cross section of society" at a hotel, it opens these dilemmas of human isolation, insecurity, identity, and class to a more universal interrogation. Similarly, *The Winslow Boy* (1946) examines both a family's particular judicial case and the moral and political implications of the issues that that case addresses. Rattigan's plays examine larger human themes within a drama that focuses on portraying particular characters and their situations with feeling and insight. This dramatic aesthetic allowed him to be one of the first English playwrights to stage implicit homosexual themes. Both the heterosexual Major in *Separate Tables* and Hester Collyer in THE DEEP BLUE SEA (1952) were conceived of as homosexual protagonists. Hester embodies Rattigan's interest in examining unrequited, socially unsanctioned love and the need to reconcile the impossibility of satisfying that physical need with the heroism of continuing to find a purpose in life.

Innovations in the 1950s

During the 1950s, particularly following the defection of Guy Burgess and Donald MacLean, homosexuality became much more widely discussed in political and artistic circles. Despite the overall political negativity toward homosexuality, the very fact of its being discussed seemed to encourage its dramatic representation (doubtless encouraged by simultaneous developments in American theater). In 1958, the nineteen-year-old SHELAGH DELANEY wrote *A Taste of Honey* in direct response to what she saw as Rattigan's overly repressed treatment of homosexuality in *Variations on a Theme* (1958). Delaney directly addresses themes characteristically censored or sublimated in English drama: pregnant by a Negro sailor who has deserted her, the overtly independent Jo "settles down" with the homosexual Geof before expressing her female independence and deciding to bring the child up with her mother, free of male influence. Delaney has come to be associated with a "new drama" that gave itself the prerogative to label its contemporaries and predecessors as antiquated and socially irrelevant, no matter the social context in which they wrote. The injustice of the critical complacency that has accepted such presumptions has yet to be fully acknowledged with a more serious consideration of Rattigan's work in particular.

A Taste of Honey is significant for demonstrating the influence of another dramatic development: the incorporation of music hall traditions within spoken drama. Director Joan Littlewood's Theatre Workshop, founded in 1945 and based at the Theatre Royal in London, did much to promote the perceived aesthetic of BERTOLT BRECHT and to associate that aesthetic with specifically English left-wing concerns. This interest in Brecht was further encouraged by the visit of the Berliner Ensemble to London in 1956. ANN JELLICOE's *The Sport of My Mad Mother* (1958) went so far as to abandon words as the primary means of invoking meaning. Influenced both by ANTONIN ARTAUD's Theater of Cruelty and Brecht, Jellicoe's play was designed to appeal to the audience primarily through rhythm, noise, and music to ritualize and thus universalize patterns of movement and sound. John Osborne's THE ENTERTAINER (1957) at the Royal Court was one of the first commercially successful English plays to acknowledge some Brechtian influence. Unlike the generally pastichelike productions of the Theatre Workshop, *The Entertainer* integrates the music hall tradition within its narrative to tell the tale of the decline of music hall performer Archie Rice. By invoking a theatrical tradition that had become increasingly associated with expressing left-wing ideology, Osborne focused his play both on Archie Rice and on the metaphoric representation of an England in social decay.

This interest in Brechtian production aesthetics, evocation (if not full articulation) of left-wing ideology, and use of visual and musical effects to ensure an emotional impact found its most powerful exemplification in the works of John Arden. Unlike Osborne, Arden does not grant his music hall pieces a narrative justification; instead, he integrates the music hall tradition to establish levels of irony and pathos within the greater framework of his drama. Each scene in *Live Like Pigs* (1958), despite a naturalistic setting, is framed by a music hall ballad to suggest a greater metaphorical significance to staged events. Arden's most difficult and controversial play of the period, SERGEANT MUSGRAVE'S DANCE (1959), was among the most ambitious productions of the Royal Court Theatre. Detailing the arrival of a band of deserted soldiers to a mining town, Arden at first invokes the audience's sympathy for the soldiers' predictably anti-establishment resentment of the army and its regimens. When, however, Sergeant Musgrave reveals his "plan," to restore a moral order by compensating for the death of five natives at the hands of the army with the death of twenty-five civilians of the town, Arden effectively complicates any clear identification with the pacifist, revolutionary, or establishment ideologies variously articulated throughout the play. This complication is further ensured by staging that threat directly at the audience in the shape of a Gatling gun: Arden could equally be querying the moral standards of the audience by implicitly accusing them of complicity in the maintenance of establishment standards, attacking the audience's theatrical expectations and standards, or merely attempting to shock that audience into a recognition of the brutality of any and all violence. Despite the fact that the play's first production was disastrous, the work itself deserves a place as an equally, if not more, important marker of "revolutionary" English drama as *Look Back in Anger*. Arden aligned Osborne's initial interest in representing the working class, emotional expression, and youth with a much more expressionistic dramatic style and politically polemical (if enigmatic) tone. Although Arden has since distanced himself from West End theater and more explicitly allied himself with Marxist drama, the political and aesthetic influence of his plays of the 1950s can be discerned in the plays of EDWARD BOND, DAVID HARE, and SARAH KANE.

While Osborne's play signaled an energy of emotion that allied itself to particular social circumstances, it is itself relatively conservative in its technique and notably unspecific in its ideas. In contrast, ARNOLD WESKER's *Roots* trilogy (*Chicken Soup with Barley*, 1958; *Roots*, 1959; *I'm Talking About Jerusalem*, 1960) devotes itself to a much more realistic representation of working-class setting (small rooms and houses in East London and Norfolk), situation (political rallies vying for attention with teatime), and dialogue. Like Arden, Wesker further distances himself from the plays of their imminent predecessors by asserting the importance of dramatizing not only the working class but also various aspects of regional life without caricature.

Despite the differences in their dramatic aesthetic, Wesker and Osborne are often associated with each other in discussions of the "new" drama of the 1950s. This critical association bears tribute to one of the defining aspects of the theater of the late 1950s: the emergence of the voice of the playwright (rather than the actor) as defining the dramatic experience. The anger of Osborne's hero came to be equated with the anger of Osborne himself; Osborne embodied a new spirit of drama that expressed itself primarily in appeals to the similar subjectivity of audience members. Similarly, Ronald in Wesker's working-class trilogy is a thinly disguised anagram of Arnold and effectively undergoes a development from enthusiastic socialist to reconciled artist prepared to recognize, if not actively address, social difficulties within the limited framework of his own familial, artistic, and social context.

Furthermore, the fact that such popular playwrights as Priestley, Rattigan, and Eliot could, as Rattigan noted, be instantly "dismissed, sacked by the critics" after *Look Back in Anger* indicates the increasing importance of the theater critic (rather than the audience that was still enjoying the plays of Coward, Eliot, Priestley, and Rattigan) as determinant of dramatic success. Kenneth Tynan's ultimately equivocating review of *Look Back in Anger* nonetheless established Osborne's reputation and Tynan himself as the mitigator of the educated dramatic taste. The critical revaluation of theater from sensitive, at times philosophical, entertainment to a deliberately shocking, political, emotional, and ultimately subjective experience defined the development of English drama from 1940 to 1960 and paved the way for the political engagement of HOWARD BARKER, Hare, and Brenton, the absurdist examinations of Stoppard, and the psychological and linguistic explorations of Pinter.

FURTHER READING

Browne, Terry. *Playwrights' Theatre: The English Stage Company at the Royal Court*. London: Pitman, 1975.

Duff, Charles. *The Lost Summer: The Heyday of the West End Theatre*. London: Heinemann, 1995.

Elsom, John. *Post-War British Theatre*. Rev. ed. London: Routledge, 1979.

Hinchcliffe, Arnold P. *Modern Verse Drama*. London: Methuen, 1977.

Innes, Christopher. *Modern British Drama: The Twentieth Century*. Cambridge: Cambridge Univ. Press, 2002.

Rabey, David Ian. *English Drama Since 1940*. London: Pearson, 2003.

Rebellato, Dan. *1956 and All That: The Making of Modern British Drama*. London: Routledge, 1999.

Taylor, John Russell. *Anger and After: A Guide to the New British Drama*. Harmondsworth: Penguin, 1963.

Irene Morra

1960–1980

In 1957 Prime Minister Harold Macmillan famously said, "Most of our people have never had it so good," and compared to the privations of World War II and its aftermath, he was right. The Butler Education Act of 1944, followed by the formation of the National Health Service in 1948, meant that a new generation of healthy and well-educated children came of age in the 1960s. In addition to free health care and compulsory education up until the age of sixteen, the development of the contraceptive pill meant the new generation was to experience a degree of sexual freedom unimaginable by their parents. The 1966 Sexual Offences Act decriminalized homosexuality between consenting adults over the age of twenty-one, the death penalty was abolished in the previous year, and Britain was still in a time of full employment.

The State of the Nation, 1960–1980

In spite of these lifestyle improvements, 1960s England was riven with political instability and unrest. In the wake of the postwar consensus, which saw the two major political parties in agreement over the main aspects of policy, a rift had emerged. Political opinion was divided over Suez, the Common Market (the 1960s version of the debate about Britain's entry into Europe), and Britain's burgeoning nuclear armory (the Campaign for Nuclear Disarmament began in 1958). The 1960s saw four general elections in a decade; each time the victorious party was voted in with the smallest of majorities. The privately educated gentleman politician epitomized by Winston Churchill (who died in 1965) was superseded by the grammar school boy, a figure who could identify with the newly affluent working classes. As John Seed points out:

> [W]hile Macmillan and Home [the previous Conservative prime ministers] posed as Edwardian gentlemen on their grouse moors in plus-fours, Wilson was a pipe smoking northerner, a self-proclaimed supporter of Huddersfield Town with traces of a Yorkshire accent. (Seed, 1992)

Wilson represented the newly modernized Labor Party and oversaw a period of comparative stability from his election in 1964 until the Conservative victory of 1970. The 1970s, by way of comparison, were a time of civil unrest: they saw the beginning of British occupation of Northern Ireland, the miners' strikes, the three-day week (to help cope with the fuel shortages), the Winter of Discontent (mass industrial protests, some of which prevented the National Theatre being opened on time), and the deterioration of race relations as outlined in David Edgar's *Destiny* (1976). The beginning of Margaret Thatcher's office in 1979 signaled the death knell for subsidized theater; political theater was stifled through the stripping of subsidy, and the commercial theater of the West End enjoyed a renaissance, thanks to a boom in musicals.

The National Theatre and the Royal Shakespeare Company

The years 1960 to 1980 represent an extraordinary period of activity and diversity within English drama. The success of the English Stage Company at the Royal Court during the 1950s was followed in the next decade by the formation of the National Theatre (NT) company and the transformation of the Shakespeare Memorial Theatre into the Royal Shakespeare Company (RSC). In addition, the men whose artistic vision fueled these government-subsidized centers embarked on an extraordinary round of musical chairs, which ensured the succession of influential posts in the theater resembled the succession to the throne.

In 1960 Peter Hall assumed the directorship of the Shakespeare Memorial Theatre, then persuaded chairman Fordham Flower to change the name to the RSC (effective from 1961), to run down the theater's reserves so that it could become eligible for subsidy, and to lease a theater to form a permanent base in London (first, the Aldwych, then the Barbican). Two years later, Laurence Olivier formed the National Theatre (NT) Company, thus realizing the hope cherished by English theater for over a century, although the company was not to have a permanent decade until well into the 1970s, by which time the NT would be under the directorship of Peter Hall (who took over from Olivier in 1973). Hall, in turn, was succeeded at the RSC by Trevor Nunn, who also became director of the NT in 1997. Meanwhile, Joan Littlewood continued to experiment at the Theatre Workshop, scoring a notable hit with *Oh What a Lovely War!* in 1963 and unwittingly setting a precedent for political protest in plays that would reverberate through the 1960s and 1970s. In addition, the emphasis on the visual demonstrated in *Oh What a Lovely War!* preempted the way in which spectacle would reclaim its place on the English stage during the next decade in the work of Peter Brook and PETER SHAFFER.

The West End and the Subsidized Theater

In spite of the hype that surrounds the New Wave "explosion" of the 1950s, the new theater had very little immediate impact on the commercial sector of English theater, chiefly located in London's West End, however the increase in government subsidy and the formation of the NT and the RSC changed that. The subsidized theater began to challenge the hegemony of the West End, many of its plays transferred to West End theaters, and the companies catered to a new, politically aware audience. A good illustration of this shift is Peter Shaffer's *The Royal Hunt of the Sun* (1964), one of the defining theatrical moments of the 1960s. A believer in "total theater," Shaffer's extraordinarily ambitious play depicts the colonization of the Incas by the Spanish, encompassing battle scenes, sacrifices, torture and mutilation, a procession of gold, and crucially, the climbing of the Andes. Shaffer's earlier play *Five Finger Exercise* (1958) had been a West End hit, and as a result, *The Royal Hunt of the Sun* was initially offered to legendary theatrical impresario Hugh "Binkie" Beaumont. Beaumont refused, allegedly on the grounds that the Andes scene would be too difficult to stage, but he passed the script on to the NT, of which he was a board member. National Theatre associate director John Dexter (formerly of the Royal Court) read the play and recognized that it provided the NT with a golden opportunity to showcase its talents. The play premiered at the Festival Theatre in Chichester before moving to the Old Vic (the NT's base while the South Bank complex was under construction) and was hailed by the critics as: "as close as this imperfect world is ever likely to get to the *Gesamtkunstwerk* of which Richard Wagner dreamed, in which every element, every force that the theatre could provide would fuse in one overwhelming experience" (Elsom, 1981). Shaffer was to repeat this success, again with John Dexter directing, with EQUUS (1973).

At the other end of the artistic spectrum, JOE ORTON was one of the few "new" dramatists to be produced predominantly in the commercial sector. His anarchic FARCES, with their coded references to homosexuality and Winston Churchill's penis (*What the Butler Saw*, 1967) caused a furor along with the "dirty plays" produced by the RSC, but Orton continued to survive in the mainstream and was even commissioned to write a screenplay for the Beatles. Conversely, TOM STOPPARD's career had its roots firmly in the subsidized sector, from the beginnings of his career with ROSENCRANTZ AND GUILDENSTERN ARE DEAD (NT, 1967), *Jumpers* (NT, 1972), and TRAVESTIES (RSC, 1974), up to later works such as ARCADIA (1993) and THE COAST OF UTOPIA (2002).

The Theatres Act of 1968 and the End of Censorship

Arguably the most significant event of this period is the abolition of theater censorship in 1968. The Lord Chamberlain's office examined playscripts for "suitability" and suggested cuts or amendments to be made before a license for performance could be issued. Plays containing scenes of or references to adultery, homosexuality, blasphemy, "invidious" representations of living people, or unflattering references to the monarchy or politicians, swearing, and subject matter likely to jeopardize relations with a foreign power were all subject to censorship. Until 1968 theaters circumvented these restrictions either through ingenious innuendo (for example, Orton) or by staging the plays on a "club" basis, since the Lord Chamberlain had no power to censor private performances. The Lord Chamberlain's power limited theater's ability to present contemporary life and issues, and as such, it came under ferocious assault during the postwar period with its new emphasis on the "kitchen-sink," "ANGRY YOUNG MAN" experience. A number of decisive events led to the government's decision to overturn censorship on the stage, the first of which was the "dirty plays" controversy, followed by the Lord Chamberlain's failure to bring a public prosecution against the Royal Court for *A Patriot for Me*, and culminated in the token fine extracted from the English Stage Company (ESC) for SAVED violating the rules of club performance. In addition, the growth of television in Britain during the 1960s meant that material the Lord Chamberlain could prevent being seen onstage could be broadcast to the nation, once again reinforcing the archaism inherent in this position.

Dirty Plays

As well as new versions of Shakespeare and reviving forgotten classics, Peter Hall had an additional ambition for the RSC—to produce stimulating new work by new writers. Among the first of these was David Rudkin's *Afore Night Come* (RSC, 1962), in which a tramp—an increasingly familiar figure on the English stage since Hall's production of WAITING FOR GODOT (Arts, 1955) and HAROLD PINTER's THE CARETAKER (1960)—is not merely menaced or beaten in his sleep but brutally murdered. Next came Peter Brook's experimental Theater of Cruelty Season featuring PETER WEISS's MARAT/SADE (1964). Weiss was inspired by BERTOLT BRECHT, Brook by ANTONIN ARTAUD, and the fusion of the two provided a landmark piece of theater, violent, sexually explicit, and politically subversive; the play was an affront to the gentility of the well-made play and significantly challenged prevailing assumptions about the style and subject matter of the RSC. In an interview, theater impresario and RSC governor Emile Littler gave voice to this shock and disgust: "These plays do not belong, or should not, to the Royal Shakespeare. They are entirely out of keeping with our public image and with having the Queen as our Patron" (Elsom, 1981). Littler's outrage, however, was not unconnected with his position of impresario: the appearance of large-scale, high-quality productions by subsidized companies was a source of bitterness and concern for the commercial West End who feared that subsidized plays would adversely affect their profits. Peter Brook's next major work for the RSC was US (1966), a critical examination of the Vietnam War and U.S. involvement in it; it highlighted the RSC's commitment to experimental theater regardless of its royal patronage. Ironically, the Theater of Cruelty season convinced one unsuccessfully commercially produced playwright—Harold Pinter—to give his next work to the RSC and, in doing so, unwittingly form a lifelong professional association with Peter Hall. Hall subsequently directed *The Collection* (1962, RSC), THE HOMECOMING (1965), and OLD TIMES (1971) and invited Pinter to be an associate director at the NT when he assumed the post in 1972. Hall continued to direct Pinter's work at the NT, reaching a career high with *No Man's Land* in 1975, featuring the most famous actors on British stage (Olivier excepted), Ralph Richardson and John Gielgud.

A Patriot for Me

Already enshrined in theater history for causing a watershed in British theater with *Look Back in Anger* (1956), John Osborne was to make history again as the author of *A Patriot for Me* (1965) at the Royal Court. The play's depiction of a homosexual sex scene and a transvestites' ball aroused the Lord Chamberlain's ire, as expected. The reader's report commented: "The present text seems to be a perfect example of a piece which might corrupt, since it reveals nearly all the details of the homosexual life usually left blank even in the newspaper reports." To avoid the Lord Chamberlain's restrictions, George Devine turned the Court into a club theater, requesting the audience to sign up in advance and pay a membership fee. The Lord Chamberlain gave an interview in *The Sunday Times* condemning the practice of one-off club theaters, but the performance went ahead anyway, and the director of public prosecutions refused to approve a prosecution. This refusal was to prove a significant turning point in the battle against censorship.

Saved

Shortly after Brook's experiments with the Theater of Cruelty, EDWARD BOND was also following the Artaudian prescription of a "succession of violent stage images" with *Saved*, first performed at the Royal Court in 1965. *Saved* is frequently cited in accounts of postwar British drama because of the torturing and stoning to death of a baby and the indifference with which this act is perpetrated and that also characterized the family's response to it. William Gaskill, the artistic director of the Royal Court, planned to stage the play during his inaugural season; the script was submitted to the Lord Chamberlain's office, who insisted on drastic cuts before a license would be granted. Gaskill, like Devine before him, decided to stage the play as a members-only production and was prosecuted by the Lord Chamberlain for breaching the licensing laws (a member of the Lord Chamberlain's staff was not asked for his membership card). The case ended with a nominal fine, the judiciary's leniency seen as a further indictment of the Lord Chamberlain's archaic role. The prosecution kick-started a concerted campaign against censorship by theater professionals. In 1967 a joint parliamentary committee recommended that it should be abolished, and their recommendations finally became law on September 26, 1968.

New Voices: The 1970s

The end of censorship gave playwrights and directors a new freedom. The anti-authoritarian attitudes that characterized 1960s Britain could now be articulated. Sex, swearing, and less-than-flattering representations of the monarchy, the government, and their political allies became the order of the day as a new generation of predominantly middle- and working-class writers and actors tried to express the contemporary living experience. Along with Pam Gems (*Loving Women, Dusa, Fish Stas and Vi*), CARYL CHURCHILL gave women a significant and sustained voice on the stage for the first time since the Restoration, exploring the boundaries of gender and sexuality in CLOUD NINE (1979) and women's experiences during the civil war in *Light Shining on Buckinghamshire* (1976). David Edgar, DAVID STOREY, and Trevor

Griffiths wrote about the working-class experience in a newly politically aware era and also articulated the gap that left educated children distanced from their less fortunate parents.

The plays of HOWARD BRENTON (contemporary and collaborator of David Hare) epitomize the politically committed zeitgeist of the period. *The Churchill Play* (Nottingham Playhouse 1974), written to commemorate Winston Churchill's centenary, is a typically iconoclastic depiction of the "great man" and his contribution to the country. The play is concerned with the tensions between an idealist and a pragmatist in the Churchill internment camp over the production of a play to be put on for a visiting Parliamentary Select Committee. All the received wisdom about Churchill is questioned during the course of the play. In the opening scene, for example, one of the "guards" around Churchill's coffin refutes the sentiment that Churchill was responsible for an Allied victory in World War II: "People won the War. He just got pissed with Stalin."

In the same year, Brenton was commissioned to write the first new piece of work for performance in the newly built National Theatre complex, and in 1976 *Weapons of Happiness* was first performed in the National Theatre's Lyttleton Theatre, directed by David Hare. The play's appearance demonstrated to the public that the NT was committed to producing new and challenging works, and it demonstrated to the political dramatists that "going mainstream" was not synonymous with "selling out." The play signaled the beginning of Brenton's and, in particular, Hare's long association with the NT, which Brenton famously compared to "an armoured charabanc parked within the National's walls" (Morley, 1976).

Brenton went on to cause even greater controversy when he wrote *The Romans in Britain*, also produced at the NT, directed by Michael Bogdanov. The play parallels the Roman colonization of Britain with the British occupation of Northern Ireland and features a homosexual rape and horrific scenes of torture and violence, as well as overt political commentary on the Troubles. A loophole in the Theatres Act of 1968 allowed Mary Whitehouse, chair of the Viewers and Listeners Association, to prosecute Bogdanov for "procuring an act of gross indecency" under the Sexual Offences Act, despite the fact that she had never seen the play. The case was terminated, but as Shellard (1999) notes, it

> set a potentially disastrous legal precedent. The immunity from prosecution for simulating events that performers held to be sacrosanct was now thrown into doubt, and to this day no one has dared to stage *The Romans in Britain* again for fear that the case might once more be tested.

The fate of *The Romans in Britain* accurately prophesied a bleak future for subsidized theater in Britain in the 1980s.

FURTHER READING

Acheson, James, ed. *British and Irish Drama Since 1960*. London: Macmillan, 1993.

Brook, Peter. *Threads of Time*. London: Methuen, 1999.

Bull, John. *New British Political Dramatists*. London: Macmillan, 1984.

———. *Stage Right*. London: Methuen, 1994.

Elsom, John. *Post-war British Theatre Criticism*. London: Routledge, 1981.

Eyre, Richard, and Nicholas Wright. *Changing Stages*. London: Bloomsbury, 2000.

Hall, Peter. *Peter Hall's Diaries*. London: Hamish Hamilton, 1983.

Innes, Christopher. *Modern British Drama 1890–1980*. Cambridge: Cambridge Univ. Press, 1991.

Morley, Sheridan. "The Man Behind the Lyttleton's First New Play." *The Time*, July 10, 1976.

Seed, John. "Hegemony Postponed: The Unravelling of the Culture Consensus in Britain in the 1960s." In *Cultural Revolution? The Challenge of the Arts in the 1960s*. ed. by Bart Moore-Gilbert and John Seed. London and New York: Routledge, 1992.

Shellard, Dominic. *British Theatre Since the War*. New Haven, Conn.: Yale Univ. Press, 1999.

Kate Dorney

1980–Present

In the wake of the ascent to power of Margaret Thatcher's Conservative Party, the political, historical, and economic changes of the era and corresponding attitudes and consequences became reflected in the dramaturgy, dramatic texts, and theatrical styles of the 1980s and 1990s. For an extended range of British playwrights, theater became a fulcrum for change and reaction.

Enduring Influence of Brecht

BERTOLT BRECHT's epic stagecraft had been brought to the London stage in the 1950s, and it continued to profoundly influence the British theater well into the last decades of the 20th century. Anti-illusionistic paradigms were conceived to convey satire, historical immediacy, and ethical crisis at a universal level. British counterparts to Brecht and his German anti-expressionist stagecraft continued to adapt his principles to the British stage while extending beyond them toward new innovative concepts and productions.

Predominant among the heirs of Brecht have been Christopher Hampton, JOHN ARDEN, EDWARD BOND, David Edgar, HOWARD BRENTON, and DAVID HARE. Brecht himself appears as a character in Hampton's 1982 play and 1983 film *Tales from Hollywood*, based on Hampton's own fictionalized historical vision in which he imagines the Viennese writer ÖDÖN VON HORVÁTH to have survived the 1938 accident that killed him in Paris before he could depart from war-threatened Europe for the United States to join other German writers in exile in Hollywood.

The 1982 production *Little Gray Home in the West* was a revival of *Ballygombeen Bequest* (1972) by John Arden and his collaborator Margaretta D'Arcy, Marxist playwrights who had brought to English theater of the 1950s, 1960s, and 1970s proletarian anti-illusionistic political satire frequently compared to Brecht's. The radicalization of British theater begun with AGITATION-PROPAGANDA (agit-prop) found particular advancement in Arden's rejection of naturalistic conventional dramaturgy and his ideological view through art of history and the world.

Edward Bond adapted Brecht's techniques of political drama to the British stage for both National Theatre and left-wing fringe companies. Although far less present in British theater after the late 1970s, Bond's writing has become tremendously respected and popular in continental Europe. In Britain there have been occasional productions of his plays, such as the 1995 Young Vic revival of his 1973 classic *Bingo* about the moral blindness of Shakespeare and the complicity of artists in social injustice. The 1981 production *Restoration* was a melodramatic musical parody of traditional Restoration COMEDY and the perpetuation of oppressive class systems. *War Plays*, produced in 1985, portrayed the destruction of the world by an atomic explosion as justifiable revolutionary violence. Bond's drama is intellectual, didactic, and violent.

The Next Generation

Leading British playwrights of the next generation were HOWARD BARKER, JOHN MCGRATH, David Edgar, Howard Brenton, David Hare, Trevor Griffiths, and Peter Barnes. Departing from the direct topical, episodic caricatures and dramas of agit-prop, Barker moved on to develop a form of psychological allegory. McGrath stayed with agit-prop and wrote plays incorporating music hall cabaret technique. Edgar, however, created a new form of theatrical social REALISM by combining the forces of the personal and subjective with the ideological, objective, and historical to create a new, epic form of social realism. This method allowed a panoramic focus and narrative format, which was used by Edgar in his eight-hour adaptation of Charles Dickens's *Nicholas Nickleby* (1980); in his play about the cholera epidemic of 1854, *Entertaining Strangers* (1986); and in his political drama *Maydays* (1983), the story of ideological moves to the right of characters in the period from the post–World War II years to the early 1980s. *Pentecost* (1994), first produced in 1994 by the Royal Shakespeare Company, was about the slow uncovering of myth in a collaborative effort of comprehension, despite the tragic resolution of a hostage crisis.

Naturalistic violence and the promise of utopia characterize many of Brenton's political dramas, beginning with *Weapons of Happiness* (1976) and continuing in his major plays of the 1980s, *The Romans in Britain* (1980) and his *Utopia Trilogy*, composed of *Thirteenth Night* (1981), *Bloody Poetry* (1984), and *Greenland* (1988). In *Bloody Poetry*, parallels are drawn between the moral vacuum and alienation of artists during the conservative era of Thatcherism in Britain and events of the early 19th century. First presented at the Haymarket Theatre in 1984, *Bloody Poetry* was revived at the Royal Court Theatre in 1988 under the direction of Max Stafford Clark.

Hare and Brenton have worked as collaborators on a number of plays, including *Pravda* (1985), a satire on Australian American tycoon Rupert Murdoch's Fleet Street makeover. Both bring to their work a belief in utopianism, but Hare's plays have a more profound historical orientation. Several of Hare's dramas center on a female who is destroyed and who incarnates values discarded by the right-wing materialists and opportunists around her. The moral vacuum in the Thatcher era that Hare points to is most clearly illustrated in his 1989 play *Secret Rapture* and in *Amy's View*, presented in the Royal National Theatre's production at Lyttleton Theatre in 1997. A socialist, Sussex-raised writer educated in and influenced by the tradition of Brechtian stagecraft, Hare presents the moral dilemma imposed by the conservatism and opportunism of the Thatcher era. He underlines the fundamental inability of his own generation to counter the loss of values in modern-day Britain. His other works include a "Trilogy" composed of three political dramas, *Racing Demon* (1990), *Murmuring Judges* (1991), and *The Absence of War* (1993), and four later dramas, *Skylight* (2000), *The Judas Kiss* (1997), *The Blue Room* (1998), and *Via Dolorosa* (1990).

Comic Theater

During the period 1980–2000, comic theater became increasingly symbolic and psychological and less dominated by political satire. Yet the powerful theater of HAROLD PINTER, begun in the 1950s and 1960s, continued to be featured, linked to absurdist theater by a refusal of developed, logical characterization. Pinter portrayed diverse examples of domination and subjugation, as in THE HOMECOMING (1964) and THE BIRTHDAY PARTY (1958), respectively. His satires of the 1980s and 1990s are, however, more overtly political. The plots of his comic satires of the later 1980s identify and isolate more definitively the opposing forces of dictatorship and subjugated victims. In both *Mountain Language* (1988) and *On the Road* (1984), he explicitly polarizes his characters; those commanding authority and power enjoy omnipotence in their use of language, while the disempowered victims have no effective, logical, or coherent discourse.

The plays of both Trevor Griffiths and Peter Barnes bear the influence of JOE ORTON's comedy. Like Orton, Griffiths and Barnes use comedy as an instrument of class antagonism, but for them comedy becomes also a tool of political change. Orton's use of shock and grotesque FARCE and his one-dimensional, self-seeking characters influence much of Griffiths's and Barnes's theater. The central thesis in all of Barnes's work, including the later plays of the 1980s and 1990s, is that tradition, conventional morality, and authority are sources of loss and suffering. In his parody *Red Noses* (1985), set in the Middle Ages in the historical context of the Black Death, workers vainly attempt to trigger revolutionary change. In his 1990 play *Sunsets and Glories*, Barnes portrays the tragedy of the reclusive hermit Celestine, who becomes pope but, because of his incorruptibility, is removed from power and assassinated, only to be canonized years later. Griffiths's comedies are political satires; Marxist tactical debates; and objective, with irony and self-criticism. Often, as in *Bill Brand*

(1976), they target revolutionary theoreticians themselves. Griffiths's debate on comedy and the production of a bingo club presentation in *The Comedians* (1975), as a play within a play, were major influences on the development of British comedy.

In their revival of popular comedy and traditional comic theater, ALAN AYCKBOURN and MICHAEL FRAYN turned away from didacticism, political ideology, and radicalism. In Ayckbourn's and Frayn's drama, farce is a means of underlining the coldness of modern conventional society and its inability to relate to individual unhappiness. Ayckbourn's plays offer tart commentary on customs and behavior in modern-day society. His dialogue is reminiscent of NOËL COWARD's witty verbal exchanges. Ayckbourn's comedies take place during gatherings of family and friends; revelry is superficial, disrupted by predicaments in which main characters are driven by eccentric, obsessive behavior. Frayn's comedies portray the functioning of groups in a commercial, artistic environment as a microcosm of modern society. His comedy is frequently based on momentary liberation from the constraints and limitations of the structures that contain us. *Noises Off* (1982), Frayn's popular success of the early 1980s, juxtaposed the theatrical performance of a popular farce and the backstage drama of actors, director, and stage manager. The interplay and eventual confusion of activity on- and offstage reveal character and conflict among the actors and presenters of the theatrical play within a play.

The fresh, irreverent style of TOM STOPPARD—avowedly a political centrist—infused British comedy with a new strength. His dramas center on metaphysical and philosophic issues, comically presented with very physically overt and farcical theatrics. His style is characterized by verbal wit, visual spectacle, and farce. The discussion among spies of the theory of light in the 1988 drama *Hapgood* resembles Lord Richard Attenborough's juxtaposition of Albert Einstein and chorus girls and is a device typical of Stoppard's theater. In his plays of the 1980s, Stoppard continued to dramatize themes presented in his 1966 play ROSENCRANTZ AND GUILDENSTERN ARE DEAD: the nature of drama itself and the idea that art can be effective only obliquely. His 1984 THE REAL THING is a play within a play. Role-playing and sexual deception unravel in a complex story of adultery acted out by actors both within and outside the context of the drama they are preparing for performance. Stoppard here draws on the inner and outer parallel playing characteristic of LUIGI PIRANDELLO's drama.

THEATER COMES TO FILM

An important development of the last two decades of 20th-century theatrical history was the now well-established practice of adapting theater plays as film screenplays or television drama. Among the effective and successful writers of television drama or of stage plays later adapted for television or even cinema are Morwenna Banks, ALAN BENNETT, Alan Bleasdale, Dennis Potter, Shelagh Stephenson, and Simon Gray. A notable figure in British comic theater is Bennett, one of the collaborators on *Beyond the Fringe*, a satirical British television comedy of the early 1960s. Bennett's subjects are the banal preoccupations of the lower middle class: seaside holidays, personal and class obsessions, prejudice, and sexual repression. His work includes aesthetic, fictionalized historical dramas such as his two satires on Franz Kafka, *Kafka's Dick* (1987) and *The Insurance Man* (1987), and his short comedy *An Englishman Abroad* (1983), based on the British actress Coral Browne's visit in Moscow in the 1950s to the condemned, exiled British spy Guy Burgess. Particularly critical of the convenience of such socially sanctioned confinement is the stage play THE MADNESS OF GEORGE III (1991), first presented at the National Theatre and later adapted for a movie screenplay.

Although Bennett also writes for radio as well as for the stage, he is primarily recognized for his numerous plays for television. Among the most famous of these is the televised dramatic monologue series TALKING HEADS, featuring individuals who speak to the audience as they would to themselves, thereby subtly revealing personal crises, transitions, or self-perpetuating individual tragedies. Other well-known and popular dramas include Bennett's *A Question of Attribution* (1991), from his own 1989 play; Howard Schuman's *Selling Hitler* (1991), from the book by Robert Harris; and most notably, the 1987 television series *Fortunes of War*, adapted by Alan Plater from novels by Olivia Manning, starring Emma Thompson and Kenneth Branagh.

Simon Gray, author of many television plays and novels, is best known for his 1981 television drama based on his play *Quartermaine's Terms* (1981), which depicts a schoolteacher's naïveté and humanity as he reacts to the problems of his colleagues in a 1960s school for foreigners learning English. He is eventually fired. Gray's drama responds to the greater emphasis placed at the beginning of the Thatcher era on success and financial drive. Alan Bleasdale, another well-known writer of television plays, contributed an unforgettable 1982 BBC series called *The Boys from the Blackstuff*. Set in Liverpool, it presented a series of episodes portraying individual family struggles as workers are forced into unemployment and subsistence on national benefits while employers will, illegally, hire them only for occasional limited periods. It was a powerful statement against the economic devastation of working-class communities during the Thatcher era. David Hare's *Absence of War* (1993), later a play for BBC television, treated the rise and fall in the early 1990s of a Labour Party leader preparing himself and his party to accede to power. It is constructive nostalgia for the past; its annoyed subject, Labour Party leader Neil Kinnock, suggested, despite his having given Hare collaborative access, a lost sense of commitment and spirit.

Poetic drama was developed in the theater of PETER SHAFFER, ANN JELLICOE, David Rudkin, and Irishman SAMUEL BECKETT. Themes of betrayed idealism, the individual versus society, and nonconformist individualism dominate Shaffer's staged and filmed dramas. The existential struggle of the individual to confront, possess, and displace a divinity or divinely endowed power is central to his later work. Shaffer's poetic drama is accompanied by visual color, pageantry, and costume. In *Yonadab* (1985) gestures, visuals, and other nonverbal elements communicate in depth his thesis of irrational belief and its negation. His less successful 1982 production *Shrivings* depended on dialogue and rhetorical verbal argument. The plays of David Rudkin bear the influence of AVANT-GARDE DRAMA and, most particularly, ANTONIN ARTAUD's Theater of Cruelty. Rudkin's theater of the 1980s is epitomized by his early 1981 production *The Triumph of Death*, set in the medieval period, with graphic scenes of violence, sexual identity changes, and inversion of the symbolic moral representations of good and evil in the form of satanic and godlike characters.

Samuel Beckett's theater has been considered a continuation of SYMBOLISM in British poetic drama, influenced by W. B. YEATS's spiritual drama and abstract minimalism as well as the latter's common use of tramps and beggars as protagonists. Beckett's drama, however, is really part of continental theatrical tradition, with deep imprints of the French existentialist movement of the 1950s and 1960s, of SURREALISM, and of Artaud's Theater of Cruelty. Some of Beckett's later works were political statements. *Catastrophe* (1982) criticized VÁCLAV HAVEL's internment. *What Where* (1983) concentrates on the question of torture and a totalitarian state. Beckett uses more movement in his 1981 *Rockaby* or 1980 *Ohio Impromptu*, but characters still move rigidly so as to discourage our perception of any sense of mobility. Perspectives are contradicted by a reversal of opposing images and motions, leaving the audience with the negative view that the images of life are so contradictory that they isolate themselves and cannot be expressed.

FEMALE DRAMATISTS

During the late 1970s and the following two decades, British theater became far more inclusive. Female dramatists took a prominent role in theater, and a great number of regional, multiethnic, and lesbian and gay theater groups were established. New forms of cultural creativity gave voice to formerly silent sections of society. During the years following the 1968 French, German, and British student revolts, in the course of the development of radical, regional, and working-class theater, the common interests of writer, actor, and spectator brought about the development of alternative theater, wherein rising female, nonwhite, and nonheterosexual playwrights nurtured new creative dramatic forms and approaches to modern theater. In addition to the well-known playwright, director, and producer Ann Jellicoe, and top playwrights such as CARYL CHURCHILL, other women associated with the Women's Theatre Group rose to fame. In the late 1980s, however, funding was transferred from the national government to the regions, resulting in funding cuts and fewer theater groups. It is also important to note the restrictive effect on theater of acceptance of the Thatcher government's legislated Clause 78, which limited discussion of homosexuality in the arts and in education.

Playwright Pam Gems's work in the 1970s and, most particularly, in the 1980s portrays the puzzling reduction of women to cultural representations. In Gems's *Camille* (1984), based on Alexandre Dumas's story *The Lady with the Camellias* (*La Dame aux camélias*), Marguerite and Armand become symbols of innocence and sexual exploitation. *Loving Women* (1984) reflects the oppressive Thatcher era and the loss of traditional morality. A formerly idealistic activist gives up his principles, rejects his feminist activist lover, and marries a physically appealing conformist housewife. His former lover pursues a life of political commitment and idealism. As years pass, however, they seek to resume their former shared life of activism.

The 1980s saw the rise of a new generation of female playwrights. Women's theater changed to a more narrative, true-to-life form of storytelling and to a less direct performance-based theater. Female playwrights became more concerned with portrayal of relationships between women. Playwrights such as Charlotte Keatley, Sarah Daniels, Claire McIntyre, Timberlake Wertenbaker, Jackie Kay, Winsome Pinnock, and Deborah Levy became known through productions by women's collectives and new, small-scale theater companies. Among the most important and long-lasting successes of British women's theater are the plays of Charlotte Keatley, recipient of the Laurence Olivier Most Promising Newcomer Award for her 1990 play *My Mother Said I Never Should* (1987). Keatley concerns herself deeply with mother-daughter relationships among working-class women and with crises demonstrating the strength of working women and uneducated housewives of the lower classes. Sarah Daniels introduces a fresh, new, sharply satirical and humorous treatment of serious social issues, including pornography, reproductive and lesbian rights, incest, madness, and the inequities imposed on working-class women. She is author of the first lesbian play presented by the Royal National Theatre, *Neaptide* (1986). Her work also includes such well-known plays as *Masterpieces* (1983), *The Devil's Gateway* (1983), and *The Madness of Esme and Shaz*. The latter was produced at the Royal Court Theatre Upstairs in 1994. The Royal Shakespeare Company's sponsorship of the Women's Project brought about presentation of the work of other rising young women British dramatists, such as Deborah Levy (*Heresies*, 1986). More female playwrights, such as Caryl Churchill (THE SKRIKER, 1994), were recognized as regular contributors to mainstream theater.

The Women's Playhouse Trust was established by producer and director Jules Wright to give inclusion to both women and men in Britain's mainstream theater. It gave a base for professional development for women in the areas of playwriting, directing, costuming, composing, and choreography as well as in technical aspects of theater. The Magdalena Project, an international organization of women's theater artists, was established in 1986 by Jill Greenhalgh and Susan Bassnett. It represents a women's cross-cultural, cross-generational collaborative theater that has turned away from academic, formal traditions. In the theater of the 1990s, a more intense combination of mediums (theater, mime, and dance) was strongly supported by subsidies and funding. New alternative women's theater groups developed, including the women's writing workshops at the Drill Hall, the Place, and the Oval House theaters. British women's theater was further developed by an influx of European writers' productions, such as the Sphinx theater's production of HÉLÈNE CIXOUS's work.

New black theater companies of the 1970s and 1980s included Carib, Temba, and the Black Theatre Co-operative (presently called Nitro). Temba presented new plays, such as *Back Street Mammy* (1989), by Trish Cooke, portraying adolescent pregnancy, and Barbara Gloudon's *The Pirate Princess* (1981), with Jamaican pantomime. Yvonne Brewster directed a number of successful productions, including WOLE SOYINKA's *The Road* (1965), NTOZAKE SHANGE's *The Love Space Demands* (1991), DEREK WALCOTT's *Ti-Jean and His Brothers* (1958), and FREDERICO GARCÍA LORCA's BLOOD WEDDING (1932). Black women's theater in Britain began to achieve recognition in the mid-1980s with the establishment of Talawa Theatre, founded in 1985 by Yvonne Brewster, Mona Hammond, and Carmen Munroe. The company is known for many productions, including C. L. R. James's *The Black Jacobins* (1986), about the first Haitian revolution. Important contemporary black female playwrights include Jackie Kay, Winsome Pinnock, and MARIA OSHODI. Black women's theater has also been developed by the Theatre of Black Women, the first black women's theater company in Great Britain, formed in 1982 by Bernardine Evaristo, Paulette Randall, and Patricia St. Hilaire. Among its major productions were Ruth Harris's *The Cripple* (1987) and *Miss Quashie and the Tiger's Tail* (1987). The Black Mime Theatre Women's Troupe was begun by its director, Denise Wong, in 1984. Its productions have included *Mother* (1990), *Total Rethink* (1991), and *Drowning* (1991).

Although there is still only a limited Asian drama in Britain, modern British Indian drama has been developed by Tamasha, a theater company founded in 1989 by Kristine Landon-Smith and Sudha Bhuchar. Their major productions have included Ruth Carter's *Women of the Dust* (1993), Bhuchar's *House of the Sun* (1991), and Landon-Smith's *Untouchable* (1989). *Women of the Dust* was a study of the poor in INDIA integrating music and comedy. The most successful of British Asian touring theater companies, Tamasha runs an education program alongside each of its productions. Its pilot program TIME (Tamasha Intercultural Millennium Education Development) began as a professional development program for secondary-school drama teachers and later expanded its efforts to include students. Among rising new British Asian writers of plays, Yasmin Khan, Ravi Mangat, and Ashok Patel are the most important. Zadie Smith's multicultural London novel *White Teeth* (2000) was adapted as a television screenplay at the end of the 1990s.

FUTURE DIRECTIONS

The most notable and successful contemporary plays suggest the future direction of British theater in the new millennium. Among these are TOP GIRLS (1982), by Caryl Churchill, a portrayal of powerful women and the shadows of abuse and patriarchy marking their experience; *Hysteria* (1995), by Terry Johnson, a comic but carefully documented and shocking portrayal of Sigmund Freud and his published recantation of his analysis of female hysteria; BLASTED (1993), an audacious statement on social and individual violence and abuse by SARAH KANE; *Shopping and F**king* (1996), by MARK RAVENHILL, a black humor satire on the devaluation of human life and relationships in a consumer-driven world from the gay male perspective; *The Beauty Queen of Leenane* (1996), by London-born Irish playwright MARTIN MCDONAGH, a story demythologizing the Irish experiences of family, success, and exile; *A Hero's Welcome* (1989), by Winsome Pinnock, a portrayal of West Indian poverty and the consequential move toward immigration to Great Britain; *Monsoon* (1991), by Maya Chowdhry, a black lesbian love story scripted for film; and *Leonora's Dance* (1992), by Zindika, the story of a house of black women emigrants and their ghosts, of various generations and backgrounds, who dispossess and support each other in a continuum of dreams, poverty, and rich pagan spirituality. These fine plays represent a progressive spirit of inclusion and cultural and historical reconciliation that moves past trends forward and gives hope for the continued development of British theater.

FURTHER READING

Eyre, Richard, and Nicholas Wright. *Changing Stages: A View of British Theatre in the Twentieth Century*. London: Bloomsbury, 2001.

Godiwala, Dimple. *Breaking the Bounds: British Feminist Dramatists Writing in the Mainstream Since c. 1980*. American University Studies. Series 26, Theatre Arts. Vol. 31. New York: Peter Lang, 2003.

Patterson, Michael. *Strategies of Political Theatre: Post-War British Playwrights*. Cambridge: Cambridge Univ. Press, 2003.

Peacock, Keith. *Thatcher's Theatre: British Theatre and Drama in the Eighties*. Westport, Conn.: Greenwood Press, 1999.

Sierz, Aleks. *In-Yer-Face Theatre: British Drama Today*. London: Faber, 2001.

Trussler, Simon. *The Cambridge Illustrated History of British Theatre*. Cambridge: Cambridge Univ. Press, 2000.

Betty L. McLane-Iles and Lawrence I. Iles

EN NO GYÔJA See EN THE ASCETIC

ENQUIST, PER OLOV (1934–)

There is a literary term called "deconstruction"—propounding that it is in the tension between different interpretative levels that a piece of art comes alive. Not on any particular level pointed out by anyone. Not in a final secret revealed by a scholar, but in a field of tension.

—Per Olov Enquist, 1998

Swedish novelist, playwright, scriptwriter, and critic Per Olov Enquist was born in 1934 and brought up in a strict Lutheran environment in the far north of SWEDEN; he briefly studied at the University of Uppsala. His breakthrough as a novelist came in 1964 with *The Magnetist's Fifth Winter* (*Magnetisörens femte vinter*). Among his other novels, *The Royal Physician's Visit* (*Livläkarens besök*, 1999) has received international acclaim.

After the enormous success of his first play, THE NIGHT OF THE TRIBADES (*Tribadernas natt*), in 1975, he has divided his time between writing novels and plays. He has also written scripts for a television series about AUGUST STRINDBERG (1984) and for a film about KNUT HAMSUN (1996). Socially and politically committed, he leans toward documentary fiction. As one of the foremost writers of Sweden, he has been widely translated and performed.

After the somewhat less successful *To Phaedra* (*Till Fedra*, 1980), relating to Euripides and Racine and written in blank verse, Enquist returned to fiction in *Rain Snakes* (*Från regnormarnas liv*, 1981), subtitled "A Family Portrait from 1856." Here we meet some of the leading cultural figures in Copenhagen of that time: Johan Ludvig Heiberg, recently resigned as head of the Royal Danish Theater; his wife, the celebrated actress Johanne Luise Heiberg; and the famous writer Hans Christian Andersen. Together with the two previous dramas, *Rain Snakes* forms *A Triptych*, revealing the split between private and public lives, between domestic life and life in the limelight.

With *The Image Makers* (*Bildmakarna*, 1998) Enquist launched a play of considerable interest, not least to INGMAR BERGMAN, who has personally met the persons corresponding to the four figures in the play and who directed both the first performance at the Royal Dramatic Theater and the television presentation following it. True to Enquist's semidocumentary manner of writing, the piece describes the fictive meeting between four famous persons: the writer and Nobel Prize winner Selma Lagerlöf, the pioneering film director Victor Sjöström, the equally pioneering film photographer Julius Jaenzon, and the outstanding actress Tora Teje. Or in Enquist's words: "There are four faces on stage: an author, an actor, a director, and a photographer. They penetrate a work [Sjöström's film *The Phantom Carriage* (*Körkarlen*), based on Selma Lagerlöf's novel by the same title] from different directions, their individual vantage points are seemingly very different, but their faces often seem to merge (Åhlund, 1998). The setting is the screening room of a film laboratory in Stockholm in 1920. The four characters meet here because the director wishes to have the author approve the film he is making. As is natural, each of the four characters fights for his or her own form of presentation. Tora dreams of great roles. Julius tries to convince Selma of the importance of film photography. Victor is aware that he is a pioneer in a new art form and will be recognized as such by posterity. Selma, representing a long-canonized genre, can afford to be more modest than these three. In a postscript attached to the theater program, Enquist develops the idea underlying his play that all Lagerlöf's writings stem from a sense of guilt toward her alcoholic father, a need to cover up his misery. Family members who are in such circumstances, psychologists have discovered, tend to become "co-dependent," to use Enquist's term. Like the alcoholics themselves, they establish a pattern of concealment. Lagerlöf's fictional work, Enquist argues, is such a concealment. But in *The Phantom Carriage* she is closer to the truth than elsewhere.

Enquist's fictive portraits of Strindberg, the Heibergs, Lagerlöf, and so on, have all given rise to protests in certain quarters. The real-life figures, it is rightly claimed, were rather different from Enquist's fictive counterparts. To the author this is no valid argument. Feeling free to make the renowned historical figures function meaningfully in their fictive contexts, he presents them as, basically, representative men and women—also for our time.

PLAYS: *The Night of the Tribades* (*Tribadernas natt*, 1975); *Together* (*Chez nous*, with Anders Ehnmark, 1976); *To Phaedra* (*Till Fedra*, 1980); *Rain Snakes* (*Från regnormarnas liv*, 1981); *The Hour of the Lynx* (*I lodjurets timma*, 1988); *Magic Circle* (*Magisk cirkel*, 1994); *Tupilak* (1994); *The Image Makers* (*Bildmakarna*, 1998)

FURTHER READING

Åhlund, Jannike. "P.O. Enquist: The Words in Bergman's Faces," *Dramat* [English Issue] 1998.

Moberg, Verne. "Walking in Strindberg's Footsteps." In *Niet alleen Strindberg: Zweden op de planken / Not Only Strindberg: Sweden on Stage*, ed. by Egil Törnqvist and Arthur Sonnen. Amsterdam: Holland Festival, 1985. 34–36.

Shideler, Ross. *Per Olov Enquist: A Critical Study*. Westport, Conn.: Greenwood Press, 1984.

Syréhn, Gunnar. *Mellan sanningen och lögnen: Studier i Per Olov Enquists dramatik* [Between truth and lies: Studies of Per Olov Enquist's plays]. Stockholm: Almqvist & Wiksell Intl., 2000 [English summary, 185–204].

Egil Törnqvist

ENRICO IV

Enrico IV, a drama in three acts by LUIGI PIRANDELLO, written in the fall of 1921, premiered in Milan, ITALY, at the Manzoni Theater, on February 24, 1922, and was published in 1922. Less than a year after the success of SIX CHARACTERS IN SEARCH OF AN AUTHOR, Pirandello confirmed his international renown with a work that dissects the problematic relationships between fiction and reality, lucidity and craziness. Life, says Pirandello, makes individuals wear real and metaphorical masks that, in turn, make them captives of fixed representational paradigms held by others. Masks are the only solution to live.

Enrico IV, the protagonist, embodies this paradigm. In modern-day Italy, Marquis Di Nolli promises his mother to help cure her brother, known only as Enrico IV. Readers find out that twenty years before, during a horse-riding masquerade in historical costumes, Enrico IV fell from his horse and hit his head. When he awoke, he believed he was the character he was impersonating: Enrico IV, the 11th-century Holy Roman Emperor. From that moment, with the help of Di Nolli's wealthy mother, visitors to Enrico IV's villa (turned into a mock imperial palace) wear accurate historical clothing, impersonate historical figures, and honor him as Emperor. At the doctor's suggestion and with the help of Marchioness Matilde Spina, her lover Belcredi, and her daughter Frida, Di Nolli plans to shock Enrico IV into reality. At the original horse-riding event, Enrico IV dressed as the Emperor because Matilde Spina, whom he loved, was impersonating Matilde di Toscana. According to the doctor's plan, both Matilde and Frida will dress as Matilde di Toscana (the 11th-century Marchioness to whose castle in Canossa the Emperor went in 1077), and the age discrepancy between them will trigger Enrico IV's recovery. Unbeknown to them all, Enrico IV had recuperated twelve years after the accident and chose to continue playing the role of Emperor. On the day of Matilde di Toscana's enactment, the same day of the revelation of Enrico IV's sanity, he approaches Frida, his "young Matilde," and seizes her. In the ensuing bustle that Belcredi (who may have caused the horse-riding accident) and the others put up to free Frida, Enrico IV kills Belcredi. Enrico IV realizes he has no choice but to remain fettered to his mask of Emperor forever.

Pirandello's representation of fiction as madness, and reality as a fiction of madness, reasserts the vague borders between reality and fiction, normality and abnormality. With *Enrico IV* Pirandello also probes the moral responsibilities human beings bear in dealing with a life they have not chosen to live. The killing of Belcredi is less a vendetta against a rival than the elimination of a corrupted double who lived a life Enrico IV was not allowed to and consequently resolved not to. In this sense the drama is not real because the killing is the act of a fool (already considered such before the accident) perpetrating the comedy its hero willingly kept alive in order to escape a life-experience gap (the twelve years elapsed from his accident to his return to reason). The drama takes place in the protagonist's crushing realization of his lost youth portrayed by his seizure of Frida, an act of reappropriation out of regret for the life he has lost and his friends have lived without him. *Enrico IV* is marked by autobiographical references (Pirandello's wife's long journey into madness that ended in 1919 with confinement in an asylum; references to the Emperor studying in Bonn, as Pirandello did) that complete the catharsis of Pirandello's art: writing becomes life; episodes of his life become writing. *Enrico IV* represents Pirandello's separation from his wife and a melancholic realization of the harshness of time gone by. Pirandello utilizes a noble and austere tone that reflects on the dangers of a life that if not lived in the present can have neither a past nor a future.

To avoid confusion with William Shakespeare's *Henry IV*, *Enrico IV* was first performed in New York at the Fulton Theater on January 21, 1924, as *The Living Mask*; it was later titled *Henry IV* and *The Emperor*. Along with *Six Characters in Search of an Author*, *Enrico IV* is the play that enjoyed the most success and afforded Pirandello celebrity status. Its first English translation is *Henry IV*, by Edward Storer.

[*See also* Theatricality]

FURTHER READING

Mazzaro, Jerome. "Memory and Madness in Pirandello's Enrico IV." *Comparative Drama*, no. 26 (Spring 1992): 34–57.

Pirandello, Luigi. *Henry IV*. Tr. by Edward Storer. In *Three Plays by Luigi Pirandello*, ed. by Arthur Livingston. New York: Dutton, 1922.

Vitti-Alexander, Maria Rosaria. "Madness as Mask: Themes and Variations in Enrico IV." *PSA: The Official Publication of the Pirandello Society of America*, no. 5 (1989): 6–15.

Stefano Giannini

ENRIGHT, NICK (1950–2003)

Nick Enright, born in Newcastle, New South Wales, AUSTRALIA, was one of the most prolific and influential contributors to the Australian theater for three decades. He worked as an actor, director, playwright, film writer, adaptor, translator, lyricist, and dramaturg for many different theater companies and taught at (as well as writing plays especially for) major training institutions. In all, he wrote more than thirty theater works, half of which have enjoyed multiple revivals and major tours.

The variety of his output reveals his extraordinary versatility as a writer. His best-known music theater pieces include the frequently revived *Venetian Twins* (produced 1979), adapted from Goldoni with composer Terence Clarke in a highly idiosyncratically Australian vernacular style but with sure mastery of classical farce; and *The Boy from Oz* (produced 1998), based on the life and songs of expatriate Australian singer-songwriter Peter Allen. Translations include Molière's *Don Juan* (1984) and Pierre Augustin Caron de Beaumarchais's *Figaro* (produced 1983), while other adaptations include Australian novelist Tim Winton's epic tale of suburban family life, *Cloudstreet* (with Justin Monjo), which has enjoyed huge national and international success, touring since its premiere in 1998. One of his finest plays for young people is *A Property of the Clan* (produced 1992), based on the actual rape and murder of a teenage girl some years earlier. This play was later rewritten for adult audiences as *Blackrock* (1996) and subsequently filmed.

His plays range widely in style and theme. Light, satirical COMEDY is exemplified in the enormously popular *Daylight Saving* (produced 1990), a very funny but at times poignant play about a trendy Sydney family. Enright's treatment of the complexity of their tangled lives is strongly reminiscent of the FARCE he had encountered in his earlier adaptations of Goldoni and others. He also tackled historical subjects in *On the Wallaby* (1980), portraying rural battlers during the Great Depression, and *The Voyage of Mary Bryant* (produced 1998), dealing with the daring attempt to escape from the penal colony of New South Wales by a convict woman. Also portraying real-life characters is *Mongrels* (1991), whose central characters are based on Australian playwrights Peter Kenna and Jim McNeil. This is widely regarded as one of Enright's best and most mature plays in its deeply disturbing examination of the rivalry and friendship between the two writers and in its exploration of Irish Catholicism in Australia. He later turned to examinations of aspects of his own upbringing as a Catholic in *St. James Infirmary* (produced 1992) and *Good Works* (1994); these are not autobiographical plays as such, but the struggle of an artistic sensibility to flourish in the face of stultifying family and societal attitudes rings true.

Enright has also written successfully for radio, television, and film, most notably *Lorenzo's Oil* with film director George Miller. He won the New South Wales Premier's Literary Award for Drama in 1982 with the musical *Variations* and the Australian Writers' Guild Gold awards for *Daylight Saving* in 1990 and for *A Property of the Clan* in 1993.

SELECT PLAYS: *Venetian Twins* (1979, with Terence Clarke); *On the Wallaby* (1980); *Figaro* (1983); *Don Juan* (1984); *Carnival of the Animals* (1989); *Daylight Saving* (1990); *Mongrels* (1991); *A Property of the Clan* (1992); *St. James Infirmary* (1992); *Good Works* (1994); *Blackrock* (1996); *Playgrounds* (1996); *The Boy from Oz* (1998); *Cloudstreet* (with Justin Monjo, 1998); *The Voyage of Mary Bryant* (1998); *Man with Five Children* (2002)

FURTHER READING

Brisbane, Katharine. "Close Associations." In *Mongrels*, by Nick Enright. Sydney: Currency Press, 1994.

Kelly, Veronica. "A Form of Music—An interview with Nick Enright." *Australasian Drama Studies* 24 (April 1994).

——. "Nick Enright." In *Companion to Theatre in Australia*, ed. by Philip Parsons and Victoria Chance. Sydney: Currency Press, 1995.

Geoffrey Milne

ENSLER, EVE (1953–)

I am not sure why I was chosen. I didn't, for example, have girlhood fantasies about becoming "vagina lady" (which I am often called, sometimes loudly across a crowded shoe store).

—Eve Ensler, 2001

Eve Ensler is a playwright whose use of theater as a political tool has highlighted and perhaps even outweighed her influence as a dramatist. Born on May 25, 1953, in New York City, and raised in Scarsdale, New York, the child of a physically and sexually abusive father, her dedication to stopping violence in the lives of women can be seen as a direct result of her upbringing. Ensler received her bachelor of arts degree from Middlebury College in the mid-1970s and made her theatrical debut in 1983 with a production of *When I Call My Voices*. This was soon followed by *The Depot* in 1986 and *Cinderella/Cendrillon* in 1989.

In the early 1990s Ensler became increasingly prolific, with *Floating Rhoda and the Glue Man* (1993), *Lemonade* (1995), and *Extraordinary Measures* (1995). The surrealistic *Lemonade* follows the identity shifts of Alice, who finds and fiercely protects Bernard, a man who has mysteriously shown up in her kitchen with no memory of his previous life; the play ultimately questions how we know the people we love. *Extraordinary Measures* focuses on the relationship between Paul and an entourage of mourners in the days leading to his death from AIDS, and reflects Ensler's interest in sexuality and politics that would fully emerge in her ensuing work.

Ensler's most well known play, *The Vagina Monologues*, was completed in 1995 and ran OFF-BROADWAY at the Eastside Theatre for over three years, as well as in London's West End; by 2003 it had been produced nationally and internationally in over 800 cities. Based on Ensler's interviews with scores of different women, the play is composed of diverse monologues about the characters' most intimate parts and experiences, shaped by Ensler's galvanizing questions, such as, "If your vagina got dressed, what would it wear?" The play veers between humor, bodily affirmation, and a political critique of genital mutilation and rape. There was criticism about Ensler's claim to authorship of this collection of monologues. Nonetheless, the play garnered an Obie Award, received a Drama Desk nomination, was broadcast on HBO television in 2001, and was published in 1988 with an introduction by Gloria Steinem. The play also provided the impetus for V-Day, a global movement to stop violence against women and girls, which Ensler founded with activists from the organization Feminist.com.

Ensler's *Necessary Targets* (2001), chronicling the story of two U.S. women meeting survivors in a Bosnian refugee camp, was performed in Sarajevo with Glenn Close and Marisa Tomei. While written in a didactic form, the play was an important continuation of Ensler's earlier work. Later, her work with prisoners in the Bedford Hills (New York) Correctional Facility for Women was the subject of a documentary film produced by Ensler, *What I Want My Words to Do*, which won the Freedom of Expression Award at the 2003 Sundance Film Festival and was screened nationally on public television.

Ensler was the recipient of the 1997 Berilla-Kerr Award for Playwriting, a finalist for the Jane Chambers Playwriting Award in 1997, and received a Guggenheim Fellowship in playwriting in 1999. In May 2003 she received an honorary doctorate from her alma mater, Middlebury College.

[*See also* Feminist Drama in the United States; Identity Theater; Philosophy and Drama, 1960–Present; Political Theater in the United States; United States, 1940–Present]

PLAYS: *When I Call My Voices* (1983); *The Depot* (1986); *Scooncat* (1987); *Cinderella/Cendrillon* (1989); *Ladies* (1989); *Reef and Particle* (1992); *Floating Rhoda and the Glue Man* (1993); *Loud in My Head* (1993); *Chamomille Tea* (1994); *Extraordinary Measures* (1995); *Lemonade* (1995); *The Vagina Monologues* (1995); *Conviction* (1999); *Necessary Targets* (2001); *The Goody Body* (2004)

FURTHER READING

Ensler, Eve. *The Vagina Monologues: The V-Day Edition.* New York: Villard, 2001. V-Day. http://www.vday.org/ [Web site contains information about V-Day, its mission, and its history].

Zeisler, Andi. "Eve Ensler on" Good "Bodies and Bad Politics." *Mother Jones* (November–December 2004). http://www.motherjones.com/arts/qa/2004/11/11_100.html.

Gwendolyn Alker

THE ENTERTAINER

The Entertainer is JOHN OSBORNE's cynical assessment of Britain's declining status during the Suez Crisis of the mid-1950s. Following the success of his previous play LOOK BACK IN ANGER (1956), which established his reputation as an "Angry Young Man," Osborne wrote his next play for the most prominent figure of the British theater, Sir Laurence Olivier. Famous for playing such Shakespearean heroes as Hamlet, Henry V, and Richard III, Olivier ironically achieved perhaps the greatest success of his career by portraying a tawdry, untalented music hall comedian, Archie Rice, whose career and personal life are unraveling. *The Entertainer* opened at the Royal Court Theatre on Sloane Square in April 1957. After a successful London run, the play moved to Broadway and then was made into a film directed by Tony Richardson in 1960. The play succeeded in shocking its audience on several levels—by having its famous leading actor portray a pathetically unfunny comedian, by having an actress appear naked in a music hall tableau as "Britannia," and by depicting the end of the British Empire as a shabby whimper.

British audiences were shocked by Osborne's equation of British politicians in the Suez Crisis with a bumbling comedian. The challenge for Laurence Olivier as Archie Rice was to unlearn a lifetime of theatrical skills. The play alternates scenes of the dreary family life of Archie with flashes of his depressing stage performances. In his first routine, Archie offers a few feeble jokes and sings, "Why should I care? Why should I let it touch me?"

Archie's family is symbolic of a dysfunctional Britain. His father, Billy, apparently a retired music hall entertainer, functions as a kind of Greek chorus: "Anyway, I keep telling him—it's [the music hall] dead already. . . . It was all over, finished, dead when I got out of it." Archie's wife is a pathetic alcoholic. The fortunes of Archie's younger son, Mick (never seen in the play), help to push the plot along. Captured by the Egyptians, Mick briefly becomes a tabloid sensation but then is killed in action. His futile heroism contrasts sharply with Archie's bad personal and professional behavior. The subsequent death of Archie's father allows Osborne to link the passing of a generation of talented Englishmen with the pointless sacrifice of young heroes like Mick. In the play's last scene, Archie sings one of his characteristically self-indulgent songs ("We're all out for good old Number One") and waits for the hook to yank him offstage.

Osborne's equation of Archie with the British of the 1950s seems less audacious now than it did half a century ago. His protest against the national lack of direction still has resonance; but his appeals to traditional British values now seem desperate and reactionary, and Osborne's protest dramas, such as *Look Back in Anger*, *Inadmissible Evidence* (1964), and *Luther* (1961), seem musty. *The Entertainer* will be remembered as a personal triumph for Laurence Olivier and as a snapshot of a moment of national self-doubt.

[*See also* England, 1940–Present]

FURTHER READING

Orme, Steve. Review of *The Entertainer. The British Theatre Guide* (2003). http://www.britishtheatreguide.info/reviews/entertainer-rev.htm.

Osborne, John. *The Entertainer.* New York: Bantam, 1960.

Byron Nelson

ENTERTAINING MR SLOANE

> *Entertain Mr Sloane now. Give him the benefit of your experience. (Pause) You want to learn some manners. That's what you want.*
> —Kath, Act 1

JOE ORTON's first stage play premiered at the New Arts Theatre, London, on May 6, 1964, and was produced by Michael Codron. The play satirizes both family values and previous theatrical incarnations of them, most notably HAROLD PINTER's *The Room* and THE BIRTHDAY PARTY. The play centers on a beautiful youth, Mr Sloane, who is blackmailed into being the shared sexual plaything of a middle-aged brother (Ed) and sister (Kath) after he murders their father to prevent himself from being identified for a previous murder. The scandal that greeted the play was fanned by Orton writing letters to the *Daily Telegraph* under the assumed names of Edna Welthorpe and Peter Pinnell (among others), deploring the morally depraved nature of the play. "I myself was nauseated by this endless parade of mental and physical perversion." Both the letters and the play's dialogue illustrate Orton's unerring ear for self-important rhetoric and the struggles of the ill-educated to express themselves in a more sophisticated manner.

Entertaining Mr Sloane begins as a parody of Pinter: the predatory stranger on the domestic hearth, the garrulous landlady, the shadowy "boss" figure, and the timorous old man. However, as Kath shows the handsome prospective lodger around the house she shares with her father, it becomes clear that the secrecy that characterizes the Pinteresque lodger/landlady encounter is entirely absent. Kath and Sloane are soon on intimate terms, and the tame innuendo of the "succulent" fried bread in *The Birthday Party* that passes as flirting between Meg and Stanley is transformed and superseded in *Sloane* by the aging but highly sexed Kath and the young, virile, and opportunistic Sloane. On Sloane's first visit Kath confides: "I've been doing the washing today and I haven't a stitch on . . . except my shoes. . . . I'm in the rude under this dress. I tell you because you're bound to have noticed."

Kath's apparently artless confession marks the beginning of her relationship with Sloane, much to the disgust of her father and the jealousy of her brother Ed. Ed and Sloane's first meeting is a victory of Orton's innuendo over the Lord Chamberlain's keen-eyed censorship. Ed begins by asking Sloane about his childhood in the orphanage, moves on to whether or not he exercises naked and wears "leather next to the skin," proclaims that he "sets great store by morals," and then announces:

> I've a certain amount of influence. . . . I've two cars. Judge for yourself. I generally spend my holidays in places where the bints have got rings through their noses. (*Pause*) Women are like banks, boy, breaking and entering is a serious business. Give me your word you're not vaginalatrous?

Ed and Kath compete for Sloane's affections, offering "modern" luxuries such as foam rubber pillows and brushed nylon t-shirts—reflecting Orton's skill at encapsulating the desires and aspirations of the working classes in 1960s Britain.

FURTHER READING

Bull, John, and Frances Gray. "Joe Orton." In *Essays on Contemporary British Drama*, ed. by Hedwig Bock and Albert Wertheim. Munich: Hueber, 1981. 71–96.

Coppa, Francesca. Introduction to *Fred and Madge/The Visitors: Two Plays*, by Joe Orton. London: Nick Hern Bks., 1998.

De Jongh, Nicholas. *Not in Front of the Audience: Homosexuality on Stage*. London: Routledge, 1992.

——. *Politics, Prudery and Perversions. The Censoring of the British Stage 1901–1968*. London: Methuen, 2000.

Lahr, John. *Prick Up Your Ears; The Biography of Joe Orton*. New York: Knopf, 1978.

——, ed. *The Orton Diaries*. London: Methuen, 1989.

Orton, Joe. *The Complete Plays*. London: Methuen, 1976.

Kate Dorney

EN THE ASCETIC

En the Ascetic (*En no Gyōja*, 1916), a Japanese play by TSUBOUCHI SHŌYŌ, renders the vicissitudes of the eponymous Buddhist hermit-monk, legendary founder of the mountain-dwelling priests (*yamabushi*) in the late 7th century, who practiced sorcery through unstinting esoteric disciplines. Falsely accused by someone jealous of his magical powers, En was reportedly exiled to the island of Oshima in 699.

The play's action ensues from En's Robin Hood–like vanquishing of the evil, half-human, half-animal divinity Hitokotonushi, who had been tormenting villagers in the mountains near Nara. That apparently black-and-white conflict acquires multiple shades of gray, when En's disciple Hirotaru violates his master's ascetic strictures and, tempted by a beautiful woman, ultimately betrays him. Rumors swirl that En purveys heretical doctrines and casts spells on the imperial house. In the play's signature scene, the redoubtable En passionately asserts the supremacy of the self in standing for one's convictions. When an official comes to arrest him, he staunchly refuses to give in, even though the authorities threaten to behead his mother. The standoff concludes with a cataclysm that transforms En into a white cloud floating above the fray.

Although the play was performed with standard *kabuki* declamation and physical movement, it was a distinct departure from traditional texts in portraying psychological aspects of the characters' attitudes and feelings. Tsubouchi demonstrated that a play text could stand on its literary merits and serious ideas. He was influenced by HENRIK IBSEN's use of tension, though not, as with Ibsen, to heighten overt social conflict but to emphasize lyrically his characters' inner spiritual conflicts. In the larger-than-life En, beset by betrayal, the play also has overtones of William Shakespeare's Prospero (Tsubouchi translated *The Tempest* in 1915) and FRIEDRICH NIETZSCHE's *Zarathustra*.

Personal references deepen the play's psychological dimensions. The hermit-monk stands in as Tsubouchi and Hirotaru as Shimamura Hōgetsu, the disciple with whom Tsubouchi cofounded the Literary Arts Society (Bungei Kyōkai) in 1906. The temptress stands in as Matsui Sumako, the company's famous actress. Tsubouchi, like En, felt betrayed when Shimamura embraced different ideas about theater reform and, though married, carried on a torrid affair with Matsui. The morally conservative Tsubouchi felt compelled to expel Matsui from the Literary Arts Society in 1913. Shimamura also left, and the company disbanded two months later.

While *En the Ascetic* has been called the great masterpiece of Japanese drama in the Meiji (1868–1912) and Taishō (1912–1926) periods and is regarded as Tsubouchi's best play, with its plodding density and fantastical hero it has not aged well and is daunting to stage. Yet, in 1926, it was the first play by a Japanese playwright produced by OSANAI KAORU at Tsukiji Little Theatre (Tsukiji Shōgekijō). In its combination of traditional *kabuki* elements with the psychological aspects that Tsubouchi gleaned from Shakespeare and Ibsen, it was a critical step in demonstrating that a new theater not expressly Western could be created in JAPAN. Translated into French in 1920, it became the first modern Japanese play to be rendered into any Western language.

[*See also* Shingeki]

FURTHER READING

Keene, Donald. *Dawn to the West: Japanese Literature in the Modern Era—Poetry, Drama, Criticism*. New York: Henry Holt, 1984.

Ortolani, Benito. *The Japanese Theatre: From Shamanistic Ritual to Contemporary Pluralism*. Princeton, N.J.: Princeton Univ. Press, 1990.

Powell, Brian. *Japan's Modern Theatre: A Century of Continuity and Change*. London: Japan Library, 2002.

Rimer, J. Thomas. *Toward a Modern Japanese Theatre: Kishida Kunio*. Princeton, N.J.: Princeton Univ. Press, 1974.

Tsubouchi, Shōyō. *L'Ermite: Légende dramatique en trois actes* [The hermit: Dramatic legend in three acts]. Tr. by Takamatsu Yoshie. Paris: Société Littéraire de France, 1920.

John K. Gillespie

ENVIRONMENTAL THEATER

The fundamental principle of environmental theatre is to begin with an empty space, without a preconception of where the audience or the performers will be or how they will relate.

—Shank, *Beyond the Boundaries*, 2002

The term *environmental theater* primarily refers to a theatrical movement that dates from the late 1960s and early 1970s, alongside the worldwide strikes and riots of 1968. Rather than referring to a specific canon of texts, it defines work that seeks to redefine the actor/audience dynamic by activating the entirety of the theater space. Largely a response to the presumed bourgeois structures of proscenium framed drama, environmental theater is predicated on a conceptual shift from the specified places of textual drama to the intersubjective space of performance.

Environmental theater draws from a wide variety of sources. While directly building from art movements such as HAPPENINGS, action painting, Fluxus, and New Dance (particularly the work at New York's Judson Church), it refers as well to a long history of RELIGION-based performance. Environmental practitioners often took inspiration from anthropological work examining worldwide traditions of ritual performances in which there is no clear demarcation between spaces for the actors and the audiences. Some environmental work, such as ROBERT WILSON's 1972 durational production at the Shiraz Festival, *Ka Mountain and Guardenia Terrace*, relied on the interaction between performers and spectators in site-specific found/natural space.

The other tradition of environmental theater constructs its own spaces to reject the formality of proscenium theater. This includes the work of ARIANE MNOUCHKINE, whose theatricalization of the French Revolution, *1789*, used the entirety of the space at the Cartoucherie, allowing the audience to cluster around groups of actors, as well as the LIVING THEATRE, whose productions of such works as *Paradise Now* and *Mysteries and Smaller Pieces*, while often taking place in orthodox theaters, repeatedly shattered the convention of the fourth wall.

The major figure associated with the development of environmental theater is Richard Schechner, whose seminal work with The Performance Group as well as his positions as professor at New York University and editor of TDR (formerly *Tulane Drama Review*)—where he published "Six Axioms for the Environmental Theatre" (1968)—developed both practice and theory. Schechner's best-known productions, from the 1968 *Dionysus in '69* to the 1970–1972 *Commune*, allowed the audience to sit throughout the Performing Garage on and around a variety of platforms and offered them chances to participate at particular moments throughout the performances.

Other important practitioners of the environmental movement include Peter Schumann's Bread and Puppet Theater, whose *Domestic Resurrection Circus* in Glover, Vermont, ran annually from 1974 through 1997; Andre Gregory; and the dance work of Trisha Brown and Meredith Monk. The work of ecotheater practitioners such as Canadian composer R. Murray Schafer and the success of site-specific work such as Fiona Templeton's *You—The City* (1988) and Joe and Dan Corcoran's *Tony and Tina's Wedding* (1988) demonstrate the continuing impact of the environmental theater movement.

[*See also* Poor Theater]

FURTHER READING

Fuchs, Elinor. *The Death of Character: Perspectives on Theater After Modernism*. Bloomington: Indiana Univ. Press, 1996.

Kirby, Michael. *The Art of Time: Essays on the Avant-Garde*. New York: Dutton, 1969.

McNamara, Brooks, Richard Schechner, and Jerry Rojo. *Theatres, Spaces, Environments: 18 Projects*. New York: Drama Bk. Specialists, 1975.

Schechner, Richard. *Performance Theory*. New York: Routledge, 1988.

——. *Environmental Theater*. New York: Applause, 1994.

Shank, Theodore. *Beyond the Boundaries: American Alternative Theatre*. Ann Arbor: Univ. of Michigan Press, 2002.

Josh Abrams

EPIC THEATER

The world of today can be described to the human beings of today only as a world that can be changed.

—Bertolt Brecht, *Schriften zum Theater* [Writings to the theater], 1955

Epic theater is most strongly linked with German poet, playwright, and dramaturg BERTOLT BRECHT; however, the term originated in conjunction with the innovations of Brecht's contemporary and associate ERWIN PISCATOR. Beginning in 1920, when he founded the "Proletarian Theater" in Berlin, then later as director of the Volksbühne and other theaters, Piscator used the stage to agitate for communist ideals by forging a distinctive style that incorporated film projections and political sloganeering into dramatic productions. Brecht, who collaborated with Piscator as a dramaturge in the 1920s, used his colleague's term for politically engaged stagecraft but also called his own vision "dialectical theater" to distinguish his particular dramatic view.

Brecht viewed his own plays and those of others that he staged as raw material to be reworked to address the political situation of the time and place in which they were produced; in the same spirit, he revised his theory throughout his career. Fundamentally, however, his craft and concerns remained consistent. Brecht's epic theater called for a form of drama that makes viewers stop and think about how social circumstances exercise pressure on—and even shape—characters and their actions. To this end, Brecht advised directors and actors to obstruct the audience's ability to suspend disbelief and "get lost" in the world onstage. By drawing attention to the fact that the seemingly inevitable situations in which dramatic personae find themselves are in fact not, Brechtian dramaturgy seeks to prompt viewers not just to have an emotional involvement in the play but also to develop an intellectual relationship with what they witness. The *Verfremdungseffekt* (imperfectly translated as "ALIENATION EFFECT") that epic theater provokes is actually a means of encouraging a higher degree of audience engagement. The framing devices that stand in the way of unreflective emotional cathexis prompt spectators to think about possibilities for action that characters cannot discern and thus to consider how they themselves might act in the scenes and situations depicted. By training theatergoers in perspectivism, Brecht suspends the dividing line between actors and audience; this engaged perspectivism is intended to transform spectators into actors for social change.

To this end, Brecht developed techniques that reconfigured onstage action and the performer-spectator relation. *Gestus* refers to how actors perform in ways that communicate not just the personal quality of their roles but also the social positioning that shapes these identity formations (for example, a peasant eats in a different manner than a nobleman); the term also describes how performance can highlight how character choices foreclose other possible actions (e.g., when Mother Courage haggles over her son's ransom). *Epic structure* is opposed to the Aristotelian form of drama, which strives for an organic integration of parts and a cathartic effect; each scene forms its own whole and presents a dilemma to be deliberated by the audience on the basis of actions performed by characters. *Historicization* refers to the way that plays foreground the social and cultural conditions surrounding events onstage; characters' actions should be portrayed as the result of choices made in particular circumstances, not as matters of fate. Other means that Brecht employed to disrupt illusionary theater included captions displayed onstage that divulged plot developments; placards that instructed the audience (not) to respond to the play in certain ways; and in general, a sparse, brightly lit performance space with exposed machinery and without elaborate props. Actors were instructed not to identify with the characters they played but to act in a way that prevented emotional involvement and invited commentary and criticism. Brecht's stagecraft also incorporated the styles of non-European and folk theaters in an attempt to defy audience expectations.

Epic theater continues in latter-day works that seek to replace what Brecht called "culinary theater" (that is, productions offered merely to serve as objects of delectation for the audience) with critical engagement with prevailing social realities and cultural norms. Exponents include HEINER MÜLLER and Peter Stein in GERMANY; EDWARD BOND, CARYL CHURCHILL, and Trevor Griffiths in ENGLAND; the San Francisco Mime Troupe and RICHARD FOREMAN in the UNITED STATES. The tradition inaugurated by Piscator and Brecht uses the stage to present open-ended processes rather than polished products. An engaged audience is as important a component in the theater as the dramatic text and performers.

[*See also* Learning Plays; Realism; Russia and the Soviet Union, Dramatic Criticism; Russia and the Soviet Union, Set Design]

FURTHER READING

Esslin, Martin. *Brecht: A Choice of Evils*. London: Methuen, 1984.

Innes, Christopher. *Modern German Drama: A Study in Form*. Cambridge: Cambridge Univ. Press, 1979.

Kleber, Pia, and Colin Visser, eds. *Reinterpreting Brecht: His Influence on Contemporary Drama and Film*. Cambridge: Cambridge Univ. Press, 1990.

Reinelt, Janelle G. *After Brecht: British Epic Theater*. Ann Arbor: Univ. of Michigan Press, 1994.

Rouse, John. *Brecht and the West German Theatre: The Practice and Politics of Interpretation*. Ann Arbor: Univ. of Michigan Research Press, 1989.

Thomson, Peter, and Glendyr Sacks, eds. *The Cambridge Companion to Brecht*. Cambridge: Cambridge Univ. Press, 1994.

Willett, John. *The Theatre of Erwin Piscator: Half a Century of Politics in the Theater*. London: Methuen, 1978.

Erik Butler

EQUUS

"Account for me," says staring Equus. "First account for Me!"
—Dr. Dysart, Act 2

PETER SHAFFER's *Equus* has become one of the most provocative and acclaimed plays of modern times. Premiering in London in 1973 and transferring to New York in 1974, *Equus*—the Latin word for "horse"—received extravagant praise for its thrilling theatricality and profound thematic concerns. Among its numerous accolades were the Outer Critics Circle Award, the New York Drama Critics Best Play Award, the Los Angeles Drama Critics Award, and the 1975 Tony for best play. A compelling movie version (1976) earned Shaffer an Oscar nomination for best film script.

In different ways, all of Shaffer's dramas concern themselves with critical metaphysics, particularly questions regarding the existence and nature of God. With *Equus* that quintessential puzzle is brilliantly projected onto a spellbinding "detective story." Riveting suspense emerges when Martin Dysart, a middle-aged child psychiatrist in a provincial hospital, agrees to investigate why Alan Strang, a seventeen-year-old village boy, inexplicably stabbed out the eyes of six horses at a nearby stable. As someone committed to ease pain and heal bodies, Dysart dutifully searches for answers to heal Alan and send him back into society.

Conflict in *Equus* emerges as a desperate contest between a psychiatrist seeking answers and a fugitive patient hiding truths masking innermost beliefs and passions. The story develops through alternating scenes depicting Dysart's interviews with Alan and flashback enactments of crucial events. The play's thirty-five scenes, in two acts, are performed without break.

One remarkable set allows for the flexibility required. A square wooden platform, encompassing a circular turntable, is enclosed on three sides by a wooden rail, creating a quasi-boxing ring but more significantly a sports arena for combat. Some audience members are seated upstage and on the sides, echoing amphitheaters from ancient Greece but also medical dissecting rooms. Audiences serve both as witnesses and chorus figures for the actions portrayed.

Dysart's sleuthing uncovers Alan's blurred melding of sexual awakening with his unique "worship" of a horse-divinity called Equus. Through the boy's abreacting past incidents, we learn the blinding of the six horses with a horse pick related to Alan's first sexual experience with a girl in the stables. Sexual and religious passions became intermingled with his obsession regarding horses, generating intolerable tensions within Alan. The horse mutilations resulted. With this knowledge, Dysart is able to resolve Alan's psychological problems—but at a price: the removal of the youth's quirky grasp of life that includes "unnormal" passion. The remedy for Alan means the excision of a natural part of his persona. Dysart explains: "Passion, you see, can be destroyed by a doctor. It cannot be created."

In "curing" Alan, Dysart must acknowledge his own fundamental uncertainties. If each human's life is unique and sacred, how can he presume to purge Alan's—or anyone's—individual God and understanding of the universe? At the end, Dysart becomes captive of Equus, who demands, "Why Me? . . . Account for Me!" Dysart is left the same unanswerable questions concerning God as faced Alan.

FURTHER READING

Buckley, Tom. "'Write Me,' Said the Play to Peter Shaffer." *New York Times Magazine* (April 13, 1975): 20 ff.

Gianakaris, C. J. *Peter Shaffer*. New York: St. Martin's, 1992.

Glenn, Jules. "Alan Strang as an Adolescent: A Discussion of Peter Shaffer's *Equus*." *International Journal of Psychoanalytic Psychotherapy* (1976): 473–487.

Klein, Dennis A. "Peter Shaffer's *Equus* as a Modern Aristotelian Tragedy." *Studies in Iconography* 9 (1983): 175–181.

Lounsberry, Barbara. "God-Hunting: The Chaos of Worship in Peter Shaffer's *Equus* and *The Royal Hunt of the Sun*." *Modern Drama* 21 (1978): 13–28.

Plunka, Gene A. "The Existential Ritual: Peter Shaffer's *Equus*." *Kansas Quarterly* 12 (Fall 1980): 87–97.

C. J. Gianakaris

ERDGEIST *See* EARTH SPIRIT

ERDMAN, NIKOLAI (1900–1970)

Russian playwright, screenwriter, and poet Nikolai Robertovich Erdman's two major plays, *The Warrant* (*Mandat*, 1925) and THE SUICIDE (*Samoubiitsa*, 1929–1930), renewed the indigenous, post-revolution Russian mix of dark COMEDY, TRAGEDY, and satire. Both reflected the fragmented influences of a comic tradition established by Nikolai Gogol, Aleksandr Sukhovo-Kobylin, and ALEKSANDR OSTROVSKY, while incorporating the stylistics of contemporary journalistic and political theater, such as nightclub skits, theatrical parodies, and AGITATION-PROPAGANDA theater, which turned morning newspaper headlines into texts for evening performances. Figures of influence such as MAKSIM GORKY and ANATOLY LUNACHARSKY proclaimed their innovative nature. Poetic in form, they revealed a distinctive voice that played on the paradoxes of language to reveal a philosophy of man's alienation in the modern world.

Aligning himself with the imagist poets, led by Sergei Yesenin, Erdman published several well-crafted poems between 1919 and 1923. From 1922 to 1932 he wrote dozens of sketches, songs, short plays, and full-length revues, often with Vladimir Mass, for the small theaters, music halls, and cabarets that mushroomed during the New Economic Policy (NEP), Vladimir Lenin's strategy to revive the shattered Soviet economy through capitalism. This period, the Soviet Union's version of the Roaring Twenties, spawned a genre, NEP satire, with which Erdman is sometimes linked, though not entirely accurately because he was more poet than satirist. Many of the Erdman-Mass collaborations—including dozens of mocking fables that, though unpublished, became extremely popular—provoked the wrath of the authorities.

The Warrant (also known in English as *The Mandate*) is a TRAGICOMEDY about a hapless man who fakes a Communist Party identification (the warrant of the title) in order to be safe, should the communists remain in power, while arranging to marry a wealthy man's daughter in case the tsar should retake the throne. The intricate plot twists and witty dialogue built on multiple puns made this one of the most popular productions of VSEVOLOD MEYERHOLD, inducing many to label it the "first Soviet play." One researcher counted 336 outbursts of laughter at a performance in 1926.

The Suicide further developed Erdman's poetically structured, philosophically tinged brand of comedy. However, its underlying mood of disillusionment and its image of an individual nearly being crushed by the social machine were unacceptable to Soviet censors. It was struck down by a series of bans between 1930 and 1932, which contributed to Erdman being sent into Siberian exile (1933–1936). This blow essentially drove Erdman out of the theater. He failed to complete a third full-length play, *The Hypnotist* (*Gipnotizyor*, 1934–1942) of which only scraps remain, although he occasionally wrote librettos for operettas or dramatizations of novels. From 1938 until his death, he primarily wrote scripts for feature and animated films, many of which were highly successful. In the 1960s, Erdman was a friend and unofficial adviser to YURY LYUBIMOV at the Taganka Theater. The world premiere of *The Suicide* in SWEDEN in 1969 ensured Erdman's place as one of the most important Russian playwrights of the 20th century.

[*See also* Russia and the Soviet Union]

PLAYS: *The Six-Story Adventure* (*Shestietazhnaya avantyura*, lost, 1923); *The Destruction of Europe on Holy Square* (*Gibel' Evropy na Strastnoi ploshchadi*, 1924); *Housework Bondage* (*V kabale domashnego khozyaistva*, with Nikolai L'vov, 1924); *Moscow from a Point of View* (*Moskva s tochki zreniya*, with Vladimir Mass, Viktor Tipot, David Gutman, 1924); Interludes and songs for *Lev Gurych Sinichkin* (after Dmitry Lensky, 1924); *The Warrant* (*Mandat*, 1925); *Odysseus* (*Oddissei*, with Mass, 1928); Interludes for Carlo Gozzi's *Princess Turandot* (with Mass, 1928–1932); *The Suicide* (*Samoubiitsa*, c. 1929–1930; first produced in Sweden, 1969); *Boccaccio* (with Mass, 1930); *Orpheus in Hell* (*Orfei v adu*, with Mass, 1930); *The Belle Helene* (*Prekrasnaya Yelena*, with Mass, 1931); *St. Magdalene's Salon* (*Salon Svyatoi Magdaleny*, with Mass, 1931); *A Meeting About Laughter* (*Zasedaniye o smekhe*, with Mass, 1932); *The Music Store* (*Muzykal'ny magazin*, with Mass, 1932); *The Tragedy of Hamlet, Prince of Denmark* (*Tragediya o Gamlete, printse datskom*, with Mass, 1932); Four interludes for Shakespeare's *Hamlet* (with Mass, 1932); *Mother* (*Mat*, after Maksim Gorky, 1934); *The Hypnotist* (*Gipnotizyor*, lost, c. 1934–1942); *Private Shultz* (*Ryadovoi Shul'ts*, with Mikhail Vol'pin, 1942); *The Village of Stepanchikovo and Its Inhabitants* (*Selo Stepanchikovo i ego obitateli*, after Fyodor Dostoevsky, 1957); *Hero of Our Time* (*Geroi nashego vremeni*, after Mikhail Lermontov, with Yury Lyubimov, 1964)

FURTHER READING

Freedman, John. *Silence's Roar: The Life and Drama of Nikolai Erdman*. Oakville, Canada: Mosaic Press, 1992.

Gotzes, Andrea. *Der Beitrag Nikolaj Erdmans zur russischen Komodie* [Nikolai Erdman's contribution to Russian comedy]. Mainz: Liber Verlag, 1994.

The Major Plays of Nikolai Erdman: The Warrant *and* The Suicide. Tr. and ed. by John Freedman. Amsterdam: Harwood Acad. Pub., 1995.

A Meeting About Laughter: Sketches, Interludes and Theatrical Parodies by Nikolai Erdman with Vladimir Mass and Others. Tr. and ed. by John Freedman. Amsterdam: Harwood Acad. Pub., 1995.

Segel, Harold B. *Twentieth-Century Russian Drama from Gorky to the Present*. Rev. ed. New York: Performing Arts Journal Publications, 1993.

John Freedman

ERIK XIV

Erik XIV, a historical play in four acts by AUGUST STRINDBERG written and published in 1899, was first performed at Svenska teatern in Stockholm and published the same year. It is the third part of the so-called Vasa trilogy, the earlier parts being MASTER OLOF and GUSTAV VASA. The three plays are thematically very loosely connected and share some of the same characters.

As the title makes clear, *Erik XIV* deals with Gustav Vasa's eldest son and successor on the throne, 1560–1568, best known in Swedish history for his dependence on the ruthless procurator Göran Persson; his marrying Karin Månsdotter, a woman of the common people; and his insane killing of members of the noble Sture family.

When the drama opens Erik has proposed to Elizabeth I of England. When she refuses him, he turns in rancor against the Sture family. He then legalizes his liaison with Karin Månsdotter at a nightmarish wedding banquet to which the rabble has been invited. The feast comes to an end when his half brothers, Dukes Johan and Carl, arrive. Erik is taken prisoner, and the two dukes, hitherto friends, suddenly appear to be rivals for the throne.

The main conflict—the rivalry between Erik and Johan—is caused by Erik's striving to maintain and, if possible, increase his power and Johan's opposite endeavor to deprive him of this power in order to enlarge his own.

A decade after the play was written, Strindberg (1966) characterized its double protagonist thus:

> A characterization of a characterless human being: that is my Erik XIV. . . . Göran Persson's history has been written by his enemies; I had to take him as a man of principle, and I have not concealed the evil man's good little qualities.

In the beginning of the play, the king is constantly referred to as insane. At the end he seems rather the product of an insane world. As Johan puts it: "I think the world has gone mad!" What constitutes the madness is sententiously clarified by the third brother, Carl, in the final words of the play: "the struggles of life never end!" *Erik XIV* is unconventional in its open-ended indication of a *perpetuum mobile*. As Evert Sprinchorn (1982) observes: "It is not customary to end a history play, especially [not] the last one in a trilogy . . . in the midst of the struggle and with the state on the verge of chaos and dissolution."

Parties in conflict do not normally show much understanding for each other. The impression of objectivity is much greater when an audience gets to know the motives and reasoning of both parties than if it is informed only about those of one of them. In this respect, *Erik XIV* must be regarded as a mainly subjective drama, not unlike THE FATHER.

[*See also* Sweden]

FURTHER READING

Johnson, Walter. *Strindberg and the Historical Drama*. Seattle: Univ. of Washington Press, 1963.

Lamm, Martin. *August Strindberg*. Tr. and ed. by Harry G. Carlson. New York: Blom, 1971.
Ollén, Gunnar. *Strindbergs dramatik* [Strindberg's dramaturgy]. Stockholm: Sveriges Radios förlag, 1982.
Sprinchorn, Evert. *Strindberg as Dramatist*. New Haven: Yale Univ. Press, 1982.
Strindberg, August. *Open Letters to the Intimate Theater*. Tr. and intro. by Walter Johnson. Seattle and London: Univ. of Washington Press, 1966.
Törnqvist, Egil. *Strindbergian Drama: Themes and Structure*. Stockholm: Almqvist & Wiksell Intl., 1982.

Egil Törnqvist

DIE ERMITTLUNG See THE INVESTIGATION

ERVINE, ST. JOHN (1883–1971)

John Greer Ervine was born on December 28, 1883, in the working-class Belfast suburb of Ballymacarret in Northern IRELAND. He adopted the "St." when he began his writing career. The son of William and Sarah Greer, Ervine's father died when he was three years old; as a result, he grew up under the tutelage of his Grandmother Greer. He attended Westbourne School in Belfast, but his family's financial situation stood in the way of advancing his education. At the age of seventeen, Ervine found work in an insurance office, first in Belfast and then in London, where he joined the Fabian Society and commenced his writing career. This included a stint as reviewer for A. R. Orange's weekly review *The New Age*. He gained the attention of W. B. YEATS with *The Magnanimous Lover*, a one-act play, and as a result, his first full-length play, *Mixed Marriage*, was produced at the Abbey Theatre in 1911. Ervine married Leonara Mary Davis that same year, a fellow proponent of the Fabian Reform Committee.

Four years later, Ervine would become manager of the Abbey Theatre, a position that would complicate the Irish literati's original vision for Dublin's dramatic scene. Ervine's perception of the Abbey's role was quite different than that of Yeats and Lady Augusta Gregory, for he did not see the theater as a voice for a specifically Irish national identity. In fact, he argued that no drama of merit was being written in his homeland and showed a disregard for the peasant plays that the Abbey tended to produce. It was during his tenure as Abbey Theatre manager, however, that his highly acclaimed TRAGEDY JOHN FERGUSON was produced. Amid controversy and the departure of a number of players who subsequently formed a rival touring company, The Irish Players, he resigned from his post in July 1916.

An ardent Unionist who greatly opposed the Home Rule movement, Ervine's politics complicated his position in a national theater, and after exiting the Abbey, he left Dublin and joined the British army. As a lieutenant in the Royal Dublin Fusiliers, a severe injury in 1918 led to the amputation of one of his legs. Following his active duty, Ervine worked for *The Morning Post* and *The Observer* as a drama critic and also served as guest drama critic for the New York *World*. The 1920s saw a number of his comedies produced in London's West End, including *Mary, Mary, Quite Contrary* (1923), *Anthony and Anna* (1925), and *The First Mrs. Fraser* (1929). Ervine returned to the Abbey stage in 1936, when one of his most popular plays, *Boyd's Shop*, was first produced on February 19 and enjoyed a run on Dublin's premier stage. Ervine's literary status was not solely relegated to the realm of playwriting. He also published novels and biographies—such as his highly acclaimed study on his idol GEORGE BERNARD SHAW (1956) and various prose and nonfiction pieces.

Ervine's ties with his native Ireland were not completely severed. When Yeats founded the Irish Academy of Letters in 1932, he was one of the first members. In addition, he was granted an honorary doctorate by Queen's University, Belfast, and was employed as professor of dramatic literature at the Royal Society of Literature from 1933 to 1936.

PLAYS: *The Magnanimous Lover* (1911); *Mixed Marriage* (1911); *John Ferguson* (1915); *Mary, Mary, Quite Contrary* (1923); *Anthony and Anna* (1925); *The First Mrs. Fraser* (1929); *Boyd's Shop* (1936)

FURTHER READING

Ervine, St. John. *Selected Plays of St. John Ervine*. Ed. by John Cronin. Gerrards Cross: Colin Smythe, 1988.

Rebecca Steinberger

ESSEX GIRLS

Finkin' of 'avin' a baby.
—Karen, Act 2

Essex Girls, Rebecca Prichard's first play, was first performed at the Royal Court Theatre's 1994 Coming On Strong season. Roxana Silbert directed the play, which launched Prichard's reputation for indicting the limited choices that underprivileged young women face.

Essex Girls focuses on the all-female characters' cultural and financial poverty. "Essex Girls" are stereotyped as promiscuous, binge-drinking, chain-smoking, unintelligent blondes, and Prichard's "Girls" have some of these characteristics. Audiences are tempted to laugh at their low discourse and limited perceptiveness—much of the dialogue, which reveals characters' naïveté, is very funny—are titillated by the uniformed girls' precocious interests in sex. But the desperateness of the characters' situations ensures that laughter and titillation change to melancholy awareness of the claustrophobia of working-class, teenage girlhood.

Structurally, the play is simple and effective: one act is set in a comprehensive school's restroom, featuring three unstudious girls in desperate need of the lavatory, passing the time garrulously; the second act is set in a young single mother's run-down apartment. Women suffer in this play. One of the schoolgirls, Hayley, narrates an incident when a couple copulating in a car attracted an excited audience. Afterward, the man is treated like a hero, whereas the woman is pelted with missiles and mocked. The schoolgirls condemn the unfortunate woman, not realizing that their response perpetuates sexism. Another schoolgirl, Diane, possibly hints at domestic violence. After being struck by Hayley, she says: "God, you're as bad as my . . ." Prichard leaves Hayley's sentence unfinished, as if a revelation about home violence was nearly uttered.

The second act has no plot-based link with the first act but is linked thematically. The young single mother is Kim, the slightly older sister of Kelly, the third girl from act 1. Kim's friend Karen comments on the excrementlike smell of Kim's living quarters, thus establishing a link to the act 1 girls' comments about the school toilets' odor. Kim has debts from fines acquired because of trivial thieving, a baby who she cares little for (she refuses to breastfeed him and lets him stay wet, ignoring his cries). The baby's father offers only violence. She is financially and spiritually broken, trapped. Her situation is the natural consequence of the reckless, dropout mentality that the girls of act 1 are sinking into. Kim hardly comprehends the horror of her situation. In response to the possibility that Karen is "finkin' of 'avin' a baby," she says that having a child when very young " 'Sall right" (is all right)—her situation is evidently not "right" to us.

The two-act structure of *Essex Girls* is influenced by CARYL CHURCHILL's dramaturgy in plays such as CLOUD NINE. Affinities with EDWARD BOND's work are also apparent: the fractured, harsh dialogue and the blatant disaffection of the working-class characters recalls SAVED. For one fleeting moment, Kim even considers killing the baby.

FURTHER READING

Aston, Elaine. *Feminist Views on the English Stage: Women Playwrights, 1990–2000.* Cambridge: Cambridge Univ. Press, 2003.

Aston, Elaine, and Janelle Reinelt. "A Century on View: From Suffrage to the 1990s." In *The Cambridge Companion to Modern British Women Playwrights*, ed. by Elaine Aston and Janelle Reinelt. Cambridge: Cambridge Univ. Press, 2000. 1–3.

Prichard, Rebecca. *Essex Girls.* In *Coming on Strong: New Writing from the Royal Court Theatre.* London: Faber, 1995.

——. "Plays by Women." In *State of Play: Playwrights on Playwrighting*, ed. by David Edgar. London: Faber, 1999.

Reviews of the "Coming on Strong" season, including *Essex Girls. Theatre Record* 14.21 (1994).

Sierz, Aleks. *In-Yer-Face Theatre: British Drama Today.* London: Faber, 2001.

Kevin De Ornellas

ESTONIA

Estonian drama was born on the crest of national awakening in 1870 with the folk plays of Lydia Koidula (1843–1886), the best of which is *Such a Bumpkin* (*Säärane mulk*, 1871). Theater and drama were parts of adopting forms of "high culture" for a rising nation whose earlier peasant culture had been based on folklore. For more than thirty years, simple village comedies with stereotypical characters remained the staple of numerous amateur groups. Attempts at creating more serious plays invariably ended with inferior MELODRAMAS.

The next stage came with the formation of the first professional companies in 1906 and the arrival of mature REALISM. It was introduced by August Kitzberg (1855–1927), generally regarded as the greatest Estonian dramatist. Kitzberg echoed the dramatic events of the abortive 1905 revolution in his *In the Whirlwind* (*Tuulte pöörises*, 1906); created a haunting figure in the rebellious heroine of *The Werewolf* (*Libahunt*, 1911); and presented a character of monumental greed and stubbornness in *The God of Mammon* (*Kauka Jumal*, 1912). At the same time, he continued to exploit a lighter vein in folk plays such as *The Puve Farm* (*Püve talus*, 1910). The new realm of city life was memorably treated by Eduard Vilde (1865–1933) in his *Elusive Miracle* (*Tabamata ime*, 1912), the drama of a failed artist, and in his brilliant COMEDY *The Hobgoblin* (*Pisuhänd*, 1913), where a poor writer outwits a rich businessman by using the latter's money in order to marry his daughter.

The first period of political independence (1918–1940) saw a remarkable rise in the number of theaters and native plays. By the end of the period Estonian plays and dramatizations already formed nearly half of the general repertoire. In the 1920s the Estonian arts were influenced by various modernist tendencies. In the drama these were mostly manifested in certain symbolist or expressionist features. In the 1930s, however, the growth of native drama was accompanied by a widespread return to more realism. Most authors now used the drawing-room comedy/drama format for urban surroundings and a somewhat renewed folk-play convention for the village milieu. The most influential dramatist of the period was the prolific Hugo Raudsepp (1883–1952) with his comedies. The best among them are *Mikumärdi* (1929; name of a farm), which largely effected the turn to native subjects and realism, and the character play *The Sluggard* (*Vedelvorst*, 1932). A. H. Tammsaare (1878–1940), otherwise known as the greatest Estonian novelist, also wrote two outstanding plays: *Judith* (*Juudit*, 1921) is an unconventional reading of the biblical story, and *The King Feels Cold* (*Kuningal on külm*, 1936) presents a fantastic satire of contemporary demagoguery.

World War II brought about a division of the young Estonian culture into home and exile branches, as numerous intellectuals and artists fled to the West. While in many artistic fields the exile production outweighed that of the home branch for nearly twenty years, the dispersal of small Estonian communities with their amateur groups all over the world left drama a relatively marginal genre. The first fifteen years of Soviet occupation (1940–1991) were totally desolate. Terror, rigid censorship, and strict ideological control reigned unabated. The only dramatist to accommodate Stalinist precepts successfully was August Jakobson (1904–1963), whose plays extended into all "socialist" countries but quickly disappeared after Joseph Stalin's death in 1953.

During the slow post-Stalinist liberalization of the late 1950s, modest realism and occasional lyricism reappeared in depictions of everyday life and were mainly represented by Juhan Smuul (1922–1971), whose folk play *Kihnu Jõnn* (1965), with the colorful title character a self-taught sea captain, has continued to be popular. New features could also be seen in the first plays of Egon Rannet (1911–1983), who later became more melodramatic and ideologically more rigid, and in the prolific work of Ardi Liives (1929–1992). Much more sophisticated plays with sometimes absurdist elements were written from the late 1960s onward by Paul-Eerik Rummo, *The Cinderella Game* (*Tuhkatriinumäng*, 1969), and Mati Unt, *Phaethon, Son of Helios* (*Phaeton, päikese poeg*, 1968). Features of the realistic play alternated with surrealistic effects in the work of Enn Vetemaa, the most popular playwright of the 1970s, notably in his comedies *St. Susanna, or The School of Masters* (*Püha Susanna ehk Meistrite kool*, 1974) and *Once Again Woe from Wit* (*Jälle häda mõistuse pärast*, 1975). Forceful realism and open theatricality combined in the dramas of Vaino Vahing (b. 1940), such as *Summer School* (*Suvekool*, 1972) and *The Testament* (*Testament*, 1983), as they also did in the more intellectual plays of Rein Saluri, *Guests* (*Külalised*, 1974). By the end of the 1970s general stagnation and ideological restrictions had become more evident.

One reaction to growing oppression was returning "to the roots," to subjects taken from national history. Certain taboos concerning the events of World War II in Estonia were first tentatively touched upon in Jaan Kruusvall's *Cloudcolors* (*Pilvede värvid*, 1983). Mikhail Gorbachev's glasnost (openness) and the crumbling of censorship in the late 1980s brought along such plays as Kruusvall's *The Parish House of Vaikuse* (*Vaikuse vallamaja*, 1987) and Saluri's *The Going* (*Minek*, 1988), both dealing with another taboo subject, that of the traumatic Stalinist deportations of the 1940s.

The reestablishment of political independence in 1991 first saw considerable economic difficulties and a substantial drop in theater attendances, but soon the public slowly started to return. The most outstanding oeuvre of the 1990s were the visionary and philosophical plays of Madis Kõiv, whom the theaters long considered technically unstageable. They include dramas based on personal memories, like *Returning to Father* (*Tagasitulek isa juurde*, 1993), and those based on historical and biographical material, like *A Philosopher's Day* (*Filosoofipäev*, 1994). Recent years have seen numerous younger arrivals. Attention has especially centered on Andrus Kivirähk, who often exhibits a fantastic streak, *An Estonian Funeral* (*Eesti matus*, 2002), and actor-dramatist Jaan Tätte, with his strong scenic feeling and lyricism, *The Bridge* (*Sild*, 2000).

FURTHER READING

Nirk, Endel. *Estonian Literature: Historical Survey with Biobibliographical Appendix*. 2d ed., enlarged. Tallinn: Perioodika, 1987.

Rähesoo, Jaak. *Estonian Theatre*. 2d ed., rev. Tallinn: Estonian Theatre Union, 2003.

Jaak Rähesoo

EURYDICE

Jean Anouilh composed *Eurydice*—an updated version of the legend of Orpheus's descent into the underworld—during the early years of World War II. Scholars group this play with Anouilh's adaptations of ANTIGONE and *Medea* into an informal trilogy of ancient Greek legends retold in the playwright's questioning modernist voice. In all three of these works, Anouilh calls upon the timelessness of classical myth to articulate an ambivalent vision of the plight of humanity within a compromised modern world.

In Anouilh's three-act retelling, the musician Orpheus is an itinerant accordion player who roams the French countryside by rail with his father (an unskilled harpist) in search of tolerant audiences. Early one morning in a provincial railway station café, he encounters Eurydice, a supporting actress in a second-rate theater company. Both are young, passionate, dissatisfied, and stifled—Orpheus by obligations to his hapless and talentless father and Eurydice by her domineering mother, a persistent suitor named Mathias, and the sternly controlling Dulac, traveling manager of her company. The two melancholy artists fall instantly in love and escape together to a Marseilles hotel room to begin a new life of devotion. Dulac arrives at the hotel to reclaim Eurydice, revealing himself to Orpheus as her former lover. But Eurydice has already sneaked away from her beloved—choosing to flee rather than shatter her new husband's idolatry with the uncomfortable truths of her past with Dulac. A policeman soon arrives to tell of Eurydice's death in an accident, as she departed from Marseilles by autobus.

The play's final act melds NATURALISM with the supernatural, as a mysterious guide named M. Henri leads Orpheus back to the station café for a reunion with his deceased wife. A new partnership is assured for the lovers, provided that Orpheus can refrain until sunrise from looking directly at his beloved. With his idealized image of Eurydice now tainted by knowledge of her impure history, Orpheus cannot restrain his accusatory glance. He looks at Eurydice—not out of love (as the legend has it) but from heartbreak, despair, and disillusionment. The play ends with M. Henri coaxing Orpheus toward his own death and a new reunion with Eurydice in the afterlife. Only through death can he escape all earthly sordidness and recapture his uncompromised vision of the girl he once worshipped. Orpheus's suicide stands as the tragic consequence of modern society's hostility toward all mortal strivings for purity and transcendence.

First performed in 1942, *Eurydice* was not as popular with reviewers or Parisian audiences as *Antigone* or Anouilh's other wartime dramas. Critics fault the play for its overarching pessimism, its lack of stylistic unity, and its inconsistent treatment of the traditional legend. (An unfinished, unpublished Anouilh work titled *Orpheus* adheres more closely to the customary Greek narrative.) English versions of *Eurydice* have been produced under the titles *Point of Departure* (at London's Lyric Hammersmith, 1950) and *Legend of Lovers* (on Broadway at the Plymouth Theater, 1951).

[*See also* France]

FURTHER READING

Marsh, Edward. *Jean Anouilh: Poet of Pierrot & Pantaloon*. London: W. H. Allen, 1953.

McIntyre, H. G. *The Theatre of Jean Anouilh*. London: Harrap Pub., 1981.

Pronko, Leonard. *The World of Jean Anouilh*. Berkeley: Univ. of California Press, 1961.

Thody, Philip. *Anouilh*. London: Oliver & Boyd, 1968.

Jonathan Shandell

EVEN WISE MEN ERR, OR EVEN A WISE MAN STUMBLES *See* THE SCOUNDREL

EVE OF RETIREMENT

THOMAS BERNHARD'S (1931–1989) *Eve of Retirement* (*Vor dem Ruhestand*, 1979) takes place in the late 1970s. The protagonist, Rudolf Höller, a retiring chief justice and former assistant commander of a Nazi concentration camp, annually celebrates the birthday of Heinrich Himmler, the head of the Gestapo. To mark the occasion, Höller dons his old SS uniform and forces his anarchist younger sister into a camp inmate's striped shirt.

Bernhard wrote the play for his preferred director CLAUS PEYMANN in response to the political situation in West GERMANY at the time, when the Nazi past of several leading politicians had just come to light. Most notorious among them was Hans Filbinger, the archconservative governor of the state of Baden Württemberg, where Peymann headed the State Theater of Stuttgart. A judge during Adolf Hitler's regime, Filbinger sentenced deserters to death even after the war had ended. (ROLF HOCHHUTH's play *Men of Law* [*Juristen*, 1979] documents Filbinger's Nazi career and eventual demise.) Filbinger was one of the leading politicians to push for the radical restriction of civil liberties and for barring anyone from federal employment who had even the slightest contact with peaceful protest groups. During Filbinger's governorship and Peymann's tenure in Stuttgart, the leading members of the radical Baader-Meinhof group were on trial in Stuttgart. When Peymann and his theater company collected money to help pay one prisoner's dental bills, Filbinger forced the director to resign. Bernhard completed his script in time for Peymann's last season in Stuttgart, 1978–1979.

Ostensibly a political play, *Eve of Retirement* dramatizes the perversion of traditional family values. Rudolf Höller lives with his sisters, Vera and Clara, in the same house his family has inhabited for many generations and acts according to the same principles, such as love and pride of family and fatherland. Rudolf is as loyal to his sisters as he is to his superiors. He executed his tasks as assistant concentration camp commander with the same conscientiousness he devotes to his responsibilities as a judge after the war. His love of nature energized Rudolf's fight against the construction of a chemical plant across from the family home; Himmler had similarly prevented the construction of a poison gas plant on the same site during World War II. Without families of their own, the Höller children cast themselves as a nuclear family. Rudolf and Vera take care of their paraplegic sister Clara, injured as a child in an American bombing attack. Like parents, Rudolf and Vera sleep together, if only once a year, on Himmler's birthday. The safety of the family bound by perverted Nazi ideals can be assured only in the radical exclusivity of incest.

A "political play" about unreformed Nazis, *Eve of Retirement* features the familiar Bernhard archetype, obsessed by one idea. Hubris no longer leads to actions that bring about catharsis. Instead, it is an incurable mental condition. After the catastrophes of the 20th century, balance can no longer be restored. The melodramatic ending of *Eve of Retirement* is consistent with Bernhard's universe, which, like SAMUEL BECKETT's, has been drained of all meaningful life. In such a world, existence consists of mere performance acts of varying degrees of virtuosity.

[*See also* Austria]

FURTHER READING

Bernhard, Thomas. *Eve of Retirement*. Tr. by Gitta Honegger. In *Contemporary German Plays II*, ed. by Margaret Herzfeld-Sander. The German Library, vol. 97. New York: Continuum, 2002.

Honegger, Gitta. *Thomas Bernhard: The Making of an Austrian*. New Haven, Conn.: Yale Univ. Press, 2001.

Malkin, Jeanette R. "Pulling the Pants Off History: Politics and Postmodernism in Thomas Bernhard's *Eve of Retirement*." *Theatre Journal* 47, no. 1 (1995): 105–119.

Gitta Honegger

EVREINOV, NIKOLAI (1879–1953)

Nikolai Evreinov was a Russian playwright and theater director who was influenced by the 19th-century philosophies of the human will and by the traditions of medieval theater and commedia dell'arte. Evreinov sought to destroy the conventional distinctions between life and theater through the celebration of life's essential theatricality. He embraced all antinaturalistic theater forms and espoused his own brand of MONODRAMA, in which all aspects of stage setting and character are filtered through the consciousness of a central protagonist so as to redefine the audience's perception of reality.

Evreinov's reputation as a dramatist is based on a handful of works, although he wrote about thirty plays. *A Merry Death* (*Vesyolaya smert'*, 1908) best illustrates his debt to the Italian COMEDY of masks and the contemporary symbolist drama of ALEKSANDR BLOK. The dying Harlequin has invited Pierrot and the latter's faithless wife Columbine to a last supper. Fearing cuckoldom, Pierrot seeks to advance the moment of Harlequin's death by turning the clock back two hours. As midnight approaches, Death appears in the shape of a beautiful girl with whom Harlequin performs a joyful dance before he dies and an embittered Pierrot announces that "the FARCE is over." A good example of monodrama is *In the Stage-Wings of the Soul* (*V kulisakh dushi*, 1912), which also contains elements of the medieval morality play. The stage setting is the soul itself and with action lasting "half a second." The characters are a professor, his Rational and Emotional Entities (M1, M2), and their respective Concepts of "Wife" and "Dancer." A third, Subliminal, Entity (M3) sleeps, while a huge heart and a skein of nerves pulsate throughout. The unusual treatment of banal adultery anticipates SAMUEL BECKETT's *Play* (1963) and concludes with the suicide of M2 and the awakening of M3 as the nerves sunder and the heart stops. A Porter tells M3 that he must change trains as the action has arrived at the town of "Everyman."

The Fourth Wall (*Chetvyortaya stena*, 1915) is a satire on Stanislavskyan NATURALISM (Evreinov's bête noire), in which a rehearsal of an operatic version of *Faust* is subjected to an increasingly veristic interpretation, even introducing a literal "fourth wall" with a window through which the action is fleetingly glimpsed. Evreinov's links with LUIGI PIRANDELLO are traceable in *The Beautiful Despot* (*Krasivy despot*, 1906), whose action anticipates *Henry IV* (1922) and in which a democrat-turned-despot assumes the role of an early-19th-century landowner and imposes his will on others to join him in re-creating the past in the present. In *The Main Thing* (*Samoye glavnoye*, 1921), staged by Pirandello in 1924, the protagonist is again a Harlequin figure who assumes various roles and expounds Evreinov's theories to a group of actors rehearsing *Quo Vadis?* He persuades some of them to transport a theatrical illusion of hope into a local lodging house of suicidal inmates (a satirical gibe at MAKSIM GORKY's THE LOWER DEPTHS) while seeking, with limited success, to demonstrate that "the main thing" is the need to infuse life with the power of theater.

Evreinov's last plays, written after leaving Russia in 1925 and eventually settling in Paris, are *The Ship of the Righteous* (*Korabl' pravednykh*, 1927), which deals with his experience of the 1917 revolution, and *The Theatre of Eternal War* (*Teatr vechnoy voiny*, 1928), in which students are taught the arts of deception and hypocrisy in order to survive.

[*See also* Russia and the Soviet Union]

PLAYS: *The Basis of Happiness (Fundament schast'ya, 1902); Styopik and Manyuroshka a.k.a. Styopik and Manya (Styopik i Manyuroshka, 1905); The Beautiful Despot (Krasivy despot, 1906); A Merry Death (Vesyolaya smert', 1908); A Representation of Love (Predstavleniye lyubvi, 1909); The Government Inspector, a Directorial Spoof (Revizor, rezhissyorskaya buffonada, 1911); School for Stars (Shkola etualey, 1911); The Happy Gravedigger (Schastlivy grobovshchik, 1912); In the Stage-Wings of the Soul a.k.a. The Theatre of the Soul/Backstage of the Soul (V kulisakh dushi, 1912); The Kitchen of Laughter, or the International Wit Competition (Kukhnaya cmekha, ili mirovoy konkurs ostroumiya, 1914); The Fourth Wall (Chetvyortaya stena, 1915); The Main Thing a.k.a. The Chief Thing (Samoye glavnoye, 1921); The Radio-kiss (Radio-potselui, 1926); The Ship of the Righteous (Korabl' pravednykh, 1927); The Theatre of Eternal War a.k.a. The Unmasked Ball (Teatr vechnoy voiny, 1928)*

FURTHER READING

Carnicke, Sharon M. *The Theatrical Instinct: Nikolai Evreinov and the Russian Theatre of the Early Twentieth Century*. New York: Peter Lang, 1989.

Collins, Christopher. *Theater as Life/Life as Theater: Five Modern Plays by Nikolai Evreinov*. Ann Arbor: Ardis, 1973.

Evreinoff, Nicolas. *The Theatre in Life*. Ed. and tr. by Alexander I. Nazaroff, with an intro. by Oliver M. Sayler. London: Harrap, 1927.

Evreinov, Nikolai. "Intro. to Monodrama" [*Vvedeniye v monodramu*]. In *Russian Dramatic Theory from Pushkin to the Symbolists*, ed. and tr. by Laurence Senelick. Austin: Univ. of Texas Press, 1981.

——. "The Fourth Wall." In *Russian Satiric Comedy: Six Plays*, ed. and tr., with an intro. by Laurence Senelick. New York: Performing Arts Journal Pubs., 1983.

Golub, Spencer. *Evreinov: The Theater of Paradox and Transformation*. Ann Arbor: UMI Res. Press, 1984.

Nick Worrall

EXPRESSIONISM

Expressionism was part of the broad reaction in Europe against NATURALISM and its deterministic outlook. The symbolists in FRANCE in the 1890s sought to restore what the naturalists had shunted to one side—man's soul or spirit. The futurists in ITALY a few years later turned their backs on the past, embraced the dynamism of the machine age, and regarded war as the means to greatness. The expressionists in GERMANY, beginning about 1910, opposed the man-against-man doctrine implicit in naturalism with a belief in the spiritual kinship of all humankind. Together these "isms" constituted a major cultural upheaval and an artistic revolution that can be seen in retrospect as culminating politically in the horrors of World War I while remaining influential throughout the 20th century.

As the term suggests, *expressionism* put the subjective feelings of the artist above the impressions made on him by the outside world. The movement was especially strong among painters and poets and playwrights who ardently proclaimed that the emotions and passions more accurately reflected the nature of the human being than scientific laws and rational thought. Painter Henri Matisse in 1908 insisted that the term *impressionism* "could not be retained for the new school of painting, which shuns the first impression and deems it much too illusory. . . . What I am seeking for, above all, is 'l'expression.' "

Unlike the symbolists, who hoped to capture the world of spirit behind the material world, the expressionists saw this spirit as suffusing human society. Where the symbolists, turning inward, had little concern with political man, the expressionists saw a need for a total reform of society and called for a brotherhood of man. Franz Werfel's poem "To the Reader" ("An den Leser") set the tone in its last lines: "Oh, that it might for once happen that we brothers would embrace one another!" This was written in 1910 when the major European nations were preparing for war.

Some plays written at the end of the 19th century have elements of expressionism in them. AUGUST STRINDBERG's *TO DAMASCUS*, Part 1 (1898) is a very subjective work in which the real world often dissolves into a dreamlike place when seen through the eyes of the protagonist who dominates virtually every scene. "Before, all I saw was objects and movements, forms and colors. Now I see meanings and connections. Life, which was all nonsense before, now begins to make a kind of sense. Where I formerly saw only chance and chaos, I now see plan and purpose" (act 1).

FRANK WEDEKIND's *Awakening of Spring* (1891) assails bourgeois society for its hypocrisy, and its final scene breaks completely with the conventions of realistic drama. OSKAR KOKOSCHKA's *Murderer, Only Hope of Woman*, first performed in 1909, presents a radical distortion of reality in its depiction of the war of the sexes. But these works lacked some of the features that distinguish full-blown expressionism.

These can be seen in two of the earliest expressionist works: REINHARD SORGE's *The Beggar* (*Der Bettler*, printed in 1912) and WALTER HASENCLEVER's THE SON (printed in 1914). In Sorge's drama, the Poet-hero revolts first against society, then against his family. He poisons his insane father, and when his girlfriend gives birth to new life, he becomes the prophet of a new evangel, his obligation being to change the world by speaking through "the symbols of eternity." Significantly, this drama was written when Sorge renounced FRIEDRICH NIETZSCHE and became a convert to Catholicism.

In Hasenclever's play, the hero studying at a university quarrels with his father about the value of an academic education. In the confrontation, the father dies of a heart attack, and the son steps over his body, ostensibly to become an active participant in the world outside the ivory tower.

These plays were not intended to be transcriptions of reality. Rather, they were like X-ray pictures, revealing what lay beneath social and political tensions. Whereas the symbolists in France wanted to suggest the immaterial spirit behind the physical world, the expressionists in Germany wanted to penetrate the social community to its deepest level.

To do this, they scorned the methods of realistic drama. They used speech that was either lyrical and ecstatic or inarticulate and primal. In the last act of Sorge's *The Beggar*, the protagonist exclaims, "Oh, tears! Tears!—Oh, bliss!—THE LIFE ETERNAL!!! And I cannot live it! I know it, I cannot live it!—Oh, curses! Curses! To be damned by words! Yes, I am damned by words! I must become a maker of Symbols!"

Expressionist plays dispensed with characterization. The actors represented types, the essence of human beings, not individuals. The characters were often designated as the Man, the Woman, the Stranger. The plays tended to be MONODRAMAS (*Ich-drama*) with one person dominating the action and providing the center from which the world is seen. The plots often consisted of a series of scenes that represented stations in a spiritual progress (station-drama), a technique deriving from late medieval religious drama and reinvented by Strindberg in *To Damascus*.

The plays that are most purely or thoroughly expressionistic feature a revolt against the older generation, the birth of a new order through the love of a woman, and a political revolution either implied or made explicit, as in ERNST TOLLER's *Man and the Masses* (*Masse-Mensch*, 1921). World War I, which confirmed the worst fears of the early expressionists, brought a deluge of expressionistic plays. Sons blamed their fathers for the insane horrors of trench warfare and the bombing of civilians, while the Russian Revolution of 1917 encouraged political activism. What the first expressionists had pictured in a highly stylized way became reality. Mere reformation of society was not enough; what was necessary was a rebirth of the human spirit, a purging of the old materialistic and Darwinist motivations. Some plays, like Toller's *TRANSFIGURATION* (*Die Wandlung*, 1919; tr. 1935), were a direct reflection of the chaos and horrors of war.

After the war the expressionist movement lost its force, and the movement ended as quickly as it had arisen. In the period 1912–1916 the first truly expressionist plays were written and printed but not performed. In the last years of the war new methods of production brought expressionism onstage, and there followed a deluge of expressionist plays and productions. Then, about 1922, expressionism was superseded by the NEW OBJECTIVITY, a movement that rejected the hyperemotionalism and subjectivism characteristic of the expressionists.

Expressionist plays have not fared well, since they were too much bound up with special circumstances, both political and psychological: the frenzy of the war and the dominance of the father figure in German culture. However, the stage productions of these plays required new techniques, and these have been the lasting heritage of the movement. It took some time before designers and directors discovered how to present these subjective works effectively. The production of *The Son* in Mannheim in 1918, directed by Richard Weichert, is usually considered the first truly expressionist staging of an expressionist play. GEORG KAISER'S *FROM MORNING TO MIDNIGHT* was written in 1912, printed in 1916, but not staged until 1919—a time lapse indicating how far in advance of designers the dramatists were.

However, once the artists figured out how to stage these groundbreaking works, their technical innovations came to overshadow the playscripts. While most of the plays have faded, the new techniques have become standard in the theater and given playwrights greater freedom, allowing them to escape from the constraints of realistic theater.

A stage direction in Sorge's *The Beggar* calls for floodlights, with one side of the stage brightly lighted, the other in darkness. Splitting the stage this way by means of light eliminated conventional and cumbersome scene changes. Unique at the time, but a common technique within a few years, it allowed for a flow of scenes, one dissolving into another, a cinematic technique, impacting on the eye as much as on the ear.

In addition to creating stage space by means of light, the expressionist artists designed sets that represented a subjective view of reality. Jagged and angled lines and the brilliant use of color, combined with an intensely emotional delivery of lines, brought about a new kind of theatrical poetry, unlike anything ever seen or heard before. German critic Kasimir Edschmid put the expressionist position succinctly: "The world is here; it would be absurd to repeat it (Macgowan, 1921)".

The excitement generated in America by these new methods can be sensed in *Continental Stagecraft* (1922), a handsomely illustrated book by Kenneth Macgowan and ROBERT EDMOND JONES, both friends of EUGENE O'NEILL. Quickly seizing on these new theatrical possibilities, the young O'Neill wrote *THE EMPEROR JONES* (1920) and *THE HAIRY APE* (1922). In the next few years, ELMER RICE'S *THE ADDING MACHINE* (1923), JOHN HOWARD LAWSON'S *PROCESSIONAL* (1925), and SOPHIE TREADWELL'S *MACHINAL* (1929) helped to make the 1920s the decade of creative experimentation in American drama, thanks in no small measure to the expressionists.

[*See also* Apocalypse in Modern Drama; Futurism, Italian; Symbolism]

FURTHER READING

Bablet, Denis, and Jean Jacquot, eds. *L'Expressionnisme dans le théâtre européen* [Expressionism in the European theater]. Paris: Centre national de la Recherce Scientifique, 1971.

Macgowan, Kenneth. *The Theatre of Tomorrow*. New York: Boni and Liveright, 1921.

Matisse, Henri. "Notes d'un peintre" ["Notes of a Painter"]. *La Grande Revue*, Dec. 1908.

Patterson, Michael. *The Revolution in German Theatre 1900–1933*. Boston: Routledge, 1981.

Sokel, Walter H., ed. *An Anthology of German Expressionist Drama*. Garden City, N.Y.: Anchor Bks., 1963.

Evert Sprinchorn

F

FADREN *See* THE FATHER

THE FALL OF THE CITY

Poet and essayist ARCHIBALD MACLEISH wrote his verse plays *The Fall of the City* (1937) and *Air Raid* (1938) for radio. They manifested his theories and program for poetry as "public speech" (MacLeish, 1941) for what he later termed "the imaginative ear." These experimental and propagandistic dramas sent the word, unencumbered by visuals of casting or staging, to the vast audience of CBS radio. Borrowing elements of both the expressionistic and classical theater, they called America to war against the fascist atrocities in SPAIN and the Japanese and German march of conquests. Compressing the issues to "the inwardness of human action," the two intense half hours chart the enervating, dehumanizing effects of waiting—with fascinated anticipation in *Air Raid* and with terror in *The Fall of the City*.

The Fall of the City starts with a palpable terror in an unnamed "City," at once any East Coast town and the Aztec capital of MEXICO. The characters are limited to their functions. The Conqueror is coming, preceded by the iconic omen of a Dead Woman and the reports of two Messengers like those of Greek TRAGEDIES. A tension builds over how the Crowd will respond. The Orator proposes more discussion and nonresistance; the Priests propose prayer and sacrifice. Unspecified, these personifications invite the audience to identify with the politicians, priests, and city. "The Voice of the Announcer"—central to the dramatic process—uses the familiar "we" when describing events professionally in his five-beat lines but cannot fully resist the pull of the terror, speeches, and Crowd. After a Studio Director identifies "this city" the world is watching, he "sends" us to join the Announcer (Orson Welles) in the "great square" for the rest of the play.

From his "terrace" the Announcer states he is overlooking "ten thousand" faces, and "the shuffle and hum" of the vast crowd "fills the background." The audience, with the crowd, is waiting at noon for the Dead Woman. She predicts that the free city-state will submit: "The city of masterless men / Will take a master. / There will be shouting then: / Blood after!" The prophecy puzzles the Crowd. "They are milling around us," reports the Announcer, "like cattle who smell death." The first Messenger has raced to warn us. "There has come the conqueror!" In every country he has taken, "[t]hey die as do animals," shamefully. The Orator counsels, "This conqueror unresisted / Will conquer no longer"; words will win. The Crowd relaxes, even dances, till the second Messenger describes the approaching conqueror as so famously ferocious he needs no enemies to defeat. "That touched them!" observes the Announcer. "That frightened them!" The Priests turn the frenzied crowd toward God and a human sacrifice, which the old General interrupts with his call to fight for freedom and resist to the last inch. But the citizens know the city is doomed: "Masterless men / Must take a master!" Huge and armored the Conqueror enters the square. They cheer. He opens his helmet, and it is hollow; there is no one there. "The people invent their oppressors." So: "The city has fallen."

FURTHER READING

Donaldson, Scott, with R. H. Winnick. *Archibald MacLeish: An American Life*. Boston: Houghton, 1992.

Drabeck, Bernard A., and Helen E. Ellis, eds. *Archibald MacLeish: Reflections*. Amherst: Univ. of Massachusetts Press, 1986.

MacLeish, Archibald. *A Time to Speak* [essays]. Boston: Houghton, 1941.

John G. Kuhn

THE FAMILY REUNION

> *[N]ot a story of detection, / Of crime and punishment, but of sin and expiation.*
>
> —"Agatha," Part 2

A play in two acts, composed between 1934 and 1939, and first performed in March 1938, T. S. ELIOT's *The Family Reunion* is a hybrid; on the surface it looks like a conventional country house mystery, filled with stock English upper-class "types" (the men's club uncle, the colonial administrator retired from INDIA, the iron-willed matriarch, the feckless sons who wreck automobiles), while its core is deeply religious. The play's theatrical language is also an uneasy mixture, part mystical verse, part colloquial modern dialogue. The critical consensus through the years suggests it is much more effective seen than read.

If the theme is the sin of lovelessness, the plot concerns Harry's return to his ancestral home, the blatantly named Wishwood, after an eight-year absence. His mother, Amy, has assembled the family for a reunion on the occasion of what will be her last birthday (there is the cliché of the family doctor who privately warns the son of his mother's weak heart); the group includes Mary, the no-longer-young woman Harry was to have married, and the pivotal character of Agatha, Amy's youngest sister who reveals that years before she had a passionate love affair with Amy's husband. Harry's parents' loveless marriage (we learn that his father plotted to kill his mother while she was pregnant with Harry) was echoed in Harry's own loveless marriage; his wife's death is a puzzle: how did she fall overboard during their ocean voyage—did she jump? Or, as Harry claims, did he push her? Whether he actually murdered her remains unclear, but the murderous wish is quite enough for him to be haunted by Aeschylean Furies. Harry ultimately discovers that they are the Eumenides, whose function will be not to hound him to death but to lead him into a new and redeemed life.

This link to the *Oresteia* is unconvincing, although the presence of the "bright angels" in the drawing room, revealed to us, is the most theatrical element of the play but, judging by past reviews, the most problematic in production (should they be in evening dress? or a crowd of surreal ghouls? or huge spectral figures looming over the audience?). Most intriguing is T. S. Eliot's clever and comic use of the Chorus of befuddled aunts and uncles who try to understand what is going on, find it quite incomprehensible, and lament, "Why do we feel embarrassed, impatient, fretful, ill at ease, / Assembled like amateur actors who have not been assigned their parts?"

Peter Brook's 1956 production starred Paul Scofield, and his performance, Eliot wrote, transformed Harry from "an insufferable prig" to a sympathetic haunted man. Adrian Noble directed a Royal Shakespeare Company revival in 2000 (the Stratford production transferred to London and then to New York), which had the critics on both sides of the Atlantic held by the play's power while often exasperated by Eliot's pretensions. Lyndall Gordon, Eliot's biographer, sees the play as an autobiography of Eliot's disastrous first marriage to Vivienne. Helen Gardner, in her book on *Four Quartets*, sees *The Family Reunion* as a failed attempt to dramatize the subject of the redemption of the modern personality, the same subject that in Christian terms drives most of Eliot's later greater poetry. As Harry says, "You bring me news / Of a door that opens at the end of a corridor, / Sunlight and singing; when I had felt sure / That every corridor only led to another, / Or to a blank wall."

[*See also* Religion and Drama]

FURTHER READING

Browne, E. Martin. *The Making of T. S. Eliot's Plays*. London: Cambridge Univ. Press, 1969.

Donoghue, Denis. *The Third Voice, Modern British and American Drama*. Princeton, N.J.: Princeton Univ. Press, 1959.

Eliot, T. S. *Poetry and Drama*. Cambridge: Harvard Univ. Press, 1951.

Gardner, Helen. *The Art of T. S. Eliot*. 1950. New York: Dutton, 1979.

Weales, Gerald. *Religion in Modern English Drama*. Philadelphia: Univ. of Pennsylvania Press, 1960.

Toby Zinman

FAR AWAY

In CARYL CHURCHILL's play *Far Away*, first performed in November 2000 at the Royal Court Theatre in London, the fraying of the social fabric in the domestic, artistic, work-related, and geopolitical spheres leaves the characters in an apocalypse where the entire human and natural worlds are regarded as potential enemies. All of creation has joined the battle—animals, plants, rivers; even the weather has landed on one side or the other. Who is on whose side is arbitrary and fluctuating, depending on how useful one is presently made to appear; new reasons for hatred and new opportunities for alliance proliferate. In act 1, a woman answers her young niece's questions when the girl, staying the night in a strange place, is unable to sleep. This quotidian domestic scene gradually becomes a horror show as the brutality of what is happening outside the house (children being delivered in trucks, beaten, herded into a garage, with blood all over the place) is slowly revealed. From the outset, we are witness to and implicated in the power of language to cover violence and bloody details with banal explanations. The aunt translates and contains what her niece sees into a comprehensible scenario. The scene uncannily demonstrates how quickly moral and political imperatives can be redirected, how easily what one sees can be transformed to suggest that there is nothing to see.

In act 2, the prohibition on seeing and knowing has gone much further. The girl, now a young woman, learns how not to ask questions about what is taking place offstage, out of the public view. The social blinding, in which our eyes are used against us, leads to a spectacle of violence where a procession of brutalized, chained, and silent prisoners is dressed up and paraded wearing visually stunning, gigantic handcrafted hats. Violence is aestheticized while the increasingly robust demand for the magnificent and outrageous hats materializes the labor, booming business, and industrial profits that accompany ritualized violence and mass murder.

The bizarre shapes and riotous proportions of the props of act 2 dress up the ways in which humans and things become expendable, subject to death and destruction at the whim of another. In the play's startling final act, Churchill troubles the easy and misleading comforts of wars that are waged "far away," offstage, "over there," elsewhere. As the young woman, seeking refuge, returns to her aunt's home, we discover the dangers of the aunt's phenomenal storytelling ability, of the power to produce lies that pass for moral values. *Far Away* takes the last of its frequently unsettling turns when the aunt determines, "The cats have come in on the side of the French." Species after species become part of the mayhem as the domestic merges with the national, nations divide against each other and within themselves, and even the deer, seduced and corrupted by capitalist consumption, invade and terrorize the shopping malls. In *Far Away* Churchill's prescient staging of the world's current geopolitical situation urges us to attend to the ways in which our moral sensibilities depend on our ability to interrogate the emergence and vanishing of the human at the limits of what we can see, hear, and know.

[*See also* England, 1980–Present]

FURTHER READING

Chaudhuri, Una. "Animal Rights: Performing Beyond the Human." In *Critical Theory and Performance*, ed. by Janelle G. Reinelt and Joseph R. Roach. Rev. ed. Ann Arbor: Univ. of Michigan Press, 2006.

Churchill, Caryl. *Far Away*. New York: Theatre Communications Group, 2000.

Dymkowski, Christine. "Caryl Churchill: Far Away . . . But Close to Home." *European Journal of English Studies* 7, no. 1 2003: 55–68.

Kerry Moore

FARCE

As a genre seldom defined, farce is often described, but the description usually carries a note of mockery: it treats this genre as a failure to live up to the witty standards of COMEDY. But primitive farce coexisted with early comedy or could have preceded it as knockabout humor played in the open air, before indoor theaters came into being. The two genres have features in common; they both plan to amuse spectators, and moments of farce may streak into and out of moments of pure comedy. Or farce may add a bitter note or satire to a comedy or to a MELODRAMA or, in rare instances, to a TRAGEDY—the knocking at the gate in *Macbeth*.

Genres are, after all, art forms and therefore may decline to behave within boundaries. But comedy depends in general on language and ideas, on intentional wit exerted at the expense of other persons, while farce is the medium of bumblers and depends on clumsiness, which appears to be free of malicious intentions even as it toys with collisions and physical accidents. Audiences swiftly recognize that actors in farce demonstrate their agility and acrobatic gifts, as when a farcical character ducks under a punch or turns a stumble into a somersault.

The figures of farce make fun of themselves rather than being mocked by others. They fall. They get names wrong. They misunderstand orders and make fools of themselves—but by accident not deliberately. Playing the fool belongs in their repertory. Farce is the obverse of tragedy, in which the roles bring on themselves death or ruin, the distant opposite of laughter. Actors with a bundle of farcical tricks up their sleeves or below their cloaks will be suitable for casting as lawyers or presidents or wealthy businessmen because they puncture their own dignity in performance. If actors who specialize in farce do not, as is often observed, create impersonations of great range or subtlety, they may nonetheless create impersonations drawn with powerful satirical strokes, at ease with the sort of eminent insolence that could not be enacted by a person schooled in literal REALISM. A staple of farces is a clumsy acrobat in or on an oversized bed situated in an undersized bedroom.

Since the 1860s farces have grown new limbs: tragifarces. These present a nightmare come to waking life. For instance, a man named La Brige is accused in Georges Courteline's *Article 330* (1891) of committing an "offense against decency." In an anticipation of Franz Kafka's *The Trial* (1925), La Brige, an exacting man who battles the absurdities of legal procedure, becomes known ironically in France as "the friend of the law." Since he moved into his apartment, a moving sidewalk constructed right outside it means that La Brige has revealed his bare backside to 13,687 witnesses. He committed this act unintentionally, probably when changing into pajamas and changing back into daytime garments. But the judge does not want to know about good or bad intentions and callously sentences La Brige to thirteen months at hard labor, a fine, and costs.

In another tragifarce, written half a century later, ARTHUR ADAMOV's academic criminal in *Professor Taranne* is accused by a group of small children of having publicly exposed himself. The audience never learns explicitly that the professor did commit the "crime," and so one can interpret the play as precisely the sort of material that occupies routine nightmares, whether or not based on a truthful report: (1) the topic is shameful, and (2) the victim is blameful, being an exacting man and therefore all the more liable to undergo dreams that haunt him. In both cases, we laugh at his plight all the more because we "feel for" him.

Prior and later-19th-century farces by Eugène Labiche almost all have a nightmarish element, from *An Italian Straw Hat* (1851), about the disruption of a wedding ceremony, to *Monsieur Perrichon's Trip* (1860), in which the protagonist falls into a split in SWITZERLAND's Great Glacier and has to be rescued by one of the two young men pursuing his daughter, to *The Piggy Bank* (1864), the adventures of a batch of neighbors from a village who take a day off to spend their piggy banks in Paris. All three farces by Labiche and collaborators put the villagers in strange, baffling settings. A nightmare also occurs in Courteline's most popular farce, *Boubouroche* (1893), a caricature of a booby who treats his mistress to her own apartment, where she hides (and he finds) a boyfriend in her closet.

Farces irrepressibly flowed during the 1800s–1900s from French quills wielded by Eugène Scribe, VICTORIEN SARDOU, and most boldly, GEORGES FEYDEAU, who in one season had six of his thirty-nine plays running at once in Paris. Feydeau employed farce as a medium of punishment. He tastelessly mocked the speech and activity of foreigners, people with goiters and other blemishes and deformities, ignorance, excessive behavior (he was an incurable gambler himself, in the stock market), marriage, women, men, children, illiteracy, and other targets he plucked from his tireless imagination.

Along with its extension into tragifarce, farce broadened its scope and, with the dawn of the 1900s, had already invaded social, sexual, political, and other serious topics. The lyrics of WILLIAM SCHWENCK GILBERT emerged as nonsense that made powerful sense—or impeccable—nonsense in the vein of Lewis Carroll or Edward Lear.

Sergeant: . . . When the enterprising burglar's not a-burgling
Police: Not a-burgling,
Sergeant: When the cut-throat isn't occupied in crime
Police: 'Pied in crime,
Sergeant: He loves to hear the little brook a-gurgling
Police: Brook a-gurgling,

Sergeant: And listen to the merry village chime
Police: Village chime,
Sergeant: When the coster's finished jumping on his mother
Police: On his mother. . . .
Sergeant: He loves to lie a-basking in the sun
Police: In the sun,
Sergeant: Ah, take one consideration with another
Police: With another,
Sergeant: A policeman's lot is not a happy one.

Along with its more widespread artistry, farce acquired new types of dialogue, less slangy, considerably more suave, at times understated, and not quite as gentle as it sounded. OSCAR WILDE, more prodigiously than any other farceur, played with wit so cleverly that it was tantamount to a new form of farce. The farces of N. F. Simpson, HAROLD PINTER, and JOE ORTON, making their initial reputations in London, remounted a succession of attacks on middle-class standards and beliefs. Audiences occasionally seemed unsure of whether to allow themselves to laugh and how explosively. In Simpson's *A Resounding Tinkle* (1957) a suburban family has a visit once a week from a "cleaning woman" who eats up all leftover food. In Pinter's early *The Dumb Waiter* (1960), a hit man casually discusses a woman he and his hit-man partner have murdered: "She wasn't much to look at, I know. But still, it was a mess, though, wasn't it? What a mess. Honest, I can't remember a mess like that one. They don't seem to hold together like men, women. A looser texture, like. Didn't she spread, eh? She didn't half spread. Kaw!" These sentences are so depersonalized that they are funny to anyone who dares to laugh at such grisly humor.

In France the intricate but distinctive tragifarces of SAMUEL BECKETT, Boris Vian, EUGÈNE IONESCO, and JEAN GENET stretch the genre, like Wilde's, into verbal territory where they seem to resist any definition one imposes on them.

[*See also* Tragicomedy]

FURTHER READING

Bentley, Eric. "Farce." In *The Life of the Drama*. New York: Atheneum, 1964.
Bermel, Albert. *Farce: A History from Aristophanes to Woody Allen*. New York: Simon & Schuster, 1982.
Davis, Jessica Milner. *Farce, the Critical Idiom*. London: Methuen, 1978.

Albert Bermel

FASSBINDER, RAINER WERNER (1945–1982)

Best known for the more than forty films that made him a leader of the New German Cinema in the 1970s, Rainer Werner Fassbinder spent much of his early career writing, adapting, directing, and acting in plays. His theatrical work remained closely linked to his cinematic oeuvre and provided it with significant inspiration.

Fassbinder was born on May 31, 1945, in Bad Wörishofen, West GERMANY. Following an early departure from high school, he enrolled in drama classes, which he found equally oppressive. However, a performance of ANTIGONE by Munich's Action-Theater (in the manner of the LIVING THEATRE) convinced him that the stifling theatrical tradition he abhorred could be revitalized through radical techniques. Shortly after joining the Action-Theater, Fassbinder came to dominate the collective through the energy and manipulation characteristic of his dealings with coworkers. His authorial debut occurred in 1968 with *Katzelmacher*, a play dedicated to MARIELUISE FLEIßER and influenced by her realistic, critical recasting of the VOLKSSTÜCK. Through a series of brief dialogues, *Katzelmacher* portrays the reactions of small-town Bavarians to the perceived economic and sexual threat of a foreign guest worker, revealing the jealousy, sadism, despair, and institutional and individual mistreatment of the outsider that preoccupied Fassbinder throughout his life and art.

The Action-Theater, known for its politically charged plays, was dissolved and reconstituted as the antitheater; many of its members continued working with Fassbinder in subsequent dramas and films. *Pre-Paradise Sorry Now* (1968) intertwines six narrative scenes about a famous murderer couple with nine dialogues between the pair, nine liturgies linking religious and cultural cannibalism, and fifteen "scenes about the fascistoid underpinnings of everyday life." The ability to arrange the last three groups of scenes in any order illustrates Fassbinder's experimentation with form and his emphasis on conveying domination through dialogue. Though it alludes to the Living Theatre, this play presents a disillusioned anti-utopia mired in the present.

In 1969, Fassbinder produced two feature-length films. Although he began to gain national attention for his films and devote more time to the cinema, Fassbinder remained active in the theater through 1975. *The Bitter Tears of Petra von Kant* (*Die bitteren Tränen der Petra von Kant*, 1971) deals with a lesbian relationship. Issues of domination and the inability to love typify his depictions of both homosexual and heterosexual relations. In *Bremen Freedom* (*Bremer Freiheit*, 1971), a historical TRAGICOMEDY about a male-dominated society, the heroine futilely attempts to liberate herself by poisoning her tormentors. The controversy surrounding Fassbinder's last play, *Garbage, The City and Death* (*Der Müll, die Stadt und der Tod*, 1975), prevented its performance during his lifetime. Although the drama can be seen in terms of Fassbinder's continuing analysis of the psychology of victimization, it sparked accusations of anti-Semitism.

Fassbinder's frenetic pace finally caught up with him, and on June 10, 1982, he died from a drug overdose in his Munich apartment. Though sometimes criticized for a lack of unity or hurried production, his experimental dramas constituted an exciting antidote to the tired theater of his day, providing imaginative and daring representations of social and emotional exploitation in West Germany.

PLAYS: *Only a Slice of Bread: Dialog About an Auschwitz Film (Nur eine Scheibe Brot: Dialog über einen Auschwitzfilm*, 1966); *Waterdrops on Hot Stones (Tropfen auf heiße Steine*, 1966); *Ajax* (1968); *The American Soldier (Der amerikanische Soldat*, 1968); *For Example Ingolstadt (Zum Beispiel Ingolstadt*, 1968); *Iphigenie at Tauris (Iphigenie auf Tauris*, 1968); *Katzelmacher* (1968); *Anarchy in Bavaria (Anarchie in Bayern*, 1969); *The Beggar's Opera (Die Bettleroper*, from the John Gay play, 1969); *The Coffeehouse (Das Kaffeehaus*, 1969); *Pre-Paradise Sorry Now* (1969); *Werewolf (Werwolf*, 1969); *The Bitter Tears of Petra von Kant (Die bitteren Tränen der Petra von Kant*, 1971); *Bremen Freedom (Bremer Freiheit*, 1971); *Garbage, The City and Death (Der Müll, die Stadt und der Tod*, 1975); *The Burning Village (Das brennende Dorf*, 1970); *Blood on the Cat's Neck (Blut am Hals der Katze*, 1971)

FURTHER READING

Barnett, David. *Rainer Werner Fassbinder and the German Theatre*. Cambridge: Cambridge Univ. Press. 2005.

Elsaesser, Thomas. *Fassbinder's Germany. History Identity Subject*. Amsterdam: Amsterdam Univ. Press, 1996.

Fassbinder, Rainer Werner. *Plays*. Ed. and tr. by Denis Calandra. New York: PAJ, 1985.

Hayman, Ronald. *Fassbinder: Film Maker*. New York: Simon & Schuster, 1984.

Jansen, Peter W., and Wolfram Schütte, eds. *Fassbinder*. Tr., with a new article, by Ruth McCormick. New York: Tanam Press, 1981. Originally published as *Fassbinder*. Munich: Carl Hanser, 1974; exp. 5th ed. Frankfurt: Fischer, 1992.

Thomsen, Christian Braad. *Fassbinder: The Life and Work of a Provocative Genius*. Tr. by Martin Chalmers. London: Faber, 1997.

Watson, Wallace Steadman. *Understanding Rainer Werner Fassbinder: Film as Private and Public Art*. Columbia: Univ. of South Carolina Press, 1996.

Calvin N. Jones

THE FATHER

The Father (Fadren) is a TRAGEDY in three acts by AUGUST STRINDBERG. Written and published in 1887, it was first performed the same year at the Casino Theater in Copenhagen. It became Strindberg's first play performed outside Scandinavia when it premiered in 1890 at Otto Brahm's Freie Bühne in Berlin.

Taking his deteriorating marriage to Siri von Essen and his fear for his own mental sanity as a subject, Strindberg wrote *The Father* in Bavaria in early 1887. By that time he had become an atheist. Proud of his new piece, he told his publisher: "*The Father* is the modern tragedy and therefore quite remarkable. This because the fight is fought between the souls, 'the battle of the brains,' not with dagger and lingonberry juice as in [Friedrich Schiller's] *The Robbers*. The young Frenchmen still seek the formula, but I have found it!" (Strindberg, 1981). Strindberg refers to the discussion about the new formula caused by ÉMILE ZOLA's *Naturalism in the Theater (Le naturalisme au théâtre*, 1881), which Strindberg had read. In August 1887, he had sent his own French translation of *The Father* to Zola for approval, but the leader of NATURALISM found it too abstract to fit the new movement. The scanty information both about the characters' past and about their present surroundings was clearly at odds with the strivings of the naturalists to stress heredity and environment as determining factors. An article by Paul Lafargue, in which matriarchy was considered man's original social structure, made Strindberg fear that the emancipation movement of his time was a sign that matriarchy was about to return. Using the "theater as a weapon," *The Father* was his warning.

The play is about a married couple—Adolf, a cavalry captain, and Laura—who disagree about their daughter Bertha's upbringing. When Adolf claims that he alone has the right to decide the girl's future, Laura begins to oppose him. She first spreads a rumor that he is mentally ill; then she makes him suspect that he is not Bertha's father; finally, she threatens to declare him incapable of managing his own affairs. As a result, Adolf, after having shown signs of madness, has a stroke from which he, according to the Doctor, will never recover. Laura is now free to bring up her daughter as she likes.

Because paternity was much more difficult to establish in the 1880s than it is today, the males in the audience had more reason to identify with the Captain's worry. However, this does not mean that *The Father* is outdated. Still one of Strindberg's most frequently performed plays, its vitality rests neither on the question of paternity nor on the conflict about the daughter—although productions in our divorce era have sometimes stressed this aspect—but rather in the battle of the sexes. *Willpower* is a key word in the text.

The Father is a highly subjective play, in which the Captain's point of view in various ways dominates those of the other characters. He is on stage more often than the others and has a greater number of lines. Since his concern for Bertha—mama's baby, papa's maybe—is central, we empathize with him rather than with the others. He also is intellectually superior. The Captain struggles against a collective antagonist—the women in his house and later the Pastor and the Doctor—who by manipulation, cowardly opportunism (the men), and sheer force defeat him. What makes *The Father* a rather special drama is that the Captain and Laura, in addition to being individuals, are portrayed as prototypes of the male and female sex. To demonstrate this, Strindberg has them use generalizing statements about the genders—for example: "A man has no children. Only women have children, and so the future belongs to them, while we die childless." He also provides a mytho-historical background (Hercules-Omphale, Samson-Delilah), demonstrating how man has always fallen victim to the stratagem of woman—as do all the men in the play. Strindberg took care to show that the Captain's misogyny grows in the course of the play as a reaction to the increasing pressure from the women around him. The misogyny is also tempered by his love for Bertha (the child) and the Nurse (the mother figure) and his past love for Laura. At the end, it is demonstrated how history repeats itself (*l'histoire se repète*). As the Captain clarifies, it is not only *a* man who is disarmed by *a* woman; it is the female defeating the male.

Yet rather than being a thesis play about the battle between the sexes, *The Father* is an interiorized drama, dealing with the Captain's psychic constitution, his unusual—hence not so archetypal—susceptibility to doubts about his paternity. Thus modern critics have tended to see the Captain as a victim less of Laura's manipulations than of his own psyche. Viewed in this way, Gunnar Brandell (1971) notes, the ending becomes ambiguous. "Have we witnessed the destruction of a strong spirit by means of hostile forces or the disintegration of a soul from within, a psychic murder or a psychic suicide?" What these critics suggest is that *The Father*, far from being a naturalistic play, is essentially a subjective drama anticipating those of the post-*Inferno* period.

An often-quoted passage from one of Strindberg's letters around this time is, in fact, very much in the mood of the later period. It reads:

> It seems to me as if I'm walking in my sleep; as if my life and writing have got all jumbled up. I don't know if *The Father* is a work of literature or if my life has been; but I feel as if, probably quite soon, at a given moment, it will suddenly break upon me, and then I shall collapse either into madness and remorse, or suicide. Through much writing, my life has become a shadow life; I no longer feel as if I am walking the earth but floating weightless in an atmosphere not of air but darkness. (Strindberg, 1992)

FURTHER READING

Jacobs, Barry. "Psychic Murder and Characterization in Strindberg's *The Father*." *Scandinavica* 8, no. 1 (1969): 19–34.

Brandell, Gunnar. *Drama i tre avsnitt* [Drama in three parts]. Stockholm: Wahlström & Widstrand, 1971.

Lunin, Hanno. *Strindbergs Dramen* [Strindberg's Plays]. Emsdetten: Lechte, 1962.

Strindberg, August. *August Strindbergs samlade verk*. Stockholm: Almqvist & Wiksell, 1981 *et seq*.

Strindberg's Letters, 1. Toby Michael Robinson. Chicago: Univ. of Chicago Press, 1992.

Törnqvist, Egil. *Strindbergian Drama: Themes and Structure*. Stockholm: Almqvist & Wiksell Intl., 1982.

Egil Törnqvist

FATHERLESSNESS See PLATONOV

THE FATHER RETURNS

The Father Returns (*Chichi Kaeru*), a Japanese one-act SHINGEKI play (approximately twenty-five minutes in performance) by KIKUCHI KAN, went unnoticed when it was first published in a literary magazine in 1917. The numerous theater groups aiming to establish modern drama at the time ignored it, and only a production by a progressive *kabuki* actor's company unlocked its potential. Performed first in 1920, it soon became regarded as a model of a one-act drama.

The curtain opens on a family that is seen to be respectable but not well-off. It is a family that has endured twenty years of financial struggle, because the head of the household—the father of the title—had disappeared with his mistress and all their money two decades before. The audience is given to believe that the eldest son, Ken'ichirō, has shouldered most of the burden, and the play focuses on him as the one most embittered by the experience. He has two siblings, a brother and a sister, and the brother reports that someone resembling the father has been seen on the streets of their town. A man's voice is heard at the front door, and there follows a bizarre conversation as the mother, offstage, greets her long-lost husband with conventional phrases that she might have used to a husband returning from a long business trip. When he comes onto the stage, however, his interaction with Ken'ichirō is anything but conventional. The father wants to return to the family, but Ken'ichirō rejects him, telling him they have no father. While the others show sympathy for their aged and broken visitor, Ken'ichirō persists in refusing him, and in great sorrow he leaves. At this point, Ken'ichirō breaks, and the play ends as he and his brother dash out to find their father.

Kikuchi hoped his play was not overstated and presented conflicts that were Japanese, contemporary, and dramatic. *The Father Returns* had a Western model, but critical response at the time of its first productions noted how much the theme chimed with contemporary Japanese society. The new rational individualism gives way to fundamental emotions, something spectators from every social class could respond to. The continuing popularity of this play after the war established that Kikuchi had achieved the right formula; technical features had been cannily borrowed from his Irish model, but no one reacted to *The Father Returns* as if it were a foreign play. It is something quite rare in modern Japanese drama: a play written first for publication as a piece of literature, taken up by *kabuki* actors, and then effortlessly crossing the border into more realistic types of production. The early 1920s seemed to be the right period for this to happen, but this phenomenon was rare afterward.

[*See also* Japan]

FURTHER READING

Itō Sei et al., eds. *Gendai Nihon Gikyoku-shū* [Anthology of modern Japanese drama]. Vol. 5. Tokyo: Hakusuisha, 1955.

Keene, Donald. *Dawn to the West: Japanese Literature of the Modern Era*. Vol. 5, *Poetry, Drama and Criticism*. New York: Henry Holt, 1984.

Nihon Kindai Engekishi Kenkyûkai, ed. *Nijisseiki no Gikyoku, Nihon Kindai Gikyoku no Sekai* [Plays of the twentieth century: The world of modern Japanese drama]. Tokyo: Shakai Hyōronsha, 1998.

Brian Powell

FEAR AND MISERY IN THE THIRD REICH

"No single work of Brecht's is more important than *Fear and Misery in the Third Reich*, of which *The Private Life of the Master Race* is the stage version. Both for its intrinsic merits and for its interest as a portrait and interpretation of Nazi Germany it will probably be his best-known piece." The exaggeration in this comment by ERIC BENTLEY (1989) is understandable, given that it was made in the notes to the 1944 English-language edition of the play when World War II was still raging. Since then, other works by BERTOLT BRECHT (1898–1945) have proven more popular. The urgency of *Fear and Misery in the Third Reich* (*Furcht und Elend des Dritten Reiches*) has diminished as the historical events it depicts have receded from memory. Nevertheless, it remains a compelling demonstration of how to bring complex historical events to the stage successfully and is a milestone in the development of DOCUMENTARY DRAMA.

Work on the play began in July 1937 and was completed by the following spring. Brecht wanted to show what life in GERMANY was like under the Nazi dictatorship between the 1933 seizure of power and the onset of the Spanish Civil War in 1936. To accomplish this, Brecht rejected the approach Friedrich Schiller (1759–1805) took when confronted by the challenge of representing the totality of the Thirty Years' War. Schiller had made the career of Count Albrecht Wallenstein the organizing device for his trilogy of historical dramas. Brecht's alternative to centering the action on one hero was to have no single character whatsoever. Twenty-four episodes, minidramas as short as two minutes, are presented serially. All levels of society become visible in these snapshots: workers, farmers, professors, students, soldiers, and ordinary people. Each episode captures a moment that reveals how the Nazi dictatorship exercised control down to the most intimate spheres of people's lives. A single word or gesture, whether intended as opposition or merely misconstrued as such by a spy, a neighbor, or a fellow worker, could bring imprisonment, torture, and death.

While informing those who had never experienced the everyday terror imposed by the totalitarian state, Brecht could not neglect the affective dimension of the theater if the work was to find an audience. Each of the vignettes is captivating because the characters appear as vivid individuals, even when they are anonymous. Brecht also wanted to provoke the members of the audience into critical reflection, into analysis of the causes and logic of fascism. Thus the scene "Serving the People" shows how an SS man, tired from beating his prisoner, nonetheless is compelled to go back to the work of whipping by his superior, whom he fears. Everyone could become a victim in turn. In "The Jewish Woman," Judith Keith's blunt monologue is heard by no one except the audience: "What sort of people are you, yes, you too! You discover the quantum theory and the Trendelenburg position, but let savages tell you you're supposed to conquer the world but can't have the wife you want." The direct address accuses the audience for their complicity. The didactic element is reinforced by the short poems that preface each episode. The rhymed sestets jar by contrast with the raw violence, creating the ironic alienation Brecht termed *Verfremdung*. Various scenes also convey practical instructions on how to forge solidarity and continue resistance.

[*See also* Alienation Effect]

FURTHER READING

Bentley, Eric. "*The Private Life of the Master Race*." *Critical Essays on Bertolt Brecht*. Ed. by Siegfried Mews. Boston: Hall, 1989.

Fehervary, Helen. "Enlightenment or Entanglement: History and Aesthetics in Bertolt Brecht and Heiner Müller." *New German Critique* 8 (Spring 1976): 80–109.

Kuhn, Tom. "The Politics of the Changeable Text: *Furcht und Elend des III. Reiches* and the New Brecht Edition." *Oxford German Studies* 18–19 (1989–1990): 132–149.

Lyon, James K. "Brecht's Sources for *Furcht und Elend des III. Reiches*: Heinrich Mann, Personal Friends, Newspaper Accounts." *Brecht Yearbook / Das Brecht-Jahrbuch* 26 (2001): 294–305.

Arnd Bohm

FEDERAL THEATRE PROJECT

The Federal Theatre Project (FTP) came into being in the summer of 1935, when the relief rolls in American cities included thousands of unemployed theater professionals. Harry Hopkins, head of the Works Progress Administration (WPA), argued that unemployed theatrical people got just as hungry as other unemployed people. He viewed professional theater workers, painters, musicians, and writers as part of America's wealth, a resource he did not want the country to lose. As a result, the Arts Projects of the WPA offered people an anchor, for a brief period, that enabled them to preserve their skills and dignity. An unforeseen benefit of this money-for-work arrangement was that it brought the American artist face-to-face with the American people, which *Fortune* magazine (May 1, 1937) described as an astonishing and exciting state of affairs for both sides.

At its peak the Federal Theatre employed 12,700 people—more than nine out of every ten from relief roles; $9 out of every $10 had to be spent on wages. Roughly half of the workers were actors. The others were writers, designers, theater musicians, dancers, stagehands, box-office workers, ushers, maintenance workers, accountants, and secretaries. Expenditures from appropriated funds in the first two years of the Project were approximately $25 million, only half the cost of a battleship, as the Federal Theatre's director, Hallie Flanagan, was fond of reminding critics unused to the idea of expending federal money for support of the arts. In return, the Federal Theatre Project presented over 42,000 performances of drama, COMEDY, circuses, vaudeville, marionette shows, and musical revues. Only a small proportion of the audience was ever called upon to pay an admission charge at the box office, thereby making live theater accessible to a vast new audience, particularly, young people.

Hallie Flanagan was sworn in as national director of the Federal Theatre Project on August 27, 1935, her fortieth birthday. From the outset, she emphasized that unique local and regional theatrical expression would be developed, not a New York conception of theater, nor a theater dependent on ideas and directions emanating from Washington. The FTP plan would be structured like the federal government; the general policy and program would be outlined in Washington, but the job of carrying it out would rest with the states, "national in scope, regional in emphasis and American in idea," as Flanagan (1965) put it.

Flanagan's unique qualifications for the job of national director of the Federal Theatre included theatrical experience at Grinnell College, where she wrote and directed plays; the University of Iowa, where she worked with E. C. Mabie; GEORGE PIERCE BAKER's "47 Workshop" at Harvard; her Guggenheim Fellowship, which she had used to study theater abroad; and a successful stint at Vassar College, where she taught and directed the Vassar Experimental Theatre. This kind of background was exactly the reason Harry Hopkins had chosen his former classmate at Grinnell as the national director. He felt strongly that the FTP had to be an "American job, not just a New York job."

In her hands, the Federal Theatre's national program developed along several lines. She was not so much concerned with finding hit shows, although that did happen, as with developing a comprehensive dramatic program that included classical plays, plays from abroad, cycles of plays by GEORGE BERNARD SHAW and EUGENE O'NEILL, WILLIAM SCHWENCK GILBERT and Arthur Seymour Sullivan operas, dance productions, and new American plays. She encouraged plays about legendary historical figures like John Bunyan, Davy Crockett, John Brown, and Abraham Lincoln and plays that dealt with whole periods of American development, such as plays about the problems of industrial and economic life. So at a time when theaters were dark across America, plays began to be performed not only in city theaters but in parks and hospitals, in public school and armories, in circus tents and universities, and in prisons and reformatories.

This was an agonizing period of beginnings, of testing bureaucratic procedures for running a theater, a gigantic undertaking in itself, but also for new and innovative theater activities, such as the Bureau of Research and Publications, the *Federal Theatre Magazine*, the Living Newspaper, and the Negro theater, all originating in New York but nationwide in scope. Flanagan pointed out that these activities had never been tried in this country before or anywhere else, for that matter. Immediate difficulties with censorship in New York with *Ethiopia*, the first Living newspaper, and in Chicago with *Model Tenements* cast gloom throughout the Project and caused many to wonder if Hopkins's often-repeated promise of an uncensored theater were possible after all. Even the first New York productions were nervous and faltering efforts, but *Chalk Dust*, an attack on America's school system, *Triple a Plowed Under*, the first living newspaper, MURDER IN THE CATHEDRAL, T. S. ELIOT's verse drama, needed no apologies. The production of the voodoo *Macbeth* in Harlem meant that the Federal Theatre had four big productions in operation by the end of March 1937. *Macbeth*, produced by John Houseman and directed by Orson Welles, won almost universal acclaim.

Hallie Flanagan herself worked tirelessly as she sought to put into effect the hard-won lessons of the first year. In the South, she encouraged productions of contemporary problems, antiwar plays, living newspapers on regional themes, children's plays, and plays on religion. The following year the Federal Theatre produced *Altars of Steel* by Thomas Hall-Rogers, a Birmingham author. Produced in Atlanta, the play stressed the need for economic freedom in the South and rapid development of its teeming resources. Praised, blamed, fought over, the play and the furor it created made it clear, not only in the South but across the country, that playwrights and audiences were keenly interested in plays with social and economic dimensions. In New York 60,000 people bought tickets for *Power*, a living newspaper on the Tennesse Valley Authority, before it opened. In the West, the Southwest Theatre Unit worked collaboratively on a cycle of plays about California, using local and regional history. Many critics found their first play, *The Sun Rises in the West*, more challenging than anything else produced by the Los Angeles Federal Theatre.

After John Houseman's departure from Harlem to head the new 891 Classical Unit, the Negro unit produced *Turpentine*, a play about the conditions in the Florida turpentine camps. The Negro experience in America was also of sufficient interest for the Federal Theatre to produce *How Long Brethren*, which dramatized in dance form Lawrence Gellert's *Negro Songs of Protest*, songs he gathered in the South during his assignment to the Atlanta unit. Helen Tamiris and her group danced seven episodes of Negro life, which drew raves from critics and audiences. *Dance Magazine* called it the best group choreography of the season and gave it an award. In 1938, Chicago produced Theodore Ward's *Big White Fog* which offered audiences the alternatives of Garveyism, black capitalism, or socialism in the struggle to survive the dense fog of white domination. After ten weeks of a successful run, the play was moved to a South Side high school, where it soon closed, clearly a case of de facto censorship.

What had become vigorous theater activity during the first two years of the Project took place always in the shadow of impending cuts. Flanagan's perpetual battle from first to last was the right of the Federal Theatre to choose its own plays.

Cuts, unrelenting attempts at censorship, and continuing reorganizations wore out young and old alike, hobbling and seriously undermining innovative work. On June 10, 1937, the order went out to cut the New York project by 30 percent. Subsequently, THE CRADLE WILL ROCK was prevented from opening. In addition, the publication of the *Federal Theatre Magazine* was stopped. Plans for the summer caravan season in the parks also seemed in jeopardy, but finally five trucks went rolling out to the boroughs of Richmond, Brooklyn, Queens, the Bronx, and Manhattan. Brooks Atkinson called these occasions festivals, with thousands of people filling the hillsides experiencing live theater. Even this kind of success did not prevent the dismissal of over a thousand people from the Project by the end of the summer.

The year 1938 was the year of the birth of the House Un-American Activities Committee (HUAC) whose members were quick to learn that attacks on theater made good press. The Federal Theatre was its favorite target and was depicted as a communist-controlled project wracked with controversy and mayhem. In the end, HUAC destroyed the Federal Theatre Project, and at midnight on June 30, 1939, the FTP rang down curtains for the last time all across the country. Maurice Clarke, New York City director, tells of hurrying back to his office after hearing the news of the Project's demise to find workmen breaking down partitions and axing chairs and tables. Puppeteers in California were ordered to burn their marionettes. The Project was ended because Congress, who had created the government-sponsored theater, killed it, not as an economic move, not because of a human issue or cultural issue, but because the Federal Theatre had become an important political issue that was too costly for Franklin Roosevelt to fight.

FURTHER READING

Flanagan, Hallie. *Arena*. New York: Blom, 1965.

Kruger, Loren. *The National Stage*. Chicago: Univ. of Chicago Press, 1992.

Mathews, Jane DeHart. *The Federal Theatre, 1935–1939*. Princeton, N.J.: Princeton Univ. Press, 1967.

Lorraine A. Brown

FEFU AND HER FRIENDS

I enjoy betting it won't be a real bullet.

—Fefu, Part 3

In 1977 MARIA IRENE FORNES completed and directed *Fefu and Her Friends* at the Relativity Media Lab in New York City, produced by the New York Theatre Strategy. The initial production garnered Fornes her third Obie and marked her return to public production after an intense yet publicly fallow period of reworking her aesthetic. The play was subsequently presented in 1978 by the American Place Theatre and later produced over forty times at universities in the United States and abroad. *Fefu* is widely acknowledged as Fornes's masterpiece and marks her further development as a playwright, as it combines her earlier skills with structure, action, clarity, and intensity of dialogue with a darker, more disturbing spectrum of emotion.

Fefu and Her Friends tells the story of eight women—friends, lovers, and ex-lovers—who are invited to Fefu's house. Set in 1935, the play veers between the REALISM of an intimate family drama and the language, narrative, and staging of experimental theater. The women gather to strategize for an education fund-raiser, yet that goal remains tangential until the third of the play's three parts. Instead, the play highlights the interactions of the group, moments of social violence against women, and the strength and difficulties of female intimacy. In part 1, Fefu plays a sadistic game with her husband wherein she shoots at him not knowing if the gun is loaded; in parts 2 and 3, Cecilia and Paula struggle with their discomfort and fraught romance. Throughout, a central focus is on Julia, who has been mysteriously paralyzed in a hunting accident, even though she has not been directly hit by a bullet.

Critical commentary on *Fefu* has focused on the original staging of part 2, in which the audience was divided into four separate groups to watch the various scenes in different areas of the Relativity Media Lab. The intimacy of this staging brought the audience into close contact with the actors, and it became a significant example of Fornes's penchant for using found objects and spaces. In this section of the play, spectators were most profoundly affected by Julia's monologue, in which she acts out a violent interrogation by unseen judges who bully her into declaring the inhumanity of the female gender. The monologue showed Fornes's ability to let her characters convey luminous truths at the borders of madness. The ending continued to play with truth and absence: as Fefu steps outside and shoots a rabbit, a spot of blood appears on the forehead of Julia, who is seated onstage. The lights fade as Fefu reenters, and she and the other women surround Julia, who seems to have perished as a result of Fefu's violent act.

Critics have disagreed in particular on the meaning and significance of the play's ending, as well as the play in general. Analyses from the early 1980s stressed the play's rejection of realism, and the unified presence of an all-women cast. Discussions from the late 1980s to the early 1990s suggested a more fragmented, complex understanding of the gender dynamics of the play and the violence of the ending. In retrospect, *Fefu* can be seen as a critique of feminist essentialism long before the debate surfaced in the mid to late 1980s.

[*See also* Feminist Drama in the United States; Gay and Lesbian Drama]

FURTHER READING

Austin, Gayle. "The Madwoman in the Spotlight: Plays of Maria Irene Fornes." In *Making a Spectacle: Feminist Essays on Contemporary Women's Theatre*, ed. by Lynda Hart. Ann Arbor: Univ. of Michigan Press, 1989.

Fornes, Maria Irene. *Fefu and Her Friends*. New York: PAJ Publications, 1990.

Kent, Assunta Bartolomucci. *Maria Fornes and Her Critics*. Westport, Conn.: Greenwood Press, 1996.

Pevotts, Beverly Byers. "Review of *Fefu and Her Friends*." In *Women in American Theatre*, ed. by Helen Krich Chinoy and Linda Walsh Jenkins. New York: Theatre Communications Group, 1987.

Wolf, Stacy. "Re/Presenting Gender, Re/Presenting Violence: Feminism, Form and the Plays of Maria Irene Fornes." *Theatre Studies* 37 (1992): 17–31.

Gwendolyn Alker

LES FELUETTES

See LILIES

LES FELUETTES OU LA RÉPÉTITION D'UN DRAM ROMANTIQUE

See LILIES

FEMALE PARTS

This group of four one-woman monologues, first performed together by a British actress in 1981, is drawn from the famous collection of plays *All House, Bed and Church* (*Tutta casa, letto e chiesa*, 1977) by FRANCA RAME and DARIO FO. Since 1977, Rame has performed *All House* over 1,000 times all over ITALY and in many cities (e.g., New York, Paris, and Moscow). *All House* marks a turning point for Rame, who with this publication begins to appear as co-author with her husband, Nobel laureate Dario Fo. Yet most critics consider the monologues to be primarily her invention, given Rame's goal to play fully developed female characters. Her interest in women's subaltern condition, the main theme of *Female Parts*, fuels Rame's own literary and professional self-affirmation. At the same time, her ensuing international recognition rides the crest of the 1970s Italian and international women's movements.

These four monologues explore the exploitation and entrapment of women in the workplace, family, and bedroom. Except for the tragic "Medea," the monologues rely on Rame's expertise as a brilliant comic actress. Irony, slapstick, and wordplay draw the laughter and sympathies of the audience.

The first play, "Waking Up," is a satire on women's double work (*doppio lavoro*) and the double exploitation that occurs when dehumanizing factory work is added to women's unpaid labor of housework and child care. Fo and Rame's longtime Marxist concerns with the downtrodden and the exploitation of the proletariat are here rewritten through a feminist lens. The regimentation of the factory time clock invades both the dreams of the protagonist and the frantic morning routine of getting herself and her baby ready while her left-wing husband sleeps on.

The 1970s Italian women's movement grew out of the class struggles of the 1960s, as women realized that their comrades were unwilling to take equality beyond the workplace and into the family, home, and bedroom. This is evident in the third monologue, "The Same Old Story," which starts with a woman complaining to her radical, left-wing lover during sex about his sexual technique and his lack of sexual and emotional sensitivity. Later, she accidentally gets pregnant and relates a story of abuse and liberation to her baby daughter in the form of a grim yet farcical fairy tale.

The motif of entrapment becomes literal in "A Woman Alone." The protagonist is locked in her house every day by her jealous husband. Dressed in a negligee, symbol of her sexual servitude to the men around her, and trapped in her role as drudge, she finally explodes into a flurry of vindictive killings, reflecting Rame's comic-grotesque theater.

The issue of maternity, present in all these stories, becomes dominant in Rame's reworking of Aeschylus's *Medea*. For many 1970s feminists, motherhood was a hindrance to women's self-actualization and thus incompatible with feminism. Here, in a language derived from southern Italian dialects and reminiscent of poetic verse, Medea decides that she will not accede to her husband's demands nor to her women neighbor's pressures to abdicate her role as wife and mother to make way for a younger woman. Transforming the traps of societal prejudices and motherhood, Medea decides to kill her children, and face death herself, in order to destroy the patriarchal laws of servitude, sacrifice, and selflessness that mothers, indeed women, are taught to obey.

FURTHER READING

Montgomery, Angela. "The Theatre of Dario Fo and Franca Rame: Laughing All the Way to the Revolution." In *Twentieth-Century European Drama*, ed. by Brian Docherty. New York: St. Martin's, 1994. 203–220.

Valeri, Walter, ed. *Franca Rame: A Woman on Stage*. West Lafayette, Ind.: Bordighera, 2000.

Verduyn, Lucia Monique. "Franca Rame e la ricerca di una nuova immagine della donna in *Tutta casa, letto e chiesa*" [Franca Rame and the search for a new image of woman in *All House, Bed and Church*]. *Studi d'italianistica nell'Africa australe* 7, no. 8 (1994): 83–98.

Wood, Sharon. "*Parliamo di donne*: Feminism and Politics in the Theater of Franca Rame." In *Dario Fo: Stage, Text, and Tradition*, ed. by Joseph Farrell and Antonio Scuderi. Carbondale: Southern Illinois Univ. Press, 2000. 161–180.

Tommasina Gabriele

FEMINIST DRAMA IN THE UNITED STATES

Simply because there are still a lot more men than women in charge of our theaters: producing, directing, managing, and fund raising. That's where the power and money are in this country. . . . Men aren't used to identifying with women. . . . In terms of the people who make decisions about play production, the closer these dreams are to their version of themselves, the more chance they'll want to sit through a play or to find money to produce it.

—Beth Henley, in *Betsko and Koenig*

Explicitly feminist drama emerged in the United States as a distinct genre in the late 1960s and the 1970s. It developed in the context of continuing gender inequities in all areas of life despite the ongoing influence of the radical politics of the 1960s. During this period, the second wave of U.S. feminism took root, directly resulting in the creation of organizations, activities, and a general activism in personal and professional environments. In theater, the feminist movement begat playwrights, actors, and producers as well as the formation of many feminist theater groups.

There was an earlier phase of U.S. feminism during the Progressive Era (1896–1920) that also produced noteworthy female playwrights. ZONA GALE, SUSAN GLASPELL, SOPHIE TREADWELL, Marion Craig Wentworth, and RACHEL CROTHERS all wrote during this time. The word "feminism" was sometimes used as a critical criterion to evaluate plays such as when critic and playwright Florence Kiper examined a New York theater season in 1914 "from a feminist viewpoint." But the close association of certain kinds of playwriting with feminism really occurred during the second wave of feminism in the 1960s when a new, large, and outspoken generation of playwrights emerged. Feminist dramatists, and even many who eschewed being designated such, began writing plays that focused on the social and political status of women by portraying the details of their lives. In these plays, women were no longer mostly mothers, lovers, wives, daughters, or prostitutes but complex characters engaged in a broad range of professional and personal activities with conflicting desires and tragic flaws wrought by sex, race, gender, and class.

Feminist dramatists sought to create significant roles for women, explore the spiritual and material conditions of their daily lives, and reconfigure the representation of females onstage by paying attention to the ideological implications of their dramas. They often wrote female characters that exploded the sanctioned notions of womanhood in all its forms. They investigated the patriarchal nature of language and questioned traditional dramatic structures, often abandoning the traditional dramatic arc of plot development in favor of narratives without denouement.

Not only individual authors but also new theater groups emerged and flourished. Among these were At the Foot of the Mountain (1971–1976), Circle of The Witch (Minneapolis, 1973–1978), Front Room Theater Guild (1980–1987), It's All Right to Be Woman Theater (1969–1976), Lilith (1974–1986), Spiderwoman Theater (1975–), SPLIT BRITCHES (1981–), and Woman's Experimental Theater (1977–1986). These groups were formed explicitly to explore radical methods of collective theater making. Some of these companies created scripts collectively; others called on playwrights. Playwrights associated with these companies got the opportunity to develop the representation of female subjectivity in the context of workshops and rehearsals. This resulted in a particular kind of dramatic text, simultaneously both deeply personal and political and tied to specific groups and their actors. For both playwrights and company members, the idea was to stage their own images of themselves without the intervention or critical apparatus of male perspectives, prerogatives, or criticism. Equally important was writing a celebration of women's lives in the form of creating positive roles and role models for women.

Some of the methods of feminist dramatists were adapted from experimental theater groups, especially the OPEN THEATER but also the LIVING THEATRE and The Performance Group. All these companies worked to reduce or eliminate the separation of performer and spectator. They developed specific exercises to enable actors to actively contribute to the devising, performing, and staging of new plays. Also important to the feminist playwrights were techniques adapted from feminist consciousness-raising groups, the AGITATION-PROPAGANDA (agit-prop) techniques of antiwar protests, the theoretical writings of BERTOLT BRECHT, the theatrical manifestos of ANTONIN ARTAUD, and the psychophysical theater of Jerzy Grotowski. Combining elements of all these techniques into new processes for creating artistic work, feminist dramatists began to erode enfranchised negative assumptions about women, their experiences, their abilities, their bodies, and their intelligence.

One second-wave feminist playwright is MEGAN TERRY, who set the gold standard with her *Approaching Simone* (1970), concerning Simone Weil, an activist in the French Resistance during World War II. Drawing on her work with the Open Theater, Terry has the play's fifteen characters continually transform not only into different characters but also into different aspects of Weil. But despite these innovative techniques, Terry's characters remain basically realist. Terry herself characterizes her work at this time as a kind of "magic realism."

Feminist dramatists of Terry's era were able to combine realist devices, dream, fantasy, and illusion into a creative flow in a world where the characters were discovering who they were. Feminist writers sometimes distrusted unadulterated REALISM because it represented the offstage world as if it were the natural order of things. For some feminist playwrights, the contradictions and inadequacies of theatrical realism resulted in discontent with traditional conventions of representation. Gender and race began to be examined as social constructions. In combining certain realist conventions with new techniques of personal statement, textual montage, and radical staging encoded in the plays, the writers were able to tell the "true" story of women's lives in radically new ways.

For other feminist playwrights of the second wave, the conventions of realism with its simulated domestic settings were something to be used to their own ends. The stage directions for MARSHA NORMAN's Pulitzer Prize–winning 'NIGHT MOTHER (1983) calls for a realistic stage set with the magazines, ashtrays, candy dishes, and needlework in the living room. Even the clocks in the house, in the kitchen and living room, are set at the time the performance begins and run in real time for the duration of the play. But even here there is a door meant to be a focal point that opens on nothingness.

Patricia Schroeder (1996) has argued that realistic details, narrative structure, and dialogue enable feminist playwrights to expose the entrapment of women and pitch their work to a wide audience already familiar with the conventions of the form. The question feminist playwrights ask is, Can women be effectively and truthfully represented onstage apart from the sign systems of prevailing hegemony? Disrupting and revising the aesthetic and ideological assumptions of the conventions of realism is a major contribution of feminist dramatists.

At its outset, second-wave feminist drama seemed to be the domain of white, middle-class women. But feminist playwrights around the world have long cut their own paths. In the United States during the 1920s, African American playwrights ANGELINA GRIMKÉ and Mary Burill explored specifically female issues, as did Amelia Rosselli in ITALY, Shiguré Hasegawa in JAPAN, and Zinaida Gippius in RUSSIA. More recently in the United States, NTOZAKE SHANGE, Pearl Cleage, Kathleen Collins, ALICE CHILDRESS, and Robbie McCauley have explored domestic violence, male betrayal and dominance, interracial relationships, and sexual violence. Their characters dance, start communities, serve men, love, and recover from abuse after confronting its pain and alienation. Cherríe Moraga, MARIA IRENE FORNES, and MIGDALIA CRUZ have written about Chicano/Latino households, the ways in which women never know one another, and the way poverty and race delimit the options in people's lives.

Wakako Yamauchi, Momoko Iko, Jessica Hagedorn, Velina Hasu Houston, Genny Lim, and Elizabeth Wong portray the struggles of Asian Americans to define their identities in a country that devalues their presence. TINA HOWE, Marsha Norman, PAULA VOGEL, BETH HENLEY, WENDY WASSERSTEIN, and Jane Wagner to different degrees and in different ways have all written about both the limitations and the possibilities of "domestic life" for women and what these reveal about the condition of being female. Lesbian playwrights HOLLY HUGHES, Cheryl Moch, Peggy Shaw and Lois Weaver, and Jane Chambers delve into sexuality and gender. Catherine Filloux is among a younger generation of writers exploring the condition of women in the context of being members of a global community.

Taken as a whole, "feminist playwriting" cannot be reduced to a single concern, style, or "typical case." What unites all these writers with their diverse interests, styles of writing, sexual orientation, and position on gender and politics is a determined refusal to cave in to outmoded historical models of playwrighting privileging the point of view of male subjects. Their work brought about a new aesthetic based on the continuing struggle to transform social realities and bring the truth of millennial identities to the stage.

FURTHER READING

Betsko, Kathleen, and Rachel Koenig. *Interviews with Contemporary Women Playwrights*. New York: Beech Tree Books, 1987.

Brown, Janet. *Taking Center Stage: Feminism in Contemporary U.S. Drama*. Metuchen, N.J: Scarecrow, 1991.

Charlotte, Canning. *Feminist Theaters in the U.S.A.* New York: Routledge, 1996.

Laughlin, Karren, and Catherine Schuler, eds. *Theatre and Feminist Aesthetics*. Cranbury, N.J: Associate Univ. Press, 1995.

Murphy, Brenda. *American Women Playwrights*. New York: Cambridge Univ. Press, 1991.

Schroeder, Patricia. *The Feminist Possibilities of Dramatic Realism*. Cranbury, N.J: Associate Univ. Press, 1996.

Shafer, Yvonne. *American Women Playwrights 1900–1950*. New York: Peter Lang, 1997.

Carol Martin

FEN

My mother wanted to be a singer. That's why she'd never sing.
—Val, Scene 21

Fen (1982) scrutinizes disintegrating relationships and personalities in rural East Anglia, ENGLAND. As the play opens, a previous century's barefoot boy scares crows from a field, an image that gives way to a late-20th-century Japanese businessman explaining the corporate ownership of the land. He in turn gives way to Val and her fellow farm laborers, nearly all women, as Val decides to leave her husband and the fens for her lover Frank and London. But Val finds that she cannot bear being without her children. Val's co-worker Angela, meanwhile, tortures her stepdaughter, who joins with Val's daughters in taunting the individualist Nell. The farm owner himself is under pressure, being forced to sell. The village elders tell of still harder times in the past, and after an unsuccessful suicide attempt, Frank kills the willing Val with an ax. The final image of the play is Val's embittered mother, May, singing through a closed mouth a song she is unwilling to sing aloud.

Fen has had critical success since its first performance by the JOINT STOCK THEATRE GROUP. And though occasionally labeled "strident," the play's many revivals in both England and the United States testify to CARYL CHURCHILL's ability to write viscerally compelling socialist-feminist drama. Like Churchill's *Serious Money*, *Fen* critiques corporatization; like TOP GIRLS, it relies on anachronism in its staging of women's lives. However, it is devoid of the lightheartedness of those plays. Written in twenty-one scenes of terse prose, *Fen*'s breaks with REALISM include Tewson's confrontation by a hostile 19th-century phantom and the appearance of Val's ghost immediately after her death, an apparition that does not surprise her killer at all. The last scene, in fact, is a mélange of troubling images and events from different centuries, some described by the dead Val.

Although *Fen* registers unease at contemporary economic developments, it also reminds us of the physically taxing and emotionally limiting conditions that have always accompanied that romanticized institution, the English farm. The play, inspired by Mary Chamberlain's history *Fenwomen* (1975), emphasizes as well the paralyzing nature of gender roles in rural life. As immobilized by domestic obligations as they are by lack of economic opportunities, *Fen*'s women find contentment neither at work nor at home. There are only two options for those who reject the sort of violent breakaway Val attempts: passive acceptance of wretchedness, as with grandmother Shirley and born-again Alice, or the sacrifice of social status, as for ostracized, defiant Nell. *Fen* suggests that the women's traditional domestic responsibilities serve an external purpose as well as a household one: they tie the women, serflike, to the fens where their families live—and where the landowners can exploit them. Likewise, rural impoverishment binds them to psychologically crippling families without whom they cannot survive financially. In her introduction to the play, Churchill (1985) writes that for her it is inseparable from Annie Smart's original set design of a potato field in a kitchen, a staging that encapsulates *Fen*'s intertwined social prisons.

FURTHER READING

Churchill, Caryl. *Plays: Two*. London: Methuen, 1985.

Kritzer, Amelia Howe. *The Plays of Caryl Churchill: Theatre of Empowerment*. London: Macmillan, 1991.

Rabillard, Sheila. "*Fen* and the Production of a Feminist Ecotheater." *Theater* 25, no. 1 (1994): 62–71.

Suzanne Penuel

FENCES

You can't tell me nothing about Death. Death ain't nothing but a fastball on the outside corner.

—Troy Maxson, Act 1

AUGUST WILSON's *Fences* is one of the most highly praised American dramas of the 20th century. The play was written in 1983 but is set in a black tenement in Pittsburgh during the 1950s. While the play has the elements of a family drama, it is rich with SYMBOLISM and poetry. It was first staged at the O'Neill Theatre in 1983 and produced at the Yale Repertory Theatre in 1985. It opened on Broadway at the 46th Street Theatre on March 26, 1987, and ran for 525 performances on Broadway. The play's poetry and exploration of the theme of the sins of the father visiting the son link it to other major American dramas of the 20th century, including ARTHUR MILLER's DEATH OF A SALESMAN and EUGENE O'NEILL's LONG DAY'S JOURNEY INTO NIGHT.

Set at the beginning of the civil rights movement, *Fences* tells the story of Troy Maxson and his family. A gifted black athlete, Troy was unable to make a living as a baseball player because he played when the sport was strictly segregated. As the play begins, Troy's bitterness is firmly entrenched. He is bitter toward the whites who denied him the opportunity to play and is unable to recognize that times are beginning to change. Troy's anger at his past and his concerns for his son's future dominate the tone of the play. Troy's son Cory is also a talented athlete, and he is awarded an athletic scholarship to play baseball in college, but Troy insists that his son find a practical trade rather than go to college. It is Troy's insistence on self-sacrifice over personal fulfillment that ultimately leads to confrontation with his son. Troy sees the relationship between father and son as the relationship between employer and employee. Ultimately, the father denies the son the opportunity for advancement and is unable to provide the paternal affection his son so desperately seeks. As the story unfolds, Troy loses the family he has sworn to protect, and in the final scene, he confronts death only to experience further loss. However, through the character of Rose, Troy's wife, Wilson imparts a sense of hope for a better future for the characters.

While the play deals with issues of race, *Fences* does not simply decry the injustice of racism. Rather, Wilson succeeds in portraying the complexity of family relationships in the shadow of racism. For all his faults, Troy is a responsible father who is devoted to the financial security of his family. Wilson's use of poetic imagery gives the play a theatrical depth that transcends the clichés of the traditional family drama. Troy Maxson had spent the better part of 1957 building a fence around their yard at his wife's request, yet it is the metaphorical meaning of the fence that is more important to the play. Troy is striving to keep death out and his family in. American iconic images such as baseball and the picket fence resonate in an entirely new way in *Fences*.

The success of the play was immediate, with both audiences and critics. The play was the most successful in Wilson's cycle of plays about the 20th-century African American experience. It was awarded four Tony Awards (including Best Play) and Wilson's second Pulitzer Prize for Drama.

FURTHER READING

Bogumil, Mary L. *Understanding August Wilson*. Columbia: Univ. of South Carolina Press, 1999.

Nadel, Alan, ed. *May All Your Fences Have Gates: Essays on the Drama of August Wilson*. Iowa City: Univ. of Iowa Press, 1994.

Shannon, Sandra Garrett. *August Wilson's Fences: A Reference Guide*. Westport, Conn.: Greenwood Press, 2003.

Ellen Anthony-Moore and Christopher Moore

FENNARIO, DAVID (1947–)

Canadian playwright David Fennario was born David William Wiper in Montreal in 1947. He studied at Dawson College and has served as writer-in-residence at the Centaur Theater in Montreal. Fennario grew up in the Point St. Charles section of Montreal, a district in which working-class Canadians and recent immigrants have created a rich and sometimes volatile cultural mix. Early in his life, Fennario recognized the paradox in the residents' capacity for hard work and their inability to find any sort of lasting financial security. Not surprisingly, his plays express a Marxist outrage at the economic exploitation of the working class. This political purpose, in combination with his interest in the political and cultural survival of French CANADA, has characterized almost all of his work for the stage, though in several of his most recent plays he has focused on more sensational incidents from the regional history.

Fennario's first play, *On the Job* (1975), established his theatrical voice. Focusing on a group of workers at a clothing factory, the play explores the crisis that develops when they are asked to work through much of their holiday to fill a late order from a major department store. The paradox is that while this order is a boon for the factory and thus ultimately benefits the workers themselves, it is also an exploitation of the workers by the factory management and by the economic system as a whole.

Fennario's most popular and critically acclaimed play has been BALCONVILLE (1979), for which he received the Chalmers Award for the best Canadian play of the year. In addition to providing a vivid depiction of working-class culture, the play has attracted much attention because it is bilingual. As its characters gather on the balconies of their apartments, some speak in English and others in French. There is no attempt to translate for anyone in the audience who is not bilingual. Described as an allegory of the major political issue affecting the future of Canada, the play directly illustrates the irony that French Canadians are more frequently bilingual and bicultural than residents of the "English" provinces; so the French Canadian separatist movement does not necessarily represent an isolationist mentality.

SELECT PLAYS: *On the Job* (1975); *Nothing to Lose* (1976); *Toronto* (1978); *Without a Parachute* (1978); *Balconville* (1979); *Changes* (1980); *Moving* (1983); *Doctor Thomas Neill Cream: Mystery at McGill* (1985); *Joe Beef: A History of Pointe St. Charles* (1985); *The Murder of Susan Parr* (1989); *The Death of Rene Levesque* (1991); *Banana Boots* (1994)

FURTHER READING

Blades, Margaret W. "Anglophobes, Francophobes, and the Language Question in *Balconville*." *Selecta: Journal of the Pacific Northwest Council on Foreign Languages* 12 (1991): 8–12.

Byrnes, Terry. "David Fennario." In *The Matrix Interviews: The Moosehead Anthology*, 8, ed. by Robert E. N. Allen and Angela Carr. Montreal: DC Books, 2001. 159–168.

Gilman, Marvin. "Fennario and Ryga: Canadian Political Playwrights." *Australasian Drama Studies* 29 (October 1996): 180–186.

Reid, Gregory J. "David Fennario Turned Rhapsodist: The Rebirth of the Author in Performance." *Essays in Theatre/Etudes Theatrales* 18, no. 1 (November 1999): 63–77.

——. "Mapping Jouissance: Insights from a Case Study in the Schizophrenia of Canadian Drama." *Comparative Drama* 35, nos. 3–4 (2001–2002): 291–318.

Martin Kich

FERBER, EDNA (1885–1968)

Born on August 15, 1885, in Kalamazoo, Michigan, Edna Ferber spent her early years in Iowa, a year in Chicago, and then her family moved to Appleton, Wisconsin. Ferber (1939) wrote, "Appleton represented the American small town at its best . . . curiously modern and free in the best sense of the words." The Ferber family was a theatergoing family, and Edna repeatedly wrote in her autobiographies that she was "stage-struck."

Ferber's writing career began at age seventeen, as a newspaper reporter, making rounds on foot. In 1910, she had her first short story published. With her stories of Emma McChesney, a traveling saleswoman, Ferber gained great popularity. They were first published in national magazines and collected in books; then in collaboration with George V. Hobart, a play, *Our Mrs. McChesney*, was produced on Broadway, on October 19, 1915, and ran for 151 performances.

Ferber's short story "Old Man Minick" caught the attention of GEORGE S. KAUFMAN, and he and Ferber began a collaboration, starting with *Minick*, which would last for six plays. *Minick* was first produced by Antoinette Perry, on September 24, 1924.

Ferber-Kaufman's next project was *The Royal Family*. First produced by Jed Harris on December 28, 1927, it is a COMEDY-drama of three generations of theater actors, loosely based on the Barrymore family. It remains one of the most popular plays by the collaborators. DINNER AT EIGHT (1932) and STAGE DOOR (1936) followed during the Depression. The first is a comic-serious portrayal of the lives of people invited to or preparing for a dinner at a house on New York's Park Avenue. The second is about young aspiring women trying to find opportunities to act on Broadway. These last three plays represent the best of the Ferber-Kaufman collaboration.

The next two plays—*The Land Is Bright* (1941) and *Bravo!* (1948)—were unsuccessful. Ferber commented that the former was meant to be a "Wake up!" call to the Americans regarding the war in Europe and Adolf Hitler's treatment of Jews. Ferber (1966) and Kaufman "wanted terribly to say something that they deeply felt should be said."

About the collaboration, Kaufman's biographer Howard Teichmann (1972) wrote, "With Miss Ferber, Kaufman plays always had a larger variety of plot and a broader spectrum of color and characterization. . . . Ferber made him dig deeper into what he called 'the rich, red meat of playwrighting.' "

Despite the success of the best of her plays, Ferber's reputation as a writer rests primarily with her novels. *So Big* (1924) won a Pulitzer Prize. Other novels like *Show Boat* (1926), *Cimarron* (1930), *Saratoga Trunk* (1941), *Giant* (1952), and *Ice Palace* (1958) are still widely popular with their stories of strong, independent women in panoramic settings.

When she died on April 16, 1968, in New York City, the *New York Times* ran a front-page obituary, saying her books "were vivid and had a sound sociological basis" and placed her "among the best-read novelists in the nation." Also, without doubt, she was among the best American women playwrights of the 20th century.

[*See also* United States]

PLAYS: *Our Mrs. McChesney* (with George V. Hobart, 1915); *The Eldest* (1920); *$1200 a Year* (with Newman Levy, 1920); *Minick* (with George S. Kaufman, 1924); *The Royal Family* (with Kaufman, 1927); *Dinner at Eight* (with Kaufman, 1932); *Stage Door* (with Kaufman, 1936); *The Land Is Bright* (with Kaufman, 1941); *Bravo!* (with Kaufman, 1948)

FURTHER READING

Ferber, Edna. *A Peculiar Treasure*. New York: Doubleday, 1939.

——. *A Kind of Magic*. New York: Doubleday, 1963.

Gilbert, Julie. *Ferber: Edna Ferber and Her Circle*. New York: Applause, 1999.

Goldstein, Malcolm. *George S. Kaufman: His Life, His Theater*. New York: Oxford Univ. Press, 1979.

Shafer, Yvonne. *American Women Playwrights 1900–1950*. New York: Peter Lang, 1997.

Teichmann, Howard. *George S. Kaufman: An Intimate Portrait*. New York: Atheneum, 1999.

Misako Koike

FEYDEAU, GEORGES (1862–1921)

Georges Feydeau was the premier practitioner of a peculiar craft, the boulevard FARCE. He created extremely successful commercial entertainment aimed at the particular circumstances of his time and place. He absorbed the formulas of the well-made play (*pièce bien-faîte*) and popular vaudevilles, then applied them with mechanical precision, heightened absurdity, and subversive intent to such titillating material as marriage, adultery, impotence, divorce, and passion.

Feydeau was admittedly uninterested in creating literature, observing, "Literature being the antithesis of theater, theater is the image of life, and . . . so to make characters speak in a literary manner is sufficient to destroy them" (Gidel, 1988). Instead, he created a commodity better than anyone else, for an audience eager to pay for it.

The stage was an unlikely path for this child of privilege, born in Paris on December 8, 1862, and christened Georges Léon Jules Marie Feydeau. His father was a financier and man of letters whose circle included such luminaries as Charles Baudelaire and Gustave Flaubert. Until eleven, Georges was tutored at home. He left this rarified atmosphere when his father died, and his mother remarried a leading drama critic.

Feydeau wrote and performed his way through school, then entered the world of Parisian salons with a series of monologues and sketches. At twenty, he saw successful productions of his first one-acts. A stint in the army afforded him time to work on *The Ladies' Tailor* (*Tailleur pour dames*), which became his first hit in an 1886 production at the Renaissance Theatre.

Subsequent years of disappointment left Feydeau broke and ready to try acting for money. Instead, a rapid series of successes culminated in a revival of *The Ladies' Tailor* in 1892. Marriage to an heiress helped facilitate a life of indolence bounded by the theater and his permanent table at the popular café Maxim's.

Over the next decade and a half, Feydeau rose to ever-greater prominence, observed through a haze of cigar smoke and champagne bubbles, to the accompaniment of laughing ladies of the evening. A melancholy man whose home life was crumbling, he translated it all into play after play of absurdity and abandon—including his masterpieces *Hôtel Paradiso* (*L'Hôtel du libre-échange*, 1894), *An Absolute Turkey* (*Le Dindon*, 1896), *The Lady from Maxim's* (*La Dame de chez Maxim*, 1899), and *A FLEA IN HER EAR* (*La Puce à l'oreille*, 1907).

In 1909 his wife sent him packing. By 1916 Feydeau had faded from view, and the war years left his plays out of favor. He lived in isolation in a hotel, producing intermittently, until syphilitic madness convinced him that he was Napoleon III, and he was confined to an asylum in Rueil-Malmaison, where he died on June 6, 1921. Feydeau wrote in a tradition stretching from Menander through Molière and Pierre Augustin Caron de Beaumarchais to OSCAR WILDE—and even Ray Cooney (*Run for Your Wife*) today. Enormously popular in his day, Feydeau continues to define farce, and his plays remain a theatrical staple from the Comédie Française to Broadway and the West End.

SELECT PLAYS: *Wooed and Viewed* (*Par la fenêtre*, 1881); *Love and Piano* (*Amour et piano*, 1883); *The Ladies' Tailor* (*Tailleur pour dames*, 1886); *Champignol Despite Himself* (*Champignol malgré lui*, 1892); *The Happy Hunter* (*Monsieur chasse*, 1892); *Cat Among the Pigeons* (*Un Fil à la patte*, 1894); *Hotel Paradiso* (*L'Hôtel du libre-échange*, 1894); *An Absolute Turkey* (*Le Dindon*, 1896); *The Lady from Maxim's* (*La Dame de chez Maxim*, 1899); *Chemin de Fer* (*La Main passe*, 1904); *The Sprout* (*Le Bourgeon*, 1906); *A Flea in Her Ear* (*La Puce à l'oreille*, 1907); *Look After Lulu* (*Occupe-toi d'Amélie*, 1908); *Léonie Is Ahead of Time* (*Léonie est en avance*, 1911)

FURTHER READING

Corvin, Michel. *Le Théâtre de Boulevard* [Boulevard theater]. Paris: Presses Universitaires de France, 1989.

Gidel, Henry. *Théâtre Complet de Georges Feydeau* [Complete theater of Georges Feydeau]. Paris: Bordas, 1988.

——. *Georges Feydeau*. Paris: Flammarion, 1991.

Pronko, Leonard C. *Eugène Labiche and Georges Feydeau*. New York: Grove, 1982.

Shapiro, Norman R. *Feydeau First to Last*. Ithaca, N.Y.: Cornell Univ. Press, 1982.

Gavin Witt

FIELD DAY THEATRE COMPANY

In 1980 the Field Day Theatre Company was established by BRIAN FRIEL and Stephen Rea in Derry, Northern IRELAND.

Although it was initially conceived as a theater company, it soon added publishing to the group's activities. The poets Seamus Heaney, Tom Paulin, and Seamus Deane and filmmaker David Hammond joined its board of directors—and Field Day then began to publish pamphlets and prepare an anthology of Irish writing, in addition to producing new plays.

It was inaugurated with the premiere of Friel's TRANSLATIONS in 1980 and thereafter produced at least one play every year until 1991. These include some of the most important works in the modern Irish canon, such as THOMAS KILROY's *Double Cross* (1986) and Stewart Parker's *Pentecost* (1987).

The company has strongly influenced the development of Irish theater, and with the Druid Theatre of Galway, it inspired the growth of a strong regional theater. Yet its most important achievement has been intellectual rather than theatrical. The group was founded as a response to the Northern Irish Troubles, which seemed intractable throughout the 1980s. It set out to explore a depoliticized "Fifth Province" of the mind (to add to the four geographical provinces that comprise Ireland), in which the cultural assumptions, myths, and stereotypes that underlay the Troubles could be interrogated and demystified. Much of the company's rhetoric and ideology found its way into the Good Friday Agreement of 1998, which attempted to bring peace to Northern Ireland. This project was advanced by the publication of pamphlets that examined Ireland from rewarding new perspectives, comparing it with postcolonial countries and prerevolutionary Russia. These publications were complemented by productions of plays by ATHOL FUGARD and ANTON CHEKHOV. Certainly during its early years, the intellectual and theatrical activities of Field Day were closely intertwined.

However, the theatrical importance of Field Day declined after 1990, when, having produced four of his five previous plays with the company, Friel decided that *Dancing at Lughnasa* would premiere at the Abbey Theatre in Dublin. Friel's subsequent resignation in 1994 severely undermined the company's ability to produce new drama. This problem was intensified by the increasing international profile of many of Field Day's directors. The success of the company may therefore partially account for its theatrical decline: its activities raised the profile of its members, who were in turn attracted to lucrative posts abroad, where they exercised less control over the day-to-day running of the company. It has not produced any new work since 1995.

This decline has, however, been met with an increase in its publishing activities. A three-volume *Field Day Anthology of Irish Literature* was published in 1991, to which two subsequent volumes, focusing on women's writing, were added in 2002. It also publishes an important series of monographs. Although a variety of factors have made it impossible for Field Day to maintain the quality of its theatrical output, the group remains one of the foremost intellectual movements in Ireland.

FURTHER READING

Deane, Seamus, ed. *Ireland's Field Day*. South Bend, Ind.: Univ. of Notre Dame Press, 1986.

Richards, Shaun. "To Bind the Northern to the Southern Stars: Field Day in Derry and Dublin." In *Theorizing Ireland*, ed. by Claire Connolly. London: Palgrave Macmillan, 2003.

Richtarik, Marilyn. *Acting Between the Lines: The Field Day Company and Irish Cultural Politics, 1980–1984*. Oxford: Oxford Univ. Press, 1995.

Patrick Lonergan

FIERSTEIN, HARVEY (1954–)

I don't know how much acceptance or clout I have in the [gay] community, and I don't think there was a turning point. I've always been openly gay long before I was well-known, and that's just the way I live my life. There are people in the community with whom I do have clout and there are people in the community who hate everything I stand for. You just live your life.

—Harvey Fierstein, in an on-line chat, 1996

Playwright, performer, and gay activist Harvey Forbes Fierstein was born on June 6, 1954, in Brooklyn, New York, where he was raised and educated, graduating from the Pratt Institute in 1973 with a bachelor of fine arts degree in art. In the 1970s he worked as a drag performer in a number of New York City nightclubs. His first appearance in a play came in 1971: he was an asthmatic lesbian cleaning woman in Andy Warhol's sole stage production *Pork*. This was followed by roles in over sixty OFF- AND OFF-OFF-BROADWAY productions. Fierstein has written and staged a series of plays during this time, including *In Search of the Cobra Jewels* (1973); *Freaky Pussy* (1975), about a gang of prostitutes living in a subway toilet; and *Flatbush Tosca* (1976). These were all inspired by Ridiculous Theater models and as of 2003 remained unpublished.

Fierstein first gained widespread attention with the production of his play *Torch Song Trilogy* (1982). Developed in the late 1970s as a series of three interconnected one-act plays, *Torch Song Trilogy* has a semiexperimental structure and takes an aggressive, in-your-face attitude associated with "downtown" New York. The first play of the contemporary gay theater movement, *Torch Song Trilogy* moved to Broadway in 1982 and was the first popular American play to deal with homosexuality. A coming-out drama that teaches acceptance of homosexuality, it also raises volatile issues from gay bashing to gay adoption. It featured the gruff, gravely voiced Fierstein in a starring role as Arnold Beckoff, a drag performer who aspires to live with dignity and raise a family. With 1,222 performances, the COMEDY-drama was one of the longest-running plays ever produced on Broadway, and it garnered Fierstein two Tony Awards for Best Play and Best Actor in a Play. Fierstein wrote the screenplay and starred in the film version of the play as well, which was released in 1988.

Fierstein's other Broadway credits include his play *Safe Sex* (1987), in which he also acted and which deals with AIDS. He also wrote the books for two musicals: *Legs Diamond* (1988) and *La Cage aux Folles* (1983), for which he won another Tony Award. Fierstein earned another Tony in 2003, as well as a Drama Desk Award, for his drag role as Edna Turnblad in the musical *Hairspray*. His off-Broadway credits include *Forget Him* (1988) and *Spookhouse* (1984), a black comedy in which a gay social worker tries unsuccessfully to force a mother living in a Coney Island spookhouse to take back her teenage son, who has raped and set fire to an eight-year-old girl.

Fierstein has also done a considerable amount of acting work in film and television. Always out and outspoken, Fierstein has also been a visible and active spokesman for gay rights and AIDS causes, in addition to his status as a noted playwright and performer.

[*See also* Gay and Lesbian Drama]

PLAYS: *In Search of the Cobra Jewels* (1973); *Freaky Pussy* (1975); *Flatbush Tosca* (1976); *Cannibals Just Don't Know Better* (1978); *Torch Song Trilogy* (1982); *La Cage aux Folles* (book for musical, 1983); *Spookhouse* (1984); *Safe Sex* (1987); *Legs Diamond* (book for musical, 1988); *Forget Him* (1988)

FURTHER READING

Curtin, Kaier. *"We Can Always Call Them Bulgarians": The Emergence of Lesbians and Gay Men on the American Stage*. Boston: Alyson, 1987.

de Jongh, Nicholas. *Not in Front of the Audience: Homosexuality on Stage*. New York: Routledge, 1992.

Powers, Kim. "Fragments of a Trilogy: Harvey Fierstein's Torch Song." *Theatre* 14, no. 2 (Spring 1983): 63–67.

Joe E. Jeffreys

FIFTEEN STRINGS OF CASH

In 1955 Chen Jing and members of a major Zhejiang province traditional opera troupe adapted *Fifteen Strings of Cash* (*Shiwu guan, kunqu*) from a story of the same name written by early Qing dramatist Zhu Hu. The music and acting styles of this "newly arranged historical drama" follow the styles of *kunqu*, one of the oldest and most refined types of traditional Chinese theater. While the original took two days to perform, the new version takes only a single evening and boasts an exciting rise to a climax and satisfying denouement. The Beijing premiere took place on May 17, 1956, and was followed by a performance in Shanghai.

The plot is a good example of a "righted injustice," a common theme in traditional Chinese theater, including theater in the People's Republic of CHINA. The villain Lou the Rat accuses a young woman and her male friend of murdering her stepfather, a bibulous butcher, in order to steal fifteen strings of cash from him. Lou the Rat has himself committed these crimes. A venal magistrate sentences the daughter and her friend to death, but the "pure official" Kuang Zhong investigates the murder-robbery and, by playing on Lou the Rat's superstition and stupidity, gets him to confess to the crimes and rights the injustices.

Few items of rewritten traditional drama drew more attention from the Chinese authorities in the 1950s than this one. Several major leaders attended the Beijing premiere, including Chinese Communist Party (CCP) chairman Mao Zedong (1893–1976) and premier Zhou Enlai (1898–1976). Zhou participated in a forum on the drama, also held on May 17, 1956, and praised it for giving a new luster to *kunqu* art and showing how historical drama can play an educational role in today's world. China's main newspaper *People's Daily* (*Renmin ribao*) ran an editorial the day after the Beijing premiere, praising the play for bringing *kunqu* back to life. The editorial also noted that the drama had a strong "people's flavour" and high ideological and artistic content.

During the 1950s, the CCP carried out extensive drama reform. The aims were to revive the traditions as part of the artistic creation of the Chinese people while reforming the dramas themselves to emphasize the positive features of the masses, including women, and of the "pure officials" who were prepared to take the side of the poor and oppressed, and to condemn feudal morality and corrupt officials. Applied to *Fifteen Strings of Cash*, the effort was both ironic and difficult. Although Kuang Zhong was regarded as positive in the 1950s, Mao changed his policy against the "pure officials" at the time of the Cultural Revolution, condemning them on the grounds that they deceived the masses by pretending to offer support while actually exploiting them. Kuang Zhong was among those condemned. The characterization in *Fifteen Strings of Cash* also did not sit well with drama reform. For instance the character of Lou the Rat is strongly negative, yet he is definitely very poor, and when he introduces himself to the audience, he says he has neither goods nor land and relies on gambling to make a living.

FURTHER READING

Chu Su-Chen. [Rev. by Chou Chuan-Ying, Wang Chuan-Sung, Chu Kuoliang, and other members of the Chekiang Kunchu Opera Company, with final version by Chen Sze.] *Fifteen Strings of Cash: A Kunchu Opera*. Tr. by Yang Hsien-Yi and Gladys Yang. Peking: Foreign Languages Press, 1957 [translation of the play and commentary].

Lopez, Manuel D. *Chinese Drama: An Annotated Bibliography of Commentary, Criticism and Plays in English Translation*. Metuchen, N.J.: Scarecrow, 1991.

Scott, A. C. *Traditional Chinese Plays*. Vol. 2. Madison: Univ. of Wisconsin Press, 1969.

Colin Mackerras

FIFTH OF JULY

You've no idea of the country we almost made for you. The fact that I think it's all a crock now does not take away from what we almost achieved.

—June Talley, Act 1

Fifth of July, the last play of LANFORD WILSON's Talley family trilogy, was the first to be written, and it achieved popular and critical success on Broadway in 1978, running for 168 performances at the Circle Repertory Theatre. Wilson's snapshot of family life in small-town Missouri (according to Christopher Bigsby in *Contemporary American Playwrights* [1999]) is a metaphor "for a society that seemed to him to be in decline, its institutions in a state of decay, its private and public relationships under stress." Set in 1977, the play concerns a small group of friends and relatives who gather for a weekend at the old Talley farmhouse in Lebanon to observe Independence Day, celebrate a birthday, and scatter the ashes of a family member. However, the weekend becomes an opportunity to resurrect and hash out old wounds in a bid to stake out territory for the future. The protagonist, Kenneth Talley, one of a quartet of ex–flower children, is a Vietnam vet who lost his legs in the war. He is emotionally as well as physically crippled, and his injury is an inescapable reminder of the betrayal of his youthful ideals, not least by his "friend" John who ran off to Europe, leaving Ken to face the draft alone. Each of the characters has his or her own problems to resolve, and as with many Wilson dramas, at stake are issues of inheritance, particularly with regard to land and family.

As the title indicates, *Fifth of July* is about the morning after, something that applies to the characters in the play and to the nation as a whole. The Fourth of July marks the founding of the nation and its independent spirit; the following day America needs to account for what it has done with its heritage. Ken is trying to sell the historic family property and, in doing so, escape his past and give up on his future, an idea symbolic of Wilson's concern that the nation has sold itself out and destroyed its inheritance. Wilson characteristically draws on his own background for inspiration, but the Talley family is representative of any American family. The family home in the nation's heartland is just a shadow of its former self and just as hollow as the characters that inhabit it.

Wilson's other plays in the Talley trilogy, *Talley's Folly* (1980, Pulitzer Prize) and *Talley and Son* (1981), extend the metaphor, turning the clock back to examine where things went wrong with the previous generation of Talleys. In these plays, Wilson presents America as a nation on the brink of victory in World War II, set to take its place as a superpower leading the West into the modern era. However, underlying the vision of a strong and righteous country, Wilson reveals that moral and cultural decay has already set in. Against the backdrop of national victory, the Talley family is rapidly heading for defeat at the hands of modern capitalism, war, and bigotry: despite two sons fighting in Europe, the Talleys still shun outsiders, most prominently Sally's beau, Matt Friedman.

Sally differs from the rest of her family because, as Talley writes, "she remembers the old hope" and is suspicious of modern values. Appearing in all three plays, Sally presents the way forward. This is realized in *Fifth of July* when the good from the past is used to fertilize the future; Sally's decision to own and put a stake on her heritage is symbolized by her decision to scatter Matt's ashes over the Talley estate. In turn, Ken is persuaded not to sell the family home; John and his modern capitalist values are expelled; and at the close of the play, the future of the Talley family, and by extension, the nation, looks bright.

[*See also* United States, 1940–Present]

FURTHER READING

Barnett, Gene. *Lanford Wilson*. New York: G. K. Hall, 1987.

Bigsby, Christopher. *Contemporary American Playwrights*. Cambridge: Cambridge Univ. Press, 1999.

Bryer, Jackson R., ed. *Lanford Wilson: A Casebook*. New York: Garland, 1994.

Busby, M. *Lanford Wilson*. Boise, Idaho: Boise State Univ. Press, 1987.

Olivia Turnbull

FIN DE PARTIE

See ENDGAME

FINLAND

Three gigantic gatekeepers guard the first steps of modern Finnish dama. They are HENRIK IBSEN, NORWAY, who revealed the cruelty and secrets of society; AUGUST STRINDBERG, SWEDEN, who knew how to move his characters between heaven and hell; and ANTON CHEKHOV, RUSSIA, who gave his characters the gift of dreaming and the bitter experience of knowledge and disappointment.

BIRTH OF DRAMA IN FINLAND

The second half of the 19th century had seen the birth of dramatic literature in Finland, both in Finnish and in Swedish. The founding father was Aleksis Kivi (1834–1872), who wrote a Shakespearean TRAGEDY about the Kalevala hero Kullervo (1864), still probably the best of its kind, and two comedies that belong to the classical repertoire, *The Cobblers* (*Nummisuutarit*, 1864) and *The Engagement* (*Kihlaus*, 1866). At the same time, there was a connection to classical Greek drama in the last work of J. L. Runeberg (1804–1877), a tragedy called *The King of Salamis* (*Kungarne pä Salamis*, 1863). Its main subject is the question of legitimate power and its ethical consequences. Runeberg wrote in Swedish, and so did Josef Julius Wecksell (1838–1907), whose historical drama *Daniel Hjort* (1863) about the fight for freedom under Swedish rule has a Shakespearean structure and a rich poetical imagery.

The first playwright to represent the ideas of modern drama was Minna Canth (1844–1897). She was well read in European contemporary literature and had great influence in cultural and political matters. In addition, she was a mother of seven and a shopkeeper. In her plays she wanted to fight against social evils, especially in women's lives. *The Worker's Wife* (*Työmiehen vaimo*, 1885) attacked the patriarchal legislation that bound a woman's economy to her husband. Later, in *The Parson's Family* (*Papin perhe*, 1891) and *Anna-Liisa* (1895), she saw the conflict in the generation gap between parents and children and found a possibility of reconciliation in a liberal humanism and a LYOV TOLSTOY–influenced practical Christianity.

The beginning of the 20th century was in Finland politically hard and led through oppression and threat toward World War I, Finland's independence, and the Civil War in 1918. The question of identity became dramatically challenging when the young republic had to see face-to-face opposite political forces, the White and the Red. Simultaneously, the idea of the strong symbolical meaning of theater and drama, reflecting the human situation and the universal problems of humankind, captured many writers. They were usually active in many genres, writing poetry as well as novels and plays. One of the most productive was Eino Leino (1878–1926), who published several volumes of *The Masks* (*Naamioita*, 1905–), containing almost twenty plays with various subjects: contemporary PROBLEM PLAYS, symbolical verse plays *The Chess-Play* (*Shakkipeli*, 1909), historical plays from the Middle Ages, and plays based on folklore and the Kalevala. Leino's plays expressed the dreams of a new nation but also its disappointments and betrayal. His most important plays based on folklore, *The War of Light* (*Sota valosta*, 1900) and *The King of Carelia* (*Karjalan kuningas*, 1917), contain both nostalgic memories of a lost world of purity and idealism and the urge for deeper understanding of man and his struggle.

Leino was the greatest poet of his time, and this can be seen and heard in the dialogue of his plays, often full of powerful images and rhythms but rather difficult to be given life onstage. With his theatrical ideas, he paved the way to the drama of EXPRESSIONISM, represented by Lauri Haarla (1890–1944) in Finnish and Runar Schildt (1888–1925) and Hagar Olsson (1893–1978) in Swedish. Haarla was interested in history, especially in the ruptures of Swedish-Finnish relations (Juudas) but also in the problems of the civil war (*The Brother-Murderer* [*Velisurmaaja*, 1927]). Schildt wrote a couple of fine psychological studies of people who felt they were on the wrong side of the political border and were destroyed because of their choices (*The Great Role* [*Den stora rollen*, 1923]). Olsson, politically radical, found her characters in the modern world of technology and preparation for war. In S.O.S. (1928) the basic question is the responsibility of a scientist developing chemical weapons and his moral growth with the help of love. In *The Snowball War* (*Lumisota*, 1939), Olsson develops a political conflict between the foreign minister of a small country and the political leaders of a neighboring big country. The play bore such a strong resemblance to the reality of the year 1939 that its rehearsals were interrupted by the authorities.

Woman playwrights have been numerous and important in Finland. They have a common field of interest, the family and the situation of women, but they use a wide variety of settings and psychological insight and have a sensitive ear for both COMEDY and tragedy. The pioneering work of the 19th century by Minna Canth was followed by Maria Jotuni (1880–1943) and Hella Wuolijoki (1886–1954). Jotuni wrote ten plays, starting with a family play in Ibsen's footsteps carrying a strong feeling of doomsday and betrayal but also focusing on social matters and characters from traditional folk comedy. She continued on both lines: her comedies about matrimonial errors and false dreams about happiness and money—*The Man's Rib* (*Miehen kylkiluu*, 1914), *The Golden Calf* (*Kultainen vasikka*, 1918), and *The Henpecked Husband Wife* (*Tohvelisankarin rouva*, 1924)—have become the cornerstones of the Finnish repertoire, not least because of their intelligent, sharp, and humorous dialogue. Later she wrote two full-length tragedies based on the biblical conflict of Saul and David, *I Am Guilty* (*Olen syyllinen*, 1929), and a popular episode in Finnish medieval history, *Klaus, the Lord of Louhikko* (*Klaus, Louhikon herra*, 1943). For her, life was full of moral questions, and the only lasting value was hidden in the relationship between a mother and her son—a theme that Jotuni elaborated throughout her entire writer's career.

Wuolijoki also felt the importance of the family, but her approach was more socially determined. She praised the courage and vision of women in an agrarian society. Because of her political activities, she went by the male pseudonym Juhani Tervapää—for example, in *Hulda of Juurakko* (*Juurakon Hulda*, 1937), later filmed as *The Farmer's Daughter in Hollywood*.

Life as buying and selling has become a constant theme in modern Finnish drama, especially when women playwrights discuss the tension between the official sphere of life and the inner feelings of the individual character. The agrarian structure of the society gave women a relatively independent role, and Wuolijoki wrote several plays centered on the character of the Housewife of Niskavuori, who reigned over her husband, children, and property but at the same time became more and more lonely. Wuolijoki's social activity and political empathy led her to shelter BERTOLT BRECHT during his visit as a refugee through Finland to the United States in the early 1930s. Wuolijoki was a brilliant storyteller, and she collaborated with Brecht to create the idea and characters of Brecht's *Puntila and His Man Matti* (*Herr Puntila und sein Knecht Matti*, 1941).

Quite different was the idea of agrarian people in the comedies of Maiju Lassila (1868–1918). He used several pseudonyms and wrote his comedies as entertainment, full of slow thinking and quick acting, unchanging values, and materialist stereotypes.

The 1930s was a period of light comedy, much influenced by American film and schematized human relations. Some writers, such as Mika Waltari (1908–1979), preferred to mirror the present time in a distant historical setting (*Akhnaton* [1934], a preliminary work of great postwar novel *Sinuhe the Aegyptian* (*Sinuhe, Egyptilšinen*). In familiar comedies the conflicts were superficial and easily solved when parents and children, lovers and friends, walked together toward the happy end, even when they did not recognize it.

Ilmari Turja (1901–1998), Arvi Kivimaa (1904–1984), Serp (Seere Salminen, 1894–1977), and Agapetus (Yrjš Soini, 1896–1975) were all active in various areas of the theater world, as editors, critics, journalists, and economists. Their plays followed popular European trends, although they were usually set in Finland and especially in an artist or academic society. A frequent subject was the independence and autonomy of woman. The characters were familiar and harmless, and common values were easily shared by the public.

DRAMA AFTER WORLD WAR II

World War II brought a change both to the subject material and structure of Finnish drama. The experience of the war was too near to be dramatized, but the changing values and political consciousness formed a new background in the 1950s and 1960s. Psychological interest was combined with moral questioning, and the conflict was often seen in an absurd light. The most important postwar playwrights were Eeva-Liisa Manner (1921–1995), Paavo Haavikko (1931–), and Veijo Meri (1928–). *The Burned Orange* (*Poltettu oranssi*, 1968) by Manner has become a classic with existential depth and touching human portraits. It shows her philosophical concern for man's destiny and future and the destructive forces that distort the mind and life of its main character, a young girl, Marina. The play uses horse imagery and symbols with the same vivacity as PETER SHAFFER in *EQUUS*. In *New Year's Eve* (*Uuden vuoden yö*, 1964–1965) Manner creates a crisis of the intellectuals within a nightmarish world similar to EDWARD ALBEE's *WHO'S AFRAID OF VIRGINIA WOOLF?* Manner was a great modernist poet who often elaborated her themes in the form of radio play.

Haavikko is also a great poet, and his remarkable drama production contains sharp surgical cuts to people's moral and economic conflicts. His main subjects are power, money, and women. He uses Finland's history as an allegory of the present world (*Agricola and the Fox* [*Agricola ja kettu*, 1968]) or takes an episode of the war and shows the paradoxical relations between private and public life (*Airo and Brita* [*Airo ja Brita*, 1998]). One of his best-known works is the television series *Iron Age* (*Rautaaika*, 1982), which uses the content of the Kalevala epic but gives characters and settings roles that are absolutely modern in their decorative primitivity.

Meri easily sees the absurdity in human relationships and develops them in a serious and comical way (*Soldier Jokinen's Wedding Permission* [*Sotamies Jokisen vihkiloma*, 1965]). He chooses characters who cannot meet the challenges of the restless world and are surprised by the unexpected (*Aleksis Kivi*, 1975). A great deal of Meri's philosophy is to be found between his ironic lines, in contrast to Haavikko's more open-ended method.

The period of the political music drama was rather short but not without consequences. Its emblem became *The Lapua Opera* (*Lapualaisooppera*, 1966) by Arvo Salo (1932–), who found inspiration for its structure in *West Side Story* and for its contents in the international antinuclear and peace movement. Young politically active poets and musicians invaded especially small-group and student theaters, and the plays followed each other in quick tempo. The cabaret form became strong especially in plays written in Swedish by Bengt Ahlfors (1937–), Johan Bargum (1943–), and Claes Andersson (1937–). Finnish poets such as Marja-Leena Mikkola (1939–) and Aulikki Oksanen (1944–) created a song tradition that is still active.

The return to a more analytical dramatic form took place in the 1980s in the works of Pirkko Saisio (1949–) and Ilpo Tuomarila (1948–). Saisio, both a playwright and an actress, has used her own working-class background to describe how economic circumstances influence the speculations and dreams of a family (*The Concrete Night* [*Betoniyš*, 1981–1982]). She has a sensitive and fearless way of discussing the political awareness and mistakes of the young communists of the 1970s (*The Children of Baikal* [*Baikalin lapset*, 2002]) or the thirst for life and fear of emptiness of modern man and woman (*The Insensibility* [*Tunnottomuus*, 2004]).

In Ilpo Tuomarila's many plays, one finds a connection with Meri's absurdist worldview. One of his early successes is *Gehenna Night* (*Yössä Gehennan*, 1984), a play about two great classics of Finland's literature, Aleksis Kivi and J. J. Wecksell. Instead of writing a eulogy, Tuomarila sets the drama in a mental asylum, in which both writers were also kept in reality. He has written a controversial play about Marshal Herman Gšring and about the women in the Finnish Civil War (*The Hennala Brass Band* [*Hennalan torvisoittokunta*, 1998]), revealing the traumatic memories of that period. Jouko Turkka (1942–) has done most of his work as a director and as headmaster of the Finnish Theatre Academy. In his plays he uses mercilessly living models and creates an atmosphere that makes body language the most important thing on the stage.

REALISM is still one of the main directions of Finnish drama, and Reko Lundán's (1969–) plays show how realism can be combined with dreams or with violence. He describes people who could as well be on the stage as in the audience, and he represents a new kind of social criticism (*You Did Not Have Names* [*Teillä ei ollut nimiä*, 2001]; *Useless People* [*Tarpeettomia ihmisiä*, 2004]).

The historical subjects have not disappeared, but they have been set in a new light with the help of postmodernist, feminist, or psychoanalytical thinking. Laura Ruohonen has written plays of strong and unusual women such as *Olga* (1995) and *Queen C.* (*Kuningatar K.*, 2002–2003). At the same time, there has also been a revival of old forms with new contents, even Shakespeare, as in Juha Lehtola's (1966–) *The Othello Gig* (*Othellohyrrä*, 2003). Many writers of the youngest generation have been educated at the Finnish Theatre Academy as directors or dramaturges. They have developed an ear for a trendy sentence and, like Michael Baran (1963–), an ability to see the comical and tragic side of life in modern society (*The Paradise* [*Paratiisi*, 2004]). How can you combine spiritual values with hard business culture? is a question Juha Jokela (1970–) develops in *Mobile Horror* (2003). Pasi Lampela's comments on family life and media reality (*The End of Innocence* [*Viattomuuden loppu*, 2003]) make the audience think on the lost hopes and hopeless dreams people still have in a physically and spiritually uncertain, strange world.

FURTHER READING

Koski, Pirkko. *Kaikessa mukana. Hella Wuolijoki ja hänen näytelmänsä* [*Active in All Matters. Hella Wuolijoki and Her Plays*]. Helsinki: Otava, 2000.

Niemi, Irmeli. "Modern Women Playwrights in Finland." *World Literature Today* 54, no. 1 (1980): 54–57.

——. *Arki ja tunteet: Maria Jotunin elämä ja kirjailijantyš* [*Everyday Life and Feelings. Maria Jotuni's Life and Work*]. Helsinki: Otava, 2002.

Schoolfield, George C., ed. *A History of Finland's Literature*. Vol. 4 of *Histories of Scandinavian Literature*. Lincoln: Univ. of Nebraska Press, 1998.

Kai Laitinen, *Suomen kirjallisuuden historia* [History of Finland's literature]. Helsinki: Otava, 1981.

Irmeli Niemi

THE FIRST HOUSE OF BEIJING DUCK

Set in Beijing, CHINA, *The First House of Beijing Duck* (*Tianxia diyi lou, huaju*) by He Jiping dramatizes the rise and fall of a famous roast duck restaurant during the turbulent decade from 1917 to 1928, when competing warlords dominated the Chinese political scene. Rich in local color and steeped in tradition, this play belongs to the category of Beijing-flavored plays pioneered by LAO SHE (1899–1966). Like the teahouse in Lao She's play *Teahouse*, He Jiping's restaurant is a microcosm of Chinese society. Chang Gui, a waiter and the central character in He's play, is reminiscent of Lao She's teahouse proprietor: both are "little people" trying to make a living in hard times. Although He does not make a direct connection between the fortunes of her characters and the political situation, as Lao She did, her evocation of life in old Beijing makes her play a worthy successor to Lao She's masterpiece and an outstanding example of Chinese realistic drama in the post-Mao era.

As a play whose subject is food, *The First House* pays tribute to the importance of food in Chinese culture. The playwright spent two and a half years in a roast duck restaurant to immerse herself in the Chinese culinary art. The rituals of cooking and serving the roast duck described in great detail in the play are rooted in the Chinese cultural tradition.

Besides its cultural importance, the art of cooking is compared to the art of government in the play. A receptionist at the restaurant tells the cooks that their work is similar to that of the prime minister who was called "chef of the state" in ancient times. Furthermore, in times of political uncertainty, food seems to be the only constant in people's lives. A policeman who delivers official flags to the restaurant with every change of government remarks, "No matter who are in power—emperors, presidents, revolutionaries, or warlords—people will always eat roast ducks."

The art of cooking is also a metaphor for life itself because the five flavors—sweet, sour, bitter, spicy, and salty—cooks use to season dishes are also the flavors of life. This analogy is borne out by the life experiences of the characters: the receptionist is a scholar fallen on bad times, Chang Gui dies in humiliation after a lifetime of devoted service, manager Lu Mengshi is dismissed after ten years of hard work, Lu's assistant and mistress is left to fend for herself when Lu returns to his wife. The play ends with Lu's question: "Such a great house, who are its masters, who are its guests?" And the audience is reminded that "no banquet lasts forever."

This play won critical acclaim when the Beijing People's Art Theater premiered it in 1988. It has also been performed in Hong Kong, Taipei, and Singapore and restaged in Beijing in 2002. He Jiping graduated from the Central Drama Institute in Beijing and worked as a scriptwriter for the BPRT before moving to Hong Kong in 1989. A prolific writer, she has written five plays and seven film and television scripts.

FURTHER READING

He Jiping. "*Tianxia diyi lou xiezuo zhaji*" [Notes on writing *The First House of Beijing Duck*]. *Zhongguo xiju*, no. 9 (1988): 42–43.

——. *The First House of Beijing Duck*. In *Chinese Drama After the Cultural Revolution, 1979–1989*, ed. and tr. by Shiao-ling Yu. Lewiston, N.Y.: Edwin Mellen Press, 1996. 423–484.

Qiu Liuyi. "*Tianxia diyi lou de lishi wenhua yishi*" [Historical and cultural consciousness in *The First House of Beijing Duck*]. *Xiju pinglun* (*Drama Review*), no. 5 (1988): 4–5.

Zhang Ziyang. "*Tianxia diyi lou bian*" [Debates on *The First House of Beijing Duck*]. *Zhongguo xiju*, no. 11 (1988): 10–12.

Shiao-ling Yu

FISCHEROVÁ, DANIELA (1948–)

A graduate of Prague's Film Academy, Daniela Fischerová, born on February 13, 1948, in Prague, CZECHOSLOVAKIA, is not only a respected playwright but a successful writer of screenplays, radio plays, and stories for children and adults. Her plays almost always include elements of fantasy, myth, and deliberate theatricality. Prior to the Czech's Velvet Revolution of 1989, her themes clearly reflected issues of power and oppression, but her later plays relate to broader humanistic concerns.

The Hour Between Dog and Wolf (*Hodina mezi psem a velkem*, 1979), a lively work about François Villon's defiance of feudal authority, was banned after its fourth performance and not shown again until 1990. Presented in the form of a trial, the play makes use of song and dance, startling anachronisms, and rapid shifts of time and place in its celebration of individuality. A feudal setting is also present in *A Legend* (*Baj*, 1987), a provocative reworking of the Pied Piper story to include the tribulations of a medieval village subject to the Inquisition.

Princess T (*Princezna T*, 1984) is another work that reflects the stresses in Czechoslovakia at the time it was written. Fischerová presents a highly imaginative variation of the Princess Turandot story; in her version, the Princess refuses suitors because she does not want to extend the despotic rule of her father but rather to survive him and improve the lot of her people. Ironically, she falls in love with one suitor and helps him win her hand, only to discover that he has made a deal with her father to strengthen the tyrannic power of the monarchy, a stratagem that she is powerless to fight. The exotic setting of the action is theatrically supplemented by a lively, clownlike chorus of three who address the audience, cynically comment on the action, and even take part in it.

In the 1990s, Fischerová wrote *The Massage Table* (*Masážní stul*, 1992), a witty contemporary morality in one act that related directly to one aftermath of the Velvet Revolution, namely, the process of screening (*lustrace*), which revealed those who collaborated with the previous regime's secret police. One such person, a guilt-ridden woman, is tempted by a Devil to continue similar activity, but she refuses and is immediately relieved of her psychosomatic insomnia. The Devil, like the chorus in *Princess T*, is a comic figure who jokes with the audience.

Two other plays reveal Fischerová's continued interest in issues of morality, conscience, and responsibility. *Sudden Misfortune* (*Náhlé neštestí*, 1993) is a dialogue between two patients in a psychiatric clinic who reflect the identities of Job and Niobe and thereby give voice to questions of religious beliefs and the existence of God and free will, as well as to viewpoints of each one's gender. *Fantomima* (1996) was originally conceived as a pantomime but later evolved into a fuller action with two life-size mannequins and two live characters (their bizarre alter egos) and a fantasy trial probing contemporary values and mores, including questions of each person's ultimate responsibility to others.

PLAYS: *The Hour Between Dog and Wolf* (*Hodina mezi psem a velkem*, 1979): *Princess T* (*Princezna T*, 1984); *A Legend* (*Baj*, 1987); *The Massage Table* (*Masážní stul*, 1992); *Sudden Misfortune* (*Náhlé neštestí*, 1993); *Fantomima* (1996)

FURTHER READING

Barr, Alan. *Modern Women Playwrights of Europe*. New York: Oxford Univ. Press, 2001.

Hron, Madelaine. "The Enduring Desire to Write: An Interview with Daniela Fischerová." *Central Europe Review* 2, no. 42 (December 4, 2000). http://www.ce-review.org/00/42/interview42_fischerova.html.

Jarka Burian

FITCH, CLYDE (1865–1909)

[T]o amuse and interest is the thing.

—Clyde Fitch, 1902

William Clyde Fitch was born on May 2, 1865, in Elmira, New York, to William and Alice Clark Fitch. Owing to the elder William's career in the Union Army, the family moved a great deal, but they eventually settled in Schenectady, New York. As a child, Clyde showed a propensity toward dramatics and writing, and during his years at Amherst College, from which he graduated in 1886, he fully explored theater as both performer and playwright. Although his father was adamant that he take up architecture, Fitch insisted on moving to New York to try his hand at writing. *New York Times* drama critic Edward A. Dithmar introduced him to actor Richard Mansfield, who was seeking someone to write a play for him based on the character of Beau Brummell, a subject well suited to the sensibilities of the young playwright who was noted as somewhat of a "dandy."

Beau Brummell opened at the Madison Square Theatre on May 17, 1890, marking a promising beginning to Fitch's remarkable playwriting career. From then on, until his untimely death from appendicitis on September 4, 1909, in Chalons-sur-Marne, France, the dramatist wrote a steady stream of creative work, turning out over thirty original plays and twenty adaptations of foreign works or dramatizations of novels. Despite the range and variety of his plays and his remarkable prolificacy—in 1901 he had four plays running in New York at the same time—his works were not viewed as hastily written; indeed, one writer observed that his plays exhibited "a superior mastery of the dramatist's craft." Throughout his career, however, in spite of enormous public approval, Fitch agonized over the barbs of critics and their often lukewarm response to his work.

Among Fitch's important works, *Nathan Hale* (1899), which interwove historic incidents with a romance, and *Barbara Frietchie* (1899), a romantic Civil War TRAGEDY, were both well received. Beginning with *The Climbers* (1901), a satirical COMEDY of manners, much of Fitch's later work depicts characters with extreme traits. Richard Sterling in *The Climbers* has poor judgment in business dealings and resorts to dishonest transactions; in *The Girl with the Green Eyes* (1902), Jinny Austin's unreasoning jealousy drives her to attempt suicide; THE TRUTH focuses on Becky Warder, whose compulsive lies almost destroy her marriage. In his last play, *The City* (1909), Fitch aimed for a drama of larger ideas, showing the corrupt influences of a big city on a family from a small town. Produced at the Lyric Theatre after Fitch's death, *The City* ran for 190 performances and was hailed as his masterpiece.

Although much of Fitch's work now seems contrived with barely-believable characters, in his day many of his plays were considered "marvels of truthful portraiture and realistic action." All but one of Fitch's original plays used distinctly American subject matter, and his use of detail gave authentic aspects to his work; indeed, by examining Fitch's worlds, one may find a clear reflection of American life as it was from 1890 to 1910.

SELECT PLAYS: *Beau Brummell* (1890); *The Moth and the Flame* (1898); *Barbara Frietchie* (1899); *The Cowboy and the Lady* (1899); *Nathan Hale* (1899); *Captain Jinks of the Horse Marines* (1901); *The Climbers* (1901); *The Last of the Dandies* (1901); *The Way of the World* (1901); *The Girl with the Green Eyes* (1902); *Her Own Way* (1903); *Her Great Match* (1905); *The House of Mirth* (1906, with Edith Wharton from her novel); *The Truth* (1907); *The City* (1909)

FURTHER READING

Bell, Archie. *The Clyde Fitch I Knew*. New York: Broadway, 1909.

Fitch, Clyde. *The Knighting of the Twins and Ten Other Tales*. Boston: Roberts Brothers, 1891.

——. *A Wave of Life*. New York: Mitchell Kennerley, 1891.

Hornblow, Arthur. "Mr. Clyde Fitch—An Interview." *Theatre* 1 (1901): 10–13.

Moses, Montrose J., and Virginia Gerson, eds. *Plays by Clyde Fitch*. Vols. 1–4. Boston: Little, Brown, 1915.

——, eds. *Clyde Fitch and His Letters*. Boston: Little, Brown, 1924.

"A Talk with Clyde Fitch." *New York Times* (January 28, 1900): 16.

Sherry D. Engle

FIVE LESBIAN BROTHERS

Some critics and scholars call them a theater collective, others a derisively funny, AVANT-GARDE ensemble. All agree they are Maureen Angelos, Babs Davy, Dominique Dibbell, Peg Healey, and Lisa Kron and that as the Five Lesbian Brothers their plays—*Voyage to Lesbos* (1990), *Brave Smiles . . . Another Lesbian Tragedy* (1992), *The Secretaries* (1993), and *Brides to the Moon* (1996)—are integral not only to America's modern queer theater scene but also to the world of theatrical COMEDY. Their plays have been produced by WOW Café (New York), Theatre Rhinoceros (San Francisco), Alice B. Theatre (Seattle), and New York Theatre Workshop (New York), to name a few, and have garnered them a *Village Voice* Obie Award, a New York Dance and Performance Award, and a New York Press Award as Best Performance Group.

Forming their company in 1989, the Five Lesbian Brothers (FLB) come out of New York City's early 1980s East Village performance scene. Like their predecessors, SPLIT BRITCHES and the Ridiculous Theatrical Company, FLB collaboratively create plays that appropriate, parody, and subvert cultural stereotypes (whether by emulating lesbian pulp novels, Hollywood films of the 1950s and 1960s, television, or current advertising fads) to dramatize both queer and female identities. The world and characters of their plays are shown as being overdetermined by straight society. Seen as such, FLB challenge their audiences to consider the ways in which identity is fluid and performative.

Their most well known play, *The Secretaries*, is a satirical and biting tale about secretaries who work in a Lumber Mill and who set out to destroy the patriarchal power structure by killing the male lumberjacks for their coats, hilariously bringing home the not unreasonable conspiracy theory that even men's clothes are better made than women's. Performed through the many rituals of the secretarial pool, which include secretly calling out the commands of their word processing, collecting used tampons to regulate each other's menstrual cycles, and dieting on Slimfast shakes to maintain a size-ten body, the secretaries, under the control of their charismatic leader Susan Curtis, stage what Peggy Phelan has referred to as "a horror film in order to expose the deeper horror of how commonplace the killing of women in film and everyday life has become" ("The Serious Comedy of Hope: Introducing the Five Lesbian Brothers" in Five Lesbian Brothers, 2000).

Perhaps what is most remarkable is the wide array of audiences FLB plays have reached. The plays are regarded as well-made comedies that have traveled beyond queer-festival circuits to full productions mounted by regional theaters and by new generations of theater companies. As performance artist Holly Hughes writes in her introduction to *The Five Lesbian Brothers/Four Plays* (2000), "The Five Lesbian Brothers have developed an astonishing body of work that reads as 'real' theatre,' even though it was made in a community far off the cultural radar screen."

Since 1996, FLB have had successful careers touring in solo performances, lecturing at universities, as well as remounting their plays. In 2005 their newest work, *Oedipus at Palm Springs*, premiered at New York Theatre Workshop and then toured around the United States.

[See also Gay and Lesbian Drama]

FURTHER READING

Cvetkovich, Ann. "In the Archives of Lesbian Feelings: Documentary and Popular Culture." *Camera Obscura*–49 17, no. 11 (2002): 107–147.

Falzoi, Jill Christine. *Between Women: Inverting the Audience. Four Feminist Performances*. New York: New York Univ. Press, 2001.

Five Lesbian Brothers (Theater Troupe). *Five Lesbian Brothers/Four Plays*. Intro. by Holly Hughes. New York: Theater Communications Group, 2000.

Solomon, Alisa. "Five Lesbian Brothers NO WHINING!" *American Theatre* 15, no. 7 (1998): 61.

Jessica Kaplow Applebaum

A FLEA IN HER EAR

Helped perhaps by a felicitous title, *A Flea in Her Ear* (*La Puce à l'oreille*, 1907) remains among the best known of GEORGES FEYDEAU'S FARCES in the English-speaking world. It manages to employ most of the devices common to his DRAMATURGY. Here are physical disabilities exploited for comic potential, infidelity intended and merely suspected, jealous wives and overpossessive husbands, mistaken identities, secret letters, slamming doors, and slapstick violence.

The play revolves around a central couple with a troubled marriage, Victor-Emmanuel and Raymonde Chandebise. They are in turn beset by other troubled couples, amorous aggressors, incompetent hirelings, and unwitting dupes. A sudden conjugal diminution and a pair of suspenders in the morning mail have convinced Mme Chandebise that her husband is unfaithful—when he, in fact, is struggling with impotence. She persuades her friend Lucienne to write an anonymous love letter to Chandebise, inviting him to an assignation that night at a seedy hotel. Chandebise shares the letter with his own friend, Tournel, who resolves to go in his stead. Lucienne's husband, an excitable Spaniard with a penchant for duels, also sees the letter and recognizes the handwriting.

All of which, of course, ensures that everyone will show up at the hotel, itself populated by a roster of misfits and obsessives including the masochistic, drunken porter Poche—played, in one of Feydeau's mischievous calculations, by the actor playing Chandebise. To the inevitable series of catastrophic mistaken identities the author adds a sadistic hotelier, a randy Englishman, a deaf old uncle, a naïf with a cleft palate, and a rotating bed.

Feydeau's plays, high-intensity comic machines fueled by lust, offer mathematically structured, endlessly repeatable exercises at the brink of disaster, based on the haute bourgeoisie who watched them. His characters are the quintessential monomaniacs farce requires, observed with all the satirical bitterness of a Ben Jonson or a Juvenal. To the hypocritical strictures—class, gender, and morality—of Belle Époque Paris, he added the complicating catalysts of deceit and carnality.

He simply determined which characters should absolutely not meet; then, as he put it, "I throw them together as quickly as possible." Repeat this dynamic to its logical extremes, then stage with wild abandon. Furthermore, experience as a performer and the sensibilities of a choreographer meant that Feydeau—who acted his plays aloud as he composed—added stage directions to hone the action precisely and oversaw the staging of many of his successful works. An audience hungry for this sort of titillation (Feydeau's heyday also saw the rise of such enticements as the Folies Bergére and Can-Can dancers) flocked to his plays.

Despite a triumphant 1907 premiere in Paris at the Théâtre des Nouveautés, *A Flea in Her Ear* had largely disappeared by the time World War I sent Feydeau's reputation into a tailspin. Only in 1944 did a significant Parisian revival reintroduce the work into the French repertoire. Similar rediscoveries in ENGLAND and America in the 1960s cemented the play's place in the canon. As recently as 1999, a star-studded revival (directed by neo-vaudevillian Bill Irwin) played in New York to fresh laughter.

FURTHER READING

Feydeau, Georges. *From Marriage to Divorce: Four One-Act Plays*. Tr. by Peter Meyer. Bath: Absolute Classics, 1998.

Marcoux, J. Paul. *Five by Feydeau*. New York: Peter Lang, 1994.

McLeish, Kenneth. *Feydeau Plays: Two*. London: Methuen, 2002.

Pronko, Leonard C. *Georges Feydeau*. New York: Frederick Ungar, 1975.

Gavin Witt

FLEIßER, MARIELUISE (1901–1974)

Although the titles of her first two plays stress an affinity to her Bavarian hometown, Marieluise Fleißer offered a bold alternative to the socially affirmative representations of most regional literature. Her critical version of the VOLKSSTÜCK destroys the illusion of an intact idyll by depicting lower-middle-class characters who face an alienation they do not comprehend arising from conditions they feel powerless to change. The adolescents in *Purgatory in Ingoldstadt* (*Fegefeuer in Ingolstadt*, 1924), for example, engage in a repetitive cycle of domination and violence: packs gang up on outsiders by imitating the authoritarian norms of the church and school that dominate them. The effect is intensified through Fleißer's language, a sparse rendering of dialect-flavored speech that provides complex characterization and indirect commentary. Frequently used as a weapon rather than a means for achieving insight, the characters' language reveals the extent to which patterns of authority have been internalized, even when the institutions themselves remain offstage.

Fleißer, born on November 23, 1901, in Ingolstadt, GERMANY, was the daughter of a smith and member of the first generation of German women to attend the university in large numbers, studied theater in Munich, and later moved to Berlin as a result of her association with BERTOLT BRECHT. Although she did not adopt Brecht's dramatic theories or techniques, her first play, which received favorable reviews by leading critics, was performed on his recommendation. Brecht encouraged her to write *Soldiers in Ingolstadt* (*Pioniere in Ingolstadt*, 1928), about the relationship between young women in a small town and soldiers temporarily stationed there. Like *Purgatory in Ingolstadt*, its carefully constructed dialogue reveals patterns of domination from which the characters are unable to escape. When Brecht took over the 1929 Berlin production, the consequences were not entirely favorable for Fleißer. Brecht's staging emphasized certain sexual features to provoke the establishment, and the resulting furor made Fleißer unwelcome in her hometown. Disillusioned, she retreated into an unfortunate relationship with a journalist; *The Deep-Sea Fish* (*Der Tiefseefisch*, 1929) portrays the whole experience.

After the Nazis came to power, her books were burned, and she married an Ingolstadt merchant who reneged on his promise to allow her time for writing. Her work during this "inner exile" thus proceeded slowly. She wrote a conventional historical drama, *Charles Stuart* (*Karl Stuart*, 1938), and a COMEDY in dialect, *Of Sturdy Stock* (*Der starke Stamm*, 1944).

Despite scattered performances, Fleißer's dramas were basically forgotten after World War II until interest in her early work was rekindled a few years before her death (on February 1, 1974, in Ingolstadt, West Germany) by a new generation of playwrights, including FRANZ XAVER KROETZ, Martin Sperr, and RAINER WERNER FASSBINDER, who encouraged new performances of her dramas and attested to her influence on their own work. A writer of novels, stories, and essays as well as plays, Fleißer continues to attract considerable interest as a woman who became one of Germany's important 20th-century authors.

PLAYS: *Purgatory in Ingolstadt* (*Fegefeuer in Ingolstadt*, 1924); *Soldiers in Ingolstadt* (*Pioniere in Ingolstadt*, 1928); *The Deep-Sea Fish* (*Der Tiefseefisch*, 1929); *Charles Stuart* (*Karl Stuart*, 1938); *Of Sturdy Stock* (*Der starke Stamm*, 1944)

FURTHER READING

Case, Sue-Ellen, ed. *The Divided Home/Land: Contemporary German Women's Plays*. Ann Arbor: Univ. of Michigan Press, 1992.

Colvin, Sarah. *Women and German Drama: Playwrights and Their Texts, 1860–1945*. Rochester, N.Y.: Camden House, 2003.

Hoffmeister, Donna L. *The Theater of Confinement: Language and Survival in the Milieu Plays of Marieluise Fleißer and Franz Xaver Kroetz*. Columbia, S.C.: Camden House, 1983.

Jones, Calvin N. *Negation and Utopia: The German Volksstück from Raimund to Kroetz*. New York: P. Lang, 1993.

Schmidt, Henry. *How Dramas End: Essays on the German Sturm und Drang, Büchner, Hauptmann, and Fleisser*. Ann Arbor: Univ. of Michigan Press, 1992.

Calvin N. Jones

THE FLIES

JEAN-PAUL SARTRE's first play was written and produced during World War II at the time of the German Occupation of FRANCE. Charles Dullin not only directed but took on the role of Zeus in the play's premiere, which opened in 1943 at the Théâtre de la Cité-Sarah Bernhardt in Paris. Though Sartre had already begun to establish his reputation as an existential writer, the original audience was less responsive to the play's philosophical debates than the thinly veiled political message urging resistance against authoritarian oppression. (Its classical subject matter apparently duped the Nazi censors into approving the play.) Though *The Flies* (*Les mouches*) has not enjoyed a very successful stage history, it is considered one of Sartre's greatest theatrical works, as much for its historical significance as for its political and philosophical grappling with the meaning of freedom—the central concept in Sartre's existential thought.

The Flies reimagines the Orestes's revenge myth from a TRAGEDY of fate into a tragedy of freedom. Destiny does not dictate that Orestes kill his mother Clytemnestra and Aegisthus for the murder of his father, King Agamemnon; Orestes consciously chooses his vengeful course of action. His motive is no longer bloodlust. Instead, he is moved toward this crime out of a sense of public duty. The townspeople of Argos have been living in a state of penitent submission ever since Agamemnon was assassinated. Flies hover thickly in the air as a reminder of the collective guilt shared by the population for not intervening in the murder of their king. What's more, Orestes's sister Electra is treated like a common servant in the royal household yet is still expected to perform her role in the ceremonies of the Day of the Dead, a national holiday of atonement created by Aegisthus to keep the public in a state of fearful subservience.

In defiance of Aegisthus's authoritarian misery and in the face of divine disapproval (Zeus unabashedly enjoys the benefits of a cowed population), Orestes kills his father's murderers. The question is, Will he have the strength to bear the burden of his freely committed crime? Unlike Electra, who buckles under the pressures of guilt and conformism, Orestes recognizes the value of his independent act of resistance. Renouncing remorse, he seeks to be an example to the people of Argos, who for too long have let themselves be suppressed by a status quo determined to conceal their fundamental liberty from them.

The Flies' situational analogy with the French dilemma of resistance versus collaboration during the German Occupation is only too clear. The mythological setup, however, allows Sartre to both convey and transcend his play's historical imperative. On the one hand, the playwright urges his audience to resist the enemy of oppression at any cost. On the other, he allows himself license to approach the problem philosophically. "Human life begins on the far side of despair," Orestes says to Zeus, recognizing that it takes a radical stripping away of false certainties for humanity to comprehend its capacity for self-determination. Each of us must take responsibility for our free will, and only by doing so can we work toward the greater freedom of the community.

[*See also* Philosophy and Drama]

FURTHER READING

Howells, Christina. *Sartre—The Necessity of Freedom*. Cambridge: Cambridge Univ. Press, 1988.

Kern, Edith, ed. *Sartre—A Collection of Critical Essays*. Englewood Cliffs, N.J.: Prentice-Hall, 1965.

McCall, Dorothy. *The Theatre of Jean-Paul Sartre*. New York: Columbia Univ. Press, 1969.

Murdoch, Iris. *Sartre—Romantic Rationalist*. London: Vintage, 1999.

Sartre, Jean-Paul. *What Is Literature?* Tr. by Bernard Frechtman. London: Methuen, 1950.

——. *Sartre on Theater*. Tr. by Frank Jellinek. New York: Pantheon Bks., 1976.

——. *Basic Writings*. Ed. by Stephen Priest. London: Routledge, 2001.

Thody, Philip. *Jean-Paul Sartre: A Literary and Political Study*. London: Hamish Hamilton, 1960.

Wood, Philip R. *Understanding Jean-Paul Sartre*. Columbia: Univ. of South Carolina Press, 1990.

Charles McNulty

FLIGHT

A play in eight "Dreams" by MIKHAIL BULGAKOV written between 1926 and 1928, *Flight* (*Beg*) was not performed until 1957. The play focuses on civilian and military members of the so-called Whites fighting, or in flight from, the revolutionary Reds during the Russian Civil War. The action occurs between October 1920 and the following year, and the play charts the fate of those combatants and noncombatants on the White side who are being driven off the Crimean peninsula into the Black Sea by the Red Army (which only makes a fleeting appearance in the first scene), like the cockroaches into a bucket of water (to cite one of the play's central images).

The main character is Khludov, a White general, haunted by the specters of those he has had tortured and killed to the point where he becomes slightly crazed and begins to suffer from hallucinations. The main sympathies of the audience are with two other central figures, Serafima and Golubkov, both in flight from the violence of civil war and who meet by chance, fall in love, and also have a chance encounter with Serafima's husband, Korzhukin, who is revealed to be a conscienceless coward. Following the defeat of the White forces, Khludov, Serafima, Golubkov, and another White general, Charnota, succeed in making their way to Constantinople and, in some cases, to Paris.

The nightmarish, expressionist quality of the play is apparent from the outset where the "First Dream," set in a monastery, consists of a series of uncanny theatrical metamorphoses as a pregnant peasant woman turns out to be the disguised General Charnota, and monks appear and disappear through floors and walls like ghosts. Analogies are established between the monks and the cockroaches, which later figure in a fairground race (the title *Beg* has connotations of a race in Russian). The "Second Dream" takes place at a railway station, where sound and light combine to turn the place into a hellhole where a waiting room becomes an interrogation center, and an insane White officer sings snatches of an aria from Tchaikovsky's *The Queen of Spades*. A scene in a counterintelligence office involving the threat of torture is followed by one in a palace, where Khludov recounts a childhood dream about cockroaches falling into a bucket of water.

The "Fifth Dream," in Constantinople, depicts the humiliation of the former Whites now reduced to street trading and prostitution. The central image is of a cockroach race, which has been rigged in advance and which concludes with a brawl between disappointed punters. The penultimate scene in Paris emphasizes the sense of unreality through its amplification of theatrical metaphors as Charnota, clad in yellow underpants, engages in a wild gambling bout with Korzhukin, now living in luxurious sin with Charnota's former mistress, Lyuska, who is masquerading as a French lady of leisure attended by a Russian manservant playing the part of a French flunkey. The eighth and last "Dream" reunites Serafima with Golubkov in Constantinople, where Khludov decided to return to RUSSIA and face the music. Golubkov concludes, "None of it happened, we imagined it all."

Joseph Stalin read the play in 1929 but felt it was unacceptable as it stood, asking that a final scene or two be added justifying the Bolshevik cause. Bulgakov felt unable to oblige, and the play was banned.

FURTHER READING

Bulgakov, M. *Flight*. Tr. by Carl R. Proffer and Ellendea Proffer. In *Early Plays of Mikhail Bulgakov*. Bloomington: Indiana Univ. Press, 1972.

Curtis, J. A. E., ed. and tr. *Manuscripts Don't Burn: Mikhail Bulgakov—A Life in Letters and Diaries*. London: Bloomsbury, 1991.

Henry, Barbara. "Reality and Illusion: Duality in Bulgakov's Theatre's Plays." In *Bulgakov the Novelist-Playwright*, ed. by L. Milne. Luxembourg: Harwood Acad. Pubs., 1995.

Wright, A. Colin. *Mikhail Bulgakov: Life and Interpretations*. Toronto: Univ. of Toronto Press, 1978.

Nick Worrall

FO, DARIO (1926–)

Dario Fo was not born into a theatrical family but proclaimed his debt to the *fabulatori* (storytellers) active around Lake Maggiore in northern ITALY, where he was born in 1926. He was a student of architecture in Milan, the city with which his subsequent life and career were identified, in the bracing days of the Liberation, when previously banned literary, artistic, and political ideas began to circulate. Like others of his generation, Fo adopted a pro-communist stance, being particularly impressed by the writings on popular culture of Marxist thinker Antonio Gramsci. He frequented the newly founded Piccolo Teatro, where the director Giorgio Strehler was steering Italian theater in a new course, although later relations between the two were strained.

His debut as writer-performer came with a series of comic radio monologues, *Poor Soul* (*Poer nano*), which overturned traditional plots, making, for example, Goliath a harmless, genial giant provoked by a simpering, attention-seeker by the name of David. He graduated to variety theater, where he met the actress FRANCA RAME, whom he married in 1954. Their subsequent lives and careers are inseparable, and her influence on him is incalculable. Rame came from a family company of touring players with a theatrical lineage dating from the 17th century. Their style was based on improvisation; their repertoire consisted of parody, COMEDY or popular versions of classic works, including William Shakespeare; and their audience was precisely the popular audience Fo himself was to seek during his most politically committed years.

With two well-known actors, Fo established a company that put on two highly successful cabaret-style shows, *A Poke in the Eye* (1953) and *Madhouse for the Sane* (1954), where the songs and sketches varied from nonsense numbers to satires on the holders of political and financial power. In the same years, he wrote and recorded many whimsical-absurdist songs—the musical element was to remain important in much of his later theater—and in 1955 moved to Rome to break into the world of cinema. Although he contributed to several scripts, he wrote and performed in only one film of his own, *The Screwball*. Judged a failure at the time, it was subsequently reassessed more favorably by critics. Returning to Milan and to theater in 1958, the couple set up the Fo-Rame company to stage one-act FARCES written by Fo. Farce was to remain his preferred genre all his life, but since SAMUEL BECKETT and EUGÈNE IONESCO had made farce the dominant genre in European theater, Fo was taken by contemporary critics as the Italian exponent of the absurd. In fact, his style of farce had older, more popular, and less intellectual roots. He was never in sympathy with the AVANT-GARDE, which he viewed as elitist. The two programs, each of four farces, showed him as actor-author and demonstrated twin sides of his creativity. *Thieves, Mannequins and Naked Women* (Milan, 1958) consisted of four wholly original, mildly satirical pieces, while the four plays in *Comic Finale* (Turin, 1958) were reworkings of situations staged over the years by the Rame family company. All Fo's theater looks at his own day but is firmly grounded in tradition.

The couple now found the doors of Italy's major theaters open to them. The period from 1959 until 1967 has been dubbed Fo's "bourgeois period," a description that refers more to the venues in which the company performed than to the content of the works themselves. In every phase of his development, satire was his forte, and as the political-satirical edge became increasingly overt and acerbic, the company drew the ire of the censors, who still had the right to see all scripts before they reached the stage. Large sections were routinely blacked out. In these years, Fo turned out a play a year, a comedy rather than a farce, even if the distinction is a fine one. "The choice of comedy involves a more complex structure. While farce is based from beginning to end on a theatrical mechanism using one single device, comedy has a structure articulated according to the storyline, so the devices can be multiple," he wrote (qtd. in Farrell, 2001). The plots of Fo's comedies are often a chain of sometimes tenuously related situations, many of which, especially those devised in rehearsals rather than plotted at a desk, are indistinguishable from knockabout farce. *Archangels Don't Play Pinball* (1959), the first of his plays to be given a precise social setting, moves from a rundown neighborhood where a naïve scoundrel, played by Fo, is duped into forming a relationship with a good-hearted local prostitute, played by Rame, onto a ministry where civil servants stand alongside a mass-production line, fulfilling their duties with the mechanical precision of puppets. The following year's play, *He Had Two Pistols and White and Black Eyes*, was set in a mental hospital run by a monastic order, an easily recognizable, satirical image of Italy run by a clerical-political establishment.

The couple's celebrity status was acknowledged by an invitation to present Italy's leading television light-entertainment program, *Canzonissima*, a mixture of comedy sketches and songs. Fo's sketches were not the expected lighthearted pieces but fiery political exposés, provoking hostile articles and questions in Parliament and leading to the couple walking off the set when a sketch on striking workers was refused. The incident caused a sensation all over Italy and secured their reputation as radical firebrands. They returned to theater with *Isabella, Three Caravels and a Con-man* (1963), overtly about Christopher Columbus but focusing at a deeper level on dissident intellectuals, like Fo himself with the broadcasting authorities, whose heads are turned by invitations to walk the corridors of power.

His patience with the constraints of comedy and with the audiences he was attracting was wearing thin, and in 1968, the year of student demonstrations and social turbulence, he broke with "bourgeois theater" to set up a cooperative, Nuova Scena, and to play in an alternative circuit of unconventional venues where he hoped to attract a new audience of working-class people. "I was tired of being the *giullare* [jester] of the bourgeoisie, on whom my satirical sallies had the effect of an alka-seltzer, and decided to become the jester of the proletariat," he declared (Farrell, 2001). Farce would once again be his style, and the new theater would be popular and explicitly political, but it was typical of the complexity of Fo's beliefs that at exactly the moment he announced his dedication to revolutionary Marxism, he chose as his model the *giullare*, a medieval performer. *Comic Mysteries* (*Mistero buffo*, 1969), the principal work he performed with Nuova Scena, demonstrated his stance as political revolutionary and theatrical traditionalist. The choice of medieval material baffled many members of the cooperative, who had expected a more contemporary, didactic work.

Fo was increasingly attracted to the burgeoning extraparliamentary movement, and in 1970 he left Nuova Scena to set up a new company, La Comune, whose advocacy of revolution allowed him to include the "reformist" Communist Party among the targets for his scorn. The first work was *ACCIDENTAL DEATH OF AN ANARCHIST* (1970), a farce that was an exposé of the sinister maneuverings of the Italian police and authorities after the bombing at Piazza Fontana in Milan that left sixteen dead. A madman with a genius for impersonation conducts an investigation into the arrest and death in custody of Pino Pinelli, an anarchist who died mysteriously in police custody after being slanderously blamed for the outrage. No other playwright could make farce out of such black material, and no previous farceur had shown any interest in political propaganda. Fo, who always wrote at speed, produced many plays to illustrate problems of the day and drew huge crowds all over Italy. However, there were further schisms, and the cooperative dissolved in 1973, to be re-formed as a more conventional organization owned by Fo and Rame.

The couple, still the target of official bile and frequently in court on a number of charges, continued to produce radical theater. The mass political movement for which he had become unofficial spokesman was disintegrating, and Fo's interest widened to social as well as explicitly political issues. *Mum's Marijuana Is the Best* (1976) deals with the problem of drugs in society, but the main focus of the new theater was on the role of women in society. Fo wrote and Rame performed a series of one-woman shows collected under the title of FEMALE PARTS (first performed 1977). Fo returned to one-man, storytelling performance with *Story of a Tiger* (1977), based on a tale he learned in CHINA. He paid a debt to figures and writers he recognized as theatrical masters by performing a Harlequin show at the Venice Biennale in 1985 and by directing plays by Molière and devising a show from the works of the Renaissance actor-author Ruzante (Angelo Beolco). He also accepted invitations to direct opera, particularly those of Gioacchino Rossini, whom he viewed as fellow heir of commedia dell'arte. Political passion was far from spent, as is clear from *The Devil with Tits* (1997), a scathing comedy on the corruption scandals that shook Italy in the late 1990s.

During the run of that show came the announcement that he had been awarded the Nobel Prize for Literature. The citation by the Swedish Academy declared that he "emulates the jesters of the Middle Ages in scourging authority and upholding the dignity of the poor. . . . Fo is an extremely serious satirist with a multifaceted oeuvre." He continued writing and performing and used the enhanced prestige conferred by the award to raise environmental questions. His monologue on Saint Francis of Assisi (1999) drew, to general surprise, the gratitude of the Vatican for ensuring that religious questions were still aired. Fo is one of 20th-century Italian theater's great satirists and comic spirits, and even when the causes he espoused are forgotten, the deft union of tradition and innovation, the vivacity of his inventiveness combined with a passion against injustice, will guarantee him a lasting place in theater history.

SELECT PLAYS: *The Virtuous Burglar* (*Non tutti i ladri vengono per nuocere*, 1958); *Archangels Don't Play Pinball* (*Gli arcangeli non giocano a flipper*, 1959); *Isabella, Three Caravels and a Con-man* (*Isabella, tre caravelle e un cacciaballe*, 1963); *Seventh: Steal a Little Less* (*Settimo: Ruba un po' meno*, 1964); *Toss the Lady Out* (*La signora è da buttare*, 1967); *Comic Mysteries* (*Mistero buffo*, 1969); *Accidental Death of an Anarchist* (*Morte accidentale di un anarchico*, 1970); *Can't Pay? Won't Pay!* (*Non si paga! Non si paga!* 1974); *All Bed, Board and Church* (*Tutta casa, letto e chiesa*, 1977); *Story of a Tiger* (*Storia della tigre*, 1977); *Trumpets and Raspberries* (*Clacson, trombette e pernacchi*, 1981); *Elizabeth: Almost by Chance a Woman* (*Quasi per caso una donna: Elisabetta*, 1983); *The Open Couple* (*Coppia aperta, quasi spalancata*, 1983); *The Pope and the Witch* (*Il Papa e la strega*, 1990); *Johan Padan and the Discovery of America* (*Johan Padan a la descoverta de le Americhe*, 1991); *The Devil with Tits*, also translated as *The Devil in Drag* (*Il diavolo con le zinne*, 1997)

FURTHER READING

Behan, Tom. *Dario Fo: Revolutionary Theatre*. London: Pluto, 2000.

Farrell, Joseph. *Dario Fo and Franca Rame: Harlequins of the Revolution*. London: Methuen, 2001.

Farrell, Joseph, and Antonio Scuderi. *Stage, Text, and Tradition*. Carbondale: Southern Illinois Univ. Press, 2000.

Mitchell, Tony. *Dario Fo: The People's Court Jester*. London: Methuen, 1999.

Joseph Farrell

EN FOLKEFIENDE See AN ENEMY OF THE PEOPLE

FOOL FOR LOVE

It was like we knew each other from somewhere but we couldn't place where. But the second we saw each other, that very second, we knew we'd never stop being in love.

—Eddie

Of *Fool for Love* (1982), playwright SAM SHEPARD says, "I was determined to write some kind of confrontation between a man and a woman, as opposed to just men . . . this one is really more about a woman than any play I've ever written" (Dugdale, 1989). As Shepard reveals the passion between May and Eddie, he also delves into the elusive nature of a love relationship—its commingling of illusion and reality, jealousy and obsession, memory and truth.

The one-act play takes place in a seedy motel room at the edge of the Mojave Desert where May is getting ready for a date, and Eddie, a rodeo stuntman, has just arrived, having traveled 2,480 miles with his pickup and horses to find her. During their fifteen-year relationship, Eddie has left May over and over again, most recently for the glamorous Countess, who is chasing him and shoots out the windshield of his truck. May's new date, Martin, a mild-mannered groundskeeper for the local high school, arrives at the height of Eddie and May's brutal argument and learns that they have been lovers since their teens. May and Eddie share the same father, the Old Man, who sits at the edge of the stage, rocking in his chair, swigging whiskey, and who is visible only to his children.

Through extended monologues, Eddie, May, and the Old Man reveal the interrelationships of these obsessive, and often delusional, romantic triangles. Eddie tells his story of going on a long walk of silent bonding with the Old Man, arriving at May's family's house, watching his father embrace May's mother, and then falling in love with May himself. As Eddie had repeated the Old Man's example, May tells us that she similarly followed in her mother's footsteps and became obsessed with Eddie and, finally, that Eddie's mother "blew her brains out" when she realized that the half-siblings were lovers. The Old Man believes that his love for their two mothers was benign—"the same love, just got split in two, that's all"—and cannot admit to the destructive power of need and jealousy. May's story "doesn't hold water," complains the Old Man. "That's the dumbest version I ever heard in my whole life. She never blew her brains out. Nobody ever told me that. Where the hell did that come from? . . . I wanna' hear the male side a' this thing." But Eddie declines to defend his father's behavior, affirms May's account of her mother's obsessive love for the Old Man, and reveals that she took her life with the Old Man's shotgun.

May and Eddie are drawn into a final, sustained kiss but are abruptly pulled apart as the Countess's Mercedes careens through the parking lot, sets Eddie's trailer ablaze, and scares away his horses. Eddie goes "out to look," but May gives him up as gone. After May leaves, the Old Man retreats to his fantasy, pointing to an empty space where he admires a picture of country music star Barbara Mandrell: "That's the woman of my dreams. That's who that is. And she's all mine. Forever."

Fool for Love was first performed in San Francisco in a 1983 Magic Theater production directed by the author, whose highly physical approach can be discerned from the stage directions of the published script. The production, which starred Kathy Baker and Ed Harris, was moved to New York, where it had a long and successful run OFF-BROADWAY, Shepard winning the Obie for both his writing and direction. Reviewing the play for the *Village Voice* (June 7, 1983), Michael Feingold remarked that Shepard's "awesomely rich and dense" vision "continually breaks the naturalistic frame without ever devaluing it as a way of finding and rooting the strongest emotions."

[*See also* United States, 1940–Present]

FURTHER READING

Dugdale, John. *File on Shepard*. London: Methuen, 1989.

Hart, Lynda. *Sam Shepard's Metaphorical Stage*. New York: Greenwood Press, 1987.

Shepard, Sam. *Fool for Love and The Sad Lament of Pecos Bill on the Eve of Killing His Wife*. San Francisco: City Lights Books, 1983.

Wilcox, Leonard, ed. *Rereading Shepard: Contemporary Critical Essays on the Plays of Sam Shepard*. New York: St. Martin's, 1993.

Mary Fleischer

FOON, DENNIS (1951–)

Dennis Foon, one of CANADA's foremost playwrights for young audiences, was born in Detroit, Michigan, on November 18, 1951, to Alvin Nathan and Shirley Weiss Foon, the youngest of three sons. Attending Cooley High School in central Detroit in the 1960s, Foon witnessed a racially divided environment fraught with discrimination and bigotry. His experience with racial tension and polarization later prompted him to examine systematic racism and its impact on children. As a playwright, Foon acknowledges that writing is a way for him to explore personal issues rooted in his troubled youth.

From 1969 to 1973, Foon attended the University of Michigan, majoring in religious studies. In 1973, he won a creative writing fellowship to the University of British Columbia in Vancouver, Canada. In 1975 Foon and Jane Howard Baker founded Vancouver's Green Thumb Theater for Young People. During the first phase (1975–1978) of Foon's career, his plays were more experimental in nature, using common children's themes, such as myth, folktales, and native legends. In 1978 Foon became conscious of the dearth of dramatic works that examined children's lives and reflected their real concerns, and he began to write and produce plays that focused on the concerns and plight of young audiences. As drama critic Sarah Gibson-Bray states in "The Mirror Game" (1996), "Foon's most significant contribution to the arts in Canada has been as a pioneer playwright who has helped to forge a new, realistic, issue-oriented, dramatic and theatrical genre christened 'child advocacy theatre.' "

Some of Foon's most influential works include *New Canadian Kid* (1981), *Skin* (1984), *Invisible Kids* (1985), *Liars* (1986), *Mirror Game* (1988), *Seesaw* (1993), *War* (1994), *Little Criminal* (1996). These plays, based on Foon's meticulous research and interviews with hundreds of young subjects, social workers, teachers, and police officers, portray with compelling credibility the increasingly perilous world of children who must endure systematic racism, school bullying, the trauma of divorce, and dysfunctional families.

In 1987 Foon left Green Thumb to pursue freelance playwriting and directing projects. In recent years, he has been mainly writing young adult novels and television and movie scripts.

Foon's pioneering work in child advocacy drama has garnered him many awards, including two Writers Guild of Canada: Top Ten Award (*Torso*, 2003; *Little Criminals*, 1997), Gemini Award for Best Screenplay (*Little Criminals*, 1997), two Canadian Chalmers Awards for Best Children's Play (*Skin*, 1987; *The Short Tree and The Bird That Could Not Sing*, 1995), and a British Theatre Award for Best Production for Young Audiences (*Invisible Kids*, 1986).

For more than two decades, Foon has helped to reform the Canadian theater for young audiences and has been at the forefront of creating a new genre of theater: plays that use adult actors to demonstrate the emotional depth and complexity of characters and portray the real lives and concerns of young people.

SELECT PLAYS: *Heracles* (1978); *Hotsy Totsy* (1978, co-creator); *Raft Baby* (1978); *The Windigo* (1979); *The Hunchback of Notre Dame* (1981, adaptation); *New Canadian Kid* (1981); *Feeling Yes, Feeling No: A Child Sexual Abuse Prevention Programme* (1982, co-writer); *Trummi Kaput*

(1982, adaptation of Volker Ludwig's play); *Children's Eyes* (1983); *Skin* (1984); *Invisible Kids* (1985); *Afternoon Tea* (1986); *Liars* (1986); *Bedtimes and Bullies* (1987, adaptation of Volker Ludwig's play); *Mirror Game* (1988); *Seesaw* (1993); *The Short Tree and The Bird That Could Not Sing* (1994); *War* (1994); *Little Criminal* (1996); *Chasing the Money* (1999)

FURTHER READING

Doolittle, Joyce. "The West Coast's Hardy Perennial: Green Thumb." *Canadian Theatre Review* 37 (Spring 1983): 59–65.

Gibson-Bray, Sarah. "Skin and Liars: Two Plays by Dennis Foon." *Canadian Theatre Review* 69 (Fall 1989): 88–89.

——. "The Plays of Dennis Foon—Playwright for Young Canadians." Ph.D. diss., Univ. of Toronto, 1992.

——. "The Mirror Game: Reflections of Young Canadians in Dennis Foon's Child Advocacy Drama." *Canadian Children's Literature* 82, no. 22 (1996): 40–56.

McDonald, Marci. "Foon, Dennis (profile)." *Maclean's* (January 22, 1996).

Pendergast, Sara, and Tom Pendergast, eds. *St. James Guide to Children's Writers*. 5th ed. Detroit: St. James Press, 1999.

Lei Zhang

FOOTE, HORTON (1916–)

There's been some changes, haven't there? Your daddy's dead, the Robedauxs moved, you're mama married again—a lot of changes. Well, we have got to get used to change, son. All of us.

—George Tyler, Act 2, *Roots in a Parched Ground*

Horton Foote was born in 1916 in the east Texas town of Wharton, which became the basis for his imaginary Harrison. The upheaval surrounding the region's transformation in the Civil War's aftermath from land of King Cotton to wildcat oil, abandoned farms, and urban sprawl from cities like Houston gave substance to Foote's prolific, highly nuanced, and unabashedly "realistic" writing career, the upheaval being firmly anchored in the study of family life as formative and sustaining, with strong autobiographical elements therein.

After graduating from high school, Foote went on to study elocution in Dallas and acting at the Pasadena Playhouse. From there he moved to New York City to train at the Daykarhanova School for Acting. Foote has remarked that he first began writing plays to provide parts for himself while working with the American Actors Company. Writing soon took over, and in the 1940s the playwright began to work with the autobiographical material based on his childhood in Wharton. *Out of My House* (1942), presented at the Provincetown Playhouse in Greenwich Village, received the first substantial critical recognition of his work, and *Only the Heart* (1944) was his first production on Broadway.

In the 1950s, during the "Golden Age of Television," Foote was able to work steadily as a dramatist for such programs as *Studio One*, *Playhouse 90*, and the *U.S. Steel Hour*. One remarkable play from this period is *The Trip to Bountiful* (1953), which relates the story of one Mrs. Watts, who returns home, after years of ugly life in the city, to her country town to regain her spirit and moral strength. Although she must go back to the city to live out her life, she is transformed by the trip home.

The death of his mother and father spurred Foote to tell their story and begin composition (1974–1978) of the nine plays, which comprise the ambitious *The Orphans' Home Cycle*. Generally acknowledged as Foote's major achievement, it has been compared to that planned by EUGENE O'NEILL and William Faulkner's Yoknapatawpha saga. Consisting of both one- and two-act plays that are meant to stand alone as single dramas, the *Cycle* tells the story (one among many) of Horace Robedaux, beginning with his father's death at age ten and his maturation into husband, father, and patriarch. The range of the plays in the *Cycle* is impressive: coming-of-age small-town chronicle, *Roots in a Parched Ground*; savage, lethal black COMEDY, *Convicts*; social satire and heartbreak, *Lily Dale*; marriage studies, *Courtship* and *Valentine's Day*; and minor-key domestic TRAGEDY, *1918*.

Later years saw a sustained course of dramatic writing and recognition and awards, in spite of continued suggestions over the years that his work was sentimental and nostalgic with flat language and dullness of action. Production of the *Cycle* plays throughout the country was followed by a Signature Theatre season devoted to his work (New York City, 1994–1995). One of the plays in that series, *The Young Man from Atlanta*, won the Pulitzer Prize in Drama (1995). Foote also won an Academy Award for Best Original Screenplay for the film *Tender Mercies* (1983).

SELECT PLAYS: *Only the Heart*, (1944); *The Trip to Bountiful* (1953); *The Traveling Lady* (1954); *Flight* (1956); *The Orphans' Home Cycle* (including *Roots in a Parched Ground*, *Convicts*, *Lily Dale*, *Courtship*, *Valentine's Day*, *1918*, *Cousins*, and *The Death of Papa*, 1974–1978); *In a Coffin in Egypt* (1979–1980); *The Man Who Climbed the Pecan Trees* and *The Road to Home* (1982); *The Widow Claire* (fourth part of the *Cycle*, 1982); *The Habitation of Dragons* (1988); *Dividing the Estate* (1989); *Children of Pride* (1991); *Night Seasons* (1993); *Talking Pictures* (1994); *Laura Dennis* (1995); *The Young Man from Atlanta* (1995); *Vernon Early* (1998); *The Day Emily Married* (2000)

FURTHER READING

Foote, Horton. *Farewell: A Memoir of a Texas Childhood*. New York: Scribner, 1999.

——. *Beginnings: A Memoir*. New York: Scribner, 2001.

Porter, Laurin. *Orphan's Home: The Voice and Vision of Horton Foote*. Baton Rouge: Louisiana State Univ. Press, 2003.

Watson, Charles S. *Horton Foote: A Literary Biography*. Austin: Univ. of Texas Press, 2003.

Wood, Gerald C. *Horton Foote and the Theater of Intimacy*. Baton Rouge: Louisiana State Univ. Press, 1999.

Stanley R. Richardson

FORCED UP MOUNT LIANG

Forced Up Mount Liang (*Bishang Liangshan*) is a *jingju* ("Capital theater") written by Yang Shaoxuan in Yan'an in northern Shaanxi Province. He was aided by members of the Central Party School of the Chinese Communist Party (CCP), before Mao Zedong's 1949 takeover of CHINA. The premiere took place late in 1943 and was performed by the Mass Arts Research Association, an amateur group of the Central Party School's teachers and students. Based on the novel *Outlaws of the Marsh* (*Shuihu zhuan*), and other material, the story is set during the turbulent times of the end of the Northern Song Dynasty (960–1127). The core of the plot relates how low-level military official Lin Chong joins Mount Liang's rebels, the novel's heroes. Involved in Lin Chong's ideological conversion to the anti-Song rebellion, besides Lin, are Li Tie, Li Xiaoer, and Lu Zhishen.

Forced Up Mount Liang has a significant place in the history of CCP-sponsored traditional opera. In May 1942 Mao had put forward radical views on the arts in his "Talks at the Yan'an Forum on Literature and the Arts." He had called for the arts to reflect class struggle and to serve the interests of the masses, rather than those of the ruling classes or the elites. Mao saw a performance of *Forced Up Mount Liang* and on January 9, 1944, wrote a letter to the troupe, congratulating them for "restoring the true face of history," which was "created by the people." Mao said that formerly "lords and ladies, old and young, ruled the stage, but you have reversed this reversal of history" by putting the masses back in control of the stage. He expressed his delight and confidence that "this beginning would mark the commencement of the period of revolution of the old dramas" (Mao, 1999).

Forced Up Mount Liang is also significant as the first major work belonging to the genre "newly written historical dramas" (*xinbian lishi ju*)—newly written and composed musical dramas in a traditional Chinese opera style and set in the 19th century or before. Since 1943, the CCP has made this genre specifically its own, with its writers and composers creating many pieces in various traditional opera styles, especially Beijing Opera. Newly written historical dramas differ significantly from the old, traditional operas. In addition to being written now by authors whose identities are known, they often have elaborate settings, in contrast to the bare stage of Chinese traditional theater. The plots of newly written historical dramas rise to a climax, unlike the episodic features of traditional dramas.

Like all dramas set before the CCP's birth, *Forced Up Mount Liang* was banned during the Cultural Revolution of 1966–1976. However, with the arrival of a new ideological atmosphere following Mao's death, traditional theater was publicly revived in May 1977, and several scenes from *Forced Up Mount Liang* were restaged. Apart from *jingju*, it has been adapted to many other traditional regional styles.

FURTHER READING

Mackerras, Colin. *The Performing Arts in Contemporary China*. London: Routledge, 1981.

Mao Zedong. "Talks at the Yan'an Forum on Literature and the Arts" and "A Letter after Seeing *Bishang Liangshan*." In *Chinese Theories of Theater and Performance from Confucius to the Present*, ed. and tr. by Faye Chunfang Fei. Ann Arbor: Univ. of Michigan Press, 1999. 129–142.

Colin Mackerras

FORDRINGSÄGARE *See* CREDITORS

FOREMAN, RICHARD (1937–)

Richard Foreman is one of half a dozen auteur directors who dominated the AVANT-GARDE theater scene of New York from the Richard Nixon era through the turn of the millennium. The playwright, director, and scenic designer was born on June 10, 1937, in New York City and was raised in the comfortable suburb of Scarsdale, New York. As a teenager, he rebelled, at least spiritually, against his conservative environment, and he has said he remembers "sitting around the swimming pool at [his] father's golf club," fantasizing about writing a school essay titled "Why I Think Communism Is Good." Subversive impulses notwithstanding, Foreman went on to receive his bachelor of arts degree from Brown University and a master of fine arts degree in playwriting from the Yale School of Drama. His interest in experimental theater first began after he left Yale, when he moved back to New York City in 1962. He soon fell under the influence of other experimental artists, particularly filmmakers, and in 1964 he helped cinema director Jonas Mekas establish the Cinematheque, where, in 1968, Foreman would stage *Angelface*, the first play of what he called his Ontological-Hysteric Theatre.

Over the years, Foreman became known for writing and directing plays that question traditional ideas of character, plot, and presence. The figures onstage, dressed in eclectic combinations of clothes apparently culled from secondhand shops, are as apt to evoke Hasidic Jews as they are the court of Louis XIV. Whether they lurk or dance about the stage, they seem to embody facets of Foreman's own neuroses about sex and death.

Foreman counts among his main influences two theater artists whose work bears little immediate resemblance to his own: BERTOLT BRECHT and GERTRUDE STEIN. Like Brecht, Foreman uses ALIENATION techniques, but Foreman's scenic design clutters the stage with makeshift props that look like they might have come out of an eccentric's attic—baby dolls, plastic skulls, stuffed horses, and striped poles. Strings crisscross the stage; letters from the Hebrew and Latin alphabet may be stuck to the walls; perhaps a wall of Plexiglas separates the actors from the audience. Intermittently, stage lights will take aim at and momentarily blind the audience. From Gertrude Stein, Foreman has taken the ideas of the "continuous present" and the "landscape play," dispensing with the traditional unwinding of linear narrative and instead exploring states of mind remarkable for their complexity, irony, and oblique sense of cause and effect.

Early in his career, Foreman lacked a permanent venue, and much of the small audience would leave during the course of a performance. By 1972, though, he won a Rockefeller Fellowship for playwriting, and in 1992, he was able to move into a permanent space in a wing of St. Mark's Church in New York's East Village. He has won three Obie Awards for Best Play as well as an Obie for Sustained Achievement. In 1995, he won a MacArthur Fellowship. He has also successfully staged plays written by other playwrights, most notably VÁCLAV HAVEL's *Largo Desolato* at the New York Shakespeare Festival, for which his directorial work won an Obie in 1986.

[*See also* Chance; Happenings and Intermedia; Philosophy and Drama; Political Theater in the United States; Surrealism]

SELECT PLAYS: *Pain (T)* (1974); *Rhoda in Potatoland* (1975); *The Cure* (1986); *Film Is Evil: Radio Is Good* (1987); *Symphony of Rats* (1988); *The Mind King* (1992); *Pearls for Pigs* (1997); *Bad Boy Nietzsche* (1999); *The Gods are Pounding My Head* (2005).

FURTHER READING

Davy, Kate. *Richard Foreman and the Ontological-Hysteric Theatre*. Ann Arbor: UMI Res. Press, 1981.

Rabkin, Gerald. *Richard Foreman*. Baltimore: Johns Hopkins Univ. Press, 1999.

Robinson, Marc. *The Other American Drama*. Cambridge: Cambridge Univ. Press, 1994.

Daniel Mufson

THE FOREST

The Forest (*Les*, 1871) is a COMEDY by ALEKSANDR OSTROVSKY set on the country estate of the aristocrat Raisa Gurmyzhskaya, a widow in her fifties. She is selling her forests to the lumber profiteer Vosmibratov, professing to use the cash for charitable purposes. In actual fact, Gurmyzhskaya plans to use the money for herself, which she also intends to do with the inheritance she is going to steal from her nephew and heir Gennady. She also declares that her ward, Aksyusha, must marry Bulanov, who will benefit by the girl's dowry, as will Gurmyzhskaya, who has set her own lascivious sights on the snivelling good-for-nothing. Meanwhile, Vosmibratov cheats Gurmyzhskaya out of 1,000 rubles—the sum agreed upon for the sale of two tracts of forest—while she rejects his proposal of a dowry of 3,000 rubles for Aksyusha to marry his own son, Pyotr, despite the fact that the couple love each other.

Enter the nephew Gennady, a professional actor whose stage name is The Unfortunate, accompanied by a comedian, Arkashka, called The Fortunate. Poor and unemployed, Gennady has come to visit his aunt, pretending to be a retired army officer, attended by Arkashka as his valet. With a good deal of sound and fury, Gennady recovers for his aunt the 1,000 rubles owed her by Vosmibratov, but she promptly makes a gift of it to Bulanov. Meanwhile, Gennady is unable to help Aksyusha, who asks for 2,000 rubles as a dowry to marry Pyotr. The tragedian then adopts a theatrical disguise and inveigles from his aunt a single payment of 1,000 rubles in return for renouncing his inheritance forever. However, hearing Gurmyzhskaya announce her engagement to Bulanov, and also refusing to give her ward a penny, Gennady uses his 1,000 to pay the, now-reduced, price of Aksyusha's dowry. The happiness of Aksyusha and Pyotr is achieved, and so is the incongruous pairing of Gurmyzhskaya and Bulanov. The now-penniless actors depart on foot, as they arrived.

In *The Forest*, Gurmyzhskaya's and Vosmibratov's domestic tyranny has assumed tendencies peculiar to the new mercantile age. They are devastating the forest for cash, and her estate is appropriately named "Treestumps." The comedy focuses on the contrast between the poor wandering actors and the hypocritical gentry, the noble ideals of literature and the wild mores of the Russian backwoods. True, the comedian admits the few books he carries in his backpack are FARCES, but the tragedian uses Friedrich Schiller's eloquence to berate his aunt at the end. Gennady's famous parting lines are: "Comedians? No, we are artists, noble artists—it's you who are the comedians. If we love, then we show it;—if we give help, then down to our last hard-earned penny. And you? You discuss all your lives the welfare of society, the love of mankind. And what have you done?—Whom have you comforted? You comfort only yourselves. You are the comedians, the clowns, not we."

According to D. S. Mirsky (1958), of all Ostrovsky's plays, this is the one in which humanity's essential nobility is asserted, but it also contains "the most unsweetened types of cynical and complacent meanness and selfishness in the whole of Russian literature."

FURTHER READING

Hoover, Marjorie L. *Alexander Ostrovsky*. Boston: Twayne, 1981.

Mirsky, D. S. *A History of Russian Literature*. New York: Knopf, 1958.

Ostrovsky, Alexander. *The Forest*. In *Five Plays*, ed. and tr. by Eugene K. Bristow. New York: Western, 1989.

Rahman, Kate Sealey. *Ostrovsky: Reality and Illusion*. Birmingham Slavonic Monographs No. 30. Edgbaston, Birmingham, U.K. Univ. of Birmingham Press, 1999.

Liisa Byckling

FORMALISM

A literary movement that originated in Russia and existed during the years immediately before and after the October Revolution of 1917, the term "formalist" was originally applied by members of the Moscow Linguistic Circle and the Society for the Study of Poetic Language (Opoyaz), two Russian literary-critical groups who formed similar ideas regarding the primacy of form in literary analysis. Individuals associated with the movement were Roman Jakobson, Boris Eichenbaum, Jurij Tynyanov, and Viktor

Shklovsky. Arguing that literature was not a reflection of reality but a semiotically organized signification of it, the formalists argued that literature created a "vision" of an object, not a means of knowing it.

Closely associated with structuralism (a movement that partly evolved from formalism), formalism attempts to separate the meaning of a work of art from the work itself. Following the direction begun by Russian literary societies, Soviet filmmakers of the 1920s, Sergei Eisenstein in particular, were instrumental in the development of formalism through their use of montage as a filmmaking device. Since then, formalism has been applied to a range of arts, including painting and theatrical production, and holds that an artwork's meaning exists primarily through form or language, rather than content or subject. A variety of movements in the theater, all aimed at challenging or stretching the boundaries between form and content, have emerged and continue to develop into the 21st century.

Early-20th-century theater directors such as VSEVOLOD MEYERHOLD, Alexander Tairov, and STANISŁAW WITKIEWICZ began implementing formalist techniques that sought to eliminate traditional relationships between performer and spectator as well as between theatrical form and meaning. Concerned with the "destruction of NATURALISM," Meyerhold experimented with the significance of objects and gestures, introduced stylized settings and exaggerated lighting, and gave primary attention to the movement of the human form through space. BERTOLT BRECHT's *Verfremdungseffekt* or "ALIENATION EFFECT" realized through practical work the early Russian formalist theory of "defamiliarization," forcing the audience to reconsider objects and relationships that have become naturalized. Both directors eliminated the use of the traditional stage curtain as a way to bridge the gap between actor and spectator. In America in the 1960s, "HAPPENINGS" were staged that further explored form as divorced from traditional meaning, content, or narrative. With Happenings, scripts were absent, "found" spaces were used rather than theaters, the relationship between the audience and the performer was radically altered to include interaction and voyeurism, and there was an increased emphasis on movement and visual imagery. Later works of the LIVING THEATRE (Julian Beck and Judith Malina), the OPEN THEATER (Joseph Chaikin), and the work of RICHARD FOREMAN and the Ontological-Hysterical Theatre made significant advances in formalist techniques.

Particularly relevant in the area of scenic design, formalist theories were advanced through the writings of Adolphe Appia and Gordon Craig and have been realized in the 20th and early 21st centuries in the work of ROBERT WILSON, Meredith Monk, Laurie Anderson, and other performance artists who emphasize external and visual elements.

[*See also* Russia and the Soviet Union]

FURTHER READING

Appia, Adolphe. *Music and the Art of Theater*. Coral Gables: Univ. of Miami Press, 1962.

Bennet, Tony. *Formalism and Marxism*. London: Methuen, 1979.

Erlich, V. *Russian Formalism: History and Doctrine*. The Hague: Mouton Press, 1955.

Kiebuzinska, Christine. *Revolutionaries in the Theater: Meyerhold, Brecht and Witkiewicz*. Ann Arbor: UMI Res. Press, 1988.

Kirby, Michael. *A Formalist Theater*. Philadelphia: Univ. of Pennsylvania Press, 1987.

Quadri, Franco, Franco Bertoni, and Robert Stearns. *Robert Wilson*. New York: Rizzoli Intl., 1998.

Steve Earnest

FORNES, MARIA IRENE (1930–)

Maria Irene Fornes' life and work in the theatre defies classification . . . she has built a body of work and created an aesthetic that runs against the conventions of what an American playwright's (and director's) career "should" be.

—Delgado and Svich, *Conducting a Life*, 1999

Maria Irene Fornes, playwright, director, and teacher, is one of the most important and enduring yet underacknowledged theater practitioners to come out of the OFF-OFF-BROADWAY movement of the 1960s. A playwright whose work defies the simplicity of any single label, Fornes has alternatively been called AVANT-GARDE, an absurdist, a realist, a feminist, and a nonfeminist. Born on May 14, 1930, in CUBA, Fornes immigrated to the UNITED STATES with her mother and siblings at the age of fifteen. She began her artistic career as a painter and spent numerous years in Paris during the early 1950s, where she attended the original 1954 Roger Blin production of SAMUEL BECKETT's *WAITING FOR GODOT*. While Fornes did not begin writing until 1960, she was and remains influenced by this production and the intensity and minimalism of Beckett's aesthetic. Critics have noted her attention to the visual spectrum and detail as indicative of her earlier career in the visual arts.

Fornes began writing in an attempt to help Susan Sontag (then her roommate) overcome writer's block. Despite little formal training in the theater, Fornes wrote prolifically beginning in the early 1960s: *Tango Palace*, her first well-known play (1963), depicted a Beckettian confrontation between the clownish Isidore and the earnest and youthful Leopold and was premiered under the direction of Herbert Blau at the San Francisco Actor's Workshop. Two years later, *The Successful Life of 3* garnered Fornes her first Obie Award (1965). During these formative years, Fornes worked with many of the important theater groups of the era: she observed work at the Actors' Studio, and while she was impressed with Lee Strasberg's techniques, she cared less for his aesthetic; she also joined Joseph Chaikin's OPEN THEATER in late 1963. She found the Judson Poets' Theatre and began directing her own work such as the Obie Award–winning

Promenade (1965, with music by Al Carmines), an absurd, carnivalesque critique of class and military culture, centered on two escaped convicts named 105 and 106.

During the mid- to late 1960s, Fornes honed her political commentary and satire with *A Vietnamese Wedding* (1967), an antiwar play that ironically never directly mentions war, and *Dr. Kheal* (1968), whose title character emerges out of the contradictory notions of to kill and to heal. Fornes's early plays demonstrated her commitment to paradox and complexity, a compelling yet sparse use of dialogue, and great attention to the visual intricacies of production. In 1968, Fornes completed *Molly's Dream*, which would be her last published work for many years. She was dissuaded from directing the play but felt that the ensuing production avoided the literalness that her text intended. Consequently, Fornes decided that she would henceforth direct all her own plays, and she has directed virtually every premiere production of her plays since the late 1960s. Fornes has become a well-known director in her own right, directing plays by Pedro Calderón, HENRIK IBSEN, ANTON CHEKHOV, and others.

Toward the end of the 1960s, Fornes, ADRIENNE KENNEDY, Julie Bovasso, and other avant-garde women playwrights formed the Women's Theater Council (WTC); because of a lack of funding, this group soon merged with such male playwrights as ED BULLINS and SAM SHEPARD to form the New York Theater Strategy, of which Fornes was the managing director from 1973 to 1979. Fornes used this time to rework her aesthetic and emerge with a more mature and intimate aesthetic, most graphically demonstrated by the 1977 production of her acknowledged masterpiece FEFU AND HER FRIENDS. With *Fefu*, Fornes began her most prolific and profound period of writing and directing. *The Danube* (1981) tells of a cross-cultural love affair set against the creeping pollution of nuclear war; *Mud* (1983) is a violent, sparse, yet beautiful story of Mae's struggle to find humanity amid the lecherous and dependent weight of two men, Lloyd and Henry. Positioned on a bare outcropping of red mud invoked by the title, this play is one of Fornes's finest. Her characters, simultaneously cretinlike and immature, capture the essence of individual spirit in a manner that avoids both stereotyping and any play of generalities. Originally produced at the Padua Hills Festival in Los Angeles, *Mud* earned an Obie in its subsequent New York production at the Theater for the New City. *Sarita* (1984, with music by Leon Odenz) details the sexual passion of a young girl and her ultimately destructive relationship with her older lover, Julio.

In *The Conduct of Life* (1985), which also won an Obie Award, Orlando, a Latin American army lieutenant, holds hostage and repeatedly rapes a young street girl, Nena, while his wife Leticia assiduously fails to acknowledge the relationship. What remains gripping about these and other characters is not so much their startling violence but the playwright's ability to find strength amidst a character's frailty, affection amid savagery. In *The Conduct of Life* such tension is crystallized in Nena's monologue toward the end of the play, in which she responds to the ongoing sexual torture by telling Leticia, "I want to conduct each day of my life in the best possible way. I should value the things I have. And I should value all those who are near me." Such generosity in the face of abuse is not only astonishingly profound; it is demonstrative of Fornes's ability to give her characters depth in the face of, rather than in spite of, their circumstances.

Although Fornes has been criticized for rarely investigating her Cuban heritage in her plays, one of her greatest influences has been as a teacher and mentor to younger Latina and Latino playwrights through the Hispanic Playwrights Lab, which she founded and led at INTAR (International Arts Relations) Hispanic Arts Center in New York City from 1981 to 1991. Fornes developed much of her work during this decade through her involvement with this group, and the lab was integral for nurturing some of the most well known Latino dramatists of the 1990s: Cherríe Moraga, Milcha Sanchez-Scott, MIGDALIA CRUZ, EDUARDO MACHADO, Nilo Cruz (who later won the Pulitzer Prize in 2003), Edit Villareal, Caridad Svich, Bernardo Solano, Ela Troyano, and others.

Fornes has also been criticized for making contradictory statements about the feminist implications of her work. Yet she has been embraced by many academics as a preeminent feminist playwright and director, and she frequently confronts issues of gender, sexuality, and violence in her dramas. Plays such as *Fefu and Her Friends*, *Abingdon Square*, and *Mud* suggest that Fornes addresses social ills through the individual experiences of her characters. A commitment to the organic process of character development and theater making has made it difficult to categorize her work, or even to define a signature style, and Fornes has repeatedly eschewed most theoretical and political labels. Fornes connects her work to Ibsen, Beckett, JEAN GENET, and EUGÈNE IONESCO and yet also claims her Cuban roots as a significant force in her work. She situates herself within the noncommercial, off-off-Broadway movement and is one of the few who have sustained careers in that community. Overall, Fornes can be regarded as an artist who uses pinpoint simplicity to convey emotional complexity, finds beauty in the filth of human experience, and brilliantly employs Brechtian techniques, ENVIRONMENTAL THEATER, found objects, ABSURDISM, and other elements in order to crystallize her idea of theatrical performance.

Fornes's later plays include *Abingdon Square* (1987) in which Marion is trapped between her need for her older husband and her desire for a younger man. First produced by the Women's Project in New York City, it won Fornes another Obie. The following year *What of the Night?* (1988) was short-listed for the Pulitzer Prize. Probably due to her constant pushing against the limits of theatrical representation, Fornes has never developed a strong mainstream audience. Although drama theorists have found it difficult to write definitively about her work, since the 1980s Fornes has increasingly drawn attention in academic circles. In total, Fornes has won nine Obie Awards, including one for Sustained Achievement in theater in 1982. She has received a Distinguished Artist Award from the National Endowment for the Arts (NEA), grants from the Rockefeller and Guggenheim foundations, has taught in numerous universities throughout the United States and in Latin America, and was a Theatre Communications Group (TCG) / Pew artist-in-residence at Women's Project and Productions. In perhaps the strongest tribute to her increasing visibility, Fornes's plays were the focus of the 1999–2000 Signature Theatre's season and also the occasion for her to direct the premiere of *Letters from Cuba* (2000), Fornes's first play to directly confront her Cuban heritage.

[See also Feminism Drama in the United States; Gay and Lesbian Drama]

SELECT PLAYS: Tango Palace (1963); The Widow (1963); Promenade (1965); The Successful Life of 3 (1965); The Office (1966); The Annunciation (1967); A Vietnamese Wedding (1967); Dr. Kheal (1968); Molly's Dream (1968); The Red Burning Light (1968); The Curse of the Langston House (1972); Aurora (1974); Cap-a-pié (1975); Washing (1976); Fefu and Her Friends (1977); Lolita in the Garden (1977); In Service (1978); Eyes on the Harem (1979); Evelyn Brown (A Diary) (1980); The Danube (1981); A Visit (1981); Mud (1983); No Time (1984); Sarita (1984); The Conduct of Life (1985); Drowning (1985); Art (Box Plays) (1986); Lovers and Keepers (1986); A Matter of Faith (1986); The Mothers (1986); Abingdon Square (1987); What of the Night? (1988); Oscar and Bertha (1991); Terra Incognita (1991); Enter the Night (1993); Ibsen and the Actress (1995); Manual for a Desperate Crossing (1996); The Summer in Gossensass (1997); The Audition (1998); Letters from Cuba (2000)

FURTHER READING

Chaudhuri, Una. "Maria Irene Fornes." In *Speaking on Stage: Interviews with Contemporary American Playwrights*, ed. by Philip C. Kolin and Colby H. Kullman. Tuscaloosa: Univ. of Alabama Press, 1996.

Delgado, Maria M., and Caridad Svich, eds. *Conducting a Life: Reflections on the Theatre of Maria Irene Fornes*. Lyme, N.H.: Smith & Kraus, 1999.

Fornes, Maria Irene. "I Write These Messages that Come." *The Drama Review* 21, no. 4 (1977): 25–40.

Keyssar, Helene, ed. *Feminist Theatre and Theory*. New York: St. Martin's, 1996.

Moroff, Diane Lynn. *Fornes: Theater in the Present Tense*. Ann Arbor: Univ. of Michigan Press, 1996.

Robinson, Marc, ed. *The Theater of Maria Irene Fornes*. Baltimore: Johns Hopkins Univ. Press, 1999.

Gwendolyn Alker

FORSSELL, LARS (1928–)

In our times the betrayer becomes a tragic person and consequently is not unsympathetic

—Lars Forssell, 1962

After his debut in 1949, Swedish poet, dramatist, and member of the Swedish Academy Lars Forssell soon established himself as one of the leading poets of his generation with a wide formal range in his many volumes of poetry. Exceedingly versatile and internationally oriented, Forssell has shown a great interest in various media: film, radio, cabaret, popular songs, cartoons. In 1953 he published his monograph *Chaplin*. As a translator he has devoted himself to Ezra Pound's *Cantos*, HENRIK IBSEN'S PEER GYNT, and some of Molière's plays.

As a dramatist he played a leading role in SWEDEN in the 1950s and 1960s. *The Coronation* (*Kröningen*) is a verse drama modeled on Euripides' *Alcestis*. Forssell's Admetus is a selfish king reluctant to face reality, constantly donning different masks in want of identity. In the *quart d'heure* (fifteen minutes) *Charlie McDeath* (1962), inspired by ventriloquist's dummy Charlie McCarthy, and subtitled "A Tragedy in One Act," Forssell interestingly varies the situation in AUGUST STRINDBERG'S MONODRAMA THE STRONGER by making the dummy seem to be the stronger character, although all lines come from his manipulator, the Ventriloquist. *Mary Lou* (1962) is set in a broadcasting studio. As the lights change from red to green, Mary Lou alternates between her everyday self and her microphone personality, yet the border between the two remains suggestively obscure. THE SUNDAY PROMENADE (*Söndagspromenaden*), Forssell's most successful play, begins as a COMEDY but ends as a TRAGEDY when the charming central character exchanges his fictive family games in his small-town drawing room—arguably a symbol of Sweden—for the reality of the world outside. That power corrupts not only the oppressor but also the oppressed is an important theme in *The Girl in Montréal* (*Flickan i Montréal*, 1967). Marie, the girl, sells herself to Monsieur D in order to survive. Stand-up comedian Lenny Bruce serves as a model for the cabaret artist in *The Goat* (*Show*, 1971). The Goat—the English title refers to the nickname of the main character—is another self-centered character, more concerned with ideas than with people; he ruins his message by using insulting language, being a drug addict, and committing a double murder.

Forssell has also, inspired more by BERTOLT BRECHT than by Strindberg, tried his hand at historical drama. The rather conventional *The Madcap* (*Galenpannan*, 1964) is about the Swedish king Gustavus IV Adolphus who was deposed in 1809 and later called himself Gustafsson. In *The Madcap* he is a somewhat-Chaplinesque character. Like most Forssell protagonists, Gustavus Adolphus is unable, or unwilling, to see life in the raw. He also has a tendency to be right at the wrong time. *Christina Alexandra* (1968) deals with the 17th-century Swedish virgin queen who Strindberg examines in *Christina*. Christina is a self-centered prisoner of her own ego. Her childish innocence is contrasted with her coldness and lust for power. *The Hare and the Buzzard* (*Haren och vråken*, 1978), partly based on Pedro Calderón de la Barca's *The Mayor of Zalamea*, is set in mid-18th-century Sweden—the "age of freedom." The hare of the title stands for the oppressed in society; the buzzard for the oppressors.

A central role is played by Ulla Winblad, known to every Swede as the tavern nymph in Carl Michael Bellman's famous *Fredman's Epistles* (*Fredmans Epistlar*, 1790), a collection that combines poetry with epic, drama, and music. To some, the play pleads for the right of the oppressed to rebel, even at the cost of human lives, whereas others see it as noncommittal in this respect.

The typical Forssell protagonist is a complex figure combining likable and disagreeable traits. He has lost all faith in anything outside of himself and is totally incapable of loving others. He feels that all ideologies have eventually betrayed humanity, and he believes that disengagement from all personal loyalties and commitments to values is the only strategy for coming to terms with the absurdities of existence. As a betrayer, he is, Forssell claims, a true representative of our times.

SELECT PLAYS: *The Fool Attached to His Bells* (*Narren som tillhörde sina bjällror*, 1949); *The Coronation* (*Kröningen*, 1956); *Charlie McDeath* (*Charlie McDeath*, 1962); *Mary Lou* (*Mary Lou*, 1962); *The Sunday Promenade* (*Söndagspromenaden*, 1963); *The Madcap* (*Galenpannan*, 1964); *The Girl in Montréal* (*Flickan i Montréal*, 1967); *Christina Alexandra* (1968); *The Goat* (*Show*, 1971); *The Hare and the Buzzard* (*Haren och vråken*, 1978); *The Rockblaster and His Daughter Eivor* (*Bergsprängaren och hans dotter Eivor*, 1989).

FURTHER READING

Carlson, Harry G. "Lars Forssell—Poet in the Theater." *Scandinavian Studies* 37 no. 1, (1965): 31–57.

McKnight, Christina S. "Lars Forssell: The Jester as Conscience." *World Literature Today* 55 (1981): 210–215.

Syréhn, Gunnar. *Osäkerhetens teater: Studier i Lars Forssells dramatik* [The theater of uncertainty: Studies in Lars Forssell's plays]. Uppsala: Lundequistska, 1979 [English summary, 181–186].

——. *Makten och ensamheten: Studier i Lars Forssells historiedramatik* [Power and loneliness: Studies in Lars Forssell's History plays]. Stockholm: Almqvist & Wiksell, 1985 [English summary, 215–223].

Egil Törnqvist

FOSSE, JON (1959–)

"When I write a play I reduce, and concentrate, and this reductive concentration makes possible the sudden outbursts of a kind of unspoken intense wisdom, which is both sad and funny."

—Jon Fosse

Jon Fosse was born in 1959 in Strandebarm, on the west coast of NORWAY. His dramatic work has attracted international attention and is now performed frequently worldwide. Before turning to the dramatic genre with the play *Someone Is Going to Come* (*Nokon kjem til å komme* 1992), Fosse had established himself as a writer of novels, poems, short stories, children's literature, and essays. Influences on his work can be traced to philosophers like FRIEDRICH NIETZSCHE, Martin Heidegger, Theodor Adorno, and Jacques Derrida and to the modernist drama of SAMUEL BECKETT.

Fosse's dramas are characterized by a linguistic sensibility and materiality; there is an emphasis on rhythm, euphony, repetition, and silence. The characters speak an extremely simple language, and their utterances are often abbreviated and unfinished. Their attempts at addressing each other often result in accusations, helpless monologues, and failed dialogue. They are emotionally bound to family and sexual relationships but are ultimately lonely, homeless, and alienated. Usually the plot conflict is uncomplicated and allows the plays to appear as miniatures of the dramatic complexity found in HENRIK IBSEN. Through its minimal form and linguistic focus, Fosse's dramatic work provokes philosophical reflection even though it is firmly embedded in psychological relationships.

The first play of his to be performed, *And We'll Never Be Parted* (*Og aldri skal vi skiljast*, 1993), was commissioned by the theater of Bergen, in an attempt to promote new Norwegian drama. The play introduces some of the main features of Fosse's aesthetics. A lonely woman tries to restore a lost relationship while she talks to her absent former husband or lover, to herself, and to the things around her. Haunted by loss and mourning, she tries to cope with her existential fear through clinging to things like a glass, a vase, a cushion. Her language becomes a fragile line on which she balances between a longing for company and communication and a tragic experience of being left totally alone. This language theme is more openly discussed in *The Name* (*Namnet*, 1994).

Fosse continually pushes his characters into existential border situations, where they confront the reality of death in life. In *The Child* (*Barnet*, 1995), written for the Ibsen Festival at Nationaltheatret in 1996, a married couple experiences the reality that their child is born dead. During the night at the hospital, Fredrik faces a new dimension in his life and starts thinking of God. In *Someone Is Going to Come* (performed 1996) a man and a woman buy a house near the sea and believe that they can withdraw from other people in order to be "lonely together." Instead, they are invaded by the Other, materialized by the landlord and by remaining objects from his grandmother, who died in the house. The setting in *Autumn Dream* (*Draum om hausten*, 1998) is a churchyard where a family gathers to bury the grandfather and where death captures other family members as well.

Fosse's modernist plays do not primarily offer reflections of our social and political circumstances; instead, they present a more profound interpretation of basic human conditions. This is perhaps a reason why his renewal of the contemporary drama has met broad universal approval.

PLAYS: *Someone Is Going to Come* (*Nokon kjem til å komme*, 1992); *And We'll Never Be Parted* (*Og aldri skal vi skiljast*, 1993); *The Guitar Man*

(*Gitarmannen*, 1994); *The Name* (*Namnet*, 1994); *The Child* (*Barnet*, 1995); *Mother and Child* (*Mor og barn*, 1996); *The Son* (*Sonen*, 1996); *Nightsongs* (*Natta syng sine songar*, 1997); *A Summer's Day* (*Ein sommars dag*, 1997); *Autumn Dream* (*Draum om hausten*, 1998); *Sleep My Baby Sleep* (*Sov du vesle barnet mitt*, 1999); *Visits* (*Besøk*, 1999); *When the Light Fades and All Is Dark* (*Medan lyset går ned og alt blir svart*, 1999); *Afternoon* (*Ettermiddag*, 2000); *Winter* (*Vinter*, 2000); *Beautiful* (*Vakkert*, 2001); *Death Variations* (*Dødsvariasjonar*, 2002); *The Girl on the Sofa* (*Jenta i sofaen*, 2003); *Purple* (*Lilla*, 2003)

FURTHER READING

Sætre, Lars. "Dramatic Meaning—and Beyond. Jon Fosse's Late Modernity in *Autumn Dream*." In *I skriftas lys og teatersalens mørke. Ei bok om Ibsen og Fosse*, In the Light of the Text and in the Dark of the Theater. [A book about Ibsen and Fosse], ed. by Gunnar Foss. Kristiansand: Norwegian Academic Press, 2005.

Svich, Caridad. "In Conversation: Trusting in Theatre: Jon Fosse." *The Brooklyn Rail* (June 2004). http://www.thebrooklynrail.org/theater/june04/fosse.html.

Unni Langås

FOUR SAINTS IN THREE ACTS

GERTRUDE STEIN's opera libretto *Four Saints in Three Acts* was written in 1928 for composer and friend Virgil Thomson (1896–1989). Thomson set a number of Stein's poems to music and also composed her last opera, *The Mother of Us All*, which was completed after her death in 1946.

Bonnie Marranca calls *Four Saints* "a joyful miracle play" in which Stein's life is juxtaposed to the life of St. Theresa of Avila. This equation of "saint" and "artist" posits a new cosmology for the 20th century in which art becomes a form of RELIGION. As in many of her plays, Stein incorporates into the text of the play her own experience of writing it, undercutting her own title by continually revising the number of saints in it and staging a discussion of the number of its acts. (There prove to be four.) Although there is focused interplay between St. Theresa and St. Ignatius, *Four Saints* defies conventions of narrative, character, and conventional dialogue, and Stein's STAGE DIRECTIONS are characteristically not distinguished from text intended to be spoken. However, its exuberant poetry, its complex and self-conscious consideration of the play as a landscape, in which a saint's garden plot and the plot of the play are laid out simultaneously, and its gentle humor make *Four Saints* one of Stein's most popular plays. One of its lines, "Pigeons in the grass alas," became a national catchphrase.

The first of Stein's works to be staged, *Four Saints in Three Acts* received an auspicious and popular premiere in 1934, inaugurating the Wadsworth Atheneum and coinciding with Stein's lecture tour of America. Music was by Virgil Thomson, scenario (based on Stein's text) by Maurice Grosser, and directed by John Houseman with designs (including cellophane scenery) by the painter Florine Stetteheimer and choreography by Frederick Ashton. This production moved to Broadway and also toured to The Sullivan Opera House in Chicago, playing sixty performances in a year. It was revived in a revised form in 1952, directed by Grosser. The premiere is notable for several reasons: it redefined "opera" in the popular imagination, suggested a new, open model for collaboration between artists, constituted the first popular success for the AVANT-GARDE American theater, and marked the first occasion of an all-black cast being hired for reasons that were not called for in a script. It also—in its playful visual style, its accessible, through-composed music, and its free approach to Stein's text—constituted a template for future productions of her work.

Four Saints in Three Acts has been subsequently performed in numerous productions, including as a monologue (by Julian Sawyer) and in a number of movement theater versions, including a 1972 version at the Vivian Beaumont Theater in New York, with direction and choreography by Alvin Ailey, and a version adapted by postmodern choreographer Mark Morris in 2000. ROBERT WILSON directed a production for the Houston Grand Opera in 1996.

[*See also* Feminist Drama in the United States; Philosophy and Drama]

FURTHER READING

Houseman, John. *Run-through, a Memoir*. New York: Simon & Schuster, 1980.

Marranca, Bonnie. "Presence of Mind," *Performing Arts Journal*, Vol. 16 No. 3 (Sept. 1994).

Stein, Gertrude. *Last Operas and Plays*. Baltimore: Johns Hopkins Univ. Press, 1995.

Watson, Steven. *Prepare for Saints: Gertrude Stein, Virgil Thomson, and the Mainstreaming of American Modernism*. Berkeley: Univ. of California Press, 1995.

Mark Lord

FRANCE

EARLY 1800S

Two dates offer useful approximations for the beginning of "modernity" in French theater. The first is 1791 when, in the wake of the French Revolution, government censorship of theaters was annulled and the exclusivity of the privileges enjoyed by the Comédie-Française was revoked. The second is 1830, the year not only of the July Revolution but also of the *Bataille d'Hernani*—the dramatic fight over the play *Hernani* by Victor Hugo (1802–1885). Its opening night (February 25, 1830) provides a snapshot of modernity's arrival. At the premiere, the pit and stalls of the augustly conservative Théâtre-Français were filled with traditionalist supporters of classical drama, while the galleries were packed with Hugo's raucous and forward-looking admirers. Hugo's metrical irregularities, disregard for Aristotelian unities, and deliberate violation of accepted standards of decorum in the script for *Hernani* triggered a riot between the proto-romantics in the galleries and the disgruntled dramaturgical conservatives in the stalls and pit. Among the staunch allies of Hugo was Théophile Gautier (1811–1872), who appeared in his pink satin doublet, not the incendiary red waistcoat of legend. Boos, shouts, and cheers could be heard from an audience split between old and young, restriction and freedom, tradition and innovation.

The events of the opening marked public and press acknowledgment of Hugo's abandonment of classical unity and *bienséance* (good taste and decorum) in favor of character development, poetic originality, and the rejection of arbitrary genre distinctions. The mixing of genres was emerging as typical of the *drame romantique* (romantic drama), a genre that Hugo had defined three years before the opening of *Hernani* in what stands today as romantic theater's manifesto, the substantial preface to his play *Cromwell*. In it, Hugo asserts that the *drame* (a term much rarer then than *drama* is today) is a result of the combination of two aspects of reality, the grotesque and the sublime. These can coexist brilliantly in a work of art, he argues, as they do in William Shakespeare's theater; Hugo sought to make them do just that in plays such as *Cromwell* and *Hernani*. The success of the *drame romantique* would be exemplified by scripts of much higher literary quality than those of the MELODRAMA that had been flourishing since the 1790s. Other romantic playwrights such as Alexandre Dumas père (1802–1870) in *The Tower of Nesle* (*La Tour de Nesle*, 1832), Alfred de Musset (1810–1857) in *Lorenzaccio* (1834), and Alfred de Vigny (1797–1863) in *Chatterton* (1835) sustained the literary quality of romantic drama in the early 19th century.

Their successes did not stop, however, the continuing development of melodrama. Hugo and other romantic dramatists reacted, in part, to the excesses of early-19th-century melodrama, but the age of melodrama and *comédie larmoyante* (earful or sentimental COMEDY) would survive to the point where it would, paradoxically, react against romantic theater's own immoderation. Later melodrama stripped ROMANTICISM of its philosophical and poetical underpinnings and relied instead on spectacle, improbable plot twists, and simplistic moralizing to titillate and captivate a vast audience of mixed social classes.

It still embodied many of the ideas of the most famous early melodramatist, René Charles Guilbert de Pixérécourt (1773–1844), which had been disseminated among later followers who saw *drame romantique* as lacking in moral rigor and grossly irreverent toward classical rules of unity and structure. Pixérécourt had at one time been acclaimed (with an allusion to one of France's greatest classical dramatists) as the "Corneille of the Boulevard" because his plays dominated the popular entertainment of Paris' Boulevard du Temple—a thoroughfare so lined with theaters offering sensational plays that it was nicknamed the "Boulevard du Crime." Pixérécourt wrote over 120 plays, fifty-nine of them melodramas, as well as manifestos defining the principles of the genre: *The Melodrama* (*Le Mélodrame*, 1818) and *Last Reflections on the Melodrama* (*Dernières Réflexions sur le Mélodrame*, 1843).

In his vision, good and evil are in a constant struggle embodied in conventional and opposite character types—persecuted heroines versus unscrupulous villains, star-crossed young lovers versus wicked old jealous husbands—and surrounded by additional mysterious characters whose identities can only be revealed with unpredictable *coups de théâtre* (theatrical surprises), volatile confrontations, and sudden denouements (resolutions). Pixérécourt's melodramas, manifestly modern in their sensationalism, violence, pathos, and comic excesses, were to classical TRAGEDY what FARCE was to classical comedy. His success had spread quickly across Europe with *Coelina, or the Child of Mystery* (*Cœlina, ou l'Enfant du mystère*, 1800). The play gained immediate international fame and by 1802 was already translated into English, as *A Tale of Mystery*, by Thomas Holcroft (1745–1809), who would be credited with introducing melodrama to ENGLAND. The continental popularity of the genre Pixérécourt made famous is demonstrated by the fact that between 1800 and 1823 over 450 melodramas were produced in France.

The frequent supposition that melodrama waned because of the triumph of REALISM is not wholly accurate. There were other factors. Although mid-19th-century realist drama offered it a challenge, melodrama survived a long time. It was the later advent of cinema that distracted audiences with a new source of excess and illusion. Later still, television would replace cinema with made-for-television dramas, sitcoms, and supremely "melodramatic" soap operas with implausible coincidences and oversentimental appeals. Despite this shift of medium, the influence of the melodramatic aesthetic on the modern theater remains paramount. Elements of action, disaster, triumph, physical pantomime, and heroism, all placed within the skillfully crafted structure of the *pièce bien faite* (well-made play) that gained popularity in the middle of the 19th century, have not lost their power in the theater even today. The American scholar Peter Brooks suggests that melodrama constituted an essential response to the French Revolution and secularization, cutting across traditional literary genres and still surviving as "an important and abiding mode in the modern imagination" (Brooks, 1976).

The continuing influence of melodrama on the French theater, while *drame romantique* waxed and waned, and realism made headway, was accompanied at midcentury by reforms in playwriting, stage directing, acting and by new views of theater's political role. The period was marked by profound cultural upheaval: the birth and crib death of the Second Republic, the rise of positive science, the burgeoning Industrial Revolution, and in France, the seesaw between republicanism and dictatorship. Although romanticism had been opposed by advocates of "reason" as it was inherited from the Enlightenment, this vestigial midcentury reason turned out to be far different from classic French Cartesianism: it had now become a pragmatic reason of the individual, responsive to and influenced by a bourgeois ethos. While the Second Empire can be seen as a repressive, highly centralized, and authoritarian regime, it was also a regime that sought to increase France's uncertain prosperity through economic expansion, industrialization, urbanization, the commercialization of agriculture, the greater integration of provincial society into the national whole, and the development of the modern bureaucratic state. Such swift and fierce modernization had huge consequences for the theater. Semifeudal, aristocratic, and largely agricultural social order had begun to give way to an industrialized and bourgeois order with transformed certainties, changed social and psychological makeup, and new desires for entertainment and pleasure. The bourgeois ethos became almost schizophrenic, at once wanting to see social traditions upheld on stage and yet also participating eagerly in a ruthless, even comic, obsession with money, influenced by the economic ideologies moving into dominance.

Two corresponding orientations mark this ambivalent period: the *comédie-vaudeville* inherited from Eugène Scribe (1791–1861), and the neo-melodramatic genre of the boulevards. Scribe had been one of France's most prolific dramatists, flooding the theater with over 400 comedies, farces, and dramas. He was mocked even in his day for supposedly keeping separate files of opening gambits, plot surprises, witty rejoinders, puns, stage effects, and so on, which he would simply line up to churn out his works, many of them in the *comédie-vaudeville* mode. *Comédie-vaudeville* differed from melodrama in using settings and situations from daily life, rather than exotic locales, and inserting popular songs (the original meaning of the word *vaudeville*) into the action. Modern sketch comedy, musical revues, and sitcoms all owe something to the genre. Whether for *comédie-vaudeville* or melodrama proper, Scribe's scripts were built upon solid templates for surefire entertainment, and he, with Pixérécourt, ensured the long life of the "well-made play," influential even today.

MID-19TH CENTURY

The neo-melodramatic genre was dominated midcentury by three figures: Alexandre DUMAS FILS (1824–1895), Eugène Labiche (1815–1888), and VICTORIEN SARDOU (1831–1908). All three, to varying degrees, helped move melodramatic story lines away from the exotic locales and situations of Pixérécourt toward the more recognizable territory of middle-class drawing rooms and high-society settings. All three also wrestled with the strictures of the "well-made play," as it had been pioneered by Scribe and further developed by Emile Augier (1820–1889), in opposition to romanticism.

Augier emphasized the doctrine of "common sense" and proposed *pièces à thèse* (thesis plays) deviating from the romantic model and glorifying the virtues of the bourgeoisie by assuring the middle-class audience that Enlightenment principles would be able to solve any social problem. Second Empire society would be scrutinized by Augier in such plays as *Shameless* (*Les Effrontés*, 1861), which tackles the emerging influence of journalism on public life, and *Mr. Poirier's Son-in-Law* (*Le Gendre de M. Poirier*, 1854), dealing with political corruption. Augier's *Giboyer's Son* (*Le Fils de Giboyer*, 1862) treats the figure of a wealthy courtesan but never achieved the renown afforded the same subject by Dumas fils.

Dumas's *Lady of the Camellias* (*La Dame aux camélias*, 1852) caused a scandal by offering a sympathetic treatment of a prostitute, much as Hugo had in his drama *Marion Delorme* (first produced in 1831). *The Demi-Monde* (*Le Demi-Monde*, 1855) remains the best comedy by Dumas fils, with a sharp analysis of contemporary manners exposing the bourgeoisie's all-consuming, but conflicted, relationship to money. *The Question of Money* (*La Question d'argent*, 1857) deals with the accumulation of wealth, while THE ILLEGITIMATE SON (*Le Fils naturel*, 1858), his first thesis play, treats issues in public and private lineage—a theme that allowed Dumas fils, himself the illegitimate son of Dumas père, to draw on the social repercussions of his own career. Both Augier and Dumas can be placed among the first "realists" because they depicted contemporary social types and conditions that they had actually observed rather than imagined, and the language and sentiments of their characters, while heightened, are recognizably modeled on those of actual society.

Eugène Labiche perfected French farce. "Of all the subjects which offered themselves to me," Labiche wrote, "I have selected the bourgeois being. Essentially mediocre in his vices and in his virtues, he stands half-way between the hero and the scoundrel, between the saint and the profligate." The *Mr. Perrichon's Trip* (*Voyage de M. Perrichon*, 1860) remains Labiche's comic farce par excellence, looking back both to the wit of Molière (1622–1673) and the satire of Pierre de Beaumarchais (1732–1799).

Sardou's successes continued as late as the 1900s and were often tied to actors. In 1887 Sardou wrote *La Tosca* for Sarah Bernhardt (1844–1923). She was one of the era's most influential actors, referred to with awe as a *monstre sacré* (sacred monster), along with the actors Constant Coquelin (1841–1909) and Mounet-Sully (1841–1916), who triumphed in France and abroad in both classical and modern plays. In 1900 the text for *La Tosca* provided Giacomo Puccini with the libretto for his opera. The skillful stagecraft of the well-made play that Sardou built on continued to be imitated not only in France but by playwrights across Europe and America, where the model was disseminated by frequent translation, imitation, and undisguised plagiarism.

As the second half of the 19th century marched on, however, the ploys that dominated "well-made" DRAMATURGY became patently insufficient. Emerging theater makers and theatergoers grew weary of the well-made play's repetitive structural gambits, stereotyped heroes, facile emotionalism, tired moral conundrums, and problematic lack of *vraisemblance* (plausibility and exemplary trueness to life). Added to this were the distraction and competition offered by other literary and artistic forms: the novel, prose fiction, and even photography were gaining more influence, triggering a crisis in how theater was viewed. The low end of the appetite for melodramatic sensationalism could be satisfied by the lurid butchery of the Grand Guignol, but the seriousness of the *drame* seemed to contribute to theater's weakening appeal for the middle class when confronted with competition from other art forms. Comedy had once helped the theater to triumph but needed new life.

It arrived with satirical parody, a genre that had a brief but vivid life and that brought two collaborators to considerable fame: Ludovic Halévy (1834–1908) and Henri Meilhac (1831–1897). Their joint work is divided generally into three types: comedies, farces, and operettas. Their farces were light sketches of contemporary Parisian life, consisting of complicated middle-class intrigues with beguiling comic characters. The two writers had little success in more serious comedy, with the exception, perhaps, of *Frou-Frou* (1869), which remains their unique *succès de larmes* (weeping or sentimental success). The operettas *Orpheus in the Underworld* (*Orphée aux Enfers*, 1858), *Beautiful Helen* (*La Belle Hélène*, 1864), and *Life in Paris* (*La Vie Parisienne*, 1866), all with music by Jacques Offenbach (1819–1880), are their most celebrated works. Such operettas became famous due in part to the fact that they allowed young composers to showcase developing musical talent in a popular mode, and Offenbach's range of styles was well suited to match Halévy and Meilhac's roguish tone. After Offenbach's death, the pair would go on to provide libretti for such famous operas as Georges Bizet's *Carmen* (1875) and Jules Massenet's *Manon* (1884, Meilhac alone).

The brief age of satirical parody ended after the disaster of the Paris Commune in 1871. Between March 26 and May 30, workers had established a government of their own within the city of Paris—the "Commune"—to protest the French government's subjection to Prussia after the French defeat in the Franco-Prussian War. At the end of May, the national government, based not in Paris but in Versailles, sent its armies to storm the barricades set up by the workers in Paris, and some 30,000 Parisians were killed in the debacle. Theatrical satire, and drama in general, now seemed frivolous to the Parisian bourgeoisie. Drama would flourish again in a more serious mode after a decade had passed, and memories of the Commune would reappear explicitly a century later during the upheavals of 1968; but, for the moment, drama was replaced by a swelling vogue for prose writers with a condescending mistrust of drama. Authors such as the Goncourt brothers openly expressed their dislike of theater's artificialities and simplistic plot devices. Edmond Goncourt (1822–1896) maintained that drama was no longer part of literature because as an art it was bound to rely on other arts and doomed to recycle its own formulaic stories ad nauseum. This may have been true of some works in 19th-century France, but elsewhere in Europe playwrights such as HENRIK IBSEN, ANTON CHEKHOV, and AUGUST STRINDBERG were rejuvenating interest in the stage's capacity to represent contemporary reality. Their plays treated formerly taboo subjects such as venereal disease, poverty, divorce, and women's rights in intimate stories that called real life to account onstage. The realism and directness in handling daily existence with which these Scandinavian and Russian playwrights approached theater eventually caught the attention of a French theater enthusiast soon to become director, manager, and theater critic: ANDRÉ ANTOINE (1858–1943).

Antoine was a practical-minded employee of the gas company who, once he became a theater director, would be known for hanging slabs of bleeding meat in a production of *The Butchers* (1888) and importing Norwegian cedar for his production of A DOLL'S HOUSE (1889). More important was the role he played in introducing global reforms to the theater. Placing himself in opposition to the rigid training of the Paris conservatory system, Antoine founded his own company and named it the Théâtre Libre (Free Theater), following Hugo's expression *théâtre en liberté* (theater at liberty); its first season in 1887 showcased a program of four one-act plays. The Théâtre Libre became an influential experiment whose work resonated across Europe despite the fact that it was essentially a small, amateur theater club, funded through private subscriptions. Antoine's immediate inspiration was the work he saw in Brussels by the Meiningen Company, which produced authentic historical dramas in period costumes. Antoine championed the use of the box set with the "fourth wall" constantly borne in mind and the room arranged so that the fourth wall could simply be removed later for public performance. He also discouraged actors from declaiming their text in favor of more natural speech patterns and acting, and he replaced footlights with more modern lighting. Considered the first modern theater director, Antoine devoted over two decades to his passion. After the Théâtre Libre, he founded the Théâtre Antoine in 1897, then directed the Théâtre de l'Odéon from 1906 to 1914.

The epithet "modern" is important here if we consider the definition Roland Barthes gave to the term when speaking of Gustave Flaubert's writing: it is "the realization of the totality of the work of representation." Antoine was the first director to sign his name to the totality of the work involved in theater making; he was, in other words, the first modern director in France. Previously, the work of the director had been divided into tasks occupied by the *régisseur* (stage manager), the stage director, the stage designer, and so on. Antoine's innovations were crucial in four major areas: he strove for the independence of the theatrical arts, revolutionized decor and theater space, reformed styles of acting, and encouraged young playwrights.

When Antoine arrived on the decaying theatrical scene, he found the larger intellectual world grappling with the influence of ÉMILE ZOLA (1840–1902). Zola's theories inspired Antoine to seek innovations parallel to those that had influenced the novel a few years earlier. The theater would now be informed by the discoveries of experimental science and recent philosophical investigation, including the positivism of Auguste Comte (1798–1857), the evolutionary theory of Charles Darwin (1809–1882), the experimental medicine of Claude Bernard (1813–1878), and the theory of milieu of Hippolyte Taine (1828–1893). The naturalist theater that resulted attempted to apply the scientific method to stage realism. In this way, drama drew upon direct observation of the human behavior found in precise settings at specific historical moments. In practical terms, NATURALISM underlined the importance of heredity and environment on the psychological makeup of dramatic characters and redefined the plasticity of the stage by subjecting decor to the exact and precise documentation provided by science.

Reproducing a *tranche de vie* (slice of life) became Antoine's modus operandi. What is interesting in this theatrical ideal is not so much the attempt to adhere closely to empirical truth as the struggle to represent reality in all its crudity and harshness onstage when new thematic possibilities were opened up by scientific candor about contemporary life. The arrival of the underprivileged masses as theater spectators, the role of collectivities and syndicalism, the world of industrial work and workers, the effects of machine and technical logic on daily life, and new understandings of economics and capitalist forces all fed the dramatic imagination of the period.

Zola's writings on theater, collected in *Naturalism in the Theater* (*Le naturalisme au théâtre,*), gave Antoine support in his battle against theatrical artifice, a project with a profound political agenda. Politics and polemics were inherent in naturalism, as evidenced by Zola's role in *l'affaire Dreyfus* (the Dreyfus affair), which had such a large impact on turn-of-the-century France. Alfred Dreyfus (1859–1935), a Jewish officer in the largely anti-Semitic French army, was falsely accused in 1894 of leaking strategic information to the Germans. He was tried twice and found guilty twice on the basis of forged evidence. In 1898 Zola wrote to the president of the republic his now famous "*J'accuse*" (I accuse) letter protesting Dreyfus's treatment, and the affair became a national scandal. Under the pressure of the scandal, the French president pardoned Dreyfus after the second trial in 1899, but Zola's letter had prompted revelations of major fault lines in French society: Republicans, socialists, and anticlerical secularists were supporters of Dreyfus, while militarists, royalists, nationalists, and Roman Catholics were opponents.

The Dreyfus affair called attention not only to the problem of anti-Semitism in France but also to politics as a media-manipulated, even media-generated, spectacle. More specifically, the Dreyfus affair allowed naturalism, confined until then to the realm of aesthetics and social commentary, to be politicized. Zola had first described the relationship between art and naturalism in the 1866 essay *My Hates* (*Mes Haines*), which includes the celebrated statement, "The work of art is a corner of nature seen through a temperament." At the end of the century, Zola was writing, "The Republic will be naturalist or will not be at all," thus expanding naturalism's scope to include the ideological and the political. This had particular resonance for the theater. The stage was now seen not only as a platform where nature can be reproduced, represented, and analyzed but also one where politics can be debated and ideologies disputed.

Many theater critics and historians believe that naturalism offered no renewal of dramatic art or dramaturgy and that naturalist texts remain rudimentary when compared to steps toward realism taken by the novel in the hands of Flaubert and Honoré de Balzac or to advances in the visual arts. The stage nonetheless saw adaptations of many famous naturalist novels such as Zola's THÉRÈSE RAQUIN (1873) and *The Drinking Hole* (*L'Assommoir*, 1879). Other naturalist plays such as the Goncourt brothers' *Henriette Maréchal* (1865), and the adaptation in 1888 of their novel *Germinie Lacerteux* (1864), enjoyed tremendous success. Urban capitalism was scrutinized in plays like *The Vultures* (*Les Corbeaux*, 1882) by Henri Becque (1837–1899). Other theatrical experiments revealed new playwrights with specifically modern preoccupations, including Paul Hervieu (1857–1915), EUGÈNE BRIEUX (1858–1932), Henri Lavedan (1859–1940), Albert Guinon (1863–1923), and Émile Fabre (1869–1955).

TURN OF THE 19TH CENTURY

Naturalism had a paradoxical relationship to other aesthetic movements at the end of the century. Although it is often contrasted with SYMBOLISM, it is important to note that many symbolists were politically associated with the same naturalists whose aesthetic choices clashed with their own. Antoine seemed to be able to create around himself a widely inclusive AVANT-GARDE, not unified as a movement or school of thought but responding to the psychological climate and sensitivities of the belle epoque with an array of different orientations.

A vogue of foreign influence, and the increased financial protections allowed by international legislation covering copyright, translation, and publishing rights, triggered a renewal of interest in writing for the stage. In the final decade of the century, drama was again on the rise, reinvigorated not only by the naturalists, whose fundamental medium was the novel, but also by playwrights associated with poetry and symbolism. Naturalism's preoccupations with social issues gradually gave way to what became known as the *théâtre d'idées* (theater of ideas). The *théâtre d'idées* movement transformed the stage into a tribune for social commentary and reform. Eugène Brieux, who followed in the footsteps of Dumas fils and Augier, critiqued the traditionalism of French society. His play *The Red Robe* (*La Robe rouge*, 1900) opened the century with a demonstration of how individual interest and corruption pervade the administration of justice; his play *Blanchette* (1892) treats the education of girls as an urgently pressing issue for a progressive society.

More critical than Brieux was Paul Hervieu, whose tragic sense of the conflict between civilization and nature exposed problems related to marriage, divorce, and family in *In Chains* (*Les Tenailles*, 1895) and *Labyrinth* (*Le Dédale*, 1903), as well as those related to women's rights in *The Law of Man* (*La Loi de l'Homme*, 1897). Less rhetorical and more illustrative than Hervieu was François de Curel (1854–1929), who perfected the *drame psychologique* (psychological drama) by moving away from the pure abstraction characteristic of the theater of ideas to what de Curel called *austère psychologie* (psychology laid bare). His theater experimented with the suggestive power of images and the relationship between modern reality, science, and capital. His notorious play *The New Idol* (*La Nouvelle Idole*, 1899) raises the question of the moral limits on scientific power and frames the worship of science as a dangerous new form of religious zealotry.

At the same time that turn-of-the-century playwrights used tragic modes to express fin de siècle uncertainty, a comedic trend with a vaudevillian inflection developed. GEORGES FEYDEAU (1862–1921), the most famous vaudeville writer since Labiche, perfected the art of the fast-paced bedroom farce, putting cuckolds, philanderers, and marital conflict onstage. Feydeau's most famous work is *A FLEA IN HER EAR* (*La Puce à l'oreille*, 1907), a minutely regulated, fast-paced comedy about the misadventures of Raymonde, an adulterous wife. She puts her husband Victor's fidelity to the test by having another woman write him a love note—a standard comic plot trigger still in wide use. Many of Feydeau's theatrical situations still persist in modern-day comedies, including adulteries, infidelities, mistaken identities, and general sexual frustration grappling with social mores that restrict and taunt desire at the same time.

Although the comedy writers of the belle epoque were mostly at odds with symbolists such as Stéphane Mallarmé (1842–1898) and ANDRÉ GIDE (1869–1951), many prominent symbolists recognized the great comic talent of Georges Courteline (1858–1929). Even the Comédie-Française, not known for favoring contemporary playwrights, introduced one of Courteline's most famous plays, *Boubouroche* (1893), into its repertoire as early as 1910. Credited with being the greatest humorist in French literature since Molière, Courteline chronicled the lives of the French middle and lower-middle classes in the late 19th century and provided a social analysis of the hypocrisy of Parisian life. Many other playwrights also used comedy to bridge, or avoid, the divide between symbolism and naturalism. EDMOND ROSTAND (1868–1918) revived the fluent verse composition and dramaturgical expansiveness of Hugolean romanticism but added a touch of satire. His *CYRANO DE BERGERAC* (1898), with its heroic yet pathetic protagonist—a role written for the comic actor Constant Coquelin—remains the most revived French play of the late 19th century. Also active and influential during the period was Sacha Guitry (1885–1957), who wrote over 150 plays in prose or verse. Among his most celebrated works are *Nono* (1905) and *A Good Match* (*Un Beau mariage*, 1911), dominated by his trademark irony and wit.

The turn of the century also saw the rise of women playwrights. Most notable among them is Marie Lenéru (1875–1918), who enjoyed wide recognition and had many of her plays produced at the Comédie-Française. Propelled to fame with her first play, *The Emancipated* (*Les Affranchis*, 1907), influenced by François de Curel's theater and championed by the Parnassian poet, critic, and novelist Catulle Mendès (1841–1909), Lenéru triumphed over many adversities. Not only did she surmount gender bias, but she also overcame obstacles associated with her own hearing and vision impairment. Her play *Woman Triumphant* (*La Triomphatrice*, 1914) was accepted at the Comédie-Française on the eve of World War I but did not see the stage until after the war, a few months before her premature death in 1918. While *Woman Triumphant* dealt with the issue of careers for women writers, the play *Peace* (*La Paix*, written in 1917 and produced posthumously in 1928) treated issues of pacifism and antimilitarism through the character of a British woman, Stanley, who refuses to marry a French general on the grounds that a pacifist cannot betray her political principles, even for personal reasons.

Marguerite Eymery assumed the pseudonym Rachilde (1860–1953) and was a prominent literary figure in her time. She wrote over sixty works of fiction, poetry, criticism, memoir, and drama under the influence of the decadent trend of the belle epoque. In her play *Madame Death* (*Madame la mort*, 1891), Rachilde illustrates important issues in women's history and delineates significant features of turn-of-the-century French society. Although she wrote a polemical pamphlet against suffrage for women, Rachilde also wrote many plays and fiction texts dealing with gender inversion, female sexual desire, sadomasochism, and other taboo subjects. These provoked, at times, condemnation for obscenity or willful inattention because of their eccentricity. The neglect of the work of Lenéru, Rachilde, and other women playwrights, then and now, is part of a long theatrical history of gender bias and timidity in the face of work expressing social discontent. A renewed examination of the work of these women playwrights provides a more accurate view of how the theater of ideas critiqued sexual identity and gender politics.

While playwrights of the theater of ideas continued to engage in social critique, playwrights associated with symbolism focused on the symbiotic relationship between art and life. Theatrical symbolists shared with the avant-garde in other arts a strong interest in mysticism, the dream world, and metaphysics. While symbolists considered Charles Baudelaire (1821–1867) and, later, Mallarmé to be their literary forefathers, they were also inspired by innovators in the theater arts from across Europe, including Adolphe Appia (1862–1928), Edward Gordon Craig (1872–1966), VSEVOLOD MEYERHOLD (1874–1942), FILIPPO TOMMASO MARINETTI (1876–1944), Alexander Tairov (1885–1950), and Tristan Tzara (1896–1963).

Among the French innovators who formulated new theories of stage directing, stage design, and acting methods were the founders of two experimental theaters, Paul Fort (1872–1960), who founded the Théâtre d'art in 1890, and Aurélien-Marie Lugné-Poe (1869–1940), who founded the Théâtre de l'Oeuvre in 1893. Fort and Lugné-Poe encouraged young authors and theater practitioners to experiment with form and themes where language provided the chief means of creating a magical atmosphere. The results fused together all elements of theater, including language, movement, songs, decor, and lighting in a unified production style. MAURICE MAETERLINCK (1862–1949) was one of these authors whom Lugné-Poe brought into the limelight. Called the "Belgian Shakespeare" (more for his role as national playwright than any dramaturgical characteristics), Maeterlinck developed a spiritual vision that pushed aside mundane daily life and the realist stage and promoted instead a suggestive and exalted ambiguity that was to become emblematic of theatrical symbolism. His lyrical dramas were characterized by fatalism, mystical drive, fairy-tale atmosphere, and an obsession with death, all accentuated by depersonalized characterization, resulting in marionettelike stage personae. The love drama *Pelléas and Mélisande* (*Pelléas et Mélisande*, 1892), produced with great success by Lugné-Poe, examines the mysteries of love and existence through symbols in a dream world that suggests, rather than reproduces, reality.

EARLY 20TH CENTURY

With a similar emphasis on poetry, though inspired by the mystical Catholic renaissance of the early 20th century, PAUL CLAUDEL (1868–1955) wrote mysteries and epic dramas of sophisticated literary quality depicting religious and moral struggle within individual consciences. Claudel's protagonist in *Golden Heads* (*Tête d'Or*, 1890), Simon Agnel, asks existential questions in violently poetic language and articulates his desire to conquer the world although faced, ultimately, with death. *The Tidings Brought to Mary* (*L'Annonce faite à Marie*), a mystery deriving from the medieval Christian tradition, is set in 15th-century Champagne. It opened in Paris in 1912 at Lugné-Poe's Théâtre de l'Oeuvre and brought to the stage the dialectical struggle between mystical devotion and material pleasures. THE SATIN SLIPPER (*Le Soulier de satin*, 1924), influenced by both the Spanish and the Shakespearean traditions, is an epic drama recounting the adventures of Rodrigue and his beloved, Doña Prouhèze. The poetic charge of Claudel's theater is so great that he is able to convey the universal mystery of creation without ever neglecting the physical elements involved in communicating a story from the stage. It comes as no surprise that a director like Jean-Louis Barrault (1910–1994), known for his work with physical theater and focused on the plasticity of the mise-en-scène (direction, directorial conception) was seduced by the corporeal attributes of Claudel's poetic language and produced many of his plays.

As a more intense focus came to be placed on the language of drama and experiments in form, theatrical space and stage design fell under the influence of various artistic movements, including cubism, FUTURISM, suprematism, DADAISM, constructivism, and SURREALISM. Cubism, which stood at the time as a revolutionary break with traditional figurative painting and launched the era of abstract art, involved seeing the world from multiple, yet simultaneous, points of view, forcing a complete reappraisal of form, space, and color. This was translated for the theater when spectators were asked to construe meaning by perceiving multiple, incongruent elements onstage, which it was their job to add up into a comprehensible whole. In playwriting, cubist tendencies are seen in the theater of GUILLAUME APOLLINAIRE (1880–1918), though his work is chiefly associated with surrealism. Suprematism, formulated in 1913 by the Russian artist Kasimir Malevitch (1878–1935), reached France by joining forces with cubism to focus on nonobjective form, austere geometry, and abstractions extrapolated from the world of the familiar. Futurism, expounded by Filippo Marinetti and others in ITALY between 1909 and 1916, coincided with the rise of fascist nationalism, though Marinetti published its manifesto in Paris in 1912. In the theater, futurism insisted on a commitment to new mechanical technologies and depictions of the dynamic violence of modern city life. Constructivism began in RUSSIA as a movement of geometric abstraction influenced by revolutions in science, technology, and social and political thought. Between 1913 and 1922, it had a major influence on theater architecture. Finally, dadaism pitted the world of the irrational against the rational as a form of protest against definable "meaning" or bourgeois "coherence" in a work of art.

All of these movements left their mark on the stage early in the century without forging any globally unified school or dogma. The lack of dogmatic principles, however, did not mean there was no program of reform. A new breed of directors inspired by these artistic movements understood totality in the theater experience to be the chief way of moving theater practice forward in ways that would be even more spectacular—and controversial—than those of the relatively sober, poetic, and abstemious symbolists like Maeterlinck and Claudel. Growing awareness among members of the educated public of the views of Sigmund Freud (1856–1939) on the unconscious and the interpretation of dreams helped to propel ALFRED JARRY (1873–1907) and Guillaume Apollinaire into the limelight of controversy at the turn of the century, though their personalities alone would have been sufficient to create a maelstrom of interest around them.

Jarry began writing plays at the age of fifteen while in high school. Working with his fellow pupils at the Lycée de Rennes, he soon gave the theater one of its most memorable texts, *Ubu the King* (*Ubu Roi* part of the UBU TRILOGY). What started as a prank satire of a physics teacher became a manifesto for a new theater combining scathing irony with highly charged theatricality. The grotesque and hyperbolic role of Ubu the King, a distant parody of Shakespeare's *Macbeth*, made Firmin Gémier

(1869–1933), an actor, director, manager, and pupil of Antoine, famous for the first time. The opening word of the play—the provocative expletive *Merdre!* which mischievously adds an extra "r" to the center of a commonplace French vulgarity—triggered widespread scandal among the outraged, riotous, and sometimes enthusiastic crowd during the premiere at the Théâtre de l'Oeuvre on December 10, 1896.

The pure theatricality of *Ubu* was at home at the Théâtre de l'Oeuvre. Lugné-Poe, the theater's director, imposed an aesthetic rigor on production that almost did away with any realistic representation of objects. Regularly paced, impersonal diction underlined the monotony of verbal exchanges from everyday life, and narration recited by pallid actors whose movements were unusually slow replaced mimetic action. Paradoxically, it was this stripping down of the artifice of the stage that heightened theatricality as a key concept in the modern theater. Generally defined, *theatricality* has always been the process by which it is possible to transform an everyday situation into a stage fiction. Led by practitioners like Lugné-Poe, modern theatricality began to move away from excessive artifice and mimetic illusion toward the stage as a space where meaning is achieved by what is particular to a specific live performance without evaluating that performance for the skill with which it reproduces "real life."

Surrealism, the newest nonrealist movement to attract a substantial following in the arts and theater, was enthusiastic about this new understanding of pure theatricality. The word *surrealism* was not coined by the man who is regarded as the "Pope of Surrealism," the French poet André Breton (1896–1966) but by Guillaume Apollinaire, the poet and dramatist whose play THE BREASTS OF TIRESIAS (*Les Mamelles de Tirésias*) triggered a huge scandal in 1917. A satire of hotly debated feminist issues introduced by the Scandinavian theater of the 1890s, *The Breasts of Tiresias* recounts the story of Thérèse, who wants to become a man and leave to her husband the responsibility for pregnancy and repopulation of their country. *Tiresias* is a parody, targeting theatrical conventions by mixing the rhythm of vaudeville theater with the absurdity of contemporary reality and making use of artificially tragic declamation. In the preface to *Tiresias*, Apollinaire calls for the unity of all the arts in a new kind of expression that resembles the notion of total theater first introduced by opera composer RICHARD WAGNER (1813–1883).

Symbolism's poetic drive and surrealism's affinity for absurdity had to be matched on the practical level by a revolution in theater scenery, space, and architecture. The influence of "isms" from the visual arts has already been noted. Early in the century, the Englishman Edward Gordon Craig published an essay titled "The Art of the Theatre" (1905) detailing how theater should strive for simplicity, abstraction, and essence to unify the spectator's experience. He would develop the idea further in his own designs for the stage and republication of an expanded version of the essay as *On the Art of the Theatre* (1911), widely read on the Continent. Theater designers responded by building stages without a proscenium arch and by creating open, revolving, or elevator stages. In addition to these architectural shifts, the total theater formula brought about an enhanced relationship between the playwright, the director, and the actor, a three-way conversation that gained complex aesthetic, critical, and ideological significance throughout the 20th century.

Growing awareness of PSYCHOANALYSIS sustained both symbolism and surrealism. The work of Freud and his followers allowed theater practitioners, and audience members, to take for granted that socially unacceptable instincts, feelings, and behavior are buried in the subconscious and that the dream world cohabits with and sometimes invades the world that we view as real. "Truth" thus becomes even more difficult to reach since our own minds are part of the mystery that obscures it. There were great riches here for the new theater, and some artists came to believe that theater, like psychoanalysis itself, could be used to illuminate the contents of the unconscious. Both Jarry and Apollinaire pushed to an extreme the gap between surface appearances and suppressed realities, the rational and the irrational, the conscious and the unconscious, the objective and the subjective worlds. They did so theatrically: instead of attempting to represent the internal, unconscious conflicts within the mind, they opted to cover their stage characters and actions with a mask of artificiality so audacious that the audience had to presume that what was hidden behind the mask was all the more complex, disturbing, or illuminating. Thus what was unacknowledged and unspoken in the theater, the "SUBTEXT," became in their hands even more important than what was consciously articulated, the "text."

Such an excess of playful surface artifice led to numerous scandals. The most famous surrounded the production in 1917 of *Parade* (better translated as *Sideshow* or *Barker's Booth* than by the English word *parade*), a ballet based on a libretto by JEAN COCTEAU (1889–1963), who also did programs and publicity, with choreography by Léonide Massine (1896–1979), settings and costumes by Pablo Picasso (1881–1973), and music by Erik Satie (1866–1925). The result was a multi-arts ballet created by the Ballets Russes of Serge Diaghilev (1872–1929), the same year as *Tiresias*.

Parade stands as a supremely influential experiment in total theater. Satie introduced extramusical elements into his jazz score—sound splashes, lottery wheels, sirens, typewriters, pistol shots—in order to give *Parade* the burlesque atmosphere of a sideshow booth enticing spectators to enter. Three Company Managers arrive onstage in turn, introducing various acts as "coming attractions." The managers are costumed in heavy cubist style, indicating that they, the commercial minds who run the show, are imprisoned by artificiality; while the actors, who have to provide entertaining illusions at the managers' command, embody human reality. *Parade* set Paris on its ear and provoked riots in the streets. One member of the audience exclaimed, "If I had known it was going to be so stupid I would have brought the children!" Satie and Cocteau faced a libel suit labeling them "cultural anarchists" and resulting in jail time of eight days. All of this launched Cocteau gloriously on a career of fame, aestheticism, and scandal.

WORLD WAR I PERIOD

The striking experimentation of the time disguised the central fact that theater, like culture at large, had lost its dream that science and progress would flourish for all foreseeable time to come. The unprecedented sophistication of the weaponry in World War I, resulting in previously inconceivable casualty rates, brought the dreamers down to earth and put an end to the optimism that had dominated the various avant-gardes of the century's first decade. On the practical level, many theaters in France were closed when actors were called up or went on tour as entertainers for the troops; casts had to be filled with students from the Conservatoire. Popular entertainment escaped into a boulevardian ahistorical bliss that hearkened back to Scribe. As the war intensified, some theater artists left France for America in order to keep their work alive and their companies afloat. New movements like EXPRESSIONISM, influenced by the psychological and physical devastation caused by the war, migrated from GERMANY to France and elsewhere in Europe. The most notable expressionist in France was HENRI-RENÉ LENORMAND (1882–1951), who started writing for the theater in 1905 with *White Madness* (*La Folie blanche*), a play he later disavowed. He triumphed in 1919 with *Time Is a Dream* (*Le Temps est un songe*), influenced by Freud, LUIGI PIRANDELLO, and Ibsen, in which he didactically exposes pathological psychology. Other playwrights such as Paul Raynal (1885–1964) and Steve Passeur (1899–1966) resorted to a darkly cynical comedic style highlighting industrialism's threat to the individual will.

The war was not the only factor that affected the theater, because film was tugging at its audiences. In France, however, unlike in the UNITED STATES, the impact of film production was moderate. Motion pictures presented some competition for spectators, but the more serious theatrical endeavors retained their appeal since they were preoccupied with serious themes not easily conveyed by the relatively unsophisticated cinema of the time. From 1919 to 1939, with France recovering from the traumas of World War I, theater went in search of new writing, acting, and directing talent. Among the new innovators was the landmark reformer JACQUES COPEAU (1879–1949). Copeau advocated bringing out the poetic dimension of the text in accordance with the wishes of the author and the will of the actor. He saw the actor as the most important theatrical element, the primary "living presence" capable of giving voice to the text; and in order to highlight the "true beauty and poetry" of the French language on the stage, Copeau proposed the notion of the *tréteau nu* (naked trestle), or pared-down platform stage, without additional trickery. To put his ideas into action, he took over a derelict neighborhood theater and turned it into the Théâtre du Vieux-Colombier, following Craig's architectural prescriptions for the ideal theater. The result was an auditorium with about 400 seats, a forestage, architectural steps leading up to a bare platform stage, and a set of basic curtains that could be moved on rods to indicate changes in scene. The "first" Vieux-Colombier was open in 1913 and 1914. It had to close during World War I while Copeau, medically exempted from military service, pursued his researches and even took his company to New York City for over forty productions between 1917 and 1919. Returning to France, he opened the "second" Vieux-Colombier in 1920 after rebuilding the auditorium, which had housed refugees during the war. He closed this second Vieux-Colombier suddenly in 1924 in order to found a theater school in Pernand-Vergelesses near Dijon. Although Copeau was interested in Antoine's previous innovations, he rejected the principles of realistic and naturalistic representation and promoted instead the central capacity of the director to translate the playwright's script into a new form of "stage poetry."

THE INTER WAR PERIOD

After World War I, many artists and theater practitioners formed alliances and wrote manifestos outlining a vision for theater in the face of the postwar crisis. Four directors heavily influenced by Copeau—Georges Pitoëff (1884–1939), Gaston Baty (1885–1952), Charles Dullin (1885–1949), and Louis Jouvet (1887–1951)—allied themselves publicly with the creation of the Cartel des quatre (Four-Man Cartel, 1927–1939). They agreed that their companies, which performed in many theaters throughout Paris, would share certain marketing and infrastructure expenses as a way of competing against the Boulevard-influenced commercial theater, would provide each other with moral support against the power of Paris' theater critics, and would stay in constant communication to avoid repertoire overlaps. Viewed as the intellectual avant-garde by critics and the general Parisian audience, the Cartel cultivated young authors such as JEAN GIRAUDOUX (1882–1944), Jean Cocteau, Jean Sarment (1897–1976), ARMAND SALACROU (1899–1989), and JEAN ANOUILH (1910–1987). By 1939, when the Cartel came to an end, the four directors, while still noncommercial, had come to represent the theatrical establishment rather than the avant-garde. Three of them, Baty, Dullin, and Jouvet, joined by the still-productive Copeau, began working at the Comédie-Française. Pitoëff was not invited to work at the national theater because he was not French.

Copeau had promoted a form of theater in which language was the primary element. Cocteau responded soon after *Parade* and took Paris by storm with *Wedding on the Eiffel Tower* (*Les Mariés de la Tour Eiffel*, 1921), a play combining neoclassical style and oddball characters. Cocteau would cultivate the clash between genre expectation and linguistic register, between classical models and street-life characters, throughout his career. His retelling of the Oedipus tale, THE INFERNAL MACHINE (*La Machine infernale*, 1932), was influential for years to come because of its revival of Greek mythology, which would reappear in his own work as well as that of Giraudoux, Anouilh, and JEAN-PAUL SARTRE (1905–1980). What the modern French theater found in the classics was not antiquated mythology but an opportunity to adapt, or even corrupt, myth in order to handle contemporary social and political realities. This mythological revival was fertile, but it augmented a sense of crisis in theater writing, because playwrights now found it hard to propose totally original themes or to gain attention with works solely about contemporary reality.

Giraudoux, writing between the wars, triumphed with theater that was remarkably literary. The characters in his plays, from *Siegfried* (1928) to THE TROJAN WAR WILL NOT TAKE PLACE (*La Guerre de Troie n'aura pas lieu*, published in English as *Tiger at the Gates*, 1935), display a classical purity and preciosity of style in their language that would be rejected by the absurdists to come. A similar destiny was reserved for the theater of HENRY DE MONTHERLANT (1895–1972), who also neglected action while emphasizing language. He is seen today as one of the French theater's last tragedians because of the way his characters combine Corneillian honor with Racinian complexity.

The Dead Queen (*La Reine morte*, 1942), Montherlant's most widely known play, used the ceremonial and at times highly artificial diction of its royal protagonists to convey noble and profound skepticism in the face of tragic disillusionment and death. But the sense of tragedy conveyed by his plays could not compete with that in the real wartime lives of his audience, who seemed to face the defeat of the humanist project.

In fact, modern French theater can almost be defined as an attempt to liberate the stage from that predominant humanist project, "the dead word of the absent author," as ANTONIN ARTAUD (1896–1948) put it, and from the mimetic realism with which it was traditionally paired. Artaud himself wrote only two full-length plays, which enjoyed very little success on stage; his brief sketch JET OF BLOOD (*Jet de sang*, 1925) provides such a vision of gore and surrealistic sexual trauma that it had to wait until 1964 for its first production. Still, Artaud remains today one of the most influential theatrical figures of the 20th century. Important modernist ideas are often tied to him: the questioning of our ability to represent the real; the ensuing disintegration of the stage persona; the insistence on the autonomy of the stage; the independence of mise-en-scène as an absolute art; the unique, irreducible, and ephemeral aspect of the theatrical event; and finally, the insistence on the symbiosis of the actor's body and voice in a totalized "emotional athleticism." In Artaud's view, what constitutes overall stage harmony is more important than texts and dialogues, because that harmony embodies the sacred and cathartic meaning of the spectator-actor relationship. These principles, outlined in Artaud's famous manifesto *The Theater and Its Double* (*Le Théâtre et son double*, written 1932, published 1938), are interwoven with Asian aesthetics and metaphysics inspired by Balinese and Javanese dance forms. It remains fruitless to search for conceptual coherence in Artaud's vision, however. He dreams of what he calls, in his famous phrase, a "Theater of Cruelty" that can carry the spectator off in a frenetic trance induced by "contagion" rather than by identification with a psychologically realistic protagonist. But his dream remains a disjointed utopia sitting at the furthest limit of what is conceivable or playable onstage. Artaud's work is important largely because his compelling formulations fired the imagination of theater practitioners for decades to come. It becomes more coherent if we view him as an advocate of 19th-century romantic ideals, addressing us from the imaginary spot where the poetic absolutes of romanticism and the self-reflexivity of symbolism are synthesized, where Lord Byron meets Mallarmé.

It is worth noting that while experimental theater was spreading across Europe, there was a systematic attempt to rediscover and breathe fresh life into the classics. Despite the scandalous uproars of various avant-gardes and the dramaturgical revolutions longed for by Artaud, there were in France, during the twenty years between the creation of the Cartel in 1927 and that of the Avignon Festival in 1947, repeated pushes to revive the classics at the highest levels. Modern playwrights from Giraudoux to Sartre, from Montherlant to ALBERT CAMUS (1913–1960), pursued the renewal of theater's civic role, and this included a role for the classics. The classics chosen by Louis Jouvet for revival announced the preoccupations of the forthcoming *théâtre engagé* (politically engaged theater) of Sartre, Camus, and Anouilh. One new play from between the wars proved to be a prophetic model of the politically engaged theater to come, *Knock, or, The Triumph of Medicine* (*Knock ou le Triomphe de la médecine*, 1923) by JULES ROMAINS (1885–1972). Without advocating any particular ideological stance, it staged the problem of individual freedom confronting the hysteria of fascism.

WORLD WAR II PERIOD

During World War II, the necessity of seeming to evade ideological stances while scheming to reveal them became a dramaturgical necessity. Classic plays or classicizing themes could be used for many purposes by all sides—"all" rather than "both," because there were more sides than simply Germany, on the one hand, and France, on the other. France itself was divided after the Nazi invasion into two zones, the "free" zone, including Paris and the Atlantic coastline, under the jurisdiction of the puppet French government of Maréchal Philippe Pétain (1856–1951) based in Vichy, and the remaining southern zone, the playground of the French Resistance. During the German Occupation of Paris from 1940 until the Liberation in 1944, theater activity remained rich and diverse, encouraged by the occupying authorities in order to give the impression that cultural life was normal. Theaters continued to function despite frequent blackouts and interruptions by air-raid sirens. But this relative freedom to operate theater companies was not matched by a freedom to choose content: censorship of topics and themes was tight. This was one of several reasons that playwrights and directors returned to the apparently safer classics and to classically inspired themes. Cocteau, for example, rewrote a tale derived from Tasso, *Renaud and Armide* (*Renaud et Armide*, 1941); it was performed in 1943 at the Comédie-Française and exemplifies the escapist art without a political stance encouraged by the governing regime. Other dramatic works under the occupation emerged as more politically meaningful despite the tight grip of the censors. Anouilh's rendering of the myth of ANTIGONE (1943) shows the ambiguous nature of politics in the theater of the time. Parisian spectators saw in the figure of Antigone an example of resistance to tyranny (and thus of the French Resistance itself) and in the figure of her enemy Creon a veiled apology for the violence of despotic realpolitik—of "collaboration," in contemporary terms. The Nazis could see in Antigone's stubbornness an insistence on millennia-old Aryan traditions of piety and patriotism. The fact that all sides among the occupation's political divisions could claim the ideological platform of *Antigone* underscores how theater can provide structural reconciliation between contesting forces even in charged political circumstances.

Similar paradoxes appeared throughout politically aware theater during World War II. The existentialist and political theater of Camus and Sartre—their theater of ideas—helped to frame the crisis of the modern subject within a larger discourse concerning the human condition, freedom, and freedom's ominous consequences. Despite these new themes, their plays were, for the most part, conventional in form: Sartre's THE FLIES (*Les Mouches*, 1943), Camus's CALIGULA (1944), and Anouilh's *Antigone*, like the less politically charged plays of Montherlant, all have classical structures.

Sartre's version of this conventional-yet-engaged mode was the existentialist theater, which continued to develop over the course of fifty years. Sartre's plays constituted *théâtre engagé* because of their attempts to make social change and address issues of spectatorship and class. Because of their engagement with the real at a specific historical juncture, they have also been described as neorealist theater. Because Sartre used them to expose, in practical terms, key concepts from his own philosophical investigations as well as more general issues of the human condition, including freedom of choice, and the consequences of exercising that choice, they are also "philosophical theater." For Sartre, theater was always a means to a didactic end, despite his disclaimer that "theater is not the basis for any thesis, nor is it inspired by any preconceived idea. What it tries to do is to explore the [human] condition in its entirety and present contemporary humans with a portrait of themselves, their problems, their hopes and struggles" (Sartre, 1973). Sartre defined his theater as a "theater of situations placing the character under extreme conditions and forcing them to make a choice where death is one of the options." Existentialist slogans like "Man is condemned to be free" and "Existence precedes essence" had particular resonance in his theater since situational theater could reveal any flaws inherent in the thesis it represents. In the same Sartrean mode, *Who Shall Die?* (*Les Bouches inutiles*, 1945) by Simone de Beauvoir (1908–1986) is an example of *théâtre à thése* (theater with a thesis), debating issues of freedom and resistance while fascist ideologies grow.

POST—WORLD WAR II

After the war, the growing legend of the French Resistance pervaded the theater, standing in for all resistance serving to protect human dignity from the humiliation of political oppression and invasion. Sartre's *Death Without Burial* (*Morts sans sépulture*, 1946) and *Dirty Hands* (*Les Mains sales*, 1948) deal with the anguish experienced by characters who realize they have to be agents of history. Both plays emphasize the moral ambiguity of revolutionary processes by setting two visions of history in opposition: one based on a form of puritanical idealism requiring heroic sacrifice in the name of an absurd ideal, and the other based on a humanistic pragmatism that finds itself siding, at times, with bourgeois conservatism in order to save the world from widespread destruction. By rejecting ethical absolutes, Sartre raises the moral paradox that conforming in ultimate and absolute ways to binding morals may make it difficult to achieve a valid ethical system. The paradox threatens to result in total anarchy on the political level and profound malaise on the individual level. His play NO EXIT (*Huis clos*, 1944) confirms the malaise by depicting a nightmarish hell where three individuals are trapped in a bland salon from which there is no exit. In this *huis clos* (dead end), the consciousness of one character has no choice but to apprehend the consciousness of the others in the salon; the results lead to a famous existentialist declaration by one of the trapped characters: "L'enfer, c'est les Autres" (Hell is other people). In addition to its philosophical value, the play also announces some of the preoccupations of the *nouveau théâtre* (new theater) by finding dramatic tension in an absurd situation, soon to be expanded and multiplied in the plays of the Theater of the Absurd.

There are many links between existentialism and the absurd, the most important of which is the origin of the two movements in the theater of the avant-garde. There are many distinctions between them, as well, applying to dramatic and narrative structure, ideology, subjectivity, language, the body, and space. While existentialism employs all the conventional tools of drama (character, plot, three-act or five-act structures, and so on) to convince the audience of the irrationality of the human condition, the Theater of the Absurd seems to fragment and implode such traditional theatrical apparatus, thus demonstrating practically that the existentialist theater could only talk about theoretically. Martin Esslin first formulated this claim in his book *The Theatre of the Absurd* (1961); he neglects, however, to consider the parallels between the two approaches. Esslin's view that the Theater of the Absurd is a meeting place between form and content does not distinguish the absurd from the realistic theatrical models it purports to critique. Esslin also neglects the fact that both existentialist and absurdist theater dwell obsessively on the antagonisms between the subject's intent and the chaos the subject encounters in the world. One example of a theater that straddles these tendencies is that of Camus.

Sartre used to call Camus the "Descartes of the Absurd" because Camus succeeded in combining existential angst with the Kantian categorical imperative as he tried to explain the contradictions of consciousness and the intricacies of existence. Camus's rendering of the events of the French Resistance (in which he had been active) reveals the problem. His play *State of Siege* (*L'Etat de siège*, 1948), directed by Jean-Louis Barrault, brought Camus to the same level of renown as Sartre as a dramatist of existentialism, but his work was even more political because it calls upon individuals to dissociate themselves completely from totalitarianism. *The Just* (*Les Justes*, 1949) foretells the preoccupations of Camus's philosophical essay *The Rebel* (*L'Homme révolté*, 1951), in which he seeks to formulate a new ethics opposed to terror. Camus's theater analyzes the mechanisms that condemn individuals to imprisonment within the abyss of their own freedom. The quintessential figure of this condemnation is the emperor protagonist in Camus's *Caligula* (1944), who suddenly discovers the absurdity of existence. Caligula sees that the absurd is "a childishly simple and obvious truth" but that it requires, nonetheless, a rebellion—even if the rebel's powerful position as emperor might make him seem immune to despair and even if the rebellion is futile. Camus's theater moved the preoccupations of politically committed theater from the local and national politics of Europe to the larger universal issues of freedom and ALIENATION. Such a giant mission for the existentialist and absurdist theater opened the way for avant-garde experiments, but it did not change the fact that theatergoers remained largely bourgeois. It was not until the founding of the Théâtre national populaire or TNP (National People's Theater) by Jean Vilar (1912–1971) at the end of the 1940s that the question of audience composition and the need to increase theatergoing across social classes became central to French theatrical debates.

The idea of a national and popular theater had been, on and off during the first three decades of the century, the project of Firmin Gémier, the actor who created the role of Ubu and who became a prominent director and theater administrator. Gémier emphasized and popularized the practice of touring companies—including the Théâtre National Ambulant (National Mobile Theater) of 1911, transported on eight steam-driven tractors—as a way to share successful theatrical events outside Paris, but his attempts were doomed by lack of funding and support. After the brief election of the Popular Front in 1936, the tenets of the popular theater were revived, but again without long life because of the quick collapse of the leftist government. The Popular Front ideology left behind one major achievement, however: the reconstruction in the heart of Paris' 16th arrondissement of the Palais de Chaillot, with an auditorium of 2,800 seats waiting to be filled.

During World War II, Jacques Copeau championed the necessity of a true people's theater in France. In a booklet published in Paris in 1941 during the German Occupation, Copeau contends that a popular theater suitable for all social classes is in tune with the tradition of the small experimental theaters from the period between the two world wars. The concerns of Copeau, like those of other members of the Cartel (Pitoëff, Baty, Dullin, and Jouvet), were that the audience be provided with more than just a luxury commodity, that they also be offered a "living theater" supplying reasons "for belief, for hope, for fulfillment" (Copeau, 1974). Many of the principles of the *théâtre populaire*, not unlike those of André Antoine's turn-of-the-century Théâtre Libre, dealt with reforming the outdated repertoire while redefining the plasticity of the mise-en-scène. New dramatic writing by contemporary authors had to be encouraged, and playhouses had to allow for more democratic access. Theater companies were invited to abandon their traditional buildings, seen as the domain of the bourgeoisie, and seek more truly grassroots and popular theatrical spaces outside the capital. This became known as "decentralization" when five regional Centres dramatiques were established between 1946 and 1952 outside of Paris, appealing to the working class and rural communities across France unaccustomed to attending plays. The leaders of decentralization, Jean Dasté (1904–1994), Charles Dullin, and Jean Vilar, were all involved in this migration and popularized the practice of touring to small villages.

Many of the directors working in this web of popular theater activism knew each other and had worked together. Vilar had studied under Dullin, who had worked with Gémier, while Dullin was greatly influenced by Copeau and his concept of the *tréteau nu* (naked treatise)—a concept that was artistically justifiable but also logistically and financially helpful to a touring popular theater. Vilar's founding of the Avignon Festival in 1947 emphasized similar minimalism by producing theater in the open air without decor and against a preexisting backdrop—the giant, awe-inspiring inner courtyard wall of the Papal Palace in Avignon—with actors mingling among the spectators before and after the play. As noted by prominent theater critic Bernard Dort, 1947 marked a significant transition to new forms of theater making in France. The founding of the Avignon Festival encouraged a new breed of writers to provide a much-needed supply of new texts. The year 1947 also brought the official end of the last phase of the Cartel's influence, the founding of the Centre dramatique de l'Est where Jouvet introduced playwright JEAN GENET (1910–1986), and a new collaboration among the celebrated actors Maria Casarès (1922–1996) and Gérard Philipe (1922–1959) and Vilar under the aegis of the TNP.

The French scholar Jean Caune places Vilar "at the intersection between Gémier, the initiator of a popular theater in France, and Copeau, its prophet" (Caune, 1992). Vilar was concerned with sensitizing the audience while modifying its class composition. To encourage a popular audience to join, or replace, the bourgeoisie, he introduced practical reforms: simpler pricing and seating hierarchies, no more tipping of ushers, free transportation for group bookings, and earlier start times for evening performances. Some of these reforms provoked widespread outrage among the theater elite who were scandalized by the arrival in droves of the "unwashed masses" seeking to share a pleasure that had been reserved previously for the decadent few.

The inaugural performances of the TNP in 1951 were held not at Chaillot (then serving as a meeting place for the plenary sessions of the United Nations) but at the Théâtre national de Suresnes, in a predominantly working-class and communist suburb west of Paris. On the program within the first season were Jean Vilar's productions of BERTOLT BRECHT's MOTHER COURAGE and Pierre Corneille's *Le Cid*, two significantly different, even contradictory, plays: one was modern, translated, controversial; the other classic, in French, and familiar to French audiences from school days. Vilar's *Mother Courage* production, like Brecht's 1949 Berlin production, took on nationalist resonance. Vilar chose Brecht to politicize popular theater and enlarge its significance beyond that of community theater or public festival, toward a theater committed to the "enlightenment of the popular masses" from a socialist perspective. This resulted in accusations that Vilar was a communist. The popular theater movement could not be sustained after this, due in part to the departure of Vilar but also because of heightened cultural polemics resulting from political polarization during the transition from the Fourth to the Fifth Republic in 1958, which placed Charles de Gaulle (1890–1970) in power. France's sense of cultural unity also suffered from the continuing Algerian War of Independence (1954–1962), which happened to fall immediately after France's 1954 withdrawal from Indochina. In such circumstances, a national people's theater suffered from uncertainty as to what constituted the French nation—and just who the people were to whom it belonged. Colonial and postcolonial issues would survive in the theater long beyond the TNP, however: both Algeria and Indochina would return in the lives and works of the next two generations of playwrights.

While the TNP sought to reform spectatorship, the avant-garde movement continued pushing the limits of what was acceptable in writing and on the stage. The critic and theater historian Geneviève Serreau has proposed the collective label *nouveau théâtre* (new theater, like the "*nouveau roman*" or "new novel") for this avant-garde syndrome (Serreau, 1966). Playwrights such as Roger Vitrac (1899–1952), NATHALIE SARRAUTE (1900–1999), JEAN TARDIEU (1903–1995), Georges Schéhadé (1905–1989), SAMUEL BECKETT, ARTHUR ADAMOV (1908–1970), Jean Genet, JEAN VAUTHIER (1910–1992), EUGÈNE IONESCO, Romain Weingarten (1926–), and FERNANDO ARRABAL (1932–) each represent in their own way different tendencies within it. At times the movement challenged theatrical conventions in writing and acting; at other times it opposed or even offended its audience. In *Qu'est-ce que la littérature?* (What Is Literature? 1947), Sartre wrote that "by definition, the author writes against his readers." This new oppositional antitheater, the Theater of the Absurd, brought about a radical transformation of form and structure through two major orientations: one the "tragic farce" dominated by Ionesco (1912–1994) and the other, the *jeu pur* (pure play) represented by Beckett (1906–1989).

Ionesco's success came with THE BALD SOPRANO (*La Cantatrice chauve*, 1948), based on the idiotic and disconnected phrases found in textbooks for learning to speak English. When it premiered in 1950 at the Théâtre des Noctambules, directed by Nicolas Bataille, only three people were in the audience. Since 1957, *The Bald Soprano* and THE LESSON (*La Leçon*, 1951), playing almost daily, have become the two plays with the longest uninterrupted runs ever in world theater. *The Bald Soprano* carries the subtitle *anti-pièce* (antiplay), underscoring the philosophy of negation espoused by Ionesco as early as 1934 when, influenced by Tristan Tzara's negativity, he published a book of essays titled *Non*. Ionesco's theater stresses the absurdity of bourgeois values and the life they dictate and posits that human endeavor is futile since the world is ruled by fortuitous action. Ionesco's theater is related to the absurdist tradition of humor but otherwise abandons its philosophical tenets; it is more in the tradition of surrealist and dadaist provocation than absurdist despair.

The "pure play" of Beckett responds to both traditional views of drama and the experimental energy of avant-garde theaters. Instead of using a story involving conflict as the basis for action and character revelation, Beckett made inaction and static waiting the nexus of his plays. The quintessential example of this is WAITING FOR GODOT (*En attendant Godot*, 1953). The Irish-born Beckett, like Ionesco, chose to write in the adopted language of French in order to rid himself of as much cultural baggage as possible and sustain his position of "outsider." The play enjoyed immediate word-of-mouth success after its premiere in front of a small audience at the Théâtre de Babylone in January 1953, in a production directed by Roger Blin (1907–1984). Parisian spectators were shocked to see the play's impoverished landscape through the eyes of Estragon and Vladimir, two metaphysical clowns waiting for Godot's arrival. Some critics were puzzled, others outright bored or scandalized, but many found themselves exhilarated by seeing the world in a new way. Similar theatrical asceticism is maintained in ENDGAME (*Fin de partie*, 1957) where Hamm and Clov debate the incommensurability of communication. Although Beckett's theater is antirealistic to an extreme, it is not entirely devoid of influence from the objective world. The claustrophobic atmosphere resembles the moods of war and its inherent terror, boredom, imprisonment, despair, confusion, and gallows humor. But the language that expresses these moods is not that of realism. Neither formal nor colloquial, Beckett's language struggles with silence until the latter finally prevails. The theater of Beckett pushes the conditions that make representation possible to their logical limits and takes refuge in pure play and even pure "voice," the last remaining element of dramaturgy. In this light, one can understand why Beckett wrote scripts for the radio such as ALL THAT FALL (*Tous ceux qui tombent*, 1957) and *Embers* (*Cendres*, 1959), since radio offers a medium where the expressive elements of language confound the materiality of the theatrical event.

1960s

Many of these radical views on language and space were further explored by later playwrights. The revolution of the absurd was, at once, a reaction to classical dramaturgy, a rejection of psychological realism, and a questioning of language's ability to represent—though such thoroughgoing abandonment of drama's fundamental tools pushed the theater into yet another crisis. This time the crisis became so widespread that the critic and theater historian Robert Abirached had to pronounce "the death of character" and the wholesale destruction of the language of representation. When the language of drama is itself put into question, it turns into a drama about language and a form of theater that became known as *logo-drame*.

Nathalie Sarraute theorized this problem in relation to the novel in her book of essays *The Age of Suspicion* (*L'Ere du soupçon*, written in 1932, published in 1956), in which she analyzes the role of the author at a time when linear and cohesive narrative is no longer necessarily the object of writing; and she applied the principles to her theatrical writing. In her plays, she emphasized language's inability to translate the authenticity and fluidity of human thought, motility, sensibility, and action. Her theater explores the world of the unsaid and the unnamable reality of characters devoid of physical or historical continuance. Characters with names such as *Il* (He), *Elle* (She), *On* (One), "H1," and "H2," and plays with titles such as *Silence* (1967), *The Lie* (*Le Mensonge*, 1967), *It Is There* (*Elle est là*, 1975), and *Just for Nothing* (*Pour un oui ou pour un non*, 1982) point to the fact that theatrical elements of speech, character, space, or temporality are mere schemas for understanding a reality that is usually obscured rather than revealed by the commonplaces of conversation.

A number of writers of this period, including MICHEL DE GHELDERODE (1898–1962), Arthur Adamov, and ROBERT PINGET (1919–1997), focused their attention to varying degrees on the impossibility of communication. In them, the breakdown of any meaningful flow of messages leaves the only potential for dialogue in the mundane exchanges of daily life. Adamov's *Spring '71* (*Printemps 71*, 1963) mixes ironic despair with a Marxist analysis of the ideological consequences of the breakdown of social solidarity; the result is an originally modern treatment of the 1871 Paris Commune.

On the fringe of the absurd and the *nouveau théâtre* developed another movement, influenced by contemporary experiments in poetry. JACQUES AUDIBERTI (1899–1965), Jean Tardieu, Georges Schéhadé, and Romain Weingarten (1926–) are representative of this stage revival of spoken poetry. Their work demonstrates the possibility of mixing poetic lyricism with humor and dramatic irony. This poetic variant of the absurd resulted in an extraordinary collaborative relationship between the poet-turned-playwright Henri Pichette (1924–2000) and renowned actor Gérard Philipe. In their productions of *The Epiphanies* (*Les Epiphanies*, 1947) and *Nucléa* (1951), directed by Jean Vilar, Pichette used multiple voices reciting lyrical poems. These poetic experiments seduced the public with their erotic sensibilities, in particular Audiberti's *The Evil Spreads* (*Le Mal court*, 1948) and Schéhadé's *Evening of the Proverbs* (*La Soirée des proverbes*, 1954), where dreamers are awakened by the power of stage words heard in an ephemeral theatrical event.

While the absurd posited various challenges to traditional forms, a phenomenon was brewing on the sidelines that soon took center stage and acquired mythical proportions: the life and work of Jean Genet. Genet's work can only be understood when it is viewed in relationship to the author's life. His plays bring together the contradictory drives of crime and innocence, blasphemy and mysticism, and obscenity and ritual. THE MAIDS (*Les Bonnes*, 1947) opened the way for a modernization and redefinition of tragedy. THE BALCONY (*Le Balcon*, 1956) is a macabre parody of theatricality and a critique of the artificiality of social relations, while THE BLACKS (*Les Nègres*, 1958) is a celebration of theatrical illusionism in a flamboyant, carnivallike atmosphere of sacrificial excess. What Artaud had theorized in the 1930s about the Theater of Cruelty seems to have been realized in Genet's work, though Genet claimed to be uninfluenced by him. Genet's theatrical excesses led in 1961 to THE SCREENS (*Les Paravents*), one of the most scandalous French plays of the modern period. Produced in 1966 at the Odéon by Roger Blin and Barrault, *The Screens* represents today the most important play of the antitheater tendency, with its enigmatic, funerallike atmosphere and its ironic dramatization of existence after death. Genet's paradoxical theater merges Brecht's self-reflexivity and hyperillusionism with Pirandello's joy in theatrical artifice for artifice's sake.

Throughout the 1960s many playwrights continued the creative battle on two fronts: one more political, inspired by Brecht; the other more ritualistic, deriving from Artaud. ARMAND GATTI (1924–), Eduardo Manet (1930–), and JEAN-CLAUDE

GRUMBERG (1939–) can be aligned with Brecht, while Vauthier, Audiberti, and Arrabal followed Genet and Artaud. Vauthier's *Blood* (*Le Sang*, 1970), a tragic story of revenge and murder, was performed as a ceremonial comedy filled with dance and parody similar to Genet's *The Blacks*. Audiberti's *The Loner* (*Le Cavalier seul*, 1963) is a dreamlike contemplation of the ritual struggle between good and evil. What these various post-absurd experiments had in common is a rejection of realism and a concern with a disintegrating subject whose tragedy is no longer expressed through nostalgic lamentation but through polyphonic and polysemous voices and images. Without a central integrated subject, the stage is transformed into a celebratory spectacle of all the arts, including marionettes, animated projections, mimes, dance, and opera.

Late 1960s theoretical trends in PHILOSOPHY, social, and political science were reflected in theater's rediscovery of its role in public education through festive rituals emphasizing the sacred and communal aspects of the theatrical event. "Communal" often translated into "collective creation," in which the very act of devising the playscript became a systematic exploration by actors, directors, dramatists, and other members of theatrical companies, who often relied on improvisations to contribute to the creative writing process. This important revolution within the theater community was overshadowed by a much larger public revolution during the dramatic and spectacular events of May 1968.

It is no accident that one of the primary symbolic venues for those events, second only to the street itself, was a national theater, the Théâtre de l'Odéon. Jean-Louis Barrault, director of the theater at the time, opened its doors and allowed protesting students to enter. They occupied the Odéon and turned its stage into a platform for their demands, though it became more of a festive space than a revolutionary one: the students partied, made love backstage, and proclaimed revolutionary rhetoric into the microphone, encouraged by the presence of Julian Beck of the LIVING THEATRE who had earlier been invited to perform at the Odéon but who now joined the students. Barrault lost his position for having allowed the students access to the building. André Malraux, then minister of culture, accused him of siding with the revolution against a government that was the main subsidizer of state-funded national theaters, including the Odéon itself. Stories and filmic documents of the events make May 1968 look like a form of utopian theater. On the one hand, there was the practical triumph of apparently universal solidarity among workers and students united in a single struggle; on the other, there was the dissemination of a theoretical Rousseauian ideal of the "natural" in which the stage became a platform for "truthful testimonies" uttered by "genuine workers" talking about "real oppression" and exploitation.

The interventionist performances that ensued can be considered a form of *théâtre vérité* (documentary theater, or DOCUMENTARY DRAMA), integrating direct accounts, improvisations, workshops, and manifestos. The theater became a "forum" in AUGUSTO BOAL's sense of the term (Boal, 1985), demanding an end to the division between art for the elite and other forms of communal activity, a forum where the community was invited to participate actively in direct action rather than in the mere representation of action. Many playwrights felt the need to liberate theater from cultural and class biases.

Spanish-French playwright Fernando Arrabal, who participated in the student uprising in Paris, proposed a new theater that he called *théâtre de guerilla* (GUERRILLA THEATER), characterized by baroque excess and aggressive, even savage, speech directed at the audience. His play THE ARCHITECT AND THE EMPEROR OF ASSYRIA (*L'Architecte et l'empereur d'Assyrie*, 1967) tells the story of two men stranded on a desert island who engage in sadomasochistic role-playing games until one finally devours the other in a cannibalistic ritual. After guerrilla theater, Arrabal developed *théâtre panique* (Theater of Panic) in a manifesto written with Alexandro Jodorowsky (1930–) and Roland Topor (1938–1997). The Theater of Panic combines the absurd with the Theater of Cruelty, resulting in "une manière d'être régie par la confusion, l'humour, la terreur, le hasard et l'euphorie" (a way of existing governed by confusion, humor, terror, chance and euphoria). A similar note of exuberant anarchy was struck by the works of the Argentine-French cartoonist and playwright Raul Damonte, known as COPI (1939–1987), who added the issue of sexual identity into his hyperactive dramatic mix.

1970s

Despite the unparalleled energy of the period, the 1960s ended with a sense of disillusionment as the revolution of May 1968 seemed to fade away without permanent results. The highly mediatized visibility of the protesters, however, revealed two important aspects of France's political and cultural landscape. First, the modern state in France emerged as an *état-spectacle* (the state as spectacle), a public entity made visible in part because of the theatrical metaphor, enacted throughout the events, whereby politics are constituted by the spectacular unveiling of a mediatized picture of them. Second, this theatricalization of politics underscored a paradox within specifically political theater: it proved to be a force that can challenge spheres of power and knowledge just as much as it can sustain them. For the theater community, May 1968 made possible two major practical developments: first, through the work of collective theater companies such as the Théâtre du Soleil, the Folidrome, and the Théâtre de la Salamandre, the sacred aspect of the theatrical event as a festive ritual was rediscovered; second, writers, directors, and other theater practitioners were brought physically together, allowing them to make each other's acquaintance and establish professional relations. Examples abounded afterward of directors working in close collaboration with playwrights: in 1969 Roger Planchon (1931–) directed his own play *Monstrous* (*L'Infâme*), while, in the same year, Jerzy Grotowski directed Arthur Adamov's play *Off Limits*; a year later the director and writer Marcel Maréchal (1937–) triumphed directing Vauthier's *Blood*. This rise in collaboration transformed the director into the new star of the theater, filling the gap left as the stature of authors faded following their time in the limelight after World War II. There were some exceptions to this diminished awareness of writers, notably MARGUERITE DURAS (1914–1996) and Armand Gatti (1924–). Both of them challenged the idea that there were no more stories to tell after the violent events of the war and the political and social turmoil of the 1960s.

For Duras, the response to history's failure came in the form of paroxysmal violence, revealed in the theater by multiple stage voices and fragmented narrative continuity. In Duras's theater, violence is internalized by characters to the point where it becomes unbearable, transforming their world into spectacle. Through obsessive repetition, the characters have to relive the incursion of their past or their internal mnemonic world into the present to such an extent that the constant repetition impedes their ability to tell their story. Duras's play *India Song* (1973) pulls apart the narrative by splintering the retelling of a simple love story among four onstage and offstage voices. *Savannah Bay* (1983), written for the actress Madeleine Renaud (1900–1994) in the later years of her career, underscores how a simple event—a Piaf song, in this case—can trigger uncontrollable links to memory in the listener. The play recounts a story of unfulfilled love, loss, and exile surrounding a young woman who commits suicide shortly after giving birth. It is as though the violence of the past inhabits one character for a moment, then moves on to the next character, splintering stage personae into fragments that contradict or torture one another.

While the violence in Duras's theater is internal, Gatti sees the need to expose the consequences of historical and political violence on the stage externally. His theater deals with events from recent history, such as the Holocaust or the Vietnam War. Dubbed a "theater of the last chance," Gatti's work explores the brutality of the post-Auschwitz condition in *théâtre éclaté* (theater blown apart or blown open). In *The Second Life of the Tatenberg Camp* (*La Deuxième existence du camp de Tatenberg*, first produced in Lyon in 1962), Gatti explores two totally different realities: that of a Baltic Jew, Ilya Moïssevitch, a survivor of the concentration camps; and that of Hildegarde Frölick, a German war widow who is trying to reconstruct the circumstances surrounding the death of her husband, a corporal in the German infantry executed unjustly for dereliction of duty on the way to Stalingrad. Gatti's figures are victims of historical violence, but their recollection of it can only be approached indirectly, through theatrical metaphors, because of the grave insufficiency of words to construct an understanding of genocide and crimes past. Spectators do not need to see torture scenes or gas chambers to understand their trauma; and, in any case, the terrible reality of the camps cannot be contained in language and familiar forms of drama. Similar engagements with history and memory are present in the theater of Jean-Claude Grumberg. His *The Workshop* (*L'Atelier*, 1979) is the story of Jewish seamstresses who survived the Nazi Occupation and now sew together after the war. The play shows the paradoxes inherent in a post-Auschwitz community, one in which physically demanding labor distances workers from the horrific past and offers some respite from the guilt of survival.

The most famous example of theater's new post-1968 stance was the Théâtre du Soleil, under the guidance of ARIANE MNOUCHKINE (1939–). For more than three decades, Mnouchkine, who founded her company in 1964, has been considered the leader of the French theatrical avant-garde. In 1970, following the 1968 upheaval in public power structures, her company, which started as a student troupe, grew from nine to sixty artists and moved to a former munitions factory, La Cartoucherie, in the Bois de Vincennes on the southeastern edge of Paris. Since then, other important theater companies have moved to the Cartoucherie complex, including the Théâtre de la Tempête, Thèâtre de l'Epée de Bois, Théâtre de la Chaudron, and Théâtre de l'Aquarium.

Ideologically, the Théâtre du Soleil is close to Brecht's EPIC THEATER, but Mnouchkine departs from Brecht in her understanding of theater as at once political and historical, sacred and contemporary, classical and mythological, with only the proportions changing from production to production. The actors of the Théâtre du Soleil are trained in various techniques, including the non-Western NŌ, *kabuki*, Bunraku, and *kathakali* traditions. The resulting spectacle resembles a carnival or athletic event where movement and gesture are dominant. Despite the carnival atmosphere, Mnouchkine believes that verbal communication with the audience should be simple and direct, and playwrights who work with the Théâtre du Soleil must keep this in mind.

The first big success of the Théâtre du Soleil dates back to 1967 with *The Kitchen* by British playwright ARNOLD WESKER, performed in French at the former Cirque de Montmartre. This was followed by a series of aesthetic and thematic cycles focused on the French Revolution (*1789*, *1793*); Shakespeare (*Richard II*, *Henry IV*); Molière (*Don Juan*, *Molière*, *Tartuffe*); classical Greek tragedy (*The House of Atreus* [*Les Atrides*]); and finally in collaboration with HÉLÈNE CIXOUS (1937–), episodes from Asian history. Cixous, known for her feminist and novelistic work, began writing plays for the Théâtre du Soleil in 1984. The first was THE TERRIBLE BUT UNFINISHED HISTORY OF NORODOM SIHANOUK, KING OF CAMBODIA (*L'Histoire Terrible mais inachevée de Norodom Sihanouk roi du Cambodge*, produced in 1985), which tells the story of King Sihanouk's 1955 accession to power in CAMBODIA, the invasion of Vietnam, the 1979 overthrow of Pol Pot, and the ensuing clash of ideologies resulting from France's colonial history and America's flawed foreign policy. Other plays by Cixous combine an analysis of history with emancipatory spectacle that unites people in the face of tragedy.

The collaboration of Cixous and Mnouchkine is a rare and formidable example of a successful partnership between a playwright and a director during a period that has often seen a tug of war between the two roles. Due in part to a sharp decline in government subsidies for the theater, and also to the growing stardom of certain directors, the last two decades of the 20th century came to be viewed as a difficult period for playwrights. It became commonplace in French theater circles to declare the era of the playwright at an end, replaced by collaborative forms of creation or by the era of the director.

In the 1970s many playwrights responded in specific ways to this schism by creating what came to be known as the *théâtre du quotidien* (theater of daily life). This trend was influenced by authors and filmmakers from Germany and AUSTRIA for whom the fragmentation of everyday life and thus the fragmentation of its representation onstage were key. The *théâtre du quotidien*'s mandate was to expose the inherent violence of the mediated and media-saturated society of the late 20th century. MICHEL VINAVER's *Overboard* (*Par-dessus bord*, 1969) deals with the world of commerce and business—a world that Vinaver knows well, having been an executive with the international corporation Gillette. His theater is split between disillusionment with late capitalism's routine and repetitive labor and the need to sustain perfect symbiosis with that labor despite disillusionment. The *théâtre du quotidien* rejects the romantic vision of the playwright or artist as a redeemer on a mission to save humanity from metaphysical collapse; it proposes, instead, that the playwright underline the cracks in the established order through ironic distancing and the use of derisive humor and show how artificial the supposed "realism" of the arts has always been when compared to the nonlinear kaleidoscopic reality we live in. The works of RENÉ KALISKY (1936–1981), Jean-Paul Wenzel (1947–), and Michel Deutsch (1948–), like those of Vinaver, show how the routine of the modern condition crushes the individual even when the individual appears to be in communion with it.

LATE 20TH CENTURY

Although the 1970s saw many new plays, the decade came to be viewed as an era of stagnation for the dramatic arts in France. The 1980s reversed the trend, but without restoring power to the playwright; instead, directors continued as the stars of the theater. Many theater companies in the early 1980s, aided by the cultural policies of France's minister of culture, Jack Lang (1939–), used the advantages provided by the Socialist government of President François Mitterand (1916–1996) to revitalize production. Symbolic proof of this was the way in which the productions by Patrice Chéreau (1944–) of the plays of BERNARD-MARIE KOLTÈS (1948–1989) at the Théâtre des Amandiers in Nanterre (on the northwestern outskirts of Paris) often used huge, costly sets, despite the fact that the works of Koltès, one of the few notable playwrights to emerge during the 1980s, are equally, perhaps even more, compelling on a bare stage. The theater of Koltès, unlike many postmodernist theater projects, is not apolitical. Koltès's entire body of work, from *The Night Just Before the Forests* (*La Nuit juste avant les forêts*, first produced 1977) to *Roberto Zucco* (first produced 1990), the last play he wrote before his death from AIDS, handles the status of the individual faced with restraints imposed by cultural, moral, and political regimes.

New or newly prominent directors such as Peter Brook (1925–), Jacques Lasalle (1936–), Mnouchkine, Patrice Chéreau, and Robert Lepage (1957–) have responded to the requirements of new writing by molding a postmodern drama defined by its new language, heterogeneity, and multiperspectivism, intensely theatrical precisely because of its pluridisciplinary framework. Playwrights of the last two decades such as Hélène Cixous, Valère Novarina (1942–), Daniel Lemahieu (1946–), Eugène Durif (1950–), Enzo Cormann (1953–), and YASMINA REZA (1959–) use every resource at their disposal to come to terms with end-of-millennium despair and ideological stagnation at a moment when concepts of community and ritual are severely challenged.

The essential plurality of 21st-century French theater now goes beyond the facts of writing and staging to that of global origins. Under the current influences of multiculturalism and *écriture plurielle* (collective writing), contemporary Francophone theaters emphasize extraterritoriality, *errance* (erring or wandering, both personal and cultural), diaspora, and migration. Francophone playwrights from around the world such as AIMÉ CÉSAIRE (1913–), Andrée Chedid (EGYPT and Lebanon, 1920–), Driss Chraïbi (Morocco, 1926–), René Depestre (Haiti, 1926–), Sylvain Bemba (Congo, 1934–), MICHEL TREMBLAY (Québec, 1942–), Alioune Badara Bèye (Senegal, 1945–), Julius-Amédé Laou (Martinique, 1950–), Ahmed Madani (Algeria, 1952–), MICHEL MARC BOUCHARD (Québec, 1958–), and Yehuda (Jean-Bernard) Moraly (ISRAEL) have underscored the performance of difference by dramatizing the interlocking issues of ethnicity, race, class, and gender.

FURTHER READING

Boal, Augusto. *Theatre of the Oppressed*. New York: Theatre Communications Group, 1985.

Bradby, David. *Modern French Drama: 1940–1990*. 2d ed. New York: Cambridge Univ. Press, 1991.

——— and Annie Sparks. *Mise en Scène: French Theatre Now*. London: Methuen, 1997.

Brooks, Peter. *The Melodramatic Imagination*. New Haven, Conn.: Yale Univ. Press, 1976.

Caune, Jean. *La Culture en action: De Vilar à Lang* [The culture in action: Of Vilar with Lang]. Grenoble: P. U. de Grenoble, 1992.

Copeau, Jacques. *Registres du Vieux-Colombier I* [Registers of Vieux-Colombier I]. Paris: Gallimard, 1974.

Esslin, Martin. *The Theater of the Absurd*. 1961. Garden City, N.Y.: Anchor Doubleday, 1969.

Grossvogel, David I. *20th Century French Drama*. New York: Columbia Univ. Press, 1961.

Knapp, Bettina L. *French Theater Since 1968*. Farmington Hills, Mich.: Gale, 1995.

Lamar, Celita. *Our Voices, Ourselves: Women Writing for the French Theatre*. New York: P. Lang, 1995.

Mounsef, Donia, and Josette Feral, eds. *Transparency of the Text: Contemporary writing for the Stage. Yale French Studies*, Volume 112 (Fall 2007).

Pavis, Patrice. *Theatre at the Crossroads of Culture* Tr. by Loren Kruger. New York: Routledge, 1992.

Sartre, Jean-Paul. *Qu'est-ce que la littérature* [What is literature?]. In *Situations II*. Paris: Gallimard, 1948.

——. *Un Théâtre de situations* [Theater of situations]. Paris: Gallimard, 1973 [all translations mine].

Serreau, Geneviève. *Histoire du nouveau théâtre* [History of the new theater]. Paris: Gallimard, 1966.

Donia Mounsef

FRASER, BRAD (1959–)

Born in Edmonton, Alberta, CANADA in 1959, Brad Fraser has been winning awards as a playwright since the age of seventeen. His plays challenge the tradition of the "well-made play" as well as conventional conceptions of identity and sexuality. Uncompromising and quirky, Fraser has created a career out of pushing the boundaries of taste for both the gay and heterosexual communities. In his plays, as in person, he has defied public opinion about concepts of gender and morality. His works transform theatrical REALISM into vibrant productions that are fast-paced, jump from scene to scene, and use nudity and explicit sexual content for much of their dramatic impetus and punch. Fraser defies concrete definitions of sexual orientation; many of his characters are sexually ambiguous individuals who are difficult to categorize and, while being oversexed, present sexuality in a way that is undeterminable.

An active member of the Alberta theatrical community for many years, Fraser became internationally recognized with his production of *Unidentified Human Remains and the True Nature of Love* in 1989. *Unidentified* takes place in Edmonton in 1989. The play follows the lives of twenty-somethings who are looking for meaning in their lives while a serial killer terrorizes the city. *Unidentified* explores the difficulty to feel any true sense of love in a world that has been desensitized to shock or emotion. The production was extremely successful and performed throughout Canada and abroad; *Unidentified* was adapted into a successful film version by Denis Arcand in 1994.

Fraser's next work, *The Ugly Man* (1990), later performed in America and Europe, presented an even more cynical worldview. Based on the Jacobean revenge tragedies, the play is extremely violent and sexually explicit with uncompromising acts of violence and degradation. The play, directed in French by the Quebecois director Derek Goldby at the Quat'Sous in Montreal, created a sensation in the artistic community about the radical wave of new anglo-Canadian playwrights and their graphic representation of modern life.

Poor Super Man (Ensemble Theatre, Cincinnati, 1994, Mark Mochahabeess) was written in 1994 at the height of the AIDS pandemic when Fraser was losing many of his own friends to the disease. It presents a love affair between a Gay man and a Straight man. David, the Gay male in the play, the last survivor of all of his friends, is extremely angry by the circumstances of his life. Other characters include a transsexual going through a sex change while dying of AIDS. The play ends tragically, like much of Fraser's work, but continues his exploration of sexual experimentation and relationships that blur the boundaries of sexual orientation and identity.

In addition to his work in the theater, Fraser has adapted several works for film and television. He is a co-producer and writer for Showtime's *Queer as Folk* and hosts the talk show *Jawbreaker*. Fraser is also celebrity spokesperson for The AIDS Network in Edmonton.

[*See also* Gay and Lesbian Drama]

SELECT PLAYS: *Unidentified Human Remains and the True Nature of Love* (1989); *The Ugly Man* (1990); *Poor Super Man* (1994); *Martin Yesterday* (1998); *Outrageous* (co-written by Joel Miller, 2000); *Snake in Fridge* (2000)

FURTHER READING

Blumberg, Marcia. "Queer(y)ing the Canadian Stage: Brad Fraser's Poor Super Man." *Theatre Research in Canada* 17, no. 2 (Fall 1996): 175–187.

Dvorak, Maria. "Le Polar de la Génération X" [The whodunnit of Generation X]. *Etude Canadiennes/Canadian Studies* (1998): 115–123.

Glaap, Albert-Reiner. *Anguished Human Relations and the Search for Love: Plays by Canadian Writers Brad Fraser, Judith Thompson, and Dianne Warren*. Trier: Wissenschaftlicher Verlag Trier, 1998.

Holly Maples

FRAYN, MICHAEL (1933–)

Born in London on September 8, 1933, Michael Frayn completed his baccalaureate work at Emmanuel College, Cambridge, in 1957. He began his writing career as a journalist, reporting for the Manchester *Guardian* from 1957 to 1959 and writing columns for the *Guardian* and then for the *Observer* from 1959 to 1968. In 1970 he received a National Press Club Award for distinguished reporting for a series of articles on CUBA.

Frayn has subsequently produced a substantial body of work both as a playwright and as a novelist. His plays have been characterized by their knowing observation, their energy, their wit, and increasingly, their imaginative staging. His recurring subjects have included the strains on the relationships between men and women, the personalities of journalists and the ways in which the news is "made," and the forced camaraderie of the "working holiday."

He has received many honors for both his plays and his novels. For *Noises Off* (1982), a FARCE about the staging of a farce, he has received the Best Comedy of the Year Award from the *Evening Standard* and the Society of West End Theater Award for best COMEDY of the year. For *Benefactors* (1984), a study of two couples, with incisive observations about romantic and political idealism and the compromises that are rationalized as pragmatism, Frayn received the Best Play of the Year Award from the *Evening Standard*, the Society of West End Theatre Award for best play of the year, the Laurence Olivier Award for best play, the *Plays and Players* Award for best new play, and the New York Drama Critics' Circle Award for best new foreign play. For *Copenhagen* (1999), a historical play about a momentous meeting in 1941 between the German physicist Werner Heisenberg and the Danish physicist Niels Bohr, Frayn received the *Evening Standard* Award for Best Play of the Year and the Antoinette Perry (Tony) Award for best play.

Trained in Russian during his term of compulsory military service, Frayn has adapted five of ANTON CHEKHOV's plays to the contemporary stage: THE CHERRY ORCHARD (1978), THREE SISTERS (1985), *Wild Honey* (1984), THE SEAGULL (1986), and UNCLE VANYA (1987).

Among Frayn's novels, *The Tin Men* (1965), *The Russian Interpreter* (1966), and *Spies* (2002) stand out. For *Spies*, a coming-of-age story set in World War II, Frayn has received both the Whitbread Award for best novel and the Commonwealth Writers Prize for the best book from Eurasia.

[*See also* England, 1940–Present]

SELECT PLAYS: *Zounds!* (with John Edwards, 1957); *Black and Silver* (1970); *Chinamen* (1970); *Mr. Foot* (1970); *The New Quixote* (1970); *The Two of Us* (1970); *Sandboy* (1971); *Alphabetical Order* (1975); *Clouds* (1976); *Donkey's Years* (1976); *Balmoral* (1978); *The Fruits of Enlightenment* (1979); *Make and Break* (1980); *Noises Off* (1982); *Benefactors* (1984); *Number One* (1984); *Exchange* (1989); *Look Look* (1990); *Here* (1993); *Copenhagen* (1999)

FURTHER READING

Kahan, Marcy. "Michael Frayn." BOMB 73 (Fall 2000): 54–59.

Rose, Paul Lawrence. "Frayn's *Copenhagen* Plays Well, at History's Expense." *Chronicle of Higher Education* 46, no. 35 (May 5, 2000): B4–B6.

Staub, August W. "The Scientist as Byronic Hero: Michael Frayn's *Copenhagen*." *Journal of Dramatic Theory and Criticism* 16, no. 2 (Spring 2002): 133–141.

Stewart, Victoria. "A Theatre of Uncertainties: Science and History in Michael Frayn's *Copenhagen*." *New Theatre Quarterly* 15, no. 4 (November 1999): 301–307.

Worth, Katharine. "Farce and Michael Frayn." *Modern Drama* 26, no. 1 (March 1983): 47–53.

Martin Kich

FREEMAN, DAVID (1945–)

Born in Toronto on January 7, 1945, Canadian playwright David Freeman has had cerebral palsy since he was an infant. He completed a B.A. in political science at McMaster University. His writing has been supported with grants from the Ontario Council for the Arts and the CANADA Council.

Not surprisingly given his own history, Freeman's early work exhibits his interest in the psychological effects of physical disabilities. But, in his later work, Freeman's focus has shifted to the ways in which the detrimental consequences of our overly commercialized, materialistic culture have been manifested in increasingly commonplace psychological problems.

For the various productions of his first staged work, the powerful one-act play *Creeps* (1971), Freeman has received the Chalmers Award for the best Canadian play of the year, the New York Drama Desk Award for the best new playwright, the Los Angeles Critics Circle Award, and the first prize from the Edinburgh Festival. Set mainly in the restroom of a vocational shop for the physically disabled, the play focuses on four young men whose responses to their disabilities and to the repetitive menial work they are being trained to do provide, in total, a very complex depiction of their circumstances. Furthermore, in their expressions and demonstrations of bitter cynicism, resentment, apathy, diligent application, contentment, and private ambitions, Freeman shows how these characters define themselves as much by their own impressions of each other as by the broader society's stereotypes of them.

In contrast to the provocative NATURALISM of *Creeps*, *You're Gonna Be Alright, Jamie-Boy* (1974) is an absurdist fable about a couple named Ernie and Fran who wish their family life were as harmonious and heartwarming as that portrayed in the television series *The Waltons*. Instead, their son has had to be institutionalized for serious psychological problems, their daughter is slipping into alcoholism, and their son-in-law is impotent. At the family gathering that is the play's focal event, everyone has gathered around the television from which the programming is transmitted like a tranquilizer. Of course, when the television screen goes blank and the picture cannot be restored, it is only a short while before the numbingly affable conversation devolves into a cacophony of resentments, ridicule, complaints, and accusations.

Freeman is also the author of the autobiography *Stage Voices* (1978).

SELECT PLAYS: *Creeps* (1971); *Battering Ram* (1972); *You're Gonna Be Alright, Jamie-Boy* (1974); *Jesse and the Bandit Queen* (1975); *Flytrap* (1976); *Hell's Angels* (an opera for which Freeman wrote the text, prod. 1986)

FURTHER READING

Donnelly, Pat. "Disabled Need Right to Work, Not Right to Die, Playwright Says." *Gazette* (Montreal) (February 18, 1995): C1.

Guernsey, Otis L., ed. "*Creeps*, by David Freeman." In *The Best Plays of 1973–1974*. New York: Dodd, 1974.

——. "*Jesse and the Bandit Queen*, by David Freeman." In *The Best Plays of 1975–1976*. New York: Dodd, 1976.

Martin Kich

FRENCH, DAVID (1939–)

Born in Coley's Point, Newfoundland, on January 18, 1939, Canadian playwright David French grew up primarily in Toronto. After graduating from high school, he studied acting at the Al Saxe Studio in Toronto, at the Pasadena Playhouse in California, and at the Lawlor School of Acting in Toronto. For half a decade, he worked primarily as an actor and then began writing plays for radio and for television. As he made the transition to writing plays for the stage, he supported his family by working for several years in the post office.

Although he had lived in Newfoundland only until he was seven years old, the island is the focal geographical and cultural location for much of French's work. Specifically, French's cycle of plays about the Mercer family—*Leaving Home* (1972), *Of the Fields, Lately* (1973), *Salt-Water Moon* (1984), *1949* (1988), and *Soldier's Heart* (2001)—depict the experiences of Irish immigrants to provincial Newfoundland who then become transplants to the much more cosmopolitan city of Toronto. For *Of the Fields, Lately*, French received both the Chalmers Award and the Governor General's Award. In addition, *Leaving Home* was a finalist for the Chalmers Award, and *Salt-Water Moon* was a finalist for the Governor General's Award.

The first two plays of the cycle explore the conflicts between Jacob Mercer and his son Ben, as Ben first chooses to make his own way in the world and then as he confronts his father's physical and psychological decline. At the beginning of *Leaving Home*, Ben's brother Billy is getting married to his pregnant high school girlfriend. Ironically, the girl's mother, Minnie Jackson, had once been romantically involved with Jacob. In the third play in the cycle, *Salt-Water Moon*, French provides a prequel to *Leaving Home*, depicting Jacob's determination to marry Mary Snow, a relatively straight-laced Protestant from a respectable family, rather than Minnie, who is a vivacious Roman Catholic with a scandalous air about her. Although *Salt-Water Moon* captures the romantic intensity of the early years of Jacob and Mary's marriage, it establishes the ways in which their differences in temperament had a corrosive effect on their family life over the long term.

For JITTERS (1979), a wild COMEDY about the turmoil that very nearly wrecks the rehearsals of a new play, French also received the Chalmers Award. The most popular of French's plays, *Jitters* has been widely staged in CANADA and beyond.

SELECT PLAYS: *Leaving Home* (1972); *Of the Fields, Lately* (1973); *One Crack Out* (1975); *Jitters* (1979); *The Riddle of the World* (1981); *Salt-Water Moon* (1984); *The Forest* (1987); *1949* (1988); *Silver Dagger* (1992); *That Summer* (2000); *Soldier's Heart* (2001)

FURTHER READING

Maufort, Marc. "Celebrating Paradises Lost: Echoes of Eugene O'Neill in David French's 'Mercer Cycle.'" *Études Canadiennes/Canadian Studies* 49 (December 2000): 97–107.

Nunn, Robert. "The Subjects of *Salt-Water Moon*." *Theatre History in Canada/Histoire du Theatre au Canada* 12, no. 1 (Spring 1991): 3–21.

Zimmerman, Cynthia. "David French." In *Profiles in Canadian Literature*, 4, ed. by Jeffrey M. Heath. Toronto: Dundurn, 1982. 117–124.

Martin Kich

FRIEL, BRIAN (1929–)

Confusion is not an ignoble condition.

—Hugh, Act 3, *Translations*

Brian Friel is one of the leading Irish playwrights of the 20th century. He has achieved international success with plays that blend intellectual analysis with bittersweet humor, and theatrical experimentation with popular appeal.

Friel was born in 1929 to a Catholic family in County Tyrone in Northern IRELAND. His first success as a writer was in the pages of *The New Yorker* and *The Saturday Evening Post*, for which he wrote short stories throughout the 1950s. Between 1958 and 1963, he began to attempt drama: four radio plays were broadcast by the BBC, and three apprentice plays were produced, although Friel is prepared to acknowledge only *The Enemy Within* (1962).

The key moment in Friel's early career occurred in 1963 when he was invited to the Tyrone Guthrie Theatre in Minneapolis. This experience transformed Friel's writing, offering him a distance from "inbred, claustrophobic" Ireland that brought him self-confidence and a "necessary perspective" about his work.

The result of this visit was *Philadelphia, Here I Come!* Premiered at the 1964 Dublin Theatre Festival, the play portrays Gar, a young Irishman, on the night before his immigration to America. The play's main innovation was that Gar was played by two actors, one representing his public self and the other his inner thoughts. *Philadelphia* shows Friel's interest in the clash between public and private, his love of theatrical artifice, and his fascination with the role of America in Irish life. Throughout the 1960s, his plays returned to these themes, while also exploring love and relationships.

While Friel's reputation was growing, the political situation in Northern Ireland was deteriorating: optimism created by the emergence in 1967 of a Civil Rights movement for Catholics gave way to despair at the growth of sectarian violence. The situation reached its lowest point in 1972, when the British army opened fire on a Civil Rights march in Derry, killing thirteen civilians. This event profoundly affected Friel, who quickly wrote *The Freedom of the City*, a dramatization of Bloody Sunday and the controversial public enquiry that followed it. The play's political content was criticized when it premiered in 1973, but Friel continued to write about the Northern Irish Troubles for much of the following two decades.

Not all of his work during this period was explicitly political. *Aristocrats* (1979) brilliantly charts the declining status of a wealthy Catholic family in Donegal and owes a great deal to ANTON CHEKHOV, whose work Friel would later adapt. And although *Faith Healer*, a series of three linked monologues, was unsuccessful on its 1980 New York debut, it is now regarded as one of Friel's best works.

The year 1980 also saw the production of *Translations*, Friel's treatment of colonialism and language in 19th-century Ireland. This was the premiere production by FIELD DAY THEATRE COMPANY, which was established by Friel and others as a response to the Troubles. Although Friel experienced periods of writer's block during the 1980s, both of his original plays—*The Communication Cord* (1982) and *Making History* (1988)—were produced by Field Day.

In 1990, Friel decided not to offer his latest play, *Dancing at Lughnasa*, to Field Day, and it was instead produced at the Abbey Theatre in Dublin. A partially autobiographical play about five sisters living in Donegal in the 1930s, it presents its story in two ways—the everyday lives of the women are performed naturalistically onstage, while a narrator, Michael, comments on the action. The contrast between the story being performed by the women and the story being narrated by Michael makes *Lughnasa* one of Friel's most poignant works. Audiences responded enthusiastically to it, and it toured throughout the world during the early 1990s.

After Friel's resignation from Field Day in 1994, his plays took on a more somber, reflective tone—particularly in *Give Me Your Answer, Do!* (1997), a harsh consideration of the value of writing. In 1999, the Irish theater marked Friel's seventieth birthday with a "Friel Festival" of his best plays. While that event was intended to celebrate a long and brilliant career, it has not signaled an end to Friel's writing—since 2000, he has written well-regarded adaptations of Chekhov and Leos Janacek.

The importance of Friel to the Irish stage is inestimable. His work is popular with audiences and critics, and it is almost impossible to find a younger Irish writer whose work is free of his influence. Friel's plays therefore have not just dominated Irish drama; they have significantly determined its development.

PLAYS: *This Doubtful Paradise* (1959); *The Enemy Within* (1962); *Philadelphia, Here I Come!* (1964); *The Loves of Cass Maguire* (1966); *Lovers* (1967); *Crystal and Fox* (1968); *The Gentle Island* (1971); *The Freedom of the City* (1973); *Volunteers* (1975); *Living Quarters* (1977); *Aristocrats* (1979); *Faith Healer* (1980); *Translations* (1980); *The Three Sisters* (after Chekhov) (1981); *The Communication Cord* (1982); *Fathers and Sons* (1987); *Making History* (1988); *Dancing at Lughnasa* (1990); *The London Vertigo* (after Macklin) (1992); *A Month in the Country* (1992); *Wonderful Tennessee* (1993); *Molly Sweeney* (1994); *Give Me Your Answer, Do!* (1997); *Uncle Vanya* (after Chekhov) (1998); *The Yalta Game* (2001); *Two Plays After: The Bear and Afterplay* (2002); *Performances* (2003)

FURTHER READING

Andrews, Elmer. *The Art of Brian Friel*. London: Macmillan, 1995.

Maxwell, D. E. S. *Brian Friel*. Lewisberg, Pa.: Bucknell Univ. Press, 1973.

Peacock, Alan, ed. *The Achievement of Brian Friel*. Gerrards Cross: Colin Smyth, 1993.

Pine, Richard. *Brian Friel and Ireland's Drama*. London: Routledge, 1990.

Patrick Lonergan

FRIENDS

Friends (*Tomodachi*, 1967), a Japanese SHINGEKI drama by ABE KŌBŌ, premiered at Tokyo's Kinokuniya Hall on March 15, 1967, in a production directed by Naruse Masahiko. Abe once said of his inspiration for it, "Prosaic posters of smiling family-like groups inspire me with terror" (Shields, 1996). The play, perhaps Abe's best known, is an excellent example of the Japanese postwar AVANT-GARDE and illustrates the influence of the Theater of the Absurd on his writing.

Friends opens with a family of eight knocking on the apartment door of a Man. When the Man opens the door, the family enters and promptly moves in. Despite his protests, they begin to settle in. The Man calls the police, but the family remains unconcerned. The Father explains to the Man that they are there to ease his loneliness. The police arrive to investigate, urge the Man to settle matters amicably, and leave when they decide there has been no injury. A series of discussions follows, in which the family uses circular logic and verbal sparring to convince the Man that he owes them money that they have already stolen from him. The Man's Fiancée calls him on the telephone, and in return for their silence during the phone call, the Man agrees to let them spend the night.

The second act opens with Eldest Son meeting the Fiancée in the park and planting seeds of doubt in her mind about the fidelity and commitment of the Man. The Man appears and is chastized by his Fiancée for his secrecy. She only agrees to believe him if she can bring a reporter by the house to verify his story and expose the family, but the reporter is impressed by the family's generosity and praises them. Later, the Middle Daughter exposes her older sister's plot to escape the family with the Man, but after more semantic maneuvering, the Man admits he has grown used to the family and has no desire to leave.

Upon hearing this, the Father immediately places him in a cage, insisting that his assertion was too enthusiastic. The final scene of the play has the Middle Daughter sympathizing with the Man, offering him milk, and giving him the key to his cage. As soon as he gets the key, however, he collapses and dies, a victim of the poisoned milk, and the family moves on to its next encounter.

Abe adapted the basic plot of *Friends* from an earlier short story titled "The Intruders" ("Chinnyūsha," 1952). The play was awarded the Tanizaki Jun'ichirō Prize in 1967 and underwent a revision in 1974, with Abe adding a third son to the family unit. *Friends* contains many of the themes that Abe's work is known for, including social isolation, absurdist COMEDY, and the dangers of complacency. Abe's work is a break from the traditional realistic theater of his time, incorporating surrealist situation and circular logic. Audiences have also seen it as an allegory on the destruction of freedom by "well-meaning" tyrants.

[*See also* Japan]

FURTHER READING

Abe Kōbō. *Friends*. Tr. by Donald Keene. New York: Grove, 1969.

——. *Friends*. In *Contemporary Japanese Literature: An Anthology of Fiction, Film, and Other Writing Since 1945*, ed. by Howard Hibbett and tr. by Donald Keene. New York: Knopf, 1977.

Shields, Nancy. *Fake Fish: The Theater of Kobo Abe*. New York: Weatherhill, 1996.

David Jortner

FRISCH, MAX (1911–1991)

Max Frisch ranks among the few German-language playwrights of the 20th century who have achieved an international reputation. Although he was a cosmopolitan and traveled extensively, and although he was often critical of his homeland, he remained Swiss and would die in Zurich, the city of his birth. Two of his dramas, *The Firebugs: A Learning-Play Without a Lesson* (also translated as *The Fire Raisers: A Morality Without a Moral* [*Biedermann und die Brandstifter: Ein Lehrstück ohne Lehre*], 1958) and ANDORRA (1957), were immediate successes, utterly in tune with the mood that prevailed in the late 1950s, one compounded of existentialist cynicism, anxieties about the Cold War, and nagging guilt about the Holocaust. Even if they are no longer performed as regularly in commercial venues, these plays remain influential, canonical texts, not least because they are widely read in schools and universities. Frisch's reputation was further solidified by his novels: *I'm Not Stiller* (*Stiller*, 1954); *Homo Faber: A Report* (*Homo Faber. Ein Bericht*, 1957); and *A Wilderness of Mirrors* (*Mein Name sei Gantenbein*, 1964).

At first glance Frisch would seem not to have written much, especially when compared to more prolific writers. But looks deceive. For one thing, Frisch's career as a playwright started late. Although he had always wanted to be a writer and had even dashed off a spate of plays while a student (his first drama *Steel* [*Stahl*, 1927] was turned down by MAX REINHARDT), it was not until 1944 that he wrote two plays, *Santa Cruz* (performed 1946) and *Now They're Singing Again* (*Nun singen sie wieder: Versuch eines Requiems*, performed 1945), at the instigation of Kurt Hirschfeld, dramaturg at the Zurich Schauspielhaus. From then until just before his death, Frisch wrote for the theater at regular intervals. Until 1954 he was also a practicing architect, a profession that had a profound impact on his worldview.

Frisch was one of those writers who continually rewrite and revise their works even after they have been published and achieved success. As a result, there are often several different versions of his texts with the same title. *The Firebugs* was initially published as a radio play, then as a short version for the premiere, and finally as the familiar longer version with the epilogue. In addition, most of the plays are anticipated in prose sketches or synopses in Frisch's diaries, which he kept from the 1940s and which are a considerable part of his published literary output. The versions are substantial enough that each title actually indicates several different works, each of which deserves to be considered in its own right, rather than being subsumed into one. This multiplies the number of plays several times.

Frisch's compulsion to revise is symptomatic of his tendency to return to the same problems over and over again. A small number of topics recur: the quest of individuals for authenticity; the inability of men to understand and love women; the failure of human beings to learn from their past; the dangers of abstract analytical thought; the pleasures of ordinary life; and the need for humor as an instrument of survival. Many of his characters are obsessed with returning to the past, with creating the past in the act of remembering. And yet the attempt seems futile. As Frisch's Don Juan remarks: "I am startled when I look back at my life, I see myself like a swimmer in a stream, without a track." Like BERTOLT BRECHT—whom Frisch met in 1947 and from whom he learned much—Frisch did not set out primarily to entertain. His plays always analyze some problem, even if they decline to provide solutions, as the subtitle to *The Firebugs* emphasizes by declaring itself to be "a learning-play without a lesson."

Frisch's first play, *Santa Cruz*, is a dream play that explores the theme of self-realization. In the program notes for the premiere, Frisch cautioned the audience against trying to find an actual Santa Cruz on the map. The same caution should apply to all of his subsequent plays, but many readers still thought that they could identify CZECHOSLOVAKIA in *The Firebugs* or SWITZERLAND in *Andorra*.

Paradoxically, however, Frisch was also a politically engaged writer with strong views on important social issues of the day. This dimension came through in *Now They're Singing Again*, the first of his dramas to be performed. The play deals explicitly and movingly with the legacy of World War II and constitutes one of the earliest contributions to what would subsequently be called *Vergangenheitsbewältigung*, the discourse on how to come to terms with GERMANY's violent history. Frisch's next play, *The Great Wall of China* (*Die Chinesische Mauer: Eine Farce*, 1946), confronted the threat of nuclear war and questioned whether art or literature could make a difference in a world where "[t]he deluge is becoming feasible. . . . It depends on us whether there is humanity or not."

Gradually Frisch came to rely on individual figures as the organizing element in constructing his dramas. In *When the War Was Over* (*Als der Krieg zu Ende war*, 1949), the antiwar message is conveyed through the love affair between a German woman and a Russian soldier during the early years of the occupation. *Count Oderland: A Street Ballad in Twelve Scenes* (*Graf Öderland: Eine Moritat in zwölf Bildern*, 1949–1951) depicts a public prosecutor who has become convinced that the bureaucratic state is the antithesis of a liberal society, but he cannot escape its reach. Similarly, the title figure of *Don Juan; or, The Love of Geometry* (*Don Juan oder die Liebe zur Geometrie: Komödie in fünf Akten*, 1952–1953) is trapped by a society that cannot tolerate anyone who rejects the prevailing norms. Don Juan would rather do geometry and play chess than have sex, but ultimately he is compelled to get married. Conversely, Mr. Biedermann is only too happy to conform, even when the group he aligns himself with consists of terrorists plotting to blow up his house and his world. Finally, in *Andorra* the main character Andri first resists the community's biased opinion of him, only to be killed at their hands once he has accepted and internalized the identity they have imposed on him.

After the successes of *The Firebugs* and *Andorra*, Frisch wrote two plays that found less favor, perhaps because they are too cerebral. *Biography: A Game* (*Biografie: Ein Spiel*, 1966–1967) anticipates postmodernist techniques of metacommentary about its own situation in a genre. Kürmann, a behavioral scientist, is given the opportunity to revise his identity by playing through several different versions of his life. The aim is not to let him select a self but to show the contingency and variability of personal identity. As Frisch (1976) said: "The biography of Mr. Kürmann, which is banal, is not the theme of the piece, but rather his relationship to the fact that over the course of time one inevitably gets a biography." The play inevitably invites comparison to LUIGI PIRANDELLO's classic SIX CHARACTERS IN SEARCH OF AN AUTHOR.

Frisch's next work, *Triptych: Three Scenic Panels* (*Triptychon*, 1978), consists of three loosely connected "panels" in which the question of identity is explored from the perspective of those whose options for establishing a new self have run out, namely, the dead. The first panel takes place after a funeral, where the dead man exists through others' memories, over which he has no control. The second consists of a conversation among some dead characters, who now have all the time necessary for reinventing themselves but lack the opportunity. In the last panel a lover tries to imagine an alternative outcome to the affair with his dead mistress but ends up replaying their final conversation; nothing changes.

Frisch's final dramatic project was again political and controversial. It developed out of the debates about whether or not Switzerland should end conscription. Frisch's contribution, *Switzerland Without an Army? Small Talk* (*Schweiz ohne Armee? Ein Palaver*, 1989) was written as a dialogue, then performed in Zurich and Lausanne as *Jonas and His Veteran* (*Jonas und sein Veteran*), arousing predictable outrage.

In contrast to his willingness to be daring and provocative with his ideas, Frisch was fairly conservative when it came to language and staging. However, this did not weaken the impact of his plays. If anything, the straightforward representations of bizarre situations served to heighten the sense that the world is fundamentally absurd. The realm of the dead in *Triptych* is a disarmingly idyllic setting. The matter-of-factness with which the Andorrans report their prejudices hints at an insanity lurking just below the surface.

One aspect of Frisch's work that should not be overlooked is its humor. While dark, it is often hilarious, as the following examples suggest. Don Juan would have eloped except that the candidate turns out to be his intended bride. Mr. Biedermann gives the arsonists matches because, he reasons, true arsonists would surely bring their own. Janos in the underworld hopes that "[t]he coming revolution will make us immortal, even if we don't live to see it."

SELECT PLAYS: *Now They're Singing Again* (*Nun singen sie wieder: Versuch eines Requiems*, 1945); *The Great Wall of China* (*Die Chinesische Mauer: Eine Farce*, 1946; rev. 1972); *Santa Cruz* (1946); *When the War Was Over* (*Als der Krieg zu Ende war*, 1949); *Count Oderland: A Street Ballad in Twelve Scenes* (*Graf Öderland: Eine Moritat in zwölf Bildern*, 1949–1951; rev. 1961); *Don Juan; or, The Love of Geometry* (*Don Juan oder die Liebe zur Geometrie: Komödie in fünf Akten*, 1952–1953; rev. 1961); *A Lance for Freedom* (*Eine Lanze für die Freiheit*, (1955); *Andorra* (1957, 1961); *The Firebugs: A Learning-Play Without a Lesson* (*Biedermann und die Brandstifter: Ein Lehrstück ohne Lehre*, 1958); *The Great Rage of Philip Hotz* (*Die große Wut des Philipp Hotz*, 1958); *Biography: A Game* (*Biografie: Ein Spiel*, 1966–1967); *Triptych: Three Scenic Panels* (*Triptychon*, 1978; rev. 1981); *Jonas and His Veteran* (*Jonas und sein Veteran*, 1989)

FURTHER READING

Butler, Michael. "Reflections of Mortality: Max Frisch's *Triptychon: Drei szenische Bilder*." In *Transformations in Modern European Drama*, ed. by Ian Donaldson. Atlantic Highlands, N.J.: Humanities Press, 1983. 147–161.

Frisch, Max. *Gesammelte Werke in zeitlicher Folge, Band V. 2 1964–1967.* Ed. by Hans Mayer with Walter Schnitz. Frankfurt: Suhrkamp, 1976.

Hoak, Mary Lucille. "French Influences on the Dramas of Bertolt Brecht, Max Frisch, and Heiner Mueller (Switzerland, Germany)." Ph.D. diss., Univ. of Tennessee, 1999.

Kieser, Rolf. "Taking on Aristotle and Brecht: Max Frisch and His Dramaturgy of Permutation." In *Theatrum mundi: Essays on German Drama and German Literature. Dedicated to Harald Lenz on His 70th*

Birthday, ed. by Edward R. Haymes. Munich: W. Fink, 1980. 185–197.

Pickar, Gertrud Bauer. *The Dramatic Works of Max Frisch*. Bern: Lang, 1977.

Probst, Gerhard F., and Jay F. Bodine, eds. *Perspectives on Max Frisch*. Lexington: Univ. of Kentucky Press, 1982.

Ruppert, Peter. "Brecht and Frisch: Two Theaters of Possibility." *Mosaic: A Journal for the Interdisciplinary Study of Literature* 15, no. 3 (1982): 109–120.

Arnd Bohm

FRÖKEN JULIE See MISS JULIE

FROM MORNING TO MIDNIGHT

One of GEORG KAISER's most acclaimed and influential plays, *From Morning to Midnight* (*Von Morgens bis Mitternachts*, written 1912, published 1916 premiered in Munich 1917) has been widely regarded as representative of German EXPRESSIONISM. With its symbolic imagery, character types rather than individuals, and its pathos-laden, fragmented language, the play broke with the tradition of REALISM onstage. Its "hero," a nameless cashier, escapes from his robotlike, monotonous existence to embark on a quest for meaning in a dehumanized world. Critics saw in the play's episodic structure and rapid tempo a link to the cinema; an expressionist film based on the play was produced in 1920.

A small-town bank employee awakens from his machinelike routine when an exotic Italian woman enters the bank to withdraw money. Believing her to be an impostor, the cashier embezzles the sum she requests and hopes to flee with her to a new life. When he discovers his mistake, he seeks to escape the law in the anonymity of a big city where he uses the stolen money to experience intense, passionate living. His torturous search for meaning is presented in the form of a modern mystery drama, patterned after AUGUST STRINDBERG's TO DAMASCUS (1898). At the beginning of the cashier's journey, Death appears to him in the shape of a skeletal tree in a snowfield, but the protagonist brazenly takes up the challenge and tells Death to return at midnight. In the space of a single day, the protagonist races through the modern metropolis, but at each station (a bicycle race, a dance hall), he is disappointed. At his final stop, the Salvation Army, where he seeks faith, love, and expiation of guilt, he discovers only greed. The cashier realizes too late that he has served Mammon, a false god. Betrayed to the police by his supposed beloved, he commits suicide, falling against a cross in the background, with the final words "Ecce homo" on his lips.

Translated into English in 1920, *From Morning to Midnight* was successfully produced in New York in 1922. American commentators acknowledged the significance of the "new method" that Kaiser brought to the theater. For reviewer Gilbert Seldes, the play was "a way of revelation for the cluttered and floundering theater of our time" (*The Dial*, 1922), while another wrote that "its savagery seemed at times to bewilder the audience" (Crawford, 1922). Interpretations of the play have shifted from socioethical readings to more recent views of the play as social satire.

[*See also* Germany]

FURTHER READING

Chick, Edson M. "Civilization's Discontents: Kaiser, Brecht, Dürrenmatt, and the Satiric Tradition." In *Dances of Death: Wedekind, Brecht, Dürrenmatt, and the Satiric Tradition*. Columbia, S.C.: Camden House, 1984. 81–124.

Crawford, J. "Expressionism on Broadway." *Drama* 12 (September, 1992): 342.

Eben, Michael. "Georg Kaiser's *Von Morgens bis Mitternachts* and Eugene O'Neill's *Emperor Jones*: Affinities in Flight." In *Georg Kaiser Symposium*, ed. by Holger A. Pausch and Ernest Reinhold. Berlin: Agora, 1980. 263–276.

Sheppard, Richard William. "Unholy Families: The Oedipal Psychopathology of Four Expressionist 'Ich-Dramen.' " *Orbis Litterarum* 41, no. 4 (1986): 355–383.

Willeke, Audrone B. *Georg Kaiser and the Critics: A Profile of Expressionism's Leading Playwright*. Columbia, S.C.: Camden House, 1995.

Audrone B. Willeke

THE FRONT PAGE

Critic Brooks Atkinson wrote of *The Front Page* by Ben Hecht and Charles MacArthur in 1941 that it "is to journalism what *What Price Glory?* is to the marines—rudely realistic in style but romantic in its loyalties, and also audaciously profane" (Atkinson, 1941). Certainly no journalism COMEDY, before or since, managed to capture the American imagination with as much aplomb and success as this raucous, dark, fever-pitched FARCE, the most celebrated work in Hecht and MacArthur's long-lived collaboration, which also produced *Ladies and Gentlemen* and *The Twentieth Century*.

Set in the smoky pressroom of the Chicago City Courthouse, the play follows the attempt of hotshot reporter Hildy Johnson to quit journalism once and for all, while his editor, the charming and ruthless Walter Burns, does everything in his considerable power to keep his star reporter on the job. To make matters worse, a convicted murderer (and accused communist) has escaped the incompetent and graft-ridden city officials and seeks asylum with the beleaguered Hildy, who knows a headline story when one crawls right into his rolltop desk.

Premiering at the Times Square Theatre under the direction of GEORGE S. KAUFMAN in 1928, this play was one of four smash hits brought to Broadway by producer Jed Harris and reflected an exuberant explosion of American theater. The 1927–1928 Broadway season was the largest in history with 280 productions, partially the result of the growing centralization (and commercialization) of Manhattan theaters and of a growing candor among American playwrights. Bitter battles over censorship had been fought and won by theaters in the late 1910s and early 1920s, leaving writers free to express an emergent cynicism in American culture. John Gassner wrote that the theater of the 1920s "nourished itself on all the absurdities of the age: yellow journalism, publicity-fanned murder trials, racketeering, prize fighting, prohibition-dodging, and bootlegging" (Gassner, 1949), almost all of which appear in *The Front Page*. This turbulent history gave rise to the development of a uniquely American style of unsentimental, hard-boiled, wisecracking farce, realistic, skeptical, irreverent, and robust; *The Front Page* is certainly one of the most spectacular plays of this tradition.

Written for the commercial theater, *The Front Page* nevertheless has exhibited a remarkable posterity. Many critics and playgoers of 1928 were offended by the play's frankness of language and openness about sexuality; modern readers might also have difficulty with its unapologetically sexist and racist dialogue. Nevertheless, the play has inspired a great number of adaptations and spin-offs on both stage and screen, notably Howard Hawks's 1940 film *His Girl Friday*, starring Cary Grant as Burns and Rosalind Russell as a female Hildy, who adds a sizzle of sexual SUBTEXT. Of the play's relative importance to American theater history, critic Irving Wardle wrote in 1972 that *The Front Page* is "surely as fine a comedy as [America] has ever produced," and playwright TOM STOPPARD said of the play that "it's the 'only' American comedy of the 1920s in the way that *The Importance of Being Earnest* is the 'only' English comedy of the 1890s" (both quoted in Hecht, 2002).

FURTHER READING

Atkinson, Brooks. Introduction to *Sixteen Famous American Plays*. Ed. by Bennett A. Cerf and Van H. Cartmell. New York: Garden City Pubs., 1941.

Gassner, John, ed. *Twenty-five Best Plays of the Modern American Theatre*. New York: Crown, 1949.

Hecht, Ben. *Charlie: The Improbable Life and Times of Charles MacArthur*. New York: Harper, 1957.

——. *The Front Page: From Theater to Reality*. Ed. by George W. Hilton. New York: Smith & Kraus, 2002.

MacAdams, William. *Ben Hecht: The Man Behind the Legend*. New York: Scribner's, 1990.

MacArthur, Charles. *The Stage Works of Charles MacArthur*. Ed. by Arthur Dorlag and John Irvine. Tallahassee: Florida State Univ. Foundation, 1974.

Michael M. Chemers

FRUEN FRA HAVET See THE LADY FROM THE SEA

FRÜHLINGS ERWACHEN. EINE KINDERTRAGÖDIE See SPRING AWAKENING

FRY, CHRISTOPHER (1907–2005)

British-born playwright and poet Christopher Fry wrote verse TRAGICOMEDIES and romances primarily with religious or historical themes that begin darkly and progress toward a more or less happy conclusion. His works, exemplified by his greatest success THE LADY'S NOT FOR BURNING (1948), show the poetic influence of William Shakespeare and T. S. ELIOT. Fry's plays also sparkle with the brilliant wit, wordplay, and hyperbole of the COMEDIES of the Restoration, OSCAR WILDE, and GEORGE BERNARD SHAW and express the playwright's great fascination for the natural world.

Fry was born Christopher Fry Harris on December 18, 1907, in Bristol, ENGLAND. His father, an Anglican missionary, destroyed his health with overwork and died when Fry was three. His mother (whose mother's surname was Fry) and aunt, both devoutly religious, raised Fry and a younger brother in the city of Bedford and exposed him from an early age to mythology, Shakespeare, the Bible, and John Bunyan's *The Pilgrim's Progress*. Intimacy with his mother's family compelled him to change his name to Fry. Fry was first a schoolteacher but soon rejected that profession to become an actor with repertory companies. He composed for music hall revues, and directed, before devoting himself to playwriting.

Fry's first published play, *The Boy with a Cart* (1938), a religious verse drama based on the legend of St. Cuthman and the "sorrows" that culminate in his building of a church, was part of the 1930s revival of English poetic drama. This revival began in 1928 at the first theater festival in Canterbury Cathedral with John Masefield's religious verse drama *The Coming of Christ*. Eliot's MURDER IN THE CATHEDRAL fueled the verse-drama movement with its reception at the Canterbury Festival in 1935 and greatly influenced *The Boy with a Cart* in character presentation. Eliot's subsequent call for the secular English theater to reclaim its first language, poetry (rejected in the Restoration and forgotten by the eras of theatrical REALISM and NATURALISM), spurred the verse-drama renaissance and its most notable playwrights: W. H. AUDEN, CHRISTOPHER ISHERWOOD, Eliot, and Fry.

Fry's blank verse *The Lady's Not for Burning* starred John Gielgud, Pamela Brown (for whom Fry wrote the play), and Richard Burton and won the playwright international acclaim. *Venus Observed* (1949), about an aging duke seeking a second wife in order to forget the first, starred Laurence Olivier. The Australian Episcopal hierarchy condemned *A Sleep of Prisoners* (1951), Fry's finest religious play about prisoners confined to a church. By 1955, however, the verse-drama movement began to wane in popularity, and although he continued writing plays, including his take on Thomas à Becket in *Curtmantle* (1961), Fry never matched his earlier success.

In addition to writing original works, Fry also translated plays by JEAN ANOUILH and JEAN GIRAUDOUX and collaborated on screenplays, most notably *Ben-Hur* (1951). Fry died on June 30, 2005, in Chichester, England.

PLAYS: *She Shall have Music* (with Monte Crick and F. Eyton, 1934); *Open Door* (1936); *The Boy with a Cart* (1938); *Robert of Sicily: Opera for Children* (libretto, 1939); *Seven at a Stroke: A Play for Children* (libretto, 1939); *Thursday's Child: A Pageant* (1939); *The Tower* (1939); *A Phoenix Too Frequent* (1946); *The Firstborn* (1948); *The Lady's Not for Burning* (1948); *Thor, with Angels* (1948); *Venus Observed* (1949); *A Sleep of Prisoners* (1951); *The Dark Is Light Enough: A Winter Comedy* (1954); *Curtmantle* (1961); *A Yard of Sun: A Summer Comedy* (1970); *One Thing More, or Caedmon Construed* (1986)

FURTHER READING

Fry, Christopher. *Can You Find Me: A Family History*. Oxford: Oxford Univ. Press, 1978.

Leeming, Glenda. *Christopher Fry*. Boston: Twayne, 1990.

Roy, Emil. *Christopher Fry*. Carbondale: Southern Illinois Univ. Press, 1968.

W. Douglas Powers

FUGARD, ATHOL (1932–)

The basic device has been that of Challenge and Response. As writer-director I have challenged, and the actors have responded, not intellectually or merely verbally but with a totality of Being that at the risk of sounding pretentious I can only liken to a form of Zen spontaneity.

—Athol Fugard, "Introduction to Statements," *Modern African Drama*, 2004

Born Harold Athol Lanigan Fugard on June 11, 1932, to an Afrikaner mother and a father of Liverpool-Irish ancestry in the small village of Middelburg in SOUTH AFRICA's Cape Province, Fugard has distinguished himself as one of AFRICA's prominent writers of all times. Like his contemporaries—WOLE SOYINKA and NGUGI WA THIONG'O—Fugard's works combine the practices of playwriting and directing with long-standing theories of performances and their sociopolitical efficacies in Africa's complex histories. Dominated by existentialist themes, his plays generally explore issues of social and political ALIENATION and the determined struggle of human beings to achieve full and effective citizenship in the historically determined social and political contexts they find themselves. Combining acting with directing and writing, Fugard's contribution to modern African drama lies not only in the highly inventive dramatic structures of his plays, and in his brilliance in understating the existential despair of living in a dangerously hierarchical society like apartheid South Africa, but also in developing a unique process of creating plays with actors through what he calls "Challenge and Response."

Fugard was informally trained in theater through several amateur and later professional productions in an atmosphere where the making of theater was as arduous as it was a politically dangerous cultural practice. He produced, wrote, performed, and directed at university but dropped out shortly before graduation. The issue of the race and classes of his audiences provided a basis for exploring themes of social and cultural segregation in South Africa. Fugard not only wrote for mostly integrated audiences; he even endangered himself by performing with black actors on the same stage despite restrictive laws.

Fugard's plays seek certain senses of "truthfulness" with which individuals in their social contexts understand and contest their realities without necessarily performing with the certainties of ideological partisanship. Fugard has acknowledged his obsession with the Orestes story and how he literally used it as a palimpsest to explore core existential issues in his numerous plays set in South Africa. His plays engage their social contexts by raising questions not only about marginalization but also about how others are conscripted into witnessing and living with extreme dehumanization. Having lived in a country in which D. F. Malan, the first Afrikaner prime minister and a major facilitator of the separate and unequal development called "apartheid" declared, "The difference in colour is merely the physical manifestation of the contrast between two irreconcilable ways of life, between barbarism and civilization, between heathenism and Christianity" (Kuper, 1957), it is hardly surprising that the efficacies of his plays are mostly judged against such a backdrop. The political, economic, and cultural manifestations of apartheid were enshrined in several draconian laws and statutes Fugard critically examined in many of his plays. He wrote most of his plays during an epoch when play scripts had to be submitted to township authorities to safeguard against treason; when permissions for performances were rarely given; and when the gathering of any crowd, particularly a racially integrated one, was a source of state anxiety.

The textual settings of his plays are sparse and highly minimalist. The casts are usually small (with the exception of *No-Good Friday*, which has eleven characters) and mobile: his characters are visually stark but deeply complex in their thoughts and actions, and the plays generally use multiple and overlapping narrative structures to tell their stories. While the subjects of his plays work out the basis of their individual identities as well as developing nonrestrictive social relationships, it is how Fugard has extended such a thematic preoccupation to the making of theater that has attracted more critical attention.

His collaborative work began to be more formalized when he and his wife Sheila, also a writer, formed the Circle Players in Port Elizabeth. Apart from working with such eminent actors as Zakes Mokae, encounters with the Serpent Players from New Brighton, which began in 1966 and eventually blossomed in the making of SIZWE BANSI IS DEAD and *The Island* in 1972, gave Fugard the opportunity to further extend his Orestes literary thesis and minimalist acting formulas akin to that of late Polish director Jerzy Grotowski.

[*See also The Blood Knot; "Master Harold" . . . and the boys*]

PLAYS: *Klass and the Devil* (1956); *The Cell* (1957); *No-Good Friday* (1958); *Nongogo* (1959); *The Blood Knot* (1961); *Hello and Goodbye* (1965); *The Coat* (1966); *People Are Living There* (1968); *Boseman and Lena* (1969); *Orestes* (1971); *Sizwe Bansi Is Dead* (co-authored with John Kani and Winston Ntshona, 1972); *Statements After an Arrest Under the Immorality Act* (1972); *The Island* (co-authored with John Kani and Winston Ntshona, 1973); *Master Harold . . . and the Boys* (1982); *The Road to Mecca* (1984); *My Children, My Africa!* (1989); *Playland* (1992)

FURTHER READING

Kuper, Leo. *Passive Resistance in South Africa*. New Haven: Yale Univ. Press, 1957.

Orkin, Martin. *Drama and the South African State*. Manchester: Manchester Univ. Press, 1991.

Vandenbroucke, Russell. *Truths the Hand Can Touch: The Theatre of Athol Fugard*. New York: Theatre Communications Group, 1985.

Walder, Dennis. *Athol Fugard*. London: Macmillan, 1984.

Awam Amkpa

FUGLEELSKERNE *See* THE BIRD LOVERS

FUKUDA TSUNEARI (1912–1994)

Japanese critic, SHINGEKI playwright, translator, and director Fukuda Tsuneari was a seminal figure in the cultural politics of postwar JAPAN. He was one of a number of Tokyo-born conservative intellectuals who challenged Marxism in their search for spiritual values with which to fill the vacuum created by Japan's defeat in 1945. At the elite Imperial University of Tokyo in the 1930s, Fukuda wrote his graduating dissertation on the ethics of D. H. LAWRENCE and later translated the novelist. Like Lawrence, Fukuda railed against the egoism of modern society, was skeptical about Christianity, and insisted on the need to separate literature from politics.

In 1950, Fukuda enjoyed his first theatrical success with *Typhoon Kitty* (*Kiti Taifū*), which satirizes the intellectual life of the day. His 1952 drama *The Man Who Stroked the Dragon* (*Ryū wo Nadeta Otoko*) is influenced stylistically by T. S. ELIOT's *The Cocktail Party* (1949), and his 1956 play *Light and Dark* (*Meian*) is a poetic drama that explores the problem of accent in Japanese speech. This interest in language was probably at the expense of a sense of time or place. Fukuda was always conscious of his country's past and was involved in various initiatives to protect native traditions. In 1946, he unsuccessfully opposed reform of the Japanese writing system.

Fukuda was also the leading Shakespearean of his generation. In 1953, Fukuda saw a production of *Hamlet* at the Old Vic in London, starring Richard Burton and directed by Michael Benthall, and determined to re-create the experience in his own translation. His 1955 *Hamlet* set the agenda for William Shakespeare production through to the 1970s, and his translation is still praised as both lyrical and vivacious. Fukuda eventually translated some nineteen of the plays, ever despairing at the difficulties of finding rhetorical equivalents for Shakespeare's language. He had a holistic view of drama and language, writing that "however remarkable the character of human beings and however intense their individuality, they are still just components (*bubun*) [in the wider scheme of things]" (Fukuda, 1981).

Fukuda could be authoritarian as a director, but he worked with three of the most influential *shingeki* companies of postwar Japan: the Literary Theatre (Bungakuza), Cloud (Kumo), and Pleiades (Subaru); he helped found the last two. In 1963, he founded the Contemporary Japanese Playwrights Association, and in 1964 he invited Benthall to direct a production of *Romeo and Juliet* for Kumo. Fukuda received the prestigious Yomiuri Literary Prize in 1960 and 1967.

SELECT PLAYS: *The Last Trump* (*Saigo no Kirifuda*, 1948); *King of the Castle* (*Kenrui Dasshu*, 1950); *Typhoon Kitty* (*Kiti Taifū*, 1950); *The Man Who Stroked the Dragon* (*Ryū wo Nadeta Otoko*, 1952); *A Modern Hero* (*Gendai no Eiyū*, 1952); *On the Cliff* (*Gake no Ue*, 1955); *Light and Dark* (*Meian*, 1956); *Akechi Mitsuhide* (1957)

FURTHER READING

Fukuda Tsuneari. *Watashi no Engeki Kyōshitsu* [Lessons in drama]. Tokyo: Shinchōsha, 1961.

——. *Engeki Nyūmon* [Introduction to drama]. Machida: Tamagawa Univ. Press, 1981.

Kawachi Yoshiko. "The Stage Translation of Shakespeare in Japan." In *Shakespeare and Cultural Exchange*. Tokyo: Seibidō, 1995.

Keene, Donald. *Dawn to the West—A History of Japanese Literature*. Vol. 4, *Poetry, Drama, Criticism*. New York: Henry Holt, 1984.

Ortolani, Benito. "Fukuda Tsuneari: Modernization and Shingeki." In *Tradition and Modernization in Japanese Culture*, ed. by Donald Shively. Princeton, N.J.: Princeton Univ. Press, 1971.

Daniel Gallimore

FUKUDA YOSHIYUKI (1931–)

Fukuda Yoshiyuki is a Japanese SHINGEKI playwright (stage, radio, and television) and director. Fukuda's early work was as production assistant to one of the most famous *shingeki* directors, Okakura Shirō. *Shingeki* had always been anticommercial, but in the 1950s Okakura and Fukuda collaborated in commercial theater work, and this is said to have contributed to the rich visual and musical elements in Fukuda's *shingeki* plays. The common thread running through Fukuda's best-known plays is his reworking of stories from the past to give them contemporary political relevance.

Fukuda's writing for *shingeki* followed a similar trajectory to that of KINOSHITA JUNJI, by whom he was influenced. His first play, like Kinoshita's, was rigorously realist in method, and having had severe doubts about it, he was more experimental thereafter. *Long Lines of Grave Markers* (*Nagai Bohyo no Retsu*, 1957) narrated the heroic stand of a Tokyo University professor against the military authorities in 1938. In 1960 Fukuda joined many other *shingeki* people in the mass demonstrations against the renewal of the JAPAN-U.S. Mutual Security Treaty, and out of this came an experiment in cooperative theatrical creativity (involving a variety of elements such as individual narratives of personal experience, free discussion, *sprechtchor*), which proved to Fukuda that intense political experience could be translated to the stage (*Record No. 1* [*Kiroku Nanba-1*, 1960]). From this time on Fukuda confronted in his plays the political issue with which he was preoccupied—how to dislodge the Japan Communist Party from the leadership of the Left.

Fukuda's energy in creating total theater out of *shingeki* led him to a metatheater experiment, *Oppekepe-* (1964), in which he dramatized the start of the SHINPA (a variety of theater that appeared in Japan during the Meiji era) movement. *Oppekepe-* was an immensely popular satirical song performed by KAWAKAMI OTOJIRŌ in 1891 in the wake of the small-scale oppositional drama that was the origin of *shinpa*. Kawakami played patriotic theater at the time of the Sino-Japanese War (1894–1895), and Fukuda, in his play, gives him an opponent who is antiwar. This main theme is supplemented by so many subthemes that *Oppekepe-* gave the impression of being somewhat undisciplined.

Fukuda's most famous play, *Where's Hakamadare?* (*Hakamadare wa Doko da?* 1964), is also multifaceted, but it is a more controlled work, and its varied but carefully crafted DRAMATURGY presages much of the antirealist, anti-*shingeki* theater of the later 1960s. Hakamadare was a medieval Robin Hood/savior figure and is portrayed here as the only hope of some impoverished and downtrodden peasants. Driven to desperation by the general retribution that will follow a violent act of protest against authority by one of their number, they leave their village and go in search of Hakamadare. By proclaiming themselves to be a Hakamadare band and robbing the rich to give to the poor, as he would have done, they hope to force him to declare himself. Eventually someone does and then demands their obedience and allegiance. His vision for the new world they have been seeking, however, involves a superstructure of high-flown ideals and a secret infrastructure of terror. The villagers kill him and resume their search.

SELECT PLAYS: *Long Lines of Grave Markers* (*Nagai Bohyo no Retsu*, 1957); *Record Number 1* (*Kiroku Nanba-1*, 1960); *Oppekepe-* (*Oppekepe-*, 1964); *Where's Hakamadare?* (*Hakamadare wa Doko da?* 1964)

FURTHER READING

Fukuda Yoshiyuki. *Dorama no Mukō no Sora* [Drama beyond the sky]. Tokyo: Yomiuri Shinbun, 1995.

Goodman, David G. *Japanese Drama and Culture in the 1960s: The Return of the Gods*. Armonk, N.Y.: M. E. Sharpe, 1988.

Ōyama Isao. *KindaiNihon Gikyoku-shi* [History of modern Japanese drama]. Vol. 4. Yamagata: Kindal Nihon Gikyoku-shi Kankōkai, 1972.

Brian Powell

FURCHT UND ELEND DES DRITTEN REICHES *See* FEAR AND MISERY IN THE THIRD REICH

FURCHT UND ELEND DES III *See* FEAR AND MISERY IN THE THIRD REICH

FURUHASHI TEIJI (1960–1995)

Furuhashi Teiji was a Japanese playwright and director and founder of the Kyoto-based company "dumb type" in 1984 with fellow graduates of Kyoto Prefectural College of Arts. The group worked as a collective to pursue a radically new stage vocabulary. Although Furuhashi was heir to the first three post-1960s generations of playwrights, his work is startlingly different both from theirs and from that of his fourth-generation contemporaries. Still, his minimalism, self-conscious theatricality, and use of silence are somewhat reminiscent of BETSUYAKU MINORU, TERAYAMA SHŪJI, and OTA SHŌGO, respectively. When Furuhashi died of AIDS in 1995, JAPAN lost perhaps its most creative theater auteur since Terayama died in 1983.

The first major production of dumb type, *PLEASURE LIFE* (1988), a performance-art installation, put the context of daily life onstage in the form of a square matrix rigged with a variety of sensors. The performers enacted quotidian rhythms by an endless process of repetition and aberration, repeatedly scurrying through the matrix, deviating unexpectedly when fatigue forced lapses in concentration. In its enactment of the boredom of leisure as controlled by a wired world, it eerily anticipated the thematic direction of Japanese plays in the 1990s.

Furuhashi and his collaborators built on that approach in *S/N*—"S" meaning signal and "N" noise—completed in 1994. The work explores the public perception of homosexuality and AIDS in a self-conscious, metatheatrical style. It begins with an "abnormal" person—a minority—dancing the tango. What is normal? Furuhashi applies this question to human prejudices. A wall doubling as a projection screen divides order (Sound) from chaos (Noise). A performer atop the wall is unable to see his image on the screen and therefore, like a body casting no shadow, is at pains to ascertain his presence. The screen continuously projects naked bodies, close-ups of the other performers, and AIDS-related quotes from assorted media and social thinkers. Performers in front of the screen are branded homosexual or

HIV-positive. At some point, they shed their clothes, climb the wall, and leap off the other side. Just as the performer above the screen has lost the sense of self as connected to others, the gay victims of AIDS teeter toward the chaos of extinction, near at hand, and away from the order of love and life, just out of reach.

Amid this volatile emotional backdrop, Furuhashi himself speaks about his sex life and how he contracted AIDS, but truth and fiction blur. The spectators are left to teeter on their own metaphorical S/N wall: is this a "true confession" or a contrived "play"? In this sense the performance turns self-consciously inward, stimulating questions about what theater is, how it is made, and what it means to watch it. Certainly, S/N could never be performed the same way twice. Reversing convention, Furuhashi regards the text as merely traces of the performance rather than the performance arising from the text.

S/N had a highly praised international debut at the Adelaide Theatre Festival in 1994 and in Japan was recognized by the Yomiuri Theatre Grand Prize.

[*See also* Gay and Lesbian Drama]

SELECT PLAYS: PLEASURE LIFE (1988); p/H (1990); S/N (1994)

FURTHER READING

dumb type. *Memorandamu Furuhashi Teiji* [Furuhashi Teiji remembered]. Kyoto: Ritorumoa, 2000.

Furuhashi, Teiji. *S/N*. Tr. by dumb type. In *Half a Century of Japanese Theater II: 1990s Part 2*, ed. by Japan Playwrights Association. Tokyo: Kinokuniya, 2000.

John K. Gillespie

FUTURISM

Futurism, a 20th-century art movement, confined itself largely to Italy and Russia, although adherents were found in other countries.

ITALIAN

> *We want to free this land from its smelly gangrene of professors, archaeologists, ciceroni, and antiquarians. For too long has Italy been a dealer in second-hand clothes.*
>
> —Filippo Tommaso Marinetti, "Founding and Manifesto of Futurism," 1909

Italian futurism, at the forefront of the call for radical artistic and societal change, was ultramodernist when modernism was just beginning. FILIPPO TOMMASO MARINETTI, "the caffeine of Europe," launched the explosive "Founding and Manifesto of Futurism" on the front page of *Le Figaro* in 1909. Futurists built on the energy of newly unified (1861) ITALY to reinvent art and culture in every field, including theater, visual art, music, poetry, architecture, declamation, and film. Their central concerns—speed, innovation, conflict, aggression, machines, and nationalism—reflected their desire for Italians, "faithful slaves" of a glorious cultural history, to join the modern world.

Inspired by technological inventions such as the telegraph, telephone, train, bicycle, automobile, airplane, and cinema, as well as cultural developments in PSYCHOANALYSIS, anarchism, cubism, symbolist synesthesia, and the Nietzschean idea of the superman, futurists embarked on a wholesale rejuvenation of Italian art and culture. Masters of the incendiary polemic, they wrote over fifty manifestos between 1909 and 1916. In addition, futurists employed performance as a form of "cultural combat" that would lead artists "to participate, like the workers or soldiers, in the battle for world progress." Theatrical innovations encompassed costume, set, and light design; playwriting; acting; music and sound; as well as new "tactilist" and olfactory elements and Fedele Azari's aerial theater, which used planes as actors.

Futurist theater began with Marinetti's dramatic tribute to ALFRED JARRY, *King Revel* (*Le Roi Bombance*), performed at the Théâtre de l'Oeuvre in 1909. That same year saw the first *serate*, evenings featuring declamations of manifestos, exhibitions of paintings, recitations of poetry, and music by Luigi Russolo's noise instruments (*intonarumori*). The "Variety Theater," launched in 1913, drew on these riotous and often violent evenings by insisting that the audience not "remain static like a stupid *voyeur*, but join noisily in the action" (Kirby, 1971). Inspired by the "strong and healthy danger" found in music halls, cabarets, and circuses, the Variety Theater concentrated on pure spectacle by eliminating plots, characters, and logical connections between acts and introducing acrobatic feats, parodies of classics, and "all the new significations of light, sound, noise, and language" (Kirby, 1971).

Futurist theater sought "incessantly to invent new elements of astonishment" (Kirby, 1971). It pitted itself against conventional "*passéist*" theater that "exalts the inner life, professorial meditation, libraries, museums, monotonous crises of conscience, stupid analyses of feelings" (Kirby, 1971) and supplanted psychology with *fisicofollia* (body-madness). The Synthetic Theater, launched in 1915, focused on simultaneity, brevity, and speed. It abolished standardized technique and worries about verisimilitude by creating autonomous, alogical, dynamic works. Through this theater, the futurists developed the *sintesi*, sketches "synthesizing facts and ideas in the smallest number of words and gestures" (Kirby, 1971). Francesco Cangiullo's emblematic *Detonation: Synthesis of Modern Theater* (1915) consisted of a minute of silence and one gunshot. Others concretely represented abstract states, such as Fortunato Depero's *Colors* (1916), which used colored, mobile shapes as characters and onomatopoeic sounds as dialogue.

Futurists fused scenic, lighting, and costume design with performers, replacing organic figures and painted backdrops with "electro-mechanic architecture" and creating entire pieces in which automated constructions operated in conjunction with lights, noise, and smells. For Igor Stravinsky's *Fireworks* (produced by the Ballets Russes in 1917), Giacomo Balla designed illuminated groups of mechanical shapes, whose asymmetrical colors and shadows dynamically translated the music into concrete spatial language. Costume designs, such as those by Enrico Prampolini and Fortunato Depero, enveloped human actors in pliable polyhedral steel and cardboard costumes that propelled the performer and the costume into new harmonies of movement.

Other futurist innovations included what are probably the first AVANT-GARDE films, including *Vita Futurista* (1916) and Marinetti's "Words-in-Freedom," a poetic innovation replacing syntax and traditional grammatical conventions with original typefaces, arrangements, and dynamic rhythms. Futurism stimulated an enormous array of artists, including Umberto Boccioni, Gino Severini, and Carlo Carrà in painting and sculpture; Russolo in music; Antonio Sant'Elia in architecture; and Carlo Bragaglia in photo and cinema. It also fostered the creation of new forms, such as Balla and Depero's "plastic complexes," dynamic, four-dimensional, abstract mechanical objects.

Most theatrical developments in the European avant-garde find a precedent in Italian futurism. The futurists influenced later movements such as DADAISM, SURREALISM, and Fluxus in their use of the manifesto to generate publicity and polemics. Russian futurism, Italy's Grotesque Theater, and the Theater of the Absurd would have been unthinkable without these "antineutralist," forward-looking, "innovators and intellectual snipers of the world" (Kirby, 1971) that revitalized Italian culture from 1909 to World War II.

[*See also* Guerrilla Theater; Happenings and Intermedia; Performance Art]

FURTHER READING

Apollonio, Umbro, ed. *Futurist Manifestos*. New York: Viking, 1973.

Berghaus, Günter. *Italian Futurist Theatre, 1909–1944*. New York: Oxford Univ. Press, 1998.

Humphreys, Richard. *Futurism*. New York: Cambridge Univ. Press, 1999.

Kirby, Michael, and Victoria Nes Kirby. *Futurist Performance*. New York: Dutton, 1971.

Marinetti, F. T. *Let's Murder the Moonshine: Selected Writings*. Tr. by R. W. Flint and Arthur A. Coppotelli. Los Angeles: Sun & Moon Press, 1991.

Taylor, Christiana J. *Futurism: Politics, Painting, and Performance*. Ann Arbor, Mich.: UMI Res. Press, 1979.

Tisdall, Caroline, and Angelo Bozzolla. *Futurism*. New York: Oxford Univ. Press, 1978.

Kimberly Jannarone

RUSSIAN

He who does not forget his first love will not recognize his last.
—"A Slap in the Face of Public Taste," 1912

In 1912, members of a group called Hylaea, who would later call themselves cubo-futurists, published a manifesto titled "A Slap in the Face of Public Taste," which outlined the basic tenets of Russian futurism. The treatise attacks Aleksandr Pushkin, Fyodor Dostoevsky, and LYOV TOLSTOY and ridicules the popular symbolists and realists as tied to the past. The authors of the treatise call for a rejection of tradition, common sense, and good taste in favor of the development of a new vocabulary to capture the spirit of modernity and urbanism. Signers of the treatise included David Burliuk, Alexander Kruchenykh, VLADIMIR MAYAKOVSKY, and Victor (Velimir) Khlebnikov, who were among the key poets, playwrights, and painters at the center of Russian futurism. The manifesto shocked public as well as literary and artistic communities and established the futurists' often contradictory program of antiaestheticism, buffoonery, infantilism, and dynamism that would soon extend into dramatic writing and theatrical staging. Mayakovsky became the prominent artist associated with futurism in Russian theater through his declarations against tradition and his work as a theorist, playwright, actor, and director.

Although several futurist dramas by Victor Khlebnikov and Elena Guro (Eleonora Genrikhovna von Notenberg) were published earlier, Russian futurism made its debut in the theater in December 1913 in the Luna Park Theatre in St. Petersburg. Advertised as "The First Futurist Productions in the World," the bill included Vladimir Mayakovsky's TRAGEDY *Vladimir Mayakovsky* and Alexander Kruchenykh and Mikhail Matyushin's opera *Victory Over the Sun*. The latter centers on the capture of the sun, representing rationalism and order, by a group of futurist strongmen, who help to free the world from conventional logic and traditional thought. The play is characterized by such futurist principles as the use of clever neologisms, illogical situations and language, and emphasis on endless progress and modernization. Significantly, the production was designed by Kasimir Malevich, who applied cubist principles to the costume designs and set designs.

Mayakovsky's drama centers on the misunderstood poet himself and his encounters with various abstract versions of himself during and after an apocalyptic overthrow of the traditional world. The play develops in a nonlinear, achronological manner, presents abstractions such as Man with One Eye and One Leg and Old Man with Scrawny Black Cats, and contains many illogical and absurd images and ideas. Mayakovsky not only wrote and directed the play, but he performed in the lead role. Pavel Filonov designed bright panels in a childlike manner for the prologue and epilogue, and Iosif Shkolnik created cubist cityscapes for the two acts. Except for Mayakovsky, the amateur actors represented their characters with cardboard cutouts, moving only in straight lines facing the audience.

The two productions, the only futurist productions before the Revolution, largely confounded the public, but they helped establish futurist principles for the theater, which included the use of highly stylized movement and speech patterns, antiprofessionalism and antiaestheticism, cubist design, buffoonery and absurdity in the text and staging, and dynamism as an organizing principle.

While they shared similar techniques, the Russian futurists proclaimed sovereignty from Italian Futurism. In fact, most of the Russian futurists maintained distance from F. T. MARINETTI when he visited St. Petersburg in 1914 to strengthen ties with the Russians. Though he admitted that there were formal similarities between the work of the Russians and Italians, Mayakovsky often stressed the distinction between the aims of the groups. He and his colleagues characterized the Italians as warmongers interested in destruction, while they viewed the Russian movement as constructive.

Though before the Revolution Russian futurism was identified with a small group of artists, it eventually influenced the practices of numerous Russian theater artists including VSEVOLOD MEYERHOLD, Sergei Eisenstein, and Nikolai Foregger. Meyerhold became associated with futurism in 1918, when he staged Mayakovsky's MYSTERY-BOUFFE, a satirical cycle drama, in celebration of the Bolshevik Revolution. Meyerhold incorporated elements of commedia dell'arte, circus clowning, acrobatics, and accelerated pace into the production of the play. This marked the first effort to apply futurist principles to the Bolshevik cause. Futurism soon exploded onto the theatrical scene in RUSSIA as artists like Meyerhold, Eisenstein, and Foregger sought to develop a mechanized theater that emphasized highly disciplined, rhythmic, and acrobatic movement. After the production of *Mystery-Bouffe*, the leading Russian futurist directors increasingly turned to classical plays for material, which marked the decline of futurism in Russian drama.

[*See also* Realism; Symbolism]

FURTHER READING

Braun, Edward. "Futurism in the Russian Theatre, 1913–1923." In *International Futurism in Arts and Literature*, ed. by Gunter Berhaus. Berlin: De Gruyter, 2000. 75–99.

Markov, Vladimir. *Russian Futurism: A History*. Berkeley: Univ. of California Press, 1968.

Mayakovsky, Vladimir. *The Complete Plays of Vladimir Mayakovsky*. Tr. by Guy Daniels. New York: Washington Square Press, 1968.

Proffer, Ellendea, and Carl R. Proffer. *The Ardis Anthology of Russian Futurism*. Ann Arbor: Ardis, 1980.

Rudnitsky, Konstantin. *Russian and Soviet Theatre: Tradition and the Avant-Garde*. Tr. by Roxane Permar. Ed. by Lesley Milne. London: Thames & Hudson, 1988.

Valleri Robinson Hohman

GABRE-MEDHIN, TSEGAYE See TSEGAYE GABRE-MEDHIN

GALDÓS, BENITO PÉREZ See PÉREZ GALDÓS, BENITO

GALE, ZONA (1874–1938)

Zona Gale was born on August 26, 1874, in Portage, Wisconsin. After graduating from the University of Wisconsin (from which she later received a Master of Literature degree), Gale began her professional writing career as a reporter. Over the course of her life, Gale published twenty-two volumes of fiction in addition to poetry and essays. Her seven plays, several adapted from her novels and short stories, form a small part of her literary canon.

Among Gale's early works were the popular "Friendship Village" stories, romanticized tales of a benevolent community. Most of her writings are set in the Midwest, and she is often grouped with regionalists like Sherwood Anderson and Sinclair Lewis. A committed social activist, Gale was a vocal supporter of women's suffrage and a drafter of the 1923 Wisconsin Equal Rights Law. Not surprisingly, her political views permeate her literary canon. Gale's best works are realistic novels and plays that strip off the facade of small-town geniality to show the petty tyrannies underneath.

MISS LULU BETT (1919) was a best-selling short novel before Gale turned it into a play of the same title. Drawing on her knowledge of women's limited options in rural America, Gale created in *Miss Lulu Bett* a satirical yet realistic portrayal of the plight of the "spinster." The play opened at the Belmont Theatre in New York on December 27, 1920, to generally positive reviews. Even after a controversial revision of the ending, *Miss Lulu Bett* went on to a long run and was awarded the Pulitzer Prize for Drama, making Zona Gale the first woman to win this award. Three years later Gale had less success with *Mister Pitt* (a dramatization of her 1918 novel *Birth*), the story of a hapless, socially inept condiment salesman. It received some critical support but was faulted for choppy construction and an inarticulate protagonist. *Mister Pitt* ran on Broadway for only six weeks.

Plays like *Uncle Jimmy* (1922), *The Clouds* (1932) and *Faint Perfume* (1934, adapted from her 1923 novel) were not professionally produced, although some proved popular with amateur groups. *The Clouds* is a brief COMEDY with an unbelievable plot but a clear message: the Cloud sisters are determined that their niece Lily will "have a life" away from the town they've come to despise. Similarly, *Faint Perfume* is one of Gale's most negative portrayals of how village life stifles gentle, creative spirits. These are all minor works, however, and Zona Gale's single lasting contribution to the American dramatic canon is *Miss Lulu Bett*. As several recent revivals testify, this surprisingly modern satire of small-town despotism remains a potent social critique as well as an engaging stage comedy.

[*See also* United States, 1860–1940]

PLAYS: *The Neighbors* (ca. 1914); *Miss Lulu Bett* (1920); *Uncle Jimmy* (1922); *Mister Pitt* (1924); *The Clouds* (1932); *Evening Clothes* (1932); *Faint Perfume* (1934)

FURTHER READING

Derleth, August. *Still Small Voice: The Biography of Zona Gale*. New York: Appleton-Century, 1940.

Londré, Felicia Hardison. "Zona Gale." In *Notable Women in the American Theatre*, ed. by Alice M. Robinson et al., 322–325. New York: Greenwood Press, 1989.

Schroeder, Patricia R. "Realism and Feminism in the Progressive Era." In *The Cambridge Companion to American Women Playwrights*, ed. by Brenda Murphy, 31–36. Cambridge: Cambridge Univ. Press, 1999.

Shafer, Yvonne. *American Women Playwrights, 1900–1950*. New York: Peter Lang, 1995.

Simonson, Harold P. *Zona Gale*. New York: Twayne, 1962.

Williams, Deborah Lindsay. *Not in Sisterhood: Edith Wharton, Willa Cather, Zona Gale, and the Politics of Female Authorship*. New York: Palgrave, 2001.

Judith E. Barlow

GALSWORTHY, JOHN (1867–1933)

John Galsworthy was born on August 14, 1867, at Kingston Hill, Surrey, ENGLAND, to a Devonshire farming family that had made a comfortable fortune in property in the 19th century. His father was a solicitor. Educated at Harrow and New College, Oxford, Galsworthy also became a lawyer in 1890. Galsworthy specialized in marine law and voyaged around the world, during which he encountered Joseph Conrad, then mate of a merchant ship; they became lifelong friends. Galsworthy found the law lacking and uninspiring and began writing. For his first works, the short story collection *From the Four Winds* (1897) and the novel *Jocelyn* (1898), both published at his own expense, he used the pseudonym John Sinjohn. *The Island Pharisees* (1904) was the first book to appear under his own name.

The Man of Property (1906) began the novel sequence known as *The Forsyte Saga*; other works in the series are "Indian Summer of a Forsyte" (1918, in *Five Tales*), *In Chancery* (1920), *Awakening* (1920), and *To Let* (1921). The novels investigate the multigenerational lives of a large, upper-middle-class family at the turn of the century. The Forsytes are a rabidly ambitious and successful family, eager to capitalize on and expand their place in the world of the wealthy and powerful. The saga investigates the ethical and moral implications of the pursuit of wealth, power, and property. The works challenge the then-accepted moral superiority of the wealthy, while invoking the nuance of humanity through fecund character and place descriptions. Much of Galsworthy's work seems to be in the vein of "writing what he knows" in that his works reflect on the family structure bound by property management and lawyers. Galsworthy's work shows an investment in exposing the comfort and pleasures of middle-class values. In *The Man of Property*, Galsworthy marks the relation between masculine ownership of property and masculine ownership of women (as property).

Galsworthy was also a successful dramatist; his plays, written in a naturalistic style, usually examined controversial ethical or social problems. *The Silver Box* (1906), like many of his other works, has a legal theme and illustrates that law and justice do not go hand-in-hand. It shows the particularities of the disparity in the application of the law based on class privilege (or lack thereof). *Strife* (1909) revisits the issue of class-based relations, this time through a study of industrial relations. *Justice* (1910), a realist play depicting prison life, forced its audience to encounter the despair and degradation of prison and led to prison reform. Galsworthy also wrote verse.

A televised version of *The Forsyte Saga* was broadcast by the BBC and achieved immense popularity in Great Britain in 1967 and later in the United States, reviving interest in Galsworthy.

Galsworthy was awarded the Nobel Prize a year before his death on January 31, 1933, in Grove Lodge, Hampstead.

SELECT PLAYS: *The Country House* (1907); *The Patrician* (1911); *The Mob* (1914); *The Freelands* (1915); *The Skin Game* (1920)

FURTHER READING

Barker, Dudley. *The Man of Principle: A Biography of John Galsworthy*. New York: Stein & Day Publishers, 1969.

Dupre, Catherine. *John Galsworthy. A Biography*. New York: Coward, McCann & Geoghegan, 1976.

Gindin, James. *John Galsworthy's Life and Art*. London: Macmillan, 1987.

Marrot, H. V. *Life & Letters of John Galsworthy*. New York: Charles Scribner's Sons, 1936.

Sternlicht, Sanford. *John Galsworthy*. Boston: Hall, 1987.

Shanté T. Smalls

GAMBARO, GRISELDA (1928–)

Griselda Gambaro was born in Buenos Aires, ARGENTINA, on July 28, 1928, into a family of limited economic means. She taught herself drama and literature by going to the public library and reading authors like EUGENE O'NEILL, ANTON CHEKHOV, and LUIGI PIRANDELLO. After finishing high school in 1943, she worked in a publishing company. She married sculptor Juan Carlos Distefano with whom she had two children.

She received her first success with *Madrigal in the City* (*Madrigal en ciudad*), a collection of short stories for which she received a prize from Argentina's National Endowment for the Arts (1963). She collaborated with the Instituto Torcuato di Tella, which was known for groundbreaking experimental art, music, and theater, but it closed in 1971 as a result of political repression.

Gambaro was forced into exile in SPAIN in 1977 after her novel *To Earn One's Death* (*Ganarse la muerte*) was banned by the regime of President Rafael Videla. In Europe, she became engaged in the feminist movement of FRANCE. Her concerns about women's social situation and specific problems in the world would surface in her work. Gambaro became more and more involved in women's issues, and in the 1980s she wrote *From the Rising Sun* (*Del sol naciente*, 1984) and *Antígona furiosa* (1986). They include strong female characters who evolve from victims to active fighters against oppression, making a vivid commentary on the situation in Argentina, human nature, and the need for a new social order. They become powerful models who reject the confines of stereotypical female roles.

She returned to Argentina in 1980 and became an active member of the Teatro Abierto [OPEN THEATER], a creative outlet against governmental repression. After losing the Falkland Islands to Great Britain, the dictatorship lost power and Argentina started to enjoy a period of freedom and democracy. In 1987, she published one of her most political works, INFORMATION FOR FOREIGNERS (*Información para extranjeros*), in which she makes a passionate stand against violence, torture, and human passivity when facing a horrific situation.

In Gambaro's plays there is an intense exploration of the dramatic language and the nonverbal elements that are a part of theatrical performance. Gambaro's style includes black humor with a focus on the absurd political situation in Argentina in the 1960s, 1970s, and 1980s. She never sets her plays in a specific time or place, and the action never follows a logical or linear structure. These surreal settings contribute to a terrifying atmosphere that forces the audience to feel uncomfortable and think about what they are watching.

[*See also* Avant-Garde Drama; Identity Theater; Poor Theater]

SELECT PLAYS: *The Walls* (*Las paredes*, 1963); *The Blunder* (*El desatino*, 1965); *The Camp* (*El campo*, 1967); *The Siamese Twins* (*Los siameses*, 1967); *Saying Yes* (*Decir Sí*, 1974); *From the Rising Sun* (*Del sol naciente*, 1984); *Antígona furiosa* (1986); *Information for Strangers* (*Información para extranjeros*, 1987); *Sucede lo que pasa* (1987)

FURTHER READING

Betsko, Kathleen, and Rachel Koenig. *Interviews with Contemporary Women Playwrights*. New York: Beech Tree Books, 1987.

Garfield, Evelyn Picón. *Women's Voices from Latin America: Interviews with Six Contemporary Authors*. Detroit, Mich.: Wayne State Univ. Press, 1985.

Kozilowski, Thomas. "Griselda Gambaro." *Gale Contemporary Authors Online*. http://www.gale.com (February 8, 2003).

Marting, Diane E., ed. *Spanish American Women Writers: A Bio-Bibliographical Source Book*. New York: Greenwood Press, 1990.

Partnow, Elaine T., ed., with Lesley Ann Hyatt. *The Female Dramatist*. New York: Facts on File, Inc., 1998.

Paloma Asensio

THE GAME OF LIFE

Glass and light, say I, glass and light. Oh, how I would like to find the bottom.
—Ivar Kareno, Act 1

At the beginning of his career in the 1890s, KNUT HAMSUN published six novels, one collection of short stories, and three plays. The plays, *At the Gates of the Kingdom* (*Ved Rigets Port*, 1895), *The Game of Life* (*Livets Spil*, 1896), and *Evening Glow* (*Aftenrøde*, 1898), make up the Kareno trilogy.

At the Gates of the Kingdom takes place in the 1880s and 1890s in the academic and pseudo-intellectual circles of the Norwegian capital, Kristiania (later Oslo), where Ivar Kareno, the main character of the trilogy, is desperately trying to get his controversial philosophical dissertation published. Ten years later, in *The Game of Life*, Kareno has moved to a rural parish in the northern part of NORWAY, Hamsun's own Nordland, where he tutors the two boys of the local trader, Mr. Oterman. After ten more years, in *Evening Glow*, the now fifty-year-old Kareno is back in the capital, trying to make a political career.

The first and the last parts of the trilogy are variations on the traditional bourgeois-realist play of ideas. As expressions of ideological conflicts, these plays are rather limited in perspective. *The Game of Life*, however, is quite different, both in shape and content. It is a sort of early dream play, related both to symbolist and expressionist traditions. Kareno's journey to northern Norway represents a journey into the subconscious, the mysterious world of Nordland. The landscape and the people there become symbols of the unconscious.

The action takes place over the period of a year; the four acts correspond with the four seasons. Besides tutoring the two boys, Kareno is occupied with writing his "metaphysics." To support his writing project, a strange tower with a cupola of glass is built near the ocean. The tower is an ambiguous symbol, suggesting philosophical and intellectual aspiration, but it is also a principal phallic symbol, related to a wish for potency and erotic appreciation. Kareno believes strongly that in the tower "with the help of an optical forgery he can neutralize [his] earthly power of cognition" and hurl his "soul to the coast of eternity."

But Kareno is also obsessed with Mr. Oterman's daughter, the seductive Teresita. The action in *The Game of Life* appears chaotic and unreal. Ships are wrecked in the middle of the night, Mr. Oterman is driven to madness by his workers, a plague is approaching from the north, blasts sound night and day from the marble quarry, Teresita is shot by the mysterious messenger, Thy (also called Justice), and the Northern Lights become red. In the end, Mr. Oterman sets fire to Kareno's tower to prevent the publication of his "metaphysics," but he is unaware that his two sons are in the tower. They both die in the fire.

The thematic aspects of the play center on the human subconscious but also include the passion for life, demonic sexuality, human pride and arrogance, God's punishment, and the human fear of His punishment.

FURTHER READING

Arntzen, Even. "Skrifta i vold. Eit intertekstuelt sveip over Hamsuns Kareno-trilogi" ["Writing with the Devil Close Behind. An Intertextual View at Hamsun's Kareno-Trilogy"]. In *Norsk Litterær Årbok 1990* [*Norwegian Literary Annual 1990*], ed. by Hans H. Skei and Einar Vannebo. Oslo: Det Norske Samlaget, 1990. 61–75.

Grabowski, Simon. "Kareno in Nordland: A Study of *Livets Spil*," *Edda* (1969): 297–321.

Even Arntzen

GANGULI, USHA (1945–)

Usha Ganguli, born on August 20, 1945, in Jodpur, Rajasthan, began her career as a Bharatanatyam dancer but took up acting in 1970, appearing in a production of FRANZ XAVER KROETZ's *Request Concert* in Kolkata. In 1976 she formed her own theater company, Rangakarmee. Ganguli describes Rangakarmee as "a politically committed group that delves into forms of exploitation and oppression, political, economic, social, and sexual, unraveling the mechanisms at work." Ganguli describes her own work as "theatre with a cause" and her audience as "the average citizen" of Kolkata, the "person who is bogged down by his daily life and helplessness." Rangakarmee attempts, she says, to provide "a space in some corner of his over-exploited mind, to question." She is interested in "realistic" theater that portrays the real lives of ordinary individuals (Mee, 2001).

Rangakarmee began by adapting classics such as HENRIK IBSEN's *A DOLL'S HOUSE* and MAKSIM GORKY's *Mother* (*Maa*), about an uneducated woman who takes over a son's responsibilities and was performed for factory workers. Subsequent productions have included *Beti Ayee*, a Hindi translation of Jyoti Mhapsekar's Marathi play *A Daughter is Born* (*Mulgi Zhali Ho!*), which opens with a song in honor of Jotiba Phule, who promoted education for women; a production of Mahesh Elkunchwar's *Holi*, which, Ganguli says, "portrayed the emptiness, the inherent frustration of teenagers who are trying to come to terms with themselves"; and *For Myself* (*Nijer Jonne*) about a fourteen-year-old Hindu girl who is displaced from Pakistan and exploited as a servant in INDIA until she finds her inner strength.

Rangakarmee made its name nationally with their 1999 production of *RUDALI*, adapted from the novel by Mahasweta Devi. Since then, Ganguli has produced *Himmat Mai*, an adaptation of BERTOLT BRECHT's *MOTHER COURAGE*, and *Freedom* (*Mukti*). She has also written *Kashinama*, which is set in Varanasi and exposes the corruption underlying the socioeconomic changes of the last century. "The story mirrors the entire nation where politicians have transformed religion into savage fanaticism," she says. "Rampant globalization has robbed the common life of its simplicity and has given birth to perverse greed and wild hypocrisy." Thus, Ganguli sees the play as a critique of contemporary politics and society.

Rangakarmee functions as other Kolkata theater groups do: it is composed of theater enthusiasts best described as amateurs with professional standards of performance and production. They subscribe to an alternative, experimental, noncommercial ethic, unlike "professional" commercial theater. Rangakarmee is an unusual phenomenon in the Bengali group theater scene in Kolkata because they perform in Hindi (Ganguli's first language) for a largely Bengali-speaking audience.

Not only does Ganguli write, she also directs and acts in almost every one of Rangakarmee's productions. She has won several awards for her acting and received the Dayavati Modi Shree Shakti Samman in 1998 for her contributions to the theater.

FURTHER READING

Ganguli, Usha. *Rudali*. Kolkata: Seagull Foundation for the Arts, 1997.

Katyal, Anjum. "The Metamorphosis of *Rudali*." *Seagull Theatre Quarterly* 1 (1994): 5–11.

——. "The Metamorphosis of *Rudali*." In *Muffled Voices: Women in Modern Indian Theatre*. Delhi: Shakti Books, 2002.

Mee, Erin, ed. *DramaContemporary: India*. Baltimore: Johns Hopkins Univ. Press, 2001.

"*Rudali*: Questions of Language and Audience." *Seagull Theatre Quarterly* 1 (1994): 12–24.

"*Rudali*: The Making of a Production." In *Seagull Theatre Quarterly* 1 (1994): 25–34.

Erin B. Mee

GAO XINGJIAN (1940–)

Born in Ganzhou, Jiangxi Province, in 1940, Gao Xingjian studied French at Beijing Foreign Languages Institute from 1958 to 1962. Upon graduation from the university, he worked as a translator for China's Book Import and Export Company in Beijing. In 1978 he was transferred to the Chinese Writers' Association as a translator. The same year he began to publish. From 1981 to 1987, he worked as the scriptwriter for Beijing People's Art Theatre (Beijing renmin yishu juyuan). The year 1982 saw the premiere of his play *The Alarm Signal* (*Juedui xinghao*), and 1983, *The Bus Stop* (*Chezhan*), two plays that heralded experimental theater in CHINA. Gao's theatrical experiments were greeted with critical acclaim as well as political misgivings in China of the 1980s. His last major play of this period, *Wild Man* (*Yeren*, 1985) was withdrawn from public performance shortly after its premiere in Beijing, and Gao was suspended from publishing for more than a year. In 1987, Gao emigrated to France as a political refugee and became a French citizen in 1998.

Gao's post-emigration work is banned in China. Nonetheless, he continues an active and productive career as playwright, director, critic, novelist, and artist. His stage plays published abroad include the acclaimed *The Nether City* (*Mincheng*, 1987), *Classic of Mountains and Seas* (*Shanhaijing zhuan*, 1989), *Fugitives* (*Taowang*, 1989), *Between Life and Death* (*Sheng si ji*, 1991), *Dialogue and etortl* (*Duihua yu fanji*, 1992), *Weekend Quartets* (*Zhoumuo sichong zou*, 1992), *Sleepwalker* (*Yeyou shen*, 1993) and *Snow in August* (*Bayue xue*, 1997).

Gao Xingjian (1988) aims at creating a "total theater" (*quanneng juchang*). While the concept of "total theater" originally comes from ANTONIN ARTAUD, Gao Xingjian means more specifically a blend between spoken drama and operative theater. The two theatrical traditions had been meticulously kept apart in China after 1949, when KONSTANTIN STANISLAVSKY's acting system and later SOCIALIST REALISM were officially endorsed. Gao's expands on "spoken drama (*huaju*)" to include more body language, sound effect, and symbolic acting. Starting with *The Alarm Signal*, Gao stripped the stage of almost all props so as to abandon the illusion of REALISM. On this bare stage, he resorts to symbolic action to create a dynamic space of imagination. His more recent plays and productions borrow extensively from Beijing opera. In 1995, he invited choreographer Jiang Qing to direct his plays *The Other Shore* (*Bi'an*, published in 1986) and *The Nether City*. *Snow in August* premiered as a Peking opera.

Gao Xingjian uses the theater as a space and means to reflect on existential issues, for which French existential theater provides an important source of inspiration. *The Bus Stop*, for one, is conspicuously modeled after SAMUEL BECKETT's *WAITING FOR GODOT* in plot as well as narrative structure. The play reduces verbal language to incoherent and fragmented utterances. Instead of providing summaries and explanations for each and every utterance and action as commonly found in overtly didactic plays, Gao makes it necessary for the audience to accept the entire play as a semantic unit and make their own abstractions. Variously regarded as a pioneer of the Theater of the Absurd in China or "modern Zen theatre" (Zhao, 2000), Gao's experimental theater amounted to a reinvention of the contemporary Chinese stage.

Some of the issues explored in his theater, such as the obtainment of self-knowledge and the relationship between human beings and nature, are carried over to his nondramatic prose. The Swedish Academy awarded Gao Xingjian the Nobel Prize for Literature in 2000 "for an œuvre of universal validity, bitter insights and linguistic ingenuity, which has opened new paths for the Chinese novel and drama."

PLAYS: *The Alarm Signal* (*Juedui xinghao*, 1982); *The Bus Stop* (*Chezhan*, 1983); *Wild Man* (*Yeren*, 1985); *The Other Shore* (*Bi'an*, 1986); *The Nether City* (*Mincheng*, 1987); *Classic of Mountains and Seas* (*Shanhaijing zhuan*, 1989); *Fugitives* (*Taowang*, 1989); *Between Life and Death* (*Sheng si ji*, 1991); *Dialogue and Retotl* (*Duihua yu fanji*, 1992); *Weekend Quartets* (*Zhoumuo sichong zou*, 1992); *Sleepwalker* (*Yeyou shen*, 1993); *Snow in August* (*Bayue xue*, 1997)

FURTHER READING

Gao, Xingjian. *Dui yizhong xiandai xiju de zhuiqiu* (*In Pursuit of a Modern Theater*). Beijing: Zhongguo xiju chubanshe, 1988.

——. *The Other Shore: Plays by Gao Xingjian*. Hong Kong: The Chinese Univ. Press, 1999.

Lee, Mabel. "Gao Xingjian's *Lingshan/Soul Mountain*: Modernism and the Chinese Writer," *HEAT* 4 (1997): 128–157.

Sen, M. "The Theater of the Absurd in Mainland China: Gao Xingjian, *The Bus Stop*." *Issues & Studies* 258 (August 1989): 138–148.

Tam, Kwok-kan, ed. *Soul of Chaos: Critical Perspectives on Gao Xingjian*. Hong Kong: The Chinese Univ. Press, 2001.

Tay, William. "Avant-Garde Theater in Post-Mao China: *The Bus Stop* by Gao Xingjian." In *Worlds Apart: Recent Chinese Writing and Its Audiences*, ed. by Howard Goldblatt. Armonk, N. Y.: M. E. Sharpe, 1990. 111–118.

Zhao, Henry Y. H. *Towards a Modern Zen Theatre: Gao Xingjian and Chinese Theatre Experimentalism*. London: School of Oriental and African Studies, 2000.

Donghui He

GARCÍA LORCA, FEDERICO (1896–1936)

Federico García Lorca is preeminent among a generation of playwrights—RAMÓN MARÍA DEL VALLE-INCLÁN, Miguel de Unamuno, Azorín (José Martínez Ruiz), and Jacinto Grau—who sought to revitalize Spanish theater in the AVANT-GARDE era. A multifaceted and charismatic intellectual with deep social convictions, Lorca treated the arts primarily as a tool for communing with the masses. He founded and directed SPAIN's first university theater troupe, La Barraca (1932–1936), and brought open-air productions of Spain's classics to townspeople throughout the country.

These activities reveal the popular spirit that informs Lorca's poetry of the 1920s—*Poem of the Deep Song* (*Poema del cante jondo*), *Songs* (*Canciones*), and *Gypsy Ballads* (*Romancero gitano*)—and most of his theater. In his historical play, *Mariana Pineda*, he portrays Granada's legendary heroine who was assassinated for her liberal ideals in 1831 by monarchist troops. Under Valle-Inclán's influence, Lorca cultivated the FARCE, producing two major examples of this genre, *The Shoemaker's Wonderful Wife* (*La zapatera prodigiosa*, 1926–1933) and *The Love of Don Perlimplín and Belisa in the Garden* (*El amor de don Perlimplín con Belisa en su jardín*, 1924–1931), while modeling his minor pieces on the Andalusian puppet tradition that he helped to perpetuate through his own outdoor productions. The intermingling of tradition and modernity that characterizes these farces becomes the hallmark of BLOOD WEDDING (*Bodas de sangre*, 1932), *Yerma* (1933–1934), and THE HOUSE OF BERNARDA ALBA (*La casa de Bernarda Alba*, 1936), his 1930s masterpieces centered on Lorca's foremost concern: the ill-fated struggle to realize one's desire within a repressive social order. He structured their plots according to the traditions of Greek TRAGEDY and Andalusian custom while using conventions of avant-garde poetry.

Exposure to the nation's major artists and intellectuals during the 1920s while living in Madrid influenced Lorca toward more cosmopolitan modes of writing. Close ties to Luis Buñuel (filmmaker) and Salvador Dalí (artist) brought him under the influence of SURREALISM. These developments anticipate Lorca's turn toward the more extreme avant-garde style of *Poet in New York* and *The Public*, his poetry and play he composed in New York and Cuba in 1929 and 1930. Such incursions into the irrational world of the poet's subconscious represent an unleashing of sexual inhibitions that challenged prevailing social codes and made *The Public*'s staging in Spain unimaginable during Lorca's lifetime.

Lorca's wavering between tradition and modernity is constant throughout his career. Over time, however, his inherently lyrical theater supplanted poetry as his primary means of communicating with the masses, especially during the reformist years of the Second Republic (1931–1939). Assassinated in the first weeks of the Spanish Civil War (August 1936) by insurgent troops loyal to Francisco Franco, Lorca received scant attention under the ensuing dictatorship (1939–1975), while abroad he was cast as the symbol of tragic Spain. Lorca's revival since Franco's death has been essential to the nation's reconstruction of its collective memory.

[*See also* Theatricality]

PLAYS: *The Butterfly's Evil Spell* (*El maleficio de la mariposa*, 1919); *The Billy-Club Puppets* (*Títeres de la cachiporra: Tragicomedia de don Cristóbal y la seña Rosita*, 1922); *Mariana Pineda* (1923)

DRAMATIC DIALOGUES: The Love of Don Perlimplín and Belisa in the Garden (El amor de don Perlimplín con Belisa en su jardín, 1924–1931); Buster Keaton Takes a Walk (El paseo de Buster Keaton, 1925–1928); Chimera (Quimera, 1925–1928); The Maiden, the Sailor, and the Student (La doncella, el marinero y el estudiante, 1925–1928); The Shoemaker's Wonderful Wife (La zapatera prodigiosa, 1926–1933); The Public (El público, 1930–1931); The Puppet Play of Don Cristóbal (El retablillo de Don Cristóbal, 1931); When Five Years Pass (Así que pasen cinco años, 1931); Blood Wedding (Bodas de sangre, 1932); Yerma (1933–1934); Comedy Without a Title (Comedia sin título, unfinished, 1935); Doña Rosita, the Spinster (Doña Rosita la soltera o el lenguaje de las flores, 1935); The House of Bernarda Alba (La casa de Bernarda Alba, 1936)

FURTHER READING

Allen, Rubert. *Psyche and Symbol in the Theater of Federico García Lorca. Perlimplín, Yerma, Blood Wedding*. Austin: Univ. of Texas, 1974.

Edwards, Gwynne. *Lorca. The Theatre Beneath the Sand*. London, New York: Marion Boyars, 1995.

Fernández Cifuentes, Luis. *García Lorca en el teatro: La norma y la diferencia* [García Lorca in the Theater: The Norm and the Difference]. Zaragoza: Prensas Universitarias, 1986.

Gibson, Ian. *Federico García Lorca: A Life*. New York: Pantheon Books, 1989. Originally published as *Federico García Lorca* (Barcelona: Ediciones Grijalbo, 1985).

Higginbotham, Virginia. *The Comic Spirit of Federico García Lorca*. Austin: Univ. of Texas Press, 1976.

Newton, Candelas. *Understanding Federico García Lorca*. Columbia: Univ. of South Carolina Press, 1995.

Stainton, Leslie. *Lorca: A Dream of Life*. London: Bloomsbury, 1998.

Bernardo Antonio González

GARRO, ELENA (1920–1998)

Elena Garro, renowned for her contributions to Mexican literature and to women's writing in particular, was born in Puebla, MEXICO, on December 11 or 12, 1920, to the Spaniard José Antonio Garro and the Mexican Esperanza Navarro. The author grew up in the capital and state of Guerrero, Mexico, but spent the larger part of her adulthood and artistic career abroad, moving often because of the political assignments of her husband, the influential Mexican intellectual and author Octavio Paz, to whom she was married from 1937 until the early 1960s.

The experiences that inform Garro's writing are diverse, increasing her appeal to audiences worldwide; her works have been widely translated into English and other languages. In addition to academic pursuits at the Universidad Nacional Autónoma de México, Garro held the position of choreographer for the Theater of the University of Mexico at the age of seventeen, worked at one point as a screenwriter, and worked extensively as a journalist. In addition, Garro's travels carried her to the United States, Japan, Switzerland, Paris, and Spain, with periodic returns to Mexico. The author's experiences in Mexico and Spain often found her in the presence of significant political events in which she partook actively, identifying with the plight of the oppressed. These experiences and Garro's personal interest in the plight of the marginalized are reflected in both her prose and dramatic works, and eventually led to a self-imposed exile after she found herself incarcerated in 1968 in Mexico for suspected participation as an instigator in the Students' Movement.

Although she received many literary awards for her endeavors in prose throughout her publishing career—the Premio Xavier Villaurrutia in 1963 for the novel *Memories of Things to Come* (*Los recuerdos del porvenir*), the 1981 Grijalbo Award for *Testimonies about Mariana* (*Testimonios sobre Mariana*), and the Sor Juana Inés de la Cruz Award in 1996 for *Look for My Obituary* (*Busca mi esquela*)—the genre with which Garro felt most comfortable was drama. It is in her theatrical works that she excels in her ability to erase the lines between reality and fiction, thereby constructing alternative realities in which her characters escape their oppression and gain a voice in and control over their destiny. Garro's unconventional techniques for depicting temporal and spatial relations further facilitate her characters' journey toward self-definition. The mythical dimensions she creates give freedom not only to her characters, but also to herself, allowing her to subvert traditional representations of societal roles and literary symbols.

Although Garro's trademark may be her ability to create a mythical realm for her characters, there is no escaping the historical and political reality of oppression and alienation that she depicts as the motivating force behind the desire to flee to another dimension. At the same time that she creates an escape for the oppressed, she forces the dominant culture, often seen as responsible for society's injustices, to reflect on its actions and examine its conscience.

Garro's works clearly vocalize the desires of the marginalized and the oppressed, particularly women, leading many to consider her one of the most influential feminist writers of Mexican literature, although the desires she communicates can apply to any group alienated by injustice from the larger population. Garro routinely expresses women's quest for freedom from the strictures of patriarchal society and its dominant institutions of Catholicism and dictatorial governments.

The later years of Garro's personal life were plagued by illness and poverty that parallel the existence of many of her fictional characters. Her choice to live in isolation, cut off from the reality of convention and tradition, contributed to the formation of a personality that some might call eccentric, but that perhaps allowed her to identify more closely with the needs of those for whom she speaks in her works. In the last years of her life, Elena Garro returned to Mexico, where she died in Cuernavaca on August 22, 1998.

SELECT PLAYS: *Felipe Ángeles* (1954); *The Pillars of Doña Blanca* (*Los pilares de doña Blanca*, 1957); *A Solid Home* (*Un hogar sólido*, 1957); *Wandering Off the Point* (*Andarse por las ramas*, 1957); *The Wise King* (*El rey mago*, 1957); *Enchantment, General Store* (*Encanto, tendajón mixto*, 1958); *Ventura Allende* (1958); *The Move* (*La Mudanza*, 1959); *The Lady on Her Balcony* (*La señora en su balcón*, 1960); *The Lady Simpleton* (*La dama boba*, 1963); *The Dogs* (*Los Perros*, 1965); *The Tree* (*El Arbol*, 1967); *The Trace* (*El Rastro*, 1981); *Benito Fernández* (1981); *Parada San Ángel* (staged 1993); *Socrates and the Cats* (*Sócrates y los gatos*, staged 2003)

FURTHER READING

Cypess, Sandra Messinger. "Visual and Verbal Distances in the Mexican Theater: The Plays of Elena Garro." In *Woman as Myth and Metaphor in Latin American Literature*, ed. by Carmelo Virgillo and Naomi Lindstrom. Columbia: Missouri Univ. Press, 1986.

Larson, Catherine. "Recollections of Plays to Come: Time in the Theatre of Elena Garro." *Latin American Theatre Review* 22, no. 2 (Spring 1989): 5–17.

Rojas-Trempe, Lady. "Elena Garro dialoga sobre su teatro con Guillermo Schmidhuber" [Elena Garro Talks about Her Theater with Guillermo Schmidhuber]. *Revista Iberoamericana* 55.148–149 (1989): 685–690.

Southerland, Stacy. "Elusive Dreams, Shattered Illusions: The Theater of Elena Garro." In *Latin American Women Dramatists: Theater, Texts,* and Theories, ed. by Catherine Larson and Margarita Vargas. Bloomington: Indiana Univ. Press, 1998.

Stoll, Anita K., ed. *A Different Reality: Studies on the Work of Elena Garro*. Lewisburg, Penn.: Bucknell Univ. Press, 1990. 38–58.

Winkler, Julie A. *Light into Shadow: Marginality and Alienation in the Work of Elena Garro*. New York: Peter Lang, 2001.

Stacy Southerland

GATTI, ARMAND (1924–)

Provocative and collective based, Armand Gatti's theater depicts both contemporary events and historic struggles. Born on January 26, 1924, in Monte Carlo, Gatti's passion for political theater can be traced to his difficult youth in the south of FRANCE as the son of Italian immigrants. In 1942, Gatti joined the Resistance movement. One year later he was arrested and deported to a German labor camp. His brief time there profoundly affected his life and art. Of his imprisonment, David Bradby (1984) writes that "Gatti was a survivor who talked. Much of his work was an attempt to exorcise the ghosts that haunted him from this period." Upon Gatti's return to France, he began an important career as a reporter for *Le Parisien Libéré* and was named journalist of the year in 1954. Missions to South America and China, as well as his regular coverage of the trials of French collaborators during this period, provided him with material for the plays he began to write in the late 1950s, as well as a global interest and dramatic perspective that persist to this day.

Relying on the premise that theater retains its power to effect social change, and that the structure of a play must be revolutionary, Gatti quickly established himself as a didactic playwright, writing overtly political plays to be performed in factories and other nontraditional places. In contrast with the static dramas of SAMUEL BECKETT and the gestural and linguistic kaleidoscopes of JEAN GENET and EUGENE IONESCO, Gatti's stage works are orchestrated, Brechtian spectacles employing dramaturgical collage, projections, song, puppets, and other distancing mechanisms. Unlike BERTOLT BRECHT, however, whose best work analyzed contemporary dilemmas in historic locations, Gatti turns just as often to current events and figures for dialectical fodder: Vietnam, Che Guevara, and the student riots of May 1968, among others. One of his best known plays, *The Passion of General Franco* (*La Passion du Général Franco*, 1969), portrays the Spanish dictator Francisco Franco as seen by those he exiled, a subject inspired as much from Gatti's personal experience in Toulouse with the exile community as by the historical record. Gatti is also interested in rupturing notions of continuous time; in *The Imaginary Life of the Garbage-Collecter Auguste-Geai* (*La Vie imaginaire de l'éboueur Auguste Geai*, 1962), for example, four eponymous Augustes at different ages exist and sometimes interact simultaneously.

Gatti made a greater mark during the turbulent 1960s. In a departure from his earlier EPIC THEATER, he wrote a series of mini-plays during the riots of May 1968. One of them, *A Day in the Life of a Hospital Nurse, or, Why House Pets?* (*Pourquoi les animaux domestiques? ou La journée d'une infirmière*, 1970), portrayed the exhausting day of a nurse and housewife. The play was performed in hospitals, hostels, and worker's clubs and remained widely performed well into the 1970s. Gatti also formed a street theater troupe in May 1968 and, using puppets, acted out moments from the history of the Paris Commune.

Believing that his audience should be as well-informed as possible about the events of a play, Gatti often organizes discussions around the performances, modifying the play according to audience response. He does not seek consensus, and no text is definitive. Although he remains relatively unknown in the English-speaking world, he continues to write plays, screenplays, poems, essays, and criticism.

SELECT PLAYS: *The Second Life of Tatenberg Camp* (*La Deuxième Existence du Camp de Tatenberg*, 1962); *Public Song Before Two Electric Chairs* (*Chant public devant deux chaises électriques*, 1964); *V. like Vietnam* (*V. comme Vietnam*, 1967); *The Three Suns of St. Blaise Street* (*Les Treize Soleils de la rue Saint-Blaise*, 1968); *The Passion of General Franco* (*La Passion de Général Franco*, 1969); *A Day in the Life of a Hospital Nurse, or, Why House Pets?* (*Pourquoi les animaux domestiques? ou La journée d'une infirmière*, 1970); *Rosaspartakus Seizes Power* (*Rosaspartakus prend le pouvoir*, 1971); *The Stork* (*La Cigogne*, 1971); *The Unicorn* (*La Licorne*, 1984); *The 7 Possibilities for Train 713 Departing from Auschwitz* (*Les 7 possibilités du train 713 en partance d'Auschwitz*, 1987)

FURTHER READING

Bradby, David. *Modern French Drama: 1940–1980*. Cambridge: Cambridge Univ. Press, 1984.

Champagne, Lenora. *French Theatre Experiment since 1968*. Ann Arbor, Mich.: UMI Research Press, 1984.

Gatti, Armand. *Armand Gatti: Three Plays (The Second Life of Tatenberg Camp, The Stork, A Day in the Life of a Hospital Nurse)*. Tr. by Joseph Long. Sheffield, England: Sheffield Academic Press, Ltd., 2000.

Knowles, Dorothy. *Armand Gatti in the Theatre: Wild Duck Against the Wind*. London: Athlone Press, 1989.

Kate Bredeson

GAY AND LESBIAN DRAMA

Gay and Lesbian Drama is a designation for plays that reflect the lives and experiences of gay, lesbian, bisexual, transgender, and queer people. Although the concept of gay and lesbian drama grew out of the Gay Liberation movement of the late 1960s and 1970s, the category is often stretched to include plays from previous eras depicting gay and lesbian lives, as well as contemporary "queer" theater that has entered the cultural mainstream.

On the modern popular stage, plays that attempted to present gay and lesbian characters usually met with censorship, including Sholom Asch's YIDDISH drama *God of Vengeance* (1907), about the daughter of a wealthy brothel owner who falls in love with one of her father's prostitutes; Edouard Bourdet's

The Captive (1926), about a girl lost to the sinister allure of lesbianism; and MAE WEST's *The Drag* (1927), which shocked and titillated audiences with a bevy of drag queens and a deceitful cad murdered by his abandoned male lover. To stop such "dirty" plays from appearing on Broadway, New York passed the Wales Padlock Law, which allowed police to shut down theaters that presented plays "depicting or dealing with . . . the subject of sex degeneracy or sex perversion."

Subsequently, the existence of gay characters was often implied rather than explicit, but those "in the know" recognized "deviancy" in the sophisticated aesthetes of NOËL COWARD's DESIGN FOR LIVING (1933) and the insidious upper-class patron of a working-class ward in Mordaunt Shairp's *The Green Bay Tree* (1933). More explicit was THE CHILDREN'S HOUR (1934), LILLIAN HELLMAN's acclaimed drama about the turmoil caused when a young girl accuses two of her teachers of being lovers. In the play's final act, one of the teachers acknowledges that she is a lesbian and commits suicide. The homosexual as dangerous and/or doomed was evident in two French plays with lesbian characters: NO EXIT (1944) by JEAN-PAUL SARTRE and THE MAIDS (1947) by JEAN GENET.

During the Cold War, which saw the persecution of gays and lesbians under McCarthyism as well as the first gay rights organizations, homosexuality was usually presented as a pathological condition that led to misery and death. Gay characters in TENNESSEE WILLIAMS's major plays are dead by suicide or murder before the curtain rises: Blanche's husband in A STREETCAR NAMED DESIRE (1947), Brick's football buddy Skipper in CAT ON A HOT TIN ROOF (1955), and Sebastian Venable, a predatory tourist killed and devoured by a pack of boys in SUDDENLY LAST SUMMER (1958). Another strategy for discussing homosexuality while avoiding actual homosexuals on stage was to present a character falsely accused of being gay, such as Tom Lee, the sensitive youth brought to "manhood" by a caring headmaster's wife in Robert Anderson's *Tea and Sympathy* (1953).

The possibility of a completely "uncloseted" theater began to be realized OFF-OFF-BROADWAY in the 1960s, particularly at The Caffe Cino, a Greenwich Village coffeehouse and performance space that became home to many gay and lesbian playwrights, including Tom Eyen, MARIA IRENE FORNES, William M. Hoffman, MEGAN TERRY, Doric Wilson, LANFORD WILSON, and Jeff Weiss. John Vaccaro's Play-House of the Ridiculous was the proving ground for CHARLES LUDLAM, who went on to found his own Ridiculous Theatrical Company, where he wrote, directed, and starred in plays that explored the artistic possibilities of camp, mixed highbrow and lowbrow art forms, incorporated drag performance, and often "queered" classic plays, most notably *Camille* (1973).

Groundbreaking works from the 1960s include Lanford Wilson's portrait of a demented drag queen in *The Madness of Lady Bright* (1964), AMIRI BARAKA's exploration of teenage homosexual desire across racial lines in *The Toilet* (1964), and ED BULLINS's depiction of a violent "bull dyke" in *Clara's Ole Man* (1965). In Britain, JOE ORTON eroticized dangerous young men of "questionable" sexuality in dark comedies like ENTERTAINING MR. SLOANE (1964) and LOOT (1966), while Frank Marcus depicted the dissolution of a sadomasochistic relationship between a butch actress and her childlike lover in *The Killing of Sister George* (1965). A defining moment in gay drama came in 1968 with the success of Mart Crowley's *The Boys in the Band*, which ran for 1,000 performances off-Broadway. The play presents eight gay men (and one potential closet case) at a birthday party, going from camp frivolity to vicious bitchiness before ending on a note of hope for self-acceptance. Coinciding with the Stonewall Riots, which involved conflicts between the police and gays in June 1969 in New York City and the repeal of stage censorship laws in the United States and Britain, Crowley's play is often credited with opening the door for honest and sympathetic gay characters in mainstream theater.

The 1970s saw the emergence of community-based theater companies dedicated specifically to gay and lesbian plays for gay and lesbian audiences, including The Other Side of Silence (TOSOS) and The Glines (New York), Theatre Rhinoceros (San Francisco), Out and About (Minneapolis), Buddies in Bad Times (Toronto), and the Gay Sweatshop (London). Certain plays became staples of the growing "purple circuit," including *T-Shirts* (1978) by Robert Patrick, *Last Summer at Bluefish Cove* (1980) by Jane Chambers, and *Street Theater* (1982) by Doric Wilson. Plays such as Hosanna (1973) by Canada's MICHEL TREMBLAY and Rents (1979) by Britain's Michael Wilcox were also revived frequently by gay theaters. Lesbian companies such as Lavender Cellar (Minneapolis) and Red Dyke Theatre (Atlanta) also flourished, and playwrights dealing with lesbian themes achieved wider recognition, including CARYL CHURCHILL, Maria Irene Fornes, Susan Miller, Cherrie Moraga, and Joan Schenkar. Gay characters appeared more frequently, if not always less stereotypically, in mainstream hits of the 1970s like *A Chorus Line* (1975), *Chicago* (1975), *Gemini* (1976) by Albert Innaurato, *Streamers* (1976) by DAVID RABE, and *Deathtrap* (1978) by Ira Levin.

The first gay play to go from the "gay ghetto" to major Broadway success was HARVEY FIERSTEIN's *Torch Song Trilogy* (1982). Fierstein's three one-act plays about a drag queen's search for romantic and domestic happiness were originally produced at La Mama, ETC in the late 1970s before going to Broadway and winning the 1983 Tony Award for Best Play and running for 1,222 performances. Also successful on Broadway, often breaking stereotypes and challenging homophobia, were BENT (1979) by MARTIN SHERMAN, *The Dresser* (1980) by Ronald Harwood, *La Cage aux Folles* (1983) by Fierstein and Jerry Herman, *Breaking the Code* (1986) by Hugh Whitemore, and *M. Butterfly* (1988) by DAVID HENRY HWANG. Charles Ludlam achieved his greatest success in the 1980s with *The Mystery of Irma Vep* (1984), and his influence was evident in the plays of Charles Busch, who mixed drag spectacle with film parody in *Vampire Lesbians of Sodom* (1984) and *Psycho Beach Party* (1987).

AIDS had an enormous impact on gay theater, as it took the lives of many theater artists and became the subject of plays by gay and gay-friendly playwrights. As David Román has documented, noncommercial community-based theaters played a unique role in breaking the silence and stigmatization in the early days of the AIDS crisis. LARRY KRAMER's polemical *The Normal Heart* (1985) and William Hoffman's elegiac *As Is* (1985) both found popular success and are often credited with changing the national conversation around AIDS. AIDS is also central to two of the most celebrated works of the 1990s: TONY KUSHNER's "gay fantasia on national themes" ANGELS IN AMERICA (1993) and Jonathan Larson's musical celebration of East Village bohemians, lesbians, and transsexuals, *Rent* (1996).

As the gay rights movement has entered the political mainstream, playwrights concerned with gay and lesbian issues have found homes in more mainstream theaters. Subscription-based regional and off-Broadway theaters have become regular venues for gay and lesbian plays, including new works by Claudia Allen, William Finn, Richard Greenberg, David Greenspan, Lisa Kron, CRAIG LUCAS, TERRENCE MCNALLY, Paul Rudnick, Nicky Silver, Jonathan Tolins, PAULA VOGEL, and Chay Yew. Yet dozens of queer-specific theaters continue to thrive, perhaps most notably the WOW Café, founded in New York in 1982, which has been the home to some of the most influential artists in lesbian theater, including Peggy Shaw, Lois Weaver, and Deborah Margolin (collectively known as SPLIT BRITCHES), HOLLY HUGHES, Sarah Schulman, and the FIVE LESBIAN BROTHERS. Solo performance art has been an important form for theater artists outside of the mainstream, expressing more diverse perspectives on queer lives, as seen in the works of Luis Alfaro, Kate Bornstein, Claire Dowie, Marga Gomez, Tim Miller, the Pomo Afro Homos, and Carmelita Tropicana.

The work of both mainstream and fringe theater artists continues to shatter the myth of a single "gay experience," and gay and lesbian drama now speaks with so many voices in so many styles that the work has become impossible to pigeonhole. Recent trends range from the documentary plays of Moisés Kaufman to the transgender rock and roll of *Hedwig and the Angry Inch* (1998), from the violence of SARAH KANE and MARK RAVENHILL's "in yer face" dramas to gay puppets finding love in the musical *Avenue Q* (2003). The theater, which has been called "the queerest art," remains the richest venue for the dramatic exploration of gay, lesbian, bisexual, and transgender lives.

FURTHER READING

Clum, John M. *Still Acting Gay: Male Homosexuality in Modern Drama*. New York: St. Martin's Griffin, 2000.

Curtin, Kaier. *"We Can Always Call Them Bulgarians": The Emergence of Lesbians and Gay Men on the American Stage*. Boston: Alyson Publications, 1987.

Harbin, Billy J., Kim Marra, and Robert A. Schanke, eds. *The Gay and Lesbian Theatrical Legacy: A Biographical Dictionary of Major Figures in American Stage History in the Pre-Stonewall Era*. Ann Arbor: Univ. of Michigan Press, 2005.

Martin, Carol, ed. *A Sourcebook of Feminist Theatre and Performance*. London: Routledge, 1996.

Román, David. *Acts of Intervention: Performance, Gay Culture, and AIDS*. Bloomington: Indiana Univ. Press, 1998.

Senelick, Laurence. *Lovesick: Modernist Plays of Same-Sex Love, 1894–1925*. London: Routledge, 1999.

Sinfield, Alan. *Out On Stage: Lesbian and Gay Theatre in the Twentieth Century*. New Haven: Yale Univ. Press, 1999.

Solomon, Alisa, and Framji Minwalla, eds., *The Queerest Art: Essays on Lesbian and Gay Theater*. New York: New York Univ. Press, 2002.

Jordan Schildcrout

GEARY, DAVID (1963–)

David Geary was born on September 9, 1963, Feilding, Taranaki. After completing a Bachelor of Arts at Victoria University, he trained at the NEW ZEALAND Drama School and worked as a professional actor. His more interesting and ambitious plays have dealt with aspects of gender and sexuality. *Pack of Girls* (produced 1991), an extremely funny farce about a women's rugby team, was praised for its perceptive exploration of gender issues. The play ends with the audience being made to join in the after-match function.

With its emphasis on theatrical performance and male sexuality, *Backstage with the Quigleys* (produced 1992, cowritten with Tim Spite and Mick Rose) about sibling rivalry, anticipates Geary's most complex work, *Lovelock's Dream Run* (1993), which was a highlight of the 1992 Australasian Playwrights' Workshop. *Lovelock* is set in the generically named Boys' High School, and its precocious thirteen-year-old protagonist offends all that the school stands for: Howard is inept at sports and a homosexual. He is bullied mercilessly. To survive, he creates an elaborate fantasy world around the famous athlete Jack Lovelock. Not only does this allow Geary to explore the intersection between history and myth, in particular the mythology around national heroes, but it also provides the cue for some wonderful theatrical invention: Howard's schoolmates are subsumed into and enact his imaginings, which include the 1936 Olympic Games and Adolf Hitler, a Berlin cabaret, and the famous aviatrix, New Zealander Jean Batten.

Geary (1993) stipulates that the play "should never lose as one of its levels of reality the sense of a bunch of schoolboys putting on a play." Although this generates much comedy, the play moves toward a tragic denouement: Lovelock insists on repudiating Howard's misconceptions about him, and the school determines to expel the rebel. However, in a moving, even exhilarating finale, Lovelock rescues Howard and embraces the fabricated persona he had previously rejected: "I can't go back now. You showed me a world far more exotic than my own. One where

I was more beautiful, more decadent, more of a fascist . . . And I like it here."

Geary returned to farce with *The Learner's Stand* (produced 1994), set mainly in a woolshed at the national shearing competition. One of the shearers is a transvestite who has fled Wellington's red light district. Georgina Beyer, who has since achieved fame as the first (self-confessed) transsexual Minister of Parliament in the world, appeared in the Auckland production.

A native of the Manawatu, Geary has a close association with Palmerston North's Centrepoint Theatre. Among the plays commissioned by Centrepoint is *The Farm* (produced 1997) about Jim and Maggie who are faced with the threat of the loss of their farm, and two Russian cycling tourists who turn up unexpectedly on the doorstep.

PLAYS: *Gothic but Staunch* (1988); *Kandy Cigarettes* (1988); *Dry, White and Friendly* (a collaboration, 1989); *The Rabbiter's Daughter* (co-written with Tim Spite and Mick Rose, 1993); *Savage Hearts/Manawa Taua* (co-written with Wiremu Davis, 1994); *King of Stains* (1996); *Ruapehu* (1996)

FURTHER READING

Dale, Judith. "Ladies sheilas girls dolls babes fluff . . ." *Illusions* 18, no. 2 (Summer 1991): 37–39.

Garrett, Simon. "Seeing what's going on: recent plays by Ken Duncum and David Geary." *Illusions* 23 (Winter 1994): 46–48.

Geary, David. *Lovelock's Dream Run*. Wellington, New Zealand: Victoria Univ. Press, 1993.

Edmond, Murray. "Lovelock's False Start." *Illusions* 20 (1992): 42–44.

Shipman, R. "Theatre but staunch." *Stamp* 31 (April 1992): 12–13.

Young, Stuart. " 'So much more the man': *Lovelock's Dream Run* and the Re-fashioning of Masculinity in New Zealand Drama." *Landfall* 192 (Spring 1996).

Stuart Young

GELBER, JACK (1932–2003)

The American playwright, director, and teacher Jack Gelber, born on April 12, 1932, in Chicago, Illinois, is best known for his drama *The Connection*, which was produced and performed by the Living Theatre in New York City on July 15, 1959. *The Connection* won Gelber three Obies, including one for the best play of the 1959–1960 season, and it was adapted to film by director Shirley Clarke 1961. Gelber's career is also distinguished by the award of another Obie for his direction of ARTHUR KOPIT's *The Kid* in 1973.

In a highly realistic but nonnarrative style, *The Connection* tells the story of a group of junkies waiting for their dealer—their "connection," called Cowboy—to arrive with heroin, their "shit." The plotless, improvisational quality of the acting, the jazz-inflected cadences of the dialogue, and the live jazz played onstage were groundbreaking at the time. Street culture and street language were freely used. During intermission the actors solicited money from the audience, ostensibly for drugs. Gelber's play helped put experimental theater on the map of American cultural imagination. Even as the play rattled audiences and critics alike, it kept them coming for a record OFF-BROADWAY run of 722 performances.

Gelber's hip irreverence and aggressive defiance of theatrical and social conventions emerged against the conservative culture of 1950s America. In all his plays, he used profane language and attempted to dismantle the comfortable division between actors and audience. *The Apple* (1961) begins in the lobby with the character Tom accusing the audience of bullying him while he offers them swigs from his pint bottle. *Sleep* (1972), set in an experimental sleep laboratory, explores masculine dreams of race and desire in a play in which dream characters, bells, and off-stage voices create a world between waking and dreaming. First performed at the Living Theatre, the original cast included James Earl Jones and Julian Beck. Gelber died on May 9, 2003, in New York City.

[*See also* Happenings and Intermedia; Political Theater in the United States; United States, 1940–Present]

PLAYS: *The Connection* (1960); *The Apple* (1961); *Square in the Eye* (1966); *The Cuban Thing* (1969); *Sleep* (1972); *Barbary Shore* (adaptation of a novel by Norman Mailer, 1973); *Farmyard* (adaptation of a play by Franz Xaver Kroetz, 1976); *Rehearsal* (1976); *Starters* (1980); *Big Shot* (1988); *Magic Valley* (1990); *Dylan's Line* (2003)

FURTHER READING

Aronson, Arnold. *American Avant-Garde Theatre*. London: Routledge, 2000.

Shank, Theodore. *American Alternative Theatre*. London: Macmillan Press, 1982.

Carol Martin

GENET, JEAN (1910–1986)

Jean Genet, ward of the French state, vagabond, novelist, dramatist, and political journalist, moved from the lowest margins of French society to the highest realms of its cultural life through a career marked by petty crime, sexual and literary notoriety, and efficacious networking. By the end of his life he was viewed in FRANCE as one of its most significant 20th-century writers and throughout the world as France's most famous homosexual.

His mother was unmarried and described herself as a governess when she gave birth to Jean Genet on December 19, 1910, in Paris; the father was never identified. Seven months later she gave the child up to the government office for welfare children and never again had contact with him. Jean was placed with a foster family in the village of Alligny-en-Morvan.

His foster family treated Genet warmly by the standards of the day; he became a choirboy and a gifted student in the Alligny public school. With other boys, he formed intense erotic friendships. At about the age of ten, he began the petty thieving (candy, books) that continued throughout the first half of his life. At the end of the 1922–1923 school year, he received the highest grades in the region in his primary school examination. Because of his illegitimate origins, his education ended here, and he was assigned to an apprenticeship in typography near Paris. This lasted only ten days before he ran away; he was found by the police a week later in Nice.

Genet's escapade to Nice at the age of fourteen marked the beginning of some twenty years of repeated cycles of vagabondage, theft, prostitution, arrest, trial, evaluation by the authorities, incarceration, and expedient military service, followed at each turn by release or escape and a return to petty crime. Two longer periods within this repeated cycle influenced him deeply. The first was his incarceration from 1926 through 1929 at Mettray, a penitentiary colony for boys run according to relatively enlightened work-based principles. Genet ran away only once during those two and a half years and romanticized Mettray throughout his life.

He finally left by enlisting in the French army initiating the second influential period made up of various military assignments. These included duties in the eastern Mediterranean and northern Africa, beginning with eleven months in Syria in 1930 and eventually placing him in Algeria and Morocco. He deserted the military in 1936 and, now a fugitive, made a last grand criminal tour, surviving on thievery and prostitution in France, Italy, Albania, Yugoslavia, Austria, Czechoslovakia, and Poland. Without legal status in any of these countries, he was repatriated and put in a military prison in Marseilles in 1938. His official discharge from the military was because of "mental imbalance" and "amorality" After he was freed, he continued to commit petty crimes and cycled in and out of French prisons until 1944. By then he had gained enough support from prominent French literary figures to keep him out of prison for good.

That support came about because of his literary reputation. During prison stays, he had begun writing novels, poetry, screenplays, and dramatic texts. By the end of 1942, he had completed *Our Lady of the Flowers* (*Notre Dame des Fleurs*), a pornographic novel (as Genet would later call it) about the Montmartre homosexual milieu. The central character is the drag queen Divine, whose criminal adventures include scenes of explicit sex amidst a parade of underworld types. The narrator, named Jean Genet, tells the story in lush prose, thick with metaphors evoking Christian mystical writing, chivalric tales, and the French Decadents—all of it punctuated regularly with graphic homosexual encounters. "I should like to address to you," the narrator tells us, "a book laden with flowers, with snow-white petticoats and blue ribbons." The paradox of a sexy underworld dressed up in flowers fired Genet's reputation: after the clandestine publication of *Our Lady of the Flowers* in 1943, respectable literary figures read it for its pornography, but could discuss it out loud because of its style.

The publication came about through JEAN COCTEAU, the homosexual artist and pundit. Genet and Cocteau met in 1943, and Cocteau read Genet's manuscript of *Our Lady of the Flowers*. Cocteau was shocked at first, but soon described the novel in his journal with a mixture of praise and envy, where he called it "the Genet bomb" (Cocteau, *Journal 1942–1945*, p. 271.) He was right: *Our Lady of the Flowers* signaled the demise of French literature's coy, aristocratic mode of handling homosexuality.

Within the year, Cocteau found legal help for Genet and arranged to get Genet's novel published in a luxurious edition designed for a monied, furtive homosexual audience. Genet was imprisoned one more time in 1943 for theft, but once released in March 1944, his new connections and reputation ensured that he never went back to prison again.

His social and intellectual world now expanded rapidly. In May 1944, he met JEAN-PAUL SARTRE in a café society that included Simone de Beauvoir, Roger Blin, ALBERT CAMUS, Pablo Picasso, Jacques Prévert, and Alberto Giacometti. Sartre and Beauvoir adopted Genet immediately. Between Cocteau's older Right Bank circle of artists and writers, vaguely aristocratic and largely homosexual, and Sartre's younger Left Bank circle of intellectual celebrities, connected professionally to publishing and academia, Genet was now exceedingly well connected. The power of his new network was made clear when, in 1948, after old legal problems threatened Genet with life imprisonment, Sartre and Cocteau wrote a letter asking that Genet be pardoned. The letter was also published in a literary review and accompanied by a manifesto signed by prominent French intellectuals. The publicity surrounding the pardon augmented the Genet legend.

Between his final release from prison in 1944 and his presidential pardon in 1949, Genet solidified his reputation with four more novels, three of which, like the earlier *Our Lady of the Flowers*, were so autobiographical that even now they are sometimes viewed as memoirs. His second novel, *Miracle of the Rose* (*Miracle de la Rose*), was published in 1946 and again has "Jean Genet" as the narrator. Throughout the novel, roses appear as visual replacements for any object provoking intense emotion in the narrator—chains, scars, blood, kisses, penises—and while the sexual encounters remain graphic, hagiography, medieval allegory, and heraldic chivalry provide a more consistent system of imagery than in *Our Lady*. Also more explicit is the theme of saintly abnegation, by which Genet claims to speak for the lowest of the low in society. The narrator's final words place him on an ascetic pilgrimage: "I say no more and walk barefoot."

Genet's most shocking novel, *Funeral Rites* (*Pompes funèbres*), was published clandestinely in 1947. The pornography has become more scatological, Joan of Arc is seen menstruating, and Adolf Hitler himself has sex in its pages with a French boy. Genet, remarkably, uses the circumstances of World War II without giving the war itself any political meaning; it merely provides a shift in the male landscape of France.

Also in 1947, Genet published the novel *Querelle* (*Querelle de Brest*) in a clandestine edition with erotic drawings by Jean

Cocteau. Set in the port city of Brest, it is his least autobiographical novel, and follows the murders and copulations of the sailor Querelle as he swaggers toward sex with the closeted commanding officer, who is in love with him. Genet's last novel, *The Thief's Journal (Journal du voleur)*, published clandestinely in 1948, is based on Genet's criminal vagabondage throughout Europe during the 1930s. In it Genet again makes explicit his desire to speak for the bottom of the social scale: "If I cannot have the most brilliant destiny, I want the most wretched one, not to live in a wasteland, but to make something new out of a subject matter that is so rare."

Theater artists were powerfully represented in Genet's new social circles. Cocteau and Sartre were both playwrights, and Roger Blin, who socialized among them, was one of Paris's leading directors. Despite Genet's lack of apprenticeship in the business of the stage, he was now offered shortcuts to major production. This sudden access to the top meant that his experiments in staging lurid or aggressive material were readily indulged, but his lack of experience, both as audience member and as playwright, put him at risk for chronic insecurity as a playwright.

The first of Genet's plays to be published was *Deathwatch (Haute Surveillance)*, appearing in 1947. It was the second of his plays to be produced when it was staged two years later, codirected by Genet with Jean Marchat. In *Deathwatch*, a trio of prisoners fight about the prison power hierarchy and their repressed mutual desires. Despite its resemblance to the novels, Genet's script does not make it clear why the three prisoners are interacting so vehemently—something that becomes obvious for an audience only if actors bring enough carnal appeal and sexual tension to the performance to embody the motives the dialogue omits. THE MAIDS (*Les Bonnes*), Genet's most frequently revived play, was both published and staged in 1947. Nine years elapsed before another of Genet's plays was published, and ten years (after the 1949 *Deathwatch* staging) before another was produced in France—a gap resulting from Genet's unproductive depression in the early 1950s. THE BALCONY (*Le Balcon*) was published in 1956 and first performed in Paris in 1960, after initial stagings in London and Berlin. THE BLACKS: A CLOWN SHOW (*Les Nègres: Clownerie*) was published in 1958 and produced in 1959. THE SCREENS (*Les Paravents*), the last of Genet's plays to be produced while he was alive, was published in 1961 and first staged in Paris in 1966. Since Genet's death in 1986, some of his prose works have been adapted for the theater, and an early abandoned script, *Splendid's*, about a mobster takeover of a luxury hotel, has been rediscovered and staged. Other abandoned works have been published posthumously, and additional theater-related material, perhaps even lost titles, may yet come to light.

Although theater historians sometimes place Genet among the Absurdists, his plays have little in common with the intellectual preoccupations of SAMUEL BECKETT, ARTHUR ADAMOV, or EUGENE IONESCO. Instead, they are obsessed with hierarchies of power and the way underclasses mimic those who dominate them socially, while also threatening those who dominate them socially—issues that are more volatile than the existential anguish of the Absurdists and that require a complacent bourgeois audience to produce their unnerving effects. That the first two of Genet's plays reached the stage on bills with GEORGES FEYDEAU and JEAN GIRAUDOUX, and that his final play, *Les Paravents*, received a premiere at the Odéon-Théâtre de France, indicates that Genet had, during his lifetime, exactly the middle-class audiences who would react most defensively to his taunts.

The presidential pardon in 1949 was soon followed by a second legend-making event: the 1952 publication of Jean-Paul Sartre's study, *Saint-Genet, comédien et martyr (Saint Genet, Actor and Martyr)*. The title takes a cue from the hagiographical imagery of Genet's novels and points to Genet's self-conscious performance of his outlaw identity, something which Sartre analyzes as a model of existential self-definition and freedom. Sartre's view that Genet deliberately enacted his adult identity is unassailable, but his postulate that the child Genet chose to be a thief because he was called one is more dubious, and his corollary that Genet chose to be homosexual now seems to be nonsense, though tolerable if we understand Sartre to mean that Genet chose to *label* himself a homosexual, by which Genet was a pioneer. Whatever the limitations of Sartre's study, it defined the legend of Genet still recognized today.

Once Genet's novels had been published, his plays were reaching production, and he had achieved financial stability and fame, the depression he had long suffered from deepened. Sartre's book didn't help because Genet felt it "turned him into a statue" (Cocteau, *Le Passé Défini*, p. 391). Genet experienced something of a renewed creative burst for his second group of plays (*Le Balcon*, *Les Nègres*, and *Les Paravents*), but after that his literary output diminished for nearly fifteen years to a few essays, hypothetical movie scenarios, and never-fulfilled plans for a large multigenre work to be called *La Mort (Death)*.

Otherwise, the years from 1952 through 1968 were filled with querulous social and professional relations and leapfrogging love affairs. Throughout these two decades Genet was nostalgic for marginalization and re-created it through travel. The 1950s saw him travel widely throughout Europe, the eastern Mediterranean, and North Africa. In the 1960s he expanded his itineraries to include India, Pakistan, Thailand, China, and Japan.

He did not visit the United States until 1968. That spring, Genet had participated, to some degree, in the Paris demonstrations by students and workers against the French government. Perhaps because of that, the American men's lifestyle magazine, *Esquire*, invited him to cover the Democratic Convention in Chicago later that summer. Genet seemed eager to do it, sneaking into the country because the U.S. government had refused him a visa. The resulting article, however, was politically incoherent: it focused on the attractiveness of the Chicago cops, whom Genet described repeatedly as divine athletes with superbly attractive thighs.

Two years later, in 1970, he was invited back to the United States by the Black Panthers. Genet spent two months traveling with them, meeting American cultural stars and speaking on behalf of imprisoned Panther leader Bobby Seale. In October 1970, the Paris representative of the Palestinian Liberation Organization (PLO) invited him to visit Palestinian refugee camps in Jordan for a week. Genet went and stayed for six months, becoming so enthralled with the fedayeen—the refugee Palestinian fighters who lived in camps and engaged in amorphous revolt against Israel and Jordan—that he returned to the area six times through 1984.

Two important works resulted from Genet's relationship with the fedayeen during the last fifteen years of his life. The essay "Quatre Heures à Chatila" ("Four Hours in Shatila"), Genet's most important work of journalism, appeared in early 1983. During a return trip to the Middle East in 1982, he happened to be in Beirut when a Jordanian Christian militia massacred Palestinians in the nearby camps at Sabra and Shatila. Genet was one of the first Westerners to enter Shatila only two days later, stumbling through the corpse-filled streets which he later described in the essay.

A little over a year later, Genet returned to the Middle East for the last time. He had been diagnosed with throat cancer in 1979, and the treatments were taking their toll. Since his first stays among the fedayeen in 1970, he had worked sporadically on a sprawling text about them, including in it his memories of the Black Panthers. The Shatila experience gave him the resolve to finish the book despite his waning health. The result was the memoir *A Prisoner of Love* (*Un Captif amoureux*). There are similarities with the autobiographical novel *Journal du voleur*, but now a few women move into the foreground, and Genet sounds like a different man. He has nearly eliminated overt sexual content and considers his own impulses with a new humility that keeps the focus on the fedayeen. In depicting them, Genet approaches a lucidity about human mortality that is almost Homeric: "the fedayeen . . . are tracer bullets, knowing their traces vanish in the twinkling of an eye."

Genet was next. He finished *A Prisoner of Love* and gave it to his publisher in November 1985. In December, *The Balcony* was staged at the Comédie Française for the first time. In the new year, Genet was able to correct galleys for *A Prisoner of Love* despite the cancer, but didn't live to see publication: he died on April 15, 1986, in Paris. A few days later, he was buried on the coast of Morocco in Larache, home of his last lover. *A Prisoner of Love* was published in France one month later.

Two major social changes have affected the meaning of Genet's work since his death in Paris. The first, affecting the novels, is the ongoing normalization of homosexuality. As homosexual rights continue to grow within middle-class Western society, Genet's presumption that his sexuality is the mark of absolute marginalization faces fossilization.

The second affects all of Genet's major plays except, perhaps, *The Balcony*. The impact of these plays depends on a sense of threat to the European middle classes, and the threat is embodied in characters who are underprivileged women, blacks, or North Africans—groups who, at the time of Genet's writing, constituted social underclasses. Fifty years later, these groups can speak for themselves in the arts and need not depend on Genet's patronizing depictions of them. In fact, the process of bypassing him began as far back as 1964, when LORRAINE HANSBERRY began work on *The Whites* (*Les Blancs*) as a rebuke to *The Blacks*.

These interpretive issues do not diminish Genet's historical importance, which lies broadly across the cultural, rather than within the tradition of any one art form, and comes from his unequivocal identification of himself to all audiences as homosexual. Genet could label himself this way because, starting as a social outsider, he had nothing to lose, and ending as a literary insider, he had a role for making the identification pay. Countless public figures have described themselves as homosexual in the decades since Genet became famous, but Genet did it first.

[*See also* Absurdism; Gay and Lesbian Drama; Philosophy and Drama, 1860–Present]

PLAYS: *Deathwatch* (*Haute Surveillance*, published 1947, premiered 1949); *The Maids* (*Les Bonnes*, 1947); *The Balcony* (*Le Balcon*, published 1956, premiered 1957); *The Blacks: A Clown Show* (*Les Nègres: Clownerie*, published 1958, premiered in Paris, 1959); *The Screens* (*Les Paravents*, published 1961, premiered 1964); *Splendid's* (published 1993, premiered 1994)

FURTHER READING

Cocteau, Jean. *Le Passé Défini: Journal 1951–1952, Vol. 1.* Paris: Gallimard, 1983.

——. *Journal 1942–1945.* Paris: Gallimard, 1989.

Dichy, Albert, and Pascal Fouché. *Jean Genet, Essai de chronologie 1910–1944* [Jean Genet, Chronological Essay, 1910–1944]. Paris: IMEC (Institut Mémoires de l'Edition Contemporaine), 1988.

Durham Scott, ed. *Genet: The Language of the Enemy* (*Yale French Studies*, No. 91). New Haven: Yale Univ. Press, 1997.

Giles, Jane. *Criminal Desires: Jean Genet and Cinema* (*Persistence of Vision*, Vol. 2). London: Creation Books, 2002.

Hankins, Jérôme, ed. *Genet à Chatila* [Genet in Shatila]. Paris: Solin, 1992.

Sartre, Jean-Paul. *Saint Genet, comédien et martyr.* Paris: Gallimard, 1952. English translation, *Saint Genet: Actor and Martyr.* New York: Braziller, 1963.

White, Edmund. *Genet: A Biography.* New York: Knopf, 1993.

David Pelizzari

GENGANGERE *See* GHOSTS

GERMANY

In the 1860s the groundwork for German unification was laid. After the failure of the bourgeois revolutions of 1848–1849, the liberal bourgeoisie turned more to the areas of economics and culture, including the theater, than to politics. The unsettled problem of national unification was resolved through the diplomacy and power politics of Prussian prime minister Otto von Bismarck (1815–1898). The Franco-Prussian War of 1870–1871 led to the founding of the German Empire; in January 1871, the King of Prussia, William I (1797–1888), was crowned German Emperor, and Bismarck was appointed Chancellor. The new, Prussian-dominated state excluded AUSTRIA, previously a major player in German affairs. Unlike the German nation-state, the dual monarchy of Austria–Hungary constituted a multicultural entity that, like the German Empire, came to an end at the conclusion of World War I.

IMPERIAL GERMANY, 1871 TO 1918

The political prominence of the German Empire in Europe and the economic boom that followed the Franco-Prussian War did not immediately result in new impulses in the theater. In the 1870s and 1880s, the historical drama, chiefly represented by Ernst von Wildenbruch (1845–1909), and the well-made play, an import from France, dominated. Whereas the historical dramas were chiefly produced at theaters subsidized by various courts and cities, the French plays and those of their German imitators found their audience in commercial venues. The court theater of George II, Duke of Saxe-Meiningen (1866–1914), was widely acclaimed for its "realistic" productions and painstaking attention to the details of staging. The highly influential composer RICHARD WAGNER (1813–1883) postulated in his theory of the *Gesamtkunstwerk* (total work of art) the fusion of all the elements that contribute to a staged work in order to transport the spectator from the humdrum here and now. In 1876, the Bayreuth Festspielhaus, a theater exclusively dedicated to staging Wagner's operas, opened with his most famous work, the tetralogy *The Ring of the Nibelung* (*Der Ring des Nibelungen*, 1853–1874), an event that has been interpreted as the artistic equivalent of the founding of the empire.

Germany still lacked a central cultural hub comparable to London or Paris. Only gradually did the new capital Berlin begin to assume its role as Germany's principal theater venue. In 1883, the Deutsches Theater was established with a regular ensemble, but a sudden, radical transformation of the theater scene occurred in October 1889 when GERHART HAUPTMANN's "social drama" BEFORE DAYBREAK (*Vor Sonnenaufgang*) opened at Berlin's Freie Bühne (Free Stage), a venue modeled after the Théâtre Libre in Paris and dedicated to the promotion of modern plays. Modernists and traditionalists engaged in a pitched battle; overnight Hauptmann became the leading representative of a new movement, NATURALISM. "Modern" German literature had arrived.

Various developments fostered the advent of naturalism. The rapid economic expansion and industrialization that benefited bourgeois entrepreneurs was accompanied by the formation of impoverished proletarian masses living in the squalor of large tenement houses, particularly in Berlin. Karl Marx (1818–1883) had formulated the theoretical foundations of socialism; the Social Democratic Party was established in 1869 and withstood Bismarck's attempts to suppress it. The "social question" remained an issue. Scientific advances, including the theory of evolution developed by Charles Darwin (1809–1882) and promoted in Germany by Ernst Haeckel (1834–1919), contributed to skepticism regarding a divinely ordered universe and encouraged a scientific and empirical worldview. FRIEDRICH NIETZSCHE (1844–1900) proclaimed that "God is dead"; Christian ethics were no longer applicable. ÉMILE ZOLA (1840–1902), the influential theoretician and practitioner of the French school of naturalism, applied scientific methods of close observation and, in deterministic fashion, focused on such ills of modern society as poverty, alcoholism, prostitution, and incest. Norwegian dramatist HENRIK IBSEN dealt critically with many aspects of bourgeois society and occupied a prominent position in naturalist theater.

Hauptmann's *Before Daybreak* displays some of the major tenets of naturalism. Alfred Loth, who is motivated by charity, rationality, and a social conscience, chances upon a sordid milieu of moral deprivation, gross materialism, and pervasive alcoholism in a nouveau riche peasant family in a Silesian village. Only the youngest daughter, Helene, has remained unaffected, but she is preyed upon by her drunkard father. Loth appears to be her savior, but he ultimately abandons her because he is convinced that alcoholism is hereditary and that their future offspring would be at great risk. Loth's decision, which causes Helene to commit suicide (offstage), has been condemned by critics as doctrinaire and narrow minded; however, it is consistent with a deterministic worldview in which heredity and milieu are decisive factors.

Hauptmann was supported by OTTO BRAHM, one of the cofounders of the Freie Bühne. As director of various Berlin theaters, Brahm developed a naturalist style of presentation. With a series of plays, Hauptmann established his permanent reputation: *The Coming of Peace* (*Das Friedensfest*, 1890), a family drama in the vein of Ibsen; *Lonely Lives* (*Einsame Menschen*, 1891), a play in which the irresolute male protagonist has to decide between a traditionally brought-up woman and an emancipated one; and his principal naturalist drama, THE WEAVERS (*Die Weber*), which depicts the Silesian weavers' uprising against their exploiters in the 1840s and innovatively dispenses with the traditional, individual protagonist in favor of a collective of weavers. In *The Beaver Coat* (*Der Biberpelz*, 1893), praised as an outstanding German COMEDY, a resourceful and down-to-earth washerwoman plans to acquire social status and material wealth by fencing stolen goods. Her misdeeds pale in comparison to the ineptitude, arrogance, and authoritarianism of a bureaucrat who is bent on exposing suspected enemies of the state rather than on apprehending common criminals. Traditional moral values have been inverted: it is no longer the criminally inclined individual that is a menace to a fundamentally just society; rather, the social system poses a danger to those who seek justice.

Hauptmann continued to write in a naturalist mode well into the 20th century, but he also turned fairly early to non-naturalist dramas. In his most popular play, the neoromantic German fairy tale drama in verse, *The Sunken Bell* (*Die versunkene Glocke*, 1896), as well as in *Hannele* (*Hanneles Himmelfahrt*, 1893) and in the glass-works fairy tale *And Pippa Dances!* (*Und Pippa tanzt!*, 1906) "real" and ideal, imaginary worlds coexist.

Arno Holz (1863–1929), one of the foremost theoreticians of German naturalism, collaborated with Johannes Schlaf (1862–1941) on *The Selicke Family* (*Die Familie Selicke*, 1890), a family drama staged by the Freie Bühne. In true naturalist fashion, the father's alcoholism is the chief source of the family's misery; all the characters are caught in a web of circumstances from which they cannot escape. HERMANN SUDERMANN scored a non-controversial hit with the November 1889 Berlin premiere of *Honor* (*Die Ehre*). Sudermann adapted the time-honored motif of the "fallen" woman: honor has become an antiquated concept and a salable commodity. In *Magda* (*Heimat*, 1893), Sudermann addressed the issue of female emancipation—generally viewed favorably by naturalists. Although *Heimat* relies on melodramatic effects, the play achieved considerable international recognition.

Virtually forgotten today, Max Halbe (1865–1944) gained instantaneous public acclaim with *Youth* (*Jugend*, 1893). Halbe's programmatic title and the play's sensuous, lyrical elements indicate its affinity with the aspirations of the young generation of artists who voiced their opposition to the historicizing and monumentalizing tendencies of officious art in the journal *Youth* (1896–1940) and sought to advance the stylized, ornamental aesthetics of *Jugendstil* (Art Nouveau) in architecture, interior design, the applied arts, and literature.

As early as 1891, the versatile Viennese writer Hermann Bahr (1863–1934) posited that naturalism would be replaced by a "nervous ROMANTICISM" emphasizing the sensitive individual's psyche. Actually, the countermovements to naturalism such as neoromanticism, impressionism, and *Jugendstil* began to emerge almost simultaneously with naturalism. Although the early dramas of Austrians HUGO VON HOFMANNSTHAL and, to a lesser extent, ARTHUR SCHNITZLER are infused with neoromantic and impressionist elements, FRANK WEDEKIND struck out in a different direction and combined social satire with a vitalistic orientation that flew in the face of both conventional morality and Hauptmann's social compassion.

Wedekind's *SPRING'S AWAKENING* (*Frühlings Erwachen*, 1891) was subject to censorship and not produced until 1906 on account of its open treatment of adolescent sexuality and its savage indictment of the oppressive world of adults whose narrow-mindedness and insensitivity lead to suicide and a botched abortion with fatal consequences. Yet there is an optimistic, albeit grotesque, ending. A masked gentleman representing the life force exhorts the dead girl's despondent seducer to abandon moral scruples and to embrace life to the fullest. *EARTH SPIRIT* (*Der Erdgeist*, 1895) and *Pandora's Box* (*Die Büchse der Pandora*, 1904) feature Lulu as an unfettered, animalistic sexual being, impervious to bourgeois social taboos, who is murdered by Jack the Ripper. In *The Marquis of Keith* (*Der Marquis von Keith*, 1901), the amoral confidence man and adventurer Keith prevails over the idealistic moralist Scholz. In reducing characters to representatives of abstract principles, Wedekind foreshadowed EXPRESSIONISM; in his social satire, he influenced CARL STERNHEIM.

Sternheim's cycle of comedies, *Scenes from the Heroic Life of the Middle Classes* (*Aus dem bürgerlichen Heldenleben*), satirizes the materialism, greed, and prejudice of the middle classes. In *THE UNDERPANTS* (*Die Hose*), Theobald Maske skillfully exploits a potential éclat, his wife's loss of her underpants in public. Maske hides his ruthlessness and acquisitiveness behind the mask of an upright civil servant. Schippel, the protagonist of *Paul Schippel Esq.* (*Bürger Schippel*, 1913), is shunned by respectable middle-class society because of his dubious, proletarian origins, but nevertheless manages to become a member of the bourgeois establishment. Sternheim's innovative use of language, a kind of *Telegrammstil* (telegram style) that trims down communication to its barest essentials, was adopted by some expressionists; his technique of presenting characters as social types rather than individuals similarly anticipates expressionism.

Expressionism, a term derived from art history, was a literary phenomenon almost exclusively confined to the German-speaking countries. It denotes an intense but relatively short-lived movement that began around 1910, whose major tenets include a profound rejection of the social order of the Wilhelmine Empire; the utopian desire to change the world via literature and the theater; and the hope for a general regeneration of humankind, a hope fostered by the cataclysm of World War I and the subsequent revolutionary turmoil. The expressionists proclaimed the birth of the "new man" (rather than "woman"; women were ordinarily confined to subordinate roles) who had cast off the shackles of the past. Inasmuch as expressionist plays written before the war were, in large part, not produced until its end or thereafter, and since expressionist drama flourished during the postwar years, the movement pertains essentially to the Weimar Republic and will be discussed under that heading. Some of the later plays of the Swedish dramatist AUGUST STRINDBERG, especially his *A DREAM PLAY* (*Ett drömspel*, 1902), which required surprising stage effects, exerted their influence on expressionist aesthetics and techniques.

THE WEIMAR REPUBLIC, 1919 TO 1933

At the end of World War I, Germany became a republic named after the town in which, in February 1919, a democratic constitution was ratified. The republic had to struggle with considerable social, economic, and political problems ensuing from the lost war; these problems, in turn, were exacerbated by the harsh conditions imposed by the victorious allies in the Treaty of Versailles of June 1919. Owing to the enormous reparation payments, the currency collapsed and inflation was rampant. At the same time, the breakdown of the old order gave rise to revolutionary fervor and utopian hopes that are, to some extent, reflected in expressionist drama.

The first genuinely expressionist drama, *The Beggar* (*Der Bettler*) by REINHARD JOHANNES SORGE, was published in 1912 and staged posthumously in 1917 in a stunning Berlin production by the famed director MAX REINHARDT. The play discards all naturalistic stage conventions; it presents a "dramatic mission" in which a youthful poet strives for a purely spiritual self-realization and articulates his striving in long and lyrical monologues. The father, as the representative of the scientific-technological establishment, is poisoned by his son. Patricide was a favorite motif in expressionist drama; it highlighted and personalized the conflict between the fathers' generation as stalwart defenders of the patriarchal order and that of the sons yearning for liberation and self-fulfillment. THE SON (*Der Sohn*) by WALTER HASENCLEVER, a manifesto of rebellious youth, and the programmatically entitled *Patricide* (*Vatermord*) by ARNOLT BRONNEN, which caused a scandal at its 1922 Berlin premiere, offer variations on the motif.

GEORG KAISER, a most prolific, versatile, and successful author with more than seventy dramas to his credit, attained his breakthrough with the 1917 Frankfurt/Main premiere of the expressionist *Verkündigungsdrama* (a drama that allegorically and symbolically proclaims the birth of the "new man"), *The Burghers of Calais* (*Die Bürger von Calais*), in which a prominent citizen sacrifices his life so that the enemy may spare the community. In a different vein, Kaiser's best-known play, FROM MORNING TO MIDNIGHT (*Von morgens bis mitternachts*), depicts the development of a lowly bank clerk in *Stationen* (stages) that lead him from a small provincial town to the capital. Yet the fraudulently obtained money does not enable him to experience the intensity of life that he seeks. Utterly disenchanted, he commits suicide; his attempts to transform his nameless fellow citizens into free human beings have been thwarted by their narrow-mindedness, subservience to authority, and materialistic orientation.

The experience of war and exposure to or involvement in the postwar revolutionary disorder is a recurrent theme in German drama at this time. In the tragedy *Naval Battle* (*Seeschlacht*, 1918), Reinhard Goering (1887–1936) explores the fate of five nameless sailors who are confined to the turret of a battleship and killed without finding out how to prevent future slaughter. *A Generation* (*Ein Geschlecht*, 1917) by Fritz von Unruh (1885–1970) features a mother figure who, appalled by the wartime misdeeds of her sons, seeks to wrest leadership from men in order to establish a new world without war. Kaiser's *Gas* trilogy—*The Coral* (*Die Koralle*, 1917), *Gas* (1918), and *Gas II* (1920)—is completely devoid of stage realism. It is a forceful indictment of the type of rampant technological progress that leads to mass annihilation, such as the production of the poisonous gas that was used in the trenches of World War I. ERNST TOLLER, in *Masses and Man* (*Masse Mensch*, 1920), questions the legitimacy of using force, albeit somewhat abstractly through the use of dream scenes. A female pacifist-socialist leader is pitted against the revolutionary masses clamoring for bloodshed to obtain social justice.

Expressionism began to decline with the political and economic stabilization of the Weimar Republic around 1923, a stabilization that resulted in a brief phase of relative prosperity and tranquility. The economic recuperation of the mid-1920s was accompanied by an astonishing flourishing of the arts and the theater, a period often nostalgically referred to as the Golden Twenties. Berlin offered a vibrant theater scene with an extraordinary number of venues and companies, renowned directors, famous actors and actresses, and well-known theater critics. The waning of expressionist pathos and utopianism and its gradual replacement by the unpretentious style and emphasis on the here and now of NEW OBJECTIVITY (*Neue Sachlichkeit*) is evident in Kaiser's turn to comedy—a subgenre totally incompatible with expressionism. This signified an implicit admission of failure: idealistic proclamations from the stage were not likely to set in motion substantial social changes. The legacy of expressionism was primarily evident in acting techniques and stage designs that challenged and revolutionized naturalist conventions.

New Objectivity consisted of diverse tendencies rather than a fairly uniform movement. Even before the general decline of expressionism, there had been deviations from the expressionist norm. In his first major drama, BAAL, BERTOLT BRECHT polemicized against the depiction of playwright Christian Dietrich Grabbe (1801–1836) as a misunderstood, lonely genius in *The Lonely One* (*Der Einsame*, 1918) by HANNS JOHST. The protagonist of Brecht's DRUMS IN THE NIGHT (*Trommeln in der Nacht*) rejects all idealistic notions of remaking the world by fighting on the barricades in support of the revolutionary Berlin Spartacus movement, opting instead for material comforts. Brecht advocated a productive approach to such new mass-culture phenomena as film, radio, revues, and sporting events like bicycle races and boxing matches, which in part emanated from the United States. But in his exploration of the big city in *In the Jungle of Cities* (*Im Dickicht der Städte*, 1923), Brecht conveyed the individual's alienation and lack of human contact in the jungle of the cold, semi-mythical city of Chicago. Although the comedy *A Man's a Man* (*Mann ist Mann*, 1926) takes place in an exotic setting, Brecht's experience of the modern "asphalt city" of Berlin and its urban mass society with its attendant loss of individuality is reflected in the play. Technical innovation, one of the hallmarks of New Objectivity, is carried to an extreme in that Brecht applies the principle of mechanical montage to a human being: a meek and gentle dockworker is transformed into a ferocious "human fighting machine."

The interwar revival of the VOLKSSTÜCK (popular drama) tradition significantly contributed to a new, realistic orientation in the German theater. The 1925 Berlin premiere of *The Merry Vineyard* (*Der fröhliche Weinberg*) by CARL ZUCKMAYER was a resounding success. Zuckmayer's figures, patterned after the down-to-earth, dialect-speaking inhabitants of his wine-growing home region on the Rhine, display an infectious zest for life. In contrast to Zuckmayer's conservative *Volksstück* and its preindustrial world populated by simple and unsophisticated but basically good-natured folk, MARIELUISE FLEIẞER depicts the lower-middle-class milieu of her Bavarian hometown as repressive and exploitative. In *Purgatory in Ingolstadt* (*Fegefeuer in Ingolstadt*, 1926), two outsiders experience the full brunt of the townspeople's narrow-mindedness and prejudice. Similarly, *Soldiers in Ingolstadt* (*Pioniere in Ingolstadt*) dramatizes the sexual exploitation of an innocent and naïve maid by a soldier. Brecht, who was involved in the rehearsals for the 1929 Berlin performance, provoked a formidable theater scandal by having actors simulate sexual intercourse in an enclosure onstage. As a result, Fleißer was declared persona non grata in her native town and broke off her relationship with Brecht.

ÖDÖN VON HORVÁTH established his reputation as a playwright with a series of critical *Volksstücke* during the final phase of the Weimar Republic. In *The Italian Evening* (*Italienische Nacht*, 1931), Horváth shows Communists and Social Democrats fighting each other rather than forming a united front against the Nazis and their increasing threat to the republic. TALES FROM THE VIENNA WOODS (*Geschichten aus dem Wiener Wald*), Horváth's best-known play, is the story of a victimized woman who is forced to return to her fiancé, a brutal butcher, and a dismal life. The "heavenly" music of the younger Johann Strauss's (1825–1899) waltz, from which Horváth derived the play's title, ironically evokes notions of Viennese charm and lightheartedness.

The economic crisis and its attending political radicalization fostered a new type of drama, the *Zeitstück*, which concentrated on addressing contemporary sociopolitical affairs. The narrow focus on topical issues, however, usually prevented the *Zeitstück* from generating lasting appeal. The Communist physician FRIEDRICH WOLF declared that "art is a weapon" in the struggle for social justice. His controversial *Cyanide* (*Cyankali*, 1929), about an unemployed, pregnant young woman who dies from a botched, illegal abortion, is a fierce indictment of the German antiabortion law that penalized working-class women who could least afford to feed additional children. The 1927 staging of Toller's *Hoppla, We're Alive* (*Hoppla, wir leben!*) by ERWIN PISCATOR employed technical innovations such as film, radio transmissions, and simultaneous scenes to great effect. Yet Toller's protagonist, a revolutionary activist who had been incarcerated in an insane asylum, perceives the new world as dominated by pragmatism and cynicism. His ideals shattered, he commits suicide.

None of the playwrights of the Weimar Republic had a greater impact on the future development of drama and theater than Brecht. Around 1926, he began to read Karl Marx; his studies of Marxism coincided with the gradual evolution and theoretical formulation of the concept of EPIC THEATER. Retrospectively, Brecht deemed the August 1928 Berlin premiere of THE THREEPENNY OPERA (*Die Dreigroschenoper*), a collaborative effort with composer Kurt Weill (1900–1950), a "most successful demonstration of the epic theater" in that visual, short scene descriptions were designed to minimize suspense, and special song lighting and the illumination of the organ were intended to prevent the seamless merging of speech and singing in an effort to foreground the act of performance. Yet the astonishing popularity of the "opera" is largely attributable to its "culinary," entertaining qualities. Weill's catchy tunes, foremost among them the ever-popular "Mack the Knife," tended to overshadow the intended social criticism. As a monument of Weimar popular culture, *The Threepenny Opera* has been credited with being the perfect vehicle for expressing the effervescent spirit and artistic vibrancy of the Golden Twenties.

Brecht's attempts to transform the spectator into a critical, rational viewer who would obtain novel, liberating insights by observing human beings as changeable was dependent on the ALIENATION EFFECT, his widely discussed key concept. Brecht posited that the audience, whose perception had been dulled by the habitual observation of recurring phenomena, should be enabled to perceive new possibilities and social solutions via representations of our everyday world in unfamiliar, estranging ways. Between approximately 1928 and 1931, Brecht turned to the LEARNING PLAYS (*Lehrstück*) in which he dispensed with "culinary" elements altogether and foregrounded the plays' Marxist orientation. He sought to create a new kind of theater in which the distinction between actors and audience was abolished. The complex drama *Saint Joan of the Stockyards* (*Die heilige Johanna der Schlachthöfe*) constituted a return to the epic mode. Written during the worldwide economic crisis that resulted from the Wall Street stock market crash of October 1929, the play was not produced until after Brecht's death. In its condemnation of capitalism in the United States, the play is a far cry from Brecht's former enthusiasm for a vigorous, youthful America that provided important impulses in technology, mass entertainment, and sports.

The thriving and diverse cultural scene and the novel theater practices of the Weimar Republic came to an abrupt end when, on January 30, 1933, Adolf Hitler (1889–1945) was appointed chancellor of a coalition government and began instituting radical and far-reaching measures that profoundly altered the political and cultural landscape.

THE THIRD REICH, 1933 TO 1945: DRAMA AND THEATER IN EXILE

The vast majority of successful German dramatists were of leftist or liberal persuasion. After the cultural *Gleichschaltung*—the Nazis' euphemistic term for enforced adherence to ideological principles—there was no place for representatives of what the Nazis perceived as the decadent, cosmopolitan, democratic, and urban Weimar culture. The burning of the Reichstag, the parliament building, in February 1933 was used by the Nazis as a pretext for increasing the terror against political opponents, and the public book burning of May 1933 highlighted the fascists' cultural intolerance. A virtually unprecedented exodus—for political, racial, and other reasons—of artists and intellectuals who had significantly shaped the Berlin theater scene ensued; among them Bertolt Brecht, Walter Hasenclever, Ödön von Horváth, Georg Kaiser, Erwin Piscator, Max Reinhardt, Carl Sternheim, Ernst Toller, Friedrich Wolf, Kurt Weill, and Carl Zuckmayer.

The gap left by the exiles was filled by lesser talents; Johst and Bronnen were among the few adherents of Nazism whose work had been acknowledged during the Weimar Republic. Johst's *Schlageter* (1933) turned the protagonist into a martyr for the national cause of Germany's "reawakening" and became one of the most frequently performed plays in the Third Reich. Yet endeavors to create a genuinely National Socialist type of drama largely failed. The *Thing-Spiel*, based on the Germanic tradition of meting out justice in a public forum, was designed for open-air performances to attract huge masses and foster a sense of community. The *Thing-Spiel* was surpassed by the painstakingly orchestrated, vast political rallies that showed Nazi aesthetics most impressively. Theaters proper, on account of the comparative paucity of convincing new plays, tended to concentrate on the classics and on entertaining fare. Non-Nazi artists who remained in Germany had to walk a tightrope between accommodation and subtle acts of opposition; director/actor Gustaf Gründgens (1899–1963) is a case in point.

Exile proved to be a severe challenge for theater practitioners and playwrights because of their dependence on the German language. Hence, Austria—until the *Anschluss* by Nazi Germany in 1938—and the German-speaking part of neutral SWITZERLAND became favorite destinations. The Zurich Schauspielhaus in particular evolved into a premier theater institution by staging a number of plays by exiles, among them Wolf's *Professor Mamlock* (1934), the most frequently performed exile drama, in which a Jewish physician, a conservative and loyal citizen, is barred from his clinic by a ruthless Nazi upstart and commits suicide. During World War II, when Brecht was no longer in Europe, the Schauspielhaus premiered three of his best-known plays written in exile: the first version of THE LIFE OF GALILEO (*Leben des Galilei*), MOTHER COURAGE AND HER CHILDREN (*Mutter Courage und ihre Kinder*), and THE GOOD WOMAN OF SETZUAN (*Der gute Mensch von Setzuan*).

Other venues in which German-language plays could be produced and troupes that could perform them were created by the exiles themselves in the larger cities of approximately twenty-five host countries. The exiled playwrights' desire to enlighten audiences about conditions in Germany and to attack Nazism made plays that could be produced in the language of the respective host country potentially more effective. Brecht's parable play about the divisiveness of racial theories, *Roundheads and Pointed Heads* (*Die Rundköpfe und die Spitzköpfe*), eventually premiered in 1936 in Copenhagen in a Danish translation. In *Señora Carrar's Rifles* (*Die Gewehre der Frau Carrar*), a play about the Spanish Civil War, and FEAR AND MISERY OF THE THIRD REICH (*Furcht und Elend des Dritten Reiches*), Brecht made a deliberate effort to deemphasize "epic" elements in favor of a more realistic portrayal of the threat emanating from fascism. Both dramas were performed by and for German exiles in Paris, in 1937 and 1938, respectively.

After the outbreak of World War II, most European countries were threatened by Nazi invasion and could no longer provide a sanctuary for exiles. Hence, overseas destinations, especially the United States, became a desirable refuge. Yet establishing a successful career proved to be a formidable challenge. Reinhardt's Hollywood Workshop for Stage, Screen and Radio failed to thrive. Piscator, after his sojourn in the Soviet Union, achieved a measure of recognition with his New York City Dramatic Workshop, in which exiles and American artists developed experimental approaches to theater. Despite Brecht's unceasing productivity, he was unable to gain a foothold either in Hollywood, which he detested, or on Broadway. Generally more successful were actresses and actors with experience in both the theater and film, such as Elisabeth Bergner (1897–1986) and Peter Lorre (1904–1964).

After the battle of Stalingrad in 1943 and the Allied invasion of Normandy in June 1944, the tide of war in Europe began to turn. In German cities, devastated by Allied bombings, theater performances continued until the fall of 1944, when theaters were ordered closed so that all endeavors might be directed toward the war effort. With the end of the war approaching, the surviving exiles began to face the question of whether, how, and when to return and what to expect from the homeland they were forced to leave and that had gone so terribly astray.

POSTWAR, DIVIDED GERMANY, 1945 TO 1989

Germany's unconditional surrender in May 1945 ended World War II, and the country was divided into four occupation zones by the victorious American, British, French, and Soviet Allies; similarly, Berlin (in the Soviet occupation zone) was divided into four sectors. More than ten million Germans fled or were expelled from the territories east of the Oder and Neisse rivers, aggravating the dire economic situation in bombed-out cities without a functioning infrastructure, housing, and food. The catastrophic defeat of Nazi Germany and its legacy of both wholesale physical destruction and moral decline gave rise to the thesis of the "zero hour," which posited a completely new beginning for the nation and those who had survived the war. Yet the Nuremberg Trials of Nazi war criminals, conducted by an international tribunal in 1945 and 1946, served as a reminder that the past continued to cast its long shadow.

Despite the necessity of surviving, in many cities theaters began reopening in the fall of 1945; astoundingly, more than one hundred new productions were mounted by the end of the year. In addition to the classics, entertaining, lighter fare attracted audiences. The cultural policies of the occupation authorities served to promote plays from their respective countries; in the American zone dramas were intended to serve the purpose of reeducation and instilling democratic values. Plays by a wide range of international authors who had been banned in Nazi Germany became part of the postwar repertoire.

One of the first postwar indigenous plays, *The Illegals* (*Die Illegalen*) by Günther Weisenborn (1902–1969), premiered in a (West) Berlin theater in March 1946. It thematized resistance to the Nazi regime based on the author's personal experiences. A far greater impact was achieved by WOLFGANG BORCHERT's impassioned *The Man Outside* (*Draußen vor der Tür*, 1947), which recalls expressionism in its emotional intensity and subjective vision, and in its protagonist's progress through a number of stages (*Stationen*). Borchert gave voice to the despair and existential anguish of the "lost generation" of young men returning from a war that they had survived, but that had robbed them of their youth. Confronted with and rejected by what Borchert rather incongruously depicts as a satiated postwar society, his protagonist faces a life of hopelessness and despair.

An encompassing view of the Nazi past was provided by returnee Zuckmayer in *The Devil's General* (*Des Teufels General*, 1946), the most heatedly debated drama of the postwar years. Protagonist General Harras of the Luftwaffe is faced with the moral predicament of despising Hitler, on the one hand, and of supporting Hitler's war effort via his expertise on the other. In the end, he submits to "divine judgment" by flying a malfunctioning airplane and is killed in the ensuing crash. Zuckmayer was criticized for both his sympathetic portrayal of fellow traveler Harras and his ambivalent treatment of the resistance movement. Nevertheless, the play was instrumental in initiating an intense discussion about coming to terms with the Nazi past. Brecht likewise returned with a hit; his *Mr. Puntila and His Man Matti* (*Volksstück, Herr Puntila und sein Knecht Matti*, 1948) was staged to great acclaim in West Germany—ironically, in part because of the erroneous assumption that it lacked the ingredients of class antagonism.

The developing political, ideological, and economic tensions among the antifascist Allies that found expression in the Soviets' attempt to blockade the Western powers' access to Berlin (except by air) in 1948 and 1949 resulted in the Cold War, during which the two parts of Germany eventually developed into junior partners of their former enemies, the United States and the Soviet Union, respectively. The establishment of two German states in 1949, the Federal Republic of Germany (FRG, on the territory of the U.S., British, and French postwar occupation zones) with Bonn as its capital and the German Democratic Republic (GDR, on the territory of the Soviet occupation zone) with East Berlin as its capital, manifested the division of Germany that was to last approximately forty years and resulted in distinctly different developments in the cultural realm.

THE FEDERAL REPUBLIC OF GERMANY, 1949 TO 1989

The currency reform of 1948 and the economic aid under the auspices of the Marshall Plan created the conditions for an enormous postwar reconstruction effort. The "economic miracle" as well as the political stability under patriarchal Chancellor Konrad Adenauer (1876–1967) encouraged large segments of the population to focus on material prosperity and to ignore attempts to come to grips with the legacy of the Third Reich. Despite the prevalence of mass media in postwar West Germany, the theater soon reclaimed its place. In divided Germany, Berlin lost its central role as theater capital; Düsseldorf, Hamburg, Munich, and other cities gained recognition as regional centers.

During the first decade of its existence, the Federal Republic did not produce promising new playwrights. The revitalization of the theater in German-speaking countries began in the mid-1950s with the emergence of Swiss authors FRIEDRICH DÜRRENMATT and MAX FRISCH. Events of major significance—including the construction of the Berlin Wall in 1961, the end of the economic boom, and the series of trials against concentration camp personnel in the early 1960s—resulted in a reorientation of drama that assumed a decidedly political edge. Martin Walser (1927–) linked the recent past and present in his "German chronicle" *The Rabbit Race* (*Eiche und Angora*, 1962) in which he scathingly satirized the propensity of some Germans to willingly serve various regimes and to adapt to different political systems.

DOCUMENTARY DRAMA, which was based on the selective use of authentic records, became prevalent in the early 1960s; it modified the model Piscator used during the Weimar Republic. In fact, after his return from exile, Piscator produced three of the most significant documentary dramas at West Berlin's Freie Volksbühne: *The Deputy* (*Der Stellvertreter*, 1963) by ROLF HOCHHUTH, *In the Matter of J. Robert Oppenheimer* (*In der Sache J. Robert Oppenheimer*, 1964) by HEINAR KIPPHARDT, and THE INVESTIGATION (*Die Ermittlung*, 1965) by PETER WEISS. Hochhuth's *The Deputy* unequivocally condemns Pope Pius XII for failing to speak out publicly against the extermination of the Jews in Nazi concentration camps. According to Eric Bentley in his *The Storm over The Deputy* (1964), the play *The Deputy* almost certainly caused "the largest storm ever raised by a play in the whole history of the drama"; Constantin Costa-Gavras (1933–) recently directed a film adaptation, *Amen* (2003).

Hochhuth emphasized the individual's moral responsibility in the historical process, but he tended to view complex issues in personal terms, as in *Soldiers* (*Soldaten*, 1967), *Jurists* (*Juristen*, 1980), and *Female Doctors* (*Ärztinnen*, 1980). *Soldiers* probes the ethics of the indiscriminate saturation bombing of German cities and wholesale killing of civilians during World War II and implicates Sir Winston Churchill (1874–1965). In *Jurists*, a member of the younger generation fiercely accuses those wartime military judges who condemned German soldiers to death for minor infractions but were able to continue their careers in postwar West Germany. *Female Doctors* draws attention, albeit in sensationalist fashion, to the unsavory connections between the pharmaceutical industry and physicians who prescribe inadequately tested medication for profit.

Kipphardt's *In the Matter of J. Robert Oppenheimer* explores the ethical dimensions of constructing weapons of mass destruction on the basis of the Atomic Energy Commission's protocol about the investigation of the physicist Oppenheimer. Weiss, however, a returnee from Sweden, is considered the chief representative of documentary drama in Germany. His MARAT/SADE (*Die Verfolgung und Ermordung Jean Paul Marats dargestellt durch die Schauspielgruppe des Hospizes zu Charenton unter Anleitung des Herrn de Sade*) became an international triumph. The drama presents a play within a play in which two historical figures, the revolutionary Jean Paul Marat (1744–1793) and the representative of extreme individualism, the Marquis de Sade (1740–1814), advocate antithetical political and philosophical views. The setting of the insane asylum and the performance of the inmates provide a rich array of theatrical devices ranging from pantomime and melodrama to intellectual discussions conducted with great virtuosity, as evidenced in the 1964 Royal Shakespeare Company production by Peter Brook (1925–) and the subsequent film version (1966).

In *The Investigation*, Weiss abandoned "total" theater in favor of an approach that was strictly documentary and relied on verbal means, albeit in the form of an "oratorio." Weiss used the protocols from the 1963–1964 Frankfurt/Main trials against the guards at Auschwitz to raise the public's awareness about the magnitude of the crimes committed. His increasing commitment to socialism led Weiss to lend his moral support to the Vietcong in the play *Discourse on the Progress of the Prolonged War of Liberation in Viet Nam* (*Viet Nam–Diskurs*, 1968).

After a hiatus of more than thirty years, the *Volksstück* experienced yet another significant revival; Fleißer and Horváth, whose plays had been banned during the Nazi period, served as models. The *Volksstück* shared with documentary drama a focus on concrete social problems, but presented a perhaps more limited scope by concentrating on the lower middle classes and Germany's rural population. Martin Sperr (1944–2002) in *Hunting Scenes from Lower Bavaria* (*Jagdszenen aus Niederbayern*, produced 1966) exposed the rejection and persecution of outsiders, among them a homosexual, in a Bavarian village. The multitalented, enormously prolific RAINER WERNER FASSBINDER is perhaps best known as the chief representative of the New German Cinema. Yet Fassbinder also served, albeit briefly, as a theater director and wrote a considerable number of plays and adaptations. His first drama, *Katzelmacher* (1968), is provocatively titled with an untranslatable, derogatory dialect term used to characterize Italians. But it is a Greek rather than an Italian guest worker who is in danger of becoming the victim of the young male villagers in the play. In the end, the victim turns into a potential victimizer himself when he refuses to collaborate with a Turk. Fassbinder's most controversial play, *Garbage, the City and Death* (*Der Müll, die Stadt und der Tod*) was, after several abortive attempts, scheduled to premiere posthumously in 1985, but members of the Jewish community in Frankfurt/Main, who objected to the negative representation of a Jewish developer, physically prevented the performance from taking place.

FRANZ XAVER KROETZ, the most important representative of the postwar German *Volksstück*, turned out plays in rapid succession and, by the mid-1970s, had become one of the most frequently produced West German playwrights. Kroetz offered naturalistic depictions (with an admixture of the abnormal) of people seemingly on the fringes of society who are frequently unable to articulate their problems, such as unwanted pregnancies, abortions, and the like. Their inability to communicate predisposes them to become either victims or perpetrators of violence. But *The Nest* (*Das Nest*, 1975) features an active protagonist: a worker who reports his boss for polluting the environment. In *Mensch Meier: A Play of Everyday Life* (*Mensch Meier*, 1978), Kroetz continued to articulate emancipatory tendencies: the wife and son of a domestic tyrant learn to live independently by severing their familial ties. In the 1980s, Kroetz engaged in some moderate aesthetic experimentation: *Neither Fish nor Fowl* (*Nicht Fisch nicht Fleisch*, 1981) contains a scene derived from the theater of the absurd in an otherwise realistic plot.

Although documentary drama had contributed to questioning the underpinnings of the prevailing conservatism and restorative tendencies of postwar society, the so-called student revolt of 1968 caused far-reaching changes in relations between the sexes, education, attitudes toward foreigners, and participatory democracy. Although the rebellious students ultimately failed to radically alter the political system, their movement contributed to a general democratization of society. Inasmuch as students resorted to happenings of a theatrical nature via sit-ins and love-ins, (unconventional) theater assumed a significant public dimension but did not spawn any noteworthy plays. In fact, GÜNTER GRASS in his piece of "dialectic theater" *Max* (*Davor*, 1969) inveighs against the students' ritualized protests and happenings and advocates a policy of enlightenment and unspectacular measures as an alternative, yet constructive, means of opposing the war in Vietnam.

Attempts to democratize the society extended to the institution of the theater. Most notably, director Peter Stein (1937–) formed a company at the West Berlin Schaubühne that practiced teamwork and was based on egalitarian principles. Initially of a pronounced political bent, Stein later veered in a more apolitical direction and succeeded in establishing his theater as the foremost West German institution. He staged plays by PETER HANDKE and, especially, BOTHO STRAUSS, an erstwhile dramaturge and translator at the Schaubühne who became one of the most significant playwrights in the last decades of the 20th century. The Schaubühne presented Strauss's *Three Acts of*

Recognition (*Trilogie des Wiedersehens*, 1978; which was also produced at the New York Shakespeare Festival in 1982), premiered Strauss's first great success, *Big and Little* (*Groß und Klein*, 1978), and produced *The Park* (*Der Park*, 1984). Strauss's achievement is generally considered to have provided a panoramic view of West German society by representing chance encounters with characters whose banal, inconclusive stories allude to an underlying layer of deeper significance.

Unlike the practitioners of documentary drama and the *Volksstück*, the dramatists of the 1970s and 1980s cannot be said to have a common ideological or aesthetic platform. Whereas Handke may exemplify a neoromantic "New Sensibility" and Strauss offers a kind of mythical realism, ELFRIEDE JELINEK assumes an aggressively feminist position and THOMAS BERNHARD savagely criticized his homeland Austria. Hungarian-born playwright and director GEORGE TABORI established an experimental studio in Germany in which he promoted nonauthoritarian, supportive cooperation between actors and director, the very antithesis of the then fashionable *Regietheater* (director's theater) that allowed prominent directors to realize their vision on stage, often at the expense of the text, authorial intent, and spectators' expectations.

The entirely unexpected opening of the Berlin Wall on November 9, 1989, followed by the subsequent demise of the GDR and Germany reunification, considerably changed the conditions under which the theater had operated in divided Germany.

THE GERMAN DEMOCRATIC REPUBLIC, 1949 TO 1990

Owing in large measure to the lack of resources and the significant reparations that the GDR was obliged to pay to the Soviet Union, economic recovery here proceeded considerably more slowly than in the FRG. Nevertheless, Chairman Walter Ulbricht (1893–1973) and his Sozialistische Einheitspartei Deutschlands (SED; Socialist Unity Party), which completely controlled the government and determined cultural policy, considered theater an important medium worthy of substantial subsidy. This support enabled a comparatively large number of stages with high professional standards. Their chief function consisted of propagating the dominant ideology of Marxism-Leninism and contributing to the development and strengthening of the socialist order; deviations from the party line usually resulted in harsh punishment. Only gradually did the theater begin to serve as a venue for criticizing the shortcomings of life in the GDR, criticism that otherwise could not be articulated publicly.

In January 1949, Brecht's exile play *Mother Courage and Her Children* (*Mutter Courage und ihre Kinder*) opened at the Deutsches Theater in East Berlin with Brecht's actress wife, Helene Weigel (1900–1971), in the leading role, a significant theatrical event that brought into sharp focus the contradictory tendencies attending the formation of a new, socialist theater. Wolf, who returned to Germany from the Soviet Union and was a practitioner of "Aristotelian," cathartic theater, criticized Brecht's play as being too pessimistic, but in the long run *Mother Courage* prevailed and became an international triumph. Wolf's objections highlighted Brecht's dilemma after taking up permanent residence in East Berlin in May 1949: on the one hand, he was considered one of the chief cultural representatives of the GDR; on the other, he was constantly running the risk of being accused of violating the norms of the official aesthetic doctrine, Socialist Realism. The opera *The Trial of Lucullus* (*Das Verhör des Lukullus*), originally a radio play written at the beginning of World War II, met with stern criticism for alleged "formalist" and pacifist tendencies on the part of Brecht and his collaborator, composer Paul Dessau (1894–1979).

Brecht had opted for East Berlin in part because of the prospect of having at his disposal a theater of his own. He envisioned a representative role, one that could transcend the political division of Germany, by having his plays staged in both the East and the West. The vehicle for promoting his design was the Berliner Ensemble, a troupe that developed eventually into one of the GDR's premier cultural institutions. In light of the material devastations of the war and the ideological remnants of Nazism, Brecht considered his chief responsibility to rebuild the repertory with socially progressive plays from the German and international stage via adaptations and "model" productions. Guest appearances by the Berliner Ensemble in Paris and London paved the way for Brecht's work to be esteemed in the West as modern classics. Brecht's ascendancy was briefly interrupted by various West German boycotts of his plays in the 1950s and early 1960s; these boycotts did not succeed in permanently damaging his reputation.

In the late 1950s, younger dramatists became prominent in the GDR. Peter Hacks (1928–2003) encountered difficulties but gradually became one of the most productive and, particularly in the 1970s, frequently performed GDR playwrights in both parts of Germany. In *Worries and Power* (*Die Sorgen und die Macht*, 1960), Hacks appeared to conform to the official demand that literary and theatrical projects concern themselves with the sphere of productive labor, yet the conversion of a factory worker from an outsider to a follower of party discipline is motivated by love rather than ideology. Hope for a more liberal cultural policy as a consequence of the construction of the Berlin Wall in 1961, a measure that effectively stopped the mass flight of GDR citizens to West Berlin and then (via plane) to the FRG, were soon dashed. In 1965, Hacks's *Moritz Tassow*, in which an agricultural worker prematurely initiates the redistribution of land without the blessing of the party, had to be withdrawn after a few performances.

Similarly, the early plays of HEINER MÜLLER, which in their dialectic structuring are indebted to Brecht, addressed the problems of socialist reconstruction within the milieux of workers and engineers, farmers, refugees, and party functionaries. Müller was by no means opposed to the goals of socialism, but his critical view did not in all cases conform to the required optimistic outlook. *The Scab* (*Der Lohndrücker*, 1956), a collaborative effort with his first wife, Inge Müller (1925–1966), that depicts the difficulties an activist worker encounters in his heroic efforts to prevent an interruption in the production of fireproof bricks, was produced in 1958. Yet the comedy *The Resettled Woman, or Life in the Country* (*Die Umsiedlerin, oder Das Leben auf dem Lande*), which deals with the difficult process of forming agricultural collectives, was immediately banned after its premiere in 1961 and not produced again until 1975. In the 1970s, Müller abandoned contemporary subjects and began writing plays in a mythical-historical as well as apocalyptic vein, among them the forceful and violent Shakespeare adaptation DIE HAMLETMASCHINE, which was first produced in 1979 in Paris. These dramas, reminiscent of the theater of cruelty in the manner of ANTONIN ARTAUD, established Müller's international fame. In the 1980s, he was allowed to travel freely and began collaborating with the renowned director of the Theater of Images, Robert Wilson (1941–), on various projects.

In 1971, Ulbricht was succeeded by Erich Honecker (1912–1994), who instituted a (temporary) liberalization in cultural policies from which scriptwriter Ulrich Plenzdorf (1934–) benefited with his widely debated—in both East and West—*The New Sufferings of Young W.* (*Die neuen Leiden des jungen W.*, 1972), an adaptation of an epistolary novel by Johann Wolfgang von Goethe (1749–1832). In a series of filmic flashbacks, the young protagonist asserts his right to self-realization in a strictly regimented society by wearing blue jeans, letting his hair grow long, and listening to jazz; he does not, however, question the legitimacy of the GDR or the party. The expatriation of singer/poet Wolf Biermann (1936–) in 1976 ended the brief period of comparative freedom of expression and resulted in an exodus of artists, among them THOMAS BRASCH, whose play *Rotter* (1977), the story of a perennial fellow traveler who easily adapts to various political systems, was performed in the West.

The dramas of Volker Braun (1939–) reflect—despite the author's firm commitment to the GDR—the development of East German society in a critical vein. Because of Braun's critical stance, the production of his plays and the publication of his other texts were often delayed. In *The Transitional Society* (*Die Übergangsgesellschaft*, 1987), an adaptation of THE THREE SISTERS (1904) by ANTON CHEKHOV (1860–1904), Braun articulated, particularly in a fantastic sequence of scenes, the desire of large segments of the population to escape a narrow and confined existence. This desire was fueled by the reform efforts of Mikhail S. Gorbachev (1931–), who advocated *perestroika* (the rebuilding of society) and *glasnost* (openness in public affairs) in the Soviet Union. The GDR leadership continued to insist, however, that the Soviet reforms were not applicable to the GDR. CHRISTOPH HEIN used Arthurian legends in the comedy *The Knights of the Round Table* (*Die Ritter der Tafelrunde*, 1989) as a historical model to demonstrate the potential for change—a radical and unanticipated change that began with the opening of the Berlin Wall and was followed by the demise of the GDR.

REUNITED GERMANY, 1990 TO PRESENT

Reunification exposed East German theater to the pressures of economics and the marketplace. Particularly in Berlin, where during the Cold War the East–West competition for intellectual and artistic superiority had resulted in the duplication of cultural and academic institutions, there appeared to be an overcapacity of theater venues. The West Berlin Schillertheater, one of the largest stages in the old and new capital, was closed in 1993. Conversely, the Berliner Ensemble was able to continue its existence through subsidies granted by the Berlin city government. At the same time, GDR writers in general were subject to scrutiny by Western critics who somewhat disingenuously charged them with having been instrumental in stabilizing the failed regime via carefully veiled criticism and insufficient candor. Notable dramatists of the former GDR such as Braun, Hein, and Müller, who had criticized their state during its existence, responded to reunification with skepticism and foreboding. Braun's *Bohemia on the Sea* (*Böhmen am Meer*, produced 1992) uses the title of the play as a metaphor for unfulfilled utopian hopes and implies the failure of the experiment of reunification. An aggressively negative view was presented by the West German Hochhuth in his *Wessis in Weimar: Scenes from an Occupied Country* (*Wessis in Weimar. Szenen aus einem besetzten Land*)—*Wessis* is a derogatory term for West Germans—a play that premiered in 1993 to both enthusiastic acclaim and fervent rejection at the Berliner Ensemble under the direction of Einar Schleef (1944–). Hochhuth cast East Germans in the role of helpless, exploited victims. A more ambivalent view was taken by the West German Strauss, who in *Final Chorus* (*Schlußchor*, 1991) alluded to the nation as a mythical rather than a political entity.

Surprisingly, Brecht, who during the 1950s and early 1960s had served in the West as a scapegoat for the sins of the GDR system, escaped the attacks that his successors had to endure. In 1995, Müller mounted a spectacular Berliner Ensemble production of Brecht's exile play THE RESISTIBLE RISE OF ARTURO UI (*Der Aufstieg des Arturo Ui*) that depicts Hitler's rise to power as the ascendancy of a gangster in the manner of Al Capone. On the occasion of Brecht's 100th birthday in 1998, the media paid unprecedented attention to the playwright and thereby cemented his position as the foremost German dramatist of the 20th century and as one of the most influential innovators and practitioners of the theater. Berlin continued to offer exciting theatrical fare; in the 1990s, under the direction of Frank Castorf (1951–), the Volksbühne in the eastern part of the city began to offer highly unconventional productions that tended to use the text of plays very freely. Strauss, the most frequently produced contemporaneous German dramatist, continues to be productive; both *Unexpected Return* (*Unerwartete Rückkehr*; 2002), a play about a cuckolded husband who masochistically seeks belated revenge, and *Violation* (*Schändung*, 2006), based on William Shakespeare's *Titus Andronicus*, had their German premieres at the Berliner Ensemble that since the 1999/2000 season has been under the artistic direction of Claus Peymann (1937–).

Among the playwrights who have emerged in reunified Germany, Albert Ostermaier (1967–) emphasizes Brecht's role as an agent provocateur (rather than an innovator of the theater) in his play with the unidiomatic title *The Making Of B.– Movie* (produced 1999). Since 1995 Ostermaier's dramas have been produced on a regular basis; *Death Valley Junction* (2000) shows a couple searching for their true selves in scenes bordering on the surreal. Other younger dramatists who have established their reputations during the 1990s include Dea Loher (1964–) and Theresia Walser (1967–). Loher's *Life on the Praça Roosevelt* (*Das Leben auf der Praça Roosevelt*) premiered in 2004; it incongruously but skillfully combines comedy and death and is, perhaps, indicative of a new trend in German drama and theater, that is, the renewed attention devoted to the representation of human nature rather than to abstract concepts.

FURTHER READING

Benson, Renate. *German Expressionist Drama: Ernst Toller and Georg Kaiser.* New York: Grove Press, 1984.

Bentley, Eric. *The Storm over The Deputy.* New York: Grove Press, 1964.

Calandra, Denis. *New German Dramatists: A Study of Peter Handke, Franz Xaver Kroetz, Rainer Werner Fassbinder, Heiner Müller, Thomas Brasch, Thomas Bernhard and Botho Strauss.* London: Macmillan, 1983.

Garten, Hugh Frederick. *Modern German Drama.* 2nd ed. London: Methuen, 1964.

Haas, Birgit. *Modern German Political Drama 1980–2000.* Rochester, NY: Camden House, 2003.

Osborne, John. *The Naturalist Drama in Germany.* Manchester, England: Manchester Univ. Press, 1971.

Patterson, Michael. *German Theatre Today: Post-War Theatre in West and East Germany, Austria, and Northern Switzerland.* London: Pitman, 1976.

Rennert, Hellmut Hal, ed. *Essays on Twentieth-Century German Drama and Theater: An American Reception 1977–1999.* New York: Lang, 2004.

Willett, John. *The Theatre of the Weimar Republic.* New York: Holmes & Meier, 1988.

Siegfried Mews

GESCHICHTEN AUS DEM WIENER WALD

See TALES FROM THE VIENNA WOODS

GHASHIRAM KOTWAL

The most radical and controversial of VIJAY TENDULKAR's plays, *Ghashiram Kotwal* (1972) presents a unique blend of history, politics, and myth. Based on an 18th-century historical legend, the story centers on Nana Phadavis, the chancellor of the Brahmin rulers of Pune called the Peshwa (whom the British defeated to establish their rule over INDIA), and his corrupt officer Ghashiram. Ghashiram trades his daughter to the lascivious Nana for power, which he uses to avenge himself on others. Nana in turn uses Ghashiram to achieve his own political ends and destroys him when he is no longer needed. Significantly, the play includes a British agent watching Nana—yet another despotic power that will overcome the devious Nana.

Although the play locates the themes of state power and violence in the brahminical Peshwa Raj of 17th- and 18th-century Maharashtra, it was not a historical play. Ghashiram and Nana personify the unchanging aspects of politics: corruption, violence, brutality, greed, hypocrisy, intrigue, treachery, and immorality. *Ghashiram Kotwal* is Tendulkar's comment on contemporary politics and on how politicians always trample the common people. Tendulkar's vision of human beings as beasts and of politics as an eternal process of creating despots finds its darkest expression in this play.

Structurally, the play was very innovative with a blend of several forms of traditional theater, such as *kirtan*, *dashavatar*, *khele*, and ancient and contemporary musical and dance traditions. A chorus of twenty-four actors playing Brahmins dance, sing, and form various set pieces such as a wall, a house, a garden, a road. This use of dance and music to tell such a gruesome tale was a fantastic experiment on the Marathi stage. The language is also extraordinarily innovative: it is steeped in irony, sacrilegious word play, juxtaposition of sacred and profane expressions, and uses diverse caste dialects of Marathi (both ancient and modern) to represent a wide variety of speech rhythms. It is by far the most theatrical play on the modern Indian stage.

First performed by the Progressive Dramatic Association in Pune on December 16, 1972, the play sparked unprecedented controversy. First, the Association itself banned the play on the grounds that it was anti-Brahmin, that it projected a false image of Maratha history, and that it would invite abusive social reactions (a prediction that later proved true). Most of the actors resigned to form Theatre Academy, which revived the play on January 11, 1974. When the production was invited to tour Europe, the Theatre Academy was directed by the Bombay court to publicly declare before every performance in Europe that the play was not historically accurate. Tendulkar and the actors were threatened with dire consequences if they persisted with the performances, which, of course, they courageously did.

The Theatre Academy went on with the performances of *Ghashiram Kotwal* for a considerable period after this and gradually the controversies subsided at least outwardly. However, *Ghashiram Kotwal* remains one of the most powerful and theatrical plays on the Indian stage.

FURTHER READING

Bhalla, Neela. *Ghashiram Kotwal: Essays and Annotations.* Delhi: Worldview Publications, 2001.

Gokhle, Shanta. *Playwright at the Centre: Marathi Drama from 1843 to the Present.* Calcutta: Seagull, 2000.

Pandey, Sudhakar, and Freya Barua, eds. *New Directions in Indian Drama.* Delhi: Prestige Books, 1994.

Tendulkar, Vijay. *Collected Plays in Translation*. Delhi: Oxford Univ. Press, 1983.

——. *Vijay Tendulkar*. Delhi: Katha, 2001.

——. *Ghashiram Kotwal*. Tr. by Jayant Karve and Eleanor Zelliot. Calcutta: Seagull, 2002.

Maya Pandit

GHELDERODE, MICHEL DE (1898–1962)

The Belgian playwright who renamed himself Michel de Ghelderode was born Adémar Adolphe Louis Martens, on April 3, 1898, in Ixelles, BELGIUM. Associated with French theater because he wrote in French, he gained widespread popularity only after Paris was infected with "acute Ghelderoditis" (*la ghelderodite aigüe*) following a controversial 1949 production of *Chronicles of Hell* (*Fastes d'enfer*).

Ghelderode was one of four children in a household of modest means. A life-threatening case of typhus in 1914 ended his formal education and postponed his required military service until 1919, after the end of World War I. In 1921 he accepted a teaching position, the first of several short-lived jobs. Two years later he was hired as a clerk, the job that supported his writing efforts for over twenty years. In 1924 Ghelderode married Jeanne-Françoise Gérard, whom he met two years earlier during a brief stint working at a bookstore.

Ghelderode's first productions were provided by De Vlaamsche Volkstoneel (The Flemish People's Theater), a traveling troupe. Dutch translations of his early plays toured throughout Flanders, Limburg, and the Netherlands between 1926 and 1932.

Ghelderode borrowed from many forms and sources—from biblical narratives and the medieval morality play, to commedia dell'arte, medieval farce, vaudeville, fairground theater, and the paintings of his contemporary James Ensor. Famously called "our man in the 16th century" by Lionel Abel, many of Ghelderode's dramas rely on the themes, forms, and even settings of the late medieval period and early Renaissance. *Christophe Colomb* (1927), *Red Magic* (*Magie Rouge*, 1931), and *Mademoiselle Jaïre* (1945–1935) are only a few examples. Like FERNAND CROMMELYNCK, Ghelderode was fascinated by medieval Flanders and the paintings of Pieter Breughel and Hieronymus Bosch. In addition to his plays intended for actors on the stage, he also wrote puppet and radio dramas.

His plays also reveal a debt to the symbolism of MAURICE MAETERLINCK, the atmosphere of Edgar Allen Poe, and the theatrical lawlessness of ALFRED JARRY. They are filled with dark mysticism, coarse humor, and psychically damaged figures. The spirit is in constant conflict with the flesh as he dramatizes death, the devil, gluttony, and lust through plays that often feature clergy, clowns, and Lucifer. Sexual and scatological humor is a frequent strategy, as when the literal and figurative flatulence of the priests provide the climax to *Chronicles of Hell*. The dark mysticism, sometimes even nihilism, of his plays has an affinity with the kind of spectacle advocated by ANTONIN ARTAUD—full of dreamlike mystery and irrationality, and devoid of didacticism.

Ghelderode died on April 1, 1962, in Schaerbeed, just as his work was gaining an international reputation. Martin Esslin characterizes Ghelderode, along with JACQUES AUDIBERTI, JEAN VAUTHIER, and others, as part of the poetic AVANT-GARDE. He acknowledges their relationship to the absurdists, but sees their dreamlike lyricism as reliant on linguistic associations and therefore essentially different from the works of EUGENE IONESCO, JEAN GENET, and SAMUEL BECKETT. Some contemporary critics and audiences find troubling racial and gender politics in his plays. Today, despite their author's global reputation and their intense theatricality, Ghelderode's plays are staged infrequently outside of Belgium, mostly in university settings or by experimental companies.

SELECT PLAYS: *Piet Bouteille* (1925); *The Death of Dr. Faust* (*La Mort du Docteur Faust*, 1926); *Christophe Colomb* (1927); *Images of the Life of St. Francis of Assisi* (*Images de la vie de Saint Francis d'Assise*, 1928); *The Massacre of the Innocents* (*Le Massacre des Innocents*, 1929); *Chronicles of Hell* (*Fastes d'enfer*, 1929); *Barabbas* (1932); *The Women at the Tomb* (*Les Femmes au Tombeau*, 1934); *Pantagleize* (1934); *Red Magic* (*Magie Rouge*, 1935); *The Blind Men* (*Les Aveugles*, 1936); *Hop, Signor!* (1938); *Mademoiselle Jaïre* (1942); *The School for Buffoons* (*L'École des bouffons*, 1942); *Lord Halewyn* (*Sire Halewyn*, 1943)

FURTHER READING

Beyen, Roland. *Ghelderode*. Paris: Seghers, 1974.

——. *Bibliographie de Michel Ghelderode* [Bibliography of Michel Ghelderode]. Bruxelles: Palais des Académies, 1987.

Dukore, Bernard F., and Daniel C. Gerould. *Avant-Garde Drama: A Casebook*. New York: Bantam Books, Inc., 1969.

Esslin, Martin. *The Theatre of the Absurd*. New York: Anchor Books, 1961.

Ghelderode, Michel de. *Seven Plays, Volumes I and II*. Tr. by George Hauger. New York: Hill and Wang, 1960, 1964.

——. *Théâtre complet* [Complete Plays], Vols. I–VI. Paris: Gallimard, 1950–1982.

Parsell, David B. *Michel de Ghelderode*. New York: Twayne Publishers, 1993.

Wendy A. Weckwerth

GHOSTS

. . . now this long, loathsome comedy is over.

—Mrs. Alving, Act 1

After publishing *A DOLL'S HOUSE* (1879), in which Nora Helmer in the end feels obliged to leave her husband and children, HENRIK IBSEN wrote *Ghosts* (*Gengangere*) about a family in which the wife has chosen to stay.

Helene Alving, widow of Captain Alving, late Court Chamberlain, has been careful to cover up the truth about her depraved husband and is about to celebrate the dedication of an orphanage built on a part of the estate and named after him. Her son Osvald, a painter, has arrived from Paris, and Pastor Manders, an old friend of the family, is visiting from the nearby town. The Pastor is struck by the son's likeness to his late father, but Mrs. Alving is eager to minimize any paternal inheritance. Reproached by Pastor Manders for sending her son away from home before he was seven, Mrs. Alving explains that the intention was to protect Osvald from detrimental influence of his father. Yet it becomes increasingly clear that Osvald has acquired the tastes of his father: smoking, drinking, and lusting after Regine, Mrs. Alving's maid, just as the Chamberlain had been after her mother.

The real reason for Osvald's homecoming is bad health; implicit references are made to a hereditary venereal disease which will make him a nursing case, and he has made his mother promise to terminate his life with morphine when that happens. Mrs. Alving decides to tell him the truth, that his father was also the father of Regine. The Orphanage burns down, uninsured. The effect of Osvald's exertion trying to put out the fire is the final outbreak of the disease.

The entire action takes place in the garden room at Rosenvold. At the back, the room opens on a conservatory that is walled with large panes of glass through which can be seen the garden and a gloomy fjord landscape, veiled by rain. The arrangement presents itself metaphorically as a greenhouse, with plants inside getting the appropriate amount of water and care, while plants on the outside are exposed to natural conditions.

Ghosts is the only play by Ibsen referred to as a family drama. There are five characters; fewer than in any other of his plays: a mother, her son, his half-sister, a carpenter, and a friend of the family. They represent very different social positions. Mrs. Alving is liberal minded, well informed about intellectual currents, but also a killjoy occupied by fulfilling her duties. Osvald knows he is ill without understanding why. Regine is a social climber. Engstrand the carpenter is a hypocrite, engaged in activities of a dubious nature, and clever in obtaining his aim. Pastor Manders is a conservative clergyman, afraid of scandal, naïve, and easily fooled.

The pattern of the plot is reminiscent of a classical Greek TRAGEDY of fate, in particular the tragic irony of *King Oedipus*. The efforts of Mrs. Alving to protect her son and remove every trace of her late husband are not founded on the perception of truth, and can only lead to the reaffirmation of the chamberlain's moral and physical decay in the character of Osvald. Mrs. Alving is gradually forced to recognize not only the inevitable heredity but also her own share of the guilt: She did not respond properly to the joy of living in the young lieutenant she once married. As a modern writer Ibsen felt it was his mission to move boundaries; he had observed obsolete beliefs and worn-out conventions that yet retained the power to haunt people's minds. And so he created Mrs. Alving, a modern woman who feels haunted, and who is heroically determined to fight everything that is defunct, but who does not know enough to avoid tragedy in her own house.

The publication of *Ghosts* in Scandinavia met with violent reactions. Ibsen had expected protests from conservative critics, but he was surprised by the vehemence of the response even from liberal papers. People were shocked by what they felt was a derogatory presentation of a man of the church, and they were extremely provoked by the play's implicit reference to such issues as promiscuity among respectable citizens visiting Paris, a case of venereal disease affecting an upper-middle-class family, and the idea that incest probably did occur in many apparently "decent" families. The dramatic concentration of the action contributed to the extraordinary impact on the readers.

Ghosts was first presented by an amateur group of Scandinavian immigrants in Chicago in 1882, but no permanent theater ventured to stage the play publicly until 1890, when it was produced in Bergen. Since then *Ghosts* has acquired a permanent place in world theater.

[*See also* Naturalism; Philosophy and Drama, 1860–1960; Problem Plays; Realism]

FURTHER READING

Aarseth, Asbjørn. *Peer Gynt and Ghosts. Text and Performance.* Houndsmill and London: Macmillan Education, 1989. Chaps. 6–9, 50–75.

Chamberlain, John S. *Ibsen: The Open Vision.* London: Athlone Press, 1982. Chap. 3, "Ghosts: The Vision Blurs," 71–103.

Fergusson, Francis. *The Idea of a Theater. The Art of Drama in Changing Perspective.* Princeton, N. J.: Princeton Univ. Press, 1949. Chap. 5, "Ghosts: The Tragic Rhythm in a Small Figure," 159–174.

Northam, John. "Ghosts," in *Ibsen. A Critical Study.* Cambridge: Cambridge Univ. Press, 1973. 76–112.

Sprinchorn, Evert. "Science and Poetry in Ghosts: A Study in Ibsen's Craftmanship." *Scandinavian Studies* 51 (1979): 354–367.

Asbjørn Aarseth

THE GHOST SONATA

The Ghost Sonata (*Spöksonaten*) is a CHAMBER PLAY by AUGUST STRINDBERG, written and published in 1907 for his Intimate Theater in Stockholm. Together with TO DAMASCUS and A DREAM PLAY, *The Ghost Sonata* foreshadowed both EXPRESSIONISM and ABSURDISM and is generally recognized as Strindberg's most important contribution to the development of modern drama.

A student who has just saved people from a collapsing house and a crippled old man (Jacob Hummel) meet outside a fashionable house. The Old Man enables the Student, who is clairvoyant, to enter the house and become acquainted with the Young Lady, Adèle, who is living there and who is, in fact, Hummel's illegitimate daughter. Inside the house the Student is confronted with the Colonel, who poses as Adèle's father, and the Mummy, her mother, who lives in a closet. At the "ghost supper" they and a few invited guests are unmasked by Hummel, who has come uninvited. Then he in turn is unmasked by the Mummy and forced to hang himself in the closet. Disillusioned, the Student, by expressing doubts about Adèle's virginity, "kills her with words," as it says in the notes for the play. He is remorseful and prays that she may be carried to a better life after death. The play ends with the following spectacular stage direction:

> The room vanishes. Böcklin's painting The Isle of the Dead appears as the background. Music, soft, tranquil, and pleasantly melancholy is heard from the island.

The underlying idea is that life on earth is painful and illusory and that when we die, we are rescued from a pseudoexistence and returned to the original one. To make this idea dramatically effective, Strindberg turns his protagonist, the Student, into an outsider who only gradually gains insight into the true state of events. Ultimately, *The Ghost Sonata* is a parable depicting the pilgrimage of humanity and a station drama in which each station corresponds to a state of mind. In the first, the Student sees the beautiful facade of the house. Having entered the house, he detects its many shortcomings. Still believing in the saving grace of love, he discovers that even the beloved Young Lady is "sick at the source of life"; that is, tainted by Original Sin. After the three earthly stations—each characterized by "the treacherous hope"—a fourth station, death, remains where hope, in the biblical words of the Student, "may not maketh ashamed!"

Just as the three earthly stations are identified with youth, middle age, and old age, so the Student is a youthful version of the Old Man—toward the end he continues, as it were, Hummel's destructive behavior—and the Young Lady, a youthful version of the Mummy, the statue of the Mummy as young is the connecting link. Strindberg portrays each individual's age-determined development from innocence to guilt as a repetition of the original Fall.

Because life on earth is a shadow life, a mirage, it follows that we are all ghosts, whereas those who appear as ghosts in the play, although dead, are the truly living. The title also alludes to Beethoven's Piano Sonata No. 17 in D minor, usually called "The Tempest"; in a letter to his German translator, Strindberg refers to this as the *Gespenster* (ghost) sonata. He had earlier used the sonata in CRIMES AND CRIMES to indicate the pangs of conscience afflicting the protagonist.

In a prologue written for the opening of his Intimate Theater, Strindberg refers to the journey that mankind must undertake "from the Isle of the Living to the Isle of the Dead." He alludes to Arnold Böcklin's once-fashionable paintings, copies of which at his request had been placed at either side of the stage in the theater. As Northam observes, *The Ghost Sonata* displays a striking visual correspondence between the House of Life in the opening of the play and the Isle of the Dead at the end of it, giving prominence to the Student's—and humanity's—final question: Will the beautiful Isle of the Dead prove to be genuine, or will it be yet another delusion?

In line with modern thinking is the idea that verbal communication, far from conveying truths, serves to hide the truth. A number of striking visual images foreshadow the visual metaphors of the absurdists: the spider-like Hummel in his "battle wagon" surrounded by beggars; the Colonel who, when stripped of his uniform, proves to be held together by an iron corset; the Milkmaid's bottles, representing maternal love, contrasting with the vampiric Cook's soya bottle "with the scorpion-like lettering."

[*See also* Philosophy and Drama, 1860–1960; Symbolism]

FURTHER READING

Brandell, Gunnar. "Questions without Answers: On Strindberg's and Ibsen's Dialogue." In *Structures of Influence: A Comparative Approach to August Strindberg*, ed. by Marilyn Johns Blackwell. Chapel Hill: Univ. of North Carolina Press, 1981. 79–91.

Bryant-Bertail, Sarah. "The Tower of Babel: Space and Movement in *The Ghost Sonata*." In *Strindberg's Dramaturgy*, ed. by Göran Stockenström. Minneapolis: Univ. of Minnesota Press, 1988. 303–315.

Lunin, Hanno. *Strindbergs Dramen* [*Strindberg's Plays*]. Emsdetten: Lechte, 1962. 245–268.

Northam, John. "Strindberg's *Spook Sonata*." In *Essays on Strindberg*, ed. by Carl Reinhold Smedmark. Stockholm: Beckman, 1966. 39–48.

Sprichorn, Evert. *Strindberg as Dramatist*. New Haven: Yale Univ. Press, 1982.

Törnqvist, Egil. *Strindberg's The Ghost Sonata: From Text to Performance*. Amsterdam: Amsterdam Univ. Press, 2000.

Egil Törnqvist

GIACOSA, GIUSEPPE (1847–1906)

Born into an upper-class family in Piedmont, ITALY, Giuseppe Giacosa took his university degree in Turin with a specialization in law, although contact with groups interested in literary realism and with the *scapigliati*, who followed literary experiments originating in France, contributed to his literary development in drama as well as poetry and the narrative. His first theatrical works oscillate between lyrical intimacy and a late-Romantic taste for the legendary and historical settings, which reappear in *The Game of Chess* (*Una partita a scacchi*, 1873) and *Brother in Arms* (*Il fratello d'armi*, 1877), as well as the later *The Lady of Challant* (*La signora di Challant*, 1891). His early dialogue is far from any natural speech and dulled by literary echoes and stylistic references to 19th-century MELODRAMA and traditional forms of Martellian (fourteen-syllable) verse.

Following French models, he experimented with *commedia brillante* (brilliant comedy) based on "dramatic proverbs" and wrote *Don't Cast Pearls Before Swine* (*A can che lecca cenere non gli fidar farina*) and *Don't Count Your Chickens Before They're Hatched* (*Non dir quattro se non l'hai nel sacco*), both in 1872. In these works Giacosa refined his taste for lively conversation reflecting the upper middle class with a touch of irony regarding *gli amori di commedia* (loves in plays) and the masks that impede authentic relationships among characters. Such themes, also developed by the late Giovanni Verga and then taken up by LUIGI PIRANDELLO, appear in Giacosa's major works, although they already strengthen the successful *The Husband Lover of the Wife* (*Il marito amante della moglie*, 1876), set in the 18th century and informed by the lessons of dramatist Carlo Goldoni, the founder of modern Italian comedy.

Both Giacosa's activity as journalist (which in 1901 took him in the direction of the Milanese *Lettura*) and that of romantic-realistic narrator led him toward a more natural and less stereotyped realism, attentive to traditions and local practices: *Stories and Lands of Valdaosta* (*Novelle e paesi valdostani*, 1886). His early mawkish sentimentalism matured into a more concentrated and intense intimacy of Chekhovian caliber, and his settings became anchored to concrete places: landscapes or interiors meticulously described and proposed as correlative symbols of the characters and their inner life. These plays move past the naturalistic models of ÉMILE ZOLA, HENRY BECQUE, and ANDRE ANTOINE, toward a proto-crepuscolarism: dialogue became more allusive and almost whispered, versification gradually abandoned in favor of prose, the stage occupied with themes of silence and absence. He opened a dialect with modern European aestheticism—from OSCAR WILDE to GABRIELE D'ANNUNZIO (who dedicates one of his *Faville del maglio* [sparks from the hammer] to Giacosa), evoked as emblems of an art that reflects life's falsifications.

Truth in Giacosa, at his best, is no longer a solid and evident given, as in NATURALISM, but the result of a difficult and sorrowful journey through the illusions that hide it. The theater ceases to be a place of disguise, and instead Giacosa stages the fall of masks with which the individual hides his shortcomings from himself and from others. These themes unite in profundity Giacosa's most successful prose dramas *Luisa* (1879), *Sad loves* (*Tristi amori*, 1887), *Rights of the soul* (*I diritti dell'anima*, 1894), *Like the leaves* (*Come le foglie*, 1900), and the libretti for Puccini's operas, written in collaboration with Luigi Illica, *La Bohème* (1896), *Tosca* (1900), and *Madame Butterfly* (1904).

PLAYS: *Sitting at the Piano* (*Al pianoforte*,1870); *Better the Devil You Know Than the Devil You Don't Know* (*Chi lascia la via vecchia per la nuova, sa quel che lascia, e non sa quel che trova*, 1870); *Don't Cast Pearls Before Swine* (*A can che lecca cenere non gli fidar farina*, 1872); *Witty People* (*La gente di spirito*, 1872); *Don't Count Your Chickens Before They're Hatched* (*Non dir quattro se non l'hai nel sacco*, 1872); *Stale Story* (*Storia vecchia*, 1872); *The Game of Chess* (*Una partita a scacchi*, 1873); *Night Surprises* (*Sorprese notturne*, 1875); *The Triumph of Love* (*Il trionfo d'amore*, 1875); *Mountain Downpours* (*Acquazzoni in montagna*, 1876); *The Husband Lover of the Wife* (*Il marito amante della moglie*, 1876); *Brother in Arms* (*Il fratello d'armi*, 1877); *Luisa* (1879); *The Red Count* (*Il conte rosso*, 1880); *The Thread* (*Il filo*, 1883); *The Mermaid* (*La sirena*, 1883); *The Paw of the Cat* (*La zampa del gatto*, 1883); *Surrendering at Discretion* (*Resa a discrezione*, 1886); *Tardy Repentance* (*La tardi ravveduta*, 1886); *Stories and Lands of Valdaosta* (*Novelle e paesi valdostani*, 1886); *Sad Loves* (*Tristi amori*, 1887); *Intermezzi and Scenes* (*Intermezzi e scene*, 1888); *The Lady of Challant* (*La signora di Challant*, 1891); *Rights of the Soul* (*I diritti dell'anima*, 1894); *Like the Leaves* (*Come le foglie*, 1900); *The Stronger* (*Il più forte*, 1904)

FURTHER READING

Barsotti, Anna. *Giuseppe Giacosa*. Firenze: La Nuova Italia, 1973.

Doroni, Stefano. *Dall'androne medievale al tinello borghese. Il teatro di Giuseppe Giacosa* [*From the Medieval Manor Hall to the Bourgeois Lounge. The Theater of Giuseppe Giacosa*]. Roma: Bulzoni, 1998.

Finotti, Fabio. "*Come le foglie* di Giuseppe Giacosa: maschera e verità" ["Giuseppe Giacosa's *Like Falling Leaves*: Mask and Truth"]. In *La maschera e il volto. Il teatro in Italia* [*The Mask and the Truth. The Italian Theater*], ed. by Francesco Bruni. Venezia: Marsilio, 2002. 355–374.

Gedda, Lido. *Giuseppe Giacosa commediografo e narratore* [*Giuseppe Giacosa as a Dramatist and Narrator*]. Torino: Trauben, 2000.

Nardi, Piero. *Vita e tempo di Giuseppe Giacosa* [*Life and Times of Giuseppe Giacosa*]. Milano: Mondadori, 1949.

Fabio Finotti

GIDE, ANDRÉ (1869–1951)

André Gide was a moralist, novelist, and playwright whose work tracks his personal struggle between the formidable pressures of religious, social, and sexual conventions and his lifelong belief in the individual's right to chart his or her own moral course. Born in Paris on November 22, 1869, as an only child, Gide was caught between his mother's Catholic influence and his father's Huguenot upbringing. Gide's interest in writing stemmed from his childhood when, after his father's death, he came under the influence of several women in his household who encouraged him to explore nature and independent learning. This early education fostered his love of natural beauty and enjoyment of analysis, but once he entered the École Alsacienne in Paris, Gide had trouble adapting to rules. As a youth, he began sexual experimentation with other children, particularly those he considered most "natural." At the same time, he continued to be fascinated by Christianity, and carried a copy of the New Testament in his pocket and engaged in ascetic practices to mortify the flesh. By the age of twenty, however, Gide dropped his zealous rituals in rejection of the conventional dichotomy between body and soul.

Gide's novels, plays, journals, and essays reflect his continual exploration of humanity's moral position in society, particularly as it relates to contradictory themes, such as obedience and freedom, marriage and homosexuality, Protestant self-restraint and classical humanism. In keeping with his complicated relationship with Christianity, Gide accepted the Gospels but disallowed the interpretations of Saint Paul and the institution of the Church. Christian conventionality, he believed, discouraged the individual from developing his or her authentic self. In Greek mythology, however, he found models of heroic authenticity. Gide recognized the theater's power as a forum for moral instruction but opposed the use of realism, faulting it for reinforcing the status quo. His vision of the theater was inspired by the idealism of the Greek protagonists, whose pursuit of truth and virtue were motivated not by religious piety, but by the desire for self-fulfillment.

Gide was influenced by FRIEDRICH NIETZSCHE and the SYMBOLISTS, especially Stéphane Mallarmé. Selected major works include *Fruits of the Earth* (*Les Nourritures terrestres*, 1896), *The Immoralist* (*L'Immoraliste*, 1902), *Lafcadio's Adventures* (*Les Caves du Vatican*, 1914), *The Pastoral Symphony* (*Le Symphonie pastorale*, 1919), *Dostoevsky* (1923), *If It Die . . .* (*Si le Grain ne meurt . . .*, 1926), *The School for Wives* (*L'École de femmes*, 1929), and *Oedipe* (1931). Among the pivotal moments that shaped his personal and professional life were two trips to Algeria, the first with Paul-Albert Laurens in 1892 and the second in 1894, during which he met OSCAR WILDE and acknowledged his homosexuality.

Gide's mother died in May 1895, and in October of that same year he married his cousin, Madeleine Rondeaux. In 1909 he co-founded the Nouvelle Revue Française with a circle of like-minded writers. Catherine Gide, his daughter with Elisabeth van Rysselberghe, was born in 1923. In 1925–1926 Gide traveled to Congo and Chad, leading to the publication of two works of social criticism, *Travels in the Congo* (*Voyage au Congo*) in 1927 and *Back from Chad* (*Retour du Tchad*) in 1928. He published his *Oeuvres complètes* (in fifteen volumes) from 1932 to 1939, and in 1936 he traveled to Soviet Russia, putting an end to his fascination with Communism. Madeleine Gide died in 1938, and André returned to Tunisia and Algeria from 1942 to 1945. Gide received the Nobel Prize for Literature in 1947 for *The Vatican Cellars* (*Les Caves du Vatican*). He died in Paris on February 19, 1951.

[*See also* France]

PLAYS: *Philoctete* (1898); *King Candaules* (*Le Roi Candaule*, 1901); *Saul* (1903); *The Return of the Prodigal Son* (*Le Retour de l'enfant prodigue*, 1907); *Robert* (1929); *Oedipe* (1931); *Persephone* (1934)

FURTHER READING

Andregide.org. "Online Center for Gidian Studies." http://andregide.org (June 15, 2003).

Gide, André. *My Theater*. Tr. by Jackson Matthews. New York: Knopf, 1952.

McLaren, James C. *The Theatre of André Gide: Evolution of a Moral Philosopher*. New York: Octagon Books, 1971.

O'Brien, Justin. *Portrait of André Gide: A Critical Study*. New York: Knopf, 1953.

San Juan, Jr., E. *Transcending the Hero, Reinventing the Heroic*. New York: Univ. Press of America, 1988.

Kristin Johnsen-Neshati

GILBERT, SKY (1952–)

Openly gay playwright, performer, journalist, activist, and drag queen extraordinaire, Sky Gilbert is a powerful force in the gay community of Toronto, CANADA. Born Schuyler Lee Gilbert, Jr., in Norwich, Connecticut, in 1952, he has lived in Toronto, Ontario, since 1965. Gilbert has shaped the radical transformation of how the gay and lesbian community has been represented on the stage since the 1970s. Gilbert's plays are a pastiche of MELODRAMA, burlesque, and vaudeville genres, similar to the works of CHARLES LUDLUM.

Co-founder and artistic director of Buddies in Bad Times in 1979, Gilbert and his colleagues dedicated their theater company to performing works by or about gays and lesbians. As the company developed, they also included the works of writers who brought issues of gender, women's rights, and social justice to the theater. Throughout the 1980s their productions became increasingly radical, experimenting with style, plot, and genre.

Gilbert's plays *The Post Man Only Rings Once* (1985), *Drag Queens in Outer Space* (1990), *Play Murder* (1993, Chalmers Award nominee), and *Drag Queens on Trial* (1994), among others, were produced across Canada, the United States, and Europe.

Gilbert's work is often confrontational, and he has been considered a maverick within artistic and political spheres. He challenged notions of respectability and the need for respectability—or the outer display of it—prevalent within gay culture. Gilbert believes that the AIDS pandemic has psychologically, as well as physically, harmed individuals; in much of his work, Gilbert illustrates what he has found as an unhealthy and hypocritical response to life within the gay community. By presenting a controversial and highly critical take on society, Gilbert remains a pariah of gay culture; as he describes his position, "I am used to being demonized for my ideas within the gay community."

Outside of his theatrical company, he has achieved recognition as a director of films and as an actor. In 1987 he directed *Anything Goes* and OSCAR WILDE's *Salome* for the Shaw Festival. In 1985 he received the Pauline McGibbon award for directing. He has performed at many venues in Toronto. In 1987 he was nominated for a Dora Mavor Moore award for his performance in *The Edge of the Earth is Too Near*, directed by Violette Leduc, and he was awarded the Dora Mavor Moore award twice for his plays *The Whore's Revenge* and *Suzi Goo: Private Secretary* in 1990 and 1992.

From 1996 to the present, Gilbert has been recognized for his nontheatrical writing. He has several books of poetry and two novels in print and is a regular columnist for Toronto's alternative *Eye Weekly* magazine. Through his writings, Gilbert constantly challenges ideas of morality and psychological reactions to the AIDS pandemic within the gay community. Often controversial, his work remains a self-described "thorn in the side of the gay community."

[*See also* Gay and Lesbian Drama]

SELECT PLAYS: *Lana Turner Has Collapsed!* (1980); *The Postman Only Rings Once* (1985); *Drag Queens in Outer Space* (1990); *The Whore's Revenge* (winner of the Dora Mavor Moore Award, 1990); *Suzie Goo: Private Secretary* (winner of the Dora Mavor Moore Award, 1991); *Play Murder* (1993); *Drag Queens on Trial* (1994); *Strange Little Monsters* (1995); *Jim Dandy* (1996); *Ten Ruminations on an Elegy* (1996); *Schubert Laid* (1998); *The Birth of Caper G. Schmidt* (2000)

FURTHER READING

Gilbert, Sky. "Steal Well: Racial and Ethnic Diversity in the Club Queer World." *Canadian Theatre Review* 103 (Summer 2000): 25–27.

——. "Politics and Playwrights Discuss the Nature, Social Role, and Reception of Political Theatre." *Canadian Theatre Review* 115 (Summer 2003): 52–56.

——. "Political Theatre: Because We Must. Reflections." *Canadian Theatre Review* 117 (Winter 2004): 25–28.

Holly Maples

GILBERT, WILLIAM SCHWENCK (1836–1911)

W. S. (William Schwenck) Gilbert is most remembered for his contributions to the Savoy Operas, a series of widely successful comic operas he produced with composer Arthur Seymour Sullivan. As playwright, librettist, and humorist, he remains one of Great Britain's most important theater figures and a major comic wit. His works with Sullivan were among the highlights of the Victorian stage and provided a foundation for popular musical theater in the 20th century.

Gilbert was born in London on November 18, 1836, the child of a modestly wealthy retired naval surgeon. He flirted unsuccessfully with his military commission during the Crimean War, and after a similarly aborted career in law, turned to parody, establishing himself as a contributor to *Fun*, a humor periodical.

Between 1861 and 1871, Gilbert's burlesque reviews (comic theater critiques in dialogue form), caricatures, and Bab Ballads (satirical rhymes that targeted everything from human nature to Victorian society) led to full-scale opera burlesques, beginning in 1866 with *Dulcamara*. His greatest successes before meeting Sullivan were *The Palace of Truth* (1870), a romantic parody of high society, and *Pygmalion and Galatea* (1871), a blank verse version of the legend that enjoyed several successful revivals.

The efforts of composer Frederic Clay, a close friend of Sullivan, and John Hollingshead brought the two independently successful artists together on their first project, *Thespis, or The Gods Grown Old* (1871). Despite its commercial failure (it ran only one month), Gilbert and Sullivan produced a second work, *Trial by Jury* (1875). This immediately successful take on a breach-of-promise lawsuit led to a number of increasingly elaborate collaborations, including *H.M.S. Pinafore* (1878), *The Pirates of Penzance* (1879), *Patience* (1881), *Iolanthe* (1882, the first of these to be produced for the newly built Savoy Theatre), *The Mikado* (1885), and *The Gondoliers* (1889). Their working relationship eventually soured, and although Gilbert continued to enjoy considerable financial reward from revivals and tours of their productions, the team produced no major successes after 1889 and did not collaborate at all after 1896. Sullivan died four years later; Gilbert died in 1911, after rescuing a drowning girl.

In an 1883 autobiographical sketch, Gilbert suggested that the Savoy Operas were a relatively minor chapter in his career, and certainly, the artist produced a large body of work before, during, and after his twenty years of successful ventures with Sullivan. Nonetheless, it is these fifteen works that have exerted the most influence on nearly 130 years of musical theater and comic drama.

PLAYS: *Dulcamara* (1866); *Harlequin Cock-Robin* (1867); *Robert the Devil* (1868); *An Old Score* (1869); *Ages Ago* (1869); *The Gentleman in Black* (1870); *Our Island Home* (1870); *The Palace of Truth* (1870); *The Princess* (1870); *Great Expectations* (1871); *Pygmalion and Galatea* (1871); *Thespis* (1871); *Creatures of Impulse* (1872); *Randall's Thumb* (1872); *The Happy Land* (1873); *The Wicked World* (1873); *Charity* (1874); *On Guard* (1874); *Ought We to Visit Her?* (1874); *Broken Hearts* (1875); *Trial by Jury* (1875); *Dan'l Druce* (1876); *Engaged* (1877); *The Sorcerer* (1877); *H.M.S. Pinafore* (1878); *The Ne'er Do Well* (1878); *Sweethearts* (1878); *The Wedding March* (1878); *Gretchen* (1879); *The Martyr of Antioch* (1880); *The Pirates of Penzance* (1880); *Tom Comb* (1880); *Foggert's Fairy* (1881); *On Bail* (1881); *Patience* (1881); *Reveillon* (1881); *Iolanthe* (1882); *Princess Ida* (1884); *The Mikado* (1885); *The Ruddigore* (1887); *Brantinghame Hall* (1888); *The Yeoman of the Guard* (1888); *The Gondoliers* (1889); *Haste to the Wedding* (1892); *The Mountebanks* (1892); *Rosencrantz and Guildenstern* (1893); *Utopia, Limited* (1893); *His Excellency* (1894); *Comedy and Tragedy* (1895); *The Grand Duke* (1896); *The Fortune Hunter* (1897); *The Fairy's Dilemma* (1904); *Fallen Fairies* (1909); *The Hooligan* (1911)

FURTHER READING

Ffinch, Michael. *Gilbert and Sullivan*. London: Weidenfield and Nicolson, 1993.

Goodman, Andrew. *Gilbert and Sullivan's London*. Tunbridge Wells: Spellmount Ltd., 1988.

Orel, Harold, ed. *Gilbert and Sullivan: Interviews and Recollections*. Iowa City: Univ. of Iowa Press, 1994.

Pearson, Hesketh. *Gilbert: His Life and Strife*. London: Methuen & Co., 1957.

Steadman, Jane W. *W. S. Gilbert: A Classic Victorian and His Theatre*. Oxford: Oxford Univ. Press, 1996.

Ben Fisler

GILLETTE, WILLIAM (1853–1937)

William Hooker Gillette was the son of United States Senator Francis Gillette. Born on July 24, 1853, in Hartford, Connecticut, he left home in 1873 to pursue a career on the stage, appearing in St. Louis and New Orleans before making his New York debut as Colonel Sellers in Mark Twain's *The Gilded Age*.

Gillette was best known for playing roles in his own works, especially Beene (also listed as "Blane") in *Held by the Enemy*, nearly 1,800 performances as Dumont/Thorne in SECRET SERVICE, and over 1,300 performances in the title role of *Sherlock Holmes*.

In *Held by the Enemy*, a northern officer stands trial for espionage, while the prosecutor tries to establish that he was framed by a renegade southern officer. The northerner is engaged to a woman who is in love with the southerner, and in a battlefield hospital, she offers herself in marriage to the prosecutor, who is also a physician, if he'll agree not to betray the northerner. The treatment of love and honor echoes some romantic European precedents. After his escape, the northerner returns to prevent the physician from taking advantage of the young woman, who is finally free to marry the man she truly loves. One of the more popular Civil War dramas, the *Boston Evening Transcript* argued that it was deserving of attention beyond its intrinsic merits simply because it was an American play.

Secret Service also involves an espionage intrigue during the Civil War. A northern spy enters Richmond disguised as a southern officer and surreptitiously uses the Confederate telegraph office to send a message. He loves a Confederate general's daughter, who compromises herself to help him, but when the southern army wins the battle, they send the spy to prison rather than execute him.

Sherlock Holmes uses Conan Doyle's characters and story motifs, borrowing fragments of selected tales, but the style of the dialogue is more Gillette's than the original's, except when he quotes entire passages. Yet the title character retains his knack for deduction, and Gillette borrows memorable moments from the Holmes canon: a false alarm of fire to compel someone to reveal the hiding place of crucial evidence, an example of the detective's ability to confound Watson, and Holmes donning an impenetrable disguise to earn the sympathy due to a helpless old man. His adversary is, of course, the redoubtable Professor Moriarty.

Gillette's other notable roles included Hopkins in *The Professor*, Douglas Winthrop in BRONSON HOWARD's *Young Mrs. Winthrop*, the secretary in *The Private Secretary*, Billings in *Too Much Johnson*, and the title role in J. M. BARRIE's THE ADMIRABLE CRICHTON.

On November 14, 1913, Gillette delivered his famous lecture, "The Illusion of the First Time in Acting," advocating his cool, restrained, and realistic approach in contrast to the emotionalism and bombast that some audiences preferred. A contemporary observer noted that Gillette seemed to do nothing on stage, but always held the audience's interest; his work was subdued but natural. Gillette died on April 29, 1937, in Hartford.

[*See also* United States, 1860–1929]

PLAYS: Esmerelda (with Frances Hodgson Burnett, 1881); *The Professor* (1881); *The Private Secretary* (also known as *Digby's Secretary*, 1884); *Held by the Enemy* (1886); *She* (1887); *Legal Wreck* (1888); *Robert Elsmere* (1889); *All the Comforts of Home* (1890); *Mrs. Wilkinson's Widows* (1891); *Settled Out of Court* (1892); *Ninety Days* (1893); *Too Much Johnson* (1894); *Secret Service* (1895); *Because She Loved Him So* (1898); *Sherlock Holmes* (1899); *Clarice* (1905); *The Painful Predicament of Sherlock Holmes* (1905); *The Red Owl* (1907); *Samson* (1908); *Ticey, or, That Little Affair of Boyd's* (1908); *Among Thieves* (1909); *The Robber* (a revision of *The Red Owl*, 1909); *Electricity* (1910); *The Dream Maker* (1921); *Winnie and the Wolves* (1923)

FURTHER READING

Cook, Doris E. *Sherlock Holmes and Much More*. Hartford: Connecticut Historical Society, 1970.

Cullen, Rosemary, and Don B. Wilmeth, eds. *Plays by William Hooker Gillette*. Cambridge: Cambridge Univ. Press, 1983.

Gillette, William. "The Illusion of the First Time in Acting." In *Papers on Acting*, ed. by Brander Matthews (1915). New York: Hill and Wang, 1958.

Nichols, Harold J. "William Gillette: Innovator in Melodrama." *Theatre Annual* 31 (1975): 7–15.

Schuttler, Georg W. "William Gillette: Marathon Actor and Playwright." *Journal of Popular Culture* 17 (1983): 115–129.

Jeffrey D. Mason

GINZBURG, NATALIA (1916–1991)

Easily considered a voice of the 20th century, Natalia Ginzburg's writing career spans and documents nearly sixty years of Italian history. Ginzburg is traditionally acclaimed for her simple, realistic prose, and for her ability to portray, through the family, a microcosm of changing Italian culture. A chronological reading of her work shows a marked experimentation with genre, from the short story to the epistolary novel. We also see the evolution of gender roles within the family, demonstrated by Ginzburg's use of the narrating "I." That *voice*, that narrating "I," in successive decades, develops into a distinct female narrating self until the period spanning 1966–1973, when that single-voiced "I" gives way to multiple first-person perspectives—still in relation to the family—in Ginzburg's plays. Ginzburg writes that her purpose in writing the plays and the epistolary novels was to get inside more "I's" so that she might provide a panoramic view. The plays provide an interesting contrast of autobiographical voices in both dialogue and monologue.

Natalia Ginzburg was born Natalia Levi in Palermo, Sicily, ITALY, where her father was teaching at the University of Palermo. In 1919 the family moved to Torino, where it remained for several years. Ginzburg was born into a family with strong socialist affinities that was active in the anti-fascist movement of the *ventennio*. Her father was a secular Jew and her mother a secular Catholic. In 1938 she married Leone Ginzburg, who was exiled to Abruzzo between the years 1940–1943. She had three children with him. Leone Ginzburg left Natalia and their children in Abruzzo in 1943 so that he might fight in the Resistance in Rome: he was captured in November 1943 and died in the Regina Coeli Prison in February 1944. Natalia later (1951) married Gabriele Baldini and moved to Rome with him, where she died.

Ginzburg worked as an editor for Einaudi publishing house for many years. She published her first novella *The Road to the City* (*La strada che va in città*, 1942) while the family was in exile, and until her death in 1991 wrote novels, plays, short stories, and three collections of essays in which she commented on culture and politics (many of these essays appeared initially in the newspapers *La Stampa*, *Corriere della sera*, *Il Mondo*, and *L'Unità* between 1968 and 1974. Keenly active in politics and social engagement, in 1983 Ginzburg was elected deputy to Parliament with the group "Independents of the Left."

Ginzburg published two collections of plays: *I Married You for Fun and Other Comedies* (*Ti ho sposato per allegria e altre commedie*, 1968), which includes *I Married You for Fun* (*Ti ho sposato per allegria*, 1965), *Strawberries and Cream* (*Fragola e panna*, 1966), *The Secretary* (*La segretaria*, 1968) and *The Classified Ad* (*L'inserzione*, 1968), and *Sea Town and Other Comedies* (*Paese di mare e altre commedie*, 1973), which includes *Sea Town* (*Paese di mare*, 1968), *Dialogue* (*Dialogo*, 1971), *The Wrong Door* (*La porta sbagliata*, 1968), and *The Wig* (*La parrucca*, 1973). Although better known and critically received for her narrative prose in the form of the novel (*Family Sayings*, (*Lessico famigliare*, 1973) and *The Dry Heart* (*É stato così*, 1947)), Ginzburg's plays merit consideration since they occupy a distinct phase of one of Italy's most important modern cultural figures. Of all Italian writers, her plays, and in particular those of the first collection *I Married You for Fun*, are the most read and studied by students of Italian in the United States. Several reasons account for this: the accessibility of the language; the unique juxtaposition of the different narrating "I's" and the slice of modern Italian life they portray—a bourgeois society in decline and its attendant counterculture of relaxed sexual and social mores; rejection of the family (often in the form of matrophobia); and psychological issues of depression, guilt, and identity crisis. The period of 1965–1973 marks a moment of intense social upheaval, political terrorism, and reevaluation of the family.

One might read the first collection of plays as if they were one, and constants are repeated among them: the poisoned relationship between the couple; the bourgeois mother (of the male who has chosen as a partner someone quite the opposite); the young woman, often termed a "stray," a free spirit often incapable of taking care of herself; her own mad mother closed away in a room and from whose destiny the young woman flees; and the ever present servant. While names, characters, and configurations in these plays change, these elements remain. In *I Married You's* Giuliana, we have the example of a daughter who refuses her mother's fate, only to find herself in a more desolate and desperate situation. Other female characters, like Teresa in *The Classified Ad*, similarly attempt to disidentify from the mother figure, only to replicate a similar situation of spousal abuse, loneliness, and near madness.

Although some of the plays of the first collection were performed, their lasting value lies in the form of dramatic literature, and as a meditation of an existential and social state of being by a keen observer of society and human relationships.

PLAYS: *I Married You for Fun* (*Ti ho sposato per allegria*, 1965); *Strawberries and Cream* (*Fragola e panna*, 1966); *The Secretary* (*La segretaria*, 1968); *The Classified Ad* (*L'inserzione*, 1968); *Sea Town* (*Paese di mare*, 1968); *Dialogue* (*Dialogo*, 1971); *The Wrong Door* (*La porta sbagliata*, 1968); *The Wig* (*La parrucca*, 1973); *The Armchair* (*La Poltrona*, 1984); *The Interview* (*Intervista*, 1988)

FURTHER READING

Anderlini-D'Onofrio, Serena. *The "Weak" Subject*. Madison, N.J.: Fairleigh Dickinson Univ. Press, 1998.

Jeannet, A. M., and G. Sanguinetti Katz, eds. *Natalia Ginzburg: A Voice of the Twentieth Century*. Toronto: Univ. of Toronto Press, 2000.

Picarazzi, Teresa. *Maternal Desire: Natalia Ginzburg's Mothers, Daughters, and Sisters*. Madison, N.J.: Fairleigh Dickinson Univ. Press, 2002.

Teresa Picarazzi

GIRAUDOUX, JEAN (1882–1944)

Born in Bellac, Haute-Vienne, FRANCE, on October 19, 1882, Hippolyte Jean Giraudoux was educated in the classical, rational tradition. After obtaining his baccalaureate in 1900 and spending two years at the Lycée Lakanal, he was accepted at the École Normale Supérieure, the training ground of French intellectuals, where he specialized in German literature. Before receiving his Diplôme d'Études Supérieures, he studied in Munich, where he learned to appreciate Germany's poetic spirit. As an exchange student at Harvard two years later, he learned to appreciate the social and sartorial graces.

Upon returning to Paris, Giraudoux was a journalist for *Le Matin*, and the *Paris Journal*, and the *Revue Française*. But he was destined to be a diplomat and began his career in the consular service in 1910 until it was interrupted by World War I. After the war, he resumed his diplomatic career, which culminated in his appointment as the Foreign Ministry's Press Chief in 1924 and the head of the central office of wartime propaganda in 1939. After the military collapse of France in World War II, he accepted a post as Curator of Historical Monuments, but resigned in discomfort with the Vichy government's movement toward Nazi collaboration. When he died in the throes of acute internal pain on January 31, 1944, it was rumored that he had been poisoned by the Gestapo, though this proved unfounded.

Giraudoux was a prolific and highly reputed man of letters, winning the Prix Balzac for his novel *Siegfried and the Man from Limousin* (*Siegfried et le Limousin*) in 1922. In addition to fifteen dramas, he wrote two screenplays, four volumes of short stories, ten novels, and eleven volumes of essays and memoirs.

Biographers point out the relationship between Giraudoux's life and literary works. His education as a rationalistic idealist began in his peaceful, well-ordered provincial home and community and was reinforced in his formal schooling. But the experience of war and the dissolution of the Third Republic shattered his world of possibility and promise. A tension between the ideal and the real provides the central conflict in his writings.

At forty-six, Giraudoux adapted his novel into his first play, *Siegfried*, the antinationalistic story of an amnesiac French soldier who becomes the leader of a German community. Produced successfully at the Comédie des Champs-Élysées in 1928, it marked the beginning of a productive, lifelong collaboration with actor-director Louis Jouvet, whom Giraudoux credits with transforming his literary plays into theater pieces.

His sparkling boudoir COMEDY *Amphitryon 38* (the thirty-eighth version of the myth of Jupiter's seduction of Alcemena, wife of Amphitryon, whom the god impersonates) was another success in Paris in 1929—and in London and New York as well, when adapted by S. N. BEHRMAN for Alfred Lunt and Lynn Fontanne in 1937.

In *Judith*, Giraudoux transformed the biblical widow who slays the enemy general Holofernes to save her people into a flirtatious young virgin who becomes a woman in Holofernes's bed and kills him because ideal love is impossible. The play was disappointing in its 1931 Paris production. But the author redeemed himself with *Intermezzo* (1933), the tale of another young idealist—a schoolmistress who abandons her world of dreams and her association with a benevolent Spirit to become fully human and marry the Controller of Weights and Measures. This antiphilistine fantasy was well received in Paris, but not on Broadway in a 1950 Maurice Valency adaptation entitled *The Enchanted*.

In 1935 Giraudoux wrote one of his most popular plays, THE TROJAN WAR WILL NOT TAKE PLACE (*La Guerre de Troie n'aura lieu*), a paradoxical analysis of the fateful moments leading up to the Trojan War, which after almost being averted, breaks out as the result of a lie and a misunderstanding. This pacifist drama, written on the eve of World War II, solidified his position as a major dramatist. It enjoyed London and New York runs in 1955 in a CHRISTOPHER FRY translation entitled *Tiger at the Gates*.

The idealistic *jeune fille* (seen in *Intermezzo* and *Judith*) was revived in *Electre* (1937), a modernization of the Greek legend in which the heroine chooses ruin for her city rather than a national well-being based on lies. The play had notable success in Paris, but not abroad. In ONDINE (1939), another *jeune fille* is faced with the choice between dreams of perfection and harsh reality. Based on a story by the German romantic writer La Motte-Fouqué, it features a water sprite that loves, marries, and is betrayed by a mortal.

Sodome et Gomorrhe (1943), a pessimistic study in conjugal incompatibility, reflects both the political context of the Holocaust and the domestic context of Giraudoux's own matrimonial troubles.

With *The Madwoman of Chaillot* (*La Folle de Chaillot*), produced posthumously in Paris in 1945, where it ran for nearly 300 performances, Giraudoux returned to a more optimistic worldview. In this poetic extravaganza featuring an elderly eccentric heroine, he satirizes greed and celebrates a fantastic liberation from the villainous profiteers and unscrupulous opportunists of modern society. It was his most successful American production: the Maurice Valency adaptation ran for 368 performances in 1949, followed by a tour and a return engagement. It also played London in 1951. A musical version starring Angela Lansbury, *Dear World*, ran for 132 performances on Broadway in 1969.

Giraudoux's last play, *Pour Lucrèce*, was produced posthumously in 1953 by Jean-Louis Barrault at the Marigny. Another variation on a classical tale—Livy's *Lucretia*—it relates the tragic story of Lucile, a superhumanly pure woman who is tricked into believing that she was raped while unconscious and poisons herself in shame. Even when her virtue is "restored" by the trickster's confession, Lucile is content to be leaving a world so foul. Under the title *Duel of Angels*, a Christopher Fry adaptation featuring Vivien Leigh opened in London in 1958 and traveled to New York in 1960.

Of Giraudoux's ten full-length original dramas, seven have protagonists who are (usually young) women, and the other three have female protagonists who share equally the spotlight with male protagonists. These implacable, outspoken heroines have pure intentions, intuitive (sometimes supernatural) powers, and clear missions that often involve the overthrow of injustice or corruption. They yearn for the ideal—whether justice or love or truth—and thus are almost always doomed to fail. Yet their very yearning is an affirmation, a sign of hope in the human condition.

Some critics fault Giraudoux for artificiality and affectation and decry his writing as precious. Others defend his "polite" theater, seeing his eloquent use of language as both fitting for a diplomat and characteristic of classical French writers. They praise his playful intelligence, his wit and whimsy, his rich poetry, and his gentle irony.

Though Giraudoux's characters are drawn from the world of fairy tale, biblical legend, and classical mythology, they are human and recognizable in their responses to a world that, in spite of its ancient or fantastical setting, is very like our own.

SELECT PLAYS: *Siegfried* (1928); *Amphitryon 38* (1929); *Judith* (1931); *Intermezzo* (1933); *The Trojan War Shall Not Take Place* (also known as *Tiger at the Gates, La Guerre de Troie n'aura lieu*, 1935); *Electre* (1937); *Ondine* (1939); *Sodome et Gomorrhe* (1943); *The Madwoman of Chaillot* (*La Folle de Chaillot*, 1945); *Duel of Angels* (*Pour Lucrèce*, 1953)

FURTHER READING

Giraudoux, Jean. *Four Plays, Vol. 1: The Madwoman of Chaillot. The Apollo of Bellac, The Enchanted, Ondine*. Adapted by Maurice Valency. New York: Hill and Wang, 1958.

——. *Three Plays, Vol. 2: Siegfried, Amphitryon 38, Electra*. Tr. by Phyllis LaFarge with Peter H. Judd. New York: Hill and Wang, 1964.

Korzeniowska, Victoria B. *The Heroine As Social Redeemer in the Plays of Jean Giraudoux*. New York: Peter Lang Publishing, 2001.

LeSage, Laurent. *Jean Giraudoux: His Life and Works*. University Park: The Pennsylvania State Univ. Press, 1959.

Mankin, Paul. *Precious Irony: The Theatre of Jean Giraudoux*. The Hague: Mouton and Co., 1971.

Raymond, Agnes G. *Jean Giraudoux: The Theatre of Victory and Defeat.* Amherst: Univ. of Massachusetts Press, 1966.

Patricia Montley

THE GIRL OF THE GOLDEN WEST

It pictures with perfect fidelity the characters, life, and manners of my own dearly loved California in the golden days of '49.

—David Belasco, 1929

The Girl of the Golden West by DAVID BELASCO inspired four movie versions and an opera while faithfully portraying an American frontier that never existed. Dependent on highly sentimentalized characters and implausible situations, the play succeeded through the spectacular stage effects that were the hallmark of its author.

Belasco (1853–1931) was born in San Francisco and toured the northern California countryside as a young actor. These early experiences supplied the creative spark for his play about The Girl, a virtuous saloon keeper, who falls in love with a highwayman and saves him from a hangman's noose.

This four-act MELODRAMA opened at the Belasco Theatre in Pittsburgh on October 3, 1905, and moved to the Belasco Theatre in New York on November 11 with Blanche Bates in the title role.

Set in the fictional mining camp of Cloudy Mountain, the play purports to present an accurate picture of a 1849 California mining camp. The original production opened with a stunning panorama that scrolled down, rather than from side to side, disclosing first The Girl's lonely mountain cabin and then the Polka Saloon below.

The action begins in the Polka, where we meet a colorful assortment of miners with names like Bucking Billy, Handsome, Happy, Sonora, and Trinidad, as well as examples of racial stereotypes like an "oily, greasy, unwashed" Mexican and a "lazy, shifty" Indian. Though Belasco assures us "I know the period Forty-Nine as I know my alphabet," The Girl reminds one of Snow White surrounded by the Seven Dwarfs, her honor protected by a chivalrous pack of otherwise drunken miners who consider themselves "her boys."

The fly in the ointment is the villain, Jack Rance, both gambler and sheriff, appropriately waxen of skin and black of mustache, who seeks to add The Girl to his list of conquests. The Girl, though strong and independent, lets us know she is seeking real love, so she spurns him. The month before on the road to Monterey, she had seen a man on horseback and fallen in love at first sight. Now this man, Dick Johnson, walks into her saloon. Johnson, however, is really the "road-agent Ramerrez," who plans to rob the miners.

In act 2, The Girl and Johnson repair to her cabin where the play quickly reaches its climax. As they talk, a storm builds outside, wind wailing and snow blanketing the stage in one of Belasco's trademark effects. Snowbound, Johnson reveals he was forced into banditry but remains pure of heart. They pledge their love, but Rance shoots Johnson as he attempts to escape. The Girl and Rance then play poker for Johnson's life, and The Girl wins the game by hiding her losing cards in her bosom and drawing aces from her stocking.

In act 3, The Girl teaches school and saves Johnson from a lynch mob, and the brief act 4 finds them "on the boundless prairies of the West," concluding with a breathtaking sunrise that took three months and $5,000 to perfect.

Giacomo Puccini turned Belasco's play into an opera, *La Fanciulla del West*, which premiered five years later with Arturo Toscanini conducting, Belasco directing, and Enrico Caruso in the role of Dick Johnson.

[*See also* United States, 1860–1929]

FURTHER READING

Belasco, David. *The Theatre Through Its Stage Door.* New York: Harper and Brothers Publishers, 1919.

——. *Six Plays.* Boston: Little, Brown, and Company, 1929.

Marker, Lise-Lone. *David Belasco: Naturalism in the American Theatre.* Princeton, N.J.: Princeton Univ. Press, 1975.

Timberlake, Craig. *The Life and Work of David Belasco: The Bishop of Broadway.* New York: Library Publishers, 1954.

Winter, William. *The Life of David Belasco.* Freeport, N.Y.: Books for Libraries Press, 1918.

Philip Zwerling

GLASPELL, SUSAN (1876–1948)

Dramatist and fiction writer Susan Glaspell rose to theatrical and literary prominence simultaneous with the advent of U.S. modernism. A founding member of the groundbreaking Provincetown Players, Glaspell figured centrally in the development of United States DRAMATURGY throughout the first decades of the 20th century. At the height of her career, critics deemed Glaspell among the most important playwrights in America, and in ENGLAND, they compared her favorably to HENRIK IBSEN, GEORGE BERNARD SHAW, and ANTON CHEKHOV.

Glaspell was born on July 1, 1876, in Davenport, Iowa, where she grew up and attended Drake University. Following graduation in 1899, she embarked on a journalistic career but after two years chose to devote herself to creative writing. Glaspell soon gained a reputation as a local colorist, publishing short stories in such magazines as *Harper's* and *Ladies' Home Journal*. Glaspell's first novel, *The Glory of the Conquered* (1909), introduced themes that would dominate her writing: the struggles of women as artists and intellectuals, and the pressure of social conventions on women's competing roles as wives and professionals.

Through the Monist Society, a group devoted to progressive movements, Glaspell met George Cram ("Jig") Cook, whom she married in 1913. They moved east to live in communities of like-minded artists and political activists. In the summer of 1915, in Provincetown, Massachusetts, they and some friends staged *Suppressed Desires*, a spoof on Freudian psychology written by the couple. The event was so successful that Cook urged others in their circle to contribute plays; the next summer the group produced more one-acts, including one by EUGENE O'NEILL. At Cook's urging, the friends decided to form a theater that rejected the aesthetics and commercialism of Broadway and began producing in Greenwich Village that fall. The Provincetown Players committed themselves to developing stylistically and topically adventurous new work by American playwrights. From 1915 to 1922, the Players staged eleven plays by Glaspell (two co-authored with Cook), including TRIFLES, her best known drama and a foundational text for feminist criticism; *Inheritors*, her most forceful political play; and *The Verge*, her most experimental and perhaps strongest overall work.

In 1922, disenchanted with the commercial direction the Players had taken, Cook moved to Greece with Glaspell, where he died two years later. Glaspell soon returned to the States. Her play ALISON'S HOUSE, produced by Eva Le Gallienne's Civic Repertory Theatre, won the Pulitzer Prize in 1931. With her companion Norman Matson, she co-authored *The Comic Artist*, produced on Broadway in 1933. From 1936 to 1938, Glaspell headed the Midwest Play Bureau, nurturing local dramatists as part of the FEDERAL THEATRE PROJECT. She returned to Cape Cod in the last decade of her life, where she wrote her final play, *Springs Eternal*, which was neither published nor produced. She died of a pulmonary embolism on July 27, 1948, in Provincetown, Massachusetts.

[*See also* United States, 1860–1929]

PLAYS: *Suppressed Desires* (with George Cram Cook, 1915); *Trifles* (1916); *Close the Book* (1917); *The Outside* (1917); *The People* (1917); *Tickless Time* (with George Cram Cook, 1918); *Woman's Honor* (1918); *Bernice* (1919); *Inheritors* (1920); *The Verge* (1921); *Chains of Dew* (1922); *The Comic Artist* (with Norman Matson, 1928); *Alison's House* (1930); *Springs Eternal* (1943–1944)

FURTHER READING

Ben-Zvi, Linda, ed. *Susan Glaspell: Essays on Her Theater and Fiction*. Ann Arbor: Univ. of Michigan Press, 1995.

——. *Susan Glaspell: Her Life and Times*. New York: Oxford Univ. Press, 2005.

Gainor, J. Ellen. *Susan Glaspell in Context: American Theater, Culture, and Politics, 1915–1948*. Ann Arbor: Univ. of Michigan Press, 2001.

Ozieblo Rajkowska, Barbara. *Susan Glaspell: A Critical Biography*. Chapel Hill: Univ. of North Carolina Press, 2000.

Papke, Mary. *Susan Glaspell: A Research and Production Sourcebook*. Westport, Conn.: Greenwood Press, 1993.

J. Ellen Gainor

THE GLASS MENAGERIE

Oh, Laura, Laura, I tried to leave you behind me, but I am more faithful than I intended to be! I reach for a cigarette, I cross the street, I run into the movies or a bar, I buy a drink, I speak to the nearest stranger—anything that can blow your candles out!—for nowadays the world is lit by lightning! Blow out your candles, Laura—and so good-bye. . . .

—Tom, Scene VII

TENNESSEE WILLIAMS's lyrical 1944 "memory play" firmly established him as a major voice in American theater. Often described as autobiographical, this delicate, poetic drama is based only loosely on Williams's relationship with his domineering mother and fragile sister. A quintessential American play, *The Glass Menagerie* has influenced several generations of dramatists, from WILLIAM INGE and Robert Anderson to BETH HENLEY and TONY KUSHNER, and it remains one of Williams's most frequently produced works.

As a self-avowed "stage magician," Tom Wingfield reflects back on his life with his mother and sister, conjuring scenes from the past. At the height of the Great Depression, the sensitive Tom has aspirations of becoming a writer, but financial exigencies force him to work in a St. Louis factory. Amanda, his mother, is an unhappy woman who was deserted by her husband years before. Ill-equipped to cope with the hard realities of her reduced circumstances, Amanda struggles to make ends meet and worries about the future of her repressed daughter, Laura. Amanda enrolls Laura in a business school hoping she might learn stenographic skills, but under the pressure of a time test Laura becomes physically ill and ceases to attend the class. Frustrated, Amanda pressures Tom to bring home a "gentleman caller" for Laura in a desperate hope that she might find security in a marriage.

Despite practical pressures, Amanda frequently retreats into either real or imagined memories of herself as a romantic Southern belle receiving seventeen gentlemen callers. Fearing that Tom may give in to his desire to escape the factory, Amanda cannot help nagging him about everything from taking his job more seriously to the proper way of chewing his food. Tom strives to be patient with Amanda for Laura's sake, but often flees to the movies or into the oblivion of alcohol. Laura, too, frequently escapes into a fantasy world listening to old Victrola records her father left behind and collecting glass figurines. Among these, a unicorn is her favorite; as a unique and fragile creature herself, she relates to the symbolism of the unicorn's distinguishing horn.

Amanda's browbeating finally convinces Tom to bring Jim O'Connor, his factory co-worker, home to dinner. Amanda's enthusiastic preparations extend to digging out her old cotillion dress, in which she appears to greet Jim in a scene Williams crafts with both poignancy and absurdity. Laura and Jim discover they were high school classmates and when they are left alone, Laura touchingly recalls the crush she had on Jim. She fondly remembers his good-humored teasing, revealing feelings for him that have remained with her. Laura shows Jim her glass menagerie and he impulsively kisses her, exuberantly swinging her about the room in an impromptu dance. They knock over the table containing Laura's glass figures and the prized unicorn loses its horn. It is now, as Laura ruefully notes, "just like all the other horses." Jim apologizes, making a hasty departure after confessing that he is engaged to another girl. Amanda angrily turns on Tom for his blunder and they argue bitterly. Tom, as Amanda has predicted and feared, storms out the door never to return. As the play ends, Tom is again seen in the present reflecting back with sadness, explaining that despite geographic distance and the intervening years he has been unable to extinguish the memory of his sister.

The Glass Menagerie demonstrates Williams's characteristic use of poetic language mixed with both theatrical and realistic elements, from carefully selected symbols to EPIC THEATER–inspired projected titles and other nonrealistic devices. The play also established a dominant Williams theme: the struggle for survival of the sensitive or artistic soul in a harsh and unreceptive world. Williams's unparalleled skill at constructing unforgettable characters is fully evident in *The Glass Menagerie*, as is his ability through character, language, and theatrical embellishments to create a unique and dramatically compelling world of the play.

The Glass Menagerie was recognized as a masterpiece from the time of its original production in December 1944. There have been at least four films and numerous Broadway revivals.

The Glass Menagerie, like other mid-20th-century classics of American drama—including EUGENE O'NEILL's LONG DAY'S JOURNEY INTO NIGHT, THORNTON WILDER's OUR TOWN, ARTHUR MILLER's DEATH OF A SALESMAN, and Williams's own A STREETCAR NAMED DESIRE—is one of the enduring works of the Broadway theater. It is also the play most responsible for establishing American lyric REALISM, a dramatic style that dominated the U.S. stage throughout the second half of the 20th century.

[*See also* United States, 1940–Present]

FURTHER READING

Bigsby, C. W. E. "Entering *The Glass Menagerie*," *The Cambridge Companion to Tennessee Williams*, ed. by Matthew C. Roudané. Cambridge: Cambridge Univ. Press, 1997. 29–44.

Bloom, Harold, ed. *Tennessee Williams's The Glass Menagerie (Modern Critical Interpretations)*. New York: Chelsea House, 1988.

Kolin, Philip C. "Black and Multi-Racial Productions of Tennessee Williams's *The Glass Menagerie*." *Journal of Dramatic Theory and Criticism* 9, no. 2 (1995): 97–128.

Parker, R. Brian, ed. *The Glass Menagerie: A Collection of Critical Essays*. Englewood Cliffs, N. J.: Prentice-Hall, 1983.

Presley, Delma E. *The Glass Menagerie: An American Memory*. Boston: Twayne, 1990.

Siebold, Thomas, ed. *Readings on The Glass Menagerie*. San Diego, Ca.: Greenhaven Press, 1998.

James Fisher

GLENGARRY GLEN ROSS

We're just 'talking' about it.

—Aaronow, Act 1

The most critically acclaimed play of DAVID MAMET's long and distinguished career, *Glengarry Glen Ross* was first presented at London's National Theatre in 1983. The U.S. premiere was produced at the Goodman Theatre in Chicago, and subsequently transferred to Broadway's Golden Theatre, where it ran for 378 performances, earning a Tony Award nomination and the 1984 Pulitzer Prize for Drama. It has since been produced by countless professional and university theaters worldwide, was adapted as a film in 1992, and revived on Broadway in 2005.

Based loosely on Mamet's own experience working in a Chicago real estate office, the two-act, seven-character play depicts the competition and camaraderie among a group of middle-aged salesmen. Hustling to sell, sight unseen, parcels of land in far-off developments with such fanciful names as Glengarry Highlands, the salesmen live in a state of constant tension. Old-timers Levene, Moss, and Aaronow find their livelihood threatened by competition from a younger, more ruthless generation. Act 1 consists of three loosely connected scenes, each a two-person conversation in a Chinese restaurant, which introduce the characters and their circumstances. Fear of losing their jobs leads the older men to contemplate a desperate crime, stealing the prized sales leads from their office and selling them to a competitor. Act 2 is a single continuous scene in the real estate office; the crime has been committed and all the characters converge to discover the culprit.

The whodunit aspect of the play is secondary, however, to Mamet's critique of corporate greed and cutthroat competition. The masculine bonding and cooperative goodwill of the older characters is set in opposition to the every-man-for-himself ethic of the younger generation, Roma and Williamson. Though the play shows the latter view triumphing over the former, it is clear that something of great value has been lost in the changing of the guard. Critics have frequently compared *Glengarry Glen Ross* to ARTHUR MILLER's DEATH OF A SALESMAN in its depiction of flawed, but essentially good men left behind by a changing business environment. Mamet's take on this phenomenon was particularly timely during the mid-1980s, an era marked by the public celebration of wealth and greed, as well as by several high-profile insider trading scandals in the United States. Mamet himself has compared the policies of the real estate office in *Glengarry* to those of the administration of Ronald Reagan, because in each case "one can only succeed at the cost of the failure of another."

Perhaps more than any other of Mamet's works, *Glengarry Glen Ross* offers the strongest synergy between its subject matter and Mamet's linguistic dexterity. As salesmen selling a worthless and intangible product, the characters in the play are uniquely dependent on their skill at manipulating language. They use words to persuade, cajole, deceive, and intimidate their potential customers and each other. The rapid-fire dialogues of the first act have the rhythm, precision, and aggressiveness of a fencing match, whereas the more chaotic second act demonstrates how quickly a position built solely on words can erode.

FURTHER READING

Dean, Anne. *David Mamet: Language as Dramatic Action*. Rutherford, N. J.: Fairleigh Dickinson Univ. Press, 1990.

Kane, Leslie, ed. *David Mamet's Glengarry Glen Ross: Text and Performance*. New York: Garland, 1996.

Nightengale, Benedict. "Glengarry Glen Ross." In *The Cambridge Companion to David Mamet*, ed. by Christopher Bigsby. Cambridge: Cambridge Univ. Press, 2004. 89–102.

Roudané, Matthew C. "Something Out of Nothing." In *David Mamet in Conversation*, ed. by Leslie Kane. Ann Arbor: Univ. of Michigan Press, 2001. 46–53.

Henry Bial

GLOVER, SUE (1943–)

More important than myth/legend is the idea of confinement: I like my characters cut off, marooned spatially or psychologically, or both. But I don't play this consciously.

—Sue Glover, 2000

Born in Edinburgh, SCOTLAND, in 1943, Sue Glover is one of a group of Scottish women playwrights, including LIZ LOCHHEAD and RONA MUNRO, who emerged during the 1980s. In the wake of the failed devolution referendum (on Scottish home rule) of 1979 and amidst the conservative political and cultural ferment associated with British prime minister Margaret Thatcher's "conviction politics," there arose an impetus to reassess the nation and what it meant to be Scottish. Glover's writing reveals the larger political picture through a focus on personal histories.

Sue Glover has written widely for radio and television, including fifty episodes of the television soap opera *Take the High Road*. Her television adaptation of her early play, *The Bubble Boy* (1980), won awards at festivals in Chicago and New York. Mastery of characterization, narrative, and dramatic structure has enabled her to play with form, incorporating techniques derived from Scotland's oral tradition to challenge accepted versions of Scottish history and culture. Her "history" plays, notably *The Straw Chair* (1988) and BONDAGERS (1991), employ elements of myth, folktale, storytelling, and ballad and are suffused with skillfully used language—English, Scots-English, Scots Gaelic, and dialect. Glover seeks to question the value assigned by a patriarchal society to women's stories and utterance.

Glover's work was among the earliest to break out of the domestic and urban settings of much 20th-century Scottish drama into the open spaces of land, sea, and sky, which dominate the struggle by her characters to know themselves and their place within the wider landscape. In the plays *The Seal Wife* (1980), *The Straw Chair* (1988), and *Shetland Saga* (2000), Glover uses the image of the sea to explore female sexuality, its power, and the fear it engenders. *The Seal Wife* herself is one of the mythical Selkies, who has shed her sealskin to love a man onshore, with tragic results, while *The Straw Chair* tells the story of Rachel, Lady Grange, the rebellious wife of an 18th-century aristocrat, who discovered her husband's Jacobite sympathies, refused to be silenced, and was banished to the remote island of St. Kilda. A young woman, Isabel, newly married to a minister, arrives on St. Kilda. In Rachel's reckless disregard for convention and struggle for freedom and the confident engagement of the island women with their environment and ancient culture, she finds a path to her awakening sexuality, which is expressed in her burgeoning love for the sea. The environment shapes the characters, nurturing or destroying them as ruthlessly as do the gender roles thrust on them by society. The price paid by individual women for rebellion against these roles is starkly portrayed in Rachel's final disintegration.

The transformative power of communication between different cultures is an ongoing theme in Glover's work. In *The Straw Chair* characters speak in a mixture of Gaelic and English, and Isabel, growing in confidence, learns Gaelic. In *Shetland Saga*, the characters converse in English, which Glover uses to render both Bulgarian and English. A skeleton crew aboard a Bulgarian trawler impounded in Shetland, left without pay or supplies, scrabbles for survival; the crew's hopes and aspirations affect the Shetlanders, who variously feed them, love them, or resent them. As the fate of the ship, *Ludmilla*, and her crew is decided elsewhere, the women in the play—Bulgarian and Shetlander alike—are driven to violent action to protect their dreams. As trawlerman Svetan and local girl Mena grow closer, their use of language converges.

Sue Glover's more recent work continues to examine characters who are "cut-off." In 2005, her radio play *The Doll's Tea Set* deals with an exploration of traumatic childhood memory. She is also developing a script for the Royal National Theatre Studio around the lives of destitute and delinquent boys aboard a Victorian "ship of correction."

SELECT PLAYS: *The Bubble Boy* (1980); *An Island in Largo* (1980); *The Seal Wife* (1980); *The Straw Chair* (1988); *Bondagers* (1991); *Sacred Hearts* (1994); *Artist Unknown* (1996); *Shetland Saga* (2000)

FURTHER READING

Bain, Audrey. "Loose Canons: Identifying a Women's Tradition in Playwriting." In *Scottish Theatre since the Seventies*, ed. by Randall Stevenson and Gavin Wallace. Edinburgh: Edinburgh Univ. Press, 1996.

Horvat, Ksenija, and Barbara Bell. "Sue Glover, Rona Munro and Lara Jane Bunting: Echoes and Open Spaces." In *Contemporary Scottish Women Writers*, ed. by Aileen Christianson and Alison Lumsden. Edinburgh: Edinburgh Univ. Press, 2000.

Poggi, Valentina, and Margaret Rose. *A Theatre That Matters: Twentieth-Century Scottish Drama and Theatre*. Milan: Editzioni Unicopli, 2000.

Scullion, Adrienne. "Contemporary Scottish Women Playwrights." In *Modern British Women Playwrights*, ed. by Elaine Aston and Janelle Reinelt. Cambridge: Cambridge Univ. Press, 2000.

Triesman, Susan. "Transformations and Transgressions: Women's Discourse on the Scottish Stage." In *British and Irish Women*

Dramatists since 1958, ed. by Trevor R. Griffiths and Margaret Llewellyn-Jones. Buckingham: Open Univ. Press, 1993.

Barbara A. E. Bell

GOLDEN BOY

Golden Boy (1935) maintains much of CLIFFORD ODETS's left-wing political outlook in its exploration of the callous and destructive exploitation of the talents of its sympathetic central figure, Joe Bonaparte. Odets himself now seems far less a revolutionary radical and far more a noncontroversial social liberal.

The main difference between this and the earlier Odets dramas is the direct intrusion of the outside world in scenes other than the close intimacy of the family apartment. Settings vary from the Bonaparte home to the boxing manager's office, the gymnasium, and the dressing room. No longer is the circle inhabited only by relatives or neighbors; it has expanded to bring in members of a social culture completely alien to that of the Bonapartes. It is one they cannot understand, and though Joe attempts to become part of it, he never totally succeeds. There is much that attracts Joe—the immediacy of money and the availability of the high-powered cars he has always admired—but his gradual seduction by the allure of the fight game leads to his ultimate destruction. The abstraction of a Depression faced and fought by the families of *Awake and Sing!* or *Paradise Lost* has been replaced by the visible world into which Joe leaps, over his head.

It is, of course, obvious to those closest to him that Joe can never be a part of this world he has chosen. His brokenhearted father is well aware of his son's terrible mistake, but one of the strongest points is made by Tokio, the trainer, who tells him flatly, "Your heart ain't in fightin' . . . your hate is." This statement strikes at the play's central theme that one's decisions should be in keeping with one's inner nature. But the validity of this view is challenged: How can that inner nature succeed in providing the material things one desperately wants, but which seem to demand contrary actions to acquire? In other words, why starve in the attic, so to speak, when a prosperous life can be achieved if you so choose?

Golden Boy is Odets's clear indictment of a society that provides its greatest material rewards to those who rely on brute power and physical strength, with few rewards and little encouragement offered within the aesthetic areas of art or music. The irony lies in the fact that Joe Bonaparte, who performs so easily in the fight ring, is really not a fighter. The requisite killer instinct that can rouse the crowd is subsumed by his skills as a boxer, which wins the fight but does little to please the fans. Joe is fully aware of the brute he has become, and as Tokio well knows, he hates the new persona that is destroying his inborn sensitive nature. He takes vengeance on himself in his vicious and fatal attack on the Chocolate Drop, ending with broken hands and no prospects of ever playing the thousand dollar violin his father has given him. He is now, in the words of the gambler Eddie Fuseli, a bum. He has not only killed a hapless opponent, he has killed himself. Moreover, the irony is doubled as he and his sweetheart, Lorna, speed off in Joe's other great achievement, the fast car, to a fatal crash.

On stage and screen, *Golden Boy* remains one of Odets's major successes. It can be taken on a narrow level as a social lesson involving a sensitive character who recognizes, too late, that there is more in life than material achievement. But that is much too simple. *Golden Boy* offers a far broader comment on a society incapable of adequately sustaining the talents of those devoted to beauty and humaneness while callously exploiting, rewarding, and too often killing those who reveal the savagery so frequently just beneath the surface.

[*See also* The Group Theatre; Political Theater in the United States]

FURTHER READING

Clurman, Harold. *The Fervent Years: The Story of the Group Theatre and the Thirties*. New York: Hill and Wang, 1945, 1957.
Goldstein, Malcolm. *American Drama and the Theatre of the Great Depression*. New York: Oxford Univ. Press, 1974.
Weales, Gerald. *Clifford Odets, Playwright*. New York: Pegasus, 1971.

Jordan Miller

GOLDFADEN, AVROM (1840–1908)

Avrom Goldfaden was, more than any other single figure, responsible for the creation of the modern, professional YIDDISH THEATER. Traditionally, Judaism viewed theater as anathema—the "seat of scoffers," as the sages put it (Psalms 1:1). Goldfaden was born on July 12, 1840, into an environment where those views were in the process of loosening. He grew up in a household that blended traditional and modern learning.

Goldfaden was the surname the writer took after he began writing professionally. He was born Avrom Goldenfodem in Volhynia, RUSSIA, son of a respected watchmaker who gave Avrom and his other three sons a traditional Jewish education mixed with secular learning. In his teens, Avrom attended a government-run rabbinical academy in Zhitomir (currently in western Ukraine). While there, he published poetry in Hebrew and Yiddish and began writing dramas—a short sketch and a full-length COMEDY, *Aunt Sosya* (*Di mume Sosya*, 1869). He also played the title role, to great acclaim, in a school production of Solomon Ettinger's *Serkele*. Such writing and performing were of little practical use, however, since no professional Yiddish theater existed at the time.

After graduating from the seminary, Goldfaden tried various jobs, including starting a Yiddish newspaper in ROMANIA, which the government closed after a few months. In Jassy, Romania, Goldfaden came in contact with performers who included his songs in their repertoire, and by the end of 1876, he was writing sketches and plays for them. He and his new troupe were soon touring Romania with such works as *The Capricious Bride* (*Di kaprizne kale*, 1876), *Grandmother and Granddaughter* (*Di bobe mitn eynikl*,

1877), and *Shmendrik* (also known as *The Comical Wedding*, 1877). Many of his earliest plays sharply satirized religious extremism and intolerance within the Jewish community.

Goldfaden turned out a tremendous number of plays, and his growing company made its way eastward into Russia. The best of his plays from the late 1870s and early 1880s were the musical comedies *The Sorceress* (*Di kishefmakherin*, 1877) and *The Two Kuni-Lemls* (*Di tsvey Kuni-Leml*, 1880) and the operettas *Shulamis, or The Daughter of Jerusalem* (*Shulamis, oder bas yerushalayim*, 1881) and *Doctor Almasado, or the Jews in Palermo* (*Doctor Almasado, oder di yidn in Palermo*, 1881), in which the author/composer marries Jewish characters, subject matter, and textual and musical references to Western dramatic structures and musical modes. The latter works reflected a radical change in the fortunes of Eastern European Jews after the assassination of Tsar Alexander II in 1881. His successor, Alexander III, enacted a series of repressive measures that made life more difficult than ever for Russian Jews, sparking an exodus that would transform Jewish life in Eastern Europe and around the world.

In this climate, Goldfaden turned from writing satires to works adapted from Jewish legend and history. Best known in the latter category was *Bar Kokhba, or the Son of the Stars* (*Bar Kokhba, oder der zun fun di shtern*, 1883), based on the story of a second-century Jewish zealot who led a suicidal revolt against the Roman Empire. The play became a staple of the Yiddish theatrical repertoire, and its subversive allegorical message may have been partly responsible for provoking the Russian ban on Yiddish theater in 1883. In grand spectacles like *Shulamis* and *Bar Kokhba*, Goldfaden's sure hand at creating vivid characters and his skill as a composer are as evident as in his early comedies, but he significantly widens his range of devices, with an array of exotic character types, spectacular tableaux, and even wild animals. These works struck a chord with audiences coming to terms with an increasingly hostile world.

Goldfaden would continue writing plays and poems until the end of his life, but at a slower pace than in his early career. The best of his later works included the biblically inspired operettas *King Ahasuerus* (*Kenig Akhashveyresh*, 1887) and *The Binding of Isaac* (*Di Akeydes Yitskhok*, 1887) and his six-act epic, *The Messianic Era?!* (*Meshiekhs tsaytn?!*, 1891), which reflected his increasing commitment to Zionism later in life. With a one-act play based on the exploits of King David, *Some of My People* (*Ben Ami*, 1907), he also made a brief attempt to do for Hebrew theater what he had done for Yiddish theater.

Goldfaden's death on January 9, 1908, was a valediction rather than an ending. The most popular of his plays were ubiquitous on Yiddish stages worldwide and inspired a tradition of reinterpretation. AVANT-GARDE productions of his work were staged in major cultural centers like Moscow, Warsaw, and New York, and later generations of playwrights found ways to adapt his work to new aesthetic and political circumstances. Notable among these efforts are Mikhl Weichert's *Trupe Tanentsap* (*The Tanentsap Troupe*, based on *The Two Kuni-Lemls*), Itsik Manger's *Hotsmakh-shpil* (*Hotsmakh Play*, based on *The Sorceress*), and Shmuel Halkin's reworking of *Shulamis* and *Bar Kokhba* along Soviet lines. At least as important, Goldfaden's music became so popular that many of his best-known songs, like "Raisins and Almonds" ("*Rozhinkes mit mandlen*"), became widely regarded as folk melodies.

SELECT PLAYS: *Aunt Sosya* (*Di mume Sosya*, 1869); *The Capricious Bride* (*Di kaprizne kale*, 1876); *The Recruits* (*Di rekrutn*, 1876); *Grandmother and Granddaughter* (*Di bobe mitn eynikl*, 1877); *The Capricious Bride, or, Pauperson and Hungerman* (*Di kaprizne kale, oder kaptsnzon et hungerman*, 1877); *The Sorceress* (*Di kishefmakherin*, 1877); *The Two Kuni-Lemls* (*Di tsvey kuni-lemls*, 1880); *Doctor Almasado, or the Jews in Palermo* (*Doktor Almasado, oder di yidn in Palermo*, 1881); *Shulamis, or the Daughter of Jerusalem* (*Shulamis, oder bas yerushalayim*, 1881); *Bar Kokhba, or the Son of the Stars* (*Bar Kokhba, oder der zun fun di shtern*, 1883); *The Binding of Isaac* (*Di Akeydes Yitskhok*, 1887); *King Ahasuerus* (*Kenig Akhashveyresh*, 1887); *The Messianic Era?!* (*Meshiekhs tsaytn?!*, 1891); *Son of My People* (*Ben Ami*, 1907)

FURTHER READING

Adler, Jacob. *A Life on the Stage*. Tr. by Lulla Rosenfeld. New York: Alfred A. Knopf, 1999.

Berkowitz, Joel, ed. *Yiddish Theatre: New Approaches*. London: Littman Library of Jewish Civilization, 2003.

Rosenfeld, Lulla. *Bright Star of Exile: Jacob Adler and the Yiddish Theatre*. New York: Thomas Y. Crowell, 1977.

Sandrow, Nahma. *Vagabond Stars: A World History of Yiddish Theater*. New York: Harper & Row, 1977. Reprint Syracuse Univ. Press, 1999.

Joel Berkowitz

GOLL, YVAN (1891–1950)

> *The function of art is not to make life easy for the bloated bourgeois . . . Art, insofar as it aims to educate, ameliorate, or be somehow effective, has to kill off the everyday citizen, terrify him as the mask does the child, as Euripides did the Athenians who could only stagger on their way out. Art must turn man into a child again.*
>
> —Yvan Goll, 1920

Yvan Goll (also known as Iwan Lassang, Tristan Torsi, Johannes Thor, and Tristan Thor) challenged aesthetic traditions and bourgeois conceptions his entire life and was associated with most AVANT-GARDE movements of the early 20th century, including Italian FUTURISM, German EXPRESSIONISM, DADAISM, French Orphism, and SURREALISM. Goll is best known for his poetry, which includes *Jean sans Terre* (*La Chanson de Jean sans Terre*, 1936–1939) and, together with his wife Claire Goll, *Love Poems* (*Poèms d'amour*, 1925), but he also wrote three Expressionist dramas, as well as novels and essays. Goll published in German, French, and English and collaborated with many artists throughout his career.

Born Isaac Lang on March 29, 1891, in Saint-Dié, FRANCE, Goll, a Jewish socialist-pacifist, lived in exile for much of his adult life, moving to SWITZERLAND from Alsace-Lorraine in 1915 to avoid military service after receiving a doctorate in law in Strassburg in 1913. In Switzerland, Goll became friends with Romain Rolland (1866–1944) and published antiwar poems and articles in leading German Expressionist publications.

Through altered states of consciousness and by rejecting logic and syntax, Goll sought to discover insights into the human condition and wrote two Expressionist-Surrealist plays. In the preface to *The Immortals* (*Die Unsterblichen*, 1920), Goll writes of the need for a more meaningful theater beyond the world of the five senses and external form, one capable of "slaying workaday man." He rejects realism for the distorting mirror of the grotesque and its ability to shock the spectator, liberate repressions, and gain access to the "superreal." Through exaggerated and disconnected scenes of the bizarre and the grotesque, *The Immortals* demonstrates the meaninglessness of life and the inadequacies of rational faculties to explain the world. In the preface to *Methusalem, or the Eternal Bourgeois* (*Methusalem, oder Der ewige Bürger*, 1922), Goll cites superrealism and illogic as the newest weapons of the modern satirist. Gestures and everyday dialogue atrophy into meaningless drivel through seemingly disconnected scenes, casting the communicative power of language into doubt. Absurd phrasings and bizarre proclamations parody the self-serious attitudes of literary and political causes. All of Goll's dramas lack formal logic and traditional dramatic structure, so that they themselves reflect the absurdity of the human condition, prefiguring the absurd theater of SAMUEL BECKETT and EUGENE IONESCO.

In 1919 Goll moved to Paris, became involved in Dadaism and Surrealism, and wrote some of his best poetry. After emigrating to New York in 1939, he published the French-American journal *Hemispheres* (*Hémisphères*, 1943–1946), his lyric cycle *Fruit from Saturn* (1945), and the English translation of *Love Poems* (1947) among other works. His highly regarded posthumous lyric collection *Dream Herb* (*Traumkraut*, 1951) marked his return to the German language. Goll died of leukemia on March 27, 1950, in Paris.

[*See also* Germany]

PLAYS: *The Immortals: Two Pranks* (*Die Unsterblichen: Zwei Possen*, 1920), *Methusalem, or the Eternal Bourgeois: A Satiric Drama* (*Methusalem, oder Der ewige Bürger: Satirisches Drama*, 1922); *The Stall of Augias* (*Der Stall des Augias*, 1924)

FURTHER READING

Brandt, George W., ed. *Modern Theories of Drama: A Selection of Writings on Drama and Theatre 1850–1990*. Oxford: Oxford Univ. Press, 1998. 171–175.

Goll, Iwan. *Dichtungen. Lyrik, Prosa, Dramen* [Literature: Lyric, Prose, Dramas]. Ed. by Claire Goll. Darmstadt, Germany: Luchterhand, 1960.

Goll, Yvan. "Preface to *Die Unsterblichen* (*The Immortals*, 1920)." Tr. by George W. Brandt. In *Modern Theories of Drama: A Selection of Writings on Drama and Theatre, 1850–1990*. Ed. by George W. Brandt. Oxford: Oxford Univ. Press, 1999. 171–173.

Schaefer, Dietrich. "Iwan Goll." In *Expressionismus als Literatur. Gesammelte Studien* [Expressionism as Literature: Collected Studies]. Ed. by Wolfgang Rothe. Bern, Switzerland: Francke, 1969. 426–436.

Sokel, Walter Herbert. *The Writer In Extremis: Expressionism In Twentieth-Century German Literature*. Stanford, Ca.: Stanford Univ. Press, 1959.

Christa Spreizer

GOMBROWICZ, WITOLD (1904–1969)

Witold Gombrowicz gradually emerged as one of the most widely produced Polish playwrights of the late 20th century. He was born in Maloszyce, POLAND, on August 4, 1904. As a result of immigrating to ARGENTINA and FRANCE after 1939 and decades of censorship of his works in communist Poland, by the late 1960s, Gombrowicz enjoyed the distinction of being a playwright with an international reputation whose works were almost exclusively produced abroad and in translation. He died on July 24, 1969, in his flat in Vence, in southeastern France. His works began to assume a central place in the Polish repertory in the mid-1970s, and a major revival of interest in his works both at home and abroad began with Poland's break from the Soviet bloc and the fall of the Berlin Wall in 1989. A biannual International Gombrowicz Festival was established in Radom in 1993.

Gombrowicz authored four plays: *Ivona, Princess of Burgundia* (*Iwona, ksiezniczka Burgunda*, 1938), *The Marriage* (*Slub*, 1944), *Operetta* (*Operetka*, 1966), and *History* (*Historia*, 1975). His plays have proven consistently popular in GERMANY, where *Ivona* and *The Marriage* have also provided the libretti for operas by the composers Boris Blacher and Volker David Kirchner. Decades after his plays entered the repertories of Stockholm's Royal Dramatic Theater and La Comédie Française in Paris, Gombrowicz's *The Marriage* was belatedly produced in Warsaw's National Theater in 1998, followed by *Operetta* in 2000.

The playwright also authored a collection of short stories (1933), a three-volume *Diary* (*Dziennik*, 1953–1969), and a variety of autobiographical sketches, most notably *A Kind of Testament* (*Entretiens avec Dominique de Roux*, 1968). The history of the stage adaptations of Gombrowicz's short stories, novels, and other writings roughly parallels that of his plays, with the earliest examples appearing in West Germany, France, and ITALY in the late 1960s. Among the most notable was Tadeusz Kantor's landmark production *The Dead Class* (Umarla klasa, 1975).

The defining paradox of Gombrowicz is his appeal as both a classical and an AVANT-GARDE writer, and his works have consistently enjoyed theatrical success in both categories over the decades. Critics in the 1960s immediately linked his work to SAMUEL BECKETT, EUGENE IONESCO, and JEAN GENET, comparisons which he vigorously rejected. The only playwrights whose influence he acknowledged were William Shakespeare, Johann Wolfgang von Goethe, and ALFRED JARRY. Major directors of Gombrowicz's work in both Poland and Western Europe (including Jerzy Jarocki, Jorge Lavelli, Ernst Schröder, and INGMAR BERGMAN) have acknowledged their attraction to the playwright's combination of Shakespearean theatrics, substructure, and parody. Gombrowicz's dramas are generally devoid of any specific Polish references and details, and function instead as complex metaphorical constructions. Gombrowicz possessed a strong philosophical bent, and Camus and others acknowledged him as a precursor to the French existentialists.

PLAYS: *Ivona, Princess of Burgundia* (*Iwona, ksiezniczka Burgunda*, 1938); *The Marriage* (*Slub*, 1944); *Operetta* (*Operetka*, 1966); *History* (*Historia*, 1975)

FURTHER READING

Cioffi, Kathleeen M. *Alternative Theatre in Poland 1954–1989*. Amsterdam: Harwood Academic Publishers, 1996.

Esslin, Martin. *The Theatre of the Absurd*. 2d ed. London: Pelican Books, 1968.

Kott, Jan. "On Gombrowicz." In *The Theater of Essence*, ed. by Kott. Evanston, Ill.: Northwestern Univ. Press, 1984.

Milosz, Czeslaw. *The History of Polish Literature*. London: The Macmillan Company, 1969.

Thompson, Ewa. *Witold Gombrowicz*. Boston: Twayne, 1979.

Ziarek, Ewa Plonowska, ed. *Gombrowicz's Grimaces: Modernism, Nationality, Gender*. Albany: State Univ. of New York Press, 1998.

Allen J. Kuharski

GOODNIGHT DESDEMONA (GOOD MORNING JULIET)

ANN-MARIE MACDONALD's rich and clever parody *Goodnight Desdemona (Good Morning Juliet)* premiered in Toronto, CANADA, in 1988 at the Annex Theatre and toured with a revised script two years later, when it won the Governor General's Award for Drama.

The heroine of the play is Constance Ledbelly, a timid assistant professor at Queen's University who is infatuated with Professor Claude Night, who has manipulated Constance into writing his academic articles for him. Constance is still working on her doctoral dissertation, which proposes that William Shakespeare took the plots for his TRAGEDIES *Othello* and *Romeo and Juliet* from an unknown comic source text in which a wise fool rights the wrongs of the main characters, giving the tragedies happy endings. Disappointed by Claude's lack of interest in her and disillusioned by academic life, Constance finds herself magically transported into the text of *Othello*, where she immediately reveals Iago's treachery, thereby saving Desdemona's life and averting the tragedy. Constance is awed by Desdemona, whom MacDonald depicts as a female warrior, the embodiment of bravery and adventure.

Iago, his first plan thwarted, turns his machinations on Desdemona, convincing her that Othello has been unfaithful to her with Constance. Desdemona, with the same propensity for jealousy that Othello has, promptly decides to murder Constance, who inadvertently escapes by entering the text of *Romeo and Juliet*. Disguised as a young boy named Constantine, Constance announces Romeo and Juliet's marriage to Tybalt, ending the fateful duel before it begins. Without their tragic circumstances to hold them together, Romeo and Juliet lose interest in each other and fall in love with Constance. Determined to die for love, Juliet nearly convinces Constance to end her own life while Desdemona, who has arrived from Cyprus, learns of Iago's deceit and tries to persuade Constance to kill Iago. In the end, Constance fulfills her role as the wise fool by encouraging both women to let go of the tragic tendencies that drive them, and she returns to her world with renewed confidence and self-knowledge.

MacDonald begins her play with a dumbshow and a prologue, and ends it with an epilogue, imitating Shakespeare's style even as she inverts Shakespeare's plots. *Goodnight Desdemona (Good Morning Juliet)* is written almost entirely in iambic pentameter, and lines from *Othello*, *Romeo and Juliet*, and *Hamlet* are sprinkled throughout the text, often reassigned to fit the intricate new plot. While MacDonald's play carries the tragic elements of Shakespeare's plays to comic extremes, the changes are firmly rooted in a thorough knowledge of Shakespearean drama. The play explores the fickle nature of love, the perils of hero-worship, and the comic potential of cross-dressing. Even the attraction that Desdemona and Juliet express for violence and tragic love have their basis in Shakespeare's text and provide development for the character of Constance. Through her interaction with Desdemona and Juliet, Constance discovers the warrior and the lover in her own personality, making the play both a sensitive portrayal of Constance's journey of self-discovery and an intelligent adaptation of *Othello* and *Romeo and Juliet*.

FURTHER READING

Dvorak, Marta. "Goodnight William Shakespeare (Good Morning Ann-Marie MacDonald)." *Canadian Theatre Review* 79 (1994): 128.

Fortier, Mark. "Shakespeare with Difference: Genderbending and Genrebending in Goodnight Desdemona." *Canadian Theatre Review* 59 (1989): 47.

Hengen, Shannon. "Towards a Feminist Comedy." *Canadian Literature* 146 (1995): 97.

Mackay, Ellen. "The Spectre of Straight Shakespeare: New Ways of Looking at Old Texts in Goodnight Desdemona and Mad Boy Chronicle." *Canadian Theatre Review* 111 (2002): 10.

Novy, Marrianne. "Saving Desdemona and/or Ourselves: Plays by Ann-Marie MacDonald and Paula Vogel." In *Transforming Shakespeare*, ed. by Novy. New York: St. Martin's Press, 1999.

Porter, Laurin. "Shakespeare's 'Sisters': Desdemona, Juliet, and Constance Ledbelly in Goodnight Desdemona (Good Morning Juliet)." *Modern Drama* 38, no. 3 (1995): 362.

Stone-Blackburn, Susan. "Recent Plays on Women's Playwriting." *Essays in Theatre* 14, no. 1 (1995): 37.

Jennifer Flaherty

THE GOOD WOMAN OF SETZUAN

BERTOLT BRECHT began writing *The Good Woman of Setzuan* (*Der gute Mensch von Sezuan*) in SWEDEN in March 1939, completing it in FINLAND in January 1941. Two years later, the play premiered in Zurich, SWITZERLAND. Its first production in GERMANY, under the direction of Benno Besson, took place in Rostock in 1952. Ironically, Brecht himself never staged this work, described by some as his most popular play.

One of a number of works shaped by Brecht's enthusiasm for Asian theater, the play makes use of many of the presentational conventions of classical Chinese drama, including direct address to the audience, schematic characterization, disguise, and the free intermixture of human and divine personages.

Set in prerevolutionary CHINA, the action begins when Wong, the water seller, informs us that he is expecting the arrival of a party of gods. Immediately a divine trio appears on a mission to find at least one good person, thus refuting the atheists who say the "world must be changed because no one can *be* good." Only Shen Te, the prostitute, fills the bill, for which the gods reward her with 1,000 dollars.

She buys a tobacco shop, but is immediately besieged by spongers who quickly devour her capital. Faced with ruin, the kindhearted Shen Te transforms herself into Shui Ta, a hard-hearted fictional cousin who clears the shop of the hangers-on and brings order to the business.

Shen Te meets and falls in love with an unemployed pilot who cynically tries to squeeze money out of her to advance his career. Soon finding herself pregnant and beset on all sides by demands for money, Shen Te again assumes the mask of Shui Ta, who now opens a tobacco factory in which he employs—and exploits—all the former spongers. Eventually, however, people begin to wonder what has become of the good Shen Te. Shui Ta, accused of her murder, is brought to trial and vilified as a thief, liar, blackmailer, and cheat, only to be exposed as Shen Te, the good woman herself. Thus unmasked, she sadly informs us that the gods' injunction—" To be good and yet to live . . . to be good to others / And myself at the same time"—is impossible in this predatory world.

The Good Woman of Setzuan is the product of a remarkable period in Brecht's career, the years between 1938 and 1942, during which he also wrote THE LIFE OF GALILEO (*Leben des Galilei*, 1938–1939) and MOTHER COURAGE AND HER CHILDREN (*Mutter Courage und ihre Kinder*, 1939). These three plays, written in exile as fascism first threatened then conquered most of Europe, are darkly pessimistic visions of human possibility. They are also among the half dozen plays on which Brecht's international reputation principally rests. Like a number of his major characters, such as Kattrin in *Mother Courage* and Grusha in THE CAUCASIAN CHALK CIRCLE (*Der kaukasische Kreidekreis*, 1944), Shen Te is handicapped by her goodness, too virtuous to survive in the jungle of the world. Marxist critics have called this jungle capitalism and have assumed that Brecht intended *The Good Woman of Setzuan* as an explicitly political statement. But the play's open-endedness has led others to regard it as a more generally poetic parable about the moral torment inherent in human affairs.

[*See also* Alienation Effect; Avant-Garde Drama; Epic Theater; Expressionism]

FURTHER READING

Fuegi, John. *The Essential Brecht*. Los Angeles: Hennessey & Ingalls, 1972.

Mews, Siegfried, ed. *Critical Essays on Bertolt Brecht*. Boston: G.K. Hall, 1989.

Willett, John. *The Theatre of Bertolt Brecht: A Study from Eight Aspects*. 2nd ed. New York: New Directions, 1960.

Martin Andrucki

GORDIN, JACOB (1853–1909)

Jacob Gordin was nearly forty years old when he wrote his first play, but his two decades of work as a professional playwright would transform the YIDDISH THEATER. Born on May 1, 1853, Gordin grew up in a Mirgorod, Ukraine, household more influenced by secular learning than by traditional Jewish observance. Gordin would become active in religious and political groups grounded in Jewish faith, but with a socialist, utopian bent. As a young man he worked a wide variety of jobs, from dock worker to theater critic, before emigrating from RUSSIA—as rumor has it, just one step of the tsarist police, who sought to arrest him for revolutionary activity.

When he arrived in New York in 1891, Gordin found work writing for the Yiddish newspaper and supplemented his income by writing plays. At this point, professional Yiddish theater had existed for only a generation, and the Yiddish theater in New York was only a decade old. In contemporary sketches and later memoirs, Gordin repeatedly expressed his disdain for what took place on Yiddish stages. "Everything I heard and saw there," he remarked, "was far from Jewish life: coarse, unaesthetic, false, mean, and vulgar" (Berkowitz).

Gordin, like his fellow Russian intellectuals, admired not the musicals and MELODRAMAS that dominated the Yiddish theater until the early 1890s, but the more naturalistic, socially engaged dramas by such non-Yiddish writers as GERHART HAUPTMANN, HENRIK IBSEN, and MAKSIM GORKY. Gordin's first drama, *Siberia* (*Sibirye*, 1891), followed the efforts of its protagonist to start a new life after escaping from a Siberian prison camp. Critics like Abraham Cahan, the highly influential editor of the *Jewish Daily Forward*, heaped praise on Gordin for his coherent plot, natural Yiddish dialogue that was sharply different from the Germanized language then common to Yiddish theater, and the play's treatment of serious issues.

Among audiences and actors, Gordin was an immediate popular success. Another early play, *The Jewish King Lear* (*Der yidisher kenig Lir*, 1892), initially alienated actors, who were concerned that Gordin was eliminating the lines of business and stock characters that had brought them success before.

Many of Gordin's best roles were written with the dominant New York Yiddish actors specifically in mind. Gordin demanded fidelity to the text, and these actors gave it to him (at least most of the time). His actors needed real-life situations, but also grand speeches and effective dialogue, which Gordin wrote in abundance. And he did not entirely break with established Yiddish stage traditions; his early plays, in particular, contain numerous songs, and he always provided work for comic character actors. At their best, such characters can be both poignant and funny, but Gordin had an unfortunate tendency to abuse such devices as characters' verbal tics.

Gordin's reputation, however, was based on the power of his melodramas and his TRAGEDIES, and his ability to tackle social and intellectual problems such as the nature of Jewish identity and belief in the modern world, childbirth out of wedlock, adultery, exploitation of factory workers, and other matters that preoccupied his audiences. He brilliantly married Western drama to Jewish concerns, adapting the work of William Shakespeare, Friedrich Schiller, Hauptmann, Ibsen, LYOV TOLSTOY, Johann Wolfgang von Goethe, Franz Grillparzer, and others into Yiddish with great success. Such adaptations established a paradigm that would be imitated by many of Gordin's followers, who learned from him how to do more than simply change a Christian name to a Jewish one; Gordin found creative ways to find parallels in the Jewish milieu to the dramatic situations he found in his sources.

Because of his sometimes radical views, Gordin became a favorite target for religiously traditional commentators, but most critics found his dramas a welcome antidote to the musicals and melodramas so prevalent on the Yiddish stage. Many of Gordin's characters became tests of actors' abilities, and his plays helped lay the bedrock for theater companies with artistic ambitions. Gordin's work also enjoyed great popularity on film, including accomplished versions of *Mirele Efros* (1898), *God, Man, and Devil* (*Got, mentsh, un tayvl*, 1899), and *Homeless* (*On a heym*, 1907) in the 1930s and 1940s. Gordin died on June 10, 1909.

SELECT PLAYS: *Siberia* (*Sibirye*, 1891); *The Jewish King Lear* (*Der yidisher kenig Lir*, 1892); *The Pogrom in Russia* (*Der Pogrom in rusland*, 1892); *The Wild Man* (*Der Vilder mentsh*, 1893); *The Lithuanian Luria Brothers* (*Di Ltvishe brider Lurye*, 1894); *The Russian Jew in America* (*Der Rusisher yid in amerike*, 1895); *Mirele Efros* (1898); *The Slaughter* (*Di shkhite*, 1899); *God, Man, and Devil* (*Got, mentsh un tayvl*, 1900); *The Oath* (*Di shvue*, 1900); *Sappho* (1900); *The Kreutzer Sonata* (*DerKreytser sonate*, 1902); *Khasye the Orphan Girl* (*Khasye di yesoyme*, 1903); *The Truth* (*Di varhayt*, 1903); *Elisha ben Abuye* (1906); *Homeless* (*On a heym*, 1907); *On the Mountains* (*Af di berg*, 1907); *Dementia Americana* (1908)

FURTHER READING

Adler, Jacob. *A Life on the Stage*. Tr. by Lulla Rosenfeld. New York: Alfred A. Knopf, 1999.

Berkowitz, Joel. *Shakespeare on the American Yiddish Stage*. Iowa City: Univ. of Iowa Press, 2001.

Rosenfeld, Lulla. *Bright Star of Exile: Jacob Adler and the Yiddish Theatre*. New York: Thomas Y. Crowell, 1977.

——. *Vagabond Stars: A World History of Yiddish Theater*. New York: Harper & Row, 1977. (Reprint, Syracuse Univ. Press, 1999.)

Joel Berkowitz

GORKY, MAKSIM (1868–1936)

Maksim Gorky was born in Nizhnii Novgorod, RUSSIA. Russian political activist, publicist, novelist, short story writer, and dramatist, Gorky is least acknowledged for his contribution to Russian and international theater. Among his best-known prose works, his three-volume autobiography—*Childhood* (*Детство*, 1912), *In the World* (*Влюдях*, 1916), *My Universities* (*Мои университеты*, 1923)—presents the figure on which his reputation rested: the self-made, self-educated fighter for people's rights and enemy of the privileged classes. Born into a family whose livelihood depended on their small business as fabric dyers, Aleksei Peshkov (his real name; his nom de plume translates as "Maksim the Bitter") soon met emotional and material hardship. The death of his father and mother left him in the care of his grandparents at an early age. The failure of the business and the disintegration of the extended family meant his grandfather soon put him out to work. From then on, the young Gorky became little more than a vagrant, traversing much of the Volga region in search of work.

He became a voracious reader and searcher after education. He determined to be a writer and submitted short stories to the newspaper in Samara, and then obtained a post as an editor in Nizhnii Novgorod (renamed "Gorky" in Soviet times). By this time he was also involved with radical groups, was under police surveillance, and had begun his career as a politically engaged writer. After two highly successful novels, Gorky began his theatrical career just as he was being fêted as the demanding new voice of the aspirations of a politically and socially aware Russia. Introduced to the MOSCOW ART THEATRE (MAT) by ANTON CHEKHOV, who acted as an informal mentor to him, Gorky was commissioned to write a play and produced two, both performed in 1902, *Philistines* (*Meshchane*) and THE LOWER DEPTHS (*Na dne*). Over the next thirty years, he would produce a further fourteen plays that were published and performed, as well as an unfinished one and another discovered after his death.

Gorky came to the theater at a point when the MAT, through the efforts of KONSTANTIN STANISLAVSKY and Vladimir Nemirovich-Danchenko, was at the peak of its early success. MAT's reputation was aesthetically revolutionary, a new-wave theater allied to quality performance and design standards that met the demands for theatrical REALISM and NATURALISM of the period.

Gorky brought political and social consciousness, as well as his own brand of theatrical radicalism, to this heady mix. Philistines attacked the materialist, socially uncaring lifestyles of the old merchant classes, now the capitalist backbone of Russia, while *The Lower Depths* argued a case for the social inclusion of an underclass whose only home was the doss-house. Staged in Berlin by MAX REINHARDT in 1903, *The Lower Depths* established Gorky as a provocative international playwright. Both plays caused uproar: the wealthy middle classes who patronized the theater felt under attack, and the theater space was claimed by a new belligerent social type and voice. Theater changed its social role: no longer did the audience find itself mirrored on the stage, but it was now confronted by other social groups. Gorky, however, went further and began to attack the inactivity of the educated, affluent classes (the intelligentsia) who were failing to bring social change to Russia in SUMMERFOLK (*Dachniki*, 1904), *Children of the Sun* (*Deti solntsa*, 1905), and *Barbarians* (*Varvary*, 1905).

This potent mixture of politics and aesthetics remains central to Gorky's plays, even though he was to witness intense political change in his lifetime. By 1906, he was in exile for his involvement in revolutionary activity. He went to America, where he completed *Enemies* (*Vrgai*, 1906, revised in 1935–1936), which turns on a confrontation between the owning and working classes. The press surrounded him with scandal for traveling with his mistress, the actress Mariya Andreyeva, and America rejected him. Italy was to provide a refuge from 1907 to 1913, then again after the 1917 revolution, from 1923 to 1933. During his first exile, Gorky produced a further eight plays: *The Last Ones* (*Polsednie*, 1907) targeted the Russian police, and *Eccentrics* (*Chudaki*, 1910) and the unfinished *Yakov Bogomolov* (1916–1917, written in Russia but spiritually part of this group) targeted the intelligentsia. Russian traders and capitalists were targeted by the remaining five: *Vassa Zheleznova* (1910, revised in 1935), *The Reception* (*Vstrecha*, 1910), *The Zykovs* (*Zykovy*, 1913), *Counterfeit Coin* (*Fal'shivaya moneta*, 1913, revised in 1926), and *The Old Man* (*Starik*, 1915)—the last, a bid to save Russia from a Dostoevskian vision of humiliation and suffering.

It might appear that the 1917 Revolution brought everything that Gorky had fought for, but his blend of radicalism with aesthetics brought him new trouble. His satire, *Workaholic Slovotekov* (*Rabotiaga Slovotekov*, 1920), caused friction with the new Soviet leadership, which was intensified by his fight for Russia's artistic heritage to be preserved and for victims of the new regime to be helped rather than ousted. This led to his second exile. On the face of it, his final three plays laid the foundation for the SOCIALIST REALISM that he and Andrei Zhdanov were to introduce in 1934 as Joseph Stalin's formulators of cultural policy. However, these plays also raise many questions about Stalin's Russia. *Yegor Bulychyov and the Others* (*Egor Bulychyov i drugie*, 1931) and *Dostigaev and the Others* (*Dostigaev i drugie*, 1932) chronicle the overthrow of the middle class in 1917, and *Somov and the Others* (*Somov i drugie*, 1931, unpublished in Gorky's lifetime) focuses on the 1928 show trial of a group of technical experts for sabotaging Soviet industry. The historical account of the period may be accurate, but the drama also depicts a regret that the talent and strength of now discredited groups have to be wasted, while new sources of heroism have still to be located. In 1935–1936, after the declaration of the policy of socialist realism, its insistence on "engineering human souls" (in Stalin's and Zhdanov's words; Zhadnov, p. 21), and its glimpse of the Socialist Utopia to come (this last romantic aspect undoubtedly derived from Gorky), we find him reediting *Enemies* to make it conform with the new demands and completely redrafting *Vassa Zheleznova* to sharpen its attack on the degenerate capitalist class and to include an unconvincing revolutionary heroine.

Gorky's relationship with Stalin was publicly presented as adulatory on both sides; privately, as the archives are beginning to show, Gorky stood up for Stalinism's victims where he could, but after his return to Russia in 1933, he lived under close police surveillance. Recent evidence suggests that Gorky's death in 1936 came about, by poisoning, on Stalin's orders.

SELECT PLAYS: *Philistines* (also known as *The Merchant Class* or *The Petty Bourgeoisie*; *Meshchane*, 1902); *The Lower Depths* (*Na dne*,1902); *Summerfolk* (*Dachniki*, 1904); *Barbarians* (*Varvary*, 1905); *Children of the Sun* (*Deti solntsa*, 1905); *Enemies* (*Vragi*, 1906, revised in 1935–1936); *The Last Ones* (*Poslednie*, 1907); *Eccentrics* (also known as *Queer People* or *Country Folk*; *Chudaki*, 1910); *The Reception* (also known as *Children*; *Vstrecha*, 1910); *Vassa Zheleznova* (1910, revised in 1935); *Counterfeit Coin* (*Fal'shivaya moneta*, 1913, revised in 1926); *The Zykovs* (*Zykovy*, 1913); *The Old Man* (*Starik*, 1915); *Workaholic Garrulous* (*Rabotiaga Slovotekov*, 1920); *Somov and the Others* (*Somov i drugie*, 1931); *Yegor Bulychyov and the Others* (*Egor Bulychyov i drugie*, 1931); *Dostigaev and the Others* (*Dostigaev i drugie*, 1932)

FURTHER READING

Gorky, Maxim. "'Soviet Literature' in Maxim Gorky, Karl Radek, Nikolai Bukharin, Andrey Zhdanov and Others." In *Soviet Writers' Congress 1934—The Debate on Socialist Realism in the Soviet Union*. London: Lawrence & Wishart, 1977. 27–69. Reissue of H.G. Scott, ed., *Problems of Soviet Literature*. London: Martin Lawrence, 1935.

——. "Literary Portraits." In *Collected Works in Ten Volumes*, Vol. IX, ed. by Nikolai Zhegalov. Moscow: Progress Publishers, 1982.

——. *Selected Letters*. Tr. and ed. by Andrew Barrett and Barry P.Scherr. Oxford: Oxford Univ. Press, 1997.

Marsh, Cynthia. *File on Gorky*. London: Methuen Drama, 1993.

——. *Maxim Gorky: Russian Dramatist*. Oxford, Bern: Peter Lang, 2006.

Scherr, Barry S. *Maxim Gorky*, Boston: Twayne's World Authors, 1988.

Troyat, Henri. *Gorky: A Biography*. Tr. by Lowell Blair. London: W.H. Allen, 1991.

Yale Theatre 7, no. 2 (1976), Special issue on Gorky.

Yedlin, Tovah. *Maxim Gorky. A Political Biography*. Westport, Conn.: Praeger, 1999.

Zhdanov, A. A. "Soviet Literature—the Richest in Ideas. The Most Advanced Literature" (Speech to the Soviet Writers' Congress, 1934). In *Soviet Writers' Congress, 1934—The Debate on Socialist Realism* in the Soviet Union. London: Lawrence and Wishart, 1977. Reissue of H.G. Scott, ed., *Problems of Soviet Literature*. London: Martin Lawrence, 1935.

Cynthia Marsh

GOROSTIZA, CARLOS (1920–2004)

Carlos Gorostiza was born in Buenos Aires, on June 7, 1920. After completing his secondary education he began his artistic career writing poems that appeared in small literary magazines. He was also a puppeteer, an acrobat, and an actor with the theatrical groups La Estrella Grande and La Máscara. From this grass-roots beginning, his relationship with the theater grew into a highly productive career. Critics agree that Gorostiza is the creator of the new Argentine theater that emerged in the 1940s called *teatro independiente argentino*. He led the generation of new amateur playwrights of his time with his innovative style of realistic theater, which confronted the social and personal topics of everyday life.

The premiere in 1949 of THE BRIDGE (*El puente*), both written and directed by Gorostiza, set an immediate radical precedent in Argentine theater. Gorostiza featured characters drawn from suburban Buenos Aires. Creating for them personas that were both deeply emotional and rebellious, he was heavily influenced by the theater of MAKSIM GORKY and BERTOLT BRECHT. The paramount importance of *The Bridge* can perhaps best be appreciated by the fact that, since its premiere, Gorostiza has never stopped directing. *The Case about the Man with the Black Suitcase* (*El caso del hombre de la valija negra*, 1951) is a police drama deeply soaked with the realist language of its characters. In *Madness's Bread* (*El pan de la locura*, 1958), Gorostiza returns to the existentialist language that characterized his first play. In *The Others* (*Los prójimos*), in the very closed environment of a building, Gorostiza analyzes the evolution of characters confronted with violence and death in the street. This play was awarded the first Premio Nacional de Teatro in 1966.

With the takeover by the military dictatorship (1976–1983), the world of culture in ARGENTINA was subjected to censorship. Argentine playwrights were forced to stretch their ingenuity to dodge the censors. During these sad times, Gorostiza undertook two ambitious and rebellious projects. Between 1976 and 1979, he belonged to the theatrical organization Grupo de Trabajo, an association of playwrights and directors who planned to sustain and develop the Argentine theater. He premiered *Madness's Bread* (written in 1958 but premiered in 1976) and *The Dear Brothers* (1978).

When the dictatorial regime started to weaken in 1980, a group of playwrights, actors, directors, set designers, and critics, including Gorostiza, founded the renowned Teatro Abierto (OPEN THEATER), a resistance movement that aimed to premiere plays by both famous and amateur playwrights. During this time, Gorostiza premiered *The Extras* (*El acompañamiento*, 1981). When Argentina adopted democracy, Raúl Alfonsín rose to power (1983–1989), and Gorostiza was named Secretary of Culture. He never stopped writing and directing. One of Gorostiza's most recently renowned plays, *Airplanes* (*Aeroplanos*, 1989), explores the human language.

Carlos Gorostiza has also excelled in other literary genres. In 1999, he won the *Premio Planeta* (one of SPAIN's most prestigious awards given to novels written in Spanish) for his novel *Vuelan las palomas*. Other significant novels written by Gorostiza include *Cuerpos presentes* (1981), *El basural* (1985), and *La buena gente* (2001).

SELECT PLAYS: *The Bridge* (*El puente*, 1949); *The Case about the Man with the Black Suitcase* (*El caso del hombre de la valija negra*, 1951); *Balthazar's Watch* (*El reloj de Baltasar*, 1955); *The Enchanted Code* (*La clave encantada*, 1956); *Madness's Bread* (*El pan de la locura*, 1958); *Living Here* (*Vivir aquí*, 1964); *The Others* (*Los prójimos*, 1966); *What Are We Playing?* (*¿A qué jugamos?*, 1969); *The Dear Brothers* (*Los hermanos queridos*, 1978); *The Extras* (*El acompañamiento*, 1981); *We Must Put Out the Fire* (*Hay que apagar el fuego*, 1982); *Daddy* (*Papi*, 1983); *The Red Suit* (*El frac rojo*, 1988); *Airplanes* (*Aeroplanos*, 1990)

FURTHER READING

Gorostiza, Carlos. *Teatro* [Theater]. 3 vols. Buenos Aires: Ediciones de la Flor, 1996.

Guerrero Zamora, Juan. *Historia del teatro contemporáneo* [History of Contemporary Theater]. Barcelona: Juan Flors, 1967.

Guiano, José Carlos, ed. *Teatro argentino contemporáneo 1949–1969: Antología* [Contemporary Agentinian Theater, 1949–1969: Anthology]. Madrid: Aguilar, 1970.

Pelletieri, Osvaldo, ed. *El teatro y los días: Estudios sobre teatro argentino e iberoamericano*. Buenos Aires: Galerna; Facultad de Filosofía y Letras, 1995.

Solórzano, Carlos. *Teatro latinoamericano del siglo XX*. Buenos Aires: Nueva Visión, 1961.

Tirri, Néstor. "El viraje de Gorostiza." In *Realismo y teatro argentino* [Realism and Argentinian Theater], ed. by Tirri. Buenos Aires: La Bastilla, 1973.

Benito Gómez and Jorge Herreros

GOSET

See MOSCOW STATE YIDDISH THEATRE

GOW, MICHAEL (1955–)

Michael Gow was born in Sydney, New South Wales, on February 14, 1955, and was educated at the University of Sydney, where he became a member of the Sydney University Dramatic Society. He is one of AUSTRALIA's most prominent contemporary playwrights and has worked as a director in major state theater companies.

A string of successful plays written during the 1980s and 1990s were received favorably by both audiences and critics. *Away* (1986) is one of the most often performed contemporary Australian plays; it is Gow's most awarded play and is widely studied. It examines the peculiarly Australian ritual of the annual Christmas summer holiday at the beach, using this background to contrast the experiences of three different families. The role of the family in contemporary life is a recurring theme in Gow's plays. This can be seen in his first play, *The Kid* (1983), as well as in *On Top of the World* (1987) and *All Stops Out* (1991). His plays also tend to examine the social pressures that are felt by young people. Sometimes this extends to physical illness, as with Tom from *Away* who is dying of leukemia; other times, young people are alienated from the general community.

Gow has also made a significant contribution to Australian theater as an actor and director. He started his career in 1970 working with the Australian Theatre for Young People. His influence on the Australian national theater scene is epitomized by his work with a wide range of theater companies. He has also contributed to the Sydney and Adelaide Arts Festivals. He served as associate director of the Sydney Theatre Company (STC) from 1991 to 1993 and, since 1999, as the Artistic Director of the Queensland Theatre Company (QTC). While working for STC, Gow's productions included William Shakespeare as well as contemporary works. His productions with QTC have included a season of his own epic adaptation of Henry Handel Richardson's classic novel *The Fortunes of Richard Mahoney* for the Brisbane Festival in 2002.

Gow twice directed *Away* for STC, and he directed a version of *Sweet Phoebe* in 1994 that subsequently toured to England. Gow has also directed the premiere seasons of *Furious* and *Live Acts On Stage*. Gow's work for television includes writing the screenplays for *Art'n Life* and *Edens Lost*; the latter winning an Australian Film Institute Award for best Mini-Series in 1988.

Away received a New South Wales Premier's Literary Award, a Sydney Theatre Critics Circle Award, and a Green Room Award in 1986. It also received the Australian Writers' Guild AWGIE for Best Play in 1987. *Furious* was awarded a Sydney Theatre Critics Circle Award in 1992, and *Sweet Phoebe* won the New South Wales Premier's Literary Award in 1995.

SELECT PLAYS: *Away* (1986); *Europe* (1987); *1841* (1988); *All Stops Out* (1991); *Live Acts On Stage* (2002)

FURTHER READING

Pearson, John. "An Interview with Michael Gow." *Southerly* 52, no. 2 (1992): 116–131.

Radic, Leonard. *The State Of Play: Revolution in the Australian Theatre Since the 1960s*. Ringwood: Penguin, 1991.

Simon, Luke. *Michael Gow's Plays: A Thematic Approach*. Sydney: Currency Press, 1991.

Webby, Elizabeth, ed. "Away." In *Modern Australian Plays*, ed. by Webby. Sydney: Sydney Univ. Press, 1990. 54–64.

Delyse Ryan

GRACE-SMITH, BRIAR (1966–)

Primarily known as a playwright, Briar Grace-Smith is also an actor, short story writer, poet, and screenwriter. Since the mid-1990s her most well-known plays have contributed significantly to valid representations of self and identity which she sees as an important task of Maori Theater in NEW ZEALAND: *Ancestral Women* (*Nga Pou Wahine*, 1997) received an Award for Best New Zealand Short Play and *Stars* (*Purapurawhetu*, 1999), which toured nationally and internationally, won Best New Zealand Play in 1997. She received the inaugural Arts Foundation of New Zealand Laureate Awards in 2000.

Grace-Smith's experience in the cultural interstice (her heritage is Nga Puhi, Ngati Wai, and Scottish), her acting and writing with Maori collectives Te Ohu Whakaari and He Ara Hou, and her continued associations with Taki Rua Productions, inform her DRAMATURGY, creating representations of Maori characters and their social contexts that shift away from cultural stereotypes and provide alternative sites of identification for young Maori audiences.

Set in both rural and urban locations, *Ancestral Women*, *Flat Out Brown* (produced 1996), *Don't Call Me Bro* (produced 1996), and *Stars* examine modern-day constructions of Maori individual and community identity. The historical context of her sixth play, *Roaring Thunder* (*Haruru Mai*, produced 2000), explores similar thematic terrain but reflects upon the cultural issues prevalent in 1960s New Zealand. Through the experiences of its World War II veteran, antihero Silas, it also comments on the relationship between Maori and Pakeha at that time. Maori and Pakeha affinities and dissonances are examined in the tension between rural and urban, traditional and modern lives, and in explorations of family and genealogy.

Ancestral Women is the first solo play to be written for a Maori woman actor. Six characters, including a male, contribute to the telling of Kura's story as she attempts to channel memories of her dead mother and an ancestress figure, Waiora, into a realization of cultural identity. Maori perceptions of the indelible connection between ancestors and their descendants are effectively theatricalized through the embodiment of all characters in one actor.

Of her nine plays written between 1995 and 2003, and excepting the co-written *The Sojourns of Boy* (produced 1999), *Stars* best exemplified Grace-Smith's playwriting technique. Structured on a Maori story entwined in a woven tukutuku panel, the play's 1990s gothic setting in a small, rugged, coastal community is reenergized by the mysterious appearance of the mystical Kui/Aggie Rose, who unravels the deadening secret behind the sadness that has enveloped the place. *Stars*' haunted setting, its movement between the community's past and present, and the presence of ghostlike figures and voices are characteristic also of *Roaring Thunder* and *Potiki's Memory of Stone* (produced 2003). In *Fish-Skin Suit* (produced 2001), a television drama set in a fantastical seaside village, Grace-Smith's child narrator, accompanied by his prophetic grandmother-queen, watches his forlorn mother and an Elvis-impersonating goldfish learn about love.

Set in landscapes alive with natural and supernatural phenomena, Grace-Smith's plays reorient conventional understandings about the interaction between people, historical time, and geographical space. Her other plays are *Sacred Waters* (*Waitapu*, produced 1996) and *When Sun and Moon Collide* (produced 2000).

PLAYS: *Don't Call Me Bro* (1996); *Flat Out Brown* (1996); *Sacred Waters* (*Waitapu*, 1996); *Ancestral Women* (*Nga Pou Wahine*, 1997); *Stars* (*Purapurawhetu*, 1999); *Roaring Thunder* (*Haruru Mai*, 2000); *The Sojourns of Boy* (co-written with Jo Randerson, 1999); *When Sun and Moon Collide* (2000); *Potiki's Memory of Stone* (2003)

FURTHER READING

Chamberlain, Jenny, and Natasha Brinsden. "Playing up." *North and South* 168 (2000): 58–69.

Dale, Judith. "'On the beach': questions of identity in recent Maori drama." *Illusions* 26 (1997): 39–42.

Livesey, Anna. "Briar Grace-Smith: Something to Say." *Skirt* (2000): 3–6.

Welch, Denis. "Claiming a Space." *Listener* 6 (March 1999): 36–37.

Mei-Lin Te-Puea Hansen

EL GRAN CIRCO EUCRANIANO See THE GREAT USKRANIAN CIRCUS

EL GRAN GALEOTO See THE GREAT GALEOTO

GRANVILLE-BARKER, HARLEY (1877–1946)

Harley Granville-Barker, actor, writer, director, and producer, wielded significant influence on modern drama and was a major contributor among the NEW DRAMATISTS. Composed of several strains of thought, New Drama instigated two trends: presenting relevant social and ethical issues on stage and moving away from Victorian realistic sets and toward more abstract ones. Granville-Barker is also credited with creating director's theater, which holistically combined fundamentals of theater production—DRAMATURGY, acting, scenic, costume, sound, and lighting design.

Granville-Barker was born on November 25, 1877, in London. He started his theater career as an actor at the age of fourteen. The following year he made his London debut with Sarah Thorne and the Theatre Royal. His striking presence made him a local celebrity. By 1900, he had joined the experimental theater company, the Stage Society, after growing tired of conventional theatrical productions. Through his work with the Stage Society, Granville-Barker met GEORGE BERNARD SHAW, who would become a long-time collaborator, and William Poel and Ben Greet.

Not content to play merely one side of the stage, Granville-Barker produced his own work, *The Marrying of Ann Leete*, in 1902, and in 1904 directed his first Shakespearean production. He quickly became a theatrical Renaissance man, occupying the role of producer, director, and manager with his business, Barker-Vedrenne Management. The management company produced plays for no more than £200 ($400) each—a revolutionary approach to theater production. The company produced almost 1,000 performances in three seasons at the Court Theatre; 700 of them were Shaw productions, and many starred Granville-Barker in the lead.

In 1906, Granville-Barker married his leading lady from the Court Theatre productions, Lillah McCarthy. The two took over management of the Little Theatre in 1911 after Granville-Barker's two failed attempts to bring his experimental work to the Savoy Theatre and The Duke of York's Theatre. The first play produced there was Shaw's *Fanny's First Play*. The play was a commercial success, running for over 600 performances, even though Shaw is said to have called it a "potboiler."

In 1915 Granville-Barker and McCarthy toured New York, where his productions of William Shakespeare's *Midsummer Night's Dream* and Shaw's *Androcles and the Lion* were presented at Wallack's Theatre. Lillah returned to England, and the company moved on to present plays by Euripides at Ivy League universities. During this tour, Granville-Barker met and fell in love with American novelist and poet Helen Huntingdon. He contacted Shaw, demanding that he obtain Lillah's consent to a divorce. Lillah was devastated.

Granville-Barker's decision to end his marriage effectively ended his acting career and his friendship with Shaw, whose socialism Helen Huntingdon found unacceptable. The couple moved to Paris and collaborated in translating Spanish plays. He also wrote his famous and influential *Prefaces to Shakespeare* (1927–1948). Granville-Barker died in Paris on August 31, 1946.

[*See also* Dramatic Criticism; England, 1860–1940; *The Voysey Inheritance*]

SELECT PLAYS: *The Voysey Inheritance* (1905); *Prunella* (1906); *Waste* (1906); *The Madras House* (1909)

FURTHER READING

Chinoy, Helen Krich, and Toby Cole, eds. *Directors on Directing: A Source Book of the Modern Theater*. Indianapolis, Ind.: Bobbs-Merrill, 1953.

Menzer, Paul. "That Old Saw: Early Modern Acting and the Infinite Regress." *Shakespeare Bulletin* 22 (2004).

Purdom, C. B. *Harley Granville Barker: Man of the Theatre, Dramatist, and Scholar*. London: Salisbury Square, 1955.

Reynolds, Paige. "Chaos Invading Concept: Blast as a Native Theory of Promotional Culture." *Twentieth Century Literature*, 46 (2000).

Wilson, A. E. *Edwardian Theatre*. London: Arhtur Baker, 1951.

Shanté T. Smalls

GRASS, GÜNTER (1927–)

Günter Grass was born on October 16, 1927, in Danzig (now Gdańsk) POLAND. A prolific artist in many media and Nobel laureate in literature, he is perhaps least known for his dramas, but these play an important role in his artistic development as blueprints for his larger and more acclaimed works.

This is especially true of the dramas that predate the notoriety earned by his novels. These earlier plays appear to be totally surrealistic and virtually impossible to understand. But if one works backward from the vantage point of the later novels, one sees they are laboratories for themes to be more fully developed in fiction.

Typical of these is *Flood* (*Hochwasser*, 1957), in which actors wearing rat masks deal with the adverse effects of high water. From the vantage point of Grass's novels *Dog Years* (*Hundejahre*, 1963), one sees floods as a symbol for the flow of history that washes evil onto our shores; and from *The Rat* (*Die Rättin*, 1986), one sees anthropomorphic postapocalyptic rats comment on the reasons the human race destroyed itself.

This is also true of *Mister, Mister* (*Onkel, Onkel*, 1958), a play about children finding a pistol, which is similarly illuminated by the novel *Local Anesthetic* (*Örtlich Betäubt*, 1969), involving juvenile Nazi gangs and their postwar equivalents. *Only Ten Minutes to Buffalo* (*Noch zehn Minuten bis Buffalo*, 1958), a play about Moby Dick, prefigures the naval warfare sections of *The Tin Drum* (*Die Blechtrommel*, 1959). *The Wicked Cooks* (*Die bösen Köche*, 1961) contains imagery that is spelled out in *The Flounder* (*Der Butt*, 1977), a cookbook tracing the genesis of human evil—reduced to the formula of starvation vs. nutrition—from the beginning of time.

Later plays that paralleled the publication of the novels are far easier to understand because they are essentially dramatizations of material from the novels. These include *Thirty-Two Teeth* (*Zweiunddreißig Zähne*, 1959) and *Lil' Goldmouth* (*Goldmäulchen*, 1963), material from both of which concerns an artist in the novel *Dog Years* whose teeth are knocked out by Nazi thugs and subsequently replaced by gold, an evocation of the gold teeth harvested by Nazis from Holocaust victims. *Max, A Play* (*Davor*, 1969) is a scenic reworking of an entire novel *Local Anasthetic*, involving a young man who plans to burn his dachshund Max to protest the use of napalm in Vietnam.

One play stands independent of the novels: *The Plebeians Rehearse the Uprising* (*Die Plebejer proben den Aufstand*, 1966). It imagines BERTOLT BRECHT rehearsing William Shakespeare's *Coriolanus* in his theater in Berlin, even as the uprising of workers on June 17, 1953, is brutally repressed by Soviet tanks. Brecht fails to recognize the need to leave the realm of art, even temporarily, to help solve problems in the real world. But rather than being a criticism of Brecht, it is an apology for Günter Grass, who has always effectively managed to keep one foot in the world of politics.

[*See also* Germany]

SELECT PLAYS: *Flood* (*Hochwasser*, 1957); *Mister, Mister* (*Onkel, Onkel*, 1958); *Only Ten Minutes to Buffalo* (*Noch zehn Minuten bis Buffalo*, 1959); *Thirty-Two Teeth* (*Zweiunddreißig Zähne*, 1961); *The Wicked Cooks* (*Die bösen Köche*, 1961); *Lil' Goldmouth* (*Goldmäulchen*, 1963); *The Plebeians Rehearse the Uprising* (*Die Plebejer proben den Aufstand*, 1966); *Max, a Play* (*Davor*, 1969)

FURTHER READING

Cunliffe, W. Gordon. *Günter Grass*. New York: Twayne, 1969.
Jurgensen, Manfred. *Über Günter Grass* [About Günter Grass]. Bern: Franke, 1974.
Keele, Alan Frank. *Understanding Günter Grass*. Columbia: Univ. of South Carolina Press, 1988.
Lawson, Richard. H. *Günter Grass*. New York: Ungar, 1985.
Miles, Keith. *Günter Grass*. New York: Barnes and Noble, 1975.
Tank, Kurt Lothar. *Günter Grass*. New York: Ungar, 1969.

Alan Keele

GRAY, JOHN (1946–)

Born in Ottawa on September 16, 1946, Canadian playwright John Gray earned a bachelor of arts degree at Mount Allison University in Newfoundland and a masters' degree in theater at the University of British Columbia. The founding director of the Tamahnous Theater in Vancouver, Gray subsequently worked as a freelance director in the mid-1970s, directing some forty productions at venues throughout CANADA.

Known for his experiments within the genre of the musical, Gray has been most concerned with the influences of popular culture on the daily lives of ordinary Canadians. Gray's most enduringly popular and most critically acclaimed play has been BILLY BISHOP GOES TO WAR (1978). The play focuses on the World War I flying ace, dramatizing his transformation from a rambunctious Canadian lad into a national hero and then a folk icon. Bishop's character has had historical and theatrical appeal because, although he had no intention of becoming a hero, he was able when necessary to draw on some inherent capacity to act heroically. Likewise, after he had been packaged as a hero, he was willing to play the role to the hilt, but always with a knowing wink and a nod. Technically the play is of interest because, aside from an accompanist who serves as a sounding board, the musical is a one-man show, with a single actor portraying not only Billy Bishop but also a dozen and a half supporting characters.

Three of Gray's other plays have also received significant notice. In *18 Wheels* (1977), he depicts the subculture of the long-distance hauler, which has figuratively linked the widely separated communities of the Canadian plains in the same way that the highway system itself has connected them literally and geographically. In *Rock and Roll* (1981), he uses the reunion in middle age of a small-time rock band based in a small Canadian town. Rather than suggesting how the hit songs of an era have shaped the social milieu for individuals coming of age in that era, Gray's play suggests that the local manifestations of the popular culture may have a more direct and lasting influence, even if they are largely derivative. *Don Messer's Jubilee* (1984) explores the rationale for the cancellation of a popular but seemingly anachronistic television show set in the Canadian "provinces." Gray works around the convoluted ironies inherent in the cancellation of a regional production with a proven national appeal because it no longer reflects the national culture.

SELECT PLAYS: *Godiva Was a Lady* (1967); *Salty Tears on a Hangnail Face* (1974); *18 Wheels* (1977); *Billy Bishop Goes to War* (1978); *Rock and Roll* (1981); *Balthazar and the Mojo Star* (1982); *Better Watch Out, You*

Better Not Die (1983); *Don Messer's Jubilee* (1984); *The B. C. Review* (1986); *Local Boy Makes Good* (1987); *Health: The Musical* (1989)

FURTHER READING

Bessai, Diane. "Discovering the Popular Audience." *Canadian Literature* 118 (Autumn 1988): 7–28.

Miller, Mary Jane. "Billy Bishop Goes to War and Maggie and Pierre: A Matched Set." *Theatre History in Canada / Histoire du Theatre au Canada* 10, no. 2 (Fall 1989): 188–198.

Yardley, M. Jeanne. "Unauthorized Re-Visions of the Billy Bishop Story." *Textual Studies in Canada / Etudes Textuelles au Canada* 3 (1993): 86–96.

Martin Kich

GRAY, SPALDING (1941–2004)

I am to some extent an inverted Method actor in the sense that I use autobiographic emotional memory to play myself rather than some other character. When it works, and it has for years, I'm able to transform what might be considered a psychopathology (divided or schizoid personality) into a creative act. The presentation of self in a theatrical setting.

—Spalding Gray (in Mark Russell's *Out of Character: Rants, Raves and Monlogues from Today's Top Performance Artists*, 1997)

Spalding Gray reinvented the dramatic monologue as a popular technique of late-20th-century American performance. Although Gray began his theater career as a trained and highly disciplined actor, he found himself drawn both to solo performing and to writing his own texts based on episodes from his own life. The result was a series of more than eighteen monologues chronicling American life in the second half of the 20th century. (The exact number of monologues is difficult to pinpoint because Gray developed each of them as works in progress, sometimes under different titles or in combination with other monologues.) The pieces range in tone from hilariously understated COMEDY to near TRAGEDY, but always involve an intimation of spiritual transcendence.

Born on June 5, 1941, in Providence, Rhode Island, Gray was a classic son of New England whose otherwise typical middle-class upbringing was deeply influenced by his Christian Scientist mother, who committed suicide when Gray was twenty-six. Although dyslexic and a perennially poor student, Gray studied theater and speech at Emerson College in Boston, where he studied William Shakespeare by listening to recordings of the Royal Shakespeare Company.

Gray's sure sense of voice, cadence, and dry humor served him well in his initial attempts at an acting career, first in summer stock and regional theater, including a 1967 stint at the Alley Theater in Houston. That same year Gray moved to New York City, where he performed OFF-BROADWAY in Robert Lowell's *Endecott and the Red Cross* (1967) and in Tom O'Horgan's *Tom Paine* (1968).

Gray joined Richard Schechner's AVANT-GARDE Performance Group in 1970, performing in *Makbeth* (1970), *Commune* (1970), MOTHER COURAGE (1975), and JEAN GENET'S THE BALCONY (1979). Gray next became a founding member of the Wooster Group, which emerged from the Performance Group in 1975, under the direction of Elizabeth LeCompte. The Wooster Group's first production, *Sakonnet Point* (1975), written by Gray and LeCompte, was the beginning of Gray's autobiographical journey, telling the story of his upbringing by means of the deconstructionist techniques the Wooster Group was then developing into its signature style. *Rumstick Road* (1977) and *Nayatt School* (1978) followed in the same vein, finally coalescing as a trilogy, *Three Places in Rhode Island*.

Gray emerged from the Wooster Group in 1978 to focus on his monologues for the next twenty-six years. In *Sex and Death to the Age 14* (1979), the first solo performance, Gray described how such varying influences as Wallace Stevens, Robert Lowell, and the audiotapes of Baba Ram Dass inspired him to articulate his own 1960s journey in search of self.

Although his solo performances emerged in the Off-Off-Broadway world, Gray continued to work as an actor on Broadway, on television, and in film. His role as an American diplomat in Roland Jaffe's 1984 movie *The Killing Fields* led Gray to create *Swimming to Cambodia* (1985), a hilarious and sometimes horrific meditation about filmmaking, the Vietnam War, and Gray's own continuing search for enlightenment, which won him an Obie Award. Gray's notable acting roles range from the Stage Manager in the 1988 Broadway production of THORNTON WILDER'S OUR TOWN (1988) to a recurring role as Fran Drescher's psychologist in the television sitcom *The Nanny* (1998). Gray wrote one novel, *Impossible Vacation* (1993), but quickly returned to the dramas of his own life. "When I'm doing my monologue, I'm in my element," he said in a 1997 interview; "I am most me when I'm on stage" (Associated Press, 2004).

The arc of Gray's monologues begins with serious uncertainty and self-doubt (*Sex and Death to Age 14*) and proceeds to follow Gray's development as an artist and complicated human being to moments of familial bliss as a husband and father (*Morning, Noon, and Night*). Ever obsessed with doubt and mortality, Gray was heavily shaken, and physically injured, by a 2001 automobile accident. He characteristically turned this experience into material for a new monologue, *Life Interrupted* (2002), but was increasingly beset by depression, and ended his life in January 2004 in New York City.

Gray was the first and in some ways most successful of the solo performance artists to emerge from the New York avant-garde theater scene of the 1980s, and his contribution to American theater—re-creating the introspective monologue as a new means of dramatic performance—was recognized by general acclaim from audiences, critics, and fellow theater makers.

[*See also* Happenings and Intermedia; Performance Art; Political Theater in the United States; United States, 1940–Present]

PLAYS: *Scales* (1966); *Three Places in Rhode Island: Sakonnet Point* (1975); *Rumstick Road* (1977); *Nayatt School* (1978); *Booze, Cars and College Girls* (1979); *India and After (America)* (1979); *Point Judith: An Epilog* (1979); *Sex and Death to the Age 14* (1979); *Nobody Wanted to Sit Behind a Desk* (1980); *A Personal History of the American Theatre* (1980); *47 Beds* (1981); *Interviewing the Audience* (1981); *8 x Gray* (1982); *In Search of the Monkey Girl* (1982); *Travels Through New England* (1984); *Rivkala's Ring* (1985); *Swimming to Cambodia, Parts 1 and 2* (1985); *Terrors of Pleasure: The House* (1985); *Monster in a Box* (1991); *It's A Slippery Slope* (1995); *Gray's Anatomy* (1996); *Gray on Gray* (1997); *Morning, Noon and Night* (1999); *Life Interrupted* (also known as *Black Spot*, 2002)

FURTHER READING

Associated Press. "Actor-Writer Spalding Gray Missing." *Stamford Advocate*, Jan. 13, 2004.

Gray, Spalding. "About *Three Places in Rhode Island*." *The Drama Review* 23, no. 1 (T81, 1979).

——. *Life Interrupted: The Unfinished Monologue*. New York: Crown, 2005.

Merchant, Diane Allene. "Mirrors of the Self: The Myth of Narcissus in the Monologues of Spalding Gray." Ph.D. diss., Ohio State Univ., 1996.

Schechner, Richard. "My Art in Life: Interviewing Spalding Gray." *The Drama Review* 46, no. 4 (T176, 2002).

John Bell

THE GREAT DIVIDE

Hailed as a "virile story of the West" in a review in The Rochester Herald (August 24, 1915), WILLIAM VAUGHN MOODY's *The Great Divide* was first produced as *The Sabine Women* at the Garrick Theatre in Chicago in 1906. Margaret Anglin, who played the lead role of Ruth Jordan, was instrumental in bringing the play to New York, where it opened as *The Great Divide* on October 3, 1906, at the Princess Theatre.

A primitive frontiersman and a refined society lady clash on the rugged terrain of developing Arizona in this lyrical drama. Ruth Jordan and her brother Philip are trying to recuperate their family fortune by farming cactus fiber in the desert. One night, when Ruth is alone in the cabin, three drunken men break in and attempt to attack her. Seeing it as her only chance for protection, Ruth offers to marry the strongest of the men. To her horror, Stephen Ghent accepts her offer and pays the other men gold for her.

When next we see the two, love and temperance have reformed Ghent, who is busy planning a magnificent family ranch near his successful gold mine, but Ruth, now with child, remains tormented by the thought that she has been sold. Ruth's family members have been searching for her since her disappearance, and when they finally locate her, she leaves with them and departs the West. Though she blames Ghent for the failure of her family business and the defiling of her moral self, Ruth has fallen in love with his brute genius and primitive ways. Her feelings become clear to her when Ghent appears at her family home in Massachusetts and reveals that he has refinanced the family fortune and wants desperately to reunite the family.

The gripping drama was well received by both audiences and critics, who embraced the play's "American-ness." In the play, the clash between rural, Western values and urban, Eastern culture eventually leads to an altogether new undertaking, a kind of modern sensibility. Self-reliance, the shedding of inhibition, and the cultivation of the individual spirit are advocated by the drama's happy resolution. Critics consider the play's distinctive combination of philosophical lyricism with realistic settings and characters to mark a turning point in the American theatrical tradition.

On the night of the play's premiere, rights to the production had not yet been established. Anglin carried out a tense negotiation with Moody's agents as the performance proceeded, and the audience was forced to wait an hour between the second and third acts while contracts were settled. Anglin and Henry Miller, who played Ghent, took the production to New York, where it ran for 238 performances at the Princess Theatre and 103 performances at Daly's Theatre. The production went on to the Adelphi Theatre in London and the Theatre des Arts in Paris.

[*See also* United States, 1860–1929]

FURTHER READING

Brown, Maurice F. *Estranging Dawn: The Life and Works of William Vaughn Moody*. Carbondale: Southern Illinois Univ. Press, 1973.

Hall, Roger A. *Performing the American Frontier, 1870–1906*. Cambridge: Cambridge Univ. Press, 2001.

Halpern, Martin. *William Vaughn Moody*. New York: Twayne, 1964.

Henry, David Dodds. *William Vaughn Moody, A Study*. New York: Folcroft, 1973.

Mason, Daniel Gregory, ed. *Some Letters of William Vaughn Moody*. New York: Houghton Mifflin, 1913.

Quinn, Arthur Hobson. *A History of the American Drama from the Civil War to the Present Day*. New York: F. S. Crofts, 1936.

Leah R. Shafer

THE GREAT GALEOTO

The Great Galeoto (*El gran Galeoto*) is considered to be JOSÉ ECHEGARAY's best-known work. It opened on March 19, 1881, in the Teatro Español in Madrid to an overwhelmingly enthusiastic reception from both the audience and the press. An intriguing sequence of events, each more extreme and frustrating than the last, and the intense display of emotion from its characters appealed to the bourgeois audiences of SPAIN's Restoration period. Although the play is embedded within a sociological problem play representing the dire consequences of calumny, the melodramatic excess for which Echegaray is known remains this play's prevailing characteristic.

The Great Galeoto begins with a prologue in which Echegaray introduces the theme and characters. Echegaray reportedly added this prologue after writing the play, for fear that the audience would not understand the central theme of the play: the disastrous consequences of spiteful gossip. Written in prose, it is in this Prologue that we first meet Ernesto, both as a character and as the author of a play called *The Great Galeoto*. The main body of the play is written in verse.

Ernesto is a young man who has been taken in by his deceased father's best friend, don Julián, and his much younger wife, Teodora. The threesome live happily as a family until rumors start flowing about a hidden desire between Ernesto and Teodora, who are much closer in age. At first, don Julián defends the innocence of his wife and his charge, but then begins to suspect, with the encouragement of his spiteful brother, that there might be some truth behind the rumors. Don Julián later dies as a result of wounds received during a duel, but not before he discovers the love between the young characters.

The discovery is not don Julián's alone, for as the play progresses, Ernesto and Teodora realize, horrified, that they do love each other. Gathering a fainting Teodora in his arms, Ernesto defiantly claims that he will now take care of her and that rumor will have finally become truth. As he dares those present to spread the news, he cries that they are to blame for this infamy: these are the consequences of the seemingly insignificant act of gossip. Echegaray named this play after the knight who brought Lancelot and Queen Guinevere together. Ernesto reminds the audience that in *The Divine Comedy*, Francesca and Paolo are reading this part of the legend when they share their first kiss. Here, it is society itself that has served as the intermediary, or the Galeoto, to the end result, whether by exposing hidden desires or merely suggesting them.

The problem of calumny, however, is not the most compelling element of this play; that belongs to the intrigue, the intense emotion, and the unjust suffering of Teodora. As the play closes, we see the continued melodramatics of a playwright who attempted to align himself with the more naturalist European authors of his day, like HENRIK IBSEN and AUGUST STRINDBERG.

[*See also* Naturalism]

FURTHER READING

Cabrales Arteaga, José Manuel. "El teatro neorromántico de Echegaray" [The Neoromantic Theater of Echegaray]. *Revista de Literatura* 51, no.101 (January–June 1989): 77–94.

Castilla, Alberto. "Una parodia de *El gran Galeoto*" [A Parody of *El gran Galeoto*]. *Hispanófila* 26: 3, 78, (May 1983): 33–40.

Ibarra, Fernando. "La aventura parisiense de *El gran Galeoto*" [The Parisian Adventure of *The Great Galeoto*]. *Revue de Litterature Comparée* 46 (1972): 428–437.

Jerelyn Johnson

THE GREAT GOD BROWN

Why am I afraid to live?

—Dion, Prologue

The Great God Brown by EUGENE O'NEILL was first produced by Kenneth Macgowan, ROBERT EDMOND JONES, and O'Neill on January 23, 1926, in New York, and was directed and designed by Jones.

Billy Brown is a regular guy, rich in cliché and poor in imagination, a mockery of American materialism, while Dion Anthony is a tormented Dionysian soul. Brown loves Margaret, but she marries Dion, who turns out to be a failure as a conventional husband, father, and provider. For solace, he turns to Cybel, who joins Anna Christie, Abbie (in DESIRE UNDER THE ELMS), and Josie (in A MOON FOR THE MISBEGOTTEN) as another of O'Neill's landmark blends of whore, wife, mother, and goddess.

The play presents O'Neill's most highly developed use of masks to explore the conflicting aspects of character. Dion's first mask, when he is just seventeen, is "a fixed forcing of his own face—dark, spiritual, poetic, passionately supersensitive, helplessly unprotected in its childlike, religious faith in life—into the expression of a mocking, reckless, defiant, gaily scoffing and sensual young Pan." Alone, he removes his mask, revealing his face as "shrinking, shy and gentle, full of a deep sadness." He feels everything intensely but covers his pain by mocking others. Seven years later, the "real" face has "grown more strained and tortured, but at the same time, in some queer way, more selfless and ascetic," while the mask is "older, more defiant and mocking, its sneer more forced and bitter, its Pan quality becoming Mephistophelean." The Jungian combination of a Dionysiac anti-Christ and an ascetic St. Anthony, he is excruciatingly aware of his divided personality; in one scene, he takes off the mask and reads a blessing to it.

To Margaret, Dion is as thrilling as Brown is boring. Her first mask is a transparent duplicate of her "real" face, "but giving her the abstract quality of a Girl," and her later masks are clearly the faces she chooses to put before the world.

Brown makes a mundane but substantial success of his building and architecture firm, and he wears no mask. When Dion dies, Brown takes on his mask and from then on plays three roles: his "true" self, the mask of Dion, and a new "Brown" mask he wears as his public self. He even manages to persuade everyone else that Dion is still alive and still working for him as a draftsman. He allows the mask of Brown to die so that he may more fully become Dion, but he can't make it work, telling Cybel that he is Dion's "murderer and murdered." In the end, Brown dies, having taken the burden of Dion's suffering and vulnerability, and when the police captain pulls out his notebook to take his report, Cybel tells him that the deceased's name is "Man," and he gruffly asks, "How d'yuh spell it?"

The play traces O'Neill's struggle toward staging interior monologue and toward finding the actual self beneath the performed self, possibly working from FRIEDRICH NIETZSCHE's idea that only through ecstatic performance can the individual approach his symbolic potential. The action recalls Johann Wolfgang von Goethe's *Faust* in Dion's transformation from mischievous Pan to mocking Mephistopheles and in the innocence of Margaret as an analogue for Marguerite. From another perspective, the play is a Christian parable about two sinners who stray through pride and envy but return to God in death. Stark Young criticized the writing as "often obvious, sometimes flat, poor poetry" (Houchin), but Richard Dana Skinner, in *Commonweal*, praised O'Neill for beginning "to fathom the meaning of earthly suffering" (Houchin).

[*See also* United States, 1860–1929]

FURTHER READING

Ben-Zvi, Linda. "Exiles, *The Great God Brown*, and the Specter of Nietzsche." *Modern Drama* 24 (1981).

Elliot, Thomas S. "Altar Ego: O'Neill's Sacrifice of Self and Character in *The Great God Brown*." *Eugene O'Neill Review* 18 (Spring–Fall 1994).

Hardin, Michael. "Fair Maiden and Dark Lady in *The Great God Brown*: Inverting the Standard Representations." *Eugene O'Neill Review* 22 (Spring–Fall 1998).

Houchin, John H., ed. *The Critical Response to Eugene O'Neill*. Westport, Conn.: Greenwood Press, 1993.

Toczyski, Suzanne C. "The Memory of Naked Ages: Charles Baudelaire, Eugene O'Neill and *The Great God Brown*." *Eugene O'Neill Review* 23 (Spring–Fall 1999).

Jeffrey D. Mason

THE GREAT REBELLION

The Great Rebellion (Mahabidroha) by UTPAL DUTT extols and analyzes what British historians have called the Sepoy Mutiny of 1857. Demanding a new look at Indian history, Dutt calls the same event the "Great Rebellion," the first war for INDIA's independence. The first scene, set in 1840, serves as a prologue to the play, depicting the rising resentment against British rule among the Indian *sepoys* (soldiers, from the Farsi *sepahi*). This resentment eventually led to the rebellious outbreak at Meerut in 1857, which British historians called the Sepoy Mutiny, and later Indian historians recognized as the Great Rebellion, the first War of Independence.

The narrative begins with the story of a weaver, Budhan Singh, whose refusal to raise the price of his handmade fine cloth—as ordered by the British—costs him his right thumb and the destruction of his family. His son Bishen escapes. Seventeen years later (shown on stage with the help of projected legends), Bishen and his own son Kalu are members of the British Indian Army, under their new names, Heera and Lachman Singh—both apparently loyal to their British masters but nursing their anger. In the meantime, a rumor circulates that the grease for the cartridge of Enfield rifles used by the Indian soldiers, both Hindus and Muslims, is made of the fat of cows and pigs—a sacrilege for both communities. Brigadier Archdale Wilson, a senior British officer, tries to convince the Indian soldiers this is just an unsubstantiated rumor. However, Waziran, a courtesan at the British camp who also serves as an informant for the Indian soldiers, confirms the truth of the rumor and causes the uprising to break out spontaneously on May 21, eleven days before schedule. All of Heera Singh's effort to organize the unplanned outbreak into a planned offensive—with ultimate authority vested in the titular Mughal Emperor Bahadur Shah—is ruined by a clique of native princes and merchants who betray the uprising. Heera Singh is framed and sentenced to death. He is recognized, too late, by his wife Kasturi and son Lachman. The play ends with the arrest of Emperor Bahadur Shah by the British on September 21, and the death sentence of his heir, which promises to end the Mughal line.

Drawing mainly from the journalistic despatches of Karl Marx and Friedrich Engels, written between 1853 and 1859 for the *New York Daily Tribune* on the Rebellion of the Indian soldiers, Dutt's play mixes fact with fiction, creating emotional drama out of cold historical minutiae and larger-than-life events. Nandi Bhatia sees in the play "an alternative interpretation [of events] . . . that explores the discursive links between the politics of economics, class, gender, nationalism and colonialism" (2004).

The play was first performed as *The Bullet (Tota)* in Delhi, in February 1973, by the People's Little Theatre. It was restaged as *The Great Rebellion (Mahabidroha)* in 1985 in Calcutta, and was taken on tour to the German Democratic Republic in the same year. It continued to be performed off and on until Dutt's death in 1992. Although it has not been performed since Dutt's death, it remains one of the most important works in Indian theater and continues to provide a model for historically based plays.

FURTHER READING

Bharucha, Rustom. "The Revolutionary Theater of Utpal Dutt." In *Rehearsals of Revolution: The Political Theater of Bengal*, ed. by Bharucha. Honolulu: Univ. of Hawaii Press, 1983.

Bhatia, Nandi. "Colonial History and Postcolonial Interventions: Staging the 1857 Mutiny as 'The Great Rebellion.'" In *Acts of Authority / Acts of Resistance: Theater and Politics in Colonial and Postcolonial India*, ed. by Bhatia. Ann Arbor: Univ. of Michigan Press, 2004.

Chaudhuri, Sashi Bhushan. *Theories of the Indian Mutiny, 1857–1859: A Study of the Views of an Eminent Historian on the Subject*. Calcutta: Calcutta World Press, 1965.

Dutt, Utpal. *Towards a Revolutionary Theatre*. Calcutta: M.C. Sarkar & Sons, 1982.

———. *Great Rebellion*. Calcutta: Seagull Books, 1986.

Gunawardana, A. J. "Theatre as a Weapon: An Interview with Utpal Dutt." *The Drama Review* 15, no. 2 (T50, Spring 1971).

Jacob, Paul, ed. "Interview with Utpal Dutt." In *Contemporary Indian Theatre: Interviews with Playwrights and Directors*, ed. by Paul Jacob. New Delhi: Sangeet Natak Akademi, 1989.

Sudipto Chatterjee

THE GREAT USKRANIAN CIRCUS

MYRNA CASAS began to dramatize Puerto Rican identity with the modalities of a well-made play and then experimented with

AVANT-GARDE forms. Her trajectory evolved again with the recursive techniques of *Not All of Them Have One* (*No todas la tienen*, 1974, revised 1994), *The Great USkranian Circus* (*El gran circo eucraniano*, 1988, translated into English 1997, published 2004), and *This Country Does Not Exist* (*Este país no existe*, 1993). The characters in all three are actors mounting a play; the action of *This Country* completes the denouement of *Circus*; Gaby, the ambiguous heroine of *Not All*, becomes the divided Gabriela José of *Circus*. The trilogy converts the failure to mount a successful production into a parody of theater. As the characters unmask the artful guises of theater, the action invites spectators to probe the falseness in their lives.

The Great USkranian Circus relies on metadrama to question PUERTO RICO's claim as *La Isla del Encanto* (The Isle of Enchantment). The double structure of circus-comedy and actor-character alludes to the political and psychic confusion of the people. No one refutes Gabriela José's assertion that "This country is full of doubts." A symbol of the island, the circus houses rootless migrants with no more family than the other performers. As they travel the island, the actors discover that the people depend on welfare programs, and that crime, drugs, and politics have driven them crazy.

The oscillating behavior of the actor-characters reveals their fractured identity and family ties. The dual name of Gabriela José implies conflict between her female and male personas. An able administrator, she pines for the son she abandoned in childhood but suppresses her emotions when a young man who could be her son visits the circus. The shame of being a vagabond prevents her from unmasking.

The spontaneous scenes manifest the sorrows of the actors as individuals; the inner skits frame broader social issues. The inserted scenes of "Miracle on Providence Street" ("El Auto de la Providencia"), the play-within-a-play, subvert the religious goals of morality plays by portraying three bitter marriages; the satire suggests that the new Puerto Rican deity is money, not love. Other vignettes spear government bureaucrats with biting humor. The clash between theater and life spins a whirlpool of dizzying images. *Circus* simulates a house of mirrors that projects grotesque figures. The opening call of the circus barkers to passersby to see their souls on stage underscores the continuity of circus mirroring society.

Despite its humor and hyperbole, *Circus* reflects the desolation of Puerto Ricans; they are depicted as nomads, their home a tent. By extension, the tent covers the fiction of the island's political status. The Estado Libre Asociado emerges as a euphemism to hide the indignity that Puerto Rico is neither a state nor free. Gabriela José insists on pronouncing the title "US-krainian" not "Ukrainian," an indictment of geopolitics that also accents the idea of cranium—brain. The title suggests the dual marginalization of Puerto Ricans: demeaned by Americans as dark people with a foreign language and culture, and rejected by their Latin American brothers as "gringos." Both *Circo* and *Este país no existe* challenge the audience to restage the past and reassert *boricua* identity. In 1988, the Theater Critics' Circle of San Juan selected *Circus* for their National Dramaturgy Award, and Joseph Papp produced it in the New York Theater Festival.

FURTHER READING

Cajiao Salas, Teresa, and Margarita Vargas. "Women's Voices in Hispanic Theater." In *International Women Playwrights: Voices of Identity and Transformation*, ed. by Anna K. France and J. P. Corso. Metuchen, N. J.: Scarecrow Press, 1993. 213–221.

Casas, Myrna. *The Great USkranian Circus*. Tr. by Teresa C. Salas and Margarita Vargas. In *Women Writing Women: An Anthology of Spanish American Theater of the 1980s*, ed. by Salas and Vargas. Albany: State Univ. of New York Press, 1997.

——. *El gran circo eucraniano* [The Great USkranian Circus]. San Juan, Puerto Rico: Editorial Plaza Mayor, 2004.

Panico, Marie. J. "Myrna Casas: Nacional y trascendente" ["Myrna Casas: National and Universal"]. *Alba de América: Revista Literaria* 7, nos. 12–13 (July 1989): 411–418.

Stevens, Camilla. "Traveling Troupes: The Performance of Puerto Rican Identity in Plays by Luis Rafael Sánchez and Myrna Casas." *Hispania* 85, no. 2 (May 2002): 240–249.

Unruh, Vicky. "A Moveable Space: The Problem of Puerto Rico in Myrna Casas's Theater." In *Latin American Women Dramatists: Theater, Texts, and Theories*, ed. by Catherine Larson and Margarita Vargas. Bloomington: Indiana Univ. Press, 1998.126–142.

Vargas, Margarita. "Regional Identity in Myrna Casas's *El gran circo eucraniano*." *Latin American Theatre Review* 36, no. 2 (Spring 2003): 5–19.

Wilma Feliciano

GREECE

In 1860 the Greek independent state was barely thirty years old. The national uprising of 1821 against the Ottoman ruler had led, after a decade of fierce war and arduous negotiations, to the establishment of a small kingdom at the end of the Balkans. However, with the vast majority of the Greeks still living in lands outside the new country, and the originally acknowledged borders short and uncertain, social stability and economic prosperity could not be attained. Therefore, until the early 20th century, Greece was caught up in a laborious process of augmenting its territorial boundaries, defining its political and social status, and constructing its national identity.

SERVING THE NATION, 1860 to 1922

The social and cultural life of the new state was, in many respects, aligned with the aspirations of the national cause. The implement of Megali Idea, the reunion of all Greeks in a country that would include the great economic and cultural centers of the Byzantine period, was the dominant ideology until 1922 and exerted a great influence on the contemporary imagery and rhetoric. In general, 19th-century playwriting frequently endorsed a nationalistic discourse, not only because the political situation often dictated it, but also because it was an effective means of achieving several other objectives: advancing Hellenism, controlling the language, and fostering drama as a primarily literary activity.

In the early 19th century, when neo-Hellenic drama began to emerge, neoclassical TRAGEDIES influenced by Voltaire, Pietro Metastasio, and Vittorio Alfieri and COMEDIES in the mode of Molière and Carlo Goldoni dominated dramatic production. Heroic deeds and courageous characters such as Achilles and Leonidas were chosen to serve the evidently instructive and patriotic purposes of this predominantly CLOSET DRAMA. Celebrated Byzantine emperors as well as emblematic figures and memorable incidents from the recent war against the Turks also became popular *dramatis personae* and dramatic themes, thereby establishing a thriving tradition of historical drama that lasted for more than a century.

In parallel, the comic and satiric compositions that focused on everyday life and contemporary customs reinforced the idea of *couleur local* in Hellenic DRAMATURGY. All these trends and genres inherent in the Greek drama of the 1860s and 1870s resulted in an amalgam of classicism and ROMANTICISM, which is best exemplified in the plays written by Demetrios Vernardakis (1833–1907), especially *Maria Doxapatri* (1858), and to a lesser degree by Spyridon Vassiliadis (1845–1874) and Demetrios Paparigopoulos (1845–1873). Until the 1890s the most difficult task for Greek playwrights was not merely to integrate into their dramas differing features from old and new aesthetic movements, but also, on the ideological level, to bring together East and West—or, essentially, the past and the future. This complex target was particularly harsh because innovative efforts were usually snared by the regulating mechanisms that Greek society had already acquired.

In the second half of the 19th century, annual literary contests were sponsored by wealthy merchants and bankers and organized by the country's major educational institution, Athens University. In most of these competitions, serious drama was heralded as high poetry and entrenched in uncompromising morality, purity of language, and classical models. The support for tragedies written in verse and in *katharevousa*, a purist idiom of contemporary literati, was necessary to promote a drama dissociated from the stage but in full accordance with the canon woven and imposed by the newly established academia. However, despite the ambivalent popularity of such dramas in the Greek state, they also had a specific role and place on the stage.

Theatrical activity, until at least 1870, was a rather limited part of the new state's cultural life, residing mostly with foreign visiting companies devoted to opera. A considerably undersized city compared with other European capitals, Athens did not even have a winter playhouse. Greek theater companies had to travel in the Balkans, Eastern Europe, and the Ottoman Empire—wherever there was sufficient Greek population to attend their performances and cover their expenses. For the numerous Greeks living in prosperous, multicultural centers such as Odessa, Istanbul (Constantinople), Izmir (Smyrne), and Alexandria, these troupes were a way to strengthen their link with the motherland and to safeguard their national traits. All patriotic plays were, consequently, a major attraction for these ethnic communities until the 1922 war, and the subsequent population migration in the East Mediterranean and curtailing of national expectations.

The call for patriotism and the emphasis on national character were not reserved for tragedy and high drama. Popular genres and commercial theater also adopted the cause, sometimes aggressively sometimes more subtly. Greek musical comedy and MELODRAMA—such as *komeidyllion* and *dramatic idyll* by the creative mind of Demetrios Koromilas (1850–1898) and *epitheorissi*, a type of revue—as well as comedies of manners and satires, all shaped and exemplified Greek identity by repeatedly illustrating, advancing, or ridiculing various social and ethnic groups, regional customs and dialects, and images of urban life. At the same time, these dramatic forms exposed Greek drama to REALISM.

SOCIAL DRAMA, 1880 to 1950

The realistic movement reached the shores of Greek theater life in the dusk of the 19th century and was soon fully embraced. By the 1880s, a new generation of authors and artists was introducing innovation in literature and culture. The flourishing of comic musical drama and its variations in the late 19th century drew from the earlier comic tradition of Byzantios and Hourmouzis, but much more clearly illustrated matters of everyday life and criticized contemporary reality.

The most important development, though, was in serious drama, and as in Europe, HENRIK IBSEN became the standard. Playwrights such as GRIGORIOS XENOPOULOS (1867–1951), Giannis Kambyssis (1872–1901), Demetrios Tagopoulos (1867–1926), and Kalliroi Parren-Siganou (1859–1940) with her drama *The New Woman* (*H nea gynaika*, 1907) upheld the doctrines of realistic and naturalistic dramaturgy, discussing in their pieces issues of marriage and adultery, woman's role in society, social oppression, and class tension. Innovation gradually spread through all aspects of theater life: well-informed essays on Scandinavian, German, and Russian literature and dramaturgy appeared in papers and journals; French melodramas and well-made plays stopped to monopolize the stage; Greek popular vernacular, *demotiki*, gradually replaced *katharevousa* in serious drama and performances; new companies were founded as the vigorous independent theater movement spread; inspiring directors from the European capitals, such as Konstantinos Christomanos, Thomas Oikonomou, and Fotos Politis, started to work in Greek theater.

The decline of neoclassical tragedy and historical drama and the emergence of domestic and social drama opened the door to other innovative efforts. More authors—among them Paulos Nirvanas (1866–1937), Pantelis Horn (1881–1941), Spiros Melas

(1882–1966), and Demetris Bogris (1890–1964)—experimented in the early 20th century with realism as well as SYMBOLISM. Their pioneering work linked Greek drama with the European AVANT-GARDE and fertilized Greek theater with the seeds of modernism, clearly apparent in the dramatic works of the distinguished poets and novelists Costis Palamas (1859–1943), Nikos Kazantzakis (1883–1957), and Aggelos Sikelianos (1884–1951). As early as 1903 Palamas wrote his only play, *Trisevgeni*, a poetic drama on the impulses of human nature as exposed in its heroine's clash with the values and attitudes of her environment. Trisevgeni's uncompromising character and her bleak destiny found eager disciples in Kazantzakis's and Sikelianos's protagonists in the 1930s and 1940s. Their rebellious and adamant behavior emphasizes individual will, free judgment, unrestrained spirit, and at times superhuman forces. Kazantzakis's often legendary heroes, dressed in messianic garb, recall the past and defend personal ideals against corrupt and oppressive institutions, while Sikelianos's highly symbolic language and metaphysical visions pursue self-awareness and spiritual redemption.

However, Kazantzakis's and Sikelianos's closet drama was a rather small part of the dramatic production in the period between the wars. The popular genres of the late 19th century attracted theatergoers, so more such plays were written in abundance. Comedy, *epitheorissi* (Greek revue based on short sketches and stereotypical characters), music spectacles, and especially operettas continued to confirm the strength and influence on economy and politics that the Greek middle class had gradually gained.

POLITICAL UPHEAVAL, 1936 to 1967

The extensive defeat of the Greek army in Asia Minor in 1922 not only signaled the deplorable end of an enduring dream, but also forced Greece to contend with its wavering political system and an urgent humanitarian crisis. More than a million refugees, persecuted and destitute, arrived in the homeland, which had been deeply segregated by the relentless clash between the king and the prime minister. In the following years, governmental and constitutional changes sustained a climate of uncertainty and repression. Under these circumstances, Greece proved vulnerable to the rise of fascism in Europe, and in 1936, a fascist dictatorship was imposed. After a long period of political and social tension, authoritarianism and warfare ensued.

The dictatorship immediately forced censorship and strict ideological control over drama and theater. Quite reasonably, *epitheorissi* was the genre that mostly felt such restrictions. With the outbreak of World War II, a heavily patriotic rhetoric stormed dramatic and theatrical production, but soon the German occupation forced relentless surveillance and rigid examination on all pieces printed and performed. New plays for the commercial theater were still written and produced, but only indirectly and at great risk could they express the anxieties of the age. On the contrary, the anti-Nazi feelings overwhelmed all sketches and plays composed and performed in the mountainous villages, where an uncompromising guerrilla war against the fascists went on. In these shells of resistance, improvisation and popular legends held the community to the sacred duty of liberation and at the same time shaped the idea of a people's theater that prevailed in the strongholds of the Communists through the years of the dire civil war (1946–1949).

During this same period of restraint, war, and propaganda, the foundations for modern Greek theater and drama were built. Small, avant-garde theater companies, with Karolos Koun's Theatro Technis (Art Theatre) as the unrivaled leader, paved the way for a new era in original drama. Theatro Technis was founded in 1942 and, despite the short intervals of closure and economic disparity, remained the crèche for new dramatists, until at least Koun's death in 1988. A group of the so-called postwar generation—including Giorgos Sevastikoglou, IAKOVOS KAMBANELLIS, Demetris Kehaidis, Loula Anagnostaki, and Giorgos Skourtis—had their plays premiered at Theatron Technis. Koun's meticulous direction enhanced the features in this new Greek drama, which focused on the politics of everyday life and spoke for the needs and feelings of ordinary people.

The realism of postwar drama drew from ANTON CHEKHOV's depth in the depiction of the characters and from TENNESSEE WILLIAMS's atmospheric scenery and psychological intensity. The emphasis on social and political issues meant to unravel the agonies of lower classes and to address the existential crisis brought on by the ceaseless conflicts. The emergence of the Theatre of the Absurd also influenced how contemporary playwrights dealt with reality: Kehaidis, *The Engagement Ring* (*H vera*, 1972) and *Backgammon* (*To tavli*, 1972), and Skourtis, *The Nunnies* (*Oi Ntantades*, 1974). Gradually Greek drama moved from collectivity to individualism, from general codes to marginal behaviors, and from the outer world to the inner sentiments.

In parallel, comedy dominated the commercial stage with plays that usually featured either the poor and honest laborer dazzled by rapid urbanization, or the desires and goals of what was shown as an apolitical middle class. These comedies, regularly written by the collaborative teams of Asimakis Gialamas (1912–2004) and Kostas Pretenteris (1926–1976) and of Alekos Sakelarios (1913–1991) and Xristos Giannakopoulos (1909–1963), were often adapted for the cinema with huge success.

THE YEARS OF DEMOCRACY

When democracy was reestablished in 1974, Greek society had first to heal the wounds from the earlier turbulent phases of its political life. During the 1970s and for most of the 1980s, freed from earlier restrictions, drama was dominated by political and social issues as it attempted to rehabilitate aspects of recent history and to conciliate with painful losses and difficult choices (consider, for example, Anagnostaki's *The Victory*

[H niki, 1978]). Progressively, a new concept of the political appeared; it focused on personal relationships and the merging of identities, and it left behind the restrictions of specificity and historical accuracy (Giorgos Dialegmenos, *Do Not Listen to the Rain* [*Min akous ti vrohi*, 1989]). Greek playwrights of the postwar period also renovated their dramatic discourse, abandoning the rationality and realistic representation of the earlier days (Kambanellis, *The Invisible Group* [*O aoratos thiasos*, 1988]).

Peace and stability prompted a break with the past that became more obvious in the 1990s. Dramatic production ceased to proclaim homogeneity and obedience to traditional aesthetic norms and specified expressive means. Contemporary Greek dramatists started questioning the nature and limits of their art and its relation to the world around (Andreas Staikos, *1843*, 1990). Old plays and writers now subvert the notion of creativity and renegotiate the conditions of human experience (Kambanellis, *In Ibsen Land* [*Sti hora Ibsen*, 1996], Akis Demou, *. . . and Juliet* [*. . . kai Ioulietta*, 1994] and *Margueritte Gautier Travels Tonight* [*H Margarita Gautier taxideuei apopse*, 2004]). Fragmentation and improvisation together with the use of other art forms dislocate dramatic plot and characterization (Elena Pega, *Emperor's New Clothes* [*Ta kainourgia rouha tou autokratora*, 1998]). Greek drama of the new millennium, experimental and diversified, crossed the bridge to POSTMODERNISM.

FURTHER READING

Bacopoulou-Halls, Aliki. *Modern Greek Theatre: Roots and Blossoms*. Athens: Diogenis, 1982.

Constantinidis, Stratos E. *Modern Greek Theatre: A Quest for Hellenism*. Jefferson, N.C.: McFarland and Company, 2001.

Giorgos, Michailidis. *Neoi ellines syggrafeis* [Modern Greek Playwrights]. Athens: Kaktos, 1975. [Γιώργος, Μιχαηλίδης. *Νέοι έλληνες θεατρικοί συγγραφείς*. Αθήνα: Κάκτος, 1975.]

"Modern Greek Drama." *Journal of Modern Greek Studies* 14, no. 1 (May 1996).

Sideris, Giannis. *The Modern Greek Theatre*. Tr. by Lucille Vassardaki. Athens: Difros, 1957.

Spathis, Dimitris. "To neoelliniko theatro" [The Modern Greek Theatre]. In *Ellada: Istoria kai Politismos* [Greece: History and Civilization], vol. 10. Thessaloniki: Malliaris, 1983. [Σπάθης, Δημήτρης. «Το νεοελληνικό θέατρο». Στο *Ελλάδα: Ιστορία και Πολιτισμός*, τ. 10. Θεσσαλονίκη: Μαλλιάρης, 1983.]

Valsa, M. *Le théâtre grec moderne de 1453 à 1900* [Modern Greek Theater from 1453 to 1900]. Berlin: Academie Verlag in Berliner Byzantinische Arbeiten, 1960.

Ioulia Pipinia

GREEN, PAUL (1894–1981)

Playwright, poet, essayist, composer, and human rights activist Paul Green remains one of the most revered native sons of the American South. Born on March 17, 1894, near Lillington in Harnett County, North Carolina, Green attended and later taught at the University of North Carolina in Chapel Hill, where he wrote scores of plays, screenplays, and essays, and originated a new form of historically based dramatic works.

Green had six plays produced on Broadway. His first Broadway hit, IN ABRAHAM'S BOSOM, won a Pulitzer Prize. Other awards include the North Carolina Award for Literature, the National Theatre Conference plaque, a citation from the American Theatre Association, the Frank P. Graham Award, and two Guggenheim Fellowships. He was named North Carolina's dramatist laureate by the General Assembly in 1979.

Green affiliated with the Carolina Playmakers shortly after its inception in 1918 and was mentored by founder Frederick Koch. There, Green's interest in the concerns of ordinary people, primarily those in the South, fueled a desire to create drama that would affect the lives of the people who saw it. This focus, coupled with his belief in the power of music, dance, lighting, and language prompted his development of a vital new form he called the Symphonic Outdoor Drama. The first of this type, *The Lost Colony*, presented in Manteo, North Carolina, in 1937, has continued every year since, except during World War II. Many others, such as *The Common Glory*, *Wilderness Road*, *Cross and Sword*, *Drumbeats in Georgia*, *Louisiana Cavalier*, and *The Lone Star*, ran for many years in their respective communities. Those still in production include *The Stephen Foster Story* (now *Stephen Foster: The Musical*), *Texas*, and *Trumpet in the Land*. These, and others written to mark specific historical events, incorporate the elements of Green's symphonic drama to tell a story of special significance to the locale where they are presented. To this day, they remain an exciting part of tourism in many areas.

Green's liberal political convictions are evident in his artistic endeavors. During the height of segregation, Green brought novelist Richard Wright to Chapel Hill to collaborate on the dramatic adaptation of his book, *Native Son*. Green was one of the few playwrights providing significant roles for African American actors at the time. His social activism led to pioneering efforts in drama, and he remained committed to issues of social justice, integration, and human rights throughout his life. Green died on May 4, 1981, in Chapel Hill, North Carolina. The Paul Green Foundation, established in 1982, perpetuates his vision by continuing to nurture the arts and support human rights.

[*See also* United States, 1860–1940]

SELECT PLAYS: *In Abraham's Bosom* (1926); *The House of Connelly* (1931); *Johnny Johnson* (music by Kurt Weill, 1936); *The Lost Colony* (1937); *Native Son* (from the novel by Richard Wright, 1941); *Wilderness Road* (1955); *The Confederacy* (1958); *The Stephen Foster Story* (now *Stephen Foster: The Musical*, 1959); *Cross and Sword* (1965); *Texas* (1966); *Trumpet in the Land* (1970); *Drumbeats in Georgia* (1973); *Louisiana Cavalier* (1976); *We the People* (1976); *The Lone Star* (1977)

FURTHER READING

Adams, Agatha Boyd. *Paul Green of Chapel Hill*. Ed. by Richard Walser. Chapel Hill: Univ. of North Carolina Press, 1951.

Green, Elizabeth Lay. *The Paul Green I Know*. Chapel Hill: North Carolinian Society Imprints, 1978.

Green, Paul. *Home to My Valley*. Chapel Hill: Univ. of North Carolina Press, 1970.

Kenny, Vincent. *Paul Green*. Twayne's United States Authors Series. New York: Twayne, 1971.

Roper, John Herbert. *Paul Green, Playwright of the Real South*. Athens: Univ. of Georgia Press, 2003.

Judith Midyett Pender

THE GREEN PASTURES

MARC CONNELLY's *The Green Pastures*, based on Roark Bradford's *Ol' Man Adam an' His Chillun* (1928), opened on February 26, 1930, at the Mansfield Theatre in New York City. Connelly directed it himself. It was hailed as "a miracle of folk art" (Brown, 1929) and "the finest achievement of the American theatre in one hundred years" (Woollcott, 1930).

The play consisted of two parts and eighteen scenes—chronicling the Biblical tales of Adam, Eve, Cain, Noah, and Moses—with an all-black cast of one hundred actors. In the lead role of God was the unforgettable, sixty-five-year-old Shakespearean actor, Richard B. Harrison, hailing from a black Chicago family of erstwhile slaves. Bradford's southern sketches were geared to the Old Testament through the Louisiana black folk idiom, which Connelly took the trouble to learn and incorporate. Visualizing God as a benevolent, white-haired patriarch, Mr. Deshee, a preacher, addresses his Sunday class of restless children with his mellifluous meditations on the Bible, highlighting the metamorphosis of Jehovah himself.

The overwhelming success of *The Green Pastures* must be attributed to the African American contribution to the American theater during the Harlem Renaissance. Connelly's play belongs to the tradition of white Anglo-American DRAMATURGY, which subscribed to the belief that "one undiscovered country in emotional America was Negro country" (Hackett, 1917). Beginning with Ridgely Torrence's *Three Plays for a Negro Theatre* (1917) and EUGENE O'NEILL's *THE EMPEROR JONES* (1920) and *ALL GOD'S CHILLUN GOT WINGS* (1924), the new theater interest included as well "a purposive folk fantasy with a religious and spiritual edge" (Raghavacharyulu, 1966) that is revealed in PAUL GREEN's *IN ABRAHAM'S BOSOM* (1926) as well as in *The Green Pastures*, both recipients of the Pulitzer Prize.

In both parts of the play, Jehovah's motive for "walkin' de earth in de shape of a natchel man" is a reformative one. Each time, his outrage at sinful reality moves him to punish mankind, first with the deluge and second with his own renunciation from the responsibility of a deliverer. Ironically, in the end he undergoes a change of mind through his encounter with Hezdrel—an apocryphal, heroic character created by Connelly and played by the same actor who played Adam—who convinces God that man can be better understood through suffering than through wrath. God sees the point. The play concludes not only with the epiphanic vision of the Crucifixion, but also with man's compassion for that act of sacrifice: "Oh, dat's a terrible burden for one man to carry!"

In this classic, Connelly moves beyond theology to a religion for all times. Maxwell Anderson sees in the play the same spiritual theme and lesson that was operative in Aeschylus's *Orestia*: "that God must learn and grow and change or his rigid justice will become an injustice in the end" (Anderson, 1947).

[*See also* United States, 1929–1940]

FURTHER READING

Anderson, Maxwell. *Off Broadway: Essays About the Theatre*. New York: Sloane, 1947.

Atkinson, Brooks. "The Green Pastures." In *The American Theatre As Seen by Its Critics, 1752–1934*, ed. by Montrose J. Moses and John Mason Brown. New York: Norton, 1934.

Brown, John Mason. "The Ever Green Pastures." In *Dramatis Personae*, Brown. New York: Viking Press, 1929.

Fergusson, Francis. "*The Green Pastures* Revisited." *Bookman* 73 (May 1931).

Hackett, Francis, article in *The New Republic* referring to Ridley Torrence's *Three Plays for a Negro Theatre* (1917), quoted in Edith J. R. Isaacs, *The Negro in the American Theatre*, New York: Theatre Arts Inc., 1946.

Krumbleman, John T. "Marc Connelly's *The Green Pastures* and Goethe's *Faust*." *Studies in Comparative Literature* (Fall 1962).

Raghavacharyulu, D. V. K. "The Drama in the 1920's," in *Renaissance in the Twenties*, American Literature Symposium, United States Information Service, Bombay, India (March 1966).

Woollcott, Alexander, article in *The Ladies Home Journal* after *The Green Pastures* opened at the Mansfield Theater in New York on February 26, 1930, quoted in Beatrice Paul Hirschl, "McKeesport Was Home to Areas's First Pulitzer Dramatist," *Pittsburgh Tribune Review* (May 5, 2002).

Rupendra Guha-Majumdar

GREGORY, LADY (1852–1932)

> *Monday, 6 September 1926. I suppose it is cancer. Thank God, if so, that is only now it has come when I have I think done my work.*
> *29 January 1930. (Re Irish Declaration of Independence, for 26 counties excluding the north of Ireland.) I myself wish full independence could have been given, even though greater material loss had come to us—to my class.*
> —Lady Gregory, *Journals*, 1926

Lady Gregory (Isabella Augusta Persse), playwright, folklorist, and a director of the Abbey Theatre, Dublin, was born on March 15, 1852, in Roxborough, County Galway, one of thirteen children in a Protestant, landowning family. It was a prosperous estate in a famine-wasted part of IRELAND. Her education was that of a well-born young lady—French and etiquette—in addition to the Bible lessons given by her evangelical mother. In 1880, she married the sixty-three-year-old landlord of a neighboring estate, Sir William Gregory, formerly Governor of Ceylon, who died in 1892.

She met W. B. YEATS in London in 1894 and advanced her friendship with the poet during his 1896 stay at her home, Coole Park. Thereafter, he was a regular summer resident for twenty years. In the 1890s Gregory became more and more sympathetic to the cause of Irish nationalists. In 1897 Yeats, Gregory, and her neighbor Edward Martyn planned to start the Irish Literary Theatre (1897–1901). Yeats and Gregory were central to the development of the Irish National Theatre Society and the Abbey Theatre, of which she was a director, playing an active managerial role until the last years of her life.

The opening play of the Irish national theater, CATHLEEN NI HOULIHAN (1902), is largely Gregory's work, though credit for authorship was taken by Yeats. She quickly revealed a talent for writing folk plays, especially COMEDIES and histories, in an Hiberno-English dialect called Kiltartanese after a townland near Coole Park. As a playwright, she had more than one string to her bow. She could write nationalist propaganda plays like *Cathleen ni Houlihan* (1902), *The Rising of the Moon* (1904), and *The Gaol Gate* (1906); light comedies about the people of her fictive village Cloon like *Spreading the News* (1904) and *Hyacinth Halvey* (1906); and TRAGEDIES based on Irish history or saga like *Dervogilla* (1907), *Kincora* (1909), and *Grania* (1911). Her translations of Molière's work into Kiltartanese are less satisfactory, but they reveal an important source of her comic attitude toward life. Her dramatic work tapered off in quality and finally in quantity from 1912.

For the Abbey Theatre she was an essential breadwinner, as she wrote scores of actable plays that drew a regular audience. Her plays had a formative influence on the language and themes of J. M. SYNGE's plays. She was a stalwart in the management of the Abbey Theatre, steering it through both financial and political problems from its beginnings until shortly before her death on May 22, 1932, in Galway. She backed up Synge, whom she did not like, and SEAN O'CASEY, whom she did, when their plays were under attack. Without her assistance, Yeats could not have managed, either as playwright (she wrote a good deal of the prose dialogue in many of his plays) or as theater director. Finally, she was instrumental in popularizing the notion that the people in the west of Ireland are fanciful, innocent, and simple, and the truest of Irishmen.

SELECT PLAYS: *Cathleen ni Houlihan* (with W. B. Yeats, 1902); *The Pot of Broth* (with W. B. Yeats, 1902); *Twenty-Five* (1903); *Spreading the News* (1904); *Kincora* (1905); *The Canavans* (1906); *The Doctor in Spite of Himself* (1906); *The Gaol Gate* (1906); *Hyacinth Halvey* (1906); *Dervogilla* (1907); *The Jackdaw* (1907); *The Rising of the Moon* (1907); *The Unicorn From the Stars* (with W. B. Yeats, 1907); *The Workhouse Ward* (1908); *The Image* (1909); *The Miser* (1909); *The Travelling Man* (1910); *Grania* (1911); *The Cat and the Moon* (with W. B. Yeats, 1926)

FURTHER READING

Gregory, Lady. *Lady Gregory's Journals*. Ed. by Daniel Murphy. Gerrards Cross, Bucks.: Colin Smythe, 1978.

Kohfeldt, Mary Lou. *Lady Gregory: The Woman Behind the Irish Renaissance*. London: Deutsch, 1985.

McDiarmid, Lucy, and Maureen Waters, eds. *Lady Gregory: Selected Writings*. New York: Penguin, 1995.

Pethica, James. "'Our Kathleen': Yeats's Collaboration with Lady Gregory in the Writing of *Cathleen ni Houlihan*." *Yeats Annual* 6, ed. by Warwick Gould. London: Macmillan, 1988. 3–31.

——. "Patronage and Creative Exchange: Yeats, Lady Gregory, and the Economy of Indebtedness." In *Yeats and Women*, ed. by Deirdre Toomey. London: Macmillan, 1988. 60–94.

Saddlemyer, Anne, and Colin Smythe, eds. *Lady Gregory: Fifty Years After*. Gerrards Cross, U.K.: Colin Smythe, 1987.

Tóibín, Colm. *Lady Gregory's Toothbrush*. Dublin: Lilliput, 2002.

Adrian Frazier

GREIG, DAVID (1972–)

David Greig, born in Edinburgh in 1972, is widely recognized as one of the most exciting new British playwrights. An Edinburgh native, much of his success also originated at the Fringe and International Festival there; in particular his work has been closely linked with The Traverse Theatre. In addition to solo work, Greig is a founding member of the collaborative company SUSPECT CULTURE, begun in the early 1990s.

Part of what critics have called a Scottish Renaissance in drama since the late 1990s, Greig's plays rarely talk openly about SCOTLAND. Instead, the world of his drama is very much the impersonal and sterile environment of places that could be found as easily in Florida as in Fife. Greig's plays live under the influence of postmodern thought, the tricky set of concepts that articulate what life is like in the late 20th and early 21st centuries. Particularly relevant to Greig's drama are two ideas: globalization and the related concept that in a world saturated with images, data, and ever quicker means of communicating, true human connection has become rarer and more difficult.

In an early solo effort, *Europe* (1994), Greig explores these themes powerfully. Set in a "small decaying provincial town in Europe," the play studies the inertia, fears, and aspirations of the inhabitants. The town once took its importance from the border, but as borders come to mean less and less, the future of the town seems uncertain. Fret, the manager of the train station, oversees a building where trains no longer stop as they rush toward "more beautiful" and "more important places." The station becomes the center of the drama, and trains shooting by are images of movement in a static place. The sense of being nowhere and everywhere permeates the play, and the weight of memory and history are heavy in a town that holds no future, only the possibility of escape.

Two years later in *The Architect*, Greig takes up a different way of exploring communities under threat, here through the grotesque Black family. Leo Black is the patriarch of a chronically dysfunctional family; his marriage is failing and his children seek casual sex in the hope of finding companionship. He is also, according to a local activist, the architect of a dysfunctional tower block–housing estate that should be demolished. The architect proves incapable of planning and designing a life for himself and his family, and he and his tower block end in ruin. But it is perhaps the failure to communicate rather than to imagine that destroys the Blacks.

This theme is important in Greig's work, finding its most striking investigation in *The Cosmonaut's Last Message to the Woman He Once Loved in the Former Soviet Union* (1999). Here a scattered sequence of scenes, ultimately connected through the plight of a manned Soviet satellite marooned in space, explores a myriad of miscommunications and language barriers, failed "signals." What Greig portrays here, as elsewhere, is a stage full of people profoundly and deeply connected but unable to talk to each other.

SELECT PLAYS: *The Time Before and the Time After* (1993); *Caledonia Dreaming* (1997); *Danny 306 + Me (4 Ever)* (1999); *The Speculator* (1999); *Victoria* (2000); *Casanova* (2001); *Outlying Islands* (2002); *San Diego* (2003)

FURTHER READING

Logan, Brian. "It's Easier to Bring a Belgian Play to London Than a Scottish One." *The Guardian* (April 26, 2000).

Rebellato, Dan. "Introduction." *David Greig, Plays: 1*. London: Methuen, 2002. ix–xxiii.

Reinelt, Janelle G. "Performing Europe: Identity Formation for a 'New' Europe." *Theatre Journal* 53, no. 3 (October 2001): 365–387.

Simard, Jean-Pierre. "Rupture et continuité: Le Théâtre écossais au passage du millénaire." *Cycnos* 18, no. 1 (2001): 133–144.

Paul Gleed

GRIEG, NORDAHL (1902–1943)

The action can take place in China today. In India tomorrow. In Palestine 2,000 years ago.

—Grieg, Introduction to *Barabbas*, 1927

In his youth Nordahl Grieg was a sailor, journalist, poet, and a student of literature. He traveled extensively in Europe. In 1927 he was a war correspondent in CHINA, observing the fighting between Western imperialists, Russian communists, and Chinese nationalists. His first novel, *The Ship Sails On* (1924), provoked international debate on social conditions among sailors. Grieg's early plays are technically weak but not without talent. *Barabbas*, written in China, focuses on the choice between Barabbas, the rebel who can liberate his people from the Romans, and Jesus, who represents mildness and foregiveness. Grieg's interest in political and ethical principles rather than in historical conflicts is manifest.

The cynicism of mass media—in an age when air traffic was new and both newspaper editors and adventurous individuals would go far to get attention—is the subject of *The Atlantic* (1932). A technical novelty in this play is the use in the final scene of radio transmission to the crowd on the stage from the reporter on board the plane trying to cross the ocean.

Grieg spent 1933 and 1934 in the Soviet Union, studying Russian theater and film. He returned to NORWAY a Communist. His next play, OUR POWER AND OUR GLORY, presents Bergen shipping magnates during the boom of the Great War, juxtaposing greedy shipowners and exploited sailors facing the threat of German submarines. The performance in 1935 was Grieg's greatest theatrical success, although the play was politically controversial. Equally controversial but less stirring was *But Tomorrow*, about conflicts among the owners of a chemical plant facing a request for production changes (making poison gas instead of fertilizer) because of the threat of war.

As a playwright Grieg preferred contemporary ideological conflicts. His sympathies are as a rule clearly expressed, mostly through lyrical imagery, whereas character development and dramatic motivation are less convincing. His inclination for monologues with a lyrical touch sometimes tends to reduce the dramatic tension. His last play, *The Defeat* on the final stage of the Parisian Commune in 1871 fighting for survival against government troops, has more individualized characters than the earlier plays.

When the Germans invaded Norway in 1940, Grieg was quick to join the resistance, going to ENGLAND as a reporter. In 1943 he accompanied a Lancaster bomber crew over Berlin. The plane was shot down and no one survived. Grieg's patriotic stand had a positive effect on the reception of his poetry and drama after the war.

PLAYS: *Barabbas* (1927); *A Young Man's Love* (*En ung manns Kjærlighet*, 1927); *The Atlantic* (1932); *Our Power and Our Glory* (1935); *But Tomorrow* (1936); *The Defeat* (1937)

FURTHER READING

Borgen, Johan. "Nordahl Grieg som dramatiker" ["Nordahl Grieg as a Playwright"]. *Nordahl Grieg 1902—1 Novemberv 1952* [*Nordahl Grieg 1902—November 1, 1952*]. Special Issue of *Kvinnen og tiden*. Oslo 1952

Engberg, Harald. *Nordahl Grieg og tidens drama* [*Nordahl Grieg and the Drama of His Time*]. Copenhagen: Aschehoug, 1946.

Naess, Harald S. "Introduction." *Five Modern Scandinavian Plays. The Library of Scandinavian Literature*, Vol. 11, ed. by Erik J. Friis. New York: Twayne, 1971.

Asbjørn Aarseth

GRIFFITHS, LINDA (1953–)

Canadian actress and playwright born in Montreal in 1953, Linda Griffiths won five Dora Mavor Moore Awards, a Gemini Award, and two Chalmers Awards.

After studying at the National Theatre School, she began her dramatic career as founding member and Artistic Director of Twenty-Fifth Street House Theatre in Saskatoon, CANADA, and was one of the writers of the popular collective creation, *Paper Wheat* (1978). In the spring of 1974, she met PAUL THOMPSON, who became her long-term collaborator. In 1979 they worked together on the collective *Les Maudits Anglais*.

Griffiths joined the Theatre Passe Muraille in 1979, where she produced her controversial MAGGIE AND PIERRE (co-written with Thompson), a two-act, one-person, three-character show. The play premiered on February 14, 1980, putting Griffiths in the national spotlight for her critically acclaimed tour de force solo performance, for which she won her first Dora Moore Award in 1981. The play also won the award for the Outstanding New Play. Subtitled "A Fantasy of Love, Politics and the Media," *Maggie and Pierre* tells the story of a torrid love affair between Margaret Sinclair and Pierre Trudeau, thirty years her senior and formerly Canadian prime minister. The play was published in 1980 and adapted for television in 1983. In 1996, it was revived for a Playwrights Union benefit, and in 1997 for a run at Passe Muraille.

O.D. on Paradise (co-written with Patrick Brymer) premiered in 1982 at Twenty-Fifth Street. This comedy about Canadian couples on vacation in Jamaica won Griffiths her second Dora Mavor Moore Award for outstanding new play. She won a Los Angeles Actor's Guild of America Award for her title role in John Sayles's film *Lianna*, an ACTRA Award and Gemini nomination for her performance in the CBC television miniseries *Empire Inc*. Her next play, *Jessica*, premiered at Passe Muraille in 1986. Directed by Griffiths and Clarke Rogers, the play won another Dora Mavor Moore Award for outstanding new play, a Floyd S. Chalmers Canadian Play Award, and the Quinzaine International Festival Award for Best Canadian Production in Quebec City. Griffith's next play, *The Darling Family* (1991), was nominated for a Governor General's Award and made into a feature film. *A Game of Inches* (1991) was co-written and co-directed with Sandra Balcovske. In 1997 Griffiths formed her own company, Duchess Productions, which produced a tour of *Alien Creature*, as well as developing and associate-producing *The Duchess*, *Alien Creature*, and her latest project, *Chronic* (2003 at Factory Theatre).

SELECT PLAYS: *Brother Andre's Heart* (1993); *Spiral Women and the Dirty Theatre* (1992); *The Duchess* (1998); *Alien Creature: a visitation from Gwendolyn MacEwan* (2000); *Chronic* (2003)

FURTHER READING

Bennet, Susan. "Performing Lives: Linda Griffiths and Other Famous Women." *Performing National Identities: International Perspective on Contemporary Canadian Theatre*, ed. by Sherill Grace and Albert-Reiner Glaap. Toronto: Univ. of Toronto Press, 2003.

Johnston, Denis W. *Up the Mainstream: The Rise of Toronto's Alternative Theatres 1968–1975*. Toronto: Univ. of Toronto Press, 1991.

Miller, Mary Jane. "*Billy Bishop Goes to War* and *Maggie and Pierre*: A Matched Set." In *Theatre History in Canada / Histoire du Theatre au Canada* 10, no. 2 (Fall 1989). 188–198.

Rogers, Clarke. "Introduction." *Dangerous Traditions: A Passe Muraille Anthology*, ed. by Judith Rudakoff. Winnipeg: Blizzard, 1992. 143–144.

Rudakoff, Judith, and Rita Much. *Fair Play: Twelve Women Speak: Conversations with Canadian Playwrights*. Toronto: Simon & Pierre, 1990. 13–36

Magda Romanska

GRIMKE, ANGELINA WELD (1880–1958)

If then, white women of this country could, see, feel, understand just what effect their prejudice and the prejudice of their fathers, brothers, husbands, sons were having on the souls of colored mothers everywhere, and upon the mothers that are to be, a great power to affect public opinion would be set free and the battle [over racism] would be half won.

—Angelina Weld Grimke, "Rachel: The Reason and Synopsis" (1920)

Poet, essayist, short-fiction writer, and playwright Angelina Weld Grimke holds a prominent place in American theater history. As the first female African American playwright to be published and produced for the stage—and whose work was performed by professional African American actors in 1916—Grimke opened the stage for LORRAINE HANSBERRY, ADRIENNE KENNEDY, NTOZAKE SHANGE, and future generations of talented black female artists.

Grimke was born on February 27, 1880, into a prominent biracial family. Her father, Archibald Grimke, was the black son of white slaveholder Henry Grimke and his slave Nancy Weston. Archibald would go on to receive a law degree from Harvard and to have a career as lawyer, diplomat, essayist, and vice president of the National Association for the Advancement of Colored People (NAACP). He married Sarah Stanley, a white woman of middle-class background, but when Angelina was three, her mother would abandon both her and her father.

On receiving a degree in physical education from Boston Normal School of Gymnastics (now Wellesley College), Grimke followed her father to Washington, D.C., where she taught gymnastics at Armstrong Manual Training School and then English at Dunbar High School—an institution that supported the careers of many talented writers of the Harlem Renaissance. Although Grimke mostly wrote poetry and short fiction, it is her play *Rachel* that remains her most controversial work. Written in 1916, it was produced by the NAACP as a rallying piece against D. W. Griffith's film, *Birth of a Nation*, in Washington D.C.

Rachel, one of the United States's earliest antilynching plays, centers on a young African American woman who lives in a northern city with her mother, Mrs. Loving, her brother Tom, and her adopted son Jimmy. The drama of the play centers on the internal struggles Rachel faces as she realizes the extent to which the United States's racist culture both overtly and subconsciously inflicts psychical and psychological damage not only on her loved ones, but on her whole race. By learning her mother's secret—that Rachel's father and eldest brother were lynched for publicly admonishing that very crime, Rachel, whose one desire in the world is to fulfill the ideal role of mother and house maker, realizes that the only true freedom she could have ever given her children would be to have never brought them into the world.

Grimke was part of a generation of female African American playwrights whose primary focus was to dramatize the domestic repercussions of lynching. Setting her play in a middle-class home, Grimke examines the crime of lynching as a means of exploring the overlooked gendered complexities in African American family life. The lynching of black men was not only a heinous crime directed at black manhood, it also left mothers, wives, and daughters traumatized. Through Rachel's belief in a woman's right to reproductive control, Grimke challenges the racist society she lives in, and makes an amazingly modern argument for black women.

Grimke's radical choice to have her main character decide never to have children was read by many critics as an overtly propagandistic statement of auto-genocide and was criticized by both the African American and white communities. Grimke authored a response published in the *Competitor*, an African American periodical of the early 1920s: "Since it has been understood that *Rachel* preaches racial suicide, I would emphasize that that was not my intention. To the contrary, the appeal is not primarily to colored people, but to whites." Speaking of racism as a force, a contamination from which no person of color could take one clean, deep breath, Grimke continued, "Now the purpose of *Rachel* was to show how a refined, sensitive, highly strung girl, a dreamer and an idealist, the strongest instinct in whose nature is a love for children and a desire some day to be a mother herself—how this girl would react to this force."

Knowing that theater audiences were primarily composed of educated whites, Grimke used the platform of the stage to appeal to white women. Believing that the issues behind motherhood would appeal to women's consciousness irrespective of race, her play asked mothers to consider their role beyond the private domestic sphere, as a political force. Grimke died in 1958.

[*See also* United States, 1860–1940]

PLAY: *Rachel* (1916)

FURTHER READING

Abramson, Doris E. "Angelina Weld Grimke, Mary T. Burrill, Georgia Douglas Johnson, and Marita O. Bonner: An Analysis of Their Plays." *Sage* 2, no.1 (Spring 1985).

Brown-Guillory, Elizabeth. *Their Place on the Stage: Black Women Playwrights in America*. Westport, Conn.: Greenwood Press, 1988.

Harris, Will. "Early Black Women Playwrights and the Dual Liberation Motif." *African American Review* 28, no.2 (Summer 1994).

Haskins, James. *Black Theater in America*. New York: Thomas Y. Crowell, 1982.

Hester, Michelle. "An Examination of the Relationship Between Race and Gender in an Early Twentieth Century Drama." *The Journal of Negro History* 79, no. 2 (Spring 1994).

Keyssar, Helene. "Rites and Responsibilities: The Drama of Black American Women." In *Feminine Focus: The New Women Playwrights*, ed. by Enoch Brater. New York: Oxford Univ. Press, 1989.

McKay, Nellie. "Black Theater and Drama in the 1920s: Years of Growing Pains." *Massachusetts Review* 28, no. 4 (1987).

———. "'What Were they Saying?': Black Women Playwrights of the Harlem Renaissance." In *The Harlem Renaissance Reexamined*, ed. by Victor Kramer. New York: AMS, 1987.

Storm, William. "Reactions of a 'Highly-Strung Girl': Psychology and Dramatic Representation in Angelina W. Grimke's Rachel." *African American Review* 27, no. 3 (Autumn 1993).

Jessica Kaplow Applebaum

GROTESCO CRIOLLO

In his famous preface to *Cromwell* (1827), Victor Hugo refers to modern theater as that which "links the ugly with the beautiful, the deformed with the harmonious, the grotesque with the sublime." It was in ITALY, following the premiere of LUIGI CHIARELLI's *The Mask and the Face* (*La mascara y el rostro*) in 1916, and in large part in the work of LUIGI PIRANDELLO, that this *teatro del grostesco* (THEATER OF THE GROTESQUE) took shape.

Given the flood of Italian immigrants who poured into the Argentine Republic during the first decade of the 20th century, it is not surprising that a sort of *grotesco criollo* (creole grotesque) emerged. Prefigured in comedic sketches (SAINETES), such as Carlos M. Pachero's *The Costumed* (*Los difrazados*, 1906), the masterful development of the genre is seen in the work of playwright ARMANDO DISCÉPOLO (1887–1971).

Grotesco criollo represents the internalization of the *sainete*. If indeed the *sainete*—a very popular genre in its day—is set in the patio and given over to prodigious amounts of humor and an examination of the external environment, the *grotesco criollo* concentrates its locus of action and scenery in an interior setting, the tenement house (that decrepit hovel where Buenos Aires's immigrant populations were crowded together).

The humor of the *sainetes* is replaced by the tragicomic quality of *grotesco criollo*, where the failure and the defeat of its characters strongly alludes to the general breakdown of liberal optimism, of the processes of immigration, and of the dream of "an ARGENTINA for all those that want to inhabit its soil," in the words of the Magna Carta. In this way, it serves as the elegy to liberalism's abstract universalist appeals, the criticism of an exaltation of individualistic values, and the stark portrayal of a class-based society, immersed in a crisis that the economic crash of 1929 and the military coup of 1930 would only exacerbate. It dramatizes a world where earning a living through hard work is no longer a viable option and, consequently, submerges its inhabitants in a mire of stagnation and anomie.

As bitter confirmation of the communal divisions that it saw plaguing society, *grotesco criollo* is distinguished by its opaque dialogue, riddled with the slang of Buenos Aires (the argot of those cocksure swaggerers who popularized the tango) and linguistic turns in *cocoliche* (a pidgin Spanish spoken by Italian immigrants). This approach to language creates scenarios wherein natives and immigrants merely pretend to understand one another. The impossibility of true communication (even between family members and loved ones), combined with the animalism that characterizes Discépolo's protagonists as well as the discovery that certain trade skills have become obsolete, all reveal the mechanisms of social contradiction that had been set in motion and had, by that time, come to seem irreversible.

Discépolo scripted a number of well-known *grotesco criollos*. *Mateo* (1923), based on ANTON CHEKHOV's short story "The Sadness," portrays the plight of a carriage conductor driven to desperation with the disappearance of his traditional world and the arrival of the automobile. *The Hurdy-Gurdy* (*El organillo*, 1925), written in collaboration with Enrique Santos Discépolo (1901–1951), details the process by which the immigrant Saverio becomes infected by the corruption of his environment and exploits Felipe, the hurdy-gurdy of the title. *Babylon* (*Babilonia*, 1925) paints a brutal portrait of the divisions between "those above" (the privileged classes) and "those below" (the poor). *Stefano* (1928) relates the tale of a failed musician who can no longer support his family. *Cremona* (1932) is, in the author's own words, "the story of a good man who doesn't amount to anything, as is the case with many good men." And *The Watchmaker* (*Relojero*, 1934) centers on the dissolution of the family of the brothers and protagonists, Daniel and Bautista.

Other notable *grotesco criollo* playwrights include Francisco de Filippis Novoa, Alejandro Berutti, Alberto Novión, and Rafael José de Rosa, the last of whom occasionally collaborated with Discépolo. It is also worth noting that Roberto Arlt's dramatic and narrative works are injected with certain *grotesco criollo* elements, and that Enrique Santos Discépolo masterfully adapted the genre's pessimistic streak to tango lyrics in such musical themes as "Cambalache" and "Yira Yira." Beginning in the 1960s, there was even talk of a *neogrotesco*, as seen in the work of playwrights like GRISELDA GAMBARO, Eduardo Pavlovsky, and Roberto Cossa. Yet this term applies only to the more general aesthetic characteristics of these plays and ignores the specific historical circumstances that prompted—and indeed defined—the rise of *grotesco criollo*.

FURTHER READING

Galasso, Norberto. *Discepolín y su época* [Discepolín and His Age]. Buenos Aires: Jorges Alvarez, 1967.

Ghiano, Juan Carlos. *El grotesco en Armando Discépolo* [The Grotesque in Armando Discépolo]. Buenos Aires: Ediciones Culturales Argentinas, 1965.

Kaiser-Lenoir, Claudio. *El grotesco criollo: estilo teatral de una época* [Grotesco Criollo: Theater Style of an Age]. La Habana, Cuba: Casa de Las Américas, 1977.

Ordaz, Luis. "Armando Discépolo o el 'grotesco criollo' " [Armando Discépolo and the 'Grotesco Criollo']. In *Historia de la literatura argentina. Tomo 3: Las primeras décadas del siglo* [History of Argentine Literature. Volume 3: First Decades of the Century.]. Buenos Aires: Centro Editor de América Latina, 1981.

Viñas, David. *Grotesco, inmigración y fracaso: Armando Discépolo* [The Grotesque, Immigration and Failure: Armando Discépolo]. Buenos Aires: Corregidor, 1997.

Norberto Cambiasso (Tr. by Gabriel Milner)

THE GROUP THEATRE

In 1931 a band of young actors and directors led by Harold Clurman, Lee Strasberg, and Cheryl Crawford broke away from the Theatre Guild to form their own production company. They were to function as a unified whole in all aspects of staging, adopting as their professional designation The Group Theatre.

The Group's concept as a professional theater company in which all members were equal was a new idea in the American theater. It was, however, based on the well-established tradition of the MOSCOW ART THEATRE under KONSTANTIN STANISLAVSKY, who developed the principle of ensemble acting, in which all performers were on the same level, able and willing to perform any roles, large or small. To accomplish this all actors and directors would receive the same pay, and no one could achieve dominance or stardom. As developed by the Group, with its emphasis on Stanislavsky's insistence on bringing individual life experience into each character portrayal to convey a sense of realistic immediacy, this was to become known as Method Acting.

The Group attempted to hold to two ideals: The first was the belief that the audience must become emotionally involved in the performance beyond the conventional empathetic response. The second was the firm conviction that social conditions, however deplorable, could always be improved by human action. Moreover, because the productions were to reflect the actual social patterns of the time, the Group consciously tried to avoid plays deemed too romantic or farcical.

The first production, PAUL GREEN's *The House of Connelly* (1931), displayed the Group's determination to follow their restrictive ideals, bringing them in direct conflict with the parent Theatre Guild, which had given them the play. Green's emphasis on the decadence of the South, culminating in a murder by two black retainers, was unacceptable. Green was persuaded to alter the conclusion to reflect a more promising future. The Guild did not agree, and withdrew much of its initial support. Even so, the play in its altered and more optimistic ending, had a successful, if limited, run.

Four subsequent failures during the 1931–1932 season reduced the Group to virtual penury. Claire and Paul Sifton's 1931, heralded as the first "proletarian" play, was an episodic allegory designed to shock and anger, but went nowhere. MAXWELL ANDERSON's ponderous verse TRAGEDY, *Night Over Taos*, about Spanish feudalism in New Mexico quickly faded, as did two plays attempting to expose the flaws in American society, JOHN HOWARD LAWSON's *Success Story* and Dawn Powell's *The Long Night*.

Nothing was attempted in the 1932–1933 season, but in September 1933, the Group produced SIDNEY KINGSLEY's intense naturalistic MELODRAMA, *Men in White*. This portrayal of the lives of doctors in a large metropolitan hospital amid corruption, suffering, and death seemed directly counter to the more proletarian views of many Group members, but its immediate success saved the floundering organization from oblivion. With coffers now full, the Group was able to emerge as an important part of the New York theater for the next half-dozen years.

In January 1935, the Group began its successful involvement with CLIFFORD ODETS, whose plays fit precisely into the Group's left-wing philosophy. His first, *WAITING FOR LEFTY*, was the season's sensation, presented together with Odets's heavily propagandistic anti-Nazi drama, *Till the Day I Die*, now long forgotten.

In *Waiting for Lefty* the bare stage was set with simple wooden chairs to resemble a union hiring hall, and actors planted in the audience reacted from time to time to what was occurring onstage. The illusion of an actual meeting of New York taxi drivers debating a proposal to strike was highly effective. A series of brief spotlighted vignettes performed within the circle of chairs portrayed the debilitating effect of the Depression, in the course of which one character is urged to read the *Communist Manifesto*, or better yet, to go to Russia where you will be lifted from the gutter and where everybody calls you comrade. When Lefty, the leader for whom all have been waiting, is reported murdered, the ensuing call to "Strike! Strike!" created a wave of emotion throughout the theater as audience and actors seemed ready to rush into the street and man the barricades.

In *AWAKE AND SING!* (February 1935), Odets's portrayal of a lower-middle-class family struggling against the deepening Great Depression was an excellent vehicle for the Group's principle of ensemble acting. No single character stands apart from the rest. All are equally affected by the forces of the depressed society, from the son who cannot afford a pair of black and white shoes, to the hapless father who cannot support the family, to the grandfather who sees salvation in the Communist way of life, all subjected to the true head of the household, the matriarch who desperately fights to hold everybody together. But true to the Group's philosophy, the play ends with a ringing assertion that life is worth the living if we all awake and sing as the prophet Isaiah affirms. *Paradise Lost* continues the Depression theme as the family faces eviction with their furniture out on the street. It is a bit more complicated than *Awake and Sing*, involving one son who is mixed up in criminal activity and another suffering from a fatal disease, further compounded by their father's suffering from a business partner's fraudulent dealings. The play seems to blame the Depression less and human failings more, with the open Communist line left to a minor character. And it further submits to the Group's social philosophy with a lengthy final scene in which husband and wife stand close together, declaring a positive future in which no man stands alone. The curtain descends on the Group's optimistic assertion that adversity can be conquered by human effort and determination.

The next two Odets plays, GOLDEN BOY and *Rocket to the Moon*, avoided espousing the Communist line, but both continued to emphasize the effects of the Depression. *Golden Boy* (1937), the more successful of the two, provides more dramatic emphasis on a single individual than Odets's earlier plays, centering around the young and talented violinist who is faced with a choice between the limited rewards of an artistic career and the monetary abundance of the prize ring, where his talents as a boxer bring instant gratification, but eventually destroy him. The effects of the Depression may be oblique in this case, but they still remain a powerful force.

Rocket to the Moon (1938) dwells on the drab, unpromising life of a struggling dentist involved with his attractive assistant many years his junior. He cannot afford an air conditioner for his sweltering office; she cannot afford to buy stockings. Their sorry little affair may be a symbolic rocket skyward, but it cannot succeed, and he must face a continued passionless life with a wife equally struggling to survive emotionally.

These two plays, while maintaining the Group's emphasis on a society gone awry, do not quite, in the end, live up to the positive attitude that society's ills can be countered by determined human effort. The sordid world of professional boxing can turn its participants, in one character's words, into "bums," and can kill. The clandestine office "romance" offers no way out, and the situation at the end is as depressing as that at the beginning. But these Odets plays continued to enhance the reputation of the Group, even though the financial rewards were limited. The last Odets play, *Night Music*, staged in 1940 quickly failed.

In 1936, the Group produced two highly stylized plays with strong statements against war. Paul Green's biting satire on the mindless nature of warfare in *Johnny Johnson* used for the first time on the American stage the music of Kurt Weill. A kind of innocent "natural"man forced into an army he cannot understand, Johnny attempts to end the war by subjecting the generals to laughing gas and rendering them incapable of fighting. When his plan fails, he is put in an insane asylum, suffering from "peace monomania." A far grimmer attack on war's madness was Irwin Shaw's *Bury the Dead*, in which a group of slain soldiers refuse to be buried, despite a direct order from their commanding officer to lie down and stay dead.

WILLIAM SAROYAN'S *MY HEART'S IN THE HIGHLANDS* (1939) was a short, mystical, almost dreamlike play, that made use of expressionistic staging quite removed from the Group's reliance on a realistic approach. The story of a nine-year-old boy, his impecunious poetry-writing father, and an old man who plays the title song on a bugle dwells on the point that the spiritual can overcome the material in human existence. Audiences were more than a little bewildered by it all. *Thunder Rock*, also 1938, by Robert Ardrey, ventured into metaphysical fantasy about a lighthouse inhabited by ghosts. Neither of these plays met with any particular success.

In the decade between 1931 and 1940, The Group Theatre produced twenty-three plays of widely varied nature with widely varied success. They sought to express American life as seen by American writers. Unlike the parent Theatre Guild, which long continued as a major producing company, the Group in its short and often difficult existence made its permanent mark on the American theater. Foremost, of course, was the success of the principle of ensemble acting, which produced through success and failure some of the most significant names in the business.

The most lasting impact of the Group has been the Actors' Studio, formed in 1947 by Group alumni Elia Kazan, Cheryl Crawford, and Robert Lewis. Its training of a select few in the philosophy and style of Method Acting, especially as developed by Lee Strasberg, has produced an unparalleled roster of acting talent including Marlon Brando, Eli Wallach, Robert DeNiro, Gregory Peck, and Sidney Poitier. In the area of directing and playwriting have emerged EDWARD ALBEE and DAVID MAMET.

[*See also* Political Theater in the United States; United States, 1929–1940]

FURTHER READING

Clurman, Harold. *The Fervent Years: The Story of the Group Theatre and the Thirties*. New York: Hill and Wang, 1945, 1957.

Goldstein, Malcolm. *American Drama and the Theatre of the Great Depression*. New York: Oxford Univ. Press, 1974.

Himelstein, Morgan Y. *Drama Was a Weapon: The Left Wing Theatre in New York. 1929–1941*. New Brunswick: Rutgers Univ. Press, 1963.

Smith, Wendy. *Real Life Drama: The Group Theatre and America, 1931–1940*. New York: Knopf, 1990.

Weales, Gerald. "The Group Theatre and Its Plays." In *American Theatre (Stratford-upon-Avon Studies 10)*. New York: St. Martin's Press, 1967.

Jordan Miller

GRUMBERG, JEAN-CLAUDE (1939–)

Born in Paris on July 26, 1939, French actor, playwright, and screenwriter Jean-Claude Grumberg's early life was marked by trauma. A Jew whose father was deported when he was a child, he spent the war in hiding. He did not learn until later that deportation meant death. Such revelations became the basis for much of his drama.

Grumberg entered the theater world as an actor in the company of Jacques Fabbri. He wrote his first plays in the late 1960s, quickly gaining a reputation for treating difficult subjects with a sense of humor and grace. From among these early plays, *Amorphe d'Ottenburg*, originally performed at the Odéon in 1971, has since entered the repertoire of the Comédie Française, which is unusual for a contemporary playwright. It was the first of his many plays that focused on anti-Semitism and violence in a historical context.

Known in the United States chiefly for a trilogy of plays about Jewish life before, during, and after World War II, Grumberg deals with the Holocaust in each play from a personal—yet oblique—perspective. In *Dreyfus* (1974), he manipulates theatrical time and illusion to great effect. Set in a community center in an imagined Lodz, Poland, circa 1930, the play shows a group of amateur actors attempting to stage a play about anti-Semitism in 1895 France, which is undermined by the group's personal lives, their complacence, and the apparent danger just outside the door.

In *The Workroom* (*L'Atelier*, 1976), Grumberg sets the play in a garment shop in Paris after the war where Jews and non-Jews, struggling daily to make ends meet, must cope with the aftermath of the Holocaust and its impact on their relationships.

In the third play, *The Free Zone* (*Zone Libre*, 1990), he presents the lives of a family of Jews who leave Paris in 1942 for the "free zone," the unoccupied section of south-central France. Despite the relative safety of the countryside, the family must disguise their identity. The constant threat of betrayal, however, has an uncanny effect on the family, for we see them at their best and worst. Remarkably, Grumberg presents a complete picture of their experience, finding humor and pathos in the face of disaster. His achievement is one of shifting focus from the enormity of the Holocaust to the conflicts of daily survival, which become more vivid in its shadow.

Grumberg's later plays continue to explore Jewish experience, shifting tone or context to underscore his interest in urgent social or political themes. Sometimes he deemphasizes autobiographical or realistic elements to distort the view of his subject, as in *Perchance to Dream* (*Rêver peut-être*, 1998), which involves an actor accused of murder while rehearsing Hamlet. Still, his central concern tends to be the volatile dynamics between society and the "Other."

[*See also* France]

PLAYS: *Michu* (1967); *Tomorrow, a Window on the Street* (*Domain une fenêtre sur rue*, 1968); *The Brawl* (*Rixe*, 1968); *Mathieu Legros* (1969); *Amorphe d'Ottenburg* (1971); *Dreyfus* (1974); *On the Way Back from the Fair* (*En r'venant d'l'expo*, 1975); *The Workroom* (*L'Atelier*, 1979); *On Vacation* (*Les Vacances*, 1981); *The Indian under Babylon* (*L'Indien sous Babylone*, 1983); *The Others* (*Les Autres*, 1985); *Chez Pierrot* (1990); *The Free Zone* (*Zone Libre*, 1990); *Dirty Linen* (*Linge sale*, 1992); *Commemorations* (*Commémorations*, 1994); *Mama Returns, Poor Orphan*

(*Maman revient, pauvre orphelin*, 1994); *Adam et Ève* (1997); *Perchance to Dream* (*Rêver peut-être*, 1998); *The Little Violin* (*Le Petit Violon*, for younger audiences, 1999); *Sleep, Child . . . Sleep* (*L'Enfant do*, 2002); *Marie of the Frogs* (*Marie des grenouilles*, for younger audiences, 2003)

FURTHER READING

Bradby, David. *Modern French Drama 1940–1980*. Cambridge: Cambridge Univ. Press, 1984.

Fuchs, Elinor. *Plays of the Holocaust*. New York: Theatre Communications Group, 1987.

Skloot, Robert. *The Theatre of the Holocaust*. Madison: Univ. of Wisconsin Press, 1982.

Michael Kinghorn

GUANTANAMO: "HONOR BOUND TO DEFEND FREEDOM"

Detainees, not prisoners of war.

—Donald Rumsfeld, Act 2

As part of its War on Terror, following the terrorist attacks on the UNITED STATES of September 11, 2001, the U.S. military captured hundreds of prisoners in Afghanistan, labeled them as Taliban or Al-Qaeda suspects, and herded them into indefinite detention at Guantánamo Bay, Cuba. The subtitle of *Guantanamo: "Honor Bound to Defend Freedom,"* an unusually effective political drama that opened at the Tricycle Theatre, London, in May 2004, is the slogan of the soldiers who run the Guantánamo camp. The appropriation of this phrase by the authors, journalist Victoria Brittain and novelist Gillian Slovo, is highly ironic because they lambast what they see as the United States's flagrant violation of the prisoners' human rights, including that of freedom.

There is no invented dialogue in the play. The story is narrated by numerous monologues: material derives from interviews held by the authors with former British prisoners, their families, and other interested parties; further dialogue is taken from broadcasted statements made by politicians. Donald Rumsfeld, U.S. Secretary of Defense, defends the prisoners' brutal incarceration, appearing disingenuous and bumbling, as if improvising excuses in reaction to media questions. He asserts that the men are "illegal combatants" with no entitlement to the Geneva Convention; they are "detainees, not prisoners of war."

The British prisoners have been released, but their bitterness continues: during their imprisonment without trial, they were interrogated violently, fed badly, starved of exercise and mental diversion, stuck in appalling, insect-infested cells (cages), and left baffled about the charges against them. They were released only because of their status as British citizens; other detainees are not so privileged. These events are harrowingly described by their relations, by the released prisoners themselves, and through the reading of prisoners' letters.

The play has moments of high FARCE—a British policeman's inability to take fingerprints; the naïveté of one uneducated prisoner—but the tone is always grim. Anxieties are expressed about western democracies, which the authors regard as tainted because of the U.S. government's disregard for prisoners' rights (and the British government's indifference). The possible anti-Islamic agenda of America is alleged, as is the suspicion that Guantánamo is a model for future policies. Resonant comments are made by a 9/11 victim's brother, Tom Clark. His sister would have supported a ruthless assault on the terrorists, he argues, but one handled justly to ensure that the guilty, not the innocent, suffer. The authors maintain that America's enemies actually gain support because of the brutal treatment of Muslim detainees. Another irony is articulated by a former British prisoner, Wahab Al-Rawi. His family left Iraq because of torture and persecution by Saddam Hussein's supporters. They emigrated to the West, only to find that democracies use similar methods.

After its successful Tricycle run, *Guantanamo* moved to London's larger New Ambassadors Theatre, attracting further critical and public acclaim. In August 2004, a Culture Project production of the play began at New York's 45 Bleecker Street Theatre.

FURTHER READING

Brittain, Victoria. "Questions and Lies." *The Guardian* (May 24, 2004) <www.guardian.co.uk/arts/features/story/0,11710,1223144,00.html>.

Brittain, Victoria, and Gillian Slovo. *Guantanamo: "Honor Bound to Defend Freedom."* London: Oberon, 2004.

Conover, Ted. "In the Land of Guantánamo." *New York Times Magazine* (June 29, 2003) <www.tedconover.com/gitmo.html>.

Coveney, Michael. "Why Guantanamo is a Political Play Too Far." *The Observer* (June 6, 2004) <http://observer.guardian.co.uk/review/story/0,,1232214,00.html>.

[Various]. Reviews of *Guantanamo: 'Honor Bound to Defend Freedom'*. *Theatre Record* 24, no. 11 (2004): 683–687.

Kevin De Ornellas

GUARE, JOHN (1938–)

You've got to be aware of everything on that stage, because everything on that stage is going to be called playwriting.

—John Guare, *The Playwright's Art*, 1995

John Guare was born on February 5, 1938, in New York City, and raised in the borough of Queens by parents who "liked to see shows" and often took their son with them. He also had two great uncles who had toured in vaudeville. Guare's interests in playwriting appeared early: by age eleven he had already "done a couple of plays," and local newspapers heralded him as a "prodigy." Educated at Georgetown University and the Yale School of Drama, he graduated in the early 1960s, just as the OFF-OFF-BROADWAY movement began. And so, like SAM SHEPARD, LANFORD WILSON, and other of his contemporaries, he wrote shorter plays, freely and experimentally, for performance at Caffe Cino and other Off-Off-Broadway venues.

The dramatist's first major success, the full-length *House of Blue Leaves*, opening in New York in 1971, concerns a failed tunesmith, his deranged family, and the 1965 visit of the Pope to New York. The play contains many of the signature elements of Guare's later work: a flamboyant theatricality, relentless plotting, and outrageous characters that nonetheless reveal emotional substance in extreme situations. The farcical and often violent mayhem of the plotting derives from biographical and topical experience, and the DRAMATURGY often breaks into song or direct address to the audience.

Frank Rich in the *New York Times* referred to *Six Degrees of Separation* (1990) as a "master work . . . an extraordinary high comedy." Others noted the play's intellectual pleasures, social profundity, and swirling ideas. Based on a statistical theory that everyone on earth is separated by only six other people, the play picks up on mistaken and assumed identities, class and manners, and runs with a direct-address brio and interrogatory exposition that is remarkable.

Guare's Nantucket series, a project under way from the 1980s through the early 2000s, marks a shift in focus in that biographical elements are mixed with historical material, specifically events that followed the Civil War. *Lydie Breeze* (2000), a play in two parts staged at the New York Theatre Workshop, was an extensive reworking of two dramas from the early 1980s. Depicting the experiences of three Union soldiers and a nurse who fled from the disaster of Cold Harbor to attempt a communal life on Nantucket, the drama uses 19th-century events to consider the failure of 20th-century idealism. The steady and sometimes hallucinatory plotting combines absurd humor, heartbreak, and emotional generosity.

The offstage villain in the Nantucket plays is General Ulysses S. Grant ("the butcher of Cold Harbor"), and he becomes the central figure in *A Few Stout Individuals* (2003). This play takes place in 1885, when Grant is bankrupt, living in a Manhattan brownstone, dying of throat cancer, and trying to complete his memoirs, which will hopefully provide his family with money. Barely able to speak, and often in a drug-induced hallucinatory state, he is continually "encouraged' by his wife, family, and his publisher, Samuel Clemens. Yet another character is Grant's valet, who was a soldier at Cold Harbor and is intent on revenge.

Guare's early stylistic gifts continue in his later dramas, and the range and complexity of his materials indeed allows the plays a depth and power that anchors the brio and panache of the dramatic method itself.

[*See also* United States, 1940–Present]

PLAYS: *Theatre Girl* (1959); *The Toadstool Boy* (1960); *The Golden Cherub* (1962); *Did You Write My Name in the Snow?* (1963); *To Wally Pantoni, We Leave a Credenza* (1965); *The House of Blue Leaves* (1966); *The Loveliest Afternoon of the Year* (1966); *Something I'll Tell You Tuesday* (1966); *Muzeeka* (1967); *Cop-Out* (1968); *Home Fires* (1969); *A Day for Surprises* (1970); *Kissing Sweet* (1971); *Two Gentlemen of Verona* (a rock musical after Shakespeare, with Mel Shapiro and Galt McDermott, 1971); *Optimism: or, The Misadventures of Candide* (with Harold Stone, after Voltaire, 1973); *Rich and Famous* (1974); *Marco Polo Sings a Solo* (1976); *Landscape of the Body* (1977); *Take a Dream* (1978); *Bosoms and Neglect* (1979); *In Fireworks Lie Secret Codes* (1979); *Gardenia* (1982); *The Nantucket Series: Lydie Breeze* (1982); *Women and Water* (1984); *Gluttony* (1985); *The Talking Dog* (1985); *Moon Over Miami* (1989); *Six Degrees of Separation* (1990); *Four Baboons Staring at the Sun* (1992); *The General of Hot Desire* (1998); *Chaucer in Rome* (1999); *Greenwich Mean* (1999); *Lake Hollywood* (1999); *New York Actor* (1999); *Lydie Breeze* (revised version): *Part I, Bullfinch's Mythology*; *Part II, The Sacredness of the Next Task* (2000); *A Few Stout Individuals* (2003); *His Girl Friday* (after Ben Hecht and Charles MacArthur, 2003)

FURTHER READING

Bryer, Jackson R., ed. *The Playwright's Art: Conversation with Contemporary American Dramatists*. New Brunswick, N.J.: Rutgers Univ. Press, 1995.

DiGaetani, John Louis, ed. *A Search for a Postmodern Theater: Interviews with Contemporary Playwrights*. New York: Greenwood Press, 1991.

Marranca, Bonnie, and Gautam Dasgupta, eds. *American Playwrights: A Critical Survey, Volume One*. New York: Drama Book Specialists, 1981.

Savran, David, ed. *In Their Own Words: Contemporary American Playwrights*. New York: Theatre Communications Group, 1988.

Stanley R. Richardson

GUARNIERI, GIANFRANCESCO (1934–2006)

Actor, playwright, director, screenwriter, and songwriter Gianfrancesco Sigfrido Benedetto Martinenghi de Guarnieri was born in Milan, ITALY, on August 6, 1934. His parents, renowned conductor Edoardo de Guarnieri and harpist Elza Martinenghi de Guarnieri, finding it more and more difficult to work under the fascist regime of Benito Mussolini, immigrated to BRAZIL in 1936. In the early 1950s, as a high school student in Rio de Janeiro, Guarnieri became an activist in a number of different student political organizations. In 1954, Guarnieri moved to São Paulo, and founded a theater group, Teatro Paulista do Estudante (Student Theatre of São Paulo) that would radically transform Brazilian theater through their desire to foster an awareness of national realities and to promote Brazilian culture.

It was only in 1958, with his play THEY DON'T WEAR BLACK TIE (*Eles não usam black-tie*, 1956), that Guarnieri found the way to do this. The staging of *They Don't Wear Black Tie* would be a turning point for Brazilian drama. For the first time in the history of Brazilian theater, a play brought the concerns of the working class to center stage, presenting the struggle against economic exploitation from the workers' point of view. A tremendous hit, Guarnieri's play inaugurated a wave of new works by Brazilian playwrights that focused on themes directly related to the social and political realities of the time.

Guarnieri's next play, *Gimba, President of the Brave* (*Gimba, Presidente dos valentes*, 1958), focuses on those who live on the periphery of society. It tells the story of a notorious *malandro*, Gimba, who decides to break away from his criminal past and move West with his lover, Guiô, to work as a simple farmer. Surrounded by the police at the shantytown, he surrenders and is summarily executed. A success both in Brazil and in Europe, *Gimba* won an award at the International Festival of Nations in Paris in 1960.

The Seed (*A Semente*, 1961) also deals with a labor strike. However, whereas *Black Tie* presents an idealistic view of the world, *The Seed* is a darker drama. The play lays out the difficulties of the revolutionary process, deepened by the narrow-minded policies of the Communist Party.

After the military coup in 1964, Arena staged a series of plays of resistance denouncing the political situation of the country. Together with AUGUSTO BOAL (1931), one of Arena's directors, Guarnieri wrote two musicals, *Arena Narrates Zumbi* (*Arena conta Zumbi*, 1965) and *Arena Narrates Tiradentes* (*Arena conta Tiradentes*, 1967).

After December 1968, the repression and censorship intensified dramatically with the promulgation of *Institutional Act #5* (*Ato Institucional nº 5*), a decree ending political parties and organizations, terminating the political mandates of House and Senate representatives, and exiling scores of critics of the government. Many were imprisoned, tortured and "disappeared." Guarnieri, like other playwrights, turned to what he called "theatre of occasion," that is, a theater that he would not have written under different circumstances. Making broad use of metaphors to address the political reality of Brazil, he wrote plays such as *A Shout Caught in the Air* (*Um grito parado no ar*, 1972) and *Point of Departure* (*Ponto de partida*, 1976), the latter a one-act fable in response to the 1975 torture and murder of journalist Wladimir Herzog by the regime's political police.

Recent works include *The Secret Struggle of Maria da Encarnação* (*A luta secreta de Maria da Encarnação*, 2001), a musical epic that revisits contemporary Brazilian history through the narrative of a woman's life, and a play about Che Guevara (2003). Throughout his career, Guarnieri won dozens of awards for Best Actor and Best Playwright, and in 2003 he was awarded the prestigious Vitae Foundation Fellowship to write his memoirs.

PLAYS: *They Don't Wear Black Tie* (*Eles não usam black-tie*, 1956); *Gimba, President of the Brave* (*Gimba, Presidente dos valentes*, 1958); *The Seed* (*A Semente*, 1961); *Arena Tells Zumbi's Story* (*Arena conta Zumbi*, with Augusto Boal, 1965); *Bar* (*Basta!*, 1972); *A Scream Halted in the Air* (*Um grito parado no ar*, 1972); *Starting Point* (*Ponto de partida*, 1976); *History of a Citizen Without Any Importance* (*Crônica de um cidadão sem nenhuma importância*, 1979); *The Secret Struggle of Maria da Encarnação* (*A Luta Secreta de Maria da Encarnação*, 2001)

FURTHER READING

Guarnieri, Gianfrancesco. "Depoimento." In *Depoimentos V*. Rio de Janeiro: MEC—Serviço Nacional de Teatro, 1981.

Khoury, Simon. "Entrevista com Gianfrancesco Guarnieri" [Interview with Gianfrancesco Guarnieri]. In *Atrás da áscara*, Vol. I. Rio de Janeiro: Editora Civilização Brasileira, 1984.11–72.

Magaldi, Sábato. *Um palco brasileiro—o Arena de São Paulo*. São Paulo: Editora Brasiliense, 1984.

Mostaço, Edelcio. *Teatro e política: Arena, Oficina e Opinião*. São Paulo: Proposta—Secretaria de Estado da Cultura, 1982.

Prado, Décio de Almeida. *Apresentação do teatro brasileiro moderno: crítica teatral, 1947–1955*. São Paulo: Editora Martins, 1956 (1st ed.).

——. "Guarnieri revisitado" [Guarnieri Revisited]. In *O melhor teatro de Gianfrancesco Guarnieri*. São Paulo: Global Editora, 2d ed., 2001. 5–16.

Ana Bernstein

GUERRILLA THEATER

> *The guerrilla fighter needs full help from the people of the area. . . . From the very beginning of the struggle he has the intention of destroying an unjust order and therefore an intention, more or less hidden, to replace the old with something new.*
>
> —Che Guevara, *Guerrilla Warfare*, 1961

Guerrilla Theater, a term first coined during the mid-1960s by Peter Berg, one of the writer/directors of The San Francisco Mime Troupe, is based on the philosophies of Cuban freedom-fighter Che Guevara regarding guerrilla warfare. Central to Guevara's philosophies, and to the goals of guerrilla theater, is the commitment to empower the oppressed in the fight for revolutionary sociopolitical change.

During the mid- to late-1960s, the director and founder of The San Francisco Mime Troupe, R. G. Davis, published a series of journal and magazine articles attempting to define guerrilla theater and to promote its ideas. Alternative theaters across the country quickly adopted the term to describe their own work in the l960s and 1970s, including El Teatro Campesino (Fresno), Los Angeles Bodacious Buggerilla, The Street Players Union (Boston), The City Street Theatre (New York City), The East Bay Sharks (Berkeley), The Soul and Latin Theatre (New York City), and The Concept East Theatre (Detroit).

Theater companies like these fought for a new sociopolitical order and sought to act as a voice for the populace. Though deeply influenced by ANTONIN ARTAUD's Theater of Cruelty, BERTOLT BRECHT's EPIC THEATER, and most importantly, the writings of Che Guevara, guerrilla theater grew out of specific dissatisfaction with the American government. In his articles, Davis vehemently argues that the American government promotes "superficial values" and is "oppressive, repressive, and nonaesthetic." Therefore, Davis writes, "The motives, aspirations, and practice of U.S. theater must be readapted in order to teach, direct towards change, and be itself an example of change."

According to Davis, the adaptation begins with the structure of the theater group itself. The guerrilla theater group should operate as an equal collaboration, instead of a corporate- or government-style ladder structure. Davis also insists that the group operate with a high level of morality, and that there be no distinction between private and public behavior. Ideally, the group should include members of the community in which social change is sought, promoting connection with the audience. In direct opposition to the bourgeois theater, guerrilla theater is noncommercial and explicitly for the people. Performers, directors, and designers are typically regular people, not professionals.

Throughout the 1960s and 1970s, guerrilla theater took on a wide array of sociopolitical issues, in particular protests against the Vietnam War and against capitalism. Much of the work done in the early sixties was shocking to audiences in a way that it would not be today. Performances included a high level of experimentation, nudity, profanity, and taboo subjects.

Guerrilla theater performances strip theater to its most essential requirements, the actor and the audience, using a minimum of advertising, set pieces, props, and costumes. Performances often occur in public places, such as neighborhood streets, city parks, and community centers. Therefore, the audience for guerrilla theater is the general public, many of whom have never been to the theater before. An ideal setting for guerrilla theater, according to Davis, is the university, which is not encumbered by commercialism in the same way that the professional theater is. The public setting poses some challenges, one of which is the possibility of violence, especially when the performance occurs during a large-scale protest. Davis acknowledges this possibility, but argues that theatrical representation should remain separate from real life. He writes, "When we actually cross the picket line, punch the cop, throw the real firebomb, tear down the fence, sit in front of the truck, we are not doing theater."

From its beginnings, guerrilla theater has been in a state of flux. The definition of the term itself is increasingly difficult to pin down, as the lines between guerrilla theater, alternative theater, theater of social protest, and agitation propaganda theater are blurry at best. Over time, the term has become a catchall for theater groups with sociopolitical agendas. Writing about guerrilla theater in 1970, Davis refers to the movement in the past tense. However, theater groups promoting social change throughout the world still adopt the term and its radical stance today.

[*See also* Agitation–Propaganda; Avant-Garde Drama; Living Theatre; Political Theater in the United States; Poor Theater]

FURTHER READING

Davis, R. G. *The San Francisco Mime Troupe*. Palo Alto, Ca.: Ramparts Press, 1975.

Estrin, Marc. "Guerrilla Theatre from The American Playground." *The Drama Review* 13, no. 4 (Summer 1969): 72.

Guevara, Che. *Guerilla Warfare*. New York: Monthly Review Press, 1961.

Lesnick, Henry, ed. *Guerrilla Street Theater*. New York: Bard/Avon, 1973.

Malpede, Karen Taylor, ed. *People's Theatre in Amerika*. New York: Drama Book Specialists, 1973.

Schechner, Richard. "Guerrilla Theatre: May 1970." *The Drama Review* 14, no. 3 (T47 1970):163–168 .

Schevill, James. *Break Out! In Search of New Theatrical Environments*. Chicago: Swallow Press, 1973.

Weisman, John. *Guerrilla Theater: Scenarios for Revolution*. Garden City, N. J.: Anchor Books, 1973.

Kelly Carolyn Gordon

GUGLANI, MADAN MOHAN *See* RAKESH, MOHAN

GUO MORUO (1892–1978)

Born to a wealthy and educated family in 1892 in Sichuan Province, CHINA, Guo Moruo pursued a wide range of career interests and achievements. He was an extraordinary Chinese playwright, writer, translator, poet, historian, archeologist, philologist, politician, and social activist. He was possibly the most versatile and productive Chinese intellectual of the last century. He was Chinese vice premier, the Minister of the Chinese Ministry of Culture and Education, President of the Chinese Academy of Science, and a member of the Central Committee of the Chinese Communist Party.

Guo Moruo was well trained in Chinese classics and the Confucian ideology in his childhood, as well as in science and the Western humanities. In his early twenties, he went to JAPAN where he studied medicine and became proficient in English, Latin, and German and translated many literary canonic works. He had a great penchant for foreign writers and poets including Percy Bysshe Shelley and Johann Wolfgang von Goethe, who greatly influenced his writing.

His plays were influenced by Chinese historical accounts, mostly with legendary women figures as protagonists. His plays generally centered on the subjects of nationalism, humanism, antifeudalism, heroism, woman's liberation, and ROMANTICISM. The narrative of his plays was impressively lyrical, poetic, metaphorical, philosophical, and political. The best of his theatrical writings was *Qu Yuan*, a five-act spoken drama inspired by the story of a great ancient poet (c. 343–c. 290 B.C.). In the play, the Queen of Qin (221–206 B.C.), on behalf of an evil ambassador, plotted to discredit him. Chan Juan, Qu Yuan's admirer and maid, devoted her young life to rescuing him. This love-plus-hero tearjerker extolled loyalty, self-sacrifice, nobility, and heroism, while exposing the seamy side of both the ruler and the society of the time.

Empress Wu (*Wu Zetian*), originally written in 1960 and revised from five acts to the four in 1962, was another woman-centered play, this one depicting a powerful image of the first empress in Chinese history. Neglecting the everlasting debates over this controversial figure, Guo Moruo reversed the orthodox verdict on the Empress of Tang Dynasty (B.C.E. 618–907) and celebrated her leadership and achievements in his dramatic imagination and representation. Many critics regarded Guo's theatrical eulogy of Empress Wu as, in part, his tribute to and support of Jiang Qing, the wife of Mao Zedong, the leader of China.

Guo's overwhelmed political sensibility manifested in his later theatrical works and in his other literary writings discredited him as a great playwright, particularly after the People's Republic came to power in 1949. He turned himself to the studies of history, archeology, and philology in his later years. He died on June 12, 1978, in Beijing, China.

SELECT PLAYS: *Zhuo Wenjun* (1923); *Wang Zhaojun* (1924); *Twin Flowers* (*Nie Ying*, 1925); *Gao Jianli* (1942); *Qu Yuan* (1942); *The Tiger Tally* (*Hu fu*, 1942); *Wild Cherry Blossoms* (*Tangdi zhi hua*, 1942); *The Gallbladder of the Peacock* (*Kongque dan*, 1943); *Construction* (*Zhu*, 1946); *Cai Wenji* (1959); *Empress Wu* (*Wu Zetian*, 1960); *Zheng Chenggong* (1963)

FURTHER READING

Chen Xiaomei. "Twentieth-Century Spoken Drama." In *The Columbia History of Chinese Literature*, ed. by Victor Mair. New York: Columbia Univ. Press, 2001.

Guo Moruo. *Selected Works of Guo Moruo: Five Historical Plays*. Beijing: Foreign Languages Press, 1984.

Lee, Leo Ou-fan. *The Romantic Generation of Modern Chinese Writers*. Cambridge: Harvard Univ. Press, 1973.

Roy, David Tod. *Kuo Mo-jo [Guo Moruo]: The Early Years*. Cambridge: Harvard Univ. Press, 1971.

Wagner, Rudolf. *The Contemporary Chinese Historical Drama*. Berkeley, Los Angeles, and Oxford: Univ. of California Press, 1990.

Wang Xunzhao and Lu Zhengyan, eds. *Guo Moruo Yanjiu ziliao* [The materials of Guo Moruo studies]. Beijing: Zhongguo shehui kexue chuban she, 1986.

Ping Fu

GUO QIHONG (1940–)

Born in 1940 in Chaozhou, Guangdong Province, CHINA, Guo Qihong graduated in 1961 from Zhongshan University as a student of Wang Jisi, a renowned scholar of classical Chinese plays. After graduation, he was assigned to Beijing and worked as playwright with the China Pingju Troupe (Zhongguo pingju yuan), the Beijing Jingju Troupe (Beijing jingju yuan), the Northern Kunqu Troupe (Beifang kunqu yuan), and the Beijing People's Arts Troupe (Beijing renmin yishu juyuan, the best spoken drama troupe). He has written about fifty plays in the forms of *pingju*, *kunqu*, *jingju*, and *huaju* as well as television series.

His best works are historical plays (*xinbian lishi ju*), written since the 1980s. *Reminiscences of the Southern Tang* (*Nantang yishi*), staged by the Northern Kunqu Troupe in 1987, is about Li Yu, the famous emperor poet. *Sima Xiangru*, produced by the Shanghai Kunqu Troupe in 1995, retells the well-known love story between Sima Xiangru and Zhuo Wenjun. The spoken drama *Li Bai the Poet* (*Li Bai*, *huaju*, 1991) and *The Proud Son of Heaven* (*Tian zhi jiaozi*, 1993) written for the Beijing People's Arts Troupe, focus on the Tang poet Li Bai and the Wei-Jin poet Cao Zhi, respectively. These four plays have earned the playwright, troupes, and leading actors a significant number of awards at both national and municipal levels.

Like most contemporary playwrights, Guo looks at well-known historical figures from new perspectives. At the same time his work remains faithful to the traditional cultural aura attending each personage. The best known of his plays is *Reminiscences of the Southern Tang*, which examines the value and meaning of life by comparing the success and failure between the two real historical figures: Li Yu, the last emperor of the Southern Tang Dynasty, and Zhao Kuangyin, the founding emperor of the succeeding Song Dynasty. Li Yu was a big loser, who lost his empire and was captured alive by Zhao Kuangyin, but a great lover, who has also been recognized as one of the greatest *ci* poets throughout history. Some of his best poems are still being memorized and recited by Chinese people. Zhao was historically praised as heroic and righteous. Legends and a literary story told how he, before becoming the emperor, accompanied a beautiful lady named Jing Niang for thousands of miles without making any amorous advance to her even though she was romantically suggestive.

Guo's play makes these two figures interact. Under his pen, the winner envies the loser for his true feeling in poetry and love. Though gaining a whole country, Zhao feels lonely as he witnesses the deep love between Li and Li's wife during the house arrest. It is easy for him to possess Li's beautiful empress, but Zhao can never win her heart. Out of envy and fear—because Li's poetry still inspires his former subjects not to succumb to the Song—Zhao has Li poisoned. But he immediately shows remorse and regret and orders Li's rescue, but of course, it is too late. The play shows great sympathy for the poet emperor, working some of his famous poems into the theatrical aria, and affirms the value of life and love lived and experienced by the couple overflowing with enthusiasm. As a contrast, Zhao is depicted as an emotionally suppressed human being. The question paradoxically remains: who is the real winner or loser? The play opens a new channel for multileveled interpretations or DECONSTRUCTION of the traditional value system.

Guo has also joined other playwrights in a new trend of adapting Western classics into *xiqu* plays. He wrote *Thebes* (*Tebai cheng*) for a large production by the Beijing Heibei Bangzi Troupe in 2002. Based on Aeschylus's *Seven against Thebes* and Sophocles's *Antigone*, the play sets the story in the Spring and Autumn and combines Chinese poetry, costume, and acting style with the concepts of Greek TRAGEDY.

Guo's plays have been praised by most critics for the literary quality in their lyrics and content. His drama reads as well as it plays.

SELECT PLAYS: *Sima Qian the Historian* (*Sima Qian*, *jingju*, 1979); *Pingju Opera Star* (*Pingju huanghou*, *pingju*, 1983); *Reminiscences of the Southern Tang* (*Nantang yishi*, *kunqu*, 1986); *Li Bai the Poet* (*Li Bai*, *huaju*, 1991); *The Proud Son of Heaven* (*Tian zhi jiaozi*, *huaju*, 1993); *Sima Xiangru* (*kunqu*, 1994); *Thebes* (*Tebai cheng*, *Hebei bangzi*, 2002)

FURTHER READING

Guo Qihong. *Guo Qihong juzuo xuan* [Selected Plays by Guo Qihong]. Beijing: Zhongguo xiju chubanshe, 1992.

——. *Tebai cheng* [Thebes]. *Xin juben* [New Playscripts] 5 (2002)—: 4–14.

Xie Boliang. "Guo Qihong de lishi renwu ju" [Guo Qihong's Plays of Historical Figures]. In *Zhongguo Dangdai xiqu wenxue shi* [A History of the Contemporary Xiqu Literature]. Beijing: Zhongguo shehui kexue chubanshe, 1995. 285–294.

Wenwei Du

GUO SHIXING (1953–)

Guo Shixing, a prominent Chinese playwright, was born in Beijing, CHINA, in 1953. As with a majority of his contemporaries, Guo's education was interrupted by the Cultural Revolution (1966–1976). He had barely finished his middle school when he was assigned to do farm work in Helongjiang Province in 1969. Returning to Beijing in 1973, Guo worked in a factory from 1974 to 1979. For the next fifteen years, he served as a staff correspondent covering cultural events for *Beijing Evening News* (*Beijing wanbao*). This experience allowed him to participate in, among other things, GAO XINJIAN's theater experiments as a witness and critic, which led to his friendship with Gao and continuous cooperation with Lin Zhaohua, the director of Gao's experimental work of the 1980s.

In 1989, Guo Shixing finished writing his first play *Fishman*, which was not approved for public performance until 1997. His first three plays, known as *Trilogy of Dilettantes* (*Xianren sanbuqu*), were directed by Lin Zhaohua: *Birdmen* (*Niaoren*) in 1991, *Chessman* (*Qiren*) in 1994, and *Fishman* (*Yuren*) in 1997. In 1994, Guo Shixing was appointed the scriptwriter for the Beijing Experimental Theater (renamed the National Theater Company of China in 2002). His more recent plays include *A Street of Bad Talk* (*Huaihua yitiaojie*, 1998) and *Toilet* (*Cesuo*, 2004).

Guo Shixing appears to many as a successor to LAO SHE. Like Lao She, Guo Shixing draws his characters and themes locally (in most of his plays) and takes his departure point from the specifics of everyday life. His *Trilogy of Dilettantes* in particular focuses on leisurely activities such as fishing, chess playing, and birdkeeping, activities that have provided traditional entertainment for Beijing residents. The comparison, however, ends here. Guo shuns the slice-of-life representation that characterizes Lao She's theater. Instead, he makes psychological, cultural, and environmental inquiries into everyday life. According to Guo Shixing, he owes a major source of inspiration to *Zen Buddhism and Psychoanalysis* co-authored by D. T. Suzuki and E. Fromm and to the plays of FRIEDRICH DÜRRENMATT. Dürrenmatt-style paradox is fondly used as a framing structure in Guo Shixing's plays, which question the norms of Chinese culture. His *Trilogy of Dilletantes*, for example challenges the very idea of leisurely pursuit or dilettantism, which in Chinese culture is conceptually associated with individual freedom. His plays illustrate the intricate relationship between individual agency and submission that underlies leisure culture, hobbies, or dilettantes.

In *Chessman*, for example, the chessmaster has confined himself for fifty years to the world of chess, in which he looks for self-fulfillment. When he eventually examines his experience in perspective, he is shocked to discover that the chess table he presides over actually controls his life. The chessman concludes that he has sacrificed too much to become a connoisseur: "I have warmed up the stone-carved chess set with fifty years of my life while my own flesh is turning cold." Paradoxically, he allows chess to be his master because of his aspiration for independence. Guo Shixing describes his plays as allegorical, indicating that this paradox has wider cultural and existential applications and is by no means limited to chess games. Indeed, with the exception of *Toilet*, temporal space is rarely specified in Guo Shixing's plays.

Guo Shixing is the most insightful and innovative playwright in mainland China since Gao Xingjian. Gao Xingjian strove to blur the boundary between realistic and symbolic theater in his attempt to create an alternative theater to the social realist mode of stage presentation. Consequently, a hybridized theater that blends different theatrical conventions, as well as dramatic and nontheatrical arts, has been widely practiced in China since the mid-1980s. In contrast, Guo revisits and revitalizes the verbal theater with cultural and existential inquiries as well as drives critics to redefine what can be represented on the stage by presenting hobbies, language and toilets as subjects. His works are both highly acclaimed and criticized in China for the challenges they present to critics, among other audiences.

SELECT PLAYS: *Birdmen* (*Niaoren*, 1991); *Chessman* (*Qiren*, 1994); *Fishman* (*Yuren*, 1997); *A Street of Bad Talk* (*Huaihua yitiaojie*, 1998); *Toilet* (*Cesuo*, 2004)

FURTHER READING

Cheung, Martha, and Jane Lai, eds. *An Oxford Anthology of Contemporary Chinese Drama*. Hong Kong: Oxford Univ. Press, 1997.

Conceison, Claire. "The Occidental Other on the Chinese Stage: Cultural Cross-Examination in Guo Shixing's *Bird Man*." *Asian Theatre Journal* 15, no. 1 (Spring 1990): 87–100.

Donghui He

GURNEY, A. R. (1930–)

The people I write about are not as threatening as they once were. They're now perceived as another ethnic group. They're no longer thought to hold the keys to the kingdom.

—A. R. Gurney, 1983

American playwright Albert Ramsdell (A. R.) Gurney, Jr., was one of the most prolific and successful American playwrights of the second half of the 20th century. Gurney was born on November 1, 1930, in Buffalo, New York, and after serving in the Korean War, he enrolled in the Yale School of Drama in 1955.

At Yale, A. R. Gurney began to develop a singular American theatrical voice focused on the White Anglo-Saxon Protestant (WASP) culture of the Northeast. His earliest efforts included

Love in Buffalo (1958), which was the first musical ever produced at Yale. His first New York production was *The David Show* in 1968. In 1971, his play *Scenes From An American Life* was awarded a Drama Desk Award. The play is a collection of comic vignettes aimed at the powerful elite of 20th-century America. Gurney had his first major commercial success with *The Dining Room* in 1982. Like much of Gurney's work, *The Dining Room* mixes both humor and pathos with a vivid theatrical imagination. Focused on the elite WASP culture of New England, the play consists of eighteen vignettes in which six actors play over fifty roles. As the vignettes unfold, Gurney's detailed insight into American ritual and this dying culture becomes increasingly apparent. Both wryly comic and touchingly human, the play ran for 552 performances OFF-BROADWAY.

In 1988, Gurney had several successes. Both *Love Letters* and *The Cocktail Hour* opened successfully in New York. Begun by Gurney as a writing exercise, *Love Letters* would develop into one of the most produced plays of the 1990s. The two-person play follows an evolving and complex fifty-year relationship between a lawyer and an artist, without the aid of a complex set or design elements. The two actors simply sit side by side at a desk and read the play. The accessibility and purity of the play has attracted numerous celebrities in productions worldwide. *The Cocktail Hour* revisits the themes of generational and family conflict in a New England family during the 1970s, focusing on a young playwright and his parents.

Gurney's award-winning COMEDY *Sylvia* (1995) presents the character of an aggressive dog that comes between a man and his wife. The play found both commercial and critical success. Other notable works include *Another Antigone* (1986), *The Golden Age* (1981), *The Middle Ages* (1977), *Far East* (1998), *A Cheever Evening* (1994), and the libretto for *Strawberry Fields* (1999). More recently in *The Fourth Wall* (2001) and *O Jerusalem* (2003), Gurney successfully uses his theatrical agility to concentrate on contemporary political and social issues in America, as well as the conventions of theater itself. More overtly political than his previous work, these plays mark yet another stage in the steady evolution of a singular American artist. In addition to commercial success, Gurney has been awarded an Obie and two Lucille Lortel awards, as well as awards from the National endowment for the Arts, the Rockefeller Foundation, and the New England Theatre Conference.

[*See also* United States, 1940–Present]

PLAYS: *Three People* (1956); *Love in Buffalo* (1958); *Turn of the Century* (1958); *The Bridal Dinner* (1962); *The Comeback* (1965); *The David Show* (1966); *The Rape of Bunny Stuntz* (1966); *The Golden Fleece* (1968); *The Open Meeting* (1969); *The Problem* (1969); *The Love Course* (1970); *Scenes From American Life* (1970); *The Old One-Two* (1973); *Children* (1974); *Who Killed Richard Cory?* (1976); *The Middle Ages* (1977); *The Wayside Motor Inn* (1977); *The Golden Age* (1981); *What I Did Last Summer* (1981); *The Dining Room* (1982); *Another Antigone* (1986); *The Perfect Party* (1986); *Sweet Sue* (1986); *The Cocktail Hour* (1988); *Don't Fall for the Lights* (1988); *Love Letters* (1988); *White Walls* (1988); *The Old Boy* (1991); *The Snow Ball* (1991); *Later Life* (1993); *Cheever Evening* (1994); *Sylvia* (1995); *Overtime* (1997); *Far East* (1998); *Labor Day* (1998); *Ancestral Voices* (1999); *Strawberry Fields* (1999); *Buffalo Gal* (2001); *Fourth Wall* (2001); *O Jerusalem* (2003); *Strictly Academic* (2003); *Big Bill* (2004)

FURTHER READING

Arvid Sponberg. *A. R. Gurney*. New York: Routledge, 2003.

Ellen Anthony-Moore and Christopher Moore

GUSTAV VASA

Gustav Vasa, a historical play in five acts by AUGUST STRINDBERG, was first performed at Svenska teatern in Stockholm, SWEDEN, in 1899, and published the same year. It is the second part of the so-called Vasa trilogy, following MASTER OLOV (1872).

Using William Shakespeare as a precedent, Strindberg noted when he wrote *Master Olof* that a historical drama does not essentially differ from a contemporary one. As he would later state (Strindberg, 1909):

> Even in the historical drama, the purely human is of major interest, and history the background; souls' inner struggle awaken more sympathy than the combat of soldiers or the storming of walls; love and hate, torn family ties, more than treaties and speeches from the throne.

King Gustav Vasa (c. 1495–1560), liberator and founder of the Swedish national state, was much admired by Strindberg, who portrayed him in several of his works. About his role in the play bearing his name, Strindberg writes in his *Open Letters to the Intimate Theater*:

> The destiny of Gustav Vasa begins like a legend or a miracle story, develops into an epic, and is impossible to survey completely. To get this gigantic saga into one drama is impossible, of course. Therefore the only answer was to find an episode. That was the one centering in the rebellion led by Dacke. The king was then in his second marriage with children by two wives, and at the height of his power. But Providence wanted to test him and temper its man, to whom the building of the kingdom was entrusted, and for that reason it struck him with all the misfortunes of Job. That time of despair gives one the best opportunity to depict the great human being Gustav Vasa with all his human weaknesses.

The so-called bell feud (1532–1533) and its consequences dominate the first part of the drama, whereas the circumstances around the Dacke rebellion (1542–1543) prevail in the latter part. These events, covering some ten years, have been compressed to occur in five days between autumn and midsummer.

In *Gustav Vasa* political issues alternate with private ones. The political issues dominate in acts 1, 3, and 5, which concern the king's dealings with the people of the province of Dalarna, with the merchants of Lübeck—both groups claiming "to have provided Sweden with a king," and with the people of the province of Småland, Dacke's province. The private issues are addressed in acts 2 and 4 in the form of three father-son relationships—Gustav and Erik, Herman and Jakob, Olaus and Reginald—as well as in the erotic relationships between Jakob and Agda and between Erik and Karin. Whereas the erotic relations are rather loosely tied to the main action, the sons' rebellion against their fathers mirror the central conflict of the play between the father of the nation and his defiant subjects.

The prolonged wait for the king's judgment in act 1, for his own appearance in act 3, and for the peripety effectuating a good nemesis at the end of the play, are some of the more spectacular elements in *Gustav Vasa*, the most popular and best constructed of Strindberg's historical dramas.

FURTHER READING

Johnson, Walter. *Strindberg and the Historical Drama*. Seattle: Univ. of Washington Press, 1963. 94–113.

Lamm, Martin. *August Strindberg*, tr. and ed. by Harry G. Carlson. New York: Blom, 1971. 327–358.

Ollén, Gunnar. *Strindbergs dramatic [Strindberg's Plays]*. Stockholm: Sveriges Radios förlag, 1982.

Strindberg, August. *Öppna bref till Intima Teatern [Open Letters to the Intimate Theater]*. Stockholm: Björck & Börjesson, 1909.

Egil Törnqvist

DER GUTE MENSCH VON SEZUAM See THE GOOD WOMAN OF SETZUAN

GUY DOMVILLE

On Saturday, January 5, 1895, HENRY JAMES's play *Guy Domville*, opened at London's St. James Theatre. James was a well-established novelist, critic, and short-story writer by the time he began *Guy Domville* in June 1893, but sales for his novels were dwindling and he hoped for a financial success. Although he had written a small number of plays, until then, he had had no real success in drama. One of the dozen completed plays James produced over his career, *Guy Domville* was a turning point in James's later development as a writer.

James's philosophy of playwriting came from the ideas of 19th-century French dramatist Eugene Scribe and the critic Francoise Sarcy about the "well-made play." This form has a strict structure that unfolds through cause and effect; the protagonist experiences good and bad fortune alternatively; the subject must be important, such as adversity between the sexes; there is usually a secret and a misunderstanding; the end of the play must resolve all issues. *Guy Domville* follows this formula.

Set in the West of England in 1780, the play examines the tension between a man dedicated to high, pure ideals and the corrupting nature of society. It opens and closes at Porches, the country home of the young widow Mrs. Peverel. The second act is set in Richmond at the Domville estate. On the eve of Guy's departure for Bristol, where he is to take up his vows as a priest in the Catholic Church, Lord Devenish arrives to announce the death of Guy's distant relative, leaving Guy the last of the Domvilles. He begs Guy to abandon the Church and marry, so the family will not die out.

Mrs. Peverel had employed Domville as a tutor for her son Geordie, and although Guy and Mrs. Peverel feel passion for one another, his dedication to a monastic life had prevented them both from declaring their feelings. Frank Humber, Mrs. Peverel's neighbor, is courting the widow, who has been holding him in abeyance. Humber asks Guy to plead his case with the widow, which Guy does. Meanwhile, unbeknownst to Guy, Devenish has promised to marry the widow Domville if she can get Guy to marry her daughter Mary. Mary does not know yet that Devenish is really her father. Mary is in love with a naval lieutenant, George Round, but her mother and Devenish have thwarted the affair.

In act 2, Guy, who has become more sophisticated in the ways of the world, is about to wed Mary. Round appears and Mary breaks off with Guy after telling him the truth. In act 3, Guy returns to Porches, and for a moment, it appears that he has come to proclaim his love to Mrs. Peverel. Instead, he declares his intention to return to the Church, and the play ends without us knowing if Mrs. Peverel will accept Humber.

James frustrated the audience's romantic notion that Domville should find happiness in love. The idea that he would renounce worldly pleasure and live as an ascetic dedicated to sacred ideals did not fit their notion of an evening's entertainment. Although James would continue to write occasionally for the stage, after *Guy Domville*, he focused largely on writing fiction.

[*See also* England, 1860–1940]

FURTHER READING

Edel, Leon. "Henry James: The Dramatic Years" and "*Guy Domville*, Editor's Foreword." In *The Complete Plays of Henry James*, ed. by Edel. Philadelphia and New York: Lippincott, 1949.

——. *The Life of Henry James. The Middle Years: 1882–1895*. Philadelphia and New York: Lippincott, 1962.

——. *The Life of Henry James: The Treacherous Years: 1895–1901*. Philadelphia and New York: Lippincott, 1969.

James, Henry. *Guy Domville: Play in Three Acts*. Philadelphia and New York: Lippincott, 1960.

Murphy, Brenda. "James's Later Plays: A Reconsideration." *Modern Language Studies* 13, no. 4 (Fall 1983): 86–95.

Ellen Rosenberg

H

HAI RUI BAGUAN, JINGJU

See Hai Rui's Dismissal

HAI RUI'S DISMISSAL

Hai Rui's Dismissal (*Hai Rui baguan, jingju*), a Beijing opera by Wu Han (1909–1969), a prominent historian and deputy mayor of Beijing in 1966, depicts the cause and process of Hai Rui's (1515–1587) dismissal from office from June 1569 to January 1570. An honest and upright official of the Ming dynasty and widely known for his bravery and impartiality in his fight against the corrupt officials of the time, Hai Rui was appointed Censor-in-Chief of Nanjing. He went to the post in plain clothes and learned of a number of serious offenses by Xu Ying, son of Xu Jie, a retired prime minister who once pleaded for Hai Rui's release when Hai Rui offended the emperor. After a thorough investigation, Hai Rui found Xu Ying guilty and ordered his death to redress the wrong and to uphold justice. Failing to persuade Hai Rui after repeated efforts, Xu Jie resorted to bribery with his connections in the capital and finally had Hai Rui replaced by Dai Fengxiang. As Dai and Hai confronted each other toward the end of the play, Hai Rui insisted on executing Xu Ying before he handed over his official seal. The play thus ends with Xu Ying executed as Hai Rui left office.

The play was largely faithful to the historical fact with only some minor changes (e.g., history records that Xu Ying was banished, not executed) to stress Hai Rui's resolve in fighting against official corruption. It was first staged in Beijing in February 1961 and again in 1965. The production of the play coincided with the internal struggle among senior Chinese Communist party officials, particularly between Mao Zedong and the then defense minister Peng Dehuai. After Peng wrote to Mao, complaining about the latter's economic policy during the Great Leap Forward, he was dismissed for his "anti-Party activities." As a result, the play was regarded by some as a veiled critique of Mao, a charge that even Mao himself acknowledged on December 21, 1965, when he remarked that

> . . . the crux of *Hai Rui's Dismissal* was the question of dismissal from office. The Emperor Jiaqing (of the Ming Dynasty, 1522–1566) dismissed Hai Rui from office. In 1959 we dismissed Peng Dehuai from office. And Peng Dehuai is "Hai Rui," too.

A Mao-endorsed newspaper article by Yao Wenyuan, one of "the Gang of Four," accused Wu Han of using the past to satirize the present, which was widely regarded as the opening shot of the Cultural Revolution. With the publication of Yao's article, an initially academic debate about the merits and demerits of the historical play was quickly turned into a political campaign. Wu Han, as a victim of the campaign, was cruelly persecuted to death on October 11, 1969.

[*See also* China]

FURTHER READING

Ansley, Clive M. *The Heresy of Wu Han: His Play "Hai Jui's Dismissal" and Its Role in China's Cultural Revolution.* Toronto: Univ. of Toronto Press, 1971.

Pusey, James R. *Wu Han: Attacking the Present through the Past.* Cambridge: Harvard Univ. Press, 1969.

Smith, Chester Leo, ed. *The Dismissal of Hai Jui: An Epic Tragedy, by and of Wu Han.* Los Angeles: Bede, 1968.

Unger, Jonathan. *Using the Past to Serve the Present: Historiography and Politics in Contemporary China.* Armonk, N.Y.: M. E. Sharpe, 1993.

Wagner, Rudolf G. *The Contemporary Chinese Historical Drama: Four Studies.* Berkeley: Univ. of California Press, 1990.

Yao Wenyuan. "On the New Historical Play *Hai Rui's Dismissal.*" *Wenhuibao* (November 10, 1965).

Hongchu Fu

THE HAIRY APE

> *Aw, yuh make me sick! Yuh don't belong!*
> —Yank, Scene 1

After The Emperor Jones (1920), *The Hairy Ape* was Eugene O'Neill's second major experiment with expressionism, and it demonstrated his interest in Georg Kaiser's From Morning to Midnight (1916). In a letter to Kenneth Macgowan (December 24, 1921), O'Neill wrote:

> I don't think the play as a whole can be fitted into any of the current "isms." It seems to run the whole gamut from extreme naturalism to extreme expressionism—with more of the latter than the former. I have tried to dig deep in it, to probe in the shadows of the soul of man bewildered by the disharmony of his primitive pride and individualism at war with the mechanistic development of society. (Bogard, 1988)

The Provincetown Players produced the play on March 9, 1922, with Louis Wolheim in the role of Yank.

In the firemen's forecastle of an ocean liner, drunk, half-naked men are packed together like animals. "The treatment of this scene, or of any other scene in the play, should by no means be naturalistic. The effect sought after is a cramped space in the bowels of a ship, imprisoned by white steel . . . The ceiling crushes down upon the men's heads. They cannot stand upright."

Yank is "broader, fiercer, more truculent, more powerful, more sure of himself than the rest," and the others fear and respect him. He favors whiskey over beer, sailing ships over steamers, and home over the forecastle. He has no patience with class consciousness and "Salvation Army-Socialist bull."

On the promenade deck, Mildred describes herself as "a waste product in the Bessemer process," the wealthy granddaughter of a steel baron who uses her influence to insist on a tour of the stokehole. The heat of the furnaces quickly melts her arrogance, and as Yank rails against the officer who blows the signal whistle, beating his chest like a gorilla, she whimpers, "Oh, the filthy beast!"

Back in the forecastle, Yank ponders what he senses is a profound insult, and another man suggests that she reacted as though she'd seen a hairy ape escaped from the zoo. Yank embraces the name, but he resolves to confront the "skoit" that gave it to him.

Yank undertakes a journey through New York, outraging the Fifth Avenue gentry, crossing the membership of the waterfront office of the International Workers of the World, and finishing at the zoo, where he frees a gorilla that crushes him to death. Yank insists on the validity and primacy of sheer power: steel, dynamite, and the engines that drive the ships. Yet he searches for a way to "belong," to fit in, and as he dies in the gorilla cage, the directions read, "And, perhaps, the Hairy Ape at last belongs." In O'Neill's vision, the machine inevitably uses people and so reduces them to cogs; his is a highly deterministic perspective that leaves little room for hope or freedom.

Stark Young called the play "a fine example of dramatic rhythm" (Houchin, 1993) and Alexander Woollcott described it as "a bitter, brutal wildly fantastic play of nightmare hue and nightmare distortion" (Miller, 1965).

[*See also* United States, 1860–1929]

FURTHER READING

Bak, John S. "Eugene O'Neill and John Reed: Recording the Body Politic, 1913–1922." *Eugene O'Neill Review* 20 (Spring–Fall 1996):17–35.

Bogard, Travis. *Contour in Time: The Plays of Eugene O'Neill*. New York: Oxford Univ. Press, 1972. Rev. ed. New York: Oxford Univ. Press, 1988.

Houchin, John H., ed. *The Critical Response to Eugene O'Neill*. Westport, Conn.: Greenwood Press, 1993.

Miller, Jordan Y. *Playwright's Progress: O'Neill and the Critics*. Chicago: Scott, Foresman, 1965.

Murray, Keat. "O'Neill's *The Hairy Ape* and Rodin's 'The Thinker'." *Journal of Evolutionary Psychology* 19 (March 1998): 108–115.

Nickel, John. "Racial Degeneration and *The Hairy Ape*." *Eugene O'Neill Review* 22 (Spring–Fall 1998):33–40.

Plunka, Gene A. "Eugene O'Neill's *The Hairy Ape* and the Legacy of Andrew Carnegie." *Eugene O'Neill Review* 23 (Spring–Fall 1999): 31–48.

Jeffrey D. Mason

HALAC, RICARDO (1935–)

Ricardo Halac was born in Buenos Aires in 1935 and grew to become a highly prominent figure in the Argentine theater of the dictatorial period, 1976 to 1983. He addresses the social anguish and feeling of failure experienced by the Argentine people in 1973 during the disappointing period of *Peronismo* and the *coup d'état* that occurred a few years later in 1976. Halac criticizes the middle class for lacking a vision of the future and for holding an individualistic conception of success.

His theater introduced an aesthetic debate about DECONSTRUCTION in the social sector. The theater, according to Halac, must construct a polyvalent world in which society changes according to a level of fair and egalitarian values. Halac was influenced by BERTOLT BRECHT's didactic sense of theater. Brecht exercised a tremendous influence in Halac after they met in 1957 in Berlin, where Halac studied on a grant from the Goethe Institute. Artistically, Halac also breaks with the "imitative logic" or realistic strategy of the theater that preceded him and, through playful dialogue, elevates his own theater to a new artistic level.

Initially considered part of a reflexive, social REALISM movement, Halac started to win recognition in ARGENTINA in 1961 with his first play *Loneliness for Four* (*Soledad para cuatro*). He progressively evolved toward a more critical social realism, with his two plays, *End of December* (*Fin de Diciembre*, 1965) and *Star of Dawn* (*Estela de Madrugada*, 1965), borrowing from traditional and modern theatrical genres such as the Theater of the Absurd, EXPRESSIONISM, and the Spanish SAINETE. His main contribution resides in his idea of criticizing the social concerns by invoking the *GROTESCO CRIOLLO*, a grotesque interpretation of Argentine contemporary society.

Halac was very active in the 1970s. In 1971 he began writing for the leftist newspaper *La opinion* in addition to plays and novels. In 1975 he became involved in the visual media, adapting to the screen his own novel *The Single Man* (*El soltero*, 1977), a metaphor of freedom. After he filmed the movie and appeared on a television program, he received a death threat and emigrated to MEXICO.

Halac's play *The Weaning* (*El destete*, 1977), which premiered in 1978, reveals the failure of his generation to stop the ascension to power of the right-wing dictatorship. The political dimension of life during this period, "the process," is revealed in *A Wonderful Job* (*Un trabajo fabuloso*, 1978), a harsh and realistic play about a father forced to prostitute himself as a transvestite. From this time forward, Halac's works became an inspiration to groups like Teatro Abierto, which Halac helped create and develop. It grew into a cultural movement that worked successfully to undermine the dictatorship and to encourage the ideal of democracy. The Argentine government censored Halac's 1982 play, *The Silver Pearl* (*La perla del plata*), for its criticism of the dictatorship. During this time, Halac also wrote *Noise of Broken Chains* (*Ruido de Rotas Cadenas*, 1983), which speaks about the new class of poor and outcast Argentines that emerged after the military dictatorship, and *Far Away Promised Land* (*Lejana Tierra prometida*, 1982), an allegory of the mothers of Plaza de Mayo and their struggle to retrieve their "disappeared" children.

With the advent of democracy in Argentina, Halac was named Director Nacional de Teatro and Director del Teatro Nacional Cervantes. Halac is currently heavily involved in promoting theater in Argentina.

SELECT PLAYS: *Loneliness for Four* (*Soledad para cuatro*, 1961); *End of December* (*Fin de Diciembre*, 1965); *Star of Dawn* (*Estela de Madrugada*, 1965); *Second Time* (*Segundo tiempo*, 1976); *The Single Man* (*El soltero*, 1977); *The Weaning* (*El destete*, 1977); *A Wonderful Job* (*Un trabajo fabuloso*, 1978); *Far Away Promised Land* (*Lejana Tierra prometida*, 1982); *Noise of Broken Chains* (*Ruido de Rotas Cadenas*, 1983); *The Sosa Echagüe Duet* (*El duo Sosa Echagüe*, 1986); *Long Live Anarchy* (*Viva la anarquía*, 1992); *One Thousand Years, One Day* (*Mil años, un día*, 1993); *Frida Kahlo, the Passion* (*Frida Kahlo, la pasión*, 1996); *Gypsy Moon* (*Luna Gitana*, 2002)

FURTHER READING

Arancibia, Juana, and Zulema Mirkin, eds. *Teatro argentino durante el proceso, 1976–1983* [*Argentine Theater During the Process, 1976–1983*]. Buenos Aires: Vinciguerra, 1992.

Banham, Martin, ed. *The Cambridge Guide to the Theatre*. Cambridge: Cambridge Univ. Press, 1995.

Giella, Miguel Angel. "Teatro Abierto 1981: de la desilusión a la alienación" ["Open Theater 1981:From Disillusion to Alienation"]. In *De Dramaturgos: Teatro Latinoamericano Actual* [*Of Playwrights: Contemporary Latin American Theater*], ed. by Giella. Buenos Aires: Ediciones Corregidor, 1994.

Glickman, Nora, and Gloria F. Waldman, eds. *Argentine Jewish theater: a critical anthology*. London: Associated Univ. Presses, 1996.

Pellettieri, Osvaldo. "Ricardo Halac y sus veinticinco años de realismo" ["Ricardo Halac and His Twenty Five Years of Realism"]. *Latin American Theatre Review* (Spring 1987).

Woodyard, George. "Making America or Making Revolution: the Theatre of Ricardo Halac in Argentina." In *Theatre Matters, Performance and Culture in World Stage*, ed. by Richard Boon and Jane Plastow. London: Cambridge Univ. Press, 1998.

Juana Arancibia and Benito Gómez

HALFWAY HOUSE

MOHAN RAKESH's third and last complete full-length play, *Halfway House* (*Aadhe Adhure*), was written in 1968. Its first performance by the theater group Dishantar was held on March 2, 1969, in Delhi. The play has since been translated into many Indian languages as well as English and may be the most produced play in INDIA over the last thirty years. This is because of its theme, its apparently simple but very sharp diction, its immense theatrical potential, its small cast of two men and three women, and its modest production requirements.

Halfway House narrates the story of one household—husband, wife, two daughters, and a son who are condemned to live together in the same hell. The husband has gone to seed and has become a parasite on his wife, who is so disgusted with him in particular and with life in general that she desperately gropes for some exit from her hell. The eldest daughter has been married for some time, but her condition replicates her mother's. The younger daughter is constantly provoked to throw tantrums because of the overwrought atmosphere in the home. The son is pent up with rage and hatred for everyone.

The play is about the values that govern this family, and the class to which this family belongs. With an incisive scalpel, Rakesh exposes the utter rottenness of the value system that governs the middle class. At one point, the husband leaves the house in complete disgust, perhaps with the intention of never returning to its hell. Toward the end of the play, a conversation takes place between the wife and a Fourth Man:

> Fourth Man: He [husband] won't come back. He's weak, but not that weak. He is attached to you, but not that attached. He's not as helpless either, as he thinks. If he'd look around he would see that a whole world is before him. I'll try and open his eyes to it.
>
> Woman: Do, please do. You'll not only help him, you will also be helping me.

Before the Fourth Man completes his next dialogue, the son enters and asks for the walking stick for his father, who has returned.

Its agony is reminiscent of EUGENE O'NEILL's *LONG DAY'S JOURNEY INTO NIGHT* and its brutal bickering of EDWARD ALBEE's *WHO'S AFRAID OF VIRGINIA WOOLF?*. Through a brilliant theatrical device Rakesh makes another very significant point that would not have been possible had he treated the play in a strictly realistic fashion: the actor who speaks the prologue also plays four other men, including the husband. This illustration, that the same man can put on different masks depending on the situation in which he finds himself, lifts the "area of experience" to a much higher plane.

The two most remarkable qualities of *Halfway House* are Rakesh's success in capturing a fundamental truth about the Indian middle class and the intensely dramatic language he employs. The simple diction has a powerful effect. Because of these two qualities, the critic J. D. Sethi rightly said that *Halfway House* breaks new ground in dramatic literature.

FURTHER READING

Jain, N. C. "Some Recent Significant Plays." *Enact* 25, 26 (January, February 1969).

Kumar, Nita N. "*Halfway House*: A House Divided." In *Many Indias Many Literatures*, ed. by Shormishtha Panja. Delhi: Worldview Publications, 1999.

Nigam, R. L. "*Aadhe Adhure*: A Comment." *Enact* 32–33 (August–September 1969).

Rakesh, Mohan. "Why Plays?" *Enact* 13, 14 (January, February 1968).

——. *Halfway House*. Ed. by Dilip K. Basu and tr. by Biindu Batra. New Dehli: Worldview Publications, 1999.

Sethi, J. D. "Rakesh's *Aadhe Adhure*: A Breakthrough." *Enact* 27 (March 1969).

Rajinder Nath

HALL, ROGER (1939–)

Roger Hall has written a series of boulevard COMEDIES in the vein of Alan Ayckbourn and NEIL SIMON and become NEW ZEALAND's most commercially successful playwright. Although his best work achieves complex, even poignant characterization and witty dialogue, he can settle for the stereotypes and easy one-liners typical of the stage revues and television satire to which he contributed in the 1960s and 1970s. From 1977 to 1995 he taught playwriting at the University of Otago.

After writing several pieces of television drama, Hall turned to stage plays in the mid 1970s. His first two plays remain his greatest successes. *Glide Time* (1977), set in the stores department of a branch of the public service, ensured the financial security of both Playmarket and Wellington's fledgling Circa Theatre and then received another thirteen productions in its first year. It spawned several radio and television series, which ran until 1985. A sequel, *Market Forces*, was produced in 1996, in which the government department has become a state-owned enterprise, a consequence of the radical economic restructuring initiated by the government in the 1980s.

Middle-Age Spread (1978) is a bleaker play about three couples at a suburban dinner party, punctuated by flashbacks of an affair between the host and one of the guests. Although now over, the affair is announced to the company by another guest, Reg. It then comes to light that the host's daughter is pregnant by Reg's son. The play ran for fifteen months in London in 1979–1980, winning an award for best comedy of the year, and was made into a film in 1979. Hall has written a sequel to this play: *Spreading Out* (2004) revisits the characters nearly thirty years on, in their retirement.

Occasionally, Hall has ventured into different territory and genres. *State of the Play* (1979), about a playwriting seminar run by a once-successful dramatist, satirizes the formulae of the well-made play that Hall so deftly manufactures. It becomes quite serious when the seminar's participants are required to role-play their relationships with their fathers. Hall has also collaborated on pantomimes and musicals, including *Footrot Flats* (1984), a musical based on Murray Ball's extremely popular cartoon strip about Wal's farm. In 1986 Hall rewrote ANTON CHEKHOV'S THREE SISTERS as *Dream of Sussex Downs*, relocating the action to 1950s Wellington among English expatriates who long for England. *A Way of Life* (2001) is a saga tracing the story of three generations in a farming family.

Hall has continued with formulaic satires and FARCES that tap astutely into the topical issues and social phenomena that resonate with middle-class New Zealand. In *The Share Club* (1988), a group of neighbors seek to make money on the booming share market; in *After the Crash* (1988), the same group of neighbors tries to restore their financial fortunes after the 1987 share market collapse. *By Degrees* (1993) explores women's experiences of university; *Social Climbers* (1995) features a group of women teachers stranded in a tramping hut for three days; and in *Taking Off* (2004) four middle-aged women set off belatedly on their "O.E." (overseas experience).

SELECT PLAYS: *Prisoners of Mother England* (1980); *The Rose* (1981); *Fifty Fifty* (1982); *Hot Water* (1983); *Multiple Choice* (1983); *The Hansard Show* (1986); *Mr Punch* (1989); *Conjugal Rites* (1990); *You Must Be Crazy* (produced 1990); *C'mon Black* (1996); *The Book Club* (1999); *You Gotta Be Joking* (produced 1999); *Take A Chance on Me* (2001)

FURTHER READING

Groves, David. "The State of Hall's Play." *Act* 3, no. 8 (1978): 61–63.

Hall, Roger. *Glide Time: A Play in Four Acts Set in the Public Service*. Wellington, N.Z.: Victoria Univ. Press, 1977.

——. *Middle-Age Spread*. Wellington, N.Z.: Victoria Univ. Press, 1978.

——. *State of the Play*. Afterword by Ian Fraser. Wellington, N.Z.: Victoria Univ. Press, 1979.

——. *Bums on Seats: The Backstage Story*. Auckland, N.Z.: Viking, 1998.

Stuart Young

HAMLETMACHINE

I'm not Hamlet. I don't take part anymore. My words have nothing to tell me anymore . . . I won't play along anymore.

—"Actor of Hamlet," Part 4

Hamletmachine (*Die Hamletmaschine*), a dense COLLAGE of nine pages divided into five parts that can take up to four hours to perform, was written by HEINER MÜLLER in 1977 and published the same year in the journal *Theater Today* (*Theater heute*). The play was first staged in 1979 by Jean Jourdheuil at the Théâtre Gérard Philippe in Saint Denis, FRANCE, and continues to be one of Müller's most frequently produced works.

Müller once confessed that a *Hamlet* adaptation had been a long-cherished dream of his. By altering William Shakespeare's original, Müller transforms the title character into an inactive, failed intellectual who is unable to respond to the repeated calls for a revolution in the German Democratic Republic. The origins of Hamlet's stagnation, loss of hope, and bleak vision in *Hamletmachine* lie in his conflict with the fundamentals of European civilization. Müller was well aware of the discrepancies between the imagined utopia and the failing practices of Communism in his country. His play opens with Hamlet, his back to the ruins of Europe, contemplating history. His soliloquy reflects his inactivity and reveals his inability to find a single spatial or temporal reference point for political action. Accordingly, he becomes an onlooker to the depressing events in the GDR. His language becomes a mere "BLABLA," a confusing collection of statements.

Instead of a clear and linear plot, *Hamletmachine* provides a complex of disjunctive, clashing images and scenes. Müller uses inflammatory rhetoric and metaphors to provoke his audience. For example, when Ophelia is transformed into Electra, she declaims: "I choke between my thighs the world I gave birth to . . . Long live hate and contempt, rebellion and death." The actor playing Hamlet shares Hamlet's aspirations and his desire to change political conditions. He enters the play after Hamlet's resignation and the announced refusal of his existence. However, even though he is sent in to stand up for Hamlet and his views, he, too, soon loses hope and becomes alienated from both himself and society. Hence, the existence of a stable or meaningful Hamlet is questioned for a second time in the play. When the character subsequently splits the heads of Karl Marx, Vladimir Lenin, and Mao Zedong with an ax, "Snow" and the "Ice Age" follow, suggesting that the end of Communism signals the stopping of time, the failure of a political solution.

Ophelia, who also assumes the role of Medea, provides a contrast to Hamlet, the inactive intellectual. She enjoys her freedom of speech by protesting oppression until she is wrapped in gauze, placed in a wheelchair, and silenced. At that moment Hamlet and Ophelia are transformed into a single character. Müller underlines the intertextual dimension of history and identity by having his own photograph torn to pieces on stage and deconstructing the autonomy of the writer as he opens his text to other texts and voices, signaling that the autonomy of any text proves to be nothing but a mere illusion.

[*See also* Avant-Garde Drama; Germany]

FURTHER READING

Dudley, Joseph M. "Being and Non-Being: The Other and Heterotopia in *Hamletmachine*." *Modern Drama* 35, no. 4 (1992): 562–570.

Girshausen, Theo, ed. *Hamletmaschine. Heiner Müllers Endspiel* [Hamletmachine: Heiner Müller's End Game]. Cologne: Prometh Verlag, 1978.

Kalb, Jonathan. "On *Hamletmachine*: Müller and the Shadow of Artaud." *New German Critique* 73 (1998):47–66.

Nash, Douglas. "The Commodification of Opposition: Notes on the Postmodern Image in Heiner Müller's *Hamletmaschine*." *Monatshefte* 81, no. 3 (1989):298–311.

Petersohn, Roland. *Heiner Müllers Shakespeare-Rezeption* [Heiner Müller's Reception of Shakespeare]. Frankfurt am Main: Peter Lang, 1993.

Zurbrugg, Nicholas. "Post-Modernism and the Multi-Media Sensibility: Heiner Müller's *Hamletmachine* and the Art of Robert Wilson." *Modern Drama* 31, no. 3 (1988):439–453.

Natasa Masanovic

DIE HAMLETMASCHINE

See HAMLETMACHINE

HAMSUN, KNUT (1859–1952)

The point is this: Ibsen's characters have all too often been only instruments that represent and stand for concepts and ideas. And about concepts and ideas one can talk an awful lot of twaddle.

—Knut Hamsun, 1891

Norwegian writer Knut Hamsun was awarded the Nobel Prize for Literature in 1920. Although his reputation rests almost entirely on his novels, Hamsun was the author of six plays, all written before 1911.

Born on August 4, 1859, in Lom, NORWAY, as a young man the self-educated Hamsun lived in the UNITED STATES for several years during the 1880s, making a living as a peddler, clerk, and streetcar conductor. His life as a wanderer became the basis for his early novels, notably *Hunger* (*Sult*, 1890), *Mysteries* (*Mysterier*, 1892), and *Pan* (1894), that portray the world as a series of fleeting impressions in the mind of the narrator. These works struck a new note in Scandinavian literature and made a sharp break with the dominant school of psychological realism.

Hamsun made his quarrel with the older school of writers perfectly clear in three public lectures delivered in 1891, with HENRIK IBSEN, by then world famous, sitting in the front row. Ibsen and the realistic writers of his generation were declared not only passé but also uninformed. Hamsun remarked that when one "goes through the main contents of their collected works, the total impression one has is that they are intended more for the less developed people than for the better developed." The following year Ibsen wrote THE MASTER BUILDER, an autobiographical and symbolistic drama in which the hero fears that the younger generation will surpass him.

Hamsun's own plays are conventional in form and lack the experimentation of his early novels, although they have a greater political content. The Kareno trilogy pictures three stages in the life of the hero. In the first play, *At the Gates of the Kingdom* (*Ved Rigets Port*, 1895), the young idealist Ivar Kareno is writing a treatise on the weaknesses of democracy. He is so occupied with this work that he loses his wife to a political rival and his property to his creditors. In the second play, THE GAME OF LIFE (*Livets Spil*, 1896), Kareno is supporting himself as a tutor and living in a glass cupola, an ivory tower for himself but, as he sees it, a lighthouse for the rest of the world. He falls in love with his patron's daughter, and after that, one catastrophe follows another. The daughter is accidentally slain by a demented man known locally as "Justice"; a fire not only destroys Kareno's manuscripts but also burns to death the two boys he was tutoring. In the final play, *The Evening Sky* (*Aftenrøde*, 1898), Kareno's wife, now wealthy, returns to him, and he abandons his old ideals and joins the democratic government. In the last scene, Kareno is seen telling his daughter a fairy tale about a proud young man who was true to his ideals and remained unbowed.

Dramatically, the best of Hamsun's plays is his last, *In the Grip of Life* (*Livet ivold*, 1910), which, like his early novels, renders what he called "the subjective logic of the blood," the impulses and desires that undermine rational behavior. In Hamsun's own case, this subjective logic drew him to admire Adolf Hitler's dictatorship and the Nazis' racism. When the Germans invaded Norway in 1940, Hamsun gave them his support. After the war, he was tried, found guilty of treason, and put under virtual house arrest. His plays had no lasting success, and they have seldom been revived. Hamsun died on February 19, 1952, near Grimstad, Norway.

PLAYS: *At the Gates of the Kingdom* (*Ved Rigets Port*, 1895); *The Game of Life* (*Livets Spil*, 1896); *The Evening Sky* (*Aftenrøde*, 1898); *Munken Vendt* (1902); *Queen Tamara* (*Dronning Tamara*, 1903); *In the Grip of Life* (*Livet ivold*, 1910)

FURTHER READING

Beyer, Harald. *History of Norwegian Literature*. New York: New York Univ. Press, 1956.

Downs, Brian W. *Modern Norwegian Literature 1860–1918*. Cambridge: Cambridge Univ. Press, 1966.

Ferguson, Robert. *Enigma: The Life of Knut Hamsun*. London: Richard Cohen, 1987.

Evert Sprinchorn

HANDKE, PETER (1942–)

When will people finally recognize the falsity, the nasty untruth of things supposedly earnest in the realms of theater? This isn't an aesthetic question; it's a question about truth. Perhaps, then, an aesthetic question, indeed.

—Peter Handke, from the essay "Straßentheater und Theatertheater," 1968

One of the preeminent cultural and critical voices in the German-speaking world today, Peter Handke first gained wide public attention at the meeting of the prestigious Gruppe 47 (Group 47) at Princeton University in 1966. There he launched a verbal offensive against the programmatic "new REALISM" in German literature, brazenly dismissing the bulk of work produced by his established peers as "ridiculous" and "impotent." Focusing upon the commanding reality of language itself in literature and everyday experience, Handke's defense of linguistic FORMALISM proved pivotal in directing German-language writers away from the predominantly theme-based orientation of postwar German literature and toward greater stylistic freedom and experimentation.

Born on December 6, 1942, in Griffen, AUSTRIA, Handke was raised by an ethnic Slovenian mother and a German stepfather in a rural, working-class home in southern Carinthia. He studied law at the University of Graz before embarking on his writing career. His first works—essays, short stories, and radio plays—appeared in the journal *manuskripte* in the early 1960s. Following the appearance of his first novel, *The Hornets* (*Die Hornissen*, 1966), Handke's first major play, OFFENDING THE AUDIENCE (*Publikumsbeschimpfung*, 1966), was staged in Frankfurt by CLAUS PEYMANN, marking the first of many collaborations between the two. By unconventionally turning attention from the stage action toward the theatergoers themselves, *Offending the Audience* became an overnight success and a pop-cultural sensation. Three companion pieces, which Handke called *Sprechstücke* (speech plays), were written and produced shortly thereafter: *Prophecy* (*Weissagung*, 1966), *Self-Accusation* (*Selbstbezichtigung*, 1966), and Calling for Help (*Hilferufe*, 1967). Like *Offending the Audience*, the speech plays challenge representational conventions of the theater by suggesting that those present, both onstage and off, as well as the rest of society, all subscribe to roles determined by cultural scripts and linguistic formulae.

The problem of language takes center stage in Handke's best-known play, KASPAR (1966), loosely based on the story of Kaspar Hauser, a so-called wild child discovered in early-19th-century Nuremberg who became the object of scientific study and popular intrigue. Handke's Kaspar is indoctrinated into the world of words and sentences by anonymous voices emitted from a loudspeaker. Once Kaspar has acquired the ability to both comprehend and speak, he arrives at the ultimate recognition that language has, in fact, trapped him, separating him from immediate experience of the world.

Handke's silent play, *My Foot My Tutor* (*Das Mündel will Vormund sein*, 1969), keeps with the socialization theme evident in *Kaspar*, as two characters, a ward and a warden, carry out the roles of master and slave without the aid of spoken language. The dubious role of speech is again the focus in *Quodlibet* (1969), which consists of lines intentionally murmured and muted so they remain vague and merely suggestive to the audience. In the early 1970s, *The Ride across Lake Constance* (*Der Ritt über den Bodensee*, 1970) and *They Are Dying Out* (*Die Unvernünftigen sterben aus*, 1973) signaled something of a departure from the openly abstract schemata of Handke's previous plays, yet still remained grounded in the rubric of experimental drama. In *The Ride across Lake Constance*, characters take their names from European film and theater stars and are presented in almost marionettelike fashion, depicting actions and behaviors often contradictory to their own words. *They Are Dying Out* also presents figures resembling caricatures, but offers a more realistic stage setting, a corporate office in which the audience witnesses the brutish behavior, self-alienation, and ultimate self-destruction of the protagonist, Herr Quitt.

Handke's first play of the 1980s, *A Walk through the Villages* (*Über die Dörfer*, 1981) constitutes a further stylistic turn. Premiered at the 1982 Salzburg Festival under the direction of filmmaker Wim Wenders, *A Walk through the Villages* features an Austrian everyman, Gregor, and a mythical muse-like figure, Nova. Handke's previous deconstructive focus is transformed in this work into a postmodern, reconstructive mission to establish an epic dimension to his art. In subsequent texts, the initially speechless Kaspar is resurrected in *Voyage to the Sonorous Land, or The Art of Asking* (*Das Spiel vom Fragen, oder die Reise zum Sonoren Land*, 1989) as a neoclassical, childlike Parsifal, and the minimalist, silent power game of *My Foot My Tutor* evolves into a wordless choreography of the everyday and the fantastic in *The Hour We Knew Nothing of Each Other* (*Die Stunde da wir nichts voneinander wußten*, 1992).

In the 1990s, Handke gained notoriety for his controversial support of SERBIA during the wars of Yugoslav secession, authoring two plays aimed at the conflict: *Preparations for Immortality: A Royal Drama* (*Zurüstungen für die Unsterblichkeit. Ein Königsdrama*, 1997) and *Voyage in the Dugout, or The Play about the Film about the War* (*Die Fahrt im Einbaum, oder Das Stück zum Film vom Krieg*, 1999). The latter serves as a platform for Handke's accusations of conceptual straitjacketing and propagandizing on the part of the Western media in its coverage of the wars.

In 2006 Handke's play *Voyage to the Sonorous Land, or The Art of Asking* was canceled by the Comédie Française in Paris because he delivered a eulogy at the funeral of Slobodan Milošević, who had been on trial for war crimes during his presidency in Yugoslavia. In response, Handke said he was not an apologist for Milošević, "But I know the truth. But I watch. I feel. I remember. I question."

SELECT PLAYS: *Kaspar* (1966); *Offending the Audience* (*Publikumsbeschimpfung*, 1966); *Prophecy* (*Weissagung*, 1966); *Self-Accusation* (*Selbstbezichtigung*, 1966); *Calling for Help* (*Hilferufe*, 1967); *My Foot My Tutor* (*Das Mündel will Vormund sein*, 1969); *The Ride across Lake Constance* (*Der Ritt über den Bodensee*, 1970); *They Are Dying Out* (*Die Unvernünftigen sterben aus*, 1973); *A Walk through the Villages: A Dramatic Poem* (*Über die Dörfer. Dramatisches Gedicht*, 1981); *Voyage to the Sonorous Land, or The Art of Asking* (*Das Spiel vom Fragen, oder Die Reise zum Sonoren Land*, 1989); *The Hour We Knew Nothing of Each Other: A Play* (*Die Stunde da wir nichts voneinander wußten. Ein Schauspiel*, 1992); *Preparations for Immortality: A Royal Drama* (*Zurüstungen für die Unsterblichkeit. Ein Königsdrama*, 1997); *Voyage in the Dugout, or The Play about the Film about the War* (*Die Fahrt im Einbaum, oder Das Stück zum Film vom Krieg*, 1999); *Subday Blues: A Station Drama* (*Untertagblues. Ein Stationendrama*, 2003); *Voyage to the Sonorous Land, or The Art of Asking* (*Das Spiel vom Fragen, oder die Reise zum Sonoren Land*, 2006)

FURTHER READING

Firda, Richard. *Peter Handke*. New York: Twayne, 1993.

Klinkowitz, Jerome, and James Knowlton. *Peter Handke and the Postmodern Transformation: The Goalie's Journey Home*. Columbia: Univ. of Missouri Press, 1983.

Nägele, Rainer, and Renate Voris. *Peter Handke*. Munich: Beck, 1978.

Pütz, Peter. *Peter Handke*. Frankfurt: Suhrkamp, 1982.

Renner, Rolf Günter. *Peter Handke*. Stuttgart: Metzler, 1985.

Schlueter, June. *The Plays and Novels of Peter Handke*. Pittsburgh: Univ. of Pittsburgh Press, 1981.

Marton Marko

THE HANDS OF GOD

The Hands of God: A Miracle Play in Three Acts (*Las manos de Dios*, 1956), by Guatemalan playwright CARLOS SOLÓRZANO, dramatizes the conflict between experience and religion in a village devastated by drought, injustice, and fear. Beatriz, the heroine, must liberate her brother, imprisoned for criticizing the local Boss. When her appeals to the Jailer and the Priest fail, she inadvertently conjures up the Devil, her alter ego. His solution is to steal the jewels in the Church to bribe the Jailer to release her brother. The Priest discovers the theft and instigates the people to kill her. The heroine fails to free her brother, but her challenge to God and the Boss symbolizes her triumph over dogma and death. When she snatches the jewels from the hands of God, Beatriz leaves the wooden image as empty as the values it represents.

The play represents timeless stories of sacrifice and salvation, the heroic quest, the rebellions of Satan and Prometheus, the Cosmic Tree as World Axis, and the day of wrath unleashed by a vengeful God. The set depicts the trinity of peasant life—Church, State, and poverty. The ornate church clashes with the funereal landscape; a skeletal tree at center stage becomes the site of the heroine's martyrdom. The dirty jail with a twisted sign manifests the sordidness of the civil administration. Lighting effects, mood music, and pantomimes project Beatriz's despair as the Devil guides her through the process of self-awareness necessary to determine her destiny.

Like the set, the characters are expressionistic. The exhausted peasants bear their burdens stoically. Always fearful, they form a silent chorus that comments on the action with doleful pantomimes. They come alive briefly during the trial scene; as the Priest and the Devil battle for the soul of Beatriz, the chorus sways between resignation and rebellion. The Priest warns them that God punishes defiance. An icy wind howls as they attack her, then beat themselves for the double sin of listening to then rejecting their would-be redeemer.

Beatriz incarnates both a supplicant and a rebel. Unable to stir the mercy of her fellow sufferers, she implores God for guidance, but He remains silent. The Devil helps her. Identifying himself with Prometheus and Galileo—rebels punished for helping humanity—he counsels action instead of faith and defends his moral integrity: "to find another answer to life that would not always smash against the closed doors of death, of nothingness."

A heroine in the classic mold, Beatriz struggles with her faith, perceives a new truth, and propels the tragedy. Motivated by love and emboldened by instinct, she defies Church and State to vindicate her soul. Her triumph, however, is bittersweet. The social-religious structure remains intact, and the jewels will return to the hands of God. Yet bound to the tree of death, the protagonist exhorts the Devil to continue the fight for spiritual and personal freedom.

The Hands of God provoked controversy in MEXICO. Instead of affirming divine goodness, it challenges human beings to love themselves more than God. Love, not sacrifice, is the miracle that sustains life.

FURTHER READING

Bravo-Elizondo, Pedro. *Las manos de Dios: el encadenamiento de Promoteo, Teatro hispanoamericano de crítica social [The Hands of God: The Binding of Prometheus, Hispanoamerican Theater of Social Criticism]*. Madrid: Playor, 1975.

Castagnino, Raúl H. *Las manos de Dios, Semiología, ideología y teatro hispanoamericano contemporáneo [The Hands of God, Semiology, Ideology and the Contemporary Hispanoamerican Theater]*. Buenos Aires: Nova, 1974. 107–124.

Feliciano, Wilma. "Myth and Theatricality in Three Plays by Carlos Solórzano." *Latin American Theatre Review* 25, no. 1 (Fall 1992): 111–121.

Rosenberg, John R. "The Ritual of Solórzano's *Las manos de Dios*." *Latin American Theatre Review* 17, no. 2 (Spring 1984):39–48.

Solórzano, Carlos. *Teatro [Theater]*. Mexico City: Difusión Cultural, UNAM, 1992.

——. *Crossroads and Other Plays by Solórzano*. Tr. and ed. by Francesca Colecchia. Rutherford, N.J.: Fairleigh Dickinson Univ. Press, 1993.

Wilma Feliciano

THE HANGMAN

The Hangman (*Bödeln*), a one-act play by PÄR LAGERKVIST, is a dramatization of his eponymous novella (1933). It was first performed at Den Nationale Scene in Bergen, NORWAY, in 1934, and published in 1946. The play, directed by the Swede Per Lindberg, was a tremendous success, as was Lindberg's production at the National Theater in Oslo. His production in Stockholm was not as well received.

Like the novella, the play is divided into two parts. The first takes place in a medieval tavern, the second in a modern restaurant. Straddling the two, the Hangman is found sitting at the same table throughout. He does not say a word until the end when he gets up and delivers a long, concluding monologue. Originally planned as a two-act drama, Lindberg persuaded the author that the emotional impact on the stage would be much stronger if the play was performed without an intermission.

The Hangman is portrayed as a scapegoat. As a symbol, he is a projection of all that is evil in humanity. He assures the people in the restaurant that he has been with humanity from time immemorial, and his presence throughout the play testifies to this; that their God "is long since dead"; and parodying the Christmas gospel, that he is now their Christ, with the Hangman's mark on his forehead, sent down to "bring war on earth, and to men an evil will!" Lagerkvist's Hangman has been compared to the Erinyes in classical Greek drama, those bloody tools of the gods who persecute criminals, especially murderers. But if evil is eternal, so is its opposite, here symbolized by the Woman who enters toward the end and sits down next to the Hangman. Dressed like a beggar and ignored by the guests, her symbolic role is indicated by her stillness and the halo of light that surrounds her. "I, too, live in this world you think calls only for you," she assures the Hangman.

The two scenes form tightly knit contrasts and parallels. As parallels—strengthened in Lindberg's productions by having the same actors take parts in both scenes—they not only give a certain thematic unity to the play, but also stress the indelibility of human evil, in fact suggesting that evil has grown more powerful in the course of time. In the medieval tavern, the Hangman, immediately recognized by his blood-red robe, is sitting at the same table but somewhat removed from the other guests, who keep a respectful distance from him. In the restaurant, although he apparently sits alone at the table, he is constantly approached by the other customers, who rather disrespectfully address him. The medieval belief in God and the Devil has been replaced by a worship of the brutal strength in man himself. Another difference between the venues is that, while the crowd in the tiny tavern is socially quite homogeneous, the huge restaurant displays a marked class society: the rich guests are contrasted with the poor beggars, who are literally marginalized. A third difference is that the natural light and storytelling in the tavern give way to loud jazz music and decadent, psychedelic violet-blue-green light from a mirror ball in the ceiling of the restaurant.

A mixture of epic and dramatic ingredients, the play contains no less than ten different stories, each one dealing with an execution. Nine of these belong to the medieval part, the tenth, climactic one—the Hangman's crucifixion of his "brother" Jesus—to the Hangman's final monologue. The modern part is significantly lacking in stories. Some of the stories are visualized in the form of tableaux above the heads of the storytellers and their listeners, rather like flashbacks in a film.

In connection with the Bergen premiere, Lagerkvist noted, "*The Hangman* has been written because violence is now being preached as a religion. It has something to say to anyone who places himself on the side of violence, whether it is Nazism, Fascism or Bolshevism" (Lagerroth, 1978). In the text, only the outstretched arms of the soldiers make one think especially of Nazi GERMANY. Yet by opting for a black orchestra, Lagerkvist could broaden the idea of social discrimination and at the same time disguise the Jewish pogrom connotations in this part. In Lindberg's productions, Nazilike uniforms, *Heil* greetings, and the sound of the Nazi party song "Horst Wessel" turned the play into a somewhat more timely product than was intended by the author.

FURTHER READING

Lagerroth, Ulla-Britta. *Regi i möte med drama och samhälle: Per Lindberg tolkar Pär Lagerkvist [Direction As Encounter Between Drama and Society: Per Lindberg Interprets Pär Lagerkvist]*. Stockholm: Rabén & Sjögren, 1978. 278–322.

Mjöberg, Jöran. *Livsproblemet hos Lagerkvist [Lagerkvist and the Problem of Life]*. Stockholm: Bonniers, 1951. 149–157.

Oberholzer, Otto. *Pär Lagerkvist: Studien zu seiner Prosa und seinen Dramen [Pär Lagerkvist: Studies in His Prose Works and Dramas]*. Heidelberg: Carl Winther Universitätsverlag, 1958. 126–130.

Törnqvist, Egil. *Svenska dramastrukturer [Swedish Drama Structures]*. Stockholm: Prisma, 1973. 85–107.

Egil Törnqvist

HANG THUN HAK (1924–1975)

Cambodian author and politician Hang Thun Hak was influenced by the introduction of western theater techniques by Frenchman Guy Porée in Phnom Penh in the years just after World War II. Porée served as cultural attaché to the monarchy and, with the support of Queen Kossamak, worked with Cambodian artists to develop a Cambodian modern spoken drama (*lakhaoun niyeay*).

Born in 1924, Hang Thun Hak, who would come to be called the second Molière, studied theater in Paris. He returned to CAMBODIA in 1951 and was with guerilla forces in the jungle until 1953. He then taught at Lycée Sisowath, where he translated William Shakespeare and created new work with his students, who were developing the modern drama of the then French colony. He shifted to the newly instituted National Theatre School in the mid 1950s, where he directed, taught acting, and developed plays as the nation moved toward independence. Among the works he created there was *Balatay*, an adaptation of Hamlet set in Cambodia. He initiated the theater curriculum at the Royal University of Fine Arts after its founding in 1965 and served as director of the school.

His largest work was *Life of Buddha* (1957) for the 2,500th birthday of the Buddha, a large and collaboratively developed piece. In addition to creating such pageants for government events, he also collaborated on works that critiqued corruption: *Dancing Stone (Thma Raom)* attacked the complicity of government officials in the illegal marketing of Khmer antiquities on the international art market. *Ethical Girl (Kanya Chareya)* showed an upper-class girl who confronts the culture of bribery through which her father, a high-placed Cambodian, enriches himself. This politically engaged work, using realistic situations and Western-style acting, was popular in Phnom Penh in the late 1950s. The cleanly directed and fully scripted works contrasted with the traditional drama where dialogue was more improvised. The polished presentation appealed to urban audiences. Drama was a vital tool used by intellectuals in the discourse about the fate of the nation. But such works caused controversy as well. Performers were threatened by police censorship after some of Hang's plays, but the queen protected artists from arrest.

Among the government posts Hang held were director of the University of Fine Arts, Minister of Culture, and even President of the Republic of Cambodia for a short period prior to the 1975 accession of the Khmer Rouge. Hang Thun Hak's theater work grew from and served his engaged political practice. He was murdered along with other important Lon Nol regime officials by the Khmer Rouge when they entered Phnom Penh in 1975.

PLAYS: *Life of the Buddha* (collaboratively created, 1957), *Balatay*

FURTHER READING

Daravuth, Ly, and Ingrid Muan. *Cultures of Independence: An Introduction to Cambodian Arts and Culture in the 1950s and 1960s*. Phnom Penh: Reyeum, 2001.

Foley, Kathy, and Tony Shapiro. "Cambodia." In *Cambridge Guide to Asian Theatre*, ed. by James Brandon. Cambridge: Cambridge Univ. Press, 1993.

Kathy Foley

HANSBERRY, LORRAINE (1930–1965)

> *Life was not a struggle—it was something that one did. One won an argument because, if facts gave out, one invented them—with color! The only sinful people in the world were dull people. And, above all, there were two things which were never to be betrayed: the family and the race.*
>
> —Lorraine Hansberry, 1960

Playwright Lorraine Vivian Hansberry was born on May 19, 1930, in Chicago, Illinois, and grew up in a family where political activism, community service, and black pride were givens. Her father Carl worked with the NAACP (National Association for the Advancement of Colored People). Her paternal uncle William Leo was a Howard University professor and a noted scholar of African history who brought Hansberry into contact with African students and exiles at a time when liberation movements were emerging across AFRICA. Paul Robeson was among a number of important and influential blacks who visited the Hansberry home.

A standout student at Chicago's Englewood High School, Hansberry came to appreciate the struggles of poorer black students and to understand the meaning of her own middle-class privilege. After attending the University of Wisconsin at Madison for two years, she moved to New York City in 1950 to pursue a career in writing. By 1951 she was contributing to Paul Robeson's radical *Freedom* magazine. She studied African history under W. E. B. DuBois and taught black literature at the Jefferson School of Social Science. In 1953 she met her future husband, Robert Nemiroff, on an antidiscrimination picket line. Hansberry was also active with the Student Nonviolent Coordinating Committee (SNCC) and produced a volume titled *The Movement: Documentary of a Struggle for Equality* (1964). Hansberry unabashedly expressed her social and political convictions through her creative work, making her a precursor to BLACK ARTS MOVEMENT artists of the 1960s and early 1970s. Her developing black feminist consciousness is also evident in her work.

Hansberry's best-known work, *A Raisin in the Sun* (1959), focuses on an extended black family's struggle to emerge both figuratively and literally from their overcrowded and stifling socioeconomic conditions. The play opened on Broadway in 1959 to critical acclaim, making Hansberry the first black woman to have a play produced on Broadway. *A Raisin in the Sun* won a Drama Critics' Circle Award—the first time a black writer had received that honor.

Following Hansberry's success with *Raisin*, NBC commissioned *The Drinking Gourd* (1960), a drama about slavery's dehumanizing effects. In 1961 she completed *What Use Are Flowers?*, a play that imagines the aftermath of a nuclear holocaust. Both of these plays are collected together with Hansberry's third major drama, *Les Blancs*—a play about pan-African liberation—in *Les Blancs: The Collected Last Plays of Lorraine Hansberry* (1972). *The Sign in Sidney Brustein's Window* (1965), her second major drama, ran for 101 performances on Broadway before closing on the same night that Hansberry died of pancreatic cancer, at the age of thirty-four. Although Hansberry and Nemiroff divorced before her death, he served as her literary executor and continued to produce material based on her work long after her death.

PLAYS: *A Raisin in the Sun* (1959); *The Sign in Sidney Brustein's Window* (1964); *To Be Young, Gifted, and Black*, (1969, adapted by Robert Nemiroff); *Les Blancs* (1970, adapted by Robert Nemiroff); *The Drinking Gourd* (1972); *What Use Are Flowers?* (1972)

FURTHER READING

Bond, Jean Carey, ed. "Lorraine Hansberry: Art of Thunder, Vision of Light." *Freedomways: A Quarterly Review of the Freedom Movement* 19, no. 4 (special issue, 1979).

Carter, Steven R. *Hansberry's Drama: Commitment Amid Complexity*. Urbana: Univ. of Illinois Press, 1991.

Cheney, Anne. *Lorraine Hansberry*. New York: Twayne, 1984.

Hansberry, Lorraine. *Les Blancs: The Collected Last Plays of Lorraine Hansberry*. New York: Vintage Books, 1972, 1994.

Nemiroff, Robert, ed. *To Be Young, Gifted, and Black: Lorraine Hansberry in Her Own Words*. New York: New American Library, 1969.

Lovalerie King

HAPPENINGS AND INTERMEDIA

The genre of "happenings" emerged in the 1950s and flourished in the 1960s and early 1970s. It is a fundamentally intermedia and interdisciplinary disposition for its creators—painters, musicians, actors, dancers, sculptors, and cinematographers—and a flexible agency for its audience.

Although its origins lie in medieval pageantry and *commedia dell 'arte lazzi*, the AVANT-GARDE events of the Italian futurists and Zurich dadaists transgressed boundaries between author, performer, and spectator. Happenings attempted to liberate structures of theater and drama such as place, time, and character, resulting in a nonmatrixed approach. No longer autonomous, spectators found themselves in nonstatic, often interventionist positions. The uncertainty about whether any given fragment of text or action was intended constitutes another potential disruption of the traditional matrix of theater, text, and performance.

In 1952 at Black Mountain College, North Carolina, composer John Cage used collage techniques to mount the first happening with poet Charles Olson, dancer Merce Cunningham, and tech artist Robert Rauschenberg. Allan Kaprow coined the genre with his *18 Happenings in 6 Parts* (1959). His *Household* (1964) transgressed several conventions: It played outdoors in a landfill. The set was ready-made; spectators were participants: From trash, men built themselves a tower, and women, a nest. Characters were not identifiable. Costumes (and clothes!) were anathema. The men covered a car wreck in jam, it was licked by the women, and subsequently demolished by the males and set on fire to loud jubilation. Automobiles had a special attraction. Sculptor Claes Oldenburg's *Autobodys* (1963), performed in various parking lots, explored the meaning of the ubiquitous icon. Jim Dine's *The Car Crash* (1960) was an enigmatic response to the artist's experience in a car accident. Other happenings artists working in the UNITED STATES include Carolee Schneeman, Meredith Monk, Al Hansen, and Robert DeForest Whitman.

Meanwhile in Europe, the Vienna *Aktionisten* transgressed multiple taboos. Hermann Nitsch's *Abreaktionsspiele* and *Orgien Mysterien* actions featured blood, organs, and animal carcasses, often still steaming. Nitsch, Günther Brus, Otto Muehl, and Rudolf Schwarzkogler pushed happenings into the public arena of controversy. In an *Aktion* at Vienna University (1968), Brus undressed, cut himself with a razor blade, urinated in a glass, drank it, smeared his body with feces, and masturbated, singing Austria's national anthem. Arrest followed. German artist Wolf Vostell's *décollages*, on the other hand, were urban interventions using real life situations. *Ligne Petite Ceinture* (1962) invited people to board a circular bus route to take in Paris's acoustic and visual structures. Joseph Beuys, a German Fluxus member, created events that were introspective and mystical, focusing on material, texture, and sound. In the United Kingdom, Adrian Henri, JOHN ARDEN, and the interventionist group People Show operated around Liverpool and York, while Jeff Nuttall and Mark Boyle (*Son et Lumière for Bodily Fluids*, 1966) performed in London. Dutch Theater Proloog's *Aktie Tomaat* disrupted classical productions in established theaters.

The 1968 political upheaval in FRANCE and BELGIUM inspired artists around the Situationist movement (Jean Jacques Lebel) to produce interventionist street theater, which has recently reemerged in protests at political summits. The Paris-based Panic Theatre around FERNANDO ARRABAL and Alexandro Jodorowsky organized outrageous *ephémères* (*Sacramental Melodrama*, 1965), which soon became part of Arrabal's scripted dramas. With audience response reintegrated as a structural component of performance, the happening became a convention for groups like the LIVING THEATRE, The San Francisco

Mime Troupe, Richard Schechner's Performance Group, and Les Trétaux Libres (Geneva–Paris). Numerous plays of the 1960s and 1970s, including PETER HANDKE's infamous *Publikumsbeschimpfung* (1966), lean heavily on the genre.

Happenings evolved into PERFORMANCE ART and body art installations by the early 1970s. Italian Pierre Manzoni and New Yorker Vito Acconci pioneered the latter, focusing on the body and its functions. Chris Burden's *Shoot* (1971), in which a friend shot him in the arm, took this physicality further, as did French performers Gina Pane and Orlan (who turned plastic surgery into video art). Korean Nam June Paik pioneered the use of video in performance. American Bruce Naumann, Lebanese-born Mona Hin, and German performer Ulrike Rosenbauch turned it into an established genre. More recently, performance artists Karen Finley, Coco Fusco, and Tim Miller have eschewed technology and returned to non-techno-based media like foodstuffs, mass-produced clothing, and family pictures. Computer-mediated theater or cyber-performance, on the other hand, embrace technology, producing a hybrid form in which mouse clicks give spectators agency. Since *Hamnet* (1993) and The Palace's *WAITING FOR GODOT* (1997), digital media artists Stelarc, Andrea Polli, and Avatar Body Collision have embarked in altogether new directions for multimedia performance, further challenging hierarchies of liveness and presence.

[*See also* Dadaism; Futurism, Italian]

FURTHER READING

Carlson, Marvin. *Performance: A Critical Introduction*. London: Routledge, 1996.

Causey, M. "Postorganic Performance: The Appearance of Theatre in Virtual Spaces." *Cyberspace Textuality: Computer Technology and Literary Theory*, ed. by M. L. Ryan. Indianapolis: Indiana Univ. Press, 1999.

Foster, Stephen C., ed. *"Event" Arts and Arts Events*. Ann Arbor: UMI Research Press, 1988.

Goldberg, RoseLee. *Performance Art From Futurism to the Present*. New York: Harry Abrams, 1988.

Henri, Adrian. *Total Art: Environments, Happenings, and Performance*. New York: Praeger, 1974.

Kirby, Michael, ed. *Happenings. An Illustrated Anthology*. New York: Dutton, 1965.

Phelan, Peggy, and Jill Lane, eds. *The Ends of Performance*. New York: New York Univ. Press, 1998.

Sandford, Mariellen R. *Happenings and Other Acts*. London: Routledge, 1995.

Piet Defraeye

HAPPY DAYS

I don't see the play at all clearly, but a little more so. The figure is a woman as far as I can see. Bright light, flowers and a large handbag containing all vital necessities from revolver to lipstick. Would like to try it in English but fear it will have to be in French again.

—Samuel Beckett, in a letter to Alan Schneider, September 1960

Within two weeks of this letter, SAMUEL BECKETT had embarked in English on his new play, titled *Female Solo*. Beckett misdated his drafts and later thought it had taken him a year and a half to write, but it was published in New York in the summer of 1961 and received its first performance there in September of that year. Beckett's intensive work on the text lasted for some six or seven months, at most.

On the first typescript version he produced, Beckett wrote a one-word instruction to himself, underlined twice: "Vaguen." The scorched mound of earth in which Winnie is gripped to her waist and the blazing light that relentlessly burns down on her were given the realistic origin of missile strikes described in some of the newspaper reports that Willie, who lives in a burrow at the back of the mound, reads aloud. Beckett ruthlessly stripped out of his text these and many other details that might attach his play to a realistic or recognizable world. The only world relevant to a Beckett play is the one the audience shares with the players. Beckett's key strategy is the avoidance of explicitness—the effect of this is to transfer the onus of interpretation to the audience.

Happy Days offers its audience, at one level, a portrait of a marriage. Willie is mostly uncommunicative and he has a taste for sexual innuendo and titillation. His emunctory (nose-cleaning) habits are disgusting—at least Winnie finds them so. Winnie is committed to keeping herself "nice," insofar as her extraordinary circumstances permit, and she fills the time between bell-induced waking and sleeping with a constant loquacity. She has few resources—a large black shopping bag containing the props she uses literally to sustain her: toothbrush, nail file, lipstick, hand mirror, and a revolver Willie gave her years ago in case he might use it to put himself out of his misery. This she leaves out of the bag (all the other props are returned at the end of her day), so it is right beside her face in the second act. She also has a stock of half-remembered scraps of poetry she employs consolingly. The strain of maintaining her cheerful demeanor sometimes makes her falter in her speech.

Winnie's situation worsens greatly for the short second act as she is now buried to her neck, with only the most local movement possible. Still she persists in putting on a brave face, but sorrow and anguish intrude with increasing frequency. The play ends in a tableau of astonishing ambiguity: Willie appears from behind the mound—"dressed to kill," as the stage direction puts it—and attempts to climb the mound. Winnie wonders if he wants to touch her face, kiss her, or is he after "something else." Beckett intensifies the ambiguity by shifting the verb tenses in her penultimate utterance: "Oh this is a happy day, this will have been another happy day! [*Pause*.] After all. [*Pause*.] So far."

FURTHER READING

Harmon, Maurice, ed. *No Author Better Served: The Correspondence of Samuel Beckett and Alan Schneider.* Cambridge: Harvard Univ. Press, 1998.

Knowlson, James, ed. *Happy Days: The Production Notebook of Samuel Beckett.* London: Faber and Faber, 1985.

Pountney, Rosemary. *Theatre of Shadows: Samuel Beckett's Drama 1956–1976.* Gerrard's Cross, U.K.: Colin Smythe, 1988.

Gerry Dukes

HARE, DAVID (1947–)

David Hare is one of the most respected, prolific, formally inventive, and internationally produced of contemporary playwrights. Part of the 1960s generation of New Left playwrights in Britain (including CARYL CHURCHILL, David Edgar, Trevor Griffiths, and HOWARD BRENTON, with whom Hare has frequently collaborated), Hare's plays successfully wed the EPIC THEATER of BERTOLT BRECHT with the more proximate influences of postwar British dramatists like JOHN OSBORNE and HAROLD PINTER. From his early days as a gadfly of the Fringe circuit through his long association with the National Theatre, Hare has used his work as a moral compass, documenting the social malaise and creeping conservatism he believes has gradually overtaken English society since 1945.

After graduating from Jesus College, Cambridge, Hare co-founded Portable Theatre with Tony Bicât in 1968 as a way of touring plays to regions ill-served by resident theater companies. At Portable, and later at JOINT STOCK (which he co-founded in 1975), Hare learned to work collaboratively and in a number of different styles, writing and directing corrosive satires about the institutional power structures that govern private lives. Notable successes during this period include: *Slag*, Hare's first full-length solo play, about three idealistic schoolteachers; *England's Ireland*, a group effort outlining the history of England's political intervention in Northern Ireland; and *Knuckle*, a critique of capitalism masquerading as a Raymond Chandleresque thriller that first garnered Hare widespread attention, winning him the John Llewellyn Rhys Prize.

Hare solidified his reputation as one of Britain's leading dramatists by writing and directing *Plenty* for the National Theatre in 1978, beginning an association with the institution that continues to this day. *Plenty* tells the story of Susan Traherne, a British counterintelligence operative in France during World War II who is unable to adjust to postwar life in England. In a series of twelve nonchronological scenes that culminate with the Suez Canal crisis of 1956, Hare parallels Susan's descent into madness with England's trading of its wartime political ideals for baser domestic appetites, asking how one voices dissent in an age of increasing economic prosperity and social conformity. It is a question Hare would pose again during the 1980s within the explicit context of Thatcherism, and that he would investigate definitively in a trilogy of plays written in the early 1990s exploring Britain's corrupt and crumbling public institutions: *Racing Demon*, about the Anglican church and winner of an Oliver Award as Best Play; *Murmuring Judges*, about the judiciary; and *The Absence of War*, about the Labour Party.

Plenty is also notable for the star-making role it affords its lead actress, one of a series of prominent female roles Hare has written over the course of his career: from Joanne, Elise, and Ann in *Slag* to Frances and Madeleine in *The Breath of Life*. What each of these "difficult," occasionally unsympathetic, but always compelling characters reveals is that the political in Hare's work is balanced by the personal. We witness a similar dialectic operating in *Wetherby*, *Paris by Night*, and *Strapless*, three original films written and directed by Hare between 1985 and 1990 that also feature indelible female protagonists.

In 1998 Hare scored a theatrical hat trick when three of his plays opened successively in London and then subsequently transferred to Broadway. *The Judas Kiss* starred Liam Neeson as an OSCAR WILDE paralyzed by romantic inertia. In *The Blue Room*, Hare freely adapted ARTHUR SCHNITZLER's classic REIGEN (*La Ronde*, 1900), updating its daisy-chain of sexual liaisons as a star vehicle for Nicole Kidman. Finally, Hare himself took to the stage in *Via Dolorosa*, a moving monologue about the cultural, religious, and ideological divisions encountered by the playwright on a trip to ISRAEL and PALESTINE. At the end of this remarkable year, Hare was knighted for his services to the theater.

Hare continues to produce exciting and challenging work at a staggering pace, supplementing his own new plays (*My Zinc Bed*, *The Breath of Life*, *The Permanent Way*) with acclaimed adaptations of classic plays and contemporary novels (Michael Cunningham's *The Hours*; Jonathan Franzen's *The Corrections*).

[See also England, 1940–Present]

PLAYS: *Inside Out* (with Tony Bicât, 1968); *How Brophy Made Good* (1969); *Slag* (1970); *What Happened to Blake* (1970); *Deathshead* (1971); *Lay By* (with Howard Brenton et al., 1971); *The Rules of the Game* (adaptation of Luigi Pirandello's play, 1971); *England's Ireland* (with Tony Bicât, Howard Brenton, et al., 1972); *The Great Exhibition* (1972); *Brassneck* (with Howard Brenton, 1973); *Man above Men* (1973); *Knuckle* (1974); *Fanshen* (1975); *Teeth 'n' Smiles* (with Tony Bicât and Nick Bicât, 1975); *Deeds* (with Howard Brenton, Ken Campbell, and Trevor Griffiths, 1978); *Licking Hitler* (1978); *Plenty* (1978, screenplay 1985); *Dreams of Leaving* (1980); *A Map of the World* (1982); *Saigon: Year of the Cat* (1983); *Pravda* (with Howard Brenton, 1985); *Wetherby* (1985); *The Bay at Nice* (1986); *Wrecked Eggs* (1986); *The Knife* (with Tim Rose Price and Nick Bicât, 1987), *The Secret Rapture* (1988, screenplay 1994), *Paris by Night* (1989); *Strapless* (1989); *Racing Demon* (1990); *Heading Home* (1991); *Murmuring Judges* (1991); *The Absence of War* (1993); *Damage* (adaptation of Josephine Hart's novel, 1993); *The Life of Galileo* (adaptation of Bertolt Brecht's play, 1994); *Mother Courage and Her Children* (adaptation of Bertolt Brecht's play, 1995); *Skylight* (1995); *Amy's View* (1997); *Ivanov* (adaptation of

Anton Chekhov's play, 1997); *The Blue Room* (adaptation of Arthur Schnitzler's play *La Ronde*, 1998); *The Judas Kiss* (1998); *Via Dolorosa* (1998); *My Zinc Bed* (2000); *Platonov* (adaptation of Anton Chekhov's play, 2001); *The Breath of Life* (2002); *The Hours* (adaptation of Michael Cunningham's novel, 2002); *The Permanent Way* (2003); *The Corrections* (adaptation of Jonathan Franzen's novel, 2004); *Stuff Happens* (2004); *The Vertical Hour* (2006)

FURTHER READING

Boon, Richard. *About Hare*. London: Faber, 2003.

Dean, John Fitzpatrick. *David Hare*. Boston: Twayne, 1994.

Donesky, Finlay. *David Hare: Moral and Historical Perspectives*. Westport, Conn.: Greenwood Press, 1996.

Homden, Carol. *The Plays of David Hare*. Cambridge: Cambridge Univ. Press, 1995.

Oliva, Judy Lee. *David Hare: Theatricalizing Politics*. Ann Arbor: UMI Research Press, 1990.

Page, Malcolm. *File on David Hare*. London: Methuen, 1990.

Zeifman, Hersh, ed. *David Hare: A Casebook*. New York: Garland, 1994.

Peter Dickinson

HARRIGAN, EDWARD G. (1844–1911)

I have sought above all to make my plays like pages from actual life.

—Edward Harrigan, "Holding the Mirror Up to Nature," 1903

Born on October 26, 1844, in New York City, Edward Green Harrigan, playwright, actor, and director, ranks among the 19th-century American theater's most prolific and popular figures. As half of the COMEDY team of Harrigan and Hart, lyricist for over two hundred songs by David Braham, and manager of four successful New York theaters, he stood among America's most respected theater artists. William Dean Howells and others praised his work, citing his writing, directing, and acting skills. "Mr. Harrigan accurately realizes in his scenes what he realizes in his persons; that is, the actual life of this city . . . Consciously or unconsciously, he is part of the great tendency toward faithful representation of life which is now animating fiction" (*Harper's*, July 1886). Audience reactions, too, confirmed Harrigan's talents; fourteen of his plays ran more than one hundred performances.

Harrigan's career began on variety stages in the late 1860s. While on tour, he teamed with Tony Hart and began developing the unique style that he would hone for the next thirty years. Drawing upon the conventions of 19th-century popular entertainment—minstrel shows, variety, MELODRAMA, and burlesque—Harrigan created scripts that depicted the lives of New York City's immigrant poor and celebrated them in comedy, music, and dance. The team's first hit, *The Mulligan Guard Ball*, showcased Harrigan as Irish immigrant Dan Mulligan, a Lower East Side saloon owner whose conflicts with his German and African-American neighbors provided the play's hilarious action. Between 1879 and 1884, Harrigan wrote eight more Mulligan Guard plays. *Cordelia's Aspirations*, considered his best by critics, dramatized the Mulligans's disastrous move uptown to Madison Avenue. In the series' last play, *Dan's Tribulations*, Harrigan's hero happily returned to the Lower East Side.

Harrigan's plays set the standard for late 19th-century American comedy. In the 1870s, immigrants and other working-class New Yorkers flocked to his theaters on Lower Broadway and helped to establish his reputation. As he expanded his range to full-length musical comedies in the early 1880s, he attracted the attention of the critical establishment, which proclaimed that only Harrigan truthfully depicted New York's immigrant masses. Financial success followed, and as Harrigan moved his theater further uptown, his audience grew to include middle- and upper-class New Yorkers. By the beginning of the 1890s, he had firmly established his position on the legitimate stage. The December 1890 opening of *Reilly and the Four Hundred* at his sumptuous Harrigan's Theatre was the triumph of his career.

In *Dramas from the American Theatre 1762–1909*, Richard Moody (1966) commented that Harrigan "not only served his era, he now serves the social and theater historian. No dramatist, novelist, or short story writer of his time committed himself so completely to the dark streets, back alleys, water fronts, and crowded tenements of New York." Not only can scholars use his plays to better understand New York's immigrant culture, but they may also find in his work the vitality of American theater in the late 19th century. Harrigan died on June 6, 1911, in New York City.

[*See also* United States, 1860–1929]

SELECT PLAYS: *The Little Fraud* (1871); *Mulligan Guard Ball* (1879); *Mulligan Guard Nominee* (1880); *Mulligan's Silver Wedding* (1881); *Squatter Sovereignty* (1881); *McSorley's Inflation* (1882); *Cordelia's Aspirations* (1883); *Dan's Tribulations* (1884); *The Investigation* (1884); *Old Lavender* (1885); *Reilly and the Four Hundred* (1890); *Under Cover* (1903)

FURTHER READING

Davidson, June, and Alicia Kae Koger. *Harrigan, Hart and Irish-American Musical Comedy*. Boston: Irish Studies Program, Northeastern Univ., 1989.

"Edward Harrigan's Comedy," *Harper's Monthly*, Vol. LXXIII (July 1886), 315–316.

Kahn, E. J. *The Merry Partners. The Age and Stage of Harrigan and Hart*. New York: Random House, 1955.

Koger, Alicia Kae. "A Critical Analysis of Edward Harrigan's Comedy." Ph.D. diss., Univ. of Michigan, 1984.

——. "Harrigan's Company." In *American Theatre Companies, 1749–1887*, ed. by Weldon Durham. Westport, Conn.: Greenwood Press, 1986. 275–279.

Moody, Richard, ed. *Dramas from the American Theatre, 1762–1909*. Cleveland: World Publishing Co., 1966.

——. *Ned Harrigan. Corlears Hook to Herald Square*. Chicago: Nelson Hall, 1980.

Williams, William. *'Twas Only an Irishman's Dream. The Image of Ireland and The Irish in American Popular Song, 1800–1920*. Urbana: Univ. of Illinois Press, 1996.

Alicia Kae Koger

HART, MOSS (1904–1961)

Everything is apple pie.

—Moss Hart

Even though Moss Hart is mostly known for his enduring collaboration with GEORGE S. KAUFMAN, with whom he wrote many plays, Hart also produced many other librettos, plays, and musical revues himself. Born on October 24, 1904, in New York City, Hart began working for Augustus Pitou, a theatrical producer, by age fourteen to provide financial support to his family. Two years later, he advanced to secretary, a position that helped him write his first play, a MELODRAMA, *The Hold-Up Man*.

In 1930 Hart wrote his first noteworthy play, *ONCE IN A LIFETIME*, under the pseudonym of Robert Arnold Conrad. This comedy caught the attention of Sam H. Harris, a Broadway producer who promised to stage the play on the condition that Hart would rewrite it with George S. Kaufman, a prestigious playwright. During the course of a partnership that lasted eleven years, they wrote many other plays, including the serious drama *Merrily We Roll Along* (1934) and the Pulitzer Prize winner *YOU CAN'T TAKE IT WITH YOU* (1936). After this play, Hart and Kaufman decided to write more serious drama; among these works are *I'D RATHER BE RIGHT* (1937), a social satire on the New Deal, *The Fabulous Invalid* (1938), which used the history of a single playhouse to represent the New York stage since 1900, and *The American Way* (1939), a patriotic play about a German immigrant and his family who manage to remain loyal to their country. The long-term collaboration of Kaufman and Hart came to an end in 1940 with the failure of their play *George Washington Slept Here*.

Another reason why Hart decided to separate from Kaufman was his desire to be recognized in his own right. His first solo effort was *Lady in the Dark* (1941). His next play, *Winged Victory* (1943), was based on his personal flight experience during World War II. *Christopher Blake* (1946) deals with the distress of a boy whose parents get divorced. *The Climate of Eden* (1952) was based on the novel *Shadows Move Among Them* by Edgar Mittelholzer. Its protagonist is a tormented young man who blames himself for the unavoidable death of his wife, and thus flees to a British Colony in which he progressively comes to terms with himself when he falls in love with another woman.

Hart was also producer and director of the plays of others with remarkable success, including Irving Berlin's *Miss Liberty* (1949) and Frederick Loewe and Alan Jay Lerner's *My Fair Lady* (1956) and *Camelot* (1960). His autobiography, *Act One* (1959), has been described as one of the best accounts of a life in the theater. Hart died on December 20, 1961, in Palm Springs, California, and was inaugurated into the Theater Hall of Fame in 1972.

[*See also* United States, 1929–Present]

SELECT PLAYS: With George S. Kaufman: *Once in a Lifetime* (1933); *Merrily We Roll Along* (1934); *You Can't Take It With You* (1936); *I'd Rather Be Right* (1937); *The Fabulous Invalid* (1938); *The American Way* (1939); *The Man Who Came to Dinner* (1939); *George Washington Slept Here* (1940). As sole playwright: *Lady in the Dark* (1941); *Winged Victory: The Air Force Play* (1943); *Christopher Blake* (1946); *Light Up the Sky* (1949); *The Climate of Eden* (1952)

FURTHER READING

Bach, Steven. *Dazzler. The Life and Times of Moss Hart*. New York: Knopf, 2001.

Goldstein, Malcolm. *George S. Kaufman, His Life, His Theater*. New York: Oxford Univ. Press, 1979.

Hart, Moss. *Act One. An Autobiography*. New York: Random House, 1959.

Estefania Olid-Peña

HARTE, BRET (1836–1902)

Bret Harte was the first writer who combined the American Western tradition with the REALISM of late-19th-century fiction. His work made use of Western characters (Native Americans, Chinese, pioneers, miners, gamblers), dialect and landscape, all of which contributed to the local color that was popular in both fiction and drama. He wrote to formula, combining sentiment, MELODRAMA, and coincidence; his whores were good-hearted and his gamblers were always gentlemen. His portraits of the Chinese in California were controversial; he intended to write satire of the racist stereotype, but when readers took it at face value, he created the character of Wan Lee, who was so sophisticated he looked down on the Americans, perhaps reflecting Harte's fundamentally Eastern view of the California frontier.

Born on August 25, 1836, in Albany, New York, Harte moved to California in 1854 and spent several years working as a teacher, tutor, miner, apothecary clerk, expressman, and printer, publishing his first poem in *Golden Era* in 1857. He wrote stories while working as an editorial assistant and typesetter, including "The Luck of Roaring Camp" (1868), "The Outcasts of Poker Flat" (1869), and "Plain Language from Truthful James" (1870). *The Luck of Roaring Camp and Other Sketches* (1870) was the first of many volumes of Harte's work, and in 1871, the author left San Francisco and returned to the East Coast, where William Dean Howells paid him well for his contributions to the *Atlantic*.

Harte's play, *Two Men of Sandy Bar*, opened on August 28, 1876, at the Union Square Theatre in New York. Including elements of three of Harte's stories—"Mr. Thompson's Prodigal," "The Idyl of Red Gulch," and "The Iliad of Sandy Bar"—it entertained its audience with Don José, the serape-clad lord of the rancho; the profane, stammering, and verbose Colonel Culpepper Starbottle; and Hop Sing, a Chinese laundryman who informs his acquaintances that "me plentee washee shirtee"—all colorful stereotypes painted from the playwright's memories of California in the 1850s.

Harte collaborated with Mark Twain on *Ah Sin*, opening May 7, 1877, in Washington, D.C. The story involves a group of unsuccessful miners and a rich judge's daughter who hopes to reward the man who saved her life; a murder charge ends in a madcap trial.

Harte wrote or collaborated on thirteen plays; the two discussed above and *Sue* (1896) with T. Edgar Pemberton were the only three produced. Harte lived in Europe from 1878 until his death on May 5, 1902, in Camberley, Surrey, England.

PLAYS: *Two Men of Sandy Bar* (1876); *Ah Sin* (with Mark Twain, 1877); *Sue* (with T. Edgar Pemberton, 1896)

[*See also* United States, 1860–1929]

FURTHER READING

Duckett, Margaret. *Mark Twain and Bret Harte*. Norman: Univ. of Oklahoma Press, 1964.

Meserve, Walter J. "The American West of the 1870s and 1880s as Viewed from the Stage." *Journal of American Drama and Theatre* 3 (Winter 1991): 48–63.

Moy, James S. "Bret Harte and Mark Twain's *Ah Sin*: Locating China in the Geography of the American West." In *Marginal Sights: Staging the Chinese in America*, ed. by Moy. Iowa City: Univ. of Iowa Press, 1993. 23–34.

Nissen, Axel. *Bret Harte: Prince and Pauper*. Jackson: Univ. Press of Mississippi, 2000.

Scharnhorst, Gary. *Bret Harte*. New York: Twayne , 1992.

——. Gary. *Bret Harte: Opening the American Literary West*. Norman: Univ. of Oklahoma Press, 2000.

Jeffrey D. Mason

HASENCLEVER, WALTER (1890–1940)

Let the theater be expression, not play!

—Walter Hasenclever, in his essay "Das Theater von Morgen" ("Theater of Tomorrow"), 1916

A prolific and versatile author, Walter Hasenclever (also known as Axel Kjellström) wrote lyric poetry, dramas, COMEDIES, essays, and two novels, but is best known for his early Expressionist play THE SON (*Der Sohn*, 1914).

Hasenclever was born on July 8, 1890, in Aachen, GERMANY. Despite a childhood of material wealth, he suffered horribly at the hands of his father. Sent to Oxford and then Lausanne to study law, he ended up in Leipzig studying philosophy and literature and became a leading member in the Leipzig circle of literary EXPRESSIONISM. Hasenclever wrote for Berlin and Leipzig dailies and published the lyric collections *Cities, Nights, and People* (*Städte, Nächte und Menschen*, 1909–1910) and *A Youth* (*Der Jüngling*, 1913) while tweaking the nose of the academic establishment. In 1914 he completed *Der Sohn*, which made him famous.

A war volunteer, Hasenclever feigned mental illness after the 1916 Dresden performance of *Der Sohn* and procured a prolonged stay and eventual medical discharge at a Dresden sanatorium. While there he befriended the severely wounded OSKAR KOKOSCHKA. Hasenclever's antimilitarist and pacifist leanings were evident in his lyric cycle, *Death and Transfiguration* (*Tod und Auferstehung*, 1917), and his antiwar drama *Antigone* (1917), a veiled attack on Kaiser Wilhelm II, which advocated the Expressionist ideals of peace, brotherhood, and spirituality.

The youthful hubris of *Der Sohn* and the antimilitarism of *Antigone* gave way to disillusionment and withdrawal from political action in *The Decision* (*Die Entscheidung*, 1919). In *Humanity* (*Die Menschen*, 1920) Hasenclever sought to "discover new dimensions and a new language for the stage" with a severe Expressionist style: speech becomes staccato utterances, and pantomime, light, and silence rather than words convey meaning. The mystical and parapsychological are prominent in the play *Beyond* (*Jenseits*, 1920) and in an adaptation of selected works of the mystic Emmanuel Swedenborg (1688–1772) entitled *Heaven, Hell, Spiritual World* (*Himmel, Hölle, Geisterwelt*, 1925).

Hasenclever's retreat from the everyday ended when he became the Paris correspondent for a Berlin daily (1924–1929). His enthusiasm for the French led to the successful boulevard comedies *A Distinguished Gentleman* (*Ein besserer Herr*, 1926) and *Marriages are Made in Heaven* (*Ehen werden im Himmel geschlossen*, 1928).

Hasenclever refused to emigrate to New York despite his left-wing reputation and his anti-fascist comedy *Napoleon Intercedes* (*Napoleon greift ein*, 1930). He spent 1930–1939 in uneasy exile in France, Yugoslavia, England, and Italy; his works were burned in Germany in 1933, and he was arrested twice in Fascist Italy. Hasenclever's later plays include the "comedy" *Conflict in Assyria* (*Konflikt in Assyrien*, 1938), a revisiting of the Book of Esther. Of his two autobiographical novels, *Error and Passion* (*Irrtum und Leidenschaft*, 1934–1939) and *The Outlaws* (*Die Rechtlosen*, 1939–1940), the latter details his experiences in an internment camp, Les Milles at Aix-en-Provence, France, where he committed suicide on August 15, 1940.

SELECT PLAYS: *Kingdom: Tragedy of a Human Idea* (*Das Reich. Die Tragödie einer Menschenidee*, 1909); *Nirvana* (*Nirwana*, 1909); *The Son* (*Der Sohn*, 1914); *The Savior* (*Der Retter*, 1916); *Antigone* (1917); *Humanity* (*Die Menschen*, 1918); *The Decision* (*Die Entscheidung*, 1919); *Beyond* (*Jenseits*, 1920); *Gobseck* (1922); *A Distinguished Gentleman* (*Ein besserer Herr*, 1926); *Murder* (*Mord*, 1926); *Marriages are Made in Heaven* (*Ehen werden im Himmel geschlossen*, 1928); *Curtains* (*Kulissen*, 1929); *Napoleon Intercedes* (*Napoleon greift ein*,1930); *A Bird Flies By* (*Kommt ein Vogel geflogen*,1931); *Christopher Columbus or the Discovery of America* (*Christoph Kolumbus, oder die Entdeckung Amerikas*, with Kurt Tucholsky, 1931–1932); *The Frogking* (*Der Froschkönig*,1931–1932); *Of Hearts and Minds* (*Sinnenglück und Seelenfrieden*,1932) *Münchhausen* (1934); *Marriage Comedy* (*Ehekomödie*, 1937); *Conflict in Assyria* (*Konflikt in Assyrien*, 1938)

FURTHER READING

Elwood, William R. "Hasenclever's *Sinnenglück und Seelenfrieden* as Metaphor for Suicide." *Text & Presentation: The Journal of the Comparative Drama Conference* 12 (1992): 15–21.

Hamburger, Käte. "Antigone." In *Sophocles: The Classical Heritage*, ed. by R. D. Dawe. New York: Garland, 1996. 251–268.

Löb, Ladislaus. " 'The Second Time as Farce?' Hasenclever's *Der Sohn* and Schiller's *Don Carlos*." *The Modern Language Review* 88, no. 2 (1993) 375–388.

Spreizer, Christa. *From Expressionism to Exile: The Works of Walter Hasenclever (1890–1940)*. Rochester: Camden House, 1999.

Christa Spreizer

HASHMI, SAFDAR (1954–1989)

[W]e believe that street theatre is doing something which is of singular significance. At a time when all forms of community entertainment are as fast disappearing, when the video and TV have started marketing encapsulated entertainment to be consumed at the level of the nuclear family or the individual, street theatre is once again reviving art which can be enjoyed at the community level . . . In this sense it is already playing the role that a fully developed and popular theatre should.

—Safdar Hashmi, from the essay "Jana Natya Manch: The First Ten Years of Street Theatre, October 1978–October 1988," in *The Right to Perform*, 1989

Safdar Hashmi made this statement on January 2, 1989, just six weeks before he was killed by industrialists' goons in Sahibabad, an industrial area on the outskirts of Delhi, INDIA, during a performance of *Holla Bol*, a street play written in support of local industrial workers demanding better wages. Born on April 12, 1954, in Delhi, India, Hashmi—a writer, director, actor, and full-time member of the Communist Party of India—was dedicated to creating a political theater "that would effectively express the emotions and concerns of India's working class" (1989). In 1973 he helped to found Jana Natya Manch (Janam), which produced protest street theater. Hashmi defines street theater as a "militant political theatre of protest. Its function is to agitate the people and to mobilize them behind fighting organizations" (1989).

Janam's first piece, the thirteen-minute play *Machine*, has had an enormous impact on the street theater movement. *Machine* was inspired by a situation at a nonunionized chemical factory: workers wanted a place to park their bicycles and a place to get a cup of tea. Management refused to grant their demands, and the workers went on strike. Guards fired on the strikers, killing six workers. *Machine*, which was first performed on October 15, 1978, is still being performed around the country in a wide variety of languages and adaptations.

Although members of Janam wrote their plays collaboratively, Hashmi did most of the writing. Janam has performed plays addressing a wide range of subjects: *Killers* (*Hatyarey*, 1978), was about the Hindu-Muslim riots in Aligarh. *Stratagems of the DTC* (*DTC Ki Dhandhli*, 1979) dealt with a more pedestrian urban problem of the Delhi Transport Corporation's exorbitant fare hike. *Woman* (*Aurat*, 1979), one of Janam's most often performed plays, argues that "women's struggle for equality is only a part of the broader united struggle of the working classes." During the state of emergency imposed by Indira Gandhi in June 1975 and lasting twenty-one months, Janam performed a number of plays challenging the government.

Engaged primarily in activist street theater, Hashmi also worked in other genres, including two plays for the proscenium stage—a Hindi adaptation of MAKSIM GORKY's *Enemies* (1983) and *Moteram's Satyagraha* (*Moteram ka Satyagraha*, 1988), the latter written collaboratively with HABIB TANVIR—and numerous songs, poems, and plays for children, the script for a television series, and documentary films.

By the time Hashmi died, Janam had given 4,300 performances of more than twenty-two plays in ninety cities for more than two and a half million people. Most of these plays have been widely translated and/or adapted from Hindi and are still being performed.

Safdar Hashmi's birthday, April 12, is celebrated in India as National Street Theatre Day, and every year on the anniversary of his death, a street play and political rally is held at the site of the attack.

FURTHER READING

Hashmi, Safdar. *The Right to Perform: Selected Writings of Safdar Hashmi*. New Delhi: Janam, 1989.

van Erven, Eugene. *A Playful Revolution: Theatre and Liberation in Asia*. Bloomington: Indiana Univ. Press, 1992.

Jana Natya Manch [People's Theatre Forum]. *People's Art in the Twentieth Century: Theory and Practice*. Ed. by Editorial Board. Delhi: Jana Natya Manch, 2000.

Sudipto Chatterjee

HASSAN, NOORDIN (1929–)

. . . the world watches whatever we're doing; and the world has tremendous influence.

—"Siti," Section 44 in *Children of This Land*, 1989

Noordin Hassan, winner of Malaysia's prestigious National Writer Laureate Award in 1993, was born in Penang, MALAYSIA on January 18, 1929. He studied at the Kirby Teacher Training College in ENGLAND and attended classical Western theater. Upon his return to Malaysia, he wrote *No Return Ending* (*Tak Kunjung Kembali*, 1953), a realistic drama about an Indonesian freedom fighter. Until 1969, he explored theater independently, including SURREALISM; plays from this period include the classical *Surai Cambai* (1954), the dance drama *Hot Rains on Malacca* (*Hujan Panas di Bumi Melaka*, 1962), and *In Three Colors* (*Dalam Tiga Warna*, 1962) about Indonesian President Sukarno. In 1962 Hassan returned to London to study, this time watching innovative theater.

In 1970, he directed his landmark music drama, IT IS NOT THE TALL GRASS BLOWN BY THE WIND (*Bukan Lalang Ditiup Angin*), which won Malaysia's Literary Award for drama in 1972. The play deals with issues arising in the aftermath of the ethnic riots of May 13, 1969. A clear break with the realistic theater, the work features a Greek style chorus, surrealistic design, traditional Malay theater, and a Brechtian structure. The nonrealistic style disguises the sensitive nature of Hassan's discourse as he criticizes government leaders.

Hassan's experimental techniques and use of Indigenous models caught the imagination of Malay playwrights over the next decade. He also espouses Islamic sentiment, creating several public pantomimes for the *musabaqah* occasion that marks the journey of Prophet Muhammad from Mecca to Medina. *The Five Pillars Stand Shining Upright* (*Tiang Seri Tegak Berlima*, 1973) supports the *Rukunegara*, the five national principles formulated after 1969 to help resolve ethnic issues; the title refers to the five pillars of Islam. *Door* (*Pintu*, 1974) deals with drug addiction among troubled youth; the door of choice can bring blessings to those who follow the Islamic path. *Don't Kill the Butterflies* (*Jangan Bunuh Rama-Rama*, 1979) depicts a mystical journey. 1400 refers to the Islamic year (C.E. 1981) when the play was staged. The protagonist, Dollah, abandons animistic practices to pursue a pure form of Islam. Drawing on Hassan's concept of *teater fitrah* (theater of faith), 1400 addresses how Malays should approach the new Islamic century.

Children of This Land (*Anak Tanjung*, 1989) uses a play-within-a-play format, reminiscent of PETER WEISS's MARAT/SADE. A college student, Siti, helps villagers improvise a play about national history. Finally, the village leader, who holds extreme religious views, is arrested for corruption. The play rejects fanaticism and envisions Islam as a religion of peace and progress. Siti reassures her village friend that the Malay way of life is not in danger, that those who are industrious have nothing to fear, and that as Muslims they must be just to those who hold alternative beliefs. Ultimately, Siti stresses, "the world watches whatever we're doing." In demonstrating cooperation between Malays and Chinese, the play is more multiethnic in its content than earlier works. *Masks* (*Peran*, 1991) critiques political corruption. Other 1990s plays include *Riddles* (*Sirih Bertepuk Pinang Penari*, 1992) and *Tonight the Turtle Cries* (*Malam Inin Penyu Menangis*, first staged in 1994). *By the Olive* (*Demi Zaitun*), staged in 2004, deals with characters of high status whose circumstances take a turn for the worse.

Noordin Hassan's is a multidimensional theater that can appeal to audience members on various levels. His drama provides pure entertainment as well as sophisticated intellectual content, and he has increasingly embraced a religious, social mission.

SELECT PLAYS: *Hot Rains Fall on the Land of Malacca* (*Hujan Panas di Bumi Melaka*, 1962); *In Three Colors* (*Dalam Tiga Warna*, 1962); *Struggle* (*Gelutan*, 1964); *Surai Cambai*; *It Is Not the Tall Grass Blown by the Wind* (*Bukan Lalang Ditiup Angin*, 1970); *The Five Pillars Stand Shining Upright* (*Tiang Seri Tegak Berlima*, 1973); *Door* (*Pintu*, 1974); *Don't Kill the Butterflies* (*Jangan Bunuh Rama-Rama*, 1979); *1400* (1981); *Cindai* (1987); *Anak Tanjung* (1989); *Masks: A Malay Play* (*Peran*, 1991); *Riddles* (*Sirih Bertepuk Pinang Menari*, 1992); *Tonight the Turtle Cries* (*Malam Ini Penyu Menangis*, 1994); *By the Olive* (*Demi Zaitun*, 2004)

FURTHER READING

Hassan, Noordin. *Mana Setangginya?: Kumpulan Drama Pilihan* [*Where Is the Incense?: A Collection of Selected Plays*]. Kuala Lumpur: Dewan Bahasa dan Pustaka, 2000.

——. "Speech on Receiving the Seventh National Literary Award." Tr. by Hawa Abdullah. *Malay Literature* 8, no. 2 (1995): 1–5.

——. "Theatre of Faith." Tr. by Faizal Yamimi Mustaffa. *Malay Literature* 8, no. 2 (1995).

Ishak, Solehah. *Histrionics of Development: A Study of Three Contemporary Malay Playwrights*. Kuala Lumpur: Dewan Bahasa dan Pustaka and Kementerain Pendidikan Malaysia, 1987.

——. "Teater Fitrah and '1400.'" *Malay Literature* 8, no. 2 (1995): 234–255.

——. "Solehah Ishak Interviews Noordin Hassan." *Malay Literature* 8, no. 2 (1995):256–273.

Nur Nina Zuhra [Nancy Nanney]. *An Analysis of Modern Malay Drama*. Shah Alam, Malaysia: Birtoteks, MARA Institute of Technology, 1992. 157–168.

Nancy Nanney

HAUPTMANN, GERHART (1862–1946)

One weakness is [my] inability to let one voice speak isolated from the polyphony of voices in my mind . . . There were always a lot of voices inside me that wanted to speak, and I saw no other possibility to create some order than to write polyphonic movements: dramas.

—Gerhart Hauptmann, in his speech "Die Sendung des Dramatikers" ["The Mission of the Dramatist"] to the Akademie der Wissenschaften [Academy of Sciences] in Vienna, 1905

The Swedish Academy awarded Gerhart Hauptmann the Nobel Prize for Literature in 1912, citing his "fruitful, varied, and outstanding production in the realm of dramatic art." Formulated at the beginning of the 20th century, the Academy's words of praise remain valid today. Aside from BERTOLT BRECHT, Hauptmann is the only modern German dramatist to attain enduring world fame.

Born on November 15, 1862, in Ober-Salzbrunn (currently Szczawno Zdrój, POLAND), the German province of Silesia where his father owned a hotel, Hauptmann encountered a variety of social classes throughout his youth: aristocratic families from RUSSIA, Poland, and GERMANY that frequented the hotel; dialect-speaking employees and local farmers; and workers in the nearby coal-mining district. Hauptmann's Silesian background influenced him deeply and plays an important role in many of his works.

Hauptmann's education was limited. The small town in which he grew up had very little to offer in terms of culture, and Hauptmann was a poor student who barely managed to pass his graduation exams. His parents sent him to an uncle's estate to study agriculture, but farm labor proved too hard. He then entered an art academy in Breslau to study sculpture, but this ended in failure as well. Although his formal education during these years was disappointing, other influences were shaping his future as an author. At his uncle's estate, he learned of and was moved by the religious ideas of Pietism. In Breslau he was in contact with a group of young radicals who read socialist tracts by Karl Marx (1818–1883) and Friedrich Engels (1820–1895). Even more important for Hauptmann's career as a writer was his engagement to Marie Thienemann in 1881. She was the daughter of a wealthy widow, and her money was vital to the poor, unsuccessful artist who continued to search for a suitable vocation. Hauptmann studied briefly at the universities of Jena and Berlin, but never received a degree. He subsequently attended an art school in Dresden to further his career as a sculptor, but never was able to establish himself as a studio artist. Despite, or maybe because of, these disappointments, Hauptmann started devoting more time to writing.

Supported by his wife's money, Hauptmann moved to Berlin, the center of German NATURALISM at the time. In 1886 a group of young intellectuals formed the Akademische Vereinigung (Academic Alliance), whose literary members, in turn, formed a second society called Durch (Across), the aim of which was to create "modern" literature, a literature depicting men and women of flesh and blood and reflecting the growing interest in social questions. Aestheticism and imitation of the classics were anathema to the group. Hauptmann became one of its leading members, as did Arno Holz (1863–1929) and Johannes Schlaf (1862–1941), the co-authors of *Papa Hamlet* (1889), the first German work written according to the new naturalist principles. In 1898 members and associates of Durch formed the Freie Bühne (Free Stage) theater club, which was decisive for the development of naturalist drama in Germany.

Major literary influences on the members of Durch were ÉMILE ZOLA (1840–1902), HENRIK IBSEN, LYOV TOLSTOY (1828–1910), and Fyodor Dostoevsky (1821–1881). Zola provided the theoretical foundation with writings such as *The Experimental Novel* (*Le Roman expérimental*,1880) and *Naturalism in the Theater* (*Le naturalisme au théâtre*, 1881). For Hauptmann, however, Ibsen and Tolstoy were stronger influences. Given the naturalist's commitment to a "scientific literature" recognizing the importance of socioeconomic and biological factors, the works of Karl Marx, Friedrich Engels, and Charles Darwin were equally important.

In 1888 Hauptmann experienced his literary breakthrough with the novella *Flagman Thiel* (*Bahnwärter Thiel*). The novella is generally considered a masterpiece of naturalism and seems to follow every rule of the movement. Social concerns are powerfully present in the description of Thiel's life as a poor railroad worker. Poverty, child abuse, and neglect are central themes, and heredity and environment play decisive roles in the development of the story. However, naturalist techniques are not an end in themselves, but rather the means to get to something much deeper: the human predicament. Despite its strong naturalist tendencies, *Flagman Thiel* is a mixture of established (e.g., REALISM) and emerging (e.g., SYMBOLISM and Impressionism) literary styles, combined with a significant amount of mysticism and transcendence. Such an admixture would come to characterize Hauptmann's subsequent works as well.

After the success of *Flagman Thiel*, Hauptmann turned to drama, and in 1889 his first play, BEFORE DAYBREAK (*Vor Sonnenaufgang*) had its tumultuous premiere. During the next twelve years, Hauptmann wrote fourteen plays. All were performed and reached a wide audience, not only in Germany but in the rest of Europe and in the United States as well. Although Hauptmann continued to write until his death—he authored more than forty plays, twenty novels, and many short stories and poems—his fame and importance to world literature are largely based on the dramas written between 1889 and 1911.

The family TRAGEDIES *The Coming of Peace* (*Das Friedensfest*, 1890) and *Lonely Lives* (*Einsame Menschen*, 1891) show strong influences from Ibsen's plays, in particular GHOSTS and ROSMERSHOLM. Both of Hauptmann's family tragedies pose the question whether a family and its individual members can overcome the constraints of social and genetic heritage. In *The Coming of Peace* (the plot is taken from information FRANK WEDEKIND gave Hauptmann in confidence), the Scholz family comes together at Christmas in hope of forgiving old animosities. It initially appears as if forgiveness will prevail, but the reconciliation is only temporary. When an old father-son conflict is revived, the father dies of a stroke. However, the audience is left with the possibility of a new beginning. The son's fiancée and her mother represent a contrast to the Scholz family. Mother and daughter try to convince the son, Wilhelm, that it is possible to break away from established patterns and start something new. Whether or not this is possible remains an open question. The play's ending—Wilhelm and his fiancée are seen entering the room where the father lies dead—does not provide a conclusive answer.

In *Lonely Lives* (*Einsame Menschen*, 1891; Hauptmann based the plot on his brother's marital problems), the theme shifts from a hopelessly dysfunctional family to a more traditional generational conflict: Johannes Vockerat, a self-centered academic, is trying to escape the confines of his conservative upper-middle-class family, but he possesses neither the will nor the strength to do so. His hopes focus instead on an outsider, the young female student Anna Mahr, who comes to stay with the family. With her he can share his intellectual ideas and utopian goals, something he is unable to do with his wife and the rest of his family. His wish to have a purely intellectual relationship with Anna turns out to be a fantasy, however, and she must leave the family. Johannes leaves the stage as well, but it is not entirely clear whether he commits suicide by drowning himself.

THE WEAVERS (*Die Weber*, 1893) brought Hauptmann his international breakthrough. More than any of his other plays, this one has been cited as proof that Hauptmann harbored socialist political views. *The Weavers* has always been popular in socialist countries. Vladimir Lenin's sister translated the drama into Russian, and in the Soviet Union and the German Democratic Republic, it was hailed as a masterpiece of socialist art. Käthe Kollwitz's graphic cycle *A Weaver Rebellion* (1898) has further contributed to this reputation. Hauptmann, however, never considered himself a socialist, and many critics have even seen an antisocialist message in *The Weavers*.

With Hauptmann's reputation as a serious naturalist firmly established, his next play, *Hannele* (*Hanneles Himmelfahrt*, 1893), a dream poem in two acts, surprised many. Hauptmann uses naturalist techniques to portray the inhabitants of a poorhouse, including the dying young girl Hannele. But for Hannele the reality of the poorhouse is not the most important thing. In her final moments, she is in a dream world, a paradise, where all her longings and aspirations come true. The beauty of Hannele's dreams and the transcendence they promise stand in stark contrast to naturalist dogma and are accentuated by Hannele's language. Rather than speaking the uneducated dialect that would have corresponded to her social status, she speaks poetically in High German.

If some of Hauptmann's readers and audiences were surprised by the neo-ROMANTICISM and symbolism of *Hannele*, others may have been even more surprised by his success with COMEDY. Having tried his hand at comedy in 1892 with *Colleague Crampton* (*Kollege Crampton*, 1892), Hauptmann's second comedy, *The Beaver Coat* (*Der Biberpelz*, 1893) has earned its place as one of Germany's greatest comedic texts. *The Beaver Coat* combines all of the necessary ingredients for a good comedy. While it is a critical satire of the political situation in Wilhelmine, Germany, it is at the same time a character comedy in the tradition of Molière. The main character is Mother Wolff, a petty thief who steals a beaver coat. Hauptmann's Mother Wolff has attained the same elevated status in Germany as William Shakespeare's Falstaff in England or Molière's Miser in France. Even though she is scheming and shrewd, Mother Wolff is portrayed with great humor and sympathy. Like Robin Hood, she steals only from the rich, and she steals only to move her family into a better social situation. Her popularity stems from her ability to fool the local magistrate, von Wehrhahn, the epitome of a German bureaucrat. Rather than finding the responsible thief, von Wehrhahn is preoccupied with finding political suspects. The play's ending has been controversial, since Mother Wolff is neither caught nor punished. Perhaps this ending became increasingly burdensome to Hauptmann, since he wrote a sequel, *Conflagration* (*Der rote Hahn*, 1901), in which we meet Mother Wolff ten years later. In the meantime, everything in *The Beaver Coat* has been brutalized. Although Mother Wolff has climbed the social ladder, she has deteriorated both personally and psychologically. She has remarried a shoemaker and police spy, and she has moved from poaching and petty theft to arson. Her once sympathetic presence has been transformed, and in the end justice seems to prevail: Mother Wolff dies before she meets the magistrate.

With *The Sunken Bell: A German Fairy Tale Drama* (*Die versunkene Glocke. Ein deustsches Märchendrama*, 1897), Hauptmann demonstrated yet another dramatic style. The play is written entirely in verse and the content has shifted away from the social-political to the personal-artistic. Using German folklore as a backdrop, Hauptmann presents the bell founder Heinrich, a symbol of the creative artist struggling between failure and success. The symbolism and neoromanticism of *Hannele* has been refined and fully developed here, and like *The Weavers*, *The Sunken Bell* was a big international success. The drama was performed in many major U.S. cities and widely praised by the critics. As in several of Hauptmann's plays, the protagonist is torn between two women, his wife Magda and the elfin Rautendenlein, a young nymph who inspires him both creatively and erotically. Many critics have pointed out that Heinrich's vacillation between Madga and Rautendenlein closely mirrors the marriage crises Hauptmann himself experienced from 1893 to 1904.

In 1893 Hauptmann met an eighteen-year-old actress and violinist named Margarethe Marschalk with whom he began a relationship. When his wife found out, she took their three children and went to America in 1894. In an attempt at reconciliation, Hauptmann soon followed her. This was Hauptmann's first trip to America, where several of his plays had already been staged. Apart from dealing with his family conflict, Hauptmann was able to attend the controversial premiere of *Hannele* in New York. Hauptmann and his wife were reunited for some time, but when they returned to Germany, Hauptmann resumed his relationship with Marschalk, with whom he fathered a son in 1900. In 1904 he finally divorced his wife and married Marschalk.

In 1900 Hauptmann wrote another drama depicting a suffering artist, *Michael Kramer*. The importance of this drama lies above all in the fact that it deeply moved and influenced some of Hauptmann's fellow authors. Thomas Mann (1875–1955), Rainer Maria Rilke (1875–1926), Bertolt Brecht, and James Joyce (1882–1941) all considered it a masterpiece. Joyce learned German to read Hauptmann in the original, and in 1901 he translated *Before Sunset* and *Michael Kramer* into English. Many critics have shown that Hauptmann influenced Joyce's work, "The Dead" and *Ulysses* in particular.

Themes from *The Sunken Bell* and *Michael Kramer* are developed further in *And Pippa Dances* (*Und Pippa tanzt!*, 1906). The play is subtitled *A Glassworks Fairy Tale* (*Ein Glashüttenmärchen*) and uses Silesian fairy tales and myths to create an atmosphere in which the quest for artistic and emotional freedom takes center stage. As in so many of Hauptmann's plays, this one looks pessimistically at the possibility of attaining such freedom in the real world. Those characters who already possess artistic creativity and make beautiful glass, like the Venetian Tagliazoni and the brute Huhn, squander their talents through destructive behavior and come to untimely deaths. Those who are searching for artistic and emotional freedom, like Tagliazoni's young daughter Pippa and the apprentice Michael Hellriegel, also fail: Pippa dies and a blinded Michael disappears into a fantasy. Only the magician Wann is capable of sustaining his creativity, but he, of course, is only a fairy tale figure.

A discussion of Hauptmann's most important works would not be complete without mentioning *Drayman Henschel* (*Fuhrmann Henschel*, 1897), *Rose Bernd* (1903), and *The Rats* (*Die Ratten*, 1911), all of which are social dramas in the naturalist tradition. *Drayman Henschel* appears to be a dramatization of *Flagman Thiel*, albeit with recast characters and settings. Henschel has climbed the social ladder, but his predicament is the same as Thiel's. After his wife's death, Henschel marries a seductive young woman who turns out to be destructive and unfaithful. She abuses and neglects both her own illegitimate child and Henschel's child by his first wife. In the end, Henschel commits suicide.

Rose Bernd is a family tragedy in which a young woman is trapped and ultimately destroyed by the male-dominated society around her. The plot is based on a story that Hauptmann heard as a juror at the trial of a young woman accused of perjury and infanticide. Hauptmann used the actual events as an outline for the plot, but then recast the setting and the characters to create a drama uniquely his own. The title figure is a peasant girl impregnated by the landowner for whom she works, and she is later raped by a scheming machinist. When her condition is revealed, she is deserted by all, including her father who does not want the reputation of his family to be destroyed. Left alone and without any hope of support, Rose kills her newborn child. Many critics see *Rose Bernd* as a modern *bürgerliches Trauerspiel* (bourgeois tragedy), a German dramatic tradition in which a young woman is sacrificed to class conflicts, bourgeois conventions, and male domination.

As much as *Drayman Henschel* and *Rose Bernd* seem to reemphasize the naturalist style of Hauptmann's early dramas, *The Rats* does so even more. Whereas the former plays are both set in Silesia, the latter takes place in a rat-infested working-class district in Berlin. Just as in *Rose Bernd*, the main character in *The Rats* is a woman, Mrs. John, but in contrast to Rose, Mrs. John desperately wants a child, which she then buys from a poor Polish maid, Pauline. Pauline, however, soon changes her mind and wants her child back, but Mrs. John is not ready to give up the child. Thus, she steals a sickly child from a drug addict and gives it to Pauline, so as to keep the child she bought. When her deception is discovered and the child is taken away, Mrs. John commits suicide. Intertwined with Mrs. John's tragedy is a comic story line played out in an apartment above the Johns. Here, a former theater director and a young acting student are plotting how to achieve success in the theater. *The Rats* was initially received rather coolly by both audiences and critics. On account of its expressionist and grotesque tendencies, however, the drama has proven to be one of Hauptmann's most modern and influential plays.

Of Hauptmann's later dramas, *Before Sunset* (*Vor Sonnenuntergang*, 1932) and *The Atriden Tetralogy* (*Die Atriden-Tetralogie*, 1940–1944) are of particular importance to understanding the totality of Hauptmann's life and work. In 1932 Hauptmann turned seventy and was celebrated as Germany's greatest author. In the same year, *Before Sunset* premiered. The main character in the play, a seventy-year-old man, has fallen in love with a much younger woman and is hoping for a second youth. But his grown children do everything in their power to destroy the relationship so that they alone can inherit the old man's estate. Devastated by his children's cruelty, he kills himself. The pessimism of *Before Sunset* foreshadows not only the sad final years of the author himself, but also of German culture as he knew it. When Adolf Hitler came to power the following year, Hauptmann remained in Germany, unlike Thomas Mann, Brecht, and other well-known authors. He was thus subjected to harsh criticism from Mann, for example, who argued that by not going into exile, Hauptmann gave tacit support to the Nazi regime. However, Hauptmann was never a member or supporter of the Nazi Party. With time he became increasingly isolated and pessimistic, a development that is expressed in his last work, *The Atriden Tetralogy*, a dramatic rendition of the Agamemnon tale.

During the very last years of his life, Hauptmann saw the total destruction of Germany, and he was particularly devastated by the Allied bombing of Dresden. Hauptmann died a broken man on June 6, 1946, in Agnetendorf (currently Jagniatków), Poland.

SELECT PLAYS: *Before Daybreak* (*Vor Sonnenaufgang*, 1889); *The Coming of Peace* (*Das Friedensfest*, 1890); *Lonely Lives* (*Einsame Menschen*, 1891); *The Weavers* (*Die Weber*, 1892); *The Beaver Coat* (*Der Biberpelz*, 1893); *Hanneles Himmelfahrt* (1893); *Florian Geyer* (1896); *The Sunken Bell* (*Die versunkene Glocke*, 1896); *Drayman Henschel* (*Fuhrmann Henschel*, 1898); *Michael Kramer* (1900); *Schluck and Jau* (1900); *Conflagration* (*Der rote Hahn*, 1901); *Henry of Auë* (*Der arme Heinrich*, 1902); *Rose Bernd* (1903); *And Pippa Dances!* (*Und Pippa tantz!*, 1906); *Griselda* (1909); *The Rats* (*Die Ratten*, 1911); *Indiphodi* (1920); *Before Sunset* (*Vor Sonnenuntergang*, 1932); *The Atriden Tetralogy*: *Iphigenia in Aulis*; *Agamemnon's Death*; *Electra*; *Iphigenia in Delphi* (*Die Atriden-Tetralogie*; *Iphigenie in Aulis*; *Agamemnons Tod*; *Elektra*; *Iphigenie in Delphi*, 1940–1944)

FURTHER READING

Cowen, Roy C. *Der Naturalismus* [Naturalism]. Munich: Winkler Verlag, 1981.

Guthke, Karl S. *Gerhart Hauptmann*. Munich: Francke Verlag, 1980.

Maurer, Warren R. *Understanding Gerhart Hauptmann*. Columbia: Univ. of South Carolina Press, 1992.

Sprengel, Peter. *Gerhart Hauptmann: Epoche-Werk-Wirkung* [Epoch, Works, Reception]. Munich: C.H. Beck, 1984.

Kerstin T. Gaddy

HAVEL, VÁCLAV (1936–)

Probably the best-known Czech of the last fifty years, Václav Havel gained international fame first as a playwright, then as a political dissident, and finally as a philosophic statesman. Born on October 5, 1936, in Prague, Havel was intermittently imprisoned in the 1970s and 1980s for challenging the Communist regime in CZECHOSLOVAKIA. He emerged as an obvious choice for President once that regime had been dismantled at the end of 1989.

As a literary person, he has written many theoretical and critical studies in addition to more than a dozen plays. His theater career began in the 1950s and included work with legendary actor/writer Jan Werich and director Alfred Radok before his sustained collaboration with director Jan Grossman at Prague's Theatre on the Balustrade in the 1960s, where Havel served as dramaturge and resident playwright. His first major play for this theater, *The Garden Party*, (*Zahradní slavnost*, 1963), contained several elements that were to become characteristic of his later work: an intricately structured plot and a satirical, absurdist theme centered in a character's confrontation with a nameless, highly bureaucratic institution. By intuitively adapting to the convoluted procedures and language of the bureaucracy, Hugo Pludek achieves a lofty position but loses his identity. THE MEMORANDUM (*Vyrozumění*, 1956), an earlier play, presents a power struggle within a similar anonymous institution over the introduction of a new "scientific" language (Ptydepe) for interoffice communications. A highly calculated symmetrical plot eventuates in the defeat of a manager whose self-proclaimed humanistic ideals are totally ineffectual in coping with the dehumanized workings of the bureaucracy.

Perhaps reflecting the more liberal time of its writing, *The Increasing Difficulty of Concentration* (*Stížena možnost soustř edění*, 1968) moves the action into a domestic setting, the home of a philosophizing and philandering sociologist who is trying to manage his marriage, a mistress, and an affair with his secretary concurrently. The precise, repetitive plotting becomes ever more intricate and farcical as time and action become erratic and characters echo each other's lines in a frenzied scene of blurred identities, before the play ends with a brief dialogue repeating that of the opening scene. With these three plays, Havel's association with the Theatre on the Balustrade and Grossman ended for more than twenty years as Havel's works were banned during the Normalization era following the crushing of the Prague Spring of 1968.

During the 1970s Havel wrote three full-length plays and three one-acts, none produced in a Czech theater until the 1990s. Of three full-length plays, most effective is *The Beggar's Opera* (*Žebrácká opera*, 1972), a nonmusical comedic work based on John Gay's 18th-century satiric musical. Its lively biplay among the scoundrels Macheath, Peachum, and Lockit echoes Havel's interest in deceitful maneuverings and power struggles. *Mountain Hotel* (*Horský hotel*, 1972) is a remarkable instance of Havel's talent for orchestrating complex cyclical plots involving caricatured figures but lacks a sufficiently engaging central action. *The Conspirators* (*Spiklenci*, 1971), perhaps Havel's weakest play, deals with four conspirators' failed efforts to gain power after the overthrow of a dictator.

Each of the three one-act plays, collectively called the Vaněk plays because of their recurring central figure, involves an encounter between a self-effacing dissident, Vaněk, and three sets of characters symptomatic of the Normalization era. In *Private Viewing* (*Vernisáž*, 1975), Vaněk visits a married couple who indirectly seek his approval for their newly prosperous and trendy lifestyle that resulted from compromises with the new regime. *Audience* (1975) has Vaněk working in a brewery and parrying the pressures and requests of a corrupt but vulnerable manager. In *Protest* (1979), the subtlest of the three plays, Vaněk visits a friend, ostensibly a critic of the regime, who wants to avoid putting himself on the line in a protest action on behalf of one of their colleagues. Realistic and straightforward in structure, all three plays depict the ethical evasions and venalities that characterized the Normalization era.

Havel wrote three other full-length plays, all after his release from his longest detention, 1979–1983. Like the one-act plays, all three are relatively more realistic in tone and offer more textured characterizations than the early plays of the Grossman era. *Largo Desolato* (1983) is an intensely autobiographical, tragifarcical portrait of a celebrated but insecure dissident at the edge of a breakdown from the pressures of the regime to recant some of his positions and the pressures of his friends and followers to live up to their idealized image of him. Havel makes effective use of his already developed skills of complex plotting and stage business to heighten the tension between critical ethical issues and comedic human frailties. *Temptation* (*Pokoušení*, 1985) is a satirical, contemporary treatment of the Faust story, once again using a vaguely defined scientific institute as its chief setting. The very name of the chief character, Faustka (little Faust), conveys Havel's slant: Faustka, a would-be defier of the establishment, is the victim of his own inherent flaws. His dabbling in black magic produces a jaded devil (Fistula) who turns out to be in the employment of the institute, suggesting that even in the mid-1980s Havel still regarded the Communist regime as a formidable though grotesque force built in part on the weaknesses of its challengers.

Havel's last major play, *Urban Renewal* (*Asanace*, 1987) bears few of the features that marked his early absurdist, schematically orchestrated plots, although some remnants of those techniques remain. The emphasis is on more fully developed, emotive characters (a team of architectural engineers) engaged in planning the rehabilitation of a run-down section of the city mandated by an ineffectual but strong administration. The heart of the play is the seeming liberation from the administration, leading to a euphoric celebration by the architects, which in turn is squelched by a new administration with a new mandate, thus recalling the events of the Prague Spring and its harsh demolition, which resulted in the Normalization era. Ironically, some two months after the play's premiere in Zurich, the events triggering the Velvet Revolution and its euphoric aftermath occurred in Prague. The aftermath included a revived democratic regime with Havel as its president, one who put aside playwriting during his tenure. Václav Havel's first new book since leaving the presidency in 2003, released in 2006, is a combination of notes, interview and diary titled *Prosím stručně* (*Briefly, Please*).

SELECT PLAYS: *The Memorandum* (*Vyrozumění*, 1956); *The Garden Party*, (*Zahradní slavnost*, 1963); *The Increasing Difficulty of Concentration* (*Stížena možnost soustředění*, 1968); *The Beggar's Opera* (*Žebrácká opera*, 1972); *Mountain Hotel* (*Horský hotel*, 1972); *Audience* (1975); *Private Viewing* (*Vernisáž*, 1975); *Protest* (1979); *Largo Desolato* (1983); *Temptation* (*Pokoušení*, 1985); *Urban Renewal* (*Asanace*, 1987)

FURTHER READING

Goetz-Stankiewicz, Marketa. *The Silenced Theatre: Czech Playwrights without a Stage*. Toronto: Univ. of Toronto Press, 1979.

——. "Shall We Dance? Reflections on Václav Havel's Plays," *Cross Currents* 10 (1991): 213–222.

Havel, Václav. *Disturbing the Peace*. New York: Knopf, 1990.

Trensky, Paul I. *Czech Drama Since World War II*. White Plains, N.Y.: M.E. Sharpe, 1978.

——. "Václav Havel's Temptation Cycle." *Czechoslovak and Central European Journal*, 10, 2 (Winter 1991):84–95.

Jarka M. Burian

HAYAVADANA

GIRISH KARNAD's *Hayavadana* (*The One With The Horse's Head*, 1971), is the first modern play incorporating both dramaturgical and technical elements of traditional performance, but written for actors trained in modern theater, to receive national attention in INDIA. When *Hayavadana* was published in 1971 it was immediately hailed as an important play: noted scholar Suresh Awasthi singled it out as an example of what could be done creatively with folk forms in an urban setting, and he credited Karnad with having evolved "a new dramatic form" (1989). The review of B. V. Karanth's 1972 Hindi-language production in Delhi hailed it as "not only an event of Delhi's theatre season but an event of the Indian theatre itself" and "a pointer towards the form the emerging theatre might take" (Kaushal 1972a). It is one of the most visible examples of the theater of roots; it is produced often, has been written about extensively, and is widely imitated. It is one of the most important plays of the post-independence period.

Hayavadana's central plot is based on a tale found in *The Ocean of Story* (*Kathasaritsagara*), a collection of 11th-century Sanskrit stories, and on its further development in Thomas Mann's German novella *The Transposed Heads: A Legend of India* (*Die vertauschten Köpfe: Eine indische Legende*, 1940). Girish Karnad's play focuses on Padmini, who is attracted to Kapila, her bookish husband Devadatta's sexy friend. In a jealous fit, Devadatta cuts off his own head. Kapila finds the body and, knowing he will be blamed for Devadatta's suicide, beheads himself. Terrified of the gossip that will surely ensue, Padmini appeals to the goddess Kali for help. Kali agrees to restore the men to life, and tells Padmini to put the heads back on their bodies. But Padmini, desiring to possess the man of her dreams—the one with Devadatta's mind and Kapila's body—"accidentally" switches the heads, leading to the central question of the story: which man is her husband, the one with Devadatta's head, or the one with his body? When a *rishi* (great sage) announces that the head is the supreme limb of the body, and that the man with Devadatta's head is therefore her husband, Padmini feels that she has the best of both worlds and happily goes home with the new Devadatta. Kapila exiles himself to the forest. In *The Ocean the Story*, this head-body split occurs between body and soul; in Mann's novella, the dichotomy is between intellect and emotion; in Karnad's play, the conflict is between self and other, and it is placed in a postcolonial context.

The play is named for Hayavadana, a man trying to unite his horse head with his man's body. When Hayavadana appears in act 2, he has managed to acquire a horse's body, but he still has a human voice. He tries to lose this by singing patriotic songs such as *Sare Jahan se Acchha Hindustan Hamara* (Our India is better than the whole world) and *Jana Gana Mana* (the national anthem), which he sings most often because he has noticed that people who sing the national anthem have lost their voices! Thus Hayavadana expresses his dilemma in terms of nationalism and Indianization. For this reason, *Hayavadana* can be seen as a play that comments on the divided self of the postcolonial subject, but it is also a play about a woman in love with two men in a society that restricts her to one. And at its basic narrative level, *Hayavadana* is a play about a woman who wants the perfect man. Ultimately, however, the play suggests that personal survival and happiness lie not in dissecting human identity, and that national identity lies not in singing the national anthem, but in the celebration of complexity and the integration of difference.

Hayavadana has had many famous productions, including B. V. Karanth's Kannada-language production in Bangalore (1972), his Hindi-language production in Delhi (1972), Satyadev Dubey's Hindi-language production staged in Mumbai and Delhi (1972), a Hindi-language production staged by Rajinder Nath in Kolkata (1972), a tri-lingual production (in English with songs in Kannada and Telugu) directed by Yamuna Prabhu and Lakshmi Krishnamurthi for the Madras Players in Chennai (1973), and a Marathi-language production directed by Vijaya Mehta in Mumbai (1973). *Hayavadana* continues to be performed in theaters and colleges all over India and the world.

[See also *Tughlaq*]

FURTHER READING

Awasthi, Suresh. "'Theatre of Roots': Encounter with Tradition." *The Drama Review* 33, no. 4 (1989).

Dhanavel, P. *The Indian Imagination of Girish Karnad: Essays on* Hayavadana. Delhi: Prestige Books. 2000.

Dodiya, Jaydipsinh, ed. *The Plays of Girish Karnad: Critical Perspectives*. Delhi: Prestige Books. 1999.

Karnad, Girish. "Interview with Kirtinath Kurtkoti. In *Contemporary Indian Theatre*." Delhi: Sangeet Natak Akademi, 1998.

Kaushal, J. N. "Last Month in Delhi: *Hayavadan*." *Enact* 63 (1972).

Mee, Erin. "*Hayavadana*: Model of Complexity." In *Girish Karnad's Plays: Performance and Critical Perspectives*. Ed. Tutun Mukherjee. Delhi: Pencraft International, 2006.

Erin B. Mee

HAYES, KATE SIMPSON (1856–1945)

Born in Dalhousie, New Brunswick, in 1856, Catherine Ethel Hayes was the third daughter of Irish Catholic immigrants. Patrick was a lumber merchant and owned a general store; financial misfortune caused him to seek work abroad, and in 1869 he was killed in a Wisconsin lumber camp. Anna, was "a highly cultivated woman" (Morgan, 1898) from whom her daughter learned a love of literature. Kate's first literary accolades came at sixteen when the editor of the *St. Croix Courier* read her play and hired her to write a children's column. She took a second class certificate in music, trained as a public school teacher, and at twenty-three taught in Prince Arthur's Landing, Ontario. After briefly working as governess in Prince Albert, Saskatchewan, she married C. Bowman Simpson, the son of a mill owner and Ontario senator, and had two children with him.

At twenty-nine, she left Simpson and moved to Regina. There she conducted a ten-year love affair with parliamentarian and editor Nicholas Flood Davin. She was employed by Davin as *The Regina Leader's* first woman reporter and through his assistance gained the post of first woman librarian in western Canada. Hayes supported herself and her children (she had two more with Davin) largely through her journalism and freelance writing. For ten years, until 1906, she edited the women's page of the *Winnipeg Free Press*; in 1910 she briefly edited a similar page for the *Ottawa Free Press*. Hayes helped found the Canadian Women's Press Club and was its first secretary and second president. Between 1904 and the outbreak of World War I, she was immigration agent for the Canadian Pacific Railway. Around 1920 Hayes moved to Victoria, British Columbia, where she wrote a daily advice column for *The Winnipeg Tribune*. She also contributed articles to *MacLean's*, *The Daily Colonist*, *Saturday Night*, and *The Campbellton Graphic*.

Hayes wrote and published many literary works under a variety of *noms de plum*, including Ivy, Betty Vincent, Elaine, Marka Wöhl, Yukon Bill, and her most commonly used Mary Markwell. Her theatrical output was at its peak in Regina during her association with the Literary and Musical Association, which she and Davin helped establish. With them, in 1886, she made her debut as an actor; her second stage appearance was in the FARCE *Turn Him Out*, and she later took the role of Lady Teasel in *School for Scandal*. Her flamboyant Regina plays—*A Domestic Disturbance* (1892), *A Divorce for $50* (1893?), and *A Duplicate Man* (1897)—all enjoyed performances, but none are extant. These parlor farces irreverently poke fun at illegitimacy, divorce, and adultery, issues at the heart of her affair with Davin. Although she gained literary recognition with *The Writ* (1921) and won tenth place in a Montreal playwriting competition, only three of her plays are still in existence: *Midnight Express* (1927), *Slumberland Shadows* (1895), and *The Anvil* (1927). More play fragment than play, *Midnight Express* treats melodramatic themes similar to those of the Regina farces. The latter two are more ambitious and deal with racial relations and immigration on the prairies. Generically, they represent very different forms of Hayes's dramatic output, the one being a children's fairy play and the other a melodramatic problem play for adults. Hayes died in 1945 in Victoria, British Columbia.

[*See also* Canada]

SELECT PLAYS: *A Domestic Disturbance* (1892); *A Divorce for $50* (1893?); *Slumberland Shadows* (1895); *A Duplicate Man* (1897); *The Writ* (1921), *The Anvil* (1927); *Midnight Express* (1927)

FURTHER READING

Bird, Kym. "Mothers of a New and Virile Race: Liberalism and Social Purity in the Life and Works of Kate Simpson Hayes." In *Redressing The Past: The Politics of Early English-Canadian Women's Drama, 1880–1920*, ed. by Bird. Montréal: McGill-Queen's Univ. Press, 2004. 92–137.

Koester, C. B. *Mr. Davin M.P.* Saskatoon: Western Producer Prairie Books, 1980.

Maguire, Constance Anne. "Convention and Contradiction in the Life and Ideas of Kate Simpson Hayes, 1856–1945." M.A. thesis, Univ. of Regina, 1996.

Morgan, Henry James. *Canadian Men and Women of the Time: A Handbook of Canadian Biography*. Toronto: Briggs, 1898.

O'Neill, Patrick B. "Nineteenth-Century Theatre in Regina." *Prairie Forum* 21, no. 1 (1996). 1–16.

Kym Bird

HAY FEVER

NOËL COWARD's early play *Hay Fever* (1924) not only brought him stardom, but remains one of the best-loved plays in his long and multifaceted career. One critic, writing for *The Era*, called it "the gayest, brightest and most amusing entertainment in London" when it was first produced in 1925 (Morley, 1979).

Coward claimed that this play was written in three days, shortly after a trip to New York. This trip brought him first-hand experience with the fast pace of Broadway shows, which he employed in this COMEDY. He also became a regular guest at the evening parties of playwright Hartley Manners and his actress wife Laurette Taylor. Coward remembered in his autobiography *Present Indicative* that evenings spent at the couple's New York City home were often devoted to "acrimonious games" that brought about "shrill arguments concerning rules." The games, the subsequent arguments, and the people became the inspiration for this comedy about unconventional people who lead an existence of total self-absorption.

The plot of *Hay Fever* is almost nonexistent—in fact, its production was delayed because producers and actors found the plot too thin. The play unfolds during a weekend at the Bliss family's country home, where each of the four family members have invited a guest of the opposite sex, without notifying the others. They arrive one by one, but the family does not seem to care whether they are having a good time. Every one of the family is totally involved in his or her own world. Judith, although retired from the London stage, experiences her life as scenes in a play; David studies real human life for the sake of authenticity in his novels; the two children, Simon and Sorel, are artists living more in a fantasy world than in reality. Forgetting all about their individual guests, members of the Bliss family get entangled with different people at different moments, enjoying themselves but bringing confusion to all the guests. Finally, in the midst of quarreling and making up, the family hears the slamming of the front door, and realizes that their guests have left them to their own madness.

Coward borrows the Edwardian theme of sexual intrigue, the house party, but plays with the code of behavior that holds the party together. Instead of having the characters behaving with good manners, the Bliss family's manners are governed by charm, a trademark of Coward's plays. The Blisses are charming personalities because they are forever playing roles. Judith fashions moments of her real life after great scenes she has played, and her family is ready to step into the fantasy at any time. The Bliss family's egocentric enjoyment of the weekend contrasts with the guests' confusion to emphasize the gap between the fictional world of charm and the real world of manners.

Hay Fever heralds a series of Coward successes such as PRIVATE LIVES (1930), DESIGN FOR LIVING (1933) and BLITHE SPIRIT (1941). Through his succinct and simple conversational exchange, Coward shifts the comic attention to the situation rather than the quality of one-liners. By this he creates his own kind of comedy which is different from the language-oriented OSCAR WILDE.

[*See also* England, 1860–1940; Gay and Lesbian Drama]

FURTHER READING

Coward, Noel. *Present Indicative*. London: Heinemann, 1937.
Gray, Frances. *Noel Coward*. London: Macmillan, 1987.
Lahr, John. *Coward the Playwright*. Berkeley: Univ. of California Press, 1982.
Morley, Sheridan. "Introduction" to *Collected Plays: Volume 1*, by Noel Coward. London: Methuen, 1979.
Russell, Jacqui. *File on Coward*. London: Methuen, 1987.

Amy Lee

HAZEL KIRKE

Hazel Kirke opened on February 4, 1880, at Madison Square Garden in New York City, a theater that author STEELE MACKAYE had redesigned. Originally titled *The Iron Will*, the play ran for a total of 486 performances, and during the 1882–1883 season, fourteen different companies toured the show.

The four-act play is set in a small English town. When Hazel Kirke was fourteen years old, her father Dunstan promised her in marriage to Squire Rodney, an older man who had bailed Dunstan's mill out of financial trouble. The play begins seven years later, and we discover that bride-to-be Hazel has fallen in love with Arthur Carrington, a young man who has been staying in the Kirke household since Dunstan rescued him from drowning. Arthur loves Hazel, too, but both try to conceal their feelings.

The Kirkes don't know that Arthur is really Lord Travers and that he is engaged to a woman of his own class, Lady Maude. Like Hazel, Arthur was betrothed out of duty to his father, who was responsible for the loss of Lady Maude's family fortune.

Hazel and Arthur finally declare their love for one another, but Dunstan disowns her: "I cast thee out adrift, adrift forever from thy feyther's love, and may my eyes never more behold thee." Rodney, however, does not resent Hazel's decision, declaring, "I love ye still, God help me; love ye too well to ask anything save your own happiness."

Arthur and Hazel elope and are married just across the border in Scotland, a fact that makes the legality of their marriage questionable. Behind Arthur's back, his mother tells Hazel that her marriage is a fraud, driving Hazel back to her father's house. Poetic justice is served, however, by the immediate onstage death of Arthur's mother.

Meanwhile, Hazel's father has gone blind and is now in danger of losing the mill, though he refuses to ask Rodney for help again. Hazel returns and wants to make things right, even considering Rodney's proposal to marry and live together in chastity. Dunstan remains unbending and Hazel decides to commit suicide. At the last moment, she is saved by Arthur, and a letter arrives which confirms that the lovers are legally married. Dunstan blesses the marriage and the family is reconciled.

As is typical of a MELODRAMA, the plot is sensationalistic and highly emotional, offering comic relief in the parallel courtship of Arthur's friend Pittacus Green and Hazel's cousin Dolly. The language features local color, and the play leans toward a new American REALISM in its frequently naturalistic dialogue and in the absence of a traditional villain. It is not so nearly realist, however, as some other late-19th-century American plays, such as JAMES A. HERNE'S MARGARET FLEMING (1890) or WILLIAM GILLETTE'S SECRET SERVICE (1896).

The play requires several major scene changes, all of which were accomplished with the elevator stage Steele MacKaye had invented and recently installed at Madison Square Garden. Indeed, the play can be understood in part as a vehicle for MacKaye's stage innovations.

FURTHER READING

Kelly, James E. *Faces and Scenes from Hazel Kirke: as represented at the Madison Square Theatre, Twenty-fourth Street, near Broadway, New York*. New York: Art Interchange, 1881.

MacKaye, Percy. *Epoch: The Life of Steele MacKaye, Genius of the Theatre.* New York: Boni & Liveright, 1927.

Mackin, Dorothy. *Melodrama Classics: Six Plays and How to Stage Them.* New York: Sterling, 1982.

McLennan, Kathleen Ann. "American Domestic Drama 1870–1919: Individualism and the Crisis of Community." Ph.D. diss., Univ. of Wisconsin, Madison, 1987.

Murphy, Brenda. "The State of the Art: The American Theatrical Scene in the 1880s." In *American Realism and American Drama, 1880–1940*, ed. by Murphy. Cambridge: Cambridge Univ. Press, 1987.

Woodard, Debra J. "The Plays of Steele MacKaye: The Beginning of a Movement Toward Realism." Ph.D. diss., Northwestern Univ., 1981.

DeAnna M. Toten Beard

HEAD OF MARY

Head of Mary: A Nagasaki Fantasia (Maria no Kubi: Nagasaki Gensokyoku), a Japanese SHINGEKI play by TANAKA CHIKAO, is a Roman Catholic drama about survivors of the atomic bombing of Nagasaki. It was first performed in February 1959 by the New Man (Shinjinkai) troupe under the direction of the playwright.

Blown by strong winds away from the Mistsubishi Munitions factory, its intended target, the atomic bomb that was dropped on Nagasaki on August 9, 1945, exploded directly above the Urakami Cathedral, the largest Roman Catholic church in Asia. The cathedral was demolished, the worshippers inside killed, and the statues of the Virgin Mary and saints that stood outside toppled and scorched. In the Head of Mary, Tanaka Chikao explores the implications of this event by imagining a group of atomic bomb survivors who plot to retrieve fragments of the statue of the Virgin from the ruins and rebuild it in their private shrine as their personal intercessor and object of veneration. The plot is an allegory of the efforts by Christians in Nagasaki to reconstitute their faith after the atomic bombing, but it is also a universal metaphor for the difficulties of rebuilding faith after all the horrors of the 20th century.

The group formed to steal the statue of Mary is led by Shika, a woman who works as a nurse by day and prostitute by night. Shika is a survivor whose face is disfigured by a large keloid. Her faith in the Virgin is what drives the group: "Mary! Selfless Mary!" she prays, "when women die in sin as we, / When women live in sin as we, / Only you, who have escaped sin, / Can see into the reaches of our soul." Shika's faith is opposed by Yabari, a student in his early twenties, who advocates political activism. When Yabari tries to convince Shika that she should put herself and her disfigurement at the service of the movement to ban nuclear weapons, she retorts, "Absolute justice cannot be found in politics. / Nor in existence; / Nor absolute freedom either." Absolute justice is what she craves, and only God can provide that.

A secondary plot concerns Shinobu (Endurance) and Jigoro (Gigolo), sworn enemies who are reconciled in the face of impending death. They teach each other the vacuousness of their respective life strategies—hatred and nihilism—and realize together the need "to go beyond."

In the surreal last scene of the play, Shika and her co-conspirators struggle to move the head of Mary, the last remaining piece of the icon. They fail, but the head suddenly speaks to them: "I'll let you suckle at my breast. I'll let you drink to your hearts' content. My milk is so sweet, oh so sweet! First drink, then I'll listen to your prayers. So come, come!" It is the nurturing voice of succor, but the head does not budge. In the end, the believers' efforts to reconstruct their faith, although incomplete, are rewarded.

FURTHER READING

Hayashi Hirochika. "Tanaka Chikao *Maria no Kubi*" [Tanak Chikao's *Head of Mary*]. In *Nijusseiki no Gikyoku II: Gendai Gikyoku no Tenkai* [Twentieth Century Plays II: The Evolution of Contemporary Plays], ed. by Nihon Kindais Engekishi Kenkyukai. Tokyo: Shakai Hyoronsha, 2002. 162–165.

Rimer, J. Thomas. "Four Plays by Tanaka Chikao." *Monumenta Nipponica* 31, no. 3 (1976): 275–298.

Tanaka Chikao. *The Head of Mary*. In *After Apocalypse: Four Japanese Plays of Hiroshima and Nagasaki*, ed. and tr. by David Goodman. Cornell East Asia Papers 71. Ithaca: Cornell East Asia Program, 1994. 109–181.

David G. Goodman

HEARTBREAK HOUSE

At your age I looked for hardship, danger, horror, and death, that I might feel that life in me more intensely. I did not let the fear of death govern my life; and my reward was, I had my life.

—Captain Shotover, Act 2

Heartbreak House: A Fantasia in the Russian Manner on English Themes written by GEORGE BERNARD SHAW in 1916–1917, was first performed in New York at the Garrick Theatre in 1920 and in London at the Royal Court Theatre in 1921. Although it had a mixed early reception, the play is widely recognized as one of Shaw's major achievements as a dramatist and has repeatedly proven its theatrical strength over the decades since its first production. As Richard Watts, Jr., a reviewer for the *New York Post*, remarked of one production, the play "always seems to have something new to say to the generation seeing it" (Oct. 19, 1959).

In some ways *Heartbreak House* presents large public issues: Shaw described it in his Preface as a portrait of "cultured, leisured Europe before the War." The inhabitants of Shaw's "house without foundations" represent a society on the brink of apocalyptic doom, playing futile, childish games of flirtation and humiliation of others, and unable to control the drifting ship of state. But the work also reflects, in a number of subtle and disguised ways, some of Shaw's own comic and painful experiences in the period leading up to World War I, especially his associations with Erica Cotterill, the intelligent young cousin of Rupert Brooke, and with the actress Mrs. Patrick Campbell, who are recalled in the characterizations of Ellie Dunn and Hesione Hushabye, respectively. In the Preface Shaw emphasizes the intellectual and social origins of the malaise that resulted in the catastrophe of World War I, but the Preface is much more historically specific than the play, where very much to the foreground in dialogue and action are the cruel, manipulative, and often childish games pursued in the duel of sex. The capitalist Boss Mangan and the offstage character, the colonial governor Sir Hastings Utterword, evoke powerful and threatening contexts of exploitative capitalism and brutal, imperialistic systems of racial subordination.

In the composition of *Heartbreak House*, Shaw continually conducts witty and parodic dialogues with other texts, works belonging to several genres and ranging in time from *The Iliad* through Shakespearean TRAGEDY to early 20th-century plays by ANTON CHEKHOV. Analysis of the intertextual relations of *Heartbreak House* shows that the numerous echoes of other texts and literary motifs in the play are creatively transformed in Shaw's treatment of them into quite different keys. The many literary burglaries that can be detected in the play are Shavianized in distinctive and amusing ways.

The play is set in the shiplike house of the ancient retired sea Captain, Shotover, an eccentric, rum-drinking weapons inventor. Like King Lear, with whom Shaw associated the character, Shotover has two "demon daughters,: Hesione, who lives in the house with her handsome but ineffectual husband, Hector, and Ariadne, who is revisiting her childhood home after a long period abroad. The main thread of action in the play concerns the fortunes of Ellie Dunn, a young friend of Hesione who progresses from heartbreaking disillusionment about a romance with Hesione's husband, Hector (posing as a romantic character called "Marcus Darnley") to a "spiritual" marriage with Shotover after the collapse of a proposed marriage of convenience with Mangan. The play ends sensationally but anticlimactically with the "Beethoven music" of a bombing raid that almost destroys Heartbreak House. It passes, leaving the house intact and the characters disappointed.

In the structural organization of *Heartbreak House* and in the depiction of its characters, Shaw adopted disconcerting and destabilizing strategies. The form of the play is quite remote from the dramatic model established in the 19th-century well-made plays, with their carefully developed, intricate plots, and denouements in which all the threads of narrative are carefully drawn together. In contrast, Shaw's "fantasia" develops as a kaleidoscopic series of encounters, coquetry and sexual passes, stratagems, snatches of philosophy, quarrels, and character assassinations. Most of the narrative motifs generated in the course of the play remain unresolved. Characters are presented in deeply ambivalent lights, in one moment seen as "heartbroken imbeciles" and in the next as "rather a favourable specimen of what is best in . . . English culture."

In some ways *Heartbreak House* can be seen as an expression of Shaw's frustration. The political causes for which he had fought were, temporarily at least, swept aside by the *force majeur* of a great war between imperial foes. His pamphlet "Common Sense About the War" did nothing to alter the course of events; rather, it succeeded in bringing down on his head an enormous amount of hostile invective, as well as social ostracism. But the self-delighting artistry of *Heartbreak House*, its exuberant comedy and pungent satire, and its masterly organization of extraordinarily complex dramatic materials all suggest a stance of gaiety and poise rather than defeat and disappointment.

FURTHER READING

Gibbs, A. M. *Heartbreak House: Preludes of Apocalypse*. New York and Ontario: Twayne Publishers & Maxwell Macmillan Canada, 1994.

Kruse, Axel. "Bernard Shaw's *Heartbreak House*: The War in 'Neverland.'" *Sydney Studies in English* 13 (1987–1988): 100–119.

Weintraub, Stanley. *Bernard Shaw 1914–1918: Journey to Heartbreak*. London: Routledge & Kegan Paul, 1971.

Wright, Anne. *Literature of Crisis, 1910–1922*. London: Methuen, 1984.

A. M. Gibbs

HEDDA GABLER

But, good God Almighty . . . people don't do such things!
—Judge Brack, Act 4

Hedda Gabler (1890), a play in four acts by HENRIK IBSEN, was first performed at the Munich Hoftheater in January 1891 and met with a mixed reception. Many critics regarded Hedda as an enigmatic monster without any roots in empirical experience, and yet this character soon became one of the most coveted roles in world drama.

By the title, Ibsen is indicating that the main character is the daughter of her father, General Gabler, more than she is the wife of Jørgen Tesman. Brought up without a mother, Hedda has developed a militaristic and aristocratic way of thinking, as well as a masculine pattern of behavior, that complicates her role as a woman in 19th-century society. The General's pistols are heirlooms, which also provide Hedda with a symbolic connection to a masculine role. By contrast her husband, Jørgen Tesman, has been raised by two aunts who have passed on to him feminine, compassionate values, symbolically represented by the slippers he likes to wear. Much of the conflict in *Hedda Gabler* is built around differing social values. The paternally fixated Hedda is portrayed by Ibsen as a product of Victorian norms bordering on frigidity, which recalls other decadent female figures at the turn of the century, a mixture of *femme fatale* and *femme d'enfant*.

Returning from their honeymoon, the newlyweds settle in a villa that Judge Brack, a friend of Hedda's, with his own agenda, has helped them to buy. Hedda suffers under the petit bourgeois sphere, carrying within her an unfulfilled longing for beauty, which she used to speak of as "vine leaves in the hair." Jørgen, holding a scholarship in cultural history, is hoping to win a professorship at the local university. He is surprised to find that an old acquaintance of Hedda and himself, Ejlert Løvborg, is back in town, apparently recovered from his alcohol problems. He has published a brilliant study of cultural history, has just completed a new manuscript on the forces shaping the future civilization, and through the efforts of Thea Elvsted, is about to regain social respectability. It is obvious that he could become a rival for the vacant chair. Invited to Brack's place for some drinks, Løvborg gets drunk and loses his manuscript. With the intention of saving it for return to Løvberg, Jørgen gives it to Hedda. The next morning Løvborg, desperately looking for his manuscript, comes to the Tesman household. To Hedda he talks about ending his life. She grasps this opportunity and encourages him to do it "in beauty," giving him one of General Gabler's dueling pistols. Jealous of Thea's positive influence on Løvborg, Hedda burns the "child" of Thea and Løvborg in the stove.

At first, the news of Løvborg's death pleases Hedda, but when Brack tells her that the shot had fatally wounded Løvborg in the groin, seeming to indicate an accident rather than a suicide, she is disgusted that everything in her surroundings is transformed into something ugly and ridiculous. The originally positive connotations attached to the vine leaf symbolism are negated. Brack's knowledge that Løvborg has been killed with one of the Gabler pistols puts Hedda under pressure to comply with his erotic demands. Hedda is driven into a corner from which she can see no escape. Jørgen and Thea, engaged in reconstructing Løvborg's manuscript from earlier drafts, have no use for her. Since she dreads the scandal and will not give in to Brack's advances, she shoots herself in the temple with another of her father's pistols.

There is a pervasive irony in the fact that, in the end, it is Hedda who realizes the death in beauty that she had chosen for Løvborg to perform. In her fatal coupling of ideal, beauty, and suicide lies implicitly a fundamental criticism of the prevailing petit bourgeois conditions of life that allow no room for anything but the degrading and ridiculing of all higher efforts. Yet ultimately Hedda's free, courageous act takes on an ambivalence, since it seems more forced upon her by circumstance than the chosen response to a distaste for life that lets suicide appear as dying in beauty.

FURTHER READING

Arup, Jens. "On Hedda Gabler." *Orbis litterarum* 12 (1957): 3–37.

Durbach, Errol. "The Apotheosis of Hedda Gabler." *Scandinavian Studies* 43, no. 2 (1971): 143–159.

Northam, John. "*Hedda Gabler*." In *Ibsenårbok 1968–69* [*Ibsen Annual 1968–69*]. Oslo: Universitetsforlaget, 1969. 60–81.

Olsen, Stein Haugom. "Why does Hedda Gabler marry Jørgen Tesman?" *Modern Drama* XXVIII (1985): 591–610.

Sprinchorn, Evert. "Ibsen and the Immoralists." *Comparative Literature Studies* 9, no. 1 (1972): 58–79.

——. "The Unspoken Text in *Hedda Gabler*." *Modern Drama* 36 (1993): 353–367.

Theoharis, Theoharis C. "*Hedda Gabler* and 'The Dead.' " *ELH: Journal of English Literary History* 50 (1983): 791–809.

Knut Brynhildsvoll

HEIBERG, GUNNAR (1857–1929)

. . . but when two human souls come together, one of them must wait for the other, and at times the other must also wait, and they remain at a standstill and get no further. But when two human bodies come together, it is like locking out the holy and throwing away the key.

—Abel, Act 3, *The Balcony*

Gunnar Heiberg was born November 18, 1857, in Kristiania (now Oslo). He was the most important Norwegian playwright in the decades following HENRIK IBSEN and was a leading theater director and critic in his time. He combined critical REALISM with impulses from impressionism and neoromanticism in a modern, lyrical, symbolic dramatic form. Inspired by Ibsen's prose dramas, Heiberg soon modified his approach, creating COMEDIES, TRAGICOMEDIES, satires, and stylized plays that broke up the standard plot structure.

Working as a journalist for *Dagbladet* (1880–1882) and *Verdens Gang* (1890–1903), Heiberg wrote articles on politics and the theater and is said to have turned theater criticism into an art form. While at the Bergen Theatre, he directed the world premières of THE WILD DUCK and ROSMERSHOLM. As a stage director he was insightful and inventive.

Heiberg's first drama was the problem play *Aunt Ulrikke* (*Tante Ulrikke*, 1884), celebrating the free, oppositional spirit in a female character. *King Midas* (*Kong Midas*, 1890) is a camouflaged portrait of BJØRNSTJERNE BJØRNSON and his moralism. Truth and freedom are pronounced as ideals, expressed in a tragicomic dramatic form. Both plays were rejected by the Christiania Theater because of their radicalism and their attack on Bjørnson, but *Kong Midas* was staged at The Royal Theater in Copenhagen, over Bjørnson's protest. This was a great victory for Heiberg and triggered a heated debate in NORWAY. From then on, Bjørnson actively opposed Heiberg both as a playwright and as a stage director. Heiberg later wrote the satirical play *Bed of State* (*Paradesengen*, 1913), a satire on Bjørnson's public image.

One of Heiberg's most original plays is *The Balcony* (*Balkonen*, 1894), which celebrates passion and love as the ultimate meaning of life. This theme, combined with the radically stylized, symbolical form of the play, made it unacceptable to the Christiania Theater. It enjoyed a successful premiere in Copenhagen with Heiberg directing. In Norway the play triggered a feud about the relationship between art and morality.

Heiberg's lyrical drama, *Love's Tragedy* (*Kjærlighedens tragedie*, 1904), is a tragic treatment of the difference in love and passion between men and women. He also wrote several plays with more political content, including the Aristophanic comedy *The People's Council* (*Folkeraadet*, 1897) and the satirical *I Will Fend for My Country* (*Jeg vil værge mit land*, 1911). Both deal with Norwegian equivocation over the breakup of the Norway–Sweden union in 1905. *Harald Svan's Mother* (*Harald Svans mor*, 1900) is a satirical drama about mawkish press ethics.

Heiberg received a writer's grant from the Norwegian Parliament in 1891 and 1892, and was awarded the public status of poet laureate, and the accompanying annual stipend, beginning in 1923. He died in Oslo on February 22, 1929.

Several of Heiberg's plays have been translated into German, and some into French and Finnish. His collected plays appeared in Russian translation in 1911.

PLAYS: *Aunt Ulrikke* (*Tante Ulrikke*, 1884); *King Midas* (*Kong Midas*, 1890); *Artists* (*Kunstnere*, 1893); *The Balcony* (*Balkonen*, 1894); *The Garden of Gert* (*Gerts Have*, 1894); *The Big Prize* (*Det store Lod*, 1895); *His Majesty* (*Hs. Majestæt*, 1896); *The People's Council* (*Folkeraadet*, 1897); *Harald Swan's Mother* (*Harald Svans Mor*, 1899); *Love for One's Neighbor* (*Kjærlighed til næsten*, 1902); *Love's Tragedy* (*Kjærlighedens tragedie*, 1904); *I Will Fend for My Country* (*Jeg vil værge mit land*, 1912); *Bed of State* (*Parade-sengen*, 1913); *In Freedom's Cage* (*I frihetens bur*, posthumously, 1929)

FURTHER READING

Beyer, Harald. *A History of Norwegian Literature*. Tr. by Elinar Haugen. New York: New York Univ. Press, 1956. 254–257.

Downs, Brian W. *Modern Norwegian Literature 1860–1918*. Cambridge: Cambridge Univ. Press, 1966.

Nygaard, Knut. *Gunnar Heiberg—Teatermannen* [*Man of Theater*]. Bergen: Universitetsforlaget, 1975.

Skavlan, Einar. *Gunnar Heiberg*. Oslo: Aschehoug, 1950.

Vigdis Ystad

THE HEIDI CHRONICLES

We're all concerned, intelligent, good women. [*Pauses.*] *It's just that I feel stranded. And I thought the whole point was that we wouldn't feel stranded. I thought the point was that we were all in this together.*

—Heidi, Act 2

The Heidi Chronicles won the Tony Award and the Pulitzer Prize for Best Play of 1989, solidifying the reputation of its author WENDY WASSERSTEIN as a major American playwright. Wasserstein's previous COMEDIES (*Uncommon Women and Others*, [1977], *Isn't it Romantic*, [1981]) addressed the conflicts between the traditional values and personal ambitions facing modern women, but in the more ambitious and serious *Heidi*, she traced the evolution of the women's movement and its aftermath over twenty-four years, explicitly linking the personal crises faced by her protagonist with the political currents of successive eras.

Heidi Holland is an art history professor specializing in neglected female painters. (Each of the play's two acts begins with a prologue of Heidi lecturing on slides of some of these artists' works for her class.) Beginning with a 1965 high school dance, the play follows her through the next two decades. In college she begins a turbulent noncommittal romance with the charmingly arrogant publisher Scoop that typifies the problems she will continue to have in relationships. When Scoop marries at the end of act 1, he admits he has settled for someone inferior, but one whose ambitions would not compete with his own—as opposed to Heidi, who refuses to compromise her career and life's work to serve a husband.

Her platonic friendship with the gay doctor Peter, though sexually unconsummated, remains the solitary Heidi's most intimate attachment, and the social obstacles faced by homosexuals offer a counterpoint to her own. By the play's end, Heidi accepts her choice not to settle down since she has achieved the success and stature in her field for which she strove. But she does adopt a baby and hopes her daughter will grow up in a world offering more choices and fewer limitations than she herself has faced.

The changes in American society are reflected in the journeys of the characters on stage. Some ultimately sell out, such as Scoop, a full-throated 1960s radical who goes on to publish a trendy magazine. Heidi's childhood friend Susan goes from women's rights activist and collective farmer to a glitzy television executive developing sitcoms about successful "post-feminist" women of the 1980s. Heidi's awakening consciousness of feminism in the 1970s is dramatized in a women's support group scene and a demonstration she leads at a museum for the inclusion of female artists. Yet when asked later to give a speech on the topic "Women: Where are They Going?", she pleads ignorance and becomes exasperated, not at male domination but at the failure of women to support each other.

The Heidi Chronicles marked the beginning of Wasserstein's fruitful collaboration with director Daniel Sullivan (who would direct her next two plays). After a workshop at Sullivan's Seattle Repertory Theatre in April 1988, the play opened OFF-BROADWAY at Playwrights Horizons later that year. That production transferred to Broadway in 1989, marking Wasserstein's Broadway debut.

[*See also* Feminist Drama in the United States; Identity Theater]

FURTHER READING

Barnett, Claudia, ed. *Wendy Wasserstein: A Casebook*. New York: Garland, 1999.

Bryer, Jackson R., ed. *The Playwright's Art: Conversations with Contemporary American Dramatists*. Jefferson, N.C.: MacFarland, 1991.

Kolin, Philip C., and Colby H. Kullman, eds. *Speaking on Stage: Interviews with Contemporary American Playwrights*. Tuscaloosa: Univ. of Alabama Press, 1996.

Wasserstein, Wendy. *The Heidi Chronicles and Other Plays*. San Diego: Harcourt Brace Jovanovich, 1990.

Garrett B. Eisler

HEIJERMANS, HERMAN (1864–1924)

Internationally, Herman Heijermans is the most famous Dutch playwright of the period from 1860 to 2004. Born in Rotterdam on December 3, 1864, to a journalist father in a bourgeois Jewish family, he early became aware of social inequalities. His body of work—over sixty-five plays, as well as an impressive number of novels, prose works, and many reviews—are imbued with his socialist convictions. He was critical of the establishment of his time, expressing his views on capital and the Catholic Church. His dramas have been translated into many languages, among them Russian and Hebrew, and his plays have been performed worldwide.

As a young man Heijermans was trained in banking, but he spent all his spare time writing. He wrote his first play, *Happiness* (*Geluk*), for his parents' twenty-fifth wedding anniversary in 1882. After a number of failures in commercial trading, he made a definitive choice to be a playwright, but to make a living he had to continue writing as a journalist.

His first literary work, *A Low-Down Trick* (*Een jodenstreek*), appeared in 1892 in the literary magazine *De Gids*. His first play, *Dora Kremer*, followed in 1892. Disappointed over the bad reviews, Heijermans sought revenge later that year by publishing *Ahasverus*, using the pseudonym Ivan Jelakowitch. The play deals with the pogroms in Russia and economic and human misery. Jelakowitch was supposed to be a Russian Jew who died in London after escaping from the pogroms. It received much better reviews, and in light of the international recognition it received, Heijermans disclosed his real identity.

As a confirmed socialist, he objected to what he perceived as a growing individualism. He made a stand for the working class. He portrays his characters naturalistically, as in *Ghetto* (1898), *Ora et labora* (1903), *Result* (*Uitkomst*, 1907), and *Eva Bonheur* (1919). What he offers in his dramas, that his contemporaries do not, is his focus on the static situation of the characters. His most famous piece, *In Good Hope* (*Op hoop van zegen*, 1900), portrays the history of fishermen and their families in a Dutch fishing village and tells the story of how an unscrupulous ship owner sends his fishermen to sea in an unseaworthy ship. After the shipwreck, he collects the insurance money while the poor fisher families are left without recompense.

His writing style is naturalistic, giving detailed descriptions of both the physical and mental traits of his characters. He used the 19th century theory of temperaments: the character Dora is a prototype of the "nervous" temperament. The stage notes say: "The colour of her face is pale, not unhealthy. The speed in her movements refers to a nervous temperament. She is slightly impatient when she speaks." Such author's notes aside, much of the characterization, like social class and mood, is made within the dialogue.

In the next years, until his death, the majority of his plays were inspired by social issues and the working class (like *Ora et labora* [1901], or *Glück auf* [German for "With happiness too," 1911]) or the surpressed emotional lives of the petit bourgeoisie (*Links* [*Schakels*, 1903]). For a large part of his own life, he was pursued by financial problems and was writing for a living. His last few plays, like *The Flying Dutchman or The Big Bet* (*De Vliegende Hollander of de grote weddenschap*, 1924), a story of survivors of a plane crash, and also *Of Old, the Morningstar* (*Vanouds 'de Morgenster,'* 1924) were considered less important. The comic plays were said to be geared toward a larger audience, but his plays were performed decades after his death. For his centennial in 1964, a new edition of his complete works for stage was published.

[*See also* Netherlands]

SELECT PLAYS: *A Low-Down Trick* (*Een jodenstreek*, 1892); *Dora Kremer* (1892); *Ahasverus* (pseud. Ivan Jelakowitch, 1893); *Ghetto* (1898); *In Good Hope* (*Op hoop van zegen*, 1900); *Ora et labora* (1903); *Links* (*Schakels*, 1903); *Result* (*Uitkomst*, 1907); *Glück auf* (1911); *Eva Bonheur* (1917); *The Wise Tomcat* (*De wijze kater*, 1918); *Of Old, The Morningstar* (*Van ouds De Morgenster*, 1923)

FURTHER READING

Goedkoop, Hans. *Geluk. Het leven van Herman Heijermans* [*Happiness. The Life of Herman Heijermans*]. Amsterdam, Antwerpen: De Arbeiderspers, 1996.

Kemperink, Mary. *Nederlands toneel in het Fin de sciècle* [*Dutch Theater at the Fin de Siècle*]. Amsterdam: Amsterdam Univ. Press, 1995.

Neck Yoder, Hilda van. *Dramatizations of social change: Herman Heijermans' plays as compared with selected dramas by Ibsen, Hauptman and Chekhov*. The Hague: Martinus Nijhoff, 1978.

Zalm, Rob van der. "9 april 1898—Herman Heijermans' politieke scherts in één bedrijf" ["The 9th of April—Herman Heijremans Political Jest in One Act"]. In *Een theatergeschiedenis der Nedelanden. Tien eeuwen drama en theater in Nederland en Vlaanderen* [*A Theater History of the Netherlands. Ten Centuries of Drama and Theater in the Netherlands and Flanders*], ed. by R. L. Erenstein et al. Amsterdam: Amsterdam Univ. Press, 1996.

Lucia van Heteren

HEIN, CHRISTOPH (1944–)

Hardly known in the English-speaking world, Christoph Hein was one of the leading playwrights in the German Democratic Republic (GDR) and continues to be active as a writer, playwright, and essayist. His career and literary production are closely linked to the history of the communist GDR (1949–1990). Because his father, a pastor, was considered bourgeois, Hein, born on April 8, 1944, in Heinzendorf, GERMANY, could not pursue a regular education but eventually was allowed to study philosophy. In 1971 he began work as a DRAMATURG at East Berlin's

Volksbühne under Benno Besson; he began to write plays and, despite the continual censorship, was able to get some premieres in the GDR. In West Germany, he was primarily known as a novelist after the publication of *The Distant Lover* (*Drachenblut*, 1983).

Like many of the younger generation of East German writers, Hein struggled between wanting to be a good citizen and wanting to criticize the social and economic problems that were increasingly evident in the GDR by the late 1960s. The so-called "real existing Socialism" could not deliver on its promises for an egalitarian society. The main themes of Hein's works are the growing alienation of individuals under a system that is too rigid, the discrepancy between the rhetoric of Marxist theorists and reality, the inner conflicts of intellectuals such as himself, and the frustrations of political idealists.

In contrast to Hein's courage in bringing sensitive issues to the stage, in his theatrical practice he tended to follow rather than innovate, looking to BERTOLT BRECHT, William Shakespeare, and the 18th-century playwright J. M. R. Lenz for models. His most successful play, *The True Story of Ah Q* (*Die wahre Geschichte des Ah Q*, 1983) was adapted from a story by the Chinese Socialist Lu Xun (1881–1936). It is a sardonic take on the *trahison des clercs*, the betrayal by intellectuals of the realm of independent thought when they take part in actual political events. Ah Q and Wang pretend to be thinking but are actually fantasizing. Their ivory tower is a temple with a roof that leaks while they talk of the coming revolution and enjoy saying the word "anarchy," which neither can define.

Passage (1987) is also about people who think too much because they cannot act. Haunted by Walter Benjamin's 1940 death as well as by the film *Casablanca* (1942), Hein focuses on a group of refugees waiting at the Spanish border to get out of Vichy France. One of them commits suicide. The final words of one protagonist—"We want to wait just a minute more"—leave the fates of the others hanging in the air.

Hein's diagnosis in *The Knights of the Round Table* (*Die Ritter der Tafelrunde: Eine Komödie*, 1989) that the governing elite of the GDR was too old and sclerotic to be able to grasp and cope with rapid change proved entirely accurate. Half a year after the play premiered in April the Berlin Wall came down in November 1989 and by October 1990 the two Germanies were united. Disappointed by the widespread rejection of all further socialist experiments and worn down by serious illness, Hein did not produce another drama until 1995. *Randow: A Comedy* (*Randow: Eine Komödie*) is a quite unfunny biting satire reflecting the grim cynicism that had replaced the initial enthusiasm buoyed by unification. The action focuses on a large villa located in the Randow region on the new German border with Poland. Anna Andress, an artist separated from her alcoholic husband, is the sole occupant. Before unification no one really wanted the crumbling house, but now the sinister Fred R. Paul, a blend of gangster and neo-Nazi based in Cologne, directs a campaign of brutal intimidation against Anna until she decides to move away. The political allegory is a blatant accusation against the West German occupation of both the land and history of the GDR. Not surprisingly, it met with negative responses from West German critics.

Hein published four more plays in 1999 in the collection *Pieces* (*Stücke*). Three deal with the shadows of history. In *Bruch: Play in Four Acts* (*Bruch: Schauspiel in vier Akten*), set in the early 1950s, the retired surgeon Theodor Bruch fantasizes about opening a clinic, to be financed by drawing on his great reputation, but amidst the postwar ruins the past is bankrupt. Bruch's illegal operation that kills a desperate female patient represents the monstrosities caused by of clinging to the old order. Just as grotesque are the delusions of the former knights of the Round Table in *Outlawed: Comedy in One Act* (*In Acht und Bann: Komödie in einem Akt*), which follows up on *Knights of the Roundtable*. A decade has passed; outside the prison Mordred reigns; inside Arthur and four of his knights practice running democratic meetings so they will be ready to govern when restored to power. Their notions are as preposterous as ever and only Parzival, who has taken up gardening, has any grasp of reality.

Two short pieces depict history as seen from below. *Gatecrashers: Comedy* (*Zaungäste: Lustspiel*, though lost in translation are the puns on "fence sitting" as well as on *teichoskopia*, the description of events from the perspective of onlookers as in book three of *The Iliad*) reports on events of May 1968 when the university's St. Pauli Church was blown up by GDR authorities. The hypocritical interactions of the characters expose the mechanisms which rendered citizens into impotent observers of their own oppression. *Heaven on Earth: Comedy* (*Himmel auf Erden: Lustspiel*) is the ironic name of a sleazy strip club. An early quitting time gives two bricklayers a chance to explore what is advertised as an exotic realm of lust and pleasure. However, at eleven in the morning they only encounter the stark reality of exorbitant charges and the totally unexotic woman who recognizes one of them as a former classmate. Hein's use of dialect—Low German here and Saxon in *Gatecrashers*—lends color but also limits the range of reception by audiences.

On the whole Hein has had more success with prose than with plays since unification. This has led to the interesting phenomenon of adaptations of his novels for the stage. Although the titles are unchanged, the adaptations are actually done by other playwrights: *Taking the Land* (*Landnahme*), adapted by Anna Badora and Andrea Koschwitz, premiere 2004; *Horn's End* (*Horns Ende*), adapted by Armin Petras, permiere 2006; *In His Early Childhood a Garden* (*In seiner frühen Kindheit ein Garten*, adapted by Jens Graß, premiere 2006). Hein has also written the libretto for an opera, *Noah* (*Noach*), composed by Sidney Corbett (premiere 2001).

SELECT PLAYS: *Hungry Hennecke* (*Vom hungrigen Hennecke*, 1974); *Schlötel or What's the Use* (*Schlötel, oder Was solls*, 1974); *Cromwell* (1978); *The Business of Mr. John D.* (*Die Geschäfte des Herrn John D.*, 1979); *Lassalle Asks Mr. Herbert about Sonya* (*Lassalle fragt Herrn

Herbert nach Sonja, 1980); *The New Menoza, or History of the Kumbanian Prince Tandi* (*Der neue Menoza, oder Geschichte des kumbanischen Prinzen Tandi*, 1982); *The True Story of Ah Q* (*Die wahre Geschichte des Ah Q*, 1983); *Passage* (1987); *Knights of the Round Table* (*Die Ritter der Tafelrunde*, 1989); *Randow* (1994): *Heaven on Earth* (*Himmel auf Erden*, 1999); *Onlookers* (*Zaungäste*, 1999); *Outlawed* (*In Acht und Bann*, 1999); *Rupture* (*Bruch*, 1999); *Siegfried and Sieglinde* (*Siegfried und Sieglinde*, with Gert Heidenreich, 1999); *Mother's Day* (*Mutters Tag*, 2002); *On the History of the Human Heart, or Mr. Schubart Tells Mr. Lenz a Novel Which Took Place Right Amongst Us* (*Zur Geschichte des menschlichen Herzens, oder Herr Schubart erzählt Herrn Lenz einen Roman, der sich mitten unter uns zugetragen hat*, 2002)

FURTHER READING

Jackman, Graham, ed. *Christoph Hein in Perspective*. Amsterdam, Atlanta: Rodopi, 2000.

McKnight, Phillip. *Understanding Christoph Hein*. Columbia: Univ. of South Carolina Press, 1995.

Menke, Timm. "The Reception of Lenz in the Final Years of the German Democratic Republic: Christoph Hein's Adaptation of *Der neue Menoza*." In *Space to Act: The Theater of J.M.R. Lenz*, ed. by Alan C. Leidner and Helga S. Madland. Columbia, S.C.: Camden House, 1993. 150–161.

Niven, Bill. "A Play about Socialism? The Reception of Christoph Hein's *Die Ritter der Tafelrunde*." In *"Whose Story?": Continuities in Contemporary German-Language Literature*, ed. by Arthur Williams, Stuart Parkes, and Julian Preece. Bern: Peter Lang, 1998. 197–218.

——, and David Clarke, eds. *Christoph Hein*. Cardiff: Univ. of Wales Press, 2000.

Richter, Eva. "The Collapse of the Old and Hope of the New Order in Hein's *Knights of the Round Table*." *Studies in Medievalism* 6, Supplement (1996): 231–238.

Robinson, David W. *Deconstructing East Germany: Christoph Hein's Literature of Dissent*. Rochester: Camden House, 1999.

Arnd Bohm

HELDENPLATZ

When CLAUS PEYMANN, the artistic director of Vienna's Burgtheater, commissioned THOMAS BERNHARD to write a play commemorating the fiftieth anniversary of AUSTRIA's 1938 annexation to Nazi GERMANY, Bernhard at first hesitated. He suggested instead that all of the Viennese stores that had been "Arianized" by the Nazis should once again display the sign they hung during the Third Reich, proclaiming their establishments "free of Jews." Such an act, Bernhard contended, would aptly dramatize the city's legacy of guilt.

Heroes' Square (Heldenplatz) is the large square next to the Imperial Palace in the city center where throngs of Austrians cheered Adolf Hitler's triumphant arrival in Vienna in March 1938. The political controversies occasioned by Bernhard's 1988 play were triggered months before its Burgtheater opening, when newspapers published excerpts of the drama's blistering diatribes against Austria, its Socialist government, the hypocritical powermongering of the Catholic Church, and the nation's persistent anti-Semitism. This was not the first time that a Bernhard text caused a national uproar in Austria. What was especially shocking with regard to *Heldenplatz*, however, was the fact that in this text the invectives were uttered by a Jew, who turned out to be as cantankerous, misanthropic, and authoritarian as Bernhard's previous characters and, even worse, was as Austrian as the culture that persecuted him.

Heldenplatz begins after the tragedy of the suicide of Professor Josef Schuster. He and his family recently returned to Vienna from Cambridge, England, where they had found refuge following Hitler's rise to power. Shocked to experience a form of Austrian anti-Semitism even worse than that of fifty years ago, Professor Schuster jumps to his death from his apartment window facing the Heldenplatz.

Bernhard's drama demonstrates most strikingly the act of internalizing another's speech and the performative force of hate speech. The professor's housekeeper has memorized the things he has told her, from his literary and musical preferences to the way he wants his shirts ironed and folded, from his own social and political biases to his attitudes toward his brother, his wife, and his children. Listening to the professor, the housekeeper has appropriated his values and viewpoints, including some of his most questionable ones. Quoting him, she embodies him. His surviving brother, Robert, in turn, has internalized some of the worst anti-Semitic clichés by quoting them to others. Upon learning that Olga, his niece, was spat on in the street by a stranger, Robert was sure it happened "just because he can see she is a Jew."

Robert Schuster's strong reaction suggests that he is still traumatized by the past, by the enforced wearing of the yellow Jewish Star of David. His response also raises problematic questions. What, or perhaps more to the point, who distinguishes Olga as a Jewish woman? Is it Robert? If so, what are his feelings about her apparently obvious racial traits? Or is this matter indicative of the author's own Freudian slip? All the while, the professor's widow keeps hearing in her memory the masses shouting "Heil Hitler" on the Heldenplatz.

In their rantings against Austria, the Schusters not only reveal their profound connection to the country but also, for better or worse, their love for the culture that terrifies them.

FURTHER READING

Bernhard, Thomas. *Heldenplatz*. Tr. and intro. by Gitta Honegger. *Conjunctions* 33 (Fall 1999): 307–408.

Heldenplatz: Eine Dokumentation [*A Documentation*]. Vienna: Burgtheater, 1989.

Honegger, Gitta. *Thomas Bernhard: The Making of An Austrian*. New Haven: Yale Univ. Press, 2001.

Gitta Honegger

HELLMAN, LILLIAN (1905–1984)

Lillian Hellman is one of the UNITED STATES's most famous, important, and controversial dramatists. Her plays, several of which have been turned into popular films, are regularly revived throughout the world. Among many other honors, Hellman was elected to the American Academy of Arts and Sciences and served as Vice President of the National Institute of Arts and Letters. When she died, the *New York Times* ran her obituary on the front page.

Born on June 20, 1905, to a German Jewish family in New Orleans, Hellman spent much of her childhood shuttling between her hometown and New York City. She dropped out of New York University, worked for a publishing firm, then became a script reader for Metro-Goldwyn-Mayer. Her first produced drama was a striking success, running 691 performances in New York. THE CHILDREN'S HOUR (1934) explores what happens when two headmistresses at a boarding school are accused of being lesbians. The play introduced several themes that would dominate Hellman's work: the dangers of self-righteousness, the power of public opinion, the uselessness of good intentions without accompanying actions, and the need to accept responsibility for one's life.

Hellman's second play, *Days to Come* (1936), lasted only six performances. While *Days* offers an incisive analysis of class differences and capitalist paternalism, it is overburdened with plot and dull characters. She fared much better with her next critique of capitalism, THE LITTLE FOXES, which opened in New York in 1939. *Foxes* is set in the South at the turn of the 20th century and traces the machinations of the three grown Hubbard siblings—Ben, Oscar, and Regina—as they jockey for power and money. The family, the town, and by implication the whole country are ravaged by the Hubbards' greed as well as by the passivity of the more ethical characters who are reluctant to confront them. *The Little Foxes*, which enjoyed a long initial run, is the most frequently revived of her works. A brilliantly theatrical drama, *Foxes* (on stage and on screen) has attracted such stars as Tallulah Bankhead, Bette Davis, Elizabeth Taylor, and Anne Bancroft.

Still fascinated by the avaricious "foxes," Hellman went back in time to write *Another Part of the Forest* (1946), a look at the Hubbards in 1880. *Forest* introduces the family patriarch, Marcus, who despite his pretensions to culture, is a brutal father and husband. Marcus made his fortune betraying his neighbors during the Civil War and serves as a dangerous role model for his three children. *Another Part of the Forest*, which the playwright herself directed, received mixed notices. Brooks Atkinson complained that it combined "blackmail, insanity, cruelty, theft, torture, insult, drunkenness, with a trace of incest thrown in for good measure," but others were more receptive, and over the years some critics have preferred *Forest* to *Foxes* (Wright, 1986).

In the late 1930s and 1940s, concerns about the Depression began to be replaced by the growing Nazi threat. Spurred by her liberal politics and her heritage (although she was not religious, she said that being Jewish "suddenly became very important to" her with the advent of Nazism [Bryer, 1986]), Hellman wrote two plays about American involvement—or lack of involvement—in world events. *Watch on the Rhine* (1941) won the playwright her first Drama Critics Circle Award and brought the European war home to Americans. When the Farrelly family, safely lodged in their country house near Washington, D.C., discover that they are sheltering a Nazi informer, they realize that no one's hands are clean: ignoring evil makes one culpable, even when the source of that evil is thousands of miles away. Another play about the Nazi era, *The Searching Wind* (1944), proved less successful. Moving back and forth over a period of two decades, *The Searching Wind* exposes the disastrous cowardice of politicians, journalists, and private citizens. Once again Hellman allows her characters no excuses: not even fear for the safety of loved ones can justify Alex Hazen's attempts to appease the Nazis, his father-in-law's cowardly withdrawal from public life, or Cassie Bowman's duplicity.

Although *The Autumn Garden* (1951) had only a moderate run, many critics consider it Hellman's best work. More than a few dubbed *Garden* "Chekhovian," primarily because it centers on middle-aged characters dissatisfied with their lives but unwilling or unable to change them. Hellman admired Russian writer ANTON CHEKHOV—she later edited a volume of his letters—and *Garden* is certainly more loosely plotted than her earlier plays. But where Chekhov shows compassion for the bemused inhabitants of his theatrical world, Hellman treats hers more harshly. If her characters lead wasted lives, the fault is largely their own. Taking a cue from her previous plays, Hellman contrasts the aimlessness of Americans with the decisiveness of their European counterparts.

Neither *Montserrat* (1949), based on Emmanuel Roblès's grisly moral parable about loyalty and treachery in 19th-century Venezuela, nor *The Lark* (1955), Hellman's adaptation of JEAN ANOUILH's drama about St. Joan, is great theater, although the latter proved popular with audiences. It is not surprising that Hellman was concerned with issues of betrayal and martyrdom while the House Un-American Activities Committee (HUAC) was conducting its inquisition against Americans accused of leftist sympathies. When Hellman herself was subpoenaed by the Committee, she refused to testify against her friends and colleagues. Several months after her HUAC appearance, Hellman directed a revival of *The Children's Hour*, her play about lives ruined by rumors, accusations, and parochialism.

Lillian Hellman's solo foray into the musical world, *Candide* (1956), closed after seventy-two performances. Hellman was never comfortable with the collaborative aspects of the theater, working with directors and actors, and adding a composer and lyricist exacerbated her uneasiness. Many critics complained that Hellman's book was too "heavy" for a COMEDY, although John Chapman considered it "strong, clear and humorous" (Chapman, 1956). In fact, Hellman's text is biting and eminently playable, providing a splendid spoof of the American musical: despite war, famine, the Inquisition, earthquakes, shipwrecks, kidnapping, and imprisonment, the young lovers are eventually reunited. In 1956 the public was not yet ready for Hellman's send-up of this most American of dramatic genres.

Except for *My Mother, My Father and Me* (1963), a humorless comedy adapted from a Burt Blechman novel, Hellman's final play was *Toys in the Attic* (1960). *Toys* grew from an anecdote, told to Hellman by longtime companion Dashiell Hammett, about a feckless young man who surprises those around him when he apparently achieves prosperity. In a revealing comment Hellman (1973) admitted, "I can write about men, but I can't write a play that centers on a man. I've got to tear it up, make it about the women around him, his sisters, his bride, her mother." *Toys* is a Freudian-Gothic work focused on two bored, overworked maiden sisters, Carrie and Anna Berniers, who try to live their lives through their weak brother, Julian. When Julian seems no longer to need their support, the threads binding their lives come undone with nearly tragic consequences. The popular *Toys* earned Hellman her second Drama Critics Circle Award.

After she left the theater, Lillian Hellman went on to become a successful writer of memoirs: *An Unfinished Woman*, *Pentimento*, *Scoundrel Time*, and *Maybe* (the last labeled simply "a story"). All of these provoked great controversy, and she was accused of prevarication, distortion, and outright lying. *Scoundrel Time*, Hellman's history of the HUAC days, angered many people because she saved her strongest censure for fellow liberals who passively watched the political witch-hunt. Consistent to the end, Hellman chastised those who failed to stand up to evil—just as she had in such plays as *The Children's Hour*, *The Little Foxes*, and *Watch on the Rhine*. Hellman spent her last years embroiled in lawsuits and public battles with writers Mary McCarthy and Martha Gellhorn, as well as others who either challenged her veracity or were offended by her confrontational style. Hellman died on June 30, 1984, in Martha's Vineyard, Massachusetts.

Hellman's plays won two Drama Critics Circle Awards, presented by the critics themselves, but despite several nominations she never received the establishment accolade of a Pulitzer Prize. Since her death more attention has been paid to Hellman the public figure than Hellman the dramatist. Although no major study of her theater work has appeared, she has been the subject of several largely unsympathetic biographies and, ironically, a number of stage plays. Some critics dismiss Hellman's carefully crafted early works as "MELODRAMA," while others recognize that she deliberately uses melodramatic devices to develop character and deepen themes. Materialist feminists accuse realistic drama, Hellman's favored style, of reifying the very social ills it would condemn. Many other feminist scholars, however, argue that Hellman successfully employs realism to expose the inequities in a patriarchal, capitalist society. These diverse viewpoints suggest that Hellman's theatrical canon merits the same close critical scrutiny to which her life has been subjected. As countless revivals around the globe testify, actors and audiences already recognize the power of Lillian Hellman's dramas.

[*See also* Feminist Drama in the United States]

PLAYS: *The Children's Hour* (1934); *Days to Come* (1936); *The Little Foxes* (1939); *Watch on the Rhine* (1941); *The Searching Wind* (1944); *Another Part of the Forest* (1946); *Montserrat* (adapted from Emmanuel Roblès's play, 1949); *The Lark* (adapted from Jean Anouilh's play, 1955); *Candide* (musical, based on Voltaire's novel, 1956); *Toys in the Attic* (1960); *My Mother, My Father and Me* (based on Burt Blechman's novel *How Much?*, 1963)

FURTHER READING

Bryer, Jackson, ed. *Conversations with Lillian Hellman*. Jackson: Univ. Press of Mississippi, 1986.

Chapman, John. "*Candide* an Artistic Triumph." *New York Daily News*, Dec. 3, 1956: 44.

Estrin, Mark W., ed. *Critical Essays on Lillian Hellman*. Boston: G.K. Hall, 1989.

Falk, Doris V. *Lillian Hellman*. New York: Frederick Ungar, 1978.

Griffin, Alice, and Geraldine Thorsten. *Understanding Lillian Hellman*. Columbia: Univ. of South Carolina Press, 1999.

Hellman, Lillian. *Pentimento*. Boston: Little Brown, 1973.

——. *An Unfinished Woman*. Boston: Little Brown, 1969.

Lederer, Katherine. *Lillian Hellman*. Boston: Twayne, 1979.

Rollyson, Carl. *Lillian Hellman: Her Legend and Her Legacy*. New York: St. Martin's, 1988.

Wright, William. *Lillian Hellman: The Image, The Woman*. New York: Simon and Schuster, 1986.

Judith E. Barlow

HENLEY, BETH (1952–)

Beth Henley, born on May 8, 1952, in Jackson, Mississippi, to a lawyer and an actress, earned a bachelor of fine arts degree at Southern Methodist University, where in 1972 she wrote her first play, *Am I Blue*, a one-act faintly reminiscent of TENNESSEE WILLIAMS's *This Property Is Condemned*. She has also written several screenplays.

Like her contemporaries TINA HOWE and WENDY WASSERSTEIN, Henley's preferred genre is COMEDY. Her plays are a mélange of black humor and pathos peopled with eccentric characters. Henley's comedy often arises from the juxtaposition of the extraordinary with the mundane: a wife who shoots her husband and then makes lemonade; a seamstress who hears voices through her eyes. *Crimes of the Heart*, her first professionally produced play, won the Pulitzer Prize and the New York Drama Critics Circle Award for Best American Play of 1981. It is a dark but compassionate comedy about three sisters confronting the losses and failures of their lives. Later plays met with mixed critical reaction, in both the mainstream and academic worlds. Feminist scholars were divided about the relevance of her work to the feminist movement. Many condemned her reliance on traditional climactic plot structure and her portrayal of dysfunctional female characters who failed to provide positive, independent role models for women. Her portrayals of female relationships seem to fulfill an old stereotype: sisters, mothers, and daughters are frequently antagonistic.

The early plays—*Crimes of the Heart* (1979), *The Wake of Jamey Foster* (1982), *Miss Firecracker Contest* (1984), *The Debutante Ball* (1985), and *The Lucky Spot* (1986)—all take place in small southern towns. Henley is generally regarded as a Southern writer of the Gothic school, although later plays such as *Abundance* (1989) and *Family Week* (2000) are set outside the South. The grotesque and even the violent have a predominant role throughout her works: death, disease, and deformity define events and characters. Her point of departure is often a cultural or life marker—a birthday in *Crimes of the Heart*, a death in *The Wake of Jamey Foster*, a marriage in *Abundance*. In due course, the event goes awry.

Her style has grown more loosely structured over time and her vision, more pessimistic. In *Abundance*, the story of two 19th-century mail-order brides in the Wyoming territories, Henley first explored a more fragmented composition. She continued her experimentation with *Signature*, a play that deals with the decline of American culture. Set fifty years in the future and partly written in an invented language, it reflects aspects of science fiction. *L-Play* is a dramatization of the human condition written in twelve unrelated scenes, each exploring a word beginning with the letter L, such as love or loss.

Henley is an imaginative, playful writer who enjoys employing parody. For example, *The Debutante Ball* uses Wildean epigrams (although less successfully than OSCAR WILDE) and borrows elements of THE IMPORTANCE OF BEING EARNEST, as well as Tennessee Williams's A STREETCAR NAMED DESIRE. The final scene of *The Debutante Ball*, featuring the debutante's mother in a bathtub in full view of the audience, her nude body covered with psoriasis, complaining about "the ravages of time," evokes Blanche DuBois and her offstage baths. In 1995, she was awarded a new play initiative grant from the Nederlander Organization and the Roundabout Theatre.

[*See also* United States, 1940–Present]

PLAYS: *Crimes of the Heart* (1979); *Am I Blue* (1982); *The Wake of Jamey Foster* (1982); *The Miss Firecracker Contest* (1984); *The Debutante Ball* (1985); *The Lucky Spot* (1986); *Abundance* (1989); *Signature* (1990); *Control Freaks* (1992); *Revelers* (1994); *L-Play* (1996); *Impossible Marriage* (1998); *Family Week* (2000)

FURTHER READING

Andreach, Robert J. "The Missing Five Years and Subjectivity in Beth Henley's *Abundance*." *Southern Quarterly* 39, no. 3 (Spring 2001): 141–150.

Bryer, Jackson R., ed. *The Playwright's Art: Conversations with Contemporary American Dramatists*. New Brunswick, N.J.: Rutgers Univ. Press, 1995.

Fesmire, Julia A., ed. *Beth Henley: A Casebook*. London: Routledge, 2002.

Guerra, Jonnie. "Beth Henley: Female Quest and the Family Play Tradition." In *Making a Spectacle*, ed. by Lynda Hart. Ann Arbor: Univ. of Michigan Press, 1989.

Shepard, Alan Clarke. "Aborted Rage in Beth Henley's Women." *Modern Drama* 36 (1993): 96–108.

Jane Baldwin

HERNÁNDEZ, LUISA JOSEFINA (1928–)

Luisa Josefina Hernández has written some fifty plays and an equal number of novels, almost all produced or published. Born in Mexico City in 1928, she studied drama at the National University (UNAM) under RODOLFO USIGLI and succeeded him as chair of the Department of Dramatic Literature. Her early works rely on psychological REALISM to probe the stultifying effects of social mores on individuals. Her protagonists are mainly professional women forced to sacrifice happiness to convention. Although men inflict much of the pain, they suffer in equal measure.

Hernández is a master of dramatic form. Two early realist plays, *Sugarcane Fire Water* (*Aguardiente de caña*, 1951) and *Corner Pharmacy* (*Botica Modelo*, 1954), won national prizes. Structured as a farcical fantasy, *The Spirits* (*Los duendes*, 1952) uses humor to examine a dysfunctional family. In *Deaf-Mutes* (*Los sordomudos*, 1953), a wealthy family rebels against a tyrannical father. The mystical *Dance of the Big Complex Rooster* (*Danza del urogallo múltiple*, 1971) explores human and divine love in a ritualized setting. Written as dramatic exercises for students, *The Street of Grand Occasion* (*La calle de gran ocasión*, 1985) comprises two series of lyrical scenes that question all aspects of society.

The theme of suffocating conformity climaxes with *Fallen Fruit* (*Los frutos caídost*, 1955), winner of the INBA prize in 1958, and *Royal Guests* (*Los huéspedes reales*, 1958), winner of the Bellas Artes Prize in 1968; these are her most acclaimed plays. In *Royal Guests*, a mother coerces her daughter into an arranged marriage; impotent to protect his child, the father commits suicide. Celia, the apparently liberated heroine of *Fallen Fruit*, is a professional woman with two children by two husbands. On the verge of another divorce, she returns to her ancestral home to sell her property and thwart the seductions of a suitor. She yields to the family, rejects the suitor, and stays in a loveless marriage for the children, knowing she will rot like the fruit in the title. By contrast, *The Order of the Factors* (*El orden de los factores*, 1983) features a single mother and physician who defies opprobrium to love again; here marriage becomes an act of solidarity.

In the 1960s, Hernández turned to nonrealistic forms to plumb Mexico's history of injustice against its nonwhite populations. Three major plays derive from documented incidents, two from its mythic past. *Fictitious Peace* (*La paz ficticia*, 1960) excoriates the government of Porfirio Díaz for selling Indian lands to foreign investors. *History of a Ring* (*La historia de un anillo*, 1961) begins with an Indian maid falsely accused of a crime and ends in a massacre. *The Mulatto's Orgy* (*La fiesta del mulato*, 1968) re-creates the trial of a colonial mulatto who aspired to ascend in a society bound by caste and class. *Popul Vuh* (1966) and *Quetzalcóatl* (1967) honor the feats of ancient heroes; by analogy, they encourage the audience to compare the exemplary behavior of the heroes to present norms. Other anti-illusionist plays followed this quintet.

Hernández refutes the label of feminist writer, arguing that in MEXICO men and women share the same problems: poverty, education, and jobs. Convinced that truth can change society, she unmasks characters and mores to reveal hypocrisy. In 2002 the Mexican government awarded her its highest honor, the National Prize for Sciences and Arts.

PLAYS: *The Legal Ambiance* (*El ambiente jurídico*, 1950); *Agony* (*Agonía*, 1951); *It's Raining Outside* (*Afuera llueve*, 1952); *Corner Pharmacy* (*Botica Modelo*, 1953); *Deaf-Mutes* (*Los sordomudos*, 1954); *Fallen Fruit* (*Los frutos caídos*, 1955); *Royal Guests* (*Los huéspedes reales*, 1958); *The King's Daughter* (*La hija del rey*, 1959); *Fictitious Peace* (*La paz ficticia*, 1960); *The Spirits* (*Los duendes*, 1960); *History of a Ring* (*La historia de un anillo*, 1961); *The Street of Grand Occasio—Dialogues* (*La calle de gran ocasión—diálogos*, 1962); *White Harps, Golden Rabbits* (*Arpas blancas, conejos dorados*, 1963); *Popul Vuh* (1966); *Quetzalcóatl* (1967); *The Mulatto's Orgy* (*La fiesta del mulato*, 1968); *The Dance of the Big Complex Rooster* (*Danza del urogallo multiple*, 1971); *Apostasy* (*Apostasía*, 1974); *Pavane of Aranzazu* (*Pavana de Aranzazu*, 1975); *Caprices and Nonsense by Goya* (*Caprichos y Disparates de Goya*, 1979); *Certain Things* (*Ciertas cosas*, 1980); *The Order of the Factors* (*El orden de los factores*, 1983); *The Wedding, Temperate Zone* (*Las bodas, Zona Templada: un díptico*, 1999); *The Dandy from Abroad, The Lover, Ferment and Sleep, Three Dogs and a Cat* (*El galán de ultramar, La amante, Fermento y sueño, Tres perros y un gato: Teatro*, 2000)

FURTHER READING

Bisset, Judith. "Luisa Josefina Hernández y Estela Portillo Trambley: La expresión dramática de una voz femenina: Semejante o distinta?" ["Luisa Josefina Hernández and Estela Portillo Trambley: Dramatic Expression of a Feminine Voice: Similar or Distinct?"]. *Ollantay* 1, no. 2 (July 1993): 14–19.

Cohen, Deb. "Defining and Defying 'Woman' in Four Plays by Luisa Josefina Hernández." *Latin American Theatre Review* 30, no. 2 (Spring 1997): 89–102.

Feliciano, Wilma. "Entrevista a Luisa Josefina Hernández: 'El teatro es mi oficio, no mi hobby'" ["Interview with Luisa Josefina Hernández: 'Theater Is My Job, Not My Hobby'"]. *Gestos* 14, no. 28 (November 1999): 135–139.

——. "El nacimiento de México en *Popul Vuh* de Luisa Josefina Hernández" ["The Birth of Mexico in *Popul Vuh* of Luisa Josefina Hernández"]. In *Teatro latinoamericano para niños* [*Latin American Theater for Children*], ed. by María Mercedes Jaramillo. Medellín, Colombia: Universidad de Antoquia, 2002. 285–337; includes text of *Popul Vuh*.

Knowles, John K. "The Labyrinth of Form: Luisa Josefina Hernández." In *Dramatists in Revolt*, ed. by Leon F. Lyday and George W. Woodyard. Austin: Univ. of Texas Press, 1976. 133–145.

Krugh, Janis Lynne. "Solitude and Solidarity: Major Themes and Techniques in the Theater of Luisa Josefina Hernández." Dissertation Abstracts International 47, no. 6 (December 1986): 2174A.

Wilma Feliciano

HERNE, JAMES A. (1839–1901)

Born James Ahern (or A'Hern) on February 1, 1839, in Cohoes, New York, he began as an actor with his first major role, George Shelby in *Uncle Tom's Cabin* at the Adelphi Theatre in Troy, New York, in 1859. He changed his name to Herne soon afterward, probably to avoid the era's anti-Irish bigotry. He quickly moved from lines of business to a range of parts, and his popularity enabled him to avoid Civil War service; he paid for a substitute when he joined the John Ford company in Baltimore, briefly becoming a friend and drinking companion of John Wilkes Booth.

Herne's early career coincided with the shift from the oratory typified by Edwin Forrest to a more natural approach, observing commonplace speech and mannerisms and incorporating them in his characterizations. He readily adopted the new style, and his interest in natural action influenced both his later playwriting and directing.

Following a series of domestic complications, Herne relocated to San Francisco and eventually became manager of Maguire's New Theatre. He began adapting (often, more accurately, appropriating) novels for performance, acting in several, and he likely met DAVID BELASCO when the two played in Herne's *Oliver Twist* adaptation. Despite Belasco's fondness for MELODRAMA and Herne's urge for REALISM, the two collaborated for more than five years. And in spite of ongoing reforms of copyright law, each freely appropriated popular novels and even other plays. Among the plays Herne used was Henry Leslie's *The Mariner's Compass*, which became his greatest financial success, first as *Chums* (1879) then retitled as *Hearts of Oak*, which he revived throughout his career. His partnership with Belasco ended with a dispute over *Hearts of Oak*, but Herne profitably toured the play from 1880 to 1886. He then lost most of the proceeds on the disastrous *"The Minute Men" of 1774–1775*, a romance nearly as awkward as its title.

Herne attracted attention from Hamlin Garland, WILLIAM DEAN HOWELLS, and other realists, initially through his 1888 sea play and temperance drama *Drifting Apart*. The play marked a transition for Herne and American dramatic form, as it presented a moral TRAGEDY, yet avoided melodrama's standard sensationalism. In *MARGARET FLEMING*, Herne came closest to a new theatrical realism—presenting moral complexity, social issues, and internal motivation—despite his use of sentimental plot devices. His later plays, such as *Shore Acres* (1892)and *Sag Harbor* (1899), retreated from socially significant themes to rely on realistic setting and character action, while his plots retained sentimental hyperbole and audience-pleasing conclusions.

Attacked by critics who favored sentimentality, Herne drew praise from realists, who favorably compared him to HENRIK IBSEN. In "Art for Truth's Sake in the Drama," Herne argued for drama as a realistic art: "Its highest purpose has ever been to perpetuate the life of its time. [. . . T]he larger the truth, the higher the art." He insisted, "that which is in touch with contemporaneous life adheres closest to truth." Herne died in Chicago on June 2, 1901. Few of his original scripts remain; even the current version of *Margaret Fleming* is a reconstruction.

[*See also* United States, 1860–1929]

PLAYS: *Charles O'Malley* (adaptation, 1874); *Oliver Twist* (adaptation, 1874); *Rip Van Winkle* (adaptation, 1874); *Robert Macaire* (adaptation, 1877); *Chums* (later *Hearts of Oak*, adaptation, 1879); *The Millionaire's Daughter* (adaptation, 1879); *Marriage by Moonlight* (adaptation, 1879); *Within an Inch of His Life* (adaptation, 1879); *"The Minute Men" of 1774–1775* (1886); *Mary, the Fisherman's Child* (later *Drifting Apart*, 1888); *Fall River* (with Hamlin Garland, not produced, 1890); *Margaret Fleming* (1890); *Coon Hollow* (not produced, 1891); *My Colleen* (1892); *Shore Acres Subdivision* (later *Uncle Nat*, then *Shore Acres*, 1892); *The Volunteers* (1892); *The Reverend Griffith Davenport* (later *Griffith Davenport*, adaptation, 1899); *Sag Harbor* (1899)

FURTHER READING

Denison, Patricia D. "The Legacy of James A. Herne: American Realities and Realisms." In *Realism and the American Dramatic Tradition*, ed. by William W. Demastes. Tuscaloosa: Univ. of Alabama Press, 1996. 18–36.

Durham, Weldon B. "James A. Herne." In *American Playwrights, 1880–1945*, ed. by William W. Demastes. Westport, Conn.: Greenwood Press, 1995. 145–155.

Edwards, Herbert J., and Julie A. Herne. *James A. Herne: The Rise of Realism in the American Drama*. Orono: Univ. of Maine Press, 1964.

Herne, James A. "Art for Truth's Sake in the Drama." *The Arena* 17 (February 1897): 361–370. Reprinted in *American Drama and its Critics*, ed. by Alan S. Downer. Chicago: Univ. of Chicago Press, 1965. 3–9.

Jones, Betty Jean. "James A. Herne: The Rise of American Stage Realism." Ph.D. diss., Univ. of Wisconsin, Madison, 1983.

Perry, John. *James A. Herne: The American Ibsen*. Chicago: Nelson-Hall, 1978.

Robinson, Alice M. "James A. Herne and his 'Theatre Libre' in Boston." *Players* 48 (1973): 202–209.

Ron West

HEROES' SQUARE *See* HELDENPLATZ

HEWETT, DOROTHY (1923–2002)

Dorothy Hewett is one of AUSTRALIA's greatest literary figures, writing more than twenty plays, five collections of poetry, and four novels. Born in Perth on May 23, 1923, Hewett spent her childhood in rural Western Australia and her later life in Sydney with her husband, the writer Merv Lilley, and their five children. Her autobiography *Wild Card* (1990) covers the period 1923–1958. Hewett received a top award with her Bachelor of Arts in 1940 and an Honorary Doctorate of Literature in 1995. Between 1941 and 1996, she won seven poetry prizes, three literary prizes, two Australian Writers Guild awards for *Bon-Bons and Roses For Dolly* (1974) and for *Golden Valley* (1982), and the Special Award in the New South Wales Premier's Literary Awards (2000). Hewett worked as a journalist and lectured in universities in Australia and the UNITED STATES. She made a major contribution to Australian culture as a writer and as an activist aware of working-class inequality.

In Hewett's drama, women characters rebel against social convention and explore artistic and sexual freedom. Her plays deal with complex political concerns, often delivered with comedy and pathos. In presentation, they range from realistic reflections on ordinary people's lives to nonrealistic revelations of a character's interior experience. Because some of the earlier plays were groundbreaking explorations of intimate female experience, they were controversial and often inaccurately deemed autobiographical.

The Chapel Perilous (1972/1997) is widely studied as a feminist classic and a chronicle of 20th-century Australian political events. The play intersperses vivid images, poetry, and realistic dialogue to present Sally Banner's inner and outer struggles, her school days in the 1930s, her love affairs, her lesbian love for Judith, and her marriages to men. The adventurous Sally wants to be a writer, but when her parents and boyfriend try to control her, she attempts suicide. Later her communist sympathies put her in conflict with the state. Sally leaves her husband Thomas and their baby for Michael, but finally resolves that she has been on a journey of self-discovery.

Hewett's feminist sympathies were evident in *Mrs Porter and the Angel* (produced 1969), which rejects middle-class suburbia in absurdist form. By her stylistic approaches, her political purpose avoids didacticism. Hewett's well-known realist plays are *This Old Man Comes Rolling Home* (produced 1967), about the working class Dockerty family; *The Golden Oldies* (1976), again about domesticity and three generations of women; and *The Tatty Hollow Story* (1976), about sexual freedom. She wrote children's dramas, including *Song of the Seals* (1985). Her musical dramas include the popular *The Man from Mukinupin* (1985) about the white and Aboriginal inhabitants of a small Australian rural town set during World War I. *The Fields of Heaven* (produced 1982) is concerned with migrant experience. Her last plays are the *Jarrabin Trilogy* (written 1997), about a Western Australian rural town between 1920 and 1970, and the politically relevant but emotionally moving *Nowhere* (2001), about three homeless people, one an Indigenous woman. Hewett's drama has layered and philosophically complex dialogue that integrates repetition, song, and references from popular culture and literature. Hewett's plays combine poetry and social commentary. She died on August 25, 2002.

[*See also* Australia, New Wave Drama; Australia, Women Playwrights, 1980–1990s]

SELECT PLAYS: *This Old Man Comes Rolling Home* (1967); *Mrs Porter and the Angel* (1969); *The Chapel Perilous* (1972); *Bon-Bons and Roses For Dolly* (1974); *Catspaw* (1974); *Joan* (1975); *Pandora's Cross* (1975); *The Golden Oldies* (1976); *The Tatty Hollow Story* (1976); *Golden Valley* (1982); *Christina's World* (1983); *The Man from Mukinupin* (1985); *Song of the Seals* (1985); *The Rising Of Pete Marsh* (1988); *Zoo* (1991); *Jarrabin Trilogy* (1997); *Nowhere* (2001)

FURTHER READING

Bennett, Bruce. *Dorothy Hewett: Collected Essays*. Fremantle: Fremantle Arts Centre Press, 1995.

Hewett, Dorothy. "Writer's View." *Theatre Australia* IV, no. 2 (1979): 15–16.

Williams, Margaret. *The Feminine as Subversive*. Sydney: Currency, 1992. 153–177. (Includes an extensive bibliography.)

Peta Tait

HE WHO GETS SLAPPED

He Who Gets Slapped (*Tot, kto poluchaet poshchechiny*, 1915) is generally considered the best of LEONID ANDREEV's nearly thirty plays. It emerged out of the playwright's reaction against the "bestiality," violence, and cruelty of World War I. It also engages in a sharp polemic with such literary epigones as Mikhail Artsybashev.

The action of the play takes place in a French circus. Andreev counterposes the circus as a world of purity and genius with the corruption of the surrounding civilization. In the world of the circus, performers such as Consuela, the "Queen of the Tango on Horseback," pursue their craft selflessly. But this ideal world is not free from the grip of the outside world. Baron Regnart's interest in the circus devolves into his desire for Consuela. The circus remains a sanctuary from the outside world, and it offers a refuge for the main character, who will be known only as "He Who Gets Slapped." Although distrusted at first, "He" persuades Papa Briquet, the director of the circus, to take him on as a clown. The slaps "He" receives mimic the blows he received in the outside world, where he had achieved great success as a scholar only to have his ideas stolen and bowdlerized by his protégé, who then ran off with his wife.

"He" turns his back on the world in no small part because he and Consuela recognize in one another a kindred spirit. Together with Baron Regnart, they form a romantic triangle that bears a strong resemblance to the triangles in ALEKSANDR BLOK's plays *A* PUPPET SHOW, *The Unknown Woman*, and *The Rose and the Cross*. "He" kills Consuela to save her from the baron. To everyone's surprise, this does not end the battle: Regnart shoots himself, and "He" poisons himself to pursue Consuela into the next life. Murder and suicide seem the logical outcome of the opposition between the ideal world of the circus and the mundane reality that surrounds it.

He Who Gets Slapped enjoyed considerable success on the stage. I. F. Schmidt's production at the Moscow Dramatic Theater and Nikolai Petrov's at the Aleksandrinsky Theater, both in the autumn of 1915, were followed by stagings throughout RUSSIA, even into the first years after the Revolution. Neglected through much of the Soviet era, *He Who Gets Slapped* has been staged with some regularity since the 1970s.

[*See also* Avant-Garde Drama; Symbolism]

FURTHER READING

Andreyev, Leonid. *He Who Gets Slapped*. In *An Anthology of Russian Plays*, Vol. II, 1890–1960, ed., tr., and intro. by F. D. Reeve. New York: Vintage Books, 1963.

Barratt, Andrew. "Leonid Andreyev's *He Who Gets Slapped*: Who Gets Slapped?" In *Russian Theatre in the Age of Modernism*, ed. by Robert Russell and Andrew Barratt. London: Macmillan, 1990.

Kaun, Alexander Samuel. *Leonid Andreyev: A Critical Study*. New York: B.W. Huebsch, 1924. Reissued by New York: Books for Libraries, 1969.

Newcombe, Josephine Marjorie. *Leonid Andreyev*. Letchworth: Bradda, 1972; New York: Frederick Ungar, 1973.

Woodward, James B. *Leonid Andreyev: A Study*. Oxford: Oxford Univ. Press, 1969.

Timothy C. Westphalen

HEYWARD, DOROTHY (1890–1961)

HEYWARD, DUBOSE (1885–1940)

With a poet's sympathetic understanding and eloquence, DuBose Heyward (born August 31, 1885, in Charleston, South Carolina; died June 16, 1940, in Tryon, North Carolina) wrote his novel *Porgy* (1925) about Charleston's poor, fading, but fascinating Gullah community. A 1924 newspaper item about someone trying to outrun police in a goat cart had caught his imagination, not as a joke but as a man with a self-determined dignity. The author, his right arm and upper body visibly handicapped by polio, (Hutchisson, 2000) had found his character, story, and setting. One summer the crippled, lonesome Porgy would defeat the enviably strong, murderous, and attractive stevedore Crown to win his moments with Bess, before the larger criminal and racist societies pulled them apart.

Heyward's wife Dorothy (born Dorothy Hartzell Kuhns, June 6, 1890, in Wooster, Ohio; died November 19, 1961, in New York City) saw a play in the successful novel and drafted a dramatization with a more upbeat ending (Porgy set out for New York after Bess). DuBose developed and polished the Gullah-flavored dialect, dialogue, and spirituals. George Gershwin, impressed by the novel, told DuBose and Dorothy that he saw an opera in it but urged them to go ahead with the play (Alpert, 1990). The

Heyward's play *Porgy*, with its large Afro-American cast, ran 367 performances in 1927–1928.

Dorothy Heyward's *Nancy Ann* had won a playwriting prize and a 1924 production. Her other light COMEDIES, the musical *Jonica* written with MOSS HART and *Cinderelative* with Dorothy DeJagers, opened and closed in 1930. In her pious 1943 drama *South Pacific* (with Howard Rigsby), a torpedoed sailor returns to combat despite his homeland's mistreatment of blacks. In 1932 the Heywards had started but dropped a script about Denmark Vesey's unsuccessful slave rebellion in Charleston (Hutchisson, 2000). Reworked by Dorothy as *Set My People Free*, it opened November 3, and closed November 27, 1948. While *New York Times*' critic Brooks Atkinson's reviews on the fourth and the fourteenth praised the production, Atkinson also remarked that she derived the "formula for Negro plays" from her *Porgy* of twenty years before. DuBose, too, mined their *Porgy*'s formula; his 1933 film script for EMPEROR JONES (1933) is weakened by the lengthy chronological and realistic social documentary that showcases Paul Robeson's voice and body before introducing a solid version of O'Neill's expressionistic play itself. Heyward's MELODRAMA *Brass Ankle* (1931), with an apparently all-white cast, preaches tolerance as it dreadfully resolves the "problem" of miscegenation.

Both Heywards adapted DuBose's novel *Mamba's Daughters* into a successful, melodramatic vehicle for Ethel Waters. In *Mamba's Daughters* (1939) singing is an alternative to violence, especially for big, gullible Hagar. For twenty years Mamba raises granddaughter Lissa in Charleston as a lady, while illiterate Hagar, separated from her daughter, works on an island plantation to finance her upbringing and vocal studies. Lissa, inheriting Hagar's beautiful voice, stars in a national broadcast where she sings her mother's prison song (Jerome Kern's "Lonesome Walls"). In the 1929 novel, Lissa's musical ascent took her to the Metropolitan Opera, where Heyward's spokesman witnesses the dream of an opera starring a black cast. Not till 1985 would that Met dream come true for their Porgy.

Adapting the Heywards's play *Porgy*, the 1935 collaboration of DuBose on book and lyrics with George and Ira Gershwin as composer and lyricist produced PORGY AND BESS, the formally and socially controversial masterpiece of the American musical theater. Opera or musical? Condescending stereotypes or people sympathetically portrayed? In a fresh, *verismo* mode, *Porgy and Bess* represents a single, severely restricted, historic, and homogenous community realistically—insofar as possible with an observant but idealistic poet's script, such glorious songs and music, and a now long parade of great Afro-American voices to act and sing it. It has secured its place in the repertories of JAZZ as well as in opera houses around the world.

[*See also* United States, 1860–1940]

PLAYS: *Nancy Ann* (1924); *Porgy* (from the novel by DuBose Heyward, 1927); *Cinderelative* (with Dorothy DeJagers, 1930); *Jonica* (with Moss Hart, 1930); *Brass Ankle* (1931); *Porgy and Bess* (music by George Gershwin, lyrics by Ira Gershwin, 1935); *Mamba's Daughters* (from the novel by DuBose Heyward, 1939); *South Pacific* (with Howard Rigsby, 1943); *Set My People Free* (1948)

FURTHER READING

Alpert, Hollis. *The Life and Times of Porgy and Bess: The Story of an American Classic*. New York: Alfred A. Knopf, 1990.

Hutchisson, James M. *DuBose Heyward: A Charleston Gentleman and the World of "Porgy and Bess."* Jackson: Univ. Press of Mississippi, 2000.

Schiff, David. "The Man Who Breathed Life into 'Porgy and Bess.'" *New York Times* (March 5, 2000): Sect. 2, pp. 35, 38.

Standifer, James. "The Tumultuous Life of 'Porgy and Bess.'" *Humanities* (November–December 1997): 8–12, 51–54.

John G. Kuhn

HIGHWAY, TOMSON (1951–)

Tomson Highway was born near Brochet, Manitoba, CANADA, in a tent on his father's trapline and spent his first six years living the traditional nomadic lifestyle of the northwestern Cree people, traveling the traplines of Northern Manitoba. At the age of six, he was sent to a Catholic boarding school before attending high school in Winnipeg, Manitoba, where he learned English. Highway earned a Bachelor of Music degree from the University of Western Ontario in 1975 and a Bachelor of Arts degree in 1976. He holds three honorary degrees and has been writer in residence at a number of universities in Canada.

Highway's social conscience and experience in both the Catholic residential schools and in foster care as a teenager have led him to concentrate his efforts and talents within Native groups in Canada. He began writing plays at the age of thirty. Early in his development as a playwright, Highway worked with native theater companies in a variety of capacities, eventually garnering success, both within and without the Aboriginal community, for his play *The Rez Sisters* (1986), winner of the Dora Mavor Moore Award for best new play in Toronto in 1986. His next mainstream success was *DRY LIPS OUGHTA MOVE TO KAPUSKASING* (1989), another Dora Mavor Moore Award winner. Highway was instrumental in the foundation of Native Earth Performing Arts, a professional Aboriginal theater company, and in 1994 he became the first Aboriginal writer to be inducted into the Order of Canada.

Highway's dramatic oeuvre concerns itself with the contemporary experience of the Aboriginal people in Canada, and in particular with transformation, healing, spirituality, and sexuality. The residential schools that many Aboriginal children were forced to attend have had far-reaching, damaging effects on Highway's community. After struggling to recuperate from the abuse and forced assimilation policies of Canada in the 1950s and 1960s, Highway finds expression and recovery in music and language, storytelling and community. Highway's plays present the tricky negotiations of a people who have had to learn to live in two worlds. Central to the expression of these concerns in his plays is the presence of Nanabush, a trickster figure that is prominent in much Aboriginal storytelling. Just as the trickster figure frequently challenges humans with the essential contradictions of their existence, Highway's plays present audiences with challenging and often contradictory emotions—sorrow and humor, bawdiness and grief, violence and compassion—that lead ultimately to acceptance.

Highway has been inspired by other Canadian playwrights such as JAMES REANEY and MICHEL TREMBLAY, for example; however, Highway's work displays an artistic direction of his own by frequently addressing two topics that traditionally have not been explored by Aboriginal writers, homosexuality and misogyny. For Highway, the trickster figure becomes an important device through which many traditional and imposed gender roles are explored and challenged, including sexual ambiguity. Highway's numerous two-spirited characters (the trickster figure is neither male nor female, or is both at once) can be understood not only within the tradition of trickster narratives, but also as a method of resistance against the homogenizing forces of colonial discourse.

PLAYS: *The Sage, The Dancer and the Fool* (1984); *A Ridiculous Spectacle in One Act* (1985); *The Rez Sisters* (1986); *Aria* (1987); *Annie and the Old One* (1988); *New Song . . . New Dance* (1988); *Dry Lips Oughta Move to Kapuskasing* (1989); *Kiss of the Fur Queen* (1998); *Cariboo Song* (2001); *Ernestine Shuswap Gets Her Trout* (2001); *Johnny Nation Superhero* (2001); *Dragonfly Kites* (2002); *Comparing Mythologies* (2003); *Rose* (2003); *Fox on Ice* (2003)

FURTHER READING

Dickenson, Peter. *Here is Queer: Nationalisms, Sexualities and the Literatures of Canada*. Toronto: Univ. of Toronto Press, 1999.

Doran, Gregory Killen. *Saying Good-bye to Tonto: The Changing Representation of Natives in Canadian Drama*. DAI. thesis, Univ. of New Brunswick, 1995.

Enright, Robert. "Let Us Now Combine Mythologies: The Theatrical Art of Tomson Highway." *Border Crossings* 1, no. 4 (December 1992): 22–27.

Favel, Fred. "Born of the Sky: Tomson Highway: Cree Playwright, Novelist, Pianist." *Transition* (November–December 1998).

Jolene Armstrong

HINDLE WAKES

It isn't because I'm afraid of spoiling your life that I'm refusing you, but because I'm afraid of spoiling mine!

—Fanny Hawthorn, Act 3

Anarchist and women's rights advocate Emma Goldman highly praised STANLEY HOUGHTON's *Hindle Wakes* when it first appeared, mainly because of its heroine Fanny Hawthorn, a Lancashire weaver's daughter who sneaks away with the son of the mill's owner, Alan Jeffcote. In contrast to the Victorian understanding of womanhood, Fanny is represented as strong-willed, independent, and driven by the same erotic urges that surge through adolescent men. Goldman felt that such a character who asserts her "right to satisfy, if she so chooses, her emotional and sex demands like any other need of her mind and body" could enlighten an audience so that "the relation of the sexes will lose the shallow romanticism and artificial exaggeration [of the past] and assume a . . . healthy and normal expression."

The plot is complicated by the fact that Fanny's father Christopher and Alan's father Nathaniel grew up together, and while the former remains a laborer, the latter has moved up the social ladder to become a wealthy, powerful mill owner. When Fanny's seaside affair is discovered at the Hawthorn home, Christopher hurries to tell Nathaniel, who grudgingly agrees that the two should marry, despite Alan's severe reluctance to give up his advantageous engagement to the socially prominent Beatrice, whom he claims to love. Surprisingly, Fanny shares this view of their weekend together, refusing her parents' demands, the Jeffcotes's entreaties, and finally Alan's proposal because she is "afraid of spoiling" her life. Relying on the trade she has learned in the mill and her stamina, Fanny vows to live on her own and thus claim the right to determine her future.

Despite what critic A. E. Morgan (1969) called the "sordid material" of its premise, many critics praised *Hindle Wakes* as Houghton's most mature play, especially its "freshness" of dialogue in comparison to that of ARTHUR PINERO and HENRY ARTHUR JONES. Audiences too made the play's initial run in 1912 (and numerous tours) a sensation. Its early success came in part from the novelty of seeing a New Woman character arising from the ranks not of the middle or upper classes but of the working class, especially one expressing such viewpoints about a sexual tryst.

Yet, within the play, Fanny's bold assertion of equal rights has little effect. Indeed, her feminism enables the male characters to wriggle out of their "honorable" obligations, allowing Alan to return to the girl he wishes and allowing Nathaniel the prosperous marital union he desires between Alan and Beatrice. The social order seems intact, with the classes kept apart and serious consideration of the moral double standards toward women by those in positions of social power precluded.

The serious intellectual content of the Shavian style debate that forms the center of the play is softened further by Houghton's deft comic style. Despite some odd somber elements (including the drowning of one of Fanny's girlfriends), the play mostly maintains a light tone, what George Rowell (1968) calls a "dry, dour humour" in characterization and language, that has ensured numerous revivals of *Hindle Wakes* on stage, film, and television since its scandalous premiere.

[*See also* England, 1860–1940]

FURTHER READING

Chothia, Jean. *English Drama of the Early Modern Period, 1890–1940*. New York: Longman, 1996.

Goldman, Emma. *The Social Significance of the Modern Drama*. Boston: Gorham, 1914.

Morgan, A. E. *Tendencies of Modern English Drama*. New York: Scribner, 1924.

Rowell, George, ed. *Late Victorian Plays, 1890–1914*. London: Oxford Univ. Press, 1968.

Christopher Wixson

HIRATA ORIZA (1962–)

Hirata Oriza (1962–), Japanese playwright, director, and critic, together with IWAMATSU RYŪ, Suzue Toshirō, and Matsuda Masataka, is one of the leading contemporary playwrights in the so-called quiet theater (*shizuka na engeki*) movement, a reaction to the frenetic, festive nature of most Japanese theater during the 1980s, and he is its most articulate exponent. The son of a playwright and a clinical psychologist, Hirata was born and raised in Tokyo. He published his first book in 1981 about his adventures on a solo around-the-world bicycle tour when he was sixteen; he began writing plays in 1982 as a freshman at International Christian University. His theater company Seinendan (Youth Group), founded the same year, has used the Komaba Agora Theatre as its base of operations since 1986.

Hirata has written more than thirty plays, most of which he directed for Seinendan; in addition, two of the major SHINGEKI companies, the Literary Theatre (Bungakuza) and Theatre Circle (En), have commissioned works by him. He frequently directs and adapts works by other playwrights, including Matsuda Masataka, ŌTA SHŌGO, and BETSUYAKU MINORU. He has published a number of popular books on drama theory, the Japanese language, and cultural policy. As a teacher, he has conducted theater workshops for school students and people with disabilities. Since 2000 he has taught theater at Obirin University. He was director of the Japan Playwrights Association from 1993 to 2002 and is currently director of the Japan Society for Theatre Research. He has been actively touring abroad since 1990—to North America, Europe, Australia, Southeast Asia, and Oceania—and has been involved in a number of co-productions with Korean and French artists. Together with Korean playwright Kim Myung-Hwa, he won the second Asahi Theatre Award for *Across the River in May* (*Sono Kawa o Koete Gogatsu*, 2002).

Noted for their slice-of-life REALISM, all of Hirata's plays are concerned with what it means to be Japanese in the world today. His first important drama, *Citizens of Seoul* (*Seoul Shimin*, 1989), about the Japanese annexation of Korea in 1910, was drawn in part from his own experiences as a foreign student in Seoul in the mid-1980s. TOKYO NOTES (*Tōkyō Nōto*, 1994) portrays a family's confrontation with divorce and old age and is set in 2004 as a war in Europe threatens to engulf the world. *Kings of the Road* (*Bōken'ō*, 1996), based partly on Hirata's own experiences as a traveler in the late 1970s, features a group of Japanese backpackers in an Istanbul hostel; it ends with the sun setting over the Golden Horn and, by implication, on the West itself. *A Night Longer than the Sea* (*Umi yori Nagai Yoru*, 1999), his play about the collapse of a citizens' movement, and his series of parodies on the classic puppet and *kabuki* revenge play, *Chūshingura* (1999), set in contemporary times and turning the loyal masterless samurai into office ladies or schoolchildren on an excursion, demonstrate an increasing mastery of dramatic structure and a penetrating critique of Japanese ways of conflict resolution.

[*See also* Japan]

SELECT PLAYS: *Citizens of Seoul* (*Seoul Shimin*, 1989); *The Scientifically Minded* (*Kagaku Suru Kokoro*, 1990); *Tokyo Notes* (*Tōkyō Nōto*, 1994); *Kings of the Road* (*Bōken'ō*, 1996); *Chūshingura* (1999); *A Night Longer than the Sea* (*Umi yori Nagai Yoru*, 1999); *Citizens of Seoul 1919* (*Seoul Shimin 1919*, 2000); *Across the River in May* (*Sono Kawa o Koete Gogatsu*, 2002)

FURTHER READING

Hasebe Hiroshi. "The Sense of Being Alive: Japanese Theater in the 1990s." Tr. by Mari Boyd. In *Half A Century of Japanese Theater I: 1990s Part 1*, ed. by Japan Playwrights Association. Tokyo: Kinokuniya, 1999. 11–24.

Hirata Oriza. *Engeki Nyūmon* [Introduction to Theater]. Tokyo: Kōdansha, 1998.

———. "Citizens of Seoul" [Seoul Shimin]. Tr. by John D. Swain. In *Half A Century of Japanese Theater I: 1990s Part 1*, ed. by Japan Playwrights Association. Tokyo: Kinokuniya, 1999. 25–101.

———. *Geijutsu Rikkoku Ron* [How Art Can Build a Country]. Tokyo: Shūeisha, 2001.

———. "*Tokyo Notes*: A Play by Hirata Oriza." Tr. and intro. by M. Cody Poulton. *Asian Theatre Journal* 19 (Spring 2002): 1–120.

M. Cody Poulton

HIRSCHBEIN, PERETZ (1880–1948)

Yiddish and Hebrew playwright, novelist, and essayist Peretz Hirschbein was born in 1880 in a watermill in a rural part of the Grodno District, RUSSIA (now POLAND). As a teenager he discovered contemporary Hebrew literature, and soon Hirschbein was writing poetry. At eighteen he went to Vilnius, then a center of Jewish culture, where he fell in with a circle of Hebrew writers and began writing Hebrew plays and Yiddish short stories, supporting himself as a Hebrew teacher. His first play, *Miriam*, a naturalistic drama about a prostitute, was written in this period, but it was not until he moved to Warsaw in 1904 and earned the support of Y. L. Peretz and H. N. Bialik, leading figures of Yiddish and Hebrew literature, respectively, that he published it in a journal edited by Bialik. The NATURALISM of his early plays and the fact that several take place in cellars led the Hebrew writer Reuven Brainin to dub him "The Poet of the Cellar" (Niger, 1941).

In 1906 he ceased writing Hebrew literature and published his first Yiddish play, *Across the River* (*Af yener zayt taykh*), a symbolist work that earned him the nickname "the Yiddish MAETERLINCK." A period of great productivity ensued, during which he wrote the folkloric plays *The Vow* (*Der tkies-kaf*, 1908) and *The Earth* (*Di erd*, 1908), his first play about nature. In Odessa in 1908, at Bialik's urging, he founded the Dramatic Troupe under the Direction of Peretz Hirschbein, commonly known as the Hirschbein Troupe. This troupe was dedicated to raising the standard of the Yiddish repertoire and of Yiddish acting. Though the troupe survived for only two years, it inspired the foundation of the most important Yiddish theater companies, including the Vilna Troupe and the Yiddish Art Theater.

Hirschbein first came to the UNITED STATES in 1911 and wrote more plays in a folkloric style including *The Empty Inn* (*Di puste kretshme*, 1914) and *A Secluded Corner* (*A farvorfn vinkl*, 1915). He traveled extensively, began writing travelogues, and wrote his most important and successful play, *Green Fields* (*Grine felder*, 1916), an idyllic portrait of a family of rural Jewish farmers. The dialogue is at once lyrical and naturalistic, the characters vivid, and their interactions subtle. This play became one of the most frequently performed pieces in the Yiddish repertory.

Hirschbein married the Yiddish poet Esther Shumiatcher in 1920 and continued to travel and write plays and travelogues. In 1940 he settled in Los Angeles, where he spent the rest of his life until his death in 1948. Many of his plays were translated and performed in English and other languages. Film versions were made of *The Vow* and *Green Fields*.

Hirschbein's importance is twofold: Alongside the works of playwrights David Pinski, Leon Kobrin, and Ossip Dymov, Hirschbein's plays are central to YIDDISH THEATER's Second Golden Era in the first decades of the 20th century. In addition, the legacy of his troupe led to the modernization of the repertoire and style of acting in the Yiddish theater.

PLAYS: *Children* (*Yeladim*, 1905); *In a Cellar* (*Bemartef*, 1905); *Lonely Worlds* (*Olamot bodedim*, 1905); *Miriam* (1905); *Villainy* (*Nevala*, 1905); *Walking and Burning* (*Holchim uchavim*, 1905); *From Across the River* (*Fun yener zayt taykh*, 1906); *Graveyard Flowers* (*Kvorim blumen*, 1906); *Of Friends and Strangers* (*Fun eygene un fremde*, 1906); *In the Dark* (*In der finster*, 1907); *Twilight* (*Demerung*, 1907); *The Earth* (*Di erd*, 1908); *The Intellectual* (*Der inteligent*, 1908); *The Vow* (*Der tkies-kaf*, 1908); *At the Crossroads* (*Afn sheydveg*, 1911); *At the Shore* (*Bam breg*, 1911); *Joel* (*Yoyl*, 1911); *The Last* (*Der letster*, 1911); *Down the Wide Road* (*Tsum breytn veg*, 1914); *The Empty Inn* (*Di puste kretshme*, 1914); *Bebele* (1915); *Elijah the Prophet* (*Elyohu hanovi*, 1915); *Raisins and Almonds* (*Rozhinkes mit mandlen*, 1915); *A Secluded Corner* (*A farvorfn vinkl*, 1915); *The Blacksmith's Daughters* (*Dem shmids tekhter*, 1916); *A Blizzard* (*A zaverukhe*, 1916); *The Child of the World* (*Dos kind fun der velt*, 1916); *Green Fields* (*Grine felder*, 1916); *A Life for a Life* (*A lebn far a lebn*, 1916); *On the Threshold* (*Afn shvel*, 1916); *Sparks* (*Funken*, 1916); *When the Dew Falls* (*Ven es falt der toy*, 1916); *A Dream of the Time* (*A kholem fun der tsayt*, 1919); *Two Cities* (*Tsvey shtet*, 1919); *In the Shadow of Generations* (*In shotn fun doyres*, 1921); *Frost-flowers* (*Frostblumen*, 1922); *Levi Yitskhok* (1923); *What Do Demons Know* (*Sheydim veysn vos*, 1924); *The Mouse and the Bell* (*Di moyz mitn glekl*, 1925); *Hands* (*Hent*, 1928)

FURTHER READING

Liptzin, Sol. *The Flowering of Yiddish Literature*. New York: Thomas Yosselof, 1963.

Niger, Samuel, and Mendl Elkin, eds. *Perets Hirshbeyn*. New York: Astoria, 1941.

Rollansky, Samuel, ed. *Perets Hirshbeyn: teater, veltrayzes, zikhroynes* [Theater, Travels, Memoirs]. Buenos Aires: Zlotopioro Hnos., 1967.

Sandrow, Nahma. *God, Man, and Devil*. Syracuse: Syracuse Univ. Press, 1999.

Zylbercwajg, Z. "Perets Hirschbeyn." In *Leksikon fun yidishn teater* [Lexicon of the Yiddish Theater], Vol. 1. New York: Trio, 1931. 613–628.

Benjamin Sadock

THE HISTORY BOYS

History is just one fucking thing after another.
—Rudge, Act 2

ALAN BENNETT's play, first performed May 2004 at the Littleton Theatre in London, investigates the collision of sexuality, knowledge, history and performance. Set in a Northern England sixth-form boys' school in the 1980s, the play bursts with buried quotations and historical allusions including Rudyard Kipling, T. S. ELIOT, W. H. AUDEN, and Philip Larkin. The classroom functions as allegorical and material meditation on independent thought, the role and value of education, and the utility of knowledge in the English marketplace. The play explores two teachers' multiple positions: the utilitarian preparing the boys for university entrance exams, and the humanist who presents living, breathing complexities over staid facts—invoking learning's erotics and the classroom's homoerotics.

Act 1 opens to the future world outside the classroom, where a wheelchair-bound Irwin addresses a group of political strategist Members of Parliament (MPs). Irwin pragmatically suggests the MPs affect contrived paradox, not earnestness: " 'the loss of liberty is the price we pay for freedom' type thing." Hector's ribald entrance into the classroom occurs in juxtaposition to Irwin's performance. The boys remove his leather motorcycle gear with flare, announcing the articles' names *en Français*. The exchanges are swift and robust: Hector and the boys use language coyly, proficiently, humorously, and erotically. Their possession and expression of knowledge bridges social, economic, cultural, and sexual arenas.

The Headmaster wants the boys to attend Oxford and Cambridge universities and wonders how to achieve this, setting him in conflict with Mrs. Lintott who asserts facts need no presentation. She queries, "a sprig of parsley? An umbrella in the cocktail?" A fresh, young Irwin arrives from Oxford to teach the boys how to "perform" knowledge, while Hector teaches covertly in the overt classroom setting: behind a locked door, memorizing poetry, famous movie scenes, Posner's passionate singing. The classroom's passion materializes in the boys' taking turns riding pillion on Hector's motorcycle. The boys never tell; the Headmaster's wife sees Hector fondling a boy's genitals.

Act 2 begins with wheelchair-bound Irwin, five years older. He's taping a television show about monastic life, addressing history, time, desire, and waste. His anecdote about rags, used for wiping monks' bottoms, and their hallowed contemporary value, exposes how articles are revered for enduring, not for their usage or importance. This act contemplates the gains of history, facts, and knowledge and their shared erotic investments. Posner, the singing ingénue, who has failed out of Cambridge, asks Irwin what happened between him and Daikin—the beautiful, black-haired straight boy who manipulates the desires of Posner and Irwin. The scene returns to the classroom where Hector and Irwin share a session devoted to the Holocaust. Irwin spins various angles of interpretation—truthful or not; Hector questions the appropriateness of eating sandwiches and drinking Coke at Auschwitz or Dachau. Posner and Irwin's eyes meet, both fixed on Daikin. Mrs. Lintott provocatively asserts, "History is a commentary on the various and continuing incapabilities of men." Daikin propositions closeted Irwin through the guise of subjunctive history—what might or might not have happened. Their date never takes place—the motorcycle accident that kills Hector leaves Irwin crippled. This play, while exploring male homoerotics in the classroom and in education, is not a play about homosexual love and possibility; rather it rehearses desires, thwarted, unrealized and failed. In *The History Boys* history is an accident, a subversive collision of opposing views on life, education and sexuality.

[*See also* England, 1960–Present]

FURTHER READING

Bennett, Alan. *The History Boys*. New York: Faber, 2004.

Kerry Moore

HOBSON'S CHOICE

Well, by gum.

—Will, Act 3

Because of the enduring success of his 1915 COMEDY, *Hobson's Choice*, Harold Brighouse referred to himself in his autobiography as a "one-play playwright." In essence, the play, set in 1880, is a happy-ending version of *King Lear*. The priggish Henry Hobson owns a boot shop in Salford, Lancashire that is staffed by his three daughters. Through carelessness, inefficiency, and devotion to alcohol, he neglects the business, infuriating his hardworking eldest daughter, Maggie. Other than Maggie, Hobson's main asset is the talented shoemaker, William (Will) Mossop, but this low-paid doormat is harshly exploited by his irresponsible employer. Recognizing his good faith and commercial potential, the independent, assertive Maggie marries Will against her father's aggressive patriarchal declarations. Further defying Hobson, Maggie sets up a rival business with her husband.

Maggie's business acumen combines with Will's exquisite craftsmanship and customers flock to them, severely diminishing Hobson's share of the market. At his lowest ebb in act 3, Hobson, citing medical advice, pleads for one of his three (now all married) daughters to return to look after him and the business. The two younger daughters selfishly refuse. But Maggie, the Cordelia-like daughter, will return to assist her father—with conditions attached. Using evidence against Hobson, Maggie and a newly assertive Will threaten to disgrace Hobson unless he agrees to hand over half of the business to them. With no choice—Hobson's choice—Hobson accepts. The play ends with Will and Maggie running a shop that will be successful with Hobson as a sleeping partner. Because of Maggie and Will's rescue, he enjoys a lucrative retirement.

The play was first performed in New York in late 1915. It opened in June 1916 for 246 wartime performances at London's Apollo Theatre. The play has had a multifaceted afterlife, including notable revivals in 1922, 1950, 1952, and 1975. Brighouse turned the play into a novel, and a 1960s musical version, *Walking Happy*, received hostile reviews.

With his depiction of the maligned Will Mossop, Brighouse may have been intent on condemning the injustice and stupidity of the poor employment conditions open to such lowly figures. But in later appropriations of the play, Will's rise is seen to demonstrate the possibility for advancement through diligence in capitalist Britain. In a 1953 film version, Will is seen to be literally led away from the squalor of his mother's terraced council home by Maggie. In an exhilarating 2003 British-Indian adaptation by Tanika Gupta, Will, now called Ali, is a hapless, humble asylum seeker, an immigrant of the lowest caste. But under the direction of the Maggie-figure, Durga, he transforms into a dynamic, prepossessing executive, thereby implying that any motivated citizen can rise to economic independence in multicultural, 21st-century Britain. Brighouse's original text gives the last word to Will. Surveying Hobson's shop, which he now co-owns, he gazes in awe over the premises and, in northern English idiom, asserts with disbelief, "Well, by gum."

FURTHER READING

Brighouse, Harold. *Hobson's Choice: a Three-Act Comedy*. London: Constable; New York: Doubleday, Page, 1916.

——. *Hobson's Choice*. London: Samuel French, 1924.

——. *Hobson's Choice, in a New Adaptation by Tanika Gupta*. London: Oberon, 2003.

Mandelbaum, Ken. *Not Since Carrie: 40 Years of Broadway Musical Flops*. New York: St. Martin's, 1991. 186–188.

Smigel, Libby. "Harold Brighouse." In *British Playwrights, 1880–1956: a Research and Production Sourcebook*, ed. by W. W. Demastes and K. E. Kelly. London and Westport, Conn.: Greenwood, 1996. 67–80.

Tyson, B. F. "Harold Brighouse." In *The Dictionary of Literary Biography, Vol. 10, Part 1: Modern British Dramatists, 1900–1945*, ed. by Stanley Weintraub. Detroit: Gale, 1982. 75–80.

Kevin De Ornellas

HOCHHUTH, ROLF (1931–)

Plays that deny that individuals–which by no means need to be heroes—, can act or that, out of cowardice or ignorance, they can fail to act [. . .], are reduced to harmlessness, because it is the individual alone with whom the spectator can identify.

— Rolf Hochhuth, in "Reading Büchner in Order to Save Marx," 2001

Rolf Hochhuth was trained in the book trade and worked for years as a reader and an editor for big publishing companies. Born on April 1, 1931, in Eschwege, GERMANY, Hochhuth began his career as a freelance author in 1963 with his DOCUMENTARY play *The Deputy* (*Der Stellvertreter*).

While launching his career, *The Deputy* also initiated what would become a permanent trademark of Hochhuth's theater productions. Although he attracts enormous public attention and initiates lively public debate on account of the topics he chooses for his plays—the role of the Catholic Church during fascism in *The Deputy*; the undermining of the Geneva Convention in *Soldiers* (*Soldaten*, 1967); militarism and the arms race in *Lysistrata and NATO* (*Lysistrate und die Nato*, 1973); the colonial attitudes of West Germans toward the East Germans in *Wessis in Weimar* (*Wessis in Weimar*, 1993), to name just a few—Hochhuth's craftsmanship as a playwright is often called into question by those critics who have called his works "superficial and tendentious" (Bekes, 2001). Hochhuth's primary interest in the content seems to prevent a critical distance from it. It may appear that Hochhuth is building a case for his particular point of view, a fact attested to by the wealth of material he incorporates into his plays. Hochhuth himself, however, would not consider such a reaction negative criticism of his approach but rather an affirmation of it. Hochhuth works in the tradition of the German dramatists Gotthold Ephraim Lessing (1729–1781) and Friedrich Schiller (1759–1805) for whom the protagonist functions as the bearer of a message or a set of ideas. From this follows the tragic conflicts of Hochhuth's leading characters: they either become martyrs following through on their ideas or they get caught in the conflict between what they perceive as their role in history and the personal, moral guilt that comes as the cost of their actions. Hochhuth can thus be seen as the antipode to his contemporary HEINAR KIPPHARDT.

Hochhuth's *The Deputy* and Kipphardt's *In the Matter of J. Robert Oppenheimer* (*In der Sache J. Robert Oppenheimer*, 1964) catapulted documentary theater onto German stages, but the two authors approach their historical subject matter from opposite directions. Whereas Kipphardt focuses on the model character of the historic moment, Hochhuth personalizes and moralizes the historical events, highlighting moral freedom as well as the importance of individual responsibility and accountability at important moments in history. Hochhuth turns the stage back into a "moral institution" (Schiller) and a "secular pulpit" (Gottsched) in the spirit of the German Enlightenment. Thus, from the very beginning, the tradition of documentary theater in Germany never had as much to do with attempts at greater objectivity through the incorporation of authentic materials as it did with authorial intentions as disparate as those of Hochhuth, Kipphardt, and PETER WEISS, whose works form the high point of this period in postwar German theater.

PLAYS: *The Deputy* (*Der Stellvertreter*, 1963); *Soldiers: An Obituary for Geneva* (*Soldaten. Nekrolog auf Genf*, 1967); *Guerillas: A Tragedy in 5 Acts* (*Guerillas. Tragödie in 5 Akten*, 1970); *The Midwife: A Comedy* (*Die Hebamme. Komödie*, 1971); *Lysistrata and NATO: A Comedy* (*Lysistrate und die Nato. Komödie*, 1973); *Distant Relatives: A Monologue* (*Entfernte Verwandte. Monolog*, 1976); *Death of a Hunter* (*Tod eines Jägers*, 1977); *Men of Law: Three Acts for Seven Actors* (*Juristen: drei Akte für sieben Spieler*, 1979); *Female Physicians: Five Acts* (*Ärztinnen. 5 Akte*, 1980); *Judith: A Tragedy* (*Judith. Ein Trauerspiel*, 1984); *Immaculate Conception: A Chalk Circle* (*Unbefleckte Empfängis. Ein Kreidekreis*, 1988); *Summer 1914: Danse Macabre* (*Sommer 1914. Ein Totentanz*, 1989); *Wessis in Weimar: Scenes from an Occupied Country* (*Wessis in Weimar. Szenen aus einem besetzten Land*, 1993); *Effi's Night: A Monologue* (*Effis Nacht. Monolog*, 1996); *Unemployed* (*Arbeitslose*, 1999); *The Right to Work* (*Das Recht auf Arbeit*, 2000); *Serenade* (*Nachtmusik*, 2000); *Hitler's Dr. Faust* (2001); *Gas Stove and Enemas, or the Great-Grandmother of the Diet Cook: Requiem and Farce Each in One Act* (*Gasherd und Klistiere, oder Die Urgroßmutter der Diätköchin. Requiem und Posse jeweils in einem Akt*, 2002)

FURTHER READING

Barton, Brian. "Dokumentartheater in der Bundesrepublik Deutschland. Die Modelle. Hochhuth: Dokumente in klassischem Muster" [Documentary Theater in the Federal Republic of Germany: Models. Hochhuth: A Classic Example of Documents]. In *Das Dokumentartheater* [Documentary Theater]. Stuttgart: Metzler, 1987. 94–101.

Bekes, Peter. "Rolf Hochhuth." In *Kritisches Lexikon zur deutschsprachigen Gegenwartsliteratur* [*Critical Encyclopedia of Contemporary German-Language Literature*], ed. by Heinz Ludwig Arnold. Munich: Text und Kritik, 2002. 72nd Supplement. 1–16 and A–T.

Marx, Patricia. "An Interview with Rolf Hochhuth." *Partisan Review* 31 (1964): 363–376.

Ward, Margaret E. *Rolf Hochhuth*. Boston: Twayne, 1977.

Friedemann J. Weidauer

HOFMANNSTHAL, HUGO VON (1874–1929)

This is how we act our parts out,
Acting plays of our own making,

Early-ripe and sad and tender,
The commedia of our spirit,
What we feel as time slips by us,
Ugly facts in pretty guises.
—Hugo von Hofmannsthal, Prologue to Arthur Schnitzler's *Anatol* (1892)

Hugo von Hofmannsthal's legacy as a playwright is difficult to assess. A broader audience knows him primarily as the co-founder of the Salzburg Festival and for his opera librettos for German composer Richard Strauss (1864–1949). Although his output for the stage was rich and varied, including lyrical verse plays, serious dramas, COMEDIES, and ballet scenarios, many projects remained unfinished, and now only a handful of his plays are performed.

Hofmannsthal was born on February 1, 1874, in Vienna, AUSTRIA, into a family that embodied the promise of multi-ethnic integration within the Habsburg Empire: his paternal great-grandfather, a Jewish textile merchant from Bohemia, had attained a patent of nobility for services to the Austrian throne. His descendants converted to Catholicism, consolidated economic success, and intermarried with people of Austro-German and Italian stock. Prodigiously gifted, young Hofmannsthal grew up sheltered by social and material privilege, in the precarious world of a vanishing cosmopolitan lower aristocracy. In 1890, as a sixteen-year-old high-school student writing under a pseudonym, he caused a sensation with masterful poems that gained the respect and admiration of fellow writers of the *Jung Wien* (Young Vienna) circle, the coffee-house representatives of fin-de-siècle modernism, including the dramatist ARTHUR SCHNITZLER, the novelist Richard Beer-Hofmann (1866–1945), and the critic Hermann Bahr (1863–1934). In mature and exquisite language, these poems addressed issues that would preoccupy Hofmannsthal throughout his life: existential questions concerning time and change, the instability of the self, the possibility of human contact, and the limits of language as a means of communication.

Between 1892 and 1894, Hofmannsthal studied law at the University of Vienna. Following mandatory military service (1894–1895), he pursued a doctorate in Romance literatures (1898) and further academic qualifications, yet in 1901 he abandoned an academic career and became a freelance writer. The same year, he married Gertrud Schlesinger, daughter of a banker of Jewish descent who had himself converted to Catholicism, and the couple settled in Rodaun, outside Vienna, where they lived for the rest of Hofmannsthal's life.

The crisis marking the transition from admired *Wunderkind* poet to mature author found its most prominent expression, and a kind of resolution, in the prose essay "Ein Brief" (1902, known as the "Lord Chandos Letter"). The most significant document of the fin-de-siècle *Sprachkrise* (Language Crisis), it has been interpreted as articulating the comprehensive identity crisis of the modern subject effected, among others, by FRIEDRICH NIETZSCHE's (1844–1900) value skepticism, Ernst Mach's (1838–1916) empirio-criticism, and Sigmund Freud's (1856–1939) emerging depth psychology. In response, Hofmannsthal asserts a sphere of experience outside conceptual thought and discursive language, involving a near mystical sense of unity with the world—the basis for his shift from poetry toward drama as a social art form based in, and concerned with, human interaction. His breakthrough as a playwright came in 1903 with the successful first production of his TRAGEDY *Elektra* in Berlin, inaugurating a lifelong collaboration with famed theater impresario and fellow Austrian MAX REINHARDT, which secured Hofmannsthal a firm position in the cultural elite of prewar Europe.

Apolitical and conservative, Hofmannsthal watched his world of refinement and cosmopolitan goodwill collapse in the cataclysm of World War I. He joined the Austrian military in July 1914 and, from 1915 to 1917, traveled on diplomatic missions to occupied territories to conduct official patriotic propaganda work. In the fall of 1917, Hofmannsthal and others launched the idea of a festival at Salzburg as a source for the spiritual renewal of Austro-Bavarian culture, based on a shared Catholicism nostalgically idealized as an organic antidote to the dry secularism of North German (Prussian) modernity. The festival opened auspiciously in July 1920 with an outdoor performance of Hofmannsthal's morality play *Everyman* (*Jedermann*, 1911) in front of the Salzburg cathedral, but the venture quickly turned into vacuous commercial ritual and snobbish tourist attraction. Despite such setbacks, for years Hofmannsthal devoted himself in countless essays and lectures to combating the political fragmentation of an increasingly contentious reality, aligning himself with the forces of "conservative revolution," intellectuals aiming to salvage the legacy of Christian humanism against the assault of both the radical Left and Right, Bolshevism and the emerging Nazi movement. Deeply alienated by the political tensions of the interwar period, Hofmannsthal withdrew into pessimistic introspection. In July 1929, his eldest son, Franz, committed suicide. Two days later, on July 15, Hofmannsthal died from a stroke in Rodaun near Vienna, Austria.

Hofmannsthal's early short plays, like *Yesterday* (*Gestern*, 1891) and *Death and the Fool* (*Der Tor und der Tod*, 1983), set themselves in opposition to the socially engaged NATURALISM prevalent at the time and championed by dramatists like HENRIK IBSEN and GERHART HAUPTMANN. In a manner reminiscent of Francophone and Italian SYMBOLISM, the plays are set in a vaguely premodern feudal world, written in stylized evocative verse, and centered on isolated male protagonists in a threshold situation in which they come to realize the human consequences of their aestheticist self-absorption. Subsequent verse plays, like *Madonna Dianora* (*Die Frau im Fenster*, 1898), and magical or oriental fairy tales like *The Emperor and the Witch* (*Der Kaiser und die Hexe*, 1897) and *Sobeide's Wedding* (*Die Hochzeit der Sobeide*,

1899), add a modicum of action to the monologic presentation of psychic dispositions. Yet structural problems persist; for instance, in the tensions between everyday reality and the magical underground world of the mines in the sprawling, unfinished five-act drama *The Mine at Falun* (*Das Bergwerk zu Falun*), begun around 1899.

Seeking to overcome the solipsism and the dramaturgical limitations of his early plays, Hofmannsthal turned to traditional models for guidance. Sometimes, as in his 1902 version of Thomas Otway's (1652–1685) Jacobean tragedy *Venice Preserv'd* (1682), the many changes (including inventing new characters) raise the question of whether such reworkings can still be called translations or adaptations, or whether they should be regarded as original works in their own right. Yet such projects helped Hofmannsthal address problems of plot structure by refining what he called *Konfiguration*, the carefully balanced arrangement of characters whose different positions reflect the complexities and nuances of a thematic issue in a kind of dramatic kaleidoscope.

The line of reworkings of ancient Greek dramas began in 1894 with an adaptation of Euripides's *Alkestis* and culminated in 1903 with *Elektra*, which endowed Sophocles's mythical heroine with a nuanced psychology modeled on Freud's *Studies on Hysteria* (1893–1895). Enhanced by ecstatically charged verse, the result is a thoroughly gripping drama at once powerfully archaic and thoroughly modern. Subsequent efforts at emulating ancient Greek drama, including *Oedipus and the Sphinx* (*Oedipus und die Sphinx*, 1904) and *King Oedipus* (*König Oedipus*, 1910), performed in arenas throughout Europe under Reinhardt's direction as a mass spectacle, were artistically less successful. When Strauss expressed an interest in setting *Elektra* to music, the playwright eagerly obliged, accommodating the composer's pragmatic suggestions in revising his stage play into an opera libretto that was performed to great critical acclaim in Dresden in 1909. Thus began the extraordinary creative partnership of two distinct artistic temperaments that yielded as a first original result *The Rose Bearer* (*Der Rosenkavalier*, 1911), a nostalgic musical comedy set in an idealized 18th-century Vienna of Empress Maria Theresia (1717–1780). It became a sensational success.

In the Strauss operas, Hofmannsthal explored the reciprocal transformation of individuals in an encounter with others, which he called *das Allomatische* (coined in opposition to "the auto-matic"), exemplified in *The Rose Bearer* in the love-at-first-sight between two young people, Sophie and Octavian, and the Marschallin's wistful renunciation of her love for Octavian. Similar transformations occur for the title character in *Ariadne on Naxos* (*Ariadne auf Naxos*, first version 1912, revised version 1916), a complex pastiche of elements from commedia dell' arte and serious heroic opera; for the Empress in *The Woman Without a Shadow* (*Die Frau ohne Schatten*, 1919), a mystical romantic fairy tale; for Menelaos in *The Egyptian Helen* (*Die ägyptische Helena*, 1928), a comedic mythological opera based on motifs from Homer, Euripides, and Johann Wolfgang von Goethe; and for Arabella and her suitor Mandryka in the final Hofmannsthal-Strauss opera, *Arabella* (1929; performed posthumously in 1933), a conversation piece set among the declining aristocracy of 1860s Vienna. The beauty of Hofmannsthal's lyrical language often inspired Strauss to unprecedented creative heights, yet the ravishing music does not always manage to assuage convoluted plot structures, clarify arcane symbolism, or make philosophically suspect ideas more palatable.

Hofmannsthal's problematic conservatism is evident in the serious plays emulating the Austro-Spanish Catholic tradition, including medieval allegories and works by the Spanish Baroque Golden Age dramatist Calderón (Pedro Calderón de la Barca, 1600–1681) and Austrian playwright Franz Grillparzer (1791–1872). As early as 1897 with *The Little World Theater, or the Fortunate Ones* (*Das kleine Welttheater, oder Die Glücklichen*), Hofmannsthal projected a hope that Catholicism could provide cohesion to a world fraught with conflict. Likewise, the religious allegory *Everyman* reworks the famous English medieval mystery play to restore a sense of community by reminding the audience of a common humanity. It was to become the centerpiece of the Salzburg Festival, where it is still performed annually. The play Hofmannsthal wrote specifically for the festival, *The Salzburg Great Theatre of the World* (*Das Salzburger Große Welttheater*, 1922), a variation of Calderón's *El gran teatro del mundo* (1635), has fared less well.

To many of Hofmannsthal's contemporaries, the religious world-as-theater metaphor suggesting that humans should accept their divinely ordained "roles" within the social order smacked of reactionary political appeasement. Hofmannsthal seems to exhibit a despairing sense that the only response to the threat of barbarism in modernity would be a return to organicist notions of order and community based on shared spiritual (if not downright religious) values. That this belief is highly ambivalent is evidenced by the tortured genesis of his most ambitious serious drama, *The Tower* (*Der Turm*, first version 1925, second version 1928). It began in 1901 with a translation of Calderón's *Life as a Dream* (*La vida es sueño*, 1635) and emulated Grillparzer's reworking of Calderón, *A Dream of Life* (*Der Traum ein Leben*, 1831). The five-act tragedy depicts the oedipally charged, gruesome story of Sigismund, the Polish prince whose father keeps him imprisoned in a tower for fear of a prophecy of insurrection. A hoped-for reconciliation with the father fails, and upon his release, Sigismund cannot survive in a corrupt and violent world. In the second version, Sigismund, having come to accept his dungeon as a sheltering cocoon, refuses to leave his prison, a reflection of Hofmannsthal's own increasing historical pessimism.

If the serious dramas seem to negate the notion of fruitful autonomous action, the comedies assert that meaningful human connection is possible. They highlight *das erreichte Soziale* (the social dimension attained), for which love in general, and marriage in particular, serve as emblems—in a mundane version of the metaphysics of marriage propagated in the opera libretti. Hofmannsthal's early efforts in the genre, *Sylvia in the 'Star'* (*Sylvia im 'Stern'*, 1907) and *Cristina's Journey Home* (*Cristinas Heimreise*, 1908), place memorable characters in tensions between frivolous erotic flirtation and existentially serious commitment. A series of translations/adaptations of plays by Molière (1622–1673) refined the art of conversation in sophisticated, multilayered comedies of manners.

The line culminates in two late masterpieces set in more contemporary environments. *The Difficult Man* (*Der Schwierige*, 1921) achieves a balance of *Konstellation* (in the intricate arrangement of refracted sets of complementary characters) and *Konversation* (in dialogic exchanges that appear casual yet convey complex philosophical and psychological subtexts). "Difficult" Hans Karl, a recluse lacking a stable sense of self, despairs of existentially connecting with another person until the woman he loves, whom he awkwardly tries to woo on behalf of another man, reaches out to him in a gesture of intuitive understanding that transcends language. A kind of companion piece, *The Incorruptible Man* (*Der Unbestechliche*, 1923), originally a character study for the legendary Viennese comic actor Max Pallenberg (1877–1934), hinges on an old servant who sets his philandering master's marital conflicts aright according to premodern notions of the absolute sanctity of marriage. The comedy, whose central character and moral backbone bears the telling name Theodor ("gift of God"), aims to restore an irretrievable status quo, the supposedly organic social order of feudal subservience.

At their best, Hofmannsthal's stage works—opera libretti, serious dramas, and comedies—provide thankful opportunities for performers and intriguing food for thought for readers and viewers alike.

SELECT PLAYS (arranged chronologically by date written): *Yesterday* (*Gestern*, 1891); *The Death of Titian* (*Der Tod des Tizian*, 1892); *Death and the Fool* (*Der Tor und der Tod*, 1893); *Alkestis* (1894; set to music as opera by Egon Wellesz, 1923); *The Little World Theater, or the Unfortunate Ones* (*Das kleine Welttheater, oder Die Glücklichen*, 1897); *The White Fan* (*Der weiße Fächer*, 1897); *The Emperor and the Witch* (*Der Kaiser und die Hexe*, 1898); *Madonna Dianora* (*Die Frau im Fenster*, 1898); *The Adventurer and the Lady Singer* (*Der Abenteurer und die Sängerin*, 1899); *Sobeide's Wedding* (*Die Hochzeit der Sobeide*, 1899); *The Mine at Falun* (*Das Bergwerk zu Falun*, 1899–1925); *A Dream is Life* (*Das Leben ein Traum*, 1901, an adaptation of Calderón); *Venice Preserv'd* (*Das gerettete Venedig*, 1902, an adaptation of Thomas Otway); *Elektra* (1903, an adaptation of Sophocles); *Oedipus and the Sphinx* (*Oedipus und die Sphinx*, 1904); *King Oedipus* (*König Oedipus*, 1905, an adaptation of Sophocles); *Sylvia in the "Star"* (*Sylvia im 'Stern'*, 1907); *Cristina's Journey Home* (*Cristinas Heimreise*, 1908); *Marriage Against One's Will* (*Heirat wider Willen*, 1910, an adaptation of Molière); *Everyman* (*Jedermann*, 1911); *The Rose Bearer* (*Der Rosenkavalier*, 1911); *Ariadne on Naxos* (*Ariadne auf Naxos*, 1912); *The Burgher as Nobleman* (*Der Bürger als Edelmann*, 1912, an adaptation of Molière); *The Nuisances* (*Die Lästigen*, 1916, an adaptation of Molière); *The Woman without a Shadow* (*Die Frau ohne Schatten*, 1919); *The Difficult Man* (*Der Schwierige*, 1921); *The Salzburg Great Theater of the World* (*Das Salzburger große Welttheater*, 1922, an adaptation of Calderón); *The Incorruptible Man* (*Der Unbestechliche*, 1923); *The Tower* (*Der Turm*, 1925, an adaptation of Calderón and Grillparzer); *The Egyptian Helena* (*Die ägyptische Helena*, 1928); *Arabella* (1929)

FURTHER READING

Bennett, Benjamin. *Hugo von Hofmannsthal: The Theatres of Consciousness*. Cambridge: Cambridge Univ. Press, 1988.

Broch, Hermann. *Hugo von Hofmannsthal and His Time: The European Imagination, 1860–1920*. Tr., ed., and intro. by Michael P. Steinberg. Chicago: Univ. of Chicago Press, 1984.

König, Christoph. *Hofmannsthal: Ein moderner Dichter unter den Philologen* [Hofmannsthal: A Modern Poet Among Philologists]. Göttingen, Germany: Wallstein, 2001.

Kovach, Thomas A., ed. *A Companion to the Works of Hofmannsthal*. Rochester: Camden House, 2002.

Le Rider, Jacques. *Modernity and Crises of Identity: Culture and Society in 'fin de siècle' Vienna*. Tr. by Rosemary Morris. New York: Continuum, 1993.

Meyer, Mathias. *Hugo von Hofmannsthal*. Stuttgart: Metzler, 1993.

Ward, Philip M. *Hofmannsthal and Greek Myth: Expression and Performance*. Oxford: Peter Lang, 2002.

Christian Rogowski

HŌJŌ HIDEJI (1902–1996)

Hōjō Hideji was an employee of the Japanese Railway company, director, and one of Japan's best-known playwrights for the commercial theater. He wrote consistently for SHINPA, Shinkokugeki ("new national drama," actually the name of a company) from the beginning of World War II until shortly before his death.

In his spare time from work with the railway company, Hōjō studied playwriting under OKAMOTO KIDŌ and Hasegawa Shin. From Okamoto, by this time the leading SHIN KABUKI playwright, Hōjō learned the stagecraft necessary for work in larger theaters, and he acquired a conscientious attitude toward popular content from Hasegawa, who in the late 1920s established the parameters for Japanese popular fiction and drama. On Okamoto's death in 1939, Hōjō became a full-time playwright. Productions of his early work attracted attention for their solid DRAMATURGY and sensitivity to both the actors' talents and the audiences' moods. This was especially true of *Honored Sir* (1940), performed by *shinpa*, in which Hōjō wrote with simple candor of the hesitation of two old lovers (the captain of industry who is referred to as honored sir [*kakka*] and a local girl) to meet, when the former's visit to a village after many years presents the opportunity.

During the war Hōjō wrote *kokumingeki*—plays the government intended would help the war effort. *Tanna Tunnel* (1942) is regarded as a model of such plays. It certainly praised a spirit of self-sacrifice on the part of some tunnel workers, but Hōjō imbued the play with his genuine interest in their motivation.

Emotional sincerity and fine crafting were the hallmarks of Hōjō's postwar playwriting, particularly evident in *Chess Master* (1947), a series of three plays written for *shinkokugeki*, in which Hōjō describes the single-minded struggle of a chess player to become a master, the devotion of his wife in supporting him through setbacks, and the mutual love that binds them together. These plays, set in contemporary Japan, helped *shinkokugeki* to reconnect with its audiences, now that its "feudal" history plays were temporarily unacceptable.

Postwar *shinkokugeki*, *kabuki*, and *shinpa* have much to thank Hōjō for. They all benefited from plays that brought out the best in their actors. *Behind the Flower Garden* (1960) provided *shinpa*'s leading *onnagata* Hanayagi Shōtarō with the possibility of playing both male and female leads: the sexually instinctual lover and the superhumanly forgiving wife of a husband tragically at the mercy of his emotions. Hōjō did much to bolster *kabuki* in the early 1950s. As Japan was struggling to lift itself from immediate postwar deprivation, Funahashi Seiichi (in 1951) and Hōjō (from 1953) brought the romantic 11th-century classic *Tale of the Genji* to the stage. Hōjō wrote ten plays based on this work and greatly helped the new generation of *kabuki* actors in their efforts to bring *kabuki* to a wider range of age groups. His role in founding and being active in the revived Nihon Engeki Kyōkai, an organization devoted to the improvement of all aspects of the performing arts, testifies to his commitment to the Japanese theater. To the end of his life, Hōjō was a consummate participant in commercial theater who directed his own plays with a detailed regard to all aspects of production.

[*See also* Japan]

SELECT PLAYS: *Honored Sir* (*Kakka*, 1940); *Chess Master* (*Ōshō*, 1947); *Behind the Flower Garden* (*Hyakkaen Ura*, 1960); *Taro* (*Tarō*, 1970)

FURTHER READING

Ōyama Isao. *Kindai Nihon Gikyoju-shi* [History of Modern Japanese Drama], Vols. 3 and 4. Yamagata: Kindai Nihon Gikyoju-shi Kankōkai, 1971.

Tanabe Akio. *Hōjō Hideji: Shijō no tatsujin* [Hōjō Hideji: Master of Poetic Feeling]. Osaka: Henshū Kōbō Noa, 1994.

Brian Powell

HOLIDAY

On November 26, 1928, PHILIP BARRY's sparkling high comedy, *Holiday*, produced and directed by Arthur Hopkins, opened at Broadway's Plymouth Theatre and began a run of 229 performances.

The action occurs in the Fifth Avenue family home of self-made industrialist Edward Seton. Lovely daughter, Julia, brings home her fiancé, Johnny Case, acquired in a whirlwind romance while on a ski trip. Upon arrival in New York, Johnny realizes he has fallen for an heiress. Basic beliefs concerning financial responsibility force him to face a conflict between love and integrity. Case has never viewed the accumulation of wealth as an end in itself; an idea shared by the other Seton daughter, Linda. Linda's remark, "What good's all this jack we've got anyway—unless to get us a superior type of husband?" reveals her attitude toward wealth. Like Edward, Johnny has earned his money the hard way and does not need Julia's. He intends to spend some time enjoying the fruits of his labor while he is young; Julia, however, shares her father's attitude toward wealth and is appalled that Johnny would abandon his success in business just when he's beginning to amass a fortune. Linda becomes the advocate for Johnny's point of view and, while helping him win over other family members, falls for him herself.

The sparkling dialogue and witty, well-turned-out characters who populate this comedy deftly clarify a contemporary conflict. The values of a generation of Americans who defined themselves by the fortunes they amassed do not seem fulfilling to their free-spirited children. Typically, Barry affords each side of the conflict reasonable examination as he leads his characters to the kind of self-knowledge that allows for an equitable resolution. Like most wealthy Americans just before the crash of 1929, Barry's characters face no problem so difficult that intelligent, self-possessed individuals cannot find a way to resolve it equitably. While Barry pokes fun at stuffy patriarch Edward and his entire clan, he clearly admires each of his creations in one way or another. By refraining from harsh ridicule, Barry distinguishes his comedies of manners from their European predecessors.

Barry's favorite actress, sporty and boyish Hope Williams, played the feisty fast-talking Linda Seton. This character epitomizes a signature creation often referred to as "the Barry Girl." Miss Williams enjoyed most career success when collaborating with Barry on this and other roles of this type. Portrayal of the Barry Girl also catapulted Williams's understudy, Katharine Hepburn, to stardom when she earned the role of Linda Seton in the film version of *Holiday* and, later, Tracy Lord in THE PHILADELPHIA STORY.

FURTHER READING

Broussard, Louis. *American Drama: Contemporary Allegory From Eugene O'Neill to Tennessee Williams*. Norman: Univ. of Oklahoma Press, 1962.

Gassner, John. "Philip Barry: A Civilized Playwright." In *The Theatre in Our Times: A Survey of the Men, Materials, and Movements in the Modern Theatre*, ed. by Gassner. New York: Crown, 1954.

Midyett, Judith A. "The Comedy of Equitable Resolution: S.N. Behrman and Philip Barry." Ph.D. diss., Univ. of Georgia, 1987.

Roppolo, Joseph Patrick. *Philip Barry*. Twayne's U.S. Authors Series. New York: Twayne, 1965.

Judith Midyett Pender

HOLLINGSWORTH, MARGARET (1939–)

Born in 1939 in Sheffield, ENGLAND, Margaret Hollingsworth immigrated to CANADA in 1968 and eventually settled in British Columbia. Her work has often received more interest in academic circles than in professional ones. For example, she self-published an anthology of four short plays, *Endangered Species*, and at the time of publication, not one of the plays had received a professional production. And yet this collection is one of the works that Ric Knowles writes about in *Theatre of Form* and uses in his formulation of the "dramaturgy of the perverse," a term he uses to describe a type of DRAMATURGY that "perverts" Aristotelian and modernist forms of containment (also included are playwrights such as JUDITH THOMPSON, GEORGE F. WALKER, and DANIEL MACIVOR).

Hollingsworth's plays usually engage with but inevitably subvert REALISM, an approach that has been variously described as "magic realism" (Maufort, 2000) or as a "feminist absurd" (Derkeson, 2002). Early plays such as *Ever Loving* or *Islands* have a principally linear and realistic form, but later experimental plays, especially those in *Endangered Species* such as *Poppycock* and *Prim, Duck, Mama and Frank*, initiate challenges to form, character, and linear time. The manipulation of form is often linked to themes in Hollingsworth's plays. In *WAR BABIES*, for example, Hollingsworth queries the individual's responsibility within a global context and links this to the relationship between fiction and truth as she uses the device of the play-within-a-play as an aesthetic vehicle for her political concerns.

Social action and humanist concerns resonate throughout Hollingsworth's plays and are often linked to another major thematic consideration: the choices and desires of women. The focus of Hollingsworth's plays is often literally on the lives of women. In *Ever Loving*, the lives of three war brides are followed, exploring their desires as their lives intersect. In the more experimental *Poppycock*, a play developed through a clown workshop, Hollingsworth looks at the historical women in the shadows of Adolf Hitler, Pablo Picasso, and Ezra Pound, using imaginative and imagistic ways of conveying their relationships. Hollingsworth's plays often give voice to the unconsidered and unspoken, often seen in the lives of women. Multiple realities are made apparent through various stylistic devices. For example, Hollingsworth frequently uses the device of the inner voice to bring to the foreground the psychological split of many of her (usually female) characters. In *Apple in the Eye* and *Diving*, for example, two short one-act plays, the conflict between private desires and public pressures is made concrete through this device as offstage male voices compel the actions of the women onstage. *In Confidence*, a play of essentially two intersecting monologues, gives attention to a subject often overlooked: the lives and desires of older women as they contemplate both their life choices and their friendship.

Although principally a playwright, Hollingsworth has also written essays, short stories, and most recently, a novel, *Be Quiet* (2004), inspired by the life of Canadian West Coast painter Emily Carr. Throughout her career, Hollingsworth has been a consistent and vocal advocate for the rights of women writers.

SELECT PLAYS: *Alli Alli Oh* (1975); *Operators* (1978); *Ever Loving* (1980); *Mother Country* (1980); *Bushed* (1981); *The Apple in the Eye* (1983); *Diving* (1983); *Islands* (1983); *War Babies* (1984); *Poppycock* (1987); *The House that Jack Built* (1988); *It's Only Hot for Two Days in Kapuskasing* (1988); *Prim, Duck, Mama and Frank* (1988); *Alma Victoria* (1989); *In Confidence* (1994); *Commonwealth Games* (1996)

FURTHER READING

Derksen, Celeste. "A Feminist Absurd: Margaret Hollingsworth's *The House that Jack Built*." *Modern Drama* 45, no. 2 (Summer 2002): 209–230.

Hollingsworth, Margaret. "Musings on the Feminist Muse: New Year's Day, 1990." In *Language in her Eye*, ed. by Libby Scheier, Sarah Sheard, and Eleanor Wachtel. Toronto: Coach House, 1990. 142–145.

Knowles, Ric. "The Dramaturgy of the Perverse." *Theatre Research International* 17, no. 3 (1992): 226–335.

——. *The Theatre of Form and the Production of Meaning: Contemporary Canadian Dramaturgies*. Toronto: ECW Press, 1999.

Maufort, Marc. "Redrawing the Boundaries of Poetic Realism in Margaret Hollingsworth's Drama." *Canadian Theatre Review* 101 (Winter 2000): 40–43.

Parker, Dorothy. "Alienation and Identity: The Plays of Margaret Hollingsworth." *Canadian Literature* 118 (Autumn 1988): 97–113.

Rudakoff, Judith, and Rita Much. "Margaret Hollingsworth Interview." In *Fair Play: 12 Women Speak*, ed. by Rudakoff and Much. Toronto: Simon and Pierre, 1990. 88–104.

Marlene Moser

HOLLINGSWORTH, MICHAEL (1950–)

Although identified in the theater world as a playwright and director, Michael Hollingsworth's extensive work with video, music, and design more properly locates him as participating in what art historian Leo Steinberg terms "inter-art traffic"—an interaction of visual forms, performance, and text. Hollingsworth learned to write for video (both prerecorded and live) and for many years created video and performance spectacles in which cameras, lights, monitors, musical instruments, amplifiers, and technicians were part of the design.

When Hollingsworth began working on his elaborate multipart play cycle *The History of the Village of the Small Huts*, he stripped the theatrical experience to its barest means: actor, costume, and light. Exploiting theater's limits, Hollingsworth's multipart cycle reduces the means and then radically hyperbolizes what remains: an actor becomes scores of grotesque characters; costumes and props often swell to elaborate proportions (larger-than-life-sized wigs, exaggerated costumes in vibrant primary colors, a gigantic copy of Niccolò Machiavelli's *The Prince*); and a black box is punctured with light in which the scenes and characters are positioned in *tableaux vivants*. Against this black void the performers align themselves with thousands of computerized lighting cues.

Celebrated for enlivening Canadian history, *The History of the Village of the Small Huts* dramatizes Canada's history from Donnacona and Cartier to Mulroney and George H. W. Bush in parodic satires. Incorporating theatrical formats—including mystery plays, *commedia dell 'arte*, puppet theater, MELODRAMA, operetta, and multimedia—provides a sense of time to this elaborate historical project. Hollingsworth's ferociously paced theatrical style moves hundreds of characters through years of time and miles of wilderness. For a small theater company, the *History Plays* are unusually grand in scale and scope and filled with artistic challenges.

Born in Wales in 1950, since 1976 Hollingsworth has been working and collaborating with VideoCabaret International, the company he co-founded with performance artist Deanne Taylor. The presence of technology (as both form and content) and the audience as participant provide the structure for most of their work, along with a sustained interest in fusing performance, music, and graphics in a cabaret format. From its inception, the company has worked with very little financial backing. VideoCabaret and its associated artists make their art out of what is around them; their aesthetic is part *arte povere* and part theatrical extravaganza. The company's projects involve movement between historical precedents and contemporary influences—a fusion of sources ranging from John Milton to rock and roll. In the jarring juxtapositions between past and present, parodies of European theatrical formats, and the illustrated pictorial history approach to the past, Hollingsworth's massive *History Plays* challenge the lack of depth of our understanding of CANADA's history and comment on the capacity to embrace and pilfer the creativity of other cultures without developing and sustaining its own.

For their work on *The History Plays*, the company's artists have received more than fifty Dora Mavor Moore nominations and awards, a pair of Chalmers Awards for Creation and Excellence in the Arts, and two Harold Awards.

PLAYS: *Strawberry Fields* (1972); *Clear Light* (1973); *Broken Record* (1977); *Cheap Thrills* (1977); *Punc Rock* (1977); *Electric Eye* (1978); *Trans-World* (1978); *1984* (1979); *The History of the Village of the Small Huts* (1985–1999)

Kerry Moore

THE HOMECOMING

HAROLD PINTER's complex and enigmatic early play, *The Homecoming*, has continued to mystify audiences since its world premiere at the Aldwych Theatre in London in 1965. The play was originally performed by the Royal Shakespeare Company under the direction of Pinter's longtime collaborator Peter Hall; in 1973 it was turned into a film, also directed by Hall.

The Homecoming narrates twenty-four hours in an all-male, working-class house in North London. The household is composed of Max, patriarch of the family and retired butcher, his brother Sam, a chauffeur, and Max's two grown sons, Lenny, a pimp, and Joey, a demolition worker and boxer. Their daily communication is a litany of sexual abuses, exchanged as an exercise of power. One night, after everyone has gone to bed, the third son, Teddy, a philosophy professor at some American university, returns after six years for a brief visit, bringing his wife Ruth. Lenny wakes up and immediately involves Ruth in sexual power games.

To Lenny's surprise, he meets his match in Ruth. The next day Ruth calmly endures Max calling her a "tart" and a "pox-ridden slut," an abusive outbreak that culminates in the memorable lines with which he reminds his sons, "I've never had a whore under this roof before. Ever since your mother died." When the mood finally cools down, Teddy is welcomed and Ruth adulated as a mother, with three sons of her own at home. During the course of the afternoon, first Lenny and then Joey start kissing and touching Ruth, who consents. The family decides to keep Ruth on and have her work as a prostitute in one of Lenny's flats. Ruth accepts in a businesslike manner, and after a feeble resistance, Teddy leaves to return to the States.

Critics of *The Homecoming* have not been able to agree on the play's meaning, a puzzle all the more perplexing because of the simplicity of the play's plot. *The Homecoming* could well be considered an absurd COMEDY or a TRAGICOMEDY, but there is disagreement on whether it should be considered realist or surrealist. Much hinges on attitudes toward women's agency within a sexist culture. In this setting of unabashed misogyny and contested familial hierarchies, the motivations of the sole female character, Ruth, are difficult to understand. Hardly a victim in that all-male jungle, she is under no pressure when she accepts the brothers' flirtations and eventually their offer to stay and fill the mother-whore role so frequently evoked by the men during the play. But she shows little enthusiasm either. Her philosopher husband, who, we infer, has tried to escape this stifling culture, lacks the agency to alter it.

Much rides on whether Ruth's actions result from a free choice among rival lifestyles or from a propensity to return to preestablished patterns of abuse. In practice, which of the two interpretations dominates will depend on the performance of the actress playing Ruth. Under the second interpretation, the title of the play could in fact refer ironically to the homecoming of Ruth, rather than of Teddy, back into the loins of a family bent on living out an incestuous nightmare.

[*See also* England, 1960–1980]

FURTHER READING

Batty, Mark. *Harold Pinter*, Horndon, Tavistock, and Devon, England: Northcore House in association with British Council, 2001.
Esslin, Martin. *The Peopled Wound: The Work of Harold Pinter*. Garden City, N.Y.: Doubleday, 1970.
Hinchcliffe, Arnold. *Harold Pinter*. New York: St. Martin's, 1967.
Lahr, John., ed. *A Casebook on Harold Pinter's "The Homecoming."* New York: Grove, 1971.
Peacock, D. Keith. *Harold Pinter and the New British Theatre*. Westport, Conn.: Greenwood, 1997.
Raby, Peter, ed. *The Cambridge Companion to Harold Pinter*. Cambridge: Cambridge Univ. Press, 2001.

Jacobia Dahm

HONGLOU MENG

See DREAM OF THE RED CHAMBER

HONG SHEN (1894–1955)

Born in December 1894 in Wujin county, Jiangsu province, CHINA, Hong Shen went to middle schools in Shanghai and Tianjin. After graduating from Tsinghua University in 1916, he attended Ohio State University and then went to Harvard University to study under Professor GEORGE PIERCE BAKER as one of "Baker's Dozen"—thirteen students chosen to study playwriting each year.

Returning to China in 1922, Hong Shen published the play *Yama Zhao* (*Zhao yanwang*), which established his reputation in modern Chinese drama. Later he adapted OSCAR WILDE's LADY WINDERMERE'S FAN for a Chinese play under the title *Madam's Fan* (*Shao nannan de shanzi*), which enjoyed tremendous popularity. In 1930 Hong Shen joined the Star Motion Picture Company and produced one of China's first sound films. An active member of the left-wing Dramatists League in the 1930s, Hong Shen took part in many political activities. He also wrote quite a few film scripts and three plays—*Wukui Bridge* (*Wukui qiao*), *Fragrant Rice* (*Xiang daomi*), and *Green Dragon Pond* (*Qinglong tan*)—that formed his *Trilogy of the Countryside*. After 1949 he worked mainly as a cultural administrator until his death in August 1955.

According to many, as well as to Hong Shen himself, his contribution to modern Chinese drama lies more in his drama theory and stage direction than in his playwriting. As an active reformer of Chinese drama, Hong Shen abolished the traditional Chinese dramatic custom of women's roles being taken up by men, helped establish a complete system of theater directorship on the modern Chinese stage, and was the first to propose using the term *huaju* (spoken drama) for modern Chinese plays. He avidly applied the drama theory and techniques he learned abroad to Chinese theater. His writings—such as *The Art of Filmic and Dramatic Performance* (*Dianying xiju biaoyan yishu*), *Playwriting and Film Script Writing* (*Dianying xiju de bianju fangfa*), and *Introduction to Modern Theater* (*Xiandai xiju daolun*)—have since become the pioneering works for the theory of modern Chinese film and drama.

In terms of his playwriting, *Yama Zhao* remains one of his most-well-known plays. Influenced by EUGENE O'NEILL's EMPEROR JONES in applying expressionist techniques such as the stream of consciousness on stage, he vividly portrayed the protagonist's psychology and hallucination under pressure in order to lay bare the evils committed by warlord soldiers. But the *Trilogy of the Countryside* is perhaps Hong Shen's most important and representative work. The three plays center around a series of conflicts between peasants and local landlords, showing the misery and hardships that the peasants in the 1920s and 1930s had to bear, which ultimately led to their fight for a better life. The simple and clear-cut structure plus the characterization have made the trilogy a great success.

SELECT PLAYS: *Yama Zhao* (*Zhao yanwang*, 1922); *Wukui Bridge* (*Wukui qiao*, 1930), *Fragrant Rice* (*Xiang daomi*, 1931); *Green Dragon Pond* (*Qinglongtan*, 1932); *Smuggling* (*Zousi*, 1936); *Weather Forecast via Early Cockcrows* (*Jiming zao kantian*, 1946)

FURTHER READING

Dong Limin and Fang Quanlin. *Hong Shen: Jiliu zhong de nahan* [Hong Shen: A Voice from the Rapids]. Shanghai: Shanghai jiaoyu chubanshe, 1999.
Han Binsheng. *Da zai, Hong Shen: Hong Shen ping zhuan* [A Great Hong Shen: Commentaries and a Biography of Hong Shen]. Beijing: Zhongyang wenxian chubanshe, 2000.
Hong Shen. *Yama Chao* [Zhao Yanwang]. Tr. by Carolyn T. Brown. In *Twentieth-Century Chinese Drama: An Anthology*, ed. by Edward M. Gunn. Bloomington: Indiana Univ. Press, 1983. 10–40.
Sun Qingwen and Hong Shen. *Hong Shen yanjiu zhuanji* [A Special Collection of Studies of Hong Shen]. Hangzhou: Zhejiang wenyi chubanshe, 1986.

Hongchu Fu

HOROVITZ, ISRAEL (1939–)

If the man I am met the man I was, there'd be a fist fight.

—Brackish, in *Park Your Car in Harvard Yard*, Sequence Four

Born on March 31, 1939, into a Jewish family in the predominantly Catholic community of Wakefield, Massachusetts, Arthur Israel Horovitz wrote his first novel, *Steinberg, Sex, and the Saint*, at age thirteen and his first play, *The Comeback* (1958), at age nineteen, for which he himself originated the role of the son. He has continued to create plays, screenplays, and novels, compiling a body of work that has met with commercial and critical success (to varying degrees) both in the United States and abroad, especially in FRANCE. His Jewish upbringing in an otherwise gentile region has strongly colored his view of the world from an outsider's perspective.

In the early 1960s, Horovitz became a fellow at the Royal Academy of Dramatic Arts in London and in 1965, playwright-in-residence at both the Royal Shakespeare Company and the Aldwych Theatre. Returning to the UNITED STATES, he almost immediately helped to launch the Eugene O'Neill Memorial Theatre Foundation in Waterford, Connecticut. He subsequently founded the New York Playwrights Lab and the Gloucester Stage Company (in his native Massachusetts), and continues to serve as artistic director of both.

He lists among his earliest influences seeing LORRAINE HANSBERRY'S *A RAISIN IN THE SUN* and freely admits admiration not only for the work of ARTHUR MILLER and THORNTON WILDER, but also for patently absurd pieces from EUGÈNE IONESCO and SAMUEL BECKETT. His own output ranges greatly, from the early NATURALISM of *The Indian Wants the Bronx* (the 1966 play that made his reputation) to fantastic flights of imagination, as with the huger-than-huge fish story, *Mackerel* (1978).

Horovitz's prolificacy might partly result from his mastery of short-form plays, especially one-acts, as well as MONODRAMAS and monologues. Still, his oeuvre contains many longer pieces and screenplays, not the least of which are several grouped pieces that form trilogies, tetralogies, and still longer sets.

Subjects in his plays have long been loosely grouped around geographical connections, as in his "Gloucester Plays," a sequence of more than a dozen plays set in and around Gloucester, and the "Quannapowitt Quartet." Other relationships can be found among activities, especially sports, that Horovitz has used as controlling ideas in plays such as *The Former One-on-One Basketball Champion* (1977), *Sunday Runners in the Rain* (1980), *Marathon* (2003), and *One Under* (1997). Horovitz's interest in competition no doubt owed something to his own lifelong commitment to long-distance running, a commitment he shared with his wife, Gillian Adams-Horovitz, herself a British marathon champion. Another subject arresting Horovitz's consciousness, and the world's, has been the terrorist attacks of September 11, 2001, which prompted three 2002 plays: *Ten Minutes Older, 3 Weeks after Paradise*, and *Speaking Well of the Dead*.

French connections in his career have included Eugène Ionesco, whose daughter, Marie-France, provided a literal translation of her father's play *The Man with the Suitcases* (*L'Homme aux valises*) for Horovitz's 1977 adaptation, *Man with Bags*. The playwright's relationship with Samuel Beckett began with an arranged meeting and led to a friendship and several pieces consciously in Beckett's style, especially *Spared* (1976) and *Cappella* (1978). He maintained a relationship with the theater scene in France throughout his career, overseeing translated productions of many of his works. Horovitz has been critically recognized with several awards, including two Obies in the late 1960s for *The Indian Wants the Bronx* (1966) and for a double bill of *The Honest-to-God Schnozzola* and *Leader* (1969).

[*See also* United States, 1940–Present]

SELECT PLAYS: *The Indian Wants the Bronx* (1966); *It's Called the Sugar Plum* (1967); *Acrobats* (1968); *Rats* (1968); *Leader* (1969); *Hero* (1971, revised as *Dr. Hero*, 1972); *Shooting Gallery* (1971); *The Alfred Trilogy* (1972–1977); *The Former One-on-One Basketball Champion* (1977); *Man with Bags* (adapted from Ionesco, 1977); *Mackerel* (1978); *The Primary English Class* (1979); *Sunday Runners in the Rain* (1980); *Park Your Car in Harvard Yard* (1984); *Speaking Well of the Dead* (2002)

FURTHER READING

DiGaetani, John L., ed. *A Search for a Postmodern Theater: Interviews with Contemporary Playwrights*. Westport, Conn.: Greenwood Press, 1991.

Kane, Leslie, ed. *Israel Horovitz: A Collection of Critical Essays*. Westport, Conn.: Greenwood, 1994.

Witham, Barry B. "Images of America: Wilson, Weller and Horovitz." *Theatre Journal* 34, no. 2 (May 1982): 223–232.

Jay Malarcher

HORSE AND BAMBOO THEATRE

Founding artistic director of the Horse and Bamboo Theatre, Bob Frith trained as a painter in Manchester and London, ENGLAND, and in 1972 set up a workshop in Rossendale in Lancashire. In 1974 Frith worked with a group to create a festival celebration commemorating Palmer's shipyard and the series of events that led to the Jarrow March, the famous unemployment and hunger march of 1936. With the success of this piece, he gradually became aware of other performance groups that were interested in pushing the boundaries of visual representation in performance.

In 1976 he worked with John Fox and Welfare State, a company known and celebrated for its large-scale outdoor performance events. After his Welfare State experience, Frith founded Horse and Bamboo in 1978 with a site-specific performance entitled *The Ballad of Ellen Strange*. The Horse and Bamboo Theatre can be described as a puppet and mask company with a strong visual style and a focus on community arts and global issues. In 1982 Frith created *The Woodcarver Story*, a work in homage to childhood hero Harry MacDonald. Other acknowledged influences include the artists Claus Oldenburg and Red Grooms, as well as the Welfare State.

In 1979 Horse and Bamboo launched its first touring group with a piece entitled *Pictures from Breughel*. This tour experimented with using horses, and for the next twenty years their horse-drawn theater became their unique signature. The tours took place every summer to reach an audience that did not normally go to the theater. Their geographic focus on rural areas combined with a deliberate avoidance of art centers, cities, and festivals was a defining feature of their commitment to reaching a nontraditional audience. The three-month summer horse-drawn tours continued with new shows each year until 1999. In 1991 the company added a second tour with motor vehicles that made it possible for them to tour for up to seven months.

In 1981 Horse and Bamboo developed a second company project, Guided Imagery, workshops and residencies for people with special needs, to complement their performances.

In 1992 and 1993 *A Strange (and Unexpected) Event!* focused on the Mexican printmaker J. G. Posada. The piece was set during the Mexican Day of the Dead. In 1994 they made a work based on American avant-garde filmmaker Maya Deren's journey to Haiti to study voudoun. In 2000 and 2001 they were inspired by the paintings and etchings of Paula Rego and created *The Girl Who Cut Flowers.* In 2002 they focused on the paintings and drawings of Charlotte Salomon in a stunning work entitled *Company of Angels: The Story of Charlotte Salomon.*

In 1995 and 1996 their piece *Visions of Hildegard* was based on the life of Hildegard of Bingen. And in 1998 they staged *Harvest of Ghosts,* their first outdoor show since 1981. This was a unique cross-cultural collaboration with Sam Ukala, a Nigerian playwright, director, and African folk theater specialist. Ukala's nine-month residency with the company resulted in a fusion of Horse and Bamboo's established style of mask and puppet theatre with West African folk theater traditions. *Harvest of Ghosts* depicted the events in Nigeria leading up to execution of the playwright and environmentalist, Ken Saro-Wiwa.

Lesley Ferris

HORVÁTH, ÖDÖN VON (1901–1938)

People accuse me of being too coarse, too disgusting, too uncanny, too cynical . . . but they overlook the fact that my only intention is to depict the world just as it unfortunately is.

—Ödön von Horváth, 1932

Two years prior to the election in 1933 of Adolf Hitler to head the German government, Ödön von Horváth received the prestigious Kleist Prize, and his dramas were enjoying great critical and popular success. Denounced by the Nazis as a "cultural Bolshevik" for his commitment to democratizing social and cultural institutions, Horváth was forced into exile and his plays banned from the stages of the Third Reich. Following his untimely death (Horváth was killed by a falling branch during a storm in Paris), his works seemed doomed to oblivion. However, when the post–World War II generation came of age in the 1960s, impelling German society to question the Nazi past more pointedly, Horváth's works experienced a widespread renaissance. They now belong to the standard repertoire of the German-speaking stage and have inspired a new generation of dramatists to create a VOLKSSTÜCK (popular drama) addressing contemporary sociopolitical conditions.

Horváth was born Edmund (Ödön) Josef von Horváth on December 9, 1901, in Fiume, then part of the Austro-Hungarian monarchy (now Rijeka, Croatia), the eldest son of a civil servant in the Hungarian Ministry of Trade. The author's early biography reads like a geography lesson in the Habsburg Empire: between his birth in Fiume and his high school graduation in Vienna in 1919, Horváth lived in Belgrade, Budapest, Pressburg (currently Bratislava), and Munich. Residing in various central and eastern European cities provided Horváth with a sense of geographical and linguistic particularity as well as a sense of social uprootedness and displacement, phenomena that would all come to inform his dramas in significant ways. Horváth died on June 1, 1938, in Paris.

Horváth's works include three novels and various short prose pieces, but he is primarily known as a leading dramatist of the interwar period whose plays revitalized the tradition of the *volksstück*. Like his contemporaries CARL ZUCKMAYER, MARIELUISE FLEIẞER, and to a lesser extent, BERTOLT BRECHT, Horváth strove to reclaim for the *Volksstück*—and its attending theatrical institution, the *Volkstheater* (popular theater)—the popularity they enjoyed in 19th-century Vienna. Working both within and against the *Volksstück* tradition, Horváth aimed to create a broad-based and socially critical form of theater committed to dramatizing "issues of the people . . . seen through the people's eyes."

For Horváth, "the people" signified in large part the petite bourgeoisie, that class of small shopkeepers, tradesmen, and peasant proprietors who seemed particularly displaced by the social, economic, and political upheavals resulting from World War I and the dissolution of the German and Austro-Hungarian monarchies. Unable to make the transition to mass production and to find their way among the nascent republican institutions of the interwar period, the majority of the petite bourgeoisie clung tenaciously to their dream of rising into the ranks of the more affluent and secure middle class when in fact they had already undergone precisely what they feared most: economic proletarianization. The resulting discrepancy between the sociocultural aspirations of the petite bourgeoisie and their actual economic circumstances and prospects is central to Horváth's DRAMATURGY, finding its concrete expression in what Horváth himself called a "Demaskierung des Bewusstseins" (unmasking of consciousness).

An important contributor to the long Austrian tradition of *Sprachskepsis*—literally "language skepticism," questioning the extent to which language functions as an accurate and adequate means of communication—Horváth paid particular attention to issues of language use. His dialogues are marked by frequent silences; in those moments, he claimed, the characters' conscious and subconscious collide. Whereas many characters in the 19th-century *Volksstück* speak in dialect, challenging the linguistic conventions of the classical theater, the majority of Horváth's characters speak a kind of socio-lect, which serves to underscore their precarious social, economic, and cultural position. Horváth called it *Bildungsjargon* (educated jargon), a constructed language that frequently includes unnecessarily complicated syntax, tautologies, phrases borrowed from the mass media, and erroneous quotations from cultural giants—for instance, when the neighborhood butcher misquotes Wolfgang von Goethe in TALES FROM THE VIENNA WOODS (*Geschichten aus dem Wiener Wald*, 1931).

Horváth's cast of characters includes half-hearted democrats and committed fascists (*The Italian Evening* [*Italienische Nacht*, 1930]), unemployed chauffeurs (the male protagonist in *Casimir and Carolina* [*Kasimir und Karoline*, 1931]), and traumatized soldiers who have returned from World War I (*Don Juan Comes Back from the War* [*Don Juan kommt aus dem Krieg*, 1936]). His figures frequently express their false consciousness in the form of egotistical self-pity, kitschy sentimentalism, and an unconsciously felt need to brutalize others. Unable to understand the exact causes of their socioeconomic misery and perceiving themselves largely as the victims of some inexplicable fate, they seek in turn to victimize those who try to find an alternative to the oppressive confines of the status quo. Thus, for example, the neighborhood residents in *Tales from the Vienna Woods* collectively act to abort Marianne's attempt to liberate herself from the day-to-day physical and psychological brutality she suffers from her father, her fiancé, and the extended "family" that is the neighborhood.

The patriarchal domination that eventually leads to Marianne's forced submission also informs Horváth's *Faith, Hope and Charity* (*Glaube Liebe Hoffnung*, 1932), a *Volksstück* he co-authored with Lukas Kristl, a court reporter in Munich. The drama's protagonist, Elisabeth, had previously sold women's undergarments, and the play begins with her unsuccessful attempt to sell what will eventually become her corpse to obtain sufficient funds for a new traveling saleswoman's license. In the course of the drama, she becomes the victim of a male bureaucracy intent on self-advancement and the irresponsible and inhumane administration of the law. The "gigantic struggle between the individual and society," which Horváth considered central to all of his dramas, ends in this case with the protagonist's suicide.

Horváth's attempts to refunctionalize the institution of the theater encompassed more than the form and content of individual dramas; he also advocated democratizing the rituals associated with attending a play. For instance, he called for abolishing dress codes in the theater, arguing that more people would attend, even in economically difficult times, if they were able to wear whatever they wanted, since a significant number of potential theatergoers stayed away simply because they did not have a nice suit.

SELECT PLAYS: *Murder in the Mohrengasse* (*Mord in der Mohrengasse*, 1923); *The Belle Vue* (*Zur schönen Aussicht*, 1926); *Revolt in Cōte 3018* (*Revolte auf Cōte 3018*, 1926); *The Cable Railway* (*Die Bergbahn*, a reworking of *Revolte auf Cōte 3018*, 1927); *Sladek, oder Die schwarze Armee* (1928); *A Sexual Congress* (*Rund um den Kongreß*, 1929); *The Italian Evening* (*Italienische Nacht*, 1930); *Casimir and Caroline* (*Kasimir und Karoline*, 1931); *Tales from the Vienna Woods* (*Geschichten aus dem Wiener Wald*, 1931); *Faith, Hope and Charity* (*Glaube Liebe Hoffnung*, 1932); *Back and Forth* (*Hin und her*, 1933); *Stranger from the Seine* (*Die Unbekannte aus der Seine*, 1933); *Heavenwards* (*Himmelwärts*, 1934); *Pigheaded* (*Mit dem Kopf durch die Wand*, 1935); *Don Juan Comes Back from the War* (*Don Juan kommt aus dem Krieg*, 1936); *Figaro Gets a Divorce* (*Figaro läßt sich scheiden*, 1936); *Judgment Day* (*Der jüngste Tag*, 1936); *Village of No Men* (*Ein Dorf ohne Männer*, 1937); *Pompeii* (*Pompeji*, 1937)

FURTHER READING

Bance, Alan. "Ödön von Horváth: Sex, Politics and Sexual Politics." *German Life and Letters* 38, no. 3 (1985): 249–259.

Bruns, Dirk. "Horváth's Renewal of the Folk Play and the Decline of the Weimar Republic." *New German Critique* 18 (1979): 107–135.

Huish, Ian. *Horváth: A Study*. London: Heinemann, 1980.

Krischke, Traugott. *Horváth auf der Bühne 1926–1938. Eine Dokumentation* [Horváth on the Stage, 1926–1938: A Documentation]. Vienna: Edition S, 1991.

Lunzer, Heinz, and Victoria Lunzer-Talos. *Horváth: Einem Schriftsteller auf der Spur* [Horváth: On the Trail of the Author]. Salzburg: Residenz, 2001.

Craig Decker

HOSANNA

Set in a crumbling furnished bachelor apartment in downtown Montreal during the turbulent 1970s, *Hosanna* is one of MICHEL TREMBLAY's most successful plays. The piece explores the relationship between cohabitating couple Hosanna, an aging drag queen, and her handsome, though now overweight, lover, Cuirette. After fleeing her roots and her reputation as a social misfit in Ste. Eustache, a small town in rural Quebec, Hosanna comes to Montreal. Hairdressing by day and performing in the local drag clubs by night, she scrapes by on a modest living. The play opens around 4 A.M., after she is publicly humiliated at a Halloween party when, fed up with her constant insults and superiority, the other drag queens in town put her in her place once and for all.

Hosanna functions both as an examination of gender and of how it is played out in gay relationships. The couple spends the first act arguing about their roles within the relationship in and out of bed. After four years together, the two have fallen into a comfortable, though unsatisfying pattern of Hosanna bringing in the money and Cuirette cleaning the apartment and cooking. Hosanna tells him that while she may be wearing a dress, she is in fact the "man" of the house. He tells her that even when she tries to act like a man she ends up "behaving exactly like a woman," especially in bed. During the second act, Hosanna recounts the story of her evening. Over the course of the play, she sheds her drag, removing her dress, makeup, and wig, until she reveals herself naked to Cuirette at the end, asking to be accepted as a man. Despite their constant arguing, there is a powerful love between the two, and their struggle to make their relationship work after four years together is touching.

The play had its debut at the famous Théâtre de Quat 'Sous in Montreal, Quebec, on May 10, 1973. The English language premiere was produced at Tarragon Theatre in Toronto, Ontario, May 15, 1974, and its Broadway premiere followed later that year at the Bijou Theatre. The title role was played by Richard Monette and his companion by Richard Donat. The piece has subsequently been translated into several languages and has been performed at theaters around the world.

Hosanna was Tremblay's most successful play since his debut work, *Les Belles Soeurs*, and is considered one of the most important works in both the French Canadian and queer canons. He has remained a central figure, and perhaps the premiere *enfant terrible* in the Quebec theater scene since the 1960s. Like many of his other works, *Hosanna* is written in *joual*, a dialect of French unique to Quebec. While Tremblay uses the language in a frank and brutal way, it is never done for shock value, but rather to show the beauty of the working class speech with which he grew up.

Like his use of language, his portrayal of gay characters was unapologetic and virtually unheard of at the time in a society heavily controlled by the Catholic Church. He was simultaneously considered a hero of both the queer and working class communities, and he became a household name by the mid-1970s.

[*See also* Canada, French Language]

FURTHER READING

Barrette, Jean-Marc. *L'univers de Michel Tremblay: dictionnaire des personnages* [*The Univers of Michel Tremblay: Dictionary of Personalities*]. Montréal: Presses de l'Université de Montréal, 1996.

Boulanger, Luc. *Pièces à conviction : entretiens avec Michel Tremblay* [*Work of Conviction: Interview with Michel Tremblay*]. Montréal: Leméac, 2001.

David, Gilbert. *Le Monde de Michel Tremblay: des Belles-Soeurs à Marcel poursuivi par les chiens* [*The World of Michel Tremblay: The Sisters in Law to Marcel Pursued by Hounds*]. Montréal: Cahiers de théâtre jeu. And Carnières, Belgium: Editions Lansman, 1993.

Usmiani, Renate. *Michel Tremblay*. Vancouver: Douglas & McIntyre, 1982.

Chris Dupuis

DIE HOSE *See* THE UNDERPANTS

HOUGHTON, WILLIAM STANLEY (1881–1913)

William Stanley Houghton's plays fill three substantial volumes—*The Works of Stanley Houghton*, edited by his fellow north-English playwright, Harold Brighouse. The volumes contain Brighouse's account of Houghton's life, a number of full-length and one-act plays, an unfinished novel, *Life*, together with literary criticism and miscellaneous newspaper articles. For decades, Brighouse's collection was the last word on Houghton's career, but research done in the 1960s by Marcel Gaberthuel and in the 1980s by Paul Mortimer revealed new information about Houghton's life. More crucially, further unperformed and unpublished manuscript plays (and some previously unknown short fiction) were discovered. Despite these finds, and the quantity and (albeit inconsistent) quality of Houghton's plays, he is generally forgotten; other than HINDLE WAKES (1912), his plays rarely attract theatrical revivals or critical comment. Although his large dramatic oeuvre is multifaceted, his plays often attack pretensions of manner and foolish, self-interested conduct. His comic and serious plays sometimes dramatize the lack of choices open to young women and regularly expose gulfs of comprehension between generations.

Born in Ashton-upon-Mersey, Cheshire, England, on February 22, 1881, Houghton left school at age sixteen to enter his father's cotton business, where he stayed until 1912. He was a keen writer from his teens and performed in over seventy amateur productions during the 1910s. His first play to be performed, the one-act *The Dear Departed*, was played by Annie Horniman's repertory company (established in 1907) at the Manchester Gaiety Theatre in November 1908. The same company staged his first full-length play, *Independent Means*, at the Gaiety on August 30, 1909.

The Horniman-Houghton association flourished. *The Younger Generation* (1910) transferred from Manchester to London's Haymarket Theatre and then to the Duke of York Theatre, where its success prompted an American tour and later revivals. *Hindle Wakes* was premiered at London's Aldwych Theatre on June 16, 1912, and by Houghton's death at age thirty-two, had seen over 1,800 performances in Chicago, Manchester, New York, and elsewhere. Houghton moved south to London during this breakthrough year and was soon invited to join the Dramatists' and Savage Clubs. His subsequent plays failed. The last two Houghton plays to be performed during his lifetime were *Trust the People* and *The Perfect Cure*. The former, apparently written hurriedly, survived for forty-four performances at London's Garrick Theatre but was critically slated; *The Perfect Cure* was withdrawn, embarrassingly, after only four performances at London's Apollo Theatre. Unsettled by good and bad critical reception, commercial pressures, and increasing illness after 1912, Houghton moved to Paris and then to Venice, but returned to Manchester in late 1913. Appendicitis, influenza, and meningitis overwhelmed him, and he died on December 10, 1913 in Manchester.

[*See also* England, 1860–1940]

SELECT PLAYS: *The Intriguers* (1906); *The Reckoning* (1907); *The Dear Departed* (1908); *Marriages in the Making* (1909); *The Young Generation* (1909); *Ginger* (1910); *Partners* (1911); *Hindle Wakes* (1911); *The Hillarys* (1912); *The Perfect Cure* (1912); *Trust the People* (1912)

FURTHER READING

Bain, Ted. "Stanley Houghton." In *British Playwrights, 1880–1956: A Research and Production Sourcebook*, ed. by W. W. Demastes and K. E. Kelly. Westport, Conn.: Greenwood , 1996. 213–224.

Charlton, H. B. "William Stanley Houghton." In *The Dictionary of National Biography, 1912–1921*, ed. by H. W. C. Davis and J. R. H. Weaver. London: Humphrey Milford and Oxford Univ. Press, 1927. 271–273.

Chothia, Jean. *English Drama of the Early Modern Period, 1890–1940*. London : Longman, 1996. 75–79, 307.

Houghton, W. Stanley. *The Works of Stanley Houghton*. Ed. by Harold Brighouse (3 vols.). London: Constable, 1914.

Mortimer, Paul. "W. Stanley Houghton: an Introduction and Bibliography." *Modern Drama* 28 (1985): 474–489.

Wisenthal, J. L. "A. A. Milne." In *The Dictionary of Literary Biography*, Vol. 10, Part 1: *Modern British Dramatists, 1900–1945*, ed. by Stanley Weintraub. Detroit: Gale Research Company, 1982. 231–234.

Kevin De Ornellas

HOUSE OF AMERICA

BOYO: Hey, the other thing about John Cale was, he's Welsh.
SID: No, he's not, he's American, New York Band.
BOYO: I'm telling you he comes from Ponty or somewhere.
SID: Bullshit, Boyo, talking crap.
BOYO: You ask Cat next time you see him.
. . .
SID: Cat, what does he know, the only deaf piano tuner in the country, and I don't care if Cale came from fucking Ystrad, he's living in New York now, and I bet you that's where he'll stay, huh, can you imagine Lou Reed walking 'round Ystrad—all right Lou, how's it going, wus, on the Wild Side—not cool enough for him, no way, probably never even heard of Wales.
—Act 1

House of America by EDWARD THOMAS is a play of enduring popularity. First staged in 1988, it was revised and toured Britain in 1989. It won various awards, including the *Time Out* Critics Award, was revised again and produced in 1992, and toured the world in a radically rewritten form in 1997. The play was made into a film first screened at the British Academy Television Awards (BAFTA) in October 1996. In 1997 it was shown at the Sundance Festival, U.S.A., the first Welsh film ever to be screened at Sundance. In October 1997 it opened in general release in the United Kingdom and won numerous BAFTAs including Best Film and Best Director.

In a style Thomas describes as "heightened NATURALISM," *House of America* deals with the disaffection of many South Walian communities in the 1980s. The play tells the story of the Lewis family, whose failure to come to terms with their deprived environment leads to a mental escape into an imaginary "otherworld." Thus, it depicts the morbid defeatism of a minority culture in the face of a figurative and literal erasure of place through cultural domination symbolized by open-cast mining.

The brothers Sid and Boyo fail to get one of the Mickey Mouse jobs offered at the mine and are stuck at home. Sid and his sister Gwenny invent a game in which they play Jack Kerouac and Joyce Johnson and pretend to be "on the road" in an imaginary America, the antithesis of the Wales they hate. Tragedy is triggered when the mine advances toward the house: Mother, a bold caricature of the stereotype of the Welsh "mam," flees into a half-pretended madness to escape the inevitable discovery of the body of her husband, whom she had killed some ten years earlier and who had not, as she had pretended, gone to America. As the mine unearths the corpse, Sid and Gwenny, unable to cope, take their game to its logical conclusion. When Boyo discovers that Gwenny is pregnant, he kills Sid in a rage and Gwenny kills herself.

The play takes up the theme of confinement versus escape, which had been explored in J. O. Francis's *Change* (1920), EMLYN WILLIAMS's THE CORN IS GREEN (1938), and GWYN THOMAS's THE KEEP (1960). Unlike these plays, however, escape, whether it is to America or simply to a better life elsewhere, has become impossible. The characters can only escape into make-believe, a route that leads to madness and death. This is, Thomas implies, a failure of the imagination as much as a consequence of Anglo-American cultural and economical domination in postcolonial Wales. Yet the play's violent ending fractures its realist framework, and the play becomes a tragedy. Sid gains an epic stature and, by implication, becomes a Welsh (tragic) hero. The 1977 revision and the film stress this reading by refashioning Sid as a James Dean–esque "rebel without a cause." The play and particularly the film have attracted a cult following and can be seen as an expression of a new Welsh identity in the late 1990s.

FURTHER READING

Davies, Hazel Walford, ed. *State of Play: Four Playwrights of Wales*. Llandysul, Wales: Gomer, 1998.

Rhys, Martin. "Keeping it in the Family: *Change* by J. O. Francis, *The Keep* by Gwyn Thomas and *House of America* by Ed Thomas." In *Dangerous Diversity: The Changing Faces of Wales*, ed. by Andrew Hiscock and Katie Gramich. Cardiff: Univ. of Wales Press, 1998. 150–177.

Thomas, Ed. "House of America." In *Three Plays*, ed. by Brian Mitchell. Bridgend, Wales: Seren, 1994. 11–100.

Williams, Daniel. "Harry Secombe in the Junkshop: Nation, Myth and Invention in Edward Thomas's *House of America* and David Mamet's *American Buffalo*." *Welsh Writing in English: A Yearbook of Critical Essays* 4 (1998): 133–158.

Alyce von Rothkirch

THE HOUSE OF BERNARDA ALBA

The House of Bernarda Alba (*La Casa de Bernarda Alba*) was written by FEDERICO GARCÍA LORCA in 1936, the year when the Spanish Civil War started after the fascist coup d'état. Many critics have seen in Bernarda, the main character in the play, the anticipation of that fascist Spain where the moral of Catholicism was articulated inside politics.

It is the third and final rural play of Lorca's tragic trilogy about Andalusia. The play is about Bernarda Alba and her family: her senile mother María Josefa and her daughters Angustias, Magdalena, Amelia, Martirio, and Adela. Bernarda is an ultra-Catholic, authoritarian woman who is a tyrant toward her mother and daughters. The whole plot takes place in the suffocating atmosphere of Bernarda's house, which evokes the inside of a convent. The story starts with the burial of Bernarda Alba's husband and the preparation for the arranged marriage of her eldest daughter, Angustias, with Pepe el Romano. In this oppressive atmosphere, we witness the breakdown of the daughters' sexual repression and the rivalry among them caused by Pepe's presence; he is the object of desire for all of them. The TRAGEDY occurs when Adela, the youngest daughter, confesses to her mother that she has had sexual relations with Angustias's fiancé. Bernarda lies to Adela by saying that she has killed Pepe el Romano when he was trying to approach the house. Desperate, Adela locks herself in her room and hangs herself. The play ends with Bernarda insisting that her daughter has died a virgin and ordering silence, the culmination of her constant obsession to maintain the family's honor.

The House of Bernarda Alba is unique within Lorca's trilogy in showing a female character who consummates sexual relations with her lover and actually breaking the prevailing code of honor. It is also unique in having a female character dying. Adela's death by suicide to oppose the established power reminds us of the tragic figure of Sophocles' *Antigona*. However, Adela's tragic death is not an effective act of rebellion. On the contrary, Bernarda uses Adela's death to reinstate order at her home, imposing silence and announcing publicly that the family's honor is intact. This implies that for Lorca, the concept of destiny and the fight against power, symbolized by the characters in Classical tragedies, is not only ineffective but also forms part of the mechanism used by power to maintain itself.

Finally, contrary to what might be the general consensus, *The House of Bernarda Alba* and, in fact, all Lorca's rural tragedies do not represent a faithful reflection of the social codes of the popular class in rural Andalusia. Sons and daughters that would not accept a fixed marriage would just run away with their lovers to free themselves from the family demands. This escape was socially accepted and did not represent a serious problem. In other words, Lorca manipulates the popular codes to establish a correlation between classical tragedy, anthropological manifestations, Catholicism, and the political interests of the bourgeoisie. In this sense, Lorca follows the surrealist view strongly marked by Sigmund Freud's psycho-anthropological studies.

[*See also* Spain]

FURTHER READING

Anderson, Reed. "Christian Symbolism in Lorca's *La casa de Bernarda Alba*." In *Homenaje a Antonio Sánchez Barbudo: Ensayos de literatura española moderna [Tribute to Antonio Sánchez Barbudo: Examinations of Modern Spanish Literature]*, ed. by Benito Brancaforte, Edward R. Mulvihill, and Roberto Sanchez. Madison: Univ. of Wisconsin, 1981. 219–30.

Domenech, Ricardo. *La casa de Bernarda Alba' y el teatro de García Lorca* [The House of Bernarda Alba and the Theater of García Lorca]. Madrid: Cátedra, 1985.

Frigolé, Joan. *Un étnólogo en el teatro. Ensayo antropológico sobre Federico García Lorca [An Ethnology in the Theater. An Anthropological Examination of Federico García Lorca]*. Barcelona: Muchnik, 1995.

Gabriele, John P. "Mapping the Boundaries of Gender: Men, Women and Space in La casa de Bernarda Alba." *Hispanic Journal* 15, no. 2 (1994): 381–392.

García-Posada, Miguel. *Realidad y transfiguración artística en 'La casa de Bernarda Alba' [Reality and Artistic Transfiguration in 'The House of Bernarda Alba']*. Madrid: Cátedra, 1985.

Morris, C. Brian. *García Lorca: La casa de Bernarda Alba*. London: Grant & Cutler with Tamesis, 1990.

Urbina, Eduardo. *De Calderón a Lorca: El tema del honor en 'La casa de Bernarda Alba' [From Calderón to Lorca: The Theme of Honor in 'The House of Bernarda Alba']*. In *Approaches to the Theater of Calderón*, ed. by Michael D. McGaha. Washington, DC: Univ. Press of America, 1982. 259–70.

Maribel Parra-Domínguez

HOWARD, BRONSON (1842–1908)

Born on October 7, 1842, in Detroit, Michigan, Bronson Crocker Howard was the son of a merchant who was elected mayor of Detroit in 1849. After studying at Yale, he worked as the drama critic for the Detroit *Free Press*. His first play was *Fantine*, an adaptation of the Cosette episode of *Les Miserables*, and its production inspired him to go to New York, where he wrote for the *Tribune* and the *Post* before achieving his first theatrical success in 1870 with the COMEDY SARATOGA. He offered light commentary on social behavior in *Young Mrs. Winthrop*, *One of Our Girls*, and *Aristocracy*; in *The Henrietta*, he depicted Wall Street and a young financier's scheme to engineer a stock market crash for his own benefit.

In *The Banker's Daughter* (originally *Lilian's Last Love*), a young woman agrees to marry a wealthy man to forestall the financial ruin of her father, who betrays her by failing to inform the husband that his daughter knows about their business relationship and is actually in love with an artist. When the artist dies in a duel over her honor, her husband realizes the truth from her reaction and sends her back to her father. Only their love for their young daughter ultimately reunites them.

In 1886, Howard delivered a lecture at Harvard University that explained the guiding principles behind his revision of *Lilian's Last Love* into *The Banker's Daughter*. The first version of the play ends with Lilian's pathetic death, whereas the second closes on her reconciliation with her husband; in both, the action builds from the decision of a banker to trade his daughter for financial security.

> The death of a pure woman on stage is not "satisfactory." . . . The death . . . of a woman who is not pure . . . is perfectly satisfactory, for the reason that it is inevitable . . . The wife who has once taken the step from purity to impurity can never reinstate herself in the world of art on this side of the grave; and so an audience looks with complacent tears on the death of an erring woman. But Lilian had not taken the one fatal step which would have reconciled an audience to her death. She was still pure, and every one left the theatre wishing she had lived. (Howard, 1914)

Howard's theory of "satisfactory" drama encoded the attitudes of the Gilded Age (the period from the Civil War to World War I) toward relations between the sexes and their expression on the stage; he and his audience sought the security of stable sexual politics. Like other writers, Howard sought to depict men and women not as they were, but as they were hoped to be—to present the ideal as the reality—a duty that provided increasing challenge as the changing perceptions of the waning century eroded the earlier forms of MELODRAMA and spurred the trend towards realism. The difficulty was acute with regard to the depiction of women because even the most proper woman would be played by an actress, a paradox that engaged Howard's attention:

> Nothing can be conceived more absolutely unlike a delicate, beautiful, and refined woman in a drawing-room, than the painted young creature, with dark shadows about her eyes and flagrant carmine on her lips and cheeks, who looks, to her companion on the stage, like a gaudily painted wooden doll. (Howard, 1900)

In order to give their audience a stage world that reflected not the reality they endured but the ideal they desired, Howard's actors turned gesture and facial expression into languages as formal and as strictly designed as the plays they presented. Howard himself defined acting as an artificial semblance of behavior, not the behavior itself; a seeming instead of an actuality:

> The painter appeals to the eye by artificial, not by natural, means. So, the actor's art is to make the people in an audience . . . think that he is moving, speaking, and appearing like the character assumed: and, in nine cases out of ten, the only way to make them think this is to be not doing it; to be doing something else. (Howard, 1900)

He thought of the actor's face as a mask:

> A raised outer corner of the eyebrow, for instance, for a social Mephistopheles in evening dress, with a crush hat . . . carries the idea of evil to the modern audience. It has taken its place with the downward stroke for melancholy, the permanent frown, and other traditional lines of the face, most of them based on nature, but, on the stage, as truly artificial and conventional as the old Greek mask. (Howard, 1900)

In Howard's hands, love was not passion but high sentiment, and his idealization linked him with the genteel tradition of arts and letters, a movement that unintentionally clarified the gulf between the reality and the ideal by trying to hide mankind's less refined impulses. Love was "the universal passion," but love also implied lust and a physicality that required denial; that is, the subject was compelling but fraught with danger, and therefore all the more fascinating.

Howard's was a theater of affirmation, not of provocation; his form and content were mutually interdependent, the artificial theatrical style and the Scribean DRAMATURGY forming a synergism with the idealized metaphysics of society and sexual relations that the culture wished to express, making the play an attempt to reconcile the contradictions between the phenomenal and mimetic aspects of its performance. Howard's theory of "satisfactory" drama is therefore more a rationalization than a rationale, an attempt to preserve the conventions that protected the ideals of the Gilded Age.

Howard died on August 4, 1908, in Avon, New Jersey. He is best remembered for SHENANDOAH, a leading Civil War drama that subordinates the military and political conflict to the dramatic imperative to preserve two intersectional romances. The climactic scene was Sheridan's famous ride to rally his troops at Cedar Creek.

Howard helped strengthen the profession of playwriting by organizing his fellow dramatists into the American Dramatists Club and working toward stronger copyright laws to ensure that playwrights would earn royalties.

[*See also* United States, 1860–1929]

PLAYS: *Fantine* (1864); *Feds and Confed, or Taking the Oath* (1869); *Saratoga* (1870); *Diamonds* (1872); *Drum Taps* (1873); *Lilian's Last Love* (1873); *Brighton* (1874); *Moorcroft, or The Double Wedding* (1874); *The Banker's Daughter* (a revision of *Lilian's Last Love*, 1878); *Hurricanes* (1878); *Old Love Letters* (1878); *Wives* (1879); *Fun in a Green Room* (1882); *Young Mrs. Winthrop* (1882); *One of Our Girls* (1885); *The Henrietta* (1887); *Met by Chance* (1887); *Baron Rudolph* (1881); *Shenandoah* (1888); *Aristocracy* (1892); *Peter Stuyvesant* (with Brander Matthews, 1899)

FURTHER READING

Bloomfield, Maxwell. "Mirror for Businessmen: Bronson Howard's Melodramas, 1870–1890." *Midcontinent American Studies Journal* 5 (Fall 1964): 38–49.

Felheim, Marvin. "Bronson Howard, 'Literary Attaché.'" *American Literary Realism* 2 (Summer 1969): 174–179.

Gottlieb, Lois C. "The Antibusiness Theme in Late Nineteenth Century American Drama." *The Quarterly Journal of Speech* 64 (1978): 415–426.

Howard, Bronson. *The Autobiography of a Play*. New York: Dramatic Museum of Columbia University, 1914.

——. The Banker's Daughter *and Other Plays*. Ed. by Allan G. Halline. *America's Lost Plays* X. Princeton: Princeton Univ. Press, 1941.

——. "Our Schools for the Stage." *Century Magazine* 61 (November 1900): 30.

Mason, Jeffrey D. "*Shenandoah* (1889) and the Civil War." In *Melodrama and the Myth of America*, ed. by Mason. Bloomington: Indiana Univ. Press, 1993. 155–186.

Ryan, Pat G. "The Horse Drama, With Supernumeraries: Bronson Howard's Semi-Historical *Shenandoah*." *Journal of American Drama and Theatre* 3 (1991 Spring): 42–69.

Jeffrey D. Mason

HOWARD, SIDNEY (1891–1939)

Sidney Coe Howard helped move American drama from its provincial nature toward the social thesis plays of the 1930s. He proved adept at melding COMEDY, MELODRAMA, and REALISM believably in scenes where the action moves rapidly and emotions are kept closely in line.

Born on June 26, 1891, in Oakland, California, Howard attended public school in Oakland and then traveled in Europe, returning home in 1910 after contracting tuberculosis. After a year of convalescence, he enrolled at the University of California at Berkeley, where he wrote several plays, both alone and in collaboration. After graduating in 1915, Howard enrolled in GEORGE PIERCE BAKER's playwriting workshop at Harvard, where in 1916 he received his M.A. degree.

Howard volunteered in the Ambulance Corps in France and the Balkans. Once the United States entered the war, he joined the Air Service as a fighter pilot, becoming a squadron captain in France and a war hero.

As a *Life* literary editor, he wrote and adapted plays. His experience as an investigative journalist and fiction writer prepared him to be a theatrical social critic. Howard proved capable, reliable, and natural, with an easy yet meticulous writing style. Although his dramatic topics were not innovative, critics praised his ability to focus on characters, revealing something natural and essential about the human condition. John Gassner stated:

> If Howard's preference for letting life speak for itself led at times to flatness . . . it nevertheless gave his work considerable conviction and plain humanity. The adjectives "solid" and "sound" are apt to crop up in descriptions of his best writing. He himself claimed only a modest role for playwriting, maintaining that the merit of a play lay in its providing good parts for acting rather than in distinction of content or writing.

THEY KNEW WHAT THEY WANTED (1924) centers on an old Italian-American in Northern California who accepts his young mail-order wife's brief adultery because she never truly committed to "her mistake." Before the THEATRE GUILD produced this breakthrough play, sixteen managers rejected the future Pulitzer Prize winner. Krutch (1957) suggested the play makes life's compromises palatable. Howard's other important plays include *Ned McCobb's Daughter* (1926), hailed by Brooks Atkinson for its "flavorsome" dialogue; *The Silver Cord* (1926), praised by Mantle as the "finest of the [New York] dramas" and by Krutch for its Freudian overtones; *The Late Christopher Bean* (1932), Atkinson's mixed review called it both "undisciplined" and "a funny comedy with a hilarious conclusion"; *Dodsworth* (1934), another popular adaptation and "an extremely good play," according to Lockridge; and *Yellow Jack* (1934), an adaptation of Chapter 11 of Paul de Kruif's *The Microbe Hunters*, garnered mixed reviews. Although Krutch praised it, others found it more a lecture than a play.

Although the Theatre Guild produced his early plays, professional difficulties ended that relationship in the late 1920s, and the playwright accepted Samuel Goldwyn's offer to write movies. He subsequently won Academy Awards for *Arrowsmith* in 1931 and *Gone With the Wind* in 1939.

Shortly before his death on August 23, 1939, on his farm in Tyringham, Massachusetts, he founded the Playwrights' Company with MAXWELL ANDERSON, S. N. BEHRMAN, ELMER RICE, and ROBERT SHERWOOD to ensure productions of their plays.

[*See also* United States, 1860–1940]

PLAYS: *Cranbrook Masque* (1916 Detroit); *Casanova* (adaptation of Lorenzo de Azertis's play, 1921); *Swords* (1921); *S.S. Tenacity* (translation of Charles Vildrac's *Le Paquebot Ténacité*, 1922); *Sancho Panza* (adaptation of Melchior Menyhért Lengyel's *Sancho Panza Király sága*, 1923); *Bewitched* (with Edward Sheldon, 1924); *They Knew What They Wanted* (1924); *The Last Night of Don Juan* (translation of Edmond Rostand's *La Derniere nuit de Don Juan*, 1925); *Lexington* (1925); *Lucky Sam McCarver* (1925); *Michael Auclair* (translation of Charles Vildrac's *Michel Auclair*, 1925); *Morals* (translation of Ludwig Thoma's *Morality*, with Charles Recht, 1925); *Ned McCobb's Daughter* (1926); *The Silver Cord* (1926); *Olympia* (translation of Ferenc Molnár's play, 1928); *Salvation* (with Charles MacArthur, 1928); *Half Gods* (1929); *Lute Song* (1930 Stockbridge, 1946 New York adaptation of *Pi-Pa-Ki*, with Will Irwin and music by Raymond Scott); *Marseilles* (adapted from Marcel Pagnol's *Marius*, 1930); *One, Two, Three* (translation of Ferenc Molnár's *One, Two, Three, President!*, 1930); *The Late Christopher Bean* (adapted from René Franchois's *Prenez garde à la peinture*, 1932); *Alien Corn* (1933); *Dodsworth* (adaptation of Sinclair Lewis's novel, 1934); *Ode to Liberty* (adapted from Michel Duran's *Liberté Provisoire*, 1934); *Yellow Jack* (from Chapter 11 of de Kruif's book *The Microbe Hunters*, 1934); *Paths of Glory* (adapted from Humphrey Cobb's novel, 1935); *The Ghost of*

Yankee Doodle (1937); *Madam, Will You Walk?* (one draft, produced posthumously, 1953)

FURTHER READING

Bordman, Gerald. *American Theatre: A Chronicle of Comedy and Drama, 1914–1930*. New York: Oxford Univ. Press, 1995.

Gerwirtz, Arthur. "Sidney Howard." In *American Playwrights, 1890–1945: A Research and Production Sourcebook*, ed. by William W. Demasters. Westport, Conn: Greenwood Press, 1982. 171–182.

Krutch, Joseph Wood.: *The American Drama since 1918*. New York: George Braziller, 1957.

Meserve, Walter J. "Sidney Howard and the Social Drama of the Twenties." *Modern Drama*, 6 (December 1963): 256–266.

Murphy, Brenda. *American Realism and American Drama, 1880–1940*. Cambridge: Cambridge Univ. Press, 1987.

White, Sidney Howard. *Sidney Howard*. Boston: Twayne, 1977.

Andrew Longoria

HOWE, TINA (1937–)

Born in New York City on November 21, 1937, into an economically privileged and cultured family, Tina Howe was educated at prestigious finishing schools and received a bachelor of arts degree from Sarah Lawrence College. She married the historian and novelist Norman Levy.

In 1960 she spent a year in Paris, where she was exposed to EUGÈNE IONESCO's absurdist work. Ionesco's one-acts with their farcical grotesqueries have parallels in Howe's plays, all of which are COMEDIES and several of which, *Museum* (1976) and *The Art of Dining* (1979), for example, portray a similar anarchic world. Her characters, mainly drawn from the upper classes, reflect her own background. *Coastal Disturbances* (1986) and *Prides Crossing* (1997) in particular are reminiscent of ANTON CHEKHOV, but decaying Boston Brahmins replace decaying Russian gentry. Many of her works are zany descendants of comedies of manners. A number of them, including *Approaching Zanzibar* (1989), *The Art of Dining*, and *Museum* take place in public spaces—a cross-country camping trip, a restaurant, and a museum—settings that allow for interactions among a great many characters who are often strangers to each other.

Although Tina Howe entered the theater at the point when women's drama was about to explode, she was ambivalent about feminism. Growing up, she preferred her father to her eccentric, overbearing mother, and at school she was intimidated by the cruelty of the other girls. In the 1970s, she joined and was disappointed by a women's consciousness-raising group; she did not share many of their concerns, nor did they relate to hers—how to balance writing and motherhood. Through her plays, she has explored the various permutations of the role of art and the female artist in contemporary society.

Her earliest theater experiences taught her that critics regarded certain subjects as off limits to women. She became more of a feminist as she realized the extent to which her gender defined her work, not only in the eyes of critics and audiences, but also in her own focus. *The Nest* (1969), her first professionally produced play, outraged reviewers with its presentation of a ritualized (and comedic) rape of a male character by a woman, whereas the converse, in Ionesco's THE LESSON, had apparently been acceptable. Her second play to be produced, *Museum*, is a satirical investigation of the nature and world of art. Its episodic—or for some, nonexistent—plot structure that includes forty-four characters baffled critics, and the play was a commercial failure. Her next play, *The Art of Dining*, which combines REALISM, SURREALISM, and vaudeville-like turns, also focuses on creativity; it too met with critical incomprehension.

Howe continued experimenting with form, in part to win mainstream acceptance, and succeeded with *Painting Churches* (1983), an ostensibly realistic play. Its themes are familiar in Howe's work: art, eating obsessions, dysfunctional relationships. But missing is the chaotic and extravagant comedy that animated her earlier plays. In later works, such as *Approaching Zanzibar* and *Pride's Crossing*, Howe depicts fragile characters struggling with disappointment and loss in a hostile world.

Although her plays have received mixed and sometimes even antagonistic reviews, Howe has received a New York Drama Critics' Award, an Outer Critics' Circle Award, an Obie Award, and a Tony nomination.

[*See also* Feminist Drama in the United States; United States, 1940–Present]

PLAYS: *Closing Time* (1959); *The Nest* (1969); *Birth and After Birth* (1973); *Museum* (1976); *The Art of Dining* (1979); *Appearances* (1982); *Painting Churches* (1983); *Coastal Disturbances* (1986); *Approaching Zanzibar* (1989); *Swimming* (1991); *Teeth* (1991); *One Shoe Off* (1993); *Pride's Crossing* (1997); *The Divine Fallacy* (1999); *Women in Flames* (2000); *Rembrandt's Gift* (2001); *Such Small Hands* (2003)

FURTHER READING

Backes, Nancy. "Body Art: Hunger and Satiation in the Plays of Tina Howe." In *Making a Spectacle: Feminist Essays on Contemporary Women's Theatre*, ed. by Lynda Hart. Ann Arbor: Univ. of Michigan Press, 1989.

Barlow, Judith E. "The Art of Tina Howe." In *Feminine Focus: The New Women Playwrights*, ed. by Enoch Brater. New York: Oxford Univ. Press, 1989.

——. "Tina Howe." In *Speaking on Stage: Interviews with Contemporary American Playwrights*, ed. by Philip C. Kolin and Colby H. Kullman. Tuscaloosa: Univ. of Alabama Press, 1996.

Bigsby, Christopher. *Contemporary American Playwrights*. Cambridge: Cambridge Univ. Press, 1999.

Lamont, Rosette C. "Tina Howe's Secret Surrealism: Walking a Tightrope." *Modern Drama* 36, no. 1 (March 1993): 27–37.

Jane Baldwin

HOWELLS, WILLIAM DEAN (1837–1920)

William Dean Howells was a major American literary figure of the 19th and early 20th centuries and the leading critical spokesman for literary REALISM in the United States between 1880 and 1900. Born on March 1, 1837, in Martin's Ferry, Ohio, Howells wrote thirty-five novels and eight volumes of criticism. His primary significance is as a realistic novelist, literary critic, influential editor of *Atlantic Monthly*, and columnist for *Harper's*, but Howells also authored at least thirty-six plays and sixty pieces of drama criticism.

As a drama critic, Howells consistently articulated the realist aesthetic that he translated from fiction to the stage. In a late 19th-century theater that favored ROMANTICISM, sensationalism, and MELODRAMA, Howells insisted that playwrights should strive to present a direct reflection of life on the stage in all aspects of the drama, including character, dialogue, and setting, with as little artificiality, convention, and arbitrariness in the action as possible. A great admirer of HENRIK IBSEN and GEORGE BERNARD SHAW, he wrote six articles about Ibsen and was an early and avid champion of the Shavian PROBLEM PLAY, defending the right of Europeans to write honestly about every aspect of life at a time when Shaw's plays were being closed down as "immoral" in many American cities.

Closer to his heart were the American playwrights he saw as producing a homegrown realism out of the melodrama and sentimentality of American theater in the 1880s and 1890s. His praising of JAMES A. HERNE'S *MARGARET FLEMING* in 1890 is widely seen as the moment when literary status was conferred on American realistic drama. His regular critical essays in *Harper's* identified and applauded what he saw as the elements of an emerging realism in the plays of BRONSON HOWARD, EDWARD HARRIGAN, and CLYDE FITCH: psychological characterization, natural dialogue without "literosity," and plots that dispensed with the sensational conventions of melodrama in a conscious attempt to create an illusion of reality on the stage by representing the action of everyday life. Herne, Fitch, AUGUSTUS THOMAS, and WILLIAM GILLETTE acknowledged the direct influence of Howells's ideas on their efforts at writing realistic drama, and his influence is evident in the work of such early 20th-century playwrights as RACHEL CROTHERS, EDWARD SHELDON, and LANGDON MITCHELL as well.

Howells's own plays exhibit many of the qualities he was seeking in his contemporaries. Like those in his fiction, the characters in Howells's plays, beginning with the one-act FARCE *The Parlor Car* in 1876, speak dialogue that is often witty and clever but still sounds like normal speech, even to a 21st-century ear. Known for his psychologically realistic characterizations in novels of the 1880s, Howells brought the same principles of character to his serious plays, as well as an attention to detail in his stage directions that helped to establish setting as an integral element in the esthetics of American domestic realism.

The better-known of Howells's plays are a series of twelve one-act society farces that he published in magazines between 1876 and 1900. The plays form a sophisticated situation COMEDY series based on a close-knit circle of upper-middle-class Back Bay Boston friends. The characters are loosely modeled on the people in Howells's own life, particularly two couples, Howells and his wife Elinor and their close friends, Livy and Samuel Clemens. Each play revolves around an incident in the characters' daily lives that is suggested in the play's title—*The Sleeping Car* (1882), *The Elevator* (1884), *The Garroter* (1885), *The Mouse Trap* (1886), *Five O'clock Tea* (1887), *A Likely Story* (1888), *The Albany Depot* (1889), *A Letter of Introduction* (1892), *Evening Dress* (1892), *The Unexpected Guests* (1893), *A Masterpiece of Diplomacy* (1894), and *The Smoking Car* (1898). Howells used the deceptively innocent form of the farce to assault some of the basic assumptions of upper-middle-class American society, particularly exposing the contradictions in the moral position of a social group that professes to believe in truth, but that could not function without constant falsehood and deceit.

Howells also made use of the traditional comic types of the trickster and the gullible fool to attack the fundamental corruption of this social order, portraying himself through Roberts as the victim of the jokes of Campbell, the Mark Twain character, who constantly exposes the hypocrisy and deceit that make the social group function. As may be noted from the titles, Howells also focused on the general social anxiety produced by the increased mechanization of modern life at the turn of the century. The introduction of such innovations as the elevator, the sleeping car, and the telephone cause disruptions in the old social rules that govern this society and have to be accommodated somehow if the group is to think of itself as "modern" and yet survive as a group defined by etiquette and social norms. Although these one-act plays did not receive many professional productions, they were widely read and often produced by amateur theater groups well into the 20th century.

In the professional theater, Howells collaborated with actor-manager Lawrence Barrett, who toured with *A Counterfeit Presentment* in the 1870s. This play was ahead of its time in making a serious dramatic problem of a stock comic device, mistaken identity. Even more AVANT-GARDE in its time, Howells's unproduced *Out of the Question* (1877) anticipated the genre that Shaw was to define in 1891 as the "drama of discussion." In contrast to the then typical well-made play, this play about the pervasive effect of social class in America is centered in the discussion of an issue rather than the construction of the plot. After he developed his unique form of situation comedy, Howells concentrated his playwriting efforts on the Roberts-Campbell series, but he returned to the discussion play toward the end of his career. Two short magazine plays written in his seventies are *The Night Before Christmas* (1910), which exposes the social hypocrisy of Christmas gift-giving and the commodification of the Christmas holiday that he observed in 1910, and *True Hero:*

Melodrama (1909), which attacks romantic self-sacrifice, a perennial target of his realistic fiction as well as his plays. Howells died on May 11, 1920, in New York City.

[*See also* United States, 1860–1929]

PLAYS: *The Parlor Car* (1876); *Counterfeit Presentment* (1877); *Out of the Question* (1877); *The Sleeping Car* (1882); *The Register* (1883); *The Elevator* (1884); *The Garroters* (1885); *The Mouse Trap* (1886); *Five O'Clock Tea* (1887); *A Likely Story* (1888); *The Albany Depot* (1889); *Samson* (1889); *Evening Dress* (1892); *A Letter of Introduction* (1892); *Bride Roses* (1893); *The Unexpected Guests* (1893); *A Masterpiece of Diplomacy* (1894); *A Previous Engagement* (1895); *An Indian Giver* (1897); *The Smoking Car* (1898); *Room Forty-Five* (1899); *The Mother and the Father* (1900); *Her Opinion of His Story* (1907); *Saved, An Emotional Drama* (1908); *A True Hero, Melodrama* (1909); *The Impossible, a Mystery Play* (1910); *The Night Before Christmas, a Morality* (1910); *Parting Friends, Tragedy* (1910); *Self-Sacrifice, a Farce Tragedy* (1911)

FURTHER READING

Arms, George, Mary Bess Whidden, and Gary Scharnhorst, eds. *Staging Howells: Plays and Correspondence with Lawrence Barrett*. Albuquerque: Univ. of New Mexico Press, 1994.

Howells, William Dean. *Complete Plays*. Ed. by Walter J. Meserve. New York: New York Univ. Press, 1960.

——. *A Realist in the American Theatre: Selected Drama Criticism of William Dean Howells*. Ed. by Brenda Murphy. Athens: Ohio Univ. Press, 1992.

Murphy, Brenda. *American Realism and American Drama: 1880–1940*. Cambridge: Cambridge Univ. Press, 1987.

Brenda Murphy

HOYT, CHARLES H. (1859–1900)

Charles Hale Hoyt was born on July 26, 1859, in Concord, New Hampshire. He worked as the drama critic for the Boston *Post* (1878–1883) before turning to playwriting. He became a major writer of FARCE and satire that generally showcased society and were filled with realistic characters. Hoyt saw theater as a business, becoming not only a writer but a producer, songwriter, and theater owner who made almost $500,000 per year with his ventures. He became the proprietor of the Madison Square Theater in New York City and, as a writer of farces, was probably the most financially successful playwright of the Gilded Age. He also served two terms in the New Hampshire state legislature (1893–1894 and 1895–1896).

For his plays, songs, and musicals, Hoyt drew on his own early experiences and always gave the audiences what they wanted, never worrying about critics. He spoofed small town life in *A Rag Baby* (1884), his father's one-time occupation in running a hotel in *A Bunch of Keys* (1882), corrupt politicians in *A Texas Steer* (1890), prohibition in *A Temperance Town* (1893), and the all-American favorite, baseball, in *A Runaway Colt* (1895). Though his plays were never seen as literary masterpieces, they were extremely popular with the masses, always dwelling on themes approachable by the common person. That his songs commented on and perhaps furthered the simple plots of his farces did have an influential effect on the concept of the revue and the American musical—more because of his financial success than any literary value.

A Trip to Chinatown (1891) opened in New York City after almost one year of touring. It had a simple plot and provided a tight evening of recognizably American entertainment, an important step in the development of the musical COMEDY. Its run of 657 performances held the New York record for almost three decades. *The Passing Show* (1894) was the first American revue, offering the combination of music, dance, women, and satire that was to distinguish this important Broadway genre into the early 1930s. Two songs from *A Trip to Chinatown* became huge hits and are still widely familiar—"After the Ball" and "The Bowery," the latter used in the 1945 film *Sunbonnet Sue* and the basis for a ballet sequence in the John Phillip Sousa biographical film, *The Stars and Stripes Forever*. The song was so popular in its day that it was blamed for the decline in Bowery realty prices.

Hoyt's first wife, Flora Walsh, died in 1892. His second wife, Caroline Miskel Hoyt, whom he married in 1894, was a rising young star of the stage, renowned for her beauty and charm. On October 2, 1898, Caroline died at the age of twenty-five giving birth to a son who also did not survive; the New York newspapers gave prominent coverage to Hoyt's loss. The playwright never recovered and was for a while confined to a sanatorium in Hartford, Connecticut. On the night he died—November 8, 1900, in Charlestown, New Hampshire—theaters in New York went dark.

[*See also* United States, 1860–1929]

PLAYS: *A Rag Baby* (1884); *A Tin Soldier* (1886); *A Hole in the Ground* (1887); *A Brass Monkey* (1888); *A Midnight Belle* (1889); *A Trip to Chinatown* (1891); *A Parlor Match* (1893); *A Milk White Flag: And Its Battle Scarred Followers on the Field of Mars and in the Court of Venus* (1894); *A Temperance Town* (1894); *A Texas Steer* (1894); *A Black Sheep* (1896); *A Runaway Colt* (1896); *A Contented Woman* (1897); *A Day and Night in New York* (1898); *A Winsome Widow* (posthumous, 1912)

FURTHER READING

Hoyt, Charles H. "When Someone Pulls the String" sung by Harry Conor in Hoyt's *A Stranger in New York*. Sheet Music Supplement to the *New York Journal* (Sunday, October 3, 1897). New York: Charles Hoyt. http://parlorsongs.com/content/p/pulstrng.htm.

Hunt, D. *The Life and Works of Charles H. Hoyt*. Birmingham: Univ. of Alabama Press, 1946.

McNamara, Brooks. *The New York Concert Saloon*. Cambridge: Cambridge Univ. Press, 2002.

Brian Sajko

LOS HUÉSPEDES REALES See ROYAL GUESTS

HUGHES, HOLLY (1955–)

Few performance artists—no matter how skilled or funny—intend simply to entertain; they mean to provoke, to raise questions, to implicate their audiences."

—Holly Hughes, 1998

Holly Hughes's plays and solo performance pieces are characterized by a love of language. This takes the form of puns, richly descriptive passages, and an abundance of well-turned phrases. Born in 1955 and raised in Saginaw, Michigan, Hughes graduated from Kalamazoo College in 1977 with a major in art. She moved to New York City in 1979 and soon got involved with the WOW Café, a lesbian performance space in the East Village. Her first play, *The Well of Horniness*, premiered at WOW in 1983. A blend of film noir, camp, and lesbian eroticism, it was dubbed "dyke noir" by the *Village Voice*, as were her two subsequent plays, *The Lady Dick* (1984), a detective drama set in a lesbian bar called The Pit, and *Dress Suits to Hire* (1987), a two-woman drama written for Lois Weaver and Peggy Shaw of the SPLIT BRITCHES theater company. *Dress Suits* was the first of Hughes's plays to be presented in a venue for audiences of both men and women.

In 1989, Hughes premiered her first autobiographical solo, *World Without End*. The piece centers on Hughes's relationship to her mother, who had died a few years before. The graphic language, particularly concerning mother-daughter eroticism, discomfited many while demonstrating the performance artist's proclivity for delving into dark and unsettling places.

Her career took an unexpected turn in 1990 when she and three other writer-performers—Tim Miller, Karen Finley, and John Fleck—were denied grants from the National Endowment for the Arts (NEA), despite unanimous approval by a peer review panel. All four of the performers dealt explicitly with issues of sexuality in their performances. They were dubbed "The NEA Four" and became a symbol of the so-called culture wars that raged in the late 1980s and early 1990s in relation to the federal funding of controversial art. Hughes became a nationally known name, although her notoriety closed as many doors as it opened. She received hate mail and death threats, and often found that the protracted legal battle distracted her from developing her artistic work.

Nevertheless, she continued to write and perform solo shows that toured the United States, including the provocatively titled *Clit Notes* (1994), a queer meditation on her father, shame, lesbianism, and performance art. In 2000 she debuted *Preaching to the Perverted*, which chronicled her experience as one of the NEA Four, and particularly the 1998 Supreme Court decision allowing the NEA to make funding decisions based on "general standards of decency" (National Endowment for the Arts v. Finley. 524 US 569 (1998)).

Hughes has taught playwriting and performance composition at a number of different schools including New York University, Barnard College, and Yale. She has collaborated with students to create original scripts through the workshop process. These include *The Mystery Spot* (1997), a DECONSTRUCTION of childhood family vacations, presented at her alma mater, Kalamazoo College; and *After a Fashion* (2003), a look at how fashion forms identity, created with students at the University of Michigan.

[*See also* Gay and Lesbian Drama; United States, 1940–Present]

PLAYS: *The Well of Horniness* (1983); *The Lady Dick* (1984); *Dress Suits to Hire* (1987); *World Without End* (1989); *No Trace of the Blonde* (1993); *Clit Notes* (1994); *Cat o' Nine Tails* (1997); *The Mystery Spot* (1997); *Preaching to the Perverted* (2000); *After a Fashion* (2003)

FURTHER READING

Carr, C. *On Edge: Performance at the End of the Twentieth Century*. Hanover, N.H.: Wesleyan Univ. Press, 1993.

Hart, Linda, and Peggy Phelan, eds. *Acting Out: Feminist Performances*. Ann Arbor: Univ. of Michigan Press, 1993.

Hughes, Holly. *Clit Notes: A Sapphic Sampler*. New York: Grove, 1996.

Hughes, Holly, and David Román, eds. *O Solo Homo: The New Queer Performance*. New York: Grove, 1998.

Dan Bacalzo

HUGHES, LANGSTON (1902–1967)

James Langston Hughes, born on February 1, 1902, in Joplin, Missouri, to James and Carrie Hughes, was a distinguished and influential African American poet who also excelled in the field of drama, having written more than fifty stage works, a number of which reached Broadway. Hughes's theatrical writings include MELODRAMA, folk COMEDY, historical plays, poetic dramas, musicals, librettos, cantatas, lyrics, radio plays, and gospel song-plays. His comic works show his understanding of black urban and rural culture from which he drew characters whose foibles were ironic reflections of African American personal and social relations. His political works show his support of the working classes and the racially oppressed, whose plight could be revealed through agit-prop and other forms. Furthermore, his interest in blues, JAZZ, and gospel led to various musical works. Hughes died on May 22, 1967, in New York City.

Hughes's most important asset as a playwright was his gift for observing social interaction. He observed black life in Lawrence, Kansas, where he attended primary school; in Cleveland, Ohio, where in 1916 he was a student at Central High School; and in other locations such as Chicago, Washington, D.C., and Harlem, where he journeyed in 1921 to attend Columbia University and was later part of the Harlem Renaissance group of young writers, including Countee Cullen, ZORA NEALE HURSTON, and Claude McKay. During his teens, Hughes traveled to MEXICO to visit his father, a period that influenced his first published play, *The Gold Piece* (1921). In Harlem, where he would reside for a good portion of his life, he saw such stage productions as the all-black Broadway musical *Shuffle Along* (1921). He studied the craft of playwriting in 1929 through a brief residence at Jasper Deeter's Hedgerow Theater in Moylan, Rose Valley, Pennsylvania. As an apprentice playwright, Hughes was aware of such African American dramatists as Willis Richardson and Hurston. In part, Hughes was responding to the prominence of white dramatists, such as MARC CONNELLY and EUGENE O'NEILL, who wrote about black situations.

Soviet theater was a significant influence on Hughes's political dramas. He was among a group of African Americans who journeyed to Moscow in 1931, where he was exposed to the work of KONSTANTIN STANISLAVSKY, Nikoloai Gogol, and especially VSEVOLOD MEYERHOLD. Furthermore, the social upheaval of the Great Depression, with its grinding poverty and international left-wing politics, helped to shape Hughes's creative projects, although African American folk humor was also a primary influence. Among his early works were *Mule Bone: A Comedy of Negro Life* (1930), in collaboration with Hurston and set in Eatonville, Florida. The play, which Hughes (1940) thought would be "the first real Negro folk comedy," was eventually staged in 1991 at New York's Ethel Barrymore Theater. *Scottsboro, Limited* (1931), an agit-prop work, supported the wrongfully accused black men of the infamous Scottsboro Case, and MULATTO, written in 1930 and staged in 1935, was a melodrama about race relations in the South. *Mulatto* received mixed reviews by prominent Broadway critics, and in its day, it was the longest-running Broadway production by an African American. Like many American playwrights of the 1930s, such as CLIFFORD ODETS, Hughes was drawn to the Left, whose message is evident in *Harvest* (1934), about migrant workers, and *Angelo Herndon Jones* (1935), named after labor organizer Herndon.

Hughes was associated with Karamu Theater in Cleveland (1936–1939), the New Negro Theater in Los Angeles (1939), and the Skyloft Players in Chicago (1941–1942). Karamu Theater, a program sponsored by Karamu House with its Gilpin Players, staged a series of Hughes plays including such comedies as *Little Ham* (1935), *When the Jack Hollers* (1936), written in collaboration with Arna Bontemps, and *Joy to My Soul* (1937), and several more serious works, including *Emperor of Haiti* (1936), *Troubled Island*, *Front Porch* (1938), and *Mulatto*. Reviewed in the Cleveland press, a number of these productions were both praised and questioned regarding their representations of black life.

Under the direction of Louise Thompson Patterson and supported by the International Workers Organization, the Harlem Suitcase Theater in 1938 staged Hughes's poetic drama, and perhaps his most important nontraditional play using poetry, *Don't You Want to Be Free?* chronicling the African American experience from slavery to the segregation era. During the same year, the Harlem Suitcase Theater also staged a series of Hughes's one-act skits including *Limitations of Life*, which satirized the Fannie Hurst novel and Hollywood film *Imitation of Life* (1934), *The Em-Fuehrer Jones*, satirizing THE EMPEROR JONES and fascism, and *Colonel Tom's Cabin*, which mocked Harriet Beecher Stowe's *Uncle Tom's Cabin* (1852). The Skyloft Players performed his historical play *The Sun Do Move* (1942), and the New Negro Theater revived *Don't You Want to Be Free?*

The Organizer, a blues opera with music by James P. Johnson and a political message, was performed in 1940 at Carnegie Hall. As a LIBRETTIST, Hughes collaborated with another noted African American composer, William Grant Still, adapting *Emperor of Haiti* (*Troubled Island*), about the downfall of Haitian leader Dessalines, to operatic form to be staged in New York in 1949. During World War II, Hughes had written race-conscious, patriotic works such as *For This We Fight* (1943) and later provided lyrics for the ELMER RICE–Kurt Weill Broadway opera *Street Scene* (1947). After 1950, when the Red Scare prevailed, Hughes no longer emphasized left-wing politics. During the Cold War, Hughes wrote more extensively for the musical stage, possibly because musical works were generally less political. In 1953 Hughes had been called before the McCarthy Committee, where Hughes disavowed his connection with the Left. This followed his well-received adaptation of *Mulatto* as the New York opera *The Barrier* (1950), scored by Jan Meyerowitz; Hughes later collaborated with Meyerowitz on the opera *Esther* (1956).

Two of Hughes's most important New York musicals with comedic themes were set in Harlem, *Simply Heavenly* (1957) and *Tambourines to Glory* (1963), the latter a gospel play with music by Jobe Huntley. *Simply Heavenly* featured comic figure Jesse B. Semple of Hughes's newspaper column and stories. *Tambourines to Glory* presented the black church in a playful yet somewhat critical manner. During the Civil Rights Era in the 1960s, Hughes turned again to gospel music to portray religious themes, as in *Black Nativity* (1961), which became a popular Christmas production. His longtime interest in racial themes is reflected in *Jericho-Jim Crow* (1963), and one of his last musical works, *The Prodigal Son* (1965), used the Biblical story to address social issues in the black community. The recognition of the black gospel play as a genre may be attributed in part to Hughes's influence.

[*See also* United States, 1860–1940]

PLAYS: (not including musical works) *The Gold Piece* (1921); *Mulatto: A Play of the Deep South* (1930); *Mule Bone: A Comedy of Negro Life* (1930); *Scottsboro, Limited: A One-Act Play* (1931); *Harvest* (also titled *Blood on the Fields*, 1934); *Angelo Herndon Jones* (1935); *Little Ham* (1935); *Emperor of Haiti* (also titled *Troubled Island*, 1936); *Mother and Child* (1936); *Soul Gone Home* (1936); *When the Jack Hollers* (1936); *Joy to My Soul* (1937); *Colonel Tom's Cabin* (1938); *Don't You Want to Be Free?* (1938); *The Em-Fuehrer Jones* (1938); *Front Porch* (1938); *Hurrah, America!* (in collaboration with Louis Douglas, 1938); *Limitations of Life* (1938); *Scarlet Sister Barry* (1938); *Young As We Is* (1938); *Booker T. Washington in Atlanta* (radio play, 1940); *Young Black Joe* (in collaboration with Charles Leonard, 1940); *Brothers* (radio play, 1942); *The Sun Do Move* (1942); *For This We Fight* (1943); *Pvt. Jim Crow:*

A Radio Script (1943); In the Service of My Country (radio play, 1944); St. James: Sixty Years Young, An Anniversary Panorama (1955); Ballot and Me: The Negro's Part in Suffrage, An Historical Sequence (1956)

FURTHER READING

Duffy, Susan, ed. *The Political Plays of Langston Hughes*. Carbondale: Southern Illinois Univ. Press, 2000.

Hughes, Langston. *The Big Sea*. New York: Hill and Wang, 1940.

McLaren, Joseph. *Langston Hughes: Folk Dramatist in the Protest Tradition, 1921–1943*. Westport, Conn.: Greenwood, 1997.

Rampersad, Arnold. *The Life of Langston Hughes*. 2 vols. New York: Oxford Univ. Press, 1986, 1988.

Sanders, Leslie Catherine, ed. *Gospel Plays, Operas, and Later Dramatic Works. The Collected Works of Langston Hughes*. Vol. 6. Columbia: Univ. of Missouri Press, 2004.

Sanders, Leslie Catherine, ed., with Nancy Johnston. *The Plays to 1942: Mulatto to The Sun Do Move. The Collected Works of Langston Hughes*. Vol. 5. Columbia: Univ. of Missouri Press, 2002.

Smalley, Webster, ed. *Five Plays by Langston Hughes*. Bloomington: Indiana Univ. Press, 1963.

Joseph McLaren

HUGHIE

He's out of the racket. I mean, the whole goddamned racket.
I mean life.
—Erie

Hughie by EUGENE O'NEILL premiered at the Dramatiska Teatern in Stockholm on September 18, 1958; José Quintero directed the first American production on December 22, 1964. The one-act was the only one O'Neill completed out of a planned series of seven or eight plays to be entitled *By Way of Obit*. In 1942, he explained to George Jean Nathan that each play would consist of a monologue that would depict both the speaker and the subject of his eulogy (Bogard, 1988).

The play is virtually an extended monologue by Erie Smith, "a Broadway sport and a Wise Guy—the type of small fry gambler and horse player, living hand to mouth on the fringe of the rackets. Infesting corners, doorways, cheap restaurants, the bars of minor speakeasies, he and his kind imagine they are in the Real Know, cynical oracles of the One True Grapevine." The time is just a couple of hours before dawn on a summer night in 1928, and Erie has come to the front desk of the third-rate hotel where he lives. His foil is the night clerk, who neither thinks nor acts but "simply droops and stares acquiescently at nothing."

Erie is returning from a four- or five-day drunk that began with the funeral of the former night clerk, a man he called "Hughie." Erie tells the clerk how he left his parents' home in Pennsylvania and learned how to make his way as a sport and a ladies' man. Hughie was a sucker, he explains, an easy mark for Erie's stories and enthralled when Erie took him to the track. A salesgirl got Hughie to marry her and then disapproved of Erie when Hughie brought him to their cheap flat for dinner. Erie fascinated Hughie: "The bigger I made myself the more he lapped it up. I went easy on him at first. I didn't lie—not any more'n a guy naturally does when he gabs about the best he wins and the dolls he's made." Erie visited Hughie in the hospital and came to the funeral with a hundred-dollar horseshoe of roses. He wishes Hughie were alive so he could "tell him I win ten grand from the bookies, and ten grand at stud, and ten grand in a crap game!" Since Hughie went into the hospital, Erie hasn't won a single bet. "That ain't natural. I've always been a lucky guy—lucky enough to get by and pay up, I mean."

The night clerk finally starts asking Erie questions about Arnold Rothstein, and even though that famous gambler barely acknowledges the "small fry," Erie assures the clerk that when Arnold plays poker, one white chip is worth a hundred dollars. Erie proposes, "How about shootin' a little crap?" and the curtain falls as they play, back and forth, with Erie's money and Erie's dice: "His soul is purged of grief, his confidence restored."

Hughie offers an alternative perspective on the pipe dream that O'Neill explored so thoroughly in THE ICEMAN COMETH.

FURTHER READING

Bernstein, Samuel J. "*Hughie*: Inner Dynamics and Canonical Relevance." *Eugene O'Neill Review* 22 (Spring–Fall 1998): 77–104.

Bogard, Travis and Jackson R. Bryer, eds. *Selected Letters of Eugene O'Neill*. New Haven: Yale Univ. Press, 1988.

Maufort, Marc. "Exorcisms of the Past: Avatars of the O'Neillian Monologue in Modern American Drama." *Eugene O'Neill Review* 22 (Spring–Fall 1998): 123–136.

Shea, Laura. "An E(e)rie Sound: The Stage Directions in O'Neill's *Hughie*." *Eugene O'Neill Review* 23 (Spring–Fall 1999): 134–140.

Vorlicky, Robert. " 'No Use Gabbin' Here All Night': Male Talk and Silence in *Hughie*." *Eugene O'Neill Review* 19 (Spring–Fall 1995): 81–94.

Jeffrey D. Mason

HUIS CLOS See NO EXIT

THE HUNCHBACK OF AOMORI

The Hunchback of Aomori (*Aomori-ken no Semushi Otoko*, 1967) was the initial production by TERAYAMA SHŪJI's experimental theater troupe Tenjō Sajiki (The Peanut Gallery). One of the most innovative plays of the ANGURA movement, its production heralded the beginning of Terayama's theatrical revolution. Although hugely popular with audiences, the critics were astounded and confused by this complex reworking of *Oedipus the King*.

The play evokes an exotic, superstition-filled Aomori, the rural prefecture of Terayama's birth where time seems to have stopped. In the original production, even before the performance began, old-time circus music and incense filled the lobby, evoking a lost childhood world filled with itinerant performers and mysterious Buddhist rituals. In front of a pop-art rising sun, a bizarre family posed with a wall clock and a stuffed hawk, as though frozen in a commemorative photo from the early 20th century. The cast included the outrageous, male transvestite chanteuse Maruyama (later Miwa) Akihiro (who also played the high camp, god-like, transvestite "mother" in Terayama's *Mink Mary* [*La Marie-Vison*, 1967]) wearing an old-fashioned Western gown, a dwarf, a hunchback, a naked female snake charmer, a proper butler, and an eighteen-year-old female chanter of *naniwabushi* (old tales recited to *shamisen* music).

A hunchbacked thief, abandoned at birth, is caught stealing food from the local mansion. The grotesque, rich, and bitter dowager Matsu (played by Maruyama), who may or may not be his mother, makes him her sex slave. Years ago, her master's son had raped her. As a servant, she was forced to abandon the deformed baby. The narrator—who claims to have been in love with the now dead hunchback—chants this tale of the past while a chorus of crippled men and old women whisper rumors and magical incantations. Did Matsu murder her hunchbacked lover to conceal incest, or did she kill her baby shortly after birth? Since the town's registry of births and deaths vanished long ago, the truth is unknowable.

Like Oedipus, the deformed baby (whose hunched back equals Oedipus's scarred feet) had been saved by the servant ordered to kill him. The grown boy may have unknowingly returned to sleep with this queenly mother. Like the Greek original, the tale unfolds backwards; however, there is no father in Terayama's version.

Sexually provocative mothers and other females frequent Terayama's plays. They reflect his complex relationship with his mother and the impossibility of JAPAN's spiritual and social integration with its own past and with the West (especially America). The West is depicted as simultaneously rapist, master, mother, whore, savior, and betrayer. Japan is the innocent yet deformed child lacking a sense of identity. In some plays (such as *The Dog God* [*Inugami*] or *Heresy* [*Jashūmon*]), the boy rapes and/or murders the temptress.

Terayama viewed his plays as performance, not as literature. Like BERTOLT BRECHT, he utilized unorthodox staging devices and multiple points of view to distance the audience. Like ANTONIN ARTAUD, he immersed the audience in bizarre sensual experiences to free imagination. As a Japanese artist, he made creative use of Japan's popular and classical performance traditions. In these and other ways, his work questions the meaning of Japanese identity in the modern world.

FURTHER READING

Terayama Shūji. *Terayama Shūji no Gikyoku*. [Collected Plays of Terayama Shūji]. 9 vols. Tokyo: Shichōsha, 1969–1972 (vols. 1–4); 1969–1987 (vols. 1–9).

——. *The Hunchback of Aomori* [Aomori-ken no Semushi Otoko]. Tr. by Carol Fisher Sorgenfrei. In Carol Fisher Sorgenfrei, *Unspeakable Acts: The Avant-Garde Theatre of Terayama Shūji and Postwar Japan*. Honolulu: Univ. of Hawaii Press, 2005.

Carol Fisher Sorgenfrei

HUNGARY

The emergence of modern Hungarian drama was part and parcel of the modernization of the country. In the last quarter of the 19th century, having achieved social and economic liberalization as well as a large degree of independence within the Hapsburg Empire, Hungary moved with dizzying speed into the 20th century, creating one of the urban marvels of fin de siècle Europe: Budapest. The city's rapidly growing middle class demanded a culture native in origin, cosmopolitan in spirit, and national in flavor.

The theater rose to the occasion with a new breed of playwrights whose work enjoyed huge success both at home and abroad, especially on Broadway. Foremost among these playwrights was FERENC MOLNÁR, author of such COMEDIES as *The Devil* (1907), *The Guardsman* (1910), and *The Play's the Thing* (1926). His masterly command of dramatic structure, his witty, sophisticated dialogue, and his penchant for pitting illusion against reality have invited comparisons with OSCAR WILDE and LUIGI PIRANDELLO, while his insight into the sexual impulses behind middle-class respectability betray the influence of Sigmund Freud. With a few exceptions, such as Menyhért Lengyel's internationally successful TRAGEDY, *Typhoon* (1909), based on the clash of Eastern and Western world outlooks, comedy became the reigning theatrical form of Hungary during this period. Little room was left in theaters for the tragically nuanced social criticism of such playwrights as Sándor Bródy, Zoltán Thury, and Imre Földes, who held up to their audiences a less than flattering mirror. This accounts also for the failure of the premiere of *Liliom* (1909), considered Molnár's finest play by many critics.

The bourgeois comedy proved so vital that its golden age lasted into the mid-1920s, outliving the cataclysm of World War I and its aftermath. The theater was influenced by the Budapest cabaret, whose leading writer was Jenö Heltai, and together these venues absorbed the new attitudes and turns of phrase of a multiethnic urban citizenry.

It was not only the successful who made use of the new urban idiom. Others, such as Ernö Szép, Géza Csáth, and Milán Füst, who used the new linguistic possibilities in service of dramatic genres other than middle-class comedy, fared less well, and turned to, or back to, fiction. Dezsö Szomory, attacked by critics for his bold use of Budapest slang and his coinages, remained undaunted, writing linguistically daring historical as well as social dramas. During the heyday of bourgeois comedy, European intellectual and artistic trends resonated in other Hungarian literary forms and art, but made little or no headway in the theater. Béla Balázs became known as a symbolist playwright thanks only to Béla Bartók's use of his *Bluebeard's Castle* (1910) as a libretto. Tibor Déry's brilliant Dadaist plays, especially *The Giant Baby* (1926), remained an isolated phenomenon, unperformed for decades. Gyula Háy's Brechtian historical satire, *God, Emperor, Peasant* (1931), directed in Berlin by MAX REINHARDT, was not produced in Hungary at the time. Only the proto-absurdist cabaret pieces of Frigyes Karinthy placed the AVANT-GARDE on the Hungarian stage.

The underside of Budapest's glittering café society was urban squalor and catastrophic rural poverty. By the 1930s, plays with a social conscience began gaining some ground on stage, thanks largely to the work of László Németh, whose noble-minded heroes were bent on confronting grave social problems, but were undone by class or family interests. Such manifestations remained scant, however, and could not meaningfully broaden the palette established by bourgeois comedy. By now, and for the rest of the interwar period, Hungarian drama seemed fixed in a well-worn, often hackneyed, pattern.

The outcome of World War II placed Hungary in the Soviet camp, and literary expression was subjugated to Communist doctrine. Following Joseph Stalin's death in 1953, a reform movement led by writers culminated in the Revolution of 1956, which was crushed by Soviet tanks and followed by a period of severe repression. In the early 1960s, the regime of János Kádár sought legitimacy by gradually loosening its dictatorial grip. Compulsory artistic norms were abandoned, writers were permitted freer expression within ever-broadening limits, and Hungarian drama embarked on a remarkably fruitful period that lasted into the 1980s. The lack of freedom, which determined so much of life and its conflicts, was dealt with by playwrights in metaphor and parable, and audiences drew strength and reassurance from these "coded" messages. In contrast to the period between the wars, now the audience and the theatrical profession were not an obstacle but an encouragement to the advancement of modern Hungarian drama. This conspiratorial aspect of the theater, however, was not lost on the authorities, and certain plays were banned from production or publication for years. Among these were Hungary's first absurdist plays, Miklós Mészöly's *The Window Washer* (1957) and *Bunker* (1959), Imre Sarkadi's existentialist *Simeon Stylites* (1960), Sándor Weöres's mythical *Octopus* (1965), István Csurka's satirical *Deficit* (1968), and ISTVÁN ÖRKÉNY's grotesque *Stevie in the Bloodbath* (1969). Despite such setbacks, Hungarian drama during these decades, as the country moved from "hard" to "soft" dictatorship, rose to—indeed surpassed—the challenge of the times.

Many plays questioned whether personal integrity is possible in a system whose ideology is belied by reality. Such plays as Sarkadi's above-mentioned *Simeon Stylites*, István Csurka's *Who's Paying for the Party?* (1961), and Károly Szakonyi's *Sophie, My Love* (1963) are about the moral crisis of the post-1956 intellectual, constrained to become a supporter of the ruling class. *I Bear Fire* (1970), a contemporary social play by Miklós Hubay in which he characteristically alludes to ancient sources, in this case Prometheus, is also about a ruinously disillusioned generation. Indeed, disillusionment, self-destruction, and loss of moral balance became central problems in such plays. At the same time, the nuances and abuses of power and the possibilities open to the individual at the mercy of power were examined in a number of grotesque and absurdist comedies, such as István Örkény's groundbreaking THE TOTH FAMILY (1967), Gábor Görgey's *Jumping the Gun* (1968), and István Eörsi's *Tombstone and Cocoa* (1969). Tibor Gyurkovics, Károly Szakonyi, and Ferenc Karinthy contributed lyrically grotesque pieces in the tradition of the Budapest comedy. Endre Fejes and Ákos Kertész are known for their socially conscious NATURALISM; Gyula Hernádi and László Gyurkó, for their abstract parables. Many plays of this period tend to question the stable order of reality through the disintegration of the personality or of traditional dramatic structure. In Örkény's *Stevie in the Bloodbath*, recent history is represented in scenes that follow one another in free association, while the unity of the hero, played by four actors, vanishes.

Simultaneously, the Hungarian tradition of the historical drama, which assumes a stable moral order in which human action can make a difference for better or worse, went on. László Németh's lofty historical dramas treat the simultaneous triumph of an idea and the demise of its bearer. Gyula Illyés's *Minion* (1963), set in 5th century Rome, shows the corrupting influence of moral compromise with authority. Magda Szabó has successfully applied anachronistically modern, de-heroicized dialogue to historical topics in such plays as *A Bright Shining Day* (1974), about the power struggles surrounding the founding of the Hungarian state in the 9th century. Transylvania, a province of present-day ROMANIA with a large Hungarian population, has contributed to the tradition of the historical drama through the work of GÉZA PÁSKÁNDI, András Sütö, and János Székely. Since Stalinism survived in Romania until 1989, and the Hungarian minority was additionally subjected to severe nationalist pressure, there was even greater reason for these playwrights to treat social, political, and national issues in highly allegorical ways. Páskándi's absurdoid *Sojourn* (1970), Sütö's sweeping, poetic *Star at the Stake* (1975), and Székely's intricately intellectual *Protestants* (1976) are set during the Protestant Reformation, a period that Transylvanian playwrights frequently turned to, for it was a time when nuances in matters of faith could become questions of life and death, salvation and damnation—a rich source for a people struggling to save its identity. Nor were these dramatic clashes of ideas and principles lost on audiences in Hungary.

In the late 1970s a new generation of Hungarian playwrights began creating a drama with a fundamentally new outlook. Their work, which critics have termed *hiánydramaturgia* (drama of deficiency), is based on the absence of a moral order that could lend meaning to human action. Deficiency is what their characters suffer from: the lack of a meaningful past, of ideals, of possibilities, of love, of personal space, of a coherent personality. These young playwrights were not caught in the moral crises of their fathers, whose reluctant compromises with authority influenced so many plays. Nor were they impressed by the heroism of the individual confronting authority in so many historical dramas of the previous period. Their predecessors had directly experienced their era's cataclysms and hopes for change. For the younger generation, the 1968 invasion of CZECHOSLOVAKIA only confirmed the hopelessness of change, the seeming permanence of their situation. Their world could not give a dramatic character a point of orientation, internal or external, for or against which struggling might be worthwhile.

The main representatives of this movement were Péter Nádas, Géza Bereményi, Mihály Kornis, and GYÖRGY SPIRÓ. Nádas's extraordinary trilogy, *House Cleaning* (1977), *Encounter* (1979), and *Burial* (1980), becomes increasingly abstract and multivalent as communication is replaced by ritual, until even ritual cannot be sustained. On one level, *Burial* represents the end of theater itself; no wonder Nádas, a celebrated novelist, wrote nothing else for the stage. Bereményi's *Halmi* (1979) reincarnates William Shakespeare's Danish Prince into a contemporary Hungarian antihero for whom inaction is the only response to the morally tainted world of his father's various embodiments. *Hallelujah* (1979) is Kornis's rhapsodic depiction of a generation—his—that experienced the 1950s as children. The play's basic situation is simple enough: a man is waiting for his father in a room with his grandfather; but time and place are in a constant dreamlike flux, and the dialogue is an agglomeration of linguistic debris. When the awaited father finally arrives, nothing is clarified. Spiró's *Chikenhead* (1985), a hypernaturalistic look into the consciousnesses of characters at the squalid margins of society, exposes modern man's catastrophic lack of connection to others and himself. The momentum these four writers brought to drama was carried forward with new outlooks and styles by György Schwajda, András Forgách, Ottó Tolnai, Pál Békés, László Márton, András Nagy, and other playwrights. In his intellectual essay-dramas, Nagy probes figures from cultural history, such as Kierkegaard and Alma Mahler.

Following the change of regime in 1989, drama gradually lost its capacity to influence public morale. The threat to the community by the political system came to an end, and the tacit conspiracy between audience, playwright, and theater lost its raison d'être. The impulse to deal with the problems of contemporary Hungarian society, though it remains strong in the ever-growing oeuvre of György Spiró, is not very evident in the work of the youngest playwrights. Among the few exceptions are *Mausoleum* (1995) by Lajos Parti Nagy and *Géza-Boy* (2000) by János Háy. But *Headman's Holiday* (1999) by Kornél Hamvai, about an insignificant common man stumbling about against the backdrop of the French Revolution, the import of which totally escapes him, reveals the emergence in drama of a new kind of relationship between the individual and society, the individual and history. Most plays of the previous decades treated the public sphere as intruding upon or determining the private. In most plays of the 1990s, however, the individual in his private sphere is at the center of the playwright's attention, often blurring the line between interior and exterior, as in *Wonderful Wild Animals* (1999) by László Garaczi and in plays of Vera Filó.

In contemporary Hungarian theater, it is all but impossible to identify a common generational voice or thematic concern. The relationship between playwright and theater has also undergone a transformation. Decentralization has brought into being a number of small venues where writers, dramaturges, and directors work more closely than ever before in creating stage texts. Many promising young playwrights have emerged in this new context, among them Ákos Németh, Attila Lörinczy, István Tasnádi, Zoltán Egressy, and Péter Kárpáti. It remains to be seen whether the current state of seeming transition becomes permanent, or leads to new, identifiable directions.

FURTHER READING

Bécsy, Tamás. *Kalandok a drámával, Magyar drámák 1945–1989* [Adventures with Drama, Hungarian Dramas 1945–1989]. Budapest: Balassi Kiadó, 1996.

Csáki, Judit, ed. *Modern Hungarian Theatre*. Budapest: ITI Hungarian Center, 1999.

Czigány, Lóránt. *The Oxford History of Hungarian Literature*. Oxford: Oxford Univ. Press, 1984.

Ézsiás, Erzsébet. *Mai magyar dráma* [Hungarian Drama Today]. Budapest: Kossuth Könyvkiadó, 1986.

Müller, Péter P., and Anna Lakos, eds. *Collision: Essays on Contemporary Hungarian Drama*. Budapest: Hungarian Theatre Museum and Institute, 2004.

Radnóti, Zsuzsa. *Cselekvés-nosztalgia* [Longing for Action]. Budapest: Magvetö Könyvkiadó, 1985.

——. *Lázadó dramaturgiák* [Dramaturgies in Revolt]. Budapest: Palatinus, 2003.

Eugene Brogyányi

HURSTON, ZORA NEALE (1891–1960)

While White people strive to achieve restraint, we strive to pile beauty on beauty and magnificence on glory.

—Zora Neale Hurston, in a letter to Lewis Gannett, 1934

Best known as a novelist, anthropologist, and folklorist, two-time Guggenheim Fellow Zora Neale Hurston also dramatized her first-hand experiences of marginalized black Americans.

Born on January 7, 1891, in Notasulga, Alabama, Hurston was raised in rural Florida. She traveled to New York City in 1925, joining writers like Countee Cullen and LANGSTON HUGHES in the Harlem Renaissance and bringing the work of black writers to a national audience for the first time. While other authors wrote about urban middle-class blacks, emphasizing their similarities to whites, Hurston accentuated the differences, concentrating on the unique southern African American culture of voodoo, mule camps, and juke joints.

She graduated from Barnard College in 1928 and trained with Franz Boas for a career in anthropology. Committed to bringing African American folklore to a popular audience, she wrote several novels, most notably *Their Eyes Were Watching God*, but found that theater allowed her to bypass white editors and publishers and tell her story whole and unadulterated.

Her 1925 play *Color Struck* tackled the controversial theme of color consciousness within the black community. Written in dialect for an all-black cast, the play's centerpiece is an elaborate cakewalk contest, combining spectacle, music, and dance. In its powerful conclusion the main character allows her color prejudice to destroy her only chance for happiness. As Hurston wrote to Hughes in 1928, she hoped to initiate "a real Negro art theatre . . . to act out the folk tales, however short, with . . . abrupt angularity and naiveté" (Kaplan, 2002).

In 1931, Hurston collaborated with Langston Hughes to turn one of her unpublished stories into a full-length play entitled *Mule Bone: A Comedy of Negro Life*. It dramatizes a quarrel between two rival churches in the rural south whose members come to blows. The plot turns on whether or not the mule bone wielded by one congregant in the dispute can be considered a weapon. Townspeople decide the donkey is father to the mule, Samson slew 1,000 Philistines with the jaw bone of an ass, and "de further back on de mule you goes de mo' dangerous he gits . . . by de time you gets clear back tuh his hocks he's rank pizen."

Although the battling churches reconcile in the end, *Mule Bone* led to an embarrassingly public squabble between Hurston and Hughes over authorship. As a result it was neither performed nor published in their lifetimes.

Hurston's career declined after the war. A charge of child molestation in 1948 drew national notoriety before she was vindicated. In the 1950s, Hurston grew increasingly isolated by her conservative politics, naming former friends as Communists to the House Unamerican Activities Committee and opposing the U.S. Supreme Court's decision to end school segregation. Late in the decade, she went to work as a maid for a white family, pawned her typewriter, and went on welfare. At her death on January 28, 1960, in Fort Pierce, Florida, she was buried in an unmarked grave in a segregated cemetery. In 1975, Pulitzer Prize–winning novelist Alice Walker placed a headstone on Hurston's grave and began recapturing her reputation for a new generation.

[*See also* United States, 1860–Present]

PLAYS: *Meet The Mama* (1925); *Spears* (1925); *Color Struck* (1926); *The First Ones* (1927); *Cold Keener* (1930); *De Turkey and de Law* (1930); *Fast and Furious* (1931); *The Great Day* (1931); *Mule Bone* (1931); *Sermon in the Valley* (1931); *Spunk* (1935); *Polk County* (1944)

FURTHER READING

Boyd, Valerie. *Wrapped in Rainbows: The Life of Zora Neale Hurston*. New York: Scribner 2003.

Hemenway, Robert. *Zora Neale Hurston: A Literary Biography*. Urbana: Univ. of Illinois Press, 1977.

Kaplan, Carla, ed. *Zora Neale Hurston: A Life in Letters*. New York: Doubleday, 2002.

Philip Zwerling

HUSAIN, SHAHAROM (1919–)

Don't forget, Tanjung,
God makes man equal,
no differences,
'tis man who differentiates . . .
—The Hunchback, Act 4, *The Hunchback of Tanjung Puteri*, 1961

Playwright Shaharom Husain was born in MALAYSIA, on November 4, 1919, and earned his bachelor's degree from Universiti Nasional Jakarta in 1972. He spent much of his adulthood in Johor writing novels, historical studies, and plays, for which he is known. An admirer of William Shakespeare and GEORGE BERNARD SHAW, Husain worked as a history teacher at the Sultan Idris Teacher Training College in Tajung Malim, Perak, and the Malay Teacher Training College in Johor Bahru, where he wrote and produced plays. His early work was undertaken in the 1930s and during the Japanese occupation of Malaya (1940–1945). One of his earliest plays, *Lawyer Dahlan* (1939–1940), which he directed in 1943, is contemporary in theme and setting and deals with the changes wrought by modernization in Malay society. Husain approaches drama as an educational as well as an aesthetic medium to promote social progress and a respect for justice. He sees playwriting as a didactic art.

Husain's major mark on modern Malaysian drama is in the development of *sandiwara* (literally "drama"). The *sandiwara* style of playwriting, popular in Malaysia in the 1950s and early 1960s, is an adaptation of Indonesian drama that deals with both historical and modern themes. *Sandiwara* plays also reflect the influence of Shakespeare. Husain's forte is the historical drama, sometimes composed in poetic verse, that re-creates exciting episodes in Malay history. Husain uses history symbolically to express present-day aspirations; he relates historical figures to the issue of Malay nationalism and independence, illustrating the ill effects of feudalism and colonialism on Malay society. He also explores the nature of freedom on a personal and societal level. Husain's historical dramas often deal with his home state of Johor and nearby Singapore. *The Tiger of Johor* (*Harimau Johor*, 1962), for example, portrays a model warrior, Nong Mutalib, who serves his people loyally. In *Tun Fatimah or the Secret of the Fall of Malacca* (*Tun Fatimah atau Rahsia Kejatuhan Melaka*, first performed in 1953 and published in 1964), Husain presents an ideal female warrior, the consort of Sultan Mahmud Syah, who resisted Portuguese colonization at the beginning of the 16th century.

In his best-known play, *The Hunchback of Tanjung Puteri* (*Si Bongkok Tanjung Puteri*, 1961), Husain finds as much fault with Malay leaders who sold out Malaya to the British as with the British colonizers themselves. Si Bongkok, a hunchback pirate reminiscent of the Hunchback of Notre Dame, displays a complex, rebellious personality. His attempts to seduce Tanjung Puteri, who symbolizes the nation, are unsuccessful. This beautiful woman is arrogant on account of her country's attractions and wealth; in the climactic scene of the play, she is killed. The free-spirited Si Bongkok is defeated by Warrior Putih (the White Warrior), the would-be hero who is himself tainted by dealings with the British. Because his counterparts are less than ideal, Si Bongkok transforms into a tragic figure rather than simply an outright villain. Thus, in Husain's skillful hands, *sandiwara* plays become thought-provoking, multilayered works that have a lasting place in Malaysia's modern theater history.

PLAYS: *The Sword of Admiral Bentan* (*Keris Laksamana Bentan*, 1940); *The Sea Devil* (*Hantu Laut*, 1948); *The Dagger of the Riau Warrior* (*Badik Panglima Riau*, 1956); *Tun Seri Lanang* (1958); *Family and Neighbors* (*Keluarga dan Tetangga*, 1960); *The Vow of the Youth of This Land* (*Sumpah Pemuda-pemudi Tanahair*, 1960); *The Foundation of the Malay Government* (*Tonggak Kerajaan Melayu Johor*, 1961); *The Hunchback of Tanjung Puteri* (*Si Bongkok Tanjung Puteri*, 1961); *Kuala Kubu Karam* (1961); *Harimau Johor* (*The Tiger of Johor*, 1962); *The Golden Bowl* (*Balang Mas*, 1964); *Tun Fatimah* (1964); *Wak Cantuk* (1965); *The Successful Warrior* (*Satria Jaya*, 1968); *The Worn-out Minister* (*Bendahara Tepok*, 1983); *Seri Nara* (1984); *The Path to Happiness* (*Meniti Bahagia*, 1985)

FURTHER READING

Ahmad Kamal Abdullah, et al. "Drama." In *History of Modern Malay Literature*, Vol. II. Kuala Lumpur: Dewan Bahasa dan Pustaka, 1992. 264–269.

Husain, Shaharom. "Activities of the Culture, Arts, Language and Literature Club." Tr. by Solehah Ishak. *Malay Literature* 12, nos. 1 and 2 (1999): 1–28.

——. "Solehah Ishak Interviews Shaharom Husain." *Malay Literature* 12, nos. 1 and 2 (1999): 29–45.

Nur Nina Zuhra (Nancy Nanney). *An Analysis of Modern Malay Drama*. Shah Alam, Malaysia: Biroteks, MARA Institute of Technology, 1992. 64–68.

Nancy Nanney

HWANG, DAVID HENRY (1957–)

David Henry Hwang is the only Asian American playwright of the 20th century to have his work produced on Broadway. His career began when New York City's Public Theater, under the artistic direction of theater luminary Joseph Papp, presented his play *F.O.B.* in 1980. The play addresses tensions between American-born Asian Americans and recent immigrants, while simultaneously interweaving characters from Chinese mythology. Originally written while Hwang was a senior at Stanford University, *F.O.B.* was well received and won an Obie Award. The Public Theater went on to produce several more of the playwright's works, including *The Dance and The Railroad* (1981), *Family Devotions* (1981), and the double bill *Sound and Beauty* (1983), consisting of the one-acts *The Sound of a Voice* and *The House of Sleeping Beauties*.

Hwang is best known for his 1988 work *M. Butterfly*, which garnered him his most important critical success: three Drama Desk Awards, three Outer Critics Circle Awards, and three Tony Awards, including Best New Play. It tells the tale of Frenchman René Gallimard, who had a twenty-year affair with Beijing Opera star Song Liling without ever realizing that she was, in fact, a man. The play addresses issues of gender, sexuality, and racial stereotyping in complex and theatrically compelling ways. At the heart of the play's conflict is the presumption that Gallimard did not recognize his lover's true gender. Hwang suggests this conflict results from the West's idea of the Orient as submissive and passive. However, it should be noted that this is not merely an abstract delusion on the part of Gallimard; it is a critique of larger historical and cultural trends within East-West relations.

Following *M. Butterfly*, Hwang came to be seen as a leading voice in an emerging Asian American theater scene. This became apparent during the protests surrounding the 1991 U.S. premiere of *Miss Saigon*. Hwang was a vocal opponent of casting Caucasian actor Jonathan Pryce in the role of the Engineer, without giving an adequate chance for an Asian American actor to audition for the role. Hwang's next effort as a playwright attempted to utilize his experiences during the *Miss Saigon* controversy to craft a FARCE on racial identity, *Face Value* (1993). However, the play was not well received and closed in previews.

It was several years before Hwang once again aimed for the Great White Way. *Golden Child* was workshopped extensively prior to its Broadway run. The 1998 production was nominated for a Tony Award but did not repeat the success of *M. Butterfly*. Hwang expanded his Broadway repertoire to include musicals, first as the co-librettist for Disney's *Aida* (2000) and later as the author of the revised book to the Richard Rodgers and Oscar Hammerstein musical, *Flower Drum Song* (2002).

In nearly all of his works, Hwang has explicitly addressed Asian American issues. His detractors have complained that his use of Asian cultural forms has been superficial, simply providing an exotic flavor for white audiences. However, critics have recognized that Hwang has provided mainstream representations of Asian Americans that subvert both stereotypes and expectations.

[*See also* Identity Theater; United States, 1940–Present]

PLAYS: *F.O.B.* (1980); *The Dance and the Railroad* (1981); *Family Devotions* (1981); *The House of Sleeping Beauties* (1983); *The Sound of a Voice* (1983); *As the Crow Flies* (1986); *Rich Relations* (1986); *M. Butterfly* (1988); *1,000 Airplanes on the Roof* (libretto, 1988); *Bondage* (1992); *Face Value* (1993);

Trying to Find Chinatown (1996); *Golden Child* (1998); *Peer Gynt* (adaptation, 1998); *Aida* (co-librettist, 2000); *The Silver River* (libretto, 2000); *Flower Drum Song* (libretto, 2002); *Yellowface* (2006)

FURTHER READING

Kondo, Dorinne. *About Face: Performing Race in Fashion and Theater.* New York: Routledge, 1997.

Lee, Josephine. *Performing Asian America: Race and Ethnicity on the Contemporary Stage.* Philadelphia: Temple Univ. Press, 1997.

Moy, James. *Marginal Sights: Staging the Chinese in America.* Iowa City: Univ. of Iowa Press, 1993.

Shimakawa, Karen. *National Abjection: The Asian American Body Onstage.* Durham, N.C.: Duke Univ. Press, 2002.

Dan Bacalzo

HWANG MEI-SHU (1930–)

Hwang Mei-shu (1930–) was born in Mainland CHINA and moved to Taiwan as a teenager near the end of World War II. He received a bachelor's degree from the Tamkang University in Taiwan and a master's degree from the National Taiwan Normal University. In 1976 he received a doctorate in theater from Florida State University in the UNITED STATES. From 1976 to 1995 he was a professor at the Graduate School of Western Languages and Literature, Tamkang University. He was a founding member of the *Tamkang Review*, a distinguished literary journal in Taiwan. Retired from Tamkang University, he is now teaching at Chinese Culture University in Taiwan. He immerses himself in drama development, participating in theatrical activities in Taiwan and drama conferences in Asia. He is a playwright, a translator of plays, and a theater critic.

Hwang has written eight plays. Among these, *The Fool Who Wins an Ass* was first performed in English at Florida State University in 1973 and *Cathay Visions* at Mankato State University (now affiliated with Minnesota State University) in 1986. Purdue University also staged *Cathay Visions* in January 2004. *Good Heavens!* was premièred in Korea in 1983. *The Comedy of Mr. Allman Yang* (1983) has been performed in Taiwan, Korea, and Malaysia.

As Martha Cheung and Jane Lai pointed out (*An Oxford Anthology of Contemporary Chinese Drama*, 1997), Hwang is fascinated with a particular state—"you dream that you are dreaming, and then think that you are awake when in fact you are still in a dream." This dream-within-a-dream form indeed shaped his play *Cathay Visions (Empty Cage)*.

In *Cathay Visions*, after the visionlike or apparitionlike characters being invoked to deliver their views, the real-life characters—an old Chinese man and his family—function as chorus to comment, sing, and deliver the lines with a chanting quality. The arrangement of music, the use of mime and magic, and the characters' movements and gestures combine to create the surreal atmosphere of the play. *Cathay Visions* is an example of the experimental work undertaken by a group of Taiwanese playwrights since the late 1970s.

Hwang Mei-shu's position within political, aesthetic, and philosophical contexts could be reflected in his words, "Time passed, cross-strait relations changed, and the older generation's hatred slowly faded . . . As for the generations who were born and raised in Taiwan, the Communists were never part of the life experience that often inspires new works." Some of his plays are based on the fusion of folklore stories, Beijing Opera, and regional drama, transforming those traditional dramas into a style of modern spoken drama.

Hwang Mei-shu translated a series of the Irish playwright WILLIAM BUTLER YEATS's plays into Chinese, introducing the western plays to Taiwan. He has also been influential in introducing Taiwan drama to the West as he translated several important Chinese plays into English.

PLAYS: *The Fool Who Wins an Ass* (1973); *Good Heavens!* (1981); *The Comedy of Mr. Allman Yang* (*Yang Shiren de xiju*, 1983); *Cathay Visions* (*Empty Cage*, 1986); *Marvels of the Heart* (*Xin de chuanqi*, 1986); *Simply Outrageous* (*Qi you ci li*, 1986)

FURTHER READING

Hwang Mei-shu. *Cathay Visions (Empty Cage)*. Tr. by Hwang Mei-shu. In *An Oxford Anthology of Contemporary Chinese Drama*, ed. by Martha P.Y. Cheung and Jane C.C. Lai. Hong Kong: Oxford Univ. Press, 1997. 455–499.

——. "Is There Tragedy in Chinese Drama? An Experimental Look at an Old Problem." *Tamkang Review* 10, no. 2 (1979): 211–226.

——. "A Brief Introduction to Peking Opera." *Tamkang Review* 12, no. 3 (1982): 315–330.

——. "Peking Opera: Simplicity out of Necessity." *Tamkang Review* 13, no. 3 (1983): 267–278.

Wang, Li-ji. "Pointing to the Moon: Zen Influences in Three Plays by Hwang Mei-shu." Ph.D. diss., Brigham Young Univ., 1993.

Iris Hsin-chun Tuan

I

I AM MY OWN WIFE

Doug Wright's play *I Am My Own Wife* premiered at Playwrights Horizons in New York City on May 27, 2003. After moving to Broadway in the fall of 2003, it garnered the 2004 Tony Award for Best Play, as well as the 2004 Pulitzer Prize for Drama.

Based on personal interviews, letters, East German secret police files, and official news sources, *I Am My Own Wife* explores the extraordinary life of Charlotte von Mahlsdorf (1928–2002), an East German transvestite who grew up in Nazi Germany. Originally born Lothar Berfelde, Mahlsdorf became one of the most remarkable personalities to surface in the decade after Germany's unification. Her story is compelling not only because she overcame nearly impossible historical odds (an abusive father, the massive destruction of World War II, two repressive regimes, and, after 1989, the violent homophobia of disillusioned skinheads), but also because she seemed unscathed by her heroic fight: a kindly, grandmotherly figure with a quirky passion for 19th-century mass-produced furniture, which she displayed for over forty years in her private, self-made museum.

Though the play allows its audience to experience the same delight that Wright experienced during his interviews with Mahlsdorf, it also confronts its protagonist's darker underside: not only might some of her stories (of murdering her father, of surviving an SS firing squad in the last days of the war) not be true, but there is clear evidence in her secret police files that she worked as an unpaid informant for the East German secret police and informed on a close personal friend and fellow gay antiques dealer. Because Mahlsdorf resisted self-reflection in real life, the play embodies the moral struggle where it really took place: in the act of writing the play, which is subtitled *Studies for a Play About the Life of Charlotte von Mahlsdorf*. As Wright, who appears as a character in the play, confesses to his childhood friend John near the play's conclusion, "I need to believe in her stories as much as she does! I need to believe that . . . a little boy . . . navigated a path between the two most repressive regimes the Western World has ever known—the *Nazis* and the *Communists*—in a pair of heels. I need to believe that things like that are true." In grappling with the complexity of its heroine, the play offers a rich meditation on the meaning of history, the ethics of curating another person's life, and our very human need for storytelling.

While Mahlsdorf's stories are enthralling, Wright's storytelling techniques make this "one-woman show, performed by a man" equally mesmerizing. Written for Jefferson Mays, who played Mahlsdorf and the thirty-five other characters, *I Am My Own Wife* eschews monologues in favor of dialogues, leaving the uncanny impression that there are usually several characters—even several actors—on stage at the same time. Though Wright uses documentary theater techniques pioneered by Moisés Kaufman (*The Laramie Project*), who collaborated on this play as its director, he also acknowledges taking liberties with the documentary evidence. Like his heroine, he also knows what it takes to tell a great story.

[*See also* Gay and Lesbian Drama; United States, 1940–Present]

FURTHER READING

Wright, Doug. *I Am My Own Wife: Studies for a Play About the Life of Charlotte von Mahlsdorf*. New York: Faber, 2004.

Jeffrey Schneider

IBSEN, HENRIK (1828–1906)

In these times every work of creative writing should attempt to move the frontier markers.

—Album of the author Sacher Masoch, 1882

Henrik Johan Ibsen was born on March 20, 1828, to the merchant Knud Ibsen and his wife Marichen Altenburg in the small town of Skien on the southeast coast of Norway. The family was originally well off, but because of financial setbacks in 1834 the father had to sell his properties in town, and the family moved in 1835 to a farm in the countryside. Eventually the farm was sold as well, and in 1843 the family had to move back into the town, where they rented a modest apartment. The early experience of social decline may have contributed to a certain inwardness of character in the young Ibsen, combined with considerable social ambitions.

One of his main pleasures as a boy was to present puppet shows to the children of the area. He attended local schools and received basic education in history, religion, German, and other common subjects. At the end of 1843 the young man left his parents' home and traveled to Grimstad, another coastal town farther south, where a position had been found for him as a pharmacy apprentice. His intention was to go on to medical studies, and in Grimstad, where he stayed six years, he started to prepare for the university entrance examination. He also developed his literary and artistic interests, reading, writing, and painting. In 1846 a maidservant at the pharmacy gave birth to a boy and claimed Ibsen as the father, who accepted his responsibility and had to contribute paternity payments for fifteen years.

Several lyrical poems date from this period, the earliest one written in 1847. In 1849 he completed his first play, *Catiline*, a verse drama in three acts about the tragic fate of a Roman aristocrat who conspired against the Republic and died in 62 B.C.

Ibsen was inspired by the revolutionary atmosphere following political events in Europe in 1848 (the February Revolution). His historical sources were speeches by Cicero and Catiline's biography by Sallust—texts on his Latin syllabus. Contrary to these sources, Ibsen's presentation of Catiline is mainly sympathetic; he is a brave leader, but not flawless. His ambition is to restore ancient Roman virtues to the morally decaying people, but he is betrayed, his army is defeated, and he himself is slain by the demonic Furia after he has fatally wounded his loving wife Aurelia.

Encouraged by two young Grimstad friends, Ibsen presented his play to the Christiania Theater, but it was rejected. Printed under the pseudonym of Brynjolf Bjarme at the cost of the author (supported by one of his friends), *Catiline* was published on April 12, 1850, the day Ibsen left Grimstad on board a ship bound for the Norwegian capital of Christiania (now Oslo). The critical reception was on the whole encouraging, because an original play by a Norwegian writer was a rarity around 1850. The sale of the book, however, was extremely limited.

On his journey leaving Grimstad, Ibsen visited his family in Skien. This was the last time he saw them. His feelings for them were complicated, and as three of them had joined a local pietistic sect, he felt even more estranged, although he did exchange letters with his sister Hedvig on a few occasions.

In Christiania Ibsen made another effort to reach the stage, and this time he succeeded. *The Burial Mound* (*Kjæmpehøien*), a one-act play in blank verse, was accepted by the theater and presented to the public on September 26, 1850. It presents a dramatic confrontation between representatives of two civilizations on a shore of Normandy. Norse Vikings on an avenging expedition meet an old Christian hermit and his adopted daughter and discover that the hermit is their former king, believed to have been slain in an earlier encounter. Similar plots can be found in plays by Adam Gottlob Oehlenschläger and William Shakespeare. Ibsen was not proud of his achievement, and the text remained unpublished in his lifetime. Still, the fact that a play of his had been performed meant increased respect in literary circles, as well as free admission to productions at the theater.

By this time the young man was less determined to study medicine. At the university entrance exam he received insufficient grades in Greek and mathematics, so he was not qualified to begin his studies unless the grades were improved at a second try. He was admitted to the Students' Union, however, and even became the editor of its handwritten journal. At the same time he joined two older friends in editing a satirical weekly magazine. Here Ibsen published theater reviews, some poems, and one political satire, *Norma; or, The Love of a Politician* (*Norma eller en politikers kjærlighed*, 1851). In May 1851 Ibsen had seen a performance of Vincenzo Bellini's opera *Norma*, and he made it his model for an unpretentious joke in three short acts targeting the current political debates in the National Assembly.

During the summer the young writer also contributed to the left-wing newspaper of the labor unions. The founder of the unions and the editor of the newspaper (a friend of Ibsen) were both arrested and charged with subversive activity. They had to serve time in prison and at hard labor, seven years altogether. Ibsen was not apprehended, but he was shocked. After that he kept his political views to himself.

In the fall of 1851 the famous violin virtuoso Ole Bull arrived in Christiania from Bergen, where in 1850 he had founded a permanent theater and hired Norwegian actors. He did not obtain state support for his theater, so the Students' Union organized a fund-raising musical entertainment for which Ibsen wrote a verse prologue. This brought the two men together, and Ibsen was offered the post of stage instructor, as well as house author, at the theater. He accepted and arrived in Bergen in late October 1851.

The position Ibsen was to hold at the Bergen Theater for almost six years was that of an assisting manager, partly stage director and partly house author. In the latter capacity he was expected to write prologues for special occasions and plays. The contract did not specify how many plays, but there was an understanding that Ibsen was to have a new play ready every fall, to be performed on January 2, the anniversary of the theater.

In the spring of 1852 the theater board awarded Ibsen a travel grant for a three-month study tour to DENMARK and GERMANY, where he could acquaint himself with all aspects of theater production in eminent theaters in Copenhagen and Dresden. Because of letters of recommendation he was well received at the Royal Theater in Copenhagen. He was given free admission, met directors and writers, and had the chance to see twenty- four productions, including Shakespeare's *King Lear*, *Romeo and Juliet*, *Hamlet*, and *As You Like It*. In Dresden he did not get free admission, and his reports to the theater board in Bergen are less informative, but he did see *Hamlet* again, and probably other Shakespeare plays, such as *A Midsummer Night's Dream*.

A book by a young German drama critic, Hermann Hettner's *Das moderne Drama*, was just out in 1852, and Ibsen read it on his tour. Hettner's views of historical TRAGEDY, as well as of romantic fairy-tale COMEDY, include a favorable evaluation of Shakespeare's work in these genres, which agreed well with Ibsen's own preferences at the time. After his return to Bergen he completed a fairy-tale comedy, St. *John's Night* (*Sancthansnatten*), to be performed on January 2, 1853. Oehlenschläger had written *St. John's Night's Play* (1803), but the plot of Ibsen's play was more like that of Shakespeare's *A Midsummer Night's Dream*, with its device of interpenetration of the real and the fairy-tale world, and the problem of the young characters in finding their true partners. The reception was not favorable, and the play was not printed during Ibsen's lifetime.

For the following year's theater anniversary Ibsen presented a revision of *The Burial Mound*. Moving the location of the encounter from Normandy to an island near Sicily, he sharpened the contrast between the brutal and vigorous north and the mild and soft south. The response was not particularly encouraging.

Hettner's book, with its chapter on historical tragedy as a promising and challenging kind of drama for contemporary audiences, probably made Ibsen especially eager to find a subject for such a drama in the history of Norway. The 1520s and 1530s, the age when Norway became a region under Danish rule for many years to come, were studied by scholars in the early 1850s, and in their publications Ibsen found recorded events and characters he could use. In the fall of 1854 he completed *Lady Inger* (*Fru Inger til Østeraad*), a historical tragedy in five acts. It is a prose play about a powerful but indecisive widow in her castle on a dark and stormy night receiving guests and envoys with different political interests and varying diplomatic abilities. The widow has several daughters, but her ambition is to prepare the way for her secret, illegitimate son, raised in SWEDEN, to the vacant Norwegian throne. Among the visitors is a young Swede, whom the lady thinks is her son's rival. She orders him killed and discovers too late that he was her son.

Most of the characters are historical, but the secret son is fictional. Ibsen's main interest was not to illustrate a historical situation, but to present a female character in a central position and to explore her actions and the expressions of her internal conflict at a fateful moment of dynastic and national significance. The plot is complex, with accidental encounters, mistaken identity, and a letter coming into the wrong hands, devices that suggest influence from Eugène Scribe and "the well-made play." The 1855 production did not meet the rather high expectations of the theater, although the critics noted a promising poetic quality in the dialogue. The response of the audience was reserved, but Ibsen was satisfied with what he had achieved. For several years he would occasionally refer to *Lady Inger* as his best play.

The mid-1850s saw an increasing interest in folk ballads and other national traditions, and Ibsen had witnessed the success of Danish playwrights who used music, song, and dance in a medieval setting. He followed their example in *The Feast at Solhaug* (*Gildet på Solhaug*, 1856), a three-act play with a 14th-century action colored by ballad fragments and archaisms. A minstrel who is loved by two sisters is returning home. The sister who has married while the minstrel was away is now rich but unhappy. With so many romantic clichés, the play could not fail to succeed on stage. The critics were friendly, although some later accused the playwright of not being independent enough. *The Feast at Solhaug* was Ibsen's first theatrical success. The Stockholm performance in 1857 was the first of an Ibsen play outside Norway.

Gradually Ibsen gained self-confidence and became more sociable. People with literary interests had approached him earlier, such as the Society of 22nd December, where he was invited to become a member, and where he in November 1855 read a paper on "W. Shackspear and His Influence on Nordic Art." The manuscript has not survived. Some days after the performance of *The Feast at Solhaug* the young playwright was invited to a party at the home of the vicar H. C. Thoresen, whose second wife, Magdalene Thoresen, a playwright herself, was a prominent figure in the literary circles of Bergen. Here Ibsen met Suzannah Thoresen (1836–1914), the daughter of the vicar by his first wife. Henrik and Suzannah were engaged some weeks later and married in 1858. In 1859 their son Sigurd was born.

In 1850 Ibsen had been working on a play based on a folktale from a remote valley in western Norway after the Black Death of 1349. The title was *The Grouse in Justedal* (*Rypen i Justedal*), and nearly two acts were completed before he gave it up. In 1856 he incorporated the central character, Alfhild, the only survivor of the plague in the valley, into a new play based on ballad material, *Olaf Liljekrans*, a romantic drama in three acts. The conflict is typical of the nineteenth century—young people opposing the parents' plans for an arranged marriage, with romantic love triumphing in the end. The first performance on January 2, 1857 was less well received than that of *The Feast at Solhaug*, and the text was not printed until the first edition of Ibsen's *Collected Works* (1902).

Some weeks later Ibsen read a second paper to the Society of 22nd December: "On the Heroic Ballad and Its Significance for the Poetry of Our Time." The manuscript was enlarged and printed in May 1857. It deals with the aesthetic advantages of the ballads, as opposed to the old sagas, as material for dramatic poetry. Having completed two ballad plays, he argues in favor of the ballad style. His ideas on the difference of verse and prose as applied in drama also indicate that he had been giving serious attention to these issues in relation to his own work.

Ibsen's five-year contract with the Bergen theater expired in April 1857 and was renewed for another year. In Christiania a Norwegian theater had been established in 1852, and now Ibsen was offered the post of artistic director. He accepted and was released from the Bergen contract in July 1857.

In the fall of 1856 Oehlenschläger's *The Vikings in Miklagard* had been played at the Bergen theater, and the work on this production may have led Ibsen to search for suitable saga material for a play of his own. Several Icelandic sagas were available in Danish translation. Ibsen found that *Volsunga saga* contained events and characters he could transform into drama, but elements from *Njál's saga*, *Egil's saga*, *Laxdœla saga*, and others can also be found. *The Vikings at Helgeland* (*Hærmændene paa Helgeland*), a play in four acts, completed in Christiania in 1857, was printed in 1858. Oehlenschläger had used blank verse; Ibsen preferred a prose strongly colored by the terse saga style. The most striking character in the play is a woman, Hjørdis, who has been deceived in love and has developed a vindictive temper, while her foster sister Dagny is a conciliatory character. The two are reminiscent of the female opponents in *Catiline*, Furia and Aurelia.

Ibsen had high hopes for a success this time. He offered the play to the main theaters in Christiania and Copenhagen. The Christiania Theater rejected it, apparently for economic reasons, while the Copenhagen Theater gave aesthetic grounds for its rejection, arguing that the brutality of the ancient society, while acceptable in the sagas, would be unpleasant on stage. Ibsen had to take his Viking play to his own theater. The rejection by the Christiania Theater led to a newspaper debate on the repertory policy of the Danish management at the oldest theater in Christiania, and most contributors supported Ibsen. When the play finally was presented on November 24, 1858, to a Norwegian audience, the response was prolonged applause. Even the critics were on the whole positive, more than one claiming that this was the best play written in Norway so far. The success was a lasting one. No other play by Ibsen written before 1864 reached a higher number of performances during his lifetime.

Yet Ibsen had a hard time being in charge of the Christiania Norwegian Theater. The building was small, the ensemble was mainly trained in playing musical comedies and other types of light entertainment, and the economic situation of the theater was not promising. Even the salary he was entitled to could not always be paid. He had plans to write new plays; one of them was to make an opera libretto out of *Olaf Liljekrans*, but he gave it up. He had joined a group of friends, "the Dutchman's circle," scholars and writers who met at the home of Paul Botten-Hansen, an editor and university librarian. The members were critically talented rather than creative and were more attracted to wit and irony than to positive ideas. Ibsen wrote a couple of poems, but on the whole these years were the most difficult ones in his life. Other writers, such as BJØRNSTJERNE BJØRNSON, had received public travel grants, but Ibsen's applications had been rejected. The Christiania Norwegian Theater was closed down in the summer of 1862, and Ibsen had to accept a poorly paid post at the Christiania Theater as an aesthetic adviser. He was depressed and had alcohol problems, but his wife managed to turn his mind back to creative work.

In 1862 he was granted some money by the university; the idea was to collect popular ballads and tales on the western coast. He traveled, mainly on foot, up the Gudbrandsdal, across the mountains to Sogn, and northward through the fjord region, returning home after a couple of months. Some texts were printed from this travel. The impressions he had received from the mountain and fjord scenery turned out to be mental resources he used in his literary work for as long as he continued to write.

In 1860 Ibsen had worked on a prose comedy in a contemporary Christiania setting; the title was *Svanhild*, after the name of the main character, a young girl. In 1862 he made a new start on this project, but changed to verse and found a new title, *Love's Comedy* (*Kjærlighedens komedie*). In this play Ibsen gave free rein to his talent for misanthropic satire. The young poet Falk, in love with Svanhild, wants to preserve his love unimpaired, and so he decides to leave her. The aesthetic attitude to life is underlined by ironic and partly grotesque presentations of couples in various kinds of relationships, from youthful infatuation to marital exhaustion. An artist should take care not to get involved in the trivialities of life. This antisocial cynicism claiming that marriage is bound to have a crippling effect on love was not well accepted by readers, and the play had to wait for more than ten years before it reached the stage in 1873.

Attending a choral festival in Bergen in 1863, Ibsen met old friends, among them the enthusiastic and generous Bjørnson, and this had a remarkable effect on his productivity. On his return he resumed work on a prose drama in five acts based on the saga of King Haakon Haakonsson during the 13th-century civil war. THE PRETENDERS (*Kongs-Emnerne*, 1863) is focused on the rise to power of the young Haakon and the increasing frustration of his father-in-law Skule Baardsson, the duke who has been governing the country and who considers himself the best-qualified statesman. The third protagonist is the cunning Bishop Nikolas, who, in order to secure his own power, seeks to balance the king and the duke against each other, so that neither is the more powerful. The central character is Skule, brooding over the question of who has the right to reign. Covering a number of locations and a quarter of a century and with an impressive range of characters, *The Pretenders* is the most Shakespearean of Ibsen's works. It is also his most successful historical play. First performed at the Christiania Theater in January 1864, it was a turning point in Ibsen's career.

A trip to ITALY was now what he longed for, and friends organized a fund-raising campaign that, together with an allowance by the National Assembly, enabled Ibsen to leave Norway for Rome in the spring of 1864. His wife and son followed him in the fall. For twenty-seven years Ibsen stayed abroad, in Italy and Germany. He was able to observe life and art in areas with venerated cultural traditions. Yet Norway continued to occupy his artistic imagination more than anything else. He dropped Norwegian history and instead turned his attention to his contemporaries. Apparently the geographic distance made it easier for him to address his people as an intellectual moralist. He had seen hypocrisy, spineless politicians, and words without deeds. Traveling through Prussia in 1864, he witnessed the army celebrating the victory over Denmark. A convinced adherent of a Scandinavian union, he blamed the loss of Danish territory on Norwegian and Swedish cowardice.

The resentment that was growing in him inspired the new work he started in Rome, an epic poem about Brand, a clergyman who accuses his people of moral slackness and lack of will. After a year of strenuous work and little progress he decided to write BRAND as a dramatic poem. Now the work advanced quickly and was finished in the fall of 1865. He approached a Danish publisher, Fredrik Hegel of Gyldendal, and after some delay *Brand*, a dramatic poem in five acts, was published in March 1866.

The radical and eloquent moralism voiced by Brand is no doubt inspired by the existentialist philosophy of Søren Kierkegaard. Like Abraham in Kierkegaard's *Fear and Trembling*, Brand is prepared to sacrifice his own son. This uncompromising attitude was controversial, but the poem appealed to a large part of the readership in the 1860s, probably on aesthetic as much as on ethical grounds, and the reception was unprecedented in Scandinavia. The book ran to four printings before the end of 1866, and the author was awarded a poet's pension by the National Assembly. His economic situation was no longer a concern. Although scenically conceived, *Brand* was not written as a play. The whole of it was adapted for the stage and presented in Stockholm in 1885. The performance lasted nearly seven hours.

Ibsen's next work, PEER GYNT, also a dramatic poem in five acts (1867), is generally regarded as a counterpart to *Brand*. Both poems are written in verse, deal with ethical and philosophical issues, and have a Norwegian male as the central character. Yet there are important differences. Brand is true to his fjord parish, while Peer Gynt is constantly on the move, running away from his obligations, partly avoiding consequences of his acts and partly tempted to seek his fortune in brighter-looking circumstances. Originally a folk hero in a Norwegian tale, Peer is transformed into a man of many professions and disguises, but without a spiritual core, and toward the end in danger of being annihilated because of a lack of identity.

Peer Gynt belongs to the tradition of *Everyman* and Johann Wolfgang Goethe's *Faust*. Kierkegaard's philosophy of identity is one element, and so is Georg Wilhelm Friedrich Hegel's view of Egyptian mythology. Wit and irony are more abundant in this than in any other work by Ibsen. On the whole, *Peer Gynt*, whether read as a poem or seen as a play (adapted for the stage and performed for the first time in 1876 at the Christiania Theater, accompanied by Edvard Grieg's music), has been received as a masterpiece of dramatic creation.

In Rome Ibsen had been frequenting the Scandinavian Club, where he met a number of artists and writers and was informed about matters at home. In summer most Scandinavians stayed in cooler areas away from the city, and Ibsen came to know several smaller towns in the hills or along the coast, such as Genzano, Ariccia, Sorrento, Casamicciola, and later Amalfi. In 1868 he left Italy and moved with his family to Dresden, where he wrote his next play, *The League of Youth* (*De unges forbund*, 1869), a prose comedy in five acts. It is a political satire targeting certain liberal politicians whose main object, in Ibsen's opinion, was self-promotion. In the central character, Stensgaard, some critics saw a malicious portrait of Bjørnson, and this affected the reception negatively. Liberal critics claimed that he had deserted them, but Ibsen responded (in a poem),

You say I've become a "conservative."
I remain as I was, every day I live.

He preferred to be above political parties; the liberals were exposed mainly because their side was the more aggressive one in these years. Twenty years earlier Ibsen had entertained radical views, even sympathizing with the labor unions. Over the years he had privately developed an anarchist attitude in politics, not often revealed. In a letter to Georg Brandes of May 18, 1871, he complains that the Paris Commune has "spoiled my excellent state theory—or rather nonstate theory," although he still thinks that it has a sound core. In religious issues he insisted on remaining independent, an observer rather than a believer. In 1869 he was informed by his sister about the death of their mother. Writing back, he comments on his long silence: "I look into myself; there is where I fight my battles, now conquering, now suffering defeat. But I cannot write about all this in a letter. Make no attempts at converting me. I will be honest; what is to come, will come."

A literary celebrity in the Scandinavian countries by now, Ibsen was invited to Stockholm in 1869, where Carl XV decorated him with the Vasa Order and appointed him royal representative at the opening of the Suez Canal. He went via Paris and Marseilles; this and the return trip were his only visits to FRANCE, and the couple of months in Egypt was his only trip outside Europe. A year later he was a revered guest in Copenhagen and received the Order of Dannebrog. In 1873 he attended the Vienna World Exhibition, representing Norway and Denmark as a member of an international art jury. He visited Norway in 1874 and was honored correspondingly.

For some years Ibsen had planned to collect and revise his lyrical poems. The volume of *Poems* (*Digte*, 1871) contained a selection of fifty-five poems, about one-third of his total lyrical production. Most of his efforts in these years were dedicated to the work on his world historical play, EMPEROR AND GALILEAN (*Kejser og Galilœer*, 1873), in two parts of five acts each. He had studied the writings of several historians on the life and short reign of the Roman emperor Julian around A.D. 360. As a writer of historical tragedies, Ibsen had been attracted to characters who choose to stand up against current historical forces and who are doomed to failure. This was the destiny of Catiline, of Lady Inger, and of Duke Skule, and it happened also to Emperor Julian, who turned against Christianity and persecuted the Christians, thereby forcing believers to find new spiritual strength. In this way Julian is presented as a tool of history.

According to Hettner, a historical drama should deal with something that was seen as relevant to the contemporary audience. In the 1870s Europe witnessed several imperial events—Queen Victoria of the British Empire, the fall of Napoleon III of France, the rise of William of Prussia, and others. Another factor was the debate stirred by philosophers critical of the Christian religion. Ibsen felt that he had presented not only a play, but a historical analysis of the final stage of the Roman Empire as well. When the University of Uppsala in Sweden in 1877 prepared for its 400th anniversary, Ibsen was asked if he would accept nomination as an honorary doctor. He was proud to accept and insisted from then on that he be addressed as "the Doctor." He had achieved the position of a man of learning. The critical reception of *Emperor and Galilean* did not confirm his own evaluation. Yet this play was the first of Ibsen's works to be translated into English in full length (by Catherine Ray in 1876). It was first performed in Leipzig in 1896, but not many times after that.

In the 1870s Ibsen spent time revising some of his early plays for a second edition. Significant changes were made in *Lady Inger* (1874) and *Catiline* (1875). Moving from Dresden to Munich in 1875, he observed changes in critical opinion. Historical drama was no longer in the foreground of public interest. Two modern prose plays by Bjørnson had been well received in 1875. Ibsen had met the young Danish critic Georg Brandes; of their correspondence only Ibsen's letters are preserved, but it is well known that Brandes urged him to present controversial issues and make the theater take part in the modernization of European culture.

While sympathetic to the ideological campaign of Brandes, Ibsen was more preoccupied with the questions of dramatic form. The drafts to his next play, PILLARS OF SOCIETY (*Samfundets støtter*, 1877), bear witness to a new strategy. The four acts were originally planned in four different locations; in their final form they all take place in the spacious garden room of Consul Bernick's house. The new DRAMATURGY, with interior scenes prevailing, has a detailed scenography. This is partly an effect of improved stage light with the use of gas and around 1880 electricity in European theaters. Ibsen made the scenographic elements thematically significant. *Pillars of Society* represents a first step in this direction.

The structural pattern of Ibsen's modern prose plays is organized on the basis of narrow versus open space, either in the form of a house interior as opposed to the world outside or as a contrast between the limited social sphere of the action and the larger community represented by visitors. A recurrent device is a visitor or some reminiscence from the past that affects the events of the present. In *Pillars of Society* the rear wall of the garden room is of glass, so the stage can include the outside. In this way the scenography adds to the complexities of the dramatic action. In the first play of this series the family problem is solved after some shocking revelations, whereas the end of most of the later plays is more catastrophic.

The reception of *Pillars of Society* was unanimously positive, particularly in Germany, and Ibsen's fame was by 1877 established beyond the Scandinavian countries. In 1878 the family moved to Rome (where they stayed until 1879, before going to Munich) because of Sigurd's university studies, and Ibsen started a new play, A DOLL'S HOUSE (*Et dukkehjem*, 1879), which was to make him a controversial playwright. The idea expressed in the former play of a citizen's home being like a glass cabinet is here transformed into a children's toy; the flat of the Helmers is metaphorically seen as a doll's miniature home. The spiritual awakening of Nora makes her realize that as a grown-up human being she can no longer stay in the doll's house. Nevertheless, a woman choosing to leave her husband and children was bound to provoke strong reactions. The play and its author met indignant protests.

Ibsen's response was to write a new play, GHOSTS (*Gengangere*, 1881), in which he suggests a possible outcome if the wife decides to stay in the house in spite of the moral decay of the husband. Again the scenography indicates a rear wall of glass, so that Mrs. Alving's garden room becomes a greenhouse, a sphere of protection. She cannot avoid the fatal consequences, however. Because of some unheard ideas and a hypocritical minister, the reaction among readers was almost unanimous rejection, and for nine years no permanent theater would produce the play. Later generations of critics and spectators have praised it as one of the most forceful European dramas.

The vehement protests triggered another response from the playwright, a comedy that appeared only a year later: AN ENEMY OF THE PEOPLE (*En folkefiende*, 1882). Ibsen had been accused of bringing moral pollution to the public stage, letting his characters hint at unspeakable conditions such as venereal disease and incest. In the new play the doctor of a spa has discovered that the water is polluted, but instead of receiving thanks when he informs the authorities about necessary measures, he is fired from his job and persecuted by the mob. The focus changes from physical to ideological pollution, and the political loser becomes the moral winner.

In Rome Ibsen met a young Danish writer, J. P. Jacobsen, who was the translator of Charles Darwin's *On the Origin of Species*. Earlier, as in *Peer Gynt*, Ibsen had stressed the essential difference between men and animals, but the knowledge of Darwin's work made him emphasize the similarities, for example, in Doctor Stockmann's lecture in act 4 of *An Enemy of the People*. The device is used in a more subtle way in the next play, THE WILD DUCK (*Vildanden*, 1884), where the Ekdals keep rabbits, hens, pigeons, and a duck in the attic of their flat. Darwin discusses the effects of domestication on these species, whereas Ibsen's play refers to the caged animals in their miserable indoor existence deprived of a life in natural surroundings—a parable of the kind of life led by the members of the Ekdal family, as well as the chamberlains at the dinner party in act 1. The demand for uncompromising truth is in this play replaced by a question concerning the necessity of illusion in some instances. *The Wild Duck* sold well and was performed without delay in several Scandinavian cities. Yet the public and the critics were confused; there seemed to be no central character one could identify with.

The political situation of Norway during the early 1880s had been marked by a growing liberal opposition to the conservative, royally appointed government on the issue of parliamentarism. The Liberals insisted that cabinet ministers were to be held accountable to the National Assembly, whereas the Conservatives defended the constitutional practice of separating the legislative and the executive powers. The fierceness of the struggle was abhorrent to Ibsen, who spent three summer months in Norway in 1885 before moving to Munich, after five years in Rome (from 1881 to 1885). The action of ROSMERSHOLM (1886), the first play of the Munich trilogy, takes place in a somber mansion where the ancestors seem to watch the present inhabitants from their portraits on the walls. The last descendant of the family, who is determined to keep aloof from party politics, has developed an ambitious plan to instigate nobility of character in human beings, but events of the past that led to the suicide of his wife have made him doubt his spiritual power. His lady friend is also affected by the past. They can both restore their freedom from guilt only by going the way the late Mrs. Rosmer went. It would seem that Ibsen in this play is trying to achieve the same sense of unavoidability as can be found in Greek tragedies. Again the response was one of uncertainty.

In THE LADY FROM THE SEA (*Fruen fra havet*, 1888) the majority of the acts are played in open-air decorations. The contrast between narrow and open space is marked through various degrees of confinement, ranging from the stagnant carp pond in the garden to the fjord in the background with mountain ranges, with references to the ocean beyond as the sphere of freedom. The mentally suffering Ellida Wangel is healed when she is given the freedom to choose between staying in her marriage or leaving town together with her onetime fiancé. Her well-being is a matter of acclimatization, a central concept in Darwin's work as well. The play reveals a Darwinian influence also in some references to the origin of life in the sea.

Georg Brandes had discovered the philosophy of FRIEDRICH NIETZSCHE in 1888 and published the following year his essay about the German philosopher. Ibsen sensed the importance of Nietzsche's cultural criticism, and there are traces of these ideas in most of the plays he wrote in the 1890s. In HEDDA GABLER (1890) social rank is essential to the central character. The general's daughter has married a scholar with limited means and feels trapped. The distinction between master and servant is both social and intellectual. Hedda entertains some obsolete conceptions about beauty and honor and is frustrated when her ambitions to be able to control the life and death of others are thwarted, while others threaten to control her instead. The play was welcomed by female critics who saw Hedda as a truthful representation of a woman left without a meaningful task in a male-dominated society, whereas some male critics regarded her as a monster.

In 1891 Ibsen decided to end his self-imposed exile and settle in Christiania. By now his fame as a playwright was well established in France and England and growing in the United States. He preferred a quiet life with regular habits, devoted to writing plays and publishing a new one every other fall. Since the mid-1870s he had stopped publishing new poems. He took some interest in young writers and artists, people who were moving in new directions. The position of an aging architect facing impatient young people is presented in the next play, THE MASTER BUILDER (*Bygmester Solness*, 1892). The mental strength of the main character seems to give him a mysterious kind of power over his environment, particularly over young women. In Hilde, however, he faces his superior, who by an act of will is able to drive him on toward a catastrophic end. This may be an attempt by Ibsen to make dramatic use of Nietzsche's concept of will to power.

In this and the other last plays the protagonist—a middle-aged or aging man who has achieved a certain position—is led to reflect on his life and career, testing his conscience, because of reproaches presented by his female companion. In LITTLE EYOLF (*Lille Eyolf*, 1894) the man and wife have to go through a painful process of mourning after their only son has drowned. The reproach is mutual, but they are sincere and manage to reach reconciliation. The central character of JOHN GABRIEL BORKMAN (1896) is old and beyond self-reproach. He has been waiting in vain to be called on to resume his leading position in the bank, but when he finally walks out into the winter landscape, he does not survive. The sculptor Arnold Rubek in the dramatic epilogue WHEN WE DEAD AWAKEN (*Når vi døde vågner*, 1899) also ends his life in the snow, in a fatal attempt to consummate a relationship that in his youth had been the basis of his artistic creativity.

Ibsen had not intended the epilogue to be his final play; it was merely the last one of the series of modern prose plays. He had further plans. His health failed, however, and his last years were marred by an inability to write. He died on May 23, 1906, in Christiania. At his death he was generally regarded as the world's leading playwright.

Ibsen's influence on 20th-century drama is not easily defined. He knew theatrical technique from the inside, and he was a keen observer of contemporary currents in moral philosophy. He developed a drama form that is unsurpassed in combining powerful dramatic illusion and rich poetic significance. The construction of plot and character in his mature plays does not aim at clear-cut solutions. The ambiguity, as well as the universal issues presented, remains open to new approaches in a way that has continued to vitalize modern theater, as well as modern drama, in many corners of the world. Ibsen the father of modern drama managed to move the frontiers without losing contact with readers and theater audiences.

PLAYS: *Catiline* (1850); *The Burial Mound* (1850); *Norma; or, The Love of a Politician* (1851); *St. John's Night* (1853); *Lady Inger* (1855); *The Feast at Solhaug* (1856); *Olaf Liljekrans* (1857); *The Vikings at Helgeland* (1858); *Love's Comedy* (1862); *The Pretenders* (1863); *Brand* (1866); *Peer Gynt* (1867); *The League of Youth* (1869); *Emperor and Galilean* (1873); *Pillars of Society* (1877); *A Doll's House* (1879); *Ghosts* (1881); *An Enemy of the People* (1882); *The Wild Duck* (1884); *Rosmersholm* (1886); *The Lady from the Sea* (1888); *Hedda Gabler* (1890); *The Master Builder* (1892); *Little Eyolf* (1894); *John Gabriel Borkman* (1896); *When We Dead Awaken* (1899)

FURTHER READING

Bradbrook, M. C. *Ibsen the Norwegian*. London: Chatto, 1966.

Clurman, Harold. *Ibsen*. New York: Macmillan, 1977.

Jæger, Henrik. *Henrik Ibsen, 1828–1888: A Critical Biography*. Tr. by William Morton Payne. Chicago: McClurg, 1890.

Koht, Halvdan. *Life of Ibsen*. Tr. by Einar Haugen and A. E. Santaniello. New York: Blom, 1971.

McFarlane, James. *Ibsen and Meaning: Studies, Essays and Prefaces, 1953–87*, Norwich: Norvik Press, 1989.

Meyer, Michael. *Ibsen*. Garden City, N.Y.: Doubleday, 1971.

Asbjørn Aarseth

ICELAND

The history of Iceland goes back only to the second part of the 9th century A.D., the time of settlement. The history of Icelandic theater is even younger; the history of theater in the modern sense is younger yet. The year 1860 can serve as a portal as good as any. Before 1860 one can note some worthwhile COMEDIES in the vein of Ludvig Holberg and Molière, especially Sigurður Pétursson's (1759–1827) *Hrólfun* and *Narfi*, written at the end of the 18th century as part of the revelries of the Latin School, which were based on the boy bishop tradition and the feast of fools of medieval times. But it was not until 1860 that a continuous flow of playwriting existed together with an intense theater activity in the awakening commercial and fishing villages around the coast, in the rural areas, and in the schools.

FOR PURPOSE OR PLEASURE?

During the 19th century, theater in Iceland was amateur theater. The tradition of singing, reading aloud, or other forms of entertainment in the isolated farms around the country was replaced by theater in the small villages and towns, to which people flocked when new fishing methods opened access to new jobs and new modes of life. In the sixty years from 1860 to 1920 the whole society underwent radical changes, from being predominantly rural, suffering from Danish commercial monopoly, to becoming a modern state with towns and villages along with the countryside, culminating when Iceland was proclaimed a sovereign state in 1918. Recent research has shown that this feeling of progress manifested itself in a theatrical ecstasy. During these sixty years one can trace rigorous activities in all the approximately fifty villages; as soon as the number of inhabitants reached 100, they put on a play, and many of these plays were Icelandic.

The most influential animator behind this movement was a painter, Sigurður Guðmundsson (1833–1874), who returned to Reykjavík from his studies at the Academy in Copenhagen, DENMARK, and immediately became involved in the theater representations in the capital, then a town of no more than 4,000 people. He inspired his pupils to write dramas and pointed to the history of Iceland, exceptionally well documented, and its rich folklore and folktales as suitable subject matters. The first to answer the call was a pupil at the Latin School in Reykjavík, Matthías Jochumsson (1835–1920), who later became a leading poet and author of the national anthem. Jochumsson's play *The Outlaws* (*Útilegumennirnir*), later renamed *Skugga-Sveinn* after one of its leading characters, was first presented in 1862, became an instant success, and has been popular with Icelandic audiences ever since. The play, set in the 17th century, has a pure, naïve tone that gives it a poetic and comic quality that has made it a candidate for the title "the national play," if such a title exists. Another of Sigurður Guðmundsson's pupils was Indriði Einarsson (1851–1939), who in 1871, then also a pupil at the Latin School, wrote another play with themes from the folk tradition of elves or the hidden people, titled *New Year's Eve* (*Nýársnóttin*). Even more than *Skugga-Sveinn*, this play corresponded to the nationalistic feelings of the last decades of Icelanders' struggle for independence.

Until the arrival of Sigurður Guðmundsson all theater activities had been looked upon as pastime and mere entertainment. For him, however, they had another meaning as well: the theater was a means of educating the people, opening the eyes of the audience to the life and thoughts of other civilizations, an aesthetic enjoyment, and not least a token of a healthy national identity.

PLAYWRITING IS BORN

The example of Matthías Jochumsson and Indriði Einarsson inspired others, and a flow of "school plays" followed. Set in rural surroundings, these plays were a sort of comedy of manners and can be seen partly as a continuation of the pattern laid out by Sigurður Pétursson, partly as a nationalistic-romantic illustration of Sigurður Guðmundsson's ideals. The latter may be even more the correct description of plays by a number of rural playwrights who appeared from the 1860s to the 1890s, reacting to the tendency of the Danish merchants in the commercial villages to play Danish vaudevilles in Danish.

Both Matthías Jochumsson and Indriði Einarsson later wrote a handful of plays, some of them based on historical themes, as Sigurður Guðmundsson had emphasized, using Shakespeare's chronicle plays as good examples. Matthías Jochumsson's masterwork in this genre was *Jón Arason* (1900), on the fate of the last Catholic bishop in Iceland, who was beheaded in 1550. Some claim that Indriði Einarsson's *Sword and Crozier* (*Sverð og bagall*, 1899), with themes from *Sturlunga saga*, is his best play. Both needed a bigger stage than was at hand in 1900.

But the scene was changing. In 1897 Leikfélag Reykjavíkur (the Reykjavík Theater Company) was founded, and this group, in contrast to former amateur groups and others in the bigger towns and villages such as Akureyri and Ísafjörður that came into existence during this period, had a different aim, that of producing what it labeled theatrical arts, comparable to theater in neighboring countries. This ambition was parallel to other developments in the changing society, such as the opening of a university in 1911 and the establishment of a supreme court in 1920 and a national bank. This development went hand in hand with growing urbanization and the arrival of trawlers that revolutionized the fisheries and drew many farmworkers from the countryside to the towns and villages. This was also the age of the awakening labor movement, and as in FINLAND and IRELAND, the establishment of a worthwhile ambitious theater was interwoven with the endeavors of the labor movement and the Good-Templar Order. The idea of a national theater was born.

One of the main tasks of a national theater is usually to promote national playwriting, and to deserve such an official theater, one must show that there is an existing drama tradition mirroring the society where it is built and a theater group capable of presenting plays in an adequate manner. It became the task of the Reykjavík Theater Company to prove to decision makers that these conditions were met. It changed course in the choice of repertoire from Danish vaudevilles and classical comedies to the plays of the day, realistic bourgeois dramas of HENRIK IBSEN, BJØRNSTERJNE BJØRNSON, HERMAN SUDERMANN, and others. Even the old romantic-nationalistic drama had to give way, and one of its chief apostles, Indriði Einarsson, wrote the first realistic Ibsen-inspired urban drama, *The Ship Goes Down* (*Skipið sekkur*), presented by the Reykjavík Theater Company in 1903.

THE ICELANDIC PERIOD

There were two ways of proving that the praise of the Icelandic press bestowed on this young theater was not simply an outburst of provincial chauvinistic feeling: that of touring abroad, as, for example, the Abbey Players in Ireland did, and as was customary within the Scandinavian countries, where the language did not bar or discourage the audience from attending, or that of writing worthwhile plays that tempted foreign companies. The latter was what occurred. Around 1910 new winds were blowing, symbolistic and neoromantic, with a taste for the exotic. At first some of the existing Icelandic plays were translated into foreign languages without being staged abroad. Then two young Icelandic would-be dramatists, JOHANN SIGURJONSSON (1880–1919) and Guðmundur Kamban (1888–1945), turned to writing simultaneously in Danish and Icelandic, and that broke the ice. After an unprecedented success in Reykjavík at its first production at Christmas 1911, Sigurjonsson's *Eyvind of the Mountains* (*Fjalla-Eyvindur*) was hailed as the most important event of the Copenhagen season in May 1912 and then triumphed in many European countries in following seasons.

Guðmundur Kamban's first plays were in the same neoromantic vein. Although they were set in modern times, the critics spoke of the sagalike heroines and the poetic atmosphere and language. *Hadda Padda* (1914) was first performed at the Royal Theatre in Copenhagen with considerable success and then was acclaimed in Reykjavík a few months later. It has a rural setting and concerns a crime of passion. His second play, *The Wrestling of the Kings* (*Konungsglíman*), describes the new urban milieu of the growing capital, Reykjavík, with its political battles. Both plays, in spite of the lyrical tone, bear witness to the fact that Sigmund Freud has arrived on the scene and treat moral issues, a trait that Kamban followed throughout his career.

In 1915 Kamban went to New York, possibly with the dream of becoming an author in the English language to gain a wider audience. That came to nothing, and he returned to Copenhagen in 1917, where he worked as a writer and theater director (and incidentally Iceland's first film director) for the rest of his life.

Kamban's stay in America left a deep impression on his development as an author, and moral problems were predominant in most of his plays. These include *Marble* (*Marmari*, 1918), in which he satirizes American society, taking charity foundations and child labor as examples and advocating a new approach to punishment. This play, in contrast to all his other plays, was never produced during Kamban's lifetime; a production in Germany was stopped when the Nazis took over, and the first production was in Reykjavík in 1945. Kamban's masterpiece, however, is the realistic drama *We Murderers* (*Vér morðingjar*, 1919, first produced in Copenhagen that same year), a well-made play set in New York and a Strindbergian tale of innocence and guilt, of jealousy and crime. Surprisingly, this well-made play is not as well known as it deserves to be.

The period 1907–1920 has been called the Icelandic period in the theater history of Iceland. Every season offered a couple of newly written plays. Apart from the plays of Kamban and Sigurjonsson, some new authors followed in their neoromantic footsteps, whereas Indriði Einarsson continued with some plays in his former antirealistic style (the best of these being the verse drama *Dansinn í Hruna*, 1921, first produced in 1925, based on a folktale equivalent to the dance at Kölbigk), and the otherwise realistic novelist Einar Hjörleifsson Kvaran (1859–1938), who from time to time worked as a stage director, wrote a popular historical play, *Magistrate Leonhard* (*Lénharður fógeti*, 1913), which coincided with the feeling of strengthened national identity in the wake of independence.

The exports of Icelandic playwriting to other countries, however, came to a halt. There may be several reasons, but World War I hindered many plans of producing these plays. After the war it was obvious that the old world had collapsed, and a new world had to be built with a new identity. Exotic neoromanticism was not valid any more; the plays of LUIGI PIRANDELLO (introduced in Reykjavík in 1926) and the German expressionists better corresponded to that search for identity. Johann Sigurjonsson never became the international classic he possibly was gifted to be, and he and Kamban today have to content themselves with being classics on the Icelandic stage.

TOWARD A NATIONAL THEATER

In 1922 a bill was passed in the old Icelandic Parliament (established in 930) on building a full-fledged National Theater. However, it took more time than anticipated and was at last inaugurated in 1950. The period from 1920 up to the opening of the National Theater was not a period of flourishing drama in Iceland. Few of the plays presented have survived their first production or are likely to be revived. One of them is Davíð Stefánsson's (1895–1964) *The Golden Gate* (*Gullna hliðið*, 1941), a humorously charming folktale about a woman who tried to get her beloved and frail husband to heaven at the risk of her own damnation that has remained immensely popular with Icelandic audiences in several revivals and is in fact competing with *Skugga-Sveinn* as the "national play." Another of a very different sort is Sigurður Nordal's (1886–1974) *Ascension* (*Uppstigning*), which plays with roles in society and with dreams and reality in a JOHN BOYNTON PRIESTLEY–like form.

Unfortunately the opening of the National Theater did not change the situation for the better. The most prolific arrivals were those of Agnar Þórðarson (1917–2006), who mainly wrote for the theater in the 1950s and 1960s and was at his best in realistic comedies (*Atomic Power and Sexual Attractions* [*Kjarnorka og kvenhylli*, 1956]), and the brothers Jónas Árnason (1923–1998) and Jón Múli Árnason (1921–2002) with *Delerium búbonis* (1959), the first of many successful musicals. An important event was the turn of Nobel Prize novelist Halldór Laxness (1902–1998) to playwrighting. He had written his first play in 1933, at the opening of the National Theater a dramatization of his *Bell of Iceland* became a hit, and now he tried his hand at writing directly for the stage. These plays included the satiric *The Silvery Mood* (*Silfurtúnglið*, 1954), *The Chimney Play* (*Stompleikurinn*, 1961), *The Sewing Factory the "Sun"* (*Prjónastofan Sólin*, 1966), and, the most successful, *The Dove Banquet* (*Dúfnaveislan*, 1966). These highly original and somewhat controversial plays were influenced by the reigning ABSURDISM of these days, also with some side glimpses to BERTOLT BRECHT, but with a tone and color and humor of their own. All are satires, where, for instance, the frugal attitude of Taoism is confronted with the greed of the consumer society where everything is for sale. Several of Laxness's novels have been adapted for the stage, including the successful *Christianity Under the Glacier* (1970).

THE NEW WAVE

But at the beginning of the 1960s a wave of new playwrights emerged. It is customary to attribute this new era to the first performance of Jökull Jakobsson's (1933–1978) play *Hard-a-Port* (*Hart í bak*) in 1962, but the same season also saw the first performances of Oddur Björnsson's (1932–) one-act plays at the independent Gríma group, and the role of Halldór Laxness in the process should not be overlooked. *Hard-a-Port* was produced by the Reykjavík Theater Company, running for three successive seasons and beating all former public records. Indeed, it was the Reykjavík Theatre Company that took the lead once more with a consistent policy of promoting new Icelandic plays, with the motivation that it was the duty of the theater to mirror its own society. Other theaters, the National Theatre, the professional theater in Akureyri, numerous independent theater groups, and even the sixty amateur groups around the country in due course followed the pattern. New Icelandic plays have been a significant part of the repertoire for nearly half a century, in many seasons constituting up to 40 percent of what was offered and often being the plays that drew the biggest audience. And the audience is large, in some seasons outnumbering the total population.

These plays are extremely varied, and there is no way of talking about an "Icelandic school" in playwriting. But at the same time as they are part of international world drama, influenced by absurdism, Bertolt Brecht, the democratically rooted social criticism of emerging groups, especially in the 1970s and 1980s, and the experiments of avant-garde movements, it cannot be denied that they mirror modern Icelandic society quite effectively.

And this society is in most ways different from the rural community encountered in 1860, based mainly on agriculture, or the community around 1900, when fishing and fishing products more and more made their impact and remained important until recently. From being one of the poorest nations, Iceland now ranks among the most prosperous per capita, with a complex and diverse society. Fishing is still the greatest source of exports, but only ten percent of the population makes a living on fishing. The economy has many pillars (energy and software, to mention two of the newest). Culture has its share in this development, not as an ornament to economic and political development but as a participant and stakeholder.

Dramatists have noted the waves and winds and painted corresponding pictures. Many of the generation after World War II were highly influenced by absurdism, including the previously mentioned Oddur Björnsson with, for example, his one-act play *Yolk-Life* (*Jóðlíf*, 1965), *A Grand Ball* (*Dansleikur*, 1974), and *The 13th Crusade* (*13. krossferðin*, 1993), but at the same time he is a political moralist and philosopher (and his humor is very special). Guðmundur Steinsson (1925–1996) started his career with political satires inspired by the Cold War and the fact that in Iceland there was a foreign military base, which divided the whole nation into two blocs. In his later works, such as *Viva Espana!* (*Sólarferð*, 1976) and especially *A Brief Respite* (*Stundarfriður*, 1978), one of the most resounding successes in Icelandic theater of that period, he draws a picture of the alienation and lack of tenderness in our career-minded times expressed not least through the inarticulation of the language of the characters. In his original version of the biblical Adam and Eve theme,

The Garden Party (*Garðveislan*, 1982), Christ is portrayed by a black woman.

Jökull Jakobsson's style, after a realistic Chekovian beginning, was also influenced by the absurdists, although he soon, like HAROLD PINTER, found his own way with an ambiguous dialogue contemplating time and space and the role of the individual in society, as seen by himself or others. Outstanding among this popular playwright's works are his chamber trilogy *Domino* (1972), *Room 213* (*Herbergi 213*, 1974), and *In a Strong City* (*Í öruggri borg*, 1980), with its delicate balance of reality and unreality; the tender *A Light of the Candle* (*Kertalog*, 1974), which takes place in a lunatic asylum; and the ambitious *The Song of Mylai* (*Sonur skóarans og dóttir bakarans*, 1978), where the global conscience of mankind is echoed through the Vietnam War.

More realistic in style is Birgir Sigurðsson (1937–), who in his *Day of Hope* (*Dagur vonar*, 1987) wrote a powerful, well-made domestic drama. Ólafur Haukur Símonarson (1947–), one of the most prolific of this succession of playwrights, is also less experimental with form and style, but no less impressive. Standing out in his oeuvre is *The Sea* (*Hafið*, 1992, later a film with the same title), a poignant description of a society in transition. Mention should also be made of his play about and for teenagers, *Hoolaballoo* (*Gauragangur*, 1993), and his latest play, *The Green Land* (*Grœana landið*, 2004), on the process of becoming old.

The brothers Jónas and Jón Múli Árnason continued their collaboration with many musicals, including *The Iron Head* (*Járnhausinn*, 1964), but Jónas alone wrote several highly successful satirical comedies with an Irish-like humor. Outstanding among them were *Dead Still* (*Koppalogn*, actually two one-acts, 1966); *You Remember Jörundur* (*Þið munið hann Jörund*, 1969), about a Danish adventurer who made himself a king in Iceland during the Napoleonic Wars; and *Operation Shield Rock* (*Skjaldhamrar*, 1975), about espionage in Iceland during World War II. Satire and humor are also among the many-sided theater personality Kjartan Ragnarsson's (1945–) qualities. Among his works, the black comedy *The Missing Teaspoon* (*Týnda teskeiðin*, 1977) deserves a mention, as does the highly successful musical *Fatherland* (*Land míns föður*, 1985), which he wrote with composer Atli Heimir Sveinsson, and his dramatizations of the novels of Halldór Laxness and Þórbergur Þórðarson. Several other successful playwrights deserve a mention, such as Svava Jakobsdóttir (1930–2004), Nína Björk Árnadóttir (1941–2000), Vésteinn Lúðvíksson (1944–), and Þórunn Sigurðardóttir (1944–).

The list is long. The poet Sigurður Pálsson (1948–) has several plays to his credit, including the ingenious *Someone at the Door* (*Einhver í dyrunumr*, 2000), and so has Árni Ibsen (1948–) with his highly original farces and comedies, including *Heaven* (*Himnaríki*, 1995) and *Forever* (*Að eilífur*, 1997). Of a different kind is his deeply felt *Elín Helena* (1993), which is about a search for identity. A search for identity is also the theme of Hrafnhildur Hagalín Guðmundsdóttir's (1965–) plays *I Am the Maestro* (*Ég er meistarinn*, 1990) and *Easy Now, Elektra* (*Hœagan, Elektra*, 2000). Most of the plays mentioned and several others have been produced outside Iceland in recent years.

Among the younger generation of playwrights, many deserve a mention. These include Þorvaldur Þorsteinsson (1960–), Hávar Sigurjónsson (1958–), Bjarni Jónsson (1966–), and Jón Atli Jónasson (1972–).

FURTHER READING

Einarsson, Sveinn. "Íslensk leikritun." In *Íslensk leiklist*, vol. 2. Reykjavík: Hið íslenska bókmenntafélag, 1996.

——. *A People's Theatre Comes of Age*. Reykjavík: Háskólaútgáfan, 2006.

Ibsen, Árni. "Íslensk leikritun frá upplýsingu til fullveldis." In *Íslensk bókmenntasaga*, vol. 5, ed. by Halldór Guðmundsson. Reykjavík: Mal og menning, 1996.

Kress, Helga. *Guðmundur Kamban: Æskuverk og ádeilur*. Studia Islandica 29. Reykjavík: Bókaútgáfa Menningarsjóðs, 1970.

Sigurðardóttir, Fríða Á. *Leikrit Jökuls Jakobssonar*. Studia Islandica 38. Reykjavík: Bókaútgáfa Menningarsjóðs, 1980.

Sveinn Einarsson

THE ICEMAN COMETH

I know now from experience what a lying pipe dream can do to you.

—Hickey, Act 1

The Theatre Guild produced EUGENE O'NEILL's *The Iceman Cometh* on October 9, 1946. The action was set in 1912 in Harry Hope's saloon, "a cheap ginmill of the five-cent whiskey, last-resort variety" on the downtown West Side of Manhattan, based on various Hell's Kitchen dives of O'Neill's youth but especially on the flophouse run by "Jimmy the Priest," where the playwright lived between voyages in 1912. The back room is dark, crowded, and grimy, and it serves as home for a gathering of the lost.

Larry Slade scratches his lice without noticing them; his "gaunt Irish face" recalls other O'Neill characters, and his pipe dreams "are all dead and buried." Hugo Kalmar is an anarchist who is "through with the Movement" because he "saw men didn't want to be saved from themselves, for that would mean they'd have to give up greed, and they'll never pay that price for liberty." Joe Mott, a "colored" man, takes pride in the many occasions when white men accepted him into their games and fights. "Jimmy Tomorrow" was once a gentleman but started drinking when he found his wife sleeping with another man. Harry is a bag of bones with "the face of an old family horse," but also a "softhearted slob" and "a sinner among sinners, a born easy mark for every appeal." His other roomers include his brother-in-law, a police lieutenant, a lawyer, a Boer soldier, a British infantry captain, a pair of streetwalkers, and both of his bartenders.

Young Don Parritt hopes to understand his past by finding Larry, who was once his mother's lover. He asks what the men do for a living; Larry explains, "They manage to get drunk, by hook or crook, and keep their pipe dreams, and that's all they ask of life. I've never known more contented men."

Hickey is a traveling salesman who has been their favorite crony, but they are shocked when he tells them that he has stopped drinking. He does not condemn "the stuff," because "it's given me too many good times," and he will not try to peddle "some brand of temperance bunk" to anyone else, but "I finally had the guts to face myself and throw overboard the damned lying pipe dream that'd been making me miserable," and he found—so he claims—that he did not need to drink any more. He urges them to stop kidding themselves about what they might do tomorrow and face the present with honesty. He offers not pity that lets a man keep lying to himself, but sympathy that is "after final results that will really save the poor guy, and make him contented with what he is, and quit battling with himself, and find peace for the rest of his life." Hickey is a messianic figure come to offer salvation to the damned.

They try to celebrate Harry's sixtieth birthday, but they resent Hickey for inducing them to doubt themselves. Larry asks him, "Did this great revelation of the evil habit of dreaming about tomorrow come to you after you found your wife was sick of you?" Most of the men try to face their demons, but much to Hickey's exasperation, they are miserable in consequence. He finally confesses that he killed his wife as the only way to make up for the suffering he had brought her and to "free her from the misery of loving me." The police take him away, and the roomers once again find pleasure and oblivion in drink and fellowship. Only Larry sits apart, watching in anguish as Parritt throws himself out of an upper-story fire escape to atone for having betrayed his mother.

The play echoes HENRIK IBSEN'S *THE WILD DUCK* in the exploration of the destructive effect of living a lie, and it anticipates SAMUEL BECKETT'S *WAITING FOR GODOT* in the characters' weary sense of stasis. O'Neill stages the godless world of FRIEDRICH NIETZSCHE, yet the casting structure and the nature of the gathering evoke the Last Supper of Christian tradition. In terms of Greek TRAGEDY, the three principal actors are Hickey, Slade, and Parritt; Harry Hope is the *choregos* (leader of the chorus); and the others constitute the chorus.

In *The New York Times* (October 10, 1946), critic Brooks Atkinson called it "a dark and somber play" and announced that O'Neill had "plunged again into the black quagmire of man's illusions and composed a rigadoon of death." Eric Bentley, of *The Atlantic Monthly* (November 1946), saw two stories, Hickey's and Parritt's, and explained that "human wrecks, then kept afloat only by pipe dreams, form a kind of choral setting." According to Richard Watts, Jr., in the *New York Post* (May 9, 1956), the play argued that "some sort of illusions are necessary in a bleak world and . . . some men are lost without them."

[*See also* Apocalypse in Modern Drama; Naturalism; Philosophy and Drama, 1860–1960; Realism; United States, 1940–Present]

FURTHER READING

Diggins, John Patrick. " 'The Secret of the Soul': Eugene O'Neill's *The Iceman Cometh*." *Raritan* 19 (Summer 1999): 63–76.

Dugan, Lawrence. "O'Neill and the Wobblies: The IWW as a Model for Failure in *The Iceman Cometh*." *Comparative Drama* 36 (Spring–Summer 2002): 109–124.

Manheim, Michael. "The Transcendence of Melodrama in O'Neill's *The Iceman Cometh*." In *Critical Essays on Eugene O'Neill*, ed. by James J. Martine. Boston: G. K. Hall, 1984. 145–158.

Murphy, Brenda. "The 'Genius' as Iceman: Eugene O'Neill's Portrayal of Theodore Dreiser." *American Literary Realism* 34 (Winter 2002): 135–145.

Raleigh, J. H., ed. *Twentieth Century Interpretations of "The Iceman Cometh": A Collection of Critical Essays*. Englewood Cliffs, N.J.: Prentice-Hall, 1968.

Vera, Yvonne. "Observation as System in Eugene O'Neill's *The Iceman Cometh*." *Modern Drama* 39 (Fall 1996): 448–456.

Jeffrey D. Mason

IDENTITY THEATER

Identity theater explores the problematic nature of identity politics and the question of an individual's sense of location or dislocation in relation to a dominant cultural, social, and political structure. Designed to address the experience of marginalized groups from within the perspective of the group itself, identity theater gives performative voice to their concerns and offers counternarratives to mainstream discourses about those groups and their place in the larger society. These theaters work to undo stereotypical representations of the particular group, to provide new personal and cultural histories that have previously been silenced or rendered invisible, and to serve as pedagogical interventions in the public sphere. In bringing to light and contesting sociopolitical parameters, these theaters investigate questions of power and offer possibilities for alternative social paradigms. As an active method of cultural dialogue, identity theater can forge new alliances within and across communities.

There is a long history to the development of identity theater, but in the last few decades this genre has been fueled by a number of convergences ranging from the profound impact of the civil rights and Black Power movements in the UNITED STATES in the 1960s to a growing internationalism in the contemporary world. Artistic factors include the history of interests in combining politics and art through the work of, for example, the surrealists and AUGUSTO BOAL. The surrealists promulgated a collaborative artistic practice through the use of games that allowed for input from all the participants. This approach provided techniques for bringing together bits and pieces of multiple perspectives into a transformed communal space. Augusto Boal's theatrical work, designed as performance forums for the disenfranchised, also engenders a space for other voices.

Many identity theaters draw on an amalgamation of theatrical techniques and practices, including traditional ones from their respective cultures, in order to stage questions of identity and to create new processes of representation. Additionally, transnational exchange among artists has increased interest in identity theater as a means both of articulating local histories and of building alliances across geographic boundaries. Contemporary identity theater in the United States has come to include a wide variety of works, such as those by African American, Asian American, Hispanic American, feminist, and disability theater practitioners. Numerous diasporic theaters are also emerging from the African, Caribbean, and South Asian experience. While much identity theater work has gained national and international renown, considerable work has been done and is being done that has not yet been properly archived and analyzed.

One of these diasporic theaters, Tara Arts—the preeminent South Asian theater, based in London, ENGLAND—had its genesis in 1976 in response to the murder of a young South Asian boy. Interested in educating the general British population about the presence and history of the South Asian Britons in England, the company performs many works based on collections of oral histories or revisions of Indian stories within contemporary England. The trilogy *Journey to the West* (2001) chronicles the difficult journey of South Asians from India to East Africa to work as indentured servants on the railroads in the early 1900s, their later flight from Kenya in the 1960s and 1970s to England, and life in Britain in 2000. The work gives voice to numerous personal, cultural, and political histories. It also reflects the hybridity of the South Asian imagination in Britain. In the last section of the trilogy—contemporary England—characters are both Indian and British, both Hindu and Muslim, and the dialogue often includes what director Jatinder Verma has called "Binglish" in order to capture more fully the "double consciousness" (W. E. B. DuBois's term) of their lives.

The use of multiple performance techniques and community-based interventions can be seen in a wide variety of identity theaters. These projects intend to contest the dominant culture's instantiation of ethnic identity, gender, and normative bodies. In so doing, identity theaters provide a powerful forum for challenging, critiquing, and revising the status quo in favor of a greater inclusiveness.

[*See also* Black Arts Movement; Feminist Drama in the United States; Gay and Lesbian Drama]

FURTHER READING

Bean, Annemarie, ed. *A Sourcebook of African-American Performance: Plays, People, Movements*. Worlds of Performance. New York: Routledge, 1999.

Canning, Charlotte. *Feminist Theaters in the U.S.A.: Staging Women's Experience*. New York: Routledge, 1996.

Geiogamah, Hanay, and Jaye T. Darby, eds. *American Indian Theater in Performance: A Reader*. Los Angeles: UCLA American Indian Studies Center, 2000.

Hill, Errol. *The Theater of Black Americans*. New York: Applause, 1987.

Kuppers, Petra. *Disability and Contemporary Performance: Bodies on Edge*. New York: Routledge, 2004.

Lee, Josephine. *Performing Asian America: Race and Ethnicity on the Contemporary Stage*. Philadelphia: Temple Univ. Press, 1997.

Uno, Roberta, ed. *The Color of Theater: Race, Culture, and Contemporary Performance*. New York: Continuum, 2002.

Kanta Kochhar-Lindgren

IDIOT'S DELIGHT

During the mid-1930s ROBERT E. SHERWOOD pondered the world around him—Harbin, Manchuria, under siege by Japan in 1933 waiting for the bombs to fall, his own disillusionment as he waited in Reno for his divorce, the sad group of American chorus girls in Budapest, the frightened governments, and the "little people" bringing about their own destruction. His reaction in 1935 was *Idiot's Delight*, written for Alfred Lunt and Lynn Fontanne. The opening of *Idiot's Delight* in New York on March 24, 1936, was a fine success, the actors receiving nineteen curtain calls. Sherwood was at first pleased and then, after the reviews, angry: "God damn it—" he wrote in his diary, "why do they deliberately close their ears to everything of importance that is said in a comedy? You'd think it was a crime to state unpleasant truths in an entertaining way." The play ran for 300 performances and won a Pulitzer Prize.

Business is terrible at the Hotel Monte Gabriele, an Italian winter resort near highways into Switzerland and Austria and an Italian airfield. From among its few patrons Sherwood exposes the problems and arguments that he wants his audience to consider. Dr. Waldersee, a German scientist working on a cure for cancer, sees himself as "a servant of the whole damn stupid human race." Mr. and Mrs. Cherry, the English honeymooners, want only quiet and "to hell with all the rest." Dumptsy, a waiter, worries about his family in the war. Quillery, a French radical socialist, rails at the prospect of "mass murder—mass suicide" and at Achille Weber, the self-satisfied munitions maker who attributes war to the "spontaneous combustion of the dictatorial age" and defends his business as giving people what they want. Into this group of strong opinions toward war—the scientist, the Communist, the isolationist, the professional soldier, the common man, the arms provider—Sherwood introduces Weber's companion, the mysterious Irene, who speaks of "poor-dear God, playing Idiot's Delight. The game that never means anything and never ends," and the entertainer Harry Van with his dancers, Les Blondes.

In act 2 the serious comments of Quillery, Irene, and Weber are balanced by Harry's flamboyant act with Les Blondes. There is also the suggestion that Irene and Harry may have met previously at the Governor Bryan Hotel in Omaha. With war imminent, Sherwood's final act of *Idiot's Delight* sends Dr. Waldersee back to Germany to join the "obscene maniacs!" The Cherrys will return to England.

Dumptsy will join the army. Quillery has already been executed. Weber departs; but Irene, with a passport issued by the League of Nations, which has no value, must remain, as does Harry. As the bombs fall, and Harry plays "Onward, Christian Soldiers" on the piano in "a slow solemn tempo," they both sing loudly.

Early on, Sherwood expressed concern that his play might lose its purpose should Adolf Hitler and Benito Mussolini die; later he had other problems when he realized that his deliberate mixture of sensation and bitter irony had again failed to reach his audiences. And the failure bothered him. But in spite of objections from the mayor of Omaha, the city censor of Memphis, who found "objectionable language," the Lord Chamberlain's Office in London, and M-G-M censors, *Idiot's Delight* was toured successfully by the Lunts and made into a successful movie for which Sherwood wrote the screenplay.

[*See also* United States, 1929–1940]

FURTHER READING

Brown, John Mason. *The Worlds of Robert E. Sherwood: Mirror to His Times, 1896–1939*. New York: Harper, 1965.

Meserve, Walter J. *Robert E. Sherwood: Reluctant Moralist*. New York: Western, 1970.

Mordden, Ethan. *The American Theatre*. New York: Oxford Univ. Press, 1981.

Walter J. Meserve

I'D RATHER BE RIGHT

It happened
I felt it happened
I was awake
I wasn't blind
I didn't think
I felt it happened
now I believe in matter over mind.
—Lorenz Hart, 1937

I'd Rather Be Right, a musical COMEDY by Richard Rodgers (music) and Lorenz Hart (lyrics), with a book by MOSS HART and GEORGE S. KAUFMAN, produced by Sam H. Harris, opened at the Alvin Theatre on November 2, 1937, and ran for 289 performances. This play brought the song-and-dance man (and playwright) George M. Cohan, playing the role of Franklin D. Roosevelt, back to Broadway after an absence of ten years. A social satire about the New Deal, *I'd Rather Be Right* brings to the stage not only the president, but also the chief justice, the Supreme Court, the entire cabinet, and Roosevelt's own mother.

The protagonists of this hilarious political play are Peggy and Phil, an ordinary couple who hope to get married. While this young and distraught pair is sitting on a bench to hear a concert in Central Park in New York City on the Fourth of July, Phil falls asleep and dreams that he and his fiancée meet by mere chance Franklin D. Roosevelt (FDR) strolling cheerfully in the park. In his dream Phil complains to the president that his boss will not give him a raise unless Roosevelt balances the budget. Phil says that if he could get an increase in pay, he and Peggy would have enough money to get married. Roosevelt seems resolved to increase the national budget and face the countrywide economic crisis on behalf of these new friends. In his closing monologue Roosevelt vows to see the couple married and bids farewell. The play ends when Phil wakes up and, taking Roosevelt's advice, resolves to ask Peggy to marry him.

The plot of *I'd Rather Be Right* was considered to be audacious because it portrayed the head of state in a peculiar way. The general public and the press enjoyed the sharp and highly irreverent jests about the president, the Supreme Court, and the cabinet. Specifically, the Supreme Court, described by the president as the "nine old men," is unmercifully mocked by him because they voiced objections to the president's ideas. The songs include "A Homogeneous Cabinet," "Have You Met Miss Jones?" "Take and Take and Take," "A Baby Bond," "Labor Is the Thing," and the song that gives the play its name, "I'd Rather Be Right." The title comes from a popular saying ("I'd rather be right than president") that became identified with Roosevelt, although it dates from a speech by Henry Clay. This musical, then, is a lampoon of the politics and follies of the age of the Depression. It addressed selected public issues of the nation—FDR's political doctrine and specifically the tax programs. In an age of economic instability and social change, *I'd Rather Be Right* helped American audiences forget, for a brief moment at least, about the main worries in their lives. This musical was popular also because it allowed Americans to look for entertainment within the largely humorless world of the Depression.

[*See also* United States, 1929–1940]

FURTHER READING

Bach, Steven. *Dazzler: The Life and Times of Moss Hart*. New York: Knopf, 2001.

Goldstein, Malcolm. *George S. Kaufman: His Life, His Theater*. New York: Oxford Univ. Press, 1979.

Nolan, Frederick. *Lorenz Hart: A Poet on Broadway*. New York: Oxford Univ. Press, 1994.

Estefania Olid-Peña

ILAGAN, BONIFACIO (1951–)

Bonifacio Ilagan creates an engaged theater that carries messages of political and social commitment. During the Ferdinand Marcos era in the PHILIPPINES he was forced to go underground, was arrested, and was tortured by the regime. When he was released, he returned to his writing.

Born in 1951, Ilagan attended the University of the Philippines, where he was part of the Mobile Theatre troupe in 1968–1969. He taught at the Philippine High School for the Arts and was instrumental in founding a number of theater groups. In the 1960s and 1970s Filipino theater was evolving from realistic productions in English to performances in the vernacular that were presented in the streets. Ilagan's first play, *Strike! Strike* (*Welga! Welga!* 1971), was a move toward this socially engaged theater and one of the first Filipino plays to deal with union issues. The plot pits the hero, Ador, against the traitorous union negotiator, Ignacio, who is selling out the union members to his American boss. Ador rallies the union members, helping them see their struggle in the context of the whole nation throwing off imperialism. The production came at the peak of the nationalist movement just before martial law was imposed in 1972. Ilagan went underground when Marcos declared martial law, but was arrested in 1974 and held for twenty-two months before being released.

Ilagan's best-known work is *The People's Worship*, which was first commissioned for a 1976 performance in Hong Kong for the National Council of Churches in the Philippines. The play was translated into Tagalog as *Pagsambang bayan* in 1977 and directed by activist-artist Behn Cervantes. Based on the structure of a Catholic mass, the piece sought to build solidarity between all the elements opposed to the dictatorial regime. Using the story of the Good Samaritan (the victim in the play is attacked by characters representing imperialism, feudalism, and capitalism), the priest prepares his mass. Peasants, workers, students, tribal groups, and professionals make up the congregation as the priest transforms himself, abandoning his liturgical garments and putting on the clothes of the common man. The mass included a communion and the collection of an offering for the disenfranchised. The play was translated into local languages and staged all over the country. After the death of political reformist Benigno Aquino at the hands of the Marcos government, the play was restaged, but accusations in new productions grew more strident, preparing the way for Marcos's fall. The director, author, and musical director were each imprisoned for periods, and the play was performed over 100 times.

Ilagan's 1981 production of *The United States Versus Cruz, Abad, and Tolentino* was a restaging of the trial of these three "seditious" playwrights of 1900 who protested the loss of Filipino freedom to American imperialism. The piece included a staging of Juan Abad's *I Am Not Dead* (*Hindi aco patay*, 1902), wherein the dead hero rises from his funeral bier to rouse patriotic struggle. The playwrights and directors of the martial law period identified heavily with these banned poets of 1900 who, despite imprisonment and fines, still stood up to call for freedom.

After Marcos's ouster in 1986 Ilagan's political themes continued. *Termites on Wood* (*Anay sa kahoy*, 1987) shows patriot Manuel Quezon opposing the American governor general Leonard Wood. Ilagan's *Revolution* (*Himagsik*) is an adaptation of national hero and martyr José Rizal's *Subversion* (*El filibusterismo*). For Ilagan, theater is a weapon. He calls for unity and justice in the face of tyranny and economic injustice.

PLAYS: *Fire of Race* (*Alab ng Lahi*, 197?); *Strike! Strike!* (*Welga! Welga!* 1971); *The People's Worship* (1976), translated as *Pagsambang Bayan* (1977); *Katipunan: Children of the People* (*Katipunan: Mga anak ng bayan*, 1978), revised as *The People's Cry* (*Sigaw ng bayan*, 1978); *Though Heavens Grow Dark* (*Langit ma'y magdilim*, 1979); *The United States Versus Cruz, Abad, and Tolentino* (*Estados Unidos bersus Cruz, Abad, at Tolentino*, 1981); *Sexy Dancers* (1982); *Red Earth* (*Pulanlupa*, 1985); *Termites on Wood* (*Anay sa kahoy*, 1987); *Revolution* (*Himagsik* [adapted from José Rizal's *The Subversive* (*El filibusterismo*)]; *Game of Pretend* (*Juego de prendar*, 1989); *To Love Again* (*Pag-ibig*, 1991); *Away Layas*, adapted from the Australian play, 1993)

FURTHER READING

Cultural Center of the Philippines. *CCP Encyclopedia of Philippine Art.* Vol. 7, *Philippine Theater*. Manila: CCP, 1994.

Fernandez, Doreen. *Palabas: Essays on Philippine Theater History*. Quezon City: Ateneo de Manila Univ. Press, 1996.

Jit, Krishen. "The Philippines: Modern Drama." In *The Cambridge Guide to Asian Theatre*, ed. by James Brandon. Cambridge: Cambridge Univ. Press, 1993.

Tiongson, Nicanor. *Dulaan: An Essay on Philippine Theater*. Manila: Cultural Center of the Philippines, 1989.

Kathy Foley

THE ILLEGITIMATE SON

Alexandre DUMAS FILS's first "thesis play" (*pièce à thèse*), *The Illegitimate Son* examined the effects of illegitimacy, a subject then considered taboo in society and on the stage.

Clara, the impoverished, unwed mother of baby Jacques, is left by the child's father to marry a bourgeois woman. Twenty years later Jacques and the wealthy Hermine are engaged, but a family friend informs the Marquise, Hermine's guardian, of Jacques's illegitimacy: he was the result of an affair between Hermine's uncle Charles (the Marquise's son) and the embroiderer Clara. When Jacques is told of his heredity, he confronts his mother and "new" father, who refuses to recognize the marriage to Hermine. The following year, however, Charles finds himself consumed with political ambition; he strikes a bargain to adopt Jacques, in effect recognizing his son and allowing the marriage. Nevertheless, when Jacques returns home after fulfilling an important mission for the government, he refuses to take his father's name, choosing instead to keep the one he has made for himself.

Called a pioneer of prose drama and the "father of modern social drama," Dumas fils laid the groundwork for the NATURALISM of HENRIK IBSEN, EMILE ZOLA, and ANTON CHEKHOV. Having found previous forms inadequate, Dumas concluded that moral instruction must accompany mere observation. *The Illegitimate Son* had its premiere during a period of unprecedented prosperity, stability, and material indulgence. "We're headed for universal prostitution," Dumas proclaimed, and in his 1868 preface to the play he summarized his intentions with the new form:

"Let us inaugurate the *useful* theatre, at the risk of hearing the cries of the apostles of *art for art*, three words absolutely devoid of meaning. All literature that does not have in view perfectibility, moralization, the ideal, the useful, in a word, is stunted and unhealthy, born dead." His play's "usefulness" can be seen in what critics have called "abnormal" logic and a "forced" denouement. It is clear that Clara and Jacques are powerless to improve their positions, but in Dumas's rectified world, Jacques serves his country and attains a stature illegitimate children do not typically attain. To Dumas, himself a "natural" child, this is morally logical; it was certainly no more illogical than Jacques's being robbed of happiness by the circumstances of his birth. In act 2, in the face of his father's refusal, Jacques makes Dumas's thesis clear: "All my life is shattered, my future is lost, my heart is condemned for a fault that is not my own; it is yours and you throw its consequences on me with cold logic and social egoism. But watch, monsieur, your conclusions can drive us to overthrow the most sacred natural laws."

Departing from the traditional five-act model, Dumas condensed his action into four acts, accelerating his "logical" premises: we reach the conclusion—Jacques's moral nobility—before we can debate the hypotheses. Dumas wrote in a true-to-life language peppered with wit, puns, and colloquial analogies; he substituted action for literature. Despite the author's desire to instruct, it was these qualities, rather than moral edification, that captivated audiences for more than 200 performances.

[*See also* Comedy; France]

FURTHER READING

Chandler, Frank Wadleigh. *The Contemporary Drama of France*. Boston: Little, Brown, 1920.

Filon, Augustin. *The Modern French Drama*. Tr. by Janet E. Hogarth. London: Chapman, 1898. Originally published as *De Dumas à Rostand: Esquisse du mouvement dramatique contemporain*. Paris: Fayard, 1898.

Schwarz, H. Stanley. *Alexandre Dumas fils, Dramatist*. New York: New York Univ. Press, 1927.

Smith, Hugh A. *Main Currents of Modern French Drama*. New York: Holt, 1925.

Taylor, F. A. *The Theatre of Alexandre Dumas fils*. London: Oxford Univ. Press, 1937.

Matt Di Cintio

I LOVE YOU, BABY BLUE

Despite the popular conception of a "Toronto the good," Friday evenings in Toronto in the mid-1970s were largely devoted to the clandestine programming known as the *Baby Blue* movies: soft-core pornography that aired at midnight on one of Canada's longest-running television stations. These mild skin flicks brought in nearly sixty-five percent of the station's viewers and an even more astonishing forty-eight percent of the viewing public.

Theater throughout time and across the globe has served as both a social mirror and commentator, and much the same was true in Toronto on January 15, 1975. *I Love You, Baby Blue* was the fourteenth collective creation produced by the cornerstone alternative theater company Theatre Passe Muraille. Under the direction of PAUL THOMPSON, *I Love You, Baby Blue* developed as a variety of scenes, each detailing and exploring various sexual realities in Toronto. From Yonge Street massage parlors to swinging couples to a trio of singers extolling the virtues of the vibrator, no subject was left untouched.

I Love You, Baby Blue opened at the Bathurst Street United Church (the space used by the company) to receptions both favorable and confrontational. After its first week the production faced pressure from the Metro Toronto Police morality squad to modify the performance's language and content. While this proved a disappointing reaction to a piece that hoped to enlighten the Toronto audience to their collective sexuality—thereby encouraging dialogue and discouraging sexual shame—the knee-jerk call for censorship seemed an almost fitting and anticipated reaction in light of the pervasive attitude the production was speaking out against. With the soft-core porn of City-TV drawing a large sample of the Toronto public, it was clear that a certain margin of Toronto reality was being kept behind closed doors. Furthermore, "Toronto the good" was being unfairly categorized, with a far-reaching reality being forsaken for a more savory image, not to mention the label "good" being synonymous with suppressing one's nature.

In the preface to the published text of *I Love You, Baby Blue*, Thompson describes the scope of the production and the wide audience it reached: "The show didn't focus on any particular generation or group. We had couples of fifty bringing their twenty-year-old children to the thing. We had people in psychology, counselors who try to help marriages, etc., coming to the show and recommending it to their clients as a basis for their discussions." In the tradition of collective creation, *I Love You, Baby Blue* successfully addressed a particular Canadian attitude, whether organic or bestowed, and facilitated around it a buzz of truth.

The morality squad that had previously been satisfied with a few script changes returned to a later performance where it served the stage manager and actors, as well as Thompson, with summonses to appear in court under the charge of presenting an immoral theatrical performance. After a twelve-week run seen by over 26,000 audience members, *I Love You, Baby Blue* fell victim to the censors and closed on April 18, 1975.

[*See also* Canada]

FURTHER READING

Bessai, Diane. *Playwrights of Collective Creation*. Toronto: Simon & Pierre, 1992.

Brissenden, Connie, ed. *I Love You, Baby Blue*. Toronto: Press Porcepic, 1976.

Campbell, Maria, and Linda Griffiths. *The Book of Jessica: A Theatrical Transformation.* Toronto: Coach House Press, 1989.

Johnston, Denis William. *Up the Mainstream: The Rise of Toronto's Alternative Theatres, 1968–1975.* Toronto: Univ. of Toronto Press, 1991.

Renaud, Andrea. *The History of Theatre Passe Muraille from 1968–69 to 96.* Toronto: Theatre Passe Muraille Archives, 1996.

Sarah Cervinka

THE IMPORTANCE OF BEING EARNEST

The Importance of Being Earnest: A Trivial Comedy for Serious People, first produced on February 14, 1895, is the most often revived of OSCAR WILDE's four COMEDIES. The extent to which the characters treat important things as trivial, and trivial things as important gives the play a deliriously farcical quality.

Two young men of wealth and idleness both pretend to be someone named Ernest in order to win the hands of Gwendolen Fairfax (Algernon's cousin) and Cecily Cardew (Jack's ward), who insist on marrying a man of that name. Upon being introduced, the girls suspect that they are both engaged to the same Ernest; later they believe that they are in fact engaged to different men, neither of whom is named Ernest. Christening ceremonies seem the only route to wedding ceremonies, but in the denouement it transpires that Jack had been named Ernest before being mislaid by Miss Prism, an absent-minded, novel-writing governess, in the cloakroom of a London train station. There he was found and adopted by Cecily Cardew's father. The play ends with love matches all around, including one between Miss Prism and a doctor of divinity, Revd. Canon Chasuble, who is hilariously prone to, and terrified of, double entendres.

For all its hell-bent focus on getting couples to the altar, the play's most charismatic character is the flamboyantly dissolute Algernon Moncrieff. He explains early in act 1 his theory of how to live well: it is by means of Bunburying. He has invented an ailing friend called Bunbury who lives in the country, so that whenever a social or moral obligation appears on his horizon in the city, he pleads the necessity to attend the deathbed of Bunbury. Actually, he goes off to riotous pleasures in country houses. The double life of Algernon seems at the least to involve extramarital pleasures, and possibly homosexual ones. He insists that Bunbury will be as necessary after marriage as before. The undercurrent of disrespect for monogamy, religion, society, and every other totem and taboo races through every speech by every character, save for that of the redoubtable Lady Bracknell. She gives a defense of the status quo so absurd that it never need have an attacker. Her habit of repeating with alarm and incredulity some word in the speech of the previous character makes her an immensely enjoyable figure on stage.

Originally the play was written in four acts, but George Alexander, the producer, insisted on dropping act 4, in which Algernon flees arrest for debt. Wilde was not pleased by the cut, but the three-act version has been overwhelmingly preferred by producers of revivals.

In company with his producer, Wilde coached the original casts of his plays into a style of acting appropriate to his work; this style became a staple of the English comedy of manners. All of the farcical speeches in the play were pronounced by the characters with debonair earnestness. None of them showed that they were conscious of the absurdity of their utterances; they paid heed only to perfection of accent and articulation. A cracking pace was kept up from start to finish. In a theater for a production of one of Wilde's comedies, the only people who do not laugh are the ones on stage, and they never do.

The most obvious antecedents of the play are to be found in Restoration comedies, especially those of Anglo-Irishman William Congreve, whose works were both republished and popularly revived during Wilde's youth. The light operas of W. S. GILBERT and Arthur Sullivan have similarly satirical frolics, and similar imperturbability on the part of absurd characters. Writers for the English stage, especially NOËL COWARD, have continued the tradition. But before or after Wilde, no writer has equaled the brilliance of epigram with which he endowed his characters except, on occasion, his compatriot, GEORGE BERNARD SHAW.

[*See also* England, 1860–1940]

FURTHER READING

Beckson, Karl, ed. *Oscar Wilde: The Critical Heritage.* London: Routledge, 1970.

Craft, Christopher. *Another Kind of Love: Male Homosexual Desire in English Discourse, 1850–1920.* Berkeley: Univ. of California Press, 1994.

Gagnier, Regenia, ed. *Critical Essays on Oscar Wilde.* New York: G. K. Hall, 1991.

Powell, Kerry. *Oscar Wilde and the Theatre of the 1890s.* Cambridge: Cambridge Univ. Press, 1990.

Adrian Frazier

IN ABRAHAM'S BOSOM

Got to keep studying, got to keep climbing.
—Abraham McCranie, Scene 3

Subtitled *The Tragedy of a Southern Negro, In Abraham's Bosom* is widely considered to be PAUL GREEN's most powerful folk drama. An emotional study of an African American seeking to transcend his racial bondage through education, this was Green's first full-length play, as well as his first Broadway production and the winner of the 1927 Pulitzer Prize. The seven-scene play ran for 200 performances, starting at the Provincetown Players' Greenwich Village Theatre in December 1926, then moving uptown to the Garrick Theatre. The *New York Times* praised the premiere as a "sincere and powerful tragedy written with courage, understanding, logic and humor," while critic

Brooks Atkinson later described it as the "most penetrating, unswerving tragedy in town," noting also that "Negro plays are in the wind just now." Green, renowned for his realistic studies of rural Southern life, including white farmers and the disintegrating antebellum society, grew up amid the oppression, poverty, and bitter racism of the postwar South, cultural deprivations that deeply and permanently affected him.

Spanning about two decades, *In Abraham's Bosom* depicts the efforts of its central character, Abraham McCranie—the mulatto son of a white planter and one of his slaves—to make a better life for himself through books and learning and to found a school to lead his people, like a new Moses, out of the land of oppression. As he tells his only diligent pupil, "Got to keep studying, got to keep climbing." The play also exposes how Abe helps ensure his own defeat through his passion, temper, and impracticality, with his ideals thwarted not only by whites but also by the passivity of the blacks themselves. As one says, "The colored's place is down at the bottom." In the end, even his own son, Douglass, who has become a criminal and a drunk, betrays his father.

Early in the play Colonel McCranie does get Abe a small schoolhouse, but when Abe beats one student for misbehaving, it is closed down. Abe embarks with his wife and child on a series of itinerant jobs, continuing to get into trouble with his preaching and defiance of authority. Eventually they return to the farm, where Abe's half brother Lonnie, the late colonel's legitimate son, has agreed to let Abe work the cotton fields. Abe neglects his duty in his educational zealotry, which culminates in a final speech that is thwarted by a crowd of white supremacists—tipped off by Douglass—who run off the black audience and then proceed to beat and threaten Abe. Returning home, Abe encounters Lonnie, who informs him that he has taken away Abe's crop, and in a fit of madness Abe kills him. When the crowds descend on Abe's cottage for revenge, he goes out to try and reason with them but is shot dead.

Interestingly, Green's stage directions set the play "somewhere in the southern part of the United States," even though the action clearly takes place in North Carolina. This ambiguity perhaps suggests Green's recognition of the tragically broad extent of segregation and discrimination.

[*See also* United States, 1860–1929]

FURTHER READING

Avery, Laurence G., ed. *A Southern Life: Letters of Paul Green, 1916–1981*. Chapel Hill: Univ. of North Carolina Press, 1994.

Kenny, Vincent S. *Paul Green*. New York: Twayne, 1971.

Paul Green Foundation. http://www.paulgreen.org/.

Roper, John Herbert. *Paul Green: Playwright of the Real South*. Athens: Univ. of Georgia Press, 2003.

Watson, Charles S. *The History of Southern Drama*. Lexington: Univ. Press of Kentucky, 1997.

Karen Blansfield

IN A LAND OF SILENCE

Written by Zong Fuxian when he was a worker and amateur playwright in Shanghai, *In a Land of Silence* (*Yu wu sheng chu, huaju*) depicts events that unfolded in April 1976 when thousands upon thousands of people poured into Tiananmen Square in Beijing, CHINA, to mourn the death of Premier Zhou Enlai and voiced their indignation at the perverse acts of the Gang of Four, who were still in power. Borrowing playwriting technique from CAO YU in following the three unities in drama, the play depicts a series of events that take place within nine hours in the same household.

Mei Lin, a veteran revolutionary persecuted and once imprisoned during the Cultural Revolution for being a "traitor," comes to the home of her former comrade and colleague He Shifei for help. Ouyang Ping, Mei's only son, and He Yun, He Shifei's daughter, who is now an officer in the Beijing Municipal Public Security Bureau, were lovers previously, but Ouyang broke off their relationship years ago so that his antirevolutionary family background would not cause trouble for He Yun's political future. Unbeknownst to each other, Ouyang is now a counterrevolutionary activist and hence a fugitive for his role in the underground collection and circulation of *The Collection of Tiananmen Poetry of 1976*, while He Yun is none other than the one who has been put in charge of the case. As the truth gradually comes out that He Shifei is the one who betrayed Mei and sent her to prison, a series of conflicts ensues concerning love, political loyalty, and family solidarity. When the curtain falls, Ouyang calmly awaits arrest together with his mother and all others in the He family, leaving He Shifei alone desperately lamenting his eventual political downfall.

Considered simple in its plot line, artificial in its dramatic conflict, and crude in DRAMATURGY by some, the play was immensely popular when it was premiered in Shanghai in September 1978 because of its political sensitivity. In both Beijing and Shanghai the play was simultaneously staged in more than forty theaters. Particularly striking and provocative for the audience at the time was the reading aloud onstage of some of the antiofficial poems and the retelling of the bloody scenes involved in the circulation of the poems at a time when such activities were still banned and hence highly risky. The success of the play was therefore more due to its timing than to its own theatrical merit. The courage with which the play depicts the political event occurring in the spring of 1976 before it was officially rehabilitated echoed the voice and conscience of the millions of people in China then. While the play anticipated the downfall of the Gang of Four with the reverse of the verdict on the April fifth movement, it acted as a powerful and subversive appeal to people's emotions concerning the outcome of the Cultural Revolution. Because of its popularity, the play quickly led to a theater boom in 1979 with a number of plays on the aftermath or the "wounds" of the Cultural Revolution. Zong Fuxian went to work with the Shanghai Writers' Association in 1985 and became a professional writer.

FURTHER READING

Cao Yu, Zhao Xun, and Zong Fuxian. "Yuwu shengchu sanren tan" [Three dramatists on *In a Land of Silence*]. *Renmin xiju* [People's drama] 1 (1979): 16–20.

Chen, Xiaomei. *Acting the Right Part: Political Theater and Popular Drama in Contemporary China*. Honolulu: Univ. of Hawaii Press, 2002.

Shanghai xi ju xue yuan xi ju wen xue xi, ed. *Huaju "Yu wu sheng chu" zhuanji* [*A special collection of essays on the play* In a Land of Silence]. Shanghai: Shanghai xiju xueyuan xiju yishu she, 1979.

Yan, Haiping, ed. *Theater and Society: An Anthology of Contemporary Chinese Drama*. Armonk, N.Y.: M. E. Sharpe, 1998.

Zong Fuxian. *In a Land of Silence*. Tr. by Shu-ying Tsau. In *Twentieth-Century Chinese Drama: An Anthology*, ed. by Edward M. Gunn. Bloomington: Indiana Univ. Press, 1983. 409–447.

——. "Yu wu sheng chu" [When all sounds are hushed]. *Chinese Literature* 4 (1979): 3–56.

Hongchu Fu

INDIA

India as it is currently configured is the most populous democracy in the world. It is also one of the most culturally diverse. Each of India's twenty-six states has its own political and social history and its own language—there are seventeen nationally recognized Indian languages and more than 1,652 recognized dialects. Hindi is the official national language of the country, but it is not spoken by a majority of the population. Each state has its own performing arts traditions and its own regional theater, with the result that scholars often write about regional theaters (such as Bengali theater and Marathi theater) in terms that refer simultaneously to the area, culture, language, thematic preoccupations, and often style. This cultural and geographic survey traces the rise of modern theater in India, outlines its major movements, highlights some of the most influential plays, productions, and playwrights, and discusses some of the most important issues faced by theater practitioners in India today. It also provides historical context for entries on individual plays and playwrights.

THEATER IN INDIA IN THE 19TH CENTURY: COLONIZATION AND DECOLONIZATION

Modern theater in India began as a colonial enterprise in three ports set up by the British East India Company: Calcutta (now Kolkata), Bombay (now Mumbai), and Madras (now Chennai). Unlike Delhi (the seat of Mughal power) or Kochi (which has a history of trade with China and the Middle East that predates the arrival of the British in that area by centuries), Kolkata and Mumbai were small villages until the British arrived. Mumbai was established as a "frontier outpost against the Maratha power" (Mehta, 1960) and only developed into a commercial and industrial center in the early to mid-1800s. Kolkata grew out of three villages. It was one of the earliest British colonial settlements and was used as the central clearing place and port for "extraction"—the exportation of raw materials back to ENGLAND for manufacturing. In the 19th century the British introduced modern theater to these cities in three ways: by touring productions to entertain their expatriate communities, by supporting productions of English plays staged by the expatriates themselves, and by teaching English drama in Indian universities. The spread of English drama was part of colonizing Indian culture—it was designed not only to shape artistic activity, but to impose on Indians a way of understanding and operating in the world. Two things happened: the urban middle class (particularly those who had to work with the British) learned to despise their own ritual, classical, and popular performances, thereby losing touch with them, and they learned to appreciate Western plays—"spoken dramas" that were performed on proscenium stages for a ticket-buying public at times that were not related to annual festivals, harvests, or religious occasions. While the British did have an enormous influence on modern theater in India, it is also true that several scholars have overemphasized the colonization of modern Indian theater and the "destruction" of "indigenous" theatrical genres in order to give a clear framework for what is known as the theater of roots—the theatrical manifestation of a post-independence nationwide search for a common "national" identity, a way of defining India as a unified, unique, nation *in opposition to* colonial (Western) theater. In reality 19th-century theater almost always appropriated, undermined, adapted, and redirected elements and attitudes of the colonial culture that tried to suppress it. Thus, modern drama in India is characterized by hybridity.

The Development of Modern Theater in Mumbai

In *English Drama on the Bombay Stage in the Late Eighteenth Century and in the Nineteenth Century* (1960), when Kumudini Mehta details the history of English theater in Mumbai, she is really telling the story of the Indianization of the English-language theater in Mumbai. She tells how, during the course of the 19th century, Indians in Mumbai gradually took over English playhouses and the production of English and English-language plays. But in doing so she shows how 19th-century Indian writers and theatergoers absorbed English aesthetics and sensibilities.

The Bombay Amateur Theatre, Mumbai's first theater, was founded in 1776 (Mehta, 1960). The Amateur Theatre's audience in 1820 was "society:" merchants, the officers of several European regiments, a few barristers, and civilians. The theater imported to Mumbai in the early 1800s by traveling theater companies, as well as the theater staged by amateur residents, was intended to provide entertainment and escape for the staff, soldiers, officers, and attendant civilians stationed there. Physically, these theaters (like the ones built in Kolkata) were exact copies of their English counterparts: they had a pit, gallery, dress boxes, painted perspective scenery, painted backdrops, wings, footlights, a front curtain, and chandeliers. These theaters in physical structure, as well as in choice of presentations, were designed to remind their audiences of home and homeland. While inside, audiences were in (a) British space.

The earliest evidence of Indians in the audience at the Bombay Amateur Theatre is a record of the purchase of a dress-box seat by Balcrustnath Sunkerset on August 3, 1821. Later, on December 13, 1822, Hormusjee Bomanjee and Sorabji Framji each bought two tickets to see Richard Sheridan's play *The Rivals* (Mehta, 1960). Indians began to attend the English theater in increasing numbers, and in 1830, when the Amateur Theatre needed money, eleven of the fifty donors were Indian—among them Bomanjee and Jugonath Sunkersett. When the Amateur Theatre went bankrupt and was demolished, Sunkersett donated the land on which it was later rebuilt. Significantly, the land he donated was in his own neighborhood. When the rebuilt Amateur, known thereafter as the Grant Road Theatre, opened on February 10, 1846, there were more Indians in the audience than there had been at the Amateur Theatre. "The European residents did not conceal their disappointment in a Theatre nestling in the heart of what was then called the Black Town. But the Indians living in Girgaum and Kalbadevi found it conveniently close. They crammed the Pit and filled it to crushing" (Mehta, 1960).

The rising number of Indians attending the theater empowered the Indian audience to control the theatrical experience. For example, just after the Grant Road Theatre opened, a rumor circulated that Mrs. Deacle, who had come from Kolkata to run the theater, intended to reserve the front row of boxes exclusively for Europeans, apparently because the red turbans of the Parsis obstructed their view. The Parsi audience, "sensitive to any suggestion of segregation in the theatre," boycotted the performance on February 21, 1846, and Mrs. Deacle, not wanting to alienate large numbers of patrons, abandoned any plans of "providing an extra pit for Indians or of reserving the front boxes for Europeans" (Mehta, 1960). As time went on, the opinion of Indian spectators mattered more and more, and it began to influence the selection of plays (Mehta, 1960).

A letter to the *British Indian Gentleman's Gazette* pointed out that Mrs. Deacle was likely to bring about "by her performances, that which moral philosophers with their lectures on ethics, and Missionaries with their sermons on Christianity, have sought and labored for, for ages" (quoted in Mehta, 1960). In other words, English-language drama was successfully disseminating the values of the British Empire. Sunkersett (who donated the land for the Grant Road Theatre) and Jamsetjee Jeejeebhoy, one of the eleven Indians who donated money to the Amateur Theatre, were two of the three Indian members chosen by the Bombay Native Education Society to serve on the Board of Education when it was formed in 1840. Both Sunkersett and Jeejeebhoy

> wanted their countrymen to share the knowledge and training, which they discerned to be in a large measure the secret of the superior efficiency of the nations of the West. They collaborated closely with the Government in every major undertaking in the social and cultural arena. Their interest in the fortunes of the Theatre can be understood in the context of their general keenness in imbibing the intellectual values of the West. (Mehta, 1960)

Sunkersett and Jeejeebhoy supported the theater for the same reason they set up an English educational system in Mumbai: they wanted to master the knowledge and values of the West.

In the 1860s and 1870s students at the new British colleges who were studying William Shakespeare in their classes began to form dramatic societies. They were encouraged by their professors and coached by the professional English actors who toured to or settled in Mumbai. The Parsi Elphinstone Society (named after Mountstuart Elphinstone [1779–1859], governor of Mumbai from 1819 to 1827 and the founder of Elphinstone College) inaugurated its club in 1861 with light pieces such as *Lovers' Quarrel* and *Bengal Tigers*, but these societies soon began to change the taste of theatergoers in Mumbai with their regular annual presentations of Shakespeare.

Interest in Shakespeare led to an interest in classical Indian plays, and in the latter half of the 19th-century dramatic literature provided a means for asserting an Indian identity. When British touring companies brought Shakespeare productions to India, they also brought the idea that a playwright best represented British civilization (see Karnad, 1998). At the same time the reverence with which Oriental scholars such as Max Müller (1823–1900) and Monier Williams (1819–1899) treated India's classical philosophy, sculpture, literature, and drama contributed to a renewed interest in Sanskrit drama as a way of asserting cultural parity with the British. The Indian middle class looked for a Sanskrit dramatist who could function as an equivalent to Shakespeare, and found one in Kalidasa (dates uncertain, between 150 B.C.E. and 500 C.E.), whose plays were translated and performed with "unprecedented frequency" in the late 19th century (Karnad, 1998). The Kalidas Elphinstone Society, an amateur dramatic club formed by students at Elphinstone College in Mumbai, became famous in the 1870s for its production of Monier Williams's translation of Kalidasa's *Shakuntala Recognized* (*Abhijnanashakuntala*).

Actually, interest in Indian plays dates back to 1843, when Vishnu Amrit Bhave, known as Vishnudas Bhave (1819/1824–1901), wrote *Sita Chooses a Husband* (*Sita swayamvara*; Sita is the heroine of the epic *The Ramayana*). Rumor has it that a company of *dashavatar* performers (a genre of performance based on the ten incarnations of Vishnu) from Karnataka visited Sangli in 1842 and performed at a temple. The raja of Sangli saw this performance and, thinking that this type of entertainment would add to the culture of the court, asked Bhave (the court's storyteller and poet) to create a refined version of a *dashavatar* play. In

Playwright at the Centre: Marathi Drama from 1843 to the Present (2000) Shanta Gokhale calls *Sita Chooses a Husband* "the first non-traditional, non-folk, non-ritualistic dramatic performance in Marathi" and "the first performance in Marathi that could be called a play" (Gokhale, 2000). *Sita Chooses a Husband* was staged for the court on November 5, 1843. A description of the play gives a good sense of the theater in 1843:

> The stage setting of the play was very simple. It consisted of a piece of red cloth hung at the back and a few wooden properties. . . .
>
> At the beginning of every scene . . . the *sutradhara* [literally "holder of the strings"; the sutradhar was the company manager/stage manager] sung [*sic*] a song giving in outline the events to be acted and the players spoke the dialogue, which was not written but roughly decided beforehand. . . . All the characters, except the demons, sang songs appropriate to the mood of the scene. The Sutradhara and the members of the chorus not only provided instrumental music but often joined in the singing. The entries of the demons were a noisy and spectacular affair. The red-painted faces of the inhuman characters looked fierce when lit up by naked torches. (Bapu Rao Naik, 1961)

The sutradhar was obviously a central figure in the evening. Most significantly with respect to later developments, actors were allowed to improvise their lines. Although the play is clearly Bhave's, it retains quite a number of the features, characteristics, and structural elements of the *dashavatar* that inspired it.

Ten years later, on March 9, 1853, another of Bhave's plays, generally acknowledged as "the first ticketed 'native' play to be performed in an English-style proscenium theatre in Mumbai" (Gokhale, 2000), opened for the first of five performances at the Grant Road Theatre. A review of the play appeared in the *Bombay Times* on March 11, 1853:

> The God and Goddess of wisdom seemed quite at home, too, while sitting on chairs and couches, and the combat between Luxuman [Lakshmana] and Indrajit was carried on (the weapons being bows and the combatants dancing fiercely round each other) in an English-looking parlor. . . . Scenery and the other similar accessories that so much aid the effect of a dramatic presentation were . . . almost entirely overlooked; and we recommend more attention being paid to these matters for the future. (quoted in Gokhale, 2000)

Here again the play retains some of the characteristics of the *dashavatar*, although the fact that it took place on one of the theater's stock sets (with Lakshamana and Indrajit battling it out in an English parlor) meant that Bhave-style plays would soon begin to be influenced by English theater.

Bhave's next play, *King Gopichand (Raja Gopichand)*, which was written in Hindi to make it more accessible, was performed at the Grant Road Theatre on November 26, 1853. The *Bombay Times* called this the first performance of a play by an Indian for an Indian audience. However, it seemed "crude" to the theater's increasingly English-educated Indian audience schooled in Shakespeare, mainly because of the play's stylistic affinities to the *dashavatar* Bhave had seen, and to *tamasha* (popular entertainment of Maharashtra, performed in Marathi). Although *tamasha* had been patronized by the Maratha armies and later by landlords, the raja of Sangli, who was a Brahmin, thought that it was unsuitable for court performances because of its erotic songs and dances, performed by women. Gokhale (2000) suggests that the real reason he found it unsuitable is that the satiric interludes were aimed at the establishment. Nonetheless, Bhave understood that he was being asked to adapt *dashavatar* and *tamasha* to create something more "refined." He cut the dances and minimized the battle scenes, but kept the *lavani* (a type of song in the *tamasha* repertoire, often used to express erotic sentiment), to which he added *keertans* (a form of temple storytelling through song) and various forms of classical music (Gokhale, 2000). These "refinements" were not enough for sections of the Grant Road audience who were learning to eschew traditional performance full of songs and dances and based on mythological stories drawn from *The Mahabharata* and *The Ramayana*.

In 1871 students at Deccan College in Pune performed a translation of Narayanbhatta's *Venisamhar*. Krishnaji Parashuram Gadgil, a student at the college, wrote the prologue in rhymed iambic pentameter. The prologue clearly indicates the attitude these new Shakespeare scholars had learned to take toward indigenous popular performance:

> Though some might laugh us out and set at naught,
> Because they see no feats no duels fought
> No freakish monkey, no delirious yell,
> No Lanka's tyrant fierce with fury fell,
> No absurd songs, no din, no wild attire,
> No meaningless uproar, no senseless ire;
> Let them, what can they, indiscretion's tools,
> In turn we laugh them down and deem them fools.
> Illiterate players have usurped the stage,
> With scenes obscene depraved this rising age.
> (quoted in Gokhale, 2000)

To Gadgil, traditional performances based on the story of Rama were obscene and depraved. Among this group of Indians, colonialism had thoroughly done its work.

Consequently, when members of the college dramatic societies wanted a new kind of "Indian" drama, they began by translating Shakespeare from English and Kalidasa from Sanskrit. Eventually they began to write and produce their own plays (in their own languages) modeled on Shakespeare (Gokhale, 2000; Mehta, 1960). Vinayak Janardan Kirtane (1840–1891), a student at Elphinstone College, wrote the first play to use history rather than mythology as its subject. Written in 1857, the same year as the First War of Independence or the Great Rebellion *The Elder Madhavrao Peshwa (Thorle Madhavrao Peshwe)* was one of the first great nationalist plays (the first of many that sprang up after the rebellion), and it marked the beginning of Marathi dramatists' commitment to serious political issues. This was probably inevitable, given the fact that on August 2, 1858, with the passing of the Government of India Act, the British Crown formally took over from the British East India Company and began direct rule over India. At the very beginning of the play the sutradhar announces that he will not transport the audience to the present Maratha Durbar (court) because he does not want to "take them to a place where people from other isles hold command" (quoted in Gokhale, 2000). In *The Elder Madhavrao Peshwe* Kirtane took the colonial theatrical form and used it as a vehicle for anticolonial sentiment, simultaneously valorizing and disrupting its authority.

The Elder Madhavrao Peshwe gave rise to an entire body of dramatic writing in prose—in other words, to plays without songs (Gokhale, 2000). However, eight years later, when the *Belgaum Samachar* reviewed another production of the play, it noted: "Many people did not like it because it was made up entirely of dialogues" (quoted in Gokhale, 2000). This back-and-forth between those who wanted more songs and those who wanted fewer or no songs eventually led to a split between the straight or "bookish" play and the *sangeetnatak*, which literally means "music drama" and is described as either opera or musical theater.

The *sangeetnatak* was extremely popular until it was wiped out by the film industry in the 1930s. It was performed in three languages (Gujarati, Urdu, and Hindi) for a linguistically and culturally diverse audience. But because it played to several communities, Gokhale (2000) claims that it had no stake in any one community's culture or social life, which meant that its appeal was based on pure entertainment, on "flamboyant devices and sensationalism." The first *sangeetnatak* in Marathi, *Shakuntala* (1875 or 1880), had 209 songs taken from an enormous variety of sources: "keertan, lavanis, devotionals, lullabyes, bhoopalis, ovis, folk songs from Karnataka and Gujarat, ghazals, dadras, and thumris" (Gokhale, 2000). However, playwright Balwant Krishna Kirloskar (1843–1885) reduced the role of the narrator (the sutradhar) and had characters sing their own thoughts and feelings. The characters were not archetypes, but individuals. Structurally *Shakuntala* was an interesting mixture of "Indian" and "Western" dramaturgy.

Marathi theater set itself up in opposition to the pure entertainment of the *sangeetnatak*. Marathi theater spoke to a relatively homogeneous audience and quickly became a platform for addressing social issues of one community. From there it became a staging ground for the nationalist movement. Although many people still wanted songs (and dances), these gradually gave way to the straight play as the best medium for a political theater.

However, overtly political theater became problematic all over the country after 1876. Sudipto Chatterjee (1998) persuasively argues that the stage in 19th-century Kolkata was a place where a new vision of the state was rehearsed and produced. Certainly the stage in both Bengal and Maharashtra was a place where anticolonial sentiment was expressed. The most famous example of an anticolonial play is *The Mirror of Indigo Planters* (*Nil darpan*, 1860), about the ruthless exploitation of indigo cultivators, who were forced to cultivate indigo by British indigo planters. *The Mirror of Indigo Planters* caused riots at one of its performances in Lucknow because the British audience objected to the way the planters were portrayed in a scene in which a white planter rapes an Indian peasant (see Guha, 1974, and Rao and Rao, 1992). Indigo planters sued the English translator, James Long, on the grounds that the play gave planters a bad name. Long's trial generated a great deal of publicity for both the play and the issue it portrayed and established *Indigo Planters* as the first nationalist drama in India. It also marked the moment when both British and Bengali audiences became acutely aware of the power of drama as a tool for resistance in the struggle for independence. In his defense, Long compared *Indigo Planters* to the best social dramas in dramatic history and noted that "the Drama is the favorite mode with the Hindus for describing certain states of society, manners, customs" (quoted in Bhatia, 1996).

British authorities began to fear that other "subversive" productions were being written and staged. They were right: *Indigo Planters* inspired a wave of anticolonial plays. Upendra Nath Das's *Surendra and Binodini* (*Surendra-Binodini*, 1875) "showed a European Magistrate McCrindle sexually assaulting a maid, Birajmohini, who jumps out of the window to save her honor" (Bhatia, 1996). *The Trial of* Gaekwar (*Gaekwar-durpan*), staged on June 17, 1875, challenged the purported objectivity and fairness of the British legal system by depicting the "farcical trial of Malhar Rao Gaekwar of Baroda, who was forced to abdicate his throne on 27 April, 1875 on [trumped-up] charges of attempting to poison Colonel Phayre, a British resident of Baroda" (Bhatia, 1996). A third play performed in 1875, Dakshina-Charan Chattopadhyay's *The Tea Planter's Mirror* (*Chakar-darpan*), attacked "the cruel and licentious behavior of British planters towards the natives on the tea plantations in Assam" (Bhatia, 1996). This play also threw a very public light on British economic and political policy.

Theater was deemed dangerous enough to prompt the Dramatic Performances Act of 1876, which empowered the government of Bengal to prohibit dramatic performances that were "scandalous, defamatory, seditious, obscene or otherwise prejudicial to the public interest" (Bhatia, 1996; see also Pandhe, 1978; Rao and Rao, 1992). The Dramatic Performances Act of 1876 made it difficult for playwrights to attack British rulers openly, so they turned to historical dramas and attacked Muslim rulers who, reportedly, were generally understood to represent the British (see Bhatia, 1996). Playwrights also turned women into symbols of the nation. For example, Girish Chandra Ghosh's 1889 play *Profulla* portrayed a wealthy merchant's wife as "mother

India." The rape of a Hindu woman became a metaphor for the violation of the motherland. (This strategy was later exploited by the British, who began to ban plays ostensibly because of their treatment of women rather than their overt criticism of the British Raj.) Playwrights also cloaked their attacks in adaptations of Shakespeare and in mythological stories (see Bhatia, 1996).

The partition of Bengal in 1905 caused a new wave of protest plays, followed by yet another backlash of government censorship. So when Krishnaji Prabhakar Khadilkar (1872–1948) wrote what is now considered to be one of the most important political plays in Marathi, he cloaked its message in a story from *The Mahabharata*. *The Slaying of Keechaka* (*Keechaka-vadham*, 1907) was written, according to scholar Rakesh Solomon, to support the Nationalist wing of the Indian National Congress. The Nationalist wing, led by Bal Gangadhar Tilak (1856–1920) and Aurobindo Ghosh (1872–1950), advocated opposing British rule by any available means, including violence. The liberal wing, led by Gopal Krishna Gokhale (1866–1915), advocated peaceful resistance by working within colonial law. (These two stances were later reconciled by Mohandas Gandhi in *satyagraha*, which literally means "truth action" and is a legitimate form of political action by the people against the injustices of the state. It was both peaceful and unlawful). In *The Slaying of Keechaka*

> the heroic Pandavas' unjust and temporary servitude echoes the Indians' subjugation under colonial rule, Keechaka's molestation of the chaste and beautiful Sairandhri (i.e. the disguised Draupadi) represents the abuse of Mother India by Lord Curzon (Viceroy 1899–1905); Kankabhata's (i.e. the disguised Yudhisthira's) caution resembles the liberals' ineffective constitutional approach; and Ballaba's (i.e. the disguised Bhima's) violent punishment of Keechaka suggests the efficacy of the Nationalists' methods. (Solomon, 1994)

The production used many elements of Sanskrit performance, including an opening *puja* (literally, sacred offerings) and concluding prayer. But it also used painted scenery, front curtains, and painted drops and was performed on a proscenium stage.

The Slaying of Keechaka was banned in 1910. While the authorities were keeping such a close eye on the Marathi stage, Bhargavram Vitthal Warerkar (1883–1964), known as "Mama" or "Uncle" Warerkar, approached the owner of a *tamasha* company and asked for permission to write several political plays that never would have passed the censors. Warerkar wrote four *tamasha* plays about patriots such as the Rani of Jhansi (c. 1830–1858), who led an uprising to protest the British annexation of her land after the death of her husband and was killed fighting in the first war of independence, and Vasudeo Balwant Phadke (1845–1883), who led a violent campaign against British rule in 1879 aimed at establishing an Indian republic. Warerkar was proud of his *tamasha* plays because he was able to spread news of the nationalist movement to a nonliterate audience. Tilak also used traditional performance to spread nationalist sentiment. In the late 1800s Tilak expanded a popular Ganesh festival by several days to include *bhajans* (devotional tunes) to Ganesh, who is primarily worshipped as the remover of obstacles. Tilak mobilized Ganesh in the fight against the obstacle of British rule:

> O Ganesh, bring an end to all obstacles. Take away this illusion, for we are all oppressed by the *Kali yuga* [the dark age, or British rule]. . . . [O]ur motherland calls to you. Do not abandon us, but ward off this peril. Give us the *modaka* [a kind of dessert, which is Ganesh's favorite food] of self-rule as your *prasada* [blessing]. (quoted in Courtright, 1985)

While sections of the elite were learning to despise traditional performance in the theater, other people were using it to avoid censorship and to speak to "the masses" in a way that prefigured the work of the Indian People's Theatre Association in the 1940s (discussed later).

Meanwhile, "bookish" plays were increasingly popular, which meant that actors had to learn their lines and no longer improvised in and around a story, as they had in Bhave's first play. An 1874 ad for a performance in the *Belgaum Samachar* promised that "the actors will generally speak according to the book" (quoted in Gokhale, 2000). At the same time, stagecraft was changing:

> The drop curtain in the old mythological plays used to bear crudely drawn, gaudily colored representations of deities—Ganapati, Maruti or Shankar-Parvati. But when "bookish" plays were performed, an attempt was made to convey to the audience the exact locations of the scenes, such as roads, temples, gardens, palaces, hills, jungles or rivers, by means of curtains depicting them as faithfully as possible. Since some of these plays dealt with contemporary subjects and since, meanwhile, education in the new English techniques of painting had become available, skills in curtain painting improved. The greatest change was visible in the settings. Earlier a garden used to be represented by means of a few branches stuck on the stage; but now, in addition to the gardens painted on curtains, real trees, potted shrubs and plants would be placed on stage to complete the illusion of the real. (quoted in Gokhale, 2000)

Sets got further and further away from the bare stage of Sanskrit drama or the open-air three-quarter thrust with a handheld half curtain that was customary in many genres of traditional performance.

According to Gokhale (2000), Mama Warerkar was "the first dramatist to declare his commitment to 'modernity.' " Dedicated to using drama as a social tool, he turned for formal inspiration to HENRIK IBSEN. In 1931 he wrote *The Golden Spire* (*Sonyacha kalas*), a play about mill owners' exploitation of labor. Gokhale says:

> The form of the play was "new," that is, Ibsenian. This meant there was unity of time and space and a single narrative line. No characters were introduced by way of comic relief. The play began with the exposition which caught the main protagonists just before the dramatic crisis, the middle of the play developed the crisis and brought it to a head, and the end resolved it. (Gokhale, 2000)

Although Warerkar threw in a few songs and painted his characters in black and white, he demonstrated that the Shakespearean structure "could be effectively replaced by a tighter structure of three acts" (Gokhale, 2000).

Gokhale claims that the first "modern" play in Marathi is *School for the Blind (Andhalyanchi shala)*, produced on July 1, 1933 by Natyamanwantar. Natyamanwantar was

> formed with the specific purpose of bringing modern drama to the Marathi stage. What constituted its modernity in the eyes of the playmakers and their critics was not simply the number of songs, but the structure of the play, the stage design and the acting style. A "modern" play was expected to have a cohesive structure of three single-scene acts, a theme that reflected an engagement with the human condition, a credible plot and rounded characters, dialogue that would serve a dramatic purpose while sounding conversational, a real-seeming stage set, a natural acting style and, above all, women playing the roles of women. (Gokhale, 2000)

By 1933 "modern plays" had been conflated with "NATURALISM," and the two had become synonymous.

Marathi plays in the 1930s were for the most part "social realist" plays. However, GIRISH KARNAD, one of India's most influential 20th-century playwrights, has pointed out some of the problems these playwrights encountered. First, they set their plays in the living room. While the Western living room symbolizes all that is important to the Western bourgeoisie, Karnad says, space in a traditional Indian home is organized according to

> caste hierarchy as well as the hierarchies within the family. Whether a person is permitted inside the compound, allowed as far as the outer verandah, or admitted into the living room depends on his or her caste and social status. And it is in the interior of the house, in the kitchen, in the room where the gods are kept, or in the backyard, where family problems are tackled, or allowed to fester, and where the women can have a say. Thus the living room as the location of dramatic action made nonsense of the very social problems the playwright set out to analyze, by distorting the caste dimensions as well as the position of women in the family. (Karnad, 1994)

Western REALISM distorted the issues and therefore weakened the plays.

The Development of Modern Theater in Kolkata

The history of modern theater in Kolkata is remarkably similar to the history of modern theater in Mumbai. But because histories of Indian theater in the last fifty years have either created or perpetuated false and useless distinctions between so-called folk theater, so-called classical theater, and so-called modern theater, it is worth examining why these "categories," which are now entrenched, arose. A discussion of 19th-century Bengali theater adds greater clarity to a discussion of the split between modern theater and traditional performance that occurred under colonial rule, while offering a more complicated picture of which aspects of Indian theater are seen as "Western," which are seen as "Indian," and why.

In 1753 the first English theater opened in Kolkata. It was called the Playhouse and was followed in 1775 by the New Playhouse, which catered to Governor General Warren Hastings and other Englishmen of rank and produced plays by Thomas Otway (1652–1685, author of *Venice Preserved*), William Congreve (1670–1729, author of *The Way of the World*), Richard Brinsley Sheridan (1751–1816, author of *The School for Scandal*), and George Farquhar (1678–1707, author of *The Beaux Stratagem*). On May 1, 1789, Mrs. Emma Bristow opened a theater in her Chowringhee residence that catered to the city's elite. She produced *The Poor Soldier*, *Julius Caesar*, *The Sultan*, and *The Padlock*. In 1813, with the support of Sanskrit scholar H. H. Wilson (1786–1860) and Dwarkanath Tagore (1794–1846, grandfather of Rabindranath Tagore), the Chowringhee Theatre opened. Several of its actresses came from the London theater, and it presented not only the classics (Shakespeare, Sheridan, and Oliver Goldsmith), but contemporary English plays. In 1839 the Sans Souci Theatre opened. The Sans Souci is famous for its 1848 production of *Othello*, starring Baishnav Charan Auddy in the title role. As theater historian Sushil Mukherjee says: "A Bengali youth in an English play in an English theatre catering to an English audience in the middle of the nineteenth century is certainly a memorable event" (Mukherjee, 1982). Nonetheless, these playhouses, like their counterparts in Mumbai, were set up for the entertainment of Kolkata's British residents.

Meanwhile, as in Mumbai, Bengalis were beginning to attend, perform in, and write their own plays—although the first play in Bengali was actually done by the Russian Herasim Lebedeff (1749–1817), who in 1795 translated an English play (*The Disguise*) into Bengali and produced it with a cast of Bengali actors. Playwright/historian Adya Rangacharya notes that this was a significant event because for the first time "a play without songs and dance, a play having nothing to do with Indian tradition . . . was brought to the notice of the audience" (Rangacharya, 1971).

Although an editorial appeared in *Samachar Chandrika* calling for "a [Bengali] theatre in the English model" (Mukherjee, 1982) as early as 1826, the plea was not answered until 1851, when Jogendrachandra Gupta wrote *Kirtivilas*. *Kirtivilas* has been described as the "first TRAGEDY in Bengali modeled on the English tragedies" (Rangacharya, 1971). In 1859 Michael Madhusan Dutta (1824–1873) arrived on the scene with his first play, *Sharmistha* (centered on the character Sharmistha). Dutta is credited with modernizing Bengali drama by breaking away from the structure of Sanskrit drama and introducing the form and formalities of English theater—he was the first person to use blank verse in Bengali literature (Mukherjee, 1982; Banerjee, 1989). Clearly, in Kolkata, as in Mumbai, 19th-century Indian theater modeled itself on colonial forms. Dutta noted that his plays were written "for that portion of my countrymen who think as I think, whose minds have been more or less imbued with Western ideas and modes of thinking" (quoted in Banerjee, 1989).

Mehta, Gokhale, Mukherjee, and Sudipto Chatterjee all begin their histories of Indian theater with the first English plays and playhouses. Because the English educational system taught the superiority of English culture, "native theater," of which *tamasha*, *dashavatar*, and *jatra* (a genre of popular theater in Bengal, Bihar, and Orissa) are just three examples, was devalued. So the very term "theater" was colonized. It came to refer only to scripted plays and their productions on formal proscenium stages. It did not include what we now call performance, which was excluded from the history of theater in modern India. Amitava Roy's objection to the categorization of genres such as *jatra* as theater is based specifically on this anglicized separation of theater and performance. "The term 'folk theatre' is itself a misnomer," he writes. "What we do on the proscenium stage is 'theatre,' what our 'folks' have been doing throughout the centuries is best termed 'performance'" (Roy, 1995). Of course he is right, but this is precisely the mind-set that allows this entry to begin with a statement that could be read as an implication that the British brought theater to India, which is far from the truth.

In *The Parlour and the Streets* (1989) Sumanta Banerjee outlines the colonization of upper-class theater culture in Kolkata. Banerjee shows how the divide between high/English/urban culture and low/Indian/rural culture was created. Understanding this split is key to understanding 20th-century Indian theatrical movements. In charting the increasing division between elite and popular culture in Kolkata, based upon an increasing cultural divide between the emerging middle class and the lower class during the 19th century, Banerjee begins by defining the elite in Kolkata as

> composed predominantly of *banians* and *dewans* (intermediaries helping the East India Company to conduct business and administration in relation to the indigenous people) at the beginning; absentee landlords (rentiers appointed by Lord Cornwallis as government agents to collect rents from landed estates under the Permanent Settlement) at a later stage; and as we reach the end of the nineteenth century, a middle class consisting of professionals who were products of an English colonial education system. (Banerjee, 1989)

The lower classes, or "lower orders," as Banerjee refers to them, consisted of "migrants who came to Calcutta from the neighboring villages in search of jobs" (Banerjee, 1989). The lower classes, then, made up the most recent arrivals to the city: the people with the closest, or most recent, ties to rural life.

By the end of the 18th century the Bengali upper class began to realize that the English had firmly established themselves as rulers. In order to improve their economic opportunities, they decided to give their children an English education, and in 1816 a group of "respectable Hindus" met at the house of Chief Justice Sir E. Hyde East to establish Hindu College. An English education was the way to climb the social ladder. Increasingly members of the new Indian middle class "felt education in English language and norms alone could set them apart socially from their humble origins and associations" (Banerjee, 1989). The *bhadralok* (a new class of absentee landlord created by the Permanent Settlement Act of 1795), in order to create their own "distinct cultural forms that could be representative of [their] newly acquired economic status and educational position" (Banerjee, 1989), dissociated themselves from the cultural expressions of the lower classes—from "urban folk culture" with its connections to rural life. The term *geinya*, or rustic simpleton, became a popular put-down. Urban culture became increasingly associated with the upper class and with an English education, while rural culture was increasingly associated with the lower classes. Similarly, "rural" was coming to mean "simple," while "urban" was becoming synonymous with "sophisticated." The 19th-century scholar Dwarkanath Vidyabhushan stated that "traditional folk literary forms" were not "fit for treating any profound subject." He went on to say that "for serious profound compositions, compound words and well-articulated letters are necessary" (quoted in Banerjee, 1989).

Like their counterparts in Mumbai, college-educated Bengalis were learning a "healthy" contempt for their own literature and indigenous culture. John Drinkwater Bethune (chairman of the Education Council), in a letter to a young Bengali, wrote: "By all that I can learn of your vernacular literature, its best specimens are defiled by grossness and indecency" (quoted in Banerjee, 1989). Bethune spoke of cleansing the Bengali language of "grossness and indecency," but he—and other Englishmen—were attacking Bengali culture as a whole, including performance. Soon educated Bengalis began to attack *jatra*. In 1855 one *bhadralok* wrote: "Who that has any pretension to polite taste will not be disgusted with the vulgar mode of dancing with which our play commences; and who that has any moral tendency will not censure the immorality of the pieces that are performed?" (quoted in Banerjee, 1989).

English authorities had by this time adopted Thomas Babington Macauley's plan to create among Bengalis "a class of persons, Indian in blood and color, but English in taste, in opinions, in morals, and in intellect" (Macauley, 1835). Clearly, with respect to theater, they had succeeded. The alternative to the unanglicized *jatra* was the anglicized modern urban theater.

Meanwhile, *jatra* was pushed out to the countryside. As Banerjee suggests,

> Calcutta's popular culture became increasingly marginalized and faced virtual extinction by the turn of the twentieth

century. . . . [T]he *jatra-walas* lost a chunk of their middle class patrons to the new spectacle of the theatre mounted by the bhadraloks. . . . [T]he jatras somehow managed to linger on among the lower orders till the educated gentry launched a concerted campaign against their public performances on grounds of "obscenity." They then sought refuge in the Bengal countryside, where they hoped to rediscover the ties that led to their birth. . . . Quitting the gas-lit urban atmosphere, the kobi songs, tarjas and panchalis [literally, "five-edged debate," a kind of storytelling] descended on the dimly-lit village stage in evenings ringing with the chirp of crickets. (Banerjee, 1989)

Clearly, as they move from gaslight to torches, and as crickets become one of the accompanying instruments, the exiled popular performances also take on a more rural quality. This explains the separation between the rural culture of "the folks" and urban "Westernized" middle-class culture.

However, an 1886 treatise on *jatra* written by Bengali babu Bhubancandra Mukhopadhyay shows that *jatra* had changed in order to compete with the popularity of modern theater:

With the secular quality of life in Calcutta and with the traditional caste-line fast disintegrating under the impact of colonial free enterprise, the nature of the traditional, devotional jatra itself had started to make way for thematically more generalized performances that would attract all sorts of audiences. Several professional jatra companies had emerged that found welcome consumers among the Calcutta audiences. This, in turn, defined popular taste and very soon secular jatra-plays became the norm and rage of the town. A large section of the babu class received these plays well and patronized them. (quoted in Sudipto Chatterjee, 1998)

Sudipto Chatterjee argues that a new "hybridized" *jatra* emerged, one that incorporated elements of the modern theater.

Similarly, Chatterjee claims that modern drama was so popular because it incorporated elements of *jatra*.

The public theatre, despite an apparent disdain for jatra, was nonetheless being influenced by it, especially by imbibing the musicality and histrionic acting style of the folk form and molding it to fit its requirements to attract/address a larger audience. (Sudipto Chatterjee, 1998)

In the late 19th century the direction of Bengali theater—whether it should be modeled on the East or on the West—was a huge topic of debate. As an article published in the literary journal *Madhyastha* recounts:

Some members of our modern educated community believe that theatre does not require songs at all. They have subjected themselves to such a belief after having noted the lack of songs in the European theatre. However, they have failed to contemplate that India is not Europe, European society and our own society are very different, European tastes and our tastes are credibly independent of each other. (quoted in Sudipto Chatterjee, 1998).

Popular taste agreed with the pronouncement in *Madhyastha*. In 1893 Girish Chandra Ghosh (1844–1912), a producer, director, actor, designer, composer, and playwright, produced his own translation of *Macbeth*. It was a dismal failure because it had no songs, and because it faithfully reproduced English stagings of the play. Several other Shakespeare translations were panned. Scholars think that this might have been because Shakespeare was too "foreign." However, Chatterjee points out that

when the principles of Shakespearean drama were applied unannounced to indigenous dramas, the plays were well received. In other words, the Bengali audience did not object to hybridity, but disliked direct imports. The blind respect for everything Sanskrit and/or Shakespearean had given way to a firm basis for an indigenous aesthetics that fed on both the foreign and the native. (Sudipto Chatterjee, 1998)

Ghosh's work is interesting because it proves that modern Indian drama, while influenced by colonial drama, was always re-creating itself on its own terms. Ghosh's work prefigures the work of the Indian People's Theatre Association and the theater of roots in the 20th century.

20th-CENTURY THEATER IN INDIA

Struggle for Independence: The Indian People's Theatre Association

The first conscious, programmatic break with realism came in 1942 when the Indian People's Theatre Association (IPTA), the cultural wing of the Communist Party, was formed in Mumbai and Kolkata with the self-expressed purpose of mobilizing "a people's theatre movement throughout the whole of India as the means of revitalizing the stage and the traditional arts and making them at once the expression and organizer of our people's struggle for freedom, cultural progress and economic justice" (quoted in Pradhan, 1979). So IPTA was following the precedent already set by Tilak and Warerkar (a founding member of IPTA) in their work with Ganesh festivals and *tamasha*.

IPTA had two overlapping goals: they used *jatra* (in Bengal), *tamasha* (in Maharashtra), and *burrakatha* (dramatic ballad singing popular in Andhra Pradesh) to spread awareness among the largely nonliterate rural population of India's subjugation under the English. They also employed these popular entertainments as a way of legitimizing genres of theater denigrated by the English and the English-educated Indian elite. The result was a raised consciousness in the countryside, as well as a democratization of the urban theater. For the first time peasants appeared on the modern stage both as actors and as leading characters. IPTA productions provided both a venue and a forum for urban and rural performers and their respective performance genres to work together. IPTA's goal was nothing less than uniting the upper and lower classes by employing them both in common projects (Bhatia, 1997; Bannerji, 1984; Bhattacharya, 1983).

Most important, however, IPTA overtly linked performance to anticolonial politics. IPTA's most famous production is *New Harvest* (*Nabanna*, 1944), written by Bijon Bhattacharya (1917–1978) and directed by the famous Bengali director Sombhu Mitra (1915–1997), about the Bengal famine of 1943. Nandi Bhatia, in her article "Staging Resistance," notes that *New Harvest* was "more than a play about famine. It is also an attempt on the IPTA's part to expose the sordid reality that the famine was not a natural disaster but a man-made calamity" (1997). *New Harvest* was a stridently anti-imperialist play.

Despite its successes, IPTA was threatened by inherent contradictions. Although several of IPTA's productions were written by T. K. Salmarkar, a "member of a working class family" (Pradhan, 1979), most of the plays IPTA presented were—like *New Harvest*—actually written, directed, and performed by the urban elite. In an article titled "Language and Liberation" Hemani Bannerji points out that most writers (and directors) were "equally removed from the countryside and the city slums" and therefore presented plays "neither created by the people nor narrated in their own voices" (Bannerji, 1984). In other words, IPTA often presented (despite its very good intentions) a middle-class version of a working-class reality. Despite its drawbacks, IPTA is possibly the most important and influential theatrical movement of the 20th century in India.

Decolonizing Theater: The Theater of Roots

The theater of roots movement is a postindependence effort to decolonize the aesthetics of modern Indian theater by challenging the visual practices, performer/spectator relationships, dramaturgical structures, and aesthetic goals of colonial performance—which is to say ways of perceiving, ways of interacting, and ways of structuring experience. Many late 19th-century and early 20th-century productions resisted colonial laws and practices in their subject matter, but the roots movement is important because it challenged colonial culture by reclaiming the aesthetics of performance and by addressing the politics of aesthetics. It began shortly after India's independence in 1947 when playwrights and directors, in an effort to decolonize their work, turned to their "indigenous" roots in religious ritual, classical dance, popular entertainment, martial arts, and Sanskrit aesthetic theory. Habib Tanvir, a member of IPTA and one of the first directors to use popular performance in his productions for aesthetic, as well as political reasons, felt that 200 years of "alien" rule had destroyed India's cultural identity. In 1961 Tanvir called for "our own plays about our own problems in our own forms." He was followed by Girish Karnad, Kavalam Narayana Panikkar, Vijay Tendulkar, Ratan Thiyam, Vijaya Mehta, Neelam Mansingh Chaudhury, Chandrasekhar Kambar, B. Jayashree, Satish Alekar, A. Mangai, K. Kaladharan, Arjun Raina, and Maya Rao, among many others.

The roots movement is significant in that it is the first conscious effort to make a body of work for urban audiences that is different from both modern European theater and traditional Indian performance. Some of the roots work is a fusion of European and Indian dramaturgical structures and practices. In fact, Manipuri director Thiyam (1948–) has defined the roots movement as "a kind of synthesis between modern [Western] techniques and stage-craft on the one hand and ancient Indian traditions on the other" (Thiyam, 1999a). Some critics of the movement see a weakness in this attempt to fuse urban theater with traditional performance because urban theater is not rooted in the needs, calendar, and culture of a particular community. Other critics attack the movement on the basis of relevance. For example, Marathi playwright Mahesh Elkunchwar has asked what relevance traditional performance has in an urban environment: "How can I, with my urban sensibility largely molded by Western thought, hope to relate to them?" (quoted in Gokhale, 2000). Marxist director, playwright, and critic Safdar Hashmi objects to the use of traditional performance in modern theater because he claims that it brings along "the traditional content with its superstition, backwardness, obscurantism, and its promotion of feudal values" (quoted in van Erven, 1992). However, the assertion of the roots movement as a whole is that it is possible to combine contemporary political and social themes with stage practices derived from traditional Indian performance for an urban community.

Although the origins of the roots movement lie in the impulses and experiments of individual artists, these impulses were formalized, institutionalized, and later prescribed by the Sangeet Natak Akademi (the National Academy of Music, Dance, and Drama in Delhi) and scholar-bureaucrats attempting to define an "Indian" theater. The assumptions about theater and culture that gave rise to the movement were articulated by Jawaharlal Nehru, formalized in the government policy that established the Sangeet Natak Akademi, and embedded in the Sangeet Natak Akademi's mission statement and activities that were designed to create a "national" theater. What the Sangeet Natak Akademi actually created was not a single "national theatre" as the title of their 1972 seminar "Emergence of The National Theatre" suggests, but a group of artists spread across the nation who used "indigenous" performance in the making of their modern theater. In an effort to promote the spread of the roots movement as a truly "Indian theatre" the Sangeet Natak Akademi established a Scheme of Assistance to Young Theatre Workers in 1984 to "support the endeavors of young theatre workers engaged in exploring and [developing] a theatre idiom indigenous in character, inspired by the folk/traditional theatre of the country" (*Annual Report*, 1986–1987). For ten years the Sangeet Natak Akademi produced a theater festival in each of four geographical zones. An "expert committee" selected the best of those productions for an annual Theatre Festival in Delhi that was designed to present and represent the best of "Indian theatre." Five years later the Sangeet Natak Akademi could legitimately claim that the scheme, with its twenty-five festivals (twenty regional, five national) of 134 performances (ninety-eight regional, thirty-six national) of plays in twenty-one languages (including several plays written in dialects that until then had not been used for full-length plays) directed by ninety young directors from ninety theater companies involving 2,500 actors and stagehands, judged by sixty experts, and performed for 200,000 audience members had "made significant contributions to all areas of theatre activities" (Awasthi, 1989). However, the scheme provoked numerous criticisms. Marathi playwrights Satish Alekar (1949–) and Mahesh Elkunchwar publicly objected to the scheme on the grounds that a government organization was inappropriately supporting a specific style of theater. The Scheme of Assistance to Young Theatre Workers turned the theater of roots from a movement into a style, prompting criticism that directors tended to use traditional performance as a "glove or a coat to be put on and taken off at will" (Roy, 1995). The goal of creating an "Indian" theater using traditional performance was also criticized by Safdar Hashmi, who pointed out that "Indianness cannot be a matter of form alone. It [must] be a matter of intention, of perception. . . . A play cannot become Indian merely by looking Indian" (Hashmi, 1989).

CONTEMPORARY THEATER: MANY BRANCHES

In the 1980s the roots movement was an overwhelming presence in the Indian theater scene. Today it is just one of many branches of theater. Several branches of theater that are currently addressing issues of cultural and social importance are the English-language theater, women's theater, street theater, children's theater, and Dalit theater. Of course, theater is always more fluid than it is made out to be on paper and many productions belong to more than one of these categories, which are themselves only useful as tools for organizing an article.

English-Language Theater

English is dismissed by some in India as a foreign language and, until recently, plays written in English have stayed on the fringes of the theater scene because they have been associated with mindless British drawing-room COMEDY and English-speaking elite. However, playwrights MAHESH DATTANI and Manjula Padmanabhan have changed this. Dattani takes as his subject the complicated dynamics of the modern urban family. His characters struggle for some kind of freedom and happiness under the oppressive weight of tradition, cultural constructions of gender, and repressed desire. Dattani is concerned with the "invisible issues" in Indian society, including incest and homosexuality. In several plays he takes issues surrounding homosexuality out of the closet and places them on stage for public viewing and dialogue.

Padmanabhan has taken on a variety of issues, such as violence against women and the riots in Mumbai and Gujarat (in *Hidden Fires*, a collection of monologues performed and published in 2003). Her most famous play is *Harvest*, which won the 1997 Onassis Award for Theatre and focuses on the international organ trade. In *Harvest*, the lead character Om signs up to be an organ donor for an American woman named Ginni, because there are no other jobs available for him in Mumbai. Ginni pays him to lead a "clean" and "healthy" life (terms *she* defines) so she can harvest healthy organs whenever she needs them. Ginni begins to control every aspect of Om's life, from when and what he eats to who he sees and how he uses the bathroom. In fact, Ginni begins to control the entire family. *Harvest* is a personalization of the politics of organ donation in a global economy and a play about how the "first" world cannibalizes the "third" world to fulfill its own desires. *Harvest* is an exceptional play because it focuses both on questions of individual moral choice and the social structures that make those choices seem necessary. Through Om's wife, Jaya, who refuses to participate in an economy of greed and degradation, the play ultimately suggests the possibility of a world in which there are no sellers and buyers, only partners.

Women's Theater

Nineteenth-century nationalist constructions of India confined women to the home. Partha Chatterjee traces the way the discourse of nationalism created a dichotomy between outer and inner that, when applied to daily life, "separate[d] the social space into *ghar* and *bahir*, the home and the world" (1993). *Bahir* belonged to the men, who had to make adjustments in their style of dress, their language, and their mannerisms in order to work with colonial administrators. "In the world," Chatterjee asserts, "imitation of and adaptation to Western norms was a necessity; at home, they were tantamount to annihilation of one's very identity" (1993). *Ghar*, the home, became the domain of women, and it came to represent "one's inner spiritual self, one's true identity" (1993). Mothers became the gatekeepers of "authentic" Indian culture, and, as such, their purity had to be protected. As a result, their movement was circumscribed, and the presence of women onstage was seen as a transgression of respectability (see Bhatia, 1996).

This social prohibition still operates. As a result, many women find it difficult—but enormously liberating—to join theater groups. In a series of interviews grouped together under the title "In Her Own Words: Actresses Speak" (1996) several actresses spoke about staying up all night to finish their "chores" and "duties" before rehearsal so no one could accuse them of neglecting their familial responsibilities. They spoke about their families' attempts to discourage them from acting. And they spoke about the prejudices they encounter—for example, not being thought of as directors (or leaders) and not having the same access to formal training. However, they spoke of the emotional support they got from other actors, the "inhibitions" they overcame, and the sense of power they acquired through theater. "I had to spend twenty-four hours within four walls, couldn't talk to anyone," one woman said.

"Theatre gave me the scope to interact with people. This is what I keep coming for." Another woman said, "Theatre is a very important part of a woman's life, because it gives her what life and society don't give her." A third woman said, "I came to realize that [through theater] I . . . could make everybody listen to what I thought of them." One participant in a theater workshop held for sex workers in Kolkata said: "If I can put my sad tale before society, it eases my burden. I feel lighter, more peaceful" ("'Amra Ananda Payi,'" 1996).

Many women in India resist the term "feminist" because they feel that it refers primarily to the concerns of middle-class white women in the United States and not to the issues they face on a daily basis. They prefer the more expansive term "women's theater," of which there are many types. There are solo performances retelling *The Mahabharata* from the point of view of the main female character Draupadi, adaptations of BERTOLT BRECHT's MOTHER COURAGE, plays about adolescent women, USHA GANGULI's adaptation of RUDALI about a woman's fight for survival, TRIPURARI SHARMA's work with *khayal* (a genre of popular theater from the Indian state of Rajasthan) and *nautanki* (an operatic drama performed in the Indian states of Rajasthan, Uttar Pradesh, and Punjab) artists on the subject of "woman," and A. Mangai's street theater piece *The New Born* (*Paccha mannu*, 1996), which deals with female infanticide and the abortion of female fetuses and was designed to be performed in districts outside Chennai where female infanticide and the abortion of female fetuses are prevalent.

The New Born presents a series of formative moments between a woman's birth and her first childbirth. Mangai's premise is that the rituals of socialization are the moments in which patriarchy is inscribed onto and embedded in the consciousness of girls and young women. Mangai and her actors "collected the songs and ritual practices of ceremonies conducted during puberty, marriage and first pregnancy" (Mangai, 1998). Then they rewrote and recontextualized those to re-present the experiences of women in the area. For example, Mangai placed a popular all-female puberty ritual in the play, but she changed the lyrics to the song and the context in which it was performed. Mangai says that the song and the ceremony both serve to imprison the girl, to end her freedom, and to place her under the ever more watchful eye of her family. In Mangai's production the girl ends up entangled in a net. In this way Mangai literalizes and stages the way women get entangled in their gender roles through socialization. Because it is other women who imprison the girl in the net, Mangai's staging demonstrates the way women are complicit in replicating the patriarchal system. Mothers are often the ones who, in passing on accepted traditions, trap their own daughters. By turning the private rituals of women into public forums of debate, Mangai also focuses on forms of performance that, as she says, are "never recognized as performance" (2002a). *The New Born* is an interesting and important contribution to "women's theater" because women's rituals are simultaneously the form, subject, and means of communication.

STREET THEATER

Most of the street theater done today grew out of the work IPTA did in the 1940s. As its own movement, street theater gained momentum in the 1970s with the work of BADAL SIRCAR and Safdar Hashmi. Sircar began performing in the streets to reach audiences that either would not or could not come to a theater hall to see a performance. He eventually created what he called Third Theater, which is neither urban proscenium theater nor traditional performance, but a third kind of theater (he calls it *anganmancha*, which literally means courtyard stage). Sircar's company Shatabdi performs without sets, lights, costumes, sound, or makeup in the street, in bare rooms, and in courtyards—anywhere that is free. He charges one rupee as a token entrance fee, but waives that for anyone who cannot afford to pay. Thus he has freed himself from the constant struggle to raise money and has created a modern people's theater. Sircar's real strength, according to scholar Rustom Bharucha, is that he goes beyond easy political statements and simple analyses of topical events. Sircar deals with "the individual caught in the network of politics," and "he never fails to emphasize that his spectators are responsible for the world they live in" (Bharucha, 1983).

Hashmi dedicated himself to creating a political theater "that would effectively express the emotions and concerns of India's working class" (quoted in van Erven, 1992). Hashmi defines street theater as a "militant political theatre of protest. Its function is to agitate the people and to mobilize them behind fighting organizations" (Hashmi, 1989). His company's first piece, the thirteen-minute play *Machine*, has had an enormous impact on the street-theater movement. *Machine* was inspired by a situation at a nonunionized chemical factory: workers wanted a place to park their bicycles and a place to get a cup of tea. Management refused to grant their demands, and the workers went on strike. Guards fired on the strikers, killing six workers. *Machine*, which was first performed on October 15, 1978, is still being performed around the country in a wide variety of languages and adaptations. Both street theater and Third Theatre have contributed significantly to what Hashmi has called the "democratization" of Indian theater.

Street theater is obviously closely connected to theater for development, a term that encompasses various kinds of theater performed or initiated by government organizations and nongovernmental organizations (NGOs) working with Dalits, women, children, sex workers, and other marginalized populations to educate people with respect to family planning, hygiene, the building of latrines, sexual health, HIV/AIDS, female infanticide, gender, and caste concerns. Theater for development is generally employed as a tool to reach people in areas with low literacy rates and is didactic in nature.

Children's Theater

Vijay Tendulkar, one of India's most important playwrights, asserts that theater has the power to change the world only when it is aimed at children. You cannot change adults, he argues, so if you want to make an impact, you have to do theater for children while they are still children. Children's theater is a well-respected stream of Indian theater. In fact, students at the University of Calicut's School of Drama in Kerala choose between specializations in directing, acting, and children's theater, and the National School of Drama has a special Theatre-in-Education wing devoted to educating children through theater. Although there are the usual number of fairy tales, there is quite a bit of very serious theater aimed at young audiences. For example, Natrang Jammu works regularly with children. Its piece *Mere hisse ki dhoop kahan hai* teaches children about the impact of overpopulation. Another play, *Aaj ki aurat*, performed in Delhi in 1995, deals with issues of the girl child, dowry, and gender discrimination. *Ek ekke ek*, produced by Indian Mime Theatre, uses mime, dance, and music to examine the adult world from the children's point of view. Other groups use theater workshops for what they call "personality development." For example, Srijan in Jodhpur encourages children to think for themselves and to develop self-confidence by improvising and performing their own scripts. Nandikar, one of Kolkata's better-known theater groups, started a project called In Search of Children's Theatre in 1992. Its first project involved children from slum areas and used theater as a tool for self-expression and collective cultural action. Salaam Balak Trust in Delhi, which is dedicated to helping street children, has a similar ongoing project: one of its activities is to help children improvise plays that detail their experiences on the street. These plays are performed in front of government offices in Delhi as a way of raising awareness of their plight and the related issues of village poverty. These are only a few examples of the huge number of productions aimed at educating, empowering, and challenging the young and the underprivileged.

Dalit Theater

"Dalit" means "ground down" or "depressed" in Marathi and is the term used by politicized ex-Untouchables to describe themselves with respect to the oppression they have endured. Dalit theater is closely connected to the Dalit movement, which began as a political movement among the Mahars, a caste of Untouchables in Maharashtra. The Mahars traditionally worked in their villages as watchmen and messengers and as the people responsible for removing dead cattle and other animals. They could not eat with members of a higher caste or drink water from the same well; they were prevented from entering temples at all and from entering certain other buildings through the front door; and they were denied access to education. However, the Mahars were also the singers, dancers, comedians, and drummers of *tamasha*. As such, they have their own oral tradition of stories and songs.

In the 1920s Dr. B. R. Ambedkar emerged as the "father" of the Dalit movement. A lawyer, writer, reformer, and politician, Ambedkar worked to educate and politicize Mahars in Maharashtra and to fight for their rights. He founded newspapers to unify Untouchables, and educational organizations that to this day run colleges in several major cities. He also championed reserved seats for Untouchables in the legislature. In 1956 Ambedkar led millions of Untouchables in a mass conversion from Hinduism to Buddhism. This conversion was a rejection of everything associated with caste Hinduism—Hindu mythology and notions of rebirth, pollution, and untouchability—in favor of a religion that did not legitimize caste hierarchy. Thus Untouchables became Dalits. "Dalit," says poet Arjun Dangle, "is not a caste but a realization" (Dangle, 1992). In the 1960s Dalits began to write about their experiences: Dalit poetry, novels, and autobiographies began to appear, and in the 1970s this outpouring of work was recognized as Dalit Sahitya, or literature of the oppressed. Dalit Sahitya is a socioliterary movement that demands, through literature, social change and economic justice. Dangle defines Dalit Sahitya as that "which acquaints people with the caste system and untouchability in India, [with] its appalling nature, and [with] its system of exploitation" (Dangle, 1992). Many people think of Dalit Sahitya as the most important literary movement of the last fifty years in India.

In the theater, politically active Dalits stopped participating in *tamasha* (which takes its plots from Hindu mythology) after the Buddhist conversion. They reconstructed *tamasha* so that it focused on the life of Ambedkar and on the Buddhist conversions, and they called it Ambedkari Jalsa. They performed Jalsas to spread the teaching of Ambedkar and to create greater political awareness among both the Untouchables (those who had not yet converted to Buddhism or become politically active) and Dalits. Although Jalsas are rarely performed these days, a piece called *Ambedkari Jalsa*, directed by Prakash Tribuwan of Dalit Theatre in Aurangabad, was performed in 1991 as part of the Sangeet Natak Akademi's Scheme of Assistance to Young Theatre Workers in a festival held at Jodhpur.

Premanand Gajvi, whose play *A Sip of Water* (*Ghotbhar pani*) about the politics of drinking water has been performed over 1,000 times in villages all over Maharashtra, has talked about the marked absence of "modern" plays in Dalit literature. He attributes this in part to a lack of funds available to Dalit writers. "What we get," he says, are "tamasha-type plays presented raw, so to say—under trees in villages" (Gajvi, 1998). There is some criticism of Dalit theater: that it focuses exclusively on oppression, which gives it a narrow focus and tone; and that it only addresses the Dalit community. However, Gajvi notes that two Dalit plays—Texas Gaekwad's *Wait, Rama's Reign Is on Its Way* (*Thamba Ramrajya yet ahe*) and DATTA BHAGAT'S ROUTES AND ESCAPE ROUTES (*Wata palwata*)—"have made a mark." The impact of Dalit theater on society as a whole, and on theatrical culture in particular, remains to be seen. But Dalit theater and Dalit writers are receiving more and more attention in national theater festivals and in publication.

WORKING CONDITIONS IN CONTEMPORARY INDIAN THEATER

Clearly there is a great deal of theater being done all over India, but it is done in extremely difficult circumstances. Most actors working in noncommercial urban theater are not paid, cannot rehearse full-time, and have little or no formal training. There are both professional and commercial theater companies and theaters in most cities. For example, one company has given more than 2,000 performances of its farce about three young roommates (one blind, one mute, and one deaf) all over Maharashtra. However, the vast majority of urban theater in India is "amateur," when viewed from an economic perspective. Some of this amateur theater is done in connection with universities, some is done for amusement and entertainment or as an excuse for socializing, and some is done as a way to launch a career in film or television. Most of it, however, is best described as amateur theater with professional standards of performance and production, mounted by companies composed of theater experts and enthusiasts who have other jobs to pay the rent. Although some groups get a substantial percentage of their income from ticket sales and others rely on corporate sponsorship, many rely on the limited funding available from the Sangeet Natak Akademi and state arts academies. Panikkar's company Sopanam and Thiyam's company Chorus Repertory Theatre offer two other models of survival.

Sopanam

Panikkar has his own company, Sopanam. In 1991 he had a multiyear grant from the Ford Foundation that allowed him to pay his actors and also provided funds to bring in experts to do workshops with the actors in various traditional genres. In other words, Panikkar's actors were well paid and well trained. However, the only rehearsal space they could find was the outdoor courtyard of a school near Panikkar's house, which meant that they could only rehearse in the evenings when the school was empty. Rehearsal hours were shorter for the women, who had to leave early in order to be home before dark. In 1992 his Ford Foundation grant ended, and Panikkar had to support his company on grants from the Department of Culture and on the money the company made from performances.

The grant from the Department of Culture covered only eight actors. But the Department of Culture only provided Rs. 750 per actor per month, and Panikkar had more than eight actors in the company (the cost of a round-trip bus ride from the center of Thiruvananthapuram to Panikkar's house was Rs. 10 in June 2004). In an effort to generate income for the company, Panikkar wrote a television serial, which also provided an opportunity for his assistant director to direct and for his actors to be seen on television. As a result, many of Panikkar's leading actors left the company to try to make it in television. Although many of them have since returned, turnover for financial reasons remains a big problem.

In 1993 Panikkar took on a number of new actors, but without the Ford Foundation money, there was neither the time nor the resources to train them intensively. They had to learn by doing and by taking small "tutorials" here and there from the senior actors. Furthermore, the actors had to take on other jobs to support themselves: Sujatha tutored students in Hindi, G. Ayyappan taught dance to young children, Krishnakumar had a job at local Milma (milk) stand, and P. Gopinath taught *kalarippayattu* (a martial art) at a school two hours outside Thiruvananthapuram, which meant that he missed rehearsal twice a week. The length of the rehearsal day was shortened to accommodate the actors' work schedules.

Panikkar has since built a theater behind his house where he can rehearse whenever he wants, and the Department of Culture has increased both the number of company members it will support and the amount of that support. In 2003 it funded nineteen actors at Rs. 3,000 per month each. Sopanam now rehearses from 9 A.M. to 6 P.M. six days a week. However, it still is not easy: Panikkar's house is far away from the center of the city, and it takes the actors an hour to get there by bus. Furthermore, one of Panikkar's best actors, who has been with the company for over thirteen years, got married in 2002 and quit the company to get a better-paying job so he can support his family.

Chorus Repertory Theatre

Thiyam's Chorus Repertory Theatre is structured differently. When Thiyam founded the company in 1976, he realized that he would have to invent a new company structure if it was going to survive. He set up a collective in which all members are responsible for growing the vegetables they eat, raising chickens, and cooking meals for the group. A similar ethic applies to theatrical projects: everyone has administrative duties and artistic responsibilities such as building props, costumes, and set pieces. "Chorus is not like any other repertory company," Thiyam says.

> Apart from theatre it is involved in many other issues like environment and water conservation. . . . Every actor has to learn carpentry, tailoring, light design and stage design. Actors at Chorus develop and craft their own properties, which gives them a strong sense of belonging. The attempt is to develop artists with a holistic attitude toward the theatre. We discourage specialization, which ultimately harms the cause of theatre. (Thiyam, 1994)

In 1980 the Chorus Repertory Theatre received a token grant from the Sangeet Natak Akademi and a grant from the Department of Culture that covered the salaries of seven members of the company. It bought a piece of land and started a fishery and a piggery. However, the fish were swept away by floods, and the pigs disappeared. "Survival is a game for the company," writes Kavita Nagpal:

Ratan has created an efficient team of technicians who are in demand in and around Manipur and the precious money they earn goes to help its sagging fortunes. Ratan hires out his own services as designer at various festivals. The company manages to raise about Rs. 25,000 a year through these "extra-curricular" activities. (Nagpal, 1998)

Thiyam often takes as long as a year and a half to develop a new production, exploring the text through improvisation and spending several weeks on sound patterns alone, but farming continues throughout the rehearsal period. Although the company has now toured the world, receives grant money from a variety of government arts organizations, and has completed a 200-seat brick theater complex, Thiyam does not want anyone to forget the three years they rehearsed in his home, the six times their interim rehearsal space washed away in the monsoons, or the year their crops flooded and all their chickens drowned. Several of Thiyam's twenty-seven actors have been with the company since 1976, and the majority have been company members for over seventeen years. His challenge now is to establish a pension scheme for the older members of his company who will soon have to retire.

Neither Sopanam nor Chorus Repertory Theatre has a "season" as such. Both companies produce one or sometimes two new productions a year, which do not have a "run," but are performed as isolated presentations. For example, a Sopanam production might be presented for one night in Delhi at the Bharat Rang Mahotsav and then not again for several months. However, the piece will stay in the repertory for years. For example, Panikkar first presented Bhasa's play *The Middle One (Madhyama vyayogam)* in 1978, and it is still being performed.

TRAINING

The most famous institution for theater training in India is the National School of Drama (NSD) in Delhi. Originally established in 1959 under the auspices of the Sangeet Natak Akademi, it became an independent school in 1975, with a curriculum based on that of the Royal Academy of Dramatic Arts (RADA) in England. The curriculum has since been modified by directors B. V. Karanth (who introduced the study of several genres of traditional performance) and Ratan Thiyam, but much of the structure set up by the NSD's first director, Ebrahim Alkazi, remains in place. The school offers a three-year actor-intensive training program for students aged eighteen to thirty. In the first year all students take classes in dramatic literature, aesthetics, theory of acting, mime and movement, martial arts and yoga, music, and stage technique. In the second and third years students can specialize in acting or theater techniques and design.

There are also training programs in other cities around the country. For example, the School of Drama at the University of Calicut was established in 1978 "for the practice and preservation of an alternative theatre culture." Students in the three-year bachelor of theater arts (B.T.A.) program can specialize in directing, acting, or children's theater. Women complain, however, that the men get all the directing opportunities, and that they are seen only as actors even when they want to specialize in directing. Rabindra Bharati University also offers a three-year B.A., but students there complain that attendance (on the part of both students and teachers) is low, and that many of them are self-taught. A handful of other colleges and universities offer programs in theater, but the majority do not. Most companies are left to train their own actors either in workshops or as part of rehearsal.

CONCLUSION

From this brief survey of modern Indian theater (its major movements, plays, productions, and issues) it is clear that although modern theater in India began as a colonial enterprise, it quickly defined itself on its own terms and has since been a vital part of the social, cultural, and political life of the nation.

A brief description of several productions presented in 2004 at the now-annual Bharat Rang Mahotsav (National Theatre Festival) organized by the National School of Drama gives an idea of the range of work being produced today. Between March 20 and April 8, 2004, the festival presented seventy-five productions by seventy-three companies (eight of them from foreign countries) in nineteen languages. The festival included a feminist rewriting of a story from *The Mahabharata* by Tripurari Sharma, a solo piece about outsourcing and the call centers that have sprung up around Bangalore and Delhi, the Sanskrit play *Charudattam*, the play *Riot* (inspired by Shashi Tharoor's novel), a multilingual, multimedia rewriting of *Macbeth* titled *Mr. and Mrs. Macbeth*, new plays by Usha Ganguli and Kavalam Narayana Panikkar, *Ei Ngaoba Natte* about the violence in Manipur, a piece combining Brecht's *Antigone* with video documentation of the riots in Gujarat, and a piece performed in "body language" that investigates the dialogue between movement and sound, body and soul, tradition and modernity. This sampling of a few of the many productions presented around the country proves that Indian theater is some of the most vital, important, and varied in the world.

FURTHER READING

"'Amra Ananda Payi': Theatre and the Sex Workers of Kalighat: A Documentation." *Seagull Theatre Quarterly* 9 (1996): 3–36.

Annual Report. Delhi: Sangeet Natak Akademi, 1986–1987.

Awasthi, Suresh. "'Theatre of Roots': Encounter with Tradition." *TDR* 33, no. 4 (1989): 48–69.

Banerjee, Sumanta. *The Parlour and the Streets: Elite and Popular Culture in Nineteenth Century Calcutta*. Kolkata: Seagull Bks., 1989.

Bannerji, Hemani. "Language and Liberation: A Study of Political Theatre in Bengal." *Ariel* 15 (1984): 131–144.

Bapu Rao Naik. "The Beginning, 1843–1880." In *The Marathi Theatre, 1843 to 1960*. Mumbai: Popular Book Depot, 1961.

Bharucha, Rustom. "Government Policy: Anatomy of Official Cultural Discourse." In *Rasa: The Indian Performing Arts in the Last Twenty-five Years*. Vol. 2. Kolkata: Anamika Kala Sangam, 1995.

——. *Rehearsals of Revolution: The Political Theater of Bengal*. Honolulu: Univ. of Hawaii Press, 1983.

Bhatia, Nandi. *Acts of Authority, Acts of Resistance: Theater and Politics in Colonial and Postcolonial India*. Ann Arbor: Univ. of Michigan Press, 2004.

——. "Staging a Change: Modern Indian Drama and the Colonial Encounter." Ph.D. diss., Univ. of Texas at Austin, 1996.

——. "Staging Resistance: The Indian People's Theatre Association." In *The Politics of Culture in the Shadow of Capital*, ed. by Lisa Lowe and David Lloyd, Durham, N.C.: Duke Univ. Press, 1997. 432–460.

Bhattacharya, Malini. "The IPTA in Bengal." *Journal of Arts and Ideas* (January–March 1983): 5–22.

Bhattacharya, P. K. *Shadow Over Stage*. Kolkata: Barnali, 1989.

Chatterjee, Partha. *The Nation and Its Fragments*. Princeton: Princeton Univ. Press, 1993.

Chatterjee, Sudipto. "The Colonial Stage(d)." Ph.D. diss., New York Univ., 1998.

——. "From Colonial Jatra to Native Theatre: Hybrid Aesthetics of Nineteenth Century Bengali Theatre." *Seagull Theatre Quarterly* 31 (2001): 24–32.

——. "The Nation Staged." In *Imperialism and Theatre*, ed. by J. Ellen Gainor. London: Routledge, 1995.

Courtright, Paul. *Ganeśa: Lord of Obstacles, Lord of Beginnings*. New York: Oxford Univ. Press, 1985.

Dangle, Arjun, ed. Poisoned Bread: Translations from Modern Marathi Dalit Literature. Bombay: Orient Longman, 1992.

Das Gupta, Hemendra Nath. *The Indian Stage*. Kolkata: M. K. Das Gupta, 1944.

Deshpande, G. P. "Fetish of the Folk." *Economic Times* (23 December 1984).

Gajvi, Premanand. "The Here and Now Are Important: An Interview with Premanand Gajvi." Seagull Theatre Quarterly 19 (1998): 50–57.

Gokhale, Shanta. *Playwright at the Centre: Marathi Drama from 1843 to the Present*. Calcutta: Seagull Bks., 2000.

Guha, Ranajit. "Neel-Darpan: The Image of a Peasant in a Liberal Mirror." *Journal of Peasant Studies* 2, no. 1 (1974): 1–46.

Hashmi, Safdar. *The Right to Perform*. Delhi: Sahmat, 1989.

"In Her Own Words: Actresses Speak." *Seagull Theatre Quarterly* 9, nos. 55–65 (1996).

Jacob, Paul, ed. *Contemporary Indian Theatre: Interviews with Playwrights and Directors*. New Delhi: Sangeet Natak Akademi, 1989.

Jain, Nemichandra. *Indian Theatre: Tradition, Continuity, and Change*. New Delhi: Vikas, 1992.

Kanhailal, H. "Theatre Is Only a Link Between Heritage and Community." *Seagull Theatre Quarterly* 14/15 (1997): 41–51.

Karnad, Girish. "The Arts and Social Change in India." In *Indian Culture in Motion*. Amsterdam: Royal Tropical Institute, 1998.

——. *Three Plays*. Delhi: Oxford Univ. Press, 1994.

Khilnani, Sunil. *The Idea of India*. New York: Farrar, Straus, Giroux, 1998.

Lal, Ananda, ed. *The Oxford Companion to Indian Theatre*. New Delhi: Oxford Univ. Press, 2004.

Macauley, Thomas Babington. "Minute on Education. 2 February." 1835. In *Macauley: Poetry and Prose*, selected by G. M. Young. London, 1952. 729.

Mangai, A. "Cultural Intervention Through Theatre: Case Study of a Play on Female Infanticide/Foeticide." *Economic and Political Weekly* 33, no. 44 (1998): 70–72.

——. Interview with the author. June 25, 2002a.

——. " 'Let Me Live'—Cry the Baby Girl, in the Cradle and in the Womb: *Paccha Mannu*—An Interventionist Theatre Experience." In *Muffled Voices: Women in Modern Indian Theatre*, ed. by Lakshmi Subramanyam. New Delhi: Shakti Bks., 2002b. 215–230.

Mangai, A., S. Raja Samuel, and Mina Swaminathan. "Confronting Discrimination: Some Approaches to the Issue of Female Infanticide." *Search Bulletin* (July–September 1998): 64–74.

The Marathi Theatre: 1843 to 1960. Mumbai: Popular Book Depot, 1961.

Mee, Erin, ed. *DramaContemporary: India*. Baltimore: Johns Hopkins Univ. Press, 2001.

Mehta, Kumudini Arvind. *English Drama on the Bombay Stage in the Late Eighteenth Century and in the Nineteenth Century*. Bombay: Univ. of Bombay, 1960.

Mukherjee, Sushil. *The Story of the Calcutta Theatres, 1753–1980*. Kolkata: K. P. Bagchi, 1982.

Nagpal, Kavita. "Pre-text." In *Chakravyuha*, by Ratan Thiyam. Calcutta: Seagull Bks., 1998.

Pandhe, Pramila, ed. *Suppression of Drama in Nineteenth Century India*. Kolkata: India Book Exchange, 1978.

Pradhan, Sudhir. *Marxist Cultural Movement in India: Chronicles and Documents; 1936–47*. Kolkata: National Book Agency, 1979.

Rangacharya, Adya. *The Indian Theatre*. New Delhi: National Book Trust, 1971.

Rao, Amiya, and B. G. Rao. *The Blue Devil: Indigo and Colonial Bengal*. Delhi: Oxford Univ. Press, 1992.

Rea, Kenneth. "Theatre in India: The Old and the New; Part Three." *Theatre Quarterly* 8, no. 32 (1978): 47–66.

Roy, Amitava. "Folk Is What Sells Well." In *Rasa: The Indian Performing Arts in the Last Twenty-Five Years*. Vol. 2. Kolkata: Anamika Kala Sangam, 1995.

Solomon, Rakesh. "Culture, Imperialism, and Nationalist Resistance: Performance in Colonial India." *Theatre Journal* 46 (1994): 323–347.

Tanvir, Habib. "The Indian Experiment." In *Theatre in India*. Cochin: Kerala Sangeetha Nataka Akademi, 1977.

——. "Use of Music and Dance in Contemporary Dramatic Performances." *Natya* 5, nos. 1–2 (1961): 57–59.

Theatre in India. Cochin: Kerala Sangeetha Nataka Akademi, 1977.

Thiyam, Ratan. "The Audience Is Inside Me." *Seagull Theatre Quarterly* 14/15 (1997): 62–72.

——. "I Communicate to the World." Interview with Meenakshi Shedde. *Times of India* (November 27, 1997).

——. "Indian Theatre—In Search of Identity." In *Bengali Theatre: 200 Years*, ed. by Utpal K. Banerjee. Delhi: Ministry of Information and Broadcasting, Government of India, 1999a. 220–226.

——. Interview with Shamsul Islam. *Economic Times* (Mumbai) (March 29, 1994).

——. "Uttar-Priyadarshi: Theatre of Manipur." *International Gallerie* 2, no. 2 (1999b): 41–49.

van Erven, Eugène. *The Playful Revolution: Theatre and Liberation in Asia*. Bloomington: Indiana Univ. Press, 1992.

Vatsyayan, Kapila. *Some Aspects of Cultural Policies in India*. Paris: UNESCO, 1972.

——. *Traditional Indian Theatre: Multiple Streams*. New Delhi: National Book Trust, 1980.

Erin B. Mee

INDONESIA

Theater has played a vital role in Indonesia, the world's largest Islamic country, where over 580 languages are spoken by numerous distinct ethnic groups. About sixty percent of the population lives on the island of Java, where Jakarta, the capital and epicenter of modern theater, is located.

Far from being culturally unified, the country is a creation of the mid-20th century. In 1945 the former Dutch East Indies became a constitutional democracy when the Republic of Indonesia declared its independence after 350 years of Dutch rule. However, the government has often fallen short of constitutional ideals. Ethnic and religious differences continue to dominate the cultural climate at the start of the 21st century, despite the government's efforts to develop a unified national culture.

The birth and development of modern Indonesian theater are tied to the country's political and intellectual movements of the 20th century. The use of Bahasa Indonesia, a form of Malay adopted as the national language in the early 20th century as part of the independence movement, is one of the identifying markers of modern Indonesian theater. Unlike "traditional" theater that uses regional languages and is geared toward local communities, modern Indonesian theater is performed in the national language and presented in major urban centers for diverse audiences. Using the common language, modern playwrights are able to address social, political, and religious issues for wider audiences than their own local ethnic groups. This helps forge what anthropologist Benedict Anderson calls "an imagined community" where a common language unites disparate groups and facilitates a sense of nationhood.

The term "modern theater" (*teater moderen*) came into use in Indonesia in the 1960s and is now used to describe Indonesian-language theater as early as 1885. This early modern theater, called *bangsawan*—based on a Parsi theater from Bombay, INDIA—was brought to Sumatra and Java from Penang, Malaya, by traveling troupes.

Bangsawan was familiar because it shared characteristics of local traditional performances such as *wayang* (shadow puppetry) and *topeng* (masked dance drama) that integrate spoken or chanted dialogue, drama, dance, improvisation, and music. These total theater forms also feature "clown" characters and contemporizing devices to criticize or promote current issues and events. But *bangsawan* and its subsequent incarnations (*komedi stamboel* or Malay opera) introduced new elements as well. Unlike traditional theater, *bangsawan* was secular and commercial, using the Indonesian language rather than local dialects. It also introduced a director, used a proscenium stage, and employed texts from nontraditional sources, including *1,001 Nights*, *Zorro*, *The Count of Monte Cristo*, and the local story named after its heroine, *Nyai Dashima*.

Tonil (from the Dutch *toneel* or plays) was the term given to a new noncommercial theater linked to the independence movement from the 1920s to the 1950s. Rustom Effendi's *Bebasari* (1926), an allegory in verse about the struggle against colonialism, is hailed as the first truly modern Indonesian play. It shows a heroic Indonesian youth freeing the imprisoned Princess Bebasari (representing Indonesia) from an ogre king (the Dutch). Spurred on by a burgeoning Indonesian nationalist movement spearheaded by cultural and religious organizations, *Bebasari* represents a more "intellectual" style of play that emerged in the 1920s and 1930s. These nationalist plays are linked with the historically significant 1928 Youth Congress where nationalists took an oath proclaiming "One Country, One Nation, One Language." Indonesian, primarily a trade argot, was chosen as the common medium. Many of the major playwrights, including Sanusi Pane (1905–1968), Mohammad Yamin (1903–1962), and Armijn Pane (1908–1970), were nationalists who wrote allegories ostensibly on historical subjects but actually about current nationalistic themes. Generally these plays recounted the hero's travails as he followed a disastrous path, dying tragically in an unfair world. Sanusi Pane's *The New Man* (*Manusia baru*, 1940) was the first play to deal directly with common, contemporary social problems between laborers and colonial management, attempting to find a suitable resolution by pointing out the personal responsibility of individuals on both sides.

In the 1950s modern Indonesian theater focused on drama, reflecting the influence of Western drama, especially those practices that were current in the Soviet Union, where many young intellectuals studied during the Sukarno era. The result was an emphasis on the importance of the script and a KONSTANTIN STANISLAVSKY–style approach to acting based on psychological realism. Productions of European, American, and Russian playwrights in translation were frequent. What came to be called *teater moderen* was born.

The popularization of the term *teater* (theater) followed the 1955 founding of the Indonesian National Academy of Theatre (Akademi Teater Nasional Indonesia, ATNI) in Jakarta. Several theater troupes subsequently used the word in their groups' names, such as Studiklub Teater Bandung, founded in 1958 and headed by Suyatnya Anirun and Jim Lim, and Teater Populer, headed by Teguh Karya from 1968. Until then, the word *teater* had only been used to name buildings, not to describe a performance practice. There is no indigenous word for "theater" in Bahasa Indonesia, nor for "modern" (*moderen*) or "traditional" (*tradisionil* or *tradisional*). It was only with the adoption of the term *teater moderen* that the concept of "traditional" theater was reflected in the language. Until then, all "theater"—traditional and modern—was considered a type of *tontonan* (literally, a watching) or *pertunjukan* (literally, a showing), what in English we would call "performance."

In the late 1960s a confluence of events precipitated a shift toward a new theater movement that shapes modern Indonesian theater into the 21st century. Influences during this period came from the Western bloc as President Suharto allied his New Order government (1966–1998) away from the Soviets. In the 1960s both Western and Eastern theatrical experimentation was characterized by a return to roots. The transition in Indonesia came with a 1968 performance: a *mini-kata* (minimal word) piece by a young poet named RENDRA (1935–), shortly after he returned to Jakarta from study in New York.

Bip Bop baffled its audience. Its surrealistic staging, nonlinear narrative, and use of nonsense words, as exemplified by the title, were unlike anything anyone had dared to stage. It was clearly modern but did not follow any of the conventions of naturalistic theater associated with *teater moderen*. Instead, with its emphasis on visuals, sound, movement, and improvisation, there were elements that connected it more clearly to traditional performance styles.

Fiscal support for this radical experimentation helped it advance. Also in 1968 a new art center, Taman Ismail Marzuki (TIM), opened in Jakarta as a component of Suharto's national development policy, which mandated the cultivation and promotion of a national culture highlighting the "pinnacle" artistic achievements of various cultures across the archipelago. TIM, which was state funded, showcased performances from across Indonesia and abroad. It quickly became a meeting ground where artists of traditional and modern dance and theater and foreign artists all interacted, not only revitalizing the traditional performing arts, but fostering creative experimentation between traditional and modern performing arts. TIM provided modern theater practitioners with funding and a relatively unrestricted forum for free expression, a unique circumstance in Indonesia, where, under Suharto, social and political criticism were severely curtailed.

In this post-1968 period four pioneering modern dramatist-directors created their companies. Their most significant original plays are noted here.

Rendra and his Bengkel Teater (literally, Theater Workshop) produced *The Mastodon and the Condors* (1973), *Prince Reso* (1986), and *The Ritual of Solomon's Children* (1986). Exemplifying Rendra's hard-hitting political critique, the group's best-known production, *The Struggle of the Naga Tribe* (1975), depicts a village facing exploitation from a foreign mining project supported by government development planners.

ARIFIN C. NOER (1941–1995) and his Teater Ketjil (literally, Little Theater), founded in 1968, are best known for a poetic-metaphysical style that is found in MOTHS (1970), which tells of a dehumanized menial worker who is haunted by a childhood tale of a magic mirror that promises happiness. Their other notable productions include *The Bottomless Well* (1964), *The Clouds* (1969), *The Madun Orchestra Plays I–IV* (1974–1989), *Interrogation I: In God's Image* (*Interogasi I: Dalam Bayangan Tuhari*, 1984), and *In His Image or Interrogation II* (*Dalam Bayangan atau Interogasi II*, 1990).

PUTU WIJAYA (1944–), who founded the Teater Mandiri (literally, Independent or Self-Sufficient Theater) in 1972, has written and directed *Ouch* (1974), *Lo!* (1975), *Crazy* (1980), *Geez* (1981), *Roar* (1982), *Shame* (1988), *Yell* (1991), and *War* (2002). Beginning with *Ouch*, Putu initiated what he called "stupid theater" (*teater bodoh*) by portraying a group of marginalized people facing disturbing moral, ethical, and social dilemmas. His reportage style allowed the audience to draw their own conclusions.

NANO RIANTIARNO (1949–) founded Teater Koma (literally, Comma/Coma Theater) in 1977. This group, characterized by its professional and high-energy productions, has staged Riantiarno's many original plays and adaptations, including *Paper House* (1977), *Time Bomb* (1982), THE COCKROACH OPERA (1985), *Sampek Engtay* (1989), *Succession* (1990), *The Three Gods and the Butterflies* (1992), and *Semar Fights Back* (1995). Riantiarno's plays typically depict the plight of the disenfranchised in modern urban Indonesia.

Although each of these four writer-directors comes from a different part of the country, they have several things in common. Each had an accomplished acting career before founding his own theater group. Each published essays and books and worked for major magazines, journals, and newspapers. In addition, each received national and international awards for their plays, poetry, or novels. When they began their theatrical careers, they were all well versed in Western drama theory. but following Rendra's model, after 1968 they each made a conscious shift in their work back toward indigenous sources even though none had any formal traditional performance training. Their turn to traditional sources happened in several ways and led to the production of experimental works that deviated from Western-style naturalistic staging. Sometimes these deviations included deliberate use of traditional elements such as costumes and setting, as was seen in Rendra's adaptation of Western classics, including *Oedipus Rex* (1969) and *Lysistrata* (1976). Sometimes, as in the work of Riantiarno, the difference was on a more structural level, with the integration of music, singing, and dance found in traditional theater. Traditional forms of folk storytelling, or *dongeng*, have also had a profound influence on their plays, particularly in the works of Noer and Wijaya. Their plays and productions often mingled the fantastic with the ordinary, presented archetypal characters who did not "develop" throughout the course of the drama, featured "clown" characters, freely adapted and played with traditional stories and epics, and presented non-Aristotelian plots.

Sometimes, however, the distinguishing "traditional" characteristic has been even more fundamental, stemming from a traditional spirit that guided how the performance was created from start to finish, how the cast members interacted with their director, and how the performers interacted with the audience, even when the script was a Western play in translation. Experimentation with traditional elements by these directors and playwrights was undertaken, in part, as a way for them to get in touch with their "roots," drawing upon the appeal and role of regional *tontonan*. They also use traditional elements to counteract the Western-borrowed naturalistic conventions of *teater moderen* that had been popularized by the national acting academies. By using traditional elements in their productions, theater practitioners capitalize on and experiment with the tradition's associative powers and popularity rather than replicate traditional forms. The more technical aspects and histories of the various genres are generally less relevant than how traditional theater functions—or is imagined to function—in society, particularly as an educational tool and as an acceptable vehicle for social criticism. Heavy censorship persisted throughout the New Order era, but in many instances even blatantly political theater was successfully presented within the sanctuary of TIM and through using traditional theatrical tropes, such as clown characters. Despite this, there have been cases of censorship, closings, and banning involving all four of these directors, as well as others.

By the late 1980s a second generation of directors and playwrights emerged in this "new tradition," along with a perceptual shift toward an intellectual preoccupation with the postmodern. This is most notably seen in the works of Budi S. Otong and Afrizal Malna (Teater Sae) and Dindon (Teater Kubur, literally, Buried Theater). RATNA SARUMPAET (1949–) (Satu Merah Panggung, literally One Red Stage), a former member of Rendra's Bengkel Teater, stands out as one of a very few successful female directors and political activists in the theater community.

Although modern theater has been primarily active in Jakarta, there have been several regional theater artists of note who have written and mounted productions in Indonesian, including Suyatna Anirun and playwright Saini K. M. (Studiklub Teater Bandung, West Java); Wisran Hadi (Bumi Teater, literally, Earth Theater, Sumatra); Aspar Paturusi (Sulawesi); and Akhudiat (Surabaya). In central Java there are several theater groups that perform modern theater in Javanese, including Kenthut Bambang Widoyo's Teater Gapit (literally Pinch Theater); Fajar Suharno's Teater Dinasti (literally Dynasty Theater); Jujuk Prabowo's Teater Gandrik (literally Ecstatic Theater); and Azwar AN's Teater Alam (literally, Natural World Theater). Traditional theater's artists too have modernized significantly in Bali, where the work of I Wayan Dibia, Sidja, and I Ketut Kodi is notable, and other locales. However, despite creativity and innovation, *teater moderen* directors and playwrights throughout Indonesia have had to struggle to create a steady and significant audience base in the face of declining funding and competition with other modern secular entertainments, such as film, television, and the Internet.

Cobina Gillitt

THE INFERNAL MACHINE

"He shall slay his father. He shall marry his mother." So intones The Voice, the narrator of *The Infernal Machine*, a four-act adaptation of Sophocles' *Oedipus Rex* by JEAN COCTEAU, as the curtain rises on the ramparts of Thebes, where a young soldier boasts of his intention to challenge the Sphinx, who devours all who cannot answer her secret question. This same soldier has reported seeing the ghost of King Laius, who has returned to warn his widow Jocasta and the seer Tiresias; the two soon appear to question the young soldier. The ghost of Laius calls to them, but no one hears him until Jocasta has gone.

Act 2 rises on the Sphinx, in the guise of a young woman. Tired of her murderous interrogations, she is bemoaning her fate when Oedipus arrives. The Sphinx soon entices him to answer her dreaded riddle: what animal walks on all fours in the morning, two feet in the afternoon, and three in the evening? Half in love with the arrogant Oedipus, she tells him the answer (man) and collapses at his feet. Triumphant, he carries her body, now that of a monster, to Thebes.

Oedipus and Jocasta are celebrating their wedding night as act 3 begins. Tiresias comes to give them his blessing, but Oedipus insists on staring into the prophet's eyes and is nearly blinded with pain. Jocasta has an equally terrifying moment when she sees the scars on Oedipus's feet—the marks correspond to the mutilations of her own lost child—although her new husband reassures her by recounting the way he was wounded as an infant.

Seventeen years have passed in relative calm: the royal household boasts four children. But act 4 begins with the arrival of a messenger who brings news not only of Polybus's death (Oedipus's ostensible "father"), but also the revelation of a secret: Oedipus was a foundling adopted by a shepherd. Jocasta begins to panic. Oedipus then muses that at least he did not kill Polybus and describes the location of the accident that killed Laius. Jocasta, past hope, hangs herself with a scarf. The shepherd who found the infant Oedipus appears to confirm the worst: Oedipus has indeed killed his father and married his mother. He blinds himself with Jocasta's earrings and is led out of the city by his daughter Antigone, shadowed by his wife's ghost.

Like all of Cocteau's interpretations of classic myths, *The Infernal Machine* mixes social COMEDY, domestic FARCE, and mysterious symbolism to arresting effect. STAGE DIRECTIONS call for raucous jazz sound cues, and Jocasta, a kind of aging socialite, refers to Tiresias as "Zizi" and speaks in what Cocteau slyly calls "the international accent of royalty." As for Oedipus, his narcissism is closer to that of Orpheus than to the behavior of a classical hero; he is not even granted the triumph of solving the Sphinx's riddle, since she gives him the answer herself. Cocteau's Boulevard satire diminishes the story's tragic grandeur, with the odd effect that the characters seem more modern but less sympathetic. His interest lies in the evocation of the "infernal machine," his sense of life not as a series of existential choices, but as fatalistically determined by a supreme justice.

The Infernal Machine premiered in Paris on April 10, 1934. The play received its best reviews from conservative critics, who praised Cocteau for his "good taste." Later critics have been divided; some call the play Cocteau's masterpiece, while others, such as biographer Frederick Brown, dismiss the play as being "composed of old spare parts ingeniously riveted together with gimmicks" (1968).

[*See also* Expressionism; France; Surrealism]

FURTHER READING

Brown, Frederick. *An Impersonation of Angels: A Biography of Jean Cocteau*. New York: Viking, 1968.

Cocteau, Jean. *Diary of an Unknown*. Tr. by Jesse Browner. New York: Paragon House, 1988.

——. *The Infernal Machine*. Tr. by Albert Bermel. In *The Infernal Machine, and Other Plays*. Norfolk, Conn.: New Directions, 1963.

Fergusson, Francis. *The Idea of a Theater*. Princeton: Princeton Univ. Press, 1949.

Oxenhandler, Neal. *Scandal and Parade: The Theater of Jean Cocteau*. New Brunswick, N.J.: Rutgers Univ. Press, 1957.

Charlotte Stoudt

INFORMACIÓN PARA EXTRANJEROS

See INFORMATION FOR FOREIGNERS

INFORMATION FOR FOREIGNERS

In *Information for Foreigners* (*Información para extranjeros*), a play by Argentine playwright GRISELDA GAMBARO, a "guide" shows the different rooms of a nonspecified building to a group of visitors. What appears to be a mere tour of the structure turns into a true journey into the world of torture. A systematic reelaboration of language occurs, in all its expressive dimension: the actors' performance and the public's reaction are developed in the play through a grotesque vision of cruelty and torture, physical and psychological, whose purpose seems to be to analyze the limits and possibilities of language as a weapon against the individual and the world considered "real" or "secure." Torture turns into a subliminal element, always present and threatening.

Information for Foreigners uses almost all the elements present in popular culture, but it distorts them, depriving them of that layer of sentimentalism that keeps them away from our ability to utter a compromised reaction, and throws them at us, like a slap on the face.

Gambaro's play is not addressed to those who are already informed of what is going on in the building's symbolic space. It is for those who have closed their eyes to what is really happening, and the cruelty that seems to seep from *Information* is nothing but our point of view. Our own ignorance is our torture.

During the so-called dirty war in ARGENTINA, the majority of the public reacted with a passive attitude to what was happening, subordinate to power. *Information* is a whole allegory of what was going on at that moment in the country, and to realize that, it is necessary to create a conscious awareness in the public.

The play is organized like some sort of vignette strip, which the public that is present goes on visiting following the direction of the guide, who chooses each vignette in an arbitrary way. This particular use of the "atmospheric" theatrical space has an essential influence on the feeling provoked in the spectator. The fact that the group is placed in some sort of nightmarish labyrinth where horrible things happen in every corner has much to do with the allegory created by Gambaro, and it also allows the space itself to take on a life of its own, turning into another element that participates in the personal torture that each spectator should feel after facing what he or she sees.

The guide himself gets lost in his own building. Perhaps the play is trying to convey here the arbitrary nature of dictatorial power, in which the dictator loses touch with reality, and with it the credibility that could give him an apparent control over things. The citizen/spectator starts to get the feeling that the guide is someone who in truth does not know what he is doing anymore and has lost reference over his own role in the "building." Somehow, the space is transformed into an element, first, of psychological anguish, of threatening environment, and then, of blatant demonstration of the inherent flaws of the building's established system.

The guides are in charge of showing the public attending the show what is going on in the building, as Argentina's political leaders would be doing with their citizens: showing them the scene as they see it. However, they provoke a reaction of disbelief, of the scene's horror: it does not agree with what the guides are showing, or with their attitude, thoroughly dehumanized. Here the concept of "official story," of double meaning, comes into play: what they tell us and what is really going on. The guides' position eventually breaks apart. It is in the spectator's hands to react to it. That is Gambaro's hope.

[*See also* Poor Theater]

Paloma Asensio

INGE, WILLIAM (1913–1973)

A play should be admired for the experiences it gives, not for the idea a playgoer comes away remembering. [The playgoer] should feel richer within himself, more responsive, more aware.

—William Inge, 1954

William Inge was one of the most promising dramatists of the early 1950s, but to many critics, he never succeeded in rising above the second tier of 20th-century American dramatists. Unlike the works of EUGENE O'NEILL, ARTHUR MILLER, and Inge's mentor, TENNESSEE WILLIAMS—the playwrights who dominated mid-20th-century U.S. drama—Inge's sensitive, realistic depictions of emotionally and sexually repressed characters in small-town Kansas settings never broke new ground in form, language, or style. Inge simply conformed to the lyrical realism Williams had pioneered, and with a mastery of that form, Inge found critical approval throughout the 1950s. After 1960 his plays failed to find favor in part because his attempts at experimentation were ineffective and more so because the moral questions and sexual yearnings of his plays seemed locked into the conservative, tightly repressive 1950s.

Inge, born in Independence, Kansas, was the youngest son of Luther Clayton and Maude Sarah (Gibson) Inge. He received a B.A. degree from the University of Kansas at Lawrence in 1935, and his theatrical career essentially began when he acted in tent shows in rural Kansas, starting in 1932. In 1938 Inge completed an M.A. in English at George Peabody College for Teachers before taking a job teaching English at Stephens College in Columbia, Missouri. His interest in theater was heightened when he became a close friend of legendary stage actress Maude Adams, who was also teaching at Stephens. Inge began Freudian psychiatric analysis in this period, attempting to confront his homosexuality and struggle with alcoholism. Freudian theory provided a foundation upon which Inge constructed his characters when he began writing plays, and, together with his admiration for Williams's dramatic techniques, Inge developed an effective formula he exploited in all of his successful plays in the 1950s.

As a critic for the *St. Louis Star-Times*, he traveled to Chicago to interview a new playwright, Tennessee Williams, and to see the premiere of Williams's THE GLASS MENAGERIE. Inspired by Williams's artistic model, Inge wrote his first play, *Farther Off from Heaven* (1945), which was staged by the Margo Jones Theatre in Dallas, Texas. His major theatrical breakthrough came when the prestigious THEATRE GUILD produced his drama *Come Back, Little Sheba* in Westport, Connecticut, in 1949. In 1950 a Broadway production of *Come Back, Little Sheba* was mounted and won the George Jean Nathan Award for Inge. A drama of lost dreams and failed ambitions, *Come Back, Little Sheba* focused on the unhappy marriage of Doc and Lola Delaney. Their "shotgun" marriage twenty years before ended Doc's hope of becoming a real doctor, and Lola's unsuccessful pregnancy leaves her emotionally starved, directing her attentions to her lost dog, Sheba, who disappeared some months before the play's beginning. When a young woman, Marie, becomes a boarder in their home, Doc's passions are aroused, while Lola takes an interest in the young woman's future. They are unable to fulfill their needs through Marie and remain mired in the marriage that symbolizes their lost dreams.

In 1953 Inge's next play, PICNIC, opened on Broadway to enthusiastic reviews. Its plot concerned the unsettling impact of a virile drifter on three generations of women living in a small, rural Kansas town. *Picnic* ran for an impressive 477 performances and won the Pulitzer Prize, the New York Drama Critics' Circle Award, and the Donaldson Award.

Inge followed *Picnic* with *Bus Stop* (1955), a COMEDY-drama featuring Kim Stanley as the "chanteuse" Cherie, who spends a night trapped by a blizzard in a roadside café in Kansas with a group of travelers. She improbably finds love with a rowdy cowboy who must learn to put aside his pride to win her. *Bus Stop* won critical plaudits and a run of 478 performances. Inge's drama *The Dark at the Top of the Stairs* opened on Broadway in 1957 for a run of 468 performances. The play deals with a 1920s Oklahoma family, each of whose members faces fears, especially the young son, who is afraid of the closed, dark attic in the family home. Unhappy marriage, anti-Semitism, and small-town proprieties versus looming modernity are explored by Inge through his strength at characterization.

Inge's impressive string of theatrical successes during the 1950s ended abruptly with his 1959 play *A Loss of Roses*, which closed after a mere twenty-five performances on Broadway. Changing tastes were at least part of the problem, because New York stages increasingly featured experimental works. Inge's personal fortunes were improved by the critically applauded film version of *The Dark at the Top of the Stairs*, which was released in 1960, followed by *Splendor in the Grass*, a hugely popular movie scripted by Inge, who won an Academy Award for Best Original Screenplay.

After 1960 Inge's plays continued to meet with critical and commercial apathy even though Inge began to experiment with form, particularly the challenges of the absurdist plays that were finding productions in this period. Inge's *Natural Affection* (1963) folded after thirty-six performances, and *Where's Daddy?* (1966) managed only twenty-one performances, both driven from the stage by a chorus of critical disapproval. In 1968 Inge began occasional stints teaching theater arts at the University of California at Irvine. Depression over the failures of his recent plays and novels, his continuing struggle with alcoholism, and inner conflicts about his sexuality led him to take his life on June 10, 1973.

Inge remains an exemplar of post–World War II Broadway drama, with themes and characters exuding a bolder brand of realism and an emphasis on sexual and psychological issues. *Come Back, Little Sheba, Picnic, Bus Stop,* and *The Dark at the Top of the Stairs* continue to find frequent revivals on professional and amateur stages, ensuring Inge's reputation as one of the finest American dramatists of the 1950s.

[*See also* United States, 1940–Present]

PLAYS: *Farther Off from Heaven* (1945); *Come Back, Little Sheba* (1950); *To Bobolink, for Her Spirit* (1950); *Picnic* (1953; later revised as *Summer Brave*); *Bus Stop* (1955); *The Dark at the Top of the Stairs* (1957); *Glory in the Flower* (1958; later revised as *Bus Riley's Back in Town*); *A Loss of Roses* (1959); *The Mall* (1959); *The Tiny Closet* (1959); *The Boy in the Basement* (1962); *Bus Riley's Back in Town* (1962); *An Incident at the Standard Arms* (1962); *Memory of Summer* (1962); *People in the Wind* (1962); *Rainy Afternoon* (1962); *A Social Event* (1962); *The Sounds of Triumph* (1962; later revised as *The Strains of Triumph*); *Summer Brave* (1962); *Natural Affection* (1963); *Where's Daddy?* (1966); *The Call* (1968); *The Disposal* (1968; later revised as *The Last Pad*); *A Murder* (1968); *Midwestern Manic* (1969); *I'm a Star* (1970); *The Love Death* (1970); *Margaret's Bed* (1973)

FURTHER READING

Leeson, Richard M. *William Inge: A Research and Production Sourcebook.* Westport, Conn.: Greenwood Press, 1994.

McClure, Arthur F. *William Inge: A Bibliography.* New York: Garland, 1982.

McClure, Arthur F., and C. David Rice, eds. *A Bibliographical Guide to the Works of William Inge (1913–1973).* Lewiston, N.Y.: Edwin Mellen, 1991.

Sarotte, Georges-Michel. "William Inge: 'Homosexual Spite' in Action." In *Like a Brother, like a Lover,* tr. by Richard Miller. Garden City, N.Y.: Anchor/Doubleday, 1978. 121–133.

Shuman, R. Baird. *William Inge.* Rev. ed. Boston: Twayne, 1989.

Voss, Ralph F. *A Life of William Inge: The Strains of Triumph.* Lawrence: Univ. Press of Kansas, 1989.

James Fisher

INNAURATO, ALBERT (1947–)

A Yale-educated playwright whose most successful works were written and produced in the 1970s and early 1980s, Albert Innaurato, born on June 2, 1947, in Philadelphia, Pennsylvania, is the recipient of two Obies. Although his plays have been produced on Broadway and internationally, they have nevertheless often been considered too gratuitous or bizarre to have broad or enduring appeal.

Innaurato's most successful play, *Gemini* (1976)—also considered his most commercial work—ran for four years on Broadway, but failed to make the crossover to the regional circuit. Drawing on Innaurato's own Italian Catholic upbringing in South Philadelphia, it tells the story of Francis Geminiani, a Harvard undergraduate on scholarship who returns home to his ethnic, blue-collar neighborhood to work out his sexual identity. In many ways *Gemini* was a forerunner to the popular "gross-out" comedies that became a Hollywood staple in the 1990s, and its popular success was assured by the gratuitous use of foul language, ethnic stereotypes, and deliberately crude antics, which included throwing food at the audience. Critics were more skeptical. While Innaurato's sensitive and realistic handling of Francis's sexuality was praised, parallel story lines concerning the outrageous antics of his cartoonlike neighbors and father were criticized for turning the narrative into an uneven mixture of REALISM and burlesque. The play's reception set the trend for Innaurato's career. By 1980, although *Gemini* was the longest-running drama on Broadway, many reviewers censured its strong language, overcrowded narrative, and lack of resolution. It consequently had limited appeal elsewhere and has been revived only sporadically in the years since.

Despite its mixed reception, *Gemini*'s audacity is considered modest next to Innaurato's other works. These commonly deal with such hard-hitting themes as overeating, self-mutilation, and sexual perversity, often within an Italian American context. *The Transfiguration of Benno Blimpie* (1973), first produced in New Haven, Connecticut, later earned Innaurato his second Obie and received two OFF-BROADWAY productions. It was nonetheless greeted by vehement and conflicting reviews. The surreal, almost expressionistic piece takes the audience on a harrowing journey through the tortured life of the grotesquely obese narrator, who decides to eat himself to death as a result of the degradations and humiliations his body has called forth. Innaurato's treatment of the subject matter, which also explores issues of pedophilia and homosexuality, is brutal and uncompromising. Although Innaurato called it a black COMEDY, it was considered by many to be sexually perverse and offensive. Other works continued the trend. *Earth Worms* (1974), for example, involves a trio of nuns who alternately play rock-and-roll music and mutilate paper dolls in an effort to coerce a sexually confused young man into self-mutilation. *The Idiots Karamazov* (1974), which Innaurato co-authored with fellow playwriting student CHRISTOPHER DURANG while both were at Yale, is an anarchic parody of Western literature. Loosely based on Fyodor Dostoevsky's classic, the play burlesques a who's who of literary characters from Anaïs Nin to EUGENE O'NEILL. While it impressed Robert Brustein, founding director of the Yale Repertory and American Repertory Theatres, enough to be premiered at the Yale Repertory Theatre, the use of excess, crude humor, and sexual references gained Innaurato a reputation for perversity that dogged his career and, with the exception of *Dreading Thekla* (1997), saw him cease playwriting by the 1990s.

[*See also* United States, 1940–Present]

PLAYS: *Urlicht* (1971); *I Don't Genarally Like Poetry but Have You Read "Trees"?* (1972); *Life Story of Mitzi Gaynor; or, Gyp* (1973); *The Transfiguration of Benno Blimpie* (1973); *Earth Worms* (1974); *The Idiots Karamazov* (co-written with Christopher Durang, 1974); *Gemini* (1976); *Ulysses in Traction* (1977); *Passione* (1980); *Coming of Age in Soho* (1984); *Gus and Al* (1987); *Magda and Callas* (1988); *Dreading Thekla* (1997)

FURTHER READING

Durang, Christopher, and Albert Innaurato. *The Idiots Karamazov.* New York: Dramatists Play Service, 1981.

Innaurato, Albert. *Best Plays of Albert Innaurato.* New York: Gay Presses of New York, 1987.

——. *Bizarre Behavior: Six Plays.* New York: Avon Bks., 1980.

Olivia Turnbull

INOUE HISASHI (1934–)

Inoue Hisashi, a Japanese playwright and a Catholic, was born in Yamagata Prefecture and graduated from Sophia University in Tokyo. Although he came of age with the first generation of post-1960 "little theater"—ANGURA and SHŌGEKIJŌ—playwrights, he has been more popular than experimental in theme and stagecraft and is properly appreciated in his own category. Heir to the satirical *gesaku* (popular literature) tradition of the Edo period (1603–1868), he distrusts *junbungaku* (pure literature) in favor of FARCE, parody, and impish humor. A prolific playwright, he formed his own theater troupe, Komatsuza, in 1984. Also an accomplished novelist, he won the Naoki Prize for *Handcuffed Double Suicide* (*Tegusari shinjū*, 1972) and the Yomiuri Literary Prize and Japan Science Fiction Award for *The People of Kirikiri* (*Kirikiri-jin*, 1981). His renown in JAPAN is pervasive, augmented by frequent television appearances as an all-purpose pundit.

Inoue's common-man touch is evident in *Make-up* (1983), a one-actress play. The leader of an itinerant *shitamachi no kabuki* (blue-collar *kabuki*) troupe, while applying makeup for her role as an adopted son who locates his real mother, relates eerily similar details of her own life; someone who might be her son appears later on. The bittersweet laughter she provokes happens while a bulldozer ominously approaches to demolish the seedy theater for a new store. Reflecting the anguish of both play and play-within-a-play, her makeup becomes increasingly smeared. The play, perhaps Inoue's best known, effectively renders human despair over confused identities and lost opportunities. Its fame is partly attributable to the versatile Watanabe Misako, who originally defined the role and has performed it several hundred times throughout Japan.

Inoue often leverages pan-Japanese values only to question them subtly, as if he were writing in thin ink that suddenly, despite all the laughter, thickens. This approach informs his many plays dramatizing the lives of famous Japanese writers. In *A Headache, Shoulder Pain, and Higuchi Ichiyō* (1984), for example, Komatsuza's first production, the poverty of Ichiyō's brief existence (1872–1896) ostensibly causes her aches and pains. The play appeals to Japanese in part for its Buddhist undergirding—the wish for a happy afterlife—that taps the Japanese subconscious. Enduring hardship by interacting with a ghost, Ichiyō is spiritually in the afterworld even before her death. These traditional inclinations are punctuated by such great wit and laughter that the spectator is hardly aware of a more gently rendered notion—in Ichiyō's yearning to gain more freedom through writing, we realize that her headache and shoulder pain emerge less from poverty than from how Japanese society treats women.

In *Flowers in the Dark* (1987), ostensibly a rumination about the ideal Shinto shrine, Inoue exercises a similar subtlety and stimulates tear-shedding laughter by appropriating the Japanese familiarity with shrines as places to access vaguely grasped patron deities and gain peace of mind. Thus lulled, the spectator is shaken upon realizing that Inoue, perhaps for the first time on the Japanese stage, breaks taboo in gently questioning the role of Shinto, Japan's indigenous religion, in galvanizing people for World War II.

SELECT PLAYS: *Japanese Bellybuttons* (*Nihonjin no heso*, 1969); *Great Doctor Yabuhara* (*Yabuhara kengyō*, 1973); *The Strange Testament* (*Chin'yaku seisho*, 1973); *Kobayashi Issa* (1979); *The Theatre Train of Iihatōbo* (*Iihatōbo no geki-ressha*, 1980); *Make-up* (*Keshō*, 1983); *A Headache, Shoulder Pain, and Higuchi Ichiyō* (*Zutsu katakori Higuchi Ichiyō*, 1984); *The Impudent Crybaby Ishikawa Takuboku* (*Nakimushi namaiki Ishikawa Takuboku*, 1984); *History of the Common People of the Shōwa Era* (*Shōwa shomin den*, 1988) (this trilogy consists of *Twinkling Constellation* [*Kirameku seiza*, 1985], *Flowers in the Dark* [*Yami ni saku hana*, 1987], and *Snowed In* [*Yuki ya kon kon*, 1988]); *Still Human* (*Ningen gōkaku*, 1992)

FURTHER READING

Inoue, Hisashi. *Make-up.* Tr. by Akemi Horie. *Encounter* 52, no. 5 (May 1989): 8–18.

——. *Maquillages* [Makeup]. Tr. by Patrick de Vos. Paris: Éditions L'Harmattan, 1986.

Nihon Kindai Engeki-shi Kenkyūkai, ed. *Nijusseiki no gikyoku III: Gendai gikyoku no henbō* [Twentieth-century plays III: The metamorphosis of modern Japanese plays]. Tokyo: Shakai Hyōronsha, 2002.

Ozasa, Yoshio. *Dōjidai engeki to gekisakkatachi* [Contemporary plays and playwrights]. Tokyo: Gekishobō, 1980.

——. *Gendai engeki no mori* [The forest of contemporary theater]. Tokyo: Kōdansha, 1993.

Senda Akihiko. *The Voyage of Contemporary Japanese Theatre.* Tr. by J. Thomas Rimer. Honolulu: Univ. of Hawaii Press, 1997.

John K. Gillespie

THE INSECT COMEDY

The Insect Comedy (*Ze života hmyzu*) was the third play on which Josef and KAREL ČAPEK worked together. Begun before R.U.R., but not produced until a year after the latter's premiere, *The Insect Comedy* was written in 1919–1921, published in 1921, and first produced in Brno on February 3, 1922. Its better-known premiere occurred in the Prague National Theatre on April 8, 1922, directed by K. H. Hilar with designs by Josef Čapek, who was a noted artist. Within the same year it was produced in London, New York, and other theater centers. Its most celebrated Czech production of the past half century was designed by Josef Svoboda in 1965 for the National Theatre.

The play has been called a philosophic revue because of its several discrete sections, its colorful and dynamic action, and its thought-provoking themes. Karel Čapek himself referred to it as a "mysterium in an entirely old and naive sense. And as in a medieval mystery [play] . . . certain moral concepts are here personified by insects." The play begins with a prologue that establishes the insect realm and introduces the chief human character, an unnamed, good-natured, intoxicated vagrant who witnesses the three main actions: narcissistic butterflies gossip, versify, and play at love; various soil-bound insects hoard dung balls and kill neighbors to feed their own young, only to have their larvae eaten in turn by parasites; and an industrialized and militant ant world divided into red and yellow camps invents weapons of mass destruction and plunges into war over possession of a few square feet of dirt between clumps of grass.

The vagrant comments to the audience on the ongoing actions. He is attracted initially by the amusing and positive aspects of what he sees but eventually appalled by the waste and destructiveness involved. Able to relate to much of what he observes, he gains insight into his own misspent life. The culminating event of his education is the birth of a chrysalis, who has been joyfully proclaiming throughout the play the great tidings of her birth-to-be from her cocoon. The tramp awakens after the ant sequence and witnesses a dance of fragile moths celebrating the glory of life, and they are joined by the now-liberated chrysalis. The vagrant himself awkwardly starts to dance, only to notice the ephemeral moths perishing one by one, including the former chrysalis. He himself is stricken by an unseen mortal force but struggles against it, declaring that he has at last learned how to live. His death throes are observed and commented on by two lisping snails, to whom his final moments are simply a momentary distraction. The painful bleakness of the action is redeemed by two elements. Čapek provides an epilogue of simple country folk for whom life is reaffirmed in their daily work and a recently born child. Throughout the play, moreover, Čapek imbues much of the action with wit, humor, and sheer vitality.

[*See also* Avant-Garde Drama; Czechoslavakia]

FURTHER READING

Bradbrook, Bohuslava R. *Karel Čapek: In Pursuit of Truth, Tolerance, and Trust*. Portland, Ore.: Sussex Academic Press, 1998.

Harkins, William E. *Karel Čapek*. New York: Columbia Univ. Press, 1962.

Jarka M. Burian

AN INSPECTOR CALLS

An Inspector Calls epitomizes the popular middlebrow socially aware writings of JOHN BOYNTON PRIESTLEY. The central message of the play is that individuals in society have responsibility for one another.

The play opens with the Birling family in the dining room of their comfortable home, celebrating the engagement of Sheila Birling to one Gerald Croft, in a move that will also create a business alliance or cartel and will represent social advancement for the Birlings. Placing the action in 1912 gives Priestley the opportunity to combine sledgehammer irony with distaste in his depiction of Arthur Birling, the paterfamilias, who speaks of the "absolutely unsinkable" *Titanic*. It is Birling's line that "a man has to . . . look after himself and his own," however, that immediately precedes and perhaps prompts the arrival of the mysterious Inspector Goole. The inspector announces the suicide of a young woman and then proceeds to conduct a series of interviews with those present, in the course of which he demonstrates that each of them has contributed to the girl's death. Although no single one of their actions has been outstandingly damaging or cruel, each has been callous, selfish, or blindly unhelpful, and the cumulative effect has been catastrophic for the girl. The inspector leaves the family to reflect on what they have done. Despite having been convinced by the inspector while he was present, the reaction of the senior Birlings and of the fiancé, Gerald Croft, is that the entire affair has been a hoax and can now be disregarded. The younger Birlings recognize that this visitation has been significant, however, and that their own past actions have been culpable. Priestley ends the play with a telephone call announcing that a young woman has committed suicide, and that a police inspector is on his way to speak to the family about their responsibility in the matter. Whether this second visit has been brought on their own heads by the display of indifference by Croft and the senior Birlings remains a matter for speculation on the part of the audience.

The social significance of the play is simultaneously universal and specific to the immediate postwar era. Britain at that time was perceived to have the opportunity to create a more just and equitable society without having recourse to the totalitarianism that had prevailed in the Eastern bloc. The fear was that the demands of the class that owned the means of production might outweigh these new demands for social and economic justice. Priestley was concerned to underline the extent to which we are all implicated in this matter. The name of the dead girl—Eva Smith—belongs in a sense to Everywoman. Meanwhile, the wordplay on Inspector/specter Goole/ghoul suggests a supernatural presence, perhaps that of a universal social conscience. Priestley's overall view seems to be an optimistic one. It is notable that it is the younger family members—the voice of the future—who recognize the need for greater social awareness in the future.

The play's first London production in 1946 was not received enthusiastically by the critics. However, it is reckoned that the play has been in production somewhere in the world continuously ever since. In particular, Stephen Daldry's 1992 production for the National Theatre in London transferred with immense success to a series of commercial venues in both London and New York and was still running nearly ten years later. In any case, the play clearly retains a power to communicate its central ethos to a modern audience.

[*See also* England]

FURTHER READING

Brome, Vincent. *J. B. Priestley*. London: Hamilton, 1988.

Cook, Judith. *Priestley*. London: Bloomsbury, 1997.

Klein, Holger. *J. B. Priestley's Plays*. Basingstoke: Macmillan, 1988.

Andrew Wyllie

INTERCULTURALISM

It is precisely the merit of a [Eugenio] Barba or [an Ariane] Mnouchkine never to reduce or destroy the Eastern form from which they gain inspiration, but to attempt a hybridization . . . situated at the precise intersection of the two cultures and the two theatrical forms.

—Patrice Pavis, 1998

Intercultural performance rests between the devil of cultural imperialism on one side and the angel of cultural dialogue on the other. At its best, intercultural performance is a hybrid event that combines performance traditions and representational strategies from disparate cultures without eliding cultural specificity and in order to inspire social, cultural, and political change. Like much AVANT-GARDE art, interculturalism is revolutionary in scope and vision, but in practice can fall short of its goals. Most discussion of intercultural performance focuses on Western artists incorporating (or appropriating) Third World practice; more recently, postcolonialist performers have created intercultural performances that comment on the history and impact of this often exoticizing tradition.

Intercultural performance is linked to PERFORMANCE STUDIES, especially the anthropological explorations of ritual and drama associated with Edward Spicer (the Yaqui Indian deer dance), Victor Turner (West African Ndembu rituals systems), and Richard Schechner (South Asian dance-drama). Grounded in the anthropology of performance, interculturalism translates cultural practice and cultural values between its producers and for its audiences. Intercultural performance also includes more traditional drama, prefigured by playwright/theorists such as W. B. YEATS, BERTOLT BRECHT, ANTONIN ARTAUD, and WOLE SOYINKA, all of whom merge non-Western theatrical traditions with Western dramatic conventions.

British director Peter Brook's *Mahabharata* (1985) and French director ARIANE MNOUCHKINE's *Les Atrides* (1990) are salient examples of the promise and pitfalls of intercultural performance. Brook, who staged William Shakespeare in AFRICA and JAPAN and worked with El Teatro Campesino, produced a nine-hour dramatization of the 90,000-stanza Hindu epic featuring an international and ethnically diverse cast and a variety of performance styles and techniques. His production was roundly criticized for its implication that cultural parallels are more relevant than cultural differences; his *Mahabharata* elided the specificity of both Indian performance traditions and Hindu lore. Mnouchkine's adaptation of the *Orest-ia*, on the other hand, was generally understood as deconstructing Western epistemologies of the East as Other. Mnouchkine's performance strategies, which included laying bare the production process and offering artifacts for preperformance education and purchase, grappled with the history of Western appropriation. Other interculturalist Western directors include Eugenio Barba (*Faust*, 1987) and Lee Breuer (*The Warrior Ant*, 1988). Playwright DAVID HARE's *A Map of the World* (1983) engages interculturalism through realist conventions.

Postcolonialist intercultural projects have suggested how marginalized cultures might "perform back." For example, Coco Fusco and Guillermo Gómez-Peña's *Two Amerindians Visit* (1992) featured the performers as caged natives of a "primitive" and imaginary South American tribe. These performances, held in natural history and art museums, referenced the history of displaying nonwhites in circuses, world's fairs, and other exhibitions. Dramatists DAVID HENRY HWANG (*M. Butterfly*, 1989) and LUIS VALDEZ (*Zoot Suit*, 1978) successfully brought their postcolonialist interculturalism to mainstream stages.

[*See also* Deconstruction; Postmodernism]

FURTHER READING

Berghaus, Gunter, and Richard Gough, eds. "On Ritual." Special Issue, *Performance Research* 3, no. 3 (Winter 1998).

Chaudhuri, Una. "Beyond a 'Taxonomic Theater': Interculturalism After Postcolonialism and Globalization." *Theater* 32, no. 1 (2002): 33–47.

Fusco, Coco. "The Other History of Intercultural Performance." In *ReDirection: A Theoretical and Practical Guide*, ed. by Rebecca Schneider and Gabrielle Cody. London: Routledge, 2002. 266–280.

Holledge, Julie, and Jeanne Tompkins. *Women's Intercultural Performance*. London: Routledge, 2000.

Marranca, Bonnie, and Gautam Dasgupta, eds. *Interculturalism and Performance: Writings from PAJ*. New York: Performance Art Journal Bks., 1991.

Pavis, Patrice, ed. *The Intercultural Performance Reader.* New York: Routledge, 1996.

Peters, Julie Stone. "Intercultural Performance, Theatre Anthropology, and the Imperialist Critique: Identities, Inheritances, and Neo-Orthodoxies." In *Imperialism and Theatre: Essays on World Theatre, Drama, and Performance*, ed. by J. Ellen Gainor. London: Routledge, 1995. 199–213.

Schechner, Richard, and Willa Appel, eds. *By Means of Performance: Intercultural Studies of Theatre and Ritual.* Cambridge: Cambridge Univ. Press, 1990.

Kirsten Pullen

IN THE SHADOW OF THE GLEN

In the Shadow of the Glen, J. M. SYNGE's first play, was staged by the Irish National Theatre Society at Molesworth Hall, Dublin, on October 8, 1903, as part of a double bill with W. B. YEATS's verse play *The King's Threshold.* Before its production Yeats told novelist George Moore that other Irishmen had written well before Synge, but they did so by casting off IRELAND; Synge was the first man to be largely inspired by Ireland.

Based on a folktale Synge heard in the Aran Islands, the one-act play is set inside a cottage high in the mountains of Wicklow. An old man pretends to be dead so that he may catch his wife in an act of unfaithfulness with a young farmer who lives down the hill. It is a wild night, and a stranger knocks on the door seeking shelter. Left alone to mind the "corpse," the stranger is shocked to find it rise up and ask for a glass of the whiskey laid on for his own wake; then the old man asks the stranger to bring him the big stick that is behind the door. He draws the stranger into his plan to punish the wife. However, after hearing the wife, the husband, and the lover argue, the stranger takes the woman's part. When the old man tries to drive her from the cottage, the stranger romantically and poetically invites her to join him tramping on the roads, and she goes out the door with him. At the curtain the old man sits down to a drink with the young farmer.

Although brilliantly played by W. G. Fay and Maire nic Shiubhlaigh, the play was booed on its opening night, because the audience was shocked by the presentation of an adulterous wife who gets away happily into further adultery. At the end of the folktale as it had been told to Synge, the wife is beaten until her blood leaps up and splashes on the wall. Synge altered the ending in a fashion that made some Irish reviewers see the play as a feminist critique of the patriarchal family on the pattern of A DOLL'S HOUSE; significantly, his heroine was also called Nora. Synge defended the authenticity of his materials. Certainly, efforts were made in costume, props, manners, and accent to achieve naturalism in the production, but the behavior of the wife, it was argued, was not natural for an Irish country woman; Irish women were pure, Catholic, and monogamous. A debate arose on the qualifications necessary for a play to be Irish, and this debate—tinged with sectarianism (Synge's family was Protestant; his characters and most of his audience were Catholics)—cast a shadow over Synge's dramatic career and the Irish revival as a whole.

FURTHER READING

Frazier, Adrian. *Behind the Scenes: Yeats, Horniman, and the Struggle for the Abbey Theatre.* Berkeley: Univ. of California Press, 1990.

Kiberd, Declan. *Synge and the Irish Language.* 2d ed. Dublin: Gill & Macmillan, 1993.

Levitas, Ben. *The Theatre of Nation: Irish Drama and Cultural Nationalism, 1890–1916.* Oxford: Oxford Univ. Press, 2002.

Adrian Frazier

IN THE SUMMER HOUSE

> *Did you ever worry about running far away from sad things when you were young, and then later getting older and not being able to find your way back to them ever again, even when you wanted to?*
> —Lionel, Act 2

JANE BOWLES's only completed full-length play, *In the Summer House*, was written between 1943 and 1947 and then periodically revised until its Broadway opening in 1953.

Elliptical and poetic, both its subject matter and style challenged its audience. TENNESSEE WILLIAMS described *In the Summer House* as "one of those very rare plays which are not tested by the theatre but by which the theatre is tested." Bowles focuses on relationships between mothers and daughters rather than the mother/son dynamic that dominated plays by EUGENE O'NEILL, Tennessee Williams, LILLIAN HELLMAN, and ARTHUR MILLER. Instead of being plot driven, *In the Summer House* is built on a series of unresolved tensions and abrupt shifts of mood that starkly dramatize the painful isolation of Bowles's women.

Not confined to the interior spaces of most American family drama, *In the Summer House* is set mostly outdoors, in open, natural vistas that provide an expansive canvas that throws the characters into bold relief and accommodates many surreal images within the play's realistic framework.

The play is structured around three contrasting pairs of mothers (all widows) and their daughters. Gertrude Eastman Cuevas, who lives under the "shadow" of her father's abandonment and with anger toward her pleasure-seeking dead husband, rails against her daughter, Molly, who in turn retreats to her vine-covered summer house, where she daydreams. Out of economic need, and in fear of Molly's dependence, Gertrude rashly decides to marry Mr. Solares, move to Mexico, and marry off Molly to Lionel, a sweet, gloomy young man.

Mr. Solares's sister is Mrs. Fula Lopez. She and her daughter Frederica speak Spanish and have a simple closeness and physical bonding that eludes the others. The third mother, Mrs. Constable, grieves because her husband and daughter Vivian never loved her, but is timid and dominated by the vivacious and impulsive

Vivian. After Vivian is either pushed off a cliff by Molly or falls (the event is left unresolved), Mrs. Constable depends on Lionel and Molly. In act 2 Gertrude can no longer endure Mr. Solares's large family and returns to reclaim her daughter. Molly is caught between her chaste marriage with Lionel and her possessive mother and, at the urging of Mrs. Constable, flees with Lionel to St. Louis. At the end of the play Gertrude is left desperate and alone.

During its extended tryout period there were cast and director changes, and Bowles continually rewrote the play; as Broadway pressures mounted, a psychiatrist was even called in to help explain the motivations of the characters to the cast. Finally, after only eight days of full rehearsal, the production opened on December 29, 1953, at the Playhouse Theatre under the direction of José Quintero, with music by Paul Bowles, and starred Judith Anderson, Mildred Dunnock, and Jean Stapleton; it ran for fifty-five performances. *In the Summer House* received respectful reviews that acknowledged Bowles's original voice, but criticized the play for its lack of a moralizing force and its eccentric characters. Mildred Dunnock suggested that the Broadway audience was not ready for a play that centered mostly on the lives of middle-aged women and left the outcome of Molly and Lionel's romance chaste and unresolved.

Today the play's intuitive shifts of mood, its narrative gaps, and its contested relationships feel contemporary, as do Bowles's characters' search for autonomy and their rueful acceptance of its unforeseen consequences. *In the Summer House* has been revived several times in New York, most recently by the Lincoln Center Theatre in 1993, directed by JoAnne Akalaitis, featuring Dianne Wiest and Frances Conroy, with a score by Philip Glass.

[*See also* Feminist Drama in the United States; Gay and Lesbian Drama; United States, 1940–Present]

FURTHER READING

Bowles, Jane. *In the Summer House*. In *Best Plays of 1953–1954*, ed. by Louis Kronenberger. New York: Dodd, 1954.

——. *My Sister's Hand in Mine: An Expanded Edition of the Collected Works of Jane Bowles*. New York: Ecco, 1978.

Dillon, Millicent. *A Little Original Sin: The Life and Work of Jane Bowles*. Berkeley: Univ. of California Press, 1998.

Olauson, Judith. *The American Woman Playwright: A View of Criticism and Characterization*. Troy, N.Y.: Whitston, 1981.

Skerl, Jennie, ed. *A Tawdry Place of Salvation: The Art of Jane Bowles*. Carbondale: Southern Illinois Univ. Press, 1997.

Mary Fleischer

THE INVENTION OF LOVE

What a strange thing is a young man. You had better be a poet. Literary enthusiasm never made a scholar, and unmade many. Taste is not knowledge.

—AEH, Act 1

In keeping with the intellectually challenging plays TOM STOPPARD typically writes, *The Invention of Love* entertains largely through inordinate cleverness, sharply articulated language, and irresistible charm. *Invention* opened in London in September 1997 at the Royal National Theatre and arrived in the UNITED STATES in early 2000 at San Francisco's American Conservatory Theatre. Its New York debut came the following year. Reaction was positive overall, but not universally so. Opinion split on the usual issues where Stoppard's works are concerned. A majority of observers admitted to being intoxicated with the writer's originality in tackling unusual, meaty themes, all carried along in blazingly intelligent dialogue laced with keen humor. A smaller but respected group of commentators were untouched by Stoppard's cerebral approach to his subjects, wherein plot is anemic and characters are distanced from ordinary people who make up audiences.

An imaginative consideration of English poet A. E. Housman (1859–1936) provides the play's center point, and Stoppard shapes a myriad of related spin-off themes from that core. The play opens with Housman, newly dead, being ferried in a boat to the underworld by Charon, a figure from classical mythology. Housman uses the occasion to look back at his life. *Invention* thereby becomes a personal afterlife pilgrimage for Housman. Along one track Stoppard examines Housman's life as a poet and university don teaching classical literature at Oxford.

Another dimension of the work centers on Housman's personal life. Housman, author of *A Shropshire Lad*, is portrayed as a repressed homosexual. His single passion when young was for his close heterosexual friend Moses Jackson, a star athlete in college unaware for years of Housman's romantic crush. When the poet confessed his love to Jackson, the friendship was severely damaged. Rebuffed, Housman lived the remainder of his life with that regret.

Another story line informatively juxtaposed with Housman's unrequited passion is his fictional encounter with the notorious OSCAR WILDE. Whereas Housman earned distinction in a narrow field of classical letters and simple poetry, Wilde, also an actual man of letters, became a brilliant intellectual figure—world renowned and heaped with extravagant praise but also boundless scorn. Wilde played a flamboyant role as an open homosexual in the straitlaced Victorian culture, ignoring what others thought. Wilde's full-throttle lifestyle stood in sharp relief to Housman's constrained, colorless existence. Although the two men never met in life, Stoppard generates fascinating interchanges between them, providing some of the liveliest sections in the play. When challenged by Housman about the veracity of news accounts concerning his misdemeanors, Wilde refutes the basis of the question: "On the contrary, it's only fact. Truth is quite another thing and is the work of the imagination."

To shuttle between the time periods of Housman's life, Stoppard creates two separate characters performed by different actors. For ages eighteen to twenty-six, a character called "Housman" is on stage; as a seventy-seven-year-old, he becomes known as "AEH." In one marvelous scene the two figures sit next to each other on a park bench and literally converse—a man with his earlier self. Such scenes help make *Invention* resonate with provocative thought.

[*See also* England]

FURTHER READING

Demastes, William W., ed. *British Playwrights, 1956–1995: A Research and Production Sourcebook*. Westport, Conn.: Greenwood Press, 1996.

Graves, Richard Perceval. *A. E. Housman: The Scholar-Poet*. New York: Scribner, 1979.

Gussow, Mel. *Conversations with Stoppard*. New York: Grove, 1995.

Holden, Alan W., and J. Roy Birch, eds. *A. E. Housman: A Reassessment*. London: Palgrave Macmillan, 2000.

Innes, Christopher. *Modern British Drama: The Twentieth Century*. Cambridge: Cambridge Univ. Press, 2002.

Kelly, Katherine E., ed. *The Cambridge Companion to Tom Stoppard*. Cambridge: Cambridge Univ. Press, 2001.

C. J. Gianakaris

THE INVESTIGATION

When the events seem to have become incomprehensible, that is when reason has to take over. We only have this single weapon.
—Peter Weiss, 1970

PETER WEISS's *The Investigation* (*Die Ermittlung*, 1965), an "Oratorio in 11 Cantos," is based on the court documents of the Frankfurt Auschwitz trials of November 1963 to August 1965 and on Bernd Naumann's reports on the court proceedings in the *Frankfurter Allgemeine Zeitung* (Frankfurt General Newspaper). Weiss condensed tens of thousands of pages and years of hearings into a play that can be staged in one evening and provides a compelling account both of how the concentration camp was organized and of how its victims and perpetrators—who now confront each other again as witnesses and defendants—once interacted. Although Weiss has avoided the mistake of trying to represent life in the camp, the play is gripping because it reconstructs the language of the camp, a language that seems to have stuck with both victims and perpetrators even after almost twenty years have passed. The language of the camp clearly defines the roles of inmates and guards, hiding behind its impersonal bureaucratic tone the deadly machinery that was the reality of Auschwitz. The structure of the play, its eleven cantos, mirrors the physical plan of the camp and the organization of its mass murders. Through the witnesses' accounts the spectators are led from the ramp where the new victims arrive to the last stage, the ovens where the victims are burned.

Although many critics have concentrated on Weiss's fascination with Dante and the playwright's having considered modeling *The Investigation* on Dante's *Paradiso*, a more direct link to other aesthetic models can be seen in the subtitle of the play itself: it is an oratorio. We are thus reminded of Johann Sebastian Bach's *St. Matthew Passion* and *St. John Passion*. The Stations of the Cross have been reduced from twelve to eleven, but the structural backbone of Bach's work remains intact. While the bulk of the text is delivered as recitatives, they are periodically interrupted by choral passages (in the play these are collective responses by the defendants who voice their agreement with or objection to what the witnesses say) and reflective passages that resemble arias, for example, the "Canto About the End of Lili Tofler." But regardless of its possible aesthetic models, the power of this play lies in its bold attempt to explain what seems inexplicable. As Weiss himself stated, "These are crimes, committed by humans, against humans on this Earth," and the taboo surrounding representations of the Holocaust is perhaps just an excuse for avoiding confronting this simple truth. Parallel to putting on display the linguistic deformations that regulated the functioning of the camp, Weiss concentrates on Auschwitz as an extreme case of exploitation—where everything, right down to an inmate's body, is measured in terms of its value in the production process—and of capitalism's division of labor, a division that makes mass production of the "product death" possible.

[*See also* Germany]

FURTHER READING

Cohen, Robert. "The Political Aesthetics of Holocaust Literature: Peter Weiss's *The Investigation* and Its Critics." *History and Memory* 10, no. 2 (1998): 43–67.

Holub, Robert. "The Premiere of Peter Weiss's *The Investigation: Oratorio in Eleven Songs*, a Drama Written from the Documentation of the Frankfurt Auschwitz Trial, Is Staged." In *Yale Companion to Jewish Writing and Thought in German Culture, 1096–1996*, ed. by Sander L. Gilman and Jack Zipes. New Haven: Yale Univ. Press, 1997. 729–735.

Schlunk, Jurgen E. "Auschwitz and Its Function in Peter Weiss' Search for Identity." *German Studies Review* 10, no. 1 (1987): 11–30.

Friedemann J. Weidauer

IONESCO, EUGÈNE (1909–1994)

Poet, essayist, and critic Eugène Ionesco was forty, living in Paris, and working as a proofreader for a legal publishing house when he turned his hand to writing for the theater. The year before, 1948, he had tried to teach himself English using the Assimil method, *Anglais sans peine*, a conversation manual with model dialogues featuring a married couple (the Smiths) who gravely inform each other how many children they have and where in London their house stands. Their stilted dialogue crystallized everything that Ionesco felt was tired and hackneyed in realistic theater. THE BALD SOPRANO: *An Anti-play* (*La Cantatrice chauve*, 1949) was his response. Although the initial production at the Théâtre des Noctambules in May 1950 was not a great success, it came to exemplify a strand of postwar drama that critic Martin Esslin would later christen "theatre of the absurd." Revived in 1957 at the ninety-seat Théâtre de la Huchette, it was an immediate hit and is still playing at this writing, making it one of the world's longest theatrical runs.

Ionesco's account of finding the germ of *The Bald Soprano* in an English conversation manual belies his prior achievements as a writer and critic in ROMANIA. It also ignores the rich tradition of dada, surrealist, and café-theater FARCE that Ionesco knew and drew upon.

Born on November 26, 1909, in Slatina, Romania, of a French mother and a Romanian father, Ionesco came to Paris when he was a year old. When he was seven, his father returned to Bucharest to join the Romanian forces going off to war, the last news the family had of him for six years. Eugène and his younger sister were sent to live with a kindly peasant couple in the Loire valley. He remembered this interlude fondly in later life as the only period of profound joy he had ever known. In 1922 the father resurfaced, having survived the war. Moreover, he had divorced Eugène's mother, remarried, become inspector general of police in Bucharest, and successfully sued for custody of his two children. Thus it was that at age thirteen, Eugène was forced to rediscover the country of his birth and learn its language. (The ironies and pitfalls of language and its acquisition were to become a lifelong fascination for him.) His relationships with his father and stepmother were strained. After a particularly violent dispute he left his father and went to live with his mother, who was now working at a bank in Bucharest. Eugène finished high school and began to contribute poems and criticism to literary journals in Romania. In 1936 his pamphlet *No!* (*Nu!*) provoked heated discussion with its satirical attacks on leading Romanian literary figures. By this time he had taken a degree in French and was teaching at a French high school. He married Rodica Burileanu, a philosophy student, in 1936. In 1938 Ionesco obtained a French government grant to write a dissertation on the theme of death in French poetry from Baudelaire onward. When their visas finally came through in 1942, the couple came to FRANCE and eventually settled in Paris. Romania's plunge into fascism and counterplunge into communism further soured Ionesco on political ideologies of all sorts. His father later became a Communist militant; Ionesco never saw him again. The playwright never wrote a line of the planned dissertation, but the stage was set for *The Bald Soprano*.

Although Ionesco wore the absurdist label for the rest of his career, none of his subsequent plays was quite as absurd as the first. Instead of attacking the absurdity of the theater per se, they use theater to expose absurd subcurrents in other fields, including education [THE LESSON (*La Leçon*, 1950)], conformity [*Rhinoceros* (*Rhinocéros*, 1958)], and political oppression [*Exit the King* (*Le Roi se meurt*, 1962)]. While his plays now made more explicit reference to reality, the staging remained fanciful: *Amedee; or, How to Get Rid of It* (*Amédée ou Comment s'en débarrasser*, 1953) features a constantly growing corpse that knocks down walls as it progressively invades the playing space; *The New Tenant* (*Le Nouveau locataire*, 1953) shows a man becoming submerged within his possessions; *The Chairs* (*Les Chaises*, 1951) depicts an elderly couple who have hired an orator to explain their lives to a roomful of empty chairs representing the elite of their era. When the orator arrives, he turns out to be incapable of speech. A proliferation of objects is a favorite technique; in *Victims of Duty* (*Victimes du devoir*, 1952) Madeleine, the central character's wife/mistress/mother, brings on innumerable cups of coffee until the stage is covered with them; the hero's love interest in *Jacques; or, The Submission* (*Jacques ou La Soumission*, 1950) has three noses and nine fingers on her right hand. Ionesco also likes to double up names; the ten characters in *Jacques* are all called by some variant of Robert or Jacques. The heroes of four major plays between 1957 [*The Killer* (*Tueur sans gages*)] and 1962 (*Exit the King*) are all called Bérenger.

In the world of *Rhinoceros* human characters turn into rhinoceroses when they stop thinking for themselves and let other people think for them, a theatrical absurdity used to make a serious statement against totalitarianism and doctrinaire thinking. Playing the role of Jean, William Sabatier transformed himself into a stamping, snorting pachyderm without benefit of makeup or special effects—a feat duplicated by Zero Mostel on Broadway in 1960.

In *Exit the King* Ionesco's anxious obsession with death is personified in a centuries-old king whose tyrannous longevity has dried up all sources of creativity and joy in the universe, even causing planets to collide and the Milky Way to curdle. Gently but firmly, his two queens, his doctor, and—most successfully—his maid all persuade him to die. This stately dramatization of the inevitable has been compared with works by Jean Racine and William Shakespeare, but is very far from the gleefully iconoclastic "antiplay" with which Ionesco began his career. About this time he told an interviewer, "I've always made fun of myself in my writing, but I can't manage it as easily as before. I take myself more and more seriously. . . . I end up falling into a sort of trap." As the author's outlook on life darkened and his public role as a defender of individual imagination in the face of ideologies of all sorts became more pronounced, his theater became less playful.

Hunger and Thirst (*La Soif et la Faim*, 1964) is a dreamlike meditation in which the hero, driven by insatiable hunger and thirst, leaves his family to seek out his secret desires and fears. Like many of Ionesco's later plays, it premiered at the Schauspielhaus in Düsseldorf. The venerable Comédie Française gave the French-language premiere fourteen months later. Discursive and almost mystical, the play has received relatively few productions, although it did inspire a chamber opera by Violeta Dinescu.

Macbett (1972), written in a twenty-five-day sprint after eighteen months of preparation, is a DECONSTRUCTION of *Macbeth* in which all the characters, not just the eponymous Thane, seek their own undoing. Ionesco himself pointed out his debt to ALFRED JARRY's *Ubu the King* (*Ubu roi*) on this occasion.

In addition to a novel, several short stories, and his diaries, Ionesco published many essays and interviews. *Notes and Counter Notes* includes an exchange of letters with British critic Kenneth Tynan over the social obligations of playwrights, which originally enflamed the pages of the *Observer* in the summer of 1958.

Eugène Ionesco was named Transcendent Satrap in the neodadaist College of Pataphysics in 1952. He was elected to the Académie Française in 1970. Ionesco died on March 28, 1994, in Paris.

SELECT PLAYS: *The Bald Soprano* (*La Cantatrice chauve*, 1949); *Jacques, or the Submission* (*Jacques on La Soumission*, 1950); *The Lesson* (*La Leçon*, 1950); *The Chairs* (*Les Chaises*, 1951); *The Future is in Eggs* (*L'avenir est dans les oeufs*, 1951); *Victims of Duty* (*Victims du devoir*, 1952); *Amedee, or How to Get Rid of It* (*Amédée ou Comment s'en débarrasser*, 1953); *The New Tenant* (*Le Nouveau locataire*, 1953); *The Killer* (*Tueur sans gages*, 1957); *Rhinoceros* (*Rhinocéros*, 1958); *Exit the King* (*Le Roi se meurt*, 1962); *A Stroll in the Air* (*Le Piéton de l'air*, 1962); *French Conversation and Diction Exercises* (*Exercises de conversation et de diction françaises pour étudiants américains*, 1964); *Hunger and Thirst* (*La Soif et la Faim*, 1964); *Killing Game* (*Jeux de Massacre*, 1970); *Macbett* (1972); *A Hell of a Mess* (*Ce formidable bordel*, 1973)

FURTHER READING

Bonnefoy, Claude. *Conversations with Eugène Ionesco*. Tr. by Jan Dawson. New York: Holt, Rinehart & Winston, 1971.

Coe, Richard. *Eugène Ionesco*. 2nd ed. New York: Grove, 1970.

Esslin, Martin. *The Theatre of the Absurd*. Harmondsworth: Penguin, 1968.

Guicharnaud, Jacques. *Modern French Theatre from Giraudoux to Beckett*. New Haven: Yale Univ. Press, 1961.

Ionesco, Eugène. *Fragments of a Journal*. Tr. by Jean Stewart. New York: Paragon, 1990.

——. *Notes and Counter Notes*. Tr. by Donald Watson. New York: Grove, 1964.

Lista, Giovanni. *Ionesco*. Paris: Henri Veyrier, 1989.

Vernois, Paul. *La dynamique théâtrale d'Eugène Ionesco*. Paris: Klincksieck, 1972.

Robert Schneider

IRAN

The rediscovery of traditional theater in Iran has become an important cultural feature of the overall development of Iranian artistic expression. Playwrights and writers have attempted to develop new modes of artistic expression that move away from imitation of Western tradition, and to develop new theater that speaks to the cultural roots of modern Iranians.

TRADITIONAL THEATER FROM THE 16TH TO THE 19th CENTURY

After the Mongol invasion two great empires arose in the Middle East—the Ottoman, centered in Istanbul (late 13th-Century–1926) and the Safavid in Iran (1501–1723). The Safavids were succeeded after a short interim by the Qajar dynasty (1779–1924). Except for extreme northwestern AFRICA, all of the present-day Middle East was contained under the reign of these empires until World War I.

Court life dominated the wealthy classes, and all sorts of entertainments were found in the capitals of the empires. For the most part the shahs of Iran and the sultans of the Ottoman Empire were interested in patronizing the arts. They maintained performers, including actors and artists, in their courts despite general Islamic disapproval of these entertainments. At the same time, the theatrical arts flourished on a popular level outside court settings, although the historical record of these more popular forms is much less complete.

NARRATIVE FORMS

Narrative drama was well established by the 13th century among the Arab populations of the Middle East. At this time the storytellers of Baghdad organized themselves into a guild headed by a sheikh.

Storytellers were already popular at the beginning of the Ottoman Empire. They were greatly revered in the Ottoman court and are mentioned continually in accounts of the reigns of the sultans, from Bayazid Yildirim in the 15th century to World War I. *Meddahs* (eulogizers) in the Ottoman Empire were ingenious parodists and satirists. Because of their tendency to burlesque political affairs, they were subject to rigorous censorship, particularly in the 19th century. They could not use the word *sultan* nor mention riots, revolutions, or insurrections—even those of other countries. They were also prohibited from mocking the clergy.

The *meddahs* performed most often in coffeehouses in large cities. Financial arrangements varied. Occasionally tickets were sold, and the coffeehouse owner was paid rent for the use of the room. Often the proprietor would be content with the additional income brought in by the large number of customers attracted by the performance. The Iranian *naqqal* operated in a similar fashion, working from coffeehouses or occasionally from private homes. His stock-in-trade was almost exclusively Ferdowsi's *Book of Kings* (*Shahnāmeh*), although he would occasionally narrate other epics for the pleasure of the crowd. The art of the *naqqal* was codified in a 17th-century work, *The Adornment of Narrative* (*Tarāz al-akhbār*). One unusual setting for the Iranian storyteller even today is the *zurkhāneh* (house of strength), a traditional athletic club. In this setting a professional chanter, called a *murshed*, accompanies the traditional athletic exercises with a drum beat and recitations of deeds of bravery from Ferdowsi's epic. The history of *pardeh-dāri* (screen-keeping) is lost to us. Similar narrative techniques exist throughout Asia and the

Middle East, however, suggesting great antiquity. The *pardeh-dar*'s episodes from Islamic religious drama were illustrated using a giant rolled screen that was often handed down from father to son. The *pardeh-dars* would ply their trade in public markets and bazaars, collecting money as freewill public offerings for their stories. They most often would recite the events of the martyrdom of Imam Husain at Karbala and are occasionally seen even today.

Rowzeh-khāni, the recitation of the martyrdom of Imam Husain without visual aids, would not be called entertainment by strictly religious persons in Iran, but it was so classified in Safavid and Qajar Iran. The *rowzeh-khāns* even had a guild at one time. These reciters of the events of Karbala are often Islamic clergymen today, but they need not be. They receive fees for their services when reciting outside normal prayer services at public mosques, at funerals, at private family memorial services, or occasionally at private devotions. Since Safavid times, on principal Shi'a religious holidays the most famous *rowzeh-khāns* have been in heavy demand. Many became both rich and famous for their performances. In recent years their recitations have even been sold as audiotape cassettes. *Rowzeh-khāni* is noteworthy as the one narrative tradition open to women, but only for consumption by all-female audiences.

Ta'ziyeh

Religious epic drama in Iran most likely evolved under the patronage of the Safavid shahs. They themselves had origins as a religious brotherhood and were particularly interested in encouraging religious ritual. They patronized mourning ceremonies for Imam Husain on a grand scale. During their reign enormous processions of mourners in groups, called *dasteh* (groups or bands), would congregate in the streets during the first ten days of the Islamic month of Muharram. They would scourge themselves with chains and cut themselves with swords and knives while they chanted rhythmic dirges of mourning. As the size of the processions grew, they became more elaborate, with depictions of the events of the martyrdom enacted by players on "floats" situated at intervals among the mourners.

Early travelers noted these processions. The first full-fledged account was given by the English traveler William Francklin in 1787, though the Russian voyager Samuel Gotlib Gmelin noted the ceremonies and used the word "theater" to describe them in 1770, and two other travelers, Petrus Wilhelmus Salamons and Johannes Van Goch, had seen the processions without calling them "theater" sometime between 1722 and 1735. By the 19th century *ta'ziyeh* was being performed as a full-fledged dramatic form. Adrian Dupré, who was attached to the scientific body that accompanied the French mission to Persia in 1807–1809, gives an account that is essentially a description of the dramatic form as it is seen today. Manuscripts of *ta'ziyeh* dramas held privately in Iran date from the late 18th century, suggesting that the form was already well established when Dupré saw it.

Ta'ziyeh was lavishly patronized by the Qajar shahs. Huge open-air arenas called *tekiyeh* were built for royally patronized performances featuring thousands of actors and an equally large number of live animals. Members of the foreign community were regularly invited to attend. Naser od-Din Shah (1848–1896) had a *ta'ziyeh* "director" as part of his royal household. Gradually the dramas began to be performed nearly all year, not only in the court, but in cities and villages throughout the country. Shi'a communities in Lebanon and Bahrain also enacted *ta'ziyeh*, though not on such a grand scale. The processional form of the mourning ceremony continues today in Shi'a communities in INDIA and PAKISTAN.

Comic Improvisatory Theater

Comic improvisatory theater was also supported by the courts. Shah 'Abbās of Iran (1588–1629) had a famous jester, Kal 'Enayat (Bald Enayat), who performed comic entertainments in court. A miniature painting by Soltan Mohammad Naqqāsh from this period (1621) shows performers entertaining in what seems to be a court setting. One of the clowns is wearing a tall hat, and others are clothed in goatskins. In *Performance in Iran* (Namāyesh dar Irān, 1965), Bahrām Bezā'i reports that musicians from this period used to give comic performances when called on to entertain in the homes of the wealthy:

> Entertainers in *taqlid* would normally imitate the accents and personal characteristics of well known people in the towns and villages in which they performed. These people would be seen meeting and greeting each other. After a short while they would fall to arguing and making fun of each other's accents and behaviour, and the story would end with the two characters fighting and chasing each other.

THE ADVENT OF WESTERN THEATER

During the 19th century the Qājar and Ottoman empires began to come under the influence of European culture. Although many European travelers had journeyed to Middle Eastern lands in the 16th and 17th centuries, it was only in the 18th that Middle Easterners began to tour Europe with any regularity. Most cultured travelers were greatly impressed by European theater, as well as by opera. It was at this point that European-style drama began to be performed.

It is difficult to ascertain who staged the first Western-style drama in a Middle Eastern language, but a strong claim may be made for Marūn Mikhā'il al-Naqqāsh, a Maronite Christian with musical and literary talents born in Sidon in 1817. He was trained as a bookkeeper and, as a member of the Beirut Chamber of Commerce, traveled throughout the Ottoman Empire. In 1846 he traveled to ITALY, where he was greatly struck with the theater and opera. On returning to Beirut he was determined to stage a theatrical performance with the help of his family and friends, and in 1847 he wrote an original drama in Arabic heavily inspired by Molière's *L'Avare*, titled *The Miser* (al-Bakhil). Pioneers of Western-style theater in the Arabic-speaking world included Ya'qub Ṣanū',

Salīm Naqqāsh, Yūsuf Khayyāt, Sulaymān al-Qardāhī, and Ahmad Abū al Khalīl al-Qabbānī. As far as is known, none of these pioneers ever visited Iran, although their work may have been seen by Iranians traveling in Cairo or Damascus.

Farther to the east, one other early pioneer of Western-style theater did have a profound influence on the development of Iranian theater. This was Mirzā Fath 'Ali Ākhundzādeh (1812–1878). Though he lived in the Russian Caucasus, Akhundzadeh wrote in Azeri Turkish, the dialect of Azerbāijān. He composed six plays between 1850 and 1855: *Mullah Ibrāhim the Alchemist* (*Mollā Ibrāhim khalil kimiyāgar*), *Monsieur Jordan the Botanist* (*Musir Jordan, hakim-e nabātāt*), *The Vizier of the Khān of Sarab* (*Vizir-e Khān-e Sarāb*), *The Thief-Catching Bear* (*Khers-e qoldorbāsān*), *The History of a Miser* (*Sargozasht-e mard-e khasis*), and *The Rich Lawyers of Tabriz* (*Vokalāye morāfe'e-ye Tabriz*). He translated some of these plays into Russian and performed them in large cities of the Caucasus. A collection of these works, *Proverbs* (*Tamsilāt*), was published in Āzeri Turkish in 1859 and later became the first Western-style dramatic literature published in Persian in a translation by Mirza Mohammad Qarājedāghi in Tehran (1974).

The first original plays in Persian were written by Mirzā Āqā, Tabraīzī, literary government bureaucrat who visited Constantinople and encountered Ākhundzādeh's writings. Ākhundzādeh asked Mirzā Āqā to translate his works into Persian, but the latter preferred to write original works. His COMEDIES, *The Rule of Zamān Khān* (*Ashraf khān hokumat-e Zamān Khān*), *The Pilgrimage to Kerbalā of Shāh Qoli Mirzā* (*Kerbalā raftan-e Shāh Qoli Mirzā*), and *Āqā Hāshem's Love Affair* (*'āsheq shodan-e 'Āqā Hāshem*), are extremely amusing and surprisingly modern. Until recently many of Mirzā Āqā's works were attributed to Malkām Khān, a literate, rebellious politician who lived abroad. Because of the satirical nature of many of the plays, Mirzā Āqā may have been content to allow this mistake to stand.

POPULAR THEATER IN THE 20th CENTURY

Traditional theater forms declined greatly in the 20th century, but have continued to influence theatrical development in all countries in the Middle East and North Africa. An assessment of their form today is also a key to understanding something of their artistic structure in the past.

Comic Improvisatory Theater

The two principal forms of comic improvisatory theater in the Middle East, *ruhōzi* in Iran and *ortaoyunu* in TURKEY, are very similar and are probably related historically. In the 21st century they still bear a clear resemblance to each other, sharing many common features. The names of these two forms refer similarly to the location of the performances. In Iran performances were held *ru* (on) the *hōz* (courtyard pool). A bed or platform—*takht*—was placed over the pool, hence the alternate name for the form, *takht-e hōzi*. *Ortaoyunu* refers to the performance taking place in the middle (*orta*) of the courtyard (*oyunu*).

Comic improvisatory troupes in the *ruhōzi* tradition are generally composed of actors and musicians. All members of the troupe generally play one or more musical instruments and are able usually to perform a full musical program in addition to or in lieu of a theatrical performance. Many troupe members, especially those who specialize in women's roles, are also adept dancers.

All comic traditions in South and Southwest Asia emphasize the clown as a central figure, and *ruhōzi* does the same. The clown may be thought of as the central figure around whom the "text" of the performance is constructed. In *ruhōzi* the clown has no fixed name, but Rajab seems to be a common personal name assigned to him, especially when he is cast in the role of a servant. He uses blackface makeup and so is regularly referred to by performers as the *Siah*, or black. Similarly, playing the clown is called *siah-bāzi*, (blackplaying). This term is occasionally used as a synonym for the performance form itself. There is always a second principal figure in *ruhōzi*, the *hajji* (referring to a person who has made the *hajj* pilgrimage to Mecca), an elderly merchant who represents conventional morality and respectability.

The performance also depends on stock characters in addition to the clown. The most important of these are the juvenile "dandy," female figures, nobles, court figures, and a whole range of ethnic characterizations. Parallels here with *karagöz* (shadow puppet theater) are very clear and have led to speculation that live comic improvisatory drama may have developed from puppet drama.

Performances are not entirely improvisatory. However, in *ruhōzi* there is no written text. Stock plots are most commonly transmitted through rehearsal and oral transmission and are learned by troupe members. These plays are refined over years of performance and acquire slightly different realizations for each individual troupe. One important feature of performance is that the individual play story lines are interlaced with set comic routines, shticks, or, using a term from commedia dell'arte, *lazzi*. These routines are set pieces often involving pratfalls, acrobatics, and visual or verbal humor. Many involve satirizing other groups and dialects, and skill as a performer is often linked to the ability to mimic other language and ethnic groups. Performance is expandable or contractible at will. Troupes can perform the same play in half an hour or three hours, depending on necessity. The active repertoire consists of from ten to twenty pieces. Many more pieces are known by troupe members, but are not in active use. These can be resurrected if requested by patrons.

Religious Epic Theater

Religious epic theater, *ta'ziyeh* or *shabih*, continues to be performed in areas of the Middle East with large Shi'a populations: Iran, IRAQ, southern Lebanon, and Bahrain, as well as processional forms in India, Pakistan, and even places far removed from Asia where Shi'a Muslim populations exist, such as Jamaica. However, the most elaborate, full-blown dramatic performances of *ta'ziyeh* continue to be performed in Iran. Although religious themes dominate in *ta'ziyeh*, there are more than 250 known pieces, some of which are secular or comic. This leads to the conclusion that *ta'ziyeh*, with its original dramatic conventions, is first and foremost a truly unique form of theater in which religious themes have a prominent role.

Performances of *ta'ziyeh* are given both by "professional" troupes of players and by villagers in amateur performances. Many small towns and villages have erected special buildings—*hoseinieh*—specifically for the performance of mourning ceremonies during the month of Muharram. *Ta'ziyeh* is most often performed in these buildings, although an open-air playing space may also be constructed to accommodate large crowds, live animals, and dozens of players, some on horseback.

Whether the performers are amateurs or professionals hired for the occasion, the staging of *ta'ziyeh* is a community affair, with cooperative funds committed for the purpose. Performances may be long or short, but they often take place all day, particularly on the ninth and tenth days of the Islamic month of Muharram, called Tasuā and Āshurā, respectively, the latter being the day of the martyrdom of Imam Husain. A noon meal may be provided for spectators, and the performance may be preceded or followed by communal mourning ceremonies that consist of processions, religious chanting, and self-flagellation. Often persons leave a bequest in their wills to contribute financially to the annual support of these rituals.

Participants and spectators do not view *ta'ziyeh* as theater, but rather as part of ritual mourning. Nevertheless, *ta'ziyeh* has many theatrical conventions. The players do not, by convention, memorize their roles (though many have memorized them through years of repetition); rather, they read them from strips of paper held in their hands called *tumār*. The parts are not welded together in a common script, but are maintained as separate scripts with cue lines for each role, akin to "sides" used in Western theater. The "good" characters, on the side of Imam Husain, chant their lines in classical Persian musical modes and wear the color green. The "bad" characters declaim their lines in stentorian tones and wear the color red. Women's roles are taken by men, who wear black and veil their faces. The performances offer a number of roles for children, played by young boys, who are also dressed in black, but are unveiled, whether they portray male or female characters.

Several forms of staging exist, but most observe the convention of having one area for the camp of Imam Husain and another area in the same open playing space for the camp of the enemies. A third space may represent Damascus, the seat of the Umayyid governor, Yazid, who ordered the death of the martyrs. A fourth area usually contains props. When characters are not "onstage," they often do not leave the playing area, but merely retire to their playing space, drink tea, and converse. When characters move in the playing area, spaces traversed in circles or arcs represent long distances, and straight lines are short distances.

Ta'ziyeh performances suffered a decline in the 20th century. Immensely popular, they are nonetheless suspect from both a religious and a political standpoint. Religious officials were always uncomfortable with the depiction of actual historical figures on stage. Political officials did not like huge gatherings of people mourning injustice. Nevertheless, the performances continue unabated in many parts of the Shi'a world. The influence of these traditional forms is deeply felt in the modern theatrical tradition of the Middle East. Despite the importation of Western-style theater to the region in the 20th century, when native writers have attempted original work, the most successful productions have always contained elements of these traditional performance genres.

THE 20th-CENTURY RISE OF NATIONAL THEATERS

The great 19th-century empires came to an end with World War I. The Ottoman Empire was split into a dozen small states, and modern Iran emerged under the leadership of Rezā Shah Pahlavi. All of the resulting new nations looked toward Europe and the UNITED STATES as models for development. The theater was no exception. Traditional theater forms declined rapidly in favor of Western-style theater. Film and later television became important entertainment media, further speeding the decline of traditional performance forms. For the most part the national theaters that arose in the 20th-century Middle Eastern nations have been pale imitations of Western theater. Only in the last twenty years has new experimentation combining traditional forms of past centuries with modern directorial and acting styles yielded a revitalized theater in the Middle East. The first Western-style playing space in Iran was not constructed until 1886 at the Dar al Fonun secondary school in Tehran. Because of religious opposition, performances there of translations of Molière and other European authors were patronized only by the court. Nevertheless, there was an increased interest in drama during this period, and Mirza Aqa Tabrizi's example prompted many writers to experiment. Among these were Morteza Qoli Khan Fekri, Ahmad Mahmudi, Abdolrahim Khalkhāli, Afrāsiyāb Āzād, Ali Mohammad Khān Oveysi, Taqi Raf'at, and Abolhasan Forughi.

The constitutional revolution of 1906–1911 ushered in a new cultural era. The Teātr-e Melli (National Theater), built in 1911, staged the first public performances of Western-style theater—some in public parks. Gradually, other theaters began to appear in Tehran. A number of writers began to translate European stage works, and a few original plays were produced.

Ahmad Mahmud Kamàl al-Vezāreh (1875–1930) wrote a number of dramas, including *Master Nowruz, the Cobbler* (*Ostād Nowruz-e pineduz*, 1919), in which the colloquial Persian of south Tehran was used for the first time. Mirzādeh Eshqi (1893–1925) wrote six historical patriotic works, including *The Resurrection of Iranian Kings* (*Rastākhize salātin-e Iran*, 1916), which conjures up the spirits of the pre-Islamic Achaemenian kings of Iran. Hasan Moqaddam (1896–1925) wrote a mocking satire, *Ja'far Khān Has Returned from Europe* (*Ja'far Khān az Farang āmadeh*, 1922), inspired by *ruhōzi* theater, which makes light of pretentiously Europeanized Iranians speaking French-spattered Persian on their return from abroad and putting on Western airs.

Rezā Shah Pahlavi's reign (1925–1941) proved difficult for the Iranian theater because of heavy censorship. Few writers of fiction turned their talents to the stage, although the novelist Sadeq Hedayat did write two plays, *Parvin, the Daughter of Sāsān* (*Parvin dokhtār-e Sāsān*, 1928) and *Māzyār* (1933), both concerned with the Arab invasion of Iran in the 7th century A.D. During the reign of Rezā Shah women appeared on the Iranian stage for the first time.

It was only after the end of World War II that Western-style theater became established on a fully professional basis. 'Ali Nasiriān and ʿAbbās Javānmard began to stage productions in a small theatrical company, the Goruh-e Honar-e Melli (National Art Group), brought into being by Shāhin Sarkissiān (1912–1966). Both Nasiriān and Javānmard later worked with the Office of Dramatic Arts of the Ministry of Culture and Arts after its establishment in 1964. In its early days the Goruh-e Honar-e Melli produced stage adaptations of Hedāyat's stories, including *The Temporary Husband* (*Mohallel*, 1957) and *Eaters of the Dead* (*Mordeh khorhā*, 1957). Nasiriān was the first serious Iranian writer to be inspired by traditional performance forms in writing for the modern stage. He wrote several successful plays, including *The Golden Serpent* (*Afʿiye talāʿi*, 1957) and *The Wandering Nightingale* (*Bolbol-e sargashteh*, 1959). The latter, based on a folktale, was the first Iranian play to be produced in Europe (Paris, 1960). He also wrote *The Black One* (*Siyāh*, c. 1962), a play depicting the deep sadness of the blackfaced clown of *ruhōzi* comedy, and *The Theatre Company* (*Bongāh-e theatrāl*, 1974), a straight scripted version of a *ruhōzi* comedy.

The finest dramatic writer of the post–World War II years, in many people's opinion, was also one of Iran's greatest novelists and short-story writers, Gholam Hosein Sā'edi (1935–1985), who often wrote under the pen name Gohār Morād. Like many Iranian writers, Sā'edi avoided censorship by couching his work in heavy symbolism. His early plays were direct in their political comment—for example, his collection *Five Plays from the Constitutional Revolution* (*Panj namāyeshnāmeh az enqelāb-e mashrutiyat*), which depicts the plight of citizens of the city of Tabriz victimized by an uncaring upper class around the turn of the 20th century. His later plays grew more subtle and simpler.

The Clubwielders of Varazil (*Chubbedasthā-ye Varazil*, 1965) told the story of villagers threatened by hunters who first befriend them; the villagers eventually take refuge in an Islamic shrine that offers them no protection. In *Workaholics in the Trenches* (*Kārbāfakhā dar sangar*, 1960) he focuses on the conflicts that arise from rapid industrialization. Of his other plays, perhaps the best known are *"A" Without a Hat, "A" with a Hat* (*Āy bi kolāh, Āy bā kolāh*, 1967, referring to the long A in the Persian alphabet that has a "hat" over it, and also to an idiom: to have a cap put on one is to be fooled), *Woe to Be Vanquished* (*Vāy bar maghlub*, 1971), and *Honeymoon* (*Mahe asal*, 1978).

Bahrām Bezā'i (1938–) has had a varied career as a theater scholar, film director, and playwright. His *Performance in Iran* remains a definitive work on Iranian traditional theater. His plays are highly symbolic and often draw on folkloric sources. The traditional puppet theater inspired his influential play *Marionettes* (*Arusak-ha*, 1962, published in 1963), in which an unwilling hero is inspired to fight a demon in a final battle to the death for the love of a woman. The puppet theater also inspired his *Evening in a Strange Land* (*Ghorub dar diyāri gharib*, 1963) and *The Story of the Hidden Moon* (*Qesse-ye māhe penhān*, 1963). Traditional Iranian wrestling furnished the background for *Akbar the Champion Dies* (*Pahlavān Akbar mimirad*, 1965). Bezā'i has gradually included more political allegory in his writing. In *Four Boxes* (*Chahār sanduq*, 1967) he presents four characters representing different factions of society in different colors: yellow, the intellectual; green, the clergy; red, the merchant; and black, the laborer. In order to protect themselves from some unknown threat, they construct a scarecrow, who comes to life and forces them to live out their lives in separate boxes, thus preventing them from uniting to overthrow him. The clear analogy to the Pahlavi regime prevented this play from being produced during the reign of the shah. Similarly, *The Death of Yazdigerd* (*Marg-e Yazdigerd*, 1979) deals with the death of the last Sassanian king and, by extension, the death of any despot.

Sādeq Chubak (1916–) is one of Iran's best-known modern writers. Most famous for his short stories depicting the life of villagers and poor urban residents, he also wrote several influential plays, including *Sly* (*Hatkhat*, 1960) and *Rubber Ball* (*Tup-e lastiki*, 1949–1950). His novel *The Patient Stone* (*Sang-e sabur*, 1966) contains several sections in dramatic format, including a myth of creation.

Nader Ebrahimi (1936–) is a prolific writer who has produced short stories, novels, screenplays, and dramatic works, many of which seem to be literary works rather than stage pieces. Two of his plays, *The Essence of Waiting* (*Nafs-e entezār*, 1976) and *Blind Expectation* (*Entezāre kur*, 1976), have been translated into English.

Several institutions formed the backdrop for dramatic work in Iran in the 1960s and 1970s, as the regime of Mohammad Rezā Pahlavi attempted to develop the arts along European lines. A School of Dramatic Arts was founded, and a major national theater, the twenty-fifth of Shahrivar Hall, was opened with a regular theater season in both the main theater and a smaller studio. A good deal of experimental theater work was produced here. National Iranian Radio–Television also served as a major source for support of theater. The Kargāh-e Namayesh (Performance Workshop) was opened in 1969 and served as a training school for actors. Within this framework a number of plays were written and given outstanding productions by a group of talented young writers and directors. Arby Ovanessian (1942–) produced several plays by Abbās Na'lbandiān (1947–), including *Profound Research* (*Pazhuheshi zharf*, 1968), a surrealist drama in the style of SAMUEL BECKETT about a number of persons waiting for an "answer," and *Suddenly* (*Nāgāhān*, 1972), concerning the murder of an "outsider" by a group of fanatics. Bizhan Mofid wrote *A City of Tales* (*Shahr-e qesseh*, 1968), which mocked Iranian society, using actors in the guise of animals and employing traditional storytelling methods and music; and *Self-Sacrificer* (*Jān-nessār*, 1972), a satirical farce that preserves the style of traditional *ruhōzi* comedy. Esmà'il Khalaj wrote several plays dealing with village life, including *How Are You, Mash Rahim?* (*Hālet chetōr-e Mash Rahim*, 1977) and *Mrs. Flowerpot* (*Goldune Khānom*, 1977). Ashurbanipal Bābella's *Tonight Is a Moonlit Night* (*Emshab shab-e māhtāb-e*, 1974) is a *ruhōzi*-inspired satire.

The most important contribution of National Iranian Radio–Television to theatrical life in Iran was perhaps the establishment of the annual Festival of Arts in Shiraz. Under the direction of the writer and filmmaker Farrokh Gafary, the festival was a major international showcase for AVANT-GARDE Western drama and for the traditional performance arts of Asia, Africa, and Latin America.

All major postwar Iranian actors and directors produced works at the festival. The world's major avant-garde directors also produced new works, including Peter Brook, Jerzy Grotowski, ROBERT WILSON, Shuji Teriyama, Peter Schuman, Tadeusz Kantor, and André Gregory, among others. One important consequence of the festival was the artistic cross-fertilization it produced. Iranian actors and directors had the opportunity to see daring new works, such as Brook's *Orghast* (1971) and Wilson's *KA MOUNTAIN AND GUARDenia TERRACE* (1972). These directors in turn had the opportunity to be exposed to traditional performing arts, such as *ta'ziyeh* and *ruhōzi* theater, both of which were produced extensively at the festivals. *Ta'ziyeh* was first produced at the 1967 festival by director Parviz Sayyād in conjunction with theater scholar Kojasteh Kia. Sayyad had presented an earlier production in Tehran in 1965. In 1976 a series of ten highly successful *ta'ziyeh* performances using traditional performers was held at the festival under the direction of actor, director, and theater researcher Mohammad Bāgher Ghaffāri.

Ruhōzi was presented in several "modernized" forms during the eleven years that the festival was in existence. In 1977 Mohammad Bāgher Ghaffāri assembled existing traditional troupes from throughout the country for a series of highly successful performances held in a garden setting in Shiraz.

The revolution of 1978–1979 halted much of the theatrical activity that had taken place under the Pahlavi regime, making the future of theater much less certain. Theatrical training schools and regular performance in public virtually ceased in Iran. National Iranian Radio–Television, its name changed to the Voice and Vision of the Islamic Republic of Iran, on occasion produced dramas on revolutionary themes for television, but stage drama was viewed with great suspicion. Sa'id Soltanpur, a leftist writer, staged *'Abbās-Āqā, Worker* (*'Abbās-Āqā kārgar*) in 1980 but was executed by the authorities in 1981. Many Iranian writers, actors, and directors emigrated, producing works in Persian abroad. Director Parviz Sayyād toured the United States with two successful plays, *The Donkey* (*Khar*, 1983) and *Samad Goes to War* (*Samad be jang miravad*, 1984), both dealing with Iran after the revolution. Gholam Hosein Sa'edi published two plays in Paris before his death: *Mirror Polishing Chamberlains* (*Pardeh-dārān-e ā'ineh-afruz*, 1986) and *Othello in Wonderland* (*Otello dar Sarzamine Ajāyeb*, 1986). Mohammad Bagher Ghaffari staged an updated version of a traditional *ta'ziyeh*, *Moses and the Wandering Dervish* (1989), at Trinity College in Hartford, Connecticut.

In Iran traditional theater forms are reportedly making a comeback. Sturdy *ruhōzi* seems to have survived the revolution by turning its satire on the former Pahlavi regime; and *ta'ziyeh*, despite skepticism from some clerics, has undergone a full-blown revival. A government-sponsored troupe toured FRANCE in 1991, and *ta'ziyeh* performances with modern sound amplification are now seen widely in Iran. Mohammad Bagher Ghaffari later brought highly acclaimed *ta'ziyeh* performances to the Festival d'Autonne in Paris in 2000 and to the Lincoln Center Festival in New York in 2002.

FURTHER READING

Beeman, William O. *Culture, Performance, and Communication in Iran.* Tokyo: Institute for the Study of Languages and Cultures of Asia and Africa, 1982.

——. "A Full Arena: The Development and Meaning of Popular Performance Traditions in Iran." In *Modern Iran: The Dialectics of Continuity and Change*, ed. by Michael E. Bonine and Nikki R. Keddie. Albany: State Univ. of New York Press, 1981.

——. "Why Do They Laugh? An Interactional Approach to Humor in Traditional Iranian Improvisatory Theatre." *Journal of American Folklore* 94, no. 374 (1981): 506–526.

Benjamin, Samuel Greene Wheeler. *Persia and the Persians.* Boston: Ticknor, 1887.

Chelkowski, Peter J., ed. *Ta'ziyeh: Ritual and Drama in Iran.* New York: New York Univ. Press, 1979.

Faique, Mohammad. *A Complete Study of Persian Drama, 1906–1995.* Delhi: Nice Bks., 1999.

Gaffary, Farrokh. "Evolution of Rituals and Theatre in Iran." *Iranian Studies* 17, no. 4 (1984): 361–390.

Gaster, Theodore H. *Thespis: Ritual, Myth, and Drama in the Ancient Near East.* 2d ed. Garden City, N.Y.: Doubleday, 1961.

Ghaffari, Mohammad Bagher. "The Director Speaks." In *Ta'ziyeh: Ritual and Popular Beliefs in Iran*, ed. by Milla Cozart Riggio. Hartford, Conn.: Trinity College, 1988.

Ghanoonparvar, M. R. "Drama." *Iranian* (1997). http://www.iranian.com/Iranica/Nov97/Drama/index.html.

Ghanoonparvar, M. R., and J. Green, eds. *Iranian Drama: An Anthology.* Costa Mesa, Calif.: Mazdâ, 1989.

Jannati-Ata'i, Abu al-Qāsem *Bonyād-e namāyesh dar Irān* [The institution of performance in Iran]. Tehran: Chāp-e Mihan, 1955.

Kapuscinski, Gisèle, ed. *Modern Persian Drama: An Anthology*. Lanham, Md.: Univ. Press of America; New York: Bibliotheca Persica, 1987.

Lassy, Ivar. *The Muharram Mysteries Among the Azerbeijan Turks of Caucasia: An Academical Dissertation*. Helsingfors: Lilius & Hertzberg, 1916.

Pelly, Lewis. *The Miracle Play of Hasan and Hussein*. 2 vols. London: Croom Helm, 1879.

William O. Beeman

IRAQ

Iraq, which has existed as an independent state only since the end of World War I, encompasses the Tigris-Euphrates basin and the western part of Kurdistan. Theatrical activity has been present in this historic region since the beginning of civilization. As in other Middle Eastern nations, the rediscovery of traditional theater has become an important cultural feature of the overall development of art in the region as playwrights and writers attempt to develop new modes of artistic expression that move away from imitation of Western tradition, and to develop new theater that speaks to the cultural roots of modern Middle Eastern peoples.

Most of these historical forms of Middle Eastern and North African theater escaped the attention of Orientalist scholars because they existed primarily as folk theatrical tradition, with little in the way of formally recorded text. Today it is not possible to reconstruct the exact forms of the earliest historical traditions. Researchers must rely on comparisons of existing folk traditions and on historical accounts by travelers and local chroniclers to come to an understanding of the earliest theatrical forms.

Theodore Gaster, in his comprehensive study *Thespis: Ritual, Myth, and Drama in the Ancient Near East*, suggests that ritual and drama have a common religious origin in the Near East. He deals with ancient Egyptian theatrical rituals and also with ritual poems and texts from Canaanite, Babylonian, and Hittite sources—all in the Mesopotamian region. While many of the sources cited by Gaster are not written in contemporary dramatic form, these mythological texts were probably enacted in ritual context before a public audience. The most important of these texts is the epic *Gilgamesh*, which is highly theatrical in its presentation of the adventures of the great hero.

The Roman theaters extended as far as Jordan and Syria, where their ruins can be seen today. Since there is no mention of theater in the Qur'an or Ḥadīth (accounts of the actions and sayings of the Prophet Muhammad), it may be that the early Muslims had no active knowledge of theater. The general Islamic prohibition against depicting living beings, thought to be a form of idolatry, biased dramatic activity in the Islamic world toward narrative.

The word *laʿb* (also *liʿb* or *laʿib*) in Arabic means roughly "to play" and is frequently the base term for describing various forms of theatrical activity. The "hobby horse" and masked performance seem to have been widespread in the early Islamic world. Ibn al-Ṭiqṭaqā wrote in the 13th century C.E. that the last caliph of the Abbasid period, al-Mustaʿṣim, spent too much time watching *maskhara*, which may signify masked actors.

The term *ḥikāya* means both "story" and "imitation," or impersonation. Another widespread term was *khayāl*, which also indicates "dream" or "imagination." The jesters and famous clowns of the medieval courts were involved in this kind of activity. Accounts of the Abbasid court of Baghdad indicate that the *ḥikāya* was frequently enacted by entertainers of the court. This form later developed by the 11th century C.E. into a rhymed prose work, the *maqāma*, in which a narrator recounts a story, taking different roles. The *risāla* seems also to be a learned treatise composed as a dialogue, much like Galileo's *Dialogue Concerning the Two Chief World Systems*.

Present-day Iraq was part of the Ottoman Empire from the 15th century until World War I. Thus the performance forms that were active among the Ottomans also served to inspire and shape dramatic traditions in Iraq. First and foremost among these was the shadow puppet theater, known by its Turkish name, *karagöz*, literally "black eye," after the main clown figure in the tradition, who was depicted having a black eye. In EGYPT the form continues to be known by this name, pronounced in Egyptian Arabic as *ʿaraʿuz*. The purely Arabic name for the shadow theater is *khayāl a-ẓill*, shortened in this period to *khayāl*. This word later came to indicate live performances, as well as shadow puppet theater. By the 16th century another Arabic term, *muḥabbaẓ*, became widely used for actors, especially comic players. This term extended well into the 19th century, until the establishment of Westernized theater in the Arab world around 1870. The *muḥabbaẓīn* continued to be an important source of entertainment until modern times. Another source of theatrical activity in the Mesopotamian region, extending into 20th-century Iraq, is *taʿziyeh*, the epic dramatic presentation among the Shi'a Islamic population in the southern Tigris-Euphrates basin of the martyrdom of Imam Husain, grandson of the Prophet Muhammad. Husain was killed in the city of Karbala in present-day southern Iraq. *Taʿziyeh* is widely performed today in other Shi'a communities, particularly in IRAN, Bahrain, and Lebanon.

During the 19th century the Ottoman Empire, along with the Qajar Empire in Iran, came under the influence of European culture. Although many Europeans traveled to the Middle East in the 16th and 17th centuries, it was only in the 18th that Middle Easterners began to tour Europe with any regularity. Most cultured Arabic travelers were greatly impressed by European theater, including opera. It was at this point that European-style drama began to be performed in the Middle East. Modern drama in Iraq was part of this overall development.

It is difficult to ascertain who staged the first Western-style drama in a Middle Eastern language, but a strong claim may be made for Mārū n Mikhā'il al-Naqqāsh, a Maronite Christian with musical and literary talents born in Sidon in 1817. In 1846 he traveled to ITALY, where he was greatly struck with the theater and opera. On returning to Beirut in 1847 he wrote an original drama in Arabic, heavily inspired by Molière's *L'avare*, titled *The Miser* (*al-Bakhīl*). A series of other dramas followed.

The first Western-style Arabic production in Cairo was not that of al-Naqqash but the play *Operette* by Ya'qūb Ṣannū ʿ(1839–1912), staged in 1870 in the garden of a coffeehouse at Azbbakiyya, which had been built, along with the Cairo Opera House, by Khedive Ismail, who had an interest in transforming Egypt into a Europeanized state. Ṣannūʿ, known also as James Sanua, was a Cairene of Italian Jewish parentage who had studied in Italy and loved opera. In Cairo he wrote and staged a number of humorous plays in the Egyptian colloquial language, full of songs and satirical musical sketches, much like the traditional *muḥabbaẓ* but also reflecting the influence of Italian opera. Some of the plays are COMEDIES of manners, centering on stock characters such as the Nubian servant (al-Barbari), the talkative maid, and the European with faulty classical Arabic. Like those of al-Naqqāsh, the plays of Ṣannūʿ were influenced by Molière—full of scheming lovers, intrigues, mistaken identities, and pedants who abuse and misuse language, and taking love and greed as common themes.

The emergence of these modern scripted plays in Cairo (now designated by the Arabic term *al-masraḥ*, "stage") occasioned the establishment of acting troupes that toured the Arabic-speaking world. Egyptian troupes, the first being that of the impresario Jurj Abyaḍ, and subsequently those of Fāṭima Rushdī and Yūsuf Wahbī, visited Iraq in the 1920s and 1930s and created a strong interest in theater. An Iraqi actor who had studied in Europe, Ḥaqqi al-Shiblī (1913–1985), apprenticed with Fāṭima Rushdī's troupe in Cairo. He returned to Iraq, where he formed his own troupe with Egyptian and Iraqi actors. Of all the Egyptian actors, Yūsuf Wahbī achieved the greatest success as one of the most continuously popular performers in Iraq. His unprecedented influence on Iraqi theater lasted until the Iraqi revolutionary period in the 1950s.

Gradually Iraqi playwrights emerged, mostly imitating Egyptian writers such as Aḥmed Shauqī and TAUFIQ AL-HAKĪM. Perhaps the most prominent of these new Iraqi playwrights was Yūsuf al-ʿĀnī (1927–). Al-ʿĀnī was interested in theater from a very early age, when as a junior-high-school student he met Ḥaqqi al-Shiblī, who came to his school to judge oratory students. Al-ʿĀnī reports in his autobiography that al-Shiblī was not impressed by his performance, but this did not dissuade the young dramatist, who wrote and produced his first play, *The Gamblers* (*al-Muqamirūn*), in high school in 1944. In college Al-ʿĀnī established a performing troupe named Jamaʿat Jabr al-Khawātīr (the Goodwill Reconciliation Group). During this period he began an enormously productive association with fellow performers and later directors Ibrahim Jalal and Samiʿ ʿAbdul-Ḥamīd. These three artists, beginning in the 1950s, were the architects of modern theatrical development in Iraq, founding the group al-Masraḥ al-Ḥadith (the Modern Theater), which served not only as a theater production group, but also as a training ground for theater professionals. Al-ʿĀnī's dramas were reflective of the earlier *muḥabbaẓ* tradition. They were composed in colloquial Iraqi Arabic and featured the humorous clown figures of the traditional pre-Western theater.

As social conditions in Iraq began to deteriorate in the 1950s, al-ʿĀnī also grew more serious. One of his best-received plays, *I am your mother, Shakir* (*Anā ummak yā Shakīr*), in which a mother sees her children die in Iraq's nationalist struggle, but still defends the struggle itself, caused great consternation. In 1957 the Modern Theater troupe's license was revoked, sending al-ʿĀnī into brief exile. The revolution of 1958, which deposed the British-supported monarchy, also brought about the restoration of the troupe. Al-ʿĀnī's dramas, such as *Welcome to Life* (*Aḥlan bi al-ḥayāt*), which he had written in exile, were staged again. The events surrounding the revolution appear to have sobered him, and his dramas became more serious, emphasizing social reform. Other struggles with the government were eventually resolved, and al-ʿĀnī's theater company was eventually attached to the Iraqi Ministry of Culture, with him as head. His influence continued through 1978, when he produced his last significant play, *To Be or Not to Be* (*Kān yā mā kān*).

Al-ʿĀnī's output was prodigious. Some notable works from his later period are *The Ruin* (*al-Kharāba*, 1970), which invokes the *Gilgamesh* epic in Brechtian style; and the political trilogy *The Moorings* (*al-Sharī'a*, 1970–1971), *The Inn* (*al-Khān*, 1976), and *The Loom* (*al-Jūma*, 1976). Of all al-ʿĀnī's works, perhaps *The Key* (*al-Miftaḥ*, 1967–1968) is the best known. It is the only one of his works to be translated into English. The work is steeped in folklore, with a flavor of the *Thousand and One Nights*.

After Saddam Hussein took over as dictator in Iraq after 1978, theater culture declined significantly. Although al-ʿĀnī and his colleagues continued to produce new works, none was really successful. Theater, funded by the state, consisted of light comedies, plays praising Iraq's attacks on Iran, and works glorifying the Ba'athist regime. Any "leftist" productions were repressed, and actors, directors, and production personnel were arrested. After the first Gulf War in 1992, American economic sanctions against Iraq delivered the coup de grâce to live theater, since there were few resources to mount productions, and little money for the public to buy tickets. Nevertheless, al-ʿĀnī was able with great difficulty to make his way to Amman, Jordan, to give a distinguished lecture in 1996—a tribute to an exceptional life in the theater.

FURTHER READING

Abu-Hayf, Abd-Allāh. *Al-Masrah al-ʿArabi al-muʿāsir* [Contemporary Arabic drama]. Damascus: Ittihād al-Kuttāb al-ʿArab, 2002.

Al-ʿĀnī, Yūsuf, *Al-Tajrībah al-masrahiyya* [The theater experience]. Beirut: Al-Farabi, 1979.

Allen, Roger, ed. *Modern Arabic Literature.* A Library of Literary Criticism. New York: Ungar, 1987.

Aziza, Mohamed. *Regards sur le théâtre Arabe contemporain.* Tunis: Maison Tunisienne de l'Edition, 1970.

Gaster, Theodore. *Thespis: Ritual, Myth, and Drama in the Ancient Near East.* New York: Schuman, 1950.

Jayyusi, Salma Khadra, and Roger Allen, eds. *Modern Arabic Drama: An Anthology.* Bloomington: Indiana Univ. Press, 1995.

Landau, Jacob M. *Studies in the Arab Theater and Cinema.* Philadelphia: Univ. of Pennsylvania Press, 1958.

Al-Mubarak, Khalid. *Arabic Drama: A Critical Introduction.* Khartoum: Khartoum Univ. Press, 1986.

Moreh, Shmuel. *Live Theatre and Dramatic Literature in the Medieval Arab World.* Edinburgh: Edinburgh Univ. Press, 1992.

Shawool, Paul. *Al-Masrah al-ʿArabi al-ḥadīth* [Modern Arab theater]. London: Riad El-Rayyes, 1989.

Yousif, Salaam. "The People's Theater of Yusuf al-Ani—Modern Iraqi Literature in English Translation." *Arab Studies Quarterly* 19, no. 4 (1997): 65–93.

William O. Beeman

IRELAND

In the mid-19th century theaters did a lively business in Ireland, with 3,000 people attending a stage entertainment each night. Dublin's Theatre Royal, which earlier had had a monopoly, had been joined by the Queen's Royal Theatre (1844), the Athenaeum (later called the Opera House) in Cork (1866), the Gaiety in Dublin (1871), the Star of Erin Music Hall (later called the Olympia) in Dublin (1879), and the Grand Opera House in Belfast (1895). These theaters catered to a variety of tastes, through stock companies that revived popular plays and musicals, hosting touring companies from Paris, London, and New York, and putting up variety shows and pantomimes. Those who would in their maturity come to be known as specifically Irish playwrights were exposed in their youth to revivals of William Shakespeare and other classics of the English stage and to the best of contemporary global entertainments. What Ireland lacked, and had for a long time lacked, were thriving resident playwrights dealing with local themes. The attraction of London metropolitan theaters to Irish-born playwrights was overwhelming in the 17th century (William Congreve), in the 18th (Richard Brinsley Sheridan, Oliver Goldsmith), and throughout the 19th (DION BOUCICAULT, OSCAR WILDE, GEORGE BERNARD SHAW).

It was in New York with THE COLLEEN BAWN (1860) that Boucicault (1820–1890) made the "Irish play" popular. In his advertisement for this play Boucicault claims to place the Irishman before the public as he really is, and not as that blundering blockhead unable to master the English language that earlier passed as the stage Irishman. The formula for Boucicault's Irish plays required scenic views of Killarney's lakes and mountains, villainous servants, helpless colleens, wicked landlords, and a donnybrook on stage. It was MELODRAMA spectacularly Celticized for the entertainment of world audiences. In 1884 J. W. Whitbread (1847–1916), a writer of English background and a Dublin actor-manager, proclaimed the Queen's Royal Theatre the new "Home of Irish Drama." Whitbread's plays (such as *Lord Edward; or, '98*, 1894) carried the conventions of the "Irish play" in a more specifically historical and patriotic direction, frequently dramatizing the revolutionary and pathetic excitements of the failed 1798 rebellion of Irishmen against British rule. Noisy Dublin audiences booed the nasty informers of his plays and wept for their dying young heroes and heartbroken colleens.

To the degree that Oscar Wilde (1854–1900) and George Bernard Shaw (1856–1950) were influenced by theater in Dublin, it was the revivals of Sheridan and Congreve and tours of French COMEDIES at the Gaiety that mainly had an impact on Wilde, and RICHARD WAGNER and Boucicault shows that held a lasting appeal for Shaw. When these two men of letters began writing for the London stage—Wilde's LADY WINDERMERE'S FAN and Shaw's *Widowers' Houses* were running simultaneously in 1892—they did not write explicitly as Irishmen about Irish subjects. There are no Irish characters or settings in Wilde's plays, and only two of Shaw's many works feature Irish characters (JOHN BULL'S OTHER ISLAND, 1904, and *O'Flaherty, V.C.*, 1915). The role model of HENRIK IBSEN—the artist as "enemy of the people"—was inspiring to both Irish playwrights, though only Shaw was thoroughgoing in the adaptation of the PROBLEM PLAY to his own socialist purposes. The Irishness of Wilde and Shaw was noticeable to audiences, even if the characters in the plays were not themselves Irish. The celebration of wit and the mockery of English common sense as disguised self-interest were implicitly Irish attributes of the works of both Wilde and Shaw, and they were understood by contemporary audiences to be such.

Wilde's THE IMPORTANCE OF BEING EARNEST (Valentine's Day, 1895) perfectly combined the inane with the profound in making a farce of the English forms of marriage, class, property, and patriotism. Wilde's refusal to take cultural norms as natural laws may be a resident alien's response to arbitrary national customs or a homosexual's reaction to arbitrary heterosexual norms. Although Wilde's plays have a background in the Irish dramatic tradition (Congreve, Sheridan), they did not have a future in that tradition. Many characteristics of his playwriting made him inimitable. The quality of his plays depends on his genius for epigram, and genius of any kind is never easy to imitate. Furthermore, high society—wealth, class, and polished manners—was essential to the world of Wilde's plays. Because Shaw had a semi-Marxist conception of life, he was interested in many social classes and the conflict between them, not just in the manners of the well-off. As for W. B. YEATS, J. M. SYNGE, and the Abbey Theatre playwrights in their wake, a theater located in Ireland for Irish audiences had to put on stage representative Irish people, and those people were neither wealthy nor high fashioned. Finally, Wilde's imprisonment for gross indecency in 1895 turned him overnight from a man everyone envied to one everyone shunned. Only in the 1930s at the Gate Theatre did Wilde's comedies come to be popular in Ireland.

A self-conscious program for national drama in Ireland began in 1897 with a prospectus by W. B. Yeats, Edward Martyn, and George Moore for an Irish Literary Theatre. All three men were London residents of Irish birth who had written plays and failed to have them staged in London, or, if staged, failed to have them celebrated. Their goal was to write as people of Irish birth literary plays about Ireland for occasional performance in Dublin. A special license was issued by Dublin Castle for this purpose, on condition that the plays were occasional and literary (rather than commercial or rabble-rousing). The Irish Literary Theatre put on one week of plays each year from 1899 to 1901.

W. B. Yeats (1865–1939), the spearhead of the initiative, was certainly aware of the example of other national theaters in Europe. Since the 18th century national theaters had normally preceded the nation-state that they claimed to represent. They were based on the belief that Italian opera, French comedy, and metropolitan variety shows were not suitable in language, customs, or morality to their own nation. Gothhold Lessing in Hamburg, Friedrich von Schiller in Mannheim, Wojciech Boguslawski in Warsaw, and Ibsen in Christiania (now Oslo) had all written plays in local idioms for such anti-imperial national theaters. A political dimension was implicit: it was hoped that the establishment of a national theater was a halfway house to decolonization and national self-government. The Irish dramatic revival received popular support in Dublin on the belief that it would follow this familiar pattern.

A theater movement led by Irish amateur actors followed the annual appearances of the writer-led Irish Literary Theatre. W. G. Fay and his brother Frank—admirers of ANDRÉ ANTOINE's Théâtre Libre in Paris—established a continuous company after their presentation of *CATHLEEN NI HOULIHAN* by W. B. Yeats and LADY GREGORY and *Deirdre* by AE (George Russell) in April 1902. Both are one-acts; the first is a powerful propaganda play for martyrdom through physical resistance to British rule, and the second is a dreamy evocation of romantic Irish sagas. Yeats was elected president of the new Irish National Theatre Society in August 1902, a position he retained until the last years of his life. Yeats's own ambition for the movement was to develop Irish alternatives to REALISM and to society drama, not to propagandize openly for Irish self-government.

A production of Yeats's verse play *The King's Threshold* and J. M. Synge's first work to be staged, IN THE SHADOW OF THE GLEN, on October 8,1903, established the dynamic of the early years of the Irish national theater movement. *The King's Threshold* is set in ancient Ireland, where a bard is on a hunger strike to protest his exclusion as a counselor from the king's table. The play argued that for a nation to prosper, obedience must be given to poets, who are the guardians of all values. Critics immediately protested the implied subordination of politics to art. Synge's lyrical prose version of A DOLL'S HOUSE set in a peasant's mountain cabin—with the heroine walking out on her husband at the curtain—caused even more uproar, as nationalists in the audience argued that such behavior by a woman and such drama by a man were equally un-Irish. However, when the early plays of the Irish National Theatre Society were taken on tour to London, Oxford, and Cambridge, the writing was praised for its literary distinction, and the acting was celebrated for its simplicity and NATURALISM. Thereafter, the dramatic revival in Ireland continued to debate the nature of Irishness, the value of propaganda, and the importance of artistic value as measured by established metropolitan critics. The fundamental formal qualities of Irish revival plays remained romantic representations of Irish history and mythology or plays in Hiberno-English dialect set in peasant cabins. In both types of play it is often the heart of the conflict that a stranger or artist enters to disturb and challenge the nature of the society represented by the other characters, as the bard does in *The King's Threshold* and a wandering tramp does in Synge's play. Middle-class people having conversations in drawing rooms—as in the plays of Wilde, ARTHUR WING PINERO, and HENRY ARTHUR JONES—were not represented at all in the early plays of the Irish revival.

One person in the audience for *The King's Threshold* on October 8, 1903, was Yeats's friend, the London heiress Annie Horniman. Her wealth made her opinion more effectual than the opinions of other spectators, and, liking what she saw, she promised to buy a theater building for the advancement of Yeats's ideas of drama. She refurbished the Mechanics' Theatre in Dublin (formerly a music hall), and it opened on December 26, 1904, as the Abbey Theatre, given free of charge to the Irish National Theatre Society. From 1905 she subsidized the actors' salaries as well. As a result, the theater management—Yeats, Synge, and Lady Gregory—was not dependent on the popularity of its plays with local audiences.

In the first decade of the Irish revival Lady Gregory emerged as a central shaper of modern Irish theater. As mentioned earlier, she brought to life Yeats's vision of the 1898 aisling (or vision) play *Cathleen ni Houlihan*. That play takes place in a peasant cottage, a stage set that became so common at the Abbey that practically no work other than repair and repainting was required of the stage carpenter from play to play, year in and year out. Lady Gregory had visited the originals of such cottages, whether on mercy missions around her estate or collecting folklore on behalf of Yeats. She observed manners carefully and picked up turns of phrase common in the west. Out of the local "Kiltartan" speech forms she confected an artificial, comic, and poetic stage dialect. Her Irish patriotism was in harmony with that of the people across the footlights. Although she found it difficult to resist a denouement that made all difficulties vanish, the Irish dramatic revival simply could not have done without Lady Gregory. She came up with its typical stage set, stage speech, folktale plots, and plays people enjoyed. Gregory's rosy, glorified view of the Irishman of the west became a kind of state ideology in an independent Ireland that no longer had room for the class of people that dreamed it up.

Among the three directors of the early Abbey Theatre, Synge was the one rapidly recognized to be a dramatic genius, although initially a controversial one in Ireland. Drawing upon his own experience of Irish speech and customs in Wicklow and the Aran Islands, he followed Lady Gregory's example in the invention of an Irish stage dialect. Synge's shaping of sentences, however, also draws upon Jacobean dramatists and modern French poets, making his characters utter a spectacularly elaborate and beautiful speech. As thoroughly a writer for the theater as Ibsen (with whom he maintained a subconscious rivalry), Synge constantly upset audience expectations by destabilizing generic forms: shocking outcomes were treated as happy ones, such as an unhappy wife walking out the door in *The Shadow of the Glen* (1903), and tragic outcomes, such as the attempted murder of a father in THE PLAYBOY OF THE WESTERN WORLD (1907), suddenly became comic endings. He was also able to wring nobility out of simple peasant characters, as in the intensely brief TRAGEDY of a mother who loses all her menfolk in RIDERS TO THE SEA (1904).

The one totemic event in the history of theater in Ireland is *The Playboy of the Western World* and the riots that followed it, the masterpiece that once infuriated Dublin and now delights the world. In Irish theater history everything leads up to *The Playboy* and the riots or away from them. This play's performance is the standard of measurement. What other new work could instantly cause a riot, be soon recognized as a classic, go on international tour, and rapidly enter the repertory of theater companies around the world?

What goes by the name of "context"—that is, anything around the play—is better known and more vividly debated in the case of Synge's play than in that of any other Irish play. The author, the Abbey directors, the actors, the reviewers, the theater building, the whole process leading up to February 1907, the whole consequence of it, the police-protected performances, the arrests of noisemakers, the trials, the resignations of actors and authors, the revivals, the tours in the UNITED STATES, the imitations, are all lavishly examined by theater scholars insofar as the available evidence allows. The more that is known about it, however, the more elusive the dream of a totality of comprehension becomes. There is no cinematic record of the play's performance in 1907, or, what might be as valuable, of the audience's reactions. Was it really shock at the phrase about women in their "shifts" that ignited the crowd? Scholars have not reached agreement on whether Synge intended to foment trouble, whether the play's action is a heightening and celebration of Irish speech and manners or a parody of them, whether the audience ridiculously misread the play or only took offense where offense was meant, whether the play's politics are unionist, republican, antinationalist, or nonexistent, or whether Synge was a colonizer or decolonizer. People do agree, however, that the play is a masterpiece.

Once Synge's plays began to be staged by the Irish National Theatre Society, it did not take long for leading European translators and theater directors to catch up with him. Remarkably, James Joyce—at the time in Trieste—put *Riders to the Sea* into Italian, but a production by the Grand Guignol company was not permitted by Synge's heirs. Karel Mušek translated *The Shadow of the Glen* into a Moravian dialect for the Bohemian National Theatre in Prague (August 22, 1907). *The Well of the Saints* was performed in a translation by Max Meyerfeld in MAX REINHARDT's Deutsches Theater in Berlin (January 1906), the principal theater of GERMANY. *The Playboy of the Western World* was produced by the great Aurélien Lugné-Poë, famous for also introducing MAURICE MAETERLINCK and PAUL CLAUDEL, at the Théâtre de l'Oeuvre in Paris (December 12, 1913).

George Bernard Shaw's first great success came with a play written for the Abbey, but, on the pretense that it could not be properly cast within the acting company, was rejected by its management. This was *John Bull's Other Island*, which premiered at the Royal Court Theatre in London on November 1, 1904, the first of a series of Shaw hits there. Shaw's "Preface for Politicians" to the published version of the play is a classic of theater historiography, autobiographically investigating how an author may seek to create controversy and change the attitudes of an audience to a political issue. In the case of Shaw's play, the issue was Irish Home Rule, and the attitudes he originally meant to disturb were those of Irish people in Dublin. His aim was to replace nationalism with international socialism.

The play begins in the London office of two civil engineers, one an Englishman named Broadbent and the other an Irishman named Doyle. Broadbent has a plan to buy up farmland in Ireland near Doyle's home village in order to erect a modern suburban development. He takes a reluctant Doyle along as his interpreter to the strange nation. In the characterizations Shaw completely reverses stereotypes of national temperaments: the Englishman is sentimental and at the mercy of his imagination; the Irishman is fact-facing, cold-eyed, and hardworking. The differences are not owing to race, but to the Irish climate, both the natural one (endless rain) and the artificial economic one (feudalism and colonialism). The characterization of types within Ireland is equally hard-hitting, surprising, and perceptive. The tenant who now owns his land is mean-minded, domineering over landless farmworkers, and suspicious of everyone. The Irish colleen is pale and "spiritual" as a result not of purity but of poor diet. The parish priest is authoritarian and despiritualized. In the denouement of the play the bumbling but energetic Broadbent sweeps all before him—the colleen, an Irish seat in Parliament, and his property deal. Doyle is satisfied with that outcome because he does not believe in politics, but in capitalism and technological progress. A defrocked and mystic priest, Peter Keegan, transcends all the conflicting views in the play in his concluding vision of a communist paradise.

Had the Abbey opened *John Bull's Other Island* in Dublin, Shaw would certainly have gotten the controversy he sought, because the play shows no respect at all for the nationalist assumptions that Irish people are good and hard done by, and English people are bad and unwelcome visitors. But, as Shaw observes in his preface, because the play opened in London, the English audience was flattered in its belief that Englishmen will always muddle through and Britannia will rule.

Ultimately Shaw did have an influence upon Abbey Theatre playwrights, but that influence was delayed to the war years. In October 1915 Ulster playwright ST. JOHN ERVINE (1883–1971), a disciple of Shaw, was appointed director of the Abbey Theatre. His *Mixed Marriage* (1911) was a study of bigotry among the working classes in Belfast dialect. The next director of the Abbey, J. Augustus Keogh, did a whole season of Shaw's plays at the Abbey in 1916 and 1917. Some of these—such as *Widowers' Houses*—were relevant to the interests of the young socialist SEAN O'CASEY (1880–1964).

In the two decades after the death of Synge (1909) there were three dominant playwrights in Dublin, and they were all realists: LENNOX ROBINSON, T. C. Murray, and Sean O'Casey. Lennox Robinson (1886–1958) began with serious studies of the shortcomings of life in small towns, such as *The Clancy Name* (1908) and *Crossroads* (1909), and then labored to expand his range to state-of-the-nation plays, comedies, Chekhovian mood pieces, and Pirandellesque comedies. His best play, perhaps, is *The Big House* (1926), which tells the story of a Protestant landlord family trying to hold its own in Ireland from Armistice Day in 1918 to February 1923, when its grand house is burned during the Irish Civil War. As an effort to appeal sincerely for the civic value of some Irish Protestants and their heritage at a time when that class was being driven from the country by Irish republicans, Robinson's play was going against the grain of his audience's sympathies, but it did so effectively. The play's form is inspired by ANTON CHEKHOV's THE CHERRY ORCHARD, as mediated through the example of Shaw's HEARTBREAK HOUSE (1920).

T. C. Murray (1873–1959), like Robinson from County Cork, but, unlike him and nearly all other Irish playwrights at the time, a Catholic, consistently produced well-made, unsensational plays that dramatized family life in rural Ireland. *Maurice Harte* (1912), one of his best plays, is typical of his work. It depicts the mental breakdown of a young man pushed by his mother into Maynooth Seminary although he does not feel a vocation for the priesthood. No outright villains or heroes are fingered by the characterization; everyone is a decent soul; unhappiness, it is suggested, flows from the structures of the Irish family.

While Robinson and Murray were capable playwrights, with O'Casey's first play on the Abbey stage, THE SHADOW OF A GUNMAN (1923), it was apparent that he was a budding genius. O'Casey followed Synge's example in several ways. First, he made literary use of a dialect (that of the Dublin working class, rather than rural cotters). Second, he exploited, as Synge had done, the power of an unstable generic form, veering rapidly from comedy to pathos. O'Casey, however, made more extensive use than Synge of Boucicault's Irish melodramas, music-hall turns, and variety-show gags. A Shavian socialist who had become disenchanted by the alliance of the working-class movement with republican nationalism in 1916, O'Casey consistently critiqued the supposed heroism of the recent Irish struggle for independence in plays set against the War of Independence, the Civil War, and the Easter Rebellion.

O'Casey's plays offered consummate character parts. Some of the actors who flourished in those parts in Ireland and ENGLAND—such as Sara Allgood, Molly Allgood (stage name Maire O'Neill), J. M. Kerrigan, and Arthur Sinclair—had begun their careers at the Abbey Theatre in works by Lady Gregory and Synge. Sara Allgood, for instance, enjoyed a triumph as the lead in JUNO AND THE PAYCOCK (1924), which propelled her into international fame and a career in film. Younger actors also made a name for themselves in O'Casey's work, such as F. J. McCormick and Barry Fitzgerald. Fitzgerald's depiction of Fluther Good in THE PLOUGH AND THE STARS (1926) was, in the opinion of Dublin theatergoers, a high point in Irish acting. So crucial was Fitzgerald to the ensemble that republican protestors against the antimilitarism of that play planned to scuttle its performance by kidnapping him. When that plan failed, some protestors rushed the stage, from which one was punched by Fitzgerald.

After the fight over *The Plough and the Stars* (later among the most popular plays in the Abbey repertoire), O'Casey moved to England. His next play, THE SILVER TASSIE, was astonishingly rejected by the Abbey directors in May 1928. As a result, O'Casey severed his relationship with the theater. The cost to both author and theater was terrible, as O'Casey wrote no better plays afterwards, and the Abbey could not find a replacement for him. Fortunately, in 1924 the government of the Irish Free State had accepted the Abbey Theatre as a gift from Yeats and Gregory in exchange for an annual subsidy. Without this subsidy the National Theatre of Ireland would possibly not have survived the departure of O'Casey.

A successful competitor to the Abbey arose in 1928 when on October 14 MICHEÁL MACLIAMMÓIR and Hilton Edwards premiered Gate Theatre productions with PEER GYNT on the stage of the Peacock, the Abbey's studio space. This was followed by a daring production of Oscar Wilde's *Salomé* and Denis Johnston's expressionist lampoon of Irish nationalist culture, *The Old Lady Says, "No!"* The production values of MacLiammóir and Edwards's productions—both men had a professional background on the London stage—outclassed the affable character acting of the Abbey regulars. The Gate Theatre obtained an 18th-century premises, the Assembly Rooms attached to the Rotunda Hospital, and opened there in 1930. With MacLiammóir as star actor and designer and Hilton Edwards as actor and director, it developed a reputation for classy productions of William Shakespeare, Wilde, and English social comedies. A year after opening, in 1931, a sixteen-year-old American, lying that he had experience with the Theatre Guild in New York, asked for an audition. Edwards gave Orson Welles his first professional work onstage, with a lead role in *Jew Suss*. The audience rewarded Welles's over-the-top acting with ovation after ovation. Welles's mature style as an actor was quite possibly influenced by the romantic acting in the grand manner of MacLiammóir. Another actor to get his start with the Gate was James Mason, subsequently a Hollywood leading man.

Since the trauma of Synge's death in 1909, Yeats had effectively withdrawn as playwright from the theater he managed. He sought his players and audience elsewhere for a new sort of play, a mixture of CLOSET DRAMA, magical rite, and séance. Inspired by the translations of Japanese NŌ plays Ezra Pound had shown him, Yeats began to write intensely lyrical, short dance plays, opening and closing with songs. This form gave him the quality of ritual he sought, while isolating him from the demands of realism, plausibility, and intelligibility. One of his first and most impressive essays in the form was AT THE HAWK'S WELL, like several other successes, such as *Only Jealousy of Emer* (1919) and *Death of Cuchulain* (1939), based on the life of Cuchulain from the Irish heroic sagas. Like his late poetry, these verse plays are compacted of Yeats's beliefs about the afterlife, his sense of the place of the individual in history, and his struggle to order his personal life. Ordinary theatergoers looking for an entertainment like other entertainments are wholly ignored. With no advertising, no reviews, no press photographers on opening night, no scenery to build, no tickets to sell, and not many spectators desired, Yeats's new type of theater left him free of any demand other than that of his own imagination.

In the 1930s, a former senator of the Free State and wholly at odds with it, Yeats reengaged as a dramatist with the Abbey Theatre. *Words Upon the Window Pane* (November 17, 1930) is a séance play in which the medium must re-create the voices and presences of many characters, including Jonathan Swift and the two women he loved. This was an uncustomary use of realism by Yeats in order to validate views of the paranormal regarded by most people as unrealistic. The voice of Swift is flawless: tormented, majestic, and greathearted. He leaps frighteningly into contemporary life and curses its democracy, low-mindedness, and envy of greatness. Those in the Abbey audience were being harangued not just by the ghost of Swift but by the old poet Yeats as well.

The last Yeats play staged at the Abbey during his lifetime was his masterpiece, PURGATORY (August 10, 1938), appropriately as part of a two-week festival celebrating the theater's achievements over the previous forty years. Lennox Robinson, asked the next day by a priest what the play was about, wisely dodged the question. The play was not only unorthodox in its understanding of Purgatory, but obviously expresses Yeats's rage at modernity and especially modern Irish democracy in a Catholic, Gaelic state.

The action in *Purgatory* involved a calculated transgression upon the socially enforced modesty of the Irish stage. The audience watches as the two characters on stage watch a sex scene between a high-born lady and a groom from the stable, as seen in silhouette in a high window of a burned-out house. It is a shadow play of ghosts and vanishes in darkness at the moment of sexual contact, but even so the action violated the current Irish norms of representability. The censorship of publications bill (1928) had been enacted over Yeats's protests by the Irish Free State. He then prophesied that "the power to create great character or possess it cannot long survive" if authors like Synge and O'Casey were not permitted to create works that pious citizens "shudder at, something wild and ancient." Even though the censorship law did not extend to the stage, a regime of enforcement by the growing clericalism of Ireland was established throughout the cultural sphere. For decades in the future, truly transgressive characters and actions would not be permissible on the stage of the National Theatre, although Yeats got away with it one last time.

Purgatory is a fitting swan song for a half century of modern Irish drama. The best of that drama is to a large extent the work of Anglo-Irish Protestants: Wilde, Shaw, Gregory, Yeats, Synge, and Robinson. In the years following, Ireland labored to find a dramatic voice suitable to its postrevolutionary character and representative of the Catholic majority.

After the death of Yeats (1939) Ernest Blythe—formerly a minister of finance and then member of the Abbey board—was appointed artistic director of the Abbey Theatre. There was little that was artistic about Blythe's direction, which extended, miserably, until 1967. He declared that the National Theatre was an instrument of the national defense. His job was to prevent the intrusion of foreign culture and foreign morality into Ireland and to reinforce a patriotic and morally pure ethos.

During World War II Ireland was neutral, and fear of all things outside was widespread in the island. Furthermore, the government of Eamon de Valera was in favor of an aggressive program of decolonization. The Irish constitution of 1937 gave Roman Catholicism a special place, outlawed divorce, abortion, and contraception, and declared that the first language of the country was Irish, not English. One of Blythe's chief aims was to advance the use of the Irish language (most of the country and nearly all of Dublin was not Irish speaking). He required new Abbey actors to demonstrate a capacity to act in both languages. The theater's policy was to do at least a brief play in Irish every night, along with a full-length play in English. The limited number of fluent Irish speakers drastically diminished the pool from which Blythe could draw either actors or playwrights. Many of the famous actors of the O'Casey period—Sara Allgood, Barry Fitzgerald, and Arthur Shields, for instance—had already gone to Hollywood for careers in film (especially the films of Celtophile John Ford). The quality of Abbey productions declined; audience numbers declined. Then Blythe made every effort to supply plays that met the popular taste, so long as these plays did not clash with his own sense of what was Irish in sentiment and morality. He dropped the Abbey's rules of short runs, regardless of a play's popularity, and of regular revivals of all elements in its repertoire. By doing long runs of current hits, or revivals of the same classics over and over, Blythe hurt new Irish writing in two ways. First, he deprived potential young writers of familiarity with the range of the developing theatrical vocabulary for national expression; second, he reduced the demand for new plays, so that fewer young writers gained trial productions of their first efforts.

When the Irish National Theatre Society was being established, Yeats often articulated its aim: to solicit dramatic literature of the highest order in Ireland. Forced by skeptics to define both what Irish drama was and what great drama was, Yeats said that national literature was the work of writers molded by the influences that are molding their country, and great literature was "extravagant, vehement, impetuous . . . beating against the walls of the world." Between these two definitions there is certainly tension, if not a contradiction. A great Irish dramatist had to be characteristic and defiantly uncharacteristic. What Ernest Blythe would not tolerate was anything uncharacteristic. He rejected the extravagant, vehement, impetuous works submitted to him by Teresa Deevy (1903–1963), SAMUEL BECKETT (1906–1989), BRENDAN BEHAN (1923–1964), BRIAN FRIEL (1929–), THOMAS KILROY (1934–), and TOM MURPHY (1935–). The body of work by these dramatists would be enough to make any theater proud; without them the Abbey was impoverished.

Blythe was more effective in snuffing out the young talent of Teresa Deevy than in stopping these other playwrights, who found elsewhere their routes to fame. Unfortunately, she was one of the few female Irish playwrights of midcentury. Six of her plays were produced at the Abbey in the 1930s; she was a favorite protégée of Lennox Robinson. Given that Deevy was deaf from her early twenties, it is surprising that her dialogue is pitch perfect: lyrical but idiomatic, not thesis driven, and always in character. Although Deevy herself never married, her theme is typically a rebellious woman who must accept that her fate is to be married. The way in which she is confronted with this necessity is, time and again, that she is physically beaten by her husband or father or both. There is never a question, by characters or evidently by the author, that it is a man's right to batter a woman. Deevy's plays are not protest plays, but strangely Chekhovian and lyrical representations of bleak inevitabilities in the life of an Irish woman. *Katie Roche*, a 1936 play revived at the Abbey in 1975 and 1994, concerns a spirited young woman born out of wedlock now employed as a house servant. An offer of marriage and a step up in the world comes to her from a much older man, but accompanied by a demand that she give up her heart and mind to him. She does her best to pay this stiff price. In 1942, shortly after becoming director of the Abbey, Blythe rejected her three-act *Wife to James Whelan*, adding coldly that he had no further use for her plays, not at any price.

Brendan Behan had a Dublin reputation as a wit, Irish Republican Army (IRA) prisoner, and heavy drinker when he wrote *THE QUARE FELLOW*, a mordant comedy about the deathwatch in a prison before the execution of a murderer, who does not himself appear on stage. Blythe rejected it for the Abbey; neither did it fit in with the Gate Theatre's repertoire. Alan Simpson and Carolyn Swift staged *The Quare Fellow* in the tiny Pike Theatre (seating for fifty-five) in 1954. Critical acclaim brought it to the attention of Joan Littlewood and her Theatre Workshop, which revived the play in London in 1956. Its free form, black humor, and unfocused social anger made the play seem comparable to JOHN OSBORNE'S *LOOK BACK IN ANGER* (also 1956) and suggestive of a "new wave" in modern British drama. With an improvisational, collaborative style of direction, Littlewood also turned Behan's *The Hostage* (1958) into an international hit, adding local jokes as the play toured from city to city.

Samuel Beckett, though Dublin born and educated, settled permanently in Paris in 1937. About ten years later, when he began writing plays, he wrote them in French. Explaining his own relationship to Irish dramatists, Beckett said that he would upset Shaw's vast applecart for a sup at the Hawk's well, or the Saints', referring to Yeats's nō play and Synge's *Well of the Saints* (1905). Whatever affinity, however, there is between Beckett's works for the stage and the Irish tradition, Beckett rewrote the rules for theater in a postwar, death-of-God era. His experimental use of the theater as a device for the expression of life's absurdity had a vast impact on international theater, though it had little immediate bearing on Irish drama. Beckett's plays are profoundly unlike those of Yeats and Synge in that they are not set in Ireland or even in a particular historical moment, though the idiom of their English translations frequently borrows from Hiberno-English speechways. Nor is there the folklorish, storytelling quality to Beckett's dead-end narratives that one finds in most Irish drama. *WAITING FOR GODOT* (Théâtre de Babylone, January 3, 1953) and *ENDGAME* (London, 1957) could not have sensibly entered Blythe's Abbey Theatre repertoire of the 1950s.

It was left to Alan Simpson and Carolyn Swift, producers of Brendan Behan, to bring *Waiting for Godot* to Dublin at the Pike Theatre (October 28, 1955). The actors delivered the lines in an "authentic O'Casey voice," perhaps assisting the production's surprising success. It moved from the Pike to the Gate Theatre and then on tour, with a six-month run. Jokes by disillusioned and then reillusioned tramps were taken to be very Irish jokes indeed.

Beckett's world-famous works did not have an obvious impact on a generation of Irish playwrights first coming to light around 1960, including Brian Friel, Tom Murphy, and Thomas Kilroy. A sense of entrapment in an impoverished, church-dominated, family-centered country prevails in their works, in place of the metaphysical pains of Beckett's theater. Instead of "No Exit," the imperative was "Emigrate!" All three of these new Irish writers came up from the country to Dublin in the 1960s. All three were schoolteachers. Remarkably, all three wrote brilliant plays right from the start—Brian Friel's PHILADELPHIA, HERE I COME! (1964), Kilroy's *The Death and Resurrection of Mr. Roche* (1967), and Murphy's *A* WHISTLE IN THE DARK (1960). They sent their plays to Ernest Blythe at the Abbey, and he rejected them all. They had absorbed history and begun to escape from it. That was too much for the warriors of Blythe's generation, but it was just what audiences turned out to want in Dublin, New York, and London.

Murphy was the first of the three to gain recognition, when *Whistle in the Dark* was played by the Theatre Workshop at the Stratford East Theatre in 1960 before transferring to London's West End. In later plays, such as *A Crucial Week in the Life of a Grocer's Assistant* (1969), Murphy gave a stinging representation of the emptiness of life in a small town, a town like Tuam, County Galway, Murphy's birthplace. In *Whistle in the Dark* an Irish man has left that emptiness behind for a job and marriage in Coventry, England, but his family pursues him, with all the inherent violence of Irish patriarchy. The drunken father loves to goad his drunken sons into fights, whether brawls in the street with other gangs or donnybrooks in the household; it is an outlet, because none feels that he is worth anything. In the end the protagonist tries to kill his father and winds up killing his brother instead. This mere summary suggests why the play has been thought to be an influence on the work of HAROLD PINTER (e.g., THE BIRTHDAY PARTY); the energy and brutality of the dialogue make the case for influence stronger still. The complete obliteration of idealism about the Irish peasant from the west spelled the end of romantic nationalist theater in Ireland.

Brian Friel had established himself as a writer of short stories, often published in the *New Yorker* in the 1950s, before he began to write for the stage. From the start he was interested in the stories that characters tell themselves so that they may go on living, or so that they do not need to come to grips with reality and the need for individual change. Friel also possessed a gift for finding aspects of theater, ones not shared with other forms of expression, that enable the subject to be uniquely explored on stage. For instance, in *Philadelphia, Here I Come!* Friel split the protagonist—Gar O'Donnell, a Donegal young man about to emigrate to the United States—into "Private Gar" and "Public Gar," played by two different actors, so that the private self can comment on the foolishness of the public self and argue with it. Gar's problem is that Ireland is stagnant, but his destination, America, while rich, is vulgar and empty of spiritual values. In spite of all that is found wanting in Ireland, it is treated by Gar with anticipatory nostalgia. The play enjoyed a tremendous success in New York. Friel would remain America's favorite contemporary Irish playwright, as Murphy would remain England's.

Thomas Kilroy's work was not, at the start, and it did not become, typical of contemporary Irish drama. If Friel has an affinity for New York, and Murphy for London, Kilroy's affinity might be for a European capital such as Paris. The Irish trend was for contemporary, narrative, realist drama of character, often nationally self-involved, if not self-infatuated. Kilroy's work is historical, scenic, and full of artifice, often deeply critical of nationalism and aesthetically experimental in a European manner. In order to cast a light on present conflicts between the exceptional individual and society, he often put on stage historical figures—Hugh O'Neill, Matt Talbot in the great *Talbot's Box* (1977), Lord Haw-Haw and Brendan Bracken in the perhaps greater *Double-Cross* (1986), Constance Wilde in *The Fall of Constance Wilde* (1997), and *Blake* (2002). A Kilroy play cannot be mistaken for a short story told directly to the audience; it communicates an experience only to be understood in theatrical terms.

Kilroy makes use of theater's "wonderful box of tricks": discoveries, sound effects, masks, symbolic lighting, multiple acting levels, stilts, puppets, actors doubling parts, choruses, stage attendants as part of the cast. This is especially the case in the 1997 production of *The Fall of Constance Wilde*, where the central triangle of "real" characters—Oscar Wilde, Constance Wilde, and Lord Alfred Douglas—is conducted about the stage and supplied with props by "Six Attendant Puppeteers." Kilroy carries on that dream of Yeats, the founder of the Irish National Theatre: a total theater that combines all the arts and, while dealing with issues both national and philosophical, addresses itself through the senses to the intellect. The playwright admits, as a member of an individualist and artistic minority, to a sense of kinship with Anglo-Irish writers—a minority, aloof from the sweep of history, creating amid their various works a sense of personality and playfully using a language happily shared with Anglo-Saxons and Anglo-Americans. Kilroy's version of Anglo-Irish modernism is modified by Joan Littlewood and Peter Brook, whose groundbreaking productions he saw during 1950s summers in England while working to make money to get through University College, Dublin.

On July 18, 1951, the Abbey Theatre burned. For the time being, the National Theatre Society took up temporary premises in the home of Irish melodrama, the Queen's Theatre. Government funding for a new building was delayed again and again, but fifteen years later a new Abbey Theatre opened on the same site. It is a modernist block of a building (Tomás Mac Anna: "four walls dead as mutton"). Although the seating capacity is comparable to that of the original building, the stage is far wider, seventy-two feet as compared with twenty-one feet. It also does not have the old building's wraparound, horseshoe balcony, which had provided intimacy with the audience and a visible representation of social class. Along with the new theater came new management, as Ernest Blythe's hold upon the Abbey at last gave way. The door was opened to the new playwrights of the 1960s.

The new lighting rigs, stage machinery, and wide stage of the Abbey permitted Tom Murphy, Brian Friel, and Thomas Kilroy to experiment with more open concepts of stage space. By the 1980s new directors such as Patrick Mason—alive to trends in Polish, English, and French theater—gave exciting productions of major plays at the Abbey. Murphy's *The Gigli Concert* (1983) was one of the highlights of 20th-century Irish theater. It concerns a "dynamatologist"—really a charlatan psychiatrist—named J. P. W. King. Although he has almost no business, the Irish Man, a rich, vulgar property developer, appears at his door, seeking help. He has been stricken with an obsession: he wants to be able to sing like the opera star Beniamino Gigli. In the end it is King himself, whose life has gone to pieces and come to nothing, who opens his mouth and spreads his arms as an aria by Gigli blasts out from the theater sound system.

Murphy enjoyed a creative relationship with the director of a small theater in Galway, Garry Hynes at the Druid. One of his best plays, *Bailegangaire* (1985), received its first production there with the Abbey great Siobhan MacKenna in the lead role of Mommo, a senile old Mother Ireland figure in a bed on center stage, telling over and over the story of a laughing contest that ended in the destruction of her family. Murphy tapped into the blackness of traditional Irish culture in the west, so that the play is both folklorish and modernist.

The Irish Arts Council developed a strategy in the late 1970s for the diversification of theater within the country. Although the Abbey Theatre still took the lion's share of the subsidy, other theater companies also won regular awards, including the Gate Theatre, Galway's Druid Theatre, An Grianán in Donegal, Island Theatre in Limerick, Passion Machine in Dublin, Red Kettle in Waterford, and many, many others. Simultaneously the Abbey moved away from a stock company of actors with civil service appointments and lifetime job security. Instead, actors and other theater professionals circulated among various theaters on short-term contracts. The life of theater in the nation was no longer restricted to the National Theatre itself. A show might begin in Waterford, tour the main cities of the country, come up for a production on the main stage at the National Theatre, and then go on tour. Contrariwise, Irish playwrights might—as they have done from Kilroy and Murphy through CONOR MCPHERSON and MARTIN MCDONAGH—have a play first staged in London and then see it toured back to Ireland before being revived in a new production in a regional theater. The number of new theaters has dramatically increased the demand for new plays, and many talented playwrights arose to supply them. They include FRANK MCGUINNESS, Vincent Woods, Martin McDonagh, MARINA CARR, Sebastian Barry, Marie Jones, Christina Reid, Gary Mitchell, Conor McPherson, Mark O'Rowe, and Loughlin Deegan.

One of the new Irish theater companies was created as an "intervention" in the "Troubles" of Northern Ireland. This new company was FIELD DAY, founded in 1980 by Brian Friel and actor Stephen Rea. Its purpose was to investigate the supposedly fixed cultural identities of Protestant and Catholic, settler and native, in a liberating fashion, through plays first staged in Derry, then toured around Northern Ireland, frequently arriving in the autumn at the Dublin Theatre Festival for the tour's conclusion. Brian Friel (three plays), Tom Kilroy (two plays), Stewart Parker, Seamus Heaney, Terry Eagleton, Derek Mahon, and Tom Paulin all contributed work. The most successful productions were Friel's *TRANSLATIONS* (1980) and Kilroy's *Double Cross* (1986). Field Day stopped producing plays after 1992.

From 1991 to 1994 Garry Hynes was artistic director of the Abbey Theatre, a period in which she staged some explosive productions of classics such as *The Plough and the Stars*, which had become embalmed in museumlike traditions of interpretation. Returning to the Druid in 1994, she directed the most successful productions of new plays to come from any small English-language theater in the world for that period. It is difficult to ascribe Hynes's directorial style to a particular influence; she describes it as "straight on." She is a first-rate reader of the stage potential of a script, a coach who gets actors to give more than pat performances, a conductor who gets a high-paced rhythm out of the ensemble, and a canny employer of highly gifted professional designers; all the production values, as a result, are superior. A touchstone playwright for her is Synge, so it is appropriate that one of the gifted new playwrights she discovered is a postmodernist whose plays appear to be black-humored, punk parodies of Synge's world—Martin McDonagh. In January 1996 McDonagh's *Beauty Queen of Leenane* opened in Galway and then won prize after prize in London and New York, including four Tony Awards in 1998. This was the first of a "Leenane trilogy" from McDonagh's pen and Hynes's theater, including the rather Beckettian *A Skull in Connemara* and Murphy-like *Lonesome West*. Each play is horrible and funny, a high-speed sequence of brilliant gags.

Hynes and the Druid Theatre also premiered a play by Marina Carr (1964–), whose first significant play, *Low in the Dark*, was staged in Dublin at the Project Arts Centre in 1989; her second, third, and fourth plays appeared at the Peacock or Abbey theaters. In those plays she wrote herself from a woman's point of view first into and then out of the absurdist outlook of Beckett. Eventually, she said, she wanted "a different starting point, to write a classical tragedy" as opposed to an absurdist view. Hynes's production of *On Raftery's Hill* (Town Hall Theatre, Galway, May 2000) had this "Greek idea of destiny and fate" that Carr sought. A mythically awful farm in rural Ireland is run as a dictatorship by Red Raftery. His son lives in the cattle shed. Dead animals lie rotting all about the 300-acre farm. This seems a black-humor parody of rural idiocy, and funny to make an audience laugh out loud, until at the end of act 1 Red Raftery, throwing her on the kitchen table, rapes his eighteen-year-old daughter, who in act 2 is revealed to be the child of Raftery's incest with her elder sister. This jaw-dropping exposé of vicious patriarchy in Ireland was not the popular success of McDonagh's plays, or even of Carr's earlier work, but its primal, gothic, tragic quality is a new note in Irish drama.

Several elements give a remarkable coherence to the styles of contemporary Irish drama. The first element is the quality and range of the canon of modern Irish drama as a whole. Irish playwrights do sometimes imitate contemporary trends in theater from other countries. The annual Dublin Theatre Festival, now in its fifth decade, brings to Ireland a sampling of the best theater elsewhere, and that has an impact. The work of DAVID MAMET, for instance, is a little-mentioned but quite significant influence on young playwrights. But contemporary Irish playwrights normally find their inspiration and vocabulary of stage expression within the Irish canon itself. The degree of interreference among Irish plays has continued up to the present, as illustrated by the ways McDonagh and Carr have recently drawn upon both Synge and Beckett.

Second, there is an overarching preference for classic realism in contemporary Irish drama. This is manifest in many adaptations of the works of Chekhov (especially by Brian Friel and Thomas Kilroy) and the works of Ibsen (primarily by Frank McGuinness). In these new versions Irish writers have freed the works of Chekhov and Ibsen from the traditional, genteel performance style imposed on the English stage. Instead, the plays are provided with a suggestively Irish milieu.

Third, Irish plays are characterized by what Nicholas Grene (1999) has called a tradition of "storytelling in a confined space." He traces an origin of the tradition to *The Playboy of the Western World*, in which Christy Mahon again and again tells the people in a Mayo pub the story of how he killed his father, and walks out at the end with that same father, now saying how in the future he will make his way in the world by telling stories about the foolish people in Mayo pubs. Often in more recent decades storytelling is a direct presentation of character to audience, rather than part of a simulation of conflict among characters as witnessed by the audience through an invisible fourth wall. In *Faith Healer* (1979), for instance, Brian Friel presents four monologues by three characters (the faith healer himself speaks twice), but the protagonist's gift and death both remain mysterious. This storytelling form is replicated in Conor McPherson's *This Lime Tree Bower* (1995), in which two brothers and their sister's boyfriend take turns describing their parts in a robbery; again, overexplanation leads to mystery. With *The Weir* (1998), McPherson was commissioned by the Royal Court Theatre, London, to write a play in which the characters talk to each other rather than to the audience. He provided a wildly successful play in which characters tell one another ghost stories in a Leitrim pub (an obvious allusion to the setting and action of *The Playboy*). The tales become truly threatening to the one woman present, who then herself tells a heartbreaking tale of picking up the telephone to hear on the other end the voice of her darling dead little girl, who had been drowned in a swimming pool. Eventually it is by telling one another stories that all the characters achieve some escape into community from a sense of terrifying isolation in the world.

The soliloquy has been taken on by other young Irish playwrights as well, such as Vincent Woods, Michael West, and Eugene O'Brien. Why is the form so popular, even dominant? The custom of storytelling is established in Ireland; the writers are good at it; theater audiences enjoy the sense of community with actors; large casts are unnecessary; Irish actors excel in voice and characterization, rather than in physical theater; set requirements are limited and easily transportable (crucial for touring shows): the monologue play has all these advantages.

In the 140 years of this survey of Irish drama, the remarkable development is the proliferation of playwrights. Initially, one impetus for Irish authors to write plays was to overcome what they took to be the misrepresentation of Ireland on the English stage. The subject of their plays, as a result, was to answer dramatically the questions, What is Ireland? and What is an Irish person? It was a given that Ireland was a problem to be assessed at home and explained abroad. These colonial anxieties of an English-speaking people were one basis of Irish drama. Yet the Irish Free State, in spite of its support for one national theater, curtailed the freedom of theatrical expression in midcentury on account of the same postcolonial anxieties. Only a dogmatically Catholic, Gaelic, and morally superior Irish people was to be dramatized, and then within strictly understood native traditions. Fuller funding by the Arts Council for a variety of theaters, without a sniping censorship, has enabled new waves of Irish writers to flourish since the 1970s.

Yet there is something else, not covered by political and economic factors, that may give an Irish character to Irish drama. That factor may be indicated by considering a playwright thus far ignored in this survey, John B. Keane, a pub owner in Listowel, County Kerry. Like all the best Irish plays from 1940 to 1970, Keane's first play, *Sive*, was rejected by Ernest Blythe at the Abbey—"too melodramatic," Blythe declared. Its 1959 debut in an amateur performance by the Listowel Drama Group won the All-Ireland drama competition in Athlone. John B. Keane continued to be denied an Abbey production until the 1980s, but still he became the most popular Irish playwright through the multitude of amateur theaters around the country. Keane is melodramatic, but only as Shakespeare is melodramatic. The Shakespeare of Listowel is also lyrical, full of splendid oaths, real passions, fate, and prophecy. Keane's sensitivity to country characters, oral traditions of narrative and belief, and pleasure in entertaining the crowd indicates something fundamentally theatrical about Irish culture. Furthermore, the amateur tradition that first recognized his genius (as the Irish professional theater now does by means of revivals of *Sive*, *Big Maggie*, *The Field*, and *Sharon's Grave*) is rooted in the pleasure people take in pretending to be someone else on stage for the enjoyment of their friends. This fundamental pleasure in role playing and storytelling on stage seems the heart of what remains a thriving, if relatively young, tradition of national theater in Ireland.

FURTHER READING

Frazier, Adrian. *Behind the Scenes: Yeats, Horniman, and the Struggle for the Abbey Theatre*. Berkeley: Univ. of California Press, 1990.

Grene, Nicholas. *The Politics of Irish Drama*. Cambridge: Cambridge Univ. Press, 1999.

Morash, Christopher. *A History of Irish Theatre, 1601–2000*. Cambridge: Cambridge Univ. Press, 2002.

Murray, Christopher. *Twentieth-Century Irish Drama: Mirror up to Nation*. Manchester: Manchester Univ. Press, 1997.

Welch, Robert. *The Abbey Theatre, 1899–1999*. Oxford: Oxford Univ. Press, 1999.

Adrian Frazier

ISHERWOOD, CHRISTOPHER (1904–1986)

Christopher William Bradshaw-Isherwood, British playwright and novelist, was born in 1904 in Cheshire, ENGLAND, the son of successful farmers who became landed gentry. His father, an army officer, was killed during World War I. Isherwood attended St. Edmund's Preparatory School, where he met his lifelong friend and sometime collaborator, poet W. H. AUDEN. Isherwood studied at Repton School and in 1925 at Corpus Christi College, Cambridge, without graduating. He moved to Berlin, Germany, in 1929 with Auden and spent nine years there writing, teaching English, tutoring, and enjoying the creative and sexual freedom that came from casting off his upper-class values.

Isherwood is best known for *The Berlin Stories*, his fictionalized accounts of his pre–World War II experience in Germany. These stories were the inspiration for the most famous works based on his writings, the stage play *I Am a Camera* and the musical *Cabaret*. *The Berlin Stories*, made up of two novels, *Mr. Norris Changes Trains* and *Goodbye to Berlin*, depict the glittering and grotesque metropolitan life of German cafés, nightlife, and vices in pre-Nazi years. The stories explore bold individualism, bohemianism, and the political climate of changing GERMANY in the early 20th century.

In 1938 Isherwood and Auden traveled to CHINA and recorded in *Journey to a War* (1939) their experiences in the country ravaged by civil war and a Japanese invasion. He and Auden emigrated to the UNITED STATES, and Isherwood became an American citizen in 1946. Isherwood settled in California, where he taught and wrote for Hollywood films. Unlike his army officer father, Isherwood explored pacifism and Quakerism and worked at a Quaker hotel in Pennsylvania during part of World War II. His exploration of mysticism introduced him to other famous spiritual explorers, including Aldous Huxley, Chris Wood, John Yale, and Igor Stravinsky. His spiritual quests led him to embrace the Hindu religion. Isherwood translated several Hindu scriptural texts from Sanskrit in conjunction with his guru Swami Prabhavananda, including *The Bhagavad-Gita* and *The Yoga Aphorism of Patanjali*.

Isherwood's later books addressed the important aspects of his life, including his religion, friendships, and familial relations. He also increasingly wrote about homosexuality and homosexual desire in his later works, *The World in the Evening* (1954) and *A Single Man* (1964). Isherwood's autobiographical works led to his becoming an outspoken advocate for gay rights in 1970s America. He was one of the first internationally known figures to acknowledge publicly his homosexuality. In the retrospective autobiography *Christopher and His Kind* (1977), set in the 1930s, Isherwood examined his complex relationship with Auden, who had died a few years earlier in 1973, before the book was published. *Kathleen and Frank* (1971) was a double portrait of his parents as seen through the letters and writings of his mother and father.

Isherwood taught at Los Angeles State College, the University of California at Santa Barbara, and the University of California at Los Angeles. In 1975 he won the Brandeis Medal for Fiction. From 1953 until his death Isherwood lived with his partner, the portrait artist Don Bachardy. Isherwood died in Santa Monica, California, on January 4, 1986.

SELECT PLAYS: *The Dog Beneath the Skin* (with W. H. Auden, 1935); *The Ascent of F6* (with W. H. Auden, 1936); *Journey to a War* (with W. H. Auden, 1939)

FURTHER READING

Bachardy, Don. *Christopher Isherwood: Last Drawings*. Londen: Faber, 1990.

Berg, James J., and Chris Freeman, eds. *Conversations with Christopher Isherwood*. Jackson: Univ. Press of Mississippi, 2001.

Funk, R. W. *Christopher Isherwood: A Reference Guide*. Boston: G. K. Hall, 1979.

Schwerdt, Lisa M. *Isherwood's Fiction: The Self and Technique*. New York: St. Martin's, 1989.

Shanté T. Smalls

ISRAEL

In the 18th and 19th centuries Hebrew drama was a literary rather than a theatrical issue. All the printed plays were effectively subgenres of poetry or prose. Because Hebrew during these centuries was not a "living" language, the plays were written in a flowery style, tended toward biblical sources, and were not actually staged. A great many of the dramas that were printed served various sociopolitical functions. Among these, for example, were the different versions of *Tartuffe*.

More than any other play from the classic repertoire, Molière's *Tartuffe* has attracted numerous adaptations and translations for the Hebrew (and YIDDISH) stage. *Tartuffe* serves Hebrew drama in the *Kulturkampf* struggle of the secularists against the religious, and its production is affected by contemporary political events and conflicts. Hebrew drama has made use of several of the play's motifs, particularly that of *l'imposteur* (the hypocrite). Playwrights have chosen to assail the religious extremists, to show the lustful nature concealed beneath their masks, and thus to disclose the real character of the ultra-Orthodox community.

This motif appeared, for example, in the character of the hypocrite in Adam Hacohen Lebensohn's (1794?–1878) play *Truth and Faith* (1862), in which the hypocrite is depicted as someone who "presents himself to the people as 'holier than thou' with his vanities and deceptions . . . like the false prophets . . . who created an uproar in every generation and every nation." Molière's characters become "Jewishized" in Hebrew versions of *Tartuffe*. The playwrights tend toward satire. They provide familiar signs indicating a particular image, well known to the Jewish public, and which to the secularists represents the degenerative and hypocritical side of religion. Even in 1985 Yehoshua Sobol noted several familiar politician-rabbis as the source of inspiration for his translation-adaptation of *Tartuffe*.

At the beginning of the 20th century, with the rebirth of the Hebrew language in PALESTINE and the diaspora, a new generation of writers arose, laying the foundations for a new era in Hebrew theater, which was launched in 1918 with the establishment in Moscow of Habima, what was later to become the National Theatre of Israel. The birth of a professional Hebrew theater, as part of the general renaissance of Hebrew culture that included both written and performed drama staged during the period of settlement (1882–1948), served the purposes of secular Zionism. Israeli theater as such began at the end of the 19th century, first in schools and later in amateur theater, semiprofessional troupes, the Ohel workers' theater, and, finally, with the arrival of Habima in Palestine in 1931. Throughout this period the Hebrew stage and a great portion of its repertoire were committed to adopting Hebrew as an ideological artistic language and element in the process of creating the Hebrew settlement. Many plays about the renewal of the Hebrew settlement and its symbols were written and presented on school and community stages; most aimed at reinforcing the nationalist awareness of their creators and audiences. At their center lay the exemplary character of the Hebrew-speaking pioneer (*halutz*) and his mission of reclaiming the land. During the period before the establishment of the State of Israel, the professional theater lacked original texts and was forced to fulfill its ideological purposes with a repertoire mainly consisting of adaptations and translations. Almost eighty plays about "life in the Land of Israel" were published before 1948, and an even greater number were staged but never published. A lively dramatic activity was carried on, harnessed to the purpose of promoting the Zionist ethos.

To illustrate love for people and homeland, playwrights and directors used a variety of dramatic-theatrical semiotic systems: sets, costumes, props, songs, and music. *Chaim* by Menachem Badar (1942) is an exemplary play in that it incorporates many elements characteristic of other plays of the period. The play both depicts reality and exalts it. Badar gained a wide dramatic-theatrical education from reading plays and attending the theater. His own plays are stories of the immigration to Israel (*aliyah*) and the flight from Europe from the late 1930s to the early 1940s, and about the difficulties of integration in Palestine and the dispute with the Arabs. His work was influenced by German expressionist theater tradition and the DOCUMENTARY theater of ERWIN PISCATOR.

Chaim (a community play written for Kibbutz Tel Amal) comprises a series of scenes running through the mind of its dying hero, who has been shot by an Arab. It begins with a scene of assimilated Viennese Jewry and continues with scenes depicting the *aliyah* and the establishment of the kibbutz. Badar presents Zionism as a combination of "there" and "here," European in its sophisticated theatrical means, but local in its content and language, in which one could still distinguish the remnants of European syntax: the fancy European clothing of "there"; the outdoor Viennese decor (borrowed from productions by Piscator, who made much use of slides and lighting effects) to depict an urban jungle in which the growing Nazi movement rampaged and, in contrast with this, the kibbutz scenery that revealed an open vista of Palestine; and the internal decor too of the "kibbutz hut," whose rough doors contrast with the bourgeois interior of the Vienna scenes. The main tool is that of declaration: of the "Zionist narrative" on the foundation day of establishing a new kibbutz. Reference is also made to those "Others" whose plotting is thwarting Hebrew patriotism: the European oppressor and in particular the Arab, who objects to plowing the land at Tel-Shuk. Facing the European oppressor and against the aggressive Arab stands the exemplary (masculine!) figure of Zionism.

The playwrights and main characters in the *dor ba-haretz* (a-generation-born-on-the-land) plays written after the War of Independence (1948) and establishment of the State of Israel were of the second generation, the "*sabra* generation," the children of those who had immigrated to the Land of Israel before establishment of the state, and the children of refugees from the Holocaust. They were Hebrew speakers who had been educated according to the *halutz* idealist-Zionist pioneering ethos. Most were members of youth movements who volunteered to realize this ethos through settlement on the land and who fought in the War of Independence.

Among the works of the first "native-born" generation of playwrights (Yigal Mossinsohn [1917–1994], Moshe Shamir [1921–2004], Nathan Shacham [1925–], Aharon Meged [1920–], and others), the stalwart tie of *sabra* youth to the group and to the Land of Israel is portrayed as indigenous culture. The pathos of the *halutz* was viewed by such native sons as ludicrous, and in its place they chose to present a Zionism of action and self-sacrifice. At the same time the collectivist-Zionist ideal was shared by both generations. From the standpoint of "native-born" playwrights the "Arab question" almost did not exist, and one could define it as concealed. The only play with an Arab figure, *They'll Arrive Tomorrow* by Nathan Shacham (1950), in which an Arab is murdered on stage, was "rectified" in a later version, and the presence of the Arab characters was removed.

Until the middle of the 1960s the Ashkenazim (Jews from Europe) perceived the Mizrahim (Jews from Arab countries) as inferior and socially threatening and pressured them to assimilate into the Ashkenazi hegemonic culture. Toward the end of the 1960s, as a reaction to the cultural change undergone by the Mizrahim, their increasing protest, and the influence of the ethnic pluralism prevalent in the United States, the Ashkenazi standpoint became somewhat moderated. These changes are represented in the play *Kazablan* by Yigal Mossinsohn.

Kazablan, written in 1954, was created as a "Zionist play." This is a detective play about Kazablan, a Moroccan Jew accused of attempted murder by stabbing. In the end it is revealed that the real knife wielder was an Ashkenazi, but throughout the entire play the audience identifies Kazablan with guilt, with the knife, and with the stabbing. The play also features Kazablan's love for Rachel, an Ashkenazi girl who rejects him. The exceptionality of depicting such an ethnically mixed love story in the 1950s can be understood from the reservations shown by some of the critics.

Any romance between Kazablan and Rachel is depicted from the outset as hopeless and impossible. Rachel's recoiling from his believed violence arouses fear of the Mizrahi man. The Kazablan-Moroccan "package" also includes indirect reference to the Arab "semblance." Expressions of recoil from the aggressive Moroccan found their echo in fear of Arab aggression, emphasizing in Yiddish and Hebrew the "bestiality," aggressiveness, and "blackness" as expressed by other Israeli playwrights as well.

From the mid-1950s a silent change began to take place in the Hebrew theater's attitude to Zionism. It moderated its dealings with the subject and also altered its taste regarding the pioneering ethic. Several of the plays of this period were nostalgic attempts to return to a period of imaginary innocence. The original plays staged during these years dealt with the family, community problems, the Holocaust, and the changes taking place in the kibbutzim and also reflected the poetic experimental repertoire of the Theater of the Absurd and its influence. Yoram Matmor's play *An Ordinary Play* (1956) introduced several of the changes that had begun to take place in Israeli society after the war—a society that turned effectively from the ideals of self-realization to materialism. *An Ordinary Play* is the tale of a play that was never completed and whose protagonist, Danny, is represented by means of a wooden beam. The fighters of the earlier plays by Mossinsohn, Moshe Shamir, and Nathan Shacham were now presented as alienated from normal life after the war. An entire generation found itself having to confront a new and confusing reality. Matmor complicates the theatrical reality in a Pirandellesque manner by introducing a play-within-a-play, thereby questioning (more in form than in content) the realism of a *sabra* playwright, as well as the validity of the Zionist narrative.

Beginning in the 1960s, a new profession entered Israeli culture: that of playwright. The earlier playwrights had mainly been writers who also wrote plays. The important playwrights of this new generation are Nissim Aloni, Chanoch Levin, Yehoshua Sobol, Hillel Mittelpunkt (1949–), and Shmuel Hasfari. Nissim Aloni (1926–1998) was a poet in the theater who succeeded in creating a stylized language for the Hebrew stage without it suffering from bombastic artificiality or facile expressions. His plays move between the "local" and the universal and reflect the influence of European theater of the 1950s and 1960s. Aloni had—and still has—a considerable effect on young Israeli playwrights. After *The King's New Clothes* (1961) Aloni directed all his own plays, as well as other entertainment programs that he wrote.

In *The American Princess* (1963), as an example, Aloni describes "A small country in newly liberated Africa. Very fanatical. Much folklore." The exemplary figure is no longer the *halutz* or *tsabar*, but an actor ("a superb actor . . . with no first name, no individuality, no face, no ego! Only plastic surgery"). Love of Zion finds itself competing with the American dream of wealth.

The most notable representative of Israeli drama is Chanoch Levin (1943–1999). Levin wrote fifty-six plays, of which thirty-three were staged in his lifetime, twenty-four under his own direction. He began as a satirical writer, criticizing Israel society after the 1967 war. Later he wrote CHAMBER PLAYS and FARCES in the spirit of the Theater of the Absurd, operatic philosophical plays such as *The Agonies of Job* (1981), and a caustic play, *Murder* (1997), that combined all his previous works in a critique of the Israeli-Palestinian conflict.

The sketch "Samatocha" in Levin's *The Queen of Bathtub* (1970) created a new prototype of Arab character in Israeli drama. Samatocha the Arab is a waiter and dishwasher at an Israeli café. He is "smart and obedient and doesn't harm the Jews. He knows how to stand on his own two feet, just like us!" The Jews know that Samatocha will not plant any bombs and is not a terrorist, and they are complacent with their own image: they are not primitive types who cannot distinguish between a bomb-planting Arab and a harmless one; and they let him get back to the kitchen to wash the dishes. The dependence on the Arab, because of his willingness to work at menial jobs, is what saves Samatocha from clashes: "Don't hurt the Arab, there's a pile of dirty cups in the kitchen." The sketch presents for the first time on an Israeli stage the economic exploitation of the Arabs that took place when the restrictions imposed by the military government were lifted and they were able to enter the Israeli labor market and find employment in jobs at which Israeli Jews were unwilling to work. The sketch also reveals the attention paid to the security threat after the 1967 war, with the escalation in Palestinian terrorist activity. The contempt expressed by the Jewish characters at the Arab's downfall is mixed with fear of his revenge for the humiliation and exploitation—a fear that would increase in the following years as the conflict worsened. *The Queen of Bathtub* aroused criticism and even controversy, apparently expressing concern over a split in the Jewish-Zionist consensus regarding the Arab question, which had lost its status in Israeli cultural concepts—and in a public theater.

Murder (1997) differs from all of Levin's earlier plays in locating the conflict at the center and incorporating a Palestinian figure, as well as in its fragmented structure. *Murder* is a text in which incongruity is the central issue. There is order in the disorder and logic in the illogic of the play. The logic, which is beyond the pattern of the plot, design of the characters, dialogue, or genre, is the murderous logic of the dispute with the Palestinians.

Yehoshua Sobol (1939–) is a playwright of great technical skill in a range of styles, with an international career as writer and director. *Night of the Twentieth*, one of Sobol's early plays, was first staged at the Haifa Municipal Theatre in 1976. It deals with the night of October 20, 1920, on the eve of the settlement in Mansurin of a group of young immigrants to the Land of Israel. The play depicts a night watch; one long uninterrupted conversation through the night. The argument is not only ideological, but an expression of conflict between contrasting characters. At its center, from the perspective of 1976, lies the question of what should be chosen that night: redeeming a man (saving a man's life) or realizing the Zionist settlement dream.

Several of the plays from the 1980s and 1990s pointedly raise the question of the relationship between Zionism and Judaism. Sobol has a particularly interesting view of his own Jewish identity as an Israeli. He has been dealing with Judaism in all its aspects for the last three decades, examining it by means of different tools: first, using satire (*Status Quo Vadis*, 1973; *Repentance*, 1977) and later in plays examining Israeli reality and history. Since the production of *Wars of the Jews* (1981), a play about the destruction of the Second Temple, Sobol has turned the tension between his Jewishness and his Israeliness into a central theme in both his own original works and those that he has translated. His background in philosophy is notable in his approach, which is influenced by the traditions of the Jewish Enlightenment. He adopts from Judaism those same values, images, and historical events that he perceives to be of a positive nature, while rejecting and criticizing its darker sides of destructive, extremist nationalism, of superstition, and of the religious political establishment.

Sobol uses the period of the Second Temple as a model for a destructive society, and he warns against the fact (particularly in *The Jerusalem Syndrome*, 1987) that Israeli society is attempting to adopt this model, which has two paths: that of Orthodoxy, demanding that the state's citizens be cut off from all that is enlightened and liberal; and that of self-destruction, of extreme Jewish nationalism. Sobol, seen by religious circles as "an Israel-hating Jew," deals in his plays with figures on the legitimate border of Judaism, such as the anti-Semitic Jewish philosopher Otto Weininger in *Soul of a Jew* (1982), and he dedicated his play *Solo* (1991) to Baruch Spinoza, a Jewish philosopher rejected by the Jewish community of Amsterdam.

By the 1990s all that was left to the secular Zionist center was, in the main, nostalgia for the past. The play *Village* (1996) by Sobol offers an interesting contrast to the dystopian vision that he presented in *The Jerusalem Syndrome*. Sobol's nostalgic patriotism in this play does not seek a solution to the polarity and ideological crisis that Israeli society is undergoing, but retreats to the paradise of a political end of childhood, in which the secular Zionist dream has begun to be realized. *Village*, like ANTON CHEKHOV'S THE CHERRY ORCHARD, is about painful change. Both works show their audience that a real return to the past is not possible; only, perhaps, to return and dream about it. Through the eyes of a child experiencing love and death for the first time in his life, the play presents a small village at the end of World War II, before establishment of the State of Israel. It offers slightly nostalgic memories of the "beautiful" and tragic Land of Israel, which must pay the price of her fallen sons in order to establish the Hebrew state.

Shmuel Hasfari (1954–) is an important representative of the third generation of Israeli playwrights. Hasfari's *Kiddush* (1985, revised in 1995) is a realistic play depicting the secular/religious schism from the "anthropological" aspect, without any secular figures appearing onstage.

Hasfari wanted to show onstage the change that had occurred among those same Zionist Jews who were attempting to bring together the two religions—the traditional and the Zionist. In *Kiddush* he follows the ritual Sabbath eve blessings in one such family and depicts a process showing the rising political power of the group to which it belongs, accompanied by extremism and the realization of a dream of power. After the Six-Day War the religious father in the play says: "When I think about my son becoming a paratrooper in the holy places: in Nablus, Hebron, the city of the fathers . . . Jericho . . . it's like a dream."

The theatrical chronicle *Kiddush* is a synecdochical reflection of a family representing a particular social group. The father, a shabby religious clerk who in the past had also voted for a secular party, demonstrates in his own way the revolution that had begun among the religious Zionists. The realistic imaginary world depicts this process, and the end of the play illustrates his abandonment, his internal contradiction, and the hopelessness of his chances. The son not only becomes secular but also emigrates from Israel to the United States, thus discarding both religions, the Jewish and the Zionist. The end of the play is broken up into almost Beckettian scenes in which the characters speak to themselves, to tape recorders, or on the telephone: an end in which those same grotesque elements that had accompanied the characters from the beginning of the play as background music now proliferate and take over the performance.

Toward the end of the 1980s new voices began to be heard in Israeli drama, particularly those of women. Women playwrights have begun to gain a place in mainstream theater, slowly changing the depiction of women. The most outstanding among them are Miriam Kainy (1942–) and Edna Mazya (1950–). From the very outset of her career Kainy designed a different image for her female characters. In the early phase of her work she challenged the centrality of the Israeli man in the theatrical narrative, introducing the Arab male as a potent rival to the Jewish-Israeli male (who is portrayed as suffering from impotence). Alona and Ayala, respectively, in Kainy's plays *The Return* (1973, revised in 1975) and *Like a Bullet in the Head* (1981) prefer the Arab to the Jew. The choice of an Arab is not coincidental, but rather a demonstrative act, since the Arab man is seen as the polar opposite of the Jewish-Israeli male on the map of Jewish-Israeli culture.

Two plays present women who have been written out of male history: *Babatha* by Miriam Kainy, staged in 1987, and *The Maid of Ludomir* by Yossefa Even-Shoshan (1965–), staged in 1996, with the subtitle *The Story of Hannah Rachel Werbermacher, the Maid of Ludomir, Who Wanted the Soul of a Man.* Hannah Rachel was a historical figure (1892–1915) who openly claimed the right to study Torah and Talmud, which in her time was permitted only to men. She breaks her engagement, fearing that married life will frustrate her desire to study, and gives up family life, which the male narrative has perceived as woman's main goal.

Babatha returns the audience to Judea, sixty-two years after the Romans destroyed the Second Temple and at the outbreak of the Jewish rebellion against the Romans (132–135 C.E.). The play is based on thirty-five authentic documents discovered by archeologist Yigael Yadin (1917–1984), which describe Babatha's struggle against the male monopoly over her life and, no less important, over her property. When Babatha is widowed, she is forced to appoint guardians for her son despite the fact that she is his sole support. The guardians steal her property, all the while claiming to represent her son's interests. Since there is not a single man whom she can trust, she decides to protect the property, which she had acquired through her own hard work. In contrast to the male narrative, in which the woman plays a passive role, these two playwrights have created an alternative female narrative in which the women are active, take charge of their own lives, and confront the reality that seeks to restrict them.

Edna Mazya is an extremely successful playwright and director. Among her plays is *Games in the Back Yard* (1993), based upon a case of rape dealt with by two courts of law, which received particularly wide public notice. The genre of the play approaches that of television. Mazya wrote an action drama with a dramatic climax: in the final scene the rape is enacted, and a verdict of "guilty," as ruled by the playwright, is declared. The events in *Games in the Back Yard* take place on two parallel levels. The first is the seduction of the girl by four youths, which leads to rape by three of them, while their leader, whom she also fancies, is "satisfied" by merely "directing" the event. The second level is that of the rape trial, in which the youths' defense attorneys finally attack the rape victim and her attorney. It ends in the conviction of the rapists. The actors who play the four youths are also the four defense attorneys, and the rape victim is also the prosecuting attorney. The defense attorneys perform a sort of second rape while cross-examining the girl, disclosing her past wild behavior. The prosecuting attorney too is exposed to verbal sexual aggression from her professional colleagues. In *Herod* (2000) Mazya tells the story of King Herod from the perspective of the women involved, Mariamme his wife and Cleopatra, who are not only depicted as strong and characterized in detail, but are also accorded "equal time" with the men.

At the beginning of the 21st century a significant change appears to be taking place in the way in which women are presented in Hebrew theater. The number of active women playwrights whose plays are presented in mainstage and fringe theaters has grown considerably, occasionally equaling the number of ongoing productions of plays written by men. This change has in turn brought about an increase in the number of women characters depicted on the stage, as well as a change in their roles in the plot and the amount of dialogue allotted to them. Women (both playwrights and characters) no longer deal only with confrontations with the masculine world, but with their own perspective as women and with the nature of their lives.

FURTHER READING

Abramson, Glenda. *Drama and Ideology in Modern Israel*. Cambridge: Cambridge Univ. Press, 1998.

Ben-Zvi, Linda, ed. *Theater in Israel*. Ann Arbor: Univ. of Michigan Press, 1996.

Kohansky, Mendel. *The Hebrew Theatre: Its First Fifty Years*. Jerusalem: Israel Universities Press, 1969.

Urian, Dan. *The Arab in Israeli Drama and Theatre*. Amsterdam: Harwood, 1997.

———. *Judaic Nature of Israeli Theatre: A Search for Identity*. Amsterdam: Harwood, 2000.

———. "Mizrahi and Ashkenazi in the Israeli Theatre." *Arabic and Middle Eastern Literatures* 4, no. 1 (2001): 19–36.

Dan Urian

ITALY

In many spheres of cultural and political life the adjective "anomalous" has been attached to Italy, and no brief description could be more apt for Italian theater in the mid-19th century, at the moment of unification. The age–old paradox of Italy as a country of enormous theatrical vitality yet one which produced few playwrights whose work deserved to enter the national, let alone international, repertoire retained all its validity. The main divergence from the European norm was that in Italian theater, as had been the case since the heyday of commedia dell'arte, the central figure was the actor rather than the author. The fame of Italian actors in the 19th century was worldwide, and even when they toured and performed in countries whose language they did not speak, they were feted and imitated. The other distinctive feature was that inside Italy, at the level of both popular and bourgeois theater, touring companies rather than fixed repertory companies were the spine of theatrical activity. In consequence, no history of theater in Italy can ever be merely a chronicle of plays and writers.

The touring companies were of two types, the provincial nomadic troupe that did not necessarily perform in recognized theater spaces, and the grand urban companies, often clustered around an established celebrity figure. There is no knowing how many such small touring troupes there were in total, but they operated in all regions of Italy. They offered a genre of improvised performance that had its roots, however remote, in commedia dell'arte, and that de facto made the writer redundant. One company can be taken as representative. The Rame family-company, which in the 20th century produced FRANCA RAME (1929–), started life in the 18th century as puppeteers, but when in the 20th century cinema threatened their livelihood, they switched to live theater. They operated only in Lombardy and northern Italy, and Franca Rame has described how the company would arrive in a town, research the legends associated with it or with the patron saint of the place and be in a position to mount an improvised performance by the evening. The principal figure in this genre of theater production was the *capocomico* (literally, head actor), who was often the company owner and who normally combined the tasks of lead performer, designer, script manager, and director. There were different types of *capocomico*, some of whom relinquished performance for the administration of the company, but, at his best, he can be regarded as the equivalent of the contemporary figure of actor-manager in British and American Victorian theater. Figures such as Edwin Booth in New York and Beerbohm Tree in London have much in common with Ernesto Rossi and Tommaso Salvini of Italy, except that the former pair relied on theatrical writing which was not pre-made in their image and likeness. In Italy, the *capocomici* commissioned work in accordance with their own view of their abilities, or recreated existing drama for their own needs. They set the tone for the troupe, decided on the works to be staged, and attended to the crucial work of allocating parts and arranging scenes. The standard repertoire ranged from popular versions of classic, perhaps Shakespearean, theater to instant improvised dramas. The lack of detailed archives makes it impossible to reconstruct accurately the standards and skills of these companies, and both contemporary critics and later pundits are unreliable, the former often reformers prejudiced against the touring companies and its practitioners and the latter frequently 20th-century zealots for popular theater who made their predecessors the object of sentimental recollection. The indisputable fact is that they were integral to the actor-centered tradition of theater specific to Italy.

The newly united Italian state did inherit theaters in the big cities from the statelets that it superseded, but rarely could it find the funds to sponsor a permanent company of a high standard. The Real Compagnia Sarda, established in 1821 with its base in Turin, was briefly an exception, but its grant was removed by Camillo Cavour's government in 1852, and the company finally collapsed in 1855. There were other attempts to establish companies based in one theater, but none prospered. The fortunes of the standard company depended on a figure known immodestly to history as the *grande attore* (great actor), but who was also a *capocomico* in the terms already discussed. The first such figure was Gustavo Modena (1803–1861), but it was with the trio in the succeeding generation that the *grande attore* came indisputably into his or her own. Adelaide Ristori (1822–1906) is there to ensure that the tradition was not exclusively male, and she was in no sense inferior in power and prestige to the others, Ernesto Rossi (1827–1896) and Tommaso Salvini (1829–1915). Nothing is more transitory than performance, but contemporary accounts suggest that they fully merited the description "great." HENRY JAMES wrote fulsomely of the slightly later Ermete Zacconi (1857–1948), noting his reserve and restraint, qualities he had not anticipated, while Salvini achieved a deeper immortality through the impact on KONSTANTIN STANISLAVSKY of his meticulous, preperformance efforts to think himself into a role. The Russian director and theorist observed Salvini while the Italian was on tour in Russia, recording the time Salvini took at every stage in his preparation for *Othello*, and noting, crucially for theories of acting that Stanislavsky was to develop, that he was as attentive over the state of mind as over details of costume and makeup. Through Stanislavsky the Italian style of performance influenced the craft of acting in the western world throughout the 20th century.

Salvini's presence in Moscow is an indication of the international fame all these "great actors" attained. Ristori, for example, performed in Warsaw in Friedrich von Schiller's *Mary Stuart*; but while she used Italian, her co–performers spoke in Polish. Both she and Rossi accomplished the tour de force of playing in English, even though neither spoke the language. The *New York Mail* (August 28, 1921) greeted the Sicilian actor Giovanni Grasso (1875–1936) with an article quoting Enrico Caruso, who described Grasso as "the greatest dramatic actor of all time." For performances both at home and abroad, Italian performers had no substantial national repertoire to fall back on, so while works of Vittorio Alfieri appeared occasionally on the stages, and those of Carlo Goldoni less frequently, it was William Shakespeare who occupied the position of honor. The TRAGEDIES, a reliable source of grand passions and poses, were preferred to the COMEDIES, but the Shakespeare offered to Italian audiences was a Bard reshaped to demonstrate the brio of the principal actor. Salvini, for instance, cut the scene where Othello by chance overhears conversations between Iago and Cassio or Bianca since he viewed it as incompatible with grandeur; he also moved the killing of Desdemona offstage. Ristori had *Macbeth* rewritten to give greater weight to the part of the queen of Scotland and even considered retitling the play *Lady Macbeth*.

This self-centered narcissism that disregarded the havoc wreaked on the subtleties and complexities of the original work was also apparent in the dealings of the *grande attore* with contemporary writers. A play script was like the marble awaiting the sculptor's chisel, as is apparent from the best-documented case involving Adelaide Ristori and the playwright Paolo Giacometti (1816–1882). Giacometti was experienced in turning out biographical-historical works, such as the *Michelangelo Buonarroti* that was a vehicle for Salvini, so he was happy to accept a commission from Ristori, who, about to embark on a tour of the United States in 1867–1868, wanted to round off a regal repertoire that already contained three queens, Queen Elizabeth of England, Mary Queen of Scots, and Lady Macbeth. Her performance as Schiller's Mary won special praise, and she commissioned from Giacometti a matching piece on Marie Antoinette. Being in the position of a noblewoman hiring a tradesman, she chose the subject, imposed the approach to be adopted, recommended the appropriate historical works to be consulted, laid down the required characterization, and dictated the direction of individual scenes. Giacometti complied with her orders, continually altering his text until it was deemed acceptable. When the work was finally produced in 1868, it had become, in accordance with the views of the actress but in contradiction to the radical outlook of the author, a hymn of praise to the *ancien régime* and a rejection of the values of the French Revolution.

As a writer, Giacometti was one of a generation of solid craftsmen who had to struggle to find a hearing, and whose works are now routinely filed, sometimes unjustly, under the patronizing tag "bourgeois writers." However, Giacometti chose the unexpectedly challenging theme of divorce for *Civil Death* (1861), his best-known work. The protagonist, Corrado, sentenced to life imprisonment, is reluctant to see his wife condemned to a life of loneliness and, since she was denied the prospect of divorce and eventual remarriage to the man she loves, abandoned to the status of "civil death." He chooses suicide, a solution that is both a form of redemptive sacrifice for him and a reproach to Italian society for banning divorce. The didactic intention is made explicit in the finale, when the Ibsenite doctor who acts as the chorus figure issues a call to the country's legislators to pay heed. The work may well have been inspired by the domestic situation of Giacometti himself who, after separating from his wife, found himself unable to marry the woman with whom he had co–habited but the melodramatic denunciations of society and the grand passions of the finale provided an ideal vehicle for Rossi in its first production and for Salvini in its revival. The contemporary Achille Torelli (1844–1922) made his mark in 1867 with *Husbands*, written when the author was only twenty-three and giving him a success he never repeated. Emma is of aristocratic birth, but marries for love the bourgeois lawyer, Fabio. The woman's name carries deliberate echoes of Emma Bovary, and like her French counterpart, the Italian Emma is bored by her husband's dedication to his routine office work, but unlike the French Emma, she sets out to earn her husband's love. By the ending, when she announces her pregnancy, she has done so, but in the process she has also learned to accept the bourgeois ethic that allocates to the wife a domestic role of noninterference with her husband's career. The more conventional adulterous triangle made its appearance in *Sad Loves* (1887) by GIUSEPPE GIACOSA (1847–1906), where yet another Emma moves in semiaristocratic circles but this time gives way to sexual temptation. The unity of the family prevails as the illicit lovers part and the wronged husband forgives his errant wife, ensuring that the bourgeois family ethic prevails. MARCO PRAGA (1862–1929), a vigorous upholder of the rights of the playwright against the interference of the *grand attore* with the playwright's scripts, offered the new middle class the chance to see themselves on stage in various plays, and in *The Virgins* (1889) he challenged the traditional notion that lost female virginity was an affront to male honor and an insuperable obstacle to the marriage contract.

The references to Emma Bovary recall the impact all over Europe of REALISM, whose Italian variant took the name *verismo* and whose main exponents were Sicilian. *Verismo* was a strong force in opera, where composer Umberto Giordano proclaimed his *Andrea Chenier* a verist work, as did Pietro Mascagni with his *Cavalleria rusticana* (1883). The original *Cavalleria rusticana* was adapted from one of his own short stories by GIOVANNI VERGA (1840–1922), a Sicilian writer whose discovery of French realism sanctioned his switch from modish novels to sterner works depicting the life and culture of the dispossessed among whom he had grown up. Both *Cavalleria rusticana* and *The She–Wolf* (*La lupa*), his two most performed plays, are set among the poor of Sicily and deal with the brutal consequences of the workings of such elemental forces as love, jealousy, the code of honor, and superstition. Verga was playing to bourgeois audiences and insisted that standard Italian was the only vehicle for his work, but dialect theater enjoyed a vogue in all the regions of Italy. The most significant of the various dialect theaters was the Sicilian, and its theatrical capital was Catania. The founding work of Sicilian Dialect Theater was *The Mafiosi of the Vicaria* (*I mafiusi di la Vicaria*), first performed in 1863, jointly authored by Gaspare Mosca and the *capocomico* Giuseppe Rizzotto. The principal figure in this movement in Sicily was Nino Martoglio (1870–1921), playwright and director, who set up several companies, often in an effort to bring together the two leading actors of the time, both of whom gained international renown, Giovanni Grasso (1873–1930), as a tragic or dramatic actor, and Angelo Musco (1872–1937), as a comic performer. It has been said that Sicily was the epicenter of European theater in the 19th century, and the career of these two actors could serve as a metaphor of wider changes in cultural sensibility. Grasso enjoyed fame early in the century, but reforms brought about in part by Luigi Pirandello's notions of *umorismo* (humor) meant that the comic talents of Musco provided a more suitable vehicle for the new theater. Through Pirandello, whose earliest works were in dialect, Sicilian theater influenced European, especially French, drama.

Elsewhere, too, dialect theater flourished, perhaps as a re-assertion of local sentiment in reaction to political unification. The only work of Vittorio Bersezio (1828–1900) that has endured is *Le miserie di Monsú Travet*, a depiction of the gray life and eventual rebellion of an impoverished Turinese clerk. The twin plays by the Milanese Carlo Bertolazzi (1870–1916) that make up *El nost Milan* focus on the refusal of a poor man to tolerate insults inflicted on his daughter. This work was revived with great success by Giorgio Strehler in the 1970s at the Piccolo Teatro in Milan. The dialect theater of Venice, which could trace its origins back to Carlo Goldoni in the 18th century, continued to flourish, as did the more derivative dialect theater of Genoa.

The success of Verga's masterpiece in its own time was due in no small measure to the willingness of Eleonora Duse (1858–1924) to take the part of Santuzza, the abandoned and jealous peasant girl. Verga was prepared to modify his work to ensure the approval of the great actress. The already-mentioned Ermete Zacconi played alongside her. The arrival of these two is indicative of a generational shift among actors: the terminology, if little else, changed, with *mattatore* replacing *grande attore*. This term is strange even in Italian, and its roots are disputed. It might be a dull pun on *matto* (mad) and *attore* (actor), or it might contain some reference to the Spanish matador. In any case, the *mattatore* bestrode the stage like his predecessor, with the crucial difference that he or she had greater, but not unlimited, respect for writers. Duse, one of the first international superstars, was the object of an admiring article by GEORGE BERNARD SHAW, who saw her in London and compared her technique favorably with that of Sarah Bernhardt. Tragedy was not the forte of the newcomers, who were instead at ease with the more nuanced demands of Europe's "new drama." Zacconi played Osvald in HENRIK IBSEN'S *GHOSTS* on numerous occasions throughout his life. Duse won praise for her emotional, sensual performance in ALEXANDRE DUMAS *FILS*'S MELODRAMA *The Lady of the Camellias*, but played Nora in Ibsen's *A DOLL'S HOUSE* with greater subtlety. She had the intellectual vision and range to detect the value of both the realist theater of Verga and Giacosa and the poetic drama of GABRIELE D'ANNUNZIO. However, in spite of the enhanced willingness to work with new authors, there was no change in the power system. The *mattatore* remained in control. Even Ibsen, it is now known, was subject to alteration to suit the needs of the *mattatore*, although the changes were not as radical as those imposed by the previous generation on William Shakespeare. Productions still required, to the irritation of many playwrights, the presence of the prompter, who from his box read out a script that the actors repeated. Learning lines was not always part of the actor's craft.

The fin de siècle controversies over decadence and aestheticism were made more contentious in Italian theatrical circles by anxious talk of the need for "modernization." The works of Ibsen, AUGUST STRINDBERG, and Shaw, as well as the operas of RICHARD WAGNER, created a crisis in contemporary culture, revolutionizing audience expectations, and the feeling began to grow that Italy was excluding itself from these developments. The two principal points of contention concerned the desirability of dethroning the actor, or traditional *capocomico*, and replacing him with the figure of the director, for whom there was not as yet any accepted word in Italian, and the need for the introduction in Italian cities of a new institution to be known as the *teatro stabile*, where *stabile* was the opposite of touring. The new ideal was of a theater stably based in one venue, with a permanent company and a planned season, in the manner of the repertory theaters in Germany or Britain.

The two issues overlapped, since the *capocomico* was responsible for leasing theater buildings suitable for a program dictated by his own company requirements, and these were unlikely to be innovative. Questions of interest, as well as of principle, were involved, and the debate dragged on for decades. Settlement of both questions was reached only in the 1940s, after the liberation of Italy from fascism. The first tentative initiatives were not encouraging. In 1898 Domenico Lanza founded the Teatro d'Arte in Turin, and in 1905 the critic Eduardo Boutet set up the Drammatica Compagnia in Rome, but both ventures were short lived. Virgilio Talli (1858–1928), a multitalented man of the theater who left his imprint on generations of actors, has been viewed by some as a protodirector. He established several important companies with other actors and was responsible for bringing to the stage the writers of the so-called grotesque school, as well as LUIGI PIRANDELLO and D'Annunzio, but when he retired from the stage, it was to set up in Milan a school for actors.

Gabriele D'Annunzio (1863–1938) brought to the Italian stage his own brand of extravagant, lush, multitextured poetic theater. T. S. ELIOT would later write of the necessity and impossibility of poetic theater, but his solutions to those problems had nothing in common with those of D'Annunzio. D'Annunzio's imagination required a poetic never-never land that made almost acceptable his grandiloquence, his cult of the superman, his demand that as poet he was called to respect only those laws, literary or moral, that his creativity sanctioned, his disregard for the problems of staging, and for the expectations of audiences. His plays are now out of favor and perhaps would not have found audiences in his lifetime had it not been for the powerful performances of the two greatest actresses of the day, Eleonora Duse, his lover in the years 1896–1904, and Sarah Bernhardt in France. D'Annunzio had little sense of theatrical time or momentum, his plotting was often strained, and his works all exhibit his idiosyncratic, decadent poetics, together with his unscrupulousness over plagiarism. The first piece, *The Dead City* (*La città morta*, 1896), was inspired by Heinrich Schliemann's excavations in Mycenae but was constructed around a typically D'Annunzian erotic, exotic plot featuring a fey poet in charge of the archeological dig, his blind wife, and his young lover. *Francesca da Rimini* (1901), a much-extended version of Dante's story of the tragic lovers, draws heavily on a couple of works of academic history. *The Martyrdom of Saint Sebastian* (*Le martyre de Saint Sébastien*, 1911), written in French during the period in which creditors had forced him into (gilded) exile, is in many ways his most representative work, since the theme allowed him to wallow in his taste for voluptuous sensuality and sadistic violence overlaid with a touch of spurious spirituality.

D'Annunzio had no followers in theater, but he had many parodists, including FILIPPO TOMMASO MARINETTI (1876–1944), who, the year before he launched the founding manifesto of futurism (1909), published, in French, his pamphlet *The Gods Depart, D'Annunzio Remains* (*Les dieux s'en vont, D'Annunzio reste*), in which he mocks D'Annunzio's overblown style. D'Annunzio was a bête noire in the futurist attempts to sweep away the heritage of the past and to revolutionize all the arts, including theater, in the light of a new aesthetic of movement, dynamism, flight, speed, élan, and all that could go under the name of modernity. With an intoxicating mixture of exuberance and harlequinade, it proclaimed war "the world's only hygiene," called for highways to be built over the canals of Venice, and even advocated the abolition of moonlight. Marinetti was drawn to theater, which could not in any case have been omitted from this outpouring of energy. It is common to regard ALFRED JARRY'S *Ubu the King* (*Ubu roi*, 1898) as the first expression of the European *avant-garde*, and the first works of Marinetti, who was bilingual and frequented innovative artistic circles in Paris, were in French. He made his debut with *King Bombance* (*Le roi Bombance*, 1905), whose title may have been an act of homage to Jarry's epoch-making work, and *Electrical Dolls* (*Poupées électriques*, 1909), forerunners of absurdist theater. In *King Bombance* cuisine is used as a metaphor of sorts for revolution versus order, with no obvious winner. Béchamel, a cook, and the Poet-Idiot stand by while the starving people devour the corpse of the king, who will rise again, but so too will the revolutionaries who had died of starvation in the stinking recesses around the castle. *Electrical Dolls* is divided conventionally into three acts and unfolds in a grand hotel near a house where an engineer named Wilson is at work on experiments, but its characters are puppets, creatures who were to recur in the new antinaturalist theater. In this case the puppet is a female who regresses to childhood but kills herself when faced with the male responsible for the death of the first woman.

After its birth in FRANCE, FUTURISM flourished in Italy, where it inspired many subsequent Italian avant-garde movements. Its influence on what, however paradoxically, can be called the tradition of iconoclasm, on those waves of antinarrative, antirealist, self-consciously provocative, irrationalist, absurdist theater that mark 20th-century theater making in Italy, was immense. Since it relied on performance rather than on dramatic literature, it was also in intuitive harmony with the dominant Italian tradition of theater. There were several distinct aspects to the contribution to theater of Marinetti personally and of the futurists collectively. Marinetti's prefuturist plays, the futurist manifestos, and the futurist theatrical events—they fit no accepted genre—all made a contribution.

The futurists were prolific publishers of manifestos. The essence of their radical approach to drama is contained in *Variety Theater* (1913), *Futurist Synthetic Theater* (1915), and *Theater of Surprise* (1921), although there were sections dedicated to theater in other manifestos, for instance, *Dramatic and Synoptic Declamation* (1916). They proclaimed their "deep disgust with contemporary theater because it wavers stupidly between historical reconstruction (medley or plagiarism) and the photographic reproduction of our daily life." In contrast to the beliefs of Verga and the verists, they asserted that theater had no obligation to resemble day-to-day life, but should reflect only itself. There would be no loss, they believed, if Shakespeare were boiled down to a single act, and they pondered the advantages of having Victor Hugo's *Hernani* "performed by actors tied in sacks up to their necks." The classics could maintain their place, but only if they were "prostituted, plagiarized or parodied." The only established genre that drew any approbation was the previously despised variety theater or music hall (the manifesto on variety theater was first published in London), which showed greater zest, energy, panache, and inventiveness than bourgeois theater. Variety theater was "born of electricity and fed on speed and modernity," and it alone showed itself capable of "seeking the audience's collaboration." The theater they wanted was some kind of carnival reversal of established order, one that would irritate, provoke, and outrage the spectators, but would simultaneously stimulate their active participation.

The first of the futurist events, called simply "*soirées*" or "evenings," took place in Trieste in 1910, and they were repeated in various theaters all over Italy. Their ideas found form in an ideal of synthetic theater, set out in the 1915 manifesto that was signed by three futurist artists, including Marinetti. A synthesis, which had much in common with the vaudeville sketch, had to be brief and incisive, could be grotesque or bizarre, and was comic in its improbability but was not required to be witty, logical, or linear or to make any point. The characters were stripped of all psychological plausibility, while the situation had no logical development or connection with history or society. The syntheses were designed to provoke outrage and succeeded in their aim. One particularly celebrated piece was titled *Decision*, with the subtitle *Tragedy in 58 Acts, of Which the First 57 Have Been Cut*. All that remained was the final decision, conveyed in few words by the one character featured, to take his life. The others had been cut along with the scenes in which they appeared. Theater had been effectively dismantled.

More or less contemporary with futurism was the THEATER OF THE GROTESQUE, which burst onto the scene in 1916 with the production in Rome of *The Mask and the Face* (*La maschera e il volto*), by LUIGI CHIARELLI (1880–1947). The group's name came from the play's subtitle, *A Grotesque in Three Acts*. Others who identified themselves as Grotesques included Luigi Antonelli (1882–1942), Enrico Cavacchioli (1885–1954), and, more tentatively, Pier Maria Rosso di San Secondo (1887–1956). Some critics would add early Pirandello, and the influence of this theater on him is beyond dispute. Grotesque theater represents the first appearance of a new vein of black, quasi-tragic comedy, an outlook explained by Chiarelli as a realization that even at the most tragic moments, human beings are plagued by a sense of their own ridiculousness. The new theater was greeted with enthusiasm by political thinkers such as Antonio Gramsci and Piero Gobetti, both of whom were ardent theater critics, as a liberating force that undermined and satirized the comfortable bourgeois vision. In his first play Chiarelli held up to scorn the very code of honor that had led to tragic outcomes in Verga's theater. Paolo proclaims that if his wife were to commit adultery, his need to maintain his honor would compel him to kill her, but when she admits infidelity, he is incapable of carrying out the threat but pretends to do so, and even goes to the lengths of having himself put on trial for murder. Antonelli's *The Man Who Met Himself* (1918) also deals with adultery, but committed two decades previously by a woman now dead. On an enchanted island her husband has the opportunity to meet himself as he was at that time and perhaps avoid the event, but the struggle to be other than himself is a failure.

Another of Antonelli's plays, *The Master* (1933), was produced by Luigi Pirandello (1867–1936), who, along with Carlo Goldoni, is one of only two Italian playwrights to have an unquestioned place in any canon of world drama. Pirandello came late to theater and was already well established as a novelist, poet, and essayist when, in 1910, Nino Martoglio encouraged him to write a play for performance by the Sicilian *capocomico* Angelo Musco. Adopting a practice that was to become common, Pirandello offered adaptations of two of his short stories. His first fully staged work, *Sicilian Limes*, was in Sicilian dialect. Previous plays by Pirandello, which can be classed as juvenilia, had appeared only in literary magazines, but he had discussed drama in essays in which he showed little sympathy for the collaborative effort that is intrinsic to theater. In the essay *Illustrators, Actors, and Translators* (1908) he put all three of these figures on the same level as unwanted, obstructive trespassers on terrain that was not theirs as of right. Pirandello's ideal was direct communication between author and audience: "Unfortunately, there always has to be a third, unavoidable element that intrudes between the dramatic author and the creation in the material being of the performance: the actor. As is well known, this is an unavoidable limitation for dramatic art (qtd. in Bassnett and Lorch, 1993)." These views may even have been responsible in part for the unsympathetic portrait of the actors in *SIX CHARACTERS IN SEARCH OF AN AUTHOR*. In 1915, annoyed at a production of *If Not Thus* that distorted his meaning, he threatened to give up theater entirely. He was dissuaded by Martoglio, and although he worked closely with actors in the years 1925–1928 when he had charge of a company of his own, the Teatro d'Arte, he never formally renounced the idiosyncratic doubts expressed in the earlier essay.

Pirandello was an amalgam of conflicting forces—humorist of tragic themes, Sicilian and Italian, realist and antirealist, antidirector and director, philosopher and antiphilosopher, Fascist adherent and non-Fascist (but never anti-Fascist) writer, playwright at odds with actors and even with theater itself. There are schools of criticism built on each of these aspects of his output, but Pirandello needs to be seen in the round. The theoretical works fundamental to appreciating his distinctive philosophy are his 1908 essay *On Humor* and the preface to the definitive 1925 version of *Six Characters*. In the first he distinguishes between the comic, which is spontaneous and unsympathetic, and the humorous, which is reflective and compassionate. In the same essay, he sets out the intellectual groundwork for a new poetic based on the willing acceptance of a godless and bleak cosmos, in which tragedy is impossible. The preface establishes the basic terms of what came to be known as *Pirandellismo*, a semiphilosophical outlook intrinsic to his theater, involving questions over the oneness or multiplicity of personality, the nature of truth, the reliability of words, and the ontological clash between life and form.

Like his Swedish counterpart, August Strindberg, Pirandello began as a realist but abandoned realism in favor of a literature that gave freer rein to imagination and greater license to explore intangible dimensions of life. According to Pirandello, "The realists limit art to the pure and simple imitation of nature: they do not claim to say anything: they want to represent nature as it is. But why repeat with a lesser, human voice what nature says with its powerful voice?" His three undisputed masterpieces—RIGHT YOU ARE (IF YOU THINK SO) (Milan, 1917), *Six Characters in Search of an Author* (Rome, 1921), and *Henry IV* (Milan, 1922)—were premiered in an arc of five years. *Six Characters* exercised enormous influence on European, especially French, theater, but in spite of his international prestige, Pirandello struggled to find an audience and venues at home, and in his last years many of his plays were premiered abroad.

Pirandello joined the Fascist Party in 1924 at the moment when Mussolini, following international condemnation of his involvement in the murder of the Socialist member of Parliament Giacomo Matteotti, was at his weakest. He remained a member all his life, even though he refused to write in accordance with Fascist aesthetic principles, which were much more favorable to D'Annunzio. Fascism is normally regarded as an embarrassing interlude in the history of Italian theater, as in most other spheres, but the Duce gave a certain prominence to theater and advocated the establishment of "theaters for twenty thousand," as well as of itinerant troupes, the so-called wagons of Thespis. In conjunction with the playwright Giovacchino Forzano (1884–1970), Mussolini claimed co-authorship of grandiose, patriotic scripts that featured such personages as Napoleon and Julius Caesar.

Fascism could not stamp out the debates over the direction of Italian theater, particularly in the latter years when preparations were under way for the inevitable post-Fascist era. The long-debated questions of *teatro stabile* and of the introduction of the director acquired greater urgency as part of a process of renewal. Aurélien Lugné-Poë, Georges Pitoeff, and Louis Jouvet, who would later make a substantial contribution to the young Piccolo Teatro in Milan, were already active on the French stage, as were MAX REINHARDT in Germany and VSEVOLOD MEYERHOLD in Russia. Silvio D'Amico (1887–1955) emerged as the most forceful advocate of reform, damning the *capocomico* as a mere tradesman, deficient in the technique and sensibility to graft onto his craft the elusive higher quality called art. D'Amico envisaged the director as visionary and co-coordinator, charged with ensuring narrative flow and coherence, imposing balance between script and performance, and paying due attention to the psychological and emotional consistency of character. "Yesterday's theater was entrusted to the performer. . . . Today, however, the co-coordinator has arrived, the *metteur-en-scène*. Yesterday it was the *grande attore*, the *mattatore* who relegated the poet to second rank to put himself on display (and there is no knowing yet in which rank the author has finished)" (D'Amico, 1930). The last remark is significant. The author still had no central role in Italy's new theater.

The foundation of the Piccolo Teatro on May 14, 1947, in a Milan still caught up in the exhilaration of the liberation, was as important in 20th-century Italian theater as the premiere of Pirandello's *Six Characters*. It provided the model for the *teatro stabile* over the length and breadth of Italy and consolidated the role of the director. The Piccolo was the joint creation of Giorgio Strehler (1921–1997) and Paolo Grassi (1919–1981), the former in charge of artistic policy and the latter of administration and "cultural operations." Their vision ensured that Italy would have permanent theaters, subsidized by the state and able to mount a planned season of drama. They shared the ideal of theater as a public service with a social and moral function, accessible to all. Strehler was a director of genius who had the privilege of being able to produce few works but to keep them on the program for many years. Eclectic in style, he was no experimentalist and did little to encourage new writing in Italy. His preference was to work and rework a few scripts from a classical canon. In his celebrated productions of Goldoni's *Harlequin, Servant of Two Masters*, he sought a fusion of commedia dell'arte techniques and modern physical theater, while with his successive versions of Pirandello's late myth *The Mountain Giants* he found a key to make a demanding literary work a piece of captivating visual theater. After his productions of THE THREEPENNY OPERA and THE LIFE OF GALILEO, BERTOLT BRECHT saw him as his favored successor, although Strehler himself later changed tack.

Three principal strands can be detected in the theater of postwar Italy: director's theater, the avant-garde, and theater that was, broadly, traditional. Two other directors of unusual ability, Luchino Visconti (1906–1976) and Luigi Squarzina (1922–), were, along with Strehler, responsible for the shift of power away from the performer toward the director. Visconti, who made his theatrical debut with his 1945 production of JEAN COCTEAU's *Les parents terribles*, enjoyed parallel careers as theater, opera, and cinema director. There seemed to be two souls in Visconti, one that laid bare harsh social reality (he was a Communist) and one that relished the opulence of style and splendor (he belonged to the nobility). Squarzina was also a playwright whose works include *Three Quarters of the Moon* (1955) and *The Five Senses* (1987), while as director he worked with the actor Vittorio Gassman in the Teatro d'Arte Italiano, producing the first complete and reliable Italian *Hamlet* (1952) after the excesses of the great actors. Squarzina is most closely associated with Genoa's *teatro stabile*, and in all his theatrical activities he showed himself an acute, if disenchanted, observer of society.

It may seem odd to number EDUARDO DE FILIPPO (1900–1984) and even more the avowed Marxist DARIO FO (1926–) among the traditionalists, but as actor-authors and practitioners of popular theater, they stand in a line that stretches back to the commedia dell'arte. As a Neapolitan, De Filippo has the tradition of Pulcinella behind him and belongs to the one city responsible in the late 19th and 20th centuries for the production of a mass of dramas of a high level. His precursors include Antonio Petito (1822–1876) and Raffaele Viviani (1888–1950), as well as his father, Eduardo Scarpetta (1853–1925), all actor-authors, even though the remarkable Petito was illiterate and had initially to dictate his pieces. De Filippo's brother Peppino was also an actor-author, and his sister Titina an actress, and there are now two companies in Naples managed by descendants of Eduardo and Peppino and one run by a Scarpetta. For all these writers, the principal character in their drama is invariably Naples itself, with its teeming life, vivacity, granite-hard humor, stoicism, and refusal of resignation, but Eduardo De Filippo brought to the highest level the knack of disconcertingly mingling comedy and tragedy. Viviani in *The Lane* (1920) had depicted scenes of brutal violence in knockabout style, and Scarpetta was the author of *Misery and Nobility* (1888), perhaps the finest of all Neapolitan plays and one that drew the praise of that most exacting of critics, Benedetto Croce. Scarpetta preferred to focus on the Neapolitan bourgeoisie, but in this play he entered a powerful protest, dressed as comedy, against the hunger and grinding poverty of the underclass. A starving family ends up silently observing the excesses at a wedding feast in a mansion they have entered in disguise. De Filippo too dealt with social injustices in his theater, but stopped short of overt political protest. The family, with its tensions and conflicts, is the site of virtually all his drama. A history of Italian society could be drawn by reference to the problems featured generation after generation. He never surpassed his *Napoli milionaria!* (1945) or *Filumena Marturano* (1946), both set in a Naples devastated by war.

If De Filippo fought shy of political involvement in his theater, Dario Fo felt no such inhibition. Fo made his debut in postwar Milan with his actress wife, Franca Rame (1929–), and first attained fame in the 1950s with a series of comedies, later tagged "bourgeois." In 1968 he broke with that style of theater to write and perform explicitly political theater with a touring cooperative he founded. Fo is a more complex character than the conventional description of him as "political playwright" would indicate, and a dramatist whose creative habitat is tradition. At the very moment of siding with the revolutionary politics of the post–1968 movement, he adopted as his model the medieval *giullare* (jester). If Fo was a political revolutionary, he has remained a theatrical conservative. His two best-known works from this period illustrate the twin springs of his talent. COMIC MYSTERY (1969), a series of sketches from medieval sources, demonstrates his obsession with popular culture from all ages and provides a platform for his bravura performance skills, while ACCIDENTAL DEATH OF AN ANARCHIST (1970), a farce that was a counter inquiry into neo-Fascist intrigue in contemporary Italy, gave proof of his ability to transform the headlines of the day into theater. With Fo, farce became a vehicle for political protest. In 1997 he was awarded the Nobel Prize for Literature.

Fo had no sympathy for experimental theater, which he regarded as elitist, but Italy is home to the most flourishing avant-garde in Europe. Some critics distinguish between the historical pre-avant-garde (the futurist generation), the avant-garde as such (the 1950s to the 1970s), and a contemporary post-avant-garde. The universally acknowledged master in this field is Carmelo Bene (1937–2002), even if with Bene it is difficult to separate genuine achievement from rodomontade and the urge to be a mere enfant terrible. He pillaged the classics to produce provocative stage works that were parody, pastiche, or even kitsch. His work included three versions of Pinocchio and several adaptations of Shakespearean drama, including six separate productions of *Hamlet*, of which *Hommelette for Hamlet* (1987) was the most striking. Music and melodrama were an intrinsic part of his output, and from 1966 his debt to ANTONIN ARTAUD was generously acknowledged. In an unexpected way he too was an actor-author, although his productions consisted entirely of extravagant, often obscene reworkings of traditional material. Carlo Quartucci (1931–), who forged productions according to the physical space in which they were presented, and Memè Perlini (1944–), who preferred to stage extracts, or "frescos," were among the more inventive creators of avant-garde theater, while contemporary director-writer-performers in the post-avant-garde, whose work is close to what is known elsewhere as PERFORMANCE ART, include Federico Tiezzi, whose company Carozzone later rebranded itself Magazzini Criminali, and Giorgio Barberio Corsetti, whose Gaia Scienza later became Compagnia Teatrale. None invites interpretation, and all operate at the contact point between rationalism and irrationalism, but it is curious how frequently in their search for the new they hark back to Shakespeare and classical theater.

The now firmly established *teatri stabili* rarely provide a home for new writing, but there are several writers who have made an important contribution to theatrical life. Vittorio Franceschi (1936–) produced militant texts for Dario Fo's Nuova Scena cooperative, but later authored *Checkmate* (1990), a delicately observed study of insanity. Umberto Marino (1952–) has moved between screen and stage with works such as *The Station* (1987), a modern version of the white knight/black knight conflict. Giuseppe Manfridi (1956–) has seen many plays produced in many countries and brings a lyrical tone to unlikely subjects, as with *Hooligans* (1986). Paolo Puppa (1945–) has moved from being a theater historian to author of a series of monologues presenting classical myth as modern dilemmas. Pia Fontana (1949–) has a sharp ear for dialogue and a taste for seemingly humdrum plots that suddenly explode to lay bare underlying tensions, as she did with *The Yell* (1996). Naples remains true to its own traditions and has produced a clutch of dialect writer-performers, including Ruggero Cappuccio (1965–), Antonio Scavone (1947–), and Enzo Moscato (1948–), who runs his own company in the manner of the old *capocomici*. These writers are as talented as their contemporaries in other European countries, but have to struggle without the institutional support available elsewhere. For all its problems and defects, Italian theater is still bristling with its own anomalous life.

FURTHER READING

Alexander, Alfred. *Giovanni Verga: A Great Writer and His World.* London: Grant & Cutler, 1972.

Bassnett, Susan, and Jennifer Lorch, eds. *Luigi Pirandello in the Theater: A Documentary Record.* Philadelphia: Harwood Academic Publishers, 1993.

Caesar, Ann Hallamore. *Characters and Authors in Luigi Pirandello.* New York: Oxford Univ. Press, 1998.

D'Amico, Silvio. *Tramonto del grande attore* [Twilight of the Actor]. Milan: A. Mondadori, 1929.

Farrell, Joseph. *Dario Fo and Franca Rame: Harlequins of the Revolution.* London: Methuen, 2001.

Farrell, Joseph, and Paolo Puppa, eds. *A History of Italian Theatre.* New York: Cambridge Univ. Press, 2006.

Giannachi, Gabriella, and Nick Kaye. *Staging the Post-Avant-Garde: Italian Experimental Performance after 1970.* New York: Peter Lang, 2002.

Kirby, Michael. *Futurist Performance.* New York: Dutton, 1971.

Tisdall, Caroline, and Angelo Bozzolla. *Futurism.* London: Thames and Hudson, 1977.

Woodhouse, John. *Gabriele D'Annunzio: Defiant Archangel.* New York: Oxford Univ. Press, 1998.

Joseph Farrell

IT IS NOT THE TALL GRASS BLOWN BY THE WIND

NOORDIN HASSAN's landmark Malaysian music drama *It Is Not the Tall Grass Blown by the Wind* (*Bukan lalang ditiup angin*) premiered in 1970 at the Sultan Idris Teacher Training College in Tanjung Malim, Perak, and won MALAYSIA's first Literary Award for drama (1972). Written in response to the ethnic riots of May 13, 1969, the play addresses the deep-rooted causes of this Malaysian tragedy.

This experimental work rejected the realism of the preceding decade. Inspired by the promise of a newly independent nation, playwrights of the 1960s created social dramas with clear plot lines and positive resolutions. The riots challenged assumptions about progress and exposed irrational aspects of human nature. The play rejects straightforward chronology and simple cause and effect. Scenes shift between past, present, and future via thematic fragments expressed in poetry, proverbs, songs, music, dance, symbolic action, and dialogue. Western elements (for example, a Greek-like chorus) are featured along with the traditional *boria* (comic sketches and call-and-response procession). Noordin eliminated the customary curtain, prompting the audience to ponder the surrealistic set: a floating human eyeball, torn cloth on branches, and a broken Daliesque clock. As the play begins, the chorus chants: "The booming sound is indeed rain / It is not the tall grass blown by the wind." What one hears is not simply wind; rather, it is a concrete occurrence that must be addressed. The "sound" is the tragedy of May 13.

Two story lines are enacted. The main story features the weak Pak Leman, who, defeated in a cockfight, pawns his family and village. An astrologer says that he must take responsibility for reversing his fate, or his progeny will continue to experience the cycle of suffering. Rural Malays themselves must work to overcome recurrent poverty. They cannot wait for fate—or others. The second story line deals with the astrologer's prophecy. Hadi and Kintan are a young couple. Hadi and other farmers reject a life of exploitation from one generation to the next and plan to take up arms against Culan, their oppressive landlord. Kintan pleads for a peaceful resolution. Her father, Ihsan, who deserted his family years before, returns and promises to help financially, but the people do not trust him. Culan takes what he wants: he detains Ihsan and Kintan. The farmers capture Culan and free his two captives, but the landlord's guards save Culan, killing Ihsan and Kintan in the process. Here the prophecy ends as we return to the story of Pak Leman. If Pak Leman does not alter his fate, the future of the Malay villagers will remain bleak.

Some do not interpret the prophecy as a future prospect but as an allegory of May 13. From this perspective, Pak Leman represents a leader whose ineptitude plagues the community. The play ends with a series of questions detailing the overall issue: What will Pak Leman do? Noordin addresses the Malay leadership, asking what they will do to alleviate poverty, ignorance, and ill will. That Noordin chose to present these questions in an allegorical manner is partly a consequence of the politically charged times in which he wrote. The penetrating message and novel production style inspired the artists of the following decade.

[*See also* Malaysia]

FURTHER READING

Abdullah, Ahmad Kamal, Hashim Awans, Ramli Isin, Sahlan Mohd. Saman, and Zakaria Ariffin. *History of Modern Malay Literature.* Vol. 2. Tr. by Khidmat Terjemahan Nusantra (Nusantra Translation Service), Hason Rashid, and Noor Rashidah Abdul Hamid. Kuala Lumpur: Dewan Bahasa dan Pustaka and the Ministry of Education Malaysia, 1992.

Dahaman, Ismail. "Bukan Lalang Ditiup Angin." *Dewan Masyarakat* (October 1970): 26–29.

Nur Nina Zuhra (Nancy Nanney). *An Analysis of Modern Malay Drama.* Shah Alam, Malaysia: Biroteks, MARA Institute of Technology. 1992.

Nancy Nanney

IT PAYS TO ADVERTISE

The popular comedy *It Pays to Advertise* opened on September 8, 1914, at the Cohan Theatre in New York. The play was the only collaboration between its two playwrights, Roi Cooper Megrue and Walter Hackett, and it represented another in the string of successes produced by George M. Cohan and Sam Harris. Critics and audiences embraced the production; the *New York Times* called *It Pays to Advertise* "continuous fun," noting that "not often in the course of a season is it given to the first-nighters to roar so heartily." *It Pays* enjoyed a run of 399 performances and gave Louise Drew, John Drew's daughter, a critical success in the supporting role of a phony French countess.

Billed as "a farcical fact in three acts," the story concerns Cyrus Martin, a successful soap manufacturer known as "The Soap King," and his efforts to encourage his spoiled but good-hearted son Rodney to make good on his own. When Rodney tells the elder Martin that he loves the old man's stenographer, Mary, the father turns Rodney out of the house and fires Mary as well. Mary, however, is in fact cooperating with Rodney's father—the elder Martin would like Mary and Rodney to become a couple.

Rodney soon hits on the idea of entering the soap field himself. He succeeds by using the factual part of the "farcical fact"—the power of advertising. He teams up with theatrical agent Ambrose Peale, who convinces Rodney that with the right advertising campaign, they will not even need to produce a product. They come up with the perfect name for the soap and the perfect slogan: "13 Soap—Unlucky for Dirt." They generate further interest by charging the exorbitant rate of $1.00 per cake of soap, ten times the price the elder Martin charges, using the logic that the public will automatically think that a product is better if it is more expensive. When Rodney's father must contend with increasing orders for the nonexistent competing soap, he buys out his son, thus clinching the happy ending.

Although *It Pays* was not Broadway's first advertising comedy, it did provide the New York stage with the most comprehensive (and successful) portrait of how important and all-pervasive advertising had become by 1914. This was largely a result of the creative efforts of copywriters, a career that had only come into existence at the turn of the century. When Peale "sells" Rodney on the need to advertise, he rattles off a litany of then-popular real-life advertising slogans to make his case, as well as numerous statistics—"facts, not farce," the program assured theatergoers.

New York advertising agencies immediately saw the opportunity for placing "tie-in" ads in the programs. "If, after seeing this 'Farcical Fact in Three Acts' you'd like to hear the facts without farce about what Advertising can do," one such ad began. In a short time any play with a contemporary setting that featured a character like Cyrus Martin, who did not believe in advertising, would scarcely have been believable.

[*See also* United States, 1860–1929]

FURTHER READING

Blum, Daniel. *A Pictorial History of the American Theatre, 1900–1950.* New York: Greenberg, 1950.

Megrue, Roi Cooper, and Walter Hackett. *It Pays to Advertise.* Novelized by Samuel Field. New York: Grosset, 1915.

The New York Times Theater Reviews, 1912–1919. New York: New York Times and Arno Press, 1975.

Turner, E. S. *The Shocking History of Advertising!* New York: Dutton, 1953.

Michael Schwartz

IVANOV

Ivanov represents a transitional moment in the career of ANTON CHEKHOV as he moved away from plays of direct action, such as his first large-scale drama, PLATONOV, to the mature style of his four masterpieces, THE SEAGULL, UNCLE VANYA, THE THREE SISTERS, and THE CHERRY ORCHARD. *Ivanov* troubled Chekhov, and he was never completely satisfied with it. Over the course of fourteen years, he revised the play many times, and no fewer than seven complete versions are known.

Chekhov sought to portray in Ivanov the disillusionment and moral weariness of a generation, whose idealism rose and fell with the reforms of Aleksandr II. The playwright conceived of Ivanov as an apotheosis of the so-called superfluous man (*lishnii chelovek*). Like Aleksandr Griboedov's Chatsky, Aleksandr Pushkin's Onegin, Mikhail Lermontov's Pechorin, and Ivan Turgenev's Rudin, Ivanov is a disaffected nobleman whose idealism has waned and whose failure to find a meaningful role in society leads to self-destructive tendencies. Chekhov's handling of his material is instructive. By the 1880s the very notion of a superfluous man was in danger of becoming a hackneyed stereotype. In his ongoing revolt against the well-made play that dominated the stage at this time, Chekhov desired to portray real life in his drama and reacted against stereotypes, attempting to articulate both Ivanov's distinct individuality and his psychological development. From the beginning, critics felt intuitively that *Ivanov* was innovative. To no small degree, this innovation owes to the growing objectivity of Chekhov's technique. As the playwright wrote to his brother, "There are no villains or angels in my play (although I couldn't resist throwing in a couple of clowns). I have not condemned anyone, nor have I vindicated anyone." The author stands, as it were, at a remove from his characters and, for the first time, allows the drama to arise out of the characters' autonomy. Although imperfectly realized in *Ivanov*, this technique made possible the masterpieces that followed.

Ivanov, in its first version, premiered on November 19, 1887, at Korsh's Theater in Moscow. Both audiences and critics responded positively to the play's love triangle, which finds Ivanov unable to deal with either his dying wife Anna (also known as Sarra Abramson) or the young, idealistic Sasha. Some criticism was directed at the curious ending: Insulted by the young Dr. Lvov, Ivanov lies down on a couch and dies while the other characters go on talking for some time before they realize what has happened.

Chekhov extensively revised *Ivanov* for the production at the Imperial Aleksandrinsky Theater in St. Petersburg. Aside from numerous stylistic alterations, Chekhov's aim was threefold: First, he highlighted Ivanov's weariness and disillusionment; second, he reconceived the character of Sasha, in part to make it a more substantive role for the famous actress Maria Savina, in part to provide Ivanov a stronger foil to play off of; and third, he transformed the last act in order to provide what he thought would be a more realistic ending in the form of Ivanov's suicide. However, contemporary critics chided Chekhov for his handling of psychological motivation throughout this period and often cited Ivanov's suicide as a negative example. Most later commentators have vindicated the playwright.

[*See also* Russia and Soviet Union]

FURTHER READING

Chekhov, Anton. *The Plays of Anton Chekhov*. Tr. by Paul Schmidt. New York: HarperCollins, 1997.

Gilman, Richard. *Chekhov's Plays: An Opening Into Eternity*. New Haven: Yale Univ. Press, 1995.

Magarshack, David. *Chekhov the Dramatist*. New York: Hill & Wang, 1960.

Pavis, Patrice. "*Ivanov*: The Invention of a Negative Dramaturgy." In *The Cambridge Companion to Chekhov*, ed. by Vera Gottlieb and Paul Allain. Cambridge: Cambridge Univ. Press, 2000.

Timothy C. Westphalen

IWAMATSU RYŌ (1952–)

Iwamatsu Ryō, Japanese playwright, director, and actor, is noted for his versatility and radical change from comic improvisation to "quiet theater" (*shizuka na engeki*). He has inspired playwright-directors HIRATA ORIZA and Miyazawa Akio.

Born in Nagasaki, Iwamatsu majored in Russian at the Tokyo University of Foreign Languages and Studies. In 1976, after training at the Azabu Actors Gym, run by the Freedom Theater Company (Jiyū Gekijō), he joined the Tokyo Battery Theater (Tokyo Kandenchi), known for improvisational theater. Until 1986 he served as director, compiling the actors' comic improvisations into performance. From 1985 to 1987 Iwamatsu was also involved in the unusual performance unit Radical Gaziberibimba System, founded by the well-known actors Takenaka Naoto and Itō Seikō. The unit promoted a new intellectual humor in contrast to the humor based on wordplay and nonstop action prevalent in the 1980s and the harsh satirical humor of the decade before that.

Iwamatsu the playwright emerged when the Tokyo Battery Theater turned to script-based theater. Iwamatsu's debut play, *Tea and a Lecture* (1986), is part of his neighborhood trilogy, which includes *Kitchen Lights* (1987) and *Romance Is Banned* (1987). *Tea and a Lecture* features three middle-aged men leading slovenly lives without tension. The play is considered to be one of the pioneering works in quiet theater, which provided an antithesis to the dominant trend of comic-frenetic theater in the 1980s. An established subgenre of little theater (ANGURA AND SHŌGEKIJŌ) by the mid-1990s, quiet theater portrays the minutiae of existence in a stringently nondramatic manner and reveals the unspoken and even the unspeakable in daily life.

Iwamatsu established his reputation with *Futon and Daruma* (1988), for which he was awarded the prestigious Kishida Kunio Drama Prize. Part of Iwamatsu's second trilogy, which includes *Dad's Bathing* (1989) and *Dad's Dad* (1990), *Futon and Daruma* is about the pitiably low status of the modern father.

Before leaving the Tokyo Battery Theater in 1992, Iwamatsu became the resident playwright-director of the Takenaka Naoto Group (Takenaka Naoto no Kai) in 1990. His best-known work with Takenaka is *The Man Next Door* (1990), inspired by François Truffaut's film *The Woman Next Door*. Again part of a series, this time about men, it is about an optician who is already jaded with the affair he is having with the wife of his friend, who knows but feigns ignorance.

Iwamatsu himself denies that his plays are "quiet." His characters can harbor great inner violence that sometimes spills out into acts of aggression. For example, in *An Umbrella and Sandals* (1996), produced by Iwamatsu, Inc., tension escalates among young people staying at a hotel and results in murder. Iwamatsu received the Kinokuniya Theatre Award for *The Sisters Who Keep Doves* (1993) and *A Man Breaking Down* (1994) and the prestigious Yomiuri Literary Award for *TV Days* (1997).

[*See also* Japan; Shingeki]

SELECT PLAYS: *Tea and a Lecture: On the Moral Value of Indifference* (*Ocha to sekkyō: Mukanshin no dōtokuteki-kachi o megutte*, 1986); *Kitchen Lights: People and Their General Tendencies* (*Daidokoro no hi: Hito to sono ippansei no chōkō ni yosete*, 1987); *Romance Is Banned: A Violent Seizure of Futility and Honesty* (*Ren'ai go-hatto: Muda to shōjiki no gekiteki hossa o megutte*, 1987); *Futon and Daruma* (*Futon to daruma*, 1988); *Dad's Bathing* (*Otōsan no kaisuiyoku*, 1989); *Dad's Dad* (*Otōsan no otōsan*, 1990); *The Man Next Door* (*Tonari no otoko*, 1990); *The Ice-cream Man: The Remarkable Recreation of the Middle Class* (*Aisu-kuriimu Man: Chūryū-kaikyū no gekiteki kyūsoku*, 1992); *Ichigao Hill: The Three Legendary Brothers of the Rainbow* (*Ichigao no saka: Densetsu no niji no san kyōdai*, 1992); *The Sisters Who Keep Doves* (*Hato o kau shimai*, 1993); *A Man Breaking Down* (*Kowareyuku otoko*, 1994); *The Modesty of Moonlight* (*Gekkō no tsutsushimi*, 1994); *An Umbrella and Sandals: The Festivities and Tragedy of the End of Youth* (*Kasa to sandaru: Seishun no owari no saien to sangeki no monogatari*, 1996); *TV Days* (*Terebi deizu*, 1997); *The Caprice of Water* (*Mizu no tawamure*, 1998)

FURTHER READING

Hasebe Hiroshi. *Nusumareta riaru: 90 nendai engeki wa kataru* [The stolen real: Japanese theater of the 1990s speaks]. Tokyo: Aspect, 1998.

Iwamatsu Ryō. *Futon and Daruma* [*Futon to daruma*]. Tr. by Yuasa Masako. Leeds: Alumnus, 1992.

——. *The Man Next Door* [*Tonari no otoko*]. In *Half a Century of Japanese Theater*, vol. 3, *1980s, Part 1*, tr. by Yuasa Masako, ed. by Japan Playwrights Association. Tokyo: Kinokuniya, 2000. 15–71.

Kazama Ken. *Shōgekijō, minna ga hiirō no sekai: Gendai engeki no fūkei* [In little theater everyone's a hero: The landscape of contemporary theater]. Tokyo: Seikyūsha, 1993.

Mari Boyd

IZUMI KYŌKA (1873–1939)

Izumi Kyōka, Japanese playwright and novelist, was born Izumi Kyōtarō (Kyōka was a pen name) in Kanazawa, JAPAN, and spent most of his adult life in Tokyo. A romantic, he rejected NATURALISM, the dominant literary and theatrical movement in Japan during the first decade of the 20th century, and was deeply skeptical of most modern trends in society. Kyōka's literature can roughly be divided into two kinds: sentimental realism and supernatural fantasy. Traditional folkways, theater, and narrative inform much of his best work, casting an otherworldly light on even the more conventional stories and plays; his unique, almost surrealistic literary style distinguishes his writing from the ranks of most popular fiction and drama of that time. He wrote more than a dozen original plays, as well as several excerpts and adaptations of his own fiction. While the adaptations from his fiction are quite melodramatic, his original plays are daringly symbolist and at times even seem to anticipate ABSURDISM or ANTONIN ARTAUD's Theater of Cruelty. He wrote most of his plays during the Taishō era (1912–1926), a great age for drama in Japan.

Kyōka first came to prominence in the mid-1890s with a series of highly melodramatic stories, such as *The Surgery* (1895), that harshly criticized the treatment of women, the poor, and other marginalized people. With *Taki no Shiraito*, in 1894, KAWAKAMI OTOJIRŌ staged the first SHINPA dramatization of a Kyōka story. Many others, such as *The Vigil's Tale* (1906), *A Woman's Pedigree* (1908), and *The White Heron* (1910), followed. Typically these works featured a passionate geisha or prostitute in doomed love with an ineffectual intellectual. From the 1920s until the 1960s many of these works also saw film treatments (sometimes multiple). Increasingly disenchanted with others' versions of his work, Kyōka began to write his own plays. *Shinja the Great* (1904), an uneasy amalgam of sentimental romance and bizarre fantasy, was his first effort. His translation (with German scholar Tobari Chikufu) of GERHART HAUPTMANN's *Märchendrama* (fairy-tale play) *The Sunken Bell* in 1907 helped form Kyōka's dramaturgy of the fantastic, but the traditional theater, NŌ as well as *kabuki*, also provided ready inspiration. During a time when Japanese models were increasingly being rejected, he was one of the first playwrights to attempt a synthesis of Western and native dramatic modes. Kyōka found a loyal audience among other writers such as Tanizaki Jun'ichirō (1886–1965) and KUBOTA MANTARŌ, who later adapted and directed many of the *shinpa* versions of his work. But many of his best plays, including *The Sea God's Villa* (1913), *The Castle Tower* (1917), and *The Wild Rose* (1923), were not staged until after his death. Kyōka's melodramatic fiction has provided staple fare for the *shinpa* theater down to the present day, but since the 1960s a more avant-garde coterie of playwrights and directors, such as KARA JŪRŌ, TERAYAMA SHŪJI, TADASHI SUZUKI, Ninagawa Yukio, and Miyagi Satoshi, have staged his more experimental work. Kabuki female role specialist Bando Tamasaburō V has long championed Kyōka, regularly starring in *shinpa* productions; he has also directed two film versions of his work, *The Surgery* (1990) and *The Castle Tower* (1995).

[*See also* Shingeki; Shin kabuki]

SELECT PLAYS: *Shinja the Great* (*Shinja daiō*, 1904); *Demon Pond* (*Yashagaike*, 1913); *Ruby* (*Kōgyoku*, 1913); *The Sea God's Villa* (*Kaijin bessō*, 1913); *Beloved Wife* (*Koi nyōbō*, 1914); *The Castle Tower* (*Tenshu monogatari*, 1917); *Nihonbashi* (1917); *The Wild Rose* (*Yamabuki*, 1923); *Polytheism* (*Tashinkyō*, 1927; a modern adaptation of the Nō play *The Iron Crown* [*Kanawa*])

FURTHER READING

Inouye, Charles Shirō. *The Similitude of Blossoms: A Critical Biography of Izumi Kyōka*. Cambridge, Mass.: Harvard Univ. Press, 1998.

Izumi Kyōka. *Kyōka zenshū* [Complete works of Kyōka]. 29 vols. Tokyo: Iwanami Shoten, 1973–1976.

Poulton, M. Cody. *Spirits of Another Sort: The Plays of Izumi Kyōka*. Ann Arbor: Univ. of Michigan Press 2001.

M. Cody Poulton

J

JACOB, MALOU (1948–)

Abolish corruption? There will always be corruption. No matter who sits up there. If you compare corruption in higher places, ours is petty theft.

—*Anatomy of Corruption*, 1992

Playwright and filmmaker Malou Lordes Leviste Jacob was born in Calapen, Mindoro, the PHILIPPINES, on February 4, 1948. She attended schools in Davao and college in Manila before obtaining a Masters of Arts in television production from City University of New York. Returning to the Philippines, she worked for *Metro Manila*, a television magazine. She has created video documentaries and served as associate artistic director for the Visual, Literary, and Media Arts Department at the Cultural Center of the Philippines, as well as developing her skills as a playwright.

Joining the PHILIPPINE EDUCATIONAL THEATRE ASSOCIATION (PETA) in 1969, she became one of its significant authors. Her first play was *The Weighing Scale Is Tilted* (*Timbangan ay tagilid*, 1971). One of her most important works is *Juan Tamban*, which was produced by PETA in 1978. The play was inspired by a newspaper article about a child who ate cockroaches to draw attention to his situation. Jacob's play was a well-researched and moving piece created in celebration of the International Year of the Child. It shows a graduate-student social worker, Marina, who faces the realities of the disenfranchised Juan Tamban, a child whose mother dreams of education for him and whose father urges him toward crimes to increase the family income. This moving portrait of contemporary social problems combined realistic characterization with stylization of set and staging. Audiences identified with the middle-class heroine who moves from studying the boy to becoming his defender in the legal system. The play was effective in pointing out inequities in the Marcos era's distribution of resources. It won the Don Carlos Palanca Memorial Award for literature (1979) and the National Book Award (1985).

Another important work produced by PETA was *Macli-ing Dulag*, named after the hero Macli-ing, which opened on April 15, 1988. The story focused on the plight of the indigenous Cordillera people, whose way of life is threatened by the Chico River Dam. The script portrayed the ongoing betrayal of indigenous peoples' rights in both the contemporary and historical context.

Jacob's *Anatomy of Corruption* (*Anatomiya ng korupsyon*) was produced by Tanghalang Pilipino, the resident company of the Cultural Center of the Philippines, in 1992 and was revived in November 2003 at the Women's Playwright International Festival in Manila. It examines the dynamics of the Filipino legal system, where bribery is rife. The naïve heroine abjures the petty dishonesties, which are part of the communal life of a legal office, and finds herself first ostracized and then subject to dismissal because her hard work and honesty upset the status quo. In a play that is half protracted skit and half incisive social critique of Filipino office and social behaviors, Jacob shows that minor dishonesties lay the groundwork for a culture of corruption that plagues the nation. The Brechtian humor makes this a popular piece, which continued to tour in 2003.

Jacob's background in television documentary is apparent in her approach to drama. She seeks out situations that illustrate major problems in Filipino political and social life and then crafts characters and situations that draw the audience's attention to the inequities and injustices implicit in society.

PLAYS: *The Weighing Scale Is Tilted* (*Timbangan ay tagilid*, 1971); *It Hurts!* (*Aidao*, 1972); *Juan Tamban* (1978); *The Protracted Indecision in the Short Life of a Petitbourgeois* (*Ang mahabang pagdadalawang isip sa maikling buhay ng isang beti-burgis*, 1980); *Macli-ing Dulag* (1988); *Pepe* (1990); *Anatomy of Corruption* (*Anatomiya ng korupsyon*, 1992); *Teresa* (1993)

FURTHER READING

Cultural Center of the Philippines. *CCP Encyclopedia of Philippine Art*. Vol. 7, *Philippine Theater*. Manila: CCP, 1994.

Fernandez, Doreen. *Palabas: Essays on Philippine Theatre History*. Quezon City: Ateneo de Manila Univ. Press, 1996.

Jacob, Malou. *Anatomiya ng korupsyon* [Anatomy of Corruption]. Manila: Babaylan Women's Publishing Collective, Institute of Women's Studies, St. Scholastica College, 1992.

Jit, Krishen. "The Philippines: Modern Drama." In *The Cambridge Guide to Asian Theatre*, ed. by James Brandon. Cambridge: Cambridge Univ. Press, 1993.

Tiongson, Nicanor. *Dulaan: An Essay on Philippine Theatre*. Manila: Cultural Center of the Philippines, 1989.

Kathy Foley

JAMES, HENRY (1843–1916)

Henry James's work as a dramatist is usually thought of as an unsuccessful episode in his better-known career as a novelist and critic. Nevertheless, James's appropriation of a "dramatic" approach to writing is significant both in his own work and as an influential element of his creative precepts. During his lifetime four of his plays—*The American*, GUY DOMVILLE, *The High Bid*, and *The Saloon*—were performed; his *Collected Plays* contains twelve complete plays and fragments of unfinished and unproduced works.

James was born in New York in 1843, and his love of the theater was established in his childhood—he attended plays growing up in the UNITED STATES—and blossomed when he was a young adult in Europe. Early in his writing career he published some dramatic pieces in periodicals, but James's theatrical interests were soon eclipsed by his success in writing novels and short fiction. However, in 1875 James moved to Paris and delighted in the theater he found there, remarking approvingly that "the Parisian theatre-going public seizes an artist's intention with extraordinary alertness" (*Parisian Sketches*, 1957). He often reiterated his nostalgia for the sensitivity of the French audience when faced with an English theatergoing public that was not fully attuned to the subtle moral drama James produced.

James's lifelong fascination with the theater developed into a more direct professional interest in the 1890s, when he became disillusioned with his novels' poor sales and turned to writing plays. In 1890 he dramatized his 1876 novel *The American*, which was well received and signaled a five-year period in which James battled to make a name for himself as a playwright. It concluded with the infamously hostile reception of *Guy Domville*, which opened on its first night in 1895 to scorn and derision from the audience, James appearing on stage at the end to a torrent of abuse. The play was afterwards defended by GEORGE BERNARD SHAW and others, but James's dreams of being a successful playwright were irrevocably damaged.

James did not give up writing drama after *Guy Domville*, but did return to fiction as his primary interest. His attempts to secure production of his plays continued to develop into drawn-out rounds of negotiations with stage managers and lead actors, which often ended with the embryonic productions never actually being performed. Two volumes of *Theatricals* (1894 and 1895) were published containing works of this sort; a production of *Summersoft*, written for Ellen Terry in 1895, was also dropped. *The High Bid* and *The Saloon* (an adaptation of James's story "Owen Wingrave") were produced in 1908 and 1911, respectively, and other works were staged after his death in London in 1916.

James's plays evoke the subtle, nuanced world of his novels, representing moral dilemmas of the privileged classes and usually focusing on their sense of vocation or emotional relationship with art. James is often unfavorably compared with French contemporaries or with HENRIK IBSEN and George Bernard Shaw, but Susan Carlson places James in "a tradition of comedies of manners at the turn of the century" (Carlson, 1985) within which James examines manners and morals in typically delicate, yet searching, depictions of social consciousness.

PLAYS: *Daisy Miller* (1882); *The American* (1890); *Tenants* (1890); *The Album* (1891); *The Reprobate* (1891); *Disengaged* (1892); *Guy Domville* (1893); *Summersoft* (1895); *The High Bid* (1907); *The Saloon* (1908); *The Other House* (1908); *The Outcry* (1909)

FURTHER READING

Carlson, Susan. *Women of Grace: James's Plays and the Comedy of Manners*. Ann Arbor: UMI Research Press, 1985.

Edel, Leon. *Henry James: The Middle Years, 1884–1894*. London: Hart-Davis, 1963.

Greenwood, Christopher. *Adapting to the Stage: Theatre and the Work of Henry James*. Aldershot: Ashgate, 2000.

James, Henry. *The Complete Plays of Henry James*. Ed. by Leon Edel. London: Hart-Davis, 1949.

——. *Parisian Sketches: Letters to the "New York Tribune," 1875–1876*. Ed. by Leon Edel and Ilse Dusoir Lind. New York: New York Univ. Press, 1957.

——. *The Scenic Art: Notes on Acting and the Drama, 1872–1901*. Ed. by Allan Wade. London: Hart-Davis, 1949.

Joanne Knowles

JAPAN

When Japan opened to the West after 1868, the country already had a thriving theater—the actor-centric and highly physicalized *kabuki*. Exposure to Western culture showed the Japanese another type of theater, and some, like TSUBOUCHI SHŌYŌ, thought *kabuki* should change. These changes were manifested in three new genres: SHIN KUBUKI peopled traditional *kabuki* plays with psychologically believable characters; SHINPA primarily depicted the new age but owed much to *kabuki*'s presentational style; and SHINGEKI took Western NATURALISM and REALISM as its dramatic models and created plays that were true to Japanese society.

Acting was a major problem for the new genres, and performance has to take place alongside sensitivity to the changing age in any survey of modern Japanese theater. KAWATAKE MOKUAMI's plays of the 1880s reflected modern technology but were written for *kabuki* actors. Tsubouchi Shōyō wrote new historical *kabuki* plays in the early 1900s that incorporated some elements of character development, but he, too, consciously utilized the *kabuki* actor's special skills. The onnagata (player of female roles) presented an impossible challenge to aspiring actresses, a problem that continued well into the 1910s. Shinpa introduced actresses, but retained the onnagata. Even early *shingeki* sometimes had men playing women.

So was *kabuki* acting to the yardstick? OSANAI KAORU and *kabuki* actor Ichikawa Sadanji II used *kabuki* actors for plays by HENRIK IBSEN and MAKSIM GORKY in their Free Theater (Jiyū Gekijō) from 1909, whereas Shōyō and *shingeki* director Simamura Hōgetsu trained amateurs for their Literary Arts Society (Bungei Kyōkai), beginning with a production of *Hamlet* in 1911. These two companies began the *shingeki* movement in earnest.

During the 1910s Nakamura Kichizō and Nagata Hideo used consciously naturalist plays to expose the conflicts produced by the new meritocratic and industrializing society. Some playwrights wrote for *shingeki* in symbolist or humanist vein, while others simply experimented with a new medium. The plays that made an impact in performance, however, were those taken up by progressive *kabuki* actors, such as TALE OF SHUZENJI (1911) by OKAMOTO KIDŌ and THE FATHER RETURNS (1920) by Kikuchi Kan. Audiences thrilled to the depiction of new interpersonal relations that transcended the dictates of the characters' social status.

Kabuki and *shinpa* were commercial theater. For every highlight, such as the two successes mentioned above, many more plays simply provided the familiarity and repetition that audiences expected as part of the theatrical experience. Other commercial enterprises started during this time: TAKARAZUKA REVUE COMPANY (which began as the Takarazuka Girls Opera and had its first public performance in 1914), with its all-female musical routines that developed into romantic extravaganzas; and Shinkikugeki (literally, "new national drama," but actually the name of just one company), in which ex-*shingeki* actors offered realistic sword fights but kept "half-a-step ahead" in the literary quality of the plays.

Some playwrights were not happy having only commercial outlets and welcomed the first contemporary European-style theater, the Tsukiji Little Theater, in 1924. However, the Tsukiji company, led by OSANAI KAORU and Hijikata Yoshi, excluded these writers and for two years concentrated exclusively on Western plays. *Shingeki* was gradually co-opted by intellectuals who brought a left-wing ideology to their work.

Expressionist playwrights such as Akita Ujaku and MURAYAMA TOMOYOSHI shifted toward a more obvious socialist message, as the proletarian drama movement progressed. Highlighting Japan's social problems of rural and urban poverty, usually by analogy to confound the censors, Murayama, Fujimori Seikichi, and other proletarian playwrights sought a new DRAMATURGY in which every line carried a political purpose. Notwithstanding some signal successes, the proletarian drama movement was forced out of existence in 1934 because its narrow Communist stance and AGITATION-PROPAGANDA format were deemed a threat by Japan's conservative masters.

The 1930s saw parallel developments in *shingeki*: a deliberately nonpolitical theater and socialist-realist drama. In 1932 a group of writers led by Kishida Kunio and Iwata Toyoo founded the magazine *Playwriting* (*Gekisaku*), which encouraged a shift back to basics in playwriting with attention to language and to complex psychological shading. This venture resulted in the founding of Literary Theater (Bungakuza) in 1938; Literary Theater still exists and—along with Haiyūza and Mingei—was one of three *shingeki* groups that dominated the genre in the 1950s and 1960s. However, the most substantial *shingeki* performances of the late 1930s were those of two (covertly) left-wing companies playing socialist-realist works by writers such as KUBO SAKAE and Hisaita Eijirō. These works eschewed overt extrapolation from single events to some grand revolutionary design and detailed their focus on social problems exacerbated by human failings. *Shin kabuki*, meanwhile, had been enriched by the trenchant dialogue of MAYAMA SEIKA, who used his historical research to achieve compelling realization of the stark choices faced by famous historical figures.

The two socialist-realist companies put up artistic resistance to 1930s militarism, but they were forced to disband in 1940. Literary Theater was allowed to continue, although the liberal view of man presented in its productions of contemporary French drama was suspect. Commercial drama—*kabuki*, *shinpa*, Takarazuka, Shinkokugeki, and the half-*kabuki*, half-*shingeki* Zenshinza (whose members joined the Japan Communist Party after the war)—were encouraged by the military authorities to continue performing. The government fostered drama of the nation (kokumingeki) plays to keep up morale, and small troupes roamed the countryside performing them. Some of the best were written by HŌJŌ HIDEJI, who became the mainstay of postwar commercial playwriting.

Literary Theater director MORIMOTO KAORU wrote *A WOMAN'S LIFE* in the last months of the war. The play recounts the story of a woman who suffered as a child because of the Sino-Japanese War and whose great personal achievements thereafter came to nothing because of World War II. *Shingeki* fans risked their lives to see it. It kept a creative light flickering until liberation for *shingeki* (but restriction for "feudal" *kabuki*) came with the Occupation. As the Japanese began to search for the values that had sustained them before militarism, KINOSHITA JUNJI caught, and reinforced, the mood of the times with his folktale plays (minwageki), especially TWILIGHT CRANE (1949). Both it and KATŌ MICHIO's poetic *Naotake* (1951) presaged different dramaturgical approaches in the 1950s, including MISHIMA YUKIO's recasting of NŌ plays and TANAKA CHIKAO's surreal HEAD OF MARY (1959) set in Nagasaki (one of many plays, by Koyama Yūshi, with the atomic bombing as a major theme).

Despite this variety, young theater people of the 1960s saw *shingeki* as a realism-bound, stultified re-creation of its prewar forebear and revolted against it. Established *shingeki* figures were ignored or rejected by the ANGURA movement. Playwright/directors like KARA JŪRŌ reintroduced the centrality of the actor's body, long subordinated to the text by *shingeki*. SATOH MAKOTO borrowed indiscriminately from other entertainment genres, including *kabuki*, in his taboo-breaking attacks on the establishment, including the emperor system. Theaters themselves were rejected: both Kara and Satoh used tents and TERAYAMA SHŪJI performed in the streets of Tokyo. Some of their generation, notably directors SUZUKI TADASHI and Ninagawa Yukio, took their brand of theater abroad. ŌTA SHŌGO found drama not in movement and sound, but in the silences that characterize much of human interaction. BETSUYAKU MINORU (and ABE KŌBŌ), in more contemplative mode, used deliberate logical absurdities to expose man's greatest anxieties.

Angura's political anger was rooted in the widespread feelings of frustration in the wake of the ultimately unsuccessful demonstrations against the 1960 Japan-U.S. Mutual Security Treaty. However, as Japan prospered in the 1970s and 1980s, the mood changed. The political radicalism of *angura* continued into the 1970s (most of its leaders are active in the twenty-first century), but the use of COMEDY to express serious social issues made an appearance, epitomized by TSUKA KŌHEI. It became usual to refer to this stream as the little theater (*shōgekijō*) movement, although the term had been used earlier in reference to *angura*. Playwrights of the 1980s, led by NODA HIDEKI and KŌKAMI SHŌJI, further developed the tendency toward less confrontational theater. Their young audiences, enjoying Japan's great prosperity, wanted to be entertained, and playwrights like WATANABE ERIKO and OHASHI YASUHIKO responded with kaleidoscopic productions full of references to contemporary youth culture, often set in a science-fiction or fantasy world. The 1980s saw a bewildering variety of theater, with multiple and rapidly changing stimulation of the senses a common method of presentation. That a reaction should set in once the economic bubble burst in 1989 was perhaps inevitable, and the "quiet theater" of dramatists such as IWAMATSU RYŌ and HIRATA ORIZA in the 1990s brought reflection, even realism, back to Japan's modern theater.

Japanese theater since 1968 has shown an inexhaustible capacity to challenge, supersede, and create. What is extraordinary about the early twenty-first century in this theater is that, alongside the very newest manifestations, almost all types of theater that have been "superseded" are still available. Such energy to create and determination to retain finally brought widespread international recognition in the 1980s and 1990s, and Japan has entered this century as a central player in global theater.

FURTHER READING

Goodman, David G. *Japanese Drama and Culture in the 1960's: Return of the Gods*. Armonk, N.Y.: M.E. Sharpe, 1988.

Japan Playwrights Association, ed. *Half a Century of Japanese Theater*. 5 vols. Tokyo: Kinokuniya, 1999.

Keene, Donald. *Dawn to the West: Japanese Literature of the Modern Era*. Vol. 2, *Poetry, Drama and Criticism*. New York: Henry Holt, 1984.

Poulton, M. Cody. *Spirits of Another Sort: The Play of Izumi Kyōka*. Ann Arbor: Center for Japanese Studies, Univ. of Michigan, 2001.

Powell, Brian. *Kabuki in Modern Japan, Mayama Seika and His Plays*. Basingstoke: Macmillan, 1990.

——. *Japan's Modern Theater: A Century of Continuity and Change*. London: Japan Library, 2003.

Rimer, J. Thomas. *Toward a Modern Japanese Theater: Kishida Kunio*. Princeton, N.J.: Princeton Univ. Press, 1974.

Rolf, Robert, et al., ed. and trans. *Alternative Japanese Drama: Ten Plays*. Honolulu: Univ. of Hawaii Press, 1992.

Brian Powell

JARRY, ALFRED (1873–1907)

Alfred Jarry was born in Laval, FRANCE, and began his career as a playwright and provocateur as a schoolboy when he entered high school in Rennes in 1888 and became friends with two brothers named Morin. Together they wrote a play titled *The Poles* (*Les polonais*), parodying an unpopular physics teacher named Hebert (nicknamed "Ebé" in the play), and produced it with marionettes. After moving to Paris to study at the Lycée Henri IV, Jarry continued to work on this piece and a sequel, which eventually became the plays *Ubu the King* (*Ubu roi*) and *Ubu the Cuckold* (*Ubu cocu*). After a medical discharge from the army, Jarry became an administrative assistant to the director Aurélien Lugné-Poë at his Théâtre de l'Oeuvre, which championed symbolist drama. Soon afterward he convinced Lugné-Poë to stage *Ubu the King* for a two-night run.

The premiere, on December 10, 1896, was directed by Lugné-Poë and featured masks and sets created by Jarry and Henri Toulouse-Lautrec, among other artists. It resulted in the most violent theatrical uproar since Victor Hugo's *Hernani* (1830). The character of Ubu had grown from a schoolboy satire to a full-scale attack on Boulevard drama, the French bourgeoisie, and European rationalism in general. He remained Jarry's most famous creation. A third play, *Ubu Enchained* (*Ubu enchaîné*, 1899), and two editions of *Ubu's Almanac* (*Almanach illustre du Père Ubu*, 1899 and 1901) followed, and Jarry increasingly incorporated the character's features, referring to himself as "Père Ubu," wearing the character's grotesque costumes, and speaking in the curious, uninflected accent he had urged the actor Firmin Gémier to use in the premiere.

Jarry's art and life seem to have been dedicated to blurring the distinction between the two. Weakened by poverty, malnutrition, alcoholism, and ether, Jarry died on November 1, 1907, in Paris.

In the theater Jarry was a fierce opponent of NATURALISM and all other middle-class models of theatrical representation. In place of the illusion of external reality, he championed exaggerated, artificial movement and voice, masks, and abstract settings to force the spectator's imagination into action. Like the symbolists, he looked for a truer reality in the realm of human consciousness; like many of them (and others, such as Edward Gordon Craig), he was fascinated with the puppet as an alternative to the acting style of stars such as Sarah Bernhardt; unlike them, Jarry grounded consciousness in the human body, looked to popular entertainment forms such as the Grand Guignol (the French equivalent of the puppet Punch), and approached his thesis from a comic standpoint.

Although his reputation had faded by the time of his early death, he became a model for succeeding generations of the AVANT-GARDE: in France he has been claimed as an influence by artists including JEAN COCTEAU, André Breton, and ANTONIN ARTAUD (who named his theater after Jarry); EUGÈNE IONESCO and the film director René Clair were among the founders of a College of Pataphysics in the late 1940s. Père Ubu has survived as a modern archetype of mindless authority for theater artists and audiences confronting repressive or inhuman experiences ranging from the atomic bomb to South African apartheid.

[*See also* Absurdism; Ubu Trilogy]

PLAYS: *Ubu the King* (*Ubu roi*, 1896); *Ubu the Cuckold* (*Ubu cocu*, unfinished during Jarry's lifetime, first published 1944); *Ubu Enchained* (*Ubu enchaîné*, 1899); *Ubu up the Hill* (*Ubu sur la butte*, revision of *Ubu roi*, 1901); *Les Silènes* (free adaptation of Christian Dietrich Grabbe's *Jest, Satire, Irony, and Deeper Significance*, first published 1926)

FURTHER READING

Esslin, Martin. *The Theatre of the Absurd*. 3rd ed. Harmondsworth: Penguin, 1980.

Innes, Christopher. *Avant Garde Theatre, 1892–1992*. London: Routledge, 1993.

Jarry, Alfred. *Selected Works of Alfred Jarry*. Ed. by Roger Shattuck and Simon Watson Taylor. New York: Grove, 1965. [Contains all of Jarry's writings on the theater.]

——. *The Ubu Plays*. Ed. by Simon Watson Taylor. New York: Grove, 1969.

——. *The Ubu Plays*. Tr. by Kenneth MacLeish. London: Nick Hern Bks., 1997.

Shattuck, Roger. *The Banquet Years: The Origins of the Avant Garde in France, 1885 to World War I*. New York: Random, 1969.

Walter Bilderback

JAZZ

There is a cruel contradiction implicit in the art form itself. . . . [T]he jazzman must lose his identity even as he finds it.

—Ralph Ellison, 1964

Jazz musicians fused European harmonies and African polyrhythms from New Orleans to Chicago during the 1910s. Initially considered a threat to democracy, jazz is now a veritable philosophy of individual freedom and community vision. To drama it has supplied decoration, titillation, subject matter, formal models, and excellent playwrights.

"Jazz Age" entertainment exploited it as a titillating emblem of decadence. Rarely was there concern with authenticity. The putatively cutting-edge dance-club setting and score of 1920's *Jim Jam Jems* shore up well-worn musical-COMEDY routines. *Out of Step* (1925) explores how, in the words of one reviewer, "the lure of syncopation" intensifies youthful "impatience with the ways of business." Jazz panic swept the West during the 1920s: Avery Hopwood's jazzy sex farces were condemned in the press, while the 1928 Vienna production of Ernst Krenek's "jazz opera" *Jonny spielt auf* was sabotaged by Austrian nationalists.

Even among modernist enthusiasts, jazz was still emblem and idiom of Western decline. T. S. ELIOT experimented with syncopated rhythms in *The Waste Land* (1922). His incomplete *Sweeney Agonistes* (1926) is arguably the first jazz drama on the modernist side. Edith Sitwell's *Façade* (1923) may precede it, if we are willing to consider it dramatic. Less world-weary, Noble Sissle and Eubie Blake's smash hit *Shuffle Along* (1921) brought jazz dance to Broadway, stardom to Florence Mills and Josephine Baker, and renewed success to James P. Johnson, Fats Waller, and others.

Jazz was also embraced as the spirit of progressive modernity. In the Soviet Union, Blue Blouse troupes set propaganda to jazz. GERTRUDE STEIN invoked it as "a something that was nothing but a difference in tempo between anybody and everybody including all those doing it and all those hearing and seeing it." Stein's use of jazz influenced Julian Beck and Judith Malina's LIVING THEATRE. Their 1959 production of JACK GELBER's *The Connection* was the first successful marriage of jazz, drama, and theater. A generation of jazzmen sat on the production, including Jackie MacLean and Archie Shepp. Joseph Chaikin, who played Leach in the play for part of its run, founded the Open Theatre in 1963 and developed "jamming," a "traveling within the rhythms" that brought the form to the theater games of Viola Spolin.

The modes and musical heroes of post–World War II jazz (John Coltrane, Dizzy Gillespie, Miles Davis, Charlie Parker, Thelonius Monk, Charles Mingus) sparked the first jazz movement in the arts, the BLACK ARTS MOVEMENT (1965–1976). Playwrights and musicians literally shared the stage, underlining the role of jazz as conceptual, critical, and formal key and marking the movement as, in Kimberly Benston's words, "a nearly total reimagining of western history and metaphysical presumption," (Benston, 2000). In *Blues People* (1963) LeRoi Jones (AMIRI BARAKA) asserts that jazz synthesizes African tradition and modernist innovation to oppose colonialism. Ben Caldwell's agit-prop play *The Job* (1968) is more pragmatic, concluding with "[o]ne of those 'black nationalist' characters" clubbing a white employment officer to death with his saxophone. ED BULLINS and Robert Macbeth's New Lafayette Theatre used jazz as ornament, structure, and attitude in *Goin' a Buffalo* (1969) and *The Electronic Nigger* (1968). Archie Shepp was musician and playwright; *Junebug Graduates Tonight* (1971) shifts dramatic modes rapidly, not unlike his music. The 1968 Chelsea Theatre production of Baraka's *Slave Ship* was scored by Shepp; *A Black Mass* (1968) by Sun Ra. Both stand as significant monuments to the effort to challenge traditional dramatic mimesis and open the form to the significatory potential available to musicians after Coltrane.

Jazz was everywhere during the Cold War, helped in part by U.S. cultural tours: It was inspiration and threat across AFRICA, lingua franca in the underground clubs of VÁCLAV HAVEL's Prague, soundtrack for Buenos Aires's Di Tella Institute. Jazz continues today in drama and theater, as heard in the work of SAM SHEPARD (*Suicide in B-flat*, 1976), AUGUST WILSON (*Ma Rainey's Black Bottom*, 1984), Thulani Davis (*X*, 1986), Aishah Rahman (*Unfinished Women Die in a No-Man's Land While a Bird Dies in a Gilded Cage*, 1977), and South African Xoli Norman

(*Hallelujah!* 2001; *Our Father, Ma's Got the Blues*, 2002). But it has also modeled the move "beyond drama" into PERFORMANCE ART and INTERCULTURALISM. At first derided, it is now celebrated as "America's music," as well a challenge to the very notion of "America."

FURTHER READING

Baraka, Imamu Amiri. *Blues People: Negro Music in White America*. New York: William Morrow, 1963.

Belgrad, Daniel. *The Culture of Spontaneity: Improvisation and the Arts in Postwar America*. Chicago: Univ. of Chicago Press, 1998.

Benston, Kimberly. *Performing Blackness: Enactments of African-American Modernism*. New York: Routledge, 2000.

DeVeaux, Scott. *The Birth of Bebop: A Social and Musical History*. Berkeley: Univ. of California Press, 1997.

Ellison, Ralph. *Shadow and Act*. New York: Random House, 1964.

MacAdams, Lewis, *Birth of the Cool: Beat, Bebop, and the American Avant-Garde*. New York: Free Press, 2001.

Rosenthal, David H. *Hard Bop: Jazz and Black Music, 1955–1965*. New York: Oxford Univ. Press, 1992.

Mike Sell

JELINEK, ELFRIEDE (1946–)

Elfriede Jelinek was born on October 20, 1946, in Mürzzuschlag, AUSTRIA. Her self-performances and literary works reflect the struggle of Austria's first post–World War II generation to construct an identity from the devastation it inherited. Like her fellow Austrian writers THOMAS BERNHARD (1931–1989) and PETER HANDKE (1942–), Jelinek set out to smash the hypocrisies of a society that tried to establish a continuity to the cultural achievements of the Hapsburg Empire.

Though Jelinek joined Austria's Communist Party in 1974 and remained a member until 1991, it is rage rather than ideology that drives her work. If anything, her Communist affiliation served to reinforce her oppositional stance toward mainstream Austrian politics. While BERTOLT BRECHT'S (1898–1956) politicized DRAMATURGY was an early model, Jelinek was much more influenced by the linguistic skepticism and critique of language that have historically distinguished Austrian thinkers and artists.

Jelinek's breakthrough play, *What Happened After Nora Left Her Husband; or, Pillars of Societies* (*Was geschah, nachdem Nora ihren Mann verlassen hatte oder Stützen der Gesellschaften*, 1977), is a Marxist-feminist sequel to HENRIK IBSEN'S (1828–1906) play PILLARS OF SOCIETY. In Jelinek's version Nora becomes a factory worker, but her liberation is the romantic illusion of a privileged woman. What counts as freedom to her constitutes drudgery for working-class women.

Like Bernhard, whom she succeeded as Austria's most prestigious scourge, Jelinek thrives on hyperbole, which she extends well beyond the speech act into over-the-top physical actions exploiting pornography with as much gusto as outrage. In her play *Clara S.: A Musical Tragedy* (*Clara S. musikalische Tragödie*, 1981), the young, piano-playing daughter of Clara Schumann (1819–1896) is fondled in full view of her father's obliging mistresses by the famous Italian writer and Benito Mussolini protégé GABRIELE D'ANNUNZIO (1863–1938). During dinner the child is discovered under the table with her head in his crotch. The romantic myth of (phallic) genius, absurdly propped up by women and Fascist fantasies, is graphically deflated by images of sexual indulgence and impotence. Female genius is accepted only in the little-girl prodigy, soon devoured by her mentor. Only the stunted child-woman remains, her sexuality exploited, her gifts ingested by her teachers.

Jelinek's own *wundergirl* biography enters most of her work. Her ambitious mother raised her to become a concert pianist. Her 1983 novel *The Piano Teacher* (*Die Klavierspielerin*) depicts the stifling relationship between a tyrannical mother and a daughter drilled to excel at the piano who ends up a spinsterish, self-mutilating piano teacher with voyeuristic obsessions and sadomasochistic fantasies that she finally acts out on a flirtatious student. Jelinek's mentally ill father haunts her mammoth performance piece *A Piece on Sports* (*Ein Sportstück*, 1998; the title also suggests "an athletic feat," an apt description of the work), in which she introduces herself as the character Elfie-Elektra. Einar Schleef's (1944–2001) seven-hour production at Vienna's Burgtheater (1988), which included a chorus of over forty actors performing several thirty- to fifty-minute nonstop speeches to strenuous physical exercises, constitutes a high point in her career as a playwright.

With increasing radicalness, Jelinek has staged language itself as the eerily undying agent in the construction of national myths and in the self-destruction of consumer society. Women play a major part in perpetuating such undying myths. The play *Illness; or, Modern Women* (*Krankheit oder moderne Frauen*, 1984) features women as the undead returning in various domesticated erotic constellations, sucking the blood even from their own children.

Over the years Jelinek has developed an intricate system, laced with puns and etymological word games, of quoting from classical texts, advertising slogans, political commentaries and propaganda, and headlines and mediaspeak. Text is texture, a complex linguistic net that can be cast around any issue: from Martin Heidegger's (1889–1976) affinity for nature and the Nazis to Austria's exploitation of tourists and fear of strangers (*Totenauberg*, 1992); from the Nazis' obsession with the perfect Aryan body to the contemporary fitness mania (*A Piece on Sports*); from Austria's most catastrophic glacier railway accident (*In the Alps* [*In den Alps*], 2002) to its spectacular dam in the same mountain range that was originally built by Adolf Hitler's slave laborers and completed after the war by foreign workers (*Das Werk*, 2002 [literally *The Plant*, also suggesting work and its product]); from Jackie Onassis to Snow White to Marilyn Monroe (*Death and the Maiden I–V*, 2002) to the Iraq War (*Bambiland*, 2003). As Jelinek has responded to topical issues with increased rapidity, the individual performance texts have become nearly indistinguishable. Though triggered by public concerns, her stage language has become almost impenetrably private, a development that has made Jelinek the darling of GERMANY's leading AVANT-GARDE directors, who see in her texts starting points for their own imagistic spectacles.

Though Jelinek has received numerous prestigious awards, it was only after Thomas Bernhard's death in 1989 that she became Austria's most prominent literary celebrity. With her knack for designer clothing, her photo shoots with exotic animals, and her razor-sharp public statements, Jelinek has constructed herself as a postmodern intellectual femme fatale. She received the Nobel Prize for Literature in 2004.

SELECT PLAYS: *What Happened After Nora Left Her Husband; or, Pillars of Societies* (*Was geschah, nachdem Nora ihren Mann verlassen hatte oder Stützen der Gesellschaften*, 1977); *Clara S.: A Musical Tragedy* (*Clara S. musikalische Tragödie*, 1981); *Burgtheater* (1982); *Illness; or, Modern Women* (*Krankheit oder Moderne Frauen*, 1984); *President Evening Breeze* (*Präsident Abendwind*, 1987); *Clouds. Home* (*Wolken.Heim*, 1988); *Death/Valley/Summit* (*Totenauberg*, 1992); *Rest Area* (*Raststätte*, 1994); *Stick, Cane, and Pole* (*Stecken, Stab und Stangl*, 1996); *he not as him* (*er nicht als er*, 1998); *A Piece on Sports* (*Ein Sportstück*, 1998); *Doesn't Matter* (*Macht nichts*, 1999); *The Farewell* (*Das Lebewohl*, 2000); *Death and the Maiden I–V* (*Der Tod und das Mädchen I–V*, 2002); *In the Alps* (*In den Alpen*, 2002); *The Plant* (*Das Werk*, 2002); *Bambiland* (2003); Ulrike Maria Stuart (2006)

FURTHER READING

Jelinek, Elfriede. *Clara S.: A Musical Tragedy*. Tr. by Kan Moulden. In *Women's Words, Women's Works: An Anthology of Contemporary Austrian Plays*, ed. by Udo Borgert. Riverside, Calif.: Ariadne Press, 2001.

——. *Totenauberg (Death/Valley/Summit)*. Tr. by Gitta Honegger. In *DramaContemporary: Germany*, ed. by Carl Weber. Baltimore: Johns Hopkins Univ. Press, 1996.

Janz, Marlies. *Elfriede Jelinek*. Stuttgart: J. B. Metzler, 1995.

Johns, Jorun B., and Katherine Arens, eds. *Elfriede Jelinek: Framed by Language*. Riverside, Calif.: Ariadne Press, 1994.

Gitta Honegger

JELLICOE, ANN (1927–)

Ann Jellicoe, born on July 15, 1927, in Middlesbrough, Yorkshire, ENGLAND, wanted to work in theater from the age of four. When she left Central Drama School, she began teaching drama students; at the same time she set up and ran the Cockpit Theatre, an experimental theater club of the pre-1956 era.

Jellicoe joined the Royal Court Theatre as a reader, then became a member of the Writers' Workshop. During that time she worked closely with Keith Johnson, and it was as a result of this collaboration that an AVANT-GARDE, improvisationally driven theater praxis was formed. Her first play, *The Sport of My Mad Mother* (1958), was a succès d'estime, a critical failure, and played to empty houses: it brought Jellicoe to prominence and became an emblem of Royal Court writers' solidarity against the uncomprehending scorn of critics used to more standard West End fare. After that she decided to write a commercial success: her next play, THE KNACK (1961), became a well-regarded film. Other plays followed: *Shelley* (1965) and *The Giveaway* (1969). However, *The Knack* and *Sport* remain her best-known works.

Her work is characterized by physicality and strength of dialogue. *The Sport of My Mad Mother* is a fantastical piece in which absurdist dialogue is mixed with physical theater; it depicts young teenage delinquents. *The Knack* is a far more technically sophisticated piece that deals with the complicated relationships in a sexual triangle; although its topic is sexual relations of the (burgeoning) 1960s, its form owes something to the romantic comedies of earlier eras.

Jellicoe was literary manager of the Royal Court (1973–1975). Upon moving to the countryside with her husband, photographer Roger Mayne, she began writing plays for local schools, leading to her Jellieplays for children (1975). The Colway Theatre Trust was founded in 1979. The community theater work that it produced was unique. It pioneered a new model of theater, in which local writers, actors, and audiences transformed their relationship by taking local themes and using local talent to produce top-quality, locally produced, professionally directed plays. Rural themes and settings attracted small-town and rural audiences.

Despite a long and varied career, there is an underlying consistency in Ann Jellicoe's work. Her career parallels the development of academic feminism: from being a pioneering woman director to being the first (and, initially, only) woman in the Writers' Workshop at the Royal Court and to the development of a community theater trust in which women's participation is encouraged, and in which many key women writers have played a prominent role. Today she says that she finds women more interesting to write about than men. "Women are what interest me." Her writing is antiliterary: she has reacted against the proscenium arch and professional tradition in postwar British theater, moving to work in contexts with people and producers that develop a new understanding of the relationship between actors and audience. Her theater theory reflects this interest; she describes the audience as a thing in itself, a collective entity with its own ways of reacting. She also has sought to bring theater into new areas, such as the rural regions, and introduce new ways of working into different countries, such as SWEDEN.

SELECT PLAYS: *The Sport of My Mad Mother* (1958); *The Knack* (1961); *Shelley* (1965); *The Giveaway* (1969)

FURTHER READING

Jellicoe, Ann. *Community Plays: How to Put Them On*. London: Methuen, 1987.

——. *The Knack; The Sport of My Mad Mother*. London: Faber, 1985.

——. *Some Unconscious Influences in the Theatre*. Cambridge: Cambridge Univ. Press, 1967.

——. *Three Jelliplays*. London: Faber, 1975.

Jüngst, Heike. *Frauengestalten und Frauenthemen bei John Arden und Margaretta D'Arcy: Mit Vergleichskapiteln zu Ann Jellicoe, Arnold Wesker, John McGrath und Caryl Churchill*. Frankfurt am Main: Peter Lang, 1996.

Snyder, L. "Learn to Play the Game: Learning and Teaching Strategies in Ann Jellicoe, *The Knack*." *Modern Drama* 37, no. 3 (1994): 451–460.

Kerry Kidd

JENKIN, LEN (1941–)

> *You know, it's a fact, and it goes to show you. You work at it, and work at it, and you get a little older and you figure out what you've bought with all that effort. You bought death. Somehow you got it backwards. It's life you been trying to buy. Death you're supposed to get for free.*
>
> —Man, *Limbo Tales*

Len Jenkin is a master of the funny-house, mythic, quintessentially American landscape. He writes a vision of America that is analogous to Nathanael West's narrative world (*Day of the Locust*), reconfigured into the dramatic form. Informed by Theater of the Absurd, his plays are typically dense multilayered concoctions in which the various outsiders, cast-offs who inhabit the American hinterland's substrata, bump into and glance off each other or pass like ships in the night. His settings are selected for their American flavors—a car on a highway at night, cheap hotels, detective agencies, and seedy diners and bars. The plays generally are episodic in structure and are long on atmosphere, one that shuttles on a continuum between film noir and Lewis Carroll. The central characters are lost souls who, having reached a dead end in their lives, find second wind by the plays' end, or, alternatively, who are careening through mad, futile quests.

At the more naturalistic end of the spectrum is a play such as *American Notes*, that is set in a cheap motel where the isolated denizens include a woman deposited there by her boyfriend who awaits his return, a down-and-out man abandoned by his wife and kids, and a semiretarded handyman called Chuckles. The deposited woman's errant boyfriend, meanwhile, is a reporter who is visiting an aberrant professor, who is obsessed and haunted by flying saucers. *American Notes* works with the imagery of human disappearance and other manifestations of the uncanny, as well as existential loneliness.

At the more far-out end of the stylistic spectrum is a play such as *My Uncle Sam*, one of Jenkin's masterpieces. The title character, "My Uncle Sam," is a purveyor of old-fashioned gag toys. He is commissioned by the woman he loves, Lila, to go on a quest to find her brother, who had stolen her share of their inheritance. It turns out that he is one of a slew of such fiancés to be sent off on the same mission, and that a group of dangerous thugs are also out there in search of Lila's brother. Sam's travels take him to all manner of wacky places, where he encounters a plethora of weird types, ultimately putting himself up against himself. In the end, when Lila, the woman he risked his life for, offers herself, he walks away from her, winding up a lonely old man in a hotel room. This surrealistic puzzle of a play works with coincidence and circularity of time.

Equally brilliant, *Dark Ride* pits a jeweler from whom a Thief has stolen a particularly special precious gem and a man who is translating the Book of the Yellow Ancestor against an optical lens grinder and a retired general, all of whose paths intersect wildly. The action culminates at a World Oculists' Convention. Here, as elsewhere, Jenkin manages to suggest the existence of a spiritual, esoteric quest, the seriousness of which his sardonic, offhanded style manages not to entirely undermine.

Somewhere in between is *Limbo Tales*, three playlets in one, which charts a Driver out on a highway driving to intercept his main squeeze before she leaves her house to intercept him. Elsewhere, an encyclopedia salesman is holed up in a motel with the voices of lost souls raining down on him. The lives in the playlets cannily intersect. With his intricate labyrinthine works, Jenkin succeeds in suggesting cosmic patterns, as well as both the grandeur and bathos of human existence. The Manager of a miniature golf course in *My Uncle Sam*, who may or may not be Lila's brother, says in self-irony about Lila's brother: "He helped me build this place. Every hole a different planet. In fact, it was his idea to have only eight holes. 'Leave out the earth,' he says. 'Too dull.'" Jenkin manages to find the invisible life lurking in the most banal terrestrial settings.

Born on April 2, 1941, in Brooklyn, New York, Len Jenkin holds a doctorate in English from Columbia University and teaches at the New York University Tisch School of the Arts. He was associate artistic director of the River Arts Repertory Company in Woodstock, New York, and has received a number of awards, including a National Endowment of the Arts grant, a Rockefeller grant, an Obie, and a Guggenheim. His plays have been widely produced at such New York theaters as the New York Shakespeare Festival and Soho Rep, as well as such venues as the Magic Theatre in San Francisco and the Mark Taper Forum in Los Angeles.

[*See also* United States, 1940–Present]

SELECT PLAYS: *Kitty Hawk* (staged 1972); *Grand American Exhibition* (staged 1973); *Mission* (staged 1975); *Gogol: A Mystery Play* (staged 1976, published 1986); *Kid Twist* (staged 1977); *The Death and Life of Jesse James* (staged 1978); *New Jerusalem* (staged 1979); *Limbo Tales* (staged 1980, published 1982); *Dark Ride* (staged 1981, published 1982); *Five of Us* (staged 1981, published 1986); *Candide; or, Optimism* (staged 1982, published 1983); *A Country Doctor* (staged 1983, published 1999); *The Birds* (staged 1984); *My Uncle Sam* (staged 1984, published 1984); *Madrigal Opera* (staged 1985); *American Notes* (staged 1986, published 1988); *A Soldier's Tale* (staged 1986); *Poor Folks Pleasure* (staged 1987); *Careless Love* (staged 1991, published 1993); *Pilgrims of the Night* (staged 1991, published 1999); *Like I Say* (staged 2003, published 1999); Margo Veil (staged 2005)

FURTHER READING

Fuchs, Elinor, and Una Chaudhuri, eds. *Land/Scape/Theater*. Ann Arbor: Univ. of Michigan Press, 2002.

Gerard, Jeremy. "Len Jenkin's Magic Ride." *Soho Weekly News* (November 17, 1981).

Stuart, Jan. "A Dreamscape from the Dark Side of America." *New York Times* (February 14, 1988).

David Paul Willinger

JEPSEN, ERLING (1956–)

We are not as straight-forward as we pretend to be. But we cling to the order we have tried to create in a world, where it is impossible to create order.

—Erling Jepsen

Danish playwright Erling Jepsen (born on May 14, 1956, in Gram) represents the province as a geographic, social, and mental area, populated by individuals who play subordinate parts in their own lives. Jepsen made his debut at the age of twenty-one in 1977 with a radio drama and has since been a full-time playwright (in 1999 he also began to write novels). Jepsen attracted great attention in 1980 with the television play *Polle-Boy Comes Home* (*Polledreng kommer hjem*), which introduced some significant themes: the fragility of average normality, the parents' wish to control the son. By the critics he was immediately proclaimed "the new Panduro" (with his television dramas Leif Panduro [1923–1977] had been almost a kind of national psychotherapist).

Jepsen's first plays involved rather absurd components. Turning to his own provincial background, Jepsen developed an increasing authenticity in dialogue, environment, and situations, narrated with an almost Ibsenian accuracy, although the menacing unpredictability of the subconscious was a permanent fellow player. Lack of understanding and grotesque expressions of callousness and insensibility often cause humorous effects in his plays. In *A Dangerous Man* (*En farlig mand*, 1987) Jepsen depicts the outsider's, the psychiatric patient's, direct and indirect challenge of benevolent normality. This theme is played out in the two radio dramas *The Trip to the Mental Hospital Sankt Hans* (*Rejsen til Sankt Hans*, 1996) and *At Sankt Hans* (*På Sankt Hans*, 1998), including a significant Oedipus motif in the tense confrontation with the father figure. The father conflict ends in tragedy in one of his most successful plays, *Muhammad Ali Never Lets You Down* (*Muhammed Ali svigter aldrig*, 1997), which takes place in a small province home the night of the fight between Cassius Clay and Joe Frazier. The fight goes wrong for Clay, as it does for the father who wants to repair the relationship with his son. In his pathetic frustration the father fakes a suicide; driven by guilt, the son actually does commit suicide.

In the plays from the late 1990s on, the dreamlike dimension, the imagination, manifests itself as a force in its own right, and Jepsen experiments more freely with the form. Thus *The Snowflake and the Eyeball* (*Snefnugget og øjeæblet*, 1999) is about normal suburban people's displacement from everyday reality. The imaginative outsider is treated in *The Man Who Asked for Permission to Be on Earth* (*Manden som bad om lov til at vææare her på jorden*, 2000), with its flowing borders between real and imagined, which even lead the main character to accept guilt because he cannot exclude that he theoretically might have committed the murder. *Anna and the Law of Gravitation* (*Anna og tyngdeloven*, 2001) is based on an actual scandal: without academic degrees a charismatic lady managed to be nominated director of an important museum of modern art. Jepsen recognizes her for her courage and creativity. The metatheatrical technique, including the author meeting his main character, and the political satire were, however, criticized for being rather schematic.

SELECT PLAYS: *The Return of Paul-boy* [television-play] (*Polledreng kommer hjem*, 1981); *A Dangerous Man* (*En farlig mand*, 1987); *A loving Transfer* [television-play] (*En kærlig omstingning*, 1994); *When it Only Comes From the Heart* (*Når bare det kommer fra hjertet*, 1995); *The Journey to Saint John's Asylum* [radio-play] (*Rejsen til Sankt Hans*, 1996); *Muhammad Ali Never Lets You Down* (*Muhammed Ali svigter aldrig*, 1997); *The Snowflake and the Eyeball* (*Snefnugget og øjeæblet*, 1999); *The Man Who Asked Permission to Stay Here on Earth* (*Manden som bad om lov til at være her på jorden*, 2000); *Anna and the Law of Gravitation* (*Anna og tyngdeloven*, 2001); *The Man from Estonia* (*Manden fra Estland*, 2004)

FURTHER READING

Bøg, Pernille. "Drama på drengen." In *Klangbund for Drama*, ed. by Bent Holm. Copenhagen: Teatervidenskab, 2002.

Branth, Janicke. Foreword to *Snefnugget og øjeæblet*, by Erling Jepsen. Gråsten: Drama, 1999.

Theil, Per, and Lise Garsdal. *Hvem der? Scener fra 90erne*. Copenhagen: Høst og Søn, 2000.

Bent Holm

THE JET OF BLOOD

Written in 1925, *The Jet of Blood* is a short play by ANTONIN ARTAUD that represents his early attempt to envision a "theater of cruelty," later articulated in *The Theater and Its Double* (originally published in 1938).

The play begins with a young man and woman solemnly declaring their love for each other, but their bliss is interrupted when the sky falls. A more grotesque scene of desire follows as a lewd knight gropes a buxom wet nurse in an attempt to recover papers filled with Swiss cheese while the nurse alludes to the incestuous nature of the relationship between the two young people. The young man reappears in search of his love and gets no help from "society," a parade of types that includes, among others, a priest, a cobbler, a judge, a bawd, and a beadle. Finally God himself gets into the act, cursing the bawd and setting her hair aflame until she bites his wrist, from which splatters a jet of blood. The wrathful deity strikes nearly everyone dead with a bolt of lightning, leaving the young man and the bawd to watch in horror as the wet nurse, now flat-chested, brings the body of the young woman on stage. The wet nurse lifts her skirts as we see "a multitude of scorpions crawl out from beneath [her] dress and swarm between her legs. Her vagina swells up, splits, and becomes transparent and glistening, like a sun." The young man and the bawd run off. The young girl gets up, dazed, and remarks: "The virgin! Ah, that's what he was looking for."

A dreamlike succession of shocking images and sudden meteorological calamities, *The Jet of Blood* is often interpreted as a "family romance," Sigmund Freud's term for the libidinal and aggressive dynamics played within the family structure. In this view, Artaud's five-page play depicts an idealistic young man's encounter with illicit desire (for his sister, the young woman); the child's need to split his or her parents into demoniac or impotent identities (the knight verses the beadle; the bawd verses the wet nurse); and the trauma of the primal scene (the wet nurse's swelling genitals). In Artaud, however, the battle lines are always cosmic; even God is at war with the forces of the flesh.

The play is also a reaction to ARMAND SALACROU's one-act *The Glass Ball* (1924), which features the characters of the young lovers, the knight, and the wet nurse and the theme of disillusionment; additionally, there are echoes of GUILLAME APOLLINAIRE's THE BREASTS OF TIRESIAS (the wet nurse's collapsing mammaries) and ALFRED JARRY (the absurdist social satire). Critics have argued to what degree *The Jet of Blood* is intended as a parody, but all agree that the piece is an early experiment in creating a theater in which "violent physical images crush and hypnotize the sensibility of the spectator . . . paroxysms will suddenly burst forth, will flare up like fires in different spots" (Artaud, *The Theater and Its Double*, 1958).

The Jet of Blood was never performed during Artaud's lifetime, although Peter Brooke staged a London production during his famous 1964 "Theater of Cruelty" season.

FURTHER READING

Artaud, Antonin. "The Jet of Blood." In *Theater of the Avant-Garde, 1890–1950: A Critical Anthology*, ed. by Bert Cardullo and Robert Knopf. New Haven: Yale Univ. Press, 2001. 373–381.

———. *The Theater and Its Double*. Tr. by Mary Caroline Richards. New York: Grove, 1958.

Barber, Stephen. *Antonin Artaud: Blows and Bombs*. London: Faber, 1993.

Cohn, Ruby. "Artaud's *Jet de sang*: Parody or Cruelty?" *Theatre Journal* 31 (1979): 312–318.

Charlotte Stoudt

JEWEL

In *Jewel*, a one-woman show written in 1987 by Canadian playwright JOAN MACLEOD, the heroine Marjorie Clifford remarks that "the best way to live that anyone had ever come up with" is with "no heart and no memory." For Marjorie, a young thirty-something woman struggling to come to terms with her own widowhood, this could not be more true.

The date is St. Valentine's Day, 1985, exactly three years to the day after the *Ocean Ranger* oil rig went down off the coast of Newfoundland, taking her husband Harry with it. The core of this play, however, is that Harry is still very much alive for her. By playing with the one-person convention, MacLeod leads us to believe that Harry is actually there listening to Marjorie. "Wanna dance?" she asks him when the radio pipes up. "C'mon, dance with me."

He has lived on for a long time in his wife. At one point she spins a tale of fooling around with a kid who drives a grain truck in the area. "Just wanting to make you jealous," she explains. However, she continues to have her most significant relationship with the one who "got through" her defenses and actually loved her—her husband.

Gradually her life unfolds. In the Peace River Valley of Alberta we see her endure "Valentines through the ages." There were Valentine cards, school dances, and sleepovers as a teenager, romances at college, and then life as a young wife. However, everything was not perfect, as her father-in-law "compliments" her on her cheeks, "all glowy and red. I like that in a woman. Looks freshly slapped."

With elegant passages of writing, MacLeod explores the helpless rage after such a tragedy and the need to assign blame, to have a sole human target on whom to concentrate the anger and exact revenge.

It comes as no surprise that MacLeod is a published poet, since *Jewel* reads as an extended lyrical poem or ballad. Steeped in lush metaphors and meaning-potentized analogies, MacLeod—who originated the role of Marjorie when actress Tantoo Cardinal withdrew "for personal reasons" days before opening night at Toronto's Tarragon Theatre—has written a fire-infused character eloquently drawn and real to the mind.

The journey of this play is the cathartic release Marjorie experiences through retelling her stages of grief and anger. By tapping into our collective sense of mourning, Marjorie reminds us that there is life after death. Finally, she takes her "jewel"—her wedding ring—off her finger and is now free to begin anew.

FURTHER READING

Hood, Sarah B., ed. "The Shape of the Playwright." *CanPlay: Playwrights Guild of Canada News Magazine* 22, no. 4 (Fall 2004).

MacLeod, Joan. *Amigo's Blue Guitar*. Burnaby: Talonbooks, 1997.

———. *The Hope Slide/Little Sister*. Burnaby: Talonbooks, 1999.

Much, Rita, and Judith Rudakoff, eds. *Fair Play: 12 Women Speak; Conversations with Canadian Playwrights*. Toronto: Simon & Pierre, 1990.

Christine L. Estima

JIN YUN (1938–)

Jin Yun (Liu Jin Yun) was born in Xiongxian in Hebei Province in 1938 and graduated from the Chinese Department of Beijing University in 1963. He worked in the countryside for sixteen years as a middle-school teacher and a party official on various levels. He became a playwright of the Beijing People's Art Theater in 1982 and was appointed its first vice president and party secretary in 1992. His familiarity with rural life in northern CHINA was reflected in his world-renowned play *The Nirvana of Gou'er Ye* (*Gou'er Ye niepan*), first premiered by the Beijing People's Art Theater in 1986 and later performed in Singapore, Hong Kong, and the United States.

Critics celebrated *The Nirvana of Gou'er Ye* as having skillfully combined Brechtian theater, Beijing-flavored plays, and expressionist, symbolist, and realist styles. The play broke with the conventional image of happy peasants grateful to Mao Zedong for emancipating them from the old society in 1949, as previously portrayed on the Maoist stage. The work depicts the broken dream of Gou'er Ye, who, during the land reform in the early 1950s, was allotted three acres of land and the arch over the gateway from the property of Qi Yongnian, the detested village landowner. Unlike other Maoist stories, however, Gou'er Ye does not give up his newly acquired land to the state later on when urged to do so. He declares: "I do not want public meetings and whatever glory it might have granted me. I only want my land, my cart, and my horse." He goes insane when his dream of owning his own land is suddenly shattered. During more than thirty years of madness that follow, Gou'er Ye lives in his dream world, in which he feeds his own horses and tills his own land, which now in reality belong to the collective. In his hallucination he talks to the ghost of Qi Yongnian, imagining himself as owning more property than Qi Yongnian had ever dreamed of.

During the economic reform in the 1980s, however, Gou'er Ye is told that he can now own his own land and horses, which cures him of his insanity. The restored Gou'er Ye, however, can never comprehend what happened in the previous thirty years, nor does he care to find out. However, to clear the ground for his son's marble factory, the arch over the gateway given him during land reform—the symbol of the old power of Qi Yongnian and of his triumph over the former landlord—is condemned for destruction. Gou'er Ye burns down the arch and leaves home to search for his own paradise, where he can be left alone with his own dreams. Gou'er Ye's two silent withdrawals into his own world erase the official rural history of the People's Republic of China that glorified the liberated peasants and cast doubt on the bountiful future promised in the post-Mao period. In this play Jin Jun effectively presents his reflections on the characteristics of Chinese peasants. Their passion for their own land illustrates their hardworking spirit, perseverance, and endurance; it also reveals their ignorance and narrow-mindedness, rooted in isolated rural environments. Theater critics also commended the outstanding performance of Lin Liankun, a well-known actor from the Beijing People's Art Theater specializing in Beijing-flavored plays. Critics agreed that Lin's contribution made the play an artistic whole and helped continue the Beijing-styled plays inherited from earlier dramatists such as LAO SHE and directors such as Jiao Juyin.

FURTHER READING

Chen, Xiaomei, *Acting the Right Part: Political Theater and Popular Drama in Contemporary China*. Honolulu: Univ. of Hawaii Press, 2002.

——, ed. *Reading the Right Text: An Anthology of Contemporary Chinese Drama*. Honolulu: Univ. of Hawaii Press, 2003.

Jin Yun. *Jin Yun juzhuo ji* [selected plays of Jin Yun]. Beijing: zhongguo lüyou chubanshe, 1993.

——. *Uncle Doggie's Nirvana* [*Gou'er Ye niepan*]. Tr. by Ying Ruocheng. In *An Oxford Anthology of Contemporary Chinese Drama*, ed. by Martha P. Y. Cheung and Jane C. C. Lai. Hong Kong: Oxford Univ. Press, 1997. 89–147.

Lin, Haipo. *Jiushi niandai zhongguo xiju yanjiu* [A critical study of Chinese drama in the 1990s]. Beijing: Beijing guangbo xueyuan chubanshe, 2002.

Pan, Ping. "Triumphant Dancing in Chains: Two Productions of Chinese Huaju Plays in the Late 1980s." *Asian Theatre Journal* 16, no.1 (Spring 1999): 107–120.

Yan, Haiping, ed. *Theater and Society: An Anthology of Contemporary Chinese Drama*. Armonk, N.Y.: M. E. Sharpe, 1998.

Xiaomei Chen

JITTERS

In *Jitters* DAVID FRENCH presents a comical and endearing look at the regional Canadian theater. The play follows the exploits of a theater company that is preparing a new play. *Jitters* highlights the insecurities of theater folk and satirizes the attitudes some Canadian theatrical types have about only revering plays that can make it in New York. It was first performed at the Tarragon Theatre in Toronto in 1979. Ironically, *Jitters* itself was popular enough to be moved to the UNITED STATES, although it never quite made it to New York.

Jitters opens on a run-through of a new play by a regional Canadian theater company. The cast will have four preview performances, and then the play will officially open. Unfortunately, the two leads do not get along at all. Jessica Logan is a seasoned actress who has been successful in the United States and is therefore revered in Canadian theatrical circles. Patrick Flanagan is a Canadian actor who has never worked in the United States. Flanagan is jealous of Logan's reputation, and the two bicker constantly. The other members of the theater company are an extremely quirky bunch as well. Tom Kent is a younger actor who has little stage experience and even less self-discipline. Phil is a longtime actor who experiences terrible bouts of stage fright and cannot seem to remember his lines. The company learns that a

New York producer and a New York critic will be in attendance on opening night, and this heightens the tension and brings out the worst in many of the cast members. The rehearsal is plagued with constant interruptions, and it eventually dissolves into pandemonium due to a mishap with a cigarette lighter.

Act 2 begins on opening night of the play as the cast is getting ready for the performance. The company is getting worried because Phil and Tom have not arrived yet. Phil shows up late with a black eye, and Tom shows up drunk. Phil gets locked in the bathroom, and Tom accidentally knocks himself out trying to get Phil out. The scene in the dressing room erupts into chaos as the curtain falls on act 2.

Act 3 takes place the following day. The cast is working on the script and getting ready for a brush-up rehearsal. They are also discussing the opening-night reviews. The local critic has raved about Phil's performance because he has mistaken Phil's inability to remember his lines for a brilliant acting choice. Unfortunately, Jessica has received the worst review. The New York critic has not yet made it to the show, however, so there is still a possibility that Jessica will receive a good notice. The critic calls and informs the director that he will be attending the performance that night. *Jitters* ends as things once again disintegrate into pandemonium.

In *Jitters* French deftly combines scenes of character COMEDY with farcical elements. The witty, humorous banter is often interspersed with interludes of broad physical comedy. Although *Jitters* has often been an audience pleaser, it has received mixed reviews from the critics. Some believe that it is a finely crafted play, while others consider it flawed since an audience must be familiar with theatrical conventions to fully appreciate all the humor contained in the piece. The play received the Floyd S. Chalmers Canadian Play Award in 1980.

[*See also* Canada]

FURTHER READING

Conolly, L. W., ed. "Jitters." In *Canadian Drama and the Critics*. Rev. ed. Vancouver: Talonbooks, 1995. 248–255.

David French. (http://www.davidfrench.net/). Accessed August 26, 2004. [David French's official website, with a biography and information about French's plays, critical reception of his works, and his most recent projects.]

Donovan, Pat. "A Play Within a Play, Just for Laughs." *Buffalo News* (April 1, 2000): C-12.

Beth A. Kattelman

JOAQUIN, NICK (1917–2004)

I realize now what impelled me to start writing was a desire to bring in the perspective, to bring in the grandfathers, to manifest roots.
—Nick Joaquin

Although Nick Joaquin was primarily a journalist, novelist, and nonfiction writer, he authored the most often produced Filipino play, *Portrait of the Artist as Filipino: An Elegy in Three Scenes*, and other scripts. He was an independent voice ready to question political authority and the fashions of the age. Rather than seeing the Filipino as subjugated by the colonial process, he sees him or her as a creative force selecting features from the colonial reality to develop something unique. He was bred in the American colonial period, and his work highlights the Hispanic past.

Joaquin was born in Manila, the PHILIPPINES, in 1917, the fifth of ten children of a cultured Hispanic lawyer. With the death of his father when Joaquin was twelve, the dream of a religious vocation was put aside for labor as a baker and then a printer. He began writing in the 1930s to give voice to the Filipino experience that was missing in that Americanized era after the U.S. accession of the islands in 1898. During the 1940s Japanese occupation the family lived hand to mouth.

His sister-in-law, Sarah K. Joaquin, had a theater troupe for which Joaquin stage-managed in the 1940s. With her encouragement he wrote *Portrait of the Artist as Filipino*, which was published and broadcast as a radio drama in 1952. The landmark production (1955) by Barangay Theatre Guild, directed by Lamberto Avellana, starred Daisy Avellana and Naty Crame Rogers. It was made into a film in 1965 and translated into Filipino (*Larawan*, 1969). Roland Tinio directed a musical version in 1994. A notable 2002 production replaced the sisters with brothers, allowing a new reading with muted homosexual implications.

The title alludes to James Joyce. The play examines the fate of the Hispanic Philippines in the onslaught of American culture and the havoc of war through the prism of a single family. The narrator stands amid the ruins of postwar Manila and, using flashbacks, reveals the experiences of a pair of sisters and their artist father who live in Intramuros, "the walled city," before World War II. Themes of cultural disintegration and dissonance are at the core of the work.

Joaquin returned to theater in the 1970s when martial law closed his *Asian-Philippines Leader*. He translated the *Complete Poems and Play of José Rizal* (1976) and wrote the play *The Beatas* (1976), which dealt with a 17th-century religious community of laywomen. Their struggle against patriarchy referred to Ferdinand Marcos's arbitrary rule. He adapted his short stories for theater: "Three Generations" became *Father and Sons* (1977), and "Summer Solstice," *Tatarin* (1978).

Named National Artist in 1976, Joaquin refused to be co-opted by the dictatorial Marcos government. As Marcos sought to create a new history that would glorify the precolonial past, Joaquin critiqued the endeavor. As radicals called for a return to Tagalog language only and searched for Asian roots in the post-Marcos period, Joaquin continued writing in English. In 1996 he received the Ramon Magsaysay Award for Journalism, which cited him for "exploring the mysteries of the Filipino body and soul in sixty years of inspired writing." He died April 29, 2004 at his home in San Juan, Metro Manila.

SELECT PLAYS: *Portrait of the Artist as Filipino* (1952, produced 1955); *The Beatas* (1976, staged 1978); *Fathers and Sons* (1977); *Tatarin* (1978); *Camino Real* (1983)

FURTHER READING

Cultural Center of the Philippines. *CCP Encyclopedia of Philippine Art.* Vol. 7, *Philippine Theater;* vol. 9, *Philippine Literature.* Manila: Cultural Center of the Philippines, 1994.

Fernandez, Doreen. *Palabas: Essays on Philippine Theatre History.* Quezon City: Ateneo de Manila Univ. Press, 1996.

——. "Philippine Theatre in English." http://www.geocities.com/icasocot/dgfernandez_theatre.html.

Lanot, Marra PL. *The Trouble with Nick, and Other Profiles.* Quezon City: Univ. of the Philippines Press, 1999.

Mojares, Resil. "Nick Joaquin Biography for the 1996 Ramon Magsaysay Award for Journalism, Literature." http://www.rmaf.org.ph/Awardees/Biography/BiographyJoaquinNic.htm.

San Juan, E., Jr. *Subversions of Desire: Prolegomena to Nick Joaquin.* Quezon City: Ateneo de Manila Univ. Press, 1988.

Kathy Foley

JOHN BULL'S OTHER ISLAND

John Bull's Other Island was written by GEORGE BERNARD SHAW in 1904 and was first performed at the Royal Court Theatre, London, in the same year. The play satirically subverts a wide spectrum of romantic stereotypes of the Irish national character and presents a fine comic portrait of the John Bullish liberal Englishman. Although it had a mixed reception from many critics in 1904, who mistook its lack of conventional plot complications for a lack of structure, it attracted a great deal of notice. Max Beerbohm, Shaw's successor as theater critic on the *Saturday Review,* countered the judgment of other contemporary reviewers by praising Shaw's effortless skill in dramatic technique in the work and his "instinct for the theatre." The British prime minister of the day, Arthur J. Balfour, saw the play no fewer than five times. On March 11, 1905, a special performance was held for King Edward VII, who is said to have laughed so heartily at the play that he broke his chair. The play had 121 performances at the Court Theatre during the Vedrenne-Barker seasons and later was greatly appreciated by audiences in Dublin, where it was first presented in 1907 at the Theatre Royal. Plans for an earlier production in Dublin—possibly as the first work to be performed at the newly founded Abbey Theatre in 1904—broke down, mostly because it was technically beyond the casting and technical resources of the new theater, and less for the reason Shaw gave in the preface that it was "uncongenial to the whole spirit of the neo-Gaelic movement." W. B. YEATS, with whom Shaw corresponded about this project, was equivocal in his pronouncements on the play.

The action begins in the London civil engineering office of the ludicrously sentimental, but jovial and effective Englishman, Broadbent, and his clever and acerbic Irish partner, Doyle, then moves to the small village of Rosscullen in IRELAND, where Broadbent has business interests. Doyle's act 1 denunciations of Ireland and exposure of a fake stage Irishman, Tim Haffigan (who is revealed to have been born in Glasgow), anticipate the subsequent intimately knowledgeable, unsentimental view of village life on the "other island." Broadbent is the subject of much merriment among the villagers, but he carries all before him with his conquest of the heart of Nora O'Reilly, his preselection for the parliamentary seat of Rosscullen, and his plans to turn the village into a Garden City with tourist attractions. His relentless materialism is countered by the philosophical and spiritual visions of Keegan, a defrocked priest whose loyalties lie with a broader conception of religion than that represented by the village's unimaginative Father Dempsey. "Every dream is a prophecy: every jest is an earnest in the womb of Time," declares Keegan after he has expressed his philosophical idea of a totally unified culture, in which conceptual divisions between human and divine, church and state, work and play are all dissolved. Autobiographical dimensions are discernible in Shaw's portrayal of all three of the main male characters, Broadbent, Doyle, and Keegan. The preface to the play includes forceful condemnation of religious bigotry and "the curse of nationalism," as well as some noteworthy reflections by Shaw on the differences between the national characteristics of the English and Irish.

[*See also* England]

FURTHER READING

Gibbs, A. M. "Light in the Celtic Gloom: *John Bull's Other Island.*" In *The Art and Mind of Shaw: Essays in Criticism.* London: Macmillan, 1983.

Grene, Nicholas. "Stage Interpreters." In *The Politics of Irish Drama.* Cambridge: Cambridge Univ. Press, 1999.

McDowell, F. P. W. "Politics, Comedy, Character and Dialectic: The Shavian World of *John Bull's Other Island.*" *PMLA,* 82, no. 2 (1967).

A. M. Gibbs

JOHN FERGUSON

Set in the farmland of County Down, IRELAND, in 1885, *John Ferguson* by ST. JOHN ERVINE is the story of a fiercely religious man's attempts to reconcile the tragedies that befall him with his faith in a higher power.

John Ferguson lives with his wife Sarah, son Andrew, and daughter Hannah on a modest farm. Once a vigorous man, Ferguson is now in poor health, which has forced him to turn over the farm to his son. As a result of Andrew's poor farming skills, Ferguson is in danger of losing the farm. Ferguson's only hope is that his brother in America will send money to pay off the mortgage held by a brutal local miller named Witherow. When no saving letter comes, all hope appears lost until James Caesar offers to supply the needed funds if Hannah will marry him. Although the salvation the marriage promises is tempting, Ferguson refuses to pressure his daughter into marrying a man she despises, even after she consents to sacrifice her happiness for the welfare of her family.

After Witherow rapes Hannah, who had gone to try and change his mind, Caesar flies into a murderous rage. Ferguson cannot prevent Caesar from going after Witherow, and Andrew refuses to try; he too wants his sister's honor avenged. Ferguson has lived with faith in God's will. "It's His work to judge, not ours!" Ferguson tells his son. The next morning Caesar returns a broken man. He was too cowardly to kill Witherow and spent the night hiding in the bushes, ashamed of his inability to act. However, word comes that Witherow is indeed dead. Caesar protests his innocence, but circumstantial evidence compels the police to arrest him, and it appears that he will be executed. When a letter arrives from America containing the money from Ferguson's brother, Hannah is bitter. "God's late, da!" she tells her father. Ferguson cannot believe that God made a mistake; there has to be a reason. His faith is profoundly shaken when Andrew confesses to Witherow's murder. Since he cannot let an innocent man suffer for his crime, Andrew will turn himself in. John begs him to save himself and not go, but Andrew is adamant. Ferguson and Sarah are left to contemplate the workings of God. The play ends with him reading aloud the Bible's account of David hearing of the death of his son: "Would God I had died for thee, O Absalom, my son . . . my son."

A realistic TRAGEDY with elements of classic MELODRAMA, *John Ferguson* featured a title character of indomitable faith. Unfortunately for Ferguson, his faith neither prepared him for the misfortunes of life nor offered him succor when he was unable to defend his family from those misfortunes. Faith for John Ferguson only served to help dull his sorrow. The play was first performed on November 30, 1915, at the Abbey Theatre in Dublin while Ervine managed the theater. After a successful run in Ireland, *John Ferguson* crossed the Atlantic and in 1919 became the first success for the New York–based THEATRE GUILD, saving the organization from bankruptcy and helping initiate its career as a major creative force in 20th-century American theater.

FURTHER READING

Eaton, Walter Pritchard. *The Theatre Guild: The First Ten Years.* Freeport, N.Y.: Bks. for Libs., 1970.

Ervine, St. John G. *John Ferguson.* In *British and American Plays, 1830–1945*, ed. by Willard Higley Durham and John W. Dodds. New York: Oxford Univ. Press, 1947. 378–423.

Hogan, Robert, Richard Burnham, and Daniel P. Poteet. *The Modern Irish Drama: A Documentary History.* Vol. 4, *The Rise of the Realists, 1910–1915.* Irish Theatre Series 10. Dublin:. Dolman Press, 1979.

Hogan, Robert, and Michael J. O'Neill, eds. *Joseph Holloway's Abbey Theatre: A Selection from His Unpublished Journal, Impressions of a Dublin Playgoer.* Carbondale: Southern Illinois Univ. Press, 1967.

Malone, Andrew E. *The Irish Drama.* London, 1929. Repr., New York: Blom, 1965.

Maxwell, D. E. S. *A Critical History of Modern Irish Drama, 1891–1980.* Cambridge: Cambridge Univ. Press, 1984.

Richard K. Tharp

JOHN GABRIEL BORKMAN

The dreamland of our lives, yes. And now it's a land of snow.
—Ella Rentheim, Act 4

The eponymous main character in *John Gabriel Borkman*, HENRIK IBSEN's second-to-last play, is generally judged as Ibsen's most despicable antihero, and the play as a whole as one of his most pessimistic works. An egoistic desire for personal wealth, power, and honor, which even leads him to betray the woman he loves, is Borkman's moral crime, which Ibsen seems not only to analyze in his dramatic laboratory, but also to condemn in the name of higher values. And yet John Gabriel Borkman belongs to those dramatic personae that never stop fascinating.

In his younger days John Gabriel Borkman was a flamboyant bank director with great powers and even greater industrial plans and visions. But he embezzled the bank's money in order to finance his plans, was caught and convicted, and spent several years in prison and eight years in total isolation on the first floor of the big house that belongs to Ella Rentheim, the woman he betrayed for her own sister, Gunhild. Ella has allowed Borkman and his wife to live there while she has taken their son, Erhart, into her care and fostered him in another part of the country. When the play opens, Ella, who is mortally ill, makes her entrance on a cold and snowy winter night with a particular aim in mind: she wants to adopt Erhart so that her name may live after her death. The struggle between the two sisters over Erhart forms the surface conflict of the play and is brutally solved when Erhart departs, together with the sensual and experienced Mrs. Wilton, for a life of presumed happiness and joy under a warmer climate. But Ella's visit has broken John Gabriel's isolation and disturbed his endless rumination over past visions of power and honor. Exploring the past in a manner typical of Ibsen, the play brings the conflict between the moral values of love and power to a climax in the final scene, in which Ella and John Gabriel have reached their favorite place high up on the hillside, overlooking the city and the fjord, and where they used to talk enthusiastically about Borkman's grandiose plans. Now this place is snowy and barren, but in a poetic and powerfully nostalgic final speech Borkman is able to express his inner dreams and aspirations once more, before a hand of ice and metal breaks his heart, as the dialogue metaphorically puts it. The curtain falls upon the two old women standing like "two shadows over the dead man."

The painter Edvard Munch once called *John Gabriel Borkman* "the most powerful snow landscape in Nordic art." The monumentality of the play is difficult to conceal, even when we agree on the moral shortcomings of its main character and conclude that Ella's severe judgment in the final scene may be Ibsen's judgment as well.

[See also Norway; Philosophy and Drama, 1860–1960; Symbolism]

FURTHER READING

Lyons, Charles R. "The Function of Dream and Reality in *John Gabriel Borkman*." *Scandinavian Studies* 45 (1973).

Madsen, Peter. "Nature's Revenge: The Dialectics of Mastering in Late Ibsen." In *Proceedings: VII International Ibsen Conference*. Oslo: Centre for Ibsen Studies, 1994.

Northam, John. "*John Gabriel Borkman* and the Swansong." *Contemporary Approaches to Ibsen* 8 (1994).

Atle Kittang

JOHNSON, GEORGIA DOUGLAS (1877–1966)

I was persuaded to try [drama] and found it a living avenue.
—Georgia Douglas Johnson

Georgia Douglas Johnson was born on September 10, 1877, in Atlanta, Georgia. She was already heralded as the "foremost woman poet of her race" in 1925 when she wrote the first of thirty plays, all realistic one-acts on racial themes, nine of which are extant. Today she is recognized as an important Harlem Renaissance figure: the leading playwright of lynching dramas, as well as other woman-centered plays; a poet who published three volumes of verses that reflect the genteel values of Victorian womanhood; a novelist and short-story writer; and a mentor and catalyst for numerous African American writers and artists of the 1920s and 1930s.

Five of Johnson's extant plays focus on lynching, particularly as it affects African American mothers. *A Sunday Morning in the South* illustrates a mother's powerlessness and the complicity of a white woman as an innocent boy is dragged from his home and lynched as hymns sound from a neighboring church. In *Safe* a young mother who witnesses a lynch-mob murder strangles her newborn son to keep him safe. The mother in *Blue-Eyed Black Boy* is able to save her son from lynching through a desperate appeal to the white governor, who is revealed to be the boy's father. All these plays were rejected by the FEDERAL THEATRE PROJECT. Two others, submitted to the National Association For the Advancement of Colored People (NAACP) in 1938, address attempts to pass an antilynching law. Both *And Yet They Paused* and *A Bill to Be Passed* include a painful description of an offstage lynching and a scene of congressional debate. In the latter play the bill is successfully passed. The public resisted facing American terrorism, and none of these plays was published or produced in Johnson's lifetime.

Johnson dealt with black history, color hierarchy, miscegenation, motherhood, and spiritualism in folk, comic, and history plays that were more palatable to her contemporaries. *Blue Blood* was awarded honorable mention in the Urban League's *Opportunity* magazine play contest, produced by the Kwigwa Players, and published in a one-act-play collection. In a comic game of one-upmanship that turns serious, two mothers brag about the high-class "blue blood" of their children, who are about to wed each other. The horrified mothers learn that the betrothed share the same white father, who raped both women. Apprised of the secret, the bride elopes with a dark-skinned suitor, and disgrace is avoided. *Plumes*, a folk TRAGEDY, won first place in the *Opportunity* contest, was produced by the Harlem Experimental Theatre, and was published all in 1927. A poor mother wonders whether to spend the fifty dollars she has saved on an operation that a money-hungry doctor cannot guarantee will save her daughter's life. Ashamed of the shabby funerals given for her husband and other child, she dreams of spending the money on a fancy funeral with plumed horses that will demonstrate her love.

Johnson's home in Washington, D.C., was a meeting place for dozens of Harlem Renaissance writers. She died there on May 14, 1966.

[See also United States]

SELECT PLAYS: *A Sunday Morning in the South* (1925); *Blue Blood* (1926); *Plumes* (1927); *Safe* (c. 1929); *Blue-Eyed Black Boy* (c. 1930); *Frederick Douglass* (c. 1935); *William and Ellen Craft* (c. 1935); *And Yet They Paused* (c. 1938); *A Bill to be Passed* (c. 1938)

FURTHER READING

Donlon, Jocelyn Hazelwood. "Georgia Douglas Johnson." In *Black Women in America: An Historical Encyclopedia*. ed. by Darlene Clark Hine. New York: Carlson Publishing, 1993. 1:640–642.

Fletcher, Winona. "From Genteel Poet to Revolutionary Playwright: Georgia Douglas Johnson." *Theatre Annual* 30 (1985): 41–64.

Hull, Gloria T. *Color, Sex and Poetry: Three Women Writers of the Harlem Renaissance*. Bloomington: Indiana Univ. Press, 1987.

McKay, Nellie. "What Were They Saying? Black Women Playwrights of the Harlem Renaissance." In *The Harlem Renaissance Re-examined*, ed. by Victor A. Kramer and Robert A. Russ. Rev. and exp. ed. Troy, N.Y.: Whitston, 1997. 151–166.

Perkins, Kathy A, and Judith L. Stephens, eds. *Strange Fruit: Plays on Lynching by American Women*. Bloomington: Indiana Univ. Press, 1998.

Stephens, Judith. "Lynching, American Theatre, and the Preservation of a Tradition." *Journal of American Drama and Theatre* 9, no. 1 (1997): 54–65.

Shauna Vey

JOHST, HANNS (1890–1978)

I am a German! . . . We Germans still don't have a national art. Culture has always stood in the way of our greatest leaders: Antiquity, the Romans, the Orient. With the passion of my entire being I aspire to an art that will become the expression of my people.
—Hanns Johst, 1920

Hanns Johst was a prolific, if somewhat limited, expressionist dramatist, poet, and novelist before dedicating himself to molding the arts in the service of National Socialist ideology. The leading Nazi dramatist, he held the highest cultural positions, including Prussian councilor of state (1933–1945), president of the Nazi Professional Literary Association (1933–1945), and president of the Academy of German Poetry (1935–1945), as well as the rank of SS brigade leader. Classified a "Mitläufer" or low-level "fellow traveler" after World War II, Johst was reclassified a "Hauptschuldiger" or major Nazi criminal after he challenged the verdict; he was incarcerated for three years and forbidden to practice his profession for ten years.

Johst was born on July 8, 1890, in Seerhausen, GERMANY. After a difficult period as a nurse in an epileptic hospital, he abandoned his goal of becoming a Lutheran missionary to study medicine and then philology and art history in Munich, Vienna, and Berlin before volunteering in World War I. His experiences became the subject of his one-act play *The Hour of Dying* (*Die Stunde der Sterbenden*, 1914). Although this play was never performed, Johst did find an outlet for his works in such leading expressionist journals as *Action* (*Aktion*), *Literary Echo* (*Das literarische Echo*), *New Program* (*Die neue Rundschau*), and *Literary World* (*Die literarische Welt*). His poems appeared in the anthology *Proclamation* (*Verkündigung*, 1921).

Johst's one-act antiwar play *Dawn: A Roguish Play* (*Morgenröte: Ein Rüpelspiel*, 1917), included in Franz Pfemfert's *Action Book 1917* (*Das Aktionsbuch 1917*), and his antiwar novella *Johann Schuster* (1915) were followed by a trilogy of generally well-received plays on the expressionist theme of the socially misunderstood individual: the ecstatic scenario *The Young Man* (*Der junge Mensch*, 1916), the nine-scene *The Lonely One: A Human Decline* (*Der Einsame: Ein Menschenuntergang*, 1917), and *The King* (*Der König*, 1920). *Der Einsame* focuses on the tragic life of the revolutionary writer Christian Dietrich Grabbe (1801–1836), whom Johst portrays as a prophet of despair. BERTOLT BRECHT used *Der Einsame* as a negative model for his parody of the expressionist sense of mission in BAAL.

Johst's embrace of the right wing after the war and his goal to create a "German" literature free of "culture" is evident in his rejection of creative experimentation in the novel *Crossroads* (*Kreuzweg*, 1922) and his glorification of nationalist values in *Knowledge and Conscience* (*Wissen und Gewissen*, 1924). The sturdy qualities of the German *Volk*, used as comedic vehicles in *Straw* (*Stroh*, 1916) and *The Foreigner* (*Der Ausländer*, 1916), become dramatic purpose in *Prophets* (*Propheten*, 1923). In *Thomas Paine* (1927) Johst perverts the legacy of the American Revolutionary War hero and author of *The Rights of Man* into a glorified Adolf Hitler-like cultural malcontent.

Johst's most infamous play, *Schlageter* (1933), glorifies Leo Albert Schlageter (1894–1923), who committed sabotage in the French-occupied Rhineland and was later captured and executed. The play was dedicated to Hitler, and at the conclusion the audience rose to sing the German national anthem and the "Horst Wessel Song" in a striking example of Nazi cult theater, which sought the seamless merging of nationalist propaganda with political action. *Schlageter* was performed throughout Nazi Germany. Johst died on November 23, 1978, in Ruhpolding, West Germany.

PLAYS: *The Hour of the Dying* (*Die Stunde der Sterbenden*, 1914); *The Foreigner* (*Der Ausländer*, 1916); *Straw* (*Stroh*, 1916); *The Young Man* (*Der junge Mensch*, 1916); *Dawn: A Roguish Play* (*Morgenröte: Ein Rüpelspiel*, 1917); *The Lonely One: A Human Decline* (*Der Einsame: Ein Menschenuntergang*, 1917); *The King* (*Der König*, 1920); *Changers and Traders* (*Wechsler und Händler*, 1923); *Prophets* (*Propheten*, 1923); *The Cheerful City* (*Die fröhliche Stadt*, 1925); Mr. Monsieur (Der Herr Monsieur, 1926), Marmelade (1926); *Thomas Paine* (1927); *Schlageter* (1933)

FURTHER READING

Gadberry, Glen W. "Dramatic Contraries: The Paine Histories of Hanns Johst and Howard Fast." In *Text and Presentation: Comparative Drama Conference Papers*, ed. by Karelisa Hartigan. Lanham, Md.: Univ. Press of America, 1989. 61–72.

Ritchie, J. M. "Johst's *Schlageter* and the End of the Weimar Republic." In *Weimar Germany: Writers and Politics*, ed. by Alan F. Bance. Edinburgh: Scottish Academic Press, 1982. 153–167.

Russell, Susan. "Masculinity Staged: Gender in Fascist and Anti-Fascist German Theater." *Journal of Dramatic Theory and Criticism* 17, no. 1 (2002): 87–106.

Christa Spreizer

JOINT STOCK THEATRE GROUP

Wanting to give each member of the touring company a full part to play in the production process, director Max Stafford-Clark, manager David Aukin, and playwright DAVID HARE founded the *Joint Stock Theatre Group England* in 1973. The founders sought greater control over their creative process, as well as a more collaborative environment for developing new plays. Soon after being founded, Joint Stock began gaining attention for its work. Its first production, *The Speakers* (1974), was able to tour thanks to a grant from the Arts Council. Notable productions include Hare's *Fanshen* (1975); HOWARD BARKER's *Victory* (1983); HOWARD BRENTON's *Epsom's Downs* (1977); CARYL CHURCHILL's *Light Shining in Buckinghamshire* (1976), CLOUD NINE (1979), and FEN (1983); Barrie Keefe's *A Mad World, My Masters* (1977); and Stephen Lowe's *The Ragged Trousered Philanthropists* (1978). With more than thirty productions, Joint Stock worked with many of Britain's leading playwrights. Through the reputation of the company's acting and the playwrights it worked with, Joint Stock gained recognition in the fringe theater movement. Facing commercial pressure, the company disbanded in 1989.

As Joint Stock began its work, the company soon discovered a unique creative process. Joint Stock found the benefit to an extended workshop period that could last three to four weeks. Each project began with an idea or theme usually proposed by the writer/director team. The company conducted research that was shared in lengthy discussion. Although the company used conventional book research, many actors also participated in field research, taking jobs that would allow them to observe everyday people. As part of the research process, the company participated in improvisational workshops that brought to life bits of their research. During this time all members of the company—actors, designers, director(s), and writer—contributed material. After this period the company usually separated while the playwright worked independently on the text of the play, shaping and structuring the material generated by the company collectively. Once the writer had put together a text, the Joint Stock process began to look more like a conventional rehearsal, albeit a longer rehearsal, as the company rehearsed the script for production. A typical timeline for a Joint Stock production included four weeks for research, a nine-week gap for the writer during which the actors were not paid, and a rehearsal period of up to seven weeks. This extensive workshop and rehearsal period allowed the actors to develop highly nuanced and developed characters, earning the company a strong reputation for its acting.

Four central principles guided how Joint Stock managed itself as a collective: those creating the work had the most say in the collective; equal pay for all; productions played as long as they rehearsed; and the tour had to be equally as long as the London run. Other issues relating to the management and operation of the company were flexible and often created tensions between the directors and the actors.

[*See also* England, 1960–Present]

FURTHER READING

Ritchie, Rob, ed. *The Joint Stock Book: The Making of a Theatre Collective*. London: Methuen, 1987.

J. Briggs Cormier

JONAH

The feeling of desperation, the sense of being trapped in a monstrous machine from which there is no escape—Nicolae Ceauşescu's ROMANIA—found its most dramatic expression in MARIN SORESCU's play *Jonah* (*Iona*). Written in 1968, at the beginning of Ceauşescu's cruel and repressive regime, the play is an allegory that reflects on more than twenty years of Communist rule that was to end only after another twenty years with the dictator's violent demise in 1989.

The play is a monologue in which Jonah, like the biblical character, is trapped in the belly of a big fish. He is desperate and hungry, but, unlike the biblical character, Sorescu's Jonah tries to keep up his spirits by conducting a philosophical discussion with his alter ego. At times in a light tone, he reflects on the human condition and how the very existence of the self is determined by invisible powers represented by the impregnable walls of this immense fish in whose belly Jonah is trapped. Moreover, unlike the biblical Jonah, he is not a rebel refusing to fulfill his mission. Sorescu's Jonah is not chosen by God to exhort his generation's transgressions. This Jonah is no more than a simple fisherman who suffered what one may consider a work accident. He is caught by the very fish he may have been trying to catch. However, he is anything but passive and tries various ways to escape. He tries unsuccessfully with his pocketknife to poke holes in the impregnable walls of the fish. He casts nets to catch fish to feed himself, and the little fish he keeps in an aquarium for his amusement. Yet all he finds in his net are dry stones—dry stones in a sea full of fish.

Sorescu's Jonah dares to think and raise questions about the human condition in a world where all questions are answered by the presumed authority of the majority. He dares to reflect on life in a world in which reflection is forbidden and futile. Time must be spent in hard work for the betterment of socialist society.

By the time Marin Sorescu wrote his play at the age of thirty-four, he was already a well-known poet who had published several volumes of poetry, some of which had earned prestigious literary awards. The play was an immediate success and has been translated into many languages, including English. Asked about symbolism in the play, Sorescu provides an answer in his preface to the published edition: "To all these questions I cannot give an answer. All I know is that I wanted to write something about a lonely man, a terribly lonely man. I believe that the most frightening moment in the play is when Jonah loses his echo. He shouts 'Jo-nah' and the echo is only responding with half of his name 'Jo-' which in another language means: I. That is all I can remember" (translation by Mosha Yassur). Jonah sees no other escape from his terrible loneliness and the oppressive stench in the bowels of the fish than by committing suicide with the very pocketknife with which he had tried to poke a hole in the wall of the fish.

FURTHER READING

Holban, Ioan. "Marin Sorescu." In *Istoria literaturii române: Portrete contemporane*. Vol. 1. Iasi: Editura Princeps Edit, 2003.
Sorescu, Marin. *Iona: Teatru*. Bucharest: Editura Fundatiei "Marin Sorescu," 2003.

Moshe Yassur

JONES, HENRY ARTHUR (1851–1929)

> *In that new world which is shaping round us will the drama sink to the level of a childish pastime, effete, inane, inoperative, contemptible, the mere toy of the unthinking crowd, or will it take its place as a recognized and honored art, with boundaries as wide, and significance as profound and immeasurable, as human life itself?*
>
> —Henry Arthur Jones, 1892

Henry Arthur Jones was an early advocate of modern English drama. With his roots in MELODRAMA, Jones nevertheless moved toward pertinent, socially conscious drama. His lectures in the

1880s and 1890s called for the development of a national drama that could be taken seriously, and although his own plays did not always reflect his ideal, he created a movement that GEORGE BERNARD SHAW was to pick up at the turn of the century, encouraging that drama be treated as literature and art, not mere entertainment.

Born in 1851 in Grandsborough, Buckinghamshire, England, Jones left school at age thirteen to work for an uncle. At age eighteen he moved to London, where he developed his affinity for the theater. He attended the theater regularly in order to learn how plays were constructed. Married to Jane Eliza Seely in 1875, Jones had his first production, *Hearts of Oak*, in Exeter in 1879.

His first success was *The Silver King* in 1882, a play mired in controversy, with collaborator Henry Herman disputing financial compensation. Jones was not proud of the play, a true melodrama with mistaken identities, a wrongly accused hero, escapes, and ultimate reunion and redemption. The characters are types and the action is predictable, but it represents a move away from melodramatic tactics, avoiding the reliance on spectacle that is a predominant trait of melodrama. It was followed by *Saints and Sinners* in 1884, a play that Jones thought was high drama but was still distinctly melodramatic. Its many stage constructs of asides and soliloquies, coupled with clear character types, place this play in the melodramatic tradition, yet the fact that it treated religion on the stage set it apart from other standard melodramas. *Michael and His Lost Angel* (1896) failed miserably both popularly and critically, yet Jones held it as one of his favorite plays. *The Case of Rebellious Susan* (1894) and *Mrs. Dane's Defence* (1900) were two of his most popular plays, dealing with morality and revolving around the sexual double standard endorsed by the Victorian mind-set. Similarly, *The Hypocrites* (1906) explores how class can exclude morality; lower classes must be held to more stringent moral standards than the upper classes. His later plays tended to move from standard melodrama to the well-made play with social consciousness.

As a nondramatic writer he wrote *Renascence of the English Drama* (1895), a collection of essays on the state of drama in England. Perhaps more influential than his plays were his crusades for dramatic literature to be accepted as literature. He worked to change the casual approach to the publication of dramatic literature in the 19th century. He insisted that an author needed to write for reading, as well as for performance. Additionally he called for both dramatists and audiences to create and demand REALISM on the stage. He encouraged sexual and religious subjects to be given a place in the English theater. In this crusade he was joined by George Bernard Shaw, with whom he developed a friendship that would fall apart with differences over World War I. Although after the war they were again friends, the relationship was henceforth tainted. Jones died in London in 1929.

Jones's plays became dated quickly, and his reputation suffered as a result. Today they seem didactic and overly moralizing. Nevertheless, he remains responsible for moving English theater forward. The combination of his own dramatic risk taking (religious and sexual themes and avoidance of spectacle) and his theoretical campaigns (calls for reform and demands for a literary drama) place Jones as a leader in the development of the modern drama.

[*See also* England, 1860–1940]

SELECT PLAYS: *Hearts of Oak; or, A Chip off the Old Block* (1879); *The Silver King* (written with Henry Herman, 1882); *Breaking a Butterfly* (with Herman, 1884); *Saints and Sinners* (1884); *The Middleman* (1889); *Judah* (1890); *The Case of Rebellious Susan* (1894); *The Masqueraders* (1894); *Michael and His Lost Angel* (1896); *The Liars* (1897); *Mrs. Dane's Defence* (1900); *The Hypocrites* (1906); *The Evangelist* (1907); *Dolly Reforming Herself* (1908)

FURTHER READING

Cordell, Richard A. *Henry Arthur Jones and the Modern Drama*. New York: Long & Smith, 1932.

Griffin, Penny. *Arthur Wing Pinero and Henry Arthur Jones*. New York: St. Martin's, 1991.

Jones, Doris Arthur. *The Life and Letters of Henry Arthur Jones*. London: Gollancz, 1930.

Lindroth, Colette. "Henry Arthur Jones." In *British Playwrights, 1880–1956: A Research and Production Sourcebook*, ed. by William W. Demastes and Katherine E. Kelly. Westport, Conn.: Greenwood Press, 1996.

Angela Courtney

JONES, LEROI *See* BARAKA, AMIRI

JONES, ROBERT EDMOND (1887–1954)

Robert Edmond Jones was born on December 12, 1887, in Milton, New Hampshire, the son of a farmer. He showed an interest in drawing and painting at an early age. At Harvard he designed scenery for student productions and discovered the work of Gordon Craig. After postgraduate study and a year of teaching he went to Europe, where he spent the 1913–1914 season as a behind-the-scenes observer at MAX REINHARDT's Deutsches Theater. Soon after his return to America he was invited to design scenery for the Stage Society's 1915 production of Anatole France's *The Man Who Married A Dumb Wife*. His simple, boldly colored set created an immediate sensation. He quickly emerged as the leading designer of the "New Stagecraft" in America, a movement that rebelled against "commercialism and traditionalism" and dedicated itself to quality drama and European-influenced staging practices.

Jones's imaginative designs and visionary ideas heralded the dawn of a new era for the American mise-en-scène. His leadership and skill helped the innovations that had swept Europe early in the century emerge from the realm of the semiprofessional "little theaters" and into the Broadway mainstream. His most innovative period came during the late 1910s and 1920s, when he collaborated on a series of plays with the producer-director Arthur Hopkins. Both men were idealistic and gifted; they were determined to establish a theatrical alternative to the long-standing tradition of elaborately realistic stagings in the manner of Herbert Tree or DAVID BELASCO. Together they sought to create productions that were, according to Jones, "more vivid, newer, more audacious, with more imaginative resources" than any that had gone before. Jones's suggestive sets, informed by the influence of Craig, Adolphe Appia, Leopold Jessner, and Freudian and Jungian psychology, evoked the essential mood of a play. For most productions he also designed lighting and costumes, and he occasionally directed. His mood-inducing settings and dramatic chiaroscuro lighting effects were with few exceptions critically well received.

Jones's designs for William Shakespeare's *Richard III* and *Hamlet*, starring John Barrymore, were among the earliest and most artistically acclaimed uses of the unit set on Broadway. *Hamlet* featured a massive flight of stairs center stage, beyond which rose a towering Gothic arch. His expressionistic settings for *Macbeth*, starring Lionel Barrymore, featured three giant silver masks above the heath and disturbingly slanted and distorted arches. A good scene, Jones later wrote, "is not a picture. It is something seen, but it is something conveyed as well: a feeling, an evocation."

Jones was closely associated with the Provincetown Players and the THEATRE GUILD. He designed a number of plays by EUGENE O'NEILL, including *ANNA CHRISTIE*, *THE HAIRY APE*, *ALL GOD'S CHILLUN GOT WINGS*, *DESIRE UNDER THE ELMS*, *MOURNING BECOMES ELECTRA*, and *THE ICEMAN COMETH*. Among his noteworthy later productions was Paul Robeson's 1943 *Othello*.

Jones's designs were widely influential in the American theater through his own work and his impact on younger designers such as Jo Mielziner and Donald Oenslager. He was also influential as a writer and lecturer. His book *The Dramatic Imagination* features many of his visionary ideas about the stage. Jones died on November 26, 1954, in Milton, New Hampshire.

[*See also* United States, 1860–1940]

FURTHER READING

Jones, Robert Edmond. *The Dramatic Imagination*. New York: Duell, Sloan & Pearce, 1941.

———. *Towards a New Theatre: The Lectures of Robert Edmond Jones*. Ed. by Delbert Unruh. New York: Limelight, 1992.

Macgowan, Kenneth, and Robert Edmond Jones. *Continental Stagecraft*. New York: Harcourt, 1922.

McDermott, Dana Sue. "The Apprenticeship of Robert Edmond Jones." *Theatre Survey* 29 (November 1988): 193–212.

———. "Creativity in the Theatre." *Theatre Journal* (May 1984): 213–230.

Pendleton, Ralph, ed. *The Theatre of Robert Edmond Jones*. Middletown, Conn.: Wesleyan Univ. Press, 1958.

Michael A. Morrison

JOURNÉE DE NOCES CHEZ LES CRO-MAGNONS

See WEDDING DAY AT THE CRO MAGNONS'

JOURNEY'S END

Journey's End is a compelling, if now somewhat dated, account of warfare, based upon playwright ROBERT CEDRIC SHERRIFF'S own experience as a captain in the East Surrey regiment during World War I. Set in a trench at Saint-Quentin, France, during a German offensive early in 1918, the play explores the relationships between a group of British officers on this exposed front line.

Sherriff uses the figure of Raleigh, a new eighteen-year-old officer fresh out of English public school, to lead the audience into the dark reality of the war. He quickly becomes a part of the animated community but just as quickly loses his schoolboy keenness and adopts a mature, necessary weariness. He joins the besieged company of his friend and cricketing hero Stanhope and finds him dramatically changed by the experience of war. Stanhope, once the quintessential gilded youth, is now wearily drowning his neuroses and his nerves in drink: as the compassionate Osborne tells Raleigh, "You mustn't expect to find him—quite the same . . . It—it tells on a man rather badly." The responsibility of leadership in this hellish place has made him tired and disillusioned; he depends on whiskey to forget anything but the present and to bolster his authority and drown his fears. While on the one hand Sherriff's characters are now recognizable types of the officers, gentlemen, and other ranks of the British war movie, on the other, they are distinguished by their all-too-human frailties.

Although the play is predicated on character study, its three-act structure reflects the increasing anxiety in the soldiers across three tension-filled days that lead, inexorably, to death and awful destruction. The play ends with a hopeless push across no-man's-land, and the audience is left with no doubt as to the futility of the loss of a generation of young men.

Rejected by London's commercial managements, *Journey's End* was picked up by the Stage Society, a group dedicated to presenting new and important plays that seemed unlikely to reach the commercial West End stages. As was typical, the new play was to be presented for just two performances—a Sunday evening and a Monday afternoon between another production and often between other engagements by the actors. *Journey's End* opened on December 9, 1928, at the Apollo Theatre in a production directed and designed by James Whale and featuring Laurence Olivier in the lead role of Stanhope. The critical response was hugely positive. Influential critic James Agate gave over his entire week's radio broadcast to the play, and its reputation was secured. The success of the initial short run by the Stage Society led to the commercial production by Maurice Browne at the Savoy Theatre in 1929 (where it ran for more than 590 performances), a hugely successful Broadway production in the same year (it ran for 485 performances), and a film version also directed by Whale in 1930.

Although touched by a whiff of MELODRAMA, *Journey's End* captured a distinctive and, at the time, unfamiliar authenticity about the wartime experience of a generation. It deals rather allusively with the homosocial aspects of contemporary English values—the public school system, the cult of sporting fairness, and the responsibilities of the "officer class"—but, above all, its clear-eyed and generally unsentimental approach to the horrors of the trenches marked it as something highly original, and it was an influential catalyst for a raft of new serious dramatic writing about the war.

While recognizing its "genuine poignancy," Stephen MacDonald (*The Guardian*, October 16, 2003) identifies one of its key problems, "its emasculated language [that] smacks too little of the St Quentin trenches in 1918 and rather too much of the West End stage in 1928." It is a fair criticism.

None of Sherriff's subsequent work achieved the remarkable and influential success of this phenomenal play.

[*See also* England, 1860–1940]

FURTHER READING

Barker, Clive, and Maggie B. Gale, eds. *British Theatre Between the Wars, 1918–1939*. Cambridge: Cambridge Univ. Press, 2000.

MacDonald, Stephen. "Journey's End" *Guardian* (October 16, 2003).

Pellizzi, Camillo. *The English Drama: The Last Great Phase*. London: Macmillan, 1935.

Sherriff, R. C. *No Leading Lady: An Autobiography*. London: Gollancz, 1968.

Adrienne Scullion

JUNE MOON

There are no hidden meanings, no complicated psychological claptrap—the play is there to be acted and enjoyed.

—Anne Kaufman Schneider, 1984

Even though the songs of the play *June Moon* were composed by RING LARDNER, the play itself was written by both Lardner and GEORGE S. KAUFMAN. Based on Lardner's short story "Some Like 'Em Cold," this COMEDY opened on October 9, 1929, at the Broadhurst Theatre and ran for 273 performances. A comedy in a prologue and three acts, set in the late 1920s, *June Moon* satirizes the songwriters and performers of New York's Tin Pan Alley, which was the popular-music-publishing center of the world from around 1885 to the 1920s. In fact, Lardner and Kaufman pay so much attention to examining the working life of Tin Pan Alley that the play loses its main focus after act 1.

The play opens with the meeting of Fred Stevens, a gullible songwriter from Schenectady, and Edna Baker, a naïve dental assistant, who are traveling in the parlor car of a train headed for New York City. From this encounter Fred and Edna begin a relationship, and Fred finds the inspiration for the title of his next song, "June Moon." In his path to success Fred encounters Paul Sears, a frustrated composer who managed to produce just a single hit in his entire career. Paul's wife, Lucille, is an ambitious "woman who expected more from life than it has given her" and whose husband cannot satisfy her constant money needs. Eileen, Lucille's younger sister, is a single and attractive girl who opens Fred's eyes to the new world of nightclubbing and fast living and eventually persuades him to get engaged to her. He leaves Edna behind.

Even though Fred seems to be content with his relationship with Eileen, he cannot stop thinking about the girl he met on the train who reminded him of his mother. Unlike Eileen, Edna not only has been the inspiration for his hit "June Moon," but she also represents the sort of girl he would like to marry. The play closes happily with the reconciliation between Fred and Edna. In *June Moon* Lardner and Kaufman "point maliciously at our June and moon rhymes while at the same time they allowed their moronic hero to have his fool's success" (Teichmann, 1972).

The way all the characters use their words is refreshing. In this respect Kaufman incorporated a technique for changing the flow of dialogue and overlapping speeches in a way that became known as the wisecrack. Even though most of the reviewers of the time praised *June Moon*, the critic for the *New York Times* (October 10, 1929) was cautious in his evaluation of the play: "After the first act the story becomes conventional and the enjoyment lies in the broadness of the comedy."

[*See also* United States, 1860–1929]

FURTHER READING

Brantley, Ben. "Revival with Contradictions: Fluff Underlaid by Sadness." *New York Times* (January 11, 1997): L11.

Canby, Vincent. "June Moon Is a Boon with Its Own Kick." *New York Times* (January 26, 1997): sec. 2, 5+.

Goldstein, Malcolm. *George S. Kaufman: His Life, His Theater*. New York: Oxford Univ. Press, 1979.

Lembke, Russell W. "The George S. Kaufman Plays as Social History." *Quarterly Journal of Speech* 33, no. 3 (1947): 341–347.

Patrick, Walton R. *Ring Lardner*. New York: Twayne, 1963.

Simon, John. "Copping Out." *New York* 30, no. 4 (1997): 49–50.

Teichmann, Howard. *George S. Kaufman: An Intimate Portrait*. New York: Atheneum, 1972.

Yardley, Jonathan. *Ring: A Biography of Ring Lardner*. New York: Random, 1977.

Estefania Olid-Peña

JUNO AND THE PAYCOCK

I ofen looked up at the sky an' assed meself the question—what is the stars, what is the stars?

—Captain Boyle, Act 1

The background to *Juno and the Paycock*, a play by SEAN O'CASEY, is the civil war in IRELAND in 1922–1923 between the Free Staters and the Republicans, or Irregulars ("Diehards"), who rejected the Treaty of 1921 granting independence to most of the country but leaving the six northern counties under British rule. The viciousness of the civil war is described in the fourth book of O'Casey's autobiography, *Inishfallen Fare Thee Well* (1949). Though the play is dominated by the character of Juno, effectively the head of the impoverished Boyle household, O'Casey's initial purpose was to focus on her son Johnny, broken by the wars since 1916. As the play opens, news is provided of the death in an ambush of Robbie Tancred, a Republican and formerly Johnny's comrade. One of the three plots centers on the mystery of who betrayed Tancred to the Free Staters, but Johnny's terror indicates his guilt. Crippled by his involvement in the fight for freedom, Johnny is a study of a man who has lost his nerve, as well as his loyalty. O'Casey points up the folly of Johnny's political sacrifice when he has Juno reply to his boast that it was all a matter of principle: "Ah, you lost your best principle, me boy, when you lost your arm; them's the only sort o' principles that's any good to a workin' man" (act 1). When the Irregulars come to take Johnny away for "questioning," that is, execution, at the end of act 2, his plea that he has done enough for Ireland is met with the chilling reply that no man can do enough for Ireland. The politics of the play indicate a modern TRAGEDY.

The other two plots deal with the domestic as opposed to the public sphere, though O'Casey, as always, expertly interlocks both. When "Captain" Jack Boyle suddenly inherits a large sum of money, the hopes of the family seem realized, and they borrow to celebrate. O'Casey's characterization is so strong that both Juno and the Captain seem universal figures: she the hard-pressed manager of the household and he the hard-drinking waster. O'Casey elevates the women in his plays to heroic status while exposing the faults and vanities of the men. While the Captain dodges work and feeds on illusions, Juno does menial work to put bread on the table. Juno emerges as the real head of the family, and when she eventually decides to leave the Captain, O'Casey challenges conventional morality and asserts women's rights. At this point her unmarried daughter Mary is pregnant, and Juno makes her decision when the Captain fails to appreciate Mary's position. For the most part the audience is invited to find the Captain hilariously entertaining, and his association with the parasitic Joxer Daly, while providing a form of male bonding against family responsibilities, creates some of the best scenes in the play. But there is a sense also in which the Captain is judged and found wanting. In the party scene in act 2 he shows total indifference to the sufferings of Mrs. Tancred and all the other mothers in the tenement who have lost men in the civil war. His sublime apathy can be a means of getting an audience to understand the need to care. That lesson has to be borne in mind if the final scene of the play is to convey more than the same laughter evoked earlier by the antics of Joxer and the Captain.

Comic creation though he is, then, Captain Boyle betrays the family. When the will turns out to be a "washout" and no money is forthcoming, the Captain refuses to face reality and buries himself in fantasies of his own past. Betrayal is also at the heart of the third plot, involving Mary's seduction and abandonment by the schoolteacher Bentham, just as betrayal is obviously the key to Johnny's tragedy. Commonplace as Mary's story is, O'Casey provides it with a tragic outline reminiscent of HENRIK IBSEN's plays. In the opening stage directions she is described as a woman at the mercy of two conflicting forces, her environment and her innate determination to fulfill her potential. It is no accident that Ibsen's plays are among the books she is reading, though her father tosses them aside as children's books. In Bentham's rival, Jerry Devine, we see also the Ibsenist theme of failure of love, as when Mary admits her pregnancy, he is revealed as shallow and conventional. Thus O'Casey takes Ibsenist NATURALISM and transforms it into Irish TRAGICOMEDY. The result is a masterpiece.

FURTHER READING

Ayling, Ronald, ed. *O'Casey: The Dublin Trilogy; A Casebook*. London: Macmillan, 1985.

Kearney, Colbert. *The Glamour of Grammar: Orality and Politics and the Emergence of Sean O'Casey*. Westport, Conn.: Greenwood Press, 2000.

Malone, Maureen. *The Plays of Sean O'Casey*. Carbondale: Southern Illinois Univ. Press, 1969.

Murray, Christopher. *Sean O'Casey*. A Faber Critical Guide. London: Faber, 2000.

Scrimgeour, James R. *Sean O'Casey*. Boston: Twayne, 1978.

Christopher Murray

K

KAISER, GEORG (1878–1945)

The poet shows a way. He reveals the possibilities of a new humanity. The others must walk this path, must understand these possibilities.

—Georg Kaiser, 1921

Georg Kaiser has been characterized as "the leading dramatist of German EXPRESSIONISM (Koenigsgarten, 1939)," although only a small part of his large dramatic output (he wrote over seventy plays) belongs to that category. Born on November 25, 1878, in the provincial city of Magdeburg, GERMANY, the fifth of six sons, Georg Kaiser disappointed his bourgeois family by his lack of interest in formal study. Leaving secondary school after the tenth grade, he became an apprentice in the book trade. In 1899 he sailed to Buenos Aires, ARGENTINA, where he worked as a clerk in the office of a German firm, while in his free time he read the works of Arthur Schopenhauer, FRIEDRICH NIETZSCHE, and Feodor Dostoevsky. He returned to Germany in poor health in 1901, claiming that he had contracted malaria. However, medical records show that he was treated in a Berlin sanatorium for a nervous breakdown. During the following seven years of convalescence Kaiser remained financially dependent on his parents and brothers, but at this time he defined his life's goal to become a dramatist. His early literary attempts were TRAGEDIES in the style of GERHART HAUPTMANN's naturalist plays, as well as COMEDIES and social satires influenced by FRANK WEDEKIND and CARL STERNHEIM.

Marriage in 1908 to the daughter of a wealthy merchant enabled Kaiser to live comfortably for about ten years and to finance private printings of his early plays. Although the staging of two expressionist plays in 1917, *The Burghers of Calais* (*Die Bürger von Calais*) and *FROM MORNING TO MIDNIGHT* (*Von Morgens bis Mitternachts*), finally brought Kaiser recognition, he was unable to cover his debts. Forced to sell his property, he moved with his wife and three young children to a furnished house. Under financial pressure, Kaiser and his wife pawned furniture and art objects belonging to their landlords. Before the owners could reclaim the objects, Kaiser and his wife were arrested, convicted of embezzlement, and briefly imprisoned (1920–1921). In the national press the Kaiser affair quickly became a political scandal: conservative critics who had objected to Kaiser's pacifist views and his alleged socialist sympathies used the incident to dismiss him and the entire modern movement in the arts as hopelessly decadent. Turning his back on a society that had humiliated him, Kaiser lived with his family in isolation at his country home in the village of Grünheide near Berlin. Even as his stage successes multiplied in Germany and abroad during the 1920s and 1930s, he refused to attend the performances of his plays, claiming that the reception of his works by the public did not concern him. The popularity of his plays increased after he moved from expressionist tragedies to write comedies and musical plays in collaboration with composers such as Kurt Weill. Kaiser's status as one of Germany's most performed playwrights changed suddenly after 1933, when the Nazis accused him of "cultural Bolshevism" and forbade the publication and performance of his works. However, Kaiser's decision to leave Germany and his family in 1938 was motivated by personal reasons as well: he was joined in Swiss exile by his mistress Maria von Mühlfeld and their daughter Olivia (born in 1927). Until his death on June 4, 1945, in Ascona, SWITZERLAND, Kaiser continued to write plays, most of which were first published in a postwar, six-volume edition of his collected works. Although his dramas experienced only a short-lived revival on German-speaking stages after World War II, literary scholars accord him a significant position in the development of German drama.

Kaiser's important dramas can be grouped into three types: expressionist plays, comedies/musicals, and antifascist plays. His expressionist works established his reputation as a theatrical innovator. Kaiser based *The Burghers of Calais* on a historical event—the siege of the French city of Calais by the English under Edward III in 1347—in order to send a pacifist message to Germans in the midst of war. Eustache de Saint-Pierre and six other prominent citizens of Calais volunteer to die as hostages so that the city and its harbor might be spared. The controversy surrounding the play has centered on one main concern: whether Saint-Pierre's suicide at the end is the symbolic birth of a saintly "New Man," or whether it represents flawed ethical values. In *From Morning to Midnight* an unnamed cashier embezzles a large sum of money and tries to make up in one day all that his conformist life has lacked. Kaiser's reputation as a social critic is based for the most part on his two *Gas* dramas. The protagonist of *Gas I* (1917/1918), an unnamed Billionaire-Son, tries to use the wealth inherited from his capitalist father to save humanity from the destructive effects of technology. He proposes to his workers that they return to a simple, agrarian existence. Tragically, his opponent, the Engineer, persuades the workers to continue the technological race for world supremacy. In *Gas II* (1918/1919) his grandson, the Billionaire-Worker, again tries and fails to rally the masses to his idealistic cause; he is unable to prevent total warfare that leads to the annihilation of the human race. In these two plays Kaiser presents many of the issues that confront modern civilization: obsession with technical progress, exploitation and alienation of labor, socialist reforms, totalitarianism, and militarism. If for "gas" we substitute the word "atom," as Ernst Schürer (1971) has suggested, Kaiser's vision appears remarkably prophetic. Critics such as Bernhard Diebold (*Der Denkspieler Georg Kaiser*, 1924) recognized Kaiser's expressionist plays as technical masterpieces: dramas with calculated structures, rapid tempos, abstract figures, antithetical symbolism, and an appeal to the intellect that reflects the "modern, American Age of the Machine." Diebold coined the term *Denkspieler* (player with ideas) to describe what he saw as Kaiser's lack of ideological commitment, reflected in the absence of solutions to the problems portrayed.

The most frequently performed of Kaiser's plays were the comedies and musicals that he wrote after his release from prison. *Colportage* (*Kolportage*, 1923/1924) is a satire on class society, a story of mixed identities and stock characters: a count's son is exchanged for the son of a beggar; a wealthy American idealist trumps the arrogant European aristocrats. In collaboration with the composer Kurt Weill, Kaiser wrote a number of successful musical dramas: *The Protagonist* (*Der Protagonist*, 1920), the one-act comic opera *The Czar Has His Picture Taken* (*Der Zar läßt sich photographieren*, 1927), and *Silver Lake* (*Der Silbersee*, 1932). The most substantial of these, *Der Silbersee*, subtitled *A Winter's Tale in Three Acts*, reveals Kaiser's antifascist views, but his message is that of idealistic self-renewal and brotherhood, rather than political engagement.

Kaiser's increasingly pessimistic view of human nature, compounded by the rise of fascism, led him to write a number of plays that question the causes of militarism and political fanaticism. *The Leatherheads* (*Die Lederköpfe*, 1927/1928) uses expressionist pathos to condemn tyranny and warfare. It is based on the conquest of Babylon by the Persian king Darius as recounted by Herodotus. Zopyrus, an ambitious general serving Darius, mutilates himself so horribly that he must wear a leather mask to conceal his face. Zopyrus's mask symbolizes the loss of humanity through the fanaticism of war. In Swiss exile Kaiser wrote another antiwar play, this time with a contemporary Japanese setting: *Private Tanaka* (*Der Soldat Tanaka*, 1940). When Tanaka, a war hero, returns home on a visit, he learns that his parents had been forced to sell his sister to a brothel in order to pay the taxes. Humiliated and enraged, Tanaka kills both his sister and the sergeant who had asked for her sexual services. Though condemned to death, Tanaka does not plead for mercy; rather, he demands that the emperor apologize to him. The play ends with the sounds of his execution. With *Tanaka* Kaiser expressed faith in ordinary people to stand up for the truth when they realize that their leaders have betrayed them. However, in one of his last plays, *The Raft of the Medusa* (*Das Floß der Medusa*, 1942), Kaiser expressed his bitter disillusionment with human nature. The plot is based on a wartime disaster: Allan, the leader of thirteen refugee children lost at sea in a lifeboat, tries to lift their spirits and encourages cooperation to ensure that all will survive. His opponent, Ann, however, driven by superstitious fear, convinces the children to sacrifice the youngest one, because thirteen is a "bad omen." In a development reminiscent of William Golding's *Lord of the Flies*, the children reveal that the forces of humanism and civilization are powerless against the primitive fear, hatred, and hunger for power that drive human beings to kill one another.

Kaiser is important for the development of 20th-century drama, and for BERTOLT BRECHT'S EPIC THEATER in particular, because Kaiser turned away from an aesthetic of empathy and catharsis to one of rational participation by the spectators. His plays intend to stimulate thought by shaking the spectators out of their lethargy, by not giving them answers. This intellectual orientation is the common basis of both Kaiser's and Brecht's theoretical positions.

SELECT PLAYS: *David and Goliath* (*David und Goliath*, 1905/1906); *The Ghost Comes Home* (*Der mutige Seefahrer*, 1910); *From Morning to Midnight* (*Von Morgens bis Mitternachts*, 1912); *The Burghers of Calais* (*Die Bürger von Calais*, 1912/1913); *The Coral* (*Die Koralle*, 1916/1917); *The Fire in the Opera House* (*Der Brand im Opernhaus*, 1917–1918); *Gas I* (*Gas*, 1917–1918); *Alcibiades Saved* (*Der gerettete Alkibiades*, 1917/1919); *Gas II* (*Gas: Zweiter Teil*, 1918/1919); *The Protagonist* (*Der Protagonist*, 1920, music by Kurt Weill); *The Flight to Venice* (*Die Flucht nach Venedig*, 1922); *Side by Side* (*Nebeneinander*, 1923); *Colportage*, (*Kolportage* 1923/1924); *The Czar Has His Picture Taken: A Farcical Opera in One Act* (*Der Zar läßt sich photographieren: Opera buffa in einem Akt*, 1927, music by Kurt Weill); *One Day in October* (*Oktobertag*, 1927); *The President* (*Der Präsident*, 1927); *The Leatherheads* (*Die Lederköpfe*, 1927/1928); *Two Neckties* (*Zwei Krawatten*, 1929, music by Mischa Spoliansky); *Silver Lake: A Winter's Tale in Three Acts* (*Der Silbersee: Ein Wintermärchen in drei Akten*, 1932, music by Kurt Weill); *Private Tanaka* (*Der Soldat Tanaka*, 1940); *Raft of the Medusa* (*Das Floss der Medusa*, 1942)

FURTHER READING

Arnold, Armin, ed. *Georg Kaiser*. Stuttgart: Klett, 1980.

Benson, Renate. *German Expressionist Drama: Ernst Toller and Georg Kaiser*. London: Macmillan, 1984.

Diebold, Bernhard. *Der Denkspieler Georg Kaiser*. Frankfurt: Frankfurter Verlags-Anatalt, 1924.

Koenigsgarten, Hugo F. "Georg Kaiser: The Leading Playwright of Expressionism." Tr. by Cedric Hentschel. *German Life and Letters* 3 (3), 1939: 195–205.

Pausch, Holger A. and Ernest Reinhold, eds. *Georg Kaiser: Eine Aufsatzsammlung nach rínem Symposium in Edmonton/Kanada*. Berlin: Agora, 1980.

Schürer, Ernst. *Georg Kaiser*. New York: Twayne, 1971.

Shaw, Leroy R. *The Playwright and Historical Change: Dramatic Strategies in Brecht, Hauptmann, Kaiser, and Wedekind*. Madison: Univ. of Wisconsin Press, 1970.

Willeke, Audrone B. *Georg Kaiser and the Critics: A Profile of Expressionism's Leading Playwright*. Columbia, S.C.: Camden House, 1995.

Audrone B. Willeke

KALISKY, RENÉ (1936–1981)

Belgian playwright, essayist, and television scenarist René Kalisky was born in 1936 in Brussels of Polish Jewish immigrants; his father perished in Auschwitz. He married Mechthild Bäke, a German-born sculptor whose father had been a prosperous Nazi. Kalisky's theater was published in toto by the distinguished Parisian publisher Gallimard, a unique distinction for an as yet unknown playwright. Productions then followed. Kalisky was awarded the coveted Belgian Triennial Award Prize for Drama in 1975. All ten of his plays were written in the last twelve years of his life; he died of cancer in Paris in 1981.

Kalisky addressed his keen intellect to the problem of how to write for the theater in a way that went beyond BERTOLT BRECHT's distancing effect and LUIGI PIRANDELLO's theatricalism, both of which he admired but felt had led to a dead end. He thus devised and attempted to apply his theory of "Super-Play and Super-Text," which evidently posited a secondary level of action over the text. In *The Passion According to Pier Paolo Pasolini* (*Le passion selon Pier Paolo Pasolini*, 1977), therefore, actors represent characters in the movies of the Italian cineast Pier Paolo Pasolini, reenact fragments from the films, quote from them, and quarrel among themselves over the films' value. Kalisky manipulates a kind of theatrical time that can telescope, go in reverse, or simply rise above passing time to a still point.

Kalisky typically used a famous historical or literary character as a focal point, although in three cases, *Aida Defeated* (*Aïda vaincue*, 1982), *Jim the Lionhearted* (*Jim le téméraire*, 1972), and *Falsch* (1983), the principal characters he deployed were taken from his own family.

In the didactic *Trotsky, Etc.* (1969), he breaks stage reality into three parts, alternating scenes of torture of Trotsky's supposed followers in Russia with those of Trotsky and his wife in Mexico before his assassination, and finally an imaginary trial of Trotsky (as opposed to Josef Stalin's show trials) where judges condemn him for his transgressions, notably the slaughter of the sailors at Kronstadt. *Skandalon* (1970), written as a radio play, is about the cyclist Fausto Coppi and alternates scenes of action with choric passages that rise to a relentless, thumping rhythm. His most playable (and most conventional) play, *On the Ruins of Carthage* (*Sur les ruines de Carthage*, 1980), has only three characters, two of whom are specialists in the field of ancient Carthaginian history who engage in a dialectical dispute over their respective rights to a university seat based on their radically different approaches to history (the third character is a young female urchin who is amanuensis to one of the historians). In effect, it is a combat between the old, humanistic point of view and the bloodless "new man." In this case the "Super-Play" is the additional level of metaphor, in that the modern-day historians are reenacting the antique struggle between Romans and Carthaginians in which the North African civilization ultimately went up in smoke, suggesting the cyclic and repetitive nature of history.

Kalisky was fascinated by World War II, which marked his entire life, leading him to write *The Picnic of Claretta* (*Le pique-nique de Claretta*, 1973), a theme and variations on Benito Mussolini's life. It also provides the context for Kalisky's most powerful work, *Jim the Lionhearted*. In this play of towering poetry and great originality he pits a character resembling his own brother Jim, who had been transformed into something like an idiot savant by the experience of the war, against an Adolf Hitler whom Jim calls up in imagination, befriends, and sees through to his debacle, in the role of the despot's companion. It is indicative of Kalisky's audacity that he dramatizes an obscure Jew, even in imagination, having an intense fascination for Hitler that borders on admiration, whom Hitler then accepts as a trusted adviser. In this respect Jim reveals a masochistic adoration for his tormentor. Using his antinaturalistic method, Kalisky evokes a dream/memory space that allows for scenes of narrow intimacy alternating with those that disgorge lofty political and racial proposals and the seamy, pseudomystical underpinnings of National Socialism. The play oscillates between expressionistic distortion and character-based farce. In this irreverent vision he flies in the face of most other versions of the Holocaust that have been put forth thus far.

The play in which his theory of supertext is most successfully integrated concerns another Old Testament story, that of David and Saul. Although *Dave on the Beach* (*Dave au bord de mer*, 1977) seems to be about a rich Israeli real estate speculator and his family picnicking on the beach, to be visited by the interloper, Dave, freshly arrived from Brooklyn, United States, the characters periodically pierce through to the biblical layer, a time frame that is always simultaneously available for them to enter. The real estate man, Saul, is attempting to change the outcome of the story and win where the biblical David did, but fails in his project.

[*See also* Belgium]

PLAYS: *Trotsky, Etc.* (1969); *Skandalon* (1970); *Jim the Lionhearted* (*Jim le téméraire*, 1972); *The Picnic of Claretta* (*Le pique-nique de Claretta*, 1973); *Dave on the Beach* (*Dave au bord de mer*, 1977); *The Passion According to Pier Paolo Pasolini* (*Le passion selon Pier Paolo Pasolini*, 1977); *Aida Defeated* (*Aïda Vaincue*, 1980); *On the Ruins of Carthage* (*Sur les Ruines de Carthage*, 1980); *Europa* (1988); *Falsch* (1991)

FURTHER READING

Glasheen, Anne-Marie, ed. "Four Belgian Playwrights." *Gambit* 42–43 (1986).

Willinger, David. "Belgium." *Western European Stages*. Vol. 13, no. 1. (Winter 2001).

——, ed. *An Anthology of Contemporary Belgian Plays, 1970–1982*. Troy, N.Y.: Whitston, 1984.

David Paul Willinger

KALLOL See THE WAVE

KAMBANELLIS, IAKOVOS (1922–)

Fifty years of playwriting and a large number of widely successful plays allow Iakovos Kambanellis to be named the father of postwar Greek drama. Born on an island between the two world wars, he lived his early years in indigence and hard work. During World War II he was arrested by the Nazis and in 1943 was sent to the concentration camp in Mauthausen, where he stayed imprisoned until the end of the war. When he returned to Athens, fascinated by the modernist attempts at Karolos Koun's Theatron Technis (Art Theater), he turned to playwriting. His drama *Dance on the Wheats* (*Horos pano sta stahia*), the first to be performed by a small AVANT-GARDE company in 1950, is a poetic allegory influenced by FEDERICO GARCÍA LORCA's lyrical style. His experiences of the German atrocities and the agonies of the postwar world provided the material for his subsequent plays *Odysseus, Return Home* (*Odyssea gyrna spiti*) and *Our Father the War* (*O mpampas o polemos*), both acerbic critiques of warfare and its absurdity, as well as innovative dramatic efforts. Parody and satire remained in his dramatic quiver, but it was later in the 1950s and under the influence of American REALISM that Kambanellis produced his most significant plays, which, moreover, fostered developments in Greek theater. In pieces such as *The Seventh Day of Creation* (*Evdomi mera tis dimiourgias*), *The Courtyard of Miracles* (*I avli ton thavmaton*), and *The Age of Night* (*I ilikia tis nyhtas*), his heroes' enduring dilemmas and psychological discrepancies are embedded in the deadlocks, the segregation and turmoil, and the civil war inherited by Greek society. Winners and losers entrapped in an atmosphere of suspicion and despair watch their dreams fading in a gloomy daily routine. Through the depiction of everyday life and the portrayal of characters from different social classes and political convictions, Kambanellis filled the need for a modern Greek drama that would speak to contemporary audiences and would renegotiate the imperatives of patriotism, ideology, and brotherhood. The staging of these dramas by Koun at his Art Theater added to the plays' popularity and granted the playwright acceptance and recognition.

The political upheaval and the military dictatorship in 1967 forced Kambanellis to use satire and music in spectacles such as *Our Big Circus* (*To megalo mas tsirko*) to veil his sharp political hints against the repression of the junta. The return of democracy in 1974 did not eradicate his interest in political developments and their impact on Greek society. However, the growing stability allowed Kambanellis to focus on the manners and beliefs that had, after all these changes, prevailed and to discuss the alterations in traditional social structures and codes of behavior. The transition from collective memory to individual experience and complex personal relations is better exemplified in the plays written in the 1990s, especially *In Ibsen Land* (*Sti hora Ibsen*) and *Last Act* (*I teleutaia praxi*). Furthermore, these last efforts manifest Kambanellis's intention to comment not only on recent history and a constantly changing reality but also on the nature of writing and the dramatist's role in the construction of such a reality.

[*See also* Greece]

SELECT PLAYS: *Dance on the Wheats* (*Horos pano sta stahia*, 1950); *The Seventh Day of Creation* (*Evdomi mera tis dimiourgias*, 1956); *The Courtyard of Miracles* (*I avli ton thavmaton*, 1957); *The Age of Night* (*I ilikia tis nyhtas*, 1959); *An Unnamed Tale* (*Paramythi horis onoma*, 1959); *The Angel's Neighborhood* (*I geitonia ton aggelon*, 1963); *Odysseus, Return Home* (*Odyssea gyrise spiti*, 1966); *Viva Aspasia* (1966); *Our Big Circus* (*To megalo mas tsirko*, 1973); *The Table's Four Legs* (*Ta tessera podia tou trapesiou*, 1978); *Our Father the War* (*O mpampas o polemos*, 1980); *The Invisible Group* (*O aoratos thiasos*, 1988); *The Road Is Crossing By* (*O dromos perna apo messa*, 1990); *In Ibsen Land* (*Sti hora Ibsen*, 1996); *Last Act* (*I teleutaia praxi*, 1997)

FURTHER READING

Kalaitzi, Glykeria. "O dramatourgos tis metapolemikis peripeteias" [The dramatist of the postwar adventure]. *Theatrika Tetradia* 25 (March 1995): 19–29.

Kambanellis, Iakovos. *Theatro* [Plays]. 7 vols. Athens: Kedros, 1978–1998.

Pephanis, Giorgos. *Iakovos Kambanellis: Diadromes se megali hora* [Iakovos Kambanellis: Routes in a great land]. Athens: Kedros, 2000.

Tsatsoulis, Dimitris. "Iakovos Kambanellis. The Patriarch of Post-War Greek Theatre." *Ithaca* 9 (May–June 2001): 19–21.

Ioulia Pipinia

KANE, SARAH (1971–1999)

Sarah Kane, initially vilified by the press because of the violence of her first play, BLASTED, was later credited with heralding a new era of confrontational, innovative playwriting in England and with writing one of the most important British plays of the 1990s.

Kane was born on February 3, 1971, in Brentwood, in suburban Essex County, east of London. She grew up in a Kelvedon Hatch evangelical Christian household. At seventeen she rejected her family's religion, though biblical allusions tinge her writing.

In 1989 she enrolled in the B.A. program in drama at Bristol University. There she acted in and directed a number of works, including plays by William Shakespeare, SAMUEL BECKETT, HOWARD BARKER, and CARYL CHURCHILL, before graduating in 1992 with a first-class honors degree. In the fall of 1992 she enrolled in the M.A. program in playwriting at Birmingham University, but left before completing the degree. Birmingham nonetheless propelled her trajectory as a writer: there she wrote the first act of *Blasted*. In March 1994 she moved to London, where she became a literary associate at the Bush Theatre, reading a profusion of new scripts while finishing what would prove to be her most important work.

Kane's debut on January 18, 1995, the press night for *Blasted*, was surely one of the most notorious in recent theater history. *Blasted* ignited a firestorm in the press that raged for months as many critics decried the graphic violence that erupted in the play's Leeds hotel room, ravaging its three characters, the stage space, and audience complacency.

The furor over *Blasted* was never matched in Kane's tragically brief career, but neither was it forgotten. In May 1996 *Phaedra's Love*, Kane's audacious improvisation on Seneca, premiered at the Gate Theatre under Kane's own direction, but reviewers relished the opportunity to revisit *Blasted*. Though more critics now saw reason to praise her, others continued to launch attacks. Perhaps reacting to this hostility, Kane used the pseudonym Marie Kelvedon for the March 1997 reading of the poetic and allusive four-hander, *Crave*. That same year controversy swirled again when the television screening time for her short film, *Skin*, was changed from 9:30 P.M. to 11:35 P.M. because of the programmers' squeamishness about the film's confrontation with racism and violence.

When *Cleansed*, a meditation on institutional atrocities and the need for love, opened at the Royal Court Theatre Downstairs in April 1998, Kane faced the public quite literally when she took over the role of Grace, replacing an injured actress. The year 1998 also saw the premiere of *Crave*. When it toured, Kane took the stage in Maastricht, playing the role of C.

Losing her fierce battle with depression, Kane committed suicide in King's College Hospital, London, on February 20, 1999.

If Kane's work was not given astute attention in England because of the shock of her images when they first challenged audiences in the mid-1990s, at the turn of the century the desire to psychoanalyze her and her plays would prove equally detrimental to rigorous and balanced criticism, as was the case with the posthumous premiere of *4:48 Psychosis* in June 2000. In 2001 the Royal Court devoted the season to Kane, opening the possibility that her work might be viewed in England with the same discernment that it had been enjoying in Europe since it first exploded on the English stage.

[*See also* England; Postmodernism]

PLAYS: *Blasted* (1995); *Phaedra's Love* (1996); *Cleansed* (1998); *Crave* (1998); *4:48 Psychosis* (2000)

FURTHER READING

Rebellato, Dan. "Sarah Kane: An Appreciation." *New Theatre Quarterly* 15, no. 3 (August 1999): 280–281.

Sellar, Tom. "Truth and Dare: Sarah Kane's *Blasted*." *Theater* 27, no. 1 (1996): 29–34.

Sierz, Aleks. *In-Yer-Face Theatre: British Drama Today*. London: Faber, 2001.

Urban, Ken. "The Ethics of Catastrophe: The Theatre of Sarah Kane." *PAJ: A Journal of Performance and Art* 23, no. 3 (September 2001): 36–46.

Leslie Durham

KANIN, GARSON (1912–1999)

The word is playwright—W-R-I-G-H-T—like wheelwright. A play is not so much written as wrought. It's designed and built and shaped; it's carved out.
—Garson Kanin

Garson Kanin was born on November 24, 1912, in Rochester, New York, and began his long career in the theater during the Great Depression. Unlike many who suffered the effects of the Depression, Kanin found work as an actor on Broadway. But it was his role as assistant to the legendary producer, director, and writer George Abbott that led to his lifelong career in the theater. Kanin recognized Abbott's enormous talents and dedicated himself to learning from him. After a brief and frustrating period in Hollywood as a director, Kanin returned to Broadway in 1948 as the playwright of the classic COMEDY *Born Yesterday*. The play captures the wit and insight that are evident in all of Kanin's work and is one of the most successful American theater comedies ever written. Telling the story of Harry Crock, a tycoon who hires a journalist to educate his dim mistress, Kanin's play takes a uniquely American spin on GEORGE BERNARD SHAW'S *PYGMALION*. The play weaves political and social satire within the framework of a traditional love story. Keen wit and dark themes intertwine in this critically successful play. Kanin adapted his drama for a highly successful 1950 film version, which won an Academy Award for Judy Holliday.

Kanin wrote a series of collaborative screenplays with his wife, actress Ruth Gordon, including the comedies *Adam's Rib* (1950) and *Pat and Mike* (1953). Kanin's plays include *The Rat Race* (1949), *The Smile of the World* (1949), *Come On Strong* (1962), and *A Gift of Time* (1962). *The Rat Race* tells a story of a young woman in despair in New York who meets an optimistic saxophone player from the Midwest. Critics celebrated *Come On Strong* as a chilling and engrossing story of the inner workings of show business. In 1956 he directed the Broadway debut of the moving Holocaust drama *The Diary of Anne Frank*, which was nominated for a Tony Award. Steeped in research, Kanin's version of the story about a young girl who lives hidden in an attic with her family to escape capture by the Nazis is written not merely as a tragedy, but also as a tale of bravery and the resilience of the human spirit. Kanin also served as director of ROBERT E. SHERWOOD'S Pulitzer Prize–winning drama *IDIOT'S DELIGHT* and the musical *Funny Girl*, based on the life of comedienne Fanny Brice. In 1961 Kanin received two Tony Award nominations for the musical *Do Re Mi*. The musical, which tells of the adventures of the luckless Hughie Cram, was adapted from Kanin's novella of the same name and ran for over 400 performances on Broadway.

With a libretto by Kanin, music by Jule Styne, and lyrics by the acclaimed team of Betty Comden and Adolph Green, the show achieved a success that marked yet another example of Kanin's skill as a collaborator. In total, Kanin was involved in more than thirty Broadway productions. He also authored fourteen novels and numerous articles and short stories. Kanin died on March 13, 1999, in New York City.

[*See also* United States, 1929-Present]

PLAYS: *Born Yesterday* (1946); *The Rat Race* (1949); *The Smile of the World* (1949); *The Live Wire* (1950); *Do Re Mi* (1960); *The Good Soup* (1960); *Come On Strong* (1962); *A Gift of Time* (1962); *Remembering Mr. Maugham* (1966); *Dreyfus in Rehearsal* (1974); *Peccadillo* (1985); *Happy Ending* (1989)

FURTHER READING

Kanin, Garson. *Hollywood*. New York: Viking, 1974.

——. *It Takes a Long Time to Become Young*. Garden City, N.Y.: Doubleday, 1978.

Ellen Anthony-Moore and Christopher Moore

KAPAI-KAPAI *See* MOTHS

KARA JŪRŌ (1940–)

Kara Jūrō is a Japanese playwright and director and one of the leading figures in the ANGURA AND SHŌGEKIJŌ theater movement of the 1960s. Kara's drama searched for new forms. As a socialist, Kara in his plays resisted establishment governmental, social, and cultural programs that he felt were perpetuating JAPAN's militaristic past. Growing up in Asakusa, the entertainment district of old Tokyo, Kara was influenced by *kabuki* and turned to some of its scenic elements, such as the *hanamichi* walkway, and acting techniques such as cross-gender performance to engage more fully with the spectator, revive a sense of theatrical play, and privilege the body of the actor. In 1963 Kara founded the Situation Group (Shichueishon no Kai), which later became the Situation Theatre (Jōkyō Gekijō). In 1967 the company began performing in a red tent. In 1969 Kara won the Kishida Kunio Drama Prize for his play THE VIRGIN'S MASK.

One type of place where Kara set up the red tent was the grounds of Shinto shrines. Performing at a shrine recalled an actor's onetime religious function, as well as wartime manipulation of Shinto and the emperor system for nationalistic purposes. Performing a play critical of Japan's wartime actions, such as *The Virgin's Mask*, at a Shinto shrine raised uncomfortable questions for many Japanese. Furthermore, Kara drew on the premodern outcaste status of actors, labeled "riverbed beggars," as resistance against the established theatrical practices of SHINGEKI. Using a tent allowed actors and their performances to escape the boundaries of conventional social and theatrical behavior. The mobile tent also created theatrically exciting moments. For example, with the tent on the bank of a pond, the back wall could open directly onto the water for actors to make entrances and exits.

The Situation Theatre, like many of the characters in Kara's plays, was nomadic. The company toured overseas in the 1970s, while the characters often wander in search of identity.

Characters in *The Virgin's Mask* are "beggars for a body." In *John Silver, the Beggar of Love* (1970) the characters want physical love and a meaningful social existence. The characters search for a messianic figure to replace the emperor and lost wartime identity. In *The Vampire Princess* (1972) and *Matasaburō of the Winds: Kara Version* (1974), the characters wander in search of their past. In *The Vampire Princess* corpses of aborted babies represent the past, while in *Matasaburō of the Winds* it is puppetlike fighter pilots. In both plays blood represents an inescapable cultural and political heritage.

As early as 1979 other troupes were performing Kara's plays in venues other than the red tent. In that year the Seventh Sick Ward (Dainan Byōtō) produced *Two Women*, a play about Japan's loss of traditional cultural anchors. The Situation Theatre was officially disbanded in 1987, but Kara continues to use the red tent in producing new plays with Kara Group (Karagumi).

SELECT PLAYS: *John Silver* (*Jon Shirubaa*, 1965); *Pettycoat Osen* (*Harumaki Osen*, 1967); *The Virgin's Mask* (*Shōjo kamen*, 1969); *John Silver, the Beggar of Love* (*Jon Shirubaa, ai no kojiki*, 1970); *Vampire Princess* (*Kyūketsuki*, 1971); *A Tale of Two Cities* (*Nitō monogatari*, 1972); *Bengal Tiger* (*Bengaru no tora*, 1973); *Matasaburō of the Winds: Kara Version* (*Kara-ban kaze no Matasaburō*, 1974); *The Phantom Salesman* (*Maboroshii no seerusuman*, 1974); *Seeing-Eye Dog* (*Mōdō-ken*, 1974); *Kara's Exercises for Actors* (*Kara-ban haiyū shūgyō*, 1977); *Princess Snake* (*Hebihime-sama*, 1977); *Two Women* (*Futari no onna*, 1979); *The Golden Bat* (*Ōgon bato*, 1981); *The Secret Garden* (*Himitsu no hanazono*, 1982); *Jenny the Wanderer* (*Sasurai no Jenii*, 1988); *The Grave of the Music Box* (*Orugōru no haka*, 1992)

FURTHER READING

Goodman, David. *Japanese Drama and Culture in the 1960's: The Return of the Gods*. Armonk, N.Y.: M. E. Sharpe, 1988.

Kara Jūrō. *Tokkenteki nikutai ron* [The Privileged Body Theory]. Tokyo: Hakusuisha, 1997.

——. *Waga seishun furōden*. [Confessions of my vagrant youth]. Authors' Autobiographies 20. Tokyo: Nihon Zusho Sentaa, 1994.

Ortolani, Benito. *The Japanese Theatre: From Shamanistic Ritual to Contemporary Pluralism*. Rev. ed. Princeton, N.J.: Princeton Univ. Press, 1995.

Powell, Brian. *Japan's Modern Theatre: A Century of Change and Continuity*. London: Japan Library, 2002.

Rolf, Robert T., and John K. Gillespie, trs. and eds. *Alternative Japanese Drama: Ten Plays*. Honolulu: Univ. of Hawaii Press, 1992.

John D. Swain

KARNAD, GIRISH (1938–)

> *My generation was the first to come of age after India became independent of British rule. It therefore had to face a situation in which tensions implicit until then had come out in the open and demanded to be resolved without apologia or self-justification: tensions between the cultural past of the country and its colonial past, between the attractions of Western modes of thought and our own traditions, and finally between the various visions of the future that opened up once the common cause of political freedom was achieved. This is the historical context that gave rise to my plays and those of my contemporaries.*
>
> —Girish Karnad, 1994

Girish Karnad was born on May, 19, 1938, in Matheran, near Mumbai, INDIA. He wrote his first play, *Yayati* (named after a character in the epic *Mahabharata*) in 1961 during a crisis brought on by his first trip abroad: an identity crisis in which, through the very act of going to England to study, Karnad felt that he had to choose between a future in England and a future in India. King Yayati is cursed for a moral transgression: he is transformed into an old man while still fairly young. Yayati persuades one of his sons to trade places with him, but for the son old age brings neither knowledge nor wisdom—it is simply punishment for an act he did not commit. "[L]ooking back," Karnad writes, "I am amazed at how precisely the myth reflected my anxieties at that moment, my resentment with all those who seemed to demand that I sacrifice my future" by returning home to India. Although the theme of the play came from an Indian story, Karnad felt forced to use a Western dramaturgical structure—which he had learned from HENRIK IBSEN and JEAN ANOUILH—because there was, according to him, "no dramatic structure in [his] own [modern theatrical] tradition to which [he] could relate." In an attempt to find an indigenous structural model for his work, Karnad turned to traditional Indian performance.

Karnad's second play, TUGHLAQ (named after Sultan Muhammad bin Tughlaq, 1964), made him famous, but it was with his third play, *The One with the Horse's Head* (HAYAVADANA, 1971) that he was able to bring together an Indian story with a dramaturgical structure adapted from traditional Indian performance. Karnad has said that "the basic concern of the Indian theater in the post-independence period has been to try to define its 'Indianness.'" *Hayavadana* is one of the first modern Indian plays using traditional performance to receive national attention. It established Karnad as one of India's most important playwrights because it provided a model for decolonizing Indian theater. Noted theater scholar Suresh Awasthi has hailed *Hayavadana* as a play that "reversed the colonial course of contemporary theatre" (Awasthi, 1989).

In *Play with a Cobra* (*Naga-Mandala*, 1988) Karnad continues to use traditional performance in order to make strong political and social statements about contemporary life by weaving together two folktales that deal with the position of women in a patriarchal society. Because these are women's tales, told in domestic contexts, Karnad notes that they "express a distinctly woman's understanding of the reality around her" (Karnad, 1994), which is reflected and given voice in the play. Karnad is one of the first people to use women's folktales as the basis for a play.

Death by Beheading (*Tale-Danda*, 1989) focuses on a movement which promoted equality and neutralized caste and gender discrimination and was quashed by Hindu fanatics. Karnad uses the 12th-century story to comment on the rise of Hindu fundamentalism in India in the 1980s.

Karnad has said, "The energy of folk theatre comes from the fact that although it seems to uphold traditional values, it also has the means of questioning those values" (Karnad, 1994). *The Fire and the Rain* (*Agni Mattu Male*, 1993) opens with an elaborate *yajna*, a fire sacrifice intended to preserve the world from physical and moral chaos. However, the moment after he presents this Brahminic ritual, Karnad begins to turn it upside down: this is not a reverent play espousing Brahmin ideals. On the contrary, *The Fire and the Rain* exposes the hypocrisy and brutality of Brahmin priests and the failure of religion. On a personal level it reveals the ways in which jealousy can destroy a family—and, by extension, an entire community and the cosmos itself.

Karnad's plays often begin with a ritual that changes the spectators' relationship to what they see on stage. For example, *Hayavadana* begins with a *puja* (literally, sacred offering) to Ganesh, the presiding deity of performance. Although it is always performed as a reference to a ritual, Karnad intended the Ganesh *puja* to be an actual *puja*, and several spectators, used to seeing a Ganesh *puja* at the beginning of a performance, responded to it as such. If it functions as an actual *puja*, then Karnad begins a play with a ritual offering to a *murthi*, or manifestation of a deity. Ganesh appears not as a character, or a representation of a deity, but as the deity himself. Consequently Karnad plays with the way some spectators perceive, interpret, and relate to the levels of "reality" on stage. Theater is, in many situations, about temporarily transforming "as if" into "is" in the mind of the spectator: theater presents a situation "as if" it is real, and spectators suspend their disbelief and respond to it as real—always knowing that they are actively involved in the transformation process. When Karnad begins *Hayavadana* by presenting Ganesh himself, he begins an "as if" experience with an "is." Thus the play is seen through the real(ity) that the ritual brings to the stage. In other words, when Karnad conflates the two systems spectators have to deal with the real ("as if" and "is"), he changes the way spectators expect to engage with the play, thereby changing the spectators' relationship to what they see. In *The Fire and the Rain* Indra (god of the firmament, a personification of the atmosphere, and lord of the rains) appears in several forms as part of the *yajna*. At one level he is a mythological figure. At another level he appears as a character within the play.

And at another level he is a *murthi*. By placing Indra onstage in the context of a staged ritual, Karnad has asked his spectators to practice "complex seeing," or seeing that simultaneously acknowledges several different realities. He then asks spectators to apply complex seeing—and complex thinking—to everything they see.

Tughlaq and *Hayavadana* have become landmarks of modern Indian theater. Karnad's plays have been translated into many languages and are performed in theaters and colleges all over India and abroad. He has received many awards, including the Sangeet Natak Akademi Award, the Natya Sangha, and the Bharatiya Jnanpith, India's highest literary award.

PLAYS: *Yayati* (1961); *Tughlaq* (1964); *The One With The Horse's Head* (*Hayavadana*, 1971); *Play With A Cobra* (*Naga-Mandala*, 1988); *The Fire and The Rain* (*Agni Mattu Male*, 1993); *The Dreams of Tipu Sultan* (2000); *Bali: The Sacrifice* (2002); *Macaulay's Children*

FURTHER READING

Awasthi, Suresh. " 'Theatre of Roots': Encounter with Tradition." *TDR* 33, no. 4 (1989): 48–69.

Karnad, Girish. "The Arts and Social Change in India." In *Indian Culture in Motion*. Amsterdam: Royal Tropical Institute, 1998.

——. *Collected Plays*. 2 vols. New Delhi: Oxford Univ. Press, 2005.

——. *Three Plays*. Delhi: Oxford Univ. Press, 1994.

Mukherjee, Tutun, ed. *Girish Karnad's Plays: Performance and Critical Perspectives*. New Delhi: Pencraft International, 2006.

Erin B. Mee

KARVAŠ, PETER (1920–1999)

On the contrary, any attempt to fix and canonize knowledge on theatre, on its origin and its development, any attempt to consider certain rules of theatre production the only correct, definite and unshakable ones, would lead to the blind alley of idleness.
—Peter Karvaš, 1948

Peter Karvaš, one of the most important Slovak writers, whose plays have been translated into seventeen languages, was a pioneering theorist of drama and theater and a professor at the Academy of Music and Dramatic Arts in Bratislava.

Karvaš was born on April 25, 1920, in Banská Bystrica, in the Czechoslovak Republic. After the occupation of Bohemia by the Nazis, Karvaš had to abandon his studies in Prague and return to SLOVAKIA. There he worked as a photographer, editor, and DRAMATURG until he was briefly interned in a labor camp because of his Jewish origin. He participated in the Slovak National Uprising in 1944; his parents were murdered by the Nazis. After the reunification of CZECHOSLOVAKIA in 1945 he finished his studies at Comenius University in Bratislava. He was one of the leading dramatists during the first twenty years of the Communist era in Czechoslovakia. In the period of "normalization" after the Soviet invasion in 1968, he was prevented from participating in public life, although the ban was not total. He died on November 28, 1999, in Bratislava, Slovakia.

Karvaš first attracted attention with his early existentially tuned novels and short stories, *There Are No Ports* (*Niet prístavov*, 1946) and *Low-Voiced* (*Polohlasom*, 1947). His play *People from Our Street* (*Ludia z našej ulice*, 1950) documents his gradual acceptance of Communist ideology, but in *A Scar* (*Jazva*, 1963) he criticizes the recent past, the cult of personality, and the abuse of power. His sharp sense of humor appears in his comic sketches and satires *A Book of Relieve* (*Kniha úl'avy*, 1970) and *In the Nest* (*V hniezde*, 1981), by many considered to be the apex of his prose.

In his best work for the theater—he was also a major writer for radio, television, and film—Karvaš effectively combined rational construction of the narrative with convincing characters, and a moral dimension with emotional intensity. Themes of pretense and abuse of power dominate *A Big Wig* (*Vel'ká parochňa*, 1964). Manipulation of the public and people's fear of the authorities reach a high point in ABSOLUTE PROHIBITION (*Absolútny zákaz*, 1969). In *Midnight Mass* (*Polnočná omša*, 1959) Karvaš presents the model situation of a bourgeois family, engaged in Aryan racial policies and collaboration with a clergy-controlled fascist regime. To save lives and property, the family has to sacrifice their youngest son, who is a partisan. In *Antigona and the Others* (*Antigona a tí druhí*, 1961) the classic story is set in a concentration camp before the end of the war. A small group of Communists tries to organize a revolt and bury their comrade despite a prohibition. Gradually they die in an unsuccessful fight with fascist oppression. Karvaš depicts the relations of the individual to the authorities in an overwhelming existential situation that reveals the human being's failure but also his ability to preserve his honor. In his most valuable theoretical work, *Introduction to the Basic Problems of Theater* (*Úvod do základných problémov divadla*, 1948), Karvaš deals with the sociology and aesthetics of theater, the development of dramatic structure, and the spectator's psychology from a structuralist position.

PLAYS: *A Lighthouse* (*Maják*, 1944); *Meteor* (1945); *Union for Five "P"* (*Spolok pre piatich "P"*, 1945); *A Play About a Poet* (*Hra o básnikovi*, 1946); *Hannibal in Front of Gates* (*Hanibal pred bránami*, 1947); *A Bastion* (*Bašta*, 1948); *A Return to Life* (*Návrat do života*, 1948); *People from Our Street* (*L'udia z našej ulice*, 1950); *Heart Full of Joy* (*Srdce plné radosti*, 1953); *Patient One Hundred Thirteen* (*Pacient stotrinásť*, 1955); *Diplomats* (*Diplomati*, 1958); *Midnight Mass* (*Polnočná omša*, 1959); *Grandfather Koloman's Resurrection* (*Zmŕtvychvstanie deduška Kolomana*, 1960); *Antigona and the Others* (*Antigona a tí druhí*, 1961); *A Scar* (*Jazva*, 1963); *A Big Wig* (*Vel'ká parochňa*, 1964); *Experiment Damokles* (1967); *Absolute Prohibition* (*Absolútny zákaz*, 1968); *The Twentieth Night* (*Dvadsiata noc*, 1971); *A Private Party* (*Súkromná oslava*, 1986); *The Backyard Door* (*Zadný vchod*, 1987); *A Foggy Morning* (*Hmlisté ráno*, 1987); *Heaven Hell* (*Nebo peklo*, 1987); *A Night Visit* (*Nočná návšteva*, 1987); *Zero Hour* (*Nultá hodina*, 1987); *Patriots from the Town Yo* (*Vlastenci z mesta Yo*, 1988)

FURTHER READING

Blaho, Jaroslav, and Andrej Mat'ašík. "Slovak Republic." "In Vol. 1. *The World Encyclopedia of Contemporary Theatre*. Ed. by Don Rubin. With Regional editors Péter Nasy and Philippe Rouyer. New York: Routledge, 1994.

Darovec, Peter. "Peter Karvaš." In *Portréty slovenských spisovatel'ov* [Portraits of Slovak writers], ed. by Ján Zambor. Vol. 1. Bratislava: Univerzita Komenského, 1998.

Hradileková, Katarina, ed. *Prozaický svet Petra Karvaša* [Prosaic world of Peter Karvaš]. Bratislava: Literárne informačné centrum, 2000.

Krnová, Kristína, ed. *Osobnosť a dielo Petra Karvaša* [Personality and Work of Peter Karvaš]. Banská Bystrica: Univerzita Mateja Bela, 1992.

Lajcha, Ladislav. *Dramatický svet Petra Karvaša* [Dramatic world of Peter Karvaš]. Bratislava: Národné divadelné centrum, 1995.

Juraj Sebesta

KASPAR

It is not true that the conditions are as they are represented; on the contrary, it is true that the conditions are different from their representation.

—The "Prompters"

Kaspar, PETER HANDKE's first full-length play, is a philosophically well-informed investigation into language and convention. It owes its name to Kaspar Hauser, a historical figure said to have turned up mysteriously in Nuremberg in 1828, unable to say anything except his name and the sentence "I want to become a horseman like my father once was." Similarities between the historical Kaspar and Handke's character, however, extend little further than their names (in his preface to the play Handke states that he has no intention of simply retelling Hauser's story), because the play is much more concerned with the dynamics of language acquisition.

Described by Handke as a kind of "speech torture," *Kaspar* details the way in which language acquisition—particularly through the processes of speaking and being spoken to—may influence both spatial and social orders. To this end, Handke's work follows the single protagonist, Kaspar, as he is introduced to a world that is in many ways a linguistic production. Early in the play one finds Kaspar repeating the sentence "I want to be a person like somebody else once was" while moving awkwardly around the stage. Disembodied voices—or "Einsager" ("prompters")—soon interrupt this recitation to give Kaspar words for the things around him, while adding that one can take comfort in words that relate directly to objects. Shortly thereafter Kaspar becomes silent, but eventually submits to the linguistic rules the "prompters" provide. As he becomes increasingly comfortable with language, as well as with the "prompters'" prescriptions for social behavior, a quintet of ill-behaved Kaspar-like figures appears on stage, signaling a loss of individuality. Kaspar's language acquisition is then made to seem more anxiety-provoking than reassuring, in part because he senses a separation between words and their referents, but also because his experience of the world becomes limited by the sentences provided for him.

Further emphasizing the way in which the individual can be made to correspond with the conventional, the printed text itself takes on a noticeably unusual format, consisting of two columns of text running side by side. Kaspar's lines appear in the left-hand column; the lines for the "prompters" are printed to the right. Handke's extensive stage directions appear in both columns.

Kaspar was first performed in May 1968 at both the Theater am Turm in Frankfurt and the Städtische Bühne in Oberhausen. At that time a particularly acute wave of political disturbance—including robberies, terrorist bombings, and assassination attempts—was developing in West GERMANY, and there can be little doubt that the reception of Handke's play was influenced at least in part by the social events that were taking place alongside it. To be sure, with its investigation of the relationship between language and social rule following, *Kaspar* was by nearly all accounts a success. It won Handke the well-respected GERHART HAUPTMANN Prize and, in addition to being named Play of the Year by the journal *Theater heute* (Theater Today), eventually led critic Jack Kroll to declare Handke "the hottest young playwright in Europe." Considered a major literary achievement, *Kaspar* was the most frequently produced play in Germany, AUSTRIA, and SWITZERLAND during the 1968–1969 season.

[*See also* Avant-Garde Drama]

FURTHER READING

Hill, Linda. "Obscurantism and Verbal Resistance in Handke's *Kaspar*." *Germanic Review* 52 (1977): 304–315.

Klinkowitz, Jerome, and James Knowlton. *Peter Handke and the Postmodern Transformation*. Columbia: Univ. of Missouri Press, 1983.

Nägele, Rainer. "Das Unbehagen in der Sprache: Zu Peter Handkes *Kaspar*" [Language and its discontents: On Peter Handke's *Kaspar*]. *Basis* 6 (1976): 78–96.

Read, Malcolm. "Peter Handke's *Kaspar* and the Power of Negative Thinking." *Forum of Modern Languages* 29, no. 2 (1993): 126–148.

Andrea Brewer

KATŌ MICHIO (1918–1953)

Katō Michio, Japanese novelist, SHINGEKI playwright, critic, director, and scenario writer, while not a prolific playwright for the stage, is remembered for one play, *Nayotake*, which offered something new to *shingeki* in the early years after World War II. Katō was an active writer for radio and a well-known translator of JEAN GIRAUDOUX, WILLIAM SAROYAN, ALBERT CAMUS, and JEAN-PAUL SARTRE. He cut his own life short by hanging himself.

Born into an academic family, Katō studied English literature, majoring in William Shakespeare and Ben Jonson, at Keiō University and continued with graduate work, which included learning ancient Greek. He drafted *Nayotake* (his first play) toward the end of the war and left it in JAPAN as a literary testament when he was sent (in 1944) to New Guinea as an interpreter. While he was away, established literary figures such as Kishida Kunio and Iwata Toyoo read *Nayotake* and were very impressed with it as a piece of dramatic literature. Strangely, it was taken up by *kabuki* actors first in 1951 (by Onoe Kikugorō VI's company) and was only performed by the Literary Theatre (Bungakuza), the *shingeki* company to which Katō had belonged, in 1955, two years after his death.

Nayotake, as literature and in performance, thrilled with its celebration of youth and pure love. The story of Fumimaro, the young nobleman who may have been the author of the 10th-century fable *The Tale of the Bamboo Cutter* (*Taketori monogatari*), the play charts his hopeless love for the maiden Nayotake, who is the daughter of a worker in bamboo. A wicked minister who had schemed to have Fumimaro's father sent far from the capital, snatches Nayotake from him and puts her beyond his reach. Fumimaro wanders disconsolate through a misty bamboo grove and sees her as a phantom, a princess born from a bamboo, who is carried off by a messenger from the moon. Fumimaro sets off for the uncivilized east of Japan, where he writes the story of the bamboo cutter's daughter.

Katō used several dramaturgical devices that in combination made this play memorable in *shingeki* history: an evocative classical language, a consistent poetic tone, and some choral speaking. To Japanese audiences in the bleak postwar period, a hero whose dream is dashed in the real world but who finds fulfillment within himself seemed to have an admixture of tragedy, fantasy, and hope to which they could respond deeply. *Nayotake* was revived at Japan's New National Theater (2000) under the direction of Kimura Kōichi, one of Japan's foremost *shingeki* directors. Other plays, though interesting and innovative in themselves, have not fared as well. Katō's antiwar play *Episode: A Tropical Fantasy* was written in 1948 and premiered in 1949, but it is in 1953 that the narrator (a military interpreter in the South Seas, as Katō was) is speaking about his experiences just before the end of the war. Katō Michio's brief flash of creative brilliance in Japanese theater led Kishida Kunio to comment on his suicide in 1953 that his colleagues would for years continue to see him in a corner of the green room.

SELECT PLAYS: *Episode: A Tropical Fantasy* (*Episo-do*, 1948); *Nayotake* (1951); *Rags and Jewels* (*Boro to hōseki*, 1952)

FURTHER READING

Asai Kiyoshi et al., eds. *Shin kenkyū shiryō, gendai Nihon bungaku* [New research materials, contemporary Japanese literature]. Vol. 6. Tokyo: Meiji Shoin, 2000.

Ochi Haruo. *Kindai bungaku no tanjō* [Birth of modern literature]. Tokyo: Kōdansha, 1975.

Yashiro Seiichi. *Kishutachi no seishun* [The standard-bearers in their youth]. Tokyo: Shinchōsha, 1985.

Brian Powell

KAUFMAN, GEORGE S. (1889–1961)

George S. Kaufman was one of the most successful playwrights in the history of American theater, dominating commercial Broadway COMEDY during the 1920s and 1930s. Born on November 16, 1889, in Pittsburgh, Pennsylvania, he later took an acting class at the Alveine School of Dramatic Art and worked as the manager of a stock company in Troy, New York. His work first appeared in print in 1909, when Franklin Pierce Adams accepted a brief contribution for his humor column in the *Evening Mail*, and in 1912 the *Washington Times* hired him to edit his own column. He moved to New York City, worked for the *Tribune* and the *Evening Mail*, and in 1917 joined the staff of the *New York Times* as a drama reporter. He took a playwriting course at Columbia University, and after writing four unproduced plays, he accepted a job with producer George C. Tyler as a play "doctor" for *Someone in the House*, which opened on September 9, 1918.

In 1919 he became a member of Alexander Woollcott's so-called Round Table at the Algonquin Hotel, an informal lunch group that included such wits as Dorothy Parker, Harold Ross, Robert Benchley, Heywood Broun, ROBERT E. SHERWOOD, and MARC CONNELLY, who became Kaufman's collaborator on *Dulcy*. The team's next hit was *Merton of the Movies*, a spoof of the silent film industry that established a pattern Kaufman would use again: a tale of the fortunes of an innocent, foolish protagonist who pursues a naïve dream, can not imagine his own failure, and through sheer luck succeeds against all probability. Their other plays included BEGGAR ON HORSEBACK, an expressionistic comedy.

The playwright met Harpo Marx in 1924, and he and Morrie Ryskind subsequently wrote two Broadway musicals for the Marx Brothers: *The Cocoanuts* and *Animal Crackers*. Both were later made into movies, and Kaufman was one of the principal writers on the Marx Brothers film *A Night at the Opera* (1935). All three pieces ran to a pattern composed of predictable intrigue and thin stories designed to support the clowning of the brothers, combined with a casting structure of stock characters: ingenue, juvenile, villains, detective, and a dim-witted society dowager. Kaufman and Ryskind also worked with George and Ira Gershwin on *Strike Up the Band*, *Of Thee I Sing*, which won the Pulitzer Prize, and *Let 'em Eat Cake*.

Kaufman's first directing assignment was THE FRONT PAGE (1928), and because his theatrical career was doing so well, he resigned his job at the *New York Times* in 1930. He ultimately directed forty professional productions, including twenty-two of his own plays, as well as John Steinbeck's *Of Mice and Men* (1937) and *My Sister Eileen* (1940).

MOSS HART asked Kaufman to collaborate on revising his early version of ONCE IN A LIFETIME, which opened on September 24, 1930, with Kaufman in the role of Lawrence Vail. Their later successes included the Pulitzer Prize–winning YOU CAN'T TAKE IT WITH YOU, I'D RATHER BE RIGHT, and *The Man Who Came to Dinner*. In 1951 Kaufman won a Tony Award for directing *Guys and Dolls*.

The foundation of his approach to playmaking shows clearly in the cast list of *The Old Home Town* (an early version of *The Deep, Tangled Wildwood*), where he designates the various characters as leading man and woman, character man and woman, juvenile, ingenue, comedian, comedienne, heavy, and "wise bit." When he and Hart sought examples of pre-1920s American drama to use in *The Fabulous Invalid*, they chose plays by George Broadhurst, Frank Craven, Roi Cooper Megrue, and Bayard Veiller, popular dramatists whose work is now virtually forgotten. Kaufman combined his theatrically conventional sensibility with a flawless ear for the wisecrack, a perfect sense of comic timing, and a knack for using sentiment and affirming the American dream, but without becoming maudlin. His memorable plays are more farcical than comedic, sacrificing a truly satirical point of view while presenting a wittily derisive attitude through parody and caricature. Kaufman died on June 2, 1961, in New York City.

Recent professional revivals include *Dinner at Eight* (Lincoln Center Theatre, 2002), *The Royal Family* (Theatre Royal, Haymarket, 2001), *The Man Who Came to Dinner* (Roundabout Theatre Company, 2000), and *Once in a Lifetime* (Atlantic Theatre Company, 1998).

[*See also* United States, 1860–Present]

SELECT PLAYS: *Dulcy* (with Marc Connelly, 1921); *Merton of the Movies* (with Connelly, 1922); *Beggar on Horseback* (with Connelly, 1924); *The Butter and Egg Man* (1925); *The Cocoanuts* (with Morrie Ryskind, music and lyrics by Irving Berlin, 1925); *The Royal Family* (with Edna Ferber, 1927); *Strike Up the Band* (music and lyrics by George and Ira Gershwin, 1927); *Animal Crackers* (with Ryskind, music and lyrics by Bert Kalmar and Harry Ruby, 1928); *June Moon* (with Ring Lardner, 1929); *Once in a Lifetime* (with Moss Hart, 1930); *Of Thee I Sing* (with Ryskind, music and lyrics by George and Ira Gershwin, 1931); *Dinner at Eight* (with Ferber, 1932); *Let 'em Eat Cake* (with Ryskind, music and lyrics by George and Ira Gershwin, 1933); *Merrily We Roll Along* (with Hart, 1934); *Stage Door* (with Ferber, 1936); *You Can't Take It with You* (with Hart, 1936); *I'd Rather Be Right* (with Hart, lyrics by Lorenz Hart and music by Richard Rodgers, 1937); *The Fabulous Invalid* (with Hart, 1938); *American Way* (with Hart, music by Oscar Levant, 1939); *The Man Who Came to Dinner* (with Hart, 1939); *George Washington Slept Here* (with Hart, 1940); *The Solid Gold Cadillac* (with Howard Teichmann, 1953)

FURTHER READING

Gaines, James R. *Wit's End: Days and Nights of the Algonquin Round Table.* New York: Harcourt, 1977.

Goldstein, Malcolm. *George S. Kaufman: His Life, His Theater.* New York: Oxford Univ. Press, 1979.

Hart, Moss. *Act One.* New York: Random, 1959.

Mason, Jeffrey D. *Wisecracks: The Farces of George S. Kaufman.* Ann Arbor: Univ. of Michigan Research Press, 1988.

Meredith, Scott. *George S. Kaufman and His Friends.* Garden City, N.Y.: Doubleday, 1974.

Teichmann, Howard. *George S. Kaufman: An Intimate Portrait.* New York: Atheneum, 1972.

Jeffrey D. Mason

DER KAUKASISCHE KREIDEKREIS

See THE CAUCASIAN CHALK CIRCLE

KAWAKAMI OTOJIRŌ (1864–1911)

Kawakami Otojirō was a Japanese playwright, actor, director, and producer and a flamboyant pioneer whose radical theater reforms branded him a publicity monger, charlatan, and national disgrace. He was also the esteemed actor-manager of the first Japanese theater company to visit the West.

During the topsy-turvy politics of the Meiji period (1868–1912) Kawakami advocated for a democratic constitution and was arrested 180 times for his subversive political diatribes. He joined the "youth theater" (*sōshi shibai*) of political progressive Sudō Sadanori. In 1889 Kawakami shot to fame with his patter-song diatribe *Oppekeppebushi*.

Kawakami's progressive attitudes made his productions the most successful of the new SHINPA. Just two weeks into the Sino-Japanese War, Kawakami visited the front, returning to stage *Otojirō Kawakami's Battlefield Report* (*Kawakami Otojirō senchi kembunki*, 1894), a stirring jingoistic spectacle. Although he was castigated by TSUBOUCHI SHŌYŌ for "pandering to the tastes of the vulgar" (Komiya, 1956), Kawakami helped redefine *kabuki* as a classical theater.

Kawakami married Sadayakko, a famous geisha. They built the Kawakami-za, a modern theater, in 1896, but it soon failed. Partially to escape crushing debts, they toured the West in 1899–1901 as the "Imperial Japanese Theatrical Company." They performed *shinpa* and pseudo-*kabuki* for Japanese on America's West Coast and later staged amalgams of *kabuki* dance plays in major American cities and Paris.

More hack than playwright, Kawakami displayed a genius for adapting well-known classics and contemporary events into popular concoctions. He reworked political novels, both Japanese (*The True Story of Itagaki's Misfortunes* [*Itagakikun sōnan jikki*, 1891]) and Western (*A Beautiful Tale of Statesmanship* [*Keikoku bidan*, 1891], based on the Spartan War), as well as docudramas based on contemporary events such as *Strange* (1894), based on a scandalous poisoning. In America he adapted *shinpa* and *kabuki* plays, always including ferocious battles, a passionate dance by Sadayakko, and hara-kiri suicides, playing to Western stereotypes of the Japanese. His centerpiece was *The Geisha and the Knight* (Geisha to bushi, 1899), combining the savage swordfights of *Sayaate, a Duel* with the dancing maiden turned jealous snake of *Dōjōji*. Always attuned to the news, Kawakami rewrote a dance play to congratulate Admiral George Dewey for his victory in the PHILIPPINES (1899) and created a Japanese *Sappho* (1900) to mark Daudet's play's victory in a historic obscenity trial. After seeing Henry Irving and Ellen Terry's *The Merchant of Venice*, he crafted *Shylock* (*Sairoku*, 1900), featuring a fisherman in the judgment scene, intended as a searing indictment of Western capitalism. Despite the publicity he generated, his artistic results were generally unfavorable.

Kawakami introduced Western ideas into Japanese theater practice. His troupe produced Nipponized versions of Western classics, having Hamlet enter on a bicycle and *Othello* (*Osero*, 1902) set in Formosa (Taiwan). He and Sadayakko founded the first academy for actresses. In 1911 they helped build the Imperial Theatre in Osaka, but months later Kawakami died.

Kawakami and Sadayakko's timely vision, accommodation to circumstance, and vigorous self-promotion led to formidable accomplishments. They stimulated others to mount authentic Shakespearean and modern productions. In the West they spurred a boom in kimono, inspired Giacomo Puccini and Isadora Duncan, and established Japanese theater as worthy of international recognition.

[*See also* Japan; Shin Kabuki]

Precise records of Kawakami's authorship are not available. The plays listed here are those, attributed to him or in which he is believed to have had an authorial, advisory, or adaptor's hand.

SELECT PLAYS: *A Beautiful Tale of Statesmanship* (*Keikoku bidan* [joint authorship], 1891); *The True Story of Itagaki's Misfortunes* (*Itagakikun sōnan jikki* [joint authorship], 1891); *Otojirō Kawakami's Battle Report* (*Kawakami Otojirō senchi kembunki*, 1894); *The Geisha and the Knight* (also known as *Geisha and the Samurai*; *Geisha to bushi*, 1899); *Sappho* (1900); *Shylock* (*Sairoku*, 1900); *A Tragedy Abroad* (*Yōkōchū no higeki*, 1901); *Othello* (*Osero*, 1902); *Hamlet* (*Hamuretto*, 1903)

FURTHER READING

Berg, Shelley. "Le Rêve Réalisé." *Dance Chronicle*, 18, no. 3 (1995): 343–404.

——. "Sada Yacco: The American Tour, 1899–1900." *Dance Chronicle* 16, no. 2 (1993): 147–196.

Downer, Leslie. *Madame Sadayakko: The Geisha Who Seduced the West*. London: Review, 2003.

Kano, Ayako. *Acting like a Woman in Modern Japan: Theatre, Gender, and Nationalism*. New York: Palgrave, 2001.

Kawakami Otojirō and Kawakami Sadayakko. *Jiden: Otojirō Sadayakko* [Autobiography of Sadayakko]. Ed. by Sōtetsu Fujii. Tokyo: San'ichi Shobo, 1984.

Komiya, Toyotaka, ed. *Japanese Culture in the Meiji Era*. Vol. 3, *Japanese Music and Drama in the Meiji Era*. Tr. and adap. by Edward Seidensticker and Donald Keene. Tokyo: Obunsha, 1956.

Salz, Jonah. "Intercultural Pioneers: Otojirō Kawakami and Sada Yakko." *Journal of Intercultural Studies* 20 (1993): 25–74.

Toshiba-EMI Limited. *Yomigaeru Kawakami Otojirō: Oppekepe* Return to Otojirō Kawakami: Oppekepe. TOCG 5432 [CD-ROM]. 1997.

Jonah Salz

KAWATAKE MOKUAMI (1816–1893)

Kawatake Mokuami was a Japanese *kabuki* playwright whose career was split between the Tokugawa shogunate and that of modern JAPAN in the wake of the Meiji Restoration (1868), when the nation was exposed to Western civilization. Straddling these eras, Kawatake struggled to bring the traditional dramaturgy of *kabuki* into line with modern ideas at a time when reformists were urging that *kabuki*—embarrassing because of its association with fantasy, brothels, and bloodshed—adopt the rationalism of Western theater. Kawatake never fully succeeded in bridging the gap between old-time *kabuki* and modern drama, but his attempts were revolutionary and led the way to the acceptance of more psychologically and rationalistically acceptable genres, including SHIN KABUKI, SHINPA, and SHINGEKI. Kawatake was both the last traditional exponent of old-time *kabuki* and Japan's first modern playwright.

Before the Meiji period (1868–1912) Kawatake (known for much of his career as Kawatake Shinshichi II) had risen to the top of the Edo playwriting world, especially after 1854 when he began a series of collaborations with the star Ichikawa Kodanji IV, for whom he wrote a number of popular bandit plays (*shiranami mono*); Kawatake remained the representative playwright of bandit plays into the Meiji era. During the Meiji era he continued to be associated with great actors, writing plays suited to their specific interests and talents, such as history plays (*jidaimono*) for Ichikawa Danjūrō IX and domestic dramas (*sewamono*) for Onoe Kikugorō V. He displayed special mastery in domestic dramas, vividly capturing the daily life and language of his native city under both its old name (Edo) and new (Tokyo) and even pioneering a completely new kind of domestic drama—"cropped-hair plays" (*zangiri mono*)—that reflected the changing cultural mores of Meiji Japan, with men wearing Western-style haircuts and carrying umbrellas and pocket watches. The plays—such as *Plovers of the Island* (1881)—remained rooted in *kabuki* techniques, but did their best to illustrate the dizzying changes in the offstage world with which the Japanese were then contending. His numerous other innovations included adapting Western literature for *kabuki*. In 1879, for example, he wrote *Money Is Everything in This World*, an adaptation of Edward Bulwer-Lytton's *Money*. But he continued to write standard Edo-style domestic plays as well, some of them among *kabuki*'s most popular, such as *The First Flowers of Ueno* (1881).

Similarly, Kawatake broke new ground in historical dramas, creating for Danjūrō IX a number of "living history" (*katsureki geki*) plays that abandoned the slapdash and (because of censorship) veiled treatment of history—which privileged theatricality over archeological correctness—in favor of plays whose characters, speech, and behavior were based on scholarly research. A still-performed one is *Takatoki* (1884). Neither "cropped-hair" or "living history" genres left much that is still performed, but they pointed the way to 20th-century dramaturgy.

Kawatake dominated Meiji *kabuki*. He was the most prolific *kabuki* dramatist, with 360 plays. He wrote in every genre, including dance-dramas based on NŌ, such as *Earth Spider* (1881), and topical plays about contemporary political events, including one in which the Japanese hero was modeled after former American president Ulysses S. Grant, then visiting Japan.

SELECT PLAYS (popularized versions of the titles are given in several cases): *Two Lions* (*Renjishi*, 1872); *Sakai's Drum* (*Sakai no taiko*, 1873); *Shinza the Barber* (*Kamiyui Shinza*, 1873); *The Tokyo Daily News* (*Tōkyō nichinichi shinbun*, 1873); *Encouragement of Virtue, Chastisement of Vice* (*Kanzen chōaku*, 1877); *The Woman Student* (*Onna shosei*, 1877); *Chronicles of the Later Three Years of War in the North* (*Gosannen ōshū gunki*, 1879); *Money Is Everything in This World* (*Ningen banji kane no yononaka*, 1879); *Strange Tales of Wanderings Abroad: A Western Kabuki* (*Hyōrū kidan seiyō kabuki*, 1879); *Earth Spider* (*Tsuchigumo*, 1881); *The First Flowers of Ueno* (*Kumo no magō Ueno no hatsuhana*, 1881); *Plovers of the Island* (*Shimachidori*, 1881); *The Renowned Banzui Chōbei* (*Kiwametsuki Banzui Chōbei*, 1881); *Benkei Aboard Ship* (*Funa Benkei*, 1883); *The Demon Ibaraki* (*Ibaraki*, 1883); *Fishmonger Sōgorō* (*Sakanaya Sōgorō*, 1883); *Takatoki* (1884); *Brush Seller Kōbei* (*Fudeya Kōbei*, 1885); *The Kaga Tobi Firefighters* (*Kagatobi*, 1886); *Viewing the Autumn Foliage* (with Morita Kanya XII; *Momijigari*, 1887); *The Balloonist: The Palace on High People Are Talking About* (*Fūsen-nori uwasa no takadono*, 1891)

FURTHER READING

Brandon, James R., and Samuel L. Leiter, eds. *Kabuki Plays on Stage*. Vol. 4, *Restoration and Reform, 1872–1905*. Honolulu: Univ. of Hawaii Press, 2003.

Kawakami Shigetoshi. *Kawatake Mokuami*. Tokyo: Yoshikawa Hiro Bunkan, 1956.

Kawatake Mokuami. *The Love of Izayoi and Seishin: A Kabuki Play*. Tr. by Frank T. Motofuji. Rutland, Vt.: Tuttle, 1966.

Keene, Donald. *Dawn to the West: Japanese Literature of the Modern Era*. Vol. 2, *Poetry, Drama, Criticism*. New York: Holt, Rinehart & Winston, 1984.

Leiter, Samuel. *New Kabuki Encyclopedia: A Revised Adaptation of Kabuki Jiten*. Westport, Conn.: Greenwood Press, 1997.

Rimer, J. Thomas. "Mokuami's Evil One and Her Modern Counterpart." In *Pilgrimages*. Honolulu: Univ. of Hawaii Press, 1988. 59–70.

Samuel L. Leiter

KAZANBICHI

See LAND OF VOLCANIC ASH

THE KEEP

After GWYN THOMAS had successfully written short pieces for radio, George Devine at the Royal Court Theatre, London, suggested that he write a full-length stage play. The result is the loosely autobiographical *The Keep*, a comic play set in 1954, in which the characters consistently fail to become independent and live their own lives. "Keep" means "prison" in the dialect of South Wales, and the male characters, father Ben Morton and his five sons Constantine, Russell, Wallace, Oswald, and Alvin, are locked in a mental prison of their own making. Constantine, whose name recalls the Roman emperor of the same name but whose abbreviation Con also suggests the trickery of the confidence man, has secured low-level jobs for each of his brothers and has thus emotionally chained them to himself and the house. The four brothers are less than grateful but do not have enough stamina to leave. Only Miriam, their sister and housekeeper, can stand up to Con, but her sense of duty keeps her bound to the Morton household. Matters come to a head when Con plans to mount a plaque in honor of their dead mother: Miriam reveals that their mother had not died in an accident but had escaped to live a new life in America. Thus the cliché of the self-sacrificing "Welsh mam" is turned on its head because Mam is the person who "saw a door and walked through it." At the end of the play Miriam is set to follow her mother's example, leaving her brothers and her shell-shocked father to fend for themselves.

The play was first performed at the Royal Court Theatre in London in 1960. It subsequently went to the Piccadilly Theatre, where it ran for about a month. It was enthusiastically received and became a repertory favorite. The play's weakness lies in its plotting, and the characters have a tendency to all sound like Gwyn Thomas himself. The reasons for its success, though, are its sharp, witty dialogue and its situation COMEDY. Furthermore, the peculiar atmosphere of small-town resignation, the lack of individual spirit, and the thwarted escape from a prison that is as much mental as it is material are recurring themes of Welsh drama and literature. Already in J. O. Francis's *Change* (1920) and in EMLYN WILLIAMS's THE CORN IS GREEN (1938), escape is the only way the characters can fulfill their true potential. In the 1980s the characters' inability to escape in ALAN OSBORNE's drama and in ED THOMAS's HOUSE OF AMERICA becomes pathological. The centrality of the theme of confinement versus escape has its roots in the keen sense of cultural inferiority that is the result of Wales's postcolonial status and its long history of economic depression. *The Keep* is thus not only a play of enduring appeal but an astutely observed representation of South Wales in the 1950s.

[*See also* England]

FURTHER READING

Rhys, Martin. "Keeping It in the Family: *Change* by J. O. Francis, *The Keep* by Gwyn Thomas and *House of America* by Ed Thomas." In *Dangerous Diversity: The Changing Faces of Wales*, ed. by Katie Gramich and Andrew Hiscock. Cardiff: Univ. of Wales Press, 1998. 150–177.

Thomas, Gwyn. *A Few Selected Exits*. Bridgend: Seren, 1985.

Alyce von Rothkirch

KEJSER OG GLAILŒR *See* EMPEROR AND GALILEAN

KELLY, GEORGE (1887–1974)

George Kelly, born on January 16, 1887, in Philadelphia, Pennsylvania, was the seventh of ten children of an Irish immigrant father and an American mother. The Kelly children rose from relative austerity to become influential in entertainment, construction, and politics. Kelly's working-class, Irish Catholic upbringing is reflected in the conservative moral perspective presented in his plays.

Kelly was also a skilled draftsman. He worked in the construction business for several years before following his true passion and embarking on an acting career at the age of twenty-four. Kelly's interest in writing grew from the necessity of finding better material as an actor in vaudeville sketches. Even in his early writing Kelly demonstrated an ear for authentically re-creating American idioms and a talent for comic social commentary.

Kelly's first full-length play, *The Torch Bearers*, satirizes the little theatre movement in America in the 1920s. Kelly's play is a comic indictment of the rapidly emerging amateur theatrical troupes that some felt were responsible for the degradation of theater. His next play, *The Show-off*, like *The Torch Bearers*, was developed from Kelly's early vaudeville sketches. *The Show-off* and its comic antihero, Aubrey Piper, secured the playwright's reputation for crafting recognizable characters distinctively drawn from the American middle class. Controversy arose when *The Show-off* was passed over for the Pulitzer Prize despite its recommendation from the play committee. This slight was mended two years later with the awarding of the 1926 Pulitzer to *Craig's Wife*. Less comic than his earlier works, *Craig's Wife* reflects a more direct influence of European REALISM, the well-made play, and social thesis plays, particularly those of HENRIK IBSEN and AUGUST STRINDBERG. The play critiques the moral bankruptcy of marrying for economic security versus marrying for love. Kelly's severe portrayal of the play's title character garnered him undue repute as a misogynist. *Craig's Wife* was the last of Kelly's commercially successful plays.

Kelly refused to pander to changing commercial tastes, adhering to his predilection for moral chastisement of what he considered societal ills. Having lost faith in theater's ability to enlighten its audience, Kelly made a brief and unsuccessful attempt at writing for the Hollywood film industry. After five years in California he returned to New York, but he never recaptured the critical or commercial success of his early career. He took responsibility for directing his plays throughout his career and was considered to be an insightful and demanding director.

Preferring to let his dramatic works speak for themselves, Kelly shunned interviews and seldom offered commentary beyond the moral attitudes presented in the plays. Little is known of his personal life before, during, or after his brief period of success. Family biographer Arthur Lewis speculates that Kelly was homosexual, though there are no personal statements either to support or deny this on Kelly's behalf. Kelly died on June 18, 1974, in Bryn Mawr, Pennsylvania.

[*See also* United States, 1860–1929]

SELECT PLAYS: *The Torch Bearers* (1922); *The Show-off* (1924); *Craig's Wife* (1925); *Behold the Bridegroom* (1927); *Daisy Mayme* (1927); *Philip Goes Forth* (1931); *Reflected Glory* (1936); *The Deep Mrs. Sykes* (1945); *The Fatal Weakness* (1946)

FURTHER READING

Graves, Mark A. *George Kelly: A Research and Production Sourcebook*. Westport, Conn.: Greenwood Press, 1999.

Hirsch, Foster. *George Kelly*. Boston: Twayne, 1975.

Hutchinson, Peter Wood. "A Re-evaluation of the Works of George Kelly." Ph.D. diss., Univ. of Southern California, 1972.

Lewis, Arthur. *Those Philadelphia Kellys*. New York: Morrow, 1977.

Maisel, Edward. "The Theater of George Kelly." *Theater Arts* (February 1947): 41.

Miller, Jordan Y., and Winifred L. Frazer. "George Kelly's Portrayal of Painful Delights." In *American Drama Between the Wars: A Critical History*. Boston: Twayne, 1991. 185–191.

Tanney, Michael Joseph. "An Analysis of the Plays of George Kelly." Ph.D. diss., Tulane Univ., 1973.

Craig Willis

KEMP, JENNY (1949–)

Jenny Kemp, born in Melbourne, Victoria, on March 11, 1949, is one of AUSTRALIA's leading writer-directors in innovative performance. Over a twenty-five-year career, up to 2006, Kemp has created nine original works and four collaborative works and also teaches writing and directing. She lives in Melbourne with her partner, the writer and theater lecturer Richard Murphet, and their son.

Kemp's works are strongly visual, with poetic segments. Although Kemp also works as a professional director of more conventional plays, her writing does not present a realist story with characters. Her published writings in the productions that Kemp directed herself are discussed here. Importantly, her scripts also outline the design for visual images and effects. Kemp's performances are expressions of interior worlds and suggest memories, dreams, and imagined places. In *Call of the Wild* (produced in 1989) the paintings of Paul Delvaux could be glimpsed as the performers glided through the set's two levels and painted building facade. The elegant female performers wore hats, long gloves, and skirts as if they were attending a garden party, except that they were also bare-breasted; a male character recited in French and Spanish from a novel.

While each of Kemp's performances is centered on one female identity, her distinctive technique is to have this one identity acted by up to four performers in order to portray experience over time, at different ages, and events happening in contrasting places. Her work presents subjective experience that relives reality out of order, and other people appear to be projections of the central presence rather than fully developed personalities. In *Remember* (produced in 1992) a sexual assault is a reoccurring memory for Moderna Two in hospital; while her earlier life living with Jack before the assault enacted by Moderna One is remembered as a sequence of events. A domestic conversation is contrasted with stanzas about mythological worlds, so that the domestic conversation becomes poeticized. This is further heightened by staging that interweaves the mythic through domestic worlds. Kemp uses repetition in lines and scenes, and some images and themes even continue into subsequent performances. *The Black Sequin Dress* (1996) draws on the stylistic elements of previous works, including Delvaux's paintings. In a nightclub and a railway tunnel, as well as other less specific places, Woman 1, Woman 2, Woman 3, and Woman 4 relive moments of one life or possibly each other's lives; they fall and lie prone, possibly dead. The motif of Undine's descent into an underworld is contrasted with a Man trying to cross the river Styx. A train journey and concerns about time return in *Still Angela* (2002). Three performers play Angela at different stages in her life. She goes to the Australian desert. The interior world of Angela, which is realized through visual images as much as spoken words, is comparable with the work's central motif of seeing a landscape from a train window. Identities in Kemp's texts are ambiguous and fluid, captured momentarily in images; they are reminiscent of how a mind might experience memories.

SELECT PLAYS: *Call of the Wild* (1989); *Remember* (1992); *The Black Sequin Dress* (1996); *Still Angela* (2002)

FURTHER READING

Fensham, Rachel, and Denise Varney. *The Doll's Revolution: Australian Theatre and Cultural Imagination*. With Maryrose Casey and Laura Ginters. Melbourne: Australia Scholarly, 2005.

Kemp, Jenny. *Call of the Wild*. In *Performing the Unnameable*, ed. by Richard James Allen and Karen Pearlman. Sydney: Currency, 1999. 7–24.

McDonald, Helen. *Erotic Ambiguities*. London: Routledge, 2001.

Tait, Peta. *Converging Realities: Feminism in Australian Theatre*. Sydney: Currency, 1994.

Varney, Denise, and Rachel Fensham. "'Help Me, I'm Drowning!' Calls the Man in Jenny Kemp's *The Black Sequin Dress*: Heterosexual Masculinity in Feminist Performance." *Australasian Drama Studies* 34 (April 1999): 68–85.

Peta Tait

KENNEDY, ADRIENNE (1931–)

I'd often stare at the statue of Beethoven I kept on the left-hand side of my desk. I felt it contained a "secret." I'd do the same with the photograph of Queen Hatshepsut that was on the wall. I did not then understand that I felt torn between these forces of my ancestry . . . European and African . . . a fact that would one day explode in my work.

—Adrienne Kennedy, 1987

Adrienne Lita Hawkins was born in Pittsburgh in 1931 and grew up in a middle-class neighborhood in Cleveland, Ohio, where her parents moved when she was four. She kept diaries as a child and studied writing formally when she matriculated at Ohio State University, where life for blacks and whites was segregated. The experience of institutional segregation left an indelible impression on her and became a vital inspiration for her plays. She graduated with a degree in education in 1953 and married Joseph C. Kennedy. Together they had two sons and divorced in 1966. After moving to New York City, Kennedy studied creative writing at Columbia University, the American Theatre Wing, and Circle in the Square Theatre School. Kennedy's experimental narratives use powerful imagery to dramatize racial conflict, the struggles of black female identity, and the collective history of blacks in America.

Kennedy began writing her first and best-known play, *Funnyhouse of a Negro*, while traveling in AFRICA and ITALY with her family in 1961. The stark contrast between African and European history provided the foundation for the play and its ambivalent attitude toward race. Much of the play's imagery was inspired by African masks and the people and landscape of West Africa, as well as the social and political transformation that accompanied Ghana's liberation from British colonialism. When she returned to New York City a year later, Kennedy submitted *Funnyhouse* to Circle in the Square School, where it received a workshop production under the auspices of playwright EDWARD ALBEE. The play enjoyed a successful OFF-BROADWAY run and garnered an Obie Award for Best Play in 1964.

Funnyhouse focuses on the character Sarah, also called Negro, a young woman who aspires to be a poet. Sarah was conceived after her black father, a missionary in Africa, raped her white mother. She is haunted by the vision of her father, whose brutal violence becomes emblematic of her fear of "blackness" in the play: "black is evil and has been from the beginning." This split heritage leads to a confusion regarding Sarah's identity. She attempts to confront the implications of her biracial ancestry and the cruelty that engendered her, striving to separate the parts of herself shaped by her mother and father, those derived from European culture and African history. Seemingly plotless, *Funnyhouse* is a surreal, dreamlike narrative that combines autobiography with the historical past to convey black feminist themes and aspects of the African American struggle.

At the center of the stage is Sarah's room, dominated by the "astonishing white repulsiveness" of the statue of Queen Victoria. In the funnyhouse of Sarah's mind she is tormented by iconic figures of Western culture that also include the Duchess of Hapsburg and Jesus Christ. *Funnyhouse* employs a signature technique that Kennedy used in several later plays. The voice and consciousness of Sarah are distributed over various personae who speak in white accents, revealing her multiple and uncertain identities. Historical figures are used as extensions of the central character, all of whom at different points in the play "speak" for Sarah. These other personifications of the main character consist of Queen Victoria and the Duchess of Hapsburg, both of whom aspire to be the epitome of whiteness and represent the protagonist's impersonations of white culture. Sarah's other selves also include Patrice Lumumba, the president of the Republic of the Congo until his assassination in 1961, and Jesus, a disappointing savior embodied as a hunchbacked, yellow-skinned dwarf. Early in the play the protagonist says that these voices provide "a stark fortress against recognition of myself." These diverse characters evoke Sarah's fiercely conflicted attitude toward her own racial and sexual history. Kennedy has said that it was her greatest breakthrough as a writer when her main characters began to have other selves.

The desire to unite the contradictions in Sarah's character only fragments her more. Her hair falls out, littering the stage; she is beleaguered by a vision of her father as a dead man with an axe through his head. Sarah drifts aimlessly through rooms—Hapsburg chambers, hotels, Victorian castles, a room on the Upper West Side of Manhattan cluttered with dreams of a piano, European antiques, and Oriental carpets. Nothing soothes her emotional pain, and she is unable to find a restful home. The play's final image shows Sarah hanged, as if her suicide is the only way she finds to express herself. The play is an endless hall of dense imagery and textural language that refract and distort the protagonist and accentuate her terror about racial difference and femininity.

Many of the characters that appear in Kennedy's work are taken from American popular culture and the historical past, including Charlie Chaplin, Galilei Galileo, Ludwig van Beethoven, and Leonardo da Vinci. Kennedy's plays are typically structured as one-acts, elaborating a complex tapestry that breaks from conventional notions of dramatic narrative, character, and setting.

The cast for *The Owl Answers* (1965) includes characters with multiple identities built into their names. The protagonist is "She who is Clara Passmore who is the Virgin Mary who is the Bastard who is the Owl." Clara is an avid reader of *Jane Eyre*, and the play's action concerns the conflict between her English heritage and her "blackness." Her father, a character named "Goddamn Father who is the Richest White Man in the Town who is the Dead White Father who is Reverend Passmore," encourages her to repudiate her black self: "He came to me in the outhouse. . . . He told me you are an owl, ow, oww, I am your beginning, ow. You belong here with us owls in the fig tree, not to somebody that cooks for your Goddamn Father." Historical figures form part of the cast, including Geoffrey Chaucer, William Shakespeare, and William the Conqueror, who compose a chorus of white, male British tradition that disputes Clara's claim to English ancestry.

Like many of her plays, *A Movie Star Has to Star in Black and White* (1976) has characters composed of various personae and explores the fragmented psyche of a black female protagonist named Clara, who fails to unite the splintered elements of her identity. The play opens as the Columbia Pictures Lady appears in a magnificent spotlight and introduces the "film's" stars. The actors are made up to resemble movie stars, including Bette Davis, Marlon Brando, Montgomery Clift, Shelley Winters, Paul Henreid, and Jean Peters. A system of projections is used, and films such as *Voyage Out*, *Viva Zapata!*, and *A Place in the Sun* are superimposed on Clara's own troubled narrative. After the near-fatal accident of her brother, Wally, Clara is united with her divorced parents. In light of their failed marriage, the pregnant Clara is distressed by her own marital conflicts and torn between her ambitions as a writer and her desires for motherhood and family. Movie stars, playing parts from film roles, speak for the protagonist and make up much of her personal history. They also represent exalted social roles that neither Clara, her husband Eddie, nor Clara's parents can live up to. Clara plays only a bit part in her own life story. As a writer, she seeks to author her life's script and play a more active, starring role.

Kennedy's work uses intertextuality and frequently employs multimedia. Clips from old black-and-white movies are often projected as part of a story, slides are shown, and headlines are read aloud. She sometimes creates a play from topical news, as with *An Evening with Dead Essex* (1973), which deals with the Mark Essex shootings when a black ex-navy man left six people dead and fifteen wounded after sniping from the rooftop of a New Orleans Howard Johnson's in 1972. Her dramas are composed of poetic language, rich metaphors, and mythic associations. The dialogue is rhythmic, lyrical, and repetitious.

The broader dramatic impact of Kennedy's work consists of a shift in emphasis away from events and external circumstances into a character's private, interior state of mind. Kennedy's characters are often more like apparitions or amalgams of various emotions. She creates an imaginative world through stream of consciousness and the use of unconscious symbolism. Another major breakthrough for her as a dramatist came with the incorporation of dream imagery into her plays. She was deeply influenced by the use of symbolism by writers such as Charlotte Brontë, Charles Dickens, F. Scott Fitzgerald, and T. S. ELIOT.

Another characteristic of Kennedy's work resides in her unusual and imaginative use of theatrical space. The fate of Kennedy's characters is inevitably bound up with that of the rooms they inhabit. Hers is a theater possessed by an unstable setting, with the capacity of rooms to solidify characters and reinforce their place in society or else threaten them and sever them from life. The playwright was also influenced by Martha Graham, whose dance choreography, popular in the 1950s, deemphasized narrative and supported the simultaneous occurrence of many things onstage. The work of Pablo Picasso and surrealist filmmakers such as JEAN COCTEAU and Luis Buñuel further inspired Kennedy. She enjoyed the Hollywood magazine *Modern Screen* while growing up in Cleveland. Favorite playwrights include TENNESSEE WILLIAMS, FEDERICO GARCÍA LORCA, and EUGENE O'NEILL, particularly his use of the long, internal monologue.

The drama cycle *The Alexander Plays* (1992) includes *She Talks to Beethoven*, *The Film Club*, *The Dramatic Circle*, and *The Ohio State Murders*.

The Ohio State Murders concerns Suzanne Alexander, an eminent African American writer who returns to her alma mater to discuss the use of violent imagery in her work. The protagonist is doubled, extending Kennedy's familiar distribution of personae over antithetical selves. Suzanne is both a playwright serving as narrator in the present and a college student of half a century ago at a recently desegregated institution of higher learning. The play is presented as a series of flashbacks that recall the sinister forces of racial hatred and ostracism that characterized the student's college days.

In 1991, while Kennedy was working on *The Ohio State Murders*, her son, Adam Kennedy, was beaten and arrested by a white police officer and later won a civil lawsuit. *Sleep Deprivation Chamber* (1996), first performed at the New York Shakespeare Festival and co-written with Adam, was inspired by this violent incident. The play is about Teddy, a young African American who is stopped late one night by the police as he approaches his home in Arlington, Virginia. Without provocation the policeman viciously beats and arrests Teddy, charging him with assault. The Kennedys interweave Teddy's trial with his mother's tender letters written in his defense.

Motherhood 2000 (1994) revisits the brutal and senseless police beating of Kennedy's son from the viewpoint of a black woman writer. The play is set in the apocalyptic future of New York City where food is scarce and hordes of homeless refugees cross the Hudson River from New Jersey. In Riverside Park a group of homeless men performs a Miracle Play, repeating the same performance every night, the crucifixion of Jesus Christ. These men are discovered to be the same ones who turned the writer's son into a martyr, the very policeman who beat him playing the Savior. The mother joins the cast, playing the role of a soldier in a new version of the Passion Play that ends abruptly when she smashes her son's aggressor on the head with a hammer.

Kennedy's bold, autobiographically inspired work dramatizes the perils of blackness in America and has had a strong influence on the BLACK ARTS MOVEMENT. Her plays explore the struggle to resolve the anxieties of African American female identity within the larger cultural context of black experience in white America.

[*See also* United States, 1940– Present]

SELECT PLAYS: *Funnyhouse of a Negro* (1964); *The Owl Answers* (1965); *A Rat's Mass* (1966); *The Lennon Play: In His Own Write* (with John Lennon and Victor Spinetti, 1967); *A Lesson in Dead Language* (1968); *A Beast Story* (1969); *Boats* (1969); *Sun: A Poem for Malcolm X Inspired by His Murder* (1969); *An Evening with Dead Essex* (1973); *A Movie Star Has to Star in Black and White* (1976); *Black Children's Day* (1980); *A Lancashire Lad* (1980); *Orestes and Electra* (1980); *The Ohio State Murders* (1992); *She Talks to Beethoven* (1992); *Motherhood 2000* (1994); *June and Jean in Concert* (1995)

FURTHER READING

Bryant-Jackson, Paul K., and Lois More Overbeck, eds. *Intersecting Boundaries: The Theatre of Adrienne Kennedy*. Minneapolis: Univ. of Minnesota Press, 1992.

Burke, Sally. *American Feminist Playwrights*. New York: Twayne, 1996.

Diamond, Elin. "Adrienne Kennedy." In *Speaking on Stage*, ed. by Philip C. Kolin and Colby H. Kullman. Tuscaloosa: Univ. of Alabama Press, 1996.

Kennedy, Adrienne. *People Who Led to My Plays*. New York: Knopf, 1987.

Keyssar, Helene. *Feminist Theatre*. London: Macmillan, 1984.

Kolin, Philip C. *Understanding Adrienne Kennedy*. Columbia, S.C: Univ. of South Carolina Press, 2005.

Meigs, Susan. "No Place but the Funnyhouse." In *Modern American Drama: The Female Canon*, ed. by June Schlueter. Rutherford, N.J.: Fairleigh Dickinson Univ. Press, 1990.

Olauson, Judith. *The American Woman Playwright: A View of Criticism and Characterization*. Troy, N.Y.: Whitson, 1981.

Robinson, Marc. *The Other American Drama*. Baltimore: Johns Hopkins Univ. Press, 1997.

Wilkerson, Margaret B. "Adrienne Kennedy." In *Dictionary of Literary Biography*, vol. 38, *Afro-American Writers After 1955*. Detroit: Gale, 1985.

Molly Castelloe

KERR, LOIS REYNOLDS (1908–2001)

Canadian playwright and journalist Lois Reynolds Kerr was born in Hamilton, Ontario, CANADA, in 1908. She attended the University of Toronto. In 1930 her play *Open Doors* won a national playwright's competition. It was produced a year later by Toronto Little Playhouse. The award opened doors for Kerr, leading to her appointment with the *Globe*, Toronto's major newspaper of that time. From 1930 to 1937 she worked as a journalist at the *Globe*'s women's department. Kerr's experiences at the *Globe* became the main source of inspiration for her later plays, many of which depict the working environment of newspaper rooms, specifically, the women's departments. In 1933 Kerr joined Playwrights' Studio Group. Founded in 1932 by Dora Smith Conover, Rica McLean Farquharson, and Leonora McNeilly, the group focused on producing original Canadian plays. Its members also included Marjorie Price, Virginia Coyne Knight, Winnifred Pilcher, Arthur Burrows, Jameson Field, and Margaret Ness. From 1932 to 1940 the group wrote and produced over sixty plays, most of them staged at Hart House Theatre.

As with many of her plays, Kerr's next two COMEDIES, *Among Those Present* (the title is based on a 1921 silent film) and *Nellie McNabb*, her most popular comedy, draw on Kerr's journalistic background and her experiences as a single working woman. Both were produced at Hart House Theatre in 1933 and 1934, respectively, and both deal with the world of the women's department of 1930s newspapers. Another play, *Guest of Honour* (produced in 1936), also takes place in the journalistic milieu. Kerr's last full-length play staged with the Playwrights' Studio Group was an espionage comedy, *X.Y.7.* (produced in 1939). But in 1940 she returned to the group to participate in the wartime revues *Well, Of All Things* and *Keep It Flying*, staged to raise funds in support of the war.

In 1950 Kerr moved to Vancouver, British Columbia, where family responsibilities and lack of an appropriate producing outlet prevented her from working in the theater until 1960. Her Vancouver plays include *No Reporters Please!* (which won honorable mention in 1970 at the Pacific Writers Conference in Seattle) and *O Woman!* These were produced by the University Women's Club in Vancouver (a women's club founded by Dr. Evlyn Farris on May 11, 1907) in 1969 and 1972, respectively. Kerr died in Vancouver on December 5, 2001. Acquired between 1982 and 1999 and donated by John Kerr in 2002, a large collection of Kerr's private correspondence, diaries, scrapbooks, photographs, and slides, as well as manuscripts of stage and television plays, playbills, and reviews is available at the University of Calgary archives.

PLAYS: *Open Doors* (1930); *Among Those Present* (1933); *Nellie McNabb* (1934); *Guest of Honour* (1936); *No Reporters Please!* (1969); *O Woman!* (1972)

FURTHER READING

Benson, Eugene, and L. W. Conolly, eds. *The Oxford Companion to Canadian Theatre*. Toronto: Oxford Univ. Press, 1989.

Reynolds, Lois. *Nellie McNabb, a One-Act Farce Comedy*. Canadian Playwright Series. Toronto: French, 1937.

Wagner, Anton, ed. *Canada's Lost Plays*. Vol. 3, *The Developing Mosaic: English-Canadian Drama to Mid-Century*. Toronto: Canadian Theatre Review, 1980.

Magda Romanska

KHAN-DIN, AYUB (1961–)

Ayub Khan-Din was raised in Salford, Manchester, ENGLAND, the primary setting of his best-known play, *East Is East* (1996). Indeed, the setting is just one of the many autobiographical elements in the play. Its main character, George Khan, is based on Khan-Din's own father, a small-time entrepreneur who was as enthused about his economic possibilities in England as he was disturbed by the erosion of his children's sense of their ethnic heritage. Khan-Din's own family was even larger than the Khan family of the play; he was one of ten children. After an undistinguished record in secondary school, Khan-Din became a hairdresser in Manchester and, by his own admission, had almost no natural or acquired talent for the job. After reading David Niven's memoir *The Moon's a Balloon*, he was, however, inspired to apply for admission into the drama program at Spalford University. There he worked on several early drafts of *East Is East*.

Set in the early 1970s, *East Is East* focuses on George Khan, a Pakistani immigrant to the United Kingdom who marries an English woman, has six children, and makes a success of a fish-and-chips shop. Yet, as his children grow up and assimilate into British culture, he becomes increasingly disturbed by their behavior and increasingly authoritarian. When his eldest son embarrasses him by rejecting an arranged marriage while the ceremony is already in progress, George demonstrates his obstinacy by arranging marriages for two of his other four sons. Although he has no desire to return to PAKISTAN, George demands that his wife and children behave as if the family were living in Pakistan. He becomes increasingly obsessed with the idea of moving them into a community with a large concentration of Pakistani immigrants. There he believes that their immersion in their cultural heritage will make them feel more Pakistani than British, and their segregation from the surrounding British culture will diminish its appeal and influence. George Khan's insistence on his patriarchal right to shape his children's lives well into their adulthood is a reflection of his fundamental uneasiness as an immigrant. He cannot accept that his decision to emigrate from Pakistan to the United Kingdom and to raise his children there has unavoidably given him and his family "hyphenated" identities. Ironically, his desire to retreat into the familiar customs and expectations of his home culture offers no protection against, or even any feasible response to, ingrained British racism toward non-European immigrants. On the surface much of the play is comical, but it explores important themes with great seriousness.

Khan-Din has written two subsequent plays for which he has received mixed notices, *Last Dance at Dum Dum* (1999) and *Notes on Falling Leaves* (2004). For his screenplay for the film adaptation of *East Is East* (1999), Khan-Din received a British Independent Film Award for Best Screenplay, an Asia Award for Film and Television, and the London Film Critics' Circle Award for Best Screenplay. The film also received the Alexander Korda Award for the Best British Film of the Year. He has also acted onstage and in films; his most memorable performance to date has been in the film *Sammy and Rosie Get Laid*.

PLAYS: *East Is East* (1996); *Last Dance at Dum Dum* (1999); *Notes on Falling Leaves* (2004)

FURTHER READING

Ahmad, Shazia. "Din's Own Story." *American Theatre* 17 (May/June 2000): 54–55.

Klobah, Loretta Collins. "Pakistani Englishness and the Containment of the Muslim Subaltern in Ayub Khan-Din's Tragi-comedy Film *East is East*." *South Asian Popular Culture* 1 (October 2003): 91–108.

Reitz, Bernard. "'Discovering an Identity Which Has Been Squashed': Intercultural and Intracultural Confrontations in the Plays of Winsome Pinnock and Ayub Khan-Din." *European Journal of English Studies* 7 (April 2003): 39–54.

Wolf, Matt. "East Is East and West Is an Off Broadway Stage." *New York Times* (May 23,1999): sec. 2, 5.

Martin Kich

KHARMS, DANIIL IVANOVICH (1905–1942)

Daniil Ivanovich Kharms (a pseudonym of D. I. Yuvachyov) was a Russian poet, prose writer, children's author, and playwright whose short, starkly eccentric plays, dialogues, verses, stories, and anecdotes stand at the beginning of what is known as the Russian absurd. His first poem dates to 1922, but he began writing in earnest in 1925, often under pseudonyms. "Kharms" is a mystification apparently incorporating the English words "charm" and "harm" and, perhaps, the Sanskrit "dharma." Most of the few works published in Kharms's lifetime were written for the children's journals *Yozh* and *Chizh* and the children's branch of Molodaya gvardia (Young Guard) publishing house, all located in his native city of Leningrad (St. Petersburg at his birth). He was a founding member of OBERIU (an imperfect acronym for Ob'edinenie real'nogo iskusstva, or Association for Real Art), a heterogeneous group of writers unified by their unconventional, often absurdist tendencies. This short-lived association (1928–1930) and Kharms's active role in it were significant for the development of Russian literature and drama. His best-known play, *Yelizaveta Bam* (1928), was written for the debut of OBERIU and is considered one of its seminal works. Twice arrested (1931, for "anti-Soviet" literary activity; 1941, for doubting aloud that the Soviet army could defeat the Germans), he died in a prison psychiatric ward where he may have simulated insanity to avoid execution.

Kharms's output is so unorthodox that it is impossible to count his plays. Over eighty works are composed primarily, though not exclusively, of dialogue, and over half of those are barely longer than a page and cannot be called traditional "plays." His whimsical, iconoclastic works employing word and sound play were often literary travesties: *Vengeance* (1930) spoofs Goethe's *Faust*; *Don Juan* (1932) lampoons Hamlet's "to be or not to be" monologue; *Pushkin and Gogol* (1934) burlesques the reverence commonly granted these writers.

My Mother Is All in Clocks (1926), combining texts by Kharms and Alexander Vvedensky, was his first dramatic script. Mixing drama, circus, dance, and painting, it was performed at the Institute of Artistic Culture (InKhuK), run by Kazimir Malevich. *The Comedy of the City of Petersburg* (1927), his largest drama, is a cheerfully ludicrous, yet melancholy, fantasy wherein Tsar Nikolai II meets a member of the Young Communist League, Peter the Great, Famusov from Aleksandr Griboyedov's play *Woe from Wit*, and a Man Resembling a Sausage. Fragmentary and plotless, it mingles farce with serious poetry while parodying and referencing works by ALEKSANDR BLOK, VLADIMIR MAYAKOVSKY, Aleksandr Pushkin, ANTON CHEKHOV, and others. Aside from the puppet play *The Shardam Circus* (1935), *Yelizaveta Bam* is his only other large drama. In it two strangers arrive to arrest Yelizaveta, who appears to be falsely accused of murder and has been deprived of the right to speak about anything. But neither plot nor meaning is the point in this jubilant tour de force of puns, gags, and nonsensical linguistic gymnastics that make up one of the most inventive and enigmatic Russian plays of the 20th century. Kharms defined his own sensibility in his notebooks in 1937: "Only 'nonsense' interests me; only that which has no practical significance. Life interests me only in its inept manifestations."

[*See also* Avant-Garde Drama; Chance; Collage; Russia and the Soviet Union]

SELECT PLAYS: *My Mother Is All in Clocks* (*Moya mama vsya v chasakh*, with Aleksandr Vvedensky, 1926); *The Comedy of the City of Petersburg* (*Komediya goroda Peterburga*, 1927); *Yelizaveta Bam* (1928); *Guidon* (*Gvidon*, 1930); *Vengeance* (*Mest'*, 1930); *Don Juan* (1932); *Nikolai II* (1933); *Fakirov* (c. 1933–1934); *Pushkin and Gogol* (*Pushkin i Gogol'*, 1934); *The Unsuccessful Show* (*Neudachniy spektakl'*, 1934); *The Shardam Circus* (*Tsirk Shardam*, 1935); *Yevstigneyev Laughs* (*Yevstigneyev smeyotsya*, c. 1935–1936); *Multifaceted Research* (*Vsestoroneye issledovaniye*, 1937)

FURTHER READING

Kharms, Daniil. *Daniil Kharms and the Poetics of the Absurd: Essays and Materials*. Ed. by Neil Cornwell. New York: St. Martin's, 1991.

——. *Elizabeth Bam*. In *Eight Twentieth-Century Russian Plays*, tr. by Timothy Langen and Justin Weir. Evanston, Ill.: Northwestern Univ. Press, 2000.

——. *Incidences*. Ed. and tr. by Neil Cornwell. London: Serpent's Tail, 1993.

——. *The Man with the Black Coat: Russia's Literature of the Absurd; Selected Works of Daniil Kharms and Alexander Vvedensky*. Ed. and trans. by George Gibian. Evanston, Ill.: Northwestern Univ. Press, 1997.

——. *The Plummeting Old Women*. Introd. and tr. by Neil Cornwell. Dublin: Lilliput Press, 1989.

Nakhimovsky, Alice Stone. *Laughter in the Void: An Introduction to the Writings of Daniil Kharms and Alexander Vvedenskii*. Vienna: Wiener Slawistischer Alamanach, 1982.

John Freedman

KILROY, THOMAS (1934–)

To base one's identity exclusively upon a mystical sense of place, upon the accident of one's birth, seems to me a dangerous absurdity. To dedicate one's life to the systematic betrayal of the same notion seems to be just as absurd.

—Thomas Kilroy

Thomas Kilroy may be best known as one of IRELAND's leading playwrights, but he is also one of the country's most distinguished scholars. Born in County Kilkenny in the southeast of Ireland in 1934, Kilroy first established a reputation as an academic. His influential article "Groundwork for an Irish Theatre" was published in 1959, the year he completed his M.A. at University College Cork; and he spent the subsequent decade teaching—at Notre Dame, Vanderbilt, and McGill universities, as well as University College Dublin. In 1975 he was appointed professor of English at University College Galway, a post he held until 1989. His 1991 article "A Generation of Playwrights" is an indispensable treatment of the aesthetics and politics of his many contemporaries, such as BRIAN FRIEL, Hugh Leonard, John B. Keane, and TOM MURPHY.

His first play, *The Death and Resurrection of Mr Roche*, was premiered at the 1968 Dublin Theatre Festival. A dark COMEDY concerning a group of men struggling to come to terms with a rapidly urbanizing Ireland the play provoked much negative coverage for its frank treatment of homosexuality. Yet it found an audience in Ireland and transferred to London in 1969. Its treatment of loneliness shows Kilroy's ability to present characters with real emotional depth; and its representation of homosexuality demonstrates his interest in bringing to the stage elements of Irish life that have been suppressed or ignored—one of the dominant characteristics of his work.

During the 1970s Kilroy's reputation as a writer grew steadily. His novel *The Big Chapel* was shortlisted for the Booker Prize in 1971, and he produced a series of well-received plays at the Abbey Theatre throughout the decade.

In 1986 his most significant play, *Double Cross*, was produced by FIELD DAY THEATRE COMPANY (of which Kilroy became a board member in 1988). It presents two Irishmen, Brendan Bracken and William Joyce, who occupied opposite sides during World War II. The play considers the instability of identity and complicates the issue of national allegiance by having both characters played by the same actor. An excellent example of the intellectual curiosity present throughout Kilroy's work, *Double Cross* also shows his interest in theatrical experimentation.

Kilroy's next play for Field Day, *The Madame MacAdam Travelling Theatre* (1991), was also set during World War II, but was harshly criticized, with the result that Kilroy stated that he would no longer write plays. Fortunately, he reversed this decision and premiered *The Secret Fall of Constance Wilde* at Dublin's Abbey Theatre in 1997. Presenting the trial and death of OSCAR WILDE from the perspective of Wilde's wife, the play was a powerful treatment of the place of the theatrical in everyday life. *The Shape of Metal*, possibly his finest work to date, premiered at the Dublin Theatre Festival in 2003.

SELECT PLAYS: *The Death and Resurrection of Mr Roche* (1968); *The O'Neil* (1969); *Tea and Sex and Shakespeare* (1976); *Talbot's Box* (1977); *Double Cross* (1986); *The Madame MacAdam Travelling Theatre* (1991); *The Secret Fall of Constance Wilde* (1997); *The Shape of Metal* (2003)

FURTHER READING

Dubost, Thierry. *Le Théâtre de Thomas Kilroy*. Caen: Presses Universitaires de Caen, 2001.

Murray, Christopher. "Words Elsewhere: The Plays of Thomas Kilroy." *Eire-Ireland* (Summer 1994): 123–138.

Roche, Anthony, ed. Special issue on Thomas Kilroy. *Irish University Review* 32, no. 1 (Spring/Summer 2002).

Patrick Lonergan

KING CHULALONKORN

See RAMA V

KINGSLEY, SIDNEY (1906–1995)

Born Sidney Kirshner in New York City on October 22, 1906, Sidney Kingsley was just twenty-six years old in 1933 when his first play, MEN IN WHITE, stamped him as a playwright to watch. Although he had just eight more plays produced over twenty-nine years, five of his nine works became critical and popular successes. He maintained a high reputation through the early 1950s, but as his realistic style fell out of fashion, he was increasingly seen as well meaning but lacking in nuance and innovation.

The criticisms of his work are not without merit. His characters are often underdrawn, his plotting schematic, and his dialogue stilted and, to the modern ear, dated. Even contemporary critics who liked his plays recognized these flaws, yet in his best work they usually found them offset by his narrative drive, his acute observation (the product of prodigious research), and especially his passion for social and political justice.

Kingsley attended Cornell University, flirted with acting, then worked in the film industry while beginning *Crisis*, the play that would become *Men in White*. The piece is set in a large-city hospital and, in threading the relationship of an older doctor and his protégé through several plots and subplots, celebrates the selflessness of those who sacrifice normal lives in the service of humankind. It is more a slice of life than a plausible, persuasive narrative, yet as Joseph Wood Krutch wrote in the *Nation*, it is "so immediately interesting, so completely absorbing, that one forgets to ask whether or not it is 'significant' or 'important.'" Staged on Broadway by the young GROUP THEATRE, it won the Pulitzer Prize for Drama.

Two years after *Men in White*, Kingsley's second play had its Broadway debut on a striking set that located New York's East River in the Belasco Theatre orchestra pit. Transpiring on a slum wharf abutting the rear of a swanky new apartment house, DEAD END decries the causative effects of poverty as it interweaves events in the lives of six obstreperous, foul-mouthed urchins with the story of a bitter, out-of-work architect who encounters a childhood acquaintance turned vicious gangster.

Though encumbered with cardboard adult characters and unlikely romantic relationships, *Dead End* was Kingsley's most popular play: It won generally favorable reviews, ran for 687 performances, and energized debate about the eradication of poverty. The boys who played the urchins, a combination of professional actors and real street kids, reproduced their roles in the film version.

Kingsley's next two plays were less successful. But he had another hit with *The Patriots* (1943), which argues for a democracy of conflicting views by dramatizing eleven years of debate between Thomas Jefferson and Alexander Hamilton (with George Washington serving as referee) about the nature of the new American republic. *The Patriots* is Kingsley's weakest major play. Its characters, especially the largely villainous Hamilton, have little flesh and blood, and its dialogue often consists of speechifying. (Some, in fact, was lifted from actual speeches and other sources.) Yet its message of unity struck a chord in wartime America, and the New York Critics' Circle named it the best play of the season.

Kingsley's verisimilitude of setting was again on display in *Detective Story* (1949), transpiring over four hours in the detective squad room of a New York police precinct. The play is populated by a sprawling array of officers and miscreants, but the focus is on one violent, morally unyielding detective, McLeod, whose insistence on prosecuting a heartless abortionist and a pathetic petty thief with equal zeal ends in tragedy, an implicit rebuke to those who would give the police unchecked power. *Detective Story* again lacks much characterization, and the dying conversion at its end is hard to credit. But its crackling dialogue, its plenitude of action, and its colorful depiction of its exotic milieu make it immensely playable. It won mostly enthusiastic notices and ran for 581 performances.

Kingsley's last major play, *Darkness at Noon* (1951), was both the flip side of *The Patriots* and a deepening of the police-state theme of *Detective Story*. Adapted from Arthur Koestler's novel, it deals with a onetime revolutionary leader in Stalinist Russia who is falsely imprisoned and comes to realize that his inhumane excesses have created the merciless regime that now proposes to execute him. Some felt that the play diminished the novel, and because much of it is set in a prison where inmates communicate solely by tapping on the walls (and then voicing their messages), it is difficult to stage effectively. But in general the critical response was favorable, and *Darkness* won Kingsley his second Critics' Circle best-play award.

Kingsley failed to find either critical or popular success with his last two produced plays, the second of which appeared in 1962. He remained active in the theater, however, notably as a longtime member and officer of the Dramatists Guild, until his death on March 20, 1995, in Oakland, New Jersey.

[*See also* Avant-Garde Drama; Naturalism; Realism; United States, 1929–Present]

PLAYS: *Men in White* (1933); *Dead End* (1935); *Ten Million Ghosts* (1936); *The World We Make* (1939); *The Patriots* (1943); *Detective Story* (1949); *Darkness at Noon* (1951); *Lunatics and Lovers* (1954); *Night Life* (1962)

FURTHER READING

Kingsley, Sidney. *Sidney Kingsley: Five Prizewinning Plays*. Ed. by Nena Couch. Columbus: Ohio State Univ. Press, 1995.

MacNicholas, John, ed. *Dictionary of Literary Biography*. vol. 7, *Twentieth-Century American Dramatists*. Detroit: Gale, 1996.

Smith, Wendy. *Real Life Drama: The Group Theatre and America, 1931–1940*. New York: Knopf, 1990.

Clifford A. Ridley

KINOSHITA JUNJI (1914–)

Kinoshita Junji, Japanese SHINGEKI playwright, was raised in Tokyo and Kumamoto and studied English literature, specializing in Elizabethan theater, at Tokyo University. By the 1950s he had become perhaps the leading figure in modern Japanese theater and the foremost commentator on its issues. Beyond his plays for stage and radio, he published record albums titled *Group Readings from Tales of the Heike: Tomomori* (*Heike monogatari ni yoru gundoku—Tomomori*) in 1969, a complete translation of William Shakespeare in the 1970s, and several works of criticism. For his powerful and provocative dramatic situations, he has been called the ARTHUR MILLER of JAPAN. His plays can be divided into two types: folktale plays (*minwageki*) and plays dealing with historical and political issues (*gendaigeki*).

Inspired by the work of the famous ethnographer Yanagita Kunio, Kinoshita's folktale plays were a lyrical departure from the relentless REALISM of orthodox *shingeki*. To stage them, Kinoshita helped found a theater group, the Grapes Society (Budō no Kai) in 1947. In 1950 the group staged Kinoshita's TWILIGHT CRANE, its signature piece that ultimately overshadowed his career; the play became more famous than the playwright.

Kinoshita intended such plays to counterbalance the rabid urbanization and commodification of postwar Japan. Informed by folk wisdom, they expose the foibles of humans, once guileless, but now beguiled by the temptations of capitalism—in short, by greed. Kinoshita dots his relatively simple dialogue with regional expressions, thereby lending his characters a common touch. While that approach and his tendency to weave a didactic point into the action may be obvious on one level, eliciting immediate response even from children, his folktale plays are in fact quite complex and easily sustain several levels of interpretation.

By contrast, his historically grounded plays, tinged with Georg Wilhelm Friedrich Hegel's theory of history, emerge from actual events, are structured by complex ideas, and are resolutely literary. Kinoshita is more interested in ideas and situations than in character and motivation. Typically his main characters are types or models confronted by an overwhelming array of opposing forces; how they resist sparks the action. For example, in *Between God and Man—A Judgment on War Crimes* (1972), about the Tokyo war crimes trials in 1946–1947 and the twenty-eight defendants, he illuminates the problem of moral awareness when confronted by the need to make choices, even when those choices might lead to destruction. The collective situation, not the character of each defendant, is pivotal. Questions posed include the following: In a time of war, how is one to be a good Japanese? How is the guilt of a nation to be defined? Does the war crimes court even have jurisdiction over the defendants?

As with his folktale plays, Kinoshita has a didactic bent here. He aimed to move passive spectators to actively confront those critical questions and make their own judgments. To that end, the twenty-eight defendants in *Between God and Man* are never on stage but are seated among the spectators. That technique drives home Kinoshita's point: even though the war crimes trials offer no possibility of reaching an impartial decision, the spectators have themselves become the defendants and are thus moved to consider the critical questions posed by the play on an individual but especially on a national level.

SELECT PLAYS: *Wind and Waves* (*Fūrō*, 1939); *The Story of Hikoichi* (*Hikoichi-banashi*, 1946); *Twilight Crane* (*Yūzuru*, 1949); *Ascension of a Frog* (*Kaeru shōten*, 1951); *Okinawa* (1961); *A Man Called Ottō* (*Ottō to yobareru Nihonjin*, 1962); *The Winter Season* (*Fuyu no jidai*, 1964); *Between God and Man—A Judgment on War Crimes* (*Kami to hito to no aida*, 1972); *Requiem on the Great Meridian* (*Shigosen no matsuri*, 1978)

FURTHER READING

Keene, Donald. *Dawn to the West: Japanese Literature in the Modern Era*. Vol. 2, *Poetry, Drama, Criticism*. New York: Holt, Rinehart & Winston, 1984.

Kinoshita Junji. *Between God and Man—A Judgment on War Crimes: A Play in Two Parts*. Tr. by Eric J. Gangloff. Tokyo: Univ. of Tokyo Press; Seattle: Univ. of Wash. Press, 1979.

——. *Gikyoku no Nihongo* [Japanese language in the drama]. Vol. 12 of *Nihongo no sekai* [The world of Japanese]. Tokyo: Chūō Kōronsha, 1982.

——. *Requiem on the Great Meridian and Selected Essays*. Tr. and ed. by Brian Powell and Jason Daniel. Tokyo: Nan'undō, 2000.

Ortolani, Benito. *The Japanese Theatre: From Shamanistic Ritual to Contemporary Pluralism*. Rev ed. Princeton, N.J.: Princeton Univ. Press, 1995.

Powell, Brian. *Japan's Modern Theatre: A Century of Change and Continuity*. London: Japan Library, 2002.

John K. Gillespie

KIPPHARDT, HEINAR (1922–1982)

> *There are people today who are prepared to protect freedom to the extent that nothing of freedom remains.*
>
> —J. Robert Oppenheimer, Scene 4, *In the Matter of J. Robert Oppenheimer*

Heinar Kipphardt was born on March 8, 1922, in Heidersdorf, GERMANY. A psychiatrist by training, he not only wrote plays for the stage but also produced those of others as chief dramatic adviser for the Deutsches Theater in East Berlin (1950–1959) and for the Kammerspiele in Munich (1970–1971). Both assignments ended involuntarily when Kipphardt became the victim of the politics of culture on both sides of the Iron Curtain. In East Germany he had been accused of "neglecting the position of the working class" and showing signs of "a lack of trust in the right politics of the Party." The progressive hardening of the party's line in terms of cultural politics caused Kipphardt to leave East Germany in 1959. His assignment for Munich's Kammerspiele ended in the wake of staging a play by the East German dissident Wolf Biermann (1936–), *The Dra-Dra* (*Der Dra-Dra*, 1970), because Kipphardt had dared to compare West German politicians to the parasitic powermongers of the state he had left twelve years earlier. Perhaps it was his political position—which he described as, "to advocate Marxism as a critical and open science that seeks its practice"—that made him a gadfly in both Germanys. Nevertheless, his plays, and in particular his DOCUMENTARY DRAMA *In the Matter of J. Robert Oppenheimer* (*In der Sache J. Robert Oppenheimer*, 1964), made him famous on both sides of the Atlantic. Kipphardt died on November 18, 1982, in Munich, West Germany.

In the Matter of J. Robert Oppenheimer shows the title character as the type of scientist who creates moral dilemmas for himself through the success of his own work. In the course of the hearings before the Atomic Energy Commission that make up the body of the text of the play, and as he is being questioned about his loyalty to the state that employs him, he himself begins to question his loyalty toward his friends in his dealings with the FBI; he begins to question his opportunism in putting the importance of being able to do his work before his loyalty to his friends. He becomes tormented by the conflict between working on the atomic bomb and, at the same time, trying to prevent its use for military purposes. Above all, he questions the morality of a science that is practiced in the service of other interests, represented here by the military. As in his other plays, Kipphardt successfully avoids psychologizing the conflicts and works at bringing out the "nucleus and meaning" of historic moments such as this one that lend themselves to comparisons with other such moments. Thus it is only logical that Kipphardt employs dramatic techniques similar to those of BERTOLT BRECHT, adding to the text spoken on the stage such elements as quotes from other sources, historic film footage, and newspaper clippings. The intended effect is not empathy and identification with the protagonist, but a distanced and critical stance that allows the audience to see the relevance of the historic event for their own time.

SELECT PLAYS: *Decisions: Scenes* (*Entscheidungen: Szenen*, 1952); *Desperately Seeking Shakespeare: A Satiric Comedy in Three Acts* (*Shakespeare dringend gesucht: Eine satirische Komödie in drei Akten*, 1953); *The Rise of Alois Piontek: A Tragicomic Farce* (*Aufstieg des Alois Piontek: Eine tragikomische Farce*, 1956); *The Chairs of Mr. Szmil* (*Stühle des Herrn Szmil*, 1961); *The General's Dog* (*Hund des Generals*, 1962); *In The Matter of J. Robert Oppenheimer* (*In der Sache J. Robert Oppenheimer*, 1964); *Joel Brand: The Story of a Business Deal* (*Joel Brand: Die Geschichte eines Geschäfts*, 1965); *The Night the Boss Was Butchered* (*Nacht in der der Chef geschlachtet wurde*, 1967); *The Soldiers, Based on Jacob Michael Reinhold Lenz* (*Soldaten, nach Jacob Michael Reinhold Lenz*, 1968); *Sedan Anniversary: A Montage of Materials from the 1870 War* (*Sedanfeier: Montage aus Materialien des 70er Krieges*, 1970); *März, an Artist's Life* (*März, ein Künstlerleben*, 1980); *Brother Eichmann* (*Bruder Eichmann*, 1983)

FURTHER READING

Barnett, David. "Documentation and Its Discontents: The Case of Heinar Kipphardt." *Forum for Modern Language Studies* 37, no. 3 (2001): 272–285.

Karbach, Walter. *Mit Vernunft zu rasen: Heinar Kipphard; Studien zu seiner Ästhetik und zu seinem veröffentlichten und nachgelassenen Werk* [Racing with rationality: Heinar Kipphardt; Studies of his aesthetics and his published and posthumous works]. Oberwesel: Hermann, 1989.

Steiner, Carl. "Heinar Kipphardt, Robert Oppenheimer and Bruder Eichmann: Two Plays in Search of a Political Answer." In *Amerika! New Images in German Literature*, ed. by Heinz D. Osterle. New York: Peter Lang, 1989. 199–211.

Friedemann J. Weidauer

KISAH PERJUANGAN SUKU *See* THE STRUGGLE OF THE NAGA TRIBE

KISHIDA RIO (1950–2003)

Kishida Rio, Japanese playwright and director, trained for the law at Tokyo's Chūo University, but joined the Theatre Laboratory of playwright TERAYAMA SHŪJI's Tenjō Sajiki (a name derived from the Japanese title of the French film *Les enfants du Paradis*) in 1974. She became Terayama's trusted collaborator in AVANT-GARDE theater and wrote with him such plays as *Shintoku-maru: Poison Boy* (1978) and *Lemmings* (1983).

Kishida is one of a new wave of women playwrights in the 1980s who were also directors, actors, and heads of their own theater companies. Included in this dynamic group are Kisaragi Koharu, WATANABE ERIKO, and Ichidō Rei of the all-woman company Blue Bird (Aoi Tori, founded in 1974). In 1978 Kishida founded With the Help of My Big Brother Theatre (Ka-i Gekijō). In 1981 Kishida launched the theater group Kishida Company (Kishida Jimusho), and two years later she joined forces with director Wada Yoshio's Optimists' Troupe (Rakuten-dan) to form Kishida Jimusho + Rakuten-dan (1983–1993). Her company is now called Kishida Rio Company (Kishida Rio Kanpanii).

Although not strictly a feminist, Kishida portrays the predicament of women in a male-dominated society as a structural problem of the nation as a whole. She contends that "denying the Emperor System and patriarchal authority [is] a way for women to restore themselves to themselves . . . we must kill the system" ("Kyōdo Tōron," 2001). This critical stand is evident in her signature work, *Thread Hell* (1984). A girl is searching for her mother and a place to call home. At a thread-spinning factory she is promised a new family registry, but the place turns out to be a front for a house of prostitution. She and the thread spinners entrap the pimps in the winds and windings of thread hell and take over the business. A metaphor for JAPAN's problematic modernization, the play depicts female exploitation through poetic symbolism and rhythmic dialogue rendered in traditional seven-five meter. For this play Kishida won the 1985 Kishida Kunio Drama Prize, the most prestigious award in modern Japanese drama. In 1992 it was produced at Australian theater festivals.

In the 1990s Kishida was an important figure in the growing internationalization of theater and cultural exchange. She entered a new collaborative period, this time with foreign artists. She and director TADASHI SUZUKI were instrumental in launching the Heiner Müller Project between GERMANY and Japan. Kishida also established the Theatre Across Borders series in 1992 and began experimentation for a new Asian theater. She collaborated with Korean director Lee Yun-tek in the first Japanese-Korean production, *Happy Days* (1993), which employs the languages of both countries to expose the ravages of Japan's colonial policy in Korea. Her subsequent work, *Lear* (1997), with Singaporean director ONG KENG SEN, was more radical. Performers from six Asian countries were enlisted, the cumulative effect being to highlight Asian diversity sans harmony. This production toured Berlin and major Asian cities. In their second collaboration, *Desdemona* (2000–2001), Kishida devised a script from the performers' improvisations that radically deconstructed William Shakespeare's *Othello* from an Asian woman's perspective.

[*See also* Angura and Shōgekijō; Shingeki]

SELECT PLAYS: *Shintoku-maru: Poison Boy* (*Shintoku-maru*, with Terayama Shûji, 1974, revised 1997); *Knock* (*Nokku*, with Maboroshi Kazuma, 1975); *The Law of Gravity* (*Inryoku no hōsoku*, with Terayama, 1976); *Anatomische Tabellen* (*Kaitai shinsho*, 1978);

Foundling's Tale (*Sutego monogatari*, 1978); *December Chronicles* (*Rōgekki*, 1979); *The Floating Bridge of Dream* (*Yume no ukihashi*, 1980); *Weird Love Songs: O-shichi* (*Koiuta kuzushi: Higaku o-shichi*, 1982); *Lemmings* (*Remingu*, with Terayama, 1983); *New Heretics Gate* (*Shin Jashūmon*, with Terayama and others, 1983); *Thread Hell* (*Ito jigoku*, 1984, revised 1987, 1990); *Love Trilogy* (*Koi sanbusaku*, 1985–1987); *The Last House, Temporary Home: The Biography of Kawashima Yoshiko* (*Tsui no sumika kari no yado—Kawashima Yoshiko-den*, 1988); *Cat and Canary* (*Neko to kanaria*, 1990); *Hide and Seek* (*Kakurenbo*, 1990); *A Mid-Summer Night's . . . Dream?* (*Manatsu no yoru no . . . yume?* 1990); *Our Eves* (*Watakushi-tachi no ibu*, 1992); *Happy Days* (*Sewori chotta* or *Sewoli-chota*, 1993); *Bird! Bird! Blue Bird!* (*Tori yo tori yo aoi tori yo*, 1994); *Love: Part 4* (*Koi sono yon*, 1994); *Lost Angels* (*Maigo no tenshi*, 1996); *Lear* (with Ong Keng Sen, 1997); *Eternity: Part I* (*Towa Part I*, 2000); *Desdemona* (with Ong Keng Sen, 2000–2001); *Eternity: Part II* (*Towa Part II*, 2001); *Sky, Sky, Langit* (*Sora hanur langit* or *Sora hanuru langit*, 2001)

FURTHER READING

Kishida Rio. *Thread Hell* [*Ito Jigoku*]. Tr. by Carol Fisher Sorgenfrei. In *Half a Century of Japanese Theater*, Vol. 4, 1980s, Part 2, ed. by Japan Playwrights Association. Tokyo: Kinokuniya, 2002. 161–221.

"Kyōdo tōron: Engeki ni totte 'tennō-sei' to wa nani ka?" [Panel discussion: What is the significance of the emperor system for theater?). *Shiatā Ātsu* [Theater Arts] 13 (April 2001): 8–31.

Nishidō Kōjin. *Doramachisuto no shōzō: Gendai engeki no zen'ei-tachi* [Portraits of dramatists: The avant-garde of modern Japanese theater]. Tokyo: Renga Shobō Shinsha, 2002.

Scholz-Cionca, Stanca, and Samuel L. Leiter, eds. *Japanese Theatre and the International Stage*. Leiden: Brill, 2001.

"Tokushū: Watakushi-tachi no ibu" [Special edition: Our eves]. In *KAZE Booklet No. 3*. Tokyo: Tokyo Engeki Shūdan Kaze, 1992.

Mari Boyd

KITAMURA SŌ (1953–)

Kitamura Sō is a Japanese playwright and director whose motto is "risk your life for the sake of laughter." His plays have a light, dry humor with many literary references. Influenced by KARA JŪRŌ, Kitamura's dramas draw inspiration from other works worldwide and are eminently playable by actors. Kitamura began his career in Nagoya in 1973 and became one of the first playwright-directors in JAPAN to become successful working outside metropolitan Tokyo or Osaka.

Kitamura's humor often is based on his characters seemingly having no identity of their own, but using identities of figures from various sources, such as literature (the 20th-century Japanese author Miyazawa Kenji in *The Kenji Incident*, 1992), the movies (the Marx Brothers in *Duck Soap*, 1987), or the Bible (Christ in *Ode to Joy*, 1979). The plays are set in vaguely determined spaces such as "somewhere in Kansai [near Osaka] after a nuclear holocaust," "on a rooftop," or "the countryside of Iwate." The combination of vague identities and indeterminate locations allows Kitamura to have his characters behave in ways that may not be consistent with conventional expectations.

Miyazawa Kenji was highly respected for his Buddhist faith and efforts to increase the agricultural productivity of his native Iwate Prefecture. Physical farm work undermined his health, and he died in 1933 at age thirty-seven. In *The Kenji Incident* Kitamura poses the question, "What if Miyazawa was a scoundrel who faked his death and ran off to a life of dissipation in Tokyo?" The answer is an irreverent interpretation of Miyazawa's life and work in Iwate. Kenji in the play is a lost soul interested only in his own profit.

A Hino Terumasa song inspired *Ode to Joy*. It also seems to be an attempt by Kitamura to exorcise some of his own demons. He wrote it in just two days in 1979 during a bout of neurosis. The play takes place in Japan after a nuclear war with no known cause or foreseeable end. Two itinerant performers, Gesaku and Kyōko, wandering aimlessly through the blasted landscape, encounter another character walking to Jerusalem. His name, Yaso, is close to the Japanese pronunciation of Jesus. Christlike miracles provide food, but eventually they part ways.

The humor in *Duck Soap* starts with the mispronunciation of the Marx Brothers's movie *Duck Soup*. The play satirizes corporate culture and theater when a pair of gangsters, trying to muscle in on the profits of the Duck Soap Company, stumble into a rehearsal of the company's drama club.

The characters in *People on the Roof* search for their identity on a rooftop in a modern city. Their search is limited to the roof itself. They simply drop off if they search beyond those boundaries. In an area the size of a NŌ stage Kitamura explores social limits and theatrical space.

Kitamura's humorous confrontations of human frailties and worldly pitfalls usually produce a sense of optimism.

[*See also* Angura and Shōgekijō; Shingeki]

SELECT PLAYS: *Ode to Joy* (*Hogi uta*, 1979); *A Blue Comet Night* (*Aoi suisei no ichiya*, 1982); *Eleven Boys* (*Jūichinin no shōnen*, 1982); *Boiled Down to Love and Death* (*Ai to shi o nitsumete*, 1983); *The Mechanical Apple* (*Kikaijikake no ringo*, 1983); *The Night of the Milky Way Express a la Kitamura* (*Sōkō: Ginga tetsudō no yoru*, 1986); *Duck Soap* (*Duck Soap*, 1987); *Duck Soap 2* (*Duck Soap 2*, 1988); *People on the Roof* (*Okujō no hito*, 1990); *The Kenji Incident* (*Kenji no jiken*, 1992); *The Great Kenji Incident* (*Kenji no dai jiken*, 1995)

FURTHER READING

Japan Playwrights Association, ed. *Half a Century of Japanese Theater*. Vol. 4, 1980s, Part 2. Tokyo: Kinokuniya, 2002.

Kazama Ken. *Shōgekijō no fūkei* [The Little Theater Landscape]. Tokyo: Chūō Kōronsha, 1992.

Powell, Brian. *Japan's Modern Theatre: A Century of Change and Continuity*. London: Japan Library, 2002.

Senda Akihiko. *The Voyage of Contemporary Japanese Theatre*. Tr. by J. Thomas Rimer. Honolulu: Univ. of Hawaii Press, 1997.

John D. Swain

KLOP See THE BEDBUG

THE KNACK

The play is the structure that allows everything to happen.
—Ann Jellicoe

Performed in 1961 at the Arts Theatre in Cambridge, England, and directed by Keith Johnstone, *The Knack* by ANN JELLICOE is a risqué COMEDY set at the beginning of the Swinging Sixties in which, as one of the characters confesses, "we're all more or less total sexual failures." An unusual play of manners, it blends comic situation with genuine moments of fear. The plot revolves around three young men, Tom, Colin, and Tolen, who share a house, and the attempts made by Colin and Tolen to get one young woman into bed. Tensions inevitably arise, fueled by the cramped living conditions of the postwar national housing shortage. Colin is young and inexperienced, a stereotypical schoolteacher; Tolen, a sinister, protofascist figure with a fixation with authority who claims to have five hours of sexual intercourse a day, takes advantage of him and offers to tutor him. This is "the knack," the way to get women.

While Colin listens in awe, Tom, the third flatmate, attempts to intervene, pouring scorn on Tolen's ideas and adding that it is unlikely in the extreme that changing his diet to milk and meat will do the trick. At this point a young woman (Nancy) arrives, seeking the YWCA. Tolen decides to demonstrate his prowess. Beds are moved and doors blocked as the rest of the play explores Tolen's attempts to seduce her, Colin's attempts to imitate him, and Tom's equally purposeful and increasingly frantic attempts to get in the way. Nancy succumbs, and Tolen laughs and leaves her. Nancy, who is only seventeen, faints and then cries "Rape!" The final act of the play turns upon the question of how to prevent Nancy from going to the authorities, and how to convince her that she has in fact not been raped. Subversively, rape becomes a signifier not just of male domination and aggressiveness, but also of adolescent sexuality. Tom's comment "If he wants to keep her quiet he must rape her. That's the only thing that will satisfy her" darkens the mood significantly and creates a significant chill in the final scene.

The play has a surreal quality, reminiscent of the Writers' Workshop techniques produced at the Royal Court, of which Jellicoe was a member. Tom's attempts to distract Colin and Nancy range from pretending that his bed is a piano to moving chairs onto the wall and, eventually, telling bad jokes and talking nonsense. Repeatedly, Jellicoe's dialogue veers away from the realistic, exploding into ABSURDISM and large-scale comic relief. Sometimes these exchanges carry significant themes. A deeply symbolic exchange takes place near the end: while Tom cries "Parley," and Nancy stands on a stepladder refusing to listen, Tolen's cry is "Force!"

In this play sexual politics run deep. In a stunning twist at the end, the worm turns: Colin gets the girl and demands that Tolen cease to molest her. Nancy, who appears in search of a protector, plays along. The play is well formed, witty, and precise. Unsurprisingly, it remains one of Jellicoe's most popular plays.

[*See also* England]

FURTHER READING

Jellicoe, Ann. *Community Plays: How to Put Them On*. London: Methuen, 1987.

——. *The Knack. The Sport of My Mad Mother*. London: Faber, 1985.

——. *Some Unconscious Influences in the Theatre*. Cambridge: Cambridge Univ. Press, 1967.

Jüngst, Heike. *Frauengestalten und Frauenthemen bei John Arden und Margaretta D'Arcy: Mit Vergleichskapiteln zu Ann Jellicoe, Arnold Wesker, John McGrath und Caryl Churchill*. Frankfurt am Main: P. Lang, 1996.

Snyder, L. "Learn to Play the Game: Learning and Teaching Strategies in Ann Jellicoe, *The Knack*." *Modern Drama* 37, no. 3 (1994): 451–460.

Kerry Kidd

KNUTZON, LINE (1965–)

To me it is very concrete. People call me odd and peculiar and surrealistic and things like that, but to me it is pure and simple reality.
—Line Knutzon, 2000

Danish playwright Line Knutzon, born on March 3, 1965, in Odense, DENMARK, left school early and performed in small roles in film and television. She had her breakthrough with *The Splinter in the Heart* (*Splinten i hjertet*, 1991) about two youngsters and a "closet mother" placed at their disposal by the local authorities. She made her mark as the most significant and successful representative of a new generation's frustration and confusion after the collapse of the intelligible world of the previous decades, related to the ideas of the parents. Line Knutzon belongs to the third generation of a family of actors and stage directors. Her grandfather, Per Knutzon, staged KJELD ABELL's *The Melody That Disappeared*.

Her style was from the very beginning dynamic, comic, sometimes almost farcical, mixed up with poetic expressions of indignation and desperation in a particular combination of ABSURDISM and grotesque REALISM, fragments of fairy tales, and subconscious metaphors. The painful process of leaving childhood, of growing up deprived of evident authorities against whom to rebel, and of meeting the opposite sex is a significant motive in her dramatic universe. To these mental pressures corresponds a scenographic confinement: the outside world conceived as a threat. Gradually more direct satire appears, against, for example, narcissism, and against the superficiality of the media, and similarly the characters represent problems related to a more mature age. Knutzon has written seven plays for the stage and six radio dramas. The first plays implied only three or four characters and a rather loose, associative dramaturgical composition. With *First of All You Are Born* (*Først bli'r man jo født*,

1994), written while she was playwright-in-residence at Aarhus Theatre, the motive of breaking isolation is played through by six characters and in a more complex structure. But poetic monologues are still a characteristic part of all her plays. She took a position as a "mature" playwright with SOON THE TIME WILL COME (*Snart kommer tiden*, 1998), a play about time and consciousness of death. With *Two-Legged Torben* (*Torben Toben*) from 2000, Knutzon presented a grotesque political parable about a man who is about to eat up the whole world. Her plays have been translated into, among other languages, English, French, German, and Italian. In 2004 *First of All You Are Born* was staged in New York.

PLAYS: *The Splinter in the Heart* (*Splinten i hjertet*, 1991); *Invisible Friends* (*Usynlige venner*, 1992); *Well, That's the New* (*Det er så det nye*, 1993); *First of All You Are Born* (*Først bli'r man jo født*, 1994); *Harriet's Ascension* (*Harriets himmelfart*, radio drama, 1995); *Mâvens and Peder in the Spotlight of the Media* (*Mâvens og Peder i mediernes søgelys*, radio drama, 1998); *Mâvens and Peder on a Canoe Trip* (*Mâvens og Peder på kanotur*, radio drama, 1998); *Soon the Time Will Come* (*Snart kommer tiden*, 1998); *Two-Legged Torben* (*Torben Toben*, 2000); *The Air the Others Breathe* (*Den luft, de andre indånder*, 2001); *Mâvens and Peder Lose Their Tongues* (*Mâvens og Peder mister mælet*, radio drama, 2002); *Mâvens and Peder Meet Mâvens and Peder* (*Mâvens og Peder møder Mâvens og Peder*, radio drama, 2002); *The Fairytale About Einar* (*Eventyret om Einar*, radio drama, 2003)

FURTHER READING

Bille, Karen-Maria. "Floundering but Not Fooled." *Danish Literary Magazine* 7 (1994).

Hesselaa, Birgitte. *Vi lever i en tid: Line Knutzons dramatik*. Copenhagen: Borgens, 2001.

Theil, Per, and Lise Garsdal. *Hvem der? Scener fra 90erne*. Copenhagen: Høst og Søn, 2000.

Bent Holm

KŌKAMI SHŌJI (1958–)

Kōkami Shōji is a Japanese playwright and artistic director who, together with playwright NODA HIDEKI, was a major figure in the lively comic-frenetic theater that arose in the 1980s. He launched the theatrical troupe the Third Stage (Dai San Butai) in 1981 while still a student at Waseda University in Tokyo.

His career can be divided into three periods: the first was centered on his *Chronicles of Planet Earth* plays (1981–1985), which are about postnuclear war devastation and dystopias; the second was a time of expansion (1986–1991), when he and his troupe members forged into television, film, and other media, the culmination of which was his troupe's London production of *Angels with Closed Eyes, International Version* (1991); and the third period (1992–2001) was one of creative collaboration with talented artists from other performance genres. In this most recent active phase, Kōkami attended a yearlong actor-training course at the Guildford School for Music and Drama, London, in 1997, as part of the Agency of Cultural Affairs Arts Program. In 2001 he "sealed" his Third Stage troupe for ten years and is now working mainly through Kōkami@network, his production team established in 1999.

Considerable disagreement has attended the critical assessment of Kōkami's theater. Nonetheless, the 1987 revival of his best-known work, *With a Sunset like the Morning Sun* (1981), which won the Kinokuniya Theatre Award Group Prize, gained him critical acclaim, and in 1995 he received the prestigious Kishida Kunio Drama Prize for *Snufkin's Letter* (1994), thus establishing his reputation.

His major themes are social oppression, alienation, and the temptation to conform. He portrays contemporary urban youth caught in a conformist society dominated by late capitalism. Kōkami employs the image of a "soft, expansive wall" to suggest the insidious control exercised by authorities; even those who revolt are only being "permitted" to rebel within the city's flexible boundaries.

His lighthearted performance style belies the seriousness of his message. Attuned to pop culture, Kōkami targets the Japanese MTV generation. Across a bare stage his actors dash about in outrageously colorful costumes while engaging in wordplay, jokes, metatheatrical allusions, and parody. His shows are complex, alogical structures of short, fast-paced scenes, often connected by lively dance sequences and song.

His signature work, *With a Sunset like the Morning*, is an example. Kōkami portrays the desperation of the city dweller, who, unable to form close ties with others, wastes his life in pursuing frivolity. The characters bound vigorously between the two "worlds" of the Tachibana Toys Company and SAMUEL BECKETT's WAITING FOR GODOT. Suddenly the characters are revealed to be patients in a role-playing therapy session at a hospital. This unexpected development opens up the suspicion that other worlds could appear just as randomly, thus endlessly destabilizing fictive meaning and structure. Without the hope of ever creating significant meaning, the characters are left to share their loneliness and hone their time-killing skills.

[See also Angura and Shōgekijō; Japan; Shingeki]

SELECT PLAYS: *Dancing in the Plastic Night Under the Midnight Sun* (*Purasuchikku no byakuya ni odoreba*, 1981); *Rules to Sleep in the Universe* (*Uchū de nemuru tame no hōhō ni tsuite*, 1981); *With a Sunset like the Morning Sun* (*Asahi no yōna yūhi o tsurete*, 1981, revised 1983, 1985, 1987, 1991); *The Electric Sheep Whistles for the Carnival* (*Denki hitsuji wa kānibaru no kuchibue o fuku*, 1982); *Déjà Vu* (*Deja Byū*, 1983, revised 1986); *The Relay Runner* (*Rireiyā*, 1983); *Modern Horror* (*Modan horā*, 1984); *Angels with Closed Eyes* (*Tenshi wa hitomi wo tojite*, 1988); *Pilgrim* (*Pirugurimu*, 1989); *Angels with Closed Eyes, International Version* (*Tenshi wa hitomi o tojite, intānashonaru bājon*, 1991); *Trance* (*Toransu*, 1993); *Snufkin's Letter* (*Sunafukin no tegami*, 1994); *The Relay Runner III* (*Rereiya III*, 1996); *Lullaby: A Hundred Years of Song* (*Rarabai: Matawa hyakunen no komori-uta*, 2000)

FURTHER READING

Daisan Butai, ed. *Daisan Butai: Third Stage Private Data Book*. Tokyo: Hakusuisha, 1996.

Kazama Ken. *Shōgekijō no fūkei: Tsuka, Noda, Kōkami no geki sekai* (The landscape of little theater: The theater of Tsuka, Noda, and Kōkami). Tokyo: Chūkō Kōronsha, 1992.

Kōkami Shōji. *Angels with Closed Eyes, International Version* Tr. by A to Z Network Inc. Tokyo: Hakusui-sha, 1991.

——. *Lullaby: A Hundred Years of Song* [*Rarabai: Mata wa hyakunen no komori-uta*]. Tr. by Mari Boyd. In *Half a Century of Japanese Theater*, vol. 3, 1980s, Part 1, ed. by Japan Playwrights Association. Tokyo: Kinokuniya, 2001. 223–314.

Senda Akihiko. *The Voyage of Contemporary Japanese Theater*. Tr. by J. Thomas Rimer. Honolulu: Univ. of Hawaii Press, 1997.

Mari Boyd

KOKOSCHKA, OSKAR (1886–1980)

Born in Pöchlarn, AUSTRIA, and known today primarily as an important painter and graphic artist, Oskar Kokoschka also played a significant role in theater history. There he is known as one of the founding figures of expressionist drama. His five expressionist plays, from the period between 1907 and 1919, are deceptively short. Their compact, dense language and strong visual effects make a profound impression on the audience. The plays' central themes are the agonistic relationships beween men and women. As in expressionist art and poetry, the surface veneer of polite society is stripped away, so that a raw reality is exposed in stark, often grotesque forms.

Expressionist theater wanted to shock, and it did. Just as the public recoiled from what it saw in expressionist visual art as deformed representations of nightmare visions, it was appalled by the form and content of Kokoschka's plays. The first to be performed also became the most notorious: *Murderer, Hope of Women* (*Mörder, Hoffnung der Frauen*, 1909). The title accurately summarizes the drama's contents. In one unbroken scene the Man and the Woman abuse each other verbally, and he tortures her physically. Although other contemporary playwrights had depicted the modern war of the sexes on stage, Kokoschka's drama, ending with the woman's death and the killing of the chorus, was an early example of what ANTONIN ARTAUD (1895–1948) would later describe as the "theater of cruelty."

Kokoschka's other plays deal with the same issues. Some of the dramas contain moments of optimism and even humor. *The Burning Bush* (*Der brennende Dornbusch*, 1911) uses imagery of light and dark, of fire and radiance, to suggest how sexual desires might be sublimated into love. Contemporary discussions about the changing role of women in society are reflected in *Sphinx and Strawman* (*Sphinx und Strohmann*, 1907), as when Mr. Rubberman proclaims: "Joy reigns supreme, conscience is dead. Yes, marriage reform, marriage reform and let us make love in front of scientists!" This play is also notable for Kokoschka's innovations in staging. For example, a series of Gentlemen appear only as their heads pop through holes painted on a canvas. Such exorbitant theatricality led to an important crossover to Dada; the play was the first to be staged by the Zürich dadaists in 1917, with Hugo Ball (1886–1927) as one of the performers. Kokoschka was increasingly drawn to more symbolic dramas. *Job* (*Hiob*, 1917) removed the male-female theme from the immediate present to the plane of biblical myths. *Orpheus and Eurydice* (*Orpheus und Eurydike*, 1919), the longest and most complex of these plays, used mythology to work through the repercussions of Kokoschka's own affair with Alma Mahler (1879–1964).

Kokoschka's only other play, *Comenius*, was written between 1936 and 1938 but not published until 1972. Based on the life of Jan Amos Komenský (1592–1670), a Czech theologian and philosopher who worked for peace during the Thirty Years' War, this play is a fairly traditional historical drama. Against the background of the violent 20th century, the play's pessimism regarding progress toward a world without war seems all too reasonable.

[*See also* Dadaism; Expressionism]

PLAYS: *Sphinx and Strawman* (*Sphinx und Strohmann: Komödie für Automaten*, 1907; 1913 as *Sphinx und Strohmann: Ein Curiosum*); *Murderer, Hope of Women* (*Mörder, Hoffnung der Frauen*, 1909); *The Burning Bush* (*Schauspiel*, 1913; 1919 as *Der brennende Dornbusch, Schauspiel*); *Job* (*Hiob, Ein Drama*, 1917); *Orpheus and Eurydice* (*Orpheus und Eurydike, Schauspiel*, 1919); *Comenius* (first version, 1938; second version, 1972)

FURTHER READING

Diethe, Carol. *Aspects of Distorted Sexual Attitudes in German Expressionist Drama: With Particular Reference to Wedekind, Kokoschka, and Kaiser*. New York: Peter Lang, 1988.

Knapp, Bettina. "Oskar Kokoschka's *Murderer, Hope of Womankind*: An Apocalyptic Experience." *Theatre Journal* 35, no. 2 (1983): 179–194.

Kokoschka, Oskar. *Plays and Poems*. Tr. by Michael Mitchell. Riverside, Calif.: Ariadne, 2001.

Lucas, W. I. "Oskar Kokoschka." In *German Men of Letters: Twelve Literary Essays*, ed. by Alex Natan. London: Wolff, 1963. 3:37–52.

Nicholls, Peter. *Modernisms: A Literary Guide*. Berkeley: Univ. of California Press, 1995.

Rothe, Daria. "Kokoschka's *Comenius*." *Cross Currents* (1983): 211–221.

Schvey, Henry I. *Oskar Kokoschka: The Painter as Playwright*. Detroit: Wayne State Univ. Press, 1982.

Arnd Bohm

KOLTÈS, BERNARD-MARIE (1948–1989)

At the time of his death from AIDS in 1989, Bernard-Marie Koltès was widely considered the most important new voice in French drama. His major plays have since become modern repertory classics, translated into more than thirty languages and performed the world over.

Born in 1948, Koltès grew up in a devout Catholic family in Metz in eastern FRANCE and rarely saw his father, a professional soldier stationed in Indochina and Algeria for most of the 1950s. He attended the Jesuit school of Saint-Clément, located in the middle of the Arab ghetto of Metz, during the height of the Algerian War (1958–1962). He would return to the events of these turbulent years in *Return to the Desert* (*Le retour au désert*, 1988), which treats France's complex relationship to its collective memory of the war. His early interests included Arthur Rimbaud, cinema, and classical organ. Apart from the pleasure of discovering William Shakespeare in English, he remained indifferent to theater until, he would claim, he saw actress Maria Casarès perform Seneca's Medea in Strasbourg in 1969. He thereupon briefly enrolled at the Centre dramatique de l'Est in Strasbourg and then founded Le Théâtre du Quai with fellow students. Among his earliest dramatic efforts, written and staged for this theater, were adaptations of MAKSIM GORKY (Bitterness [*Les amertumes*]), Fyodor Dostoevsky (*Drunken Process* [*Procès ivre*]), and the Song of Songs (*The March* [*La marche*]). After some experiments with radio drama, *Heritage* (*L'héritage*) and *Silent Voices* (*Des voix sourdes*), Koltès wrote a novel (*La fuite à Cheval très loin dans la ville*) and two more adaptations, *Day of Murders in the Story of Hamlet* (*Le jour des meurtres dans l'histoire d'Hamlet*) and *Sallinger*, which combined themes and characters from stories by American fiction writer J. D. Salinger. Set in New York, a place of mythic fascination for Koltès, *Sallinger* deals with America's uneasy relationship with outsiders. After a three-year absence from the theater, a time of extensive international travel and a move to Paris, Koltès wrote the one-act monologue *The Night at the Edge of the Forest* (*La nuit juste avant les forêts*) for actor Yves Ferry and directed it to great success at the Off Festival at Avignon in 1977. Upon his return from a trip to Latin America in 1979, he wrote the play that became his most celebrated and widely known work, *Black Battles with Dog* (*Combat de nègre et de chiens*), which exposes the legacy of colonial exploitation, crime and punishment, and the ensuing struggle for justice in the modern world. *Combat* had its premiere outside France at La Mama Theatre in 1982, in a translation by Matthew Ward, under the direction of Françoise Kourilsky.

A year later *Combat* caught the attention of preeminent director and filmmaker Patrice Chéreau, who, frustrated by a lack of important new playwrights in French theater, soon brought Koltès to lasting fame on the Parisian stage and publication by the prestigious Editions de Minuit. In their ongoing collaboration Chéreau directed four of Koltès's major plays at his theater, Amandiers-Nanterre, and at the Théâtre du Rond-Point. Besides *Black Battles with Dog* and *Return to the Desert*, he directed *West Pier* (*Quai Ouest*, 1985), which deals with complex family relations set on the western piers of Manhattan against the backdrop of poverty, immigration, and urban violence, and *In the Solitude of the Cotton Fields* (*Dans la solitude des champs de coton*, 1986), a fantastical duet of aggression, desire, and despair between the generically named "The Dealer" and "The Client."

Shortly before his death Koltès completed his final play, ROBERTO ZUCCO, inspired by the life of serial killer Roberto Succo and the dramatic trajectory of Shakespeare's Hamlet. It was produced posthumously at Berlin's Schaubühne in 1990, under the direction of Peter Stein. Among Koltès's unpublished works are the screenplay *Nickel Stuff*, inspired by the persona of film star John Travolta, and the plays *Coco*, (*Rêve égaré*), and *The March* (*La marche*).

Koltès's theater combines an ultra-modernist appeal with an edgy restlessness. The *London Times* has described him as "a creator of a mythology of the underworld, a champion of the underdog and the lone wolf, and a pioneer of a wholly new style of dramatic writing." At the crossroads between JEAN GENET's epic ritualism and Jean Racine's passionate incantations, Koltès's theater simultaneously cultivates and denounces stage illusion and challenges identity and difference in a powerful language that reinvents the need for TRAGEDY and myth. His world is one of enigmatic encounters, bewildering, unconscious violence, migrating bodies, and spatial spareness; it is a fascinating and discomforting vision of postindustrial society that questions the ubiquitous specter of desire set against the ruins of contemporary subjectivity.

[*See also* Gay and Lesbian Drama]

PLAYS: *Bitterness* (*Les amertumes*, 1970); *Drunken Process* (*Procès ivre*, 1971); *The March* (*La marche*, 1971); *Heritage* (*L'héritage*, 1972); *Lifeless Tales* (*Récits morts*, 1973); *Silent Voices* (*Des voix sourdes*, 1973); *Day of Murders in the Story of Hamlet* (*Le jour des meurtres dans l'histoire de Hamlet*, 1974); *The Night at the Edge of the Forest* (*La nuit juste avant les forêts*, 1977); *Sallinger* (1977); *Black Battles with Dog* (*Combat de nègre et de chiens*, 1980); *The Blood Knot* (*Le lien du sang*, translation of Athol Fugard's *The Blood Knot*, 1982); *West Pier* (*Quai Ouest*, 1985); *In the Solitude of the Cotton Fields* (*Dans la solitude des champs de coton*, 1986); *Tabataba* (1986); *Return to the Desert* (*Le retour au désert*, 1988); *The Winter's Tale Le Conte d'hiver* (translation of Shakespeare's *The Winter's Tale*, 1988); *Roberto Zucco* (1989)

FURTHER READING

Alternatives théâtrales 35–36 (Brussels) (February 1994).

Bident, C. *Bernard-Marie Koltès, généalogies*. Tours: Farrago, 2000.

Desportes, Bernard. *Koltès, la nuit, le nègre et le néant*. Charlieu, France: La Bartavelle, 1993.

Koltès, Bernard-Marie. *Une part de ma vie: Entretiens, 1983–1989*. Paris: Editions de Minuit, 1999.

"Koltès: Combats avec la scène." *Théâtre Aujourd'hui*, no. 5 (March 1996).

Ubersfeld, Anne. *Bernard-Marie Koltès*. Arles: Actes Sud, 2001.

Donia Mounsef

KON, STELLA (1944–)

Before the mid-1980s Stella Kon somewhat mockingly described herself as "SINGAPORE's greatest never-produced playwright." Although Kon had won Singapore's National Playwriting Competition three times for her plays *The Bridge* (1977), *Trial* (1982), and *Emily of Emerald Hill* (1981), none of her works had been produced in Singapore. This changed in 1986 when her dramatic monologue *Emily of Emerald Hill* ran successfully in Singapore and then moved to the Edinburgh Festival. In spite of her impressive output as a dramatist, Kon's reputation still rests largely on the success of this much-loved work, which remains the country's most produced play.

Born in Edinburgh in 1944, Kon spent her formative years in Singapore in a large, multigenerational household dominated by her grandmother, the matriarch of a prominent Peranakan family. Her grandfather, Seow Poh Leng, had been an amateur actor with a great love for William Shakespeare, while her mother, Kheng Lim, was a noted Singaporean actress in the 1950s. After graduating from the University of Singapore, Kon spent much of her adult life in MALAYSIA and the United Kingdom, writing most of her plays while living as an expatriate. She returned to Singapore permanently in 1986.

Two of Kon's earliest published plays, *Z Is for Zygote* and *To Hatch a Swan* (1971), examined the phenomena of reproductive engineering and surrogate motherhood, respectively. The plot of *Zygote* seems especially prescient in that the quota system imposed on prospective mothers in the play is eerily close to the policies Prime Minister Lee Kuan Yew sought to implement years later to ensure that well-educated mothers reproduced at a higher rate.

Kon's *Emily of Emerald Hill* marked a significant turning point in the nation's theater in that the language, concerns, and characterization of the play's protagonist are all uniquely Singaporean. *Emily* demonstrated that Singaporeans could speak eloquently onstage using the idioms of their own speech rather than the false tones of British "received pronunciation." The work's protagonist, Emily Gan, is of Peranakan stock, a culture that developed in the 19th century when imported Chinese laborers married local Malay women. In the play Emily, the matriarch of a large and prominent Peranakan family not unlike Kon's, interacts with unseen characters and recounts her life's triumphs and tragedies in a series of flashbacks that extend from the 1930s, when Emily is a young bride, into her old age. In Singapore the work's appeal lies in its cultural specificity, while its overseas success rests on Kon's deft exploration of larger, more timeless themes such as the conflict between generations and the difficulty of overcoming past trauma.

By the late 1990s Kon had largely abandoned playwriting. Her remarks at a 1998 theater conference suggest why: "The theatre for which I was writing is no longer practiced in Singapore today. Actor's theatre, writer's theatre, my mother's tradition of British Shakespearean theatre, is a dead letter." Since that time however, Kon has emerged as a prolific writer of new Singaporean musicals, of which five have been staged in just a few short years. In addition to her work as a dramatist, Kon is also a poet, short-story writer, and novelist.

SELECT PLAYS: *To Hatch a Swan* (1971); *Z Is for Zygote* (1971); *Runner of Marathon* (1975); *The Bridge* (1977); *Emporium* (1977); *Emily of Emerald Hill* (1981); *Trial* (1982); *Dragon's Teeth Gate* (1985); *Silent Song* (1986); *Human Heart Fruit* (2002); *Exodus: A Journey of Faith* (musical book and lyrics, 2003); *Lost in Transit* (musical book and lyrics, 2005); *One Voice* (original version titled *Victorian Days*, musical book and lyrics, 2006); *Peter and Pierre* (musical book and lyrics, 2006); *Red Lanterns* (original version titled *Blue Willow House*, musical book and lyrics, 2006)

FURTHER READING

Gilbert, Helen, and Jacqueline Lo. "Performing Hybridity in Post-colonial Monodrama." *Journal of Commonwealth Literature* 32, no. 1 (1977): 5–19.

Kon, Stella. "Cross Cultural Influence in the Work of a Singapore Writer" and "The Migrant." In *Perceiving Other Worlds*, ed. by Edwin Thumboo. Singapore: Times Academic Press, 1991. 305–317; 318–319.

——. *Emily of Emerald Hill*. Singapore: Pan Pacific Publishing, 2000.

Le Blond, Max. "Stella Kon." In *Encyclopedia of Post-colonial Literatures in English*, ed. by Eugene Benson and L.W. Conolly. London: Routledge, 1994.

Peterson, William. *Theater and the Politics of Culture in Contemporary Singapore*. Middletown, Conn.: Wesleyan Univ. Press, 2001.

William Peterson

KONGS-EMNERNE See THE PRETENDERS

KOPIT, ARTHUR (1937–)

> *We need new plays that will upset the audiences. We want to upset you enough to make you want to talk about it afterwards.*
>
> —Arthur Kopit, 2002

Born on May 10, 1937, in New York, New York, Arthur Kopit became a writer at Harvard, where he had several plays produced while he was an undergraduate. He wrote *Oh, Dad, Poor Dad, Mamma's Hung You in the Closet and I'm Feelin' So Sad* (1960) in the summer after graduation, and when a student theatrical society produced it the following year, Boston critics lauded his writing, thus launching his career. The play received its professional premiere in London, where it garnered less-than-enthusiastic reviews, but New York embraced Kopit's mordant wit, and the OFF-BROADWAY production in 1962 was far more successful. Director Jerome Robbins deftly mined the characters' psychological obsessions, and the play proved to be the theatrical equivalent of pop art's dethroning of abstract expressionism. *Oh, Dad* broke with and lampooned the 1950s obsessions with Freudianism, hidden meanings, "momism," and the psychological fascination with secrecy. *Oh, Dad* announced the weltanschauung of a new era.

Kopit followed *Oh, Dad* with a string of one-acts, including *The Day the Whores Came Out to Play Tennis* (1960), which presciently presaged the fears and bewilderment of middle-class male America faced with a rising tide of feminism. At the height of the Vietnam War, Kopit used America's past to comment on its present with *Indians*, a COLLAGE of memory and reality ostensibly about Buffalo Bill and the winning of the American West. The play evoked and derided the effects of white, American imperialism toward other races. First produced in London by the Royal Shakespeare Company in 1968, and the following year by the Arena Stage in Washington, D.C., *Indians* quickly moved to Broadway, where it enjoyed a substantial run. Robert Altman directed a 1976 film version from a screenplay by Kopit and Alan Rudolph.

Kopit's generation grew up with radio drama, and he has acknowledged the medium's role as "possibly the most important influence on whatever voice I have." His plays challenge audiences to collaborate by mentally filling out the visual frame, and this tendency reached its apogee thus far with *Wings*, the tale of a former aviatrix imprisoned by a stroke. Researched at the institution in which his own father underwent rehabilitation for a similar condition, the drama was originally written for National Public Radio's *Earplay* series in 1977, was translated to the stage at the Yale Repertory Theatre in 1978, and was produced on Broadway in 1979. Although it is grounded in intensely personal circumstances, *Wings* nonetheless highlighted Kopit's sensitivity to contemporary concerns as it limned the articulation of the tongue-tied during the shallowness of the 1970s.

End of the World with Symposium to Follow (1984) grappled with the inability of a fictional author to write about the nuclear arms race, a task that Kopit himself had seriously undertaken and researched while the issue captivated the American public during the Ronald Reagan era. In Kopit's writing, characters often wrestle with moral positions, both practical and artistic. *Road to Nirvana* (originally *Bone-the-Fish*, 1989) is a savage attack on the changing artistic mores of not-for-profit theaters in the 1990s. Kopit himself had wrestled with some of the same questions and withdrew a pair of plays under the title *Asylum* (1963) after five off-Broadway preview performances. He also tangled with the University of Minnesota after he was awarded a Rockefeller grant for production at the Guthrie Theatre, but then learned that the Guthrie's commitment to new works relegated the authors to invitational staged readings. *BecauseHeCan* (originally *Y2K*, 1999) continued Kopit's tendency to link his writing to contemporary concerns.

Kopit's stage adaptations include a version of HENRIK IBSEN's *GHOSTS* (1982) and books for the musical *Nine* (1982), based on Federico Fellini's movie *8½*, and *High Society* (1998), a reworking of PHILIP BARRY's *THE PHILADELPHIA STORY*. With his *Nine* collaborator, Maury Yeston, Kopit adapted Gaston Leroux's novel *The Phantom of the Opera* into a musical, *Phantom* (1991). Written before the Andrew Lloyd Webber extravaganza, the Kopit-Yeston version has been produced in numerous theaters around the country and abroad.

[*See also* United States, 1940–Present]

PLAYS: *Don Juan in Texas* (with Wally Lawrence, 1957); *Gemini* (1957); *On the Runway of Life You Never Know What's Coming Off Next* (1957); *The Questioning of Nick* (1957, 1974); *Across the River and Into the Jungle* (1958); *Sing to Me Through Open Windows* (1958, subsequently a curtain-raiser to *Oh, Dad* but withdrawn during previews in New York); *The Day the Whores Came Out to Play Tennis* (1960); *Oh, Dad, Poor Dad, Momma's Hung You in the Closet and I'm Feelin' So Sad* (1960); *Asylum; or, What the Gentlemen Are Up To, Not to Mention the Ladies* (1963); *Mhil'daim* (1963); *As for the Ladies* (1964); *The Conquest of Everest* (1964); *The Hero* (1964); *Chamber Music* (1965); *An Incident in the Park* (1968); *Indians* (1968); *What's Happened to the Thorne's House* (1972); *Louisiana Territory; or, Lewis and Clark—Lost and Found* (1975); *Secrets of the Rich* (1976); *Wings* (1978); *Good Help Is Hard to Find* (1981); *Ghosts* (adaptation, 1982); *Nine* (book) (1982, revival 2003); *End of the World with Symposium to Follow* (1984); *Road to Nirvana* (originally *Bone-the-Fish*, 1989); *Phantom* (book) (1991); *High Society* (book) (1998); *BecauseHeCan* (originally *Y2K*, 1999); *Chad Curtiss, Lost Again* (2001); *Discovery of America* (2002)

FURTHER READING

Auerbach, Doris. *Sam Shepard, Arthur Kopit, and the Off Broadway Theater.* Boston: Twayne, 1982.

Dieckman, Suzanne Burgoyne, and Richard Brayshaw. "Wings, Watchers, and Windows: Imprisonment in the Plays of Arthur Kopit." *Theatre Journal* 35, no. 2 (Fall 1988).

Kelley, Margot Anne. "Order Within Fragmentation: Postmodernism and the Stroke Victim's World." *Modern Drama* 34, no. 3 (September 1991).

Lahr, John. "Arthur Kopit's 'Indians': Dramatizing National Amnesia." *Evergreen Review* 13, no. 71 (October 1969).

Louis Scheeder

KORNFELD, PAUL (1889–1942)

The melody of a great gesture says more than the highest consummation of what is called naturalness.
—Paul Kornfeld, 1913

A member of the Prague circle, which included Franz Kafka (1883–1924) and FRANZ WERFEL, Paul Kornfeld made far-reaching theoretical and practical contributions to German expressionist drama. Kornfeld, who was born on December 11, 1889, in Prague, then part of the Austro-Hungarian Empire, grew up steeped in literature, philosophy, and Jewish theology: his great-grandfather, Ahron Kornfeld, was a noted Talmudist; Kornfeld's father, the owner of a textile firm, was a man of letters. In 1916 Kornfeld moved to Frankfurt to try his luck as a freelancer.

Kornfeld is best known for his essay "The Soulful and the Psychological Individual" ("Der beseelte und der psychologische Mensch," 1918), the main ideas of which also appear in the epilogue to his drama *The Seduction* (*Die Verführung*, 1913) titled "To the Actor" ("An den Schauspieler"). It is a strident rejection of psychological REALISM and especially NATURALISM. An important tenet of EXPRESSIONISM, Kornfeld's essay calls for a new theater that does not feign reality; in order to transcend causality, the materialism of Wilhelmine GERMANY, and its repression of the human spirit, the expressionist actor should embrace the fact that he is acting and should be "nothing but a representative of thought, feeling, or fate!" Thus he will find his way to human "essence." *The Seduction* and the mystery play *Heaven and Hell* (*Himmel und Hölle*, 1919) are influenced by the spirituality, mysticism, and dream consciousness of Emanuel Swedenborg (1688–1772) and AUGUST STRINDBERG.

Well regarded and popular, Kornfeld switched from expressionist TRAGEDY to COMEDY in 1920 when both expressionism and Kornfeld's fame were at their peak. From 1920 to 1926 Kornfeld wrote a drama, many essays, and three comedies that put his ecstatic expressionist beginnings in perspective: In *The Eternal Dream* (*Der ewige Traum*, 1922) he eases up noticeably on the serious business of love and soulful expressionist longing; in *Palme; or, The Offended One* (*Palme oder Der Gekränkte*, 1924) the sensitive expressionist hero transmutes into one who easily offends and is offended by others; in *Kilian; or, The Yellow Rose* (*Kilian oder Die gelbe Rose*, 1926), Kornfeld's most successful comedy, he pokes fun at literary salon culture. In 1925 Kornfeld began working as a DRAMATURG for MAX REINHARDT in Berlin, left briefly in 1928 for a position as dramaturg in Darmstadt, then returned to Berlin, where he wrote for the leftist *The Diary* (*Das Tage-Buch*).

Kornfeld's conviction that art should transcend reality led him to underestimate the political realities of 1930s Germany. His three-act tragedy *Sweet Jew* (*Jud Süfl*, 1930) details the rise and fall of Josef Süfl-Oppenheimer, the financial adviser to Duke Karl Alexander of Württemberg, but there is no intimation of the plight of the Jews at the time, nor is a solution offered for Oppenheimer's conviction for treason and the popular, anti-Semitic rejoicing at his hanging.

Kornfeld left Berlin for Prague in 1932 and remained there rather than escaping the continent for England. In 1941 he was arrested and taken to Lodz concentration camp, where he died in April 1942.

PLAYS: *The Seduction* (*Die Verführung*, 1913); *Heaven and Hell* (*Himmel und Hölle*, 1919); *The Eternal Dream* (*Der ewige Traum*, 1922); *Palme; or, The Offended One* (*Palme oder Der Gekränkte*, 1924); *Sakuntala* (1925); *Kilian; or, The Yellow Rose* (*Kilian oder Die gelbe Rose*, 1926); *Smither Buys Europe* (*Smither kauft Europa*, 1928); *Sweet Jew* (*Jud Süß*, 1930)

FURTHER READING

Pazi, Margarita. "Paul Kornfeld: Tagebücher von 1905 bis 1921" [Paul Kornfeld: Diaries, 1905–1921]. In *Österreichische Tagebuchschriftsteller* [Austrian Diarists], ed. by Donald G. Daviau. Vienna: Schaumberger, 1994. 191–236.

Puzo, Madeline. "Who Was Jud Süss?" *American Theatre* 13, no. 10 (1996): 16–18, 61.

Schneider, Karl Ludwig. "Theorie und Praxis des expressionistischen Dramas bei Paul Kornfeld" [Theory and practice of Paul Kornfeld's expressionist dramas]. In *Studien zur deutschen Literatur: Festschrift für Adolf Beck zum siebzigsten Geburtstag* [Studies in German literature: Festschrift for Adolf Beck on his seventieth birthday], ed. by Ulrich Fülleborn and Johannes Krogoll. Heidelberg: Winter, 1979. 278–283.

Christa Spreizer

KOUKA, HONE (1967–)

Since Hone Kouka graduated from Te Toi Whakaari (NEW ZEALAND Drama School) in 1990, he has contributed his skills as a playwright, screenwriter, actor, and director to the development of Maori drama. In 1994, as Taki Rua Theatre's co–artistic director, he, along with Colin McColl, led the Wellington-based collective toward the establishment of a permanent bicultural management and artistic structure. It was under Kouka's directorship in 1998 that the controversial decision was made to discard Taki Rua's venue in favor of a production-company model to provide Maori practitioners with increased opportunities to tour their plays, nationally and internationally.

Kouka's playwriting career, already set in motion by a solo performance of his play *Life Principle* (*Mauri tu*, 1991) and followed by the co-written, award-winning *Hide 'n Seek* (produced in 1992), was bolstered in 1994 by the formation of Te Roopu Whakaari, Taki Rua's own theater company. Kouka's first production with Te Roopu Whakaari, *The Warrior People* (*Nga tangata toa*, 1994), rewrites *The Vikings at Helgeland* in a historical Maori context, accentuating HENRIK IBSEN's rugged geography, larger-than-life characters and events, and the supernatural. Set mainly on the east coast of the North Island (Kouka's home ground) shortly after World War I, Kouka's revision relates the tale of a family's collapse when warrior woman Rongomai enacts revenge upon her foster father and seeks satisfaction of her desperate, destructive love for returned war hero Taneatua.

A commission from the 1996 New Zealand International Festival of the Arts resulted in the compact and carefully drawn *The Homeland* (*Waiora*, 1996). It uses *waiata* (song/chant) and *haka* (rhythmic posture dances) to tell the story of a *whanau* (family) that, in 1965, moves from its home on the east coast of the North Island to a sawmill town in New Zealand's South Island. Here the *whanau* struggles to settle in while trying to maintain its Maori language, *waiata*, and *whanau* connections. Tracked by a chorus of ghostly Maori ancestors who, like memories from the characters' pasts, interfere with their activities and relationships, the *whanau* is forced to decide whether it should sacrifice its cultural beliefs and practices in order to flourish in its new home. Subsequently revised to heighten its exploration of familial love, the dangers of loss, and relationships with home, *Waiora* toured to Britain and Hawaii in 1997.

Less critically acclaimed than *Waiora*, perhaps because of Kouka's shift to a dialogically reduced, largely gestural dramatic style, is *Home Fires* (produced in 1998), the second play in a trilogy (with *Waiora* and *The Prophet*; rehearsed reading, 2003) that examines the effects of migration. After their sister's drowning, two siblings (sisters in the first production, brothers in the second in 2002), confront the geographic distance and emotional and spiritual schisms that have developed between them. Having completed his first novel, *The Warmth of the Sun*, Kouka is also writing screenplays.

SELECT PLAYS: *Life Principle* (*Mauri tu*, 1991); *Hide 'n Seek* (co-written, 1992); *Remembrance of Things to Come* (co-written, 1992); *Vehicle, Conveyance* (*He waka*, co-written, 1992); *Five Angels* (1993); *Pulling-together* (*Whakakotahi*, 1994); *Warrior People* (*Nga tangata toa*, 1994); *Brother, Sister* (*Tuakana, tuahine*, 1995); *King Hits* (1995); *The Homeland* (*Waiora*, 1996); *Grey* (1997); *Home Fires* (1998)

FURTHER READING

Amery, Mark. "Strength to Strength." *Listener* 29 (August 1998): 38–39.

Kouka, Hone. Introduction to *Ta Matou Mangai*, ed. by Hone Kouka. Wellington: Victoria Univ. Press, 1999.

Kouka, Hone, and Howard McNaughton. "Ta Matou Mangai/Our Own Voice: A Discussion." In *(Post)Colonial Stages: Critical and Creative Views on Drama, Theatre and Performance*, ed. by Helen Gilbert. West Yorkshire, UK: Dangaroo Press, 1999. 109–123.

Peterson, William. "Reclaiming the Past, Building a Future: Maori Identity in the Plays of Hone Kouka." *Theatre Research International* 26, no. 1 (2001): 15–24.

Mei-Lin Te-Puea Hansen

KRAMER, LARRY (1935–)

Larry Kramer is a playwright, film scenarist, novelist, and political activist. Born on June 25, 1935, in Bridgeport, Connecticut, he grew up in Maryland, the son of a Jewish American father (a lawyer) and a Russian Jewish mother. Although many of his screenplays remain unproduced, he came to fame as the scenarist for Ken Russell's cult classic, *Women in Love* (1970), and later *Lost Horizon* (1971). His controversial novel *Faggots* (1978) gave him credentials as a commentator on the gay scene, and he authored one sprawling play, *Sissies' Scrapbook*, adapted into a more streamlined, but dramatically less effective work, *Four Friends*, which was something of a failure. It was with the onset of the AIDS crisis that his cantankerous nature and apostolic style found its most effective arena.

In the face of shrill opposition from both gay and straight camps, Kramer struggled to bring the AIDS emergency to the attention of the world, siring in the process two extraordinary organizations, the Gay Men's Health Crisis (GMHC) and AIDS Coalition to Unleash Power (ACT UP). Kramer did not hesitate to make a pest of himself for the cause of lifestyle change and adequate medical and governmental response to the emergency. His vocation as a daring playwright was firmly established with *The Normal Heart*, the first full-length play about AIDS, a genre that, in later years, came to boast hundreds of such works; Kramer's subsequent works have also centered on the subject of AIDS.

The Normal Heart chronicles the early days of political response to the growing health crisis. After years of barren, anonymous encounters the central character, Ned, enjoys a meteorically passionate relationship that is nipped in the bud when his lover Felix brings act 1 to its climax with the admission that he has a purple lesion that will not go away. Act 2 ends with a deathbed marriage ceremony between Felix and Ned, officiated by Dr. Brookner. In between, Kramer alternates scenes of Dr. Brookner's struggle to get funding for her research; scenes of the internecine struggle within the gay community for power and over which tactical approach to use; scenes about Ned and Felix's simultaneously developing and crumbling relationship; and scenes of Ned and his brother Ben, all encounters of unbearable, soul-baring intensity.

The Normal Heart became the New York Public Theatre's longest-running hit and went on to enjoy 600 productions internationally. Kramer followed up this heart-rending masterpiece with a riotous topical political farce, *Just Say No*, which posits a collision between the two power figures who most nearly epitomize the politics of the 1980s: Ronald Reagan (who never appears onstage) and the mayor of New York City, Ed Koch. Their respective agendas relating to homosexuality and AIDS are unmasked and held up for ridicule. Both political figures appear to share the same Achilles' heel: homosexuality. In the president's case, it is his son, "Junior," who is trying to live a consummated existence as a gay man in the gay mecca "Appleberg" (read New York City). In the case of Koch (called "Mayor" in the play), it is his meticulously concealed lover, Gilbert Perch, a functionary who, when Mayor's ardor cooled and when Perch threatened to go public with the enormity of a certain growing health crisis, was drummed out of the "Department of Sex and Germs" by none other than his sugar daddy. Kramer manages to stuff Gilbert Perch, Junior, and Nancy Reagan ("Mrs. Potentate"), who is in quest of hot sex with younger men, into the same apartment with other unlikely characters. Their hilarious evasions and collisions provide the stuff of the play, in which Kramer lambasts the official cover-up of the AIDS crisis through satire.

His fourth play, *The Destiny of Me*, is a towering domestic drama based on much autobiographical material. Ned (the same Ned as in *The Normal Heart*) is in the hospital with AIDS, submitting to excruciating experimental treatments, as he relives his early life in his dysfunctional family. As a sensitive young man in a home where his father bitterly opposes accepting his gayness, and Ben, the brother he looks up to, urges him to "cure" himself through psychotherapy, his only source of sympathy is his dynamic, but elusive mother, who uses her great resources of energy in organizational work that is an escape hatch from the domestic quagmire. Despite the stormy dissonance of the childhood scenes and the ominous horror of the hospital scenes, Ned does ultimately achieve some measure of reconciliation with his brother Ben, who offers him acceptance in the present day. *The Destiny of Me* confirms and extends Kramer's ability to draw compelling, memorable characters and to construct successive scenes of great dramatic power, mixing the pathos with eruptions of impossible hilarity.

[*See also* Gay and Lesbian Drama; United States, 1940–Present]

PLAYS: *Sissies' Scrapbook* (1973); *Four Friends* (1974); *The Normal Heart* (1983); *Just Say No* (1988); *The Destiny of Me* (1989)

FURTHER READING

Clum, John. *Acting Gay: Male Homosexuality in Modern Drama*. Rev. ed. New York: Columbia Univ. Press, 1994.

——, ed. *Staging Gay Lives: An Anthology of Contemporary Gay Theater*. Boulder, Colo.: Westview Press, 1995.

Kramer, Larry. *Reports from the Holocaust: The Making of an AIDS Activist*. New York: St. Martin's, 1989.

Paller, Michael. "Larry Kramer and Gay Theatre." In *We Must Love One Another or Die: The Life and Legacies of Larry Kramer*, ed. by Lawrence D. Mass. London: Cassell, 1997.

Willinger, David. "The Abnormal Talent: Larry Kramer's Electro-Shock Treatment for the World Theatre." In *We Must Love One Another or Die: The Life and Legacies of Larry Kramer*, ed. by Lawrence D. Mass. London: Cassell, 1997.

David Paul Willinger

KRAPP'S LAST TAPE

> *Nothing to say, not a squeak. What's a year now? The sour cud and the iron stool.* [Pause.] *Revelled in the word spool.* [With relish.] *Spooool! Happiest moment of the past half million.* [Pause.] *Seventeen copies sold, of which eleven at trade price to free circulating libraries beyond the seas. Getting known.* [Pause.] *One pound six and something, eight I have little doubt.*
>
> —Krapp

In December 1957, while at his cottage in Ussy, SAMUEL BECKETT heard a broadcast on BBC Radio of the Irish actor Patrick Magee reading extracts from the novel *Molloy*. Beckett was very taken by the qualities of Magee's voice and almost immediately began to draft a monologue for the voice under the title *Magee Monologue*. The play was first published in the *Evergreen Review* in New York in the summer of 1958 and received its first production, with Magee playing Krapp, in London in October of that year.

It is Krapp's custom to mark "the awful occasion" of his birthday by recording a retrospect of the year just gone and by listening to "passages at random" from a tape recorded on a similar occasion in the past. On this occasion, having consulted his ledger containing an index to his collected reels of tape, he chooses one recorded thirty years earlier.

The Krapp the audience sees in the play is ill kempt and dishevelled, constipated, and given to overindulgence in bananas and booze. American and British published texts specify features that render him faintly clownish and ridiculous. The productions Beckett had a direct involvement in tended to deemphasize these, making Krapp a more pitiable character. Krapp's evident relish for words is established early—it emerges that he is an unsuccessful writer—so it is surprising that when he hears the word "viduity" spoken by the pompous voice of his earlier self, narrating the death of his mother, he has to consult a dictionary for its precise meaning. With extraordinary economy Krapp is revealed as a man who uses words to insulate himself from the gross and painful facts of experience.

A similar economy is manifest in the stage setting. Downstage, off-center, Krapp's table with a solitary light directly above it. Upstage, a cubbyhole where he keeps his machine, boxes of tapes, ledger, and dictionary and to which he retreats at timed intervals to drink. As he settles to listen to the earlier tape, he knocks a box off the table and, with a violent gesture, sweeps the ledger and the other boxes to the floor. In his own productions Beckett substituted tin boxes for the cardboard ones specified in the text, so that when they fell there was an explosion of sound. The audience's reaction to Krapp's noisy boorishness is soon modified by the realization that, as he moves to and from his cubbyhole, he must literally tread on the records of his past life.

As the tape runs on, the narrative switches to the crucial moment when Krapp saw "the vision at last," when his artistic vocation became clear to him. Three times Krapp winds the tape forward, with increasing impatience, until he reaches his account of a moment of intimacy with a girl in a punt on a lake. He carefully removes the tape from the machine and loads a fresh one to record his customary retrospect, but he finds that he has little to say. He rips the tape, his last, from the machine and flings it to the floor with the rest of the discarded recordings and loads the earlier one to listen to the lyrical evocation yet again. With modest means—an actor, his recorded voice, and a few hundred words—the play communicates bitter regret, loss, and self-loathing.

[*See also* Apocalypse in Modern Drama; Philosophy and Drama, 1860–1960]

FURTHER READING

Beckett, Samuel. *The Theatrical Notebooks of Samuel Beckett*. Vol. 3: *Krapp's Last Tape*. Ed. by James Knowlson. London: Faber, 1992.

Cohn, Ruby. *A Beckett Canon*. Ann Arbor: Univ. of Michigan Press, 2001.

Gerry Dukes

KRAUS, KARL (1874–1936)

The dramatic work of art has no business on the stage. The theatrical effect of a drama should go as far as arousing one's wish to see it performed: more than that destroys the artistic effect.
—Karl Kraus

Karl Kraus, born April 28, 1874, in Jitschin, Bohemia, then a part of the Austro-Hungarian Empire; Austrian journalist and playwright, is known primarily as the editor and chief writer of *Die Fackel* (*The Torch*), a journal he founded and ran throughout its existence (1899–1936). As both dramatist and theater critic, Kraus was most strongly influenced by the performances he attended at Vienna's famed Burgtheater as a young man. He greatly admired 19th-century actors such as Josef Lewinsky and Charlotte Wolter and lamented that their skills and personalities were, in his view, lacking among 20th-century Viennese performers. Kraus believed that Austrian newspapers corrupted the cultural and moral life of the nation, and he sensed that corruption most acutely in the theater because Viennese dailies such as the *Neue Freie Presse* (New Free Press), where he had worked as a young man, often employed critics who were themselves directors or dramatists. Such men often unabashedly promoted their own works and frequently disparaged those who operated outside their tightly knit circles.

Kraus is better known for his poetry and essayistic polemics against contemporary Austrian culture and politics than for his dramas. A satiric approach marks his engagement with all these genres. He saw satire as a way to purify the German language he felt was corrupted by the press; the return of language to purer origins, he believed, would, in turn, purify social and cultural mores. The satiric technique in Kraus's dramas was largely inspired by Johann Nestroy (1801–1862), famous for his biting and irreverent COMEDIES. Kraus also admired Nestroy's contemporary Ferdinand Raimund (1790–1836), as well as William Shakespeare and the operettist Jacques Offenbach (1819–1880). Kraus frequently recited the works of these four men in his Theater der Dichtung (Theater of Poetry), where Kraus gave one-man readings without scenery or makeup, using only music to enhance the dramatic effect of his performances.

Kraus authored six dramas. *The Last Days of Mankind* (*Die letzten Tage der Menschheit*, 1918–1919) is an enormous antiwar drama. Kraus was sickened by the mendacity, corruption, and jingoism that fed AUSTRIA-HUNGARY's participation in World War I, and savagely indicted his own nation, GERMANY, and the Allies in this play, frequently by quoting directly from real-life politicians, journalists, and soldiers. Though rarely performed because of its volume, it is Kraus's only theatrical work still widely read and studied today. Its non-Aristotelean structure influenced BERTOLT BRECHT'S EPIC THEATER. Rather than using the traditional Aristotelean model of cohesive acts building toward a climax, *The Last Days of Mankind* consists of seemingly random scenes, some lengthy and some as short as a one-line blackout, some humorous, others tragic, and some grotesquely mixed with respect to emotional tenor.

Kraus's works were staged infrequently even in his lifetime because he deliberately wrote them as literary dramas, to be read rather than performed. His other dramas are so narrowly focused on events and personages contemporary to Kraus that they are virtually ignored today. They primarily satirize Viennese literature and politics, though *Dream Theater* (*Traumtheater*, 1924) is a eulogy to the actress Annie Kalmar. Among the major themes in Kraus's plays are the putative venality of the Viennese press, police brutality, political-military deception, and the supposed epigonism of Kraus's Austrian contemporaries.

PLAYS: *The Last Days of Mankind* (*Die letzten Tage der Menschheit*, 1918–1919); *Literature; or, We Shall See About That* (*Literatur oder Man wird doch da sehn*, 1921); *Cloudcuckooland* (*Wolkenkuckucksheim*, 1923); *Dream Play* (*Traumstück*, 1923); *Dream Theater* (*Traumtheater*, 1924); *The Unconquerables* (*Die Unüberwindlichen*, 1928)

FURTHER READING

Grimstad, Kari. *Masks of the Prophet: The Theatrical World of Karl Kraus*. Toronto: Univ. of Toronto Press, 1982.

Timms, Edward. *Karl Kraus, Apocalyptic Satirist: Culture and Catastrophe in Habsburg Vienna*. New Haven: Yale Univ. Press, 1986.

Zohn, Harry. *Karl Kraus*. New York: Twayne, 1971.

John D. Pizer

KRIZANC, JOHN (1956–)

Born in 1956 in Lethbridge, Alberta, Canada, playwright and screenwriter John Krizanc is best known for his innovative dramatic works TAMARA (1981) and *Prague* (1984). His work often incorporates overtly political themes, though he himself purportedly espouses no particularly strong personal political beliefs. With his ENVIRONMENTAL play *Tamara* Krizanc gained a reputation as a dramatist with a penchant for exploring the nexus between audience and actor and between the script and the larger climate in which the script is allowed to live.

Set in Italy in the late 1920s during the Benito Mussolini regime and based upon actual events as recorded in Aelis Mazoyer's diary, *Tamara* explores what occurs in the mansion of Italian poet GABRIELE D'ANNUNZIO when Polish artist Tamara de Lempicka comes to paint his portrait. *Tamara* is an audience migratory work wherein the audience is broken into small groups and all the action happens concurrently, with many story lines playing out at once in different "rooms" of the theater's stage. Playgoers are encouraged to move about freely, following whichever characters and story lines pique their interest, changing their minds whenever they wish. The spectators, in essence, become creators, shaping their texts by their viewing choices. Since all the action takes place simultaneously, audience members are encouraged to share notes and information with each other at intermission and after the show in an attempt to piece together this "whodunit." The audience, in a sense, becomes a character, and audience members are catapulted out of their seats and into the drama, working as hard as the actors in making meaning out of the show's more than 100 scenes. *Tamara* has been successfully staged all over the world, including Toronto, Warsaw, and Lisbon, with especially long runs in New York (four years) and Los Angeles (ten years). For his work with *Tamara*, Krizanc was awarded the Dora Mavor Moore Award in 1982.

On the heels of *Tamara*, Krizanc's next work, *Prague*, also achieved great critical acclaim. Again an overtly political text, this show is more traditional in presentation, but still fresh and savvy in its message. Krizanc's two-act drama focuses on the backstage world of the Bread and Dreams Theatre Company as it attempts to stage *The Magnificat*, a drama that dances perilously close to affronting the ruling Communist Party with its message denouncing government oppression. *Prague* is filled with intrigue, deception, falsehoods, and opportunism and explores what happens when art meets state and whether such a thing as a state-owned art can ever really exist.

Krizanc's work on *Prague* has been favorably compared with writers such as VÁCLAV HAVEL and TOM STOPPARD. *Prague* earned Krizanc the Floyd S. Chalmers Canadian Play Award (1985) and the Canadian Governor General's Award for Drama (1987).

Krizanc's corpus of work also includes successful projects on the large and small screen. Among his screenwriting credits are the television miniseries *Dieppe* and work on the television series *Due South*, *Traders*, and *DaVinci's Inquest*, where he also served as writer/producer. He has also co-scripted the motion picture *Men with Brooms* (2002).

[*See also* Canada]

PLAYS: *Crime of Innocence* (1976); *Uterine Knights* (1979); *Tamara* (1981); *Prague* (1984); *The Half of It* (1989); *The Gist* (2001)

FURTHER READING

Blumenthal, Eileen. "*Tamara* from the Ground Floor Up." *New York Times* (November 29, 1987): H7.

Garebian, Keith. "Success or Excess?" *Performing Arts and Entertainment in Canada* 26, no. 1 (1990): 13.

"Krizanc, John." In *Contemporary Authors*, vol. 187. Detroit: Gale, 2000.

"Krizanc, John." In *Contemporary Literary Criticism*, vol. 57. Detroit: Gale, 1990.

"Krizanc, John." In *Encyclopedia of Canadian Theatre*. http://www.canadiantheatre.com.

Kate Maurer

KRLEŽA, MIROSLAV (1893–1981)

All my plays of that time, all those symbolic danses macabres, innumerable masses of murders, suicides, apparitions, that anxious unfolding of images in a furious tempo, all that dashing of the deceased, the dead, the prostitutes, the burning angels and gods, the graves overturned, the underworld revived, all those armies retreating, that blood and fires, the bells tolling and the conflagrations and the madness of a frantic chase, all that was a search for the so-called dramatic action in a completely wrong direction: in the quantitative.

—Miroslav Krleža, 1928

Croatian writer Miroslav Krleža wrote poems, short stories, novels, and essays on politics, art, and culture—a huge oeuvre, which earned him the status of a major figure in Croatian public life after World War II. Theater, however, was his primary interest. While still a schoolboy, he wrote romantic historical TRAGEDIES that he later destroyed, but he continued nevertheless to write plays, seventeen in total, into the last decade of his career.

Born on July 7, 1893, in Zagreb, CROATIA, to a bourgeois family of modest income and respectable genealogy, he managed to get a solid education, not only in Austro-Hungarian military schools in Pecs and Budapest, but also on his own as an avid reader. Back in Zagreb he worked as a journalist and published his first play, *Legend* (*Legenda*, 1914), which marked the beginning of his first, expressionist phase—a group of plays sometimes referred to as "the Legends"—stemming from his experience of World War I and embracing the unfinished cycle on giants (Jesus, Michelangelo, Christopher Columbus, Immanuel Kant, Francisco de Goya): *Masquerade* (*Maskerata*, 1914), *Croatian Rhapsody* (*Hrvatska rapsodija*, 1917), *Cristoval Colon* (*Kristofor Kolumbo* in later versions; 1918), *Kermes* (*Kraljevo*, 1918), *At Dusk* (*U predvecerje*, 1919), *Michelangelo Buonarroti* (1919), and *Adam and Eve* (*Adam i Eva*, 1922), to which, according to certain classifications, can be added *Arethaeus; or, The Legend of St. Ancilla, the Bird of Heaven* (*Aretej ili legenda o sv. Ancili, rajskoj ptici*, 1959), *Saloma* (1963), and *The Road to Heaven* (*Put u raj*, 1970) of his later antinaturalistic phase.

At first Krleža had problems getting his plays produced at the Croatian National Theatre, primarily for aesthetic reasons—his stage directions were considered unrealizable on stage—but also for political ones, because Krleža inclined to the Left and promoted the AVANT-GARDE cultural matrix in his literary journal *Flame* (*Plamen*, 1919).

The transition to the "qualitative DRAMATURGY" of Nordic provenance—as Krleža himself insisted—that dominated in the late 1920s and the 1930s was marked by plays still partaking of expressionist typology and treating the cruelty of war—*Galicia* (*Galicija*, 1922), later rewritten as *In the Camp* (*U logoru*, 1934) and again as *Galicia* (1977); *Golgota* (1922); and *Vucjak* (1923)—but with a much sharper sociohistorical consciousness than was the case with his early "scenic visions."

Although in the early 1950s Croatian theaters welcomed productions of all his plays, and later adaptations of his nondramatic work as well, Krleža's most acclaimed dramatic legacy was for many years the Glembay trilogy—*Honorable Glembays* (*Gospoda Glembajevi*, 1928), *In agony* (*U agoniji*, 1928), and *Leda* (1932). It is an anamnesis of the rise and decline of a nouveau riche Croatian family, much in the style not only of HENRIK IBSEN and AUGUST STRINDBERG, but also of European modernist genealogical novels, since the trilogy forms a cycle with the "prose" *The Glembays* (*Glembajevi*, 1928), which embraces short stories focused on individual members of the family.

Before his withdrawal from theater life Krleža revised and complemented almost all of his plays, publishing for the first time some that existed in earlier versions (*Saloma*) and writing new ones, such as the bitterly metahistoriographic *Arethaeus*—magnificently produced, as was *Kristofor Kolumbo*, at the Dubrovnik festival (both plays directed by Georgij Paro)—and *The Road to Heaven*, a screenplay derived from the adaptation of his short story "Cricket Under the Waterfall" ("Cvrcak pod vodopadom," 1937) and a short dialogical fragment *Finale: An Essay in Quinquagicentennial Synthesis* (*Finale: Pokušaj pedesetovjekovne sinteze*), published in the collection of his essays *Ten Gory Years* (*Deset krvavih godina*, 1937). Krleža died on December 29, 1981, in Zagreb, Croatia.

Krleža is the only Croatian writer who is the subject of a personal encyclopedia, which includes entries on his numerous literary, philosophical, and political readings and references, as well as on his lasting stylistic and structural influence on Croatian modern literature, especially playwriting.

PLAYS: *Legend* (*Legenda*, 1914); *Masquerade* (*Maskerata*, 1914); *Croatian Rhapsody* (*Hrvatska rapsodija*, 1917); *Cristoval Colon* (*Kristofor Kolumbo* in later versions, 1918); *Kermes* (*Kraljevo*, 1918); *At Dusk* (*U predvecerje*, 1919); *Michelangelo Buonarroti* (1919); *Adam and Eve* (*Adam i Eva*, 1922); *Galicia* (*Galicija*, 1922); *Golgota* (1922); *Vucjak* (1923); *Honorable Glembays* (*Gospoda Glembajevi*, 1928); *In agony* (*U agoniji*, 1928); *Leda* (1932); *In the Camp* (*U logoru*, 1934); *Arethaeus; or, The Legend of St. Ancilla, the Bird of Heaven* (*Aretej ili legenda o sv. Ancili, rajskoj ptici*, 1959); *Saloma* (1963); *The Road to Heaven* (*Put u raj*, 1970)

FURTHER READING

Fotez, Marko, et al., eds. *Dani hvarskog kazališta, eseji i grada o hrvatskoj drami i teatru: Miroslav Krleža*. Split: Cakavski sabor, 1981.

Senker, Boris. *Hrvatski dramaticari u svom kazalištu*. Zagreb: Hrvatski centar ITI, 1996.

Visković, Velimir, ed. *Krležijana*. Zagreb: Leksikografski zavod "Miroslav Krleža," 1999.

Lada Cale Feldman

KROETZ, FRANZ XAVER (1946–)

With the controversial premiere of his one-act plays *Home Work* (*Heimarbeit*) and *Stubborn* (*Hartnäckig*) in 1971, Franz Xaver Kroetz burst onto a West German theatrical scene that had largely been marked by Brechtian drama, absurdist plays, and DOCUMENTARY theater. Kroetz, however, found his model in the recently revived socially critical VOLKSSTÜCK (popular drama) of MARIELUISE FLEIẞER and ÖDÖN VON HORVÁTH, which portrayed in stark REALISM and laconic speech the bleak lives of the lower middle class. To Kroetz (born on February 25, 1946, in Munich, GERMANY), a school dropout who supported himself with odd jobs and acting at a rural farmers' theater, Fleißer and Horváth were worth emulating because they portrayed "the people that matter" through powerful scenic techniques that reduced dialogue to the essentials.

In his early plays Kroetz goes even farther than his predecessors in his hyperrealism and refusal to indicate any possibility for change in the lives of his characters, members of the rural underclass who speak Bavarian dialect in scenes marked as much by silence as by speech. The demonstrations at the premiere of *Home Work* and *Stubborn* were prompted by the plays' content, and Kroetz's repeated onstage portrayals of such subjects as abortion, masturbation, sexual intercourse, and infanticide have continued to provoke strong public reaction. But it would be wrong to characterize Kroetz mainly in terms of content, since the language and construction of his plays are equally significant. In contrast to the neoromantic dramas of "new subjectivity" that were beginning to appear at the same time, Kroetz's dramas seem starkly naturalistic, yet they contain a significant degree of abstraction and an artistically constructed language that conveys the characters' vulnerabilities more than it mimetically transcribes dialect. *Farmyard* (*Stallerhof*, 1971), which solidified Kroetz's reputation on the national stage, is typical of his early period in its portrayal of a retarded thirteen-year-old girl made pregnant by a hapless, aging farmhand. After driving the farmhand away, the farmer and his wife are unable to carry out their plans to abort their daughter's child, and the play ends with the onset of her labor pains. Many critics recognized that Kroetz intended to express both compassion for the underclass and a commitment to change the socioeconomic system that has devastated their lives. But because his techniques seemed merely to display these bleak lives while withholding commentary, and because he depicted extreme cases among socially marginal groups unable to understand or articulate their own situation, his early plays tended to invite interpretations that denounced the characters themselves or fatalistically viewed their conditions as unavoidable. However, Kroetz's productivity (premieres of twelve different plays between 1971 and 1973), his provocative thematics, and critics' recognition of his dramatic techniques soon made him the most widely performed German playwright of the 1970s and the recipient of numerous prizes.

To avoid stylistic repetition and the tendency of audiences to overlook the political intent of his plays, Kroetz began searching for new methods. He also joined the German Communist Party in 1972 and remained a member until 1980. One result was agit-prop techniques and more explicit criticism in *Global Interest* (*Globales Interesse*, 1972) and *Munich's Children* (*Münchner Kindl*, 1973), but Kroetz recognized the insufficiencies of such formulaic approaches. His more successful *Upper Austria* (*Oberösterreich*, 1972) resembles the early plays by withholding commentary and depicting the effects of economic conditions on domestic life, but it goes in a new direction by portraying people from a higher social station who are somewhat more articulate and aware. Although they are less likely than his early characters to resort to violence, they are nonetheless still mired in clichés that prevent their escape from the illusory dreams of consumer society. Kroetz carries the possibility of a positive outcome even further in *The Nest* (*Das Nest*, 1974), in which a worker realizes the potential for change through union solidarity. *Upper Austria* and *The Nest* were both televised nationwide, allowing Kroetz to reach the mass audience he explicitly seeks. In addition to his work in and for the theater, Kroetz has written radio and television plays, novels, essays, and travel diaries.

The skeptical Kroetz did not stick with the positive solution of *The Nest*, however. *Neither Fish nor Fowl* (*Nicht Fisch nicht Fleisch*), which received the Play of the Year award in 1981, explores the connections between the private sphere, the workplace, and gender relations through two couples more typical of contemporary Germans. Through parallel and mirror images of the characters and their views, four different perspectives and possibilities are explored. The play also demonstrates Kroetz's willingness to go beyond his "kitchen-sink realism" and incorporate new forms: in an expressionistic water scene, visual images provide a metaphorical dimension to the conflict. Though the play offers a critique of capitalism and its exploitative use of technology, the final scene, in which a nurturing mother feeds the others, led some to view Kroetz's concept of the family as basically conservative. In fact, however, the ending remains open, reflecting Kroetz's view that theater should dramatize questions, rather than answer them. *Farmers Die* (*Bauern sterben*, 1984/1985), a bleak passion play about the death of the family farm, strays even further from realism in its use of surreal images and abstraction: though it deals with a topical theme, it seems to indicate that the theater is no place for political solutions. In *The Poet as Pig* (*Der Dichter als Schwein*, 1986/1988), *Timeache* (*Zeitweh*, 1988), and *Peasant Theater* (*Bauerntheater*, 1989) Kroetz dramatizes his own creative crisis with author figures who agonize over the problem of finding a proper synthesis between the aesthetic and the political; the plays' self-reflexivity and grotesque scatology have limited their success. *I Am the People* (*Ich bin das Volk*, 1993) portrays a broader social spectrum through a series of scenes representing xenophobia, fascist tendencies, and cowardice in a newly unified Germany. The variety in his later plays—ranging from an intense emotional duel between two fictionalized political figures over corporeal decay and the inability to effect change in a world of starving children in *The End of Mating* (*Das Ende der Paarung*, 1999) to more fanciful stagings involving puppets and birds as characters in *Native Daughter* (*Die Eingeborene*, 1999) and *Mourning Furies* (*Die Trauerwütigen*, 2001)—indicates that Kroetz has continued his search for an adequate dramatic means to portray the political and the quotidian in the lives of contemporary Germans. However, after the negative reaction to his last play, *Ballerinas and Channel Surfers* (*Tänzerinnen und Drücker*, 2006), Kroetz announced in June 2006 that he was "depressed and burned out" and planned to give up writing.

SELECT PLAYS: *Wild Game Crossing* (*Wildwechsel*, 1968); *Home Work* (*Heimarbeit*, 1969); *Stubborn* (*Hartnäckig*, 1970); *Farmyard* (*Stallerhof*, 1971); *Ghost Train* (*Geisterbahn*, 1971); *Request Concert* (*Wunschkonzert*, 1971); *Upper Austria* (*Oberösterreich*, 1972); *Munich's Children* (*Münchner Kindl*, 1973); *The Nest* (*Das Nest*, 1974); *Neither Fish nor Fowl* (*Nicht Fisch nicht Fleisch*, 1981); *Farmers Die* (*Bauern sterben*, 1984/1985); *Peasant Theater* (*Bauerntheater*, 1989); *I Am the People* (*Ich bin das Volk*, 1993); *The End of Mating* (*Das Ende der Paarung*, 1999); *Ballerinas and Channel Surfers* (*Tänzerinnen und Drücker*, 2006)

FURTHER READING

Calandra, Denis. *New German Dramatists*. New York: Grove, 1983.

Hoffmeister, Donna L. *The Theater of Confinement: Language and Survival in the Milieu Plays of Marieluise Fleisser and Franz Xaver Kroetz*. Columbia, S.C.: Camden House, 1983.

Jones, Calvin N. *Negation and Utopia: The German Volksstück from Raimund to Kroetz*. New York: Peter Lang, 1993.

Mattson, Michelle. *Franz Xaver Kroetz: The Construction of a Political Aesthetic*. Oxford: Berg, 1996.

Walther, Ingeborg C. *The Theater of Franz Xaver Kroetz*. New York: Peter Lang, 1990.

Calvin N. Jones

KUBO SAKAE (1900–1958)

Kubo Sakae, JAPAN's leading Marxist dramatist of SHINGEKI plays, was born in Sapporo on Japan's northernmost island of Hokkaido. He majored in German literature at Tokyo University, where he wrote a senior thesis on the historical plays of the German expressionist GEORG KAISER. Despite his elite education, Kubo never lost touch with his rural roots, which shaped his sensibility and his work.

After graduation Kubo joined the literature department of the Tsukiji Little Theater (Tsukiji Shōgekijō), which had been founded in 1924 as Japan's first theater dedicated to the production of modern plays. During his tenure Kubo translated more than thirty modern German works, including plays by Kaiser, FRANK WEDEKIND, and GERHART HAUPTMANN. His translation of Johann Wolfgang von Goethe's *Faust, Part I*, was his crowning achievement as a translator.

Kubo regarded himself as a disciple of OSANAI KAORU, one of the founders of the Tsukiji and an advocate of theatrical REALISM. Kubo dedicated his most important play, *LAND OF VOLCANIC ASH* (1937–1938), to Osanai, and in 1947 he published a book-length biography of his mentor.

To Kubo, the future form of realism was Marxist, which is to say that it would apply the techniques of the social sciences to the depiction of society. After the Tsukiji dissolved into warring factions following Osanai's untimely death at the age of forty-seven in 1928, Kubo emerged as the leading theorist and dramatist of the politically engaged group. Although he was a Marxist, he was not doctrinaire, and he refused to conform to the orthodoxy of socialist realism, which became Communist dogma in 1932. Kubo objected to SOCIALIST REALISM on the grounds that it did not allow sufficient room for understanding local conditions.

Kubo's ideal was to achieve "a unification of scientific theory and poetic form." "Our realism," he wrote in 1934, "captures the innermost truths of man and society and, cutting through all facades, shows how—while antagonistic, contradictory, and interacting in complex ways—they develop toward a higher stage of unity. Without reducing them to stereotypes and without vulgarization, we clarify them in terms of the typical form of [class] conflict and formulate them with artistry and style" (quoted in Sugai, 1971). *Land of Volcanic Ash* is the monumental work in which Kubo tried most successfully to realize this ideal.

Kubo was imprisoned twice during the war for his leftist views. In 1947 he wrote about his wartime experience in the introspective play *Apple Orchard Diary*. *The Weather in Japan*, a play about politics and science in the occupation period, followed in 1953. Kubo suffered from severe depression and died by his own hand in 1958.

SELECT PLAYS: *The Battles of Coxinga Retold* (*Shinsetsu Kokusenya gassen*, 1930); *Blood Petition at Goryōkaku Fortress* (*Goryōkaku kessho*, 1933); *Land of Volcanic Ash* (*Kazanbaichi*, 1937–1938); *Apple Orchard Diary* (*Ringoen nikki*, 1947); *The Weather in Japan* (*Nihon no kishō*, 1953)

FURTHER READING

Gangloff, Eric J. "Kinoshita Junji: A Modern Japanese Dramatist." Ph.D. diss., Univ. of Chicago, 1973.

Goodman, David G. Introduction to *Land of Volcanic Ash*, by Kubo Sakae. Rev. ed. Tr. by David G. Goodman. Cornell East Asia Papers 40. Ithaca, N.Y.: Cornell East Asia Program, 1993.

Inoue Yoshie. *Kubo Sakae no sekai* [The World of Kubo Sakae]. Tokyo: Shakai Hyōronsha, 1989.

Murakami Ichirō. *Kubo Sakae ron* [On Kubo Sakae]. Tokyo: Kōbundō, 1959.

Sugai Yukio. *Kindai Nihon engeki ronsōshi* [A history of debates in modern Japanese theater]. Tokyo: Miraisha, 1979.

Uno Jūkichi, Kuno Osamu, et al., eds. *Kubo Sakae kenkyū* [Kubo Sakae Studies]. 11 vols. Tokyo: Kubo Sakae Kenkyū, 1959–1988.

David G. Goodman

KUBOTA MANTARŌ (1889–1963)

Kubota Mantarō, Japanese playwright, novelist, poet, and director, was known as "the poet of Asakusa," Tokyo's working-class neighborhood. Kubota's delicate and understated plays combined an old-fashioned morality and sensibility with a modern, Western REALISM. Born into a family of artisans, Kubota made his debut while still an undergraduate at Keiō University (where he later taught literature), publishing his first short story and play in *Mita Literature* (*Mita Bungaku*) in 1911. He claimed that Kinoshita Mokutarō's (1885–1945) *Izumiya Dye Shop* (1911), a play notably lacking in strong plot or dramatic conflict, helped him discover his own voice in *Eventide* (1911), his debut play about tradespeople on the night of a festival. He came into his own as a dramatist with *Rainy Skies* (1920), and his best work was produced during the 1920s and 1930s. He also distinguished himself as a director and DRAMATURG for the *SHINPA* theater. His dramatizations of popular novels by IZUMI KYŌKA, Satomi Ton, Tanizaki Jun'ichirō, and Higuchi Ichiyō are still staples of the *shinpa* repertory.

From 1926 until 1938 he was also a director of theater and music programming for NHK, JAPAN's national broadcasting network. He was a skilled director and dramatist for both *shinpa* and *kabuki*, and his association with SHINGEKI dated from Aoyama Sugisaku's brilliant direction of his masterpiece, *The Odera School* (a play compared at the time with ANTON CHEKHOV'S THE CHERRY ORCHARD), at the Tsukiji Little Theater (TLT, Tsukiji Shōgekijō) in 1928. In 1932 Kubota teamed up with Tomoda Kyōsuke and his wife, Tamura Akiko, the two leading *shingeki* actors of prewar Japan, to establish the Tsukijiza theater company. After Tomoda's death in military action in China in 1937, Kubota, together with Kishida Kunio, founded the Literary Theater (Bungakuza), still today the leading *shingeki* theater company. He directed the first production of MORIMOTO KAORU'S *A WOMAN'S LIFE* during the air raids of 1945.

Though Kubota was blessed with a wide circle of friends and professional associates, domestic hardship—the family business folded, his marital life was difficult, and he was burned out twice, first by the Great Earthquake of 1923 and second by the firebombs of 1945—colored his plays, which are typically elegies to a passing way of life and feature good-natured and honorable but feckless characters faced with insolvency or betrayal, such as *Brief Night*'s Isaburō or Principal Odera of *The Odera School*. Kubota was an accomplished haiku poet, and his motto was "art is thrift"; he was a master of the pause, of the ellipse, the implied. Kikuchi Kan complained when he first read *The Odera School* that he kept waiting for something to happen, but nothing ever did—the play was all exposition and no action—but the success of the TLT's staging put the lie to the claim that Kubota's work was CLOSET DRAMA. Kubota studiously avoided theme, political message, or dramatic conflict in his work, but few dramatists could surpass his deft dialogue or sensitivity in capturing the sentiments of the common Japanese.

SELECT PLAYS: *Eventide* (*Kuregata*, 1911); *Rainy Skies* (*Amazora*, 1920); *Each to His Own* (*Kokorogokoro*, 1922); *Unhappiness* (*Fukō*,

1924); *Brief Night* (*Mijikayo*, 1925); *The Odera School* (*Odera gakkō*, 1928); *Leaving Home* (*Kadode*, 1931); *At the Fishing Hole* (*Tsuribori nite*, 1935); *Autumn Flowers* (*Akikusa-banashi*, 1946)

FURTHER READING

Kubota Mantarō. *Kubota Mantarō zenshū* [The complete works of Kubota Mantarō]. 15 vols. Tokyo: Chūō Kōronsha, 1967.

Powell, Brian. *Japan's Modern Theatre: A Century of Change and Continuity*. London: Japan Library, 2002.

Toita Yasuji. *Kubota Mantarō*. Tokyo: Bungei Shunjū, 1967.

M. Cody Poulton

KUO PAO KUN (1939–2002)

The life and work of Singaporean playwright and theater practitioner Kuo Pao Kun reflects his country's rich ethnic and cultural diversity, its complex history, and its sometimes treacherous politics. As SINGAPORE's most important and influential playwright, Kuo created a body of work in both English and Mandarin that expresses the social, political, and linguistic complexity of Singaporean life in the last half of the 20th century. As an influential director and teacher of theater, Kuo trained two decades of Singaporean theater artists.

Born in CHINA's Hebei Province, Kuo went to Singapore at age ten to live with his father when the country was still a British colony. A fluent speaker of Mandarin and English, as a teenager Kuo was exposed to drama in both languages. Kuo's theater training continued in AUSTRALIA, where he graduated from the National Institute of Dramatic Art (NIDA) in 1964 with a diploma in production. Upon returning to Singapore in 1965, Kuo, along with his wife, Goh Lay Kuan, founded the influential Singapore Performing Arts School (later renamed the Practice Performing Arts School). Kuo's overtly political work in the late 1960s and early 1970s brought him into conflict with Singapore's authoritarian government, resulting in four years of detention (1976–1980) under the country's Internal Security Act.

In the following decade Kuo quickly rose to prominence with two much-produced dramatic monologues that reflected the conflict between the individual and the state in the newly prosperous, small island nation. THE COFFIN IS TOO BIG FOR THE HOLE (first produced in 1984), though ostensibly about the problems an eldest son faces when trying to bury his grandfather in a coffin too large for the regulation-sized cemetery plot, cuts to the core of what it means to confront an inflexible bureaucracy. *No Parking on Odd Days* (first produced in 1986) uses Singapore's then-Byzantine system of parking coupons and cryptic signage to dramatize a relationship between father and son as they both ultimately make the necessary concessions to live comfortably in a highly regulated society.

Kuo's work is also significant for its ability to embrace the multiple identities of ordinary Singaporeans. Kuo's *Mama Looking for Her Cat* (produced in 1988) uses English, Tamil, Malay, and Mandarin, as well as the Chinese dialects of Hokkien, Cantonese, and Teochew, to reflect the increased social isolation of a Hokkien-speaking woman who finds herself unable to communicate in a meaningful way with her children as they grow up.

During the 1990s Kuo wrote a number of plays that excavated the country's past while indirectly pointing out how core values have been compromised by wealth, modernity, and decades of social engineering and tight political control. *Lao Jiu* (produced in 1990) incorporated the dying art form of Hokkien hand puppetry to explore the conflict between tradition and modern life, while *Descendants of the Eunuch Admiral* (produced in 1995) used castration as a metaphor to underscore the sacrifices made to achieve material success. Kuo's ability to uncover and examine those personal, political, historical, and linguistic forces that have contributed to the making of contemporary Singapore is also what makes his plays resonate well in other cultural contexts where identity is increasingly fluid, complex, and multicultural.

SELECT PLAYS: *Hey, Wake Up!* (1968); *The Struggle* (1969); *The Spark of Youth* (1970); *Growth* (1974); *The Little White Sailing Boat* (1982); *The Coffin Is Too Big for the Hole* (1984); *Kopitiam* (1986); *No Parking on Odd Days* (1986); *The Silly Little Girl and the Funny Old Tree* (1987); *Day I Met the Prince* (1988); *Mama Looking for Her Cat* (1988); *The Eagle and the Cat* (1990); *Lao Jiu* (1990); *oZero01* (1991); *The Evening Climb* (1992); *Descendants of the Eunuch Admiral* (1995); *Geylang People in the Net* (1997); *The Spirits Play* (1998)

FURTHER READING

Jit, Krishen. Introduction to *The Coffin Is Too Big for the Hole, and Other Plays*, by Kuo Pao Kun. Singapore: Times Books International, 1990. 7–28.

Kuo Pao Kun. "Between Two Worlds: A Conversation with Kuo Pao Kun." In *9 Lives: 10 Years of Singapore Theatre, 1987–1997*, ed. by Sanjay Krishnan. Singapore: Necessary Stage, 1997. 126–142.

——. "Time/Space with a Simple Gesture." *Drama Review* 38, no.2 (Summer 1994): 59–63.

Kwok Kian Woon and Teo Han Wue, eds. *Kuo Pao Kun: And Love the Wind and Rain*. Singapore: Selectbooks, 2002.

Peterson, William. "Kuo Pao Kun." In *Contemporary Dramatists*, ed. by Thomas Riggs. 6th ed. New York: St. James Press, 1999. 375–377.

——. *Theater and the Politics of Culture in Contemporary Singapore*. Middletown, Conn.: Wesleyan Univ. Press, 2001.

William Peterson

KUREISHI, HANIF (1954–)

Hanif Kureishi (also spelled Kereishi), playwright, fiction writer, and essayist, was born in Bromley, ENGLAND, on December 5, 1954. With an English mother and a Pakistani father, Kureishi inherited a mixed racial and cultural experience. Kureishi studied philosophy at the University of London and wrote pornography under the pseudonym Antonia French to support himself.

Kureishi's view on writing is that it is a substitute for, rather than a reflection of, experience: an "instead of" rather than a "reliving." With this caveat, it may be said that much of his best-known work, including *Borderline*, *My Beautiful Laundrette*, *Sammy and Rosie Get Laid*, *The Buddha of Suburbia*, and *The Black Album*, portray the experiences of interracial and intercultural tension.

Kureishi's first play, *Soaking the Heat* (1976), was staged at the Royal Court Theatre Upstairs. *The King and Me* (1980) and *The Mother Country* (1980) were produced at the Soho Poly and Riverside studios, respectively. *Outskirts* (1981) won the George Devine Award; in the same year *Borderline* opened at the Royal Court Theatre. Kureishi became writer-in-residence at the Royal Court in 1982. *Birds of Passage* (1983) opened at Hampstead Theatre, an adaptation of BERTOLT BRECHT's MOTHER COURAGE (1984) was staged at the Barbican, and *Sleep with Me* (1999) was produced at the Royal National Theatre.

Kureishi's script for the film *My Beautiful Laundrette* (1985) established his fame. Directed by Stephen Frears, the screenplay was nominated for BAFTA Best Screenplay Award. It won the New York Film Critics' Best Screenplay Award and an Oscar nomination for best screenplay. The plot, based on the homosexual relationship of an Asian and a Briton, engages with a world of drug dealers, cocktail bars, and conflict. *Sammy and Rosie Get Laid* was Kureishi's next film, released in 1988. More diffuse and more polemical, it deals with the relationship between Sammy, an Asian, and Rosie, a Briton. *London Kills Me* (1991) was both written and directed by Kureishi. The film *My Son the Fanatic* (1998) was adapted from his short story.

His radio plays include *You Can't Go Home* (1980) and *The Trial* (1982), from Franz Kafka's novel of the same title.

Kureishi's debut novel *The Buddha of Suburbia* (1990) has autobiographical overtones and won the Whitbread Award for the best first novel. The plot of his second novel, *The Black Album* (1995), explores the reactions of the Asian Muslim community in England in the aftermath of Salman Rushdie's *The Satanic Verses*. *Intimacy* (1998) and *Gabriel's Gift* (2001) followed. Kureishi's most recent novel, *My Ear at His Heart*, was published in 2004.

Kureishi has two collections of short stories to his credit, *Love in a Blue Time* (1997) and *Midnight All Day* (1999). In 1995 he published *The Faber Book of Pop*, which he edited with Jon Savage.

Foremost among his influences Hanif Kureishi acknowledges WOLE SOYINKA, JAMES BALDWIN, Richard Wright, and V. S. Naipaul. From them he learned that discrimination was not his uniquely personal experience, and that it was possible to express and communicate this experience.

PLAYS: *Soaking the Heat* (1976); *The King and Me* (1980); *The Mother Country* (1980); *You Can't Go Home* (radio play, 1980); *Borderline* (1981); *Outskirts* (1981); *The Trial* (radio play, adapted from Kafka's novel, 1982); *Birds of Passage* (1983); *Mother Courage* (adapted from Brecht's play, 1984); *Sleep with Me* (1999)

FURTHER READING

Kaleta, Kenneth C. *Hanif Kureishi: Postcolonial Storyteller*. Austin: Univ. of Texas Press, 1998.

Sudha Shastri

KUSHNER, TONY (1956–)

I think that people do go to art in general as a way of addressing very deep, very intimate, very mercurial and elusive, ineffable things in a communal setting. It ends a certain kind of inner loneliness. Or it joins one's own loneliness with the inner loneliness of many other people. And I think it can be healing.

—Tony Kushner

"Not since [TENNESSEE] WILLIAMS has a playwright announced his poetic vision with such authority on the Broadway stage. [Tony] Kushner is the heir apparent to Williams's romantic theatrical heritage: he, too, has tricks in his pocket and things up his sleeve, and he gives the audiences 'truth in the pleasant disguise of illusion.' And, also like Williams, Kushner has forged an original, impressionistic theatrical vocabulary to show us the heart of a new age," wrote critic John Lahr (*The New Yorker*, May 31, 1993) in response to Kushner's acclaimed ANGELS IN AMERICA, a two-play epic on American life in the last decades of the 20th century. Viewing that era as the twilight of an America built by European immigrants who, by the mid-1980s, were dying away, Kushner wonders what will replace their values, politics, religions, and aspirations. His background is that of a gay Jewish man for whom a new socialism might provide a new path, a view in stark contrast to the Reaganesque neoconservatism of the 1980s, the period in which Kushner found recognition as one of the most promising dramatists on the American stage.

Kushner was born in New York City on July 16, 1956, although he spent his childhood in Lake Charles, Louisiana. He was the son of classically trained musicians William and Sylvia (Deutscher) Kushner, who named him after Tony Bennett. During his childhood Kushner's mother appeared in semiprofessional theater productions that left an indelible impression on her precocious literature-, music-, and history-loving son.

In 1974 Kushner moved to New York City to study English literature at Columbia University. On completion of a bachelor's degree in 1978, Kushner worked as a switchboard operator at the United Nations while immersing himself in the New York theater scene. Shortly thereafter he enrolled at the Tisch School of the Arts at New York University to train as a stage director under the mentorship of BERTOLT BRECHT specialist Carl Weber. During this period he also began to write plays.

Completing a master of fine arts degree in directing in 1984, Kushner embarked on a professional career with directing stints at various regional theaters. He also adapted Johann Wolfgang von Goethe's romantic TRAGEDY *Stella*, wrote several children's plays, and completed other original plays, including

Hydriotaphia; or, The Death of Dr. Browne (1987), and a free adaptation of Pierre Corneille's *L'illusion comique*, retitled *The Illusion* (1988). This poetic evocation of the joys and sufferings of love in all its guises was well received and became a staple of regional theaters throughout the United States.

Kushner's first important play, *A Bright Room Called Day* (1987), viewed the rise of the Nazis as seen through the eyes of a group of artists and filmmakers in Berlin during the years 1932–1933. Adopting the episodic structure he admired in Bertolt Brecht's plays, Kushner juxtaposed the drama's 1930s scenes, which included a visit from the Devil, with interludes set in the mid-1980s in which Zillah Katz, an angry Jewish feminist and leftist political activist, equates the rise of the Nazis to that of Ronald Reagan and the American neoconservatism of that period. Critical response to the first New York production of the play in 1991 was largely negative, and many reviewers found the Hitler-Reagan comparison extreme.

Critics did a complete about-face the following year, when Kushner's *Angels in America: A Gay Fantasia on National Themes; Part One: Millennium Approaches* opened at New York's Walter Kerr Theatre after acclaimed runs at San Francisco's Eureka Theatre (where artistic director Oskar Eustis had commissioned the play), Los Angeles's Mark Taper Forum, and the Royal National Theatre of Great Britain. *Millennium Approaches* was the most acclaimed American play of the 1990s, winning Kushner the Pulitzer Prize for Drama, as well as a Tony Award for Best Play, an Olivier Award for Best Play (during its run at the Royal National Theatre of Great Britain), and virtually every critics' award. The eight actors in the Broadway production each played multiple roles, sometimes switching genders to underscore the play's unapologetic depiction of the complexities of sexuality. Kathleen Chalfant, for example, played Joe's mother Hannah, Ethel Rosenberg, an elderly male rabbi, and Roy Cohn's male doctor. Nearly four hours in length, *Millennium Approaches* again used a Brechtian structure, weaving together numerous episodes focusing on the struggles of two fictional couples and one historical figure, Roy Cohn. Rejecting the homosexual label when he learns that he is dying of AIDS, Cohn continues his backstairs political maneuverings, which include using the name of First Lady Nancy Reagan to acquire a batch of a new drug, AZT. Cohn also hopes to place Joe Pitt, a young Mormon lawyer, at the Justice Department to do his bidding. Despite his marriage to Harper, a Valium-addicted Mormon woman with an extraordinary imagination, Joe is losing a battle with his latent homosexuality. Joe and Harper's paths cross with those of a gay couple, Prior and Louis, who are also in a crisis. Prior is HIV-positive, and Louis, a verbose Jewish intellectual with socialist politics, realizes that he may not have the strength of character to help Prior. Cohn is visited by a specter from his past, Ethel Rosenberg, whom Cohn was instrumental in bringing to execution as a Soviet spy along with her husband, Julius, in the early 1950s. Prior, too, receives a visitation from an Angel who crashes through his apartment roof calling Prior a "prophet" and announcing "The Great Work begins" as the play ends.

In *Millennium Approaches* Kushner uses the intimacies of the personal lives of this small band of characters to illuminate a broad spectrum of universal issues on social, political, religious, and moral subjects. Love and betrayal, conservative versus liberal, homophobia and racial bigotry, the search for hope in seemingly hopeless situations, compassion and forgiveness, the need for community and caring for the "other," transgression and victimhood, the power of imagination, the meaning of history, and the inevitability of change are all explored within a Brechtian structure, but also with a warm humanism typical of American lyric REALISM in the manner of Tennessee Williams. Lyricism in language was wedded by Williams to frank realities of relationships and human desires, and the result was an American realism that pervaded mid-20th-century American plays, at its best in works by Williams, WILLIAM INGE, and others. Kushner, similarly poetic in his use of language, adds a bolder theatricality to other aspects of the play than Williams typically attempted. Kushner turned to many inspirations for *Angels in America*, from Walter Benjamin's theory of history and Brecht's EPIC THEATER to Williams, Kushner's contemporaries in gay-themed drama (from HARVEY FIERSTEIN to LARRY KRAMER), and a host of American and European literary voices.

Kushner returned to *Angels* with *Perestroika*, a second play nearly four hours in length. It picks up exactly where *Millennium Approaches* ends, with the Angel's encounter with Prior. Where *Millennium Approaches* deals, in part, with the paralysis and fear behind the traumas suffered by the characters and the fact that all have to face up to adjusting to new circumstances, *Perestroika* finds the characters moving toward the feared changes. For some, acceptance and growth is possible; for others, it is not. Joe's mother, Hannah, arrives to find Harper lost in Central Park and hallucinating. Joe is nowhere to be found, so Hannah takes charge. She finds employment at New York's Mormon Welcome Center, where Harper spends her empty days watching repeated showings of a diorama depicting a 19th-century Mormon family headed across the Great Plains in a covered wagon. When the figures come miraculously to life—the Mormon father, for example, looks suspiciously like Joe, and the Mormon mother speaks of her unspeakable suffering as the devastated Harper seeks to understand her own pain—Kushner ties together the strands of American history and human experience to posit that although it is not easy, it is possible to "live past hope," as Prior states later in the play.

Prior becomes ill on the street in front of the Mormon Welcome Center, and Hannah takes him to the hospital, where, after they project stereotypical views on each other, a friendship is formed. Prior helps Hannah understand Joe's dilemma and gay life, while Hannah provides comfort to the lonely Prior, who, in occasional hallucinatory bouts, is visited by two of his ancestors—"prior Priors"—one from the Middle Ages and another from the 17th century, both of whom have died in previous plagues. Prior is also frequently visited by the Angel, who tells him that God disappeared at the time of the 1906 San Francisco earthquake and has left the celestial beings, who are beautiful but unable to take action, without guidance. They have turned to Prior, but he chooses to go on living despite his physical and emotional pain. He returns to his life, and in a strained meeting with Louis, who returns after an unhappy affair with Joe, their friendship is renewed, but not their intimate union.

Cohn lies in a hospital bed nursed by none other than Belize, Prior's friend. The encounter of this flamboyantly gay African American with the bigoted Cohn provides some hilarity, but also a demonstration of compassion and forgiveness as Belize, who finds Cohn repugnant, advises him on treatments. Dying, Cohn is again visited by the ghost of Ethel Rosenberg, who revels in telling him that he has been disbarred. When Cohn dies, Belize enlists the repentant Louis to help him steal Cohn's ill-gotten supply of AZT for Prior. Harper, having recovered from her delirium, confronts Joe. She leaves him, taking only a credit card, and flies off to San Francisco to begin a new life journey. *Perestroika*'s final scene finds Prior, Louis, Belize, and Hannah enjoying a pleasant afternoon at Central Park's Bethesda Fountain. It is 1990, and this group of survivors constitutes a new family—one Kushner sees as capable of change and embracing the pain of their lives through community and the grace bestowed by compassion.

Perestroika won the Tony Award for Best Play, as well as numerous critics' awards. In 2003 both parts of *Angels* were filmed for a six-hour film for HBO directed by Mike Nichols and with a stellar cast led by Al Pacino, Meryl Streep, and Emma Thompson.

Kushner's next play, *Slavs! Thinking About the Longstanding Problems of Virtue and Happiness* (1994), is constructed out of characters and two scenes originally intended for *Perestroika*. A seriocomic vaudeville about the collapse of the Soviet Union, it focuses on the relationship of a young lesbian woman employed as a guard at a facility in which the brains of the dead "great thinkers" of the Soviet experiment are stored. Kushner explores the irreparable social consequences of the failure of the Russian brand of socialism, introducing a speechless child, Vodya, damaged by the Chernobyl nuclear disaster. As well, some old Bolsheviks debate the relative merits of various political theories and end with Lenin's famous question, "What is to be done?" First produced at the Humana Festival of New Plays at the Actors Theatre of Louisville, *Slavs!* was one of a number of short plays Kushner occupied himself with during the late 1990s.

In the first decade of the new millennium Kushner was working on several works, including *Henry Box Brown, or, The Mirror of Slavery*, the first in a three-play cycle on economic history to be staged at the Royal National Theatre of Great Britain. Kushner centers the play on a historical figure, Henry Brown, an African American slave who shipped himself out of slavery in a crate, after which he lectured in England on the economic forces that perpetuated slavery. Kushner continues to adapt classic dramatic works and in 1999 revised his early play *Hydriotaphia; or, The Death of Dr. Browne* for regional theater productions, beginning at Houston's Alley Theatre. This "epic FARCE" also makes use of a historical figure, Sir Thomas Browne, a 17th-century philosopher, writer, scientist, and, in Kushner's view, seminal capitalist. Inspired in part by EDWARD BOND's *Bingo*, the play is set on the day of Browne's death and brings together the various participants in his life. All indict Browne as a grasping businessman who has thrown local peasants off some common lands he has converted into a profitable quarry. Browne's unloving wife, Dorothy, doubts the value of her husband's life as he dies and the quarry machines collapse into a great pit, stopping their eternal pounding as Browne's heart stops.

Kushner has also completed a libretto, *St. Cecilia; or, The Power of Music*, for an unproduced opera based on a Heinrich von Kleist story, continues to revise his early adaptation of Goethe's *Stella*, and is developing several screen and television plays. In late 2001 the New York Theatre Workshop went into rehearsals for Kushner's *Homebody/Kabul*, a drama about an English family caught up in the tragedies of AFGHANISTAN under the Taliban. The play was an expansion of a one-woman monologue Kushner had written for actress Kika Markham, who performed it at London's Chelsea Centre in the summer of 1999. As the expanded version went into rehearsals, the attacks of September 11, 2001, occurred, and the play took on even greater relevance. As with *Angels in America*, Kushner again tapped into events of immediate import. *Homebody/Kabul* won the Obie Award for Best OFF-BROADWAY Play and several critics' prizes, but Kushner continued to revise it in preparation for a production at Chicago's Steppenwolf Theatre in the summer of 2003, under Frank Galati's direction. An HBO film version went before the cameras in 2003.

That same year Kushner busied himself with adapting librettos for two chamber operas, *Brundibar* and *The Comedy on the Bridge*, both designed by Kushner's close friend Maurice Sendak and produced by the Chicago Opera Theatre in the spring of 2003, followed by a critically-acclaimed New York production at the New Victory Theater in 2006. Kushner also published a one-act play, *Only We Who Guard the Mystery Shall Be Unhappy*, in the *Nation* and presented it as a reading in a number of venues. It is a satiric drama that finds President George W. Bush's wife, Laura, escorted by an Angel into a classroom to read to the children, all of whom turn out to be dead Iraqi children killed in American bombings. Mrs. Bush ruminates on the ability of her husband to sleep soundly despite his culpability in the deaths of children. Kushner was also at work on another play, *The Intelligent Homosexual's Guide to Capitalism and Socialism with a Key to the Scriptures*, which takes stock of gay politics in the early 21st century.

Kushner wrote the libretto and lyrics for an original musical drama, *Caroline, or Change*, which, with music by Jeanine Tesori, opened to good reviews at New York's Public Theatre under the direction of George C. Wolfe in late 2003. The production, with slight changes, moved to Broadway in early 2004, where it received six Tony Award nominations. An imaginatively autobiographical work, *Caroline, or Change* is set at the time of the civil rights movement and President John F. Kennedy's assassination. A middle-aged African American maid, Caroline Thibodeaux, works for a Jewish family in a drama of the individual struggles of race and ethnicity set against a time of great social change. Caroline, who has a difficult life as a divorced mother of four, cannot negotiate the changes inherent in the times, but her teenage daughter Emmie is able to imagine a brighter future and, with her siblings, moves boldly into the unknown future.

Kushner also completed an as-yet unnamed screenplay about EUGENE O'NEILL and, in collaboration with Eric Roth, wrote the screenplay for *Munich* (2005), which was directed by Steven Spielberg. The action is set in the immediate aftermath of the 1972 murder of Israeli athletes at the Munich Olympic Games and follows the small hit squad sent out by Israel to kill those who planned and carried out the murders. The script ruminates on the cost of vengeance. Kushner received Academy Award and Golden Globe nominations and garnered generally positive reviews, although some Jewish organizations felt the film was too critical of Israel.

In the summer of 2006, Kushner's adaptation of Bertolt Brecht's MOTHER COURAGE, directed by George C. Wolfe and starring Meryl Streep and Kevin Kline, won rave reviews at New York's Shakespeare in the Park festival. The production brought Kushner's long interest in Brecht full circle, as the play offered parallels between the issues depicted and current events surrounding the Iraq War.

At age fifty, and despite a diverse résumé of theatrical accomplishment, Tony Kushner continues to explore the social, moral, political, and spiritual issues of the late 20th and early 21st centuries, drawing from literary traditions and history that, for him, provide texts for living in the present and moving into the future.

[*See also* Apocalypse in Modern Drama; Gay and Lesbian Drama; Identity Theater; Philosophy and Drama, 1960–Present; Political Theater in the United States; United States, 1940–Present]

SELECT PLAYS: *A Bright Room Called Day* (1987); *Hydriotaphia; or, The Death of Dr. Browne* (1987, revised 1998); *The Illusion* (1988, revised 1990; freely adapted from Pierre Corneille's *L'illusion comique*); *Angels in America: A Gay Fantasia an National Themes* (1991–1992); *Slavs! Thinking About the Longstanding Problems of Virtue and Happiness* (1994); *Grim(m)* (1995); *"It's An Undoing World," or, Why Should It Be Easy When It Can Be Hard? Notes on My Grandma for Actors, Dancers, and a Band* (1995; one-act); *Notes on Akiba* (1995; one-act); *East Coast Ode to Howard Jarvis* (1996; one-act, originally written as a screenplay); *Reverse Transcription: Six Playwrights Bury a Seventh, a Ten-Minute Play That's Nearly Twenty Minutes Long* (1996; one-act); *St. Cecilia; or, The Power of Music* (1997; opera libretto); *Terminating, or Lass Meine Schmerzen Nicht Verloren Sein, or Ambivalence* (1997; one-act); *Caroline, or Change* (1998; revised 2003; libretto for opera with music by Jeanine Tesori); *Homebody/Kabul* (2001); *Brundibar* (2003; opera libretto); *Only We Who Guard the Mystery Shall Be Unhappy* (2003; one-act); *But the Giraffe* (2006)

FURTHER READING

Barrett, Amy. "The Way We Live Now: 10-07-01; Questions for Tony Kushner." *New York Times* (October 7, 2001): sec. 6, 230.

Brask, Per, ed. *Essays on Kushner's Angels*. Winnipeg: Blizzard, 1995.

Fisher, James. *The Theater of Tony Kushner: Living Past Hope*. New York: Routledge, 2001.

——, ed. *Tony Kushner: New Essays on the Art and Politics of the Plays*. Jefferson, N.C.: McFarland, 2006.

Geis, Deborah R., and Steven F. Kruger, eds. *Approaching the Millennium: Essays on "Angels in America."* Ann Arbor: Univ. of Michigan Press, 1997.

Kushner, Tony. "A Modest Proposal." *American Theatre* (January 1998): 20–22, 77–89.

——. "Notes About Political Theatre." *Kenyon Review* 19 (Summer/Fall 1997): 19–34.

——. *Thinking About the Longstanding Problems of Virtue and Happiness: Essays, a Play, Two Poems, and a Prayer*. New York: Theatre Communications Group, 1995.

——. "Three Screeds from Key West: For Larry Kramer." In *We Must Love One Another or Die: The Life and Legacies of Larry Kramer*, ed. by Lawrence D. Mass. New York: St. Martin's, 1997. 191–199.

James Fisher

L

LABUTE, NEIL (1963–)

I am trying to examine the "ground zero" of our lives.

—Preface to *The Mercy Seat*

American playwright, director, and filmmaker Neil LaBute was born in 1963 in Detroit, Michigan, grew up in Spokane, Washington, and attended Brigham Young University, where he earned his bachelor's degree in theater and film. He also studied at New York University and the University of Kansas and participated in a writers' workshop at the Royal Court Theatre and the Sundance Institute's Playwrights' Lab. While he was at Brigham Young, LaBute joined the Church of Jesus Christ of Latter-Day Saints, but in late 2004 he formally broke ties with the church. Moving easily between the worlds of theater and cinema, LaBute's work has earned praise for its sharp and witty dialogue while drawing harsh criticism for alleged misogyny.

His unflinching look at the dark side of American life has invited comparisons with DAVID MAMET and SAM SHEPARD, but he has also cited the influence of contemporary British writers, such as CARYL CHURCHILL, whose technique of overlapping dialogue is frequently used, and HOWARD BARKER, whose "theatre of catastrophe" can be seen in LaBute's refusal of sympathetic protagonists or moral retribution.

LaBute's characters often make choices in erotic relationships based on either superficiality or sheer sadism. *In the Company of Men* chronicles the efforts of two businessmen who make an attractive deaf woman the subject of a cruel contest. His film adaptation of the play established LaBute as a major voice for both stage and screen. In THE SHAPE OF THINGS (also adapted for film) an art student transforms her ostensible boyfriend as if he is a sculpture. In *Fat Pig* a man is torn between two lovers, one overweight and the other attractive; his friends' endorsement is a major factor in his choice.

The three playlets gathered together as *Bash*, subtitled *Latterday Plays* (as in Latter-Day Saints), focus on Mormon characters who fall horrifyingly short of their religious community's ethical standards. The confessional monologues *Iphigenia in Orem* and *Medea Redux* adapt Greek myths of infanticide to a Mormon context, bracketing the overlapping monologues of a young couple in *A Gaggle of Saints*, who fondly recall a romantic weekend in New York, the man revealing his participation in a homophobic homicide.

One of the first plays to address the terrorist attack of September 11, 2001, *The Mercy Seat* is set on the day after the disaster, as a man ignores the incessant cell-phone calls of his wife as he hides in the apartment of his boss and lover, faced with the decision to go back to his life or start anew.

Controversial, challenging, and always compelling, LaBute's dark COMEDIES of manners reveal a tragic undercurrent in the American psyche. His plays offer a glimpse—but never a critique—of contemporary mores. It is this refusal to pass judgment that has earned LaBute the scorn of many, while others have lavished praise on him for his rejection of "political correctness." Whether the moral shortcomings of his characters are an appeal to divine justice, an effort to acknowledge the presence of everyday evil, or simply misanthropic revelry, LaBute's plays never fail to provoke and disturb.

[*See also* United States, 1940–Present]

PLAYS: *In the Company of Men* (1992); *Bash: Latterday Plays* (1999); *The Shape of Things* (2001); *The Distance from Here* (2002); *The Mercy Seat* (2002); *Autobahn* (2004); *Fat Pig* (2004); *This Is How It Goes* (2005); Some Girl(s) (2006); Wrecks (2006)

FURTHER READING

Baitz, Jon Robin. "Neil LaBute." *Bomb* 83 (Spring 2003): 56–61.

Goldsmith, David. "The Shape of Things." *Creative Screenwriting* 10, no. 3 (May–June 2003): 51–54.

Limsky, Drew. "Sexual Warfare in Naturalist Cinema: The Films of Todd Solondz and Neil LaBute." *Excavatio: Emile Zola and Naturalism* 13 (2000): 276–280.

Schilliner, Liesl. "Is Neil LaBute Getting . . . Nice?" *New York Times* (May 2, 2004): late ed., sec. 2, 7.

Steyn, Mark. "Desensitized Beyond Belief." *New Criterion* 18, no. 1 (September 1999): 38–42.

David Kilpatrick

THE LADY FROM THE SEA

Once you've really become a land animal, then there's no going back again—into the sea. Or the life that belongs to the sea.

—Ellida, Act 5

HENRIK IBSEN's *The Lady from the Sea (Fruen fra havet)*, a play in five acts, was published in Copenhagen in November 1888. The action takes place by a fjord on the northwest coast of NORWAY. In the preliminary notes it is stated that human beings are akin to the sea, are bound by the sea, and must return to it. The play portrays a married couple who succeed in overcoming problems from the past and decide to start life afresh. The first performance took place in Christiania (now Oslo) in February 1889. The critics were at a loss to form any consensus on its interpretation, and this lack of agreement, in particular concerning the final scene, still prevails today. By some critics it is considered as obscure, and by others as too obvious in its symbolism.

Ellida Wangel is married to the district medical officer, a former widower with two daughters from his first marriage.

She is restless and dissatisfied, mentally unbalanced after the death of her newborn infant. Her relationship with her husband is in a rut. She is longing to get away: to the vast expanse of the sea from which she came—as the lighthouse keeper's daughter—and to a seaman she had met before she got married. The memory of this unknown man exerts a strong power over her, although he has committed a murder and run away. In act 3 the stranger turns up in the flesh and asks her to break with her husband and his family and go with him.

The experienced doctor and husband intervenes in Ellida's crisis. At the end of a long dialogue, not unlike a case of psychoanalytic therapy, he allows her to choose freely between the stranger and himself. She apparently steps out of her world of false illusions and decides to stay as his wife and to take on the role of mother to his daughters.

Ellida's decision has challenged the critics ever since the play appeared. The ending has provoked modern feminists. Ellida is one of a series of women striving for freedom in Ibsen's oeuvre. The searchlight is focused on the woman's role in a premodern society. This is brought out particularly clearly in the relations between the two daughters and the other men in the drama. The men behave as "guardians" and are patronizing toward the women, depriving them of their autonomy. Through the daughters' "choices" the options are listed: a marriage of convenience with financial stability, or life "in the open air," outside the community.

In a general sense the play sets up the idea of living freely and naturally as the opposite picture to the civilized, enclosed, and regulated kind of life. The nature versus culture dichotomy is reflected in the choice of topography and symbolic means, with reference to the fundamental idea of ROMANTICISM. At the same time there is on the psychological level a disturbingly modern description of the split mind and of mental conflicts that Sigmund Freud was later to explore in his studies of the subconscious.

[*See also* Philosophy and Drama, 1860–1960; Symbolism]

FURTHER READING

Johnston, Brian. "The Turning Point in *The Lady from the Sea*." In *Text and Supertext in Ibsen's Drama*. University Park: Pennsylvania State Univ. Press (1989). 193–233.

Saari, Sandra. "Giving Voice: The Emergence of a Female Story in Ibsen's *The Lady from the Sea*." Pt. 1. In *Ibsen at the Centre for Advanced Study*, ed. by Vigdis Ystad. Oslo: Scandinavian Univ. Press, 1997. 248–260.

Stanton-Ife, Anne-Marie V. "A Woman's Place/Female Space in Ibsen's *Fruen fra Havet*." *Scandinavica* 35, no. 1 (1996): 29–52.

Templeton, Joan. "The Acclimatization of Ellida and Bolette Wangel: *The Lady from the Sea*." In *Ibsen's Women*. Cambridge: Cambridge Univ. Press, 1997. 194–203.

Astrid Sæther

THE LADY ON HER BALCONY

The Lady on Her Balcony (*La señora en su balcón*) has distinguished itself as one of the most popular of the one-act plays by the Mexican author ELENA GARRO with its engaging plot and innovative use of time, space, and memory. Its popularity is evidenced by the increasing frequency with which it has been performed worldwide in recent years. This work remains accessible to a wide audience because of its timeless theme—the search for one's true self—and societal, cultural, and historical context, a culture dominated by a deeply rooted, oppressive patriarchal tradition and its expectations for men's and women's behavior, with which many easily identify.

The work begins with a fifty-year-old Clara sitting on her balcony, reflecting on the most influential events and people in her life and searching for the moment she abandoned her life's ambitions and resigned herself to accepting a role assigned to her by others, one devoid of the freedom to choose and act according to her own will. The work exemplifies Garro's penchant for playing with time and space as she structures it achronologically, moving between the present and past through a series of flashbacks as the older Clara recalls her life at different stages during her youth.

Images of entrapment and monotony abound, lending the work a strong symbolic unity and rendering Garro's stance on women's struggles in an oppressive society obvious and undeniable. Everywhere Clara turns—from a childhood school lesson that quashes her creativity and discourages her desire to travel to the mandates of a husband who is as unhappy in his monotonous routine as she is in hers and who ridicules her when she expresses her dreams—she hears the message that there is no escaping the rules that dictate a woman's place in society. Nevertheless, throughout the work Clara is sustained by her dream of the mythical, ideal city of Nineveh that promises an alternative reality where all that is lacking in Clara's present world exists and awaits her. It is there that she expects to find the freedom now lost and inaccessible to her because of the strictures of society and to be able to live in accordance with the desires of her true self, which she finds that she has denied throughout her life in order to please others.

The work comes full circle in its final moments as Garro brings the reader back to Clara on her balcony, facing a critical decision at this juncture in her life. Clara attains a moment of complete self-awareness in which she acknowledges her responsibility for her current circumstances and realizes that she has been searching in the wrong place for what she was lacking, looking for completion of self in others when the answer always lay within her.

Clara's final, suicidal act is at once tragic and liberating, reflecting the ironic truth that death will become the time and space in which she can truly begin to live. Her death is tragic in the most traditional sense, reflecting Clara's pessimism regarding the possibility that the freedom to be herself and follow her dreams can be attained only through death because things on this earth will not change within her lifetime. It is liberating and empowering when considered in a historical context in which her ancestors committed suicide to avoid death from their conquerors, indicating that Clara finally realizes that she does in fact have control over her destiny and can act to follow a path of her choosing rather than passively acquiescing in the demands of others, thereby allowing her to be true to her inner self and travel to a dimension where she believes that Nineveh and its freedoms exist. Clara at fifty: "I have nothing left but myself. I am leaving you forever. . . . I went away on a trip and came back to myself. . . . Now I know that all I need is to flee from myself to reach [Nineveh]. . . . All that's missing now is the great leap to enter the silver city" (Garro, 1990).

[*See also* Mexico]

FURTHER READING

Garro, Elena. *The Lady on Her Balcony*. In *A Different Reality*, tr. by Beth Miller, ed. by Anita K. Stoll. Lewisburg, Pa.: Bucknell Univ. Press, 1990. 59–68.

——. *La señora en su balcón*. In *Tercera antología de obras en un acto*. Mexico: Colección Teatro Mexicano, 1960. 25–40.

Southerland, Stacy. "Elusive Dreams, Shattered Illusions: The Theater of Elena Garro." In *Latin American Women Dramatists: Theater, Texts, and Theories*, ed. by Catherine Larson and Margarita Vargas. Bloomington: Indiana Univ. Press, 1998.

Stoll, Anita K., ed. *A Different Reality: Studies on the Work of Elena Garro*. Lewisburg, Pa.: Bucknell Univ. Press, 1990.

Winkler, Julie A. *Light Into Shadow: Marginality and Alienation in the Work of Elena Garro*. New York: Peter Lang, 2001.

Stacy Southerland

THE LADY'S NOT FOR BURNING

A world unable to die sits on and on
In spring sunlight, hatching egg after egg,
Hoping against hope that out of one of them
Will come the reason for it all.
—Thomas Mendip, Act 1

The Lady's Not for Burning (1948) by CHRISTOPHER FRY is a whimsical verse drama set in the year 1400 in the house of Hebble Tyson, the mayor of a small market town. While a witch-hunting mob riots outside Tyson's house, Thomas Mendip, a recently discharged soldier, climbs through a window. Weary and disillusioned by his war experience, Mendip claims to have murdered a local beggar and demands to be hung for his crime. Tyson is skeptical of Mendip's claims and regards him as a nuisance until the arrival of another stranger, Jennet Jourdemayne. She seeks sanctuary from the mob outside, which accuses her of being a witch and of turning the same beggar into a dog. Tyson, suspecting that Jourdemayne has bewitched Mendip into falsely confessing to the murder, detains them both and sentences Jourdemayne to be executed the following morning.

Later that night Mendip and Jourdemayne are present, under house arrest, during the engagement party for Tyson's nephew, Humphrey. Jourdemayne's beauty and wit charm the party guests, and soon all regret the pronouncement of death upon her. Mendip declares his love for Jourdemayne and renounces his death wish. In a romantic deus ex machina the supposedly dead beggar, Skipps, arrives on the scene, considerably drunk. Freed from suspicion of witchcraft and murder, Jourdemayne and Mendip slip away as the authorities turn a blind eye to their escape.

Fry wrote *The Lady's Not for Burning* for the Arts Theatre, London, where it was produced in 1948. In 1949 a revised version was presented at the Globe Theatre, starring John Gielgud and Pamela Brown. The play was a surprise commercial and critical hit and was hailed as a triumph for the verse-drama movement, although some observed that the verse decorated a rather thin plot. Fry's poetry is joyful and witty, in keeping with the light tone of this, the "spring" play of his four-play "seasons cycle," which also includes *Venus Observed* (1949, autumn), *The Dark Is Light Enough* (1954, winter), and *A Yard of Sun* (1970, summer).

The play's critical reception suffered in the wake of the "kitchen-sink" REALISM ushered in by JOHN OSBORNE's LOOK BACK IN ANGER in 1956; verse drama suddenly seemed precious and out of touch. In retrospect, however, *The Lady's Not for Burning* appears to be the dainty precursor of Osborne's revolutionary piece; both are essentially static plays whose heroes are angry young men and gifted orators proclaiming their disillusion with the fallen world. In Mendip, the nihilistic war veteran who hopelessly embraces death, Fry almost creates an absurdist hero. But the themes of this spring COMEDY are rebirth and redemption, and so Mendip is ultimately saved by Jourdemayne's love. Since its initial productions in London and in New York (1951) the play has had two major revivals, one by the Prospect Theatre Company in 1978 and the other at the Chichester Theatre Festival in 2001.

[*See also* England, 1940–1960]

FURTHER READING

Innes, Christopher. *Modern British Drama, 1890–1990*. Cambridge: Cambridge Univ. Press, 1992.

Leeming, Glenda. *Christopher Fry*. Boston: Twayne, 1990.

Melissa Dana Gibson

LADY WINDERMERE'S FAN

Lady Windermere's Fan: A Play About a Good Woman, OSCAR WILDE's first successful play, opened at St. James's Theatre, London, on February 22, 1892. The theater's manager, George Alexander, commissioned Wilde to write a modern play; the author thought that he could "beat the [ARTHUR WING] PINEROS and the HENRY ARTHUR JONESES" after a few weeks' work. Wilde drew freely upon the situations common to these authors, and from their originals in the French well-made plays of VICTORIEN SARDOU. The precision and wit of the dialogue, however, and the double concealment in act 3 hark back to William Congreve's plays and Richard Brinsley Sheridan's *School for Scandal*. The stock situations of the lost child, the woman with a past, lost personal property, confrontations between rival women, concealment within closets, and melodramatic recognitions are all employed, but the plot is not resolved in the customary fashion. Instead of reinforcing the moral status quo, the denouement casts doubt on morality and, like HENRIK IBSEN's plays, suggests that ideals are illusions. Good girls (like Lady Windermere) do naughty things, and women with bad reputations (like Mrs. Erlynne) may have both goodness and sense.

The least attractive characters in the play are the straight and proper ones, Lord and Lady Windermere, who seem bereft of cleverness. The two most attractive characters in the play are the witty ones, Mrs. Erlynne and Lord Darlington. Yet they are types upon whom proper society looks down, the divorced woman living under an assumed name and the man-about-town who courts his best friend's wife. Mrs. Erlynne is a woman of such reputation that the young Lady Windermere—it is her twenty-first birthday—will not have her in the house, not knowing that it is her own mother against whom she bars the door. Yet because Mrs. Erlynne has herself learned for twenty years what it is to be cast out and despised, and because she has brains, she is able to save her daughter from a similarly scandalous doom. When Lady Windermere leaves her fan, a birthday present from her husband, in Lord Darlington's apartment, and it is discovered by Lord Windermere, Mrs. Erlynne steps forward to say that it was she who took the fan by mistake from the Windermeres' house and dropped it by mistake at Darlington's, thus saving her daughter from the discovery of an intention to be unfaithful. The "good" woman is saved by the "bad," and Lady Windermere learns that "there is nothing so unbecoming in a woman as a Nonconformist [Protestant] conscience." She keeps her flirtation a secret from her husband and reconciles with him on the new basis of nonjudgementalism: "I don't think now," she tells her husband, "that people can be divided into the good and bad."

[*See also* England, 1860–1940]

FURTHER READING

Ellmann, Richard. *Oscar Wilde*. New York: Knopf, 1988.

Gagnier, Regenia. *Idylls of the Marketplace: Oscar Wilde and the Victorian Public*. Aldershot: Scolar, 1987.

Powell, Kerry. *Oscar Wilde and the Theatre of the 1890s*. Cambridge: Cambridge Univ. Press, 1990.

Adrian Frazier

LAGERKVIST, PÄR (1891–1974)

Our time, in its lack of balance, its heterogeneity, and through the violent expansion of its conflicting forces, is baroque and fantastic, much more fantastic than naturalism is able to portray it.

—Pär Lagerkvist, 1918

Swedish poet, novelist, and dramatist Pär Lagerkvist is best known for such novels as *The Dwarf* (*Dvärgen*, 1944), set in Renaissance Italy, and *Barabbas* (1950), later dramatized by the author, dealing with the robber who was released instead of Jesus. Lagerkvist was elected to the Swedish Academy in 1941 and received the Nobel Prize for Literature in 1951.

Barabbas is the first of six novels set in the Holy Land at the time of Jesus or, in one case, centuries before in classical Delphi. Far from being historical novels in any strict sense, they deal, as always with Lagerkvist, with timeless and fundamental human questions: the meaning of life, the significance of death, the question of good and evil.

During World War I, while living in DENMARK, Lagerkvist showed considerable interest in medieval and Indian drama, as well as in AUGUST STRINDBERG's post-*Inferno* plays. He was then, for a short period, theater critic for the Stockholm newspaper *Svenska Dagbladet*.

The result of this interest can be seen in his first play, *The Last Man* (*Sista mänskan*, 1917), a doomsday "oratorium" peopled by incarnated attitudes rather than characters. Much more stageable are the three short one-act plays titled *The Difficult Hour* (*Den svåra stunden*, 1918), all three describing the moment of death. In the first, the arrogant Man of Tails, victim of a railway accident, is confronted with his rival whose death he has caused, the modest Man with a Hunchback. The dark tunnel where they meet is at once the place of the accident and the space between life and death. The scenery similarly visualizes both the accident and the victim's subjective experience of it. The second one-act shows a dying man surrounded by hallucinatory figures reliving in chaotic fashion his past life. In the third, a little boy with a lit candle is wandering around in the dark realm of the dead. When the tiny flame of life has gone out, he dies and all is darkness. Equally innovative is the one-act *The Secret of Heaven* (*Himlens hemlighet*, 1919), published in the collection *Chaos* (*Kaos*). At the center of this single-space station drama (i.e.: a drama where the single setting can be divided into a number of stations, from medieval drama) Lagerkvist places an erotic triangle situation. The young man who enters the semiglobe filled with cripples—an image of the (postwar) world—does not know whence he has come or where he is going. His movement corresponds to a search for meaning. When his love for a young girl finds no response, he jumps from the globe. What we come across in these early plays is underpinned in Lagerkvist's essay "Modern Theater" ("Modern teater," 1918), in which Ibsenite NATURALISM is seen as a thing of the past and the nonillusionism of Strindberg's late plays as the promising foreboding of the drama of the future. Yet, unlike Strindberg, Lagerkvist pleads for a drama that does not give priority to the spoken word but integrates the dialogue into the audiovisual totality of the presentation. Of importance, he writes, is that "everything is directed to one purpose—the liberation of a single mood, a single feeling whose intensity increasingly grows and grows" (Lagerkvist, 1918).

In several of his later, somewhat more realistic plays Lagerkvist stresses the duality of man. In *The King* (*Konungen*, 1946), set in ancient Babylonia, the duality concerns two like-named characters of contrasting disposition, Amar-Azu and Iream-Azu, one succeeding the other as a king. In *Victory in the Darkness* (*Seger i mörker*, 1939) it concerns two stepbrothers, a relationship indicating both correspondences and differences. In *The Man Who Lived His Life Over* (*Han som fick leva om sitt liv*, 1928) it is about the protagonist Daniel's two lives, which turn out to be less different than Daniel had hoped.

The political situation in Europe in the 1930s caused Lagerkvist to take a clear stand earlier than any other writer in Scandinavia. THE HANGMAN (*Bödeln*, 1946), based on the novella of the same title, is at once a timely and a timeless drama: timely when seen as an attack on the new dictatorships in Europe, timeless in its assertion that the hangman, the tool of evil, is eternal. In *The Man Without a Soul* (*Mannen utan själ*, 1936) the author combines an immediate political concern with a broader one, what he termed "fighting humanism."

Midsummer Night's Dream in the Workhouse (*Midsommardröm i fattighuset*, 1941) portrays old blind Jonas, who sees reality as an obstacle to man's happiness. His granddaughter Cecilia hopes for a brighter future. Their dreams about "the great, eternal midsummer realm of love" are set off against the misery surrounding them. In *The Philospher's Stone* (*De vises sten*) the obsession of Albertus, a Faustian alchemist, and Simonides, a rabbi, prevents both men from leading a meaningful life and proves destructive for their children. Formally more original is the "stage oratorio" *Let Man Live* (*Låt människan leva*, 1949), in which fourteen characters, ranging from Christ and Socrates to a World War II resistance fighter and an American Negro, each of them a victim of man's readiness to condemn his fellows, address the audience.

[*See also* Sweden]

PLAYS: *The Last Man* (*Sista mänskan*, 1917); *The Difficult Hour* (*Den svåra stunden*, 1918); *The Secret of Heaven* (*Himlens hemlighet*, 1919); *The Invisible One* (*Den osynlige*, 1923); *The Man Who Lived His Life Over* (*Han som fick leva om sitt liv*, 1928); *The Man Without a Soul* (*Mannen utan själ*, 1936); *Victory in the Darkness* (*Seger i mörker*, 1939); *Midsummer Night's Dream in the Workhouse* (*Midsommardröm i fattighuset*, 1941); *The Hangman* (*Bödeln*, 1946); *The King* (*Konungen*, 1946); *The Philosopher's Stone* (*De vises sten*, 1947); *Let Man Live* (*Låt människan leva*, 1949); *Barabbas* (1953)

FURTHER READING

Bergman, Gösta M. *Pär Lagerkvists dramatik*. Stockholm: Norstedt, 1928.

Buckman, Thomas. "Pär Lagerkvist and the Swedish Theatre." *Tulane Drama Review* 6 (Winter 1961): 60–89.

Lagerkvist, Pär. "Modern Theatre: Points of View and Attack." 1918. In *Modern Theatre: Seven Plays and an Essay*. Ed. by Thomas R. Buckman. Lincoln: Univ. of Nebraska Press, 1966.

Mjöberg, Jöran. *Livsproblemet hos Lagerkvist*. Stockholm: Bonnier, 1951.

Oberholzer, Otto. *Pär Lagerkvist: Studien zu seiner Prosa und seinen Dramen*. Heidelberg: Carl Winter, 1958.

Sjöberg, Leif. *Pär Lagerkvist*. Columbia Essays on Modern Writers, 74. New York: Columbia Univ. Press, 1976.

Spector, Robert Donald. *Pär Lagerkvist*. New York: Twayne, 1973.

Egil Törnqvist

LAI SHENG-CH'UAN (1954–)

Lai Sheng-ch'uan (Stan Lai) is not only one of the most influential dramatists and directors in contemporary Taiwanese theater, but also one of the most important figures in Chinese-language theater around the world. He was born on October 25, 1954, in Washington, D.C., but moved back to Taiwan with his family when he was twelve. After receiving his doctorate degree in dramatic arts from the University of California at Berkeley, he returned to Taiwan and dedicated himself to teaching and creating theater. In 1984 he founded the Performance Workshop (Biaoyan Gongzuo Fang). Its premiere production of *The Night We Became Xiangsheng Comedians* (*Na yiye women shuo xiangsheng*, 1985) was a landmark in contemporary theater in Taiwan.

The Night We Became Xiangsheng Comedians set the standard for the group's theatrical works. The script was created collaboratively through improvisation by Lai and his ensemble actors. The themes are deeply connected with social, political, and cultural issues in contemporary Taiwan. The theatrical style combines tongue-in-cheek humor with thought-provoking philosophical observations, slapstick, and traditional Chinese art. *Xiangsheng* (cross-talk), a two-person stand-up COMEDY form, is one of the many traditional art forms that is disappearing in modern Taiwan, where traditional art, like traditional values, must compete with modernization and Westernization. In this play two minor entertainers are forced to perform *xiangsheng* in place of two famous masters of the art. From their first pathetic attempts to their final magical transformation (they "become" the master performers), the two entertainers comment on important moments in modern Chinese history. Since the founding of the People's Republic of CHINA (PRC) in 1949, Taiwan has been "home" for three major groups: mostly Mandarin-speaking new diasporic Chinese or "mainlanders" (those who came from mainland China in 1949, along with their descendants); earlier generations of Taiwanese- and Hakka-speaking diasporic Chinese (those who came before 1949, along with their descendants); and descendants of the native groups that populated the island before the beginning of Chinese immigration. Even as the three groups coexist and compete for resources, the question of the connection (tenuous or not) with the PRC has been grounds for a major political debate. The confusion, tension, and nostalgia of Lai's play reflect the problems that Taiwan has faced in its recent transitional period: in the process of gaining economic strength and political independence, what is Taiwan losing?

Secret Love for the Peach Blossom Spring (*Anlian taohuayuan*, 1986) marks the ensemble's next success. This Pirandellian play involves two theater groups sharing a rehearsal space as they prepare completely different productions. The juxtaposition of tragic and farcical elements, REALISM and Beijing opera stylization, and the technique of "metatheater" once again illustrates Taiwan's unique situation: the negotiation between old "mainlanders" and younger generations, and a conversation between nostalgia and modernization. A film version of this play, titled *Peach Blossom Land* (*Anlian taohuayua*), directed by Lai, appeared in 1991. He also directed the film *The Red Lotus Society* (*Feixia ada*, 1994).

Lai is active and prolific. He has co-created and produced dozens of plays in the past two decades. The most famous among these are *Journey to the West: A Modern Chinese Opera* (*Xiyou ji*, 1987), *Look Who's Cross-Talking Tonight* (*Zhe yiye, shei lai shuo xiangsheng?* 1989), *Strange Tales of Taiwan* (*Taiwan guaitan*, 1991), *The Complete History of Chinese Thought: Cross-Talk Version* (*You yiye, tamen shuo xiangsheng*, 1997), *You, Me, He, Him* (*Ni he wo he ta he ta*, 1998), *Millennium Teahouse* (*Qianxi ye, women shuo xiangsheng*, 2000), and the eight-hour epic play *A Dream Is like a Dream* (*Ru meng zhi meng*, 2000). Although his plays are usually set in contemporary Taiwan, they usually concern universally "Chinese" issues, and he tours his productions to other Chinese-speaking regions. He is regarded as one of the most successful and established contemporary Chinese-speaking directors.

SELECT PLAYS (By Lai Sheng-Ch'uan and the Performance Workshop): The Night We Became Xiangsheng Comedians (Na yiye women shuo xiangsheng, 1985); Secret Love for the Peach Blossom Spring (Anlian Taohuayuan, 1985); The Story of Yuanhuan (Yuanhuan wuyu, 1986); Journey to the West: A Modern Chinese Opera (Xiyou ji, 1987); Look Who's Cross-talking Tonight? (Zhe yiye, shei lai shuo xiangsheng?, 1989); Strange Tales of Taiwan (Taiwan guaitan, 1990); Red Sky (Hongsede tiankong, 1994); The Complete History of Chinese Thought: Cross-talk Version (You yiye, tamen shuo xiangsheng, 1997); I, Me, He, Him (Ni he wo he ta he ta, 1998); A Dream Is Like a Dream (Ru meng zhi meng, 2000); Millennium Teahouse (Qiani ye, women shuo xiangsheng, 2000)

FURTHER READING

Chung, Mingder. "The Little Theatre Movement of Taiwan (1980–89): In Search of Alternative Aesthetics and Politics." Ph.D diss., New York Univ., 1992.

Lai Shengchuan. *Lai Shengchuan juchang* [The theater of Lai Shengchuan]. Taipei: Yuanzun wenhua qiye gufen youxian gong si, 1999.

——. *Pining . . . in Peach Blossom Land* [*Anlian taohuayuan*]. Tr. by Martha P. Y. Cheung. In *An Oxford Anthology of Contemporary Chinese Drama*, ed. by Martha P. Y. Cheung and Jane C. C. Lai. Hong Kong: Oxford Univ. Press, 1997. 375–453.

Daphne Lei

LAND OF VOLCANIC ASH

Land of Volcanic Ash (*Kazanbaichi*, 1938), a SHINGEKI play by KUBO SAKAE, is widely regarded as the supreme achievement of SOCIALIST REALISM in JAPAN. The play was first performed by the New Cooperative (Shinkyō) troupe.

Land of Volcanic Ash is a forbidding work. It is seven acts long, requires two nights to perform, has a cast of fifty characters, and occupies more than 250 pages in English translation. The subject is dry: it presents in minute detail the economic and social life of an agricultural town and its environs on Japan's northernmost island of Hokkaido during the famine years of 1935–1936. The style is prolix. Full-scale war had broken out with CHINA in July 1937, and freedom of expression was being severely curtailed in Japan. In order to avoid censorship, Kubo was forced to make his arguments indirectly, which added to the play's length and complexity.

Despite all these factors, *Land of Volcanic Ash* thrilled its original audience and was restaged twice after the war. It has been widely anthologized and is considered a modern classic. A journal titled *Kubo Sakae Studies*, whose contributors included many of Japan's leading postwar intellectuals, published eleven issues between 1959 and 1988.

There are many interrelated subplots in *Land of Volcanic Ash*, involving, among others, destitute charcoal burners, political activists, and exploitative landlords. The main story line concerns a young agronomist named Amamiya Akira, the star pupil of a leading scholar, who marries his mentor's daughter, is placed in charge of a local agricultural station, and is destined for success until his research leads him to conclusions that bring him into conflict with his professor and the entire social and political establishment. Amamiya's struggle to maintain his intellectual integrity in the face of overwhelming opposition is what holds the diverse strands of the play together.

The issue at stake is the appropriate fertilizer for use on the volcanic ash soil of the Tokachi plain, where the play takes place. Amamiya's research leads him to believe that the fertilizer sold by the local flax company, which does not contain potassium, is poorly suited to local conditions. Thinking that it will increase their yields, Amamiya encourages farmers to use potassium fertilizer, but this only puts them at odds with the business establishment and alienates them from their peers. Amamiya concludes that the only way to maximize agricultural results and achieve social justice is through collectivization, but he is horrified when he realizes that this conclusion is the same as the Communist view and in line with the policies of the Soviet Union. Despite these self-doubts and the consequences for his personal life and career, Amamiya ultimately decides to stick to his scientific guns. At the end of the play he departs for an academic conference in Sapporo, where he will make his findings public.

Kubo's ideal was to achieve, in his words, "a unification of scientific theory and poetic form." For all its flaws, *Land of Volcanic Ash* achieves this goal better than any other contemporary work.

FURTHER READING

Inoue Yoshie. "Kubo Sakae *Kazanbaichi*" [Kubo Sakae's *Land of Volcanic Ash*]. In *Nijusseiki no gikyoku I: Nihon kindai giyoku no sekai* [Twentieth-century plays I: The world of modern Japanese plays], ed. by Nihon Kindai Engekishi Kenkyūkai. Tokyo: Shakai Hyōronsha, 2002. 335–344.

——. *Kubo Sakae no sekai* [The world of Kubo Sakae]. Tokyo: Shakai Hyōronsha, 1989.

Kubo, Sakae. *Land of Volcanic Ash*. Tr. by David G. Goodman. Rev. ed. Cornell East Asia Papers 40. Ithaca, N.Y.: Cornell East Asia Program, 1993.

Murakami Ichirō. *Kubo Sakae ron* [On Kubo Sakae]. Tokyo: Kōbundō, 1959.

Uno Jūkicihi, Kuno Osamu, et al., eds. *Kubo Sakae kenkyū* [Kubo Sakae studies]. 11 vols. Tokyo: Kubo Sakae Kenkyū, 1959–1988.

David G. Goodman

LANGER, FRANTIŠEK (1888–1965)

František Langer was a physician devoted to the cause of independence for CZECHOSLOVAKIA who served on the Russian front with the Czech legionnaires in World War I. He shared with KAREL ČAPEK a dedication to the democratic, liberal principles of the Czechoslovak Republic. As a dramatist, Langer was very popular in the 1920s and 1930s with his well-composed, usually realistic plays depicting ordinary urban Czechs with fidelity to their often idiosyncratic mannerisms of speech and behavior. Although Langer was primarily a writer of social COMEDIES, his palette included darker tones as well.

His first real success was *Camel Through a Needle's Eye* (*Velbloud uchem jehly*), a Shavian-like work celebrating an enterprising lower-class city girl who not only becomes a successful entrepreneur but marries the son of a millionaire and is entrusted with her father-in-law's holdings. *The Wrong Side of the Tracks* (*Periferie*, 1925), probably Langer's most important work, has a similar urban setting but a Dostoevskian action of crime and guilt involving a young man who accidentally kills a well-to-do customer of his prostitute girlfriend, but is not in any way suspected of the crime. Wracked by his conscience, proclaiming his guilt but to no avail, he finally finds release from his torment by killing once more, in a manner that will assure his arrest and conviction. It is his beloved that he slays, with her willing consent and assistance, in order to ease his torment. Langer handles the inherently lurid action with restraint, compassion, and even touches of humor.

In *The Turnabout of Ferdyš Pištora* (*Obrácení Ferdyše Pištory*, 1929) Langer turns again to whimsical, ironical social comedy in depicting a likeable safecracker who is hailed as a hero for saving a young boy from a burning villa that caught fire while Ferdyš was inside it during a safecracking attempt. Temporarily converted to an almost aggressive do-gooder, Ferdyš strenuously tries to convert others to a moral life, but finally his common sense makes him settle for a more everyday life as a married man.

The Mounted Patrol (*Jízdní hlídka*, 1935) presents more serious material: the desperate struggle of the Czechoslovak legionnaires in World War I to fight their way out of Russia in order to join in the conflict on the western front. Rejecting an attractive offer by the Red Army to join it, they continue to battle for the cause of their own homeland-to-be. Langer remains objective in his depiction of the clash of the two politically defined positions of brave men even though his heart is with the Czechs and Slovaks.

Of Langer's other works, two warrant mention. *Angels Among Us* (*Andeli mezi námy*, 1931) deals sympathetically and somewhat fancifully with the issue of euthanasia; and *Prisoner Number Seventy-Seven* (*Sedmdesátka*, 1937) ingeniously employs a theater-in-theater device in presenting three different versions of the same crime in order to clear a woman imprisoned for murder.

SELECT PLAYS: *Camel Through a Needle's Eye* (*Velbloud uchem jehly*, 1923); *The Wrong Side of the Tracks* (*Periferie*, 1925); *The Turnabout of Ferdyš Pištora* (*Obrácení Ferdyše Pištory*, 1929); *Angels Among Us* (*Anděli mezi námy*, 1931); *The Mounted Patrol* (*Jízdní hlídka*, 1935); *Prisoner Number Seventy-Seven* (*Sedmdesátka*, 1937)

FURTHER READING

Vocadlo, Otokar. "Theater and Drama of Czechoslovakia." In *The Theater in a Changing Europe*, ed. by T. H. Dickinson. New York: H. Holt, 1937.

Jarka M. Burian

LAOS

Laos, in Southeast Asia, was a Thai vassal state in the early 19th century when the French established a protectorate. The artistic traditions of the four million national Lao are shared by the thirteen million Lao of northern THAILAND. Most theater grows from indigenous storytelling or courting games. Sung storytelling by a male chanter (*mawlum*), accompanied by a *kaen* (a bamboo panpipe), told *jataka* (tales of Buddha's previous births), local epics, or historical tales in verse. The *Wetsundwn* (*Vesswantara*), which tells of Prince Wetsundwn, who is so generous that he gives away his wife and children, is the most popular *jataka*. Buddhist reading of *jataka* and other tales in palm-leaf manuscripts (*aan*) and preaching of sermons (*tet*) are other theatrical roots, as is *pa-nyah*, a courting game in which males and females exchange sung poetic verse dialogue. Amateur jousts developed into professional in *lum glawn*, a form in which two singers sing love poetry at temple festivals and other events, besting each other via wit and improvisation.

Royal dramatic forms followed the models of the Khmer and Thai. In the court of Luang Prabang drama and dance included female court dance, male masked dance-drama, and shadow play. In the 20th century most of the training of the royal troupe came from Thai experts. Excerpts were the norm rather than full-length dance dramas. In the post-1945 period Katherine Bond's research noted the following: major repertoire items included *Fon Nang Keo* (similar to the Khmer *Apasara* dance), *Phra Lak, Phra Lam* (the dance of Laksmana and Rama), *Fon Ling* (the dance of the monkey Hanuman), and *Fon Yak* (the dance of the ogre King Totsakan/Rhawana) (Bond and Pathammavong, 1992). Episodes such as the *Abduction of Sita* from the Rama epic might be presented. After independence in 1955 court performers continued to be patronized by the royal family until 1975, when King Sisavong Vathana vacated the throne as the Marxist government assumed power at the climax of the Southeast Asian war.

Drama that involves multiple performers playing characters in an extended narrative is largely a phenomenon of the last eighty years. Thai *likay* troupes toured in the 1920s. Lao groups were inspired to take *likay*'s flashy costumes, wing and drop scenery, repertoire, and stock character types and combine them with *kaen* and *mawlum* singing. This mixed genre came to be called by different names, including *likay lao* (Lao *likay*) and *mawlum plun* (spontaneous *mawlum*). Since around 1940 the form has often been called *lum luang* (sung story).

Performances take place on temporary outdoor stages. Scenery represents general locales such as a court, a forest, or a town. Immovable microphones, which make the singing audible, are the focal points of the performance. The slight staging of action never takes the actors far from the microphone.

In the 1950s Ouane Southathamma of Khorat was a major *khru* (teacher/troupe leader) who performed stories drawn from Lao history in Vientiane. Members of this troupe helped form the Natasin (Lao National School of the Arts) in 1956 under the leadership of Lao-French Branchard de la Broche, and U.S. Agency for International Development funding supported the project (Bond and Pathammavong, 1992). In 1969–1970 a troupe led by Sommay Lommonty in Viengsay called its performances *lakon lam* and introduced a fuller orchestra, modern songs, and modern stories, including revolutionary narratives such as *Return of the Voice of Justice* (*Sithong i plia*). In the 1990s only one of the ten extant *lam luang* troupes received support from the People's Democratic Republic of Laos (Rattanavong, 1992).

[*See also* Avant-Garde Drama, Southeast Asia]

FURTHER READING

Berval, René de. *Kingdom of Laos*. Saigon: France-Asie, 1959.

Bond, Katherine, and Kingsavanh Pathammavong. "Contexts of *Dontrii Lao Deum*: Traditional Lao Music." In *Selected Reports in Ethnomusicology, vol. 9, Text, Context, and Performance in Cambodia, Laos, and Vietnam*, ed. by Amy Catlin and Therese Mahoney. Los Angeles: UCLA Department of Ethnomusicology, 1992. 131–148.

Compton, Carol. *Courting Poetry in Laos*. DeKalb: Northern Illinois Univ., Center for Southeast Asian Studies. 1979.

Miller, Terry. "Laos." In *The New Grove Dictionary of Music and Musicians*, ed. by Stanley Sadie. London: Grove, 1980.

Rattanavong, Houmphanh. "The *Lam Luang*, a Popular Entertainment." In *Selected Reports in Ethnomusicology, vol. 9, Text, Context, and Performance in Cambodia, Laos, and Vietnam*, ed. by Amy Catlin and Therese Mahoney. Los Angeles: UCLA Department of Ethnomusicology, 1992. 187–191.

Kathy Foley

LAO SHE (1899–1966)

Lao She, a pseudonym of Shu Sheyu, was born Shu Qingchun, of Manchu descent, in February 1899 in Beijing. Graduating from Peking Teachers' College in 1918, he started his teaching career as principal of an elementary school. From 1924 to 1929 he taught Chinese at the School of Oriental and African Studies at the University of London, where he began writing novels in his spare time. He returned to CHINA in 1931, where he continued to write and teach at various universities. During the second Sino-Japanese War (1937–1945) Lao She headed the All-China Anti-Japanese Writers Federation. In 1946–1947 Lao She traveled to the UNITED STATES on a cultural grant from the U.S. State Department, lecturing and overseeing the translation of several of his novels. Upon his return to China in 1949, he took part in various cultural activities and assumed posts in numerous literary and political committees. He was also honored as a "People's Artist" and a "Great Master of Language" by the Beijing municipal government. With the onset of the Cultural Revolution, Lao She fell victim to the persecution. When he could no longer bear the insult and humiliation, he drowned himself in Taiping Lake in Beijing on August 24, 1966.

Influenced by his childhood experience in old Beijing's streets, teahouses, and theaters, Lao She had a special penchant for folk arts of various kinds, including drama. He began playwriting during the early years of the second Sino-Japanese War. The plays he wrote during the 1930s and 1940s were almost all satirical COMEDIES that vividly caricatured the various ugly aspects of life revealed by people during that time. Lao She excelled in storytelling because of his unusual insight into the subtle linguistic nuances of the vernacular that people used in old Beijing. He saw humor in the everyday experiences of life, and he could laugh at himself and get points across with humor, often tinted with his own brand of satire. Lao She's plays after 1949 were more mature. The most important were *Dragon Beard Ditch* (*Longxu gou*, 1950) and *The Teahouse* (*Chaguan*, 1957). *Dragon Beard Ditch* shows a sea change in life taking place for people in the Dragon Beard Ditch area in Beijing by depicting the vicissitudes of fate for members of four households in the same courtyard. The artistic images of several characters with their varying mental activities made the play a huge success. But *The Teahouse*, a play in three acts, remains the acme in Lao She's playwriting. Abandoning the traditional dramatic structure with a major plot running through, it displays some slices of life of people of various social strata during the late Qing, early Republican, and post–World War II periods. With each act of the play showing one historical period, it truthfully re-creates the social climate in various historical periods. *The Teahouse* is known for its power in characterization, especially for its use of local Beijing dialect, which is terse, lively, and yet meaningful. Because of its huge success and influence both at home and abroad, the play has since become one of the masterpieces on the modern Chinese stage.

SELECT PLAYS: *Lingering Fog* (*Canwu*, 1939); *The Issue of Face* (*Mianzi wenti*, 1941); *Fang Zhenzhu* (1950); *Dragon Beard Ditch* (*Longxu gou*, 1950); *The Teahouse* (*Chaguan*, 1957); *Divine Fists* (*Shenquan*, 1961)

FURTHER READING

Kao, George, ed. *Two Writers and the Cultural Revolution: Lao She and Chen Jo-hsi*. Hong Kong: Chinese Univ. Press, 1980.

Lao She. *Dragon Beard Ditch* [*Longxu gou*]. Tr. by Liao Hongying. Beijing: Foreign Languages Press, 1956. Also in *Modern Drama from Communist China*, ed. by Walter J. Meserve and Ruth I. Meserve. New York: New York Univ. Press, 1970. 43–103.

——. *Teahouse* [*Chagua*]. *Chinese Literature* 12 (1979): 16–96. Also tr. by John Howard-Gibbon. Beijing: Foreign Languages Press, 1980.

Towery, Britt. *Lao She, China's Master Storyteller*. Waco, Tex.: Tao Foundation, 1999.

Vohra, Ranbir. *Lao She and the Chinese Revolution*. Cambridge, Mass.: Harvard Univ. Press, 1974.

Wang, David Der-wei. *Fictional Realism in Twentieth-Century China: Mao Dun, Lao She, Shen Congwen*. New York: Columbia Univ. Press, 1992.

Hongchu Fu

LAPEÑA-BONIFACIO, AMELIA (1930–)

Amelia Lapeña-Bonifacio has been an important figure in the "Asianization" of Filipino theater and a pioneer in children's and puppet performance. She received an A.B. in English literature from the University of the Philippines and did graduate work at the University of Wisconsin at Madison on a Fulbright grant. Her 1972 monograph explored the "seditious" playwrights of the early 1900s who were banned by the American government for their patriotic attacks on the American occupation. The work resurrected an important part of Filipino theater history and helped inspire a new generation of playwrights to take up the nationalist torch. In the 1970s, as part of this new nationalism, artists were returning to vernaculars from English as the medium of theater. Simultaneously they were rejecting the psychological REALISM learned from American theater and seeking new models. Lapeña-Bonifacio was part of this movement of using Filipino languages and adapting Asian theatrical models. Her work normally focuses on Filipino themes or myths while turning to the rich narrative structures and performing techniques of Asian genres for ideas. Although some critics have felt that the attempts to link the PHILIPPINES with Asian models are forced, most agree that Lapeña-Bonifacio's choices as a playwright and director make for visually gripping and challenging theater.

Japanese NŌ was a model for *Journey of Sisa* (*Ang paglalakbay ni Sisa*, 1976). In it she used *nō*'s pattern of the ghost play and summoned back the spirit of the madwoman in national hero José Rizal's controversial novel *Touch Me Not* (*Noli me tangere*). Using nō-like chanting, the woman retraces the hardships of her life. Another work from the same period, *Magic Hat* (*Madyik na sombrero*, 1976), was influenced by Japanese *kyogen*'s comic excesses.

Lapeña-Bonifacio has a deep interest in performance for children, and much of her work since the 1970s has been for this audience. Leading Teatrong Mulat (Awakening Theater), the puppet company she founded in 1977, she has written and directed many pieces that blend dance, music, and visual elements with text. The company, associated with the University of the Philippines, now includes multiple generations of her family. *Wayang golek* rod puppetry of Java, *wayang kulit* shadow puppetry, *bunraku*, and other Asian puppet techniques are a regular part of her puppet productions. A number of her works explore myths of different ethnic groups. They function to build awareness of local culture in the face of globalization. Lapeña-Bonifacio is a university professor of the University of the Philippines, where she taught in the writing program and led the creative writing center for over a decade. She serves as the national representative for Union International de la Marionette (UNIMA) and devotes much of her time to educational performances.

SELECT PLAYS: *Journey of Sisa* (*Ang paglalakbay ni Sisa*, 1976; puppet version, 1998); *Magic Hat* (*Madyik na sombrero*, 1976); *Abadeja: Our Own Cinderella* (*Abadeja: Ang ating Sinderela*, 1977?); *The Trial* (*Ang paghuhukom*, 1978); *Monkey and Turtle* (*Ang pangong an tssonggo*, 1980); *Sepang Loca and Others* (1982); *A Fish So Tiny* (*Isda mon siya't malut*, 1983); *Puppet Passion Play* (*Papet pasyon*, 1985); *Pipit Birds and Snake* (*And mga pipit at an ahas*, 1989)

FURTHER READING

Tiongson, Nicanor. *Dulaan: An Essay on Philippine Theatre*. Manila: Cultural Center of the Philippines, 1989.

Kathy Foley

LARDNER, RING (1885–1933)

For him music and theater became a single interest. He would have preferred to spend all his time and energy on it than on the journalism that was his living or the sort of stories on which his fame rests.

—Donald Elder, 1956

Mostly known for his work as a journalist, Ring Lardner was also a short-story writer with a particularly sharp sense of humor with which he depicted, mocked, and satirized the American way of life. Raised in a well-off family, Lardner, who was born on March 6, 1885, in Niles, Michigan, studied mechanical engineering at the Armour Institute of Technology in Chicago, following his father's request. After working as a freight agent and a bookkeeper in his hometown, Lardner took a position as a reporter for the *South Bend Times* covering baseball games in 1905. For the next thirteen years he continued his work as a sportswriter for the *Chicago Inter-Ocean*, the *Chicago Examiner*, the *Chicago Tribune*, and the *Boston American*. In 1911 he married Ellis Abbott, the daughter of a lumber manufacturer, with whom he had four sons.

After working as a war correspondent in Europe during World War I, Lardner wrote "A Busher's Letters Home," twenty-six sketches in epistolary form by Jack Keefe, a fictitious baseball rookie who sends letters to one of his friends. Six of these letters were published in the compilation of short stories *You Know Me Al* (1916). His popularity as a short-story writer increased after the publication of *How to Write Short Stories* in 1924, which was included in the collection of stories *Round Up* in 1929.

In addition to his sketches and satires, Lardner composed song lyrics. During the years before the Great Depression, Lardner poured most of his effort into theater. After working under contract for the Century Theatre of Morris Gest for a short period of time with hardly any success, Lardner was not discouraged in his attempt to go on writing plays. Most of Lardner's plays and skits, written between 1919 and 1928 and mainly published in magazines, were either unproduced or rejected. He also wrote several nonsense or Dada plays, including *Abend di Anni Nouveau* and *The Tridget of Greva*. Among his many other plays are *Beautiful Katie* (previously called *Going South*), *Carmen*, *Cinderella*, *Not Guilty*, *The Operating Room*, and *The Other World*. He wrote plays in collaboration with other playwrights: *Elmer, the Great* (1928), the story of a baseball player, with George M. Cohan; and JUNE MOON (1929), a COMEDY about a composer who fled his hometown in order to look for fame and success on Broadway, with GEORGE S. KAUFMAN. After 1930 Lardner's health began to deteriorate; he died of a heart attack on September 25, 1933, in East Hampton, New York, at the age of forty-eight.

[*See also* United States, 1860–1929]

SELECT PLAYS: *The Bull Pen* (1922); *Rip Van Winkle Jr.* (1922); *Thomson's Vocation* (1922); *The Tridget of Greva* (1922); *I Gaspiri* (or *The Upholsterers*) (1924); *Taxidea Americana* (1924); *Clemo Uti—"The Water Lilies"* (1925); *Cora; or, Fun at a Spa* (subtitled *An Expressionist Drama of Love, Death and Sex*, 1925); *Orpheus in the Underworld* (1925); *Abend di Anni Nouveau* (1928); *All at Sea* (1928); *Dinner and Bridge* (1928); *Elmer the Great* (1928); *June Moon* (1929); *Quadroon—A Play in Four Pelts Which May All Be Attended in One Day or Missed in a Group* (1931)

FURTHER READING

Elder, Donald. *Ring Lardner*. Garden City, N.Y.: Doubleday, 1956.

Goldstein, Malcolm. *George S. Kaufman: His Life, His Theater*. New York: Oxford Univ. Press, 1979.

Patrick, Walton R. *Ring Lardner*. New York: Twayne, 1963.

Yardley, Jonathan. *Ring: A Biography of Ring Lardner*. New York: Random, 1977.

Estefania Olid-Peña

LATVIA

The beginnings of Latvian drama date back to the national revival movement of "young Latvians" in 1868. Since the invasion of German crusaders in the 12th century, the German nobility had retained cultural, economic, and political privileges in Latvia. The national liberation was simultaneously a rejection of German supremacy and an adaptation of many German cultural institutions, since most "young Latvians" had been educated in GERMANY. The interest shown in drama as an art form was one manifestation of the rising ambition to create a national literature. Ādolfs Alunāns (1848–1912) was largely responsible for bringing to the stage the life of Latvian peasants. His plays, mostly adaptations or translations from the German, tended toward the MELODRAMA and could be brought under the category of VOLKSSTÜCK (folk play).

Modern Latvian drama begins with Aspazija (Elza Rozenberga, 1865–1943), the first outstanding romantic poet-playwright, who found her themes in mythology and in regional history (*The Vestal* [*Vaidelote*, 1894]; *The Silver Veil* [*Sidrabašidrauts*, 1903]), as well as protesting against the injustices of woman's position in society, creating a remarkable study in social conscience, *The Lost Rights* (*Zaudētās tiesības*, 1895). In 1903 Aspazija was joined by another woman writer, Anna Brigadere (1861–1933), who wrote her first play, *Tom Thumb* (*Sprīdītis*), based on Latvian fairy tales.

A new interest in man's inner life became visible in the plays of Rūdolfs Blaumanis (1863–1908), who inherited the tradition of stories about peasant life and displayed interest in moral and psychological problems. His dramas (*The Indrāns* [*Indrāni*, 1904];

On Fire [*Ugunī*, 1905]) are concerned more with individual destinies than with general moral or social principles. Blaumanis's most frequent theme is the conflict of moral values within the human soul. Combining cast-iron theatrical construction with unusually deep insight into the conscious and unconscious impulses of the characters, Blaumanis wrote the first TRAGEDY in Latvian, *The Prodigal Son* (*Pazudušais dēls*,1893). The hero is a young man caught in a tension between the possible and the impossible. The COMEDY *The Tailor's Days in Silmači* (*Skroderdienas Silmačos*, 1904) is the most beloved Latvian play; written as a folk play, it contains the people's vital humor, songs, and dancing. In his last period Blaumanis, like HENRIK IBSEN, made a move in the direction of symbolic drama, which is evident in *A Saturday Evening* (*Sestdienas vakars*, 1908), a one-act play of almost mystical character.

Between 1918 and 1940 Latvia enjoyed twenty years of political independence. The leading playwright of this period was RAINIS (Jānis Pliekšāns, 1865–1929), who offered a new, highly metaphoric mode of expression. But it is the craftsmanlike REALISM of Jūlijs Pētersons (1880–1945) and Elīna Zālīte (1898–1955) that best represents Latvian drama between the two world wars. Since they followed the principles of VICTORIEN SARDOU's well-made play, their work depended on the exploitation of successful formulas and a wide arsenal of effective devices. Pētersons was at his best in drawing-room comedies (*The Stray Kitten* [*Pieklīdušais kaķēns*, 1931]), Zālīte in drawing-room melodramas (*Roses in Autumn* [*Rudens rozes*, 1939]).

The most successful plays of the period, notably *The Jester* (*Āksts*, 1938) about the life and death of William Shakespeare, were written by Mārtiņš Zīverts (1903–1990). Although a preparedness to challenge conventional morality is always present in Zīverts's plays, they leave a sense of pathetic melodrama. Each play is built around a central situation, and the characters are not highly developed, but are sustained by the sheer force of the dramatic action. Two works that established Zīverts as the leading playwright during the years of the following German occupation (1941–1944) were *Münchhausen's Wedding* (*Minhauzena precības*, 1941), an elaborately sophisticated comedy about German adventurer Baron Münchhausen, and *Power* (*Vara*, 1944), a tragedy about Mindaugas, the medieval unifier of feudal Lithuania, who established a strong centrally governed state capable of fighting off Teutonic invaders.

Andrejs Upīts (1877–1970) is celebrated as the leader of NATURALISM in Latvian literature. Although his major literary importance is for his monumental series of novels, he also maintained a considerable interest in the theater. His best-known plays are his three historical tragedies *Mirabeau* (*Mirabo*, 1926), *Joan of Arc* (*Žanna d'Arka*, 1930), and *Spartacus* (*Spartaks*, 1943), in which the crowd is the hero.

After Latvia's incorporation into the Soviet socialist regime in 1940, Latvian drama was committed to the tight boundaries of SOCIALIST REALISM. Vilis Lācis (1904–1966), Anna Brodele (1910–1981), and Arvīds Grigulis (1906–1989) in their plays presented the moral superiority of Communists over "class enemies" and "former people." In accordance with the theory of "conflictless drama," their plays glorified labor's achievements and the desired Commmunist future.

Joseph Stalin's death in 1953 was followed by the "thaw" period in the arts. Gunārs Priede (1928–2000), Pēteris Pētersons (1923–1998), Harijs Gulbis (1926–), and Pauls Putniņš (1937–) belong to the first generation of postthaw dramatists in Latvia. Priede's play *Summer of the Younger Brother* (*Jaunākā brāļa vasara*, 1955) was marked by a "new lyricism" and "rehumanization." He created a new form of intimate play of conscience and crisis; there were no more clear-cut victims and villains. In the following decades Priede's postthaw optimism gave way to a critical perspective on the historical past (*The Mushrooms Smell Fresh* [*Smaržo sēnes*, 1967]; *The Centrifuge* [*Centrifūga*, 1985]) and attempts to capture the essence of contemporaneity (*The Thirteenth* [*Trīspadsmitā*, 1966]; *The Blue One* [*Zilā*, 1972]; *The Snow-Covered Mountains* [*Sniegotie kalni*, 1986]) by using "Chekhovian" principles—misdirection, noneventfulness, and partially stated meaning. Gulbis possessed an acute ear for dialogue, and his subject matter ranged from the problems of youth (*Bear's Lullaby* [*Aijā žūžū, bērns kā lācis*, 1968]) to the search for roots (*The Cīrulīši Farmstead* [*Cīrulīši*, 1975]). Putniņš was successful in two distinct styles, that of folk play (*Tiny Small Brushwood Rods* [*Paši pūta, paši dega*, 1972]) and that of social problem play (*The Sweet Burden of Faithfulness* [*Uzticības saldā nasta*, 1981]). Pēteris Pētersons (the son of Jūlijs Pētersons) stood somewhat aside from his "brothers-in-arms." An outstanding director and theoretician, he wrote verse dramas about the difficulties experienced by the artist in reconciling the tensions of his personal and professional lives. Since much of Pētersons's work was ill suited to the stage, verbose, and lacking action, his success as a dramatist was largely due to the fact that he directed almost all his plays himself, from *The Bastard* (*Bastards*, 1975) to *Fēlikss and Felicita* (*Fēlikss un Felicita*, 1997).

It was not until the 1970s that new dramaturgical forms appeared, giving expression to the modern sense of anguish and despair. Jānis Jurkāns's (1950–) hyperrealistic plays (*A Clock with a Cuckoo* [*Pulkstenis ar dzeguzi*, 1977]; *The Humming-Bird* [*Kolibri*, 1980]; *The Ravens* [*Kraukļi*, 1987]) were rendered with purposeful nontheatricality and ambiguity. In one of his best plays, the medieval ballad *Virtuss* (*Virtuss*, 1978), Jurkāns looked to the theater of the past to focus upon the moral dilemma of an individual using violent means to accomplish a public good. Lelde Stumbre (1952–) initiated enigmatically realistic dramas in claustrophobic, rural (*The Red-Haired Servant* [*Sarkanmatainais kalps*, 1987]; *Jānis, Jānis*, 1984) or modern urban (*The Murderer and the Murderer* [*Slepkava un slepkava*, 1994]) settings. They definitely contained elements of SURREALISM and ABSURDISM. Stumbre portrayed a world that was simultaneously real and unreal, a world where people eat, drink, sleep, work, love, and suffer—and then walk into a pine tree (*The Crown* [*Kronis*, 1989]) or turn into birds (*Feathers* [*Spalvas*, 1995]) or dissolve into a puddle like sugar cubes in hot tea (*It's Raining* [*Līst*, 1993]). Poet and playwright Māra Zālīte (1952–) was the one who fulfilled Pēteris Pētersons's dream of bringing poetry back to the modern stage. Her verse dramas were noted for their originality of poetic diction and power of social and political vision. Zālīte draws upon Latvian folklore and primitive religion (*Māra's Room: Full* [*Pilna Māras istabiņa*, 1983]), diverse literary contexts (*The Trial* [*Tiesa*, 1984] is based on Garlieb Merkel's historical essay "Die Letten"; *Margarēta*, 1999, on Johann Wolfgang von Goethe's *Faust*; *The Living Water* [*Dzīvais ūdens*, 1987] on Blaumanis's unfinished play), and popular legends (in *Kaupēns, My Dear!* [*Kaupēn, mans mīļais!* 1998]. Zālīte tells the story of an ambitious highway robber and murderer from the 1920s, Kaupēns, who takes from the Poet his bride [representing Latvia itself], thus provoking the Poet to undertake the role of judge and hangman). Though the problems of contemporary Latvia may not be immediately evident, *Kaupens* sensitively echoes the moods of Latvian society under the situation of economic and spiritual crisis.

After the dissolution of the Soviet regime in 1991, a group of new dramatists emerged, including Lauris Gundars (1958–), Egīls Šņore (1954–), and Inga Ābele (1972–). The best drama comes from the young Ābele. Her plays appear realistic on the surface, belying their vivid theatricality and close relationship with psychoanalytic theory. Ābele gained international acclaim with her first play, *The Dark Deer* (*Tumšie brieži*, 2000), a piercing study of the spiritual emptiness that lies at the core of contemporary life in Latvia. The dark deer, like the wild duck in Ibsen's play, are both real deer and a symbol of the heroine's situation. Alienated from their environment, Ābele's characters struggle toward some kind of transcendental experience.

FURTHER READING

Ekmanis, Rolfs. *Latvian Literature Under the Soviets. 1940–1975*. Belmont, Mass.: Nordland, 1978.

Silenieks, Juris, and Alfreds Straumanis. "Latvian Drama." *Baltic Drama. A Handbook and Bibliography*. Ed. by Alfreds Straumanis. Prospect Heights, Ill.: Waveland Press, 1981. 113–380.

Straumanis, Alfreds, ed. *Bridge Across the Sea: Seven Baltic Plays*. Prospect Heights, Ill.: Waveland Press, 1983.

——, ed. *Fire and Night: Five Baltic Plays*. Prospect Heights, Ill.: Waveland Press, 1986.

——, ed. *The Golden Steed: Seven Baltic Plays*. Prospect Heights, Ill.: Waveland Press, 1979.

Valda Čakare

LAWLER, RAY (1921–)

Ray Lawler was born in Melbourne, Victoria, AUSTRALIA, on May 23, 1921. His *Summer of the Seventeenth Doll* (produced in 1955) has an iconic status in Australian theater that is unlikely to be challenged. At a time when the "great Australian play" seemed as urgent but unlikely a discovery as its counterpart in fiction, *Summer* burst on the scene, looking for all the world like a harbinger of great things to come. It had all the right ingredients: a recognizably Australian vernacular, a distinctively local geographic mythology (the juxtaposition of warm and hedonistic north with cool and morally serious south), engaging characters, and, above all, international certification; the triumph of the play's London production gave the imprimatur of the colonizing power to Australia's emergent postcolonial drama.

The success of Lawler's play, both in its premiere season with Melbourne's Union Theatre Repertory Company (UTRC), foundational to the Melbourne Theatre Company, and in its subsequent national and international tours, was built on conspicuous virtues in the writing that in part reflected Lawler's own background as an actor with the UTRC and with other fringe groups in Melbourne. Its humor and authentic conversational rhythms made it immediately appealing to audiences. But the enduring power of *Summer* resides in its particular combination of local, cultural iconography and widely recognizable themes of loss (of youth, of hope, of sustaining illusions). Roo and Barney, the two cane cutters who come down from far north Queensland, "like a coupla kings," to spend the summer with their barmaid girlfriends in Melbourne, confront in the seventeenth year of that ritual the realization that this will be the last. Everything unravels—one of the "girls," Nancy, has opted for marriage and has been replaced in the unconventional foursome by the censorious Pearl; the "boys" have less money to splash around, because Roo has lost the job at which he was once preeminent; and finally, Olive, whose love for Roo seems so fierce, is affronted by his proposal of a marriage that would for her make their love just like everybody else's.

For Lawler, it proved a hard act to follow. He went to live in ENGLAND in 1957, taking the usual pilgrimage for the successful colonial author, but the cultural specificity on which his creative imagination seemed to be founded made it hard for him to do substantial work without the commissions or return journeys that put him directly in touch with his roots: *The Piccadilly Bushman* (produced in 1957) dealt prophetically with this problem, its central expatriate Australian continually lamenting that he is a man between cultures who belongs to neither; *The Man Who Shot the Albatross* (produced in 1971), a vehicle for another expatriate, the actor Leo McKern, dramatizes the history of Bligh and the *Bounty*; and finally, the two plays that marked his permanent homecoming and confirmed the mythic status of *summer*, *Kid Stakes* (1976) and *Other Times* (1977), are two "prequels" that tell the stories of the first and ninth summers and animate the character of Nancy, who is such a potent absence from the seventeenth. The staging of the three plays as a trilogy in 1978 was a celebration of *Summer* and a coming of age in Australian theater.

SELECT PLAYS: *Hal's Belles* (1946); *Cradle of Thunder* (1949); *Summer of the Seventeenth Doll* (1955); *The Piccadilly Bushman* (1959); *The*

Unshaven Cheek (1963); *A Breach in the Wall* (1970); *The Man Who Shot the Albatross* (1972); *Kid Stakes* (1975); *Other Times* (1976); *Godsend* (1982)

FURTHER READING

Carroll, Dennis. *Australian Contemporary Drama*. 2d ed. Sydney: Currency, 1995.

Fitzpatrick, Peter. *After "The Doll": Australian Drama Since 1955*. Melbourne: Edward Arnold Australia, 1979.

McCallum, John. "The Doll and the Legend." *Australian Literary Studies* 3, no. 2 (1983): 33–44.

Sumner, John. *Recollections at Play: A Life in Australian Theatre*. Melbourne: Melbourne Univ. Press, 1993.

Peter Fitzpatrick

LAWRENCE, DAVID HERBERT (1885–1930)

David Herbert (D. H.) Lawrence was a critic, novelist, painter, and poet and arguably one of the most influential figures in 20th-century English literature. Lawrence, a provocateur, turned the mores of his day on their ear with his keen investigation of the human condition, sex, intuition, and the cruelty of the industrial age. Most famous for his ribald novel *Lady Chatterley's Lover* (1928), he also wrote poems addressing the physical and inner life of plants and animals. Other works are bitterly satirical and express his outrage at the puritanism and hypocrisy of English society. Lawrence, a rebellious and polemical writer, expressed radical views and regarded sex, the unconscious, and nature as cures to the weaknesses of modern industrialized society. Lawrence's doctrines of sexual freedom incited obscenity trials that deeply impacted the relationship between literature and society.

Lawrence was born in 1885 in Nottinghamshire, ENGLAND. In 1914 he eloped with Frieda von Richthofen, who left her husband and children for him, and they traveled extensively around the world together. Lawrence's fourth novel, *The Rainbow* (1915), which contained swearwords and talked openly about sex, was banned in England. Lawrence's frank descriptions of sexual relations between men and women upset many people, and over 1,000 copies of the novel were burned. His reputation and the censorship that followed made it difficult for Lawrence to get published; his paintings were also confiscated from an art gallery.

During World War I Lawrence and Richthofen were unable to obtain passports and were constantly harassed by the authorities. Richthofen, cousin of the legendary "Red Baron" von Richthofen, was viewed with great suspicion by English authorities. They were accused of spying for the Germans and officially expelled from Cornwall in 1917. The Lawrences were not permitted to emigrate until 1919, when their years of wandering began. In 1924 the New York socialite Mabel Dodge Luhan gave Lawrence and Richthofen the Kiowa Ranch in Taos in return for the original manuscript of *Sons and Lovers*. Lawrence felt that New Mexico liberated him from his contemporary era of civilization. After severe illness in MEXICO he discovered that he was suffering from life-threatening tuberculosis.

Lawrence's best-known work, *Lady Chatterley's Lover*, first published privately in Florence, ITALY, in 1928, tells of the love affair between a wealthy, married woman and a man who works on her husband's estate. A war wound has left her husband impotent and paralyzed. The woman has a brief affair with a young playwright and then enters into a passionate relationship with her husband's gamekeeper. She becomes pregnant, her husband refuses to give her a divorce, and the lovers wait for a better time when they can be united. *Lady Chatterley's Lover* was banned in Britain and the UNITED STATES for being pornographic. In Britain it was published in unexpurgated form in 1960 after an obscenity trial at which defense witnesses included E. M. Forster, Helen Gardner, and Richard Hoggart.

D. H. Lawrence died in Vence, FRANCE, in 1930. Richthofen (d. 1956) moved to the Kiowa Ranch and built a small memorial chapel to Lawrence; his ashes lie there.

FURTHER READING

Ellis, David. *D. H. Lawrence: Dying Game, 1922–1930*. Cambridge: Cambridge Univ. Press, 1998.

Fernihough, Anne. *D. H. Lawrence: Aesthetics and Ideology*. Oxford: Oxford Univ. Press, 1993.

Kinkead-Weekes, Mark. *D. H. Lawrence: Triumph to Exile, 1912–1922*. Cambridge: Cambridge Univ. Press, 1996.

Shanté T. Smalls

LAWRENCE, JEROME (1915–2004), AND ROBERT E. LEE (1918–1994)

Drummond: Do you think a sponge thinks?
Brady: If the Lord wishes a sponge to think, it thinks.
Drummond: Does a man have the same privileges that a sponge does?
Brady: Of course.
Drummond: This man wishes to be accorded the same privilege as a sponge! He wishes to think!
—Inherit the Wind, Act 2

The fifty-year writing partnership of Jerome Lawrence and Robert E. Lee was one of the most productive collaborations in 20th-century American theater. As a team they wrote sixteen full-length stage works of great variety, plus many more short plays for radio. Their diverse oeuvre ranged from historical dramas of conscience to lighthearted social COMEDIES, from ambitious literary adaptations to lavish musicals. Throughout all their work, though, runs a fervent optimism in the dignity of the individual and in freedom of thought. Such idealism proved popular in both the commercial Broadway theater of the 1950s and in the later regional theater movement—the rise of which they were intricately involved with via their founding of the American Playwrights Theatre (1965–1980), a nationwide network supporting the production of new plays.

Jerome Lawrence Schwartz was born in Cleveland, Ohio, on July 14, 1915; Robert Edwin Lee (no relation to the famous Civil War general) was born in nearby Elyria, Ohio, on October 15, 1918. In the 1930s both embarked, independently, on careers in radio. Lawrence moved west to write entertainment television programming for CBS and NBC in Hollywood. Lee, after working for local Ohio stations, ended up at the advertising agency Young and Rubicam in New York, writing and directing radio commercials. The two men first met in New York in January 1942 and quickly formed a partnership, writing their first radio play, *Inside a Kid's Head*, within weeks. After being drafted into World War II later that year, they both were among the founders of the Armed Forces Radio Service, for which they produced coverage of live events (such as V-E and V-J Day commemorations) and created original programming (including *Mail Call*).

The team made their break into live theater soon upon their return from the war. After their first two plays went unproduced, they were hired to write the book of the musical comedy *Look, Ma, I'm Dancin'!* (1948). While moderately successful, it did not lead directly to more theatrical interest in Lawrence and Lee's writing, so they both returned to radio.

It was during this time that they painstakingly developed their masterpiece *Inherit the Wind*, a fictionalized drama of the 1925 "Monkey Trial," which contested the teaching of evolution in public schools in Dayton, Tennessee. After its rejection by several commercial producers, the play was finally premiered by regional theater pioneer Margot Jones on January 10, 1955, in Dallas, Texas, where audiences were stirred not only by its riveting courtroom theatrics, but also its daring commentary on freedom of speech in the age of McCarthyism. Word quickly spread to New York, and a Broadway production opened that April and ran for over two years.

Inherit the Wind was the first of many Lawrence and Lee plays to draw contemporary lessons from American history: *The Gang's All Here* (1959) was a thinly veiled look at the corrupt Harding administration of the 1920s; the antiwar meditation *The Night Thoreau Spent in Jail* (1970), while never opening on Broadway, was one of the most widely produced plays in regional theater during the Vietnam era; and their final collaboration, *Whisper in the Mind* (1994), examined an unlikely friendship between Benjamin Franklin and the 18th-century Austrian hypnotist and medical eccentric Anton Mesmer.

Lawrence and Lee's work in other genres was equally prolific. Typical of their eclecticism, they immediately followed *Inherit the Wind* in 1956 with the musical *Shangri-La*, based on James Hilton's novel *Lost Horizon*. Their popular adaptation of Patrick Dennis's 1955 best-selling comic memoir *Auntie Mame* took the form of both a play (1956) and a musical (1966). Even their seemingly lighter work always focused on outsiders and nonconformists—from the persecuted Jewish journalist in *Only in America* (1959) to the defiantly hedonistic Auntie Mame herself. Dreamers, misfits, and gadflies figured prominently among their protagonists; *The Incomparable Max* (1971) and *Jabberwock* (1972) celebrated the satirists Max Beerbohm and James Thurber, respectively.

While both men wrote some plays and other works on their own—Lawrence's one-act *Live Spelled Backwards* (1966), Lee's adaptation of John Reed's *Ten Days That Shook the World* (1973)—Lawrence and Lee's names are inextricably linked together in the history of American theater. While not all their plays have achieved the longevity or commercial success of *Inherit the Wind* and *Auntie Mame*, they all embody their authors' unique mix of intellectual striving, crusading liberalism, and historical perspective.

Robert E. Lee died on July 8, 1994. Jerome Lawrence died on February 29, 2004.

[*See also* United States, 1940–Present]

SELECT PLAYS: *Look, Ma, I'm Dancin'!* (1948); *Inherit the Wind* (1955); *Auntie Mame* (1956); *Shangri-La* (1956); *The Gang's All Here* (1959); *Only in America* (1959); *A Call on Kuprin*, also known as *Checkmate* (1961); *Diamond Orchid*, also known as *Sparks Fly Upward* (1965); *Mame* (1966); *Dear World* (1969); *The Night Thoreau Spent in Jail* (1970); *The Incomparable Max* (1971); *Jabberwock: Improbabilities Lived and Imagined by James Thurber in the Fictional City of Columbus, Ohio* (1972); *First Monday in October* (1975, revised 1978); *Whisper in the Mind* (1990, revised 1994)

FURTHER READING

Adler, Thomas P. *American Drama, 1940–1960: A Critical History*. New York: Twayne, 1994.

Bigsby, C. W. E. *Modern American Drama. 1945–1990*. Cambridge: Cambridge Univ. Press, 1992.

Jordan, Richard Tyler. *But Darling, I'm Your Auntie Mame! The Amazing History of the World's Favorite Madcap Aunt*. Santa Barbara, Calif.: Capra Press, 1998.

Sheehy, Helen. *Margo: The Life and Theatre of Margo Jones*. Dallas: Southern Methodist Univ. Press, 1989.

Woods, Alan, ed. *The Selected Plays of Jerome Lawrence and Robert E. Lee*. Columbus: Ohio State Univ. Press, 1995.

Garrett B. Eisler

LAWSON, JOHN HOWARD (1894–1977)

Born on September 25, 1894, in New York City, John Howard Lawson was one of America's most outspoken political playwrights during the 1920s and 1930s. His interest in politics developed after he served as a volunteer ambulance driver in World War I; in Europe he met writers John Dos Passos and Ernest Hemingway. His firsthand experience of the brutality of war shaped his worldview and inspired his acceptance of Marxist and socialist ideals that would surface thematically in his work as a playwright and screenwriter.

Before the war Lawson wrote two unproduced plays, *Standards* (1915) and *Servant-Master-Lover* (1917). His first staged play was the expressionist *Roger Bloomer*, the story of a young midwestern man who discovers disappointment, decadence, and decay in New York City. The play features such typical expressionist devices as extreme subjectivity and nightmare sequences. Lawson claimed little contact with European experimental drama, though *Roger Bloomer* has much in common with FRANK WEDEKIND's protoexpressionist play *SPRING AWAKENING*.

His next play, *PROCESSIONAL*, met with great success and remains Lawson's best-known work. Its exuberant combination of JAZZ music, vaudeville performance, dancing, and social commentary made it ideal for its times. Although *Processional* is largely expressionistic in technique, it reveals Lawson's Marxist politics more clearly than *Roger Bloomer*.

In 1927 Lawson co-founded the New Playwrights' Theatre in Greenwich Village with Dos Passos and others. The company's mission was to bring overtly leftist theater to the working classes, and its first season included Lawson's political farce *Loud Speaker* and his Communist history play *The International*. Lawson himself felt that *The International* was "the most interesting and significant experiment in form and content which I have attempted." The group hoped to serve a politicized workers' audience, but Lawson commented years later that "no such audience was visible in 1927, but the need for it determined the activity of the New Playwrights." Lawson's plays and the work of the New Playwrights' Theatre helped set a precedent for political dramatists of the 1930s such as CLIFFORD ODETS.

Lawson's stage success, primarily with *Processional*, led to offers from Hollywood. He shifted his attention west and over the next two decades wrote almost thirty screenplays, including *Dynamite* (1929), *Blockade* (1938), *Sahara* (1943), *Action in the North Atlantic* (1943), and *Cry the Beloved Country* (1951). Always a proponent of the rights of workers, including writers, Lawson helped found the Screen Writers' Guild in 1933.

In 1934 Lawson openly joined the American Communist Party, an act that led to his being called before the House Un-American Activities Committee in 1947. Lawson was one of the famous "Hollywood Ten" who refused to answer the committee's questions. Blacklisted in Hollywood, he moved to Mexico. He continued to write screenplays (sometimes uncredited or under the pseudonym Edward Lewis), and he toured the United States to give lectures on film. He also authored one of the earliest texts to explore the art of screenwriting, *Theory and Technique of Playwriting and Screenwriting* (1936). Lawson died of Parkinson's disease in 1977.

[*See also* United States]

SELECT PLAYS: *Roger Bloomer* (1923); *Processional* (1925); *Nirvana* (1926); *The International* (1927); *Loud Speaker* (1927); *Success Story* (1932); *Gentlewoman* (1934); *The Pure in Heart* (1934); *Marching Song* (1937)

FURTHER READING

Carr, Gary L. *The Left Side of Paradise: The Screenwriting of John Howard Lawson*. Ann Arbor: UMI Res. Press, 1984.

Chambers, Jonathan. "The Dilemma of Commitment: John Howard Lawson's *Marching Song*." *Journal of American Drama and Theatre* 12, no. 1 (Winter 2000): 1–21.

——. *Messiah of the New Technique: John Howard Lawson, Communism, and American Theatre, 1923–1937*. Carbondale: Southern Illinois Univ. Press, 2006.

——. "To Break Down the Walls of the Theatre: John Howard Lawson's *Roger Bloomer*." *Journal of American Drama and Theatre* 14, no. 3 (Fall 2002): 34–52.

Mishra, Kshamanidhi. *American Leftist Playwrights of the 1930's: A Study of Ideology and Technique in the Plays of Odets, Lawson, and Sherwood*. New Delhi: Classical, 1991.

Valgemae, Mardi. "John Howard Lawson." In *Accelerated Grimace: Expressionism in the American Drama of the 1920s*. Carbondale: Southern Illinois Univ. Press, 1972.

DeAnna M. Toten Beard

LAZARUS LAUGHED

The Pasadena Community Players produced the premiere of EUGENE O'NEILL's *Lazarus Laughed* on April 9, 1928, under the direction of Gilmor Brown, with Irving Pichel as Lazarus and a cast of over 170 wearing 400 costumes and 300 masks.

O'Neill expanded the experimental use of masks he initiated in *THE GREAT GOD BROWN* (1926); the opening scene shows a chorus wearing forty-nine different masks, each a combination of period of life (boyhood/girlhood, youth, young manhood/womanhood, manhood/womanhood, middle age, maturity, old age) and character type (simple and ignorant, happy and eager, self-tortured and introspective, proud and self-reliant, servile and hypocritical, revengeful and cruel, and sorrowful and resigned). Only Lazarus, free of the fear of death, wears no mask.

The story of Lazarus appears in John 11; Jesus reassures the sister of the dead man with a passage fundamental to Christian theology: "I am the resurrection, and the life: he that believeth in me, though he were dead, yet shall he live: And whosoever liveth and believeth in me shall never die." The biblical account concludes with the dead man walking out of his crypt, but O'Neill takes the story much further.

Life is affirmation; in order to raise Lazarus, Jesus looked into his face until the man answered, "Yes," and as Jesus walked away, Lazarus "began to laugh softly like a man in love with God." To the great wonder of the others, he preaches that there is no death. The orthodox faction scorns him as a sinner and his followers as idolaters. The antagonists brawl over the news that Jesus has died on the cross, but Lazarus explains, "Even a Son of Man must die to show men that Man may live! But there is no death!"

Caligula hopes to learn from Lazarus a secret for renewing youth, and he taunts him with the idea that he will be Caesar and Death, laughing because men fear him. He sends his legions to massacre Lazarus's followers, but they die laughing. The aged Tiberius fears death, and Pompeia goads him to demand that Lazarus repeat his miracle by raising Miriam from the dead after she poisons her. Holding his wife in his arms, Lazarus realizes that loneliness is nothing more than fear of life. Tiberius burns Lazarus alive, but he continues to laugh. In a rage, Caligula murders Tiberius and begs Lazarus to help him.

In *Billboard*, H. O. Stechan compared the play with Greek TRAGEDY and suggested that "O'Neill's point seems to be to demolish the idea of the grim reaper of time-honored Christian theology. Men may die, he infers, but Man never does; wherefore life is eternal." He reported that the immense production enjoyed the participation of many volunteers and that the art department at the University of California contributed the masks. Pichel played the title role in a "stereotyped Christ-like manner, which hardly seems to be the Dionysian sort of man the author had in mind."

The *New York Times* (April 10, 1928) observed that the play "is based on the dying Dion's last speech" in *The Great God Brown*, which asserts that Man conquers through laughter. O'Neill "makes concession of faith in a guiding Omnipotence, affirms his belief in life beyond the grave and makes a plea for men to love life and laughter and to forget sorrow and death."

[*See also* United States, 1860–1929]

FURTHER READING

Cunningham, Frank R. "A Newly Discovered Fourth Production of O'Neill's *Lazarus Laughed*." *Eugene O'Neill Review* 22 (Spring–Fall 1998): 114–122.

Han, Kim. "*Lazarus Laughed*: Dionysus and the Birth of Tragedy." *Journal of English Language and Literature* 37 (Winter 1991): 993–1005.

Rollyson, Carl E., Jr. "Eugene O'Neill: The Drama of Self-Transcendence." In *Critical Essays on Eugene O'Neill*, ed. by James J. Martine. Boston: G. K. Hall, 1984. 123–137.

Sarlós, Robert K. " 'Write a Dance': *Lazarus Laughed* as O'Neill's Dithyramb of the Western Hemisphere." *Theatre Survey* 29 (May 1988): 37–49.

Jeffrey D. Mason

THE LEAGUE OF NATHANS

JASON SHERMAN's first stage success, *The League of Nathans* (written in 1992) premiered at Theatre Passe Muraille in Toronto, produced in association with Orange Dog Theatre. It won the Floyd S. Chalmers Canadian Play Award. A revised version opened in Winnipeg in 1996. It has subsequently been performed frequently in CANADA.

The play introduces the character Nathan Abramowitz, a quasi-surrogate for the author: a young, liberal Canadian writer struggling with his relationship to Judaism and Zionism. As a boy, in 1973 Nathan formed the League of Nathans with two friends, Nathan Isaacs and Nathan Glass. The league has its own complex set of rituals satirizing the Judaic tradition, such as a secret chant that starts "Putzes, petsels, schmendrik schlong / Mine's nine hundred miles long" and finishes "Granpa was a goy, Bubbie was a yid / I'm a fatalistic atheistic mixed-up kid."

Each of the Nathans has a distinct personality. Glass is the grandson of a fighter in the Warsaw Ghetto uprising and a Zionist. Isaacs is a joker, more concerned with girls than religion. Nathan Abramowitz is ironic, ambivalent about his upcoming bar mitzvah, fascinated by the mystical kabbala, and devoted to his wisecracking and wise grandfather. After high school the three grow apart, partly as a result of Glass's sudden move to Israel in 1980. The action of the play starts and ends in 1993, with Isaacs and Nathan receiving telegrams from Glass, convening a "final meeting of the League" at a Spanish synagogue. Isaacs is now a used-car salesman in Winnipeg, married to his high-school sweetheart. Nathan is a writer building a name for himself, separated from his Christian wife and their children, and still ambivalent about his Jewishness. Glass, who does not appear until near the end of the play, is now a West Bank settler who considers all Arabs and Palestinians "terrorists."

As in all of Sherman's plays, time is extremely fluid. In the last scene of act 1 Nathan moves back and forth between a conversation in 1993 with Isaacs and Glass's revelation that he has witnessed the murder of a young Arab gas-station attendant, the reason for his flight to Israel. The scene is dramatic, although Sherman's later play *Reading Hebron* denies the sort of direct psychological causality that is implied between Glass's adolescent trauma and his adult fanaticism.

In the end, after Nathan and Glass have a confrontation in the Spanish synagogue, Nathan discovers that the reunion has been a plan hatched by the seemingly guileless Isaacs to force Nathan to confront his demons. As in all his best plays, Sherman raises unanswerable questions about what constitutes moral behavior in the contemporary world. Although he obviously rejects Glass's fanaticism, the reader or viewer can understand it. And although Nathan is the most fascinating character onstage, the play seems to ask whether Isaacs, beneath all his jokes about boobs and apparent complacency about his middle-class suburban life in western Canada, might not have the most complex moral vision of the three former friends.

FURTHER READING

Donahue, Lauri. "Nathans Playwright Takes Chances." *Western Jewish Bulletin* (February 27, 1994). http://www.jewishbulletin.ca/archives/Feb04/archives04Feb27-06.html.

Sherman, Jason. *Jason Sherman: Six Plays*. Toronto: Playwrights Canada Press, 2001.

Walter Bilderback

LEARNING PLAY

"Learning play" is how BERTOLT BRECHT (1898–1956) translated the German term *Lehrstück*. Canonical examples of Brecht's *Lehrstücke* include *The Baden-Baden Cantata of Acquiescence* (*Das Badener Lehrstück vom Einverständis*, 1929), *The Flight Over the Ocean* (*Der Ozeanflug*, 1929, also known as *Der Flug der Lindberghs* and *Der Lindberghflug*, 1), *The Exception and the Rule* (*Die Ausnahme und die Regel*, 1930), THE MEASURES TAKEN (*Die Maßnahme*, 1930), *He Who Says No* (*Der Neinsager*, 1931), and *He Who Says Yes* (*Der Jasager*, 1931), relatively short works that all appeared in quick succession between 1929 and 1934. THE MOTHER (*Die Mutter*, 1931) expands the format of the *Lehrstück* into a full-length play. More than any of Brecht's other works, the learning plays have aroused hostile responses in critics. In particular, *The measures Taken* has earned the epithet "notorious" because it tells the story of a young Communist agitator who assents to being killed at the hands of the other agitators to advance their cause. Audiences accustomed to dramas depicting heroic struggles by individuals against the collective find such a plot both strange and morally outrageous.

To grasp Brecht's intentions, it is helpful to keep in mind the distinction between theater as performance and the wide range of uses to which those performances may be put. They can be religious celebrations (Greek TRAGEDY), can entertain (COMEDIES), can provide information (history plays and documentaries), can sell products (advertising), and can reinforce bonds of community (patriotic festivals), to name some obvious possibilities. In Brecht's theory, as it developed out of his involvement with the use of theater in the Weimar Republic to educate workers about social issues, the primary function of performance was to get people to think critically about the world and their situation in it. This meant more than disrupting the illusions offered in the commercial theater. Rather than remaining passive consumers of entertainment, the members of the audience, as well as the actors and the director, had to learn to ask their own questions about the problem depicted on the stage, instead of simply relying on the questions posed by the dramatist. To quote Brecht, "The learning play is essentially dynamic; its task is to show the world as it changes (and also how it may be changed)" (*New York Times*, November 24, 1935). Unlike the catharsis of classical tragedy, which restores the spectators to what they once were, the *Lehrstück* spurs the spectators to become what they have never been and to do what they have not yet undertaken.

The didactic function of the theater has a strong tradition in GERMANY, going back to the reforming programs of the 18th-century Enlightenment. For example, Gotthold Ephraim Lessing's (1729–1781) masterpiece *Nathan the Wise* (*Nathan der Weise*, 1779) teaches a lesson about religious tolerance more than it entertains. The Brechtian *Lehrstück* is thus hardly an aberration and has exerted profound influence on German-speaking playwrights after 1945. Although MAX FRISCH (1911–1991) ironically subtitled *The Firebugs* (*Biedermann und die Brandstifter*, 1958) a "learning play with nothing to teach," the play has all the characteristics of a *Lehrstück*. The East German playwright HEINER MÜLLER (1929–1995) appropriated and refined the *Lehrstück*, while the Austrian PETER HANDKE (1942–) wittily turned the *Lehrstück* against itself in OFFENDING THE AUDIENCE (*Publikumsbeschimpfung*, 1966).

[*See also* Alienation Effect; Epic Theater]

FURTHER READING

Bathrick, David, and Andreas Huyssen. "Producing Revolution: Heiner Müller's *Mauser* as Learning Play." *New German Critique* 8 (Spring 1976): 110–121.

Fehervary, Helen. "Enlightenment or Entanglement: History and Aesthetics in Bertolt Brecht and Heiner Müller." *New German Critique* 8 (Spring 1976): 80–109.

Kalb, Jonathan. "*The Horatian*: Building the Better *Lehrstück*." *New German Critique* 64 (Winter 1995): 161–173.

Mueller, Roswitha. "Learning for a New Society: The *Lehrstück*." In *The Cambridge Companion to Brecht*, ed. by Peter Thomson and Glendyr Sacks. Cambridge: Cambridge Univ. Press, 1994. 79–95.

Nelson, G. E. "The Birth of Tragedy out of Pedagogy: Brecht's 'Learning Play' *Die Maßnahme*." *German Quarterly* 46, no. 4 (1973): 566–580.

Schoeps, Karl-Heinz. "Brecht's *Lehrstücke*: A Laboratory for Epic and Dialectic Theater." In *A Bertolt Brecht Reference Companion*, ed. by Siegfried Mews. Westport, Conn.: Greenwood Press, 1997. 70–87.

Arnd Bohm

LEBEN DES GALILEI *See* THE LIFE OF GALILEO

LEE, ROBERT E. *See* LAWRENCE, JEROME, and ROBERT E. LEE

LEE KUO-HSIU (1955–)

Lee Kuo-hsiu is a key figure in the rise and flourishing of Taiwan's LITTLE THEATER MOVEMENT from the early 1980s to the present. Through his work as artistic director of the Taipei-based Ping-Fong Acting Troupe, he has brought thirty-four different plays to the stage, writing, directing, and starring in most of them. Among the major playwrights in Taiwan, he has one of the strongest articulations of what it means to live in Taiwan in the contemporary era. Although Mandarin is the dominant language in his works and his own mother tongue, he also uses Taiwanese, Hakka, and other languages frequently heard on the island. Lee has also innovated in artistic direction, building the largest theater company in Taiwan in terms of full-time staff. His 1991 play *National Salvation Corporation Ltd.* ran for a record-shattering seventy performances in a market where less than half of that constitutes a long run. Through both artistic and administrative skills Lee has played a major role in extending the ethos of the little theater movement into a professional, commercially viable theater.

In background and training, Lee is unusual among leading artistic directors of modern theaters in Taiwan in the local nature of his exposure to theater. Most of the others have had significant experience abroad, and many have earned advanced degrees in theater from American or European universities. Lee, whose postsecondary training was in television broadcasting, learned about theater through participation in the limited theatrical activities available in Taiwan at the time, joining his school drama club in 1974 and performing with the Gengxin Experimental Theater in early 1980. Later that year the Gengxin group became the Lan-ling Theater Workshop and presented the first hit of the little theater movement, *Lotus-Pearl's New Match*, with Lee giving an acclaimed comic performance. In 1985 Lee performed in another landmark play with another group he co-founded, Performance Workshop's *Chinese Comedy in the Late 20th Century*. The following year, on October 6, 1986, Lee founded a group of his own, the Ping-Fong Acting Troupe.

Lee's most significant plays explore timely local themes, both the serious and the lighthearted, through comic means. His signature *Can Three Make It?* series, which began with a breakthrough production in 1987, explores topics ranging from cross-straits relations and widespread emigration to pornographic films and illicit love affairs. The series takes its name from Lee's experiment in presenting a play with a limited number of actors, each portraying multiple roles. That challenge is also incorporated into the "Fong-Ping" series, which chronicles the travails of a fictional theater troupe by that name. In 2000 Lee, who had previously mounted few revivals of earlier works, chose to celebrate the new millennium by reviving all three plays from the series, *Collapse of "The Great Wall," Shamlet*, and *The Apocalypse of Beijing Opera*. In addition to his work with Ping-Fong, Lee now teaches directing and playwriting at the university level, passing his largely self-taught skills on to the next generation of theater artists in Taiwan.

SELECT PLAYS: *Can Three Make It? Part I (Sanren xingbuxing I*, 1987); *Can Three Make It? Part II—City Panic (Sanren xingbuxing II—Chengshi zhi huang*, 1988); *Far away from Home (Xi chu yangguan*, 1988); *Collapse of "The Great Wall" (Banli changcheng*, 1989); *National Salvation Corporation Ltd. (Jiuguo zhushi huishe*, 1991); *Shamlet (Shamuleite*, 1992); *Can Three Make It? Part III—Oh! Three Diverged Paths (Sanren xingbuxing III—OH! Sanchakou*, 1993); *The Classified (Zhenghun qishi*, 1993); *The Kingdom of Paradise (Taiping tianguo*, 1994); *The Apocalypse of Beijing Opera (Jingxi qishilu*, 1996); *Can Three Make It? Part IV—Play Hard (Sanren xingbuxing IV—Changqi wanming*, 1997); *Can Three Make It? Part V—Empty City (Sanren xingbuxing V—Kongcheng zhuangtai*, 1999); *Can Three Make It? Part VI—Incredible Country (Sanren xingbuxing VI—busiyi de guo*, 2001); *Wedding Memories (Hong nü'er*, 2003); *Last Night When the Stars Were Bright (Zuoye xingchen*, 2005)

FURTHER READING

Chung, Mingder. "The Little Theatre Movement of Taiwan (1980–89): In Search of Alternative Aesthetics and Politics." Ph. D. diss., New York Univ., 1992.

Diamond, Catherine. "Reflected and Refracted: Metatheatrics in Taiwan." *Journal of Dramatic Theory and Criticism* 9, no. 2 (1995): 85–95.

Lee Kuo-hsiu. *National Salvation Corporation, Ltd*. In *An Oxford Anthology of Contemporary Chinese Drama*, ed. by Martha P. Y. Cheung and Jane C. C. Lai. Hong Kong: Oxford Univ. Press, 1997.

Weinstein, John B. "Directing Laughter: Modes of Modern Chinese Comedy, 1907–1997." Ph. D. diss., Columbia Univ., 2002.

——. "Multilingual Theatre in Contemporary Taiwan." *Asian Theatre Journal* 17, no. 2 (2000): 269–283.

John Weinstein

LENORMAND, HENRI-RENÉ (1882–1951)

Henri-René (H. R.) Lenormand wrote some two dozen plays between 1919 and 1938 in a "well-made" mode that he used equally well for both drawing-room drama and exotic foreign intrigue. Within a framework of middle-class values he offered sophisticated depictions of racial and social minorities, sexuality across racial lines and between adults and children, mental retardation, depression, and alcoholism that nonetheless allowed his audiences to sustain some identification with his protagonists, making him one of the most praised French playwrights between the two world wars.

Despite setting his plays in locales that could invite exotic, detailed settings, Lenormand praised the pared-down, abstracted productions of Georges and Ludmilla Pitoëff, who debuted many of his plays in Geneva. Lenormand also worked with Gaston Baty, who, with Georges Pitoëff, Charles Dullin, and Louis Jouvet, constituted the Cartel des quatre (1927–1939), an alliance among the most intellectual directors in Paris to sustain each other's productions against the financial dominance of the popular Boulevard theaters.

In *The Simoom (Le simoun*, 1920)—named after the relentless wind of the North African desert—the protagonist, Laurency, left France twenty years earlier when rejected by his wife Yvonne, with whom he was obsessively in love. He is now a colonial trader in the Algerian Sahara, living with a half-Arab, half-Spanish mistress. His daughter, whom he has never seen, suddenly arrives. The local Agha, in order to stabilize relations with Laurency, wishes to have Laurency's daughter marry his son. But Laurency refuses because he himself is obsessed with his daughter's resemblance to his lost wife Yvonne and has begun to desire her incestuously—to the point of eventually trying to act on his desire. All these relationships end in tragedy the night of a terrible simoom, validating the Arab-Spanish mistress's earlier pronouncement: "Nature is delirious and there is nothing one can do to calm it."

In *The Coward* (*Le lâche*, 1925) the young French painter Jacques feigns tuberculosis in order to spend World War I in a Swiss sanatorium rather than on the battlefield. The other pan-European denizens of the sanatorium, some of them actually ill, others similarly feigning in order to act as spies for either the French or the Germans, soon suspect Jacques's fraud. Eventually they use this knowledge to blackmail him into spying for the French government, but when he is caught red-handed by the German side, he betrays his original French blackmailers and offers his information to the Germans. Jacques believes that he has gotten away with all his frauds (tuberculosis, spying, counterspying) even after he returns to a tranquil postwar life—until the original blackmailers turn up after the war to execute him for his betrayal.

Lenormand was hailed in his time as a bringer of Freudianism to the stage—though it should be understood that the term *Freudianism* was loose code for "unconventional desire." Now his work seems less psychological than sociological, depicting the European middle class gradually losing control of its fate through the external side effects of colonialism and the internal damage of psychological and social repression. The influence of his colonial and sexual candor can still be seen in the late 20th-century works of BERNARD-MARIE KOLTÈS. Lenormand's two-volume memoir *Les confessions d'un auteur dramatique* (1949 and 1953) treats his career and travels, providing a valuable picture of FRANCE, America, Asia, and AFRICA in the first half of the 20th century.

SELECT PLAYS: *Time Is a Dream* (*Le temps est un songe*, 1919); *Failures* (*Les ratés*, 1920); *The Simoom* (*Le simoun*, 1920); *The Dream Doctor* (*Le mangeur de rêves*, 1922); *The Red Tooth* (*La dent rouge*, 1922); *In the Shadow of Evil* (*A l'ombre du mal*, 1924); *Man and His Phantoms* (*L'homme et ses fantômes*, 1924); *The Coward* (*Le lâche*, 1925); *Love the Magician* (*L'amour magician*, 1926); *A Secret Life* (*Une vie secrète*, 1929); *Asie* (1931); *The Madwoman of the Skies* (*La Folle du ciel*, 1937); *Satan's Realm* (*Terre de Satan*, published 1942)

FURTHER READING

Blanchart, Paul. *Le théâtre de H.-R. Lenormand: Apocalypse d'une société*. Paris: Revue International d'Art Dramatique, 1947.

Jones, Robert Emmet. *H.-R. Lenormand*. Boston: Twayne, 1984.

David Pelizzari

LEOW PUAY TIN (1957–)

there once was a something . . . a something like a
temple on a hill, a well of sweet water. . . .
where is it now?
—Prologue, *Three Children*

Born in 1957 and raised in Malacca, MALAYSIA, actor/playwright/director Leow Puay Tin has achieved theatrical prominence in Kuala Lumpur and SINGAPORE and has had work staged in Hong Kong, the PHILIPPINES, JAPAN, AUSTRALIA, EGYPT, GERMANY, and the UNITED STATES. She received an M.F.A. in playwriting from the University of Hawaii (1986) and an advanced diploma in voice studies at the Central School of Speech and Drama in London (1990). Employed as a journalist and voice instructor at the National Academy of Art in Kuala Lumpur, she was a member of the Five Arts Center, a collective dedicated to shaping a Malaysian identity in the performing and visual arts. Currently she teaches voice and speech at the experimental Practice Performing Arts School in Singapore.

She first gained recognition as an actress in 1984, when she performed the title role in STELLA KON'S 1983 MONODRAMA about a Singapore matriarch, *Emily of Emerald Hill*. Leow has since created several monodramas of her own, including *Two Grandmothers* (1987). Leow, who writes in English, probes the Malaysian experience in the areas of family, women, and the single life. She experiments with shifting voices, nonlinearity, storytelling, songs, and chants. She draws upon both contemporary and traditional Southeast Asian aesthetics. In recent work she has created collaboratively with directors, performers, designers, and crew, exploring multimedia, art installations, audience participation, found spaces, and multiple languages.

In 1992 her full-length *Three Children* was staged in Kuala Lumpur. In this experimental psychological drama three young adults revisit their childhood to understand better their present. Through humor, borrowings from the Hokkien street opera Leow loved in her youth, live music, and the assistance of a narrator, the three siblings express what it was like to grow up on Kappan Road in Malacca. They transform into various personae, recreating bizarre and harsh stories from their past, some obviously conceived by a child's imagination.

Leow received critical acclaim for her monodrama *A Modern Woman Called Ang Tau Mui* (1993). The piece concerns an unmarried working-class woman nearing middle age who cleans toilets in an urban shopping complex. Seeking to be a happy modern woman, Ang Tau Mui shops incessantly and emulates movie idol and singer Lin Dai, a popular Hong Kong film star of the 1950s and 1960s. Eventually Ang Tau Mui realizes the futility of her dreams; her demise raises social and psychological issues relevant to contemporary Malaysian society. The drama unfolds through narration, monologue, memories, dreams, and songs from Chinese opera and the 1960s. It was staged in Adelaide and Melbourne for the Third International Women Playwrights Conference in 1994.

Leow's *Family* was first presented in Singapore in 1992. It was later performed in Kuala Lumpur in 1998 and at the Festival der Geister Kunsthaus Tacheles in Berlin in 1999. This play, which draws upon the classical Chinese tale of the Yang Clan Women Warriors, covers the 20th-century saga of three generations of a Chinese-Malaysian family whose success is due to the female members of the family. In Leow's most recent play, *Dinner for Two at the Best of Restaurants* (2002), a middle-aged couple engage in an unusually frank conversation while dining out at an expensive restaurant. Leow Puay Tin is an engaged, vital presence in contemporary Malaysian and Singaporean theatre.

PLAYS: *Two Grandmothers* (1987); *Family* (performed 1992); *Three Children: A Play* (Singapore, 1992); *A Modern Woman Called Ang Tau Mui* (1993); *The Window* (1995); *The Dakini Reading Project* (2000); *Ganesh Kalyanana* (2001); *Dinner for Two at the Best of Restaurants* (2002); *Songs and Monologues for the Landmines Project* (in progress)

FURTHER READING

Hasham, Joe. "Childhood Days Relived." *Sunday Star* (Malaysia) (February 9, 1992).

Lee, Kit. "Perfect Union of Three Children." *New Straits Times* (November 28, 1988).

Lord, Richard. "Broken Dreams, from Top to Bottom." *Quarterly Literary Review Singapore* 2, no. 2 (January 2003). http://www.qlrs.com.

Nur Nina Zuhra (Nancy Nanney). "Puteri Li Po, *Emily of Emerald Hill*, and *Three Children*: Imaginative Reconstructions of a Chinese Past." *Malay Literature* 7, nos. 1 and 2 (1994): pp. 32–47.

Peterson, William. *Theater and the Politics of Culture in Contemporary Singapore*. Middletown, Conn.: Wesleyan Univ. Press, 2001.

Nancy Nanney

LES See THE FOREST

THE LESSON

Subtitled *A Comic Drama*, *The Lesson*, EUGÈNE IONESCO's second produced play, can be read as a satire on pedantry and authoritarian education, as a denunciation of arbitrary power and its mystifications, or as a sadomasochistic rite in which learning is eroticized and virginity is fatal.

The doorbell rings on an empty stage; the Maid comes to open the door and admit the Student, a self-assured eighteen-year-old. She has come for a private lesson; she wants to prepare for the "total doctorate" exam that takes place in three weeks' time. When the Professor enters ("between fifty and sixty, small white beard"), he is timid and excessively polite. As he instructs, however, he becomes more and more sure of himself. The Student progressively loses her assurance, which is beaten out of her by the Professor's imperious pedagogy. The lesson is interrupted at regular intervals by the Maid, who comes to warn the Professor not to excite himself. The Professor ignores the warnings. He has discovered that the Student has memorized the products of all possible multiplication problems but has no notion of subtraction. "You have to subtract, too. It's not enough to merely integrate. You must also disintegrate. That's life. That's philosophy. That's science. That's progress and civilization."

Despite another warning from the Maid, the Professor goes on to philology, explaining that a dozen (real and imaginary) European languages are so closely derived from "neo-Spanish" as to be indistinguishable one from another. Only the most profound study will allow one to know which language one is speaking. The Student complains that she has a toothache, but the Professor, increasingly tyrannical and domineering, ignores her. He berates her for her ignorance. Taking up a knife—which the author stipulates may be "invisible"—the Professor dances around the Student, asking her to repeat the word *knife* over and over. (In French the word *couteau* has two syllables and becomes an orgasmic chant.) She can do nothing except complain that the pain from her tooth has spread to her entire body. In an apoplexy of sexual and pedagogic ecstasy, he stabs her. (Ionesco allows in a footnote that he may do this either with the knife itself or merely with the word *knife*.) The Student sprawls on her chair, her legs apart. The Professor stands in front of her, facing upstage. "His whole body is visibly convulsed."

The Maid reenters, scolds him, then helps him disguise the crime. "We'll bury her at the same time as the thirty-nine others." The Maid will contact her lover, the curate, for help in conducting forty burials. "Nobody will ask any questions—they're used to it." The Maid has been identified with the church, whose complicity with authoritarian regimes is a matter of record, but the play has also been interpreted philosophically as a dramatization of subjects killed by the words we create for them. The strong, symmetrical action is a tour de force for the principal duo, but the role of the Maid provides vital shaping and punctuation to the ritualized murder. A revival has played continuously since 1957 at the ninety-seat Théâtre de la Huchette in Paris, one of the world's longest theatrical runs. Danish choreographer Flemming Flindt created a ballet version of *The Lesson* in 1963.

[*See also* France]

FURTHER READING

Coe, Richard. *Eugène Ionesco*. 2nd ed. New York: Grove, 1970.

Esslin, Martin. *The Theatre of the Absurd*. Harmondsworth: Penguin, 1968.

Guicharnaud, Jacques. *Modern French Theatre from Giraudoux to Beckett*. New Haven: Yale Univ. Press, 1961.

Ionesco, Eugene. *Notes and Counter Notes*. Tr. by Donald Watson. New York: Grove, 1964.

Lista, Giovanni. *Ionesco*. Paris: Henri Veyrier, 1989.

Robert Schneider

LIANG BINGKUN (1936–)

With only a few years of formal schooling, Liang Bingkun, born in Beijing in 1936, learned to write in a workshop established by the Communist Party in the early 1950s to train future artists and writers for the new CHINA. Liang honed his writing skills at a variety of jobs in the theater, as actor, lighting technician, secretary, and managerial assistant. His plays before the 1980s, mostly co-authored and written in the socialist realist mode, include *Braving the Waves* (*Chengfeng polang*, 1961), and *This is also the Frontline* (*Zhe ye shi qiankian*, 1976). In 1981, after a lengthy stay at a factory, he wrote *Who Is the Strongest of Us All* (*Shui shi qianxian*), tackling political and social issues facing the nation. The hero of the play, Yuan Zhicheng, is the ambitious head of a state-owned textile factory and an upright party member. His effort to expand the factory is repeatedly thwarted by a minor official, Section Chief Ni, who works in the company that monopolizes electricity supply in the city. Yuan refuses to brown-nose Ni and deliver the expected bribery. As a result, his factory experiences two mysterious blackouts. Instead of offering support, Yuan's superior, head of the Textile Bureau, removes Yuan from his post in an attempt to placate the section chief. *Who Is the Strongest of Us All* is one of the first attempts in Chinese theater to address the problem of corruption. The story of Yuan Zhicheng's frustrating but heroic battle against the entrenched bureaucracy plagued by rampant bribery, complacency, and nepotism found a sympathetic audience within a party that worried about the effect of corruption on its ability to lead and a supportive audience among ordinary people who were outraged by the abuse of power at various levels of the government.

The play earned Liang Bingkun the fame that had eluded him for more than two decades, winning the coveted national award of Excellent Play, as well as the first prize given to dramatic literature by the Municipal Government of Beijing. The artistic strength of the play lies in its tight structure, intriguing plot, and lively dialogue. Riding on its success, Liang wrote several plays in quick succession in the 1980s. *Wang Jianshe Becomes an Official* (*Wang Jianshe dangguan*, 1983), *The Moment of Labor Pain* (*Zhentong de shike*, 1984), *The End of Night Is Morning* (*Yewan guoqu shi zaochen*, 1987), and *New Residence* (*Xin ju*, 1989) all deal with challenges of life in the era of economic reform. He continued to write into the 1990s, though none of his later work enjoyed the same kind of success as *Who Is the Strongest of Us All*. His favorite subject is factory life, a result of many years spent working and living among workers. A prolific writer, Liang Bingkun has created some forty plays and many essays, short stories, and literary reportage, as well as a critical work on playwriting. A collection of his plays was published by the China Theater Press in 1988.

SELECT PLAYS: *Braving the Waves* (*Chengfeng polang*, with Zhu Lin, Lan Tianye, and Mei Qian, 1961); *This Is also the Battlefront* (*Theli ye shi qianxian*, with Duan Lianjun, 1976); *Who Is the Strongest of us All* (*Shui shi qiangzhe*, 1981); *Disaster of Lies* (*Huang huo*, with Zhao Zixiong, 1981); *Wang Jianshe Becomes an Official* (*Wang Jianshe dang guan*, 1983); *Times of Labor Pain* (*Zhentong de shike*, 1984); *End of Night Is Morning* (*Yewan guoqu shi zaochen*, 1986); *New Residence* (*Xin ju*, 1989)

FURTHER READING

Liang Bingkun. *Who's the Strongest of Us All?* Tr. by Shun Cheng. In *An Oxford Anthology of Contemporary Chinese Drama*, ed. by Martha P. Y. Cheung and Jane C. C. Lai. Hong Kong: Oxford Univ. Press, 1997. 3–88.

Lin Zhaohua. "Paiyan *She shi Qiang Zhe* de tihui" [Reflections on Rehearsing *Who Is the Strongest of Us All*]. *Juben* [Play scripts] 1 (1982).

Li Shusheng. "Zhongguo wenlian lilun yanjiushi zuotan *Shei shi qiang zhe*" [Panel Discussion of *Who Is the Strongest of Us All* at the Research Institute of Theories of the All-China Literary Association]. *Juben* [Play scripts] 2 (1982).

Zhao Xun. "Ba wenyi de denghuo ran de geng liang xie—Ping huaju *Shei shi qiang zhe*" [Let the Light of Art Burn More Brightly—On the play *Who Is the Strongest of Us All*]. *Juben* [Play scripts] 2 (1982).

Li-hua Ying and Cai Xingshui

LIANG SHANBO YU ZHU YINGTAI, ZHEJIANG YUEJE See THE STORY OF THE BUTTERFLY-LOVERS

LIBRETTISTS

The years between the two world wars saw significant changes in the American musical theater, not the least of which was a major development in the librettos for stage musicals. Always the least impressive aspect of most Broadway musicals, the "book" was often the work of hacks or a team of journeymen hired to find a plausible story to loosely string together the songs, dances, and comic routines. In the early years of the new century George M. Cohan had made progress by structuring his musicals with a tight, serviceable story, and the books of P. G. Wodehouse and Guy Bolton for Jerome Kern's Princess Theatre musicals of the 1910s brought a lightness and playful sophistication to the musical COMEDY story line. But it was in the 1920s that the libretto made distinct efforts to be more than a drawn-out sketch used to highlight the songs and stars.

Otto Harbach (1873–1963) was the first to take libretto writing seriously. He was born Otto Abels Hauerbach in Salt Lake City and worked his way through college to become an English teacher. When he went to New York to study at Columbia, lack of funds forced him to drop out, and he took up journalism and then scriptwriting for musicals. From the beginning, Harbach (he changed his Teutonic-sounding name during World War I) tried to make the librettos more literate, giving the stories a firm structure and insisting on a logical progression of events. His early successes, such as *Three Twins* (1908) and *Madame Sherry* (1910), written with composer Karl Hoschna, were still silly musical comedies, but at least they made sense. When Harbach scripted the operettas *The Firefly* (1912) and *Katinka* (1915), the plots were the usual preposterous tales of street singers who become opera stars and princesses in disguise, but his lyrics and characterizations were a step above the norm. It was only when Harbach started working with Oscar Hammerstein II (1895–1960) that his ideas for more logical and literate librettos started to come alive.

Hammerstein came from a theatrical dynasty but was trained for the law profession. The stagestruck youth started writing musical shows at Columbia and by 1920 had his first Broadway credit. Harbach took Hammerstein under his wing, taught him how to structure a libretto, and even suggested that the songs should tie in with the plot and characters. This early form of integrated musical intrigued both men, and they made valiant efforts to realize their ambition in musicals such as *Rose-Marie* (1924). While that show might appear to be typical operetta to modern audiences, it was very bold for its time, and the complicated (but logical) plot and the way the songs fit into the story line was a significant achievement. The two men attempted to carry their ideas further but failed with traditional musicals such as *Sunny* (1925) and *Song of the Flame* (1925). Ironically, it was Hammerstein, and not his teacher, who achieved the goal of writing the first "musical play" when he and composer Jerome Kern created *Show Boat* (1927). Hammerstein's sprawling, epic tale (based on EDNA FERBER's novel) was the most ambitious libretto yet seen on the American stage, and his lyrics seemed to flow right out of each situation and character. *Show Boat* was a triumph of musical theater writing that even Hammerstein himself would not be able to improve upon until his musicals with Richard Rodgers in the 1940s and 1950s.

While other librettists of the period may not have had such lofty ambitions about scripting musicals, there were some who certainly had innovative ideas about what a musical can do. Herbert Fields (1897–1958) wrote the librettos for many of the Rodgers and Hart musicals, and he was tireless in his cockeyed experimentation. He also came from a theatrical dynasty and, like Hammerstein, began his theater career writing shows at Columbia. There was something brash about the Fields librettos; they are a mixture of Roaring Twenties optimism and collegiate irreverence. Consider *Dearest Enemy* (1925), which used an episode from New York City history to create a lighthearted musical comedy. When the Redcoats occupy Manhattan, Mrs. Robert Murray detains the officers in her mansion while the colonial troops escape to join George Washington and his army at Harlem Heights. It was a refreshing idea for a musical and, accented by some delightful Rodgers and Hart songs, seemed very daring. *Peggy-Ann* (1926) was even bolder, using the recent German style of EXPRESSIONISM in its plot. The title heroine escapes her dreary boardinghouse existence by fantasizing about fighting pirates and marrying dashing heroes. Fields populated his script with talking animals, oversized props, and plenty of Freudian clichés that were satirized. Fantasy was also used effectively in *A Connecticut Yankee* (1927), a playful take on modern man in medieval Camelot, based on Mark Twain's tale.

Fields also wrote librettos for the other up-and-coming songwriters of the period. For Cole Porter he penned the sophisticated *Fifty Million Frenchmen* (1929), which lampooned Americans abroad, and *DuBarry Was a Lady* (1939), the Twain plot reset in the court of King Louis XV of France. He wrote several hits in the 1940s with his sister Dorothy Fields (1905–1974), but his experiments in the 1920s and 1930s cannot be underestimated. What Hammerstein and Harbach were attempting in serious musicals, Fields was doing with musical comedy.

In the genre of operetta Dorothy Donnelly (1880–1928) stands out as one of the finest librettists of the period. Operettas flourished on Broadway in the 1920s, and, until the Depression put them out of business, it was a genre that all the great songwriters and librettists attempted at least once. Donnelly began as an actress who essayed roles in serious dramas by HENRIK IBSEN, W. B. YEATS, and GEORGE BERNARD SHAW. But by the 1920s she turned to libretto writing and scripted two of the era's most popular shows. *Blossom Time* (1921) was a musical biography of Franz Schubert, with Sigmund Romberg turning the classic pieces into operetta song hits. It was a lush and passionate musical, and Donnelly constructed a logical (if largely fictitious) plot with engaging characters. Even finer was *The Student Prince* (1924), a romantic tale about a German prince who falls in love with a tavern waitress. In a standard operetta she would be a princess in disguise or, in Cinderella fashion, would rise to the top of society. But Donnelly's libretto is all the more poignant for having the lovers part when circumstances beyond them dictate what they must do. Romberg's music soars with passion, but there are also some brains in *The Student Prince*, a reason it remains one of the few operettas of the period that can be revived without difficulty today.

Not many American playwrights were able to cross over from plays to musicals with equal success, but GEORGE S. KAUFMAN (1889–1961) did so for much of his long career. By 1923 he was contributing to musical librettos, usually broad comedies such as the Marx Brothers vehicles *The Cocoanuts* (1925) and *Animal Crackers* (1928). But his talent lay in the wisecrack and his satirical point of view, and both were best realized in two important musical satires of the 1930s. *Strike Up the Band* (1930) was about a warmongering industrialist who convinces America to go to war with Switzerland over the tariffs on Swiss cheese. The musical was a sharp spoof of international relations and American big business. George and Ira Gershwin provided the score, and they worked so well with Kaufman and co-writer Morrie Ryskind that they reunited for *Of Thee I Sing* (1931), the American theater's greatest musical satire and the first musical to win the Pulitzer Prize. Domestic politics was the subject this time as a beauty contest was used to hype an election, a party's platform was based on love, and a president faced impeachment for marrying the wrong girl. It was all exaggerated enough to be fun and accurate enough to be pointed. *Of Thee I Sing* was also well plotted, and the extended musical sequences by the Gershwins made the whole show very integrated. The time was also right for such a satire. A few years later, when the same team went even further in the acerbic sequel *Let 'em Eat Cake* (1933), the satire making fun of homegrown dictators seemed less funny in the depths of the Depression, and the show quickly closed. Kaufman wrote many more successful plays after 1940 (especially with Moss Hart), but his musical satires of the 1930s will remain a high point for American libretto writing.

MATURITY: THE 1940s, 1950s, and 1960s

Although many new librettists came on the scene during the war years, it was veteran Oscar Hammerstein who created the modern, mature libretto with his collaborator, composer Richard Rodgers. Beginning with *Oklahoma!* (1943), Hammerstein's book and lyrics for a series of musical plays brought about an integration of story, character, songs, and even dance that had not been previously seen on Broadway. The score grew out of the characters and the situation in such a way that the musical was a unified whole. A musical number from one show could not be plugged into another, any more than a song written for one character could not be given to another in the same play. The rural simplicity of *Oklahoma!* led to the more complex *Carousel* (1945), the experimental *Allegro* (1947), the adult wartime musical *South Pacific* (1949), the exotic and moving *The King and I* (1951), and other works. The Rodgers and Hammerstein model for a musical play dominated Broadway for over thirty years, and it remains the accepted form for most American musicals.

Librettist-lyricist Alan Jay Lerner (1918–1986) came to prominence in the 1940s and best represented the artists who followed in Hammerstein's footsteps. The heir of a wealthy clothing retail business, the Lerner Shops, the well-educated, world-traveled Lerner preferred the theater over the garment industry and wrote intelligent, witty, and highly romantic scripts, often collaborating with composer Frederick Loewe on the score. After some promising failures, the team found success with *Brigadoon* (1947), a fantasy set in Scotland that had the whimsy of a J. M. BARRIE play and the lush ROMANTICISM of old-time operetta. Lerner's original librettos for *Brigadoon* and *Paint Your Wagon* (1951) illustrated his talent for musical storytelling, but it was his adaptation of George Bernard Shaw's drawing-room comedy PYGMALION into the Broadway classic *My Fair Lady* (1956) that crowned his career. It was here that Hammerstein's ideas of total integration of story, song, and character reached a high point as Shaw's original play and Lerner's dialogue and lyrics all blended into a new and unified whole. Lerner's libretto for the ambitious *Camelot* (1960) was not as successful, though his dramatization of T. H. White's mammoth fantasy novel *The Once and Future King* into a musical play had its moments of brilliance as well. Although he continued to write original and adapted librettos for another twenty years, Lerner rarely found success. Efforts such as *On a Clear Day You Can See Forever* (1966), *Coco* (1969), *Carmelina* (1979), and *Dance a Little Closer* (1983) often contained superior lyric writing, but Lerner's libretto-writing skills failed him. Yet when he was at his peak, Lerner brought a polish and sophistication to the Broadway libretto that sometimes even surpassed Hammerstein's.

But there were still musical comedies, shows that did not have the pretensions of Rodgers and Hammerstein's and Lerner and Loewe's musical dramas. The team of Betty Comden (1915–) and Adolph Green (1915–2002) concentrated on lighter fare, and, as librettists and lyricists, they shone for over forty years. Both born New Yorkers who had ambitions of becoming performers, they began in nightclubs, where the team often wrote their own material. Their first Broadway show, *On the Town* (1944), was slight on plot (three sailors on leave in New York City find romance during a twenty-four-hour period) but vivacious in its broad characterizations and sassy lyrics set to Leonard Bernstein's music. In subsequent musical comedies such as *Wonderful Town* (1953), *Bells Are Ringing* (1956), and *On the Twentieth Century* (1978), Comden and Green wrote both librettos and lyrics, tying the shows together with Hammerstein precision but with a lighter, less reflective spirit. Sometimes the duo wrote only the libretto, as in the popular *Applause* (1970), and other times they just contributed songs, as in *Peter Pan* (1954); regardless, a Comden and Green musical was always a bright and comic display of talent. Equally adept at comedy librettos was Abe Burrows (1910–1985), a writer from radio and television who scripted such musical comedy successes as *Guys and Dolls* (1950), *Can-Can* (1953), *Silk Stockings* (1955), and *How to Succeed in Business Without Really Trying* (1961). Burrows had an ear for quirky dialogue, brash characters, and economical plotting. In most of his works the exuberance of the songwriter's score is matched by his book scenes. Burrows's librettos combine the slaphappy comedy of the pre-*Oklahoma!* shows with the structure of the Rodgers and Hammerstein model.

Four noteworthy librettists who concentrated on comedy as well emerged in the 1960s. Michael Stewart (1929–1987) was also a New Yorker who began by contributing comedy sketches for television. His first Broadway effort, *Bye Bye Birdie* (1960), illustrated how he could tell a comic tale in a breezy and unpretentious way. Stewart displayed a lighter, more delicate touch in his librettos for quieter musicals such as *Carnival* (1961), *Mack and Mabel* (1974), and *The Grand Tour* (1979), but he is best known for his big, brassy shows such as *Hello, Dolly!* (1964), *Barnum* (1980), and *42nd Street* (1980). Few librettists wrote efficient, tight-knit, multiscene musicals as well as Stewart could. Joseph Stein (1912–) had an up-and-down career, but, unlike most librettists, one can detect a theme running throughout all his librettos. Stein usually focuses on a community or group of similarly circumstanced people in his librettos. His first Broadway musical was *Plain and Fancy* (1955), a genial show about an Amish community in Pennsylvania. *The Body Beautiful* (1958) was about members of the boxing profession, *Juno* (1959) takes place in a Dublin neighborhood in 1922 during the Irish Republican Army troubles, *Zorba* (1968) was set in a little village in Crete where the habitants tell the story of the Greek visitor Zorba, *The Baker's Wife* (1976) took place in a small French town where the baker stops making bread when his wife runs off with another man, and *King of Hearts* (1978) focused on the inmates of a French insane asylum who take over their abandoned town during World War I. Few of these musicals were hits (*The Baker's Wife* did not even make it to New York), but Stein's greatest success, *Fiddler on the Roof* (1964), was also about a community: the Russian village of Anetevka. In each libretto the characters are shaped or hindered by the members of their social circle. In *Fiddler on the Roof* the town itself is the major character. Stein's script has some very serious and complex issues, but basically the musical follows the form of a comedy, in this case, a folk comedy. The writing is whimsical at times, but it also goes deep, making *Fiddler on the Roof* as unique as it is accomplished.

Peter Stone (1930–2003) was born in Los Angeles and grew up in the world of movies (his father was a film producer and writer) but ended up on Broadway in the 1960s as well. After some admirable failures such as *Kean* (1961) and *Skyscraper* (1965), he found acclaim for his literate, lively libretto for *1776* (1969). Few musicals have as much book as this re-creation of the debates leading to the ratification of the Declaration of Independence, and there are sections where half an hour goes by without a song. But Stone's dialogue sparkles, and what was an unlikely prospect for a Broadway show became a hit. His other librettos range from the escapism of *My One and Only* (1983) and *The Will Rogers Follies* (1991) to the more character-oriented *The Woman of the Year* (1981) and *Titanic* (1997). Stone was also a much-favored play doctor who assisted in saving several other musicals. Rarely inspired, he was a shrewd and practical writer who knew how musicals worked. In a similar way, comic writer Larry Gelbart (1923–) has often been more clever than inspired. Yet his comedy is first rate, and he has found success in writing for television, films, and the stage. His most important musical comedy contributions were *A Funny Thing Happened on the Way to the Forum* (1962), co-written with Burt Shevelove, and *City of Angels* (1989). The former was a well-crafted adaptation of several Roman plays by Plautus into a seemingly loose but tightly structured libretto. Gelbart and Shevelove managed to keep the classical form even as they used American vaudeville techniques. In *City of Angels* Gelbart was in the genre of parody, but again the script is so complex and intricate that this spoof of a 1940s detective yarn encompassed cinematic elements even as it played off old musical comedy traditions.

Perhaps the most ambitious librettist of the postwar years was Arthur Laurents (1918–). Like Hammerstein, he was interested in complex storytelling; but unlike the older writer, Laurents wanted to experiment and find new subjects and new ways to write Broadway musicals. He was born in Brooklyn and, after a quality education, began to write plays and screenplays, mostly social dramas. Laurents's first foray into the musical form was *West Side Story* (1957), a bold project conceived with director-choreographer Jerome Robbins that retold William Shakespeare's *Romeo and Juliet* in terms of contemporary gang warfare in Manhattan. The script was uncompromising as it blended vigorously with Leonard Bernstein's music and Stephen Sondheim's lyrics to create a musical TRAGEDY of sorts. More conventional but just as accomplished was Laurents's libretto for *Gypsy* (1959), a fable about show business that contained incisive character studies and used an episodic format to build to an emotional climax. Although none of Laurents's later scripts found as much success as these two, some of his later efforts were just as daring, such as his cockeyed look at insanity in *Anyone Can Whistle* (1964) and the musical-social history of African Americans through the ages in *Hallelujah, Baby!* (1967). In addition to being a prominent writer, Laurents foreshadowed an age of experimental musical theater.

EXPERIMENTATION: THE 1970s, 1980s, and 1990s

The most innovative force in the American musical theater during the last three decades of the 20th century was composer-lyricist Stephen Sondheim. He did not script the librettos for his works, but each musical was a brave experiment that encouraged his librettist to attempt to write in a unique and often dangerous way. George Furth (1932–), for example, is an actor and sometime playwright. When he was asked to turn a series of his one-acts about contemporary Manhattan into the musical *Company* (1970), the result was so new, so unprecedented, that it seemed that only a fresh set of eyes could have conceived it. In fact, it was Sondheim and director Harold Prince who probably brought the boldness to the project, but it was Furth who wrote the superb libretto. *Company* was the first fully realized concept musical, a type of theater that does not rely as strongly on plot and characters as on an idea. The musical is about how marriages survive, why some people resist the commitment of marriage, and how fragile our connection is to those who provide companionship. These themes are explored in brief dialogue sections, musical numbers that cross over time and space, and scenes that only take place in a character's imagination. The success of *Company* opened the door for *A Chorus Line* (1975), *Nine* (1982), *Jelly's Last Jam* (1992), and other later concept musicals. Furth's only other significant libretto was *Merrily We Roll Along* (1981), an experiment that failed in many ways but was another daring project: the story of youth's eventual disillusionment told in reverse order. Sondheim was again the composer-lyricist, and again the result was dangerous.

Sondheim's other librettists have been James Goldman, Hugh Wheeler, James Lapine, and John Weidman, and each has contributed similarly innovative scripts for highly experimental works. Goldman (1927–1998) was a television writer and playwright whose libretto for Sondheim's *Follies* (1971) has continued to cause controversy. A haunted look at the past as two middled-aged couples review their mistakes and lost dreams, it took the form of a reunion of show people, but the whole musical was a metaphor for uncomfortable self-realization. Sondheim's score, filled with accurate and pointed pastiche numbers, was easily appreciated, but Goldman's book was what challenged audiences. It is still challenging today as *Follies* is revived and rethought by new audiences. Hugh Wheeler (1912–1987) was an English-born mystery writer and playwright who provided librettos for two of Sondheim's most acclaimed works: *A Little Night Music* (1973) and *Sweeney Todd, the Demon Barber of Fleet Street* (1979). Both shows have a seemingly traditional, linear format (neither are concept musicals), but there is little else that is conventional about either. The former is a waltzing portrayal of love and lust among some upper-class Swedes at the turn of the last century. While reviving the genre of operetta, the musical deconstructs it as well, exposing the despair behind all the frivolity. Wheeler's comedy-of-manners libretto is rich with wit and pathos. *Sweeney Todd*, on the other hand, is operetta as grim social commentary. The Victorian tale, about a mass murderer and his cohort Mrs. Lovett, who serves pies made of human flesh, is in itself a bold choice for a Broadway musical. But Wheeler's book and Sondheim's score blend to create a poetic nightmare that is as funny as it is disturbing. The "musical thriller" may be Sondheim's masterpiece, and Wheeler played no small part in its formation.

James Lapine (1949–) brings a younger and more absurd flavor to the Sondheim musical. He made his reputation as an author and director of quirky OFF-BROADWAY plays, not from a Broadway musical background, and his librettos are refreshingly unaware of old traditions. *Sunday in the Park with George* (1984) explores the process of artistic creation, in this case Georges Seurat's famous pointillist painting. The characters are mostly types, and the plot is secondary; the concept here is how and why an artist creates, and the musical is as enthralling as its subject. *Into the Woods* (1987) is more linear and less abstract, but just as probing. The first act re-creates some familiar and new fairy tales; the second act explores the moral consequences of the characters' actions. *Passion* (1994) may be the most conventional of the Sondheim-Lapine collaborations: a dark love triangle in which obsession both creates and destroys its participants. John Weidman (1946–) is another younger writer who brings a fresh perspective to Sondheim's musicals. *Pacific Overtures* (1976) is history as a concept musical. The story of the opening of Japan in 1853 and its subsequent indoctrination into Western ways was told in vignettes that used both *kabuki* and Broadway theater techniques. Weidman's libretto is episodic and yet takes time to dwell on seemingly unconnected details. Like a delicate Japanese screen, it is general and specific at the same time. History was also treated in an unusual way in *Assassins* (1991), a surreal look at the various men and women who have assassinated or attempted to kill U.S. presidents over the years. Sondheim's score pastiched different styles of American popular music, and Weidman played off our preconceived notions of what motivates a person to assassinate. It is one of the musical theater's most complex and disturbing (also funniest, which makes it more disturbing) works.

The Sondheim musicals were not the only dark and challenging examples between 1970 and the millennium. Librettists working with other composers also experimented. Among the noteworthy writers were William Finn (1952–), a composer-lyricist whose modern, frantic musicals are sung through, so he is, in essence, the librettist. Nervy and funny works such as *March of the Falsettos* (1981), *Falsettoland* (1990), and *A New Brain* (1998) illustrate a superb artist who, perhaps more than any other recent theater artist, is interested in contemporary life and its many joys and pitfalls. Just as ambitious is composer-lyricist Michael John LaChiusa (1962–), whose widely different musicals are also sung through. His comedy of sexual manners, *Hello, Again* (1993), jumps through history to dramatize a chain of sexual encounters. His other disarming pieces include the triptych musical *First Lady Suite* (1993), a *Medea* variation called *Marie Christine* (1999), and the JAZZ-infiltrated *The Wild Party* (2000). On the more conventional side, librettists Thomas Meehan (1929–) and TERRENCE MCNALLY (1939–) have found critical and popular success writing musicals in the traditional, linear format. Meehan co-wrote the scripts for three long-run musical comedies: *Annie* (1977), *The Producers* (2001), and *Hairspray* (2003). McNally, an acclaimed playwright, turned to musicals halfway through his career and scripted such memorable shows as *Kiss of the Spider Woman* (1993), *Ragtime* (1998), *The Full Monty* (2000), and *A Man of No Importance* (2002). But conventional or experimental, the importance of the librettists cannot be diminished, and they will continue to play an important role in a vital American musical theater.

FURTHER READING

Bordman, Gerald. *American Musical Theatre: A Chronicle*. 3d ed. New York: Oxford Univ. Press, 2001.

Ewen, David. *The New Complete Book of the American Musical Theatre*. New York: Holt, Rinehart & Winston, 1970.

Gänzl, Kurt. *The Encyclopedia of the Musical Theatre*. 2d ed. New York: Schirmer Bks., 2001.

Gottfried, Martin. *Broadway Musicals*. New York: Abrams, 1979.

Green, Stanley. *The World of Musical Comedy*. 4th ed. New York: Da Capo, 1984.

Hischak, Thomas S. *Boy Loses Girl: Broadway's Librettists*. Lanham, Md.: Scarecrow, 2002.

Thomas S. Hischak

LIEBELEI

Fond!—He?—I was nothing more to him than a diversion—and he died for another—!

—Christine, Act 3

One of ARTHUR SCHNITZLER's most performed plays, *Liebelei* (translated as both *Light-o' Love* and *Flirtation*) was written in 1894, premiered in 1895 at Vienna's Burgtheater, and remained in the repertory until 1910. In 1918 it was revived and performed in various theaters until 1930. Since World War II *Liebelei* has often been on the program of Austrian theaters.

The characters in this play seem familiar from ANATOL: well-to-do, young bachelors seeking out *süße Mädel* (sweet young girls) for diversion. However, in moving from the episodic COMEDY of his first success to the serious drama of *Liebelei*, Schnitzler differentiates character types of *süße Mädel*. In *Liebelei* Christine and Mizi are both young, unmarried women from the poorer classes who live in the suburbs, yet they interpret the rules of social convention differently. Whereas Mizi knows that she is just a flirtatious adventure for Theodor and pursues their affair accordingly, Christine, as the cultured daughter of a widowed musician, is full of romantic idealism and believes in true love. She thus takes her relationship with Fritz quite seriously, despite Mizi's warning that their kind of girls will always be left by such men. Typically, "their kind" must be resigned to marrying a pedantic, moral, middle-class man and to a marriage in which love plays no role.

Although Fritz is not unwilling to begin a dalliance with Christine, initially he is still preoccupied with the affair he has been pursuing with a married woman. Never taking Christine's feelings into consideration, Theodor encourages Fritz to use her as a mere diversion because he fears that Fritz's affair is becoming dangerous. Indeed, the husband arrives, confronts Fritz, and challenges him to a duel while the two young couples are enjoying a flirtatious evening together. When Fritz visits Christine in her modest but comfortable home before the duel, the enjoyment of this fleeting moment gives him a sense of eternity. Still, as W. E. Yates (1992) notes, Fritz is enjoying the *moment*, which is "an aesthetic experience, not a moral commitment." In this potentially eternal moment, however, Fritz also recognizes that he has deceived and betrayed Christine, not only because her understanding of the social rules differs from his or Mizi's and Theodor's, but also because he will die for another woman. When Fritz is subsequently killed in the duel, Christine realizes that she meant nothing to him—although he meant the world to her. *Liebelei* ends with a distraught Christine leaving home and her father lamenting that he will never see her again. Critics have almost always interpreted this as an implied suicide, though Schnitzler does not directly specify it as such, thus leaving the ending open.

With *Liebelei* Schnitzler created a masterpiece of dramatic tension that moves from cheerful, flirtatious interactions between the two couples in act 1 to the tragic ending of act 3. Schnitzler not only empathetically deals with the situation of women, but also criticizes the senselessness of the (illegal) duel. Although early critics often viewed *Liebelei* as immoral, its lasting success demonstrates that it indeed is a powerful commentary on turn-of-the-century Viennese mores and social conventions, attesting to Schnitzler's perceptive creativity.

[*See also* Austria; Germany]

FURTHER READING

Lorenz, Dagmar, ed. *A Companion to the Works of Arthur Schnitzler*. Rochester, N.Y.: Camden House, 2003.

Ossar, Michael. "Individual and Type in Arthur Schnitzler's *Liebelei*." *Modern Austrian Literature* 30, no. 2 (1997): 19–34.

Yates, W. E. *Schnitzler, Hofmannsthal, and the Austrian Theatre*. New Haven: Yale Univ. Press, 1992.

Elizabeth G. Ametsbichler

THE LIFE OF GALILEO

In a series of loosely connected scenes spanning the years 1609–1642, BERTOLT BRECHT's *The Life of Galileo* (*Leben des Galilei*) depicts the 17th-century astronomer at work, at home with family and friends, and also in conversation and confrontation with representatives of ITALY's ruling elite. Brecht completed his first version of the play, titled *The Earth Moves/Life of Galileo* (*Die Erde bewegt sich/Leben des Galilei*) in exile in DENMARK in 1939. In 1945–1946 he collaborated with the actor Charles Laughton (1899–1962) on an English-language version, *Galileo*. The final version, for his East Berlin theater company, the Berliner Ensemble, was completed in 1956 and is a German translation of the English-language version bearing the title *Leben des Galilei*. After the dropping of the first nuclear bomb, Brecht made changes to his initial version, placing greater emphasis on the central theme of the play. Historically, both feudalism and capitalism have not granted science the freedom to be practiced for the well-being of all members of society, since the respective governmental rulers, church leaders, and business interests have frequently dictated which projects could be pursued in order to further their own power or material gain. Advocating a science free of such constraints, Brecht's play foreshadows a society in which science facilitates the liberation of all classes from material need.

The play is chiefly about the role of science and teaching in future social formations. As we have seen in the course of the 20th century, socialist societies have never been able to deal with the social leverage that scientists hold through their control of intellectual property. Hence these societies had to offer them positions of privilege to keep them from going elsewhere. The scientists, in turn, were always easily tempted by the riches society could offer them, even if it meant pursuing science harmful to humanity as a whole. While agricultural and industrial property can be socialized—by choice or by force—and transferred to the possession of the state, intellectual property, in contrast, typically cannot. In this play Brecht works to find a way out of this impasse. Science has to come up with a method that takes it out of the hands of the few and puts it into the hands of the masses. As we witness the maturation of the naïve Andrea Sarti, the lower-class boy who has become Galileo's student and subsequent heir to his method of research and teaching, we also witness the emergence of a new type of scientist, one who enables the masses to advance the progress of science rather than excluding them from the process. This is one of the main lessons Sarti learns from his teacher Galileo.

The other is Galileo's method of doing research, which in Brecht's view represents a universal method for all sciences, as well as for the arts. It is a way of looking at natural, social, and aesthetic processes as if for the first time, by adopting a point of view in which nothing seems "natural." Galileo's research and teaching method not only constitutes a new, socialized way of doing science, but also embodies Brecht's own theory and practice of the theater, a theater committed to teaching the spectator how to analyze processes and discover the forces behind them.

The play is also about how science continues to decenter the human being. Just as Galileo's teachings took the planet inhabited by humans out of the center of the universe, so Charles Darwin (1809–1882), Karl Marx (1818–1883), and Sigmund Freud (1856–1939) decentered what had previously been thought of as the autonomous, self-determined individual at the center of human actions. This decentering, Brecht thought, would also pave the way for the development of the human species into a truly social one, thus dissolving the contours of the bourgeois individual.

Finally, one can speculate that the play is also about the Moscow trials (1936–1938) that were occurring as the first version of the play was taking shape. If this is not the case, then the drama points to Brecht's own ideological blind spots, that is, the fact that he could have believed that those trials bore no similarities to what Galileo, the avant-garde thinker, faced when confronted by the guardians of orthodoxy. If Galileo's fate in the face of the Inquisition did not remind Brecht of the dangers some of his own friends were facing in a Soviet Union dominated by the paranoid Joseph Stalin (1879–1953), then we are left to think that the view of things Brecht intended to teach others sometimes failed the playwright himself.

FURTHER READING

Paulsell, Patricia R. "Brecht's Treatment of the Scientific Method in His *Leben des Galilei.*" *German Studies Review* 11, no. 2 (1988): 267–284.

Suvin, Darko. "Heavenly Food Denied: 'Life of Galileo.'" In *The Cambridge Companion to Brecht*, ed. by Peter Thomson and Glendyr Sacks. Cambridge: Cambridge Univ. Press, 1994. 139–152.

White, John J. *Brecht: Leben des Galilei*. London: Grant & Cutler, 1996.

Friedemann J. Weidauer

THE LIFE OF MAN

The Life of Man (*Zhizn' cheloveka*, 1906) is often seen as the point at which LEONID ANDREEV broke with REALISM and the group around MAKSIM GORKY at the Znanie publishing house. According to some commentators, Andreev's reaction to the 1905 revolution led to a rapprochement with the poetics of Russian SYMBOLISM.

Andreev originally conceived of *The Life of Man* as the first of a cycle of plays that would deal with the life of man and humanity: "After *The Life of Man* comes 'human life,' which will be depicted in four plays: *Tsar Hunger, War, Revolution,* and *God, the Devil, and Man.*" Of these, only *The Life of Man* and *Tsar Hunger* were realized, but Andreev's remarks suggest the philosophical breadth of his original conception.

Andreev wrote *The Life of Man* in only twelve days while he was living in Berlin in the autumn of 1906. From his pen issued a new dramatic form that many heralded as a new type of drama. Andreev abandoned development of dramatic conflict as such. In its stead he placed stylized tableaux of representative moments in a human life. A mysterious character identified only as "Someone-in-gray" begins the play by delivering a prologue. He argues that the protagonist, called simply "Man," will complete "a circle of iron predestination" in the course of his life. The five tableaux that follow chart "Man's" course around this circle, but they also reveal his inner rebellion against the life into which he is born in the first tableau. At each stage of his life Man grows, develops, and matures to a chorus of commentary in the background. A group of old midwives at his birth, the company of his peers at the height of his success, and a band of drunkards at his death help shape the gray norm of life for the audience. Against this background Man sets himself apart, struggling through poverty and want to achieve success as an architect. His success proves short lived when his son is killed by a random act of violence. Man counters the law of inevitability set forth by "Someone-in-gray" with a curse, his only weapon in an unequal battle. Yet at his death Man attains some measure of victory by not acquiescing.

The play and the new dramatic form that encased it drew the attention of some of Russia's leading directors. VSEVOLOD MEYERHOLD staged *The Life of Man* at the Komissarzhevskaia Theater. The production elicited praise from some symbolists, ALEKSANDR BLOK and Andrei Bely in particular, but met a torrent of vituperation in the press. Andreev was not wholly satisfied with Meyerhold's staging, even though he readily acknowledged its merits. He pinned his hopes on KONSTANTIN STANISLAVSKY and the MOSCOW ART THEATRE. Stanislavsky himself remained ambivalent about that production, but it garnered extravagant praise in the press, and many saw it as a turning point in the history of the theater. Konstantin Mardzhanov's production, which toured through Kharkov, Kiev, and Odessa, called forth an intense reaction from reactionary political groups, which actually tried to shut down the performances. After a long period of neglect during the Soviet era, *The Life of Man* has again attracted attention after perestroika.

[*See also* Russia and the Soviet Union]

FURTHER READING

Andreyeff, Leonid. *The Life of Man*. In *Plays*, tr. by C. L. Meader and F. N. Scott. London: Duckworth, 1915.

——. *The Life of Man*. Tr. by Thomas Seltzer. In *Representative Continental Dramas—Revolutionary and Transitional*, ed. by Montrose J. Moses. Boston: Little, Brown, 1924.

Kaun, Alexander Samuel. *Leonid Andreyev: A Critical Study*. New York: Huebsch, 1924. Repr., New York: Bks. for Libs., 1969.

Newcombe, Josephine Marjorie. *Leonid Andreyev*. Letchworth: Bradda, 1972; New York: Ungar, 1973.

Woodward, James B. *Leonid Andreyev: A Study*. Oxford: Oxford Univ. Press, 1969.

Timothy C. Westphalen

LIFE WITH FATHER

HOWARD LINDSAY enjoyed reading aloud to his wife, the actress Dorothy Stickney, whose eyesight was weakened by a childhood illness. Reciting passages from Clarence Day, Jr.,'s memoir *Life with Father*, Lindsay became convinced that there was a play in it, although dramatizing it would be difficult since it was not an ordered, sequential biography but an informal series of casually related episodes. The pieces first appeared separately in the *New Yorker*, *Harper's*, and The *New Republic*. The problem for the dramatist was to stitch these pieces together so artfully that none of the seams would show.

Lindsay and his partner Russel Crouse spent almost a year talking it out, never writing a line, then wrote the play in seventeen days. Lindsay would pace around his brownstone acting out dialogue while Crouse typed it. Still, it was a true collaboration. They could not remember which author wrote which lines or evolved a scene.

Life with Father is easily summarized. In the late 1880s an upper-middle-class couple, Clarence and Vinnie Day, live in a lovely house in midtown Manhattan with their four sons, who range in age from six to seventeen. Father is volatile but loving and tries to rule the house in a benevolently authoritarian way. Such plot as there is revolves around Mother Day's determination to have Father—whose parents had neglected the ritual in his childhood—consent to be baptized, and the need of the oldest son, Clarence, Jr., to acquire a suit of his own since he can do nothing in the hand-me-down from his father that the elder Day would not do, such as kneel at the feet of the girl he fancies. In the end Mother triumphs, and Clarence, Jr., kneels in his new suit.

One may wonder how such a slight piece became what is still the longest-running nonmusical play on Broadway. Opening at the Empire Theatre on November 8, 1939, with Mr. and Mrs. Lindsay as the Days, it continued for 3,224 performances, closing at the Alvin on July 12, 1947. Two highly profitable touring companies were formed soon after the New York opening. Lindsay found several reasons for the longevity, calling it "such a purely American play that I feel it has a sort of subdued patriotic appeal. . . . Then, too, children like it because they see their elders in a state of perpetual strife and uproar, a circumstance unfailingly amusing to the young. Then it is a COMEDY of historic manners, and it is immaculately clean." *New York Times* critic Brooks Atkinson called it a perfect comedy, "Father is a representative parent with a warm regard for his sons and a real affection for his wife. If Mr. Lindsay and Mr. Crouse were less discerning as playwrights, Father might have emerged as a cheapjack bully to be played only for laughs. But they treat him with relish and respect."

Considering its phenomenal initial reception, the play has not had an impressive afterlife, with only one New York revival, a twenty-two-performance limited run at the City Center in 1967. There were countless productions by regional and summer theaters, colleges and amateur groups, but it is rarely produced today.

[*See also* United States, 1929–1940]

FURTHER READING

Atkinson, Brooks. "The Play: Clarence Day's 'Life with Father' Dramatized by Howard Lindsay and Russel Crouse." *New York Times* (November 9, 1939): 26.

Shipley, Joseph T. *Guide to Great Plays*. Washington, D.C.: Public Affairs Press, 1956.

Taubman, Howard. " 'Father' Looks at 'Life': Long-Running Play's Co-Author Recalls Its Beginnings." *New York Times* (October 16, 1967): 58.

Woollcott, Alexander. "What the Doctor Ordered." *Ladies' Home Journal* (May 1941): 20–21, 55–56.

Roderick Bladel

LI JIANWU (1906–1982)

Born on August 17, 1906, in Shanxi Province, CHINA, Li Jianwu is generally viewed as a productive Chinese modern writer, dramatist, literary critic, and great translator of the first half of the 20th century. He was born into a family educated and talented in letters. In 1925 he entered Tsinghua University in Beijing, first majoring in Chinese literature and later transferring to the Western Literature Department. In 1931 he went to FRANCE to study French literature. After he returned to China from France, he held a number of academic positions.

Li came to prominence as a writer after producing a large number of prose writings, novels, literary critiques, and particularly the dramas that he adapted or translated from the masterpieces of French and Russian drama. His unique translation skills gained him a good reputation in the Chinese circle of translation, literature, and drama.

His original dramas of the late 1930s and the 1940s were a remarkable contribution to 20th-century Chinese theater. The majority of Li's plays were greatly conditioned by the social reality and political scenario of early-20th-century China. For most of the time he remained a writer of straightforward, single-act plays of Ibsenesque REALISM. Many of his plays presented vivacious pictures of implacable conflicts and confrontations between evil and virtue, the oppressed common people and the oppressing power of feudalism and imperialism. His dramatic appeal lay in compassionate understanding of and a great sensitivity toward mostly poor rural people, as he conveyed successfully to his audiences the universally amusing and simultaneously agonizing quality of ordinary human nature under both mundane circumstances and wartime surroundings. For instance, *Liang Yunda*, a one-act play of rural passion, told a daunting yet moving story of murder—a son (Liang Yunda) killed his father for a fortune at other people's instigation. The play presented the son's internal struggle and constant shift between his evil desire and unraveling guilt. Li's marvelous presentation of the son's unraveling state of mind owes much to his well-sprung dialogue, which included dialectisms appropriate to the location and plain vulgarisms natural to the people who utter them. Li Jianwu was a fine playwright writing for the local audience and his people. He died on November 24, 1982, in China.

SELECT PLAYS: *Liang Yunda (Liang Yunda*, 1934); *The Role Model (Yisheng zuoze*, 1936); *The New Pedant (Xin xuejiu*, 1937); *The Springtime (Zhe bu guo shi chuntian*, 1937); *Thirteen Years (Shi san nian*, 1939); *The Signal (Xinhao*, 1942); *Lilien (Huang hua*, 1944); *The Horse Thief (Caomang ji*, 1945); *The Autumn (Qiu*, 1946); *The Youth (Qingchun*, 1948)

FURTHER READING

Gunn, Edward. "Shanghai's 'Orphan Island' and the Development of Modern Drama." In *Popular Chinese Literature and Performing Arts in the People's Republic of China, 1949–1979*, ed. by Bonnie S. McDougall. Berkeley: Univ. of California Press, 1984. 36–53.

Han Shishan. *Li Jianwu*. Beijing: Zhongguo huaqiao chubanshe, 1999.

Li Jianwu. *It's Only Spring; and, Thirteen Years*. Tr. by Tony Hyder. London: Bamboo/UNESCO, 1989.

——. *Li Jianwu daibai zuo* [The representative works of Li Jianwu]. Ed. by Li Yifei. Beijing: Huaxia chubanshe, 1999.

——. *Li Jianwu juzuo xuan* [The selected plays of Li Jianwu]. Beijing: Zhongguo xiju chubanshe, 1982.

——. *Li Jianwu xiju pinglun xuan* [The selected drama criticism of Li Jianwu]. Beijing: Zhongguo xiju chubanshe, 1982.

——. *Springtime* [*Qingchun*]. Tr. by David Pollard. In *Twentieth-Century Chinese Drama: An Anthology*, ed. by Edward M. Gunn. Bloomington: Indiana Univ. Press, 1983. 174–227.

Pollard, D. E. "Li Chien-Wu and Modern Chinese Drama." *Bulletin of the School of Oriental and African Studies* 39, no. 2 (1976): 346–388.

Ping Fu

LILIES

First produced in French as *Les feluettes ou La répétition d'un drame romantique, Lilies; or, The Revival of a Romantic Drama* is perhaps the best-known and most successful play of Quebec playwright MICHEL MARC BOUCHARD. Set in the tiny town of Roberval, Quebec, the play starts with Simon Doucet having invited Bishop Jean Bilodeau to a secret meeting. The year is 1952, and the two have not seen each other for forty years, since they were classmates together at Lac-Saint-Jean Catholic School. While Bilodeau has risen in the ranks of the church, earning his place as a respected member of the community, Simon has been languishing in prison for a murder he did not commit. Having finished his sentence, he has assembled a collection of other wrongly accused convicts to perform a play for Bilodeau, taking us back in time to 1912 to tell the story of the events leading up to the murder. Using the popular device of a play-within-a-play, Simon tells the story of his relationship with Count Vallier de Tilly, a young French nobleman, who has recently moved to the town.

Lilies is a complex play, exploring gay sexuality and its repression under the Catholic Church. The piece echoes Bouchard's own life and his strict upbringing in a very religious small town. Simon and Vallier have been lovers for some time, which infuriates Bilodeau, whose own repression prevents him from ever accepting his desires. He constantly quotes his mother, who never appears in the play, about the religious implications of their homosexuality and the scandalous production of their school play, *The Martyrdom of Saint Sebastian*. After a severe beating from his father when he comes to suspect his budding homosexuality, Simon is left with marks resembling Saint Sebastian's arrow wounds. He announces to Vallier that their affair has come to an end and that it is time for him to "think about girls." He decides to marry Lydie-Anne de Rozier, an attractive French woman more than ten years his senior. Vallier later confronts him with his desire, and Simon admits that his pending marriage is a sham. The two make a pact of suicide, like the characters in *Saint Sebastian*, only to have it disrupted by Bilodeau.

The play was first produced in French at Salle Fred-Berry, in Montreal, Quebec, on September 10, 1987, and was directed by André Brassard. The English-language production, translated by Linda Gaboriau, premiered in Toronto, Ontario, at Theatre Passe Muraille on February 1, 1991, and was directed by Brian Richmond. Since then it has been produced by companies across CANADA and in Europe, Asia, and South America. In 1996 Bouchard adapted the play to a film version.

FURTHER READING

Cloutier, Raymond. *Le beau milieu: Chronique d'une diatribe; Propos sur la diffusion du théâtre au centre-ville de Montréal et chronique des réactions du milieu et des médias*. Outremont, Quebec: Lanctot, 1999.

Huffman, Shawn. "L'affect en cachot: La sémiotique des passions et le théâtre québécois d'enfermement chez Michel Marc Bouchard, Normand Chaurette et René-Daniel Dubois." Graduate thesis, Univ. of Toronto, 1998.

Chris Dupuis

LILL, WENDY (1950–)

Playwright and politician Wendy Lill was born in Vancouver, British Columbia, in 1950, though she grew up largely in London, Ontario. Lill did not become a full-time writer until her mid-thirties. After graduating from York University in Toronto in 1970, she wrote while working in various jobs (including being a consultant to the Canadian Mental Health Association in the northern Ontario town of Kenora) before moving to Winnipeg, Manitoba, where she became a full-time writer for CBC Radio in 1979.

Her first play, *On the Line* (1982), addressed the exploitation of female immigrant garment workers in Winnipeg. Encouraged by her rapport with Kim McCaw, director of the Prairie Theatre Exchange, Lill wrote four more plays during her Winnipeg years. *The Fighting Days* (1984) explores the suffragette movement during the early 20th century and critically investigates the multiple perspectives and voices of women activists such as Nellie McClung and Francis Beyn. THE OCCUPATION OF HEATHER ROSE (1986) addresses hegemonic social issues as a well-meaning "white" nurse attempts, yet fails, to "do good" on a remote Native reserve. *Sisters* (1989) is a searing drama about a nun who burns down a school for indigenous people. It examines the disciplinary structures of schools that exist as much to repress the potential of those who go to them as to educate. *All Fall Down* (1993) presents a female day-care worker wrongly accused of sexual abuse by a child psychiatrist. Lill's adaptation of a short story by Antigonish author Sheldon Currie, *The Glace Bay Miners' Museum*, premiered in 1995. This play, concerning a working-class Cape Breton woman, Margaret, whose memories of her life are concretely embodied in her collections of unusual but everyday objects, brought Lill her widest audience yet. Social issues remain in focus in CORKER (1998), where the intertwining links between the family and the social bond are exposed when, in an attempt to improve the system, Merit and Leonard nearly destroy their family.

Lill has also written extensively for radio, magazines, film, and television. She has received two Alliance of Canadian Cinema, Television and Radio Artists (ACTRA) awards, a Golden Sheaf award (for her film *Ikwo*), a Chalmers award, a Gemini award, and four nominations for the Governor General's Literary Award for Drama (*The Occupation of Heather Rose*, *All Fall Down*, *The Glace Bay Miners' Museum*, and *Corker*). Lill has become increasingly involved in political activity in Nova Scotia; in 1997 she ran successfully for a seat in Parliament from Dartmouth, representing the New Democratic Party, CANADA's liberal-socialist third party, from 1997 to 2004. Additionally, she has served as board member with a day-care center and cofounder of the Eastern Front Theatre Company in Dartmouth, Nova Scotia (1993). Her concern for the community is embedded in her plays that focus on localized incidents, but extend to broader audiences and communities. Lill's socially conscious plays align her with JOAN MACLEOD, LINDA GRIFFITHS, MARGARET HOLLINGSWORTH, and SHARON POLLOCK (among others), who continue to give voice to women and feminist issues in Canada.

PLAYS: *On the Line* (1982); *The Fighting Days* (1984); *The Occupation of Heather Rose* (1986); *Memories of You* (1988); *Sisters* (1989); *All Fall Down* (1993); *The Glace Bay Miners' Museum* (1995); *Corker* (1998)

FURTHER READING

Coates, Donna. "Pot Shots to Parting Shots: Wendy Lill's *The Fighting Days*." In *Women, the First World War and the Dramatic Imagination: International Essays (1914–1999)*, ed. by C. Tylee and R. Athfield. Lewiston, N.Y.: Edwin Mellen, 2000. 171–190.

Glaap, Albert-Reiner. "Personal Conflict and Personal Concern in Wendy Lill's *The Occupation of Heather Rose*." *Contemporary Theatre Review* 5 (1996): 135–138.

Nicholas Birns

LI LONGYUN (1948–)

Li Longyun was born in Beijing, CHINA, in 1948 to a working-class family. When he graduated from high school in the summer of 1966, the Cultural Revolution broke out. He and hundreds of thousands of city youth were sent to the Great Northern Wilderness to reclaim the wasteland. In 1979 he was admitted to Nanjing University as a graduate student, studying under the well-known playwright CHEN BAICHEN. Since 1982 he has worked at the Beijing People's Art Theater as a playwright.

During the literary thaw after the Cultural Revolution, Chinese playwrights began to search for new ways of expression to free Chinese drama from the restrictions of the past thirty years. Some of them took modern Western drama, such as the Theater of the Absurd and the EPIC THEATER of BERTOLT BRECHT, as their model. Others revived the tradition of critical realism from the May Fourth period as their guiding principle. Li Longyun belongs to the latter group. His play *Small Well Lane* (*Xiaojing hutong*) is a good example of social criticism combined with local color, a formula first used in LAO SHE's play *Teahouse* (1957). Set in a small alley in Beijing, the play reexamines Chinese political history from the late 1940s to the early 1980s. It shows how the painful experiences of the residents during the Great Leap Forward and the Cultural Revolution contrast sharply with the grandiose visions of their leaders. In the last act the author calls for a community-based democracy—election of the neighborhood committee by the residents—as a safeguard against future disasters. He also voices the wishes of common people living at the bottom of Chinese society: "What do regular folks want? They only want to live, to live a quiet and peaceful life."

When this play was first staged in 1983, it was criticized for focusing only on the bad things the Communist Party did. To prove his critics wrong, Li revised the last act four times to make the ending brighter. Although the controversy over *Small Well Lane* centered on its political content, its strength lies in the human drama it depicts. The author's familiarity with the inhabitants and language of Beijing's back streets enabled him to create a true-to-life portrayal of these characters and to speak for these men and women who have no voice of their own.

The play *Wilderness and Man* (*Huangyuan yu ren*) depicts the experiences of a group of "sent-down" youth in the Great

Northern Wilderness. The action takes place in an imaginary Kingdom of Luomahu, and the time is described as "the space between man's two changes of faith." To emphasize this change, one character in the play is split into two persons: one in the present and another one fifteen years later. This character's transformation from his former self to his future self underlines the theme of man's search for a new faith and a new identity. Unlike most other literature about the subject of the "sent-down" youth, which emphasizes the hardships endured by the young people, this play is a meditation on man's fate and man's relationship with nature.

PLAYS: *There Is a Small Courtyard* (*You zheyang yige xiaoyuan*, 1979); *Small Well Lane* (*Xiaojing hutong*, 1981); *Not Far from the Old Summer Palace* (*Zheli bu yuan shi Yuanming Yuan*, 1982); *Wilderness and Man* (*Huangyuan yu ren*, 1987); *Under the Red Banner* (*Zheng hongqi xia*, 1999); *Call Me Brother, and I Will Be Moved to Tears* (*Jiao wo yisheng ge, wo hui lei luo ru yu*, 2002); *Myriad Twinkling Lights* (*Wanjia denghuo*, 2003)

FURTHER READING

Chen Baichen. "Guanyu *Xiaojing hutong* de tongxin" [Correspondence concerning *Small Well Lane*]. In *Huangyuan yu ren: Li Longyun juzuo xuan*, by Li Longyun. Beijing: Zhongguo shehui kexue chubanshe, 1993. 5–20.

Dong Jian. "Cong minsu huajuan kan lishi fengyun: Lun Li Longyun chuangzuo de tese." In *Zhonguo dangdai juzuojia yangjiu* [Studies of contemporary Chinese dramatists]. Beijing: Wenhua jishu chubanshe, 1986. 1: 117–135.

Li Longyun. *Huangyuan yu ren: Li Longyun juzuo xuan* [Wilderness and man: A collection of Li Longyun's dramatic works]. Beijing: Zhongguo shehui kexue chubanshe, 1993.

——. *Small Well Lane*. Tr. and ed. by Hong Jiang and Timothy Cheek. Ann Arbor: Univ. of Michigan Press, 2002.

——. *Xiaojing hutong* [Small Well Lane]. In *Zhongguo dangdai shi da zheng ju* [Ten contemporary Chinese serious plays], ed. by Wang Jisi et al. Nanjing: Jiangsu wenyi chubanshe, 1993.

——. *Zheng hongqi xia: huaju juben* (Under the Red Banner: A Spoken Play). Beijing: Minzu chubanshe, 2000.

Shiao-ling Yu

LINDSAY, HOWARD (1889–1968), AND RUSSEL CROUSE (1893–1966)

Howard Lindsay brought far more theatrical experience to his first collaboration with Russel Crouse than his partner when they revised the book of the Cole Porter musical *Anything Goes* in 1934. His first theater job as assistant stage manager and actor lasted three years. A turning point came in 1913 when he was hired by the actress and manager Margaret Anglin to be in crowd scenes for films for 50 cents a day. He remained five years and attributed his real professional education to her. Valentine in *Twelfth Night* was his first role on Broadway in 1914. He joined the army in 1918 and staged military entertainments in FRANCE. After the war he directed nineteen plays and musicals on Broadway.

It took Lindsay only twenty years of trying before he had a play produced: *Tommy* in 1927, written in collaboration with Bertrand Robinson. Almost all of his writing was collaborative, with many adaptations. He wrote three other plays before his partnership with Russel Crouse.

Crouse was a newspaper reporter in the Midwest from age seventeen, and was already thirty-five and a columnist for the *New York Post* before he played an eight-line role in *Gentlemen of the Press*. His first writing assignment in the theater was with Oscar Hammerstein II on the book of *The Gang's All Here*, which ran for three weeks. *Hold Your Horses* ran for eleven weeks. Crouse had less than a year of theatrical experience before *Anything Goes*.

A maritime disaster led to the Lindsay-Crouse partnership. *Anything Goes*, written by Guy Bolton and P. G. Wodehouse, was originally a COMEDY about a ship burning at sea. When the SS *Morro Castle* burned and sank in September 1934, the script had to be revised before it could go into rehearsal. Neither Bolton nor Wodehouse was available for the revision, so the musical's director, Howard Lindsay, was asked to do it. Recovering from influenza, he insisted on a collaborator to help him. Crouse was hired because a friend of Cole Porter had a dream about Crouse and recommended him.

Lindsay and Crouse went on to write fourteen more plays and musicals together, almost all of which were critically and financially successful, none more than their masterpiece, LIFE WITH FATHER (1939). Lindsay directed most of them and acted occasionally. They also produced plays written by others, including *Arsenic and Old Lace*, *Hasty Heart*, and *Detective Story*. They worked on films, such as their adaptation of *The Sound of Music* (1959), for which they won a Tony Award. They received a special Tony commemorating their twenty-five-year partnership in 1959. *State of the Union* (1945) was awarded the Pulitzer Prize. None of it might have happened without a shipwreck, a dream, and a case of influenza.

[*See also* United States, 1929–Present]

PLAYS BY HOWARD LINDSAY: *Tommy* (with Bertrand Robinson, 1927); *Your Uncle Dudley* (with Bertrand Robinson, 1929); *Oh, Promise Me* (with Bertrand Robinson, 1930); *She Loves Me Not* (adapted from the novel by Edward Hope, 1930); *A Slight Case of Murder* (with Damon Runyon, 1935)

PLAYS BY RUSSEL CROUSE: *The Gang's All Here* (with Oscar Hammerstein II and Morris Ryskind, 1931); *Hold Your Horses* (with Corey Ford, 1933)

PLAYS BY LINDSAY AND CROUSE: *Anything Goes* (a revision of an earlier version by Guy Bolton and P. G. Wodehouse, with music by Cole Porter, 1934); *Red. Hot and Blue!* (with music by Cole Porter,

1936); *Hooray for What* (with music by Harold Arlen and lyrics by E. Y. Harburg, 1937); *Life with Father* (adapted from stories by Clarence Day, Jr., 1939); *Strip for Action* (1942); *State of the Union* (1945); *Life with Mother* (adapted from stories by Clarence Day, Jr., 1948); *Call Me Madam* (with music by Irving Berlin, 1950); *Remains to Be Seen* (1951); *The Prescott Proposals* (1952); *The Great Sebastians* (1956); *Happy Hunting* (with music by Harold Karr and lyrics by Matt Dubey, 1956); *The Sound of Music* (with music by Richard Rodgers and lyrics by Oscar Hammerstein II, 1959); *Tall Story* (adapted from the novel *The Homecoming Game* by Howard Nemerov, 1959); *Mr. President* (with music by Irving Berlin, 1962)

FURTHER READING

Croner, Ted. "The Mind of the Playwright: A Conversation with Lindsay and Crouse." *Esquire* (July 1957): 36–38.

Crouse, Russel, and Howard Lindsay. "Life with Lindsay and Crouse." *New York Times Magazine* (January 13, 1966): 16, 54.

Roderick Bladel

LINNEY, ROMULUS (1930–)

The theatre can do things that no other art form can—it can put something that seems unbearable in front of you, and you are bettered by it.

—Romulus Linney, 2004

Romulus Linney is an American playwright closely identified with not-for-profit theater, both in New York and around the United States. In spite of his election to the American Academy of Arts and Letters, two Obie awards, one for *Tennessee* (1979) in 1980 and one for sustained excellence in 1992, and his status as the first playwright to whose work the Signature Theatre devoted an entire season, Linney has remained underrated and underrecognized by critics.

Born on September 21, 1930, in Philadelphia, Pennsylvania, Romulus Zachariah Linney V was reared in and around Madison, Tennessee, where he absorbed the cadences of Appalachian speech and the King James Version of the Bible. His childhood profoundly influenced his writing, and he has said, "Everything I have written goes back to when I was a child in some way or other." He graduated from Oberlin College and the Yale School of Drama, where he studied acting and directing before becoming a writer.

Linney's writing may be grouped into three broad categories—historical, personal, and Appalachian. Plays such as *Holy Ghosts* (1974), *Tennessee*, *Heathen Valley* (1986), and *Sand Mountain* (1986) are set in a quasi-mythic Appalachia, in which themes of sex and religion are presented in a mountain-gothic style. *Old Man Joseph and His Family* (1977) traces the life of Jesus to the age of fourteen, drawing on the Apocrypha, the ancient tales not included in the New Testament. In all these plays Linney employs a lyrical, homespun language as a medium for an inner, personal reality, not merely for local color. The working language of the ordinary endows his characters with dignity and humor. While they might live lives of desperation and poverty, Linney never patronizes them as they struggle with each other, with their God, and with the land itself.

Linney's personal plays, such as *April Snow* (1983), in which three mature artists have their hearts broken by young people, and *The Love Suicide at Schofield Barracks* (1972), his only Broadway production to date, display an intense emotional reality and dark, almost Freudian motives that are redolent of 1950s acting training, which perhaps reflect the influence of Linney's tenure as a stage manager at the Actors Studio.

In the historical works, including his first major achievement, *The Sorrows of Frederick* (1966), Linney creates emotional connections with historical subjects by focusing on cathartic experiences at the intersection of life and history. In *Childe Byron* (1977) the poet and his daughter battle over their estrangement; *2* (1990) recounts the friendship between Hermann Goering and one of his guards during the Nuremberg trials, at which Goering initially bested prosecutor Robert Jackson in cross-examination; *Democracy* (1974) and *Esther* (1974), each adapted from novels by Henry Adams, detail the wheelings and dealings of Washington corruption. A recurring theme in all of Linney's work is that of the lone battler against authority, as in *Three Poets* (1989), which looks at the lives of Komachi, a 9th-century Japanese poet; Hrosvitha, the 10th-century Saxon nun; and 20th-century Russian poet Anna Akhmatova. Linney has also written three novels (two of which he has adapted for the stage) and numerous short stories.

[*See also* United States, 1929–Present]

SELECT PLAYS: *The Sorrows of Frederick* (1966); *The Love Suicide at Schofield Barracks* (1972); *Democracy* and *Esther* (adapted from novels by Henry Adams, 1974); *Holy Ghosts* (1974); *Appalachia Sounding* (1975); *Childe Byron* (1977); *Old Man Joseph and His Family* (1977); *Just Folks* (1978); *The Captivity of Pixie Shedman* (1981); *El Hermano* (1981); *F.M.* (1982); *Gardens of Eden* (1982); *Goodbye, Howard* (1982); *April Snow* (1983); *Laughing Stock* (1984); *Wrath* (1985); *Heathen Valley* (adapted from his own novel, 1986); *Sand Mountain* (1986); *A Woman Without a Name* (1986); *Precious Memories* (also known as *Unchanging Love*, adapted from a short story by Anton Chekhov, 1988); *Yancey* (1988); *Three Poets* (includes *Komachi*, *Hrosvitha*, *Akhmatova*, 1989); *2* (1990); *Ambrosio* (freely adapted from Matthew Lewis's 18th-century gothic novel, 1992); *Shotgun* (1994); *Spain* (1994); *True Crimes* (a retelling of Tolstoy's *Power of Darkness*, 1996); *Mock Trial* (1997); *Stars* (1997); *Gint* (adapted from Ibsen's *Peer Gynt*, 1998); *A Lesson Before Dying* (based on the novel by Edward J. Gaines, 2000)

FURTHER READING

Fleming, John. "Facing the Holocaust: Romulus Linney's Examination of Goering at Nuremberg." *Journal of American Drama and Theatre* 11, no. 1 (Winter 1994).

Hurley, Daniel F. "Down in the Valley, the Valley So Low." *Appalachian Journal: A Regional Studies Review* 16, no. 1 (Fall 1988).

——."The Low-Down on a High Place: Family Matters in Heathen Valley." *Appalachian Journal: A Regional Studies Review* 20, no. 2 (Winter 1993).

Schlatter, James F. "Storyteller in the Wilderness: The American Imagination of Romulus Linney." *Southern Quarterly: A Review of Arts in the South* 32, no. 2 (Winter 1994).

Louis Scheeder

LION IN THE STREETS

Lion in the Streets is one of JUDITH THOMPSON's most formally experimental plays. Scenes are linked, not through any explicit content, but through a gesture, a character, an action, or a moment. The play has been described as a "relay" or "daisy-chain," with reference to the almost accidental linkages between scenes. The audience's guide is Isobel, the ghost of a young Portuguese girl, murdered in the neighborhood seventeen years ago. The play is her journey toward her own recognition of her death and, in the final scene of the play, her absolution of the man who murdered her. The other scenes, in their tangential links to Isobel, are of people in her downtown Toronto neighborhood: parents complaining about too much sugar at a day-care center; a woman confronting an inoperable cancer; a man's ambiguous realization and denial of homosexual desires.

The play conveys the sense of a community in distress, individuals often trapped by social roles or their own psychic repressions. Just as the form has the sense of a relay or a handing off, the roles that the characters play also are switched from hero to victim or from victim to oppressor. Sue, for example, is a young woman who at first proves to be Isobel's helper. She rescues Isobel from attacks by other children in the first scene. In a subsequent scene, however, Sue finds out that her husband is having an affair. She tries to get him to come back to her by performing a desperate, public striptease and is humiliated when she is rejected. These shifts in power are clearly linked to the stories that characters tell about themselves and the roles that they take with respect to this narration. Ric Knowles, in "The Achievement of Grace" (1991), describes how the "duelling narratives" pit one character against the other. In this way *Lion in the Streets* makes clear the relationship between narrative and identity: roles can shift according to the way that characters construct their identities through the stories they tell. As in other Thompson plays, Robert Nunn (2001) notes how the shifts between characters and narratives can be cast in a psychoanalytic reading of the play, because the boundaries between inside and outside and self and other are constantly shifting.

Despite the fragmented nature of the play, and Isobel's surreal journey, the individual scenes themselves are exquisitely rendered slices of life. Thompson's ear for dialogue and precise observation of human nature make for compelling interactions between characters. Her particular style in this play combines this keen REALISM with moments of magical and imaginative transformation as Scarlett, a woman with advanced cerebral palsy, gets up from her wheelchair and dances about the room, or as a man transforms into Isobel's mother. Catholic iconography and references are used throughout the play and provide a kind of mythological background for Thompson's storytelling. In this play, as in others, Thompson juxtaposes extremes in the human experience, from loss to hope, from terror to joy, from humiliation to transcendence, shaping the quotidian into the poetic.

[*See also* Canada]

FURTHER READING

Harvie, Jennifer. "Constructing Fictions of an Essential Reality; or, 'This Pickshur Is Niiice': Judith Thompson's *Lion in the Streets*." *Theatre Research in Canada* 13, nos. 1–2 (Spring/Fall 1992): 81–93.

Knowles, Ric. "The Achievement of Grace." *Brick* 41 (Summer 1991): 33–38.

——."The Dramaturgy of the Perverse." *Theatre Research International* 17, no. 3 (1992): 226–235.

——." 'Great lines are a dime a dozen': Judith Thompson's Greatest Cuts." *Canadian Theatre Review* 89 (Winter 1996): 8–18.

Nunn, Robert. "Judith Thompson's Marginal Characters." In *Siting the Other: Re-visions of Marginality in Australian and English-Canadian Drama*, ed. by Marc Maufort and Franca Bellarsi. Brussels: P. Lang, 2001. 311–323.

Wilson, Ann. "The Culture of Abuse in *Under the Skin, This is for You, Anna*, and *Lion in the Streets*." In *Contemporary Issues in Canadian Drama*, ed. by Per Brask. Winnipeg: Blizzard, 1995. 160–170.

Marlene Moser

LITHUANIA

Lithuanian theater can be traced back to its pagan past, when a *vaidila*, or a person who was a combination priest, actor, and minstrel bard, was wreathed and masked for his performance in religious rituals and folk festival celebrations. The role of the *vaidila* evolved over the centuries, and in the Middle Ages he was identified as the chief performer of romantic allegories, miracle plays, and the elaborate street theaters common to the period. After 1795, when Lithuania (which by then had merged with POLAND) fell under Russian rule, theater was inextricably tied to a national yearning for independence, the kindling of Lithuanian patriotism, and resistance to what the citizens recognized as czarist oppression.

By the end of the 19th century the czarist regime forbade literature in the Lithuanian language, one of the reasons for the late emergence of a Lithuanian national DRAMATURGY. At that time thousands of disobedient Lithuanians had been executed for rioting against the Russian Empire, while others were refused the right to their land, schools, writing, and language. RUSSIA's repression, however, led to a resistance movement that held patriotic performances on farms, in rural barns, or on village threshing grounds, where intellectuals and peasants alike gathered to flame the passions of liberation in the people. This new form of theater, called "threshing-house" or "barn theater," also fueled Lithuania's national independence movement.

After 1918, when the modern independent state of Lithuania was founded, theater, as if it had fulfilled its patriotic mission, became a representative and a necessary attribute of the young state. Between the two world wars theater in Lithuanian thrived as a vehicle for artistic expression. This is the "classical" period of Lithuanian theater, when writers such as Maironis (1862–1932), Vincas Krėvė-Mickevičius (1882–1954), Vincas Mykolaitis-Putinas (1893–1967), and Balys Sruoga (1896–1947) wrote TRAGEDIES and dramas based mainly on national history. Petras Vaičiūnas (1890–1959), one of the most popular playwrights of this period, wrote well-made plays about actual events in a distinctively realistic style. During the Soviet occupation in 1940 many Lithuanian playwrights and artists were killed, repressed, or exiled to the West. Writers such as Antanas Škėma (1911–1961), Algirdas Landsbergis (1924–2004), and Kostas Ostrauskas (1926–) adapted modern Western theater techniques to express the painful experience of exile. In 1941, under German occupation, theater in Lithuania virtually disappeared, along with many of its most talented writers, who were executed or sent to concentration camps. One of the more popular plays to survive from this period that is still frequently produced is Škėma's *Ataraxia*, appreciated for its portrayal of people in the midst of occupation, death camps, and forced exiles who manage to find peace and mutual respect for each other in spite of the violence.

The renaissance of Lithuanian drama started in the Khrushchev era when Juozas Grušas (1901–1986) staged his historical play *Herkus Mantas* about the Prussian struggle against the Teutons. Written in 1957, it broke many Soviet taboos. From that time on Lithuanian drama became more influenced by a spiritual resistance against the totalitarian regime. Though Grušas and Justinas Marcinkevičius (1930–) used traditional techniques in their plays, with some innovative elements, Kazys Saja (1932–) is generally considered the first to use the modern dramatic techniques of the time in his plays. By mixing allegorical subjects with sarcasm, he was popularly recognized as one of the new Lithuanian writers. Later Juozas Glinskis (1933–) was influenced by ANTONIN ARTAUD's Theatre of Cruelty. This, combined with his nonconformism, was reason enough for the Soviet censorship to prohibit some of his pieces. In the 1960s and 1970s Saulius Šaltenis (1945–) created a very special kind of drama by presenting onstage an array of simple small-village people, whom he described with lyricism, irony, tenderness, and nostalgia. His nonheroic leading characters had great care for simple values and real feelings in an epoch blanched with propaganda.

In the thirty years from about 1957 to 1988 Lithuanian drama developed rapidly, mastering both contemporary subjects and techniques. Lithuanian playwrights strongly influenced their readers and especially their audiences, and they played a preeminent role in preparing the renewal of independence in 1988. Because of this, the most interesting of them (Saulius Šaltenis, Kazys Saka, Juozas Glinskis, and Vidmantí Jasukaitytė) became members of Parliament, editors of big newspapers, or ministers and ceased writing plays. Between 1988 and 1993 the most important and most interesting dramas in Lithuania were not staged in the theater because the favorite works of critics were adapted to reflect dramatically every period of crisis. Therefore, during this period many Lithuanian theaters "discovered" Western dramas. These "discoveries" and the playwrights' silence were the main reasons why so few Lithuanian plays appeared onstage in the seasons immediately after Lithuania's liberation from the Soviets.

A number of female playwrights emerged in the 1970s and 1980s. Ema Mikulėnaitė (1935–), Gražina Mareckaitė (1939–), Vidmantė Jasukaitytė (1948–), and Jurga Ivanauskaitė (1961–) brought an impressionistic line of writing to Lithuanian playwriting and also highlighted feminist issues of the period. Other new writers include Sigitas Parulskis (1965–) and Mark Zingeris (1947–). Parulskis's *From the Life of the Dead Soul* deals with the spiritual state of society and its people after the Communist era and in its combination of the comic and the grotesque is indicative of the new wave of Lithuanian writers. Likewise, Zingeris's *Around the Fountain* illustrates the impact of Lithuania's reemergence into contemporary Europe and the attempts of the people caught up in extreme social turmoil to maintain their dignity.

Lithuanian theater, earlier isolated from world theater processes and suppressed by the rigor of SOCIALIST REALISM, has seen a rebirth of the so-called theater of relativity promoted by aggressively independent directors nourished by a new sense of aesthetic freedom. Where in its incipient stages Lithuanian theater was grounded in the dogmatism of socialist realism promoted by KONSTANTIN STANISLAVSKY, in the new Lithuania an antinaturalist movement inspired by the influence of BERTOLT BRECHT, VSEVOLOD MEYERHOLD, Evgenij Vachtangov, and Michail Chevhov has recently provided a deeper knowledge of technique and brought new energy to the contemporary Lithuanian stage.

In the autumn of 1988 a festival of Lithuanian drama was organized at the Shiauliai dramatic theater where every Lithuanian theater company presented new work or plays that had been banned, including texts by exiled Lithuanian playwrights. This festival was very important both as a cultural and a political event, stimulating a growing independence movement.

One problem for Lithuanian writers is that they are acutely aware of working in a small language, and this linguistic stricture is sometimes frustrating because Lithuanian writers can only be read or performed by and for Lithuanian audiences, and their works are seldom translated. As a result, many writers are concentrating on nonverbal performances or are moving away from their native language, many into English.

FURTHER READING

Johnson, Jeff. "Kaunas Mažasis Teatras." *Slavic and East European Performance* 18, no. 3 (Fall 1998): 24–27.

——. "Kauno Jaunimo Kamerinis Teatras." *Slavic and East European Performance* 20, no. 3 (Fall 2000): 43–47.

——. "Psycho-drama in the Disco-rama: Tonino Guerra's *Fourth Chair* at Kaunas Mažasis Teatras." *Slavic and East European Performance* 19, no. 3 (Fall 1999): 78–82.

Jeff Johnson

LITTLE EYOLF

Rita: Oh, let's just live our lives out together, as long as we can!

Allmers: Live our lives out, yes. But with nothing to fill them. Waste and emptiness altogether, everywhere I look.

—Act 3

HENRIK IBSEN's three-act play *Little Eyolf* has been characterized as one of his "psychopathological" plays. The characters are introduced as Alfred Allmers, man of letters, his wife Rita, their son Eyolf, aged nine, Alfred's half sister Asta, the road builder Borghejm, who wants to marry Asta, and the strange figure of the Rat-Wife. Eyolf is the family's problem: he is disabled after a fall from a table and has to use a crutch. Eyolf drowns at the end of act 1. The floating crutch and Eyolf's large open eyes seen deep down in the sea are central images suggesting the parents' sense of guilt as they go through a painful process of mourning. Finally they manage to find a joint task. They will open their home to poor children in the neighborhood, the ones who taunted Eyolf and failed to get help when he was drowning. Alfred has abandoned his plans to write a philosophical essay on human responsibility, while Rita changes her appearance, as well as her attitude to social problems.

Little Eyolf deals with a marriage in crisis. The women are portrayed as dependent on men and lacking freedom, even though they are materially well off. The child is the victim of the parents' irresponsibility. The climate in terms of psychology and ideas belongs to an age of great change. The revelation of latent conflicts, the charged tensions between the characters in triangular relationships, and the myth of the family that is unveiled preempt in poetic form insights that Sigmund Freud was later to formulate theoretically in the area of PSYCHOANALYSIS.

A clue to the understanding of the drama is the fact that Asta's half brother used to call her Eyolf when they were small. The two lost their parents early. In order to secure Asta's future, Alfred married the wealthy Rita, but it is Asta to whom he is sexually attracted. He transfers his forbidden love to the child. Rita has to stand sharing Alfred with Eyolf—or with Asta. Rita is jealous and wishes the child dead. She wants her husband's undivided attention, denying the effect of what Alfred calls "the law of change." After Eyolf's death they invite Asta to stay in his place. In this way the triangle can continue, without the characters' realizing the true nature of their relationship. Asta rejects the invitation and leaves with Borghejm. As a parting gift she presents Alfred with a bouquet of water lilies, a clearly symbolic act.

An allegorical element is the Rat-Wife, who has the function of detecting and removing vermin. Indirectly she leads Eyolf to his death. The Rat-Wife adds a fairy-tale dimension to the play.

Little Eyolf is concerned with relationships and expectations established on a false basis, but it is also about the necessity to have something to live for. Contrasting the individual's joy of living with demands for commitment to fellow human beings adds an altruistic tone to the themes of the play. The harmonious ending with the couple reaching an agreement has been considered by some critics as not credible, while others have stressed the theme of the "law of change" and have chosen to read the final lines at face value.

[*See also* Norway]

FURTHER READING

Durbach, Errol. " 'Children of Paradise': Alf, Hedvig, and Eyolf as 'Conceptions of Immortality.' " In *Ibsen the Romantic*. Athens: Univ. of Georgia Press, 1982. 71–103.

Jacobs, Barry. "Ibsen's *Little Eyolf*: Family Tragedy and Human Responsibility." *Modern Drama* 27, no. 4 (1984): 604–615.

Templeton, Joan. "Women Who Live for Love." In *Ibsen's Women*. Cambridge: Cambridge Univ. Press, 1997. 278–291.

Astrid Sæther

THE LITTLE FOXES

In her memoir titled *Pentimento*, LILLIAN HELLMAN observes that *The Little Foxes* "was the most difficult play I ever wrote." Partly based on the playwright's maternal ancestors, it required extensive historical research and went through at least eight drafts. *The Little Foxes* opened at the National Theatre in New York on February 15, 1939. After running for 410 performances on Broadway, it toured the country for years and remains the most frequently revived Hellman play. Reviews were mixed but largely positive; one critic dubbed *Foxes* a "simple MELODRAMA," while another pronounced it a "fine and important American drama." *Foxes* was adapted into both a popular movie and an opera.

The Little Foxes focuses on the Hubbard siblings, Ben, Oscar, and Regina. The year is 1900, and the South is rapidly becoming industrialized; the Hubbards are closing a deal for a mill that will make them rich but further exploit the poor townspeople. As a married woman, Regina has no financial control and summons her ailing husband, Horace Giddens, home from the hospital in a futile attempt to persuade him to participate in the project. When Horace has another heart attack, Regina callously allows him to die. Aware that her brothers have stolen Horace's bonds to help fund their scheme, Regina blackmails them into giving her 75 percent of the family's share of the venture. Her victory is diluted, however, by her idealistic daughter, Alexandra, who vows to leave her mother and fight against the forces of avarice.

The Little Foxes is a realistic play in the anticapitalist tradition of the Depression-era stage. Although Hellman freely uses such melodramatic elements as a broken medicine bottle, she avoids stock villains and heroes: as she explains, she wanted "the audience to recognize some part of themselves in the money-dominated Hubbards." Even well-meaning characters such as Horace and Oscar's wife, Birdie, are guilty of appeasing the Hubbards. The words of the black servant Addie sum up Hellman's moral: "There are people who eat the earth and eat all the people on it. . . . And other people who stand around and watch them eat it. . . . Some-times I think it ain't right to stand and watch them do it." For Hellman, good intentions are never enough. Further, the battle for supremacy between the men and Regina, one of the dramatist's greatest creations, reveals the complex interrelationship between capitalism and gender roles. In order to compete in this male-dominated world, Regina must learn to be even more devious and destructive than they are.

Hellman had envisioned *The Little Foxes* as part of a trilogy. Although she never wrote the sequel, she said that she had intended it to focus on Regina and a "disappointed, a rather angry" Alexandra in the 1920s. But before Hellman became "tired" of the characters, she completed *Another Part of the Forest* (1946), a look at the young Hubbards and their parents in 1880. *Forest* shows how the siblings learn avarice from their father, Marcus, an arrogant man who abuses his wife and sons. *Forest* is an effective drama but no match for *The Little Foxes* in sheer theatrical force.

[*See also* United States, 1860–1940]

FURTHER READING

Barlow, Judith E. Foreword to *The Little Foxes*, by Lillian Hellman. In *Plays by American Women, 1930–1960*, ed. by Judith E. Barlow. New York: Applause Bks., 1994.

Estrin, Mark W., ed. *Critical Essays on Lillian Hellman*. Boston: G. K. Hall, 1989.

Griffin, Alice, and Geraldine Thorsten. *Understanding Lillian Hellman*. Columbia: Univ. of South Carolina Press, 1999.

Hellman, Lillian. *Three: An Unfinished Woman, Pentimento, Scoundrel Time*. Boston: Little, Brown, 1979.

Lederer, Katherine. *Lillian Hellman*. Boston: Twayne, 1979.

Rollyson, Carl. *Lillian Hellman: Her Legend and Her Legacy*. New York: St. Martin's, 1988.

Judith E. Barlow

LITTLE HAM

LANGSTON HUGHES's association with Karamu House in Cleveland resulted in the production of a number of his plays by the Gilpin Players, the drama group named after the legendary African American actor Charles Gilpin. *Little Ham*, which opened on March 24, 1936, is a three-act COMEDY set in Harlem and centered on Hamlet Hitchcock Jones and his romantic entanglement with two female characters, Mattie Bea and Tiny Lee, the proprietor of a beauty parlor. The production featured Festus Fitzhugh as Ham and Irene Reese as Tiny Lee. The play employs dialogue that shows the wit and humor inherent in black vernacular.

Ham, who shines shoes at the Paradise Shining Parlors, gets caught up in the numbers-running game, which is controlled by downtown white gangsters, who use the shoeshine parlor as a front. As the play progresses, Tiny's beauty parlor is the setting for much of the action involving a range of Harlem characters, among them a follower of Father Divine (an actual Harlem minister), a "Harlem racketeer," a "chorus girl," a "West Indian," and a "Lodge Lady." The play depends on increasing conflict between Tiny and Mattie Bea, exemplified in their verbal battle over Ham. His false arrest for allegedly abusing Mattie Bea leads the play into its closing act, set in the legendary Savoy Ballroom in Harlem, where the romantic complications are resolved through a Charleston contest that becomes the final battle, expertise in dancing. When Tiny and Ham win the contest, their romantic fate is sealed as they plan for a prosperous future in the beauty salon business. Ham realizes that it is fortunate when "a man's got the woman he loves" (*Little Ham*, 1935).

Reviewed in such Cleveland newspapers as the *Cleveland Plain Dealer* and the *Cleveland News*, *Little Ham* received favorable comments regarding its presentation of Harlem life, its humor, and its JAZZ elements. Writing for *Variety*, Glenn Pullen (April 8, 1936) recognized Hughes's status as a poet and novelist and was apparently more appreciative of Hughes's folk comedy representations than of his serious racial depictions in *Mulatto*. William McDermott (*Cleveland Plain Dealer*, March 25, 1936) thought that Hughes had replicated Harlem's dance life effectively, but there were also negative remarks concerning the play's ending.

Certain African American critics objected to Hughes's presenting Harlem in supposed stereotypes. At the source of the critical debate was the use of humor to portray African Americans. Harry C. Smith, for example, maligned Hughes's achievement, and a later evaluation by noted African American critic Darwin Turner objected to its "exotic elements" and its failure to show the "serious" side of the community. However, literary critic Fannie Hicklin recognized that humor in *Little Ham* did not erase the underlying social realities of African American life.

[*See also* United States, 1860–1940]

FURTHER READING

Hughes, Langston. *Five Plays*. Ed. by Webster Smalley. Bloomington: Indiana Univ. Press, 1963.

——. *The Plays to 1942: Mulatto to The Sun Do Move*. Ed. by Leslie Catherine Sanders with Nancy Johnston. Vol. 5 of *The Collected Works of Langston Hughes*. Columbia: Univ. of Missouri Press, 2002.

McLaren, Joseph. *Langston Hughes: Folk Dramatist in the Protest Tradition, 1921–1943*. Westport, Conn.: Greenwood Press, 1997.

Nichols, Charles H., ed. *Arna Bontemps–Langston Hughes Letters, 1925–1967*. New York: Dodd, 1980.

Rampersad, Arnold. *The Life of Langston Hughes*. 2 vols. New York: Oxford Univ. Press, 1986, 1988.

Turner, Darwin. "Langston Hughes as Playwright." *College Language Association Journal* 11 (June 1968): 301–302.

Joseph McLaren

LITTLE THEATER MOVEMENT

Little theater, or small theater (*xiao juchang*), in the Chinese context describes a late-20th-century phenomenon in "spoken drama" or modern theater. Differentiated from traditional operatic theater, as well as the mainstream of modern theater, little theater identified itself as an intellectual theater. The premiere of *The Alarm Signal* (*Juedui xinghao*) in 1982 is generally accepted as its inauguration. Directed by the Beijing People's Art Theatre's art director, Lin Zhaohua (1936–), *The Alarm Signal* explores an alternative theatricality from the then-dominant socialist realist mode of representation. Stripping the stage of naturalistic stage setting and action, Lin borrows the spatial structuring from traditional operatic theater in the form of symbolic actions. In narrative structure and thematic interest Lin draws largely from French existential theater, placing his emphasis on existential and philosophical inquiries. A majority of his 1990s productions consist of reinterpretation of classics of European theater, including an expressionist production of *Hamlet* and an ANTON CHEKHOV/SAMUEL BECKETT synthesis THREE SISTERS; WAITING FOR GODOT (*San jiemei; Dengdai geduo*, 1998—*Three Sisters* and *Waiting for Godot* are staged simultaneously on the same stage).

Drama critics retroactively categorize experimental/small theater of the 1980s as exploration theater. In the meantime, the 1990s saw the proliferation and diversification of small theaters. Mou Sen (1963–), the director of the independent Drama Workshop (Xiju chejian), is noticeable for his borrowing from nondramatic arts. This aspect of his stage experiment is exemplified by *File O* (*Ling dang'an*, 1994), which was premiered in Brussels in 1994. Using a personnel archive as a central metaphor, the play unveils the discursive formation of one's official and personal identity in Chinese society. The fragmentation of the individual that is embedded in the social identity construction is played out as much by the characters mechanically reciting their life stories as by stage apparatus such as wires and fences that visualize segmentation, confinement, and forced selection. Mou Sen's stage experiments, which borrow heavily from performing arts, come close to AVANT-GARDE theater of the West.

Meng Jinghui (1965– born in Beijing) led the most dynamic branch of small theater in the 1990s. A Central Drama Academy graduate, Meng started with reproductions of the Theater of the Absurd by European playwrights such as Samuel Beckett's *Waiting for Godot*, EUGÈNE IONESCO'S THE BALD SOPRANO, JEAN GENET'S THE BALCONY, and HAROLD PINTER'S *The Dumb Waiter*. Meng retains the existential skepticism of the original but relocates the plays in a contemporary Chinese setting, which enhances the sense of alienation and absurdity in an everyday understanding of the world. A comparable carnival playfulness is applied in Meng's contemporary touch-up of a classical Chinese theatrical piece, *Si Fan* (*Si fan*, 1998).

At the prime of his career, Meng Jinghui openly challenges intellectual elitism. Meng characterizes his stage work as "something new, non-existent . . . something different from state-run theatre, from those taught at drama academy" (2000). In practice, he combines popular song, street talk, and amateur-style performance. His signature work of this period includes a production of THE ACCIDENTAL DEATH OF AN ANARCHIST (*Yi ge wuzhengfu zhuyi zhe yiwai siwang*, 1998) and *Rhinoceros in Love* (*Lian'ai de xiniu*, 1999).

[*See also* China]

FURTHER READING

Meng, Jinghui. *Xianfeng xiju dang'an* [Archive of avant-garde theater]. Beijing: Zuojia chubanshe, 2000.

Yu, Shiao-Ling S., ed. and tr. *Chinese Drama After the Cultural Revolution, 1979–1989*. Lewiston, N.Y.: Edwin Mellen, 1996. [Contains *The Alarm Signal* and commentary.]

Donghui He

LIU CHING-MIN (1956–)

Born in Hsinchu (Xinzhu), Taiwan, on September 16, 1956, Liu Ching-min (who has adopted the name Liu Ruo–yu) is one of the most influential female playwrights and theater practitioners in contemporary Taiwan. During the experimental theater movement of the 1970s and 1980s she was a key player in the Lan Ling Ensemble (Lan Ling Jufang, the leading experimental group at that time). After earning a B.A. in drama at Chinese Culture University (1981), she went to the UNITED STATES and studied with Jerzy Grotowski. The Grotowski experience, with its concept of "POOR THEATER" and its system of physical training, has had a major impact on her works.

One of the basic concepts of Grotowski's "poor theater" is returning to the basic resources—the actor's body. Liu started as an actor; her major acting credits include *A New Match for Hezhu* (*Hezhu xinpei*, 1979) and *Secret Love for the Peach Blossom*

Spring (Anlian taohuayuan, 1986). Liu's acting approach combines the movements of Beijing opera, folk dance, slapstick, and acrobatics. This style appears very different from the acting in earlier spoken drama in Taiwan, which relied on a rather declamatory style, with very limited physical movement.

An emphasis on the body certainly plays an important part in Liu's own theater experimentation. In 1988 she founded the U Theatre in the mountains outside Taipei (U stands for the Chinese character *you*, which means both "excellence" and, in ancient China, "actor"). U Theatre is both physical and metaphysical. Her actors receive vigorous and unique training—a combination of physical training and spiritual cultivation. Tai chi, dance, folk arts, drumming, martial arts, Zen Buddhism, and meditation are all part of her way of "doing" theater. Liu's theater is born from "doing," rather than from "thinking" or "planning." Her philosophy of "doing" theater puts the emphasis on rehearsal, improvisation, and learning from and growing with the self and the environment. The creation of the performance is a long process, sometimes years long, and the performance itself is a kind of pilgrimage that emphasizes spiritual growth and self-cultivation. The group members have traveled in mountainous areas in Taiwan on foot and visited INDIA and the Himalayas. While most experimental theaters are located in the trendy parts of Taipei, Liu has taken her audiences to parks, temple spaces, or remote mountain areas—very often, going to a U performance is itself a kind of pilgrim's progress. With her use of natural resources and space and her emphasis on the actor's body and spiritual cultivation, Liu indeed offers a unique theater experience for her audiences.

After the drumming master Huang Zhiqun (Huang Zhiwen) joined the group in 1993, drumming became an important part for actors' training and path for self-cultivation. "Sacred Drumming of U" (Youren shengu) thus became the synonym for the group since then.

Highlights of Liu's works with U Theatre include *The Water Mirror* (*Shuijing*) series (1992–1993). *The Sword of Dandelion* (*Pugongying zhi jian*, 1994) is the story of a swordsman's self-cultivation and self-discovery. In *The Sound of the Ocean* (*Tinghai zhi xin*, 1997) actors use various types of drums and other percussion instruments to represent all types of water, such as streams, rivers and oceans. *Flower with Smile* (*Nian hua*, 2002) is the story of a warrior's spiritual pursuit and Buddhist enlightenment. She also tours internationally with her pieces and generally receives strongly positive responses.

SELECT PLAYS (by Liu Ching-Min and U-Theatre): *Notes from the Underground/Faust* (*Dixiashi shouji Fushide*, 1988); *The River Journey, I and II* (*Shuo jihua*, 1989–1990); *The Water Mirror* (*Shuijing*, 1992–1993); *The Sword of Dandelion* (*Pugongying zhi jian*, 1994); *Growing Flowers* (*Zhonghua*, 1997); *The Sound of the Ocean* (*Tinghai zhi xin*, 1997); *Song of the Wilderness* (*Kuangye zhi ge*, 1999); *Flower with Smile* (*Nian Hua*, 2002); *Dance with You* (*Yuni gongwu*, 2006)

FURTHER READING

Chung, Mingder. "The Little Theatre Movement of Taiwan (1980–1989): In Search of Alternative Aesthetics and Politics." Ph.D. diss., New York Univ., 1992.

Liu, Ching-min. *Mother's Water Mirror*. Tr. by Jane C. C. Lai and Martha P. Y. Cheung. In *An Oxford Anthology of Contemporary Chinese Drama*, ed. by Martha P. Y. Cheung and Jane C. C. Lai. New York: Oxford Univ. Press, 1997. 559–580.

Liu, Ching-min, and Li Gufang. "Yishu zhuiqiu shifou hui ganrao lingxing xiuxing" [Will pursuit of art interfere with spiritual cultivation?] [Conversation between Liu Ching-min and Lin Gufang] (June 28, 2004). http://www.utheatre.org.tw/essay/list.php?page=1.

Daphne Lei

LIU SANJIE See THIRD SISTER LIU

LIVETS SPIL See THE GAME OF LIFE

LIVING THEATRE

Make something useful. Nothing else is interesting. . . . To serve the audience, to initiate experience, to make the heart pound . . . To provide the useful event that will help us.

—Julian Beck

In 1947 Julian Beck and Judith Malina established the Living Theatre, the oldest extant radical theater collective in the UNITED STATES. From 1951 to 1955 Beck and Malina's goal was "to bring poetry back into the theatre" by producing such works as GERTRUDE STEIN's *Dr. Faustus Lights the Lights* (1951). Influenced later by ANTONIN ARTAUD, ERWIN PISCATOR, and BERTOLT BRECHT, they produced JACK GELBER's *The Connection* (1959) and Kenneth Brown's *The Brig* (1963) at their 14th Street Theatre. Both productions brought recognition to them and transformed interactions between actors and spectators. *The Connection* depicted the underside of jazz musicians' and junkies' worlds. *The Brig*, which Malina staged behind a proscenium-high fence, exposed the brutality of a U.S. Marines prison. In 1963 federal authorities closed them down, citing tax evasion.

From 1964 to 1968 the Living Theatre toured Europe to acclaim and evolved "collective creations": *Mysteries and Smaller Pieces* (1964), *Frankenstein* (1965), *Antigone* (1967), and *Paradise Now* (1968). The company's anti–Vietnam War activism was a driving force behind these productions. Experimentation with drugs, sex, and a tribal lifestyle were central to the group's vision of "the peaceful, non-violent revolution." In 1968–1969 the Living Theatre returned to the United States. Audience response varied widely; some found the message and methods out of synch with political urgencies. Shortly after, it returned to Europe and split into four subgroups with different missions. In 1970 Beck and Malina's group went to BRAZIL. They created street theater with people of the shantytowns, rejecting middle-class venues and values. Thirteen months later the company was arrested on drug charges, imprisoned, and freed after international outcry. Street performance continued as a focus when the company returned to the United States and worked on the *Legacy of Cain* plays in Pittsburgh (1975). In 1984, after extensive touring in Europe, the Living Theatre presented a brief, unsuccessful run of four plays at the Joyce Theatre in New York City.

After Beck's death from cancer in 1985, Hanon Reznikov became co-director of the company with Malina. In 1989 the company opened the Third Street Theatre, where it produced poetic theater, street spectacles, and community-based performances; it closed in 1992. Since 1994 a small group of stalwarts has presented Malina's anti–death penalty *Not in My Name* in Times Square whenever an execution takes place in the United States. In 1995, with funding from the Italian government, the Living Theatre established a home in Rochetta, ITALY. The company continues to tour, co-creating *A Day in the Life of the City* with communities around the world.

FURTHER READING

Beck, Julian. *The Life of the Theatre*. San Francisco: City Lights, 1972.

Biner, Pierre. *The Living Theatre: A History Without Myths*. Tr. by Robert Meister. New York: Avon Bks., 1972.

Malina, Judith. *The Diaries of Judith Malina, 1947–1957*. New York: Grove, 1984.

——. *The Enormous Despair*. New York: Random, 1972.

Sainer, Arthur. *The New Radical Theatre Notebook*. New York: Applause, 1997.

Tytell, John. *The Living Theatre: Art, Exile, and Outrage*. New York: Grove, 1995.

Cindy Rosenthal

LOCHHEAD, LIZ (1947–)

Poet and playwright Liz Lochhead is one of SCOTLAND's most renowned contemporary literary figures. Born in Motherwell, Lanarkshire, on December 26, 1947, she was raised in a Protestant family, an experience she describes in her autobiographical piece "A Protestant Girlhood" (1977). From 1965 to 1970 she studied painting and drawing at the Glasgow School of Art, but her attention soon changed to writing. She attended various writers' groups, including that of critic and poet Philip Hobsbaum, through which she befriended fellow writers James Kelman, Tom Leonard, and Alasdair Gray.

Lochhead's first collection of poetry, *Memo for Spring* (1972), won a Scottish Arts Council award. For several years Lochhead lectured in fine art before becoming a full-time writer and leaving for Toronto as part of the first Scottish Arts Council and Canadian Writers Exchange Fellowship in 1978. That year also saw the publication of her second collection of poetry, *Islands*. A third volume, *The Grimm Sisters*, was published in 1981. The dramatic quality that marks Lochhead's poetry was to develop further, and she moved on to writing monologues, performance pieces, and revues. The Edinburgh Festival of 1982 staged her first full-length play, *Blood and Ice*, based on Mary Shelley's *Frankenstein*. Since then the festival has hosted several of Lochhead's plays, including MARY QUEEN OF SCOTS GOT HER HEAD CHOPPED OFF in 1987, *Medea* in 2000, and, most recently, *Thebans* in 2003.

Lochhead sees the theater as playing a crucial part in Scotland's modern revival. She is actively involved in the struggle for a Scottish National Theatre, which would reestablish a dramatic tradition that was brought to an abrupt end by the Reformation. In line with a wider postmodern tendency to critically reexamine historical narratives, Lochhead refuses to present a simple account of common myths. Accordingly, her adaptations of classic plays are written from a contemporary, feminist, and Scottish perspective. The results are dramatizations of characters such as Dracula, Medea, and Mary Stuart that not only explore individual predicaments but at the same time apply to modern times and, in particular, to present-day Scotland.

This contemporary political relevance is primarily achieved through the use of language. Like many Scottish writers, Lochhead puts great emphasis on the importance of finding a uniquely Scottish voice. Using a variety of registers, ranging from colloquial Scots dialects to educated "standard" English, she examines the heterogeneous nature of language. The lively dialogues that characterize her plays not only give them enormous energy, but simultaneously underscore notions of national identity, gender, and social background. Lochhead's political involvement is further illustrated by numerous, often comic allusions to present-day Scotland.

The success of her plays with international audiences at the Edinburgh Festivals demonstrates a wider appeal and relevance that extend far beyond Scottish borders. The most important reasons for the broader popularity of Lochhead's plays, however, are their extreme vigor, their variety in tone and style, and their great wit.

In addition to poetry and stage plays, Lochhead has written numerous dramatic works for radio and television and a wide range of performance pieces. She lives in Glasgow, where she teaches creative writing at the university.

SELECT PLAYS: *Blood and Ice* (1982); *Dracula* (1985); *Tartuffe: A Translation into Scots from the Original by Molière* (1986); *Mary Queen of Scots Got Her Head Chopped Off* (1987); *Quelques Fleurs* (1991); *Perfect Days* (1998); *Medea* (2000); *Miseryguts* (2002); *Thebans* (2003); *Good Things* (2004)

FURTHER READING

Crawford, R., and A. Varty, eds. *Liz Lochhead's Voices*. Edinburgh: Edinburgh Univ. Press, 1993.

Findlay, B., ed. *A History of Scottish Theatre*. Edinburgh: Polygon, 1998.

Gifford, D., and D. McMillan, eds. *A History of Scottish Women's Writing*. Edinburgh: Edinburgh Univ. Press, 1997.

Stevenson, R., and G. Wallace, eds. *Scottish Theatre Since the Seventies*. Edinburgh: Edinburgh Univ. Press, 1996.

Astrid Van Weyenberg

LOHER, DEA (1964–)

I am most interested in entirely normal and average people who—by accident, unfortunate coincidences or special circumstances—suddenly find themselves in situations unpleasant to them.

—Dea Loher, 1998

Dea Loher was born on April 20, 1964, in Traunstein, GERMANY, and grew up in a remote forest home in Bavaria, Germany. In 1983 she began her studies in German and philosophy at the University of Munich, graduating with an M.A. in 1988. That same year she turned to writing plays. Loher spent 1989 in Brazil, an experience that strongly influenced her first play, *Olga's Room* (*Olgas Raum*, 1992), which is based on historical facts. In the 1930s the Russian Comintern sent the Jewish Communist leader Olga Benario (1908–1942) to BRAZIL, whence she was deported to Germany, interned in concentration camps, and gassed to death.

Olga's Room is one example of Loher's recurring dramatization of ambivalent victim-perpetrator relationships. This theme informs *Bluebeard—Hope of Women* (*Blaubart—Hoffnung der Frauen*, 1997), a play whose name derives from the serial killer, as well as from OSKAR KOKOSCHKA's (1886–1980) drama *Murderer, Hope of Women* (*Mörder, Hoffnung der Frauen*, 1909). Loher questions whether Bluebeard initiates his crimes or is driven to commit murder by his female victims. Similarly, in *Adam Geist* (1998) the title character is at first humiliated and isolated by his surroundings and later rapes a woman with whom he has fallen in love. He is simultaneously victim and perpetrator.

Tattoo (*Tätowierung*, 1992) marked Loher's breakthrough; the play has been translated into several languages and performed in various European countries. *Tattoo* portrays the desperate relationship between an incestuous father and his sexually abused daughter. *Clara's Relationships* (*Klara's Verhältnisse*, 1999) presents protagonists in search of themselves and the meaning of life, unable to reach out to their surroundings to find answers. The play demonstrates how, despite good intentions, circumstances force the characters to make mistakes.

Leviathan (1993) presents the development of Ulrike Meinhof (1934–1976), a leader of the Baader-Meinhof terrorist group. *Stranger's House* (*Fremdes Haus*, 1995) dramatizes the turmoil a Macedonian soldier experiences fleeing to Germany. The classical Medea myth provides the backdrop for *Manhattan Medea* (1999), which takes place in present-day New York City and portrays the destiny of Balkan refugees. *The Third Sector* (*Der dritte Sektor*, 2001) depicts how a seamstress and a cook continue to humiliate each other after their employer, who had previously tormented them, passes away.

In *Magazine of Luck* (*Magazin des Glücks*, 2002) Loher experiments more with theatrical forms: the audience is asked to become involved in the play's plot. *Magazine of Luck* consists of a series of short scenes that were performed every couple of weeks at the Thalia Theater in Hamburg. These interactive, multimedia performances function as a farce of reality television, soaps, contemporary movies, and folk theater. In *Sanka*, short for *Sanitätskraftwagen* (ambulance) (2002), for instance, members of the audience receive flyers from undertakers and are then escorted as patients into an ambulance, while actors simultaneously film the audience's participation. Other plays in this series addressing current events include *War Zone* (2002), *Samurai* (2002), *The Scissors* (*Die Schere*, 2002), *Dog* (*Hund*, 2002), and *Hands* (*Hände*, 2002).

Loher refuses to accept the label "political writer," arguing that many of her contemporaries who have been categorized in this way have had short-lived successes. Loher's plays typically contain sequences of monologues that are symmetrically organized. The texts are rhythmical, highly compressed, and often intensified by passages spoken in chorus.

SELECT PLAYS: *Olga's Room* (*Olgas Raum*, 1992); *Tattoo* (*Tätowierung*, 1992); *Leviathan* (1993); *Stranger's House* (*Fremdes Haus*, 1995); *Bluebeard—Hope of Women* (*Blaubart—Hoffnung der Frauen*, 1997); *Adam Geist* (1998); *Clara's Relationships* (*Klaras Verhältnisse*, 1999); *Manhattan Medea* (1999); *The Third Sector* (*Der dritte Sektor*, 2001); *Dog* (*Hund*, 2002); *Magazine of Luck* (*Magazin des Glücks*, 2002); *Samurai* (2002); *The Scissors* (*Die Schere*, 2002); *War Zone* (2002)

FURTHER READING

Loher, Dea. *Stranger's House*. Tr. by David Tushingham. In *German Plays*, ed. by Elyse Dodgson. London: Nick Hern Bks., 1997.

Ludewig, Alexandra. "Dea Lohers Theaterstück *Adam Geist*." *Forum Modernes Theater* 15, no. 2 (2000): 113–124.

———. "Junges Theater im Deutschland der 1990er Jahre: Dea Lohers *Adam Geist*" [New German theater of the 1990s: Dea Loher's *Adam Geist*]. *New German Review* 14 (1998–1999): 55–73.

Britta Kallin

THE LONE TUSKER See OTTAYAN

LONG DAY'S JOURNEY INTO NIGHT

For a second you see—and seeing the secret, are the secret.

—Edmund, Act 4

Long Day's Journey Into Night by EUGENE O'NEILL premiered at the Dramatiska Teatern in Stockholm on February 10, 1956. José Quintero directed the first American production at the Helen Hayes Theater in New York City on November 7, 1956.

The play is O'Neill's ultimate drama of the American family and his most searing autobiographical revelation, treating guilt, jealousy, shame, dependency, responsibility, and sacrifice. Tyrone is James O'Neill; Mary is his wife, Ella; Edmund is the playwright himself; and Jamie is his older brother. The action takes place in a version of the O'Neill family's summer home in New London, Connecticut.

Edmund has developed consumption, and Jamie accuses Tyrone of relying on "a cheap old quack" because he is too stingy to pay for a "real doctor" even though he would spend any amount of money on a piece of land. The father, in turn, accuses his son of wasting his money on whores and whiskey, insisting that he found him a job as an actor only because he flunked out of college and showed no ambition for anything. Mary is returning to her morphine addiction, and Jamie blames his father for hiring "another cheap quack" who prescribed the narcotic to ease her pain after Edmund's birth. She senses that the men, always suspicious, are spying on her. When she comes down for lunch, Jamie realizes that she has been taking narcotics; he reproves her and challenges her to examine her dilated eyes in the mirror. In the next moment all three men take a drink of whiskey.

Mary feels lonely in the house that Tyrone has furnished as cheaply as possible, and she looks forward to the resumption of the theatrical season because she brings no domestic expectations to the series of second-rate hotels. Even Mary sees that Tyrone wastes his money by trying for bargains; he bought Mary an automobile neither of them really wanted, and he hired a dishonest, inexperienced chauffeur who takes kickbacks from the garage that repairs the machine. She believes that she lost her health in the endless touring of the theatrical circuit, and that Jamie carelessly but knowingly exposed Eugene, the baby they lost, to measles when she left the children with her mother in order to join her lonely husband.

Mary is drifting away, feeling the effects of her "medicine," but regretting what rheumatism has done to her once-beautiful hands and wistfully remembering when she fell in love with Tyrone as he played the role of a nobleman in the French Revolution. She pours drinks for both Tyrone and Edmund, making excuses even while she condemns Jamie for his chronic drunkenness. She remembers how often Tyrone drank so much that his friends would deposit him outside her hotel room, even on their wedding night. Edmund breaks the news to Mary: the doctor recommends that he go to a sanatorium. She refuses to believe that he is sick enough, and in frustration he refers to her as a "dope fiend" before hurrying out of the house.

Edmund returns at midnight to find Tyrone sitting in front of a whiskey bottle that is three-quarters empty. They argue over their favorite authors, Tyrone putting up William Shakespeare against Edmund's Charles Baudelaire, Ernest Dowson, Adgernon Charles Swinburne, OSCAR WILDE, Edgar Allan Poe, and EMILE ZOLA, whom he denounces as writing "morbidness and filth." Edmund, too, accuses Tyrone of risking Mary's addiction by hiring a cheap doctor and then by prolonging her agony by dragging her on tour and refusing to make a real home for her. Like Jamie, he is convinced that Tyrone does not believe that consumption is curable, so in order to save money, he is sending his son to a state-supported institution. Tyrone angrily justifies all his decisions and insists that his alleged wealth is an illusion because all his property is mortgaged. However, he cannot deny that after making the arrangements with the doctor, he bought another piece of land. Tyrone cannot forget the poverty of his childhood, his father's desertion of his mother, and the necessity to go to work at the age of ten, slaving twelve hours a day in a machine shop for fifty cents a week. He has never been able to shake his passion for the value of a dollar even though it drove him to buy "that God-damned play" (a thinly-veiled reference to THE COUNT OF MONTE CRISTO) and make easy money touring it rather than following through on his potential as a Shakespearean actor in the tradition of Edwin Booth. Edmund cherishes his memories of sailing on a square-rigger down to Buenos Aires, when he felt at one with the sea. Jamie returns, still drunk after his visit to a whorehouse, and confesses to Edmund that he has, for years, deliberately given him the wrong value system, raising booze and whores and putting down work and success. He passes out, and Tyrone returns to find him there. Mary walks in on them carrying an old-fashioned white satin wedding gown, confused over whether or not she is back at the convent where she went to school as a girl. The three men pour themselves drinks but sit motionless as Mary remembers when she fell in love with Tyrone "and was so happy for a time."

The play isolates the tormented family, first in their house and then in the fog that enfolds it, and the action brings the characters together, but they find no comfort in each other. The Tyrones struggle with their past, but they cannot escape from their guilt and resentment; they are both responsible and helpless. They become the apotheosis of the family, both intimate and alienated, and doomed never to escape. They are all dependent—on alcohol, on morphine, on land, on money, on fame, or on hypocrisy and deceit—and the action leads them to face their inability to break free. Once again O'Neill demonstrates his kinship with AUGUST STRINDBERG through his exploration of a self-destructive family and especially of an agonized marriage.

Walter Kerr (*New York Herald Tribune*, November 8, 1956) asserted that O'Neill had exorcised his agony, "leaving in its place an undefined dignity, an agreed-upon peace, a powerful sense of exhilarated completion. [The play] is a lacerating round-robin of recrimination, self-dramatization, lies that deceive no one, confessions that never expiate the crime." In the *New York Daily News* (November 8, 1956), John Chapman announced that the play "exploded like a dazzling skyrocket." Brooks Atkinson, of the *New York Times* (November 8, 1956) declared that with this play, "the American theatre acquires size and stature."

[*See also* United States, 1940–Present]

FURTHER READING

Barlow, Judith E. *Final Acts: The Creation of Three Late O'Neill Plays.* Athens: Univ. of Georgia Press, 1985.

Hinden, Michael. "*Long Day's Journey Into Night.*" *Native Eloquence.* Boston: G. K. Hall, 1990.

——. "O'Neill and Jamie: A Survivor's Tale." *Comparative Drama* 35 (2001–2002): 435–445.

Murphy, Brenda. *O'Neill: "Long Day's Journey Into Night."* Plays in Production. Cambridge: Cambridge Univ. Press, 2001.

Pao, Angela C. "Changing Faces: Recasting National Identity in All-Asian(-)American Dramas." *Theatre Journal* 53 (October 2001): 389–409.

Wallerstein, Nicholas. "Accusation and Argument in Eugene O'Neill's *Long Day's Journey Into Night.*" *Eugene O'Neill Review* 23 (Spring–Fall 1999): 127–133.

Jeffrey D. Mason

THE LONG VOYAGE HOME

'I feel homesick for farm and to see my people again.
—Olson

The Long Voyage Home by EUGENE O'NEILL was first produced by the Provincetown Players at the Playwrights' Theatre in New York on November 2, 1917. Along with *Bound East for Cardiff* (1916), *In the Zone* (1917), and *The Moon of the Caribbees* (1918), this was one of the four one-act plays later known as *S.S. Glencairn*. In these early works O'Neill established his theme of the sea and its power over the men who travel upon it. The plays reflect not only his own experience as a seaman in 1911 but also the influence of Joseph Conrad's account of the sailor's life in *The Nigger of the Narcissus*.

The *Glencairn* has paid off in London, and four of its seamen, "wiv their bloody pockets full o' sovereigns," walk into a squalid waterfront bar run by Fat Joe, a sometime labor contractor and undercover crimper—a dockside predator who kidnaps seamen and places them on ships for a bounty. Joe is especially eager to recruit a sailor for *Amindra*, a full-rigged windjammer; the men in port avoid the ship because the captain is a "slave-driver" who starves his men.

Because Ivan, the Russian peasant, says that he wants to dance with girls, Nick, the crimper's assistant, brings in two tarts, Freda and Kate. While the others dance to an accordion in the side room, Freda cozies up to Olson, a middle-aged Swede who is staying sober because he hopes to return to Stockholm as a passenger and use his two years' pay to buy a farm: "No more sea, no more bum grub, no more storms."

Ivan passes out, so Driscoll and Cocky carry him back to their boardinghouse. Freda asks for a glass of brandy and insists that Olson drink with her, but when he orders a small ginger beer, Nick adds something to it. Because Olson keeps getting up to follow his friends, Freda must work to keep him in the bar, and she persuades him to drain his glass by calling for a toast.

Two rough-looking men enter the bar, and one of them quietly mentions *Amindra*. Olson angrily remembers when he shipped out on her—"worst ship dat sail to sea." He pities the poor sailors who will work her around Cape Horn, then passes out, drugged. Joe empties his pockets, tells the roughnecks where to take Olson, and sternly instructs Nick not to leave the ship until the captain gives him Olson's first month's pay. They haul away the hapless Swede, and Joe knocks Freda down in order to retrieve the single bank note she slipped out of Olson's pocket. In the end the sea has punished Olson for even aspiring to escape to the land; he is predestined, even doomed, to sail the deep. Like the other *Glencairn* plays, *The Long Voyage Home* presents an essay in NATURALISM through its exploration of man as the bewildered subject of elemental forces well beyond his control.

[*See also* United States, 1860–1929]

FURTHER READING

Colburn, Steven E. "*The Long Voyage Home*: Illusion and the Tragic Pattern of Fate in O'Neill's *S.S. Glencairn* Cycle." In *Critical Essays on Eugene O'Neill*, ed. by James J. Martine. Boston: G. K. Hall, 1984. 55–65.

Condee, William F. "Melodrama to Mood: Construction and Deconstruction of Suspense in the *S.S. Glencairn* Plays." *Eugene O'Neill Review* 23 (Spring–Fall 1999): 8–18.

Larson, Kelli A. "O'Neill's Tragic Quest for Belonging: Psychological Determinism in the *S.S. Glencairn* Plays." *Eugene O'Neill Review* 13 (Fall 1989): 12–22.

Maufort, Marc. "Eugene O'Neill's Innovative Craftsmanship in the 'Glencairn' Cycle (1914–1917)." *Eugene O'Neill Newsletter* 12 (Spring 1988): 27–33.

Rust, R. Dilworth. "The Unity of O'Neill's *S.S. Glencairn*." *American Literature* 37 (November 1965): 280–290.

Jeffrey D. Mason

LOOK BACK IN ANGER

Pusillanimous. Adjective. Wanting of firmness of mind, of small courage.
—Jimmy Porter, Act 1

Few dramas in the modern era have influenced post–World War II theater as much as JOHN OSBORNE's 1956 play *Look Back in Anger*. Although simple in plot details and written using conventional NATURALISM, *Look Back* overflows with high-intensity emotion generated by its legendary antihero Jimmy Porter, the original "angry young man."

The symbolic opening displays a sitting room of a drab flat in an English provincial town of the 1950s. There Jimmy Porter, a young college graduate with few prospects, lives with his wife Alison and Cliff, his working-class partner in running a sweets stall. It is a Sunday morning, and while Jimmy and Cliff sit reading newspapers, Alison, dressed in a slip, stands over an ironing board, pressing clothes. From the outset, tension is created and mounts. Porter throughout derides his wife, mocking her passive manner—which he describes as "pusillanimous"—and cruelly ridicules her upper-middle-class breeding (her father is a retired officer who served in ENGLAND's distant colonies).

Alison says little, gamely trying to divert Jimmy's focus onto other subjects.

Porter's ongoing diatribe expresses his withering disdain for the stagnating apathy of England ten years after the hope-filled end of World War II. With absolute certitude he blames the British ruling establishment—epitomized by Alison's family and, by extension, their class—for society's stifling inertia. Cliff has served as a buffer between Jimmy and Alison, but even he cannot distract Porter from a determined intention to insult and humiliate Alison as representative of the problem, in his view.

Alison discovers that she is pregnant, and when her upper-class friend Helena cannot deflect Jimmy's continued verbal assaults, Alison is persuaded to return to her family until the baby is born. With Alison gone, Porter turns to her surrogate Helena, who, like Alison, experiences a love/hate attraction to Jimmy. Months pass, and after a miscarriage, Alison returns to find Helena living with Jimmy and Cliff. By then weary of Porter's unrelenting verbal attacks, Helena willingly departs. Alison moves back, and the trio resumes a dead-end existence, varied only by moments of romantic fantasy involving toy stuffed animals.

Look Back retains its punch for several reasons. Porter's lacerating polemics effectively chronicle a time soon after World War II when England's high hopes for a peaceful and economically satisfying life lost impetus. Thus Porter's university degree does him no good in a dormant economy, where no one in power seems to care. Corrosive disillusionment replaces lost idealism. Jimmy's sad remark captures the 1950s in England: "there aren't any good, brave causes left."

Osborne's drama also documents vividly the painful schism between social classes—a topic long central to British authors. Additionally, *Look Back* sets forth a fundamental battle of the sexes in a modern universe that has altered many gender ground rules. A generation gap between those living before World War II and those born afterwards is sharply contrasted in differing expectations from life. Ultimately, however, it is Jimmy's passionate language that lends the play longevity.

FURTHER READING

Dixon, Graham A. "Still Looking Back: The Deconstruction of the Angry Young Man in *Look Back in Anger* and *Dejavu*." *Modern Drama* 37, no. 3 (Fall 1994): 521–529.

Elsom, John, ed. *Post-war British Theatre Criticism*. London: Routledge, 1981.

Innes, Christopher. *Modern British Drama: The Twentieth Century*. Cambridge: Cambridge Univ. Press, 2002.

Taylor, John Russell, ed. *John Osborne: "Look Back in Anger"; A Casebook*. London: Macmillan, 1968.

Wandor, Michelene. *Look Back in Gender*. London: Methuen, 1987.

Wardle, Irving. "Looking Back on Osborne's Anger." *New Society* (June 16, 1966): 22–23.

C. J. Gianakaris

LOOT

JOE ORTON's controversial two-act play *Loot* was first produced in Cambridge, ENGLAND, in 1965, followed by a London production a year later that won the Evening Standard Drama Award for Best Play of the Year. The British censor insisted that "buggery" be expunged—homosexuality was illegal at the time—and replaced with "beggary." Also, the deceased Mrs. McLeavy had to be played by a mannequin rather than a living actor. Reception of the 1966 London production was as positive as that in Cambridge had been negative, and Joe Orton's reputation was made, both as a playwright and as an iconoclast.

Orton's six characters are Nurse Fay, who has made a lucrative career of marrying and murdering; Mr. McLeavy, who is the recently bereaved childlike innocent of the piece; Hal, who has no qualms about dumping his dead mother's body in a cupboard but cannot tell a lie; undertaker's assistant Dennis, Hal's partner in sex and crime, who also fancies Fay; Truscott, the brutal officer of the law who does not hesitate to break the law; and Meadows, Truscott's obedient underling, carrying out his every command.

On the day of the funeral Hal and Dennis rob a bank and decide to hide the loot in the coffin, Fay intensifies her pursuit of the naïve widower, and Truscott arrives at the door in pursuit of the thieves. With glass eyes popping out and dentures clacking like castanets, it is easy to imagine that the play could deteriorate into slapstick. Played according to Orton's explicit intentions, it has a sinister denouement, with the only decent, law-abiding citizen in the piece being imprisoned, while a murderous nurse, a corrupt policeman, and two felons form an alliance to keep themselves out of prison. People should never forget that there are corrupt or corruptible human beings inside the uniforms that instill trust: nurses, police, and ministers. McLeavy's fatal mistake is in believing that people will behave as they should. The play is a case study of what faith will do in the face of reality.

Orton insisted that playing *Loot* straight and realistic was essential to its effect, but many productions opt for the utterly farcical and stylized, neglecting the absurd and playing it for laughs with as much camp as possible. But laughs were not Orton's object; his primary purpose was to infuriate upper-class audiences by shocking them with his lack of decorum and by assaulting the pillars of society: education, religion, and law. In *Loot* he uses his gift for razor-sharp dialogue, his quirky wit, and his inherent irreverence and anger to jolt a complacent audience out of its deluded confidence in institutions, a confidence exhibited by mindless obedience and faith. The play's first words—"Wake up. Stop dreaming."—thus function as a thematic statement.

FURTHER READING

Lahr, John. *Prick up Your Ears: The Biography of Joe Orton*. New York: Avon Bks., 1980.

Zarhy-Levo, Yael. *The Theatrical Critic as Cultural Agent: Constructing Pinter, Orton and Stoppard as Absurdist Playwrights*. New York: P. Lang, 2001.

A. Mary Murphy

LORCA, FEDERICO GARCÍA *See* GARCÍA LORCA, FEDERICO

LORD, ROBERT (1945–1992)

A graduate of Victoria University, Wellington, Robert Lord had his first play, *It Isn't Cricket*, produced at Downstage Theatre in Wellington in 1971. *It Isn't Cricket* was then featured as part of the inaugural Australian National Playwrights Conference in 1973. After visiting the O'Neill Playwrights Conference in Connecticut in 1974, Lord was instrumental in establishing the workshopping process in NEW ZEALAND.

It Isn't Cricket signals recurring hallmarks of Lord's drama: an interest in the games people play in their relationships; a fondness for ambiguity and enigma, for playing with time and "truth"; and pared-down characterization. In other early plays the depiction of the alienation of individuals in a fragmented world resulted in an opaqueness and abstraction that found critical appreciation but not box-office success. In *Meeting Place* (1972) two women and two men, forced to confront a lifetime of lies, move through a series of combinations before ending up in homosexual couples. *Heroes and Butterflies* (produced in 1974) portrays the disintegration of social morality on a larger scale: it is set in a vaguely defined, nightmarish civil war, with a cast of sixteen.

More accessible and popular were two black COMEDIES that veer toward FARCE. In the one-act *Balance of Payments* (produced in 1972, published in 1978), which bears the influence of EDWARD ALBEE, a middle-aged couple who are supported by their son's prostitution treat the situation with amusingly incongruous propriety. This play also establishes Lord's interest in language, in particular his penchant for playing with repetitions and speech rhythms. One of four police dramas Lord wrote at the time (two for stage, two for radio), *Well Hung* (produced in 1974) draws on a famous contemporary murder investigation to satirize police corruption and brutality. It ends with a young officer hanging himself. Lord later revised the play as *Country Cops* (1988).

From 1974 Lord lived mostly in New York, where he became a leading figure in the New Dramatists group. *High as a Kite* (produced in 1979) and *Glorious Ruins* (produced in 1991) are both set in New York. In the former, a comedy of misunderstandings, Pat is fixatedly building a kite while his companions do their best to destroy it, just as they destroy their relationships. *Glorious Ruins* is a satire on the Manhattan art world.

The gentle, satirical tenor that developed in Lord's writing is applied to small-town New Zealand in two notable plays. In *Bert and Maisy* (1988) an elderly couple takes on a new lease of life when Bert brings home a young stranger; however, this unconventional arrangement provokes dismay in the local community. Lord's most successful play, *Joyful and Triumphant* (1993), premiered at the 1992 Wellington International Festival of the Arts. Subtitled *An Incidental Epic*, it traces the history of the Bishop family, and wider New Zealand culture, through a series of Christmas Days from 1949 to 1989.

In 1990 Lord returned to Dunedin. When he died, he left his cottage there to be used by writers. His other stage plays include *China Wars* (1987), set in a New England town, and *The Affair* (1987). He also wrote for radio and television, including screenplays of *Bert and Maisy* and *Joyful and Triumphant*.

SELECT PLAYS: *Glitter and Spit* (1971); *It Isn't Cricket* (1971); *Balance of Payments* (1972); *Meeting Place* (1972); *Nativity Theatre* (1973); *Heroes and Butterflies* (1974); *Well Hung* (1974; revised as *Country Cops*, 1988); *Friendship Centre* (1975); *High as a Kite* (1979); *China Wars* (1987); *The Affair* (1987); *Bert and Maisy* (1988); *Glorious Ruins* (1991); *Joyful and Triumphant* (1993); *The Travelling Squirrel (Tails of Manhattan)* (1994)

FURTHER READING

Amey, Sunny. "Robert Lord." *Act* 24 (October 1974): 6–10. [Interview with Lord.]

Lord, Robert. *Balance of Payments*. In *Can't You Hear Me Talking to You?* ed. by Alrene Sykes. St. Lucia, Queensland: Univ. of Queensland Press, 1978.

——. *Bert and Maisy*. Dunedin: Univ. of Otago Press, 1988.

——. *Country Cops*. New York: Broadway Play, 1988.

——. *Joyful and Triumphant*. Wellington: Victoria Univ. Press, 1993.

Stuart Young

LØVEID, CECILIE (1951–)

I am suspended on the edge of tradition, . . . but I don't produce my own "Løveid dream theater", I contact the institutions and the places where theater happens.

—Cecilie Løveid

Cecilie Løveid was born in 1951 and grew up in Bergen, NORWAY. Her experimental plays have renewed Norwegian drama and challenged dramatic conventions with their poetic qualities and mixture of theatrical techniques. Løveid started her career writing poems and short stories and established herself as a novelist before turning to the dramatic genre in the late 1970s. Her breakthrough came with the radio play SEAGULL EATERS (*Måkespisere*, 1982), which won the prestigious Prix Italia. Her dramatic work has developed in a dynamic cooperation with free dramatic groups, as well as big theater institutions.

Løveid's plays are characterized by a tension between a structuring narrative and elements that dissolve the epic coherence, such as dance, song, and recitals. Poetic qualities such as repetition, imagery, playfulness, and ambiguity dominate the texts, which also appear as a medley of quotations from all sorts of textual sources. In addition, different time layers confront each other in sharp contrasts, and excerpts from history are presented as co-present and antihierarchical scenes. Løveid's texts are open artworks, inviting producer and ensemble to create a visual performance with moving bodies, music, and stage effects in fulfillment of her artistic intentions.

Her work has been called a new EXPRESSIONISM, and she has been compared partly to German dramatists such as HEINER MÜLLER and BOTHO STRAUSS and partly to American AVANT-GARDE dramatists such as RICHARD FOREMAN and ROBERT WILSON, being more surrealist than the former and more realistic than the latter. In Norwegian theater it is impossible to ignore the strong influence of HENRIK IBSEN, and even though Løveid's drama insists on a different aesthetics, it nevertheless makes room for textual and technical echoes from him. Another influence is the Danish artist, director, and theater leader Kirsten Dehlholm, who started the Hotel Pro Forma performance theater, which has been central to the development of Danish theater. As postmodern works of art, Løveid's plays also frequently refer to historical epochs, such as the rococo [in *Tightrope Lady* (Balansedame)], the baroque [in *Baroque Frieze* (Barock Friise)], or the Middle Ages [in *The Rhine Daughters* (Rhindøtrene)], and have revived a premodernist scenery such as the tableau.

Løveid's dramatic work stages conflicts connected to gendered identity, family relationships, and professional ambitions. Her protagonist is often a woman, sometimes a historical figure, whose life is a struggle between sexual, intellectual, and artistic aspirations, on the one hand, and social circumstances, on the other. Susanne in *Tightrope Lady* is an archeologist who dreams of living an 18th-century life at the same time as she tries, in vain, to fulfill her obligations as a mother, a lover, and a professional. Zille Gad in *Baroque Frieze* and Hildegard von Bingen in *The Rhine Daughters* are highly gifted women who strive to combine being intellectuals with having bodily desires. Maria in *Maria Q* leaves her child in Russia, marries Vidkun Quisling, who becomes a betrayer, and lives a lonely life filled with lost illusions on the edge of insanity.

The impact of Cecilie Løveid's work is tied to the dramatic method that she has introduced. Staging her plays requires from the theater not only a textual "animation," but an active creation of a visual, plastic, and rhythmic totality.

SELECT PLAYS: *Seagull Eaters* (*Måkespisere*, 1982); *The Ice Breaks Up* (*Vinteren revner*, 1983); *Sea Swell* (*Sug*, 1983); *Lydia, Radio Play* (*Lydia, Hørespill*, 1984); *Shower, One Opera for Two* (*Dusj, 1 opera for 2*, opera, 1984); *Madame Butterfly on the Beach* (*Madam Butterfly På Stranden*, 1985); *Rational Animals* (*Fornuftige dyr*, 1986); *Double Delight* (*Dobbel Nytelse*, 1990); *Time in Between Times* (*Tiden mellom tidene eller Paradisprosjektet*, 1990); *Baroque Frieze* (*Barock Friise*, 1991); *Maria Q* (1994); *The Rhine Daughters* (*Rhindøtrene*, 1996); *Austria* (*Østerrike*, 1998); *The Right Wind* (*Den riktige vind*, 1999)

FURTHER READING

Garton, Janet. In "Cecilie Løveid (Born 1951)." In *Norwegian Women's Writing, 1850–1990*. London: Athlone, 1993. 209–228.

Thresher, Tanya. "Bringing Ibsen's *Brand* Into the Twentieth Century: Cecilie Løveid's *Østerrike*." *Scandinavian Studies* 74, no. 1 (2002).

——. "The Polymorphous Female Subject in Cecilie Løveid's *Barock Friise*." *Edda*, no. 2 (2002).

Unni Langås

THE LOWER DEPTHS

The Lower Depths (*Na dne*), a drama in four acts by MAKSIM GORKY, was written in 1902 and performed in December of the same year at the MOSCOW ART THEATRE (MAT) with an all-star cast: KONSTANTIN STANISLAVSKY as Satin, Olga Knipper as Nastya, Ivan Moskvin as Luka, and Mariya Andreyeva as Natasha. The play is set in a doss-house, and the characters all have different stories to tell of their route to destitution: illness, alcoholism, prostitution, crime, unemployment, lack of credentials, or escaping police pursuit. One particular arrival, Luka, a wanderer (probably from a forbidden religious sect), polarizes the inhabitants by his policy of offering comfort where he can, even if it means resorting to the odd lie. After a brawl in which the doss-house's owner is killed by an inmate, he disappears, fearful of police interference. Those remaining debate whether Luka was right to lie and about the desirability of their own claims to a place in a world based on lies. In drink-fueled rhetoric Satin—a murderer, cheat, and layabout—while disliking Luka's consoling lies, agrees with his concern for suffering human beings, despite his apparent cynicism: "Work? What do I want to work for? To have a full belly? (*He laughs*)." He demands that society should recognize the destitute and include them in its ranks. In a shock ending his message of hope and Luka's comforting lie seem to be overturned: an out-of-work actor hangs himself in despair, having discovered the falsehood of a promised cure for his alcoholism. Society's promises can be dangerous, the play would seem to say.

The play has been the subject of much debate, principally between those who regard Luka as the central character and those who side with Satin. Placing it in the context of Gorky's other plays of the period, especially *Philistines* and SUMMERFOLK, and in the context of the dramatic form chosen, would seem to suggest a more politically disengaged Gorky than the one claimed by those who have carved his reputation hitherto. In *Philistines*, among the capitalist "derelicts," the bird catcher Perchikhin offers a brighter option. A throwback to the wanderings of Gorky's youth, he speaks lovingly of the freedom of the open road. In contrast, *The Lower Depths* offers two oppressive options: the inescapable depths of doss-house destitution (easy to enter, almost impossible to leave) or, as Satin implies, the responsibilities and ties of a life in work (or political activity). Satin wants to be recognized as part of the human race as viewed from the relative freedom of his materially deprived life in the depths. In *Summerfolk* Gorky chooses a different path, anxiously urging the intelligentsia to employ their idealism to destroy social and political indifference.

Conceived within the spirit of true-to-life NATURALISM, the play was designed to shock its largely well-off audience. Its set, a dingy urban cellar, brought to sordid life by Viktor Simov, MAT's resident designer, was inhabited by foul-mouthed (for the time), irresponsible, but highly entertaining derelicts who brought a new stage and body language to the theater. Stanislavsky recorded his difficulties with Satin, a character far from his own experience and from other figures he had created hitherto. The debate at the center of this play is largely unresolved. The characters indulge in much storytelling, transporting the audience to their own worlds, the only means of escape from the depressing darkness of the doss-house. Perhaps Gorky is here telling a story himself, not so much transporting his audience as deflecting his own attention from the harsh realities of his doubts (political and social) about the future for humanity.

[*See also* Russia and the Soviet Union]

FURTHER READING

Annenskii, F. "Drama na dne." In *Kniga otrazhenii*. St Petersburg, 1906. Translated as "Drama at the Lower Depths," in *Russian Dramatic Theory from Pushkin to the Symbolists*, tr. and ed. by Laurence Senelick. Austin: Univ. of Texas Press, 1981. 93–106.

Erlich, Victor. "Truth and Illusion in Gorky: *The Lower Depths* and After." In *Freedom and Responsibility in Russian Literature: Essays in Honor of Robert Louis Jackson*, ed. by Elizabeth Cheresh Allen and Gary Saul Morson. Evanston Ill:, Northwestern Univ. Press, 1995. 191–198.

Gorky, M. *The Lower Depths*. In *Five Plays*, by Maksim Gorky, tr. by Kitty Hunter Blair and Jeremy Brooks. London: Methuen, 1988. 1–92.

Kjetsaa, Geir. "Ambivalence in Attitude: The character Luka in *The Lower Depths*." *Russian Literature* 24 (1988): 517–524.

Marsh, Cynthia. "Truth, Lies and Story-telling in *The Lower Depths*." *Canadian Slavonic Papers* 42, no. 4 (December 2000): 507–520.

Scherr, Barry S. "Grand Illusions: Maksim Gorky's *The Lower Depths* and Eugene O'Neill." *Irish Slavonic Studies* 21 (2000): 1–25.

Cynthia Marsh

LOYALTIES

JOHN GALSWORTHY called *Loyalties* "the only play of mine of which I was able to say, when I finished it, no manager will refuse this." It was secured by Basil Dean, whose company Reandean had staged Galsworthy's first commercial success. Given Dean's commitment to new British drama and naturalistic ensemble playing, Galsworthy could not have made a better choice. *Loyalties* opened at the St. Martin's on March 8, 1922, to record houses and ran for a year.

The title states the theme. Social climber Ferdinand De Levis is robbed at a house party and accuses a young officer, Ronald Dancy. The upper class closes ranks against the outsider. Pressure mounts on Dancy to sue; but meanwhile his guilt is becoming ever more apparent to us. He then wrecks any chance of a settlement by addressing De Levis as "damned Jew"; willing to forget the original insult, De Levis cannot forgive the racism. The money is found in the hands of Dancy's cast-off mistress, straining the loyalty of Dancy's lawyers, his wife, and his class. He sees only one escape and shoots himself.

Like the popular detective stories of the period, *Loyalties* exposes the mixed motives of the wealthied class. De Levis has exploited Dancy's shaky finances by allowing him to offload a "useless" racehorse that promptly wins £970—precisely the sum stolen. If Dancy's anti-Semitism is inexcusable, the theft reflects the self-destructive spirit of a war hero in a peacetime world that fails to value him, a situation the audience of the 1920s understood only too well. Galsworthy's even sympathies and confidently orchestrated flow of information ensure that the outcome remains unpredictable till the final curtain.

It is this element of suspense that prompted the initial glowing reviews. To read them today is to be disconcerted by flashes of kneejerk racism and a lack of response to Galsworthy's acerbic political comedy:

Margaret: There are more of the chosen in Court every day. Mr. Graviter, have you noticed those two on the jury? . . . Don't you think they ought to have been challenged?

Graviter: De Levis might have challenged the other ten.

Christopher St. John, in *Time and Tide*, did address the play's politics, suggesting that English anti-Semitism, dormant during the reign of Edward VII, had returned as a real and present danger. Meanwhile the "Gallery Girl" column in the *Star* offered a rare feminist critique. While—like many others—it found Galsworthy's characterization of Dancy's naïve young wife underpowered, it suggested that a study of marital loyalties should cut both ways. Is Dancy's suicide a betrayal of his wife rather than an attempt to shield her from disgrace? Such dissident voices would more truly reflect those of a modern audience. Although no longer controversial, the mix of documentary REALISM, social COMEDY, and well-made thriller ensures that the play retains its vitality. Galsworthy, although still to receive the Nobel Prize and writing until his death in 1933, never produced a more absorbing drama.

[*See also* England, 1860–1940]

FURTHER READING

Dean, Basil. *Seven Ages*. London: Hutchinson, 1970.

Galsworthy, John. *Five Plays* [*Strife, Justice, The Eldest Son, The Skin Game, Loyalties*]. London: Methuen, 1984.

Innes, Christopher. *Modern British Drama, 1890–1990*. Cambridge: Cambridge Univ. Press, 1992.

Frances Gray

LUCAS, CRAIG (1951–)

One of my parents once asked me, "Why are so many people in the theatre gay?" My answer: "So many people everywhere are gay."
—Craig Lucas

A playwright, screenwriter, director, and performer, Craig Lucas is best known for structurally complex works that frequently feature such devices as time leaps and simultaneous or overlapping dialogue and scenes. Abandoned in a car the day he was born, April 30, 1951, in Atlanta, Georgia, at eight months Lucas was adopted by a Pennsylvania couple. He studied theater at Boston University, where poet Anne Sexton became his mentor, and graduated in 1973. Moving to New York City, he performed in the choruses of several Broadway musicals in the late 1970s, including *Shenandoah*, *Rex*, *On the Twentieth Century*, and *Sweeney Todd*.

During the run of *Sweeney Todd* Lucas met director Norman Rene, with whom he formed a close friendship and collaborated over the years to come. Their first project together was *Marry Me a Little* (1980), a two-performer musical built around extant Stephen Sondheim songs. This was quickly followed by Lucas's plays *Missing Persons* (1981) and *Alec Wilder: Clues to a Life* (1982).

Lucas's play *Reckless*, concerning a woman about to be murdered by her husband's hit man on Christmas Eve, was first staged in 1983, although it was not acknowledged a success until a revised version was staged in 1988. *Blue Window* (1984) was the first play to bring Lucas widespread attention. It concerns seven New Yorkers, including a lesbian couple, who get ready for, attend, and then depart from a dinner party. The play won Lucas Dramalogue and Los Angeles Drama Critics awards and was filmed for public television in 1987.

Lucas returned to musical theater with the book for *Three Postcards* (1987), a chamber musical with music and lyrics by Craig Carnelia, which concerns three lifelong female friends who meet in a New York City restaurant for lunch. His next work, *Prelude to a Kiss* (1990), became his most acclaimed drama. A modern-day fairy tale, the play concerns a newlywed couple whose marriage is tested when they realize that the wife has switched bodies with a terminally ill old man whom she kissed at the wedding. The play ran on Broadway for over 400 performances and was turned into a film in 1991.

Lucas is openly gay, and in 1990 he wrote the screenplay for one of the first high-profile AIDS movies, *Longtime Companion*. His other screenwriting credits, aside from his screen adaptations of *Prelude to a Kiss* (1992) and *Reckless* (1995), include a screenplay, with Jane Smiley, for *The Secret Lives of Dentists* (2002), based on her novella *The Age of Grief*.

Lucas's plays at the turn of the century continued his investigations of language, time, and structure. They include *God's Heart* (1997); *The Dying Gaul* (1998), about a screenwriter struggling with power and money issues; *Stranger* (2000), concerning two people who meet on a plane; *This Thing of Darkness* (2002), written with David Schulner; and *Small Tragedy* (2004), about a new translation and staging of *Oedipus Rex*. Lucas has returned to musical theater with the book for *The Light in the Piazza* (2003), a love story set in 1950s Italy, with music and lyrics by Adam Guettel, which Lucas directed for the Intiman Theatre in Seattle.

[*See also* United States, 1940–Present]

PLAYS: *Marry Me a Little* (book for musical, 1980); *Missing Persons* (1981); *Alec Wilder: Clues to a Life* (1982); *Reckless* (1983); *Blue Window* (1984); *Three Postcards* (book for musical, 1987); *Prelude to a Kiss* (1990); *Bad Dream* (radio play, 1992); *God's Heart* (1997); *The Dying Gaul* (1998); *Stranger* (2000); *Miss Julie* (Strindberg translation, 2002); *This Thing of Darkness* (with David Schulner, 2002); *The Light in the Piazza* (book for musical, 2003); *Singing Forest* (2004); *Small Tragedy* (2004)

FURTHER READING

Clum, John M. *Still Acting Gay*. New York: St. Martin's, 2000.
Lucas, Craig. "A Gay Life in the Theatre." *American Theatre* (November 1990) 24–29, 68.
Mandell, Jonathan. "Opposites Make Use of Their Differences." *New York Times* (May 26, 2002) sec. 2, 5.

Joe E. Jeffreys

LUCES DE BOHEMIA *See* BOHEMIAN LIGHTS

LUDLAM, CHARLES (1943–1987)

Basically the catch phrase of my movement would be "virtuoso maximalism," the enemy of minimalism.
—Charles Ludlam

Playwright, performer, director, and theater company founder Charles Ludlam was born on April 12, 1943, in Floral Park, New York, and raised on Long Island. Ludlam became interested in theater at an early age and as a young child was greatly affected by a trip to a local carnival. By the time he was in high school, he had formed his own theater group, whose works included a NŌ play. After graduating from Hofstra University in 1965 he moved to New York City. Here he became a member of John Vaccaro's Playhouse of the Ridiculous, which produced his first play, *Big Hotel* (1966). During rehearsals for his second play, *Conquest of the Universe* (1967), Ludlam and Vaccaro came to artistic differences that led Ludlam to leave Vaccaro's company and take several other actors with him. Together they formed their own rival troupe, which eventually came to be known as the Ridiculous Theatrical Company.

Over the next twenty years the company devoted itself exclusively to producing plays written by Ludlam. Most were also directed by him and featured him in major roles, often in drag. In 1978, after playing various spaces around New York City, from gay bars and porn theaters to more established venues, the company moved into its own theater at One Sheridan Square in the West Village. The Ridiculous Theatrical Company became unique in American theater history because of its prolonged exclusive production of the plays of one author, who also directed and starred in them. Ludlam's plays, as performed by the Ridiculous Theatrical Company, are best known for their seriously subversive comedic style in which the deviant ridicules the norm, a self-reflective performance stance that was often confused with camp, and constant play with gender and traditional roles.

Ludlam's twenty-nine plays drew on a vast, eclectic range of sources for inspiration, from the classical to the popular. While his earliest dramas, such as *The Grand Tarot* (1969), based on the characters of the tarot and performed in a new order each night, possess an amorphous associative DRAMATURGY; his later works, such as *Le Bourgeois Avant-Garde* (1983), a take on Molière's *Le Bourgeois Gentilhomme* and the state of avant-garde art, and *The Artificial Jungle* (1986), a riff on EMILE ZOLA'S THÉRÈSE RAQUIN, can be considered some of the most masterful well-made plays written since VICTORIEN SARDOU and Eugène Scribe.

Ludlam and his company toured worldwide and are perhaps best known for two works. In *Camille* (1973), his adaptation of the famous DUMAS FILS MELODRAMA, Ludlam played the title character with his chest hair peeking out the top of his gowns. *The Mystery of Irma Vep* (1984), a quick-change play for eight characters played by two actors, was one of the most performed plays in America at the end of the 20th century and one of the longest-running plays in Brazil, where it ran for over seven years.

On May 28, 1987, Ludlam, who won numerous awards and grants during his lifetime, including Obie and Drama Desk awards and a National Endowment for the Arts Fellowship in Playwrighting, died in New York City of complications from AIDS. The Ridiculous Theatrical Company, under the direction of Ludlam's longtime partner Everett Quinton, continued to produce revivals and new works until the early 1990s.

[*See also* Avant-Garde Drama; Gay and Lesbian Drama; United States, 1940–Present]

PLAYS: *Big Hotel* (1966); *Conquest of the Universe* (1967); *The Grand Tarot* (1969); *Turds in Hell* (1969); *Bluebeard* (1970); *Eunuchs of the Forbidden City* (1971); *Corn* (1972); *Camille* (1973); *Hot Ice* (1974); *Jack and the Beanstalk* (1975); *Stage Blood* (1975); *Caprice* (1976); *Isle of the Hermaphrodites* (1976); *Der Ring Gott Farblonjet* (1977); *Utopia, Incorporated* (1978); *The Ventriloquist's Wife* (1978); *A Christmas Carol* (1979); *The Enchanted Pig* (1979); *Reverse Psychology* (1980); *Love's Tangled Web* (1981); *Exquisite Torture* (1982); *Secret Lives of the Sexists* (1982); *Le Bourgeois Avant-Garde* (1983); *Galas* (1983); *How to Write a Play* (1984); *Medea* (1984); *The Mystery of Irma Vep* (1984); *Salammbo* (1985); *The Artificial Jungle* (1986)

FURTHER READING

Brecht, Stefan. *Queer Theatre*. New York: Methuen, 1986.

Kaufman, David. *Ridiculous! The Theatrical Life and Times of Charles Ludlam*. New York: Applause, 2002.

Ludlam, Charles. *The Complete Plays of Charles Ludlam*. New York: Harper, 1989.

——. *Ridiculous Theatre: Scourge of Human Folly; The Essays and Opinions of Charles Ludlam*. Ed. by Steven Samuels. New York: TCG, 1992.

Joe E. Jeffreys

LUNACHARSKY, ANATOLY VASILYEVICH (1875–1933)

Anatoly Vasilyevich Lunacharsky was a Soviet bureaucrat of primary significance, a literary and theater historian of merit, and a Russian playwright of secondary importance. As the first Soviet People's Commissar of Education (1917–1929), effectively the minister of culture, he had a major impact on the conception of cultural policy in the Soviet Union's formative years. As defined by James Billington (in *The Icon and the Axe*, 1970), he was a "God-builder," one of the visionaries who "considered themselves to be merely elaborating the famous Marxist statement that philosophers should change rather than merely explain the world." In an age of extremes after the revolution, he was a moderate who favored compromise. He championed traditional art forms, as exemplified in his famous slogan of 1923, "Back to [ALEKSANDR] OSTROVSKY!" while supporting the inclusion of non-Communist writers—so-called fellow travelers'—in the cultural process. This did not stop him from leading vigorous campaigns against some writers, including MIKHAIL BULGAKOV. Removed from power shortly after Joseph Stalin became dictator, he no longer could defend such plays as THE SUICIDE by NIKOLAI ERDMAN, although he tried. In the Soviet years the philosophical voice of his early essays was replaced by a tendentious, sociological tone. His own dramas, COMEDIES, and historical and folklore-based plays were written to express his philosophical beliefs and reflected larger-than-life people struggling with the problems of heroic ages.

Interested in Marxism from age fifteen, he studied philosophy and natural science at Zürich University from 1895 to 1897 before starting to publish criticism in 1903. He was arrested several times in Russia for revolutionary activity and sat out exile in various provincial cities. After the failed 1905 revolution he immigrated to Europe in 1906. His first play, written in prison before emigration, was *The Royal Barber* (1906), a generalized fantasy about a 15th-century feudal kingdom. It was followed by one-act comedies collected as *Five Farces for Amateurs* (published in 1907) and *Faust and the City* (1910), a development of part two of Johann Wolfgang von Goethe's *Faust* that treated the notion of the genius and society. More didactic comedies were published under the heading *Ideas in Masks* (1912) but, like all his work heretofore, were not produced. Despite having broken with Vladimir Lenin between 1908 and 1910, he returned to Russia just days after him in 1917 and was appointed to the new government. Several of his plays, usually abstract dramatic studies set in the past and dealing with problems of revolution and power, began to be produced. His *Oliver Cromwell* (1921), about the Lord Protector of the Realm after the English civil war in the 17th century, was the first Soviet-era play that the tradition-bound Maly Theater produced. *Don Quixote Liberated* (begun in 1916, completed in 1924) warned against failing to be critical even in regard to friends and perhaps was his justification for allowing Aleksei Remizov (1921) and Nikolai Berdyayev (1922) to be forced into emigration. *Poison* (1925), a MELODRAMA about the conflict between a modern political figure and his son, was his only play set in a contemporary milieu.

[*See also* Russia and the Soviet Union]

SELECT PLAYS: *The Royal Barber* (*Korolevskii bradobrei*, 1906); *Five Farces for Amateurs* (*Pyat' farsov dlya lyubitelei*, 1907); *Faust and the City* (*Faust i gorod*, 1910); *Ideas in Masks* (*Idei v maskakh*, 1912); *Magi* (1919); *Ivan in Paradise* (*Ivan v rayu*, 1920); *Mitra the Savior* (*Mitra-Spasitel'*, 1920); *Tale of How Ivan the Fool Became Wise* (*Skazaniye o tom, kak Ivan-durak umnym stal*, 1920); *Vasilisa the Wise* (*Vasilisa Premudraya*, 1920); *The Chancellor and the Metal Worker* (*Kantsler i slesar'*, 1921); *Oliver Cromwell* (*Oliver Kromvel*, 1921); *Tommaso Campanella* (*Foma Kampanella*, 1921); *Temptation* (*Iskushheniye*,1922); *Arsonists* (*Podzhigateli*, 1924); *The Bear's Wedding* (*Medvezh'ya svad'ba*, after Mérimée, 1924); *Don Quixote Liberated* (*Osvobozhdyonny Don-Kikhot*, 1924); *Poison* (*Yad*, 1925); *Velvet and Rags* (*Barkhat i lokhmot'ya*, 1927); *The Banker's House* (*Bankirskii dom*, 1929); *The Baron's Whim* (*Baronskaya prichuda*, 1929); *Prologue in Esclavia* (*Prolog v Esklavii*, 1931)

FURTHER READING

Billington, James H. *The Icon and the Axe: An Interpretive History of Russian Culture*. New York: Vintage, 1970.

Fitzpatrick, Sheila. *The Commissariat of Enlightenment: Soviet Organization of Education and the Arts under Lunacharsky, October 1917–1921*. Cambridge: Cambridge Univ. Press, 1970.

Lunacharsky, Anatoly Vasilyevich. *On Literature and Art*. Tr. by Avril Pyman and Fainna Glagoleva. Moscow: Progress, 1973.

——. *Three Plays of A. V. Lunacharski: Faust and the City, Vasilisa the Wise, The Magi*. Tr. by Leonard A. Magnus and Karl Walter. New York: Dutton, 1923.

Tait, A. L. *Lunacharsky: Poet of the Revolution (1875–1907)*. Birmingham Slavonic Monographs, no. 15. Birmingham: Univ. of Birmingham, 1984.

Williams, Robert C. *Artists in Revolution: Portraits of the Russian Avant-Garde, 1905–1925*. Bloomington: Indiana Univ. Press, 1977.

Yermakov, A. A. *Lunacharsky*. Moscow: Novosti Press Agency, 1975.

John Freedman

LUO HUAIZHEN (1956–)

Luo Huaizhen was born in 1956 in Huaiyin, Jiangsu Province. He is one of the most important contemporary playwrights for the traditional Chinese theater generically termed as *xiqu*. Before his playwriting he had performed on the *huaiju* (the music drama of Northern Jiangsu) stage in his hometown in the late 1970s. His career as a playwright in the *xiqu* genres started in the mid-1980s in Shanghai after he received a short-term professional training at the Shanghai Academy of Drama. Since then he has been, on average, writing one play a year. Most of his plays have been staged in one or more *xiqu* forms.

All set in imperial CHINA with the exception of The Pawned Wife (*Dian qi*, *yongju* or Ningbo opera), Luo's plays can be divided into two categories: those that portray historical or literary female figures such as Xi Shi, Banzhsao, Li Qingzhao, and Liu Rushi and those that invent new stories from the past at the allegorical level. The former is best represented by *Xi Shi Returns to the Kingdom of Yue* (*jingju*). The popular version of the story treats Xi Shi as a patriotic heroine. In the Spring and Autumn period (770–476 B.C.) the Kingdom of Yue was defeated by the Kingdom of Wu. Xi Shi, a country beauty of Yue, was sent to the king of Wu as a concubine. Xi Shi sowed discord and hatred between the king of Wu and his officials, disarming the kingdom's ability to fight. Finally the king of Yue launched an attack and defeated the king of Wu, who committed suicide. Traditionally, Xi Shi has been eulogized as faithful, selfless, and of virtuous beauty because she obeyed the king's order to be the concubine of the enemy's ruler and finally saved her home kingdom. From a feminist point of view, Luo's play goes against the traditional portrayal of Xi Shi and poses a poignant question: "What if Xi Shi is pregnant with the child of the king of Wu?" In his play the king of Yue cannot tolerate the birth of the child and makes Xi Shi kill her own child and commit suicide. Like most of Luo's tragedies, this play is an effective critique of some traditional Chinese ethics and virtues. The second category is illustrated by *Golden Dragon and Mayfly*, in which Luo uses the concepts of Greek and Shakespearean TRAGEDIES to portray a prince who abandons his wife for the high cause of saving his father's kingdom and later, because of his flaw in personality and the obscurity of characters' identities, kills his faithful general, castrates his own son, and enlists his daughter-in-law as his concubine, leading to the deaths of all his family except for his grandson, who is likely to start the same vicious cycle. It is a political fable that questions the validity of male authority over women and explores the interrelations between the private and the public.

Luo has a well-defined mission in his playwriting: although most of his plays have been set in imperial China, the theme of each subject is consciously related to modern and contemporary society through reexamination of the past. All Luo has been doing is to contemporize or modernize the traditional theater through themes and ideology (*chuantong xiju xiandaihua*) and to "metropolitanize" or "cosmopolitanize" regional theaters (*defang xiju dushihua*). With his *huaiju* plays, Luo helped initiate a *huaiju* revival movement called Metropolitan New Huaiju (*dushi xin huaiju*), which boosted the genre up to the level of a major regional style in Shanghai and the lower Yangtze River area. Now the *huaiju* theater has even reached Beijing stages. Its audiences now include all walks of life, ranging from young college students to old peasants in the countryside.

SELECT PLAYS: *The Story of an Ancient Actor* (*Gu you chuanqi*, 1984); *Emperor's Son-in-Law: True and False* (*Zhenjia fuma*, 1986); *Heavenly Son of the Pear Garden* (*Liyuan tianzi*, 1987); *Wind and Moon by the Qinhuai River* (*Fengyue Qinhuai*, 1989); *Golden Dragon and Mayfly* (*Jinlong yu Fuyou*, 1992); *Hegemon King of Western Chu* (*Xichu Bangwang*, 1995); *Xi Shi Returns to the Kingdom of Yue* (*Xi Shi gui Yue*, 1995); *Magic Lotus Lantern* (*Baolian deng*, 1999); *Li Qingzhao the Poetess* (*Li Qingzhao*, 2000); *Meilong Zhen Restaurant* (*Meilong Zhen*, 2000); *Ban Zhao, the Female Historian of the Han* (*Ban Zhao*, 2001); *The Pawned Wife* (*Dian qi*, 2002); *Song of Eternal Regret* (*Chang hen ge*, 2004)

FURTHER READING

Du, Wenwei. "Western Influence Upon Traditional Chinese Theatre." *Mime Journal* 22 (2002–2003): 191–210.

Luo Huaizhen. *Jiushi niandai: Luo Huaizhen juzuo xuan* [The 1990s: Selected plays of Luo Huaizhen]. Shanghai: Shanghai kexueyuan chubanshe, 2002.

——. *Xi Shi gui Yue—Luo Huaizhen tansuo xiqu ji* [Xi Shi returns to the Kingdom of Yue—A collection of Luo Huaizhen's exploratory plays]. Shanghai: Xuelin chubanshe, 1990.

Wenwei Du

LUSCOMBE, GEORGE (1926–1999)

George Luscombe was a dramatic practitioner who insisted that audiences could be stimulated to challenge social inequalities through gripping theater. A director, DRAMATURG, and producer, Luscombe is regarded as an effective co-writer of the pioneering collective creations that defined the theatrical style of Toronto Workshop Productions. Born into a working-class family in 1926, Luscombe was heavily involved in left-wing theater from the 1940s onwards. As a member of the Ann Marshall–directed Toronto Co-Operative Commonwealth Drama Club, he organized song and dance shows for youth groups and for striking workers. In 1948 he joined the People's Repertory Theatre, bringing energetic, low-budget performances of recent plays to small towns throughout Ontario. Between 1950 and 1957 he gained further theatrical experience in Britain: he acted and co-organized a "fit-up" group that toured in Wales; and, crucially, he spent five years with Joan Littlewood's Theatre Workshop, being present at the establishment of the Stratford East headquarters of Littlewood's influential troupe.

Under Littlewood, Luscombe cemented his preference for theater that is committed politically, for maximum psychological and physical discipline by actors, and for plays that vibrantly fill stages with as many characters as possible. He also cemented his controversial insistence that dramatic texts are malleable assets that can be changed to suit the playing company at any particular time. This approach alienated Luscombe from playwrights who jealously revere the sanctity of their painstakingly authored scripts. After his return to CANADA, Luscombe established Toronto Workshop Productions in 1959. By 1967 the thriving company had progressed from a dingy basement into 12 Alexander Street's 300-seat venue. Luscombe remained the artistic director of the company until 1986; he was then retained in a salaried capacity, but was forced out in 1988 in an unpopular move that remains contentious. Luscombe had masterminded the success of Toronto Workshop Productions. *Hey Rube!* (1961) is the collective creation that he revived most often. The play, which self-consciously celebrates the theatrical energies of well-motivated entertainers, dramatizes the energetic resistance of a troupe of clowns who fight efforts by narrow-minded citizens to shift them from their patch.

Other successful creations involving Luscombe, all of which feature the struggles of society's lower orders, included *Mr. Bones* (1969), *Chicago '70* (which ran for one year through 1970/1971), *'Aint Lookin'* (1980), and *The Wobbly* (1983). Luscombe's commitment to the importance of place-based community is probably best illustrated by the contents of the 1974 collective creation *Ten Lost Years*. For this play, Luscombe's company appropriated material from Barry Broadfoot's collection of oral testimonies from survivors of the Great Depression of the 1930s: Luscombe's theater was always both about ordinary working people and for ordinary working people. After his traumatic ejection from Toronto Workshop Productions in 1988, Luscombe taught drama at the University of Guelph. By all accounts he was a demanding but inspirational pedagogue. Until his death on February 5, 1999, he was as outspoken about right-wing political interests and pointless bourgeois theater as he had been when he began to influence Canadian theater forty years previously.

FURTHER READING

Broadfoot. Barry. *Ten Lost Years: 1929–1939; Memories of Canadians Who Survived the Depression*. Toronto: Doubleday, 1973.

Bush, Stephen. "George Luscombe, 1926–1999: The Virtue of Intolerance." *Canadian Theatre Review* 99 (1999): 83–85.

Carson, Neil. *Harlequin in Hogtown: George Luscombe and Toronto Workshop Productions*. Toronto: Univ. of Toronto Press, 1995.

Filewood, Alan. "George Luscombe." In *The Oxford Companion to Canadian Theatre* ed. by Eugene Benson and L. W. Conolly. Toronto: Oxford Univ. Press, 1989. 314–315.

Knowles, Ric. "Drama." In *The Cambridge Companion to Canadian Literature*, ed. by Eva-Marie Kröller. Cambridge: Cambridge Univ. Press, 2004. 120–121.

Kevin De Ornellas

LYUBIMOV, YURY PETROVICH (1917–)

Yury Petrovich Lyubimov is a Russian director, actor, and adapter of nondramatic texts whose theatrical innovations and inventive use of literature at the Taganka Theater made this one of the most influential playhouses in the Soviet Union and RUSSIA in the late 20th century. Lyubimov founded the Taganka in 1964 with a historic interpretation of BERTOLT BRECHT's *THE GOOD WOMAN [Person]* OF SETZUAN, but most of his productions over the next eighteen years employed the prose and poetry of Russian writers through whom Lyubimov offered veiled and direct commentary on political and social realities in the Soviet Union. After the banning of Aleksandr Pushkin's TRAGEDY *Boris Godunov* in 1982 and a public clash with Soviet authorities while staging Fyodor Dostoevsky's *Crime and Punishment* in London in 1983, Lyubimov was stripped of his Soviet citizenship in 1984. He spent five years in exile in the West, returning to Moscow in 1989 thanks to the political changes engendered by perestroika.

By the early 1960s Soviet theater had developed a strong tradition of adapting novels, stories, and, to a lesser extent, poetry to the stage. Lyubimov, one of the first Russians to be described as an *auteur* director, was instrumental in raising this tradition to new heights. Between 1964 and 1982 he worked closely with major contemporary writers, including the two most prominent poets of the thaw era, Andrei Voznesensky (*Antiworlds*, 1965; and *Protect Your Faces*, 1970, banned after three performances) and Yevgeny Yevtushenko (*Beneath the Skin of the Statue of Liberty*, 1972), as well as the novelists Boris Mozhayev (*Alive!* banned in 1968, revived in 1989), Boris Vasilyev (*The Dawns Are Quiet Here*, 1971), Fyodor Abramov (*Wooden Horses*, 1974), and Yury Trifonov (*The Exchange*, 1976; and *The House on the Embankment*, 1980). Lyubimov's major productions involving texts from the postrevolutionary era included his dramatization of John Reed's journalistic account *Ten Days That Shook the World* (1965); an interpretation of poetry by VLADIMIR MAYAKOVSKY titled *Listen!* (1967); and one of the Taganka's most enduring shows, Lyubimov's dramatization of the novel by MIKHAIL BULGAKOV, *The Master and Margarita* (1977), which was performed for the 1,000th time in 2002. Another key source for productions at the Taganka was the literature of Russia's 19th-century golden age, particularly that of Pushkin and Dostoevsky. His production of *Before and After* (2003) was a so-called bricolage employing the poetry of twenty three-poets, including ALEKSANDR BLOK, Nikolai Gumilyov, Velimir Khlebnikov, Marina Tsvetayeva, and Iosif Brodsky.

NIKOLAI ERDMAN, a friend and unofficial adviser at the Taganka in the 1960s whose play THE SUICIDE was among the first Lyubimov staged after returning from exile, commented that in the absence of an in-house playwright at the Taganka, Lyubimov had assumed that role himself. Of Lyubimov's more than fifty productions at the Taganka, only PETER WEISS's MARAT/SADE (1998) could be said to be based on a traditional contemporary play. Lyubimov's unorthodox use of nondramatic literature allowed him to steer clear not only of SOCIALIST REALISM, but of REALISM in general, and to develop what has been called a "poet's theater" and a "theater of synthesis," in which music and movement are equal partners with spoken dialogue.

SELECT PLAYS [ADAPTATIONS]: *A Hero of Our Times*, with Nikolai Erdman (Mikhail Lermontov's novel *Geroi nashego vremeni*, 1964); *Ten Days That Shook the World*, with Yury Dobronravov, Ivan Dobrovolsky, and Sergei Kashtelyan (John Reed's memoir *Desyat' dnei, kotorye potryasli mir*, 1965); *Mother*, with Boris Glagolin (Maxim Gorky's novel *Mat'*, 1969); *What Is to Be Done?* (Nikolai Chernyshevsky's novel *Chto delat'?* 1970); *The Dawns Are Quiet Here*, with Glagolin (Boris Vasilyev's novel *A zori zdes tikhiye . . .*, 1971); *The Exchange*, with Yury Trifonov (Trifonov's novella *Obmen*, 1976); *The Master and Margarita*, with V. Dyachin (Mikhail Bulgakov's novel *Master i Margarita*, 1977); *The House on the Embankment*, with Trifonov (Trifonov's novella *Dom na naberezhnoi*, 1980); *A Raw Youth* (Fyodor Dostoevsky's *Podrostok*, 1991); *Doctor Zhivago* (Boris Pasternak's novel, 1993); *The Brothers Karamazov* (Dostoevsky's novel *Brat'ya Karamazovy*, 1997); *The Bunker* (*Sharashka*; Aleksandr Solzhenitsyn's novel *The First Circle*, 1998); *Eugene Onegin* (Aleksandr Pushkin's verse novel *Yevgenii Onegin*, 2000); *Socrates/The Oracle*, with Konstantin Kedrov (*Sokrat/Orakul*, a poetic collage, 2001); *Theatrical Novel*, with Grigory Faiman (Bulgakov's *Teatral'ny roman*, 2001)

FURTHER READING

Beumers, Birgit. *Yury Lyubimov at the Taganka Theatre, 1964–1994*. Amsterdam: Harwood, 1997.

Gershkovich, Alexander. *The Theater of Yuri Lyubimov: Art and Politics at the Taganka Theater in Moscow*. Tr. by Michael Yurieff. New York: Paragon House, 1989.

Law, Alma. "The Trouble with Lyubimov." *American Theater* (April 1985): 4–11.

Lyubimov, Yury. *Rasskazy starogo trepacha* [Tales of an old bluffer]. Moscow: Novosti, 2001.

Lyubimov, Yury, with Marc Dondey. *Le feu sacré: Souvenirs d'une vie de théâtre* [The sacred fire: Memories of a life in the theater]. Paris: Fayard, 1985.

John Freedman